HANDBOOK OF RESEARCH ON SCIENCE EDUCATION

HANDBOOK OF RESEARCH ON SCIENCE EDUCATION

EDITED BY

Sandra K. Abell

and

Norman G. Lederman

Routledge
Taylor & Francis Group
New York   London

Senior Acquisitions Editor: Naomi Silverman
Editorial Assistant: Joy Tatusko
Cover Design: Tomai Maridou
Full-Service Compositor: MidAtlantic Books & Journals, Inc.

This book was typeset in 10.5/12 pt. Palatino Roman, Italic, Bold, and Bold Italic.

First published by
Lawrence Erlbaum Associates, Inc., Publishers
10 Industrial Avenue
Mahwah, New Jersey 07430
www.erlbaum.com

Reprinted 2010 by Routledge

Routledge
Taylor & Francis Group
711 Third Avenue
New York, NY 10017

Routledge
Taylor & Francis Group
2 Park Square
Milton Park, Abingdon
Oxon OX14 4RN

Library of Congress Cataloging-in-Publication Data

Handbook of research on science education / edited by Sanda K. Abell and Norman G. Lederman.
    p. cm.
    ISBN 0-8058-4713-8 (case : alk. paper) — ISBN 0-8058-4714-6 (pbk. : alk. paper)
  1. Science—Study and teaching—Research. I. Abell, Sandra K. II. Lederman, Norman G.
    Q181.H149   2006
    507.1—dc22

2006031809

ISBN   978-0-8058-4713-0—0-8058-4713-8 (case)
ISBN   978-0-8058-4714-7—0-8058-4714-6 (paper)
ISBN   978-1-4106-1531-2—1-4106-1531-6 (ebook)

Contents

Preface ix
  Sandra K. Abell and Norman G. Lederman

PART I: SCIENCE LEARNING

1 Perspectives on Science Learning 3
   Charles W. Anderson

2 Student Conceptions and Conceptual Learning in Science 31
   Phil Scott, Hilary Asoko, and John Leach

3 Language and Science Learning 57
   William S. Carlsen

4 Attitudinal and Motivational Constructs in Science Learning 75
   Thomas R. Koballa, Jr. and Shawn M. Glynn

5 Classroom Learning Environments 103
   Barry J. Fraser

6 Learning Science Outside of School 125
   Léonie J. Rennie

PART II: CULTURE, GENDER, SOCIETY, AND SCIENCE LEARNING

7 Science Education and Student Diversity:
   Race/Ethnicity, Language, Culture, and Socioeconomic Status 171
   Okhee Lee and Aurolyn Luykx

8 Postcolonialism, Indigenous Students, and Science Education 199
   Elizabeth McKinley

9 Issues in Science Learning: An International Perspective 227
   Chorng-Jee Guo

10 Gender Issues in Science Education Research:
   Remembering Where the Difference Lies 257
   Kathryn Scantlebury and Dale Baker

11   Special Needs and Talents in Science Learning 287
        J. Randy McGinnis and Gregory P. Stefanich

12   Science Learning in Urban Settings 319
        Angela Calabrese Barton

13   Rural Science Education 345
        J. Steve Oliver

PART III: SCIENCE TEACHING

14   General Instructional Methods and Strategies 373
        David Treagust

15   Learning and Teaching in the School Science Laboratory:
        An Analysis of Research, Theory, and Practice 393
        Vincent N. Lunetta, Avi Hofstein, and Michael P. Clough

16   Discourse in Science Classrooms 443
        Gregory J. Kelly

17   Digital Resources Versus Cognitive Tools:
        A Discussion of Learning Science with Technology 471
        Nancy Butler Songer

18   Elementary Science Teaching 493
        Ken Appleton

19   Interdisciplinary Science Teaching 537
        Charlene M. Czerniak

20   High School Biology Curricula Development: Implementation,
        Teaching, and Evaluation from the 20th to the 21st Century 561
        Reuven Lazarowitz

21   Teaching Physics 599
        Reinders Duit, Hans Niedderer, and Horst Schecker

22   Teaching and Learning the Many Faces of Chemistry 631
        Onno De Jong and Keith S. Taber

23   Learning Earth Sciences 653
        Nir Orion and Charles R. Ault, Jr.

24   Environmental Education 689
        Paul Hart

PART IV: CURRICULUM AND ASSESSMENT
IN SCIENCE

25   Scientific Literacy/Science Literacy 729
        Douglas A. Roberts

26 History of Science Curriculum Reform in the United States
and the United Kingdom 781
   J Myron Atkin and Paul Black

27 Inquiry as an Organizing Theme for Science Curricula .807
   Ronald D. Anderson

28 Nature of Science: Past, Present, and Future 831
   Norman G. Lederman

29 Humanistic Perspectives in the Science Curriculum 881
   Glen S. Aikenhead

30 Systemic Reform: Research, Vision, and Politics 911
   Jane Butler Kahle

31 Review of Science Education Program Evaluation 943
   Frances Lawrenz

32 Classroom Assessment of Science Learning 965
   Beverley Bell

33 Large-Scale Assessments in Science Education 1007
   Edward D. Britton and Steve A. Schneider

PART V: SCIENCE TEACHER EDUCATION

34 Science Teacher as Learner 1043
   J. John Loughran

35 Science Teacher Attitudes and Beliefs 1067
   M. Gail Jones and Glenda Carter

36 Research on Science Teacher Knowledge 1105
   Sandra K. Abell

37 Learning to Teach Science 1151
   Tom Russell and Andrea K. Martin

38 Teacher Professional Development in Science 1177
   Peter W. Hewson

39 Science Teachers as Researchers 1203
   Kathleen J. Roth

Author Index 1261

Subject Index 1307

About the Author 1323

Preface

Although some have predicted the end of science (Horgan, 1996), the scientific enterprise thrives and scientists generate new knowledge at an incredible rate. (A recent report from the US National Science Foundation stated that over 92,000 scientific articles were published in 2001 in comparison with about 70,000 in 1991 (Hill, 2004).) Essential to the vibrancy of science, scientists continue to ask questions of the world. In the July 1, 2005 issue of the journal *Science*, the editor compiled responses from senior scientists and published the 125 questions that science "should have a good shot at answering" (Kennedy & Norman, 2005, p. 75) in the next 25 years, many from relatively young sciences such as neuroscience, genomics, biomedical science, geophysics, astrophysics, and bioengineering. According to Siegfried (2005), in that same journal issue:

> When science runs out of questions, it would seem, science will come to an end. But there's no real danger of that. The highway from ignorance to knowledge runs both ways: As knowledge accumulates, diminishing the ignorance of the past, new questions arise, expanding the areas of ignorance to explore. (p. 77).

For many years, science education researchers prided themselves on following research approaches and paradigms that approximated those of science. Thus, it is interesting to consider the similarities between science and science education. How does science education as a discipline compare? Our field has a much shorter history than that of the natural sciences. Our research has appeared in science education journals and books for fewer than 100 years. Yet we have generated a substantial body of knowledge during this time, knowledge from which new questions have emerged. Like the sciences, our questions are partly shaped by the society in which we live and partly by the research community in which we work. Research in science is guided by and builds upon prior research. However, in the science education community, researchers are often opportunistic, studying what is convenient to them rather than building on previous investigations. We believe that a handbook of research in a discipline such as science education provides a foundation upon which future research can be built.

The purpose of this volume is twofold. First, the authors look backward in time in an attempt to capture where science education has been and what we currently know. Secondly, the authors project into the future, positing research agendas for

The National Association for Research in Science Teaching (NARST) endorses the *Handbook of Research on Science Education* as an important and valuable synthesis of the current knowledge in the field of science education by leading individuals in the field.

various subfields in the discipline. When we invited authors to take part in the project, we asked that they tackle these two purposes:

> We are asking authors to write an "integrative review" of the research in each topic area. Authors will pull together the existing research on the topic and work to understand the historical trends and patterns in that body of scholarship. Authors will describe how the issue is conceptualized within the literature, how methods and theories have shaped the outcomes of the research, and where the strengths, weaknesses, and gaps are in the literature. Reviews will end with implications for practice and future research derived from the review. (S. Abell & N. Lederman, personal communication, October 15, 2002)

This book is intended as a comprehensive research handbook for the field of science education. Two research handbooks in the field were produced in the previous decade. The first, edited by Gabel (1994), the *Handbook of Research on Science Teaching and Learning*, was published in cooperation with the National Science Teachers Association. It is now over 10 years old and no longer represents the scope of research in the field. The second, edited by Fraser and Tobin (1998), the *International Handbook of Science Education*, although international in its collection of authors, did not present a comprehensive review of the research in science education. Rather it was an in-depth sampling of the work of various researchers, demonstrating a slice in time of research in the field. Both of these volumes responded to the inadequacy of the single review chapters for science education contained in general education research handbooks such as those produced by the American Educational Research Association. The work represented in this volume is international and comprehensive in scope. It provides both veteran and emerging science education researchers with a coherent synthesis of the empirical and theoretical research concerning teaching and learning in science, and paves the way for future research.

OVERVIEW OF THE BOOK

One of our first steps as editors was to map out our construction of the structure of the discipline of science education. We first created five organizing categories in which to place the research in the field: Science Learning; Culture, Gender, and Society and Science Learning; Science Teaching; Curriculum and Assessment; and Science Teacher Education. We thought that this organization would capture most, if not all, of the published science education research (although we were aware that no organizational scheme would achieve consensus among our colleagues). These organizers became the five major sections in this *Handbook*.

The more difficult step was deciding what chapters should appear within each section. The decisions we made were unique, based on our experiences as science educators and researchers. Our decisions certainly would not match the organization other researchers would impose on the field. Current trends and length restrictions led us to make strategic decisions on chapters to include or not to include. For example, given the recent importance of the literature on language and science, we included two chapters on language and science learning. However, as we envisioned, these chapters serve different purposes. The first, by William Carlsen, appears in the first section of the book, Science Learning. It is meant to be a theoretical overview of language and learning and how such theory has informed science education research. The second chapter on language and science education research appears in the third section of the book, Science Teaching. That chapter, by Gregory Kelly (once Carlsen's doctoral student), reviews classroom-based research on discourse in science education. We also made strategic decisions on chapters not to include. For example, although research on college science teaching has increased in the past decade (demonstrated in part by a dedicated strand at the annual NARST meeting), we chose to include this research by science discipline instead of by grade level, along with subject-specific studies at middle and high school levels, in the Science Teaching section of the *Handbook*. However, we decided that the research on elementary science teaching was less science discipline-specific and more age-related, and therefore deserved its own chapter.

The organization of this *Handbook* highlights other recent trends in the field. For example, the second section of the book, Culture, Gender, and Society, acknowledges the contributions of research focused on context to understanding science learners. The chapters in this section demonstrate the importance of learners' gender, culture, and special needs, as well as the larger societal context (urban, rural, postcolonial), in learning science. In the final section of the book, Science Teacher Education, we have presented a comprehensive synthesis of the research in the area of science teacher education for the first time. Twenty years ago, few studies in science education focused on science teacher learning. Currently such research comprises the largest submission to the NARST annual meeting, necessitating the development of two separate dedicated strands. The chapters in this section are thus a unique contribution to the field.

As editors, we also influenced the direction of the book in other ways. Once we had a structure for the *Handbook* in place, we brainstormed authors for the various chapters. First and foremost, we wanted authors who were leading experts in their research area, and who had published a significant quality and/or quantity of research. As veteran science education researchers with a total of 40+ years in the field, and as past presidents of NARST, our collective expertise was a good place to begin the brainstorming. However, we recognized that our expertise was limited in certain areas of the field and was somewhat North American centric. Thus we also consulted other resources during the author selection process, including the NARST annual meeting programs of recent years, other conference proceedings, and the ERIC database. In addition to selecting high profile researchers, we tried to ensure that our selection represented the international and gender diversity that exists in our research community. We believe that the final list of authors indeed meets these selection criteria.

An additional task we faced as editors was to engage thoughtful reviewers in providing feedback to authors on the first drafts of chapter manuscripts. The peer review process is critical to maintaining quality in our work. The reviewers we selected, along with the editors, provided insight and made recommendations that improved the final chapters in many ways. Some authors also involved their own colleagues in the review processes. The reviewers are acknowledged in the chapters they reviewed. Through section and chapter organization, author selection, and review work, we crafted this *Handbook*. It represents our current construction of the structure of the discipline of science education.

THEMATIC ELEMENTS

We have had the honor of interacting with many authors and reviewers to shape the contents of this book. We have had the privilege of reading all of the chapters and interpreting various themes that emerged from our reading. In this section we highlight three such themes.

One of the striking features of the field of science education as represented in the chapters in this *Handbook* is that it is influenced by the prevailing learning theory of the day. Few would argue that perspectives on learning have changed drastically over the past 100 years. Even the most superficial analysis indicates at least five "general families" of learning theory held dominance in educational matters over the past century—mental discipline, natural unfoldment, apperception, behaviorism, and cognitive science. These differing perspectives have influenced how science education researchers view learning, teaching, and the assessment of both.

A second theme of the research reviewed in this *Handbook* is that the predominance of various research methodologies change over time. Some of this fluctuation corresponds directly with changing views of learning. Early research on teaching and learning focused on the identification and exercise of various mental faculties as a direct result of the dominance of mental discipline theory. In the 1970s, process-product research methodologies clearly reflected the dominance of behavioristic learning theories. The emergence of qualitative methodologies mirrored the replacement of behaviorism with cognitive theories of learning.

A final theme that emerges from the *Handbook* chapters is that the teaching and learning of science is discipline-specific. What is considered effective instruction in a biology class is not the same as effective instruction in another class, science or otherwise. Teachers do not teach and learners do not learn biology in the same ways as they do physics or social science or humanities. This theme appears in the sections on science learners and learning, in the discipline-specific chapters on science teaching, and in the section on science teacher education. In that section, authors examine the notion of pedagogical content knowledge as a framework for science teacher education research. Lee Shulman, who invented this idea (1986), began his career as a science educator. He cautioned us not to allow the disappearance of subject matter from educational research. The existence of this *Handbook* is a testimony to the value of science subject matter in our research.

THE FUTURE OF SCIENCE EDUCATION

Much like the authors in the July, 2005 issue of *Science* demonstrate that science is alive and well, the chapters in this *Handbook* illustrate the vitality of science education as a discipline. We have learned much about science learners and learning, and science teachers and teaching, over the past 80 or so years of research. According to the chapter authors, many questions remain open for investigation. Surely many other questions we have not yet thought to ask.

As we continue to ask and investigate questions in science education, we believe it is crucial to keep a few guidelines in mind.

1. The ultimate purpose of science education research is the improvement of science teaching and learning throughout the world. We must take care that the proximate causes of our research (e.g., achieving publications that count for tenure, writing conference papers so our universities will fund our travel, preparing new researchers, getting grant dollars) do not derail us from achieving our ultimate purpose. Thus we call for rigor in design, data collection, interpretation, and write up.

2. To achieve the ultimate purpose of improving science teaching and learning, our research must be grounded in the real world of students and teachers and school systems and society. Ours is an applied field, and we must ensure that our research makes sense in the real world. Our research must address, and attempt to answer, the questions and concerns of teachers. To have educational warrant, our research must answer questions of educational importance.

3. To achieve the ultimate purpose of improving science teaching and learning, we as researchers need to be open to new theoretical frameworks, research methodologies, and strategies, even as we embrace existing tried and true methods. We are long past the paradigm wars that dominated education research in the 1980s. Mixed methods research (Chatterji, 2004; Johnson & Onwuegbuzie, 2004) is a new paradigm ripe for application to science education settings. Longitudinal studies that employ mixed methods will be essential to understanding student and teacher learning over time. In addition, theoretical frameworks that embrace postmodern thinking will help us see the world in new ways.

4. Translating our research for teachers is an essential component of our work. If we write only for other researchers, we will never achieve this ultimate goal. Teachers and researchers often describe the gap between research and practice. It is our responsibility to translate our research so that practitioners and policy makers can ultimately decide whether what has been offered is of practical value. This *Handbook* is written for researchers. We leave it to others to undertake the important work of interpreting and transforming its contents for other stakeholders.

These guidelines, along with the research agendas suggested by chapter authors, can help our field advance. Although we are not quite ready to state the 125 questions that the science education community has a shot at answering in the upcoming 25 years, the guidelines and research agendas can help science education researchers fulfill the mission, reflected in the NARST slogan, to improve science teaching (and learning) through research. If we keep our eyes on this goal, then we will continue to raise new research questions that will diminish our current ignorance while expanding the areas of ignorance yet to be explored.

Sandra K. Abell
University of Missouri, Columbia

Norman G. Lederman
Illinois Institute of Technology

REFERENCES

Chatterji, M. (2004). Evidence on "What Works": An argument for extended-term mixed-method (ETMM) evaluation designs. *Educational Researcher, 33*(9), 3–13.

Gabel, D. L. (Ed.). (1994). *Handbook of research on science teaching and learning.* New York: Macmillan.

Fraser, B. J., & Tobin, K. G. (Eds.). (1998). *International handbook of science education.* Dordrecht, The Netherlands: Kluwer.

Hill, D. L. (2004). *Latin America shows rapid rise in S&E articles* (NSF 04-336). Washington, DC: National Science Foundation Directorate for Social, Behavioral, and Economic Sciences.

Horgan, J. (1996). *The end of science: Facing the limits of knowledge in the twilight of the scientific age.* Reading, MA: Addison-Wesley.

Johnson, R. B., & Onwuegbuzie, A. J. (2004). Mixed methods research: A research paradigm whose time has come. *Educational Researcher, 33*(7), 14–26.

Kennedy, D., & Norman, C. (2005). What don't we know? (Special Section). *Science, 309* (5731), 75.

Shulman, L. S. (1986). Those who understand: Knowledge growth in teaching. *Educational Researcher, 15*(2), 4–14.

Siegfried, T. (2005). In praise of hard questions. (Special Section). *Science, 309* (5731), 76–77.

PART I

Science Learning

CHAPTER 1

Perspectives on Science Learning

Charles W. Anderson
Michigan State University

The past two decades have been an exciting time for research on science learning. During this time, science educators have created or adapted an impressive array of new research practices and conceptual tools that we can use to analyze student learning in science classrooms and in other settings. The results of those analyses have given us new insights into science learning as it occurs in individual students and in social, cultural, historical, and institutional contexts.

INTRODUCTION: PERSPECTIVES AND RESEARCH TRADITIONS

Purposes of This Chapter

The literature on science learning is diverse. It has been conducted by researchers from different cultural and intellectual backgrounds, using different methods, working in different settings. These researchers have based their work on different ideas about the nature of science, the purposes of science education, and the nature of science learning. Some aspects of this diversity are explicit and apparent to readers; for example, most research articles include descriptions of the settings and participants in the research and the methods used by the researchers. Other aspects of this diversity are harder to discern; authors can never fully reveal the assumptions that underlie their work or the intellectual influences that have shaped it.

This diversity of methods and viewpoints can make reading research on science education a frustrating experience. There seem to be no rules that everyone follows, no beliefs that everyone shares, no findings that everyone agrees on. Where is the order in this welter of confusing findings? How can we say that we are making progress in the field?

One way to find order and to see the progress in the literature on science learning is to recognize that within the broad field of science education there are groups of researchers who share common intellectual heritages and seek to build on one another's work. By recognizing the differences among those research traditions, we can see how researchers in each tradition are advancing knowledge as they understand it. We can also see how, in spite of their differences, researchers in all traditions are contributing to a collective effort that deepens and enriches our understanding of science learning.

In this chapter, I seek to provide a reader's guide that draws attention to the conceptual, methodological, and stylistic choices that the authors make in reporting research on science learning, and to how those choices are related to underlying beliefs about the nature and purposes of science education research. I have labeled these the *conceptual change tradition*, the *sociocultural tradition*, and the *critical tradition*. Rather than trying to provide historical overviews or general reviews of the literature in each tradition, I have chosen to focus on one exemplary article from each tradition, using quotations and commentary to discuss the authors' choices, the beliefs that underlie those choices, and the contributions that the tradition makes to our collective understanding of science learning.

In choosing to describe perspectives on student learning in terms of three research traditions, and in summarizing three individual articles to exemplify those traditions, I have oversimplified both the exemplary papers and the field in general. Representing research on science learning by focusing on three examples is a little like representing the visible spectrum by showing examples of the three primary colors. Subtlety and nuance are lost. Furthermore, the choice of three particular colors as primary is an accident of human physiology rather than a physical characteristic of light. Nevertheless, we continue to find the primary colors useful as we seek to understand color and color vision. I hope that these examples can be similarly useful. As with colors, there are very few pure examples of research within one of these traditions, both because the traditions themselves are multivoiced and because science educators are eclectic in their use of practices and conceptual tools from different traditions that will help them to achieve their research goals.

My choice of these three traditions is also idiosyncratic and historically situated. For example, I have included the extensive literature on uses of instructional technology in science education (e.g., Feurzeig & Roberts, 1999; Linn & Hsi, 2000; White & Frederiksen, 1998) in a broadly defined Conceptual Change tradition, though many researchers in both fields would consider the work in these fields as belonging to distinct traditions. Similarly, an author writing about perspectives on science learning in 1990 or in 2010 would probably identify traditions that are different from the ones I have chosen.

Thus the contrasts that I make among the traditions will not be very useful for classifying research studies, and I have not attempted to summarize research results. I hope, however, that by representing a range of perspectives and voices that researchers bring to the challenges of understanding and improving science learning, this chapter can help readers gain additional insights into the research itself. This chapter is not a substitute for reading research on science education, but an invitation that I hope will make the process of reading interesting and informative as we pursue our individual and collective goals in science education.

Core Goals and Issues

Research on student learning in science can be broadly characterized as focusing on the development of *scientific literacy*. Scientific communities have developed knowledge and practices that are potentially valuable to members of the general public in their roles as workers, consumers, family members, and citizens. *Scientific literacy* is a term that can be used to designate the science-related knowledge, practices, and values that we hope students will acquire as they learn science.

For researchers in science education generally, scientific literacy includes a sense of empowerment or agency in two senses. The first of these I call *social agency*. Successful learners of science can gain respect for their knowledge, skills that enable them to do useful work, and access to jobs and to communities that would otherwise be closed to them. The second I call *agency in the material world*.[1] Successful learners of science can describe and measure the world around them with precision, predict and explain phenomena, and act effectively to influence natural and technological systems. Following Sharma and Anderson (2003), I also sometimes refer to these two kinds of agency as dialogues: learners' *dialogues with nature* and *dialogues with other people*.

Researchers in science education also generally agree on one central finding about current school practice: *Our institutions of formal education do not help most students to learn science with understanding*. This is a robust finding, encompassing both large-scale studies of science achievement (e.g., Blank & Langesen, 2001; Schmidt et al., 2001), as well as thousands of smaller studies conducted in a single classroom or a few classrooms. Given any reasonable definition of scientific literacy, the research shows that neither most students in schools nor most adults are achieving it. Furthermore, the benefits of science education are not evenly distributed. In the United States, for example, there is a large and persistent *achievement gap* that separates students by race, ethnicity, and social class (Blank & Langesen, 2001; Kim et al., 2001; see Chapter 8, this volume). Similar achievement gaps exist within and among countries worldwide. This leads to a two core questions that research on science learning should address:

1. Why don't students learn what we are trying to teach them?
2. Why does the achievement gap persist?

The importance of the three research traditions examined in this chapter lies largely in the provocative and useful responses that each tradition provides to these questions. The practices and theories developed through this research give us a deeper understanding of how students learn, why they fail to learn, and how we might create educational systems that are more responsive to their needs.

Commonplaces and Contrasts

The next three sections of this chapter are devoted to an examination of the three traditions. Each section begins with a detailed examination of a single recently

---

1. I use the term *material world* to include the naturally occurring systems and phenomena that are studied by life, earth, and physical scientists, as well as technological systems created by humans.

published article that illustrates the perspectives and research methods typical of that tradition and exemplifies the kinds of insights into science learning that the tradition affords. Each section concludes with a more general look at the contributions that research in that tradition has made to our understanding of science learning, the influence of that research on policy and practice, and at the limitations of the tradition. Finally, the chapter concludes with some final thoughts on current issues and future progress in research on science learning.

As I compare and contrast the three articles and the traditions that they represent, I characterize each tradition in terms of five *commonplaces*—aspects of science learning that are explicitly or implicitly addressed by all research studies on science learning. These commonplaces are briefly described below and addressed in greater depth in the analyses of the research articles.

1. Intellectual history and related disciplines. All three traditions arise out of earlier work in science education and in related disciplines, such as psychology, sociology, linguistics, anthropology, and philosophy. The three traditions differ, though, in their intellectual roots and in the related disciplines that have most influenced them.

2. Ideas about the nature of science. Researchers in all three traditions share an understanding that our ideas about science learning and scientific literacy depend in part on our ideas about science. These traditions share an understanding that science is more than a body of knowledge or a set of methods for developing new knowledge. All three traditions share a view of science as a subculture with specialized language, values, and practices. The three traditions characterize science and scientific knowledge, though, in quite different ways, and those differences are reflected in their approaches to science learning.

3. Ideas about science learners and science learning. Researchers in all three traditions share a view of science learners as agents in their own right, who come to science learning with their own knowledge, language, beliefs, cultural practices, and roles in communities and power relationships. They recognize that learning arises out of the interactions between learners and the knowledge and practices they encounter in science classrooms. The three traditions differ, though, in their approaches to characterizing both learners and the process of science learning.

4. Research goals and methods. The most important research on student learning during this period has relied more on qualitative than on quantitative methods, and it has generally been conducted on a modest scale, focusing on individual learners, small groups, or learning in a few classrooms. The traditions differ, though, in the kinds of knowledge they seek to develop, in the degree to which they mix qualitative and quantitative methods, and in their methodological traditions and standards.

5. Ideas for improving science learning. All three traditions have convincing answers to the questions about the failures of formal science education above; they identify important barriers to successful learning that are rarely successfully addressed in school science. All three traditions have ideas about how schools and science teaching could be changed so that students would learn more successfully. The traditions, though, differ in the barriers to successful learning that they identify and in the suggestions that they develop for helping more students learn successfully.

CONCEPTUAL CHANGE TRADITION: SCIENTIFIC LITERACY AS CONCEPTUAL UNDERSTANDING

Of the three research traditions, the conceptual change tradition is the one with the longest history and the most influence within the science education community. Like all of the research traditions, it encompasses a wide variety of perspectives and practices. Many of its methods and perspectives can be traced back to the developmental research of Jean Piaget (see Chapter 3, this volume). Piaget recognized the importance of children's thinking and developed the clinical interview as a method for investigating how children make sense of the world. Many of his investigations, especially early in his career, focused on children's understanding of scientific topics. Piaget's core interests, though, were developmental and psychological, so his research did not lead directly to the conceptual change tradition.

Conceptual change research emerged when investigators began to link Piaget's methods with ideas about the historical development of scientific knowledge, notably those of Kuhn (1970) and Toulmin (1961, 1972). Posner, Strike, Hewson, and Gertzog brought these strands together in a seminal article in 1982, suggesting that individual learners had "conceptual ecologies" like those used by Toulmin to describe scientific disciplines, and that learning in individuals resembled the complex process of theory change in science.

Since conceptual change research became prominent in the early 1980s, this tradition has generated an impressive amount of research worldwide. Reinders Duit's bibliography of conceptual change studies (Duit, 2004) covers more than 500 single-spaced pages. Conceptual change researchers have described alternative frameworks for every topic in the school curriculum (see, for example, Chapter 15 of *Benchmarks for Science Literacy*, American Association for the Advancement of Science [AAAS], 1993, or the reviews by Driver, Squires, Rushworth, & Wood-Robinson, 1994).

An Example of Conceptual Change Research

One recent article that illustrates a number of important theories and practices is "Linking Phenomena with Competing Underlying Models: A Software Tool for Introducing Students to the Particulate Model of Matter," by Joseph Snir, Carol Smith, and Gila Raz (2003). This section summarizes the article and then discusses ways in which it exemplifies the perspectives and practices of research within this tradition.

Snir et al. (2003) addressed a problem in science learning that was well documented in previous conceptual change research and introduced in the first paragraph of their article:

> The particulate model of matter is one of the central ideas in modern science. It is also a central subject in the middle and high school science curriculum. Yet, as is well known, this topic is very hard for students to learn and internalize. . . . We believe that understanding the particulate model of matter is difficult because it requires that students develop an understanding of two profoundly important, but counterintuitive, ideas. The first one is the idea of the *discontinuity of matter* and the second is the idea of an *explanatory model* as a metaconcept in science. (p. 795)

As is typical in conceptual change research, Snir et al. (2003) defined the learning problem in conceptual terms and focused on a specific scientific domain, in this case theories about the nature of matter. Their focus on a specific scientific model or theory was also typical of conceptual change research. Their article was devoted to (a) helping readers to understand the depth and difficulty of this learning problem; (b) presenting a strategy for helping students achieve their learning goals; and (c) presenting and discussing data on student learning from two studies, one conducted in a laboratory and the other in a classroom setting. Their approach to each of these parts of the article is discussed below.

Understanding the Learning Problem

Although the study focused on learning by middle-school students, the article barely mentioned middle-school students—or any students at all—in its first four pages. Instead, the article begins with a prolonged explication of the historical and philosophical significance of scientific models in general and the particulate model of matter in particular. The authors quoted the Nobel Prize–winning physicist Richard Feynman:

> If, in some cataclysm, all the scientific knowledge were to be destroyed, and only one sentence passed on to the next generation of creatures, what statement would contain the most information in the fewest words? I believe it is the *atomic hypothesis* . . . that *all things are made of atoms—little particles that move around in perpetual motion, attracting each other when they are a little distance apart, but repelling upon being squeezed into one another.* In that one sentence, you will see, there is an *enormous* amount of information about the world, if just a little imagination and thinking are applied. (Feynman, Leighton, & Sands, 1963, Chapter 1, as cited in Snir et al., 2003, p. 795)

The authors then described the key features and multiple uses of particulate models of matter in current scientific practice, as well as the historical struggles of scientists to develop the particulate model in its current form. Thus the article begins with a description of how scientists' dialogues with nature led to the development of the particulate model, and how it continues to play a critical role in scientists' dialogues with nature today. The introduction continues with a discussion of "the general conception of an explanatory model," noting that scientific models are understood to be (a) not true descriptions of a system, (b) limited in scope, (c) evaluated according to their power to explain and predict observed phenomena, and (d) not unique—the same system can be modeled in more than one way. Thus the article begins with a careful explication of current scientific knowledge and practice as a goal for science education.

Snir et al. (2003) devoted the next five pages of their article to a detailed review of the research literature on attempts to teach students to use particulate models to reason about properties of materials and changes in materials. They made the case that Feynman's simply stated idea makes sense only in the context of a complicated conceptual ecology that students develop when they "make the transition from a tangible, observable continuous world to an abstract unseen one that consists of discrete particles at a microscopic level" (p. 802).

The authors argued that students could understand and use particulate models of matter only if they were building on some critical macroscopic understandings about matter (e.g., even bits of matter that are too small to weigh, have weight;

understanding of the relationships among volume, weight, and density) and on their development of some understandings about the nature and uses of models in general. They argued that previous attempts to teach middle-school students about particulate models of matter had generally tried to "take on too much too fast," paying insufficient attention to some of these critical conceptual issues.

Thus, the educational challenges involve not only deciding what part of the particulate model to teach first and what prerequisite conceptions must be in place to create these conceptual puzzles, but also how to build students' general understanding of what a model is. We believe the best approach is to involve students in explaining a series of phenomena and in evaluating the explanatory adequacy of alternative models. This approach gives students the opportunity to construct the particulate model slowly in their mind in response to puzzling but concrete phenomena (Snir et al., p. 803).

Presenting a Strategy for Helping Students Achieve Their Learning Goals

The next 11 pages of the article are devoted to detailed presentation and discussion of a software tool that the authors developed to help students accomplish their learning goals. The tool presented simulations of three critical experiments, involving (a) mixing of water and alcohol (a puzzling phenomenon, inasmuch as the volume of the mixture is slightly less than the total volume of the separate liquids), (b) thermal expansion of an iron ball, and (c) the reaction of copper and sulfur—the critical observation being that copper and sulfur always combine in the same proportions regardless of the amounts of the reactants available.

The tool focused the students' attention on key aspects of each phenomenon, then guided students through explanations of the phenomena based on four different models, a particulate model representing their learning goals and three alternative models designed to incorporate common student misconceptions. A series of screens guided students through the application of each model to each phenomenon, both illustrating how the model explained the phenomenon and comparing predictions of the model with actual experimental results. Only the particulate model consistently produced predictions aligned with the experimental results.

The authors summarized the key elements of the software (and implicitly the key elements of a strategy for conceptual change teaching about this topic) as follows:

1. It is designed to help students filter central facts from many experimental details.

2. It combines both tutorial and tool elements, while adjusting the mode to the nature of the learning. If one conceives of learning science on three levels—factual, conceptual, and metaconceptual (Snir, Smith, & Grosslight, 1993)—then we used the tutorial mode for the factual level and the tool mode for the conceptual and metaconceptual levels.

3. It allows students to compare, on the same screen, surface and model levels of description.

4. It acknowledges the existence of alternative models and students' initial ideas.

5. It facilitates the introduction of model evaluation based on consistency with a range of facts, rather than simply one observation, as a central part of the curriculum. (p. 814)

Research Methods, Results, and Conclusions

The next 10 pages of the article are devoted to presentation of data from two studies: a laboratory study in which nine American fifth- and sixth-grade students explained their thinking as they used the software and a classroom study in which 28 Israeli seventh-grade students used the software as part of a unit on matter.

In each study, the researchers carefully tracked the reasoning of individual students as revealed on pretests, posttests, and their performance as they were using the software. There were measures of retention in each study: students in the laboratory study were interviewed a week after they used the software; students in the classroom study took a delayed posttest the next year. The classroom study also included teaching about macroscopic conceptions of matter (e.g., identifying solids, liquids, and gases as matter; relationships among weight, volume, and density), demonstrations of the actual phenomena, and a control group of students who studied a similar curriculum without the software. The teachers of the experimental classes were the authors, Joseph Snir and Gilda Raz. In addition to the concepts that were the focus of this study (particulate models of matter and general understanding of models), the pretests and posttests included measures of students' macroscopic understanding of weight, volume, and density.

The results of these studies were complex, but some of the key conclusions were as follows:

1. Both the think-aloud data from students using the software and class discussions revealed that most (but not all) students engaged in the activities intended by the authors: comparing and evaluating models based on their ability to predict observed results of the experiments;

2. Focusing on seven key, tenets of the particulate nature of matter,

    In the experimental group, we found that 30% of the students had a perfect understanding of these seven simple points, compared to none in the control group. If we allow students one error, we find that 47% of the experimental students understood at least six of the seven points compared to 22% of the control students. (Snir et al., 2003, p. 823)

3. Thirty percent of the students in the experimental group wrote open-ended responses indicating that what makes the particulate model a good model is its ability to explain a wide range of phenomena. In contrast, none of the students in the control group answered in this way (p. 823)

4. Finally, the data provided evidence that students' macroscopic and microscopic understandings of matter mutually support one another. Students who by the time of the delayed posttest showed that they had a strong macroscopic understanding of matter were the ones most likely to have internalized the assumptions of the particulate model. (p. 825)

Similarly, these students were also the ones who showed the best understanding of the nature of models in general.

The article concludes with an argument that the key features of the software were responsible for the successful learning of the students in the experimental classes, and that the successful learners had undergone a fundamental long-term change in the way they viewed matter and models of matter. Their new, stable understanding included three mutually supporting components: an understanding of key macroscopic ideas about matter, understanding of key components of a particulate model of matter, and understanding of the nature and functions of models in general.

General Characteristics of Conceptual Change Research

The results in the article by Snir et al. (2003) are more detailed and the arguments more subtle than I could portray in the brief summary above. I hope, however, that the brief summary is sufficient to illustrate some of the key characteristics that their research shares with other research in the conceptual change tradition. I discuss some of those characteristics in the following sections, then conclude with some thoughts on the power and limitations of conceptual change research.

Characteristics of Conceptual Change Research

I discuss these characteristics in terms of the five commonplaces introduced at the beginning of this chapter. The first of these commonplaces, the intellectual history of the research tradition, is discussed briefly at the beginning of this section. The other four commonplaces—view of the nature of science, view of students and learning, methods, and implications for practice—are discussed briefly below.

Science as a theoretical dialogue with nature. Although conceptual change researchers recognize the importance of both aspects of scientific literacy discussed in the introduction—social agency and agency in the material world—they give primacy to agency in the material world. Snir et al. (2003) for example, characterized science as an ongoing theoretical dialogue with nature, in which scientists have developed successively more powerful models to account for a wider range of phenomena. For these authors and for other conceptual change researchers, the power of science lies both in its general use of model-based reasoning to understand nature and in the specific models that scientists have developed. Thus the task of science education is to include students in scientists' ongoing dialogue with nature and to give them access to the power of scientific ideas.

Learners as rational but inexperienced thinkers and learning as conceptual change. Like other conceptual change researchers, Snir et al. (2003) characterized the students who they worked with as coming into the research setting with their own ideas about matter. These ideas (labeled *misconceptions, naïve conceptions, alternative frameworks*, etc.) are less powerful and precise than scientific theories, but they generally work for the students' purposes and within the limits of their experience. Thus the task of the researchers is both to give students access to new experiences with the material world that are incompatible with students' naïve ideas—the three key experiments—and to help students see the power of the particulate model to account for these new experiences. This is a complex process of *conceptual change*; students learn with understanding only if they modify their conceptual ecologies to accommodate the more sophisticated scientific conceptions. Much of the detailed work of the conceptual change research program—the contents of

Duit's (2004) 500-page bibliography—has been mapping out the conceptual ecologies for specific topics and for students of different ages.

Research methods for analyzing students' conceptions.   Snir et al. (2003) used methods typical of conceptual change research—written tests, clinical interviews, and think-aloud protocols of problem solving—to construct an argument about the understanding of the students before and after instruction. In the article and its supporting literature, they took great care to describe and defend the validity of their methods for assessing the specific beliefs of the students with respect to the scientific topic of study: the particulate nature of matter and the nature and uses of scientific models.

As significant as what they included in their research description is what the authors did *not* consider essential information. They provided no information about themselves and their intellectual or cultural backgrounds. Although they noted the age and nationalities of the students, they provided no other information about their cultural backgrounds or social class. They did not investigate the students' general experience or learning styles. In these respects, too, they were typical of conceptual change researchers. They took great care to investigate the conceptual ecologies of their informants around the scientific topics they studied and to situate their research in a scientific context, but neither they nor the reviewers of their research thought it necessary to report on the social or cultural contexts of their work.

Teaching methods for conceptual change learning.   This article differs from much conceptual change research in that it focused on an instructional intervention. Although instructional studies are common in this research tradition, they are outnumbered by studies that document students' current conceptions and their responses to traditional science instruction. Those studies have almost inevitably found traditional instruction to be inadequate and have recommended instructional methods like those used by Snir et al. (2003). Their summary of the key characteristics of their software has great resonance within the conceptual change tradition, because it focuses only on the qualities that conceptual change researchers generally believe are essential for successful science learning—and missing from most science teaching. Their underlying belief is that successful student learning will be driven by situations of *conceptual conflict* like those that have driven historical advances in scientific communities, where students can see the contrast between their conceptions and alternative scientific conceptions and the superior power and precision of the scientific conceptions.

Power and Limitations of Conceptual Change Research

One reason for the popularity of conceptual change research is that it has produced productive answers to the first of our two key questions: Students fail to learn what we try to teach them because they come to school with alternative conceptual frameworks that shape their perceptions and interpretations and that are not addressed by school science. This is a productive answer in part because it suggests a course of action: Identify the students' alternative frameworks and address them explicitly in instruction. Furthermore, conceptual change researchers have developed conceptual and methodological tools that they can use to follow this course of action.

Another reason for the popularity of conceptual change research has been that it makes effective use of the intellectual resources of science educators. The primary qualifications for doing conceptual change research are knowledge and skills acquired through scientific training and educational experience. Scientific training teaches people to be attuned to rational and coherent theories as the content of discussions with professors and colleagues, so it prepares science educators to attune themselves to these kinds of meanings in students' language and thinking. Thus, conceptual change research has been a source of personal and professional growth for many scientists and science educators, opening up new dimensions of communication with students that lead to improved practices in science teaching and teacher education.

Conceptual change research has also had a substantial influence on educational policy. The authors of the U.S. national standards documents (AAAS, 1993; National Research Council, 1996) consulted conceptual change research findings in writing content benchmarks, and their recommendations for teaching practice were influenced by conceptual change research. Many textbooks now include lists of common misconceptions in their teacher's editions.

The evidence that conceptual change research can be used to improve teaching practice is sketchier than the evidence that students' alternative frameworks affect their learning, but still substantial. The article by Snir et al. (2003) is typical of much of this research in that it provides an "existence proof"—an example of successful teaching for understanding by individual teachers for a small number of students. These existence proofs show that under the right conditions many students can learn science with levels of understanding that are currently achieved by only a small elite. Furthermore, this article, like others in this tradition, emphasized the potential scalability of the teaching methods. Other teachers can be given access to the software tool, the demonstrations are easily replicable, and other students can be expected to have similar misconceptions.

There is little evidence, however, that these practices are spreading to large numbers of teachers, suggesting that there may be difficulties in taking these innovative to scale that are not addressed in the article. Some of those difficulties are inherent in any attempt to implement innovative practice on a large scale and are beyond the scope of this chapter (see, for example, Cohen & Hill, 2000; Elmore, 2002; Gamoran et al., 2003). There are questions that we could pose about the research itself. In the study by Snir et al. (2003), for example, a number of students did not achieve the learning goals. The authors reported that these were the students who had not previously mastered key macroscopic understanding of mass, volume, and density. But why did some students fail to master the prerequisite knowledge, especially in the classroom study where that knowledge was included in the instructional program? Was there some deeper source of difficulty that the conceptual change research methods did not discover?

These questions about a particular study are connected to questions about the larger conceptual change research program. For example, what might scientific literacy involve beyond conceptual understanding? A view of students as proto-scientists who understand the world on the basis of implicit theories is not the whole story. Conceptual change researchers generally recognize that scientific understanding is more than just understanding core concepts, but their data collection methods and analytical tools focus on conceptual frameworks.

Furthermore, the theories and methods of conceptual change research have produced more productive answers to the first of the two key questions posed in the introduction than to the second (about the achievement gap between students of different races, cultures, or social classes). Although conceptual change research has been done in many countries, there is little evidence that students of different cultures or social classes have significantly different conceptual frameworks, or that conceptual differences are responsible for group differences in achievement. Conceptual change teaching can improve the learning of many students, but it shows little evidence of reducing the achievement gap. For tools and methods that help us to address these unanswered questions, we will need to look to other traditions.

SOCIOCULTURAL TRADITION: SCIENTIFIC LITERACY AS PARTICIPATION IN A DISCOURSE COMMUNITY

The conceptual change tradition explains the failure of students to learn the science that they are taught in schools in terms of hidden conflicts—conflicts between scientific conceptual frameworks and the conceptual frameworks that students develop through their own experience. Sociocultural researchers are also concerned about hidden conflicts, but they see those conflicts in quite different terms.

Like conceptual change research, sociocultural research in science education brings together ideas and practices from several longstanding intellectual traditions. Both perspectives draw on developmental psychology, but on different branches in the field. Whereas conceptual change research used ideas and methods developed by Piaget, sociocultural research has depended more on the research of Lev Vygotsky and his followers (see Chapter 3, this volume). In contrast to Piaget's emphasis on how children learn from their encounters with the material world, Vygotsky focused on how children learn from their participation in activities with other people.

Sociocultural researchers also share with conceptual change researchers an interest in research on scientific communities and scientific practices. Again, however, their interests are different. Whereas conceptual change researchers focus on intellectual history and philosophy of science, sociocultural researchers focus more on analyses of the culture and language of scientific communities (e.g., Kelly, Carlsen, & Cunningham, 1993; Latour & Woolgar, 1979; Traweek, 1988). Sociocultural researchers in science education also base their research on anthropological studies of how people learn to use practices and resources from their intellectual and cultural contexts in their approaches to reasoning and problem solving (e.g., Cole, Gay, Glick, & Sharp, 1971; Lave & Wenger, 1991; Rogoff & Lave, 1984; Scribner & Cole, 1983). Finally, sociocultural researchers are influenced by sociocultural research that focuses on careful analysis of the language that people use in particular situations and its meaning in social and cultural context (e.g., Gee, 1991a, 1991b; Michaels, 1991; O'Connor & Michaels, 1993; Tannen, 1996).

Although these are longstanding lines of research, their application to problems of science education is more recent. The record of science education research in the sociocultural tradition is substantial, but there is no 500-page bibliography like Duit's (2004). An article that illustrates the concerns and analytical methods of sociocultural research in science education is "Maestro, What is 'Quality'?: Language, Literacy, and Discourse in Project-Based Science" (Moje, Collazo, Carrillo, & Marx, 2001).

An Example of Sociocultural Research

Moje et al. (2001) analyzed science teaching and learning in a bilingual seventh-grade classroom. In many ways this class exemplified the best of what our current science education system has to offer. "Maestro Tomas" was a well-qualified teacher who had close and supportive relationships with his students. The air quality and water quality units he used were developed by a team of highly qualified teachers, researchers, and curriculum developers, who were supporting Maestro Tomas as he taught the units (Krajcik, Blumenfeld, Marx, Bass, & Fredricks, 1998). In spite of these admirable aspects of the classroom, the authors saw reasons to doubt how effective the unit had been. Their paper included (a) an explanation of their theoretical approach, (b) the methods and the results of their research, and (c) a discussion of the implications of their research for science education.

Theoretical Approach

The first five pages of the article are devoted to a literature review that describes the authors' theoretical approach. Like other sociocultural researchers, Moje et al. (2001) viewed conceptual frameworks as cultural products that are embedded within practices (such as explaining phenomena in the material world) and Discourses (Gee, 1996): "ways of knowing, doing, talking, reading, and writing, which are constructed and reproduced in social and cultural practice and interaction" (p. 470). Moje et al. argued that students in science classrooms are likely to experience not only conceptual conflict, but also conflict among multiple Discourses, each associated with its own community of practice, that intersect in science classrooms:

> Although several different intersecting Discourses can be at work in any one classroom, at least three are particularly salient for this discussion: disciplinary or content area, classroom, and social or everyday Discourses. These Discourses represent distinct ways of knowing, doing, talking, reading, and writing, and yet they overlap and inform one another in important ways. For example, the Discourses of classroom instruction are informed by what teachers and student believe about the nature of knowledge in the discipline . . . Similarly, the ways that students take up classroom or disciplinary Discourses are shaped by the social or everyday Discourses they bring to the classroom. (p. 471)

Research Methods and Results

Moje et al. (2001) used these ideas to analyze science teaching and learning in a seventh-grade classroom with students drawn from populations for which conceptual change teaching has generally been less successful. This is the longest section of the article—12 pages.

The teacher of the seventh-grade class, whom we call Maestro Tomas, was a native Spanish speaker of Dominican descent who had been reared in both the Dominican Republic and the United States. All but one student in the class of 32 were Latino or Latina, and some were relatively recent immigrants to the United States; 27 of these students demonstrated some level of proficiency in both Spanish and English. The remaining five students had very recently immigrated from Spanish-speaking countries, and so we identified them as Spanish-dominant, English language learners. (pp. 474–475)

Moje et al. (2001) observed Maestro Tomas and his students as they studied two project-based units, on air quality and water quality. Typically for sociocultural research, they relied on ethnographic data collection and analysis techniques:

Primary data sources included participant observation documented in field notes, formal and informal interviews with the teacher and students, and artifact collection, . . . student writings and curriculum work sheets. All classroom sessions were audio taped, and several were also videotaped. Another level of data collection included an electronic discussion of the analyses with Maestro Tomas. (p. 475)

The authors saw "competing Discourses" as a dominant theme that emerged from their analyses:

Our analyses of the Discursive demands of the curriculum enactment in this one classroom yielded a number of themes, but the dominant theme was one of competing Discourses. Each of the Discourses in the classroom had its own rules and expectations, usually implicit, and often in conflict. Maestro Tomas and his students had difficulty recognizing and orienting themselves to the demands and practices of these competing Discourses. Some of their difficulties arose from the nature of the curriculum itself, which encouraged students to contribute information in their everyday Discourses and included texts that presented information in a variety of Discourses, such as a fictional play in which the villains are the "awful eight pollutants." Thus, the curriculum introduced competing Discourses, but privileged the scientific (via pre-and posttesting, writing assignments, and final projects). (p. 482)

For Moje et al. (2001) the problem was not so much that scientific Discourse was privileged as that the privileging was hidden: The curriculum neither explicitly compared Discourses nor made it clear that scientific discourse was the preferred mode of expression on assignments and tests.

While the use of different Discourses might be justified as a means of making the curriculum more engaging for students, one effect was that students saw fewer models of the privileged scientific Discourse than they otherwise might have. Neither was it always clear that this Discourse was meant to be privileged, nor were its rules and expectations made explicit. The effects of these ambiguities were apparent in the students' work.

For example, Maestro Tomas asked students to respond—in English or Spanish—to this prompt midway through the study of air quality:

Imagine a factory opens in your neighborhood. Write a story about what would happen to the neighborhood and how would the air be affected.

The students responded to this kind of assignment enthusiastically, but they also responded in ways that would more appropriately be labeled creative writing rather than scientific or even informational writing. Of the 32 papers produced by students, all were written as journal-like responses, suspense stories, and journal entries written by fictional characters; 23 were stories or fictional journal entries, whereas the other nine were straightforward responses to the question, written as if an entry in a journal. . . . In fact, despite Maestro Tomas's focus on writing and reading as informational tools, and despite the enthusiasm and creativity that students brought to the writing of these papers, only 11 of the 32 pieces incorporated terms or phrases drawn from the project work. (pp. 483–484)

Discussion and Implications

To resolve these conflicts in ways that enable students to master scientific discourse, Moje et al. (2001) turned to the ideas of Kris Gutierrez and her colleagues about the creation of *congruent third spaces:*

> Gutierrez et al. (1999) argued that the weaving together of counterscripts (what we have been calling everyday Discourses) with official scripts (or in this case, scientific Discourses) constructs a third space "in which alternative and competing discourses and positionings transform conflict and difference into rich zones of collaboration and learning." (Gutierrez, Baquedano-Lopez, Alvarez, & Chiu, 1999, as cited in Moje et al., p. 487)

Moje et al. further suggested criteria for the successful creation of congruent third spaces and the ways in which Maestro Tomas and his students had fallen short of this ideal:

> To develop congruent third spaces for language, literacy, and science learning in diverse classrooms, four characteristics of classroom interaction seem necessary: (a) drawing from students' everyday Discourses and knowledges, (b) developing students' awareness of those various Discourses and knowledges (cf. New London Group, 1996), (c) connecting these everyday knowledges and Discourses with the science discourse genre of science classrooms and of the science community, and (d) negotiating understanding of both Discourses and knowledges so that they not only inform the other, but also merge to construct a new kind of discourse and knowledge. Maestro Tomas and the written curriculum achieved the first step of constructing congruent third spaces for the development of scientific literacy, but needed to take that first step further. (p. 489)

General Characteristics of Sociocultural Research

Although the brief summary of the article by Moje et al. (2001) does not do justice to the interest of their results or the complexity of their arguments, it does illustrate some of the key characteristics that their research shares with other research in the sociocultural tradition. I discuss some of those characteristics below, then conclude with some thoughts on the power and limitations of sociocultural research on science learning.

Characteristics of Sociocultural Research

Many of the characteristics of sociocultural programs of research and development are apparent in the article by Moje et al. (2001). As in the section on conceptual change research, I use the commonplaces from the introduction—view of the nature

of science, view of students and learning, methods, and implications for practice—
to characterize this research tradition and compare it with the conceptual change
tradition.

Science as a discourse community.   In contrast to conceptual change researchers' emphasis on scientists' dialogues with nature, sociocultural researchers
focus primarily on scientists' dialogues with people. For Moje and other sociocultural researchers, scientists are participants in communities of practice with shared
linguistic and social norms, values, and patterns of activity. Scientists' language
and practices give them agency in both the social and material worlds. Thus, a primary task of science education is to help students control the linguistic and cultural
resources that they need to participate in this privileged Discourse.

Learning as control of multiple discourses.   Like other sociocultural researchers,
Moje et al. (2001) portrayed students as participants in multiple communities of
practice, each with its own language, values, and practices. Students entering school
have not participated in scientific communities of practices, though some students
come from home communities whose language and practices are much closer to scientific language and practice than others. Students learn science when they are able
to adopt scientific language, values, and social norms for the purposes of participating in scientific practices, such as inquiry and application of scientific concepts.

Thus there are interesting parallels and differences between the arguments of
Moje et al. (2001) and those of conceptual change researchers like Snir et al. (2003).
Researchers in both traditions attribute students' difficulties in learning science to
hidden conflicts. At this point, however, the arguments diverge. Rather than conceptual conflicts, Moje et al. saw conflicts among Discourses—"ways of knowing,
doing, talking, reading, and writing, which are constructed and reproduced in social
and cultural practice and interaction" (p. 470). In this situation, conceptual change
teaching methods, which rely heavily on rational argument within a shared scientific Discourse, are not likely to be sufficient. Maestro Tomas and his students needed
to find ways of resolving conflicts not only among conceptual frameworks, but also
among values, social norms, and ways of using language.

Research methods for analyzing learners' culture, language, and practices.   In
contrast with Snir et al. (2003), who collected data in carefully controlled settings
that would allow for a detailed analysis of students' conceptions, Moje et al. (2001)
used more naturalistic methods, seeking to understand how Maestro Tomas and his
students talked, wrote, and acted as they worked together. They sought to understand how these individuals operated within the social context of the classroom.
Rather than conceptual knowledge, their analyses of learning focused on students'
use of language, including choice of vocabulary and genre.

It is also interesting to note what these authors and their reviewers considered
essential information about their methods. In contrast with Snir et al. (2003), Moje
et al. (2001) informed readers about the linguistic and cultural backgrounds of each
author, Maestro Tomas, and all of his students.

> The research and development team was composed of two Latinas, two Latinos (one of
> whom was Maestro Tomas), and two European Americans, one male and one female. All

Latino and Latina members are fluent Spanish and English speakers, whereas the European American team members are monolingual. (Moje et al., p. 475)

They did not have formal instruments for structured data collection or detailed descriptions of their analytical methods. Thus, while the conceptual change researchers paid careful attention to the details of methods for data collection and analysis, the sociocultural researchers paid careful attention to the backgrounds, possible biases, and intellectual resources of the researchers themselves.

Teaching methods for sociocultural learning. Sociocultural researchers focus their attention on methods that help learners master language and culturally embedded practices, beginning with the problem of how teachers and students can communicate meaningfully across linguistic and cultural differences. Moje et al. (2001) focused on the development of congruent third spaces in classrooms, where everyday and scientific Discourses and knowledge can be negotiated and merged to create new understanding. Within these third spaces sociocultural conflicts can be resolved, and students from different home cultures can contribute intellectual resources to the classroom community. Although conceptual conflict is a commonly proposed mechanism for learning in the conceptual change tradition, many sociocultural researchers focus on *apprenticeship* as a metaphor for learning (e.g., Collins, Brown, & Newman, 1989; Lave & Wenger, 1991).

Power and Limitations of Sociocultural Research

Although roots of the sociocultural research tradition extend back for decades, it is only in the last 10 years that its significance has been widely recognized by science educators. Compared with conceptual change research, sociocultural research has had less influence on science education policy and practice. This can be attributed partly to its relatively short history in the field, and partly to the methodological challenges that sociocultural research presents. It has been difficult to use sociocultural methods to collect quantitative data or to translate sociocultural ideas about teaching into prescriptions for reproducible practice. [Though, like conceptual change research, sociocultural research has produced "existence proofs" of excellent teaching based on sociocultural ideas. See, for example, Heath (1983, Chapter 9), O'Connor & Michaels (1993), and Rosebery, Warren, & Conant (1992)].

Furthermore, the ideas and methods of the sociocultural tradition are less familiar and more challenging to science educators than conceptual change ideas and methods. People who, like most science educators, have trained to be scientists or science teachers have had relatively little exposure to the linguistic and anthropological concepts that are central to sociocultural research. Education in the sciences emphasizes immersion in communities of scientific practice, but not awareness of the ways in which other communities of practice differ in cultural practices, values, and habits of mind that scientists take for granted. Thus, science educators must struggle to see hidden sociocultural conflicts and to make use of the cultural resources that children bring to science learning.

The struggle is worthwhile, however, because sociocultural research produces deep and compelling insights with respect to the two questions posed in the introduction to this chapter. With respect to the first question, about why students fail to learn science, sociocultural research adds to and deepens the insights of conceptual change research. We can see that students in school must deal with hidden cultural conflicts as well as hidden conceptual conflicts. Furthermore, the methods of sociocultural research can reveal those conflicts in particular classrooms and show how they inhibit students' science learning.

With respect to the second question, about the origins and persistence of the achievement gap, sociocultural research produces compelling insights. This research tradition reveals the many ways in which scientific discourse communities are built around the language, values, and social norms of their (mostly European middle class) members. Similarly, schools privilege the language, values, and social norms of their (mostly European middle class) teachers. Thus middle-class European children enter school with significant advantages over children from other social and cultural backgrounds.

Sociocultural researchers recognize that these advantages have emotional as well as intellectual consequences and, more fundamentally, that science learning is an emotional as well as an intellectual process. Many sociocultural researchers (e.g., Kurth, Anderson, & Palincsar, 2002; Ogbu, 1992; Steele, 1992, 1999) have investigated the effects of the accumulated weight of cultural differences on students' willingness to keep trying to succeed in school. Research by sociocultural researchers on engagement and alienation helps us to understand how apparently simple unmotivated behavior has deep roots in students' cultural histories and personal development, as well as in the ways that schooling privileges other cultures and values at the expense of their own. Thus, sociocultural researchers transform the essential motivational problem of teaching from one of remedying motivational deficiencies to one of finding new and more productive ways of making use of the cultural resources that all children bring to school.

In summary, sociocultural researchers have developed analytical tools that they can apply to issues that conceptual change researchers relegate to craft. In particular, sociocultural research helps us to understand science learning as a linguistic, cultural, and emotional process, as well as a process of conceptual change.

CRITICAL TRADITION:
SCIENTIFIC LITERACY AS EMPOWERMENT

Researchers in the conceptual change and sociocultural traditions both attribute students' difficulties in learning science to hidden conflicts, either conceptual or cultural. Researchers in the critical tradition recognize the existence and importance of these conflicts, but they are centrally concerned with the ways in which these conflicts are shaped and how their outcomes are determined by power and ideology.

Critical researchers in science education are heirs to a long intellectual history of scholars who sought to show how dominant classes manipulated "truth" to their advantage, including scientific truth (e.g., Foucault, 1977; Scott, 1998). Feminist critics of science (e.g., Harding, 1991; Keller, 1985) have been especially influential among science educators. Other critical researchers in education have focused on how students in school who are not members of dominant classes have been marginalized and labeled "disadvantaged" or "at risk" (e.g., Delpit, 1995; Natriello, McDill, &

Pallas, 1990). In recent years, critical researchers in science education have combined these two strands to investigate specifically how some students are marginalized in our science education system. An article that illustrates the concerns and analytical methods of critical research in science education is "The Culture of Power and Science Education: Learning from Miguel," by Angela Barton and Kimberly Yang (2000).

An Example of Critical Research

Barton and Yang (2000) sought to understand and report on the life history and science learning of a young father, "Miguel," who was living in a homeless shelter in New York City with his wife, "Marisol," and their two children. Their article begins with a two-page vignette that describes the essential facts of Miguel's case: He was a Puerto Rican high-school dropout who never took science in high school in spite of a continuing interest in nature. He later earned a high-school equivalency diploma and supported Marisol and their children by working as an industrial painter of fire trucks. When his company downsized, however, Miguel was not able to find new employment, so his family came to the homeless shelter where Barton and Yang met and interviewed him.

The authors sought to describe and explore the implications of Miguel's life history and of the beliefs that he revealed in his interviews. After the opening vignette, their article includes a discussion of the culture of power in schools and in science education (three pages), a description of their research orientations and methods (one page), an interpretation of Miguel's story (six pages), and a discussion of the implications of cases like Miguel's for science education (four pages).

The Culture of Power

Barton and Yang (2000) positioned themselves as advocates for Miguel and in opposition to the "culture of power" that has a pervasive influence on schools and school science:

> The "culture of power" and its effects are part of nearly every institution in the United States, including the institution of schooling. . . . Delpit (1988) argues that without making the rules for the culture of power explicit, those who are not familiar with the culture of power will lack opportunities for upward mobility, be perceived as deficient, inferior, or disadvantaged, and be viewed as the cause of society's problems. (pp. 873–874)

Like other researchers taking a critical perspective, Barton and Yang (2000) saw abundant evidence that the culture of power affects science education as well as other aspects of schooling:

> Textbooks and other curricular materials often hide the people, tools, and social contexts involved in the construction of science. The result is often a fact-oriented science which appears decontextualized, objective, rational, and mechanistic (Brickhouse, 1994). Science labs and classrooms are typically structured hierarchically with the teacher and the text controlling what knowledge counts (Brickhouse, 1994). (Barton & Yang, p. 875)

Research Methods and Interpretations

Barton and Yang's (2000) critical perspective was also apparent in their explanations and justifications of their research methods. They were explicit in describing their own backgrounds and perspectives:

> As co-authors we come to this research from two different perspectives: One of us is an ethnic minority, the daughter of immigrants, bi-lingual, and raised on the west coast in a family that during her lifetime moved from "poor immigrant status" to upper-middle class professional. The other of us is a white, middle-class woman raised on the east coast with experience as a homeless individual in the same metropolitan area as the family presented in this paper. (p. 877)

For Barton and Yang (2000), ideas about the culture of power provided a critical lens for understanding Miguel's life story. Their case study of Miguel focused on "four key experiences in which culture, power, school, and science played out in Miguel's life: studying/doing herpetology, dropping out of school and school science, critiquing peer culture, and child rearing" (p. 878). Briefly, they reported the following:

Studying/Doing herpetology.   "Miguel often expressed a love of nature, and had for a while maintained his own black-market herpetology business, raising reptiles and selling them for a profit.
He was drawn to a way of explaining the world around him that went beyond books. The world—the turtles, rats, snakes, and other creatures he studied—was real life. However, the science to which Miguel referred was always outside of school, always a part of his own research into the world around him" (Barton & Yang, 2000, p. 878).

Dropping out of school and science.   Miguel's teachers and counselors placed him on a vocational track, never suggesting that taking a science course was even a possibility. In Miguel's school, science was clearly meant for people other than him. "In retrospect, Miguel believed these actions on the part of his teachers and his counselors only reinforced his belief that school science and scientific careers were not realistic options for youth from the 'hood'" (Barton & Yang, 2000, p. 879). In response, "Miguel dropped out of school when he was a junior, and when in his words, he had 'done all of the time [he] could handle'" (Barton & Yang, p. 879).

Critiquing peer culture.   Miguel's experiences led him to a complex understanding of the difficult relationships between his own culture and the culture of power. On the one hand, he recognized how the institutions of society had denied him opportunities. On the other hand, he recognized that the street culture in which he grew up, valuing "an image of toughness" and failing to look toward the future, had also prevented him from developing the knowledge and skills he needed to succeed. "As Miguel stated, 'Puerto Ricans are not respected in American culture, and in turn we [Puerto Ricans] make no effort to gain respect'" (Barton & Yang, 2000, p. 881).

Child rearing.   Miguel removed his daughter from an after-school program at the shelter and was reluctant to send her to a predominantly Puerto Rican public school, stating that he "'preferred to send [his] children to a school populated predominately by whites and run by whites.' In his opinion, 'they [Puerto Ricans] can learn from others because they are succeeding and we [Puerto Ricans] are not'" (Barton & Yang, 2000, p. 881).

Discussion and Implications

Barton and Yang (2000) told a story of frustration and disappointment. They saw the reasons for Miguel's frustration in the ability of "those in power [to] set the discursive norms and values, leaving those belonging to other cultural perspectives to be perceived as different and deficient" (p. 886). What can science educators learn from Miguel and his experiences? Barton and Yang suggested an answer, posing the question: "How might Miguel's story and our understanding of the culture of power inform efforts to promote equitable science education reforms?" (p. 885).

> We believe that part of the answer to this question lies in moving beyond the rhetoric of "science for all" to critically understanding how culture and power influence what creating an inclusive science community might mean. One way to ameliorate this situation is to examine what has been traditionally considered school science versus non-school science. The silencing of scientific knowledge that does not fall in the realm of recognized school science has resulted in exclusion of certain populations toward the formal learning of science (Eisenhart, Finkel, & Marion, 1996). (Barton and Yang, p. 886)

General Characteristics of Critical Research

This brief summary of Barton and Yang's (2000) article illustrates some of the key characteristics that their research shares with other research in the critical tradition. I discuss some of those characteristics in the following section, then conclude with some thoughts on the power and limitations of critical research on science learning.

Characteristics of Critical Research

Many of the characteristics of critical programs of research and criticism are apparent in Barton and Yang's (2000) article. As in the sections on conceptual change and sociocultural research, I use the commonplaces from the introduction—a view of the nature of science, a view of students and learning, methods, and implications for practice—to characterize this research tradition and compare it with the conceptual change tradition.

Science as inherently ideological and institutional. Researchers in all three traditions recognize that scientific truth is not absolute; scientists are inevitably limited by the perspectives and resources available to them. Conceptual change researchers see scientific truth as historically situated: Scientists of any generation are limited by the data available to them and the perspectives that they have inherited from their intellectual forbears. Sociocultural researchers see scientific truth as also culturally situated: Different cultures or subcultures decide what is true according to their own culturally specific standards and forms of argument. Critical researchers see truth as the servant of power: Dominant classes of people arrange the "rules of the game" so that their knowledge and their ways of thinking and acting are seen a superior to those of other classes. Thus claims that scientific knowledge is objective or disinterested mask the ways in which scientific knowledge and practice serve the culture of power.

Science learning as indoctrination or the development of critical consciousness. Critical researchers see students as participants in power relationships and institutions: Some students are given preferred access to the power of scientific knowledge and practice while others are excluded. They see current science education largely as a form of indoctrination: Students are taught to accept as truth knowledge that is designed to serve the interests of the powerful. They advocate an alternative kind of science learning—the development of critical literacy: Students need to learn not only how to participate in scientific communities but also to question and criticize the relationships between those communities and other powerful interests.

Research methods for discovering and analyzing ideologies and power relationships. Barton and Yang's (2000) approach to describing their backgrounds, credentials, and research methods differs from the approaches of the other focus articles in ways that reveal differences in the beliefs of the authors about what counts as significant knowledge and how knowledge claims can be validated. The authors of the other two focus articles used the traditional "scientific" passive voice in describing their methods and described themselves in the third person. They sought to reassure readers that they had taken appropriate steps to avoid bias in their reporting. For Snir et al. (2003), this meant careful attention to instruments and methods. For Moje et al. (2001), it meant triangulating among multiple data sources and submitting their knowledge claims to extensive intersubjective verification.

In contrast, Barton and Yang (2000) described their research methods in less than one page, writing in the first person. They informed readers about their backgrounds and interests so that readers could decide for themselves how to interpret the case study. Their goal was not to generate independently verifiable knowledge claims; instead they aspired to "intersubjectively shared theoretical perspectives and life experiences" (p. 877).

Underlying Barton and Yang's (2000) description of methods were different beliefs about the nature of the knowledge they produced and about their relationship with their informants, their readers, and social institutions. Critical researchers question whether "unbiased" or "fair-minded" knowledge is possible. They find bias to be inherent in our backgrounds and perspectives, so knowledge that claims to be unbiased typically serves the interests of powerful interests and institutions. Thus the fairest position researchers can take is to be honest about their perspectives, their biases, and whose interests they seek to serve.

Teaching methods to achieve critical literacy. Critical researchers have also developed ideas about how changes in the organization and ideology of schooling can be used to improve instruction, including changed power relationships in schools and the acceptance of knowledge that is currently outside the bounds of school science. They maintain that successful learning involves changes in powerful adults as well as powerless students. For examples of successful critical pedagogy, critical researchers often point to programs on the margins of the formal institutions of schooling, such as alternative schools or out-of-school programs like the one at the homeless shelter attended by Miguel's daughter (Barton, 1998) or the programs for disenfranchised poor started by Paulo Freire (1970/1993). Other critical researchers examine the practices of teachers in public schools, often minority teachers, who engage children in meaningful, important learning (e.g., Delpit, 1995; Ladson-Billings, 1994). A common theme that runs through all of these accounts of successful learning is that learners achieve critical literacy—the ability to see and criticize how power works to privilege some people and some forms of knowledge at the expense of others.

Power and Limitations of Critical Research

Critical research has had less influence on policy and practice than the other traditions, in part because critical researchers openly question the premises on which policy is made, science teaching practice is based, and science achievement is measured. In particular, they challenge science educators to think about our own roles in maintaining injustice and inequality in our schools. Researchers in all three traditions proclaim their commitments to social justice and their desire to improve the science literacy of less successful students. The conceptual change and sociocultural traditions implicitly assume that these improvements can come at little or no cost to students who are currently successful in school (including the children of science educators). The critical tradition challenges that assumption. Critical researchers point out that the competition for positions of power and influence in society has always been a zero-sum game, with losers as well as winners. Are comfortable professionals like science educators willing to work for the fundamental changes in society that would really change the relationships among those of us who are more and less powerful?

Critical researchers would respond to the two key questions posed in the introduction, about the ineffectiveness of our science education system and the persistence of the achievement, by challenging their implicit premises. Is it not possible that the science education system is doing quite well what it was designed to do— to restrict access to the true power of scientific reasoning to a small elite? The remaining students are fed a thin gruel of "facts" presented in ways that reinforce the correctness of their inferior position in society. The hidden message is that the people who produce and distribute the facts are different—smarter and better qualified than the students could ever be. It is not quite right to say that the people who benefit from the culture of power, including teachers, professors, and science educators, are deliberately making this happen. However, we are acquiescing in a system that serves our interests and the interests of our powerful sponsors far better than it serves the interests of the powerless students entrusted to our care.

In summary, critical researchers have developed analytical tools that reveal the hidden workings of the culture of power in the institutions that society has made responsible for science education and in the knowledge that they teach. In particular, critical research helps us to understand the ways in which the achievement gap is not an unfortunate accident; it persists because it serves the interests of those who benefit from their preferred access to and control over scientific knowledge.

CONCLUSION

Looking collectively at these three research traditions, where do we stand? We still must decide whether the glass—our understanding of how people learn science and how to improve science learning—is half full or half empty. On the half-empty side, it is clear that as a field we still have a lot to learn about science learning. Here are three important issues that are not fully addressed by the three focus articles or by the research traditions that they exemplify.

Relationships among Traditions

One question that we face concerns what we can understand about science learning by looking collectively at research from the three traditions. Are these traditions, like subdisciplines of biology, looking in complementary ways at different subsystems? In that case, the collective insights from the three traditions provide us with a richer and deeper understanding of science learning than we could achieve from any one of the traditions alone—the whole is greater than the sum of its parts. Or, alternatively, are the three traditions more like contending political parties or schools of thought, each rejecting the ideas of the others and arguing for the superiority of its theories and methods? In that case, we have to choose one tradition while rejecting many of the claims of the others—the whole is less than the sum of its parts.

I see our current situation as being somewhere between these two alternatives. On the one hand, there are real and important conflicts among the traditions, particularly with respect to questions of epistemology and research method. For example, critical theorists see science education communities as facing a basic choice about whose interests we will serve with the knowledge that we produce. Will we produce knowledge that reflects the perspectives and serves the interests of the powerful or the powerless in our society?

While acknowledging the importance of this question, conceptual change and sociocultural researchers are more sanguine about the possibility of producing knowledge that transcends the interests and perspectives of its sponsors. For example, Shakespeare's art and Galileo's science gave us insights into the human condition and the material world that could not have been anticipated by their wealthy sponsors. Is it not possible that, in our modest ways, science educators could do the same? Conceptual change and sociocultural researchers are also concerned that critical researchers' stances of open advocacy and relative lack of concern about procedures for verification of knowledge claims will undermine long-term programs of knowledge building. Thus each tradition holds ideas about the nature of grounded knowledge and the research methods appropriate to achieving that knowledge that are considered to be deeply problematic by practitioners of the other traditions.

The differences in perspectives among the traditions run deep, as do the common interests and concerns that lead people to do research on science learning. Resolving these differences must ultimately be a communal effort. Individual researchers may achieve syntheses that they find personally satisfying, but those syntheses can bring science educators together around common perspectives only in so far as they are accepted by the communities of practice associated with the different traditions. We should never expect differences in perspective and method to be completely resolved, but there are reasons to hope that researchers in different traditions can become increasingly respectful of one another's insights and understanding of one another's methods.

Understanding Learners' "Dialogues with Nature"

Sharma and Anderson (2003) characterized scientific communities as carrying on two simultaneous dialogues: a dialogue with nature in which scientists seek to create and understand new experiences with natural systems and phenomena, and a dialogue among people in which scientific communities submit the knowledge claims of their members to a process of collective validation. In studying science learning, all three of the research traditions discussed in this chapter have given us more insight into learners' dialogues among people than into learners' dialogues with nature. Our ideas and our language are strongly constrained by our individual and collective experiences with the material world, but none of the traditions has produced fully satisfactory accounts of the interactions among experience, individual cognition, and social communication.

Developing Prescriptions for Policy and Practice

Research on learning has given us increasingly powerful analytical tools that improve our understanding of why educational institutions fail to engender scientific literacy in many students. As a field, we have been far less successful in translating that analytical power into practical results. We need to find better ways to use this understanding as a basis for design work in science teaching and teacher education—programs and strategies that move beyond existence proofs to help large numbers of science learners. We also need better ways of using our understanding to develop arguments that influence policies and resources for science education.

Putting the Issues in Perspective

On the other hand, it is hard not to be impressed with the progress that our field has made in understanding science learning. As I write this, it has been over 25 years since I attended my first NARST Conference in 1979. The theme of that conference was "Paradigms for Research in Science Education." The three research paradigms discussed were (a) the behaviorist theory of Robert Gagne, (b) the verbal learning theory of David Ausubel, and (c) the developmental theory of Jean Piaget.

Looking back at these three theories, I can see the precursors to some of the theories that I have written about in this chapter, especially conceptual change. At the same time, I cannot help but be struck by how inadequate they look in comparison with the research described in this chapter. Those theories relied on thin, impoverished descriptions of scientific knowledge. They depended mostly on laboratory studies for their data; they largely lacked the analytical power to make sense of science learning in natural situations, inside or outside of school classrooms. They had little to say with respect to the two key questions about science learning posed at the beginning of this chapter. As a field, we have learned a lot since 1979, and we still have a lot to learn—all things considered, not a bad place to be.

ACKNOWLEDGMENTS

Thanks to Fouad Abd-El-Khalick, David Jonassen, and Ron Marx, who reviewed this chapter.

REFERENCES

American Association for the Advancement of Science. (1993). *Benchmarks for science literacy.* New York: Oxford University Press.

Barton, A. C. (1998). Teaching science with homeless children: Pedagogy, representation, and identity. *Journal of Research in Science Teaching, 35,* 379–394.

Barton, A. C., & Yang, K. (2000). The culture of power and science education: Learning from Miguel. *Journal of Research in Science Teaching, 37,* 871–889.

Blank, R. K., & Langesen, D. (2001). *State indicators of science and mathematics education 2001.* Washington, DC: Council of Chief State School Officers.

Cohen, D. K., & Hill, H. G. (2000). Instructional policy and classroom performance: The mathematics reform in California. *Teachers College Record, 102,* 294–343.

Cole, M., Gay, J., Glick, J. A., & Sharp, D. W. (1971). *The cultural context of learning and thinking.* New York: Basic Books.

Collins, A., Brown, J. S., & Newman, S. E. (1989). Cognitive apprenticeship: Teaching the craft of reading, writing, and mathematics. In L. B. Resnick (Ed.) *Knowing, learning, and instruction: Essays in honor of Robert Glaser* (pp. 453–494). Hillsdale, NJ: Lawrence Erlbaum Associates.

Delpit, L. (1995). *Other people's children: Cultural conflict in the classroom.* New York: New Press.

Driver, R., Squires, A., Rushworth, P., & Wood-Robinson, V. (1994). *Making sense of secondary science: Research into children's ideas.* New York: Routledge.

Duit, R. (2004). *Bibliography: Students' and teachers' conceptions and science education.* Retrieved September 15, 2004, from http://www.ipn.uni-kiel.de/aktuell/stcse/download_stcse.html

Elmore, R. F. (2002). Beyond instructional leadership: Hard questions about practice. *Educational Leadership, 59*(8), 22–25.

Feurzeig, W., & Roberts, N. (Eds.). (1999). *Modeling and simulation in science and mathematics education.* New York: Springer-Verlag.

Foucault, M. (1977). Truth and power. In D. Rabinow (Ed.), *Power: The essential works of Michel Foucault 1954–1984* (Vol. 3, pp. 51–75). London: Penguin.

Freire, P. (1993). *Pedagogy of the oppressed* (M. B. Ramos, Trans.). New York: Criterion (original work published 1970).

Gamoran, A., Anderson, C. W., Quiroz, P. A., Secada, W. G., Williams, T., & Ashmann, S. (2003). *Transforming teaching in math and science: How schools and districts can support change.* New York: Teachers College Press.

Gee, J. P. (1991a). The narrativization of experience in the oral style. In C. Mitchell & K. Weiler (Eds.), *Rewriting literacy: Culture and the discourse of the other* (pp. 77–101). New York: Bergin & Garvey.

Gee, J. P. (1991b). What is literacy? In C. Mitchell & K. Weiler (Eds.), *Rewriting literacy: Culture and the discourse of the other* (pp. 3–12). New York: Bergin & Garvey.

Gee, J. (1996). *Social linguistics and literacies: Ideology in discourses* (2nd ed.). London: Falmer Press.

Harding, S. (1991). *Whose science? Whose knowledge?* Ithaca, NY: Cornell University Press.

Heath, S. B. (1983). *Ways with words: Language, life, and work in communities and classrooms.* New York: Cambridge University Press.

Keller, E. F. (1985). *Reflections on gender and science.* New Haven, CT: Yale University Press.

Kelly, G. J., Carlsen, W. S., & Cunningham, C. M. (1993). Science education in sociocultural context: Perspectives from the sociology of science. *Science Education, 77,* 207–220.

Kim, J. J., Crasco, L. M., Smith, R. B., Johnson, G., Karantonis, A., & Leavitt, D. J. (2001). *Academic excellence for all urban students: Their acomplishment in science and mathematics.* Norwood, MA: Systemic Research.

Krajcik, J., Blumenfeld, P. C., Marx, R. W., Bass, K. M., & Fredricks, J. (1998). Inquiry in project-based science classrooms: Initial attempts by middle school students. *Journal of the Learning Sciences, 7,* 313–350.

Kuhn, T. (1970). *The structure of scientific revolutions* (2nd ed.). Chicago: University of Chicago Press.

Kurth, L., Anderson, C. W., & Palincsar, A. S. (2002). The case of Carla: Dilemmas of helping all students to understand science. *Science Education, 86,* 287–313.

Ladson-Billings, G. (1994). *The dreamkeepers.* San Francisco, CA: Jossey-Bass.

Latour, B., & Woolgar, S. (1979). *Laboratory life: The construction of scientific facts.* Princeton, NJ: Princeton University Press.

Lave, J., & Wenger, E. (1991). *Situated learning: Legitimate peripheral participation.* New York: Cambridge University Press.

Linn, M., & Hsi, S. (2000). *Computers, teachers, peers: Science learning partners.* Mahwah, NJ: Lawrence Erlbaum Associates.

Michaels, S. (1991). Hearing the connections in children's oral and written discourse. In C. Mitchell & K. Weiler (Eds.), *Rewriting literacy: Culture and the discourse of the other* (pp. 103–122). New York: Bergin & Garvey.

Moje, E. B., Collazo, T., Carrillo, R., & Marx, R. W. (2001). Maestro, what is "quality"?: Language, literacy and discourse in project-based science. *Journal of Research in Science Teaching, 38,* 469–498.

National Research Council. (1996). *National science education standards.* Washington, DC: National Academy Press.

Natriello, G., McDill, E., & Pallas, A. (1990). *Schooling disadvantaged children.* New York: Teachers College Press.

O'Connor, M. C., & Michaels, S. (1993). Aligning academic task and participation status through revoicing: analysis of a classroom discourse strategy. *Anthropology and Education Quarterly, 24,* 318–335.

Ogbu, J. U. (1992). Understanding cultural diversity and learning. *Educational Researcher, 21*(8), 5–14.

Posner, J., Strike, K., Hewson, P., & Gertzog, W. (1982). Accommodation of a scientific conception: Toward a theory of conceptual change. *Science Education, 66,* 211–227.

Rogoff, B., & Lave, J. (Eds.). (1984). *Everyday cognition.* Cambridge, MA: Harvard University Press.

Rosebery, A. S., Warren, B., & Conant, F. R. (1992). Appropriating scientific discourse: Findings from language minority classrooms. *Journal of the Learning Sciences, 2,* 61–94.

Schmidt, W. H., McKnight, C. C., Houang, R. T., Wang, H., Wiley, D. E., & Cogan, L. S. (2001). *Why schools matter: A cross-national comparison of curriculum and learning.* San Francisco: Jossey-Bass.

Scott, J. C. (1998). *Seeing like a state: How certain schemes to improve human conditions have failed.* New Haven, CT: Yale University Press.

Scribner, S., & Cole, M. (1983). *The psychology of literacy.* Cambridge, MA: Harvard University Press.

Sharma, A., & Anderson, C. W. (2003, March). *Transforming scientists' science into school science.* Presented at the annual meeting of the National Association for Research in Science Teaching, Philadelphia.

Snir, J., Smith, C. L., & Grosslight, L. (1993). Conceptually enhanced similations: A computer tool for science teaching. *Journal of Science Education and Technology, 2*(2), 373–388.

Snir, J., Smith, C. L., & Raz, G. (2003). Linking phenomena with competing underlying models: A software tool for introducing students to the particulate model of matter. *Science Education, 87,* 794–830.

Steele, C. M. (1992). Race and the schooling of black Americans. *The Atlantic Monthly, 269*(4), 68–78.

Steele, C. M. (1999). Thin ice: "Stereotype threat" and black college students. *The Atlantic Monthly, 284*(2), 44–54.

Tannen, D. (1996). *Gender and discourse.* New York: Oxford University Press.

Toulmin, S. (1961). *Foresight and understanding.* Britain: The Anchor Press.

Toulmin, S. (1972). *Human understanding.* Princeton, NJ: Princeton University Press.

Traweek, S. (1988). *Beamtimes and lifetimes: The world of high energy physics.* Cambridge, MA: Harvard University Press.

White, B. Y., & Frederiksen, J. R. (1998). Inquiry, modeling, and metacognition: Making science accessible to all students. *Cognition and Instruction, 16*, 3–118.

CHAPTER 2

Student Conceptions and Conceptual Learning in Science

Phil Scott
Hilary Asoko
John Leach
University of Leeds, United Kingdom

Alice is a 14-year-old high school student, and in her science classes she has been taught quite a lot about the scientific concept of energy. Prior to these lessons Alice certainly used the word "energy" in her every day speech, whether in talking about "having no energy," referring to the "high energy music" of her favorite band, or trying to reduce "energy consumption" to preserve the environment. During the lessons, Alice struggled to come to terms with some of the scientific ideas, which often seemed to go against common sense. Indeed, her teacher had warned that "this is always a difficult topic to get hold of." Nevertheless, by the end of the teaching, Alice (who is a bright girl) was able to use the idea of energy in answering questions about batteries and bulbs, chemical reactions, and photosynthesis. However, she still struggled, for example, to see how the products of an exothermic chemical reaction could have the same mass as the reactants, even though "energy has been transferred to the surroundings," and it didn't make sense to her that a soda can on her desk "has gravitational potential energy," even though it "just sits there."

It is clear that Alice has learned something about the concept of energy. How might we conceptualize what has happened to Alice in these particular lessons? What do we mean when we say that Alice has "learned something about energy"? What factors act to influence her learning? What happens to Alice's existing ideas about energy being consumed, in the face of her new learning? Why should she find some of the scientific energy ideas strange and difficult to understand?

There are many questions that might be posed about any such learning event. The aim of this chapter is to review the different approaches taken to characterizing science concept learning. We begin by providing a brief historical overview of trends in the way in which research on conceptual learning has developed over the last 40 years or so. We then introduce the key features that have guided our structuring of the review, before presenting the detailed review itself. Given the sheer volume of literature addressing student conceptions and conceptual learning in science, it is not possible to be comprehensive in coverage. Rather, we have cited studies which, in our judgment, best illustrate the key features guiding our review, including work, where possible, that has been influential in various parts of the English-speaking world.

Although there are significant and fundamental differences among some of the approaches taken to conceptualizing science learning, it is also the case that other differences arise simply because different aspects of the learning process are being addressed. Bearing this point in mind, we believe that some approaches offer potentially complementary perspectives. We return to this theme in the concluding section, where we discuss the ways in which these ideas about learning might be drawn upon to illuminate and inform science teaching and learning in classroom settings.

STARTING POINTS AND TRENDS IN CHARACTERIZING SCIENCE CONCEPT LEARNING

Perspectives on student concepts and conceptual learning in science have been heavily influenced by the seminal work of the Swiss genetic epistemologist Jean Piaget. This influence was particularly dominant during the 1960s and 1970s, as can be confirmed by looking through the citations of Piaget in papers published in the main science education journals of that period (see Erickson, 2000, p. 276). Piaget described an interactive learning process whereby an individual makes sense of the world through cognitive schemes, which are themselves modified as a result of the individual's actions on objects in the world. This model is summarized in the statement "L'intelligence organise le monde en s'organisant elle-même"[1] (Piaget, 1937). Piaget emphasized the significance of the child's social environment for knowledge development, claiming that: "Society is the supreme unit, and the individual can only achieve his inventions and intellectual constructions insofar as he is the seat of collective interactions that are naturally dependent, in level and value, on society as a whole" (Piaget, 1971, p. 368). Nonetheless, in most of Piaget's writing—and writing addressing the significance of Piagetian theorizing for science education—knowledge is portrayed as schemata in the individual's head, with little prominence being given to wider social aspects. The proposed mechanism for changes in intellectual organization as a result of interactions with the world (termed *adaptation*) involves the processes of assimilation and accommodation (Piaget, 1952). Assimilation is the process by which an individual interprets particular sensory information and in so doing includes that information in his/her existing cognitive structure. Accommodation is the process by which cognitive structure adapts in order to make sense of specific information. Assimilation and accommodation cannot be dissociated: whenever an individual interacts with sensory information, both assimilation and accommodation take place.

---

1. Intelligence organizes the world by organizing itself.

Although Piaget was primarily interested in development as a result of maturation, rather than learning as a result of instruction (Piaget, 1964), his empirical work addressed the development of children's knowledge about various aspects of the natural world, including life (Piaget, 1929); time (Piaget, 1946); and mass, weight, and volume (Piaget, 1930). Drawing upon this body of empirical work, an account of conceptual change based upon the development of content-independent logical structures was proposed (Piaget & Inhelder, 1956). Characteristic stages in the development of logical thinking were set out, based upon students' abilities to perform tasks involving skills such as conservation and seriation (the serial ordering of items). The concrete operational stage, for example, runs between approximately 2 and 12 years and is characterized by the development and coordination of conceptual schemes, including conservation, classification, and seriation. Children at the concrete operational stage are not capable of performing operations at a purely symbolic level, however; that competence is characteristic of the formal operational stage.

Piaget's work has influenced perspectives on student conceptions and conceptual learning in several ways. His account of how individuals come to know can be seen in much writing about students' conceptions, conceptual change, and personal constructivism through references to assimilation and accommodation. Piaget's methods for probing an individual's understanding, which involve an interviewer asking children questions without attempting to "lead" their responses (Piaget, 1929), have also been drawn upon in research on students' alternative conceptions. Furthermore, Piagetian stage theory has been drawn upon to inform science curriculum design and sequencing [e.g., *Science Curriculum Improvement Study* in the United States (Andersson, 1976) and *Cognitive Acceleration through Science Education* in Britain (Adey & Shayer, 1993)].

Various criticisms of the use of Piagetian theory in science education have been advanced. Carey (1985), Donaldson (1978), and Driver (1978) questioned the empirical basis on which claims for characteristic stages in logico-mathematical thinking were founded. Specific criticisms include the following: (a) tasks requiring identical logico-mathematical reasoning are made easier or more difficult by the degree of familiarity with the task's context (Donaldson); (b) tasks characteristic of a given stage can be performed by much younger children (Driver); and (c) the analysis used in Piagetian research is designed to validate existing theory rather than account for children's reasoning (Driver; Carey).

Although there has been a decline in the influence of Piagetian approaches since the 1970s, there remains a significant line of research on domain-general reasoning skills in science learning (e.g., Koslowski, 1996; Kuhn, 1991; Kuhn, Amsel, & O'Loughlin, 1988; Metz, 1997), as well as accounts of science learning that draw on Piaget's work (e.g., Adey & Shayer, 1993; Lawson, 1985; Shayer, 2003).

Perhaps the most significant break from the Piagetian account of conceptual learning in science can be traced back to the developmental psychology of David Ausubel (1968). Ausubel argued that the most significant influence on the learners' conceptual development is their existing conceptual knowledge in the target domain. During the early 1970s, a small number of empirical studies were conducted that accounted for students' science learning in terms of domain-specific factors, rather than explaining learning in terms of global logico-mathematical reasoning skills (e.g., Driver, 1973; McClosky, 1983; Viennot, 1979).

An empirical research program was subsequently developed (Novak, 1978), focusing upon the content of students' domain-specific reasoning (or students' alternative conceptions; Driver & Easley, 1978) about natural phenomena and involving researchers from around the world. Two particularly influential books in the development of research on pupils' alternative conceptions were *The Pupil as Scientist* by Rosalind Driver (1983) and *Learning in Science: The Implications of Children's Science*, edited by Roger Osborne and Peter Freyberg (1985). The latter provides an account of the work carried out by a group of researchers in the Learning in Science Project (LISP) at Waikato University, New Zealand. The "alternative conceptions" or "misconceptions" (Gilbert & Watts, 1983) movement gained further strength from a series of major international conferences organized by Joe Novak at Cornell University (Novak, 1987), and the number of publications in this field of science education research increased into the thousands (see, for example Bell, 1981; Driver, Guesne, & Tiberghien, 1985; Gunstone, 1987; Wandersee, Mintzes, & Novak, 1994). Helga Pfundt and Reinders Duit of the IPN in Kiel, Germany, developed a comprehensive bibliography, *Students' Alternative Frameworks and Science Education*, which is now in its fifth edition (Pfundt & Duit, 2000). All of the evidence suggests that there are strong commonalities in the alternative conceptions of students from different cultures, and, furthermore, these ideas about the natural world have a profound influence on what is learned as a result of science teaching, and some ideas are extremely resistant to change (Driver, 1989).

During the 1970s and 1980s, accounts of the *origins* of students' thinking about the natural world tended to be based upon a Piagetian view of the knower-known relationship, with knowledge portrayed in terms of entities in the individual's head, which developed through that individual's interactions with the material world. Such views of knowledge were later challenged (Matthews, 1992) on the grounds that they advanced an empiricist account of the generation of scientific knowledge, an argument that will be returned to later in the chapter. Furthermore, they failed to make any distinction between an individual's *beliefs* about the world and *knowledge* of the world that has been publicly warranted as reliable.

In recent years, the "discursive turn in psychology" (Harré & Gillett, 1994) has involved a shift in focus away from viewing meaning-making purely in terms of cognitive processes in the individual, toward an account of individuals as they function in social contexts. Central to this development has been the rediscovery of the work of Vygotsky and other Soviet psychologists of the sociocultural tradition.

Overall, we therefore see a trend in characterizing students' science concept learning, which takes us from the individually oriented perspectives of Piaget toward those sociocultural perspectives that bring together the individual with the social. In the following section we introduce the framework that we have drawn upon to structure our account of this development.

STRUCTURING THE REVIEW

Given the range of approaches taken to conceptualizing science learning, we have found it helpful to identify two key features that we use as organizing dimensions in developing and presenting the review. The first dimension is taken from the influential paper by Anna Sfard (1998), in which she proposed two key metaphors for learning: the *acquisition* metaphor and the *participation* metaphor.

According to Sfard (1998), human learning has been conceived of since the dawn of civilization as an *acquisition* of something; in recent decades, "the idea of learning as gaining possession over some commodity has persisted in a wide spectrum of frameworks, from moderate to radical constructivism and then to interactionism and sociocultural theories" (p. 6). Gaining possession implies that something is stored or held somewhere. Sfard makes clear that it is *concepts* that are learned and then stored in the learner's head: "Since the time of Piaget and Vygotsky, the growth of knowledge in the process of learning has been analysed in terms of concept development. Concepts are to be understood as basic units of knowledge that can be accumulated, gradually refined, and combined to form ever richer cognitive structures" (p. 5).

By way of contrast, Sfard (1998) saw the *participation* metaphor as offering a fundamentally different perspective on learning, in which "the learner should be viewed as a person interested in participation in certain kinds of activities rather than in accumulating private possessions" (p. 6). According to this perspective, "learning a subject is now conceived of as a process of becoming a member of a certain community" (p. 6).

In developing this review, we start with approaches to conceptualizing science concept learning that belong to the *acquisition* perspective and then move on to those that relate to *participation*. From the outset, it is important to recognize that the acquisition-participation dimension is *not* a continuum. The two metaphors offer fundamentally different perspectives on learning, or, as Sfard (1998) stated, "the acquisition/participation division is ontological in nature and draws on two radically different approaches to the fundamental question, 'What is this thing called learning?' " (p. 7). The majority of approaches to conceptualizing science learning that we review here relate to the acquisition perspective.

The second dimension to be addressed involves the distinction between individual and social perspectives on learning. This takes us from a starting point where the main focus is on the *individual* learner and moves toward approaches where increased account is taken of various *social* aspects of the learning process and of knowledge itself.

SCIENCE CONCEPT LEARNING AS ACQUISITION: COGNITIVE APPROACHES

Following the ideas set out in the previous section, we first consider those approaches that see science learning as involving a process of *acquisition* and focus on the *individual* in providing an account of that learning.

Learning as Conceptual Change

Recognition that prior knowledge influences learning (Ausubel 1968), together with Piagetian ideas of accommodation and assimilation, and work from the philosophy of science (Kuhn, 1970; Lakatos, 1972) all underpinned a seminal paper by Posner, Strike, Hewson, and Gertzog (1982) on conceptual change in science learning. In the paper by Posner et al., the conditions needed for a major change in thinking within a scientific field (such as the shift from an Earth-centered to a Sun-centered model of the solar system) were considered analogous to the conditions needed to bring about accommodation or conceptual change in individual learners. Posner et al. identified four conditions that must be met before such an accommodation can occur. These conditions are that a learner must first be *dissatisfied* with existing ideas and then that the new ideas must be seen as *intelligible, plausible,* and *fruitful.* Empirical evidence from students' learning about the special theory of relativity was then used to illustrate and exemplify this model of conceptual change learning. Though taking the view that learning is a rational activity, Posner et al. recognized that such accommodations might take considerable time, involving "much fumbling about, many false starts and mistakes, and frequent reversals of direction" (p. 223). The conditions of intelligibility, plausibility, and fruitfulness contribute to the status of an idea. During conceptual change the status of different ideas within a person's conceptual ecology (the range of ideas they hold) changes (Hewson, 1981; Hewson & Hennesey, 1992; Hewson & Lemberger, 2000). The implications of this model for teaching were outlined in the original paper and further discussed by Hewson, Beeth, and Thorley (1998). In addition, Scott, Asoko, and Driver (1992) outlined two broad approaches to conceptual change teaching. The first of these is based upon promoting cognitive conflict and follows from the model proposed by Posner et al., whereas in the second the learner's existing ideas are built upon and extended.

A significant point of confusion in this whole area of work concerns the different meanings that are attached to the term *conceptual change.* Sometimes *conceptual change* refers to the process of learning, and at other times it refers to the products. Furthermore, *conceptual change* sometimes refers to situations where one concept (seen as a unit of knowledge) is *exchanged* for another; sometimes where a concept is *modified* in some way, for example by differentiation into two; sometimes where the *relationship* between concepts changes; and sometimes where new concepts are *added* without loss of the original ideas. The interest in student misconceptions, or alternative conceptions, in the 1980s led to a focus on conceptual change as revolutionary, with new ideas replacing the original ones (through a process of exchange), rather than evolutionary and gradual, with the possibility of several views existing simultaneously (through a process of addition) and used in different contexts (see, for example, Sinatra, 2002).

What Changes During Conceptual Change?

Posner et al.'s (1982) model of conceptual change focused on the *conditions* under which radical accommodations occur. Alongside this, the focus of much work in developmental cognitive psychology has been on *what* changes, exploring the performance of learners at different ages and attempting to explain this in terms of the ways in which concepts are mentally represented and related and the cognitive processes by which they are acquired and change.

One of the early proponents of domain-specific approaches, Susan Carey, proposed two forms of knowledge restructuring in learning, one similar to that demonstrated in the shift from novice to expert and one analogous to that of theory change in science. In the first, "weak" restructuring, the relations between concepts are changed. In the second, "strong" restructuring, the concepts themselves change (Carey, 1985), and this is regarded as difficult to achieve. Considerable attention has been given to these latter situations where radical restructuring is needed, particularly in the context of learning physics concepts.

The idea that learning occurs as discrete concepts are formed and then linked into more complex conceptual structures has largely given way to a view that concepts are part of larger relational structures from the start. Vosniadou (1994), for example, argued that concepts are embedded into larger theoretical structures of two types, with the term *theoretical* being used to describe a relatively coherent explanatory structure. *Framework theories*, which develop from early infancy, consist of fundamental ontological and epistemological presuppositions. *Specific theories* are beliefs about the properties or behavior of objects, which arise from observation and/or are transmitted by the pervading culture. These specific theories are constrained by the assumptions of the underpinning framework theories. Specific and framework theories provide the basis for the generation of situation specific mental models in response to the demands of a particular situation. Exploration of these mental models, for example in the context of the development of ideas about astronomical phenomena or force, provides insight into the underlying theoretical base. Conceptual change, according to this perspective, is thought to occur by enrichment or revision of a specific or a framework theory, a process that requires a gradual suspension of presuppositions and their revision or replacement with a different explanatory framework (Vosniadou & Ioannides, 1998). From this perspective, misconceptions are generated on the spot, during testing, from the deeply held framework theory, rather than being deeply held beliefs.

Following the seminal work of Keil (1979), ontological categorization is also seen as being of fundamental importance in the learning of science concepts. Chi (Chi, 1992; Chi, Slotta, & de Leeuw, 1994) argued that the meaning of a concept is determined by the ontological category to which it is assigned. Misconceptions thus arise when a concept is assigned to an inappropriate ontological category, for example, seeing the concept of "heat" as belonging to the category of "matter" instead of the category "process." Chi and Roscoe (2002) distinguished between the reassignment of concepts within levels of an ontological category and change, which requires a shift from one category to another, which is much more difficult.

DiSessa and Sherin (1998) pointed out some difficulties with the "standard" model of conceptual change. They argued that the notion of "concept" needs to be replaced by more carefully defined theoretical constructs within a knowledge system, which allow us to understand how that system functions. Focusing on the cognitive processes by which we gain information from the world, they proposed entities such as "co-ordination classes" and "phenomenological primitives," or p-prims. Co-ordination classes include cognitive strategies such as selecting and integrating information and are "systematically connected ways of getting information from the world" (p. 1171). Phenomenological primitives are described as abstractions from experience that need no explanation and form primitive schemata that constitute the basis of intuitive knowledge. For example, people usually expect that greater effort produces greater results and may apply this principle across a range of contexts. Intuitive "rules" such as these have also been identified by Stavy and co-workers (Stavy & Tirosh, 2000; Tirosh, Stavy, & Cohen, 1998). They believed that many of the alternative conceptions reported in the literature are, in fact, due to the use of rules such as *more of A-more of B*, which are relatively stable and resistant to change.

All of the above utilize some form of mental model, or system that develops and changes as a result of cognitive processes. The view that evolutionary pressures have led to the development of innate dispositions to interpret the world in particular ways was discussed by Matthews (2000), who also suggested that some conceptual structures can be triggered, rather than learned in the usual sense of the word. He considered, for example, that some of the p-prims, proposed by DiSessa, have the character of triggered concepts. Drawing on connectionist theories, he suggested that certain neural networks are designed to respond quickly and thus reinforce an initial bias. Conceptual change might then be viewed as a "process by which additional cognitive structures are built that, once firmly established, can over-ride rather than merge with, the functioning of competing innate structures" (p. 528). Such innate structures might correspond or give rise to the "naïve physics" and "naïve psychology" proposed by Carey (1985) or DiSessa's naïve "sense of mechanism" (DiSessa & Sherin, 1998) and perhaps lie behind Vosniadou's (1994) framework theories and Stavy's intuitive rules (Stavy & Tirosh, 2000).

Beyond "Cold" Conceptual Change

Although Posner et al. (1982) noted that motivational and affective variables were not unimportant in the learning process, the model of conceptual change they proposed was based on a view of learning as a rational activity. Pintrich, Marx, and Boyle (1993), in their critique of "cold" conceptual change models, proposed that the conditions of dissatisfaction with existing conceptions and the intelligibility, plausibility, and fruitfulness of the new, although necessary, are not sufficient to support conceptual change. Cognitive, motivational, and classroom contextual factors must also be taken into account as the individual student in the classroom is subject to influences from the broader social setting.

Cognitive Approaches: Summary and Implications

The following fundamental insights about science concept learning are common to the majority of cognitive perspectives:

1. Individuals' beliefs about the natural world are *constructed*, rather than *received*.
2. There are strong commonalities in how individuals appear to think about the natural world.
3. A person's existing ideas about a given subject greatly influence his/her subsequent learning about that subject.

In addition, some have argued that there are more general aspects of reasoning, such as Piaget's logico-mathematical reasoning skills, or the skills described by Kuhn et al. (1988), which influence the learner's response to instruction.

These insights have significant implications for our understanding of how science concepts are taught and learned. The facts that scientific knowledge cannot be *transferred* during teaching, and that existing thinking influences learning outcomes, offer a starting point to explaining why some aspects of science are difficult to learn. Furthermore, the research into students' thinking about aspects of the natural world has been drawn upon by science educators involved in the design and evaluation of teaching sequences (see, for example, Clement, 1993; Minstrell, 1992; Psillos & Méheut, 2004; Rowell & Dawson, 1985; Stavy & Berkowitz, 1980; Tiberghien, 2000; Viennot & Rainson, 1999) and in decisions about sequencing of ideas and age placement in the science curriculum (Driver, Leach, Scott, & Wood-Robinson, 1994). Science educators have also drawn upon research into more general aspects of students' scientific reasoning in developing teaching materials focused on the general reasoning skills of students (e.g., Adey & Shayer, 1993).

If the above points constitute a shared ground among cognitive perspectives, where do the points of difference lie? One area for debate concerns the existence and relative importance of domain-general and domain-specific aspects of reasoning in accounting for conceptual learning and conceptual change in science. Thinking back to the case of Alice, some of her difficulties with learning about energy might be explained, from a domain-specific perspective, in terms of the ontology of her existing concepts ("How come the mass hasn't changed when energy has been transferred to the surroundings?"). Instruction might therefore be designed to make it plausible that energy is not a substance, and to allow Alice to compare the scientific account of energy explicitly with her prior thinking.

From a domain-general perspective, Alice's difficulties might be accounted for in terms of the prevalence of abstract entities in the scientific account of energy and Alice's capacity to operate with those abstract entities. We are not aware of research that accounts for the teaching and learning of specific conceptual content from a domain-general perspective. Rather, the instructional solution might involve teaching thinking skills, or possibly not addressing the more abstract aspects of the energy concept until Alice has developed the appropriate thinking skills.

Another area of debate is the relative coordination or fragmentation of the elements of conceptual thinking in science learners. Are Alice's ideas about energy coordinated and coherent, or fragmented and lacking in logical coherence? Depending on the answer to this question, the challenge for Alice's science teacher might involve presenting a scientific account of energy and contrasting it explicitly with students' theories, or helping students to appreciate how a single, coherent theory can explain a wide range of phenomena.

In practice, however, there may be no simple, direct relationship between perspectives on learning and strategies for teaching (Millar, 1989), and Alice's teacher might well achieve similar success as a result of using several of the above strategies. It might therefore be the case that messages for practice lie at a more fundamental level, suggesting that teaching ought to provide opportunities to probe students' developing understanding in a formative way, allowing subsequent teaching to be responsive to students' learning. Insights about how to teach conceptual content in areas such as thermodynamics, chemical change, or plant nutrition will only arise through design research (Brown, 1992), where insights about domain-specific reasoning are drawn upon in the design of teaching materials, which are then tested and developed in a cyclical process (Lijnse, 1995). Such research does not in itself rest directly upon cognitive theory.

SCIENCE CONCEPT LEARNING AS ACQUISITION: SOCIOCULTURAL AND SOCIAL CONSTRUCTIVIST PERSPECTIVES

At this point in the review we take a significant step in moving from approaches to characterizing science concept learning that focus on the individual, while recognizing the influence of the social context, to those that take the social context as an integral part of the learning process. In short, we move from cognitive to sociocultural and social constructivist approaches.

Vygotskian Perspective on Learning

A fundamental theoretical reference point for sociocultural and social constructivist perspectives on learning was provided by Lev Semenovich Vygotsky (Vygotsky, 1934/1987). Central to Vygotsky's views is the idea that learning involves a passage from social contexts to individual understanding (Vygotsky, 1978). Thus, we first meet new ideas (new to us, at least) in social situations where those ideas are rehearsed between people, drawing on a range of modes of communication, such as talk, gesture, writing, visual images, and action. Vygotsky referred to these interactions as existing on the *social plane*. The social plane may be constituted by a teacher working with a class of students in school; it may involve a parent explaining something to a child. As ideas are explored during the social event, each participant is able to reflect on and make individual sense of what is being communicated. The words, gestures, and images used in the social exchanges provide the very tools needed for individual thinking. Thus, there is a transition from *social* to *individual* planes, whereby the social tools for communication become *internalized* and provide the means for individual thinking. It is no coincidence that Vygotsky's seminal book is titled *Thought and Language* (Vygotsky, 1962).

The *social* origins of learning are thus a fundamental and integral part of Vygotsky's account, and it is the job of the teacher to make scientific knowledge available on the social plane of the classroom, supporting students as they try to make sense of it. Vygotsky brought the activities of teaching and learning together through his concept of the Zone of Proximal Development or ZPD (Vygotsky, 1978). The ZPD provides a measure of the difference between what the student can achieve working alone and what can be done with assistance. The key point here is that the student's learning is conceived of as being directly connected to, and dependent upon, the supporting activity of the teacher on the social plane.

As well as drawing attention to the social origins of learning, Vygotsky also emphasized the role of the *individual* in the learning process. The process of internalization, as envisaged by Vygotsky, does not involve the simple transfer of ways of talking and thinking from social to personal planes. There must always be a step of personal sense making. Leontiev (1981), one of Vygotsky's contemporaries, made the point in stating that "the process of internalisation is not the transferral of an external activity to a pre-existing 'internal plane of consciousness.' It is the process in which this plane is formed" (p. 57). That is, individual learners must make sense of the talk, which surrounds them on the social plane, relating that talk in a dialogic way to their existing ideas and ways of thinking.

In this respect Vygotskian theory shares common ground with the constructivist perspectives outlined earlier, which emphasize that learners cannot be passive recipients of knowledge. It is perhaps with this point in mind that those contemporary approaches to conceptualizing science learning, which draw on Vygotskian *sociocultural* theory, are often referred to as *social constructivist* perspectives.

Social Constructivist Views of Learning Science

Vygotskian theory has been directly drawn upon by a number of researchers in their development of an account of science learning (see, for example, Driver et al., 1994; Hodson & Hodson, 1998; Howe, 1996; Leach & Scott, 2002, 2003; Mortimer & Scott, 2003; Scott, 1998; Wells, 1999).

Hodson and Hodson (1998), for example, outlined a social constructivist perspective on teaching and learning science, which was "based on the Vygotskian notion of enculturation" (p. 33). They argued that this perspective provides an alternative to personal constructivist accounts of learning (see also Osborne, 1996), which they claimed often imply "that students who construct their own understanding of the world are building *scientific* understanding" (p. 34; emphasis as in original). This point takes us back to the empiricist critique of constructivism outlined earlier. Thus Michael Matthews has argued that "constructivism is basically, and at best, a warmed up version of old-style empiricism" (Matthews, 1992, p. 5). One might question whether adherents to such an empiricist view of constructivism actually exist.

Central to the social constructivist response to charges of empiricism is the fundamental epistemological tenet that areas of knowledge such as science are developed within specific social communities. Thus, Driver et al. (1994) stated:

> [I]f knowledge construction is seen solely as an individual process, then this is similar to what has traditionally been identified as discovery learning. If, however, learners are to be given access to the knowledge systems of science, the process of knowledge construction must go beyond personal empirical enquiry. Learners need to be given access not only to physical experiences but also to the concepts and models of conventional science. (p. 7)

The implications of this point are fundamental. The understandings of an individual, acquired, on the one hand, through the individual's interactions with the material world, and, on the other, through being introduced to the concepts and models of conventional science, are ontologically different. The concepts and models of conventional science embody practices, conventions, and modes of expression that are socially and institutionally agreed upon. Because scientific knowledge is the product of the scientific community, it cannot be learned through interactions with the material world alone. Such differences between empiricist interpretations of personal constructivism and social constructivist accounts of learning were discussed by Leach and Scott (2003).

Following the ideas set out in the preceding sections, social constructivist accounts of learning can be deemed to be "social" in nature on two counts: first, in the sense of specifying the social origins of learning, through the interactions of the social plane, and second in recognizing the social context of the scientific community for the development of scientific knowledge.

Learning Science as Learning the Social Language of Science

The view of scientific knowledge as a product of the scientific community maps onto Bakhtin's notion of *social languages*. For Bakhtin, a social language is "a discourse peculiar to a specific stratum of society (professional, age group etc.) within a given system at a given time" (Bakhtin, 1934/1981, p. 430). Thus science can be construed as the social language that has been developed within the scientific community. It is based on specific concepts such as energy, mass, and entropy; it involves the development of models that provide a simplified account of phenomena in the natural world; and it is characterized by key epistemological features such as the development of theories, which can be generally applied to a whole range of phenomena and situations. The social language of science is clearly different from that of geography or economics or literary criticism. Furthermore, the science that is taught in school focuses on particular concepts and models and is subject to social and political pressures, which are quite different from those of professional science (Tiberghien, 2000). From this point of view, learning science involves learning the social language of "school science" (Leach & Scott, 2002; Mortimer & Scott, 2003; see also Chapter 3, this volume).

James Wertsch (1991) suggested that the different social languages that we learn constitute the "tools" of a "mediational tool kit," which can be called upon for talking and thinking as the context demands. Furthermore, Wertsch suggested that "children do not stop using perspectives grounded in everyday concepts and questions after they master these [scientific] forms of discourse" (1991, p. 118). Thus, everyday, or spontaneous (Vygotsky, 1934/1987), ways of talking and thinking constitute an "everyday social language." Wertsch saw the learner developing disciplinary social languages alongside these everyday ways of talking and thinking. As such, this sociocultural perspective on learning clearly involves a process of conceptual *addition* (as introduced in the earlier section on cognitive science approaches) rather than replacement.

Learning as Conceptual Addition/Replacement

This formulation of learning in terms of conceptual addition and replacement is rather more complex than these simple labels might suggest. For example, can it be the case that, in conceptual addition, everyday knowledge is left intact as the learner develops a new point of view based on a particular social language, such as school science?

There is a certain ambiguity in Vygotsky's (1987) views on the possible outcome of the learning process. In some cases he seemed to suggest that scientific perspectives (Vygotsky actually uses the term *scientific* in referring to disciplinary knowledge, which includes the natural sciences) are likely to transform everyday views: "The formal discipline of studying scientific concepts is manifested in the complete restructuring of the child's spontaneous concepts. This is why the scientific concept is of such extraordinary importance for the history of the child's mental development" (p. 236).

Elsewhere, Vygotsky suggested that even with the emergence of scientific concepts, people continue to have access to everyday concepts, which they often employ:

> A child who has mastered the higher forms of thinking, a child who has mastered concepts, does not part with the more elementary forms of thinking. In quantitative terms these more elementary forms continue to predominate in many domains for a long time. As we noted earlier, even adults often fail to think in concepts. The adult's thinking is often carried out on the level of complexes, sometimes sinks to even more primitive levels. (p. 160)

So, we have a picture of scientific knowledge transforming everyday thinking on the one hand and everyday or elementary thinking being left behind on the other. It might be the case that the outcome of this meeting of social languages (everyday and school science) depends on the *context* of learning. For example, it might be argued that coming to understand a fundamental scientific principle such as the "conservation of substance" is likely to transform the thinking of the individual. It is difficult to believe that the learner will consciously revert to being a nonconserver and talk about simple everyday events in such a way (being prepared to accept, for example, that salt actually does disappear on dissolving in water). On the other hand, as one learns about air pressure, it is unlikely that air pressure explanations will replace everyday talk in terms of "sucking." Here it is likely that the individual will move between the two forms of explanation according to the perceived context of activity and application. Joan Solomon made a seminal contribution to the development of this perspective in science education with her work on "how children think in two domains" (see Solomon, 1983).

This general idea of a heterogeneity in ways of thinking (see Bachelard, 1940/1968; Berger & Luckmann, 1967; Tulviste, 1988/1991) has been developed in the context of science education in terms of a *conceptual profile* (Mortimer, 1995, 1998). The conceptual profile acknowledges the coexistence, for the individual, of different ways of conceptualizing physical phenomena in science. These different ways can range from approaches based on everyday knowledge (which might be informed by the immediate sense perception of the actual phenomenon) to sophisticated scientific ways (which might represent reality in purely symbolic models) and constitute different zones of an individual person's conceptual profile. As such, science learning can be characterized in terms of extending the zones of the individual learner's conceptual profile.

Alternative Conceptions and Everyday Social Language

The sociocultural view of learning offers an interesting perspective on the origins and status of alternative conceptions or misconceptions. From the sociocultural point of view, an alternative conception, such as the idea of a plant drawing its food from the soil, is representative of an everyday way of talking and thinking about plants. This is the way in which ordinary people talk about such things, and in this respect there is a very real sense in which the *scientific* point of view (based on the concept of photosynthesis) offers the *alternative* perspective. Viewed in this way, it is hardly surprising that the alternative conceptions or misconceptions identified by the science education community are "robust" and "difficult to change." These are not the ephemeral outcomes of the solitary musings of children trying to make sense of the natural world around them, but the tools of an everyday language that continuously acts to socially define, and reinforce, our ways of talking and thinking.

Social Constructivist Approaches: Summary and Implications

The following insights about science concept learning are common to social constructivist perspectives:

1. Learning scientific knowledge involves a passage from social to personal planes.
2. The process of learning is consequent upon individual sense-making by the learner.
3. Learning is mediated by various semiotic resources, the most important of which is language.
4. Learning science involves learning the social language of the scientific community, which must be introduced to the learner by a teacher or some other knowledgeable figure.

What perspective do these distinctive aspects of the social constructivist perspective take us to that is different from the interests and outcomes of the cognitive viewpoint? The most obvious development has been the increased attention, during the late 1980s and 1990s, to the role of the teacher and the ways in which teachers guide the discourse of the classroom to support the introduction of scientific knowledge and scientific ways of explaining (Edwards & Mercer, 1987; Mortimer & Scott, 2003; Ogborn, Kress, Martins, & McGillicuddy, 1996; Scott, 1998; van Zee & Minstrell, 1997). Through this kind of work, we have a much better grasp of the ways in which teachers make scientific knowledge available on the social plane of the classroom.

Whereas these approaches to *analyzing* teacher talk have been fruitful, we are less aware of work, informed by social constructivist perspectives, that addresses the issue of *designing* science instruction (see, for example, Hodson & Hodson, 1998; Leach & Scott, 2002). It also seems to be the case that the step of individual sense making, or internalization, has been given less attention, both theoretically and empirically in social constructivist studies.

And what about Alice and her learning the concept of energy? According to these views, Alice is learning a new social language, a new way of talking and thinking about the world. If some of the scientific ideas "that energy is not used up" appear implausible, it is because they *are* in relation to everyday ways of thinking. The obvious way to address this point is for the teacher to make clear that what is on offer is a new and powerful way of thinking and talking about the natural world—the scientific point of view. Furthermore, learning a scientific account of energy must involve an authoritative introduction of ideas by the teacher. Thereafter, Alice and her fellow students need the opportunity to talk and think with those conceptual tools for themselves.

SCIENCE CONCEPT LEARNING
AS PARTICIPATION

In this final section of the review we take the step from approaches to conceptualizing science concept learning that are based on acquisition to those that entail some form of participation.

Situated Cognition

The metaphor of learning as participation has largely arisen through a perspective on learning known as *situated cognition* (see, for example, Brown, Collins, & Duguid, 1989; Lave & Wenger, 1991; Rogoff, 1990).

The pioneering work in this field focused on the use of mathematics in the workplace and in day-to-day life. For example, Scribner (1984) analyzed the arithmetical practices of people as they worked in a dairy factory, and Lave (1988) focused on the use of arithmetic in everyday shopping. These studies and others (see Hennessy, 1993, for a comprehensive review) have identified forms of arithmetic that are radically different from those taught in school. The skilled users of these everyday forms of arithmetic vary their problem-solving approaches depending on the specific situation, and problems that appear to be structurally identical are solved with different strategies. In this sense, the strategies are seen to be directly linked to context and thereby *situated* in nature.

According to the situated cognition perspective, learning is seen as a process of enculturation, or participation in socially organized practices, through which specialized skills are developed by learners as they engage in an apprenticeship in thinking (Rogoff, 1990) or in legitimate peripheral participation (Lave & Wenger, 1991). According to Collins, Brown, and Newman (1989), the key components of the apprenticeship process include modeling, coaching, scaffolding, fading, and encouraging learners to reflect on their own problem-solving strategies. This apprenticeship leads to the learner becoming involved in the *authentic* practices of a "community of practice" (Lave and Wenger, 1991). Brown, Collins, and Duguid (1989) argued: "Unfortunately, students are too often asked to use the tools of a discipline without being able to adopt its culture. To learn to use tools as practitioners use them, a student, like an apprentice, must enter that community and its culture" (p. 33). Roth (1995a) suggested that authentic practices involve activities "which have a large degree of resemblance with the activities in which core members of a community actually engage" (p. 29).

In the context of education, situated cognition perspectives have received a lot of attention, particularly in North America and particularly in relation to mathematics education (see, for example, Cobb, Wood, & Yackel, 1991; Cobb & Yackel, 1996; Lampert, 1990). According to Cobb and Bowers (1999), "A situated perspective on the mathematics classroom sees individual students as participating in and contributing to the development of the mathematical practices established by the classroom community" (p. 5).

Situated perspectives on learning have also been drawn upon as part of a theoretical justification for "inquiry-based" approaches to science teaching and learning (see, for example, Metz, 1998; Roth, 1995b). Roth (1995a) suggested that "situated learning emphasizes learning through the engagement in authentic activities" (p. 29). He explained his use of the term "authentic" by suggesting that in classrooms focused on scientific activities, the students would (a) learn in contexts constituted in part by ill-defined problems; (b) experience uncertainties, ambiguities, and the social nature of scientific work and knowledge; (c) engage in learning (curriculum) that is predicated on, and driven by, their current knowledge state; (d) experience themselves as part of communities of inquiry in which knowledge, practices, resources, and discourse are shared; and (e) participate in classroom communities, in which they can draw on the expertise of more knowledgeable others (Roth, 1995a, p. 29; see also Wells, 1999).

Drawing explicitly upon these ideas, science instruction has been planned and implemented as the enculturation of students into practices such as field ecology (e.g., Roth & Bowen, 1995), environmental activism (e.g., Roth & Désautels, 2002), and basic scientific research (e.g., Ryder, Leach, & Driver, 1999). Although the practices described in these studies can be argued to be *authentic* in the sense that they refer to situations in which science is actually used, it is more difficult to argue that they are closely related to the everyday experience of most science learners. Furthermore, the authors' analyses of teaching focus more upon students' learning about various *practices* that involve science (the use of instrumentation and specific technical procedures, the construction of arguments, the social relationships of various communities) than upon the development of conceptual understanding by students.

Learning Science, Learning to Talk Science

Lemke (1990) offered a different perspective on learning science through participation in his book, *Talking Science: Language, Learning and Values*. This "social semiotic" approach has been highly influential in drawing attention to the fundamental importance of language in science learning. The basic thesis that Lemke proposed is that learning science involves learning to talk science: "it means learning to communicate in the language of science and act as a member of the community of people who do so" (p. 1). Lemke questioned the value of cognitive theories of concept use based on mental processes "which we know nothing about" and suggested that "we may as well cut out the 'middleman' of *mental* concepts, and simply analyse conceptual systems in terms of the thematic patterns of language use and other forms of meaningful human action" (p. 122). Consistent with this point of view, Lemke suggested that scientific reasoning is learned "by talking to other members of our community, we practice it by talking to others, and we use it in talking to them, in talking to ourselves, and in writing and other forms of more complex activity (e.g., problem-solving, experimenting)" (p. 122; see also Chapter 3, this volume, for more on language and science learning).

Multimodality: Extending Beyond Language

Although science classrooms are filled with the voices of teacher and students, it is clear that communication and learning in the classroom are achieved by more than just linguistic tools. Kress, Jewitt, Ogborn, and Tsatsarelis (2001) set out an approach to analyzing science teaching and learning, "in which the multiplicity of *modes of communication* that are active in the classroom are given equally serious attention" (p. 1). Through this "multimodal" approach, Kress et al. were able to demonstrate how the meaning of what is spoken or written does not reside purely in language, by focusing on the ways in which teacher and students use a variety of semiotic modes, "actional, visual and linguistic resources" (p. 33), to represent and communicate ideas. One of their examples offers a detailed and vivid illustration of how a teacher orchestrates a range of modes of communication to introduce the idea of blood circulation. The image that sticks in the mind is the teacher moving fluently between a diagram on the board, a model of the human body, and his own body, gesturing toward each as he develops the verbal scientific narrative (see also Scott & Jewitt, 2003).

This multimodal account of learning sits firmly in the participation camp. "We believe that 'acquisition' is an inappropriate metaphor to describe the processes of learning: it implies a stable system which is statically acquired by an individual" (Kress et al., 2001, p. 28). Rather, learning is presented as a *process* of transformation in which "students are involved in the active 'remaking' of teachers' (and others') signs" (p. 27). In other words, learning involves the students in making sense of (and thereby transforming) the multimodal events that are unfolding around them in the science classroom.

In his more recent work, Lemke has developed the social semiotics perspective introduced in *Talking Science*, along similar multimodal lines, to investigate "how we make meaning using the cultural resources of systems of words, images, symbols and actions" (Lemke, 2003, "Languages and Concepts in Science" section). As part of this analysis, Lemke made the important point not only that it is the communicative activities of teacher and students in the classroom that are multimodal in character, but that science itself also involves the use of multiple semiotic systems: "Science does not speak of the world in the language of words alone, and in many cases it simply cannot do so. The natural language of science is a synergistic integration of words, diagrams, pictures, graphs, maps, equations, tables, charts, and other forms of visual and mathematical expression" (p. 3).

Science thus consists of: "the languages of visual representation, the languages of mathematical symbolism, and the languages of experimental operations" (p. 3). Following this perspective, Lemke argued that learning science must involve developing the ability "to use all of these languages in meaningful and appropriate ways, and, above all, to be able to functionally integrate them in the conduct of scientific activity" (p. 3).

Participative Approaches: Summary and Implications

The following insights about learning are common to the participative approaches outlined above:

1. Learning is seen as a *process* of developing participation in the practices of a particular community.
2. The learner takes on the role of apprentice, whereas the teacher is seen as an expert participant.
3. That which is to be learned involves some aspect of practice or discourse.

Perhaps the biggest question to be raised in relation to the participative approaches concerns the issue of subject matter and the very aims of science education. For example, what does it mean to suggest that learning science should involve "participation in the practices of a scientific community"? What does it mean to suggest that students should "engage in the authentic practices of science"? To what extent is it possible to reconfigure the science classroom as a seat of authentic scientific practices? Is it reasonable to expect that the teacher can act as an expert practitioner within this scientific community of the classroom? What would be the aims of such an approach to science education? What would be learned?

Of course, we have already referred to examples of classroom practice where these kinds of questions have been addressed; it is clear that the kinds of investigative or inquiry-based activity suggested offer workable possibilities. But what about Alice and her quest to understand the scientific concept of energy? It stretches faith in participative methods to suggest that learning scientific concepts, the tools of science, might best be achieved through investigative methods. Here the social constructivist perspective seems to offer a more plausible and helpful way of framing possible instructional approaches.

WHAT CAN WE SAY ABOUT SCIENCE CONCEPT LEARNING IN CLASSROOM SETTINGS?

We began this chapter with a brief sketch of one student, Alice, and her learning of the scientific account of energy during science lessons in school. We return to that scenario, for a final time, to consider the ways in which the different approaches to viewing science concept learning might be drawn upon to illuminate such a teaching and learning event, addressing some of the questions listed in the introduction to the chapter. Our view is that, given the complexity of what goes on in classrooms as students learn science, it is unrealistic to expect that one "grand" theory might capture all of the activity. In this respect we follow the lead of Sfard (1998) and others (see, for example, Mayer, 2002) in drawing upon what might be regarded as complementary perspectives on learning.

As a starting point, we take the social constructivist perspective, which we believe constitutes a helpful framing or "orienting" (Green, Dixon, & Gomes, 2003) theory in bringing together the social context for learning with the individual student's response. Here the teacher occupies the pivotal role, between culture and students, in introducing the scientific social language. Given this overall framing, it is clear that learning scientific concepts is driven by teaching and that the students must engage in the act of personal sense-making during internalization.

Accepting the point of view that learning science involves learning the social language of "school science," a legitimate question to ask is, why can learning some parts of science prove to be so *difficult*? Why is it, for example, that Alice struggled to come to terms with the school science account of "energy." Why is it that the school science view often appears implausible to the learner, even if it is intelligible (Posner et al., 1982)? How can we develop and extend our *orienting* theoretical framework to address these questions?

One response relates to *differences* in social languages and is based on the idea that where there are significant differences between school science and everyday accounts of a particular phenomenon, greater "learning demands" (Leach & Scott, 2002) are created for the student. How might such learning demands be appraised? Three possible ways in which differences between everyday and school science perspectives might arise have been identified (Leach & Scott). These relate to differences in the *conceptual tools* used, differences in the *epistemological underpinning* of those conceptual tools, and differences in the *ontology* on which those conceptual tools are based.

For example, in relation to plant nutrition, students commonly draw upon everyday notions of food as something that is ingested, in contrast to scientific accounts, which describe the synthesis of complex organic molecules within plants, from simple, inorganic precursors. In the case of energy, the scientific concept is essentially a mathematical accounting device (which can be used to predict the limits of possible outcomes to physical events), whereas the everyday concept is likely to involve references to human activity and notions of energy as something that "makes things happen."

Other differences relate to the *epistemological underpinning* of the conceptual tools used. Thus, the ways of generating explanations using scientific models and theories that are taken for granted in school science are not part of the everyday social language of many learners (Driver, Leach, Millar, & Scott, 1996; Leach, Driver, Scott, & Wood-Robinson, 1996; Vosniadou, 1994). Whereas in scientific social languages, great importance is attached to developing a small number of models and theories, which can be generally applied to as broad a range of phenomena as possible, the same is not true for everyday social languages. Thus, in science, energy is an absolutely central concept, simply because it offers a generalizable way of thinking about virtually any phenomenon. In everyday contexts, where there is not the same attention to generalizability; the term *energy* might be used with different meanings in different contexts.

Learning demands may also result from differences in the *ontology* of the conceptual tools used (Chi, 1992; Chi, Slotta, & de Leeuw, 1994; Leach et al., 1996; Vosniadou, 1994). Thus, entities that are taken for granted as having a real existence in the realm of school science may not be similarly referred to in the everyday language of students. For example, there is evidence that many lower secondary school students learning about matter cycling in ecosystems do not think about atmospheric gases as a potential source of matter for the chemical processes of ecological systems (Leach et al.). There is a learning issue here that relates to the students' basic commitments about the nature of matter—initially they do not consider gases to be substantive. With regard to the energy example, in scientific social languages energy is regarded as an abstract mathematical device, whereas in everyday contexts it is often referred to as being substantial in nature: *Coal contains energy; I've run out of energy.*

From this point of view, learning science involves coming to terms with the conceptual tools and associated epistemology and ontology of the scientific social language. If the differences between scientific and everyday ways of reasoning are great, then the topic in question appears difficult to learn (and to teach). The key point here is that the concept of learning demand is framed in terms of the differences between social languages *and* draws on aspects of the "individual cognition" literature in identifying the epistemological and ontological aspects of learning demand.

In the cognitive literature, ontological recategorization (for example) is presented as a mental process, possibly as a psychological barrier to learning a specific science concept. The account of ontological barriers to successful learning presented here, however, begins by recognizing that ontological differences exist between the *social languages* of everyday talk and school science. Any ontological recategorization required of learners therefore has its origins in social language, and we can begin to address these through systematic teaching.

One might argue that all of this adds up to the same thing, and in a sense it does. The systematic teaching still requires individual cognitive effort by the student if learning is to take place. Nevertheless, it might be helpful in thinking about teaching and learning science in classroom settings, to cast the issue in terms of the aspects of learning demand to be worked on by teacher and students. In this way, there is greater clarity about what it is that needs to be taught and learned in any topic area of school science.

This realization of what it is is extended still further by Lemke's (2003) social semiotic analysis. As outlined earlier, Lemke emphasized that learning school science involves developing the ability to integrate and use all of the semiotic resources of science, pulling together the languages of visual representation, mathematical symbolism, and experimental operations. Lemke was absolutely clear in stating that it is the responsibility of the teacher to show students "how to move back and forth among the different mathematical, visual, and operational representations" (p. 5).

All of these preceding points relate to achieving greater clarity about what it is that needs to be taught if students are to come to understand and to be able to use the social language of science with its distinctive conceptual tools, epistemological and ontological framing, and range of semiotic resources. Within this account, there are also half-exposed hints about the kinds of instructional approaches that might be taken in addressing these learning targets. There is clearly a central role for the teacher in introducing these new conceptual tools and helping the students to make links to their existing ways of thinking. This communicative aspect of the teaching role, focusing on both language-based and broader multimodal approaches, has been developed in detail elsewhere (Kress et al., 2001; Lemke, 1990; Mortimer & Scott, 2003; Ogborn et al., 1996; Scott, 1998). It must also be a priority for the students to begin to use these ideas for themselves and to start talking and thinking with the scientific social language(s) if they are to engage with them meaningfully.

In these ways, we can see how Sfard's conclusion that "one metaphor is not enough" (p. 10) might be addressed, in the context of teaching and learning science contexts, as elements of theory are drawn on from the camps of both acquisition and participation.

LOOKING AHEAD:
FUTURE RESEARCH DIRECTIONS

One measure of the extent to which science education research can be regarded as a progressive field of activity concerns the impact of that research on practice (see Fensham, 2004). The picture that is painted in this review points to areas of research on science concept learning where our knowledge is extensive. Thus, as a community, we are familiar with students' typical alternative conceptions in a wide range of science topic areas; we are able to identify the main barriers to conceptual learning as scientific ideas are introduced against a backdrop of everyday ways of talking and thinking; we are aware of the ways in which learning involves both engaging in the social contexts of the classroom and steps of personal meaning making. The list can be further developed and, given the relatively short history of research in science education, is impressive in its extent. This body of knowledge is both broad and reliable and is based upon aspects of theory along with extensive empirical studies.

What remains far more problematic concerns the instructional approaches that might be taken to *advance* that learning. Put briefly, science education researchers are currently in the position where we can point with confidence to the likely conceptual starting points and challenges for students in any area of science learning, but we have rather less to say about how to shape instruction in order to help students come to terms with the scientific point of view. The challenge remains one of crossing the bridge from our insights on learning to making the link to reliable approaches to instruction.

Some argue that teaching is an idiosyncratic, highly personalised activity such that the very notions of best practice or an optimal instructional approach do not make sense. Although it is clear that teaching is a responsive activity and that to an extent it must therefore depend upon the circumstances prevailing in specific contexts (this class of children, at this time of the week, in this particular school, with this teacher), it might still be argued that some instructional approaches are likely to be more effective than others in supporting student learning. Why should this be the case? Possibly because the particular instructional approach is tightly linked to clear teaching objectives, or involves a motivating activity for the students, or challenges students' thinking in an engaging way, or allows students the opportunity to articulate their developing understandings.

Following this line of argument, the central challenge for science education researchers remains one of building upon insights about learning to develop robust guidelines (both science domain specific and general) to support instructional design. If such research activity is to have an impact upon practice in schools, then it needs to engage with the professional knowledge and expertise of practicing teachers and their priorities for professional development. This is a substantial project that has as its ultimate aim the exciting prospect of allowing students such as Alice to develop deeper insights into the power and elegance of scientific knowledge.

ACKNOWLEDGMENTS

Thanks to Michael Beeth and Beverly Bell, who reviewed this chapter.

REFERENCES

Adey, P., & Shayer, M. (1993). *Really raising standards.* London: Routledge.
Andersson, B. (1976). *Science teaching and the development of thinking.* Gothenburg, Sweden: Acta Universitatis Gothoburgensis.
Ausubel, D. P. (1968). *Educational psychology: A cognitive view.* New York: Holt, Rinehart & Winston.

Bachelard, G. (1968). *The philosophy of no: A philosophy of the new scientific mind* (G. C. Waterston, Trans.). New York: Orion Press (original work published 1940).

Bakhtin, M. M. (1981). Discourse in the novel (C. Emerson & M. Holquist, Trans.). In M. Holquist (Ed.), *The dialogic imagination* (pp. 259–422). Austin, TX: University of Texas Press (original work published 1934).

Bell, B. (1981). When is an animal not an animal? *Journal of Biology Education, 15,* 213–218.

Berger, P. L., & Luckmann, T. (1967). *The social construction of reality: A treatise in the sociology of knowledge.* London: Allen Lane.

Brown, A. (1992). Design experiments: Theoretical and methodological challenges in creating complex interventions. *Journal of the Learning Sciences, 2*(2), 141–178.

Brown, J. S., Collins, A., & Duguid, P. (1989). Situated cognition and the culture of learning. *Educational Researcher, 18*(1), 32–42.

Carey, S. (1985). *Conceptual change in childhood.* Cambridge, MA: MIT Press.

Chi, M. T. H. (1992). Conceptual change within and across ontological categories: Examples from learning and discovery in science. In R. Giere (Ed.), *Cognitive models of science: Minnesota studies in the philosophy of science* (pp. 129–186). Minneapolis: University of Minnesota Press.

Chi, M. T. H., & Roscoe, R. D. (2002). The processes and challenges of conceptual change. In M. Limon & L. Mason (Eds.), *Reconsidering conceptual change: Issues in theory and practice* (pp. 3–27). Dordrecht, the Netherlands: Kluwer Academic.

Chi, M. T. H., Slotta, J. D., & de Leeuw, N. (1994). From things to processes: A theory of conceptual change for learning science concepts. *Learning and Instruction, 4,* 27–43.

Clement, J. (1993). Using bridging analogies and anchoring intuitions to deal with students' preconceptions in physics. *Journal of Research in Science Teaching, 30,* 1241–1257.

Cobb, P., & Bowers, J. (1999). Cognitive and situated learning perspectives in theory and practice. *Educational Researcher, 28*(2), 4–15.

Cobb, P., Wood, T., & Yackel, E. (1991). Analogies from the philosophy and sociology of science for understanding classroom life. *Science Education, 75,* 23–44.

Cobb, P., & Yackel, E. (1996). Constructivist, emergent, and sociocultural perspectives in the context of developmental research. *Educational Psychologist, 31,* 175–190.

Collins, A., Brown, J. S., & Newman, S. (1989). Cognitive apprenticeship: Teaching the craft of reading, writing and mathematics. In L. Resnick (Ed.), *Cognition and instruction: Issues and agendas* (pp. 453–494). Hillsdale, NJ: Lawrence Erlbaum Associates.

DiSessa, A., & Sherin, B. (1998). What changes in conceptual change? *International Journal of Science Education, 20,* 1155–1191.

Donaldson, M. (1978). *Children's minds.* London: Croom Helm.

Driver, R. (1973). *Representation of conceptual frameworks in young adolescent science students.* Unpublished doctoral dissertation, University of Illinois at Urbana-Champaign.

Driver, R. (1978). When is a stage not a stage? A critique of Piaget's theory of cognitive development and its application to science education. *Educational Research, 21*(1), 54–61.

Driver, R. (1983). *The pupil as scientist?* Milton Keynes, England: Open University Press.

Driver, R. (1989). Students' conceptions and the learning of science. *International Journal of Science Education, 11,* 481–490.

Driver, R., Asoko, H., Leach, J., Mortimer, E., & Scott, P. (1994). Constructing scientific knowledge in the classroom. *Educational Researcher, 23*(7), 5–12.

Driver, R., & Easley, J. (1978). Pupils and paradigms: A review of literature related to concept development in adolescent science students. *Studies in Science Education, 5,* 3–12.

Driver, R., Guesne, E., & Tiberghien, A. (1985). *Children's ideas in science.* Milton Keynes, England: Open University Press.

Driver, R., Leach, J., Millar, R., & Scott, P. (1996). *Young people's images of science.* Buckingham, England: Open University Press.

Driver, R., Leach, J., Scott, P., & Wood-Robinson, C. (1994). Young people's understanding of science concepts: Implications of cross-age studies for curriculum planning. *Studies in Science Education, 24,* 75–100.

Edwards, D., & Mercer, N. (1987). *Common knowledge; the development of understanding in the classroom*. London: Methuen.

Erickson, G. (2000). Research programmes and the student science learning literature. In R. Millar, J. Leach, & J. Osborne (Eds.), *Improving science education: The contribution of research* (pp. 271–292). Buckingham, England: Open University Press.

Fensham, P. J. (2004). *Defining an identity: The evolution of science education as a field of research*. Dordrecht, the Netherlands: Kluwer Academic.

Gilbert, J. K., & Watts, M. (1983). Conceptions, misconceptions and alternative conceptions. *Studies in Science Education, 10*, 61–98.

Green, J. L., Dixon, C. N., & Gomes, M. de F.C. (2003, July). *Language, culture and knowledge in classrooms: An ethnographic approach*. Paper presented at the meeting of the Encontro Internacional Linguagem, Cultura e Cognição, Universidade Federal de Minas Gerais, Belo Horizonte, Brazil.

Gunstone, R. F. (1987). Student understanding in mechanics: A large population survey. *American Journal of Physics, 55*, 691–696.

Harré, R., & Gillett, G. (1994). *The discursive mind*. Thousand Oaks, CA: Sage.

Hennessy, S. (1993). Situated cognition and cognitive apprenticeship: Implications for classroom learning. *Studies in Science Education, 22*, 1–41.

Hewson, P. W. (1981). A conceptual change approach to learning in science. *European Journal of Science Education, 3*, 383–396.

Hewson, P. W., Beeth, M. E., & Thorley, N. R. (1998). Teaching for conceptual change. In B. J. Fraser & K. G. Tobin (Eds.), *International handbook of science education* (pp. 199–218). Dordrecht, the Netherlands: Kluwer Academic.

Hewson, P. W., & Hennesey, M. G. (1992). Making statue explicit: A case study of conceptual change. In R. Duit, F. Goldberg, & H. Niedderer (Eds.), *Research in physics learning: Theoretical issues and empirical studies* (pp. 176–187). Kiel, Germany: University of Kiel.

Hewson, P., & Lemberger, J. (2000). Status as the hallmark of conceptual learning. In R. Millar, J. Leach, & J. Osborne (Eds.), *Improving science education: The contribution of research* (pp. 110–125). Buckingham, England: Open University Press.

Hodson, D., & Hodson, J. (1998). From constructivism to social constructivism: A Vygotskian perspective on teaching and learning science. *School Science Review, 79*, 33–41.

Howe, A. C. (1996). Development of science concepts within a Vygotskian framework. *Science Education, 80*, 35–51.

Keil, F. (1979). *Semantic and conceptual development: An ontological perspective*. Cambridge, MA: Harvard University Press.

Koslowski, B. (1996). *Theory and evidence: The development of scientific reasoning*. Cambridge, MA: MIT Press.

Kress, G., Jewitt, C., Ogborn, J., & Tsatsarelis, C. (2001). *Multimodal teaching and learning: The rhetorics of the science classroom*. London: Continuum.

Kuhn, D. (1991). *The skills of argument*. Cambridge, England: Cambridge University Press.

Kuhn, D., Amsel, E., & O'Loughlin, M. (1988). *The development of scientific thinking skills*. London: Academic Press.

Kuhn, T. (1970). *The structure of scientific revolutions* (2nd ed.). Chicago: University of Chicago Press.

Lakatos, I. (1972). Falsification and the methodology of scientific research programmes. In I. Lakatos & A. Musgrave (Eds.), *Criticism and the growth of knowledge* (pp. 91–196). Cambridge, England: Cambridge University Press.

Lampert, M. (1990). When the problem is not the question and the solution is not the answer: Mathematical knowing and teaching. *American Educational Research Journal, 27*, 29–64.

Lave, J. (1988). *Cognition in practice: Mind, mathematics and culture in everyday life*. Cambridge, England: Cambridge University Press.

Lave, J., & Wenger, E. (1991). *Situated learning: Legitimate peripheral participation*. New York: Cambridge University Press.

Lawson, A. (1985). A review of research on formal reasoning and science teaching. *Journal of Research in Science Teaching, 22*, 569–618.

Leach, J., Driver, R., Scott, P., & Wood-Robinson, C. (1996). Children's ideas about ecology 2: Ideas about the cycling of matter found in children aged 5–16. *International Journal of Science Education, 18*, 19–34.

Leach, J., & Scott, P. (2002). Designing and evaluating science teaching sequences: An approach drawing upon the concept of learning demand and a social constructivist perspective on learning. *Studies in Science Education, 38*, 115–142.

Leach, J., & Scott, P. (2003). Learning science in the classroom: Drawing on individual and social perspectives. *Science and Education, 12*, 91–113.

Lemke, J. L. (1990). *Talking science. Language, learning and values*. Norwood, NJ: Ablex.

Lemke, J. L. (2003). *Teaching all the languages of science: Words, symbols, images and actions*. Retrieved September 10, 2004, from http://www-personal.umich.edu/~jaylemke/papers/barcelon.htm

Leontiev, A. N. (1981). The problem of activity in psychology. In J. V. Wertsch (Ed.), *The concept of activity in Soviet psychology* (pp. 37–71). Armonk, NY: M. E. Sharpe.

Lijnse, P. (1995). "Developmental research" as a way to an empirically based "didactical structure" of science. *Science Education, 79*, 189–199.

Matthews, M. (1992). Constructivism and empiricism: An incomplete divorce. *Research in Science Education, 22*, 299–307.

Matthews, P. S. C. (2000). Learning science: Some insights from cognitive science. *Science and Education, 9*, 507–535.

Mayer, R. E. (2002). Understanding conceptual change: A commentary. In M. Limon & L. Mason (Eds.), *Reconsidering conceptual change: Issues in theory and practice* (pp. 101–111). Dordrecht, the Netherlands: Kluwer Academic.

McClosky, M. (1983). Intuitive physics. *Scientific American, 248*, 122–130.

Metz, K. (1997). Reassessment of developmental constraints on children's science instruction. *Review of Educational Research, 65*, 93–127.

Metz, K. E. (1998). Scientific inquiry within reach of young children. In B. J. Fraser & K. G. Tobin (Eds.), *International handbook of science education* (pp. 81–96). Dordrecht, the Netherlands: Kluwer Academic.

Millar, R. (1989). Constructive criticisms. *International Journal of Science Education, 11*, 587–596.

Minstrell, J. (1992). Facets of students' knowledge and relevant instruction. In R. Duit, F. Goldberg, & H. Niedderer (Eds.), *Research in physics learning: Theoretical issues and empirical studies* (pp. 110–128). Kiel, Germany: University of Kiel.

Mortimer, E. F. (1995). Conceptual change or conceptual profile change? *Science and Education, 4*, 267–285.

Mortimer, E. F. (1998). Multivoicedness and univocality in the classroom discourse: An example from theory of matter. *International Journal of Science Education, 20*, 67–82.

Mortimer, E. F., & Scott, P. (2003). *Meaning making in secondary science classrooms*. Milton Keynes, England: Open University Press.

Novak, J. (1978). An alternative to Piagetian psychology for science and mathematics education. *Studies in Science Education, 5*, 1–30.

Novak, J. (1987). *Student misconceptions and educational strategies in science and mathematics*. Proceedings of the second international seminar. Ithaca, NY: Cornell University Press.

Ogborn J., Kress G., Martins I., & McGillicuddy, K. (1996). *Explaining science in the classroom*. Buckingham, England: Open University Press.

Osborne, J. F. (1996). Beyond constructivism. *Science Education, 80*, 53–82.

Osborne, R., & Freyberg, P. (Eds.). (1985). *Learning in science: The implications of children's science*. Portsmouth, NH: Heinemann.

Pfundt, H., & Duit, R. (2000). *Bibliography: Students' alternative frameworks and science education* (5th ed.). Kiel, Germany: Institute for Science Education at the University of Kiel.

Pintrich, P. R., Marx, R. W., & Boyle, R. A. (1993). Beyond cold conceptual change: The role of motivational beliefs and classroom contextual factors in the process of conceptual change. *Review of Educational Research, 6*, 167–199.

Piaget, J. (1929). *The child's conception of the world.* London: Routledge & Kegan Paul.

Piaget, J. (1930). *The child's conception of physical causality.* London: Routledge & Kegan Paul.

Piaget, J. (1937). *La construction du réel chez l'enfant* [The construction of reality in the child]. Neuchâte, France: Felachaux et Niestlé.

Piaget, J. (1946). *Le developpement de la notion de temps chez l'enfant* [The development of the concept of time in the child]. Paris: Presses Université France.

Piaget, J. (1952). *The origins of intelligence in children.* New York: International University Press.

Piaget, J. (1964). Cognitive development in children. *Journal of Research in Science Teaching, 2,* 176–186.

Piaget, J. (1971). *Biology and knowledge.* Edinburgh, Scotland: Edinburgh University Press.

Piaget, J., & Inhelder, B. (1956). *The child's conception of space.* London: Routledge & Kegan Paul.

Pintrich, P. R., Marx, R. W., & Boyle, R. A. (1993). Beyond cold conceptual change: The role of motivational beliefs and classroom contextual factors in the process of conceptual change. *Review of Educational Research, 63,* 167–199.

Posner, G. J., Strike, K. A., Hewson, P. W., & Gerzog, W. A. (1982). Accommodation of a scientific conception: Toward a theory of conceptual change. *Science Education, 66,* 211–227.

Psillos, D., & Meheut, M. (Eds.). (2004). Teaching-learning sequences: Aims and tools for science education research. *International Journal of Science Education, 26(5).*

Rogoff, B. (1990). *Apprenticeship in thinking: Cognitive development in social context.* Oxford, England: Oxford University Press.

Roth, W.-M. (1995a). *Authentic school science. Knowing and learning in open-inquiry science laboratories.* Dordrecht, the Netherlands: Kluwer Academic.

Roth, W.-M. (1995b). Teacher questioning in an open-inquiry learning environment: interactions of context, content and student responses. *Journal of Research in Science Teaching, 33,* 709–736.

Roth, W.-M., & Bowen, G. M. (1995). Knowing and interacting: A study of culture, practices and resources in a grade 8 open-inquiry science classroom guided by a cognitive apprenticeship metaphor. *Cognition and Instruction, 13,* 73–128.

Roth, W.-M., & Désautels, J. (2002). *Science education as/for sociopolitical action.* New York: Counterpoints.

Rowell, J. A., & Dawson, C. R. (1985). Equilibration, conflict and instruction: A new class oriented perspective. *European Journal of Science Education, 4,* 331–344.

Ryder, J., Leach, J., & Driver, R. (1999). Undergraduate science students' images of the nature of science. *Journal of Research in Science Teaching, 36,* 201–220.

Scott, P. H., Asoko, H. M., & Driver, R. H. (1992). Teaching for conceptual change: A review of strategies. In R. Duit, F. Goldberg, & H. Niedderer (Eds.), *Research in physics learning: Theoretical issues and empirical studies* (pp. 310–329). Kiel, Germany: University of Kiel.

Scott, P. H. (1998). Teacher talk and meaning making in science classrooms: A Vygotskian analysis and review. *Studies in Science Education, 32,* 45–80.

Scott, P., & Jewitt, C. (2003). Talk, action and visual communication in teaching and learning science. *School Science Review, 84,* 117–124.

Scribner, S. (1984). Studying working intelligence. In B. Rogoff & J. Lave (Eds.), *Everyday cognition: Its development in social context* (pp. 9–40). Cambridge, MA: Harvard University Press

Sfard, A. (1998). On two metaphors for learning and the dangers of choosing just one. *Educational Researcher, 27(2),* 4–13.

Shayer, M. (2003). Not just Piaget; not just Vygotsky, and certainly not Vygotsky as alternative to Piaget. *Learning and Instruction, 13,* 465–485.

Sinatra, G. M. (2002). Motivational, social and contextual aspects of conceptual change: A commentary. In M. Limon & L. Mason (Eds.), *Reconsidering conceptual change: Issues in theory and practice* (pp. 187–197). Dordrecht, the Netherlands: Kluwer Academic.

Solomon, J. (1983). Learning about energy: How pupils think in two domains. *European Journal of Science Education, 5,* 49–59.

Stavy, R., & Berkovitz, B. (1980). Cognitive conflict as a basis for teaching quantitative aspects of the concept of temperature. *Science Education, 64,* 679–692.

Stavy, R., & Tirosh, D. (2000). *How students (mis-)understand science and mathematics: Intuitive rules.* New York: Teachers College Press.

Tiberghien, A. (2000). Designing teaching situations in the secondary school. In R. Millar, J. Leach, & J. Osborne (Eds.), *Improving science education: The contribution of research* (pp. 27–47). Buckingham, England: Open University Press.

Tirosh, D., Stavy, R., & Cohen, S. (1998). Cognitive conflict and intuitive rules. *International Journal of Science Education, 20,* 1257–1269.

Tulviste, P. (1991). *The cultural-historical development of verbal thinking* (M. J. Hall, Trans.). Commak, NY: Nova Science (original work published 1988).

van Zee, E. H., & Minstrell, J. (1997). Reflective discourse: Developing shared understandings in a physics classroom. *International Journal of Science Education, 19,* 209–228.

Viennot, L. (1979). Spontaneous reasoning in elementary dynamics. *European Journal of Science Education, 1,* 205–221.

Viennot, L., & Rainson, S. (1999). Design and evaluation of a research based teaching sequence: The superposition of electric fields. *International Journal of Science Education, 21,* 1–16.

Vosniadou, S. (1994). Capturing and modelling the process of conceptual change. *Learning and Instruction, 4,* 45–69.

Vosniadou, S., & Ioannides, C. (1998). From conceptual development to science education: A psychological point of view. *International Journal of Science Education, 20,* 1213–1230.

Vygotsky, L. S. (1962). *Thought and language.* Cambridge, MA: MIT Press.

Vygotsky, L. S. (1978). *Mind in society: The development of higher psychological processes.* Cambridge, MA: Harvard University Press.

Vygotsky, L. S. (1987). *Thinking and speech* (N. Minick, Trans.). In R. W. Rieber & A. S. Carton (Eds.), *The collected works of L. S. Vygotsky* (Vol. 1, pp. 37–285). New York: Plenum (original work published 1934).

Wandersee, J. H., Mintzes, J. J., & Novak, J. D. (1994). Research on alternative conceptions in science. In D. Gabel (Ed.), *Handbook of research on science teaching and learning* (pp. 177–210). New York: Macmillan.

Wells, G. (1999). *Dialogic inquiry. Toward a sociocultural practice and theory of education.* Cambridge, England: Cambridge University Press

Wertsch, J. V. (1991). *Voices of the mind: A sociocultural approach to mediated action.* Cambridge, MA: Harvard University Press.

CHAPTER 3

Language and Science Learning

William S. Carlsen
Pennsylvania State University

In a 1998 contribution to the *International Handbook of Science Education*, Clive Sutton used the writings of Faraday, Boyle, Harvey, and others to compare the language found in historical documents with the ways in which science is represented in contemporary textbooks and classrooms. In Michael Faraday's letters to scientific contemporaries, Sutton found a voice that was personal and overtly persuasive, eschewing the third-person, "stick to the facts" register with which schoolchildren today are commonly taught to write laboratory reports. Drawing on science studies by Bazerman (1988), Lemke (1990), Medawar (1974), Shapin & Schaffer (1985), and others, Sutton (1998) recommended reduced emphasis in science education on language as a means of transmitting information and greater emphasis on language as an interpretive system of sense-making.

Only 5 years later, a survey of recent literature on language and science education demonstrates both the utility of Sutton's framework and the potential for its expansion. An overall healthy growth of that literature masks some interesting trends within that literature. Consider, for example, Figure 3.1, which plots the average annual publication rate of documents with keywords *Science Education, Language*, and either *Concept Formation* or *Culture*. Following a period of stability from about 1980 to 1995, publications related to *Concept Formation* have declined in number, while *Culture* has increased.[1] Trends like this reflect changes in the field regard-

---

1. For the sake of the narrative, I have simplified my description of the method in which the Figure 3.1 data were generated. The set described in the prose as (kw = "Science Education" AND "Language") is actually more accurately represented as ((kw = "Science Education" OR "Science Instruction") − (kw = "Programming" OR "Programing")) AND "Language". Use of the longer specification eliminated almost all of the numerous studies of computer programming (or ERIC's earlier spelling, "programing"), few of which were concerned with language as a means of oral or written communication between teachers and students engaged in science teaching and learning. My choice of keywords (and their linking algebra) followed a quantitative analysis of all ERIC citations in the aforementioned set from 1975–2002 (the most recent year that is reasonably completely indexed) and from study of the frequency distributions by date of the first 10 keyword descriptors of each of the citations. However, the data in Figure 3.1 are offered for heuristic purposes only; this is not a statistical argument!

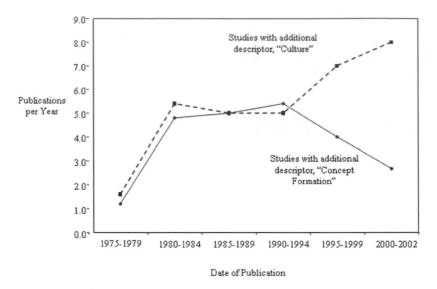

FIGURE 3–1.   ERIC citation rates for publications with keywords *Science Education, Language*, and either *Culture* or *Concept Formation*, by date.

ing what it means to learn (and to teach) science. Following a shift in emphasis from learning as individual cognitive growth to learning as individual cognitive growth in social settings, research increasingly views language as more than just a social means to individual ends.

The first section of this chapter discusses the origins of much of this newer research, beginning with four schools of thought. The roots of these perspectives grow together in a number of ways, but they also emphasize different things. The second section of this chapter reviews recent research concerning language and science learning, building to a conceptual framework based on Sutton's earlier work. The reader should note that a detailed perspective on specific studies of spoken and written discourse in science classrooms is provided by Greg Kelly in Chapter 16. A comprehensive recent review of science literacy by Yore, Bisanz, and Hand (2003) deals more extensively than I do here with the important role of writing in science learning. My aim here is to propose a framework informed by theoretical issues that are historically significant or productively emerging in science education, without covering the same ground in the same way. To do this, I first identify some of the contributions of four productive contemporary approaches to studying the role of language in science learning: the Vygotskian perspective, conceptual change theory, sociolinguistics, and situated learning.

ORIGINS OF CONTEMPORARY RESEARCH ON LANGUAGE AND LEARNING

Vygotsky

Lev Vygotsky was a contemporary of the young Piaget and closely followed his work. He concurred with many, but not all, of Piaget's conclusions. Vygotsky's most compelling contribution to science education is probably *Thought and Language* (1934/1986). Although the book says practically nothing about pedagogy, it has been productively probed for its educational implications, which are significant (Howe, 1996; Wertsch, 1985, 1991). Vygotsky distinguished between spontaneous and scientific thinking. Spontaneous concepts arise in a child's everyday experience and begin with egocentric speech, often in the company of others. Eventually, vocalized speech is internalized, evolving into inner speech. According to this view, spoken language precedes conceptualization in everyday life. Meaning actually follows speech.

According to Vygotsky, scientific thinking is special because new scientific concepts generally arise from work within a formal conceptual structure (which may be explicitly taught). Consequently, science learning is a process of moving from the linguistically abstract to the concrete, not vice versa. Children learn spontaneous concepts (e.g., what a bowl is) from their everyday experiences. Scientific concepts (e.g., what photosynthesis is) are often invisible, abstract, or otherwise inaccessible. One oft-overlooked instructional implication of this perspective is that some scientific concepts may never arise from hands-on experience, no matter how creative or time-consuming that experience may be.

Vygotsky's "zone of proximal development" (ZPD) has been used extensively by researchers and educators. The idea is appealing: The trajectory of future learning can be predicted by comparing a child's work alone with his or her work in the company of a more knowledgeable teacher or peer. Numerous studies have translated the ZPD concept into a pedagogical agenda: Engage learners in group tasks with others, on the grounds that the social setting will allow many students to stretch beyond the limits of their abilities, working alone.

Finally, in *Thought and Language*, Vygotsky noted that writing is linguistically distinct from and more demanding than speech. The developmental path of writing is more abstract, symbolic, and less likely to elicit (and be shaped by) feedback from others. A number of research and instructional projects have been built upon Vygotskian ideas, such as the Cognitive Acceleration through Science Education (CASE) project in Britain (Adey, 1999), research on elementary science instruction in Mexico (Candela, 1995), and the effects of computer-mediated communication in American science and math instruction (Charnitski & Harvey, 1999).

Some critics have charged that Vygotsky has been misappropriated for nefarious purposes like promoting sociocultural relativism, replacing formal instruction with useless hands-on experiences, and misinterpreting the ZPD as a bridge between everyday experience and scientific concepts. Vygotsky, argued Stuart Rowlands (2000), was an "out-and-out objectivist" who believed that theory precedes practice in science. Everyday experiences may be necessary for scientific concepts to develop, but they do not cause that development. Scientific ideas ascend from the abstract to the concrete (Rowlands, 2000; Rowlands, Graham, & Berry, 1999). In science there is always a critical need for formal instruction.

Conceptual Change Theory

Conceptual change theory (CCT) has long been an important paradigm in science education research. Building from work by Piaget (1929/1969) and Thomas Kuhn

(1970), the team of Posner, Strike, Hewson, and Gertzog (1982) outlined a model of science learning that accounts for the resistance of misconceptions to change and that foregrounds the interaction between individuals and the scientific communities (and theoretical perspectives) to which they are acculturated. From a sociolinguistic perspective, CCT is itself a fruitful research program; that is, it stimulates the generation of interesting questions. For example, Lavoie (1999) documented the positive effects of adding a prediction/discussion phase to the beginning of a learning cycle in secondary biology. Among the features of his experimental treatment was an insistence that students make their predictions explicit and that they publicly debate, modify, and reevaluate those predictions. The genesis of these steps from CCT is clear.

Constructivism has largely supplanted CCT in the science education research vernacular, despite the problem of its many different meanings. Nevertheless, CCT remains a viable theory and may prove—for social, philosophical, and methodological reasons—to be more long-lived. Fundamentally, constructivism is about individuals creating individual meanings, sometimes in social settings. Conceptual change theory emphasizes the congruence of individual understandings with public, often established, knowledge (see also Chapter 2, this volume). CCT also foregrounds the importance of epistemic communities (Kelly, 1997).

As Vygotsky's work is becoming more widely known, researchers and educators are seeking ways to extend CCT from the intramental to the intermental plane. Using an analysis of a chemistry lesson, Mortimer and Machado (2000), for example, discussed the evolution of their understandings of cognitive conflict (an individual, Piagetian construct) to one of public, discursive conflict, resolved dialogically. In recent years, the emphasis of many studies of conceptual development in science education has shifted from the investigation of individuals' cognitive schemata to studies of interactive discourse and the co-construction of concepts in natural language. This has required finding tools and methods better suited for documenting and analyzing the dynamics of spoken language in classrooms. This brings us to a third major approach to studying how language and learning are related: the sociolinguistic perspective.

Social Semiotics and Sociocultural Considerations

Lemke's *Talking Science* (1990), a field guide to analyzing the content of classroom discourse, clearly demonstrates the need to consider the context of spoken language. Although this principle is a sociolinguistic fundamental, Lemke drew most directly on what he labeled "social semiotics." Here and in later works (e.g., Lemke, 2001), he argued that meaning is derived in part from the cultures in which talk takes place, and that meaning-making is impeded when culture clashes arise between disciplinary cultures, as well as between more conventional social/economic/political/ethnic cultures. In fact, the science classroom sits on the border between competing cultures, such as the scientific community, which values open inquiry and disagreement, and the formal school community, which generally prefers quiet obedience. Lemke and others found that sociologies of science also offer useful tools for understanding the social work of scientists, from which implications for classroom practice can be drawn (Kelly, Carlsen, & Cunningham, 1993; Roth, 1995a).

We learn to communicate in different ways in different settings. Children who begin school without having been socialized to conventional forms of school communication may experience communicative failures that are interpreted as lack of aptitude or intelligence (Heath, 1983). Studies of language minority students demonstrate how the routine communicative expectations of majority teachers can be misinterpreted because of lack of teachers' understanding of the cultural norms and practices in their students' out-of-school lives (Au & Mason, 1983; Erickson & Mohatt, 1982). Our *discourse* consists of the words, gestures, and other signs that we use; our *Discourse* consists of all of the other things that help us make sense of language: "Different ways of thinking, acting, interacting, valuing, feeling, believing, and using symbols, tools, and objects" (Gee, 1999, p. 13). Learning may be easier when teachers strive for instructional congruence between the academic culture and the culture(s) of their students, modifying subject matter by using students' language and cultural experiences (Lee & Fradd, 1998).

Provocative but less thoroughly explored, cultural practices and language may be exploitable in addressing students' scientific misconceptions. Hewson and Hamlyn (1984) discovered that southern African Sotho and Tswana teens speak languages that predispose them to kinetic (particulate) rather than caloric (substance) views of heat. Potentially, this linguistic and cultural resource might help them avoid common misconceptions. Although later studies of Sotho college entrants could not corroborate this phenomenon (Lubben, Netshisaulu, & Campbell, 1999), further studies of the interaction of nonmajority language and science learning opportunities would be worthwhile.

Hogan and Corey (2001) provided an excellent example of classroom research from a sociocultural perspective. In addition to *Talking Science*, Groisman, Shapiro, and Willinsky (1991) offer a gentle introduction to the use of semiotics in science education research.

Situated Learning and Communities of Practice

Clearly, the concepts of situated learning, legitimate peripherality, cognitive apprenticeships, and communities of practice are having an important impact on science education research. Studies by Lave, Wenger, and others have given educational researchers much to think about and work with, even though the bulk of their work has been done in nonschool settings (Chaiklin & Lave, 1993; Lave & Wenger, 1992; Wenger, 1998). Studies of cognition in situ—of craftwork, midwifery, and other jobs—reveal how novices learn complex skills through participation in real work, initially as peripheral participants. One of the most exciting aspects of this literature is its suggestions that learning is not a process of internalizing knowledge, that it is not promoted by social activity; learning is social activity.

Wenger (1998) portrayed a claims-processing office as an environment in which work, interaction, and learning are inextricably linked. "Issues about language," Lave and Wenger (1992) wrote, "may well have more to do with legitimacy of participation . . . than they do with knowledge transmission. . . . Learning to become a legitimate participant in a community involves learning how to talk (and be silent) in the manner of full participants" (p. 105).

In some cultures and for many crafts, conventional didactic instruction would be culturally inappropriate (Jordan, 1989) and less suitable than the traditional apprenticeship model.

Roth (1995b) applied many of these ideas in his analysis of science classroom practices. Of particular interest are his demonstrations of the transformation of gestures, inscriptions, and other phenomena in shaping concepts in the public sphere, a paralinguistic process evocative of Vygotsky. In the laboratory setting, gestures, for example, may function less as evidence of conceptual understanding than as a tool for co-constructing concepts with one's laboratory partners (Roth, 2001). The utility of viewing science learning in a social fashion has also been demonstrated in studies of adult learners. For example, in an ethnographic study that took place over several years, Bowen and Roth (2002) identified the different contributions to the education of ecologists that take place in formal and informal settings, and demonstrated the importance of stories and other informal communications in shaping novices' understandings. They also argued that storytelling contributes to social cohesion in scientific communities. In other words, not only do communities of practice provide a context and a means for learning science through language, but informal language—often superficially off-task—functions to help create functioning communities. The model of apprenticeship embedded in Lave's work can also be used productively to study the learning of novice teachers in settings where they coteach, and studies conducted with this lens have the potential to inform teacher education, viewing the learning of novice and experts as reciprocal (Roth & Tobin, 2001).

TOWARD A REVISED FRAMEWORK FOR THE ROLE OF LANGUAGE IN SCIENCE EDUCATION

My goal in this section is to extend and update Sutton's 1998 framework concerning the role and function of language in science teaching and learning, focusing on four features: (a) what a speaker appears to be doing, (b) what listeners think that they are doing, (c) how language is thought to work in learning, and (d) how language is thought to work in scientific discovery.

What a Speaker Appears to Be Doing

Controlling discourse. Although of course students often speak and write, traditional teaching is characterized by an asymmetry of conversational rights that favors the teacher. Teacher questions, for example, both reflect a teacher's authority and reinforce it (Carlsen, 1991a). Questions assert sociolinguistic power (Mishler, 1978), and when teachers find themselves discussing unfamiliar subject matter, they may rely upon questioning to prevent the topic of discussion from wandering into uncomfortable territory (Carlsen, 1991b). This creates what Driver (1983) labeled as the science teachers' dilemma: teaching science as a process of inquiry and as an accepted body of knowledge poses a constant linguistic challenge. Driver wrote, "On the one hand pupils are expected to explore a phenomenon for themselves, collect data and make inferences based upon it; on the other hand this process is intended to lead to the currently accepted law or principle" (p. 3). We expect teachers to invite students to construct meaning, but we hold them accountable for the construction of the right meaning.

Fortunately, most students cooperate in the most common patterns of classroom discourse, such as variations on the Initiation-Response-Evaluation (IRE) triad that have been described by Mehan (1979), Lemke, and many others. Viewed as a language game (Wittgenstein, 1967), the IRE is both a mechanism of control and a cultural tool (Wertsch, 1991). Unfortunately, even well-intentioned control of the direction of science talk may result in a conflation of the teacher's authority as an expert with her authority as the person in charge (Carlsen, 1997; Russell, 1983; Toulmin, 1958). The resulting discourse may suggest to students that the nature of science is more certain and less susceptible to challenge than it really is. There are other cognitive hazards. Wilson (1999) cautioned: "[If] engagement in epistemic tasks in discourse is important in the construction of abstract declarative knowledge and conceptual understanding, then students may face disadvantages in classrooms in which discursive practices are teacher controlled and dominated by extensive triadic dialogue about knowledge claims provided for students by the teacher or the text" (p. 1080).

In more open-ended project-based science work, students may not understand the rules, and both order and learning may suffer. There are hazards to unguided discovery (Rogoff, 1994), but teachers who know how to play language games can transform original student moves and open them to extension, elaboration, or critique (Polman & Pea, 2001). But it is a balancing act. Hogan, Nastasi, and Pressley (1999) found that teacher-directed discourse was most effective in promoting higher-order reasoning and higher-quality explanations, but discussions among students were more generative and exploratory. Other work on the balance between restricting or expanding control has been informed by Vygotsky's ZPD concept (e.g., Blanton, Westbrook, & Carter, 2001).

Creating opportunities for meaning-making.   On a more constructive note, teachers facilitate linguistic meaning-making in many ways. Kelly and his collaborators documented the work of a science non-expert teaching science to third graders. Instead of closing down the conversation, the teacher successfully modeled and directed scientific discourse, leading her students to define science in their local context (Crawford, Kelly, & Brown, 2000).

> To become a member of a community (e.g., science classroom or research laboratory) who acts in socially appropriate ways (e.g., one who adheres to genre conventions when speaking and writeing), one must first understand the social practices of a community, that is, what counts as a valid description, explanation, inference, etc. (p. 626).

The research group found similar practices in a high school physics classroom: a teacher framing activities and coordinating sociocultural practices, thus leading his students to appropriate scientific discourse (Kelly & Chen, 1999). Coherent and jointly constructed discourse resulted in the creation of public, sociolinguistic meaning.

Of course, local meaning is not the same as scientific fact: Gravity cannot be dismissed through a classroom conversation. Science is epistemologically distinct in its empirical approaches, its forms of argument, and the demonstrable productivity of concepts and theories that would never arise spontaneously in a school setting (quantum physics, for example). Recalling Vygotsky, scientific concepts often grow from the abstract to the concrete. They are useful because they are decontextualized (Rowlands, 2000). Approached from a different direction, scientific experiments yield facts through social processes of inscription, translation, and the ultimate removal of "weasel words" that relate the empirical *who*, *what*, *when*, *where*, and *how* (Latour & Woolgar, 1986). The approaches are different, but the outcomes are the same: useful facts stripped from the particulars of their construction.

What Listeners Think They Are Doing

In inquiry-oriented classrooms, students often work in groups, and their work can be viewed as contributing to the solution of shared problems. Students can learn science and *about* science when their communication takes place through online discussions (Hoadley & Linn, 2000), computer-mediated peer review (Trautmann et al., 2003), and other modalities, but group work usually takes place face to face. Without the teacher present, the rules of the language game are altered, and the new rules must be understood by all in order to make progress. Communicative competence entails knowing how to take turns without the teacher's direction, how to hold (and yield) the floor, and how to make sense to (and of) others. These tasks are inevitably complicated by speaker differences of gender, culture, ethnicity, and so on (Philips, 1972).

The substance of science talk can be evaluated in a number of ways. Geddis (1998), for example, developed a multidimensional method for gauging the quality of discourse. High-quality discourse includes practices like giving reasons for assertions and demonstrating intellectual independence from the teacher's authority. Hogan (1999) identified metacognition as an essential element in group inquiry and conducted a study in which students in experimental classes received training in metacognition and cognitive strategies for group work. The intervention resulted in improvements in students' knowledge about metacognition and collaborative reasoning, but no difference was found in the experimental and control groups' actual collaborative behaviors. Nevertheless, the success of metacognitive strategies in individual students' learning suggests that further work along these lines may be valuable.

Epistemological beliefs may not change easily. In one study, 4 weeks of substantive inquiry about evolution produced little shift in students' epistemological frameworks, which were found to be unstable and ill-defined. The investigators in that study advocated explicit epistemic discourse coupled with inquiry (Sandoval & Morrison, 2003).

In a study of college engineering students, Kittleson and Southerland (2004) found that concept negotiation was rare, even when the instructor structured the task to promote that process. Clearly, success in channeling student discourse into productive knowledge construction is a pedagogical goal that demands much more work.

How Language Works in Learning

Making meaning.   The Sapir-Whorf hypothesis (Whorf, 1956), now largely discredited, proposed that language shapes human cognition in profound ways, so that a person's native language would shape how she perceived the world. Today it is commonly assumed by linguists that our brains are wired for language (although the details remain in dispute, such as Chomsky's (1972) theory of a universal grammar). Why then is culture—and the signifying systems that culture embodies—so important in meaning-making? From a sociocultural perspective, learning involves appropriating and using intellectual and practical tools. Much of what a student learns comes not from direct experience, but from texts that are organized to tell a disciplinary story. "From a sociocultural perspective, the use of texts as the prime vehicle for communicating knowledge can be seen as a further step in the adoption of experience-distant accounting practices for understanding the world" (Säljö, 1998, p. 49). Human knowledge is discursive in nature, reproduced through language and artifacts in social institutions like schools.

> The knowledge produced within these discourses does not remain inside the heads of individuals. . . . Rather, knowledge emerges as properties of tools and socially organized practices in which individuals participate, and which by necessity are ideological in nature—without values there can be no knowledge. . . . Knowledge is fundamentally argumentative in nature; it moves the world rather than reflects it. (Säljö, p. 53)

Wong and Pugh (2001) observed that we promote the teaching of concepts rather than facts because concepts are more integrative and thus more powerful in science. Cognitive perspectives emphasize thinking; sociocognitive perspectives highlight the role of language in stimulating and supporting thinking. John Dewey emphasized ideas rather than concepts, and being, the combination of cognition and action:

> Dewey's emphasis on being, rather than cognition, reveals an epistemological stance that locates meaning neither in the mind of the learner nor in the surrounding environment. Instead, meaning is a transactive phenomenon: it exists only in the situation created in interaction between person and world. . . . To some readers, ideas and concepts may seem synonymous and we admit that Dewey's use of the term *idea* (along with other terms), although precise, is often confusing. To begin, concepts are something that students learn: To understand is to have an accurate representation of it and to be able to apply it appropriately. The goal of conceptually oriented teaching is the construction of accurate, meaningful representations. By contrast, ideas are something that seizes students and transforms them. The goal of ideas-based teaching is to help students to be taken by an idea and to live with it, to be with it in their world. (Wong & Pugh, pp. 324–325)

Of course, meaning-making is not the only function of language in the classroom. Discourse has two distinct functions in science education: generating meaning (its generative function) and conveying meaning (its authoritative function) (McDonald & Abell, 2002; Mortimer & Machado, 2000).

Representing knowledge. A number of researchers have studied how knowledge is represented in science education settings and have developed tools that provide insights into how language functions in learning. For example, in a cross-cultural study of English and Asian-speaking children, Curtis and Millar (1988) developed a method for representing students' knowledge about scientific concepts by classifying ideas generated in a writing task. Concept mapping in diverse forms remains a popular tool for representing the relationships among concepts (Fisher, Wandersee, & Moody, 2000), and the use of concept maps has been facilitated by several different computer tools. Semantic networks, ideational networks, and other graphical diagrams have been found to be useful diagnostically and to stimulate science talk with language minority students (Anderson, Randle, & Covotsos, 2001; Duran, Dugan, & Weffer, 1998).

Building upon work on situated learning and the sociology of science, Roth (1995a) described a number of cases of both individual and collaborative knowledge construction. The assignment of group work and the use of conscription devices such as concept maps helped create conditions in which "students had to negotiate the meanings of concept labels or future courses of action. During these negotiations they externalized and objectivized their understandings so that they were open not only to public scrutiny but also to critical self-reflection. In this process, students negotiated prior understandings and invented new and not-yet experienced connections between concepts" (p. 267).

In related studies, Roth and his colleagues described the semiotic significance of graphs as signs representing objects and processes (Roth, Bowen, & Masciotra, 2002), as well as the role of gestures and rough-draft talk, which they believe support the subsequent evolution of more structured talk, iconic objects, and eventually abstract communication tools, including symbols and writing (Roth & Lawless, 2002). "Gestures are a medium on which language can piggyback in its development" (Roth & Welzel, 2001). The authors suggested that, because gestures frequently are used to refer to materials in the laboratory, students should not be sent home to write laboratory reports until they have had the opportunity to discuss the complex conceptual issues explored in the teaching laboratory.

Cultural Considerations

The interaction of culture, language, and schooling has been a productive focus of research in a number of disciplines. A great deal is known, for example, about how and why differences between the cultures and languages of school and home can be problematic for students (Au & Mason, 1983; Shultz, Erickson, & Florio, 1982). Even among speakers of the same language, problems may arise if the home register does not match the privileged formal register of schools (Bernstein, 1961). The dynamics of communication between linguistic and ethnic minority and majority speakers continues to be an active and interesting area of work (see, e.g., Moje, Collazo, Carrillo, & Marx, 2001; Stoddart, Pinal, Latzke, & Canaday, 2002). Lee's (1999) study of south Florida children's attributions of Hurricane Andrew demonstrated gender, socioeconomic, and ethnicity effects, not only with respect to what the children knew, but also where they got their information. Lee and Fradd (1996) emphasized that although culture may sometimes contribute to misconceptions, and that scientific practices like questioning and public skepticism may clash with some cultural norms, culture also provides metaphors and other linguistic resources that we are only beginning to understand.

Writing

Although my comments have focused primarily on spoken language, there is a growing literature on how writing functions in the development of knowledge. For example, Keys has shown how collaborative writing can enhance students' constructions of scientific concepts (Keys, 1994, 1999) and the quality of their reasoning (Keys, 1995). She and her colleagues developed a Science Writing Heuristic as an alternative to the traditional laboratory report and reported that it promotes students' generation of assertions from data; making connections among procedures, data, evidence, and claims; and metacognition (Keys, Hand, Prain, & Collins, 1999). Positive outcomes from interventions using diverse types of writing tasks have been reported, although the students themselves may not see writing as a tool for knowledge development (Prain & Hand, 1999).

Talking and writing yield different outcomes because of their different natures. Rivard and Straw (2000) noted:

> Talk is important for sharing, clarifying, and distributing scientific ideas among peers, while asking questions, hypothesizing, explaining, and formulating ideas together all appear to be important mechanisms during discussions. The use of writing appears to be important for refining and consolidating new ideas with prior knowledge. These two modalities appear to be dialectical: talk is social, divergent, and generative, whereas writing is personal, convergent, and reflective. (p. 588)

Both are important for doing science in classrooms: just as it is through the public processes of formal science that objectivity is pursued, via intersubjective means.

How Language Works in Science

Language is central to science. It is the medium through which claims are made and challenged, empirical methods and data are recorded, and the story of inquiry unfolds. Language is not just a vehicle for transmitting scientific information; the history of science reveals that analogies, for example, are a powerful conceptual resource for scientific discovery and understanding (Dörries, 2002). Scientific language is rich with specialized terms that have metaphorical origins (Sutton, 1992).

Compared with students, scientists, not surprisingly, hold much more sophisticated understandings about how to make knowledge claims from data. They are more likely to prioritize rhetorically the relationship between empirical evidence and conclusions, and they attribute this ability to their earlier socialization to science. In contrast, middle-school science students rely more upon their personal views to evaluate claims (Hogan & Maglienti, 2001). Nevertheless, scientists generally believe that the writing process involves knowledge telling, not knowledge building. Their writing tends to be narrowly focused on a specific genre, target audience, and approach (Yore, Hand, & Prain, 2002).

The experimental article is a specialized genre with an interesting history. For example, the detachment and emotionlessness of the form may have helped to reduce factionalism in science (Bazerman, 1988). Scientific writing is lexically dense because it is replete with colorful, invented words that reduce complex processes to singular identities (Halliday & Martin, 1993) (e.g., *photosynthesis* or *cellular automaton*). Also commonly invented are scientific discoveries, which are often reconstructed after the dust settles, fixed in time retrospectively by a scientific community (Brannigan, 1981; Woolgar, 1976). But the more startling the claim, the more likely it is that there will be dust to settle. Discursive consensus in science is not as clean or as common as is generally believed. Intellectual divergence is normal, and the interpretations of scientists may vary with their own sociocultural context (Mulkay, 1991).

Nevertheless, it would be an unusual scientific research manuscript that began with a personal statement about the investigator's gender, race, religion, or ethnicity. The official registers of science do not document an investigator's personal and social values, beliefs, and commitments, because, after all, facts speak for themselves. The status of science is attributable in part to persistent myths. As Helen Longino (1990) noted, science achieves objectivity through social means. We ought to be willing to talk about it. Furthermore, students of science need those opportunities as well. Longino (2002) offered four criteria for effective scientific discourse: (a) public venues for the critical review of methods, facts, and the interpretation of data; (b) an expectation of uptake—that investigators will respond to the substance of public criticism; (c) the existence of public standards for evaluating claims, such as the criterion that claims refer specifically to data in ways that can be generally understood; and (d) that discourse occurs in a context of tempered intellectual equality—one that recognizes inevitable differences in participants' knowledge without denying the less knowledgeable opportunities to challenge.

CONCLUSION AND IMPLICATIONS

Table 3.1 updates and extends Sutton's (1998) framework. To his two articulations of the role of language—1. a system for transmitting information, and 2. an interpretive system for making sense of experience—I have added a third column: a tool for participation in communities of practice. This third perspective reflects a contemporary emphasis on learning as a social accomplishment. Formal science is much more than Scientist A convincing Scientist B that X is true. Scientist A's conception of X is almost always the product of extensive work in a local community of practice (such as a lab group), and the proposed definition of X may have emerged there from a complex iteration of experiments, inscriptions, translations, conversations, arguments, informal talks, feedback from peers outside the group, methodological training, new experiments, etc. (see Knorr-Cetina, 1983). At the broader disciplinary level, Scientist A and Scientist B probably share assumptions and understandings that are not recognized by others. Scientist C (and her group) may be exploring the same scientific terrain with very different tools and assumptions, leading to very different conclusions. Eventually, an agonistic struggle is likely, but as Longino (1990) notes, that is the point of science. It is in the expectation and practice of public argument that science progresses. Conflict is not only permissible, it is necessary. This does not mean that science is nothing more than mob psychology. Usually arguments must be based on observable phenomena, but what counts as an observation is something we agree to agree about.

An important problem for researchers using sociocultural tools—at least in the United States—is that we are working in an era of accountability, and political forces demand "objective" measures of student learning and educational productivity. Today's emphasis on individual standardized testing is based on an assumption that learning is an individual accomplishment. One implication of a sociocultural perspective is that we need to develop better tools for evaluating learning in complex social environments. Affordable new tools for video recording and analysis

TABLE 3.1.
Changing Perspectives on the Role of Language in Science and Science Teaching

Characteristic*	Role of Language		
	A system for transmitting information (Sutton, 1998)	An interpretive system for making sense of experience (Sutton, 1998)	A tool for participation in communities of practice
1 What the speaker or writer appears to be doing.	Describing, telling, reporting.	Persuading, suggesting, ex-ploring, figuring.	Contributing to the solution of a shared problem.
2 What listeners or readers think that they are doing.	Receiving, noting, accumulating.	Making sense of another person's intended meaning.	Contributing to the solution of a shared problem.
3 How language is thought to work in learning.	Clear transmission from teacher to learner; importance of teacher's speech.	Re-expression of ideas by learner; importance of learner's speech.	Achievement of a shared understanding. Learning and language as social accomplishments.
4 How language is thought to work in scientific discovery.	We find a fact, label it, and report it to others. Words stand for things.	Our choices of words influence how we and others see things: highlighting some features and ignoring others.	Language is used to persuade, and "discovery" is often constructed only retrospectively.

*Note. "Characteristic" labels and the next two columns are based on Sutton (1998).

offer great potential for helping researchers study language as an educational outcome, not just a means. However, few science education researchers have had formal training in sociolinguistics; after all, their undergraduate training tends to occur in the sciences. It would benefit our community to support the development of graduate training programs that teach future researchers skills to work with linguistic data.

A related implication is that we need to publicly challenge the prevailing view of learning as an individual accomplishment. We must challenge that view with policymakers and parents as well as within our own research community. Strategically, support for the development of social methods of assessment is likely to require convincing the public of the social nature of real science and demonstrating that the attrition of talent from the scientific work force is in part the result of practices that represent science as the individual accomplishment of unambiguous understandings.

New tools notwithstanding, collecting data in the form of natural language is extraordinarily time-consuming and expensive. Because our community lacks useful standards for the collection, transcription, analysis, cataloging, and use of sociolinguistic data, data collected in one study are unlikely to be used again. Compounding this problem, university institutional review boards today often seek assurances that the use of video recording in precollege classrooms is minimized and that recordings are locked away or destroyed after research is conducted. The development of standards for sociolinguistic analysis in science education would be a useful effort. These standards should certainly be informed by standards in related fields. However, our needs are likely to be unique, given the gestures and other signs, texts and inscriptions, specialized tools, and shifting group composition that characterize science learning environments. We are likely to be best served by systems that could be used responsibly by researchers who have not had extensive training in linguistics. As part of such an initiative, it would be useful to develop conventions for metadata production and cataloging (e.g., through the Open Archives Initiative, www.openarchives.org), as well as mechanisms for protecting human subjects without the necessity of locking data away from other researchers. A corpus of such data would be useful in both future research and for training new researchers.

ACKNOWLEDGMENTS

Thanks to Brian Hand and William Newman, who reviewed this chapter.

REFERENCES

Adey, P. (1999). *The science of thinking, and science for thinking: A description of cognitive acceleration through science education (CASE),* Innodata Monographs No. 2. Geneva: International Bureau of Education.

Anderson, O. R., Randle, D., & Covotsos, T. (2001). The role of ideational networks in laboratory inquiry learning and knowledge of evolution among seventh grade students. *Science Education, 85,* 410–425.

Au, K. H., & Mason, J. M. (1983). Cultural congruence in classroom participation structures: Achieving a balance of rights. *Discourse Processes, 6,* 145–167.

Bazerman, C. (1988). *Shaping written knowledge: The genre and activity of the experimental article in science.* Madison: University of Wisconsin Press.

Bernstein, B. (1961). Social class and linguistic development. In A. Halsey, J. Floud, & B. Bernstein (Eds.), *Education, economy and society* (pp. 288–314). New York: Free Press.

Blanton, M. L., Westbrook, S. L., & Carter, G. (2001, April). *Using Valsiner's zone theory to interpret change in classroom practice: Beyond the zone of proximal development.* Paper presented at the annual meeting of the American Educational Research Association, Seattle, WA.

Bowen, G. M., & Roth, W.-M. (2002). The "socialization" and enculturation of ecologists in formal and informal settings. *Electronic Journal of Science Education, 6*(3), Article 01. Retrieved November 20, 2004, from http://unr.edu/homepage/crowther/ejse/bowenroth .html

Brannigan, A. (1981). *The social basis of scientific discoveries.* Cambridge, England: Cambridge University Press.

Candela, A. (1995). Consensus construction as a collective task in Mexican science classes. *Anthropology & Education Quarterly, 26,* 458–474.

Carlsen, W. S. (1991a). Questioning in classrooms: A sociolinguistic perspective. *Review of Educational Research, 61,* 157–178.

Carlsen, W. S. (1991b). Subject-matter knowledge and science teaching: A pragmatic perspective. In J. Brophy (Ed.), *Advances in research on teaching: Vol. 2. Teachers' knowledge of subject matter as it relates to their teaching practice* (pp. 115–143). Greenwich, CT: JAI Press.

Carlsen, W. S. (1997). Never ask a question if you don't know the answer: The tension in teaching between modeling scientific argument and maintaining law and order. *Journal of Classroom Interaction, 32*(2), 14–23.

Chaiklin, S., & Lave, J. (1993). *Understanding practice: Perspectives on activity and context.* Cambridge, England: Cambridge University Press.

Charnitski, C. W., & Harvey, F. A. (1999, February). *Integrating science and mathematics curricula using computer mediated communications: A Vygotskian perspective.* Paper presented at the annual meeting of the Association for Educational Communications and Technology, Houston, TX.

Chomsky, N. (1972). *Language and mind.* New York: Harcourt.

Crawford, T., Kelly, G. J., & Brown, C. (2000). Ways of knowing beyond facts and laws of science: An ethnographic investigation of student engagement in scientific practices. *Journal of Research in Science Teaching, 37,* 237–258.

Curtis, S., & Millar, R. (1988). Language and conceptual understanding in science: A comparison of English and Asian-language-speaking children. *Research in Science and Technological Education, 6,* 61–77.

Dörries, M. (Ed.). (2002). *Experimenting in tongues: Studies in science and language.* Stanford, CA: Stanford University Press.

Driver, R. (1983). *The pupil as scientist?* Milton Keynes, England: Open University Press.

Duran, B. J., Dugan, T., & Weffer, R. (1998). Language minority students in high school: The role of language in learning biology concepts. *Science Education, 82,* 311–341.

Erickson, F., & Mohatt, G. (1982). Cultural organization of participant structures in two classrooms of Indian students. In G. D. Spindler (Ed.), *Doing the ethnography of schooling: Educational anthropology in action* (pp. 132–174). New York: Holt, Rinehart & Winston.

Fisher, K. M., Wandersee, J. H., & Moody, D. E. (2000). *Mapping biology knowledge.* Dordrecht, the Netherlands: Kluwer Academic.

Geddis, A. N. (1998). Analyzing discourse about controversial issues in the science classroom. In D. A. Roberts & L. Östman (Eds.), *Problems of meaning in science curriculum.* New York: Teachers College Press.

Gee, J. (1999). *An introduction to discourse analysis.* New York: Routledge.

Groisman, A., Shapiro, B., & Willinsky, J. (1991). The potential of semiotics to inform understanding of events in science education. *International Journal of Science Education, 13,* 217–226.

Halliday, M. A. K., & Martin, J. R. (1993). *Writing science.* London: Falmer Press.

Heath, S. B. (1983). *Ways with words.* Cambridge, England: Cambridge University Press.

Hewson, M. G., & Hamlyn, J. (1984). The influence of intellectual environment on conceptions of heat. *European Journal for Science Education, 6,* 245–262.

Hoadley, C. M., & Linn, M. C. (2000). Teaching science through online, peer discussions: Speakeasy in the knowledge integration environment. *International Journal of Science Education, 22,* 839–857.

Hogan, K. (1999). Thinking aloud together: A test of an intervention to foster students' collaborative scientific reasoning. *Journal of Research in Science Teaching, 36,* 1085–1109.

Hogan, K., & Corey, C. (2001). Viewing classrooms as cultural contexts for fostering scientific literacy. *Anthropology & Education Quarterly, 32,* 214–243.

Hogan, K., & Maglienti, M. (2001). Comparing the epistemological underpinnings of students' and scientists' reasoning about conclusions. *Journal of Research in Science Teaching, 38,* 663–687.

Hogan, K., Nastasi, B. K., & Pressley, M. (1999). Discourse patterns and collaborative scientific reasoning in peer and teacher-guided discussions. *Cognition and Instruction, 17,* 379–432.

Howe, A. C. (1996). Development of science concepts within a Vygotskian framework. *Science Education, 80,* 35–51.

Jordan, B. (1989). Cosmopolitical obstetrics: Some insights from the training of traditional midwives. *Social Science and Medicine, 28,* 925–944.

Kelly, G. J. (1997). Research traditions in comparative context: A philosophical challenge to radical constructivism. *Science Education, 81,* 355–375.

Kelly, G. J., Brown, C., & Crawford, T. (2000). Experiments, contingencies, and curriculum: Providing opportunities for learning through improvisation in science teaching. *Science Education, 84,* 624–657.

Kelly, G. J., Carlsen, W. S., & Cunningham, C. M. (1993). Science education in sociocultural context: Perspectives from the sociology of science. *Science Education, 77,* 207–220.

Kelly, G. J., & Chen, C. (1999). The sound of music: Constructing science as sociocultural practices through oral and written discourse. *Journal of Research in Science Teaching, 36*, 883–915.

Keys, C. W. (1994). The development of scientific reasoning skills in conjunction with collaborative writing assignments: An interpretive study of six ninth-grade students. *Journal of Research in Science Teaching, 31*, 1003–1022.

Keys, C. W. (1995). An interpretive study of students' use of scientific reasoning during a collaborative report writing intervention in ninth grade general science. *Science Education, 79*, 415–435.

Keys, C. W. (1999). Revitalizing instruction in scientific genres: Connecting knowledge production with writing to learn in science. *Science Education, 83*, 115–130.

Keys, C. W., Hand, B., Prain, V., & Collins, S. (1999). Using the science writing heuristic as a tool for learning from laboratory investigations in secondary science. *Journal of Research in Science Teaching, 36*, 1065–1084.

Kittleson, J. M., & Southerland, S. A. (2004). The role of discourse in group knowledge construction: A case study of engineering students. *Journal of Research in Science Teaching, 41*, 267–293.

Knorr-Cetina, K. D. (1983). The ethnographic study of scientific work: Towards a constructivist interpretation of science. In K. D. Knorr-Cetina & M. Mulkay (Eds.), *Science observed: Perspectives on the social study of science* (pp. 115–140). Beverly Hills, CA: Sage.

Kuhn, T. S. (1970). *The structure of scientific revolutions.* Chicago: University of Chicago.

Latour, B., & Woolgar, S. (1986). *Laboratory life: The construction of scientific facts.* Princeton, NJ: Princeton University Press.

Lave, J., & Wenger, E. (1992). *Situated learning: Legitimate peripheral participation.* Cambridge, England: Cambridge University Press.

Lavoie, D. R. (1999). Effects of emphasizing hypothetico-predictive reasoning within the science learning cycle on high school student's process skills and conceptual understandings in biology. *Journal of Research in Science Teaching, 36*, 1127–1147.

Lee, O. (1999). Science knowledge, world views, and information sources in social and cultural contexts: Making sense after a natural disaster. *American Educational Research Journal, 36*, 187–219.

Lee, O., & Fradd, S. (1996). Interactional patterns of linguistically diverse students and teachers: Insights for promoting science learning. *Linguistics and Education, 8*, 269–297.

Lee, O., & Fradd, S. H. (1998). Science for all, including students from non-English language backgrounds. *Educational Researcher, 27*(4), 12–21.

Lemke, J. L. (1990). *Talking science: Language, learning, and values.* Norwood, NJ: Ablex.

Lemke, J. L. (2001). Articulating communities: Sociocultural perspectives on science education. *Journal of Research in Science Teaching, 38*, 296–316.

Longino, H. E. (1990). *Science as social knowledge: Values and objectivity in scientific inquiry.* Princeton, NJ: Princeton University Press.

Longino, H. E. (2002). *The fate of knowledge.* Princeton, NJ: Princeton University Press.

Lubben, F., Netshisaulu, T., & Campbell, B. (1999). Students' use of cultural metaphors and their scientific understandings related to heating. *Science Education, 83*, 761–774.

McDonald, J. T., & Abell, S. K. (2002, April). *Essential elements of inquiry-based science and its connection to generative and authoritative student discourse.* Paper presented at the Annual Meeting of the American Educational Research Association, New Orleans, LA.

Medawar, P. (1974). Is the scientific paper a fraud? In E. W. Jenkins & R. C. Whitfield (Eds.), *Readings in science education* (pp. 14–16). London: McGraw-Hill.

Mehan, H. (1979). *Learning lessons.* Cambridge, MA: Harvard University Press.

Mishler, E. G. (1978). Studies in dialogue and discourse. III. Utterance structure and utterance function in interrogative sequences. *Journal of Psycholinguistic Research, 7*, 279–305.

Moje, E. B., Collazo, T., Carrillo, R., & Marx, R. W. (2001). "Maestro, what is 'quality'?" Language, literacy, and discourse in project-based science. *Journal of Research in Science Teaching, 38*, 469–498.

Mortimer, E. F., & Machado, A. H. (2000). Anomalies and conflicts in classroom discourse. *Science Education, 84*, 429–444.

Mulkay, M. (1991). *Sociology of science: A sociological pilgrimage.* Bloomington, IN: Indiana University Press.

Philips, S. U. (1972). Participant structures and communicative competence: Warm springs children in community and classroom. In C. B. Cazden, V. P. John, & D. Hymes (Eds.), *Functions of language in the classroom* (pp. 370–394). Prospect Heights, IL: Waveland.

Piaget, J. (1969). *The child's conception of the world.* Totowa, NJ: Littlefield, Adams, & Co. (original work published 1929).

Polman, J. L., & Pea, R. D. (2001). Transformative communication as a cultural tool for guiding inquiry science. *Science Education, 85*, 223–238.

Posner, G. J., Strike, K. A., Hewson, P. W., & Gertzog, W. A. (1982). Accommodation of a scientific conception: Toward a theory of conceptual change. *Science Education, 66*, 211–227.

Prain, V., & Hand, B. (1999). Students' perceptions of writing for learning in secondary school science. *Science Education, 83*, 151–162.

Rivard, L. P., & Straw, S. B. (2000). The effect of talk and writing on learning science: An exploratory study. *Science Education, 84*, 566–593.

Rogoff, B. (1994). Developing understanding of the idea of communities of learners. *Mind, Culture, and Activity, 1*, 209–229.

Roth, W.-M. (1995a). *Authentic school science: Knowing and learning in open-inquiry science laboratories.* Boston, MA: Kluwer Academic.

Roth, W.-M. (1995b). Inventors, copycats, and everyone else: The emergence of shared resources and practices as defining aspects of classroom communities. *Science Education, 79*, 475–502.

Roth, W.-M. (2001). Situating cognition. *Journal of the Learning Sciences, 10*, 27–61.

Roth, W.-M., Bowen, G. M., & Masciotra, D. (2002). From thing to sign and "natural object": Toward a genetic phenomenology of graph interpretation. *Science, Technology, and Human Values, 27*, 327–356.

Roth, W.-M., & Lawless, D. (2002). Science, culture, and the emergence of language. *Science Education, 86*, 368–385.

Roth, W.-M., & Tobin, K. (2001). The implications of coteaching/cogenerative dialogue for teacher evaluation: Learning from multiple perspectives of everyday practice. *Journal of Personnel Evaluation in Education, 15*, 7–29.

Roth, W.-M., & Welzel, M. (2001). From activity to gestures and scientific language. *Journal of Research in Science Teaching, 38*, 103–136.

Rowlands, S. (2000). Turning Vygotsky on his head: Vygotsky's "scientifically based method" and the socioculturalist's "social other." *Science and Education, 9*, 537–575.

Rowlands, S., Graham, T., & Berry, J. (1999). Can we speak of alternative frameworks and conceptual change in mechanics? *Science and Education, 8*, 241–271.

Russell, T. L. (1983). Analyzing arguments in science classroom discourse: Can teachers' questions distort scientific authority? *Journal of Research in Science Teaching, 20*, 27–45.

Säljö, R. (1998). Learning inside and outside schools: Discursive practices and sociocultural dynamics. In D. A. Roberts & L. Östman (Eds.), *Problems of meaning in science curriculum* (pp. 39–53). New York: Teachers College Press.

Sandoval, W. A., & Morrison, K. (2003). High school students' ideas about theories and theory change after a biological inquiry unit. *Journal of Research in Science Teaching, 40*, 369–392.

Shapin, S., & Shaffer, S. (1985). *Leviathan and the air pump.* Princeton, NJ: Princeton University Press.

Shultz, J. J., Erickson, F., & Florio, S. (1982). Where's the floor? Aspects of the cultural organization of social relationships in communication at home and in school. In P. Gilmore & A. Glatthorn (Eds.), *Children in and out of school: Ethnography and education* (pp. 88–123). Washington, DC: Center for Applied Linguistics.

Stoddart, T., Pinal, A., Latzke, M., & Canaday, D. (2002). Integrating inquiry science and language development for English language learners. *Journal of Research in Science Teaching, 39*, 664–687.

Sutton, C. (1992). *Words, science, and learning.* Buckingham, England: Open University Press.

Sutton, C. (1998). New perspectives on language in science. In B. J. Fraser & K. G. Tobin (Eds.), *International handbook of science education* (Vol. 1, pp. 27–38). Dordrecht, the Netherlands: Kluwer Academic.

Toulmin, S. E. (1958). *The uses of argument.* Cambridge, England: Cambridge University Press.

Trautmann, N. M., Carlsen, W. S., Eick, C. J., Gardner, F., Jr., Kenyon, L., Moscovici, H., et al. (2003). Online peer review: Learning science as it's practiced. *Journal of College Science Teaching, 32*, 443–447.

Vygotsky, L. (1986). *Thought and language* (A. Kozulin, Trans.). Cambridge, MA: MIT Press (original work published 1934).

Wenger, E. (1998). *Communities of practice: Learning, meaning, and identity.* Cambridge, England: Cambridge University Press.

Wertsch, J. V. (1985). *Vygotsky and the social formation of mind.* Cambridge, MA: Harvard University Press.

Wertsch, J. V. (1991). *Voices of the mind: A sociocultural approach to mediated action.* Cambridge, MA: Harvard University Press.

Whorf, B. L. (1956). *Language, thought, and reality.* New York: Wiley.

Wilson, J. M. (1999). Using words about thinking: Content analyses of chemistry teachers' classroom talk. *International Journal of Science Education, 21*, 1067–1084.

Wittgenstein, L. (1967). *Philosophical investigations.* Oxford, England: Blackwell.

Wong, D., & Pugh, K. (2001). Learning science: A Deweyan perspective. *Journal of Research in Science Teaching, 38*, 317–336.

Woolgar, S. (1976). Writing an intellectual history of scientific development: The use of discovery accounts. *Social Studies of Science, 6*, 395–422.

Yore, L. D., Bisanz, G. L., & Hand, B. M. (2003). Examining the literacy component of science literacy: 25 years of language arts and science research. *International Journal of Science Education, 6*, 689–725.

Yore, L. D., Hand, B. M., & Prain, V. (2002). Scientists as writers. *Science Education, 86*, 672–692.

CHAPTER 4

Attitudinal and Motivational Constructs in Science Learning

Thomas R. Koballa, Jr.
Shawn M. Glynn
University of Georgia

This chapter examines the attitudinal and motivational constructs that are closely linked to science learning. First, we present a rationale for the study of attitudes and motivation in the context of science learning. We then discuss the history of attitude research in science education, define constructs prominent in this research, and review recent attitude research findings. We review research methods and instruments, students' attitudes toward science and factors that influence them, and interventions to change students' attitudes. Next, we focus on motivation, highlighting the historical background of theoretical orientations and discussing research on constructs of particular relevance to science education researchers. We conclude our chapter by offering recommendations for future research involving attitudinal and motivational constructs, noting implications for policy and practice.

At this point, we wish to acknowledge that it is impossible within the scope of this chapter to evaluate every significant study in the field of science education that addresses attitudinal or motivational constructs. Our goal is to provide the reader with an overview of the role these constructs play in science learning through strategic sampling of the relevant research.

Throughout this chapter we use the term *construct* to mean a scientific concept that represents a hypothesized psychological function (Snow, Corno, & Jackson, 1996). Attitudinal and motivational constructs are used to account for and infer patterns of science-related thinking, emotion, and action. They tend to be relatively enduring within a person, but have the potential to change. According to Snow et al. (1996), a construct identifies a unique dimension on which all persons differ by degree and should be represented by more than one kind of data.

Effective science instruction has the potential to improve attitudes toward science and heighten the motivation to learn science. Hands-on science activities, laboratory work, field study, and inquiry-oriented lessons tend to have these goals. Attitudinal and motivational constructs may also serve useful purposes in the context of science program evaluation and national comparisons. Of course, science instruction that is purposely developed to influence attitudes and motives may be construed as indoctrination (Koballa, 1992), raising ethical questions in some circumstances. In addition, there are attitudinal and motivational constructs that may be considered as both entry characteristics and outcomes of science instruction (Bloom, 1976). For example, motivation to enroll in elective science courses and positive attitudes toward chemistry are just as likely to be considered important instructional outcomes as they are determinants of whether a person will engage in certain science learning experiences.

An important reason for examining attitudinal and motivational constructs in science education is to understand the ways in which they affect student learning in the cognitive arena. Pintrich, Marx, and Boyle (1993) described attitudinal and motivational constructs as moderators of a learner's conceptual change and suggest that they may influence science learning in the short term and over longer periods of time. Researchers have studied these relationships intensively as individual learner differences and caution against forming expected "straightforward monotone relations" between such constructs and cognitive learning (Snow et al., 1996, p. 246). Furthermore, these relationships are influenced by contextual factors, including classroom organization, teacher authority, the nature of classroom academic tasks, and evaluation structure (Pintrich et al., 1993). These contextual factors may serve to strengthen the relations between attitudinal and motivational constructs and science learning as well as to weaken them.

Attitudinal and motivational constructs also are associated with students' actions that are considered precursors to science learning and achievement. Often, attitudes and motives are considered predictors of students' science-related decisions that affect learning, such as attending class, reading textbook assignments, and completing homework. However, the influence of attitudes and motives on science learning and achievement has tended to be difficult to document through research.

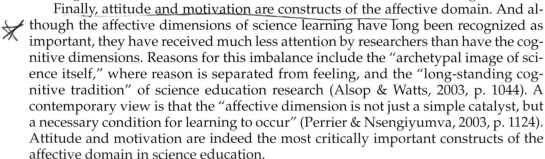
Finally, attitude and motivation are constructs of the affective domain. And although the affective dimensions of science learning have long been recognized as important, they have received much less attention by researchers than have the cognitive dimensions. Reasons for this imbalance include the "archetypal image of science itself," where reason is separated from feeling, and the "long-standing cognitive tradition" of science education research (Alsop & Watts, 2003, p. 1044). A contemporary view is that the "affective dimension is not just a simple catalyst, but a necessary condition for learning to occur" (Perrier & Nsengiyumva, 2003, p. 1124). Attitude and motivation are indeed the most critically important constructs of the affective domain in science education.

ATTITUDES

Attitudinal constructs have been part of the science education literature for more than a century; however, the interest in students' science-related attitudes among researchers and practitioners has waxed and waned over the years. According to Jones (1998), waxing interest in any research topic may result from factors ranging from convenient research paradigms and new measurement instruments to prestige of the investigator, funding priorities, and theoretical power. Waning interest, on the other hand, may result from redirection to other emerging research areas, achieving solutions to previous research problems, and research activity reaching an empirical plateau. Factors such as these have caused research on students' science-related attitudes to wax and wane.

Historical Background and Theoretical Orientations

John Dewey's philosophy served as an early inspiration for attitude research in science education. Dewey (1916) underscored the need for teaching scientific attitudes as an important aspect of educating reflective thinkers in the inaugural issue of the journal *General Science Quarterly*, which later became *Science Education*. He believed that science instruction should foster such mental attitudes as intellectual integrity, interest in testing opinions and beliefs, and open-mindedness rather than communicate a fixed body of information (Dewey, 1934). Many agreed with Dewey's thinking about scientific attitudes and translated it into practice. An early effort by Weller (1933) involved the development and use of a true-false scale to determine whether scientific attitudes could be taught. Others developed scales to measure elements of scientific attitude (Koslow & Nay, 1976) and sought to determine whether scientific attitudes can be changed by instruction (Charen, 1966).

Pioneering work on attitude measurement (Likert, 1932; Thurstone, 1928) and theoretical ideas about attitude and its relationship to behavior (Sherif, Sherif, & Nebergall, 1965) were major influences on science attitude research. In the 1960s, research on students' attitudes toward science, scientists, and science learning appeared regularly in the science education literature (e.g., Weinstock, 1967). Science educators began to distinguish "attitudes toward science" from "scientific attitudes," also called *scientific attributes*. This new label stems from the notion that scientific attitudes, such as open-mindedness, embody the attributes of scientists that are considered desirable in students (Koballa & Crawley, 1985).

The 1970s and 1980s saw a proliferation of research on students' attitudes toward science; however, research interest in scientific attitudes waned. This shift in interest from scientific attitudes to attitudes toward science was attributed to the understanding that learning about the modes of thinking associated with scientific attitudes does not mean that students will adopt them as their own (Schibeci, 1984). In other words, students may hold favorable or unfavorable attitudes toward these scientific attitudes. Attitudes came to be viewed as both the facilitators and products of science learning and research efforts focused on documenting student attitudes and their relationship to science achievement. Highlighting the research of this period was the learning theory-based program led by Shrigley (1983) that addressed the influence of persuasive messages on science attitudes and the development of Likert-type attitude scales.

Attitude research in science education began to wane in the 1990s, in part because attitude researchers seemed to reach an empirical plateau. Many studies produced results that provided little direction for improving classroom practice or advancing research in the field. For example, some studies showed favorable effects of activity-oriented instruction on students' attitudes toward science, whereas others did not (see Simpson, Koballa, Oliver, & Crawley, 1994). A second reason for the decline is that the research paradigms in social psychology and educational psychology that had influenced attitude research in science education shifted from a behavioral to a more cognitive orientation (Richardson, 1996). This shift in theoretical orientation saw attitudes aligned with affect, or feeling and belief with cognition, as exemplified in studies based on Ajzen & Fishbein's (1980) theory of reasoned action (see Crawley & Koballa, 1994). With the separation of attitudes from cognition, and the emergence of beliefs as a construct thought to explain the actions of learners, attitudes became less important.

Research on students' science-related attitudes is again receiving increased attention. The disturbing decreases in science course enrollments at the secondary and post-secondary levels, particularly in Western countries, the disdain expressed by many students for school science, and the promise of new research methods have prompted renewed interest in attitude research (Osborne, Simon, & Collins, 2003). Exemplifying this renewed interest is the special issue on affect edited by Alsop and Watts (2003) in the *International Journal of Science Education*, which included three articles that address aspects of students' attitudes.

Attitudinal Constructs

Unfortunately, issues of definition and meaning have hampered the advancement of attitude research in science education. School science is typically the focus of investigations, but often this is not made clear in reports of science attitude research. Osborne, Driver, and Simon (1998) contend that attitude researchers should consider the elements of science in society, school science, and scientific careers separately, defining them carefully. But attitude has been defined in many ways and has, unfortunately, often been used interchangeably with terms such as *interest, value, motivation,* and *opinion*. This confusion is unnecessary because quite specific definitions appear in the attitude literature (e.g., Ramsden, 1998; Schibeci, 1984; Shrigley, Koballa, & Simpson, 1988).

An attitude is "a general and enduring positive or negative feeling about some person, object, or issue" (Petty & Cacioppo, 1981, p. 7). *I love science, I hate my science teacher*, and *Science experiments are wonderful!* reflect attitudes because they express general positive or negative feelings about something. This definition distinguishes attitude from related terms such as *value, belief,* and *opinion*. Values are more complex and broader than attitudes and are more enduring (Trenholm, 1989). Examples of values are equality, justice, and symmetry in nature. Beliefs are often described as the cognitive basis for attitudes (Ajzen & Fishbein, 1980); they provide information about a person, object, or issue that may be used in forming an attitude. *Science is fun, My science teacher is smart*, and *Animal dissection should be banned* all reflect beliefs. Opinions are cast as verbal expressions of attitudes and historically have been used to represent not only attitudes but also the constructs of cognition, evaluation, and behavior (Shrigley, Koballa, & Simpson, 1988). When considered in relation to one another, a person will have far fewer values than attitudes or beliefs and many more beliefs than attitudes.

The relationship between attitude, belief, and behavior was presented in a causal model in research based on the theory of reasoned action (e.g., Crawley & Black,

1992). Attitude is the overall evaluation of a highly specific behavior that is defined in terms of action, target, context, and time. The overall evaluation of the behavior, called *attitude toward the behavior* (AB), is the affective component of the model. Attitude toward the behavior is a significant determinant of intention to engage in the behavior, the conative component of the model, called *behavioral intention* (BI). Personal beliefs, the cognitive element of the model, are the determinants of attitude. According to Simpson et al. (1994): "Each belief about the behavior links the behavior with a specific attribute (a characteristic, outcome, or event). The strength of the link between an attribute and the object (called behavioral belief, b) is weighted by the attribute's subjective evaluation (called outcome evaluation, e) through the expectancy value theorem" (p. 222). The summed product of each salient belief by its associated evaluation is the cognitive or belief-based estimate of attitude, called attitude toward the behavior (AB).

Feeling and emotion are other constructs considered in science education attitude research. According to Teixeira dos Santos and Mortimer (2003), "the word *feeling* is used to characterize the mental experience of an emotion, and the word *emotion* is used to describe the organic reactions to external stimuli" (p. 1197). Basing their definitions of these terms in the work of Damasio (1994), these researchers explain that while feelings cannot be observed, the emotions that prompt feeling are observable. The emotional states of science students and teachers that are detectable through observation of body posture, body movement, and contraction of facial musculature include anger, annoyance, joy, and satisfaction. *Mood* is the term used to describe a long-term emotional climate (Damasio, 1994; Teixeira dos Santos & Mortimer, 2003).

Reaching a universal agreement on definitions of attitude and its related terms is unlikely to occur in the near future and may even be undesirable. It is for this reason that Snow et al. (1996) recommended that it is "important not to belabor definitions unduly, even while seeking common agreement on some convenient and useful terminology" (p. 247). We suggest that science educators heed this recommendation when conducting and interpreting attitude research.

[handwritten margin note: Don't belabour definitions / no universal agreement]

Research Methods and Instruments

The methodological approaches used in studying students' science-related attitudes are increasing in their variety. While most studies continue to make use of self-report instruments that provide quantitative measures of attitude, investigators are also employing student drawings, personal interviews, and physiological expression as indicators of attitudes. Furthermore, the research methods reveal different levels of emotiveness, ranging from "the detached, statistical analysis of attitudes to the personalized, emotionally charged account[s] of teaching and learning" (Alsop & Watts, 2003, p. 1044). In this regard, it comes as no surprise that the various methodological approaches employed in the research reflect, and in a sense are limited by, the strategies used to collect and interpret attitudinal data. For example, Siegel and Ranney (2003) used quantitative modeling and Rasch analysis to develop and test the usefulness of the *Changes in Attitudes about the Relevance of Science* (CARS) questionnaire. In contrast, the ethnographic approaches highlighted in the research of Palmer (1997) and Pilburn and Baker (1993) used interviews and researchers' field notes. In the study by Teixeira dos Santos and Mortimer (2003), which is anchored in work of Damasio (1994) on emotions and feelings, videotapes of lessons were used to attend to such details as personal posture, gestures, and facial expressions in constructing understandings of emotion and attitudes. Stretching the methodological envelope of science attitude research are studies like that reported by Perrier and Nsengiyumva (2003). Basing their work on trauma recovery therapy, these researchers used data gleaned from photographs and the contents of personal diaries to construct a vivid description of the influence of inquiry-based science activities on the attitudes of orphans in war-ravaged Rwanda.

Attitude Instruments

The self-report instruments used in much of the research address one or more dimensions of attitude. An example of a unidimensional instrument is the *Attitude Toward Science Scale* (Francis & Greer, 1999), which has only 20 items and purports to measure secondary students' attitude toward science. A second example is the *Changes in Attitudes about the Relevance of Science* questionnaire (Siegel & Ranney, 2003), which includes three equally balanced versions to overcome problems associated with assessing students' attitudes over multiple intervals. In comparison, the scale developed by Pell and Jarvis (2001) includes subscales that measure the five dimensions of *liking science, independent investigator, science enthusiasm, the social context of science*, and *science as a difficult subject*. Excluding instrument development influenced by the theoretical work of Ajzen and Fishbein (1980), science attitude instruments typically address the evaluative or affective component of attitude and do not distinguish among the cognitive, affective, and conative components that constitute the attitude trilogy. Some of these instruments (e.g., West, Hailes, & Sammons, 1997) that have been designed for young children make use of smiley faces rather than words, in an effort to better capture the children's expressions of attitude. We present summary data for a sampling of recently developed attitude instruments in Table 4.1.

Instrument reliability and validity are important qualities of attitude scales. Content analysis, exploratory factor analyses, item analyses, correlations between subscales, correlations between attitude scale scores and the number of science-related subjects studied, and student interviews are among the tests and procedures used by researchers to explain the reliability and validity of their instruments (Francis & Greer, 1999; Pell & Jarvis, 2001; Siegel & Ranney, 2003). It is recognized that attitude scale construction is a multistep process that may take more than a year to complete (Bennett, Rollnick, Green, & White, 2001). In addition, instrument reliability and validity need to be reestablished when an instrument is modified or used with a population that is different from the one for which it was originally developed. Unfortunately, attitude instruments are sometimes selected for use without adequate attention to reliability and validity (e.g., Terry & Baird, 1997).

There are two limitations commonly associated with science attitude scales: (a) the limited amount of information yielded about the respondents' attitudes and (b) the inclusion of items generated by researchers who do not share the mindset of the respondents (Pilburn & Baker, 1993). These limitations have been addressed in several ways by science education researchers. One strategy involves scale

TABLE 4.1.
Summary Data for Sample Attitude Instruments

Developers and instrument focus	Instrument format	Sample items
Thompson and Mintzes's (2002) Shark Attitude Inventory measures the attitudes toward sharks of fifth-grade students through senior citizens.	Five-point Likert scale, with response options ranging from *strongly agree* to *strongly disagree* across four subscales.	I would like to touch a shark. Sharks should not be protected if protecting them makes shark fishermen lose money.
Francis and Greer (1999) developed an instrument to measure secondary school students' attitudes towards science.	A 20-item unidimensional instrument arranged for scoring on a 3-point Likert scale, with *not certain* as the midpoint response.	Science has ruined the environment. Studying science gives me great pleasure.
Pell and Jarvis's (2001) instrument assesses the attitudes to science of 5- to 11-year-old children.	Five-point "smiley" face Likert scoring scheme across five attitude subscales that include only positively worded items.	How do you feel about . . . Doing science experiments. Watching the teacher do an experiment. *Smiley scale*
Bennett, Rollnick, Green, and White's (2001) instrument measures university students' attitudes toward the study of chemistry.	Patterned after Aikenhead and Ryan's VOSTS, the multiple-choice items include response options that combine evaluation and explanation.	I like it when the lecturer gives us small tasks to do in lecture. A. I AGREE with this statement because it improves my understanding. E. I DISAGREE with this statement because it increases the noise and wastes time. X. None of the above statements reflect my view, which is . . .
The Parkinson, Hendley, Tanner, and Stable (1998) questionnaire was developed to assess the attitudes toward science of age 13 pupils in England and Wales.	Statements generated by pupils were selected for inclusion on the 34-item scale. Scoring is based on a 4-point Likert scale.	I like doing experiments in science lessons. More time should be spent on science at school.
Siegel and Ranney's (2003) Changes in Attitude about the Relevance of Science (CARS) questionnaire was designed for use with adolescents.	Three versions for repeated measures were developed. Scoring for each 20-item version is based on a 5-point Likert scale with an additional *don't understand* response option.	Science helps me to make sensible decisions. The things I do in science have nothing to do with the real world.

construction in which researchers solicit input from a sample of respondents. Crawley and Koballa (1992) questioned a representative sample of Hispanic-American students and used the students' responses to construct a scale to assess attitudes toward chemistry enrollment. Along similar lines, Bennett et al. (2001) and Ellis, Killip, and Bennett (2000) solicited student input in developing multiple-choice attitude scale items. Guided by work on the *Views on Science-Technology-Society* instrument (Aikenhead & Ryan, 1992), they used data from students to construct four or more statements for each scale item that are expressions of agreement or disagreement with the item and reasons for agreeing or disagreeing. For example, for the scale item *Scientists do a wide variety of jobs*, sample statements are: "I AGREE because they do jobs ranging from designing new medicines to being astronauts," and "I DISAGREE because scientists tend to concentrate on one thing" (Ellis et al., 2000, p. 25).

Drawing

Finson (2002) reviewed efforts since 1957 to use drawings to gather information about one aspect of students' attitudes toward science, perceptions of scientists. The image that school students hold of scientists tends to be stereotypical and rather negative, with scientists most often depicted as men with unkempt hair, wearing glasses and white lab coats, and working alone in laboratories. He concluded that Chamber's *Draw-a-Scientist Test* and the more recently developed *Draw-a-Scientist Checklist* are reliable and valid instruments for gathering data about students' perceptions of scientists and recommends that interviewing students about their drawings can enhance researchers' interpretations of students' perceptions. Finson also cautioned researchers about assuming that a student's drawing provides the definitive image of his or her perception of a scientist because students may hold multiple images of scientists that differ depending on context and recent exposure.

Interview

Other researchers have turned to student interviews as a way to overcome the limitations associated with attitude scales and to augment the data provided by the scales. In an effort to determine more about the meaning associated with students' images of scientists, Palmer (1997) interviewed upper elementary and high school students about their understandings of scientists and their work in an environmental context. From an analysis of 125 interviews, he concluded that students hold both private perceptions and stereotyped images of scientists and their work. The findings of Palmer's study suggest that drawings may not encourage students to express the full range of their perceptions about scientists. Pilburn and Baker (1993) also interviewed students with the use of a semi-structured protocol and employed a qualitative data analysis approach to gauge students' attitudes. Students were questioned about their attitudes toward science and school, academic and career goals, and what improvements they would make to science class if they were the teacher. By changing the wording of questions to suit the age of their student participants and following initial student responses with additional probing questions, Pilburn and Baker gathered attitude data from students in kindergarten through grade 12. They concluded from their work that student interviews provide useful information about students' attitudes toward science.

Attitudes and What Influences Them

Despite the limitations associated with attitude scales and other techniques used to gather attitudinal data, what they reveal provides valuable insight into students' science attitudes. A number of studies reported that although children at the primary level hold positive feelings about science, attitude scores decline as students progress through the grades (George, 2000; Jurd, 2001; Osborne et al., 1998; Reid & Skryabina, 2002). This decline, which is particularly evident in the middle school and high school years, is likely related in some way to the types of science courses in which the students are enrolled and the science self-concept that they develop as a result of these courses (George, 2000). However, it is also possible that the decline is a result of students' inability to separate their attitudes toward science from their attitudes toward school. Morrell and Lederman's (1998) investigation of the relationship between students' attitudes toward school and attitudes toward classroom science revealed a weak relationship between the two attitudes. Their findings led them to conclude that students' less-than-favorable attitudes toward science are not part of a bigger school-related attitude problem and that attitudes toward science could not be improved by addressing students' attitudes toward school. Also, in contrast to the findings of the other studies previously discussed, Morrell and Lederman found no evidence of declining attitudes toward science for older students.

Gender

Despite more than two decades of attention to issues of gender equity in science education, differences between girls and boys still persist regarding attitudes toward science. The findings of several recent studies indicate that the differences develop during the elementary school years (Andre, Whigham, Hendrickson, & Chambers, 1999; Jones, Howe, & Rua, 2000). Consistent with previous findings (e.g., Weinburgh, 1995), these studies report that girls tend to have less favorable attitudes toward science than boys, and that girls' science-related interests are more focused on the biological than physical sciences. Dawson (2000) reported similar trends in a study of primary-age boys and girls in Australia and concluded that little has changed in two decades. In contrast, Andre et al. (1999) found no differences between girls and boys in their liking of life science or physical science. However, their comparison of students' preferences for school subjects revealed that, in the elementary grades, girls prefer reading and language arts over physical science. Their findings led them to speculate that the attitudinal differences often detected between boys and girls are not a result of girls liking physical science less than boys, but their liking reading more.

Differences between boys and girls also extend to the stereotypic images that they hold of science and scientists. Boys and girls view science as a male-dominated school subject and consider science to be a male profession (Andre et al., 1999). Students in Taiwan, as is the case in other countries, are influenced by the stereotypic images of science and scientists that are often depicted in the popular media. However, the impact of these stereotypes on students' interest in a science career seems to decline as students advance in school, with girls more so than boys open to the idea of women working as scientists (She, 1998). One possible interpretation of this finding is that students hold both private perceptions of scientists and their work in addition to the public stereotypes (Palmer, 1997).

Explanations for these gender differences include both physiological and sociological functions. More credence is given to sociological factors, as indicated by the widespread support for broad-based intervention programs such as EQUALS and *Family Science* that target the science attitudes and experiences of girls. The most frequently given sociological reasons for why girls have less positive attitudes toward science than do boys include the differential cultural expectations placed on girls and boys by parents, teachers, and peers, and the different experiences in science, both in school and out of it, provided to boys and girls (Jones et al., 2000; She, 1998).

Achievement and Science-Related Decisions

A study of Australian students using data collected as part of the Third International Mathematics and Science Study (TIMSS) revealed that attitudes toward science have a strong effect on achievement (Webster & Fisher, 2000). Attitudes were found not to predict physics achievement (Willson, Ackerman, & Malave, 2000) and to be related directly to the science achievement of American students (Singh, Granville, & Dika, 2002). The narrow interpretation of attitude applied in many studies might explain the weak relationships found between attitude and achievement (Rennie & Punch, 1991), as might the narrow definitions of achievement. Research in this area still tends to corroborate Fraser's (1982) position that improving science attitudes will not necessarily lead to science achievement gains.

The influence of attitudes on students' decisions such as enrolling in elective science courses and pursuing careers in science was also examined in recent studies. The attractiveness of careers in science and higher education courses, the relevance of courses for future study and careers, self-confidence in science, and science interests are among the factors found to influence students' science course-taking and career decisions (Robertson, 2000; Woolnough & Guo, 1997). Based on a review of earlier studies that produced similar findings, Shrigley (1990) concluded that only under certain conditions should attitudes be expected to predict learners' science-related decisions. These conditions include: (a) when attitude and the decision are measured at the same level of specificity; (b) when social context and individual differences, including cognitive ones, are considered; and (c) when the person's intentions regarding the decision are known. Each of Shrigley's conditions was addressed in Butler's (1999) study, in which he sought to identify the determinants of students' intentions to perform both laboratory and non-laboratory science learning tasks in grades 4 through 8. Butler found that the students' attitudes toward the behavior were better predictors of their intentions to perform both laboratory and non-laboratory science learning tasks than either attitudes toward science or subjective norm, the element of Ajzen and Fishbein's (1980) model that measures social support for engaging in the behavior. A limitation of Butler's study was that the students' actual behaviors were not observed.

Attitude Change Interventions

Activity-based practical work (Thompson & Soyibo, 2002), learning cycle classes (Cavallo & Laubach, 2001), formally teaching ethical issues (Choi & Cho, 2002), jig-saw cooperative learning groups (De Baz, 2001), student- and teacher-constructed self-teaching resources (McManus, Dunn, & Denig, 2003), video technologies (Esca-lada & Zollman, 1998; Harwood & McMahon, 1997), inquiry-based summer camps (Gibson & Chase, 2002), and computer-assisted instruction (Soyibo & Hudson, 2000) are among the attitude change interventions evaluated in recent years. Other inter-ventions targeted the attitudes toward sciences of girls and minorities and their con-tinuation in the science pipeline. These included after-school science programs and residential summer science camps as well as year-long science courses that empha-size hands-on and performance-based learning experiences (Ferreira, 2002; Freed-man, 2002; Haussler & Hoffmann, 2002; Jayaratne, Thomas, & Trautmann, 2003; Jovanovic & Dreves, 1998; Phillips, Barrow, & Chandrasekhar, 2002).

Overall, the interventions were well planned and quite complex and incorpo-rated a host of activities believed to enhance attitudes toward science and commit-ment to the study of science. The results of these studies point to the success of some interventions, particularly those that engage learners in hands-on science activities and that stress the relevance of science through issue-based experiences (e.g., Haussler & Hoffman, 2002; Perrier & Nsengiyumva, 2003; Siegel & Ranney, 2003).

MOTIVATION

As we turn to a discussion of the role of motivation in learning science, it is impor-tant to recognize that attitudes influence motivation, which in turn influences learn-ing, and ultimately behavior. This sequence is relevant to investigating learning in many science contexts, although the relationships among these variables can be more complex and interactive than this basic sequence suggests.

It is also important to recognize that motivation has not been manipulated or assessed as frequently as attitudes by science education researchers, although his-torically science education research on learning has been significantly influenced by the theoretical orientations that researchers have adopted toward motivation. As science education researchers respond to current national initiatives to foster stu-dents' science achievement, the emphasis placed on motivation has been increas-ing, as reflected in recent articles with titles such as "Skill and will: The role of mo-tivation and cognition in the learning of college chemistry" (Zusho & Pintrich, 2003, p. 1081). Ten years ago, in the *Handbook of Research on Science Teaching and Learning* (Gabel, 1994), the word *attitude* appeared in more than 45 subject index listings and sub-listings, whereas the word *motivation* appeared only three times. The inclusion of *motivation* in the present *Handbook* in a chapter with attitudes attests to greater value being placed on the role that motivation plays in science learning.

A discussion of motivation should begin with a definition. Motivation is an in-ternal state that arouses, directs, and sustains students' behavior. The study of mo-tivation by science education researchers attempts to explain why students strive for particular goals when learning science, how intensively they strive, how long they strive, and what feelings and emotions characterize them in this process.

In this section, we discuss the research orientations and constructs that play important roles in learning science. One feature of motivation research has been the creation of many motivational constructs. Unfortunately, the constructs are often unclear in their definitions and functions, as Schunk (2000) observed:

> The field of motivation is beset with a lack of clear definition of motivational constructs and specification of their operation within larger theoretical frameworks. These problems have implications for interpretation of research results and applications to practice. . . . At times educational researchers—perhaps unwittingly—have behaved like Humpty Dumpty by renaming or defining motivational constructs to fit their theoretical models and research methodologies with insufficient attention paid to extant conceptualizations. (p. 116)

Our goal is to provide an overview of current motivation research in learning science that stresses the most widely accepted and empirically supported findings about student motivation. Cognizant of the conceptual clarity issue raised by Schunk and others (e.g., Pintrich, 2003), we have endeavored to describe, in as straightforward a fashion as possible, the orientations and constructs that are of particular relevance to science education researchers. The broad theoretical orientations that researchers adopt, either explicitly or implicitly, influence the assumptions they make about the more specific constructs they study. This point is important because researchers with different theoretical orientations often study the same constructs. They may even define them similarly but interpret them differently.

Historical Background and Theoretical Orientations

Historically, science education researchers have adopted four orientations to motivation when studying learning. We refer to these orientations as *behavioral*, *humanistic*, *cognitive*, and *social*. Although these orientations are described separately, it should be kept in mind that many science education researchers adopt aspects of more than one orientation when studying learning, with hybrids resulting, such as a *cognitive-social* orientation (Pintrich, 2003). In addition, the orientations researchers adopt often are determined by the particular topic they are studying.

Science education researchers with a behavioral orientation to motivation focus on concepts such as *incentive* and *reinforcement*. An incentive is something that makes a behavior more or less likely to occur. For example, the promise of a field trip to a quarry to study rock strata could serve as an incentive for students to perform well on a geology test. Participation in the trip itself could be the reinforcement.

Researchers have identified potential problems associated with the use of incentives and reinforcements to shape behavior in a science classroom. One major problem is that the students may not develop *intrinsic motivation* to learn. In some conditions, when students are offered incentives for doing tasks they naturally find motivating, their desire to perform the tasks can decrease (Cameron & Pierce, 2002; Deci, Koestner, & Ryan, 1999). External incentives also can focus students' attention on the incentives as ends in themselves, rather than serve as a kind of feedback on the progress students are making.

Science education researchers with a humanistic orientation to motivation emphasize students' capacity for personal growth, their freedom to choose their destiny, and their desire to achieve and excel. Humanists have used various constructs to express students' need to reach their potential. Maslow (1968, 1970) described this need as *self-actualization*. Maslow proposed that everyone has a hierarchy of needs: physiological, safety, love and belongingness, esteem, intellectual achievement, aesthetic appreciation, and self-actualization. When basic needs are satisfied, the motivation to fulfill them decreases and the motivation to fulfill the higher-level ones increases. Building upon Maslow's theory, humanists currently investigate students' *actualizing tendency* (Rogers & Freiberg, 1994) and *self-determination* (Deci, Vallerand, Pelletier, & Ryan, 1991).

[handwritten margin note: Relate to Muslm hierarchy of needs]

When science education researchers adopt a cognitive orientation to motivation, they emphasize students' goals, plans, expectations, and attributions (Glynn & Duit, 1995; Glynn, Yeany, & Britton, 1991; Schunk, 1996). An *attribution* is an explanation for the cause of a particular behavior (Weiner, 1986, 1990, 1992). When students respond to instructional events, they are viewed as responding to their attributions about these events. For example, students' motivation to achieve in a particular college biology class could be undermined by the students' attribution (true or false) that all students are receiving high grades because the instructor's grading criteria are lax.

Science education researchers with a social orientation to motivation emphasize students' identities and their interpersonal relationships in the communities that exist inside and outside of school. Students' identities are formed in their communities, and a great deal of science can be learned, both intentionally and incidentally, in them. To maintain their membership in their communities, students are motivated to learn the attitudes, values, and behaviors of those communities (Lave & Wenger, 1991). The process of *modeling* is central to the learning that takes place in those communities (Greeno, Collins, & Resnick, 1996). Science classrooms, museums, nature centers, aquariums, and even websites are being conceptualized as *learning* communities. One template for conceptualizing a science-learning community was developed by Scardamalia and Bereiter (1996), who used a computer system called *Computer-Supported Intentional Learning Environment* (CSILE) to prompt students to collaborate by posing questions and hypotheses and discussing findings. Brown and Campione (1996) developed another template that made innovative science research projects central to a classroom community.

Motivational Constructs

According to Brophy (1987), *motivation to learn* is "a student tendency to find academic activities meaningful and worthwhile and to try to derive the intended academic benefits from them" (pp. 205–206). What motivates students to learn science? We answered this question by closely examining the disparate body of research that Schunk (2000) alluded to, integrating the findings, and identifying relevant methods and instruments for the constructs. We noted that the constructs of *arousal*, *anxiety*, *interest*, and *curiosity* all have been found to play important roles, particularly in the creation of *intrinsic motivation*. We also noted that the extent to which science students are intrinsically motivated was found to be influenced by how *self-determined* they are, by their *goal-directed behavior*, by their *self-regulation*, by their *self-efficacy*, and by the *expectations* that teachers have of them.

Arousal and Anxiety

Arousal, defined as a student's level of alertness and activation (Anderson, 1990), plays an important role in initiating and regulating motivation. Arousal is a state of physical and psychological readiness for action. Too little arousal in students leads to inactivity, boredom, daydreaming, and even sleeping, and too much of it leads to *anxiety*, defined as a "general uneasiness, a sense of foreboding, a feeling of tension" (Hansen, 1977, p. 91). All students experience anxiety from time to time. Some anxiety is good in that it helps motivate science learning. Too little, however, debilitates performance, and so does too much (Cassady & Johnson, 2002).

Most researchers conceptualize anxiety as both a *state*, temporarily associated with a situation such as a science test, and a *trait*, enduringly associated with the individual. As measured by the *State-Trait Anxiety Inventory* (Spielberger, 1983), state anxiety is defined as an unpleasant emotional arousal in response to situations that are perceived as threatening. Trait anxiety, on the other hand, implies the existence of stable individual differences in the tendency to respond with state anxiety in the anticipation of threatening situations.

Interest and Curiosity

The terms *interest* and *curiosity* are often used interchangeably in the science education literature. A student who is interested or curious about a science topic has a readiness to pursue it. A student's interest in a science topic or activity is "specific, develops over time, is relatively stable, and is associated with personal significance, positive emotions, high value, and increased knowledge" (Wade, 2001, p. 245). This particular kind of interest is known as *individual* or *personal*; it should be distinguished from *situational* interest that is evoked by things in the environment that create a momentary interest. When students do poorly in science and other areas, what is the most common reason? "Lack of interest" was rated highest by more than 200 middle school students studied by Vispoel and Austin (1995). In some cases, ratings of low interest can be ego-protective—students wish to attribute their poor performance to an external, uncontrollable variable. When students do well, what is the reason? Vispoel and Austin found that middle school students rated effort highest, but interest next highest, in explaining successes. These findings indicate that students perceive interest to be a very important factor in their achievement.

According to Pintrich and Schunk (1996), interest or curiosity is "elicited by activities that present students with information or ideas that are discrepant from their present knowledge or beliefs and that appear surprising or incongruous" (p. 277). This does not mean, however, that the more discrepant the better. Researchers have found that students are most interested in science concepts and phenomena that are moderately novel to them and moderately complex (Berlyne, 1966). When students are very familiar with something, they may ignore it, and when they are unfamiliar with something, particularly if it is complex, they may not find it relevant or meaningful.

One of the most effective means of making science concepts relevant and meaningful to students is the use of analogies during instruction (Glynn & Takahashi, 1998). For example, Paris and Glynn (2004) found that elaborate analogies increased students' interest in the concepts covered in science texts, as well as their under-standing of those concepts. This finding suggests that elaborate analogies can play an important role in strategically regulating students' motivation. The analogies likely do this by establishing in students a sense of self-relevancy, or personal in-volvement. In the Paris and Glynn study, most of the students indicated that a text with analogies was interesting because it compared an abstract science concept to something more familiar to them. A typical comment was: "I know about photo-graphy, so it was more interesting when the eye was compared to a camera."

Intrinsic and Extrinsic Motivation

Motivation to perform an activity for its own sake is intrinsic, whereas motivation to perform it as a means to an end is extrinsic (Pintrich & Schunk, 1996). Intrinsic motivation derives from arousal, interest, and curiosity. Intrinsic motivation taps into the natural human tendency to pursue interests and exercise capabilities (Deci, 1996; Reeve, 1996; Ryan & Deci, 2000). Typically, students who are intrinsically mo-tivated to learn a science concept do not require physical rewards, because the process itself is inherently motivating. On the other hand, when students learn con-cepts only to earn grades or avoid detention, their motivation is primarily external (Mazlo et al., 2002). Students who are intrinsically motivated to perform a task of-ten experience *flow*, a feeling of enjoyment that occurs when they have developed a sense of mastery and are concentrating intensely on the task at hand (Csikszent-mihalyi, 2000). For example, *flow* describes the preoccupation that some students develop with a science fair project to the exclusion of other activities in their lives.

The distinction between intrinsic and extrinsic motivation is difficult to make in some instances. When studying motivational patterns in sixth-grade science class-rooms, Lee and Brophy (1996) found it useful to distinguish among students' mo-tives in multiple ways. Students are often motivated to perform tasks for both in-trinsic and extrinsic reasons. The student who constructs the science fair project may enjoy the process, particularly because the student selected the topic, but may also be motivated by the prospect of receiving a prize, an award ribbon, or entry into a higher-level science fair.

Self-Determination

Self-determination is the ability to have choices and some degree of control in what we do and how we do it (Deci et al., 1991; Reeve, Hamm, & Nix, 2003). Most people strive to be in charge of their own behavior—to be captains of their own ships. Most people are unhappy when they feel they have lost control, either to another person or to the environment. Deci (1996), in his theory of self-determination, suggested that students in particular need to feel competent and independent. He explained that intrinsically motivated activities promote feelings of competence and indepen-dence, whereas extrinsically motivated activities can undermine these feelings. Deci has found that students with self-determined motivation are more likely to achieve at a high level and to be well adjusted emotionally.

When science students have the opportunity to help design their educational activities, they are more likely to benefit from them. According to Garner (1998), "It is through this self determination, measured though it might be, that wise teachers allow each of their students to guide them to what the students find particularly enjoyable and worth learning" (p. 236). This advice is based on studies such as that by Rainey (1965), who found that high school science students who were allowed to organize their own experiments exhibited greater interest and diligence than students who were required to follow rote directions.

When students lack self-determination, it is difficult for them to feel intrinsically motivated. When they come to believe that their performance in science is mostly uncontrollable, they have developed a failure syndrome or *learned helplessness* (Seligman, 1975). Students who develop learned helplessness are reluctant to engage in science learning. They believe they will fail, so they do not even try. Because they believe they will fail, these students do not practice and improve their science skills and abilities, so they develop cognitive deficiencies. Students with learned helplessness also have emotional problems such as depression and anxiety.

Goal-Directed Behavior

A science objective or outcome that students pursue is a *goal*, and the process of pursuing it is referred to as *goal-directed behavior*, an important component of *goal theory* (Pintrich & Schunk, 1996). Goal theory builds upon an earlier *expectancy-value theory of achievement motivation* (Atkinson & Raynor, 1978), which posited that behavior is determined by how much students value a particular goal and their expectation of attaining that goal as a result of performing certain behaviors. When students endeavor to identify a substance as the objective of a chemistry lab, they are engaged in goal-directed behavior. Researchers have found that the very act of setting a goal is beneficial to students because it helps them to focus their attention, organize their efforts, persist longer, and develop new strategies (Covington, 2000; Linnenbrink & Pintrich, 2002; Locke & Latham, 1990, 2002; Midgley, Kaplan, & Middleton, 2001; Wentzel, 2000). In classrooms where students and teachers share the goals of student understanding and independent thinking, rather than the memorization and rote recall of science facts, students have higher motivation to learn (Glynn, Muth, & Britton, 1990; Nolen, 2003; Nolen & Haladyna, 1990). Recognizing this, Nicholls (1992) recommends that students be viewed as educational theorists who actively interpret and influence the classroom environment.

Science education researchers often distinguish between *learning goals* (also known as *mastery* goals or *task* goals) and *performance goals* (also known as *ego* goals). Students with learning goals focus on the challenge and mastery of a science task (Meece, Blumenfeld, & Hoyle, 1988). They are not concerned about how many mistakes they make or how they appear to others. These students are primarily interested in mastering the task and task-related strategies. They view mistakes as learning opportunities and do not hesitate to ask others for feedback and help. They are not afraid of failing, because failing does not threaten their sense of self-esteem. As a result, they set reasonably challenging goals, they take risks, and they respond to failure appropriately. When they succeed, they generally attribute it to their own effort. They assume responsibility for learning. They generally perform well in competitive situations, learn fast, and exhibit self-confidence and enthusiasm. They want to acquire mastery, often in an apprenticeship relationship. Students with learning goals are more likely to trust their teachers and adopt the goals set by their teachers as their own. They are also likely to work harder.

Meece et al. (1988) found that students with learning goals were more actively involved in science activities than students with performance goals because the latter were preoccupied with gaining social status, pleasing teachers, and avoiding extra work. Students with performance goals frequently compare their grades with others and choose tasks that are easy for them so they can maximize their grade. They work hard only on graded tasks and are often reluctant to help others achieve (Stipek, 1996). Their self-esteem is based on the external evaluation of their performance, so their esteem can be as fleeting as their last grade on a biology test. They take very few risks and restrict themselves to those skills with which they are most comfortable. If they do not receive positive external evaluations, they often develop ego-protective mechanisms such as procrastination or apathy.

In a study that examined more than 200 middle school students' motivation goals, Meece and Jones (1994) found students tended to feel greater confidence and mastery when science lessons were taught in small groups rather than in large ones. They also found that boys reported greater confidence in their science abilities than girls. More recent studies with middle school and high school students (Britner & Pajares, 2002; DeBacker & Nelson, 1999; Stake & Mares, 2001) suggest that the confidence of girls relative to that of boys is influenced by how science is being taught.

Self-Regulation

Goal setting is an important aspect of *self-regulated learning* (Schunk & Zimmerman, 1997). Students who are self-regulating know what they want to accomplish when they learn science—they bring appropriate strategies to bear and continually monitor their progress toward their goals. According to Neber and Schommer-Aikins (2002), self-regulated learning can be thought of as a cognitive activity consisting of two components, regulatory strategy use (for planning and monitoring) and cognitive strategy use (for organizing and elaborating). These components are often measured by subscales of the *Motivated Learning Strategies Questionnaire* (Pintrich & De-Groot, 1990), with items such as *In class, I ask myself questions to make sure I know what I have been studying* and *When I am studying a topic, I try to make the material fit together.*

Students' perceptions of *control* are relevant to their self-regulation and motivation to learn science. When students feel they are in control of their learning, they select more challenging tasks, they expend more effort, and they work longer on assignments (Anderman & Young, 1994; Schunk, 1996; Weiner, 1992). Students who feel they are in control are more likely to pick themselves up when they fail, attributing their failure to controllable, internal causes such as a lack of preparation. These students are adaptive and will adopt strategies to increase the likelihood of their success in the future. In contrast, students who typically feel that they are not in control of their learning focus increasingly on their own limitations and become apathetic about learning science.

Self-Efficacy

Before defining self-efficacy, it is easier to define what it is not. It is not self-concept, nor is it self-esteem (Bong & Clark, 1999). Self-concept is a more general construct that includes self-efficacy. Self-concept refers to global ideas about one's identity and one's role relations to others. According to Bong and Skaalvik (2003), "self-efficacy acts as an active precursor of self-concept development" and "self-concept is colloquially defined as a composite view of oneself" (pp. 1–2). Self-esteem is also a more general construct, and self-efficacy contributes to it. Self-esteem refers to the value one places on himself or herself. In contrast, self-efficacy is not a general personality trait or quality. It makes no sense to speak of a generally "self-efficacious" student.

Bandura (1997) defined self-efficacy as "beliefs in one's capabilities to organize and execute the courses of action required to produce given attainments" (p. 3). When science teachers use the term, they refer to the evaluation that a student makes about his or her personal competence to succeed in a field of science. For example, a student may have high self-efficacy with respect to knowledge and skills in biology, but low self-efficacy with respect to knowledge and skills in physics. In other words, self-efficacy is domain specific—and potentially task specific in a domain. Students' judgments of their self-efficacy in particular areas of science have been found to predict their performance in these areas. For example, Zusho and Pintrich (2003) found that students' self-efficacy was found to be the best predictor of grades in an introductory college chemistry course, even after controlling for prior achievement. Similarly, Joo, Bong, and Choi (2000) found that students' self-efficacy predicted their written test performance in a biology course. In their study, self-efficacy was assessed with questionnaire items similar to this one: "What grade (A through F) do you anticipate earning at the end of the term in biology?" Other questionnaires, such as the *Perceptions of Science Classes Survey* (Kardash & Wallace, 2001, p. 202), have been designed to assess self-efficacy for general science, with items such as "I have a good understanding of basic concepts in science." Given the domain-specific nature of self-efficacy, it may be that questionnaires that address a particular field of science will prove more useful than ones that address science in general.

According to Bandura (1997), a student's sense of self-efficacy is derived from sources such as mastery experiences, vicarious experiences, and social persuasion. Mastery experiences are students' actual experiences, and these have the greatest impact on their sense of efficacy in an area. Successes increase efficacy, and failures lower it. Vicarious experiences, according to Bandura, are those associated with the observation of others ("models") such as teachers, parents, peers, or characters in films (such as "Indiana Jones, archeologist"). The more that students identify with the model, the greater the model's influence on them. Social persuasion, particularly when it comes from a source that students respect, can also influence students and induce them to try harder in science. Social persuasion can reinforce students' self-efficacy in science when they have suffered a temporary setback.

Expectations and Strategies

The effect of teachers' expectations on student performance is called the *Pygmalion effect* (Rosenthal & Jacobson, 1968), named after a mythological king who created a statue and then made it come to life. Research findings on the Pygmalion effect have been mixed but generally support the view that the effect does occur and that teachers' expectations can influence student performance in science and other areas (Smith, Jussim, & Eccles, 1999). Science teachers' expectations of students, and the strategies based on these expectations, play an important role in increasing or reducing students' motivation. Researchers have found that teachers who have high expectations of students give cues and prompts that communicate to them their belief that the students can perform well (Good & Brophy, 1997; Rop, 2003). If teachers have high expectations of students, they are less likely to accept poor answers from them, and they are more likely to praise them for good answers. Teachers with low expectations of students are more likely to provide them with inconsistent feedback, sometimes praising inadequate answers, sometimes criticizing them, and sometimes ignoring them (Good & Brophy, 1997). Sometimes, if many teachers in a school adopt low expectations of the students there, a culture of low expectations can permeate the school (Weinstein, Madison, & Kuklinski, 1995).

RECOMMENDATIONS FOR FUTURE RESEARCH

The role of attitudes and motivation in learning science is a rich area for future research. As views of learning become increasingly constructivistic, it is more important than ever that researchers adopt a comprehensive view of learners that includes affective characteristics. The research reviewed in this chapter clearly shows that science learning cannot be explained solely by examination of cognitive factors. Learners' attitudes and motivation should be taken into account in explanations of science learning. Theoretical orientations and models describing meaningful relationships among affective constructs and cognition are becoming more evident in the research on science learning (Glynn & Koballa, 2007).

The research indicates that the principal means for assessing students' attitudes continues to be scales that produce quantitative scores. Instrument reliability and validity should be considered when one is choosing or modifying scales for use. We recommend that quantitative data gathered with the use of attitude scales be coupled with other forms of data, such as that collected via individual and group interviews, student drawings, log books, and photographs, to provide a more informed understanding of students' attitudes. Equally important, researchers should not be overly concerned with definitions of attitude and related constructs, but strive to seek common agreement for terms useful in their own studies. We found Teixeira dos Santos and Mortimer's (2003) use of personal posture, gesture, and voice intonation as evidence of emotion to be innovative and encourage further exploration of other physiological indicators of attitude. Building on this work, future research may include the examination of facial muscle patterns detectable through electromyographic recordings as evidence of learners' science-related attitudes (see Cacioppo & Petty, 1979).

Theoretical frameworks have not always guided attitude research in science education (Ramsden, 1998). Prominent in past research are the guiding frameworks of Hovland's learning theory approach and Fishbein and Ajzen's theories of reasoned action and planned behavior (Simpson et al., 1994). More recent attitude research has found theoretical grounding in Damasio's (1994) work on emotion and feeling and the psychotherapy of trauma recovery (Winnicott, 1970), which emphasizes the importance of play and community as elements of the learning process. These frameworks will provide guidance for continued research into the design of interventions to affect attitudes. In addition, psychologists' work on implicit attitudes (see Dovidio, Kawakami, & Beach, 2001) and the differentiated role of beliefs and attitudes in guiding behavior (called the mismatch model; see Millar & Tesser, 1992) may also contribute to the theoretical foundations for future attitude research in science education. It is clear from the research we have reviewed that diversity in theoretical orientation will lead to the use of more and different methodological approaches to investigate learners' science-related attitudes.

With respect to the role of motivation in learning science, a future direction for research is to investigate how different theoretical orientations and constructs relate to one another, rather than create new orientations and constructs simply to be innovative. *Synthesis* and *integration* should be the keywords of future motivational research in science learning (Pintrich, 2003). There is great need to clarify this area of research by examining the similar roles that orientations and constructs can play in fostering science learning (Glynn & Koballa, 2007).

We recommend that motivation researchers avoid simple categorizations such as high versus low anxiety, intrinsic versus extrinsic motivation, and learning versus performance goals. Instead, they should adopt broader perspectives that serve to synthesize orientations and constructs. For example, rather than conceptualize students as having either learning goals *or* performance, researchers should conceptualize students as having a variety of goals, depending upon the context, and endeavor to explain the relationship between students' goals and other motivational constructs such as self-determination and self-efficacy.

IMPLICATIONS FOR POLICY AND PRACTICE

Although there are certainly positive consequences of current federal initiatives designed to promote student achievement in science and other areas, there are negative ones as well. Because of an increased and often inappropriate emphasis on standardized testing, students are at increased risk of developing poor attitudes and low motivation in the area of science. Science education policy makers must come to understand that although high-stakes testing may serve to inspire some students to achieve at high levels, it serves as a deterrent to learning for many more. They are encouraged to adopt a view of learning in which "affect surrounds cognition," recognizing that "if children are not comfortable or joyful they will not learn, irrespective of how well pedagogical practices are designed" (Alsop & Watts, 2003, p. 1046). Acting from this informed view of science learning, policy makers should press state departments of education and local schools to specifically address affective elements of learning in their science curricula and associated assessment programs. Science learning experiences that are fun and personally fulfilling are likely to foster positive attitudes and heightened motivation toward science learning and lead to improved achievement. Attention to student attitudes and motivation in science curricula will prompt policy makers to become advocates for assessing affective outcomes of learning. Professional learning opportunities should be provided for teachers that will help prepare them to encourage unmotivated science students.

The research on science-related attitudes also has implications for professional practice. Teachers should consider strategies for improving students' attitudes as possible ways to increase enrollment in noncompulsory science courses and enhancing science achievement (Osborne, Simon, & Collins, 2003). Approaches to positively affecting student attitudes include instruction that emphasizes active learning and the relevance of science to daily life. When endeavoring to improve students' attitudes, teachers should consider their own cultural expectations. For example, teachers may unwittingly contribute to the persistent attitudinal differences between boys and girls. Teachers should recognize that students' enjoyment of science may be as important an outcome of school science in the long run as their scores on standardized tests.

Numerous instruments are available to assess the influence of instruction on students' science-related attitudes. When using an available measure, we recommend that teachers recognize that learners are not always willing and able to divulge their true feelings. We also encourage teachers to use interviews, photographs, and student drawings as alternatives to the use of scales and to supplement data gathered with the use of scales.

The research on motivational constructs also has many implications for practice in science education. Some of the most important of these involve the construct of self-determination, because science teachers wish to help students become independent, life-long learners. Science teachers can promote students' self-determination by providing them with appropriate challenges and feedback, by giving them leadership opportunities, by fostering students' relationships with peers and their parents, by creating a positive classroom environment, and by providing them with a role in classroom governance. The result will be greater student interest, sense of competence, creativity, learning, and preference for challenges (Matthews, 1991; Ryan & Grolnick, 1986; Williams, Wiener, Markakis, Reeve, & Deci, 1993).

Effective science teachers know students' self-determination leads to successful learning only when it is accompanied by high self-efficacy. If students have high self-efficacy in science, they will set higher goals, persist longer, expend greater effort, and endeavor to find increasingly better strategies. If students have low efficacy, they will tend to give up easily when science learning becomes difficult (Zimmerman, 2000). Students will increase their self-efficacy and improve their achievement if they adopt short-term goals to judge their progress, use specific learning strategies such as summarizing to help them focus their attention, and receive rewards based on their performance and not just their participation.

In conclusion, in this chapter we have examined the attitudinal and motivational constructs that influence science learning. We have reviewed the research conducted on these constructs, emphasizing the methods and instruments used, and the theoretical orientations in which the constructs are embedded. In addition, we have made specific recommendations for future research on these constructs and drawn implications for policy and practice.

We strongly encourage new and seasoned researchers to advance what is known about how attitudes influence motivation and how motivation influences science learning, and ultimately behavior. Ideally, all students of science should develop positive attitudes that motivate them to achieve at high levels. Their achievement should be reflected not only in their understanding of science and their development of scientific skills, but in their appreciation of the world around them. Ideally, students of science should learn to use their knowledge and skills to become caretakers of the world, preserving it and enhancing it for generations to come. We encourage science educators, who wish to help students achieve such goals, to embark on programs of research that focus upon how to best foster the growth of students' positive attitudes and their intrinsic motivation to learn science.

ACKNOWLEDGMENTS

Thanks to Thomas Andre, Frank Crawley, and Linda Winter, who reviewed this chapter.

REFERENCES

Aikenhead, G., & Ryan, A. (1992). The development of a new instrument: Views on science-technology-society (VOSTS). *Science Education, 76,* 477–491.

Ajzen, I., & Fishbein, M. (1980). *Understanding attitudes and predicting social behavior.* Englewood Cliffs, NJ: Prentice-Hall.

Alsop, S., & Watts, M. (2003). Science education and affect. *International Journal of Science Education, 25,* 1043–1047.

Anderman, E. M., & Young, A. J. (1994). Motivation and strategy use in science: Individual differences and classroom effects. *Journal of Research in Science Teaching, 31,* 811–831.

Anderson, J. R. (1990). *The adaptive character of thought.* Hillsdale, NJ: Lawrence Erlbaum Associates.

Andre, T., Whigham, M., Hendrickson, A., & Chambers, S. (1999). Competency beliefs, positive affect, gender stereotyping of elementary students and their parents about science versus other school subjects. *Journal of Research in Science Teaching, 36,* 719–747.

Atkinson, J. W., & Raynor, J. O. (1978). *Personality, motivation, and achievement.* Washington, DC: Hemisphere.

Bandura, A. (1997). *Self-efficacy: The exercise of control.* New York: Freeman.

Bennett, J., Rollnick, M., Green, G., & White, M. (2001). The development and use of an instrument to assess students' attitudes to the study of chemistry. *International Journal of Science Education, 23,* 833–845.

Berlyne, D. (1966). Curiosity and exploration. *Science, 153,* 25–33.

Bloom, B. S. (1976). *Human characteristics and school learning.* New York: McGraw-Hill.

Bong, M., & Clark, R. E. (1999). Comparison between self-concept and self-efficacy in academic motivation research. *Educational Psychologist, 34,* 139–153.

Bong, M., & Skaalvik, E. M. (2003). Academic self-concept and self-efficacy: How different are they really? *Educational Psychology Review, 15,* 1–40.

Britner, S. L., & Pajares, F. (2002). Self-efficacy beliefs, motivation, race, and gender in middle school science. *Journal of Women and Minorities in Science and Engineering, 7,* 269–283.

Brophy, J. (1987). On motivating students. In D. Berliner & B. Rosenshine (Eds.), *Talks to teachers* (pp. 201–245). New York: Random House

Brown, A. L., & Campione, J. C. (1996). Psychological theory and the design of innovative learning environments: On procedures, principles, and systems. In L. Schauble & R. Glaser (Eds.), *Innovations in learning: New environments for education* (pp. 289–325). Mahwah, NJ: Lawrence Erlbaum Associates.

Butler, M. B. (1999). Factors associated with students' intentions to engage in science learning activities. *Journal of Research in Science Teaching, 36,* 455–473.

Cacioppo, J. T., & Petty, R. E. (1979). Attitudes and cognitive response: An electrophysiographical approach. *Journal of Personality and Social Psychology, 37,* 97–109.

Cameron, J., & Pierce, W. D. (2002). *Rewards and intrinsic motivation: Resolving the controversy*. New York: Bergin & Garvy.

Cassady, J. C., & Johnson, R. E. (2002). Cognitive test anxiety and academic performance. *Contemporary Educational Psychology, 27*, 270–295.

Cavallo, A., & Laubach, T. A. (2001). Students' science perceptions and enrollment decisions in different learning cycle classrooms. *Journal of Research in Science Teaching, 38*, 1029–1062.

Charen, G. (1966). Laboratory methods build attitudes. *Science Education, 50*, 54–57.

Choi, K. & Cho, H. (2002). Effects of teaching ethical issues on Korean school students' attitudes toward science. *Journal of Biological Education, 37*(1), 26–30.

Covington, M. V. (2000). Goal theory, motivations, and school achievement: An integrative review. *Annual Reviews of Psychology, 51*, 171–200.

Crawley, F. E., & Black, C. B. (1992). Causal modeling of secondary science students intentions to enroll in physics. *Journal of Research in Science Teaching, 29*, 585–599.

Crawley, F. E., & Koballa, T. R. (1992). Hispanic-American students' attitudes toward enrolling in high school chemistry: A study of planned behavior and belief-based change. *Hispanic Journal of Behavioral Sciences, 14*, 469–486.

Crawley, F. E., & Koballa, T. R. (1994). Attitude research in science education: Contemporary models and methods. *Science Education, 78*, 36–57.

Csikszentmihalyi, M. (2000). *Flow: Beyond boredom and anxiety*. San Francisco: Jossey-Bass.

Damasio, A. (1994). *Descartes' error: Emotion, reason, and the human brain*. New York: Avon Books.

Dawson, C. (2000). Upper primary boys' and girls' interest in science: Have they changed since 1980? *International Journal of Science Education, 22*, 557–570.

DeBacker, T. K., & Nelson, R. M. (1999). Variations on an expectancy-value model of motivation in science. *Contemporary Educational Psychology, 24*, 71–94.

De Baz, T. (2001). The effectiveness of the jigsaw cooperative learning on students' achievement and attitudes toward science. *Science Education International, 12*(4), 6–11.

Deci, E. L. (1996). Making room for self-regulation: Some thoughts on the link between emotion and behavior: Comment. *Psychological Inquiry, 7*, 220–223.

Deci, E. L., Koestner, R., & Ryan, R. M. (1999). A meta-analytic review of experiments examining the effects of extrinsic rewards on intrinsic motivation. *Psychological Bulletin, 125*, 627–668.

Deci, E. L., Vallerand, R. J., Pelletier, L. G., & Ryan, R. M. (1991). Motivation and education: The self-determining perspective. *Educational Psychologist, 26*, 325–346.

Dewey, J. (1916). Methods of science teaching. *General Science Quarterly, 1*, 3–9.

Dewey, J. (1934). The supreme intellectual obligation. *Science Education, 18*, 1–4.

Dovidio, J. F., Kawakami, K., & Beach, K. R. (2001). Implicit and explicit attitudes: examination of the relationship between measures of intergroup bias. In R. Brown & S. L. Gaertner (Eds.), *Blackwell handbook of social psychology: Vol. 4. Intergroup relationships* (pp. 175–197). Oxford: Blackwell.

Ellis, J., Killip, A., & Bennett, J. (2000). Attitude? *Educational Institute of Scotland*, June, 24–25.

Escalada, L. T., & Zollman, D. A. (1998). An investigation of the effects of using interactive digital video in a physics classroom on student learning and attitude. *Journal of Research in Science Teaching, 34*, 467–489.

Ferreira, M. (2002). Ameliorating equity in science, mathematics, and engineering: A case study of an after-school science program. *Equity & Excellence in Education, 35*(1), 43–49.

Finson, K. D. (2002). Drawing a scientist: What we do know and do not know after fifty years of drawings. *School Science and Mathematics, 102*, 335–345.

Francis, L. J., & Greer, J. E. (1999). Measuring attitudes toward science among secondary school students: The affective domain. *Research in Science & Technology Education, 17*, 219–226.

Fraser, B. (1982). How strongly are attitude and achievement related? *School Science Review, 63*, 557–559.

Freedman, M. P. (2002). The influence of laboratory instruction on science achievement and attitude toward science across gender differences. *Journal of Women and Minorities in Science and Engineering, 8*, 191–200.

Gabel, D. (Ed.). (1994). Handbook of research on science teaching and learning. New York: Macmillan.

Garner, R. (1998). Choosing to learn and not-learn in school. *Educational Psychological Review, 10*, 227–238.

George, R. (2000). Measuring change in students' attitudes toward science over time: An application of latent variable growth model. *Journal of Science Education and Technology, 9*, 213–225.

Gibson, H. L., & Chase, C. (2002). Longitudinal impact of an inquiry-based science program on middle school students' attitudes toward science. *Science Education, 86*, 693–705.

Glynn, S. M., & Duit, R. (1995). Learning science meaningfully: Constructing conceptual models. In S. M. Glynn & R. Duit (Eds.), *Learning science in the schools: Research reforming practice* (pp. 3–33). Hillsdale, NJ: Lawrence Erlbaum Associates.

Glynn, S. M. & Koballa, T. R., Jr. (2007). Motivation to learn in college science. In J. Mintzes & W. H. Leonard (Eds.), *Handbook of college science teaching*. Arlington, VA: National Science Teachers Association Press.

Glynn, S. M., Muth, K. D., & Britton, B. K. (1990). Thinking out loud about concepts in science text: How instructional objectives work. In H. Mandl, E. De Corte, S. N. Bennett, & H. F. Friedrich (Eds.), *Learning and instruction: European research in an international context* (Vol. 2, pp. 215–223). Oxford: Pergamon.

Glynn, S. M., & Takahashi, T. (1998). Learning from analogy-enhanced science text. *Journal of Research in Science Teaching, 35*, 1129–1149.

Glynn, S. M., Yeany, R. H., & Britton, B. K. (1991). A constructive view of learning science. In S. M. Glynn, R. H. Yeany, & B. K. Britton (Eds.), *The psychology of learning science.* (pp. 3–19). Hillsdale, NJ: Lawrence Erlbaum Associates.

Good, T. L., & Brophy, J. E. (1997). *Looking in classrooms* (7th ed.). New York: Longman.

Greeno, J. G., Collins, A. M. & Resnick, L. B. (1996). Cognition and learning. In D. Berliner & R. Calfee (Eds.), *Handbook of educational psychology* (pp. 15–46). New York: Macmillan.

Hansen, R. A. (1977). Anxiety. In S. Ball (Ed.), *Motivation in education*. New York: Academic Press.

Harwood, W. S., & McMahon, M. M. (1997). Effects of integrated video media on student achievement and attitudes in high school chemistry. *Journal of Research in Science Teaching, 34*, 617–631.

Haussler, P., & Hoffman, L. (2002). An intervention study to enhance girls' interest, self-concept, and achievement in physics classes. *Journal of Research in Science Teaching, 39*, 870–888.

Jayaratne, T. E., Thomas, N. G., & Trautmann, M. (2003). Intervention program to keep girls in the science pipeline: Outcome difference by ethnic status. *Journal of Research in Science Teaching, 40*, 393–414.

Jones, E. E. (1998). Major developments in five decades of social psychology. In D. T. Gilbert, S. T. Fiske, & G. Lindzey (Eds.), *Handbook of social psychology* (Vol. 1, pp. 3–57). Boston: McGraw-Hill.

Jones, M. G., Howe, A., & Rua, M. J. (2000). Gender differences in students' experiences, interests, and attitudes toward science and scientists. *Science Education, 84*, 180–192.

Joo, Y. J., Bong, M., & Choi, H. J. (2000). Self-efficacy for self-regulated learning, academic self-efficacy, and internet self-efficacy in web-based instruction. *Educational Technology Research and Development, 48*(2), 5–18.

Jovanovic, J., & Dreves, C. (1998). Students' science attitudes in the performance-based classroom: Did we close the gender gap? *Journal of Women and Minorities in Science and Engineering, 4*, 235–248.

Jurd, E. (2001). Children's attitudes to science. *Primary Science Review, 66*, 29–30.

Kardash, C. M., & Wallace, M. L. (2001). The perceptions of science classes survey: What undergraduate science reform efforts really need to address. *Journal of Educational Psychology, 93*, 199–210.

Koballa, T. R. (1992). Persuasion and attitude change in science education. *Journal of Research in Science Teaching, 29*, 63–80.

Koballa, T. R., & Crawley, F. E. (1985). The influence of attitude on science teaching and learning. *School Science and Mathematics, 85*, 222–232.

Koslow, M. J., & Nay, M. A. (1976). An approach to measuring scientific attitudes. *Science Education, 60*, 147–172.

Lave, J., & Wenger, E. (1991). *Situated learning: Legitimate peripheral participation.* Cambridge, England: Cambridge University Press.

Lee, O., & Brophy, J. (1996). Motivational patterns observed in sixth-grade science classrooms. *Journal of Research in Science Teaching, 33*, 303–318.

Likert, R. (1932). A technique for the measurement of attitudes. *Archives of Psychology, 140*, 1–55.

Linnenbrink, E. A., & Pintrich, P. R. (2002). Achievement goal theory and affect: An asymmetrical bidirectional model. *Educational Psychologist, 37*, 69–78.

Locke, E. A., & Latham, G. P. (1990). *A theory of goal setting and task performance.* Englewood Cliffs, NJ: Prentice-Hall.

Locke, E. A., & Latham, G. P. (2002). Building a practically useful theory of goal setting and task motivation. *American Psychologist, 57*, 705–717.

Maslow, A. H. (1968). *Toward a psychology of being* (2nd ed.). New York: Van Nostrand.

Maslow, A. H. (1970). *Motivation and personality* (2nd ed.). New York: Harper & Row.

Matthews, D. B. (1991). The effects of school environment on intrinsic motivation of middle-school children. *Journal of Humanistic Education and Development, 30*(1), 30–36.

Mazlo, J., Dormedy, D. F., Neimoth-Anderson, J. D., Urlacher, T., Carson, G. A., & Kelter, P. B., (2002). Assessment of motivational methods in the general chemistry laboratory. *Journal of College Science Teaching, 36*, 318–321.

McManus, D. O., Dunn, R., & Denig, S. J. (2003). Effects of traditional lecture versus teacher-constructed and student-constructed self-teaching instructional resources on short-term science achievement and attitude. *American Biology Teacher, 65*(2), 93–99.

Meece, J. L., Blumenfeld, P. C., & Hoyle, R. H. (1988). Students' goal orientations and cognitive engagement in classroom activities. *Journal of Educational Psychology, 80*, 514–523.

Meece, J. L., & Jones, M. G. (1994). Gender differences in motivation and strategy use in science: Are girls rote learners? *Journal of Research in Science Teaching, 33*, 393–406.

Midgley, C., Kaplan, A., & Middleton, M. (2001). Performance-approach goals: Good for what, for whom, under what circumstances, and at what cost? *Journal of Educational Psychology, 80*, 514–523.

Millar, M. G., & Tesser, A. (1992). The role of beliefs and feelings in guiding behavior: the mismatch model. In L. Martin & A. Tesser (Eds.), *The construction of social judgment* (pp. 277–300). Hillsdale, NJ: Lawrence Erlbaum Associates.

Morrell, P. D., & Lederman, N. G. (1998). Students' attitudes toward school and classroom science: Are they independent phenomena? *School Science and Mathematics, 98*, 76–83.

Neber, H., & Schommer-Aikins, M. (2002). Self-regulated science learning with highly gifted students: The role of cognitive, motivational, epistemological, and environmental variables. *High Ability Studies, 13*(1), 51–74.

Nicholls, J. G. (1992). Students as educational theorists. In D. Schunck & J. Meece (Eds.), *Students' perceptions in the classroom* (pp. 267–286). Hillsdale, NJ: Lawrence Erlbaum Associates.

Nolen, S. B. (2003). Learning environment, motivation, and achievement in high school science. *Journal of Research in Science Teaching, 40*, 347–368.

Nolen, S. B., & Haladyna, T. M. (1990). Motivation and studying in high school science. *Journal of Research in Science Teaching, 27*, 115–126.

Osborne, J., Driver, R., & Simon, S. (1998). Attitude to science: Issues and concerns. *School Science Review, 79*, 27–33.

Osborne, J., Simon, S., & Collins, S. (2003). Attitudes towards science: A review of the literature and its implications. *International Journal of Science Education, 25*, 1049–1079.

Palmer, D. H. (1997). Investigating students' private perceptions of scientists and their work. *Research in Science and Technology Education, 15*(2), 173–183.

Paris, N. A., & Glynn, S. M. (2004). Elaborate analogies in science text: Tools for enhancing pre-service teachers' knowledge and attitudes. *Contemporary Educational Psychology.*

Parkinson, J., Hendley, D., Tanner, H., & Stables, A. (1998). Pupils' attitudes to science in key stage 3 of the national curriculum: A study of pupils in South Wales. *Research in Science and Technological Education, 16,* 165–177.

Pell, T., & Jarvis, T. (2001). Developing attitude to science scales for use with children of ages five to eleven years. *International Journal of Science Education, 23,* 847–862.

Perrier, F., & Nsengiyumva, J.-B. (2003). Active science as a contribution to the trauma recovery process: Preliminary indications with orphans for the 1994 genocide in Rwanda. *International Journal of Science Education, 25,* 1111–1128.

Petty, R. E., & Cacioppo, J. T. (1981). *Attitude and persuasion: Classic and contemporary approaches.* Dubuque, IA: Wm. C. Brown.

Phillips, K. A., Barrow, L. H., & Chandrasekhar, M. (2002). Science career interests among high school girls one year after participation in a summer science program. *Journal of Women and Minorities in Science and Engineering, 8,* 235–247.

Pilburn, M. D., & Baker, D. R. (1993). If I were the teacher . . . qualitative study of attitudes toward science. *Science Education, 77,* 393–406.

Pintrich, P. R. (2003). A motivational science perspective on the role of student motivation in learning and teaching contexts. *Journal of Educational Psychology, 95,* 667–686.

Pintrich, P. R., & DeGroot, E. V. (1990). Motivational and self-regulated learning components of classroom academic performance. *Journal of Educational Psychology, 82,* 33–40.

Pintrich, P. R., Marx, R. W., & Boyle R. A. (1993). Beyond cold conceptual change: The role of motivational beliefs and classroom contextual factors in the process of conceptual change. *Review of Educational Research, 63,* 167–199.

Pintrich, P. R., & Schunk, D. H. (1996). *Motivation in education: Theory, research, and applications.* Columbus, OH: Merrill.

Rainey, R. (1965). The effects of directed vs. nondirected laboratory work on high school chemistry achievement. *Journal of Research in Science Teaching, 3,* 286–292.

Ramsden, J. M. (1998). Mission impossible? Can anything be done about attitudes to science. *International Journal of Science Education, 20,* 125–137.

Reeve, J. (1996). *Motivating others: Nurturing inner motivational resources.* Boston: Allyn & Bacon.

Reeve, J., Hamm, D., & Nix, G. (2003). Testing models of the experience of self-determination in intrinsic motivation and the conundrum of choice. *Journal of Educational Psychology, 95,* 375–392.

Reid, N., & Skryabina, E. A. (2002). Attitudes toward physics. *Research in Science and Technological Education, 20,* 67–81.

Rennie, L. J., & Punch, K. F. (1991). The relationship between affect and achievement in science. *Journal of Research in Science Teaching, 28,* 193–209.

Richardson, V. (1996). The role of attitudes and beliefs in learning to teach. In J. Sikula, T. J. Buttery, & E. Guyton (Eds.), *Handbook of research on teacher education* (pp. 102–119). New York: Macmillan.

Robertson, I. J. (2000). Influences on choice of course made by university Year 1 bioscience students—a case study. *International Journal of Science Education, 22,* 1201–1218.

Rogers, C., & Freiberg, H. J. (1994). *Freedom to learn* (3rd ed.). New York: Macmillan/Merrill.

Rop, C. J. (2003). Spontaneous inquiry questions in high school chemistry classroom: Perceptions of a group of motivated learners. *International Journal of Science Education, 25,* 13–33.

Rosenthal, R., & Jacobson, L. (1968). *Pygmalion in the classroom.* New York: Holt, Rinehart & Winston.

Ryan, R. M., & Deci, E. L. (2000). Intrinsic and extrinsic motivations: Classic definitions and new directions. *Contemporary Educational Psychology, 25,* 54–67.

Ryan, R. M., & Grolnick, W. S. (1986). Origins and pawns in the classroom self-report and projective assessments of individual differences in the children's perceptions. *Journal of Personality and Social Psychology, 50,* 550–558.

Scardamalia, M., & Bereiter, C. (1996). Adaptation and understanding: A case for new cultures of schooling. In S. Vosniado, E. De Corte, R. Glasse, & H. Mandl (Eds.), *International perspectives on the design of technology-supported learning environments* (pp. 149–163). Mahwah, NJ: Lawrence Erlbaum Associates.

Schibeci, R. (1984). Attitudes to science: An update. *Studies in Science Education, 11*, 26–59.

Schunk, D. H. (1996). Goal and self-evaluative influences during children's cognitive skill learning. *American Educational Research Journal, 33*, 359–382.

Schunk, D. H. (2000). Coming to terms with motivation constructs. *Contemporary Educational Psychology, 25*, 116–119.

Schunk, D. H., & Zimmerman, B. J. (1997). Social origins of self-regulatory competence. *Educational Psychologist, 32*, 195–208.

Seligman, M. E. P. (1975). *Helplessness on depression, development, and death.* San Francisco: Freeman.

She, H.-C. (1998). Gender and grade level differences in Taiwan students' stereotypes of science and scientists. *Research in Science & Technology Education, 16*, 125–135.

Sherif, C. W., Sherif, M., & Nebergall, R. E. (1965). *Attitude and attitude change. The social judgment-involvement approach.* Philadelphia: W. B. Saunders.

Shrigley, R. L. (1983). The attitude concept and science teaching. *Science Education, 67*, 425–442.

Shrigley, R. L. (1990). Attitude and behavior are correlates. *Journal of Research in Science Teaching, 27*, 97–113.

Shrigley, R. L., Koballa, T. R., & Simpson, R. D. (1988). Defining attitude for science educators. *Journal of Research in Science Teaching, 25*, 659–678.

Siegel, M. A., & Ranney, M. A. (2003). Developing the changes in attitude about the relevance of science (CARS) questionnaire and assessing two high school science classes. *Journal of Research in Science Teaching, 40*, 757–775.

Simpson, R. D., Koballa, T. R., Oliver, J. S., & Crawley, F. E. (1994). Research on the affective dimension of science learning. In D. Gabel (Ed.), *Handbook of research on science teaching and learning* (pp. 211–234). New York: Macmillan.

Singh, K., Granville, M., & Dika, S. (2002). Mathematics and science achievement: Effects of motivation, interest, and academic engagement. *The Journal of Educational Research, 95*, 323–332.

Smith, A., Jussim, L., & Eccles, J. (1999). Do self-fulfilling prophecies accumulate, dissipate, or remain stable over time? *Journal of Personality and Social Psychology, 77*, 548–565.

Snow, R. E., Corno, L., & Jackson, D. (1996). Individual differences in affective and conative functions. In D. C. Berliner & R. C. Calfee (Eds.), *Handbook of educational psychology* (pp. 243–310). New York: Macmillan.

Soyibo, K., & Hudson, A. (2000). Effects of computer-assisted instruction (CAI) on 11th graders' attitudes toward biology and CAI and understanding of reproduction in plants and animals. *Research in Science & Technological Education, 18*, 191–199.

Spielberger, C. D. (1983). *Manual for the state-trait anxiety inventory (STAI).* Palo Alto, CA: Consulting Psychologists Press.

Stake, J. E., & Mares, K. R. (2001). Science enrichment programs for gifted high school girls and boys: Predictors of program impact on science confidence and motivation. *Journal of Research in Science Teaching, 38*, 1065–1088.

Stipek, D. J. (1996). Motivation and instruction. In D. Berliner & R. Calfee (Eds.), *Handbook of educational psychology* (pp. 85–109). New York: Macmillan.

Teixeira dos Santos, F. M., & Mortimer, E. F. (2003). How emotions share the relationship between a chemistry teachers and her high school students. *International Journal of Science Education, 25*, 1095–1110.

Terry, J. M., & Baird, W. E. (1997). What factors affect attitudes toward women in science held by high school biology students? *School Science and Mathematics, 97*, 78–86.

Thompson, T. L., & Mintzes, J. J. (2002). Cognitive structure and the affective domain: On knowing and feeling in biology. *International Journal of Science Education, 24*, 645–660.

Thompson, J., & Soyibo, K. (2002). Effects of lecture, teacher demonstrations, discussion and practical work on 10th graders' attitudes to chemistry and understanding of electrolysis. *Research in Science & Technology Education, 20*(1), 25–37.

Thurstone, L. L. (1928). Attitudes can be measured. *American Journal of Sociology, 33*, 529–554.

Trenholm, S. (1989). *Persuasion and social influence.* Englewood Cliffs, NJ: Prentice-Hall.

Vispoel, W. P., & Austin, J. R. (1995). Success and failure in junior high school: A critical incident approach to understanding students' attributional beliefs. *American Educational Research Journal, 32*, 377–412.

Wade, S. E. (2001). Research on importance and interest: Implications for curriculum development and future research. *Educational Psychology Review, 13*, 243–261.

Webster, B. J., & Fisher, D. L. (2000). Accounting for variation in science and mathematics achievement: A multilevel analysis of Australian data. Third international mathematics and science study (TIMSS). *School Effectiveness and School Improvement, 11*, 339–360.

Weinburgh, M. (1995). Gender differences in student attitudes toward science: A meta-analysis of the literature from 1970 to 1991. *Journal of Research in Science Teaching, 32*, 387–398.

Weiner, B. (1986). *An attributional theory of motivation and emotion.* New York: Springer.

Weiner, B. (1990). History of motivational research in education. *Journal of Educational Psychology, 82*, 616–622.

Weiner, B. (1992). *Human motivation: Metaphors, theories, and research.* Newbury Park, CA: Sage.

Weinstein, R. S., Madison, S. M., & Kuklinski, M. R. (1995). Raising expectations in schools: Obstacles and opportunities for change. *American Educational Research Journal, 32*, 121–159.

Weinstock, H. (1967). Differentiating socio-philosophical attitudes toward science from problems pertinent to science teaching. *Science Education, 51*, 243–245.

Weller, F. (1933). Attitudes and skills in elementary science. *Science Education, 17*, 90–97.

Wentzel, K. R. (2000). What is it that I'm trying to achieve? Classroom goals from a content perspective. *Contemporary Educational Psychology, 25*, 105–115.

West, A., Hailes, J., & Sammons, P. (1997). Children's attitudes toward the national curriculum at key stage 1. *British Educational Research Journal, 23*, 597–613.

Williams, G. C., Wiener, M. W., Markakis, K. M., Reeve, J., & Deci, E. L. (1993). Medical student motivation for internal medicine. *Annals of Internal Medicine, 9*, 327–333.

Willson, V, L., Ackerman, C., & Malave, C. (2000). Cross-time attitudes, concept formation, and achievement in college freshman physics. *Journal of Research in Science Teaching, 37*, 1112–1120.

Winnicott, D. W. (1970). Residential care as therapy. In C. Winnicott, R. Shepherd, & M. Davis (eds.), *Deprivation and delinquency* (pp. 220–228). London: Tavistock.

Woolnough, B. E., & Guo, Y. (1997). Factors affecting student choice of career in science and engineering: Parallel studies in Australia, Canada, China, England, Japan and Portugal. *Research in Science & Technology Education, 15*, 105–121

Zimmerman, B. J. (2000). Self-efficacy: An essential motive to learn. *Contemporary Educational Psychology, 25*, 82–91.

Zusho, A., & Pintrich, P. R. (2003). Skill and will: The role of motivation and cognition in the learning of college chemistry. *International Journal of Science Education, 25*, 1081–1094.

CHAPTER 5

Classroom Learning Environments

Barry J. Fraser
Curtin University of Technology, Australia

Because students spend approximately 20,000 hours in classrooms by the time that they graduate from university (Fraser, 2001), their reaction to their teaching-learning experiences are of considerable importance. However, despite the obvious importance of what goes on in school and university classrooms, teachers and researchers have relied heavily and sometimes exclusively on the assessment of academic achievement and other learning outcomes. Although no one would dispute the worth of achievement, it cannot give a complete picture of the educational process.

Although classroom environment is a subtle concept, it can be assessed and studied. A considerable amount of work has been undertaken in many countries in developing methods for investigating how teachers and students perceive the environments in which they work. Remarkable progress has been made over several decades in conceptualizing, assessing, and researching the classroom environment.

Researchers have carried out many dozens of studies of the relationship between student achievement and the quality of the classroom learning environment (Fraser, 1998a). These studies have been carried out in numerous different countries with tens of thousands of students. The consistent and overwhelming evidence from these studies is that the classroom environment strongly influences student outcomes. Therefore, teachers should not feel that it is a waste of time for them to devote time and energy to improving their classroom environments. The research shows that attention to the classroom environment is likely to pay off in terms of improving student outcomes.

A milestone in the historical development of the field of learning environments occurred over 30 years ago when Herbert Walberg and Rudolf Moos began seminal independent programs of research (Fraser, 1986; Fraser & Walberg, 1991; Moos, 1974). In turn, the pioneering work of Walberg and Moos built upon the ideas of Lewin (1936) and Murray (1938), presented several decades before. Lewin's field theory recognized that both the environment and its interaction with personal characteristics of the individual are potent determinants of human behavior. Lewin's formula, $B = f(P, E)$, stressed the need for new research strategies in which behavior is considered to be a function of the person and the environment.

Drawing on Murray's work, Stern (1970) formulated a theory of person-environment congruence in which complementary combinations of personal needs and environmental press enhance student outcomes. The Getzels and Thelen (1960) model for the class as a social system holds that, in school classes, personality needs, role expectations, and classroom climate interact to predict group behavior, including learning outcomes.

Psychosocial learning environment has been incorporated as one factor in a multifactor psychological model of educational productivity (Walberg, 1981). This theory, which is based on an economic model of agricultural, industrial, and national productivity, holds that learning is a multiplicative, diminishing-returns function of student age, ability, and motivation; of quality and quantity of instructions; and of the psychosocial environments of the home, the classroom, the peer group, and the mass media. Because the function is multiplicative, it can be argued in principle that any factor at a zero point will result in zero learning; thus either zero motivation or zero time for instruction will result in zero learning. Moreover, it will do less good to raise a factor that already is high than to improve a factor that currently is the main constraint to learning. Empirical probes of the educational productivity model were made by carrying out extensive research syntheses involving the correlations of learning with the factors in the model (Fraser, Walberg, Welch, & Hattie, 1987) and secondary analyses of large data bases collected as part of the National Assessment of Educational Progress (Walberg, Fraser, & Welch, 1986). Classroom and school environment was found to be a strong predictor of both achievement and attitudes even when a comprehensive set of other factors was held constant.

The field of learning environments has undergone remarkable growth, diversification, and internationalization during the past 30 years (Fraser, 1998a). A striking feature of this field is the availability of a variety of economical, valid, and widely applicable questionnaires that have been developed and used for assessing students' perceptions of classroom environment (Fraser, 1998b). Although learning environment research originated in Western countries, African (Fisher & Fraser, 2003) and especially Asian researchers (Fraser, 2002; Goh & Khine, 2002) have made many major and distinctive contributions in the last decade. For example, some of the main questionnaires that were developed in the West have been adapted (sometimes involving translation into another language) and cross-validated for use in numerous other countries.

This chapter provides access to past research on classroom learning environments and to instruments that have proved valid and useful in international contexts. The chapter begins by describing historically important learning environment questionnaires as well as contemporary instruments. In order to illustrate the application of learning environment assessments, another section is devoted to reviewing past research in six areas: (a) associations between student outcomes and environment; (b) evaluation of educational innovations; (c) differences between student and teacher perceptions of actual and preferred environment; (d) determinants of classroom environment; (e) use of qualitative research methods; and (f) cross-national studies. The chapter's concluding section provides a look forward to the next generation of learning environment research.

QUESTIONNAIRES FOR ASSESSING CLASSROOM ENVIRONMENT

Because few fields of educational research can boast the existence of such a rich array of validated and robust instruments, this section describes four contemporary instruments that have been used in both Western and non-Western countries: the Questionnaire on Teacher Interaction (QTI); the Science Laboratory Environment Inventory (SLEI); the Constructivist Learning Environment Survey (CLES); and the What Is Happening In this Class? (WIHIC) questionnaire. Before we discuss each of these instruments, some historically important questionnaires are briefly considered.

Historically Important Questionnaires

The Learning Environment Inventory (LEI) and Classroom Environment Scale (CES) were developed in the United States in the late 1960s. The initial development of the LEI began in conjunction with evaluation and research related to Harvard Project Physics (Walberg & Anderson, 1968). The CES (Moos & Trickett, 1987) grew out of a comprehensive program of research involving perceptual measures of a variety of human environments, including psychiatric hospitals, prisons, university residences, and work milieus (Moos, 1974).

The LEI was used in the Hindi language in a large study involving approximately 3,000 tenth-grade students in 83 science and 67 social studies classes (Walberg, Singh, & Rasher, 1977). Student perceptions on the LEI accounted for a significant increment in achievement variance beyond that attributable to general ability. In Indonesia, Paige (1979) used the CES and three scales selected from the LEI to reveal that individual modernity was enhanced in classrooms perceived as having greater task orientation, competition, and difficulty and less order and organization, whereas achievement was enhanced in classes higher in speed and lower in order and organization. Hirata and Sako (1998) used an instrument in the Japanese language that incorporated scales from the CES. Factor analysis of the responses of 635 students suggested a four-factor structure for this questionnaire (consisting of Teacher Control, Sense of Isolation, Order and Discipline, and Affiliation).

The My Class Inventory (MCI) is a simplified form of the LEI for use among children aged 8–12 years (Fisher & Fraser, 1981). In Singapore, Goh, Young, and Fraser (1995) changed the MCI's original Yes-No response format to a three-point response format (Seldom, Sometimes, and Most of the Time) in a modified version of the MCI that includes a Task Orientation scale. Goh et al. found the modified MCI to be valid and useful in research applications with 1,512 elementary-school students in 39 classes. In Brunei Darussalam, Majeed, Fraser, and Aldridge (2002) used the original version of the MCI with 1,565 middle-school students in 81 classes in 15 government secondary schools. When the Satisfaction scale was used as an attitudinal outcome variable instead of as a measure of classroom environment, Majeed et al. found strong support for a three-factor structure for the MCI consisting of three of the four *a priori* scales, namely, Cohesiveness, Difficulty, and Competitiveness.

Questionnaire on Teacher Interaction (QTI)

Research that originated in the Netherlands focused on the nature and quality of interpersonal relationships between teachers and students (Wubbels & Brekelmans, 1998; Wubbels & Levy, 1993). Drawing upon a theoretical model of proximity (cooperation-opposition) and influence (dominance-submission), the QTI was developed to assess student perceptions of the eight behavior aspects listed in Table 5.1. Research with the QTI has been completed at various grade levels in the United States (Wubbels & Levy) and Australia (Fisher, Henderson, & Fraser, 1995).

Goh pioneered the use of the QTI in a simplified form in Singapore with a sample of 1,512 elementary-school students in 13 schools (Goh & Fraser, 1996, 1998,

TABLE 5.1
Scale Names, Response Alternatives, and Sample Items for Four Commonly-Used Classroom Environment Instruments

Instrument	Scale names	Response alternatives	Sample items
Questionnaire on Teacher Interaction (QTI)	Leadership Helping/Friendly Understanding Student Responsibility/ Freedom Uncertain Dissatisfied Admonishing Strict Behaviour	Five point (Never-Always)	"She/he gives us a lot of free time." (Student Responsibility) "She/he gets angry." (Admonishing)
Science Laboratory Environment Inventory (SLEI)	Student Cohesiveness Open-Endedness Integration Rule Clarity Material Environment	Almost Never Seldom Sometimes Often Very Often	"I use the theory from my regular science class sessions during laboratory activities." (Integration) "We know the results that we are supposed to get before we commence a laboratory activity." (Open-Endedness)
Constructivist Learning Environments Survey (CLES)	Personal Relevance Uncertainty Critical Voice Shared Control Student Negotiation	Almost Never Seldom Sometimes Often Very Often	"I help the teacher to decide what activities I do." (Shared Control) "Other students ask me to explain my ideas." (Student Negotiation)
What Is Happening In this Class? (WIHIC)	Student Cohesiveness Teacher Support Involvement Investigation Task Orientation Cooperation Equity	Almost Never Seldom Sometimes Often Very Often	"I discuss ideas in class." (Involvement) "I work with other students on projects in this class." (Cooperation)

2000). This study cross-validated the QTI for use in a new country and found it to be useful in several research applications. Scott and Fisher (2004) translated the QTI into Standard Malay and cross-validated it with 3,104 elementary science students in 136 classes in Brunei Darussalam. An English version of the QTI was cross-validated for secondary schools in Brunei Darussalam for samples of 1188 science students (Khine & Fisher, 2002) and 644 chemistry students (Riah & Fraser, 1998). In Korea, Kim, Fisher, and Fraser (2000) validated a Korean-language version of the QTI among 543 Grade 8 students in 12 schools, and Lee and Fraser (2001a) provided further cross-validation information for the QTI with a sample of 440 Grade 10 and 11 science students. In Indonesia, Soerjaningsih, Fraser, and Aldridge (2001b) translated the QTI into the Indonesian language and cross-validated it with a sample of 422 university students in 12 classes. For example, Fisher, Fraser, and Rickards' (1997) study with a sample of 3,994 high school science and mathematics students revealed that the Cronbach alpha reliability ranged from 0.63 to 0.88 for different QTI scales at the student level of analysis.

Science Laboratory Environment Inventory (SLEI)

Because of the importance of laboratory settings in science education, an instrument specifically suited to assessing the environment of science laboratory classes at the senior high school or higher education levels was developed (Fraser, Giddings, & McRobbie, 1995; Fraser & McRobbie, 1995). The SLEI has the five seven-item scales in Table 5.1. The SLEI was field tested and validated simultaneously with a sample of 5,447 students in 269 classes in six different countries (United States, Canada, England, Israel, Australia, and Nigeria) and cross-validated with Australian students (Fisher, Henderson, & Fraser, 1997; Fraser & McRobbie). For example, based on a sample of 3,727 senior high school students from five countries, the Cronbach alpha reliability ranged from 0.70 to 0.83 for different scales when the student was used as the unit of analysis (Fraser et al., 1995).

The SLEI was further cross-validated and found to be useful in research involving both its original English form and translated versions. The validity of the English version of the SLEI was established in Singapore by A. F. L. Wong and Fraser's (1995, 1996) study of 1,592 Grade 10 chemistry students in 56 classes in 28 schools. Also, Riah and Fraser (1998) cross-validated the English version of the SLEI with 644 Grade 10 chemistry students in Brunei Darussalam.

A noteworthy program of research involving a Korean-language version of the SLEI was initiated by Kim and built upon by Lee (Kim & Kim, 1995, 1996; Kim & Lee, 1997; Lee & Fraser, 2001b; Lee, Fraser, & Fisher, 2003). For example, Lee and Fraser reported strong factorial validity for a Korean version of the SLEI and replicated several patterns from previous research in Western countries (e.g., low Open-Endedness scores and significant associations with students' attitudes).

Constructivist Learning Environment
Survey (CLES)

The CLES (Taylor, Fraser, & Fisher, 1997) was developed to assist researchers and teachers to assess the degree to which a particular classroom's environment is consistent with a constructivist epistemology, and to help teachers to reflect on their epistemological assumptions and reshape their teaching practice. The CLES has 36 items, which fall into the five scales shown in Table 5.1.

In South Africa, Sebela, Fraser, and Aldridge (2003) cross-validated the CLES among 1,864 learners in 43 intermediate and senior classes, and they used it to provide feedback that successfully guided teachers in action research aimed at promoting constructivist teaching and learning. In Texas, Dryden and Fraser (1998) cross-validated the CLES among a sample of 1,600 students in 120 Grade 9–12 science classes, and they used it to evaluate the success of an urban systemic reform initiative aimed at promoting constructivist teaching and learning. Also in Texas, Nix, Fraser, and Ledbetter (2003) cross-validated the CLES among 1,079 students in 59 classes and used it to evaluate an integrated science learning environment that bridged traditionally separate classroom, field trip, and instructional technology milieus.

Kim, Fisher, and Fraser (1999) translated the CLES into the Korean language and administered it to 1,083 science students in 24 classes in 12 schools. The original five-factor structure was replicated for the Korean-language version of both an actual and a preferred form of the CLES. Similarly, Lee and Fraser (2001a) replicated the five-factor structure of a Korean-language version of the CLES among 440 Grade 10 and 11 science students in 13 classes. Furthermore, the CLES was translated into Chinese for use in Taiwan (Aldridge, Fraser, Taylor, & Chen, 2000). In this cross-national study, the original English version was administered to 1,081 science students in 50 classes in Australia, and the new Chinese version was administered to 1,879 science students in 50 classes in Taiwan. The same five-factor structure emerged for the CLES in the two countries. Scale reliabilities (Cronbach alpha coefficients) ranged from 0.87 to 0.97 for the Australian sample and from 0.79 to 0.98 for the Taiwanese sample, with the class mean as the unit of analysis.

What Is Happening In this Class? (WIHIC) Questionnaire

The WIHIC questionnaire combines modified versions of salient scales from a wide range of existing questionnaires with additional scales that accommodate contemporary educational concerns (e.g., equity and constructivism). The original 90-item nine-scale version was refined both by statistical analysis of data from 355 junior high school science students and by extensive interviewing of students about their views of their classroom environments in general, the wording and salience of individual items, and their questionnaire responses (Fraser, Fisher, & McRobbie, 1996). Analysis of data from an Australian sample of 1,081 students in 50 classes (Aldridge & Fraser, 2000) led to a final form of the WIHIC containing the seven eight-item scales in Table 5.1. The WIHIC items are listed in an article by Aldridge, Fraser, and Huang (1999).

Although the WIHIC is a relatively recent instrument, its adoption around the world has been frequent, and already it has been translated into several other languages and cross-validated:

1. Zandvliet and Fraser (2004) used the WIHIC among 81 classes of senior high school students in Canadian and Australian internet classes, whereas Lightburn and Fraser (2002) and Robinson and Fraser (2003) used the WIHIC in teacher-researcher studies in Florida.

2. An English version was cross-validated in Brunei Darussalam with samples of 644 Grade 10 chemistry students (Riah & Fraser, 1998) and 1,188 Form 5 science students (Khine & Fisher, 2001). In Singapore, Fraser and Chionh (2000) reported strong validity and reliability for both an actual and a preferred form of the WIHIC when it was responded to by a sample of 2,310 students in 75 senior high school classes.

3. A Chinese version of the WIHIC was developed for use in Taiwan and cross-validated with a sample of 1,879 junior high school students in 50 classes (Aldridge & Fraser, 2000; Aldridge et al., 1999).

4. The WIHIC was translated into the Korean language and validated with a sample of 543 Grade 8 students in 12 schools (Kim et al., 2000).

5. The WIHIC was translated into the Indonesian language and used with both high school and university students. The validity and usefulness of the WIHIC were established for samples of 594 high school students in 18 classes (Adolphe, Fraser, & Aldridge, 2003), 2,498 university students in 50 classes (Margianti, Fraser, & Aldridge, 2001a, 2001b), and 422 students in 12 classes (Soerjaningsih, Fraser, & Aldridge, 2001a).

Dorman (2003) used confirmatory factor analysis with data collected by administration of the WIHIC to 3980 high school students in Australia, Britain, and Canada. The *a priori* factor structure of the WIHIC was supported and was found to be invariant across country, grade level, and student gender. Alpha reliability coefficients for this sample ranged from 0.76 to 0.85 for different WIHIC scales at the student level of analysis.

The WIHIC has formed the foundation for the development of learning environment questionnaires that incorporate many of the WIHIC's dimensions, but encompass new dimensions that are of particular relevance to the specific study at hand. For example, in Canada, Raaflaub and Fraser (2002) used a modified version of the WIHIC in their investigation involving 1,173 science and mathematics students in 73 classrooms in which laptop computers were used. In Australia, Aldridge and Fraser (2003) added three new dimensions (Differentiation, Computer Usage, and Young Adult Ethos) to the WIHIC to form the Technology-Rich Outcomes-Focused Learning Environment Inventory (TROFLEI) in their study of 1,035 students in 80 classes in an innovative senior high school that provides a technology-rich and outcomes-focused learning environment. In South Africa, Seopa, Laugksch, Aldridge, and Fraser (2003) used the WIHIC as a basis for developing the Outcomes-Based Learning Environment Questionnaire (OBLEQ), which they used with 2,638 Grade 8 science students in 50 classes in 50 schools in Limpopo Province. In Texas, Sinclair and Fraser (2002) modified the WIHIC for use in a study aimed at changing classroom environments among a sample of 745 urban middle-school science students in 43 classes.

RESEARCH INVOLVING CLASSROOM ENVIRONMENT INSTRUMENTS

In order to illustrate some of the many and varied applications of classroom environment instruments in science education research, this section considers six types of past research which focused on: (a) associations between student outcomes and environment; (b) evaluation of educational innovations; (c) differences between student and teacher perceptions of actual and preferred environment; (d) determinants of classroom environment; (e) use of qualitative research methods; and (f) cross-national studies.

Associations between Student Outcomes and Environment

The strongest tradition in past classroom environment research has involved investigation of associations between students' cognitive and affective learning outcomes and their perceptions of psychosocial characteristics of their classrooms. Fraser's (1994) tabulation of 40 past studies in science education showed that associations between outcome measures and classroom environment perceptions have been replicated for a variety of cognitive and affective outcome measures, a variety of classroom environment instruments and a variety of samples (ranging across numerous countries and grade levels). For example, a meta-analysis encompassing 17,805 students from four nations revealed that student achievement was consistently higher in classes that were more organized, cohesive, and goal-directed and had less friction (Haertel, Walberg, & Haertel, 1981).

McRobbie and Fraser (1993) extended learning environment research to science laboratory class settings in an investigation of associations between student outcomes and classroom environment. The sample consisted of 1,594 senior high school chemistry students in 92 classes. The Science Laboratory Environment Inventory (SLEI) was used to assess Student Cohesiveness, Open-Endedness, Integration, Rule Clarity, and Material Environments in the laboratory class. Student outcomes encompassed two inquiry skills assessed with the Test of Enquiry Skills (TOES) (Fraser, 1979b) and four attitude measures based partly on the Test of Science Related Attitudes (TOSRA) (Fraser, 1981). Simple, multiple, and canonical analyses were conducted separately for two units of analysis (student scores and class means) and separately with and without control for general ability. Past research was replicated in that the nature of the science laboratory classroom environment accounted for appreciable proportions of the variance in both cognitive and affective outcomes beyond that attributable to general ability. Science educators wishing to enhance student outcomes in science laboratory settings are likely to find useful the result that both cognitive and attitude outcomes were enhanced in laboratory classes in which the laboratory activities were integrated with the work in non-laboratory classes.

Fraser (2002) noted that Asian researchers have undertaken a wide variety of valuable studies of associations between student outcomes and students' perceptions of their classroom learning environment. These studies also covered a wide range of environment instruments, student outcomes, school subjects, and grade levels. Whereas some studies involved English-language versions of questionnaires, other studies involved learning environment questionnaires translated into various Asian languages. These studies involved samples from Singapore (Goh & Fraser, 1998; Teh & Fraser, 1995; A. F. L. Wong & Fraser, 1996), Brunei (Majeed et al., 2002; Scott & Fisher, 2004), Korea (Kim et al., 1999, 2000; Lee et al., 2003), and Indonesia (Margianti et al., 2001a).

Many past learning environment studies have employed techniques such as multiple regression analysis, but few have used multilevel analysis (Bryk & Raudenbush, 1992), which takes cognizance of the hierarchical nature of classroom settings (i.e., students within intact classes are more homogeneous than a random sample of students). However, two studies in Singapore compared the results from multiple regression analysis with those from an analysis involving the hierarchical linear model. In a study by A. F. L. Wong, Young, and Fraser (1997) involving 1,592 Grade 10 students in 56 chemistry classes in Singapore, associations were investigated between three student attitude measures and a modified version of the SLEI. In Goh's study with 1,512 Grade 5 students in 39 classes in Singapore, scores on modified versions of the MCI and QTI were related to student achievement and attitudes. Most of the statistically significant results from the multiple regression analyses were replicated in the HLM analyses, as well as being consistent in direction (Goh & Fraser, 1998; Goh et al., 1995).

Some research into outcome-environment associations involved the use of more than one classroom environment questionnaire in the same study, so that commonality analysis could be used to ascertain the unique and joint contributions made by each questionnaire to the variance in student outcomes. In Singapore, Goh and Fraser (1998) used the MCI and QTI in a study involving the achievement and attitudes of 1,512 elementary-school students. The MCI and the QTI each uniquely accounted for an appreciable proportion of the variance in achievement, but not in attitudes. Much of the total variance in attitude scores was common to the two questionnaires. A conclusion from this study was that it is useful to include the MCI and QTI together in future studies of achievement, but not of attitudes. Similarly, when Korean-language versions of the SLEI, QTI, and CLES were used in a study of science students' attitudes in Korea, generally, each classroom environment instrument accounted for variance in student outcome measures independent of that accounted for by the other instrument (Lee & Fraser, 2001a, 2001b; Lee et al., 2003).

Evaluation of Educational Innovations

Classroom environment instruments can be used as a valuable source of process criteria in the evaluation of educational innovations. For example, in an early evaluation of the Australian Science Education Project (ASEP), ASEP students perceived their classrooms as being more satisfying and individualized and having a better material environment relative to a comparison group (Fraser, 1979a). In Singapore, Teh used his own classroom environment instrument as a source of dependent variables in evaluating computer-assisted learning (Fraser & Teh, 1994; Teh & Fraser, 1994). Compared with a control group, a group of students using micro-PROLOG-based computer-assisted learning had much higher scores for achievement (3.5 standard deviations), attitudes (1.4 standard deviations), and classroom environment (1.0–1.9 standard deviations).

Oh and Yager (2004) used the CLES with 136 Grade 11 earth science students involved in two longitudinal action research studies in Korea aimed at implementing constructivist instructional approaches. Not only was it found that students' perceptions on the CLES became more positive over time, but also that changes in the CLES scale of Personal Relevance were associated with improvements in student attitudes to science. In another study, the CLES was used among 70 Korean high school teachers who attended professional development programs at the University of Iowa to monitor changes in constructivist philosophies (Cho, Yager, Park, & Seo, 1997).

Classroom environment dimensions also have been used as criteria of effectiveness in evaluating the use of laptop computers in Canadian science and mathematics classrooms (Raaflaub & Fraser, 2002), a technology-rich and outcomes-focused school in Australia (Aldridge & Fraser, 2003), the use of anthropometric activities in science teaching in the United States (Lightburn & Fraser, 2002), and the success of outcomes-based education in South Africa (Aldridge, Laugksch, Fraser, & Seopa, 2005). For example, Aldridge and Fraser's (2003) longitudinal study revealed that, over time, the implementation of an outcomes-focused, technology-rich learning environment led to more positive student perceptions of Student Cohesiveness, Task Orientation, Investigation, Cooperation, and Young Adult Ethos, but less classroom Differentiation. Despite the potential value of evaluating educational innovations and new curricula in terms of their impact on transforming the classroom learning environment, only a relatively small number of such studies have been carried out around the world.

Differences between Student and Teacher Perceptions of Actual and Preferred Environment

An investigation of differences between students and teachers in their perceptions of the same actual classroom environment and of differences between the actual environment and that preferred by students or teachers was reported by Fisher and Fraser (1983). Students preferred a more positive classroom environment than was actually present for all five environment dimensions of Personalization, Participation, Independence, Investigation, and Differentiation. Also, teachers perceived a more positive classroom environment than did their students in the same classrooms on the four of the dimensions of Personalization, Participation, Investigation, and Differentiation. The pattern in which students prefer a more positive classroom learning environment than the one perceived as being currently present has been replicated with the use of the WIHIC and QTI among Singaporean high school students (Fraser & Chionh, 2000; A. F. L. Wong & Fraser, 1996) and the WIHIC among 2,498 university students in Indonesia (Margianti et al., 2001b).

Determinants of Classroom Environment

Classroom environment dimensions have been used as criterion variables in research aimed at identifying how the classroom environment varies with such factors as teacher personality, class size, grade level, subject matter, the nature of the school-level environment, and the type of school (Fraser, 1994). Hirata and Sako (1998) found differences between the classroom environment perceptions of at-risk students (delinquent and non-attendees) and normal students in Japan. In Brunei, Khine and Fisher (2002) reported cultural differences in students' classroom environment perceptions depending on whether the teacher was Asian or Western. In Korea, Lee and Fraser (2001a, 2001b) and Lee et al. (2003) reported the use of the SLEI, CLES, and QTI in the investigation of differences between streams (science-oriented, humanities-oriented) in the student-perceived learning environment. For the first four QTI scales, the clear pattern was that the humanities stream students had less favorable perceptions than did the other two streams. Science-oriented stream students perceived their classrooms more favorably than the humanities stream students did, but less favorably than the science-independent stream students did. Overall, cooperative behaviors were more frequently displayed in the science-independent stream than in the other two streams. In contrast, opposition behaviors were less frequently displayed in the science-independent streams than in the other two streams.

Undoubtedly, the determinant of classroom environment that has been most extensively researched is student gender. Generally within-class comparisons of students' perceptions reveal that females typically have more favorable views of their classroom learning environment than do males. These studies of gender differences have encompassed numerous countries, including Singapore (Fraser & Chionh, 2000; Goh & Fraser, 1998; Khoo & Fraser, 1998; Quek, Wong, & Fraser, 2005; A. F. L. Wong & Fraser, 1996), Brunei (Khine & Fisher, 2001, 2002; Riah & Fraser, 1998), Indonesia (Margianti et al., 2001a, 2001b), and Korea (Kim et al., 2000).

Use of Qualitative Research Methods

Significant progress has been made in using qualitative methods in learning environment research and in combining quantitative and qualitative methods within the same study of classroom environments (Fraser & Tobin, 1991; Tobin & Fraser, 1998). For example, Fraser's (1999) multilevel study of the learning environment incorporated a teacher-researcher perspective as well as the perspectives of six university-based researchers. The research commenced with an interpretive study of a Grade 10 teacher's classroom at a school, which provided a challenging learning environment in that many students were from working-class backgrounds, some were experiencing problems at home, and others spoke English as a second language. Qualitative methods included several of the researchers visiting this class each time that it met over five weeks, using student diaries, and interviewing the teacher-researcher, students, school administrators, and parents. A video camera recorded activities for later analysis. Field notes were written during and soon after each observation, and during team meetings that took place three times per week. The qualitative component of the study was complemented by a quantitative component involving the use of a classroom environment questionnaire.

The qualitative information helped the researchers to provide consistent and plausible accounts of the profile of this teacher's scores on a classroom environment instrument to which her students responded. For example, the high level of perceived Personal Relevance in this teacher's class was consistent with her practice of devoting one science period a week to things that were personally relevant to students. Relatively high scores on the Critical Voice scale were consistent with observations that this teacher encouraged students to voice their opinions and suggest alternatives (Tobin & Fraser, 1998).

One of the most salient aspects of the learning environment in this study was Teacher Support. This teacher's class perceived higher levels of Teacher Support than did students in other Grade 10 classes at this school. This teacher had several features in common with the types of students whom she was teaching. She had not been a motivated learner at school and knew that students' life histories often made it difficult for them to concentrate on learning as a high priority. She was aware that social problems afflicted many students, and she was determined to make a difference in their lives. Consequently, she planned to enact the curriculum to facilitate transformative goals. She had considerable empathy for her students, was concerned with their well-being as citizens, and perceived science as an opportunity to develop their life skills. Learning to be communicative and cooperative was a high-priority goal. Getting to know her students was a priority, and meeting them at the door seemed important because it permitted brief individual interactions with almost every student. For these reasons, it was quite plausible that Teacher Support scores were high (Tobin & Fraser, 1998).

Fraser (2002) noted that the use of quantitative methods has tended to dominate Asian research into learning environments. But there are some notable exceptions in which qualitative methods have been used to advantage. Quite a few Asian studies have used qualitative methods in a minor way, such as in interviews of a small group of students aimed at checking the suitability of a learning environment questionnaire and modifying it before its use in a large-scale study (e.g., Khine, 2001; Margianti et al., 2001a, 2001b; Soerjaningsih et al., 2001a, 2001b). Lee's study in Korea included a strong quantitative component involving the administration of the SLEI, CLES, and QTI to 439 students in 13 classes (four classes from the humanities stream, four classes from the science-oriented stream, and five classes from the science-independent stream; Lee & Fraser, 2001a, 2001b; Lee et al., 2003). However, two or three students from each class were selected for face-to-face interviews in the humanities stream and the science-oriented stream. In the case of students in the science-oriented stream, interviews were conducted via e-mail to overcome practical constraints. All of the face-to-face interviews were audiotaped and later transcribed in Korean and translated into English. When the Korean transcriptions were completed, they were shown to the students for member checking. Furthermore, one class from each stream was selected for observation. While the researcher was observing, whenever possible she wrote down any salient events that occurred in the classroom. Some photographs were also taken. Field notes were made and translated into English in order to transfer the images into English. Overall, the findings from interviews and observations replicated the findings obtained with the learning environment surveys.

During observations, the researcher noted that, in classes in the science-independent stream in Korea, teachers appeared more receptive to students' talking and the lessons involved mainly group activities. Students' cooperation was natural and did not require explicit intervention from the teacher. Interviews also indicated that students from the science-independent stream were more likely to interact actively with their teachers than were students from the other two streams. It would appear that the stream in which students study influences their perceptions of their science classes.

This Korean study suggested that teacher-student interactions in senior high school science classrooms reflect the general image of the youth-elder relationship in society of "directing teachers and obeying students." It is also noteworthy that each stream's unique nature in terms of teacher-student relationships did not go beyond this societal norm.

In Hong Kong, qualitative methods involving open-ended questions were used to explore students' perceptions of the learning environment in Grade 9 classrooms

(N. Y. Wong, 1993, 1996). This researcher found that many students identified the teacher as the most crucial element in a positive classroom learning environment. These teachers were found to keep order and discipline while creating an atmosphere that was not boring or solemn. They also interacted with students in ways that could be considered friendly and showed concern for the students.

Cross-National Studies

Educational research that crosses national boundaries offers much promise for generating new insights for at least two reasons (Fraser, 1997). First, there usually is greater variation in variables of interest (e.g., teaching methods, student attitudes) in a sample drawn from multiple countries than from a single country sample. Second, the taken-for-granted familiar educational practices, beliefs, and attitudes in one country can be exposed, made "strange," and questioned when research involves two countries. In a cross-national study, six Australian and seven Taiwanese researchers worked together on a study of learning environments (Aldridge, Fraser, & Huang, 1999; Aldridge, Fraser, Taylor, & Chen, 2000; She & Fisher, 2000). The WIHIC and CLES were administered to 50 junior high school science classes in Taiwan (1,879 students) and Australia (1,081 students). An English version of the questionnaires was translated into Chinese, followed by an independent back translation of the Chinese version into English again by team members who were not involved in the original translation (Aldridge et al., 2000).

Qualitative data, involving interviews with teachers and students and classroom observations, were collected to complement the quantitative information and to clarify reasons for patterns and differences in the means in each country. Data from the questionnaires guided the collection of qualitative data. Student responses to individual items were used to form an interview schedule to clarify whether items had been interpreted consistently by students and to help to explain differences in questionnaire scale means between countries. Classrooms were selected for observations on the basis of the questionnaire data, and specific scales formed the focus for observations in these classrooms. The qualitative data provided valuable insights into the perceptions of students in each of the countries, helped to explain some of the differences in the means between countries, and highlighted the need for caution in the interpretation of differences between the questionnaire results from two countries with cultural differences (Aldridge, Fraser, & Huang, 1999; Aldridge et al., 2000).

Another cross-national study of learning environments was conducted in the United States, Australia, the Netherlands, Slovakia, Singapore, and Brunei by den Brok et al. (2003). This study, involving 5,292 students in 243 classes, was intended only to test the cross-national validity of the QTI in terms of the two-dimensional circumplex model of interpersonal behavior on which the QTI is based. Researchers found that the empirical scale locations differed from the theoretical positions hypothesized by the model and that scale positions in the circumplex differed between countries. The authors concluded that the QTI cannot be compared between countries and that further research is needed to determine whether the QTI is cross-culturally valid.

In contrast to these findings in den Brok and colleagues' cross-national validation of the QTI, Dorman (2003) reported strong support for the cross-national validity of the WIHIC when used with a sample of 3,980 students in Australia, Britain, and Canada.

Researchers from Singapore and Australia also have carried out a cross-national study of secondary science classes (Fisher, Goh, Wong, & Rickards, 1997). The QTI was administered to students and teachers from a sample of 20 classes from 10 schools each in Australia and Singapore. Australian teachers were perceived as giving more responsibility and freedom to their students than was the case for the Singapore sample, whereas teachers in Singapore were perceived as being stricter than their Australian counterparts. These differences are not surprising, given the different cultural backgrounds and education systems in the two countries. Most recently, Adolphe et al. (2003) conducted a cross-national study of science classroom environments and student attitudes among 1,161 science students in 36 classes in private coeducational schools in Indonesia and Australia.

CONCLUSION

The history of the first two decades of learning environments research in Western countries shows a strong emphasis on the use of a variety of validated and robust questionnaires that assess students' perceptions of their classroom learning environment (Fraser, 1998a). The past decade of research into learning environments in non-Western countries shows a very similar pattern. Researchers have completed numerous impressive studies that have cross-validated the main contemporary classroom environment questionnaires that were originally developed in English (SLEI, CLES, WIHIC) and Dutch (QTI). Not only have these questionnaires been validated for use in English in countries such as Singapore and Brunei, but researchers also have undertaken painstaking translations and have validated these questionnaires in the African, Chinese, Indonesian, Korean, and Malay languages. These researchers have laid a solid foundation for future learning environment research internationally by making readily accessible a selection of valid, reliable, and widely applicable questionnaires for researchers and teachers to use in a range of languages for a variety of purposes.

On the basis on the research reviewed in this chapter, the following generalizations and implications for improving science education can be drawn:

1. Because measures of learning outcomes alone cannot provide a complete picture of the educational process, assessments of the learning environment should also be used to provide information about subtle but important aspects of classroom life.

2. Because teachers and students have systematically different perceptions of the learning environments of the same classrooms (the "rose-colored glasses" phenomenon), feedback from students about classrooms should be collected in the evaluation of preservice teachers during field experience and during investigation of professional development programs.

3. Science teachers should strive to create "productive" learning environments as identified by research. Cognitive and affective outcomes are likely to be enhanced in classroom environments characterized by greater organization, cohesiveness, and goal direction and by less friction. In laboratory classroom

environments specifically, greater integration between practical work and the theoretical components of a course tends to lead to improved student outcomes.

4. The evaluation of innovations and new curricula should include classroom environment instruments to provide economical, valid, and reliable process measures of effectiveness.

5. Teachers should use assessments of their students' perceptions of actual and preferred classroom environments to monitor and guide attempts to improve classrooms. The broad range of instruments available enables science teachers to select a questionnaire or particular scales to fit personal circumstances.

In the future, there will be scope for researchers to make internationally significant contributions to the field by developing new questionnaires that tap the nuances and uniqueness of classrooms in particular countries, and/or which focus on the various information technology-rich learning environments (e.g., web-based, online learning) that are currently sweeping education worldwide (Khine & Fisher, 2003). Similarly, there is scope to adapt currently widely used paper-and-pencil questionnaires to online formats.

The most common line of past learning environment research has involved investigating associations between students' outcomes and their classroom environment perceptions. This impressive series of studies has been carried out in many countries in a variety of subject areas (science, mathematics, geography, English, and computing), at various grade levels (elementary, secondary, and higher education), and using numerous student outcome measures (achievement, attitudes, self-efficacy) and different learning environment questionnaires. Overall, these studies provide consistent support for the existence of associations between the nature of the classroom environment and a variety of valued student outcomes. These findings hold hope for improving student outcomes through the creation of the types of classroom environments that are empirically linked to favorable student outcomes.

Feedback information based on student or teacher perceptions of actual and preferred environments has been employed in a five-step procedure as a basis for reflection upon, discussion of, and systematic attempts to improve classroom environments (Sinclair & Fraser, 2002; Thorp, Burden, & Fraser, 1994; Yarrow, Millwater, & Fraser, 1997). The five steps involve (a) *assessment* of actual and preferred classroom environments; (b) *feedback* of results, including identification of aspects of classroom environments for which there are large discrepancies between actual and preferred scores; (c) *reflection and discussion*; (d) *intervention*; and (e) *reassessment* of classroom environment. Surprisingly, this important practical benefit has not yet been widely realized in science education in any country.

Whereas the use of questionnaires in learning environment research has been prolific, studies that include qualitative methods such as interview and observation have been somewhat less common. Although studies demonstrate the benefits of combining qualitative and quantitative methods in learning environment research (Tobin & Fraser, 1998), it is desirable for future learning environment research to make greater use of qualitative methods. For example, qualitative data can help researchers to make more meaningful interpretations of questionnaire data that can take into account various background, cultural, and situational variables. Although learning environment questionnaires are valuable for illuminating particular constructs and patterns, their use can also obscure other important constructs and patterns that could be revealed through qualitative methods. Researchers can also use narrative stories to portray archetypes of science classroom environments.

There is scope for researchers to adopt, adapt, or create new theoretical frames to guide the next generation of learning environment studies. For example, this could build upon Roth's (1999) advice against conceptualizing the environment as being independent of the person, and on his use of life-world analysis as a new theoretical underpinning. Roth, Tobin, and Zimmermann (2002) broke with past traditions by taking researchers into the front lines of the daily work of schools, thereby assisting in bringing about change. They proposed co-teaching as an equitable inquiry into teaching and learning processes in which all members of a classroom community participate—including students, teachers, student teachers, researchers, and supervisors. Roth and colleagues articulate co-teaching in terms of activity theory and the associated first-person methodology for doing research on learning environments that is relevant to practice.

The next generation of learning environment studies also could benefit from advances in methods of data analysis. Rasch analysis has been used to permit valid comparison of different cohorts of over 8000 science and mathematics students who responded to learning environment scales during different years of a systemic reform effort in Ohio (Scantlebury, Boone, Butler Kahle, & Fraser, 2001). In research on systemic reform, there are several important measurement problems in need of solution. For example, if we are interested in improvements in achievement or attitudes at the same grade level over several years as reform is implemented, there is a potential problem: that our samples for different years are unlikely to be strictly comparable. Similarly, changes made to evaluation instruments during the lifetime of a reform initiative can make it difficult to attribute changes to the reform rather than simply to modifications in an instrument. Finally, because all students seldom answer all items on a test or questionnaire, we need a method of calculating a valid score for each student based on the subset of items answered. Item response theory, or the Rasch model, provides a solution to all of these measurement problems.

Dorman (2003), taking advantage of relatively recent advances in techniques for validating learning environment questionnaires, has demonstrated the value of using confirmatory factor analysis within a covariance matrix framework. Using a sample of 3,980 high-school students from Australia, Britain, and Canada, Dorman found strong support for the *a priori* structure of the WIHIC and demonstrated the factorial invariance of model parameters across three countries, three grade levels, and gender. In the first use of multitrait-multimethod methodology in learning environment research, a study by Aldridge, Dorman, and Fraser (2004) involving 1,249 students used the 10 scales of the Technology-Rich Outcomes-Focused Learning Environment Inventory (TROFLEI) as traits and the two forms of the instrument (actual and preferred) as methods. Findings supported the sound psychometric properties of the actual and preferred forms of the TROFLEI.

In investigating outcome-environment associations, Goh et al. (1995) have illustrated how multilevel analysis can take cognizance of the hierarchical nature of classroom environment data in their study involving over 1,500 Singaporean students. Because classroom environment data typically are derived from students in intact classes, they are inherently hierarchical. Ignoring this nested structure can give rise to problems of aggregation bias (within-group homogeneity) and imprecision.

This chapter encourages others to use learning environment assessments for a variety of research and practical purposes. Given the ready availability of questionnaires, the importance of the classroom environment, the influence of the classroom environment on student outcomes, and the value of environment assessments in guiding educational improvement, it seems very important that researchers and teachers more often include the classroom environment in evaluations of educational effectiveness. Although educators around the world pay much greater attention to student achievement than to the learning environment, research on the classroom environment should not be buried under a pile of achievement tests.

ACKNOWLEDGMENTS

Thanks to Huei-Baik Kim and Theo Wubbels, who reviewed this chapter.

REFERENCES

Adolphe, G., Fraser, B., & Aldridge, J. (2003, January). *Classroom environment and attitudes among junior secondary science students: A cross-national study in Australia and in Indonesia.* Paper presented at the Third International Conference on Science, Mathematics and Technology Education, East London, South Africa.

Aldridge, J. M., Dorman, J. P., & Fraser, B. J. (2004). Use of multitrait-multimethod modelling to validate actual and preferred forms of the Technology-Rich Outcomes-Focused Learning Environment Inventory (TROFLEI). *Australian Journal of Educational & Developmental Psychology, 4,* 110–125.

Aldridge, J. M., & Fraser, B. J. (2000). A cross-cultural study of classroom learning environments in Australia and Taiwan. *Learning Environments Research: An International Journal, 3,* 101–134.

Aldridge, J. M., & Fraser, B. J. (2003). Effectiveness of a technology-rich and outcomes-focused learning environment. In M. S. Khine & D. Fisher (Eds.), *Technology-rich learning environments: A future perspective* (pp. 41–69). Singapore: World Scientific.

Aldridge, J. M., Fraser, B. J., & Huang, T.-C. I. (1999). Investigating classroom environments in Taiwan and Australia with multiple research methods. *Journal of Educational Research, 93,* 48–62.

Aldridge, J. M., Fraser, B. J., Taylor, P. C., & Chen, C.-C. (2000). Constructivist learning environments in a cross-national study in Taiwan and Australia. *International Journal of Science Education, 22,* 37–55.

Aldridge, J. M., Laugksch, R. C., Fraser, B. J., & Seopa, M. A. (2005). Development of a questionnaire for monitoring the success of outcomes-based learning environments in rural classrooms in South Africa. In C. S. Sunal & K. Mutua (Eds.), *Research on education in Africa, the Caribbean, and the Middle East: Forefronts in research* (pp. 9–29). Greenwich, CT: Information Age Publishing.

Bryk, A. S., & Raudenbush, S. W. (1992). *Hierarchical linear models: Applications and data analysis method.* Newbury Park, CA: Sage.

Cho, J. I., Yager, R. E., Park, D. Y., & Seo, H. A. (1997). Changes in high school teachers' constructivist philosophies. *School Science and Mathematics, 97,* 400–405.

den Brock, P., Fisher, D., Brekelmans, M., Rickards, T., Wubbels, T., Levy, J. et al. (2003, April). *Students' perceptions of secondary science teachers' interpersonal style in six countries: A study on the validity of the questionnaire on teacher interaction.* Paper presented at the annual meeting of the American Educational Research Association, Chicago, IL.

Dorman, J. P. (2003). Cross-national validation of the What Is Happening In this Class? (WIHIC) questionnaire using confirmatory factor analysis. *Learning Environments Research: An International Journal, 6*, 231–245.

Dryden, M., & Fraser, B. (1998, April). *The impact of systemic reform efforts in promoting constructivist approaches in high school science.* Paper presented at the annual meeting of the American Educational Research Association, San Diego, CA.

Fisher, D. L., & Fraser, B. J. (1981). Validity and use of My Class Inventory. *Science Education, 65*, 145–156.

Fisher, D. L., & Fraser, B. J. (1983). A comparison of actual and preferred classroom environment as perceived by science teachers and students. *Journal of Research in Science Teaching, 20*, 55–61.

Fisher, D. L., & Fraser, B. J. (2003). Emergence of learning environment research in South Africa. *Learning Environments Research: An International Journal, 6*, 229–230.

Fisher, D. L., Fraser, B. J., & Rickards, A. (1997, March). *Gender and cultural differences in teacher-student interpersonal behaviour.* Paper presented at the annual meeting of the American Educational Research Association, Chicago, IL.

Fisher, D. L., Goh, S. C., Wong, A. F. L., & Rickards, T. W. (1997). Perceptions of interpersonal teacher behaviour in secondary science classrooms in Singapore and Australia. *Journal of Applied Research in Education, 1*(2), 2–13.

Fisher, D. L., Henderson, D., & Fraser, B. J. (1995). Interpersonal behaviour in senior high school biology classes. *Research in Science Education, 25*, 125–133.

Fisher, D., Henderson, D., & Fraser, B. (1997). Laboratory environments and student outcomes in senior high school biology. *American Biology Teacher, 59*, 214–219.

Fraser, B. J. (1979a). Evaluation of a science-based curriculum. In H. J. Walberg (Ed.), *Educational environments and effects: Evaluation, policy, and productivity* (pp. 218–234). Berkeley, CA: McCutchan.

Fraser, B. J. (1979b). *Test of enquiry skills (TOES).* Melbourne, Australia: Australian Council for Educational Research.

Fraser, B. J. (1981). *Test of science related attitudes (TOSRA).* Melbourne, Australia: Australian Council for Educational Research.

Fraser, B. J. (1986). *Classroom environment.* London: Croom Helm.

Fraser, B. J. (1994). Research on classroom and school climate. In D. Gabel (Ed.), *Handbook of research on science teaching and learning* (pp. 493–541). New York: Macmillan.

Fraser, B. J. (1997). NARST's expansion, internationalization and cross-nationalization [1996 annual meeting presidential address]. *NARST News, 40*(1), 3–4.

Fraser, B. J. (1998a). Science learning environments: Assessment, effects and determinants. In B. J. Fraser & K. G. Tobin (Eds.), *International handbook of science education* (pp. 527–564). Dordrecht, the Netherlands: Kluwer.

Fraser, B. J. (1998b). Classroom environment instruments: Development, validity and applications. *Learning Environments Research: An International Journal, 1*, 7–33.

Fraser, B. J. (1999). "Grain sizes" in learning environment research: Combining qualitative and quantitative methods. In H. Waxman & H. J. Walberg (Eds.), *New directions for teaching practice and research* (pp. 285–296). Berkeley, CA: McCutchan.

Fraser, B. J. (2001). Twenty thousand hours. *Learning Environments Research, 4*, 1–5.

Fraser, B. J. (2002). Learning environments research: Yesterday, today and tomorrow. In S. C. Goh & M. S. Khine (Eds.), *Studies in educational learning environments: An international perspective* (pp. 1–25). Singapore: World Scientific.

Fraser, B. J., & Chionh, Y.-H. (2000, April). *Classroom environment, self-esteem, achievement, and attitudes in geography and mathematics in Singapore.* Paper presented at the annual meeting of the American Educational Research Association, New Orleans, LA.

Fraser, B. J., Fisher, D. L., & McRobbie, C. J. (1996, April). *Development, validation, and use of personal and class forms of a new classroom environment instrument.* Paper presented at the annual meeting of the American Educational Research Association, New York.

Fraser, B. J., Giddings, G. J., & McRobbie, C. J. (1995). Evolution and validation of a personal form of an instrument for assessing science laboratory classroom environments. *Journal of Research in Science Teaching, 32,* 399–422.

Fraser, B. J., & McRobbie, C. J. (1995). Science laboratory classroom environments at schools and universities: A cross-national study. *Educational Research and Evaluation, 1,* 289–317.

Fraser, B. J., & Teh, G. P. L. (1994). Effect sizes associated with micro-PROLOG-based computer-assisted learning. *Computers & Education, 23,* 187–196.

Fraser, B. J., & Tobin, K. (1991). Combining qualitative and quantitative methods in classroom environment research. In B. J. Fraser & H. J. Walberg (Eds.), *Educational environments: Evaluation, antecedents and consequences* (pp. 271–292). Oxford, UK: Pergamon.

Fraser, B., & Walberg, H. (Eds.). (1991). *Educational environments: Evaluation, antecedents and consequences.* Oxford, UK: Pergamon.

Fraser, B. J., Walberg, H. J., Welch, W. W., & Hattie, J. A. (1987). Syntheses of educational productivity research. *International Journal of Educational Research, 11,* 145–252.

Getzels, J. W., & Thelen, H. A. (1960). The classroom group as a unique social system. In N. B. Henry (Ed.), *The dynamics of instructional groups: Socio-psychological aspects of teaching and learning* (Fifty-Ninth Yearbook of National Society for Study of Education, Part 2, pp. 53–82). Chicago: University of Chicago Press.

Goh, S. C., & Fraser, B. J. (1996). Validation of an elementary school version of the questionnaire on teacher interaction. *Psychological Reports, 79,* 512–522.

Goh, S. C., & Fraser, B. (1998). Teacher interpersonal behaviour, classroom environment and student outcomes in primary mathematics in Singapore. *Learning Environments Research: An International Journal, 1,* 199–229.

Goh, S. C., & Fraser, B. J. (2000). Teacher interpersonal behavior and elementary students' outcomes. *Journal of Research in Childhood Education, 14,* 216–231.

Goh, S. C., & Khine, M. S. (Eds.). (2002). *Studies in educational learning environments: An international perspective.* Singapore: World Scientific.

Goh, S. C., Young, D. J., & Fraser, B. J. (1995). Psychosocial climate and student outcomes in elementary mathematics classrooms: A multilevel analysis. *The Journal of Experimental Education, 64,* 29–40.

Haertel, G. D., Walberg, H. J., & Haertel, E. H. (1981). Socio-psychological environments and learning: A quantitative synthesis. *British Educational Research Journal, 7,* 27–36.

Hirata, S., & Sako, T. (1998). Perceptions of school environment among Japanese junior high school, non-attendant, and juvenile delinquent students. *Learning Environments Research: An International Journal, 1,* 321–331.

Khine, M. S. (2001). *Associations between teacher interpersonal behaviour and aspects of classroom environment in an Asian context.* Unpublished doctoral dissertation, Curtin University of Technology, Perth, Australia.

Khine, M. S., & Fisher, D. L. (2001, December). *Classroom environment and teachers' cultural background in secondary science classes in an Asian context.* Paper presented at the annual meeting of the Australian Association for Research in Education, Perth, Australia.

Khine, M. S., & Fisher, D. L. (2002, April). *Analysing interpersonal behaviour in science classrooms: Associations between students' perceptions and teachers' cultural background.* Paper presented at the annual meeting of the National Association for Research in Science Teaching, New Orleans, LA.

Khine, M. S., & Fisher, D. (Eds.). (2003). *Technology-rich learning environments: A future perspective.* Singapore: World Scientific.

Khoo, H. S., & Fraser, B. J. (1998, April). *Using classroom environment dimensions in the evaluation of adult computer courses.* Paper presented at the annual meeting of the American Educational Research Association, San Diego, CA.

Kim, H.-B., Fisher, D. L., & Fraser, B. J. (1999). Assessment and investigation of constructivist science learning environments in Korea. *Research in Science & Technological Education, 17,* 239–249.

Kim, H.-B., Fisher, D. L., & Fraser, B. J. (2000). Classroom environment and teacher interpersonal behaviour in secondary school classes in Korea. *Evaluation and Research in Education, 14*, 3–22.

Kim, H.-B., & Kim, D. Y. (1995). Survey on the perceptions towards science laboratory classroom environment of university students majoring in education. *Journal of the Korean Association for Research in Science Education, 14*, 163–171.

Kim, H.-B., & Kim, D. Y. (1996). Middle and high school students' perceptions of science laboratory and their attitudes in science and science subjects. *Journal of the Korean Association for Research in Science Education, 16*, 210–216.

Kim, H.-B., & Lee, S. K. (1997). Science teachers' beliefs about science and school science and their perceptions of science laboratory learning environment. *Journal of the Korean Association for Research in Science Education, 17*, 210–216.

Lee, S. S. U., & Fraser, B. (2001a, March). *High school science classroom environments in Korea.* Paper presented at the annual meeting of the National Association for Research in Science Teaching, St. Louis, MO.

Lee, S., & Fraser, B. (2001b, December). *Science laboratory classroom environments in Korea.* Paper presented at the annual conference of the Australian Association for Research in Education, Fremantle, Australia.

Lee, S. S. U, Fraser, B. J., & Fisher, D. L. (2003). Teacher-student interactions in Korean high school science classrooms. *International Journal of Science and Mathematics Education, 1*, 67–85.

Lewin, K. (1936). *Principles of topological psychology.* New York: McGraw.

Lightburn, M. E., & Fraser, B. J. (2002, April). *Classroom environment and student outcomes associated with using anthropometry activities in high school science.* Paper presented at the annual meeting of the American Educational Research Association, New Orleans, LA.

Majeed, A., Fraser, B. J., & Aldridge, J. M. (2002). Learning environment and its association with student satisfaction among mathematics students in Brunei Darussalam. *Learning Environments Research: An International Journal, 5*, 203–226.

Margianti, E. S., Fraser, B. J., & Aldridge, J. M. (2001a, April). *Classroom environment and students' outcomes among university computing students in Indonesia.* Paper presented at the annual meeting of the American Educational Research Association, Seattle, WA.

Margianti, E. S., Fraser, B., & Aldridge, J. (2001b, December). *Investigating the learning environment and students' outcomes in university level computing courses in Indonesia.* Paper presented at the annual conference of the Australian Association for Research in Education, Fremantle, Australia.

McRobbie, C., & Fraser, B. (1993). Associations between student outcomes and psychosocial science environment. *The Journal of Educational Research, 87*, 78–85.

Murray, H. A. (1938). *Explorations in personality.* New York: Oxford University Press.

Moos, R. H. (1974). *The social climate scales: An overview.* Palo Alto, CA: Consulting Psychologists Press.

Moos, R. H., & Trickett, E. J. (1987). *Classroom environment scale manual* (2nd ed.). Palo Alto, CA: Consulting Psychologists Press.

Nix, R. K., Fraser, B. J., & Ledbetter, C. E. (2003, April). *Evaluating an integrated science learning environment using a new form of the Constructivist Learning Environment* Survey. Paper presented at the annual meeting of the American Educational Research Association, Chicago, IL.

Oh, P. S., & Yager, R. E. (2004). Development of constructivist science classrooms and changes in student attitudes toward science learning. *Science Education Journal, 15*, 105–113.

Paige, R. M. (1979). The learning of modern culture: Formal education and psychosocial modernity in East Java, Indonesia. *International Journal of Intercultural Relations, 3*, 333–364.

Quek, C. L., Wong, A. F. L., & Fraser, B. J. (2005). Student perceptions of chemistry laboratory learning environments, student-teacher interactions and attitudes in secondary school gifted education classes in Singapore. *Research in Science Education, 35*(2–3), 299–321.

Raaflaub, C. A., & Fraser, B. J. (2002, April). *Investigating the learning environment in Canadian mathematics and science classes in which laptop computers are used.* Paper presented at the annual meeting of the American Educational Research Association, New Orleans, LA.

Riah, H., & Fraser, B. (1998, April). *Chemistry learning environment and its association with students' achievement in chemistry*. Paper presented at the annual meeting of the American Educational Research Association, San Diego, CA.

Robinson, E., & Fraser, B. J. (2003, April). *Kindergarten students' and their parents' perceptions of science classroom environments: Achievement and attitudes*. Paper presented at the annual meeting of the American Educational Research Association, Chicago.

Roth, W.-M. (1999). Learning environments research, lifeworld analysis, and solidarity in practice. *Learning Environments Research: An International Journal, 2*, 225–247.

Roth, W.-M., Tobin, K., & Zimmermann, A. (2002). Coteaching/cogenerative dialoguing: Learning environments research as classroom praxis. *Learning Environments Research: An International Journal, 5*, 1–28.

Scantlebury, K., Boone, W., Butler Kahle, J., & Fraser, B. J. (2001). Design, validation, and use of an evaluation instrument for monitoring systemic reform. *Journal of Research in Science Teaching, 38*, 646–662.

Scott, R. H., & Fisher, D. L. (2004). Development, validation and application of a Malay translation of an elementary version of the Questionnaire on Teacher Interaction. *Research in Science Education, 34*, 173–194.

Sebela, M. P., Fraser, B. J., & Aldridge, J. M. (2003, April). *Using teacher action research to promote constructivist classroom environments in elementary schools in South Africa*. Paper presented at the annual meeting of the American Educational Research Association, Chicago, IL.

Seopa, M. A., Laugksch, R. C., Aldridge, J. M., & Fraser, B. J. (2003, April). *Assessing students' perceptions of outcomes-based learning environment in science classrooms in South Africa*. Paper presented at the annual meeting of the American Educational Research Association, Chicago, IL.

She, H. C., & Fisher, D. L. (2000). The development of a questionnaire to describe science teacher communication behavior in Taiwan and Australia. *Science Education, 84*, 706–726.

Sinclair, B. B., & Fraser B. J. (2002). Changing classroom environments in urban middle schools. *Learning Environments Research: An International Journal, 5*, 301–328.

Soerjaningsih, W., Fraser, B. J., & Aldridge, J. M. (2001a, April). *Achievement, satisfaction and learning environment among Indonesian computing students at the university level*. Paper presented at the annual meeting of the American Educational Research Association, Seattle, WA.

Soerjaningsih, W., Fraser, B., & Aldridge, J. (2001b, December). *Learning environment, teacher-student interpersonal behaviour and achievement among university students in Indonesia*. Paper presented at the annual conference of the Australian Association for Research in Education, Fremantle, Australia.

Stern, G. G. (1970). *People in context: Measuring person-environment congruence in education and industry*. New York: Wiley.

Taylor, P. C., Fraser, B. J., & Fisher, D. L. (1997). Monitoring constructivist classroom learning environments. *International Journal of Educational Research, 27*, 293–302.

Teh, G., & Fraser, B. J. (1994). An evaluation of computer-assisted learning in terms of achievement, attitudes and classroom environment. *Evaluation and Research in Education, 8*, 147–161.

Teh, G., & Fraser, B. J. (1995). Associations between student outcomes and geography classroom environment. *International Research in Geographical and Environmental Education, 4*(1), 3–18.

Thorp, H., Burden, R. L., & Fraser, B. J. (1994). Assessing and improving classroom environment. *School Science Review, 75*, 107–113.

Tobin, K., & Fraser, B. J. (1998). Qualitative and quantitative landscapes of classroom learning environments. In B. J. Fraser & K. G. Tobin (Eds.), *International handbook of science education* (pp. 623–640). Dordrecht, the Netherlands: Kluwer.

Walberg, H. J. (1981). A psychological theory of educational productivity. In F. Farley & N. J. Gordon (Eds.), *Psychology and education: The state of the union* (pp. 81–108). Berkeley, CA: McCutchan.

Walberg, H. J., & Anderson, G. J. (1968). Classroom climate and individual learning. *Journal of Educational Psychology, 59*, 414–419.

Walberg, H. J., Fraser, B. J., & Welch, W. W. (1986). A test of a model of educational productivity among senior high school students. *Journal of Educational Research, 79,* 133–139.

Walberg, H. J., Singh, R., & Rasher, S. P. (1977). Predictive validity or student perceptions: A cross-cultural replication. *American Educational Research Journal, 14,* 45–49.

Wong, A. F. L., & Fraser, B. J. (1995). Cross-validation in Singapore of the Science Laboratory Environment Inventory. *Psychological Reports, 76,* 907–911.

Wong, A. F. L., & Fraser, B. J. (1996). Environment-attitude associations in the chemistry laboratory classroom. *Research in Science & Technological Education, 14,* 91–102.

Wong, A. F. L., Young, D. J., & Fraser, B. J. (1997). A multilevel analysis of learning environments and student attitudes. *Educational Psychology, 17,* 449–468.

Wong, N. Y. (1993). Psychosocial environments in the Hong Kong mathematics classroom. *Journal of Mathematical Behavior, 12,* 303–309.

Wong, N. Y. (1996). Students' perceptions of the mathematics classroom in Hong Kong. *Hiroshima Journal of Mathematics Education, 4,* 89–107.

Wubbels, T., & Brekelmans, M. (1998). The teacher factor in the social climate of the classroom. In B. J. Fraser & K. G. Tobin (Eds.), *International handbook of science education* (pp. 565–580). Dordrecht, the Netherlands: Kluwer.

Wubbels, T., & Levy, J. (Eds.). (1993). *Do you know what you look like: Interpersonal relationships in education.* London: Falmer Press.

Yarrow, A., Millwater, J., & Fraser, B. J. (1997). Improving university and primary school classroom environments through preservice teachers' action research. *International Journal of Practical Experiences in Professional Education, 1*(1), 68–93.

Zandvliet, D. B., & Fraser, B. J. (2004). Learning environments in information and technology classrooms. *Technology, Pedagogy and Education, 13,* 97–123.

CHAPTER 6

Learning Science Outside of School

Léonie J. Rennie
Curtin University of Technology, Australia

> Unfortunately, there has been a tendency in this country to equate the term *education* with what happens in the schools or, at most, with what happens in schools, colleges, and universities. This leaves out other agencies and influences that, for better or worse and to greater and lesser degrees, may have a great impact on the knowledge, skill, understanding, appreciation, and judgment of our people: television, radio, motion pictures, the nontextbook press, the family, the back-alley gang, the teachers of private lessons, fairs and expositions, industry (through its greatly expanded training programs), the military, and the *museum*. (S. Anderson, 1968, p. 115, emphasis in original)

Fortunately, even as S. Anderson penned his chapter in 1968, a revolution had begun. Equating education with what happens in schools ignored two facts: Most people spend less of their lives in school than out of it, and they continue to learn throughout their lifetime in many places other than educational institutions. In the past, out-of-school learning for most individuals was associated with making a living and family care. Now, with more time for leisure in our society, we have the luxury of learning for interest rather than necessity, for satisfying our curiosity and enjoying ourselves. Recognizing the educational value of out-of-school learning is part of a revolution because there are so many opportunities to learn.

This chapter is about the learning of science through those out-of-school "agencies and influences" that, as S. Anderson (1968) stated, "impact on the knowledge, skill, understanding, appreciation, and judgment of our people" (p. 115). The chapter begins with an exploration of the dimensions and characteristics of such learning and so constructs a framework for the review. The subsequent overview of the research literature in the field is divided into three sections: Museums, Community and Government Organizations, and Media. Implications are then drawn for research, educational practice, and policy.

WHAT IS MEANT BY LEARNING SCIENCE
OUTSIDE OF SCHOOL?

Learning that occurs outside of school or other educational institutions has many different names: informal learning; nonformal learning; informal education; free-choice learning; learning in out-of-school contexts, settings, or environments. The term *informal* invariably refers to out-of-school contexts; for example, Crane, Nicholson, Chen, and Bitgood (1994) wrote: "Informal science learning refers to activities that occur outside the school setting, are not developed primarily for school use, are not developed to be part of an ongoing school curriculum, and are characterized as voluntary as opposed to mandatory participation as part of a credited school experience" (p. 3).

Juxtaposition of the words *informal* and *learning* has been challenged because it implies a qualitative difference between informal learning compared with formal learning. Is there a difference? In 2003, the Informal Science Education Ad Hoc Committee of the Board of the National Association for Research in Science Teaching (NARST) published a policy statement developed from a program of discussion and input from NARST members. The Committee agreed that

> Learning rarely if ever occurs and develops from a single experience. Rather, learning in general, and science learning in particular, is cumulative, emerging over time through myriad human experiences, including but not limited to experiences in museums and schools; while watching television, reading newspapers and books, conversing with friends and family; and increasingly frequently, through interactions with the Internet. The experiences children and adults have in these various situations dynamically interact to influence the ways individuals construct scientific knowledge, attitudes, behaviors, and understanding. In this view, learning is an organic, dynamic, never-ending, and holistic phenomenon of constructing personal meaning. This broad view of learning recognizes that much of what people come to know about the world, including the world of science content and process, derives from real-world experiences within a diversity of appropriate physical and social contexts, motivated by an intrinsic desire to learn. (Dierking, Falk, Rennie, Anderson, & Ellenbogen, 2003, p. 109)

If learning is an ongoing, cumulative process that occurs from experience in a range of settings, it does not make sense to try to distinguish it as formal or informal. As Walton (2000) suggested, "in the absence of physiological evidence to the contrary, all that can be said is that the learning which takes place in [science centers] is the same as learning that takes place anywhere else" (p. 50). Nevertheless, in order to mark out the boundaries for this chapter, it is helpful to distinguish between the formal and informal contexts where learning opportunities arise. Hein (1998) provided a simple distinction: "the terms 'formal' and 'informal' [refer to] a description of settings and the presence or absence of a formal curriculum" (p. 7). There are certain consistent qualitative differences in the nature of formal and informal settings or environments. For example, Falk, Koran, and Dierking (1986) compared "dimensions in which museum learning is distinct from school learning" (p. 504), but made it clear that the distinction was between the settings or contexts for learning, not between different kinds of learning. Also with a focus on museums, Bitgood (1988) compared formal and informal learning, but he discussed differences in learning environments and gave no indication that the learning was different; rather the context was different. Similarly, Wellington (1990, 1998) described the features of formal and informal learning in science in terms of differences in the settings.

These authors characterized the informal, out-of-school learning environment as one where (a) both attendance and involvement are voluntary or free-choice, rather than compulsory or coercive; (b) the curriculum has an underlying structure that is open, offers choices to learners, and tends not to be didactic; (c) the activities are nonevaluative and noncompetitive, rather than assessed and graded; and (d) the social interaction is among groups heterogeneous with regard to age, rather than constrained between same-age peers and formalized with the teacher as the main adult. In sum, compared with formal school environments, learning outside of school is learner-led and intrinsically motivated, rather than teacher-led and extrinsically motivated. Oliver Sacks (2001) identified these features as he reflected on how he learned about science in London in the late 1940s:

> My school . . . had no science and hence little interest for me—our curriculum, at this point, was based solely on the classics. But this did not matter, for it was my own read-ing in the [public] library that provided my real education, and I divided my spare time, when I was not with Uncle Dave, between the library and the wonders of the South Kensington museums, which were crucial for me throughout my boyhood and adoles-cence. The museums, especially, allowed me to wander in my own way, at leisure, going from one cabinet to another, one exhibit to another, without being forced to follow any curriculum, to attend lessons, to take exams or compete. There was something passive, and forced upon one, about sitting in school, whereas museums—and the zoo, and the botanical garden at Kew—made me want to go out into the world and explore for my-self, be a rock hound, a plant collector, a zoologist or paleontologist. (p. 57)

Besides the library, museums, zoo, and botanical garden as sources for his science learning, Sacks referred to Uncle Dave. He made much of his learning from family members, drawing attention (as did Bitgood, 1988; Falk et al., 1986; and Wellington, 1998) to the social dimension of learning outside of school. In essence, however, it is the element of volition—the freedom to choose—that characterizes the learning op-portunities in out-of-school contexts. The NARST Ad Hoc Committee decided that whatever term is used to refer to learning in out-of-school contexts (and they rec-ommended *not* using *informal*), it means "learning that is self-motivated, voluntary, guided by the learner's needs and interests, learning that is engaged in throughout his or her life" (Dierking et al., 2003, p. 109).

Science educators have strongly supported sources of out-of-school learning as important and effective complements to the science curriculum. For example, in the United States, Bybee (2001) argued that the National Science Education Standards (NSES; National Research Council, 1996) could serve as a bridge between formal and free-choice settings, stating, "the free-choice learning community must be included in any view of achieving scientific literacy" (p. 45). Others, like Hodder (1997) in New Zealand and Wellington (1998) in the United Kingdom, pointed out how sci-ence museums could contribute to the achievement of their respective national cur-riculum. The U.S. National Science Teachers Association (NSTA) adopted a Position Statement on Informal Science Education in 1998 (NSTA, 1998) outlining the bene-fits offered because it "complements, supplements, deepens, and enhances classroom science studies" (p. 30). Clearly, out-of-school learning is considered to be an important part of learning science, but what is the evidence that supports this belief?

RESEARCH ON LEARNING
SCIENCE OUTSIDE OF SCHOOL

Three important characteristics of learning are embodied in the description of learning quoted from the NARST Ad Hoc Committee (Dierking et al., 2003). First, learning is a personal process; second, it is contextualized; and third, it takes time. Some educational and psychological theories advanced about learning have not recognized these characteristics, but it turns out that they are especially significant to understanding and investigating learning outside of school. Many practitioners and researchers in out-of-school contexts now use theories of learning based in constructivist ideas (e.g., Driver & Bell, 1986; Duit & Treagust, 1998; in the museum context, see D. Anderson, Lucas, & Ginns, 2003; Hein, 1998; Roschelle, 1995) and sociocultural theory, with roots in the work of theorists such as Vygotsky (1978) and others (see also J. S. Brown, Collins, & Duguid, 1989; Lave & Wenger, 1991; Resnick, Levine, & Teasley, 1991; in the museum context, see Matusov & Rogoff, 1995; Schauble, Leinhardt, & Martin, 1997). These perspectives are not discussed here, but they are all consistent with the nature of learning as personalized, contextualized, and cumulative. These characteristics deserve some attention because of their implications for research (see Rennie & Johnston, 2004, for a more complete discussion).

Learning Is a Personal Process

Because learning is a personal process, it is different for each person. Learning involves the making of mental associations or links between new and previously acquired ideas. These changes in mental structures, or new ways of thinking about things, cause a person to react to objects or events or people in new ways. Learning results from the interpretation of experience, so for learning to occur, an individual must engage in some mental, physical, or social activity. It involves where a learner is, how that learner chooses to interact, and the nature of that interaction. The implications of this are clear: people's life circumstances, their needs, interests, and motivations determine what is attended to and what is learned. People are different, and the freedom of out-of-school contexts allows them to behave in different ways and experience different learning outcomes.

Researching learning in out-of-school contexts must take account of these implications in at least two ways. First, the learner must be central to the data-gathering process in order to capture the personal nature of learning. Photographs and videotapes of visitors using exhibits have been used to stimulate recall of their thoughts and experiences. Innovative variations in the traditional interviews and questionnaires, such as Personal Meaning Mapping (Falk, Moussouri, & Coulson, 1998), are being used to explore the diversity of learners' thinking and ideas. New digital technologies, such as wireless microphones with minidisks, facilitate recording of learners' verbal activities (e.g., Leinhardt, Knutson, & Crowley, 2003). Second, the unpredictable and varied nature of free-choice learning ensures multiple outcomes from any learning experience. Ways to measure both the expected and unexpected outcomes must be sought to get a holistic picture of what is learned and how.

Learning Is Contextualized

Although learning is a personalized process, it is rarely done alone. People are social beings. If not interacting with other people, a person usually interacts with socially constructed things, such as artifacts, language, and other socially shared and understood symbols and conventions. As Schauble et al. (1997) pointed out, "[M]eaning emerges in the interplay between individuals acting in social contexts and the mediators—including tools, talk, activity structures, signs, and symbol systems—that are employed in those contexts. Individuals both shape and are shaped by these mediators" (p. 4).

Learning is socially contextualized and shaped by the physical features of the places where meaning is made and learning occurs, an important point in terms of the rich, physical variety of out-of-school settings. Falk and Dierking (1992) formulated a framework, the Interactive Experience Model, for thinking about learning in and from these settings that tried to accommodate much of the diversity and complexity surrounding learning. More recently they built upon and refined this model, recasting it as the Contextual Model of Learning (Falk & Dierking, 2000). This model posits three contexts of importance in these settings: the Personal Context, alluded to already, concerns what individuals bring to their experience. The Sociocultural Context refers to interactions they have with other people in their social group, with staff or other unrelated groups, as well as the social and cultural features inherent in the artifacts and exhibits. The Physical Context refers to the physical surroundings. The interaction among these three contexts determines the nature and outcomes of a person's learning experience.

The Contextual Model of Learning also identified 12 critical suites of factors representing elements of the three contexts (cf. Falk & Dierking, 2000). Each factor is equally important. For convenience, they distinguish three separate contexts, but it is important to keep in mind that these contexts are not really separate, or even separable. Within the Personal Context, there are four factors: motivation and expectations; prior knowledge and experience; prior interests and beliefs; and choice and control. The Sociocultural Context includes within-group social mediation; facilitated mediation by others; and cultural background and upbringing. Factors within the Physical Context include advance organizers to content; orientation to the physical space; architecture and large-scale environmental design; design of exhibits and content of labels; and subsequent reinforcing events and experiences outside the museum. Together these 12 factors describe and emphasize the complexity of learning in museums and other out-of-school contexts.

These three contexts, and the factors inherent within them, are equally important influences on learning in any out-of-school setting. Because of this complexity, investigation of the nature of such learning requires a range of research designs and measurement techniques. Research in museums and other out-of-school settings is now guided by mixed-method research designs (Greene, Caracelli, & Graham, 1989), attention to methodological and data triangulation (Mathison, 1988; Soren, 1995), and approaches grounded in constructivist (e.g., D. Anderson et al., 2003; D. Anderson,

Lucas, Ginns, & Dierking, 2000; Falk et al., 1998; Gilbert & Priest, 1997; Stocklmayer & Gilbert, 2002) and sociocultural (e.g., Ash, 2003; Crowley & Callanan, 1998; Crowley, Callanan, et al., 2001; Leinhardt, Crowley, & Knutson, 2002; Leinhardt et al., 2003) perspectives. The ability to preserve the context of learning is critical to success (Lucas, McManus, & Thomas, 1986). The presence of a researcher or equipment to record observations may change the nature of that context and interfere with the learning experience or inadvertently cue the learner to respond in certain ways. Such reactivity is a serious issue for the researcher to consider when designing the research. Furthermore, there is an inferential gap between observing behaviors believed to indicate learning and concluding that learning has occurred, and ways must be found to bridge that gap without compromising the visitors' experience through intervention. Some researchers (e.g., Barriault, 1999; Borun, Chambers, & Cleghorn, 1996; Griffin, 1999) have proposed noninterventionist observational frameworks to identify behaviors that result in learning. Gammon (2002) produced a comprehensive synthesis of these, backed by research at the Science Museum. However, more work is needed to determine how these frameworks might be used most effectively.

Learning Takes Time

When people find themselves in new contexts, they remember knowledge and understanding gained from previous experiences and use these recollections to make meaning of their present situation. Learning occurs when people reconstruct meaning and understanding, leading to a different way of thinking, perhaps, or a different way of responding to an idea or event. Learning that occurs today depends on yesterday's learning and is the foundation for tomorrow's learning. The cumulative, iterative process of learning emphasizes the importance of time. The Contextual Model of Learning described earlier (Falk & Dierking, 2000) included time, recognizing more fully, as Falk and Dierking pointed out in 1992, that people learn from the museum experience when they "assimilate events and observations in mental categories of personal significance and character determined by the events in their lives before and after the museum visit" (p. 123). Thus learning takes time, and this makes it difficult to measure, particularly inasmuch as some learning opportunities, such as a visit to a museum, are transient events. Yet memories of them remain and can contribute to later learning (D. Anderson, 2003; Dierking, 2002; Falk & Dierking, 1997; Stocklmayer & Gilbert, 2002). Longitudinal studies, examining appropriate variables before, during, and after the learning opportunities are needed to document such learning over time.

Out-of-School Contexts for Learning Science

The opening quotation from S. Anderson (1968) listed a number of agencies and influences that facilitate learning outside of school. Lewenstein (2001) provided a more recent, but understandably similar, list of producers of science information for the public. These include government, museums, the mass media, community organizations, industry, and various nongovernment organizations and nonprofit foundations, which together have a broad range of programs and activities that directly, or indirectly, provide opportunities for learning about science throughout one's lifetime. Space prohibits an exhaustive review of each category in this chapter, so they are clustered into three sections. First, museums and related topics are given most attention because the cumulative body of research in that context provides many lessons generalizable to learning in other out-of-school contexts. In the second and third sections, relevant research on learning science from community and government organizations and the media is reviewed briefly to establish the key features of these agencies. Although prominence is given to research on school-age children, other research is included because it is important to appreciate that these settings are places that people use to support their science learning across a lifetime, often within family or all-adult groups.

LEARNING SCIENCE IN AND FROM MUSEUMS

Museums and similar institutions have always had an educational role, although the first museums, the "cabinets of curiosities" of the seventeenth and eighteenth centuries, were simply private collections, privately displayed (McManus, 1992). Even so, it is difficult to imagine that a visitor who viewed such collections of rare or unfamiliar specimens and artifacts would fail to be intrigued and to experience at least a little learning. Over several centuries, museums have developed and proliferated to a range of forms, some quite removed from the traditional natural history museums that characterized the first public institutions. Now places such as science centers, aquaria, art galleries, environmental interpretative centers, zoos, botanical gardens, planetaria, and others are included under the generic term *museum*. The definition in the Statutes of the International Council of Museums (ICOM, 2001) captures this diversity: "A museum is a non-profit making, permanent institution in the service of society and its development, and open to the public, which acquires, conserves, researches, communicates, and exhibits, for purposes of study, education and enjoyment, material evidence of people and their environment" (1974-Section II, Article 3).

In this chapter the term *museum* is used in a generic way to include the diverse range of institutions that fit the ICOM definition.

Several authors have traced the development of museums with a focus on science education (Hein, 1998; Koster, 1999; McManus, 1992; Melber & Abraham, 2002; Roberts, 1997; Schiele & Koster, 2000; Weil, 1999). Over the last four decades, the educational role of museums has become increasingly explicit. For example, the first of the three key concepts underlying the American Association of Museums' (1992) report, *Excellence and Equity*, was stated as follows: "The educational role of museums is at the core of their service to the public. This assertion must be clearly stated in every museum's mission and central to every museum's activities" (p. 8). This report emphasized the public dimension of museums and the need for both excellence (maintaining intellectual rigor) and equity (including a "broader selection of our diverse society"). From Ontario, Carter (1990) reported that community museums must formulate an interpretation and education policy to remain eligible for government funding. In Britain, the Department for Culture, Media and Sport's (2000) document, *Learning Power of Museums*, emphasized that "museums need to embrace education as a core objective in the development of mission statements, policies and action plans; similarly formal recognition of the unique educational role of museums must be reflected in the educational community's policies, plans and mission statements" (pp. 8–9). The latter part of this statement recognized the two-way commitment to education between museums and their communities, as evidenced by the British government's funding initiative to "exploit" the "learning power of museums" (p. 25).

Despite these mandates for education, in some institutions, particularly collection-based institutions such as natural history museums and zoos, there remains conflict between the dual roles of the traditional museums: research on the collections and education for the visitor (Melber & Abraham, 2002; Roberts, 1997). Koster (1999) referred to a "wide spectrum of museum philosophies [in which] the two end states seem to be (1) a curator-driven, collection-based museum with a passive stance on public programs, and (2) an audience-driven, educationally active museum that positions itself as a relevant community resource" (p. 287). Accountability pressures are moving many museums toward the second end state, a move that enhances the museum's ability to serve as a source of educational, social, and cultural change (Scott, 2003). Roberts (1997) provided an insightful analysis of the tensions created in this move, describing it as a "paradigm shift, from knowledge to knowledges, from science to narrative" (p. 3). Without doubt, such a move is transformative, because as educators become involved in exhibit development, they change the public face of the museum.

Museums and Learning: Demolishing Myths

Given that education is a recognized role of museums, do people learn from visits to museums? The unequivocal answer is yes. This does not mean that all museums are equally effective. Clearly they cannot be. Every visit does not result in immediate learning, but the potential for learning is available. There has always been some disagreement about the educational effectiveness of places like museums, disagreement that seems to be underpinned by three myths about learning in museums: (a) that playing and learning cannot occur at the same time; (b) that if learning occurs, it must happen at the museum; and (c) that what people learn is predictable and therefore easily measurable. These myths can easily be demolished based on what we know about learning in and from these settings.

Myth 1: Playing and learning cannot occur at the same time.   Play has a large research literature, with roots in anthropology, ethology, psychology, and sociology, as well as education. Commonly agreed characteristics of play are that it is enjoyable, intrinsically motivated, spontaneous, and voluntary, and it involves active exploration and engagement (Garvey, 1991; Mann, 1996; Sylva, Bruner, & Genova, 1976). Furthermore, play has been linked with creativity, solving problems, learning language and social skills, and other cognitive and social outcomes (Klugman & Smilansky, 1990; Smilansky, 1968).

In the museum context, Diamond (1996) reviewed the relationship between play and learning and concluded that museum experiences can encourage play from which learning occurs. Earlier, Hutt (1970, 1981) had distinguished between young children's exploratory activities, or investigation, and other activities that she referred to as play: "The implicit question in the child's mind during investigation seems to be 'What can this *object* do?' whereas in play it is 'What can *I* do with this object?'" (1970, p. 70, emphasis in original). Hutt's work suggested that not all playing is learning, but that much learning is associated with play. Rennie and McClafferty (1998, 2002) paraphrased Hutt's two questions as "What can this *exhibit* do?" and "What can *I* do with this exhibit?" to analyze how 3- to 7-year-old children used science center exhibits. They found that children whose play with exhibits was exploratory and investigative demonstrated higher levels of cognitive understanding than those whose play was repetitive or involved fantasy or pretense. However, symbolic or fantasy play, especially involving sociodramatic activities (when children play with others), has an important role in developing creativity and social skills (Smilansky, 1968). Clearly, playing and learning are not mutually exclusive; for children, some forms of play are, in fact, essential for learning.

Closely allied to play for older children (and even adults) is Hawkins's (1965) idea of "messing about in science." Writing for teachers, Hawkins explained how, when children are given materials and equipment and allowed to explore, test, probe, and experiment without instructions, they understood much more (and were more motivated) than if they were led immediately into formally structured investigations. Science centers are delightful places for "messing about" and the play behavior it encourages. As Semper (1990) pointed out, "Play is a serious matter in science education" (p. 6).

Science centers have been subject to the criticism that they entertain but fail to educate. Shortland (1987) famously wrote: "When education and entertainment are brought together under the same roof, education will be the loser" (p. 213). In his article, "Do science museums educate or just entertain?," Shields (1993) gathered a range of views from people employed in the science center industry, and although no one disagreed that playing and fun were important, they all had perspectives that included learning outcomes. There are strong research findings that support these perspectives. In a study conducted at the Smithsonian Institution's National Museum of Natural History, Falk et al. (1998) discovered that two motivations—education and entertainment—were given as reasons for visiting the museum by virtually all visitors and, contrary to popular belief, there was no evidence that visitors came to *either* learn or have fun, but almost without exception, visitors came to *both* learn and have fun. Individuals who self-selected to go to the museum were seeking a learning-oriented entertainment experience. As one visitor stated, "We expect to enjoy ourselves and learn new things" (p. 117).

Museum floor staff (attendants, docents, explainers, interpreters) are competent observers of visitors. Research using focus groups of museum floor staff (Rennie & Johnston, 1997), science center explainers (Johnston & Rennie, 1995), and visitors to each institution found remarkable congruence between their perceptions. Staff were adamant that both education and entertainment occurred, and visitors agreed. Griffin (1998) designed school visits that were specifically planned to match the ways in which family groups use museums. Her findings confirmed that by enabling students to have purpose, choice, and ownership of their learning processes, they enjoyed visiting museums "because they were learning *and* having fun" (p. 661, emphasis in original).

Myth 2: If learning occurs, it must happen at the museum. It is not difficult to discount this myth, given that learning is cumulative, not a series of isolated events. Early researchers who decided what the outcome of a visit should be and tried to measure it at the end of a visit frequently failed. They concluded that no learning occurred, without considering that the visit might simply have produced a readiness to learn at a later time. Some longitudinal studies (Falk, Scott, Dierking, Rennie, & Jones, 2004; Medved & Oatley, 2000; J. Stevenson, 1991) indicated that not only do visitors remember their visit experience, but in many cases they report quite outcomes some time after the visit that are different from those they report at the time of the visit, providing evidence that related learning has continued to occur. Furthermore, this learning is personalized. D. Anderson's research (Anderson et al., 2000) examined concept maps about magnetism and electricity drawn by 11- to 12-year-olds prior to their visit to a science center, after the visit, and again after some post-visit activities in the classroom. Detailed case studies of 12 children revealed that all had constructed knowledge about these topics as a result of their visit experience and the post-visit activities. Importantly, this knowledge was built in the context of the prior knowledge and understanding children brought to these experiences and thus was highly individualized.

Myth 3: What people learn is predictable and therefore easily measurable. Longitudinal studies invariably find evidence that different people learn different things. Falk and Dierking (2000) described the experiences of two women who visited a museum together and, despite doing similar things, recounted entirely different experiences. Interviews conducted five months later revealed that their museum visit had lingering influences on their subsequent activities, and again, these influences and their outcomes were quite dissimilar. Such differences are easily explained in terms of the personal context of the visit—although they were good friends, these women had different interests and motivations, and these personal differences ensured uniquely individual outcomes from the museum visit.

The experiences of these women expose the misconceptions in this third myth. People's learning is not predictable, because people are not predictable. They do not all learn the same things in the same way, because they come with different expectations and prior experiences, and the personal circumstances of their visit are different. For example, D. Anderson (Anderson et al., 2003) observed that children's learning varied from a subtle change to a recontextualizing or strengthening of something already known about electricity and magnetism, and sometimes the experience fostered personal theory building. These variations in learning not only seemed to depend upon children's prior knowledge and experience, but also embodied their personal approach to learning. Each child's knowledge was constructed and developed from a rich variety of related learning experiences that included interactions with parents and other people in enrichment and extracurricular activities; experiences at home such as reading books, watching television programs, and playing with and disassembling electric and motor-driven toys; as well as school- and museum-based experiences. Similarly, Stocklmayer and Gilbert (2002) found that adults' experiences in using exhibits were influenced by what they remembered from prior experiences, and because these memories were personally unique, so were the outcomes.

Because outcomes are personal and diverse, they are unpredictable and very difficult to measure. Much research that failed to find evidence of learning from the museum visit suffered from narrowly defined outcome measures, usually focused on some specific cognitive learning. Hence they missed the variety of affective, social, psychomotor, and other cognitive learning that occurred, which was often peripheral to the targeted outcomes, and often unexpected by exhibition designers.

Demolishing the three myths returns the focus to the nature of learning in free-choice settings. Understanding what is learned and how it is learned requires researchers to take into account the personalized, contextualized, and cumulative nature of learning. Not surprisingly, such research is challenging.

Research into Learning from Museum Visits

Research into learning from museum visits has a long history. Hein (1998) referred to a study at the Liverpool Museum in 1884, but the field did not begin to blossom until the 1960s. In the 1920s and 1930s, Robinson (1928) and Melton and his colleagues (e.g., Melton, Feldman, & Mason, 1936/1988) carried out significant research in the United States. These were carefully designed studies, examining the influence of variables such as exhibit design on visitors' learning by using quantitative approaches that featured tracking of visitors, plotting their movement, timing their actions, and formally testing their learning. Hein contrasted these early studies with the 1940s research of Wittlin (as cited in Hein, 1998), whose more qualitative approach to data collection and reporting placed less emphasis on establishing the validity and generalizability of the findings and more emphasis on the context. Wittlin focused on what visitors did and said in interviews, enabling her to obtain visitors' personal perspectives about the museum and its exhibits.

In the 1960s, visitor studies in museums tended to focus on the evaluation of exhibits and exhibitions, taking advantage of the developments in educational evaluation that accompanied the post-Sputnik science curriculum programs. Concepts such as summative and formative evaluation (Scriven, 1967) soon gained currency in the evaluation of exhibitions in museums and were supplemented by front-end evaluation (to aid in the planning of new exhibitions) and remedial evaluation (modifying the exhibit after installation). Screven (1986, 1990) and Miles and his colleagues (Alt & Shaw, 1984; Miles, 1986; Miles, Alt, Gosling, Lewis, & Tout, 1988; Miles & Tout, 1979/1994) provided insightful commentaries about evaluation research into exhibits and their effectiveness.

These evaluation studies relied upon data collected about visitors' behavior and learning in museums. In the 1970s and 1980s, their findings were built upon and extended by educational research that focused on the visitors themselves. The significance of this accumulating body of knowledge to the museum industry was recognized when, from the late 1980s, the Association of Science-Technology Centers (ASTC) began to publish a series on "What Research Says about Learning" in its newsletter.

Research into visitors' learning borrowed methodology from research into learning in schools, and consequently research designs were consistent with the educational thinking of the day. Thus the early work of Melton et al. (1936/1988), who employed pretest-posttest, control-group designs to measure carefully considered cognitive outcomes from children's museum experiences, was exemplary for its time. In 1949, Wittlin (as cited in Hein, 1998) stated her view that reliable results were possible only if they were based on controlled experiments, but her qualitative and visitor-focused reporting implied that there was some loosening in the definition of outcomes as more attention was paid to the visitors' perspectives. Surveys, observational studies, and pen-and-paper tests of knowledge continued to dominate research into the 1980s, but it was becoming increasingly urgent to recognize the active, rather than the passive, role of the visitor in the museum.

Alt and Shaw (1984) argued that "exhibits should be designed to meet the needs of visitors rather than trying to 'force' visitors to view exhibits developed largely without regard to their needs" (p. 25). This required a different approach to exhibit design, and Alt and Shaw described two studies that culminated in the visitors' view of the ideal museum exhibit. Wolf (1980) used naturalistic strategies in his evaluation studies in the Indianapolis Children's Museum. He believed that naturalistic evaluation, with its "broad, holistic view," and being "more interpretative than judgmental" in its attempts "to capture what actually occurs in museum settings" (p. 40), was a more effective way to investigate the impact on visitors. Wolf argued that there should be a focus on visitors' "current and spontaneous activities, behaviors, and expressions rather than a narrow set of pre-specified behaviors" (p. 40). These views made it clear that many evaluation measures provided ineffective recognition of the broad nature of the outcomes of museum visits. Outcomes other than cognitive had to be considered. Roberts (1989) urged that more attention be given to the affective domain, encouraging researchers to find ways of capturing "the elusive qualities of affect" (p. 6). McManus (1993) pointed out that the distinction between cognition and affect is artificial and presented evidence from her work in the Birmingham Museum of Science and Industry that "knowledge-building, meta-cognition and affect were intertwined" (p. 113).

By the 1990s, theories of learning had changed through the influence of constructivist ideas about learning and sociocultural theory, as mentioned earlier, and research in museums reflected those changes. Uzzell (1993), for example, described how, in only 15 years, visitor studies undertaken by Surrey University had moved from a behavioral to a cognitive, then to a sociocognitive focus to reflect the active constructions and interpretations made by the visitor, and the social and educational context in which they occur. Falk and Dierking (1995) provided perspectives on these theoretical changes and their implications for research. There is a substantial body of research literature, including a number of major reviews of science learning in museums and other avenues of free-choice learning (Crane et al., 1994; Falk, 2001; Falk & Dierking, 1992, 2000; Hofstein & Rosenfeld, 1996; Lucas, 1983; Ramey-Gassert, 1997; Ramey-Gassert, Walberg, & Walberg, 1994; Rennie & McClafferty, 1995, 1996), and several special issues of journals, including the *International Journal of Science Education* (Lucas, 1991), *Journal of Research in Science Teaching* (Rennie & Feher, 2003), and two issues of *Science Education* (Dierking, Ellenbogen, & Falk, 2004; Dierking & Martin, 1997). Now, in the middle of the 2000s, research on visitors' learning is an active, vibrant field. A summary of this research is presented in five parts: science museums and science centers; aquaria, botanical gardens, zoos, and interpretative centers; field trips; family visits; and museum-school-community programs.

Science Museums and Science Centers

Science museums and science centers are of particular interest to this review because of their explicit endeavor to portray science[1] and their popularity as venues for field trips and family outings. These institutions vary enormously in history, content, and purpose. McManus (1992) described the historical background to this variety, pointing out that it was not until the 1960s and 1970s that the old, established "first-generation" museums, focused on collections, research, and authoritative information, began to remodel their exhibitions to enhance communication with their visitors. The "second-generation" museums, mainly those of science and industry, were also well established and had the purpose of promoting the wonder of science as well as a training role. Their working models and hands-on elements enabled an active, communicative approach to education. The more recent "third-generation" museums were created by the move from exhibits based around objects to exhibits built to display ideas. McManus described two strands of these third-generation science museums: the thematic but non-object-based exhibitions of larger concepts, such as space, evolution, or health, and the "decontextualized scattering of interactive exhibits" (p. 164) in science centers, each exemplifying its own science concept and usually unrelated to the adjacent exhibits. The two strands often coexist in today's science centers, with the permanent, "decontextualized" exhibits rotating in the available space and themed exhibitions housed in an area dedicated to traveling displays.

Interactive exhibits, purpose-built to display some scientific and/or technological concept(s), are an important component of science centers. They are undeniably popular, so much so that "interactives," as they tend to be called, are increasingly incorporated into displays in first- and second-generation museums. Interactive exhibits are more than hands-on exhibits that visitors can touch. Touch tables in museums provide sensory experiences, feeling the difference between kangaroo fur and horse hair, for example, but involve action rather than interaction. As McLean (1993) pointed out, "interactivity is about being reciprocal" (p. 92): when the visitor does something, the exhibit offers feedback and invites further interaction. McLean described interactive exhibits as "those in which visitors can conduct activities, gather evidence, select options, form conclusions, test skills, provide input, and actually alter a situation based on the input" (p. 93). Oppenheimer's (1968) vision for the Exploratorium was driven by these aspects of interactivity. He argued for "an environment in which people can become familiar with the details of science and technology and begin to gain some understanding by controlling and watching the behavior of laboratory apparatus and machinery" (p. 206).

Of course, the fact that an exhibit is interactive does not ensure that people will learn from it. Building good exhibits, interactive or not, requires knowing the intended audience, knowing the possibilities of the venue, and knowing what makes an exhibit work, its strengths and limitations (Allen, 2004; Kennedy, 1994; McLean, 1993). Perry (1989) synthesized several theoretical positions to develop and test a

---

1. Science museums and especially museums of science and industry portray technology as well, but as the difference is not often recognized in research and rarely differentiated in the minds of the visitors, it will not be considered further (see Gilbert, 2001, for an expansion of this issue).

model for exhibit design that was attractive to visitors and both educational and enjoyable. Successful exhibits are intrinsically motivating, she argued, when they provide visitors with opportunities to experience (a) curiosity, or surprise and intrigue; (b) confidence and feelings of competence; (c) challenge, something to work toward; (d) control, a sense of self-determination; (e) play and enjoyment; and (f) communication through meaningful social interaction.

Semper (1990) provided a complementary perspective by exploring four themes in educational theory that he found relevant to the learning activity in science museums. He described (a) curiosity or intrinsically motivated learning, to which he argued too little attention has been given (see also Csiksentmihályi & Hermanson, 1995); (b) multiple modes of learning (that is, there are inviting avenues for people who learn in different ways; see also Gardner, 1993; Serrell, 1990); (c) the importance of play and exploration in the learning process (see Hawkins, 1965); and (d) the existence of different views and levels of knowledge about science and how the world works, which effective exhibits can challenge by providing entry at a variety of cognitive levels. Research confirms that visitors' understanding of the science behind the concepts or phenomena displayed depends, for example, upon how the phenomena are modeled and the range of experimentation and explanation possible (Gilbert, 2001), particularly the analogical nature of the exhibit (Falcão et al., 2004; Stocklmayer & Gilbert, 2002). In a practical way, the levels of complexity in the interactive elements of the exhibit can enhance or inhibit visitors' success in grasping the concept (Allen & Gutwill, 2004). Based on a decade of research, Allen (2004) suggested that successful exhibits should have "immediate apprehendability [sic]" (p. S20), be conceptually coherent, and cater to a diversity of learners.

The widespread use of media in museums deserves mention. Videotapes are common, and, on average, they attract about one-third of visitors. Yet, people tend to watch less than half of the content (Serrell, 2002). Videotapes are best used to extend visitors' experiences, to provide background context to exhibits, or to show animal or physical behavior unlikely to be witnessed by visitors (such as frogs catching prey and feeding; Allen, 2004). Computer exhibits, with their interactive touch screens, are attractive, and visitors expect a lot from them in terms of speed and excitement (Gammon, 1999). However, they are difficult to use in social groups of peers or families. They are now commonplace and rank low on visitors' preferences (Adams, Luke, & Moussouri, 2004), as stand-alone exhibits, computers can effectively present simulation games or scenarios where alternative choices lead to different outcomes (e.g., Falk et al., 2004).

Science centers are very popular,[2] and several comprehensive reviews of research and perspectives about science centers (McManus, 1992; Pedretti, 2002; Rennie, 2001; Rennie & McClafferty, 1996) have drawn attention to their role in communicating science. As remarked earlier, science centers have been criticized for promoting fun and enjoyment rather than education in science, but more serious criticisms were first made by Champagne (1975). After 6 hours at the Ontario Science Center with his family, he suggested that the science center failed to meet its

---

2. In 2001 ASTC estimated that there were over 158 million visits, including 47 million schoolchildren on field trips, to 445 ASTC-member science centers in 43 countries (ASTC, n.d.).

obligations to science in four ways. First, the real meaning of science was obscured—the bright and flashing displays were exciting, but no questions were asked or answers given about the important problems of the world. Second, the demonstrations contained "sloppy science"—poorly worded explanations, for example, that failed to trace the consequences of science and technological inventions and connect them with the quality of life. Third, the ethical dimensions of science and technology decisions were entirely ignored. Finally, Champagne argued that science was dishonestly portrayed as easy and unproblematic, omitting reference to the fallibility of humans and their attempts to achieve integrity in results.

If we believe that science centers should communicate an understanding of science as a genuine human endeavor, these are significant flaws, and they are not easily addressed, as shown by continued criticism (Fara, 1994; Parkyn, 1993, Ravest, 1993; Wymer, 1991) and some research evidence. Rennie and Williams (2002), for example, found that after their science center visit, some visitors were more likely to think that science was infallible and could solve all problems, consistent with Champagne's (1975) final criticism. Bradburne (2000) and his colleague, Wake, found three weaknesses in science center exhibits: they communicate principles, not processes; most fail to communicate scientific thought, focusing on conclusions rather than the journey, which includes false leads and often failures; and they mask the complex links between science and technology because they are decontextualized. Bradburne's answer was to find ways to present science as a process. One result was *Mine Games*, an exhibition at Science World in Vancouver that put the visitor at the center of social debate on science, technology, and society. According to Bradburne, "the visitors seemed ready, willing, and able to take that responsibility" (p. 45).

Mine Games is one of a genre of issues-based science exhibitions that deliberately forefront the intersections between science, technology, and society, and, to some extent, they address the challenges offered by the critics mentioned earlier. Pedretti and her colleagues researched how these exhibitions affected school visitors, finding that in focused class programs, both *Mine Games* (Pedretti, 1999) and *A Question of Truth* at the Ontario Science Center (Pedretti & Forbes, 2000) resulted in shifts in students' perspectives about the nature of science and how it sits in the sociocultural context of real lives. Adult visitors also were affected by *A Question of Truth* (Pedretti, Macdonald, Gitari, & McLaughlin, 2001; Pedretti & Soren, 2003), and they showed support for this type of exhibition. Pedretti (2004) concluded that these exhibitions enhance learning through four factors—they personalize the subject matter, evoke emotion, stimulate dialogue and debate, and promote reflexivity.

Although such exhibitions may have positive effects on the public audience, they can also be subjected to strong criticism. Molella (1999) described the backlash against *Science in American Life*, an exhibition at the National Museum of American History, which explored critical intersections between science, technology, and society through a series of historic case studies. Despite its public success, scientists felt the exhibition blurred the image of science as a pure endeavor. Molella attributed these feelings to the political climate of the day (see also Friedman, 1995). Mounting such exhibitions involves risk, but then, so does science.

Aquaria, Botanical Gardens, Zoos, and Interpretive Centers

Whereas science center exhibits are designed to display mainly physical science concepts (many dealing only with Newtonian physics), the living exhibits in aquaria, botanic gardens, zoos, and interpretive centers provide visitors with opportunities to explore biological science. Visitors differ in their responses to living things compared with preserved specimens. For example, Tunnicliffe (Tunnicliffe, 1996; Tunnicliffe, Lucas, & Osborne, 1997) found that, at the Natural History Museum, the specimens' lack of visible behavior encouraged visitors to construct their own narrative, by naming the animals, recalling knowledge about them, and commenting on structure and appearance. At the London zoo, visitors made similar comments, but often they had to locate the animal before observation could begin, and then they talked about its behavior. In both venues, Tunnicliffe found remarkable similarity in the conversations among school and family groups (Tunnicliffe et al., 1997), suggesting that much more might be done by teachers and by the institutions themselves to extend learning. Later, a comprehensive study with visitors, staff, and school groups at a New Zealand zoo (Tofield, Coll, Vyle, & Bolstad, 2003) confirmed that easily visible and active animals attracted the most attention from visitors. Furthermore, learning was enhanced considerably by pre- and post-visit activities.

Institutions housing living specimens are well placed to convey ecological and environmental messages. The zoo in the Tofield et al. (2003) study, for example, reflected its mission's emphasis on conservation education with signs conveying two types of message—information about the animals, and information about environmental and conservation matters. Adelman, Falk, and James (2000) found that visitors' experiences at the National Aquarium of Baltimore enriched their conservation-related experience, awareness, and knowledge. These positive changes persisted over time, especially with respect to the complex balance between the needs of people and nature. However, there was no evidence of increased conservation behavior, which these authors attributed to a lack of suitable reinforcing experiences.

Brody, Tomkiewicz, and Graves (2002) reported on the development of visitors' understanding of the rare geothermal and biological features of a geyser in Yellowstone National Park. Using pre- and post-visit interviews, they found that visitors constructed new knowledge and values from their prior conceptions, their experience with the environment, discussion among fellow visitors, and use of the site brochure. Values related to the beauty of this extreme environment, the need for preservation and conservation, and the commercial potential of the biotechnological use of the microorganisms. Brody et al. pointed out that effective educational programs must be cognizant of modern theories of learning, as well as the public's existing understanding of ecological concepts.

Learning Science from Field Trips

Most young people experience museums on field trips; in fact, school groups are a major audience for museums. Museum educators develop activities to link with the relevant school curricula to enable teachers to plan effective visits. Different programs are offered for different parts or levels of the curriculum or for particular exhibitions. Museums also offer programs that cater for the needs of special groups, for example, the gifted (Melber, 2003), those with disabilities (Tam, Nassivera, Rousseau, & Vreeland, 2000), and adolescents, historically "the missing audience" in museums (Lemerise, 1995). Despite these efforts, Jamison (1998) reported that many teachers are unaware of the resources and support available.

Teachers arrange field trips for a variety of reasons: to supplement or comple-ment part of the curriculum, as an enrichment experience to see things that cannot be offered in school, or sometimes as a reward for their class, with no firm educa-tional purpose in mind (Gottfried, 1980; Griffin & Symington, 1997; Jamison, 1998; Michie, 1998; Rennie, 1994). Sørensen and Kofod (2003) described (a) the "day out" tour, with no preparation and no follow-up; (b) the "classroom" tour, where stu-dents follow a docent or teacher around the venue and often do a worksheet; (c) the "inspiration" tour, when children explore the exhibits on their own to obtain ideas for their work back at school; and (d) the "learning resource" tour, when the visit is part of the work at school with before- and after-visit activities.[3] Sørensen and Kofod found that, although 80% of the 81 elementary teachers responding to their survey reported that their class visit to the Experimentarium in Denmark was re-lated to their school science, it was clear from other patterns of responses that only about 30% of visits could be classified as "learning resource" tours and 10% as "inspiration" tours. A third of teachers regarded the visit as a social event, and nearly a quarter did no pre-visit preparation. Nearly all teachers indicated that they talked about the visit in class afterward, but in less than 10% of classes did students write, draw, or report about the visit. These findings confirm other research—the minority of field trips are integrated with work back at school (D. Anderson et al., 2000; Griffin & Symington, 1997; Rennie & McClafferty, 1995).

Not surprisingly, different kinds of visits have different outcomes. Clear and compelling findings have emerged from a great deal of research about field trips (see reviews by Bitgood, 1991; Griffin, 2004; Mason, 1980; Prather, 1989; Rennie & McClafferty, 1995; Rickinson et al., 2004). Their educational effectiveness depends on how well they complement the science curriculum at school. This means that, to a large extent, their success is in the hands of teachers. Early advice intended to help teachers organize effective field trips given by museum educators (e.g., Bar-rett, 1965; Beardsley, 1975) emphasized that planning before the trip and "recapitu-lation" afterward were almost as important as the trip itself. Research has con-firmed this advice. In terms of planning, Rennie and McClafferty (2001) reminded teachers to ask themselves why they were going, to ensure that the field trip was planned to meet its purpose. These authors drew attention to both teacher and stu-dent preparation. They stressed the need for teachers to visit the intended venue and take advantage of the in-service courses, curriculum resources, and advice available from the education officers and the venue's website. Student preparation serves two purposes. First, students need orientation about the venue, so they know what to expect in terms of what they will see, their physical comfort, and the time allocated for educational tasks and for their own exploration. Second, they

---

3. Sørensen and Kofod (2003) also described a partnership between the Experimentarium and a nearby school, where students visit the science center, choose a project based on the exhibits, and pursue it to com-pletion with follow-up visits. Such partnerships are unusual but have great potential for learning.

need advance organizers for the learning objectives of the field trip so they can be self-directed in terms of achieving them during the field trip and by working toward the requirements of post-visit activities. Griffin and Symington (1997) urged teachers to include students in the planning process so they have a sense of commitment to the objectives to be achieved.

The field-trip venue is not a school classroom. The social and physical contexts, and hence the learning, are quite different. Teachers can take advantage of the new environment by helping students to orientate themselves at the venue, then allowing them sufficient time to complete structured tasks and pursue their own interests. Encouraging students to work in small groups capitalizes on the social dimension of the visit and enables them to share the responsibilities associated with learning. Group, rather than individual, worksheets are thus more effective records of students' explorations (Rennie & McClafferty, 1995). Toward the end of the visit, teachers should encourage students to regroup and ensure they have the information they need for follow-up activities. Back at school, the field trip experiences need to be revisited and built on to maximize the learning. Research still has the least to say about this aspect of field trips, but its significance has been established (D. Anderson et al., 2000; Tofield et al., 2003).

How teachers integrate the field trip with science at school depends in part on the learning objectives. Orion's (1989) high-school geology course based on field trips provides an exemplar for teachers who need to combine considerable content with first-hand experience with the subject, in this case, the geology of Israel. Astin, Fisher, and Taylor (2002) gave examples of class visits used to complete a compulsory component in a new physics course in Britain. In both cases, it is clear that prior to a field trip, the teacher must investigate the location and devise preparatory and summary activities around the field trip itself.

The Role of Docents

Docents, explainers, or education staff are available to assist school groups at many venues. Their roles may vary from leading structured tours to merely responding to questions, and teachers need to consider the role they wish docents to play during their visit. Naturally, students' patterns of behavior are quite different when they are instructed by a docent than when they are not, as Birney (1988) demonstrated in her study at a zoo and a museum in Los Angeles. When students were led by a docent, their passivity and inattention were high; when students were free to explore, these responses were replaced with activity and interaction with exhibits and peers, behaviors more likely to be associated with learning. Similarly, Cox-Petersen, Marsh, Kisiel, and Melber (2003) found that the docent-guided tours in a natural history museum in California were lecture-oriented. Although students, who were given objects to examine and some time to explore the halls, enjoyed their visit, learning outcomes were limited. More effective, inquiry-oriented, learner-centered tours led by docents (Cox-Petersen et al., 2003) or teachers (Griffin & Symington, 1997) combine initial orientation with students then moving off in small groups to pursue their own explorations. Effective guides (docents, teachers, or accompanying adults) encourage visitors to actively explore and reflect, rather than simply direct them to the "right" answer.

Despite their significant benefits, field trips can be expensive and difficult to organize. There are administrative hurdles, insurance issues, and, especially at the high school level, the need to juggle timetables (Michie, 1998; Rickinson et al., 2004; Tofield et al., 2003), so it makes sense to maximize their value by ensuring that enjoyment and education both win on the day.

Learning in Family Visits to Museums

Children visit museums in family groups, an ideal situation for play, talk, and learning from each other. Families are the most common museum-visiting group (Falk, 1998; Falk & Dierking, 1992; McManus, 1992), so it is not surprising that their behavior has been well studied. Early researchers focused on what families did in museums (e.g., Diamond, 1986; Dierking & Falk, 1994; Hilke & Balling, 1985; McManus, 1992, 1994) and constructed a general model of family visiting behavior that is still current (Kelly, Savage, Griffin, & Tonkin, 2004). Typical teaching-learning behaviors include parents acting as exhibit interpreters for children, by pointing, asking questions, and modeling exploratory behavior. Such actions might be expected to facilitate learning, especially for young children, who are likely to spend more time at an exhibit when an adult is also present (Crowley & Callanan, 1998; Crowley & Galco, 2001; Puchner, Rapoport, & Gaskins, 1997; Rennie & McClafferty, 2002).

Family behavior varies with the age of the children; older children may be left to explore alone or with their peers, and some parents are content to watch even young children rather than interact with them (C. Brown, 1995). Recognition that different patterns of behavior occurred at different types of exhibits prompted Borun and her colleagues (Borun et al., 1996; Borun, Chambers, Dritsas, & Johnson, 1997; Borun & Dritsas, 1997) to design "family-friendly" exhibits to encourage the kinds of behaviors believed to promote learning.

Recently, researchers have moved beyond observational "time and tracking" studies (Ellenbogen, Luke, & Dierking, 2004) and adopted a range of innovative methods for data collection in keeping with a sociocultural perspective on family learning. For example, paying closer attention to the nature of the conversations between parents and children in museums has revealed how parents scaffold children's scientific thinking (Ash, 2003; Crowley & Galco, 2001). This research has shown that parents help children select and process relevant evidence, generate more evidence, and provide explanations (Crowley et al., 2001).[4]

Because families remain together before and after the visit, investigation of their learning must take a longitudinal perspective. Some researchers have asked families to recall discussions and activities subsequent to their museum visit, then tried to construct how and what learning occurred. Ellenbogen (2002) obtained much information as she worked on her dissertation research. In the role of participant observer, she not only accompanied four families on their regular museum visits, but spent time in their home before and after the visits. She concluded that frameworks

---

4. How parents scaffold children's scientific thinking may be more easily studied in a science center than in the home, where the researcher would be more intrusive. Similarly, Feher and Diamond (1990) argued that science centers can be used as laboratories to study the way children learn by choice, rather than when they are constrained by expectations in the classroom.

for measuring family learning in museums (e.g., Borun et al., 1996) were constricted by the museum's agenda for assessing learning and insensitive to the variety and depth of learning conversation that actually occurred. Ellenbogen's research across multiple learning environments revealed that families who used museums frequently had their own complex motivations and agendas into which they fitted the museum visit. In this way, museums were used as tools for family members to negotiate and establish their identity as a family of learners, but on their own terms, rather than on those of the museum. Thus, the museum provided the context for learning, rather than the content. Occasional family visitors may not make the same use of their museum experience because their personal contexts and visit agendas are different, and they would be less familiar with the physical environment. However, there is evidence that families who have not traditionally used museums to meet their free-choice learning needs can learn to use these settings in personally meaningful ways that result in heightened interest and engagement in science (Dierking & Falk, 2003).

A decade ago, McManus (1992) described family members as a "coordinated hunter-gatherer team actively foraging in the museum to satisfy their curiosity about topics and objects that interest them" (p. 176). We still see this behavior pattern in museums, but the adoption of new and alternative research strategies that document the role of the museum in family life while retaining the family as the central focus of the research has resulted in a better understanding of the family as a learning institution. This learning institution utilizes the free-choice learning resources of an extensive community infrastructure, of which museums are an important part (Ellenbogen et al., 2004). Children's learning in a family context is a significant factor in their learning about science.

Other Museum-School-Community Links

Museums make a significant contribution to science education through their work with schools, teachers, and the community. The School in the Exploratorium (SITE) was one of the earliest formal links between a science center and schools. Established in 1972, it involved weekly visits for 5 or 8 weeks by fourth, fifth, and sixth graders for an extended program of "hands-on" science (Silver, 1978). By 1987, the program included a range of curriculum development and teacher professional development programs. St. John (1987) found considerable success in extended teacher change. For example, about one-third of participants said they continued to use SITE materials extensively, and 80–90% of teachers expressed improved science understanding, interest, and comfort in teaching science. Today, beyond SITE, the Exploratorium is a major provider of programs for teaching and learning, with "10,000 teachers from 37 states annually participating in Exploratorium-designed workshops" (Exploratorium, n.d.), although not all are held at the Exploratorium.

Inverness Research Associates (1996) listed 12 different kinds of programs in "informal science education institutions" (including science centers, natural history museums, aquaria, botanic gardens, planetaria, and nature centers), 5 of which were related specifically to teacher development, and others related to curriculum, materials development, and support outreach; structured and educationally supported field trips (not including regular, teacher-led field trips); preservice teacher connections; national science education programs (e.g., Challenger Centers); and local educational partnerships. At that time, Inverness Research Associates estimated that 11% of all teachers of science in the United States participated in such in-service activities each year. Programs continue to grow. Based on their 2002 survey, the Institute of Museum and Library Services (n.d.) estimated that nearly 11,000 museums in the United States provided more than 18 million hours of K–12 educational programming, spending over $1 billion in 2001–2002. A few examples will give a flavor of these activities.

Torri (1997) described a typical partnership between a museum and a nearby school to enhance K–8 science instruction. Teachers visited the museum for introduction to the programs; there were follow-up class visits and use of museum resources, some specifically written for teachers' needs. Torri stated that teachers appreciated the additional support, and the partnership was a successful innovation. Kelly, Stetson, and Powell-Mikel (2002) reported a partnership between a museum and university that benefited early childhood and elementary preservice teachers. Observation of, and working with, children visiting the museum's hands-on science facility improved the preservice teachers' understanding of young learners' abilities. In post-course surveys, the preservice teachers commented positively about their own improved confidence in science and mathematics.

Paris, Yambor, and Packard (1998) described a comprehensive museum-school-university partnership for a 6-week biology program for grades 3–5. This program was based on current research on learning with carefully designed strategies to promote intrinsic motivation and self-regulated learning. Children attended classes in the university's laboratory, used living exhibits and materials from the museum, and carried out other activities and projects, culminating in a family biology night. The children's classroom teachers were integrally involved, and university students assisted children in the laboratory as part of their own course. The program was thoroughly evaluated, showing positive increases in children's attitudes to science, problem-solving, and knowledge retention. Qualitative findings from teacher interviews and child case studies substantiated the enthusiasm of both, and the university students made similar reports. Paris et al. noted the benefits of matching the program to the state curriculum and its structuring in terms of learning theory and urged similar partnership programs.

Although not directly associated with schools, programs for volunteer exhibit interpreters provide young people with opportunities to learn about science and about people learning science, providing an ideal background for careers in teaching and science. Both the Ontario Science Center and the Exploratorium have had such programs since their inception in 1969; research with young people shows that they become better learners and educators (Nyhof-Young, 1996) and gain enduring skills in self-confidence, communication, and science learning (Diamond, St. John, Cleary, & Librero, 1987).

Museum outreach is closely related to, and often an extension of, links to schools. Many museums run programs off-site at venues such as schools, libraries, community halls, shopping centers, fairs, and festivals. D. Martin (1996) gathered descriptions of a variety of outreach programs ranging from Ulster Museum's Science Discovery Bus to Riksutsttällningar's traveling garbage museum in Sweden, to art courses by telephone from the Metropolitan Museum of Art for homebound residents of New York City, to Harborough Museum's prison outreach. Martin suggested that "outreach has become fundamental to the process of changing the role of museums within their communities, establishing relationships with new audiences, and turning museums from inward facing to outward facing organizations" (p. 38).

The opportunities provided by outreach programs are especially appreciated in remote and rural areas, where adults and children have no access to museums or similar organizations. In Australia, Garnett (2003) surveyed 63 museum-sponsored and private outreach providers of education and awareness programs in science, mathematics, engineering, and technology. Returns from 57 providers reported contacts with 421,360 students during 2002. Garnett conducted a case study in one town in each Australian state and one territory, and 207 surveys were returned from schools that had recently participated in an outreach program. The findings suggested that these programs increased students' interest and skills levels, and that presenters benefited students and teachers by demonstrating new approaches, content, techniques, and resources. Garnett concluded that provision in remote areas fell well short of need, with programs reaching only one in four children. Two-thirds of providers offered supporting websites and teacher resources, one-third offered student resources and teacher workshops, and more than half also offered programs/ exhibitions for the general public during their tours. These outreach programs are now the major providers of professional development for teachers of science outside major cities, but Garnett found that teachers in only 42 of the 207 schools believed they had access to professional development sufficient for their needs.

Rennie and Williams (2000) evaluated the impact of an Australian traveling science show. Their data included interviews with 82 teachers at 47 schools at the time of the show, 325 interviews and exit surveys from adult visitors to associated public exhibitions, and telephone interviews with 48 teachers between 4 and 8 weeks after the science show visit. The results from the teachers were similar to the findings from field trips. Very few teachers prepared their class for the visit, but about half followed up afterward by discussing what happened and what children thought about the visit. The conclusions that can be drawn are consistent with those made earlier. Although all participants were very positive about the experience, it is unlikely that the potential of these incursions into schools were fully realized in terms of students' learning of science. Most providers (and certainly this traveling science show) supply information to teachers, especially via their website, to enable them to prepare for the visit by choosing shows that can be built into their teaching program and to plan follow-up activities (a resource pack was left at the school for this purpose). Most teachers do not do these things, and for many students it is likely that the major benefit of their experience is the memory of enjoyable science activities, which may or may not be relevant to their future science activities.

Clearly, museum-school-community programs are valued, or they would not be continued, but their effectiveness is assumed rather than demonstrated. This can be attributed, at least in part, to a desire to put time, funds, and effort into the program rather than its evaluation. Despite the availability of good advice, most evaluation is usually limited to feedback sheets and head counts of participants. Self-evaluation of outreach programs is difficult, as Matarasso (1996) pointed out, because there is always a vested interest in demonstrating success. Matarasso suggested that clearly stated aims of the program should be agreed on, and indicators of their being met decided, before data gathering begins. This helps to focus the evaluation and enables it to demonstrate the outcomes. The Paris et al. (1998) and Rennie and

Williams (2000) studies were designed in this way and contributed some empirical evidence to support the potential of such programs to promote better science learning for students at school and community members at large.

LEARNING SCIENCE FROM COMMUNITY AND GOVERNMENT ORGANIZATIONS

This section considers programs that offer voluntary activities to groups of young people. Such programs are characterized by diversity. Some have a national base, such as 4-H, but others are genuinely community-based, operating in a defined geographical area. They may be offered as single events, annually, or as a regular program. Some are offered as extracurricular activities in schools, others are completely separate. An idea of their number and diversity can be obtained from a sample of what is available in Australia, a large country with a relatively small population.

The Australian Science Teachers Association's (ASTA) website (http://www.asta.edu.au/st2003/alpha-list.html) in 2003 listed 146 separate activities, competitions, programs, and events aimed at students and science teachers, sponsored or organized by a range of professional science-related associations, universities, industries, and other nongovernment organizations. These ranged from science poetry competitions, science fairs, summer schools, and work-experience placements to teacher and student awards. The annual National Science Week was not included in this list. That major event, which receives significant government funding, coordinates about 500 separate official events and activities. Rennie and ASTA (2003) analyzed the 2001 National Science Week event calendar and found that 40% were public lectures, forums, or debates; 20% school activities or competitions; 15% special exhibitions in museums or displays in public places; 5% open days/nights at science venues or to show science in industry; 5% tours or excursions; and a range of other awards, presentations, conferences, on-line activities, science theater, and so on. However, a comprehensive search for effective evaluation of the outcomes of these activities failed to provide anything beyond data for attendance/participation and subjective or self-reported assessment of the public's response.

On a broader level, the Australian government supports public science awareness-raising activities through the Science and Technology Awareness Program (STAP), replaced in 2001 by the National Innovation Awareness Strategy (NIAS). STAP and NIAS have been important sources of funding for projects aimed not only at increasing awareness of science and technology, but promoting understanding and a positive attitude toward science and technology among the Australian people. However, Gascoigne and Metcalfe (2001) noted that evaluations of STAP were positive about its role and activities but did not provide information about the effectiveness of its programs. They drew attention to the need for impact evaluation, rarely a design feature of such programs, both in Australia and internationally.

Community-Based Programs

Community-based programs are usually flexible in time and topics. They offer science-related activities at variable cognitive levels and often for a range of age groups, allowing cross-age mentoring. Although most programs are not specifically aligned to the school curricula, Nicholson, Weiss, and Campbell (1994) explained that many of them grew from a deliberate attempt to complement what was perceived as dull, teacher-directed science at school with innovative, hands-on, inquiry activities. Many such programs target minority groups and/or girls with the purpose of promoting their interest and participation in science.[5] Nicholson et al. described three categories of programs: discovery programs aimed at making science (and mathematics) interesting, thus changing attitudes and inspiring self-confidence in doing science, such as Operation SMART and Hands On Science Outreach; short-term, usually residential, science camps, providing intensive immersion in science aimed at changing attitudes and increasing participation in science; and longer term career programs, with regular participation allowing continued contact between participants and mentors.

Hands On Science Outreach (HOSO) is a good example of a community-based program because it has a long history and there has been some evaluation of its effects. HOSO was established as a local community after-school experiment in the United States in 1980 to provide a regular, recreational science option for preschool and elementary-school children (Katz, 2000). Children work in small groups with a trained adult helper (usually a parent) to engage in pleasurable, hands-on science activities in a personally supportive environment. Activity guides are provided for home use in a family situation. HOSO has grown rapidly and has received a National Science Foundation (NSF) grant to expand. HOSO's activities are consistent with the National Science Education Standards (Katz & McGinnis, 1999), and its topics are representative of the major disciplines outlined by the Standards. Katz (2000) reported several evaluations of HOSO. Participating children made significant gains in knowledge and understanding about science and perceptions of scientific activity, but long-term effects were not measured. Katz (1996) used focus groups and case studies in research with the adult leaders, finding that HOSO provided them with learning, enjoyment, and specific personal benefits.

Community-based programs are difficult to evaluate, especially their long-term effects. The evolution of programs with time and the difficulty of tracking past participants are two of the research challenges common to other out-of-school contexts. Eccles and Templeman (2002) recounted a thorough analysis and evaluation of after-school programs for youth (although with aims other than science) and concluded, with caution, that there were positive effects. More comprehensive evaluation is needed for such science-based programs to judge their effects in both the short and long term, and to examine the reasons for them. For the moment, our understanding is best informed by the findings described in the previous section, particularly for field trips, families, and museum-school-community links.

LEARNING SCIENCE FROM THE MEDIA

The media include all print and electronic means of communication to the public. Some publications and programs have explicit educational aims, ranging from *Sesame*

---

5. Examples include the Girls at the Center project (http://sln.fi.edu/tfi/programs/gac.html) linked with the Franklin Institute Science Museums and Girl Scouts of the United States and activities in Britain sponsored by sciZmic (http://www.scizmic.net).

Street to publicly funded and coordinated media campaigns for health promotion (to quit smoking, for example). Others, such as fictional stories in print or on television, have entertainment as their prime purpose. Nevertheless, all can provide learning experiences related to science.

How can we discern the learning impact of media on young people? Much research on learning from the media is based on how these avenues of communication are used in classrooms, or on the impact of particular programs, rather than on what people learn from the media in a free-choice environment. School-directed use of media, such as textbooks, television, and the Internet (including their use for homework) is not the focus here; rather it is the use of media for personal interest and information. In this section, most attention is given to television because of its pervasiveness. Print media and the Internet are also mentioned, but there is little research on their contribution to young people's learning of science in out-of-school contexts.

Print Media

Turney (1999) distinguished several genres of popular science in print: biography and autobiography both reveal much about the thinking of scientists and the way science works; sources of self-help provide information about topics of interest or relevance to the reader; dictionaries or primers for scientific literacy; and publications for intellectual entertainment that are often based on controversial issues. From a different perspective, Goldman and Bisanz (2002) described three roles for communicating scientific information: communicating among scientists, disseminating information generated by the scientific community, and formal education in science. The second is relevant here. Goldman and Bisanz divided this role into public awareness, including the press, news, advertisements, public service messages, and science fiction; and public understanding and informal learning, which includes Turney's genres and informational websites.

All of these are read by some young people, and research on the effects of reading such publications in a free-choice environment is confounded by just that; young people are *choosing* to read them. Already the personal context is positive, and although reading might be a solitary activity, most readers will share and talk over their reading with like-minded friends. Because they are already knowledgeable about the topic, interested readers find it easier to connect new information with old than does a person who is new to the topic (Goldman & Bisanz, 2002; Tremayne & Dunwoody, 2001). Given this, it is easy to imagine that reading for interest results in learning.

What research can reveal, however, is what kind of learning may occur. Most studies have been done in formal settings, often with university students, but some results are generalizable. Many public awareness communications are brief to engage the reader, but brevity risks ambiguity and oversimplification of the issues. Goldman and Bisanz's (2002) synthesis of research suggests that students have limited ability to judge the scientific status of an argument and tend not to adopt a critical stance. Of course, this varies with background knowledge, but it places the onus on journalists (and scientists) to portray science fairly to their readers. Rennie (1998) analyzed three examples and argued that this is not done well.

Computers and the Internet

Science on the Internet can range from one person's idea (or ideology) to the large and comprehensive websites of public organizations, such as the BBC, NASA, and so on. Museums have their own websites and were among the first to recognize their educational potential (Streten, 2000). As they are expected to provide authoritative information, museum websites, together with those of government agencies, science publishers, and universities, are often recommended as web-based educational resources (e.g., Bodzin & Cates, 2002; Smith, 1999; S. Stevenson, 2001). Unlike print media, websites can be updated rapidly and hence provide the public with readily accessible information on complex and controversial scientific topics (Byrne et al., 2002; Hawkey, 2001).

Museum websites are popular. Rennie and McClafferty (1996) reported that in the week beginning December 10, 1995, the Exploratorium website had 188,381 accesses. Eight years later, in the week beginning December 7, 2003, it had 800,059 page views, 8,602,363 hits, and 39,896 Mb of data transfer (R. Hipschman, personal communication, March 21, 2004). Although many hits were seeking visitor information, such as opening hours, etc., most were seeking educational or science-related information.[6] There is extensive documentation of the use of websites, but little about the learning from them. Semper (2002) wrote that "the World Wide Web and museums were made for each other" (p. 13), but, he argued, a research agenda must be developed and implemented to understand both the online audience and how the websites can support learning.

Semper, Wanner, and Jackson (2000) set out to develop a means of evaluating three online resources: (a) a step-by-step instructional sequence for dissecting a cow's eye; (b) a general informational topic on the science of cycling; and (c) flights of inspiration, based on a museum collection. Their analyses and interpretation of viewing logs and an online survey of viewers found that, for each site, 60% or more of the users were adults. The cow's eye dissection was the most popular for high school students and was used mostly in an explicitly educational setting. Cycling was the resource hit most often out of interest. Semper et al. discussed the value of the different data sources they used, which revealed previously invisible users. More research will result in further information about the learning that occurs.

Museums have embraced digital and mobile technologies with the main goal of increasing access to the collections by presenting information about exhibits and educational programs on the web (Bradburne, 2001; Institute of Museum and Library Services, 2002). They have created successful "virtual field trips" (Bradford & Rice, 1996) for virtual visitors to explore, but this may be a double-edged sword. To retain their real visitors, M. Anderson (1999) pointed out, "museums will be forced to confront the fact that the competition for leisure time demands a more aggressive case for the experience of the original" (p. 131).

---

6. The Exploratorium was the 2004 Webby Award Winner for science, an honor presented by the International Academy for Digital Arts and Sciences (2004) for achievement in technological creativity and individual achievement.

Television

Television is the most pervasive medium worldwide. Unlike books or the Internet, where the user actively chooses to read or interact, television viewing is often passive. Chen (1994) pointed out in his review of research in the field of "television and informal science education" that, despite the very high level of national funding for educational programs, there was a paucity of systematic research, and most of it was focused on NSF-funded science programs provided by the Children's Television Workshop. Some years later, Wright et al., (2001) reached the same conclusion— very little attention has been paid to the educational value of children's television viewing. Most of the challenges to research in out-of-school contexts mentioned earlier are evident in evaluation of the learning effects of television. Viewers differ in their personal and home contexts, and finding appropriate samples from which research findings may be generalized is a challenge. Data collection from people in their usual viewing context creates other problems—how does the researcher deal with channel changing, for example? Longitudinal impact studies are difficult because there are so many intervening variables. Chen (1994) also noted that summative or impact evaluation is historically absent, and the producers of most television projects do not regard it as a priority.

Chen's (1994) search uncovered only eight studies of children's or adolescents' television watching in relation to science, and four for adults. Overall, programs on science and nature were appealing and ranked high for learning potential. The findings suggested an association between watching these programs and family support and heightened interest in the subject matter and desire to read in the area. Although Chen reviewed some comprehensive studies, he concluded there was not yet a field of research and argued for a greater commitment to summative evaluation.

Some research on children's television viewing has been done by people employed in the field. Fisch, Yotive, Brown, Garner, and Chen (1997) found that although elementary school children rated two cartoon series (Cro—an educational program, and The Flintstones—a noneducational program) as having high appeal, they did not distinguish between them in terms of their educational content. Fisch et al. concluded that educational programs were more likely to be successful if they also were entertaining. Mares, Cantor, and Steinbach (1999) explored the potential of television to foster children's interest in science. Under controlled viewing conditions, fifth-grade students watched versions of programs that varied in terms of whether and how science was presented. Children learned more when the science was shown in context than when it was not. A second study in fourth- and fifth-grade classrooms suggested that greater exposure to a program resulted in more positive attitudes to science, but it seemed that children who were more interested in science were more likely to watch the same program at home as well as at school.

Longitudinal studies of children's television watching reported by Wright et al. (2001) deserve attention for their careful research design, although they did not focus on science. Two cohorts of children, aged 2 and 4 years, were studied for 3 years with the use of a combination of mother interviews, home environment visits, school readiness tests, and periodic telephone calls to document children's activities for the previous day. Statistical controls were used for some extraneous variables, and the findings suggested that children who viewed more educational programming had an advantage in school readiness compared with those who watched entertainment programs. Another study involved recontacting high school students who, 10 years earlier, had their home television viewing habits studied as 5-year-olds. Wright et al. found that the more 5-year-old children watched informative programs, the more likely they were as adolescents to have overall high grades, including in science. They attributed this to a more positive attitude toward learning. There is some relationship between these findings and earlier ones by Gibson and Francis (1993), who found teenagers' attitudes toward science to be negatively correlated with watching "soap operas" but positively correlated with watching "current awareness programs."

Long and Steinke (1996) analyzed the portrayal of science in children's educational programs and identified a variety of different images. They found that "images of science as truth, as fun, and as part of everyday life were quite evident" (p. 14). Long and Steinke inferred that viewers were encouraged to value science and the scientific community, but there was no empirical evidence to back this claim. Dhingra (2003) selected segments of network news, documentary, drama, and magazine-format science television programming to investigate how high school students understood the nature of science from these program genres. Students perceived the news and drama formats to convey uncertainty in science knowledge, whereas the documentary and magazine format conveyed an image of science as facts. Dhingra pointed out that different segments from these genres may have produced different responses, but she demonstrated that students' responses varied, and that they thought about what they had seen and made connections to other experiences in their lives, including at school.

Advertising is a ubiquitous feature of television, and the makers of advertisements are adept at finding ways to make viewers take notice of them. McSharry and Jones (2002) asked, "What better way to advertise science-based advances to the public than by television?" (p. 489). They identified 18 categories of advertisements on terrestrial (i.e., not satellite) television, of which 14 could be described as science-based, including a variety of domestic products like paints and cleaning products, and mapped them against the Science National Curriculum in England. A public survey of 196 people revealed that young people (7- to 16-year-olds) watched more science programs than adults, but all age groups watched much less science than was available (in the sample period, this was 7.21% of all programming). Furthermore, few recognized advertisements that were science-based, choosing an average of less than 4 from 14 choices. Health-care products were best recognized (by 64% of respondents), followed by food (41%). McSharry and Jones pointed out that advertisements may constitute the main exposure to science on television and urged educators to use advertising as a way to make science education relevant to children.

Television advertising, combined with other media, such as radio and print, can make a measurable difference in knowledge about an issue. Gillilan, Werner, Olson, and Adams (1996) found that after a 3-month campaign on radio, television, and in-store advertising, at least 65,000 citizens of Salt Lake City had heard of precycling (reduction of garbage by choosing goods with minimal or recyclable packaging). However, there was no evidence of behavioral change. Similarly, there is some evidence from a longitudinal study conducted by three telephone surveys that a health promotion program increased nutrition knowledge, but possible change in health-related behaviors was not measured (Chew, Palmer, & Kim, 1995). These studies were carried out with adults, and learning and behavioral change are more likely to occur when the topic has an impact on one's personal life (see, for example, Layton, Jenkins, Macgill, & Davey, 1993). The same may well apply to school-age children.

Television and other means of visual communication are changing rapidly. Old programs do not go away—instead they are repackaged into videotapes, videodiscs, CD-ROMS, DVDs, online networks, and so on. Film and television have been revolutionized by digital technology and the increasing sophistication of computer animation. Science programming has changed accordingly. Rayl (1999) suggested that "an uneasy alliance has existed between science and television" (p. 8), partly because of a historic difficulty in communicating science to the lay public. He suggested that science's increasing need for public funding has resulted in the making of expensive, high-quality programs that try to present real science and scientists, such as *Life Beyond Earth*. A genre of television programs, such as *Walking with Dinosaurs* and *Walking with Beasts*, tells stories in documentary style about digitally created prehistoric animals. These series are expensive to make (*Walking with Beasts* cost €11 million), are usually produced by a consortium, and are immensely popular (European Research News Centre, 2002). However, critics have suggested that for the sake of drama, fact and fiction are blurred in such programs, and it is not made clear to viewers what is fact and what is assumption (McKie, 2001). Furthermore, opportunities are missed to capitalize on showing how science deals with uncertainties (Rose, 2001). Separating science from fiction in television and film can be a fruitful discussion topic in science classrooms (Allday, 2003).

Bennett (1997), then head of BBC Science, warned that although production methods were sophisticated, the understanding of qualitative evaluation methods was not. More reliance was placed on robust quantitative information about viewers' habits and demographics. Like museums, television competes for "visitors" (their viewers). Bennett described how the BBC had become more audience-focused in its program provision. She provided an illustrated history of science coverage on British television, concluding that "while it was once possible to criticize science programming as deferential and portraying a universally positive view of science, this is no longer the case. In the 1990s, some of the key features of science coverage on television are the search for relevance, a focus on the impact of breakthroughs and discoveries; and a concentration on process and the narrative when covering science in documentary format" (p. 63).

Nevertheless, Bennett argued, the challenges continue: how to tap the curiosity of the audience, increase the relevance of programming, exploit the increasing interactivity of television, and retain the ability to give a sense of excitement about science.

IMPLICATIONS FOR RESEARCH, EDUCATIONAL PRACTICE, AND POLICY

This chapter began with an exploration of the meaning of learning science in out-of-school settings. Our current understanding, underpinned by constructivist and sociocultural perspectives, suggests that learning is an ongoing, personal process, shaped by the context of the learning experience. Effective learning occurs when a person is motivated to participate in the learning experience, the context is socially and physically supportive, and the linking of new learning into the person's mental structures is facilitated. These factors must be kept in mind when one considers learning in any setting, including schools, and in drawing implications for research, practice, and policy.

Implications for Research into Learning Outside of School

Recognizing that learning is personal, contextualized, and takes time provides a framework for interpreting the research findings we have reported here and providing directions for the future. It is easy to understand why early research, with narrow views of learning, produced inconclusive and partial results. Research in out-of-school settings is difficult because of the free-choice nature of the learning experience and the need to retain its context. This makes it difficult to generalize research results to other contexts and settings, and in many areas research is sparse and will probably remain so for some time. The 12 factors of the Contextual Learning Model described earlier in this chapter (Falk & Dierking, 2000) are potentially useful in this regard. Together, these 12 factors describe and emphasize the complexity of learning in museums and other out-of-school contexts. Taking account of all of them simultaneously is a nearly impossible research task. More realistically, researchers tend to tackle one or more of the factors, remain cognizant of the others, and gradually build up a holistic picture of learning outside of school.

The NARST Ad Hoc Committee set the future research agenda for learning science in out-of-school contexts (Dierking et al., 2003; Rennie, Feher, Dierking, & Falk, 2003). Six areas were suggested for extending and enhancing research in out-of-school settings. First, to accommodate the personal, self-motivated, and voluntary nature of learning, research must examine the precursors to the actual engagement in learning as well as the learning itself. Second, the physical setting must be considered by taking into account the context where learning takes place. Third, research must continue to explore the social and cultural mediating factors in the learning experience. Fourth, longitudinal research designs are required to take account of the cumulative nature of learning. Fifth, research designs must be broadened to investigate the process of learning as well as the products. Finally, innovative approaches are needed to expand the range of methods and analyses used in research. Pursuing these avenues, particularly in non-museum settings, will expand our understanding of learning outside of school.

Implications for Practice and Policy

Out-of-school contexts are undeniable sources of learning for young people, and yet there seems to be little overlap there with what happens in school. Although, for the purpose of this chapter, agencies for learning outside of school have been discussed separately, they are not separate. Rather, they merge into one continuous experience in the out-of-school environment. Korpan, Bisanz, Bisanz, Boehme, and Lynch (1997) were surprised at Canadian students' high level of involvement in science-related activities outside of school and argued that teachers should not ignore it. In the United States, Dhingra (2003) urged educators to recognize that students bring with them into the classroom television-mediated understandings about science. In England, Mayoh and Knutton (1997) observed science lessons and noted that out-of-school experiences were mentioned, on average, only once or twice a lesson, and that teachers rarely built on experiences volunteered by students. And in Botswana, Koosimile (2004) found a similar situation. In both developed and developing countries, it seems that teachers place emphasis on science concepts rather than on what students know about science and how they experience it in their everyday lives. Yet there are clear benefits for learning when teachers make use of their students' out-of-school experiences, not the least of which is capitalizing on students' interests.

The challenge for educators and policy makers is to forge closer links between formal science education and out-of-school learning. They are, as Bybee (2001) pointed out, "two components of one inclusive education system" (p. 49). Instead of quarantining school science from life outside of schools, we need to bring them together in mutually supportive ways. This review has touched on some avenues for improvement.

First, teachers can maximize the opportunities to learn from the wealth of resources available beyond the classroom door. For example, teachers can capitalize on popular media by bringing them into their classes. Freudenrich (2000) described how he uses science fiction novels, films, and television programs extensively in his physics class to motivate and maintain the interest of his students. Brake and Thornton (2003) prepared their science and science fiction degree course in a Welsh university as "a way of examining the relationship between science, technology and society" (p. 32).

Second, the evidence for learning from well-structured field trips is so strong that they should be integral to each year's science program. Research on field trips consistently concludes that effective field trips complement the in-school curriculum. Guidelines discussed earlier focused on the need for teachers to plan jointly with students and venue staff, incorporate pre-visit instruction, conduct a flexible but focused visit where students have independence and responsibility, and make use of organized, post-visit reflection. This structure has the best chance of effecting learning because it exploits the personal, contextual, and cumulative nature of learning. Furthermore, school administrators should ensure that teachers have adequate time to plan field trips, and that organizational and timetable barriers are minimized.

Third, preservice teacher education can be enhanced by experiences outside of the lecture rooms. Thirunarayanan (1997) found that preservice teachers benefited from something as simple as investigating the learning potential of a community-based science resource. In Taiwan, Chin (2004) built a semester-long course around museum visits and associated lesson planning by preservice science teachers. Participants learned science content and ways to teach it and became more willing to use a variety of resources and became aware of the importance of using different ways to assess learning outcomes. Museums are places where learning through inquiry is natural (Bybee, 2001). Especially for elementary school teachers, whose science background is often limited, they provide opportunities to learn science and to learn how to teach science in ways consistent with temporary science curricula

(Ault & Herrick, 1991; Kelly, 2000; Kelly et al., 2002). These experiences can help new teachers to feel confident and thus do more to blur the boundary between the classroom and the outside world.

Fourth, the interface between museum programs and the science curriculum is dynamic, and museum educators and interpreters, many of whom are volunteers, need support to "keep up" with educational change. Science curricula in many countries over the last decade have moved from a content focus to active inquiry, with desired outcomes much broader than increased knowledge. For example, Cox-Petersen et al. (2003) discussed the mismatch between the inquiry approach espoused by the National Science Education Standards and lecture-centered, docent-led tours. They proposed an alternative tour that focused more on inquiry learning, even in traditional galleries. Bybee and Legro (1997) pointed out the importance of museum educators using the Standards to build collaborative partnerships to improve science education, and provided examples of how this might be done. Museums, too, have recognized the opportunities provided by the new curricula to contribute to learning in science and the concomitant need to ensure appropriate training for museum professionals (Cordell, 2000; Diamond, 2000; Yorath, 1995). Lederman and Niess (1998) provided an educator's view of the urgent need for such training.

Fifth, out-of-school agencies must not shirk their role in educating community members about controversial social and scientific issues, such as global sustainability, genetically modified products, biotechnology, and so on. Pedretti's (2004) analysis of critical science exhibitions demonstrated that people's understanding of such issues can be increased, yet there remains reluctance to engage with them. From a scientist's point of view, Rose (2001) was critical of the media's role in purveying science:

> Science and technology permeate every aspect of our lives. Yet the media—BBC and newspapers alike—tend to put them into a separate box, labeled 'Science' with a capital S, parked somewhere beyond the [C. P.] Snow-line. Of course we need our dedicated programs, but if we are ever to move towards a sense of the natural and social sciences and the humanities as part of a seamless cultural web, we need to open that box and spread its contents around. (p. 118)

In order to spread those contents effectively, ways must be found to situate science in its sociocultural context—a challenge indeed for the creators of museum exhibitions, media presentations, and other out-of-school programs.

This chapter began with a plea from S. Anderson (1968) to recognize the influence of those nonschool agencies that educate our communities. These agencies form part of what has been described as the community infrastructure for science learning (Falk, 2001). Together they provide an enormous infrastructure, but not a cohesive one, with links among individual components ephemeral and ad hoc, rather than consistent and institutionalized (Luke, Camp, Dierking, & Pearce, 2001). Nevertheless, there are powerful learning opportunities available, but these diverse and pervasive sources of science learning remain, on the whole, under-researched and under-used in science teaching. Educators in schools and universities cannot ignore them while the research gets done. Instead, the value of learning science outside of school should be recognized and its benefits harnessed to complement our formal educational programs.

ACKNOWLEDGMENTS

Thanks to Lynn Dierking and John Gilbert, who reviewed this chapter.

REFERENCES

Adams, M., Luke, J., & Moussouri, T. (2004). Interactivity: Moving beyond terminology. *Curator,* *47,* 155–170.

Adelman, L. M., Falk, J. H., & James, S. (2000). Impact of the National Aquarium in Baltimore on visitors' conservation attitudes, behavior and knowledge. *Curator, 43,* 33–61.

Allday, J. (2003). Science in science fiction. *Physics Education, 38*(1), 27–30.

Allen, S. (2004). Designs for learning: Studying science museum exhibits that do more than entertain. *Science Education, 88*(Suppl. 1), S17–S33.

Allen, S., & Gutwill, J. (2004). Designing with multiple interactives: Five common pitfalls. *Curator,* *47,* 199–212.

Alt, M. B., & Shaw, K. M. (1984). Characteristics of ideal museum exhibits. *British Journal of Psychology, 75,* 25–36.

American Association of Museums. (1992). *Excellence and equity: Education and the public dimension of museums.* Washington, DC: Author.

Anderson, D. (2003). Visitors' long-term memories of world expositions. *Curator, 46,* 401–420.

Anderson, D., Lucas, K. B., & Ginns, I. S. (2003). Theoretical perspectives on learning in an informal setting. *Journal of Research in Science Teaching, 40,* 177–199.

Anderson, D., Lucas, K. B., Ginns, I. S, & Dierking, L. D. (2000). Development of knowledge about electricity and magnetism during a visit to a science museum and related post-visit activities. *Science Education, 84,* 658–679.

Anderson, M. L. (1999). Museums of the future: The impact of technology on museum practices. *Daedalus, 128,* 129–162.

Anderson, S. (1968). Noseprints on the glass or how do we evaluate museum programs? In E. Larrabee (Ed.), *Museums and education* (pp. 115–126). Washington, DC: Smithsonian Institute Press.

Ash, D. (2003). Dialogic inquiry in the life science conversations of family groups in a museum. *Journal of Research in Science Teaching, 40,* 138–162.

Association of Science-Technology Centers. (n.d.). *Highlights. ASTC Sourcebook of Science Center Statistics 2001.* Washington, DC: Author. Retrieved May 20, 2004, from http://www.astc.org/resource/case/sourcebook.pdf

Astin, C., Fisher, N., & Taylor, B. (2002). Finding physics in the real world: How to teach physics effectively with visits. *Physics Education, 37*(1), 18–24.

Ault, C. R., Jr., & Herrick, J. (1991). Integrating teacher education about science learning with evaluation studies of science museum exhibits. *Journal of Science Teacher Education, 2,* 101–105.

Barrett, R. E. (1965). Field trip tips. *Science and Children, 3*(2), 19–20.

Barriault, C. (1999, March/April). The science center learning experience: A visitor-based framework. *The Informal Learning Review, 35,* 1, 14–16.

Beardsley, D. G. (1975). Helping teachers to use museums. *Curator, 18,* 192–199.

Bennett, J. (1997). Science on television: A coming of age? In G. Farmelo & J. Carding (Eds.), *Here and now: Contemporary science and technology in museums and science centers* (pp. 51–64). London: Science Museum.

Birney, B. A. (1988). Criteria for successful museum and zoo visits: Children offer guidance. *Curator, 31,* 292–316.

Bitgood, S. (1988). *A comparison of formal and informal learning* (Tech. Rep. No. 88-10). Jacksonville, AL: Centre for Social Design.

Bitgood, S. (1991, January/February). What do we know about school field trips? *ASTC News-letter*, 5–6, 8.

Bodzin, A. M., & Cates, W. M. (2002). Inquiry dot com. *The Science Teacher, 69*(9), 48–52.

Borun, M., Chambers, M., & Cleghorn, A. (1996). Families are learning in science museums. *Curator, 39*, 123–138.

Borun, M., Chambers, M. B., Dritsas, J., & Johnson, J. (1997). Enhancing family learning through exhibits. *Curator, 40*, 279–295.

Borun, M., & Dritsas, J. (1997). Developing family-friendly exhibits. *Curator, 40*, 178–196.

Bradburne, J. M. (2000). Tracing our routes: Museological strategies for the 21st century. In B. Schiele & E. H. Koster (Eds.), *Science centers for this century* (pp. 35–85). Québec, Canada: Éditions MultiMondes.

Bradburne, J. M. (2001). A new strategic approach to the museum and its relationship to society. *Museum Management and Curatorship, 19*, 75–84.

Bradford, B., & Rice, D. (1996). And now, the virtual field trip. *Museum News, 75*(5), 30, 76–78.

Brake, M., & Thornton, R. (2003). Science fiction in the classroom. *Physics Education, 38*(1), 31–34.

Brody, M., Tomkiewicz, W., & Graves, J. (2002). Park visitors' understanding, values and beliefs related to their experience at Midway Geyser Basin, Yellowstone National Park, USA. *International Journal of Science Education, 24*, 1119–1141.

Brown, C. (1995). Making the most of family visits: Some observations of parents with children in a museum science centre. *Museum Management and Curatorship, 14*(1), 65–71.

Brown, J. S., Collins, A., & Duguid, P. (1989). Situated cognition and the culture of learning. *Educational Researcher, 18*(1), 32–42.

Bybee, R. W. (2001). Achieving scientific literacy: Strategies for insuring that free choice science education complements national formal science education efforts. In J. H. Falk (Ed.), *Free-choice education: How we learn science outside of school* (pp. 44–63). New York: Teachers College Press.

Bybee, R. W., & Legro, P. (1997). Finding synergy with science museums: Introduction to the National Science Education Standards. *ASTC Newsletter, 25*(2), 6–7.

Byrne, P. F., Namuth, D. M., Harrington, J., Ward, S. M., Lee, D. J., & Hain, P. (2002). Increasing public understanding of transgenic crops through the worldwide web. *Public Understanding of Science, 11*, 293–304.

Carter, J. C. (1990). Writing a museum education policy. *Journal of Education in Museums, 11*, 26–29.

Champagne, D. W. (1975). The Ontario Science Center in Toronto: Some impressions and some questions. *Educational Technology, 15*(8), 36–39.

Chen, M. (1994). Televisions and informal science education: Assessing the past, present, and future of research. In V. Crane, H. Nicholson, M. Chen, & S. Bitgood (Eds.), *Informal science learning: What research says about television, science museums, and community—based projects* (pp. 15–59). Dedham, MA: Research Communications.

Chew, F., Palmer, S., & Kim, S. (1995). Sources of information and knowledge about health and nutrition: Can viewing one television program make a difference? *Public Understanding of Science, 4*, 17–29.

Chin, C.-C. (2004). Museum experience—A resource for science teacher education. *International Journal of Science and Mathematics Education, 2*, 63–90.

Cordell, L. S. (2000). Finding the natural interface: Graduate and public education at one university natural history museum. *Curator, 43*, 111–121.

Cox-Petersen, A. M., Marsh, D. D., Kisiel, J., & Melber, L. M. (2003). Investigation of guided school tours, student learning, and science reform recommendations at a museum of natural history. *Journal of Research in Science Teaching, 40*, 200–218.

Crane, V., Nicholson, H., Chen, M., & Bitgood, S. (Eds.). (1994). *Informal science learning: What research says about television, science museums, and community-based projects*. Dedham, MA: Research Communication.

Crowley, K., & Callanan, M. A. (1998). Identifying and supporting shared scientific reasoning in parent-child interactions. *Journal of Museum Education, 23*, 12–17.

Crowley, K., Callanan, M. A., Jipson, J. L., Galco, J., Topping, K., & Shrager, J. (2001). Shared scientific thinking in everyday parent-child activity. *Science Education, 85*, 712–732.

Crowley, K., & Galco, J. (2001). Everyday activity and the development of scientific thinking. In K. Crowley, C. D. Schunn, & T. Okada (Eds.), *Designing for science: Implications from everyday, classroom, and professional settings* (pp. 393–413). Mahwah, NJ: Lawrence Erlbaum Associates.

Csikzentmihályi, M., & Hermanson, K. (1995). Intrinsic motivation in museums: Why does one want to learn? In J. H. Falk & L. D. Dierking (Eds.), *Public institutions for personal learning: Establishing a research agenda* (pp. 67–77). Washington, DC: American Association of Museums.

Department for Culture, Media and Sport. (2000). *The learning power of museums: A visions for museum education.* London: Author.

Dhingra, K. (2003). Thinking about television science: How students understand the nature of science from different program genres. *Journal of Research in Science Teaching, 40*, 234–256

Diamond, J. (1986). The behavior of family groups in science museums. *Curator, 29*, 139–154.

Diamond, J. (1996). Playing and learning. *ASTC Newsletter, 24*(4), 2–6.

Diamond, J. (2000). Moving toward innovation: Informal science education in university natural history museums. *Curator, 43*, 93–102.

Diamond, J., St. John, M., Cleary, B., & Librero, D. (1987). The Exploratorium's explainers program: The long term impacts on teenagers of teaching science to the public. *Science Education, 71*, 643–656.

Dierking, L. D. (2002). The role of context in children's learning from objects and experiences. In S. G. Paris (Ed.), *Multiple perspectives on children's object-centered learning* (pp. 3–18). New York: Lawrence Erlbaum Associates.

Dierking, L. D., Ellenbogen, K. M., & Falk, J. H. (Eds.). (2004). In principle, in practice: Perspectives on a decade of museum learning research (1994–2004). *Science Education, 88*(Suppl. 1).

Dierking, L. D., & Falk, J. H. (1994). Family behavior and learning in informal science settings: A review of research. *Science Education, 78*, 57–72.

Dierking, L. D., & Falk, J. H. (2003, Spring). Optimizing out-of-school time: The role of free-choice learning. *New Directions for Youth Development, 97*, 75–88.

Dierking, L. D., Falk, J. H., Rennie, L., Anderson, D., & Ellenbogen, K. (2003). Policy statement of the "Informal Science Education" Ad Hoc Committee. *Journal of Research in Science Teaching, 40*, 108–111.

Dierking, L. D., & D. Martin, L. M. W. (Eds.). (1997). Informal science education [Special issue]. *Science Education, 81*(6).

Driver, R., & Bell, B. (1986). Students' thinking and the learning of science: A constructivist view. *School Science Review, 67*, 443–456.

Duit, R., & Treagust, D. F. (1998). Learning in science—From behaviorism toward social constructivism and beyond. In B. J. Fraser & K. G. Tobin (Eds.), *International handbook of research in science education* (pp. 3–2). Dordrecht, the Netherlands: Kluwer Academic.

Eccles, J. S., & Templeman, J. (2002). Extracurricular and other after-school activities for youth. *Review of Research in Education, 26*, 113–180.

Ellenbogen, K. M. (2002). Museums in family life: An ethnographic case study. In G. Leinhardt, K. Crowley, & K. Knutson (Eds.), *Learning conversations in museums* (pp. 81–101). Mahwah, NJ: Lawrence Erlbaum Associates.

Ellenbogen, K. M., Luke, J. J., & Dierking, L. D. (2004). Family learning research in museums: An emerging disciplinary matrix? *Science Education, 88*(Suppl. 1), S48–S58.

European Research News Centre. (2002). *The secret of small screen success.* Retrieved May 22, 2003, from http://europa.eu.int/comm/research/news-centre/en/soc/02-09-special-soc05.html

Exploratorium. (n.d.). *Fact sheet 2003–04.* Retrieved May 27, 2004 from http://www.exploratorium.edu/about/fact_sheet.html

Falcão, D., Colinvaux, D., Krapas, S., Querioz, G., Alves, F., Cazelli, S., et al. (2004). A model-based approach to science exhibition evaluation: A case study in a Brazilian astronomy museum. *International Journal of Science Education, 26*, 951–978.

Falk, J. H. (1998). Visitors: Who does, who doesn't, and why. *Museum News, 77*(2), 38–43.

Falk, J. H. (Ed.). (2001). *Free-choice science education: How we learn science outside of schools.* New York: Teachers College Press.

Falk, J. H., & Dierking, L. D. (1992). *The museum experience.* Washington, DC: Whalesback Books.

Falk, J. H., & Dierking, L. D. (1995). *Public institutions for personal learning: Establishing a research agenda.* Washington, DC: American Association of Museums.

Falk, J. H., & Dierking, L. D. (1997). School field trips: Assessing the long term impact. *Curator, 40*, 211–218.

Falk, J. H., & Dierking, L. D. (2000). *Learning from museums: Visitor experiences and the making of meaning.* Walnut Creek, CA: Altamira Press.

Falk, J. H., Koran, J. J., Jr., & Dierking, L. D. (1986). The things of science: Assessing the learning potential of science museums. *Science Education, 70*, 503–508.

Falk, J., Moussouri, T., & Coulson, D. (1998). The effect of visitors' agendas on museum learning. *Curator, 41*, 107–120.

Falk, J. H., Scott, C., Dierking, L., Rennie, L., & Jones, M. C. (2004). Interactives and visitor learning. *Curator, 47*, 171–198.

Fara, P. (1994). Understanding science museums. *Museums Journal, 94*(12), 25.

Feher, E., & Diamond, J. (1990, January/February). Science centers as research laboratories. *ASTC Newsletter*, 7–8.

Fisch, S. M., Yotive, W., Brown, S. K. M., Garner, M. S., & Chen, L. (1997). Science on Saturday morning: Children's perceptions of science in educational and non-educational cartoons. *Journal of Educational Media, 23*, 157–167.

Freudenrich, C. C. (2000). Sci-fi science. *The Science Teacher, 67*(8), 42–45.

Friedman, A. J. (1995). Exhibits and expectations. *Public Understanding of Science, 4*, 305–313.

Gammon, B. (1999, September/October). Visitors' use of computer exhibits: Findings from 5 grueling years of watching visitors getting it wrong. *Informal Learning Review, 38, 1*, 10–13.

Gammon, B. (2002). *Assessing learning in museum environments: A practical guide for museum evaluators.* London: The Science Museum.

Gardner, H. (1993). *Multiple intelligences: The theory in practice.* New York: Basic Books.

Garnett, R. (2003). *Reaching all Australians.* Kingston, ACT, Australia: National Reference Group.

Garvey, C. (1991). *Play* (2nd ed.). London: Fontana.

Gascoigne, T., & Metcalfe, J. (2001). Report: The evaluation of national programs of science awareness. *Science Communication, 23*, 66–76.

Gibson, H. M., & Francis, L. J. (1993). The relationship between television viewing preferences and interest in science among 11–25-year-olds. *Research in Science and Technological Education, 11*, 185–190.

Gilbert, J. K. (2001). Towards a unified model of education and entertainment in science centers. In S. Stocklmayer, M. Gore, & C. Bryant (Eds.), *Science communication in theory and practice* (pp. 123–142). Dordrecht, the Netherlands: Kluwer Academic.

Gilbert, J., & Priest, M. (1997). Models and discourse: A primary school science class visit to a museum. *Science Education, 81*, 749–762.

Gillilan, S., Werner, C. M., Olson, L., & Adams, D. (1996). Teaching the concept of precycling: A campaign and evaluation. *The Journal of Environmental Education, 28*, 11–18.

Goldman, S. R., & Bisanz, G. L. (2002). Toward a functional analysis of scientific genres: Implications for understanding and learning processes. In J. Otero, J. A. Léon, & A. C. Graesser (Eds.), *The psychology of science text comprehension* (pp. 19–50). Mahwah, NJ: Lawrence Erlbaum Associates.

Gottfried, J. L. (1980). Do children learn on school field trips? *Curator, 23*, 165–174.

Greene, J. C., Caracelli, V. J., & Graham, W. F. (1989). Toward a conceptual framework for mixed-method evaluation designs. *Educational Evaluation and Policy Analysis, 11*, 255–274.

Griffin, J. (1998). Learning science through practical experiences in museums. *International Journal of Science Education, 20*, 655–663.

Griffin, J. (1999). Finding evidence of learning in museum settings. In E. Scanlon, E. Whitelegg, & S. Yates (Eds.), *Communicating science: Contexts and channels* (pp. 110–119). London: Routledge.

Griffin, J. (2004). Research on students and museums: Looking more closely at the students in school groups. *Science Education, 88*(Suppl. 1), S59–S70.

Griffin, J., & Symington, D. (1997). Moving from task-oriented to learning-oriented strategies on school excursions to museums. *Science Education, 81*, 763–779.

Hawkey, R. (2001). The science of nature and the nature of science: Natural history museums on-line. *Electronic Journal of Science Education, 5*(4). Retrieved August 28, 2001, from http://unr.edu/homepage/crowther/ejse/hawkey.html

Hawkins, D. (1965). Messing about in science. *Science and Children, 2*(5), 5–9.

Hein, G. E. (1998). *Learning in the museum.* London: Routledge.

Hilke, D. D., & Balling, J. D. (1985). The family as a learning system: An observational study of family behavior in an information rich setting. In J. D. Balling, D. D. Hilke, J. D. Liversidge, E. A. Cornell, & N. S. Perry (Eds.), *Role of the family in the promotion of science literacy.* Final Report for National Science Foundation Grant no. SED-81-12927 (pp. 60–104). Washington, DC: National Science Foundation.

Hodder, A. P. W. (1997). Science-technology centers in science education in New Zealand. In B. Bell & R. Baker (Eds.), *Developing the science curriculum in AOTEAROA, New Zealand* (pp. 141–155). Sydney, Australia: Longman.

Hofstein, A., & Rosenfeld, S. (1996). Bridging the gap between formal and informal science learning. *Studies in Science Education, 29*, 87–112.

Hutt, C. (1970). Curiosity and young children. *Science Journal, 6*(2), 68–71.

Hutt, C. (1981). Toward a taxonomy and conceptual model of play. In H. I. Day (Ed.), *Advances in intrinsic motivation and aesthetics* (pp. 251–298). New York: Plenum Press.

Institute of Museum and Library Services. (2002). Status of technology and digitization in the nations museums and libraries 2002 report. Retrieved October 5, 2004, from http://www.imls.gov/reports/techreports/summary02.htm

Institute of Museum and Library Services. (n.d.). *True needs true partners: Museums serving schools. 2002 survey highlights.* Retrieved May 13, 2004 from http://www.imls.gov/pubs/pdf/m-ssurvey.pdf

International Academy for Digital Arts and Sciences (2004). *The webbys.* Retrieved May 28, 2004, from http://www.webbyawards.com/main/webby_awards/top

International Council of Museums. (2001). *Development of the Museum Definition according to ICOM Statutes (1946–2001).* Retrieved December 28, 2003 from http://icom.museum/hist_def_eng.html

Inverness Research Associates. (1996). *An invisible infrastructure: Institutions of informal science education* (Vol. 1). Washington, DC: ASTC.

Jamison, E. D. (1998). *Field trip qualitative research.* St Paul, MN: Science Museum of Minnesota.

Johnston, D., & Rennie, L. (1995) Perceptions of visitors' learning at an interactive science and technology centre in Australia. *Museum Management and Curatorship, 14*, 317–325.

Katz, P. (1996). Parents as teachers. *Science and Children, 33*(10), 47–49.

Katz, P. (2000). HOSO: Play, practice, parents and time. In P. Katz (Ed.), *Community connection for science education* (Vol. 2, pp. 55–61). Washington, DC: NSTA Press.

Katz, P., & McGinnis, J. R. (1999). An informal elementary science education program's response to the national science education reform movement. *Journal of Elementary Science Education, 11*(1), 1–15.

Kelly, J. (2000). Rethinking the elementary science methods course: A case for content, pedagogy, and informal science education. *International Journal of Science Education, 22*, 755–777.

Kelly, J., Stetson, R., & Powell-Mikel, A. (2002). Science adventures at the local museum. *Science and Children, 39*(7), 46–48.

Kelly, L., Savage, G., Griffin, J., & Tonkin, S. (2004). *Knowledge quest: Australian families visit museums.* Sydney, Australia: Australian Museum and the National Museum of Australia.

Kennedy, J. (1994). *User friendly: Hands-on exhibits that work.* Washington, DC: Association of Science-Technology Centers.

Klugman, E., & Smilansky, S. (1990). *Children's play and learning: Perspectives and policy implications.* New York: Teachers College Press.

Koosimile, A. T. (2004). Out-of-school experiences in science classes: Problems, issues and challenges in Botswana. *International Journal of Science Education, 26,* 483–496.

Korpan, C. A., Bisanz, G. L., Bisanz, J., Boehme, C., & Lynch, M. A. (1997). What did you learn outside of school today? Using structured interviews to document home and community activities relating to science. *Science Education, 81,* 651–662.

Koster, E. H. (1999). In search of relevance: Science centers as innovators in the evolution of museums. *Daedalus, 128,* 277–296.

Lave, J., & Wenger, E. (1991). *Situated learning: Legitimate peripheral participation.* Cambridge, England: Cambridge University Press.

Layton, D., Jenkins, E., Macgill, S., & Davey, A. (1993). *Inarticulate science? Perspectives on the public understanding of science and some implications for science education.* Nafferton, England: Studies in Education.

Lederman, N. G., & Niess, M. L. (1998). How informed are informal educators? *School Science and Mathematics, 98,* 1–3.

Leinhardt, G., Crowley, K., & Knutson, K. (Eds.). (2002). *Learning conversations in museums.* Mahwah, NJ: Lawrence Erlbaum Associates.

Leinhardt, G., Knutson, K., & Crowley, K. (2003). Museum learning collaborative redux. *Journal of Museum Education, 28*(1), 23–31.

Lemerise, T. (1995). The role and place of adolescents in museums: Yesterday and today. *Museum Management and Curatorship, 14,* 393–408.

Lewenstein, B. V. (2001). Who produces science information for the public? In J. H. Falk (Ed.), *Free-choice education: How we learn science outside of school* (pp. 21–43). New York: Teachers College Press.

Long, M., & Steinke, J. (1996). The thrill of everyday science: Images of science and scientist on children's educational science programs in the United States. *Public Understanding of Science, 5,* 101–119.

Lucas, A. M. (1983). Scientific literacy and informal learning. *Studies in Science Education, 10,* 1–36.

Lucas, A. M. (1991). "Info-tainment" and informal sources for learning in science. *International Journal of Science Education, 13,* 495–504.

Lucas, A. M., McManus, P., & Thomas, G. (1986). Investigating learning from informal sources: Listening to conversations and observing play in science museums. *European Journal of Science Education, 8,* 341–352.

Luke, J. J., Camp, B. D., Dierking, L. D., & Pearce, U. J. (2001). The first free-choice science learning conference: From issues to future directions. In J. H. Falk (Ed.), *Free-choice education: How we learn science outside of school* (pp. 151–162). New York: Teachers College Press.

Mann, D. (1996). Serious play. *Teachers College Record, 97,* 446–469.

Mares, M., Cantor, J., & Steinbach, J. B. (1999). Using television to foster children's interest in science. *Science Communication, 20,* 283–297.

Martin, D. (1996). Outreach by museums and galleries. *Museum Practice, 1*(3), 36–77.

Mason, J. L. (1980). Annotated bibliography of field trip research. *School Science and Mathematics, 80,* 155–166.

Matarasso, F. (1996). Reconnecting audiences: The evaluation of museum outreach work. *Museum Practice, 1*(3), 40–43

Mathison, S. (1988). Why triangulate? *Educational Researcher, 17*(2), 13–17.

Matusov, E., & Rogoff, B. (1995). Evidence of development from people's participation in communities of learners. In J. H. Falk & L. D. Dierking (Eds.), *Public institutions for personal learning: Establishing a research agenda* (pp. 97–104). Washington, DC: American Association of Museums.

Mayoh, K., & Knutton, S. (1997). Using out-of-school experience in science lessons: Reality or rhetoric? *International Journal of Science Education, 19,* 849–867

McKie, R. (2001, November 11). BBC walks into a storm over natural history lessons. *The Observer.* Retrieved May 22, 2003, from http://www.observer.co.uk/uk_news/story/0,6903,591412,00 .html

McLean, K. (1993). *Planning for people in museum exhibitions.* Washington, DC: Association of Science-Technology Centers.

McManus, P. M. (1992). Topics in museums and science education. *Studies in Science Education, 20,* 157–182.

McManus, P. M. (1993). Thinking about the visitor's thinking. In S. Bicknell & G. Farmelo (Eds.), *Museum visitor studies in the 90's* (pp. 108–113). London: Science Museum.

McManus, P. M. (1994). Families in museums. In R. Miles & L. Zavala (Eds.), *Towards the museum of the future: New European perspectives* (pp. 81–97). London: Routledge.

McSharry, G., & Jones, S. (2002). Television programs and advertisements: Help or hindrance to effective science education? *International Journal of Science Education, 24,* 487–497.

Medved, M. I., & Oatley, K. (2000). Memories and scientific literacy: Remembering exhibits from a science center. *International Journal of Science Education, 22,* 1117–1132.

Melber, L. M. (2003). Partnerships in science learning: Museum outreach and elementary gifted education. *Gifted Child Quarterly, 47,* 251–258.

Melber, L. M., & Abraham, L. M. (2002). Science education in U.S. natural history museums: A historical perspective. *Science and Education, 11,* 45–54.

Melton, A. W., Feldman, N. G., & Mason, C. W. (1988). *Experimental studies of the education of children in a museum of science.* Washington, DC: American Association of Museums (original work published 1936).

Michie, M. (1998). Factors influencing secondary school teachers to organize field trips. *Australian Science Teachers Journal, 44*(4), 43–50.

Miles, R. S. (1986). Lessons in "human biology" testing a theory of exhibit design. *The International Journal of Museum Management and Curatorship, 5,* 227–240.

Miles, R. S., Alt, M. B., Gosling, D. C., Lewis, B. N., & Tout, A. F. (1988). Designing and carrying out the evaluation study. In R. S. Miles, M. B. Alt, D. C. Gosling, B. N. Lewis, & A. F. Tout (Eds.), *The design of educational exhibits* (pp. 144–170). London: Unwin Hyman.

Miles, R. S., & Tout, A. F. (1994). Outline of a technology for effective science exhibits. In E. Hooper-Greenhill (Ed.), *The educational role of the museum* (pp. 87–100). London: Routledge (reprinted from *Curation of Palaeontological Collections: Special Papers in Palaeontology, 22*(1979), 209–224).

Molella, A. P. (1999). *Science in American Life,* national identity and the science wars: A curator's view. *Curator, 42,* 108–116.

National Research Council. (1996). *National science education standards.* Washington, DC: National Academy Press.

National Science Teachers Association. (1998). Position statement: Informal science education. *Science and Children, 35*(8), 30–31.

Nicholson, H. J., Weiss, F., & Campbell, P. B. (1994). Evaluation in informal science education: Community-based programs. In V. Crane, H. Nicholson, M. Chen, & S. Bitgood (Eds.), *Informal science learning: What research says about television, science museums, and community-based projects* (pp. 15–59). Dedham, MA: Research Communications.

Nyhof-Young, J. (1996). Learning science in an alternative context: The effects on a selected group of young science educators. *Journal of Science Education and Technology, 5,* 69–75.

Oppenheimer, F. (1968). A rationale for a science museum. *Curator, 11,* 206–209.

Orion, N. (1989). Development of a high-school geology course based on field trips. *Journal of Geological Education, 37*, 13–17.

Paris, S. G., Yambor, K. M., & Packard, B. W. (1998). Hands-on biology: A museum-school-university partnership for enhancing students' interest and learning in science. *The Elementary School Journal, 98*, 267–288.

Parkyn, M. (1993). Scientific imaging. *Museums Journal, 93*(10), 29–34.

Pedretti, E. (1999). Decision making and STS education: Exploring scientific knowledge and social responsibility in schools and science centers through an issues-based approach. *School Science and Mathematics, 99*, 174–181.

Pedretti, E. (2002). T. Kuhn meets T. rex: Critical conversations and new directions in science centers and science museums. *Studies in Science Education, 37*, 1–42.

Pedretti, E. (2004). Perspectives on learning through critical issued-based science center exhibits. *Science Education, 88*(Suppl. 1), S34–S47.

Pedretti, E., & Forbes, J. (2000). A question of truth: Critiquing the culture and practice of science through science centers and schools. In D. Hodson (Ed.), *OISE Papers in STSE Education* (Vol. 1, pp. 91–110). Toronto: University of Toronto Press.

Pedretti, E., Macdonald, R. D., Gitari, W., & McLaughlin, H. (2001). Visitor perspectives on the nature and practice of science: Challenging beliefs through *A Question of Truth. Canadian Journal of Science, Mathematics and Technology Education, 1*, 399–418.

Pedretti, E., & Soren, B. J. (2003). *A Question of Truth*: A cacophony of visitor voices. *Journal of Museum Education, 28*(3), 17–20.

Perry, D. L. (1989). The creation and verification of a development model for the design of a museum exhibit. (Doctoral dissertation, Indiana University, 1989). *Dissertation Abstracts International, 50*, 3296.

Prather, J. P. (1989). Review of the value of field trips in science instruction. *Journal of Elementary Science Education, 1*(1), 10–11.

Puchner, L., Rapoport, R., & Gaskins, S. (1997, March). *Children and museum-based learning: A study of what and how young children learn in children's museums.* Paper presented at the annual meeting of the American Education Research Association, Chicago, IL.

Ramey-Gassert, L. (1997). Learning science beyond the classroom. *The Elementary School Journal, 97*, 433–450.

Ramey-Gassert, L., Walberg, H. J., III, & Walberg, H. J. (1994). Reexamining connections: Museums as science learning environments. *Science Education, 78*, 345–363.

Ravest, J. (1993, Summer). Where is the science in science centers? *ECSITE Newsletter*, 10–11.

Rayl, A. J. S. (1999). Science on TV. *The Scientist, 13*(21), 8.

Rennie, L. J. (1994). Measuring affective outcomes form a visit to a science education centre. *Research in Science Education, 24*, 261–269.

Rennie, L. J. (1998). Capacity building in science: Support the vision, renounce the tabula rasa. *Studies in Science Education, 31*, 119–129.

Rennie, L. J. (2001). Communicating science through interactive science centers: A research perspective. In S. Stocklmayer, M. Gore, & C. Bryant (Eds.), *Science communication in theory and practice* (pp. 107–121). Dordrecht, the Netherlands: Kluwer Academic.

Rennie, L. J., & The Australian Science Teachers Association. (2003). *The ASTA Science Awareness Raising Model: An evaluation report prepared for the Department of Education Science and Training.* Canberra, Australia: ASTA.

Rennie, L. J., & Feher, E. (Eds.). (2003). Informal education [Special issue]. *Journal of Research in Science Teaching, 40*(2).

Rennie, L. J., Feher, E., Dierking, L. D., & Falk, J. H. (2003). Toward an agenda for advancing research on science learning in out-of-school settings. *Journal of Research in Science Teaching, 40*, 112–120.

Rennie, L. J., & Johnston, D. (1997). What can floor staff tell us about visitor learning? *Museum National, 5*(4), 17–18.

Rennie, L. J., & Johnston, D. J. (2004). The nature of learning and its implications for research on learning from museums. *Science Education, 88*(Suppl. 1), S4–S16.

Rennie, L. J., & McClafferty, T. P. (1995). Using visits to interactive science and technology centers, museums, aquaria, and zoos to promote learning in science. *Journal of Science Teacher Education, 6*, 175–185.

Rennie, L. J., & McClafferty, T. P. (1996). Science centers and science learning. *Studies in Science Education, 22*, 53–98.

Rennie, L. J., & McClafferty, T. (1998). Young children's interaction with science exhibits. *Visitor Behavior, 12*(3–4), 26.

Rennie, L. J., & McClafferty, T. P. (2001). Visiting a science centre or museum? Make it a real educational experience. In S. Errington, S. M. Stocklmayer, & B. Honeyman (Eds.), *Using museums to popularize science and technology* (pp. 73–76). London: Commonwealth Secretariat.

Rennie, L. J., & McClafferty, T. P. (2002). Objects and learning: Understanding young children's interaction with science exhibits. In S. G. Paris (Ed.), *Multiple perspectives on children's object-centered learning* (pp. 191–213). New York: Lawrence Erlbaum Associates.

Rennie, L. J., & Williams, G. F. (2000). *Evaluation of the educational effectiveness of the Shell Questacon Science Circus program.* Perth, Western Australia: Key Centre for School Science and Mathematics, Curtin University of Technology.

Rennie, L. J., & Williams, G. F. (2002). Science centers and scientific literacy: Promoting a relationship with science. *Science Education, 86*, 706–726.

Resnick, L. B., Levine, J. M., & Teasley, S. D. (1991). *Perspectives on socially shared cognition.* Washington, DC: American Psychological Association.

Rickinson, M., Dillon, J., Teamey, K., Morris, M., Choi, M. Y., Sanders, D., et al. (2004). *A review of research on outdoor learning: Executive summary.* Retrieved September 13, 2004 from http://www.field-studies-council.org/documents/general/NFER/NFER%20Exec%20Summary.pdf

Roberts, L. (1989, September/October). The elusive qualities of "affect." *ASTC Newsletter*, 5–6.

Roberts, L. (1997). *From knowledge to narrative: Educators and the changing museum.* Washington, DC: Smithsonian Institution Press.

Robinson, E. S. (1928). *The behavior of the museum visitor* (New Series, No. 5). Washington, DC: American Association of Museums.

Roschelle, J. (1995). Learning in interactive environments: Prior knowledge and new experience. In J. H. Falk & L. D. Dierking (Eds.), *Public institutions for personal learning: Establishing a research agenda* (pp. 37–51). Washington, DC: American Association of Museums.

Rose, S. (2001). What sort of science broadcasting do we want for the 21st century? *Science as Culture, 10*(1), 113–119.

Sacks, O. (2001). *Uncle Tungsten: Memories of a chemical boyhood.* London: Picador.

Schauble, L., Leinhardt, G., & Martin, L. (1997). A framework for organizing a cumulative research agenda in informal learning contexts. *Journal of Museum Education, 22*(2&3), 3–8.

Schiele, B., & Koster, E. H. (2000). *Science centers for this century.* Québec, Canada: Éditions Multi-Mondes.

Scott, C. (2003). Museums and impact. *Curator, 46*, 293–310.

Screven, C. G. (1986). Exhibitions and information centers: Some principles and approaches. *Curator, 29*, 109–137.

Screven, C. G. (1990). Uses of evaluation before, during and after exhibit design. *ILVS Review, 1*(2), 36–66.

Scriven, M. (1967). *The methodology of evaluation.* AERA Monograph Series on Curriculum Evaluation (No. 1, pp. 39–83). Chicago: Rand McNally.

Semper, R. J. (1990). Science museums as environments for learning. *Physics Today, 43*(11), 50–56.

Semper, R. (2002). Nodes and connections: Science museums in the network age. *Curator, 45*, 13–20.

Semper, R., Wanner, N., & Jackson, R. (2000). *Who's out there? A pilot user study of educational web resources by the Science Learning Network (SLN).* Paper presented at Museums and the Web

2000 conference. Retrieved June 22, 2000, from http://www.archimuse.com/mw2000/papers/semper/semper.html

Serrell, B. (1990, March/April). Learning styles and museum visitors. *ASTC Newsletter*, 7–8.

Serrell, B. (2002). Are they watching? Visitors and videos in exhibitions. *Curator, 45*, 50–64.

Shields, C. J. (1993). Do science museums educate or just entertain? *The Education Digest, 58*(7), 69–72.

Shortland, M. (1987). No business like show business. *Nature, 328*, 213–214.

Silver, A. Z. (1978). The school in the Exploratorium. In B. Y. Newsom & A. Z. Silver (Eds.), *The art museum as educator*. San Francisco: University of California Press.

Smilansky, S. (1968). *The effects of socio-dramatic play on disadvantaged preschool children*. New York: Wiley & Sons.

Smith, D. A. (1999). Learning the web: Science magazine sites. *Journal of Computers in Mathematics and Science Teaching, 18*, 89–93.

Soren, B. (1995). Triangulation strategies and images of museums as sites for lifelong learning. *Museum Management and Curatorship, 14*, 31–46.

Sørensen, H., & Kofod, L. H. (2003, March). *School visits at science centers: It's fun, but is it learning?* Paper presented at the annual meeting of the National Association of Research in Science Teaching, Philadelphia, PA.

St. John, M. (1987). *An assessment of the school in the Exploratorium: A summary of findings*. Inverness, CA: Inverness Research Associates.

Stevenson, J. (1991). The long-term impact of interactive exhibits. *International Journal of Science Education, 13*, 521–531.

Stevenson, S. (2001). Let's get technical: Online learning opportunities for science education. *Multimedia Schools, 8*(6), 42–46.

Stocklmayer, S. M., & Gilbert, J. K. (2002). New experiences and old knowledge: Towards a model for the public awareness of science. *International Journal of Science Education, 24*, 835–858.

Streten, K. (2000). *Honored guests: Towards a visitor centered web experience*. Paper presented at Museums and the Web 2000 conference. Retrieved June 22, 2000, from http://www.archimuse.com/mw2000/papers/streten/streten.html

Sylva, K., Bruner, J. S., & Genova, P. (1976). The role of play in the problem-solving of children 3–5 years old. In J. S. Bruner, A. Jolly, & K. Sylva (Eds.), *Play—Its role in development and evolution* (pp. 244–257). New York: Basic Books.

Tam, K. Y., Nassivera, J. W., Rousseau, M. K., & Vreeland, P. (2000). More than just a field trip: Using the museum as a resource for inclusive science classrooms. *Teaching Exceptional Children, 33*, 70–78.

Thirunarayanan, M. O. (1997). Promoting preservice science teachers' awareness of community-based science education resource centers. *Journal of Science Teacher Education, 8*, 69–75.

Tofield, S., Coll, R. K., Vyle, B., & Bolstad, R. (2003). Zoos as a source of free-choice learning. *Research in Science and Technological Education, 21*(1), 67–99.

Torri, G. (1997). Museum partnerships. *Science Scope, 20*(6), 58–59.

Tremayne, M., & Dunwoody, S. (2001). Interactivity, information processing, and learning on the World Wide Web. *Science Communication, 23*, 111–134.

Tunnicliffe, S. (1996). The relationship between pupils' age and the content of conversations generated at three types of animal exhibits. *Research in Science Education, 26*, 461–480.

Tunnicliffe, S. D., Lucas, A. M., & Osborne, J. (1997). School visits to zoos and museums: A missed educational opportunity. *International Journal of Science Education, 19*, 1039–1056.

Turney, J. (1999). The word and the world: Engaging with science in print. In E. Scanlon, E. Whitelegg, & S. Yates (Eds.), *Communicating science: Context and channels* (pp. 120–133). London: Routledge in association with the Open University Press.

Uzzell, D. (1993). Contrasting psychological perspectives on exhibit evaluation. In S. Bicknell & G. Farmelo (Eds.), *Museum visitor studies in the 90s* (pp. 125–129). London: Science Museum.

Vygotsky, L. S. (1978). *Mind in society: The development of higher mental processes.* Cambridge, MA: Harvard University Press.

Walton, R. (2000). Heidegger in the hands-on science and technology center: Philosophical reflections on learning in informal setting. *Journal of Technology Education, 12*, 49–60.

Weil, S. E. (1999). From being about something to being for somebody: The ongoing transformation of the American museum. *Daedalus, 128*, 229–258.

Wellington, J. (1990). Formal and informal learning in science: The role of interactive science centers. *Physics Education, 25*, 247–252.

Wellington, J. (1998). Interactive science centers and science education. *Croner's Heads of Science Bulletin* (Issue 16). Kingston upon Thames, Surrey, England: Croner Publications.

Wolf, R. L. (1980). A naturalistic view of evaluation. *Museum News, 58*(6), 39–45.

Wright, J. C., Anderson, D. R., Huston, A. C., Collins, P. A., Schmitt, K. L., & Linebarger, D. L. (2001). The effects of early childhood TV-viewing on learning. In J. H. Falk (Ed.), *Free-choice science education* (pp. 79–92). New York: Teachers College Press.

Wymer, P. (1991, October 5). Never mind the science, feel the experience. *New Scientist, 132*(1789), 53.

Yorath, J. (1995). *Learning about science and technology in museums.* London: South Eastern Museum Service.

PART II

Culture, Gender,
Society, and
Science Learning

CHAPTER 7

Science Education and Student Diversity: Race/Ethnicity, Language, Culture, and Socioeconomic Status

Okhee Lee
University of Miami

Aurolyn Luykx
University of Texas, El Paso

Knowledge about science and technology is increasingly important in today's world. Aside from the growing number of professions that require a working familiarity with scientific concepts and high-tech tools, the future of our society hangs in the balance of decisions that must be made on the basis of scientific knowledge. Yet, the increasing diversity of the school-aged population, coupled with differential science performance among demographic groups, makes the goal of "science for all" a challenge for many nations.

Reform-oriented instructional practices hold the promise of more meaningful science learning but have yet to be widely implemented. All too often, teachers' knowledge of science and/or student diversity is insufficient to guide students from diverse backgrounds toward meaningful science learning. Limited resources often force a trade-off between providing modified instruction that takes student diversity into account and reinforcing general standards to raise the quality of instruction for mainstream students (often to the detriment of other student groups). In this way, the trend toward standardization of curricula and assessment may work against educational equity (McNeil, 2000), although efforts are made to promote both goals simultaneously (Delpit, 2003).

Standardized measures of science achievement have revealed significant gaps among students of diverse racial/ethnic and socioeconomic backgrounds. Although achievement gaps have diminished in recent decades, the gains are often disappointingly small relative to the inequities that persist (see the description below). If we start from the assumption that high academic achievement is potentially attainable by most children, then achievement gaps are a product of the learning opportunities available to different groups of students and the degree to which circumstances permit them to take advantage of those opportunities. The questions that this poses for researchers and educators are: What constitutes equitable learning opportunities, how do they vary for different student populations, and how can they be provided in a context of limited resources and conflicting educational priorities?

This chapter addresses key issues concerning student diversity and equity in science education, with a focus on how science achievement[1] relates to various factors or mechanisms. The chapter begins with conceptions of student diversity and science achievement gaps as two key constructs in this field of study. Next, it summarizes major findings in the literature with regard to the relation of science achievement gaps to curriculum, instruction, assessment, teacher education, school organization, educational policies, and students' home and community environments. Finally, it proposes an agenda for future research.

Although this chapter addresses student diversity in general, it highlights race/ethnicity, language, culture, and socioeconomic status (SES). The other chapters in this section of the *Handbook* address specific student populations that have traditionally been underserved by the education system, including girls, students in rural and inner-city settings, and students with special needs. The research studies considered for this chapter were carried out predominantly within the United States, although some studies conducted abroad (but published in English) are also considered.[2] This chapter includes studies published since 1982, in consideration of the document "Science for All Americans" (American Association for the Advancement of Science [AAAS], 1989), the release of which was a landmark for U.S. science education reform. The period between 1982 and 2003 spans the period from the years leading up to this document and to more than a decade after its release. In addition, the chapter considers primarily peer-reviewed journal articles that provide clear statements of research questions, clear descriptions of research methods, convincing links between the evidence presented and the research questions, and valid conclusions based on the results (Shavelson & Towne, 2002).

---

1. U.S. science educators and researchers generally support the goals of school science laid out in science education standards documents (AAAS, 1989, 1993; NRC, 1996): to enable students to develop an understanding of key science concepts, conduct scientific inquiry and reasoning, engage in scientific discourse, and cultivate scientific habits of mind. We acknowledge the concerns, expressed by various scholars, that science education reform in general and standards documents in particular espouse an assimilationist perspective by defining science and science achievement in terms of the Western modern science tradition, with little consideration of alternative views of science and ways of knowing from diverse backgrounds (Eisenhart, Finkel, & Marion, 1996; Lee, 1999a; Lynch, 2000; Rodriguez, 1997). However, engaging in this debate is beyond the scope of this chapter.

2. The decision to focus on the U.S. context is due to: (a) a wide range of student diversity in different countries; (b) various political, racial/ethnic, cultural, linguistic, and socioeconomic contexts in society at large and the educational systems in particular in different countries; and (c) a vast body of literature on this topic in different countries and in different languages. Despite such variations, major issues discussed about the U.S. context in this chapter have implications for issues of student diversity in other countries to the extent that non-mainstream students are marginalized from the mainstream in their societies.

STUDENT DIVERSITY

A focus on student diversity presumes that choices made with regard to curriculum, instructional practices, assessment, and school organization affect different student populations differently. Therefore, differing science outcomes may be as much a product of the ways in which policies and schools define, delimit, and manage student diversity as they are of diversity itself. Regardless of the origin or nature of students' marginalization, academic success often depends on assimilation into mainstream norms. Thus, the educational success of immigrant or U.S.-born racial/ethnic minority students depends to a large degree on acquiring the standard language and shared culture of mainstream U.S. society. For example, traditional science instruction generally assumes that students have access to certain educational resources at home and requires students living in poverty to adopt learning habits that require a certain level of economic stability.

The interplay of race/ethnicity, culture, language, and social class is complex. On the one hand, it is difficult methodologically to separate out the influences of different variables, which may cut across populations in ways that are not easily untangled (for example, when ethnic groups are internally stratified by class). On the other hand, these variables are not entirely separable, conceptually speaking; language is an important element of ethnicity, culture is partly determined by social class, and so on. Racial/ethnic identities and language proficiencies are less bounded than implied by commonly used demographic categories; they may vary within a single household or even with regard to a single individual, depending on the situation. Furthermore, although a shared language, culture, and racial background are important components of a collective ethnic identity, the relative importance of each component varies widely from one group to another.

Social theorists have proposed concepts such as "languaculture" (Agar, 1996), "class cultures" (Bourdieu, 1984), "social class dialects" (Labov, 1966), and even "Ebonics" to capture the inevitable intertwining of race/ethnicity, language, culture, and social class. Especially with regard to native speakers of non-standard dialects of English (e.g., African-American and some Hispanic and Native American populations), the influences of these different variables on student outcomes are more often conflated than systematically analyzed.

Throughout this chapter, the terms *mainstream* and *non-mainstream* are used with reference to students. Similar to contemporary usage of the term *minority* by social scientists, *mainstream* is understood to refer not to numerical majority, but rather to social prestige, institutionalized privilege, and normative power. Thus, in classroom settings, mainstream students (i.e., in the United States those who are White, middle or upper class, and native speakers of standard English) are more likely than non-mainstream students to encounter ways of talking, thinking, and interacting that are continuous with the skills and expectations they bring from home, a situation that constitutes an academic advantage for students of the former group.[3] These group-level phenomena may not apply to particular individuals or

---

3. The focus on non-mainstream students should not obscure the fact that the culture and language of mainstream students play no less a role in their educational experience. Furthermore, the mainstream language and culture can no longer be assumed to be representative of most students' experience, especially in inner-city schools or large urban school districts where non-mainstream students tend to be concentrated.

may be offset by other factors within the group, such as the vast range of proficiency levels in both the home language and English, immigration history, acculturation to mainstream society, educational levels of parents, and family/community attitudes toward education in general and science education in particular. Recognizing overall differences between groups does not justify limiting one's expectations of individual students, but does provide a framework for interpreting observed patterns and processes that occur with differing frequency among different groups (Gutierrez & Rogoff, 2003).

Varying usages of terminology often reflect different theoretical stances or disciplinary traditions. The lack of consensus around designations for different categories of students reflects the rapidly changing demographic makeup of the country, the changing political connotations of different terms, and the specific aspects of identity that researchers and/or subjects may wish to emphasize. Although this sometimes causes difficulty with regard to comparability of studies, the lack of a standard terminology to describe the overlapping dimensions of student diversity is a valid reflection of the fluid, multiply determined, and historically situated nature of identity, and the ways in which such designations are used to stake out particular claims about the location and nature of social boundaries. Although much of the science education literature (especially those studies based on quantitative analysis of student outcome data) tends to treat such categories as discrete and unproblematic, this should be understood as a necessary fiction that makes possible the management of large data sets, thus revealing "the big picture" with regard to student diversity and science achievement. In reality, the number of students whose personal circumstances cross and confound such categorical boundaries is greater than ever, and will no doubt continue to increase as those boundaries become more flexible and porous.

Terminology can be problematic in any synthesis, because some researchers use particular terms with special meanings and others invent their own terms to express specifically intended meanings. In this chapter, terms are used as they appeared in the studies in order to represent the original intentions of the researchers, to the extent that this does not confuse or conflate the ways these terms are typically used in the literature.

ACHIEVEMENT GAPS

Science outcomes are defined in broad terms that include not only achievement scores on standardized tests but also meaningful learning of classroom tasks, affect (attitudes, interest, motivation), course enrollments, high school completion, higher education, and career choices. Racial/ethnic, gender, and class disparities are evident in nearly all of these areas, suggesting that the nation's schools have far to go in terms of providing an equitable science education to all students. In the current U.S. policy context, which stresses "structured English immersion" for English language learners (or ELL students) and severely limits content area instruction in languages other than English, English proficiency becomes a de facto prerequisite for science learning. In this sense, acquisition of oral and written English, although not a "science outcome" per se, plays a large role in determining science outcomes as they are commonly measured.

Ideological and Methodological Limitations

Description of science achievement gaps must be interpreted within the context of ideological and methodological limitations in the current knowledge base. In the ideological sense, Rodriguez (1998a) argued that failure to disaggregate science achievement data may create or reinforce stereotypes about certain groups. He also addressed achievement gaps in terms of social justice in the education system at large. Contrary to the notion of meritocracy—whereby academic achievement is viewed as a direct reflection of students' ability and effort—his analysis of achievement data suggests that the educational system is structured so as to benefit those groups already in power. The students most adversely affected by the meritocracy myth come from the fastest-growing ethnic groups. According to Rodriguez, to promote participation and achievement of non-mainstream students in science, the meritocracy myth needs to be exposed and addressed.

In the methodological sense, achievement is typically measured by standardized tests administered with national and international student samples. These databases provide overall achievement results by ethnicity, SES, and gender, but contain limited information with regard to disaggregation of results, such as socioeconomic strata within ethnic groups or subgroups within broad ethnic categories (Rodriguez, 1998a). This lack of information hinders researchers' and policy makers' ability to gain insight into the causes of science achievement gaps among specific student groups. Furthermore, in the United States, ELL students were excluded from most large-scale assessments until recently. Although the 2000 National Assessment of Educational Progress [NAEP] report card was the first (since the NAEP's inception in 1969) to analyze assessment accommodations in science, the results did not disaggregate students with disabilities from limited English proficient students (O'Sullivan, Lauko, Grigg, Qian, & Zhang, 2003).

Gaps in Science Outcomes

The long-term trend assessments of U.S. students in science, as measured by the NAEP, indicate that the average score for students of every age level and race/ethnicity has increased slightly since the 1970s (Campbell, Hombo, & Mazzeo, 2000). Achievement gaps by race/ethnicity on the NAEP are gradually narrowing; the scores of Black and Hispanic students have improved since the 1970s at a slightly faster rate than the scores of White non-Hispanic students. Nevertheless, Black and Hispanic students' scores remain well below those of White students, and the gaps persist across the three age levels.

Furthermore, the growth rates of African American and Hispanic students are so minimal that (with the exception of Hispanic males) their 12th-grade achievement level still fell well below the initial 8th-grade achievement of Whites and Asian Americans (Muller, Stage, & Kinzie, 2001). Although the long-term trend assessments of NAEP science achievement by SES are not available, the 1996 and 2000 results indicate that students who were eligible for the free/reduced price lunch program performed well below those who were not eligible (O'Sullivan et al., 2003).

Rodriguez (1998a) conducted a systematic analysis of trends in science achievement by ethnicity, SES, and gender, using national databases including the National

Assessment of Educational Progress (NAEP), the National Education Longitudinal Study (NELS), the American College Test (ACT), the Scholastic Aptitude Test (SAT), and Advanced Placement (AP) exams. The results indicated improvement for all student groups in science achievement and participation, but wide gaps persisted between Anglo-European students and students from African and Latino groups (to use Rodriguez's terms). In addition, patterns of achievement gaps were alarmingly congruent over time and across studies with respect to race/ethnicity, SES, gender, and grade level.

Attitudes toward science vary among racial/ethnic groups, but this variation is not always consistent with the variation in science achievement results. In a study of four major ethnic groups of elementary, middle, and high school students in Hawaii, Greenfield (1996) reported that Filipino Americans and native Hawaiians had lower achievement and less positive attitudes toward science than Caucasian and Japanese American students. In contrast, researchers from the U.S. mainland reported that non-mainstream students have positive attitudes toward science and aspire to science careers, but have limited exposure and access to the knowledge necessary to realize this aspiration (Atwater, Wiggins, & Gardner, 1995; Rakow, 1985).

Other indicators of science outcomes include science course enrollment, college major, and career choice. Overall, minority racial/ethnic groups made gains with regard to enrollments in high school science courses, as well as bachelors', master's, and doctoral degrees awarded in science and engineering fields, but gaps persist (National Science Foundation [NSF], 2002; Oakes, 1990).

KEY FINDINGS ON STUDENT DIVERSITY AND SCIENCE OUTCOMES

Research on diversity and equity in science education is a new and developing area. Most has been published since the mid-1990s, perhaps spurred in the United States by the emphasis on the dual goals of excellence and equity laid out in *Science for All Americans* and *Benchmarks for Science Literacy* (American Association for the Advancement of Science [AAAS], 1989, 1993) and the *National Science Education Standards* (National Research Council [NRC], 1996). Prominent science education journals have increased their coverage of science-and-diversity-related topics; the *Journal of Research in Science Teaching* and *Science Education* each produced a number of special issues in recent years.

Studies have been conducted from a wide range of theoretical and disciplinary frames, including cognitive science, sociolinguistics, and sociocultural and sociopolitical perspectives. They have utilized a variety of research methods, ranging from experimental designs, to surveys, case studies, and critical ethnography. The majority of studies are small-scale descriptive studies by individual researchers. There are only a small number of intervention-based studies, and relatively few of these are on a large scale. Experimental studies are rare, relative to the many studies using qualitative methods. We found no meta-analysis of statistical research studies in the literature.

Below, we summarize key findings and selected references on issues of student diversity in science education (see Lee & Luykx, 2006, for more detailed descriptions of individual studies). Although our focus is on student diversity and science outcomes, most of the studies we reviewed did not include concrete information about student outcomes in their results. Notably absent are quantitative achievement results.

Science Curriculum

One strand of the debate over science education among diverse student groups has focused on epistemological questions, such as what counts as science? and what are scientific ways of knowing? The definition of science constitutes "a *de facto* 'gate-keeping' device for determining what can be included in a school science curriculum and what cannot" (Snively & Corsiglia, 2001, p. 6; also see Hodson, 1993; Loving, 1997; Stanley & Brickhouse, 1994). A full and nuanced account of the debate over what counts as science is beyond the scope of this chapter. While recognizing the existence of multiple views of science, we focus here on school science as defined in U.S. standards documents—the systematic search for empirical explanations of natural phenomena (AAAS, 1989, 1993; NRC, 1996).

Although appropriate instructional materials are essential for effective instruction, high-quality materials that meet current science education standards are difficult to find (NSF, 1996). In attempting to make science accessible to all students, the NSF (1998) emphasizes "culturally and gender relevant curriculum materials" that recognize "[diverse] cultural perspectives and contributions so that through example and instruction, the contributions of all groups to science will be understood and valued" (p. 29). However, efforts to develop such materials present challenges to science educators. On the one hand, they require a knowledge base of examples, analogies, and beliefs from a range of different cultures, related to specific science topics and scientific practices. Even when culturally relevant materials are developed and prove effective, their effectiveness may be limited to the particular group for which they are designed. On the other hand, materials developed for wide use, particularly those that can be accessed electronically, may be implemented across various settings. However, local adaptations are essential for such materials to be used effectively, which in turn requires expertise on the part of teachers.

The small body of literature on science curricula for diverse student groups indicates that (a) most materials currently used in U.S. classrooms are not culturally relevant to non-mainstream students and (b) cultural diversity is not adequately represented in textbooks and materials (Barba, 1993; Eide & Heikkinen, 1998; Ninnes, 2000). Materials that do incorporate experiences, examples, analogies, and values from specific cultural and linguistic groups foster higher science achievement, more positive attitudes toward science, and enhanced cultural identity among non-mainstream students (Aikenhead, 1997; Matthews & Smith, 1994).

In addition to text-based curriculum materials described above, several studies developed interactive computer-based curriculum materials. In contrast to culturally relevant materials that are designed for specific cultural groups, computer-based materials (accompanied by web-based technology) are intended for large-scale implementation, although local adaptations are necessary for effective use across educational settings. The results show the positive impact of inquiry-based, technology-rich learning environments on student outcomes as measured by standardized achievement tests in large urban school districts (Rivet & Krajcik, 2004; Songer, Lee, & McDonald, 2003).

Science Learning and Instruction

There is a rather extensive literature on science learning and instruction with non-mainstream students. The studies address a wide range of topics and employ various theoretical perspectives and research methods. This research is summarized below with regard to (a) culturally congruent instruction, (b) cognitively based instruction to promote scientific reasoning and argumentation, (c) the sociopolitical process of learning and instruction, and (d) science learning and instruction with ELL students.

Culturally Congruent Instruction

The literature on science education's relation to students' worldviews (Allen & Crawley, 1998; Cobern, 1996; Lee, 1999b) and culturally specific communication and interactional patterns (see the review by Atwater, 1994) indicates that the culture of Western science is foreign to many students (both mainstream and non-mainstream), and that the challenges of science learning may be greater for students whose cultural traditions are discontinuous with the "ways of knowing" characteristic of Western science and science instruction. The challenge for these students is "to study a Western scientific way of knowing and at the same time respect and access the ideas, beliefs, and values of non-Western cultures" (Snively & Corsiglia, 2001, p. 24).

Teachers need to be aware of a variety of cultural experiences in order to understand how different students may approach science learning (Moje, Collazo, Carillo, & Marx, 2001). Teachers also need to use cultural artifacts, examples, analogies, and community resources that are familiar to students in order to make science relevant and intelligible to them (Barba, 1993). Lee and Fradd (1998; see also Lee, 2002, 2003) proposed the notion of "instructional congruence," which highlights the importance of developing *congruence* not only between students' cultural expectations and the norms of classroom interaction, but also between academic disciplines and students' linguistic and cultural experiences. It also emphasizes the role of *instruction* (or educational interventions), as teachers explore the relationship between academic disciplines and students' cultural and linguistic knowledge, and devise ways to link the two.

Effective science instruction should enable students to cross cultural borders between their home cultures and the culture of science (Aikenhead & Jegede, 1999; Costa, 1995). According to the multicultural education literature, school knowledge represents the "culture of power," that is, the dominant society (Delpit, 1988; Reyes, 1992). The cultural norms governing classroom discourse are largely implicit and tacit, and thus are not easily accessible to students who have not learned them at home. For students who are not from the culture of power, teachers need to initially provide explicit instruction about that culture's rules and norms and gradually lead students to take greater initiative and responsibility for their own learning.

Cognitively Based Instruction

An emerging body of literature argues that the ways of knowing and talking characteristic of children from outside the cultural and linguistic mainstream are generally continuous with the ways of knowing and talking characteristic of scientific communities. The Chèche Konnen Project has promoted collaborative scientific inquiry among language minority and low-SES students in order to help them use language, think, and act as members of a science learning community (Ballenger, 1997; Rosebery, Warren, & Conant, 1992; Warren, Ballenger, Ogonowski, Rosebery, & Hudicourt-Barnes, 2001). When presented with meaningful science learning opportunities, these children employ sense-making practices—deep questions, vigorous argumentation, situated guesswork, embedded imagining, multiple perspectives, and innovative uses of everyday words to construct new meanings—that intersect in potentially productive ways with scientific practices. As students engage in scientific inquiry, teachers can identify intersections between students' everyday knowledge and scientific practices and use these intersections as the basis for instructional practices. The results indicate that low-income immigrant students or those with limited science experience are capable of scientific inquiry, reasoning, and argumentation.

Sociopolitical Process of Learning and Instruction

As an outgrowth of critical studies of schooling, a small number of studies have examined science learning as a sociopolitical process (Calabrese Barton, 1998, 2001; Rodriguez & Berryman, 2002). This literature is distinguished from that discussed above in several ways. First, it questions the relevance of science to students who have traditionally been underserved by the education system and argues that science education should begin with the intellectual capital of the learner and his/her lived experiences, not with externally imposed standards. In this way, it attempts to invert the power structure of schooling and its oppressive effects on these students. Second, it addresses issues of poverty, as well as cultural and linguistic diversity, from a critical perspective that focuses on the unequal distribution of social resources and the school's role in the reproduction of social hierarchy. Third, the researchers generally employ ethnographic methods and ground their analyses in the political, cultural, and economic history of the groups under study.

Several studies have found that science instruction often reinforces power structures that privilege mainstream students and that other students actively resist school science (Gilbert & Yerrick, 2001; Seiler, 2001; Tobin, 2000). The studies describe mistrust of schooling, of science instruction, and of science teachers among those students who have traditionally been disenfranchised and marginalized by schooling in general and science education in particular. This mistrust is exacerbated when science teachers do not expect students to succeed in science, thus presenting a serious barrier to achievement. Inquiry-based instruction is particularly trust-intensive, inasmuch as science inquiry demands skepticism, patience, and a tolerance for uncertainty and ambiguity, all of which require a certain level of trust between teacher and students (Sconiers & Rosiek, 2000). The researchers argue that building trusting and caring relationships between teachers and students is necessary in order for students to take intellectual risks, which are in turn necessary in order to develop deep understandings of science content and practices.

Science Learning and Instruction with ELL Students

A number of studies have focused on the role of language in ELL students' science learning in either bilingual or mainstreamed classrooms. Research within the United States has, unsurprisingly, focused on Spanish speakers (Duran, Dugan, & Weffer, 1998; Torres & Zeidler, 2002), whereas research in other parts of the English-speaking world has focused on students from a broad range of language communities, both immigrant and indigenous (Curtis & Millar, 1988; Kearsey & Tuner, 1999; Tobin & McRobbie, 1996). Some of the latter studies go beyond examination of language use in the classroom to consider the social, cultural, and demographic dynamics of students' language communities. Overall, the research suggests that students' limited proficiency in English constrains their science achievement when instruction and assessment are undertaken exclusively or predominantly in English.

In order to keep up with their English-speaking peers, ELL students need to develop English language and literacy skills in the context of content area instruction (August & Hakuta, 1997). Ideally, content areas should provide a meaningful context for English language and literacy development, while students' developing English skills provide the medium for engagement with academic content (Lee & Fradd, 1998). As more U.S. states adopt immersion approaches to English to Speakers of Other Languages (ESOL) instruction, ELL students must confront the demands of academic learning through a yet-unmastered language. Furthermore, teachers often lack the knowledge and the institutional support needed to address the complex educational needs of ELL students.

Recently, several studies have examined the impact of instructional interventions to promote ELL students' English language and literacy development simultaneously with science learning (Amaral, Garrison, & Klentschy, 2002; Merino & Hammond, 2001). These studies have focused on hands-on and inquiry-based science instruction, which enables ELL students to develop scientific understanding, engage in inquiry, and construct shared meanings more actively than does traditional textbook-based instruction. By engaging in science inquiry, ELL students develop English grammar and vocabulary as well as familiarity with scientific genres of writing. Furthermore, inquiry-based science instruction provides both authentic, communicative language activities and hands-on, contextualized exploration of natural phenomena, while promoting students' communication of their understanding in a variety of formats, including written, oral, gestural, and graphic (Lee & Fradd, 1998; Rosebery et al., 1992). Overall, the results indicate students' active engagement in science classroom tasks and improved achievement on standardized tests of science and literacy.

Assessment

Research on science assessment (both large-scale and classroom) with non-mainstream students is extremely limited, for various reasons. Because assessment of ELL students tends to concentrate on basic skills in literacy and numeracy, other subjects such as science tend to be ignored. Because science is often not part of large-scale or statewide assessments, and usually does not count toward accountability measures even when it is tested, research on science assessment and accommodations with diverse student groups is sparse. Given these limitations, it is unclear whether new assessment technologies and innovations present more hopes or obstacles to non-mainstream students.

Science Assessment with Culturally Diverse Groups

One way to promote valid and equitable assessment is to make science assessments relevant to the knowledge and experiences that students of diverse backgrounds acquire in their home and community environments (Solano-Flores & Nelson-Barber, 2001). This approach, which advocates tailoring assessments to specific student populations, contrasts with efforts to avoid cultural bias by making assessments as culturally "neutral" as possible. Solano-Flores and Trumbull (2003) argued that it is difficult to remove cultural bias from assessment practices because tests are inevitably cultural devices and that a more equitable and realistic approach is to consider students' cultural beliefs and practices throughout the assessment process. However, this requires more knowledge about the cultural backgrounds of specific student groups than teachers and test developers usually have access to.

Another way to promote equitable assessment is to identify more effective formats for assessing student achievement. Advocates of alternative (or performance) assessments have argued that traditional multiple-choice tests fail to measure nonmainstream students' knowledge, abilities, and skills (Ruiz-Primo & Shavelson, 1996). An important issue in using alternative assessments is their fairness to different student groups—"the likelihood of any assessment allowing students to show what they understand about the construct being tested" (Lawrenz, Huffman, & Welch, 2001, p. 280). Given the limited research on alternative science assessments with non-mainstream students, both advocates and critics have based their claims on inferences and insights drawn from related research endeavors, rather than on empirical studies that address the topic directly (see the discussion in Lee, 1999a). Furthermore, existing studies in science education show contradictory results (Klein et al., 1997; Lawrenz et al., 2001).

Science Assessment with ELL Students

Assessment of ELL students is complicated by issues such as which students to include in accountability systems, what constitutes fair and effective assessment accommodations (Abedi, 2004), and how to assess content knowledge separately from English proficiency or general literacy (Shaw, 1997). Research on these issues with regard to school science is very limited. Although efforts to ensure valid and equitable assessment of ELL students generally focus on eliminating specific linguistic effects as a way to ensure test validity, Solano-Flores and Trumbull (2003) argued that consideration of students' home languages should guide the entire assessment process, including test development, test review, test use, and test interpretation.

Regarding assessment of students with disabilities (SD) and limited English proficiency (LEP), the 2000 NAEP report is the first since its inception in 1969 to display two different sets of results: "accommodations-permitted" and "accommodations-not-permitted" (O'Sullivan et al., 2003). Accommodations included, but were not limited to, one-on-one testing, small-group testing, access to bilingual dictionaries, extended time, reading aloud of directions, and recording of students' answers by someone else. At grade 4, the accommodations-permitted results, which included slightly more SD and LEP students because of the availability of accommodations, were 2 points lower than the accommodations-not-permitted results, and this difference was statistically significant. At grades 8 and 12, there was no statistically significant difference between the two sets of results. Because of the small numbers of

SD and LEP students who were assessed at each grade level, with or without accommodations, the results were not disaggregated by SD or LEP separately.

Teacher Education

Teachers need not come from the same racial/ethnic backgrounds as their students in order to teach effectively (Ladson-Billings, 1995). Given the increasing student diversity even within individual classrooms, matching teachers with students of similar backgrounds is often not feasible. But when teachers of any background are unaware of the cultural and linguistic knowledge that their students bring to the classroom (Gay, 2002; Villegas & Lucas, 2002), or when they lack opportunities to reflect upon how students' minority or immigrant status may affect their educational experience (Cochran-Smith, 1995), there is clearly a need for teacher education that specifically addresses teachers' beliefs and practices with regard to student diversity as it relates to subject areas. Teachers must be equipped with knowledge of (a) academic content and processes, (b) ways in which academic content and processes may articulate with students' own linguistic and cultural knowledge, (c) pedagogical strategies appropriate to multicultural settings, and (d) awareness of how traditional curriculum and pedagogy have functioned to marginalize certain groups of students and limit their learning opportunities.

Teacher Preparation

Most prospective science teachers enter their teacher preparation programs with beliefs that undermine the goal of equitable education for all students and graduate without fundamentally changing these beliefs (Bryan & Atwater, 2002). A sparse but emerging literature indicates the challenges and difficulties in making fundamental or transformative changes in the beliefs and practices of prospective U.S. science teachers (who are mostly from White, monolingual English, middle-class backgrounds) with regard to student diversity (Bianchini, Johnston, Oram, & Cavazos, 2003; Luft, Bragg, & Peters, 1999; Tobin, Roth, & Zimmerman, 2001; Yerrick & Hoving, 2003). Even when changes in teacher beliefs and practices occur, such changes are demanding and slow.

Rodriguez (1998b) proposed a conception of multicultural education as integrating a political theory of social justice with a pedagogical theory of social constructivism. This approach aims to enable prospective teachers to teach for both student diversity (via culturally inclusive and socially relevant pedagogy) and scientific understanding (via critically engaging and intellectually meaningful pedagogy). The results showed promise in terms of assisting prospective teachers to critically examine their prior beliefs about what it means to be a successful science teacher. Most became aware of the importance of creating science classrooms where all students are provided with opportunities for successful learning. However, several teachers demonstrated a strong resistance to both ideological and pedagogical change.

Teacher Professional Development

Research on professional development indicates that teachers need to engage in reform-oriented practices themselves in order to be able to provide effective science instruction for their students. However, affecting changes in teachers' knowledge, beliefs, and practices in science instruction is an arduous process (Knapp, 1997). Despite the critical need for professional development of science teachers working with diverse student groups, the literature is extremely limited. A small body of studies reports the positive impact of professional development on change in teachers' knowledge, beliefs, and practices and ultimately science achievement and attitudes of non-mainstream students (Kahle, Meece, & Scantlebury, 2000).

Several studies revealed both advantages and limitations of school-wide professional development initiatives in science (Blumenfeld, Fishman, Krajcik, & Marx, 2000; Gamoran et al., 2003). On one hand, collective participation of all teachers from the same school or grade level in professional development activities allows them to develop common goals, share instructional materials or assessment tools, and exchange ideas and experiences arising from a common context. On the other hand, unlike programs composed of volunteer teachers seeking opportunities for professional growth, school-wide implementation inevitably includes teachers who are not interested in or even resist participation. Additionally, the intensity of professional development activities may be compromised because of various constraints on urban schools. Despite these hurdles, school-wide professional development can provide valuable insights for large-scale implementation (Luykx, Cuevas, Lambert, & Lee, 2005).

Teacher Education with ELL Students

Teachers of ELL students are charged with promoting students' English language and literacy development as well as academic achievement in subject areas. This may require subject-specific instructional strategies that go beyond the general preparation in ESOL or bilingual education that many teachers receive. Unfortunately, a majority of teachers working with ELL students do not feel adequately prepared to meet their students' learning needs (National Center for Education Statistics, 1999). Most teachers also assume that ELL students must acquire English before learning subject matter, though this approach almost inevitably leads such students to fall behind their English-speaking peers (August & Hakuta, 1997).

Professional development to promote science along with English language and literacy development involves teacher knowledge, beliefs, and practices in multiple areas (Wong-Fillmore & Snow, 2002). In addition to ensuring that ELL students acquire the language skills necessary for social communication in English, teachers need to promote development of both general and content-specific academic language. Furthermore, teachers must be able to view language within a human development perspective. Such an understanding would enable them to formulate developmentally appropriate expectations about language comprehension and production over the course of students' learning of English. The amalgamation of these knowledge sources should result in teaching practices that (a) engage students of all levels of English proficiency in learning academic language, (b) allow students to display learning in multiple modes, (c) provide learning activities that have multiple points of entry for students of differing levels of English proficiency, and (d) ensure that students participate in a manner that allows for maximum language development at their own level.

We found no study involving preservice science teachers of ELL students in the literature. A limited body of research indicates that professional development efforts have a positive impact on helping practicing teachers examine their beliefs and improve their practices in integrating science with literacy for ELL students (Amaral et al., 2002; Hart & Lee, 2003; Lee, 2004; Stoddart, Pinal, Latzke, & Canaday, 2002).

School Organization and Educational Policies

Policies are interpreted and mediated by educational actors at every level of their implementation, to the extent that they are sometimes implemented in ways that are directly contrary to their presumed goals. School organization, in turn, is influenced by policies mandated by the state and the school district. The literature highlights features of school organization or restructuring that influence science teaching for students from non-mainstream backgrounds (Oakes, 1990). The majority of the studies in this limited literature focus on urban education (see also Chapter 13, this volume).

School Organization

One area of research has examined the effect of tracking or ability grouping on science learning opportunities and achievement among diverse student groups (see an extensive review of the literature in Oakes, 1990). In theory, such practices separate the academically stronger from the academically weaker students; in practice, this often means segregating students by SES, racial/ethnic origin, or degree of English proficiency. Educational scholars are in general agreement that tracking or ability grouping creates a cycle of restricted opportunities, diminished outcomes, and exacerbated inequalities for students from poor and non-mainstream backgrounds; nevertheless, it remains a common practice in schools throughout the nation.

School restructuring efforts (which often address tracking, among other issues) can narrow SES and race/ethnicity-based science achievement gaps. Valerie Lee and colleagues conducted a series of studies to examine how the structure of high schools affects student learning (Lee & Smith, 1993, 1995; Lee, Smith, Croninger, & Robert, 1997). The results indicated that in schools that engaged in practices consistent with the restructuring movement, student engagement and achievement were significantly higher (i.e., schools were more effective) and differences in engagement and achievement among students from different SES backgrounds were reduced (i.e., schools were more equitable). These schools had a strong academic focus, all students took a highly academic curriculum with limited tracking options, and teachers had strong professional communities emphasizing the quality of instruction.

Spillane, Diamond, Walker, Halverson, and Jita (2001) examined how the school leadership (administrators and lead teachers in science) at one urban elementary school successfully identified and activated resources for leading change in science education. Gamoran and associates (2003) examined how teachers from elementary through high school in six school districts across the nation taught mathematics and science for understanding with diverse student groups. Both studies emphasized that strategic use of resources (human, intellectual, social, and financial) and "distributed leadership" (i.e., administrators and teacher leaders support and sustain the professional community) are essential to bringing about change in school policies and practices.

Educational Policies

All of the studies in the limited literature about policies addressing student diversity in science education focus on U.S. urban contexts. Although educational policies influence all districts and all schools, consequences are especially critical in urban schools because of the sheer number of students attending them, the array and scope of the obstacles they face, and the institutional precariousness under which they operate.

After almost a decade of high-stakes testing in reading, writing, and mathematics, school systems are now moving to include science and social studies as well. As states increasingly embrace accountability measures, high-stakes testing influences instructional practices both in subject areas being tested and in those that are not tested. When science is not part of accountability measures, it is taught minimally in the elementary grades (Knapp & Plecki, 2001; Spillane et al., 2001). When science is part of accountability measures, teachers are pressured to mold their teaching practices to the demands of high-stakes testing, sometimes leading to unintended and harmful consequences (Settlage & Meadows, 2002).

Several studies have examined systemic reform to improve science education in U.S. urban schools (see also Chapter 31, this volume). Knapp and Plecki (2001) provided a conceptual framework for renewing urban science teaching. Kahle (1998) developed an "equity metric" to monitor the progress of educational reform over time. Hewson, Kahle, Scantlebury, and Davies (2001) and Rodriguez (2001) borrowed Kahle's equity metric to assess the progress toward equity of two urban middle schools and an urban school district, respectively. Finally, Kim and colleagues (2001) examined the impact of the NSF-supported Urban Systemic Initiatives (USI) on teacher education, classroom practices, and student achievement in mathematics and science. The results indicated noteworthy gains in science achievement with non-mainstream students and strengthening of the infrastructure to sustain achievement gains.

Whereas systemic reform efforts continued from the 1990s to the present, strategies for scaling up of educational innovations have emerged more recently. Systemic reform involves restructuring various components of an educational system in interactive ways, whereas scaling up focuses on implementing effective educational innovations on a large scale. In the climate of standards-based instruction and accountability, scaling up is increasingly called for to bring about system-wide improvements (Elmore, 1996). However, scaling up compromises conceptual rigor and fidelity of implementation, because of the demands and constraints imposed by educational policies, local institutional conditions, and individual teacher practices (Coburn, 2003). Furthermore, scaling-up efforts in multilingual, multicultural, or urban contexts involve numerous challenges, due to fundamental conflicts and inconsistencies in educational policies and practices as well as lack of resources and funding. For example, Blumenfeld et al. (2000) and Fishman, Marx, Blumenfeld, Krajcik, and Soloway (2004) described the difficulties involved in scaling up technology innovations for science education in a large urban school district. They suggested that issues of scalability and sustainability be addressed in technology innovations, so that such innovations can be used widely in K–12 schools to foster deep thinking and learning.

School Science and Home/Community Connection

Several studies have examined the influences of families and home environments on students' science achievement. A challenge facing many schools, especially those serving diverse student populations, is the lack of connection between schools and students' homes and communities. This may lead to student disengagement from schooling that they see as irrelevant and meaningless to their lives beyond school. Yet, students bring to the science classrooms "funds of knowledge" from their communities that can serve as resources for science learning (Moll, 1992; Vélez-Ibáñez & Greenberg, 1988).

There is clear evidence that family support (e.g., homework supervision, learning materials and resources, and parent's educational background) influences children's achievement, attitudes, and aspirations in science (Peng & Hill, 1994). Smith and Hausafus (1998) reported that low SES, ethnic minority students whose parents communicated and enforced high expectations for science and mathematics achievement had higher test scores than similar students with less supportive parents. This result is important in the sense that such support does not require parental knowledge of science and mathematics, areas in which parents often feel inadequate.

Several studies reported the positive impacts of intervention programs to help students recognize the meaning and relevance of science and connect school science to their homes and communities. Bouillion and Gomez (2001) explored a form of "connected science," in which real-world problems (i.e., current, unresolved, and of consequence) and school-community partnerships were used as contextual scaffolds for bridging students' community-based knowledge and school-based knowledge. Hammond (2001) reported collaborative efforts in which mentor and preservice teachers worked together with immigrant students and their families and utilized the funds of knowledge that these students and their families brought to the science learning contexts. Rahm (2002) described an inner-city youth gardening program and the kinds of learning opportunities it supported. The results indicate that the intervention fostered inner-city students' active participation in science-related activities in informal settings.

The research program led by Calabrese Barton has examined science teaching and learning with urban homeless children who are most at risk for receiving an inequitable education (Calabrese Barton, 1998, 2001; Fusco, 2001). Grounded in postmodern feminism, the research program employs critical ethnography, conceived of as a methodology that emerges collaboratively from the lives of the researcher and the researched and centers on the political commitment to the struggle for liberation (Calabrese Barton, 2001). This view of "science for all" challenges the traditional paradigm whereby science lies at the center as a target to be reached by students at the margins and offers a paradigm of inclusion whereby students' experiences and identities remain in tension with the study of the world.

RESEARCH AGENDA

Considering that research on diversity and equity in science education is a relatively new and emerging field, there are multiple directions that future research might pursue. Virtually all of the areas discussed in this chapter require further investigation. However, it is necessary to prioritize in order to produce research outcomes that are rigorous, cumulative, and useful to educational practice. The suggestions below reflect those areas of research that have shown promise in establishing a robust knowledge base, as well as others in which research is limited despite the urgent need for a knowledge base.

Student Diversity

Although the studies mentioned here were selected because of their focus on diversity and equity, many do not address these issues in sufficient depth or complexity. Future research needs to conceptualize the interrelated effects of race/ethnicity, culture, language, and SES on students' science learning in more nuanced ways. Although the intersections among the multiple strands that make up student (and teacher) identities are being theorized in increasingly sophisticated ways, as are the social forces, processes, and practices that shape students' educational experiences (Levinson, Foley, & Holland, 1996), these new perspectives have rarely been applied to the area of school science.

Studies need to combine cognitive, cultural, sociolinguistic, and sociopolitical perspectives on science learning, rather than focus on one aspect to the exclusion of others. This will require multidisciplinary efforts that bring together research traditions that have too often been developed in opposition or isolation from one another.

With ELL students, future research needs to consider science learning/achievement, literacy development, and English proficiency as conceptually distinct but interrelated, and to operationalize the complex interplay of multiple variables in methodologically rigorous research designs. Science educators and researchers also need to engage more deeply the broad scholarship on classroom discourse, second language acquisition, and literacy development (see Chapters 4 and 17, this volume). Though this literature has seldom addressed school science directly, its potential contribution to science education is considerable.

Science Achievement

Another area ripe for investigation involves conceptions and measurement of science achievement. Some research programs emphasize students' agency and empowerment with regard to science, rather than more commonly recognized outcome measures based on academic achievement. These conceptions vary widely from one research program to another and tend to differ from classroom assessment practices, which continue to emphasize memorization of facts. Although science educators (researchers, teachers, policymakers, and others) share the dual goals of improving science achievement and eliminating achievement gaps, existing research programs often do not address student outcomes, especially with quantitative achievement data. Although such data should not be the sole currency of educational research, they can provide an additional perspective that confirms or complicates narrative descriptions about other types of student outcomes, which are common in many research studies.

Lack of emphasis on science in current educational policies presents a unique set of issues. On the one hand, there are few assessment instruments that are widely used in science. This obliges researchers to develop their own assessment instruments, often around authentic or performance assessments that are aligned with the goals of the research. Such instruments may be well tailored to the goals of a specific research project, but limit comparability across studies. On the other hand, the limited range of standardized tests in science makes it difficult to develop a cumulative knowledge base about student achievement in specific science disciplines or topics.

More research is also needed to examine the effectiveness of educational innovations on achievement gaps among different student groups. Such research should consider disaggregation of achievement results for the intersections of different demographic categories, as well as subgroups within categories. Longitudinal analysis of student achievement across several grade levels or beyond the K–12 years is conspicuously absent from the current literature. Finally, future research should attempt to establish (causal) relationships among educational innovations, learning processes, and student outcomes.

Diversity of Student Experiences in Relation to Science Curriculum and Pedagogy

A major area of future research should be the cultural and linguistic experiences that students from diverse backgrounds bring to the science classroom, and the articulation of these experiences with science disciplines (Lee & Fradd, 1998; Warren et al., 2001). Future research should aim to identify those cultural and linguistic experiences that can serve as intellectual resources for science learning, as well as those beliefs and practices that may be discontinuous with the specific demands of science disciplines. This will require a balanced view of non-mainstream students' intellectual resources as well as the challenges they face in learning science.

An expanded knowledge base around students' non-school experiences related to science could offer a stronger foundation for science curriculum and instruction. Students of all backgrounds should be provided with academically challenging learning opportunities that allow them to explore and construct meanings based on their own linguistic and cultural experiences. At the same time, some students may need more explicit guidance in articulating their linguistic and cultural experiences with scientific knowledge and practices. Teachers (and curriculum designers) need to be aware of students' differing needs when deciding how much explicit instruction they should provide and to what extent students can assume responsibility for their own learning (Fradd & Lee, 1999; Lee, 2002). The proper balance of teacher-centered and student-centered activities may depend on the degrees and types of continuity or discontinuity between science disciplines and students' backgrounds, the extent of students' experience with science disciplines, and the level of cognitive difficulty of science tasks. Further research could examine what is involved in explicit instruction, when and how to provide it, and how to determine appropriate scaffolding for specific tasks and students.

Another area for future research concerns the demands involved in learning science through inquiry. Although current U.S. reforms in science education emphasize inquiry as the core of science teaching and learning (NRC, 1996, 2000), inquiry presents challenges to all students (and many teachers), inasmuch as it requires a critical stance, scientific skepticism, a tolerance for uncertainty and ambiguity, and patience. These challenges are greater for students whose homes and communities do not encourage inquiry practices, or for those who have been historically disenfranchised by the social institutions of science and do not see the relevance of science to their daily lives or to their future (Gilbert & Yerrick, 2001; Seiler, 2001; Tobin, 2000). Recent research emphasizes the importance of role models, trust, and personal connections between teachers and students as the starting point for non-mainstream students' participation in science inquiry (Sconiers & Rosiek, 2000). Future research may identify essential aspects of inquiry-based teaching and learning, and how these articulate with the experiences of diverse student groups.

Teacher Education

The literature is replete with accounts of the difficulties that science teachers (who are mostly from mainstream backgrounds) experience in teaching students from non-mainstream backgrounds (see the discussion about teacher education above; also see Bryan & Atwater, 2002, and Lee & Luykx, 2006, for comprehensive reviews of the literature). Some teachers have low expectations for such students and blame students or their families for academic failure, but even those teachers who are committed to promoting equity face challenges related to student diversity in their teaching. These problems will be exacerbated as diversity within the teaching population fails to keep pace with increasing diversity among students (Jorgenson, 2000).

Teachers may not need to share the language and culture of their students in order to teach effectively; however, effective teachers should have an understanding of students' language and culture and the ability to articulate their students' experiences with science in ways that are meaningful and relevant to students as well as scientifically accurate. Some teachers may lack the cultural knowledge necessary to identify students' learning resources, but even teachers with the relevant cultural knowledge may not recognize it as such or may be unsure of how to relate their students' experiences to science (Lee, 2004). Future research may address how to design teacher education programs to enable preservice and practicing teachers to articulate science disciplines with students' linguistic and cultural practices, particularly when the discontinuities between the two domains are large. Research may also examine how teachers' knowledge, beliefs, and practices evolve as they reflect on ways to integrate these two domains. In addition, research may examine challenges in bringing about change with teachers who deride student diversity, resist multicultural views, or reproduce racism through their educational practice (Ladson-Billings, 1999).

Teacher education programs that successfully promote fundamental change in teachers' knowledge, beliefs, and practices concerning non-mainstream students tend to involve small numbers of committed teachers over an extended period of time. Effective teacher professional development requires adequate time, resources, and personal commitment on the part of both teachers and teacher educators. Future research may examine what is involved in taking effective teacher education models to scale, identifying a balance between resources required and the extent of impact on large numbers of teachers. Such research may also intersect with policies on teacher education at the state or local level, and this intersection deserves further investigation.

High-Stakes Testing and Accountability

The most dominant U.S. educational policy currently, which is particularly consequential for non-mainstream students, involves high-stakes testing and accountability (Abedi, 2004). After almost a decade of high-stakes testing in reading, language
arts, and mathematics, more U.S. states are now moving to incorporate science and
social studies as well. This trend coincides with the planned U.S. policy on science
assessment within the No Child Left Behind Act, according to which science will be
required to be included in accountability measures starting from 2007.

This policy change at the federal and state levels may bring about dramatic
changes in many aspects of science education. The culture of high-stakes testing already dominates the teaching landscape in many countries. For example, an emphasis on discrete facts and basic skills in high-stakes science testing discourages teachers
from promoting deeper understanding of key concepts or inquiry practices (Settlage
& Meadows, 2002). Also, complex issues around assessment abound, such as which
students are to be included in accountability systems, what assessment accommodations are appropriate, and how content knowledge may be assessed separately from
English proficiency or general literacy (O'Sullivan et al., 2003). A basic concern is that
ELL students' science achievement is underestimated when they are not allowed to
demonstrate their knowledge and abilities in their home language (Solano-Flores &
Trumbull, 2003). On the other hand, if science instruction is in the dominant language, simply assessing second language learners in the home language will not
guarantee an accurate picture of their science knowledge and abilities.

Future research may examine the impact of policy changes on various aspects
of science education. For example, research may address whether teaching for inquiry and reasoning also prepares students for high-stakes testing (and vice versa).
From an equity perspective, research may examine whether recent policy changes
differentially affects students from different backgrounds. More generally, research
may examine the institutional, social, and political factors that so often lead educational policies to work at cross-purposes to empirically tested "best practices" in
science education.

School Science and the Home/Community Connection

Students' early cultural and linguistic experiences occur in their homes and communities. If science education is to build upon students' experiences, it requires a
knowledge base about the norms, practices, and expectations existing in students'
homes and communities. Unfortunately, research on the connection between school
science and students' home/community environments is limited. One consequence
of this is that school science tends to be presented exclusively from the perspective
of Western modern science, without adequate consideration of how science-related
activities are carried out in diverse cultures and speech communities. Generally
speaking, the daunting task of bridging the two worlds of home and school falls
on students, who may be forced to choose one at the cost of the other. Given this
dilemma, it is not surprising that non-mainstream students are so often underserved, underrepresented, and disenfranchised in science.

Future research may examine the science-related "funds of knowledge" existing in diverse contexts and communities. It may focus on how parents and other

community members can serve as valuable resources for school-based science learn-ing, or explore various educational approaches in community-based projects that can help students recognize the meaning and relevance of science for their daily lives and for their future.

CLOSING

The literature on the intersection of school science and student diversity is currently insufficient to the task of effectively addressing persistent achievement gaps, but points in some promising directions. Deeper examination of the complex relation-ships among the various factors influencing student outcomes, combined with greater attention to the potential contributions of multiple theoretical perspectives and research methods, should produce significant and powerful additions to the existing knowledge base in this emerging field. Just as teachers must learn to cross cultural boundaries in order to make school science meaningful and relevant for all children, researchers must learn to cross the boundaries separating different theo-retical and methodological traditions if they are to disentangle the complex connec-tions between student diversity and science education.

ACKNOWLEDGMENTS

Parts of this chapter appear in our book, *Science education and student diversity: Syn-thesis and research agenda* (Lee & Luykx, 2006). The preparation of this chapter was supported in part by grants from the Department of Education Office of Educa-tional Research and Improvement to the National Center for Improving Student Learning and Achievement in Mathematics and Science (R305A60007) and to the Center for Research on Education, Diversity & Excellence (R306A60001). The find-ings and opinions expressed in this chapter do not necessarily reflect the position, policy, or endorsement of the Department of Education, OERI, or the respective na-tional centers. The authors acknowledge the electronic search of the literature by Margarette Mahotiere.
Thanks to Julie Bianchini and Randy Yerrick, who reviewed this chapter.

REFERENCES

Abedi, J. (2004). The No Child Left Behind Act and English language learners: Assessment and accountability issues. *Educational Researcher, 33*(1), 4–14.
Agar, M. (1996). *Language shock: Understanding the culture of conversation.* New York: William Morrow.
Aikenhead, G. S. (1997). Toward a first nations cross-cultural science and technology curriculum. *Science Education, 81,* 217–238.
Aikenhead, G. S., & Jegede, O. J. (1999). Cross-cultural science education: A cognitive explanation of a cultural phenomenon. *Journal of Research in Science Teaching, 36,* 269–287.
Allen, N. J., & Crawley, F. E. (1998). Voices from the bridge: Worldview conflicts of Kickapoo stu-dents of science. *Journal of Research in Science Teaching, 35,* 111–132.
Amaral, O. M., Garrison, L., & Klentschy, M. (2002). Helping English learners increase achieve-ment through inquiry-based science instruction. *Bilingual Research Journal, 26,* 213–239.
American Association for the Advancement of Science. (1989). *Science for all Americans.* New York: Oxford University Press.

American Association for the Advancement of Science. (1993). *Benchmarks for science literacy.* New York: Oxford University Press.

Atwater, M. M. (1994). Research on cultural diversity in the classroom. In D. L. Gabel (Ed.), *Handbook of research on science teaching and learning* (pp. 558–576). New York: Macmillan.

Atwater, M. M., Wiggins, J., & Gardner, C. M. (1995). A study of urban middle school students with high and low attitudes toward science. *Journal of Research in Science Teaching, 32,* 665–677.

August, D., & Hakuta, K. (Eds.). (1997). *Improving schooling for language-minority children: A research agenda.* Washington, DC: National Academy Press.

Ballenger, C. (1997). Social identities, moral narratives, scientific argumentation: Science talk in a bilingual classroom. *Language and Education, 11*(1), 1–14.

Barba, R. H. (1993). A study of culturally syntonic variables in the bilingual/bicultural science classroom. *Journal of Research in Science Teaching, 30,* 1053–1071.

Bianchini, J. A., Johnston, C. C., Oram, S. Y., & Cavazos, L. M. (2003). Learning to teach science in contemporary and equitable ways: The successes and struggles of first-year science teachers. *Science Education, 87,* 419–443.

Blumenfeld, P., Fishman, B. J., Krajcik, J., & Marx, R. W. (2000). Creating usable innovations in systemic reform: Scaling-up technology embedded project-based science in urban schools. *Educational Psychologist, 26,* 369–398.

Bouillion, L. M., & Gomez, L. M. (2001). Connecting school and community with science learning: Real world problems and school-community partnerships as contextual scaffolds. *Journal of Research in Science Teaching, 38,* 878–898.

Bourdieu, P. (1984) *Distinction: A social critique of the judgment of taste.* London: Routledge.

Bryan, L. A., & Atwater, M. M. (2002). Teacher beliefs and cultural models: A challenge for science teacher preparation programs. *Science Education, 86,* 821–839.

Calabrese Barton, A. (1998). Teaching science with homeless children: Pedagogy, representation, and identity. *Journal of Research in Science Teaching, 35,* 379–394.

Calabrese Barton, A. (2001). Science education in urban settings: Seeking new ways of praxis through critical ethnography. *Journal of Research in Science Teaching, 38,* 899–917.

Campbell, J. R., Hombo, C. M., & Mazzeo, J. (2000). *NAEP 1999 trends in academic progress: Three decades of student performance (NCES 2000-469).* Washington, DC: U.S. Department of Education, National Center for Education Statistics.

Cobern, W. W. (1996). Worldview theory and conceptual change in science education. *Science Education, 80,* 579–610.

Coburn, C. E. (2003). Rethinking scale: Moving beyond numbers to deep and lasting change. *Educational Researcher, 32*(6), 3–12.

Cochran-Smith, M. (1995). Color blindness and basket making are not the answers: Confronting the dilemmas of race, culture, and language diversity in teacher education. *American Educational Research Journal, 32,* 493–522.

Costa, V. B. (1995). When science is "another world": Relationships between worlds of family, friends, school, and science. *Science Education, 79,* 313–333.

Curtis, S., & Millar, R. (1988). Language and conceptual understanding in science: A comparison of English and Asian language speaking children. *Research in Science and Technological Education, 6*(1), 61–77.

Delpit, L. (1988). The silenced dialogue: Power and pedagogy in educating other people's children. *Harvard Educational Review, 58,* 280–298.

Delpit, L. (2003). Educators as "seed people" growing a new future. *Educational Researcher, 32*(7), 14–21.

Duran, B. J., Dugan, T., & Weffer, R. (1998). Language minority students in high school: The role of language in learning biology concepts. *Science Education, 82,* 311–341.

Eide, K. Y., & Heikkinen, M. W. (1998). The inclusion of multicultural material in middle school science teachers' resource manuals. *Science Education, 82*, 181–195.

Eisenhart, M., Finkel, E., & Marion, S. F. (1996). Creating the conditions for scientific literacy: A re-examination. *American Educational Research Journal, 33*, 261–295.

Elmore, R. (1996). Getting to scale with good educational practice. *Harvard Educational Review, 66*, 1–26.

Fishman, B., Marx, R., Blumenfeld, P., Krajcik, J. S., & Soloway, E. (2004). Creating a framework for research on systemic technology innovations. *Journal of the Learning Sciences, 13*(1), 43–76.

Fradd, S. H., & Lee, O. (1999). Teachers' roles in promoting science inquiry with students from diverse language backgrounds. *Educational Researcher, 28*(6), 14–20, 42.

Fusco, D. (2001). Creating relevant science through urban planning and gardening. *Journal of Research in Science Teaching, 38*, 860–877.

Gamoran, A., Anderson, C. W., Quiroz, P. A., Secada, W. G., Williams, T., & Ashmann, S. (2003). *Transforming teaching in math and science: How schools and districts can support change.* New York: Teachers College Press.

Gay, G. (2002). Preparing for culturally responsive teaching. *Journal of Teacher Education, 53*(2), 106–116.

Gilbert, A., & Yerrick, R. (2001). Same school, separate worlds: A sociocultural study of identity, resistance, and negotiation in a rural, lower track science classroom. *Journal of Research in Science Teaching, 38*, 574–598.

Greenfield, T. A. (1996). Gender, ethnicity, science achievement, and attitudes. *Journal of Research in Science Teaching, 33*, 901–933.

Gutiérrez, K. D., & Rogoff, B. (2003). Cultural ways of learning: Individual traits or repertoires of practice. *Educational Researcher, 32*(5), 19–25.

Hammond, L. (2001). An anthropological approach to urban science education for language minority families. *Journal of Research in Science Teaching, 38*, 983–999.

Hart, J., & Lee, O. (2003). Teacher professional development to improve science and literacy achievement of English language learners. *Bilingual Research Journal, 27*, 475–501.

Hewson, P. W., Kahle, J. B., Scantlebury, K., & Davies, D. (2001). Equitable science education in urban middle schools: Do reform efforts make a difference? *Journal of Research in Science Teaching, 38*, 1130–1144.

Hodson, D. (1993). In search of a rationale for multicultural science education. *Science Education, 77*, 685–711.

Jorgenson, O. (2000). The need for more ethnic teachers: Addressing the critical shortage in American public schools. Retrieved on September 13, 2000, from http://www.tcrecord.org/Content.asp?ContentID = 10551

Kahle, J. B. (1998). Equitable systemic reform in science and mathematics: Assessing progress. *Journal of Women and Minorities in Science and Engineering, 4*(1, 2), 91–112.

Kahle, J. B., Meece, J., & Scantlebury, K. (2000). Urban African-American middle school science students: Does standards-based teaching make a difference? *Journal of Research in Science Teaching, 37*, 1019–1041.

Kearsey, J., & Tuner, S. (1999). The value of bilingualism in pupils' understanding of scientific language. *International Journal of Science Education, 21*, 1037–1050.

Kim, J. J., Crasco, L., Smith, R. B., Johnson, G., Karantonis, A., & Leavitt, D. J. (2001). *Academic excellence for all students: Their accomplishment in science and mathematics.* Norwood, MA: Systemic Research.

Klein, S. P., Jovanovic, J., Stecher, B. M., McCaffrey, D., Shavelson, R. J., Haertel, E., et al. (1997). Gender and racial/ethnic differences on performance assessment in science. *Educational Evaluation and Policy Analysis, 19*(2), 83–97.

Knapp, M. S. (1997). Between systemic reforms and the mathematics and science classroom: The dynamics of innovation, implementation, and professional learning. *Review of Educational Research, 67*, 227–266.

Knapp, M. S., & Plecki, M. L. (2001). Investing in the renewal of urban science teaching. *Journal of Research in Science Teaching, 38*, 1089–1100.

Labov, W. (1966). *The social stratification of English in New York City.* Washington, DC: Center for Applied Linguistics.

Ladson-Billings, G. (1995). Toward a theory of culturally relevant pedagogy. *American Educational Research Journal, 32*, 465–491.

Ladson-Billings, G. (1999). Preparing teachers for diverse student populations: A critical race theory perspective. *Review of Research in Education, 24*, 211–247.

Lawrenz, F., & Huffman, D., & Welch, W. (2001). The science achievement of various subgroups of alternative assessment formats. *Science Education, 85*, 279–290.

Lee, O. (1999a). Equity implications based on the conceptions of science achievement in major reform documents. *Review of Educational Research, 69*(1), 83–115.

Lee, O. (1999b). Science knowledge, world views, and information sources in social and cultural contexts: Making sense after a natural disaster. *American Educational Research Journal, 36*, 187–219.

Lee, O. (2002). Science inquiry for elementary students from diverse backgrounds. In W. G. Secada (Ed.), *Review of research in education* (Vol. 26, pp. 23–69). Washington, DC: American Educational Research Association.

Lee, O. (2003). Equity for culturally and linguistically diverse students in science education: A research agenda. *Teachers College Record, 105*, 465–489.

Lee, O. (2004). Teacher change in beliefs and practices in science and literacy instruction with English language learners. *Journal of Research in Science Teaching, 41*, 65–93.

Lee, O., & Fradd, S. H. (1998). Science for all, including students from non-English language backgrounds. *Educational Researcher, 27*(3), 12–21.

Lee, O., & Luykx, A. (2006). *Science education and student diversity: Synthesis and research agenda.*

Lee, V., & Smith, J. B. (1993). Effects of school restructuring on the achievement and engagement of middle grade students. *Sociology of Education, 66*, 164–187.

Lee, V., & Smith, J. B. (1995). Effects of high school restructuring and size on gains in achievement and engagement for early secondary school students. *Sociology of Education, 68*, 241–247.

Lee, V., Smith, J., Croninger, J. B., & Robert, G. (1997). How high school organization influences the equitable distribution of learning in mathematics and science. *Sociology of Education, 70*, 128–150.

Levinson, B. A., Foley, D. E., & Holland, D. C. (Eds.). (1996). *The cultural production of the educated person: Critical ethnographies of schooling and local practice.* Albany, NY: State University of New York Press.

Loving, C. C. (1997). From the summit of truth to its slippery slopes: Science education's journey through positivist-postmodern territory. *American Educational Research Journal, 34*, 421–452.

Luft, J. A., Bragg, J., & Peters, C. (1999). Learning to teach in a diverse setting: A case study of a multicultural science education enthusiast. *Science Education, 83*, 527–543.

Luykx, A., Cuevas, P., Lambert, J., & Lee, O. (2005). Unpacking teachers' "resistance" to integrating students' language and culture into elementary science instruction. In A. Rodríguez & R. S. Kitchen (Eds.), *Preparing mathematics and science teachers for diverse classrooms: Promising strategies for transformative pedagogy* (pp. 119–141). Mahwah, NJ: Lawrence Erlbaum Associates.

Lynch, S. (2000). *Equity and science education reform.* Mahwah, NJ: Lawrence Erlbaum Associates.

Matthews, C. E., & Smith, W. S. (1994). Native American related materials in elementary science instruction. *Journal of Research in Science Teaching, 31*, 363–380.

McNeil, L. M. (2000). Creating new inequalities: Contradictions of reform. *Phi Delta Kappan, 81*, 729–734.

Merino, B., & Hammond, L. (2001). How do teachers facilitate writing for bilingual learners in "sheltered constructivist" science? *Electronic Journal of Literacy through Science, 1*(1). Retrieved June 25, 2004, from http://sweeneyhall.sjsu.edu/ejlts/archives/bilingualism/merino.htm

Moje, E., Collazo, T., Carillo, R., & Marx, R. W. (2001). "Maestro, what is quality?": Examining competing discourses in project-based science. *Journal of Research in Science Teaching, 38*, 469–495.

Moll, L. C. (1992). Bilingual classroom studies and community analysis: Some recent trends. *Educational Researcher, 21*(2), 20–24.

Muller, P. A., Stage, F. K., & Kinzie, J. (2001). Science achievement growth trajectories: Understanding factors related to gender and racial-ethnic differences in pre-college science achievement. *American Educational Research Journal, 38*, 981–1012.

National Center for Education Statistics. (1999). *Teacher quality: A report on the preparation and qualifications of public school teachers.* Washington, DC: U.S. Department of Education, Office of Educational Research and Improvement.

National Research Council. (1996). *National science education standards.* Washington, DC: National Academy Press.

National Research Council. (2000). *Inquiry and the national science education standards: A guide for teaching and learning.* Washington, DC: National Academy Press.

National Science Foundation. (1998). *Infusing equity in systemic reform: An implementation scheme.* Washington, DC: Author.

National Science Foundation. (2002). *Women, minorities, and persons with disabilities in science and engineering.* Arlington, VA: Author.

National Science Foundation Directorate for Education and Human Resources. (1996). *Review of instructional materials for middle school science.* Washington, DC: Author.

Ninnes, P. (2000). Representations of indigenous knowledges in secondary school science textbooks in Australia and Canada. *International Journal of Science Education, 22*, 603–617.

Oakes, J. (1990). Opportunities, achievement, and choice: Women and minority students in science and mathematics. In C. B. Cazden (Ed.), *Review of research in education* (Vol. 16, pp. 153–221). Washington, DC: American Educational Research Association.

O'Sullivan, C. Y., Lauko, M. A., Grigg, W. S., Qian, J., & Zhang, J. (2003). *The nation's report card: Science 2000.* Washington, DC: U.S. Department of Education, Institute of Education Sciences.

Peng, S., & Hill, S. (1994). Characteristics and educational experiences of high-achieving minority secondary students in science and mathematics. *Journal of Women and Minorities in Science and Engineering, 1*, 137–152.

Rahm, J. (2002). Emergent learning opportunities in an inner-city youth gardening program. *Journal of Research in Science Teaching, 39*, 164–184.

Rakow, S. J. (1985). Minority students in science: Perspectives from the 1981–1982 national assessment in science. *Urban Education, 20*(1), 103–113.

Reyes, M. (1992). Challenging venerable assumptions: Literacy instruction for linguistically diverse students. *Harvard Educational Review, 62*, 427–446.

Rivet, A. E., & Krajcik, J. S. (2004). Project-based science curricula: Achieving standards in urban systemic reform. *Journal of Research in Science Teaching, 41*(7), 669–692.

Rodriguez, A. (1997). The dangerous discourse of invisibility: A critique of the NRC's National Science Education Standards. *Journal of Research in Science Teaching, 34*, 19–37.

Rodriguez, A. (1998a). Busting open the meritocracy myth: Rethinking equity and student achievement in science education. *Journal of Women and Minorities in Science and Engineering, 4*(2, 3), 195–216.

Rodriguez, A. (1998b). Strategies for counter-resistance: Toward sociotransformative constructivism and learning to teach science for diversity and for understanding. *Journal of Research in Science Teaching, 35*, 589–622.

Rodriguez, A. J. (2001). From gap gazing to promising cases: Moving toward equity in urban education reform. *Journal of Research in Science Teaching, 38*, 1115–1129.

Rodriguez, A. J., & Berryman, C. (2002). Using sociotransformative constructivism to teach for understanding in diverse classrooms: A beginning teacher's journey. *American Educational Research Journal, 39*, 1017–1045.

Rosebery, A. S., Warren, B., & Conant, F. R. (1992). Appropriating scientific discourse: Findings from language minority classrooms. *The Journal of the Learning Sciences, 21*(1), 61–94.

Ruiz-Primo, M. A., & Shavelson, R. J. (1996). Rhetoric and reality in science performance assessments: An update. *Journal of Research in Science Teaching, 33*, 1045–1063.

Sconiers, Z. D., & Rosiek, J. L. (2000). Historical perspective as an important element of teachers' knowledge: A sonata-form case study of equity issues in a chemistry classroom: Voices inside schools. *Harvard Educational Review, 70*, 370–404.

Seiler, G. (2001). Reversing the "standard" direction: Science emerging from the lives of African American students. *Journal of Research in Science Teaching, 38*, 1000–1014.

Settlage, J., & Meadows, L. (2002). Standards-based reform and its unintended consequences: Implications for science education within America's urban schools. *Journal of Research in Science Teaching, 39*, 114–127.

Shavelson, R. J., & Towne, L. (Eds.). (2002). *Scientific research in education.* Washington, DC: National Academy Press.

Shaw, J. M. (1997). Threats to the validity of science performance assessments for English language learners. *Journal of Research in Science Teaching, 34*, 721–743.

Smith, F. M., & Hausafus, C. O. (1998). Relationship of family support and ethnic minority students' achievement in science and mathematics. *Science Education, 82*, 111–125.

Snively, G., & Corsiglia, J. (2001). Discovering indigenous science: Implications for science education. *Science Education, 85*, 6–34.

Solano-Flores, G., & Nelson-Barber, S. (2001). On the cultural validity of science assessments. *Journal of Research in Science Teaching, 38*, 553–573.

Solano-Flores, G., & Trumbull, E. (2003). Examining language in context: The need for new research and practice paradigms in the testing of English-language learners. *Educational Researcher, 32*(2), 3–13.

Songer, N. B., Lee, H-S., & McDonald, S. (2003). Research towards an expanded understanding of inquiry science beyond one idealized standard. *Science Education, 87*, 490–516.

Spillane, J. P., Diamond, J. B., Walker, L. J., Halverson, R., & Jita, L. (2001). Urban school leadership for elementary science instruction: Identifying and activating resources in an undervalued school subject. *Journal of Research in Science Teaching, 38*, 918–940.

Stanley, W. B., & Brickhouse, N. (1994). Multiculturalism, universalism, and science education. *Science Education, 78*, 387–398.

Stoddart, T., Pinal, A., Latzke, M., & Canaday, D. (2002). Integrating inquiry science and language development for English language learners. *Journal of Research in Science Teaching, 39*, 664–687.

Tobin, K. (2000). Becoming an urban science educator. *Research in Science Education, 30*, 89–106.

Tobin, K., & McRobbie, C. J. (1996). Significance of limited English proficiency and cultural capital to the performance in science of Chinese-Australians. *Journal of Research in Science Teaching, 33*, 265–282.

Tobin, K., Roth, W., & Zimmerman, A. (2001). Learning to teach science in urban schools. *Journal of Research in Science Teaching, 38*, 941–964.

Torres, H. N., & Zeidler, D. L. (2002). The effects of English language proficiency and scientific reasoning skills on the acquisition of science content knowledge by Hispanic English language learners and native English language speaking students. *Electronic Journal of Science Education, 6*(3). Retrieved June 25, 2004, from http://unr.edu/homepage/crowther/ejse/torreszeidler.pdf

Vélez-Ibáñez, C. G., & Greenberg, J. B. (1992). Formation and transformation of funds of knowledge among U.S.-Mexican households. *Anthropology and Education Quarterly, 23*, 313–335.

Villegas, A. M., & Lucas, T. (2002). Preparing culturally responsive teachers: Rethinking the curriculum. *Journal of Teacher Education, 53*(1), 20–32.

Warren, B., Ballenger, C., Ogonowski, M., Rosebery, A., & Hudicourt-Barnes, J. (2001). Rethinking diversity in learning science: The logic of everyday language. *Journal of Research in Science Teaching, 38*, 529–552.

Wong-Fillmore, L., & Snow, C. (2002). *What teachers need to know about language.* Washington, DC: Center for Applied Linguistics.

Yerrick, R. K., & Hoving, T. J. (2003). One foot on the dock and one foot on the boat: Differences among preservice science teachers' interpretations of field-based science methods in culturally diverse contexts. *Science Education, 87*, 390–418.

CHAPTER 8

Postcolonialism, Indigenous Students, and Science Education

Elizabeth McKinley
Auckland University

Science education research, particularly in the English-speaking world, has become increasingly concerned with the diversity of students in the classroom, as evidenced by increasing numbers of review articles on issues of equality and equity in the last 10 years (see, for example, Hipkins et al., 2002; Krugley-Smolska, 1996; Lee, 2003). However, much of the diversity literature does not fully address the issues of indigenous learners and their communities in postcolonial societies. This literature has tended to treat minorities as requiring similar, if not the same, solutions to what is perceived as non-participation and non-achievement in school science by these groups. As a consequence of this approach, members of various cultural groups do not recognize their struggle, or their voices and visions in the literature and rightly have been perceived to have been excluded in many cases. This review examines the science education research for indigenous students as opposed to the more homogeneous groupings of diversity, minorities, or multicultural.

The chapter focuses specifically on indigenous students' interests from international contexts and recognizes the need to establish a knowledge base to promote and support academic achievement and equity in science education for these students. In my view, the knowledge base requires the consideration of students' linguistic and cultural knowledge and experiences in combination with expectations of participation and academic achievement in science education. Furthermore, these considerations need to be seen in the light of educational imperatives of the indigenous communities themselves. There is also a global imperative of maintaining indigenous worldviews, languages, and environments to which science education research can contribute. These issues, and the complex relationships among them, are reflected in the emerging international literature on indigenous students, which recognizes that many indigenous communities have often been subject to the historical and ongoing effects of colonization, including the subjugation of their knowledge, language, and culture. Therefore, learning for indigenous communities is grounded not only on philosophical and pedagogical bases, but also on moral and political bases. As the sociologist Young (1974) and educationalist Maddock (1981) wrote over two decades ago, science education necessarily involves philosophy, sociology, history, psychology, and anthropology. Nowhere is this more so than in the circumstances of postcolonial societies where colonial rulers established formal education systems for peoples of other civilizations.

All reviews of literature are situated, partial, and perspectival, and this one is no exception, despite my use of the collective term *indigenous* to denote various peoples around the world. As Patti Lather (1999) argued, the practices of including and excluding in reviews are considered as "gatekeeping, policing, and productive rather than merely mirroring" (p. 3). First, this review surveys publications related to indigenous students and science education, mainly from the last 12 years, carrying forward from one I was involved with in 1992 (McKinley, Waiti, & Bell, 1992). Second, the review is written from the perspective of someone who identifies herself as a member of the indigenous Maori people of Aotearoa New Zealand, suggesting that I bring an "optics [that] is a politics of positioning" (Haraway, 1996, p. 257). However, I have not restricted this review to those articles written only by those who identify themselves as indigenous or separated the writers into indigenous/ non-indigenous. Although I agree with the arguments and sentiments of maintaining indigenous voice at an international level, such identity classification is difficult to determine on an international basis and is connected with each country's politics and histories. At this point in our history, such a strategy would not only exclude contributions of some countries with indigenous communities, but would also ignore some good work. Third, my own background assumes a specific context in the full range of indigenous communities. There are many characteristics regarding the nature of Aotearoa New Zealand's location, history, and circumstance that give Maori views different from those of many other indigenous communities in other countries. My partiality will undoubtedly be evident in a number of ways to many readers, not least of all to other indigenous researchers whose situations differ markedly from my own experiences. However, I hold myself accountable to a growing community of indigenous science educators with which I identify. And last, as indigenous knowledge is seen to be local in it applications, writers can have problems in getting articles on local communities accepted for peer-reviewed international journals; this was particularly true in the past. In addition, many indigenous researchers publish in local or indigenous journals or present work orally, which means that it can be difficult to get a comprehensive picture of the research being carried out. Hence, partiality should not be considered just in terms of the writer, but also in terms of science education research itself.

Overall, the research literature in the field of indigenous students in science education is very uneven in its application. Some issues have a large literature, whereas others have little or nothing written on them. This chapter is an attempt to bring some structure to the growing research literature on indigenous students' learning in science. Furthermore, not all issues raised are always of priority in indigenous communities themselves. First, I outline what I mean by *postcolonialism* and *indigeneity* in an attempt to clarify the terms and their use in this chapter. This is followed by a discussion of Indigenous Knowledge (IK) and Traditional Ecological Knowledge (TEK), two terms that are becoming more widespread in the literature.

Following these, the chapter is then divided into two broad sections that review the bulk of the literature in the field. The first section reviews the large and significant research about science as a body of knowledge with respect to culture. Included here is the philosophical debate between two positions constructed as a dichotomy—Western Modern Science (WMS) and indigenous knowledge bases (traditional and contemporary)—and their relationship to the science curriculum. The second broad section reviews literature related mainly to teaching and learning with respect to culture and covers issues such as stereotyping, curriculum contexts, learning, and indigenous pedagogy. I complete the review with a discussion of the small but growing debate considering the impact of the language of instruction and indigenous knowledge on classroom practice. Finally, I close with some comments about future directions for this research field in the light of indigenous communities' aspirations for themselves and their children, and how well science education research is meeting these aspirations.

POSTCOLONIALISM AND THE
PRINCIPLE OF INDIGENEITY

The term *postcolonialism* is controversial among many groups of researchers (see, for example, Ashcroft, Griffiths, & Tiffin, 1995; Mohanram, 1999). For many indigenous researchers the term signals that the European imperial project, and the appropriation of the "Other" as a form of knowledge, has been assigned to an historical past. Although this understanding is always present in postcolonialism, I continue to use it to highlight other meanings. The literary critic Homi Bhabha (1994) argued that postcolonialism can be used to mean "beyond"; instead of arguing using a lineal progression of before and after a point in history, another dimension is added with this alternative meaning. Although I do not want to dwell here on the more theoretical intricacies of this idea, it suffices to say that "beyond" suggests that boundaries or borders have become blurred. For example, the sustained contact between Maori and Pakeha in Aotearoa New Zealand, as with many other countries, has led to an intermingling of many things, including ancestry, cultural history, and language. Furthermore, it is simplistic and deterministic to think that there is ever a point in time where conditions change overnight. Colonialism is about many things, including the history and culture of countries involved in colonial rule, the policies that have been implemented before and after the independence of colonial states, and the personalities and beliefs of rulers and people of influence, both colonizers and colonized. Colonial discourse is complex and simplifying; it can lead to being overly simplistic in our analyses. Blurring boundaries takes us beyond the "them and us" (colonizer/colonized) position commonly found in colonial discourse. Hence, using postcolonialism in this chapter is not to imply that colonialism is over, but to affect a more complex picture of colonizing history and politics and its influence on science education research for indigenous students.

We need to keep in mind that beyondness is also contextually bound, as each country's pre- and post-contact experiences differ. Although those countries that have a history of being part of the British Empire often have points of similarity, their points of difference are just as startling. For example, whereas India was seen as the jewel of the British Empire (or crowns as evidenced in the display at the Tower of London) with its mineral wealth and spices, Aotearoa New Zealand was constructed as the farm, supplying England with primary produce to feed its burgeoning population. India managed to maintain its language and culture, while Aotearoa New Zealand's Maori became numerically decimated through imported diseases, and the language and culture became threatened. Aotearoa New Zealand became a white dominion, along with Australia and Canada, while India remained part of Asia. The colonizing histories of these countries are markedly different—colonized by the same country but at different times and places. All countries, whether numerically dominated by the colonizing peoples or not, have been left a legacy of Western European culture through institutional structures and language. For many indigenous groups, the colonizing experience is ongoing in their own country. To assume that when the administrators of colonizing countries have handed over power, colonialism stops, is to view our history too simply. As Said (1994) argued, "Even as we must fully comprehend the pastness of the past, there is no just way in which the past can be quarantined from the present. Past and present inform each other, each implies the other, each co-exists with the other" (p. 2).

It is also important to understand that imperialism, especially in the time of the Enlightenment, was both a science project and an educational movement (McKinley, 2003). Explorers sought to consciously categorize, name, and label the newly "discovered" territories and peoples, and settlers sought to modernize, develop, instruct, and civilize the natives they found. Early settlers often transplanted familiar objects from their homelands to their new settlement—from books and curricula to flora and fauna—to make their new place like home. In Aotearoa New Zealand, imported flora and fauna came to infest the landscape, causing significant (and ongoing) damage to native species, such as our flightless birds—a form of ecological imperialism (Crosby, 2004). For a science curriculum this is significant. Until the early 1970s, the New Zealand Science Curriculum was based mainly on exotic plants—ones brought in by the British settlers—deliberately planted around school playgrounds in order for the children to study them. Such a movement elevated flora and fauna, and the knowledge that is inherent in such, from the old country above that of the "new" land and so undermined the basis of Maori empirical knowledge of the world. Local knowledge came to be positioned as technical knowledge for survival and/or primitive. Today, although not as obvious, the curriculum continues this legacy in other ways. For example, a common plant, deliberately developed for its pastural qualities as a direct result of colonial settlement and the development of the land as farms, is used by Year 13 students for their plant study. The pasture plant is popular because there is a significant amount of scientific research information on it to support the students' studies, and similar research on native plants is extremely difficult to find. Ironically, Year 13 students in Maori language immersion schools continue to use it for the same reasons.

Indigeneity is a heterogeneous, complex concept that is contextually bound. For example, some groups, such as the First Nations, Inuit, Native American, Maori, and the Koorie and Torres Strait Islanders, are peoples whose colonial settlers or invaders have become numerically dominant. These indigenous groups have been termed the *cause célèbre* of postcolonial times by some writers because they have been seen as the forgotten indigenous peoples in their own countries (see Ashcroft et al., 1995). However, indigeneity also includes Third World contexts such as in Africa, South America, Southeast Asia, and India (see, for example, Semali & Kincheloe, 1999). These contexts bring with them complexities that I cannot even attempt to comprehend or unravel here or through my own experiences. Although many of these countries had Western European settlers, the white populations never attained majority by numbers (and many did not stay), but they exerted enormous influence through institutions and language (Maddock, 1981). Another group is those who claim indigenous status but who are not necessarily legally recognized as such in their own countries, for example, the Ainu people in Japan. And then there are other indigenous groups who have no land to call home, such as the Hmong people (Chang & Rosiek, 2003). The term indigenous is not necessarily used by the groups in their own countries. In Aotearoa New Zealand, Maori are known as *tangata whenua* (people of the land), but the term *indigenous* is often used in an international context to connect with other, similar groups. Hence, the term is not used here to mean the "same," but to form a collective of people who share some similarities in their aspirations and circumstances.

For many indigenous groups, the call for recognition is related to being able to live as indigenous—having access to their language, culture, and resources (such as land, forest, fisheries, and their own institutions). Furthermore, indigenous communities believe education should be about the preparation for participation of young people as both citizens of the world and for participation in their own indigenous societies. These societies—global and local—are not separate, nor is one more backward than the other. All indigenous children live in a variety of contexts and should be able to move from one context to the other with relative ease. In addition, indigenous children should expect to live with good health and a high standard of living, along with other groups in society. A number of researchers have argued that science and indigenous community development are connected (Dyck, 2001; Dzama & Osborne, 1999). Maori researcher Mason Durie (1996) drew a connection between self-determination, improved well-being, and an improved skill base among a group. He argued that self-determination reinforces a cultural identity. Dyck argued, with respect to the Canadian situation, that development is important to indigenous people's participation in science; an indigenous-determined focus means that drawing on a long-term knowledge base and experience can help a people retain a sense of continuity in an otherwise fragmented world. Castellano (2000) argued that the challenge is "to open up space for Aboriginal initiative in schools and colleges, work sites, and organisations so that indigenous ways of knowing can flourish and intercultural sharing can be practised in a spirit of coexistence and mutual respect" (p. 23).

Science education has much to contribute to the wider goals of indigenous communities, particularly in helping indigenous students to help their communities to achieve these aspirations.

Language revitalization, development, and maintenance has become an important goal for indigenous groups to pursue, particularly through the education system, which is seen by many as having a major role in indigenous language loss in many countries (see Battiste & Henderson, 2000; L. T. Smith, 1999). In times of colonization indigenous languages were targeted as an impediment to the civilization of the natives (Barnhardt, 2001; Marker, 2004; McKinley, 2003). Policies and practices of colonial rule effectively banned indigenous languages in schools in many places. As a result, these languages were relegated to community languages or were lost altogether. Furthermore, people came to believe that the colonizer's language was better and sometimes denounced their own languages in favor of it. Any language is fundamental to maintaining worldviews, cultures, and knowledge (Aoki

& Jacknicke, 2005). Furthermore, for indigenous peoples, their homelands are the only place these languages are found, unlike most immigrant groups, whose language is secure in another place. However, the teaching of indigenous languages and cultures in the education system, and in science education, does not appear to be a priority or a foregone conclusion—in fact, their place in schools continues to be contentious in many countries. Such arguments are often constructed around and bring into focus two rights that are sometimes seen to be in conflict: the democratic rights of all citizens and the rights indigenous people assert by virtue of being first peoples of the land. In most places, the individual rights tend to take precedence; unless countries value indigenous languages and find a means of negotiating these imperatives, indigenous knowledge and worldviews will be lost, despite the current resource rush on indigenous knowledge now being seen.

Focusing this chapter on indigeneity is not intended to replace concepts of diversity or multiculturalism but to sit beside them as another form of grouping that provides further insights into the issue of equity in science education research. Science education researchers have begun to recognize their role in helping indigenous communities meet these aspirations. The following section begins to explore how the science education research community has conceptualized this role by looking at terms that denote other knowledge.

INDIGENOUS KNOWLEDGE AND TRADITIONAL ECOLOGICAL KNOWLEDGE

I found few articles in science education research that attempted any explanation of the term Indigenous Knowledge (IK; also called Aboriginal or Native knowledge), though it was widely referred to in the literature. Indigenous writers Battiste and Henderson (2000) argued that there is no simple answer or any legitimate methodology to answer the question what is indigenous knowledge? (p. 35). The issues they raised center upon trying to bring together indigenous knowledge, as perceived in indigenous languages, and "Eurocentric thought" (p. 35). They highlighted three problems in defining IK. First, it is not a uniform concept across all indigenous peoples; it is diverse knowledge that is throughout many peoples and, as such, cannot be captured in the categorization of Eurocentric thought. Second, the idea of understanding IK as it is conceived in indigenous communities does not fit a Eurocentric view of culture, because no parallel word exists in some indigenous languages. And third, the act of codifying can be seen as intrusive and fragmentary as the knowledge is integral to the people and place. Kawagley (1995) expanded on this last argument by suggesting that personal context is extremely important in IK, because knowledge is created through humor, humility, tolerance, observation, experience, social interaction, and listening to conversations and interrogations of the natural and spiritual world. In fact, many indigenous writers see any attempts at definitions of IK as another way of assimilating their communities. Some definitions of IK have been published (see Battiste & Henderson, 2000) that have tended to be broad and refer to complete knowledge systems with internal validity, or they explore the epistemology involved (see Aikenhead, 1997). However, the purpose for my use of IK in this chapter is to refer collectively to the knowledges of various indigenous peoples and not to imply that these local knowledges are the same in any manner.

One of the main focuses of IK is that each group of indigenous people has constructed knowledge that reflects adaptation to a particular location or localities. Integral to such knowledge construction are people, the landscape, and the creator of all things. Furthermore, many indigenous people speak of their own specific knowledge, using their own languages, by referring to it as *matauranga Maori* (Maori), or *Qaujimajatuqungit* (Inuit), or whatever the term may be. For example, Kawagley (1995, 1999) always writes with reference to the knowledge of the Yupiaq people, of whom he is a member, and tends to askew references to IK even as a collective. Furthermore, he writes that Yupiaq knowledge is best dealt with in the native language (Kawagley, 1999). However, other indigenous writers do use the term and speak of "strands of connectedness" throughout continents at least (see Cajete, 1986, 2000). My point here is not to bring the field into paralysis, but to draw the attention of readers in the field to the specifics in the articles when any term regarding knowledge is used. The terms IK and TEK (traditional ecological knowledge) are used mainly by writers for political purposes, such as establishing connections with other groups in order to bring indigenous work to an international stage.

Some debate has occurred in the literature, mainly confined to Canada and the United States, on establishing differences between IK and TEK. Snively and Corsiglia (2001) called descriptive ecological knowledge about nature that has been gathered over years of experience by aboriginal peoples in Canada and the United States traditional ecological knowledge (TEK). One might see TEK as the "science" of IK—that IK which is validated through scientific criteria. Indigenous writers use the term as if it is part of IK, where IK is the frame of knowledge and not science (Battiste & Henderson, 2000; Cajete, 2000). Because indigenous knowledges are deeply integrated with locality (nature) and experience, along with many other characteristics, IK is difficult to separate from TEK from an indigenous point of view. In fact, the extraction of the knowledge from the knower undermines the very basis of IK.

According to indigenous writers, TEK is highly localized and social. The web between humans, the spirits, and nature in a particular locality—such as animals, plants, natural phenomena, and landscapes—form the basis of TEK. Knowledge that has been gained by indigenous peoples is empirical, experimental, and systematic, but the models and explanations do not equate to Western scientific knowledge. Battiste and Henderson (2000) suggested that TEK is a means of understanding the "web of social relationships between a specific group of people (whether a family, clan, or tribe) and a place where they have lived since their beginning" (p. 44). Hence, the knowledge is accumulative over time and is ongoing, but is not static, as often portrayed in curricula. What is traditional about TEK, argued Battiste and Henderson, is not its antiquity but the way it is acquired and used. Furthermore, in light of previous paragraphs, it must be remembered that TEK in the literature is categorized within the frame of Eurocentric thought and language, because IK in indigenous languages makes no such distinction. Any agreement on the term by indigenous writers is most likely based on political imperatives, such as concessions to the realities of working within English-language contexts and in colonized countries.

However, IK is widespread in the literature and generally used as a universal term to denote the worldviews of indigenous peoples. In keeping with Battiste and Henderson's (2000) concerns, most research articles refer to more specific descriptions of IK in local contexts and use local names. I do not intend to debate in this chapter whether IK and TEK should be different, or any advantages of having two names (and hence categories) in English. For my purposes, I will use both IK and TEK for different reasons. TEK is widely used in Canadian and U.S. literature on science education research on aboriginal students of these nations; I use it in relation to the articles that objectify it. I use IK to mean the knowledge and worldviews of indigenous communities. Philosophically, and from an indigenous point of view, the two objects are the same.

INDIGENOUS KNOWLEDGES, SCIENCE, AND CURRICULA

There is a substantial international literature that explores the relationship between indigenous and minority knowledges and Western scientific knowledge. The scientific and metaphysical nature of indigenous knowledges underlies much of the debate. A subsidiary question raised by some researchers is whether Western modern science (WMS) is a threat to indigenous knowledges (IK). This section explores debates concerning the nature of science and indigenous knowledges relevant to science education, particularly with respect to curriculum inclusion.

UNIVERSALISM, PLURALISM, AND IMPERIALISM

One of the largest (in terms of volume of literature) debates in the field of culture and science education is about the nature of knowledge. The debate connects with a wider critique (see Kuhn, 1970) that has accompanied the emergence of post-structuralist, postmodern, and postcolonial theoretical frameworks. The relevance of this literature to schools is that a universalist understanding of science informs the assumptions implicit in school science curricula about the nature of science and how science should be taught (Stanley & Brickhouse, 2001). The debate tends to be polarized into viewing science as a universal body of knowledge—a universalist position—or understanding science knowledge as a product of its culture—a pluralist (or multiculturalist) position. Holders of the universalist position argue that WMS is the paradigmatic example of science, has a universal essence, and provides knowledge that is uniquely and epistemologically far more powerful than that of any IK or traditional sciences (Loving & de Montellano, 2003). In contrast, the pluralist position stresses that all knowledges, including WMS, exist within a cultural context (Lewis & Aikenhead, 2001; McGovern, 1999; Semali & Kincheloe, 1999; Snively & Corsiglia, 2001). Pluralists argue that portraying WMS as universal has undermined indigenous knowledges, dismissing them as inadequate and inferior and making WMS elite (Jegede, 1997; McKinley, 2003; Semali & Kincheloe, 1999; Zaslavsky, 1994).

There is a sense in which this debate has been rather one-sided, in that to take a strongly universalist position is difficult without implying approval of "a politics of exclusions" (Irzik, 2000, p. 71), that is, without being seen as implicitly supporting the current inequity between groups in society. But such a construction was inevitable as researchers found ways to articulate alternative views of knowledge and apply them to curriculum subjects. However, the universalist science approach has been widespread and influential in keeping alternative views from being articulated, particularly through international journals where quantitative methodologies were the dominating ideology for a long time. These approaches tended to construct indigenous (and other minority) groups as subordinate by placing them in a position of deficit (L. T. Smith, 1999).

Semali and Kincheloe (1999) argued that the ability of WMS to present its findings as universal gives it an imperialistic power dismissive of indigenous knowledge as inadequate and inferior. Furthermore, they argued that the cultural context of WMS makes it "white" rather than "universal" science and that the conception of a universal science only arises when one fails "to appreciate the ways modernist scientific universalism excludes this 'white science' as a cultural knowledge" (Semali & Kincheloe, p. 29). This position suggests that all knowledge, including that of WMS, exists within a cultural context, and that the language (including meaning), questions, and methods used by any researcher depict a reality that reflects the cultural values, ideas, beliefs, and practices of the society with which the researcher is familiar. The pluralist position is dismissed by those who question the white science argument on the grounds that women and non-white non-Europeans have made significant contributions to scientific knowledge (Taylor & MacPherson, 1997). Furthermore, they suggested that, as a group, white men are also alienated, confused, and intimidated by science to the same extent as other groups.

Aikenhead (1997) argued that because WMS is often seen as a Western cultural icon of prestige, power, and progress, Western culture usually permeates the culture of those who engage in science. This can threaten indigenous cultures and thus cause Western science to be seen as a "hegemonic icon of cultural imperialism" (p. 15). Harding (1991, 1993, 1998), more specific in her discussion, highlighted the political utility of science to indigenous subjugation.

> Scientific and technological changes are inherently political, since they redistribute the costs and benefits of nature's resources in new ways. They tend to widen any pre-existing gaps between the haves and have-nots unless issues of just distribution are directly addressed. (Harding, 1998, pp. 50–51)

M. R. Smith (1996) argued that the threat posed by WMS to Native American children is such that it may cause for them a loss of culture. According to Smith, WMS devalues Native American science and as such causes a "progressive alienation from traditional values, family and community" (p. 2). Furthermore, George (1999) argued that IK is not found in school curricula because it is not considered to be scholarly, because of the way in which it is developed and transmitted. There is compelling evidence to suggest that imperialism and colonialism have contributed significantly to WMS's domination in school curricula to the exclusion of local knowledge. The science curriculum is the site of contestation for the inclusion of a pluralist approach to knowledge.

Contesting the Curriculum

A widespread assumption is that WMS should be part of the school curriculum for all peoples, but its place is increasingly being contested. For example, Lewis and Aikenhead (2000) asked, "How should non-Western ideas be viewed in relation to Western science? If non-Western ideas are not inferior should they be 'accepted' in science classrooms?" (p. 4). Many science education researchers argue for the inclusion of indigenous knowledges, but the debates tend to be centered around the extent to which IK/TEK should be included. In contrast, those opposing its inclusion argue that there is no place for IK unless it has been subsumed into the body of knowledge referred to as WMS, that is, unless it is made the same as WMS, in which case the status quo continues. The arguments forwarded revolve mainly around the metaphysical nature of IK. However, the arguments between IK and WMS are not as diametrically opposed as one might expect. For example, the idea that IK and WMS differ through process is agreed upon but is used to support different assertions. The following section discusses the arguments forwarded as to why IK and/or TEK should or should not be included in the curriculum. The arguments center on finding connections between the two, the proposition that IK is contemporary knowledge, that IK can enter the curriculum but not the science curriculum, and that IK has no place in the curriculum.

Finding Connections

By far the most supported argument in the literature is that IK should have a place in the science curriculum. However, many researchers suggest this can be done in a variety of ways. The admission of IK in science curricula immediately poses questions about the scientific nature of traditional indigenous bodies of knowledge; it is here where researchers have taken the opportunity to form a new object of knowledge as already outlined, that is, TEK (Corsiglia & Snively, 2000). Some researchers argue that indigenous knowledge can be taught alongside Western science as distinct but not entirely dissimilar knowledge systems within a single curriculum framework (Goes in Center, 2001; Rikihana, 1996; Roberts, 1996). In New Zealand, Roberts' approach to indigenous knowledge and Western science was to compare the similarities and differences from the perspective of Pacific knowledge bases. Aikenhead (1997) undertook a similar project with respect to Canadian First Nations knowledge bases. The argument is that both WMS and IK have an empirical database with observations of the natural world having provided information that has been accumulated over time, systematized, stored, and transmitted, either orally or in written form. Roberts argued that the differences between the two forms of knowledge are in the creation of empirical databases. In many cases, IK databases have been built up over thousands of years and include qualitative as well as quantitative information, because all observations and interactions are considered relevant. In contrast, many WMS databases are comparatively short term, primarily quantitative, and frequently obtained or supplemented by experimental data gathered under controlled conditions. WMS and IK share an ability to construct theories (models) and make predictions, and are subject to verification over time. But there are differences in the framing and testing of predictions and in the treatment of results. Another view was given by Corsiglia and Snively (2000), who argued: "Indigenous science offers important science knowledge that WMS has not yet learned to produce, and that IK and TEK are being increasingly researched in Africa because they can contribute to the eradication of poverty, disease and hunger where modern techniques are deficient" (p. 235).

They argued that if IK and TEK can make valid observations, then it is not legitimate for the science classroom to present conventional science as the only way of seeing the world. It is an acknowledgment, given with reservation, that some of the insights of science can be arrived at by other epistemological pathways.

A number of researchers have made attempts at including IK into science curricula through developing resources and writing curricula in indigenous languages (see, for example, Aikenhead, 1997; McKinley, 1996, Michie & Linkson, 1999). June George (1999), in her work in Trinidad and Tobago, took a slightly different approach and identified several ways in which school knowledge and IK are both similar and different. She presented a four-fold categorization of the relationship between the two knowledge systems. The first category is where conventional science can explain indigenous practice. For example, the indigenous practice of using a mixture of lime juice and salt to remove rust stains from clothes can be explained in conventional science in terms of acid/oxide relations. In her second category, a conventional science explanation is unavailable, but likely to be developed; for example, native plants that have pharmacological properties recognized in traditional medicine, but appropriate usage has not been verified by conventional science, although conventional science does recognize its pharmacological utility. In category three, there is a conventional science link with traditional knowledge, but the principles may be different, for example, in the relationship between sugar and diabetes, where IK claims sugars cause diabetes, WMS claims the ingestion of sugars for a diabetic can worsen the condition. Finally, in a fourth category are those aspects of IK that conventional science cannot accept. George suggested that the knowledge in categories one and three could be used in classroom programs to highlight similarities between indigenous and Western conceptions of knowledge and would increase indigenous students' engagement in learning.

IK as Contemporary Knowledge

Indigenous knowledge has been seen as knowledge that is not conversant with the modern world. Even the use of the term TEK conveys a sense of being old-fashioned. The questioning of the contemporary and continuing utility of IK is rejected by indigenous writers (see for example, Dei, 2000; Goes in Center, 2001; Kawagley, 1999; McKinley, Waiti, & Aislabie, 2004). For example, the use of Geographic Information Systems (GIS) has been taken on by indigenous communities all over the world, and many feel it has been made for us. It enables communities to analyze and organize information regarding resources, both land and people, in ways that have never been available previously, but at the same time includes "native standards, goals, and tribal wisdom" (Goes in Center, p. 121). The use of GIS to develop IK is an example of dynamism and embedding of the modern into IK.

Related to this argument is the significance of traditional knowledge to indigenous development (see, for example, Castellano, 2000; Dei, 2000; McKinley, 1997). For example, Castellano argued that the ability of indigenous Canadians to live well is inextricably linked with their traditional knowledge base, as they battle externally generated problems such as contamination of their traditional food supplies and the marginalization of rural peoples in a competitive world economy.

> The knowledge that will support their survival in the future will not be an artefact from the past. It will be a living fire, rekindled from surviving embers and fueled with the materials of the twenty-first century (p. 34).

Dei (2000) made the same argument and extended it within the context of IK and African development, as did McKinley in the New Zealand context. Lujan (2001) saw science as a tool for American Indian community development, whereas James (2001) suggested that First Nations peoples need science to understand the impact of the dominating culture's schemes on individuals and communities. The link between science and indigenous peoples is acknowledged by many. The issue is not that indigenous communities wish to shun science completely, but that science needs to be integral to development of the community, not as the controlling knowledge (Durie, 1996).

Disciplining IK

Many researchers suggest that science curricula need to be reconceptualized, going beyond presenting indigenous or subjugated knowledges as add-ons that provide interest or diversity to Western academic institutions, to integrating them into science curricula (see Aikenhead, 1996; Jegede, 1995; McKinley, 1996; Ogawa, 1997). Other researchers believe that IK should be part of the curriculum, but as a separate subject, just like art or literature (Cobern & Loving, 2000). The reason given for treating IK this way is a concern that IK could be co-opted into a universal paradigm by WMS's domination. Furthermore, IK could maintain a position of independence and continue to critique the practices of science from outside. The argument that IK and TEK, like other subjects, is not devalued by their exclusion from the science domain takes no account of colonial power and its ongoing nature in postcolonial societies. Subjects, such as history and art, are an integral part of Western societies and have had a tendency to claim a "real" history or art. These subjects have in the past excluded, and in many cases continue to exclude, knowledge from indigenous societies. As a result, many indigenous peoples learn the languages, histories, arts, nature, etc. of their colonizers in schools and have to find other means to learn about and appreciate their own knowledge and not feel ashamed. It is the tendency for WMS to establish itself as the only way of knowing that, Jegede (1995) argued, denigrates IK and creates difficulties for indigenous learners.

However, there has been some recognition that keepers of IK show a reluctance to discuss it, particularly with people who have a formal Western-style education, which affects curriculum inclusion (Castellano, 2000; Kawagley, 2001; L. T. Smith, 1999). As a result of assimilative education, economic dislocation, and government control often from external cultures, the intergenerational transmission of knowledge has been undermined to the extent that its survival is in danger. In addition, there has been some disruption of the application of IK to the demands of daily living within a language, where knowledge grows and moves on.

No Connection, No Place for IK

Taylor and MacPherson (1997) argued that the debates regarding IK and WMS should not be taking place, because they are based on a false premise, that the modifier Western suggests that science is practiced and culturally rooted only in the West. However, many of the arguments against IK inclusion in the curriculum are of a more philosophical nature. Some researchers have argued that IK does not distinguish the physical from the metaphysical (Loving & de Montellano, 2003; Yakabu, 1994). For example, Yakabu suggested that even when people in traditional societies have been well educated in science, they find it difficult to give up the traditional solutions to problems to consider new and better ones. Others suggest such a position is overstated; in the perception of students, the two domains do not have serious interference, because the two are separated by the sorts of questions asked (Durie, 1996; Thijs & van den Berg, 1995). In the New Zealand context, Durie argued that the emphasis Maori thought places on the link between the physical and the metaphysical is not so much a point of absolute difference from conventional science, but a difference in balance. He suggested that, to some extent, the debate is about semantics. More importantly, indigenous communities emphasize a holistic approach rather than the fragmentation of knowledge.

A further argument is that WMS is culture free or generic in its approach, if not its application. Inherent in this argument is that WMS is not at fault for excluding "others"; that has more to do with the public image of science. For example, in an African American context, Key (2003) argued that school science may even be seen as something foreign to all students, who can study science for years before reading about a scientist or inventor of their own ethnic group. Key suggested that if students do not identify with those who are doing the processing, they may internalize the idea that they cannot perform science. However, as science is culture-free, the students may perceive they cannot do science because of the cultural images, rather than any aspect of the subject matter. The issue of the image of what it is to be a scientist has been echoed by researchers of indigenous students, but not for the same reason (see Monhardt, 2003). The response to a lack of cultural representation among the community of scientists has usually been in finding indigenous scientists and writing about them in a resource that can be used by schools (see Martin, 1996).

Concluding Comments

A suggestion has been made that non-Western cultures be asked what concerns they have, or do not have, about WMS and whether learning about WMS is a threat to the survival of their culture and about the extent to which they wish to access Western scientific knowledge (Stanley & Brickhouse, 2001). There is little doubt, according to others, that most indigenous parents want their children to acquire the best available Western scientific knowledge, provided that such knowledge does not displace their own cultural understandings (see, for example, Corsiglia & Snively, 2000; McPherson Waiti, 1990). In Aotearoa New Zealand an emphasis on an integrated approach to economic, social, and cultural development leads to the position that there is an imperative for full Maori participation in science (Durie, 1996; McKinley, 1999). Furthermore, it is emphasized that the interface between IK and WMS allows for an expanded understanding of ourselves and the world around us. Kawagley (1995) suggested that indigenous thought sees science understandings as a quest for knowledge as well as a means to live a long and prosperous life—to be used in juxtaposing it against past experience in order to see what the future holds. Although pluralists accept the effective and reliable nature of WMS, this is not the same as saying it stands outside human conceptions. In this way, not only do IK systems have a functional significance beyond that of WMS; it is suggested that indigenous people may view science differently, which has implications for learning, in communities and classrooms, and the curriculum. The next section examines the research on learning implications of IK and/or TEK in classrooms.

IMPROVING CLASSROOM PRACTICE

The culture and science debates in the 1980s and 1990s were linked to others. Constructivism; science for all; scientific literacy; and science, technology, and society (STS) were concerned with pedagogical change and improving the learning and achievement of a wider range of students in science education by taking into account students' prior knowledge. Unfortunately, two major research projects of the 1980s that became the basis for many research studies in science education in the years that followed, the Children's Learning in Science Project (CLISP) in Britain and the Learning in Science Project (LISP) in New Zealand, never considered culture, power, and discourse as major variables in children's understanding of school science concepts or their prior knowledge at their time. However, some science educators from African and Caribbean countries working with indigenous groups published research challenging the notion that students' prior conceptual understandings of science were culture-free (see Christie, 1991; George & Glasgow, 1988; Jegede, 1988; Jegede & Okebukola, 1991; Ogawa, 1989). One argument forwarded by these writers for taking students' cultures into account in learning science was motivation—to try to get the students to enjoy science, try harder, build their self-esteem and, hence, succeed. However, there was also an attempt to consider and find ways for science education to be more inclusive of other cultural knowledge and languages (see McKinley, Waiti, & Bell, 1992). These indigenous educators challenged the personal constructivists about conceptual change and how it occurred.

The work of the indigenous educators aligns loosely with the work of those who tried to develop a sociocultural approach to teaching and learning. A few science and mathematics education researchers began to articulate a thorough critique of the assumptions underpinning personal constructivism in the research literature at the time (see, for example, Aikenhead, 1996; Cobern, 1993; O'Loughlin, 1992; Solomon, 1987, 1994; Walkerdine, 1984). The purpose of establishing a sociocultural approach was to reintroduce a cultural perspective for science education. The issues raised in this literature, often based on anthropological studies, included that which centered on meaning-making in everyday contexts. Cobern (1993, 1996), in particular, worked on establishing a worldview theory, suggesting it as a model to determine how culturally different students will engage with science meanings. Worldview theory focuses on what will appear plausible to the students and what might not. The term *worldview* has been adopted by a number of science education researchers.

However, the criticism of the sociocultural approach is that it is still situated and focused on science and how to get students acculturated into it, "to teach students the socioculturally constituted ways of knowing that underlie science so that the process of doing science is demystified" (O'Loughlin, 1992, p. 816). The approach is still favored by a number of science education researchers who explore ways to approach science critically and work within multicultural education. However, as indigenous groups assert their first people of the land status, their aspirations extend beyond what this framework appears to deliver. Even worldview theory is a model for detecting resistance to science ideas that seem counter-intuitive to the student; it does not focus on the assimilatory tendency of WMS to indigenous views of knowledge. For example, sociocultural approaches do not articulate any differences between multicultural and indigenous studies, or enculturation and assimilation (Aikenhead, 1996).

In many ways, these early studies set the scene for classroom research on culture and science education for the next 10 years. Models of culturally based pedagogy for science education have been forwarded that include notions such as "collateral learning" of both Western and traditional concepts (Jegede, 1995); or teachers as "culture brokers" who help students to master repeated "border crossings" between their own life world and that of the science classroom (Aikenhead, 1996). There have been calls for the reorganization of science programs to reflect indigenous contexts, languages, philosophies, and thoughts (McKinley, 1996; Ogawa, 1997) and the critical scrutiny of current science education practices (Ninnes, 2003). The failure of mainstream educational movements to address indigenous people's concerns has been noted, and alternative schooling movements are beginning to emerge (M. R. Smith, 1996), many from indigenous groups, such as the Maori language immersion *kura kaupapa* schools in Aotearoa New Zealand.

CULTURE AND PEDAGOGY

This section examines studies that relate to improving classroom practice for indigenous students. The reality of the situation is that most indigenous students are in cross-cultural classrooms where the teacher is not from the same culture group. Furthermore, most students attend schools where indigenous peoples, language, knowledge, and aspirations are not the norm. Hence, most of the issues that arise in this section are ones that feature of all classroom research, where so much depends on the quality of the teaching and learning. The underlying assumption in many of the studies is that indigenous students are not participating or achieving in current science education classrooms. The literature argues strongly that indigenous student participation and performance in science are undermined by low teacher efficacy; low student self-expectation; cultural stereotypes; inadequate teacher subject, pedagogic, and cultural knowledge; and conflict between the culture of home and school. However, many of these factors interact with each other and are difficult to separate out, as this section indicates. I discuss the research on improving classroom pedagogy under (1) teacher expectations and efficacy, (2) using cultural knowledge in classrooms, (3) and learning for indigenous students.

Teacher Expectations and Efficacy

Teacher expectations are seen as significant determinants of student performance. However, research has found that a deficit model often operates with respect to indigenous and minority students, that contributes to low expectations and a teacher's sense of efficacy (see, for example, Bishop & Glynn, 1999; N. Carter, Larke, Taylor, &

Santos, 2003; Dukepoo, 2001; McKinley, 1996; Poodry, 2001). Deficit thinking can manifest itself through stereotyping, seeing other cultures as inferior, and a feeling of a lack of agency on the part of the teacher. The deficit model assumes that any fault lies within the person and/or culture, such as the person not trying hard enough, or the culture militating against scientific understandings. In other words, the lack of efficacy seems to have the effect of bringing the learning of indigenous students (and others) to a point of paralysis, because teachers believe it is the student's life circumstances that prevent learning. Teachers who lack efficacy believe that trying makes little difference to the student's success. Teachers who reject that assertion believe that they can make a difference to all students and take on the responsibility to teach everybody in their classrooms (Atwater & Crocket, 2003; Bryan & Atwater, 2002; Hill & Hawk, 2000).

A lack of efficacy is not just about the teacher's agency, but also about the student's capability. Unfortunately stereotypical views of indigenous students have led to assumptions about teaching and learning for them. For example, Ninnes's (2003) work on science textbooks in Australia and Canada identified a persistence of cultural and gender stereotypes in science education in school texts. His work showed that often there was an absence of any representation of indigenous ideas and identities. If they were represented, they were presented as traditional images that the dominating white cultures had of the indigenous culture, as indigenous peoples being homogeneous, and with science knowledge privileged over IK. Furthermore, in an accompanying survey, Ninnes (2001) found that the inclusion of this material in school textbooks was mainly there to comply with state requirements. This was supported in the project carried out by McKinley, Stewart, and Richards (2004) in Aotearoa New Zealand relating to Maori cultural contexts in the science curricula of schools. Rowland and Adkins (2003) maintained that the same problem of stereotyping exists in North American multicultural science education and Native American science education. They argued that the stereotypes are based on limited research and experience and cannot accommodate within-group variance.

The ability of the student to understand and participate in science education is inextricably linked to the closeness of the relationship between the culture of school and home. For many indigenous students, there is a significant gulf rather than a closeness of cultures. Zepeda (2001) argued that school pressures reservation children to move away from tribal traditions. The effect of such movement is to isolate children from their families, communities, and identities. Indeed, the cultural gap between home and school can be such that by the time they reach university, "some Indian students fear traditional systems because they do not understand them" (Zepeda, p. 64). For Yupiaq communities, this is a problem, as they see the encroachment of Western civilization on a world that did not seek it out (Kawagley, 1999). They seek ways in which they can maintain their culture in the face of strong opposition and set up Alaska Native camps in an attempt to find more control over the changes.

Understanding of the worlds of students is a significant contributing factor toward successful teaching in low socioeconomic, multicultural New Zealand schools (Hill & Hawk, 2000). They argued that successful teachers in these schools demonstrate a good understanding of the lives of the students, and the students know and value this highly. Furthermore, successful teachers have strong interactions with students outside the classroom and place a high value on contact with parents, more often for positive rather than negative reasons. Understanding how large this cultural transition from the student's life world to that of school science is can help determine whether students achieve in science (Aikenhead, 1996; Jegede, 1995).

Using Cultural Contexts in Classrooms

Resources that connect culture with science and a teacher's ability to facilitate such resources through competent teaching have been found to be problematic (Aikenhead & Huntley, 1999; Davison & Miller, 1998; Loving & de Montellano, 2003; McKinley 1996; McKinley, Stewart, & Richards, 2004; Rowland & Adkins, 2003; Sutherland & Dennick, 2002). Researchers have argued that the inclusion of culturally relevant situations in science curricula can help to raise indigenous students' achievement (Davison & Miller; McKinley, 1997). However, this objective raises a number of concerns in the literature. For example, when Aikenhead and Huntley researched teachers' views on Western science and aboriginal science in northern Saskatchewan, Canada, they found a large number of barriers preventing any meaningful engagement with aboriginal knowledge. Teachers had not recognized Western science as cultural knowledge; had little understanding that students' preconceptions could interfere with their learning and did not provide appropriate instruction; held a deficit view of their students; gave many differing responses to cultural conflict in classrooms; and possessed insufficient resources to help with supporting aboriginal knowledge in classrooms.

In their New Zealand study, McKinley, Stewart, and Richards (2004) found that teachers in English-medium or mainstream schools tried to include Maori contexts in their science lessons. The study found that all of the teachers mentioned the same topics, despite being separated by large distances; the topics were iconic (the well-known and easily identifiable aspects of Maori culture), and teachers believed these topics met state regulations. Maori topics reportedly were included to make the students feel better about themselves by seeing Maori culture valued in classrooms and to make students interested and comfortable. The students did not see it like this at all, suggesting that the connections between cultural activities and school science are not always obvious to children who live in two worlds. Other concerns raised by teachers in this study was the effect of trying to be culturally sensitive to specific populations and not causing offense, a tendency researchers found particularly among teachers not grounded in the culture of the people whom they teach. Another concern was teachers assuming that all students who identify as belonging to an indigenous group have been exposed to the same cultural knowledge.

It would appear that resource availability is variable across various countries. For example, Loving and de Montellano (2003) argued that suitable teaching materials on science, education, and culture are not available in great number because there has been a refusal of scientists and science educators to develop accurate and valid materials dealing with the issue. As a result, alternative science materials of "dubious quality" and some examples of "blatantly bad science" (Loving & de Montellano, 2003, p. 15) have been produced. However, in a recent research project carried out in Aotearoa New Zealand, McKinley, Waiti, and Aislabie (2004) found that scientists are working with local indigenous Maori groups on science research projects and producing resources—sometimes in two languages—that can be used directly or to support resource development for teachers. This work has the potential to become an integral part of science teacher professional development. It also has the potential to help educate a wider public about Maori knowledge and its place in the curriculum.

Culture and Learning

Another issue raised for indigenous students is that of learning styles. In a recent project in New Zealand, researchers found that significant numbers of teachers thought Maori students were tactile, visual, and oral in their style of learning (McKinley, Stewart, & Richards, 2004). At the same time, the teachers suggested other characteristics related to Maori students' learning, such as liking structure and routines. This analysis by the teachers, in turn, determined their culturally relevant pedagogy. More importantly, it determined the teachers' expectations of Maori students, suggesting that such learning styles limited the achievement of these students. However, the use of learning styles associated with particular cultural groups needs to be treated with caution (Irvine & York, 1995). It is easy for teachers to draw conclusions on the basis of simplistic assumptions regarding surface characteristics of cultures as described by ethnographers and anthropologists (Kawagley, 2001; McKinley, Stewart, & Richards, 2004). Dukepoo (2001) argued that "Indians are human . . . as such, they all have different learning styles" (p. 37). Furthermore, indigenous communities have accommodated different learning styles for thousands of years (see, for example, Dukepoo, 2001; Hemara, 2000).

Some researchers have begun to explore ways of learning in indigenous communities and suggest that these ways could provide insight into classroom learning for indigenous students. Indigenous ways of knowing include knowledge as metaphysical, interdependent and balanced, constructed through indigenous languages, and dependent on personal relationships; people have specialized knowledge and passion through intergenerational teachings and social practices. Various combinations of these have been raised by several researchers, both indigenous and non-indigenous (Aikenhead, 1996; Cajete, 1986; George, 1999; Jegede, 1995; Kawagley, 1999; McKinley, 1996; Ogawa, 1995; Pomeroy, 1992; Sutherland, 1999). For example, Allen and Crawley's (1998) study of the Traditional Kickapoo Band found a worldview that differed with respect to epistemology, preferred methods of teaching/learning, values, spatial/temporal orientation, cultural rules for behavior, and a perspective of the place of humans in a natural world. They argued that this worldview prevented the Kickapoo students from being successful in science classrooms.

Furthermore, the research literature suggests there is a means by which a person comes to know in indigenous societies. For example, Sutherland (1999) wrote that for some indigenous communities in Canada, the United States, and South America, not all knowledge is accessible to everyone, and neither is all knowledge open to public scrutiny. A person may get access to knowledge previously denied when it is deemed he or she is prepared for it. This is because with the acquisition of knowledge comes responsibility to the community. Cree educator Ermine (1995) took coming-to-know further by arguing that, for aboriginal peoples, it is a process of self-actualization in relation to wholeness, "a being in connection with happenings" (p. 104). Battiste and Henderson (2000) add that indigenous languages are fundamental links to knowledge, and that transmission is both intimate and oral rather than distant or literate.

In the case of rural African students, Jegede (1995) proposed a model of collateral learning through identifying the sociocultural influences on non-Western students' learning. He argued that there are five predictors of sociocultural influences in the classroom, especially within non-Western environments, to which teachers must pay particular attention: authoritarianism, goal structure, traditional worldview, societal expectation, and the sacredness of science. Jegede argued that successful border crossing can occur through a process of collateral learning where "a learner in a non-Western classroom constructs, side by side and with minimal interference and interaction, Western and traditional meanings of a simple concept. Collateral knowledge, therefore, is the declarative knowledge of a concept which such a learner stores up in the long-term memory for strategic use in either a Western or a traditional environment" (p. 117).

Elsewhere Jegede (1998, pp. 80–86) gave a detailed description of collateral learning of which he suggested there were four main types: parallel, simultaneous, dependent, and secured.

Teaching in contexts of cultural familiarity to children and contrasting their life-worlds, using a critical analysis of science, and consciously moving back and forth between life-worlds and the science-world facilitate the type of border crossings that Aikenhead argued are essential to the successful acquisition of scientific knowledge by non-Western students (Aikenhead, 1996). Aikenhead suggested that border crossings can be facilitated in classrooms by studying the subcultures of students' life-worlds and contrasting them with a critical analysis of the subculture of science. The point being made in this theory of learning is that both teacher and student do this consciously. Aikenhead argued that border crossings would be further facilitated by the creation of a cross-cultural science and technology curriculum and a science-technology-society (STS) curriculum. He developed such units with six Aboriginal teachers in northern Saskatchewan.

Jegede (1995) argued that the cultural clash and difficulties associated with border crossing and collateral learning create an educational imperative that science education research must understand the cultural basis to learning within indigenous societies; otherwise the education of these communities will never be effective. The solution, Jegede maintained, involves restructuring science education and refocusing teacher education programs to ensure that their philosophical foundations are located and guided by the indigenous culture's imperatives. In practice, this requires an education that is accommodating, practical, and positively oriented. Nelson-Barber and Estrin (1995) argued that the way science is taught in classrooms has contributed to inadequate opportunities for Native American students to succeed. Furthermore, the process of presenting knowledge side by side and assuming all of the ideas are equally accessible to everyone needs to change. All this work suggests that teaching practices do little to recognize IK that indigenous students may have acquired in their everyday lives.

Indigenous Languages and Science Education

Historically, little research has been done with respect to student learning in indigenous languages. The range of indigenous languages, their use, and their relationship to the colonizing languages (or languages) make for some very different projects. For example, Rutherford and Nkopodi (1990) argued from the results of their study in South Africa that there should be more English language use in science classrooms of North Sotho-speaking students. They argued that the use of the vernacular hindered student learning. However, Lynch (1996), in his study in Australia and the Philippines with three distinct language groups (English, Tagalog, and B'laan), found that many alternative frameworks are linguistically and/or culturally determined. He argued that science teachers need to respond to both cultural and linguistic constructs as well as to what is accurate scientifically. He also found Tagalog and B'Laan were not sufficiently intellectualized for handling conceptual correctness for Western science. Alternative frameworks and language were investigated by Kawasaki (1996, 2002) in a comparison of Western science to Japanese views of nature through each language. He raised issues of linguistic conceptual incommensurabilities and argued that Japanese science teachers need to introduce comparative science studies to Japanese students so that they can appreciate that which belongs to both cultures, and identify science education with foreign-language education.

The issue of the critical state of indigenous languages in many countries has become part of science education. The project of teaching in indigenous languages brings with it all the attendant issues of what happens not only in our science classrooms, but also in our teacher education institutes and our science degree structures. With the development of Maori language immersion schools in the 1980s, Aotearoa New Zealand has translated their national curriculum into the indigenous Maori language (McKinley, 1995, 1996), but no other reports were found where this had occurred. Unfortunately, researchers have yet to carry out research in science education on what effect, if any, this has had on Maori children's learning. Barker (1999) cited research from the United States (Alaska) and Canada, claiming that science learning in an indigenous language can reduce the "poverty of students' thinking" (p. 58). This was extrapolated from the idea that students become familiar with two worldviews and as such can go beyond either of them to formulate new ideas. According to Atwater, the research that has been done on this has provided inconclusive results (as cited in Rowland & Adkins, 2003).

Recent research in Aotearoa New Zealand suggests the Maori philosophy that drives the Maori language immersion schools dismisses stereotypes and does not treat all Maori youth as at risk. These schools are positioned instead to determine their own academic destiny by promoting being Maori as normative—teachers are Maori, learning is in the Maori language, and Maori values and philosophies take precedent. In other words, the purpose of such schooling is to empower students and communities (Bishop & Glyn, 1999). Although the goal is ideal, the pathway brings with it multiple issues. For example, Maori immersion high schools, in particular, find it difficult to employ qualified science teachers who are proficient speakers of Maori (McKinley, Stewart, & Richards, 2004). However, it stands to reason that the development and success of such programs are essential in order to act as a wellspring for cultural contexts in English classrooms. The issue of indigenous languages and science education is an area that needs research urgently. Further-more, such projects need to reflect the long-term effort that is required to bring back languages from the brink of extinction.

COMMENTS AND CHALLENGES
FOR FUTURE DIRECTIONS

In summary, the debate in the literature is dominated by publications in favor of culturalist approaches. However, teaching practices have changed little and remain based on traditional, universalist views of the nature of science and of science edu-cation (Aikenhead, 2001; Scantlebury, McKinley, & Jesson, 2002). The resistance of school curricula to reform efforts is well documented (Blades, 1997; Hodson, 1999). This apparent paradox may be explained by examining the key role that WMS, and associated views, has played in the emergence of Euro-American culture. Further-more, WMS is supported by technocratic rationality and based on an economistic philosophy. The current position of Euro-American culture is overwhelmingly pow-erful in the contemporary global situation. However, school curricula and teaching do need to change if indigenous students are to take up their rightful place in scien-tific endeavors and contribute to the knowledge economy and world environment. Furthermore, just as science has much to offer indigenous communities, indigenous communities have much to offer science. Science education has a responsibility to help facilitate what should be a dynamic exchange. With these goals in mind, the re-search currently reviewed here shows omissions that urgently need attention.

First, there is a large amount of comment on this issue of indigenous students but a general lack of empirical studies, particularly in some areas. Second, the dis-tribution of research is uneven. For example, there is a lot of comment on philosoph-ical debates, but little research on indigenous languages and science education. Fur-thermore, there is a growing amount of work on developing indigenous contexts for classroom use, but this review found no reports on assessment for indigenous students. Many of the writers suggest research in further areas. For example, Ninnes (2003) suggested that there is a need for further research "regarding the sources of knowledge pertaining to indigenous peoples, the extent of involvement of indige-nous people in the production of texts that purport to represent their knowledges and that construct identities for them, and the effects of including material of this kind in science curricula of indigenous and other students' approaches to learning science" (p. 182).

Atwater and Crockett (2003) turned their attention to teacher education, sug-gesting that it is essential that science teacher educators and researchers examine the influence of their personal worldviews, beliefs, attitudes, and images on science learning and teaching. There is no doubt that all of these areas are important. More importantly, as researchers in the field, we need to search out and develop different frameworks for our research that match the aims of what we want to achieve.

There are a number of frameworks evident in the current research. Although a positivistic approach still exists within the field, where indigenous people are con-stituted as deficit, there is a definite and strong move away from this theorizing. However, we need to note that although the research may have moved, there are a significant number of teachers in front of indigenous students who have not. What we need to take from this as researchers is how to change thinking. Are there other conceptual frameworks we can use to target deep-seated teacher beliefs with respect to indigenous students?

Dominating the field currently are approaches derived from anthropology, such as worldviews (Cobern, 1993, 1996), collateral learning (Jegede, 1995), and border crossing (Aikenhead, 1996). The anthropological approach is a seductive one because it focuses on the culture and cultural practices of different groups and treats science as a cultural activity (Hammond & Brandt, 2004). The approach has proved to be fruitful in a number of areas, such as re-orienting our focus away from deficit theorizing, and finding a place for community voice through narrative. However, the anthropological approach has limitations for studying indigenous peoples, such as having no way to deal with issues of power and economic privilege, and having a problematic history with indigenous peoples in the past. In terms of frameworks, this may be better illustrated through a question. An anthropological approach question may be, What makes teaching and learning effective for indigenous children? But the frame does not raise the question, What makes an effective indigenous language learner and teacher of science? The latter question focuses on the imperatives of the indigenous communities concerned about language loss. However, I want to raise two further frameworks that need to be considered for our science education research.

One framework that has emerged recently was developed by postcolonial studies (see, for example, L. Carter, 2004; McKinley, 2001, 2003; Ninnes, 2003). The strengths of this approach are its deconstructive methodology; its focus on language (both borrowed from poststructural analysis); its interrogation of the self/Other relationship, such as in a colonial situation; and the interrogation of epistemologies and objects of institutional knowledge. In particular, postcolonial studies explore deep-seated ideas in the psychology of the mind, recognizing that learning from the other is a psychical event. Postcolonial theory can open up persons' anxieties about encountering difference. Furthermore, postcolonial theory analyzes these anxieties through the language used in reading the unconscious or subtext of images, print, and speech. The methodology used for this analysis is deconstruction; there is not only an unpacking of ideas, but also a displacement of them. Postcolonial theory has been criticized for being too textually based, lacking agency, and using psychoanalysis (which had been developed for practice in another field).

The second framework I want to raise is that of indigenous communities themselves (see, for example, Battiste & Henderson, 2000; James, 2001; Mihesuah & Wilson, 2004; L. T. Smith, 1999). Indigenous peoples have begun to take control of their own destiny by instigating an approach that is indigenous-focused. This approach, put simply, has three prongs. First is to decolonize the methodologies that claim to produce meaningful knowledge about indigenous people. This is being done in a variety of ways by many indigenous academics. Second is to theorize, conceptualize, and represent indigenous sovereignty. This is about treating our own knowledge and ways of knowing as something to be valued, and to profile them in our work. And last, it is about producing indigenous knowledge for indigenous peoples—setting our own research agendas and carrying out what indigenous people want, and not what others think we need.

David Clark (2004) argued that the indigenous project is about "restoring well-being to our nations" (p. 230). Well-being for indigenous peoples comes from an integrated approach to social, economic, and cultural development, and from a strong sense of identity as indigenous. I wish to leave you with two broad challenges for science education with respect to indigenous students. First, there is a need to get more indigenous students participating and achieving in science. According to our own track record, this will be a major challenge in itself. The second challenge is to find a place in our curricula and classrooms for indigenous knowledge—a place that recognizes and protects indigenous information, understanding, and wisdom. This will add to our scientific knowledge and methods. This will require some major adjustments to teacher education and science courses, and, for many, will challenge our deepest beliefs. There will be much debate and conflict, but also much excitement. As we move toward the future, the world will need people with the capacity to move between perspectives and embrace both indigenous ways and science. Our work is to help create the platform for that to happen.

ACKNOWLEDGMENTS

The author acknowledges Nga Pae o te Maramatanga/The National Institute of Research Excellence for Maori Development and Advancement for funding the project from which much of this literature is drawn, and thanks the research assistants on that project, particularly Dominic O'Sullivan and Georgina Stewart. Thanks also to William Cobern and Dawn Sutherland, who reviewed this chapter.

REFERENCES

Aikenhead, G. S. (1996). Science education: Border crossing into the subculture of science. *Studies in Science Education, 27*, 1–52.

Aikenhead, G. S. (1997). Toward a first nations cross-cultural science and technology curriculum. *Science Education, 81*, 217–238.

Aikenhead, G. (2001). Integrating Western and Aboriginal sciences: Cross-cultural science teaching. *Research in Science Education, 31*, 337–355.

Aikenhead, G., & Huntley, B. (1999). Teachers' views on aboriginal students learning western and aboriginal science. *Canadian Journal of Native Education, 23*(2), 159–175.

Allen, N. J., & Crawley, F. E. (1998). Voices from the bridge: Worldview conflicts of Kickapoo students of science. *Journal of Research in Science Teaching, 35*, 111–132.

Aoki, T. T., & Jacknicke, K. (2005). Language, culture and curriculum. In W. F. Pinar & R. L. Irwin (Eds.), *Curriculum in a new key: The collected works of Ted T. Aoki* (pp. 321–329). Mahwah, NJ: Lawrence Erlbaum Associates.

Ashcroft, B., Griffiths, G., & Tiffin, H. (Eds.). (1995). *The post-colonial studies reader*. London: Routledge.

Atwater, M., & Crockett, D. (2003). Prospective teachers' education worldview and teacher education programs: Through the eyes of culture, ethnicity, and class. In S. M. Hines (Ed.), *Multicultural science education: Theory, practice, and promise* (pp. 55–86). New York: Peter Lang.

Barker, M. (1999). The Maori language science curriculum in Aotearoa/New Zealand: A contribution to sustainable development. *Waikato Journal of Education, 5*, 51–60.

Barnhardt, C. (2001). A history of schooling for Alaska native people. *Journal of American Indian Education, 40*(1), 1–30.

Battiste, M., & Henderson, J. Y. (2000). *Protecting indigenous knowledge and heritage*. Saskatoon, SK, Canada: Purich.

Bhabha, H. K. (1994). *The location of culture*. New York: Routledge.

Bishop, R., & Glynn, T. (1999). *Culture counts: Changing power relations in education.* Palmerston North, New Zealand: Dunmore Press.

Blades, D. W. (1997). *Procedures of power and curriculum change: Foucault and the quest for possibilities in science education.* New York: Peter Lang.

Bryan, L., & Atwater, M. (2002). Teacher beliefs and cultural models: A challenge for science teacher preparation programs. *Science Education, 86,* 821–839.

Cajete, G. (1986). *Science: A Native American perspective—a culturally based science education curriculum.* Unpublished doctoral dissertation, International College, Los Angeles.

Cajete, G. (2000). *Native science: Natural law of interdependence.* Santa Fe, NM: Clearlight.

Carter, L. (2004). Thinking differently about cultural diversity: Using postcolonial theory to (re)read science education. *Science Education, 88,* 1–18.

Carter, N. P., Larke, P. J., Singleton-Taylor, G., & Santos, E. (2003). Multicultural science education: Moving beyond tradition. In S. M. Hines (Ed.), *Multicultural science education: Theory, practice, and promise* (pp. 1–19). New York: Peter Lang.

Castellano, M. B. (2000). Updating of aboriginal traditions of knowledge. In G. J. S. Dei, B. L. Hall, & D. G. Rosenberg (Eds.), *Indigenous knowledges in global contexts. Multiple readings of our world* (pp. 21–36). Toronto, Canada: University of Toronto Press.

Chang, P. J., & Rosiek, J. (2003). Anti-colonialist antimonies in a biology lesson: A sonata form case study of cultural conflict in a science classroom. *Curriculum Inquiry, 33,* 251–290.

Christie, M. J. (1991). Aboriginal science for the ecologically sustainable future. *Australasian Science Teachers Journal, 31*(1), 26–31.

Clark, D. A. T. (2004). Not the end of the stories, not the end of the songs. In D. A. Mihesuah & A. C. Wilson (Eds.), *Indigenizing the academy* (pp. 218–232). Lincoln, NE: University of Nebraska Press.

Cobern, W. W. (1993). Contextual constructivism: The impact of culture on the learning and teaching of science. In K. Tobin (Ed.), *The practice of constructivism in science education* (pp. 51–69). Washington, DC: American Association for the Advancement of Science.

Cobern, W. W. (1996). Worldview theory and conceptual change in science education. *Science Education, 80,* 579–610.

Cobern, W. W., & Loving, C. C. (2000). Defining science in a multicultural world: Implications for science education. *Science Education, 85,* 50–67.

Corsiglia, J., & Snively, G. (2000). Rejoinder: Infusing indigenous science into western modern science for a sustainable future. *Science Education, 85,* 82–86.

Crosby, A. (2004). *Ecological imperialism: The biological expansion of Europe, 900–1900.* London: Cambridge University Press.

Davison, D. M., & Miller, K. W. (1998). An ethnoscience approach to curriculum issues for American Indian students. *School Science and Mathematics, 98,* 260–265.

Dei, G. J. S. (2000). African development: The relevance and implications of 'indigenousness'. In G. J. S. Dei, B. L. Hall, & D. G. Rosenberg (Eds.), *Indigenous knowledges in global contexts: Multiple readings of our world* (pp. 70–86). Toronto, Canada: University of Toronto Press.

Dukepoo, F. (2001). The Native American honor society: Challenging Indian students to achieve. In K. James (Ed.), *Science and Native American communities: Legacies of pain, visions of promise* (pp. 36–42). Lincoln, NE: University of Nebraska Press.

Durie, M. H. (1996). Maori, science, and Maori development. *People and Performance, 4*(3), 20–25.

Dyck, L. (2001). A personal journey into science, feminist science, and aboriginal science. In K. James (Ed.), *Science and Native American communities: Legacies of pain, visions of promise* (pp. 22–28). Lincoln, NE: University of Nebraska Press.

Dzama, E. N. N., & Osborne, J. F. (1999). Poor performance in science among African students: An alternative explanation to the African worldview thesis. *Journal of Research in Science Teaching, 36,* 387–405.

Ermine, W. J. (1995). Aboriginal epistemology. In M. Battiste & J. Barman (Eds.), *First nations education in Canada: The circle unfolds* (pp. 101–112). Vancouver, BC, Canada: University of British Columbia Press.

George, J. M. (1999). Indigenous knowledge as a component of the school curriculum. In L. M. Semali & J. L. Kincheloe (Eds.), *What is indigenous knowledge? Voices from the academy* (pp. 79–94). New York: Falmer Press.

George, J., & Glasgow, J. (1988). Street science and conventional science in the West Indies. *Studies in Science Education, 15*, 109–118.

Goes in Center, J. (2001). Land, people, and culture: Using geographic information systems to build community capacity. In K. James (Ed.), *Science and Native American communities: Legacies of pain, visions of promise* (pp. 119–125). Lincoln, NE: University of Nebraska Press.

Hammond, L., & Brandt, C. (2004). Science and cultural process: Defining an anthropological approach to science education. *Studies in Science Education, 40*, 1–47.

Haraway, D. (1996). Situated knowledges: The science question in feminism and the privilege of partial perspective. In E. F. Keller & H. E. Longino (Eds.), *Feminism and science* (pp. 249–263). Oxford, England: Oxford University Press.

Harding, S. (1991). *Whose science? Whose knowledge? Thinking from women's lives.* Milton Keynes, England: Open University Press

Harding, S. (Ed.). (1993). *The "racial" economy of science: Towards a democratic future.* Bloomington, IN: Indiana University Press

Harding, S. (1998). *Is science multicultural? Postcolonialisms, feminisms and epistemologies.* Bloomington, IN: Indiana University Press.

Hemara, W. (2000). *Māori pedagogies (A view from the literature).* Wellington, New Zealand: New Zealand Council for Educational Research.

Hill, J., & Hawk, K. (2000). *Making a difference in the classroom: Effective teaching practice in low decile, multicultural schools.* Wellington, New Zealand: Ministry of Education.

Hipkins, R., Bolstad, R., Baker, R., Jones, R., Barker, M., Bell, B., et al. (2002). *Curriculum, learning and effective pedagogy: A literature review in science education.* Wellington, New Zealand: Ministry of Education.

Hodson, D. (1999). Critical multiculturalism in science and technology education. In S. May (Ed.), *Critical multiculturalism: Rethinking multicultural and antiracist education* (pp. 216–244). New York: Falmer Press.

Irvine, J. J., & York, D. E. (1995). Learning styles and culturally diverse students: A literature review. In J. A. Banks & A. Cherry (Eds.), *Handbook of research on multicultural education* (pp. 484–497). New York: Macmillan.

Irzik, G. (2000). Universalism, multiculturalism and science education. *Science Education, 85*, 71–73.

James, K. (2001). Fires need fuel: Merging science education with American Indian community needs. In K. James (Ed.), *Science and Native American communities: Legacies of pain, versions of promise* (pp. 1–8). Lincoln, NE: University of Nebraska Press.

Jegede, O. (1988). The development of science, technology and society curricula in Nigeria. *International Journal of Science Education, 10*, 399–408.

Jegede, O. (1995). Collateral learning and the eco-cultural paradigm in science and mathematics education in Africa. *Studies in Science Education, 25*, 97–137.

Jegede, O. (1997). Traditional cosmology and collateral learning in non-western science classrooms. In M. Ogawa (Ed.), *Effects of traditional cosmology on science education: Report of an international scientific research program* (pp. 63–73). Ibaraki, Japan: Faculty of Education.

Jegede, O. (1998). Worldview presuppositions and science and technology education. In D. Hodson (Ed.), *Science, technology education, and ethnicity: An Aotearoa/New Zealand perspective* (pp. 76–88). Wellington, New Zealand: The Royal Society.

Jegede, O. J., & Okebukola, P. A. (1991). The effect of instruction on socio-cultural beliefs hindering the learning of science. *Journal of Research in Science Teaching, 28,* 275–285.

Kawagley, A. O. (1995). *A Yupiaq worldview.* Prospect Heights, IL: Waveland Press.

Kawagley, A. O. (1999). Alaska native education: History and adaptation in the new millennium. *Journal of American Indian Education, 39,* 31–51

Kawagley, A. O. (2001). Tradition and education: The world made seamless again. In K. James (Ed.), *Science and Native American communities: Legacies of pain, visions of promise* (pp. 51–56). Lincoln, NE: University of Nebraska Press.

Kawasaki, K. (1996). The concepts of science in Japanese and Western education. *Science and Education, 5,* 1–20.

Kawasaki, K. (2002). A cross-cultural comparison of English and Japanese linguistic assumptions influencing pupil's learning of science. *Canadian and International Education, 31*(1), 19–51.

Key, S. (2003). Enhancing the science interest of African American students using cultural inclusion. In S. M. Hines (Ed.), *Multicultural science education: Theory, practice, and promise* (pp. 87–101). New York: Peter Lang.

Krugley-Smolska, E. (1996). Scientific culture, multiculturalism and the science classroom. *Science and Education, 5,* 21–29.

Kuhn, T. (1970). *The structure of scientific revolutions* (2nd ed.). Chicago: University of Chicago Press.

Lather, P. (1999). To be of use: The work of reviewing. *Review of Educational Research, 69*(1), 2–7

Lee, O. (2003). Equity for linguistically and culturally diverse students in science education: A research agenda. *Teachers College Record, 105,* 465–489.

Lewis, B. F., & Aikenhead, G. S. (2000). Introduction: Shifting perspectives from universalism to cross-culturalism. *Science Education, 85,* 4–5.

Loving, C. C., & de Montellano, B. R. O. (2003). Good versus bad culturally relevant science: Avoiding the pitfalls. In S. M. Hines (Ed.), *Multicultural science education: Theory, practice, and promise* (pp. 147–166). New York: Peter Lang.

Lujan, J. (2001). American Indian community development: Needs and strategies. In K. James (Ed.), *Science and Native American communities: Legacies of pain, visions of promise* (pp. 76–82). Lincoln, NE: University of Nebraska Press.

Lynch, P. P. (1996). Students' alternative frameworks for the nature of matter: A cross-cultural study of linguistic and cultural interpretations. *International Journal of Science Education, 18,* 743–752.

Maddock, M. N. (1981). Science education: An anthropological viewpoint. *Studies in Science Education, 8,* 1–26.

Marker, M. (2004). Theories and disciplines as sites of struggle: The reproduction of colonial dominance through the controlling of knowledge in the academy. *Canadian Journal of Native Education, 28*(1/2), 102–110.

Martin, P. (1996). *He tiro arotahi ki te Putaiao, te Pangarau me te Hangarau* [Maori into science, maths and technology]. Wellington, New Zealand: Te Puni Kokiri.

McGovern, S. (1999). *Education, modern development, and indigenous knowledge: An analysis of academic knowledge production.* New York: Garland.

McKinley, E. (1995). *A power/knowledge nexus: Writing a science curriculum in Maori.* Hamilton, New Zealand: University of Waikato.

McKinley, E. (1996). Towards an indigenous science curriculum. *Research in Science Education, 26,* 155–167.

McKinley, E. (1997). Maori and science education: Participation, aspirations and school curricula. In B. Bell & R. Baker (Eds.), *Developing the science curriculum in Aotearoa New Zealand* (pp. 213–226). Auckland, New Zealand: Longman.

McKinley, E. (1999). Maori science education: The urgent need for research. In G. Haisman (Ed.), *Exploring issues in science education: Research seminar on science education in primary schools* (pp. 33–40). Wellington, New Zealand: Ministry of Education.

McKinley, E. (2001). Cultural diversity: Masking power with innocence. *Science Education, 85*, 74–76.

McKinley, E. (2003). *Brown bodies, white coats: Postcolonialism, Maori women and science.* Unpublished doctoral dissertation, University of Waikato, Hamilton, New Zealand.

McKinley, E., Stewart, G., & Richards, P. (2004). *Maori knowledge, language and participation in mathematics and science education. Final report for Nga Pae o te Maramatanga.* Auckland, New Zealand: University of Auckland, National Institute of Research Excellence for Mäori Development and Advancement.

McKinley, E., Waiti, P., & Aislabie, J. (2004). *Science, matauranga Maori and schools. Final report for Nga Pae o te Maramatanga.* Auckland, New Zealand: University of Auckland, National Institute of Research Excellence for Mäori Development and Advancement.

McKinley, E., Waiti, P., & Bell, B. (1992). Language, culture and science education. *International Journal of Science Education, 14*, 579–595.

McPherson Waiti, P. (1990). A Maori person's viewpoint on the education of Maori children and in particular, science education. *SAMEpapers, 1990*, 177–201.

Michie, M., & Linkson, M. (1999). Interfacing western science and indigenous knowledge: A northern territory perspective. *SAMEpapers, 1999*, 265–286.

Mihesuah, D. A., & Wilson, A. C. (2004). *Indigenizing the academy.* Lincoln, NE: University of Nebraska Press.

Mohanram, R. (1999). *Black body.* St. Leonards, Australia: Allen & Unwin.

Monhardt, R. M. (2003). The image of a scientist through the eyes of Navajo children. *Journal of American Indian Education, 42*(3), 25–38.

Nelson-Barber, S., & Estrin, E. T. (1995). Bringing Native American perspectives to mathematics and science teaching. *Theory into Practice, 34*(3), 174–185.

Ninnes, P. (2001). Writing multicultural science textbooks: Perspectives, problems, possibilities and power. *Australian Science Teachers Journal, 47*(4), 18–27.

Ninnes, P. (2003). Rethinking multicultural science education: Representations, identities, and texts. In S. M. Hines (Ed.), *Multicultural science education: theory, practice, and promise* (pp. 167–186). New York: Peter Lang.

Ogawa, M. (1989). Beyond the tacit framework of "science" and "science education" among science educators. *International Journal of Science Education, 11*, 247–250.

Ogawa, M. (1995). Science education in a multi-science perspective. *Science Education, 79*, 583–593.

Ogawa, M. (1997). *Effects of traditional cosmology on science education: Report of an international scientific research program.* Mito, Japan: Ibaraki University.

O'Loughlin, M. (1992). Re-thinking science education: Beyond Piaget constructivism toward a sociocultural model of teaching and learning. *Journal of Research in Science Teaching, 29*, 791–820.

Pomeroy, D. (1992). Science across cultures: Building bridges between traditional western and Alaskan native sciences. In S. Hills (Ed.), *History and philosophy of science in science education* (Vol. 2, pp. 257–267). Kingston, ON, Canada: Queen's University.

Poodry, C. (2001). How to get what Indian communities need from science. In K. James (Ed.), *Science and Native American communities: Legacies of pain, visions of promise* (pp. 29–35). Lincoln, NE: University of Nebraska.

Rikihana, T. (1996). Te Matauranga putaiao hangarau me nga momo tikanga-a-iwi he tirohanga no Aotearoa. In Royal Society (Ed.), *Science, technology education, and ethnicity: An Aotearoa/New Zealand perspective* (pp. 24–29). Wellington, New Zealand: The Royal Society of New Zealand.

Roberts, M. (1996). Indigenous knowledge and Western science: perspectives from the Pacific. In Royal Society (Ed.), *Science, technology education, and ethnicity: An Aotearoa/New Zealand perspective* (pp. 59–75). Wellington, New Zealand: The Royal Society of New Zealand.

Rowland, P. M., & Adkins, C. R. (2003). Native American science education and its implications for multicultural science education. In S. M. Hines (Ed.), *Multicultural science education: Theory, practice, and promise* (pp. 103–120). New York: Peter Lang.

Rutherford, M., & Nkopodi, N. (1990). A comparison of the recognition of some science concept definitions in English and North Sotho for second language English speakers. *International Journal of Science Education, 12*, 443–456.

Said, E. (1994). *Culture and imperialism*. London: Vintage.

Scantlebury, K., McKinley, E., & Jesson, J. (2002). Imperial knowledge: science, education and equity. In B. E. Hernanadez-Truyol (Ed.), *Moral imperialism: A critical anthology* (pp. 229–240). New York: New York University Press.

Semali, L. M., & Kincheloe, J. L. (1999). *What is indigenous knowledge? Voices from the academy*. New York: Falmer Press.

Smith, L. T. (1999). *Decolonizing methodologies: Research and indigenous peoples*. Dunedin, New Zealand: University of Otago Press.

Smith, M. R. (1996). *First nations and western science in schools. Canadian society for the study in education*. St. Catherines, ON, Canada: Brock University.

Snively, G., & Corsiglia, J. (2001) Discovering indigenous science: Implications for science education. *Science Education, 85*, 6–34.

Solomon, J. (1987). Social influences on the construction of pupil's understanding of science. *Studies in Science Education, 14*, 63–82.

Solomon, J. (1994). The rise and fall of constructivism. *Studies in Science Education, 23*, 1–19.

Stanley, W. B., & Brickhouse, N. (2001). Teaching sciences: The multicultural question revisited. *Science Education, 85*, 35–49.

Sutherland, D. (1999). The treatment of knowledge. *The Science Teacher, 66*(3), 40–43.

Sutherland, D., & Dennick, R. (2002). Exploring culture, language and the perception of the nature of science. *International Journal of Science Education, 24*, 1–25.

Taylor, N., & Macpherson, C. (1997). Traditional and religious beliefs and the teaching of science in Fiji. *New Zealand Journal of Educational Studies, 32*(2), 181–205.

Thijs, G. D., & van den Berg, E. (1995). Cultural factors in the origin and remediation of alternative conceptions in physics. *Science and Education, 4*, 317–347.

Walkerdine, V. (1984). Developmental psychology and the child-centred pedagogy: The insertion of Piaget into early education. In J. Henriques, W. Holloway, C. Urwin, C. Venn, & V. Walkerdine (Eds.), *Changing the subject* (pp. 153–202). London: Methuen.

Yakabu, J. M. (1994). Integration of indigenous thought and practice with science and technology: A case study of Ghana. *International Journal of Science Education, 16*, 343–360.

Young, M. F. D. (1974). Notes for a sociology of science education. *Studies in Science Education, 1*, 51–60.

Zaslavsky, C. (1994). "Africa Counts" and ethnomathematics. *For the Learning of Mathematics, 14*(2), 3–8.

Zepeda, O. (2001). Rebuilding languages to revitalize communities and cultures. In K. James (Ed.), *Science and Native American communities: Legacies of pain, visions of promise* (pp. 57–62). Lincoln, NE: University of Nebraska Press.

CHAPTER 9

Issues in Science Learning: An International Perspective

Chorng-Jee Guo
National Taitung Unviersity, Taiwan

Student science learning lies at the heart of the interplay among science education research, policy, and practice. Science education, especially as it is practiced in schools today, is strongly influenced by several important forces. In response to these driving forces, various research-informed reform efforts in science education have been undertaken in countries all around the world in recent years. It is of both practical significance and theoretical interest to look at the impact of these driving forces on a broad array of contexts, practices, and outcomes regarding science learning across different countries.

PURPOSE, SCOPE, AND LIMITATIONS OF THIS CHAPTER

The main purposes of this chapter are to (a) identify some of driving forces for science education reform in the twenty-first century, (b) examine the conditions of science learning in select countries, and (c) suggest research problems for further investigation.

Student science learning is a major concern for the science education enterprise and is influenced by science curriculum, instruction, and evaluation. Research on science learning involves other topics such as inquiry, cooperative learning, learning environment, gender issues, curriculum reform, science teacher preparation, and professional development. However, the focus of this chapter will be student science learning from an international perspective. Studies on student science learning involve a range of subject areas, student characteristics, physical settings, and learning environments. A range of theoretical perspectives, including historical, cultural, societal, linguistic, and human perspectives, on science learning have been adopted, using research methods that are quantitative, qualitative, or a combination of the two. Many of these aspects are dealt with in other chapters of this *Handbook*.

Science learning in each country occurs in a wide range of educational, social, cultural, and political contexts; significant changes have been observed over the years. Science education reforms in many countries have involved changes in the philosophy of education, instructional goals, curriculum materials, instructional practices, and teacher education. A historical account of the contexts, processes, and outcomes of student science learning in different countries is beyond the scope of this chapter. Instead, we shall focus our attention on results that have been obtained in the recent decade from large-scale cross-national studies on student science learning.

This chapter provides an overview of the current condition of science learning from an international perspective. The emphasis is not on specific and detailed accounts of the state of science learning in individual countries. What interests us here is describing the contemporary issues of student science learning worldwide and making recommendations for research studies needed to inform the problems. Because the policies and practices of science education vary significantly across country boarders, the issues related to science learning differ in each country.

This chapter begins with a school-based model of science learning and a brief historical background of research on science learning internationally. The chapter proceeds to a review of some driving forces for the reform of science education worldwide. With these driving forces in mind, a broad overview of the current conditions, major problems, and reform measures related to science learning in various countries around the world is given. Following that overview, the contemporary issues of science learning worldwide are discussed in further detail. The chapter ends with some concluding remarks and recommendations for future research on science learning, as viewed from an international perspective.

A MODEL OF SCHOOL-BASED LEARNING IN SCIENCE

In order to organize the information in this chapter, it is desirable to have a model of school-based learning in science from an international perspective. The model is meant to provide a representation of the relationships among important factors associated with student learning at school. The model can be used as a guide for identifying research problems and formulating research questions. A number of school-based learning models have been proposed (Huitt, 1995; Proctor, 1984; White, 1988). A modified version of Huitt's model is the organizer for this chapter.

Huitt's (1995) model includes four categories: Context, Input, Classroom Processes, and Output. Huitt emphasized the importance of context variables such as school characteristics, family, community, state and federal government, TV/movies, and the global environment, because he realized that our world is rapidly changing from an agricultural/industrial base to an information base. In his model, the input variables include two subcategories: teacher characteristics and student characteristics. Teacher characteristics include values and beliefs; knowledge of students and of the teaching/learning process; thinking, communication, and performance skills; personality; and teacher efficacy. Student characteristics include study habits, learning styles, age, gender, race, ethnicity, motivation, and moral/socio-emotional/

cognitive/character developments. The classroom processes variables include teacher behavior (planning, management, and instruction), student behavior (involvement, success on academic tasks), and other processes such as classroom climate and student leadership roles. The products or output of school learning include student achievement and other desirable skills. The structure of Huitt's model is similar to the Context, Input, Process, and Product (CIPP) model of curriculum development and evaluation (Stufflebeam, 2000), although the purposes and foci are different.

For this chapter, I developed a modified version of Huitt's (1995) model of school-based learning that includes an additional component—Driving Forces (see Fig. 9–1). This added element demonstrates explicitly that, from an international point of view, there are important forces that may influence student science learning through Contexts, Inputs, and Processes of school learning. Figure 9–1 emphasizes some of the variables relevant to student science learning as discussed in this chapter. School science learning takes place in a wide context involving family, school, community, and society. It also takes place under the influence of various backgrounds, including educational policy, historical and sociocultural development, scientific and technological development, and international conditions. Input variables important to learning processes and outcomes include the science curriculum, instructional facilities and resources, teacher characteristics, and student

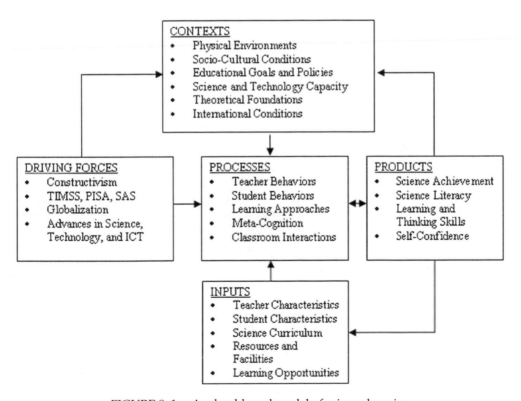

FIGURE 9–1.   A school-based model of science learning.

characteristics. The importance of processes such as student learning approaches, engagement, metacognition, perception of the context, and interaction with teachers and other students has been well documented. As for student learning outcomes, a meaningful understanding of scientific facts, concepts, principles, and theories is of course essential. Other learning outcomes, such as a better understanding of the nature of science, improved inquiry skills, and international awareness and experiences, are also important for a scientifically and technologically literate person in the twenty-first century.

The arrows in Figure 9–1 indicate possible influences of the variables in one category on those in the others. Figure 9–1 suggests the direct influence of Driving Forces on the Contexts, Inputs, and Processes of learning. Driving Forces influence Products indirectly through these variables. Likewise, student learning products or outcomes are indirectly influenced by the Contexts and the Inputs of learning. Arrows pointing toward the left in the model indicate that student learning outcomes might, to a certain extent, influence the contexts, inputs, and processes of learning.

The model of school-based learning shown in Figure 9–1 emphasizes both internal and external factors that might affect student learning outcomes. It is meant to provide broad conceptual categories while indicating possible relationships. The variables in the major categories were obtained by synthesis of the research literature. More detailed diagrams could be drawn to show how student conceptions of learning might affect their approaches to learning and, consequently, their levels of understanding (Entwistle, 1998, 2000). Of course, there are limitations to the proposed model. The scheme for separating the variables into main categories is tentative; different authors may want to group the variables quite differently for different purposes. Some variables may belong to more than one category; for instance, student study skills can be taken as an aspect of student characteristics in Inputs, while at the same time it can be considered as part of Products. Although the model could be improved, for instance, by the use of more explicit conceptual and operational definitions for the variables, it will be suitable for the purposes of this chapter.

SITUATING RESEARCH ON SCIENCE LEARNING IN AN INTERNATIONAL PERSPECTIVE

Significant change in research on student science learning has taken place since the middle of 1970s. The initial focus of these research studies was probing student understanding of natural phenomena and science concepts. The empirical findings, theoretical interpretations, and instructional implications were published in a great number of research reports, papers, books (Driver, Squires, Rushworth, & Wood-Robinson, 1994; Mintzes, Wandersee, & Novak, 1998; Osborne & Freyberg, 1985; White, 1988), and review articles (Duit & Treagust, 1998; Wandersee, Mintzes, & Novak, 1994). Results of these studies have led to research interest in constructivist approaches to teaching and learning in science. The impact of this research on science instruction, science curriculum reform, and teacher professional development is widely recognized.

van den Akker (1998) presented a historical overview of science curriculum development from an international perspective. He summarized recent initiatives and trends worldwide in improving the science curriculum. These initiatives include the development of national guidelines for science education, the emphasis on teaching key conceptual issues in depth instead of covering ever-increasing amounts of information, scientific literacy for all students, alignment of curriculum and assessment, providing more encouragement and support for teacher professional development, and the rapidly growing influence of information and communication technology. In addition, there has been an increasing emphasis on lifelong learning combined with greater emphasis on skills in problem-solving, inquiry, information and communication, and a preference for active, investigatory, and independent forms of learning. The common label for the approach characterized by these interrelated aspects is "learning to learn" (van den Akker).

Keeves and Aikenhead (1995) reviewed the historical growth of science education over the previous century and discussed developments in science curricula during recent decades in an international context. They identified five scientific and societal changes with important consequences for education, including the provision of a more general education for students at the secondary level, the recognition of the need for lifelong education, the need for each individual to acquire the skills of effective independent learning and inquiry as part of learning how to learn, the emergence of science-related social issues, and the impact of technological change. In reporting these changes, Keeves and Aikenhead made several recommendations for improving the teaching and learning of science, which are very similar to those that van den Akker (1998) suggested.

The effectiveness and appropriateness of science curriculum and science instruction for science learning have long been major interests for science education researchers. However, a distinct trend worldwide regarding research on student science learning took place in the mid-1970s. Student science learning became the research focus for a great number of research studies. Initially, much of the research interest was on student understanding of natural phenomena and science concepts. Subsequently, concerns about students' conceptions of learning, of the goals of science learning, of the nature of science, and of the subjects to be studied, and concerns about student learning and problem-solving skills have received further attention. As a result of these research efforts, constructivist approaches to the teaching and learning of science have gained wider acceptance (Tobin, 1993). The impact of this body of research on science education policy, science curriculum, science instruction and assessment, and science teacher professional development is noteworthy around the world. Constructivist notions of science teaching and learning appear to be one important factor for understanding science learning from an international perspective.

DRIVING FORCES FOR SCIENCE EDUCATION REFORMS WORLDWIDE

A new wave of science education reform has taken place in countries all around the world in recent decades. New goals of science education for citizens of the twenty-first century have been formulated and new science curricula developed, with the use of a number of strategies based on research findings and theoretical understandings about student science learning. In order to identify the conditions and problems of science learning from an international perspective, it is worthwhile to examine the driving forces that have influenced the direction and development of science education reform worldwide. Some of the most important of these are constructivist views of science learning, cross-national studies of student science learning, globalization, and advances in information technology.

Constructivist Views of Teaching and Learning Science

In spite of some debates and criticisms (Matthews, 1998; Osborne, 1996), Mathews (2000) stated that constructivism is undoubtedly a major theoretical influence in contemporary science and mathematics education, and few would dispute Fensham's (1992) claim that "the most conspicuous psychological influence on curriculum thinking in science since 1980 has been the constructivist view of learning" (p. 801). Numerous empirical studies on student science conceptions have led to the popularity of constructivist views of science teaching and learning. Based on these works, theoretical formulations of student science learning have been proposed, and suggestions for instructional interventions and teacher professional development aimed at facilitating student conceptual change and meaningful learning have been made (Bennett, 2003; Driver et al., 1994; Fensham, Gunstone, & White, 1994; Mintzes et al., 1998; Osborne & Freyberg, 1985; Tobin, 1993; White, 1988).

From an international perspective, constructivist notions of teaching and learning have had strong influences on science policy in recent years. For instance, the U.S. National Science Teachers Association (2003) Standards for Science Teacher Preparation, the mathematics component of the Curriculum Profiles for Australian Schools (Australian Capital Territory Department of Education and Training, n.d.), and the National Curriculum in England (Qualifications and Curriculum Authority, 2002) were influenced by constructivist thoughts. Cobern (1996) argued that science education research and curriculum development efforts in non-western countries could benefit by adopting constructivist views of science and science learning. Cobern's main point was that constructivist views led researchers to expect that students in different cultures will have somewhat different perspectives on science. He suggested that science education research should inform curriculum developers to make science instructional materials more sensitive to culture. Direct adoption of science textbooks, or their minor revisions, from one country to another may not work. For many non-western countries, it is a challenge to develop culturally sensitive science curriculum materials while trying to strike a healthy balance between the local culture and western science.

Cross-National Studies on Student Science Learning

In addition to constructivist notions of science teaching and learning, the latest wave of science education reform has been influenced by the results obtained in a number of recent cross-national studies on student science learning, including Trends of International Mathematics and Science Study (TIMSS), the Programme for International Student Assessment (PISA), and Science and Scientists (SAS). The results obtained by these studies provide valuable information on the states of science learning in participating countries. The studies have generated much interest among policymakers, science educators, science teachers, parents, and the general public in countries around the world. A brief description of these international comparative studies in science education is given below.

The National Academies Press (NAP) homepage (http://www.nap.edu/) provides a list of international comparative studies in education, including large-scale assessment and case studies. For science and technology (as well as for mathematics) education, a prominent example is the Third International Mathematics and Science Study (TIMSS), conducted in 1995. Subsequent iterations of the same study changed the word "Third" into "Trends." The study is now referred to by the year it was conducted. Hence the original TIMSS becomes TIMSS 1995, TIMSS-R becomes TIMSS 1999, and TIMSS 2003 remains TIMSS 2003. TIMSS is one of several studies sponsored by the International Association for the Evaluation of Educational Achievement (IEA). (Background information and downloadable reports and data files are available at http://timss.bc.edu/.) TIMSS provided not only assessment of student learning outcomes, but also information about the home, classroom, school, and national contexts within which science learning takes place.

The Organisation for Economic Co-operation and Development (OECD) has a large education sector that publishes various reports (available online at http://www.oecd.org). The OECD recently developed its own set of studies of student achievement, under the acronym of PISA. PISA works with some 40 OECD countries together with some non-OECD countries. PISA assesses in three domains: reading literacy, mathematical literacy, and scientific literacy (OECD, 1999, 2003a, 2003b, 2003c). It aims to define each domain, not merely in terms of mastery of the school curriculum, but in also terms of important knowledge and skills needed in adult life. PISA assesses students who are approaching the end of compulsory education (about the age of 15) and the extent to which they have acquired the knowledge and skills that are essential for full participation in society. The first assessment took place in 2000, with results published in 2001; PISA has continued thereafter, in 3-year cycles. Each cycle looks in depth at a major domain, to which two-thirds of testing time is devoted; the other two domains provide a summary profile of skills. Major domains by cycle are reading literacy in 2000, mathematical literacy in 2003, and scientific literacy in 2006.

The Science and Scientists (SAS) Study explored various aspects of relevance to the teaching and learning of science and technology (Sjøberg, 2000). Some 30 researchers from 21 countries collected data from about 10,000 pupils at the age of 13. The countries involved, in alphabetical order, were Australia, Chile, England, Ghana, Hungary, Iceland, India, Japan, Korea, Lesotho, Mozambique, Nigeria, Norway, Papua New Guinea, the Philippines, Russia, Spain, Sudan, Sweden, Trinidad, Uganda, and the United States. The purpose of the SAS-Study was to provide empirical input to debates over priorities in the school curriculum as well as the pedagogies that are likely to appeal to the learners.

Globalization

Progress in transportation and the use of the Internet result in frequent economic, social, and cultural exchanges internationally. There is now an increased interdependence and interrelationship among different countries around the world. Globalization is raising questions about the content, objectives, and approaches to science learning. Hallak (2001) pointed out that educational content should be designed "to meet both national demand and international concerns" (p. 3). For example, in order to get along with people from different cultural backgrounds, students should be taught to respect and understand their history and customs. In order to be well-informed citizens of the world, students should be equipped with necessary communication skills and the capability to read and speak foreign languages. Student learning experiences in science should be designed to include these important components. On the other hand, there are concerns for trying to maintain a balance between globalization and localization. For instance, Zembylas (2002) noted a number of tensions resulting from the struggle to preserve local values while incorporating global trends into the science curriculum of developing countries.

To meet the challenges of rapid globalization and the pursuit of economic and social developments in the new century, Cheng (2000a) proposed a new paradigm of school education. It is built on the concepts of contextualized multiple intelligences (referring to technological, economic, social, political, cultural, and learning intelligences), globalization, localization, and individualization in schooling, teaching, and learning. His paradigm included the formulation of a new aim for science education (Cheng, 2000b): "to support students particularly through science learning to become citizens who will be engaged in lifelong learning and will creatively contribute to the building up of a multiple intelligent society and a multiple intelligent global village" His paradigm included the formulation of a new aim for science education (Cheng, 2000b): "to support students particularly through science learning to become citizens who will be engaged in lifelong learning and will creatively contribute to the building up of a multiple intelligent society and a multiple intelligent global village" (available online at http://www.ied.edu.hk/apfslt/issue_2/foreword/index.htm).

Advances in Science, Technology, and Information Technology

Rapid development of science and technologies in the previous century resulted in not only the changing face of science, but also significant changes in industrial structures and employment markets (Hurd, 1998). These advances had noticeable influences on other aspects of society, both politically and economically. Hurd noted that some changes in the nature, ethos, and practice of science have taken place. For instance, traditional science disciplines such as biology, chemistry, physics, and earth science have become fractionated into a large number of research fields; instead of physical sciences, life sciences have become the center of attention in the twenty-first century. The fields of scientific/technological research are increasingly hybridized; science is becoming more holistic, blending the natural and social sciences.

There is an increasing awareness of the importance of knowledge to the economic and technological development of our societies. Promoting creativity and reaching for excellence in science and technology are national policy goals for increasing international competitiveness. Solid and successful science education is expected to make significant contributions toward this end. For citizens of the twenty-first century, scientific and technological knowledge and skills are crucial for actions and decisions. Meaningful and responsible participation in society assumes the ability to judge evidence and arguments associated with the socio-scientific issues that appear on the political agenda. A broad understanding of the nature, content, and methods of science and technology by the general public is important. It is imperative that students are interested in science subjects and that they have a broad understanding of basic scientific principles and ways of thinking. A comprehensive list of attributes that will enable students to adapt to the changing world of science and technology and its impacts on personal, social, and economic affairs was presented by Hurd (1998).

Advances in information and communication technologies (ICTs) have caused a revolution in living. Commercial products and services relating to ICTs, such as mobile phones, digital cameras, notebook computers, and DVDs, have found their way into all parts of our daily lives. ICT not only changes our lifestyles, but also offers tools to facilitate both teaching and learning in different settings, by incorporating a wide variety of instructional strategies, such as peer tutoring, and cooperative learning. Students and citizens of the twenty-first century need to know and be able to use ICT wisely and fruitfully. However, ICT requires considerable investment in equipment and infrastructure. Substantial costs for maintenance, training, software development, and technical support can be expected. Accessibility to ICT equipment and facilities affects the opportunities to learn at the student, school, and school district levels. Advances in ICT bring along the threat of a widening gap between developed and developing countries, with disparities in access to knowledge and information that reinforce existing disparities in resources (Lewin, 2000).

As shown in Fig. 9–1, these Driving Forces are predicted to influence the Contexts, Inputs, and Processes for student science learning. Thus, it is evident that student science learning in the 21st century will be different from the previous century in the following ways:

1. Research on science learning has led to better theoretical understandings about student learning processes. Policy-makers, curriculum developers and school teachers are becoming better informed in their efforts to improve teaching and to facilitate student science learning.

2. With results obtained from recent cross-national comparative studies such as TIMSS, PISA, and SAS, researchers in various countries can examine the conditions of student learning in science, identify goals and content areas that need to be strengthened, develop and adopt more powerful instructional strategies, and provide more supportive learning environments.

3. Demand to enhance the relevance of science learning to students' daily lives will increase as we prepare students to function competently and successfully as members of communities at local, national, and international levels.

4. The emphasis on science education to foster scientific and technological literacy for all students will increase. A wide variety of tools, resources, environments, and locations now offer new opportunities for learning science both formally and informally.

In order to provide an overview of student science learning outcomes and their influencing factors, some findings from recent cross-national studies including

TIMSS, PISA, and SAS will be described. Next, the current condition of science education in a few selected countries will be described, to illustrate the kinds of problems and issues different countries face.

FINDINGS FROM RECENT CROSS-NATIONAL STUDIES ON SCIENCE LEARNING

Results obtained from recent cross-national studies including TIMSS, PISA and SAS provide valuable information on the current conditions of science learning worldwide. These results are described in the following sections.

TIMSS

The Third International Mathematics and Science Study (now renamed as TIMSS 1995) was conducted in 1994–1995 at five grade levels (3, 4, 7, 8, and the final year of secondary school) in more than 40 countries. Extensive information about the teaching and learning of mathematics and science was collected from thousands of teachers and school principals, and more than half a million students. TIMSS also investigated mathematics and science curricula in participating countries through an analysis of curriculum guides, textbooks, and other curricular materials.

The TIMSS 1995 science achievement results for students at the primary, middle school, and high school levels were summarized by Martin, Mullis, Beaton, Gonzalez, Smith, and Kelly (1997); Beaton et al. (1996); and Mullis et al. (1998), respectively. Eighth-grade boys had significantly higher achievement than girls in about half of the participating countries, particularly in earth and physical science. The overwhelming majority of fourth-graders in nearly every country indicated that they liked science. Having educational resources in the home (e.g., computer, dictionary, own study desk, and 100 or more books) was strongly related to science achievement in every country. Students in most countries reported spending between half an hour and an hour studying or doing homework in science. In most countries, the challenge of catering to students of different academic abilities was the factor teachers mentioned most often as limiting how they taught their mathematics and science classes. Other limiting factors included a high student/teacher ratio, a shortage of equipment for use in instruction, and the burden of dealing with disruptive students.

Information from the 1995 TIMSS assessment on school contexts for learning mathematics and science (Martin, Mullis, Gonzales, Smith, & Kelly, 1999) included school characteristics, policies, and practices organized around five major topics: roles and responsibilities of schools and school principals, school organization and staffing, organization for learning mathematics and science, school resources, and school atmosphere. The combined results for three grade levels were discussed for a range of school factors and how they varied across countries. Another interesting report by Martin, Mullis, Gregory, Hoyle, and Shen (2000) presented analyses of the TIMSS 1995 eighth-grade data aimed at helping understand what makes some schools more effective than others. The results showed that school and classroom variables were related to average school achievement, even after adjustment for the home background of the students in the school. However, the strong relationship that persists between the average level of home background and adjusted student achievement also serves as a reminder that, in many countries, home background, schooling, and student achievement are closely intertwined, and that teasing out the influences of the various contributing factors remains a major challenge.

TIMSS 1999 was designed as a replicate of TIMSS 1995 at the eighth-grade level (Martin et al., 2000). Of the 38 participating countries, 26 also participated in the TIMSS 1995, which enabled these countries to measure trends in mathematics and science achievement. Six content areas were covered in the TIMSS 1999 science test: earth science, life science, physics, chemistry, environmental and resource issues, and scientific inquiry and the nature of science. Chinese Taipei and Singapore had the highest average performance, closely followed by Hungary, Japan, and the Republic of Korea. Other countries that performed well included the Netherlands, Australia, the Czech Republic, and England. Lower-performing countries included the Philippines, Morocco, and South Africa.

Boys were found to have significantly higher average science achievement than girls in 16 of the 38 countries in TIMSS 1999. This was attributable mainly to significantly higher performance by boys in physics, earth science, chemistry, and environmental and resource issues. The gender gap in science achievement was especially apparent among high-performing students, with 29% of boys on average across countries in the top achievement quarter, compared with 21% of girls.

The TIMSS 1999 report also included information on students' home environment and attitudes toward science (Martin et al., 2000). The level of home educational resources varied considerably across countries. On average, students from homes with a high level of educational resources had higher science achievement than students from homes with fewer resources. The association between home educational resources and science achievement is well documented in TIMSS. Low average student achievement in some of the less wealthy countries most likely reflects the low level of educational resources in students' homes. However, there are also other influences at work. The TIMSS 1999 results indicated that, in almost every country, there was a positive association between educational expectations and science achievement. Eighth-grade students internationally had high expectations for further education. On average across countries, more than half the students reported that they expected to finish university.

To investigate what students think of their abilities in science, TIMSS created an index of student self-concepts in the sciences (Martin et al., 2000). The results indicated that eighth-grade boys generally had more positive self-concepts in science than girls. This difference was most pronounced in countries where the sciences are taught as separate subjects. Although girls in such countries had a more favorable science self-concept in biology, this was outweighed by a more favorable self-concept for boys in physics, and to a lesser extent in earth science and chemistry.

TIMSS 1999 also created an index of attitudes toward the sciences in order to gain some understanding about eighth-graders' views about the utility of science and their enjoyment of it as a school subject (Martin et al., 2000). The results showed that, although student attitudes toward science were generally positive in countries where eighth-grade science is taught as a single subject, they were less positive in separate science countries. Attitudes were most positive toward biology and earth science, and least positive toward physics and chemistry. Eighth-grade boys generally had more positive attitudes toward science than girls, particularly in physics, chemistry, and earth science. Girls had more favorable attitudes toward biology.

In comparing achievement across countries, it is important to consider differences in students' curricular experiences. Students' opportunity to learn the content, skills, and processes tested depends to a great extent on the curricular goals and intentions inherent in each country's policies for science education. A distinction between intended, implemented, and attained curricula was made in TIMSS 1999 (Martin et al., 2000). Results indicated some discrepancies in a number of countries between the intended curriculum in science and the implemented curriculum as reported by teachers. There were many cases of topics intended to be taught to all, or almost all, students, for which teachers reported lower coverage. Interestingly, there were even more cases in which teachers reported greater topic coverage than would be expected from the intended curriculum. In all countries except Australia, Canada, and the United States, specifications for curricular goals in science existed at the national level. In 21 countries, science was taught in the eighth grade as a single general subject. In the other countries, separate courses were offered in the different science subjects.

Science teachers reported spending almost one-quarter of their class time, on average, on lecture-style presentations to the class. They reported devoting substantial percentages of their class time to student experiments (15%) and teacher-guided student practice (14%). Almost 40% of eighth-grade students in general science countries were in classes where teachers and students reported a high degree of emphasis on conducting science experiments. In contrast, emphasis on experiments was reportedly much less in separate science countries, particularly earth science and biology. Less than 10% of eighth-grade students in general science countries, and half this percentage in separate science countries, reported frequent use of computers in science class. Although there was great variation across countries, about a quarter of the students reported Internet access at school. Despite this access, only 12% on average used the Internet to obtain information for science projects on even a monthly basis (Martin et al., 2000).

Knowing basic facts and understanding science concepts received major emphasis in the official eighth-grade curricula of most participating countries, with at least moderate emphasis placed on application of science concepts. Few countries gave major emphasis to using laboratory equipment or performing science experiments, but there were some notable exceptions. Top-performing Singapore, Korea, and Japan were among the 10 countries that reported major emphasis on both. The increasing importance of technology in school curricula was reflected in the major emphasis given by 12 countries and the moderate emphasis given by 14 to "science, technology, and society." Thematic approaches were more common in science than in mathematics and received major emphasis in 13 countries. Multicultural approaches and integration of science with school subjects other than mathematics were the approaches least likely to be given major or moderate emphasis (Martin et al., 2000).

Teachers from countries in which eighth-grade science was taught as a general course were asked what subject matter they emphasized with their classes (Martin et al., 2000). In Canada, Italy, and the United States, earth science was emphasized in considerably more classrooms than in other countries. Biology was more likely than the other sciences to be emphasized in Italy and Tunisia. Countries where relatively high proportions of students had seen an emphasis on physics, chemistry, or both were Cyprus, Iran, Israel, Jordan, Korea, and South Africa.

Results from TIMSS 1999 showed that testing and assessment were widely used methods to support curriculum implementation. Belgium (Flemish) and Chinese Taipei were the only countries that reported having no public examinations in science to certify students or select them for university or academic tracks. Approximately two-thirds of the countries conducted system-wide assessments at two or three grades, primarily to inform policymakers about achievement of the intended curriculum. Instructional time designated in official curricula for science instruction increased from 11% at grade 4 to 16% at grade 8, on average across countries (Martin et al., 2000).

Internationally, 58% of eighth-grade students were taught science by female teachers and 42% by males. In most countries, at least 80% of eighth-grade students were taught science by teachers with a major in the appropriate science subject. However, teachers reported only a moderate level of confidence in their preparation to teach science. Almost 40% of students were taught by teachers who reported a low level of confidence in their preparation. Teachers' confidence in their preparation was greatest for biology, and least for earth science, environmental and resource issues, and scientific methods and inquiry skills.

Students in schools that reported being well resourced generally had higher average science achievement than those in schools where across-the-board shortages affected instructional capacity in science some or a lot. According to their principals, nearly half the students were in schools where science instruction was negatively affected by shortages or inadequacies in instructional materials, budget for supplies, school buildings, instructional space, audio-visual resources, or library materials relevant to science instruction. Schools around the world expected help from parents to ensure that students completed their homework, to volunteer for school projects or field trips, and to help raise funds and to serve on committees. One-fifth of the students attended schools where principals reported that attendance was not a problem. However, 60% were in schools where principals reported moderate attendance problems, and 19% were in schools with some serious attendance problems. The overwhelming majority of eighth-grade students attended schools judged by principals to have few serious problems threatening an orderly or safe school environment.

PISA

As a triennial survey, starting in 2000, the aim of PISA is to assess the knowledge, skills, and other characteristics of 15-year-olds in principal industrialized countries and other countries around the world (OECD, 2003a). PISA assesses literacy in reading, mathematics, and science, as well as asking students about their attitudes and approaches to learning. In the first assessment, about 315,000 students in 43 countries completed pencil-and-paper tests in their schools and filled out questionnaires about themselves. Schools also provided background information through questionnaires.

Performance in scientific literacy was marked on a single scale with an average score of 500 points and a standard deviation of 100 points. The scale measures students' ability to use scientific knowledge, to recognize scientific questions and identify what is involved in scientific investigations, to relate scientific data to claims and conclusions, and to communicate these aspects of science. About two-thirds of students across OECD countries scored between 400 and 600 points.

Performance in scientific literacy on PISA 2000 was summarized by way of countries' mean scores (OECD, 2003a). Japan, Korea, and Hong Kong–China demonstrated the highest performance on the scientific literacy scale. Other countries that scored significantly above the OECD average were Australia, Austria, Canada, the Czech Republic, Finland, Ireland, New Zealand, Sweden, and the United Kingdom. Mean scores in Belgium, France, Hungary, Iceland, Norway, Switzerland, and the United States were not significantly different from the OECD average. Except for the Czech Republic and Hungary, all low- and middle-income countries scored below the OECD average of 500 points. The range of average scores between the highest and the lowest performing countries was large: very high performing countries scored around one-half standard deviation above the OECD average, and the lowest performing countries performed 1–11/2 standard deviations below the OECD average.

Another aspect of student learning outcomes available from the results of PISA 2000 is student engagement at school. Student engagement at school is important because it can be seen as a disposition that allows one to learn, work, and function in a social institution. In the PISA study, student engagement was treated as an important school outcome in its own right. The report, *Student Engagement at School— A Sense of Belonging and Participation* (OECD, 2003b), examined PISA 2000 findings about the engagement at school of 15-year-old students. It looked at two measures: their sense of belonging in terms of whether they felt they fit in at school, and their participation in terms of classes and school attendance. PISA made it possible, for the first time in such a large international survey, to look at these characteristics alongside the performance of students in acquiring knowledge and skills.

The PISA survey found that significant proportions of students had low levels of engagement, possibly limiting their capacity to benefit from school and constraining their potential. One in four students felt that they did not belong in a school environment in at least one respect, and about one in five reported being regularly absent from school (OECD, 2003b). On the other hand, just over half of students belonged to groups that combined high engagement in school with average or high performance. Several key findings of this report are noteworthy. The prevalence of disaffected students (with a low sense of belonging or low participation) varied significantly across schools in each country. Engagement was found to link only weakly to students' social background; thus there is hope for school policy and practice to help engage more students. In addition, students in schools with strong levels of engagement tended to perform well, showing that, overall, academic performance and engagement are complementary rather than competing alternatives. However, for individual students, it was found that performance and engagement did not always go hand in hand. A quarter of students were both highly engaged and high achievers, and a similar proportion of students were highly engaged with average achievement. Students with lower levels of engagement were spread among those with high, medium, and low performance. Approximately a quarter of foreign-born students, and students from the lowest socioeconomic status or single-parent families, were more likely to be disaffected. However, those from the quarter of families with the highest socioeconomic status were not much less likely than average to show low levels of engagement. Students attending schools with a concentration of students from families with low socioeconomic status were more likely to be disaffected, suggesting probable peer effects. On the other hand, on average engagement was higher at schools with a strong disciplinary climate, good student-teacher relations, and high expectations for students. This suggests that the culture of schools plays a key role.

In addition to student engagement at school, student approaches to learning are important aspects of their learning processes. Positive student approaches to learning are necessary for success in schools and can be taken as important learning outcomes of schooling (OECD, 2003c). Students need motivation, self-confidence, and learning strategies to allow them to drive and regulate their own learning activities. The PISA 2000 analysis has shed light on the relationship between different aspects of student approaches to learning and thus on the whole process that makes students into competent autonomous learners. These findings are summarized in turn.

Student Learning Approaches as a Predictor of Student Performance

One rationale behind efforts to improve student approaches to learning is that appropriate approaches to learning have positive effects on student performance. Students who can regulate their own learning set realistic goals, select learning strategies and techniques appropriate to the demands of the task at hand, shield themselves from competing intentions, and maintain motivation when learning (OECD, 2003c). The PISA findings show a high degree of correlation between positive learning approaches and strong performance. Students' attitudes—their self-confidence and level of motivation—played an important role in adopting strong learning strategies. Positive attitudes were important for performance; they made it more likely for students to adopt fruitful learning strategies. Students' approaches to learning affected performance over and above the effect of family background (OECD). In some countries, this was most obvious for motivational variables such as interest in reading and students' self-efficacy. A large amount of the variability in performance was associated with student background: students from more advantaged backgrounds tended to have stronger characteristics as learners. To reduce social disparities in performance, it will be necessary to reduce the differences in student approaches to learning. However, only a fraction of the differences in student performance (about a fifth) were related to the variations in approaches to learning. Differences also depended on a range of other factors, including prior knowledge, capacity of the working memory, and reasoning ability. All of these factors facilitate the process of comprehension during reading; they free resources for deeper-level processing, such that new knowledge can be more easily integrated into the existing framework and hence more easily understood (OECD).

Student Learning Approaches as an Outcome

The PISA study established five student attributes that could be directly compared across cultures: students' use of memorization strategies, self-concept in reading, mathematical self-concept, self-efficacy, and preference for cooperative learning. The OECD (2003c) report presented student profiles in terms of the average strength of these learning characteristics in each country, the degree to which students clustered into groups with strengths or weaknesses across characteristics, and the learning attributes of different subgroups of the population. Comparison of the mean values of learner characteristics indicates that country differences in this respect were relatively small. Also, the differences across schools were small when compared with differences within schools: relatively few schools succeeded in promoting particularly strong approaches to learning among their students. Attention thus needs to be focused on teaching practices within schools and on system-wide change to improve classroom practices. Cluster analysis identified a group of students with particularly strong motivation, self-confidence, and learning strategies in combination as compared with a group particularly weak on these attributes. Clearly, the latter group needs targeted support, not just to help them succeed at school, but also to equip them with learning attitudes and habits that will be important in their later lives. That this clustering effect is of similar strength in all of the countries surveyed demonstrates that no country can ignore the existence of students at risk for learning.

Relationships Between Different Learner Characteristics

Effective, self-regulating learners cannot be created by the fostering of cognitive strategies alone. Learners also need to have the motivation to deploy these strategies (OECD, 2003c). In all countries, students who controlled their own learning processes and adapted them to the task at hand were characterized by a high level of confidence in their own abilities. Students were more likely to use control strategies if they were motivated to learn by concrete incentives (e.g., occupational aspirations) or specific interests. Overall, about two-thirds of the differences in the degree to which students used self-regulating strategies could be explained by differences in motivation and self-concept. Because the attitudes and learning behaviors of students were closely intertwined, an integrated approach is needed to improve these characteristics as a whole.

SAS Study

Compared with TIMSS and PISA, the SAS Study operated on a less comprehensive and ambitious scale. The project Science and Scientist was an investigation of the interests, experiences, and perceptions relevant to the learning of science by children in many countries (Sjøberg, 2000). The SAS Study was an attempt to open up for a critical discussion how to approach science teaching and learning in ways that take into consideration the cultural diversity within a country as well as differences across countries and cultures. Gender-related performance was of particular importance in the SAS Study.

The project involved 30 researchers from 21 countries. Some 9,300 children at the age of 13 answered the questionnaire. The quality of the sample varied from country to country; thus, the results should be interpreted with care. The SAS questionnaire consisted of seven questions aimed at probing student attitudes and perceptions on matters such as scientists as persons, out-of-school experiences, things to learn about, what is important for a future job, science in action, scientists at work, and me as a scientist.

Children in developing countries articulated a more positive view toward science and technology than children in industrialized countries. Some children in industrialized countries (mainly boys) portrayed the scientist as a cruel and crazy person, whereas most children in developing countries saw scientists as idols, helpers, and heroes. The low interest for learning science and technology expressed by Japanese children was remarkable. Gender differences in learning different topics of science varied among countries, but were higher in the Nordic countries (and in Japan) than in other regions. The study also provided examples to illustrate how different contexts and applications appealed differently to girls and boys.

CURRENT CONDITIONS OF SCIENCE LEARNING IN SELECTED COUNTRIES

Results obtained from TIMSS, PISA, and SAS indicate that students' learning outcomes and processes and the conditions of science learning at schools vary significantly both across countries and within a given country. Wide variations in science education practices, policies, and research in different countries are expected. Countries have different problems to be solved, and the ways in which they solve their problems may involve different purposes, approaches, and strategies. Thus it is helpful to know the current condition of science learning in different countries.

Science Education in Developing Countries

In 1990/1991, the International Institute for Educational Planning conducted a survey on the state of science education in 12 developing countries (Caillods, Gottelmann-Duret, & Lewin, 1997). The countries selected included four African countries, three Latin American countries, two Arabic countries, and three countries from the Asia and Pacific region. Focusing on science at the secondary school level, the information collected included participation in science education, curriculum organization, the conditions of teaching and learning, teaching methods, cost of science education, student achievement in science, and the destination of school leavers. Detailed discussion on the state of science education in the selected countries can be found in work by Caillods et al. (1997).

In terms of educational inputs, most African countries face a lack of financial and human resources. Even in countries where essential resources appear to be available, much remains to be done to improve the quality of education and student achievement in science. The organization of curricula and the forms and degrees of specialization in science subjects differ among countries. Factors affecting science achievement include curriculum content, the amount of time devoted to science, availability and quality of textbooks, and subject knowledge and subject-related pedagogical skills of teachers. Certain conditions of science education, such as the qualification level of science teachers, have improved almost everywhere. Most countries have made tremendous efforts to increase the participation of students in science education (Caillods et al., 1997).

Based on the findings of this survey, Lewin (2000) noted four factors that shape the policy context for science education. The first identifies questions related to participation, the second notes the importance of financial constraints, the third explores the dimensions of supply and demand for science education, and the fourth draws attention to different needs for different groups. In this context, Lewin discussed the current status and main problems of science education in developing countries.

1. There are large disparities among developing countries in gross enrollment rates at the secondary school level. Middle-income developing countries have a majority of children enrolled in the secondary grades. In contrast, some of the poorest countries have gross enrollment rates of between 5% and 10%. In many of the higher income developing countries and some of the low-income countries, female enrollment is greater than that for males. Participation rates at upper secondary are typically 30–50% of those at lower secondary, as a result of attrition, policies on mainstreaming, and availability of other options.

2. The amount spent per secondary student in different countries varies significantly. The richest countries allocate more than $5000 per child per year; the poorest less than $50. Money allocated to science education per year in the poorest countries can be as low as $1 per child. Sustainable levels of resources are low in poor developing countries. These countries may have to select students to specialize in science who will have access to facilities similar to those in richer countries.

3. Regarding the supply and demand in education and the labor market, the basic questions revolve around whether participation in science education is supply or demand constrained at different levels, and whether there is a case to increase supply or demand related to national development strategies on human resource development.

4. Lewin also discussed the different needs of five groups of stakeholders: those who will become qualified scientists and engineers, those destined to work in sub-professional roles that require or benefit from a grounding in science, the remaining general school population, members of marginalized groups with special needs of one kind or another, and those in the informal sector.

Science Education in European Countries

Sjøberg (2002) described and analyzed some of the challenges facing science and technology education in European countries by relating these challenges to their wider social setting. Keeping in mind that problems and issues may be perceived differently from different perspectives, Sjøberg pointed out the following:

1. Falling enrollment of students studying science. In many European countries, there is a noticeable decrease in the numbers of students choosing to take physics and mathematics. In many countries, there is also a growing gender gap in the choice of scientific and technological subjects at both the secondary and tertiary levels. Many countries have had a long period of steady growth in female participation in traditionally male fields of study, but this positive trend seems to have been broken in some countries.

2. Critique of large-scale international comparative studies. Comparative research in education, such as TIMSS, is important. However, the test items tend to become decontextualized and rather abstract. Sjøberg (2002) suggested complementing the data from TIMSS-like studies with open-ended and culturally sensitive information and perspectives.

3. Public understanding and attitude toward science. There is a political concern about how the general public relates to science, including the nature and level of public scientific and technological knowledge, attitudes and interests, and the degree of public support for scientific and technological research.

Sjøberg (2002) mentioned the widely the accepted notion that science curricula play important roles in developing and sustaining pupils' interest in science, and in preparing citizens for the twenty-first century. Yet, there is broad agreement about the shortcomings of traditional curricula that prevail in most countries: that science is conveyed mainly as a massive body of authoritative and unquestionable knowledge; that there is a lack of relevance and deeper meaning for the learners and their daily lives; and that students do not make the commitments necessary to learn science.

Cases of Science Education Reform Worldwide

An international workshop on reform in the teaching of science and technology, held in Beijing in 2000, presented current trends and main concerns regarding science curriculum development and implementation in selected countries in Asia and Europe (Poisson, 2001). A total of 15 countries were involved, including China, France, Hungary, India, Indonesia, Israel, Japan, Malaysia, the Netherlands, New Zealand, the Philippines, the Republic of Korea, Sri Lanka, Thailand, and the United Kingdom. Reports from each country focused on the following three aspects: (a) the status of teaching science and technology in the country under discussion, (b) the main problems that country confronts in teaching science and technology, and (c) the most recent science education reform implemented in the country. In order to illustrate the range of variation in the reports from different countries, I have decided to describe the results for China, France, Israel, Japan, New Zealand, and the United Kingdom. The selection is somewhat arbitrary; it is meant to be illustrative of the range of conditions and reforms in science education worldwide.

China. Rapid development of science and technology coupled with substantial socioeconomic growth now poses unprecedented challenges to China. Efforts are under way to enhance the content and the delivery system to reform curriculum and instruction. The main problems in the Chinese science curriculum were reported by Poisson (2001). In terms of the instructional goals, the emphasis is on science, rather than technology, and there is undue stress on acquiring knowledge; the development of student ability to apply scientific skills and knowledge to problem-solving remains neglected. The curriculum is subject-centered and knowledge-centered. For classroom practices, recitation of science prevails over science as inquiry, and teachers fail to inculcate scientific attitudes, values, processing skills, and higher-order thinking skills in their students. The separation of science into major disciplines impedes the comprehension of the interconnectedness among physics, biology, chemistry, and earth science.

Relative to science curriculum reform currently under way in China, Poisson (2001) recommended changing curriculum objectives that overemphasize knowledge transmission. The stress should be on the education of physically and emotionally healthy citizens with good characters. Desire, attitude, and ability for lifelong learning among students need to be cultivated. The tendency to structure curricula crammed with many subjects having little or no integration should be changed. Efforts must be made to ensure qualities of comprehensiveness, balance, and selectivity during the structuring of curricula. Curriculum content should be relevant to modern society and promote the development of science and technology. There should be an emphasis on integrating formal education with informal education in form and content, and on avoiding overemphasizing receptive learning, rote memorization, and passive imitation in the teaching process. Learning activities such as active participation, cooperation, exploration, and discovery should be advocated to enable students to become independent learners. Textbook content should be related to students' daily lives and be able to meet specific needs of students and schools in different areas. The variety and number of different versions of textbooks should be increased, and schools should be allowed to select their own textbooks. As for assessment, less emphasis should be placed on factual knowledge and rote memory. A new assessment system characterized by multiple methods that take into account both outcomes and processes is being established. In addition, there is an effort to replace the originally highly centralized system of curriculum management by establishing national, local, and school-level curriculum management policies. This will ensure the overall quality of basic education in China and improve its adaptability.

France.   In France, science and technology teaching takes place at all levels of schooling, but to widely differing degrees (Malleus, 2001). It is intended that everyone should have science education up to the age of 16. Science teaching takes account of the need to educate future citizens. There is constant emphasis on scientific questioning and increasing progression from the concrete to the abstract. Practical work is an expensive requirement, but one the system strives to satisfy at all levels. Information technologies have become essential in modern science teaching. Changes in the curriculum are evidence that the education system is constantly adapting to societal changes, based on continuous assessment (Malleus).

A strong tradition in France in the teaching and learning of science was to value mainly abstract studies and mathematics. Until the 1960s, the teaching and learning of physics and chemistry in France had not changed for 30 years. Pupils tended to believe that science was final, perfect, removed from reality, and not to be questioned. The introduction of practical work into the school curriculum was a difficult task. It took nearly a quarter-century to change. Change occurred as a result of giving teachers examples of new and interesting experiments, convincing teachers that pupils should not be taught science the way they themselves were taught, leading schools to build laboratories and buy equipment, and lobbying national and regional decision-makers to invest in practical work. Nowadays, assessment of new types of abilities such as problem-solving is emphasized, and links to everyday life and the environment are developed in science curricula. *Hands-on Science* for 5–12-year-olds was developed in 1995 and gradually grew and gained prestige. One important innovation was the introduction of supervised personal projects, which provided direction to pupils to understand the ultimate purpose of what they were learning. A new curriculum is under way, with the main idea of "less is more," emphasizing skills over knowledge (Malleus, 2001).

Israel.   In order to prepare the next-generation citizens for life in the twenty-first century, the goals of science and technology teaching in Israel emphasize knowledge and understanding of facts, concepts, laws, and principles that every citizen will need. Science and technology courses are expected to achieve the following objectives (Ilan, 2001): to develop creative and critical thinking, as well as understanding of research methods and enhanced problem-solving skills; to improve comprehension of the importance of science and technology knowledge that will help pupils make decisions regarding national and international issues; to help students recognize the possibilities and limitations of science and technology when applying them to problem-solving; to develop smart consumer thinking and behaviors by using a decision-making process when selecting a product or a system; to prepare individuals to take care of the environment; and to encourage the development of both individual and team learning skills and good work habits.

The characteristics and rationale of the Israeli science and technology curriculum (Ilan, 2001) are as follows. Science and technology should be integrated, while emphasizing the uniqueness of each subject; the integration of science and technology can be done in various ways; and different models should be evaluated in order to show the range of possibilities. Science and technology teachers choose their curriculum from the subjects given in the national syllabus and decide how to integrate them; they are encouraged to engage in team teaching. Students are expected to acquire the relevant knowledge, skills, and attitudes in key technology and science areas in order to be able to tackle human needs and problems. Ultimately, students should be able to follow a full process of problem-solving within a technological and scientific environment.

Japan.   In Japan, the science and technology syllabus includes scientific phenomena commonly encountered by students in day-to-day life. The aim is to train students in the practical aspects of scientific learning through laboratory and other experiments, develop their powers of observation, and hone their ability to interpret and apply their knowledge. Although the overall academic achievement of Japanese children is considered to be satisfactory, there are still problems that need to be addressed (Goto, 2001). These problems include a substantial number of children who do not fully understand the syllabus content; limited opportunities for children to develop their abilities to study, to think for themselves, to express their opinions, and to view things from different perspectives; children's inability to solve comprehensive science problems related to the environment; and children's lack of interest in science and its study.

The new curriculum and the reform of science education in Japan are aimed at the following goals (Goto, 2001): to help a child develop humanitarian values, social ability, and self-identity as a Japanese person living in the international community; to help a child develop the ability to learn and to think independently; to help a child develop his/her individuality by providing ample scope for learning opportunities; and to encourage each school to show ingenuity in developing distinctive educational activities. In addition, more specific objectives and reform measures were formulated for students at different levels. The suggested reforms at the elementary school, for instance, emphasized fostering problem-solving abilities and student understanding of the relationship between science and daily life. Life-long learning is also emphasized.

New Zealand.   In New Zealand, the major aim of science education is to help students develop knowledge and coherent understanding of living, physical material, and technology components of their environment; skills for investigating the above in scientific ways; and attitudes on which scientific investigation depends. The main problems in teaching science and technology in New Zealand are as follows (Kelly, 2001): lack of teacher confidence, knowledge of subject matter, and knowledge of subject pedagogy; lack of science facilities in primary schools; lack of an established base of teaching, learning, and assessment experience in technology; lack of familiarity with "real world" technological practice, the legacy of craft-based curricula in years 7 and 8; and the difficulties of attracting and retaining teachers, especially at the secondary level, in the physical sciences.

In New Zealand, the science curriculum was updated in 1992–1993. A curriculum assessment was planned for 2000–2002. The Ministry of Education produced resource materials and contracted providers to support the introduction of curriculum change to inservice teachers, assess learning, and monitor student progress in science (Kelly, 2001).

United Kingdom.   In the United Kingdom, the aim of the science curriculum is to stimulate pupils' curiosity about phenomena and events taking place in the world around them. Both scientific knowledge and scientific methods are emphasized. Pupils are expected to understand, to question, and to discuss how major scientific ideas contribute to technological change; affect industry, business and medicine; and improve the quality of life for all (Osborne, 2001).

The report edited by Millar and Osborne (1998) described the current state of science education in the United Kingdom. On the bright side, science is a universal curriculum for all pupils from age 5 to 16, and 80% of pupils undertake a program at age 16 that covers all of the major sciences. Science is also a core subject of the 11–16 curricula, along with English and mathematics. The current significance of science is reflected in the fact that it now occupies the curriculum high table, with literacy and numeracy, as an essential core of the primary curriculum. Moreover, there has been a general acceptance that learning science involves both knowing about the natural world and having opportunities for personal inquiry.

Although the results of TIMSS for the United Kingdom appeared to be satisfactory, Millar and Osborne (1998) noted that most students lack familiarity with the scientific ideas that they are likely to meet outside school—they lack the ability to deal effectively and confidently with scientific information in everyday contexts. School science, particularly at the secondary level, fails to sustain and develop the sense of wonder and curiosity of many young people. The apparent lack of relevance of the school science curriculum contributes to too few young people choosing to pursue courses in science and mathematics after the age of 16. Millar and Osborne suggested several reasons for these problems. There is an overemphasis on content in science curriculum, which can appear as a catalogue of ideas, lacking coherence and relevance. The science curriculum lacks a well-articulated set of aims or an agreed model of the development of pupils' scientific capability for the ages of 5–16 years and beyond. Assessment is based on exercises and tasks that rely heavily on memorization and recall, quite unlike those contexts in which learners might wish to use the science knowledge or skills in later life. The National Curriculum separates science and technology. There is relatively little emphasis within the science curriculum on discussion or analysis of the scientific issues that permeate contemporary life. Thus, science appears detached from and irrelevant to young persons' concerns and interests. There is a lack of variety of teaching and learning experiences, leading to too many dull and uninspiring lessons. The science curriculum fails to take adequate account of the range of interests and aptitudes of young people of this age.

Reform measures in the United Kingdom include the following (Osborne, 2001): the introduction of societal issues into the science curriculum; the use of more student-centered approaches; changing the assessment system to reflect the aims of the science curriculum; and increasing out-of-school and informal sources of science teaching, including the Internet and science-related television programs.

MAJOR PROBLEMS AND CONTEMPORARY ISSUES OF SCIENCE LEARNING WORLDWIDE

In view of the discussions presented in the previous sections, I now present a summary of the major problems and contemporary issues of student science learning, using Fig. 9.1 as an organizer.

Student Learning Outcomes in Science

Low student achievement in science for a portion of students, as shown in the TIMSS and PISA studies, is a major concern in many countries. Gender differences exist, with boys having significantly higher average science achievement than girls, particularly in physics, earth science, chemistry, and environmental and resource issues. Inasmuch as different students (with different needs, purposes, beliefs, social-cultural background, prior knowledge, learning experiences, learning approaches, and so on) learn science differently, a problem of both theoretical and practical interest is how to motivate, teach, and assess their learning in science so that optimal results can be obtained for students' individual development and for the benefit of society as a whole. There are gaps between the intended, the implemented, and the attained curriculum, although there is wide consensus that the goals of the science curriculum are meaning making, understanding, and conceptual change (Mintzes & Wandersee, 1998). It is also recognized that, besides achievement in the cognitive domain, student learning outcomes should include aspects such as motivation, self-concept, social-cultural and linguistic aspects, study skills, engagement, learning how to learn, global awareness, and the effective use of ICT. The desired learning outcomes are aligned with science curriculum reforms that are taking place in many countries. To improve learning outcomes, many problems must be solved, including the formulation of science education goals, the development and implementation of new curricula, the preparation and professional development of science teachers, the evaluation of science education programs, and securing financial and material resources and parent and societal support.

Learning Processes

As shown in Fig. 9–1, learning processes in classroom and school settings include many factors expected to link to learning outcomes. In order for a significant proportion of students to achieve the desired learning outcomes, the current state of science learning processes in many countries appears to be inadequate. For instance, in TIMSS 1995, students in most countries reported spending between half an hour and an hour studying or doing homework in science. In most countries, the challenge of catering to students of different academic abilities was the factor teachers mentioned most often as limiting how they taught their mathematics and science classes. Other limiting factors were a high student/teacher ratio, a shortage of equipment for use in instruction, and the burden of dealing with disruptive students. In the PISA study, significant proportions of students had low levels of engagement, which limited their capacity to benefit from school and constrained their potential in the future. The PISA findings showed a high degree of consistency within each country in the association between positive learning approaches and strong performance. But within each country, there were many students whose learning approaches were less effective.

More favorable conditions for developing student learning processes in science are required. For instance, greater attention should be paid to shaping positive learning behaviors and helping students develop effective learning approaches and metacognitive skills. To be conducive to science instruction aimed at the desired learning outcomes, more favorable teacher behaviors and classroom practices are needed. These will require, in turn, significant efforts in the preparation and professional development of science teachers.

Inputs to Learning

Student characteristics such as their prior knowledge, ability, motivation, goals, IQ, conceptions of learning, conceptions of teacher, and conceptions of the nature of science are important inputs to learning. The TIMSS 1999 results indicated that, in almost every country, there was a positive association between students' educational expectations and their science achievement. The results also indicated that eighth-grade boys generally had more positive self-concepts and attitudes in science than girls. PISA 2000 showed that students' attitudes—their self-confidence and level of motivation—played an important role in adopting strong learning strategies. Overall, about two-thirds of the differences in the degree to which students used appropriate learning strategies could be explained by differences in motivation and self-concept.

Another important input is teacher characteristics such as educational training and experience, beliefs, content knowledge, pedagogical knowledge, pedagogical content knowledge, self-confidence, instructional skills and teaching styles, and conceptions of teaching and learning. The TIMSS 1999 results indicated that eighth-grade students were taught science by teachers with a major in the appropriate science subject. However, eighth-grade science teachers reported only a moderate level of confidence in their preparation to teach science. Teachers' confidence in their preparation was greatest for biology, and least for earth science, environmental and resource issues, and scientific methods and inquiry skills.

Science curriculum and opportunity to learn are also important inputs to learning. Student opportunity to learn the content, skills, and processes in science depends to a great extent on the curricular goals and intentions inherent in a country's policies for science education. Discrepancies exist between intended and implemented curricula in science. Knowing basic facts and understanding science concepts received major emphasis in most countries. Shortcomings of traditional curricula in many countries include the fact that science is conveyed mainly as a massive body of authoritative and unquestionable knowledge, and that the curriculum lacks relevance and deeper meaning for the learners and their daily lives.

Financial, material, and human resources are also important inputs to learning. In the TIMSS studies, having educational resources in the home was strongly related to science achievement in every country. Students in schools that reported being well resourced generally had higher average science achievement than those in schools where across-the-board shortages affected instructional capacity in science. Likewise, public understanding, support, and attitude toward science are important inputs to learning.

Contexts of Learning

Important context inputs include the physical environment and social-cultural conditions at the home, classroom, and school levels. TIMSS 1995 showed that classroom variables were related to average school achievement even after adjustment for the home background of the students. The strong relationship that persists between the average level of home background and student achievement serves as a reminder that, in many countries, home background, schooling, and student achievement are closely intertwined. Teasing out the influences of the various contributing factors remains a major challenge.

The contexts of learning at classroom and school levels also involve factors such as educational goals and policies, prevailing theories of learning and teaching, educational philosophies, the scientific and technological capacities of the nation, supply and demand in education and the labor market, and other international conditions. These factors are influenced by the driving forces of science education reform shown in Figure 9.1. Important problems and issues can be raised while considering the constraints imposed on and the opportunities provided to the learning process.

CONCLUSIONS AND RECOMMENDATIONS

A global look at science learning is helpful for examining problems faced within a country, working out possible solutions, and taking necessary actions. Through an overview of the conditions of science learning worldwide, it is evident that many old problems persist, new challenges occur, and research-based reforms and policies are needed. To conclude this discussion, I present a global view of science learning in the twenty-first century. Finally, I offer some suggestion for international research studies on science learning.

A Global View of Science Learning in the Twenty-first Century

Old problems.   Across national boundaries, problems of student science learning persist. Regarding the inputs for school science, there are problems due to falling enrollment of students studying science, student lack of interest in science, lack of adequate supply and professional development of science teachers, and limited resources for science instruction. Science education policies are not well informed by research, and there is a lack of public understanding and support of science. Regarding the processes of learning science, there are problems that have to do with goals for curriculum/instruction/assessment, effective practices in science instruction and learning, and attending to student individual differences and special needs. In terms of problems related to the products of science learning, in addition to concerns about student achievement in science, other desired student learning outcomes need to be considered, including student abilities to apply scientific concepts in daily life, understanding the nature of science, attitudes toward science, and knowledge and skills for professional careers and for dealing with science-related social issues. Student learning outcomes in these areas are generally not as good as expected. It is easier to identify problems related to student learning processes and outcomes in science than to find effective methods to improve student learning, to inform teachers of research findings and teaching strategies, or to institutionalize change.

New challenges.   The purpose of learning science has changed in recent years. Students and citizens need to be well prepared for a science- and technology-oriented twenty-first century. Rather than preparing selected elites for science careers, schools now are expected to promote scientific literacy for all students. Science teaching, learning, and assessment are expected to stress meaningful learning of basic science concepts, a better understanding of the nature of science, and communication skills, critical thinking, cooperative learning, and problem-solving. Science curriculum and instruction are expected to have relevance to students' daily lives and deal with social issues. The international trends toward globalization and a knowledge economy create opportunities for international cooperation and competitiveness in science and technology. Improved science curriculum, instruction, and learning are expected to play important roles in national development and economic growth in many countries. New waves of science education reforms are sweeping the world. However, based on the lessons of previous science education reforms, it is clear that piecemeal reform attempts will not meet the new demands or solve the existing problems. What is needed is systemic reform, which involves research-informed policy-making and practice.

New opportunities.   On the research side, there is now a better theoretical understanding of student science learning from philosophical, sociological, psychological, and physiological points of view. A wide range of research methods in the qualitative and quantitative paradigms has been developed, enabling more valid, reliable, and fruitful studies of science learning. A number of international studies have been conducted, providing useful information, examples of best practices, and databases useful for secondary analysis. On the practical side, new instructional strategies, learning materials, delivery systems, learning environments, and assessment methods have been developed in recent years, often using ICT. There is a proliferation of technological tools that provide opportunities, locations, environments, and aids to science learning. Of course, the ways to make the best use of these new tools and opportunities need to be more thoroughly investigated.

Recommendations for International Research Studies on Science Learning

Sound theoretical and empirical bases are important to the improvement of student science learning and science education as a whole. In light of results obtained from international studies such as TIMSS and PISA, many important research questions may be answered meaningfully from an international perspective. Exchanging and sharing research findings among countries and international cooperation in doing research studies are important steps that the science education research community should take in the future.

Research studies with participants from more than one country can serve a number of purposes. For instance, Chabbott and Elliot (2003) pointed out three types of international comparative studies: (1) type I studies, which focus on comparing students' outcomes internationally; (2) type II studies, which are designed to inform education policy by examining specific policies and their implementation in other countries; and (3) type III studies, which are designed to increase general understanding about educational systems and processes. With the help of ICT, these studies can be more easily planned, carried out, and disseminated. Thus, a larger international community may be able to use the research results to inform science education practices and policy-making. Such studies can provide opportunities for educators and researchers from a given country to reflect on the educational goals, beliefs, and practices that they take for granted. Considering the wide range of educational, social, cultural, and historical contexts in different countries may help reduce the effects of intervening variables that plague most quantitative studies carried out in individual countries. These contexts also can provide a wider spectrum of situations to be considered in qualitative studies. Research results obtained from well-executed international studies can enhance the knowledge of what works best in different contexts, yield more reliable relationship between relevant variables, and deepen understanding of the phenomena involved.

Because of the trends in globalization and ICT, many countries face similar problems and challenges related to student science learning. Because research funds for doing science education studies are limited in most countries, international cooperation involving activities such as the exchange of research scholars and joint research studies should be encouraged. Strong commitment and support from public and private funding agencies, universities, research centers, and professional organizations are desirable.

Studies on student science learning are important in informing educational policy decisions and improving teaching/learning/assessment practices. The interest and scope of such studies may vary from individual students to groups of students, classes, schools, and countries. It is important to recognize that science education exists within historical, cultural, and institutional contexts that differ among countries. The educational goals, instructional conditions, teaching and learning practices, and students' learning outcomes in different countries also vary. From an international perspective, it is therefore important to take a systems approach in selecting research topics, priority, strategies, and methods in the planning of such international studies.

By examining important issues in science learning from an international perspective, I have tried in this chapter to provide useful information, discussion, and recommendations for the planning and execution of research studies on science learning from an international perspective. I hope that the model of school-based learning in science, the implications of the driving forces for science education reforms in the twenty-first century, and the current conditions of science learning worldwide as reviewed in this chapter will provide background information and guidance for conducting international research on science learning in the future.

ACKNOWLEDGMENTS

Thanks to Allan Harrison and Rudi Laugksch, who reviewed this chapter.

REFERENCES

Australian Capital Territory Department of Education and Training. (n.d.). *Curriculum profiles for Australian schools.* Retrieved August 1, 2004, from http://www.decs.act.gov.au/publicat/profiles.htm

Beaton, A. E., Martin, M. O., Mullis, I. V. S., Gonzalez, E. J., Smith, T. A., & Kelly, D. L. (1996). *The science achievement in the middle school years: IEA'S third international mathematics and science study (TIMSS).* Chestnut Hill, MA: Boston College.

Bennett, J. (2003). *Teaching and learning science.* London: Continuum.

Caillods, F., Gottelmann-Duret, G., & Lewin, K. M. (1997). *Science education and development: Planning and policy issues at secondary level.* Paris: UNESCO.

Chabbott, C., & Elliott, E. J. (Eds.). (2003). *Understanding others, educating ourselves: Getting more from international comparative studies in education.* Washington, DC: The National Academies Press.

Cheng, Y. C. (2000a). A CMI-tripilization paradigm for reforming education in the new millennium. *International Journal of Educational Management, 14*(4), 156–174.

Cheng, Y. C. (2000b). Foreword. A paradigm shift in science learning and teaching. *Asia-Pacific Forum on Science Learning and Teaching, 1*(2). Retrieved August 1, 2004, from http://www.ied.edu.hk/apfslt/issue_2/foreword/index.htm

Cobern, W. W. (1996). Constructivism and non-western science education research. *International Journal of Science Education, 4,* 287–302.

Driver, R., Squires, A., Rushworth, P., & Wood-Robinson, V. (1994). *Making sense of secondary science.* London: Routledge.

Duit, R., & Treagust, D. F. (1998). Learning in science-from behaviorism towards social constructivism and beyond. In B. J. Fraser & K. G. Tobin (Eds.), *International handbook of science education* (pp. 3–25). London: Kluwer Academic.

Entwistle, N. J. (1998). Improving teaching through research on student learning. In J. J. Forest (Ed.), *University teaching: International perspectives* (pp. 73–112). New York: Garland.

Entwisle, N. J. (2000, November). *Promoting deep learning through teaching and assessment: conceptual frameworks and educational contexts.* Paper presented at the meeting of the Teaching and Learning Research Programme, Leicester, United Kingdom.

Fensham, P. J. (1992). Science and technology. In P. W. Jackson (Ed.), *Handbook of research on curriculum* (pp. 789–829). New York: Macmillan.

Fensham, P. J., Gunstone, R., & White, R. (Eds.). (1994). *The content of science: A constructivist approach to its teaching and learning.* London: Falmer Press.

Goto, M. (2001). Japan. In M. Poisson (Ed.), *Science education for contemporary society: Problems and dilemmas* (pp. 31–38). Geneva, Switzerland: International Bureau of Education.

Hallak, J. (2001). Foreword. In M. Poisson (Ed.), *Science education for contemporary society: Problems and dilemmas* (pp. 3–4). Geneva, Switzerland: International Bureau of Education.

Huitt, W. (1995). *A system model of the teaching/learning process.* Valdosta, GA: Valdosta State University.

Hurd, P. D. (1998). Scientific literacy: New minds for a changing world. *Science Education, 82,* 408–416.

Ilan, M. (2001). Israel. In M. Poisson (Ed.), *Science education for contemporary society: Problems and dilemmas* (pp. 90–92). Geneva, Switzerland: International Bureau of Education.

Keeves, J., & Aikenhead, G., (1995). Science curricula in a changing world. In B. J. Fraser & H. J. Walberg (Eds.), *Improving science education* (pp. 13–45). Chicago: National Society for the Study of Education.

Kelly, F. (2001). New Zealand. In M. Poisson (Ed.), *Science education for contemporary society: Problems and dilemmas* (pp. 46–50). Geneva, Switzerland: International Bureau of Education.

Lewin, K. M. (2000). *World bank, human development network secondary education series: Mapping science education policy in developing countries.* Washington, DC: World Bank.

Malleus, P. (2001). France. In M. Poisson (Ed.), *Science education for contemporary society: Problems and dilemmas* (pp. 74–82). Geneva, Switzerland: International Bureau of Education.

Martin, M. O., Mullis, I. V. S., Beaton, A. E., Gonzalez, E. J., Smith, T. A., & Kelly, D. L. (1997). *The science achievement in the primary school years: IEA'S third international mathematics and science study (TIMSS).* Chestnut Hill, MA: Boston College.

Martin, M. O., Mullis, I. V. S., Gonzalez, E. J., Gregory, K. D., Smith, T. A., Chrostowski, S. J., et al. (2000). *TIMSS 1999 international science report: International study center.* Chestnut Hill, MA: Boston College.

Martin, M. O., Mullis, I. V. S., Gonzalez, E. J., Smith, T. A., & Kelly, D. L. (1999). *The school contexts for learning and instruction: IEA'S third international mathematics and science study (TIMSS).* Chestnut Hill, MA: Boston College.

Martin, M. O., Mullis, I. V. S., Gregory, K. D., Hoyle, C., & Shen, C. (2000). *Effective schools in science and mathematics: IEA'S third international mathematics and science study (TIMSS).* Chestnut Hill, MA: Boston College.

Matthews, M. R. (Ed.). (1998). *Constructivism in science education.* Dordrecht, the Netherlands: Kluwer Academic.

Matthews, M. R. (2000). Constructivism in science and mathematics education. In D. C. Phillips (Ed.), *National society for the study of education, 99th yearbook* (pp. 161–192). Chicago: University of Chicago Press.

Millar, R., & Osborne, J. (1998). *Beyond 2000: Science education for the future.* London: King's College.

Mintzes, J. J., & Wandersee, J. H. (1998). Research in science teaching and learning: A human constructivist view. In J. J. Mintzes, J. H. Wandersee, & J. D. Novak (Eds.), *Teaching science for understanding: A human constructivist view* (pp. 60–92). San Diego: Academic Press.

Mintzes, J. J., Wandersee, J. H., & Novak, J. D. (Eds.). (1998). *Teaching science for understanding: A human constructivist view.* San Diego: Academic Press.

Mullis, I. V. S., Martin, M. O., Beaton, A. E., Gonzalez, E. J., Kelly, D. L., & Smith, T. A. (1998). *The mathematics and science achievement in the final years of secondary school: IEA'S third international mathematics and science study (TIMSS).* Chestnut Hill, MA: Boston College.

Mullis, I. V. S., Martin, M. O., Fierros, E. G., Goldberg, A. L., & Stemler, S. E. (2000). *Gender differences in achievement: IEA'S third international mathematics and science study (TIMSS).* Chestnut Hill, MA: Boston College.

National Research Council. (1996). *National science education standards.* Washington, DC: National Academies Press.

National Science Teachers Association. (2003). *Standards for science teacher preparation* (Rev. ed.). Retrieved August 1, 2004, from http://www.nsta.org/main/pdfs/NSTAstandards2003.pdf

OECD. (1999). *Measuring student knowledge and skills: A new framework for assessment.* Retrieved August 1, 2004, from http://www.pisa.oecd.org/docs/books.htm

OECD. (2003a). *Literacy skills for the world of tomorrow: Further results from PISA 2000.* Retrieved August 1, 2004, from the OECD/PISA Web site: http://www.pisa.oecd.org/docs/books.htm

OECD. (2003b). *Student engagement at school: A sense of belonging and participation.* Retrieved August 1, 2004, from http://www.pisa.oecd.org/docs/books.htm

OECD. (2003c). *Learners for life: Student approaches to learning.* Retrieved August 1, 2004, from http://www.pisa.oecd.org/docs/books.htm

Osborne, J. (1996). Beyond constructivism. *Science Education, 80*, 53–82.

Osborne, J. (2001). United Kingdom (England). In M. Poisson (Ed.), *Science education for contemporary society: Problems and dilemmas* (pp. 99–101). Geneva, Switzerland: International Bureau of Education,

Osborne, R., & Freyberg, P. (1985). *Learning in science: The implications of children's science.* Auckland, New Zealand: Heinemann.

Poisson, M. (Ed.). (2001). *Science education for contemporary society: Problems, issues and dilemmas.* Geneva, Switzerland: International Bureau of Education.

Proctor, C. (1984). Teacher expectations: A model for school improvement. *The Elementary School Journal, 84*, 469–481.

Qualifications and Curriculum Authority. (2002). *National curriculum for England.* Retrieved August 10, 2004, http://www.nc.uk.net/index.html

Sjøberg, S. (2000). *Science and scientists: The SAS study.* Retrieved August 25, 2004, from http://folk.uio.no/sveinsj/SASweb.htm#_Toc483975184

Sjøberg, S. (2002). *Science and technology education: Current challenges and possible solutions.* Retrieved August 23, 2004, from http://folk.uio.no/sveinsj/STE_paper_Sjoberg_UNESCO2.htm

Stufflebeam, D. L. (2000). The CIPP model for evaluation. In D. L. Stufflebeam, G. F. Madaus, & T. Kellaghan (Eds.), *Evaluation models* (2nd ed., pp. 279–317). Boston: Kluwer Academic.

Tobin, K. (Ed.). (1993). *The practice of constructivism in science and mathematics education.* Washington, DC: AAAS Press.

van den Akker, J. (1998). The science curriculum: Between ideals and outcomes. In B. J. Fraser & K. G. Tobin (Eds.), *International handbook of science education* (pp. 421–447). London: Kluwer Academic.

Zembylas, M. (2002). The global, the local, and the science curriculum: A struggle for balance in Cyprus. *International Journal of Science Education, 24*, 499–519.

Wandersee, J. H., Mintzes, J. J., & Novak, J. D. (1994). Research on alternative conceptions in science. In D. L. Gabel (Ed.), *Handbook of research on science teaching and learning* (pp. 177–234). New York: Macmillan.

White, R. T. (1988). *Learning science.* Oxford: Basil Blackwell.

CHAPTER 10

Gender Issues in Science Education Research: Remembering Where the Difference Lies

Kathryn Scantlebury
University of Delaware

Dale Baker
Arizona State University

Take the fact of education. Your class has been educated at public schools and universities for five or six hundred years, ours for sixty . . . . though we see the same world we see it through different senses. Any help we can give you must be different from that you can give yourselves, and perhaps the value of that help may lie in the fact of the difference. Therefore before we agree to sign your manifesto or join your society, it might be well to discover where the difference lies, because then we may discover where the help lies also. (Woolf, 1938, p. 17)

If there is any misleading concept, it is that of coeducation: that because women and men are sitting in the same classrooms, hearing the same lecture, reading the same books, performing the same laboratory experiments, they are receiving an equal education. They are not, first because the content of education itself validates men even as it invalidates women. Its very message is that men have been the shapers and thinkers of the world, and that this is only natural. (Rich, 1979, p. 241)

In the early twentieth century, Virginia Woolf (1938) noted that men had centuries of experience with and in public education. Access to public education had only recently become available to women, and she suggested that women saw the world "through different senses." Woolf suggested that exploring those differences has provided an opportunity to improve education. For the past 40 years, gender research in science education has explored those differences. Often, curriculum choices, assessment techniques, and pedagogical practices that improve women and girls' knowledge, understanding, attitudes, and participation in science are also beneficial to the majority of their male peers. Since gaining access to science education, women and girls have overcome many obstacles, and although females perform well on various measures of science achievement, comprise at least 50% of the graduates from many undergraduate and graduate science programs, and have used their senses to conduct scientific research differently from their male colleagues, inequities in science education between females and male still exist at all levels and across different societies.

Twenty years ago, Rich (1979) challenged the equitable nature of coeducation, and educators continue to assume the stance that females and males receive equal and thus equitable education. However, in the United States, 20 years after the landmark Title IX of the Elementary and Secondary Education Act legislation that banned sex discrimination in education programs and activities, the American Association of University Women (AAUW) published a series of studies that focused on gender differences in K–12, noting that girls were "shortchanged" in the education they received and describing the environment in public schools as hostile toward females (AAUW, 1993, 1998a, 1998b; Wellesley Center for Research on Women, 1992). Other researchers observed that the U.S. educational system "failed at fairness" (Sadker & Sadker, 1994), and 30 years of gender research found similar patterns in other Western countries (Arnot, David, & Weiner, 1999; Kelly, 1998; Kenway, Willis, Blackmore, & Rennie, 1998).

Science education researchers often fail to acknowledge "where the difference lies" and to take steps to redress those gender differences. This chapter foregrounds gender issues in science education by defining the term, reviewing the influence of gender on the historical and sociocultural aspects of science education, discussing access and participation rates for females in science from an international perspective, considering the impact of educational policies that introduced standards-based teaching and high-stakes testing, and finally proposing directions for future research in the field. Our chapter focuses on research studies, and because of page limitations many examples are Eurocentric. When possible, we have used other literature reviews to support our arguments.

DEFINING GENDER

Gender and *sex differences* are terms that are used interchangeably and incorrectly (Rennie, 1998). For many, *gender* is "a polite way to talk about the sexes" (Haslanger, 2000, p. 31). However, the current trend is to use the term *sex differences* to refer to the biological dichotomy of male and female bodies, whereas *gender* is a social construction, usually based upon the biology of one's body. Studies in gender research and science education have tended to ignore the interplay of sex, the body, and biology in the social construction of gender (Gilbert, 2001). This limited focus has influenced science education researchers by establishing an oppositional stance between feminine and masculine, causing a nonexistent dichotomy[1] that limits theoretical, em-

---

1. Where relevant, throughout the chapter we highlight studies that have focused on males, however there are few studies in science. Much masculinity literature focuses on reading or males in high-risk groups, e.g., in the US. African American or low socio-economic Eurocentric males, in Australia, Aboriginals, in New Zealand, boys from Maori or Samoan groups.

pirical, and qualitative studies to exploration of gender as a "closed box" (Gilbert; Henwood & Miller, 2001). In this chapter we consider gender a social construction and have expanded the discussion to include aspects of sex differences in science education.

Recently, gender research in education has been broadened to include issues related to gay, lesbian, bisexual, and transgender (GLBT) people and masculinity. To date, there are few published studies in these areas focusing on aspects of science education. Research in this area has implications for science teacher education, teacher and student identity, the nature of the curriculum, and the safety of students as it affects their ability to learn science (Snyder & Broadway, 2004; Fifield & Swain, 2002; Kosciw, 2004; Letts, 2001).

Sex, the body, biology, and the social construction of gender have all influenced students' access to general education and, more specifically, science education, as well as the kinds of research questions scholars have asked. This chapter synthesizes the gender research, especially with regard to science education, and identifies several major issues. The first section of this chapter focuses on the historical aspects of gender research in science education. The next section discusses the current international situation for girls in science education. In the third section, we discuss sociocultural aspects, which include student attitudes; interplay of gender with race, ethnicity, sexuality, socioeconomic status, language, and religion; and science teacher education. We conclude with a discussion of the impact of policy on gender research and future research directions.

HISTORICAL PERSPECTIVE

In this section we focus on the history of science education for girls, a history that until very recently was confined to the West, and a synopsis of research into factors influencing the rates of females' participation in science. Because of space limitations, we illustrate our points with a selection of representative studies, position papers, and examples.

The History of Science Education for Girls

Many scholars have taken a historical perspective that places equity in science education in the context of the nineteenth and twentieth centuries' socially approved gender roles for middle- and upper-class women (Baker, 2001; Blair, 1998; Fry, 1988; Gaskell, 1998; Theobald, 1996; Tolley, 2003; Yates, 1998). Thus, at the beginning of the nineteenth century middle-class girls' education in the United States, the United Kingdom, New Zealand, and Australia was limited to private instruction at home or in academies where the curriculum included drawing, painting, and needlework. Society perceived studying science as a threat to a girl's health and her virtue. However, by the mid-nineteenth century, girls were attending public primary and secondary schools, but there was continued debate about whether they should be studying science and curricula focused on music, painting, modern languages, and mathematics. Charles Perry, an Australian bishop, stated that women should know only enough science for drawing-room conversation but should not study professional science. His views were reflective of the Western world, especially Cambridge intellectuals. In New Zealand, primary education for girls often took second place to their contribution to the family's economic well-being (Mathews, 1988).

By the end of the nineteenth century, more girls than boys were studying science in high school in the United States and Canada, and girls were receiving better grades than boys. However, only urban, white girls living in the northeastern United States had access to science education. All students in rural areas of the United States and Australia were less likely to attend school, as were First Peoples in Canada (Baker, 2001; Gaskell, 1998; Theobald, 1996). In the United Kingdom, lower-class girls trained to be domestics instead of attending secondary school. Middle-class girls could enroll in endowed private schools located primarily in London, Cambridge, and Oxford. These schools stressed educational achievement in subjects that included science (Blair, 1998). In New Zealand, secondary education for girls was still considered a luxury, and the curriculum reinforced traditional gender roles (Fry, 1988). European girls also had limited access to science education. For example, girls in Germany could not attend the Gymnasium, where the rigorous curriculum (including science) prepared students for university (Sime, 1997). In Poland, Marie Sklowdowska (Curie) was educated at home so that she could study mathematics and science (Quinn, 1995).

Sadly, the positive trend for girls' education in science declined in the early decades of the twentieth century in the United States, the United Kingdom, and Canada (Baker, 1998, 2001; Gaskell, 1998). The vocational education movement and the post–World War I "back-to-the-home" movement created a mechanical or university track for boys and a business or home economics track for girls. This resulted in a decrease in the number of girls taking science. There was an 80% drop in enrollment in physics in the United States between 1900 and 1928, and girls' chemistry classes focused on the home, cooking, and food adulteration (Rury, 1991, as cited in Baker, 2001). In the United Kingdom in 1902, the National Board of Education made training in housewifery mandatory and allowed girls to substitute domestic science for natural and physical science.

The Great Depression further exacerbated girls' limited access to science in the United States and the United Kingdom and reinforced traditional gender roles (Baker, 2001; Blair, 1998). Girls in the United States, but not boys, were actively discouraged from taking science to reduce the amount of materials consumed and thus the cost of education. In the United Kingdom, the National Board of Education justified a female curriculum by stating that girls' futures would be as homemakers. In the early part of the twentieth century, state governments in Australia also tried to promote a curriculum for girls that emphasized domestic skills, but there was active resistance from women teachers, parents, and girls (Yates, 1998).

The decline in girls' participation in science caused little or no concern in the United States until the mid-twentieth century, when Truman's science advisors argued for a foundation to fund science research and improve science teaching in schools (DeBoer, 1991). The result was the National Science Foundation, which funded the development of new science curricula. These curricular reform projects came under sharp criticism for a variety of reasons. They were directed by men, were based on the theories of male psychologists, and did not result in large numbers of girls choosing science or doing well in science (DeBoer). Scholars interested in gender concluded that the new curricula in the United States ignored the needs of girls. They continued their efforts to bring girls into science.

Until the 1970s, Australia offered a sex-differentiated vocational curriculum in addition to the academic secondary curriculum, and girls took fewer science courses than humanities, commercial, or domestic courses. Reports, generated in the 1970s, prompted in part by the women's movement, recommended curricula to help girls. Changes in Australia included campaigns to encourage girls to choose nontraditional careers, school-based projects, and inclusive curriculum (Yates, 1998). Canada and the United Kingdom were also involved in curriculum reform in the 1970s and 1980s that was sensitive to girls' needs. This led to guidelines for nonsexist curriculum materials, the elimination of sexist guidance materials, and an effort to increase girls' interest in science (Blair, 1998; Gaskell, 1998). Feminists in New Zealand also challenged the sexist nature of the curriculum at this time (Watson, 1988). In addition, the international organization known as GASAT (Gender and Science and Technology) was founded in 1981 to engage in research and grassroots activities to promote gender equity in science and technology worldwide. GASAT has created a global network of women and provided a forum (international conferences held every 2–3 years) for sharing ideas for promoting gender equity in science and technology.

Efforts to increase the participation of women in scientific careers have had an impact, although participation in engineering is still lagging. According to New Zealand's 1996 census, statistics engineering was the field with the largest number of male university graduates (New Zealand Bureau of Statistics, 2004). Males numbered 133,950, in contrast to females, who numbered 3,633. The gap between men and women choosing science as a field of study was much smaller. Approximately 15,742 men graduated from university in all fields of science, as compared with approximately 13,000 women. Other western countries have similar enrollment and graduation patterns in science, mathematics, engineering, and technology (SMET), and although engineering remains a highly gendered occupation, there has been a steady increase of women interested in the field (Clair, 1995).

A gender gap between the enrollment of women and men in SMET also exists in Australia. In 2003, 11% of female students were studying engineering, but 42% were studying all areas of science. Furthermore, only 55.5% of women in the natural and physical sciences and 43.1% of women in engineering were employed full-time, as compared with 73.3% of males in the natural and physical sciences and 81.4 % of males in engineering. The number of doctorates awarded to men and women in the natural and physical sciences in 2003 revealed a smaller gender gap (male = 863, female = 752) than in engineering, where men received 752 doctorates and compared with 97 females (Australian Bureau of Statistics, 2004).

Canadian statistics indicate that 15% of engineering students, 36% of mathematics and physical science students, and 58% of agriculture and bioscience students were female (Statistics Canada, 2004). In the United States, the number of women in engineering is low, but women now earn more bachelor's degrees in science than men (Mervis, 2003). In the next section, we discuss the research on factors influencing females' participation rates in science, the question of a gender gap, and how research has changed over time.

Research into Factors Influencing Rates
of Participation in Science

One of the earliest studies of gender differences was conducted by Field and Copley (1969) and focused on cognitive style and achievement differences between males and females in Australia and the United Kingdom. They concluded that there were "basic and important psychological differences between the sexes in the processing of information" (p. 10) and that the "slower development of formal operations by these girls" (p. 8) was responsible for boys' higher science achievement scores. Kelly (1978), reviewing the research of the 1960s and 1970s, also acknowledged that males performed better than females on science assessments worldwide; but she concluded that researchers did not know the causes of girls' underachievement in science and that most explanations have not been empirically tested. She then proceeded to test three hypotheses (cultural, school, attitude) to explain sex differences in International Association for the Evaluation of Educational Achievement (IEA) data. She concluded that societal/cultural expectations contributed to the magnitude of sex differences, that school experiences could limit achievement differences, provided girls studied as much science as boys, and that the relationship between liking science and achievement was stronger for boys than girls.

Kahle and Meece (1994) synthesized the gender-related research from the 1970s to early 1990s, noting the "recent concern" about the low participation of women and girls in science, and placed this research in the context of "factors underlying the differential participation of boys and girls in school science" (p. 542). While Kahle and Meece acknowledged the impact of family, cultural, and social factors on gender issues in science, they focused on school-related factors, because teachers and administrators could influence those factors. They also reviewed the research on interventions designed to increase girls' participation in science and identified areas for further research. Kahle and Meece noted that the gender gap in mathematics achievement was closing in 1988, but not in science. The most recent Third International Mathematics and Science Study (TIMSS) data (IEA, 2000) continue to support this conclusion, indicating that from 1988 to 2000 the U.S. gender gap did not decrease, except at the middle-school level. Here, the performance of girls and boys is the same, as it was found to be for six other countries (Beaton et al., 1996). In the United Kingdom, the gender gap has reversed and now favors girls (Arnot et al., 1999).

Kahle and Meece (1994) also reviewed the now controversial work of Benbow, Stanley, and colleagues; of Maccoby and Jacklin; and of other researchers looking for what were then called sex differences in cognitive abilities. They concluded that there was more evidence for attributing performance differences in mathematics and spatial ability to differential experiences (e.g., course taking, out-of-school activities) than to innate differences attributable to biological sex. Furthermore, they concluded that the differences that did exist in mathematics and spatial ability were not large enough to explain the differences in science achievement. Kahle and Meece noted that part of the gender gap could be attributed to test bias in standardized test format, and that girls had better grades awarded by high school science and mathematics teachers. These two factors often have been ignored in the discussion of differences in male and female achievement.

The cumulative effect of teacher expectations, classroom interactions, and the type of instruction, all of which favored boys, was identified as the main educational factor that influenced girls' participation in science. Intervention programs designed to increase girls' participation in science had limited impact, because they focused on single rather than multiple causes and were not grounded in theoretical models that integrated psychological and sociocultural variables (Kahle, Parker, Rennie, & Riley, 1993).

Baker (2002a), in an editorial, asked, "Where is the gender and equity in science education?" (p. 659). To answer that question, she examined articles and editorials in the *Journal of Research in Science Teaching* by decade, beginning with the 1970s. She included "articles that addressed planning for the future, setting priorities, establishing a research agenda, and describing our theoretical orientation as well as articles that took gender and equity as their main theme" (p. 659). During the 1970s and early 1980s, there was little research that addressed gender or equity. The few studies that were identified ($n = 12$) addressed sex differences in cognitive ability and implicitly or explicitly used a deficit model with male performance as the norm. In the late 1980s, Baker found approximately 20 articles that were primarily concerned with gender. These articles were less focused on sex differences and more on gender equity. This change in perspective brought about a questioning of the meaning of differences and attempts to get more girls interested in science. However, this research did not as yet question the locus of the problem. Girls, not science, had to be changed.

Race, Ethnicity and Socioeconomic Status

Kahle and Meece (1994) criticized a large portion of gender research because it was based on a deficit model that implied that girls lack the cognitive, personal, and experiential characteristics that promoted achievement in science. They called for research that focused on school and workplace barriers, paid more attention to individual differences, and examined the role of ethnicity and socioeconomic status as moderators of success. Several years later, Kenway and Gough (1998) identified the key areas of the gender and science education discourse as documenting differences in participation, attitudes, achievement, and learning strategies. They critiqued the dominant focus on differences and suggested that the research should move away from the male-female dichotomy and encompass race, ethnicity, and class. In a 2000 editorial in the *Journal of Research in Science Teaching*, Gallagher and Anderson (2000) also criticized the research in science education for excluding gender, race, class, or ethnicity.

One of the exceptions to the dominant focus critiqued by Kenway and Gough (1998) was the book *Gender, Science and Mathematics* (Parker, Rennie, & Fraser, 1996). Parker et al. included the work of many scholars, albeit from Western countries (Australia, Canada, Germany, Norway, the United Kingdom, the United States), working within a gender-inclusive perspective. Baker (1998) also synthesized the research that addressed the role of ethnicity and socioeconomic status in participation in science worldwide. She noted that until recently science was the province of white upper-class European and North American males and found that continuing inequities in the educational systems of countries serving large minority and indigenous populations (e.g., the United States, Canada, Australia, New Zealand) made it particularly difficult for girls of color to be successful in science.

Research that has focused on socioeconomic status and ethnicity has provided a more nuanced picture of girls' participation in science. The second IEA study found that the higher the educational level of parents, the more books in the home, and the smaller the family size, the higher the science achievement for all students (Baker, 1998). Also, studies have found that for some minority students, participation in science requires a large cultural shift. In the United States, this shift has been easier for African American females, who are less constrained by traditional gender roles and community than some other minority groups, such as Latinas, who are more constrained by traditional gender roles and community (AAUW, 1998a).

Concurrently with gender, race, ethnicity, and social class, culture and language were making a breakthrough in the science education literature (Baker, 2002a). These two lines of research had, for the most part, moved along on parallel tracks with few links that would bring them together. For example, Baker criticized the work of Michael Apple (1992), who wrote about economic oppression and curricular reform, but failed to mention the special effect of economic oppression on women. She also criticized the work of Michael O'Loughlin (1992), who focused on issues of culture, power, and discourse in the classroom only in relation to students of color without acknowledging the research on gender in these areas or considering the double impact of color and gender. Other authors were more sensitive to the complexities of gender in race, class, ethnic, and sociocultural contexts and struggled to avoid oversimplification. Krockover and Shepardson (1995) made a strong argument for including these "missing links" in gender research. On the other hand, many of the writers in the 1990s were concerned that issues of gender would be subsumed by issues of culture or race.

Nevertheless, the 1990s also brought official recognition that gender was an important issue in science education, and journal editors supported special issues that focused on recommendations for gender reform. The 1990s saw approximately 30 articles published in the *Journal of Research in Science Teaching* on the topic of gender. These articles went beyond describing well-known phenomena and moved toward explaining what the phenomena meant. The deficit model was discarded, and new feminist and emancipatory theories and methodologies were employed. Gender research in science education had turned a corner (Baker, 2002a).

Masculine Nature of Science

Kelly (1985) identified the masculine stereotyping of science in Western culture as a major barrier to participation not found in non-Western countries. In addition, Kahle and Meece (1994) identified gender role expectations (reinforced by parents and culture) and conflicts about balancing family, children, and a scientific career. These stereotypes and gender role conflicts continue to exist to varying degrees, depending upon context and remain a concern for women worldwide. Kenway and Gough (1998), in their critique of science education research, found that most explanations for differences blamed girls, the curriculum, or the learning environment; the explanation did not take into consideration educational politics and showed a reluctance to attribute differences to science as a masculine discourse. For example, women were largely missing from the academy until the middle of the twentieth century, and currently, issues of child care, especially release time for bearing and raising children, impede women's progress in academe. The structure of the academy within science still favors men, who often have no or minimal child-care, home, or other family responsibilities (Baker, 1998).

Despite barriers that the masculine nature of science erects for girls and women, there are some encouraging data. Baker (1998) found that girls often rejected the masculine aspects of science (de-contextualized activities, competition, mechanistic views of nature) and the tedium of school science, but not science itself. Moreover, the outcome of girls' attitudes toward science seems to depend on which attitude measures are used (Kahle & Rennie, 1993).

INTERNATIONAL PERSPECTIVES

Women and girls' participation in science in many countries is restricted by their limited access to education. In 2002, the World Bank estimated that of the 150 million children in primary school, 100 million were girls who were expected to leave before completing their education. United Nations Educational, Scientific and Cultural Organization (UNESCO) (2003) estimated that 104 million children, aged 6–11, worldwide are not in school each year and that 60 million of these children are girls. Nearly 40% of out-of-school children live in sub-Saharan Africa. For example, 90% of girls aged 15–19 in Chad have not finished primary school, and 80% in Burkino Faso have not completed primary school (Hertz & Sperling, 2004). Another 35% of the out-of-school children live in South Asia. In Laos, fewer than one in four girls attend school beyond primary years, and only 12% of girls in Cambodia are enrolled in secondary school (UNESCO).

Urban-rural disparities are striking, especially for girls. In Niger, 83% of the girls living in the capital attend primary school, compared with only 12% of rural girls. In Pakistan, three times as many boys as girls living in rural areas complete primary school, and in urban areas of Pakistan, twice as many boys as girls complete primary school (Hertz & Sperling, 2004). One-third of girls in Africa and South Asia who have completed primary school are still functionally illiterate and cannot read, write, or do simple arithmetic (Hertz & Sperling).

Data for secondary and tertiary enrollment comparisons are limited because of changes in international statistics (United Nations Development Fund for Women [UNIFEM], 2004). However, when comparing the number of females with males enrolled in secondary education, there are 82 females per 200 males attending school; the exception is Latin American/Caribbean countries, where there is one female per 100 males. For tertiary education, there are 63 females per 100 males in sub-Saharan Africa and 58 females per 100 males in South Central Asia. Overall, there are 75 females per 100 males in university in developing countries. The exceptions, where females outnumber males, are Latin American/Caribbean, Southeast Asian, and Western Asian countries. These numbers are ratios and do not represent the actual number of students enrolled, which are very small for both males and females.

Girls in developing countries who attend school face instruction that fosters gender stereotypes and discourages girls from achieving. Curriculum materials portray women as passive (i.e., in Togo, Ethiopia, Kenya). For example, curricula in

Kenya describe men as leaders, fighters, or soldiers, and women are described as breast feeders, fertile, or pregnant (Hertz & Sperling, 2004). In Nigeria, classroom interactions favor boys, who are given more time to ask and answer questions, use materials, and take leadership roles. They are also provided more time and opportunities to engage in science tasks compared with girls (United Nations Children's Fund, 2003).

Science and technology courses at all levels of education are limited in developing countries, and where they exist, enrollment is dominated by men. Among the major barriers to female participation in science are the lack of the basic prerequisite education, and the perceptions of teachers, counselors, family, and peers that science and technology are for males. Thus, half of the world's workers are in sex-stereotyped occupations (UNIFEM, 2004). In addition, cultural norms prevent even scientifically educated women in developing countries from entering the upper echelons of science (UNIFEM, 1995). Almost all of the 479 members listed as members of the Third World Academy of Science (2002) are male.

Latin America

Women in Latin America have not experienced the educational disadvantages of their sisters from other developing countries. This is attributed in part to the egalitarian attitudes of indigenous populations and a push toward industrialization. However, women at university still tend to choose professions that reflect traditional gender roles (Bustillo, 1993). Latinas' access to education steadily increased during the twentieth century until the 1980s. Primary-school enrollment for boys and girls was equal, female illiteracy rates dropped, and the number of women entering university increased. However, the economic downturn of the 1980s and the slow recovery of many countries in Latin American has placed the education of women, especially of rural women, at risk and increased the dropout rates for girls who feel that an education no longer ensures economic and social mobility (Conway & Borque, 1993).

Middle East

Throughout the Middle East (Iran, Iraq, Israel, Jordan, Oman, Qatar, and Yemen) illiteracy rates are at least twice as high for women than men, ranging from 5% to 45% for males and 16% to 77% for females. Jordan has the lowest rates (5% male, 15.7% female) and Iraq the highest rates (45% male, 77% female). Only in Israel are the illiteracy rates less than 10% for the population (3% male, 7.2 % female) (United Nations [UN], 2004a). Science is taught in Muslim countries as an integrated compulsory subject from the beginning school grades. It is also part of the curriculum in the last two or three years in secondary school. However, fewer girls than boys enroll in these courses because girls are encouraged to enroll in arts and humanities classes; there is stereotyping of science and technology as suitable only for boys, and the curriculum does not relate science to the everyday life of women (Hassan, 2000).

Change is taking place in Iran, among those women who graduate from secondary school and go on to tertiary education (Koenig, 2000). In Koenig's report, almost 60% of incoming university students were female and, unlike in the past patterns, they were choosing science. Two-thirds of the students in chemistry at the University of Isfahan were female and 56% of all students in the sciences were female. This included one in five Ph.D. students. Some observers attribute women's dedication to the gains in their science participation. However, others believe that women in Iran have fewer career options than men and so devote more time to their studies. Despite increasing female enrollments, the number of women in faculty positions in universities is still low. In 1999, women were 6% of full professors, 8% of associate professors, and 12% of assistant professors in all academic fields.

Iran was the only Muslim country to participate in TIMSS. In Iran, gender differences that occurred in science at fourth grade favored boys in earth science, but there were no gender differences in life or physical sciences, or environmental issues and the nature of science. At the eighth grade, gender differences favoring boys appeared in earth science and physics, but not in life science, chemistry, or environmental issues and the nature of science. Data for the final year of secondary education were not reported (IEA, 2000).

To avoid getting a false picture of female participation in science, it is important to look at the actual numbers rather than percentage of enrollment. Of the 18,000 students enrolled at the University of Kuwait in 1996–1997, 623 graduated with a science or science-related degree. One hundred and eighty-one of the students in the sciences were female, 142 females were in engineering and petroleum, 52 women were in medicine, and 38 women were in allied medicine fields (e.g., nursing) (Kuwait Information Office, 2002). In 1997, Jordan had 39% of female university students studying natural and applied science nationwide for a total of 12,227 women, and 19% of graduate students in these areas were women ($n = 1,719$) (Jordan Higher Council for Science and Technology, 1997). Other Middle East countries have similarly high percentages of women in science (17–75%), but absolute numbers are low (e.g., 28% represents 7,344 women in Egypt) (Hassan, 2000).

The number of female faculty in universities varies from country to country, with countries such as Syria with 7% of women in science and engineering-related fields ($n = 410$ nationwide) and Lebanon with 24% female science and engineering faculty ($n = 111$ nationwide). Overall, statistics for female faculty in Muslim countries are similar to those found in the United States, where representation in the health sciences is highest, followed by biological science; the fewest women are found on the faculties of engineering. However, the more prestigious the academic institution, the less likely it is that women will be on the faculty in senior positions, even at the level of department head, and even fewer women scientists are in policy-making positions (Hassan, 2000). This participation pattern also exists in Western academic institutions.

Turkey, although not in the Middle East, is an Islamic country, but because of its secular government, there are more women in science and there is less gender discrimination than elsewhere (Cohen, 2000). The number of years of schooling completed is 10.4 for males and 8.5 for females (UN, 2004b). Consequently, far more students are enrolled in university and more in science compared with other Muslim countries. However, a disturbing trend was noted in 1994, in the form of a shift in secondary enrollment for girls from technical and general education schools, where the curriculum focused on preparation for further education or the workplace, to schools focused on religious education that emphasized traditional women's roles

(Turkish Republic State Ministry for Women's Affairs and Social Services Directorate General on the Status and Problem of Women, 1994).

The secular nature of Turkey's government means that women have attended university and studied science and engineering since 1927. In 2002, more females ($n = 6,327$) than males (6,054) graduated from Turkish universities with degrees in mathematics and natural sciences, more females (6,263) than males (4,801) graduated with degrees in health sciences, and more than three times as many males (14,614) than females (4,850) graduated with degrees in the technical sciences such as engineering (Women Information Network in Turkey, 2004).

Seven percent of the female Turkish workforce in 2000 was employed in scientific or technical fields, as compared with 7.5% of the male workforce. However, in absolute numbers, the levels of participation of men and women were far apart. There were 653,035 women or slightly more than half the number of men ($n = 1,248,704$) employed in scientific or technical fields in 2000 (Women Information Network in Turkey, 2004).

Europe

TIMSS data for European countries indicate that gender differences in favor of males appear at the fourth grade and continue through to the final year of secondary school, with the gender gap widening at each level (IEA, 2000). Differences appear in the earth and physical sciences at fourth grade, and the Netherlands has the largest gender gap overall at this grade. Gender differences in earth science continue, and physics and chemistry are added at eighth grade. At the final year of secondary school, gender differences favoring males in science literacy emerge. Males also had significantly higher scores in physics in all countries except Latvia.

By the eighth grade, students' attitudes toward science and mathematics begin to show gender differences. More males than females believe it is important to do well in science and mathematics to get their desired job. These differences may account, in part, for the low participation rates of women in higher levels of science in Europe.

The European Union (EU) has been concerned about the low participation of women in science but does not collect gender-related data and cannot describe the extent of the problem. According to Rees (2001), what is known is that "irrespective of discipline, the proportion of female undergraduates in the discipline, and country, women leave scientific careers in disproportionate numbers at every stage, but particularly after the post-doctoral level" (p. 260). We also know that less than 10% of full professors in science in European countries are women (e.g., 6% of Germany's full professors are women) as compared with 15% in the United States. Furthermore, statistics for women scientists in industry are completely lacking (Williams, 1998). Underrepresentation is less severe in Southern European countries and Finland than in the rest of the EU (Dewandre, 2002). For example, in Portugal, women make up 48% of the researchers at all professorial ranks in the natural sciences and 29% in engineering and technology in institutions of higher education. In contrast, the Netherlands has only 8% women researchers at all professorial ranks in the natural sciences and 6% in engineering and technology in institutions of higher education (Holden, 2002).

However, the higher rates of participation in some parts of the EU do not mean that women in these countries are immune to gender discrimination. In Italy, only 13% of women as compared with 26% of men reach the most senior positions. Nor is the number of female science majors in university reflected in the number of female professors. For example, in the United Kingdom women have comprised 50% of biology majors for the past 30 years, yet women are only 9% of the full professors in biology (Dewandre, 2002). This problem will likely continue, because the rate of increase in the number of women full professors in science in EU countries is approximately .05% to 1.0% per year (Bulmahn, 1999).

Some of the barriers that EU women in science face are reflected by the consistently smaller grant awards they receive compared with men (e.g., in Denmark), demands for 2.6 times higher publication rates than for men, fewer postdoctoral fellowships (e.g., in Sweden), and the use of gender as a criterion for grant awards (e.g., in Netherlands) (Dewandre, 2002; Williams, 1998).

Asia

According to the Korean National Statistics Office (2004), 41% ($n = 250,917$) of females 15 and older were studying natural sciences compared with 13% studying engineering ($n = 247,064$). These numbers mirror the participation of women in science versus engineering in most countries. Employment numbers indicate that scientifically and technically trained women are participating in the workforce at similar rates in Korea compared with Western countries. TIMSS data for Korea indicated gender differences at the fourth grade in earth and physical science favoring males, and differences favoring males in earth science, physics, and environmental issues and the nature of science at the eighth grade. Data for the final year of secondary education were not reported (IEA, 2000).

TIMMS data for Hong Kong indicated that gender differences favoring males appeared in the physical sciences at the fourth grade (earth science, physical science) and eighth grade (earth science, physics, chemistry). Japanese data followed the same pattern. Singapore had no gender differences in any area of science at either the fourth or eighth grade. No data were available for the last year of secondary school for Hong Kong, Japan, or Singapore (IEA, 2000).

The number of women in science in Japan is quite low, reflecting traditional values and a secondary education system that reinforces women's participation in home economics while boys study technology (Kuwahara, 2001). At the tertiary level, women typically enroll in humanities or education and study topics that interest them (Ogawa, 2001). Attitudes toward science are generally positive for both males and females at the primary level, but decline in junior high school and throughout high school. Physical science, physics, and chemistry are disliked even by Japanese women studying science at university, and even more strongly disliked by men studying non-science subjects. Biology is viewed as a female subject and is only liked and taken in high school by women planning a science major at university or by males planning a non-science major at university (Scantlebury, Baker, Sugi, Yoshida, & Uysal, 2003).

Gender issues are something that Japanese culture is just beginning to address. A survey conducted in 2002 by the Japan Society of Applied Physics found that women scientists reported a glass ceiling, slower advancement than their male counterparts, and difficulties reentering the scientific workforce after having children (Normile, 2001). Another survey of university science and non-science majors (Scantlebury et al., 2003) found that women in both science and non-science majors were well aware of gender issues, but that males, especially in non-science majors, avoided answering questions concerning gender issues by responding that they did not understand the question. Initiating such surveys was a big step forward in Japan, which has little baseline data about gender issues.

In China, participation rates in physics during the 1970s were among the world's highest, with one in three women students in top Chinese universities studying physics. The number of women has dropped below participation rates in the West to less than one in ten. The high levels of the 1970s are explained by women asserting their equality and inflated numbers. The downturn in the number of women in physics has been attributed to the same gender barriers as found elsewhere, stereotypes encountered by women in physics, and current media messages that emphasize marrying a good husband and raising children (Jianxiang, 2002).

Nearly 30 years ago, the United Nations officially called for women's equal rights and access to education as a "fundamental right" (UNESCO, 2004). UNESCO's policies state that female education is a key strategy to eliminating poverty and improving development. Although females' access to science education has improved, regardless of culture or country, masculine hegemony promoting stereotypical gender roles remains a strong barrier to female's participation in science. Females in many countries are expected to place family and child-rearing responsibilities (private sphere) ahead of education or working outside the home (public sphere). Although government policies have removed the structures that promoted different science education for females and males, few countries have implemented policies to address the imbalance in domestic and family responsibilities between females and males. In the following section, we use a U.S. example of women in academic science to illustrate the dilemma women face in moving between private and public spheres.

MOVING BEYOND SCHOOL: WOMEN IN COLLEGE SCIENCE MAJORS AND CAREERS

The number of women moving into science majors and careers has increased steadily during the past few decades. In the United States, women account for 27% of doctoral degrees in the physical sciences, 31% in the geosciences, and nearly 50% in the life sciences (National Science Foundation [NSF], 2002), and they are reaching parity in several undergraduate and master's degree programs. However, women of color are especially underrepresented in academe. For example, the largest group, African American women, represent only 2% of full-time science faculty (Gregory, 2002).

There is a dearth of women faculty in the sciences at colleges and universities, and women are underrepresented at the senior ranks (NSF, 2003). Promotion and tenure rates for women science faculty are lower, compared with their male peers (Rosser & Lane, 2002). Researchers have begun to explore the reasons for the failure of universities to attract, promote, and retain women scientists and have identified a number of barriers (NSF, 2003; Rosser, 2004; Scantlebury, Fassinger, & Richmond, 2004). Although major barriers, such as access to science education, have been removed, micro-inequities between women and men scientists build to a cumulative disadvantage throughout an academic career (Valian, 1998). For example, after interviewing 50 female tenured professors in the chemical sciences, Scantlebury et al. found a pattern of "sabbatical babies." Women planned their pregnancies to coincide with a post-tenure sabbatical leave. This strategy meant that women could avoid requesting maternity leave and dealing with unsupportive administrators. The micro-inequity occurs because male scientists are more likely to use their post-tenure sabbatical to focus on their research (duties in the public sphere), rather than child-rearing responsibilities (private sphere). Although not unique to scientists, the balance of career and family is difficult for women in academe (Rosser, 2004; Scantlebury et al., 2004; Valian, 1998). For example, the structure of academe is counter to women's biological clocks, and although many institutions stop the tenure clock during maternity leave, there is an expectation that faculty will maintain their research programs at a productivity level similar to that of their peers.

Overwhelmingly, the climate for women in research science remains hostile, isolating, and un-collegial. Recent studies suggest that female graduate students and post-doctoral research associates are choosing not to enter academics because of the treatment they received and observed during their graduate school experiences (Rosser, 2004). However, several structural mechanisms are in place to counteract the negative academic environment for women. Recently, the NSF established ADVANCE (NSF, 2004) awards for institutional transformation to change the climate for faculty. Institutions receiving grants through the program have identified and are beginning to remove the institutional barriers that exist for the recruitment, retention, and promotion of women in STEM fields. For example, the Georgia Institute of Technology (2004) established a mentoring program, developed tenure and promotion training workshops that address issues of bias, and instituted more family-friendly policies that recognize that the tenure clock often is in competition with a woman's biological clock. In the United States, funding agencies are recognizing that structures exist that limit women's advancement and participation in science. ADVANCE (NSF, 2004) encourages academic institutions to identify where the difference lies and supports their efforts to change those structures that support research science and recognize the demands that the private sphere places on public lives for women and men.

SOCIOCULTURAL ASPECTS

A decade ago, Kahle and Meece's (1994) handbook chapter on gender issues in science education focused on the impact of sociocultural aspects such as home, family and teachers and teaching, the implementation of intervention programs to promote girls' participation and retention in science, and learners' individual characteristics, such as attitudes and cognitive abilities. They also proposed a need for a theoretical model that would address multiple variables and not use a deficit view of gender.

Several major changes in the sociocultural context for science education have occurred since the previous handbook chapter. First, in Western cultures, there has been a shift from allowing teachers independence with respect to how and what they teach, to a climate where teachers and students are held accountable for what is taught and learned. Second, in response to policymakers' stance on student and teacher accountability, content standards in science have been written in many countries, and countries such as the United States have introduced high-stakes tests at the state level.[2] In this section, we discuss gender issues related to student attitudes, sociocultural classroom environment, assessment and testing practices, and teacher education, with reference to research studies. Because of page limitations, we draw mainly on studies conducted in the United States.

Attitudes Toward Science

Since Kahle and Meece's (1994) chapter, two studies reviewed students' science attitudes. Weinburgh (1995) conducted a meta-analysis, and Osborne, Simon, and Collins (2003) published a literature review. Both studies reported that gender is still the major factor differentiating students' attitudes toward science and that females' participation in science has similar patterns in most Western countries. For example, girls in Britain chose not to enter undergraduate programs in the physical and computer sciences and engineering (Osborne et al.).

Recent research found that gifted girls attribute their academic success and/or failure in science to effort and strategy (Li & Adamson, 1995). These research results are consistent with an ongoing pattern identified by gender researchers in the 1980s (Kahle, 1985). Recently Jones, Howe, and Rua (2000) reported that the U.S. intervention programs of the 1980s and 1990s had little impact on the recruitment and retention of girls and women into science. This may be due to the deficit model approach that many of these programs used—that is, a "fix the girls" approach—rather than projects challenging science structures. However, we cannot ignore the social structures that affect students' science identity.

Barton (1997, 1998, 2001) has challenged science educators to rethink the concept of gender so that the field is more inclusive of all students. Brickhouse (1994) challenged the field to rethink the curriculum in order to "bring in the outsiders" and their perspectives. Gilbert (2001) called for a redefinition of the terms *science* and *gender* so that students who typically have not viewed science as part of their identity would choose to do so. Two U.S. studies that addressed science identity were contradictory. In their study of four African American middle-school girls, Brickhouse, Lowery, and Schultz (2000) found that the girls, whose teachers encouraged them to develop their science identities, also aligned themselves with the feminine stereotype of quiet, studious schoolgirl. However, Scantlebury (2005) found that teachers who had encouraged girls who challenged the feminine stereotype and engaged those girls in science, alienated quiet girls.

Sociocultural Classroom Environment

Several studies suggest that changing teachers' practice will improve students' attitudes, especially the attitudes of girls, toward science (Parker & Rennie, 2002; Weinburgh, 1995). Kahle, Meece, and Scantlebury (2000) found that middle science teach-

---

2. Prior to this time the only state that with a state-wide high stakes testing program was New York, with the Regents' exam.

ers using standards-based teaching practices positively influenced urban, African American students' science achievement and attitudes, especially those of boys. Current reforms in science education place an emphasis on standards-based teaching that provides students with opportunities to learn, which in turn should improve students' achievement. The concept of opportunity to learn (OTL) incorporates instructional strategies, curriculum materials, and the psychosocial environment to promote student achievement and attitudes (Stevens, 1993). Yet, ongoing studies of the classroom suggest that girls still have limited opportunities to learn science compared with boys.

Harwell's (2000) study of middle-school girls researched five areas: (a) girls as learners, (b) perception of the nature of science, (c) perceptions of classroom environments conducive to learning science, (d) perceptions of teachers' actions to enhance science learning, and (e) girls' suggestions for improving science learning. Sixty-four percent of the girls in the study reported that they would prefer to learn science in an active way, that is, doing science, experimentation, hands-on experiences, observations, or a combination of these approaches. However, the girls' reported preferences were in stark contrast to their classroom experiences. The results of this study reflect strong and enduring cultural patterns—nearly 80% of the girls reported that they were passive learners. Only 47% of the girls reported that their teachers used some "new" teaching approaches such as demonstrations, hands-on activities, or fieldwork.

Other studies found similar patterns. Jovanovic and King (1998) examined gender differences in performance-based assessment science classrooms; they found that boys appropriated equipment and dominated the use of resources. Girls often had passive roles, such as reading instructions and writing down results. Freedman's (2002) study showed the positive impact that laboratory experiences had on ninth-grade students' attitudes and achievement in physical science. Jones et al. (2000) focused on elementary student dyads using tools to develop their science understanding. Girls' and boys' engagement with the equipment reflected patterns first identified by Kelly (1985). Girls carefully followed teachers' directions and the "rules," whereas boys dominated resources, tinkered with the equipment, and were competitive. Girls developed social relationships while working in their dyads. Jones et al. offered the same suggestion that Kahle (1985), Kelly (1981), and others made 20 years ago—that teachers create an environment where girls have permission to tinker, take apart the equipment, and "color outside the lines" (p. 781).

During the past decade, gender research in science education has sought to tell the stories of people from groups underrepresented in science (e.g., people of color, rural, urban, economically disadvantaged). Using feminist methodologies and theoretical frames, researchers have diversified the knowledge base. For example, in K–12 settings, Parrott, Spatig, Kusimo Carter, and Keyes (2000) reported on an intervention project that targeted the intersection of poverty, race, and place of nonprivileged, middle-school Appalachian girls. They selected eight girls for in-depth study and found that the science teaching they received was often not standards-based. Teachers felt driven to a didactic approach because of the changes in educational policy that held them and their students accountable to a defined set of learning goals, which were usually established through high-stakes tests.

In urban school settings, African American girls tend to outperform their male peers on measures of science achievement (Coley, 2001; Pollard, 1993). The differences in science achievement of these students may be attributed to a number of school contextual factors that limit learning opportunities for all African American students, but especially for male students (Davis & Jordon, 1994; Selier, 2001). African American males, when compared with their female peers, have a disproportionate number of school suspensions, expulsions, and absences. In one study, home environment and peer support had a positive effect on African American girls, suggesting that high-achieving African American girls are more likely to seek support from their peers, but high-achieving African American males do not (Kahle et al., 2000). Scantlebury (2005) noted girls' roles as *othermothers* (surrogate mothers) prevented urban, African American girls from regularly attending school. In Brickhouse and Potter's (2001) study of two African American girls enrolled in a computer science program at a vocational high school, the picture was more complicated because of the interplay of gender with race and socioeconomic status.

Although some reforms have had positive outcomes, such as pushing teachers in urban schools to expect more from their students, the move toward accountability potentially has negative outcomes, because teachers teach to high-stakes tests (Henig, Hula, Orr, & Pedescleaux, 1999; Olsen, 2001). When "teaching to the test" means drilling students on repetitive examples, we run the risk of further alienating students from learning science, and the gains seen in girls' involvement with school science may be lost.

High-Stakes Test-Taking Patterns

Penner (2003) examined the gender by item difficulty for high-school students on TIMMS results from 10 countries (United States, Canada, Australia, New Zealand, Lithuania, Czech Republic, Sweden, Austria, South Africa, and Cyprus.) The effect size difference for science literacy ranged from .30 to .51 in favor of boys. A pattern emerged indicating that girls had more difficulty with harder items than boys. Although this difference is clear, the source of the difference is not. Understanding the source of differences on high-stakes testing is a major challenge in gender research and has implications for determining the success of reforms.

In the past decade, standards-based reform efforts in science education in the United States have produced national standards, a plethora of state-wide high-stakes tests, and demands by politicians, parents, and other community members for student and teacher accountability, especially related to student outcomes (National Research Council, 1996). As educational systems begin to adopt standards-based reforms and request the funds needed to implement changes, policymakers and politicians call upon educators to provide evidence and reform efforts are directly attributable for improvements in students' achievement.

Student outcome data, such as achievement scores on a state test, have become high-stakes. That is, many states require students to attain minimally passing levels on state tests for high-school graduation. Boone's (1998) research highlights a gender issue researchers should take into account when considering the impact of high-stakes testing. Boone conducted an analysis of test-taking patterns as a function of race and gender with the use of a 28-item multiple-choice science test for middle-school students. A significantly larger number of females, compared with males, and African Americans compared with white Americans, did not answer a number of items at the end of the test. As a consequence, the researchers shortened the test, removing overlapping items that tested similar content because the purpose was to document students' science achievement, not their test-taking skills.

In contrast, Lawrenz, Huffman, and Welch's (2001) study of 3,550 U.S. ninth-graders reported no gender-differentiated patterns across question types of multiple choice, open-ended format, hands-on, and full investigation. The study did not report gender by race results. And at the college level, Weaver and Raptis's (2001) study of the responses of female and male undergraduate students on multiple-choice and open-ended questions on exams associated with introductory atmospheric and oceanic sciences found no gender differences.

Often data from the high-stakes tests are disaggregated by gender or by race, but never by both gender and race/ethnicity. For example, the Council of Chief State School Officers (2004) report, *State Indicators of Science and Mathematics Education 2003*, provided data on gender or race/ethnicity distribution for students taking science and math courses, but did not disaggregate the data by gender and race. This omission makes it difficult to measure our success in supporting science achievement for all groups of students.

Single-Sex versus Mixed-Sex Science Classes

Since the late 1970s, researchers have identified the masculine hegemony of the sociocultural environment experienced in science classrooms as one reason for the lack of women and girls in science courses and careers (Ginorio, 1995; Kelly, 1985; Seymour & Hewitt, 1997). Coeducation assumes that all students receive an equal education, but Rich (1979) noted that this assumption was clearly erroneous. Based upon historical studies of the characteristics of women scientists, Rossiter (1982) found that many of these women had a single-sex schooling experience. Parents, teachers, and researchers have viewed single-sex science classes as one strategy that would provide girls the experiences they needed to succeed in science.

Several reviews of the research have challenged the idea that single-sex environments are good for girls (AAUW, 1998b; Mael, 1998; United States Department of Education, 1993). All of these reviews concluded that single-sex classrooms in the United States do not necessarily translate into higher achievement or reduced stereotyping of women's roles. Much depends upon what goes on inside the classroom. For example, Baker (2002b) found that the curriculum topics and the pedagogy employed by teachers were more important than the fact that Latino/a middle-school boys and girls were in single-sex mathematics and science classrooms. There was no clear evidence that the single-sex classroom resulted in higher achievement, but it did provide girls with a strong sense of empowerment. This finding replicated the work of Wood and Brown (1997), who found that single-sex mathematics classes had no effect on achievement. Nor did Wood and Brown or Forgasz and Leder (1996) find an effect on future course-taking. A reanalysis of data from single-sex Catholic schools (LePore & Warren, 1997; Lewin, 1999) indicated that the higher academic achievement attributed to secondary Catholic schools was the result of pre-enrollment academic differences between students in single-sex and coeducational schools rather than the single-sex environment, curriculum, or instruction.

On the other hand, the evidence is strong that single-sex environments do provide girls with a sense of empowerment, confidence to ask questions in class, an intimidation-free classroom climate, and a positive attitude toward science (Baker, 2002b; Forgasz & Leder, 1996; Parker & Rennie, 1995; Rennie & Parker, 1997; Streitmatter, 1999; Wollman, 1990; Wood & Brown, 1997). Conversely, Shapka and Keating (2003) found greater positive effects on mathematics and science achievement for girls in single-sex Canadian classrooms than on boys or girls in coeducational classrooms. Furthermore, they did not find positive effects for affect. The single-sex environments did not have an effect on students' attitudes toward mathematics, math anxiety, or perceived math competence. Parker and Rennie found positive science achievement effects for girls in single-sex classrooms in Australia.

Lee, Marks, and Byrd (1994) found that gender stereotyping was as likely to occur in single-sex boys' or girls' schools as in coeducational schools. Girls' schools reinforced academic dependence and had the least academically rigorous instruction (Lee et al.). The data for single-sex schools or classrooms in developing countries are contradictory. Mael (1998) concluded that in the United States, single-sex education had more benefits for males than females, primarily because single-sex male schools received more resources than female schools. Lee and Lockheed (1998) came to the opposite conclusion, based on studies in Africa (Beoku-Betts, 1998; Kiluvandunda, 2001), where cultural values, patriarchal religion, and male hegemony have led to a curriculum that reinforces gender stereotypes (Baker, 1998).

The instructional strategies employed may determine the success or failure of single-sex education. Parker and Rennie (2002) found that it was easier for teachers to implement gender-inclusive strategies in single-sex science classrooms than in coeducational classrooms. The single-sex classroom reduced management problems (a finding noted by Kenway et al., 1998) and allowed more time for girls to develop their hands-on inquiry skills. Teachers in all-male classrooms found that they spent more time on management problems than teaching.

Heteronormative Science Education

In the broader educational context, Kosciw (2004) found that institutions of education promote heterosexuality as the norm, which produces a caustic climate for GLBT youth and adults. GLBT youth reported high levels of verbal and physical harassment, which occurred 84% of the time within hearing of school faculty and staff. Students reported that 42% of the time adults failed to intervene. Gay boys were more likely to experience physical violence than lesbian or transgendered youth. However, all students reported missing school because of isolation and ostracism (Kosciw). Opportunities to learn for GLBT students are thus diminished because of hostile school environment and absenteeism.

The issues of GLBT in science are closely related to the preparation of teachers, the curriculum, and scientific knowledge. Letts (2001) discussed science's heteronormative masculinity and proposed introducing a critical science literacy into elementary science teacher education to counteract these dominant discourses. Fifield and Swain (2002) used queer theory to problematize science teacher education and, in particular, biology education's heteronormative stance on issues of identity and knowledge. Using personal stories, they illustrated the need for science teacher educators to reconstruct the concepts of gender and diversity for ourselves and for our students. Snyder and Broadway (2004) queered text of eight high-school biology textbooks to focus on the silence with regard to sexuality that is not heterosexuality. In reviewing high-school biology textbooks, Snyder and Broadway noted that the texts portrayed homosexuals as a high-risk group for contracting acquired immunodeficiency disease (AIDS). There was no discussion of scientists' sexual orientation, and they found that the dominant heteronormative perspective did not allow students to develop knowledge in topics such as genetics, behavior, nature of science, sexuality, or AIDS.

FUTURE RESEARCH DIRECTIONS

Consciousness raising is not any guarantee that a person will not succumb to a hidden curriculum. But still, one is in a better position to resist if one knows what is going on. Resistance to what one does not know is difficult, if not impossible. (Martin, 1994, p. 167)

Gender research in science education initially focused on "where the differences lie," and from that data, educators developed intervention programs to increase girls' skills and influence their attitudes toward science. The field has moved from this deficit model, but fewer researchers are focused on gender issues in science education. There is a possibility that girls and women will become invisible in science education research.

A literature search using the ERIC database to identify journal articles published from 1990 to 2004 with the terms *gender* and *science* generated 817 articles. Adding *race* into the keyword search decreased the number of articles to 61. An examination of these articles indicted that 15 articles were not research in science education but in areas such as library science, economics, or political science. Thus during that 14-year period, less than 6% of the research articles on gender and science included a focus on race.

The failure to consider gender and race or ethnicity is not unique to researchers. In the United States, the No Child Left Behind Act has tied state funding to student performance. Yet, Kahle (2004) reported that this critical piece of legislative policy does not require data disaggregated by gender. Requiring such data will help researchers as well as U.S. state and national legislators to critically examine the impact of this legislation and potentially prevent girls from becoming invisible once more. It will allow us to determine the interactions of gender with race and socioeconomic status to identify what works and for whom. As Baker (2002b) found in her study of single-sex classrooms, what works for Latina girls may not work for Latino boys, and the issues affecting African American girls differ from those affecting their male peers (Kahle et al., 2000; Scantlebury, 2005; Seiler, 2001).

In 1994, Kahle and Meece recommended that research on gender issues in science education also explore the impact and interaction of socioeconomic status, race, and ethnicity. Krockover and Shepardson (1995) repeated that recommendation, characterizing research on gender and sociocultural aspects, ethnicity/race, and identity as "missing links." Baker (2002a) also noted the limited research on gender, race, and socioeconomic status in an increasingly complicated field. Why have calls to examine gender and race gone largely unheeded? Perhaps the answer lies in the challenges to conducting gender research. Research that focuses on the intersection of gender with other variables must avoid oversimplification of complex settings. Ignoring the nuances and dilemmas within the field limits the development of theoretical models and frameworks that can assist researchers (Kenway & Gough, 1998; Rennie, 1998).

In an effort to keep gender in the forefront of science education, the Henry Booth Foundation in New York conducted a seminar, Nurturing the Next Generation—Research on Women in the Sciences and Engineering (Daniels, 2004). Disaggregating data (by race, SES, rural/urban) from gender research in science education remains a critical issue, especially in the determination of how gender, social class, race, and sexuality affect students' science trajectories, career decisions, and participation. Gender researchers also need to develop sophisticated survey instruments and analysis to identify micro-inequities in schooling, students' science trajectories, and career paths. Furthermore, research is needed on fostering institutional transformations to change the climate of academic science departments and understanding the transitions from community college to bachelor's, master's, and doctoral degrees.

Science teacher educators also face challenges in preparing teachers who understand the subtleties and nuances of gender affects on students' science learning and their teaching. Many schools promote cultural reproduction of stereotypical gender roles that are more inflexible and more polarized than those held by the wider society (Ruble & Martin, 1998). Those stereotypical gender roles and behaviors noted by Kahle (1985) and Kelly (1981) are still observed by researchers today. Although the percentage of girls participating in K–12 science and achievement increased in the past three decades, recent studies suggest that their involvement, engagement, and attitudes toward the subject have not (Altermatt, Jovanovic, & Perry, 1998).

Science teacher educators need to engage current and future teachers in an exploration of gender roles and their attitudes toward those roles. The subtle inequities in classrooms are barely noticed by the participants in classroom life (Kahle, 1990; McLaren & Gaskell, 1995; Spender, 1982). The acceptance and consistency of traditional gender roles in schools are often invisible to students and teachers (McLaren & Gaskell, 1995; Spender, 1982). Gender inequity is the "norm" and anything else is "not normal." Most people only consider gender inequities a problem when the inequity challenges the norm (e.g., homosexuality) or is blatant (e.g., sexual harassment).

However, we science teacher educators need to practice what we preach and examine from a gender perspective the issues that exist in our planned and enacted curriculum, pedagogical practices, enrollment patterns of students in teacher education programs, hiring policy, tenure and promotion of faculty, and policy documents that influence our field (Scantlebury, 1994).

For nearly three decades, researchers in science education have examined the hidden curriculum influencing women and girls' participation in science. More recently, we have also begun to address the exclusive impact of science's heteronormative view. Although there has been some progress in increasing the participation of girls and women in science, much remains to be done. Gender differences in participation, achievement, and attitude still exist. The social construction of gender in terms of the legitimacy of women's access to education and the heteronormative view of science in the classroom has not been challenged.

Many people remain at the margins of science, in both the developed and developing world. Science continues to promote a Western, masculine worldview that many girls and women reject. And research still faces the challenge of considering gender, race, and socioeconomic status within accountability systems that want simpler answers than we can provide.

ACKNOWLEDGMENTS

Thanks to Sharon Haggerty and Ann Howe, who reviewed this chapter.

REFERENCES

Altermatt, E., Jovanovic, J., & Perry, M. (1998). Bias or responsivity? Sex and achievement-level effects on teachers' classroom questioning practices. *Journal of Educational Psychology, 90,* 516–527.

American Association of University Women Educational Foundation. (1993). *Hostile hallways: The AAUW survey on sexual harassment in America's schools.* Washington, DC: Author

American Association of University Women Educational Foundation. (1998a). *Gender gaps: Where schools still fail our children.* Washington, DC: Author.

American Association of University Women Educational Foundation. (1998b). *Separated by sex. A critical look at single-sex education for girls.* Washington, DC: Author.

Apple, M. (1992). Educational reform and educational crisis. *Journal of Research in Science Teaching, 29,* 779–790.

Arnot, M., David, M., & Weiner, G. (1999). *Closing the gender gap. Post-war education and social change.* Malden, MA: Blackwell.

Australian Bureau of Statistics. (2004). *Education and training indicators.* Retrieved September 5, 2004, from http://.abs.gov.au/ausstats/abs@.nsf

Baker, D. (1998). Equity issues in science education. In B. Fraser & K. Tobin (Eds.), *International handbook of science education* (pp. 869–895). Dordrecht, the Netherlands: Kluwer Academic.

Baker, D. (2001). Mathematics and science. In M. Forman-Brunell (Ed.), *Girlhood in America: An encyclopedia* (pp. 453–444). Santa Barbara, CA: ABC Clio.

Baker, D. (2002a). Editorial: Where is gender and equity in science education? *Journal of Research in Science Teaching, 39,* 659–663.

Baker, D. (2002b). Good intentions: An experiment in middle school single-sex science and mathematics classrooms with high minority enrollment. *Journal of Women and Minorities in Science and Engineering, 8,* 1–23.

Barton, A. C. (1997). Liberatory science education: Weaving connections between feminist theory and science education. *Curriculum Inquiry, 27,* 141–163.

Barton, A. C. (1998). Reframing "science for all" through the politics of poverty. *Educational Policy, 12,* 525–541.

Barton, A. C. (2001). Science education in urban settings: Seeking new ways of praxis through critical ethnography. *Journal of Research in Science Teaching, 38,* 899–917.

Beaton, A. E., Martin, M. O., Mullis, I., Gonzalez, E. J., Smith, T. A., & Kelly, D. L. (1996). *The science achievement in the middle school years:* IEA'S *third international mathematics and science study (TIMSS).* Chestnut Hill, MA: Boston College.

Beoku-Betts, J. (1998). Gender and formal education in Africa: An exploration of the opportunity structure at the secondary and tertiary levels. In M. Bloch, J. Beku-Betts, & R. Tabachnick (Eds.), *Women and education in sub-Saharan Africa* (pp. 157–184). Boulder, CO: Lynne Reinner.

Blair, G. (1998). Australia. In G. Kelly (Ed.), *International handbook of women's education* (pp. 285–322). New York: Greenwood Press.

Boone, W. (1998). Assumptions, cautions, and solutions in the use of omitted test data to evaluate the achievement of under-represented groups in science-implications for long-term evaluation. *Journal of Women and Minorities in Science and Engineering, 4,* 183–194.

Brickhouse, N. (1994). Bringing in the outsiders: Reshaping the sciences of the future. *Journal of Curriculum Studies, 26,* 401–416.

Brickhouse, N. W., Lowery, P., & Schultz, K. (2000). What kind of a girl does science? The construction of school science identities. *Journal of Research in Science Teaching, 37,* 441–458.

Brickhouse, N., & Potter, J. T. (2001). Young women's scientific identity formation in an urban context. *Journal of Research in Science Teaching, 37,* 965–980.

Bulmahn, E. (1999). Women in science in Germany. *Science, 286,* 2081.

Bustillo, I. (1993). Latin America and the Caribbean. In E. King & M. Hill (Eds.), *Women's education in developing countries* (pp. 175–210). Baltimore: Johns Hopkins University Press.

Clair, R. (1995). *Scientific education of girls.* Paris: UNESCO.

Cohen, P. (2000). Muslim women in science. *Science, 290,* 55–56.

Coley, R. (2001). *Differences in the gender gap: Comparison across the racial/ethnic groups in education and work.* Princeton, NJ: Educational Testing Service.

Conway, J., & Bourque, S. (1993). *The politics of women's education: Perspectives from Asia, Africa and Latin America.* Ann Arbor, MI: University of Michigan Press.

Council of Chief State School Officers. (2004). *State indicators of science and mathematics education, 2003.* Washington, DC: Author.

Daniels, J. D. (2004). *Proceedings of nurturing the next generation—Research on women in the sciences and engineering.* New York: Henry Luce Booth Foundation.

Davis, J., & Jordan, W. (1994). The effects of school context, structure, and experiences on African American males in middle and high school. *Journal of Negro Education, 63,* 570–587.

DeBoer, G. (1991). *A history of ideas in science education.* New York: Teachers College Press.

Dewandre, N. (2002). European strategy for promoting women in science. *Science, 295,* 278–279.

Field, T., & Copley, A. (1969). Cognitive style and science achievement. *Journal of Research in Science Teaching, 6,* 2–10.

Fifield, S., & Swain H. (2002). Heteronormativity and common-sense in science (teacher) education. In R. Kissen (Ed.), *Getting ready for Benjamin: Preparing teachers for sexual diversity in the classroom* (pp. 177–189). Lanham, MD: Rowman & Littlefield.

Forgasz, H., & Leder, G. (1996). Mathematics classrooms, gender and affect. *Mathematics Education Research Journal, 28,* 153–173.

Freedman, M. (2002). The influence of laboratory instruction on science achievement and attitude toward science across gender differences. *Journal of Women and Minorities in Science and Engineering, 8,* 191–200.

Fry, R. (1988). The curriculum and girls' secondary schooling. In S. Middleton (Ed.), *Women and education in Aotearoa* (pp. 31–45). Wellington, New Zealand: Allen & Unwin.

Gallagher, J., & Anderson, C. (1999). Glimpses at our history as the century closes. *Journal of Research in Science Teaching, 10,* 1063–1064.

Gaskell, J. (1998). Australia. In G. Kelly (Ed.), *International handbook of women's education* (pp. 493–514). New York: Greenwood Press.

Georgia Institute of Technology. (2004). *NSF ADVANCE program for institutional transformation.* Retrieved October 7, 2004, from http://www.advance.gatech.edu

Gilbert, J. (2001). Science and its 'other': Looking underneath 'woman' and 'science' for new directions in research on gender and science education. *Gender and Education, 13,* 291–305.

Ginorio, A. (1995). *Warming the climate for women in academic science.* Washington, DC: Association of American Colleges and Universities.

Gregory, S. (2002). Black faculty women in the academy: History, status, and future. *Journal of Negro Education, 70,* 124–138.

Harwell, S. (2000). In their own voices: Middle level girls' perceptions of teaching and learning science. *Journal of Science Teacher Education, 11*, 221–242.

Haslanger, S. (2000). Gender and race: (What) are they? (What) do we want them to be? *Nous, 34*, 31–55.

Hassan, F. (2000). Islamic women in science. *Science, 290*, 55–56.

Henig, J. Hula, R., Orr, M., & Pedescleaux, D. (1999). *The color of school reform: Race, politics, and the challenge of urban education.* Princeton, NJ: Princeton University Press.

Henwood, F., & Miller, K. (2001). Editorial: Boxed in or coming out? On the treatment of science, technology, and gender in educational research. *Gender and Education, 13*, 237–242.

Hertz, B., & Sperling, G. (2004). *What works in girls' education: Evidence and policies from the developing world.* Retrieved September 6, 2004 from http://www.cfr.org/pdf/Girls_Education_full.pdf

Higher Council for Science and Technology. (1997). *Study of national scientific and technological requirements and potential (phase II): Scientific and technological capabilities, 1997.* Aman, Jordan: Author.

Holden, C. (2002). Euro-women in science. *Science, 295*, 41.

International Association for the Evaluation of Educational Achievement. (2000). *Gender differences in achievement.* Chestnut Hill, MA: Boston College.

Jianxiang, Y. (2002). China debates big drop in women physics majors. *Science, 295*, 263.

Jones, M. G., Brader-Araje, L., Carboni, L., Carter, G., Rua, M., Banilower, E., et al. (2000). Tool time: Gender and students' use of tools, control, and authority. *Journal of Research in Science Teaching, 37*, 760–783.

Jones, M. G., Howe, A., & Rua, M (2000). Gender differences in students' experiences, interests, and attitudes toward science and scientists. *Science Education, 84*, 180–192.

Jovanovic, J., & King, S. (1998). Boys and girls in the performance-based science classroom: Who's doing the performing? *American Educational Research Journal, 35*, 477–496.

Kahle, J, B. (Ed.). (1985). *Women in science: A report from the field.* Philadelphia: Falmer Press.

Kahle, J. B. (1990). Real students take chemistry and physics: Gender issues. In K. Tobin, J. B. Kahle, & B. Fraser (Eds.), *Windows into science classrooms: Problems associated with higher-level cognitive learning* (pp. 92–134). Philadelphia: Falmer Press.

Kahle, J, B. (2004). Will girls be left behind? Gender differences and accountability. *Journal of Research in Science Teaching, 41*, 961–969.

Kahle, J. B., & Meece, J. (1994). Research on gender issues in the classroom. In D. Gabel (Ed.), *Handbook of research in science teaching and learning* (pp. 542–576). Washington, DC: National Science Teachers Association.

Kahle, J. B., Meece, J., & Scantlebury, K. (2000). Urban African-American middle school science students: Does standards-based teaching make a difference? *Journal of Research in Science Teaching, 37*, 1019–1041.

Kahle, J. B., Parker, L. H., Rennie, L. J., & Riley, D. (1993). Gender differences in science education: Building a model. *Educational Psychologist, 28*, 379–404.

Kahle, J. B., & Rennie, L. J. (1993). Ameliorating gender differences in attitudes about science: A cross-national study. *Journal of Science Education and Technology, 2*, 321–334.

Kelly, A. (1978). *Girls and science: An international study of sex differences in school science achievement.* Stockholm: Almquist and Wiksell International.

Kelly, A. (1981). *The missing half: Girls and science education.* Manchester, England: Manchester University Press.

Kelly, A. (1985). The construction of masculine science. *British Journal of Sociology of Education, 6*, 133–153.

Kelly, G. (Ed.). (1998). *International handbook of women's education.* New York: Greenwood Press.

Kenway, J., & Gough, A. (1998). Gender and science education in schools: A review with "attitude." *Studies in Science Education, 31*, 1–30.

Kenway, J., Willis, S., Blackmore, J., & Rennie, L. (1998). *Answering back: Girls, boys and feminism in schools.* New York: Routledge.

Kiluva-ndunda, M. (2001). *Women's agency and educational policy: The experiences of the women of Kilome, Kenya.* Albany, NY: State University of New York Press.

Koening, R. (2000). Iranian women hear the call of science. *Science, 290,* 1485.

Korean National Statistics Office. (2004). *Employment, labor, wages.* Retrieved September 6, 2004, from http://www.nso.go.kr

Kosciw, J. G. (2004). *The 2003 national climate survey: The school-related experiences of our nation's lesbian, gay, bisexual and transgendered youth.* New York: GLSEN.

Krockover, G., & Shepardson, D. (1995). The missing links in gender equity research. *Journal of Research in Science Teaching, 32,* 223–224.

Kuwahara, M. (2001). Japanese women in science and technology. *Minerva, 39,* 203–216.

Kuwait Information Office. (2002). *Education.* Retrieved September 6, 2004 from http://www.kuwait-info.org/statistics/education.html

Lawrenz, F., Huffman, D., & Welch, W. (2000). Policy considerations based on a cost analysis of alternative test formats in large scale science assessments. *Journal of Research in Science Teaching, 37,* 615–626.

Lee, V., & Lockheed, M. (1998). Single-sex schooling and its effects on Nigerian adolescents. In M. Bloch, J. Beoku-Betts, & R. Tabachnick (Eds.), *Women and education in sub-Saharan Africa* (pp. 201–226). Boulder, CO: Lynne Reinner.

Lee, V., Marks, H., & Byrd, T. (1994). Sexism in single-sex and coeducational independent secondary classrooms. *Sociology of Education, 67,* 92–120.

LePore, P., & Warren, J. (1997). A comparison of single-sex and coeducational Catholic schooling: Evidence from the national longitudinal study of 1988. *American Educational Research Journal, 3,* 485–511.

Letts, W. J. (2001). When science is strangely alluring: Interrogating the masculinist and heteronormative nature of primary school science. *Gender and Education, 13,* 261–274.

Lewin, T. (1999, April 11). Amid equity concerns, girls' schools thrive. *New York Times,* pp. A1, A23.

Li, A., & Adamson, G. (1995). Motivational patterns related to gifted students' learning of mathematics, science and English: An examination of gender differences. *Journal for the Education of the Gifted, 18,* 284–297.

Mael, F. (1998). Single-sex and coeducational schooling: Relationships to socioemotional and academic development. *Review of Educational Research, 2,* 101–129.

Martin, J. R. (1994). *Changing the educational landscape: Philosophy, women and the curriculum.* New York: Routledge.

Mathews, K. (1988). White pinafores, slates, mud and manuka. In S. Middleton (Ed.), *Women and education in Aotearoa* (pp. 20–30). Wellington, New Zealand: Allen & Unwin.

McLaren, A., & Gaskell, J. (1995). Now you see it, now you don't: Gender as an issue in school science. In J. Gaskell & J. Willinsky (Eds.), *Gender in/forms curriculum: From enrichment to transformation* (pp. 136–156). New York: Teachers College Press.

Mervis, J. (2003). Scientific workforce: Down for the count? *Science, 300,* 1070–1074.

National Research Council. (1996). *National science education standards.* Washington, DC: National Academy Press.

National Science Foundation. (2002). *Science and engineering indicators: 2002.* Washington, DC: Author.

National Science Foundation. (2003). *Gender differences in the careers of academic scientists and engineers: A literature review.* Washington, DC: Author.

National Science Foundation. (2004). *ADVANCE.* Retrieved October 8, 2004, from http://www.nsf.gov/home/crssprgm/advance/start.htm

New Zealand Bureau of Statistics. (2004). *1996 census.* Retrieved September 6, 2004, from http://www.stats.govt.nz

Normile D. (2001). Academic harassment. Women faculty battle Japan's koza system. *Science, 297,* 817–818.

Ogawa, M. (2001). Reform Japanese style: Voyage into an unknown chaotic future. *Science Education, 85,* 586–606.

O'Loughlin, M. (1992). Rethinking science education: Beyond Piagetian constructivism toward a sociocultural model of teaching and learning science. *Journal of Research in Science Teaching, 29,* 791–820.

Olsen, L. (2001). Holding schools accountable for equity. *Leadership, 30*(4), 28–31.

Osborne, J., Simon, S., & Collins, S. (2003). Attitudes towards science: A review of the literature and its implications. *International Journal of Science Education, 25,* 1049–1079.

Parker, L., & Rennie, L. (1995). *For the sake of the girls? Final report of the Western Australian single-sex education project: 1993–1994.* Perth, Australia: Curtin University.

Parker, L., & Rennie, L. (2002). Teachers' implementation of gender-inclusive instructional strategies in single-sex and mixed-sex science classrooms. *International Journal of Science Education, 24,* 881–897.

Parker, L., Rennie, L., & Fraser, B. (1996). *Gender, science and mathematics.* Dordrecht, the Netherlands: Kluwer Academic.

Parrott, L., Spatig, L., Kusimo, P., Carter, C., & Keyes, M. (2000). Troubled waters: where multiple streams of inequality converge in the math and science experiences of nonprivileged girls. *Journal of Women and Minorities in Science and Engineering, 6,* 45–71.

Penner, A. (2003). International gender X item difficulty interactions in mathematics and science achievement tests. *Journal of Educational Psychology, 95,* 650–655.

Pollard, D. S. (1993). Gender, achievement, and African-American students' perception of their school experience. *Educational Psychologist, 28,* 341–356.

Quinn, S. (1995). *Marie Curie: A life.* New York: Simon & Schuster.

Rees, T. (2001). Mainstreaming gender equality in science in the European Union: The ETAN report. *Gender and Education, 13,* 243–260.

Rennie, L. (1998). Gender equity: Toward clarification and a research direction for science teacher education. *Journal of Research in Science Teaching, 35,* 951–961.

Rennie, L., & Parker, L. (1997). Students' and teachers' perceptions of single-sex and mixed sex mathematics classrooms. *Mathematics Educational Research Journal, 9,* 731–751.

Rich, A. C. (1979). *On lies, secrets, and silence: Selected prose, 1966–1978.* London: Norton.

Rosser, S. (2004). *The science glass ceiling: Academic women scientists and the struggle to succeed.* New York: Routledge.

Rosser, S., & Lane, E. (2002). A history of funding for women's programs at the national science foundation: From individual POWRE approaches to the advance of institutional approaches. *Journal of Women and Minorities in Science and Engineering, 8,* 327–346.

Rossiter, M. W. (1982). *Women scientists in America: Struggles and strategies to 1940.* Baltimore: Johns Hopkins University Press.

Ruble, D., & Martin, C. L. (1998). Gender development. In W. Damon (Editor-in-Chief) & N. Eisenberg (Vol. Ed.), *Social, emotional, and personality* (Vol. 3, pp. 933–1016). New York: John Wiley & Sons.

Rury, J. (1991). *Education and women's work.* Albany, NY: State University of New York Press.

Sadker, M., & Sadker, D. (1994). *Failing at fairness: How America's schools cheat girls.* New York: C. Scribner's Sons.

Scantlebury, K. (1994). Emphasizing gender issues in the undergraduate preparation of science teachers: Practicing what we preach. *Journal of Women and Minorities in Science and Engineering, 1,* 153–164.

Scantlebury, K. (2005). Meeting the needs and adapting to the capital of a Queen Mother and an Ol' Head: Gender equity in urban high school science. In K. Tobin, R. Elmesky, & G. Seiler (Eds.), *Improving urban science education: New roles for teachers, students, and researchers* (pp. 201–212). New York: Rowman & Littlefield.

Scantlebury, K., Baker, D., Sugi, A., Yoshida, A., & Uysal, S. (2003, March). *The cultural context of gender research in Japanese science education: Why university students "don't understand the question."* Paper presented at the annual meeting of the National Association of Research in Science Teaching, Philadelphia.

Scantlebury, K., Fassinger, R., & Richmond, G. (2004, April). *There is no crying in chemistry: The lives of female academic chemists.* Paper presented at National Association of Research in Science Teaching, Vancouver, BC, Canada.

Seiler, G. (2001). Reversing the standard direction: Science emerging from the lives of African American students. *Journal of Research in Science Teaching, 38,* 1000–1014.

Seymour, E., & Hewitt, N. (1997). *Talking about leaving: Why undergraduates leave the sciences.* Boulder, CO: Westview Press.

Shapka, J., & Keating, D. (2003). Effects of girls-only curriculum during adolescence: Performance, persistence, and engagement in mathematics and science. *American Educational Research Journal, 40,* 929–960.

Sime, R. L. (1997). *Lise Meitner: A life in physics.* Berkeley, CA: University of California Press.

Snyder, V. L., & Broadway, F. S. (2004). Queering high school biology textbooks. *Journal of Research in Science Teaching, 41,* 617–636.

Spender, D. (1982). *Invisible women: The schooling scandal.* London: Writers and Readers Publishing Cooperative Society.

Statistics Canada. (2004). *University qualifications granted by field of study, by sex.* Retrieved September 16, 2004, from http://www.statcan.ca/english/Pgdb/educ21.htm

Stevens, F. I. (1993). *Opportunity to learn: Issues of equity for poor and minority students.* Report no. NCES 93-232. Washington, DC: U.S. Department of Education, National Center for Education Statistics.

Streitmatter, J. (1999). *For girls only: Making a case for single-sex schooling.* Albany, NY: Albany State Press.

Theobald, M. (1996). *Knowing women: Origins of women's education in nineteenth century Australia.* Cambridge, England: Cambridge University Press.

Third World Academy of Science. (2002). *Programme statistics 2002.* Retrieved May 17, 2004, from http://www.ictp.trieste.it/~twas/pdf/statdig–2002.pdf

Tolley, K. (2003). *The science education of American girls: A historical perspective.* New York: Routledge Falmer.

Turkish Republic State Ministry for Women's Affairs and Social Services Directorate General on the Status and Problem of Women. (1994). *The status of women in Turkey.* Retrieved May 12, 2004, from http://www.die.giv.tr/CIN/women/status-women.htm

United Nations. (2004a). *Indicators on illiteracy.* Retrieved May 17, 2004, from http://unstats.un.org/unsd/demographic/social/illiteracy.htm

United Nations. (2004b). *Indicators on education.* Retrieved May 17, 2004, from http://unstats.un.org/unsd/demographic/social/education.htm

United Nations Children's Fund. (2003). *State of the world's children 2004.* New York: Author.

United Nations Development Fund for Women. (1995). *Missing links: Gender equity in science and technology development.* New York: Author.

United Nations Development Fund for Women. (2004). *Millennium declaration and millennium development goal.* Retrieved May 20, 2004, from http://www.unifem.org/index.php?_page_pid=10

United Nations Educational, Scientific and Cultural Organization. (2003). *Education for all global monitoring report 2003/2004.* Paris. Author.

United Nations Educational, Scientific and Cultural Organization. (2004). *UNESCO selected projects on women and gender, 1990–2002.* Retrieved May 20, 2004, from http://portal.unesco.org/shs/en/ev.php-URL_ID=4211&URL_DO=DO_TOPIC&URL_SECTION=201.html#edu

United States Department of Education. (1993). *Single-sex schooling: Perspectives from practice to research.* Washington, DC: Author.

Valian, V. (1998). *Why so slow? The advancement of women.* Cambridge, MA: MIT Press.

Watson, H. (1988). The impact of the second wave of the women's movement on policies and practices in schools. In S. Middleton (Ed.), *Women and education in Aotearoa* (pp. 97–113). Wellington, New Zealand: Allen & Unwin.

Weaver, A., & Raptis, H. (2001). Gender differences in introductory atmospheric and oceanic science exams: Multiple choice versus constructed response questions. *Journal of Science Education and Technology, 10*, 115–26.

Weinburgh, M. (1995). Gender differences in student attitudes toward science: A meta-analysis of the literature from 1970 to 1991. *Journal of Research in Science Teaching, 32*, 387–398.

Wellesley Center for Research on Women. (1992). *How schools shortchange girls: A study of major findings on girls and education.* Washington, DC: American Association of University Women.

Williams, N. (1998). EU moves to decrease the gender gap. *Science, 280*, 822.

Wollman, J. (1990). The advantage of same sex programs. *Gifted Child Today, 13*, 220–24.

Women Information Network in Turkey. (2004). *Literacy and education.* Retrieved March 26, 2004, from http://www.die.gov.tr/istatistikler.html

Wood, B., & Brown, B. (1997). Participating in an all female algebra class: Effects on high school mathematics and science course selection. *Journal of Women and Minorities in Science and Engineering, 3*, 265–278.

Woolf, V. (1938). *Three guineas.* New York: Harcourt Brace & Company.

World Bank. (2002). *Education and HIV/Aids: A window of Hope.* Washington, DC: Author.

Yates, L. (1998). *Australia.* In G. Kelly (Ed.), *International handbook of women's education* (pp. 213–242). New York: Greenwood Press.

CHAPTER 11

Special Needs and Talents in Science Learning

J. Randy McGinnis
University of Maryland, College Park

Gregory P. Stefanich
University of Northern Iowa

Every learner in science is unique, with diverse abilities. Teachers as well as educational researchers have long recognized and used that understanding to varying degrees in their teaching and research. Learners in science who differ substantially in their performances from typical learner performances (physical, cognitive, or behavioral dimensions) and who need additional services and supports are the focus of this chapter. Those learners who exceed typical performances are described as possessing special talents; those learners who do not achieve at the typical level are identified as having special needs. Both of these groups of learners require additional educational, social, or medical services to support them in learning and performing science. Professionals in the field of special education use the comprehensive term "exceptional learners" to refer to learners with learning and/or behavioral problems, learners with physical or sensory impairments, and learners who are intellectually gifted or have a special talent (Hardman, Drew, & Egan, 2002; Heward, 2000). We continue use of that nomenclature to refer collectively to learners in science with special needs and talents.

Science education researchers, interested in developing a knowledge base that would guide policymakers and teachers in achieving their goal of "science for all" (Fensham, 1985), have been attracted to studying these two groups of learners. The purpose of this chapter is to outline what is known about how exceptional learners learn science, including consideration of how the totality of science education (context, personnel, curriculum, and assessment) supports or hinders this process, and to use that understanding to make recommendations for future research directions. Included is a discussion of how certain schools of thought on learning influence the research in this area. Structurally, this chapter reviews in two parts the literature on science learning by exceptional learners. Part I focuses on the science learning population with special needs. Part II focuses on the science learning population with special talents.

THEORETICAL PERSPECTIVES GUIDING RESEARCH ON EXCEPTIONAL LEARNERS

There is no one accepted theoretical model of learning that provides a grand explanation for why learners engage science in differing ways and at varying levels of achievement. Three prevailing schools of thought on learning that have guided research on exceptional learners in science are the behavioral, developmental, and cognitive perspectives (Stefanich & Hadzegeorgiou, 2001). Although the behaviorist perspective historically has dominated research by special educators in this area, a growing number of researchers dissatisfied with that perspective, including those in science education, have been drawn to more contemporary applications of cognitive science that include an appreciation of social context (Rogoff, 1990). In addition, a fourth school of thought, a sociocultural perspective, also has its proponents.

Behavioral psychologists believe that learning consists of making connections between events (stimuli) and behaviors (responses). External forces, such as rewards and punishments, and drives, such as hunger, provide the learner motivation to make stronger connections between stimuli and behaviors, that is, to learn. Although the primary form of data valued in this theoretical perspective is observable behavior, theorists applying behaviorism to educational research have expanded on the theory to include hypotheses on mental states, including thinking, understanding, and reasoning (Bransford, Brown, Cocking, Donovan, & Pellegrino, 2000). Behaviorists assert that instruction should be based on the identification of clear outcomes and be directed toward those outcomes. Developmental psychologists believe that the thinking of children is distinctly different from that of adults. They assert that as individuals progress through life, their thinking patterns change dramatically over short periods of time and then remain somewhat stable for an extended period. A key assumption is that rates of learning vary per individual. Developmental psychologists examine the external factors (such as science instruction) that might influence an individual's rate of intellectual maturity. A cognitive science perspective examines mental functioning, in the individual and the social contexts, frequently by using technology to collect biological data on the brain. It uses a multidisciplinary approach that incorporates developmental psychology, computer science, and neuroscience, as well as other fields of study. The testing of theories of teaching and learning characterizes studies in this perspective. The sociocultural perspective is distinguished by its attention to the interaction between learners' mental functioning and their cultural, historical, and institutional settings (Wertsch & Kanner, 1992). A key assumption is that learners' mental development the result of a complex interaction among multiple factors and is not determined solely by their biological structures.

Recently, some researchers, influenced by emerging findings from brain research, have proposed that there are disrupted brain functions in some learners that can be identified and hypothetically "rewired," producing additional compensatory activation in other brain regions (Shaywitz, 2003; Shaywitz et al., 2002; Simos et al.,

2002; Temple et al., 2003). However, other researchers have challenged these tenets. Donald (2001) rejected the explanation that certain brain regions perform specialized operations. Instead, he stated that the mechanisms and connectivity for language are set by experience with countless interconnection points, or synapses, which connect neurons in various patterns. He concluded that learning and experience create and shape the brain's circuits, and, therefore, these circuits are not predetermined. Lieberman (1998) proposed that human language is a system of neuro-anatomical connections that are distributed throughout the brain. Coles (2004) argued that brain researchers have misconstrued data and have drawn conclusions to justify unwarranted beliefs. Coles stated, "Dyslexia remains no more of a proven malady among a substantial percentage of beginning readers than when Glasow ophthalmologist James Hinshelwood first discussed it as 'congenital word-blindness' at the end of the 19th century" (p. 351).

Awareness of these four schools of thought may assist researchers in making sense of the reported studies on exceptional learners in science. Although it is the nature of this scholarship area to be advocacy oriented, individual articles may include reported data (either in empirical studies or summary articles) that can be inferred to reflect one of these theoretical perspectives. For example, many researchers holding a cognitive or sociocultural perspective discuss inquiry as an important and effective/efficient feature of learning in science, whereas those taking a behaviorist perspective place an emphasis on the mastery of skills and information. Likewise, the literature on inclusion can be viewed as being founded primarily on a learning perspective that places highest value on social context and developmentalism.

PART I: SPECIAL NEEDS IN SCIENCE LEARNING

Definitions

If education is devoted to offering opportunities for all students to gain sufficient schooling to help them make life choices and become productive members of society, it is essential that all teachers have the knowledge to make appropriate adaptations so that every student with special needs or disabilities can become an active participant in the learning process. This basic statement brings to the forefront the complex nature of the issues of teaching science to students with special needs or disabilities. Because of that complexity, there has been much effort devoted recently to educating science teachers worldwide to learn how to make needed accommodations and adaptations and, therefore, to differentiate effectively the science curriculum for students with special needs (Smith & Sherburne, 2001).

To understand the scope of the problem, data from the U.S. school population provides one example: the United States Department of Education (2002) *Digest of Educational Statistics* indicated that in 2000–2001, 12.7% of the U.S. school population (6- to 21-year age group) was identified as eligible for special education services, up from 12.4% in 1995–96. The numbers, percentage of the total population and percentage of the population of students with special needs, are reported in Table 11.1.

Students with special needs are typically divided into two large categories that can overlap, those with physical impairments and those with cognitive, social-personal,

TABLE 11.1
Students with Special Needs (Ages 6–21) in the US, 2000–2001

Population	Number	Percentage of total	Percentage of special needs population
Ages 6 to 21	45,264,278	100.0	
Individuals with disabilities	5,775,722	12.8	100.0
Learning disabilities			
Specific learning disability	2,887,217	6.3	50.0
Speech-language impairments	1,093,808	2.4	18.9
Mental retardation	612,978	1.4	10.6
Emotional disturbance	473,663	1.0	8.3
Hearing impairments	70,767	0.15	1.2
Orthopedic impairments	73,057	0.16	1.3
Other health impairments	291,850	0.64	5.1
Visual impairments	25,975	0.05	0.4
Multiple disabilities	122,559	0.27	2.1
Traumatic brain injury	14,844	0.03	0.2
Developmental delay	28,935	0.06	0.5

From US Department of Education (2002).

or intellectual disabilities. The first category consists of individuals with physical impairments, many of whom are considered to have the cognitive, social, and intellectual capabilities to potentially become career scientists, mathematicians, or engineers. Approximately 24% (1,386,173) of U.S. students with disabilities would fall into this group. Approximately 19% (1,093,808) of these students have speech and language impairments that require minimal accommodation in a science classroom or laboratory. This group is still significantly underrepresented in the disciplines of science. Historically, members of this group who succeeded in science were persons of special talents and exceptional persistence.

The second category of students, 76% of the total U.S. school-age population with disabilities, consisting of 4,389,549 students with cognitive or social-personal disabilities, often experience difficulty with science in secondary and post-secondary education. Some do have potential for the highest levels of science achievement, but they need assistance to have a career in science. For the others, a reasonable goal is general science literacy as opposed to a professional career in a science field.

Exceptional Students and Issues of Race

The *National Research Council Report on Minority Students in Special Education and Gifted Education* (Donovan & Cross, 2003) indicated that minority students are over-represented in U.S. special education programs. In the report, Donovan and Cross described the percentage of minority students in special education categories as compared with the majority population. The percentages of minority students identified with a learning disability (the largest classification of all disabilities) were reported as follows: Native American and Alaska Native students 7.45%, Black students 6.49%, and Hispanic students 6.44%. In comparison, the percentage was 6.02% for White students. Percentages for developmental disabilities were 2.64% for Black students and 1.28% for Native American and Alaska Native students. Emotional disability ratios were 1.45% for Black students and 1.03% for Native American and Alaska Native students. States vary widely in how they determine students with disabilities. For example, at the extreme, the ratio for Black students being identified as developmentally delayed was 10 times higher in Alabama than in New Jersey.

The figures themselves explain nothing and hold the danger of reinforcing the notion that some groups are superior to others. A number of potential factors that can be generated to explain the performance of certain groups include poverty, family dysfunction, transience, and devaluing of academic achievement. These factors can be treated relative to the individuals involved rather than being ethnicity- or race-based. More importantly, these are mutable circumstances; appropriate interventions can serve to lessen their damaging effects.

The educational research community at times questions the labeling of students as holding special needs in science (or otherwise) by school personnel. In challenge to the research on special needs, Gray and Denicolo (1998) contested research that purported to be objective within an empirical-analytic paradigm. Instead, they advocated an alternative paradigm that attempts to challenge the normalization approach to teaching learners designated as having special needs. In science education, in a study that examined the science participation in an environmental education activity by two students who were labeled by their school as learning disabled, Roth (2002) supported Mehan's (1993) argument that the placement of learners into a special needs category resulted from how they were assessed in specific learning situations, and did not convey valid information as to their attributes across situations.

Science for All

Within the field of science education, contemporary key science education reform documents have supported science education's goal of science literacy for all, regardless of any categorization of learners' abilities (McGinnis, 2000). The primary purpose of such documents is to provide a vision of the teaching and learning of science and to provide criteria for measuring progress toward that vision. In the U.S. *National Science Education Standards* (National Research Council [NRC], 1996), students with special needs are viewed explicitly as participating (as fits their ability and interest) in inquiry-based science classrooms.

The key principle guiding the development of the U.S. *Standards* (NRC, 1996) is "Science is for all students" (p. 19). This is defined as a principle of "equity and excellence" (or "fairness") (p. 20) that strongly advocates science in schools for students with special needs. In addition, all students are to be included in "challenging science learning opportunities" (p. 20). This equity principle is reflected in Teaching Standard B: "Teachers of science guide and facilitate learning" (p. 32). In order to accomplish this, it is imperative that teachers "Recognize and respond to student diversity and encourage all students to participate fully in science learning." "Students with physical disabilities might require modified equipment; students with learning disabilities might need more time to complete science activities" (p. 37).

The equity principle is also reflected in Program Standard E (NRC, 1996): "All students in the K–12 science program must have equitable access to opportunities to achieve the Standards" (p. 221). Actions to promote this include "inclusion of those who traditionally have not received encouragement and opportunity to pursue science" by "adaptations to meet the needs of special students" (p. 221). This equity principle is further reflected in Assessment Standard D (NRC): "Assessment practices must be fair. . . . Assessment tasks must be appropriately modified to accommodate the needs of students with physical disabilities [and] learning disabilities" (p. 85). This is not only an ethical requirement, but also a measurement requirement.

Legislation Affecting the Rights of Persons with Special Needs

In addition to considering learning theory and science education policy documents, it is also necessary for researchers in this area to be knowledgeable about how legislation affects the educational rights of persons with special needs. It is informative with regard to the science education documents to note that Collins (1998) stated that policy documents such as the U.S. *Standards* were designed in a political context and were therefore "political in context, political in process, and political in intent" (p. 711). Special education in the United States found its present profile and substance through federal law, the Civil Rights movement, and resulting court cases, as well as the evolutionary influences of politics and society (Friend & Bursuck, 1999; Smith, Polloway, Patton, & Dowdy, 1998). The legislation having the greatest impact on educational practice in U.S. schools was passed in 1975. The Education for All Handicapped Children Act (1975) was passed by the U.S. Congress as PL94-142. The law required that children with special needs be provided a free and appropriate public education (FAPE) in the least restrictive environment (LRE).

The passage of this law mandated integration of students with special needs into general education classes with typical peers. The name of the law reflected the language of the day and required states to educate all students, regardless of disability (Lipsky & Gartner, 1997). The major components of this landmark legislation included FAPE for students ages 6 through 17; mandates for the creation, review, and revision of an Individual Education Program (IEP) for each student receiving special education services; a guarantee of placement in the LRE; and detailed parental rights (Sherwood, 1990; Tiegerman-Farber & Radziewicz, 1998). Public Law 94-142, a turning point for those with disabilities, addressed the issue of where students with disabilities would be educated, not simply whether they would be educated.

As a result of the passage of PL 94-142, many students with mild disabilities in the United States began a new era in the general education classroom and saw success. Students were placed in the LRE (Smith et al., 1998; Takes, 1993), or school districts created accommodations in the form of separate classes and separate schools for those with more severe disabilities. At the time, this was considered by most advocates as an equitable move forward because students with greater needs had previously been denied public education in any form.

The Regular Educator Initiative (REI) associated with PL 94-142 was viewed as a major first step in the movement to include students with special needs in typical education settings (Fuchs & Fuchs, 1994; Schumm & Vaughn, 1991; Will, 1986), even though the term *inclusion* does not appear in the law itself. Although the students who benefited most from inclusion were those with mild disabilities (Lipsky & Gartner, 1997), a major milestone was achieved in making science (and other subjects) more accessible to students with disabilities.

The U.S. Congress has passed many laws designed to deal with the rights of people with disabilities, but it has taken a long time to enact and enforce them. Legislation from PL 94-142, Senate Bill 504, the Individuals with Disabilities Education [IDEA], and the 1990 Americans with Disabilities Act [ADA] were all initiatives intended to provide equal opportunities for persons with disabilities to experience the same full and independent life available to the general population. The legislation essentially extended equal opportunity to those with disabilities so they could experience the services and opportunities that were available to the general population. IDEA mandates that those identified as eligible for special services be given a free and appropriate public education, an education in the least restrictive environment, and an individualized education program (IEP) (Turnbull & Cilley, 1999).

Other significant U.S. legislative actions related to the education of learners with special needs include:

1. *Sections 501, 503, and 504 of the Rehabilitation Act of 1973.* The major impact of this legislation was to prohibit federal agencies, federal contractors, and recipients of federal financial assistance from discriminating against otherwise qualified persons with disabilities solely on the basis of disability (Tucker & Goldstein, 1992).

2. *Section 02 Amendments, 1978 & 1979.* These amendments authorized federal agencies to provide grants to state units overseeing work with people with disabilities; establish and operate comprehensive rehabilitation centers; and make the remedies, procedures, and rights of Title VI (Civil Rights Act, 1964) available to section 504 discrimination victims.

3. *Section 504 Amendment, Civil Rights Restoration Act of 1987 [CRRA].* This amendment clarified "program or activity" to mean all of the operations of a college, university, or other post-secondary institution, and that if federal financial assistance was extended to any part of an institution, all of the operations were covered.

4. *Education for All Handicapped Children Act [EAHCA] 1975.* This act required states to provide all children with disabilities with FAPE.

5. *Americans with Disabilities Act [ADA] 1990.* This legislation required that students with special needs would be served as much as possible in the general education classroom (Smith et al., 1998); that "handicapped children" was changed to "children with disabilities"; and that two new categories of disability, traumatic brain injury and autism, were eligible categories for special education services.

6. *Individuals with Disabilities Education Act [IDEA] 1990, 1997, 2004.* This act contained provisions concerning the rights of individuals with disabilities to receive an equivalent education and the opportunity to learn with other students of all abilities. It required the participation of the regular classroom teacher in the IEP process and in the delivery of an equivalent education.

Review of the Literature

For heuristic purposes the review of the literature on special learners in science is presented in two subsections: Curriculum and Instruction, and Assessment.

Curriculum and Instruction

The literature concerning curriculum and instruction in science of learners with special needs is associated with collaboration (the sharing of the teaching responsibility among educators of different professional expertise, content and pedagogy) and with the advocacy and study of inclusion (the placement of learners with disabilities in the general classroom, including science).

Collaboration

Collaboration is a supportive system in which teachers utilize the expertise of other educators to solve problems (Pugach & Johnson, 1990). Science teachers often find themselves isolated in their efforts to serve students with special needs who are placed in their classrooms (McGinnis & Nolet, 1995). Isolation makes teachers more resistant to the changes involved with including students with special needs. Perceptions that may interfere with effective collaboration can become ingrained in professional practice. Unless they are brought to the surface, they serve as persistent bottlenecks to collegiality between professionals.

Since the Education for All Handicapped Children Act (EAHCA) was enacted in the United States in 1975, learners receiving special education services have increasingly been served in the general education setting. The traditional dual system of general education and special education fostered definitive boundaries between these two areas, with little sharing of expertise and support. The concept of inclusion represented a radical departure from the typical school setting and involved, among other things, cooperative and collaborative efforts. There is no one standard model of collaborative service; however, Bauwens (1991) described three common models: teacher assistance teams, collaborative consultation, and cooperative teaching. Of the three basic models, cooperative teaching is the more frequently implemented practice in most school districts (Reeve & Hallahan, 1994). Cooperative teaching, also generically referred to as "collaboration," involves general and special educators coordinating efforts to jointly teach heterogeneous groups of students in integrated settings to meet the needs of all students (Bauwens & Hourcade, 1997).

McGinnis and Nolet (1995) reported one possible model for science teacher preparation and science instruction when the goal was for general and special educators to work collaboratively as way of meeting the science context needs (curricular, instructional, and evaluative) of learners with disabilities. They presented a model based on earlier reported work by Nolet and Tindal (1993). It was designed to bridge the gap between the fields of special education and science education by focusing on the development of what McGinnis and Nolet termed "a new professional relationship between the practitioners" (p. 32). The model was built on the premise that if the needs of the student with disabilities were to be met in authentic school settings, then the focus of the collaboration between the general and the special educator should be on science content and the effective teaching of such knowledge. Differing aspects of expertise were identified for the general science educator (key science knowledge forms: facts, concepts, principles, and procedures). They also identified for special educators the pedagogy of students with special needs (designing instruction, implementing classroom management, and motivational strategies).

Research in instituting collaboration has found that the underlying belief system within a school building must be examined thoroughly before embarking on a mission of collaborative change. The building administration must embrace the theory and concept behind collaboration, support the teachers initiating such a change, and provide structural supports that will allow the collaboration to occur. Walter-Thomas, Bryant, and Land (1996) suggested that administrators provide administrative support and leadership, select capable and willing participants, provide ongoing staff development, establish balanced classroom rosters, provide weekly scheduled co-planning time, facilitate the development of appropriate IEPs, and pilot test classroom and school collaborative efforts.

A belief system within a school that promotes open sharing among colleagues would be most beneficial to a collaborative model. Traditionally, educators have not always been prepared to share and work in a collaborative fashion with other teachers. They have been taught to be autonomous and self-sufficient, for the most part, within their classrooms (Leithwood & Jantzi, 1990). Because of the physical separation of individuals within a building, teachers historically have learned to accept this isolation as the norm or the existing condition of work in the education field. Many teachers, however, see this condition as isolation from the peers who can provide badly needed professional support within schools filled with high-need students. A collaborative environment may help provide the support teachers feel is needed under these conditions. Many schools are thus turning toward the establishment of collegial norms.

Special and general educators can work collaboratively on making adaptations, using the student's IEP as a framework and reference (Golomb & Hammeken, 1996). Myles and Simpson (1989) found that adaptations are most successful when general education teachers are involved in making decisions about designing and implementing the adaptations for students with disabilities.

Inclusion

Mainstreaming, integration, and inclusion have all been used to describe the movement to meet the needs of learners with special needs in the general school setting. Inclusive schools are those in which students with and without special needs are educated together within one educational system (Stainback & Stainback, 1990). Research in this area is extensive. As result, this section is presented in subsections identified by their headings.

Science as an inclusive setting.   As reported by McGinnis (2000), historically teachers inclined toward inclusion (a minority of all teachers) have identified science classes as especially suited for students with disabilities (Atwood & Oldham, 1985). These teachers identify the perceived relevance of the content, the possibility for practical experiences, and the opportunity for group learning with typical peers as the strengths of science classes for inclusion purposes (Mastropieri et al., 1998). However, this perspective does not mean that most contemporary teachers in science (or otherwise) are comfortable including students with disabilities in their class-rooms (McCann, 1998; Scruggs & Mastropieri, 1994; Welch, 1989). Instead, as re-ported by Norman, Caseau, and Stefanich (1998), both elementary and secondary science teachers identify teaching students with special needs as one of their pri-mary concerns.

Contrary to the teachers' misgivings, findings reported in the special educa-tion educational research literature appear to support inclusion (including in sci-ence learning contexts) as a more desirable alternative than segregated instruction for students with disabilities. Ferguson and Asch (1989) found that the more time children with disabilities spent in general classes, the more they achieved as adults in employment and continuing education. This held true regardless of gender, race, socioeconomic status (SES), type of disability, or the age at which the child gained access to general education. Research reviews and meta-analyses known as the special education "efficacy studies" (Lipsky & Gartner, 1989, p. 19) showed that placement outside of general education had little or no positive effect for students regardless of the intensity or type of disability. In a review of three meta-analyses that looked at the most effective setting for educating students with special needs, Baker, Wang, and Walbert (1994) concluded that "students [with disabilities] edu-cated in general classes do better academically and socially than comparable stu-dents in noninclusive settings" (p. 34). Their review yielded the same results re-gardless of the type of disability or grade level.

Regarding students with severe disabilities, Hollowood, Salisbury, Rainforth, and Palombaro (1995) found that including these students in the general educa-tion classroom was not detrimental to classmates. Other researchers (Costello, 1991; Kaskinen-Chapman, 1992) found such inclusion enhanced classmates' as well as their own learning (Cole & Meyer, 1991; Strain, 1983; Straub & Peck, 1994) and yielded social and emotional benefits for all students, with self-esteem and atten-dance improving for some students considered "at risk" (Costello). This research, coupled with strong public press to change current models of delivery in schools, provided a strong impetus for major educational reform.

Some researchers have generated questions about serving mildly developmen-tally delayed students via pull-out programs because of their limited growth abil-ities (Epps & Tindall, 1987; Idol-Maestas, 1983; Polloway, 1984). Other researchers have indicated that providing adaptations within the general education classroom instead of pull-out programs may prove to be more effective (Baker & Zigmond, 1990). Current research on effective schools and effective classroom practices sup-ports the integration of students with special needs into general education classes (National Council on Disability Report, 1989).

Supporters of the early inclusion movement (1980s) cited such claims as basic rights of all individuals to have equal opportunity to life in a typical manner and attend school with typical peers, to participate as fully as possible (Ferguson, 1995; McNulty, Connolly, Wilson, & Brewer, 1996). Many researchers claimed that all stu-dents would benefit from having students with special needs in the general class-room (Fuchs & Fuchs, 1995; Lipsky & Gartner, 1998; McLeskey & Waldron, 1996; Ryndak, Downing, Morrison, & Williams, 1996; Stainback, Stainback, & Stefanich, 1996; Vaughn & Schumm, 1995). Mercer, Lane, Jordan, Allsopp, and Eisele (1996) found that teaching methods and strategies utilized in special education classrooms did not differ so drastically from those used in general classes. Service models that required the students to leave the classroom for prescriptive services denied the students much valuable instructional time and socialization in the general classroom (Sapon-Shevin, 1996). Wang and Reynolds (1996) reported that when students with disabilities left their class to attend resource or pullout programs, they incurred a risk of being negatively labeled and stigmatized.

These researchers and others have documented that adaptations are often needed if students with special needs are to receive instruction in the content areas. In meta-analyses that examined the best setting for students with special needs, Baker et al. (1994) and Stainback et al. (1996) reported that learning core subjects such as social studies, science, and mathematics is beneficial for the long term for students with disabilities, including those with severe disabilities. These researchers and others have documented that adaptations are often needed if students with special needs are to receive instruction in the content areas.

Approaches of professional organizations and the attitudes of teachers to inclusion in science.   Some professional organizations have voiced concerns over the inclusion issue. The spectrum of support for inclusive education ranges from total and unrestricted support from the Association of Persons with Severe Handicaps (1991) to cautious regard for a continuum of services while supporting inclusion (Council for Exceptional Children, 1993), concern for the provision of needed services (Learning Disabilities Association of America, 1993), and guarded caution by the American Federation of Teachers [AFT] (1994) and the National Education Association (1994) in supporting appropriate inclusion (Lipsky & Gartner, 1997; Vaughn, Schumm, Jallad, Slusher, & Saumell, 1996).

The AFT (1994) called for a moratorium on inclusion in response to expressed concerns about lack of teacher preparation addressing the need of students with disabilities in a regular classroom. Practitioners consistently cite the need for inservice opportunities to promote successful inclusion for both students with special needs (Sapon-Shevin, 1996). Research has indicated that the need for teacher inservice and skill development in serving students with disabilities through collaborative efforts is one of the most important aspects of the general educator's role in serving all students (Stainback et al., 1996; Sapon-Shevin, 1996).

Cawley (1994) reported that science teachers generally have little experience or preparation for teaching students with disabilities, and, in general, special educators have little or no exposure to science education. In a survey of special education teachers, Patton, Polloway, and Cronin (1990) found that 42% of special education teachers received no training in science; 38% of children in self-contained special education classes did not receive any instruction in science; among special educators who did teach science, nearly half devoted less than 60 minutes a week to science; and nearly 90% of the teachers surveyed depended upon a textbook for science instruction. Ysseldyke, Thurlow, Christenson, and Weiss (1987) reported that for students with mild disabilities, approximately 200 minutes of reading instruction was received for each minute of science instruction. Often when students with disabilities do receive science instruction, it is from special educators who have little, if any, training in science instruction (Gurganus, Janas, & Schmitt, 1995).

Lang (1994) found that the majority of instruction deaf students receive in science is from teachers with inadequate content preparation in the discipline. Less than 5% of teachers of deaf children reported a major in the physical sciences. Lang concluded, "Although 86% of deaf students report liking science, their academic preparation is inadequate for post-secondary education" (p. 148).

In a study focused on undergraduate science teacher preparation, McGinnis (2003) reported that teacher interns (general education and special education populations collaboratively learning pedagogy) expressed differing beliefs concerning the inclusion of students with special needs in science classrooms. A significant finding was that the general education majors were more likely to support the inclusion of students with developmental delays, whereas those majoring in special education expressed reservations. An examination of the teacher interns' epistemological perspectives of learning (cognitive-based or behavioral-based), as well as their perspectives on group participation in inclusion classroom settings, offered explanatory insight into their inclusion/exclusion decision making. In addition, McGinnis reported an analysis of the ways in which teacher interns modified their science lesson plans to include a hypothetical learner with a developmental delay. In the majority of instances where interns supported the inclusion of the learner with special needs in general science lessons, the pedagogical action taken was to have others (the students' peers or a teacher's aide), rather than the science teacher, provide the learner support in the classroom, typically addressing only social needs. It was rare for any intern to use the ideas recommended by the literature to meet the student's intellectual needs. McGinnis concluded, "As a field, science educators are in moral jeopardy without a moral perspective in making decisions on the inclusion/exclusion of students with disabilities, particularly those with developmental disabilities, in the science classroom" (p. 212).

Stefanich (1994) reported on typical learners' attitudes toward the inclusion of learners with special needs in their science classrooms. He detected a concern for fairness. Too often both teachers and students perceive that equal treatment of all students is fair. This often becomes a barrier to the acceptance of inclusion with its necessary curricular accommodations for some students.

Adaptations to facilitate inclusion and instruction of students with special needs in science.   The inclusion initiative has resulted in efforts to adapt science curriculum and instruction to provide students with special needs with rich experiences that they may not receive in traditional settings. However, because of the limited science background of many general educators, adapting science curriculum can present special challenges. According to a review of the relevant research by Scruggs and Mastropieri (1994), classroom teachers can successfully include students with disabilities in science when the following are present: administrative support; support from special educators; an accepting classroom atmosphere; effective teaching skills; student-to-student peer assistance; and disability-specific teaching skills.

When students with special needs are included for science instruction, the most commonly used approach is the content approach (Scruggs & Mastropieri, 1993). In this approach, textbooks are the primary source of curriculum and instruction. A contrasting approach is the activity-oriented approach. In this approach, the teacher may still employ direct instruction, but students are also actively engaged in the exploration of science concepts (Scruggs & Mastropieri). In the activity-oriented approach, the use of the textbook and the need for acquisition of new vocabulary is significantly decreased, and students can apply the processes of science—observation, classification, measurement, comparison, predictions, and making inferences. Activity-oriented approaches to science that address fewer topics in greater depth can be especially beneficial for students with special needs (Patton, 1995). Both content- and activity-oriented approaches can be adapted and modified to meet the diverse learning needs of students.

General education teachers do implement a wide variety of adaptations to meet student needs, but they do not always find that all types of adaptations are as readily implemented as others. The most feasible adaptations centered on using positive methods and multisensory techniques that were readily integrated into daily classroom routines (Johnson & Pugach, 1990). Adaptations less favorably rated involved dealing with students individually. Yesseldyke, Thurlow, Wotruba, and Nania (1990) found that teachers rated the following methods desirable classroom adaptations: identifying alternative ways to manage student behavior, implementing alternative instructional methodologies, using a variety of instructional materials, and using alternative grouping practices.

In many instances, it is appropriate and necessary for teachers to make curricular and instructional adaptations for students. Teachers use typical adaptations more frequently than substantial adaptations. Typical adaptations include altering the format of directions, assignments, or testing procedures. Substantial adaptations include changing the difficulty level for students, such as implementing altered objectives, assigning less complex work, and providing texts with lower reading levels (Munson, 1986). This research suggested that even though there are a wide variety of adaptation types, teachers will implement the types they are most comfortable with and understand. Teachers in effective schools feel that they have the instructional freedom to alter instruction and assignments to meet the individual needs of their students (Jackson, Logsdon, & Taylor, 1983). When teachers understand typical and substantial adaptations and believe that they have the freedom to make such adaptations, students in inclusive settings benefit.

Mauer (1996) supported the application of effective schools research in making curricular and instructional adaptations for all students, particularly those with special needs. Some characteristics of effective schools are directly related to the classroom teacher. Stefanich (1983) identified the attributes of teachers in effective schools that support the instruction of students with special needs: maintain a clear focus on academic goals; select instructional goals; perceive the students as able learners; implement an evaluation system based on individual student learning, rather than on a comparison with other students' achievements; accurately diagnose student learning needs to foster high student achievement; prepare lessons (including adaptations) in advance; meet students' needs in both academic achievement and socialization; be readily available to consult with students about issues and problems; attend staff development courses to continue your professional development; and keep parents informed and involved.

Multimodality instruction is especially critical in helping students with disabilities gain a familiarity with the content material. Scruggs, Mastropieri, Bakken, and Brigham (1993), in presenting suggestions for teaching science lessons to students with disabilities, stated that students with disabilities are likely to encounter far fewer problems when participating in activity-oriented approaches to science education. The use of multimodality approaches both in teaching and in assessment has shown positive effects (Cheney, 1989). Wood (1990) noted that strategies that lend multiple exposures to new terms and concepts enhance opportunities for all students to understand that content more fully. As a result, actual examples or models are considered to be especially helpful to students with disabilities.

Curricular adaptations are often varied according to content and grade level expectations. They can be designed for groups of students and for individual students. Booth and Ainscow (1998) suggested that one type of curricular adaptation is allowing students to participate in setting their own learning and social objectives, combined with the teachers' objectives in the same areas. The students can then evaluate their progress on their goals as well as the teacher's goals. However, Stainback et al. (1996) warned that writing separate or varying learning outcomes for one student or small groups of students can foster a sense of isolation and separateness in the general education setting.

The process by which teachers implement adaptations. In inclusive settings, instruction can be adapted to ensure the academic success of all students (Smith et al., 1998). But to do this in content areas, such as science, a match needs to exist between the student's abilities and learning preferences and the curriculum and instructional methodologies. Stainback et al. (1996) stated: "Some students exhibit learned helplessness when there is not a good match between learning objectives and student attributes" (p. 14). Making adaptations for students is one way to create that match (Salisbury et al., 1994).

If teachers are given structures and supports for implementing adaptations, they will use them effectively in the general education classroom (Fuchs, Fuchs, Hamlett, Phillips, & Karns, 1995). Scott, Vitale, and Masten (1998) reported that when these support systems are in place, teachers make the necessary adaptations for students. Udvari-Solner (1996) found that when teachers decide what adaptations need to be implemented, they engage in a personal, reflective dialog with self-questioning. This leads to these same questions being posed when they meet in a group setting with other educators and parents. Parents often desire the opportunity to work collaboratively with teachers when determining appropriate adaptations for their children (National Council on Disability, 1989). This collaboration can foster positive relations between home and school, one of the effective school correlates (Salivone & Rauhauser, 1988).

When teachers determine whether adaptations should be made, the next question to consider is, what are the goals of such adaptations? Researchers such as Salisbury and associates (1994) argued that curriculum adaptations should achieve two main goals: promote positive student outcomes and optimize the physical, social, and instructional inclusion of the student in ongoing classroom lessons and activities. Creating an inclusive science classroom is thought to be a balance of designing an accepting environment, implementing effective instructional techniques, and adapting curriculum, materials, and instruction. Inclusive science classrooms are important for students (Patton, 1995).

Designing and implementing curricular and instructional adaptations in the science classroom is similar to those in other content areas. However, science adaptations can sometimes pose special challenges due to the nature of experiments and the materials used (Stefenich, 1994). Teachers must plan lesson adaptations in advance and anticipate difficulties that students may encounter with the materials needed or the science activity.

When teachers believe that the types of adaptations are feasible and desirable, they will use them (Johnson & Pugach, 1990; Yesseldyke et al., 1990). In inclusive settings where adaptations are made, all children can learn, feel a sense of belonging, and achieve their educational and social goals (Winter, 1997). Many teachers believe that they are skilled, accommodating, and willing to serve on IEP Teams in all aspects of planning and implementation of appropriate education for students with special needs (Friend & Bursuck, 1999). However, many also now believe that mechanisms are lacking to capitalize on their skills and respect their professional talents and limitations.

The role of the general educator in the development, implementation, and evaluation of IEPs has become a critical issue in response to compliance efforts of schools to IDEA 1997 (Fuchs & Fuchs, 1994; Sapon-Shevin, 1996). Studies at the secondary level indicate that although the majority of general education teachers who had learners with special needs included in their classes felt successful, over one-third of them received no prior or ongoing preparation or professional development for inclusion, and less than one-half had been involved in development of the IEP (Rojewski & Pollard, 1993). Other findings indicated that teachers did willingly make specialized adaptations when the IEP teams advised them to do so and supported them (Fuchs, Fuchs, & Bishop, 1992; Sapon-Shevin). Research studies indicate that many teachers do not attempt to meet IEP guidelines or modify or adapt any classroom procedures or expectations for any students with disabilities (Ysseldyke et al., 1990). Other studies indicated that adapted techniques may be highly desirable, yet practice does not follow the belief in some classrooms with mainstreamed students (Lipsky & Gartner, 1989, 1997; Reynolds, Wang, & Walberg, 1987; Turnbull & Turnbull, 1998).

Assessment

Assessment is a major and necessary component of education. But the assessment of students with special needs in science and elsewhere typically leads to controversy. Some believe assessment can serve as a stimulus for education reform, whereas others think it is a deterrent to educational programs sensitive to individual differences.

Much of the controversy swirling around educational assessment exists because groups involved have different agendas, views on the validity and reliability of standardized assessments, concerns about how the results of assessment will affect the students being tested, concerns about how the results of assessment will be used to evaluate those giving instruction or delivering programs, concerns about how legislative bodies will use the information from assessments in funding and evaluating schools, concerns about the use of assessment in labeling and categorizing students, and concerns about whether the test(s) accurately assess the knowledge of the individuals and their ability to perform in tasks relating to qualifications.

Kohn (2001) asserted that school testing is driven by a top-down, heavy-handed, corporate-style version of school reform that threatens the basic premises of school improvement, and that the current high-stakes assessment system suits the political appetite for rapid, quantifiable results (Thompson, 2001). Innovations supported by best-practice research are overlooked particularly in communities where the need for developmentally appropriate practice is most needed. Eisner (2001) expressed concern that when there is a limited array of areas in which assessment occurs, students whose aptitude and interests lie in other areas become marginalized. Science is particularly vulnerable. One of the easiest ways to raise test scores may be to teach in ways not recommended by the U.S. *Standards* (National Research Council, 1996), that is, to use direct instruction to present a huge amount of declarative knowledge in a superficial fashion (Kohn, 2001).

U.S. citizens have the right to (a) equal protection under the law and (b) due process when state action may adversely affect an individual. In education, constitutional rights translate into a guarantee of equal educational opportunity (not equal outcomes). Section 504 of the U.S. Rehabilitation Act of 1973 mandated that admissions tests for persons with disabilities must be validated and reflect the applicants' aptitude and achievement rather than any disabilities extraneous to what is being measured. The Education for All Handicapped Children Act (1975) PL 94-142 mandated that all children with disabilities receive a free, appropriate public education. It also mandated due process rights, responsibilities of the federal government in providing some financial assistance, and the requirement that special education services be monitored. According to Suran and Rizzo (1983): "The tests used to evaluate a child's special needs must be racially and culturally nondiscriminatory in the way they are selected and the way they are administered, must be in the primary language or mode of communication of the child, and no one test procedure can be used as the sole determinant of a child's educational program" (p. 175).

The passage of the Americans with Disabilities Act in 1990 (PL 101-336), although intended mainly for industry, has many implications for education, specifically for the licensing/certification/credentialing process. This act requires that the test application process and the test itself be accessible to individuals with disabilities. Although a person may not be able to meet other requirements of the credentialing process, he or she may not be barred from attempting to pass the credentialing exam. The agency or entity administering the test must provide auxiliary aids and/or modification and may not charge the individual with a disability for the accommodations made. Accommodations that may be provided include an architecturally accessible testing site, a distraction-free space, an alternative location, test schedule variation, extended time, the use of a scribe, sign language interpreter, readers, adaptive equipment, adaptive communication devices, and modifications of the test presentation and/or response format (Thurlow, Yesseldyke, & Silverstein, 1993).

Concerning performance examinations in science, the facilities must be accessible and usable by individuals. Acquisition or modification of equipment or devices, appropriate adjustment or modifications of examinations, qualified readers or interpreters, appropriate modification in training materials and/or policies, and other similar modifications must be made for individuals with disabilities (42 USC 12/11, Section 101(9)), who must provide documentation of the disability.

Research has indicated a continuing lack of responsiveness by science teachers to adjust the learning environment so that students with disabilities feel a sense of success and accomplishment. In an examination of science grades for over 400 students with mild disabilities in grades 9–12, Cawley, Kahn, and Tedesco (1989) reported that 50–60% of the grades were Ds or Fs. Donahoe and Zigmond (1990) reported 69%

of the science grades for ninth-grade students with learning disabilities were D or below.

Research has indicated that teachers should be cautious in their actions as a result of interpretations of student performance on standardized assessment instruments (Darling-Hammond, 1999). The use and interpretation of evaluation instruments is a fundamental concern in student identification for special services. Indeed, the validity and reliability of tests used for classification and placement has been repeatedly challenged (Gartner & Lipsky, 1987; Stainback, Stainback, & Bunch, 1989; Wang & Wahlberg, 1988). Gartner and Lipsky described these tests as "barely more accurate than a flip of the coin" (p. 372). Addressing the relative permanence of classifications based on these tests, Gartner and Lipsky reported that less than 5% of the students are declassified and returned to the general education classroom.

Many students with special needs are unable to demonstrate their true level of understanding under traditional testing conditions. Winter (1997) advocated the use of alternative assessment strategies for learners with special needs. Jones (1992) indicated that students with learning disabilities "often fail to develop efficient and effective strategies for learning. They do not know how to control and direct their thinking to learn, to gain more knowledge, or how to remember what they learn" (p. 136). Women and/or minorities with disabilities face even more obstacles to obtaining quality education because of the compounding effect of the disability with other actions of discrimination and/or low expectations.

Conclusions

A key principle in the U.S. *National Science Education Standards* (NRC, 1996) is to provide all students in science with challenging learning opportunities appropriate to their abilities and talents. Many students who are capable of high performance in science are labeled as students with disabilities because of low performance or limitations in other areas not related to reasoning in science. Science teachers must be prepared to recognize these differences and respond to the unique learning needs of each student. Evidence indicates that both practicing and prospective science teachers note the inadequacy of their preparation to make instructional adjustments for students with disabilities.

Other limitations are evidenced when students receive instruction in science primarily from special educators, including time allocated to science, delivery of science through textbook teaching as the primary mode of instruction, and limited teacher knowledge of the science content. Science teachers themselves are generally open to typical adaptations (i.e., format of directions, assignments, and testing) but seldom make substantive accommodations (i.e., altered objectives, less complex work, alternative texts) for students.

Accommodations consistently found to improve the learning of all students are teaching through multimodality instructional approaches, allowing students opportunities to resubmit and improve assignments, and willingness to collaborate with other educators about ways to better serve the needs of all students. Modifications that allow students with disabilities opportunities to share what they have learned in both formative and summative assessments (that are required in

U.S. legislation) result in improved student participation in and commitment to the learning process.

There is no substantive empirical evidence that students with special needs process information differently than other students. Coles (2004) surmised that, after a skill is attained, brain activation changes toward that commonly found in individuals with good use of the skills. When a student has difficulty learning a skill or concept, causes can be difficult to diagnose. Effective teaching of students with special needs must be grounded in interaction between the learner and the learning environment, making efforts to understand the cognitive processing that occurs. Currently, much controversy exists as to whether exceptional learners require approaches to instruction not contained in the repertoire of general classroom teachers, or whether adaptations of well-known instructional practices are sufficient for the vast majority of students. Findings from research on student performance indicate that teachers who use greater variety in their teaching and take time to get to know their students are more effective with all students, regardless of ability.

Future Research Directions

In general, a question certain to be addressed in the U.S. courts (as the newest legislation covering the educational rights of persons with disabilities is enforced) is the extent and degree of responsibility educators have in accommodating the educational needs of students with disabilities. Research that documents the extent and efficacy of science curriculum, instruction, science teacher education context, and assessment of students with special needs is urgently needed.

Other, more specific research questions to investigate include: How have teachers (with data disaggregated by school level and by science discipline) included students with special needs (with data disaggregated by type of disability and personal characteristics) in the general science classroom? What has been the outcome of such efforts across multiple dimensions (e.g., class ecology, curriculum and instruction, and assessment)? What types of teacher professional development throughout the teacher professional continuum have been designed to prepare teachers to teach students with special needs, and what outcomes have those experiences had on the teachers' practices? What outcomes are associated with the differing approaches to teaching science to learners with special needs, and to what extent do these outcomes align with local and high-stakes assessment requirements? What sense do teachers make of adaptations for learners with special needs in science, and how does their perception of their school culture influence such understandings and actions? What strategies help teachers to make adaptations for learners with special needs in the science classroom? From the general classroom teacher's perspective, what mechanisms and strategies would support them in contributing productively at meetings for learners with special needs in their science classrooms? How are the various collaboration models between the general science teacher and the special educator enacted in school environments? To what extent and with what limitations do the various models help learners with special needs to learn for understanding as well as to perform on assessment tasks (traditional as well as alternative)? From the perspective of learners with special needs, how do they access the general curriculum in science? We wonder what new insights in research in special needs might emerge if researchers posed such questions and used alternative paradigms outside of the objectivist paradigm.

PART II: SPECIAL TALENTS IN SCIENCE

George DeBoer, in *A History of Ideas in Science Education* (1991), pointed out that in the field of science education, particularly with regard to the U.S. context, a long-standing barrier to meeting the unique needs of learners with special talents was sensitivity by educators to avoid charges of favoritism. Spurred on by concerns for national security in the post–World II period, the American Association for the Advancement of Science (AAAS) Cooperative Committee argued that, by not recognizing the special abilities in talented learners, science education was committing a double error: (a) not addressing the unique educational needs of such individuals and (b) not developing a national resource that was in high need (DeBoer). Although the record since that period has not been an unqualified success for learners with special talents in science, progress has occurred.

Learners with special talents in science previously have been referred to as "gifted." Contemporary labels seek to describe this group of learners by placing a greater focus on "creativity," "extraordinary abilities," or "talents" (i.e., observable performances in situated events, context, and domain-specific activities) rather than relying solely on superior test-taking performances (academic or IQ examinations) (Ericsonn & Charness, 1994). Maker (1993) described such a learner as a problem solver who "enjoys the challenge of complexity and persists until the problem is solved . . . [and who is capable of] a) creating a new or more clear definition of an existing problem, b) devising new and more efficient or effective methods, and c) reaching solutions that may be different from the usual, but are recognized as being effective, perhaps more effective, than previous solutions" (p. 71).

Tannenbaum (1997) proposed two types of talented individuals: performers and producers. Performers are those who excel at "staged artistry" or "human services" (p. 27); producers excel at contributing "thoughts" and "tangibles" (p. 27). Other theoreticians, such as Piirto (1999), placed attention, especially in precollegiate education, on precocity (the ability to easily do those things typically seen in older learners) as a hallmark of the talented.

As result of the multiple views of researchers, policymakers, and education professionals interested in education for the talented, between 3% and 15% of the student population can be identified as fitting into this category of learners (Hardman et al., 1999). Whitmore and Maker (1985) and Willard-Holt (1998) investigated talented learners in the population with special needs (visual, hearing, physical, and learning disabilities population) and suggested that a similar percentage would apply to the identification of the talented in that group of learners as well.

Legislation Affecting the Rights of Talented Learners in Science

In contrast to U.S. legislation that mandates educational services for learners with special needs, learners with talents in science (or any areas) have no such legal entitlement. Instead, the U.S. federal Gifted and Talented Children's Act of 1978 and the

1993 Javits Gifted and Talented Education Act provided definitions of talented learners as well as some funding to support a national research center, demonstration programs, and activities for leadership personnel throughout the United States (Gallagher, 1997). Accordingly, funding for talented learners in science is a state and local issue. The U.S. Department of Education's (1993) definition of the talented is:

1. Children and youth with outstanding talent perform or show the potential for performing at remarkably high levels of accomplishment when compared with others of their age, experience, or environment.
2. These children and youth exhibit high performance capability in intellectual, creative, and/or artistic areas, possess an unusual leadership capacity, or excel in specific academic fields. They require services or activities not ordinarily provided by the schools.
3. Children and youth with outstanding talents are present in all cultural groups, across all economic strata, and in all areas of human endeavor. (p. 3)

Review of the Literature

For heuristic purposes the review of the literature on talented learners in science is presented in two subsections: Curriculum and Instruction, and Identification of Talented Science Learners.

Curriculum and Instruction

The basic principles of education for the talented have been identified as acceleration of content delivery, selective grouping of the learners, and enrichment of the curriculum (VanTassel-Baska, 2000). Research on the study of curriculum and instruction for talented learners in science has examined two intervention models: a specialized administrative model (enrolling only talented learners) and a general education model (differentiation of instruction for all ability groups). Other studies have sought to document and understand the perspectives of all stakeholders (administrators, teachers, learners, and parents) concerned with science education for the talented.

Intervention models. Researchers have sought to understand the impact of special programs in science, such as accelerated summer experiences or specialized school science courses, designed to meet the needs of talented learners. This intervention model is the specialized administrative model. Wolfe (1985) reported an in-depth study of 23 talented learners in science who participated in the McGill Summer School for Gifted and Talented Children in Montreal. The researcher's focus was determining from the learners' perspectives what messages about science were conveyed when an instructional intervention was used. The pedagogical intervention approach focused on developing six talent areas (creativity, decision making, planning, forecasting, communication, and thinking ability) to enhance the inquiry skills of the learners. From analyses of the classroom interactions in five science lessons, Wolfe determined that only two inquiry skills were being developed in the lessons, and in such a manner as to promote an unacceptable sensationalist view of science.

Lynch (1992) examined the effectiveness of an accelerated summer program in science (biology, chemistry, and physics) at Johns Hopkins University that taught talented learners (ages 12–16) a year of content in three weeks. The study extended over six years and included 905 learners. Lynch found that the summer program effectively prepared learners to accelerate in science content, and that the learners also benefited by beginning high school sciences earlier than regularly allowed. In a similar line of investigation, Enersen (1994) surveyed a sample of talented secondary students ($N = 161$) who had attended high school summer science residencies and found that their attitude toward science increased by participation. In a follow-up survey, most students reported that they were studying or working in scientific fields (no difference between genders). Bass and Ries (1995) investigated the scientific reasoning abilities of talented students in a high school's gifted education program. The researchers designed a data collection strategy that used analogous problems and questions to measure understanding of basic scientific concepts and skills. They determined that the talented learners did not uniformly benefit from the experience; their performances varied on measures that documented their ability to solve different kinds of scientific problems.

Jones (1997) reported on a six-year pre-collegiate intervention program designed to prepare academically talented, lower socioeconomic minority learners for college. The Young Scholars Program at Ohio State University transformed the way agriculture was presented to the learners. Success was measured in achievement and in career interest. In a series of evaluation studies that measured the curricular impact on elementary-level talented learners in science, Boyce, VanTassel-Baska, Burruss, Sher, and Johnson (1997) and VanTassel-Baska, Bass, Ries, Poland, and Avery (1998) reported that problem-based learning and integration of disciplines in science benefited talented learners, as measured by increased motivation, enhanced process skills, and greater ability to make intra- and interdisciplinary connections. In an exploratory study that sought to understand how a sample of talented secondary learners displayed domain-relevant skills possessed by experts in disciplinary content knowledge, Fehn (1997) found that the talented learners in science among his sample varied most widely in critical abilities (interpretation, evaluation for bias, and synthesis). The talented science learners who had previous experience with primary sources in history performed better than those with no experience. Fehn speculated that this finding had strong implications not only for teaching the history curriculum to talented science learners, but for all instructional contexts that required such skills.

Renzulli, Baum, Hebert, and McCluskey (1999) reported on the problems of underachievement by high-ability learners. The researchers presented a new perspective and advocated a strategy to increase success for such learners. *Type III Enrichment*, an educational experience for the talented, encouraged learners to take on the role of actual investigators by studying problems of their choice. The learners were responsible for carrying out their investigations with appropriate methods of inquiry and presenting their findings to an audience. Over 80% of the learners showed gain in the areas of achievement, effort, attitude, self-regulated behavior, and positive classroom behavior. This evidence supported the work of Fort (1990), who had earlier argued for talented learners in science to be allowed to conduct independent research projects.

Another intervention model that researchers have examined is the general education model, in which talented learners in science share the experience with other learners. In a study that examined the impact of mixed-ability classes for science learning in secondary schools, Hacker and Rowe (1993) reported negative results. They found that the mixed-ability class resulted in deterioration in the quality of classroom interactions of both high- and low-ability learners. However, in a study that investigated the differentiation practices of a sample of Scottish secondary science teachers, in which differentiation was defined as teaching individual students in a class at different paces and in different ways, Simpson and Ure (1994) reported evidence of success. Success resulted when teachers shared with their learners (of varying abilities, including the talented) the management of their learning, promoted the belief that achievement can improve, used a wide range of information and support, identified a range of needs, and gave and received continuous feedback.

Perspectives of talented learners, parents, and school personnel. In addition to researchers' interest in examining the impact of intervention models, they have investigated the perspectives of talented learners, their parents, and school personnel along a range of topics. Johnson and Vitale (1988) conducted a survey study of a large sample of South Dakota sixth- through tenth-grade talented learners to measure their perceptions of science. The learners enjoyed science as a discipline and believed it should be a national priority. They thought that science made the world a better place to live, improved the standard of living and the development of the country, and helped to solve everyday problems. However, students reported that, in general, school science was not challenging.

Lynch (1990) investigated credit and placement issues for talented learners in science following accelerated summer studies in science and mathematics. She reported that although the learners and their parents appreciated the acceleration, their schools were less receptive. Schools had practical concerns about how to incorporate the summer credits into existing academic programs and appropriate course placements for the learners.

Cross and Coleman (1992) documented by survey methodology the perspectives of a high school sample ($N = 100$) of talented learners in science. The key finding was that the learners felt restrained by the pace of instruction and the science content of their science courses. They expressed frustration with the lecture-memorization instructional strategy and desired to be more challenged academically.

Identification of Talented Science Learners

The identification and description of learners who would be considered talented in science has been of interest to the research community. Brandwein (1955) wrote a widely read and influential book, *The Gifted Student as Future Scientist*, which along with presenting ideas for increasing the number of talented students in science, began the contemporary conversation on the identification of talented learners in science.

School districts' reliance on aptitude tests to select for talented science learners has drawn the interest of investigators. Piburn and Enyeart (1985) compared the reasoning ability of a large sample of elementary students (grades 4 to 8) designated as gifted ($n = 217$) and mainstreamed ($n = 91$) who were enrolled in the same science-oriented advanced curriculum. The researchers used a battery of Piagetian measures designed to assess combinatorial reasoning, probabilistic reasoning, and the ability to isolate and control variables. They found that their study sample of talented science learners was accelerated over the mainstreamed comparison group by more than two grade levels. Piburn and Enveart concluded that results had implications for how to select talented students for local enrichment programs in science. Instead of complete reliance on standardized aptitude tests, they argued for additional use of a full battery of reasoning ability tests.

Jarwan and Feldhusen (1993) studied the procedures used in selecting talented learners for state-supported residential high schools for mathematics and science. The researchers used both quantitative and qualitative research designs. They determined that the learners' home school adjusted grade-point average was the best predictor of first- and second-year grade-point averages. Their performance on the Scholastic Aptitude Test was the second best predictor. Most significantly, they determined that statistical prediction was superior to professional prediction by interview or ratings of learner portfolio files. In addition, they determined by examination of enrollment data that African American and Latino learners were underrepresented.

Conclusions

Researchers' attention has been drawn to understanding how talented learners in science can be assisted to perform to the best of their abilities in science. A limited number of studies have investigated what talented learners have gained academically from participation in specific science programs and what perceptions talented learners express about science and their schooling. Limited findings suggest that talented science learners do benefit from learning situations that decrease the focus on memorization of information and increase opportunities for problem solving and inquiry.

Although the current research in science education has not determined which type of intervention model is most effective for talented learners (acceleration or enhancement), available evidence suggests that both types of models offer benefits and challenges that call for further exploration. Summer science acceleration programs for the talented have resulted in measurable academic and attitudinal gains.

There is a paucity of research concerning the instructional and learning process for learners with special needs who also have special talents. One limitation is a lack of legal entitlement for students with special needs who meet or exceed academic proficiency requirements. Additional services to address their talents are often ascertained as a general classroom issue without the same type of IEP reporting requirements of those identified with academic learning deficiencies.

Researchers have examined possible ways to identify talented science learners. The limited research in this area suggests that complete reliance on aptitude tests is not warranted and that other measures should be considered (including interviews and reasoning ability instruments).

Future Research Directions

Because of the limited nature of research in science education for talented learners, research is urgently needed in key areas. Recommended specific research questions include: What happens to the talented female learners in science as they proceed through their educational programs (mixed-ability and high-ability groupings)? What happens to the talented learners in science with special needs as they proceed through their educational programs (mixed-ability and high-ability groupings)? What happens to the talented learners in science from different cultural backgrounds or living in poverty as they proceed through their educational programs (mixed-ability and high-ability groupings)? And, what relationship, if any, exists between the identification of talented learners in science and the types of outcomes that the talented programs in science are designed to achieve?

CONCLUDING THOUGHTS

There is continuing tension in the research of exceptional learners in science. A major reason for this tension is special education and science education researchers' use of different theoretical views on learning and teaching. Special education researchers' widespread use of behaviorism as a theoretical lens in research is often in conflict with science education researchers' more common use of cognitive and sociocultural views of learning and teaching. Science educators' strong commitment to inquiry for all in science learning and instruction, as opposed to a focus on skill and information acquisition, contributes to a discernible schism between these two fields of educational research. As a result, researchers in this area who seek cohesion will find that need unmet at this time.

Compounding the epistemological disagreement among researchers interested in understanding the learning in science by exceptional learners is the unique role of legislation in regulating the education of exceptional learners. A clear consequence of the legislative involvement is that a preponderance of researchers have focused their attention on pressing issues of curriculum and instruction within the legal and administrative contexts of schools. The hope is that future research on exceptional learners in science will be expanded to address more fundamental questions of learning theory.

ACKNOWLEDGMENTS

Thanks to Janice Koch and Sharon Lynch, who reviewed this chapter.

REFERENCES

American Federation of Teachers. (1994). *AFT resolutions: Inclusion of students with disabilities.* Washington, DC: Author.

Americans with Disabilities Act. (1990). Washington, DC: United States Department of Justice, Civil Rights Division.

Association for Persons with Severe Handicaps. (1991). Seattle, WA: Author.

Atwood, R. K., & Oldham, B. R. (1985). Teachers' perceptions of mainstreaming in an inquiry oriented elementary science program. *Science Education, 69,* 619–624.

Baker, E., Wang, M., & Walberg, H. (1994). The effects of inclusion on learning. *Educational Leadership, 52*(4), 33–35.

Baker, J. M., & Zigmond, N. (1990). Are regular education classes equipped to accommodate students with learning disabilities? *Exceptional Children, 56,* 515–526.

Bass, G. M., & Ries, R. R. (1995, April). *Scientific understanding in high ability school students: Concepts and process skills.* Paper presented at the annual meeting of the American Educational Research Association, San Francisco, CA.

Bauwens, J. (1991, March). *Blueprint for cooperation teaching.* Symposium conducted at the meeting of the Special Education Conference, Cedar Rapids, IA.

Bauwens, J., & Hourcade, J. (1997, April). *Cooperative teaching; Portraits of possibilities.* Paper presented at the annual convention of the Council for Exceptional Children, Salt Lake City, UT.

Booth, T., & Ainscow, M. (Eds.). (1998). *From them to us: An international study of inclusion in education.* London: Routledge.

Boyce, L. N., VanTassel-Baska, J., Burruss, J. D., Sher, B. T., & Johnson, D. T. (1997). A problem-based curriculum: Parallel learning opportunities for students and teachers. *Journal for the Education of the Gifted, 20,* 363–379.

Brandwein, P. (1955). *The gifted student as future scientist: The high school student and his commitment to science.* New York: Harcourt Brace.

Bransford, J. D., Brown, A. L., Cocking, R. R., Donovan, M. S., & Pellegrino, J. W. (2000). *How people learn: Brain, mind, experience, and school.* Washington, DC: National Academy Press.

Cawley, J. F. (1994). Science for students with disabilities. *Remedial and Special Education, 15,* 67–71.

Cawley, J. F., Kahn, H., & Tedesco, A. (1989). Vocational education and students with learning disabilities. *Journal of Learning Disabilities, 22,* 630–634.

Cheney, C. (1989). The systematic adaptation of instructional materials and techniques of problem learners. *Academic Therapy, 25*(1), 25–30.

Civil Rights Act. (1964). *Civil Rights Act of 1964.* Retrieved June 12, 2004, from http://usinfo.state.gov/usa/infousa/laws/majorlaw/civilr19.html

Cole, D. A., & Meyer, L. H. (1991). Social integration and severe disabilities: A longitudinal analysis of child outcomes. *The Journal of Special Education, 25,* 340–351.

Coles, G. (2004). Danger in the classroom: 'Brain glitch' research and learning to read. *Phi Delta Kappan, 85,* 344–351.

Collins, A. (1998). National education standards: A political document. *Journal of Research in Science Teaching, 35,* 711–727.

Costello, C. (1991). *A comparison of student cognitive and social achievement for handicapped and regular education students who are educated in integrated versus a substantially separate classroom.* Unpublished doctoral dissertation, University of Massachusetts, Amherst.

Council for Exceptional Children. (1993). *CEC policy on inclusive schools and community settings.* Reston, VA: Author.

Cross, T. L., & Coleman, L. J. (1992). Gifted high school students' advice to science teachers. *Gifted Child Today, 15*(5), 25–26.

Darling-Hammond, L. (1999). *Teaching for high standard, what policymakers need to know and be able to do.* Washington, DC: United States Department of Education.

DeBoer, G. E. (1991). *A history of ideas in science education: Implications for practice.* New York: Teachers College Press.

Donahoe, K., & Zigmond, N. (1990). Academic grades of ninth-grade urban learning-disabled students and low-achieving peers. *Exceptionality: A Research Journal, 1*(1), 17–27.

Donald, M. (2001). *A mind so rare: The evolution of human consciousness.* New York: Cambridge University Press.

Donovan, S. M., & Cross, C. T. (Eds.). (2003). *Minority students in special and gifted education.* Washington, DC: The National Academies Press.

Education for All Handicapped Children Act of 1975, Pub. L. No. 94-142. 20 U.S.C. 1400 et seq. (1975).

Eisner, E. W. (2001). What does it mean to say a school is doing well? *Phi Delta Kappan, 82,* 367–372.

Enersen, D. L. (1994). Where are the scientists? Talent development in summer programs. *Journal of Secondary Gifted Education, 5*(2), 23–26.

Epps, S., & Tindall, G. (1987). The effectiveness of differential programming in serving students with mild handicaps: Placement options and instructional programming. In M. C. Wang, M. C. Reynolds, & H. J. Walberg (Eds.), *Handbook of special education: Research and practice: Vol. 1. Learner characteristics and adaptive education* (pp. 231–248). New York: Pergamon Press

Ericsonn, K. A., & Charness, N. (1994). Expert performance. Its structure and acquisition. *American Psychologist, 49*, 725–747.

Fehn, B. (1997, March). *Historical thinking ability among talented math and science students: An exploratory study.* Paper presented at the annual meeting of the American Educational Research Association, Chicago, IL.

Fensham, P. J. (1985). Science for all. *Journal of Curriculum Studies, 17*, 415–435.

Ferguson, D. L. (1995). The real challenge of inclusion: Confessions of a "rabid inclusionist." *Phi Delta Kappan, 77*, 281–287.

Ferguson, P., & Asch, A. (1989). Lessons from life: Personal and parental perspectives on school, childhood, and disability. In D. Bicklen, A. Ford, & D. Ferguson (Eds.), *Disability and society* (pp. 108–140). Chicago: National Society for the Study of Education.

Fort, D. C. (1990). From gifts to talents in science. *Phi Delta Kappan, 71*, 665–671.

Friend, M., & Bursuck, W. D. (1999). *Including students with special needs: A practical guide for classroom teachers.* Boston: Allyn & Bacon.

Fuchs, D., & Fuchs, L. S. (1994). Inclusive school movement and radicalization of special education reform. *Exceptional Children, 60*, 294–309.

Fuchs, D., & Fuchs, L. S. (1995). What's special about special education? *Phi Delta Kappan, 76*, 522–530.

Fuchs, D., Fuchs, L. S., & Bishop, N. (1992). Instructional adaptations for students at risk for academic failure. *Journal of Educational Research, 86*, 70–84.

Fuchs, L. S., Fuchs, D., Hamlett, C. L., Phillips, N., & Karns, K. (1995). General educator's specialized adaptations for students with learning disabilities. *Exceptional Children, 61*, 440–459.

Gallagher, J. J. (1997). Issues in the education of gifted students. In N. Clangelo & A. D. Davis (Eds.), *Handbook of gifted education* (2nd ed., pp, 27–42). Boston: Allyn & Bacon.

Gartner, A., & Lipsky, D. K. (1987). Beyond special education: Toward a quality system for all students. *Harvard Educational Review, 57*, 367–395.

Golomb, K., & Hammeken, P. (1996). Grappling with inclusion confusion? *Learning, 24*(4), 48–51.

Gray, D. E., & Denicolo, P. (1998). Research in special needs education: Objective or ideology? *British Journal of Special Education, 25*, 140–145.

Gurganus, S., Janas, M., & Schmitt, L. (1995). Science instruction: What special education teachers need to know and what roles they need to play. *Teaching Exceptional Children, 27*(4), 7–9.

Hacker, R. G., & Rowe, M. J. (1993). A study of the effects of an organizational change from streamed to mixed-ability classes upon science classroom instruction. *Journal of Research in Science Teaching, 30*, 223–231.

Hardman, M. L, Drew, C. J., & Egan, M. W. (1999). *Human exceptionality: Society, school, and family.* Boston: Allyn & Bacon.

Heward, W. L. (2000). *Exceptional children: An introduction to special education* (6th ed.). Upper Saddle River, NJ: Merrill.

Hollowood, T., Salisbury, C., Rainforth, B., & Palombaro, M. (1995). Use of instructional time in classrooms serving students with and without severe disabilities. *Exceptional Children, 61*, 242–253.

Idol-Maestas, L. (1983). *Special educator's consultation handbook.* Rockville, MD: Aspen.

Individuals with Disabilities Education Act of 1990. 20 U.S.C. 1400–1485.

Individuals with Disabilities Education Act Amendments of 1997, PL 105-17, 20 U.S.C. 1400-et seq., 105th Congress, 1st session.

Jackson, S. A., Logsdon, S. M., & Taylor, N. A. (1983). Instructional leadership differentiating effective from ineffective low-income schools. *Urban Education, 18*(1), 59–70.

Jarwan, F. E., & Feldhusen, J. (1993). *Residential schools of mathematics and science for academically talented youth: An analysis of admission programs.* Collaborative Research Study (CRSS, 93304). Storrs, CT: University of Connecticut, National Research Center on Gifted and Talented.

Johnson, B., & Vitale, P. (1988, April). *A factor analytic study of attitudes of gifted secondary students toward science.* Paper presented at the annual meeting of the National Association for Research in Science Teaching, Lake of the Ozarks, MO.

Johnson, L. J., & Pugach, M. C. (1990). Classroom teacher's views of intervention strategies for learning and behavior problems: Which are reasonable and how frequently are they used? *The Journal of Special Education, 24*(1), 69–84.

Jones, C. J. (1992). *Enhancing self-concepts and achievement of mildly handicapped students.* Springfield, IL: Charles C. Thomas.

Jones, L. S. (1997). Opening doors with informal science: Exposure and access for underserved students. *Science Education, 81,* 663–677.

Kaskinen-Chapman, A. (1992). Saline area schools and inclusive community concepts. In R. Villa, J. Thousaud, W. Stainback, & S. Stainback (Eds.), *Restructuring for caring and effective education: An administrative guide to creating heterogeneous schools* (pp. 169–185). Baltimore: Paul H. Brookes.

Kohn, A. (2001). A practical guide to rescuing our schools. *Phi Delta Kappan, 82,* 358–362.

Lang, H. G. (1994). *Silence of the spheres: The deaf experience in the history of science.* Westport, CT: Bergan & Garvey.

Learning Disabilities Association of America. (1993). *Full inclusion of all students with learning disabilities in the regular education classroom: Position paper.* Pittsburgh: Author.

Leithwood, K., & Jantzi, D. (1990, June). *Transformational leadership: How principals can help reform school cultures.* Paper presented at the Annual Meeting of the Canadian Association for Curriculum Studies, Victoria, BC, Canada.

Lieberman, P. (1998). *Eve spoke: Human language and human evolution.* New York: Norton.

Lipsky, D., & Gartner, A. (1989). *Beyond separate education: Quality education for all.* Baltimore: Paul H. Brookes.

Lipsky, D. K., & Gartner, A. (1997). *Inclusion and school reform: Transforming America's classrooms.* Baltimore: Paul H. Brookes.

Lipsky, D. K., & Gartner, A. (1998). Taking inclusion into the future. *Educational Leadership, 56*(2), 78–82.

Lynch, S. (1990). Credit and placement issues for the academically talented following summer studies in science and mathematics. *Gifted Child Quarterly, 34,* 27–30.

Lynch, S. (1992). Fast-paced high school science for the academically talented: A six-year perspective. *Gifted Child Quarterly, 36,* 147–154.

Maker, C. J. (1993). Creativity, intelligence, and problem solving: A definition and design for cross-cultural research and measurement related to giftedness. *Gifted Education International, 9*(2), 68–77.

Mastropieri, M., Scruggs, T. E., Mantziopoulos, P., Sturgeon, A., Goodwin, L., & Chung, S. (1998). "A place where living things affect and depend on each other": Qualitative and quantitative outcomes associated with inclusive science teaching. *Science Education, 82,* 163–179.

Mauer, S. (1996). Developing effective schools. *James McMahon Institute Newsletter, 3*(2), 1.

McCann, W. S. (1998). *Science classrooms for students with special needs.* ERIC Document Reproduction Service No. ED433185. Washington, DC: Office of Educational Research and Improvement.

McGinnis, J. R. (2000). Teaching science as inquiry for students with disabilities. In J. Minstrell & E. H. VanZee (Eds.), *Inquiring into inquiry/learning and teaching in science* (pp. 425–433). Washington, DC: American Association for the Advancement of Science.

McGinnis, J. R. (2003). The morality of inclusive verses exclusive settings: Preparing teachers to teach students with mental disabilities in science. In D. Zeidler (Ed.), *The role of moral reasoning on socio-scientific issues and discourse in science education* (pp. 196–215). Boston: Kluwer Academic.

McGinnis, J. R., & Nolet, V. W. (1995). Diversity, the science classroom, and inclusion: A collaborative model between the science teacher and the special educator. *Journal of Science for Persons with Disabilities, 3*, 31–35.

McLeskey, J., & Waldron, J. L. (1996). Responses to questions teachers and administrators frequently ask about inclusive school programs. *Phi Delta Kappan, 78*, 150–156.

McNulty, B. A., Connolly, T. R., Wilson, P. G., & Brewer, R. D. (1996). LRE policy: The leadership challenge. *Remedial and Special Education, 17*, 158–167.

Mehan, H. (1993). Beneath the skin and between the ears: A case study in the politics of representation. In S. Chaiklin & J. Lave (Eds.), *Understanding practices: Perspectives on activity and content* (pp. 241–268). Cambridge, England: Cambridge University Press.

Mercer, C. D., Lane, H. B., Jordan, L., Allsopp, D. H., & Eisele, M. R. (1996). Empowering teachers and students with instructional choices in inclusive settings. *Remedial and Special Education, 17*, 226–236.

Munson, S. (1986). Regular education teacher modifications for mainstreamed mildly handicapped students. *The Journal of Special Education, 20*, 389–502.

Myles, B., & Simpson, R. (1989). Regular educator's modification preferences for mainstreaming handicapped children. *The Journal of Special Education, 22*, 479–489.

National Council on Disability. (1989, September). *The education of students with disabilities: Where do we stand? A report to the President and Congress of the United States.* Washington, DC: Author

National Education Association. (1994). *NEA policy on inclusion.* Washington, DC: Author.

National Research Council. (1996). *National Science Education Standards.* Washington, DC: National Academy Press.

Nolet, V., & Tindal, G. (1993). Special education in content area classes: Development of a model and practical procedures. *Remedial and Special Education, 14*(1), 36–48.

Norman, K., Caseau, D., & Stefanich, G. (1998). Teaching students with disabilities in inclusive science classrooms: Survey results. *Science Education, 82*, 127–146.

Patton, J. R. (1995). Teaching science to students with special needs. *Teaching Exceptional Children, 27*(4), 4–6.

Patton, J., Polloway, E., & Cronin, M. (1990). *A survey of special education teachers relative to science for the handicapped.* Unpublished manuscript, University of Hawaii, Honolulu.

Piburn, M., & Enyeart, M. (1985, April). *A comparison of reasoning ability of gifted and mainstreamed science students.* Paper presented at the annual meeting of the National Association for Research in Science Teaching, French Licks Springs, IN.

Piirto, J. (1999). *Talented children and adults* (2nd ed.). Upper Saddle River, NJ: Merrill/Prentice Hall.

Polloway, E. A. (1984). The integration of mildly retarded students in the school: A historical review. *Remedial and Special Education, 5*(4), 18–28.

Pugach, M. C., & Johnson, L. J. (1990). Meeting diverse needs through professional peer collaboration. In W. Stainback & S. Stainback (Eds.), *Support networks for inclusive schooling: Interdependent integrated education* (pp. 95–122). Baltimore: Paul H. Brookes.

Reeve, P. T., & Hallahan, D. P. (1994). Practical questions about collaboration between general and special educators. *Focus on Exceptional Children, 26*(7), 1–11.

Renzulli, J. S., Baum, S. M., Hebert, T., & McCluskey, K. W. (1999). Reversing underachievement through enrichment. Reclaiming children and youth. *Journal of Emotional and Behavioral Problems, 7*, 217–223.

Reynolds, M., Wang, M., & Walberg, H. (1987). The necessary restructuring of special education and regular education. *Exceptional Children, 53*, 391–398.

Rogoff, B. (1990). *Apprenticeship in thinking: Cognitive development in social context.* New York: Oxford University Press.

Rojewski, J. W., & Pollard, R. R. (1993). A multivariate analysis of perceptions held by secondary academic teachers toward students with special needs. *Teacher Education and Special Education, 16*, 330–341.

Roth, W-M. (2002, April). *Constructing disability in science.* Paper presented at the annual meeting of the National Association for Research in Science Teaching, New Orleans, LA.

Ryndak, D. L., Downing, J. E., Morrison, A. P., & Williams, L. J. (1996). Parents' perceptions of educational settings and services for children with moderate or severe disabilities. *Remedial and Special Education, 17*(2), 106–118.

Salisbury, C., Mangino, M., Petrigala, M., Rainforth, B., Syryca, S., & Palombaro, M. (1994). Promoting the instructional inclusion of young children with disabilities in the primary grades. *Journal of Early Intervention, 18*, 311–322.

Salvione, P., & Rauhauser, B. (1988). *School improvement specialists.* Coram, NY: Salvione & Rauhauser.

Sapon-Shevin, M. (1996). Full inclusion as a disclosing tablet: Revealing the flaws in our present system. *Theory into Practice, 35*(1), 35–41.

Schumm, J., & Vaughn, S. (1991). Making adaptations for mainstreamed students: General classroom teacher's perspectives. *Remedial and Special Education, 12*(4), 18–25.

Scott, B. J., Vitale, M. R., & Masten, W. G. (1998). Implementing instructional adaptations for students with disabilities in inclusive classrooms. *Remedial and Special Education, 19*(2), 106–119.

Scruggs, T. E., & Mastropieri, M. A. (1993). Successful mainstreaming in elementary science classes: A qualitative study of three reputational cases. *American Research Journal, 31*, 785–811.

Scruggs, T. E., & Mastropieri, M. A. (1994). Current approaches to science education: Implications for mainstream instruction of students with disabilities. *Remedial and Special Education, 14*(1), 15–24.

Scruggs, T. E., Mastropieri, M. A., Bakken, J. P., & Brigham, F. J. (1993). Reading vs. doing: The relative effects of textbook-based and inquiry-oriented approaches to science education in special education classrooms. *The Journal of Special Education, 27*, 1–15.

Shaywitz, B. A., Shaywitz, S. E., Pugh, K. R., Mencl, W. E., Fulbright, R. K., Skudlarski, P., et al. (2002). Disruption of posterior brain systems of reading in children with developmental dyslexia. *Biological Psychiatry, 52*, 101–110.

Shaywitz, S. E. (2003). *Overcoming dyslexia: A new and complete science-based program for reading problems at any level.* New York: Knopf.

Sherwood, S. P. (1990). *Principals' perceptions about regular education teacher's attitudes toward integration of students with handicaps.* Unpublished doctoral dissertation, University of Northern Iowa.

Simos, P. G., Fletcher, J. M., Bergman, J. I., Breier, B. R., Foorman, E. M., & Castillo, R. N. (2002). Dyslexia-specific brain activation profile becomes normal following successful remedial training. *Neurology, 58*, 1203–1213.

Simpson, M., & Ure, J. (1994). *Studies of differentiation practices in primary and secondary schools.* Interchange No. 30. Edinbugh: Scottish Office Education Department, Research and Intelligence Unit.

Smith, J., & Sherburne, M. (2001). *Philosophy and vision for differentiation in MCPS science (K–8).* Retrieved August 28, 2003, from http://mcps.k12.md.us/curriculum/science/instr/differentiation.htm

Smith, T. E., Polloway, E., Patton, J. R., & Dowdy, C. A. (1998). *Teaching students with special needs in inclusive settings* (2nd ed.). Boston: Allyn & Bacon.

Stainback, S., & Stainback, W. (1990). *Understanding and conducting qualitative research.* Dubuque, IA: The Council for Exceptional Children.

Stainback, W., Stainback, S., & Bunch, G. (1989). Introduction and historical background. In S. Stainback, W. Stainback, & M. Forest (Eds.), *Educating all students in the mainstream of regular education* (pp. 3–14). Baltimore: Paul H. Brookes.

Stainback, W., Stainback, S., & Stefanich, G. (1996). Learning together in inclusive classrooms: What about curriculum? *Teaching Exceptional Children, 28*(3), 14–19.

Stefanich, G. (1983). The relationship of effective schools research to school evaluation. *North Central Association Quarterly, 53*, 343–349.

Stefanich, G. (1994). Science educators as active collaborators in meeting the educational needs of students with disabilities. *Journal of Science Teacher Education, 5*, 56–65.

Stefanich, G., & Hadzegeorgiou, Y. (2001). Nature of the learner: Implications for teachers from the constructivist perspective. *Science teaching in inclusive classrooms: Theory & foundations* (pp. 23–43). National Science Foundation Grant numbers HRD–953325 and HRD 9988729.

Strain, P. (1983). Generalization of autistic children's social behavior change: Effects of developmentally integrated and segregated settings. *Analysis and Intervention in Developmental Disabilities, 3*(1), 23–34.

Straub, D., & Peck, C. (1994). What are the outcomes for non-disabled students? *Education Leadership, 52*(4), 36–40.

Suran, B. G., & Rizzo, J. V. (1983). *Special children: An integrative approach.* Glenview, IL: Scott, Foresman & Co.

Takes, M. J. (1993). *Cooperative teaching as a method of collaboration between regular and special educators in an integrated setting.* Unpublished doctoral dissertation, University of Northern Iowa.

Tannenbaum, A. J. (1997). The meaning and making of giftedness. In N. Colangelo & A. D. Davis (Eds.), *Handbook of gifted education* (2nd ed., pp. 27–42). Boston: Allyn & Bacon.

Temple, E., Deutsch, G. K., Poldrack, R. A., Miller, S. L., Tallal, P., & M. M. Merzenich, (2003). Neural deficits in children with dyslexia ameliorated by behavioral remediation: Evidence from functional MRI. *Proceedings of the National Academy of Sciences USA, 110*, 2860–2865.

Thompson, S. (2001). The authentic standards movement and its evil twin. *Phi Delta Kappan, 82*, 358–362.

Thurlow, M. L., Yesseldyke, J. E., & Silverstein, B. (1993). *Testing accommodations for students with disabilities: A review of the literature, synthesis report 4.* Washington, DC: National Center on Educational Outcome.

Tiegerman-Farber, E., & Radziewicz, C. (1998). *Collaboration decision making.* Upper Saddle River, NJ: Prentice-Hall.

Tucker, B. P., & Goldstein, B. A. (1992). *Legal rights of persons with disabilities, an analysis of federal law.* Horsham, PA: LRP Publications.

Turnbull, H. R., & Turnbull, A. P. (1998). *Free and appropriate public education: The law and children with disabilities.* Denver: Love.

Turnbull, R., & Cilley, M. (1999). *Explanations and implications of the 1997 amendments to IDEA.* New Jersey: Prentice-Hall.

Udvari-Solner, A. (1996). Examining teacher thinking: Constructing a process to design curricular adaptations. *Remedial and Special Education, 17*, 245–254.

U.S. Department of Education. (1993). *National excellence: A case for developing America's talent.* Washington, DC: Author.

U.S. Department of Education. (2002). *Annual report of IDEA (2000–2001).* Retrieved May 18, 2004, from http://www.ed.gov/about/reports/annual/osep/2002/appendix-a-pt1.pdf

VanTassel-Baska, J. (2000). Theory and research on curriculum development for the gifted. In K. Heller, F. Monks, R. Sternberg, & R. Subotnik (Eds.), *International handbook of giftedness and talent* (2nd ed., pp. 345–365). London: Pergamon Press.

VanTassel-Baska, J., Bass, G., Ries, R., Poland, D., & Avery, L. D. (1998). A national study of science curriculum effectiveness with high ability students. *Gifted Child Quarterly, 42*(4), 200–211.

Vaughn, S., & Schumm, J. S. (1995). Responsible inclusion for students with learning disabilities. *Journal of Learning Disabilities, 2*, 264–270, 290.

Vaughn, S., Schumm, J. S., Jallad, B., Slusher, J., & Saumell, L. (1996). Teacher's views of inclusion. *Learning Disabilities Research and Practice, 11*(2), 96–106.

Walter-Thomas, C., Bryant, M., & Land, S. (1996). Planning for effective co-teaching: The key to successful inclusion. *Remedial and Special Education, 17*, 255–264.

Wang, M. C., & Reynolds, M. (1996). Progressive inclusion: Meeting new challenges in special education: Bringing inclusion into the future. *Theory into Practice, 35*(1), 20–25.

Wang, M. C., & Wahlberg, H. J. (1988). Four fallacies of segregationalism. *Exceptional Children, 48*, 106–114.

Welch, M. (1989). A cultural perspective and the second wave of educational reform. *Journal of Learning Disabilities, 22*, 537–540, 560.

Wertsch, J., & Kanner, B. (1992). A sociocultural approach to intellectual development. In R. Sternberg & C. Berg (Eds.), *Intellectual development* (pp. 328–349). New York: Cambridge University Press.

Whitmore, J. R., & Maker, C. J. (1985). *Intellectual giftedness in the disabled persons.* Rockville, MD: Aspen.

Will, M. C. (1986). Educating children with learning problems: A shared responsibility. *Exceptional Children, 52*, 411–415.

Willard-Holt, C. (1998). Academic and personality characteristics of gifted students with cerebral palsy: A multiple case study. *Exceptional Children, 65*, 37–50.

Winter, S. (1997). "SMART" planning for inclusion. *Childhood Education, 73*, 212–218.

Wolfe, L. F. (1985, April). *Teaching science to gifted children: The model and the message.* Paper presented at the annual meeting of the National Association for Research in Science Teaching, French Lick Springs, IN.

Wood, K. (1990). Meaningful approaches to vocabulary development. *Middle School Journal, 21*(4), 22–24.

Ysseldyke, J., Thurlow, M., Christenson, S., & Weiss, J. (1987). Time allocated to instruction of mentally retarded, learning disabled, emotionally disturbed and non-handicapped elementary students. *The Journal of Special Education, 21*, 23–42.

Ysseldyke, J. E., Thurlow, M., Wotruba, J., & Nania, P. (1990). Instructional arrangements: Perceptions for general education. *Teaching Exceptional Children, 22*(4), 4–7.

CHAPTER 12

Science Learning in Urban Settings

Angela Calabrese Barton
Michigan State University

Last year I was interviewing a group of sixth-grade students from a high-poverty urban school in New York City. I had spent a great deal of time with them in an after-school program and thought I had a good sense of what they cared about. I had also spent time in their science class. The science class was interesting, primarily because most students held strong opinions about the teacher, Mr. Logan. Nearly all of the students I talked to believed that Mr. Logan was a good science teacher. Yet, nearly all of the students also said that they did not like science class!

As I began to probe this contradiction with the students, I said to them, "Tell me about one thing you learned in science class today." I was immediately struck by their overwhelming response: "We didn't learn anything!" On the one hand, I knew that Mr. Logan had spent time that week talking about the parts of cells and was getting the students ready to make their own cell models. I had the urge to say to this group of students, "Come on, of course you learned something! What about the cell?" On the other hand, I wanted to explore why they thought they really had not learned anything at all. What did the students really mean by their statement about *not learning*?

As I reflect on this experience, my gut reaction to the students' response is that students are learning all of the time whether they realize it or not. However, *what* students learn and *how* they learn it are open for debate. In other words, learning is oriented toward an outcome (what are students learning?) and a process (who is learning, and when, where, and why?).

When learning is referred to as a *product* it is often conflated with achievement. Indeed, the past 20 years have given rise to a number of carefully documented studies focused on student achievement as an outcome measure of student learning. It is well established that these studies have helped to quantify and clarify the very specific challenges faced in urban science education. Achievement studies have highlighted who is (and is not) achieving, demonstrating that gaps in achievement still exist between ethnic, racial, and socioeconomic groups as well as between high-poverty and non-high-poverty urban students (see also Chapter 8, this volume). Achievement studies have also spurred more focused investigations that examine reasons for differential achievement in urban centers, including access to resources, teacher qualifications, and other classroom-related barriers.

When learning is referred to as a *process*, it is often discussed relative to a given context (*What* are students learning? *Where* are students learning?) and characterization (What actually constitutes learning in these settings?). Situated cognition theories tell us learning ought to be considered as a form of participation, with individuals and contexts intertwined. This lens for understanding the process of learning underscores the importance of both culture and community. In her study of urban high school students participating in a summer gardening program, Rahm (2002) pointed out that what accumulates through participation in science is not only deepening understandings of scientific facts, but also a way of talking, acting, and becoming a member of a community. Understanding learning as a process is also important in urban science education because it influences how we understand what students are learning and the means by which they do so.

Thus, I find myself contemplating the questions: What learning matters in high-poverty urban science classrooms and who should decide when learning takes place? What does learning in these urban classrooms feel like and sound like from different stakeholders' perspectives? The students I interviewed attend a school that is labeled as failing, and they exist in a system marked by high-stakes exams, strict rules regarding behavior, and certain ways of knowing that are deemed acceptable. In addition, their teachers are not always encouraged to be attentive to their students' home languages and cultures. Their educational futures are not always determined by whether they believe they have learned something—or anything—in their science class.

FRAMING QUESTIONS

In this review, I begin by examining those studies that document the outcomes of student learning through achievement, attempting to show how these studies have laid a foundation for the characterization of who is learning (and who is not learning) science in urban centers. As part of this review, I include a discussion of those studies that draw upon achievement patterns to examine the barriers or obstacles that frame opportunities to achieve in science. Thus, the questions I take up in the first section include the following:

1. Who is learning science in urban schools?
2. What are the conditions that mediate student achievement and learning?

Second, I move on to those studies that examine the process of learning in urban science settings and examine how science learning is mediated by context, including those contextual factors that influence not only how students learn (i.e., discourse, culture, etc.) but also what students learn in the name of science instruction. As part of this review I closely examine the tools researchers use to document the "differences" in the language, culture, and practice of science that mediate learning in science classrooms. Thus, the questions I take up in this second section include these:

1. What are the primary tools that urban science education researchers employ to understand and bridge differences in what and how urban students learn science?
2. What else are students learning in science class besides science?

As these questions suggest, learning as a process cannot be divorced from the process of teaching. Therefore in my discussion of these questions, I will also take up issues of teaching relative to when and how students learn.

Before I delve into either set of questions, however, I want to backtrack for a moment to address two additional questions: First, why is it important to understand learning within a uniquely urban context? Second, what kinds of articles are included in a review on learning and urban science education and why is this so?

URBAN SCIENCE EDUCATION THROUGH RESEARCH

There has been a growing interest in urban science education studies over the past 10 years. As a result, a growing number of published articles in journals like *Science Education, Journal of Research in Science Teaching, Research in Science Education*, and the *International Journal of Science Education* have titles that include words like *urban* or *city*. As I have reported elsewhere (Calabrese Barton, 2002), urban science education research, in a broad sense, studies the intersections among students, their families and their teachers, science, schooling, and the historical, physical, environmental, social, economic, and political aspects of urban life. This perspective suggests that urban science education research is especially attentive to the forces that frame the urban context through both the research questions and methods, and that the analysis and subsequent knowledge claims made reflect a propensity for generating a specialized knowledge based around urban science education.

Therefore, I developed a list of 39 articles[1] that I believe fit into urban science education studies and that address issues of student learning. To develop this list of articles, I examined the contents of the major science education journals over the past decade for relevant studies. I then examined the reference lists in these studies, which led to additional articles. I also used the search engines ERIC, First Search, and Ingenta to conduct a refereed journal-wide search for urban science education articles. I analyzed each article for questions, research frameworks, guiding assumptions, and findings.

The selection of these articles, by the nature of what they report, places further boundaries on what is reported in this chapter. First, the majority of the articles

---

[1]For the purposes of this review, I relied only on articles published in research-oriented refereed journals, and primarily upon those articles published in the major research-oriented science education journals (*International Journal of Science Education, Science Education, Research in Science Education*, and *Journal of Research in Science Teaching*).

focus on those aspects of urban life that contribute to the great divide between those urban communities that have and those that do not. In some cases, published reports reviewed here use the word *urban* synonymously with *urban poverty* or *urban minority*. I want to avoid this assumption in this chapter. However, because of the nature of the studies published in the science education literature, urban studies have taken a decidedly focused perspective on poverty, race, and language issues. Additionally, urban schools in the United States, for example, are "more likely than ever to serve a population of low-income, minority students, given increased residential segregation and recent court decisions releasing schools across the country from desegregation orders" (Oakes, Muir, & Joseph, 2000, p. 5). Second, the vast majority of the studies I reviewed were situated in the United States. I recognize that this limitation is partly my responsibility, as I only reviewed articles available in English. To compensate for this limitation, I have tried to point out the differences in the urban issues of concern in the United States and how this may or may not differ from other geographic and national locations.

ACHIEVEMENT IN SCIENCE IN URBAN CENTERS

In contemporary educational discourse, achievement and learning are often conflated. In a detailed study commissioned by the Council of Great City Schools, Snipes, Doolittle, and Herlihy (2003) found that urban districts effective in promoting student achievement across racial and socioeconomic gaps "focused on student achievement" and encouraged teachers "to use achievement data as a tool to help them improve instructional practice, diagnose students' specific instructional needs, and increase student learning/achievement" (p. xx). As these authors suggest, conflating achievement and learning is generally the result of targeting the outcomes of the learning process, as high-stakes assessments generally do. Outcome measures of learning, however, must be part of the science learning conversation because of their profound implications for urban students. For example, recent legislation in some states in the United States has linked high-stakes outcome measures with state-endorsed diplomas, school funding, and teacher pay.

The studies reported below reveal three key findings: (a) that a significant gap exists between urban and suburban learners, and that this gap is punctuated by differential achievement between White students and students from minority backgrounds; (b) that the achievement gap is a function of the sociocultural status of learners; and (c) that the achievement gap is also a function of students' and teachers' access to resources to support the teaching and learning of science. Thus, in what follows I review studies that examine (a) urban science achievement patterns across sociocultural status and access to resources and (b) the function and form of resources in urban science student achievement and learning.

The Urban Science Achievement Gap Is a Function of Sociocultural Status

Norman and his colleagues (Norman, Ault, Bentz, & Meskimen, 2001) offered an in-depth analysis of the achievement gap between White students and Black students in urban America. This study demonstrates that there exist "multiple achievement gaps" among urban science learners and that these gaps are a complex phenomenon, sustained by a complex organization of factors that frame urban communities, such as race, ethnicity, immigration patterns, and socioeconomic status.

Using a historical macro-analysis, Norman et al. (2001) suggested that a significant gap exists between Black and White students, and that this gap has a distinctly urban–suburban undertone, given the demographic patterns that mark urban and suburban settings in the United States. However, in comparing his finding for urban Black Americans with other ethnic and racial groups over the last 100 years, Norman et al. argued that the achievement gap in urban science classrooms more likely reflects the *sociocultural* position of groups in society rather than racial differences. To make a case for achievement as a sociocultural phenomenon, Norman et al. presented an analysis of the different achievement gaps in the United States during the twentieth century. Their analysis reveals that at different times achievement gaps existed and then disappeared for a number of immigrant groups, that these groups had a low scholastic profile at the same time that they occupied a low-status position, and that as the immigrant groups became mainstreamed and assimilated, their achievement gaps diminished and they generally moved away from urban centers into more suburban locations.

Norman et al.'s study (2001) suggests that achievement gaps are complex phenomena that shift over time with changing populations and changing contexts. This study sheds light on the complex phenomenon of the achievement gap, and it raises many questions worth pursuing. First, within the urban Black population, do these same trends hold for the multiple ethnic populations? Are similar trends found for Latino populations for whom similar sociocultural barriers also exist within U.S. society? How might a micro-analysis of urban Black Americans who defy the achievement trends in the United States provide insight into how sociocultural status and school success overlap? One major implication of this study is that actual achievement gaps may be a reflection of a combination of other gaps, including a group's social and political power, knowledge of U.S. systems such as schooling, and access to resources.

The Urban Science Achievement Gap Is a Function of Resources

Most researchers are generally familiar with the chilling statistics that describe high-poverty and minority urban students' differential access to resources in U.S. schools. Students attending poor, urban schools in the United States by and large have limited access to updated scientific books and equipment and science-related extra-curricular activities (Oakes, 1990). They also have limited access to certified science teachers or to administrators who could support high-quality science teaching, such that students are either denied high-level science courses (because they are not offered) or they take courses with uncertified or unqualified teachers (Darling-Hammond, 1999; Ingersoll, 1999). High-poverty urban students are disproportionately tracked into low-level classes where educational achievement typically focuses on behavior skills and static conceptions of knowledge (Oakes, 1990). In fact, some studies have shown a complete absence of science in low-track urban science classes (Page, 1990).

The impact of differential access to resources has been particularly detrimental to urban students. Oakes' studies (1990; Oakes et al., 2000), which analyzed student scores on national exams and course-taking patterns in California, reveal that although both achievement and course-taking have increased for all groups of urban students, serious gaps remain between White and non-White students and between high-poverty and non-poverty students, and that these gaps correlate with inequalities in opportunities to learn between schools and within them (Oakes et al., 2000).

Similar studies have been conducted in Australia. Two studies in particular compare student achievement in urban versus rural settings and demonstrate the complexity of the relationship between location, resource availability, and achievement. It is worth examining these studies in detail. Using data from the Third International Mathematics and Science Study, Webster and Fisher (2000) conducted a multilevel analysis, which took into account school-, classroom- and student-level variance, to determine levels of achievement in Australian urban and rural communities and their association with location and access to resources. Although larger variances in achievement were noted at the student level when issues of socioeconomic class and sex were considered, when researchers controlled for these differences at both the classroom and school level, rural schools demonstrated statistically significant positive differences in achievement. In making sense of these differences, researchers noted that "contrary to what has been written previously, the information provided by the schools in this study shows that rural schools are more adequately resourced than urban schools." However, researchers noted that access to resources was a factor in student achievement significantly only at the student level rather than also at the school level. This study is important, and its findings suggest the need for further investigation into how achievement trends may vary when the analysis more rigorously accounts for location, such as the differences in kinds of urban and rural locations investigated.

This concern has been taken up in part by Young (1998), who, by using multilevel modeling techniques in an effort to question the generalizability of the comparison of rural with urban schools, found that the location of the school had significant effects on achievement. Her study revealed that differences in achievement were more pronounced among students from remote locations. In particular, she determined that when achievement levels were examined only in Western Australia, students attending rural and remote schools did not perform as well as those students in urban schools, nor did they have access to as many resources as students from urban schools. This study indicates the importance of general access to resources in student achievement; but it should also be noted that when these data were analyzed relative to student socioeconomic status, sex, aboriginal status, English-speaking background, and academic self-concept, the size effect of these findings is relatively small.

These two Australian studies, therefore, indicate the importance of the relationship between access to resources and student achievement in science in urban versus rural settings. However, they also show how complex student achievement relative to location is, and how models developed to explain differences need to consider the nuances of specific locations and student ability differences. Like Norman et al.'s study (2001), which demonstrates the complexities in how achievement gaps ought to be understood as both individual and group phenomena, this study also suggests that careful consideration must be given to how individual factors interrelate with broader-scale factors (i.e., classroom, school, regional, social) to confound larger effect size. In urban science education studies this is of particular importance, given that higher-level policy discussions around educational practices in urban settings, like New York, have been based on generalized large-scale learning outcomes.

Thus, this collection of studies highlights the conditions under which many high-poverty and minority urban youth attend school and the impact the conditions have on their growth and development as science learners. They also set a baseline measure of differential access and opportunity and challenge basic assumptions around how access to resources in urban contexts changes across countries and even within countries.

The Form and Function of Resources and Science Achievement

The next series of articles examines what actually counts as resources and how resources are activated in the support of opportunities to learn science.

The most comprehensive set of studies that has examined access to resources has been conducted at the school, system, and state levels. In her research on the *Equity Metric*, Kahle (1998) demonstrated a relationship between differential achievement and access to resources. The *Equity Metric* advances our understanding of how achievement suffers in under-resourced schools, such as those in high-poverty urban centers, because it quantifies a set of human, social, and material resources to make sense of how well a school is moving toward equity goals. Furthermore, rather than focusing on equity in terms of individuals or groups of individuals, the *Metric* addresses the conditions within a system (a classroom, school, or district) that define equity in science education.

The *Equity Metric* and related research provide a flexible reconceptualization of what ought to be counted as resources, including clearly understood and accepted goals for reform; responsible and accessible leadership; teachers who feel efficacious, autonomous, and respected; and a community that is supportive and involved (Hewson, Kahle, Scantlebury, & Davies, 2001). For example, application of the *Metric* reveals that even in U.S. urban schools where academic achievement plans with strong equity components were in place, students were still exposed to a science education that was inequitable along three resource fronts: lack of home resources and the cultural knowledge to succeed in schools, a lack high expectations and culturally relevant practices, and a lack of engagement in science education reform practices (Hewson et al., 2001; see also Kahle, Meece, & Scantlebury, 2000; Roychoudhury & Kahle, 1999).

These studies focused on the *Equity Metric* reveal that a combination of resource-oriented factors, which the authors believe to be unique in urban schools, consumed the attention of science teachers such that they had little time or energy to teach science.

> In successful schools, teachers assume they will have the conditions needed to support quality teaching. Try as they might, [the urban] science teachers could not focus on science teaching. Webster's [suburban] science teachers, in contrast, worked in a coopera-

tive, stable environment that provided the time and space to focus their energies on teaching science. (Hewson et al., 2001, p. 1142)

This last point is crucial to understanding the connection between student achievement and resources in urban settings, for it suggests that there are resource concerns unique to urban centers, at least in the United States. Such a conjecture is worth further study.

Spillane, Diamond, Walker, Halverson, and Jita (2001), like Kahle (1998), examined the form and function of resources as both the building and district levels. In their study, they focused more on how the activation of resources—in addition to their actual presence—is fundamental to opportunities to learn science in urban settings. Whereas Kahle and her colleagues (1998, 2000) worked to quantify resources, Spillane and his colleagues drew upon a fluid conceptualization of resources and focused on the importance of the activation processes used by school leaders to utilize available resources. Their study, which examined 13 high-poverty Chicago elementary schools' efforts to lead instructional change in science education, demonstrates the importance of framing resources in terms of how material, human, and social capital is identified, accessed, and activated. Using an in-depth case study of one of their schools, where resources for leading instruction were extremely limited and unequally distributed across subject areas—more for literacy and math, fewer to none for science—Spillane et al. showed that successful changes in school-wide science achievement were brought about by school leaders who placed value on how leaders activated resources for science instruction, developed teachers' human capital, recognized and used social capital inside and outside of school, and juggled all with an eye toward achievement and accountability measures.

Each of the authors above argues for a broader conceptualization of resources in school science settings. However, it is interesting to note that their reasons for doing so are different. Spillane et al. (2001) were interested in how teachers and leaders might use what is around them to build more equitable learning opportunities in an under-resourced subject. Kahle (1998) was interested in setting standards for adequate resources in urban schools and making a case for how some of the overlooked but extremely important resources affect student achievement. Each of these articles also makes a case for how resources inform the process of how students go about learning in urban settings. These studies reveal challenging questions about the role that resources play in student learning. Spillane et al.'s study suggests that it is possible for a broad and nontraditional repertoire of resources to positively affect school science, but it only provides us with a glimpse of the resources drawn upon by school leaders in promoting reform-based science instruction, and does not show how students may also activate a fluid resource bank. What could we also learn if more systematic attention were paid to the strategies for activation that matter to students, teachers or leaders, and to whether the employment of differing strategies matters in learning outcomes?

Thus, studies on resources in urban science education provide a baseline understanding of how urban student achievement and attitudes in the sciences are directly linked to the access and activation of resources. They urge us to consider how various conditions within schools, communities, and nations are centrally part of how resources ought to be understood and activated. Although the debate is rich and at times contentious with regard to how the identification and enactment of resources ought to be framed—as measurable quantities or fluid contexts dependent upon arrangements—such richness opens up powerful lines of questioning and research. At this point, one could also argue for including those studies that examine the use of local resources or student funds of knowledge as starting points for a curriculum (see Bouillion & Gomez, 2001; Fusco & Calabrese Barton, 2001; Seiler, 2001). However, I have decided to include studies that approximate this concern in a later section dealing more directly with the role of cultural toolkits and funds of knowledge in the *process* of student learning.

THE PROCESS OF LEARNING: ARTICULATING THE RELATIONSHIP BETWEEN THE URBAN LEARNER, SCIENCE, AND THE LEARNING ENVIRONMENT

Studies of achievement and resources in science only crack the door for understanding student learning in urban settings. Although they provide us with a framework for understanding who is succeeding in educational environments and who is not, they are unable to provide us with insight into why some high-poverty groups succeed in urban schools and others do not. They demonstrate a compelling relationship between access to resources and academic achievement, but most leave open questions around how nontraditional resources facilitate learning or the motivation to learn. In this next section, I move on to those studies that take up these questions more directly by focusing on the process of learning.

With the introduction of the ideal of scientific literacy into international science education discourse, achievement studies of urban student populations have been complemented by studies that focus on how *context* frames urban student learning in science. Situated within the broad framework of social cognition, these studies, taken as a whole, have attempted to step away from singular outcome measures in order to characterize what learning is in urban science education settings and how learning is mediated by the local context. Just as achievement studies have revealed differences in learning outcomes among differing populations within urban centers and between urban and non-urban centers, social cognition studies have revealed that successful science learning is an artifact of the learning environment created for or by students.

Even though understanding context is central to understanding the process of learning in urban science education, the investigation of context is a difficult one. It is a dynamic construction, grounded in a set of geographic and structural features as well as in the histories, cultures, experiences, and identities of those individuals who make up that context. Each of the studies described below offers either an analytic lens for making sense of student learning in science or a depiction of the link between student learning and context. Thus, the questions I take up in this section include:

1. What are the primary tools that urban science education researchers employ to understand and to bridge differences in what and how urban students learn science?
2. What else are students learning in science class?

Understanding and Bridging Differences

In this section, I examine a set of articles that present tools for making sense of student learning in urban environments. By "tools" I refer to theoretical constructs that researchers have developed or adopted to help describe and explain the process of student learning. Across the studies reviewed for this section, three categories of tools are covered: (a) appropriation frameworks, (b) congruence, and (c) legitimate participation.

Appropriation Frameworks

The studies presented in this section describe tools that provide insight into how urban students learn to appropriate or assimilate science content and culture. Each of the studies shares two ideas. First, each is grounded in the belief that science is a cultural practice, with its own ways of talking, acting, and becoming a member of a community. Second, each draws upon the idea that the process of learning to become part of the scientific culture ought to be transformative for the students, for the classroom-based scientific culture they join, and for the teachers who help to form that culture. The tools described in this section include genres, everyday sense-making, and cultural toolkits.

Genres.   Varelas, Becker, Luster, and Wenzel (2002), in their study of the oral and written work of students in a sixth-grade African American urban science class, used the framework of genres to analyze student learning. Genres, according to Varelas et al., are "staged, goal-oriented social processes" that suggest a "purposeful way of doing things in a culture" and that help students to organize ideas, experiences, and practices in ways that make sense to them (p. 581). In a typical science classroom, there are two categories of genres that frame science learning. There are student genres, which include youth genres, classroom genres, and student science genres. There are also teacher genres, which include their favored classroom genre and their own science genre. According to Varelas et al., genres can be a useful tool because they "may shed light on the fullness, complexity and richness of learning science in urban classrooms" (p. 583).

Genres may be a particularly interesting analytic framework for understanding student learning in urban contexts if we apply them to making sense of pedagogical conflict in the classroom. I see three powerful points emerging from this study. First, genres provide an explanation for why and how students often *resist* learning science. Learning science requires students to incorporate a new way of talking, knowing, and doing into their assimilatory frameworks that they use to make sense of the world. Part of learning is using one's assimilatory framework to make sense of an experience; but an equally important part of learning is allowing the assimilatory framework to be changed by that experience. Second, genres bring into focus the ways in which science learning can be facilitated or constrained by how well values and expectations overlap in the classroom. If student genres do not map onto teacher genres, then conflict may emerge and learning is hindered. Conflicts between genres can result from differences in what is valued by the teacher or the science education community, but also from the student's enculturation into a view of schooling or science that may not reflect reform-based practices. Third, the conflict generated over the meeting of genres can be instructive for both teachers and students. Situating the source of conflict within the realm of how ideas, values, and so forth are assimilated, rather than within an individual and her capabilities, opens up more empowering challenges to teachers and students.

Everyday sense-making.   The next appropriation or assimilatory framework tool is everyday sense-making. Whereas genres focus on "ways of doing things within cultures," everyday sense-making examines how what students, teachers, and science contribute to the learning environment frames the nature of that environment and the interactions that occur there.

The idea of everyday sense-making suggests that there are different cultures that frame what and how students learn science. Students' cultured understandings of science can be used as a tool for enhancing the learning process (Warren, Ballenger, Ogonowski, Rosebery, & Hudicourt-Barnes, 2001). Warren et al. argued that everyday experience and ways of talking/knowing are seen not only as discontinuous with those of science, but also as barriers to robust learning in science learning settings, negatively affecting urban students and students from minority backgrounds in their opportunities to learn science. Drawing upon sense-making, this research group attempted to reverse this trend. Using descriptive case-study analysis, they provided rich examples of students making sense of science by employing accounts of everyday experience as both a context for understanding scientific phenomena and a perspective through which to engage with new dimensions of a given phenomenon, making such accounts analytically generative. For example, Ballenger reported on how some urban learners, as a way of making sense of science, engage in "embodied imagining," where they imagine themselves in the scientific phenomenon they are trying to understand (Ballenger, 1997). Viewing student learning as a process of everyday sense-making, grounded in the cognitive, physical, and cultural dimensions of being, opens up new channels for how learning in classrooms is encouraged and understood.

Cultural toolkits.   Cultural toolkits also fit under appropriation because they offer an analytic lens for understanding how youth draw upon and activate those aspects of their capital in order to appropriate science in ways transformative to them. As Elmesky (2003) wrote, "By understanding the structure of different cultural environments in which students interact and the associated strategies of action within their cultural toolkits, teachers can become better equipped with the skills for helping their students learn science in a manner that will encourage social transformation" (pp. 32–33).

Cultural toolkits offer a unique tool for understanding how youth learn to appropriate science along three different lines of thought: identity, power, and practice. In terms of identity, Seiler (2001), in her critical ethnographic account of student learning in a lunchtime program, demonstrated how students draw upon funds of knowledge that are not necessarily part of the traditional school day to craft a new place in the discourse and community of science. Looking closely at eight African American male high school students, Seiler poignantly showed how cultural and language differences are important markers of personal and group identity and can serve as a valuable form of capital to be drawn upon in learning in the science classroom. Furthermore, what Seiler's article also brings to light is that often students do not realize that the capital to which they have access can serve them well in school and does have connections to science learning. She argued that one important outcome of her study linking resources to science learning is the importance of making sound curricular and pedagogical decisions that help students to recognize the science in their everyday activities.

In terms of power, my own research group has examined how the *activation* of resources from one's toolkit is influenced by how the activation process is understood and taken up by others within the learning setting. For example, in one publication we drew upon case studies of five urban homeless children to make two points relative to power and activation of resources (Calabrese Barton, 1998). First, more important than understanding that differential access to material, human, and social/organizational resources exists in high-poverty learning communities is understanding how "a margin–center" continuum set up by differential access is often construed as a natural rather than a created phenomenon. This continuum often leaves students with access to traditional resources on the margins of school practice. Second, students without traditional resources are institutionally set up to fail, while not having the ways in which they activate their nontraditional resources recognized in their attempts to learn science.

Finally, in terms of practices, Elmesky (2003) looked at how using a cultural toolkits framework can help teachers to re-envision the role of confrontation in science learning, and in particular the practices of what are traditionally referred to as disrespect, acting out, and violence. The author made a persuasive case that confrontational strategies of action, both verbal and physical, exist as part of a toolkit shaped within a structure that demands excellence, respect, and sometimes survival of the fittest, and utilization of such strategies in turn reinforces the structure that exists. She argued that when youth spend the majority of their time within fields structured by ideology, it is not surprising that they unconsciously engage these strategies within the classroom. However, I wonder about the overt focus on what are construed as stereotypical qualities of inner-city youth. On the one hand, this could be an attempt to shatter stereotyping by transforming our understanding of those strategies of action. On the other hand, I wonder why other more socially positive examples were not selected, or if it is necessary that teachers take into account all possible strategies of action available to students.

Implications of and questions for appropriation frameworks. Everyday sense-making strategies, like genres and cultural toolkits, are well-equipped theoretical constructs to offer new ways of understanding science learning in urban classrooms. They reveal to us the diversity of resources that youth draw upon to learn science—especially those resources not traditionally viewed as scientific. They also show us how even the most experienced teachers can struggle with the challenge of knowing what to do with students' ways of sense-making, even when they recognize them and see connections. All of these tools also clue us into some of the less spoken of challenges that teachers face when attempting to implement reform-based science education: conflicts in science class can and do emerge when the ideals of science (i.e., collaboration, shared responsibility) conflict with the ideals of schooling (i.e., individualism) or the ideals of students (individual ownership).

These appropriation or assimilation framework tools raise many questions worthy of further study. For example, to date, none of these research lenses for understanding learning take up the question of how school science and high-stakes testing require students to express certain ways of knowing and of articulating that knowing. In what ways might genres, sense-making, or cultural toolkits foster real integration of student ways of knowing with scientific ways of knowing that still enable the kind of scientific literacy valued in schools to be possible? Finally, these studies all appear to be initial studies. Although rigorous, each study is small in scale. Clearly, more broad-scale studies need to be conducted across different ethnic groups, different urban centers, different kinds of schools, and different ages of students. After all, the science demands of high school students are quite different from those of elementary school students. School science goals in science magnet schools may look different from goals in general comprehensive schools or schools with other foci. Such studies will deepen the complexity of our understanding of the import of genres, sense-making, and cultural toolkits.

Congruence

Congruence, as congruent third space (Moje, Tehani, Carillo, & Marx, 2001), instructional congruence (Lee & Fradd, 1998), and composite culture, is a framework used to describe those pedagogical practices that bridge the worlds of students with the worlds of science and school in ways meant to be empowering and relevant to students. Studies focused on congruence pay close attention to the funds of knowledge that students bring to the classroom and those required to do science well in a school setting. How those funds of knowledge are validated and applied meaningfully in the learning of science is the crux of studies that examine congruence.

Congruent third space.   In describing congruent third space, Moje et al. (2001) examined how, in urban middle school science classrooms, science learning is framed by differences in culture and discursive practices. However, they also showed that more often than not, the discourse of science is privileged over social, everyday discourse even when both are used and valued in the classroom. Moje et al.'s work challenges urban science educators to consider how the process of bridging the worlds of students and science is more complex than simply bringing both into the classroom. Rather, they argued that bridging differences is insufficient to facilitate learning among urban students, and that science learning is facilitated (or constrained) by how well discourses are *integrated*. These dynamic moments of authentic integration, otherwise known as the congruent third space, provide the mediational context and tools necessary for students' social and cognitive development.

Instructional congruence.   Similar to congruent third space is the construct of instructional congruence. Instructional congruence, according to Lee and Fradd (1998), is the process by which teachers build epistemological, cultural, and linguistic bridges between science and students. These authors asserted that instructional congruence is an important way to make science learning fair and just to second-language learners in urban settings, because it expands school science from being about not only knowledge (knowing, doing, and talking) and the habits of mind (values, attitudes), but also the languages (academic discourse, social discourse, and cultural understandings) of the students. Lee and Fradd used several examples from years of mixed-methods research in Miami-area public schools to make this point.

Composite culture.   Composite culture, developed by Hogan and Corey (2001), describes the classroom culture of science that students actually experience. These researchers argued that science learning is a process of enculturation, or of learning to take on the culture and practices of the professional science community as reconstructed by classroom life. They argued that science learning, when viewed as enculturation, can be understood as mediated by the intersections of the experiences that students bring to the classroom, the pedagogical ideals of the teacher, and the teacher's explicit understanding of how to bring together the dimensions of professional science practice and pedagogical ideals.

The researchers made the case that composite culture is a useful construct in urban classrooms, because it sheds light on how teachers and students work to negotiate common understandings of science across what are sometimes vast cultural differences. For example, in their investigation of how low-income, urban fifth-graders engage in the study of ecology, Hogan and Corey (2001) used composite culture to show that students have opportunities to experience the culture of professional science. They also used composite culture to raise questions around the role a teacher's understanding of composite culture can play in her ability to prepare her students to be successful within that culture.

Implications of and questions for congruence.   Congruence suggests that there are different cultures that frame what and how students of science learn. It provides us with a way to understand how and why tensions might arise in the learning of science, such as when there is conflict between the culture of the students and the composite culture of the science classroom.

Although the outcomes of instructional congruence and congruent third space are similar—to facilitate learning among students for whom science poses different discursive and cultural practices—the form and purpose of congruence differ. Whereas *congruent third space* refers to the learning community established when students' discourses are fully integrated into scientific discourses, *instructional congruence* refers to the pedagogical process that serves to bridge the epistemological, cultural, and linguistic practices of students and science. Moje et al.'s (2001) construct of third space creates a new shared space that exists in both the world of the home and the world of the school, where urban educators should strive to be with their students. Lee and Fradd (1998), although they did not argue that their ultimate goal was to bring youth over to the culture of science, also did not make a case for the worlds in between. Furthermore, Moje et al. paid more attention to the role that conflict in discourses might play in mediating the creation of a congruent third space and student learning, whereas Lee and Fradd did not directly address conflict.

Despite these differences, both Moje et al.'s (2001) and Lee and Fradd's (1998) research, along with Hogan and Corey's (2001) research into composite culture, carry political overtones; both articles also suggest that learning in urban classrooms is embedded with power relations that frame who is labeled scientific or capable of learning science. The findings from these studies suggest that it would be important to advance this research, to study what happens when instructional models of congruence are applied in urban schools, and to learn more about how they affect youths' achievements in science as well as their visions of what it means to do science and be a part of the scientific community.

Legitimate Participation

Those studies that I group under *legitimate participation* all make a case for how learning science in urban settings is also about being legitimate participants or valid members of or contributors to a science community. The studies that fit in this category are all grounded in the pedagogical belief that urban learners ought to be afforded formal learning opportunities to participate in authentic science or science-like experiences.

Connected science/project-based learning.   Connected science, a form of project-based learning (PBL), is both an approach to student learning and an analytical construct for understanding the design of leaning environments. As an analytical construct, connected science foregrounds the importance of the funds of knowledge that students bring to class and situates science learning within a community context. As an approach to science teaching, connected science draws upon mutually beneficial partnerships and real-world problems as contextual scaffolds for bridging students' community-based knowledge and school-based knowledge.

Connected science, as a form of project-based learning, is centered around authentic driving questions and activities that matter to students. Teachers who practice connected science, or PBL more generally, create learning environments where students socially construct knowledge based upon readily available resources. Because PBL environments shift the focus of science learning away from such indisputable, "correct" answers to debatable and refinable solutions, they create a dynamic space where power, authority, control, learning, and teaching are shifted between teacher and student (Moje et al., 2001). Although connected science has not been used to show achievement gains, PBL, in general, has been used in urban classrooms (Schnieder, Krajcik, Marx, & Soloway, 2002).

Bouillion and Gomez (2001) qualitatively reported that a connected science approach among fifth-grade urban learners and their study of ecosystems led students to a deeper understanding of ecosystems *and* a more situated understanding of the nature of science (i.e., in reporting on their understandings of ecology, students also reported on how they viewed their relationships with and in science in a connected fashion). Drawing upon connected science as an approach to student learning and an analytical construct for the design of leaning environments presents the science education community with a set of tensions with which to grapple. Finding real-world problems that meet science standards and the cultural context of the school and community raises questions of what can count as connected science. Moreover, how should the science education community constructively confront how power differences between students learning science and businesses frame how experiences and the science learning agenda are prioritized? These questions are worth further investigation.

Multiscience.   Hammond (2001) used the construct of "multiscience" to capture a kind of learning community and a vision of science similar to connected science. In an ethnographic account of a collaboration involving a team of bilingual/multicultural teacher educators, teachers, students, and community members in an urban California elementary school and their efforts to build a Mien-American garden house, Hammond described how students, teachers, and student teachers learn a new kind of science—a multiscience—by garnering a community "fund of knowledge" about the science to be studied in the classroom. Multiscience refers to the incorporation of indigenous science and personal science into Western modern science, which is a foreign culture that must be learned by all students, whether they are indigenous or mainstream. Hammond argued: "All students bring to the science classroom the indigenous science of their own culture's folklore and their own personal world view, derived from their age, gender, sociohistory, and many other factors. In order for Western science to be learned, meaningful reflection upon and dialogue with these cultures of science must occur" (p. 987).

What is particularly interesting about Hammond's (2001) construct of multiscience is its focus on collateral learning. Collateral learning suggests that when learners are confronted with conflict due to the discrepancies between formal scientific knowledge and their own indigenous knowledge, instead of holding the two contradictory systems of knowledge in parallel, conflicts are explored until they are gradually resolved, allowing both systems of knowledge to be transformed. However, although Hammond advanced the claim that students learn "to see science as accessible and relevant to their lives" and to learn to view participation in science as "centered in praxis rather than in learning for its own sake" (p. 988), she did not report on what students actually learned through their participation in the Mien-American garden house experience. Further questions for investigation include how a multiscience approach might allow for collateral learning in the nature of science as well as in a student's understanding of the concepts and processes of science.

Emergent learning experiences.   Rahm (2002) took up the question of learning as participation through her qualitative case-study exploration of emergent learning opportunities in an inner-city youth gardening program. She writes of how work, science, and community can be integrated in a community of practice around gardening in out-of-school science programs. What is important in this study from a learning science perspective is that it demonstrates not only what science youth learn as a result of their participation in the program, but also how learning science was tied to learning about doing science in authentic and applied contexts. She reported that this kind of learning moves beyond motivating students to learn science. It also captures a way of being or participating in a community that has consequences for the individual and for the community. This is a different take on learning science than is seen in other articles, because it focuses on the interrelationship between the individual and the community and the mediating role that science (or doing science) plays. It also focuses on unplanned emergent learning moments that were created by the interaction of the participants with the context. For example, Rahm reported how the participants in her study first and foremost became members of their community of practice (i.e., gardeners for City Farmers). Rahm provided a multitude of other examples that show how student talk around gardening led to several scientific investigations that were not necessarily a formal part of the program. These emergent learning opportunities were one primary reason the students described City Farmers a place where "you get to do the whole package."

Similarly, my colleagues and I (Calabrese Barton, 2001, 2003; Calabrese Barton & Darkside, 2000; Fusco, 2001; Fusco & Calabrese Barton, 2001) have drawn upon critical ethnographic accounts of urban middle and high school students learning science in a community-based science setting—a practicing culture of science learning. In our research youth transformed an abandoned lot into a community garden. Through emergent learning opportunities, we have focused on three kinds of learning. Students develop deep conceptual understandings about content knowledge, such as what plants grow and how they grow, urban pollution, and skills such as mapping, computation, measurement, observation, analysis, and the communication of results. Students also learn about the value-laden and context-embedded nature of science. Third, students learn how to be legitimate participants. In our studies, we reported on how youth underwent cultural shifts in such areas as identity (from shelter youth to caring squad) and in the production of science (from "fake" school projects to real social action).

Both sets of studies reported here, however, took place in out-of-school contexts, providing a kind of freedom in the learning environment not afforded by schools—with differing time constraints, access to materials, and adult-to-student ratios, and the obligatory-voluntary nature of the experiences.

Implications for legitimate participation.   Each of the studies presented here makes a distinction between "doing" science and "talking" science that frames learner's engagement with science. Just as Rahm's (2002) students reported that City Farmers gave them the "whole package," students in the Fusco and Calabrese Barton study (2001) remarked on how doing science made it real. Second, science learning emerged from having purpose and real-world obligation. For example, Bouillion and Gomez (2001) reported that science and science ideas emerged from doing science in the service of community, supported by a context where young people were givers and creators of a plan to improve the community. Third, each of the studies emphasized how emergent opportunities were socially oriented rather than task oriented. For example, in my own research around student's community gardening (Fusco & Calabrese Barton, 2001), students learned about qualities of soil because they wanted to transform a lot into a garden.

The implications for legitimate participation approaches to framing urban science learning are that learning as participation centralizes the embeddedness of the individual in the sociocultural world and the ways in which new knowledge is negotiated and remains situated in context. "Through participation what accumulates is not scientific facts but a way of acting, talking, and becoming a member of a scientific community" (Rahm, 2002, p. 165). Furthermore, although what authentic and meaningful science looks like differs across the articles discussed in this section—from out-of-school gardening programs to in-school project-based science—cutting across each article is an attentiveness to doing as both an epistemological and cultural bridge between the worlds of professional science and student lives. In other words, in each of these studies students learned about the culture of science and learned to appropriate it and transform it into a new culture that was inclusive of other things.

These studies guide us toward fruitful avenues of research. Hammond (2001) acknowledged that the roles of teachers and students will have to change to embrace learning environments supportive of legitimate participation. One important next step might be to explore the implications this has for classroom science. Furthermore, each of the articles presented in this section addressed the fact that the process of embracing legitimate participation changes what students may learn about or in science. One direction for further study would be to explore how such an approach might be made compatible with the instructional goals, time constraints, and logistical concerns of schooling, especially in high-poverty communities. Finally, fundamental to each of the arguments presented in this section is a shift in goals for science education—that doing science is learning science. Further investigation into the ways in which students may have opportunities to metacognitively reflect on this process is important. Also important are investigations into what kinds of authority students or community members ought to have in deciding upon the focus of a project, or in what is worthwhile and related to *their* real world.

Emergent Questions in Understanding and Bridging Difference

Many researchers make the claim that if science were to be represented differently—that if it were built upon the experiences of students—then urban students would connect to it and learn better. The studies in this section, focused on understanding and bridging differences, examine this claim from different angles and compositely suggest that this is a much more complex process than such a statement lets on. Considerations must be taken into account, not only of the funds of knowledge that students or teachers bring to the classroom, but also of how these experiences are integrated with the world of science. Furthermore, although science learning may be about the content of exploration, it is also a process of participating—of learning to do science in a community.

   However, embedded in each of these studies are tensions around culture, community, and science learning. The researchers whose work is presented here are clearly cognizant of the contradictions that emerge when the worlds of home and community are brought together with the worlds of science. What would happen if researchers also used that powerful space of contradiction to push forward our understandings of culture, power, and a just education? Finding these spaces of contradiction and using them in deeply contextual ways may help to deepen our understandings, not only of what teachers know (and need to know) and the spaces they occupy (and need to occupy), but also of what youth know (and need to know) and the spaces they occupy (and need to occupy). Furthermore, understanding the tools for bridging difference would be served by an in-depth set of policy studies that provide analyses, both content-wise and conceptually, of the major reform documents in various national contexts, that drive science for all in urban settings.

What Else Do Students Learn? Success and Participation

The previous section detailed the tools for understanding the differences between urban learners and school science and the role that understanding these differences might play in designing effective learning environments. Yet, embedded in the subtext of many of the research studies reported above is the conclusion that much goes on in a science learning community besides the learning of content. In this section of the chapter, I report on those studies that address urban learners and science from the angle of what other things the students learn as part of their science experience. As the studies outlined below indicate, studies around urban science learning shed insight into *learning to* (a) succeed and resist and (b) participate.

Learning to Succeed: The Normative Practices of Schooling and Resistance

Haberman (1991), in defining the pedagogy of poverty, argued that urban teachers work within tremendous constraints, including large class sizes, inadequate prep time, lower levels of training, inadequate classroom space, and outdated materials. These constraints result in a directive, controlling pedagogy that runs counter to reform-based practices.

A pedagogy of poverty and similar teaching models have been observed in urban classrooms and have contributed to success in science class as based upon rule following and cognitive passivity rather than conceptual learning (Griffard & Wandersee, 1999; Seiler, 2001; Seiler, Tobin, & Sokolic, 2001; Songer, Lee, & Kam, 2002; Tobin, Seiler, & Walls, 1999).

For example, Griffard and Wandersee (1999) shared qualitative case studies of two African American female biology students to make a case for a cycle of "cognitive disengagement." In this study, based primarily on observations and clinical interviews in a math and science public school, attention to behavior over learning and to academic habits over cognitive engagement appeared to be the norm that defined the academic learning environment for students. These practices taught students that success in science was based upon rule following and that academic engagement was not necessary.

Just as students in Griffard and Wandersee's (1999) article learned to be cognitively passive, students in other urban settings act upon these institutional expectations to play a role in reproducing a culture of low expectations. In a series of articles, Tobin and his colleagues (Seiler, Tobin, & Sokolic, 2001, 2003; Tobin et al., 1999) made the case that framing science success through following norms and expectations leads students to resist, which at its heart is an opposition to being controlled. Across a set of three studies, these researchers outline how the "normal practices of schooling" such as tracking, teaching to the test, and curricula geared toward minimal attainment led to a "culture of low expectations" in science for high-poverty urban students. Yet, the same students who were exposed to these low expectations helped to reproduce the culture of low expectations by engaging in multiple forms of resistance, including resistance to high expectations, learning, the teacher, and attendance, even when science instruction was being led by a competent, caring teacher. What we can read from these studies is powerful: that resistance is an active process that students use to make claim to their own space in schools and by which students and teachers negotiate control in schools—control over identity, over what schooling is about, and over relationships and respect.

At issue here is the very notion of control. School agents either knowingly or unknowingly control students by framing their participation, effort, and achievement in narrow cognitive terms. Little attention is paid to how cognitive goals may be deeply rooted socioculturally. In other words, the teachers in Tobin et al.'s (1999) studies embedded learning in a culture of respect, where respect ranges from valuing the interests that students bring to the classroom to utilizing the primary discursive practices of the students. Such differences in the currency of schooling leads students to act differently from what teachers wish from and for them, even when those wishes are well intentioned. These different actions, which often conflict with "desired" actions, are labeled resistant.

My colleagues and I (Calabrese Barton, 1998; Calabrese Barton & Yang, 2000) have drawn upon resistance and its connection to the culture of power in school science. In a case study of one young father, Miguel, we showed how, during his teenage years, he resisted the culture of school science while at the same time, as a self-taught herpetologist and businessman, he sought to create his own subculture of science in his close-knit neighborhood. For Miguel, resisting school science turned out to be both an act of self-preservation and an act of defiance. Both Miguel's peer culture and the culture of school science were restrictive, demanding conformity to a narrow set of norms that failed to connect his interests and talents to the wide range of possibilities offered by our society and economy. Miguel was placed in a position of having to choose one over the other. Yet, unlike his peer culture, schooling did *not* provide a safety net of support if he chose to conform to schooling over peer culture. What is particularly interesting to us in this case study is how science itself could have mediated this difference. As a self-taught herpetologist, an occupation highly respected among his peers, Miguel possessed the interest and capacity for a practice of science that could have bridged these two worlds.

One important issue raised by these studies that ought to be studied further is that resistance has been framed as an individual activity rather than a community action. All of these studies focus on individual students. If we begin to understand resistance as a social phenomenon, then we are offered new options for interpreting what students may be resisting and why. As Moscovici (2002) suggested in a critique of Seiler et al. (2001), what if we viewed student actions through the larger lens of becoming immersed in science rather than as resistance? Individual actions that may come across as behavior challenges or resistance to teacher direction may be a result of students actually aligning with the overarching desires of the teacher—to engage in science meaningfully. A second issue raised specifically by Seiler et al. (2003) is that labeling actions as "resistant" is culturally constrained. In other words, student actions labeled as appropriate are actions that fit neatly into what a teacher or researcher expects to see. Those student actions labeled as resistant are actions that do not fit neatly. Further investigation of how student resistance could facilitate learning could be conducted, as Seiler et al. suggested, by examining what science educators view as resistant through the lens of cultural exchange, rather than as a negative action that detracts.

Learning to Participate

Who can do science and what it means to be a legitimate participant in science is another question that has garnered attention in the focus on student learning in urban science education. In urban science education, those studies that examine what students learn about who can do science concentrate on developing two kinds of claims. First there is the claim that students come to believe in whether they can participate in science based upon their perceptions of what science is and who science is for. Part of this claim is rooted in identity studies, which suggest that learning ought to be thought of as a process of identity formation. Part of this claim is also rooted in broader sociocultural studies, which suggest that one's vision of what science is or who it is for is also grounded in community-supported expectations and practices. Second, there is the claim that science is a social, cultural, and political practice and that if urban youth are to feel they are part of science, then all of these dimensions of science must be integrated into the learning environment. Although few studies in urban science education take up the question of participation, those that do pack powerful and provocative claims.

Brickhouse and Potter's (2001) ethnographic case studies of urban girls revealed that, through the experience of marginalization in the science classroom and even in peer groups, urban girls learn that membership in a school science community is often impossible or undesirable. Using the construct of identity, Brickhouse and Potter showed us how complex the relationship between identity and success in school and in peer groups can be for urban girls. Having a science- or technology-related identity does not mean that one will necessarily succeed in school, if that science-related identity does not also reflect the values of school-mediated engagement, or if students do not have access to the resources they need to do science well. However, successful participation in school science or technology, despite a lack of resources in the home environment, can be better facilitated when students have a science-related identity they can fall back on. Indeed, one of the primary claims made in this study is that students who aspire to scientific competence, yet do not desire to take on aspects of the identities associated with membership in school science communities, face difficulties and even school failure. Brickhouse and Potter's study is important because it raises questions about how to help students retain an identity that is desirable to them in their home communities, yet also allows them to cross the boundaries of race, class, and gender in order to get access to a science culture that too often resides only in more privileged communities.

In our case study of Miguel discussed earlier in the section on resistance (Calabrese Barton & Yang, 2000), we showed how Miguel learned through experiences at home and at school that science was only for "special people" or that scientists were discovered rather than self-made. Miguel expressed a keen interest in science through the Boy Scouts and through his herpetology business, yet Miguel still believed he was not capable of becoming a scientist. He had no science role models in his low-income urban neighborhood who he reported remembering, and his teachers and counselors did not encourage his interest seriously.

Only one study to date makes an explicit examination of how school-based interventions can foster students' learning to develop positive science identities. In her study of standards-based learning among high school African American studies in Philadelphia, Seiler (2001) reported on the impact that a lunchtime science group had on the students' scientific identities. In this study, she revealed how learning science intersects with learning to participate in science. However, she also suggested that learning to participate in science is hampered because the emphasis on the acquisition of certain school-based ways of speaking and interacting in science has devalued African American students' ways of being and has inflicted symbolic violence on them. Seiler's primary finding was that when science learning opportunities reflect the funds of knowledge and the strategies of action that students bring to science, then students will be more willing to appropriate scientific discourse. As a result, she reported that students learn to begin to see themselves as scientific—as individuals who can contribute to and participate in science.

What is interesting about these participation studies is how neatly they overlap each other in terms of their findings. Yet, what could we learn if this question of participation were to be taken up more systemically? Miguel, like the students in Seiler's study, believed that science was not for him. Yet, other studies included in this review that did not focus on participation presented stories of successful participation in science among high-poverty and minority urban youth. What did the students in Rahm's (2002) study of urban gardening or Bouillion and Gomez's (2001) students of urban ecosystems learn about participation in science? Was a scientific identity as important in those learning environments as these studies suggest it to be?

Implications for "What Else" Students Learn

The studies presented in this section show that learning in science class ought to be broadly conceived to cover things other than just content and process skills. Although learning how to identify with science or about what success means are most likely much more subjective components of science education than learning content might be, the studies reviewed here suggest that how or why students achieve in science depends upon these measures. This review also shows us that few studies have been conducted within the subfield of urban science education studies that use this kind of analytic lens. What does it mean to craft a science learning community that favors the positive development of scientific identities among urban youth? What resources are necessary in this environment? How does identity formation relate to learning and to success in school-based science? What role does the teacher, the curriculum, or the school culture play in how or why students as individuals or as members of a community try on new identities or new ways of interacting in the classroom? Does understanding the forms of resistance help to guide us toward new pedagogical approaches to classroom practice? Does rethinking the production of resistant communities actually help to promote student learning in science? The studies presented here open up what has really been uncharted territory in science education worthy of exploration.

CONCLUSIONS

How do urban studies change the landscape of what learning is in urban science education in both its form and its function? Today's educational climate is marked by a propensity for high-stakes exams and outcomes-based learning. The process of learning has become obscured by its product, and little attention has been paid to just how much either context or the multiple purposes of learning matter. In the United States, policies are being written and implemented that exchange a focus on learning standards for a standard process of learning. Although science education has yet to go the way of mathematics or literacy in cities like New York or Los Angeles, where teachers are prescribed page-a-day teaching requiring teachers and students in all classroom to be on the same page of the curriculum on the same day, one could easily imagine science education moving along the same trajectory. These policies have hit urban centers hard, especially those communities within urban centers where poverty rates are high and where schools serve majority minority populations.

Two considerations are crucial. First, despite what we know about learning science in urban settings at the policy level, learning continues to be addressed primarily as a unidirectional process and product with the goal of promoting learning of science content or process. However, as this review suggests, we ought to also be considering how the science education community might reshape learning so that it is viewed as a multidirectional process/product, framed not only by content goals but also by identities, purposes and goals, and context, and why this is particularly important in urban settings. Although the studies presented in this review mark only the beginning of a potentially powerful research trajectory, as a community, science education must be diligent with regard to how these kinds of studies find their way to the policy arena.

Second, although in this review I focused on student learning, it is also important to focus on the learning of others involved in science education—parents, teachers, administrators, and policy makers—and to do so through the same multidirectional lenses utilized by the studies on student learning. Our own research into parental engagement in science education in high-poverty urban schools reveals that parents often activate innovative combinations of traditional and nontraditional resources in their efforts to learn how to engage powerfully in their children's schooling. Like the students in studies presented here, their learning also covers the content of school subjects along with the processes of schooling and how home/community does or should connect with what happens in schools (Calabrese Barton, Drake, Perez, St. Louis, & George, 2004).

Current science reform efforts are largely built upon visions of scientists, science, and the scientific community that may or may not reflect what urban youth and their teachers bring or have access to in the urban classroom. Although the ideas embedded within such policies and their ascribed practices are crucial components to any balanced approach to facilitating scientific literacy among urban students, the articles covered in this review suggest that these ideas alone may not be sufficient in supporting and sustaining meaningful learning in urban science education. Although the purpose of this review is not to answer the question of who should decide the learning agenda, the research findings presented in this review suggest that a vision for science learning must include the day-to-day practice, struggles, and meaning-making of students and their teachers as part of the portrait of learning.

ACKNOWLEDGMENTS

Thanks to Ken Tobin and Maria Varelas for reviewing this chapter.

REFERENCES

Ballenger, C. (1997). Social identities, moral narratives, scientific argumentation: Science talk in a bilingual classroom. *Language and Education, 11*(1), 1–14.

Bouillion, L., & Gomez, L. (2001). Connecting school and community with science learning: Real world problems and school-community partnerships as contextual scaffolds. *Journal of Research in Science Teaching, 38*, 899–917.

Brickhouse, N., & Potter, J. (2001). Young women's scientific identity formation in an urban context. *Journal of Research in Science Teaching, 38*, 965–980.

Calabrese Barton, A. (1998). Margin and center: Intersections of urban, homeless children and a pedagogy of liberation. *Theory into Practice, 37*, 296–305.

Calabrese Barton, A. (2001). Critical ethnography: Science education in urban settings: Seeking new ways of praxis through critical ethnography. *Journal of Research in Science Teaching, 38*, 899–918.

Calabrese Barton, A. (2002). Urban science education studies: A commitment to equity, social justice and a sense of place. *Studies in Science Education, 38*, 1–38.

Calabrese Barton, A. (2003). Kobe's story: Doing science as contested terrain. *Qualitative Studies in Education, 16*, 533–552.

Calabrese Barton, A., & Darkside (2000). Autobiography in science education: Greater objectivity through local knowledge. *Research in Science Education, 30*, 23–42.

Calabrese Barton, A., Drake, C., Perez, G., St. Louis, K., & George, M. (2004). Ecologies of parental engagement in urban education. *Educational Researcher, 33*(4), 3–12.

Calabrese Barton, A., & Yang, K. (2000). The culture of power and science education: Learning from Miguel. *Journal of Research in Science Teaching, 37*, 871–889.

Darling-Hammond, L. (1999). America's future: Educating teachers. *Education Digest, 64*(9), 18–35.

Elmesky, R. (2003). Crossfire on the streets and into the classroom. *Cybernetics and Human Knowing, 10*(2), 29–50.

Fusco, D. (2001). Creating relevant science through urban planning and gardening. *Journal of Research in Science Teaching, 38*, 860–877.

Fusco, D., & Calabrese Barton, A. (2001). Re-presenting student achievement. *Journal of Research in Science Teaching, 38*, 337–354.

Griffard, P., & Wandersee, J. (1999). Challenges to meaningful learning in African-American females at an urban science high school. *International Journal of Science Education, 21*, 611–632.

Haberman, M. (1991). The pedagogy of poverty versus good teaching. *Phi Delta Kappan, 73*, 290–294.

Hammond, L. (2001). Notes from California: An anthropological approach to urban science education for language minority families. *Journal of Research in Science Teaching, 38*, 983–999.

Hewson, P., Kahle, J., Scantlebury, K., & Davies. (2001). Equitable science education in urban middle schools: Do reform efforts make a difference? *Journal of Research in Science Teaching, 38*, 1130–1144.

Hogan, K., & Corey, C. (2001). Viewing classrooms as cultural contexts for fostering scientific literacy. *Anthropology & Education Quarterly, 32*, 214–244.

Ingersoll, R. (1999). The problem of underqualified teachers in American secondary schools. *Educational Researcher, 28*(2), 26–30.

Kahle, J. B. (1998). Equitable systemic reform in science and mathematics. *Journal of Women and Minorities in Science and Engineering, 4*, 91–112.

Kahle, J., Meece, J., & Scantlebury, K. (2000). Urban African-American middle school science students: Does standards-based teaching make a difference? *Journal of Research in Science Teaching, 37*, 1019–1025.

Lee, O., & Fradd, S. H. (1998). Science for all, including students from non-English-language backgrounds. *Educational Researcher, 27*, 12–21.

Moje, E. B., Tehani, C., Carrillo, R., & Marx, R. W. (2001). "Maestro, what is 'quality'?": Language, literacy, and discourse in project-based science. *Journal of Research in Science Teaching, 38*, 469–498.

Moscovici, H. (2003). The way I see it: Resisting teacher control or canceling the effect of science immersion. *Journal of Research in Science Teaching, 40*, 98–101.

Norman, O., Ault, C., Jr., Bentz, B., & Meskimen, L. (2001). The black-white "achievement gap" as a perennial challenge of urban science education: A sociocultural and historical overview with implications for research and practice. *Journal of Research in Science Teaching, 38,* 1101–1114.

Oakes, J. (1990). *Multiplying inequalities: The effects of race, social class, and tracking on opportunities to learn mathematics and science.* Santa Monica, CA: Rand.

Oakes, J., Muir, K., & Joseph, R. (2000, May). *Course taking and achievement: Inequalities that endure and change.* A keynote presentation at the National Institute for Science Education Annual Meeting, Detroit, MI.

Page, R. (1990). Games of chance: The lower-track curriculum in a college-preparatory high school. *Curriculum Inquiry, 20,* 249–264.

Rahm, J. (2002). Emergent learning opportunities in an inner-city youth gardening program. *Journal of Research in Science Teaching, 39,* 164–184.

Roychoudhury, A., & Kahle, J. (1999). Science teaching in the middle grades: Implications for teacher education and systemic reform. *Journal of Teacher Education, 50,* 278–290.

Schneider, R., Krajcik, J., Marx, R. W., & Soloway, E. (2002). Performance of students in project-based science classrooms on a national measure of science achievement. *Journal of Research in Science Teaching, 39,* 410–422.

Seiler, G. (2001). Reversing the standard direction: Science emerging from the lives of African American students. *Journal of Research in Science Teaching, 38,* 1000–1014.

Seiler, G., Tobin, K., & Sokolic, J. (2001). Design, technology, and science: sites for learning, resistance, and social reproduction in urban schools, *Journal of Research in Science Teaching, 38,* 746–768.

Seiler, G., Tobin, K., & Sokolic, J. (2003). Reply: Reconstituting resistance in urban science education. *Journal of Research in Science Teaching, 40,* 101–104.

Snipes, J., Doolittle, F., & Herlihy, C. (2003). *Foundations for success: Case studies of how urban school systems improve student achievement.* Washington, DC: Council of Great City Schools.

Songer, N., Lee, H., & Kam, R. (2002). Technology-rich inquiry science in urban classrooms: What are the barriers to inquiry pedagogy? *Journal of Research in Science Teaching, 39,* 129–143.

Spillane, J., Diamond, J., Walker, L., Halverson, R., & Jita, L. (2001). Urban school leadership for elementary science instruction: identifying and activating resources in an undervalued school subject. *Journal of Research in Science Teaching, 38,* 918–940.

Tobin, K., Seiler, G., & Walls, E. (1999). Reproduction of social class in teaching and learning science in urban high schools. *Research in Science Education, 29,* 171–187.

Varelas, M., Becker, J., Luster, B., & Wenzel, S. (2002). When genres meet: Inquiry into a sixth-grade urban science class. *Journal of Research in Science Teaching, 39,* 579–606.

Warren, B., Ballenger, C., Ogonowski, M., Rosebery, A., & Hudicourt-Barnes, J. (2001). Rethinking diversity in learning science: The logic of everyday languages. *Journal of Research in Science Teaching, 38,* 529–552.

Webster, B. J., & Fisher, D. (2000). Accounting for variation in science and mathematics achievement: A multilevel analysis of Australian Data: TIMSS. *School Effectiveness and School Improvement, 11,* 339–60.

Young, D. (1998). Rural and urban differences in student achievement in science and mathematics. *School Effectiveness and School Improvement, 9,* 386–418.

CHAPTER 13

Rural Science Education

J. Steve Oliver
University of Georgia

A variety of challenges are inherent in bringing together the research literature on rural science education. Perhaps the most significant challenge arises from the recognition that rural science education is not easily defined, and that it is not always easy to discern what is and what is not research on rural science education. In the same way, it has not been possible to create a useful and generalizable characterization of what is a rural school or even a rural place. Characterizations abound; finding agreement among these characterizations presents a problem. This enigmatic quality of ruralness is reflected in the way that popular writers and scholars describe not only schools, but also rural people and the places they inhabit.

Sher (1983) has written that rural schools have recognizable tendencies, such as less specialization, less equipment, and less bureaucracy than schools in non-rural sites. He has found that rural schools tend to exhibit a tendency toward teaching the basics and more reliance on the unique qualities of individual teachers, and are "more familial and relaxed in their operating style" (p. 257). These characteristics suggest that this chapter should begin with a personal story.

My earliest memories are of events on a farm in the southern Appalachian Mountains of the United States that had not seen the arrival of petroleum-powered farm equipment. That equipment had not arrived because the land was too steep, and perhaps because high-cost investment did not fit with a subsistence farming mindset. The type of farming I observed as a child has been labeled Upland Southern Mixed farming (Jordan-Bychkov, 2003) or, more simply, hill farming: "Hill farming evolved into a post-pioneer stability, becoming somewhat more market-oriented in the process. In time, it degenerated into rural poverty . . . allowing mining, logging, welfare, and tourism to play larger and destructive roles. Eventually the farming system disappeared from the countryside, perhaps about 1950 or 1960, but many vestiges remain" (p. 45).

The idyllic vision of this rural hill-farming culture persists, but the public school reality is the one of extensive poverty that Jordan-Bychkov suggested. In 1975, only 20% of America's rural population either lived or worked on farms (Sher, 1977).

Thirty years later, the percentage is smaller still. Like a few people born in the 1950s, I witnessed the end of the era when the fields were worked with only the power from the muscles of horses and people. But I knew that I was in a rural area (though people preferred to call it "the country") because things like milk cans, horse-drawn mowing machines, and wood-fired cook stoves were still used to accomplish the tasks of daily life, not as items to hold flower arrangements or umbrellas. For many, the distinction between rural and urban has been based in the availability and impact of science and technology.

The main character in Terry Kay's 1976 novel, *The Year the Light Came On*, growing up outside of Royston, Georgia, in the years just before World War II, also came to understand the distinction between rural and not. He reasoned that the world was divided between the haves and have-nots, based on access to electricity in the home. The Rural Electrification Act would be the vehicle to bring prosperity to all. Again the distinction between rural and non-rural was a correlate of the absence or presence of science and technology.

This distinction persists in some ways for rural schools today. Accounts like the one by Celis (2002), which documented a community's struggle with the conduct of a one-roomed school in Colorado, depict a variety of ways in which ruralness equates to an absence of technology. They depict rural places as pastoral, happy, and pretty, although life there is composed mostly of hard work. Celis's description of a walk from the school grounds into the mountains mirrors the myth of rural schooling from long ago where students living in isolated places walked long distances through difficult weather to arrive at school. Today that myth has many points of identification. On the negative side, it is imagined that the rural school offers the students a deficit education due to issues such as lack of science activities (Stine, 1997) and lack of a consistent curriculum (Amaral & Garrison, 2001). For the teacher, this deficit model of ruralness includes geographic isolation (Amaral & Garrison) and high teacher turnover (Barrow & Burchett, 2000).

Thus the rural school can to some degree be recognized when we are there, but the ability to provide a generalized demographic description of a rural school has grown increasingly problematic with each passing year. Many demographic definitions have been presented over the past 25 years (University of the State of New York, 1992). The U.S. Census Bureau defined rural as "a residential category of places outside urbanized areas in open country, or in communities with less than 2,500 inhabitants, or where the population density is less than 1,000 inhabitants per square mile" (Stern, 1994, cited in Horn, 1995).

One key factor that is often missing from the definitions of *rural* is the idea of isolation (Sampson-Cordle, 2001). For the schooling and living of a place to be reflective of its ruralness, it must be isolated to some degree from those areas of the world that are not rural. In the United States this rarely occurs today. Mass media, the World Wide Web, and other inlets pour in culture to essentially all sites. The availability of technology is rarely a reflection of geography. Isolation must be largely self-imposed for it to have this impact. Crockett's (1999) study of science education in an Amish Mennonite community in South Carolina illustrated the point. This fellowship-based community lives without television, radio, or computers in the home and school in order to maintain its religious beliefs. Yet at the same time, its members use technologies, including computers, that aid their business endeavors.

On the farms, there was widespread use of artificial insemination of cattle. Somehow, using technology in business is not seen as a cultural spigot.

Another factor that may characterize rural children is using education to find a new life beyond the community and home in which they were reared. This contrasts with the description by Tobin and Carumbo (2002) of an inner-city student. They discussed how the obstacles of the inner city frequently present too great a barrier for a child to "crash through":

> If Amirah were to follow this trend and crash she would add to the great divides of US schooling, urban/suburban, Black/White, and female/male. Urban, Black, female, the triple threats, must crash through the oppressive structures that characterize urban high schools to reap the promise of social transformation through science education. (p. 22)

If these are the great divides of US schooling, where does the rural school fit? Schools, whether found in the most crowded inner city or the most sparsely settled rural area, have made promises of social transformation. Whereas social transformation can be enacted within short distances of the inner city neighborhood (e.g., a new home in another neighborhood), they typically lie at great distance from the isolated rural home. Thus, the oppressive structures through which the rural child must crash are largely characterized by the fact that accomplishment equates to leaving that physical site a great distance behind. The rural child may also be a member of a minority racial group or be from a family living in poverty, but since he is not seen as one of many who have to overcome the problems of the urban setting, the problems the rural child faces seem more vague, though perhaps more manageable.

In a developing country, however, this may not be true at all. Developing countries have unique issues with regard to the problem of discerning a role for science education in their populations and in their schools. The degree to which those issues mirror the U.S. rural science education is likely a function of the similarities between industrialization and transportation. To see parallels, a look back in history of U.S. schools might be instructive.

Ghose (1982) examined out-of-school science and technology education as a means of achieving rural development in Southeast Asia. His study originated from the finding that the education provided to school children was found lacking. Ghose described the situation in this way: "Formal education was found inadequate to meet the challenge of national development in general and rural development in particular" (p. 19). These inadequacies were summed up in four points: (a) the curriculum is unsuited to agriculture, though agriculture is the primary means of making a living; (b) the curriculum tends to be "bookish in nature" and thus tends to alienate young students; (c) formal schooling tends to be inefficient in areas with high drop-out rates among students; and (d) limited economic resources do not allow formal education to be spread to everyone.

Informal science education has filled the gap in some places. Science clubs and science camps served a rural development role in some areas of Malaysia, according to Ghose (1982). They were a very important complement to formal education throughout Asia but challenging to start in rural areas. In the Philippines, science clubs played an additional community service function. Through these clubs, students conducted "analysis and resolution of community problems through out-of-school science education laboratories" (p. 22). Such clubs were also active in India.

Ghose also reported that science fairs played a community service role with the examination of realistic and relevant problems. Agriculture extension was also a force for science education and thus for "modernization" and rural development.

I hope that that this chapter illustrates how the rural science education issues in developing nations identified by Ghose (1982) in the 1980s mirror the story of rural education in the United States. This mirroring happens in two ways. First, there is the idea that science education in rural areas can have a much stronger connection to the community in which the schooling takes place. Nachtigal (1995) suggested that science projects based in the community context of the rural United States can make a significant impact on environmental and business issues of rural locations. Ghose found this to also be the case in the Philippines. Second, the history of rural science education in the United States has shown that, in the early part of the twentieth century, when electricity, good roads, and modern modes of transportation were not widely available in rural locations, students seemed primarily interested in science related to local vocations and phenomena, just as suggested by Ghose for Southeast Asia.

In many ways, this chapter is an update to the volume edited by Otto (1995), *Science Education in the Rural United States*. That volume covered a wide range of issues facing rural science education, including "[the] status of rural education, research implications, the integration of science within the science disciplines, integration with mathematics and technology, STS, distance learning, sequence which led from the definition and philosophy of rural science education, to the political implications, Native Americans, and other cultures in rural science education" (Otto, p. ix).

This volume also posed intriguing questions about the future of rural science education. The question of greatest significance seemed to be: Does the rural school offer the student a deficit education with regard to science learning? The authors of the Otto (1995) volume seemed to be in agreement that it did not. Individual papers within the volume identified areas of need such as accessing distance learning technologies, integrating curriculum across the school subjects, recognizing the role of place and context of schooling, and attending to the needs of rural science students who are members of minority ethnic and racial groups. The research compiled by Otto began to shed light on these issues, but the need remains for more attention to be focused on rural science education.

OVERVIEW OF THE CHAPTER

This description of science education research in rural schools begins with an examination of historical studies of rural science education. As a guide to the selection of these studies, I have drawn from the digests prepared by Francis Curtis and others (Boenig, 1969; Curtis, 1926/1971a, 1931/1971b, 1939/1971c; Lawlor, 1970; Swift, 1969), as well as other historical sources.

After the historical studies, the chapter moves on to an examination of studies that were conducted around the United States in the 1980s and 1990s to determine and to describe the condition of rural science teaching. In some cases, these studies contrasted rural teachers with other teachers and in other cases they did not. I emphasize in particular one study that examined the conditions of rural classrooms in eight states.

From there, I turn to the issue of what is and what is not rural research in the present-day science education literature. There have been a great many studies that use *rural* as a title word or descriptor and then simply describe the physical appearance of the school's setting. Representative examples are used to distinguish these studies from those that can more validly be described as studies of rural science education.

Following this, the chapter examines the studies that to date have been documented in the examination of the National Science Foundation (NSF)-funded Rural Systemic Initiative projects around the United States. Although these reports are not by and large published in refereed journals, they do offer insight into the present-day rural school. This is true in part because of the restrictive nature of the definition used for qualifying for inclusion in the Rural Systemic Initiative program.

The next section examines current published research that contrasts the distinctions between rural and other schools with regard to the science taught. Though few in number, these studies do make a provocative statement for understanding what a rural school is and is not in terms of student characteristics.

Science teacher education for rural schools is the theme of the next section. Though limited in scope because of a lack of published examples, this section examines both preservice and inservice science teacher education.

Finally, a summary and suggestions for future research conclude this chapter. In each section described above, I have attempted to include the research from international sources on rural science education, as well as research done in the United States. The future of rural science education research is not as obvious as it might have been in the last decades of the twentieth century. I end by considering the factors that may shape this indefinite future.

HISTORICAL STUDIES

Francis Curtis, and those who continued his work (Boenig, 1969; Curtis, 1926/1971a, 1931/1971b, 1939/1971c; Lawlor, 1970; Swift, 1969), published a series of digests to examine research in science education during the first 57 years of the twentieth century. The studies they chose for inclusion were printed as abridged versions of the original research articles in order to maximize the number included. These abridged reports emphasized findings over motivations and rationale.

Curtis (1926/1971a) described the groups to whom the digests would be of value. His description of the first group, when transferred to the science education researchers of today, was an apt description for those who will read this current handbook: "All workers in educational research, particularly in the field of the teaching of science, who need to have readily available a list of important problems in educational research together with a description of the techniques used in their solution" (p. xiii).

The relative infrequency of manuscripts in the Curtis *Digests* that dealt with rural science education was a result of a variety of factors. First, Curtis (1926/1971a) asked the National Association for Research in Science Teaching (NARST) membership to supply recommendations of articles for inclusion in the digests. He then asked that same membership to evaluate each article's value for inclusion in those volumes. Research design was an important factor in the evaluation by the NARST membership. My own experience as editor of a historical column in the journal, *School Science and Mathematics*, suggests that rigorously designed research on rural science education was quite rare. Second, there was probably not a great deal of research of any kind done on rural schools in the pre–World War II era simply because of problems with access, sample size, and efficiency.

An examination of the first digest compiled by Curtis (1926/1971a) revealed essentially no mention of rural schools. The word *rural* was contained in the title of only one article, and that article dealt with students' knowledge of agriculture. Many of the researchers stated that their data was purposely collected from high schools in cities. Curtis himself did not elaborate further.

Although not specifically identified as a study of rural schools, one study (Davis, 1923/1926) that was included by Curtis (1926/1971a) dealt with the effect of class size and its relationship to "teaching efficiency." Teaching efficiency was defined in terms of the proportion of the different grades (A, B, C, etc.) given in courses across classes of different size. This study (Davis) was conducted in schools from "very small to very large" during the 1921–22 academic year. The results were somewhat ambiguous, because although more students in small classes scored A's and B's, the author concluded that, "considering only the percentages of low marks, the best size class for science is large" (Davis, p. 94). About all we can conclude from this study is that class size and school size were on the minds of some researchers. The representation of rural science studies in the first digest indicated it was not on the minds of many.

In the second digest of science education research assembled by Curtis in 1931/1971b, an abridged version of an extensive study by Palmer (1926/1931) was included. In this work, Palmer asked teachers, beginning in 1921, to "send in the nature-study questions which had been asked by their pupils" (p. 36). In the five years that followed, the rural New York teachers who participated in the Cornell Nature Study program sent in over 7,000 questions. The most numerous categories of questions, representing over 30% of the total, related to the "habits of plants and animals." When broken down over grade level, this category of question was always the most prevalent. It seemed clear that the rural school students of that day were interested in things they encountered in their daily life.

It was often the case that research from earlier times served as a mirror for later works. For instance, the needs assessments of the 1980s and 1990s are very much in keeping with an early study reported in the *Journal of Chemical Education*, and included in the second digest, that dealt with the teaching of chemistry and other sciences in South Dakota. Written by Jensen and Glenn (1929/1931), the study reported the results of research that had used both quantitative and qualitative research methods. In the words of the authors, these were called, respectively, "statistical studies" and "visitational studies." They (1929/1931) reported:

> . . . some of the outstanding needs of small high schools are (a) a reasonable science program with a definite science sequence adapted to the needs of a given community, [and] (b) an alternation of the science subjects offered in the first and second years of high school and those offered in the third and fourth years in order to reduce the teaching load of the instructors and thus provide more time to prepare daily lessons adequately for the subjects taught. (pp. 330–331)

Also high on this list of needs was "a state law making it impossible for a Board of Education to employ a teacher to give instruction in a subject in which he is not adequately prepared" (p. 331). As with many issues in the history of science education, this has again come full circle with the creation of the U.S. presidential mandate encapsulated in the No Child Left Behind Act (U.S. Department of Education, 2002).

Curtis (1927/1931) conducted a survey of the "scientific interests of pupils enrolled in the ninth grade in small high schools and of adults living in small towns and in the country" (p. 341). Returns were received from 32 Michigan high schools in towns with a median population of 309. A sample of the responses contained an interesting expression of rural and small-town science interests. Physical science, rather than biological science, was found to "predominate," even though all of the students in the study were studying biology. Small-town and rural girls were found to have "somewhat greater" scientific interests than boys, just as "the range of the scientific interests of these country women is slightly greater than that of these country men" (p. 344). Perhaps the greatest distinction between rural and not was summed up in the finding that the issues of greatest interest to the rural dwellers were those of a "technical" nature. For instance, Curtis found that "a comparison of questions submitted in both studies, shows, moreover, that the rural dwellers ask many technical questions bearing upon horticulture or agriculture—i.e. related to their vocational life—while the city dwellers ask technical questions relatively unrelated to their vocational life" (p. 344).

Research in this vein continued into the 1930s as well. Wolford (1935/1939) conducted a study of persons living in the southern Appalachian Mountains of the United States to determine the appropriate curriculum for an eighth-grade science course. He found that, whereas city schools typically provided teachers with a description of the course of study, "teachers in small town and rural high schools must either make their own . . . or lean heavily on the adopted textbooks. They usually do the latter" (p. 49). Wolford presented findings related to parental occupations, the students' planned occupation, and reading interests. The great majority of occupational interests expressed by parents and children related to activities such as "farming, homemaking, and health, industrial, and mechanical problems peculiar to the region" (p. 50). The readings mirrored this interest in local issues.

In a study of "the teaching of biology in the secondary schools of the United States" originally published in the 1940s, Riddle, Fitzpatrick, Glass, Gruenberg, Miller, and Sinnott (1942/1969) attempted to examine all aspects of the teaching of biology. They mailed 16,000 copies of a "rather elaborate questionnaire" to teachers across the United States. However, they cautioned that rural schools and schools of the South were not adequately represented. Apparently the means to find addresses for rural science teachers was simply not adequate, even though 34.7% of replies to the survey were returned from rural science teachers. Given these deficiencies, two results stand out. First, rural teachers reported having "good school buildings" in only 62% of cases, whereas cities reported "good school buildings" in 79% of cases. Second, rural schools reported an average of 36 books on biology available to their students, whereas city schools "reported an average of 150 books of a biological nature" (p. 184).

Johnson (1950/1969) conducted a national study of science teaching in U.S. public high schools in 1947–48. He drew a stratified random sample of the 23,947 high schools with 10 or more students. He found that chemistry was typically not offered in very small schools, but that in high schools with enrollments of fewer than 100 students that did offer chemistry, approximately 25% of the 11th-graders were enrolled. In contrast, physics was much more commonly offered and enrolled about one-third of 12th-graders.

In the late 1960s, a study was conducted to examine the "differences among urban, suburban, and rural children's particular interests in science" (Clarke, 1972) as part of a larger study to examine a variety of factors that influenced elementary school science learning across Massachusetts. Clarke offered a single vague finding regarding the rural and non-rural distinction: "a significant commonality of interests exists regardless of whether the children live in urban, suburban, or rural communities" (p. 135).

Studies of science in rural schools during the first two-thirds of the twentieth century were aimed at creating understanding of a few main issues. Curricular relevance and the nature of science were frequently topics of interest. But the physical isolation of many rural schools, coupled with their small size, tended to remove them from consideration as potential research sites.

The vision of rural as pastoral and happy, yet full of hard work, was alive and well during the first half of the twentieth century. Perhaps this was the time when the daily reality of rural schooling was in the process of becoming the myth. Clearly the negative aspects of the myth—the deficit model of rural education, including the need to alternatively teach portions of the curriculum to reduce teacher work loads, the belief that rural children were interested primarily in the objects of their daily life, and the comparatively poorer quality of buildings—were to varying degrees supported by research. Although there was little research on science education in rural schools during the 1960s and 1970s, in time interest would grow.

RENEWED INTEREST IN RESEARCH ON RURAL SCIENCE EDUCATION: THE 1980S AND 1990S

Horn (1995) noted that rural education in general "enjoyed a new and more positive recognition" beginning in the mid-1970s. Before this time "literally no one in the federal government would claim responsibility for rural education" (Horn, p. 13). Recognition of the need to examine the teaching and learning in rural schools came from a variety of sources beginning in the 1980s. In 1983, U.S. Secretary of Education Bell announced the first policy on rural education (Horn). The policy was labeled the Rural Education and Rural Family Education Policy for the 1980's and was intended to ensure equal access to funds and services provided by the U.S. Department of Education (USDOE). Horn reported that this policy was announced at the annual meeting of the National Rural Education Association and simultaneously focused attention on both the organization and the problems of rural communities as seen through the eyes of educators.

Although it is not clear whether it occurred as a result of the announcement of the national policy from the USDOE, there was a complementary surge of interest and published studies on rural schools among science educators. The research that produced these reports began in the mid to late 1980s and persisted into the mid-1990s, though perhaps not much beyond. This resurgence led to the formation of a group known as the National Committee for the Study of Options for Rural Science Education (Prather & Oliver, 1991). Much of the research conducted during this resurgence came from needs assessments to determine the status of rural science education.

The largest needs assessment study was conducted by Baird, Prather, Finson, and Oliver (1994), who used a 100-item instrument developed by Zurub and Rubba (1983) and administered to 1,258 teachers in eight states. Nearly half of these teachers indicated their school as being "rural." Thus Baird et al. were able to conduct a comparison between rural and non-rural teachers. Additional needs assessments were conducted by Enochs, Oliver, and Wright (1990) in Kansas; by Carlsen and Monk (1992) in New York; and by Barrow and Burchett (2000) in Missouri. Although Carlsen and Monk (1992) found that rural teachers have less experience than urban or suburban peers, have fewer undergraduate science courses, have fewer teaching methods courses, are less likely to have a graduate degree, and are more like to teach non-science courses, the teachers in the Baird et al. study (and to a lesser degree in the Enochs et al. study) indicated remarkably similar needs across their school size and location. The top four needs identified by rural and non-rural teachers were the same and were ranked in the same order. These needs were (a) motivating students to want to learn science; (b) identifying sources of free and inexpensive materials; (c) using computers to deliver science instruction; and (d) using hands-on science teaching methods. Within the four highest ranked items, the only dissimilarity came from the higher absolute value of the need for using "computers to deliver science instruction." Science teachers in rural areas rated this need several percentage points above non-rural counterparts. As might be expected from the historical research on rural schools reported within this chapter, updating "knowledge/skills in environmental sciences" was the first item to break the parallel order between rural and non-rural teachers, taking a higher position for the rural teachers.

On the low end of the need scales were items related to issues of planning and implementing instruction. Both rural and non-rural science teachers gave low ratings to these issues. A few items across the spectrum of topics surveyed did show wide disparities between rural and non-rural science teachers. "Learning more about multicultural science education" had the greatest disparity, with 57.4% of non-rural teachers rating this as a moderate to great need, versus 46.1% of rural teachers. This was closely followed by percentages found for "maintaining student discipline." In this item, 37.7% of rural teachers rated this as a moderate to great need as compared with 47.7% of non-rural teachers.

In like manner, when identifying the frequent or serious problems in the teaching of science, rural and non-rural teachers agreed on several issues. These included insufficient student problem-solving skills, insufficient funds for equipment and supplies, inadequate laboratory facilities, and poor reading ability. Each of these was rated as a frequent or serious problem by 50–70% of each group of teachers. But several problems produced distinct response rates. Lack of science career role models and too many class preparations per day were seen as much more serious problems by rural science teachers. In contrast, large class size and lack of student interest in science were seen as more serious problems for the non-rural teachers.

Baird et al. (1994), by allowing science teachers to classify themselves as rural or not, gave wide latitude to the constitution of rural schools. This wide latitude mirrors the difficultly of creating a definition of rural schools. The variety of schools included furthers the consequential difficulty of focusing the study of rural science education. Many schools look like rural schools because they are situated in rural places or in proximity to agricultural lands and woodland expanses. But as shown in a variety of studies (e.g., Gilbert & Yerrick, 2001), these rural schools sometimes have student populations bussed from city locations who live in communities much more appropriately characterized as urban. At the same time, some validity to this system of classification is offered by the ways in which teachers rate their problems in the self-identified rural versus non-rural schools. Correspondence was found when teachers who reported their schools to be rural also identified less need for professional development related to classroom management. Likewise, validation of this self-identification of ruralness was established when those teachers also reported a greater need for professional development dealing with computers in the classroom.

WHAT IS RURAL IN A CONTEMPORARY SENSE?

One of the major problems for science educators attempting to review the research on rural education is the definition of what is and what is not rural. In many respects, this is largely an intractable problem. Rural schools frequently have physical characteristics that will be recognized when seen, but do not easily lend themselves to description. Horn (1995) saw it in this way: "The simple fact is that rural people, rural communities, and rural conditions are so diverse that one can find evidence to support nearly any characterization" (p. 3). Thus distance from a city, population density, apparent isolation, availability of resources, homogeneity of population, and similar characteristics are all considered important in some places but not in others. To complicate this factor even further, consider the following examples of research that dealt with self-described rural situations.

In the first example, Bradford and Dana (1996) titled their article "Exploring Science Teacher Metaphorical Thinking: A Case Study of a High School Science Teacher." *Rural* was not mentioned in the title but was a school descriptor applied by the authors. In the section of the manuscript regarding the participant, the school was described as being in a "rural school district in an economically disadvantaged part of a mid-Atlantic state" (p. 199). The reader learned no more about the school or the district than that single statement. It is difficult to classify this as rural research, although I do not intend this to be a negative reflection on the quality of the research.

Consider a second example. Gilbert and Yerrick (2001) titled their article "Same School, Separate Worlds: A Sociocultural Study of Identify, Resistance, and Negotiation in a Rural, Lower Track Science Classroom." This was an excellent study of how learners manipulate the classroom environment in order to "lessen the teacher's demands" for accomplishment and achievement and maneuver the teacher to accept work that was only marginal with regard to the original teacher-stated goals. Yet was this research rural? The researchers posed research questions that have the idea of "rural" at their core. For instance, their first question was: "What are key components of lower track science classroom discourse specific to rural contexts?" But the characterization of the school's ruralness seemed to disappear in the ultimate discussion of findings. Identified by the pseudonym Ridgemont High School, this school was defined as rural by its location, 10 miles from a city of 50,000. This was the only criterion for its ruralness. The article stated that the black students come from within the city limits to the rural site to "rebalance" the racial mixture of the district's schools. A central issue from the findings of the research was encapsulated in a single statement: "Instead of sharing a common discourse, lower track students and their teachers maintain separate discourses that are carved in response to and in opposition to the world view of the other" (p. 594). Did these discourse issues arise from the physically rural location of the school and its contrasts to the "in town" and "in the neighborhood" experience of the students? Quite likely the reader will be forced answer both yes and no. But the discourse issue was not really a rural school issue per se as much as an indication of a difficult mixing of socioeconomic class and racial and ethnic groups.

An older article raised a slightly different issue with regard to identifying rural science education research. Brown, Fournier, and Moyer (1977) titled their article "A Cross-Cultural Study of Piagetian Concrete Reasoning and Science Concepts among Rural Fifth-Grade Mexican- and Anglo-American Students." The authors' primary motivation came from the lack of research done with Mexican-American children at that time. They chose the rural school for this study out of convenience, as this school was willing to allow the needed testing. The children of Mexican-American heritage scored lower on both tests given, but the authors did not relate this to their ruralness. We were left to assume that rural schools of the U.S. West were simply where Mexican-American children were found.

Finally, a fourth study, which presented a picture of a rural community and ethnography of science education within this community, made an important point about rural science education research. In an article titled "Classroom and Community Influences on Youth's Perceptions of Science in a Rural County School System," Charron (1991) set the stage by writing, "Rural communities, like their urban counterparts, are composed of individuals with diverse backgrounds and points of view" (p. 671). These characteristics of individuals over long periods of time created "local universal understandings." These understandings in turn created community perspectives on schooling and the value of learning; Charron attempted to capture how these understandings "influence children's ideas about science." Within the study of this rural community, it is impossible to discern how the findings might contrast to a non-rural setting; nor was this the author's goal. We are not able to say in fact that the findings were uniquely rural, but rather were an ethnographic characterization of this particular community.

When two local parents were interviewed about the value of science, neither mother could name a single instance where she had made use of science knowledge in her daily life. Likewise, when the learners within this district's schools reported their perceptions of science, characteristics emerged that are common among students from a wide range of locations and school settings. The students perceived that a description of science equated to a "laundry" list of topics, that science was a body of facts rather than a process of discovery, and that the activity of science led to the resolution of one correct answer that all scientists can agree upon. But in one statement there was a recognizable link to historical and contemporary findings from rural schools. Charron (1991) reported that "many students seem to focus almost exclusively on natural history content when discussing science out of class" (p. 684).

Charron (1991) reported that the community, although close to a university community, "maintained a large measure of commercial and cultural separateness" (p. 673). This statement suggested agreement with the condition suggested by Shroyer and Enochs (1987) that the rural schools lie outside the "sphere of influence" of the city. Charron's conclusion that "educators need to first identify community influences, and then build upon them" marks another point of convergence with this story of research in rural schools.

In the examples above, research was conducted and defined as rural, though it is not clear that each study would meet a test of ruralness based on demographic characteristics or governmental definitions. In each case, to the degree it was knowable from the publication, the school and community did not completely meet a set of criteria, including physical isolation, and size needed for identification as rural. In most of these examples, important contributions to the research literature of science education have been accomplished. But are they rural? To answer this question we are left in the position of the teachers in the Baird et al. (1994) study, mentioned earlier, where classification as to ruralness was allowed entirely by self-report. In that case, the researchers found reasons to believe their approach to classification as rural was valid; perhaps we must allow other researchers the same freedom even when we cannot match their classification scheme to any rational typology that used quantifiable statistics or data.

Perhaps statistics and data are the real issue. As has been shown in a great deal of research across the discipline of science education over the past 20 years, qualitative assessments of science education can sometimes supersede quantitative methods for their value of description and communication of understanding. And thus qualitative methods and especially ethnographic explication may signal an end to the long search for a definition of rural education that may no longer exist.

THE RURAL SYSTEMIC INITIATIVE REFORM IN RURAL SCIENCE EDUCATION

The Rural Systemic Initiatives in Science, Mathematics, and Technology Education Program (RSI) were the third in a set of systemic reform initiatives to be created by the U.S. NSF (Russon, Paule, & Horn, 2001). Offered on a competitive basis to governmental, educational, and foundation-based groups, these grants were funded to "enhance mathematics, science, and technology education in economically disadvantaged rural areas through community development activities and instructional and policy reform" (p. 1). Thus the RSI reform was aimed at schools that were the educational institutions for concentrations of rural poor (i.e., counties with at least 30% of the school-age population living in poverty as designated by the U.S. Bureau of the Census; Horn, 2001). As such, the RSI program provided directives to its grant recipients that pointed their efforts toward "policy, leadership, and work force issues by involving communities in creating a comprehensive and sustainable system of mathematics, science and technology education that reflects current advancements in the area" (p. 1).

"Systemic reform" was a descriptive term developed by the NSF to describe an innovation in funded projects from that agency. Bruckerhoff (1998) reported that "systemic reform is the 'third wave' in contemporary educational reform" (p. 4) in the United States. Launched as a way to accomplish the government's Goals 2000 objectives, systemic reform was a product of the first Bush presidency and was created to "emphasize the federal government's leadership role in systemic educational reform" (Bruckerhoff, p. 4). The idea of systemic reform was centered on the concept of reforming education comprehensively across a system. And though "system" was defined across a range (e.g., the schools of a district, city, state, or rural region might be considered a system), changing the system was believed to be key to profound and fundamental reform. In practice, the RSI program was one component of a much larger systemic effort that included local systemic initiatives, urban systemic initiatives, and statewide systemic initiatives.

At the heart of the systemic educational reform movement was a set of essential educational elements formulated to describe the range of goals around which the participating educational systems would attempt to change. Operationalized as the "drivers" of systemic reform, and tailored to the rural educational systems involved, these six principles became the force behind the implementation and evaluation of the RSI projects. And yet, these drivers did not always represent what rural educators as well as rural residents thought of as ideal educational goals. In the words of Russon et al. (2001), "the values and beliefs of some rural residents run contrary to the tenets and assumptions of systemic reform" (p. 8). Part of this rift was based in the assumptions of the degree to which the federal government should have any impact whatsoever in rural schools. As Fenstermacher (2002) has pointed out, the federal government must, if we are to have a liberal democratic government, maintain a minimal interest in education. In the United States, the state's role in education is "deeply embodied in American history and heritage" (p. 22).

The six drivers of rural systemic reform cross the spectrum of educational provenance. These drivers were intended to be guideposts or standards about which the progress of systemic reform could be measured. Driver 1 was created to focus efforts on the implementation of standards-based curricula. Included was a companion notion that the assessment of student learning would occur across every classroom, laboratory, or other learning venue. Driver 2 focused reform efforts on the development of consistent sets of policies aimed at accomplishing high-quality science education. These polices included the need for excellent science teacher education, professional development, and administrative support toward the goal of improving achievement of all students. Driver 3 complemented Driver 2 by providing direction to the convergence of all resources, regardless of their source, and the ongoing monitoring of progress in the implementation of reform ideas. The fourth driver sought to provide a directive through which all stake-holders were brought into a single effort. Parents, policy makers, businesses, foundations, and others directed their efforts in consistent support of the systemic reform. Driver 5 was a statement regarding the need to accumulate a body of evidence, both broad and deep, so as to ensure that the program enhanced student achievement. Finally, Driver 6 spoke to the improvement of achievement of all students, including those historically underserved.

In order to create a tool for measuring how the various rural systemic projects were accomplishing the drivers, Horn and his colleagues (Russon & Horn, 1999) at Western Michigan's Evaluation Center created a list of 123 indicators. These indicators were drawn from the research literature of three areas: systemic reform, evaluation of systemic reform, and rural education literature. The indicators were then subjected to a matching process through which they were aligned with one of the six drivers. Using a two-round Delphi technique, for which the Research Advisory

Team for the RSI Evaluation project served as judges, there was ultimately an 80% agreement regarding 75 indicators from the original list with regard to their driver match.

This list of indicators was then used as the basis for both the quantitative and qualitative evaluations of the RSI projects. When used quantitatively, the indicators presented a picture of the factors that school stakeholders found most important in the accomplishment of rural systemic reform. Indicators related to Driver 1 (implementation of a standards-based curricula) tended to be rated highly by all respondents (mean = 4.06 on a 5-point scale). Interestingly, the lowest ratings for the importance of this driver came from the stakeholders of the schools of a Native American community. Those respondents in Gila River, Arizona, rated this item with a mean of only 3.68 out of 5. The highest rating was for Driver 4 (administrative support for all persons . . . to improve student achievement). With an overall mean of 4.13, 5 of 6 site visit locations rated Driver 4 the most important (Horn, 2001).

Within the evaluation data for the RSI projects, there were also indicators of the status of rural schools and the science teaching in these schools. Across the six data-reporting categories, teaching experience showed a progression toward more experienced teachers. The data reported were as follows: less than 1 year, 7.7%; 1 to 5 years, 17.1%; 6 to 10 years, 16.9%; 11 to 20 years, 25.2%; and more than 20 years, 33.1%. These figures did not stray in significant ways from the national averages, though it has been commonly reported that more experienced teachers migrate to urban/suburban districts. Demographics related to race pointed to the distinctive nature of the schools within the RSIs. Overall, just over 26% of the teachers and other school personnel were African American, and almost 70% were reported to be Caucasian/white. At the level of individual sites, wide disparities come to the fore. An eastern Kentucky site in the Appalachian RSI reported 98.6% of its personnel as white. A Mississippi delta site reported that 75.2% of its personnel were African American. Llamas (2000) reported that the Utah, Colorado, Arizona, New Mexico (UCAN) RSI included 46 Tribal Nations as well as historic communities. Within these communities, 53% of students were Native American and 25% Hispanic. A commonality among these communities also was that the sites were home to large numbers of people living in poverty. Although populations within RSI sites were often homogeneous with regard to race or ethnicity, across sites almost all major cultural and racial groups of the U.S. population were represented.

The evaluation of the RSI projects used quantitative measures to assess the impacts of the resources provided. Across the three RSIs that were first evaluated, professional development activities were rated as having had the highest impact. Specifically, the most valuable professional development resulted from those activities that were aimed at changing the way teachers perform. Close behind, however, the districts' stakeholders rated the impact of new resources and curriculum changes brought to the district (Russon, Stark, & Horn, 2000).

Findings throughout the sites validated the important role of school administrators in encouraging reform. When asked about the factors that facilitated reform, stakeholders reported that district administration and school principals were far and away the most important. Approximately 88% of respondents identified these two groups as the most important facilitators of reform. The existence of state curriculum standards ranked third, followed by the school board, computer availability, and other educational materials. In contrast, the primary barriers to systemic reform in school districts were money, lab equipment, and science materials, followed by teacher turnover, community support, and expectations for students. The other less-mentioned factors included such things as teacher preparation, teacher subject knowledge, educational materials, and other district projects. The three factors with the lowest ratings with regard to putting up barriers were state standards, school boards, and school consolidations (Russon, Stark, & Horn, 2000).

Driver 1: Standards-Based Curricula

In small rural schools, a variety of factors converged to make the accomplishment of the RSI Drivers a reality. In the area of Driver 1 (curriculum-related), small school size and the availability of human resources presented considerable challenges (Russon et al., 2001). The small school, for instance, might have been unable to offer higher level courses in mathematics or science. As Russon and his colleagues stated, these were precisely the courses favored by the advocates of systemic reform. In answer to these concerns, RSI school districts responded by using those tools and techniques available to them. Course "audits" were conducted by the RSI staff to examine the match between curricular/instructional activities of a particular teacher in a specific course and the state-level assessments for that course. At the Appalachian RSI, a web site of standards-based curriculum materials was maintained and supplemented professional development and course audits. A school district on a western Native American reservation created curricula that were not only standards-based, but also culturally relevant. In accordance with the historic farming tradition that has characterized the Gila River Indian Community, members of the community aided the school in creating a garden that was the centerpiece of the school's curriculum. The Appalachian example was clearly a product of NSF resources funneling to the district through the RSI, but the Gila River project probably happened independently of those particular resources.

Analysis of other sites within the RSI projects showed that long-term planning based on standards-based curricula was not possible in any realistic sense. One southern Mississippi county had such a high turnover rate among science teachers that it was impossible to consistently deliver a standards-based curriculum. Other rural districts in states with high-stakes testing programs reported that the curriculum was as much a mirror for the testing program as it could be made to be (Russon et al., 2001).

Driver 2: Consistent Policy

The rural school districts sampled as part of the RSI evaluation ranged across the social and political spectrum with regard to the population from which they were drawn and the governance from which their policies were built. Thus a district's ability to respond to Driver 2 (development of a coherent and consistent set of policies) was somewhat at odds with its strictures. One school district on a Native American reservation consisted of a set of schools that were overseen variously by community, district, tribal, county, state, national, and/or religious governance. Different schools within this single district were overseen by different combinations of these seven, including one school that was governed by a combination of religious and tribal boards (Russon, Horn, & Oliver, 2000).

Driver 3: Convergence of Resources

The third Driver was probably the most successful across the spectrum of RSI districts. The financial resources of the RSIs were used to bring together all resources to support science and mathematical education. The evaluators felt that "RSIs mostly worked to promote the convergence of human resources. This was primarily accomplished through professional development and directed assistance in utilizing state and federal grant funds to support a common effort to improve science and/or mathematics education" (Russon et al., 2001, p. 37).

Driver 4: Broad Support from Stakeholders

Traditionally the belief is that schools in rural areas receive the support of their communities, and clearly some do. But the full accomplishment of Driver 4 (broad-based support from parents, policy makers, institutions of higher education, business and industry, foundations, and other segments of the community) among RSI projects was rarely seen. "Some schools received an abundance of support from parents. Math and science nights were common across the RSIs, and in some cases they were well attended. In other cases, the parents were far more likely to support the football or basketball team" (Russon et al., 2001, p. 38). Likewise, some districts and RSIs were successful in bringing institutions of higher education into their sphere of financial and resource supporters. The Appalachian RSI was notable in its success in creating collaboratives with five partner institutions of higher education (Horn, Oliver, & Stufflebeam, 2000). Other RSIs had more limited success.

The UCAN RSI designed its primary approach for working within the community: "From the outset, UCAN RSI believed and acted on the premise that the 'community' as locally defined would best represent the constituents that we wanted to serve. Operationally this meant correctly identifying and working with the unit of change at the local level" (Llamas, 2000, p. 16).

Llamas went on to describe at length the means by which community partnerships and collaborations were formed in the UCAN states:

> In a similar vein, RSIs had only scattered success with business and industry partnerships. A few sites within the projects found ways to create meaningful partnerships that resulted in new resources or grants. Ultimately, the evidence related to this Driver demonstrated most effectively that school districts considered the RSIs to be a valuable addition to their pool of resources, but not a universal remedy. Discussions with school personnel showed that it was not always possible to separate the effect of RSI resources from the input of other funded and gifted projects. In some districts, there were many of these "other" projects. (Horn et al., 2000)

Driver 5: Evidence of Student Achievement

The current tenor in the United States and elsewhere requires increased student achievement as the most important justification of funding. But in the rural districts of the RSIs, many problems were encountered in the accomplishment of Driver 5. Although the body of research that had accumulated regarding rural school curricula over the past 100 years suggested the need for local relevance and applicability in science and mathematics study, there is no evidence arising from the RSIs that standardized assessments can measure this. In fact, as Russon et al. (2001) wrote in their summary to the case studies of the six RSIs under study,

> There is no clear evidence that standardized tests prepared for mass administration across all school districts in all states are related to the missions and goals of the schools, the focus of the schools' curricula, or the classroom instruction students receive. Failure to meet the standard for any one of these three conditions would invalidate the results as being a fair assessment of student achievement or even instructional/school effectiveness. (p. 39)

Driver 6: Improvement of Achievement for All Students

In the site visits of the RSI evaluation team, the results regarding Driver 6 were difficult to discern. (This is probably an example of needing to wait a bit longer before reaching a conclusion.) Because the requirements for inclusion in an RSI were that the site be an isolated rural place as well as one with a high number of students qualifying for free and reduced lunch, the ethnic and cultural variability among the students tended to be greatly reduced. In other words, these schools were typically completely or almost completely homogeneous with regard to race and ethnicity. In two study sites, the white students attended private academies, leaving the public schools almost entirely attended by African Americans (Horn, 2000). A study site on a Native American reservation was attended by an entirely Native American student body. Thus within these study sites, almost all students could be described as historically underserved.

So what can be said about the RSI evaluation data at this point in time? First and foremost, the evaluation process is ongoing, and a final report may shed light in places that the formative reports did not. But the idea that a single large-scale project can have a substantial impact on the rural poor school districts of a region that included six states and hundreds of qualifying schools may simply be too much to ask. Regardless of this, the evaluation of the rural sites for the RSI projects is providing an important source of information about the status of schools that hold the responsibility for educating rural students living in poverty.

CONTRASTING RURAL AND NON-RURAL SCHOOLS

Studies that contrast characteristics of teachers or students in rural schools with their non-rural counterparts are relatively rare. A few were mentioned in the previous "Needs Assessment" section. Three other recent studies that examined science education in rural and non-rural schools are considered here.

In 2000, Deidra Young examined the impact of ruralness on student achievement in Australia and the impact of student perceptions of their own academic ability. This longitudinal research was part of the *Western Australia School Effectiveness Study*. Involving a total of over 1000 students, data were collected during 1996 and

1997 from students in 21 schools representing 106 classrooms. Instruments included a version of the TIMSS achievement test and an instrument to measure classroom climate and academic self-concept of students (Young, 2000).

This study challenged the belief that there was a value-added component of expected student achievement that resulted from the school's special characteristics. Rather, Young (2000) found that most of the variability in the construct of student achievement occurred at the student and classroom levels.

In keeping with typical beliefs about rural schooling, Young (2000) found that "students in country schools [described as both rural and remote] appeared to be more satisfied with their schools. They felt that their teachers were more supportive, friends were more supportive and generally felt safer" (p. 212). However, with regard to achievement, the author concluded:

> . . . while rural differences were apparent to student outcomes such as science and mathematics achievement and academic self-concept, these differences were of no consequence when investigated using sophisticated multilevel modeling techniques. That is, rural students were not disadvantaged by their location. Rather, rural students were disadvantaged by their self-concept. Students in rural schools did tend to have a weaker belief in their own academic ability to perform, irrespective of their actual ability. (p. 221)

In the United States, Simpson and Marek (1988) found a somewhat different result. Building from an assumption that rural students have fewer opportunities for intellectual development, the authors conducted a study to test the hypothesis that "students attending large schools [would] show more instances of understanding . . . of the concepts of diffusion, homeostasis, classification, . . . and food production" (p. 363). They found that students attending large high schools developed greater understandings of the concepts of diffusion and homeostasis. However, with regard to the concepts of classification and food production in plants, there was no relationship of understanding to school size.

Simpson and Marek (1988) hypothesized that the difference in the learning accomplishment observed could be due to a variety of factors. One factor that figured prominently in their thinking was that the differences "could be due to a higher percent of students in large schools capable of formal operations; sound understandings of diffusion and homeostasis required students to use formal operations" (p. 372). But they also pointed to occurrences in the daily lives of the students. In the rural schools within the study, Simpson and Marek indicated that many students were children of cotton and wheat farmers. Their experiences on these farms "allowed them [the students] to develop some understandings of food production in plants and prevented instances of misunderstanding from being developed" (p. 372). The idea of the importance of teaching and learning within the local context again was thus a recurring theme.

Two researchers from Utah State University conducted a large-scale study (Fan & Chen, 1999) of the data generated by the U.S. National Education Longitudinal Study of 1988. Overall their results suggested that "rural students performed as well as, if not better than, their peers in metropolitan schools" (p. 31). Their work covered the entire curriculum and included an excellent review of the relevant literature.

Fan and Chen (1999) subdivided their analysis across racial/ethnic subcategories (e.g., Asian/Pacific, Hispanic, Caucasian, and African American), locational subcategories (e.g., rural, suburban, and urban), grade-level subcategories (e.g., 8th grade, 10th grade, and 12th grade), geographical subcategories (e.g. Northeast, Midwest, South, and West), and subject matter areas (e.g., reading, mathematics, science, and social science). The analysis used multivariate statistics to test hypotheses across these many subcategories instead of more commonly applied univariate tests. They showed that univariate tests lacked the power to discern statistical significance between the categories of variable in their data. Ultimately, they concluded: "Students from rural schools perform as well as their peers in metropolitan areas in the four areas of school learning: reading, math, science, and social studies. These results did not support the conjecture that students in rural schools nationwide are at a general disadvantage in terms of the quality of their education, at least, as reflected in their performance on a standardized achievement test" (p. 42).

This study did not allow for the inclusion of "extreme rural communities" because the data was classified according to U.S. Census categories that do not provide that degree of specificity.

RURAL SCIENCE TEACHER EDUCATION

The preparation and continued professional development of rural science teacher education have been the subjects of a variety of research efforts over recent history. These efforts have tended to focus on inservice rather than preservice science teacher education, though there has been representation across the levels. Much of what has been written regarding rural science teacher education and development is not research in the rigorous sense of the word, but rather what might be characterized as documentation and comment. The overall depiction of research on rural science teacher education is and has been one of neglect (Finson & Beaver, 1990; Shroyer & Enochs, 1987).

However, consistent throughout the literature of rural education teacher education is the idea that rural education and the context in which it occurs combine to form a core construct that must always be considered. Science teacher education designed to produce teachers for the rural areas must be cognizant of this issue. Nachtigal (1995) was speaking at least partially about teacher education when he wrote, "Science education in the rural schools, rural student and rural communities [has] not been well served by the mass production, one-best-system of schooling" (p. 116).

Yerrick and Hoving (2003) pointed to the writings of Nachtigal when they suggested that science teacher education for rural students must be cautious not to promulgate ideological positions that promote "injustices against . . . underserved students" (p. 414). These authors found that effective preservice teacher education that prepares prospective teachers to teach rural African American students in early high school physical science courses could be accomplished through a combination of strategies. These strategies include formal opportunities to make recordings of teaching sessions and conduct examinations of them; collaborative reflection; focus groups with students; "access to exemplary teaching curriculum" (p. 414); modeling alternative teaching strategies; and course readings that are helpful in creating dialogues about common problems (Yerrick & Hoving).

Inservice professional development for rural science teachers was the subject of a study by Shroyer and Enochs (1987). They worked with a group of teachers drawn from a pool of 141 U.S. school districts "outside the sphere of influence of cities with populations over 100,000 and [having] less than 600 students K–12" (p. 39). Their work began with a "needs analysis" recognizing that small schools must identify their unique needs as a first step. The program of professional development continued through "strength assessment" and then to "action planning." In the action planning phase, the teachers created a plan for implementation as a means to ensure that the reform initiatives were in keeping with the nature of this rural school.

In research on rural schools, it is often true that the rare study that takes a comprehensive look at the entire rural school is particularly enlightening. A study by Scribner (2003) accomplished this by examining teacher professional development in three rural high schools. These schools were identified based on two criteria— small dispersed school populations and seasonally based community economies. Although not specifically about science teaching, the article was highly relevant to science teacher professional development in the rural school. Scribner found that the small rural high schools did not have a departmental context as is found in larger schools. In the absence of these departments, Scribner reported that the most important context for the teachers was the classroom "or at times, their professional community external to the school" (Discussion section, paragraph 2). Interestingly, he also found that in these schools, teachers of "well-defined knowledge bases such as math and science" (Discussion section, paragraph 3) tended to focus their efforts on the transfer of conceptual knowledge. Teachers of other disciplines, specifically identified by Scribner as language and social studies, "used the content of their subject area to broadly address student needs" (Discussion section, paragraph 3). Furthermore, teachers in these schools found professional development that was locally sponsored by the school or district to be of little value, in contrast to the value they seemed to place on state "legislated" support. Overall, Scribner found that teachers were tightly wound into the student-teacher interaction of the classroom and tended to value only the "most practical and immediately applicable knowledge/skill" (Discussion section, paragraph 4) as a means to inform their practice.

These few studies of preservice and inservice teacher education represent much of the research available on science teacher education for the rural school. This paucity of research is a reflection of the field of rural science teacher education. Although there are many college and university science teacher education programs that serve areas that are largely rural, they only rarely serve areas that are exclusively rural. Thus one does not find teacher education programs aimed at producing science teachers exclusively for the rural school, but rather science teachers for the bigger markets.

Consistent themes run throughout these studies of teacher education and development. These themes center on the need for rural teachers to teach science within a frame of reference that consciously builds a curriculum with a cooperative inclusion of community, the unique student and school needs found in that community, and the inimitable capabilities of the teachers found in those schools. The aspects of these themes hark back to the characteristics of rural schools suggested by Sher (1983). Thus science education in the rural school must be constructed from the building blocks that exist in rural schools.

SUMMARY AND IMPLICATIONS

A major chapter in the life of rural U.S. schools has ended with the closing of the ERIC Clearinghouse for Rural Education and Small Schools (ERIC Clearinghouse on Rural Education and Small Schools, 2003). And yet, almost simultaneously, U.S. Secretary of Education Rod Paige announced a new recognition for the needs of rural schools: "too many rural students have not received the high-quality education they deserve. . . . Although our nation's rural schools may be physically removed from urban areas, they are no longer isolated from policy-makers" (USDOE, 2003, paragraph 5).

Perhaps it is a good moment to ask, what has really happened in rural science education? The 1970s and 1980s renaissance noted by Horn and others (Horn, 1995; Prather & Oliver, 1991), after such time when "literally no one in the federal government would claim responsibility for rural education" (Horn, 1995, p. 13), seems to have run its course. The excitement among a group of science educators, which resulted in the formation of the Committee for the Study of Options for Rural Science Education and the completion of several significant projects (for instance, Baird et al., 1994), has faded. In educational research, such conditions often signal that a rebirth is just around the corner. It is for a new group of educators to take up this torch, if it is to be taken up at all.

Rural science education research has quite often lacked the theoretical sophistication of other work, though the research of Charron (1991) and Gilbert and Yerrick (2001) provides excellent counterpoints to this assertion. Rural science education research has tended to reflect the myth of rural America with its emphasis on pragmatism and resourcefulness. The RSI program made an impact by focusing attention on the areas that are home to the rural poor. It is perhaps here, where a concentration of individuals exists and shares a set of "local-universal understandings" consisting of socioeconomic, political, cultural, and ethnic characteristics, that we find the definable rural place. But so often this definable rural place also faces a harsh reality that is mired in poverty. Thus, there is great need for the people of this place to bring forth any available pragmatism and resourcefulness to address the issues of schooling and especially science education. This is what Prather (1995) meant when he wrote, "The necessities of rural school teaching have made thoughtful and determined risk-takers of many teachers and school officials" (p. 40).

In 1935, Wolford found that rural high schools usually had to either create their own curricula or follow the textbook. He concluded that most did the latter. This was not a surprising finding in the 1930s, or in any later decade. Horn (1995) described the rural school curricula as minimal, including only what is required by the state. In those districts, the observer would expect to see science teachers following a textbook. But what else could that rural district do? Hope has persisted across the past 100 years that locally relevant curricula could be enacted in rural and small schools in the United States and throughout the world. These locally created and locally relevant curricula have been seen at various times and locations as the means to motivate learners and to address needs of the community. But the realities of standardized tests, frequent turnover of teachers, lack of material support, and lack of administrative support conspire to suppress curricula creation and enactment. And yet the hope remains alive. Perhaps best stated by Blunck et al. (1995), "Science education in rural settings may be able to provide the most conclusive and useful examples of successful reforms due to the ability of personal experiences to drive knowledge exploration in real life contexts" (p. 90).

Studies of the teachers of science in rural areas and the students in their schools have suggested a lack of difference between them and their non-rural peers. From the needs assessments, distinctions can be drawn between teachers of rural and non-rural places, but these fade into the scenery created by the similarities. Likewise with students, there are differences to be noted, but the bigger picture is one of similarity. If we look at the individual trees of this forest, we might miss the bigger picture. Clearly and quite importantly, the RSI evaluation has shown that there are unique forests, or at least groves (to fully expend the metaphor) within that sphere that stand apart from the norm where students with great educational needs are well educated. The response to these needs will quite likely come from researchers and educators who have a particular interest in a specific aspect of the rural schooling story.

And finally, where do we leave the question of technology and its potential to bring universal access to knowledge to all persons regardless of location? Finson and Dickson (1995) found that geographic isolation of rural schools became less of a barrier to student learning when distance learning technologies were employed. The World Wide Web offers a distance learning technology a quantum leap above the technologies to which Finson and Dickson referred. The day is quickly coming when the number of books in the library simply will not matter, because all of the important books will be accessed through electronic media. The day is also quickly coming when the substance of the textbook will not be the most important source of the structure of science-based curricula. Computer-based technologies that re-create the curricula with the use of animations, simulations, digital video, and hypermedia, combined with the powerful search capabilities within the World Wide Web, will offer learning opportunities that are truly new and widely available. Whether these learning opportunities are able to capture the relevance of a local community's science issues, measure outcomes with assessment tools complementary to these approaches, and not merely rely on the learner's knowledge of science facts remains to be seen.

ACKNOWLEDGMENTS

Thanks to William Baird and Jerry Horn, who reviewed this chapter. The author would also like to thank Dr. Jim Spellman, who as a graduate student assisted in the search for the research literature reviewed in this chapter.

REFERENCES

Amaral, O., & Garrison, L. (2001). Turning challenges into opportunities in science education in rural communities. *Rural Educator, 23*(2), 1–6.

Baird, W. E., Prather, J. P., Finson, K. D., & Oliver, J. S. (1994). Comparisons of perceptions among rural versus nonrural secondary science teachers: A multi-state survey. *Science Education, 78,* 555–576.

Barrow, L. H., & Burchett, B. M. (2000). Needs of Missouri rural secondary science teachers. *Rural Educator, 22*(2), 14–19.

Blunck, S., Crandall, B., Dunkel, J., Jeffryes, C., Varrella, G., & Yager, R. E (1995). Rural science education: Water and waste issues. In P. B. Otto (Ed.), *Science education in the rural United States:*

Implication for the twenty-first century (pp. 79–92). Columbus, OH: ERIC Clearinghouse for Science, Mathematics, and Environmental Education.

Boenig, R. W. (1969). *Research in science education: 1938 through 1947*. New York: Teachers College Press.

Bradford, C. S., & Dana, T. M. (1996). Exploring science teacher metaphorical thinking: A case study of a high school science teacher. *Journal of Science Teacher Education, 7*, 197–211.

Brown, L. R., Fournier, J. F., & Moyer, R. H. (1977). A cross-cultural study of Piagetian concrete reasoning and science concepts among rural fifth-grade Mexican- and Anglo-American students. *Journal of Research in Science Teaching, 14*, 329–334.

Bruckerhoff, C. (1998, April). *Lessons learned in the evaluation of statewide systemic initiatives*. Paper presented at the annual meeting of the American Educational Research Association, San Diego.

Carlsen, W. S., & Monk, D. H. (1992). Differences between rural and nonrural secondary science teachers: Evidence from the longitudinal study of American youth. *Journal of Research in Rural Education, 8*(2), 1–10.

Celis, W. (2002). *Battle rock: The struggle over a one-room school in America's vanishing west*. Cambridge, MA: Public Affairs.

Charron, E. H. (1991). Classroom and community influences on youth's perceptions of science in a rural county school system. *Journal of Research in Science Teaching, 28*, 671–688.

Clarke, C. O. (1972). A determination of commonalities of science interests held by intermediate grade children in inner-city, suburban, and rural schools. *Science Education, 56*, 125–136.

Crockett, D. (1999). *Science education in an Amish Mennonite community and school: An examination of perception and application*. Unpublished doctoral dissertation, University of Georgia-Athens.

Curtis, F. D. (1931). A study of the scientific interests of dwellers in small towns and in the country. In F. D. Curtis (Ed.), *Second digest of investigations in the teaching of science* (pp. 343–348). New York: Teachers College Press (original work published 1927).

Curtis, F. D. (1971a). *A digest of investigations in the teaching of science in the elementary and secondary schools*. New York: McGraw-Hill (original work published 1926).

Curtis, F. D. (1971b). *Second digest of investigations in the teaching of science*. New York: McGraw-Hill (original work published 1931).

Curtis, F. D. (1971c). *Third digest of investigations in the teaching of science*. New York: McGraw-Hill (original work published 1939).

Davis, C. O. (1926). The size of classes and the teaching load. In F. D. Curtis (Ed.), *Digest of investigations in the teaching of science* (pp. 93–94). New York: Teachers College Press (original work published 1923).

Enochs, L. G., Oliver, J. S., & Wright, E. L. (1990). An evaluation of the perceived needs of secondary science teachers in Kansas. *Journal of Science Teacher Education, 1*, 74–79.

ERIC Clearinghouse on Rural and Small Schools. (2003). Heartfelt thanks and farewell. *ERIC CRESS Bulletin, 15*(3), 1–6.

Fan, X., & Chen, M. J. (1999). Academic achievement of rural school students: A multi-year comparison with their peers in suburban and urban schools. *Journal of Research in Rural Education, 15*(1), 31–46.

Fenstermacher, G. D. (2002). Reconsidering the teacher education reform debate: A commentary on Cochran-Smith and Fries. *Educational Researcher, 31*(6), 20–22.

Finson, K. D., & Beaver, J. B. (1990). Rural science teacher preparation: A re-examination of an important component of the educational system. *Journal of Science Teacher Education, 1*, 46–48.

Finson, K. D., & Dickson, M. W. (1995). Distance learning for rural schools: Distance learning defined. In P. B. Otto (Ed.), *Science education in the rural United States: Implication for the twenty-first century* (pp. 93–114). Columbus, OH: ERIC Clearinghouse for Science, Mathematics, and Environmental Education.

Ghose, A. M. (1982). Out of school science and technology for rural development. In *Education for rural development* (Vol. 4, pp. 19–35). Bangkok: UNESCO.

Gilbert, A., & Yerrick, R. (2001). Same school, separate worlds: A sociocultural study of identity, resistance, and negotiation in a rural, lower track science classroom. *Journal of Research in Science Teaching, 38,* 574–598.

Horn, J. G. (1995). What is rural education? In P. B. Otto (Ed.), *Science education in the rural united states: Implication for the twenty-first century* (pp. 1–14). Columbus, OH: ERIC Clearinghouse for Science, Mathematics, and Environmental Education.

Horn, J. G. (2000). *A case study of east Feliciana Parish (Louisiana) school district and its role as a partner in the NSF-supported delta rural systemic initiative.* Kalamazoo, MI: Western Michigan University, the Evaluation Center.

Horn, J. G. (2001). *A summary of RSI school personnel's perceptions of the drivers for educational systemic reform.* Kalamazoo, MI: Western Michigan University, the Evaluation Center.

Horn, J. G., Oliver, J. S., & Stufflebeam, D. (2000). *A case study of the Cocke county (TN) school system.* Kalamazoo, MI: Western Michigan University, the Evaluation Center.

Jensen, J. H., & Glenn, E. R. (1929/1931). An investigation of types of class rooms for chemistry and other science in small high schools. In F. D. Curtis (Ed.), *Second digest of investigations in the teaching of science* (pp. 330–332). New York: Teachers College Press (original work published 1929).

Johnson, P. G. (1969). The teaching of science in public high schools: An inquiry in to offerings, enrollments, and selected teaching conditions, 1947–1948. In J. N. Swift (Ed.), *Research in science education: 1948 through 1952* (pp. 50–53). New York: Teachers College Press (original work published 1950).

Jordan-Bychkov, T. G. (2003). *The upland South: The making of an American folk region and landscape.* Santa Fe, NM: The Center for American Places.

Kay, T. (1976). *The year the lights came on.* Boston: Houghton Mifflin.

Lawlor, E. P. (1970). *Research in science education: 1953 through 1957.* New York: Teachers College Press.

Llamas, V. (2000). The four corners rural systemic initiative: Challenges and opportunities. *Rural Educator, 21*(2), 15–18.

Nachtigal, P. M. (1995). Political ramifications for rural science education in the twenty-first century. In P. B. Otto (Ed.), *Science education in the rural United States: Implication for the twenty-first century* (pp. 115–120). Columbus, OH: ERIC Clearinghouse for Science, Mathematics, and Environmental Education.

Otto, P. B. (Ed.) (1995). *Science education in the rural United States: Implications for the twenty-first century.* Columbus, OH: ERIC Clearinghouse for Science, Mathematics, and Environmental Education.

Palmer, E. L. (1931). The scientific interests of children enrolled in country schools. In F. D. Curtis (Ed.), *Second digest of investigations in the teaching of science* (pp. 36–40). New York: Teachers College Press (original work published 1926).

Prather, J. P. (1995). Rationale for an integrated approach to teaching science in rural school. In P. B. Otto (Ed.), *Science education in the rural United States: Implication for the twenty-first century* (pp. 37–38). Columbus, OH: ERIC Clearinghouse for Science, Mathematics, and Environmental Education.

Prather, J. P., & Oliver, J. S. (1991). Options for a rural science agenda. In J. P. Prather (Ed.), *Effective interaction of science teachers, researchers, and teacher educators.* SAETS Science Education Series (No. 1, pp. 45–57).

Riddle, O., Fitzpatrick, F. L., Glass, H. B., Gruenberg, B. C., Miller, D. F., & Sinnott, E. W. (1969). The teaching of biology in the secondary schools of the United States. In R. W. Boenig (Ed.), *Research in science education: 1938 through 1947* (pp. 171–186). New York: Teachers College Press (original work published 1942).

Russon, C., & Horn, J. (1999). *A report on the identification and validation of indicators of six drivers for educational system reform: For the rural systemic initiatives evaluation study.* Retrieved September 12, 2004, from http://www.wmich.edu/evalctr/rsi/indicators_drivers.pdf

Russon, C., & Horn, J. (2001). *The relationship between the NSF's drivers of systemic reform and the rural systemic initiatives.* Unpublished manuscript.

Russon, C., Horn, J., & Oliver, J. S. (2000). *A case study of Gila River Indian community (Arizona) and its role as a partner in the NSF-supported UCAN rural systemic initiative.* Kalamazoo, MI: Western Michigan University, the Evaluation Center.

Russon, C., Paule, L., & Horn, J. (2001). *The relationship between the drivers of educational reform and the rural systemic initiatives in science, mathematics, and technology education program.* Kalamazoo, MI: Western Michigan University, the Evaluation Center.

Russon, C., Stark, L., & Horn, J. (2000). *RSI survey report.* Kalamazoo, MI: Western Michigan University, the Evaluation Center.

Sampson-Cordle, A. V. (2001). *Exploring the relationship between a small rural school in Northeast Georgia and its community: An image-based study using participant-produced photographs.* Unpublished doctoral dissertation, University of Georgia, Athens.

Scribner, J. P. (2003). Teacher learning in context: The special case of rural high school teachers. *Education Policy Analysis Archives, 11*(12). Retrieved October 23, 2004, from http://epaa.asu.edu/epaa/v11n12/

Sher, J. P. (Ed.). (1977). *Education in rural America: A reassessment of conventional wisdom.* Boulder, CO: Westview Press.

Sher, J. P. (1983). Education's ugly duckling: Rural schools in urban nations. *Phi Delta Kappan, 65,* 257–263.

Shroyer, G., & Enochs, L. (1987). Strategies for assessing the unique strengths, needs, and visions of rural science teachers. *Research in Rural Education, 4*(1), 39–43.

Simpson, W. D., & Marek, E. A. (1988). Understandings and misconceptions of biology concepts held by students attending small high schools and students attending large high schools. *Journal of Research in Science Teaching, 25,* 361–374.

Stern, J. D. (1994). *The condition of education in rural schools.* Washington, DC: U.S. Department of Education, Office of Educational Research and Improvement.

Stine, P. C. (1997). Hands-on science education in rural Pennsylvania. *Bulletin of the Science and Technology Society, 17*(1), 13–15.

Swift, J. N. (1969). *Research in science education: 1948 through 1952.* New York: Teachers College Press.

Tobin, K. G., & Carambo, C. (2002, April). *Crash or crash through: Agency, structure, urban high schools and the transformative potential of science education.* Paper presented at the annual meeting of the American Educational Research Association.

University of the State of New York, Regents of the University. (1992). *Rural education: Issues and strategies.* New York: New York State Department of Education.

U.S. Department of Education. (2002). *No Child Left Behind Act.* Retrieved October 12, 2003, from http://www.ed.gov/nclb/landing.jhtml?src=fb

U.S. Department of Education. (2003). *Paige announces grants to improve rural education.* Retrieved September 12, 2004, from http://www.ed.gov/news/pressreleases/2003/11/11132003b.html

Wolford, F. (1939). Methods of determining types of content for a course of study for eighth-grade science in the high schools of the southern Appalachian region. In F. D. Curtis (Ed.), *Third digest of investigations in the teaching of science* (pp. 47–53). New York: Teachers College Press (original work published 1935).

Yerrick, R. K., & Hoving, T. J. (2003). One foot on the dock and one foot on the boat: Differences among preservice science teachers' interpretations of field-based science methods in culturally diverse contexts. *Science Education, 87,* 419–443.

Young, D. J. (2000) Rural and urban differences in student achievement in science and mathematics: A multilevel analysis. *School Effectiveness and School Improvement, 9,* 386–418.

Zurub, A. R., & Rubba, P. A. (1983). Development and validation of an inventory to assess science teacher needs in developing countries. *Journal of Research in Science Teaching, 20,* 867–873.

PART III

Science Teaching

CHAPTER 14

General Instructional Methods and Strategies

David F. Treagust
Curtin University, Australia

There is a multiplicity of instructional methods and strategies used in science classes that vary from those that are primarily didactic or teacher-centered to those that are primarily student-centered or learner-centered. A major consideration in writing this chapter was to organize these methods and strategies within some coherent framework such that readers can also locate instructional methods and strategies not described and discussed in this review.

Instructional methods and strategies can be organized in terms of the amount of direct control that teachers and instructors have over their implementation. Consequently, the organizing theme for this review is the degree of teacher-centeredness compared with student-centeredness of the methods. Six general instructional methods and strategies in teaching science in schools and universities are discussed, namely, demonstrations, classroom explanations, questioning, forms of representations, group and cooperative learning, and deductive-inductive approaches such as the learning cycle. Each of these general methods has elements of both teacher-centeredness and student-centeredness, but the order of presentation in this chapter ranges from more to less teacher-centeredness in the instruction. Strategies and teaching approaches have been omitted from this review, and it is intended that the reader can determine where omitted teaching approaches fit in the framework. Gabel (2003) has reported a similar range of effective strategies for learning science.

Four considerations over the past two decades have had a major influence on the type of instructional methods and strategies used in science classes, and these underpin the methods reviewed. The first consideration is the acknowledgment that learners construct their own individual understanding and that this can be promoted by specially designed instruction (Anderson & Helms, 2001; Duit & Treagust, 1998). Within this consideration, learners intentionally construct their own knowledge, using their existing knowledge, and thereby are able to view the world in ways that are coherent and useful to them (Sinatra & Pintrich, 2003). The second consideration is that the content of the science to be learned is acknowledged as a problematic issue. Few researchers who investigate students' learning of science comment on the problematic character of the science content itself. Rather, the accepted focus of several decades of cognitive pedagogical research has been to provide suggestions for improving the teaching and learning of particular science topics (see, for example, Fensham, 2001; Fensham, Gunstone, & White, 1994).

The third consideration that pervades the instructional methods discussed is the promise that teaching strategies and approaches aimed at enhancing student metacognition might lead to corresponding improvements in conceptual understanding of curricula (Gunstone, 1994; Hennessey, 2003). According to Baird & White (1996, p. 194), "metacognitive strategies are employed by a person in a process of purposeful enquiry and . . . comprise reflection (to determine purpose) and action (to generate information)." Consequently, there is much "promise that interventions aimed at enhancing student metacognition might lead to corresponding improvements in conceptual understanding of curricula content." Strategies such as the use of concept maps (Novak, 1996), predict-observe-explain tasks (White & Gunstone, 1992), personal logs, reflections, portfolios, and discussion have been shown to be of value in the development of metacognitive capabilities. The fourth consideration is the realization that many teachers have utilized many of the methods described here in a form of action research as they examine, implement, and evaluate these methods (see, for example, Hodson & Bencze, 1998).

Each section starts with the key theoretical and empirical issues of learning identified in the literature that underpin each type of instructional approach. This is then followed by some examples of research to illustrate the effectiveness or otherwise of each instructional approach. This short review of general instructional methods and the usefulness of these strategies discusses existing research and is intended to help readers to re-evaluate the status of these methods and strategies in science education, to ask new questions, and to spark further improvement in some new directions in research and practice related to general instructional methods and practices.

DEMONSTRATIONS

For over a century, laboratory work has been used in teaching and learning school science. With the popularity of the constructivist-informed teaching approaches since the 1980s, teachers have emphasized the role of hands-on experiences in learning science (Hofstein & Lunetta, 2004). In this chapter, the focus is on demonstrations in teaching science, which are a less expensive or a safer way of providing students with experiences of laboratory experiments. Drawing on an extensive literature review of laboratory work, White (1996) argued that this ubiquitous practice of teaching school science for more than a century did not appear to directly improve understanding of science because "imaginative practices are rare and mindless routine common in school laboratories" (p. 771). Details about the laboratory in science teaching are found in Chapter 16 and are not repeated here. Although the use of demonstrations in teaching science does not serve all of the main goals of laboratory work highlighted by Lazarowitz and Tamir (1994), such as skills, concepts, cognitive abilities, understanding the nature of science, and attitudes, it does serve to motivate students in the science classroom (White, 1996).

Demonstrations for Motivation

Laboratory demonstrations in the teaching of science can provide colorful, surprising, or dramatic effects—such as burning a piece of magnesium ribbon before a junior class of science—which motivate students but do not necessarily help them develop an understanding of the particular concept being demonstrated. Roth, McRobbie, Lucas, and Boutonne (1997) have shown that there are good reasons why students may fail to learn from demonstrations about motion, namely because students who come to the practical classes with their own ideas about motion do not observe the phenomena they studied as expected by their teacher. Similarly, the teacher expected the instructions to be self-evident but did not realize that their students did not share his theoretical perspective. Consequently, for demonstrations to be effective, research has shown the central importance of the instructor as a mediator of student learning and an interpreter of the content of science (Watson, 2000).

Demonstrations that create interest have the potential to engender learning by combining demonstrations with teachers' classroom explanations (Ogborn, Kress, Martin, & McGillicuddy, 1996). Ogborn et al. produced an interesting and thought-provoking analysis of how science teachers can utilize demonstrations in the classroom to explain science and thereby improve the level of understanding of the science concept introduced by the demonstration. Their work is discussed more fully in the section on Explanations.

Demonstrations to Increase Student Cognitive Involvement

To make demonstrations more student-centered, teachers may consider using Predict-Observe-Explain (POE) activities described by Champagne, Gunstone, and Klopfer (1985); White and Gunstone (1992); and Gunstone (1995). POE activities can be a very useful way to juxtapose demonstrations with explanations. In a POE activity, students are first asked to predict what would happen next in a demonstration. Subsequently, they have to observe the demonstrations carefully and finally to explain what they have observed. The teacher can have a follow-up group or whole-class discussion with the students to discuss their observations and explanations. One example of effective use of POEs in teaching science is Palmer's (1995) study in primary schools in which the POE technique was used by teachers to identify students' knowledge and to understand their science conceptions and their process skills development. As another example, Liew and Treagust's (1995) studied the use of POEs for the topic of heat and expansion of liquids with grade 11 physics students. Students' learning was evident in their observations and interpretations; frequently their prior beliefs, knowledge, and expectations influenced their observations, which both positively and negatively affected their new learning.

Demonstrations Enhanced by Computer Software

The use of technology in science education has been extensively discussed by Linn (2003), although her review did not directly mention demonstrations. However, three of Linn's discussion points were science visualization, science simulations, and modeling, each of which can be relevant to demonstrations. Indeed, computer technologies allow more interactive POE activities to be used in instruction to engender student understanding. As an example of these activities, Kearney, Treagust, Yeo, and Zaknik (2002) incorporated POE tasks into a multimedia computer program that used real-life digital video clips of difficult, expensive, time-consuming, or dangerous scenarios as stimuli for these tasks. Projectile motion phenomena in physics were used in designing the POE tasks in the study. The findings indicated that multimedia-supported POE tasks had a noticeable impact on the 10th- and 11th-grade classroom environment in allowing students to control the pace of their learning, to confidently discuss their learning while manipulating and observing the demonstrations.

In another study, science teachers used POE activities from an interactive computer program BioLogica (Concord Consortium, 2001) in 10th-grade classrooms to foster a deeper understanding of genetics reasoning (Tsui & Treagust, 2003). In the computer activities, students were given tasks that involved the prediction of the observable changes when they manipulated the objects in the multimedia. The findings suggested that the multiple representations of genetics in BioLogica with embedded POE tasks might have contributed to students' development of genetics reasoning by way of engendering motivation and interest. Furthermore, such POE tasks embedded in computer multimedia are likely to foster classroom social interactions conducive to co-construction of knowledge. This latter concern was evident in Kozma's (2000) study on students learning chemistry with computer multimedia; the findings suggested that the new symbol systems per se were not sufficient to aid learning and that "these new symbolic systems and their symbolic expressions may best be used within rich social contexts that prompt students to interact with each other and with multiple symbol systems to create meaning for scientific phenomena" (p. 45).

The general findings from these studies indicated that demonstrations in the form of POE tasks delivered through interactive computer multimedia can provide new learning opportunities for students in science education and have implications for authentic technology-mediated learning in science classrooms. When students became more motivated and more engaged, they were more likely to develop a better understanding of the content of science because they can play an active or intentional role in the process of learning (Bereiter & Scardamalia, 1989).

CLASSROOM EXPLANATIONS

In order to contribute to students' ability to make sense of the world, science teachers' descriptions and explanations of scientific phenomena are critically important activities in classroom teaching (Horwood, 1988). Accordingly, description is intended to provide pieces of information, not necessarily related, but explanation is intended to connect between and among pieces of information. Treagust and Harrison (1999) highlighted the importance of teachers' effective explanations in the classroom and how the expert teachers "draw creative word pictures that both appeal to and inform a diverse group like a class of students" (p. 28). As such, how to verbally explain science concepts to students and teach them how to verbalize their understanding is important. As Johnson-Laird (1983) put it, "if you do not understand something, you cannot explain it" (p. 2).

In science teachers' classroom explanations, it is very common to employ deductive and inductive strategies in an interactive way. Usually verbal or written language is used together with gestures, and sometimes the explanations may also use some actional-operational strategies, such as physical models or demonstrations (Gilbert, Boulter, & Elmer, 2000). Researchers have identified the use of language in classroom explanations as having paramount centrality for understanding science (see, for example, Yore, Bisanz, & Hand, 2003; Sutton, 1992). Furthermore, the work of Ogborn et al. represents a marriage of frameworks from the more traditional science education and those from language and communication, particularly semiotics. Ogborn et al. considered classroom explanations of science as analogous to stories and summarized four roles of language used in meaning-making during explanation of science in the classroom: (1) creating differences—the teacher explains science by making use of the differences between herself and her students (e.g., knowledge, interest, power, familiarity of the content, etc.); (2) constructing entities—the teacher explains by using some created entities or "new chunks of meanings" (e.g., *energy, heat,* or *gene*) (p. 14) about which students are to think when the teacher "talk[s] [them] into existence" (p. 14); (3) transforming knowledge—the teacher explains the constructed entities by using narratives, particularly analogies and metaphors (e.g., an eye as a camera or the pituitary gland as the conductor of the hormonal system) (see Sutton, 1992); and (4) putting meaning into matter—the teacher explains by demonstration and persuades students that things are as they are shown or by imposing meaning into the things (e.g., tissue is to be seen as cells).

The first two roles are mainly deductive strategies in which the teachers communicate to the students the concepts of science and provides some necessary contexts as motivators or advance organizers. The third and fourth roles engage the students in the use of inductive and deductive reasoning in an interactive way while the teacher emphasizes the explanation to engender student understanding of the particular concept.

Ogborn et al.'s work on classroom explanations is in line with recent interests of science educators in the use of language (e.g., Halliday & Martin, 1993; Lemke, 1990; Yore et al., 2004) and more discursive practices (e.g., Bell, 2000) in classroom instruction. Their work is also in keeping with another recent interest in Vygotskian perspectives among science educators such as Hodson and Hodson (1998) and Howe (1996), who argued for using a Vygotskian sociocultural perspective in the teaching and learning of science.

QUESTIONING

Discursive and sociocultural practices in the science classroom are relevant to instructional practices such as wait time (Rowe, 1974), dialogue patterns (Lemke, 1990), and checking student understanding in classroom discourse (Mortimer & Scott, 2000).

First, research has indicated that questioning during classroom teaching is often unproductive without wait time for students to think before answering. On the basis of an extensive review of the literature, Tobin, Tippins, and Gallard (1994) concluded that wait time (Rowe, 1974) appears to be an important factor in instruction when teachers pursue higher-cognitive-level learning in their students. Appropriate wait time during questioning affects higher-cognitive-level achievement directly by providing additional time for student cognitive processing and indirectly affecting the quality of discursive teacher-student interactions.

Second, teacher and student discourse in the classroom is affected by the way that teachers use questioning. For better meaning-making, more useful questioning has to go beyond the triadic dialogue in which the teacher asks questions, calls on students to answer them, and then evaluates their answers. In analyzing such discourse, Lemke (1990) suggested dialogues other than the triadic dialogue, such as student-questioning dialogue—a pattern in which students initiate questions on the content of the lesson and the teacher answers them; the teacher-student duolog—a prolonged series of exchanges between the teacher and one student in triadic dialogue or student-questioning dialogue; teacher-student debate—a prolonged series of exchanges in which students challenge or disagree with the teacher on the content of the lesson; true dialogue—a pattern in which the teacher and the student(s) ask and answer one another's questions and respond to one another's amendments as in normal conversation; and cross-discussion—a pattern in which students speak directly to one another about the subject matter and the teacher acts as a moderator or an equal participant without special speaking rights.

Third, to ask questions on higher-level thinking has been shown to be significant in improving the quality of classroom discourse. For example, Mortimer and Scott (2000) used the flow of discourse framework to analyze classroom talk. The framework is based on Vygotskian and neo-Vygotskian perspectives (Vygotsky, 1978; Wertsch, 1991) that classroom talk can mediate the development of meaning and understandings between teachers and students and student learning of science concepts. The importance of such analysis is that a teacher's ability to manage classroom discourse can support students' development of knowledge and meaning-making. Mortimer and Scott expanded upon the triadic dialogic pattern to a form of teacher intervention as he or she regulates and guides the classroom discourse. One form of a teacher's intervention is to support student meaning-making by asking questions to check student understanding in three ways: to ask for clarification of student ideas, to check individual understanding, and to check consensus in the class about certain ideas. As the authors argued, teacher intervention in the classroom discourse is one aspect of teacher knowledge that is often overlooked in the analysis of teaching practice.

Overall, as a general instructional strategy, questioning in classroom teaching and learning plays a very important role in determining the quality of discourse and the ways in which students learn and understand science. However, the type of questions being asked is what is important to engendering improved student learning outcomes in science (Koufetta-Menicou & Scaife, 2000).

FORMS OF REPRESENTATIONS

Many scientific phenomena, such as those studied in cosmology, geology, chemistry, or biology, are beyond the learner's temporal, perceptual, and experiential limits

(Kozma, 2000). Consequently, our understanding of these phenomena depends on "our ability to access and interact with them indirectly" (p. 12). This is an important issue in effective instruction and is dependent on the teacher's expertise in representing his or her scientific knowledge in ways appropriate to the content and the way that content should be presented to a particular of group of learners. Essentially this is the notion of pedagogical content knowledge (PCK) that Shulman (1987) has argued "represents the blending of content and pedagogy into an understanding of how particular topics, problems, or issues are organised, represented, and adapted to the diverse interests and abilities of learners and presented for instruction" (p. 8). A teacher's pedagogical content knowledge includes models, analogies, equations, graphs, diagrams, pictures, and simulations that can help the learner understand an idea. These representations may be exhibited in a variety of forms/ modes such as verbal, mathematical, visual, and actional operational. Different types of representations are used to enhance conceptual understanding, and a considerable amount of research has been conducted to investigate the effect of a single representation on learning.

Gilbert, Boulter, and Elmer (2000) considered a model in science as "a representation of a phenomenon initially produced for a specific purpose" (p. 11). From the perspectives of modeling and models in science education, Gilbert et al. delineated nine different models used in science education: a mental model, an expressed model, a consensus model, a scientific model, a historical model, a curricular model, a teaching model, a hybrid model, and a model of pedagogy. Through interactions, an expressed model is placed in the public domain by individuals or groups. According to Gilbert et al., one or more of the following six modes of representations are significant in expressed models: (1) concrete mode consisting of the use of materials (e.g., a wooden model of a car); (2) verbal mode consisting of the use of metaphors and analogies in speech (e.g., a textbook descriptions); (3) mathematical mode consisting of mathematical expressions (e.g., universal gas equation); (4) visual mode consisting of graphs, pictures, and diagrams; (5) symbolic mode consisting of visual, verbal and mathematical modes; and (6) gestural mode consisting of actions (e.g., hand movements). Each of these modes has direct application to teaching strategies, and several are discussed in more detail in this section.

ANALOGIES AND METAPHORS

Representations include analogies and their allies, particularly metaphors. According to Glynn (1991), an analogy is a process for identifying similarities between different concepts; the familiar concept is called the analog and the unfamiliar one the target. The famous seventeenth-century astronomer Johannes Kepler (cited in Polya, 1954) once wrote: "And I cherish more than anything else the Analogies, my most trustworthy masters. They know all the secrets of Nature, and they ought to be least neglected in Geometry" (p. 12). Given the historical importance of analogical reasoning in scientific discovery, insights, and explanations, analogies have been used by textbook authors and classroom teachers to explain science concepts to students. Furthermore, learning science is the reconstruction of the products of modeling (Justi & Gilbert, 2002), and analogies are at the heart of modeling.

Teachers' use of analogies, in one or several forms of representation, has been an important line of research into teaching and learning of abstract science concepts, and reasoning and problem solving, and for conceptual change (Dagher, 1995). Analogies and metaphors have been used in science education as instructional strategies to engender interest, motivation, and understanding (Harrison & Treagust, 1994; Martins & Ogborn, 1997; Venville &Treagust, 1996). Since the time before computers were used in the classroom, science teachers have been using a range of different representational techniques to present information to students, such as verbal and written language, graphics and pictures, practical demonstrations, abstract mathematical models, and semi-abstract simulations (van Someren, Boshuizen, de Jong, & Reimann, 1998).

Research has shown that analogical teaching approaches can enhance student learning. For example, the findings of the study by Treagust, Harrison, Venville, and Dagher's (1996) indicated that a teacher's use of a cart with wheels moving obliquely over different surfaces as an analogy for refraction of light in a 10th-grade physics class successfully engendered conceptual change in student learning about the refraction of light. Martins and Ogborn explored how primary school teachers used metaphors to think about scientific ideas of DNA and genetics. The results of the study indicated that these primary school teachers creatively and imaginatively assimilated and constructed metaphorical models, drawings, and analogies to understand the scientific ideas of DNA and genetics. Metaphors and analogies thus connected their everyday knowledge to scientific ideas. In another example, a cross-age study involved secondary school, undergraduate, and postgraduate students' use of analogy and anthropomorphism along with their alternative conceptions of mental models of chemical bonding (Coll & Treagust, 2002). Findings indicated that learners made use of analogy and anthropomorphism to aid their explanations of chemical bonding. Coll and Treagust suggested that teachers need not only to encourage learners to use analogy but also to carefully examine curriculum and to postpone instruction of complex models to a later stage in the students' program of study. However, when analogies were used for chemistry problem-solving in a college preparatory chemistry course, Friedel, Gabel, and Samuel (1990) showed that the use of analogies was not an appropriate teaching strategy when the teachers did not determine whether the analog was meaningful to the students or when the instructional time was too short.

In brief, despite the fact that analogies appear to be useful as strategies in teaching and learning of abstract concepts, they are "double-edged swords" (Glynn, 1991, p. 227) which, when not used cautiously, may lead to miscomprehension and misdirection. Two further problems with analogies presented in textbooks and used by classroom teachers are when teachers use analogies as mechanical clichés, that is, when they are used without thought about their meanings, and when inconsistencies between the analog and the target result in students being unable to map the shared attributes and delineate the limitations of analogies. To address these problems, Treagust, Harrison, and Venville (1998) developed a teaching model called FAR—referring to Focus, Action, and Reflection—whereby teachers overtly direct students' attention to the similarities and dissimilarities of the analog and target concept. This teaching model was developed in cooperation with science teachers based on an earlier analysis of exemplary analogies in textbooks (Glynn, 1991).

FROM MULTIPLE ANALOGIES
TO MULTIPLE REPRESENTATIONS

In view of the problems in using analogies as part of instruction, Glynn (1991) suggested using several analogies (for a single concept), which can allow students to examine the concept from more than one perspective. Each perspective (analogy) brings particular features of the concept into a clearer focus; thus students will have a more comprehensive understanding of that concept and its relationship to other concepts.

Along this line of thinking, Harrison and Treagust (2000) reported a year-long study of the role of multiple models in student learning about atoms, molecules, and chemical bonds in an 11th-grade chemistry class. The outcomes suggested that students who socially negotiated the shared and unshared attributes of common analogical models for atoms, molecules, and chemical bonds used these models more consistently in their explanation. As well, students who were encouraged to use multiple particle models displayed more scientific understandings of particles and more interactions than did students who concentrated on a single model. Harrison and Treagust proposed, among other pedagogical recommendations, that multiple models should be introduced at an early stage and consistently developed and invoked during learning discussions. In view of the weakness in the ways models were represented in this study, the authors suggested that further research be done to find out what influence the representational form of analogical models has on the effectiveness of model-based learning.

Recently, new perspectives on computer-based multiple representations used in instruction (Ainsworth, 1999) have provided a more robust framework for interpreting analogical models and their relatives such as metaphors, which have been in use for centuries as vehicles for reasoning. According to Ainsworth's (1999) conceptual analysis of existing computer-based multirepresentational learning environments (Ainsworth, Bibby, & Wood, 1997; Hennessy et al., 1995), there are three major functions that multiple external representations (MERs) serve in learning situations—to complement, to constrain, and to construct. The first function of MERs in Ainsworth's (1999) functional taxonomy is to use representations that provide complementary information or support complementary cognitive processes so that learners can reap the benefits of the combined advantages, such as using both diagrams and verbal-textual representations. The second function is to use a familiar representation to constrain the interpretation (or misinterpretation) of a less familiar representation so as to help learners develop a better understanding of the domain. The third function of MERs is to encourage learners to construct a deeper understanding of a phenomenon through abstraction of, extension from, and relations between the representations. Ainsworth's functional taxonomy of MERs has been based largely on research in mathematics (see, for example, Ainsworth et al., 1997; Larkin & Simon, 1987) and physics (see, for example, Hennessy et al., 1995). The notion of multiple representations has also been used to improve learning in other domains such as chemistry (see, for example, Kozma, 2000) and medicine (see, for example, Boshuizen & van de Wiel, 1998).

In school learning, multiple representations provide new opportunities to engender student motivation, interest, and understanding. In a recent study on the motivational aspects of learning genetics (Tsui & Treagust, 2004), a science teacher used an interactive computer program called BioLogica alongside other teaching strategies and resources to teach genetics in a 10th-grade biology class. Findings showed that MERs in the computer program intrinsically motivated the 10th-grade students in their learning of genetics, which is a linguistically and conceptually difficult topic in biology. The salient features of the MERs of the computer program identified in this study included instant feedback, flexibility, and visualization. Students' motivation was interpreted as curiosity, control, fantasy, and challenge, which were similar to Malone and Lepper's (1987) taxonomy of intrinsic motivations. The finding of this study also indicated that most students improved their genetics reasoning after instruction, indicating that computer-based MERs hold promise in providing new opportunities for learning abstract concepts in science.

LEVELS OF REPRESENTATION

One major difficulty for learning science at school is that scientific knowledge can be represented at a number of levels, some of which are not observable to the learners. Scientists must be able to represent knowledge in order to conduct research, and teachers must do so in order to teach students. Perhaps this is most important in the field of chemistry, which is difficult to learn because many concepts are abstract and are unfamiliar to students, whose personally constructed representations are often in conflict with scientifically accepted explanations (Treagust & Chittleborough, 2001). Learning of chemistry is a matter of learning about its representation at different levels, which can describe (descriptive and functional), represent (representational), and explain (molecular) chemical phenomena (Johnstone 1993).

Teachers do need to be cognizant of the three levels of representation and their meaning as follows: symbolic—comprising a large variety of pictorial representations, algebraic and computational forms; submicrosocopic—comprising the particulate level, which can be used to describe the movement of electrons, molecules, particles, or atoms; and macroscopic—comprising references to students' everyday experiences. According to Johnstone (1991), most teachers used the triangle of multilevel thought in their teaching without being aware of the demands being made on the students. In Johnstone's triangle of multilevel thought, knowledge of chemistry can generally be organized as three ideas of structure, bonding, and energy. Johnstone argued against teachers using all three levels in their teaching. To make learning easier, teachers should teach chemistry only at the macro level or at most at two levels. Johnstone also extended this triangle of multilevel thought to the teaching of physics and biology. In physics there are also three similar levels of representations: the macro (visible moving bodies), the invisible (e.g., forces, reactions, electrons), and the symbolic (mathematics, formulas). The pedagogical implications of Johnstone's notion of multilevel thought are that teachers cannot simultaneously present the three levels of representations in teaching difficult science concepts. Otherwise, students would become overloaded with information and be unable to see the connections between the levels.

In biology, too, there are three levels: the macro (plants or animals), the micro (cells), and the biochemical (DNA, etc.). Marbach-Ad and Stavy (2000) articulated Johnstone's triangle of multilevel thought to explain why genetics in biology is so difficult to teach and learn because it is difficult to understand meiosis (micro level) and the connection between meiosis and Mendelian genetics (macro level).

GROUP LEARNING AND COOPERATIVE LEARNING

As reviewed by Lazarowitz and Hertz-Lazarowitz (1998), the use of group learning in science education has been rather recent, but the learning outcomes are very promising. For science teachers, Stahl's (1996) handbook provides a comprehensive selection of highly effective and widely used cooperative learning strategies that science teachers can use in the primary and secondary science classrooms.

To encourage students to construct meaningful knowledge networks, science teachers need to provide opportunities to engage the students in motivating and interactive activities and cooperative learning activities (Treagust & Chittleborough, 2001). A review of the literature on cooperative learning indicates that most of the studies are on biology learning, and the major learning outcomes focused generally on the cognitive domain rather than on the affective domain (Lazarowitz & Hertz-Lazarowitz, 1998). Accordingly, five cooperative methods of instructions have been used in science education:

1. Learning Together and Alone (Johnson & Johnson, 1975) involves students in heterogeneous groups of four or five working together to achieve some common goal in such a way as to develop both personal and group skill.

2. The Jigsaw Classroom (Aronson, Stephan, Blaney, & Snapp, 1978). In this method, the class is divided into jigsaw groups of five (students a to e), with each student assigned a special part of a group task, and an expert group with members from those with the same part. The expert group members, after mastering their skills, return to the jigsaw group to tutor their teammates to achieve the goal.

3. Student Teams and Achievement Division (STAD) (Slavin, 1978) and Teams Games Tournaments (TGT) (De Vries & Slavin, 1978). These are the same in involving five common components: class presentation by the teacher followed by discussion, teams working on teacher-prepared worksheets, quizzes (STAD), or game/tournament (TGT);

4. Group Investigation (described in Lazarowitz & Hertz-Lazarowitz, 1998) integrates the four basic features of investigation, interaction, interpretation and intrinsic motivation. In the group investigation classroom, groups work on different but related topics using a variety of resources to generate questions, gather information and actively construct their own knowledge.

5. Peer Tutoring in Small Investigative Group (PTSIG) (Lazarowitz & Karsenty, 1990). PTSIG involves four basic features of investigation, interaction, interpretation, and intrinsic motivations combined into six stages of the model.

According to Lazarowitz and Hertz-Lazarowitz's (1998) review, previous research has shown positive results of cooperative learning in different subject areas across different academic levels in the cognitive, affective, and social domains of learning. At the primary school level, the positive learning outcomes included increased students' academic achievement, helping behavior, and peer support. At the high school level, both junior and senior students improved their learning, as demonstrated by higher cognitive achievement, more positive attitudes, greater self-esteem, more engagement on tasks, and increased motivation and enjoyment. Fraser (1998) also reported that cooperative learning promoted a positive learning environment. Similar positive learning outcomes were reported at the college level when the studies included cognitive preferences, concept learning, and gender differences.

Although cooperative learning appears to be a promising strategy for the cognitive, social, and affective development of student learning at school, teachers and researchers have to develop relevant, rich, and challenging curricula. There are several challenges of using group and cooperative strategies in supporting student learning. First, such strategies should be able to address student learning along multiple dimensions of the cognitive, affective, and social domains of learning. Second, science teachers using group and cooperative methods to address classroom learning issues have to be cognizant of any sociocultural peer effects due to ability, gender, and cultural differences (see, for example, Forman & Cazden, 1985). Third, cooperative learning involves interaction with peers in communities of learners and with computer data bases in a distributed fashion (see, for example, Brown et al., 1993; Windschitl, 1998). These challenges should be incorporated into the teacher education programs to allow pre-service teachers and in-service teachers to develop their knowledge of group and cooperative learning strategies used in their teaching.

INDUCTIVE AND DEDUCTIVE REASONING— THE LEARNING CYCLE APPROACH

The traditional textbook approach to science learning provides information and challenges students to think deductively by reasoning from cause to effect. However, this reasoning contrasts with the way that many scientists, such as geneticists, inductively reason and learn in their research work from effect to cause. Indeed, this approach is consistent with most science teaching approaches using laboratory experiments that implicitly assume that students learn by inductive reasoning. However, as previously stated, whether laboratory work will necessarily improve student learning is a contentious issue (White, 1996), and the challenge of inductive reasoning could be what makes laboratory tasks difficult for students.

The learning cycle approach has survived into the present time as an important instructional strategy (see, for example, the review by Abraham, 1998). According to Lawson, Abraham, and Renner (1989), the learning cycle originated from the work of Robert Karplus in the Science Curriculum Improvement Study (SCIS) program for U.S. elementary and junior high schools in the late 1950s and 1960s, and in Chester Lawson's work in biology education in U.S. high schools and universities during the same period. It was from Lawson's project that the famous Biological Science Curriculum Study (BSCS) project had developed during the post-Sputnik reforms in science education.

Originally known as exploration-invention-discovery (Karplus & Thier, 1967), the inquiry-based learning cycle approach consists of three phases. First, the exploration phase provides students with the experience of the concept to be developed, such as the use of laboratory experiments, which involves deductive thought. Then, in the *conceptual invention* phase, the students and/or teacher develop the concept from the data through classroom discussion, which involves inductive thinking. Finally, in the conceptual expansion phase, the student is given the opportunity to explore the usefulness and application of the concept.

The three phases in its latest version, according to Abraham (1998), are simply "inform-verify-practice" or (I → V → P). The three phases in sequence are *identification* of a concept, *demonstration* of the concept, and *application* of the concept. The common justification of using the learning-cycle approach is based on the Piagetian notions of learning new concepts through assimilation and disequilibration in the first phase, accommodation in the second phase, and conceptual expansion in the third phase. "The three distinct phases with a definite sequence and structure are necessary for the development of conceptual understanding" (Tobin et al., 1994). Through this three-phase sequencing of hands-on laboratory experiences to engender knowledge construction, the learning-cycle approach can address the concern that laboratory work is unable to improve conceptual understanding.

Two well-documented case studies using the learning-cycle approach are the studies of Renner, Abraham, and Birnie (1985) and Abraham and Renner (1986). Renner et al.'s study—conducted in three 12th-grade physics classes in a U.S. secondary school using all or some of the phases of the learning-cycle approach—highlighted the necessity of all the three phases and the importance of their sequence in concept development of physics. The content of the student investigation in Renner et al.'s study included linear motion, heat measurement in solids, static electricity, and current and magnetism. In the second case-study example, Abraham and Renner (1986) investigated different learning cycles in six classes in senior secondary school chemistry and indicated that the normal learning cycle sequence, gathering data → Invention → expansion, is the optimum sequence for achievement of content knowledge of chemical concepts associated with heat laws. Since the 1980s, many studies on the learning-cycle approach have been conducted in different domains and at different school and university levels (e.g., Jackman, 1990; Lavoie, 1999; Lawson, 2001; Libby, 1995; Marek, 2000; Odum & Kelly, 2001). Research on the learning-cycle approach has confirmed that this is an effective instructional strategy with many advantages over more traditional approaches in terms of student attitudes, motivation, process learning, and concept learning. Science teachers should make use of instructional materials with key characteristics of the learning-cycle approach (Abraham, 1998).

There are two trends in instructional strategies using the learning-cycle approach that are worth a more detailed discussion here. First, there has been an increase in the use of ICT in teaching with the learning-cycle approach (e.g., Dwyer & Lopez, 2001; Gibson, 2001; Marek, 2000). Dwyer and Lopez's study involved Australian students using the simulation software Exploring the Nardoo in all phases of the learning cycle. In this study upper elementary and middle school science students were observed, along with their teacher, using simulations as they engaged in learning-cycle lessons revolving around river ecosystems. Students were asked to address complex water management issues affecting the fictional Nardoo River and improve the environment. The simulation is intended to develope students' investigation and problem-solving skills. Findings indicated that with specific guidance in simulations, students performed better and that simulations could be used again to apply newly learned concepts in different contexts in the expansion phase of the learning cycle. Second, the learning cycle continues to be used in instructional practices at the university level (Ana G. Mendez Educational Foundation, 1987; Farrell, Moog, & Spencer, 1999; Jackman, 1990).

The most important conclusion based on research is that the inquiry-based, laboratory-based learning-cycle approach has provided students with not only hands-on experiences to learn the concepts but also the opportunity for knowledge construction from their personal experience and for application to new situations (Abraham, 1998). Nevertheless, the learning-cycle approach has its limitations, particularly when it is applied to the ICT-rich learning environment. Based largely on Piagetian psychology, the learning-cycle approach focuses on individual learning more than group learning and more on personal construction than social construction of knowledge. Although discursive practices are expected in the second phase or exploration phase, the focus is more on personal construction of knowledge developed from the data or observations in the experiments.

SUMMARY

As is apparent from this brief review, there is a wide variety of instructional methods and strategies used in the teaching and learning of science that range from those that are more teacher-centered to those that are more student-centered. Each of the six methods and strategies has a growing body of theory to support each instructional approach, and enough research has been conducted with each of these different methods and strategies to have some confidence in their effectiveness in enhancing the learning, and opportunities for learning, of students from elementary school to university. None of the approaches by themselves should be seen as a panacea that will improve science learningl but each method or strategy can be part of a successful science teacher's instructional repertoire.

ACKNOWLEDGMENTS

I wish to thank Dr. Chi-Yan Tsui for his valuable contributions to the conceptualizations that initially framed this review and for helping with the first draft of this chapter. Thanks also to Michael Abraham and Richard Gunstone, who reviewed this chapter. I hope that I have done justice to their critiques.

REFERENCES

Abraham, M. R. (1998). The learning cycle approach as a strategy for instruction in science. In B. J. Fraser & K. G. Tobin (Eds.), *International handbook of science education* (pp. 513–524). Dordrecht, the Netherlands: Kluwer.

Abraham, M. R., & Renner, J. W. (1986). The sequence of learning cycle activities in high school chemistry. *Journal of Research in Science Teaching, 23*(2), 121–143.

Ainsworth, S. E. (1999). The functions of multiple representations. *Computers & Education, 33*(2/3), 131–152.

Ainsworth, S. E., Bibby, P. A., & Wood, D. J. (1997). Information technology and multiple representations: New opportunities—new problems. *Journal of Information Technology for Teacher Education, 6*(1), 93–104.

Ana G. Mendez Educational Foundation. (1987). *Problem solving and reasoning skills cognitive development model for severely disadvantaged Puerto Rican college students: Final report.* Rio Piedras, PR: Author.

Anderson, R. D., & Helms, J. V. (2001). The ideal of standards and the reality of schools; Needed research. *Journal of Research in Science Teaching, 38*(1), 3–16.

Aronson, E., Stephan, C., Blaney, N., & Snapp, M. (1978). *The jigsaw classroom.* Beverly Hills, CA: Sage.

Baird, J. R., & White, R. T. (1996). Metacognitive strategies in the classroom. In D. F. Treagust, R. Duit, & B. J. Fraser (1996). *Teaching and learning of science and mathematics* (pp. 190–200). New York: Teachers College Press.

Bell, B. (2000). Formative assessment and science education: A model and theorising. In R. Millar, J. Leach, & J. Osborne (Eds.), *Improving science education: The contribution of research* (pp. 48–61). Buckingham and Philadelphia: Open University Press.

Bereiter, C., & Scardamalia, M. (1989). Intentional learning as a goal of instruction. In L. B. Resnick et al. (Eds.), *Knowing, learning, and instruction: Essays in honor of Robert Glaser* (pp. 361–392). Hillsdale, NJ: Lawrence Erlbaum Associates.

Boshuizen, H. P. A., & van de Wiel, W. J. (1998). Using multiple representations in medicine: How students struggle with them. In M. W. Van Someren, P. Reimann, H. P. A. Boshuizen, & T. de Jong (Eds.), *Learning with multiple representations* (pp. 237–262). London: Pergamon.

Brown, A. L., Ash, D., Rutherford, M., Nakagawa, K., Gordon, A., & Camione, J. C. (1993). Distributed expertise in the classroom. In G. Salomon (Ed.), *Distributed cognitions.* New York: Cambridge University Press.

Champagne, A. B., Gunstone, R. F., & Klopfer, L. E. (1985). Effecting changes in cognitive structures among physics students. In L. H. T. West & A. L. Pines (Eds.), *Cognitive structure and conceptual change* (pp. 163–187). Orlando, FL: Academic Press.

Coll, R. K., & Treagust, D. F. (2002). Learners' use of analogy and alternative conceptions for chemical bonding: A cross-age study. *Australian Science Teachers Journal* (48), 24–32.

Concord Consortium. (2001, October). *BioLogica.* Retrieved October 8, 2001, from http://biologica.concord.org

Dagher, Z. R. (1995). Review of studies on the effectiveness of instructional analogies in science education. *Science Education, 79*(3), 295–312.

De Vries, D. L., & Slavin, R. E. (1978). Teams-Games-Tournament (TGT): Review of ten classroom experiments. *Journal of Research and Development in Education, 12,* 28–38.

Duit, R., & Treagust, D. F. (1998). Learning in science—from behaviourism towards social constructivism and beyond. In B. Fraser and K. Tobin (Eds.), *International handbook of science education, Part 1* (pp. 3–25). Dordrecht, the Netherlands: Kluwer.

Dwyer, W. M., & Lopez, V. E. (2001, June). *Simulations in the learning cycle: A case study Involving "Exploring the Nardoo."* Paper presented at the Building on the Future. NECC 2001: National Educational Computing Conference Proceedings (22nd), Chicago.

Farrell, J. J., Moog, R. S., & Spencer, J. N. (1999). A guided inquiry general chemistry course. *Journal of Chemical Education, 76*(4), 570–574.

Fensham, P. J. (2001). Science content as problematic issues for research. In H. Behrendt, H. Dahncke, R. Duit, W. M. Komorek, A. Kross, & P. Reiska (Eds.), *Research in science education—past, present and future* (pp. 27–41). Dordrecht, the Netherlands: Kluwer.

Fensham, P. J., Gunstone, R. F., & White, R. T. (Eds.), *The content of science: A constructivist approach to its teaching and learning* (pp. 131–146). London: Falmer Press.

Forman, E. A., & Cazden, C. B. (1985). Exploring Vygotskian perspectives in education: The cognitive value of peer interaction. In J. V. Wertsch (Ed.), *Culture, communication and cognition: Vygotskian perspectives* (pp. 323–347). Cambridge: Cambridge University Press.

Fraser, B. J. (1998). Science learning environments: Assessment, effects and determinants. In B. Fraser and K. Tobin (Eds.), *International handbook of science education, Part 1* (pp. 527–564). Dordrecht, the Netherlands: Kluwer.

Friedel, A. W., Gabel, D. L., & Samuel, J. (1990). Using analogs for chemistry problem solving: Does it increase understanding? *School Science and Mathematics, 90*(8), 674–682.

Gabel (2003). Enhancing the conceptual understanding of science. *Educational Horizons, 81*(2), 70–76.

Gibson, D. (2001, October). *Collaboration through Online Personal Learning.* Paper presented at the WebNet 2001: World Conference on the WWW and Internet, Orlando, FL.

Gilbert, J., Boulter, C. J., & Elmer, R. (2000). Positioning models in science education and in design and technology education. In J. Gilbert & C. J. Boutler (Eds.), *Developing models in science education* (pp. 3–17). Dordrecht, the Netherlands: Kluwer.

Glynn, S. M. (1991). Explaining science concepts: A teaching-with-analogies model. In M. Shawn, S. M. Glynn, R. H. Yeany, & B. K. Britton (Eds.), *The psychology of learning science* (pp. 219–240). Hillsdale, NJ: Lawrence Erlbaum Associates.

Gunstone, R. F. (1994). The importance of specific science content in the enhancement of metacognition. In P. J. Fensham & R. F. Gunstone & R. T. White (Eds.), *The content of science: A constructivist approach to its teaching and learning* (pp. 131–146). London: Falmer Press.

Gunstone, R. F. (1995). Constructivist learning and the teaching of science. In B. Hand & V. Prain (Eds.), *Teaching and learning in science: The constructivist classroom* (pp. 3–20). Sydney: Harcourt Brace.

Halliday, M. A. K., & Martin, J. R. (1993). *Writing science: Literacy and discursive power.* London: Falmer.

Harrison, A. G., & Treagust, D. F. (1994). Science analogies. *Science Teacher, 61*(4), 40–43.

Harrison, A., & Treagust, D. F. (2000). Learning about atoms, molecules, and chemical bonds: A case study of multiple-model use in grade 11 chemistry. *Science Education, 84*, 352–381.

Hennessy, S., Twigger, D., Driver, R., O' Shea, T., O' Shea, T., Byard, M., et al. (1995). Design of a computer-augumented curriculum for mechanics. *International Journal of Educational Research, 17*(1), 75–92.

Hodson, D., & Bencze, L. (1998). Becoming critical about practical work: Changing views and changing practice through action research. *International Journal of Science Education, 20*(6), 683–694.

Hodson, D., & Hodson, J. (1998). From constructivism to social constructivism: A Vygotskian perspective on teaching and learning science. *School Science Review, 79*(289), 33–41.

Hofstein, A., & Lunetta, V. N. (2004). The laboratory in science education: Foundations for the twenty-first century. *Science Education, 88*, 28–54.

Horwood, R. H. (1988). Explaining and description in science teaching. *Science Education, 72*(1), 41–49.

Howe, A. C. (1996). Development of science concepts within a Vygotskian framework. *Science Education, 80*(1), 35–51.

Jackman, L. E. (1990). Effects of conceptual systems and instructional methods on general chemistry laboratory achievement. *Journal of Research in Science Teaching, 27*(7), 699–709.

Johnson, D. W., & Johnson, R. T. (1975). *Learning together and alone.* Englewood Cliffs, NJ: Prentice-Hall.

Johnson-Laird, P. N. (1983). *Mental models.* Cambridge: Cambridge University Press.

Johnstone, A. H. (1991). Why is science difficult to learn? Things are seldom what they seem. *Journal of Computer Assisted Learning, 7*, 75–83.

Johnstone, A. H. (1993). The development of chemistry teaching: A changing response to changing demand. *Journal of Chemical Education, 70*(9), 701–705.

Justi, R., & Gilbert, J. K. (2002). Models and modelling in chemical education. In J. G. Gilbert, O. De Jong, R. Justi, D. F. Treagust, & J. H. van Driel (Eds.). *Chemical education: Towards research based practice* (pp. 47–68). Dordrecht, the Netherlands: Kluwer.

Karplus, R., & Thier, H. D. (1967). *A new look at elementary school science.* Chicago: Rand McNally.

Kearney, M. D., Treagust, D. F., Yeo, S., & Zadnik, M. G. (2002). Student and teacher perception of the use of multimedia supported predict-observe-explain tasks to probe understanding. *Research in Science Education, 31*(4), 589–615.

Koufetta-Menicou C., & Scaife, J. (2000). Teachers' questions—types and significance in science education. *School Science Review, 81*(296), 79–84.

Kozma, R. B. (2000). The use of multiple representations and the social construction of understanding in chemistry. In M. J. Jacobson & R. B. Kozma (Eds.), *Innovations in science and mathematics education: Advanced design for technologies of learning* (pp. 11–46). Mahwah, NJ: Lawrence Erlbaum Associates.

Larkin, J. H., & Simon, H. A. (1987). Why a diagram is (sometimes) worth ten thousand words. *Cognitive Science, 11*, 65–99.

Lavoie, D. R. (1999). Effects of emphasizing hypothetico-predictive reasoning within the science learning cycle on high school student's process skills and conceptual understandings in biology. *Journal of Research in Science Teaching, 36*(10), 1127–1147.

Lawson, A. E. (2001). Using the learning cycle to teach biology concepts and reasoning patterns. *Journal of Biological Education, 35*(4), 165–169.

Lawson, A. E., Abraham, M. R., & Renner, J. W. (1989). *A theory of instruction: Using the learning cycle to teach science concepts and thinking skills.* Monograph No. 1. Manhattan, KS: National Association for Research on Science Teaching, Kansas State University.

Lazarowitz, R., & Hertz-Lazarowitz, R. (1998). Cooperative learning in the science curriculum. In K. G. Tobin (Ed.), *International handbook of science education* (pp. 449–469). Dordrecht, the Netherlands: Kluwer.

Lazarowitz, R., & Karsenty, G. (1990). Cooperation learning and students' self-esteem in tenth grade biology classroom. In S. Sharan (Ed.), *Cooperative learning, theory and research* (pp. 123–149). New York: Praeger.

Lazarowitz, R., & Tamir, P. (1994). Research on using laboratory instruction in science. In D. L. Gabel (Ed.), *Handbook of research on science teaching and learning* (pp. 94–128). New York: Praeger.

Lemke, J. L. (1990). *Talking science: Language, learning, and values.* Norwood, NJ: Ablex.

Lemke, J. L. (1998). Multiplying meaning: Visual and verbal semiotics in scientific text. In J. R. Martin & R. Veel (Eds.), *Reading science* (pp. 87–113). London and New York: Routledge.

Libby, R. D. (1995). Piaget and organic chemistry: teaching introductory organic chemistry through learning cycles. *Journal of Chemical Education, 72*(7), 626–631.

Linn, M. C. (2003). Technology and science education: starting points, research programs and trends. *International Journal of Science Education, 25*, 727–758.

Liew, C. W., & Treagust, D. F. (1995). A predict-observe-explain teaching sequence for learning about students' understanding of heat and expansion liquids. *Australian Science Teachers Journal, 41*(1), 68–71.

Malone, T. W., & Lepper, M. R. (1987). Making learning fun: A taxonomy of intrinsic motivations for learning. In R. Snow & M. Farr (Eds.), *Aptitude, learning and instruction: Vol. 3. Cognitive and affective process analysis* (pp. 223–253). Hillsdale, NJ: Lawrence Erlbaum Associates.

Marbach-Ad, G., & Stavy, R. (2000). Students' cellular and molecular explanations of genetic phenomena. *Journal of Biological Education, 34*(4), 200–205.

Marek, E. A. (2000). Student absences during learning cycle phases: a technological alternative for make-up work in laboratory based high school chemistry. *International Journal of Science Education, 22*(10), 1055–1068.

Martins, I., & Ogborn, J. (1997). Metaphorical reasoning about genetics. *International Journal of Educational Research, 19*(6), 48–63.

McRobbie, C. J., Roth, W.-M., & Lucas, K. B. (1997). Multiple learning environments in a physics classroom. *International Journal of Educational Research, 27*, 333–342.

Mortimer, E., & Scott, P. (2000). Analysing discourse in the science classroom. In R. Millar, J. Leach, & J. Osborne (Eds.), *Improving science education: The contribution of research* (pp. 125–142). Buckingham, UK, and Philadelphia: Open University Press.

Novak. J. D. (1996). Concept mapping: A tool for improving science teaching and learning. In D. F. Treagust, R. Duit, & B. J. Fraser (1996). *Teaching and learning of science and mathematics* (pp. 32–43). New York: Teachers College Press.

Odum, A. L., & Kelly, P. V. (2001). Integrating concept mapping and the learning cycle to teach diffusion and osmosis concepts to high school biology students. *Journal of Research in Science Teaching, 85*(6), 615–635.

Ogborn, J., Kress, G., Martin, I., & McGillicuddy, K. (1996). *Explaining science in the classroom.* Buckingham, UK: Open University Press.

Palmer, D. (1995). The POE in the primary school: An evaluation. *Research in Science Education, 25*(3), 323–333.

Polya, G. (1954). *Mathematics and plausible reasoning: Vol. 1. Induction and analogy in mathematics.* Princeton, NJ: Princeton University Press.

Renner, J., Abraham, M., & Birnie, H. H. (1985). The importance of the form of student acquisition of data in phsyics learning cycles. *Journal of Research in Science Teaching, 22,* 303–325.

Roth, W.-M., McRobbie, C. J., Lucas, K. B., & Boutonne, S. (1997). The local production of order in traditional science laboratories: A phenomenological analysis. *Learning and Instruction, 7,* 107–136.

Rowe, M. B. (1974). Wait-time and rewards as instructional variables, their influence on language, logic, and fate control: Part one-wait time. *Journal of Research in Science Teaching, 11*(2), 81–94.

Shulman, L. S. (1987). Knowledge and teaching: Foundation of the new reform. *Harvard Educational Review, 57*(1), 1–22.

Sinatra, G. M., & Pintrich, P. R. (Eds.). (2003). *Intentional conceptual change.* Mahwah, NJ: Lawrence Erlbaum Associates.

Slavin, R. E. (1978). Student teams and achievement divisions. *Journal of Research and Development in Education, 12,* 39–49.

Spivey, N. N. (1997). *The constructivist metaphor: Reading, writing and making of meaning.* San Diego: Academic Press.

Stahl, R. J. (Ed.). (1996). *Cooperative learning in science.* Menlo Park, CA: Addison-Wesley.

Sutton, C. (1992). *Words, science and learning.* Buckingham, UK, and Philadephia: Open University Press.

Tobin, K., Tippins, D. J., & Gallard, A. J. (1994). Research on instructional strategies for teaching science. In D. L. Gabel (Ed.), *Handbook of research on science teaching and learning* (pp. 45–93). New York: MacMillan.

Treagust, D. F., & Chittleborough, G. (2001). Chemistry: A matter of understanding representations. In J. E. Brophy (Ed.), *Subject-specific instructional methods and activities* (pp. 239–267). London: Elsevier.

Treagust, D., & Harrison, A. (1999). The genesis of effective scientific explanation. In J. Loughran (Ed.), *Researching teaching: Methodologies and practices for understanding pedagogy* (pp. 28–43). London and Philadelphia: Falmer Press.

Treagust, D. F., Harrison, A.G., & Venville, G. J. (1998). Teaching science effectively with analogies: An approach for pre-service and in-service teacher education. *Journal of Science Teacher Education, 9*(2), 85–101.

Treagust, D. F., Harrison, A. G., Venville, G. J., & Dagher, Z. (1996). Using an analogical teaching approach to engender conceptual change. *International Journal of Science Education, 18,* 213–229.

Tsui, C.-Y., & Treagust, D. F. (2003). Genetics reasoning with multiple external representations. *Research in Science Education, 33*(1), 111–135.

Tsui, C.-Y., & Treagust, D. F. (2004). Motivational aspects of learning genetics with interactive multimedia. *The American Biology Teacher, 66*(3), 252–261.

van Someren, M. W., Boshuizen, H. P. A., de Jong, T., & Reimann, P. (1998). Introduction. In T. de Jong (Ed.), *Learning with multiple representations* (pp. 1–5). London: Elsevier Science.

Venville, G. J., & Treagust, D. F. (1996). The role of analogies in promoting conceptual change in biology. *Instructional Science, 24,* 295–320.

Venville, G. J., & Treagust, D. F. (1997). Analogies in biology education: A contentious issue. *The American Biology Teacher, 59*(5), 282–287.

Vygotsky, L. S. (1978). *Mind in society: The development of higher psychological processes.* Cambridge, MA: Harvard University Press.

Watson, R. (2000). The role of practical work. In M. Monk & J. Osborne (Eds.), *Good practice in science teaching* (pp. 57–71). Buckingham, UK, and Philadelphia: Open University Press.

Wertsch, J. V. (1991). *Voices of the mind: A sociocultural approach to mediated action.* London: Harvester Wheatsheaf.

White, R. T. (1996). The link between the laboratory and learning. *International Journal of Science Education, 18*(7), 761–774.

White, R., & Gunstone, R. (1992). *Probing understanding.* London: Falmer Press.

Windschitl, M. (1998). A practical guide for incorporating computer-based simulations into science education. *The American Biology Teacher, 60*(2), 92–97.

Yore, L. D., Bisanz, G. L., & Hand, B. M. (2003). Examining the literacy component of scientific literacy: 25 years of language arts and science research. *International Journal of Science Education, 25*(6), 689–725.

Yore, L. D., Hand, B., Goldman, S. R., Hilderbrand, G. M., Osborne, J. F., Treagust, D. F., et al. (2004). New directions in language and science education research. *Reading Research Quarterly, 39*(3), 347–352.

CHAPTER 15

Learning and Teaching in the School Science Laboratory: An Analysis of Research, Theory, and Practice

Vincent N. Lunetta
Pennsylvania State University

Avi Hofstein
The Weizmann Institute of Science, Israel

Michael P. Clough
Iowa State University

Knowledge of the natural sciences is constructed to explain objects, phenomena, and their interactions in the natural world. With time, scientific ideas or concepts become connected by wider-ranging theories, and especially since the Renaissance, new knowledge and understanding has developed through continual, dynamic interaction between scientific theories, research, and experimental data. This complex interaction sometimes results in the rejection or modification of prior ideas and the development of newer ideas that link concepts together, in turn suggesting new methods, new interpretations of data, and new questions. Often, but not always, the data have come from carefully controlled studies conducted in scientists' laboratories. This kind of interrogation of nature often brings forth information that would not have been evident simply through direct observation of the natural world.

There are interesting similarities and differences between the ways that scientific communities develop new knowledge of the natural world and the ways that learners come to understand their world. Novice learners also construct ideas about the natural world based, in part, on observations of objects, phenomena, and their interactions. With time, these ideas also become linked and tested through the learner's experiences and his or her interactions with the ideas of others. In the process, learners come to retain and develop some concepts and explanations, to reject others, and in turn to wonder about connections to new ideas and implications. Teachers have unique opportunities in science to help students wonder about the exciting natural world, experience and observe interesting objects and phenomena, explore meaningful theoretical ideas, and grow in scientific understanding. The school science laboratory is a unique resource that can enhance students' interest, knowledge of science concepts and procedures, and knowledge of important tools and skills that can develop new understanding. Experiences in the school laboratory can also help students glimpse ideas about the nature of science that are crucial for their understanding of scientific knowledge. These are among the reasons that *laboratory activities* (*practical activities* in British Commonwealth parlance) have had a prominent place in the science curriculum since early in the nineteenth century. A classical definition of school science laboratory activities that would have been acceptable in the nineteenth century and most of the twentieth is: *learning experiences in which students interact with materials or with secondary sources of data to observe and understand the natural world* (for example: aerial photographs to examine lunar and earth geographic features; spectra to examine the nature of stars and atmospheres; sonar images to examine living systems). The development and increasingly widespread use of digital computing technologies in school science near the turn of the twenty-first century provide new tools for gathering, visualizing, and reporting data and findings as well as important new tools that can support learning. New tools also offer simulation resources for teaching and learning science. Some of these new tools and resources blur the interface between learning in the laboratory and learning with simulations that are representations of nature. In fact, work with simulations has caused some to perceive that school laboratory activities are themselves simulations of some of the things that scientists do (Lunetta, 1998). The new electronic tools and resources for teaching and learning associated with the school science laboratory also offer important new opportunities to study learning in science, and they warrant careful scholarly study by researchers in science education in the twenty-first century.

A HISTORICAL OVERVIEW

For almost 200 years, science educators have reported that laboratory activities can assist students in making sense of the natural world (Edgeworth & Edgeworth, 1811; Rosen, 1954). Over the years, many have argued that science cannot be meaningful to students without worthwhile practical experiences in the school laboratory. Unfortunately, the terms *school laboratory* or *lab* and *practical* have been used, too often without precise definition, to embrace a wide array of activities. Typically, the terms have meant experiences in school settings where students interact with materials to observe and understand the natural world. Some laboratory activities have been designed and conducted to engage students individually, and others have sought to engage students in small groups and in large-group demonstration settings. Teacher guidance and instructions have ranged from highly structured and teacher-centered to open inquiry. The terms have sometimes been used to include investigations or projects that are pursued for several weeks, sometimes outside the school, and on other occasions they have referred to experiences lasting 20 minutes or less. Sometimes laboratory activities have incorporated a high level of instrumentation, and at other times the use of any instrumentation has been meticulously avoided.

Historically, school *labs* have ranged from activities where data are gathered to illustrate a previously stated relationship to activities where students seek patterns or relationships in data they gather. In the early part of the twentieth century John Dewey and others in the progressive education movement energetically advocated an investigative and more utilitarian approach in learning. Through the 1950s, however, laboratory activities were used almost exclusively for illustrating information presented by the teacher and the textbook, and scholarly research on the educational effectiveness of the school laboratory was relatively limited.

Subsequently, in the science education reform era of the 1960s in both the United States and the United Kingdom, major science curriculum projects developed "new" curricula intended to engage students in investigation and inquiry as a central part of their science education. In that period, major curriculum projects used the learning theories of Jerome Bruner, Robert Gagne, and Jean Piaget to justify curricula emphasizing student inquiry and hands-on activities. Projects, including those of the Physical Science Study Committee and the Biological Sciences Curriculum Study in the United States and Nuffield in the United Kingdom, developed inductive laboratory activities as a fundamental part of the science curriculum. In these projects the laboratory was intended to be a place for inquiring, for developing and testing theories and assertions, and for practicing "the way of the scientist." George Pimentel (see Merrill & Ridgeway, 1969) noted that in the CHEMStudy project, the laboratory was designed to help students gain a better idea of the nature of science and scientific investigation.

For more than a century, laboratory experiences have been purported to promote central science education goals, including: the enhancement of students' understanding of concepts in science and its applications; scientific practical skills and problem-solving abilities; scientific "habits of mind"; understanding of how science and scientists work; and interest and motivation. Periodically, and particularly in the late 1970s and the early 1980s, serious questions were raised about the effectiveness of the school laboratory in promoting science learning (Bates, 1978; Hofstein & Lunetta, 1982). Questions emanated from multiple sources both within the science education community and beyond. Research on learning brought forth knowledge of learners' development and new insights about the learning of science concepts. Scholarly efforts identified serious mismatches between stated goals for science education and the learning outcomes visible in school graduates. Particularly noteworthy for laboratory learning, researchers reported that students regularly performed school science experiments with purposes in mind that were very different from those articulated by science educators for such experiences. In addition, comprehensive analyses of laboratory handbooks also provided evidence that major mismatches existed between goals espoused for science teaching and the behaviors implicit in science laboratory activities associated with major curriculum projects (Tamir & Lunetta, 1981). Lunetta and Tamir (1979) were among those who recommended greater consistency between goals, theories, and practices in the learning and teaching of science. In addition, important perspectives about the nature of science began to be applied to science education more broadly and to science laboratory activities in particular. These too fueled many concerns about the ways introductory sciences should be taught to promote learning with scientific understanding.

Nevertheless, in spite of a long series of reform efforts incorporating important elements from the history and nature of science, the predominant pattern of science teaching visible in schools through the turn of the twenty-first century has omitted the story of science. Instead, the science visible in schools has focused on "covering" knowledge of science topics and limited problem-solving skills. Within that framework laboratory activities have engaged students principally in following ritualistic procedures to verify conclusions previously presented by textbooks and teachers. In general, students have had limited freedom and time to explore and to make sense of phenomena. Objectives articulated for teaching and for student behaviors have often focused on specific tasks to be accomplished, such as "doing the density lab," rather than on the student learning that is to be accomplished, such as "learning about the relationships between mass and volume for different materials." Duschl and Gitomer (1997, p. 65) noted that teachers tend to see teaching as "dominated by tasks and activities rather than conceptual structures and scientific reasoning." Kesidou and Roseman (2002) reported that contemporary curricula did not engage students in laboratory activities consistent with goals for learning. Weiss et al. (2003, p. 1) reported that 59% of the science and mathematics lessons they observed were low in quality, often reflecting "passive learning" and "activity for activity's sake." This emphasis on dozens of tasks and activities rather than on conceptual understanding results in what Schmidt et al. (1999), analyzing the results of the Third International Mathematics and Science Study (TIMSS), called an unfocused science curriculum in the United States that is "a mile wide and an inch deep."

To complicate matters, science education studies have not always helped to distinguish between and link important ends (learning outcomes that are sought) and means to those ends (teaching resources and strategies such as specific kinds of investigative activities in the laboratory). For example, significant changes in technologies since the 1980s have offered new resources for teaching and learning, but insufficient attention has been directed to critical examination of how these new technologies can enhance or confound experiences in the school laboratory. Further complicating research into school laboratory practices have been ambiguous use of terms such as *inquiry science teaching*, which may refer to teaching science *as* inquiry (helping students understand how scientific knowledge is developed) or teaching science *through* inquiry (having students take part in inquiry investigations to help them acquire more meaningful conceptual science knowledge). Inquiry investigations conducted by novices in school science laboratories differ in important ways from authentic scientific investigations conducted by expert scientists, and to enable development of the science education field, it is important for teachers and researchers in science education to define and use central technical terms precisely and consistently. Engaging students in laboratory *inquiry*, for example, has involved activities ranging from *highly structured* laboratory experiences to *open-ended* investigations in which students explore a question they may have articulated themselves. The nature of the guidance the teacher and the curriculum materials provide for the students is very important to the learning that occurs. Unfortunately, the guidance provided for students has often not been examined or described carefully in studies of laboratory learning; careful reporting of the nature of that guidance is one important factor in good research and development of laboratory work in science education.

REVIEWS OF RESEARCH ON
THE SCHOOL LABORATORY

The uniqueness of the laboratory as a medium for learning and teaching science has caused it to be the subject of many research studies and several reviews since the 1960s. The reviews referenced in this chapter include those published by Ramsey and Howe (1969), Bates (1978), Blosser (1980), Hofstein and Lunetta (1982), Tobin (1990), Hodson (1993), Lazarowitz and Tamir (1994), and Hofstein and Lunetta (2004). These reviews are sources of many literature citations that have not been included in this chapter because of space limitations.

Prior to the reform movements of the 1960s a latent assumption of many science educators and teachers was that students learn science by verifying or applying ideas in the school laboratory that were taught earlier in class. As noted in the preceding historical overview, curriculum projects developed during the reform movement in the 1960s were intended to promote greater focus on inquiry, interest, and conceptual understanding. A tacit assumption of scientists who led the curriculum reform movement of the 1960s was that students come to understand science ideas simply by performing activities, collecting data in the school laboratory, and then generalizing from the information collected; teachers and the "teacher-proof textbook" provided guidance in the process. Important changes did occur in the development of science curricula, teaching resources, and for a time in science teacher development workshops. However, in general, science teaching has continued to be relatively didactic and focused on delivering information.

Although the 1960s reforms were based, in part, on theories of learning, relatively little research in science education in that decade looked carefully at students' understanding of science concepts, attitudes, and possible causal factors associated with students' experiences in the science classroom and laboratory. Following an extensive review of the literature on the school laboratory, Ramsey and Howe (1969) wrote that science educators had come to expect that laboratory experiences "should be an integral part of any science course." They also noted that the nature of the best kinds of experiences and how these could be integrated with more conventional class work had not been objectively assessed. They claimed that as a result, implications for teaching based on research on laboratory-classroom learning were not available (p. 75).

Between the late 1960s and the 1980s hundreds of research papers and doctoral dissertations investigated variables in settings associated with teaching in the school science laboratory. Bates (1978) reviewed 82 studies on the role of the laboratory in secondary school science programs and wrote that the question of what laboratories accomplish that could not be achieved by less expensive and less-time consuming alternatives needed more research. He wrote (p. 74):

- Lectures, demonstrations, and laboratory teaching methods appear equally effective in transmitting science content;
- Laboratory experiences are superior for providing students skills in working with equipment;

- The laboratory appears to represent significantly different areas of science learning than content acquisition;

- Some kinds of inquiry-oriented laboratory experiences appear better than lecture/demonstrations or verification-type laboratories for teaching the process of inquiry. However teachers need to be skilled in inquiry teaching methods;

- Laboratories appear to have potential for nurturing positive students' attitudes.

Many of the studies on school laboratory learning conducted between 1960 and 1980 tended to assess students' knowledge of conventional science facts. In general, the studies did not take a careful look at the nature of students' learning or their perceptions of the purposes of their laboratory work, and they did not carefully assess students' understanding of the nature of science.

Hofstein and Lunetta (1982) wrote that "Past research studies generally examined a relatively narrow band of laboratory skills and the conclusions that were drawn may apply to a narrow range of teaching techniques, teacher and student characteristics, and learning outcomes" (p. 204). They argued that many research studies conducted since the 1960s suffered from a number of weaknesses, including selection and control of variables, group size, instrumentation selected for the research studies, and control over teacher's behavior and over the students' activities provided by the laboratory. In addition, they wrote that research failed to show simple relationships between experiences in the laboratory and students' learning. Most research studies conducted on the science laboratory failed to show advantages of the laboratory over other science teaching practices, but if differences did exist they were probably masked by confounding variables, by the use of insensitive research instrumentation, and/or by poor research design. For example, only seldom was attention given to the characteristics of the student sample (e.g., cognitive development) or the crucial nature of the teacher's laboratory teaching, expectations, and assessment practices. Hofstein and Lunetta (1982) outlined the need for new research that would provide more information about the important but complex relationships between goals for learning, teacher expectations and behaviors, and student learning outcomes.

The reviews by Bates (1978) and Hofstein and Lunetta (1982) cited several studies indicating that students enjoy laboratory work in some courses and that laboratory experiences have resulted in positive and improved student attitudes and interest in science. Among the studies reviewed, Hofstein et al. (1976) reported that students in Israel rated their personal involvement in the chemistry laboratory as the most effective instructional method for promoting their interest in chemistry when contrasted with teacher demonstrations, presentations, and classroom discussions. Other studies conducted in the 1970s and 1980s made similar claims. Ben-Zvi et al. (1977), for example, reported that chemistry students' personal involvement in chemistry laboratory investigations had been the most effective medium in their chemistry classes for promoting their interest in chemistry when contrasted with teacher's demonstrations, filmed experiments, classroom discussions, and teachers' lectures. In a study that examined why students enrolled in optional advanced high school chemistry courses, one of the key reasons offered was their experience with practical activities in the chemistry laboratory (Milner et al., 1987). These results are similar to findings reported in the United States (Charen, 1966; Johnson et al., 1974; Raghubir, 1979). In Nigeria, Okebukola (1986), using the Attitude toward Chemistry Laboratory Questionnaire (Hofstein et al., 1976), reported that greater participation in chemistry laboratory activities resulted in improved student attitudes toward chemistry learning in general and toward learning in the chemistry laboratory in particular.

By early in the 1990s, the pendulum of research within the science education literature had moved away from the affective domain and toward the cognitive domain, with special attention to conceptual change. Reflecting this shift, two comprehensive reviews that were published in the early 1990s (Hodson, 1993, and Lazarowitz & Tamir, 1994) did not discuss research focused on affective variables such as attitudes and interest. Nevertheless, some science educators continued to report studies indicating that laboratory work is an important medium for enhancing attitudes, stimulating interest and enjoyment, and motivating students to learn science (e.g., Freedman, 1997; Thompson & Soyibo, 2002). In 2004, the Attitude toward Chemistry Laboratory Questionnaire was administered in a study in which two groups of students were compared (Kipnis & Hofstein, 2005). The first student group performed inquiry-type chemistry investigations, and the second group performed more conventional, confirmation-type activities. Students in the inquiry group developed more positive attitudes toward learning chemistry than did the students who experienced the conventional treatment.

Since the early 1970s, researchers have studied students' perceptions of the *classroom learning environment* and its relationship to outcomes such as student achievement and attitudes (Fraser & Walberg, 1989). A valid and reliable measure for assessing students' perceptions of the *laboratory learning environment*, the Science Laboratory Environment Inventory was developed and validated by a group in Australia and used subsequently in studies conducted in several world locations. Fraser et al. (1993) reported that Australian students' perceptions of the laboratory learning environment accounted for significant differences in the variance in students' learning of science content beyond that attributed to differences in their abilities. Fisher, Henderson, and Fraser (1997) reported significant correlations between students' perceptions of the science laboratory learning environment and their attitudes and science achievement. Similar results were reported in an Australian study by Fraser et al. (1993). A study of this kind was also conducted on high school chemistry in Israel (Hofstein et al., 2001). The study revealed that students involved in a series of inquiry-type laboratory investigations in chemistry found the laboratory learning environment to be more open-ended and more integrated with the conceptual framework they were developing than did the students enrolled in conventional laboratory courses (control). In the inquiry group the gap between the actual learning environment and the students' preferred environment was significantly smaller than in the control group. These findings suggested that some kinds of practical experiences can promote a positive, healthy learning environment.

Tobin (1990) wrote: "Laboratory activities appeal as a way of allowing students to learn with understanding and, at the same time, engage in the process of constructing knowledge by doing science" (p. 405). To attain this goal he suggested that students should be provided opportunities in the laboratory to reflect on findings, clarify understandings and misunderstandings with peers, and consult a range of resources that include teachers, books, and other learning materials. His review reported that such opportunities rarely exist because teachers are so often preoccupied with technical and managerial activities in the laboratory. Similarly, Hodson (1993) suggested that although teachers generally professed a belief in the value of student-driven, open, practical investigation, in general their teaching practices in

the laboratory failed to support that claim. He also argued that the research literature failed to provide evidence that standard school laboratory activities encouraged knowledge construction. He was critical of the research literature: "Despite the
very obvious differences among, for example, practical exercises designed to develop manipulative skills or to measure 'physical constraints', demonstration-type
experiments to illustrate certain key-concepts, and inquiries that enable children to
conduct their own investigations, there is a tendency for researchers to lump them
all together under the same umbrella title of practical work" (p. 97). Tobin (1990)
wrote that teachers' interpretations of practical activity should be elaborated, made
a part of the research design, and reported, because a laboratory session could be
open-ended inquiry in one classroom and more didactic and confirmatory in another teacher's classroom. Tobin (1990) and Hodson (1993) were among those who
wrote that, in general, science teachers failed to create an environment that encouraged students to make sense of their laboratory experiences, to reflect on their own
thinking and to explore new connections that eventually led to the desired conceptual understanding.

Based on their review of the laboratory literature, Lazarowitz and Tamir (1994)
joined the long list of authors who indicated that the potential of the laboratory as a
medium for teaching science is enormous. They wrote that the laboratory is the
only place in school where certain kinds of skills and understanding can be developed. Yet, they are among those who have written that much of what actually occurs in contemporary school laboratory work is not consistent with important purposes of those laboratory activities (Kesidou & Roseman, 2002; Hart et al., 2000).
Hodson (2001) wrote that although unique outcomes for laboratory/practical work
were articulated in the recent past, the nature of students' experiences in the laboratory and related assessment practices remained relatively unchanged.

Tibergien et al. (2001) and Sere (2002) reported work in a long-term project
(Lab-Work in Science Education) conducted in several European nations. They described similarities and differences in science education laboratory tasks in upper
secondary schools in Europe. Sere (2002) wrote: "The intention of the [study] was to
address the problem of the effectiveness of lab-work, which in most countries is recognized as being essential to experimental sciences, but which turns out to be expensive and less effective than wished" (p. 624). Information on practice was gathered through 23 case studies, surveys, and a tool that helps to map and describe the
laboratory work domain. Sere reported that the objectives typically articulated for
laboratory work (i.e., understanding theories, concepts, and laws; conducting various experiments; learning processes and approaches; and applying knowledge to
new situations) were too numerous and comprehensive for teachers to address successfully in individual laboratory sessions. In response, she suggested that the
scope of the objectives for specific laboratory activities should be limited. Science
curriculum developers and science teachers should make conscious choices among
specific learning objectives for specific laboratory activities and clearly articulate
the specific objectives for their students. Sere's "targeted lab-work" project produced a series of recommendations, including the need for each laboratory activity
to be supported by a particular strategy organized within a coherent long-term program plan with varied kinds of laboratory work. Subsequently, the Hofstein and
Lunetta (2004) review examined themes emerging at the beginning of the twenty-
first century. These themes are explored in the section that follows.

RESEARCH ON THE LABORATORY:
AN ANALYSIS OF EMERGING THEMES

Early in the twenty-first century we are in a new era of reform in science education. Once again, the content and pedagogy of science learning and teaching are being scrutinized, and new standards intended to shape meaningful science education have emerged. The National Science Education Standards (National Research Council, 1996) and other science education literature (Lunetta, 1998; Bybee, 2000; Hodson, 2001; Hofstein & Lunetta, 2004) emphasized the importance of rethinking the role and practice of school laboratory work in science teaching. To do so is timely because in recent decades we have learned much about human cognition and science learning (Bransford et al., 2000). In addition, learning through inquiry (National Research Council, 2000) has important potential for teaching science, but it also poses challenges for teachers and learners (Krajcik et al., 2001).

Recent scholarship especially relevant to the school science laboratory has focused on the following themes elaborated in this section:

- Articulating and implementing more explicit goals for student learning;
- Applying learning theory organizers
- Developing classroom communities of inquirers
- Developing students' understanding of the nature of science
- Developing inquiry and learning empowering technologies

Articulating and Implementing More Explicit Goals for Student Learning

In recent decades, educators have articulated with increasing regularity and clarity that decisions in teaching, assessment, and selection of curriculum resources should be driven by the learning outcomes sought for students. Goals for student learning continue to be explicated, most recently labeled as science standards. As noted earlier in the historical overview of this chapter, expectations articulated for school science laboratory learning since the nineteenth century have included the goals reflected in the first four bulleted items in Table 15.1. Over time, however, understanding of these goals and of how to implement them has developed substantially.

In 1983, the National Commission on Excellence in Education (1983) published *A Nation at Risk: The Imperative for Educational Reform*. This report offered recommendations for schooling in the United States that promoted the movement toward national science standards. Although the goal of promoting understanding of the nature of science has also been articulated for the better part of 100 years, in the last 20 years of the twentieth century, that goal became increasingly prominent. The *Standards* and increasing numbers of publications advocated that school science should enable graduates to understand methods of scientific inquiry, reasoning, and the nature of science (see, e.g., Duschl, 1990; Klopfer, 1969; Matthews, 1994).

Acknowledging the importance of goals for learning, science education researchers increasingly focus on factors associated with learning outcomes, and they try to examine the nature of teaching strategies and behaviors that promote the learning outcomes that are sought. Some have employed new social science research

TABLE 15.1
Principal Goals for Learning in the School Laboratory

Promote the development of students' scientific knowledge, problem-solving abilities, and habits of mind, including:

- Conceptual knowledge
- Practical skills and problem-solving abilities; now expanded to include: argumentation from data (*procedural knowledge*)
- Knowledge of how science and scientists work
- Interest and motivation
- Understanding methods of scientific inquiry and reasoning; now expanded to include the nature of science.

methodologies that can shed light on the complex factors associated with learning and teaching science in school settings. Many researchers have also sought theoretical organizers to make sense of particular strategies and to inform curriculum development, teaching, and research. These efforts have occurred while substantive changes have been under way in society, in school and technology environments, and in what we know about teaching and learning science. The importance of keeping learning outcomes in mind is illustrated in John Goodlad's (1983) extensive study of schooling. His critical analysis of observations made in over 1,000 classrooms illustrated the chasm between statements of goals for learning and what so often happens in school laboratory experiences:

> One would expect the teaching of . . . science in schools to provide ample opportunities for the development of reasoning: deriving concepts from related events, testing in a new situation hypotheses derived from examining other circumstances, drawing conclusions from an array of data, and so on. Teachers listed those skills and more as intended learnings. We observed little of the activities that their lists implied, and teachers' tests reflected quite different priorities—mainly the recall of information. The topics that come to mind as representing the natural . . . sciences appear to be of great human interest. But on the way to the classroom they are apparently transformed and homogenized into something of limited appeal. (p. 468)

Similarly, research that focused on learning in the laboratory in the late twentieth century reported that mismatches regularly occurred between teachers' perceived goals for practical work and students' perceptions of such activities (Wilkenson & Ward, 1997; Hodson, 1993, 2001). Based on evidence that the goals of instruction are more likely to be achieved when students perceive those goals, Wilkenson and Ward concluded that teachers should be much more attentive to helping students understand the general and specific goals of each laboratory activity. Furthermore, because specific learning objectives are often different from one investigation to another, students should be helped to understand the purposes for each investigation in a *pre-lab* session, and they should review those purposes in *post-lab* reporting and discussion of their findings. However, Hodson (2001) observed that teachers often do not do in laboratories what they say they intend to do. Thus, as Eisner (1985, p. 59) wrote, "In the final analysis, what teachers do in the classroom and what students experience define the educational process."

Earlier, based on analyses of student laboratory guides, Tamir and Lunetta (1981) wrote that, in spite of attempts to reform curricula, students worked too often as technicians following "cookbook" recipes in which they used lower level skills; they were seldom encouraged to discuss hypotheses, propose tests, and engage in designing and performing experimental procedures. Rarely, if ever, were students asked to formulate questions to be investigated or even to discuss sources of error and appropriate sample size. Students' performance in practical activities generally was not assessed, nor were students asked to describe or explain their hypotheses, methodologies, or the nature and results of their investigations (Hofstein & Lunetta, 1982). Science education research in the 1980s showed that students tended to perceive that following the instructions, getting the right answer, or manipulating equipment and measuring were the principal purpose for a school science laboratory. However, they failed to perceive the conceptual and procedural understandings that were the teachers' intended goals for the laboratory activities. The students often failed to understand the relationship between the purpose of the investigation and the design of the experiment. Students rarely wrestled with the nature of science and how it underlies laboratory work, including the interpretation of data; they did not connect their laboratory activity with what they had done earlier, and they seldom noted the discrepancies between their own concepts, the concepts of their peers, and those of the science community (see, for example, Champagne, Gunstone, & Klopfer, 1985; Eylon & Linn, 1988; Tasker, 1981). To many students, a laboratory activity has meant manipulating equipment but not manipulating ideas. More recent content analyses of published laboratory guides continue to suggest that students focus on relatively low-level tasks in the laboratory. For example, Domin (1998) analyzed contemporary printed chemistry laboratory guides and reported that they did not appear to actively engage students' higher level cognitive activities—such as addressing issues related to the assumptions and design underlying the investigation or the scientific justification supporting findings. To remediate discrepancies between goals for learning and the structure of labs and relevant teaching practices, research studies must be conducted to understand the sources of these discrepancies and to develop more effective practices.

To these ends, promising scholarship has ensued. Some of these efforts, linked with learning theory, have focused on helping students articulate their ideas and explanations, reason from data, and improve the quality of their argumentation in school science (Osborne et al., 2004; Kanari & Millar, 2004; Reiser et al., 2001). The research has included the development and study of new software tools designed to support student inquiry and science learning associated with the school laboratory. These activities provide insights for teachers and researchers on the nature and development of students' understanding as well as new resources for teaching and learning science. This work is elaborated later in this chapter (*Developing inquiry and learning empowering technologies*).

Applying Learning Theory Organizers

Since the curriculum reform era in the 1960s, science educators have recognized with increasing clarity the importance of identifying theories of learning that can provide guidance for research, curriculum development, and teaching. Developmental learning theory had a powerful influence on the role of the laboratory and on science education scholarship beginning in the 1960s. While more contemporary theories have been developed, developmental theory can continue to inform teachers' decisions regarding the selection and placement of laboratory experiences to promote the growth of students' reasoning abilities. For example, the three-phase Learning Cycle teaching model (Karplus, 1977; Schneider & Renner, 1980), grounded primarily in developmental learning theory, can guide teachers in providing initial exploration experiences with materials and phenomena for their students that can serve as a foundation for introducing science concepts. In the final application phase of the model, students are encouraged to explicitly link their understandings to questions and new situations. The learning cycle model was studied extensively and shown to promote many science education goals for learning (Abraham, 1982; Ward & Herron, 1980; Purser & Renner, 1983).

In the closing decades of the twentieth century a series of teaching models grounded in learning theories incorporated increasing knowledge of how people learn. These models were designed to guide teachers in selecting, planning, and sequencing their teaching, work in the school laboratory, and interactions with students to promote desired learning outcomes. Nussbaum and Novick (1982), for example, asserted that their model was an improvement on the learning cycle because it emphasized explicit identification of students' conceptual frameworks and their assumptions underlying those frameworks. A goal of their model was to help students become aware of their conceptual frameworks and assumptions and of how their frameworks differed from those of others. Like Erickson (1979), they emphasized the importance of creating conceptual conflict through laboratory experiences with observations contrary to what students tend to expect.

The Generative Learning model (Osborne and Freyberg, 1985) emphasized the need for teachers to consider their own personal explanations of the ideas the students were to study and contrast their ideas with the views of scientists on that topic. They also suggested ways teachers could ascertain the students' thinking on the topic early in the teaching sequence in order to help the students identify differences in their observations and interpretations in laboratory investigation and those of others. The *5-E model* (Bybee, 1997) advocated two phases beyond those of the learning cycle, *engagement* and *evaluation*. The engagement phase is similar to the first phase in the Nussbaum and Novick and the Osborne and Freyberg models in that it emphasizes the importance of engaging students' prior knowledge and experiences. The fifth and final *evaluation* phase reflects constructivist perspectives regarding the tenacity of learners' prior ideas; it involves assessing students' understanding via performance on a relevant task.

Research on the effects of teaching models on learning can have important implications for how teachers should implement laboratory activities. For instance, promoting students' understanding of scientific concepts demands that teachers have a rich scientific understanding of those concepts in addition to the pedagogical understanding and skills needed to use the teaching model (Tobin & Garnett, 1988). Hence, teachers' understanding of relevant science concepts is another important variable that should be, but rarely has been, examined and discussed in research studies on the laboratory. Additional empirical research is needed to examine learning outcomes more carefully and the specific elements of teaching that are most effective in promoting desired learning before, during, and following laboratory experiences.

When well planned and effectively implemented, science education laboratory and simulation experiences situate students' learning in varying levels of inquiry requiring students to be both mentally and physically engaged in ways that are not possible in other science education experiences. Teaching science as inquiry and through inquiry is at the heart of science education reform documents. Such inquiry reflects what we now know about how people learn science. Understanding how students learn and why they often struggle in learning what teachers intend is the foundation for effective teaching (Bransford et al., 2000). For instance, Driver (1997) noted:

> Our optimism about what children ought to be able to do stems perhaps from rather deep seated views about learning. And that as long as the expert tells the story clearly and that the person who is learning is listening and paying attention then they will automatically build up the understanding that the expert has. Now all our current knowledge in cognitive science, and in cognitive psychology, and in science education is telling us that simply does not happen. Children may well be listening, paying attention to what is being said or what they are reading in a book, but they are construing it in different ways to the ways that the teacher intended. And that is the issue we have to deal with.

Constructivist learning theory suggests that learners use ideas and constructs already in their minds to make sense of their experiences. Learning is an active, interpretive, iterative process (Bransford, et al., 2000). Gunstone (1991), however, wrote that helping students develop scientific ideas from practical experiences is a very complex process and that students generally did not have sufficient time or encouragement to express their interpretations and beliefs and to reflect on central ideas in the laboratory. Research on learning in the school laboratory makes it clear that to understand their laboratory experiences, students must manipulate ideas as well as materials in the school laboratory (White & Gunstone, 1992), and they must be helped to contrast their findings and ideas with the concepts of the contemporary scientific community. Manipulating materials in the laboratory is not sufficient for learning contemporary scientific concepts, and this accounts for the failure of "cookbook" laboratory activities and relatively unguided discovery activities to promote desired scientific understanding. Expecting students to develop scientific understanding solely though their laboratory experiences reflects misconceptions of the nature of science (Wolpert, 1992; Matthews, 1994) and how people learn science. Several studies suggested that although laboratory investigations offer excellent settings in which students can make sense of phenomena and in which teachers can better understand their students' thinking, laboratory inquiry alone is not sufficient to enable students to construct the complex conceptual understandings of the contemporary scientific community (Lunetta, 1998). In the laboratory, students should be encouraged to articulate and share their ideas to help them perceive discrepancies among their ideas, those of their classmates, and those of the scientific community. Driver (1995) wrote: "If students' understandings are to be changed toward those of accepted science, then intervention and negotiation with an authority, usually a teacher, is essential."

At the end of the twentieth century there was increasing understanding from cognitive sciences that learning is contextualized and that learners construct knowledge by solving genuine, meaningful problems (Brown et al., 1989; Roth, 1995;

Williams & Hmelo, 1998; Wenger, 1998; Polman, 1999). The school science laboratory can offer students opportunities to have some control of their activities, enhancing their perception of *ownership* and *motivation* (Johnstone & Al-Shuaili, 2001). It can be an environment particularly well suited for providing a meaningful context for learning, determining and challenging students' deeply held ideas about natural phenomena, and constructing and reconstructing their ideas. Though a complex process, meaningful learning in the laboratory *can* occur if students are given sufficient time and opportunities to interact, reflect, explain, and modify their ideas (Barron et al., 1998). Engaging in *metacognitive* behaviors of this kind enables students to elaborate and to apply their ideas; the process can promote conceptual understanding as well as the development of problem-solving skills. The challenge is to help learners take control of their own learning in the search for understanding while providing opportunities that encourage them to ask questions, suggest hypotheses, and design investigations, "minds-on as well as hands-on" (Gunstone, 1991). That theme has been pursued and reported in several research studies, including *Designing Project-Based Science* (Polman, 1999).

In moving students toward more "minds-on" engagement in the laboratory (including problem solving, reflecting on the meaning of data, and decision making, etc.), we now understand that teachers must sequence complex ideas and experiences (scaffolding) in ways that enable students to engage meaningfully in these activities. In doing so, teachers need to pay close attention to students' behaviors and what they are saying. They can then respond with pedagogical decisions that will help students make connections, enabling them to achieve desired learning outcomes. An important area of contemporary scholarship involves the research and development of software tools that support the scaffolding of ideas and promote dialogue. These tools are discussed in the section on Learning Technologies later in this chapter.

Emerging attention to a social constructivist theoretical framework has special potential for guiding teaching in the laboratory (e.g., Tobin, 1990; Lunetta, 1998). Social learning theory emphasizes that learning is situated in interactions with those around us, and conceptual development is associated with the medium of language. Thus, learning depends, in part, on interactions with adults and peers. Social learning theory makes clear the importance of promoting group work in the laboratory so that meaningful, conceptually focused dialogue takes place between students as well as between the teacher and students. Moreover, laboratory experiences in which students discuss ideas and make decisions can present many opportunities for teachers to observe students' thinking as they negotiate meaning with their peers. Carefully observing students' actions and listening to their dialogue creates opportunities for teachers to focus questions and make comments within learners' zones of proximal development (Vygotsky, 1978, 1986; Duschl & Osborne, 2002) that can help the students construct understandings that are more compatible with the concepts of expert scientific communities.

Developing Classroom Communities of Inquirers

The school laboratory is particularly well suited to cooperative investigation of scientific phenomena and relationships when teachers engage their students intellectually as a community of learners. The inquiring community includes students, the teacher, and occasionally expert consultants (Penner et al., 1998; Roth & Roychoudhury, 1993). The importance of promoting *cooperative learning* in the science classroom and laboratory received much attention during the 1980s (e.g., Johnson & Johnson, 1985; Lazarowitz & Karsenty, 1990). Large numbers of studies demonstrated distinct benefits in students' achievement and productivity when cooperative learning strategies were successfully utilized in the classroom-laboratory. Okebukola and Ogunniyi (1984) compared groups of students who worked cooperatively, competitively, and as individuals in science laboratories and found that the cooperative group outperformed the other groups in cognitive achievement and in process skills. Similarly, Lazarowitz and Karsenty (1990) found that students who learned biology in small cooperative groups scored higher in achievement and on several inquiry skills than did students who learned in a large group class setting. Several papers reported that the more informal atmosphere and opportunities for interaction among students and their teacher and peers can promote a healthy learning environment conducive to meaningful inquiry and collaborative learning (Tobin, 1990; DeCarlo & Rubba, 1994). In a study that compared high school chemistry students' ability to formulate questions associated with a science reading and with a science investigation, Hofstein et al. (2005) reported that students who had experience asking questions in a laboratory inquiry-focused course outperformed those in control groups in their ability to ask more and better questions.

The Lunetta (1998) and Hofstein and Lunetta (2004) reviews noted research indicating that the school laboratory offers important opportunities for interaction between students and their teacher and among peers that can be conducive to meaningful inquiry and collaborative learning that results in desired cognitive growth. Research on the school laboratory conducted early in the twenty-first century examined ways to promote and support collaboration among students while they engage in laboratory inquiry or inquiry with the laboratory data gathered by scientists (see, for example, Land & Zembal-Saul, 2003; Edelson et al., 1999). This research has resulted in the development of new software tools that promise to enhance students' inquiry and reflection on the process. Land and Zembal-Saul, for example, reported that use of Progress Portfolio software prompted learners to articulate and connect their experimental findings back to the larger driving questions. "The negotiation and struggle that ensued regarding the significance of the data promoted explanation, justification and reflective social discourse." Research and findings associated with the development of the software tools are discussed in the technology section later in this chapter.

Through the collaboration, reflection, and discussion associated with investigation, students can develop scientific knowledge, and they can begin to glimpse the collaborative nature of an expert scientific community. These are learning outcomes that are now thought to be very important in introductory science. Promoting and examining reflective social discourse in the laboratory is a particularly important area for further science education research, especially since observations of science laboratory classrooms today continue to suggest that insufficient attention is given to promoting collaboration, reflective discourse, and community negotiation.

Developing Students' Understanding
of the Nature of Science

While promoting students' understanding of the nature of science had been articulated as a science learning goal for decades, that goal acquired greater significance (see, for example, Duschl, 1990) in the last 30 years of the twentieth century
(see also Chapter 29 in this Handbook). Several reasons relevant to learning in the
school laboratory have been discussed in the literature for promoting understanding of the nature of science (Abd-El-Khalick & Lederman, 2000; McComas et al.,
1998; Matthews, 1994). Some have argued that appropriate laboratory experiences
have an important role to play in developing students' understanding of the nature
of science, whereas other evidence suggests that the relatively widespread lack of
understanding of scientific philosophical and procedural ideas by both teachers
and students has interfered with learning during laboratory inquiry. The outcomes
of laboratory investigations in which students have been expected to "discover"
accepted scientific relationships have often disappointed students, teachers, and
researchers, in part because of mistaken notions regarding the nature of science
and how people learn science concepts. Believing that students who carefully perform particular laboratory investigations will come to the same understanding as
scientists reflects a naive empiricist view of scientific knowledge (Lederman et al.,
1998; Wellington, 1981). Rowe and Holland (1990) described a student's frustration
in trying to reconcile science ideas with what is observed in the real world:

> What is this game that scientists play? They tell me that if I give something a push it
> will just keep on going forever or until something pushes it back to me. Anybody can
> see that isn't true. If you don't keep pushing, things stop. Then they say it would be
> true if the world were without friction, but it isn't, and if there weren't any friction
> how could I push it in the first place? It seems like they just change the rules all the
> time. (p. 87)

This commentary illustrates how understanding aspects of the nature of science
is crucial to helping students make sense of their school laboratory experiences. The
tendency in scientific writing and science textbooks to idealize conditions in the
natural world is counter-intuitive to everyday thinking (Cromer, 1993; Wolpert,
1992; Matthews, 1994; Toulmin, 1972).

Crucial for tapping the potential of laboratory experiences is understanding
that the underlying assumptions and theoretical frameworks that shape the understanding and concepts of the expert scientific community are often very different from ideas commonly held throughout the culture; these large differences
influence what students observe and the sense they make from their laboratory
work. Informed science educators understand that humans tried to understand
the natural world for thousands of years prior to the western Renaissance. The
subsequent development of contemporary scientific worldviews spanned hundreds of years and resulted in significant changes (paradigm shifts) in our understanding of science concepts and in our understanding of science. The long and
counter-intuitive history of science helps to explain some of the misconceptions
held regularly by students and some teachers, and the considerable challenges to

be addressed in helping novice learners to understand contemporary scientific concepts.

Making sense of school laboratory experiences often requires that learners and their teachers make conscious efforts to avoid conventional assumptions. Matthews (1994) and others have pointed out that scientific knowledge is based on several assumptions that conflict with commonly held ideas. The following widely held views, for example, can interfere with intended learning in school laboratory settings:

Processes in the natural world bring about a suitable final state. Students holding this view may search for explanations that are unnecessarily teleological, thus interfering with their understanding of contemporary scientific explanations.

Natural processes are activated and controlled by spiritual influences. This perspective is evident in the difficulty many students and some teachers have in interpreting evidence the scientific community presents in support of biological evolution.

Knowledge is fixed and unchanging. This assumption is evident in the difficulty many people have in understanding how well-accepted scientific knowledge based on sound research can be modified on the basis of new empirical evidence or the reinterpretation of evidence gathered in the past.

Scientific knowledge comes simply from observing natural phenomena. This assumption is evident in students' difficulties relating formal science concepts to the "real" world. For instance, the student's frustration with objects in motion referenced above (Rowe and Holland, 1990) illustrates how this assumption can interfere with desired science learning.

Scientific knowledge claims are validated solely by their successful predictions. Idealized science ideas do not always appear to result in accurate predictions, and some ideas that do provide accurate predictions (e.g., Ptolemaic astronomy) have been abandoned in favor of alternative ideas (e.g., Copernican astronomy). Accurate prediction is part of, but not the only factor in, developing contemporary scientific knowledge.

Many students and some teachers consciously or subconsciously maintain some or all of these assertions while learning and teaching science. If the assumptions are left unexamined, they are likely to interfere with the learning outcomes sought from school laboratory activities. Effective use of laboratory experiences, on the other hand, can help students and their teachers clarify the nature of science and how it differs from other ways of knowing. Informed and relevant discussions about the nature of science in the context of laboratory work can help students make sense of their laboratory experiences and better understand conceptual and procedural scientific knowledge. The interplay between conceptual and procedural knowledge is illustrated in Rudolph and Stewart's (1998) analysis that "conceptually understanding evolutionary biology, and science more generally, requires students to become familiar with the metaphysical assumptions and the methodological process that Darwin laid out. Theoretical context and scientific practice, in this view, are not just interdependent, but really two views of a single entity" (p. 1085).

Duschl (1987) and others have argued that effective inquiry teaching demands that science teachers have an understanding of the nature of science, that is, that an understanding of relevant philosophical presuppositions is often necessary to conduct laboratory work and to help students interpret results scientifically. Making the most of laboratory experiences requires that both teachers and students understand that many science ideas do not follow simply from observing natural phenomena. What this means for effective school laboratory experiences is that teachers must help their students come to understand the epistemological (how knowledge is constructed and justified) and ontological (nature of reality) assumptions underlying scientific knowledge and the rationale for holding those assumptions while doing science. That said, these issues are complex indeed and warrant further substantial and systematic study of their implications.

A number of recent studies relevant to the school laboratory have focused on enhancing the quality of students' argumentation from data. Kanari and Millar (2004), reporting on how students collect and interpret data, wrote that "an analysis of the sample students' performance on the practical tasks and their interview responses showed few differences in performance when investigating situations of covariance and non-covariation. . . . Investigation of non-covariation cases revealed . . . the students' ideas about data and measurement and their ways of reasoning from data. Such investigations provide particularly valuable contexts for teaching and research" (p. 748). Several of the contemporary studies that examine students' argumentation use new software tools designed to focus students' attention on the ways they justify their own assertions during science investigations. Based on data from a study utilizing such software, Sandoval and Morrison (2002) wrote: "Overall, students held a view of science as a search for right answers about the world. Yet the inconsistency of individuals' responses undermines the assumption that students have stable, coherent, epistemological frameworks. . . . Combined with previous work, our findings emphasize the crucial role of an explicit epistemic discourse in developing students' epistemological understanding." Informed use of this kind of technology tool in teaching has the potential to promote improved understanding of science concepts and perhaps of the nature of science for students. Such tools also offer a window for researchers into students' beliefs, understanding, and how students' understanding can become more scientific.

As noted earlier, research has shown that students are unlikely to develop desired understandings about the nature of science simply by taking part in inquiry experiences. Based on empirical research, Driver et al. (2000) are among those who have suggested that making argumentation a more central and explicit part of learning may improve students' inquiry abilities while supporting their epistemological development. Duschl (2000) wrote that the nature of science can be made explicit when students examine, argue about, and discuss the nature of good evidence and decide between alternatives. Others have written that students learn about the nature of science through an explicit reflective approach (Abd-El-Khalick & Lederman, 2000; Schwartz & Lederman, 2002). Sandoval and Reiser (2004) suggested "engaging students in the reasoning and discursive practices of scientists, not necessarily the exact activities of professional scientists."

Examining these issues is an important frontier area in science education scholarship. Substantive, systematic research is warranted to clarify the complex issues involved. Such research should shed light on how to use school laboratory experiences to help students understand important aspects of the nature of science and on how to help them apply their understanding of the nature of science in laboratory investigations and in the world around them. Perspectives on the relevant nature of science issues are elaborated in this *Handbook* in Chapter 28, and the development and use of software tools especially relevant to learning in the school science laboratory are discussed in the section that follows.

Developing Inquiry and Learning Empowering Technologies

In the early 1980s digital technologies became increasingly visible in school laboratories and were recognized as important tools in school science (Lunetta, 1998; Kozma et al., 2000). Much evidence now documents that using appropriate technologies in the school laboratory *can* enhance learning, and important research on learning empowering technologies is the focus of this section. That said, an initial cautionary note is fitting, since evidence also documents that inappropriate use of even simple technology tools has interfered with meaningful science learning (Olson & Clough, 2001; Hofstein & Lunetta, 2004). When a device is introduced prematurely, before students have made sense of the underlying science concepts, there is evidence that the device or tool may serve as a black box that interferes with students' perceptions of what is happening and hinder their understanding of important scientific ideas. To cite one widely viewed example, after having used a bulb holder (bulb socket) in a simple *batteries and bulbs* activity intended to illustrate electric circuits, interviewers in a very well-known video (Annenberg/CPB, 1997) showed clearly that one of the articulate and talented students in an honors high school physics class thought the bulb holder was an essential but mysterious (almost magical) part of the electric circuit. The teacher in the video had made the bulb holders available to help the students construct a simple electric circuit in the laboratory. The student interviewed, however, did not understand the construction and function of the very simple bulb holder. Her failure to have that understanding interfered with her ability to interpret simple observations, to understand the circuit as a whole, and to predict outcomes when the circuit was connected. In this powerful example, if the student had had the opportunity to connect the light bulb in a simple circuit *before* she had access to bulb holders, or if the bulb and bulb holder had been dissected prior to their use in circuits, she then might have perceived the utility and function of bulb sockets that could assist her in connecting and observing bulbs in more complex electric circuits. This video presents very clear and powerful evidence that teachers must seek information about students' understanding of laboratory materials and devices as well as their understanding of the relevant science concepts and then merge that information with the goals sought for students' learning in the laboratory-classroom.

Computer tools, of course, are far more complex and perhaps more "mysterious" than is the functioning of the simple bulb holder that was a principal source of the misunderstanding displayed in the video. Computer tools can promote learning when their role and function are understood. They can be very helpful, for example, in displaying real-time graphic representations and functional relationships. Linked to such graphic displays, the computer can serve as a powerful interfacing tool in the laboratory. However, when a student does *not* understand the purpose and functioning of that interfacing tool (perhaps, for example, if the interfacing device had been an electric current meter in the electric circuit discussed in the preceding paragraph), the use of the powerful digital interfacing tool at that particular time could have *interfered* with the student's development of the understanding sought by the teacher more than the light socket did.

Inquiry empowering technologies (Hofstein & Lunetta, 2004) have been developed and adapted to assist students in gathering, organizing, visualizing, interpreting, and reporting data. Some teachers and students also use new technology tools to gather data from multiple trials and over long time intervals (Friedler et al., 1990; Lunetta, 1998; Krajcik, Blumenfeld, Marx, & Soloway, 2000; Dori et al., 2004). Increasingly, students and their teachers use software to visualize data and functional relationships. Students can examine graphs of relationships generated in real time as an investigation progresses and examine the same data in spreadsheets and in other visual representations. They can use similar software tools such as BGuILE (Reiser et al., 2001), designed for use in biology teaching and learning, to visualize and examine relationships in scientific data gathered by expert scientists in other locations. When teachers and students properly use inquiry empowering technologies to gather and analyze data, students have more time to observe, reflect, and construct the conceptual knowledge that underlies their laboratory experiences. The associated graphics also offer visualization resources that can enhance students' experiences with authentic activities while promoting deeper conceptual understanding (Edelson, 2001). When students have the time and when the activity is valued by the teacher and by high-stakes assessment, students can examine functional relationships and the effects of modifying variables; they can also make and test predictions and explanations. Technologies that offer instantaneous display of data as it is gathered can offer opportunities through which students may be helped to understand systemic functional relationships and more holistic relationships among variables. Using appropriate high-technology tools can enable students to conduct, interpret, and report more complete, accurate, and interesting investigations. Such tools can also provide media that support communication, student-student collaboration, the development of a community of inquirers in the laboratory-classroom and beyond, and the development of argumentation skills (Zembal-Saul et al., 2002).

Two studies are among several that illustrate the potential effectiveness of particular technology in school science. Nakleh and Krajcik (1994) investigated how students' use of chemical indicators, pH meters, and microcomputer-based laboratories (MBL) affected their understanding of acid-base reactions. Students who used computer tools in the laboratory emerged with better ability to draw relevant concept maps, to describe the acid-base construct, and to argue about the probable causes of why their graphs formed as they did. Dori et al. (2004), developed a high school chemistry unit in which the students pursued chemistry investigations with the use of integrated desktop computer probes. In a pre-post design study, these researchers found that students' experiences with the technology tools improved their ability to pose questions, to use graphing skills, and to pursue scientific inquiry more generally.

In addition to developing new applications of technologies that help students gather, visualize, and analyze data, other important software tools have also been designed and developed near the turn of the twenty-first century to empower learning. As noted earlier in this chapter (*Applying learning theory organizers* section), helping students develop understanding of scientific concepts is frequently a very complex task. We now understand that teachers must sequence complex ideas and experiences in ways that enable students to engage with those ideas through a series of activities and interactions. In contemporary cognitive parlance, teachers and curriculum resources must *scaffold* complex ideas and experiences in ways that enable students to engage, interact, and reflect meaningfully in these activities in order to construct meaningful scientific knowledge. A relatively new area of contemporary scholarship in science education attempts to integrate what we know about how people learn science with the use of new computer software tools that complement and intersect learning in the school laboratory. This research is associated with the design, development, and use of interactive software tools that promote dialogue, relevant activities, and the scaffolding of scientific ideas and students' construction of scientific knowledge (Tabak, 2004; Reiser et al., 2001; Edelson, 2001; Linn, 2000). Davis and Linn (2000) wrote that prompting students (via their Knowledge Integration Environment software) to reflect on their ideas significantly increased performance and knowledge integration. Sandoval and Reiser (2004) wrote that their findings suggest that epistemic tools can play a unique role in supporting students' inquiry and are a fruitful means for studying students' scientific epistemologies.

As noted earlier in this chapter, the use of Progress Portfolio software prompted learners to articulate and connect their experimental findings back to the larger driving questions (Land & Zembal-Saul, 2003). "The negotiation and struggle that ensued regarding the significance of the data promoted explanation, justification and reflective social discourse that can be observed" and studied by teachers and researchers. Related applications of software with important potential to empower student learning include engaging students in using software presentation tools to organize, discuss, and report their investigations, data, findings, and explanations of those findings to share with others. Research on the appropriate use and development of powerful new technology tools is needed to shape the use and development of state-of-the-art technologies, teaching strategies, and curricula that can facilitate important and meaningful science learning.

TOWARD ASSESSMENT RESOURCES AND STRATEGIES

Over the years several researchers have suggested that the laboratory is not only a unique resource for teaching and learning, but also a unique vantage point for observing students' ideas and for assessing this understanding. There is some evidence that students' abilities in the laboratory are only slightly correlated with their achievement in the sciences as measured by conventional paper-and-pencil tests (Hofstein & Lunetta, 2004). These findings have suggested that students' performance, understandings, and perceptions of the science laboratory learning environment should be assessed with the use of instruments and strategies that are more closely aligned with the unique activities and goals for learning associated with the school laboratory.

In 1970, however, Grobman (1970) identified a major problem in assessing laboratory performance that persists to this day in the United States and in numerous other locations: "With few exceptions, evaluation has depended on written testing. ... There has been little testing which requires actual performance in a real situation or in a simulated situation which approaches reality ... to determine not whether a student can verbalize [or identify] a correct response, but whether he can perform an operation, e.g. a laboratory experiment or an analysis of a complex problem."

Bryce and Robertson (1985) were among several who wrote that in many countries, although students spend considerable time engaging in laboratory work, the bulk of their science assessment examines their knowledge divorced from that practical context. The hypotheses and questions students can generate from their laboratory experiences and the laboratory skills they exhibit have all too often been neglected (Van den Berg & Giddings, 1992; Tamir, 1990; Wilkenson & Ward, 1997; Yung, 2001). Gitomer and Duschl (1998) wrote that in science education, the assessment of a student's conceptual understanding has been regularly separated from the assessment of his or her procedural knowledge. They added that although discussions of performance assessment focused on laboratory inquiry skills and understanding, the limited practical assessments employed were influenced by the tradition of practical examinations; the understandings and skills examined were limited. They suggested that assessments should avoid the partitioning of curriculum experiences; curriculum, teaching, and assessment should become better integrated and holistic. The processes of science that are assessed should not be limited only to those involved in specific investigations (Millar & Driver, 1987). Gitomer and Duschl also suggested that students' prior knowledge should be assessed to assist in understanding their behavior during inquiry-type activities.

Bennett and Kennedy (2001) pointed out that because such a wide variety of goals had been articulated for science laboratory learning, it was not surprising to find disagreements in the literature about assessment methods and "what constitutes a reliable and valid assessment of practical abilities." They wrote that areas of discussion included:

- The range and nature of the skills to be assessed;
- The balance between the assessment of prescriptive and investigative tasks; and
- The extent to which the assessment should be holistic or atomistic in its approach.

The Bennett and Kennedy project considered these issues carefully in designing a new model of practical assessment in Ireland. These issues warrant the careful consideration of all test makers, teachers, researchers who inform practice, and policy makers at a time when the assessment of science standards is playing an increasingly important role in shaping the behaviors of teachers and their students in school science. The science education community must develop and use reliable assessment instruments and strategies that are well aligned with the important goals for learning in school science classrooms in general and in laboratory inquiry in particular. The instruments and strategies must also be convenient and manageable for teachers and students, whose time, of necessity, is limited.

Although new instruments must be constructed and validated guided by goals for learning- and data-based research, instruments and strategies *were* developed in the closing decades of the twentieth century to assess the dynamics, the learning outcomes, and the effectiveness of the school science laboratory objectively. Although these strategies and resources have not been widely employed by schools and policy makers, they do offer a foundation for next steps in the research and development of assessment in science education, and they are reviewed here.

Interpreting, explaining, and reporting the results of investigations have generally been important components of student activity in the science laboratory. Students' laboratory reports and behaviors can serve as important sources of data for teachers and researchers seeking to make decisions about next steps in teaching, to assess and interpret student performance, and to assess the effects of laboratory experiences on learning. Students' laboratory reports have generally included commentary on *performance* (conducting an investigation; manipulating materials and equipment; making decisions about investigative techniques; and making, organizing, and recording observations) and *analysis and interpretation* (processing data, explaining relationships, developing findings, discussing the accuracy and limitations of data and procedures, and formulating new questions based on the investigation conducted). However, they should also include students' comments on *planning and design* (articulating questions, predicting results, formulating hypotheses to be tested, and designing experimental procedures) and *application* (making predictions about new situations, formulating hypotheses on the basis of investigative results, applying laboratory techniques to new experimental situations [Giddings, Hofstein, and Lunetta, 1991], and justifying assertions). The phases of laboratory activity (italicized above) involve more than manipulation and observation skills; they are important elements of cognitively demanding *procedural knowledge* that includes understanding and sometimes developing investigative design and developing and justifying procedures and assertions about findings. A student's *procedural knowledge* in the laboratory is interwoven with the development of that student's *conceptual knowledge* and understanding of science. Kempa (1986) was one of several who suggested that these four phases of laboratory activity—planning and design, performance, analysis and interpretation, and application—also provided a valid framework for the development and assessment of practical skills.

The Lunetta (1998) and Hofstein and Lunetta (2004) reviews provided numerous citations and discussed alternative strategies for assessing students' performance and understanding in these four broad phases of laboratory activity. The strategies included assessing written and oral evidence and performance in *practical examinations, laboratory reports, portfolios, continuous assessment,* and *combinations* of these strategies in ways that now include the use of interactive digital technology tools and resources.

Practical examinations can serve as valid measures of students' understanding and skill in the *performance* and *interpretation* phases of an investigation, that is, in conducting, decision-making, observing, and making inferences from their observations. As noted in earlier reviews of the laboratory assessment literature (see, for example, Hofstein & Lunetta, 2004), examples of practical examinations reported in published research studies were more visible in the 1970s and 1980s than they were at the turn of the twenty-first century. Practical examinations on some science topics have been useful for teachers and researchers and occasionally in state examinations in some countries, but their use has generally been limited to particular laboratory activities that can be administered easily to students in a restricted time, thus limiting the scope of the activities and the breadth of the assessment. Tamir et al. (1982) developed a Practical Tests Assessment Inventory to standardize the assessment of students' written responses in the inquiry-type practical examination in biology used in Israel. The 21-category inventory included categories ranging from *problem formulation* to *application of knowledge* identified in the students' investigations.

For decades, science teachers have assessed their students' performance in the laboratory via written *lab reports* completed during or after the laboratory activity.

Such reports can offer important data for assessment, but when used in the ritualistic and mechanistic ways that have been so common in many classrooms, the conventional laboratory report reveals little about a student's thinking and understanding. Written evidence of students' thinking and understanding can also be gathered in paper-and-pencil tests designed to assess students' knowledge and understanding of investigative techniques and the scientific procedures, the concepts that underlie the laboratory activity, and their explanations of findings. To date, however, most assessments and grading systems have not examined students' understanding of the research design, the strengths and limitations of the procedures they used, the concepts in which the their findings are embedded, and their justifications for their findings. Although there are exceptions to this generalization, many more examples of effective laboratory inquiry assessment practices and carefully validated instruments associated with school laboratory learning are needed in the science education literature. The ritualistic and mechanistic assessment patterns that have been so deadly for meaningful learning in the science laboratory can be changed, of course. When science education research can be applied to inform the providers of high-stakes tests, those who provide support for classroom testing, and teachers, opportunities for more meaningful learning in the school laboratory can follow.

Especially in recent years, some science teachers and researchers have asked students to develop *portfolios* in which the students prepare and collect documents (increasingly using electronic media) throughout an investigation or unit or semester that capture the essence of their investigative work, their understanding, and their justification of procedures and assertions. Such portfolios can help students organize and make decisions about the best ways to report:

- what was investigated and investigative design;
- procedures employed and observations;
- findings and explanations;
- limitations in the findings and new questions.

Portfolios can be important sources of evidence for the assessment of students' performance, activities, understandings, and explanations. Portfolios also provide data about the students' thinking that teachers can use in making decisions about next steps in their teaching in the laboratory-classroom. Progress Portfolio software (Land & Zembal-Saul, 2003) can help students organize, monitor, reflect, and interact with others on the ideas they generate throughout designing, conducting, and determining findings in an investigation. Zembal-Saul et al. (2002) reported that "while engaging in an original science investigation Progress Portfolio assisted prospective teachers in developing elaborated explanations that were grounded in evidence and . . . [in exploring] alternative hypotheses." The Progress Portfolio software was designed "to promote reflective inquiry during learning in data-rich environments." Using such tools prompted "learners to articulate and connect their experimental findings back to the larger driving questions" and to negotiate and struggle with explaining the significance of their data. It also prompted reflective social discourse that resulted in explanation and justification (Zembal-Saul et al., 2002). Progress Portfolio is an example of software used by students in laboratory-classroom activities that can provide teachers and researchers with relatively easy electronic access to student performance data that can also contribute to the assessment of a student's development and progress. Teachers can also use that kind of information for a formative assessment to inform their teaching and their interactions with students.

In an attempt to overcome the limitations of other laboratory assessment methodologies, *continuous assessment* (Hofstein & Lunetta, 2004; Giddings et al., 1991) was designed to serve as a dynamic assessment of students' work throughout a laboratory activity. In this form of assessment the science teacher, researcher, or examiner unobtrusively observes each student during a normal laboratory session and rates him or her on the basis of a prescribed assessment protocol with defined criteria. This system was largely formalized in the United Kingdom by the Joint Matriculation Board (1979). Reflecting the contemporary position that assessment of practical work should be an integral part of the normal science course and not a separate activity, (Denby, 2004) wrote that continuous assessment of students' practical work by their teachers is now required on several occasions throughout the year in the United Kingdom; they must report the variety of practical tasks and skills students have been exhibiting in their science course. Optimally, continuous assessment provides teachers with opportunities to be more directly involved in the practical assessment of their students. However, teachers in the United Kingdom frequently treat the required laboratory assessments separately from conventional practical activities, not in the context of the normal laboratory inquiry and learning, and anecdotal evidence in the United Kingdom suggests that some students engage in very little practical work beyond what is required for their assessment. Thus, what happens in laboratory-classroom practice has often differed from the goals and visions that have been articulated for these efforts.

Science teachers have reported that assessing students during laboratory activities is quite challenging. Teachers often perceive that they do not have sufficient time or skills for evaluating when they also have multiple teaching, management, and safety responsibilities to which they must attend simultaneously (Tamir, 1989). In addition, teachers do not always believe that assessing students' performance in the laboratory should be an especially important part of science assessment. Yung (2001) wrote that teachers in his study in Hong Kong did not believe that assessment of students in the laboratory could improve their teaching and consequently their students' learning. Research examining the issues raised by Yung is needed, with larger samples of teachers in a variety of school settings to obtain more detailed information about appropriate ways to promote and sustain assessment practices that are aligned with the goals for students' learning and that can be managed successfully by teachers.

A long series of efforts have been undertaken to develop and employ multiple methods to assess students in the science laboratory and to increase the reliability and validity of those methods. Recently, Hofstein et al. (2004) used criterion-based *continuous assessment* in an *inquiry-focused* series of high school chemistry courses in Israel that included integrated laboratory activities. Teachers in the study observed individual students or groups working collaboratively. In addition, the teachers examined *hot-reports* submitted regularly by collaborating groups of students in their classes. The *hot-reports* were designed to synthesize the students' experiences, observations, analyses of data, inferences, questions, hypotheses, and plans for pursuing one or more new questions raised by their investigation. Observations of the students' performance in the laboratory, combined with assessment of the students' *hot-reports*, provided chemistry teachers with valid and wide-ranging information about their students' developing understanding and progress in the laboratory. Continuous assessment in the laboratory is now used in Israel as part of the final examination of the students in this state-approved *inquiry-focused* program. Students in the program are assessed continuously across two high school years (grades 11 and 12) on the basis of their *hot-reports* and teachers' observations of the students' performance in the laboratory. The practical assessment score, based on a performance portfolio prepared by each teacher, contributes at least 25% of each student's total final grade. It is important to note the high commitment of the state and the participating teachers to laboratory work in this project.

The project reported by Bennett and Kennedy (2001) is another showing evidence of a high commitment to laboratory work by the state, in this case in Ireland, and participating teachers. Their study was designed to "evaluate the effectiveness of a new assessment model for practical work." It involved 700 students and 30 schools in Ireland and compared students' written and practical performance associated with their laboratory work in physics and chemistry. Bennett and Kennedy reported that the model developed in their project "provided a reliable and valid assessment of a range of practical abilities, which was also economical of time and resources. Additionally, there was evidence of benefits to the examiners and teachers in terms of their own professional development." Given the substantial commitment of the state and the participating teachers to laboratory work in both the Irish and Israeli projects, it will be important to examine the effects of that commitment on long-term teacher and student behaviors and on multiple issues associated with the nature of the related science learning in years to come.

As noted earlier, limited research has focused on the complex but potentially important intersections between students' understanding of the *nature of science*, how that understanding may influence students' observations and findings in laboratory work, and how the students' understanding of the nature of science may be influenced by laboratory experiences. To develop the knowledge needed to guide relevant curriculum development and teaching decisions, it is important for researchers and teachers to have valid, reliable, and convenient measures of students' understanding of aspects of the nature of science that intersect with practical work in the laboratory. A review of nature of science instruments and associated issues is included in Chapter 28 of this *Handbook*. As noted in that chapter, assessment instruments of this kind are very difficult to develop. However, the task can be accomplished with collaboration among people with expertise in psychometrics, science education, and the philosophy, history, and sociology of science, when the need for the task is understood and supported by the constituencies involved. Research and development conducted by Fraser and a series of colleagues (Fraser, 1998) resulted in the development of the Science Laboratory Environment Inventory (SLEI), discussed earlier in this section and in Chapter 5 of this *Handbook*. Such research is also needed to serve as a foundation for developing assessment protocols that intersect the affective and cognitive domains. Once again, although busy researchers and teachers can use existing resources and strategies to assess students' conceptual and procedural knowledge, understanding of the nature of science, and attitudes associated with *laboratory* learning, the development and use of valid, reliable, and convenient assessment instruments and strategies is a very important area for further discipline-focused research in science education that will guide teaching practice and education policy.

THE SCHOOL LABORATORY: IMPLICATIONS FOR CLASSROOM PRACTICE AND RESEARCH

In *The End of Education*, Postman (1995) wrote that efforts to improve schooling require attention to the *means* for educating children, but that the "reasons" or *ends* for learning and schooling are far more important. Compelling abstract, metaphysical ends provide meaning and significantly influence education and schooling. However, practical guidance is also needed in shaping both school science reform efforts and moment-to-moment teaching decisions in the science classroom and laboratory. The bulleted goals for learning in the school science laboratory shown in Table 15.1 and discussed earlier in this chapter are important but broad. To guide teachers' pedagogical decisions and thus to improve learning in complex, busy school laboratory settings, curriculum developers and teachers need to develop more detailed objectives derived from the broader goals; more explicit objectives will also provide guidance that helps students understand the purpose for specific activities and what they need to do consistent with those purposes. Relevant research on laboratory-classroom learning can inform the development of such objectives and teaching strategies.

Selecting and Promoting Learning Goals for Focused Learning in Specific Laboratory Experiences

Education goal statements in contemporary science education reform documents such as *Project 2061: Science for All Americans* (AAAS 1989), *the National Science Education Standards* (NRC, 1996), and international standards documents reflect the broad goals discussed earlier in this chapter. These goals are best implemented in ways that are particularly relevant to local needs and resources. To these ends, more focused objectives for science laboratory learning such as those shown in Table 15.2

TABLE 15.2
More Focused Objectives for Student Learning in the School Laboratory

Identify problems for inquiry, suggest strategies for that inquiry, and successfully solve laboratory problems

Participate actively in working toward specific understanding and solutions

Exhibit creativity and curiosity in science inquiry

Exhibit interest and an internal locus of control in science inquiry

Communicate and collaborate in science inquiry

Set objectives, make decisions, exhibit analytical and reflective thinking, and self-evaluate while inquiring and investigating

Retrieve and use current scientific concepts during authentic inquiry

Demonstrate an understanding of the nature of science and its relevance for investigative design, interpreting data, and formulating findings

Make and justify decisions regarding the methodology, data collection, analysis, scientific claims, organization, and presentation of laboratory work

Demonstrate robust understanding of fundamental science concepts (*not* simply articulating isolated facts and using mathematical algorithms to solve relatively meaningless problems)

should be articulated. Promoting these more focused but still general learning outcomes demands that teachers, curriculum developers, and researchers consider how particular laboratory experiences can promote more explicit, age-appropriate, science learning objectives. They must articulate relevant objectives consistent with desired goals for learning and unique opportunities within specific laboratory activities to guide teachers' and students' decisions and behaviors. Subsequently, the success of laboratory experiences should be examined by the assessment of students' learning associated with the explicit objectives. Decisions regarding selection of laboratory activities and materials, adjustments in the curriculum, and appropriate teacher behaviors and strategies should be influenced by the information gathered from assessments targeted to explicitly stated objectives for student learning in the school laboratory.

Selecting and Scaffolding Topics, Ideas, and Laboratory Activities Appropriate for Concept Development

Important science concepts should be revisited throughout a science course in different and more complex laboratory contexts. Within a course, the selection and sequencing of topics and concepts for student investigation are factors that influence effective teachers' decisions on the selection and use of laboratory investigations. With more deliberate sequential course design and sensitive scaffolding of concepts, students can be encouraged to make more connections between concepts, materials, and contexts. Information about the students' relevant prior knowledge and skills as well as about their ability to handle abstractions, multiple variables, and alternative representations are important factors in the day-to-day decisions of effective teachers. As discussed in the *learning empowering technologies* section of this chapter, this very important area for research and development in science education has led to the production early in the twenty-first century of potentially very helpful software tools designed to support inquiry and the depth and stability of students' concepts and their networks of concepts. These tools should be used with students, and their effectiveness in promoting learning in the laboratory-classroom should be studied very carefully.

To promote conceptual and procedural understanding and engagement, particular laboratory activities must be selected for more thorough investigation in which students experience meaningful inquiry in a time frame that makes sense within the constraints of a school science course. Because in-depth, conceptually focused laboratory study usually consumes considerable time and classroom-laboratory time is of necessity limited, some laboratory activities should be selected for in-depth attention while others are treated less intensively. To conduct those activities effectively, other, less crucial school laboratory activities must be bypassed in favor of more time-efficient alternatives to laboratory teaching, such as simulations and teacher-mediated demonstrations. Many science topics are not readily amenable to first-hand examination in the school laboratory because the materials involved are dangerous to manipulate, very expensive, too large, or too small for students to examine first hand; other important phenomena may take place across time frames that are far too long or too brief to examine in real time (Lunetta & Hofstein, 1991). In deciding what science content is deserving of thorough investigation with materials in the laboratory and what content may be treated with more limited hands-on experiences, the following questions should be carefully considered:

- What are the principal learning outcomes sought for students in an investigation? Which laboratory activities can successfully promote important learning outcomes, particularly those most neglected in other school science experiences?
- To what extent is the science content in the laboratory experience (including nature of science issues) crucial for scientific literacy? To what extent does that content warrant in-depth investigation when compared with other important content?
- To what extent is the content in the laboratory experience fundamental to one or more science disciplines and extensively linked to other important science concepts? (Content that is well linked to several other important science concepts should normally have higher priority for in-depth investigation.)
- To what extent is the science content difficult to comprehend without concrete experiences that can be used to challenge and extend students' thinking?
- To what extent can students develop meaningful understanding of the important concepts and ideas through a mentally engaging demonstration or simulation, rather than in a more time-consuming, hands-on investigation with materials?
- To what extent are students likely to follow directions relatively mindlessly in pursuing the stated objectives?

In general, science knowledge (conceptual and procedural) that is central in science literacy, fundamental to one or more science disciplines, and difficult to understand without extensive hands-on and minds-on experience deserves in-depth laboratory investigation. On the other hand, "cookbook" verification activities and laboratory experiences that can be taught effectively through teacher-mediated demonstrations, appropriate simulations, and other alternative practical modes of learning and teaching are good candidates for alternative treatment or even for elimination in a conventional laboratory format. Well-conducted, mentally engaging demonstrations and simulations can often be effective and time-efficient, particularly if teachers pose effective questions and scenarios that interest and engage students cognitively. Although the learning outcomes will not be identical, demonstrations can be very appropriate and efficient alternatives to laboratory activities, especially when the instrumentation available for the laboratory normally introduces large measurement error, when special technical expertise is needed to operate those instruments successfully, or when conducting the laboratory activity successfully necessitates particularly heavy commitments of time.

Selecting Laboratory Materials to Match Goals for Learning with Students' Needs

The materials selected for use in a particular investigation often play a very important though complex role in promoting or confounding what students observe and learn. The simplicity or complexity and the novelty or familiarity of the materials and technologies to be used in the laboratory are among the important variables that teachers and curriculum developers must consider to promote meaningful learning. Using equipment and materials that students experience regularly in the world around them in laboratory investigations can help the students to understand and apply what they are learning in the laboratory. It is important to note, however, that students often bring long-standing misconceptions about the nature of familiar materials with them to school science. These misconceptions can interfere with the ways a student thinks about the materials or equipment, their functioning, and their roles as objects of investigation or as tools in the laboratory. Such misconceptions can influence students' expectations, observations, and understanding of the phenomena they are studying, as illustrated earlier in this chapter when a student's failure to understand the design and purpose of a simple light bulb socket interfered seriously with her ability to interpret a simple electric circuit. Equipment that is novel and not part of a students' prior experience can also influence their learning in the laboratory (Olson & Clough, 2001). When visitors first enter informal environments (a museum, for example), they spend substantial time becoming familiar with that environment before engaging with the exhibits (Falk & Balling, 1982; Kubota & Olstad, 1991). Similarly, when students encounter novel materials during laboratory activity, their attention focuses first on the nature of the novel materials and their functioning Olson (2004). As a result, the students may not focus on important science concepts that the teacher had intended to be a priority. When physics students use a graphing software tool for the first time, for example, their attention may be drawn to the procedures involved in using the software rather than to the graphical representations of the relationships and the concepts the graphing software was intended to illustrate and help them understand. This is but one example of the kind of issue that warrants empirical research to inform good teaching practice.

Johnstone and Wham (1982) wrote that laboratory investigations often overload students with too many variables and too much information to process, whereas Gunstone and Champagne (1990) reported that laboratory work could successfully promote conceptual change, especially if the activities focused on careful treatment of limited *qualitative* tasks. So focusing attention on describing relationships between principal variables and patterns observed in an investigation without the need to attend to multitudes of other details in an investigation can facilitate conceptual understanding at times. When materials are selected to use in laboratory activities, consideration must be given not only to the objectives articulated for students' learning, but also to their prior knowledge and understandings. Therefore, teachers need to help students verbalize their ideas, not only about the relevant science concepts, but also about the nature and function of the laboratory materials to be used in investigating their research questions. Questions that science teachers ask in the laboratory and those they ask students to address in their *portfolios* or *lab reports* can help teachers as well as students to comprehend and explain the investigative procedures and materials used, issues linked to the nature of science, and their understanding of relevant science concepts. With this information, teachers will be in a much better position to select and modify laboratory objectives and activities and to employ more sensitive teaching strategies.

Selecting and Modifying Activities to Encourage "Minds-on" Engagement in the Laboratory

As noted throughout this chapter, goals for learning in science education and knowledge of how people learn should guide teachers in selecting and modifying laboratory activities to promote those goals and the more explicit objectives derived from them. When possible, science laboratory activities should encourage students to exhibit the behaviors outlined in Table 15.3. Student behaviors like these can engage students in more meaningful laboratory activities. They are advocated in numerous papers informed by research on learning, and they can be useful for teachers in restructuring their laboratory activities to become more congruent with what we know about learning and goals for student learning. Researchers investigating school science laboratory experiences need to report the extent to which the laboratory activities and teacher-classroom environment engage students in these kinds of decision-making experiences and the effects on learning outcomes for the students.

Multiple studies confirm that the frequently observed ritualistic, even "mindless" student behaviors observed in many laboratory activities stifle students' personal engagement in decision-making in the laboratory. These kinds of activities

TABLE 15.3
Student Behaviors to Encourage in Particular Laboratory Activities

Effective laboratory activities encourage students to

1. Explicate the principal question(s) they are investigating
2. Explicate their relevant prior knowledge, e.g., predict outcomes and provide reasoning
3. Employ previously studied science ideas in more complex ways, e.g., determine the products of a chemical reaction with the use of chemical nomenclature, chemical and physical properties, and stoichiometry
4. Invent laboratory procedures. When this is not possible, students should be asked to explain the rationale for steps in the prescribed procedure.
5. Decide what data is relevant and irrelevant; explain what the data means. When students struggle to do this, teachers should ask questions that help the students make progress without making decisions for them.
6. Apply mathematical reasoning to problems. When students are told precisely when and how to use mathematical algorithms to process their laboratory data, then they are unlikely to think conceptually about what they are doing.
7. Set goals, make decisions, and assess progress. Rather than answering all student questions, teachers ask students to explain what they are attempting to do, the procedure they used, what data they collected or are attempting to collect, what meaning they are making from their data, and the reasons for their assertions.
8. Communicate their laboratory work in a clear manner. Rather than prescribe a written laboratory report or portfolio format, have small group and/or class discussions in which the students decide how best to organize and present their research questions, methods, data, interpretations, findings, and new questions. The discussion should include pros and cons of various approaches.
9. Discuss limitations in their sampling, measurement, and data
10. Make connections between science concepts and everyday phenomena. Ask questions that help students observe these relationships
11. Raise new questions suggested by their investigations
12. Reflect on the nature of science. Raise questions that have students consider fundamental assumptions underlying their laboratory work: how theory guided the design and procedures used and their interpretations of data; the role of creativity and ingenuity in their laboratory investigations

Note: Adapted from Clough (2002).

rarely uncover students' underlying beliefs; they do not encourage students to wrestle with their prior knowledge in making sense of their experiences, and they do not encourage them to reflect on their own thinking. The selection of laboratory activities that actively encourage students to wrestle with science concepts (and hence to better understand them) is one of several important and complex matters. Laboratory activities should be aligned with desired goals for learning, be within learners' zones of proximal development, and require active student engagement. When laboratory activities are outside a student's zone of proximal development, the student has little choice but to follow directions blindly, and the time invested in the laboratory activity is likely to result in learning that is far from the desired goals articulated at the outset.

Laboratory activities that engage the mind as well as the hands have students "thinking out loud, developing alternative explanations, interpreting data, participating in" constructive argumentation about phenomena, developing alternative hypotheses, designing further experiments to test alternative hypotheses, and selecting plausible hypotheses from among competing explanations (Saunders, 1992, p. 140). Students' thinking should be expressed openly and discussed to help students act on their underlying beliefs in the context of alternative explanations; the articulation of students' ideas can also enable teachers to understand and hence to help the students develop deep, scientific conceptual understanding. Because teachers have limited time to interact with all students in a laboratory class, having the students use appropriate electronic tools like Progress Portfolio while conducting their inquiry can assist in facilitating the deep understanding that is consistent with goals for learning. Again, here is an area of contemporary research on science teaching and learning that warrants careful study.

Selecting Models and Strategies to Guide Laboratory Teaching

The reviews of the school laboratory literature discussed earlier reported a mismatch between the goals articulated for the school science laboratory and what teachers and students regularly do in laboratory activities. Ensuring that students' experiences in the laboratory are aligned with stated goals for learning demands that teachers explicitly link decisions regarding laboratory topics, activities, materials, and *teaching strategies* to desired outcomes for students' learning. Effective laboratory activities require significant student engagement, thinking, and decision-making, but teachers play a crucial role in helping students have productive experiences. The teaching models and strategies teachers employ to guide their behaviors in the laboratory-classroom and the ways in which they interact with students influence the extent to which well-designed laboratory activities promote desired learning. The *learning cycle* and subsequent teaching models were designed to guide teaching that promotes learning.

Search, Solve, Create, and Share (SSCS) is a relatively open-ended teaching model (Pizzini et al., 1989) that is well suited for school science laboratory experiences. During the *search* phase, students take part in identifying researchable questions and then in refining them. In the *solve* phase, students in small cooperative groups consider ways to investigate their research questions, using procedures they have developed. In the *create* phase, the groups prepare their presentations, reporting their research questions, investigative work, results, and conclusions. Each group's presentation is shared in the final *share* phase of the strategy. Pizzini and Shepardson (1992) compared classroom dynamics in a traditional laboratory with that in a SSCS setting. They reported that in the traditional laboratory setting student behavior appeared not to be influenced by the design of the laboratory experience, whereas in the SSCS setting "student behaviors are exhibited in response to . . . the lesson structure—designing a research plan, collecting data, analyzing data, and evaluating" (p. 255). The SSCS teaching strategy helped students learn to ask researchable questions, to design a research plan, and to answer some of those questions. Whereas many teaching strategies encourage students to ask and investigate questions, some strategies like SSCS place greater direct emphasis on expecting these behaviors.

Combining different elements of recommended teaching models can help individual teachers engage students in wrestling with the meaning of laboratory observations. For instance, the *Science Writing Heuristic (SWH)* (Keys et al., 1999) can be effective in promoting thinking, negotiating meaning, and writing about science laboratory activities. The SWH strategy can be integrated with learning cycle approaches and with an SSCS problem-solving approach. The SWH strategy can help students move beyond traditional school science laboratory reports, toward more personal, expressive forms of writing while improving their science understanding (Rivard, 1994). The SWH strategy guides teachers and their students in thinking and writing, and it encourages students to elaborate the links between claims and evidence. An SWH template guides teachers in helping students to negotiate meaning with small groups and with the entire class. A student template incorporates scaffolding questions that form the heuristic: What is the question being investigated? What did I do? What did I see? What can I claim? What is my evidence? What do others say? and How have my ideas changed? These prompts encourage metacognitive behaviors consistent with how people learn and promote many goals articulated for school science laboratory activities. For instance, in a study with grade 6 students, those engaged in the SWH strategy demonstrated higher order cognitive operations when completing laboratory activities, compared with those using a more traditional laboratory report format (Grimberg et al., 2004). Effective implementation of the SWH has been shown to improve grade 7 students' performance on conceptual essay questions focusing on the big ideas of a topic (Hand et al., 2004). Similar results were obtained for freshman university chemistry students' performance on conceptual essay questions and the American Chemical Society semester 1 examination (Rudd et al., 2001; Burke et al., 2003). Based on semester final examinations, the project reported success when the SWH strategy had been used in the lectures of a university chemistry course.

Predict-observe-explain (POE) and *think-pair-share (TPS)* are examples of other teaching strategies that can be used effectively alone or in combination with teaching models described earlier to elicit students' thinking and promote minds-on, not just hands-on engagement in school science laboratory experiences. Both POE (White & Gunstone, 1992) and TPS engage students in thinking about a laboratory phenomenon and sharing their thoughts with their classmates and the teacher. POE can be used with an entire class, small groups, or individual students. Having students make a prediction often raises interest in what will be observed and investigated, and in the process, teachers can gain important insight into students' thinking (Liew & Treagust, 1995; Palmer, 1995). When observations do not match students' predictions, cognitive conflict and motivation for learning may ensue. Whether or not students' predictions match what they observe, the most important step of this strategy is the explanation the students provide for their predictions and how they account for observations that deviate from what they had predicted. TPS can be used in small groups and with the entire class when a teacher wants students to contemplate a question or phenomenon individually, then interact with other students to discuss their ideas, and finally share what they think with the teacher, group, or entire class.

A questioning strategy proposed by Penick, Crow, and Bonnstetter (1996) is well suited to school science laboratory investigations because it reminds teachers to determine explicitly what students have done and to help the students recall and use those experiences to speculate, build relationships, create explanations, and apply knowledge. The strategy can be particularly useful to teachers as they work to change their own roles and behaviors during laboratory activities, and it can guide researchers in describing the nature of student and teacher behaviors that may be related to learning outcomes. The examples shown in Table 15.4, while not an invariant step-by-step progression of questions, illustrate how the strategy is useful in the laboratory to ground questions in what students have done and to help the students bridge to more abstract concepts. Even well-written laboratory activities may not enable students to learn with the deep understanding intended by their designers when they are poorly implemented in school settings. Selecting and implementing appropriate teaching strategies can have a powerful influence on the

TABLE 15.4
Questioning Strategy for School Science Laboratory Experiences

History—Questions that relate to students' experience:
  What did you do . . .?
  What happened when you . . .?

Relationships—Questions that engage students in comparing ideas, activities, data, etc.:
  How does this compare to . . .?
  What do all these procedures have in common?

Application—Questions that require students to use knowledge in new contexts:
  How can this idea be used to design . . .?
  What evidence do we have that supports . . .?

Speculation—Questions that require thinking beyond given information:
  What would happen if you changed . . .?
  What might the next appropriate step be?

Explanation—Questions directed to underlying reasons, processes, and mechanisms:
  How can we account for . . .?
  What justification can be provided for . . .?

Note: Adapted from Penick, Crow, and Bonnstetter (1996).

extent to which learning outcomes sought for students are achieved. In addition, examining the effects of specific teaching strategies and models on student learning should be an important goal for focused research that can inform practice in science education. These are very important tasks not only for science education researchers per se, but also for science teachers and science teacher education.

ROLE OF THE TEACHER
DURING LABORATORY ACTIVITIES

As noted earlier in this chapter, contemporary science concepts rarely emerge from school laboratory experiences and data unless the students have thoughtful conversations with an informed teacher who can help them contrast their ideas with those of the scientific community. Gunstone and Champagne (1990) noted that the need for meaningful interaction and reflection in the laboratory is essentially a call for discussion, "a teaching strategy which has been widely under-used in laboratories" (p. 179).

Windschitl (2002) wrote that "Supporting student learning . . . requires special skills and conditions" (p. 145). These teaching skills are especially important when teachers work with students in the laboratory, and researchers investigating school laboratory experiences should examine and report these "skills and conditions" with special care. Laboratory activities create many opportunities in which the students can describe: what they *see*, what they are *doing*, and how they *explain* these things. Yet, asking thought-provoking questions that help students to articulate their observations, their inferences, and their explanations and to connect these with science concepts they "know" and with the concepts of experts is a particularly important and challenging task for a teacher (Driver, 1995).

Effective teachers encourage students to share their thinking by asking effective questions with appropriate wait time I and II (Rowe, 1974, 1986), carefully listening to students' ideas and asking for elaboration, acknowledging those ideas without expressing judgment, and responding with further questions and ideas that are based upon the students' comments. These skills and other complementary teacher behaviors can create mentally engaging and productive laboratory discussions conducive to meaningful science learning. These behaviors are essential *tools* that teachers use to understand students' thinking during laboratory activities and to help students piece together desired understandings. The importance of these behaviors, especially in the school laboratory, suggests that effective teaching is far more complex and challenging than most observers and even many teachers believe it to be (Clough, 2003; Windschitl, 2002).

This complexity and challenge is illustrated in a short transcript from a case study report adapted from Clough (2003) and shown in Box 15.1. The example illustrates the critical role teachers can play in learning and the importance of the pedagogical practices they use in teaching. The laboratory activity that was the context for Box 15.1 might be perceived by a layperson as simple *hands-on* learning, but to an informed teacher who is sensitive to the nuances of learning and teaching, the learning interactions visible in the dialogue are complex. A careful reading of Box 15.1 shows an expert teacher who worked to understand students' thinking, challenge misconceptions, and help the student make links to science concepts that led

Narrative Box 15–1
One Example of the Teacher's Crucial Role in the Laboratory

Dan was a "good student" who along with his classmates had successfully completed a learning cycle sequence exploring characteristics of chemical change including the conservation of mass several weeks prior to the dialogue below. In that activity, students improved their experimental design several times to prevent escape of the gas produced. With each sequential improvement the "loss" of mass resulting from gas leaking out of the system became smaller. Through these experiences, students came to the conclusion that under perfect conditions (i.e., no substances are lost or gained by the system, perfect balance, etc.) that mass would remain exactly the same before and after a chemical reaction. Dan had appeared to understand a series of activities and discussions that had taken place in the following weeks including balancing chemical reactions, the mole concept, and stoichiometry. Later, the students were enthusiastically attempting to determine the products of that prior chemical reaction using all that they had learned during the entire year in chemistry. Several days into this activity, Dan approached his teacher and the following conversation ensued:

Dan: "Mr. Smith, the mass of my system went down."
Teacher: "How do you account for that, Dan?"
Dan: "A gas was formed and gases have no mass."
Teacher: (Inwardly surprised, but maintaining an accepting and inquisitive outward appearance) "What do you think gases consist of?"
Dan: "Atoms."
Teacher: "What do you know about atoms and mass?"
Dan: "Atoms have no mass."
Teacher: (Doubly surprised and searching for a way to help Dan see his misunderstanding) "Dan, what are you made up of?"
Dan: "Atoms." (Pause, followed by a paradoxical look on his face.) "And I have mass."

In the episode, the teacher kept in mind the overarching goals he had for the students. The teacher's response to Dan reflected an understanding of how people learn and how they often struggle to fully comprehend what the teacher has in mind. To help Dan develop a more scientifically accurate concept, the teacher did not tell Dan how to interpret the data. Instead, he posed a question to have Dan elaborate on his statement. Using non-judgmental, but encouraging non-verbals, the teacher waited again (wait-time II). The teacher's hard won interaction pattern provided Dan with more time to think and talk, while giving the teacher more time to consider what his next move would be. Using positive voice-inflection with a line of questioning he thought would resolve the issue, the teacher continued the interaction while listening intently to Dan's thinking, acknowledging his ideas without judging them, and responding with questions developed from what Dan had said. The teacher reported that while Dan was telling him that *atoms have no mass*, the periodic table of elements was visible to Dan. On it, the atomic masses were clearly displayed, and they were numbers Dan had used consistently in solving stoichiometry problems. Some of those problems had explicitly addressed the mass of reactants and products in the gaseous state, and Dan had solved them successfully.

to more meaningful and comprehensive scientific understanding. Worth noting again is the need for research on learning in the school laboratory that recognizes intricate and intertwined teacher and student behaviors and more clearly articulates the roles of the teacher in promoting meaningful interaction and reflection in the development of more scientific ideas and understanding.

TOWARD APPROPRIATE QUESTIONS, METHODS, AND ASSESSMENT SCHEMES IN LABORATORY-RELATED RESEARCH IN SCIENCE EDUCATION

"At its core, scientific inquiry is the same in all fields. . . . Research . . . is a continual process of rigorous reasonings supported by a dynamic interplay among methods, theories, and findings. It builds understanding in the form of models or theories that can be tested" (Shavelson & Towne, 2003, p. 2). Unfortunately, careful scholarship and student performance data have *not* consistently driven the policies and practices associated with teaching in the school science laboratory. Our review of the literature fails to show many empirical studies that have investigated carefully the causal effects of the objectives, laboratory instructions, teaching models, and teaching behaviors experienced by students in the laboratory on the attainment of explicit objectives for learning articulated for particular laboratory activities or on the broader goals for learning articulated in contemporary science standards. Reviews in past decades have reported disappointment with studies on the laboratory, resulting from (a) failure to explicate goals and objectives for laboratory activities; (b) assessment instruments that were not well aligned with the goals of laboratory work; (c) mistaken notions regarding the nature of science; (d) failure to delineate what the teacher and students were and were not doing before, during, and after laboratory experiences; and (e) other factors discussed in this chapter. Although progress has been made, many of these problems have not been properly addressed. The laboratory presents many opportunities for promoting desired learning outcomes, but what we know about learning and effective teaching has not been visible regularly in many school laboratory settings.

Many variables interact to influence student achievement and attitudes, and searching for single cause-effect relationships in teaching and learning associated with the laboratory is contrary to the complexity that we have come to know is inherent in meaningful science teaching for human learners. Thus, employing research designs that can examine and link complex laboratory-classroom variables to learning outcomes will be a challenging but important goal. To inform practice more optimally, next steps in research on the school science laboratory should include studies that examine multiple interacting variables and research questions to ascertain the nature of their individual and composite effects on students' science learning. Research on the laboratory in school science should examine the important interacting roles of students' prior understanding of relevant conceptual and procedural knowledge, students' understanding of the nature of science, and their understanding and comfort with laboratory technologies, perceived goals and objectives articulated for laboratory learning, the roles played by curriculum materials, teachers' interactions with students, laboratory assessment systems, the teachers' scientific and pedagogical knowledge, and other relevant variables. Ultimately, the science education community should have much more *scientific* information about the nature of the individual and composite effects of these variables on students' science learning to better inform teaching practice and education policy. There is much work to be done.

Research on the school laboratory should also examine some of the very important social and ethical issues that influence teachers' decisions to engage or not to engage their students in laboratory activities. Two examples of important issues that have not been examined and discussed substantively in the literature are concerns about *laboratory safety* and about *valuing living* (*or formerly living*) materials. Busy teachers who are concerned about promoting humane and scientific habits of mind, values, and inquiry as well as safety must function within schools in which many administrators today are particularly concerned about avoiding potential controversy and litigation while operating with limited budgets. Teachers who are concerned about promoting inquiry as well as the valuing of living things must make decisions about activities to be included or avoided in science laboratory-classrooms. These decisions are made within an array of community values (anti-vivisection and immature student behavior among them) that influence those decisions. Meaningful research that can inform practice and policy must examine these kinds of issues as well as those in the domain of students' cognition.

One important part of the task is to identify appropriate research designs that can guide next steps in organizing research studies. Research questions, methodologies, and assessment instruments must be aligned in response to the problems and issues discussed in this chapter. Many studies have been conducted with the use of case-study methodologies that have provided information about effects of practices on learning in school laboratory settings. These initial steps have been informative, but it has been difficult to generalize beyond the small samples that were studied. More systematic research, sometimes with complex research designs, is warranted to yield more generalizable findings. The structure and size of many secondary and university science laboratory courses (often with multiple sections) make treatment/control research designs possible. In cases where a large number of students are enrolled, such as in college science courses, *Solomon four-group designs* (Isaac & Michael, 1987) may be appropriate, for example. Structural Equation Modeling (Gall et al., 1996; Hoyle, 1995) and other complex designs might better help science education researchers understand the role of the laboratory in conjunction with other aspects of effective teaching; contemporary social science research designs should be explored and employed. Meta-analytic studies could also provide insight into the effects of specific kinds of laboratory treatments and experiences.

Organizing for larger-scale and longer-term studies of the kind recommended here requires not only the broader expertise that is possible in well-constituted collaborating teams of researchers, but also structures for research that go beyond one classroom and teacher, beyond a single school or community, and beyond classical university science and education departments. Creating and supporting the development of competent, collaborative researchers, research teams, and larger institutional structures sensitive to school and teacher, research and development issues will be challenging. Nevertheless, these are very important tasks en route to conducting research that will properly inform and improve education practice and policy.

FOUNDATIONS FOR THE TWENTY-FIRST CENTURY: LOOKING TO THE FUTURE

In this chapter, we have reviewed and synthesized multiple activities that have fit within a definition of the school *laboratory* derived from the science education literature and articulated in the introduction to this chapter. *Laboratory activities* have been used in multiple natural science disciplines to teach students of multiple age spans in very different cultural and classroom contexts. In the many studies and varied research settings, important issues and variables intersect. However, there have been many substantive differences in the laboratory settings and in other variables reported. To develop research in the field, the science education community and especially the research community must be careful to explicate detailed descriptions of the participating students, teachers, classrooms, and curriculum contexts in research reports. Among the many variables to be reported carefully are learning objectives; the nature of the instructions provided by the teacher and the laboratory guide (printed and/or electronic and/or oral); materials and equipment available for use in the laboratory investigation; the nature of the activities and the student-student and teacher-student interactions during the laboratory work; the students' and teachers' perceptions of how the students' performance is to be assessed; students' laboratory reports; and the preparation, attitudes, knowledge, and behaviors of the teachers. What do the students perceive they are supposed to accomplish in the laboratory activity? How do they perceive their laboratory performance will be assessed? How important do the students and the teachers perceive the laboratory activities to be? Studies should clearly report the amounts of time students spend in laboratory activities and how those are integrated or separated from other work in the science course. They should distinguish clearly between long-term and short-term student investigations and indicate clearly the numbers and roles of students in each laboratory team. Because substantial differences often are present in different laboratory settings, detailed descriptions of the subjects and contextual details are especially important. To support the development of knowledge that can advance science education by informing curriculum development, teaching and assessment practices, and education policy, it is essential to define technical terms precisely to explicate knowledge in the field; it is also important to use those terms consistently in research reports and in scholarly writing.

In the introduction to this chapter, we articulated a classical definition of school science laboratory activities that would have been appropriate in the nineteenth century and most of the twentieth. We wrote that laboratory activities were learning experiences in which students interact with materials or secondary sources of data to observe and understand the natural world. We also wrote that the increasingly widespread use of digital computing technologies in school science near the turn of the twenty-first century offered not only new tools for gathering, visualizing, and reporting data, but also important simulation resources for teaching and learning science. We have written that work with simulations has helped us to understand that school laboratory activities are themselves simulations of some of the things that scientists do. To teach meaningful science successfully, teachers' decisions must be informed by substantive research on these complex issues. Because citizens in a high-technology society need to understand the important distinctions between real and virtual realities or worlds, that is one more learning outcome that will come to be expected of science education early in the twenty-first century. Experiences with real and virtual materials in school science have important roles to play in developing the needed understanding.

In the twenty-first century, students will increasingly move their science classes between experiences with actual natural phenomena and the virtual realities that model those phenomena. The distinction between real and virtual tools and phenomena is one more complex and important variable that science teachers in the twenty-first century must consider to promote scientific understanding. The powerful new electronic tools and resources blur the interface between learning in the laboratory with real materials and learning with simulations that are representations of nature. We predict that before long a new goal/standard will emerge as an expectation for science education, that is, *school graduates will discriminate between real and virtual realities*. The school laboratory will have a very important role in the teaching and learning associated with this outcome.

In the twenty-first century, students will increasingly move in their science classes between experiences with actual natural phenomena and the virtual realities that model those phenomena. On some occasions they will process and graphically display laboratory data gathered from the study of real materials, and on other occasions they will process and graphically display data generated by electronic simulations driven by models that have been created by others or by the students themselves. We have reported evidence in the chapter that digital tools in the laboratory at times can help students visualize and understand science concepts, whereas at other times they can seriously confound understanding. Curriculum developers and teachers need to be well informed about these important issues in teaching and learning, and new research is warranted to provide the information needed. The new electronic tools associated with the school science laboratory offer important opportunities for teaching and learning in science; they also offer important opportunities for the scholarly study of learning, students' understanding, and the experiences and teaching prompts that support the development of scientific understanding. For these reasons, the need has arisen for a *new* definition of the school science laboratory that will encompass the simulation of natural phenomena and be appropriate for science education in the twenty-first century.

From a 50-year perspective, considerable progress has been made in the articulation of carefully conceptualized goals for science learning and in what we know about the learning of science. Many now recognize that science curriculum development, science teaching practices, and science education policy should be guided by those goals and by that knowledge. Curriculum development and teaching methodologies reflecting theories of how people learn have begun to be tested on the basis of student performance data, but these research and development activities are not sufficient, given the need to improve education in science and the magnitude of current problems. To achieve what is needed, research and development on these important issues in science education must accelerate.

Science education scholarship to date does provide a foundation for movement toward theories and research that can guide the development of curricula and teaching practices in science education and in the laboratory. Much evidence suggests that carefully conceptualized and carefully delivered laboratory activities are very effective in helping students develop and apply science concepts and procedural knowledge. However, research results have been difficult to interpret because central goals for learning in the laboratory, assessment measures, and research methodologies have not been well aligned. Contemporary social science research designs must be used to examine complex laboratory-classroom events and an array of variables that are well grounded in theories of science learning and the extant scholarship. To examine the matrix of interacting variables, collaborative research conducted by teams of persons who bring together knowledge and skills in science education, science, and appropriate education research methodologies is warranted.

At the beginning of the twenty-first century high-stakes tests in the United States and elsewhere increasingly drive what school and state administrators, parents, teachers, and students think is important in school science. Because there is a concurrent, widespread perception that what those tests measure is not well linked with time spent on activities in the school laboratory, to expect that students' and teachers' behaviors will shift toward more effective laboratory practices is naïve unless the perceptions change. Significant discrepancies exist between what we know about learning science and current science teaching practices and policy. The policy makers who control the testing programs and those who prepare the tests must become an integral part of more functional efforts to improve the effectiveness of school science.

What we know about science learning and the goals for science learning must be reflected in the science standards, and the standards must be linked to the development of valid and reliable tests. Most assessment of students' understanding and performance in the school laboratory continues to be confined to limited, conventional measures at best. Thus, substantial research and development is needed to create more valid, comprehensive, and useful measures of students' understanding of laboratory *procedural knowledge* and its intersections with the development of students' *science concepts*, their understanding of *the nature of science*, and their *attitudes toward science and the school laboratory*; the results of those efforts must be applied in science teaching practices and policy.

Although many questions about effective school science laboratory experiences remain to be answered, this chapter makes clear that much has been learned about the teaching, curriculum, and laboratory learning environments that promote desired science education goals. This knowledge provides a foundation for research that can inform teaching and curriculum practices and science education policy. The review of literature in this chapter also illustrates the very important and complex nature of teaching in the school science laboratory. Contemporary developments in understanding the nature of science are likely analogous, in part, to contemporary developments in understanding the effects of complex science classroom events on science learning. Overarching claims (pro or con) about the value of school science laboratory experiences are misplaced as myriad variables influence learning outcomes. These interacting variables must be examined carefully to better understand the potential and realities of laboratory experiences.

Much must be done to assist teachers in engaging their students in school science laboratory experiences in ways that optimize the potential of laboratory activities as a unique and crucial medium that promotes the learning of science concepts and procedures, the nature of science, and other important goals in science education. Science education researchers, teachers, curriculum developers, administrators, and policy makers all have important roles to play in these efforts. Understanding and advancing science education learning and teaching, promoting the development of science curricula, and supporting the development of effective science teachers are very complex activities, and simplistic solutions will be naïve and inadequate. Those important activities must continually be informed and enhanced by excellent research on learning and teaching science.

ACKNOWLEDGMENTS

Thanks to Joseph Krajcik, who reviewed this chapter.

REFERENCES

Abd-El-Khalick, F., & Lederman, N.G. (2000). Improving science teachers' conceptions of nature of science: A critical review of the literature. *International Journal of Science Education, 22*(7), 665–701.

Abraham, M. R. (1982). A descriptive instrument for use in investigating science laboratories. *Journal of Research in Science Teaching, 19,* 155–165.

Aikenhead, G. S. (1988). An analysis of four ways of assessing student beliefs about STS topics. *Journal of Research in Science Teaching, 25,* 607–629.

American Association for the Advancement of Science (1989). *Project 2061: Science for all Americans.* Author: Washington, DC.

Annenberg/CPB (1997). *Minds of our own videotape program one: Can we believe our eyes.* Math and Science Collection, P.O. Box 2345, South Burlington, VT 05407-2345.

Barron, B. J. S., Schwartz, D. L., Vye, N. J., Moore, A., Petrosino, A., Zech, L., et al. (1998). Doing with understanding: Lessons from research on problem and project-based learning. *The Journal of the Learning Sciences, 7,* 271–311.

Bates, G. R. (1978).The role of the laboratory in secondary school science programs. In M. B. Rowe (Ed.), *What research says to the science teacher* (Vol. 1). Washington, DC: National Science Teachers Association.

Bennett, J., & Kennedy, D. (2001). Practical work at the upper high school level: The evaluation of a new model of assessment. *International Journal of Science Education, 23,* 97–110.

Ben-Zvi, R., Hofstein, A., Samuel, D., & Kempa, R. F. (1977). Modes of instruction in high school chemistry. *Journal of Research in Science Teaching, 14*(5), 431–439.

Blosser, P. (1980). *A critical review of the role of the laboratory in science teaching.* Columbus, OH: Center for Science and Mathematics Education.

Bransford, J. D., Brown, A. L., & Cocking, R. R. (Eds.). (2000). *How people learn: Brain, mind, experience, and school.* Washington, DC: National Academy Press.

Brown, J. S., Collins, A., & Duguid, P. (1989). Situated cognition and the culture of learning. *Educational Researcher, 18,* 32–41.

Bryce, T. G. K., & Robertson, I. J. (1985). What can they do? A review of practical assessment in science. *Studies in Science Education, 12,* 1–24.

Burke, K., Poock, J., Cantonwine, D., Greenbowe, T., & Hand, B. (2003). *Evaluating the effectiveness of implementing inquiry and the science writing heuristic in the general chemistry laboratory: Teaching assistants and students.* Paper presented at the 225th ACS National Meeting, New Orleans, March 23.

Bybee, R. (1997). *Achieving scientific literacy: From purposes to practices.* Portsmouth, NH: Heinemann.

Bybee, R. (2000). Teaching science as inquiry. In J. Minstrel & E. H. Van Zee (Eds.), *Inquiring into inquiry learning and teaching in science* (pp. 20–46). Washington, DC: American Association for the Advancement of Science.

Champagne, A. B., Gunstone, R. F., & Klopfer, L. E. (1985). Instructional consequences of students' knowledge about physical phenomena. In L. H. T. West & A. L. Pines (Eds.), *Cognitive structure and conceptual change* (pp. 61–68). New York: Academic Press.

Champagne, A. B., & Hornig, L. E. (1987). *Students and science learning.* Washington, DC: American Association for the Advancement of Science.

Champagne, A., Klopfer, L., & Anderson, J. (1980). Factors influencing the learning of classical mechanics. *American Journal of Physics, 48*(12), 1074–1079.

Charen, G. (1966). Laboratory methods build attitudes. *Science Education, 50,* 54–57.

Clough, M. P. (2002). Using the laboratory to enhance student learning. In Rodger W. Bybee (Ed.) *Learning science and the science of learning, 2002 NSTA yearbook.* Washington, DC: National Science Teachers Association.

Clough, M. P. (2003). *Understanding the complexities of learning and teaching science: The value of a research-based framework.* Paper Presented at the Association for the Education of Teachers in Science (AETS) National Conference, St. Louis, January 29–February 2.

Cromer, A. (1993). *Uncommon sense: The heretical nature of science.* New York: Oxford University Press.

Davis, E. A., & Linn, M. C. (2000). Scaffolding students' knowledge integration: Prompts for reflection in KIE. *International Journal of Science Education, 22,* 819–837.

DeCarlo, C. L., & Rubba, P. (1994). What happens during high school chemistry laboratory sessions? A descriptive case study of the behaviors exhibited by three teachers and their students. *Journal of Science Teacher Education, 5,* 37–47.

Denby, Derek. (2004). Personal communication, November 12, 2004.

Domin, D. S. (1998). A content analysis of general chemistry laboratory manuals for evidence of high-order cognitive tasks. *Journal of Chemical Education, 76,* 109–111.

Dori, Y. J., Sasson, I., Kaberman, Z., & Herscovitz, O. (2004). Integrating case-based computerized laboratories into high school chemistry. *The Chemical Educator, 9,* 1–5.

Driver, R. (1995). Constructivist approaches to science teaching. In L. P. Steffe & J. Gale (Eds.), *Constructivism in education* (pp. 385–400). Hillsdale, NJ: Lawrence Erlbaum Associates.

Driver, R. (1997). Can we believe our eyes? In Annenberg/CPB (Ed.), *Minds of Our Own Videotape Program One.* Math and Science Collection, P.O. Box 2345, South Burlington, VT 05407-2345.

Driver, R., Newton, P., & Osborne, J. (2000). Establishing the norms of scientific argumentation in classrooms. *Science Education, 84,* 287–312.

Duschl, R. A. (1987). Improving science teacher education programs through inclusion of history and philosophy of science. In J. P. Barufaldi (Ed.), *Improving preservice/inservice science teacher education: Future perspectives. The 1987 AETS yearbook.* Washington, DC: Association for the Education of Teachers in Science.

Duschl, R. A. (1990). Restructuring science education: The importance of theories and their development. New York: Teachers College Press.

Duschl, R. A. (2000). Making the nature of science explicit. In J. Millar, J. Leach, & J. Osborne (Eds.), *Improving science education: The contribution of research.* Philadelphia: Open University Press.

Duschl, R. A., & Gitomer, D. H. (1997). Strategies and challenges to changing the focus of assessment and instruction in science classrooms. *Educational Assessment, 4*(1), 37–73.

Duschl, R. A., & Osborne, J. (2002). Supporting and promoting argumentation discourse in science education. *Studies in Science Education, 38,* 39–72.

Edelson, D. C. (2001). Learning-for-use: A framework for the design of technology-supported inquiry activities. *Journal of Research in Science Teaching, 38,* 355–385.

Edelson, D. C., Gordin, D. N., & Pea, R. D. (1999). Addressing the challenges of inquiry-based learning through technology and curriculum design. *Journal of the Learning Sciences, 8,* 391–450.

Edgeworth, R. L., & Edgeworth, M. (1811). *Essays on practical education.* London: Johnson.

Eglen, J. R., & Kempa, R. F. (1974). Assessing manipulative skills in practical chemistry. *School Science Review, 56,* 737–740

Eisner, E. W. (1985). *Educational imagination: On the design and evaluation of school programs* (2nd ed.) New York: MacMillan.

Erickson, G. L. (1979). Children's conceptions of heat and temperature. *Science Education, 63,* 221–230.

Eylon, B., & Linn, M. (1988). Learning and instruction: An examination of four research perspectives in science education. *Review of Educational Research, 58,* 251–301.

Falk, J. H., & Balling, J. D. (1982). The field trip milieu: Learning and behavior as a function of contextual events. *Journal of Educational Research, 76*, 22–28.

Fisher, D., Henderson, D., & Fraser, B. (1997). Laboratory environments and student outcomes in senior high school biology. *American Biology Teacher, 59*(2), 14–19.

Fraser, B. J. (1998). Classroom environment instruments: Development validity and applications. *Learning Environments Research, 1*, 7–33.

Fraser, B., McRobbie, C. J., & Giddings, G. J. (1993). Development and cross-national validation of a laboratory classroom instrument for senior high school students. *Science Education, 77*, 1–24.

Fraser, B. J., & Walberg, H. J. (1989). *Classroom and school learning environment*. London: Pergamon.

Freedman, M. P. (1997). Relationship among laboratory instruction, attitude towards science and achievement in science knowledge. *Journal of Research in Science Teaching, 34*, 343–357.

Friedler, Y., Nachmias, R., & Linn, M. C. (1990). Learning scientific reasoning skills in microcomputer based laboratories. *Journal of Research in Science Teaching, 27*, 173–191.

Gall, M. D., Borg, W. R., & Gall, J. P. (1996). *Educational research* (6th ed.). New York: Longman.

Giddings, G. J., Hofstein, A., & Lunetta, V. N. (1991). Assessment and evaluation in the science laboratory. In B. E. Woolnough (Ed.), *Practical science* (pp. 167–178). Milton Keynes: Open University Press.

Gitomer, D. H., & Duschl, R. A. (1998). Emerging issues and practices in science assessment. In B. J. Fraser & K. G. Tobin (Eds.), *International handbook of science education*. Dordrecht, the Netherlands: Kluwer Academic.

Goodlad, J. I. (1983). A summary of a study of schooling: Some findings and hypotheses. *Phi Delta Kappan, 64*(7), 465–470.

Grimberg, I. B., Mohammed, E., & Hand, B. (2004). *A grade six case study of cognitive involvement and attitudes towards scientific inquiry using the SWH*. Paper presented at the international conference of the Association for Educators of Teachers of Science, Nashville, TN, January 8–10.

Grobman, H. (1970). *Developmental curriculum projects: Decision* points and processes. Itasca, IL: Peacock.

Gunstone, R. F. (1991). Reconstructing theory from practical experience. In B. E. Woolnough (Ed.), *Practical science* (pp. 67–77). Milton Keynes, UK: Open University Press.

Gunstone, R. F., & Champagne, A. B. (1990). Promoting conceptual change in the laboratory. In E. Hegarty-Hazel (Ed.), *The student laboratory and science curriculum* (pp. 159–182). London: Routledge.

Hand, B., Wallace, C., & Yang, E. (2004). Using the science writing heuristic to enhance learning outcomes from laboratory activities in seventh grade science: Quantitative and qualitative aspects. *International Journal of Science Education, 26*, 131–149.

Hart, C., Mulhall, P., Berry, A., Loughran, J., & Gunstone, R. (2000) What is the purpose of this experiment? Or can students learn something from doing experiments? *Journal of Research in Science Teaching, 37*, 655–675.

Hodson, D. (1993). Re-thinking old ways: Towards a more critical approach to practical work in school science. *Studies in Science Education, 22*, 85–142.

Hodson, D. (2001). Research on practical work in school and universities: In pursuit of better questions and better methods. *Proceedings of the 6th European conference on research in chemical education*. University of Aveiro, Aviero, Portugal.

Hofstein, A., Ben-Zvi, R., & Samuel, D. (1976). The measurement of the interest in and attitudes to, laboratory work amongst Israeli high school chemistry students. *Science Education, 60*, 401–411.

Hofstein, A., Levi-Nahum, T., & Shore, R. (2001). Assessment of the learning environment of inquiry-type laboratories in high school chemistry. *Learning Environments Research, 4*, 193–207.

Hofstein, A., & Lunetta, V. N. (1982). The role of the laboratory in science teaching: Neglected aspects of research. *Review of Educational Research, 52*(2), 201–217.

Hofstein, A., & Lunetta, V. N. (2004). The laboratory in science education: Foundation for the 21st century. *Science Education, 88*, 28–54.

Hofstein, A., Navon, O., Kipnis, M., & Mamlok-Naaman, R. (2005). Developing students' ability to ask more and better questions resulting from inquiry-type chemistry laboratories. *Journal of Research in Science Teaching, 42*, 791–806.

Hofstein, A., Shore, R., & Kipnis, M. (2004). Providing high school chemistry students with opportunities to develop learning skills in an inquiry-type laboratory—a case study. *International Journal of Science Education, 26*, 47–62.

Hoyle, R. H. (1995). *Structural equation modeling: Concepts, issues, and applications.* Thousand Oaks, CA: Sage.

Isaac, S., & Michael, W. B. (1987). *Handbook in research and evaluation* (2nd ed.). San Diego: EdITS.

Johnson, D. W., & Johnson, R. T. (1985). *Learning together and alone: Cooperative, competitive, and individualistic learning* (2nd ed.). Engelwood Cliffs, NJ: Prentice Hall.

Johnson, R. T., Ryan, F. L., & Schroeder, H. (1974). Inquiry and the development of positive attitudes. *Science Education, 58*, 51–56.

Johnstone, A. H., & A. Shualili. (2001). Learning in the laboratory; some thoughts from the literature. *University Chemical Education, 5*, 42–50.

Johnstone, A. H., & Wham, A. J. B. (1982). The demands of practical work. *Education in Chemistry, 19*(3), 71–73.

Joint Matriculation Board. (1979). *The internal assessment of practical skills in chemistry: Suggestion for practical work and advice on sources of information.* Universities of Manchester, Liverpool, Leeds, Sheffield, and Birmingham.

Kannari, Z., & Millar, R. (2004). Reasoning from data: How students collect and interpret data in science investigations. *Journal of Research in Science Teaching, 41*, 748–769.

Karplus, R. (1977). Science teaching and the development of reasoning. *Journal of Research in Science Teaching, 14*(2), 169–175.

Kempa, R. F. (1986). *Assessment in science.* Cambridge, England: Cambridge Science Education Series, Cambridge University.

Kempa, R. F., & Ward, J. F. (1975). The effect of different modes of task orientation on observations attained in practical chemistry. *Journal of Research in Science Teaching, 12*, 69–76.

Kesidou, S., & Roseman, J. E. (2002). How well do middle school science programs measure up? *Journal of Research in Science Teaching, 39*(6), 522–549.

Keys, C. W., Hand, B. M., Prain, V. R., & Sellers, S. (1999). Rethinking the laboratory report: Writing to learn from investigations. *Journal of Research in Science Teaching, 36*, 1065–1084.

Kipnis, M., & Hofstein, A. (2005). *Studying the inquiry laboratory in high school chemistry.* Paper presented at the European Science Education Research Association Conference, Barcelona, Spain.

Klopfer, L. E. (1969). The teaching of science and the history of science. *Journal of Research in Science Teaching, 6*(1), 87–95.

Kozma, R., Zucker, A., Espinoza, C., McGhee, R., Yarnell, L., Zalles, D., et al. (2000). The online course experience: Evaluation of the virtual high school's third year of implementation, 1999–2000. Available at www.govhs.org/Images/SRIEvals/$file/SRIAnnualReport2000.pdf

Krajcik, J., Blumenfeld, B., Marx, R., & Soloway, E. (2000). Instructional, curricular, and technological supports for inquiry in science classrooms. In J. Minstrell & E. Van Zee (Eds.), *Inquiring into inquiry: Science learning and teaching* (pp. 283–315). Washington, DC: American Association for the Advancement of Science Press.

Krajcik, J., Mamlok, R., & Hug, B. (2001). Modern content and the enterprise of science: Science education in the twentieth century. In L. Corno (Ed.), *Education across a century: The centennial volume* (pp. 205–238). NSSE: 100th Yearbook of the National Society for the Study of Education. Chicago: University of Chicago Press.

Kubota, C. A., & Olstad, R. G. (1991). Effects of novelty-reducing preparation on exploratory behavior and cognitive learning in a science museum setting. *Journal of Research in Science Teaching, 28*, 225–234.

Land, S., & Zembal-Saul, C. (2003). Scaffolding reflection and articulation of scientific explanations in a data-rich, project-based learning environment: An investigation of Progress Portfolio. *Educational Technology Research & Development, 51*(4), 67–86.

Lazarowitz, R., & Karsenty, G. (1990). Cooperative learning and student academic achievement, process skills, learning environment and self-esteem in 10th grade biology. In S. Sharan (Ed.), *Cooperative learning, theory and research* (pp. 123–149). New York: Praeger.

Lazarowitz, R., & Tamir, P. (1994). Research on using laboratory instruction in science, in D. L. Gabel (Ed.), *Handbook of research on science teaching and learning* (pp. 94–130). New York: Macmillan.

Lederman, N. G., Wade, P. D., & Bell, R. L. (1998). Assessing the nature of science: What is the nature of our assessments? *Science & Education, 7,* 595–615.

Linn, M. C. (2000). Designing the knowledge integration environment. *International Journal of Science Education, 22,* 781–796.

Liew, C. W., & Treagust, D. F. (1995). A predict-observe-explain teaching sequence for learning about students' understanding of heat and expansion liquids. *Australian Science Teachers Journal, 41,* 68–71.

Loh, B., Reiser, B. J., Radinsky, J., Edelson, D. C., Gomez, L. M., & Marshall, S. (2001). Developing reflective inquiry practices: A case study of software, the teacher, and students in Crowley, K., Schunn, C., & Okada T. (Eds.), *Designing for science: Implications from everyday, classroom, and professional settings* (pp. 279–323). Mahwah, NJ: Lawrence Erlbaum Associates.

Lunetta, V. N. (1998). The school science laboratory: Historical perspectives and centers for contemporary teaching. In P. Fensham (Ed.), *Developments and dilemmas in science education* (pp. 169–188). London: Falmer Press.

Lunetta, V. N., & Hofstein, A. (1991). Simulations and laboraory practical activity. In B. E. Wolnough (Ed.), *Practical science* (pp. 125–137). Milton Keynes, UK: Open University Press.

Lunetta, V. N., & Tamir, P. (1979). Matching lab activities with teaching goals. *The Science Teacher, 46,* 22–24.

Lunetta, V. N., & Tamir, P. (1981). An analysis of laboratory activities in Project Physics and PSSC. *School Science and Mathematics, 81,* 230–236.

Matthews, M. (1994). Science Teaching: The role of history and philosophy of science, New York: Routledge.

McComas, W. F., Clough, M. P., & Almazroa, H. (1998). The role and character of the nature of science in science education. *Science & Education, 7,* 511–532.

Merrill, R. J., & Ridgeway, D. W. (1969). *The CHEMStudy story.* San Francisco: Freeman.

Millar, R., & Driver, R. (1987). Beyond process. *Studies in Science Education, 14,* 33–62.

Milner, N., Ben-Zvi, R., & Hofstein, A. (1987). Variables that affect student enrollment in science courses. *Research in Science and Technological Education, 5,* 201–208.

Nakleh, M., & Krajcik, J. (1994). Influence of levels of information as presented by different technologies on students' understanding of acid, base, and pH concepts. *Journal of Research in Science Teaching, 31,* 1077–1096.

National Commission on Excellence in Education. (1983). *A nation at risk: The imperative for educational reform (1983).* Washington, DC: The National Commission on Excellence in Education.

National Research Council (1996). *National science education standards.* Washington, DC: National Academy Press.

National Research Council. (2000). *Inquiry and the national science education standards.* Washington, DC: National Academy Press.

Nussbaum, J., & Novick, S. (1982). Alternative frameworks, conceptual conflict and accommodation: Toward a principled teaching strategy. *Instructional Science, 11,* 183–200.

Okebukola, P. A. O. (1986). An investigation of some factors affecting students' attitudes toward laboratory chemistry. *Journal of Chemical Education, 86,* 531–532.

Okebukola, P. A. O., & Ogunniyi, M. B. (1984). Cooperative, competitive, and individualistic laboratory interaction patterns: effects on students' performance and acquisition of practical skills. *Journal of Research in Science Teaching, 21,* 875–884.

Olson, J. K. (2004). *When hands-on science makes no sense: The role of abstraction and novelty of equipment on learning.* Paper presented at the annual meeting of the North Central Association for the Education of Teachers in Science, Dubuque, IA, October 7–9.

Olson, J. K., & Clough, M. P. (2001). Technology's tendency to undermine serious study: A cautionary note. *The Clearing House, 75,* 8–13.

Osborne, J., Erduran, S., & Simon, S. (2004). Enhancing the quality of argumentation in school science. *Journal of Research in Science Teaching, 41*, 994–1020.

Osborne, R., & Freyberg, P. (1985). Learning in science: The implications of children's science. Portsmouth, NH: Heinemann.

Palmer, D. (1995). The POE in the primary school: An evaluation. *Research in Science Education, 25*, 323–32.

Penick, J. E., Crow, L. W., & Bonnstetter, R. J. (1996). Questions are the answer: A logical questioning strategy for any topic. *The Science Teacher, 63*(1), 27–29.

Penner, D. E., Lehrer, R., & Schauble, L. (1998). From physical models to biomechanics: A design based modeling approach, *The Journal of the Learning Sciences, 7*, 429–449.

Pizzini, E. L., & Shepardson, D. P. (1992). A comparison of the classroom dynamics of a problem-solving and traditional laboratory model of instruction using path analysis. *Journal of Research in Science Teaching, 29*(3), 243–258.

Pizzini, E. L., Shepardson, D. P., & Abell, S. K. (1989). A rationale for and the development of a problem solving model of instruction in science education. *Science Education, 73*, 523–534.

Polman, J. L. (1999). *Designing project-based science: Connecting learners through guided inquiry.* New York: Teachers College Press.

Postman, N. (1995). *The end of education.* New York: Vintage Books.

Purser, R. K., & Renner, J. W. (1983). Results of two tenth-grade biology teaching procedures. *Science Education, 67*, 85–98.

Raghubir, K. P. (1979). The laboratory-investigative approach to science instruction. *Journal of Research in Science Teaching, 16*(1), 13–18.

Ramsey, G. A., & Howe, R. W. (1969). An analysis of research on instructional procedures in secondary school science. *The Science Teacher, 36*, 72–81.

Reiser, B. (2002). Why scaffolding should sometimes make tasks more difficult for learners. In Gerry Stahl (Ed.), *Computer support for collaborative learning: Foundations for a computer supported collaborative learning community* (pp. 255–264). Mahwah, NJ: Lawrence Erlbaum Associates.

Reiser, B. J., Tabak, I., Sandoval, W. A., Smith, B. L., Steinmuller, F., & Leone, A. J. (2001). BGuILE: Strategic and conceptual scaffolds for scientific inquiry in biology classrooms. In S. M. Carver & D. Klahr (Eds.), *Cognition and instruction: Twenty-five years of progress.* Mahwah, NJ: Lawrence Erlbaum Associates.

Rivard, L. P. (1994). A review of writing to learn in science: Implications for practice and research. *Journal of Research in Science Teaching, 31*, 969–983.

Rosen, S. A. (1954). History of the physics laboratory in American public schools (to 1910). *American Journal of Physics, 22*, 194–204.

Roth, W. M. (1995). Authentic science: Knowing and learning in open-inquiry science laboratories. Dordrecht, the Netherlands: Kluwer Academic.

Roth, W. M., & Roychoudhury, A. (1993). The development of science process skills in authentic contexts. *Journal of Research in Science Teaching, 30*, 127–152.

Rowe, M. B. (1986). Wait-time: Slowing down may be a way of speeding up. *Journal of Teacher Education, 37*(1), 43–50.

Rowe, M. B. (1974). Wait time and rewards as instructional variables, their influence in language, logic, and fate control: Part II, rewards. *Journal of Research in Science Teaching, 11*(4), 291–308.

Rowe, M. B., & C. Holland (1990). The uncommon common sense of science. In Mary Budd Rowe (Ed.), *What research says to the science teacher: Vol 6. The process of knowing.* Washington, DC: National Science Teachers Association.

Rudd, J. A., Greenbowe, T. J., Hand, B. M., & Legg, M. L. (2001). Using the science writing heuristic to move toward an inquiry-based laboratory curriculum: An example from physical equilibrium. *Journal of Chemical Education, 78*, 1680–1686.

Rudolph, J. L., & Stewart, J. (1998). Evolution and the nature of science: On the historical discord and its implications for education. *Journal of Research in Science Teaching, 35*(10), 1069–1089.

Sandoval, W. A., & Morrison, K. (2003). High school students ideas about theories and theory change after a biological inquiry unit. *Journal of Research in Science Teaching, 40*, 369–392.

Sandoval, W. A., & Reiser, B. J. (2004). Explanation-driven inquiry: Integrating conceptual and epistemic scaffolds for scientific inquiry. *Science Education, 88*, 345–372.

Saunders, W. L. (1992). The constructivist perspective: Implications and teaching strategies for science. *School Science and Mathematics, 92*, 136–141.

Schmidt, W. H., McKnight, C. C., & Raizen, S. A. (1999). A splintered vision: An investigation of U.S. science and mathematics education: Executive summary. Retrieved September 19, 2006 from http://ustimss.msu.edu/splintrd.htm

Schneider, L. S., & Renner, J. W. (1980). Concrete and formal teaching. *Journal of Research in Science Teaching, 17*, 503–517.

Schwartz, R. S., & Lederman, N. G. (2002). "It's the nature of the beast": The influence and knowledge and intentions on learning and teaching the nature of science. *Journal of Research in Science Teaching, 39*, 205–236.

Sere, G. M. (2002). Towards renewed research questions from outcomes of the European project Lab-work in science education. *Science Education, 86*, 624–644.

Shavelson, R. J., and Towne, L. (2003). *Scientific research in education.* Washington, DC: National Academy Press.

Tabak, I. (2004). Synergy: A complement to emerging patterns of distributed scaffolding. *Journal of the Learning Sciences, 13*, 305–335.

Tamir, P. (1989). Training teachers to teach effectively in the laboratory. *Science Education, 73*, 59–69.

Tamir, P. (1990). Evaluation of student work and its role in developing policy. In E. Hegarty-Hazel (Ed.), *The student laboratory and the science curriculum* (pp. 242–266). London: Routledge.

Tamir, P., Doran, R. L., & Chye, Y. O. (1992). Practical skills testing in science. *Studies in Educational Evaluation, 18*, 263–275.

Tamir, P., & Lunetta, V. N. (1981). Inquiry related tasks in high school science laboratory handbooks. *Science Education, 65*, 477–484.

Tamir, P., Nussinuvitz, R., & Fridler, Y. (1982). The design and use of practical tests assessment inventory. *Journal of Biological Education, 16*, 42–50.

Tasker, R. (1981). Children's views and classroom experiences. *Australian Science Teachers Journal, 27*(3), 33–37.

Thompson, J., & Soyibo, K. (2001). Effect of lecture, teacher demonstrations, discussion and practical work on 10th grader's attitude to chemistry and understanding of electrolysis. *Research in Science and Technological Education, 20*, 25–37.

Tibergien, A., Veillard, L., Le Marechal, J. F., Buty, C., & Millar, R. (2001). An analysis of labwork tasks used in science teaching at upper secondary school and university levels in seven European countries. *Science Education, 85*, 483–508.

Tobin, K. G. (1990). Research on science laboratory activities: In pursuit of better questions and answers to improve learning. *School Science and Mathematics, 90*, 403–418.

Tobin, K., & Garnett, P. (1988). Exemplary practice in science classrooms. *Science Education, 72*(2), 197–208.

Toulmin, S. (1972). *Human understanding: An inquiry into the aims of science.* Princeton, NJ: Princeton University Press.

Van den Berg, E., & Giddings, G. J. (1992). *Laboratory practical work: An alternative view of laboratory teaching.* Perth: Curtin University of Technology, Science and Mathematics Education Center.

Vygotsky, L. S. (1978). *Mind in society: The development of higher psychological processes.* M. Cole, V. John-Steiner, S. Scribner, & E. Souberman (Eds.). Cambridge, MA: Harvard University Press.

Vygotsky, L. S. (1986). *Thought and language.* A. Kozulin (Ed.). Cambridge, MA: MIT Press.

Ward, C. R., & Herron, J.,D. (1980). Helping students understand formal chemical concepts. *Journal of Research in Science Teaching, 17*, 387–400.

Weiss, I. R., Pasley, J. D., Smith, P. S., Banilower, E. R., & Heck, D. J. (2003). *Looking inside the classroom: A study of K–12 mathematics and science education in the United States*. Chapel Hill, NC: Horizon Research.

Wellington, J. J. (1981). "What's supposed to happen sir?": Some problems with discovery learning. *School Science Review, 63*(222), 167–173.

Wenger, E. (1998). *Communities of practice: Learning, meaning, and identity*. New York: Cambridge University Press.

White, R. T., & Gunstone, R. F. (1992). *Probing understanding*. London: Falmer Press.

Wilkenson, J. W., & Ward, M. (1997). The Purpose and perceived effectiveness of laboratory work in secondary schools. *Australian Science Teachers' Journal*, 43–55.

Williams, S. M., & Hmelo, C. E. (1998). Guest editors' introduction. *The Journal of the Learning Sciences, 7*, 265–270.

Windschitl, M. (2002). Framing constructivism in practice as the negotiation of dilemmas: An analysis of the conceptual, pedagogical, cultural, and political challenges facing teachers. *Review of Educational Research, 72*(2), 131–175.

Wolpert, L. (1992). *The unnatural nature of science*. Cambridge, MA: Harvard University Press.

Yung, B. H. W. (2001). Three views of fairness in a school-based assessment scheme of practical work in biology. *International Journal of Science Education, 23*, 985–1005.

Zembal-Saul, C., Munford, D., Crawford, B., Friedrichsen, P., & Land, S. (2002). Scaffolding preservice science teachers' evidence-based arguments during an investigation of natural selection. *Research in Science Education, 32*, 437–463.

CHAPTER 16

Discourse in Science Classrooms

Gregory J. Kelly
Pennsylvania State University

Educational events occur through communication. Science learning can be conceptualized as students coming to know how to use specialized language, given the constraints of particular social configurations and cultural practices. Across different theoretical traditions, from the sociology and rhetoric of science to studies of classroom interaction, the importance of spoken and written discourse in the production and learning of disciplinary knowledge is becoming increasingly recognized as a salient research focus. The study of discourse, broadly defined, allows researchers to examine what counts as science in given contexts, how science is interactionally accomplished, who participates in the construction of science, and how situated definitions of science imply epistemological orientations. In this chapter, I provide a conceptual overview of the field of discourse studies in science education. My aim is not to present a comprehensive review of all studies, but rather to focus on some of the theoretical approaches, methodological orientations, and substantive findings. Through this selected review, I argue that a discourse analytic perspective provides insight into how the events that make up science education are constructed through language and social processes. The importance of viewing education through this lens of language and social processes is justified by three primary observations. First, teaching and learning occur through processes constructed through discourse and interaction. An empirical focus on the ways language contributes to learning is essential for developing theories of practice for science education. Second, student access to science is accomplished through engagement in the social and symbolic worlds comprising the knowledge and practices of specialized communities. Issues of understanding, appropriating, affiliating, and developing identities for participation in the knowledge and practices of the sciences can be understood through the study of discourse processes. Third, disciplinary knowledge is constructed, framed, portrayed, communicated, and assessed through language, and thus understanding the epistemological base of science and inquiry requires attention to the uses of language. I conclude this review with implications about how the current body of knowledge suggests future directions for research in discourse processes in science education settings.

Discourse is typically defined as language in use, or a stretch of language larger than a sentence or clause (Cameron, 2001; Jaworski & Coupland, 1999). This definition, while potentially recognizing the need to examine form and function in discourse studies, may not make obvious the relationship of language use to social knowledge, practice, power, and identity (Fairclough, 1995). Therefore, the study of discourse processes in science education should properly include a definition of discourse as using language in social contexts and, as Gee (2001a) argued, connected to social practices, "ways of being in the world . . . forms of life which integrate words, acts, values, beliefs, attitudes, and social identities as well as gestures, glances, body positions, and clothes" (p. 526). For the purposes of this review, I shall leave the definition of discourse broad and consider a range of studies that encompass the many epistemological, ideological, and social dimensions of language use. To maintain focus, I shall consider primarily discourse studies set in educational settings. Furthermore, although the majority of empirical studies related to science education use language, I shall limit my focus to those studies that specifically examine how the form, function, and/or interactional aspects of language are used in an explicit manner. Generally, this means that studies that self-identify as explicitly related to language, literacy, and discourse are more likely to be included in the review.

Studies of classroom discourse in science education have been informed by multiple theoretical traditions and apply multiple methodological orientations. Typically there is a strong tie between the theoretical positions of the researchers and the application and interpretation of a particular research approach. Each theoretical position and manifestation in research entails a certain expressive potential (Strike, 1974), offering a particular set of constructs that allows researchers to speak about certain dimensions of discourse. Furthermore, although theories of discourse may have methodological implications, there is typically flexibility within traditions as to how particular studies are conducted. In this chapter, I make reference to some clearly distinguished theory-method relationships through a review of substantive studies of classroom discourse, rather than describe a set of research methodologies for analyzing classroom discourse separate from the substantial issues of individual studies. Much of the research in science education concerned with discourse processes shows a family resemblance to one or more of a relatively limited number of theoretical traditions, including social semiotics (e.g., Halliday & Martin, 1993; Lemke, 1998), sociolinguistics (e.g., Bleicher, 1994; Carlsen, 1991a), ethnomethodology (e.g., Lynch & Macbeth, 1998; Macbeth, 2000), cognitive science and psycholinguistics (e.g., Yore, Bisanz, & Hand, 2003), rhetoric and writing (e.g., Bazerman, 1988; Keys, 1999a), and critical discourse analysis (e.g., Hughes, 2001; Moje, 1997).

This review of discourse in science classrooms is intended to provide illustrative examples of the range of perspectives and issues. I offer a view of only a limited number of the many studies that could plausibly count as studies of discourse in science classrooms. As many of the authors reviewed have noted, studies of teacher lectures, for example, are not independent of the reading and writing activities in the classroom (e.g., Lemke, 2000; Moje, Collazo, Carrillo, & Marx, 2001; Rivard & Straw, 2000). Student participation in a teacher-directed classroom typically involves attempting to make sense (or not in some cases) of a range of spoken and written texts, signs and symbols, and physical objects, all within a continually constructed set of norms and expectations, rights and obligations, and roles and relationships (Gee, 1999; Green, 1983). Similarly, learning to write science/writing to learn science typically involves participation in a range of spoken discourse practices that help make sense of the written texts contributing to the writing goal, as well as any number of participation structures (small group, whole class), cultural expectations, ways of being a student, and so forth (e.g., Kelly, Chen, & Prothero, 2000; Keys, 2000; Rivard & Straw, 2000). Indeed, any issue related to lectures, discussions, writing, or reading in science classrooms typically includes, to some degree, aspects of each of these three categories. For the purposes of this review, I have organized the chapter by studies of spoken discourse, including the topics of classroom teaching, small-group interaction, conceptual change, argumentation, and equity, and studies of written discourse, including the topics of reading and writing science. The research literature will show that there is not a clear demarcation in teacher and student discourse, nor in written and spoken discourse in all instances. Many studies could have been grouped differently.

STUDIES OF CLASSROOM SPOKEN DISCOURSE

Discourse Studies of Classroom Teaching

A landmark for discourse studies in science education is Lemke's (1990) *Talking Science: Language, Learning, and Values.* Lemke applied a social semiotic perspective to classroom discourse in a set of studies of secondary science classrooms. Lemke's work began with the premise that science lessons are social activities constructed through human action. These human actions occur with the contingencies of the moment and are generally constrained by activity structures and norms for interaction. Lemke's analysis identified both thematic and organizational patterns in science dialogues in classrooms. The thematic patterns represented the particular semantic relationships comprising the scientific knowledge discussed. This was often in the form of propositional knowledge, controlled by the teacher, with little opportunity for students to take initiatives within the conversations. The examples of classroom discourse demonstrate how these acceptable ways of talking science are tightly controlled through the enforcement of strict uses of language specific to thematic content as interpreted by the classroom teacher. The organization of the discourse often fell into a common pattern of question-answer-response, referred to by Lemke as the triadic dialogue.[1] This triadic dialogue pattern centers control of the direction and thematic content of the lesson on the teacher. Through the analysis of the organizational and thematic patterns and their relationship, Lemke put forth his central thesis that learning science is learning how to *talk* science—that is, observing, describing, comparing, classifying, discussing, questioning, challenging, generalizing, and reporting, among other ways of talking science (p. 1). Lemke explained, "students have to learn to *combine the meanings* of different terms according to accepted ways of talking science" (p. 12, emphasis in original).

---

1. This pattern has been similarly labeled IRE (initiation-response-evaluation) or IRF (initiation-response-feedback); see Cazden (2001), Mehan (1979), and Sinclair & Coulthard (1975).

Lemke (1990) argued that over time the combined effect of strict adherence to patterned language use and tight control of the nature and types of classroom conversation led to a particular ideological positioning of science. The teachers' pedagogical goal of transmitting the propositional content of the products of scientific communities left little room for justification, discussion, and re-examination of science. Students were offered little opportunity to "talk science" and practice making the language of science their own. Furthermore, the disciplinary knowledge was positioned as unassailable, difficult to learn, and reserved for a cognitive elite. Lemke's examination of the discourse processes in science classrooms posed troubling problems for educators. The portrayal of science was ideological in the sense that only one dimension of science (strict use of language in its final form) was made available to students—views of a more social and less secure science were omitted. Consequently, the students may have lost interest in science because of the ways in which science was narrowly framed in the classrooms.

Whereas Lemke (1990) studied ways that teachers talked science, Moje's (1995, 1997) research considered more explicitly how a teacher talked *about* science. By applying a critical discourse analysis framework[2] (Fairclough, 1995), Moje (1995) identified how uses of particular discourse processes (e.g., first person plural, precision in language use, demarcating science from other disciplines) positioned science and science teachers as authorities. In one particular episode described by Moje (1997), a student was requested to repeat his imprecise response three consecutive times. This example illustrated how a teacher's view of the precision required of scientific knowledge was partially responsible for a situation where the power relationships were manifested in the conversation. Rather than viewing scientific practices as a resource for understanding the social practices of a community, the discourse practices were used as a means to enforce the putative exactness and precision of scientists. In these studies, a common theme emerged regarding choices of discourse in science classrooms: The choices of discourse influenced the views of science made available to students. The framing of the disciplines of science emerged similarly in studies of teacher questions, where variables such as teacher knowledge and use of authority became pertinent (Carlsen, 1991a; Russell, 1983).

Much like the social semiotic perspective of Lemke, Carlsen (1991a, 1991b, 1992) applied sociolinguistics to consider the multiple functions of classroom conversations. Carlsen examined the role of teacher subject matter knowledge as a variable in the syntactic, semantic, and pragmatic features of classroom discourse. Carlsen found that teachers' subject matter knowledge of the scientific discipline being taught influenced the extent to which they opened up classroom conversations to student participation, the range and type of questions posed to students, and their willingness to diverge from specific, defined curriculum goals. For example, teachers' questions to students served the immediate function of eliciting a student response to a scientific topic, as well as other functions, such as maintaining control of the students and the range of discussion topics (Carlsen, 1992, 1997). Thus, questions served multiple purposes for science teachers; they had both a locutionary (literal meaning) and an illocutionary (functional meaning) force in the

---

2. Critical discourse analysis examines the role of discourse in society and culture and how discourse plays a role in sociocultural reproduction and change (Fairclough, 1995; Luke, 1995).

conversation. Carlsen's analysis of teacher questioning provided a means of examining how teacher subject matter knowledge (measured independently) influenced the science of the classroom discourse. One interesting finding of these studies was that when teachers taught less familiar subject matter they tended to ask more questions. However, rather than opening up the conversation, these questions tended to be of a lower cognitive level and were fact oriented. Thus, students were put on the defensive by the teachers' questions.

Carlsen's studies of teacher subject matter knowledge and its relationship to choices discourse expanded some earlier findings by Russell. Russell (1983) applied argumentation analysis to the study of teacher questions and found that questioning served to orient the conversation to an unjustified authority of science, rather than to an authority merited by reasons. The studies by Carlsen and Russell corroborate Lemke and Moje's views about the ideological views of science promulgated in schools. Similarly, Cross (1997) identified teachers' support of mythological accounts of science—accounts that fail to consider the problematic nature of science, the influence of funding on science, the role of personal and cultural values, and so forth. Cross attributed the uniformity of teachers' views across cultures to the science socialization processes experienced by teachers and to the professional development of science teachers.

Whereas some studies identified limits to the ways that science was made available to students, other studies showed how access to scientific knowledge and practices occurs through specific, purposeful use of language. For example, rather than finding that questions were often used to control the substance of the classroom conversation (Carlsen, 1991b; Lemke, 1990; Russell, 1983), van Zee and Minstrell (1997) provided a case study of an exemplary physics teacher (Minstrell) who used questions to engage students with scientific knowledge. In this study, the teacher used a questioning method called a *reflective toss*. Unlike the triadic dialogue controlled by the teacher, the reflective toss invited students into the conversation by building on an initial student statement. A three-part dialogic structure consisting of student statement, teacher question, and student elaboration opened up the classroom conversations to serve three emergent goals. The reflective toss served to engage students in a proposed method offered by a student, to begin a refinement process of a previously discussed method, and to evaluate an alternative method. Together these emergent goals served to create discourse events constructed to allow and encourage student participation in the cognitive processes of the lesson.

In another example of teachers using discourse processes to support student learning, Roth's (1996) study of an open-inquiry learning environment considered how teacher-questioning practices were mediated by the situational social context. In this case, the teacher used questioning to scaffold student knowledge through an engineering design unit in a grade 4/5 classroom. Unlike situations where teachers know a preconceived answer to their questions, the teacher in this study generally did not know the requested information, believed the students could provide an appropriate response, was interested in the students' point of view, and believed the students would provide an answer. A typology of the content of the teacher's questions demonstrated a range of knowledge embedded in the conversations generated from these questions. Knowledge of the natural world, design practice, and testing of the designs were central to the classroom discourse. The typology was rounded out by questions relating to students' final products and questions about the sources of knowledge used and derived from the design experience. The teacher questioning thus served to increase student competence in the requisite engineering knowledge and offered opportunities for students to appropriate the questioning practices.

Gallas's (1995) study of the "science talks" in her first- and second-grade classroom evinced the importance of paying attention to students' ideas and questions in classroom discourse. In her classroom, science was the product of a joint construction of students and the teacher(s) incorporating a child-centered, hands-on approach, emanating from children's questions. The description of these experiences in *Talking Their Way into Science: Hearing Children's Questions and Theories, Responding with Curricula* represents an important shift from engaging students in science through questioning to learning to hear children's questions as a teaching strategy. This shift represents a break in the typical power asymmetries found in science classroom discourse. By developing the norms for discourse of this sort, the classrooms became a community of inquirers "whose interests, questions, and theories emerge from the inside-out, rather than the outside in" (Gallas, p. 101). Emergent curricula were also present in studies of an experienced third- and fourth-grade teacher by Crawford, Kelly, and Brown (2000). In this and a related study (Kelly, Brown, & Crawford, 2000), children's discourse was encouraged through a series of teaching practices that situated the teacher as a co-investigator. By developing a community that valued listening and following through on students' suggestions for next moves in science investigations, the teacher created multiple opportunities for her students to engage in scientific practices and to talk through ideas as a class. Part of the students' discursive practice included generating questions for a participating scientist. In this and other examples, the research focus has shifted from teacher questioning of students to ways in which students learn to pose questions in science contexts (Gallas, 1995; van Zee, 2000).

As illustrated by the previous examples, studies of the discourse processes of science teaching offer a range of views of the inner workings of classroom life. Science can be seen as constructed through discourse processes in these empirical studies. Nevertheless, the ways that science is framed through discourse make available to students a wide range of opportunities to learn specific scientific knowledge and practices. Similarly, although the views of science made available in terms of the conceptual information, the types of permissible discourse structures, and the ways of engaging in the discourse of science show considerable diversity, many of the studies found that limited participation of students in talking science can present an ideological view of science as particularly narrow and authoritarian.

Knowledge, Discourse, and Conceptual Change

Gallas's studies speak to the issue of translating from the everyday spoken language of students to the canonical discourse patterns typically found in formalized scientific discourse. Discourse-oriented research in science education has provided examples of how to bridge from students' initial knowledge state (i.e., ways of talking about the natural world) to more robust, theoretical language characteristic of professional scientific discourse, as well as examples of how assumptions about language render the link between knowledge and discourse tenuous. For example, Dagher's (1995) study of analogies, conceived broadly to include metaphors, models, and similes, in teacher discourse in seventh- and eighth-grade science classrooms, identified different ways that teachers bridge from a familiar domain for the student learners (source) to unfamiliar domains (target). Five types of analogies were used by the teachers: compound, narrative, procedural, peripheral, and simple. Interestingly, these types of analogies were used in idiosyncratic ways, and Dagher viewed this diversity of forms of expression as a positive experience for learners. This study also cautioned researchers by suggesting differences in how students viewed analogies, as compared with researchers and teachers.

The interdependence of language use and knowledge is the subject of other discourse-orientated studies in science education. Continuing with the theme of bridging across knowledge domains, Dagher (1994) raises questions about the use of analogies and the meaning of conceptual change for educational research. She reviewed studies of analogy use from a conceptual change perspective and identified different meanings of conceptual change (e.g., replacing students' initial concepts, adding to existing knowledge, providing alternatives to existing concepts). Dagher (1994) suggested that research on uses of analogies extend beyond developing students' knowledge of target concepts and consider the ways that analogies can enhance "creativity, aesthetic appreciation, and positive attitudes" (p. 610). Similarly, Klaassen and Lijnse (1996) caution about the interpretation of classroom discourse from a purely cognitive point of view focused on student misconceptions or alternative conceptions. In this study, an exchange between a teacher and his students is interpreted from three points of view (in terms of teacher analysis, misconceptions, and alternative conceptions) that the authors view as erroneous. They proposed instead to consider the ways in which a dissenting student and her teacher miscommunicate. In the example provided, the two interlocutors in question agreed about the similarities and dissimilarities of a given situation (book-on-the-table condition) but failed to reach agreement about how to characterize the situation in terms of force acting in the relevant bodies. Klaassen and Lijnse argued that the teacher and student did not assign the same meaning to the expression "to exert a force" (p. 129), and, thus, the problem of interpretation revolves around finding common ground that forms the basis for understanding.

The relationship of conceptual change to discourse processes was also examined by Macbeth (2000), who studied the "apparatus" of conceptual change for Karen, a student participant in the Private Universe Project. As is typical of ethnomethodology,[3] Macbeth examines in great detail the practical actions and conversational sequences between Karen and a research interviewer as they participate in a discussion about light. Central to understanding the apparatus of the students' "conceptual change" is the research setting with an ensemble of technologies. This close examination called into question previous assumptions about students' native

---

3. Ethnomethodology is not a research method, but rather an orientation that focuses on the ordinary actions of people as they proceed through everyday life; it studies the methods people use in various contexts to get through the mundane activities in their given situations (Lynch, 1993; Mehan, 1979). Although few discourse studies in science education draw from this tradition, it provides an interesting contrast with other discourse studies.

conceptions and the ways in which these conceptions change through experience. Macbeth demonstrated how Karen, by finding things she could "do in the dark," showed how "perceptual 'facts' are themselves attached to local orders of activity" (p. 253). Macbeth concluded by identifying how the worlds of scientific and ordinary action are continuous and permeable, rather than separate, as sometimes assumed. In another study with an ethnomethodological orientation, Lynch and Macbeth (1998) investigated how a teacher demonstrated science to her third-grade students. In this case, the teacher was shown to position and discipline students as "witnesses" to scientific phenomena through ways of setting occasional confrontations between the students' ways of seeing and the aimed-for scientific account. This study demonstrated how the mundane discursive tasks of classroom life serve to accomplish science education as situated practice.

Research topics such as teacher framing of disciplinary knowledge, uses of language to control the subject matter, the importance of language for student sense making, and the problematic nature of conceptual change all speak to the intertwined issues of the nature of knowledge and access to knowledge for student learners. These studies identify the importance of discourse processes for understanding how science is interactionally accomplished, how access to the subject matter knowledge occurs through language, and how the disciplines of science are interpreted through ways of speaking about them. Therefore, emerging from the initial studies of science discourse in classrooms are studies centrally concerned with equity, access, and epistemology in education settings. Before synthesizing this literature and its implications for future research directions, I review studies of student (and teacher) discourse in small-group settings.

Student Small-Group Discourse

Whereas the language functions examined in teacher-directed discourse tend to center primarily on the communication of propositional information, and secondarily on the control of social situations, studies of student small-group discourse examine the interrelationship of propositional, social, and expressive functions of language (Cazden, 2001). For example, Anderson, Holland, and Palinscar (1997) studied the interwoven nature of canonical scientific discourse and the social relationships and positioning among students working on an investigation in a small group. In this example, the researchers focused on the negotiated nature of interpersonal relationships, scientific activities, and task requirements for a student, Juan, and his group of classmates. This group of five sixth-grade students observed phase changes in a "barbell apparatus" and was given the task of explaining their observations through the use of a student-designed poster and molecular models. A key finding from the study was that teachers need to develop a sense of communal activity among the students. Opportunities to engage in the scientific discourse were mediated by diverse discursive processes related to negotiation of the task. Thus, understanding access to science required an analysis of the canonical forms of science discourse in the student talk, but also required attention to the students' personal identities and ways of navigating interpersonal relationships.

The simultaneous construction of propositional, social, and expressive functions of language was further specified in a number of studies involving student small-group discourse in inquiry-oriented contexts. Hogan's (1999) study considered the sociocognitive roles taken by eighth-grade students through their science group discourse while engaged in a long-term collaborative task related to the nature of matter. This study made explicit connections among the interpersonal and the more content-oriented aspects of scientific discourse, noting how demands on students included both ways of interacting and building consensus. In this case, the demands for interactivity and consensus building proved challenging for the students and may have stood in the way of accomplishing the intellectual task. Similarly, the issues of interpersonal relationships and differential (perceived) status among students engaged in group work were central to two studies by Bianchini (1997, 1999). These two studies drew from sociological theory of expectation states and were designed to create student group work conditions aimed at eliminating disparities of access in linguistically, ethnically, and academically diverse classrooms. Through analysis of students' assessment of peer status, records of group work task behavior, rate of science discourse, and conceptual tests, Bianchini (1997) identified how some students were systematically denied access to materials and participation despite a curriculum and instructional strategy designed to ameliorate such problems. Similarly, Bianchini (1999) found that students of low status as determined by their peers (often students from groups that have historically underachieved in science, including females, Latinos, and African Americans) participated less in cooperative work groups and learned less during the units. Thus, in these studies (Anderson et al., 1997; Hogan, 1999; Bianchini, 1997) and others of student group work (e.g., Hogan, Nastasi, & Pressley, 1999; Kelly, Crawford, & Green, 2001), negotiation of the multiple social and expressive functions such as student roles, individual and collective responsibilities, the nature of the academic task, and the differential status among students were thoroughly tied to the access students had to scientific discourse and, thus, to opportunities to construct institutionally sanctioned knowledge.

Social dimensions of small-group discourse include not only ways of negotiating the interpersonal relationships entailed in group membership, but also the nature of the scientific knowledge in question. The development of explanations that count as science for a given audience is an interactional accomplishment, partially constructed by the nature of the intellectual resources, the status of the knowledge in question, the participant structures, and the goals and purposes of the activity. Herrenkohl and Guerra (1998) designed two interventions related to student roles (groups working with intellectual and audience roles, and others with just intellectual roles) to promote student engagement in the discourse practices of understanding classroom procedures, monitoring comprehension, challenging others' perspectives and claims, and coordinating theories with evidence. Analysis of the speech patterns across the three phases of the inquiry activity (introduction, small-group work, reporting sessions) revealed that students assigned audience roles during spoken reporting sessions initiated more engagement episodes and challenges than students without such role assignment. Furthermore, the teacher discourse was a major mediator of the types of student discourse (e.g., teacher attention to classroom procedures versus scientific discourse practices such as coordinating theories with evidence) and was influenced by the changes in student role taking. Other studies, such as those focused on developing student inquiry, also identify the pivotal role played by teachers' discourse practices in framing students' activity, focusing student talk on the substantial aspects of science, and allowing space for student-generated discussions (Krajcik et al., 1998; van Zee, 2000)

Research on small-group interaction poses theoretical and methodological challenges for science education. Besides the technical difficulties of recording audibly clear conversations of student talk in busy classroom settings, methodological challenges include choices related to the focus on the discourse analysis (Lemke, 1998) and identification of the relevant semiotic field, given the chosen theoretical orientation and investigative focus. For example, Roth, McGinn, Woszczyna, and Boutonné (1999) drew from multiple data sources recorded in a grade 6–7 classroom to make the argument for the importance of the discursive practices within a community and how a community of practice comes to construct those intellectual resources deemed relevant to the tasks at hand. In this case, Roth et al. (1999) identified how knowing and learning about simple machines was distributed across people, artifacts, social configurations, and physical arrangements. The opportunities for students to participate in the community involved the use of material and symbolic practices, including constructions, measurements, design, and spoken discourse. Thus, this study, like many that consider small-group interaction, recognized the embedded nature of discourse processes and the methodological importance of understanding the community practices.

Researchers concerned with the semiotic field in small-group interaction need to consider discourse broadly, as many studies of small-group work examine student discourse while engaged in hands-on or other investigations with the material world. Two studies make it clear that the multiple resources constructed in time and space in laboratory settings need to be accounted for in research transcripts of student discourse. Roth (1999) and Kelly et al. (2001) identified how hands, arms, eyes, and bodies contributed to the cognition and learning by the participating students and observing researchers. For example, Kelly et al. (2001) identified how eye gaze, bodily orientation and movement, and gestures (such as pointing and motioning) contributed to the semiotic field made available for interpretation of physical motion and graphical representation as students made sense of their own motion and that of other objects in a data acquisition microcomputer-based laboratory. This study identified how community practices provided a framework for conversations, but also how the particular microhistories of small-group interaction served to exclude certain proposed scientific explanations, leading to dissent within small groups.

Whereas laboratory experience in classroom settings has not always led to the cognitive and epistemic goals set forth by educators (DeBoer, 1991; Fairbrother, Hackling, & Cowan, 1997; Meyer & Carlisle, 1996), placing students in apprenticeships in science laboratories offers an alternative set of opportunities. For example, Bleicher (1994, 1996) took a sociolinguistic perspective to examine the cultural practices of scientific research groups with student apprentice participants. Bleicher considered the social and cultural characteristics of everyday laboratory work and how such practices influence student initiation into research groups. By focusing closely on the moment-to-moment interactions in various discursive settings (e.g., lab work, group meetings, student presentations), Bleicher identified how students enter into group practices, identify sources for their knowledge through their apprenticeship activities, and thus learn through participation in scientific inquiry.

Studies of students working in small groups in a variety of interactional contexts demonstrate both the potential to provide opportunities to engage with science not readily available in many teacher-directed events and the possible pitfalls of student-centered discourse. Much like the studies of teacher-directed discourse, examination of small-group interaction identifies two key issues for researchers: the structuring of knowledge through discourse and the potential equity concerns found in how science is constructed through discourse. These two issues surface in studies focused on argumentation and more explicitly on equity. The field of argumentation in science education is concerned with scientific knowledge, evidence, and explanation. Issues of equity transcend the interactional contexts of classroom teaching, small-group work, and writing science and show relevance in the many ways language is used in science education. A small but significant body of research has emerged that considers the ways access to scientific knowledge is mediated through discourse and, in particular, how gender, language, and cultural variation in students' experiences influence success in science. I turn to these fields before reviewing work in written discourse.

Studies of Argumentation, Explanation, and Students' Use of Evidence

Argumentation refers to the ways that evidence is used in reasoning. As an analytic tool, argumentation analysis has been applied to examine student reasoning, engagement in scientific practices, and development of conceptual and epistemic understandings (Driver, Newton, & Osborne, 2000; Jimenez-Aleixandre, Rodriguez, & Duschl, 2000; Richmond & Striley, 1996). Studies have included examination of teacher discourse (Carlsen, 1997; Russell, 1983), preservice teacher explanations (Zembal-Saul, Munford, Crawford, Friedrichsen, & Land, 2002), small-group discourse (Kelly, Druker, & Chen, 1998; Richmond & Striley, 1996), and written knowledge (Kelly & Bazerman, 2003). Rationales for the use of argumentation derive from the importance of evidence in science (Bazerman, 1988; Duschl, 1990) and the value of argumentation for unpacking the nature of claims and the warrants for knowledge. Although uses of evidence are often perceived as central for adjudicating among scientific theories, studies of classrooms show that current practices in science teaching offer students few opportunities to engage with scientific evidence, models, and socioscientific issues (Driver et al., 2000).

Research using argumentation analysis begins with a normative model. One model is Toulmin's (1958) layout of arguments. Central components of an argument following Toulmin's model are relevant data, a claim asserted by the author, and warrants supported by theoretical backing. This way of laying out an argument offers some theoretical guidance but does not attend to how the discourse features are argued *in situ*. Nevertheless, application of Toulmin's layout of arguments to teachers' discourse allowed researchers to assess the extent to which authority in the classroom was derived from evidence or social standing (Carlsen, 1997; Russell, 1983). In another application, Bell and Linn (2000) adapted the Toulmin method for analysis of student argumentation. In their study of middle-school students' argument construction, Bell and Linn sought to scaffold student knowledge integration through uses of explanation and evidence with the SenseMaker argument-building tool. This study identified a range of types of arguments formulated by students and how the nature of students' beliefs about the nature of science was associated with characteristics of the arguments.

Sandoval (2003) provided another argumentation analysis approach based on scientific explanation, in which evidence is considered in the context of building and assessing models. Sandoval's study of students' understanding of natural selection, using the ExplanationConstructor computer program (as part of the Biology Guided Inquiry Learning Environments [BGuILE] project), examined the causal claims made by students and the ways in which these claims were warranted. Results showed how students were able to adopt explanatory goals and how attention to epistemic practices in specific domains can direct student inquiry to focus on evidence. A similar model was developed by Zembal-Saul et al. (2002) to study uses of explanations by pre-service science teachers. In this study, the software associated with the BGuILE project was similarly shown to support the articulation of evidence-based arguments. Additionally, the study demonstrated ways that the arguments could be improved and the important role the instructor had in supporting students' argumentation.

Argumentation theory has also been applied to students' conversations while they are engaged in science investigations. For example, Richmond and Striley (1996) analyzed students' use of evidence in 10th-grade integrated science and found that although students were able to use evidence, the results varied across student groups. The differential opportunities for demonstrating scientific understanding were constructed in part by the emergence of the social roles of the student group members, particularly as related to the student groups' leadership roles. In another study, Jimenez-Aleixandre et al. (2000) applied argumentation analysis to student conversations about genetics. By focusing on the argumentative operations proposed by Toulmin (1958) and a set of epistemic operations, including induction, deduction, causality, and plausibility, Jimenez-Aleixandre et al. distinguished engagement in scientific practices from narrower engagement in the specified school task. In another example of the opportunities afforded by first-hand experience with phenomena, the relationship of talk and action was investigated by Abell, Anderson, and Chezem (2000). In this study, the discourse of a teacher and students during a third-grade unit focused on sound was investigated to consider ways in which teachers can place greater emphasis on evidence and explanation. Although the pedagogical goals were only partially met, the study (Abell et al., 2000) showed how students can be introduced to using evidence in arguments and how student inquiry requires both practical experiences and talk about these experiences (Mortimer, 1998).

Three studies of argumentation analysis applied to university writing extended Toulmin's (1958) model and brought into consideration more linguistically oriented methods for analyzing evidence use. Kelly and Takao (2002) introduced an analytic tool to assess university oceanography students' use of evidence in writing. Recognizing that evidence chains typically span multiple epistemic levels of claim, Kelly & Takao evaluated how students were able to tie specific claims about data representations to claims about geological features and theoretical claims about abstract entities such as terrestrial plates. This model was extended to consider the lexical cohesions tying claims together to form an argument and to recognize the rhetorical moves required of the particular academic task (Kelly & Bazerman, 2003; Takao & Kelly, 2003).

Issues of Access and Equity

Discourse plays a central role in the mediation of knowledge in classrooms. To understand the ways in which students get access to knowledge, and to consider the knowledge that counts as science in given circumstances, researchers have approached issues of equity from a language point of view. Discourse studies of classroom interaction shed light on the ways in which science is framed, who gets to speak about what regarding science, and how issues of language use, choice, and variation represent instances of identity construction. The interactional aspects of classroom life are crucial for understanding how students' opportunities to succeed in science may be limited. For example, a needs assessment of Hispanic/Latino students in elementary science classrooms in the Southwest region of the United States found that these students were less likely to have access to appropriate science materials (e.g., culturally sensitive textbooks, laboratory apparatus) and were less likely to participate in student-initiated classroom interactions, including hands-on experiences and collaborative group work (Barba, 1993). Given such inequalities, a number of scholars examined variations in culturally and linguistically diverse populations and proposed methods to ameliorate inequities in science education.

Lee and Fradd (1996) studied the interactional patterns of fourth-grade student dyads and teachers in three populations: bilingual Spanish, bilingual Haitian Creole, and monolingual Caucasian English speakers. Lee and Fradd drew from theories of cultural congruence that consider the linguistic and social competence required for participation, recognizing that discourse processes presuppose and entail values, beliefs, culturally based interactional patterns and ways of organizing knowledge. Through the use of three science tasks (weather phenomena, simple machines, and buoyancy), Lee and Fradd were able to ascertain differences in discourse patterns across the populations. These differences were found in both categories of discourse patterns, such as turn taking, unit of discourse, and nonverbal communication, as well as categories of task engagement, which included methods for completing the task, mode of teacher guidance, teacher reinforcement, and student initiative. The study pointed out that students "may have difficulty deciding when to talk, how to present their ideas, and how to demonstrate their understandings" (p. 292). These difficulties may be exacerbated when students' cultural ways of interacting are not consistent with some standard ways of using scientific discourse in a broader community. The interactional differences thus extend beyond the substantive scientific content of the conversation. In a related study for a similar student population, Lee (1999) examined how students' worldviews influenced their ways of talking about a natural disaster (Hurricane Andrew). In this case, variations were found in how students attributed the cause of the hurricane; higher SES students and Caucasian students were more likely to describe the causes of the hurricane in terms of natural forces, whereas lower SES students, girls, and African American and Hispanic students included people, nature, and supernatural forces as playing a role in causing the natural disaster (p. 214). The study by Lee shows how student-derived discourse patterns used in classrooms represent a heteroglossia of languages and cultures, and how taken-for-granted interactional patterns, not attending to the multiple ways of speaking and being, may limit access for students.

Some of the most interesting work regarding language minority students and bilingual students has emerged from the Cheche Konnen project (Ballenger, 1997; Roseberry, Warren, & Conant, 1992; Warren, Roseberry, & Conant, 1994). Cheche Konnen, Haitian Creole for "search for knowledge," was chosen for the name of a group of teachers and researchers collaborating to address issues of access in bilingual classrooms. The project draws theoretically from theories of discourse, science studies, and culture and is aimed at transforming science classrooms. For example, Ballenger's study of multigrade (5–8) bilingual Haitian students demonstrated that, by allowing students to deviate from the standard structure of classroom discussion, the teacher provided multiple opportunities for students to use everyday discourse in constructing scientific knowledge. This change in discourse pattern allowed students to interact more directly, addressing claims made by other students without the intervention of the teacher. The pedagogical foci of this and other related studies shift from transmitting knowledge to engaging students in the scientific practices of argumentation and persuasion and appropriating scientific discourse (Roseberry et al., 1992; Warren & Roseberry, 1995). Engagement in scientific practices and appropriation of scientific discourse are served by designing educational experiences derived from students' experiences and lifeworlds, such as examination of the safety of the schools' water supply or bacteria levels in a local pond. By situating students as inquirers who pose questions, find evidence, and communicate results, these studies point to directions for pedagogy that recognizes both the language diversity found in many urban U.S. schools and the usefulness of scientific concepts for problem solving.

Gender equity is also a concern for science education (Baker, 2002). While the long-standing issue of gender inequity in participation and affiliation in science has been noted (Baker, 1998), most research paradigms have examined the issue in terms of cognitive, attitudinal, and epistemic dimensions of students, teachers, and science (Kahle & Meece, 1994). Furthermore, discourse-oriented studies of classroom interaction have only begun to examine the ways in which interactional patterns in science classrooms may be discriminatory to female students. Nevertheless, gender-based interactional patterns have been considered both in teacher-student discourse patterns (Barba & Cardinale, 1991) and in small-group contexts, either as a central focus (Alexopoulou & Driver, 1997) or as part of broader equity concerns (Bianchini, 1999; Lee, 1999).

Gender differences have been identified in ways in which teachers interact with female and male students and how talk and kinds of talk are distributed among members of science classrooms. For example, in a study of teacher-student questioning interactions in secondary science classrooms, Barba and Cardinale (1991) found that female students had fewer interactions with teachers and were posed less cognitively complex questions. These questioning patterns signal views of competence among the students and may contribute to both male and female students' views about who can and should be successful in science. At the elementary school level, Kurth, Kidd, Gardner, and Smith (2002) studied the discourse patterns of two grade 1/2 combination classes in a professional development school during whole-class conversations to consider variation in the use of paradigmatic (persuasion through formulating an argument) and narrative (story-based, valued for lifelikeness) modes of discourse among students. The analysis considered variations over time, across topics (life or physical science), and by gender. This study examined discourse patterns in more detail than the study of Barba and Cardinale (1991) and led to similar results. The male and female students were not found to show qualitative differences in the uses of narrative and paradigmatic features of discourse; however, male students in both classrooms "obtained more opportunities to practice their use of narrative and paradigmatic discourse either by receiving more speaking turns or expressing more language feature per turn" (Kurth et al., p. 814). As with the case of linguistic minority students, issues of access included the interactional dimensions of discourse.

Gender differences were also found in more complex social interactions, such as those found in small-group interaction. Alexopoulou and Driver (1997) examined gender differences in the discourse of secondary school Greek students working in small groups. Both group composition (self-selected, single-sex groups) and group number (two or four members) were relevant variables. The discourse analysis, like other studies of small-group work (e.g., Bianchini, 1997; Richmond & Striley, 1996), made evident an interaction in the organization of the social activities and the discussions of the substantive science issues. Analysis attentive to gender identified how male groups used confrontation to progress through ideas, whereas female groups sought to maintain consensus among members (Alexopoulou & Driver, 1997).

The issues of gender-oriented discourse patterns intersect with other issues, such as ethnicity and class, and interestingly, in some instances, subject matter (Hughes, 2001). As differences have been found in male and female students' orientation to science, potential affiliation based on the nature of science presented (Barton, 1998), and cultural variation in discourse patterns regarding phenomena (Lee, 1999), a number of questions are raised as to how research on attitudinal and cognitive variation can be informed by detailed discourse analysis of the interactional events. Discourse analytic research methods may provide new interpretations of equity and associated constructs such as identity, agency, and attribution of success by students, teachers, and researchers.

STUDIES OF LEARNING AND TEACHING WRITING AND READING SCIENCE

Periodically, scientific literacy is put forth as a rationale for reform in science education (American Association for the Advancement of Science [AAAS], 1993; DeBoer, 1991; National Research Council [NRC], 1996). Typically, this notion of literacy is quite broad, involving understanding of science concepts, reasoning, and science-technology-society issues, and is tied to notions of citizenship. However, other research focuses more specifically on the reading and writing of science (see special issue of the *Journal of Research in Science Teaching* [Yore, Holliday, & Alvermann, 1994]). A review of literacy by Norris and Phillips (2003) sets these conceptions in clear relief. Norris and Phillips (2003) define the *derived* sense of scientific literacy as encompassed in being knowledgeable, learned, and educated in science and *fundamental* science literacy as coming from the ability to read and write on the subject of science. They argued further that scientific literacy in the fundamental sense, focused on reading and writing texts, forms a basis for understanding science in ways that serve the broader societal goals of scientific literacy. Nevertheless, what counts as the relevant texts in even relatively straightforward science lessons is interactionally accomplished and subject to the contingencies of the particular interaction context. For example, Lemke (2000) identified the multimedia literacy demands of a science lesson that include interpretation of verbal discourse of the teacher and other students; paralinguistic features such as voice quality and pacing; images from a calculator, overhead transparency, and blackboard; writing, diagrams, and mathematical symbols; and manipulation of demonstration apparatus, among others. Much like studies of classroom discourse that depend heavily on various written forms, studies of reading and writing often consider the interaction of written and spoken language (Keys, 2000; Rivard & Straw, 2000). Therefore, the question of what counts as reading, writing, and text is not as obvious as may appear at first glance. Choices regarding the textual forms of science and education lead to theoretical questions.

For the purposes of this review, I shall focus specifically on reading and writing issues identified in the literature that examine written orthographic text. The rationale for this choice is twofold. First, applying functional linguistics to textual features of written science in textbooks and professional scientific papers, Halliday and Martin (1993) identified how written science depends often on unique linguistic features such as interlocking definitions, technical taxonomies, lexical density, syntactic ambiguity, and semantic discontinuity, which pose challenges to student learning. Second, written discourse has played key roles in the history of scientific communities, particularly as related to the development of persuasive texts centered on experimental evidence (Bazerman, 1988; Harris, 1997). Within science education, research on writing in science education has created an extensive body of research (e.g., Hand & Prain, 2002; Hand, Prain, Lawrence, & Yore, 1999; Keys, 1999b, 2000; Keys, Hand, Prain, & Collins, 1999; Prain & Hand, 1999; Rivard, 1994). This research is becoming increasingly integrated with studies of classroom spoken discourse (e.g., Keys, 1997; Rivard & Straw, 2000), thus identifying the important ways in which communication systems work within particular communities of practice. Ultimately, studies of writing and reading in science merit their own extensive review, such as those found in Prain and Hand (1996) and Glynn and Muth (1994).

Reading and Science Learning

One dimension of scientific literacy concerns developing the processes associated with certain tools, procedures, and strategies involving the interpretation of written texts. The value of being able to ascertain and comprehend the meaning of science concepts from printed materials is one central component of science literacy. Issues of meaning making with such written material often center on the important role textbooks play in classroom communication (Hand et al., 1999). Parallel to comprehension, learners' relative ability to communicate ideas in clear and coherent language (to a given audience) emerges as another key dimension to scientific literacy. Meaning making with written texts and communicating through spoken and written discourse provide ways for students to develop conceptual understanding and for teachers to assess student learning.

Yore et al. (2003) provided an extensive review of literacy in science education. In this review they noted the many early studies of reading that concerned the "readability formulae, reading skills tests, text analysis, page format, and end-of-text questions" (pp. 697–698), and later studies, influenced by constructivist cognitive theories, sought to examine the many ways that reading was part of a broader communicative context of norms, practices, and actions. These later studies consider how textual materials interact with spoken discourse, readers' metacognition, and science inquiry activities (Yore et al., 2003). Therefore, the emerging view of literacy understands reading as an "interactive and constructive process for meaning making constrained by criteria for good inferences in a sociocultural context" (Hand et al., 2003, p. 612). Although it is not possible to review the full body of research on reading in science (e.g., Yore et al., 2003), I provide a short review of three bodies of literature related to reading in science: how students develop meaningful understanding from science textbooks, how text can be used to support conceptual change, and how readers understand popular reports of science.

In their 1994 review of research on reading and writing to learn, Glynn and Muth (1994) suggested that science curricula can be "placed on a continuum from text-book driven to teacher driven" (p. 1061). In this continuum, the authors suggested that the textbook can potentially serve as a reference source in a teacher-driven curriculum, or as "the engine that drives the curriculum" (p. 1062) in a textbook-driven curriculum. The teachers' outline for instruction, use of videos, transparencies, laboratory activities, among others, are all products of the textbook's design in a textbook-driven curriculum. The significance of the textbook in classroom learning extends beyond its direct influence on student comprehension of the subject matter, as it typically serves a guideline for instructional choices and for the sequencing of learning events. With the textbook having such a significant role in the learning process, the students' ability to negotiate meaning through textbook instruction becomes a crucial skill in science classroom learning (cf. comprehension of spoken discourse in Lemke, 1990). Therefore, Glynn and Muth provide analysis of three reading strategies aimed at making learning from textbooks meaningful and conceptually integrated.

Other studies of reading in science are derived from a conceptual change point of view. These studies, reviewed extensively by Guzzetti, Snyder, Glass, and Gamas (1993), involved interventions aimed at using text to promote conceptual understandings. Pedagogical strategies derived from reading research included uses of refutational texts, pedagogies aimed at activating student initial knowledge through texts, and variations of textual forms, for example, contrasts between narrative and expository texts. A general finding from these studies was that text could be used to eradicate students' misconceptions when refutational texts were used with other strategies to promote cognitive conflict. Early science education research tended to examine reading within the context of broader pedagogical practices such as the learning cycle, uses of bridging analogies, and conceptual conflict. These studies were less able to identify particular reading strategies as relevant variables because of the confounding nature of studying reading embedded in broader instructional strategies (Guzzetti et al., 1993).

An additional area of interest for research on reading in science is the use of multiple, alternative sources for texts. Much like the uses of textbooks and refutational texts, the interpretative dimensions of sense making are identified as crucial for effective uses of sources other than books. Wellington and Osborne (2001) provide a number of examples of types of texts that can be used in learning science such as newspapers, tabloids, and pamphlets from advocacy groups. The use of popular accounts, for example, can give students reason to examine issues related to the nature of science. For example, Norris and Phillips (1994) used a study of grade-12 science students reading popular reports on science to consider the issues of knowledge and expertise in interpreting texts. Although the study found that students overestimated the reported truth of scientific claims and failed to understand the extent to which science is textured, the authors point to epistemological issues involving how students' views of knowledge influence what they learn about science. Norris and Phillips argued that scientific literacy needs to include not only understanding of science concepts, but also a pragmatic understanding of how scientific texts' structures and intentions can be ascertained. Included in this understanding would be developing competence in the metalanguage of science—that is, making sense of justification and evidence in the argumentative structure of science—and understanding how to value and temper scientific expertise (Norris, 1995).

Learning to Write Science and Writing to Learn Science

Research on writing represents another dimension to discourse studies in science education. Much like the other discourse theories presented in this review, research on writing is informed by multiple theoretical traditions and offers a wealth of empirical studies examining the significance of writing on the learning process (Hand et al., 2003; Hildebrand, 1998; Keys, 1997, 1999b; Rivard, 1994). Prain and Hand (1996) presented a review of the literature on writing for learning in secondary science that provided a broad framework for understanding this literature. This review illustrated variations in thinking about written discourse. Prain and Hand argued there are three major schools of thought, modernist (advocating student use of technical scientific language), constructivist (advocating writing to bring about student understanding of scientific concepts), and postmodern (advocating genres that make visible the sociological aspects of scientific representation in written forms). They built on previous work to present an expanded model of elements for writing for learning in science that included relevant issues related to writing topic, type, purpose, audience, and method of text production. Advocates of student learning of the genre conventions of science (e.g., Halliday & Martin, 1993)—in a sense, a modernist view—and those seeking to understand the value of adhering to a scientific genre for its value in learning while incorporating constructivist pedagogy (e.g., Keys, 1999a) share a common perception regarding the value of science, for access to institutions of power or to powerful knowledge.

One specific outcome of studies of writing to learn in science was the development of the Science Writing Heuristic (Keys, 2000; Keys et al., 1999). The Science Writing Heuristic comprises two components, one oriented to helping teachers develop activities to promote laboratory understanding and another focused on assisting students in developing explanations with their peers (Keys, 1999b). In one study (Keys et al., 1999) the Science Writing Heuristic was shown to develop important attributes in student understanding, including reflection of self-understanding, meaning making with scientific data, and construction of logical-semantic relationships between events. Keys's (2000) study of an application of the Science Writing Heuristic considered how writing about investigations in a scientific genre served student learning. The study drew from the knowledge-transforming model created by Bereiter and Scardamalia (1987), which considers both the content problem space and the discourse problem space. The writing under these conditions is posited to serve student subject matter learning. Keys's study showed evidence that for some students the interaction of content and discourse influenced students' reasoning about data. The study thus poses important questions about the interaction of genre knowledge, rhetorical forms, argumentation patterns, and scientific knowledge. Prain and Hand (1999) also investigated the uses of the Science Writing Heuristic by considering students' perceptions of writing for learning. They found that students had difficulty understanding how knowledge claims were established in science and how writing could serve as an epistemological tool.

The interaction of spoken and written discourse surfaced as a key dimension in understanding student learning. Rivard and Straw (2000) used a quasi-experimental design to identify the roles of talking, writing and talking, and writing on science learning. Their study focused on middle-school ecology lessons and sought to decipher the various roles of discourse processes on student learning. By separating students into various treatments, they reported that student talk was important for sharing, clarifying, and distributing knowledge, whereas writing helped the development of more structured and coherent ideas for the participating students. Instructor roles have also been shown to influence the nature of writing and perceptions students have of the writing task. Chinn and Hilgers (2000) found that professors of college science writing could provide students with ways of relating their writing to a professional context through supportive feedback and conferencing.

Hildebrand (1998) offered an argument for expanding the academic genre of scientific writing. Her contention was that classroom science writing is hegemonic. As an alternative, she suggested that a pedagogical approach be explored that would allow individuals to apply personal perspectives to scientific writing, which would incorporate the contexts of critical, creative, affective, and feminist pedagogies. Underwriting this perspective is the notion that expanding the genre conventions could potentially address the needs and abilities of students disenfranchised by current writing practices in science classrooms. Similarly, Hanrahan (1999) documented ways that affirmational dialogue journal writing both encouraged students to participate more actively in science and provided alternative ways for students to express their concerns about science and the particular class. Hanrahan made the argument that journal writing can contribute to the development of more democratic and collaborative classrooms. Across the different perspectives there is a recognition that writing needs to be viewed from a situated perspective, acknowledging variations in the educational purposes and tasks, as well as student knowledge and background, particularly as experience with linguistic forms that may be tied to students' identity and agency (Chinn & Hilgers, 2000; Gee, 2001b).

FUTURE DIRECTIONS AND CHALLENGES FOR THE STUDY OF DISCOURSE IN SCIENCE EDUCATION

In this section, I build on lessons learned from discourse studies in science education and point to potential avenues for future research. Studies of discourse in science classrooms have contributed to understanding how learning occurs through language, how access to knowledge derives from participating in the social and symbolic worlds, and how disciplinary knowledge is constructed through language. Of the many important future directions for research in discourse studies in science education, I name six: (a) student understanding, participation, and affiliation; (b) equity and access; (c) sociocultural theories of learning; (d) language use and knowledge; (e) student achievement and policy; and (f) teacher education. After reviewing these future research directions, I note some methodological challenges for discourse studies in science education.

A common theme across studies of teacher discourse, small-group discourse, and reading and writing has been the ways in which specific linguistic features of canonical science serve to limit students' understanding, participation, and affiliation in science. Furthermore, the syntactic features of science language are not the only impediment to student understanding. The particular grammatical forms associated with science discourse do not appear to be isolated from the many other uses and purposes for language use. Thus, studies of classroom life identify how cognitive learning is embedded in and mediated through social interaction and cultural practices. The uses of language in schooling serve many purposes for speakers and hearers, with issues of student identity, cultural knowledge, and idiosyncratic ways of talking science surfacing often as unresolved topics for further investigation. Both tensions and bridging strategies were found between students' ways of talking and the thematic content of science found in teacher discourse and textbooks (Gallas, 1995; Lemke, 1990). Tensions derived from students' knowledge and discourse as compared with the ways this knowledge and discourse are valued by educational institutions proved relevant to issues of access and equity.

Issues of equity, with particular concern for examining language variation across gender, ethnicity, and class, were closely tied to understanding the relationship between students' talk and canonical science as manifested in classroom life. Discourse-oriented studies show how educational opportunity (or lack thereof) for students is socially constructed in discourses of schooling. Closely tied to issues of identity and agency (Brown, 2004; Reveles, Cordova, & Kelly, 2004), analysis of the discourses of schooling needs to consider the ways in which students are positioned among themselves, the teacher, and the putative knowledge (Hughes, 2001; Luke, 1995; Moje et al., 2001). Discourse variations and choices among repertoires of ways of speaking need to be investigated for language minority students; students of differing ethnicity, language, and culture; and others marginalized by current instructional practices.

Educational events, predominately discourse events of some sort, were shown to encompass cognitive, social, and cultural dimensions of knowing and learning. Although sociocultural theories of learning are entering the field (Duschl, 1998), there is a lack of science education research examining how sociocultural psychology can be informed by studies of science discourse processes in schooling and how the creation of new educational contexts for learning can be informed by sociocultural theory. Although the potential for fruitful interaction was indicated across instructional strategies, the research in small-group work was the most explicit about how discourse processes were framed by textual, interactional, and cultural variables (e.g., Hogan, 1999; Kelly et al., 2001; Kurth, et al., 2002; Roth et al., 1999). Understanding how learning can be viewed over time within activity systems remains an area for future research in science education.

Studies of language in use in science classrooms presuppose assumptions about knowledge. Some common background knowledge is required for participants in a discourse event to achieve some mutual understanding. Minimally, such knowledge concerns the uses of language, the nature of the conversation within the sociocultural backdrop, the purposes of the interchange, and the phenomena under consideration. Studies of classrooms have noted the ways that scientific knowledge is framed by discourse and how, in the process, science is often portrayed in an ideological manner (e.g., Lemke, 1990; Moje 1995; Sutton, 1996). Simply, discourse processes send messages about the nature of science. These messages may be mediated by choices in pedagogy. Whereas the ideological images of science have been identified to some extent, more normative visions of science have received less scrutiny. An emerging group of studies, however, considers the epistemological assumptions of classroom discourse and opens the way for implications about the pedagogies of inquiry-oriented science (Hammer & Elby, 2003; Kelly et al., 2000; Sandoval, 2003). In many cases, these pedagogies are supported by educational technology.

The body of literature on discourse processes in science education treats student acquisition and understanding of science in a variety of ways. Whether the study of teacher discourse or students' learning to write in scientific genres, student learning is central to concerns about uses of language. Although these studies often focus on the details of student uses of specialized language, there has been an absence of consideration of how such studies may influence educational policy (Hand et al., 2003). Part of the absence is due to focus. Whereas discourse studies often examine the micro-worlds of everyday life, policy concerns typically focus on broader more blunt measures of success. Therefore, an important area for research will be ways that studies of language use can influence policies that often have great influence on classroom life.

Teacher education is an important part of research in science education, although there have been relatively few studies of the discourse of teacher education. Two sorts of studies seem to emerge from this review. First, there is a need to continue studies of teacher education (e.g., Bianchini & Solomon, 2003; Zembal-Saul et al., 2002). Much of the work of teacher education has not been documented in the same detail as studies of science classroom discourse. Nevertheless, the work of teacher education has developed specialized language to accomplish the tasks of learning through teaching. The discursive work of teacher education needs to be examined. Second, there is a need to consider ways that discourse studies of spoken and written texts can be used to effectively inform teacher education. Creating a database of classroom events for examination and reflection by teachers and teacher educators would facilitate the uses of results of discourse studies to improve classroom teaching and learning.

Instructional issues such as discourse variation, access, identity, and the embeddedness of talk in social action pose methodological challenges for future research, particularly as many nations face increased pressures to produce quantifiable measures of learning. These methodological challenges are at least threefold. First, the research reviewed in this chapter made clear that understanding instances of talk required understanding the social practices of the participants, established over time, through multiple media. Therefore, as discourse studies in science education move to consider further the cognitive, social, and cultural dimensions of schooling, research methods will have to become more comprehensive in scope. These methods may require additional intellectual resources across subject matters of science, social science fields, and importantly those from the relevant community of the learners. Second, the embodied nature of discourse suggests that studies need to attend to interaction in greater detail, drawing from the intellectual resources of multiple theoretical points of view. This requires detailed analysis of verbal and nonverbal communication and the multitude of texts, images, inscriptions, and graphic representations. Third, discourse analytic work needs to find ways to tie the micromoments of interaction to institutional issues, and ultimately to educational policy. This may require the development of further systematic methods for investigation, but also strategies for communicating to those who influence education on a broad scale. Despite such challenges, the study of discourse offers much hope for improving our understanding of the ways in which science education is interactionally accomplished.

ACKNOWLEDGMENTS

The author wishes to thank Bryan Brown for helping to identify the articles presented in the review and for many conversations about students, discourse, and identity. In addition, the author wishes to thank Judith Green and Jacqueline Regev for comments on an earlier version of this chapter. Thanks also to Carolyn Wallace and Larry Yore, who reviewed this chapter.

REFERENCES

Abell, S., Anderson, G., & Chezem, J. (2000). Science as argument and explanation: Exploring concepts of sounds in third grade. In J. Minstrell & E. Zee (Eds.), *Inquiring into inquiry learning and teaching in science* (pp. 65–79). Washington, DC: American Association for the Advancement of Science.

Alexopoulou, E., & Driver, R. (1997). Gender differences in small group discussion in physics. *International Journal of Science Education, 19,* 393–406.

American Association for the Advancement of Science (AAAS). (1993). *Benchmarks for scientific literacy.* New York: Oxford University Press.

Anderson, C. W., Holland, J. D., & Palinscar, A. S. (1997). Canonical and sociocultural approaches to research and reform in science education: The story of Juan and his group. *The Elementary School Journal, 97,* 359 –383.

Baker, D. (1998). Equity issues in science education. In B. J. Fraser & K. G. Tobin (Eds.), *International handbook of science education* (pp. 869–895). Boston: Kluwer.

Baker, D. (2002). Where is gender and equity in science education? *Journal of Research in Science Teaching, 39,* 659–663.

Ballenger, C. (1997). Social identities, moral narratives, scientific argumentation: Science talk in a bilingual classroom. *Language and Education, 11,* 1–13.

Barba, R. (1993). A study of culturally syntonic variables in the bilingual/bicultural science classroom. *Journal of Research in Science Teaching, 30,* 1053–1071.

Barba, R., & Cardinale, L. (1991). Are females invisible students? An investigation of teacher-student questioning interactions? *School Science and Mathematics, 91*(7), 306–310.

Barton, A. C. (1998). *Feminist science education.* New York: Teachers College Press.

Bazerman, C. (1988). *Shaping written knowledge: The genre and activity of the experimental article in science*. Madison: University of Wisconsin Press.

Bell, P., & Linn, M. C. (2000). Scientific arguments as learning artifacts: Designing for learning from the web with KIE. *International Journal of Science Education, 22*, 797–817.

Bereiter, C., & Scardamalia, M. (1987). *The psychology of written composition*. Hillsdale, NJ: Lawrence Erlbaum Associates.

Bianchini, J. A. (1997). Where knowledge construction, equity, and context intersect: Student learning of science in small groups. *Journal of Research in Science Teaching, 34*, 1039–1065.

Bianchini J. A. (1999). From here to equity: The influence of status on student access to and understanding of science. *Science Education 83*, 577–601.

Bianchini, J. A., & Solomon, E. M. (2003). Constructing views of science tied to issues of equity and diversity: A study of beginning science teachers. *Journal of Research in Science Teaching, 40*, 53–76.

Bleicher, R. (1994). High schools students presenting science: An interactional sociolinguistic analysis. *Journal of Research in Science Teaching, 31*, 697–719.

Bleicher, R. (1996). High school students learning science in university research laboratories. *Journal of Research in Science Teaching, 33*, 1115–1133.

Brown, B. (2004). Discursive Identity: Assimilation into the culture of science classroom and its implications for minority students. *Journal of Research in Science Teaching.*

Cameron, D. (2001). *Working with spoken discourse*. Thousand Oaks, CA: Sage.

Carlsen, W. S. (1991a). Questioning in classrooms: A sociolinguistic perspective. *Review of Educational Research, 61*, 157–178.

Carlsen, W. S. (1991b). Subject-matter knowledge and science teaching: A pragmatic approach. In J. E. Brophy (Ed.), *Advances in research on teaching* (Vol. 2, pp. 115–143). Greenwich, CT: JAI Press.

Carlsen, W. S. (1992). Closing down the conversation: Discouraging student talk on unfamiliar science content. *Journal of Classroom Interaction, 27*(2), 15–21.

Carlsen, W. S. (1997). Never ask a question if you don't know the answer: The tension in teaching between modeling scientific argument and maintaining law and order. *Journal of Classroom Interaction, 32*(2), 14–23.

Cazden, C. (2001). *Classroom discourse: The language of teaching and learning* (2nd ed.). Portsmouth, NH: Heinemann.

Chinn, P. W. U., & Hilgers, T. L. (2000). From corrector to collaborator: The range of instructor roles in writing-based natural and applied science classes. *Journal of Research in Science Teaching, 37*, 3–25.

Crawford, T., Kelly, G. J., & Brown, C. (2000). Ways of knowing beyond facts and laws of science: An ethnographic investigation of student engagement in scientific practices. *Journal of Research in Science Teaching, 37*, 237–258.

Cross, R. T. (1997). Ideology and science teaching: Teachers' discourse. *International Journal of Science Education, 19*, 607–616.

Dagher, Z. R. (1994). Does the use of analogies contribute to conceptual change? *Science Education, 78*, 601–614.

Dagher, Z. R. (1995). Analysis of analogies used by science teachers. *Journal of Research of Science Teaching, 32*, 259–270.

DeBoer, G. E. (1991). *A history of ideas in science education*. New York: Teachers College Press.

Driver, R., Newton, P., & Osborne, J. (2000). Establishing the norms of scientific argumentation in classrooms. *Science Education, 84*, 287–312.

Duschl, R. A. (1990). *Restructuring science education: The importance of theories and their development*. New York: Teachers College Press.

Duschl, R. A., & Hamilton, R. J. (1998). Conceptual change in science and in the learning of science. In B. J. Fraser & K. G. Tobin (Eds.), *International handbook of science education* (pp. 1047–1065). Boston: Kluwer.

Fairclough, N. (1995). *Critical discourse analysis: The critical study of language*. London: Longman.

Fairbrother, R., Hackling, M., & Cowan, E. (1997). Is this the right answer? *International Journal of Science Education, 19,* 887–894.

Gallas, K. (1995). *Talking their way into science: Hearing children's questions and theories, responding with curricula.* New York: Teachers College Press.

Gee, J. P. (1999). *An introduction to discourse analysis: Theory and method.* New York: Routledge.

Gee, J. P. (2001a). Literacy, discourse, and linguistics: Introduction and what is literacy? In E. Cushman, E. R. Kintgen, B. M. Kroll, & M. Rose (Eds.), *Literacy: A critical sourcebook* (pp. 525–544). Boston, MA: Bedford/St. Martins.

Gee, J. P. (2001b). Identity as an analytic lens for research in education. *Review of Research in Education, 25,* 99–125.

Glynn, S., & Muth, K. (1994). Reading and writing to learn science: Achieving scientific literacy. *Journal of Research in Science Teaching, 31,* 1057–1073.

Green, J. (1983). Research on teaching as a linguistic process: A state of the art. *Review of Research in Education, 10,* 152–252.

Guzzetti, B. J., Snyder, T. E., Glass, G. V., & Gamas, W. S. (1993). Promoting conceptual change in science: A comparative meta-analysis of instructional interventions from reading education and science education. *Reading Research Quarterly, 28,* 116–159.

Halliday, M. A. K., & Martin, J. R. (1993). *Writing science: Literacy and discursive power.* Pittsburgh: University of Pittsburgh Press.

Hammer, D., & Elby, A. (2003). Tapping epistemological resources for learning physics. *The Journal of the Learning Sciences, 12,* 53–90.

Hand, B., Alvermann, D. E., Gee, J., Guzzetti, B. J., Norris, S. P., Phillips, L. M., et al. (2003). Message from the "Island Group": What is literacy in science literacy? *Journal of Research in Science Teaching, 40,* 607–615.

Hand, B., & Prain, V. (2002). Teachers implementing writing-to-learn strategies in junior secondary science: A case study. *Science Education, 86,* 737–755.

Hand B., Prain, V., Lawrence, C., & Yore, L. D. (1999). A writing in science framework designed to enhance science literacy. *International Journal of Science Education, 21,* 1021–1035.

Hanrahan, M. (1999). Rethinking science literacy: Enhancing communication and participation in school science through affirmational dialogue journal writing. *Journal of Research in Science Teaching, 36,* 699–717.

Harris, R. A. (1997). Introduction. In R. A. Harris (Ed.), *Landmark essay on the rhetoric of science: Case studies* (pp. xi–xlv). Mahwah, NJ: Lawrence Erlbaum Associates.

Herrenkohl, L. R., & Guerra, M. R. (1998). Participant structures, scientific discourse, and student engagement in fourth grade. *Cognition and Instruction, 16,* 431–473.

Hildebrand, G. M. (1998). Disrupting hegemonic writing practices in school science: Contesting the right way to write. *Journal of Research in Science Teaching, 35,* 345–362.

Hogan, K. (1999). Sociocognitive roles in science group discourse. *Journal of Research in Science Teaching, 21,* 855–882.

Hogan, K, Nastasi B. K., & Pressley, M. (1999). Discourse patterns and collaborative scientific reasoning in peer and teacher-guided discussions *Cognition and Instruction, 17,* 379–432.

Hughes, G. (2001). Exploring the availability of student scientist identities with curriculum discourse: An anti-essentialist approach to gender-inclusive science. *Gender and Education, 13,* 275–290.

Jaworski, A., & Coupland, N. (Eds.). (1999). *The discourse reader.* New York: Routledge.

Jimenez-Aleixandre, M. P., Rodriguez, A. B., & Duschl, R. A. (2000). "Doing the lesson" or "doing science": Argument in high school genetics. *Science Education 84,* 757–792.

Kahle, J. B., & Meece, J. (1994). Research on gender issues in the classroom. In D. Gabel (Ed.), *Handbook of research on science teaching and learning* (pp. 542–557). New York: Macmillan.

Kelly, G. J., & Bazerman, C. (2003). How students argue scientific claims: A rhetorical-semantic analysis. *Applied Linguistics, 24*(1), 28–55.

Kelly, G. J., Brown, C., & Crawford, T. (2000). Experiments, contingencies, and curriculum: Providing opportunities for learning through improvisation in science teaching. *Science Education, 84*, 624–657.

Kelly, G. J., Chen, C., & Prothero, W. (2000). The epistemological framing of a discipline: Writing science in university oceanography. *Journal of Research in Science Teaching, 37*, 691–718.

Kelly, G. J., Crawford, T., & Green, J. (2001). Common tasks and uncommon knowledge: Dissenting voices in the discursive construction of physics across small laboratory groups. *Linguistics & Education, 12*(2), 135–174.

Kelly, G. J., Druker, S., & Chen, C. (1998). Students' reasoning about electricity: Combining performance assessments with argumentation analysis. *International Journal of Science Education, 20*(7), 849–871.

Kelly, G. J., & Takao, A. (2002). Epistemic levels in argument: An analysis of university oceanography students' use of evidence in writing. *Science Education, 86*, 314–342.

Keys, C. W. (1997). An investigation of the relationship between scientific reasoning, conceptual knowledge and model formulation in a naturalistic setting. *International Journal of Science Education, 19*, 957–970.

Keys, C. W. (1999a). Revitalizing instruction in scientific genres: Connecting knowledge production with writing to learn in science. *Science Education, 83*, 115–130.

Keys, C. W. (1999b). Language as an indicator of meaning generation: An analysis of middle school students' written discourse about scientific investigations. *Journal of Research in Science Teaching, 36*, 1044–1061.

Keys, C. W. (2000). Investigating the thinking processes of eighth grade writers during the composition of a scientific laboratory report. *Journal of Research in Science Teaching, 37*, 676–690.

Keys, C. W., Hand, B., Prain, V., & Collins, S. (1999). Using the scientific writing heuristic as a tool for learning from laboratory investigations in secondary science. *Journal of Research in Science Teaching, 36*, 1065–1084.

Klaassen, C. W. J. M., & Lijnse, P. L. (1996). Interpreting students' and teachers' discourse in science classes: An underestimated problem? *Journal of Research in Science Teaching, 33*, 115–134.

Krajcik, J., Blumenfeld, P. C., Marx, R. W., Bass, K. M., Fredricks, J., & Soloway, E. (1998). Inquiry in project-based science classrooms: Initial attempts by middle school students. *The Journal of the Learning Sciences, 7*(3&4), 313–350.

Kurth, L. A., Kidd, R., Gardner, R., & Smith, E. L. (2002). Student use of narrative and paradigmatic forms of talk in elementary science conversations. *Journal of Research in Science Teaching, 39*, 793–818.

Lee, O. (1999). Science knowledge, world views, and information sources in social and cultural contexts: Making sense after a natural disaster. *American Educational Research Journal, 36*, 187–219.

Lee, O., & Fradd, S. H. (1996). Interactional patterns of linguistically diverse students and teachers: Insights for promoting science learning. *Linguistics and Education 8*, 269–297.

Lemke, J. L. (1990). *Talking science: Language, learning and values.* Norwood, NJ: Ablex.

Lemke, J. L. (1998). Analyzing verbal data: Principles, methods and problems. In B. Fraser & K. Tobin (Eds.), *International handbook of science education* (pp. 1175–1189). Boston: Kluwer.

Lemke, J. (2000). Multimedia literacy demands of the scientific curriculum. *Linguistics & Education, 10*, 247–271.

Luke, A. (1995). Text and discourse in education: An introduction to critical discourse analysis. *Review of Research in Education, 21*, 3–48.

Lynch, M. (1993). *Scientific practice as ordinary action: Ethnomethodology and the social studies of science.* Cambridge: Cambridge University Press.

Lynch, M., & Macbeth, D. (1998). Demonstrating physics lessons. In J. Greeno & S. Goldman (Eds.), *Thinking practices in mathematics and science learning* (pp. 269–297). Mahwah, NJ: Lawrence Erlbaum Associates.

Macbeth, D. (2000). On the apparatus of conceptual change. *Science Education, 84*, 228–264.

Mehan, H. (1979). *Learning lessons: Social organization in the classroom.* Cambridge, MA: Harvard University Press.

Meyer, K., & Carlisle, R. (1996). Children as experimenters. *International Journal of Science Education, 18*, 231–248.

Moje, E. B. (1995). Talking about science: An interpretation of the effects of teacher talk in a high school science classroom. *Journal of Research in Science Teaching, 32*, 349–371.

Moje, E. B. (1997). Exploring discourse, subjectivity, and knowledge in a chemistry class. *Journal of Classroom Interaction, 32*(2), 35–44.

Moje, E. B., Collazo, T., Carrillo, R., & Marx, R. W. (2001). "Maestro, what is 'quality'?": Language, literacy, and discourse in project-based science. *Journal of Research in Science Teaching, 38*, 469–498.

Mortimer, E. F. (1998). Multivoicedness and univocality in classroom discourse: An example from theory of matter. *International Journal of Science Education, 20*, 67–82.

National Research Council (NRC). (1996). *National science education standards.* Washington, DC: National Academy Press.

Norris, S. P. (1995). Learning to live with scientific expertise: Toward a theory of intellectual communalism for guiding science teaching. *Science Education, 79*, 201–217.

Norris, S. P., & Phillips, L. M. (1994). Interpreting pragmatic meaning when reading popular reports of science. *Journal of Research in Science Teaching, 31*, 947–967.

Norris, S. P., & Phillips, L. M. (2003). How literacy in its fundamental sense is central to scientific literacy. *Science Education 87*, 224–240.

Prain, V., & Hand, B. (1996). Writing for learning in secondary science: Rethinking practices. *Teaching and Teacher Education, 12*, 609–626.

Prain, V., & Hand, B. (1999). Student's perceptions of writing for learning in secondary school science. *Science Education, 83*, 151–162.

Reveles, J. M., Cordova, R., & Kelly, G. J. (2004). Science literacy and academic identity formulation. *Journal for Research in Science Teaching.*

Richmond, G., & Striley, J. (1996). Making meaning in classrooms: Social processes in small-group discourse and scientific knowledge building. *Journal of Research in Science Teaching, 33*, 839–858.

Rivard, L. P. (1994). A review of writing to learn in science: Implications for practice and research. *Journal of Research in Science Teaching, 31*, 969–983.

Rivard, L. P., & Straw, S. B. (2000). The effect of talk and writing on learning science: An exploratory study. *Science Education, 84*, 566–593.

Roseberry, A., Warren, B., & Conant, F. (1992). Appropriating scientific discourse: Findings from language minority classrooms. *The Journal of the Learning Sciences, 2*, 61–94.

Roth, W.-M. (1996). Teacher questioning in an open-inquiry learning environment: Interactions of context, content, and student responses. *Journal of Research in Science Teaching, 33*, 709–736.

Roth, W.-M. (1999). Discourse and agency in school science laboratories. *Discourse Processes, 28*, 27–60.

Roth, W.-M., McGinn, M. K., Woszczyna, C., & Boutonné, S. (1999). Differential participation during science conversations: The interaction of focal artifacts, social configuration, and physical arrangements. *The Journal of the Learning Sciences, 8*, 293–347.

Russell, T. (1983). Analyzing arguments in science classroom discourse: Can teachers' questions distort scientific authority? *Journal of Research in Science Teaching, 20*, 27–45.

Sandoval, W. A. (2003). Conceptual and epistemic aspects of students' scientific explanations. *The Journal of the Learning Sciences, 12*, 5–51.

Sinclair, J., & Coulthard, M. (1975). *Towards an analysis of discourse: The language of teachers and pupils.* London: Oxford University Press.

Strike, K. A. (1974). On the expressive potential of behaviorist language. *American Educational Research Journal, 11*, 103–120.

Sutton, C. (1996). Beliefs about science and beliefs about language. *International Journal of Science, 18*, 1–18.

Takao, A. Y., & Kelly, G. J. (2003). Assessment of evidence in university students' scientific writing. *Science & Education, 12*, 341–363.

Toulmin, S. (1958). *The uses of argument*. University Press: Cambridge.

van Zee, E. H. (2000). Analysis of a student-generated inquiry discussion. *International Journal of Science Education, 22*, 115–142.

van Zee, E. H., & Minstrell, J. (1997). Using questioning to guide student thinking. *The Journal of the Learning Sciences, 6*, 227–269.

Warren, B., & Roseberry, A. S. (1995). "This question is just too, too easy!" Perspectives from the classroom on accountability in science. Report no. NCRCDSLL/CAL-RR-14. (ERIC Document Reproduction Service No. ED 390658). East Lansing, MI: National Center for Research on Teacher Learning.

Warren, B., Roseberry, A., & Conant, F. (1994). Discourse and social practice: Learning science in language minority classrooms. In D. Spencer (Ed.), *Adult biliteracy in the United States* (pp. 191–210). Washington, DC: Center for Applied Linguistics and Delta Systems Co.

Wellington, J., & Osborne, J. (2001). *Language and literacy in science education*. Buckingham, UK: Open University Press.

Yore, L. D., Bisanz, G. L., & Hand, B. M. (2003). Examining the literacy component of science literacy: 25 years of language arts and science research. *International Journal of Science Education, 25*, 689–725.

Yore, L. D., Holliday, W. G., & Alvermann, D. E. (Eds.). (1994). The reading-science learning-writing connection [special issue]. *Journal of Research in Science Teaching, 31*(9).

Zembal-Saul, C., Munford, D., & Crawford, B., Friedrichsen, P., & Land, S. (2002). Scaffolding preservice science teachers' evidence-based arguments during an investigation of natural selection. *Research in Science Education, 32*, 437–463.

CHAPTER 17

Digital Resources Versus Cognitive Tools: A Discussion of Learning Science with Technology

Nancy Butler Songer
University of Michigan

Over the past two decades, computers and network technologies have become commonplace in many aspects of our work and personal lives. Despite widespread use of technology by scientists across many disciplines, computers and network technologies are often underutilized and poorly integrated into core science education activities in K–16 classrooms. How can this underutilization be explained? This chapter discusses research studies associated with technological tools for learning science relative to meaningful use of technologies in science classrooms. In particular, the chapter presents a framework for examining whether a technological tool is a cognitive tool for meaningful use of technology focused on specific audiences, learning goals, learning activities, and learning performances. To provide discussion for this perspective, examples of technologies associated with four areas of learning science are presented and discussed relative to the Cognitive Tools Framework, and implications revisit the question of underutilization of technology in science classrooms.

Technology permeates many dimensions of our work and personal lives. Evidence of this is apparent in the many instances of technology that are sometimes taken for granted or invisible to us, including cars, telephones, household appliances, and toys (Tinker & Vahey, 2002). Increasingly, institutions and industries are being dramatically altered through the integration of computers and network technologies such as the Internet. Daily business in banking, the postal service, the stock market, and neighborhood grocery stores has changed substantially as a result of computers and network technologies. With the integration of technology as an increasingly ubiquitous and essential component of our daily lives comes speculation about even more and profound alterations in how we will live, work, and play in the future. To quote *New York Times* columnist Thomas L. Friedman on technology, "Clearly it is now possible for more people than ever to collaborate and compete in real time with more other people on more different kinds of work from more different corners of the planet and on a more equal footing than at any previous time in the history of the world—using computers, e-mail, networks, teleconferencing, and dynamic new software" (Friedman, 2005, p. 8).

Like their adult counterparts, American children are also incorporating the Internet into their daily lives for many different purposes. One recent study documented that 78% of American children ages 12–17 go online on a regular basis (Levin & Arafeh, 2002). However, as research studies in education document, increasing levels of computer use do not necessarily translate into increasing use of technology in American schools. Recent studies document that in many cases across a wide range of varieties of settings, schools are struggling to implement widespread adoption of computers and network technologies into mainstream classroom activities (e.g., Levin & Arafeh, 2002; Cuban, 2001). Although policy makers and the general public generally agree that K–16 students need many and varied productive experiences learning with and by technology (e.g., United States House of Representatives, 2001; Department of Education, 2004), most educators agree that much remains to be understood relative to the productive integration of technology into today's classroom activities. Concerning the use of technology within specific content areas such as science, as discussed in this chapter, a gap exists between technology for doing science and technology for learning science. What do we know about using technology to learn science, and how can this gap be bridged and understood?

This chapter investigates whether technology is underutilized in American science classrooms and, if so, what we can learn from exemplary cases of learning science with technology to guide more widespread integration. The chapter begins with a definition of technology in schools, followed by a discussion of the possible underutilization of technology in American science classrooms. Subsequently, the chapter will present a framework for understanding the lack of utilization of technology for productive learning in science classrooms and several exemplary cases.

ARE TECHNOLOGIES UNDERUTILIZED IN SCIENCE CLASSROOMS?

According to the U.S. Department of Education (2003), technology in schools consists of six categories, including (1) computers and computer-driven equipment; (2) servers, routers, and other equipment that support wired and wireless communication; (3) telephone-based technology; (4) display equipment used in classrooms; (5) infrastructure of wires and cables; and (6) software applications and programs. This chapter uses the following working definition of technology: computers, network technologies, and education-based software associated with categories 1 and 6 above.

According to the Department of Education, American schools have nearly ubiquitous access to computers and the Internet; 99 percent of American schools are connected to the Internet, with a 5:1 student-to-computer ratio (Department of Education, 2004). In addition, computer use is widespread; 90 percent of American children between 5 and 17 use computers on a regular basis (Department of Education, 2004). Interestingly, computers are increasingly a resource that is not limited to older students or adults; one study documents the largest group of new Internet and computer users as children aged 2–5 (Department of Education, 2004).

On balance, although statistics suggest that access and use are widespread, other studies investigating meaningful use of technology to learn science or other subjects suggest that the presence of computers in schools does not necessarily imply productive use of technology within classrooms (e.g., Department of Education, 2004; Cuban, 2001). In one study, although access to computers in school was widespread, most teachers and students used computers infrequently, such as once a month or less, and the majority of uses were focused on mundane or routine tasks (Cuban, 2001).

Science education researchers provide possible explanations for the lack of widespread integration of technology into science learning activities. Concerning Internet-based materials, some researchers suggest that limited use might be a result of poor quality of available web-based science material for K–12 science learning. Linn, Davis, and Bell (2004) state that despite nearly universal Internet access in classrooms, much of the Internet-available material is of questionable scientific content or appropriateness. Others attribute low use to the limited availability of software that is well integrated into curricular programs (U.S. Department of Education, 2003) or that promotes critical thinking (Lee & Songer, 2003). In addition, classroom teachers describe a gap between building or district expectations in their use of technology and the support structures needed to successfully integrate technology into their classrooms (American Association of University Women, 2000).

Collectively, research studies suggest that although computers and network technologies are available in nearly all American schools, the literature in science education suggests that there may be many factors that contribute to the underutilization of technology in American science classrooms. One approach to teasing out the underutilization of technology is to define exemplary roles and activities for the use of technology to learn science. This approach provides one means to begin to address and overcome the barriers impeding meaningful use of technology in science classrooms.

WHAT ROLE DOES TECHNOLOGY PLAY IN SCIENTIFIC LITERACY?

A discussion of exemplary uses of technology to learn science begins with a discussion of how we define learning or knowing science. What is science literacy? As defined by the National Science Education Standards (National Research Council, 1996, 2001), scientific literacy includes both science content knowledge (declarative facts and conceptual knowledge) and reasoning knowledge such as analyzing data, building explanations from evidence, and engaging with scientific questions. In the National Science Education Standards, a central component of scientific literacy is the appropriate use of technology to support learning goals (Bransford, Brown, & Cocking, 2000; National Research Council, 1996). But what is meant by "appropriate use of technology"?

To investigate this question, we look first at how professional scientists use technology. Scientists utilize technology for many specific purposes involving working with and developing both science content and scientific reasoning skills. For example, scientists utilize computers and network technologies for advanced analysis, data modeling, and data representation. A scan of research articles from a recent edition of *Science* magazine reveals several examples of essential use of technology by scientists, including simulation modeling to explain patterns in complex ecological systems at various levels of organization (Grimm et al., 2005) and DNA analysis of ancient artifacts to characterize evidence of human evolution (Haak et al., 2005). These examples represent scientists using technology to develop both scientific content knowledge (generating patterns about complex ecological systems) and scientific reasoning skills (e.g., analyzing data; making hypotheses based on empirical data).

Similarly, students' experiences with technology in science classrooms have resulted in the productive use of technology for both content and reasoning in the form of modeling (Gobert & Pallant, 2004), data analysis, and data representation. Examples of technology to guide content development in atmospheric and environmental science and reasoning in terms of making hypotheses based on empirical data are the methods developed by Edelson and Reiser (2006) in which students use technological tools to analyze historical data on climate (WorldWatcher) or ecosystems (Galapagos Finches).

Additional examples in science education provide research-based means of technologies that can be utilized to guide the scientific reasoning we desire among K–16 students. Using technology to guide the development of reasoning can take many forms, including resources that provide (a) organized dialogue with peers and/or scientists towards collaborative understandings (O'Neill and Gomez, 1998; O'Neill, 2004), (b) scaffolded guidance in the development of scientific explanations (e.g., Explanation Constructor by Reiser, 2004), or (c) guidance in reflection on steps taken and progress within more open-ended investigations (e.g., WISE by Linn & Slotta, 2000; Knowledge Forum [formerly called CSILE] by Scardamalia & Bereiter, 1994; Symphony by Quintana et al., 2002).

A SHIFT IN RESEARCH FOCUS

An interesting commonality of the set of research studies briefly mentioned above is the emphasis on the role of technology as a resource for complex reasoning in science, including reasoning such as data analysis (e.g., WorldWatcher), the development of explanations (e.g., Explanation Constructor), or reflection (e.g., WISE). This emphasis on the role of technology as a resource for scientific reasoning is a shift from earlier studies of technology in schools that focused on counting and numbers, either amount of access to technology or amount of use. Shifting the research on technology from counting studies to quality and character of use is a major undertaking and shift in research emphasis. Why is this shift necessary or desirable?

Leaders analyzing the needs of educated citizens of the future, such as Susan Patrick, the Director of Educational Technology for the United States Department of Education, document a need to focus on the transformation of technology for educational purposes as opposed to focusing on the mere placement or integration of technology into schools, "The paper-based system does not make any sense to kids who are coming up in school. Is our educational system geared towards innovation? Do we want an 18th-century model or a 21st-century model for our schools? The 18th-century model is the one we have now. . . . The ed-tech community loves the term 'integration'. But our schools need transformation not integration" (NSTA Reports, 2005, p. 1).

Similarly, a group of researchers from diverse educational perspectives has discovered that previous examinations of the allocation of educational resources such as curricular programs provided insufficient information to explain student outcomes (e.g., Cohen, Raudenbush, & Ball, 2000). These researchers argue that a more extensive examination of the use of the materials in particular learning contexts is needed to understand the value of the learning resource and the best means of widespread incorporation. Will a similar shift in research focus toward a critique of the use of technology in particular science education settings yield new insights into the best means to overcome the underutilization of technology to learn science? Might this kind of analysis that goes beyond counting studies yield insights into what is meant by the "appropriate use of technology" (National Research Council, 1996)?

In choosing any focus, important trade-offs are required. Focusing this chapter on the quality of use of the technology as opposed to counting studies eliminates a discussion on several other topics associated with learning science with technology that might have been addressed in this chapter. This shift in focus disallows, for example, a detailed historical review of trends in technology and science education over the past several decades. Luckily, this topic is well represented elsewhere (see Linn, 2003, for a good example). Similarly, this chapter does not provide an extensive list of all of the possible technological tools that are available for teaching or learning science. On balance, this chapter focuses on a particular thesis and an associated framework for analyzing the character and quality of the use of technology for learning science. This focus sacrifices some dimensions of breadth to allow a greater discussion of depth focused around the particular perspective of the quality of the use of technologies for learning science. In addition, the chapter provides insight and discussion associated with a handful of exemplary cases of the meaningful use of technology to learn science that will help shed light on principles that might guide more widespread productive use of technology for learning science.

Digital Resources and Cognitive Tools

To begin our discussion of the use of technology for learning science, we present two critical and contrasting definitions. A Digital Resource can be defined as any computer-available information source containing facts, perspectives, or information on a topic of interest. Digital resources often contain valuable information, such as science information presented in the form of text, pictures, simulations, video, or other interactive formats. The National Aeronautics and Space Administration (NASA) article describing a newly discovered planet candidate in the constellation Hydra, *Hubble's Infrared Eyes Home in on Suspected Extrasolar Planet* (www.nasa.gov/home/hqnews/2005/jan/HQ_05012_hubble.html), is an example of a valuable digital resource. Figure 17.1 presents a sample from the NASA article digital resource.

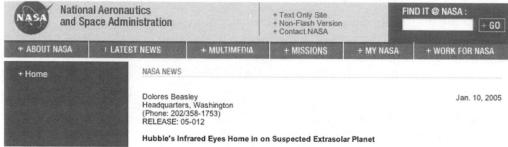

FIGURE 17–1.   NASA article describing new planet candidate as example of a digital resource.

In contrast, a Cognitive Tool is defined as a computer-available information source or resource presenting focused information specifically tailored for particular learning goals on a particular topic of interest for learning by a particular target audience. An example of a cognitive tool is the BioKIDS Sequence of CyberTracker (Fig. 17.2), a modification of the original Sequence of CyberTracker (Fig. 17.3), designed to suit the learning goals of sixth-grade students studying a particular biodiversity unit called BioKIDS (www.biokids.umich.edu).

To further define these constructs, we provide comparisons of digital resources and cognitive tools in three major areas. The first area is Audience/Knowledge. A digital resource is designed for a general audience to serve a range of possible roles. In reviewing the full NASA article available on the NASA website, it is not difficult to imagine scientists, high school students, teachers, and other adults reading this article and finding it to be of value. In contrast, a cognitive tool is designed for a specific audience and is focused on a particular knowledge goal. For example, the BioKIDS Sequence of CyberTracker is software specifically designed for the col-

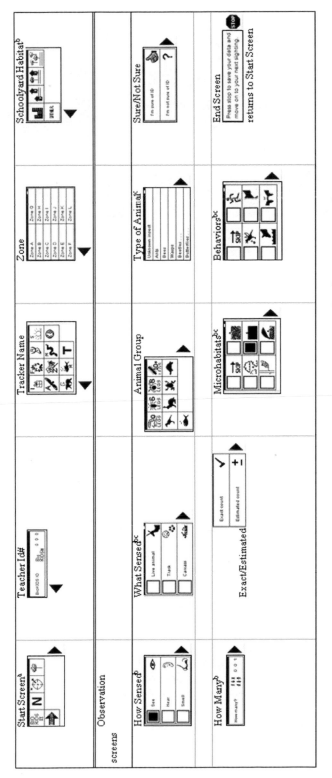

FIGURE 17–2. The BioKIDS sequence, as an example of a cognitive tool.

477

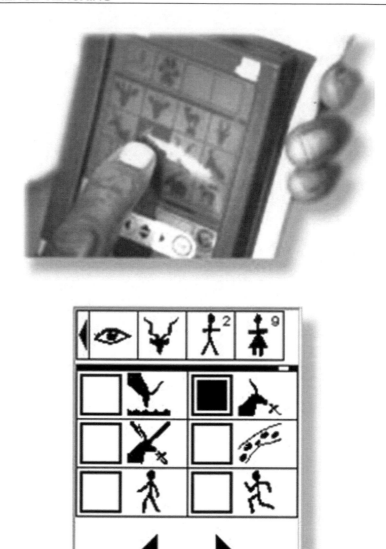

FIGURE 17–3.   Sample screens from CyberTracker sequence for gathering field-based animal data.

lection of schoolyard animal data by fifth- and sixth-graders in Midwestern states. Unlike the original CyberTracker sequence, the BioKIDS Sequence has a limited set of data types and a limited range of animals available for entry (e.g., Michigan-based animals). These limitations allow more focused data collection and more focused learning around particular curricular goals.

A second area of comparison between digital resources and cognitive tools is the area of Learning Activities. Digital Resources do not specify how the particular resource is to be used for learning. For example, the NASA article may be used by scientists for a range of purposes and by high school students for a completely different set of purposes. In contrast, cognitive tools are designed to be used in particular ways to achieve particular learning goals. Our example cognitive tool, the BioKIDS Sequence, is used by fifth- and sixth-graders to achieve specific learning goals focusing on gathering data, data analysis, and ecology that are articulated in the curricular activities aligned with the national (NRC, 1996), state, and district science education standards.

The third area of comparison is Learning Performances. As a result of the lack of specificity with regard to audience and activities, digital resources also do not specify the kinds of products learners produce as a result of working with the digital resource. With the NASA article, a high school student might use this article for a report in an astronomy class; however, the performance or outcome that student develops as a result of the use of the article will likely never be known by NASA or any source associated with the digital resource. In contrast, the products that result from the use of the cognitive tool can be examined and evaluated, as well as compared with the original predictions about audience and learning goals. With the BioKIDS Sequence, research studies provided empirical evidence of the usability and learning outcomes associated with the use of this tool (see Parr, Jones, and Songer, 2004).

An interesting outcome of the comparison of digital resources and cognitive tools in the three areas of audience, activities, and performances is what kinds of conclusions can be drawn about the value of the technology for learning. In the case of digital resources where audiences, activities, and performances are not articulated, no clean comparisons can be made between intended goals, activities, and products to determine relative "learning success" with the digital resource. It is worth noting that this lack of specificity relative to knowledge, activities, and performances might be one explanation for why some earlier studies intending to evaluate the "learning success" of technologies were not successful.

In contrast, when comparisons of audience, activities, and performances are made relative to a cognitive tool, empirical evidence can be gathered on the degree to which intended goals are demonstrated by actual outcomes. This information can serve as empirical evidence of both the effectiveness of the resource and the empirically driven redesign of the resource. With the BioKIDS Sequence, data on student accuracy of data collection, analysis, and use of data for the development of scientific explanations can be compared with the original estimations of learning goals and audience. Subsequent redesign of the cognitive tool can then be performed, resulting in stronger learning outcomes and more meaningful use of the technology.

In summary, we developed definitions of digital resources and cognitive tools and developed three areas in which we contrast digital resources and cognitive tools. The next section outlines a framework for the examination of technologies relative to their potential as a cognitive tool and the potential transformation of digital resources into cognitive tools.

Transformation via the Cognitive Tools Framework

The cognitive tools framework allows a detailed examination of a particular technological resource relative to its predicted role and value in learning science. The development of this framework draws from work in related areas, such as design of high-quality assessment instruments that are well matched to instruction (National Research Council, 2001). Similar to other frameworks and drawing on the three areas of comparison outlined earlier, the examination of a technological tool via the Cognitive Tools Framework involves an examination relative to three dimensions of the learning experience: (1) target audience and learning goals, (2 the identification of specific learning activities that are performed with the digital resource, and (3) the articulation of particular learning outcomes, such as student performances that are produced as a result of use of the technology within the particular learning context.

As outlined in the previous section, digital resources often provide a rich scientific milieu with strong but unrealized or unfocused potential as a way of learning science. An examination of a digital resource in the three focus areas outlined earlier can lead to the development of a more focused technological tool targeted for a particular audience, learning goal, task, and outcome.

In many cases, it may be advantageous for science teachers or researchers to work from these existing rich scientific resources in the development of cognitive tools for learning science. In these cases, it might be advantageous to redesign the tool in particular ways, such as transform the digital resource into a cognitive tool following the steps of the Cognitive Tools Framework. Figure 17.4 presents the cycle of activities involved in the transformation of a digital resource into a cognitive tool following the Cognitive Tools Framework.

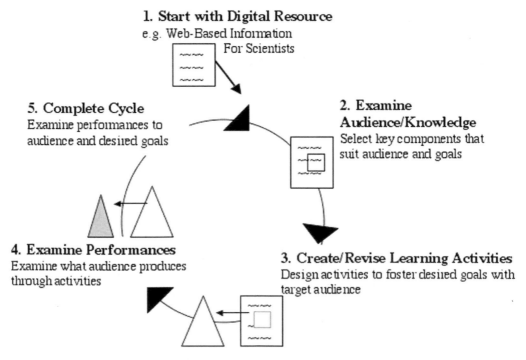

FIGURE 17–4.   Steps involved in examining or transforming a digital resource into a cognitive tool via the Cognitive Tools Framework.

The framework consists of examination in three areas. Examination relative to *Audience/Knowledge* refers to a clear definition of the target audience (age, abilities, prior knowledge, and beliefs) as well as learning goals (science content, scientific reasoning, beliefs/attitudes about science) associated with the use of the digital resource. *Learning Activities* refers to the specific tasks that the target audience will perform with the digital resource. Note that the digital learning activities must correspond directly to the audience and learning goals in the Audience/Knowledge area. *Learning Performances* refers to the specific products that are generated by the student as a result of interactions with digital learning activities. Note that digital learning performances should be a clear demonstration of the knowledge outlined in Audience/Knowledge. Correspondence between the three areas of the framework provides a stronger prediction that learning with the resource will achieve desired goals.

Why Transform Digital Resources into Cognitive Tools via This Framework?

We present the idea of transformation of digital resources into cognitive tools via the Cognitive Tools Framework as one means to examine technological resources focused on learning science. We also present this framework to use in guiding the redesign of a digital resource into a cognitive tool that may more feasibly contribute to the intended learning goals outlined.

The idea of transformation to cognitive tools builds from the work of others who developed instructional design frameworks to guide design decisions for educational technologies (e.g., Schwartz, Lin, Brophy, & Bransford, 1999; learner-centered design by Soloway, Guzdial, & Hay, 1994). In addition, this work builds from the recent trend of developing educational technologies to be tailored to specific topics, populations, or disciplines (Linn, 2003). In these studies, expertise on how individuals learn was incorporated with human-computer interface expertise on how individuals interact with technology, to produce guidelines for the design of learner-focused technologies. For example, the work by Soloway and colleagues (Soloway et al., 1994) incorporated components of learning theory such as "learn by doing" with expertise about interface design, resulting in concrete issues to be addressed when designing for learners. Some of these issues included a focus on understanding, motivation, design for a diverse audience, and software that is sensitive to learners' growth of understanding. In the work of Soloway and colleagues (1994) and others, the task of articulating guidelines for the design of technologies focusing on learners and the subsequent evaluation based on these criteria was considered essential to making informed decisions about the role of technology in learning science.

The work here also involves an analysis of software presentation and the role of technology; however, the Cognitive Tools Framework provides more specificity about the areas of necessary focus, as well as an emphasis on transformation as opposed to the nascent creation of new educational technologies.

Concerning areas of focus, an essential area for the Cognitive Tools Framework is the area of audience/knowledge. Examination of a technological resource via the Cognitive Tools framework requires a detailed understanding of knowledge to be learned and, ideally, the placement of the target concept in a sequence of concepts to be learned by the target audience. Without an articulation of the knowledge (e.g., facts, conceptual understandings, reasoning skills) and sequence of target science concepts, appropriate design decisions cannot be made that will determine whether the technology might be valuable as a learning resource within this learning environment and for the particular target audience.

Building cognitive tools from digital resources using the Cognitive Tools framework also takes into account the idea that many existing digital resources have strong educational potential that can be used as a foundation for a more focused Cognitive Tool. Many rich resources that contain excellent scientific material already exist, yet they are often unusable in their current form because of their unfocused, narrowly focused, or overly technical presentation. Guidelines for the productive reworking of these resources could expand the potential repertoire of productive learning resources for pre-college science students. In addition, transformation using the Cognitive Tools framework may be simpler than creating educational software products from scratch, particularly when a rich resource in this topic area already exists.

AN EXAMINATION OF SCIENCE LEARNING WITH TECHNOLOGY VIA THE COGNITIVE TOOLS FRAMEWORK

This section explores cases of technology in the research literature relative to the Cognitive Tools Framework. To begin this examination, it is necessary to identify the kinds of science knowledge we might wish technology to support. The National Science Education Standards suggest that in order to develop scientific inquiry abilities in K–12 education, learners should be engaging with rich scientific questions, gathering and analyzing data, formulating scientific explanations from scientific evidence, critically examining relevant data and explanations, and communicating scientific claims, evidence, and explanations to others (National Research Council, 2000).

Drawing from these dimensions of scientific inquiry, we select four areas that are considered essential in developing scientific knowledge where we believe technology can play an essential role:

a. Learners think critically and logically about scientific ideas and compare them with real-life conditions.
b. Learners critically evaluate and communicate scientific ideas.
c. Learners formulate scientific explanations from evidence.
d. Learners use appropriate tools to gather, analyze, and interpret data (National Research Council, 2000, p. 19).

In the following section, we identify categories of technologies that might be fruitful in supporting each learning dimension. The learning dimension and their associated technologies are represented in Table 17.1.

The following sections present exemplary cases of associated technologies and learning dimensions. The discussion of each case focuses on the role of the technology in the learning environment relative to the learning dimension specified and

TABLE 17.1
Learning Dimensions and Their Associated Technologies

Learning dimension	Associated technologies
Learners think critically about scientific ideas and/or compare with real life conditions	Modeling, simulations, and visualization tools
Learners critically evaluate and communicate scientific ideas	Online critique and discussion resources
Learners formulate knowledge such as scientific explanations from evidence	Online scaffolding tools
Learners using appropriate tools to gather, analyze, and interpret data	Computer-based data collection and analysis

the components of the Cognitive Tools Framework. A discussion focused on the areas of the Cognitive Tools Framework allows a review relative to the tools' use as a cognitive tool for learning science by a particular audience as opposed to digital resource. In each technology category, the cases discussed are only some of the possible resources that might have been selected from the research literature; thus this discussion is not intended to be a comprehensive review of all of the possible technologies that might have been discussed.

Thinking Critically with Modeling, Visualization, and Simulation Tools

In learning science, it is frequently not possible to manipulate objects first-hand in order to develop deep conceptual understandings of scientific concepts. Sometimes the necessary materials are very toxic or costly. Other times, resources are too large or too small to work with first hand, as when a class studies the movement of solar systems, weather systems, or individual electrons.

Digital resources transformed into cognitive tools can help science learners to experiment and think critically about real-life phenomena through study in controlled, hypothetical or virtual environments. Subsequently, learners can compare what they have learned in the hypothetical or virtual environment with real-life phenomena.

One example of a case where technology can support students in thinking critically and logically about complex systems is in the use of computer models, such as models of very large and complex three-dimensional systems. The Virtual Solar System (VSS) project supports students in the creation and analysis of three-dimensional models of the solar system that simulate the relative rotation, size, and distance between planets (e.g., Keating, Barnett, Barab, & Hay, 2002). In this study, specific curricular activities were developed to complement the visualization tools to support undergraduate students' abilities to visualize abstract three-dimensional concepts leading to more sophisticated understandings of basic astronomy concepts. Research on the development of students' explanations for the seasons, the phases of the moon, and eclipses reveals significant improvements in students' understandings of these concepts as a result of the construction and analysis of solar system models. In this case, the researchers articulated the target audience and learn-ing goals, the learning activities, and the learning performances to facilitate VSS 3D models. The models served as cognitive tools for critical thinking about sun-moon-earth concepts through students' visualization of abstract concepts about the solar system from a range of reference points or perspectives (Keating et al., 2002). Stu-dents' ability to run tests and view a three-dimensional system from a range of ref-erence points allowed students to use the cognitive tool as an interactive represen-tation of the actual scientific phenomena, which facilitated greater understanding of the scientific concepts than might be available with a non-interactive two-dimen-sional textbook picture or model. The emphasis on the needs of the audience, learn-ing goals, specific activities, and specific performances facilitated the technology's use as a cognitive tool as opposed to a mere digital resource.

Another exemplary case of a cognitive modeling tool is the case of ThinkerTools (e.g., White & Frederiksen, 1998). Grounded in theories of learning, ThinkerTools was designed with a coordination between the three elements of the Cognitive Tools Framework: audience/learning goals, activities, and performances. Middle school students are guided in physics problem solving as they are also guided in the development of metacognitive skills about their own learning process. Learning outcomes, on measures of conceptual understanding of physics, applied physics, and attitudes about science, all demonstrate significant gains. Similarly, a third mod-eling tool focused on middle and high school students creating dynamic models of plate tectonics phenomena, leading to the development of sophisticated conceptual understandings of basic geology and the value of models (Gobert & Pallant, 2004). Again, the coordination of audience/learning goals, activities, and performances facilitated the possibility of students' demonstrating strong learning outcomes with this cognitive tool.

Critically Evaluating and Communicating Scientific Ideas with Online Scaffolding Tools

Many network technologies are interactive and therefore provide possible opportu-nities for learners to critically evaluate and communicate their scientific ideas with others. Some technologies facilitate feedback and variations of tutoring, including feedback built into the tool (e.g., intelligent tutors), whereas others facilitate feed-back and communication of individuals through the tool (e.g., Scardamalia & Bere-iter, 1994). In one exemplary case, students using the interactive tool called Computer Supported Intentional Learning Environment (CSILE) demonstrated significantly higher scores on standardized tests and demonstrated greater depth in their expla-nations than students without CSILE (Scardamalia & Bereiter, 1994).

Discussion tools (e.g. online tools that provide opportunities for individuals to discuss, collaborate, or share ideas or materials) also can serve as rich examples of cognitive tools that can help learners critically evaluate or communicate their ideas about science. In one exemplary case, Guzdial and Turns (2000) discovered that computer-mediated discussions that focused specifically on topics related to class learning goals (e.g., the Audience/Knowledge area) were more effective than dis-cussions with a more open discussion format. The Multimedia Forum Kiosk (MFK; Hsi & Hoadley, 1997) supported much greater participation by a more widely representative part the class as compared with participation levels in a more traditional classroom discussion. Similarly, a tool focused on supporting ongoing conversations between mentors and students can support guidance in science concept development, reasoning skills, or more productive views of the nature of science (e.g., Bruckman, 2000; O'Neill & Gomez, 1998). In these cases, special attention to Cognitive Tools Framework areas, such as those tailored to online discussions and learning goals or tailoring activities for more anonymous participation (Hsi & Hoadley, 1997), resulted in strong desired outcomes (productive views of the nature of science, conceptual development, high participation levels).

In a contrasting case of critical evaluation and communication of scientific ideas, the Kids as Global Scientists' live prediction tool was used to support globally distributed middle school students' predictions of tomorrow's weather. Once weather data was reviewed and predictions were communicated, these predictions were evaluated relative to the actual weather outcomes through feedback by online atmospheric scientists (Lee & Songer, 2003). In this case, the online prediction environment provided opportunities not just for the development of conceptual knowledge but also for the introduction of real-time problem solving for students ("bringing real world problems into the classroom for students to explore and solve"; Bransford et al., p. 207). On balance, because of the complexity of the real-world situation, the Audience/Knowledge component of the Cognitive Tools Framework has to be carefully matched to the learner's prior knowledge and abilities for maximum effectiveness (Lee & Songer, 2003).

Formulating Knowledge Such as Scientific Explanations with Online Scaffolding Tools

A third category of technologies that can support productive learning of science is online scaffolding tools. Online scaffolding tools can provide a range of different kinds of scaffolding. Scaffolding is commonly defined as the process used by a learner to assist in solving problems or performing cognitive tasks that are too difficult to perform on their own (Wood, Bruner, & Ross, 1976; Quintana et al., 2004). In the case of technologies for learning science, scaffolds are commonly present in the form of written prompts, links, or diagrams that are built into the software to guide students in up to three different types of scientific knowledge development: conceptual knowledge development, reasoning skills such as the development of an evidence-based explanation, or understanding the nature of science.

Zembal-Saul and Land (2002) provide evidence of an online scaffolding tool that helps prospective teachers to construct scientific arguments related to physics concepts. Using the Progress Portfolio tool developed by Loh and colleagues at Northwestern University (Loh et al., 1997), teachers were provided with online guidance in two areas: the organization and reflection on evidence from experiments, and the development of scientific explanations based on evidence. An examination of the preservice teachers' performances after they used Progress Portfolio demonstrated that the cognitive tool provided valuable assistance in guiding the target audience in the interpretation of their results and in developing iterative refinements of their scientific explanations. In both of these examples, it appears that the matching of learning goals (reflection on data collected; development of strong scientific explanations) to the observed performances allowed a more detailed explanation of the ways in which the cognitive tool was and was not leading to the desired outcomes.

In two different papers, Davis (2003) and Reiser (2004) discuss research results with middle and high school students to explore differential benefits of online scaffolding tools for knowledge formulation such as scientific explanations. Davis (2003) explored different kinds of online problems to guide eighth-graders' reflection. She discovered that when working with complex problem situations, students using generic prompts developed more coherent understandings than students using directed prompts. In contrast, Reiser (2004) presents a review of research results from studies exploring online scaffolding tools. Taking a bird's-eye view of these studies, Reiser discusses two ways in which online scaffolds can assist students in learning science. These ways are to a) structure the learning task itself and b) problematize essential scientific content. Reflecting on these research results relative to the Cognitive Tools Framework, one hypothesis is that Davis's generic (2003) and Reiser's scientific content scaffolds (2004) appear to define but do not overly restrict key dimensions of the knowledge dimension, so that the learning activities and learning performances can be coupled accordingly.

Using Cognitive Tools to Gather, Analyze, or Interpret Data

The fourth area of learning science in which technology can play essential roles is in the gathering and analyzing of scientific data or information. A relatively new and promising area for the use of technology in learning science is the use of small handheld computers such as personal digital assistants (PDAs) for quick data gathering and feedback associated with teaching and learning environments. As one example of this use, in Project WHIRL: Wireless Handhelds in Reflection on Learning (Penuel & Yarnell, 2005), teachers use handheld computers and the benefits of interactivity and feedback to improve their ability to rapidly assess student learning within their classrooms.

A second example of technology for data collection and analysis is Cyber-Tracker, the tool presented earlier. CyberTracker (Fig. 17.2 and www.cybertracker.co.za) is an icon-based software tool that runs on PDA computers to support professional African animal trackers in quickly recording and identifying animals in the field. Recognizing early on the learning potential of the CyberTracker digital resource for use by middle school students, researchers began to explore the transformation of this tool into a tool better suited for use by middle school students in Michigan. The examination of how to transform CyberTracker followed the Cognitive Tools Framework.

First, researchers investigated CyberTracker for audience/knowledge. At the onset, the icon-based, data entry format of CyberTracker was a good fit for the target audience of language-diverse fifth- and sixth-graders in the Midwestern states. On balance, the learning goals were focused on ecology and the inquiry reasoning of building scientific explanations, as outlined in the National Science Education Standards (National Research Council, 1996). The original CyberTracker sequence contained prompting for data collection that was irrelevant to these learning goals.

Therefore the transformation of CyberTracker relative to audience/knowledge required little adjustment in the area of language for the target audience; however, large adjustments were necessary to focus the data collection to support content development in ecology and inquiry reasoning associated with building scientific explanations from evidence (Songer, 2006).

For all of our learning goals, the collection and organization of accurate scientific data were essential. Therefore, step three of the transformation of CyberTracker via the Cognitive Tools Framework involved the design of learning activities that focused on children's accurate data collection of animal data in their schoolyards. This transformation step involved both a reworking of the manner in which animal entries were organized in animal groups, as well as a streamlined sequence of data entry focusing on a small number of types of data focused around key unit concepts (habitats, animal group, animal, number, and zone). Figure 17.2 illustrates an example of the CyberTracker sequence after transformation via the Cognitive Tools Framework, now called the BioKIDS Sequence.

Finally, an examination of CyberTracker was performed relative to the third area of learning performances. This examination involved analysis of the products students generated from their data collection with the BioKIDS Sequence to determine if the information would support their ability to reach the desired learning goals. Figure 17.5 displays the student data collected by sixth-graders in one schoolyard in the Midwestern United States with the use of the BioKIDS sequence.

DISCUSSION

This chapter began with a discussion of the rapid integration of technology in our lives and the comparative underutilization of technology in science classrooms, despite a growing integration and use of technology by children outside of classroom walls. A majority of large-scale research on technology and science education contributes information largely associated with numbers (e.g., access, frequency of

Habitat	Animal Group	Animal	How Many?	Location (Zone)
Short grass	6 LEGS Insects	Unknown beetle	13	A
Short grass	6 LEGS Insects	Bee	2	F
Bare ground	Mammals	Norway rat	1	D
Bare ground	Mammals	Fox squirrel	1	F
In the soil	10+ LEGS Myriapods and Crustaceans	Centipede	2	E
Under rock or log	0 LEGS Annelids and Mollusks	Earthworm	1	D
In the air	6 LEGS Insects	Bee	1	A
Single tree	Birds	American robin	1	F

FIGURE 17–5. Sample habitat summary for Michigan-collected animal data.

use); few studies provide an analytical lens to help explain why technology is underutilized in science classrooms. This is the case despite high-profile requests for research studies that investigate technology designed with the principles of learning in mind:

> [T]he process of using technology to improve learning is never solely a technical matter, concerned only with properties of educational hardware and software. . . . Good educational software and teacher-support tools, developed with a full understanding of principles of learning, have not yet become the norm. Software developers are generally driven more by the game and play market than by the learning potential of their products. . . . Much remains to be learned about using technology's potential: to make this happen, learning research will need to become the constant companion of software development. (Bransford et al., 2000)

Addressing this issue of the examination of learning principle-driven technologies first hand, this chapter presents an analytical framework and a discussion of several exemplary cases designed or transformed with respect to audience, learning principles, and outcomes. Through the presentation of the analytical framework and associated cases, the chapter discusses the factors necessary in the design or transformation of learning-associated cognitive tools to learn science. The Cognitive Tools Framework identifies areas of examination necessary for either design or transformation of a digital resource into a cognitive tool, so that the technological resource can have a greater potential to contribute toward strong learning outcomes. The Cognitive Tools Framework and exemplary cases discussed present a perspective on how technological tools can be designed or transformed so that the gap in utilization in classrooms can be understood and overcome.

Each of the exemplary cases discussed illustrates means by which technologies can be designed to focus on issues of audience, knowledge, learning activities, and performances. In many of these cases, the technology was evaluated, and strong learning results that support the value of a cognitive tool as opposed to merely a digital resource were found. For example, empirical results conducted with the designed cognitive tool ThinkerTools demonstrate middle school students' significant gains on a variety of physics concepts relative to peers and older students (White & Fredricksen, 1998). Similarly, empirical results on the transformed cognitive tool the BioKIDS Sequence demonstrate high levels of usability by fifth- and sixth-grade students and strong learning outcomes, both understanding of science content and scientific reasoning (Songer, 2005; Parr, Jones, & Songer, 2004). Interestingly, although the idea of designing or transforming technologies to be cognitive tools is one that has been around for a while, a review of the literature in science education suggests that greater empirical evidence of learning outcomes relative to cognitive tools is needed.

In conclusion, we encourage additional research to examine issues associated with the design of cognitive tools for learning science, including studies that utilize quasi-experimental comparative designs to examine the relative value of different designs relative to the factors of the Cognitive Tools Framework. With the continued small amount of research studies that examine learning-focused technologies, it will remain difficult to respond to critics who claim there is little empirical evidence to support the widespread use of technology in science classrooms. Furthermore, without a solid research base on learning-focused technologies, it will be impossible to make informed decisions on how and when to use technology for learning science. We also encourage additional research to examine the potential of technology for the learning of science, such as research that couples learning research with research on software and resource design. Coupled research of this kind is necessary to understand the effective use of technology in science classrooms and the transformations necessary to develop powerful cognitive tools to advance the learning of science by all learners.

ACKNOWLEDGMENTS

Thanks to Barbara Crawford and Bob Sherwood, who reviewed this chapter.

REFERENCES

American Association of University Women. (2000). Tech-Savvy: Educating girls in the new computer age. Washington, DC: American Association of University Women.

Bransford, J., Brown, A. L., & Cocking, R. R. (2000). How people learn: Brain, mind, experience and school. Washington, DC: National Academy Press.

Bruckman, A. (2000). Situated support for learning: Storm's weekend with Rachael. The *Journal of the Learning Sciences 9*(3), 329–372.

Cohen, D., Raudenbush, S., & Ball, D. (2000). *Resources, instruction, and research.* Seattle, WA: University of Washington, Center for the Study of Teaching and Policy.

Cuban, L. (2001). *Oversold and overused: Computers in the classroom.* Cambridge, MA: Harvard University Press.

Davis, E. (2003). Prompting middle school science students for productive reflection: Generic and directed prompts. *The Journal of the Learning Sciences, 12*(1), 91–142.

Edelson, D., & Reiser, B. (2006). Making authentic practices accessible to learners. In K. Sawyer (Ed.), *The Cambridge handbook of the learning sciences* (pp. 335–354). New York: Cambridge University Press.

Freidman, T. L. (2005). *The world is flat: A brief history of the twenty-first century.* New York: Farrar, Straus & Giroux.

Gobert, J. D., & Pallant, A. (2004). Fostering students' epistemologies of models via authentic model-based tasks. *Journal of Science education and Technology, 13*(1), 7–22 (invited paper).

Grimm, V., Revilla, E., Berger, I., Jeltsch, F., Mooij, W., Railsback, S., et al. (2005). Pattern-oriented modeling of agent-based complex systems: Lessons from ecology. *Science* (310) 5750, 987–991.

Guzdial, M., & Turns, J. (2000). Effective discussion through a computer-mediated anchored forum. *The Journal of the Learning Sciences, 91*(4), 437–469.

Haak, W., Forster, P., Bramanti, B., Matsumura, S., Brandt, G., Tanzer, M., et al. (2005). Ancient DNA from the first European farmers in 7500-year-old neolithic sites. *Science* (310) 5750, 1016–1018.

Hsi, S., and Hoadley, C. (1997). Productive discussion in science: Gender equity through electronic discourse. *Journal of Science Education and Technology, 6*(1), 23–36.

Keating, T., Barnett, M., Barab, S., & Hay, K. (2002). The Virtual Solar System Project: Developing conceptual understanding of astronomical concepts through building three-dimensional computational models. *The Journal of Science Education and Technology, 11*(2), 261–275.

Lee, H. S., & Songer, N. B. (2003). Making authentic science accessible to students. *International Journal of Science Education, 25*(1), 1–26.

Levin, D., & Arafeh, S. (2002). *The digital disconnect: The widening gap between internet-savvy students and their schools.* Pew Internet and American Life Project. Retrieved November 14, 2005 from www.pewinternet.org

Loh, B., Radinsky, J., Reiser, B., Gomez, L., Edelson, D., & Russell, E. (1997). *The Progress Portfolio: Promoting reflective inquiry in complex investigation environments*. Paper presented at the Computer Supported Collaborative Learning (CSCL) meeting, Toronto, Canada.

Linn, M. C. (2003). Technology and science education: Starting points, research programs and trends. *International Journal of Science Education, 6*(25), 727–758.

Linn, M. C., Davis, E., & Bell, P. (2004). *Internet environments for science education*. Mahwah, NJ: Lawrence Erlbaum Associates.

Linn, M. C., & Slotta, J. D. (2002). WISE science. *Educational Leadership, x*(x), p. 29–32.

National Research Council. (1996). *National science education standards*. Washington, DC: National Academy Press.

National Research Council (2000). *Inquiry and the national science education standards: A guide for teaching and learning*. Washington, DC: National Academy Press.

National Research Council. (2001). Knowing what students know: The science and design of educational assessment. Washington, DC: National Academy Press.

O'Neill, K. D. (2004). Building social capital in a knowledge-building community: Telementoring as a catalyst. *Interactive Learning Environments, 12*(3), 179–208.

O'Neill, K., & Gomez, L. (1998). *Sustaining mentoring relationships on-line*. Proceedings of Computer Support for Collaborative Work 1998, Seattle, WA, pp. 325–334.

Parr, C., Jones, T., & Songer, N. B. (2004). Evaluation of a handheld data collection interface for science. *Journal of Science Education and Technologym, 13*(2), 233–242.

Penuel, W. R., & Yarnal, L. (2005). Designing handheld software to support classroom assessment: An analysis of conditions for teacher adoption. *The Journal of Technology, Learning and Assessment, 3*(5), 3–45.

Quintana, C., Reiser, B., Davis, B., Krajcik, J., Fretz, E., Duncan, R., et al. (2004). A scaffolding design framework for software to support science inquiry. *The Journal of the Learning Sciences, 13*(3), 337–386.

Reiser, B. J. (2004). Scaffolding complex learning: The mechanisms of structuring and problematizing student work. *The Journal of the Learning Sciences, 13*(3), 273–304.

Scardamalia, M., & Bereiter, C. (1994). Computer support for knowledge-building communities. *The Journal of the Learning Sciences, 3*(3), 265–283.

Schwartz, D. L., Lin, X., Brophy, S., & Bransford, J. (1999). Towards the development of flexibly adaptive instructional designs. In C. Reigeluth (Ed.), *Instructional-design theories and models: A new paradigm of instructional theory* (Vol. II, pp. 183–213. Mahwah, NJ: Lawrence Erlbaum Associates.

Soloway, E., Guzdial, M., & Hay, K. (1994). Learner-centered design: The challenge for HCI in the 21st century. *Interactions, 1*(2), 36–48.

Songer, N. B. (2005). *Persistence of inquiry: Evidence of complex reasoning among inner city middle school students*. Paper presented at the American Educational Research Association (AERA) annual meeting.

Songer, N. B. (2006). BioKIDS: An animated conversation on the development of curricular activity structures for inquiry science. In R. Keith Sawyer (Ed.), *Cambridge handbook of the learning sciences* (pp. 355–369). New York: Cambridge University Press.

Tinker, R., & Vahey, P. (2002). CILT2000: Ubiquitous computing—Spanning the digital divide. *Journal of Science Education and Technology, 11*(3), 301–304.

U.S. Department of Education. (2003). *Technology in schools: Suggestions, tools and guidelines for assessing technology in elementary and secondary education*. NCES 2003-313. Washington, DC: Technology in Schools Task Force, National Forum on Educational Statistics.

U.S. Department of Education. (2004). *Toward a new golden age in American education: How the internet, the law and today's students are revolutionizing expectations*. Retrieved November 15, 2005 from http://www.ed.gov/about/offices/list/os/technology/plan/2004/plan_pg20.html

U.S. House of Representatives. (2001). *Hearing charter: Classrooms as laboratories: The science of learning meets the practice of teaching.* Retrieved November 14, 2005, from http://www.house .gov/science/research/may10/res_charter_051001.htm

White, B. T., & Frederiksen, J. R. (1998). Inquiry, modeling, and metacognition: Making science accessible to all students. *Cognition and Instruction, 16*(1), 3–118.

Wood, D., Bruner, J., & Ross, G. (1976). The role of tutoring in problem solving. *Journal of Child Psychology and Psychiatry and Allied Disciplines, 17*, 89–100.

Zembal-Saul, C., & Land, S. (2002). *Scaffolding the construction of scientific arguments by prospective teachers using inquiry-empowering technologies.* Paper presented at the annual meeting of the American Educational Research Association, New Orleans.

CHAPTER 18

Elementary Science Teaching

Ken Appleton
Central Queensland University, Australia

This chapter is about research related to the teaching of science in the elementary school, that is, to students from 5 to 12 years of age. This age range covers grades 1 to 6 or 7 in most education systems. In some countries, particularly those with an English (UK) heritage, this level of schooling is called *primary school*; and to complicate things further, the term *middle school* is used for students aged 10 to 15 years in a number of education systems. For consistency, in this chapter I use the term *elementary school* for grades 1 to 7.

In many countries science in the elementary school is a relatively recent addition to the curriculum, in most instances having been introduced in the decade or two following World War II. Prior to this, any science was essentially nature study. Furthermore, elementary teacher preparation in universities has tended to be a more recent phenomenon and is still to be achieved in a number of countries. Elementary teacher preparation in science, particularly in universities, consequently does not have a long tradition. Because educational research tends to be done by university professors engaged in teacher preparation, research into elementary science teaching remains an emergent area. Fortunately, some research into lower secondary school science has application to the upper elementary grades and has provided a boost for research in elementary science.

Over the last few decades, there has been an increasing amount of research into elementary science teaching, so I have been necessarily selective. I have chosen to review work published over the last decade, mainly in journals, and tried to avoid major overlap with other chapters in this *Handbook*; though for some topics that cross schooling and cognate boundaries, that is unavoidable. My selection and comments naturally reflect my own views and beliefs about research and elementary science teaching.

I have organized the chapter under headings that summarize the main trends in relevant research over the last decade, which, not surprisingly, mirror some chapters in this *Handbook*. The headings are also comparable to several sections in the previous *Handbook* (Gabel, 1994), making the choice of concentrating on research during the last decade more appropriate. I have deliberately omitted a section on learning (see Chapters 2–7), though key ideas about learning surface in several sections. I begin with a consideration of trends in elementary science education research, then discuss the context for teaching and learning, moving on to consider the teacher, the curriculum, assessment, pedagogy, and finally future research directions. The research into elementary science teacher preparation and professional development has its own extensive literature (see Chapters 34–39), so it is referred to only incidentally.

TRENDS IN RESEARCH INTO ELEMENTARY SCIENCE TEACHING

Research into elementary science teaching is not immune from the pressures and influences on research into schooling more generally, and science education more specifically. The current, dominant social issues such as political demands for accountability in education, maximizing student learning outcomes, and social justice are demanding the attention of educational researchers. However, a majority of elementary science education researchers have moved to academia after commencing their careers as elementary teachers and subsequently undertaking doctoral studies. They therefore tend to have an interest in the type of research that will make a difference in the classroom. The research literature therefore abounds with investigations focusing on the pedagogical application of theories of learning, enhancing conceptual learning of science, current practices in science teaching, and ways of addressing the identified problems in elementary science teaching and learning through pre-service and in-service teacher education. Studies dealing with the larger social agendas and those that might inform policy making are less frequent. Perhaps this is understandable, given that elementary science is just one part of the overall elementary school context, so policy and social issues impinge more broadly on all aspects of the elementary school rather than just one subject. Yet a consequence of this is that elementary science education researchers are largely reactive to policy changes and do not help shape them. This is particularly significant when policy changes affect science teaching and learning in a detrimental way. In making this comment, I acknowledge that merely doing research does not guarantee that it informs policy—networking and lobbying are perhaps even more critical. But having research findings is a necessary starting point.

Over the last few decades there has been a change in the type of research conducted. With the growing popularity of constructivist views of learning in elementary science, I have noted a corresponding shift in epistemological beliefs held by elementary science education researchers from positivist views to constructivist views, and within constructivism, from cognitive to social constructivism. A consequence has been a growing tendency for researchers to select interpretive research designs rather than the experimental designs that dominated educational research 30 years ago. The shift in constructivist views has also resulted in a change from research involving clinical interviews to probe understandings to case studies of social settings and influences. This means that a change has also been under way in the type of research questions asked by researchers. Questions like, *Which teaching strategy is more effective?* and *What misconceptions do these students hold in ___?* are rare nowadays, whereas questions such as *What aspects of the teaching strategy enhance students' learning?* are more common. The trend is toward trying to understand the complexities of the learning and teaching interface. Instead of trying to control variables, there is a preference to describe how they interact. Instead of describing problems in teaching and learning, there is a preference to understand how the problems come about and how to reduce the likelihood of their occurrence. Such trends are particularly evident in the context of elementary science teaching.

THE CONTEXT FOR TEACHING AND LEARNING ELEMENTARY SCIENCE

Science in the elementary school is framed by the social and cultural context of elementary schooling. This varies considerably from country to country, despite some similarities in tradition and practice. An overriding tradition is that elementary schooling's major priorities are literacy and numeracy, with other subjects taking second place. Such traditions and perceived priorities have consequently shaped research into elementary science teaching. Inasmuch as science is a relatively new elementary curriculum area with low priority, two major research foci have been science teaching practices in the elementary school, and teacher preparation and professional development in elementary science education. Other influences on elementary science research have tended to flow from science education research in the secondary school and from research into learning. Most researchers investigating elementary science teaching have had their thinking framed by historical developments in elementary science education research and science education research generally. My own thinking has, for example, evolved from a concern for the state of elementary science teaching to an emphasis on process skills, to cognitive constructivism and emergent pedagogies, to a more social constructivist orientation, and finally to a focus on standards-based conceptual learning and teaching. Within these trends has been an ongoing and overarching interest in elementary science teacher preparation and professional development. My research practices have correspondingly evolved from quantitative, quasi-experimental studies to qualitative studies taking a constructivist perspective, with a heavy reliance on case-study techniques. Many of my colleagues throughout the world have taken a similar journey.

Understanding the context of schooling is an essential starting point for making sense of research in elementary science. Science in the elementary school is one of a number of subjects that are usually taught by a generalist teacher. Research into the social and cultural setting of science in the elementary school is consequently a subset of a vast literature that cannot be reviewed in a chapter such as this (see the special issues of *Journal of Research in Science Teaching*, volume 36 issue 3 and volume 38 issue 5).

A defining set of studies about the context of science teaching and learning was conducted by Nuthall (2001). He reported the effect on student learning in science and social studies of the intersecting variables of the instructional social setting, peer-peer social interaction, and internal cognitive processing and attending behaviors of students. He used multiple data sources from intensive and extensive observation of classroom events over several weeks, including interviews, and artefacts. He tracked conceptual development in students by identifying each concept introduced during teaching and categorizing each item of data from the focus students into the respective concept. He was thus able to construct a time-event overview of experiences for each student that influenced that student's learning of each concept. In his studies, he highlighted how each of these variables can dramatically influence the learning that occurs. Consequently, I refer to his studies in a number of places in this chapter.

Although not addressed by Nuthall, it is critical to note that students' internal cognitive processing and attending behaviors are derived from their cultural and linguistic backgrounds (Warren, Ballenger, Ogonowski, Rosebery, & Hudicourt-Barnes, 2001). These influence considerably the nature of previous experiences students bring to the learning situation and consequently what they learn (Nuthall, 1999). They also influence the types of social interactions that can occur within a small group of students (Kurth, Anderson, & Palincsar, 2002). Peer-peer interactions are largely invisible to the teacher in a busy classroom, particularly when small groups are working on activities or projects, but can either enhance or interfere with learning (Kurth et al., 2002; Nuthall, 2001; Ritchie, 2002).

It is such considerations that, I believe, have caused many researchers in elementary science education to move away from experimental and quasi-experimental studies toward qualitative ones, because these are variables that cannot be controlled and are usually hidden in experimental statistical error estimates. Nuthall (1999) makes the point, for instance, that what students learn from a lesson is not related to their ability, but to how they interact with and interpret learning experiences. Large-scale experimental designs cannot control for such a variable, but they can be identified and described with the use of qualitative data. A further example of this trend in research is presented in the next section, on the elementary science teacher.

THE ELEMENTARY SCIENCE TEACHER

Early research into elementary science teaching tended to use self-report surveys of teacher practice. Later studies have focused more on understanding classroom events from both the teachers' and students' perspectives.

Current Practice

Current practice in elementary science has been an ongoing research topic for decades, and despite huge efforts it seems that little has changed.

Teacher Avoidance of Science

That elementary teachers tend to avoid science has been an issue for a long time. For instance, Tilgner (1990) commented that the situation had not changed in 20 years, and in the decade since, there have been continuing reports along similar lines across the world (e.g., Goodrum, Hackling, & Rennie, 2001; Harlen, 1997; Harlen & Holroyd, 1997; Lee & Houseal, 2003; Osborne & Simon, 1996; Schoon & Boone, 1998). The main issues identified in research over the decades are that elementary teachers tend to have limited science subject matter knowledge, limited science pedagogical content knowledge (PCK) (Shulman, 1986), and low confidence/ self-efficacy in science and science teaching, with the consequence that many avoid teaching science. Harlen (1997) identified six avoidance strategies used by teachers:

1. avoidance—teaching as little of the subject as possible,
2. keeping to topics where confidence is greater—usually meaning more biology than physical science,
3. stressing process outcomes rather than conceptual development outcomes,
4. relying on the book, or prescriptive work cards which give pupils step-by-step instructions,
5. emphasising expository teaching and underplaying questioning and discussion,
6. avoiding all but the simplest practical work and any equipment that can go wrong. (p. 335)

Factors related to the school and/or school system, such as resources, time (both personal and class schedules), and personal and system perceptions of the importance of science in the elementary school, are cited as other reasons for limited teaching of science (e.g., Appleton & Kindt, 1997; Goodrum et al., 2001; Levitt, 2001).

Harlen also cautioned that, although some teachers are more confident about teaching science, avoidance behaviors allow them to teach a form of science with which they are comfortable, and therefore they do not see their science teaching as problematic. In self-report surveys, these teachers may appear as confident, regular teachers of science. However, King, Shumow, and Lietz (2001) found that there was a considerable discrepancy between teachers' views of their own practice in elementary science and the views of science educators who observed their teaching. What the teachers saw as inquiry, the science educators saw as expository. This has implications for research that relies solely on teachers' self-reporting of their science teaching practice.

A consequence of elementary teachers' limited science knowledge and low confidence in teaching science is a tendency for them to use teaching strategies that allow them to maintain control of the classroom knowledge flow, but which are often not appropriate ways of engaging students in science (e.g., Skamp, 1993; Woodbury, 1995). In a case study of a grade 4/5 teacher, Roth (1996) found that "the teacher's competence in questioning was related to her discursive competence in the subject-matter domain" (p. 709), but also noted the complex interaction of content knowledge and context. A naïve solution to this problem has been to demand that elementary teachers take more science content in their pre-service preparation. However, Roth noted that "subject-matter competence in and of itself was insufficient" (p. 731), and others (e.g., Morell & Carroll, 2003; Skamp & Mueller, 2001) have shown that more content knowledge, of itself, does not necessarily help teachers use strategies appropriate to recent reform initiatives (National Research Council, 1996). Schoon and Boone (1998) suggested that there may be key, fundamental misconceptions held by some elementary teachers, characteristic of a lack of understanding of foundational ideas in science, that particularly affect their self-efficacy. They suggested that misconceptions in other, more minor, ideas in science have less impact.

Even when science is taught in elementary classes, the way it is taught can be problematic. D. P. Newton and Newton (2000), for instance, concluded that there was little causal reasoning promoted in the science classes studied: "teachers' discourse was often largely confined to developing vocabulary and descriptive understandings of phenomena and situations. Often, there was little evidence of an oral press for causal understanding . . . with its persistent emphasis on reasoning, argument and explanation. The teachers who gave least time to causal questioning in their oral discourse also tended to be amongst those who did not provide a practical activity" (p. 607). Newton and Newton also noted that the more science studied in high school by the teacher, the greater the tendency for them to engage the students in causal reasoning. Such an emphasis in teaching conveys inappropriate views of the nature of science. Chinn and Malhotra (2002), for instance, argued that "the epistemology of many school inquiry tasks is *antithetical* to the epistemology of authentic science" (p. 175, emphasis in the original).

Teachers' perceptions of themselves as learners, of learning and of epistemology, also influence their teaching. For instance, Laplante (1997) reported that two grade 1 French immersion teachers tended to present science information from books during science lessons. The knowledge they presented was descriptive and anecdotal. Laplante attributed this to their epistemological beliefs about science. They saw themselves, and their students, as consumers of science, rather than inquirers in science. "They put scientists on a pedestal and consider them to be gifted with cognitive abilities they and their students do not possess" (p. 290). The tendency for elementary teachers to hold and convey inappropriate views of science has been noted by others (e.g., Watters & Ginns, 1997). These views are passed on to students. For example, grade 4 students saw science with "an inductivist, empiricist view of scientific inquiry, a view in which we approach knowledge of the world through an unbiased accumulation of data" (Varelas, Becker, Luster, & Wenzel, 2002, p. 867).

However, perceptions held by elementary teachers that they are somehow inadequate in doing and teaching science are unfounded. Harlen (1997) reported that, "[w]hat holds back teachers' understanding is not ability to grasp ideas but the opportunity to discuss and develop them" (p. 336). Indeed, Summers, Kruger, and Mant (1998), among many others, have reported how appropriate professional development can transform elementary teachers' science teaching practices. With appropriate professional development, teachers can make their own personal curriculum and pedagogical decisions for effective teaching of science and can even devise different pedagogical pathways for achieving the same learning goals for students (Kruger & Summers, 2000). However, not all teachers are able to make the same progress—not because of ability or lack of it, but because they tend to hold beliefs more or less consonant with reform moves (Levitt, 2001). Levitt categorized elementary teachers, after professional development in reform science, as being traditional, transitional (moving toward reform), or transformational (transformed their teaching to be consistent with reform initiatives). Their alignment with reform beliefs determined the extent to which their science teaching was reform-oriented.

Even if elementary teachers hold beliefs consistent with reform initiatives, they are not always able to make the transition to such teaching themselves. Ramos (1999) reported that most of the teachers she surveyed believed that constructivism was the best basis for teaching science but felt that external constraints prevented them from teaching this way. On the other hand, some teachers appear to be able to use their general pedagogical knowledge to teach science effectively (Kelly, Brown, & Crawford, 2000), despite limited knowledge and perceived constraints. Some use knowledge from other subjects: Flick (1995) reported how a teacher used language pedagogical skills to encourage discussion and exploration in science in a grade study of the solar system. Some teachers who teach science use constructivist principles such as eliciting children's ideas as a basis for their teaching, though their facility in doing this depends on their science content knowledge (Akerson, Flick, & Lederman, 2000). In their study, Akerson et al. (2000) described how the least-knowledgeable teacher of the three studied inhibited students' further sharing of ideas by the nature of her responses to the students. This, however, could be due to the fact that she was also a beginning teacher and had limited general pedagogical knowledge.

Given the incidence of science avoidance in the elementary school, it is tempting to attribute this to an anti-science attitude among teachers. However, even though many elementary teachers have limited science knowledge and avoid teaching it, Cobern and Loving (2002) reported that the teachers in their study were not "anti-science."

Making changes to the school and system context through, for example, proactive school leadership can change the teaching of elementary science in a school (Spillane, Diamond, Walker, Halverson, & Jita, 2001). In this study, school administrators successfully embarked on a deliberate process to develop the human capital within the school, with an emphasis on providing resources and improving pedagogy for science. Support from administrators and colleagues within the school as well as from personal friends/family has been identified as an important factor in helping even very capable beginning teachers to be effective in their own classroom teaching (Martinez, 1994).

The research into science teaching practices reveals a fairly depressing picture. A naïve reaction is to blame elementary teachers for not doing their job properly. However, the overwhelming majority are doing the best they can under the circumstances.

Gender Trends in Science

In the last decade, there have been relatively few studies on gender in elementary school science that give a new or different perspective (see Chapter 11 for a full discussion). Some studies show ongoing gendered preferences about science—boys toward science and physics, girls away from science and toward biology (Farenga & Joyce, 1997; Johnson, 1999; Stark & Gray, 1999). Liu and Lederman (2002) noted that girls' and boys' informal writing in science differed in both style and content. They concluded that "[g]irls seemed to personalize their knowledge more; they perceived science as a social activity involving fun and communication, appreciated the importance of science as a practical field, wrote in greater detail, and preferred to write about plants, animals, and topics relevant to their lives" (pp. 264–265). By contrast, "[b]oys' writing was condensed and formal, and contained the technical attributes normally ascribed to scientific writing. They also seemed to have a more imaginative perspective of science, to prefer informative tasks, and to write significantly more about technological applications in the physical sciences" (p. 365). It appears that socialization into such interests starts early, as parents give kindergarten girls three times as many opportunities to take part in biological activities than in physical science activities (Johnson, 1999). In a different vein, Warwick, Stephenson, and Webster (2003) reported that boys had greater difficulty expressing their understanding in writing than girls, but whether this is also a consequence of socialization is unknown. An apparent decline in boys' performance over recent years has generated controversy in the media and is an emergent research area.

Generalist/Specialist Science Teaching

One way of addressing difficulties generalists experience in teaching science is to appoint science specialists in elementary schools. However, there is limited research specifically focusing on specialist science teachers. Most reports that I have found tend to have a different research focus, such as professional development, and mention incidentally that the teacher was a specialist.

Specialists in science.   There are ambiguities in the literature in defining science specialists, as some label generalist teachers who take school leadership in science curriculum as specialists (Schwartz & Lederman, 2000; Spillane et al., 2001), some refer to generalists who have studied more science (e.g., D. P. Newton & Newton, 2000), and some think of those who take science exclusively (e.g., Owens, 2001). Those who take science exclusively also tend to be well qualified in science and elementary science and take curriculum leadership within the school for science (Schwartz & Lederman, 2000). I prefer this view of a science specialist, and call generalists who take some initiative in science, science curriculum leaders. Sometimes a school administration may deliberately invest resources in science by appointing a science specialist for the school. In some education systems, science specialists are appointed for middle school classes, but this is the exception rather than the rule.

Where specialists are appointed, it is important to choose the right people. Beeth (Beeth, 1998b; Beeth & Hewson, 1999) reported a study of an exemplar specialist teacher who achieved high-quality learning outcomes with her students. The teacher reportedly had considerable subject matter knowledge, excellent pedagogy, and extensive science pedagogical content knowledge. However, not all specialists fit this pattern. Owens (2001), for instance, had a specialist teacher in her sample of teachers who was not well qualified and held beliefs about using the textbook that were similar to those of many other generalist teachers. In fact, a generalist teacher who had the most pre-service and in-service experience in science was best able to use writing effectively within a broader inquiry framework. In this case, there was no advantage in this teacher being a specialist. In one of the few studies of any advantage in appointing science specialists, Schwartz and Lederman (2000) compared the views of science and teaching practices of elementary science specialists in grades 4 to 6 with generalist teachers' science teaching. They concluded that "elementary science specialists may be more 'effective' than elementary science teachers in implementing the reforms vision" (p. 191). Another study by Jones and Edmunds (2006) compared the effect on science in three different schools that employed specialists and science curriculum leaders. While the effect of a science curriculum leader was positive, science had a higher profile in the school where there was a specialist.

Turn teaching by generalists (swapping subjects)

In many schools there is usually little leadership support for science compared with mathematics and language arts. Leadership involvement tends to be limited to human and material resource allocation, not instructional leadership (Spillane et al., 2001). If any leadership is provided at all, it is left to classroom teachers acting as science curriculum leaders, who receive little acknowledgment or time release. These actions "reinforce the belief that science is not important" (p. 925).

A common occurrence is an informal arrangement between two or three teachers to divide subjects between them (Summers et al., 1998; Watters & Ginns, 1997), which I call turn teaching. That is, teachers who lack confidence in science may negotiate with more confident colleagues to teach their science for them. This is another form of science avoidance (Harlen, 1997).

THE ELEMENTARY SCIENCE CURRICULUM

Curriculum Influences

There are numerous influences on the curriculum that can be broadly categorized as cultural, systemic, and those internal to the teacher. Cultural influences include predominant views of science, teaching, learning, and schooling held by different community sectors, including students. Systemic influences include school traditions and practices; choices of instructional materials; and mandated curricula, standards, and testing regimes. Those internal to the teacher include aspects of teacher knowledge and self-confidence discussed above.

Cultural Influences

Research into cultural influences on the elementary science curriculum, apart from a focus on equity and "science for all," tends not to be published in mainstream science education journals. Nor have I found research into curriculum design for elementary science. Official curriculum documents issued by education systems tend to assume a "one size fits all" policy, regardless of the suitability of the curriculum for different cultural groups within their jurisdictions. Zubrowski (2002) argued for a different curriculum structure based on a social constructivist view of learning, situated cognition, but did not relate this specifically to cultural issues. In the special issue of *Journal of Research in Science Teaching* (volume 36, issue 3, 1999) on science education in developing countries, issues of curriculum and pedagogical appropriateness were raised. See also the special issues on culture and language (volume 38, issue 5, 2001) and on urban science education (volume 38, issues 8–10, 2001).

Views of "Best Practice" in Science Education

One of the few studies that considered different cultural groups was conducted by Hayes and Deyhle (2001). They suggested that notions of what science education is best for different cultural groups depend on differing views of what constitutes best practice in science education. Views of best practice are determined, in part, by cultural views of learning, teaching, and authority; available resources; and current practices.

Systemic Influences

Curriculum—scope, sequence and scheduling.   Very little has been researched in this area in recent years. Tytler and Peterson (2000) suggested that some topics in science, specifically evaporation, are too complex for young students, such as first-graders, to grasp, possibly because the necessary mental models require mastery of linguistic/conceptual tools not yet accessible to the students. Significantly, their data did not support the notion of "readiness" that is still prevalent in many early childhood settings.

There is a major implication of Nuthall's (1999) work for scheduling of science lessons in the elementary school. He found that for students to commit something to long-term memory, they need a minimum of three or four experiences with it. Furthermore, he found that a part of memory is used as a staging point before some experience is committed to long-term memory. He called this short-term memory, distinguishing it from traditional definitions of short-term memory in psychology. Significantly, memories of classroom experiences remain in this short-term memory for a maximum of two days before they are lost. By implication, to maximize student learning, science lessons (and/or homework or similar tasks) dealing with the same information need to be scheduled within two days of the previous lesson. In some education systems, science is officially scheduled for one to two hours per week, and the consequent common practice of timetabling one science class a week militates against effective science learning.

Types of Instructional Materials

Instructional materials used by elementary teachers consist of three main types: textbooks, teacher guides and resources, and supplementary materials for student use. Textbooks are common in countries such as the United States and Canada and tend to lead to heavy reliance on text reading and limited hands-on, inquiry teaching (Mastropieri & Scruggs, 1994). Teacher guides and the like, common in Britain, Australia, and New Zealand, are used as sources of activity ideas (Appleton, 2002; Appleton & Asoko, 1996). Supplementary materials such as trade books and newspapers are used generally either to supplement textbooks or activities that work, or as a basis for language-oriented science—a form of avoidance of hands-on science (Harlen, 1997).

Textbooks.   Mastropieri and Scruggs (1994) compared text-based curricula with activities-oriented curricula. They highlighted the limitations of textbooks and the advantages of hands-on activities. Texts "convey science content information through reading and interpretation of the printed word. This approach also reflects an emphasis on vocabulary learning and factual recall of text-based information . . . Activities . . . are almost exclusively paper-and-pencil tasks" (p. 82). In contrast, activities-oriented curricula depict "science as an ongoing process of exploration and discovery, rather than a content domain to be memorized. Tests . . . tend to be performance-based measures that assess student understanding of the unit's central concepts. Activities with real materials and apparatus replace paper-and-pencil activities" (p. 83). They also commented that both types of curricula require specific support for children with disabilities, though text-based curricula present particular problems for students with disabilities that influence reading ability.

In another examination of textbook elementary science, Chinn and Malhotra (2002) devised a way to analyze text-based inquiry tasks and compare them with authentic science. They concluded that "the inquiry activities in most textbooks capture few if any of the cognitive processes of authentic science" (p. 204) and that "school tasks may actually reinforce an unscientific epistemology" (p. 213). As part of this concern, they commented that textbook inquiry activities differed little from those included in other teacher resource materials, with recent innovative materials faring somewhat better: "our analysis of recent tasks developed by researchers shows that there is still room for improvement even in these outstanding, cutting-edge inquiry tasks" (p. 205). However, creative and effective use of textbooks is possible, as reported by Candela (1997).

Teacher resources.   Teacher resources can be published sets of materials or eclectic collections from a variety of sources. Published sets seem to be useful to experienced teachers, but not so useful to beginning teachers. Watters and Ginns (1997) told how a grade 4 teacher used *Primary Investigations* (Australian Academy of Science, 1994) as a resource and found it helpful, but Appleton and Kindt (1997) reported that, compared with more experienced teachers, beginning teachers tended to find the official teacher guides of limited use (Appleton, 2002). Note that when schools adopt *Primary Investigations*, they are expected to engage teachers in professional development in its use, whereas official curriculum guides are frequently distributed to teachers with limited or no professional development. Other studies have also highlighted how professional development associated with the use of teacher guides can result in effective science teaching (e.g., Appleton, 2003; Hunt & Appleton, 2003; Kruger & Summers, 2000).

Some publishers, particularly in the the United States, provide complete curriculum packages, including equipment, to accompany teacher guides. These "kit"-based materials, such as *Science and Technology for Children* (National Science Resources Centre, 2002), provide pedagogical ideas for teachers that are derived from research findings. Complete curriculum packages like this are seen as one way to minimize the difficulties experienced by elementary teachers trying to teach science. There is limited, current, independent research into the efficacy and cost-effectiveness of kit programs compared with other forms of curriculum and teacher support. This is a potentially fruitful area of research, particularly where policy direction may be needed for education systems. However, to influence policy, research designs would need to be carefully crafted.

Other resources.   Vaughan, Sumrall, and Rose (1998) reported how pre-service teachers, in-service teachers, and students all made effective use of newspapers to enhance science teaching/learning. Positive attitudes to their use were also reported, though they were found to be most effective in upper grades.

Nonfiction science books, usually called trade books, are another resource that teachers use—usually by having students do "research" into the current science topic. However, such trade books seldom focus on providing explanatory understandings (L. D. Newton, Newton, Blake, & Brown, 2002), which suits many elementary teachers' current practices.

Teacher Choice of Materials

Although the use of science textbooks is common practice in countries such as the United States and Canada, I found no studies about how teachers and schools make choices of texts to use. However, in countries such as Britain, Australia, and New Zealand, where teachers use a variety of resources, there have been a number of studies about resource selection (e.g., Appleton, 2002; Appleton & Asoko, 1996; Appleton & Kindt, 1997; L. D. Newton et al., 2002; Peacock & Gates, 2000), though only a few commented on how teachers made their choices. For instance, Appleton and Asoko (1996) reported that a teacher chose hands-on activities from resource materials, using criteria such as how manageable he thought activities would be in the classroom, whether they would teach the students something, and his perception of whether they would interest his students. As Appleton (2002) later elaborated, teachers chose such "activities that work," using these and further criteria, including whether equipment was readily available, whether there was a clear outcome or result from the activity, and the extent to which they lent themselves to integration (see below). How teachers select trade books was also the subject of a study by Peacock and Gates (2000). They reported that newly qualified teachers' selections of trade books "do not simply relate to problems of children's interaction with text, but also to teachers' perceptions of the demands placed on themselves" (p. 165). That is, they were mindful of work demands and classroom management issues. They further commented, "neither the nature and depth of the science content nor the quality of the representations of science concepts played a part in influencing their selection and use of text" (p. 165).

To explore how elementary teachers used supplementary material to their textbooks, David P. Butts, Koballa, Anderson, and Butts (1993) surveyed 125 primary (early grades) and 150 intermediate teachers over two years. They reported that some teachers supplement their textbook with other materials for alternative and additional instructional ideas:

> If teachers believe that science topics are of interest to their students and that these topics will help their students achieve goals in science that the teachers value and that are part of the expected curriculum, then teachers will find time to schedule the use of these materials with their students. The teachers' internal beliefs about what is beneficial for their students linked with the external constraints of their students' interests and the expected curriculum are the factors that govern a teachers use of instructional materials . . . teachers are not likely to use these resources if they believe that they do not fit the "gotta do's" of the expected curriculum. (p. 357)

Mandated Curricula, Standards, and Tests

Given that reform movements in elementary science education have been in progress in many countries for at least a decade, there has been limited research into how teachers are responding to these initiatives. Harlen (Harlen, 1997; Harlen & Holroyd, 1997) claimed that concerted efforts in in-service teacher education in England and Wales have resulted in some improvements in elementary science, though there is still a long way to go. In Australia, reports are beginning to emerge that show that, with extensive support, some teachers have successfully engaged with new elementary science curricula (e.g., Appleton, 2003; Hunt & Appleton, 2003; C. M. Peers & Watters, 2003). In the United States and other countries, there have been similar reports of success with helping teachers use more inquiry-based teaching (e.g., Fetters, Czerniak, Fish, & Shawberry, 2002). However, I have attended conferences such as AERA and NARST, where teachers also recount horrific stories of curriculum limitation, dispirited teachers, and jaded students constrained by so-called reform high-stakes testing regimes; but little of this has actually been published. Bianchini and Kelly (2003), in a study of the effects of the California standards, concluded that the standards were limiting curriculum and teacher flexibility. Lee and Houseal (2003) saw standards and benchmarks as an external constraint to effective science teaching. Given the limited research available, it seems that the implementation of benchmarks and testing regimes in some education systems is working against the very reform moves (National Research Council, 1996) that they are supposed to support. More research into the consequences of the reform initiatives on elementary science teaching and learning needs to be published.

Cross-Disciplinary Teaching

Cross-disciplinary teaching in science can take two forms: general science and teaching across disciplines. In general science, the traditional science disciplines are combined into science topics or themes, such as *Change*. Activities within a topic or theme may include identifiable components of traditional science disciplines, but these are subservient to the topic or theme. Arguments for general science in the elementary school tend to be based on notions of learning, curriculum philosophies, or curriculum constraints rather than research evidence of learning outcomes. Many instances of so-called general science, however, are really taught as traditional discipline strands with more contemporary names, such as "Natural and Processed Materials."

Teaching across disciplines, or, as it is more commonly called, curriculum integration, is a common feature of the elementary curriculum, particularly in some countries such as the United Kingdom, Australia, and New Zealand. Unfortunately, there is no consensus about what "integration" means (Hurley, 2001; Venville, Wallace, Rennie, & Malone, 2002), other than that some or all subjects are taught together or in association with each other in some way. In a meta-analysis of research into integration, Hurley identified five different categories (with specific reference to science and mathematics) that lie along a continuum ranging from sequential planning and teaching to the subjects being taught together in "intended equality" (p. 263). Venville et al. reported a number of similar categorizations in the literature but chose not to present their own findings as a continuum, "because of the implication that more integration is synonymous with better integration" (p. 76).

A common curriculum organization for integration has been the use of themes, like *The Sea*, or *Our Body*. Other organizers such as projects or problem solving have been suggested. However, I believe that such organizers do not readily fit the reform outcomes/standards-based science curricula that are now common. There consequently needs to be a more sustained research effort into reform-consistent integrated curricula that enhance science learning as well as learning in other subjects. This reflects the dilemma of curriculum approach conflicts noted by Venville et al. (2002), who published a recent review of research into integration from a science perspective.

Their review provides an excellent overview of research findings, so just a brief summary of their conclusions is presented here. After noting the variety of forms of integration, Venville et al. (2002) concluded that reasons for integrating subjects included epistemological, practical, and motivational arguments. Regarding the last, they raised the question of whether improved student engagement is necessarily a product of integration or some other variable such as better teaching. They also concluded that integration was "difficult to implement and maintain in school environments" because "integrated curricula challenge many aspects of established practices, rituals, beliefs and hierarchies of traditional school establishments" (pp. 76–77). In terms of student learning, integration provided benefits in motivation, interest, and development of higher order cognitive skills, at a cost of conceptual understanding of science (and other subject) content knowledge. Decisions to integrate were therefore difficult to justify from a traditional subject perspective, but could be justified from different philosophical or epistemological perspectives, such as humanism or holistic learning.

Research on integration of science with other subjects has tended to date to cluster around mathematics (Hurley, 2001; Pang & Good, 2000), language arts (Akerson & Young, 1998), and design technology (see below), with more isolated reference to science and other subjects such as art (e.g., Lach, Little, & Nazzaro, 2003), social studies (e.g., Buxton & Whatley, 2002), and physical education (e.g., Buchanan et al., 2002). A lot of published material on integration with particular subjects tends to focus on exhortations and arguments for integration, and ideas for how to do it, rather than research findings.

Integration with Mathematics

Reports of research into science and mathematics integration feature regularly in *School Science and Mathematics* (e.g., see the reviews by Hurley, 2001, and Pang & Good, 2000), a journal committed to encouraging such integration. In her meta-analysis, Hurley reported that, compared with traditional instruction, student achievement in science tended to be greatest when science and mathematics were more fully integrated. However, achievement in mathematics was more limited.

Integration with Language

Much has been written about the integration of science with language and, in particular, about the potential benefits for science achievement. This is such a central issue that a chapter has been devoted to the topic in this volume (see Chapter 3), so is not discussed further here.

Integration with (Design) Technology

There are three approaches to science and technology integration:

- Equal emphases on science and technology. Jane and Jobling (1995) described an integrated science/technology unit in grade 5. Benefits included high levels of engagement and metacognition, and integration of learning outcomes.

- Emphasis on technology. Ritchie and Hampson (1996) described an inter-linked science and technology unit, where the main focus was technology. Some science was apparently also learned, though the report did not document what.
- Science through technology. Technology as a way of accessing science was described by Benenson (2001) and Roth (2001). That is, science was taught through technology.

Information Technology

Information technology (IT) (that is, computers and the like) has been used as a pedagogical aid in elementary science (see also Chapter 17). Research reports usually recount how IT has been used to support science teaching and include an evaluation. Sometimes a contemporary theoretical stance, such as conceptual change theory or writing to learn, is adopted; sometimes there is no clear theoretical base. Evaluations vary considerably in what is evaluated and in the degree of rigor of the evaluation. IT use in elementary science tends to fall into the categories of email (Jarvis, Hargreaves, & Comber, 1997), the world wide web (Mistler & Songer, 2000), computer tutorials (Biemans, Deel, & Simons, 2001; Shimoda, White, & Frederiksen, 2002; Williams & Linn, 2002), computer tools such as word processing and publishing (Nason, Lloyd, & Ginns, 1996), and computer simulations (Barnett & Morran, 2002; Raghavan, Sartoris, & Glaser, 1998).

ASSESSMENT IN ELEMENTARY SCIENCE

Assessment in science has come under considerable scrutiny in recent years (see Chapter 32). There were two notable research projects (Bell & Cowie, 2001a, 2001b; Black, Harrison, Lee, Marshall, & Wiliam, 2002) and a comprehensive discussion (Fraser & Tobin, 1998) on classroom assessment in science worth mentioning, even though they did not exclusively focus on the elementary school. A major study of formative assessment in grades 7–10 science was reported by Bell and Cowie (1997, 2001a, 2001b). The other, by Black and associates (Black et al., 2002), looked at assessment more generally. Both studies included the effect of teacher professional development in assessment.

Formative Assessment

Teachers use formative assessment to gauge students' initial conceptions prior to teaching, their developing understandings, and progress toward learning goals, and to obtain feedback about their teaching to inform future teaching decisions (Bell & Cowie, 1997, 2001a). Others have highlighted that identifying elementary students' pre-instructional conceptions is an important part of formative assessment and is essential for deciding on subsequent pedagogy (e.g., Summers et al., 1998; Turner, 1997). Specific techniques, often adapted from research, have been used to elicit students' conceptions prior to and during a pedagogical sequence. These include concept maps (Stoddart, Abrams, Gasper, & Canaday, 2000), interviews (Turner, 1997), and drawings (Edens & Potter, 2003). Another technique for eliciting preconceptions involved showing students a cartoon illustrating a science phenomenon, in which several students commented on what they thought would happen, or why it was happening (Keogh & Naylor, 1999). Students were asked to discuss the ideas presented and decide which idea might be better. These concept cartoons, as they were called, were found to be useful for identifying student conceptions and initiating subsequent student investigation sequences.

Others have advocated identifying students' conceptions as part of the normal pedagogical sequence rather than using a specific technique prior to commencing teaching. Pedagogical approaches discussed below that do this include the 5Es (Blank, 2000), KWHL (Iwasyk, 1997), and the interactive approach (Chin & Kayalvizhi, 2002; van Zee, Iwasyk, Kurose, Simpson, & Wild, 2001; Watts, Barber, & Alsop, 1997). A more general inquiry approach incorporating several investigative techniques embedded in pedagogical sequences was outlined by van Zee et al. (2001). Another strategy reported by Palmer (1995) was POE (Predict, Observe, Explain). Students' predictions about what would happen in a particular scenario and their explanations for why they made the prediction provided insights into their initial conceptions.

A caution was sounded by McGinn and Roth (1998), which was also reflected in the study by Jones, Carter, and Rua (2000), that strategies used to elicit students' conceptions influence what is revealed of students' ideas. That is, different strategies/ techniques reveal different aspects of students' ideas. It is therefore unwise to over-rely on one specific technique for eliciting students' ideas, especially in research.

Self-Assessment

Self-assessment has not been a major focus of elementary science research. Stow (1997) described grade 4/5 students using concept maps as a self-assessment tool. Benefits included motivation (on seeing learning growth, but dependent on success-ful completion of concept maps) and metacognition, in that "children . . . analyse[d] their own thinking, enabling them to identify their strengths and weaknesses and set themselves future learning targets" (p. 15).

Summative Assessment

Traditionally, summative assessment has not been strongly emphasized in elemen-tary science. When it has been conducted, teachers have often used end-on written tests that focus on recall, or students' recordings in science notebooks. There has been, however, a trend toward conceptual learning and therefore assessment of stu-dents' science understanding (Harlen, 1998). External, benchmarked testing has been a relatively recent occurrence that has stimulated some teachers into examin-ing their own assessment practices. Many elementary teachers need considerable help in moving toward more effective assessment practices, particularly those that focus on conceptual learning.

An important principle recently advocated in assessment has been that assess-ment tasks must be authentic—that is, they should relate to the real world of the student in a meaningful way (Gitomer & Duschl, 1998; Kamen, 1996). With the no-tion of authenticity, there is the idea that assessment should be embedded as part of the pedagogy rather than tacked on at the end of a unit of work (Kamen, 1996). That is, some formative assessment can be used effectively for summative purposes (Bell & Cowie, 1997, 2001a) and documented with the use of a system such as portfolios (Gitomer & Duschl, 1998). However, change in assessment practices cannot occur in isolation from other aspects of pedagogy and teachers' views of teaching and learning. As Kamen noted, "real reform for a teacher's practice comes from a deep understanding of conceptually based science learning" (p. 875).

Assessment Techniques/Strategies

Traditional pen-and-paper tests, especially multiple-choice tests, are not necessarily the best way of ascertaining students' understanding in science. For instance, Nuthall and Alton-Lee (1995) found that students used a variety of strategies to answer test questions in science and social studies, including recall and deducing answers from related knowledge and experience. Totaled scores from such tests were not necessarily considered a measure of the students' learning. Regarding multiple-choice tests, Kamen (1996) concluded that, "[i]n many cases it is asking too much of a fourth-grade student to read a question about a difficult concept, read several answers written by someone else, and choose another person's best answer" (p. 869).

McGinn and Roth (1998) compared different assessment strategies with grade 6/7 students' understandings about levers, showing that students' responses varied according to the strategy and context. That is, the students' learning was context-dependent in a situated cognition sense. They noted that the students relied heavily on available resources in giving explanations for novel situations. Generalizations, they suggested, come after "individuals have great familiarity with a large number of contexts" (p. 829). They too were critical of standard pen-and-paper tests and suggested varied assessment techniques that contribute to the compilation of portfolios. Tytler (1998) also commented about situation-specific conceptions developed by students. This was further supported by Raghavan et al. (1998), who commented on how the assessment question used in their study showed the context-specific nature of learning. Students understood buoyancy in liquids, but some had not transferred this to fluids (balloons in air).

Jones, Carter, et al. (2000) also reported how different assessment techniques elicited different types of knowledge. Concept maps elicited pre-instructional schemas, multidimensional scaling and card sorting elicited conceptual organization for clusters of concepts, and interviews and class dyad discourse elicited processes and prior knowledge used in interpreting experiences. Choosing the most appropriate assessment techniques for the teaching/learning context is therefore critical.

Other summative assessment techniques and strategies reported include concept cartoons used by teachers for summative assessment (Keogh & Naylor, 1999) and concept maps. Stoddart et al. (2000) developed a system of analyzing concept maps for assessment purposes, using a rubric to quantify the quality of understanding demonstrated by the student in a concept map.

A Final Caution

Summative assessment is frequently in a written form, but there are some reports of gendered differences in using this medium. For example, Warwick et al. (2003) noted that boys, especially those in grade 7, had difficulty expressing their understanding in written form compared with the understanding evidenced in their speech. Boys therefore may under-perform in written assessment tasks, compared with girls, even though their understanding may be similar.

PEDAGOGY FOR LEARNING IN SCIENCE

Pedagogy that leads to conceptual learning has been a dominant focus in research into elementary science teaching. This has arisen from the misconceptions research of the previous decade, the pre-eminence of constructivist views of learning, and reform movements such as the National Science Education Standards (National Research Council, 1996). There has been limited research into affective learning, despite theoretical views and research that recognize that affect and cognition are closely intertwined (e.g., Varelas et al., 2002).

Inquiry

I have included inquiry because it is a key component of the U.S. standards (National Research Council, 1996) and because the term is used widely in the literature. However, there is considerable overlap with other sections in this chapter and other chapters in this *Handbook* (see Chapter 27), especially those dealing with specific strategies like the learning cycle (Parker, 2000). A difficulty is that there is no consensus on what constitutes inquiry, apart from attempts to define it in the standards—perhaps because it is a term that has been used extensively for many years. I personally find the notion of *working scientifically*, described in most Australian curricula (Curriculum Corporation, 1994), to be preferable. There is a close link between inquiry and the nature of science (see Chapter 28).

Butts and associates (D. P. Butts, Hofman, & Anderson, 1993, 1994), in their studies, demonstrated that hands-on experiences, of themselves, are insufficient to develop understandings in 5/6-year-olds. Specific pedagogical sequences involving exploration and discussion of ideas, "instructional conversations," are also needed. Nor does mere engagement in inquiry ensure that students will learn about the nature of science (Khishfe & Abd-El-Khalick, 2002). An explicit, reflective focus on the nature of science needs to be included as part of the inquiry pedagogy for this to occur. However, this may be a cultural phenomenon, as Liu and Lederman (2002) found that gifted grade 7 Taiwanese students "appeared to have basic understandings on several aspects of NOS . . . [Even though] science is largely taught by delivering scientific facts written in textbooks as absolute knowledge" (p. 120).

Meyer and Woodruff (Meyer & Woodruff, 1997; Woodruff & Meyer, 1997) reported that students aged 8–13 engaged in generating explanations with a form of inquiry called "consensually driven explanations." Students conducted activities and then discussed ideas/explanations in small groups; then these groups shared and justified their explanations (undergoing several cycles). Meyer and Woodruff saw this as a process of socially constructed knowledge-building.

An important part of inquiry is that the teacher is clear about the conceptual learning goals. Flick (1995) commented on how a grade 4 teacher taught inquiry with a conceptual focus, starting with students' ideas and building on these. This included her clear identification of what she wanted the students to learn. This is consistent with the research reported by Nuthall (2001).

Inquiry in the form of research-based projects is a common strategy (Nason et al., 1996), but there are uncertainties about its effectiveness (Nuthall, 1999, 2001). The learning tends to be superficial (Moje, Collazo, Carrillo, & Marx, 2001) and, according to Nason and associates, not conducive to conceptual learning, because the students focus on completing the project and therefore use superficial processing strategies. Furthermore, where students divide aspects of the task, Nuthall reports that the students only learn about the part of the task that they concentrated on, even though there may be in-group and whole-class sharing of findings.

The recent trends toward inquiry, conceptual learning, and standards have tended to cause teachers to scaffold or carefully structure lessons to maximize learning of target concepts. A cautionary note about highly structured pedagogy, however, was sounded by Tomkins and Tunnicliffe (2001), who found that, at least in some topics, sustained periods of undirected observation may later help students when formal instruction commences. This is consistent with constructivist views of learning.

Conceptual Change

The notion of conceptual change had its origins in the misconceptions research that reached its heyday during the 1980s. It emerged initially as a cognitive conflict-based teaching strategy specifically designed to address the perceived problem of students developing misconceptions (e.g., Hewson, 1981). Subsequent research led to doubts about the efficacy of such strategies, leading to reconsiderations of the notion of conceptual change. Limón (2001) provided a comprehensive review of conceptual change research, and Chapter 2 in this *Handbook* also review the area. Georghiades (2000), among others, has taken the argument beyond cognitive conflict, suggesting that a more appropriate focus would be the transfer and durability of scientific concepts, through metacognition (also see Hewson, Beeth, & Thorley, 1998). Limón outlined three ways of initiating conceptual change that have been reported: cognitive conflict, sharing and justifying ideas, and using models and analogies. I would add a fourth: scaffolding a series of learning experiences that may include a mix of these and other activities (Appleton, 1997). A discussion of these four categories is used to structure the remainder of this section.

Cognitive Conflict

Cognitive conflict originated in the Piagetian idea of disequilibrium (Piaget, 1978). Although comparative studies of teaching strategies based largely on cognitive conflict still occasionally surface, researchers over the last decade have realized the inadequacy of the strategy and have tended to include other teaching and learning experiences as well. Summarizing the situation in the special issue of *Learning and Instruction*, Caravita (2001) said that "cognitive conflict, although not disproved as the main condition producing reorganization of knowledge, is no longer seen as the result of crucial experience. It is considered as dependent on many psychological and personal factors that the instructional intervention can only partially address and control in the classroom" (p. 428).

There has also been discussion about whether misconceptions are consistent theories held by students, or are context-dependent, and therefore whether conceptual change entails major restructuring of schema. Tytler (1998) concluded that conceptual change is not necessarily a change of consistent theories, but that conceptions tend to be context-dependent and can sit alongside each other. He suggested that, because "the extension of a generalizable conception to new phenomena can involve significant difficulties related to the way situation-specific factors cue particular concepts . . . conceptual change should be viewed as a case-by-case phenomenon rather than an adjustment in mental structure" (p. 922), but this would depend on what is meant by "mental structure." For instance, the neo-Piagetian idea of minitheories suggested by Claxton (1990) would be consistent with Tytler's conclusion. Tytler also noted that older children are better at extending generalizations.

Small-Group Interaction—Sharing Ideas

In contrast to the notion that cognitive conflict is necessary for conceptual change, researchers following a more social constructivist theoretical position suggest that students sharing ideas in science is a critical part of conceptual change, or, as most of these researchers would prefer, conceptual development. For instance, Carter, Jones, and Rua (2003) suggested that giving explanations to a group partner may affect students' cognitive growth. Weaver (1996) concluded that hands-on activities combined with discussion and reflection can promote conceptual change and that learning is enhanced if students find the topics interesting and relevant to their daily lives or experience. Most reports about students sharing ideas have it as one component in a sequence of other experiences (see scaffolded instruction below). For instance, Meyer and Woodruff (Meyer & Woodruff, 1997; Woodruff & Meyer, 1997) incorporated into their pedagogical scaffold small-group work directed toward students' deriving a consistent explanation of experiences. Mutual co-construction of explanations was a key component that they claimed mirrored discourse by scientists. Barnett and Morran (2002) also described a curriculum that scaffolded grade 5 students' learning about the Earth-Moon system, using a structured sequence of activities that included opportunities for students to present their understandings to peers during class discussions and students reflecting on their own learning progress. They believed that "conceptual understanding is an evolutionary process that emerges from a complex interplay between prior understanding and the context in which learning occurs" (p. 860; see also diSessa & Minstrell, 1998). Similar approaches have been suggested by others (e.g., Beeth, 1998b; Carter et al., 2003; Fellows, 1994; Mason, 2001; Meyer & Woodruff, 1997; Woodruff & Meyer, 1997).

In mechanics, a quasi-experimental design with grade 5 students was used to explore the role of small-group interaction in conceptual change (Vosniadou, Ioannides, Dimitrakopoulou, & Papademetriou, 2001). They attributed the significant conceptual gains that they observed in the experimental group to "complex changes in . . . class dialogue . . . when the students are explaining their point of view, or when the teacher is obliged to explain what he means because these [sic] is no established common language between him and the children . . . [and] when the teacher uses empirical observations to lead children to induce theoretical abstractions" (p. 417). They referred to these processes as "negotiation of meaning" (p. 417) between teacher and students,, and between students. Whether this is possible with younger students, such as first-graders, is not so clear. Shepardson (1996) reported how a grade 1 teacher appeared to hold views that her students could not engage in this type of activity, preferring to have them engage in activities that encouraged individual work, even though they were seated in small groups. Her interactions with the students also tended to be with individuals, rather than with groups. Her discourse with students focused on observations, thinking, science ideas, and terminology, rather than developing understanding. Whether the teacher's view reflected her own perceptions of her students' capability or what they were actually capable of is consequently unclear. Other studies (see below) suggest that young students are capable of developing understanding of science ideas.

Students giving explanations to peers in small groups needs careful consideration, as this may lead to rote learning by less able pupils who defer to those they see as more capable (Nuthall, 1999) or result in disrupted learning from some students' inability to negotiate their way through peer interactions during group work (Nuthall, 2001; see below).

Models and Analogies

There is convincing evidence that, when used appropriately, analogies can enhance learning (e.g., Yanowitz, 2001). In another example, Heywood and Parker (1997) concluded that "combining, building on, moving between analogies and rigorous examination of ideas through practical activity enhances learning" (p. 882). However, they warned that the purposes of analogies may be perceived differently, depending on participants' views of learning in science, and that to be useful, the limitations of analogies must be recognized by participants.

Analogies and models can be teacher generated or student generated. Examples of effective teacher analogies used in elementary science include the following:

- Thorley and Woods (1997) described a specialist grade 5 teacher's conceptual change unit on electricity. A key component was student construction and evaluation of mental models. They concluded that analogies were valuable in helping students articulate "diffuse" theories about electricity.
- Barnett and Morran (2002) used computer models for the Earth-Moon system.
- Summers et al. (1998) reported how grade 7 students found a bicycle chain analogy for electric circuits helpful.
- Glynn and Takahashi (1998) used a text and graphic-based analogy of a cell (factory) to help grade 8 and 6 students successfully learn the functions of a cell.

Examples of encouraging the generation of student analogies include the following:

- Raghavan et al. (1998) had grade 6 students construct and test their own models of floating and sinking, using computer software.
- Penner, Giles, Lehrer, and Schauble (1997) described how grade 1–2 children constructed models of elbows. A design pedagogy was used so students could see for themselves the limitations of modeling. Penner et al. also discussed the application of the pedagogy to learning about the nature of science (specifically, modeling in science).

- Students' model building can take several other forms. Students in grades 4 and 5 who constructed their own drawings of ideas extracted from an explanatory text showed better conceptual understanding than those who copied an illustration and those who wrote a summary (Edens & Potter, 2003). Similarly, Gobert and Clement (1999) found that grade 5 students generating diagrams while reading expository text about plate tectonics reached a better understanding than those who merely read the text or who wrote summaries, even though the summaries contained more references to domain-specific information than the diagrams. Tomkins and Tunnicliffe (2001) highlighted the usefulness of students generating their own "mental models" from investigations, discussions, and reflective diaries when making predictions.

The effective use of analogies requires particular care in the development of appropriate pedagogy. For instance, Heywood and Parker (1997), who explored students' understanding of analogies of electricity, concluded that the base of the analogy must be within the students' experience for them to understand the target idea. Shepardson, Moje, and Kennard-McClelland (1994) highlighted how fifth-grade students had difficulty relating an experimental analogy on air pressure (a boiled egg being pushed into a milk bottle by air pressure) to their study of the weather. Boulter, Prain, and Armitage (1998), who reported a study of a Moon eclipse by 9–11-year-olds, commented on how students need to understand the characteristics of a model for its use to be effective:

> [A]n individual would need an understanding of what a model is, an understanding of how analogies are formed and evaluated, and a knowledge of existing conceptual models in the same or other field. The evidence is that an understanding of these notions of model is slow to develop (Grosslight et al. 1991), that many people have little idea either of what the process of drawing an analogy involves or of what other models are already available (Duit 1991). (pp. 493–494)

Furthermore, Abell and Roth (1995), in a study of grade 5 students' learning about trophic relations in a terrarium community, emphasized that it is important for students to construct their own representations, such as diagrams and analogies, before the scientific model is presented.

Scaffolded Instruction (cf. Inquiry)

Scaffolded instruction is based on the idea of cognitive development rather than cognitive change. All scaffolds begin with establishment of the students' pre-instructional conceptions and use a sequence of learning experiences that build on these ideas, usually helping students specifically consider how their ideas stand up to the evidence from investigations, the ideas of others, and scientific thinking (e.g., Abell & Roth, 1995). There also should be a focus on helping students clarify their learning goals and take ownership of their learning. For instance, Summers et al. (1998) told how a grade 7 teacher who had received intensive professional development used an effective scaffolding strategy by drawing on most of these principles. Fellows (1994, p. 999) concluded that the activities chosen must "directly relate to [the students'] initial conceptions and goal conceptions." However, scaffolded learning experiences that build on students' initial conceptions do not necessarily ensure success. For instance, Brickhouse (1994) reported limited learning of shadow phenomena with a grade 3 class, in a study of light and shadows. The pedagogical sequence was devised collaboratively by the classroom teacher and a Curriculum Development Lab researcher and was taught by both. Given the expertise that went into the planning and delivery of the unit, the issue of what might be the most effective scaffolds for particular target understandings and initial conceptions, and how teachers can make appropriate choices between competing pedagogical ideas, is a major one. This is related to the teacher's science pedagogical content knowledge, and it highlights questions of how elementary teachers with limited science PCK can teach most effectively, how science PCK is communicated to other teachers, and the extent to which teacher guides and professional development can help teachers extend their science PCK (Appleton, 2006).

Making appropriate pedagogical choices is important. For instance, Shepardson (1997) highlighted how the pedagogy and experiences provided to students determine what they learn. He suggested that planning with the "bigger conceptual picture" in mind was necessary, and specific attention needs to be drawn to aspects of the object of study on which conceptual understandings can be built. This is problematic when many elementary teachers do not have a clear idea of what the bigger picture looks like and may not have a clear idea of what the students need to attend to.

An important consideration is that the scaffold must both link several lessons and structure the detail of each lesson. Appleton (1997, 2002) emphasized that "units that work" are necessary to adequately employ constructivist strategies. This is supported by Nuthall's (1999) work on student learning. Using carefully structured learning experiences to encourage active engagement by students in thinking about activities was also advocated by D. P. Butts et al. (1993, 1994).

Different *types* of scaffold, discussed below, are required to sequence lessons in a unit, sequence detail within a lesson, and make decisions about moment-by-moment lesson transactions.

Scaffolding units of work by sequencing experiences and lessons.   Appleton (2002) suggested that there needs to be a focus on units that work that include a scaffolded lesson sequence (see, for example, Appleton, 1993; Huber & Moore, 2001). Examples such as the interactive approach are discussed below. Although cognitive conflict per se is no longer considered adequate to generate conceptual change, discrepant events that generate this have been a suggested component of a scaffolded sequence of lessons, usually as the initial lesson (e.g., Appleton, 1995; Meyer & Woodruff, 1997).

Scaffolding strategies and experiences within lessons.   Scaffolded sequences may include experiences such as students

- expressing and supporting their ideas,
- making and testing hypotheses and predictions,
- investigating in small groups,
- comparing ideas, giving scientific explanations and suggesting models, and
- presenting and debating ideas and conclusions in the whole class (Vosniadou et al., 2001).

Teacher demonstrations and explanations can also be used effectively (Shepardson et al., 1994).

Scaffolding lesson transactions.   Moment-by-moment interactions with students involve questioning, probing ideas, giving explanations, and the like (Appleton, 1997). This is a direct application of a teacher's science PCK (Appleton, 2006).

Other components of a scaffold.   Student writing can be another important component of a scaffold (see also the section on writing). In a grade 5 conceptual change unit on electricity taught by a specialist teacher, students constructed and evaluated mental models (Thorley & Woods, 1997). Students first wrote explanations and then discussed them. Thorley and Woods commented, "it was not uncommon for [the students] to change their ideas in mid-discussion. Talking allowed them the opportunity to reassess what they had written and often produced a change in their perception of the problem, concept, or definition" (p. 241).

Teacher questioning can also play a critical role (Harlen, 1998). Beeth (1998b; Beeth & Hewson, 1999) reported how a highly effective teacher used a scaffold of questions to help students think about their activity work and relate it to their existing and developing ideas. The questions, which have a metacognitive emphasis, were

1. Can you state your own ideas?
2. Can you talk about why you are attracted to your ideas?
3. Are your ideas consistent?
4. Do you realise the limitations of your ideas and the possibility they might need to change?
5. Can you try to explain your ideas using physical models?
6. Can you explain the difference between understanding an idea and believing in an idea?
7. Can you apply intelligible and plausible to your own ideas? (Beeth, 1998b, p. 1093).

Three assertions about using teacher questions were made by van Zee et al. (2001):

- "We elicited student thinking by asking questions that develop conceptual understanding" (p. 176), in order to elicit students' experiences (e.g., "What can you tell me about the moon?" [p. 177]), and diagnose and further refine students' ideas (e.g., "What is your evidence for that idea?" [p. 177]).
- "We elicited student thinking by asking students to make their meanings clear, to explore various points of view in a neutral and respectful manner, and to monitor the discussion and their own thinking" (p. 178).
- "We elicited student thinking by practicing quietness as well as reflective questioning" (p. 181), that is, by using wait time, listening to students, providing information only as needed, and encouraging students to think things out for themselves.

Scaffolded student material.   Scaffolds have been constructed with the use of written materials and/or information technology. Sneider and Ohadi (1998) reported on teachers' use of an astronomy unit (Great Explorations in Math and Science) in grades 4–5 and 7–8, with a scaffolded pedagogy embedded in the written materials used by students. Teachers were provided professional development to support their teaching. There was evidence of considerable conceptual learning in students. In another study, a curriculum designed to scaffold (my term) grade 5 students' learning about the Earth-Moon system by a carefully structured sequence of activities incorporated "class discussions, whole and small group activities, individual activities, and three-dimensional (3-D) dynamic computer models" (Barnett & Morran, 2002, p. 859). The computer models were designed to develop understandings and build on what students already knew so they could relate new ideas to existing ones and experiences. Biemans et al. (2001) also reported the use of a computer-based scaffold for activating students' prior knowledge and supporting conceptual change as they processed expository text.

A Final Caveat on Scaffolding

Scaffolding has become a popular notion in elementary science education, for many good reasons. For instance, it emerges from social constructivist views of learning that are almost universally supported, and there is research evidence that a scaffold used appropriately can enhance student achievement. However, when a scaffold is so directive that it inhibits learning for some students, there may be a problem. Warwick et al. (2003) raised this issue with respect to scaffolded writing in science used to enhance procedural understanding: "the question of 'scaffold or straightjacket' is an important one, particularly for higher ability pupils" (p. 184). Tomkins and Tunnicliffe (2001) also cautioned against the teacher being so intent and goal directed, that he/she does not listen to students and give them intellectual space: "If teachers take a less instrumental attitude to what is learned and allow a longer gestation time for considered pupil observation and familiarization, it may be conducive to allowing hypotheses to emerge more naturally. We assert that much of this 'pupil talk' or 'diary reflection', which is seemingly inconsequential, is in fact of considerable learning value" (p. 811). More research is needed on the nature and effectiveness of scaffolds for all students for units of work, lessons, and lesson interactions.

Metacognition

A different emphasis on conceptual change not included in Caravita's (2001) categorization has been made by a number of others, who have drawn on the notion of metacognition as an aid to conceptual change. Beeth (1998a) reported how a metacognitive emphasis on the perceived status of ideas, using the notions of intelligibility and plausibility (Hewson & Thorley, 1989), can aid learning (see also Beeth, 1998b; Beeth & Hewson, 1999). Others (such as Blank, 2000; Hewson et al., 1998) have also supported a metacognitive emphasis in pedagogy. A relevant series of studies on metacognition in the junior high school, the Project to Enhance Effective Learning (PEEL) (e.g., Mitchell & Mitchell, 1997), has been omitted from this review.

Writing

Writing is usually considered a complementary component to other pedagogies in elementary science and is frequently implemented in conjunction with students sharing ideas. This area has been extensively reported in the literature and is discussed in Chapter 3 of this volume. Writing, however, is an important part of the elementary school curriculum; so selected aspects of this research are touched on in this chapter. It is taken as a given that writing, used appropriately, may enhance students' conceptual learning in science. The reader may also wish to consult a comprehensive review of writing in science compiled by Rowell (1997) and the special issue of *Journal of Research in Science Teaching*.

Writing Is Difficult for Pupils

Warwick, Linfield, and Stephenson (1999) reported that elementary school students find it easier to express science understandings verbally than in writing, partially because they and teachers have different purposes in speaking and writing. Providing more structure for students' writing tasks in science can help (see also Warwick et al., 2003, below). Patterson (2001) described ways to scaffold students' science writing during different aspects of writing and added to the claims that writing enhances understanding:

> [f]or pupils at the early stages of literacy development, this research has demonstrated that support at the sentence level, through the provision of appropriate sentence connectives, can transform writing from descriptions and statements of facts to that which includes explanation. . . . Support at the text level is beneficial to pupils who are proficient at structuring sentences, but have difficulties organising their ideas into extended pieces of scientific writing. Context mapping has been shown to be an effective scaffold during the drafting stage of writing. (pp. 15–16)

In an attempt to help African American students engage more meaningfully with writing in science, Varelas et al. (2002) described a strategy that encouraged students to use genres familiar to them, such as rap songs and plays, instead of the more formal school science genres. They concluded that the strategy provided such students with an effective discourse genre that helped them construct meaning for the phenomena under study, but did not provide them with facility in scientific discourse.

Science Notebooks

Science notebooks are used extensively in elementary schools in my state, Queensland, Australia. In my numerous discussions with elementary students, many have told me that they dislike science because of the large amount of writing that they have to do. This often constitutes copying notes (frequently using headings like "Aim, Equipment, Procedure, Results, Conclusions") from the chalkboard into their science notebooks. No wonder they are bored! If this entrenched tradition of science notebooks must continue, they need to be used more effectively for student learning. Even where notebooks are constructed by students themselves, they do not necessarily enhance learning. For instance, Baxter, Bass, and Glaser (2001) examined students' notebook recording of work on electric circuits in three grade 5 classes in two schools. Videotapes of lessons were also taken. No written feedback was given to students about their writing. They found that recording in notebooks "gave little indication of the quality of student thinking or understanding" (p. 138). Not surprisingly, what the students recorded in their notebooks was dependent on the classroom context: specifically, the teachers' directions and what the teacher attended to. Their conclusion was that

> [w]e found that aspects of science instruction that teachers attend to (procedures, results) appear in some detail in students' notebooks, but the use of data recording as a platform for thoughtful reflection, hypothesis generating, and the synthesis of ideas was generally absent. Teachers use notebooks to monitor what students are doing, and students, when prompted by their teachers, use the notebooks to remind them of what they have done. (p. 138)

Similarly, other aspects of the classroom context that influence writing were reported in a study where students accessed a variety of written sources (Shepardson & Britsch, 2001). The students' journal writing was influenced by the available science texts.

Student-centered notebooks, also reported by others (Caswell & Lamon, 1998; Shepardson & Britsch, 2001; Tomkins & Tunnicliffe, 2001), can be effective if used by students as research journals to record their thinking and ideas. Usually, text is accompanied by students' drawings, diagrams (Edens & Potter, 2003), or concept maps. Computers may also be used to aid writing. In such writing tasks, consideration needs to be given to the age of the students, both in terms of their writing capability and in the ways that they interact with the world. For instance, Shepardson and Britsch (2001) described how young students contextualized their science experiences by relating to three different "worlds" or mental contexts: a) imagination, b) previous experience, and c) the science investigation itself. Although imaginative play is considered a legitimate component of informal early childhood classes, it is not usually endorsed in formal schooling, where the teacher's focus tends to be on the science investigation. Older students seem to be better attuned to the expectations of the teacher. For example, when older students were left to their own devices during a science investigation, they recorded observations including anatomical and behavioral features of animals (Tomkins & Tunnicliffe, 2001). That is, if students are familiar with a teacher-classroom culture, it is unnecessary to provide a "tight" scaffold for writing, especially in the early phases of a unit. Building on work by Gott and Duggan (1995), Warwick et al. (2003) used writing frames embedded in worksheets as prompts for grade 4, 6, and 7 students when planning investigations and recording results. They took a particular focus on teaching students about the use of evidence in drawing conclusions. The frames were varied to suit the age group. Examples of frames are (pp. 176–177):

- We are trying to find out. . . (gr. 4)
- We made the test fair by. . . (gr. 4)
- These results tell me that. . . (gr. 4)
- By carrying out these measurements we are able to find the connection between . . . and . . . (gr. 6)
- My results are accurate and reliable because. . . (gr. 7)

Warwick and associates (2003) concluded that discussion and collaboration focusing on the prompts in the frames were necessary for them to be effective—the worksheets could not just be handed to students. Furthermore, they concluded that,

> [i]t is therefore essential for the teacher to:
> - have a clear understanding of the objectives of the lesson;
> - share both the learning objectives and the assessment criteria for the session with the pupils;
> - be clear, in the structure of any writing frame, about which concepts of evidence are to be focused upon;
> - understand his/her role in scaffolding the pupils' experience through use of the writing frame; and
> - understand the central importance of social interaction to learning, and therefore to encourage pupil-pupil and pupil-teacher collaboration. (p. 182)

Even though the studies by Warwick et al. (2003) and Tomkins and Tunnicliffe (2001) differed in the degree of scaffold/support provided to students, a common component was the use of writing as a reflective tool, in which discussion played a major part.

Teacher Feedback

It is commonly accepted that the teacher should provide written feedback on elementary students' writing in science, but this presents potential difficulties for both teachers and students. Owens (2001) studied the written feedback that four grade 4/5 teachers gave to three pieces of grade 5 student writing in science. One teacher was a science specialist. Owens reported that:

- No two teachers defined or used science writing in the same ways.
- Most teachers found responding to science writing to be a frustrating process.
- All of the teachers assumed the students could read and write non-fiction science paragraphs and were uncomfortable with evidence that this might not be the case.

She further concluded, "The teachers' individual definitions of science predisposed them to either accept or reject the processes of science writing as supportive of science learning" (p. 33).

Writing to Learn

A key purpose for writing in elementary science is as an aid to arriving at conceptual understanding in science (e.g., Fellows, 1994; Mason, 2001; Tomkins & Tunnicliffe, 2001). Writing for understanding is usually part of a scaffolded sequence of experiences. Writing, however, can have multiple purposes. Mason (2001) described how students wrote on several occasions for different purposes, such as writing for prediction, expressing intuitive ideas on a topic, communicating what is temporarily understood or what puzzles, recording changes of ideas, and giving final explanations of a phenomenon. The students were told not to worry about spelling, grammar, or even how good the idea was, as this writing was for a different purpose: learning science.

A key component of writing is to clearly identify the audience, which is usually the teacher. A different audience for some grade 6 students' writing reported by Fellows (1994) was themselves: they wrote notes to themselves, in order to explain their ideas. These notes were used as a basis for discussions with others. Fellows concluded, "writing ideas to themselves to explore and share informally with peers, reflecting on the ideas to reproduce new writing, and talk about the ideas with other students appeared to be important mechanisms for conceptual change" (pp. 998–999).

Specific Strategies

A number of specific pedagogical approaches and strategies for elementary science have been reported in the literature. Some are related to conceptual change, and all have a conceptual learning focus. In this section I outline research on the use of some of these strategies.

Drama/simulations (often a specific type of model/analogy).   Bailey and Watson (1998) used a simulation game to develop ecological concepts in 11-year-olds. Affective development was an important component. A comparison of the experimental group's post-test scores on understandings with a control group suggests that the strategy was also highly successful in developing understanding. In a South African context, grade 5 students used both videotapes and comics portraying puppets working on problems and confronting common misconceptions (Rollnick, Jones, Perold, & Bahr, 1998). It was considered important to have both formats available to suit the variable resources available in South African elementary schools. The initiative was deemed successful in helping students learn science concepts. There are some parallels in this idea with Concept Cartoons (see Keogh & Naylor, 1999, below).

Small-group work.   Small-group work, preferably in a hands-on activity context, is an accepted practice in reform elementary science, partly because it is seen as analogous to high school laboratory work. However, small-group work, particularly where equipment is involved, can be difficult for some teachers because of management issues (e.g., Appleton & Kindt, 1997). Management problems can be reduced with the use of cooperative learning principles. For instance, Watters and Ginns (1997) told how a grade 4 teacher learned to use the *Primary Investigations* (Australian Academy of Science, 1994) cooperative learning strategy, involving defined roles for group members (manager, director, speaker). A confident but traditional teacher, she made the transition to small-group work in science and was enthusiastic about it. However, even though she successfully had the students working in small groups, she did not necessarily use strategies to develop understanding.

Small-group work can also be problematic for students in two ways: 1) where social interactions and/or cultural expectations subvert or interfere with learning (e.g., Gray, 1999; Kurth et al., 2002; Nuthall, 1999, 2001; Ritchie, 2002), and 2) where the students construct their own purpose, different from the teacher's, for the activity —such as to complete the worksheet or finish the activity first (Nuthall, 2001).

Tasker and Freyberg (1985) first highlighted this problem, but there has been limited subsequent research into how to resolve the issue. Both of these issues were also highlighted by Anderson, Holland, and Palincsar (1997), who noted that "interpersonal relationships among students and their interpretations of the task requirements led to the scientific activity being appropriated largely by the most academically successful member of the group" (p. 359). This raises the issue of status within groups, discussed below.

How students are grouped, and students' status within the group, are important considerations. In studies of ability-paired dyads (by reading scores), Carter and Jones (Carter et al., 2003; Carter & Jones, 1994; Jones & Carter, 1994) concluded that grade 5 students achieved best when high-ability students were paired with low-ability students. There was no difference in the science achievement of high-ability students, whether they were paired with another high-ability student or a low-ability student, but the nature of their interactions differed considerably. In both cases, they had greater opportunity for speaking and working with equipment. However, low-ability students paired with a high-ability student achieved better than when paired with another low-ability student. Low-ability dyads tended to be off-task and inattentive when the teacher gave instructions, and spent considerable time negotiating group roles.

Rath and Brown (1996) identified six ways that students engage with materials during hands-on group work. Termed "modes of engagement" (p. 1087), they are:

- Exploration—Finding out about the phenomenon and studying its basic properties.
- Engineering—Using properties of the phenomenon to make something happen.
- Pet care—A personal connection to the object of study focused on nurturing.
- Procedural—Using the phenomenon as a support for imitation and step-following.
- Performance—Soliciting attention, using the phenomenon or object of study as a prop.
- Fantasy—An imaginative play activity that builds on some aspect of the phenomenon or object of study.

They cautioned that not all modes promote conceptual learning, and there may be cross-purposes between students in a small group. Some modes of engagement used by grade 2 and 5 students are gendered (Jones, Brader-Araje, et al., 2000). In the Jones, Brader-Araje et al. study, males tended to explore/tinker, whereas females tended to follow the teacher's instructions. Social interactions within the group were related to these gendered modes of engagement, competition for materials, and competition for power and status (see also Nuthall, 2001; Ritchie, 2002).

In the elementary school, status of students can be attributed on the basis of perceived academic prowess or cultural factors. Consequently, students in the same group do not necessarily do the same thing, partially because of differences in social interactions and differences in whether and how they engage with the materials. Bianchini (1997) highlighted this in a study of a grade 6 life sciences class. Even with an experienced teacher using an accepted small-group model, access and achievement of all students was limited. She concluded that, "despite a curriculum and instructional strategy designed explicitly to meet the needs of those traditionally positioned on the periphery of science, student differences in participation and in academic achievement remained" (p. 1062). Higher-status students in a small group, despite specific steps taken by the teacher, continually excluded low-status students. In a later report, she made three recommendations for refining group work to address status issues: "the consistent implementation of interventions designed to ameliorate status differences; the strategic assignment of procedural roles to ensure student access to group materials, discourse, and decisions; and the overturning of students' conventional notions of intelligence—what they think it means to be smart" (p. 577).

Problem solving and discrepant events.   Students working on genuine, puzzling problems (not the application of algorithms) can be an important component of a scaffold, especially as an initiating activity, though they have also been used at other critical times throughout a sequence of lessons (Meyer & Woodruff, 1997). One highly effective way of generating such problems within a classroom environment is to use discrepant or counterintuitive events. Discrepant events had their origins in Piagetian (Piaget, 1978) ideas of disequilibrium. Highly refined by Suchman (1966), they have been a consistent component of science pedagogy since (e.g., Friedl, 1995; Huber & Moore, 2001). Use of discrepant events has been recommended because they can be highly motivating (Friedl, 1995; Suchman, 1966), though the pedagogy in which they are used can have different effects on students' learning (Appleton, 1995). Appleton reported that a common behavior by students experiencing a discrepant event is to try to find a solution to the perceived problem(s) by relating the event to memories and seeking information. However, the information sources and strategies that they can use are constrained by the classroom context, in particular, the teaching strategies used. For instance, although the puzzling effect of a discrepant event that is conducted as a teacher demonstration may be high, students may have limited means of gaining further information about the problem because of the constraining effect of a highly teacher-controlled strategy. If the teacher provides an explanation immediately after demonstrating the discrepant event, learning is limited. By comparison, students working in small groups with the discrepant event have the opportunity to obtain information by discussing ideas and exploring the materials directly (see, for example, Huber & Moore, 2001).

The Learning Cycle and Its Variations

The main pedagogical approach suggested in the *Science Curriculum Improvement Study* (SCIS) materials was called the learning cycle (Karplus & Thier, 1967). Over the years, this approach has remained both a valued pedagogy for inquiry and a subject of research. It has also been modified as a consequence of further consideration of constructivist ideas of learning (see below). Some argue that the approach or its variations should be used to structure a lesson (e.g., Koch, 2002); others argue that it should be used to structure a unit of work (e.g., Appleton, 1997).

The SCIS learning cycle had three main phases: exploration, concept introduction, and concept application. In revising the Learning Cycle, Barman (1997) suggested four phases: investigative, dialogue, application, and assessment, with constant evaluation and discussion being a central component. Another revision (Blank, 2000) had a metacognitive emphasis, resulting in four phases: concept exploration, concept introduction/status check, concept application/status check, and concept assessment/status check. The notion of status introduced here reflects the idea that different concepts are ascribed different levels of status by learners, with intelligibility and plausibility influencing this (see also Beeth, 1998a). A key component of Blank's first phase was students making explicit their prior knowledge of the topic, which sets the scene for later consideration of the status of their developing ideas. In a comparison study with students using the SCIS strategy, Blank concluded that, although students using the revised strategy did not show greater content knowledge, they did experience more permanent restructuring of their understandings.

Another version of the SCIS approach, called the 5Es model, has become popular for scaffolding units of work in science (Appleton, 1997) and has been used in curriculum projects like *Science for Life and Living* (BSCS, 1992) and the Australian adaptation, *Primary Investigations* (Australian Academy of Science, 1994). Derived from constructivist considerations, it has been described in detail by Bybee (1997) and has been the subject of some studies (e.g., Boddy, Watson, & Aubusson, 2003). The 5Es approach derives its name from the five phases: engagement, exploration, explanation, elaboration, and evaluation. Boddy et al. (2003) reported that "[s]tudents found the unit of work fun and interesting and were motivated to learn while others said they were interested and motivated because they were learning . . . [and that] the unit of work . . . promoted higher-order thinking" (p. 40).

Students' Questions

Using students' questions as a basis for science investigations in the elementary school is a form of curriculum negotiation and is an attempt, in part, to address the confusion over the purpose of investigations discussed earlier. This work builds on earlier studies of the interactive approach (also called question raising) in the Learning in Science (Primary) Project (Biddulph & Osborne, 1984) and has been advocated by a number of authors since (e.g., Appleton, 1997; Fleer & Hardy, 2002; Gallas, 1995).

Keys (1998) explored the reasoning strategies of grade 6 students as they created their own questions and plans for investigations. Ideas for questions came from varying the initiating activity or from the students' own imaginations. Some questions led to experimental investigations (variables), and some to descriptive investigations (describing characteristics of events). Reasoning included translating ideas embedded in the questions into physical objects/events. Keys reported that the students' ability to control variables varied, so teachers had to change their practice to encourage social interaction and encourage students to evaluate their choice of variables. Management of different groups pursuing different questions was problematic for the teachers. Another issue for the teachers was that they had to accept the fact that not all students would learn the same thing.

Others (Chin & Kayalvizhi, 2002; Gibson, 1998; Iwasyk, 1997; van Zee et al., 2001; Watts et al., 1997) have explored eliciting students' questions to initiate investigations. Grade 6 (Chin & Kayalvizhi) and grade 1 (Watts et al.) students asked questions better suited to investigations after their teachers provided examples. Group discussion also helped. The teacher providing an introductory focus was also useful (Watts et al.), though not necessary (Chin & Kayalvizhi). Iwasyk (1997) added a variation to question-raising by having kindergarten and grade 1 students also discussing answers to their questions as they investigated them. In groups, a student acted as "teacher" or "leader," and the others asked questions as part of a discussion to clarify ideas. She used a strategy, KWHL, to structure the unit—K (What do I Know about), W (What do I Want to know about), H (How can I find out about), L (What did I Learn about). KWHL was also used to elicit students' questions and encourage discussion of their answers in another study (van Zee et al., 2001). They identified four conditions that encouraged students to raise questions:

- setting "up discourse structures [KWHL, brainstorming] that explicitly elicit questions" (p. 166),
- engaging "students in conversations about familiar contexts in which they had made many observations over a long time period" (p. 168),
- creating "comfortable discourse environments in which students could try to understand one another's thinking" (p. 171), and
- establishing "small groups where students were collaborating with one another" (p. 174).

Gibson (1998) described another variation of the approach by having students suggest and discuss answers to other students' questions.

Identifying Students' Initial Ideas

This is a common theme in many teaching approaches emergent from constructivist thinking and from the 1980s misconceptions research. It is a basic plank of many approaches, such as the conceptual change approaches, as well as the 5Es, KWHL, and interactive approaches. A variety of techniques have been suggested that can be used to identify students' pre-instructional ideas for guiding subsequent teaching. Summers et al. (1998), for instance, reported how a grade 7 teacher actively sought students' ideas and used these as a basis for her teaching. There was evidence of effective learning. Other possible strategies for eliciting students' ideas include the following:

- Open-ended teacher questions can be effective (Harlen, 1998), particularly if the teacher probes students' answers for deeper explanations.
- Students raising questions provides a window into their existing ideas (Iwasyk, 1997; Watts et al., 1997). Asking them to also suggest answers/explanations provides even better windows (Gibson, 1998). See also the original work by Biddulph and Osborne (1984).
- Turner (1997) reported how teachers used interviews and observations of students' explorations to research students' ideas about food and health during professional development sessions. The teachers saw this as a useful pedagogical tool to find out what the students knew and used it to shape subsequent pedagogy.
- Keogh and Naylor (1999) reported on the use of concept cartoons to identify student conceptions, generate student discussion of ideas, and subsequent investigations exploring alternative ideas.

- Concept maps were used to identify student understandings (Stoddart et al., 2000).
- Students' drawings were used to access their ideas (Edens & Potter, 2003). Having students explain their drawings is even more effective.

FUTURE RESEARCH DIRECTIONS

The research reviewed in this chapter has demonstrated that considerable gains in our understanding about the teaching/learning nexus in elementary science have been revealed over the last decade. Given the impetus in this research, it will doubtless continue over the coming decade, with further potential to inform elementary science curriculum and pedagogy.

Over the last few years, research into the benefits or otherwise of standards reforms have begun to appear in the literature. Further work is needed, including research that has a focus on:

- curriculum design—especially integration,
- conceptual learning,
- identifying clear learning goals,
- determining appropriate scaffolds for pedagogy in different contexts,
- assessment in authentic contexts,
- reporting student progress to carers and parents,
- the validity and appropriateness of large-scale testing and possible alternatives,
- helping teachers make pedagogical shifts arising from the above, and
- ways of introducing large-scale change in elementary science teaching in education systems that are cost-effective.

As mentioned in the introduction to this chapter, there has been little research in elementary science that has been conducted to inform and shape policy. This is not to say that the research being conducted is not valuable, and cannot be used to inform policy. Perhaps one way forward is to engage in research in partnership with policy-makers so there is a greater likelihood that research questions that they feel are valuable are addressed, and they are more likely to be aware of the research findings and recognise their validity.

In preparing this review, I noticed that much of the research was conducted in upper elementary science classes, that is, was situated in the middle school. The number of studies of grades 1 to 3 was relatively small in comparison, either because fewer studies are being conducted at these grade levels, or because they are being reported in early childhood journals that I missed. If there are fewer studies, this could be because elementary science researchers:

- have a greater interest in middle school science compared with science in the early grades;
- do not feel that they have expertise in the early grades;
- find it more difficult to collect reliable data in early grades, compared with middle school grades;

- have difficulty framing worthwhile questions for research into science in early grades; or
- do not consider science learning and teaching in early grades so important and worth studying.

There clearly needs to be more research into science in the early grades (Fleer, 2006), especially to explore aspects such as curriculum integration, theoretical frameworks for research, learning in the early grades, and pedagogy to enhance learning.

ACKNOWLEDGMENTS

Thanks to Valerie Akerson and Keith Skamp, who reviewed this chapter.

REFERENCES

Abell, S. K., & Roth, M. (1995). Reflections on a fifth-grade life science lesson: Making sense of children's understanding of scientific models. *International Journal of Science Education, 17*(1), 59–74.

Akerson, V. L., Flick, L. B., & Lederman, N. G. (2000). The influence of primary children's ideas in science on teaching practice. *Journal of Research in Science Teaching, 37*(4), 363–385.

Akerson, V. L., & Young, T. A. (1998). Elementary science and language arts: Should we blur the boundaries? *School Science and Mathematics, 98*(6), 334–339.

Anderson, C. W., Holland, J. D., & Palincsar, A. S. (1997). Canonical and sociocultural approaches to research and reform in science education: The story of Juan and his group. *The Elementary School Journal, 7*(4), 359–379.

Appleton, K. (1993). Using theory to guide practice: Teaching science from a constructivist perspective. *School Science and Mathematics, 5*, 269–274.

Appleton, K. (1995). Problem solving in science lessons: How students explore the problem space. *Research in Science Education, 25*(4), 383–393.

Appleton, K. (1997). *Teaching science: Exploring the issues.* Rockhampton, Australia: Central Queensland University Press.

Appleton, K. (2002). Science activities that work: Perceptions of primary school teachers. *Research in Science Education, 32*, 393–410.

Appleton, K. (2003, July). *Pathways in professional development in primary science: Extending science PCK.* Paper presented at the Annual conference of the Australasian Science Education Research Association, Melbourne, Australia.

Appleton, K. (2006). Science pedagogical content knowledge and elementary school teachers. In K. Appleton (Ed.), *Elementary science teacher education: International perspectives on contemporary issues and practice* (pp. 31–54). Mahwah, NJ: Lawrence Erlbaum in association with the Association for Science Teacher Education (ASTE).

Appleton, K., & Asoko, H. (1996). A case study of a teacher's progress toward using a constructivist view of learning to inform teaching in elementary science. *Science Education, 80*(5), 165–180.

Appleton, K., & Kindt, I. (1997). *Beginning teachers' practices in primary science in rural areas* Research monograph. Rockhampton, Australia: Faculty of Education, Central Queensland University.

Australian Academy of Science. (1994). *Primary investigations.* Canberra, Australia: Author.

Bailey, S., & Watson, R. (1998). Establishing basic ecological understanding in younger pupils: A pilot evaluation of a strategy based on drama/role play. *International Journal of Science Education, 20*(2), 139–152.

Barman, C. (1997). *The learning cycle revisited: A modification of an effective teaching model.* Monograph 6. Washington, DC: Council for Elementary Science International.

Barnett, M., & Morran, J. (2002). Addressing children's alternative frameworks of the Moon's phases and eclipses. *International Journal of Science Education, 24*(8), 859–879.

Baxter, G. P., Bass, K. M., & Glaser, R. (2001). Notebook writing in three fifth-grade science classrooms. *The Elementary School Journal, 102*(2), 123–140.

Beeth, M. (1998a). Teaching for conceptual change: Using status as a metacognitive tool. *Science Education, 82,* 343–356.

Beeth, M. (1998b). Teaching science in fifth grade: Instructional goals that support conceptual change. *Journal of Research in Science Teaching, 35*(10), 1091–1101.

Beeth, M., & Hewson, P. W. (1999). Learning goals in an exemplary science teacher's practice: Cognitive and social factors in teaching for conceptual change. *Science Education, 83,* 738–760.

Bell, B., & Cowie, B. (1997). *Formative assessment and science education.* Research report of the Learning in Science Project (Assessment). Hamilton, New Zealand: University of Waikato.

Bell, B., & Cowie, B. (2001a). The characteristics of formative assessment in science education. *Science Education, 85,* 536–553.

Bell, B., & Cowie, B. (2001b). *Formative assessment and science education* (Vol. 12). Dordrecht, the Netherlands: Kluwer.

Benenson, G. (2001). The unrealized potential of everyday technology as a context for learning. *Journal of Research in Science Teaching, 38*(7), 730–745.

Bianchini, J. A. (1997). Where knowledge construction, equity, and context intersect: Student learning of science in small groups. *Journal of Research in Science Teaching, 34*(10), 1039–1065.

Bianchini, J. A., & Kelly, G. J. (2003). Challenges of standards-based reform: The example of California's science content standards and textbook adoption process. *Science Education, 87,* 378–389.

Biddulph, F., & Osborne, R. (1984). *Making sense of our world: An interactive teaching approach.* Hamilton, New Zealand: University of Waikato.

Biemans, H. J. A., Deel, O. R., & Simons, P. R. (2001). Differences between successful and less successful students while working with the CONTACT–2 strategy. *Learning and Instruction, 11,* 265–282.

Biological Sciences Curriculum Study [BSCS]. (1992). *Science for life and living: Integrating science, technology, and health.* Dubuque, IA: Kendall/Hunt.

Black, P., Harrison, C., Lee, C., Marshall, B., & Wiliam, D. (2002). *Working inside the black box: Assessment for learning in the classroom.* London: King's College.

Blank, L. M. (2000). A metacognitive learning cycle: A better warranty for student understanding? *Science Education, 84,* 486–506.

Boddy, N., Watson, K., & Aubusson, P. (2003). A trial of the five Es: A referent model for constructivist teaching and learning. *Research in Science Education, 33,* 27–42.

Boulter, C., Prain, V., & Armitage, M. (1998). "What's going to happen in the eclipse tonight?": Rethinking perspectives on primary school science. *International Journal of Science Education, 20*(4), 487–500.

Brickhouse, N. W. (1994). Children's observations, ideas, and the development of classroom theories about light. *Journal of Research in Science Teaching, 31*(6), 639–656.

Buchanan, A. M., Howard, C., Martin, E., Williams, L., Childress, R., Bedsole, B., et al. (2002). Integrating elementary physical education and science: A cooperative problem-solving approach. *Journal of Physical Education, Recreation & Dance, 73*(2), 31–36.

Butts, D. P., Hofman, H. M., & Anderson, M. (1993). Is hands-on experience enough? A study of young children's views of sinking and floating objects. *Journal of Elementary Science Education, 5*(1), 50–64.

Butts, D. P., Hofman, H. M., & Anderson, M. (1994). Is direct experience enough? A study of young children's views of sounds. *Journal of Elementary Science Education, 6*(1), 1–16.

Butts, D. P., Koballa, T., Anderson, M., & Butts, D. P. (1993). Relationship between teacher intentions and their classroom use of Superscience. *Journal of Science Education and Technology, 2*(1), 349–357.

Buxton, C. A., & Whatley, A. (2002, April). *Authentic environmental inquiry model: An approach to integrating science and social studies in under-resourced urban elementary schools in southeastern Louisiana*. Paper presented at the annual meeting of the American Educational Research Association, New Orleans (ERIC document reproduction services, ED464841).

Bybee, R. W. (1997). Achieving scientific literacy: From purposes to practices. Portsmouth, UK: Heinemann.

Candela, A. (1997). Demonstrations and problem-solving exercises in school science: Their transformation within the Mexican elementary school classroom. *Science Education, 81*, 497–513.

Caravita, S. (2001). A re-framed conceptual change theory? *Learning and Instruction, 11*, 421–429.

Carter, G., & Jones, M. G. (1994). Relationship between ability-paired interactions and the development of fifth graders' concepts of balance. *Journal of Research in Science Teaching, 31*(8), 847–856.

Carter, G., Jones, G., & Rua, M. (2003). Effects of partner's ability on the achievement and conceptual organization of high-achieving fifth-grade students. *Science Education, 87*, 94–111.

Caswell, B., & Lamon, M. (1998, April). *Development of scientific literacy: The evolution of ideas in a grade four knowledge-building classroom*. Paper presented at the Annual meeting of the American Educational Research Association, San Diego.

Chin, C., & Kayalvizhi, G. (2002). Posing problems for open investigations: What questions do pupils ask? *Research in Science & Technological Education, 20*(2), 269–287.

Chinn, C. A., & Malhotra, B. A. (2002). Epistemologically authentic inquiry in schools: A theoretical framework for evaluating inquiry tasks. *Science Education, 86*, 175–218.

Claxton, G. (1990). *Teaching to learn: A direction for education*. London: Cassell.

Cobern, W. W., & Loving, C. C. (2002). Investigation of preservice elementary teachers' thinking about science. *Journal of Research in Science Teaching, 39*(10), 1016–1031.

Curriculum Corporation. (1994). *A statement on science for Australian schools*. Melbourne, Australia: Author.

diSessa, A., & Minstrell, J. (1998). Cultivating conceptual change with benchmark lessons. In J. Greeno & S. Goldman (Eds.), *Thinking practices in mathematics and science learning* (pp. 155–187). Mahwah, NJ: Lawrence Erlbaum Associates.

Edens, K. M., & Potter, E. (2003). Using descriptive drawings as a conceptual change strategy in elementary science. *School Science and Mathematics, 103*(3), 135–144.

Farenga, S. J., & Joyce, B. A. (1997). What children bring to the classroom: Learning science from experience. *School Science and Mathematics, 97*(5), 248–252.

Fellows, N. (1994). A window into thinking: Using student writing to understand conceptual change in science learning. *Journal of Research in Science Teaching, 31*(9), 985–1001.

Fetters, M. K., Czerniak, C. M., Fish, L., & Shawberry, J. (2002). Confronting, challenging and changing teachers' beliefs: Implications from a local systemic change professional development program. *Journal of Science Teacher Education, 13*(2), 101–130.

Fleer, M. (2006). "Meaning-making science": Exploring the sociocultural dimensions of early childhood teacher education. In K. Appleton (Ed.), *Elementary science teacher education: International perspectives on contemporary issues and practice* (pp. 107–124). Mahwah, NJ: Lawrence Erlbaum in association with the Association for Science Teacher Education (ASTE).

Fleer, M., & Hardy, T. (2002). *Science for children: Developing a personal approach to teaching* (2nd ed.). Sydney, Australia: Prentice Hall.

Flick, L. B. (1995). Navigating a sea of ideas: Teacher and students negotiate a course toward mutual relevance. *Journal of Research in Science Teaching, 32*(10), 1065–1082.

Fraser, B. J., & Tobin, K. G. (1998). *International handbook of science education*. Dordrecht, the Netherlands: Kluwer.

Friedl, A. E. (1995). *Teaching science to children: Integrated approach* (3rd ed.). New York: McGraw-Hill.

Gabel, D. L. (1994). *Handbook of research on science teaching and learning*. New York: Macmillan.

Gallas, K. (1995). *Talking their way into science: Hearing children's questions and theories, responding with curricula*. New York: Teachers College Press.

Georghiades, P. (2000). Beyond conceptual change learning in science education: Focusing on transfer, durability and metacognition. *Educational Research, 42*(2), 119–139.

Gibson, J. (1998). Any questions any answers? *Primary Science Review, 51,* 20–21.

Gitomer, D. H., & Duschl, R. A. (1998). Emerging issues and practices in science assessment. In B. J. Fraser & K. G. Tobin (Eds.), *International handbook of science education* (Vol. 2, pp. 791–810). Dordrecht, the Netherlands: Kluwer.

Glynn, S. M., & Takahashi, T. (1998). Learning from analogy-enhanced science text. *Journal of Research in Science Teaching, 35*(10), 1129–1149.

Gobert, J. D., & Clement, J. J. (1999). Effects of student-generated diagrams versus student-generated summaries on conceptual understanding of causal and dynamic knowledge in plate tectonics. *Journal of Research in Science Teaching, 36*(1), 39–53.

Goodrum, D., Hackling, M., & Rennie, L. (2001). *The status and quality of teaching and learning of science in Australian schools.* Canberra, ACT: Commonwealth of Australia.

Gott, R., & Duggan, S. (1995). The place of investigations in practical work in the UK National Curriculum for science. *International Journal of Science Education, 18*(7), 791–806.

Gray, B. V. (1999). Science education in the developing world: Issues and considerations. *Journal of Research in Science Teaching, 36*(3), 261–268.

Harlen, W. (1997). Primary teachers' understanding in science and its impact in the classroom. *Research in Science Education, 27*(3), 323–337.

Harlen, W. (1998). Teaching for understanding in pre-secondary science. In B. J. Fraser & K. G. Tobin (Eds.), *International handbook of science education* (pp. 183–198). Dordrecht, the Netherlands: Kluwer.

Harlen, W., & Holroyd, C. (1997). Primary teachers' understanding of concepts of science: Impact on confidence and teaching. *International Journal of Science Education, 19,* 93–105.

Hayes, M. T., & Deyhle, D. (2001). Constructing difference: A comparative study of elementary science curriculum differentiation. *Science Education, 85,* 239–262.

Hewson, P. W. (1981). A conceptual change approach to learning science. *European Journal of Science Education, 3*(4), 383–396.

Hewson, P. W., Beeth, M., & Thorley, N. R. (1998). Teaching for conceptual change. In B. J. Fraser & K. G. Tobin (Eds.), *International handbook of science education* (Vol. 2, pp. 199–218). Dordrecht, the Netherlands: Kluwer.

Hewson, P. W., & Thorley, N. R. (1989). The conditions of conceptual change in the classroom. *International Journal of Science Education, 11,* 541–553.

Heywood, D., & Parker, J. (1997). Confronting the analogy: Primary teachers exploring the usefulness of analogies in the teaching and learning of electricity. *International Journal of Science Education, 19*(8), 869–885.

Huber, R. A., & Moore, C. J. (2001). A model for extending hands-on science to be inquiry based. *School Science and Mathematics, 101*(1), 32–41.

Hunt, J., & Appleton, K. (2003). Professional development in primary science: Teacher mentoring. In B. Knight & A. Harrison (Eds.), *Research perspectives on education for the future* (pp. 165–187). Flaxton, Australia: Post Pressed.

Hurley, M. M. (2001). Reviewing integrated science and mathematics: The search for evidence and definitions from new perspectives. *School Science and Mathematics, 101*(5), 259–268.

Iwasyk, M. (1997). Kids questioning kids: "Experts" sharing. *Science and Children, 35*(1), 42–46, 80.

Jane, B., & Jobling, W. M. (1995). Children linking science and technology in the primary classroom. *Research in Science Education, 25*(2), 191–201.

Jarvis, T., Hargreaves, L., & Comber, C. (1997). An evaluation of the role of email in promoting science investigative skills in primary rural schools in England. *Research in Science Education, 27*(2), 223–236.

Johnson, S. L. (1999). Discovering the potential of gifted girls: The biological and physical science interests of gifted kindergarten girls. *School Science and Mathematics, 99*(6), 302–310.

Jones, M. G., Brader-Araje, L., Carboni, L. W., Carter, G., Rua, M., Banilower, E., et al. (2000). Tool time: Gender and students' use of tools, control, and authority. *Journal of Research in Science Teaching, 37*(8), 760–783.

Jones, M. G., & Carter, G. (1994). Verbal and nonverbal behavior of ability-grouped dyads. *Journal of Research in Science Teaching, 31*(6), 603–619.

Jones, M. G., Carter, G., & Rua, M. (2000). Exploring the development of conceptual ecologies: Communities of concepts related to convection and heat. *Journal of Research in Science Teaching, 37*(2), 139–159.

Jones, M. G., & Edmunds, J. (2006). Models of elementary science instruction: Roles of science specialists. In K. Appleton (Ed.), *Elementary science teacher education: International perspectives on contemporary issues and practice* (pp. 317–343). Mahwah, NJ: Lawrence Erlbaum in association with the Association for Science Teacher Education (ASTE).

Kamen, M. (1996). A teacher's implementation of authentic assessment in an elementary science classroom. *Journal of Research in Science Teaching, 33*(8), 859–877.

Karplus, R., & Thier, H. D. (1967). *A new look at elementary school science.* Chicago: Rand-McNally.

Kelly, G. J., Brown, C., & Crawford, T. (2000). Experiments, contingencies, and curriculum: Providing opportunities for learning through improvisation in science teaching. *Science Education, 84,* 624–657.

Keogh, B., & Naylor, S. (1999). Concept cartoons, teaching and learning in science: An evaluation. *International Journal of Science Education, 21*(4), 431–446.

Keys, C. (1998). A study of grade six pupils generating questions and plans for open-ended science investigations. *Research in Science Education, 28*(3), 301–316.

Khishfe, R., & Abd-El-Khalick, F. (2002). Influence of explicit and reflective versus implicit inquiry-oriented instruction on sixth graders' views of nature of science. *Journal of Research in Science Teaching, 39*(7), 551–578.

King, K., Shumow, L., & Lietz, S. (2001). Science education in an urban elementary school: Case studies of teacher beliefs and classroom practices. *Science Education, 85,* 89–110.

Koch, J. (2002). *Science stories: A science methods book for elementary school teachers.* Boston: Houghton Mifflin.

Kruger, C., & Summers, M. (2000). Developing primary school children's understanding of energy waste. *Research in Science & Technological Education, 18*(1), 5–21.

Kurth, L. A., Anderson, C. W., & Palincsar, A. S. (2002). The case of Carla: Dilemmas of helping all students to understand science. *Science Education, 86,* 287–313.

Lach, C., Little, E., & Nazzaro, D. (2003). From all sides now: Weaving technology and multiple intelligences into science and art. *Learning & Leading with Technology, 30*(6), 32–35, 59.

Laplante, B. (1997). Teachers' beliefs and instructional strategies in science: Pushing analysis further. *Science Education, 81,* 277–294.

Lee, C. A., & Houseal, A. (2003). Self-efficacy, standards, and benchmarks as factors in teaching elementary school science. *Journal of Elementary Science Education, 15*(1), 37–55.

Levitt, K. E. (2001). An analysis of elementary teachers' beliefs regarding the teaching and learning of science. *Science Education, 86,* 1–22.

Limón, M. (2001). On the cognitive conflict as an instructional strategy for conceptual change: A critical appraisal. *Learning and Instruction, 11,* 357–380.

Liu, S. Y., & Lederman, N. G. (2002). Taiwanese gifted students' views of the nature of science. *School Science and Mathematics, 102*(3), 114–122.

Martinez, K. (1994). Postcards from the edge. In K. Smith (Ed.), *Knowledge and competence for beginning teachers* (pp. 121–140). Brisbane, Australia: Queensland Board of Teacher Registration.

Mason, L. (2001). Introducing talk and writing for conceptual change: A classroom study. *Learning and Instruction, 11,* 305–329.

Mastropieri, M. A., & Scruggs, T. E. (1994). Text versus hands-on science curriculum: Implications for students with disabilities. *Remedial and Special Education, 15*(2), 72–85.

McGinn, M. K., & Roth, W. M. (1998). Assessing students' understanding about levers: Better test instruments are not enough. *International Journal of Science Education, 20*(7), 813–832.

Meyer, K., & Woodruff, E. (1997). Concensually driven explanation in science teaching. *Science Education, 80*, 173–192.

Mistler, M. M., & Songer, N. B. (2000). Student motivation and internet technology: Are students empowered to learn science? *Journal of Research in Science Teaching, 37*(5), 459–479.

Mitchell, I., & Mitchell, J. (1997). *Stories of reflective teaching: A book of PEEL cases.* Melbourne, Australia: Monash University.

Moje, E. B., Collazo, C., Carrillo, R., & Marx, R. W. (2001). "Maestro, what is 'quality'?": Language, literacy, and discourse in project-based science. *Journal of Research in Science Teaching, 38*(4), 469–498.

Morell, P. D., & Carroll, J. B. (2003). An extended examination of preservice elementary teachers' science teaching self-efficacy. *School Science and Mathematics, 103*(5), 246–251.

Nason, R., Lloyd, P., & Ginns, I. S. (1996). Format-free databases and the construction of knowledge in primary school science projects. *Research in Science Education, 26*(3), 353–373.

National Research Council. (1996). *National science education standards.* Washington, DC: National Academy Press.

National Science Resources Center. (2002). *Science and technology for children.* Burlington, NC: Carolina Biological Supply Company.

Newton, D. P., & Newton, L. D. (2000). Do teachers support causal understanding through their discourse when teaching primary science? *British Educational Research Journal, 26*(5), 599–613.

Newton, L. D., Newton, D. P., Blake, A., & Brown, K. (2002). Do primary school science books for children show a concern for explanatory understanding. *Research in Science & Technological Education, 20*(2), 227–240.

Nuthall, G. (1999). The way students learn: Acquiring knowledge from an integrated science and social studies unit. *The Elementary School Journal, 99*(4), 303–341.

Nuthall, G. (2001). Understanding how classroom experience shapes students' minds. *Unterrichts Wissenschaft, 29*(3), 224–267.

Nuthall, G., & Alton-Lee, A. (1995). Assessing classroom learning: How students use their knowledge and experience to answer classroom achievement test questions in science and social studies. *American Educational Research Journal, 32*(1), 185–223.

Osborne, J., & Simon, S. (1996). Primary science: Past and future directions. *Studies in Science Education, 26*, 99–147.

Owens, C. V. (2001). Teachers' responses to science writing. *Teaching and Learning: The Journal of Natural Inquiry, 15*(1), 22–35.

Palmer, D. (1995). The POE in the primary school: An evaluation. *Research in Science Education, 25*(3), 323–332.

Pang, J. S., & Good, R. (2000). A review of the integration of science and mathematics: Implications for further research. *School Science and Mathematics, 100*(2), 73–82.

Parker, V. (2000). Effects of a science intervention program on middle-grade student achievement and attitudes. *School Science and Mathematics, 100*(5), 236–242.

Patterson, E. W. (2001). Structuring the composition process in scientific writing. *International Journal of Science Education, 23*(1), 1–16.

Peacock, A., & Gates, S. (2000). Newly qualified primary teachers' perceptions of the role of text material in teaching science. *Research in Science & Technological Education, 18*(2), 155–171.

Peers, C. E., Diezmann, C. M., & Watters, J. J. (2003). Supports and concerns for teacher professional growth during the implementation of a science curriculum innovation. *Research in Science Education, 33*(1), 89–110.

Penner, D. E., Giles, N. D., Lehrer, R., & Schauble, L. (1997). Building functional models: Designing an elbow. *Journal of Research in Science Teaching, 34*(2), 125–143.

Piaget, J. (1978). *The development of thought* (A. Rosin, Trans.). Oxford, UK: Basil Blackwell.

Raghavan, K., Sartoris, M. L., & Glaser, R. (1998). Why does it go up? The impact of the MARS curriculum as revealed through changes in student explanations of a helium balloon. *Journal of Research in Science Teaching, 35*(5), 547–567.

Ramos, E. (1999). *Teaching science constructively: Examining teacher's issues when teaching science.* (ERIC Document Reproduction Service No. ED436391).

Rath, A., & Brown, D. E. (1996). Modes of engagement in science inquiry: A microanalysis of elementary students' orientations toward phenomena at a summer science camp. *Journal of Research in Science Teaching, 33*(10), 1083–1097.

Ritchie, S. M. (2002). Student positioning within groups during science activities. *Research in Science Education, 32*, 35–54.

Ritchie, S. M., & Hampson, B. (1996). Learning in-the-making: A case study of science and technology projects in a year six classroom. *Research in Science Education, 26*(4), 391–407.

Rollnick, M., Jones, B., Perold, H., & Bahr, M. A. (1998). Puppets and comics in primary science: The development and evaluation of a pilot multimedia package. *International Journal of Science Education, 20*(5), 533–550.

Roth, W. M. (1996). Teacher questioning in an open-inquiry learning environment: Interactions of context, content, and student responses. *Journal of Research in Science Teaching, 33*(7), 709–736.

Roth, W. M. (2001). Learning science through technological design. *Journal of Research in Science Teaching, 38*(7), 768–790.

Rowell, P. M. (1997). Learning in school science: The promises and practices of writing. *Studies in Science Education, 30*, 19–56.

Schoon, K. J., & Boone, W. J. (1998). Self-efficacy and alternative conceptions of science of preservice elementary teachers. *Science Education, 82*, 553–568.

Schwartz, R. S., & Lederman, N. G. (2000). Achieving the reforms vision: The effectiveness of a specialists-led elementary science program. *School Science and Mathematics, 100*(4), 181–193.

Shepardson, D. P. (1996). Social interactions and the mediation of science learning in two small groups of first-graders. *Journal of Research in Science Teaching, 33*(2), 159–178.

Shepardson, D. P. (1997). Of butterflies and beetles: First graders' ways of seeing and talking about insect life cycles. *Journal of Research in Science Teaching, 34*(9), 873–88.

Shepardson, D. P., & Britsch, S. J. (2001). The role of children's journals in elementary school science activities. *Journal of Research in Science Teaching, 38*(1), 43–69.

Shepardson, D. P., Moje, E. B., & Kennard-McClelland, A. M. (1994). The impact of a science demonstration on children's understandings of air pressure. *Journal of Research in Science Teaching, 31*(3), 243–258.

Shimoda, T. A., White, B. Y., & Frederiksen, J. R. (2002). Student goal orientation in learning inquiry skills with modifiable software advisors. *Science Education, 86*, 244–263.

Shulman, L. S. (1986). Those who understand: Knowledge growth in teaching. *Educational Researcher, 15*, 4–14.

Skamp, K. (1993). Research themes, styles, purposes and future directions. In D. Goodrum (Ed.), *Science in the early years of schooling: An Australasian perspective* (pp. 43–63). Perth, Western Australia: Key Centre for Teaching and Research in School Science and Mathematics, Curtin University of Technology.

Skamp, K., & Mueller, A. (2001). A longitudinal study of the influences of primary and secondary school, university and practicum on student teachers' images of effective primary science practice. *International Journal of Science Education, 23*(3), 227–245.

Sneider, C. I., & Ohadi, M. M. (1998). Unraveling students' misconceptions about the earth's shape and gravity. *Science Education, 82*, 265–284.

Spillane, J. P., Diamond, J. B., Walker, L. J., Halverson, R., & Jita, L. (2001). Urban school leadership for elementary science instruction: Identifying and activating resources in an undervalued school subject. *Journal of Research in Science Teaching, 38*(8), 918–940.

Stark, R., & Gray, D. (1999). Gender preferences in learning science. *International Journal of Science Education, 21*(6), 633–643.

Stoddart, T., Abrams, R., Gasper, E., & Canaday, D. (2000). Concept maps as assessment in science inquiry learning—a report of methodology. *International Journal of Science Education, 22*(12), 1221–1246.

Stow, W. (1997). Concept mapping: A tool for self-assessment? *Primary Science Review, 49,* 12–15.

Suchman, J. (1966). *Inquiry development program in physical science: Teacher's guide.* Chicago: SRA.

Summers, M., Kruger, C., & Mant, J. (1998). Teaching electricity effectively in the primary school: A case study. *International Journal of Science Education, 20*(2), 153–172.

Tasker, R., & Freyberg, P. (1985). Facing the mismatches in the classroom. In R. Osborne & P. Freyberg (Eds.), *Learning in science: The implications of children's science* (pp. 66–80). Auckland, New Zealand: Heinemann.

Thorley, N. R., & Woods, R. K. (1997). Case studies of students' learning as action research on conceptual change teaching. *International Journal of Science Education, 19*(2), 229–245.

Tilgner, P. J. (1990). Avoiding science in the elementary school. *Science Education, 74,* 421–431.

Tomkins, S. P., & Tunnicliffe, S. D. (2001). Looking for ideas: Observation, interpretation and hypothesis-making by 12-year-old pupils undertaking science investigations. *International Journal of Science Education, 23*(8), 791–813.

Turner, S. A. (1997). Children's understanding of food and health in primary classrooms. *International Journal of Science Education, 19*(5), 491–508.

Tytler, R. (1998). The nature of students' informal science conceptions. *International Journal of Science Education, 20*(8), 901–927.

Tytler, R., & Peterson, S. (2000). Deconstructing learning in science—Young children's responses to a classroom sequence on evaporation. *Research in Science Education, 30*(4), 339–355.

van Zee, E. H., Iwasyk, M., Kurose, A., Simpson, D., & Wild, J. (2001). Student and teacher questioning during conversations about science. *Journal of Research in Science Teaching, 38*(2), 159–190.

Varelas, M., Becker, J., Luster, B., & Wenzel, S. (2002). When genres meet: Inquiry into a sixth-grade urban science class. *Journal of Research in Science Teaching, 39*(7), 579–605.

Vaughan, M. N., Sumrall, J., & Rose, L. H. (1998). Preservice teachers use the newspaper to teach science and social studies literacy. *Journal of Elementary Science Education, 10*(2), 1–9.

Venville, G., Wallace, J., Rennie, L., & Malone, J. (2002). Curriculum integration: Eroding the high ground of science as a school subject? *Studies in Science Education, 37,* 43–83.

Vosniadou, S., Ioannides, C., Dimitrakopoulou, A., & Papademetriou, E. (2001). Designing learning environments to promote conceptual change in science. *Learning and Instruction, 11,* 381–419.

Warren, B., Ballenger, C., Ogonowski, M., Rosebery, A. S., & Hudicourt-Barnes, J. (2001). Rethinking diversity in learning science: The logic of everyday sense-making. *Journal of Research in Science Teaching, 38*(5), 529–552.

Warwick, P., Linfield, R. S., & Stephenson, P. (1999). A comparison of primary school pupils' ability to express procedural understanding in science through speech and writing. *International Journal of Science Education, 21*(8), 823–838.

Warwick, P., Stephenson, P., & Webster, J. (2003). Developing pupils' written expression of procedural understanding through the use of writing frames in science: Findings from a case study approach. *International Journal of Science Education, 25*(2), 173–192.

Watters, J. J., & Ginns, I. S. (1997). An in-depth study of a teacher engaged in an innovative primary science trial professional development project. *Research in Science Education, 27*(1), 51–69.

Watts, M., Barber, B., & Alsop, S. (1997). Children's questions in the classroom. *Primary Science Review, 49,* 6–8.

Weaver, G. C. (1996). Strategies in K–12 science instruction to promote conceptual change. *Science Education, 82,* 455–472.

Williams, M., & Linn, M. C. (2002). WISE inquiry in fifth grade Biology. *Research in Science Education, 32*, 415–436.

Woodbury, J. M. (1995, November). *Methods and strategies of exemplary fifth grade teachers: Science as preferred and non-preferred subject.* Paper presented at the Annual meeting of the Mid-South Educational Research Association, Biloxi, MS.

Woodruff, E., & Meyer, K. (1997). Explanations from intra- and inter-group discourse: Students building knowledge in the science classroom. *Research in Science Education, 27*(1), 25–39.

Yanowitz, K. L. (2001). Using analogies to improve elementary school students' inferential reasoning about scientific concepts. *School Science and Mathematics, 101*(3), 133–142.

Zubrowski, B. (2002). A curriculum framework based on archetypical phenomena and technologies. *Science Education, 86*, 481–501.

CHAPTER 19

Interdisciplinary Science Teaching

Charlene M. Czerniak
University of Toledo

Although the topic of curriculum integration has been around for more than 100 years, its popularity among educators has been renewed in the last few years. The notion of connecting subject areas has substantial face validity, because it makes common sense. In real life, people do not separate their daily tasks into separate subjects; therefore, it seems only rational that subject areas should not be separated in our schools.

Some authors propose that the integration of subject areas helps students learn to think critically and develop a general core of knowledge necessary for success in the future (Carnegie Council on Adolescent Development, 1989). Curriculum integration advocates speak of the numerous advantages integration offers in helping students form deeper understandings, see the "big" picture, make curriculum relevant to students, build connections among central concepts, and become interested and motivated in school (Berlin, 1994; George, 1996; Mason, 1996). Advocates also maintain that curriculum integration is supported by societal reasons; traditional curriculum is not relevant to students and does not concentrate on genuine problems and issues.

Those who back curriculum integration also assert that it is anchored in psychology and human development. In defining constructivism, Brooks and Brooks (1993) remark that deep understanding is formed when students make connections between prior knowledge and new experiences—meaningful learning occurs when they see relationships among ideas. Cohen (1995) asserts that thematic teaching is supported by brain research, and Beane (1996) states that people process information through patterns and connections rather than through fragmented snippets of information.

However, after a century of calls for integrated approaches, some educators question the merit of integration and cite the paucity of research supporting it over traditional methods. Educators attempting to implement an integrated curriculum confront this critical issue and a number of other equally important ones. In this chapter, a brief history of curriculum integration is provided, and various issues are discussed, including the lack of a consistent definition of integration, the role of integration in school curriculum, advantages and disadvantages associated with integration, and problems commonly encountered in trying to implement an integrated curriculum. These issues are critical to the understanding and implementation of integration and present areas for future research that can help elucidate the value of integrated approaches.

RATIONALE

Justification can be found in the literature to support both traditional subject matter separation and integrated curriculum. Academic scholars have traditionally structured knowledge within the major disciplines recognizable today (science, mathematics, social sciences, and language arts). Some academics believe that academic disciplines are a powerful way to organize knowledge. For instance, Gardner and Boix-Mansilla (1994) declare that academic disciplines "constitute the most sophisticated ways yet developed for thinking about and investigating issues that have long fascinated and perplexed thoughtful individuals . . . (and) they become, when used relevantly, our keenest lenses on the world" (pp. 16–17). Educators who desire to keep subject disciplines separate fear that attempts to integrate subjects sometimes result in topics being left out of the curriculum and gaps in student understanding of important concepts. Berlin and White (1992) reported that Wingspread conference participants feared that the merging of the disciplines might cause people to lose important philosophical, methodological, and historical differences between the two subjects.

In contrast, others (e.g., Perkins, 1991) considered academic disciplines as "artificial partitions with historical roots of limited contemporary significance." Mason (1996) described the present-day school curriculum as moribund—a regression to the factory system, where students proceed down a hallway to the next class. Mason pointed out that although our factories today have changed, our schools remain out of sync with society and real life, where knowledge and skills are not separated. Some stress that the curriculum needs be transformed because science is divided into 25,000 to 30,000 research fields, and data generated by this research is presented in over 70,000 scientific publications (Hurd, 1991). Science is no longer differentiated by distinct disciplinary lines such as biology, chemistry, geology, and physics, and demarcations between the sciences are blurred to form new fields such as geophysics and computational chemistry. Hurd recommended that science educators integrate the science curricula, because science in daily life is not separated or compartmentalized. He argued that traditional discipline-bound, fact-laden science courses are too narrow in scope to teach students how to learn in today's world, where science, technology, and societal issues are all interrelated.

McBride and Silverman (1991) summarized literature on integration of science and mathematics dating to the early twentieth century and concluded with four primary reasons for integrating the subjects:

1. Science and mathematics are closely related systems of thought and are naturally correlated in the physical world.

2. Science can provide students with concrete examples of abstract mathematical ideas that can improve learning of mathematics concepts.

3. Mathematics can enable students to achieve deeper understanding of science concepts by providing ways to quantify and explain science relationships.

4. Science activities illustrating mathematics concepts can provide relevancy and motivation for learning mathematics. (pp. 286–287)

BRIEF HISTORY

Although disciplinary knowledge has been developed for centuries and shapes the basis for exploring a particular area of knowledge, integration of subject areas has also been discussed for over 100 years. Berlin (1994) noted that since the early twentieth century the School Science and Mathematics Association has published numerous articles on the topic. In 1903, as Moore was retiring as president of the American Mathematical Society, he provided momentum to the reform efforts of that time by devoting part of his presidential address to mathematics in secondary education. He called for "the unification of pure and applied mathematics" and "the correlation of the different subjects" (Moore, 1967). Beane (1996) summarized several historical references to integration during the progressive era in U.S. education in Kilpatrick's work in the 1920s, Hopkin's efforts in 1937, and writings of John Dewey in the 1930s. A 1927 third-grade integrated unit on the study of boats on the Hudson River in New York is outlined in Cremin's (1964) book. Bean states that the word *integration* first appeared in *Education Index* in 1936.

Hurley (1999) summarized several additional periods in U.S. history where integration was used: the core curriculum in the 1940s and 1950s, the curriculum improvement projects in the 1960s and 1970s, the science-technology-society (STS) movement in the 1980s and 1990s, the middle school movement, and most recently the national standards established by various professional organizations.

For science education, the curriculum improvement projects were a particularly important period in history where curriculum integration took a foothold. Lehman (1994) stated that numerous curriculum projects were developed with the intent to integrate science and mathematics. Examples of projects (and contemporary offshoots) designed to integrate the curriculum include the Minnesota Mathematics and Science Project (Minnemast, 1970), the Unified Science and Mathematics for Elementary Schools Project (USMES, 1973), Nuffield (1967), Lawrence Hall of Science's Great Explorations in Math and Science Project (GEMS) (Lawrence Hall of Science, 1984), Fresno Pacific College's Activities That Integrate Mathematics and Science (AIMS Educational Foundation, 1986, 1987), and the University of Chicago's Teaching Integrated Mathematics and Science Project (TIMS) (Institute for Mathematics and Science Education, 1995).

Middle School and Early Childhood Education Movement

Curriculum integration is a cornerstone of efforts aimed at creating schools focused on the developmental needs of students. The National Association for the Education of Young Children (NAEYC) and the National Middle School Association (NMSA), organizations specializing in instructional practices appropriate for the education of young children and young and early adolescents, respectively, publish numerous materials to guide teachers in the selection and use of materials for young children and adolescents. Curriculum integration is stressed in various NAEYC reports (1987), and the NMSA book titled *A Middle School Curriculum: From Rhetoric to Reality* (Beane, 1993, 1997) argues for integration around personal and social concerns that interest adolescents and young adults. *This We Believe* (NMSA, 1982, 1995) argues for developmentally responsive middle schools where curriculum is challenging, integrative, and exploratory. Numerous NMSA resources support curriculum integration (Bean, 1997; Brazee & Capelluti, 1995; Erb, 2001; Nesin & Lounsbury, 1999; Smith, 2001; Stevenson & Carr, 1993), and the *Middle School Journal* devotes considerable space to articles on curriculum integration (see, for example, the November 2001 issue).

National Standards

In the last decade, almost all national reform efforts have stressed the need to make connections among subject areas (National Council of Teachers of English, 1996; National Council of Teachers of Mathematics [NCTM], 1989, 2000; National Council for the Social Studies [NCSS], 1994; National Research Council [NRC], 1989; NRC, 1996; National Science Teachers Association [NSTA], 1996; Rutherford & Ahlgren, 1990). Integration or thematic instruction is often used as a key idea in school reform efforts. The BSCS group (1994) summarized in a questionnaire ten common reform strands, and thematic instruction is one of the common elements of reform. For example, Crane (1991) described a restructured high school science curriculum focused on four themes of change, interactions, energy, and patterns. Similarly, Greene (1991) described a science-centered reform at the elementary school level.

In the early 1990s, the NSTA's *Scope, Sequence and Coordination* project (NSTA, 1992) recommended replacing traditional high school discipline curricula with four years of integrated science. In 1996, NSTA published a position statement on interdisciplinary learning in grades PreK–4 that represented the thinking of members of a variety of professional organizations (NCTM, NCTE, IRA, NSTA, NCSS, Speech Communication Association, and Council for Elementary Science International) that met to develop guidelines for integrating curriculum. This position statement addressed some of the matters raised by Berlin and White's (1994) integrated science and mathematics model, because it focused on ways of learning and knowing, process and thinking skills, content knowledge, attitudes and perceptions, and teaching strategies.

The national standards movement in the last ten years has once again increased emphasis on integration. *Science for All Americans* states, "The alliance between science and mathematics has a long history, dating back centuries. Science provides mathematics with interesting problems to investigate, and mathematics provides science with powerful tools to use in analyzing them" (pp. 16–18). The National Science Education Standards (NRC, 1996) maintain, "Curricula often will integrate topics from different subject-matter areas—such as life and physical sciences—from different content standards—such as life sciences and science in personal and social perspectives—and from different school subjects—such as science and mathematics, science and language arts, or science and history" (p. 23). The Science Education Teaching Standards (NRC, 1996) declare, "Schools must restructure schedules so that teachers can use blocks of time, interdisciplinary strategies and field experiences to give students many opportunities to engage in serious scientific investigation as an integral part of their science learning" (p. 44). Finally, the Science Education Content Standards (NRC, 1996) state, "The standard for unifying concepts and processes is presented for grades K–12, because the understanding and abilities associated with major conceptual and procedural schemes need to be developed over an entire education, and the unifying concepts and processes transcend disciplinary boundaries" (p. 104).

NCTM (2000) emphasizes, "School mathematics experiences at all levels should include opportunities to learn about mathematics by working on problems arising in contexts outside of mathematics. These connections can be to other subject areas and disciplines as well as to students' daily lives" (p. 65).

The National Council for the Social Studies (NCSS, 1994) cautions against integration for its own sake, stressing, "Unless [programs] are developed as plans for accomplishing major social studies goals, such programs may focus on trivial or disconnected information" (pp. 165–166), but NCSS has also published resources promoting integration that is in alignment with the NCSS Standards. For example, Sandmann and Ahern's (2002) book, *Linking Literature with Life*, is a resource for integrating the NCSS standards and children's literature for middle grades. The Science-Technology-Society (STS) movement in the 1980s and 1990s also renewed the call for integration, with particular emphasis on the societal implications of science and technology.

Elementary educators viewed the whole language movement in the 1990s as a way to integrate across content areas (Willis, 1992). Others advocate the use of language arts strategies to help teachers develop science literacy (Akerson, 2001; Dickinson & Young, 1998). Dickinson and Young (1998) comment that science and language arts goals are complementary, and language arts can provide the tools for science inquiry.

Some educators claim that technology serves as a catalyst for integration across the curriculum (Berger, 1994), and recent studies suggest that technology has enhanced integration between science and mathematics by facilitating collaboration, providing real-world contexts for problem solving, removing limits on instructional time, and offering students opportunities to apply knowledge to real problems (Pang & Good, 2000).

Focus in Teacher Education

One criticism of teaching in an integrated fashion is that teachers aren't prepared to teach this way. Hurley (2003) mentioned that although there have been appeals for integrated approaches for years, it is only a recent development that integrated methods courses have been offered at universities. The need to be skilled in integrated approaches is underscored in the National Science Education Standards, which state, "Integrated and thematic approaches to curriculum can be powerful; however they require skill and understanding in their design and implementation" (p. 213).

With teacher education in mind, Hurley conducted a study examining the presence, value, and reasoning behind universities offering integrated science and mathematics methods courses. The reasons those universities reported offering integrated methods courses include new state and national standards, program reorganization, constructivist reforms, and the literature on integration. Akerson (2001) also affirms that educators have implemented integrated curricular ideas into their methods courses at universities in an effort to help teachers meet the state and national standards. Beane (1996) declared that integration is now found in university courses and even college degrees.

UNFOCUSED DEFINITION

Despite the plea for integration, many have argued that few empirical research studies support the assertion that integrated approaches are more effective than traditional, discipline-based teaching. A summary of articles from the 1991 Wingspread conference on integration found that of 423 articles summarized, 99 were related to theory and research, and only 22 were research-based articles (Berlin, 1994). Lederman and Niess (1997) echoed concerns that research supporting the use of integrated instruction or thematic curricula is almost nonexistent. Czerniak, Weber, Sandmann, and Ahern (1999) summarized literature on the integration of science and mathematics with other subject areas and concluded that there are few empirical studies to support the notion that an integrated curriculum is any better than a well-designed traditional curriculum.

A possible explanation for the dearth of empirical research on integration is a conceptual one that clouds the generation of research questions. At the fundamental level, a common definition of integration does not seem to exist that can be used as a basis for designing, carrying out, and interpreting results of research. Davison, Miller, and Metheny (1995) appealed for a definition of integration, stating, "Few educators would argue about the need for an interwoven, cross-disciplinary curriculum, but to many, the nature of the integration in many interdisciplinary projects is not readily apparent. A more pervasive problem is that integration means different things to different educators" (p. 226). Hurley (2001, 2003) concluded after a comprehensive study, however, that an agreed-upon definition of integration could not be found.

Despite Davison, Miller, and Metheny's (1995) request for clarification, this elusiveness is evident in the sheer number of words used to convey integration: *interdisciplinary, multidisciplinary, transdisciplinary, thematic, integrated, connected, nested, sequenced, shared, webbed, threaded, immersed, networked, blended, unified, coordinated,* and *fused.* Lederman and Niess's (1997) editorial in *School Science and Mathematics* explained that many educators use the terms *integrated, interdisciplinary,* and *thematic* synonymously, and this only compounds the confusion and limits the ability to adequately research the topic.

The tendency to use the words *integrated, interdisciplinary,* and *thematic* synonymously may be a result of the fact that little agreement exists regarding the definition of integration. Berlin and White (1992) reported that a group of 60 scientists, mathematicians, science and mathematics educators, teachers, curriculum developers, educational technologists, and psychologists assembled at a conference funded by the National Science Foundation (NSF) were unable, after three days of deliberation, to reach a consensus on the definition of integration of science and mathematics. The group proposed an operational definition: "Integration infuses mathematical methods in science and scientific methods into mathematics such that it becomes indistinguishable as to whether it is mathematics or science" (p. 341).

Historical references to integration (Hopkins, 1937, as cited in Beane, 1996) defined integration as problem-centered, integrated knowledge. Beane (1996) used four characteristics to define integration: (a) curriculum that is organized around problems and issues that are of personal and social significance in the real world, (b) use of relevant knowledge in the context of topic without regard for subject lines, (c) knowledge that is used to study an existing problem rather than for a test or grade level outcome, and (d) emphasis placed on projects and activities with real application of knowledge and problem solving. He maintained that other forms of integrated curriculum (such as parallel disciplines or multidisciplinary curricula) still focus on separate content areas and, therefore, are not fully integrated.

To distinguish between *integration* and other terms, Lederman and Niess (1997) defined *integration* as a blending of science and mathematics to the point that the separate parts are indiscernible. The metaphor of tomato soup was used: The tomatoes cannot be distinguished from the water or other ingredients in the soup. They defined *interdisciplinary* as a blending of science and mathematics where connections are made between the subjects, but the two subjects remain identifiable. The metaphor used is chicken noodle soup, where you can still distinguish the broth, chicken, and noodles. Jacobs (1989) described interdisciplinary as "a knowledge view and curriculum approach that consciously applies methodology and language from more than one discipline to examine a central theme, issue, problem, topic, or experience." Lederman and Niess (1997) defined *thematic* as a unifying topic used to transcend traditional subject boundaries.

INTEGRATED CURRICULUM DESIGN

Educators espousing integration have provided a variety of curriculum design options. Beane (1995) recommended that curriculum integration must have social meaning, and, therefore, design begins with "problems, issues and concerns posed by life itself" (p. 616). The notion of organizing a science and mathematics curriculum around projects as a relevant way to connect science, mathematics, and events outside of the classroom was a consensus of the NSF-sponsored Wingspread conference (Berlin & White, 1992). Venville, Wallace, Rennie, and Malone (1998) identified technology-based projects, competitions, and local community projects as forms of curriculum integration. More recently project-based science has been suggested as a methodology for curriculum integration because its key features (driving questions, student engagement in investigations, communities of learners collaborating together, use of technology, and creation of artifacts) are all congruent with integrated approaches. Rakow and Vasquez (1998) stated, "Project-based integration may be the most authentic form of cross-curricular integration because it involves students in real-world learning experiences. In project-based integration, students investigate real issues in real contexts."

Jacobs is well known for her work on curriculum integration. In 1989, she presented a continuum of curriculum design options that move from discipline-based to parallel disciplines, multidisciplinary and interdisciplinary units or courses, integrated day, and complete program integration. Underhill's (1995) editorial illustrated six perspectives on science and mathematics integration that echo some of the alternatives presented in Jacob's (1989) continuum: math and science are disjointed; there is some overlap between science and math; math and science are the same; math is a subset of science; science is a subset of math; and there is major overlap between science and mathematics. Brown and Wall (1976) presented a similar vision of science and mathematics integration in which mathematics and science (on opposite ends of the continuum) are taught for their own sake; science is guided by math; math is guided by science; or science and mathematics are blended with each other.

Davison, Miller, and Metheny (1995) identified five different models of integration: discipline specific (i.e., two or more branches of science—integrating life and chemical science), content specific (combining related objects from several disciplines—combining mathematics with science), process (using skills such as collecting data, analyzing data, and reporting results to examine real-life situations), methodological (i.e., the learning cycle model as a good way to solve problems in science), and thematic (selecting a theme, such as sharks, and teaching academic concepts around the theme). Projects such as AIMS and GEMS are good commercial examples of curricula that focus on integrating science and mathematics by using process skills, such as observing, classifying, and analyzing (Roebuck & Warden, 1998).

A similar continuum of integration for science and mathematics, ranging through independent mathematics, mathematics focus, balanced mathematics and science, science focus, and independent science, was developed by Lonning and DeFranco (1997) and Lonning, DeFranco, and Weinland (1998). They suggested that readers should ask two questions when planning an integrated curriculum: "What are the major mathematics and science concepts being taught in the activity?" and "Are these concepts worthwhile? That is, are they key elements in the curricula and meaningful to students?" (p. 214). Likewise, Huntley (1998) presented a mathematics and science continuum on which the ends of the spectrum represent separate subject area teaching and the center represents integration of the two subjects. However, Huntley extended the Lonning and DeFranco model by emphasizing that the center point, integration, occurs only when science and mathematics are dealt with in a synergistic fashion. Francis (1996) extended the mathematics and science continuum by proposing a connections matrix that integrated mathematics and science standards to integrate the curriculum.

Hurley (2001) conducted a study to determine the types of integration that have historically been used and found five major types of integration: sequenced (science and mathematics are planned and taught one preceding the other); parallel (science and mathematics are planned and taught together); partial (the subjects are taught separately as well as integrated); enhanced (one of the subjects is the major discipline being taught and the other is added to enhance the other); and total (science and mathematics are taught equally together). She found that no form of integration ever totally dominated in any period of history from the 1940s to 1990s.

RESEARCH ON INTEGRATION

Most of the literature on curriculum integration could be characterized as testimonials, how-to's, or unit/activity ideas. For example, a thematic approach is used in all K–8 classrooms where teachers report student excitement and the teacher's co-operative spirit (Peters, Schubeck, & Hopkins, 1995). School Science and Mathematics Integrated Lessons (SSMILES) are published in *School Science and Mathematics*. For example, McDonald and Czerniak (1998) describe activities developed to integrate science and mathematics around the theme of sharks. Descriptions abound of integrated methods, units, and processes used with preservice and inservice teachers and K–12 students (Francis & Underhill, 1996; Sandmann, Weber, Czerniak, and Ahern, 1999; Stuessy, 1993). Some articles discuss integrated arts and science undergraduate courses (Deeds, Allen, Callen, & Wood, 2000).

In the last five years, a greater amount of research-based literature has surfaced focusing on integration. Concerned with the lack of empirical evidence supporting the integration of science and mathematics, Hurley (2001) used mixed methodology to review 31 studies with reported outcomes conducted between 1935 and 1997. She used Study Effect Meta-analytic (SEM) methods to review the quantitative aspects of these studies, and she used grounded theory to analyze the qualitative portions of these studies. Hurley's review found quantitative evidence favoring integration and qualitative evidence revealing the existence of multiple forms of integration. Most of the published empirical research studies on integration reviewed in this chapter support its use. A number of K–12 studies sustain the notion that integration helps students learn, motivates students, and helps build problem-solving skills. Studies regarding teachers' reactions to integration focus on teacher beliefs and attitudes, subject matter knowledge, and obstacles faced when in the implementation of integrated approaches.

Student Achievement and Affective Gains

Meier, Nicol, and Cobbs (1998) state, "Without evidence that integration will produce improved student performance in mathematics and science, little change can be expected" (p. 439). This call for research that provides evidence of student performance through the use of integration has been met somewhat in the last few years.

Green (1991) reported that student achievement scores significantly improved after a year-long restructuring to connect science to all subject areas. Seventy-eight percent of students had improved NAEP scores in science, exceeding the NAEP nationwide figures. Teachers and principals also reported success with educationally disadvantaged students and indicated that real-world integration accelerated the rate of language acquisition for bilingual students. Stevenson and Carr (1993) reported increased student interest and achievement in integrated instruction. Similarly, Vars (1991) and Beane (1995) reported that interdisciplinary programs produced higher standardized achievement scores than did separate-subject curriculum. These authors also acknowledged that the interdisciplinary curriculum is frequently embedded into other reforms such as block scheduling and multi-age grouping, and therefore it is difficult to separate the effects of integration from those of other reform strategies. Zwick and Miller (1996) found that Native American students using an outdoor-based integrated science curriculum outperformed their peers using a traditional curriculum on the California Achievement Test 85 (CAT). Similarly, McGehee (2001) described the development of a problem-solving framework for interdisciplinary units used with minority students in a northern Arizona summer academy that found evidence of student success based on artifacts from student projects.

Studies that examined student gains made in curriculum improvement projects or a commercial integrated curriculum convey positive results. Shann (1977) explored the effect of the Unified Science and Mathematics for Elementary Schools (USMES) program and noted an increase in students' content knowledge and problem-solving skills. Additionally, there was an increase in students' self-worth, socialization ability, and excitement for learning. Goldberg and Wagreich (1989) report increased academic achievement in the Teaching Integrated Mathematics and Science (TIMS) program. Similarly, Berlin and Hillen (1994) report increased cognitive, motivational, and attitudinal outcomes for fourth-, fifth-, and sixth-graders using the Activities Integrating Mathematics and Science (AIMS) program.

A number of studies focused on affective gains made in the use of integrated curricula. Friend (1985) reported that students exhibited an appreciation of science as a result of an integrated mathematics/science program. McComas (1993) and Bragow, Gragow, and Smith (1995) confirmed that thematic units had a positive impact on student attitudes and interest in school. Barb and Landa (1997) state that when focused on a problem worth solving, interdisciplinary units motivate students to learn. Integrated science and reading instruction was also found to affect motivation (Guthrie, Wigfield, & VonSecker, 2000).

Hurley (2001) conducted a comprehensive study of integrated curricula from the early twentieth century to the present. Small student achievement effect sizes were found for both science and mathematics in studies from the 1930s to 1950s, and medium effect sizes were found for studies in the 1960s and 1970s (mostly curriculum improvement projects). Small effect sizes were found for studies published in the 1980s and 1990s. Student achievement effects were higher for science than for mathematics in integrated courses, especially when mathematics was used to enhance science or when the two subjects were totally integrated. Student achievement effects were higher for mathematics when mathematics was planned in sequence with science, but the subjects were taught separately—first mathematics and then science. Qualitative analyses found positive evidence for integration, attendance, student enthusiasm, and student engagement.

Hurley's (2001) meta-analyses of the effect of each type of integration on student achievement revealed differences. Sequential instruction resulted in positive effect sizes for science and mathematics, with mathematics effect sizes being larger. Parallel (but separate) integration had negative effect sizes for both science and mathematics, indicating that students achieved more in traditional instruction. Partially integrated and partially separate integration had small positive effects for science and mathematics. Enhanced instruction had a medium positive effect size for science and small effect sizes for mathematics. Total integration of science and mathematics had a large effect size for science and a small effect size for mathematics.

It may be more difficult to flesh out the effectiveness of integration on college-age students because of the limited number of integrated programs in universities, but McComas and Wang (1998) summarized a few studies of college-age students that demonstrated greater achievement or interest in science when it was presented as an integrated program rather than a traditional sequence.

Teacher Knowledge and Attitudes

A number of studies examined teachers' knowledge of and attitudes toward using integrated strategies. Although integrated techniques have been used for years in pre-K–12 schools, the integrated teacher education methods course at the university level is a more recent phenomenon. Nonetheless, studies can be found at both the preservice and inservice levels, but the findings for the effectiveness of integration are mixed.

Preservice Teachers

Conclusions from earlier studies of preservice teachers were based more on anecdotal examinations than outcome measures. For example, Lehman and McDonald (1988) studied the perceptions of preservice teachers toward integrated mathematics and science and found that preservice teachers had a greater familiarity with integration than practicing teachers, and mathematics teachers were concerned with covering the curriculum if they used an integrated approach. Lonning and DeFranco (1994) developed an integrated science and mathematics methods course, and anecdotal surveys and course evaluations indicated that students' attitudes toward the course were positive and students were enthusiastic about the course. Haigh and Rehfeld (1995) described the integration of a secondary mathematics and science methods course, and they report that surveys of students' opinions were generally favorable. Although the authors describe how they evaluated the course, no evidence is provided as to the merits of integration over separate courses.

Briscoe and Stout (1996) describe the integration of math and science through a problem-centered methods course. Using data from qualitative analyses, the authors describe problems preservice teachers had with problem solving, but it is unclear whether or how these were different from learning problem solving in separate mathematics and science methods courses. Kotar, Guenter, Metzger, and Overholt (1998) describe a teacher education model for curriculum integration that they used at California State University, Chico, but no evidence is provided about the effectiveness of the model. Conversely, Stuessy and Naizer (1996) report gains in reflection and problem solving after students completed an integrated mathematics and science methods course.

In a study of a team-taught middle-level mathematics and science methods course, Koirala and Bowman (2003) found that preservice teachers appreciated the emphasis on integration and had a better understanding of integration. An absence of integration was sometimes found because some science and mathematics concepts did not lend themselves to integration. As a result, students were frustrated at the tension between subjects. Furthermore, students at some middle schools seldom taught in an integrated fashion in their field experiences or student teaching, and these students tended to lose their appreciation for integration. In contrast, Hart (2002) studied preservice teachers' beliefs and practice after participating in an integrated mathematics/science methods course and found that beliefs and teachers' reported classroom teaching behaviors were consistent with program and reform goals.

Hurley (2003) studied methods course offerings and found that most universities reported that their integrated science and mathematics methods courses were summer courses, grant-funded projects, or experimental. Few universities had integrated courses at the time of study, but several had integrated science and mathematics Master's degree programs. Hurley's study found that surveyed universities' reported successes included teachers gaining science and mathematics concepts and reasoning, positive preservice teacher attitudes and enthusiasm, improvement in higher order thinking skills in science, improved teacher reflectivity, and success in connecting theory to practice. Failures and challenges included difficulties in communication among teaching partners, lower higher order thinking skills in math, teachers' lack of content knowledge to integrate, overcoming influence of supervising teachers in field experiences, mathematics attitudes transferring to science, concern about coverage of curriculum, and challenges with enacting reforms.

Inservice Teachers

Few studies on inservice teacher education focused on teacher knowledge or pedagogical skill. More commonly, studies reported teacher beliefs and attitudes. Again, findings are mixed regarding the effectiveness of integrated strategies.

In one of the few studies on teacher knowledge and instructional skill, Basista, Tomlin, Pennington, and Pugh (2001) evaluated an integrated professional development program and found significant gains in understanding of content and confidence to implement integrated science and mathematics in their teaching. Similarly, Basista and Mathews (2002) discovered that a professional development program for middle grades science and mathematics teachers (intensive summer institute, academic year support, and administrator workshops) increased teachers' content and integration knowledge, increased pedagogical knowledge and implementation, increased administrator awareness of science and mathematics standards, and helped support teachers as they implemented practices during the school year. Teachers in a collaborative professional development project that integrated science with mathematics, using language arts and technology, displayed increased levels of competence and confidence in the use of technology to teach science and mathematics (Cleland, Wetzel, Zambo, Buss, & Rillero, 1999).

Differential effects on students were found, depending on how the teacher implemented integrated curriculum and instruction. Waldrip (2001) found that primary teachers perceived that they implemented integration in their classrooms, but the actual level of implementation influenced the students' learning. Use of a science theme without strong connections to language and mathematics was less effective, whereas strong connections to other subject areas helped studies attain a deeper level of understanding.

To a greater extent, the research on inservice teachers focused on their beliefs, attitudes, and perceived barriers of integration. Watanabe and Huntley (1998) reported that mathematics and science educators in a NSF-funded project had many of the same beliefs about integration as other classroom teachers. Middle-level mathematics and science teachers thought that connecting mathematics and science helps students with tangible examples of mathematics, that math helps students become familiar with science relationships, and that connections provide relevancy and incentive for students.

Teachers in a Maryland NSF-funded project saw some barriers to integrated instruction, including the conflict over time in the school day and coverage of content, students not desiring to see connections between the subjects, the teacher's lack of subject matter knowledge in both subjects, and teachers feeling uncomfortable with teaching the subject for which they were not originally prepared or certified (Watanabe & Huntley, 1998). Likewise, Keys (2003) reported that despite holding similar beliefs, elementary teachers used integration to compensate for lack of knowledge to teach science, whereas secondary teachers did not consider integration because it limited the amount of time needed to cover the curriculum. Wieseman and Moscovici (2003) also describe the challenges that inservice teachers face when implementing interdisciplinary approaches.

Czerniak, Lumpe, and Haney (1999) found that teachers generally have positive beliefs concerning the use of thematic units, but negative attitudes toward integration also exist. In general, K–12 teachers believed that thematic units in the classroom have the ability to foster student excitement and interest in learning science. Although some teachers believe that integration can make science more meaningful to students because students see connections between the sciences and other subject areas, others were concerned that thematic units would water down the curriculum. Teachers were concerned that it would be time consuming and difficult to use thematic units, especially because integrated curriculum materials are not abundant. The teachers specified that a number of variables would be needed (but unlikely to be available) to help them use thematic units (resources including funding, curriculum materials, supplies and equipment; staff development; less emphasis on testing and assessment; team teaching; administrative support; and a course of study that stressed integration). Although not surprising, it was revealed that teachers of lower grade levels have greater intentions to implement thematic units in their classrooms than teachers of upper grade levels.

Finally, in a study conducted among 400 schools in Missouri, Arredondo and Rucinski (1996) discovered differences among rural and low-SES schools regarding curriculum integration. They found that a high percentage of rural, low-SES schools are not involved in any type of curriculum integration. In schools where there is a high use of integrated curriculum, teachers reported greater involvement in decision-making processes at the school—perhaps indicating their involvement in school reform efforts.

DISADVANTAGES OF CURRICULUM INTEGRATION

Critics of integration purport that there is insignificant evidence to support the belief that integrated approaches are any more effective than traditional, separate subjects. George (1996) summarized assertions about integration not corroborated by research:

1. Addresses the real-life concerns of students better than traditional curriculum
2. Presents greater opportunities for problem solving
3. Promotes student's independent learning
4. Offers more effective involvement with the environment and society
5. Provides more opportunities for student involvement in planning the curriculum along with the teacher

6. Allows teachers more opportunity to be "facilitators of learning"
7. Permits learning in greater depth; makes deeper connections
8. Presents students with opportunities to capitalize on prior learning more effectively
9. Allows for more application of curriculum outcomes to real life
10. Supplies more concrete experiences for slower learners or more enrichment opportunities for more able students
11. Encourages greater transfer or retention of learned information
12. More effectively rejuvenates and energizes career teachers with new experiences
13. Helps provide greater achievement, personal development, or harmonious group citizenship

From a theoretical perspective, Lederman and Niess (1997) commented that research on integrated instruction seems to demonstrate that science and mathematics instruction is severely restricted because the concepts included are narrowed to a specific framework. Evidence of this, they stated, is the disappointing achievement results associated with the STS approach. The argument was made that each discipline possesses unique conceptual, procedural, and epistemological differences that cannot be addressed through an integrated approach, and thus it is preferred that connections be made among topics, with each subject area retaining its own identity.

Roth's (1994) experience teaching a fifth-grade unit around the theme of 1492 supports Lederman and Niess's assertions. Roth's experiences were frustrating, because the science content was confined to the theme, and attempts to integrate science into the theme often distorted and diminished the science content she hoped to teach. Davison, Miller, and Metheny (1995) asked the following questions in reference to concerns about integration of mathematics and science: "1) To what extent can these integration efforts represent bona fide integration of science and mathematics? 2) To what extent has the integration of science and mathematics been merely cosmetic?" (p. 226).

Mason (1996) listed a number of logistical problems that may be disadvantages for using integrated strategies. For instance, mathematics concepts are sequential, and adding mathematics concepts as bits and pieces in the curriculum could confuse students if they lack the prerequisite knowledge and skills. In other words, adding mathematics here and there for the sake of integrating might leave wide gaps in the subject matter and student understanding. Additionally, Mason described a typical example of integration at the elementary school level, such as "the rain forest," and argued that students are typically asked to graph the number of endangered species. He cast doubt on the value of making dozens of graphs. Mason also asserts that many teachers, in an effort to force integration, trivialize the content. For example, "A poem about photosynthesis may not help one understand photosynthesis as a process, or poetry as a genre" (p. 266). Gardner and Boix-Mansilla (1994) concur with Mason by stating that prerequisite skills are often needed before students can use an integrated curriculum, and schools typically do not have time to both teach skills and put them in an integrated curriculum.

Thus, if integration becomes contrived and formed around trivial themes, children may not have the prerequisite background. The *Professional Standards for Teach-*

ing Mathematics state, "The content is unquestionably a critical consideration in appraising the value of a particular task" (NCTM, 1991). Despite the fact that NCTM stresses content, Roebuck and Warden (1998) declare that few curriculum materials use the content of science or mathematics as a focus of integration. Lonning and DeFranco (1997) maintain that integration is justified only when connecting science and mathematics concepts enhances the understanding of the subject areas. To avoid a shallow curriculum that lacks meaning, they suggest that some concepts and skills are better taught separately. They advised that teachers should avoid forced integration. Similarly, the National Council for the Social Studies (1994) warned:

> Integrative aspects have the potential for enhancing the scope and power of social studies. They also, however, have the potential for undermining its coherence and thrust as a curriculum component that addresses unique citizen education goals. Consequently, programs that feature a great deal of integration of social studies with other school subjects—even programs ostensibly built around social studies as the core of the curriculum—do not necessarily create powerful social studies learning. Unless they are developed as plans for accomplishing major social studies goals, such programs may focus on trivial or disconnected information. (pp. 165–166)

Several research studies support the claim that integration is no more effective than well-planned traditional curricula. St. Clair and Hough (1992) stated that few studies support interdisciplinary curriculum results in gains in student achievement. Similarly, Merrill (2001) found no significant achievement gains in high school students exposed to an integrated technology, mathematics, and science curricula.

Obstacles to Enacting Integrated Units

One of the true tests of any educational idea is that it can be successfully implemented in schools. McBride and Silverman (1991) cautioned that a number of problems must be addressed before integrated instruction becomes commonplace:

1. In most schools, students formally encounter the science and mathematics curricula organized and taught as separate subjects.
2. More instructional time is required to teach mathematics concepts through science concepts.
3. Classroom management can be more complicated when students are engaged in integrated science and mathematics activities than when they are solely engaged in whole class mathematics instruction.
4. Many teachers do not have science materials to utilize in mathematics instruction.
5. Few teachers have access to or are aware of curriculum materials that integrate science and mathematics.

Meier, Nicol, and Cobbs (1998) also pointed out that there are a number of barriers to integration: the content barrier (science and mathematics topics don't always integrate well without one subject leaving gaps), teacher knowledge barrier (secondary teachers prepared in one subject, state licensure often isn't integrated, elementary teachers have limited subject matter knowledge about how to integrate), teacher belief barrier (inservice teachers think the curriculum is already crowded; preservice teachers don't know about integrated curriculum; and math teachers are less likely to integrate than science teachers), school structure barriers (schedules, different teachers without common planning time, tracking students, supplies/materials, and assessment), and curriculum barriers (standardized tests cover separate subjects, don't measure higher order thinking skills associated with integration).

Lehman (1994) discovered that in spite of positive perceptions about integration, teachers' views do not carry over into their practice. Teachers often believed there was no time to add integrated ideas into an already overcrowded curriculum, and they were not aware of integrated resources. Similarly, Watanabe and Huntley (1998) reported that although teachers in the Maryland Collaborative for Teacher Preparation had positive attitudes about connecting science and mathematics, some had problems enacting the curriculum. Some teachers were concerned with the amount of time it took to infuse integration into an already crammed curriculum. To counter the content coverage concern, Beane (1995) maintains that the separate subject curriculum is already too dense and not everything is covered now. He argued that curriculum integration allows the most important and powerful ideas in the discipline to surface. Pang and Good (2000) mention that the current U.S. curriculum is already fragmented and unfocused, and therefore any attempts to integrate a coherent content would be difficult.

Concerns about time may be related to the structure of the school day—especially in high schools where the organization does not allow time or structure to integrate (Jacobs, 1989; Venville, Wallace, Rennie, & Malone, 1998). Unless teachers team teach (an approach popular in middle schools), they rarely have the opportunity to work with other teachers outside of their discipline (Mason, 1996). More recently, block scheduling is seen as a format that allows for reforms such as integration (Canady & Rettig, 1996).

In summarizing Lynn A. Steen's presentation at the 1991 Wingspread conference, Berlin (1994) cited inadequate teacher preparation as one cause for lack of integration. Steen declared that few science teachers, with maybe the exception of chemistry and physics teachers, have enough mathematical background to integrate advanced mathematics with science, and few mathematics teachers would be able to teach even one science subject area. Similarly, Lehman (1994) stated that less than 50% of 221 preservice and inservice teachers surveyed believed they had sufficient content background to integrate science and mathematics. Mason (1996) also suggested that many teachers do not know how to create an integrated curriculum, and, thus, teacher education may be one problem contributing to the limited implementation of integrated curriculum (Roebuck & Warden, 1998). Generally, preservice teachers do not take integrated classes in their general studies, and they do not experience integrated methods. As a result, they do not know how to integrate across the curriculum (Mason, 1996). In most states, teachers (especially secondary teachers) are licensed in specific disciplines and, therefore, do not possess the knowledge needed to integrate with other subject areas.

Student assessment is viewed as an impediment to enacting an integrated curriculum, since standardized tests measure, for the most part, disciplinary knowledge (Berlin & White, 1992; Mason, 1996). Although the standards movement (NCTM, NRC, NCSS, NCTE/IRA) is moving along disciplinary lines, it encourages integration. Standards and tests, however, do not exist for integrated ideas, and as a result, national trends will likely fail to support integration—especially with testing guidelines established in the No Child Left Behind legislation (http://www .nochildleftbehind.gov).

Finally, a few studies indicate that curriculum integration poses difficulties for teachers that might affect the quality of instruction. McGehee (2001) summarized problems that occurred among instructors teaching together and found that instructors needed to work out issues among themselves (i.e., some dominating lectures and separating their subject area). Hurley (2001) discovered that integration of science and mathematics took more time, was a challenge to teachers, and resulted in less time being spent on mathematics. She also observed that integrated courses developed by classroom teachers were less effective in affecting student achievement than commercially designed curriculum materials.

CONCLUSION

A number of implications can be drawn from this literature review. These implications provide foci for science educators to provide leadership in clarifying issues, challenging basic assumptions, and solving problems associated with integrating science with other subject areas. In spite of a plethora of literature about the benefits of curriculum integration and some recent research-based studies to support this belief, additional research would be useful to verify these benefits and determine whether the results can be used to inform school-based practices.

There continues to be a lack of consensus regarding the definition of integration. Models presented in the October 1998 special issue of *School Science and Mathematics* provide a catalyst for this discussion, but the debate continues (Hurley 2001, 2003; Pang and Good, 2000). Elucidation of definitions may help science educators eliminate confusion when discussing curriculum and instructional approaches that endeavor to integrate curriculum. Moreover, a clear-cut definition could provide the stimulus for the design and completion of further research regarding the impact of integrated curriculum.

A few STS and project-based curriculum projects focus on issues as a means to integrate across the curriculum and make science relevant to real life. However, most integrated curricula, particularly commercial curricula, concentrate on process skills and give little attention to using science or mathematics content as the curriculum's central focus. Thus, the implication is that educators continue to search for good curriculum materials that provide sufficient, high-quality science and mathematics content.

Problems regarding the structure of the school day need to be overcome before integration becomes commonplace in schools. In the last few years, many U.S. schools turned to block scheduling as a way to provide teachers, particularly at the middle, junior, and high school levels, with larger portions of time to teach (Canady, 1995; Canady & Rettig, 1996). The block schedule typically provides a 90-minute segment of time rather than the traditional 45- or 50-minute class periods, and this format may give teachers the time needed to integrate the curriculum.

Hurley (2003) identified some benefits of teacher education models designed to prepare teachers to integrate the curriculum but also noted that integrated methods courses are atypical. A few new studies support curriculum integration in professional development models (Basista, Tomlin, Pennington, & Pugh, 2001; Basista & Mathews, 2002). To better prepare preservice and inservice teachers to design and implement integrated units, they must be familiar with state and national reform recommendations, receive instruction in the integration of science and mathematics, and learn about integrated curriculum resources. It is also important that teachers experience courses where team teaching is used so that they have a better understanding of the collaborative processes needed to enact integrated strategies (Lehman, 1994; Mason, 1996).

The pressure of high-stakes standardized tests continues to be a limiting factor in implementing an integrated curriculum, and recent No Child Left Behind legislation may only exacerbate the problem. Because most standardized tests examine content separately, educators are doubtful about whether the knowledge and skills learned in an integrated fashion would transfer to these tests. One may conclude that for integration to be widely accepted in a standards environment, either standardized tests need to measure knowledge and skills associated with learning in an integrated manner or integrated units developed commercially and by teachers need to contain assessments consistent with those in the standards and on high-stakes tests.

It is paradoxical that despite the interest in integrated approaches over the last 100 years, standards today for each discipline remain separate (e.g., NCTM, NRC's *National Science Education Standards*, NCTE/IRA, and NCSS). If progress is to be made in moving integrated instruction into the mainstream, discussions need to occur among leaders of professional organizations to establish standards for integrating content areas.

Finally, Pang and Good (2000) perhaps best summarize the challenges surrounding attempts to integrate across the curriculum and the need for additional research:

> These issues suggest that integration of mathematics and science is one of the most daunting tasks educators face. There is no magic formula for completing the task except collaborative efforts among various disciplines and personnel. The more communication is opened about successes and failures of integration, the more significant progress can be made toward identifying what teachers are expected to teach and students are expected to learn through integrated curricula. In order to help all students become more scientifically and mathematically literate, a goal most reform documents advocate, more focused attention about integration of curriculum and instruction is necessary. (p. 78)

ACKNOWLEDGMENTS

Thanks to Carl Berger and Robert Lonning who reviewed this chapter.

REFERENCES

AIMS Educational Foundation. (1986). *Activities integrating math and science.* Fresno, CA: Author.
AIMS Educational Foundation. (1987). *Math + science: A solution.* Fresno, CA: Author.
Akerson, V. L. (2001). Teaching science when your principal says, "Teach language arts." *Science and Children, 38*(7), 42–47.

Arredondo, D. E., & Rucinski, T. T. (1996). Integrated curriculum: Its use, initiation and support in Midwestern schools. *Mid-Western Educational Researcher, 9*(2), 37–44.

Barab, S. A., & Landa, A. (1997). Designing effective interdisciplinary anchors. *Educational Leadership, 54*(6), 52–55.

Basista, B., & Mathews, S. (2002). Integrated science and mathematics professional development programs. *School Science and Mathematics, 102*(7), 360–370.

Basista, B., Tomlin, J., Pennington, K., & Pugh, D. (2001). Inquiry-based integrated science and mathematics professional development program. *Education, 121*(3), 615–624.

Beane, J. A. (1993, 1997). *A middle school curriculum: From rhetoric to reality.* Columbus, OH: National Middle School Association.

Beane, J. (1995). Curriculum integration and the disciplines of knowledge. *Phi Delta Kappan, 76,* 616–622.

Beane, J. (1996). On the shoulders of giants! The case for curriculum integration. *Middle School Journal, 28,* 6–11.

Beane, J. A. (1997). *Curriculum integration: Designing the core of democratic education.* New York: Teachers College Press.

Berger, C. F. (1994). Breaking what barriers between science and mathematics? Six myths from a technological perspective. In D. F. Berlin (Ed.), *NSF/SSMA Wingspread conference: A network for integrated science and mathematics teaching and learning* (pp. 23–27). School Science and Mathematics Association Topics for Teachers Series (No. 7). Bowling Green, OH: School Science and Mathematics Association.

Berlin, D. (1994). The integration of science and mathematics education: Highlights from the NSF/SSMA Wingspread conference plenary papers. *School Science and Mathematics, 94*(1), 32–35.

Berlin, D. F., & Hillen, J. A. (1994). Making connections in math and science: Identifying student outcomes. *School Science and Mathematics, 94*(6), 283–290.

Berlin, D., & White, A. (1992). Report from the NSF/SSMA Wingspread conference: A network for integrated science and mathematics teaching and learning. *School Science and Mathematics, 92*(6), 340–342.

Berlin, D., & White, A. (1994). The Berlin-White integrated science and mathematics model (BWISM). *School Science and Mathematics, 94*(1), 2–4.

Bragow, D., Gragow, K. A., & Smith, E. (1995). Back to the future: Toward curriculum integration. *Middle School Journal, 27,* 39–46.

Brazee, E. N., & Capelluti, J. (1995). *Dissolving boundaries: Toward an integrative curriculum.* Columbus, OH: National Middle School Association.

Briscoe, C., & Stout, D. (1996). Integrating math and science through problem centered learning in methods courses: Effects on prospective teachers' understanding of problem solving. *Journal of Elementary Science Education, 8*(2), 66–87.

Brooks, J. G., & Brooks, M. G. (1993). *In search of understanding: The case for constructivist classrooms.* Alexandria, VA: Association for Supervision and Curriculum Development.

Brown, W. R., & Wall, C. E. (1976). A look at the integration of science and mathematics in the elementary school—1976. *School Science and Mathematics, 76*(7), 551–562.

BSCS. (1994). Innovations in science education survey instrument. Colorado Springs, CO: Author.

Canady, R. (1995). *Block scheduling: A catalyst for change in high schools.* Princeton, NJ: Eye on Education.

Canady, R., & Rettig, M. (1996). *Teaching in the block: Strategies for engaging active learners.* Princeton, NJ: Eye on Education.

Carnegie Council on Adolescent Development, Task Force on Education of Young Adolescents (1989). *Turning points: Preparing American youth for the 21st century: The report of the task force on education of young adolescents.* Washington, DC: Carnegie Council on Adolescent Development.

Cleland, J. V., Wetzel, K. A., Zambo, R., Buss, R. R., & Rillero, P. (1999). Science integrated with mathematics using language arts and technology: A model for collaborative professional development. *Journal of Computers in Mathematics and Science Teaching 18*(2), 157–172.

Cohen, P. (1995). Understanding the brain: Educators seek to apply brain research. *ASCD Education Update, 37*(7), 1, 4–5.

Crane, S. (1991). Integrated science in a restructured high school. *Educational Leadership 49*(2), 39–41.

Cremin, L. (1964). *The transformation of the school.* New York: Vintage Press.

Czerniak, C. M., Lumpe, A. T., & Haney, J. J. (1999) Teacher's beliefs about thematic units in science. *Journal of Science Teacher Education, 10*(2), 123–145.

Czerniak, C. M., Weber, W., Sandmann, A., & Ahern, J. (December, 1999). A literature review of science and mathematics integration, *School Science and Mathematics, 99*(8), 421–430.

Davison, D. M., Miller, K. W., & Metheny, D. L. (1995). What does integration of science and mathematics really mean? *School Science and Mathematics, 95*(5), 226–230.

Deeds, D. G., Allen, C. S., Callen, B. W., & Wood, M. W. (2000). A new paradigm in integrated math and science courses: Finding common ground across disciplines. *Journal of College Science Teaching, 30*(3), 178–183.

Dickinson, V. L., & Young, T. A. (1998). Elementary science and language arts: Should we blur the boundaries? *School Science and Mathematics, 98*(6), 334–339.

Erb, T. O. (2001). *This we believe . . . and now we must act.* Westerville, OH: National Middle School Association.

Francis, R. W. (1996). Connecting the curriculum through the national mathematics and science standards. *Journal of Science Teacher Education, 7*(1), 75–81.

Francis, R., & Underhill, R. G. (1996). A procedure for integrating math and science units. *School Science and Mathematics, 96*(3), 114–119.

Friend, H. (1985). The effect of science and mathematics integration on selected seventh grade students' attitudes toward and achievement in science. *School Science and Mathematics, 85*(6), 453–461.

Gardner, H., & Boix-Mansilla, V. (1994). Teaching for understanding within and across the disciplines. *Educational Leadership, 51*, 14–18.

George, P. S. (1996). The integrated curriculum: A reality check. *Middle School Journal, 28*, 12–19.

Goldberg, H., & Wagreich, P. (1989). Focus on integrating science and math. *Science and Children, 26*(5), 22–24.

Greene, L. C. (1991). Science-centered curriculum in elementary school. *Educational Leadership, 49*, 42–51.

Guthrie, J. T., Wigfield, A., & VonSecker, C. (2000). Effects of integrated instruction on motivation and strategy use in reading. *Journal of Educational Psychology, 92*(2), 331–341.

Haigh, W., & Rehfeld, D. (1995). Integration of secondary mathematics and science methods courses: A model. *School Science and Mathematics, 95*(5), 240–247.

Hart, L. C. (2002). Preservice teachers' beliefs and practice after participating in an integrated content/methods course. *School Science and Mathematics, 102*(1), 4–14.

Huntley, M. A. (1998). Design and implementation of a framework for defining integrated mathematics and science education. *School Science and Mathematics, 98*(6), 320–327.

Hurd, P. D. (1991). Why we must transform science education. *Educational Leadership, 49*(2), 33–35.

Hurley, M. M. (1999). Interdisciplinary mathematics and science: Characteristics, forms, and related effect sizes for student achievement and affective outcomes. Doctoral dissertation, University at Albany, State University of New York.

Hurley, M. M. (2001). Reviewing integrated science and mathematics: The search for evidence and definitions from new perspectives. *School Science and Mathematics, 101*(5), 259–268.

Hurley, M. M. (2003). *The presence, value, and reasoning behind integrated science and mathematics methods courses.* Paper presented at the annual meeting of the National Association for Research in Science Teaching, Philadelphia.

Institute for Mathematics and Science Education. (1995). *Teaching integrated mathematics and science (TIMS).* Chicago: University of Illinois at Chicago, Author.

Jacobs, H. H. (1989). *Interdisciplinary curriculum: Design and implementation.* Alexandria, VA: Association for Supervision and Curriculum Development.

Keys, P. (2003). *Teachers bending the science curriculum*. Paper presented at the annual meeting of the National Association for Research in Science Teaching, Philadelphia.

Koirala, H. P., & Bowman, J. K. (2003). Preparing middle level preservice teachers to integrate mathematics and science: Problems and possibilities. *School Science and Mathematics, 103*(3), 145–154.

Kotar, M., Guenter, C. E., Metzger, D., & Overholt, J. L. (1998). Curriculum integration: A teacher education model. *Science and Children, 35*(5), 40–43.

Lawrence Hall of Science. (1984). *Great explorations in math and science (GEMS)*. Berkeley, CA: University of California at Berkeley, Author.

Lederman, N. G., & Niess, M. L. (1997). Integrated, interdisciplinary, or thematic instruction? Is this a question or is it questionable semantics? *School Science and Mathematics, 97*(2), 57–58.

Lehman, J. R. (1994). Integrating science and mathematics: Perceptions of preservice and practicing elementary teachers. *School Science and Mathematics, 94*(2), 58–64.

Lehman, J. R., & McDonald, J. L. (1988). Teachers' perceptions of the integration of mathematics and science. *School Science and Mathematics, 88*(8), 642–649.

Lonning, R. A., & DeFranco, T. C. (1994). Development and implementation of an integrated mathematics/science preservice elementary methods course. *School Science and Mathematics, 94*(1), 18–25.

Lonning, R. A., & DeFranco, T. C. (1997). Integration of science and mathematics: A theoretical model. *School Science and Mathematics, 97*(4), 212–215.

Lonning, R. A., DeFranco, T. C., & Weinland, T. P. (1998). Development of theme-based, interdisciplinary, integrated curriculum: A theoretical model. *School Science and Mathematics, 98*(6), 312–319.

Mason, T. C. (1996). Integrated curricula: Potential and problems. *Journal of Teacher Education, 47*(4), 263–270.

McBride, J. W., & Silverman, F. L. (1991). Integrating elementary/middle school science and mathematics. *School Science and Mathematics, 91*(7), 285–292.

McComas, W. F. (1993). STS education and the affective domain. In R. E. Yager (Ed.), *What research says to the science teacher, 7: The science, technology, and society movement* (pp. 161–168). Washington, DC: National Science Teachers Association.

McComas, W. F., & Wang, H. A. (1998). Blended science: The rewards and challenges of integrating the science disciplines for instruction. *School Science and Mathematics, 98*(6), 340–348.

McDonald, J., & Czerniak, C. M. (November, 1998). Scaling sharks. *School Science and Mathematics, 98*(7), 397–399.

McGehee, J. J. (2001). Developing interdisciplinary units: A strategy based on problem solving. *School Science and Mathematics, 101*(7), 380–389.

Meier, S. L., Nicol, M., & Cobbs, G. (1998). Potential benefits and barriers to integration. *School Science and Mathematics, 98*(8), 438–447.

Merrill, C. (2001). Integrating technology, mathematics, and science education: A quasi-experiment. *Journal of Industrial Teacher Education, 38*(3), 45–61.

Minnesota Mathematics and Science Project. (1970). Minneapolis, MN: Minnesota School Mathematics and Science Center.

Moore, E. H. (1967). On the foundations of mathematics. *Mathematics Teacher 60*, 360–374. A reprint of his 1902 retiring presidential address to the American Mathematical Society, originally published in *Science* (1903), 402–424.

National Association for the Education of Young Children. (1987). *Developmentally appropriate practice in early childhood programs serving children from birth through age 8*. Washington, DC: Author.

National Council for the Social Studies. (1994). *Curriculum standards for social studies*. Washington, DC: Author.

National Council of Teachers of English. (1996). *Standards for the English language arts*. Urbana, IL: Author; Newark, DE: International Reading Association.

National Council of Teachers of Mathematics. (1989). *Curriculum and evaluation standards for school mathematics*. Reston, VA: Author.

National Council of Teachers of Mathematics. (1991). *Professional standards for teaching mathematics*. Reston, VA: Author.

National Council of Teachers of Mathematics. (2000). *Principles and standards for school mathematics*. Reston, VA: Author.

National Middle School Association. (1982, 1995). *This we believe*. Columbus, OH: Author.

National Research Council. (1989). *Everybody counts: A report to the nation on the future of mathematics education*. Washington, DC: National Academy Press.

National Research Council. (1996). *National science education standards*. Washington, DC: National Academy Press.

National Science Teachers Association. (1992). *The content core*. Washington, DC: Author.

National Science Teachers Association. (1996). NSTA board endorses new position statement on interdisciplinary learning, PreK-grade 4. *NSTA Reports, 6*, 8.

Nesin, G., & Lounsbury, J. (1999). *Curriculum integration: Twenty questions—with answers*. Atlanta, GA: Georgia National Middle School Association.

Nuffield Foundation Science Teaching Project. (1967). London: Longmans.

Pang, J. S., & Good, R. (2000). A review of the integration of science and mathematics: Implications for further research. *School Science and Mathematics, 100*(2), 73–82.

Perkins, D. (1991). Educating for insight. *Educational Leadership, 49*, 4–8.

Peters, T., Schubeck, K., & Hopkins, K. (1995). A thematic approach: Theory and practice at the Aleknagik school. *Phi Delta Kappan, 76*, 633–636.

Rakow, S. J., & Vasquez, J. (1998). Integrated instruction: A trio of strategies. *Science and Children, 35*(6): 18–22.

Roebuck, K. I., & Warden, M. A. (1998). Searching for the center on the mathematics-science continuum. *School Science and Mathematics, 98*(6), 328–333.

Roth, K. J. (1994). Second thoughts about interdisciplinary studies. *American Educator, 18*(1), 44–48.

Rutherford, J., & Ahlgren, A. (1990). *Science for all Americans*. New York: Oxford University Press.

Sandmann, A. L., & Ahern, J. F. (2002). *Linking literature with life*. Silver Spring, MD: National Council for the Social Studies.

Sandmann, A., Weber, W., Czerniak, C., & Ahern, J. (Fall, 1999). Coming full circuit: An integrated unit plan for intermediate and middle grade students, *Science Activities 36*(3), 13–20.

Shann, M. H. (1977). Evaluation of an interdisciplinary, problem-solving curriculum in elementary science and mathematics, *Science Education, 61*(4), 491–502.

Smith, C. (2001). Addressing standards through curriculum integration. *Middle School Journal, 33*(2), 5–6.

St. Clair, B., & Hough, D. L. (1992). Interdisciplinary teaching: A review of the literature. ERIC Document Reproduction Service No. 373 056. Jefferson City, MO.

Stevenson, C., & Carr, J. (1993). *Integrated studies: Dancing through walls*. New York: Teachers College Press.

Stuessy, C. L. (1993). Concept to application: Development of an integrated mathematics/science methods course for preservice elementary teachers. *School Science and Mathematics, 93*(2), 55–62.

Stuessy, C. L., & Naizer, G. L. (1996). Reflection and problem solving: Integrating methods of teaching mathematics and science. *School Science and Mathematics, 96*(4), 170–177.

Underhill, R. (1995). Editorial. *School Science and Mathematics, 95*(5), 225.

Unified Science and Mathematics for Elementary Schools Project. (1973). Newton, MA: Educational Development Center.

Vars, G. F. (1991). Integrated curriculum in historical perspective. *Educational Leadership, 49*, 14–15.

Venville, G., Wallace, J., Rennie, L. J., & Malone, J. (1998). The integration of science, mathematics, and technology in a discipline-based culture. *School Science and Mathematics, 98*(6), 294–302.

Waldrip, B. (2001). Primary teachers' views about integrating science and literacy. *Investigating: Australian Primary & Junior Science Journal, 17*(1), 38–41.

Watanabe, T., & Huntley, M. A. (1998). Connecting mathematics and science in undergraduate teacher education programs: Faculty voices from the Maryland Collaborative for Teacher Preparation. *School Science and Mathematics, 98*(1), 19–25.

Wieseman, K. C., & Moscovici, H. (2003). Stories from the field: Challenges of science teacher education based on interdisciplinary approaches. *Journal of Science Teacher Education, 14*(2), 127–143.

Willis, S. (November 1992). Interdisciplinary learning: Movement to link the disciplines gains momentum. *ASCD Curriculum Update*, 1–8.

Zwick, T., & Miller, K. (1996). A comparison of integrated outdoor education activities and traditional science learning with American Indian students. *Journal of American Indian Education, 35*(2), 1–9.

CHAPTER 20

High School Biology Curricula Development: Implementation, Teaching, and Evaluation from the Twentieth to the Twenty-First Century

Reuven Lazarowitz
IIT, Israeli Institute of Technology, Haifa, Israel

This chapter is divided into two sections. The first part provides a description of the high school biology curricula taught in the twentieth century and presents the factors, which in the author's opinion, have contributed to the creation of these different study programs, based on the rationale described by Tyler (1960). The development of high school biology curricula during the past century will be depicted on the basis of two assumptions: one, that there is a high correlation among biology research, biology content structure, and biology high school curricula; and two, that new high school curricula in biology were affected by changes in society's daily life, in the high school student populations, research in science education in biology, and learning theories and pedagogy. All of these changes required modifications in the education of pre-service and in-service biology teachers; the latter issue is beyond the scope of this chapter. This section includes a short report based on selected studies of formative and summative evaluations, which investigated the implementation of the new programs in teaching biology in high school.

The second section encompasses several subjects investigated in teaching and learning biology that have had an impact on students' achievement in the cognitive, affective, and psychomotor domains. Because the new biology curricula emphasize the teaching of concepts and principles, the subjects were selected according to their relation to the "unifying themes in biology" (Schwab, 1963, p. 31), the seven levels of biological organization (Schwab, 1963, pp. 15, 16, 17), and the "fundamentals themes" in Nuffield Biology (Nuffield Foundation, 1966, p. 1). This section concludes with suggestions as to what kinds of curricula, learning materials in biology, and types of studies we need in order to address the issues of student heterogeneity in our schools, as well as their needs, interests and abilities, in order for them to master the knowledge and skills needed to cope with our highly scientific and technological society.

TYLER'S RATIONALE
FOR CURRICULUM DEVELOPMENT

Based on Tyler's Rationale for Curriculum Development, the concept of a course of study can be defined as a sequence of planned science topics to be taught in relation to a specific subject matter, for a particular age group of students, accompanied by recommendations as to what to teach in the classroom and laboratory. The planned curriculum recommends several textbooks written according to its organization, with suggested modes of instruction, learning, evaluation, and grading of students.

In 1960 Tyler published a monograph titled *Basic Principles of Curriculum and Instruction*, which was later revised by Madaus and Stufflebeam (1989). The study grew out of the problems brought on by the depression, one of which was the great increase in the number of youth attending high school (many of whom would have preferred to go to work but were unable to find employment) (Tyler, 1966). The motivation of the study was an attempt to define three key points with respect to qualitative education:

1. *Clarification of purpose*, which included a) selection of learning experiences, b) the organization of these experiences, and c) the assessment of progress toward the attainment of the school's objectives.
2. *A program's objectives should be clarified through* the learner's studies and studies of contemporary life.
3. *Objectives should then be screened through* a) the school's philosophy of education, b) theories of learning, and c) suggestions from subject matter specialists.

Four divisions of curriculum inquiry were outlined:

1. What educational purposes should the school seek to attain?
2. What educational experiences can be provided that are likely to help attain these objectives?
3. How can these educational experiences be effectively organized?
4. How can we determine whether these objectives are being met? (Tyler, 1966)

Tyler's Rationale for Curriculum Development (1966) served as a tool for analyzing high school biology curricula developed in the twentieth century.

SECTION I:
A DESCRIPTION OF THE HIGH SCHOOL BIOLOGY
CURRICULA OF THE TWENTIETH CENTURY

The Content-Oriented Curriculum in Biology

The first science study program, which we refer to as "the content-oriented curriculum," prevailed from the beginning of the twentieth century until the 1960s. It was characterized by its content structure sequence. The sequence of the science topics reflected the syllabi of the courses taught at the university level (DeHart Hurd, 1961) and represented the patterns and processes used in science research at that time, and the content knowledge structure (CKS) of any particular science as it was known.

In the field of biology the main body of knowledge included major topics such as invertebrates and vertebrates in zoology, lower and higher plants in botany, and the structure of the human body. Each organism was presented in sequence as to its morphology, anatomy, physiology, growth, development, and reproduction. Various aspects of their relationships with the environment were mentioned together within a classification approach. Each organism was introduced with a short description of the cell structure and function. This information could be found at the beginning of each textbook. Microbiology, genetics, ecology, and evolution were complementary subjects. The main biology research was aimed at learning about organisms and their classification, with the appropriate physiology aspects as far as the current knowledge in chemistry and physics permitted. This was the biology CKS of the curriculum, which was reflected in the textbooks. The textbooks depicted a sequence of cells from unicellular to multicellular organisms at different levels of sophistication.

Research in Biology that Affected the CKS

The research in cell theory, for instance, was based on a sequence of technology developments, starting with the development of microscopes and what they allowed people to see. Zacharias Janssen built the first simple microscope with only one set of lenses in 1590. Following this, in 1670 Anton van Leeuwenhoek developed a microscope that could magnify objects as much as 270 times, enabling him to see bacteria, protozoa, sperm cells, red blood cells, and yeast cells. In 1665, Robert Hooke, who was a physicist, put two sets of lenses together, thus building a compound microscope. He examined a thin piece of cork and found that it was built of walled structures; he named these empty boxes "cells." Based on these earlier technologies, in 1831, Robert Brown found that in living plant cells, small spherical structures could be detected, and he decided to call these nuclei. In 1838 Matthias Schleiden concluded that all plants are composed of cells. During the same period Theodor Schwann, while studying animal tissues, came to the conclusion that animals are also built of cells. One can see that there is a strong correlation between the technologies developed at that time and the possibility of more sophisticated research in biology. Thus, already in the nineteenth century a reciprocal impact existed between research in science and technological development. Any separation between the two, thereafter, has been artificial and the result of people's decisions alone.

Another factor that had great influence on the development of the science of biology's content structure were the advances in maritime technologies that made possible the great global expeditions led by two scientists: a) Carolus Linnaeus (1707–1778), a Swedish botanist and zoologist who firmly established the binomial system of plant and animal nomenclature in the 1750s; and b) Charles Darwin (1809–1882), a naturalist who while on the ship the *Beagle* traveled around the world between 1831 and 1836 and collected a vast number of specimens of skeletons and creatures. On his return, and based on his collections, he made public a notebook, which contained his observations on the changes of species. *Origin of Species*, published in 1859, had an enormous effect on human thought. This was the most significant book of the nineteenth century (Alexander, 1953, p. 204). Consequently, the research conducted by biologists helped them develop theories on the sequence of evolution of plants and animals, and their classification, anatomy, physiology, reproduction, and genetics. One may say that all of this research was primarily based on the two monumental works published by Linnaeus and Darwin. It also formed the biological sciences content knowledge structure that existed until the 1960s. This SCK was the foundation of the science programs taught at universities and in high school science classes, and all of the textbooks students in both places used reflected it.

Content-Oriented Curriculum and Methods of Instruction

The modes of instruction used in this type of curriculum, the first generation of the high school curriculum, were primarily expository. Teachers lectured and asked questions, while students had to listen and sometimes were allowed to answer. Student-student interactions in the learning process or any process of inquiry rarely occurred. One may therefore conclude that listening and memorization skills were emphasized rather than skills of learning, or seeking for knowledge, exchanging ideas, taking responsibility, etc. This was a teacher-centered instructional activity in which students remained passive. In the late 1980s Shulman (1987) defined the subject matter of the curriculum as content knowledge (CK). The nature of laboratory work was essentially aimed at proving what had already been learned (Lazarowitz & Tamir, 1994). Evaluation and grading procedures were based on tests with open questions in which students were asked to write their answer in a narrative mode; few tests used multiple-choice questions. The questionnaires referred mainly to the cognitive levels of knowledge and understanding. Higher cognitive levels such as application, analysis, synthesis, and evaluation were mostly ignored. Most of the examinations and tests were assessed in a summative approach and used only for grading purposes.

In Fig. 20.1, the structure of the content-oriented curriculum in biology, as it was used in many countries, is presented with its suggested sequence of the subjects to be taught in high school (grades 9–12), as was customary from 1900 to 1965. Whereas in the United States biology was taught in grade 10 only, with electives in the 11th and 12th grades, in Europe and Israel, biology was taught in 9th to 12th grades, depending on the schools' structures, their curriculum, and students' choice in what science subject to be assessed in their matriculation examinations.

	Grade
* The Cell Theory	9th
* Invertebrates: Morphology, Anatomy, Physiology, Reproduction	9th
* Vertebrates: Morphology, Anatomy, Physiology, Reproduction	10th
* Human Body: Morphology, Anatomy, Physiology, Reproduction	10th
* Botany: lower Plants and Higher Plants	9th
* Microbiology	9th - 10th
* Genetics	11th
* Ecology	11th
* Evolution	12th
* Classification of Plants and Animals	11th - 12th

Weekly time-table

Grade	classroom	laboratory
9th and 10th	2 periods	1 period
11th and 12th	3 periods	2 periods

All students in 9th and 10th grades learned Biology
In 11th and 12th grades – only those students who chose to study biology for the matriculation examinations.

FIGURE 20–1.   The content knowledge structure in biology and high school biology curriculum as it was used in Europe and Israel 1930–1970.

The Inquiry-Oriented Curriculum in Biology

In the late 1960s, a second generation of high school curriculum was developed, which we call *inquiry-oriented*. It was based on the concept of inquiry as suggested and developed in the book by Schwab and Brandwein (*The Teaching of Science as Enquiry*, 1962; see also *Inquiry* by Gagne, 1963; Rutherford, 1964). This approach had its roots in the educational and philosophical theories developed in the monumental manuscripts written by Dewey (*The Theory of Inquiry*, 1938) and by Bruner (*The Act of Discovery*, 1961). These theories were incorporated into Schwab's book *Biology Teachers' Handbook* (1963), which can be considered to be the foundation for all inquiry-oriented curricula, the Biological Sciences Curriculum Study (BSCS) textbooks, and the Invitations to Inquiry.

New High School Science Curricula

What was the trigger for the development of these new curricula? There was, and still is, a tendency to explain it by the fact that the satellite Sputnik had been launched by the Russians in the early 1960s, causing the United States to feel inferior for not having been the first country to launch a satellite. As a result, the Americans began an inquiry to find out why they had lost the race into space. They concluded that the high school science curricula did not reflect the knowledge of sciences as they had been known to scientists in the 1960s and was not being taught in the same way as science was practiced. Scientists and educators attempted to explain that the lack of updated science curricula and inadequate methods of instruction were responsible for the American "inferiority," and consequently there was a dearth of high school graduates who were well versed in the sciences. Indeed, there was a shortage of students in the science faculties, which resulted in a lack of scientists. This, together with a scarcity in research funds, led to a reduction in the numbers of researchers in the sciences and applied technology. Politicians and educators called for radical changes in high school science curricula, and adequate budgets were allocated by the American federal government for the development of satisfactory science curricula, in order to solve this problem. Can we say that Sputnik was the only factor behind the radical changes, which occurred in the second generation of high school science curricula, or were there additional reasons for these changes? The answer lies in scientific research.

Science Curricula, Technology, and Societal Issues

This chapter cannot refer to the societal issues following World War II without touching on their effect on Americans. In the United States, the aftermath of World War II saw an enormous change in students' attitudes toward the sciences and technology, because of what they thought was the misuse of technology during the war. In the postwar period, they felt that the achievements of science and technology were not being used to solve social problems or to improve the life of people living under low economic conditions. It is possible that the students' sensitivity had a significant influence on their decision about whether to study science.

Another issue that arose in the 1960s was that scientists and science educators tried to separate science from its technological applications. This trend had a huge impact on the new science curricula, which did not include any aspects of technology. This issue was addressed later in the third generation of curriculum, the problem-oriented one, where this unnatural separation between science and technology was corrected.

The Impact of Chemistry and Physics on Research in Biology

Chemistry and physics played a major role in biology research from the 1940s to the 1960s and later. Two main developments contributed to the changes in the biology CKS: one was based on biology research and the other was based on the use of advanced technology developed in chemistry (working with labeled atoms) and physics (the development of the electronic microscope). Until the late 1930s, radioactive isotopes were not commonly used to probe physiological processes below the macromolecular level. Developments in biochemistry enabled scientists to use labeled isotopes and to track the path of atoms in molecules of amino acids, proteins, nucleic acids, fats, and sugars, etc. Thus a new window of knowledge was opened, laying the foundation for molecular biology.

An example from the research in plant physiology can illustrate the impact of the use of an isotope. This example is adequate for the high school curriculum, since it can demonstrate to students how research is advancing by giving a historical view of the new methods used in the laboratory. The process of photosynthesis, until the 1940s, was taught as a process in which the chlorophyll in green plants, in the presence of light energy, liberates free oxygen and produces sugar from water and carbon dioxide. The source of the oxygen was explained to be the CO_2 molecule, which is broken down to liberate the oxygen and the carbon, and together with the molecule of water formed the skeleton of the sugar molecule. The chemical equation was very simple:

$$6CO_2 + 12H_2O \rightarrow C_6H_{12}O_6 + 6O_2 + 6H_2O.$$

It was only around 1939 when biochemists were able to add the isotope O^{18} to water and carbon dioxide, to label water H_2O^{18} and CO_2^{18}, that they were able to demonstrate that the oxygen released in photosynthesis came from water, whereas the carbohydrate that was formed contained the O from CO_2. This finding was further proved by the Hill reaction, where Hill showed that isolated chloroplasts or even fragments of them, when illuminated, can liberate oxygen from water while the hydrogen is transferred instead to the carbon dioxide, to some artificial acceptor added to the system (e.g., ferricyanide, quinone, coenzyme1):

$$2Fe^{3+} + H_2O \xrightarrow{\textit{light, chloroplasts}} 2Fe^{2+} + 2H + \tfrac{1}{2}O_2$$

(Harder, Schumacher, Firbas, & Denffer in Strasburger, 1965, p. 256).

In the 1950s the path of carbon in the photosynthesis process was described and the DNA model was suggested. The electron microscope enabled scientists to see cell ultrastructures, and organelles and membranes were more accurately described in their distinct molecular parts.

Consequently, the metabolic paths of proteins, amino acids, sugars, and fats in the cell were depicted as well, and step by step all of the physiological processes that occur in cells were described at the molecular level, parallel to the description of all of the ultrastructures, achieved with the help of the electron microscope. These two methods—labeled atoms and electron microscopy—technological in nature, when combined together made possible sophisticated biological research, changing the face of biology CKS in the middle of the twentieth century. The use of advanced technology in biological research has clearly shown the strong, inseparable relationship between science and technology. At the macro level, studies in ecology integrated with mathematical optimal methods in the framework of the ecosystem added new dimensions to field studies.

The Development of the Biological Sciences Curriculum Study in the United States

The newly accumulated body of knowledge induced changes in the corpus of the biology CKS, and scientists started to present it, using seven levels of biological organization (LBO). The seven LBO are molecular, cellular, tissue and organs, organisms, societal, communal, and biome. Unity is highest at the molecular level, common to all living creatures, and diminishes toward the last level, the biome. In contrast, diversity is lowest at the molecular level and increases through the levels, reaching the highest order of diversity at the biome level.

Figure 20.2 presents the new biology CKS in accordance with scientific research in the 1960s, together with its relationship to the cognitive learning demands of high school students.

The changes in biology CKS led to changes in curricula, and the three versions of the Biological Sciences Curriculum Study (BSCS-1968) represent the classical examples of the second generation of high school science curricula. All three versions that were developed around the seven LBO required an inquiry mode of learning and teaching. Each version emphasized the seven LBO at different levels of depth and sophistication:

a. BSCS, *Biological Science: An Inquiry into Life—The Yellow Version* (1968), emphasized developmental and evolutionary aspects of biology. In this respect this curriculum was the closest version to the content-oriented curriculum, and it is therefore understandable that it was the one most adopted by schools and teachers in the United States and other countries.

b. BSCS, *Biological Science: Molecules to Man—The Blue Version* (1968), emphasized molecular biology. It was the most revolutionary curriculum in that period.

c. BSCS, *High School Biology—The Green Version* (1968), which emphasized the ecological aspects the most, was primarily adopted by rural schools in the United States and agricultural high schools in other countries.

Figure 20.3 displays the comparative characteristics of the CKSs emphasized by the two generations (content-oriented and inquiry-oriented) of high school curricula.

In addition, other texts were developed: (a) a textbook for low academic achievers, titled *Biological Science: Patterns and Processes* (1966) (the text was minimal and

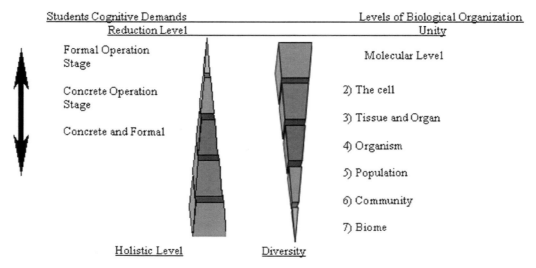

FIGURE 20–2.   The content knoweldge structure in biology from the inquiry-oriented curriculum.

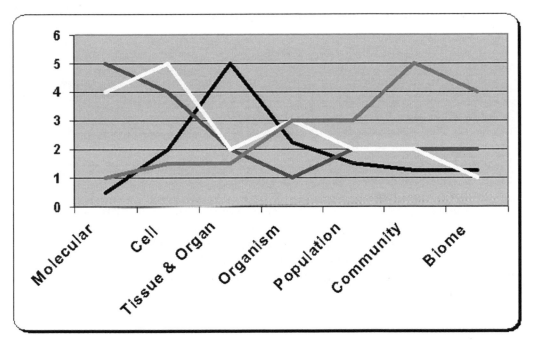

FIGURE 20–3.   The seven levels of biological organization as emphasized in BSCS—inquiry curricula vs. traditional content oriented curriculum. (Schawb, 1963, pp. 15, 16, 17).

the experiments were integrated within the text), and (b) BSCS: *Interaction of Experiments and Ideas* (2nd ed., 1970). This textbook was written in a purely inquiry mode; the experiments were integrated into the text and presented research problems in biology in a manner that required students to suggest solutions and ideas and to perform experiments in order to find answers. The textbook was developed for use in the 11th and 12th grades.

The Pedagogical Approach in the BSCS Textbooks

The content knowledge component of the BSCS textbooks emphasized the teaching of concepts and principles in biology, including a new concept, inquiry. Teachers were asked to create classroom learning environments in which students had "to search and seek" for knowledge, using the reasoning procedure and inquiry skills of scientists in their research. Students were required to use skills such as problem identification, formulation of hypotheses, planning and experimenting, collection of data and results, analysis of the results, planning, and designing and reading graphs and tables based on the results. Students were asked to draw conclusions and infer, in the hope that in this manner they would be able to identify new problems to be researched. Educators and sociologists hoped that students would use these acquired skills in their daily lives as an objective method of solving personal and societal issues. Unfortunately, no studies were carried out to establish if skills mastered in science were successfully transferred and used in daily life.

Summary of the Inquiry-Oriented Curricula

Following the Sputnik crisis and increased scientific research in biology, the science community was able to suggest new curricula. National committees consisting of scientists, educators, science supervisors, and science teachers were convened and asked for their input. The new curricula were expected to present the new achievements in sciences, and it was hoped that the committee members would be able to suggest methods of instruction and learning that would reflect the way science was carried out, researched, and studied.

Students were not required to perform pure research, but only to use inquiry skills in their learning (Schwab, 1963; Rutherford, 1964). In investigations carried out in the laboratory, students were not compelled to discover new facts unknown to science, but to seek existing knowledge in an explorative mode of learning. Later in the 1980s, Shulman (1987) called this component of any curriculum the "pedagogical content knowledge" (PCK), which was added to the content knowledge part.

The three BSCS versions were predicated on the seven levels of biological organization as presented in Fig. 20.2 and the "Unifying Themes in Biology" (Schwab, 1963, p. 31):

1. Change of living things through time: evolution
2. Diversity of type and unity of pattern in living things
3. The genetic continuity of life
4. The complementarities of organisms and their environment
5. The biological factors of behavior
6. The complementarities of structure and function
7. Regulation and homeostasis: preservation of life in the face of change
8. Science as inquiry
9. The history of biological conceptions

The Implementation of the BSCS in the United States and Evaluation Studies

The changes in biology CKS since the 1950s has had an enormous influence on high school curricula, biology education, and teaching and learning strategies. These changes required formal and summative evaluation studies, which in turn required new modes of assessment and grading as well as new tests. These tests were aimed at evaluating academic achievement; mastery of skills in the cognitive, affective, and psycho-motor domains; and attitudes and classroom learning environment, to name a few areas. The years 1960 to 1975 represent one of the most active phases in biology education in the United States. The cooperation among biology scientists in colleges and universities, science educators, and high school biology teachers reached a high level that was unknown until then.

The new biology curricula, comprising all the versions of the BSCS, additional learning material that had been developed, the second course, and the biology teachers' handbook were used in schools all over the United States. BSCS materials were used in in-service and pre-service courses in the education of high school biology teachers. DeHart Hurd (1978) called this period "the Golden Age of biological education" in the United States. Between the years 1959 and 1975, some 15 million high school students learned biology through one of the available BSCS programs. In the academic year of 1970–1971, 50% of the high school student population (of the 2,729,306 who learned biology) studied using a BSCS variant (DeHart Hurd, 1978, p. 42). The massive implementation of this new curriculum required evaluation studies, which were carried out by graduate students for their M.Sc. and Ph.D. degrees and by science educators in the United States and all over the world. In his chapter, DeHart Hurd (1978) reviewed this vast mass of studies on the implementation of the BSCS programs, as well as general studies in biology education, and succeeded in condensing all of the findings under a large number of sections.

In the present chapter, limited as we are in space, it is impossible to present all of the findings, but we strongly suggest reading the original chapter on the golden age of biology education, which includes two sections. The first one prepares the reader by providing the information needed to relate to the studies and consists of the following parts: new programs and student enrollments; growth of research in biological education; selection of investigations for review, analysis, and organization of investigations; the conceptual base for biology teaching; and developing interpretative theories. This section introduces readers to the development process and rationale of the BSCS curricula, as well as to how the studies were selected for the review.

The second section presents the nature of the studies reviewed, such as comparative analysis of learning outcomes among students enrolled in BSCS courses and those who took conventional biology programs, students' achievements, changed attitudes, inquiry skills acquired, and subject matter mastered by the methods of pre- and post-testing. The basic assumption was that teachers who adopted the BSCS textbooks and understood the goals of the theories would assimilate them, would master the required teaching behaviors, and would teach according to the inquiry mode. However, studies clearly indicated that this was not the case. Gallagher (1967) found that the individual teacher interpretation of the new method of teaching biology by inquiry actually directed their behavior in the classroom. The other studies reviewed in the second section compared BSCS with other biology curricula, teaching by inquiry, students' attitudes, the use of BSCS textbooks, students learning biology, the appropriate grade level for teaching biology, biology teachers and their education and behavior, learning conditions, the laboratory and the teaching of inquiry method, student-teacher interaction in the laboratory, and evaluation studies on the BSCS implementations in Australia, Israel, and other countries. The studies' results did not show a clear picture of the superiority of one curriculum or one method of teaching over another curriculum and mode of instruction. We can assume that the expectations of the newly implemented educational theories embedded in the BSCS program were high because of the enthusiasm.

This huge wave of studies had its advantages and disadvantages. The advantages were the immense number of studies, which provided a multitude of findings and thus helped build a body of knowledge related to the development and implementation of new curricula and the BSCS learning materials, including all of the issues related to these processes.

BSCS Curricula, Academic Achievement, and Mastery of Inquiry Skills

What might be the reasons for the fact that the studies that investigated the implementation of BSCS programs reported contradictory results? For one, numerous research projects were carried out by graduate students who were fulfilling the requirements needed to obtain their degrees, so the studies were of a one-time nature, without any continuity or sequence that could encompass connected variables and amass results that might build a body of knowledge. A complete list of results on a set of related tested variables may portray a picture in which one result may compensate for another one. The sporadic selection of the problems to be investigated simultaneously in many places actually inhibited the possibility that each science education center would specialize in the study of one variable, laterally and in depth; for example, the study of science teacher education for teaching in an inquiry mode from all possible angles and points of view was not conducted. When a new curriculum is implemented the list of variables to be studied can be very long: students' learning, achievement and mastery of skills, etc. Studies were not replicated in order to ensure more reliability than that of a single study's results. Tamir and Jungwirth (1975) suggested that longitudinal studies are needed when comparative research is carried out. When one variable alone is studied, there is a danger of ignoring other variables that may have a lateral impact on understanding and interpreting the results. For instance, while investigating a certain school population—both high and low achievers—for its academic achievement, mastery of skills, and attitudes while using any BSCS program, one might ignore other characteristics, such as cognitive stages, learning styles, learning environments, and students' preferences, choices, and needs.

Comparative Studies in Science Education

Students.   A problematic issue in any comparative study is how to compare the academic achievements of two different groups of students. For instance, how do we weigh one group of students who learned in a BSCS program (group *a*) against another group that learned biology traditionally (group *b*)? From the beginning group *a* is at a disadvantage. It must learn a new topic by a new method; group *b* has to learn the new topic only, since its members are accustomed to the traditional method of teaching and learning. The assumption that, by learning a new topic in an inquiry method, students will simultaneously master the knowledge and the inquiry skills needed to study the new topic is questionable and is not founded on research. Therefore, one cannot expect that group *a* will do better than group *b*. In the optimal situation, the two groups may well achieve the same level. In their book *The Jigsaw Classroom*, Aronson, Stephan, Sikes, Blaney, and Snapp (1978) suggested that when we want to investigate the academic achievement of students who learn in a cooperative small-groups method compared with students learning in an expository mode, we have to take care that the students should first master the needed skills of helping behavior and learning cooperatively. Only then can they learn the new topic and can their achievements be compared with those who learned by a traditional method.

Teachers. The issue of teachers is another important variable when one investigates their impact on students learning a new curriculum such as the BSCS programs. One cannot circulate an instrument on teachers' attitudes or investigate their impact on students' achievement while ignoring the teachers' past education, knowledge of science, personalities (openness vs. closeness), personal interpretations of a new CKS, and new theories and strategies of teaching, learning, and assessment as well as their attitudes toward the new method in whose development they were not involved. A single teacher cannot be an agent of change in his/her school without the cooperation of the other teachers, the principal, and other school officials or without being involved in setting the teaching timetable.

Teachers cannot be asked to introduce new curricula or new teaching strategies in their classrooms without being involved in one way or another in developing them and in the issues of the implementation process itself (from the pedagogical, educational, and administrative points of view) before they start to use them. The danger of imposing a new curriculum on teachers from top to bottom is that this will push them back from their third stage, the impact stage in their professional development in which s/he can focus on students' needs by adapting teaching modes to their learning styles. Thrusting a new curriculum onto teachers may shunt them back to the self stage (survival), in which they focus on their personal problems, classroom management and discipline, teaching a lesson, and student-teacher interaction. Such a situation invites objections, resistance, antagonism, and failure (Fuller, 1969; Bethel & Hard, 1981).

Teachers' knowledge of the classroom learning environment (learning settings) and their understanding and knowledge of the nature of their student population were also ignored in most studies, and only one variable was investigated. The interrelationships between the variables, whether constant, independent or dependent, must be taken into account when explanations and interpretations are made. This can be done only when a chain of consecutive studies on interrelated variables is carried out, and a whole picture is constructed, based on a set of study results in one science education center. Otherwise, we get broken and unrelated pieces of information that cannot contribute to the construction of a body of knowledge on a particular subject.

The Nuffield Project in Biology in the United Kingdom

The Nuffield curriculum in biology featured particular characteristics based on a different philosophical approach, which was used because of the structure of the English school system (Nuffield Foundation, 1966). The English school system consists of three parts: elementary school (1st to 5th grades), high school (6th to 10th grades), and sixth lower and upper forms (11th and 12th grades). In this chapter we refer only to the high school level. The biology curriculum was updated with the CKS of the 1960s and 1970s as then known to scientists. It had several major characteristics: it was divided into five parts for the five high school grades and two additional advanced courses for the sixth-form students who had chosen to study biology for their matriculation examinations. *The sequence of the textbooks* for every grade was as follows:

> *Nuffield Biology Text 1. Introducing Living Things (6th grade)*
>
> *Text II. Life and Living Processes (7th grade)*
>
> *Text III. The Maintenance of Life (8th grade)*
>
> *Text IV. Living Things in Action (9th grade)*
>
> *Text V. The Perpetuation of Life (10th grade)*

The structure of the course centered around 11 fundamental themes, which recur repeatedly throughout the five years (Nuffield Foundation, 1966, p. 1):

1. Cycles of matter and energy
2. Structure and function
3. Interaction of organism and environment
4. Integration and homeostasis
5. Replication
6. Variation
7. Adaptation
8. Natural selection
9. Classification
10. Man
11. Mathematical relationships and experiments.

Time allotment: During the first two years: two single periods per week. During the remaining three years: three periods per week (one double and one single)

Instructional Strategy

The synopsis of the course clearly indicates that the books were divided into five parts: the first two parts can be regarded as introductory, and the remaining three constitute the next intermediate phase. The introductory phase is characterized by a broad general approach to the subject. In the intermediate phase the treatment becomes more quantitative, with greater emphasis on experimentation and reasoning.

The learning material was written according to the expected cognitive stage of the pupils in each grade. In this way, the sophistication level of the learning material increased with the grade age. In addition, each chapter was written as a sequence of texts integrated with experiments. Accordingly, the text included concepts and principles in biology, introduced facts, and raised problems that had to be solved by the performance of an experiment. The experiment results provided answers, which, in turn, led to a new problem, which had to be solved. The activities ensured that no one could skip a text or omit performing an experiment, because the two were interconnected. Teachers and the students were requested to follow the suggested sequence.

The pedagogical approach used in the textbooks ensured that the inquiry mode of learning accompanied the learning process. Each student textbook was provided with a teacher's handbook in which, for every chapter, additional scientific information, experiments, and suggested modes of instruction were available. Thus, teachers had the needed accurate science knowledge for any particular subject and were encouraged to add more experiments to their curriculum, if time was available. They were allowed to choose the teaching strategy that matched their students' needs, their cognitive stage, and the subject being taught.

Sixth Lower and Upper Forms (11th and 12th Grades)

For the students who studied biology for their matriculation examinations, advanced courses were available based on two textbooks: 1. *Teachers' Guide to the Laboratory Guides, Volume I*. a) Maintenance of the organism; b) Organisms and populations; and *Volume II*. a) The developing organism; b) Control and co-ordination in organisms (Nuffield Advanced Science, 1970). The units covered all of the biological levels of organization and illustrated the major concepts and principles in biology, such as structure and function, organisms and their environment, processes of physiology and behavior, the genetic and evolutionary continuity of life, matter and energy cycles, homeostasis, and the development and uniqueness of the individual. In both textbooks, biological subjects and problems were presented to students who were asked to perform inquiry experiments in the laboratory.

The sequence in each subject was composed of four components: a) Principles, where items of information were presented, leading to a biological problem; b) Teaching procedure with associated materials; c) Practical problems related to the investigated subject; and d) Questions and answers, in which student-student and student-teacher interactions occur. Experimental results led to the need to read biology texts, in which more problems were raised in order to be solved. The inquiry mode of learning and performing of experiments transformed the class (no more than 12 students are in a sixth-form class) into a small group of learners who led discussions among themselves, or with the teacher. The teacher never lectured, but rather constituted a source with whom to exchange ideas and to consult, and from whom to receive support during the process of inquiry and learning.

The goals of the advanced courses were to learn rather than to be taught, to understand rather than amass information, and to find out rather than be told (Biological Science: Nuffield Advanced Science, 1970; Teachers Guide I, Young, p. VI).

The Adaptation of the BSCS, Yellow Version in Israel

The inquiry-oriented curriculum project was implemented in Israel between 1964 and 1970. *BSCS: Biological Science; An Inquiry into Life* (Yellow Version, 1968) was translated and adapted for Israeli high schools by a team of 25 biology teachers under the leadership of Professors Alexandra Poljakoff-Mayber, Clara Chen, and Ehud Yungwirth at the Department of Biology of the Hebrew University in Jerusalem, and Professor Haim Adomi from the Oranim Teachers College in Kiryat Tivon.

The CKS in biology of that period as presented in the seven levels of biological organization had raised several questions regarding pedagogical aspects of instruction. Since biology is taught in the United States in 10th grade only as an introductory course, its adaptation in Israel and Europe raised a series of problems, among them the fact that biology in the latter two countries is taught in grades 9 through 12. Following the implementation of the CKS, one of the main problems was the higher level of the learning material, especially the requirements in biochemistry knowledge, which 9th-grade students, on the one hand, were required to assimilate. On the other hand, for 11th- and 12th-graders, the need for learning material at a higher level quickly became apparent. The two main questions were: a) What should be the appropriate sequence of the LBO to be taught in the 9th, 10th, 11th, and 12th grades, respectively, since we know that all of the students in grades 9 and 10 learn biology but very few will continue to study advanced courses in biology in grades 11 and 12? and b) What are the appropriate LBO to be taught to a certain grade, when we have to match students' cognitive stages with the cognitive demands required by the learning material? Since we cannot expand on this issue in this chapter, we only mention the fact that young students who were still in the cognitive concrete operational stage found the content of the levels of biological organization at the reduced level very difficult. For them, probably the most adequate levels are the holistic ones, whereas for the students in grades 11 and 12 the reduced levels suited their cognitive stage. This problem requires a separate debate on how to match learning material to students' cognitive development, age, grades, learning theories, and learning styles.

The Implementation of the BSCS Curriculum in Israel

The teachers who implemented the BSCS chapters in their classes provided feedback that was used for the content validation process. Names of the plants and the animals were replaced by those of Israeli endemic organisms. Formative evaluation was carried out during the two years of the implementation process by Tamir and Yungwirth (1975). The formative evaluation and the feedback provided by the teachers served for the revision of the translation and adaptation of the learning material. Based on the experience of 25 teachers in their classrooms, in-service training courses were organized in four areas of the country in which teachers, who wanted to adopt the new curriculum in their schools, participated. The courses were led by biology university professors, their role being to update the participants in biology content knowledge, and by teams of biology teachers from the original group of the 25 teachers, as their pedagogical and didactic experience gained during the first two years of implementation (in instructional modes, the integration of the learning in the classroom with the performance of the experiments in the laboratory, assessment, evaluation, and grading procedure) was practical guidance for the novices. This course of action was based on Francis Fuller's (1969) findings that the implementation of a new curriculum or a new method of instruction will be successfully carried out if schoolteachers are the agents of change rather than external factors. Teachers tend to trust their colleagues, rather than experts, on learning theories, and strategies of instruction and assessment, evaluation, and grading.

The in-service training course was organized in the following manner. During the first meetings the professors and the teachers from the original group, who presented the new curriculum, were the most active participants, and the novices were passive. Thereafter, the latter began to participate actively by preparing lessons from the BSCS units, peer teaching, and performing experiments, followed by discussions regarding the implementation process in their classes. In addition, conducting laboratories as well as issues of evaluation, assessing, and grading were discussed. By the end of the course the biology professors and the original group of teachers were in the background while the participating teachers took over all the activities. Only teachers who participated in these in-service training courses, which lasted almost two months during the summer vacation, and took two more short courses of two weeks each during the academic year (during the Hanukah and Passover breaks), were allowed to join the new curriculum in biology, to implement it in their schools and have their students take the BSCS matriculation examination at the end of 12th grade. Furthermore, these teachers were provided with weekly (in five different locations) additional training sessions, at which time they heard lectures on new topics in biology and feedback on the matriculation exams. The teachers shared experiences and participated in didactical and pedagogical discussions about how to teach new topics in biology or any other issues. Teachers expressed satisfaction that opportunities were provided where they could enrich their knowledge, exchange ideas, listen, and find that they were not alone with their problems. This enabled them to seek solutions together. Later on, the Ministry of Education and Culture developed a method to recompense these teachers with an increase in their salaries according to the number of in-service courses in which they participated. It should be mentioned that almost eight years passed until the entire population of biology teachers joined the BSCS curriculum and that during these years, two curricula in high school biology and two kinds of matriculation examinations were in use. The stipulation required of the biology teachers who wanted to introduce the inquiry curriculum into their classes was their active participation in the in-service training courses and the school principals' agreement to provide an adequate laboratory schedule, equipment, biological and chemical materials, and the aid of a laboratory technician. This long period of transition ensured the successful implementation process of the Inquiry Biology-Oriented Curriculum in Israel under the leadership of Professor Tamir and his colleagues. This was a process that the teachers chose to undertake on their own and was based on learning, experience, and support, and was not imposed on them.

Consequently, there was a need to translate several chapters from the *Interaction of Experiments and Ideas* (2nd ed., 1970) for use in the 11th and 12th grades. For low academic achievers in grades 9 and 10, *Biological Science: Patterns and Process* (BSCS, 1966) was translated and adapted as well.

The Inquiry Matriculation Examinations in Biology in Israel

The new inquiry-oriented curriculum in biology required a new approach to examining students. Rather than testing for the memorization of facts and information, students were assessed on the application and mastery of inquiry skills, on higher cognitive skills such as critical thinking, problem solving, and affective skill such as responsibility in the learning process (Lazarowitz, 2000).

The matriculation examinations had four parts:

1. *A written test* (3 hours) assessed by the Ministry of Education, comprising three sections:
   a. 30 multiple-choice questions to assess students' knowledge of the seven levels of biological organization, aimed at evaluating them on the six cognitive levels (Bloom, 1956): knowledge and understanding (low cognitive levels) and application, analysis, synthesis, and evaluation (higher cognitive levels).
   b. Six to nine open-ended questions in which students were required to demonstrate knowledge of plant and animal physiology by relating an inquiry approach to the questions. Students were meant to answer the questions in a way that would show their mastery of the inquiry skills.
   c. An "unseen" section in which students were required to analyze a portion of a real research paper published in Israel, using the inquiry skills mastered in the classrooms and laboratory practical work.
2. *Laboratory work.* Performance of an unknown experiment in which students had to identify a researchable problem in biology, based on a written question. Students were required to suggest a hypothesis and an experiment to be performed in order to prove the hypothesis. Following the examiner's approval, students performed the experiment; collected data, which had to be put in tables and graphs; and analyzed the results. Students then wrote a summation in which they demonstrated biological knowledge in physiology and mastery of practical and inquiry skills in laboratory work.
3. *The identification of an unknown plant*, in which they described the structures of the flowers, stem, leaves, roots, fruits, and seeds and, by using a taxonomic key book, found the scientific names of the family, genera, and species to which the plant belongs.
4. *An ecology project.* Students selected a biology subject to be investigated during one year of field observations that were reported in a portfolio. It was assumed that students choosing a subject and studying outdoors would develop learning responsibility, along with skills of observation, data collection, and care for the environment. As a consequence, students decided on what scientific topics and data they would examine. This reduced to the minimum the anxiety factor during the oral examination. It was also expected that their motivation would increase and that they would develop positive attitudes toward nature and the environment.

Summary of the Inquiry-Oriented Curriculum Implementation

In the content-oriented curriculum the emphasis was on the sequence of biological knowledge that reflected the evolutionary and classification research in biology. The emphasis in the inquiry-oriented biology curriculum was on updating the content knowledge based on the seven levels of biological organization, from the molecular to the biome, reflecting biochemistry, biophysics, and ecological and ecosystems research in modern biology. An additional emphasis was given to the pedagogical aspects in which the pure inquiry mode of learning was recommended.

Research in biology led to changes in the CKS in biology as a subject matter, which in turn triggered modifications in the structure of the biology curriculum based on the seven levels of biological organization. Parallel to the changes in the CK and changes in the biology curriculum, changes in the nature of the student population and society occurred too. These transformations required developments in learning theories, instructional strategies, and methods of learning, evaluation, and assessment. All these have enabled teachers to not only test students' academic achievements but also their mastery of inquiry skills, attitudes toward science and understanding of the process of science, and their cognitive, affective, psychomotor, and social skills, which were assessed in the classroom and in practical laboratory work (Tamir & Glassman, 1971; Tamir, 1974; Tamir & Jungwirth, 1975; Lazarowitz & Tamir, 1994; Lazarowitz, 2000).

Inquiry Curricula and Heterogeneous Student Population

Were the BSCS programs and other curricula of the 1960s and 1970s suitable for the whole student population, which became more and more heterogeneous? What are the characteristics of a heterogeneous student population? We know that students differ in their cognitive operational stages, abilities, learning styles, preferences, choices, interests, and needs.

Although the inquiry curricula were updated in relation to the subject matter and asked for an inquiry mode in teaching and learning, they were not made suitable for a heterogeneous student population. In order for all students to function in a scientific and technological society, they had to be able to take a democratic stand on societal issues based on literacy and not on prejudices, naïve knowledge, and misconceptions. Moreover, it had to be recognized that only a small portion of students aspire to an academic career; the majority need an academic education in order to find a job in the market. The inquiry-oriented curricula did not address these issues, and a call for developing a curriculum to lead educators and students into the twenty-first century went out. Science curricula of the 1960s and 1970s represented distinct, well-defined disciplines.

In his paper, *The Crisis in Biology Education*, Yager (1982) noted that most curricula of the 1970s, the BSCS programs, the Human Science Program-HSP (BSCS), the Outdoor Biology Instructional Strategies-OBIS (Lawrence Hall of Science), the Biomedical Interdisciplinary Curriculum Project-BICP, and others were challenged regarding their appropriateness. The public was concerned about the inclusion of sensitive subjects such as sex, reproduction and social issues, and evolution, since these were the topics relevant to the students' needs. Yager (1982) mentioned that biology teachers were used to relying for the majority of their teaching on textbooks, which determined the content of their classes and directed their teaching. Biology teachers did not make curriculum decisions related to the biology programs to be used in their classrooms, and the act of selecting a textbook itself was a significant educational reform for them.

Biology Textbooks Used in High Schools

Three major textbooks were in used in high schools in the United States, *Modern Biology* (Holt, used by 40%) and the *Yellow and Green Versions* (BSCS, also used by 40%). In other countries the books used were translations of the BSCS versions in an adapted form or books written locally that used an inquiry approach. Regarding the instructional strategies practiced in the classrooms, Yager (1982) remarked that teaching science by inquiry, a major goal stated by the BSCS in the 1960s, was rarely observed in the classrooms. In the classroom teachers tended to emphasize information related to the terminology and definitions, whereas the nature of the laboratory work was demonstrations and confirmation, which was contradictory to the principles of investigation and inquiry. Biology in the school program did not relate to applications, to current issues, to individual students' needs, or to career awareness. The teachers' main concern was with the academic preparation of students, not with other aspects later raised by Yager and Hofstein (1986). In his paper, Yager (1982) stated that the optimal state of biological education would also include the need to relate to human adaptation, the inquiry process, decision making, values, and ethical and moral considerations of biosocial problems. These issues, he felt, are as important as biology content knowledge. Other aspects he mentioned were teaching and learning settings (individualized and cooperative work), new modes of testing and evaluation, and the use of biology to interpret personal and social problems and issues. The inclusion of human welfare and progress in biology teaching is also of great importance. Finally, Yager wrote that one has to see science education in a continuum change, like science itself. All of these aspects should be reflected in "a curriculum problem oriented, flexible and culturally as well as biological valid" (Yager, 1982, p. 332). Therefore, it was decided to call the third generation of biology curricula the problem-oriented curriculum. This new approach has been leading us into the new millennium.

The Problem-Oriented Curriculum in Biology

Since the 1990s, new approaches in science curricula have been started, and we now present examples of how Yager's ideas were implemented in the third generation of biology curriculum in Israel. Student populations are heterogeneous in terms of learning styles, cognitive stages, abilities, choices, preferences, and needs. In the high school student population here we have two very well-defined, main groups studying biology. In grades 10 through 12, only 15% of the students continue to study biology at the three- and five-point levels for the matriculation exams. This follows their participation in an integrated course given in a thematic approach that includes some aspects of science, technology, and society (STS) in junior high school in grades 7 and 8. Eighty-five percent of high school students do not continue to study any science or technology subjects after grade 9. With these students in mind, Harari's report (1993) recommended that every student in high school who does not choose to study a science should be provided with science and technology literacy embedded with societal aspects. It was assumed that science and technology have a reciprocal influence, and both have an impact on human life and society, the computer being one example of this. In order to produce citizens who are literate in science and technology, the goals of the curricula should give greater emphasis to societal issues and not concentrate only on preparing students for academic careers. The nature of a desired science curriculum that can fulfill students' needs was defined by Yager and Hofstein (1986). The four main goals were presented in their paper under the title *Features of a quality curriculum for school science*:

1. Emphasis on science as preparation for further academic study of a discipline has been a major focus of curricula of the past.
2. Major concerns in science are seen as a means of encountering and resolving current societal problems.
3. Means for attending to the personal needs of students.
4. Means of approaching greater awareness of career potential in science, technology and related fields, suggesting goals that may be far more important than the traditional goal of academic preparation for future courses. (Yager & Hofstein, 1986, p. 134)

Therefore, the problem-oriented curricula in biology called for a differential approach. First, it advocated a flexible curriculum, which answers the first goal in Yager and Hofstein's paper (1986). This curriculum may consist of many independent learning units from which teachers choose the units that are most appropriate for their goals, the ones they prefer to teach, and those that meet students' preferences, interests, and needs. Sometimes students can participate in this process. Any sequence of several units studied can provide the students with an entire biological picture. Each learning unit can be replaced from time to time, and each unit can be updated, so the need to change the entire curriculum at once no longer exists. This approach was suggested for students who would be taking the matriculation examination in biology at the end of 12th grade (about 15% of the high school population). Second, it recognized the need for a curriculum for the remaining 85% of students that would address Yager's other three goals: science as relevant to societal problems, and students' needs and awareness of professional career potential while learning sciences. This curriculum was built of independent units, written in a thematic content of biology, chemistry, physics, and technology with societal aspects, thus having a flavor of the STS approach. Therefore, only science and technology subjects, which could have a common background and could be integrated, were selected.

Matriculation Exams and Learning Units

The following curriculum was offered to the students who wanted to take the matriculation examination in biology. For grade 10 the following units (called basic topics) were offered:

1. Communication, regulation, and coordination in plants and animals
2. Microorganisms
3. Reproduction systems in plants, animals, and the human body
4. Processes and metabolism in the cell

5. The organism and the environment
6. Transport and mediation systems in plants and animals
7. Darwin and theories on the origin of species and evolution

Teachers and students were allowed to choose three out of seven learning units to be studied during the academic year.

The following units were offered to grade 11 and 12 students according to their level of matriculation examinations. Learning units for the three-point academic level (basic topics) were:

1. Heredity
2. Energy transformation in living creatures
3. Any two learning units not chosen in 10th grade, bringing the studies to a total of four units.

At the three-point academic level, the matriculation examinations were aimed at assessing students on a) quantitative treatment of data, b) attainment and use of inquiry laboratory skills, and c) classification and identification of plants and animals and mastery of knowledge of the four learning units. Learning units for the five-point academic level (extended topics) were:

1. Heredity
2. Regulation and mechanisms of plant development
3. Photosynthesis
4. Microorganisms
5. Cell communication
6. Physiological systems in animals: respiration and secretion

The matriculation examinations were aimed at assessing students on a) quantitative treatment of data, b) an ecology project, c) plant identification and classification, d) inquiry laboratory work, e) mastery of knowledge of three out of the six units, and e) two learning units not chosen in grade 10.

Curriculum Offered to Students
Not Taking a Science Discipline

This curriculum was built around learning units, their role being to provide students with scientific and technological literacy and mastery of skills in the cognitive, affective, and psychomotor domains. The units were written using a thematic approach, integrating biology, chemistry, physics, and societal aspects based on the STS approach (Bybee, 1987). About 20 units were developed, and teachers and students chose five of them to be studied in grades 10, 11, and 12. Each unit was structured so that it could be taught in 30 to 45 periods (two periods in the classroom and one in the lab). We present four of them here.

Human Health and Science

These learning units developed by Huppert, Simchoni, and Lazarowitz (1992) included health science subjects. The course was developed based on studies in which it was found that high school students (12 to 16 years old, girls and boys) were interested in learning subjects related to their bodies, everyday life, food, health, and the environment (Lazarowitz & Hertz-Lazarowitz, 1979; Baird, Lazarowitz, & Allman, 1984; and Bybee, 1987, who included human health and diseases in his list of the most important societal issues).

The Human Health and Science subunits were written in an STS approach for a two-year biology course, three periods per week, to be used by comprehensive high school students. The learning material consisted of five modules: a) Human Energy Expenditure, b) Organ Transplantation, c) Human Reproduction, d) Diseases of Modern Civilization, and e) Addictive Substances. Each module included the relevant biology content and physiological processes, and aspects of chemistry, physics, and technology applications, which included moral and ethical issues. The various ways of learning included laboratory work, recorded lectures, reprints of articles in science journals, computer simulations, classroom and group discussions, and films. Each module contained two learning units.

Two units from different modules are presented here to illustrate the ways in which STS was integrated:

Module 1. Human Energy Expenditure. Learning Unit B: The Fat and the Slim

STS topics	Descriptions
Biology:	Digestions and absorption. Sugar metabolism
Chemistry:	Structure of sugars and fats. Cholesterol
Physics:	Heat and temperature. Energy in food
Technology:	Recording metabolic rates. Modern agriculture technology
Society:	Obesity. Anorexia nervosa. Dietary habits. Malnutrition

Module 2. Organ Transplantation. Learning Unit A: The Heart

STS topics	Descriptions
Biology:	The cardiovascular system. Cardiovascular diseases
Biochemistry:	Neuro-hormones
Physics:	Blood pressure. Electrical activity of the heart
Technology:	Electrocardiogram. Artificial pacemakers. Heart surgery. Coronary angioplasty. Artificial heart
Society:	Organ donors. Religious, ethical, moral, and scientific rules for determination of death

A detailed description of the modules, subunits, learning topics, learning activities, assessments procedures, formative evaluation, and discussions regarding the development and implementation problems as well as the educational values of teaching biology in an STS approach may be found in Huppert, Simchoni, and Lazarowitz (1992).

Ionizing Radiation: Uses and Biological Effects

The learning unit Ionizing Radiation: Uses and Biological Effects (Nachshon, 2000) was written in a thematic and STS approach and included related subjects: a) the physics-chemistry of ionizing radiation—the particle radiation of Alpha and Beta rays, electromagnetic radiation, gamma and X-ray radioactive phenomena and background radiation; b) biological aspects—the effects of radiation on different levels of biological organization: the molecules (DNA molecules), organelles, cell, tissues, and organisms; c) the technological aspects—radioisotopes as energy and radiation sources, the food industry, science research, the range of medical uses of X-ray photography and computerized tomography (CT); and d) societal aspects and issues—uses of ionizing radiation for human needs, the use of radioisotopes for diagnosis and treatment in nuclear medicine, the use of nuclear power for electricity (advantages and disadvantages), and the use of this energy as possible weapons of mass destruction, the process of mutation, and the relationship between cancer and damage repair mechanisms and ionizing radiation's immediate effects and long-term effects, which may affect cell life cycles. The implementation and evaluation in grades 10 and 11 revealed that students' fluency and elaboration on ideas were higher while they learned in cooperative groups rather than as individuals. One-third of the students asked higher order questions, and the questions of the other students were mainly on the knowledge and comprehension levels. Half of the students were interested in the physics of ionizing radiation and activities aimed at developing creative thinking. Students preferred to learn the subjects in the thematic mode, in group activities, and most of them mentioned the importance of the diversity in instructional strategies that were used. The academic achievement of students in control groups, who learned chemistry and physics subjects in a disciplinary approach, was significantly lower, whereas the achievement of those who studied the subjects in the STS mode was higher. All students mentioned that learning about nuclear and ionizing radiation and their uses for human needs in a thematic approach and STS mode helped them to overcome their fears, which had been based on a lack of knowledge and prejudice (Nachshon & Lazarowitz, 2002).

Microorganisms

This learning unit was written in the STS approach in Arabic and Hebrew for 9th-grade Israeli and Arab students (Khalil, 2002a, 2002b). The learning unit was structured around two main biological principles: the unity of life in the world and the relationship between structure and function. The problems raised in the unit were concerned with health issues, environment, microorganisms, and drainage canalization between neighborhood villages. This unit enabled us to investigate achievement in the cognitive and affective domains as well as attitudes toward the preservation of the environment, and understanding and peace between people who live close to each other. The following topics were included in the learning unit: microorganisms and their structure, the physiological processes, microorganisms' role in the food web, carbon and nitrogen cycles, the food industry, the environment, and the level of the health of society. The unit helped students to master practical skills in laboratory work and to develop scientific thinking and problem-solving skills. The learning tasks included individual and small-group instructional settings, utilizing a variety of teaching and learning methods in the classroom and laboratory. Students read scientific essays, watched videos, played group games, went on group field trips, visited food industries, and searched for information from different sources (e.g., the Internet and libraries). The learning unit was introduced to the students in a manner designed to raise their motivation. It was practical, was connected with daily life, and dealt with societal issues. In this way the relationship among science, technology, environment, and society was emphasized. It was assumed that students would develop positive attitudes and be able to judge objectively the problems involved in the preservation of the environment, while understanding the important role of microorganisms in the life cycle. The outcomes in the cognitive and affective domains were obtained by analysis of students' portfolios written while they studyied in the classroom, in the laboratory, and during the execution of their homework. The results showed that students gained in their academic achievement, developed positive attitudes toward the environment, and understood the role that people have in preserving nature and its relation to peace (Khalil & Lazarowitz, 2002).

SECTION II:
BIOLOGY TEXTBOOKS AND HIGH SCHOOL

In his paper, Yager (1982) stated that the existing biology curriculum was textbook-centered and inflexible, and only biological validity was considered. Biological information was given in the context of the logic and structure of the discipline. While citing others, Yager mentioned that biology as it appeared in the school program was pure in the sense that few applications for it were presented, and it did not focus on individual students' needs and paid little attention to current issues and career awareness (Harms & Yager, 1981; Yager, Hofstein, & Lunetta, 1981). Citing the NSF Status Studies of 1976, Yager (1982) stated, "Biology in the school program can be characterized by one word, textbooks." The biology textbook determined the content to be taught, the order, the examples, and the applications of the content, which directed and controlled the teaching strategies. Teachers had faith in textbooks and used them 90% of the time. Teachers did not make curricular decisions about the biology programs in their classrooms, and one of their major involvements was in the "initial choice of the textbook."

Yager (1980) pointed out the need for new learning materials, which can be adapted to local situations, including new instructional strategies and models of implementation. As mentioned previously, Yager's (1982) remarks were the impetus for the development of the biology problem-oriented curricula and the learning units, geared toward students studying for biology matriculation exams or students anxious to acquire scientific and technological literacy. The learning materials in the learning units were written in an experimental mode in order to attend to the issues raised by Yager (1982) and Yager and Hofstein (1986). The learning units (textbooks) comprised a flexible and differential biology curriculum for diverse student populations. They had specific content based on the "unifying themes in biology" (Schwab, 1963), but at different levels of depth and sophistication. Teachers and students were able to choose the learning units, which included integrative topics in sciences and technology embedded with societal issues, designed to raise students' aware-ness of academic and professional careers and to help them master the cognitive and affective skills that they would need. Teachers were able decide what kind of instructional strategies, learning settings, modes of assessment, evaluation, and grading to use. The textbook remained the center of teachers' instruction and stu-dents' learning, and it is interesting to compare past studies that related to the role of textbooks with recent investigations that looked into the reasons behind teach-ers' choice of learning units that they made when making their curricular decisions, following the adoption of the biology problem-oriented curriculum.

Biology Teachers' Perceptions of the Textbooks' Role

An analysis of 22 high school biology textbooks carried out by Rosenthal (1984) revealed that between 1963 and 1983 the awareness of societal issues decreased. Nevertheless, when compared with other texts, Rosenthal mentioned that BSCS textbooks were preferential in both quantity and quality in terms of their treatment of science and society. In general, she noted that biology textbooks tended to avoid questions of ethics and values, and that the interdisciplinary nature of problems was neglected. Although between the 1960s and 1970s there was an effort to make the biology textbooks relevant to students' personal and social needs, there was, nonetheless, a decline in the emphasis on societal issues. Understanding the rela-tionships between science and society is necessary in order for citizens to be able to make decisions and deal with problems in an effective and constructive manner, which is so necessary in a highly scientific and technological society (Aikenhead, 1980). Biology teachers themselves are divided over how much attention to allocate to societal issues (Rosenthal, 1984). DiGisi and Willet (1995) reported that biology teachers modified their use of textbooks according to the academic level of the biol-ogy class they taught. They expected that students with higher academic levels would learn from classroom instruction and independent reading, and they under-stood that those with low academic levels rely only on what is taught in the class-room. Their main observation was that "biology teachers viewed both reading and inquiry activities as important to learning biology, but they appeared unsure of how to incorporate reading comprehension strategies into their science instruction" (DiGisi & Willet, 1995, p. 123). In a study conducted by German, Haskins, and Auls (1996), laboratory manuals in biology were evaluated as to how well they promoted the basic and integrated science process skills that are involved in scientific inquiry. They found that in some manuals there are some efforts to integrate science process skills, but in general they require students to use their knowledge and experience by asking questions, solving problems, investigating natural phenomena, and sug-gesting answers and generalizations.

Thus the issues raised by Yager (1982) regarding the role of textbooks and how teachers use them in their instruction are still valid today. In their paper, Stern and Roseman (2003) mentioned that the textbooks they analyzed were updated in terms of the scientific content knowledge and full of declarations regarding the cognitive goals to be mastered by the learners, but were very lacking in the inclusion of the products of the research in science education; in other words, they were in need of didactic pedagogical knowledge of how to use the content in a variety of teaching and learning strategies and learning settings. The question arises as to whether teachers can make curricular decisions choosing the learning unit and the topic to be taught and decide upon what strategies to use, so that the curriculum fit their personality as well as the students' pedagogical needs. Because schools and teachers "are still relying on textbooks as the primary source of the classroom curriculum, which strongly influence students' learning through their impact on the teachers," Stern and Roseman (2004) assumed that "curriculum material can and should play an important role in improving teaching and learning." In their opinion, textbooks that score high on the PCK, according to their criteria, should assist teachers in selecting the content and adapting the relevant pedagogical knowledge, and that this discernment and judgment will be reflected in their teaching.

Reasons for Choosing Textbooks and their Selection

What are teachers' perceptions of the textbooks, and their reasons for selecting them for their classrooms? In two studies, teachers were asked about their reasons for choosing learning units for preparing students for the matriculation exams and the criteria for their selection. In her study Agrest (2003) found that biology teachers tended to choose the subjects for the matriculation exams primarily from the basic learning units, presented in descending order: Organisms and their Environment; The Cell; Heredity; Transport and Mediation Systems in Plants and Animals; Microorganisms; Reproduction Systems in Plants, Animals, and the Human Body; Energy Transformation in Living Creatures; Evolution; Communication, Regulation, and Coordination in Organisms. The expanded learning units chosen, in descending order, were: Physiological Systems in Animals: Respiration and Secretion; Heredity; Photosynthesis; Microorganisms; Regulation and Mechanisms of the Plant Development; and Cell Communication. While the main concerns of the scientists regarding the learning units were with regard to the scientific content and the methods of scientific thinking, most of the teachers' concerns were focused on the pedagogical aspects.

In a second study, Wagner-Gershgoren (2004) clustered the teachers' criteria for choosing and evaluating biology textbooks into three groups:

1. Scientific content: The teachers attributed the highest degree of importance to the quality of the scientific content (including considerations of being up to date; precision, reliability, and trustworthiness; organization of the information; clear explanations; innovation; relevancy to the individual and daily life; interest; and quotes from studies and articles).
2. Technical aspects: The teachers attributed the highest degree of importance to the format of the book (language, aesthetics, morphological organization of the material, color and formatting of the text).
3. Didactic aspects: The teachers attributed the highest degree of importance to illustrations and organization of data (illustrations, pictures, graphs, flow charts, and schemes and tables).

All of the considerations were presented in descending order of importance.

Teaching Concepts and Principles in Biology

One of the main goals emphasized in biology curricula is the teaching of concepts and principles. When we analyze the "unifying themes in biology" (Schwab, 1963, p. 31), we find that this is a list of concepts presented in a set of biological principles. The main and ultimate expected result of any effective biology teaching and learning is the students' mastery of and ability to use biology concepts and principles in their learning. In his paper, Yager (1982, p. 331) stated that a "closer look at biology textbook reveals some important generalizations, and typical textbooks emphasize new words or concepts, often as many as 30 on a single page." A typical science textbook for middle or high school, according to DeHart Hurd, Robinson, Connell, and Ross (1981), includes 2500 new words. This amount is nearly double the number of new words required from a person of the same age when he or she is learning a foreign language. In science education literature we see studies on concept formation, concept mapping, conceptual change, misconceptions, etc. Because these studies are reviewed in other chapters, we refer here to how a concept is taught and formed in biology.

Concepts and Names

What is the definition of a concept? Is there a distinction between the word *concept* and a name of an object? Are "new words" equivalent to the word concept? When can we refer to a word as a concept and when we do refer to it as a principle? Confusion often exists in the use of all of these terms. When we talk and teach about a specific amino acid, sugar, starch, chloroplasts in the green cell of a leaf, mitochondria, a specific tissue of plants or animals, organelles in a cell, an organ, a specific system within an organism, an organism or the human body, it may be that these are "new names" for our students, a new language. Yet these new words represent objects, which can be seen, either with the help of a microscope, in a picture, or with our eyes; we can check and measure them; we can depict their characteristics or learn about their proprieties by performing chemical and other laboratory experiments. We can use our senses to learn about them, and, therefore, they are objects to which we can give names, and consequently, they are not concepts. We can learn about these objects, can classify and organize them into groups such as amino acids, organelles, cells, families genera and species, or name specific physiological processes performed by these objects or substances, respiration, photosynthesis, reproduction, and so on. These are the concepts learned, and they include names of objects, which were investigated and their specific structures, properties, characteristics, and physiological processes were identified, learned, and grouped. Each group can be given a specific name due to common characteristics of its members, which represents a mental activity. At the same time each group is different from another group, inasmuch as they differ in their characteristics. Facts are elicited through the use of discriminative mental activity, as a result of which a new grouping will form under a different umbrella and be given a different concept name. Accordingly, these are not concrete or abstract concepts. They are objects, which can be studied and their characteristics learned. There are objects for which we need technological aids in order to see and learn about them, and others that require the use of our senses, but they continue to be real at the concrete level. Students master the new words, the new language, based on experience, and they proceed to deal with and learn about them as well as use related concepts.

Models of Teaching Biological Concepts

According to Novak (1965), in order to understand a given discipline, one must do more than just memorize statements that summarize the concepts in a topic. Students have to find out how the concepts were derived and elaborated in order to meaningfully understand them so they can grasp the discipline structure. In other words, Novak understood concepts to be generalizations of aspects of the physical or biological biome, which are composed of individual facts and emotional experiences, such as the concept of osmosis or evolution, which represent a group of related facts that stand for a composite of knowledge (Novak, 1965). Concept formation, according to Novak (1965), goes through several steps: a) experience a student stores as cognitive information; b) storage of affective information; c) and the processing of all of the information. A detailed psychological description of the formation of concepts can be found in Novak's (1965) paper, and readers are invited to study this article.

According to Koran (1971), in biology, concepts represent natural objects such as mammals, invertebrates, amino acids, and autotrophs, and events such as dehydration, synthesis, oxidation, reduction. We can add physiological processes such as respiration, photosynthesis, and reproduction. When we use the term *amino acid*, it is understood that we are not referring to a single object but to a class of objects or to groups. Koran distinguished along a continuum between the concept of all amino acids and a specific amino acid. Each amino acid has COOH and NH_2 at the opposite ends of the molecule, and between them each amino acid has a different chemical structure. We can group under the concept of amino acid any compound that shows this chemical structure; a specific amino acid is a fact or object that can be studied and its characteristics learned (Koran, 1971). In the process of concept formation, two distinct activities are involved. When we group all of the organic compounds, which have at their opposite ends the chemical structures COOH and NH_2, under the name of amino acids, we are generalizing. However, when we distinguish between these molecules and a molecule of sugar, which does not possess COOH and NH_2, we are undertaking a discriminative mental activity (Mechner, 1965). These two mental activities of generalization and discrimination are the major components of concept formation. Providing adequate examples of what a concept includes is as important as providing examples of what it does not include, according to Koran (1971).

Koran, Koran, Baker, and Moody (1978), and Koran, Koran, and Baker (1980) provided many more examples of concept formation in different fields of biology, together with models of teaching using the inductive and deductive modes of instruction and learning.

Concepts and Teaching Biology

Concepts, accordingly, do not represent concrete entities but are created in the human mind, following a learning process, and are, therefore, abstract. It is obvious that we, as teachers, usually start teaching first by presenting the concept, which requires an abstract operational activity, which immediately breaks down the communication between the teacher and the students. We do not have a common language with the students, because as far as they are concerned, we are speaking a "new language" with which they have not had any prior experience. Following the introduction we proceed to present the objects or to perform an experiment, which are at the level of a concrete operational activity. Although the direction of the learning process as depicted (the deductive approach) is adequate for students who are in a formal cognitive stage and who can cope with this mode of instruction, most students are in the concrete cognitive stage, and the opposite direction is more appropriate for them. First, they have to be introduced to the object, learn about its characteristics, or perform an experiment in order to accumulate information and knowledge about it. Only then can we introduce the names of all the information mastered under the name of the concept, which represents all of the learning activities that have just occurred (the inductive approach). Topics, which are at the reduction level, such as molecules of glucose or macromolecules of starch, for example, since they are names of objects, can be taught by the inductive approach. Starch (an object) can be seen and its characteristics can be learned, being an object that is well known to students from their daily life experiences. Afterward we can relate to its components, the molecules (a concept) of glucose (an object), and as such the deductive approach is desirable. This is the way scientists investigate a phenomenon.

For instance, only after using a microscope and finding out that all organisms are built of microstructures did they refer to some common characteristics of the "cell" concept. The microstructure, the cell, represents an entire organism; when grouped together, the cells represent a structure, the tissue of an organism. Once having made these observations, scientists realized that every unicellular organism or any group of cells that form a tissue have a specific structure and perform a specific physiological activity, and that a relationship exists between the two. With this deduction, the basic principle in biology of structure and function emerged. Scientists can and do communicate among themselves using the word *cell*, without the necessity of explaining again and again all the knowledge related to this concept, because all of them know what the concept "cell" means. In essence, a concept such as a cell is an economical way of communication among people who have a common background of experience and knowledge, following a process of learning.

This is not the situation that may exist between the teacher and his/her students. The teacher has all the knowledge behind a concept, whereas for the students this is a new word, and they first have to attain this knowledge in order to be able to use the new concept. Thus, when the teacher starts to teach by first presenting the concepts to be learned by the students, instead of creating learning settings in which the learners will come into concrete contact with the objects to be studied, by observing, measuring and experimenting, perceiving and conceptualizing, they generally lose their audience. Nonetheless, even when these two steps, perception and conceptualization, are experienced in the correct sequence, students may still not attain the knowledge and grasp the concept. They must be taken through a third step application. Here learners have to show that they can use the new knowledge in a new learning situation. Only then can we say that learning has occurred. This learning process can be illustrated as follows.

First Step: Perception

This is a concrete learning process. The teacher presents a biological problem that can be solved by making observations regarding objects or by performing an experiment. Students collect information and data and construct their knowledge.

Second Step: Conceptualization

This is a formal (mental) learning activity. Students and the teacher hold class discussions, using the knowledge mastered in the perception step, and by discrimination and generalizing mental activities, they summarize the accumulated information under one name. For example, if the problem investigated is how plants nurture and they learn about the structure of leaves and perform experiments with chlorophyll, sugars, glucose, starch, solar energy, etc., they can group all of this acquired knowledge under the concept name of photosynthesis.

Third Step: Application

Students receive variegated leaves (the leaves have areas with chlorophyll that are green, and areas without chlorophyll that are albino). The question posed is: Can we find starch in both areas? In order to find an answer, students have to use their knowledge regarding the role of chlorophyll, solar energy, and the production of starch, in a new situation. Depending on how their students resolve the question, the teacher will know if their students mastered the knowledge.

Learning Difficulties in Biology

The CKS of the high schools' biology curricula is based on the seven LBO. This organization of the biological content is logical from the evolutionary point of view and represents areas of research and instruction. The concepts and principles presented in most of the LBO require students to be in the formal operational stage of learning and thinking in order to successfully cope with them. In their studies Johnstone and Mahmood (1980), Steward (1982), Finely, Steward, and Yaroch (1982) and Friedler, Amir, and Tamir (1987) reported that several biological topics were identified by their level of difficulty in terms of instruction by teachers, as well as the difficulty students encountered while learning these subjects. The concepts were water transport in organisms, osmosis and osmoregulation, the chemistry of respiration and photosynthesis, energy cycles (ATP, ADP), cell respiration, protein synthesis, mitosis and meiosis, enzyme structure and function, the chromosome theory of heredity, and Mendel's laws of genetics and multiple alleles. According to Klinckman (1970), the LBO might be one of the reasons for these difficulties. Young learners and less academically able students may be able to achieve higher scores if they study biology topics that lie within the levels of organisms, population, and community (holistic subjects). Conversely, they may encounter substantial difficulties in learning concepts related to molecules, cells, tissues, and organs. Another reason for their problems in understanding may be the abstract level of concepts such as photosynthesis, respiration, enzyme activity, dominance and co-dominance, and sex linkage.

Learning Biology and Students' Cognitive Stages

Students' ability to deal with formal concepts in a meaningful manner was found to be correlated with their cognitive operational stage. This assumption was supported by Shemesh and Lazarowitz (1989) in a study with students (ages 15 to 16). These researchers found that, following lessons on the respiratory system, results showed a positive correlation between students' cognitive stages and their achievements, and that only learners at the concrete cognitive stage made errors. Lawson and Thomson (1988) investigated students' misconceptions about natural phenomena. They hypothesized that in order to overcome their mistaken beliefs, learners must be made aware of scientific knowledge and must be able to generate the logical relationships among the evidence and alternative conceptions. The results indicated that the reasoning ability of seventh-grade students, who were assessed by having them write an essay on principles of genetic and natural selection, was the main factor related to the number of misconceptions held. These two studies indicate that relationships do exist between achievement in biology and students' mastery of formal cognitive stages. Students found to be at the concrete cognitive stage were not able to go beyond the given data in a problem situation, and the inferences they drew, even when they remembered all the necessary facts, were directly related to what they had actually observed. It seems that the lack of formal reasoning skills constrained these students' capacity to encode formal concepts and to process complex information. Only a few students at the formal cognitive stage were able to meet the high criteria of relational or extended abstract responses (Shemsh & Lazarowitz, 1989).

As such, the main question asked is, can we teach biological concepts to high school students at any age, or should one delay teaching them until they reach the appropriate formal cognitive stage, when we assume that learners will be able to cope with the concepts? To answer this question we will relate to several studies. The study by Penso and Lazarowitz (1992) looked at students (ages ranged from 17.5 to 18.5) who were given a test, which included 18 multiple-choice questions. In order to identify difficulties in learning biology and to locate the mistakes made by students in the process of choosing the correct item, they were asked to justify their choice. Their justifications were compared with a justification key prepared by the researchers. This is a method that provides teachers with a remedial teaching tool and helps students analyze their answers and master the correct knowledge. The remedial teaching can take place when the evaluated tests are returned to the students and both they and the teacher engage in a constructivist mode of learning. Students can realize that the test is used not only to give grades (as a punishment tool), but as a learning process from which all can profit. It was also determined that students can overcome test anxiety and develop positive attitudes toward the teacher, the subject matter, and, consequently, the learning process, when their justifications are compared against a justification key. All of the details of the study procedure and the biological content of the questions, the answers, and the analysis can be found in the researchers' paper (Penso & Lazarowitz, 1992).

In another study, Lawson and Worsnop (1992) reported that teaching a learning unit to high school students on the topics of evolution and natural selection yielded the following results: the instruction did not produce an overall shift toward a belief in evolution; reflective reasoning skill was significantly related to the students' initial scientific beliefs and to gains in declarative knowledge but not significantly related to changes in students' viewpoints. One of the difficulties in teaching evolution in high school is the fact that we can neither illustrate nor concretize the evolutionary process in the laboratory. In order to overcome this obstacle, Ron and Lazarowitz (1995) conducted a study among 12th-grade students in which the topic of evolution was taught in an instructional mode of cooperative groups. The topics learned were Lamarck's, Darwin's, and neutral theories; punctuated equilibria; genetics diversity; natural selection; specialization; and phylogenesis. The results showed that students' academic achievement was higher than that of the control group. The explanation for this was based on the fact that cooperative learning facilitates students' verbal interaction and construction of the knowledge, based on group products. Can ninth-grade students identified as being in the concrete operational stage learn the concept of pH, which requires formal operational ability? In their study, Witenoff and Lazarowitz, (1993) found that when the laboratory worksheets according to which students performed the experiments are restructured according to Farmer and Farrell's (1980, p. 64) suggestions, and taught in cooperative groups, they achieved significantly higher grades than the control group. It can be seen that when the cognitive operational stages of students are identified and the learning material restructured in order to fit their cognitive stage and learning style, they can succeed. Identifying students' cognitive stages not only provides additional independent variables, but also helps teachers analyze the learning difficulties their students encounter and adjust the learning material, the instructional methods, and the learning environment to their needs and thus facilitate successful outcomes. Biology teaching and learning in classrooms and in the lab present many opportunities for evaluation and grading procedures, in addition to the use of classical tests following the instruction of a unit (Lazarowitz, 2000; Lazarowitz & Tamir, 1994).

Evaluation and Grading

Finally, we relate to the issue of students' evaluation and grading. A single study performed by Welicker and Lazarowitz (1995) is presented. A learning unit on the "Cardiovascular System with Health Aspects" was implemented in 10th-grade classes, and through the learning experiences in the classroom and laboratory work, a multidimensional learning environment was created. Students were able to demonstrate a variety of competencies, which were observed by the teachers and evaluated with the use of a multidimensional performance assessment instrument. This instrument served as a tool for an authentic evaluation of students' abilities and mastery of inquiry, psychomotor, and team working skills. The multidimensional evaluation system, which was used during the process of teaching and learning in the classrooms and laboratory work, was shown to be a qualitative and dynamic tool of assessment and may provide teachers with an alternative performance evaluation in addition to summative tests.

CONCLUSIONS

In this chapter, I preferred to make a historical summary of the achievements made during the second half of the twentieth century in the development, implementation, and teaching of biology curricula in high schools all over the world and to pay tribute to the modern science educators who contributed so much to our field. The inquiry mode of teaching and learning; the study of cognitive skills and cognitive stages, conceptual change and formation; and the learning settings of individual, cooperative, and computer-assisted learning developed during the twentieth century, to mention just a few, are milestones pointing the way toward the new century. In the twenty-first century we have to grapple with the issue of teaching sciences to a heterogeneous student population in order to spread scientific and technology literacy and enable these young men and women to participate in a continually evolving society. Only by appreciating and knowing the past can one look to the future.

The reader, then, in my opinion, after reading this chapter will have a basic understanding of where research on science education has been and the directions in which it may be going.

Having said this, I point out to the reader that there are several reviews that present the topics investigated in teaching biology, some of them in specific chapters in this book and others I now mention briefly. The interested readers may look at Lawson (1988), who mentioned the research aimed at improving biology teaching. Lawson found that two major theories dominated these studies. The first, proposed by Ausubel, is a theory of verbal learning on ways students acquire specific biological concepts, and the second is Piaget's developmental theory, which focuses on ways students acquire and use general scientific reasoning patterns. The research on laboratory practical work was summarized by Lazarowitz and Tamir (1994). The research studies on teaching biology in cooperative small groups were reviewed by Lazarowitz (1995a, 1995b) and by Lazarowitz and Hertz-Lazarowitz (1988).

The topics of Concept Mapping in Biology from different angles, the nature of biology knowledge, misconceptions in biology, language, analogy and biology, concept circle diagramming as a knowledge mapping tool, and more topics are presented in *Mapping Biology Knowledge* by Fisher, Wandersee, and Moody (2000).

Recommendations

As we embark on the twenty-first century, it is becoming clear that biology curricula should serve not only the students who are pursuing academic careers, but also the remainder of students, who are the majority (almost 85%) and whose needs are different.

A differential approach in developing biology curricula, which will provide an answer to our student populations who differ so much in their needs, must be adopted. It is imperative to integrate all of the findings of our research in science education, in textbooks, in pre-service and in-service courses in a more rigorous way, so that teachers will have the tools for the instructional process to help students enjoy and profit from the learning of science and technology. If we want to be relevant to students' needs as future citizens who will have to function in a highly scientific and technological society, then an integration of the sequence of topics to be taught and learned with a new pedagogical and didactical approach should be developed, implemented, and evaluated. The pedagogical and didactical approach should include a variety of instructional strategies and learning settings. The issue of ethics and values cannot be ignored and should be integrated into textbooks and the education of biology teachers. The results of a study by Lazarowitz and Bloch

(2005) have shown that teachers, while teaching genetics, genetics engineering, molecular biology, and evolution topics, are primarily concerned with the CKS and much less with the aspects of ethics, moral, values, and societal issues, which derive from scientific research and daily life. In this troubled world, one may ask if it is not the educational role of teachers at all levels, from K to 12th grade and in the universities, to address these issues while teaching the sciences and technology, biology in particular. These new approaches are opening new frontiers for science education research in the twenty-first century and becoming more relevant to a heterogeneous high school student population.

ACKNOWLEDGMENTS

Thanks to Anton Lawson and James Wandersee, who reviewed this chapter.

REFERENCES

Aikenhead, G. S. (1980). *Science in social issues: Implications for teaching*. Ottawa: Science Council of Canada.

Agrest, B. (2003). How do biology teachers choose to teach certain topics in a high school biology curriculum without compulsory parts? Unpublished Ph.D. dissertation, Hebrew University of Jerusalem, Israel.

Alexander, G. (1953). *General biology* (6th ed.). New York: Barnes & Noble.

Aronson, E., Stephan, C., Sikes, J., Blaney, N., & Snapp, M. (1978). *The jigsaw classroom*. Beverly Hills, CA: Sage.

Baird, J. H., Lazarowitz, R., & Allman, V. (1984). Science choices and preferences of middle and secondary school students in Utah. *Journal of Research in Science Teaching, 21*(1), 47–54.

Bethel, J. L., & Hard, M. S. (1981). *The study of change: In service teachers in a National Science Foundation Environmental Science Education Program*. Paper presented at the American Research Association Conference, Los Angeles, CA.

Biological Sciences Curriculum Study. (BSCS, 1966). *Biological science: Patterns and process*. New York: Rinehart & Winston.

Biological Sciences Curriculum Study. (BSCS, 1968). *1. Biological science and inquiry into life* (Yellow version). New York: Harcourt, Brace & World; *2. Molecules to man* (Blue version), New York: Houghton-Mifflin; *3. High school biology* (Green version). New York: Rand McNally.

Biological Sciences Curriculum Study. (BSCS, 1970). *Interaction of experiments and ideas* (2nd ed.). Englewood Cliffs, NJ: Prentice Hall.

Biological Science, Nuffield Project in Biology. (1970). a. Maintenance of the organism. b. Organisms and population. In W. H. Dowdeswell (Ed.), *Advance course for the sixth form: Vol. I. Teachers' guide to the laboratory guides*. Harmondsworth, Middlesex, England: Penguin Books.

Bloom, B. S. (1956). *Taxonomy of educational objectives: The classification of educational goals*. London: Longmans.

Bybee, R. W. (1987). Science education and science-technology-society (STS) theme. *Science Education, 71*(5), 667–683.

DeGisi, L. L., & Willet, J. B. (1995). What high school biology teachers say about their textbooks use: A descriptive study. *Journal of Research in Science Teaching, 32*(2), 123–142.

DeHart Hurd, P. (1961). *Biological education in American secondary schools (1890–1960)*. Baltimore: Waverly Press.

DeHart Hurd, P. (1978). The golden age of biological education 1960–1975. In W. V. Mayer (Ed.), *BSCS, Biology teacher's handbook* (3rd ed., pp. 28–96). New York: John Wiley & Sons.

DeHart Hurd, P., Robinson, J. T., Connell, M. C., & Ross, N. R. (1981). *The status of middle and junior high school science: Vol. 2. Technical report.* Louisville, CO: Biological Sciences Curriculum Study.

Farmer, W. A., & Farrell, M. A. (1980). *Systematic instruction in science for the middle and high school years.* Reading, MA: Addison Wesley.

Finely, F., Steward, J., & Yaroch, L. (1982). Teachers' perception of important and difficult science content. *Science Education, 66*(4), 531–538.

Fisher, M. K., Wandersee, H. J., & Moody, E. D. (2000). *Mapping biology knowledge.* Dordrecht, the Netherlands: Kluwer Academic.

Friedler, Y., Amir, R., & Tamir, P. (1987). High school students' difficulties in understanding osmosis. *International Journal of Science Education, 9*(5), 541–551.

Fuller, F. F., (1969). Concerns of teachers: A development conception. *American Educational Research Journal, 6*(2), 207–226.

Gagne, R. M. (1963). The learning requirements for inquiry. *Journal of Research in Science Teaching, 1,* 144–153.

Gallgher, J. T. (1967). Teacher variation in concept presentation in BSCS curriculum program. *BSCS Newsletter,* January 8–19.

German, P. J., Haskins, S., & Auls, S. (1996). Analysis of nine high school biology laboratory manuals: Promoting scientific inquiry. *Journal of Research in Science Teaching, 33*(5), 475–499.

Harder, R., Schumacher, W., Firbas, F., & von Denffer, D. (1965). *Strasburger's textbook of botany.* London: Longmans.

Harms, N. C., & Yager, R. E. (1981). *What research says to the science teacher* (Vol. 3). Washington, DC: U.S. Government Printing Office.

Huppert, J., Simchoni, D., & Lazarowitz, R. (1992). Human health and science. A model for an STS high school biology course. *The American Biology Teacher, 54*(7), 395–400.

Johnstone, A. H., & Mahmoud, N. A. (1980). Isolating topics of high perceived difficulty in school biology. *Journal of Biological Education, 14*(2), 163–166.

Khalil, M. (2000). *Teachers' handbook: Microorganisms, a STS learning unit* (in Arabic, 76 pages, in Hebrew, 76 pages). Haifa, Israel: The Israel Science Teaching Center and the R&D Institute, IIT, Technion.

Khalil, M. (2002). *Microorganisms, a STS learning unit* (in Arabic. p. 116, in Hebrew, p. 116). Haifa, Israel: The Israel Science Teaching Center and the R&D Institute, IIT, Technion.

Khalil, M., & Lazarowitz, R. (2002). *Developing a learning unit on the science-technology-environment-peace-society mode. Students' cognitive achievements and attitudes toward peace.* Annual Meeting of the National Association of Research in Science Teaching, (NARST), New Orleans, April 7–10.

Klinckman, E. (1970). *Biology teachers' handbook.* New York: John Wiley & Sons.

Koran, J. J., Jr. (1971). Concepts and concept-formation in the teaching of biology. *The American Biology Teacher,* October, 405–408.

Koran, J. J., Jr., Koran, M. L., & Baker, S. D. (1980). Differential response to cueing and feedback in the acquisition of an inductively presented biological concept. *Journal of Research in Science Teaching, 17*(2), 167–172.

Koran, J. J., Jr., Koran, M. L., Baker, S. D., & Moody, K. W. (1978). *Concept formation in science instruction: What does research tell us?* The Science Council, Alberta Teachers Association and the National Science Teachers Association, Banff, Alberta, Canada, October 6–9.

Lawson, A. E. (1988). A better way to teach biology. *The American Biology Teacher, 50*(5), 266–277.

Lawson, A. E., & Thompson, L. D. (1988). Formal reasoning ability and misconceptions concerning genetics and natural selection. *Journal of Research in Science Teaching, 25*(9), 733–746.

Lawson, A. E., & Worsnop, W. A. (1992). Learning about evolution and rejecting a belief in special creation: Effects of reflective reasoning skill, prior knowledge, prior belief and religious commitment. *Journal of Research in Science Teaching, 29*(2), 143–166.

Lazarowitz, R., & Bloch, I. (2005). Awareness to societal issues among high school biology teachers teaching genetics. *Journal of Science Education and Technology, 14*(5/6), 437–457.

Lazarowitz, R. (1995a). Learning science in cooperative modes in junior- and senior-high school: Cognitive and affective outcomes. In E. J. Pedersen & D. A. Digby (Eds.), *Cooperative learning and secondary schools: Theory, models and strategies* (pp. 185–227). New York: Garland Press.

Lazarowitz, R. (1995b). Learning biology in cooperative investigative groups. In E. J. Pedersen & D. A. Digby (Eds.), *Cooperative learning and secondary schools: Theory, models and strategies* (pp. 341–363). New York: Garland Press.

Lazarowitz, R. (2000). Research in science, content knowledge structure and secondary school curricula. *Israel Journal of Plant Sciences, 48*(3), 229–238.

Lazarowitz, R., & Hertz-Lazarowitz, R. (1979). Choices and preferences of science subjects by junior high school students in Israel. *Journal of Research in Science Teaching, 16*(4), 317–323.

Lazarowitz, R., & Hertz-Lazarowitz, R. (1998). Cooperative learning in the science curriculum. In B. J. Fraser & K. G. Tobin (Eds.), *International handbook of science education* (pp. 449–471). Dordrecht, the Netherlands: Kluwer Academic.

Lazarowitz, R., & Penso, S. (1992). High school students' difficulties in learning biology concepts. *Journal of Biological Education, 26*(3), 215–223.

Lazarowitz, R., & Tamir, P. (1994). Research on using laboratory instruction in science. In D. Gabel (Ed.), *Handbook of research in science teaching and learning* (Vol. 3, pp. 94–128). New York: Macmillan.

Madaus, G. F., & Stufflebeam, D. L. (Eds.). (1989). *Tyler's rationale for curriculum development.* Boston: Kluwer Academic.

Mechner, F. (1965). Science education and behavioral technology. In R. Glaser (Ed.), *Teaching Machines and Programmed Learning, 11: Data and Directions* (pp. 441–507). Washington, DC: National Education Association.

Nachshon, M. (2000). *Ionizing radiation. The biological effects and uses* (p. 153). Haifa, Israel: The Israel Science Teaching Center and the R&D Institute, IIT, Technion.

Nachshon, M., & Lazarowitz, R. (2002). *Ionizing radiation, uses and effects. A thematic module for 11th grade students: Academic achievements and creativity.* Presented at the Annual Meeting of the National Association of Research in Science Teaching (NARST), New Orleans, April 7–10.

Novak, J. D. (1965). A model for the interpretation and analysis of concept formation. *Journal of Research in Science Education, 3,* 72–83.

Nuffield Advanced Science. (1970). *Biological science: 1.Teachers' guide to the laboratory guides, Volume I. a). Maintenance of the organism; b) Organisms and populations; and Volume II. a) The developing organism; b) Control and co-ordination in organisms.* Harmondsworth, England: Penguin Books.

Nuffield Foundation. (1966). *Synopsis of the Nuffield Biology Course.* London: Longmans/Penguin Books, Biological Science.

Ron, S., & Lazarowitz, R. (1995). *Learning environment and academic achievement of high school students who learned evolution in a cooperative mode.* Paper presented at the annual meeting of the National Association for Research in Science Teaching, NARST, San Francisco, April 22–25.

Rosenthal, D. B. (1984). Social issues in high school biology textbooks: 1963–1983. *Journal of Research in Science Teaching, 21*(8), 819–831.

Rutherford, F. J. (1964). The role of inquiry in science teaching. *Journal of Research in Science Teaching, 2,* 80–84.

Schwab, J. J. (1963). *Biology teachers handbook.* New York: John Wiley & Sons.

Schwab, J. J., & Brandwein, P. F. (1962). *The teaching of science as enquiry.* Cambridge, MA: Harvard University Press.

Shemesh, M., & Lazarowitz, R. (1989). Pupils' reasoning skills and their mastery of biological concepts. *Journal of Biological Education, 23*(1), 59–63.

Shulman, L. S. (1987). Knowledge and teaching: Foundation of the new reform. *Harvard Educational Review, 57,* 1–22.

Stern, L., & Roseman, E. J. (2004). Can middle school science textbooks help students learn important ideas? *Journal of Research in Science Teaching, 41*(6), 538–568.

Steward, J. H. (1982). Difficulties experienced by high school students when learning basic Mendelian genetics. *The American Biology Teacher, 44*(2), 80–84.

Tamir, P. (1974). An inquiry-oriented laboratory examination. *Journal of Educational Measurement, 11*, 23–25.

Tamir, P., & Glassman, F. (1971). A laboratory test for BSCS students—a progress report. *Journal of Research in Science Teaching, 8*, 332–341.

Tamir, P., & Jungwirth, E. (1975). Students growth and trends developed as a result of studying BSCS biology for several years. *Journal of Research in Science Teaching, 12*, 263–280.

Tyler, W. R. (1966). Dimensions in curriculum development. *Phi Delta Kappan, 48*, 25–28.

Wagner-Gershgoren, I. (2004). The development and validity of a model to set criteria for the choice and evaluation of biology textbooks. Unpublished Ph.D. dissertation, Israel Institute of Technology, Technion, Haifa, Israel.

Welicker, M., & Lazarowitz, R. (1995). *Performance tasks and performance assessment of high school students studying primary prevention of cardiovascular diseases.* Paper presented at the Annual Meeting, NARST, San Francisco, April 22–25.

Witenoff, S., & Lazarowitz, R. (1993). Restructuring laboratory worksheets for junior high school biology students in the heterogeneous classroom. *Research in Science and Technological Education, 11*(2), 225–239.

Yager, R. E. (1980). *Analysis of current accomplishments and needs in science education.* Columbus, OH: ERIC/SMEAC Clearinghouse for Science, Mathematical, and Environmental Education, Columbus State University.

Yager, R. E. (1982). The crisis in biology education. *The American Biology Teacher, 44*(6), 328–336, 368.

Yager, R. E., & Hofstein, A. (1986). Features of a quality curriculum for school science. *Journal of Curriculum Studies, 18*, 133–146.

Yager, R. E., Hofstein, A., & Lunetta, V. N. (1981). Science education attuned to social issues: Challenge for the 80s. *The Science Teacher, 48*(9), 12–13.

CHAPTER 21

Teaching Physics

Reinders Duit
Leibniz-Institute for Science Education, Germany

Hans Niedderer and Horst Schecker
University of Bremen, Germany

A deliberate subject-specific view is employed in the present chapter. We attempt to provide an overview of research on teaching and learning physics—in particular from the perspective of what is special in this domain as compared with biology, chemistry, and earth science. We would like to point to two issues where physics education appears to be "special" already.

First, according to the bibliography on constructivist-oriented research on teaching and learning science by Duit (2005), about 64% of the studies documented are carried out in the domain of physics, 21% in the domain of biology, and 15% in the domain of chemistry. There are various reasons for this dominance of physics in the research on teaching and learning. The major reason appears to be that physics learning includes difficulties that are due to the particular nature of physics. We just mention the abstract and highly idealized kind of physics (mathematical) modeling. Research on students' conceptions has shown that most pre-instructional ("everyday") ideas students bring to physics instruction are in stark contrast to the physics concepts and principles to be achieved—from kindergarten to the tertiary level. Quite often students' ideas are incompatible with physics views (Wandersee, Mintzes, & Novak, 1994). This also holds true for students' more general patterns of thinking and reasoning (Arons, 1984).

Secondly, physics clearly is the domain that is greeted with the lowest interest by students among the sciences. This is true in particular for girls (Parker, Rennie, & Fraser, 1996). It appears also that the nature of physics mentioned is at least partly responsible for these findings. Students, especially girls, perceive physics not only as very abstract, complicated, and difficult, but also as counterintuitive and incomprehensible.

The review presented draws on European views of science education, more precisely, continental European views—with German views somewhat predominant. On the one hand, the issue of scientific literacy is discussed from a position including the German idea of *Bildung*, with its emphasis on issues that are beyond functional scientific literacy (Bybee, 1997). On the other hand, European ideas of *Didaktik* (Westbury, Hopmann, & Riquarts, 2000) are used to analyze the particular role of designing the content structure of physics instruction in such a way that it meets students' perspectives (e.g., pre-instructional conceptions and interests) and the aims of instruction.

THE INTERDISCIPLINARY NATURE OF PHYSICS EDUCATION AS A RESEARCH DOMAIN

As illustrated in Fig. 21.1, physics education research is interdisciplinary in nature. There are several "reference domains" that are needed to meet the challenges of investigating and analyzing the key issues of teaching and learning physics. Philosophy and history of physics provide frameworks make it possible to identify what is usually called the "nature of physics" in the literature (McComas, 1998). Hence, these domains play a major role in discussing what is special in physics and therefore also what is special in teaching and learning physics. But also social sciences, especially pedagogy and psychology, are essential reference domains. Research and development that aims at improving practice has to address issues of physics as a specific way of knowing as well as general issues of learning. This is the underlying position of the present review.

CHARACTERISTICS OF PHYSICS EDUCATION RESEARCH

Dahncke et al. (2001) argued that there is a split in the science education community. On the one side the major focus is on science—here physics. This group usually is at home in organizations that are close to the "mother" discipline, like physical societies. Research work in this group is in most cases restricted to issues of subject matter structure or presentation techniques, more or less neglecting the way in which the ideas developed may be learned by students. On the other hand, there are science educators who try to find a balance between the mother discipline and educational issues. The latter position is the background of Fig. 21.1.

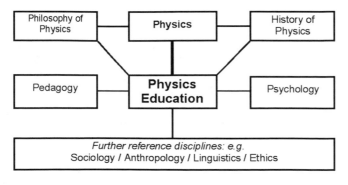

FIGURE 21-1. Reference disciplines of physics education.

Jenkins (2001) provided another distinction of research in science education, namely *pedagogical* versus *empirical*. The pedagogical tradition aims at improving practice. Research and development are intimately linked. Research is usually carried out in actual classrooms or at least in settings that are close to a classroom situation. The major concern of the empirical tradition is acquiring "objective data" that are needed to understand and influence educational practice. This distinction has much in common with the differentiation between "applied" and "basic" research. It has been argued in science education (Wright, 1993) as well as in research on teaching and learning in general (Kaestle, 1993) that basic research in education is viewed as irrelevant by practitioners and hence is in danger of widening the gap between research findings and practice. Therefore, a fine-tuned balance between the two positions is needed in research that aims to improve practice.

The German *Didaktik* Tradition

The meaning of the German term *Didaktik* should not be associated with the Anglo-Saxon meaning of *didactical*. Whereas the latter primarily denotes issues of educational technology, *Didaktik* stands for a multifaceted view of planning and performing instruction that is based on the German concept of *Bildung*. *Bildung* shares certain features of scientific literacy but also includes particular views of aims of schooling and instruction (Westbury, Hopmann, & Riquarts, 2000).

A literal translation of *Bildung* is "formation." In fact, *Bildung* is viewed as a process. Here appears to be a first significant difference to scientific literacy, which primarily denotes certain competencies, that is, outcomes of a process. *Bildung* stands for the formation of the learner as a whole person, that is, for the development of the personality of the learner. *Bildung* hence includes not only the achievement of domain-specific knowledge, but also the formation of what may be called "cross-curricular competencies" (including competencies allowing rational thinking and various social competencies). There is an emphasis on these cross-curricular competencies, which stand for a well-educated personality.

The meaning of *Didaktik* is based on the above conception of *Bildung*. It concerns the analytical process of transposing (or transforming) human knowledge (the cultural heritage) like domain-specific knowledge into knowledge for schooling, which contributes to the above formation (*Bildung*) of young people. Fensham (2001) claims that many recent attempts to improve science teaching and learning (e.g., based on constructivist perspectives) put a strong emphasis on improving the way science is taught (i.e., focus on the improvement of teaching methods and media). He thinks that science content should also be seen as problematic, that the neglected content structure for instruction should also be given attention. He is of the opinion that the *Didaktik* tradition allows such an improvement of instruction by developing a content structure for instruction that addresses students' learning needs and capabilities as well as the aims of instruction.

Briefly put, the content structure of a certain domain (e.g., physics) has to be transformed into a content structure *for* instruction. The two structures are substantially different. The physics content structure for a certain topic (like the force concept) may not be directly transferred into the content structure for instruction. It has not only to be simplified (in order to make it accessible for students), but also enriched by putting it into contexts that make sense to the learners. Two phases of this process may be differentiated. The first may be called *elementarization*. It leads to a set of "elementary" ideas comprising the key features of the content in question. For the energy concept the following elementary ideas may result: conservation, transformation, transfer, and degradation. On the basis of this set of elementary ideas the content structure for instruction is constructed. It is a key claim of the *Didaktik* tradition that both processes, "elementarization" and "construction of the content structure for instruction," are intimately interrelated to decisions on the aims of teaching the content and the students' affective and cognitive perspectives. Kattmann, Duit, Gropengießer, and Komorek (1995) have called the whole process "educational reconstruction" (for an example of the use of the model, see Duit, Komorek, & Wilbers, 1997).

The essence of the content analysis outlined in Fig. 21.2 may be well illustrated by a set of questions comprising the *Didaktische Analyse* proposed by the German educator Klafki (1969; see also Fensham, 2001):

1. What is the more general idea which is represented by the content of interest? What basic phenomena or basic principles, what general laws, criteria, methods, techniques or attitudes may be addressed in an exemplary way by dealing with the content?
2. What is the significance of the content for students' actual and future life?
3. What is the structure of the content if viewed from the pedagogical perspectives outlined in questions 1 and 2?
4. What are particular cases, phenomena, situations, experiments that allow the teacher to make the structure of the referring content interesting, worth questioning, accessible, and understandable for the students?

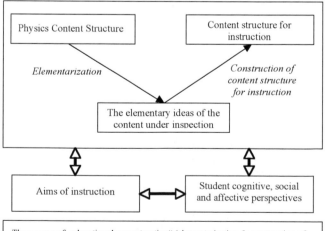

FIGURE 21–2. Educational reconstruction of physics content structure.

The concept of educational reconstruction outlined in Fig. 21.2 adds to Klafki's set of questions the idea of a fundamental interplay of all variables of instruction, namely, the *Aims*, the *Content*, the *Teaching and Learning Methods* and the *Media*, which is also a key figure of thought in the German *Didaktik* tradition (Heimann, Otto, & Schulz, 1969). In the process of instructional planning this fundamental interplay has to be taken into account. Students' perspectives must also be taken into consideration as a key point of reference for construction of the content structure for instruction and for developing the phases of instruction, the methods, and the materials and media used.

In a nutshell, the German *Didaktik* tradition as well as similar traditions in other European countries critically take the content issue into account. It is a key assumption that a content structure has to be developed which addresses students' pre-instructional perspectives and that the learning environment has to be designed in such a way that students may achieve the content in question. Improving instruction includes both critical analysis and reconstruction of content and development of supportive learning environments.

Clearly, major ideas of Shulman's (1987) approach of content specific pedagogical knowledge are in accordance with the European *Didaktik* tradition. However, whereas Shulman puts the main emphasis on teacher competencies, the *Didaktik* tradition has also developed strategies for taking the content issue seriously in instructional planning.

OVERVIEW OF THE CHAPTER

In the following chapter we first discuss major fields of research on teaching physics. The emphasis is on issues that are special for physics teaching. In the subsequent section, research on three content domains, the force concept, the electric circuit, and atomic physics, is reviewed. These three topics allow us to discuss major learning difficulties and major attempts to improve learning that are particularly relevant for physics instruction. Finally, we want to summarize major concerns and desiderata of physics education research.

TEACHING PHYSICS: MAJOR FIELDS OF RESEARCH

As detailed below, we provide a brief overview of major fields of research. We draw on the perspective of the above *Didaktik* tradition where normative research on the aims of instruction, analytical research on subject matter clarification and elementarization, as well as empirical research on teaching and learning processes are closely linked.

Aims of Instruction

The international science achievement studies TIMSS (Third International Mathematics and Science Study) and PISA (Programme for International Student Assessment) have had a strong impact on the discussion about the proper aims of instruction, in particular for lower secondary education (cf. the discussion on scientific literacy in Chapter 26). Science is seen as a major factor influencing the daily lives of individuals as well as economic progress in technology-based societies (e.g., Beaton et al., 1996, p. 7). Physics forms the basis of information technology, transport, and energy production. In order to make sensible use of technological means, to find a place in a technology-based economy, and to participate in political processes about technology-related decisions, citizens need a certain amount of physics knowledge. The PISA consortium has agreed on a notion of scientific literacy that consists of understanding basic scientific concepts, familiarity with scientific thinking and processes, and the ability to apply this knowledge in concrete situations (cf. OECD, 1999). Students should be able to identify issues that can be understood by the application of scientific knowledge, to draw conclusions from scientific investigations, and to assess the scope of scientific findings. As these competencies apply for all citizens, they have to be targeted during the obligatory phase of science education. Important physics concepts are energy, conservation/devaluation, particle/matter, and interaction.

From a European perspective, in the *upper secondary* level physics education has to contribute to three major goals of higher education: further general education (*Bildung*), scientific thinking, and providing a foundation for learning at the tertiary level. In this voluntary phase scientific literacy has to be broadened in these aspects (cf. Schecker, Fischer, & Wiesner, 2004):

- Insights into modern physics world views (basic ideas of quantum physics, relativity, nonlinear physics)
- A systematic view of the cultural and social consequences of physics and technology (e.g., in energy production and consumption)
- Awareness of the specific physics conception of the world, aiming at a small set of general and universally applicable concepts and laws
- Sustainable knowledge of standard physics procedures (e.g., using lab instruments, formal problem solving) as a basis for university studies and vocational training in science and technology

Competencies of applying physics concepts and processes have to be embedded in a proper understanding of the nature of science (NOS; cf. McComas, 1998). Standards for curriculum development based on Scientific Literacy and the NOS can be found in AAAS (1993) and in NRC (1996).

Compared with the American tradition with its pragmatic and optimistic view of science as a means for social progress, the European view as outlined above puts more weight on the contribution of scientific knowledge to the formation of students' personalities. Students have to decide the extent to which they integrate scientific thinking into their world views. This belongs to the process of *Bildung*. It includes the critical reflection on problematic outcomes of the scientific enterprise.

Science Processes and Views of the Nature of Science

Learning about science processes and the nature of science (NOS) has to be an integral part of physics education. There is a wide consensus about this thesis among science educators (see Chapter 29). Some central elements of a proper understanding of the NOS are (cf. McComas, 1998; AAAS, 1993) the following:

- Scientific knowledge has a tentative character. Scientific concepts and theories are the result of a historical genetic process.
- Observation, experimental evidence, rational arguments, and skepticism play an important role in generating scientific knowledge.
- Observations are theory-laden. There is no direct path from an experiment to a theory.

Physics is distinguished from other sciences by its extremely high level of abstraction and idealization. Complexity is strongly reduced in order to make quantitative predictions possible. For this purpose physics produces its own prototypical phenomena in lab settings. From the physics point of view the true order of nature lies beyond the "touch and show reality." The book of nature is written in the language of mathematical models. Theories should contain a very limited set of laws that are all-applicable. Before an everyday world phenomenon with its complexity of influences and parameters qualifies for a physics analysis, it has to be "cleaned." It is nearly impossible to calculate the path of a leaf falling from a tree; but it is easy to predict precisely the motion of a feather in an evacuated tube. Physics thinking does not originate from the minute observation of the world around us but from the reconstruction of this world under the assumption of theoretical principles. This shift of perspectives (cf. the following section on conceptual change) is a major factor that makes it so difficult for students to learn physics.

There are good reasons to take account of epistemological and concept-genetic aspects in physics teaching (cf. McComas, 1998). They range from a better understanding of physics concepts (e.g., Galili & Hazan, 2000) enabling students to make rational decisions in a democratic society (Driver et al., 1996).

Still, there is often a gap between the strategic aims formulated in the preambles of science curricula and the actual content of textbooks and teaching (cf. Kircher, Girwidz, & Häußler, 2000, p. 38). The NOS is seldom taught explicitly (Duit, Müller, Tesch, & Widodo, 2004). NOS items are hardly included in physics exams. Teachers do not feel competent in this domain (cf. Abd-EI-Khalick, Bell, & Lederman, 1998). Empirical studies reveal widespread misunderstandings of the NOS. Students' epistemological beliefs can be characterized as naive-empiristic: scientific theories are seen as everlasting truths, derived from precise observations and theory-free experiments. Creative speculation and theory-laden construction are not taken into account (cf. the analyses of data from TIMSS, population 3, in Köller, Baumert, & Neubrandt, 2000).

Abd-EI-Khalick, Bell, and Lederman (1998) thus strongly argue for including more NOS elements in teacher training and teaching (see also Schecker, Fischer, & Wiesner, 2004). McComas's book (1998) gives examples of how to introduce students and teachers into epistemological issues. Matthews (1994) stresses the historical perspective in teaching science. Meyling (1997) provides empirical evidence for how an explicitly epistemology-based physics course can change students' ideas toward a proper understanding of the NOS.

Conceptual Change

The dominating perspectives of research on teaching and learning science have been constructivist views of conceptual change since the 1980s (Mintzes, Wandersee, & Novak, 1997; Duit & Treagust, 2003). A problem-solving perspective on teaching and learning physics that addresses slightly different facets is provided by Maloney (1994). Both research perspectives have been rather influential in developing new teaching and learning approaches that deliberately take students' preinstructional views, beliefs, and conceptions into account (for proposals on teaching and learning physics see the following volumes: Viennot, 2001, 2003; Redish, 2003; Arons, 1997).

As mentioned above, physics is the domain in which most research studies on investigating students' conceptions and on conceptual change have been carried out. Table 21.1 presents the number of studies documented in the bibliography by Duit (2006). It becomes obvious that there is a particular emphasis on mechanics and electricity. In both domains there is a strong focus on the force concept or the (simple) electric circuit, respectively. Clearly, these subdomains are somewhat over-researched. Other domains, especially the domains of modern physics, need further attention. More details on research findings in the domains of mechanics, electricity, and atomic physics are given below. General findings of research on conceptual change are reported elsewhere. The particular difficulty of conceptual change in the process of learning physics appears to be that usually students' preinstructional conceptions about phenomena are deeply rooted in everyday experiences and are therefore in stark contrast to physics conceptions. Radical idealization and decon-textualization, the reduction to pure phenomena accompanied by particular mathematical modeling, seems to be a major hurdle for students to understand physics concepts and principles. Furthermore, in quantum physics and relativity the physics

TABLE 21.1
Number of Publications on Students' Ideas in the Bibliography by Duit (2005)

Biology—total	748
Chemistry—total	548
Physics—total	2,274
Mechanics (force)*	792
Electricity (electrical circuit)	444
Optics	234
Particle model	226
Thermal physics (heat/temp.)	192
Energy	176
Astronomy (Earth in space)	121
Quantum physics	77
Non linear systems (chaos)	35
Sound	28
Magnetism	25
Relativity	8

*Predominant concept in brackets.

view is incomprehensible in principle from everyday world perspectives. Interestingly, this also holds for the "classical" particle view, which is usually introduced in early school grades. Also here the world of the particles is fundamentally different from the world of our everyday experiences.

Viewed from the perspective of scientific literacy (Bybee, 1997), understanding physics includes understanding physics concepts and principles on the one hand and physics processes as well as views of the nature of physics on the other. As argued in the previous section, these views *about* physics are not only essential features of scientific literacy, but are also essential in understanding physics concepts and principles. Looking at teaching and learning physics from a conceptual change perspective should therefore include conceptual changes on the level of concepts and principles and on the level of processes and views of the nature of physics as well. Research has shown that students' ideas of processes (like modeling) or views of the nature of physics are "naive" in the same sense as their views of phenomena and concepts (Treagust, Chittleborough, & Mamiala, 2002). A multiple conceptual change view has to be employed (Duit & Treagust, 2003).

Students' Interests and Gender Issues

Research has shown that emotional factors play an essential role in learning science. Conceptual change, for instance, is not successful if it is based merely on "cold cognition" (Pintrich, Marx, & Boyle, 1992). A recent study on introductory electricity teaching (Laukenmann et al., 2003) has shown the significance of emotional factors. It became obvious again that positive emotions promote achievement. Interestingly, this is especially the case during the first phase of learning the new topic, where students need to be convinced that it is worthwhile to achieve the understanding intended. Kroh and Thomsen (2005) point out the significance of attitudes toward physics and students' self-concepts for learning physics. They argue that teaching and learning methods that take students' cognitive and affective variables into account and provide them with significant responsibility for their own learning will develop more positive attitudes and self-concepts and hence will result in more pleasing outcomes of instruction.

The issue of emotional factors (like interests, motivation, attitudes, and self-concept) in learning science and gender differences are more fully discussed elsewhere in the present *Handbook* (Chapters 5 and 11). Here only a few issues are added that are characteristic of physics instruction.

International comparison studies reveal that girls' achievements and interests in physics are substantially lower than those of boys (Keeves & Kotte, 1996). However, there are significant differences between the countries concerning the gap between the genders. Nevertheless, physics is usually the science domain that is greeted with the lowest interest in particular by girls. It appears that students' views of physics play a certain role. Science in general but physics in particular is seen as a male domain (Baker, 1998; Harding, 1996). Stadler, Benke, and Duit (2000) argue that girls and boys hold different (tacit) notions of what it means to understand physics. Briefly put, girls do not think that they understand a concept until they can put it into a broader (nonscientific) context. They try to understand the relations of the system of physics to the world seen as a whole. Boys, in contrast, seem to be more "pragmatic." They tend to regard physics as valuable in itself. They appear to be pleased with the internal coherence of the system of physics itself. It appears that boys' views of physics and their notions on understanding physics are somewhat nearer to the above-mentioned characteristic of radical idealization and decontextualization in physics than girls' views.

In order to improve the situation, several studies have been carried out to embed physics in contexts that make sense especially to girls, that is, to address their particular notion of understanding physics. Briefly, such studies have shown that instructional materials addressing girls' interests, such as the human body and issues of social relevance, significantly enhance girls' interests and achievement (Baker, 1998; Häußler & Hoffmann, 2002; Reid & Skryabina, 2003) and have also proved successful for boys. Research has also revealed that the way physics is taught is another major factor. Teaching strategies that enhance the self-confidence of girls, like collaborative work in single-sex groups, have also improved interests and achievement for girls and boys alike (Baker, 1998; Häußler & Hoffmann, 2002).

Labwork and Multimedia

Student work with real apparatus in the physics lab and student work with computer-based tools can be regarded as two ways of active engagement with physics phenomena. In modern teaching strategies the two modes are gradually integrated (cf. Goldberg & Bendall, 1995; Laws, 1997; Schecker, 1998). Redish (2003) describes the relevant teaching methods together with available resources.

Labwork

The experiment plays a major role in science classes. In physics instruction most of the teaching time appears to be oriented in some way toward experiments with a certain emphasis on teacher demonstrations (Duit et al., 2004). Learning with hands on in laboratory work or from demonstrations has a particular meaning for physics instruction with respect to the nature of physics. Leach (2002) has formulated empirically supported hypotheses about how students' actions during lab work are based on their image of the nature of science, thus setting up a basis for analyzing learning processes in the lab with respect to students' epistemological beliefs. It is further argued that a limited practice in which straightforward demonstration experiments dominate leads to rather limited views about the nature of science. The tension between theory with its general and sharply defined concepts and practice setting up a context with many aspects of everyday life language is a specific issue (Woolnough, 1991; Hodson 1993). In a large Delphi-type study, teachers from universities and high schools gave the following objectives high priority (Welzel et al., 1998):

For students:

A.   to link theory to practice,
B.   to learn experimental skills,

C. to get to know the methods of scientific thinking,

D. to foster motivation, personal development, and social competence.

For teachers:

E. to evaluate the knowledge of the students.

Especially with respect to objective (A), a lot of empirical work has been done. Lunetta (1998) summarized some of the findings: "To many students, a 'lab' means manipulating equipment but not manipulating ideas." He consequently speaks of a "mismatch between goals, behavior and learning outcomes." Niedderer et al. (2002) have developed a "category-based analysis of videotapes from labwork" to analyze the amount of students' talking physics during lab work. Results show that students often use lab sheets like recipes without thinking and talking physics.

Multimedia

Multimedia tools for physics instruction can be divided in six categories:

- *Micro-based labs (MBL):* probes, interfaces, and software for on-line data acquisition, evaluation, and graphing (cf. Tinker, 1996).
- *Content-specific simulation programs:* Learners vary the parameters and explore the behavior of physical systems on the basis of a given mathematical model; numerous packages are available for all domains of physics.
- *Microworlds:* Learners can set up their own simulation settings interactively by combining given object-like building blocks, such as lenses and screens on a virtual optics bench (e.g., Goldberg & Bendall, 1995; Interactive Physics, 2004).
- *Model building systems (MBS):* Students generate a quantitative model describing the behavior of a system (e.g., the motion of bodies) either by putting in a set of equations or by constructing a computer-based concept map, while the software generates the equations (cf. Schecker, 1998).
- *General tools:* For example, spreadsheets with tables and graphs.
- *Targeted tools:* For example, tools for analyzing digitized motion videos (e.g., Beichner, 1996).

Multimedia packages integrate tools from several of these categories. The tools can be bound together with nonlinear interactive multimedia hypertext to so-called hypermedia systems.

The effectiveness of multimedia tools in physics education has become a major field of empirical research. Redish, Saul, and Steinberg (1996) found significant positive effects of MBL-based tutorials in teaching mechanics. Schecker (1998) reports that the use of MBS has a positive effect on semiquantitative reasoning about force and motion. A review of the literature on teaching and learning with the computer (Urhahne et al., 2000) draws a positive picture for science. There is a general agreement that the learning effects of multimedia in science education crucially depend on the instructional approach in which the materials are embedded (e.g., Linn et al., 1993).

TEACHING PHYSICS: PEDAGOGICAL CONTENT KNOWLEDGE IN THREE DOMAINS

In this section we want to outline characteristics of teaching and learning physics by reviewing the literature in three domains, ranging from a rather basic topic—simple electric circuits—to modern physics.

Teaching Electricity

Electricity is one of the physics domains where a huge number of research studies are available (Table 21.1). Particular emphasis lies on simple electric circuits. It becomes rather obvious that simple electric circuits are neither simple for students in the early grades of school nor for those at the tertiary level as well (Duit & v. Rhöneck, 1998).

Physics Concepts

The simplest circuit of all is presented in Fig. 21.3. A bulb is connected to a battery. The same geometrical (better: topological) structure holds for all kinds of "sources" and "consumers".

There are several levels of theoretical frames to allow predictions of whether the circuit will properly work or not.

(1) *Level of connecting conditions.* "Source" and "consumer" have two connection points each; they have to be connected by *conductors* in such a way that the two connecting wires do not have direct contact (no *short circuit*). The *voltages* printed on source and consumer need to be (nearly) the same, otherwise the consumer will not work or will be destroyed. Note that voltage is simply a connecting condition. All the students need to know here is: the higher the voltage, the stronger the effect, and that voltages above 20 V are dangerous for humans.

(2) *Level of current flow.* Usually the *current* view as indicated by the two arrows in Fig. 21.3 is also seen as an essential part of theoretically framing the electric circuit

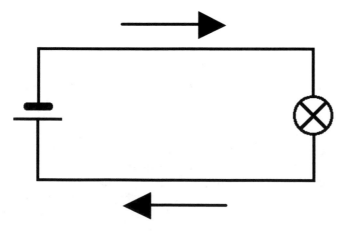

FIGURE 21–3. The simple electric circuit.

from the outset. There is a closed current flow, that is, a flow of electrically charged particles. The intensity of current is the same all over the circuit. In introductory physics instruction the particular nature of charges is usually not further discussed. There are good reasons for that because it depends on the source, the consumer, and the wires which kind of particles compose the charge flow. There is another essential feature of the current flow that needs attention in instruction. The charged flowing particles may not be viewed as moving independently from one another. Rather, the whole current flow forms a strongly coupled system—which can be compared to a bicycle chain. Whenever the current flow is changed at a certain spot the current all over the circuit is also changed.

(3) *Level of simultaneous current and energy flows.* It is important to enrich the above current flow view with the view of energy flow. If a current is flowing in the circuit of Fig. 21.3, the bulb glows. Hence energy is transported from the battery to the bulb. Therefore, every current flow is accompanied by an energy flow. Whereas the current flow is easy to locate, namely in the wire, this is more complicated for the energy flow. It seems that two different views are possible, namely energy flow in the electromagnetic field *around* the wires or *within* the wires. In any case, energy flow and current flow are fundamentally different in two regards. First, the energy flow is fast (nearly the speed of light), whereas the speed of charges (like electrons) is less than a few millimeters a second. Furthermore, the current flow is closed, the energy flow is not. Either on the path to the consumer or on the way back, energy and current flow in opposite directions.

The sketch of different levels of theoretical framing of the simple electric circuit presented above has revealed that the simple electric circuit is not so simple and easy to conceptualize also from the physics point of view. The issue of Educational Reconstruction discussed earlier (Fig. 21.2) comes into play here. The "elementary ideas" of the simple electric circuit may appear simple, but research on students' conceptions and on learning processes presented in the following show that too simple ideas may deeply mislead students in their attempts to understand the function of the electric circuit.

Students' Ideas

The following overview draws to a certain extent on the review by Duit and von Rhöneck (1998).

(1) *Everyday meanings of current.* Everyday talk about electricity is markedly different from physics talk. The meanings of words for current, for instance, are, at least in English and most major European languages, closer to the meaning of energy than to current as used in physics. Misunderstandings in class are likely if these differences are not taken into consideration.

(2) *Consumption of current.* Already students at the elementary level establish a causal connection between the battery and the bulb and explain that there is an agent moving from the battery to the bulb. The agent may be called electricity or electric current. It may be stored in the battery and is consumed within the bulb. Hence, there is no idea of conservation of electricity or current among children. A number of children think that one wire between battery and bulb suffices and that the second

wire simply serves to bring more current to the bulb. Some students believe that two different kinds of currents, called "plus" and "minus" current, travel from both sides of the battery to the bulb. In the bulb then there is a clash of the two currents producing the light ("clashing current"; Osborne, 1983) or a sort of chemical reaction. The idea of consumption of current is commonly held also by students beyond elementary level. Research has shown that it is very difficult to change this idea; it does not vanish through formal science education. It appears that the above way of talking about current is at least partly responsible for this dominance of the consumption conception.

(3) *Local and sequential reasoning.* Many students focus their attention upon one point of the circuit and ignore what is happening elsewhere. A "system" view of the current flow as described above is usually missing. An example of such local reasoning is the view that the battery delivers a constant current, independent of the circuit that is connected to the battery. Another variant of local reasoning may be called sequential reasoning. A number of students analyze a circuit in terms of "before" and "after" current passes a certain place. If, for instance, in the simple circuit of Fig. 21.3 a resistor is put into the connection leading from the battery to the bulb, students are correctly of the opinion that the bulb shines less brightly. But if the resistor is put into the other connection leading back to the battery, many students think that in this case the bulb shines as bright as before, because only the current leading back is influenced by the additional resistor.

(4) *Current and voltage.* Voltage has proved to be particularly difficult concept for students across different age levels. Before instruction voltage is usually related to the "strength of the battery" (or another source) or is viewed as the intensity of force or current. Usually there is not much progress after instruction. Many students still have severe difficulties in differentiating the two concepts.

(5) *Learning processes.* Many studies (e.g., Shipstone et al., 1988) have shown that the success of physics instruction in developing students' ideas about the electric circuit toward the physics view is rather limited. Most of these data draw on pre-post-test designs. However, there are also studies that follow the learning processes in detail. It becomes obvious that the learning pathways students follow are very complicated. There are forward and backward movements, there are parallel developments, and there are dead-end streets. In a study by Niedderer and Goldberg (1995), for instance, a group of three college students approaching the physics ideas of the electric circuit in a guided inquiry approach was involved. These students started with typical, alternative conceptions. On the *level of connecting conditions* they had many difficulties connecting a bulb to a battery in the correct way. On the *level of current flow* they viewed current as a kind of fuel that flows from the battery to the bulb and is consumed there. They further referred to previous knowledge taught in their science class on positive and negative charge. They merged these two concepts (the consumption idea and the notion of plus and minus current) in such a way that they constructed a new intermediate conception, similar to the well-known clashing currents concept which provided them with fruitful explanations. It was their own cognitive construction, which was not intended and not even realized by the teacher. During their further learning process these students developed more intermediate concepts: "Electron current" helped them to see current as moving electrons. The "electron gas pressure" idea provided a first understanding of the difference between the concepts of current and voltage. At the end of the whole teaching

sequence, however, these students still had difficulties seeing voltage as analogous to pressure *difference*, not merely to pressure.

A case study by Clement and Steinberg (2002) provided evidence that a student can start from an analogical source such as air pressure and flow and follow a learning pathway that builds a dynamically imaginable model of electric potential differences that cause current flow. There the learning pathway consisted of a series of partial models generated by dissonance-driven evaluations and revisions of the student's original model, and the student was able to apply the final model to a transfer problem. However, they still found intermittent difficulties with the distinction between potential and current.

Teaching Approaches

A substantial number of studies have been carried out investigating possibilities to guide students from their ideas to the physics concepts of the electric circuit. Basically, the same kinds of approaches as used in other science domains have also been employed here. There have been attempts to support conceptual change by specially designed multimedia learning environments and by a number of constructivist-oriented teaching and learning settings. It appears that such attempts usually (but not always) have proved superior to more "traditional" kinds of physics instruction. Still, the success is often disappointingly limited. There is, however, one exception. Almost all students, after appropriate experiences with electric circuits, are convinced that two wires are necessary to make the consumer work.

Students' pre-instructional conceptions of the electric circuit are—as outlined—in stark contrast to the referring physics concepts. Often new teaching and learning strategies start with the elicitation of students' ideas and with establishing their experiences in question. Students carry out experiments (e.g., with batteries and bulbs) and develop and exchange their views of the phenomena investigated. From such a basis the teacher tries to guide students toward the physics view. Challenging students' ideas is often a crucial period; that is cognitive conflicts play a certain role. Cognitive conflict strategies, though successful in a number of cases, bear one of several difficulties. The most important is that it is often difficult for students to experience the conflict. It may also happen that elicitation and long discussions of students' pre-instructional views may strengthen just this view. Therefore, also in the domain of electricity, various approaches have been developed that attempt to avoid cognitive conflicts. These approaches usually start from students' ideas that are mainly in accordance with the physics view and try to guide students from this kernel of conformity to the physics view via a continuous pathway. One such strategy Grayson (1996) calls "concept substitution." Instead of challenging students' views of current consumption, she provides the following reinterpretation: The view that something is consumed is not wrong at all—if seen in terms of energy as outlined above: energy is actually flowing from the battery to the bulb while current is flowing. Energy is "consumed," that is, transformed into heat and light.

Briefly summarized, understanding the simple electric circuit has proved rather difficult for students both in school and at the tertiary level. It appears that these difficulties are due at least partly to the fact that students' ideas are deeply rooted in certain everyday experiences (predominantly everyday speech about electricity, current, and electric circuits) and that these conceptions are not adequately addressed in instruction. The case of teaching and learning about electric circuits also shows that instruction may support "false" ideas. In general, the somewhat limited success of conceptual change approaches points to the issue that the content structure for instruction has to be carefully developed in a process called educational reconstruction above (Fig. 21.2). Also seemingly simple topics need substantially deep understanding of the physics "behind" that simple topic.

Teaching Mechanics

Within the domains of school physics, mechanics has the most substantial body of empirical research on students' conceptions (Table 21.1). There are various proposals for teaching approaches and a variety of multimedia tools. Nevertheless, mechanics remains one of the most difficult domains to teach and to learn. "Force" and "velocity" are subsumed by everyday interpretations of motion phenomena that differ substantially from physics concepts.

Physics Concepts

The concepts of classical mechanics—kinematics and dynamics—are *displacement, velocity, acceleration, force,* and *momentum. Mechanical energy (kinetic* and *potential energy, work*) belongs to the intersection between mechanics and thermodynamics. Mechanics is canonized by Newton's three laws. A trivialized version still found in many classrooms goes along the following lines:

1. If there are no forces acting on a body, it remains in its state of motion—at rest or with uniform velocity ("inertia").
2. The (resultant) force acting on a body is proportional to the body's mass and acceleration ($\mathbf{F} = m \cdot \mathbf{a}$).
3. To each force exerted on a body ("action") there is an equal but opposite force ("reaction").

Many students reproduce Newton's laws in similar phrases without understanding their conceptual content. $\mathbf{F} = m \cdot \mathbf{a}$ is probably the best known and least understood equation of physics. A sound way of expressing Newton's ideas is:

(1*) The motion of a body can only be changed by forces acting from outside. If there is no change, then there are either no forces at all or the vector sum of the single forces ($\mathbf{F}_R = \Sigma\mathbf{F}_i$; the resultant force) is zero.

(2*) The state of motion of a body is described by its momentum ($\mathbf{p} = m \cdot \mathbf{v}$). In order to change momentum, a resultant force has to be exerted over a certain time interval ($\Delta\mathbf{p} = \mathbf{F}_R \cdot \Delta t$).

(3*) Forces result from the interaction of bodies. Whenever a body A exerts a force on another body B, then B simultaneously exerts an equal but opposite force on A ($\mathbf{F}_{A \to B} = -\mathbf{F}_{B \to A}$).

Although the problems of teaching and learning mechanics cannot be solved simply by the use of proper formulations, the second set of laws helps to work out the conceptual core of mechanics. Law 1* opposes a widespread misunderstanding that inertia is only true in the absence of *any* force. Law 2* stresses the aspect of a *time process* of changing motion by forces. Law 3* underlines that interaction forces act on different bodies. An important aspect of conceptualizing mechanics is to distinguish clearly between the resultant force and single forces. Although the equations $F = m \cdot a$ (Newton's resultant force that changes the motion of a body) and $F = m \cdot g$ (for the single force of gravity) look very similar, the meanings of the "Fs" are completely different.

Students' Ideas

Driver et al. (1994, p. 149) summarize the empirical findings about students' ideas on force and motion in these statements:

- if there is motion, there is a force acting;
- if there is no motion, there is no force acting;
- there cannot be a force without motion;
- when an object is moving, there is a force in the direction of its motion;
- a moving object stops when its force is used up;
- a moving object has an own force within it which keeps it going;
- motion is proportional to the force acting;
- a constant speed results from a constant force.

One can add:

- friction is no "real" force but a resistance to motion;
- objects at rest or non-active objects (like tables or roads) do not exert forces;
- objects in circular motion "sense" a centrifugal force (independent of the system of reference).

These findings have been confirmed in empirical studies all over the world. They form the body of intuitive mechanics.

Research on students' ideas in mechanics was stimulated by Warren's book *Understanding Force* (1979). From a physicist's perspective Warren worked out the inherent difficulties and the conceptual stepping stones—sometimes caused by imprecise instruction. Warren developed a set of test items for university beginners that were also used in many follow-up studies with younger students (see Fig. 21.4 for an example). He showed that many students failed to solve seemingly "simple" problems.

Students are asked to mark the forces acting on the ball at points P and Q and to indicate their probable relative magnitudes (Warren, 1979, p. 34). Most students see a "force" in the direction of motion instead of a (resultant) force in the direction of the *change* of motion (in P vertically downward).

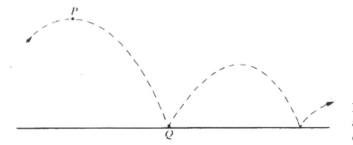

FIGURE 21–4.   Diagram from a tutorial test on student ideas of forces.

Viennot (1979) expanded on the question of how students conceptualize mechanics alternatively. She claimed that students' "spontaneous reasoning" was consistent and could be formed into an intuitive law of force in which "force" depends on velocity **v** (instead of acceleration **a**). Viennot found a coexistence between the idea of "force" as an interaction force impressed on a body and a "supply of force" stored in a body.

McCloskey (1983) drew parallels between students' "intuitive physics" and medieval "impetus theory", based on the idea that force impressed on an object can be stored in the body and is later used up in its motion. Students' impetus reasoning is very resistant to instruction. It leads to wrong predictions of the path of moving objects, like a cannon ball traveling in a straight line before the impetus is used up, so that it falls down vertically. Students even use impetus ideas when they are asked to drop a ball on a target on the ground while they are running.

Jung, Wiesner, and Engelhard (1981) worked out that "inertia" is conceptualized by students as a sort of "lameness"—a resistance to motion that has to be overcome by force. It is often associated with static friction. For students "force" has a polyvalent meaning that integrates facets of the physics concepts of energy, momentum, and Newtonian force. This is comparable to the ambivalent meaning of "force" in physics up to the mid-1850s. Students organize their mechanics knowledge in episodes (cases of force and motion) rather than in generalized principles.

There are a great number of further details on student difficulties, misunderstandings, and alternative concepts in mechanics:

- the problem of distinguishing between points of time and time intervals, which makes it difficult to understand the concepts of momentary velocity and acceleration: "If the velocity is zero, there can be no acceleration" (see, e.g., Trowbridge & McDermott, 1981).
- the misunderstanding that "action" and "reaction" refer to the same body (thus students believe that in order to cause motion, "action" must be stronger than "reaction" (see, e.g., Viennot, 1979).

A controversial issue is whether students' intuitive physics forms a systematic and coherent scheme—a sort of "alternative theory" (e.g., Viennot, 1979). diSessa (1988) strongly opposes this notion. He argues that students' knowledge consists of single loosely connected phenomenological primitives like "force as mover" or "more effort begs more result." According to diSessa, the transition to scientific understanding involves a major structural change toward systematization. In contrast, Vosniadou (2002) has argued on the basis of patterns in student responses that students construct their own narrow but coherent explanatory frameworks in mechanics. Chi, Slotta, and de Leeuw (1994) propose to organize students' thinking along ontological categories: In students' minds "force" belongs to the category "matter" (something that can be stored), while it should be re-assigned to the "constrained-based interaction" category. Jung, Wiesner, and Engelhard (1981) claim that it is more effective to address students' general categories of reasoning than to address specific alternative conceptions. Such categories are:

- functional descriptions of motion—in contrast to seeking the "cause" of motion
- relationships and *interactions* between bodies—in contrast to the *properties* of bodies

Research on students' understanding of mechanics culminated in the 1980s and has since reached a high degree of consensus. There are standardized instruments to assess students' reasoning:

- Force Concept Inventory (FCI; Hestenes, Wells, & Swackhamer, 1992)
- Force and Motion Conceptual Evaluation (FMCE; Thornton & Sokoloff, 1998)
- Test of Understanding Graphs in Kinematics (TUGK; Beichner, 1994)

Teaching Approaches

Under subject matter aspects Warren (1979, p. 13) points out that the Newtonian system of mechanics should be fully developed in terms of "real" forces. A "real" force can be attributed to a concrete body in a definable interaction which is subject to a recognizable law, such as gravitational forces caused by a planet or elastic forces caused by a deformed ball. Imaginary forces ("pseudo" forces) like centrifugal force only confuse students. Herrmann (1998) builds a mechanics curriculum around the concept of "momentum" that can be stored, shared between bodies, or flow from one body to another.

Minstrell (1992) reports on positive effects of high school mechanics courses where students are explicitly asked to express their intuitive ideas about force and motion. The students' ideas are then juxtaposed with the physics concepts. A similar strategy is presented by Schecker and Niedderer (1996) under the term "contrastive teaching." After introducing Newton's laws, the teacher poses an open-ended problem like "investigate forces in collisions." Students often make statements like "a force is transferred from body A to body B"—even though they nominally know the Newtonian definition of "force." This elicitation of students' own ideas (cf. Driver & Oldham, 1986) helps to contrast their intuitive views with the scientific notion of "force". Clement (1993) shows how students' intuitive ideas can be used as starting points ("anchors") for teaching sequences that lead to a proper understanding of related Newtonian concepts by way of "bridging analogies." Camp and Clement (1994) present a series of student activities that help them to overcome known learning obstacles.

Hake (1998) carried out a meta-analysis of studies done with the Force Concept Inventory-FCI (6,000 students involved). He found that so-called "interactive-engagement courses" score higher than "traditional" teacher-centered methods. Interactive engagement can be effectively assisted by multimedia. Laws (1997) and Thornton and Sokoloff (1990) have developed activity-based mechanics curricula that center around microcomputer-based labs with a range of new sensors, interfaces, and software. In a collaborative learning environment where students investigate "real" motion phenomena the approach leads to a considerable increase in the understanding of kinematics (Thornton, 1992). Motion in sports (like high jumping) can be analyzed by digital video tools like Videograph (cf. Beichner, 1996). The active construction of virtual microworlds from a given set of building blocks (bodies, springs, ropes, etc.) is another means of prompting students to explore mechanics phenomena (leading software package: Interactive Physics, 2004).

Teaching Atomic Physics

Teaching atomic physics concerns the introduction to various views of the "microworld" ranging from somewhat "simple" particle models to quantum mechanical views. Many research studies are available on students' views and the conceptual change processes concerning the particle model. Also, a substantial number of studies on quantum views have been carried out (Table 21.1). For both domains it turns out that students' everyday conceptions are in stark contrast to the science views. This is already true for the simple particle model which is part of every introductory science course. The microworld of particles is totally different from the world of objects in life-world dimensions. Attempts to make the microworld understandable by introducing analogies to everyday world features usually lead to major student misunderstandings. Students, for instance, tend to view the particles as if they were objects of the life world and hence attach life-world features like color or temperature to them (Duit, 1992; Scott, 1992).

The clash between everyday world views and physics concepts is even more fundamental for quantum views of the microworld. A number of quantum features in principle appear to be inconceivable by everyday world thinking. Examples are particle/wave dualism (Bohr's idea of complementarity) and Heisenberg's uncertainty principle, leading, for instance, to the consequence that it is not possible to know both the speed and location of a particle with unlimited precision.

Concerning models of the atom, students tend to have naïve realistic views. The majority see models more or less as copies of the reality (Harrison & Treagust, 1996; Treagust, Chittleborough, & Mamiala, 2002). It appears that there is not much development of such views toward awareness of the model character of atoms in lower secondary science teaching (Knote, 1975). In upper secondary physics instruction of the German Gymnasium, Bethge (1992) found that many students differentiated between a model (of an atom) and reality. However, it has to be taken into account that the German Gymnasium caters only to the top level of students and that physics instruction at this level usually includes modern physics and considerations on the philosophy of physics. This is not the case in many other countries. Briefly summarized, the domains under inspection firstly provide further examples of science views fundamentally different from students' everyday world views. Secondly, it becomes obvious that learning science concepts and principles should include the development of views about the nature of science. Here, proper understanding of particle models and models of the atom only develop if views about models develop accordingly.

Models of the Atom in Physics and Students' Ideas

The interplay between two different views—the particle view and the continuum view—characterizes scientific ideas of substance and atoms. Already the Greek philosophers (Sambursky, 1975, p. 38) held both views about the constitution of matter. Matter was either seen as consisting of tiny particles called atoms, or as a continuous "something" that fills space and is indefinitely divisible. The basic particle view was further elaborated in the eighteenth and nineteenth centuries, culminating in statistical mechanics. After 1900, various atomic models were developed, proposed different structures of positive and negative charges with respect to particle and continuum. Scientific views of the atom have grown over centuries. Certain stages of this process parallel the models constructed by students.

(1) *Atom as a ball.* In 1808, Dalton published his book *A New System of Chemical Philosophy*, in which he viewed atoms as tiny balls (Fig. 21.5). Each element had its own kind of atoms. This hypothesis was suitable to explain fundamental empirical laws about weights in chemical reactions. Later in the nineteenth century Bolzmann's theory of statistical mechanics was also based on atoms as balls. However, in this case the atoms were merely conceptualized as mass points without any other features.

(2) *Atom as a plum pudding.* In Thomson's "plum pudding" model of the atom (published 1904) the positive charge is spread out across the whole atom continuously, whereas the negative charge sits in the form of particles (electrons) in this positive charge like plums in a dough (Fig. 21.6).

A discussion of atomic models with respect to their texture, using analogies with and without a nucleus, can be valuable. Discussing fruits as analogies *with* (cherry) and *without* (kiwi) a nucleus may help students to clarify their thinking. In this respect it is interesting that Harrison and Treagust (1996) found that 76% of their students preferred space-filling models.

(3) *Atom as a nucleus with a shell.* This model was developed by Rutherford in 1911. A heavy positive nucleus is surrounded by electrons as a shell (Fig. 21.7).

Often this model is presented in science instruction. Harrison and Treagust (1996) found that 38% of lower secondary students view atoms as something with a hard center, and 50% are aware of some sort of electron clouds.

(4) *The planetary model of the atom.* A most influential model was developed by Bohr (Fig. 21.8) in analogy of the system of planets revolving around the sun.

H   **N**   **C**   **O**

FIGURE 21–5.   Four atoms of Dalton's ball model of atoms.

FIGURE 21–6.   The first three atoms of the J.J. Thomson plum pudding model.

This model is still taught in science instruction, and often it is the only model of so-called modern atomic physics students learn. About half of the students in lower secondary as well as the majority in upper secondary and in university actually see the atom as a planetary system with a nucleus being surrounded by moving electrons (Knote, 1975; Harrison & Treagust, 1996; Fischler & Lichtfeldt, 1992). As the model provides a powerful mental model by drawing an analogy to the planetary system, it has proved to be very resistant against the teaching of more advanced models (Bethge, 1992; Fischler & Lichtfeldt, 1992; Mashhadi, 1995; Taber, 2001; Müller & Wiesner, 2002).

(5) *Intermediate conceptions of the quantum atomic models.* At least in the United Kingdom and in Germany there is a certain tradition to teach quantum atomic physics beyond the Bohr model in upper secondary school. In these teaching approaches, students typically construct intermediate concepts of a quantum atomic model (Bethge, 1992; Mashhadi, 1995; Petri & Niedderer, 1998). One of these models conceptualizes smeared orbits (Fig. 21.9). A number of students at university level appear to hold such models (Müller & Wiesner, 2002).

(6) *The probability density conception of the atom.* This model is based on Born's interpretation of the Schrödinger equation (Fig. 21.10).

In this conception the Schrödinger term ψ^2 is interpreted as the probability of finding the electron at a certain distance from the nucleus: the larger the distance, the smaller is the probability. Studies have shown that students have difficulty understanding this view (Bethge, 1992; Mashhadi, 1995).

(7) *The electron cloud model of the atom.* This model consists of a nucleus as a particle and an electron cloud as a charge cloud surrounding the nucleus. Its density is calculated by the Schrödinger ψ-function (Fig. 21.11).

The charge density in this model decreases when the distance from the nucleus increases. This may be seen analogously to the distribution of the air around the

FIGURE 21–7.   The Rutherford model.

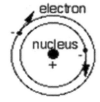

FIGURE 21–8.   Bohr's planetary model of the atom.

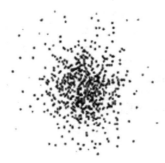
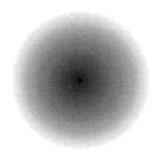

FIGURE 21–9. Smeared orbits model (Petri & Niedderer, 1998).

FIGURE 21–10. Visualization of an atom according to Born.

FIGURE 21–11. Visualization of an atom according to Schrödinger.

earth. This model of a charge cloud is called "electronium" in an approach by Herrmann (1995, 1998). Studies (Niedderer & Deylitz, 1999; Budde et al., 2002) show that the electron cloud model (electronium Fig. 21.11) is easier to learn than the Born model in Fig. 21.10. If both models are offered, students prefer the electronium model, and about 90% of them use it in the final test and in interviews.

Teaching Approaches

Various approaches of teaching and learning quantum mechanics have been developed and evaluated. *Gedankenexperimente* (thought experiments) or computer simulations to introduce the concepts of quantum physics, such as the "preparation" of samples of equal particles or the new view of "measurement", play a significant role in many approaches. In the following a brief overview of different emphases is presented.

Fischler's (1999) approach does not begin with the quantum nature of photons which is the starting point in most other courses. Right from the beginning electron diffraction experiments are carried out and interpreted. Surprising results of the experiments catch students' attention, and mechanistic interpretations of electrons are avoided. In a treatment-control-group design Fischler and Lichtfeldt (1992) found that about 20% of the students in the experimental group developed satisfactory concepts about quantum principles, whereas in the control group (starting from photons) no student reached that level. Also Müller (2003) found positive effects on understanding by introducing a more modern quantum model of the atom and by abandoning the planetary model.

In a number of approaches, major emphasis is put on explaining basic phenomena and interesting technical applications of quantum physics. Niedderer's approach (Niedderer & Deylitz, 1999) aims at understanding the size and spectra of atoms, chemical bonding, and the spectra of solids. An evaluation study (Niedderer & Deylitz, 1999) showed that—apart from problems with understanding the mathematics of Schrödinger's equation—most goals of conceptual understanding could be reached with reasonable success. As mentioned, a majority of the students preferred the "electron cloud" model to the "probability density" model.

Zollman et al. (2002) analyze objects like LEDs and gas lamps, fluorescent and phosphorescent materials, as well as the tunneling microscope. Potential energy diagrams are used to explain these materials. In the "Visual Quantum Mechanics" approach, the emphasis is on conceptual understanding and visualization as opposed to of mathematical formalisms. In an evaluation study, Rebello and Zollman (1999) observed that hands-on activities, computer visualization programs, and constructivist pedagogy enabled their students to build mental models that allowed them to explain their observations. The preliminary study also provided information about difficulties in helping students to learn abstract concepts by the approach used.

Briefly summarized, research has shown that students' understanding of particle models and quantum models of the atom may be substantially improved by approaches that are oriented toward constructivist conceptual change views of teaching and learning. However, the success rate is still somewhat limited. Much more research-based development is necessary for both domains. It appears that the above views of the German *Didaktik* tradition (see the idea of educational reconstruction in Fig. 21.2) may help in further improving the existing approaches. The content structure for instruction—seen from that perspective—has to be developed by taking into account (a) physics views of particles and atoms, (b) physics views of the nature of particles and atoms, (c) students' views of particles and atoms and of the nature of the models provided, and (d) the aims of teaching particles and atoms. From a scientific literacy perspective it appears that through adoption of the *Didaktik* tradition the purpose of teaching and learning particle views and especially quantum physics views of the atoms may also be further clarified.

OUTLOOK: DESIDERATA FOR PHYSICS EDUCATION RESEARCH

In order to improve physics teaching and learning in school as well as in other institutions, various changes in the present state of practice are necessary. Most changes are not specific to physics instruction. However, they have to be specifically designed for the particular content and content specific pedagogical issues of physics. Other necessary changes are specific for physics instruction, in particular those concerning emphases of the content taught. In the following, major concerns are briefly outlined.

General Concerns

Teachers' thinking about instruction and their teaching practices.   Teachers, of course, are the key players in education reforms (Anderson & Helms, 2001). Research has shown that (a) many teachers are not (well) informed about research findings on teaching and learning, (b) their views about "good" physics instruction are rather topic dominated, modeling of student learning is deficient, and (c) in educational practice there still appears to be a dominance of teacher-centered instruction. It is essential that teachers' thinking about instruction includes all the facets addressed in the European *Didaktik* tradition as outlined above (Fig. 21.2). In terms of Shulman's (1987) perspective, there should be a balance between content *and* content-specific pedagogical issues in teacher thinking. Instructional planning should include considerations on content issues as well as on issues of how students may be able to learn the content.

More research is needed, especially concerning the following two issues (see Chapter 39 on teacher professional development for more details):

- To investigate how teachers may be made familiar with research findings and how their views about teaching and learning physics may be improved and whether instructional practice improves accordingly. Here issues of conceptual change discussed above come into play. Changing deeply rooted views (here teachers' views) has proved to be a long-lasting process.

- In order to be able to design more efficient instructional approaches it is necessary to be familiar with the actual practice of physics instruction. So far only a few studies that allow deep insight into actual practice (e.g., by analyzing videos) are available (Duit et al., 2004). More studies on the normal practice of physics instruction are needed.

Aims and standards.   The present discussion on scientific literacy is focused on the use of physics knowledge for understanding daily life concerns and participation as citizens in decisions on science and technology. The above concept of *Bildung* adds the idea of forming the learners' personalities. It appears to be necessary to further analyze whether the actual concepts of scientific literacy are sound and can be put into practice, that is, are not just visions. A broad spectrum of research methods has to be employed, ranging from historical and hermeneutical studies on various views of scientific literacy in different areas and countries, empirical studies on the actual need of physics knowledge to understand daily life issues and to participate in society, as well as empirical studies on students' capabilities to achieve the envisioned facets of scientific literacy.

Standards have been a key concern for a number of countries since the 1990s (e.g., in the United States and Canada); in other countries (like Germany) this is a more recent issue. Standards usually attempt to make the more general concepts of scientific literacy explicit. This serves two related functions: to provide a frame for setting key issues of scientific literacy into practice and for facilitating construction of test measures that make it possible to determine the extent to which the various competencies stated are put into practice.

Standards are based on implicit or explicit models of the structure and development of competence. More research is needed:

- To design models of students' competency structures, drawing on data from achievement tests, favorably in a longitudinal perspective
- To design psychometric methods to prove the competency levels achieved

Content, processes, and views about the nature of science.   As more fully outlined above, processes and views about the nature of science are given only rather limited attention in physics teaching. Research appears to be needed to investigate the interplay of understanding content on the one hand and processes as well as views of the nature of science on the other.

Holistic approaches.   Research has shown that the outcomes of instruction (e.g., the development of achievement and affective variables) are not due simply to a single factor of the instructional arrangement but to an intimate interplay of many factors (Baumert & Köller, 2000; Oser & Baeriswyl, 2001). In other words, it does not make sense to change just one factor to improve physics instruction (e.g., introducing multimedia learning environments, new exciting experiments, or innovative teaching methods). The above idea of educational reconstruction (Fig. 21.2), which is based on the European *Didaktik* tradition, may provide a frame for designing approaches that take into account the essential interplay of the many factors determining instructional outcomes.

Physics-Specific Concerns

Physics instruction in school includes a certain canon of content that is quite similar all over the world. Interestingly, most topics of this canon concern rather "old" physics, namely physics of the nineteenth century. So-called modern physics plays a certain role only in the upper secondary levels. Most teaching approaches for quantum physics and relativity (Table 21.1) are suited only for rather gifted students. Attempts to make more recent thinking about matter, space, and time accessible to younger or less gifted students as part of their scientific literacy are rare. There is a certain irony in this situation when schools appear to be reluctant to address this issue, while popular science books on modern physics are booming. Serious attempts are needed to make key basic ideas of modern physics accessible to "normal" students. Some studies in the field of nonlinear systems have shown that this is possible (Duit, Komorek, & Wilbers, 1997).

ACKNOWLEDGMENTS

Many thanks to John Clement (University of Massachusetts) and Ron Good (Louisiana State of University), who reviewed this chapter.

REFERENCES

Abd-El-Khalick, F., Bell, R. L., & Lederman, N. (1998). The nature of science and instructional practice: Making the unnatural natural. *Science Education, 82,* 417–436.

American Association for the Advancement of Science. (1993). *Project 2061—Benchmarks for scientific literacy.* New York: Oxford University Press.

Anderson, R. D., & Helms, J. V. (2001). The ideal of standards and the reality of schools: Needed research. *Journal of Research in Science Teaching, 38,* 3–16.

Arons, A. (1997). *Teaching introductory physics.* New York: Wiley.

Arons, A. (1984). Students' patterns of thinking and reasoning. *The Physics Teacher, 22,* 21–26; 89–93; 576–581.

Baker, D. R. (1998). Equity issues in science education. In B. J. Fraser & K. G. Tobin (Eds.), *International handbook of science education* (pp. 869–895). Dordrecht, the Netherlands: Kluwer Academic.

Baumert, J., & Köller, O. (2000). Unterrichtsgestaltung, verständnisvolles Lernen und multiple Zielerreichung im Mathematik- und Physikunterricht der gymnasialen Oberstufe [Instructional planning, mindful learning and the achievement of multiple goals in mathematics and physics instruction at upper secondary level]. In J. Baumert & O. Köller (Eds.), *TIMSS/III. Dritte Internationale Mathematik- und Naturwissenschaftsstudie* (Vol. 2, pp. 271–315). Opladen, Germany: Leske & Budrich.

Beaton, A. E., Martin, M. O., Mullis, I. V. S., Gonzalez, E. J., Smith, T. A., & Kelly, D. A. (1996). *Science achievement in the middle school years. IEA's Third International Mathematics and Science Study (TIMSS).* Boston: Boston College, Center for the Study of Testing, Evaluation, and Educational Policy.

Beichner, R. J. (1994). Testing student interpretation of kinematik graphs. *American Journal of Physics, 62*, 750–762.

Beichner, R. J. (1996). The impact of video motion analysis on kinematics graph interpretation skills. *American Journal of Physics, 64*, 1272–1278.

Bethge, T. (1992). Vorstellungen von Schülerinnen und Schülern zu Begriffen der Atomphysik (Students ideas about concepts of atomic physics). In H. Fischler (Ed.), *Quantenphysik in der Schule* (pp. 88–113). Kiel, Germany: IPN—Leibniz Institute for Science Education.

Budde, M., Niedderer, H., Scott, P., & Leach, J. (2002). The quantum atomic model "Electronium": A successful teaching tool. *Physics Education, 37*, 204–210.

Bybee, R. (1997). *Achieving scientific literacy: From purposes to practices.* Portsmouth, NH: Heinemann.

Camp, C., & Clement, J. (1994). *Preconceptions in mechanics. Lessons dealing with students' conceptual difficulties.* Dubuque, IA: Kendall/Hunt.

Chi, M. T. H., Slotta, J. D., & de Leeuw, N. (1994). From things to processes: A theory of conceptual change for learning science concepts. *Learning and Instruction, 4*, 27–43.

Clement, J. (1993). Using bridging analogies and anchoring intuitions to deal with students' preconceptions in physics. *Journal of Research in Science Teaching, 30*, 1241–1257.

Clement, J., & Steinberg, M. (2002). Step-wise evolution of models of electric circuits: A "learning-aloud" case study. *Journal of the Learning Sciences, 11*, 389–452.

Dahncke, H., Duit, R., Östman, L., Psillos, D., & Pushkin, D. (2001). Science education versus science in the academy: Questions—discussions—perspectives. In H. Behrendt, H. Dahncke, R. Duit, W. Gräber, M. Komorek, A. Kross, & P. Reiska (Eds.), *Research in science education—past, present, and future* (pp. 43–48). Dordrecht, the Netherlands: Kluwer Academic.

diSessa, A. A. (1988). Knowledge in pieces. In G. Forman & P. B. Pufall (Eds.), *Constructivism in the computer age* (pp. 49–90). Hillsdale, NJ: Lawrence Erlbaum Associates.

Driver, R., Leach, J., Millar, R., & Scott, P. (1996). *Young people's images of science.* Bristol, UK: Open University Press.

Driver, R., & Oldham, V. (1986). A constructivist approach to curriculum development in science. *Studies in Science Education, 13*, 105–122.

Driver, R., Squires, A., Rushworth, P., & Wood-Robinson, V. (1994). *Making sense of secondary science—Research into childrens' ideas.* London: Routledge.

Duit, R. (1992). Teilchen- und Atomvorstellungen (Conceptions of particles and atoms). In H. Fischler (Ed.), *Quantenphysik in der Schule* (pp. 201–204). Kiel, Germany: IPN—Leibniz Institute for Science Education.

Duit, R. (2006). *Bibliography—STCSE (Students' and Teachers' Conceptions and Science Education).* Kiel: IPN—Leibniz Institute for Science Education (http://www.ipn.uni-kiel.de/aktuell/stcse/stcse.html).

Duit, R., Komorek, M., & Wilbers, J. (1997). Studies on educational reconstruction of chaos theory. *Research in Science Education, 27*, 339–357.

Duit, R., Müller, C. T., Tesch, M., & Widodo, A. (2004, April). *A video study on the practice of German physics instruction.* Paper presented at the Annual Meeting of the National Association of Research in Science Teaching (NARST), Vancouver, Canada.

Duit, R., & Treagust, D. (2003). Conceptual change—A powerful framework for improving science teaching and learning. *International Journal of Science Education, 25*, 671–688.

Duit, R., & von Rhöneck, Ch. (1998). Learning and understanding key concepts of electricity. In A. Tiberghien, E. L. Jossem, & J. Barojas (Eds.), *Connecting research in physics education.* Boise,

Ohio: ICPE—International Commission on Physics Education, ICPE Books (published on the internet: http://www.physics.ohio-state.edu/~jossem/ICPE/TOC.html).

Fensham, P. (2001). Science content as problematic—issues for research. In H. Behrendt, H. Dahncke, R. Duit, W. Gräber, M. Komorek, A. Kross, & P. Reiska (Eds.), *Research in science education—past, present, and future* (pp. 27–41). Dordrecht, the Netherlands: Kluwer Academic.

Fischler, H. (1999, March). Introduction to quantum physics—Development and evaluation of a new course. In D. Zollman (Ed.), *Research on teaching and learning quantum mechanics* (pp. 32–40). Papers presented at the annual meeting of the National Association for Research in Science Teaching (NARST) (http://www.phys.ksu.edu/perg/papers/narst/).

Fischler, H., & Lichtfeldt, M. (1992). Modern physics and students' conceptions. *International Journal of Science Education, 14,* 181–190.

Galili, I., & Hazan, A. (2000). The influence of a historically oriented course on students' content knowledge in optics evaluated by means of facets-schemes analysis. *American Journal of Physics Supplement, 68*(7), S3–S14.

Goldberg, F., & Bendall, S. (1995). Making the invisible visible: A teaching and learning environment that builds on a new view of the physics learner. *American Journal of Physics, 63,* 978–991.

Grayson, D. (1996). Improving science and mathematics learning by concept substitution. In D. Treagust, R. Duit, & B. Fraser (Eds.), *Improving teaching and learning in science and mathematics* (pp. 152–161). New York: Teachers College Press.

Hake, R. R. (1998). Interactive-engagement versus traditional methods: A six-thousand-student survey of mechanics test data for introductory physics courses. *American Journal of Physics, 66,* 64–74.

Harding, J. (1996). Science as a masculine strait-jacket. In L. H. Parker, L. J. Rennie, & B. Fraser (Eds.), *Gender, science and mathematics* (pp. 3–16). Dordrecht, the Netherlands: Kluwer Academic.

Harrison, A. G., & Treagust, D. F. (1996). Secondary students' mental models of atoms and molecules: Implications for teaching chemistry. *Science Education, 80,* 509–534.

Häußler, P., & Hoffmann, L. (2002). An intervention study to enhance girls' interest, self-concept and achievement in physics classes. *Journal of Research in Science Teaching, 39,* 870–888.

Heimann, P., Otto, G., & Schulz, W. (1969). *Unterricht, Analyse und Planung* [Instruction: Analysis and planning]. Hannover, Germany: Schroedel.

Herrmann, F. (1995). A critical analysis of the language of modern physics. In C. Bernardini, C. Tarsitani, & M. Vicentini (Eds.), *Thinking physics for teaching* [pp. 287–294]. New York: Plenum Press.

Herrmann, F. (1998). *Der Karlsruher Physikkurs* [The Karlsruhe physics course] (Vol. 1). Köln, Germany: Aulis.

Hestenes, D., Wells, M., & Swackhamer, G. (1992). Force concept inventory. *The Physics Teacher, 30,* 141–158.

Hodson, D. (1993). Practical work in science: Time for a reappraisal. *Studies in Science Education, 19,* 175–184.

Jenkins, E. (2001). Research in science education in Europe: Retrospect and prospect. In H. Behrendt, H. Dahncke, R. Duit, W. Gräber, M. Komorek, A. Kross, & P. Reiska (Eds.), *Research in science education—past, present, and future* [pp. 17–26]. Dordrecht, the Netherlands: Kluwer Academic.

Jung, W., Wiesner, H., & Engelhard, P. (1981). *Vorstellungen von Schülern über Begriffe der Newtonschen Mechanik* [Students' ideas about concepts of Newtonian Mechnanics]. Bad Salzdetfurth, Germany: Franzbecker.

Kaestle, C. F. (1993). The awful reputation of educational research. *Educational Researcher, 22*(1), 23–31.

Kattmann, U., Duit, R., Gropengießer, H., & Komorek, M. (1995, April). *A model of educational reconstruction.* Paper presented at the annual meeting of the National Association for Research in Science Teaching (NARST), San Francisco.

Keeves, J. P., & Kotte, D. (1996). Patterns of science achievement: International comparisons. In L. H. Parker, L. J. Rennie, & B. Fraser (Eds.), *Gender, science and mathematics* (pp. 77–94). Dordrecht, the Netherlands: Kluwer Academic.

Kircher, E., Girwidz, R., & Häußler, P. (2000). *Physikdidaktik* [Didactics of physics]. Braunschweig/Wiesbaden, Germany: Friedrich Vieweg & Sohn.

Klafki, W. (1969). Didaktische Analyse als Kern der Unterrichtsvorbereitung [Educational analysis as core issue of instructional planning]. In H. Roth & A. Blumental (Eds.), *Auswahl, Didaktische Analyse* (pp. 5–34). Hannover, Germany: Schroedel.

Knote, H. (1975). Zur Atomvorstellung bei Dreizehn- bis Fünfzehnjährigen [Thirteen- to fifteen-year-old students' conceptions of the atom]. *Der Physikunterricht, 4,* 86–96.

Köller, O., Baumert, J., & Neubrand, J. (2000). Epistemologische Überzeugungen und Fachverständnis im Mathematik- und Physikunterricht [Epistemological beliefs and content knowledge in mathematics and physics instruction]. In J. Baumert et al. (Eds.), *TIMSS—Mathematisch-naturwissenschaftliche Bildung am Ende der Sekundarstufe II* [TIMSS—mathematics and science literacy at the end of upper secondary school] (pp. 229–270). Opladen, Germany: Leske & Budrich.

Kroh, L. B., & Thomsen, P. V. (2005). Studying students' attitudes towards science from a cultural perspective but with a quantitative methodology: Border crossing into the physics classroom. *International Journal of Science Education, 27,* 281–302.

Laukenmann, M., Bleicher, M., Fuß, S., Gläser-Zikuda, M., Mayring, P. & v. Rhöneck, C. (2003). An investigation of the influence of emotional factors on learning in physics instruction. *International Journal of Science Education, 25,* 489–507.

Laws, P. W. (1997). Promoting active learning based on physics education research in introductory physics courses (Millikan Lecture 1996). *American Journal of Physics, 65,* 14–21.

Leach, J. (2002). Students' understanding of the nature of science and its influence on labwork. In D. Psillos & H. Niedderer (Eds.), *Teaching and learning in the science laboratory* (pp. 41–49). Dordrecht, the Netherlands: Kluwer Academic.

Linn, M. C., Songer, N. B., Lewis, E. L., & Stern, J. (1993). Using technology to teach thermodynamics: Achieving integrated understanding. In D. L. Ferguson (Ed.), *Advanced educational technologies for mathematics and science* (pp. 5–60). Berlin: Springer-Verlag.

Lunetta, V. N. (1998). The school science laboratory: Historical perspectives and contexts for contemporary teaching. In K. Tobin & B. Fraser (Eds.), *International handbook of science education, Part I* (pp. 249–264). Dordrecht, the Netherlands: Kluwer Academic.

Maloney, D. P. (1994). Research on problem solving: Physics. In D. Gabel (Ed.), *Handbook of research on science teaching and learning* (pp. 327–354). New York: Macmillan.

Mashhadi, A. (1995). Students' conceptions of quantum physics. In G. Welford, J. Osborne, & P. Scott (Eds.), *Research in Science Education in Europe* (pp. 254–266). London: Falmer.

Matthews, M. R. (1994). *Science teaching—The role of history and philosophy of science.* London: Routledge.

McCloskey, M. (1983). Intuitive physics. *Scientific American, 284*(4), 114–122.

McComas, W. F. (Ed.) (1998). *The nature of science in science education rationales and strategies.* Dordrecht, the Netherlands: Kluwer Academic.

Meyling, H. (1997). How to change students' conceptions of the epistemology of science. *Science & Education, 6,* 397–416.

Minstrell, J. (1992). Facets of students' knowledge and relevant instruction. In R. Duit, F. Goldberg, & H. Niedderer (Eds.), *Research in physics learning: Theoretical issues and empirical studies.* Kiel, Germany: IPN—Institute for Science Education.

Mintzes, J. J., Wandersee, J. H., & Novak, J. D. (Eds.). (1997). *Teaching science for understanding—A human constructivist view.* San Diego: Academic Press.

MSC Software. (2004). *Interactive physics.* Redwood City, CA: Author.

Müller, R. (2003). *Quantenphysik in der Schule* [Quantum physics in high school]. Berlin: Logos.

Müller, R., & Wiesner, H. (2002). Teaching quantum mechanics on an introductory level. *American Journal of Physics, 70,* 200–209.

National Research Council. (1996). *National science education standards*. Washington, DC: National Education Press.

Niedderer, H., & Deylitz, S. (1999, March). Evaluation of a new approach in quantum atomic physics in high school. In D. Zollman (Ed.), *Research on teaching and learning quantum mechanics* (pp. 23–27). Papers presented at the annual meeting of the National Association for Research in Science Teaching (NARST) (http://www.phys.ksu.edu/perg/papers/narst/).

Niedderer, H., Buty, C., Haller, K., Hucke, L., Sander, F., Fischer, H. E., et al. (2002). Talking physics in labwork contexts—a category based analysis of videotapes. In D. Psillos & H. Niedderer (Eds.), *Teaching and learning in the science laboratory* (pp. 31–40). Dordrecht, the Netherlands: Kluwer Academic.

Niedderer, H., & Goldberg, F. (1995). Lernprozesse beim elektrischen Stromkreis. [Learning processes in the case of the electric circuit]. *Zeitschrift für Didaktik der Naturwissenschaften, 1*, 73–86.

Organisation for Economic Co-operation and Development. (1999). *Measuring student knowledge and skills—A new framework for assessment*. Paris: OECD Publications.

Osborne, R. (1983). Towards modifying children's ideas about electric current. *Research in Science and Technology Education, 1*, 73–82.

Oser, F. K., & Baeriswyl, F. J. (2001). Choreographies of teaching: Bridging instruction to learning. In V. Richardson (Ed.), *Handbook of research on teaching* (pp. 1031–1065). Washington, DC: American Educational Research Association.

Parker, L. H., Rennie, L. J., & Fraser, B. (Eds.). (1996). *Gender, science and mathematics*. Dordrecht, the Netherlands: Kluwer Academic.

Petri, J., & Niedderer, H. (1998). A learning pathway in high-school level quantum physics. *International Journal of Science Education, 20*, 1075–1088.

Pintrich, P. R., Marx, R. W., & Boyle, R. A. (1992). Beyond cold conceptual change: The role of motivational beliefs and classroom contextual factors in the process of conceptual change. *Review of Educational Research, 63*, 167–199.

Rebello, S., & Zollman, D. (1999, March). Conceptual understanding of quantum mechanics after using hands-on and visualization instructional materials. In D. Zollman (Ed.), *Research on teaching and learning quantum mechanics* (pp. 2–6). Papers presented at the annual meeting of the National Association for Research in Science Teaching (NARST) (http://www.phys.ksu.edu/perg/papers/narst/).

Redish, E. F. (2003). *Teaching physics*. New York: Wiley.

Redish, E. F., Saul, J. M., & Steinberg, R. N. (1996). On the effectiveness of active-engagement microcomputer-based laboratories. *American Journal of Physics, 65*, 45–54.

Reid, N., & Skryabina, E. A. (2003). Gender and physics. *International Journal of Science Education, 25*, 509–536.

Sambursky, S. (1975). *Physical thought. From the pre-Socratics to the quantum physicists—an anthology*. New York: Pica Press.

Schecker, H. (1998). Integration of experimenting and modeling by advanced educational technology: Examples from nuclear physics. In K. Tobin & B. Fraser (Eds.), *International handbook of science education, Part I* (pp. 383–398). Dordrecht, the Netherlands: Kluwer Academic.

Schecker, H., Fischer, H. E., & Wiesner, H. (2004). Physikunterricht in der gymnasialen Oberstufe [Physics instruction in upper secondary schools]. In H. E. Tenorth (Ed.), *Kerncurriculum Oberstufe* (pp. 148–234). Weinheim, Germany: Beltz.

Schecker, H., & Niedderer, H. (1996). Contrastive teaching: A strategy to promote qualitative conceptual understanding of science. In D. Treagust, R. Duit, & B. Fraser (Eds.), *Improving teaching and learning in science and mathematics* (pp. 141–151). New York: Teachers College Press.

Scott, P. H. (1992). Pathways in learning science: A case study of the development of one student's ideas relating to the structure of matter. In R. Duit, F. Goldberg, & H. Niedderer (Eds.), *Research in physics learning: Theoretical issues and empirical studies* (pp. 203–224). Kiel, Germany: IPN—Leibniz-Institute for Science Education.

Shipstone, D. M., von Rhöneck, C., Jung, W., Karrqvist, C., Dupin, J. J., Joshua, S., et al. (1988). A study of secondary students' understanding of electricity in five European countries. *International Journal of Science Education, 10*, 303–316.

Shulman, L. S. (1987). Knowledge and teaching: Foundations of a new reform. *Harvard Educational Review, 57*(1), 1–22.

Stadler, H., Benke, G., & Duit, R. (2000). Do boys and girls understand physics differently? *Physics Education, 35*(6), 417–422.

Taber, K. S. (2001). When the analogy breaks down: Modeling the atom on the solar system. *Physics Education, 36,* 222–226.

Thornton, R. K. (1992). Enhancing and evaluating students' learning of motion concepts. In A. Tiberghien & H. Mandl (Eds.), *Physics and learning environments* (pp. 265–283). Berlin: Springer-Verlag.

Thornton, R. K., & Sokoloff, D. R. (1990). Learning motion concepts using real-time microcomputer-based laboratory tools. *American Journal of Physics, 58,* 858–867.

Thornton, R. K., & Sokoloff, D. R. (1998). Assessing student learning of Newton's laws: The force and motion conceptual evaluation and the evaluation of active learning laboratory and lecture curricula. *American Journal of Physics, 66*(4), 338–351.

Tinker, R. (Ed.). (1996). *Microcomputer based labs: Educational research and standards.* New York: Springer.

Treagust, D., Chittleborough, G., & Mamiala, T. L. (2002). Students' understanding of the role of scientific models in learning science. *International Journal of Science Education, 24,* 357–368.

Trowbridge, D. E., & McDermott, L. C. (1981). Investigation of student understanding of the concept of acceleration. *American Journal of Physics, 49,* 242–252.

Urhahne, D., Prenzel, M., Davier, M. V., Senkbeil, M., & Bleschke, M. (2000). Computereinsatz im naturwissenschaftlichen Unterricht—Ein Überblick über die pädagogisch-psychologischen Grundlagen und ihre Anwendung [The use of computers in science education—an overview of pedagogical and psychological foundations and their applications]. *Zeitschrift für Didaktik der Naturwissenschaften, 6,* 157–186.

Viennot, L. (1979). Spontaneous reasoning in elementary dynamics. *European Journal of Science Education, 1,* 205–221.

Viennot, L. (2001). *Reasoning in physics. The part of common sense.* Dordrecht, the Netherlands: Kluwer Academic.

Viennot, L. (2003). *Teaching physics.* Dordrecht, the Netherlands: Kluwer Academic.

Vosniadou, S. (2002). On the nature of naive physics. In M. Limon & L. Mason (Eds.), *Reconsidering conceptual change: Issues in theory and practice* (pp. 61–76). Dordrecht, The Netherlands: Kluwer Academic.

Wandersee, J. H., Mintzes, J. J., & Novak, J. D. (1994). Research on alternative conceptions in science. In D. Gabel (Ed.), *Handbook of research on science teaching and learning* (pp. 177–210). New York: Macmillan.

Warren, J. W. (1979). *Understanding force.* London: Murray.

Welzel, M., Haller, K., Bandiera, M., Hammelev, D., Koumaras, P., Niedderer, H., et al. (1998). Ziele, die Lehrende mit experimentellem Arbeiten in der naturwissenschaftlichen Ausbildung verbinden—Ergebnisse einer europäischen Umfrage [Objectives teachers relate to laboratory work in physics instruction—results of a European survey]. *Zeitschrift für Didaktik der Naturwissenschaften, 4,* 29–44 (English version available from http://www.idn.uni-bremen.de/pubs/Niedderer/1998-LSE-WP6.pdf).

Westbury, L., Hopmann, S., & Riquarts, K. (Eds.). (2000). *Teaching as reflective practice. The German Didaktik tradition.* Mahwah, NJ: Lawrence Erlbaum Associates.

Woolnough, B. (1991). *Practical science.* Milton Keynes, UK: Open University Press.

Wright, E. (1993). The irrelevancy of science education research: Perception or reality? *NARST News, 35*(1), 1–2.

Zollman, D. A., Rebello, N. S., & Hogg, K. (2002). Quantum mechanics for everyone: Hands-on activities integrated with technology. *American Journal of Physics, 70,* 252–259 (see also http://web.phys.ksu.edu/vqm/).

CHAPTER 22

Teaching and Learning the Many Faces of Chemistry

Onno De Jong
Utrecht University, the Netherlands

Keith S. Taber
Cambridge University, United Kingdom

The goal of this chapter is to review research on teaching and learning science that focuses on the specific domain of chemistry, with particular emphasis on the high school level. Many chemistry topics can be either viewed or taught from three potential perspectives that are mutually related (Fig. 22.1). First, the macroscopic perspective, focusing on substances and phenomena that can be observed with the naked eye. Second, the submicroscopic perspective, focusing on molecules, atoms, ions, and so on. Third, the symbolic perspective, focusing on formulas, equations, ionic drawings, and the like. The use of this three-cornered relationship (Johnstone, 1991) is not exclusive to the chemical domain, but it plays a more dominant role here than in the domains of the other natural sciences. Many students experience difficulties in understanding the macro/submicro/symbolic triangle and, in particular, in appreciating how and when to make the transitions between the three perspectives. Teachers do not always realize the importance of modeling the relationships here, by being explicit about the perspective being used, and the transitions being made, and helping students to overcome their difficulties.

The present chapter includes a review of studies that highlight two difficult chemical topics at the high school level. Part 1 of the chapter deals with a key topic in junior high schools: chemical reactions. Part 2 of the chapter concerns a core topic in senior high schools: atomic structure and chemical bonding. For each topic, students' main conceptual difficulties are presented. They are explained concisely by the use of another triangle: the related perspectives of teaching, chemistry content, and learning. Studies of courses designed to help students respond to their difficulties are also presented and discussed. Special attention is given to courses based on

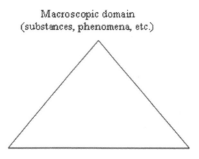

Macroscopic domain
(substances, phenomena, etc.)

Sub-microscopic domain   Symbolic domain   FIGURE 22–1. The triangle
(molecules, atoms, etc.)   (formulas, equations, etc.) of meanings.

modern perspectives on teaching and leaning, such as context-based teaching strategies and approaches incorporating a constructivist view of learning. Suggestions for priority areas for further research and curriculum development are given at several places. Finally, part 3 of the chapter presents a look to the near future of chemical education.

INTRODUCING MULTIPLE MEANINGS OF CHEMICAL REACTIONS

Multiple Meanings

In introductory chemical education, the central core content deals with chemical reactions. In elementary schools, if chemical reactions are introduced, students only have to learn the macroscopic meaning in terms of conversions of substances. High school students should also learn the submicroscopic meaning in terms of the re-arrangement of particles (molecules, atoms, ions) and the symbolic meaning in terms of chemical equations (words, iconic drawings, formulas). These students also should become able to switch mentally between these meanings in an adequate and flexible way.

This section addresses studies of students' conceptual difficulties, related to reactions that can be considered to proceed to completion, taking place in one direction. Difficulties in understanding more complex chemical reaction types can be found elsewhere, such as problems with understanding equilibrium reactions (Van Driel & Graeber, 2002) and redox reactions (De Jong & Treagust, 2002). The present section also offers some explanatory perspectives on students' difficulties. Studies of efforts to prevent and to respond to their difficulties are discussed. Suggestions for further research and course development are also given.

Students' Conceptual Difficulties

In the last two decades, numerous articles on students' difficulties in understanding the multiple meanings of chemical reactions have been published. From stud-

---

Vignette

In a junior high school class, a chemistry teacher puts a burning piece of wood in a glass with water. The burning stops.

The teacher asks:	*How is that possible?*
Student #1 answers:	*We do not understand, burning should go on because there is oxygen in the water, as we know because fish live in water.*
The teacher responds:	*But there is not enough oxygen in the water.*
Student #2 argues:	*We know that water is H_2O, so, one-third of water is oxygen, whereas it consists of oxygen for one-fifth only . . . so, teacher, how is that possible?*

In this vignette, student #2 compares water and air as providers of oxygen for a burning process. However, the student interprets the formula of water in an additive rather than from an interactive way: H_2O is seen as H_2 and O. This way of reasoning demonstrated a common difficulty in understanding symbolic representations.

---

ies and reviews, written by Ahtee and Varjola (1998), Andersson (1986), Fensham (1994), Gabel and Bunce, (1994), Johnson (2000), and Krnel, Watson, and Glazar (1998), a list of 12 of the most recurrent difficulties has been compiled and is presented below.

Regarding *the macroscopic meaning*, recurrent difficulties are the following:

- Students may fail to recognize a process as a chemical change, through lack of sufficient knowledge of substance identity. For instance, students may interpret the product of a chemical change as a mixture where the original substances still persist.
- Students may believe that during chemical changes substances are displaced without any change of their properties. This is illustrated by students who think that parts of burning wood are driven off as smoke.
- Students tend to interpret chemical reactions as a process of modification, that is, chemical changes are seen as physical changes, and properties of substances are seen as changing, whereas the substances themselves remain the same. For instance, students may believe that the black coating formed on a piece of copper metal during heating represents black or burned copper.
- Students may interpret chemical changes as a transmutation of a given substance into another substance or into energy. This is demonstrated by students who believe that burned steel wool has been turned into carbon.
- Students sometimes seem to be unaware of the interactive role of "invisible" (gaseous) reactants or products. For instance, students may believe that the mass of a rusty nail is the same as that of the nail before rusting.
- Students tend to treat properties of substances as some kind of extra substance. This can be seen in students who believe that sugar disappears when it is dissolved in water, but the sweetness remains.

Regarding *the submicroscopic meaning*, recurrent difficulties are the following:

- Students often attribute macroscopic features to molecules or atoms and attribute submicroscopic features to substances. Typical examples are: students think that a molecule of water means a small drop of the liquid and may use expressions like "substances exchange outer electrons between them."
- Students may fail to invoke atoms and molecules as explanatory constructs of chemical reactions, although they have knowledge of atoms and molecules.
- Students' ability to give a submicroscopic explanation of chemical reactions in terms of a dynamic process is often limited. For instance, students may not refer to the rearrangement of atoms, that is, breaking of bonds and formation of new bonds.

Regarding *the symbolic meaning*, recurrent difficulties are as follows:

- Students tend to perceive a formula as representing one unit of a substance rather than a collection of particles, and they tend to interpret the formulas of compounds in an additive rather than from an interactive way. This is shown by students who interpret the formula H_2O as H_2 and O.
- Students may have difficulties in understanding the meaning of formula subscripts and equation coefficients. For instance, students tend to change the subscripts while balancing reaction equations.
- Students may consider balancing chemical reactions as mainly mathematical manipulation of symbols without much insight into the chemical meaning. A typical example: students may consider $3H_2$ as six linked atoms.

The reported difficulties can be explained from several perspectives. Three perspectives offering particular insight are:

(i) The *teaching perspective*, especially the influence of the traditional chemistry curriculum structure and textbook context, and the usual teaching practice. In many chemistry courses, chemical reactions are considered predominantly at the submicroscopic and symbolic levels, without much attention to students' everyday conceptions of chemical phenomena. This situation promotes the tendency among students to consider chemical reactions as very formal processes and chemical equations as algebraic expressions. In chemistry classrooms, teachers tend to use language that may evoke confusions among students, such as using the expression "copper is formed," without indicating explicitly if this statement refers to the substance copper, the type of atoms, or the type of ions (De Jong, Acampo, & Verdonk, 1995).

(ii) The *science content perspective*, especially the abstract character of many chemistry concepts. Understanding such concepts requires formal reasoning and knowledge of models as representations of phenomena. This is not easy for many students, who are tending to see, for instance, molecules and atoms as *minima naturalia* (the Aristotelian concept of small particles) instead of theoretical model concepts (De Vos & Verdonk, 1985).

(iii)   The *learning perspective*, especially the role of the initial knowledge of students, based on daily life experiences and expressed in everyday language. Many of the students' authentic perceptions and interpretations of phenomena are often not very fruitful in a chemistry context, such as the idea that milk that has become sour is still milk (Stavidrou & Solomonidou, 1998).

Courses Developed from Modern Teaching and Learning Perspectives

The reported students' conceptual difficulties have been found among students taught quite traditional chemistry courses. Efforts to prevent and to respond to their difficulties have led to a series of chemistry courses developed from modern teaching and learning perspectives. Studies of five exemplars are given below.

- A course that included three phases of the *learning cycle*, namely explication, concept introduction, and concept application, was investigated by Cavallo, McNeely, and Marek (2003). They reported on the development of understanding among 60 junior high-school students with respect to the three levels of meaning of chemical reactions. Findings indicate significant positive shifts in understanding. A minority (about 20%) of the students, however, showed persistent conceptual difficulties, especially regarding the difference between chemical change and physical change, and the relationship between atoms and substances.

- A course that introduced a teaching strategy based on the *conceptual change perspective*, that is, confronting students with "chemical events" that evoke cognitive conflicts because of existing everyday conceptions, was investigated by Nieswandt (2001). She reported on the development of understanding among 81 junior high school students with respect to macroscopic features of substances and chemical reactions (with particular emphasis on combustion). Results show a significant "erosion" of students' everyday conceptions in favor of scientific concepts. A minority (about 25%) of the students, however, only developed "mixed" concepts, consisting of everyday concepts and chemistry explanations.

- A course that incorporated a *context-based* teaching approach by presenting chemistry concepts within the context of everyday events was investigated by Barker and Millar (1999). They reported on the development of understanding among 250 senior high school students with respect to the conservation of mass in closed- and open-system chemical reactions. Data indicate that students' reasoning improved steadily as the course progressed. Nevertheless, a minority of the students retained misunderstandings about the conservation of mass in closed systems (23%) and open systems (29%), especially for reactions including gases.

- A course that included a *constructivist view* on learning by taking students' own conceptions into account was investigated by Laverty and McGarvey (1991). They reported on the development of understanding among two classes of junior high school students with respect to macro, submicro, and symbolic meanings of chemical reactions. Results reveal good learning gains, although about 30% of the students were not able to identify particle diagrams correctly.

- A course designed from a *mix of perspectives*, namely conceptual change, context-led, and constructivist, was investigated by Solomonidou and Stavridou (2000). They reported on the development of understanding among 168 junior high school students with respect to macroscopic features of substances and various chemical reactions. Results show significant positive shifts in understanding. A minority (percentage not given) of the students, however, did not change their "concrete substance" idea toward the "unknown substance plus properties" scheme, and the "inert mixture" concept toward the "interaction between substances" concept.

Some of the reported studies cover only macroscopic features of chemical reactions (Barker & Millar, 1999; Nieswandt, 2001; Solomonidou & Stavidrou, 2000), whereas others also cover submicroscopic and symbolic features (Cavallo et al., 2003; Laverty & McGarvey, 1991). All studies report a positive development of students' understanding, but all of them also indicate conceptual difficulties, despite the use of modern course designs and teaching strategies. This raises the question: what causes the persistency of the reported difficulties in these courses?

To answer this question, knowledge of the teaching-learning processes in the classroom could be helpful. Unfortunately, four of the studies only focused on learning outcomes, by using written questionnaires, sometimes combined with some interviews, in the context of pre-test/(repeated) post-test designs. As a consequence, they are not able to report on learning processes. Fortunately, in the fifth study, not only were a pre-test/post-test design and questionnaires used, but so were other instruments, such as audio records of lessons and classroom observations (Laverty & McGarvey, 1991). This study offers a better insight into students' struggle for understanding. The researchers report how students design their own diagrammatic representations for the effect of heat on copper carbonate, why some of them mistake this decomposition for burning in air, and how they argue to find the best representation for the decomposition. In an older but still influential study of another constructivist course, De Vos and Verdonk (1985) also analyzed audiotaped classroom discussions. They found that junior high school students were able to develop primitive particle models of matter in the context of a chemical reaction, for example, for explaining the appearance of the brilliant yellow line, consisting of glittering tiny crystals in a continuous motion, when lead nitrate and potassium iodide are placed in opposite positions in a Petri dish filled with water.

In conclusion, more in-depth and longitudinal studies are needed to get a better "ecologically" valid insight into the factors and conditions that hinder or facilitate the development of students' conceptions of the multiple meanings of chemical reactions.

The Dilemma of the Course Content Structure

The five reported studies deal with courses where the choice for a particular general teaching strategy is reported, but where the course content structure is hardly indicated, especially the issue of developing the idea of chemical reactions from a macroscopic level to a submicroscopic level by an early or late introduction of the particle theory. This issue is the subject of an old but ongoing debate in chemical education.

Several scholars have proposed a delayed introduction of molecules and atoms (e.g., Ahtee & Varjola, 1998; Fensham, 1994), but others have shown that students do not naturally have a concept of substance identity that allows them to recognize chemical change in a proper way (e.g., Johnson, 2000; Stavidrou & Solomonidou, 1998). For instance, although many courses introduce the burning of substances in an early stage, students experience a lot of difficulties in recognizing and understanding this event as a chemical reaction (Watson, Prieto, & Dillon, 1997). Johnson (2002) even found that students began to accept the idea of substances changing into other substances only after a teaching unit in which atoms had been introduced. The model of atoms and changes in bonding was not the explanation for the idea of chemical change, but the means by which chemical change was acknowledged. On the other hand, it is clear that premature introduction of the concepts of molecules and atoms is not indicated, because this approach will not enable students to consider particles as a fruitful concept for explaining chemical reactions, and may induce many difficulties at the submicroscopic level, as reported before. This raises the question: how should we escape from this content-related teaching approach dilemma?

A promising way out could be the development of context-led constructivist courses that use the students' initial conceptions of substances and particles (most students have at least heard about atoms), although their conceptions are inevitably rather primitive and unscientific, to promote the development of knowledge of the multiple meanings of chemical reactions in a coherent and simultaneous way (see, e.g., Nakleh, Samarapungavan, & Saglam, 2005).

In conclusion, further research is required to get a deeper insight into the most effective course content structure for meaningful student learning of chemical reactions.

INTRODUCING MULTIPLE MEANINGS OF ATOMIC STRUCTURE AND CHEMICAL BONDING

Introduction

In chemical education at the senior high school level, one of the key concepts is chemical bonding, because knowledge of this concept allows students to make predictions, and give explanations, about physical and chemical properties of substances. For a good understanding of the bonding concept, knowledge of the structure of the atom is a prerequisite. Students who progress to learn chemistry from the high school level to the university level will meet multiple models of both concepts. Regarding atomic structure, students usually have to learn initially the shell model in terms of a positive central nucleus surrounded by shells of negative electrons. Later on, they have to learn the orbital model in terms of subshells, orbitals, and electron density patterns. Regarding chemical bonding, students usually learn first about covalent bonding (initially described as electron sharing) and ionic bonding (often implied to be equivalent to electron transfer; see below). If metallic bonding is introduced it is often presented in terms of a sea-of-electrons model. Progression toward

---

Vignette

In a senior high school class, a chemistry teacher shows a sheet including the equation for the reaction starting $H_2(g) + F_2(g)$ . . . (indicating that the reactants were in the form of molecules).

The teacher asks: *In your own words, explain why you think hydrogen reacts with fluorine?*

A student answers: *Because both atoms need one extra electron in their outside shell to have a noble gas structure, so by sharing two electrons (one from each atom) in a covalent bond, hydrogen fluoride becomes a very stable molecule . . .*

In this vignette, the student response demonstrates a confident reply, yet one that contradicts the information in the teacher's question. This is a common student response that exemplifies how students find the curriculum models of atomic structure and bonding problematic (Taber, 2002).

---

a more sophisticated understanding of these bonds types is expected later, as is knowledge of hydrogen bonding, van der Waals forces, and so forth.

This section addresses studies of students' difficulties in understanding these multiple models and offers some explanations of how these difficulties arise and ideas to prevent and to respond to them. Suggestions for further research and course development are also given.

Teaching and Learning about Atomic Structure

Students' recurrent conceptual difficulties.   In the last decade, the interest in students' difficulties in understanding the concept of atomic structure has been growing. Typical examples of recurrent difficulties are reported below (see also Justi & Gilbert, 2000). Usually, at the senior high school level, teaching about atomic structure starts with the shell model of this concept. One of the main strengths of this model is that it can act as a major explanatory device linking atomic structure to chemical behavior in terms of the periodic table. Electronic configurations expressed in symbols, such as 2.7, 2.8.2, etc., may be readily related to the period and group of the element, which in turn link to patterns of chemical behavior. Indeed the periodic table as often currently presented in chemical education is described as a table of the elements (i.e., of substances), but often presents data about atoms, sometimes juxtaposed with macroscopic properties such as melting temperature (Schmidt, Baumgärtner, & Eybe, 2003).

The shell concept is often problematic for students. First of all, the idea that the atom has a certain structure may seem to be inconsistent with prior learning. Students at the junior high school level have learned that atoms are the fundamental components of matter. However, Harrison and Treagust (1996) found that students still often appreciate this concept in only a vague way, and tend to consider these constituent particles as solid spheres. A second area of difficulties relates to learning about the construction of the atom. For instance, Harrison and Treagust (1996) reported that some students believed that an electron shell is some form of protective coating on the atom. A third area of difficulty is in appreciating the nature of interactions within the atom. For instance, Taber (1998a) showed that many high school students feel that the positively charged nucleus gives rise to a certain amount of attraction that is shared out among the electrons present. Students also tend to use alternative notions when explaining the stability of the nucleus, for example suggesting that nuclear stability is due to a force from the electrons pushing the protons together. A common alternative explanation is the conception that neutrons neutralize the charge on the protons in some way so that the protons may be collected together in the nucleus (Schmidt, Baumgärtner, & Eybe, 2003).

In a second stage of teaching about atomic structure, the shell model is replaced (or at least supplemented) by the more subtle and complex orbital model, to provide more explanatory power. Many students experience this transition as difficult to understand. As Harrison and Treagust (2000) indicated, they often initially adopt the new terminology, but still largely think in terms of shells of orbiting electrons. Even chemistry undergraduates have been found to think largely in terms of simple Bohr-type models of the atom (Cros et al., 1986). Not surprisingly, concepts such as orbital hybridization have been found to be difficult for both high school students (Taber, 2004) and undergraduates (Nakiboglu, 2003) to master.

Students' conceptual difficulties can be explained from the same three perspectives as mentioned in the previous section:

(i)   The *teaching perspective*. Teachers may be hindered by their own familiarity with ideas about atomic structure from understanding why the model presented to students is unclear for them and is often inconsistent with students' familiar notions. Furthermore, teachers often do not pay sufficient attention to the historical background and model characteristics of the shell and orbital versions of atomic structure met in the curriculum.

(ii) The *science content perspective*. The nature of the atom is very abstract. A key idea is the electrostatic interactions between the charged particles present (the electrons and the nucleus), but although necessary, this is not sufficient to understand atomic structure. Not only is quantum theory needed to appreciate why electrons should occur in shells, but the stability of the nucleus requires a completely different type of force—something that is often ignored at this level.

(iii) The *learning perspective*. Students have to learn counterintuitive ideas about the nature of atomic structure. Moreover, they have learned about electric forces and energy, but the application of these concepts to understanding the shell and orbital meaning of atoms leads to cognitive conflicts, as mentioned above.

Courses developed from modern perspectives.   Several studies have been reported about approaches to preventing and responding to students' difficulties in this area. Many conventional courses introduce atomic structure by comparison with the solar system, which is assumed to be more familiar to students. This type of teaching by analogy is very powerful when done well, but needs to focus students on both similarities and differences between the two systems. However, in practice, as Taber (2002) found, students may not have a sound appreciation of the forces at work in either the solar or atomic systems.

In a study of teaching at the junior high school level, Moran and Vaughan (2000) reported on a course, developed from a *conceptual change perspective*, that included the use of model building to make atomic structure seem more concrete for students, and that set up discussion about potential cognitive conflicts. These features seem worthy; however, the cognitive conflicts involved spotting errors in fake students' work, rather than engineering situations where the students' own ideas could be challenged by evidence. Although the authors imply that the approach was successful, they offer no evaluation of the learning outcomes.

In a study related to teaching at the high school level, Petri and Niedderer (1998) reported on a computer-assisted instruction (CAI) approach to teaching about atomic structure based around the concepts of state and orbital, and the standing wave analogy for electrons in atoms. This approach, which included a *constructivist view* on learning, uses computers to allow students to undertake mathematical modeling—yet focuses on the models produced, not the mathematics. Their case study of student learning showed that although initial, relatively limited, models of the atom continued to be used by the student, these were augmented by more sophisticated models that were closer to the target knowledge. These findings are consistent with the study of Harrison and Treagust (2000).

Understandably, there is a real debate about when and how quantum ideas ought to be taught in schools and universities. Some authors have argued that orbital concepts should be avoided completely for a longer time (e.g., Tsaparlis, 1997). Gillespie (1996) has argued that a conceptualization of atomic and molecular structure in terms of electron pair domains should be the preferred approach at the senior high school and introductory university levels.

In conclusion, the research highlights many of the difficulties students face in studying atomic structure. Unfortunately, the research does not provide clear advice to the teacher about how to proceed. In many cases, suggestions to delay the study of material may not be consistent with the prescribed curriculum. This underlines the need for further research, especially with respect to course designs that provide sufficient time for students to consolidate new ideas before being expected to develop them further.

Teaching and Learning about Chemical Bonding

Students' recurrent conceptual difficulties.   Research interest is growing in the area of students' difficulties in understanding chemical bonding. Exemplars of recurrent difficulties are reported below. At the senior high school level, students commonly develop notions of two basic types of bonding that they take forward to more advanced levels of study: covalent and ionic. The covalent bond is often defined as electron-sharing; the ionic bond is often identified with the process of electron transfer between a metal atom and a nonmetal atom. These associations may be inappropriate as students often think that the notion of electron sharing is sufficient to explain the covalent bond, and that the ionic bond is an electron-transfer event, rather than the force holding ions together.

Regarding the understanding of the *covalent bond*, Barker and Millar (2000) showed that students may think that covalent bonds are weak, because many substances of which the constituent particles are considered to be covalently bound have low melting points. Other research indicated that students might think that covalent bonds break when a piece of material is reshaped, and may assume that high viscosity is due to covalent bonds (Peterson, Treagust, & Garnett, 1989). Tan and Treagust (1999) found that some students think that substances that actually have giant molecular structures contain discrete molecules with strong intermolecular forces.

Regarding the understanding of the *ionic bond*, research has shown that students tend to think that ionic substances consist of molecules, or ion-pair units that act like molecules, even if the actual term is not used (Taber, 1997; Barker & Millar, 2000). So, for the NaCl structure (which tends to be the archetypal teaching example, and is commonly quoted by learners) students would expect each ion to be involved in two types of interaction: with the one counter-ion within the same "molecule"/ion pair, and with the five other counter-ions that are not conceptualized as part of the same structural unit (Butts & Smith, 1987). A UK survey of over 300 students showed that a "molecular" model of ionic bonding was applied—to at least some extent—by most of the students, at both the junior high and senior high levels (Taber, 1997). Some students may believe that that the "molecules" assumed to be present in NaCl break up to give ions when the salt dissolves, but others consider the molecules/ion pairs to be the solvated species (Butts & Smith, 1987).

When students have to learn about *polar bonds*, they often tend to see these as a subclass of covalent bonds (Peterson et al., 1989). So, students may suggest that substances such as HCl exist as dissolved molecules in aqueous solutions (Barker & Millar, 2000).

Students often have a quite limited understanding of the *metallic bond*. Many expect molecules or ions to be present in metallic structures and, for that reason, think that the constituent particles are linked by covalent or ionic bonds (Taber, 2003).

Students' conceptual difficulties can be examined from the same three perspectives applied earlier:

(i)   The *teaching perspective*. Scientific explanations for chemical bonding are usually considered too complex for students and are therefore not discussed with them. To fill this explanatory vacuum that exists in school chemistry, the octet framework is adopted (Taber, 1998b). This framework is based around a key explanatory principle that atoms actively seek to fill their electron shells or obtain octets of electrons, and is often described in anthropomorphic terms as what atoms want or need. Student understanding of ionic bonding provides a clear illustration of how the octet rule pervades thinking about bonding. Rather than see the ionic bond as the electrostatic attraction between any adjacent counter-ions, it is common for students to conceptualize two types of interactions. So, in NaCl, students will suggest that each sodium ion is ionically bonded only to the one chloride ion it donated an electron to (in order for the sodium and chloride atoms to obtain octet structures), and it will be attracted to other counter-ions "just by forces."

(ii) The *science content perspective*. The multiple models of chemical bonding are very abstract, especially because they include a number of abstract subconcepts, such as force, energy, electrostatic interaction, and atomic structure. Moreover, these subconcepts are related to each other in a very complex way.

(iii) The *learning perspective*. From previous lessons, students are more familiar with molecules than with ions, and the covalent bond is commonly taught before the ionic bond. For that reason, students may tend to construct their mental models of the ionic bond by analogy with the covalent case. This implies that (i) an ion is considered to be only bonded to a counter-ion with which it had exchanged an electron (in the way that in the simple covalent model atoms are only bonded when sharing electrons) and (ii) that the number of bonds formed was seen as limited by electrovalency (as in covalency, where the valency of the atom determines the number of other atoms it could be directly bonded to).

Developing research-based approaches. There are several studies that report courses informed by research into student learning difficulties in this area. In a study of teaching at the senior high school level, Barker and Millar (2000) reported on a *context-based* teaching approach that presents information about chemical bonding (and other theoretical notions) through a story line. The story line provides the context in which to introduce the concept as and when needed. Although the researchers found that the course seemed successful at teaching chemical bonding, they also found similar alternative conceptions about bonding among the students taking the course, as has been reported in the other studies discussed here.

Taber (1998b) reported a longitudinal study of teaching chemical bonding to senior high school students. He found that students often started their course with the idea that chemical bonding was always either covalent (= electron sharing) or ionic (= electron transfer). This finding can be related to research into the levels of intellectual development of students when they are introduced to these abstract concepts (e.g., Finster, 1991). They often had considerable difficulty adjusting their thinking to allow intermediate forms of bonding (i.e., polar) or accepting new categories of bond (e.g., hydrogen bonds). Unless a type of bond could be understood as a variation on the ionic or covalent case, it was often excluded from being considered a real bond and was seen as "just a force." The study also reported on the progression through the course as involving a gradual process of coming to conceptualize chemical reactions and bonding in physical terms, rather than being about atoms trying to obtain octets of electrons. The results showed that this was a difficult succession that often required more time for learning than the course allowed, so that—at best—students were left with partly developed "multiple frameworks" for chemical bonding (Taber, 2001). This result is consistent with a study of Coll and Taylor (2002), who found that undergraduates and even post-graduate chemists may still often think in terms of the limited models acquired in school.

In conclusion, there has been a good deal of research on aspects of learning about chemical bonding, although much of this simply reports findings related to the alternative conceptions of rather disparate students. Although such research can inform teaching, it often fails to suggest how fundamental improvements in teaching strategies can occur. More detailed studies, exploring individual learners over time, can provide greater insights. The studies considered here led to recommendations for teaching strategy and course content structure that may be fruitful:

- Discuss bonding in physical terms (i.e., in terms of forces) rather than octets.
- Avoid anthropomorphic or animistic language when explaining why reactions occur or bonds form.

- Present discussions of bonding in an order of increasing complexity: metals, then ionic compounds (added complication, two types of ion present), then giant covalent structures (added complication—number of bonds determined by atomic structure), then simple covalent (added complication—two types of bond present).

However, more research is needed to find out if following such recommendations can actually improve student outcomes in practice.

As new learning is only meaningful and secure when it is constructed upon suitable foundations; then there needs to be a suitable period of time before any newly acquired concepts are suitable to be relied upon as prerequisite learning for new learning. This period of consolidation may be many months (e.g., Harrison & Treagust, 2000), and yet in chemistry teaching the curriculum often requires teachers to introduce such interdependent material in a much shorter time scale. As suggested above, this is another area where more research is indicated, as it is quite possibly a major factor in many of the difficulties that students face in learning about atomic structure and chemical bonding.

A LOOK TO THE NEAR FUTURE OF CHEMICAL EDUCATION

Chemical education reform is under way in many countries. An important reason for this reform is the growing dissatisfaction with the position of many chemistry curricula: quite isolated from students' personal interest, society and technology issues, and modern chemistry. As a consequence, there is a growing interest in new issues, such as relevant and meaningful contexts (Bennett & Holman, 2002); multimedia tools, including computer software (Ardac & Akaygun, 2004); and multiple meanings of models (Justi & Gilbert, 2002). The new issues are not very specific to chemical education, but are also found in the curriculum reform of the other sciences. Most of them are elaborated in other parts of this book. Although the three exemplar issues—contexts, multimedia, and models—are already mentioned at several places in the previous sections, we will elaborate them more within the limited space available in the present chapter. First, we relate the issue of meaningful contexts and the issue of multimedia tools to the topic of chemical change. Second, we relate the issue of models to the topic of atomic structure and chemical bonding. At the end of the chapter, we briefly pay attention to the preparation of chemistry teachers for teaching multiple meanings, and, as a final note, we point out the need for a more coherent innovation of chemical education.

Teaching Multiple Meanings through Contexts

One of the most promising contributions to abolishing current curriculum isolation is the use of relevant and meaningful contexts for teaching chemistry topics (Bennett & Holman, 2002). Contexts are often considered as situations in which chemistry or other science concepts, rules, and so on, can help communicate meaning to students. They can come from several domains, such as students' personal life, social

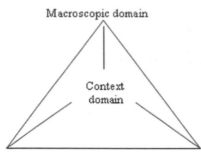

FIGURE 22–2. The tetrahe-
dron of meanings.

life, and scientific life. Mahaffy (2004) even proposes to extend the triangle of meanings into a tetrahedron by adding the context issue (Fig. 22.2).

Usually contexts are presented to students as illustrations of topics already presented as "theory," but interest in another function of contexts is growing, namely contexts as a rationale or starting point for teaching topics. However, it would be naive to expect context-based chemistry courses to provide the solutions to all problems. These courses do not seem to help all students improve their reasoning about chemical reactions (see, e.g., Barker & Millar, 1999). Studies that compare the effects of context-based chemistry teaching with more traditional teaching are quite rare. Ramsden (1997) executed such a comparative study for introductory chemistry teaching at high schools. She found that there is little difference in understanding chemical change, but there appear to be some benefits associated with the context-based approach in terms of stimulating students' interest in chemistry. Although this result may be somewhat disappointing from a cognitive development point of view, it is positive from an affective development point of view. The use of context-based approaches may not solve all of the reported problems with cognitive learning for several reasons. For instance, the contexts might have been too complex or quite unfamiliar to students, and the relation between a context and the intended accompanying concepts might not have been very meaningful to students. What is clear is that the results of existing studies suggest a need for further research in context-based chemistry teaching, especially in terms of the factors that contribute to cognitive learning outcomes.

Teaching Multiple Meanings Through Multimedia Tools

Within chemical education, there are a fast-growing number of articles on the use of multimedia tools, especially computer software with supplementary handouts. We will not review this literature, but only consider some experiences with teaching and learning the multiple meanings of chemical reactions.

Dynamic sequences of atomic and molecular interactions can be provided by computer-generated graphic representations. For instance, Garnett and Hackling (1999) reported on a short instructional intervention using a CD-ROM on balancing and interpreting chemical equations for high school students. The interactive program was designed to make extensive use of video illustrations of chemical reactions, followed by animations using dynamic graphics to show particle behavior and balancing chemical equations. Results indicate a growth of students' understanding of chemical formulas and equations as well as in their skills in balancing these equations. Although these results are interesting, the value of the study is limited because it is unknown whether this intervention offers outcomes in excess of those that can be obtained by regular instruction. A comparison between both instructional conditions is made in a study of Ardac and Akaygun (2004) of a multimedia instructional unit that relates the multiple meanings of chemical reactions. They investigated the immediate and long-term (15 months) effects of high school students using this unit and found, for both time periods, that students from the experimental group showed a higher performance level than students who received regular instruction.

Despite success stories about the use of computerized learning environments, disappointing results are also reported. For instance, Wainwright (1989) evaluated a software package as a supplement to traditional instruction in balancing and interpreting chemical equations for high school students. The experimental group received reinforcement via the computer program, while the control group used parallel worksheets for concept reinforcement. After the intervention period, the control group performed significantly higher than the intervention group.

In conclusion, although the effectiveness of multimedia tools varies, they have the potential for enhancing students' understanding of chemical reactions. They can improve students' understanding of more complex reaction types, as studies have shown for acid-base reactions (Nakleh & Krajcik, 1994), redox reactions (Williamson & Abraham, 1995), and equilibrium reactions (Russell et al., 1997). In all cases, these tools require a very careful design and should be properly embedded in an overall teaching approach. More research is required to get a good insight into their use, especially concerning the factors that explain their effectiveness.

Teaching Multiple Meanings Through Models

In chemistry, it is very common to use models to represent molecular-level structures and processes. That these models are to some extent models of models—as any molecular level description of matter is, strictly, theoretical—complicates learning for students. Much has been written about the various types of models used in science and science education (Harrison & Treagust, 1996), and "model confusion" has been identified as a particular problem for learners in chemistry (Carr, 1984).

Indeed, it has been suggested that it is useful to distinguish between at least three different types of models that are important for chemistry education: scientific, curriculum, and teaching models (Justi & Gilbert, 2000). *Scientific models* are used extensively by chemists—for example to help visualization, theory development, and problem solving. *Curriculum models* are the (often simplified) versions that are set out in syllabuses as acceptable (or even desirable) target knowledge suitable for a particular age group. The level of simplification here may reflect considerations about the learners' overall levels of cognitive development (e.g., the extent to which they are judged to be capable of formal abstract thinking), but also about their limited existing knowledge of a topic. *Teaching models* are constructed for or by teachers to help them communicate the curriculum models to students—

such as a model to help students write Lewis structures when they are learning to understand acid-base reactions at a higher school level (Quilez Pardo, 1989).

The students themselves may not even realize that the target knowledge is a model, as research shows that many students do not appreciate the meanings and roles of models and theories in science (Driver, Leach, Millar, & Scott, 1996). Indeed, studies even suggest that teachers themselves show widely varying sophistication in appreciating the importance and nature of the models they teach about and with (De Jong, Van Driel, & Verloop, 2005; Justi & Gilbert, 2002). In the present chapter, many difficulties are reviewed regarding junior high-school students' understanding of the submicroscopic meaning of chemical reactions, especially how to relate this model to the macroscopic meaning of chemical reactions. At the senior high school level, students use submicroscopic models to explain substance properties and behavior, though these are often alternative models. Indeed, it is very common for the chemical explanations produced at this level to be animistic or even anthropomorphic. Not only does research suggest that junior high school students may think that atoms are alive and grow (Harrison & Treagust, 1996), but even senior high school students may tend to believe that atoms are alive (Griffiths & Preston, 1992). Students seem to use psychological and sociological metaphors to produce explanations of chemical properties and behavior. Atoms are said to *need* and *want* full shells and to be happy once they obtain them (Taber & Watts, 1996).

Given these considerations—the centrality of models and modeling in chemistry, yet the unsophisticated understanding of models shown by students—it seems especially important that curriculum models (which will be presented to students as target knowledge, and often accordingly imbued with a high status by students) should be carefully chosen. Now it is suggested here that there are three clear criteria for any suitable curriculum model:

(i)   It must be presented at a level of complexity and abstraction that fits the developmental levels of the learners concerned.

(ii)   It must build upon conceptual foundations that are already familiar—that is, the prerequisite learning must already be in place. (This suggests that careful conceptual analysis of topics, diagnostic assessment of the range of current learning in a class, and individualized remedial instruction will be important in the effective teaching of these models.)

(iii) It must form part of a suitable progression of models that facilitates learners' subsequent learning of more advanced models.

We believe that the research that is available suggests that the curriculum models used in high school and undergraduate chemistry education often fail to meet these criteria. For example, the research of Coll and Taylor (2002) suggests that in many teaching institutions the octet explanation for bonding (found by these authors to be commonly used by undergraduate and post-graduate chemists) has such currency in the curriculum that it should be considered as a curriculum model. So, the notion of ionic bond formation as electron transfer between isolated atoms has become a standard curriculum model (see, for example, the curriculum benchmarks recommended in the United States, AAAS, 1993). This model is not only inaccurate, but closely tied to common misconceptions of the ionic bond discussed above—for example, that each sodium atom can only form a bond to one chlorine atom.

We believe that the use of the octet rule as the basis of an explanatory scheme should not be part of any curriculum model. Chemical reactions and bond formation are not explained in chemistry in terms of atoms filling their shells, and this is not a suitable simplification of actual (current) scientific thinking. Moreover, the octet framework seems to act as an impediment to learning more chemically valid models, rather than a suitable intermediate. This suggests that it does not make an appropriate curriculum model.

It might seem odd that such dubious chemical models should be presented as target knowledge in the curriculum. However, a number of studies are now suggesting that many curriculum models reflect ideas that once had scientific currency, but which have fallen into disuse (Justi & Gilbert, 2000; Tsaparlis, 1997). Some of the problems could be overcome if it was ensured that scientific models (those that may no longer be current in chemistry, but still have currency as curriculum models) are presented in their historical perspective, for instance, models of atomic structure (Justi & Gilbert, 2000), or the historical significance of the octet rule in the development of ideas about affinity and valency. Research into other chemistry topics where less attention has so far been paid to curriculum models could be very valuable. In view of the difficulties so many students have understanding the models of chemistry, as revealed in the literature reviewed in this chapter, more research into the status of the prescribed curriculum models, and how learners can be encouraged to appreciate them as models, is needed to inform both curriculum change and the teaching of chemistry itself.

Preparation of Chemistry Teachers for Teaching Multiple Meanings

Teaching chemical topics through modern student-centred courses looks attractive, but it requires teachers to have a very good insight into the topic, because these courses, especially the courses that include a constructivist view on learning, often require students to address questions where the answers are not given in the textbook. This raises the question: are prospective teachers sufficiently prepared for answering authentic questions from students about chemical topics? This question will be considered in the context of teaching the topic of chemical reactions.

At the elementary school level, prospective teachers often show conceptual difficulties, especially when they have no high school background or incomplete high school background in chemistry, as many have. For instance, prospective elementary school teachers tend to believe that mass is not conserved when a piece of paper is burned in a closed system (Ryan, Jiminez, & De Torre, 1989). They may also ignore the conservation of particles when drawing diagrammatic representations of chemical change (Gabel, Samuel, & Hunn, 1987). In more recent studies, Kokkotas, Vlachos, and Kouladis (1998) indicated that prospective elementary school teachers may attribute macroscopic properties to particles, and Del Pozzo (2001) found that they may have difficulty in interrelating macro- and submicroscopic concepts describing the composition of matter in a proper way.

At the secondary school level, prospective chemistry teachers also show conceptual difficulties, although not so many as elementary school teachers. Nevertheless, prospective chemistry teachers may show good understanding of balancing chemical equations but lack the ability to apply the concepts of conservation of mass and the same number and kind of atoms (Haidar, 1997). They may be able to draw diagrams depicting chemical reactions in terms of particles, but tend to ignore the creation of intermediate products, and to draw loosely packed representations of particles in solid ionic substances (Lee, 1999). Finally, De Jong, Ahtee, Goodwin, Hatzinikita, and Kouladis (1999) found that prospective chemistry teachers are not very familiar with current students' difficulties in understanding combustion at a macroscopic level.

Studies of courses focusing on helping prospective teachers to understand the multiple meanings of chemical reactions and to teach them are rather scarce. Kokkotas, Vlachos, and Kouladis (1998) examined a training course for prospective elementary teachers. The participants were confronted with students' authentic ideas as they are expressed when the students answer questions about the macro- and submicroscopic meaning of the composition of matter and change. Results indicate that the participants show improvement in terms of scientific understanding and knowledge of students' conceptual difficulties. In a study of a teacher training course for prospective chemistry teachers, De Jong and Van Driel (2004) reported that the participants became aware of the need to show students the relations among the multiple meanings in a much more explicit way than they initially tended to do and to ignore their own dominant orientation toward submicroscopic meanings. Moreover, they noticed the importance of the careful and consistent use of symbolic representations, for example, not using the formulas $NaCl(s)$ and $Na^+Cl^-(s)$ in the same context.

In conclusion, the reported studies show the importance of courses for teachers that pay attention to improving prospective teachers' knowledge of multiple meanings of chemical topics, and how to teach them. However, *how* prospective teachers link their "course" knowledge with their classroom practice is still not very clear. This is a general problem and requires further research.

LOOKING FORWARD

Innovations in chemical education should be carried out in a more coherent way than is currently the case. This requires the fine-tuning of at least the following components of innovations:

(i)   The development and implementation of experimental instructional materials and student courses based on new insights into teaching and learning chemical topics, especially with respect to a substantiated content structure for introducing the multiple meanings of many chemical concepts

(ii) The development and implementation of courses for chemistry teachers, to help them to acquire sufficient knowledge of new topics and appropriate competence to teach in ways that are congruent with the new approaches

(iii) The design and execution of in-depth and longitudinal studies. The purpose of this research can be twofold:
- From a theoretical point of view: to develop a better understanding of teaching and learning processes and outcomes with respect to particular chemistry.

- From a practical point of view: to develop guidelines for school and college courses and courses of teacher preparation in chemical education that are informed by research.

The integration of these three innovative steps implies an important challenge for the near future of chemical education.

ACKNOWLEDGMENTS

Thanks to George Bodner and Paul Hobden, who reviewed this chapter.

REFERENCES

A.A.A.S. (1993). *Project 2061: Benchmarks, American Association for the Advancement of Science.* (available at www.project2061.org/tools/benchol/bolframe.htm).

Ahtee, M., & Varjola, I. (1998). Students' understanding of chemical reaction. *International Journal of Science Education, 20,* 305–316.

Andersson, B. (1986). Pupils' explanations of some aspects of chemical reactions. *Science Education, 70,* 549–563.

Ardac, D., & Akaygun, S. (2004). Effectiveness on multimedia-based instruction that emphasizes molecular representations on students' understanding of chemical change. *Journal of Research in Science Teaching, 41,* 317–337.

Barker, V., & Millar, R. (1999). Students' reasoning about chemical reactions: what changes occur during a context-based post-16 chemistry course? *International Journal of Science Education, 21,* 645–665.

Barker, V., & Millar, R. (2000). Students' reasoning about basic chemical thermodynamics and chemical bonding: what changes occur during a context-based post-16 chemistry course? *International Journal of Science Education, 22,* 1171–1200.

Bennett, J., & Holman, J. (2002). Context-based approaches to the teaching of chemistry: what are they and what are their effects? In J. K. Gilbert, O. De Jong, R. Justi, D. F. Treagust, & J. H. Van Driel (Eds.), *Chemical education: Towards research-based practice* (pp. 165–184). Dordrecht, the Netherlands: Kluwer Academic.

Butts, B., & Smith, R. (1987). HSC chemistry students' understanding of the structure and properties of molecular and ionic compounds. *Research in Science Education, 17,* 192–201.

Carr, M. (1984). Model confusion in chemistry. *Research in Science Education, 14,* 97–103.

Cavallo, A. M. L., McNeely, J. C., & Marek, E. A. (2003). Eliciting students' understanding of chemical reactions using two forms of essay questions during a learning cycle. *International Journal of Science Education, 25,* 583–603.

Coll, R. K., & Taylor, N. (2002). Mental models in chemistry: senior chemistry students' mental models of chemical bonding. *Chemistry Education: Research and Practice in Europe, 3,* 175–184 (available at www.uoi.gr/cerp/2002_May/08.html).

Cros, D., Amouroux, R., Chastrette, M., Fayol, M., Leber, J., & Maurin, M. (1986). Conceptions of first year university students of the constitution of matter and the notions of acids and bases. *European Journal of Science Education, 8,* 305–313.

De Jong, O., Acampo, J., & Verdonk, A. H. (1995). Problems in teaching the topic of redox reactions: Actions and conceptions of chemistry teachers. *Journal of Research in Science Teaching, 32,* 1097–1110.

De Jong, O., Ahtee, M., Goodwin, A., Hatzinikita, V., & Kouladis, V. (1999). An international study of prospective teachers' initial teaching conceptions and concerns: The case of teaching "combustion." *European Journal of Teacher Education, 22,* 45–59.

De Jong, O., & Treagust, D. F. (2002). The teaching and learning of electrochemistry. In J. K. Gilbert, O. De Jong, R. Justi, D. F. Treagust, & J. H. Van Driel (Eds.), *Chemical education: Towards research-based practice* (pp. 317–337). Dordrecht, the Netherlands: Kluwer Academic.

De Jong, O., & Van Driel, J. (2004). Exploring the development of student teachers' PCK of multiple meanings of chemistry topics. *International Journal of Science and Mathematics Education, 2,* 477–491.

De Jong, O., Van Driel, J., & Verloop, N. (2005). Preservice teachers' pedagogical content knowledge of using particles models in teaching chemistry. *Journal of Research in Science Teaching, 42*(8), 947–964.

De Vos, W., & Verdonk, A. H. (1985). A new road to reactions, part 1. *Journal of Chemical Education, 62,* 238–240.

Del Pozo, R. M. (2001). Prospective teachers' ideas about the relationships between concepts describing the composition of matter. *International Journal of Science Education, 23,* 353–371.

Driver, R., Leach, J., Millar, R., & Scott, P. (1996). *Young people's images of science.* Buckingham, UK: Open University Press.

Fensham, P. J. (1994). Beginning to teach chemistry. In P. J. Fensham, R. Gunstone, & R. White (Eds.), *The content of science: A constructivist approach to its teaching and learning* (pp. 14–28). London: Falmer Press.

Finster, D. C. (1991) Developmental instruction: Part 2. Application of Perry's model to general chemistry. *Journal of Chemical Education, 68,* 752–756.

Gabel, D. L., & Bunce, D. M. (1994). Research on problem solving: Chemistry. In D. L. Gabel (Ed.), *Handbook of research on science teaching and learning* (pp. 301–326). New York: Macmillan.

Gabel, D. L., Samuel, K. V., & Hunn, D. (1987). Understanding the particulate nature of matter. *Journal in Chemical Education, 64,* 695–697.

Garnett, P. J., & Hackling, M. W. (1999). Improving introductory chemistry students' ability to visualise the particulate basis of chemical reactions. *Chemeda: Australian Journal of Chemical Education, 51,* 45–56.

Gillespie, R. J. (1996). Bonding without orbitals. *Education in Chemistry, 33,* 103–106.

Griffiths, A. K., & Preston, K. R (1992). Grade-12 students' misconceptions relating to fundamental characteristics of atoms and molecules. *Journal of Research in Science Teaching, 29,* 611–628.

Haidar, A. H. (1997). Prospective chemistry teachers' conceptions of the conservation of matter and related concepts. *Journal of Research in Science Teaching, 34,* 181–197.

Harrison, A., & Treagust, D. F. (1996). Secondary students' mental models of atoms and molecules: implications for teaching chemistry. *Science Education, 80,* 509–534.

Harrison, A., & Treagust, D. F. (2000). Learning about atoms, molecules, and chemical bonds: a case study of multiple-model use in grade 11 chemistry. *Science Education, 84,* 352–381.

Johnson, P. (2000). Children's understanding of substances, part 1: Recognizing chemical change. *International Journal of Science Education, 22,* 719–737.

Johnson, P. (2002). Children's understanding of substances, part 2: Explaining chemical change. *International Journal of Science Education, 24,* 1037–1054.

Johnstone, A. H. (1991). Why is science difficult to learn? Things are seldom what they seem. *Journal of Computer Assisted Instruction, 7,* 75–83.

Justi, R., & Gilbert, J. K. (2000). History and philosophy of science through models: Some challenges in the case of "the atom." *International Journal of Science Education, 22,* 993–1009.

Justi, R. S., & Gilbert, J. K. (2002). Models and modelling in chemical education. In J. K. Gilbert, O. De Jong, R. Justi, D. F. Treagust, & J. H. Van Driel (Eds.), *Chemical education: Towards research-based practice* (pp. 47–68). Dordrecht, the Netherlands: Kluwer Academic.

Kokkotas, P., Vlachos, L., & Kouladis, V. (1998). Teaching the topic of the particulate of matter in prospective teachers' training courses. *International Journal of Science Education, 20,* 291–303.

Krnel, D., Watson, R., & Glazar, S. A. (1998). Survey of research related to the development of the concept of "matter." *International Journal of Science Education, 20,* 257–289.

Laverty, D. T., & McGarvey, J. E. B. (1991). A "constructivist" approach to learning. *Education in Chemistry, 28,* 99–102.

Lee, K. L. (1999). A comparison of university lecturers' and pre-service teachers' understanding of a chemical reaction at the particulate level. *Journal of Chemical Education, 76,* 1008–1012.

Mahaffy, P. (2004). The future shape of chemistry education. *Chemistry Education: Research and Practice, 5,* 229–245 (available at www.uoi.gr/cerp/2004_October/05.html).

Moran, J., & Vaughan, S. (2000). Introducing CASE methodology at key stage 4: An example of bridging. *School Science Review, 82,* 47–55.

Nakiboglu, C. (2003). Instructional misconceptions of Turkish prospective chemistry teachers about atomic orbitals and hybridisation. *Chemistry Education: Research and Practice, 4,* 171–188 (available at www.uoi.gr/cerp/2003_May/06.html).

Nakleh, M. B., & Krajcik, J. S. (1994). Influence of levels of information as presented by different technologies on students' understanding of acid, base, and pH concepts. *Journal of Research in Science Teaching, 31,* 1077–1096.

Nakleh, M. B., Samarapungavan, A., & Saglam, Y. (2005). Middle school students' beliefs about matter. *Journal of Research in Science Teaching, 42,* 581–612.

Nieswandt, M. (2001). Problems and possibilities for learning in an introductory chemistry course from a conceptual change perspective. *Science Education, 85,* 158–179.

Peterson, R. F., Treagust, D. F., & Garnett, P. (1989). Development and application of a diagnostic instrument to evaluate grade-11 and -12 students' concepts of covalent bonding and structure following a course of instruction. *Journal of Research in Science Teaching, 26,* 301–314.

Petri, J., & Niedderer, H. (1998). A learning pathway in high-school level quantum atomic physics. *International Journal of Science Education, 20,* 1075–1088.

Quilez Pardo, J. (1989). Teaching a model for writing Lewis structures. *Journal of Chemical Education, 66,* 456–458.

Ramsden, J. M. (1997). How does a context-based approach influence understanding of key chemical ideas at 16+? *International Journal of Science Education, 19,* 697–710.

Russell, J. W., Kozma, R. B., Jones, T., Wykoff, J., Marx, N., & Davis, J. (1997). Use of simultaneous-synchronized macroscopic, sub-microscopic, and symbolic representations to enhance the teaching and learning of chemical concepts. *Journal of Chemical Education, 74,* 330–334.

Ryan, C., Jiminez, J. M. S., & De Torre, A. M. O. (1989). Scientific ideas held by intending primary teachers in Britain and Spain. *European Journal of Teacher Education, 12,* 239–251.

Schmidt, H.-J., Baumgärtner, T., & Eybe, H. (2003). Changing ideas about the periodic table of elements and students' alternative concepts of isotopes and allotropes. *Journal of Research in Science Teaching, 40,* 257–277.

Solomonidou, C., & Stavridou, H. (2000). From inert object to chemical substance: Students' initial conceptions and conceptual development during an introductory experimental chemistry sequence. *Science Education, 84,* 382–400.

Stavidrou, H., & Solomonidou, C. (1998). Conceptual reorganization and the construction of the chemical reaction concept during secondary education. *International Journal of Science Education, 20,* 205–221.

Taber, K. S. (1997). Student understanding of ionic bonding: Molecular versus electrostatic thinking? *School Science Review, 78,* 85–95.

Taber, K. S. (1998a). The sharing-out of nuclear attraction: Or I can't think about physics in chemistry. *International Journal of Science Education, 20,* 1001–1014.

Taber, K. S. (1998b). An alternative conceptual framework from chemistry education. *International Journal of Science Education, 20,* 597–608.

Taber, K. S. (2001). Shifting sands: a case study of conceptual development as competition between alternative conceptions. *International Journal of Science Education, 23,* 731–753.

Taber, K. S. (2002). *Chemical misconceptions—prevention, diagnosis and cure* (2 Vols.). London: Royal Society of Chemistry.

Taber, K. S. (2003) Mediating mental models of metals: acknowledging the priority of the learner's prior learning. *Science Education, 87,* 732–758.

Taber, K. S., & Watts, M. (1996). The secret life of the chemical bond: students' anthropomorphic and animistic references to bonding. *International Journal of Science Education, 18,* 557–568.

Tan, K.-C., & Treagust D. (1999). Evaluating students' understanding of chemical bonding. *School Science Review, 81*, 75–83.

Tsaparlis, G. (1997). Atomic orbitals, molecular orbitals and related concepts: conceptual difficulties among chemistry students. *Research in Science Education, 27*, 271–287.

Van Driel, J. H., & Graeber, W. (2002). The teaching and learning of chemical equilibrium. In J. K. Gilbert, O. De Jong, R. Justi, D. F. Treagust, & J. H. Van Driel (Eds.), *Chemical education: Towards research-based practice* (pp. 271–292). Dordrecht, the Netherlands: Kluwer Academic.

Wainwright, C. L. (1989). The effectiveness of a computer-assisted instruction package in high school chemistry. *Journal of Research in Science Teaching, 26*, 275–290.

Watson, R., Prieto, T., & Dillon, J. S. (1997). Consistency of students' explanations about combustion. *Science Education, 81*, 425–443.

Williamson, V. M., & Abraham, M. R. (1995). The effects of computer animation on the particulate mental models of college chemistry students. *Journal of Research in Science Teaching, 32*, 521–534.

CHAPTER 23

Learning Earth Sciences

Nir Orion
Weizmann Institute of Science, Israel

Charles R. Ault, Jr.
Lewis & Clark College

Great news! I've just been accepted into graduate school in geology with the opportunity to work on a terrific project. The professor I'll work with would like someone to do a photographic survey of the Lower Colorado River along the same route as traversed by an expedition of 150 years ago and documented in journals and watercolor paintings. The aim is to compare habitats and channels of today with those from the past within the context of reconstructing climate trends in western North America. The work would be very similar to what I did in Argentina on my fellowship last year, where I visited Charles Darwin's fossil collecting locales and compared his journal entries as well as sketches of landscapes made by the *Beagle*'s artist with present-day photographs. I am very excited about getting started, and I can't believe that there is a project in geology so similar to what I have dreamed about doing.

—Message from a twenty-first century graduate student

This young graduate student's excitement echoes the themes and claims developed in this chapter. The message offers a glimpse into the nature of earth science inquiry. The proposed research crosses several disciplines, though housed in the geosciences, and has importance to understanding climate change on different scales in time and space. The data include works of art found in historical literature. The reconstruction of past habitats and the extrapolation of future ones will guide human actions in response to environmental change. The project has intrinsic appeal to some, social value to many. At the dawn of the twenty-first century, earth scientists are doing multidisciplinary and interdisciplinary research serving the public good.

The image of an optimistic student captures several characteristics proposed in this chapter as representative of the earth sciences. Section 1, "Distinctive characteristics," introduces these features, arguing that they are crucial for guiding teaching and learning earth sciences. There follows a profile of earth science education worldwide, including trends evident over the past 25 years. This profile focuses on significant reforms in geosciences education undertaken at the very end of the twentieth century: the trend away from disciplinary-based science education toward an integrative, environmentally based, earth systems approach, in part a consequence of profound expectations for the science K–12 curriculum stemming from the "Science for All" movement (American Association for the Advancement of Science [AAAS], 1990).

"Learning earth sciences," Section 2 of this chapter, continues with careful attention to the empirical record of learning earth sciences in schools. Section 2 identifies the main characteristics of earth science education in the schools, such as the integration of subjects within earth sciences and between earth sciences and environmental education. Section 2 then proceeds to examine the cognitive aspects of learning earth sciences: misconceptions, spatial visualization, temporal thinking, and systems thinking. This section ends with a discussion of learning environments for the earth sciences (outdoor and indoor classrooms; the earth science laboratory) and the prospect for cultivating environmental attitudes and insights from learning earth sciences.

Today's ambitious reform agenda, guided by the principle of "science for all," scaffolds Section 3. Here the concern becomes how well, or how poorly, teachers have adapted to calls for changing their philosophies of teaching. Section 3 deals with the difficulties of reforming earth science education for science teachers who have limited content knowledge and who may lack the motivation to deal with new priorities among subjects, unfamiliar learning environments, and changes in teaching strategies.

The chapter concludes by challenging researchers to study teaching and learning in the earth sciences not only as historically practiced as a discipline-based curriculum, but also as increasingly practiced as integrated study. The conclusion acknowledges that, from a research perspective, we know very little about teaching and learning earth sciences when they have been thoroughly contextualized: for example, in the context of inquiry about changes in the climate of western North America. Such contexts value knowledge for the sake of making public policy, not only theory-building and model-testing within the earth sciences. Such contexts find promising data not only in records of sediments, but also in historical photography, journals, and art. The chapter ends, in effect, with the challenge to the next generation of researchers to embrace the implications of science for all: ambitious integration and social contextualization. At the same time, the next generation of curriculum designers must preserve distinctive characteristics of the earth sciences when setting objectives for student learning.

DISTINCTIVE CHARACTERISTICS

Every subject has something important to offer science for all. The challenge is one of establishing priorities. Essential features of what to teach ought to

1. Encompass an "intellectually honest" (Bruner, 1960, p. 33) portrait of what scientists do (e.g., date rocks radiometrically).
2. Emphasize ideas with high conceptual worth or value (Toulmin, 1972), ideas proved to advance thinking and solve problems (e.g., the law of superposition).

The host of individual fields that comprise the earth sciences, the need to integrate these subjects within schools, and the goal of contributing to science for all make characterizing distinctive features imperative. In effect, we are asking, What are the earth sciences about? and What's so important to learn from earth science? The earth sciences are simply about everything beneath our feet and above our heads, with concern for how our collective actions interact with these realms. To learn about the earth sciences is to learn about complex systems on many scales in time and space, about the interactions of these systems with each other and us with them. Learning earth sciences often means learning to think about processes linking the earth's oceans, atmosphere, land, interior, and orbit from a systems perspective. By classifying the learning concepts from the concrete to the abstract, topics from the earth sciences can be presented appropriately to students of all levels of ability, achievement, and age, from kindergarten to high school.

Let us emphasize the notion of "distinctiveness" on four levels: disciplinary, psychological, pedagogical, and sociohistorical. Characterization of the crucial features of a subject begins with attention to phenomena of interest (history of the earth, for example) that are distinctive to the discipline, then turns to cognitively distinctive challenges for learning these phenomena (psychological misconceptions about geologic time, for example). Approaches to pedagogy must demonstrate their responsiveness to such distinctive cognitive challenges (making use of outdoor learning or field study, for example). The endpoint for characterization of a subject's distinctive potential is consideration of its social and historical context: how knowing about climate change and its scale may matter in the personal and social lives of citizens, for example. Derived most explicitly from the geosciences, the use of the label *earth sciences* encompasses a host of fields and subfields in geology, hydrology, oceanography, meteorology, climatology, and even astronomy. Clearly, a definitive characterization of the crucial features of the earth sciences remains well beyond the scope of this (and perhaps any other) chapter. Nevertheless, there are heuristically useful questions to pose in the search for distinctive features of the earth sciences. These features, to repeat, are ones useful to curriculum design, framing the scope of research about teaching and learning earth sciences, and promoting science for all. For example, presumably, from learning earth sciences students acquire an intellectually honest understanding of change through earth's history across many scales. Developing a sense of scale is a distinctive feature of learning earth sciences. The concept of scale functions both psychologically and epistemologically. Psychologically, scale may present obstacles to perception and insight. Epistemologically, extrapolation of earth processes in time and space is a goal of explanation. The geologic time scale encompasses durations and changes vastly beyond the scale of human lifetimes; forecasts of global climate change must wrestle with problems of sampling and modeling on various scales. Such inquiry in the earth sciences has distinctive features; our synthesis highlights six:

1. The *historical approach*, pioneered by Charles Lyell and Charles Darwin, to scientific inquiry (e.g., Darwin's account of the reefs around coral atolls of the Pacific: the islands as a sampling distribution across space and through time of what happens to a volcanic island as it rises and subsides over immense, unwitnessed durations).

2. The concern for *complex systems* acting over the Earth as whole (e.g., the several "spheres": *hydro, geo, atmo,* and their interaction with the biosphere) as well as analysis of their subsystems on more regional and local scales.

3. The conceptualization of very *large-scale phenomena* through time and across space (e.g., "deep time" and the construction of the geologic time scale).

4. The need for *visual representation* as well as high demand upon spatial reasoning (e.g., the role of geologic maps, contour maps, and the modeling of structures and dynamic processes, such as ocean currents and storms, in three dimensions).

5. The *integration across scales* of solutions to problems (e.g., the validation of meteor impact hypotheses with evidence gathered across scales from mineral crystal to regional topography).

6. The uniqueness of *retrospective scientific thinking*. To unravel processes that took place millions of years ago, geologists have developed a distinctive way of thinking that involves retrospection. Geological inquiry applies knowledge of present-day processes in order to draw conclusions about the conditions of materials, processes, and environments of the past.

The earth sciences are both similar to and distinct from other fields of science. To the extent that earth sciences serve as concrete contexts for better understanding of basic concepts from physics, chemistry, and biology, they inherit many common challenges, for example, using operational definitions, thinking in terms of direct and inverse proportions, and overcoming pervasive misconceptions about energy, motion, particulate matter, inheritance, and adaptation (Driver, Squires, Rushworth, & Wood-Robinson, 1994; Driver, Guesne, & Tiberghien, 1985; Wandersee, Mintzes, & Novak, 1994). The readily accessible contexts for learning earth sciences may introduce young adolescents to features of scientific reasoning such as observing, hypothesizing, and drawing conclusions from evidence. At the same time, learning about the earth sciences presents distinctive challenges and opportunities.

The history and philosophy of science, when turned toward the examination of geological explanations and the concept of geologic time, reveal features of thought characteristic of the earth sciences (Ault, 1998; Brandon, 1994; Cleland, 2002; Gould, 1986; Kitts, 1977; LeGrand, 1988; Schumm, 1991). So, too, does the psychology of learning earth science concepts unveil what is cognitively distinctive about this field (Ault, 1994; Schoon, 1989; Trend, 1998, 2001b).

A strategy of compare and contrast has proved essential to forming understandings of earth's features and systems that have resulted from long and complex histories. Indeed, Gould has characterized approaches to problem solving in geology, paleontology, and evolution, from Lyell and Darwin forward, as a distinctive historical style of argument and explanation in science (Gould, 1986). The objects of explanation—such as mountain building, ice age onset, seafloor topography, storm generation, magma distillation, planetary coalescence, and earthquake frequency—have unique histories. As a consequence of individual history, each example of a basic category has, at some level of resolution, features distinct from other examples of the category (e.g., the Nile River delta is similar to, yet distinct from, other examples of deltas due to similar, thought not identical histories of formation).

This insight into the nature of categorization of rocks, volcanoes, river deltas, clouds, moons, and other objects of interest to the earth (and space) sciences contrasts with the situation easily noted in chemistry and physics, where fundamental entities come in categories whose members are quite often utterly indistinguishable from each other (Hanson, 1965): protons, atoms of carbon, electromagnetic fields. At an important level, disciplines depart from each other in how they categorize and represent what is most salient about reality, with important consequences for learning from a constructivist standpoint (Driver, Asoko, Leach, Mortimer, & Scott, 1994).

Quite obviously, most subjects are hybrids of theorizing and categorization, and the distinction between fundamental entities that have complex and distinguishing histories (for example, solar bodies) and those basic aspects of reality that differ from each other in well-determined, rule-governed ways (for example, solar energies) refers more properly to endpoints of a continuum, rather than to incommensurable opposites.

In conclusion, the distinctive features of the earth sciences stem from the centrality of historical methods of inquiry pioneered at the dawn of geology. In addition, investigating the earth depends heavily upon spatial reasoning and visual representation. The concept of scale permeates historical methods and visualization tasks, both as an obstacle to cognitive insight (phenomena happening on vast scales, well beyond the purview of human experience) and an arbiter of convincing explanation (solutions to problems on different scales must cohere). When geologic scale and historical complexity are combined with basic ideas from physical and life sciences, earth systems thinking emerges, with attention to dynamism on global scales of interest and the realization that human action affects earth systems on global scales. In brief, people acting collectively have become geologic agents, and their societies can change climates across local, regional, and global scales. Human communities consume earth resources and depend upon earth systems for the disposal of wastes. Too obviously, degradation, scarcity, and pollution reach levels that threaten human communities or interfere with vital "ecosystem services" that undergird agricultural productivity, maintain habitat and biological diversity, clean both air and water, and ameliorate climatic variation. Hence, there would appear to be no clear or useful demarcation between learning earth sciences and learning environmental sciences.

The general themes of interdisciplinary study, multidisciplinary study, environmental issues, and relationship to social responsibility invariably lie close to the surface when learning earth sciences. "Holistic" properly describes this situation. Learning earth sciences offers holistic perspectives to science for all, and this holism entails a shift from traditional science teaching.

Shifting Profiles

The stature and role of learning earth sciences in keeping with the goal of science for all has shifted in recent decades. Examples of this shift exist worldwide, and these examples answer questions such as:

1. What status does and should earth science occupy in school science?
2. How has the profile of earth science education changed in recent decades?
3. What does learning earth sciences, when linked to environmental education, offer as part of science education for all?

At the level where distinctions between earth and environmental sciences melt away, there arises another general theme of extraordinary importance: the conduct and understanding of sciences in social contexts. Citizens with knowledge of earth sciences clearly have some capacity to choose (or hold leaders accountable for choosing) policies in light of their consequences for earth systems and for society to exist in profitable harmony with earth resources.

Increased multidisciplinary and interdisciplinary research within the sciences and across other fields has had a conspicuous impact on the earth sciences. For decades a new field has grown rapidly: environmental geology. This field embraces most of the topics traditionally addressed in the earth sciences from the perspective of human interaction with natural systems (Tank, 1983; Pickering & Owen, 1994).

The time has come for science education to situate itself squarely within the educational conversation about social justice, poverty, wealth, sustainability, and the human condition. The National Science Education Standards (NSES) for the United States invite science educators to do so in the standard *Science in Personal and Social Perspective* (National Research Council, 1996). This conversation is at the same time about the nature of democratic institutions for governing the use of earth resources and affecting earth systems. The features distinctive of the earth sciences clearly align with these aims. Systems thinking, hierarchy theory, holistic explanation, and attention to scale and complexity bind learning earth sciences to environmental topics. Indeed, the environmental imperative and the role of learning earth sciences in order to achieve environmental insight has achieved a central position in the field of earth science education (Mayer & Armstrong, 1990; Brody, 1994; Mayer, 1995; Orion, 1996).

In many respects education in earth sciences has, in fact, converged upon environmental education in nations around the globe. In addition, changes in curriculum have often treated the subject more from the perspective of integration and systems (holism) rather than from the perspectives of separate disciplines (reductionism). Whether from the point of view of integrating multiple disciplines, from the acknowledgement that the phenomena of interest are complex, interacting systems, or simply in response to the imperative of educating citizens for making environmentally responsible decisions, the profile of learning earth science has changed in recent decades. It will continue to change in the direction of holism, in the sense of the multidisciplinary study of complex systems and from the standpoint of environmental concerns.

Reductionist philosophy has historically constrained the introduction of earth sciences within school science curricula by prioritizing physics, chemistry, and biology. Reduction of science literacy to competence within these three fields has allowed relatively limited time for learning earth sciences. The reductionist paradigm works quite well in keeping with the goal of science education as a preparation of a nation's new generation of scientists. From the perspective of science for all, it has serious limitations.

The shift toward a science for all paradigm places the earth sciences in a better position. The new paradigm sets the goal for science education as preparation for citizenship. Science for All Americans (AAAS, 1990) defines minimal levels of scientific literacy. The Benchmarks for Science Literacy (AAAS, 1993), which followed Science for All Americans, advocates balancing scientific knowledge, the processes of science, and the development of personal-social goals (Bybee & Deboer, 1994). The United Kingdom has adopted a similar approach in the National Curriculum for England and Wales (Department of Education and Science [DES], 1989). In the United States, the National Science Education Standards (NSES; National Research Council, 1996) encompass eight categories of content. Four are traditional categories (physical, life, earth and space, science and technology); two incorporate holistic conceptions of science (unifying concepts and processes, science as inquiry) and two examine science within wider contexts (science in personal and social lives, history and nature of science). Reform topics have equal billing with traditional subjects in the NSES.

The shift from direct instruction toward constructivist pedagogy also has influenced the profile of science education (Mintzes & Wandersee, 1998; Driver et al., 1994; Driver et al., 1985; Osborne & Wittrock, 1985; Bezzi, 1995). The constructivist approach acknowledges that individuals must construct new understandings in light of personal experience and private meanings. Constructivists recognize, in addition, the importance representations of reality (models, diagrams, equations, and category systems) play within the epistemology of a subject (Driver et al., 1994). Learners must assume personal responsibility to construct these representations and compare their thinking with that of others when in pursuit of "shared meaning" (Gowin, 1981). A constructivist might ask, "Is the concept adequate to the purpose it serves?" rather than "Is the idea true?" From a constructivist standpoint, pedagogy ought to engage students in learning meaning through the use of concepts rather than expecting them to learn ideas simply from listening to lectures and studying texts.

Conceptual change theory (Posner, Strike, Hewson, & Gertzog, 1982; Smith, 1991) has also exerted a strong influence over science teaching. Conceptual change theory recognizes that beliefs about knowledge shape student efforts to learn science. Conceptual change theory, using historical examples of major shifts in scientific conceptualizations, focuses on the adequacy of ideas. Ideas that are adequate resolve anomalies in plausible ways. In addition, they are intelligible in terms of current understanding and fruitful in the creation of new knowledge. Smith has elaborated upon conceptual change theory by describing the understanding it fosters as "usefulness in a social context" (Smith, 1991).

The concept of sea floor spreading, for instance, resolved anomalies in the pattern of magnetic fields recorded on ocean bottom rocks (a pattern detected incidentally and puzzlingly during attempts to detect enemy submarines during World War II; see LeGrand, 1988). Sea floor spreading made plausible the notion of drifting continents; the concept has proved enormously fruitful as a component (and precursor) of plate tectonic theory. Now, understandings of geologic hazards due to seismic and volcanic activity depend upon knowledge of plate tectonic theory. Public policy, from building codes to tsunami alerts, has made this knowledge useful in a social context.

Problems, projects, and issues often provide a proper context for promoting meaningful learning. No doubt many students are exposed in their daily lives or through the mass media to earthquakes, volcanoes, global atmospheric changes, journeys to Mars, ocean pollution, fresh water shortages, energy conservation, floods, hurricanes, landslides and avalanches, etc. These topics are contextual goldmines from a constructivist standpoint: opportunities to engage students in the construction of meaning through the use of concepts in personally relevant contexts.

Constructivism and holism have influenced the profile of learning earth sciences in another and very fundamental way: the growing interest in earth systems education. At least 15 countries have undertaken to reform science teaching by placing greater emphasis on the dynamic systems of the Earth (Mayer, 2002).

Earth Systems Science and Education

Earth science education worldwide has undergone a process of revival during the past decade. Since 1993 four international conferences on geoscience education have been conducted in Europe, the United States, Australia, and Canada (Stow & McCall, 1996; IGEO, 1997, 2000, 2003). At the first international conference in England participants widely supported the proposal to reinforce the environmental aspect of learning earth sciences (Carpenter, 1996; Orion, 1996; Mayer, 1996). In 1997 in Hawaii earth science educators convened again for an international conference, this time titled "Learning about the Earth as a System" (IGEO, 1997). Now, at the beginning of the twenty-first century, earth science educators accept that the purpose of earth science education for ages 5–19 is both to educate for citizenship and to prepare students to become professional geoscientists.

Orion and Fortner (2003) have argued that the earth systems approach is ideal as a holistic framework for science curricula. The starting point is the four earth systems: geosphere, hydrosphere, atmosphere, and biosphere. The study of cycles organizes earth systems education: the rock cycle, the water cycle, the food chain, and the carbon cycle. The study of these cycles emphasizes relationships among subsystems through the transfer of matter and energy based on the laws of conservation. Such natural cycles should be discussed within the context of their influence on people's daily lives, rather than being isolated to scientific disciplines. The earth systems approach also connects the natural world and technology: technology transforms raw materials that originate from earth systems.

Through the elaboration of cycles, the approach underscores that society is a natural part of the systems of the Earth and that manipulation of one part of this complex system might adversely affect people. In contrast with traditional approaches for teaching science, the earth systems approach does not sequence the curriculum using topics from physics or chemistry. Instead, this approach organizes study in terms of systems and cycles as experienced in peoples' lives. It does utilize physics and chemistry as tools for understanding science at a deeper and more abstract level within this context. However, the main educational goal is the development of environmental insight in two senses. First, we live in a cycling world that is built upon a series of subsystems (geosphere, hydrosphere, biosphere, and atmosphere) that interact through an exchange of energy and materials. Second, people are a part of nature and thus must act in harmony with its laws of cycling.

Ten years after introducing the earth systems approach, Mayer introduced Global Science Literacy (GSL; Mayer, 1997, 2002, 2003). GSL expands the argument for new science curricula for secondary schools. Instead of presenting major disciplines, Mayer argued the importance of organizing curricula with the "Earth System" concept. This approach includes teaching the methodology of system sciences and capitalizing on the cross-cultural characteristics of science.

The Earth System concept embraces holism and extends learning earth sciences into environmental, social, and political debate. However, do scientists practice holistic science? Yes; holism exists as a basic goal of research within the earth and space sciences community, as the following example illustrates.

The year 2003 witnessed in the United States the inauguration of an unprecedented multidisciplinary, earth and space science program of research: EarthScope. The National Science Foundation (NSF), the United States Geological Society (USGS), and the National Aeronautics and Space Administration (NASA) together with a number of prestigious research universities have combined resources to advance knowledge about North America's

> three-dimensional structure, and changes in that structure, through time. By integrating scientific information derived from geology, seismology, geodesy, and remote sensing, EarthScope will yield a comprehensive, time-dependent picture of the continent beyond that which any single discipline can achieve. Cutting-edge land- and space-based technologies will make it possible for the first time to resolve Earth structure and measure deformation in real-time at continental scales. These measurements will permit us to relate processes in Earth's interior to their surface expressions, including faults and volcanoes. (EarthScope Project Plan 2001, pp. 1–2)

EarthScope organizers fully expect to affect school and museum science in substantial ways, as an example of integrated science and a resource for real-world data. EarthScope is the preeminent example of "holistic" work in earth and space science. Its education and outreach components are as essential as its primary investigations because among its fundamental goals is achieving understandings of volcanoes and earthquakes needed to promote public safety, commerce, and engineering.

The profile of learning earth sciences continues to shift, as does the practice of earth and space science: from isolated, disciplinary agendas, to integrated research with outcomes of interest to the public; from separate concern for earth history and systems, to convergence upon themes essential to environmental science and education; from less reductionism to more holism; from direct instruction based upon text materials to constructivist pedagogy with access to real-world data.

LEARNING EARTH SCIENCES

Cognitive Aspects of Learning Earth Sciences

The following section describes several traditions of research about learning earth sciences. Collectively, these studies inform those whose aims are to fulfill the educational potential of learning earth sciences as part of science for all. We have grouped studies of cognitive learning in earth sciences as examples of alternative frameworks research, studies of spatial visualization, examination of temporal thinking, and investigations of systems thinking.

Alternative Frameworks of Learners Concerning Earth Sciences Concepts

The constructivist paradigm has dominated the field of science education in recent decades, producing studies of misconceptions, preconceptions, naive ideas, and alternative frameworks. Although there are relatively few published studies of students' alternative frameworks in earth sciences education, findings and patterns have emerged in four areas (see Ault, 1994, for an earlier review of this literature and related studies of "expert and novice" styles of solving earth science problems):

1. Students' conceptions of processes and mechanisms of geospheric change, including plate tectonics, the rock cycle, earthquakes, and erosion (Ault, 1984; Happs, 1985; Ross & Shuell, 1993; Bezzi & Happs, 1994; Lillo, 1994; Marques & Thompson, 1997a,b; Schoon, 1989; Gobert & Clement, 1998; Stofflett, 1994; Dove, 1997, 1999; Gobert, 2000; Kali, Orion, & Elon, 2003; Libarkin et al., 2005).
2. Students' and teachers' understanding and conceptions of the Earth's interior (DeLaughter, Stein, Stein, & Bain, 1998; Gobert & Clement, 1998; Marques & Thompson, 1997a,b; Lilio, 1994; Nottis & Ketter, 1999; King, 2000; Beilfuss, Dickerson, Boone, & Libarkin, 2004).
3. Students' and teachers' perceptions of geological deep time (Happs, 1982a,b; Marques, 1988; Oversby, 1996; Schoon, 1989; Marques Thompson, 1997a; Noonan-Pulling & Good, 1999; Trend, 1997, 1998, 2000; Dodick & Orion, 2003a, 2003b).
4. Students' and teachers' conceptions of hydrospheric processes and the water cycle (Meyer, 1987; Fetherstonhaugh & Bezzi, 1992; Brody, 1994; Taiwo, Ray, Motswiri, & Masene, 1999; Agelidou, Balafoutas, & Gialamas, 2001; Dickerson, 2003; Ben-zvi-Assaraf & Orion, 2005; Beilfuss et al., 2004).

Review of the above studies indicates that children, adolescents, and adults hold alternative frameworks in relation to almost every topic in the earth sciences. These alternative frameworks are seen across nations, cultures, and ages. Some of these frameworks emerge as students encounter difficult abstractions about the Earth in conflict with the scale of their everyday perceptions. For example, students overestimate the effect of external forces of the Earth observed directly at its surface and fail to appreciate the importance of the internal forces shaping structures. They struggle with their perceptions of geological time and spatial phenomena. Finally, they often misconceive the interior of the Earth and the state of matter within the interior of the Earth.

Review of these studies leads to another striking conclusion: the same preconceptions appear across grade levels, from kindergarten to college. These studies indicate that schooling all over the world has influenced only in a limited way the ability of students to construct scientifically sound conceptions of the Earth, congruent rather than in conflict with knowledge from the earth sciences.

Sadly, the literature suggests that many teachers hold the same alternative frameworks as their students and that even text materials foster misconceptions. Thus, it seems that earth science education in many countries is trapped in a cycle of ineffective instruction and inadequate learning—with preconceptions and misconceptions dominating learning earth sciences. Research studies about earth science education have the potential to break this nonproductive cycle.

Visualization and Spatial Reasoning

Teaching and learning earth sciences at all levels relies upon spatial reasoning. The phenomena of interest sometimes have simple geometries, though on grand scales: spiral structures of galaxies, gyres in ocean circulation, axes of synclinal folds. Sometimes the geometries are confusing: the intersection of complex topography with complicated stratigraphy, for example. Sometimes the surfaces of interest are mapped indirectly: gravitational anomalies and magnetic fields. And most confusingly, the geometries change with time.

Often earth science phenomena have challenging geometries. As a result, earth scientists use visual representations to record and study them. These representations place demand upon spatial reasoning as well. There are contour maps of a host of phenomena to master, from topography to pressure gradients, from glacial thickness to stress fields. Geologic maps contour time. Maps are two-dimensional representations yet often include data about three-dimensional structures. Seeing "through the surface" to visualize three-dimensional structure is indeed challenging. Sometimes, visualization requires skill at projecting structures from three dimensions onto two. Consider also that visual patterns among sedimentary rocks record in three dimensions events through time. In geology, visual pattern is the key to unlocking temporal puzzles.

Although the basic dependence of geoscientists on spatial abilities has long been recognized (Chadwick, 1978), the geoscience education community has only begun to explore the array of spatial reasoning abilities for learning earth sciences (McAuliffe, Hall-Wallace, Piburn, Reynolds, & Leedy, 2000). These spatial reasoning abilities may, in fact, be quite distinct from those commonly associated with tasks in learning chemistry (Dori & Barak, 2001; Pribyl & Bodner, 1987), physics (Pallrand & Seeber, 1984), and engineering (Hsi, Linn, & Bell, 1997).

The spatial objects that are studied in the geological sciences are usually large enough to walk in physically (the field learning environment). Block models can also readily represent them, as can more sophisticated renderings in a virtual setting. In the earth sciences, these blocks are visualized, but rotated, inspected, and modified to reflect temporal changes.

An understanding of deep geologic time also is associated with spatial cognition (Dodick & Orion, 2003a, 2003b). There is additional evidence that the outdoor field learning environment enhances the ability to construct a coherent narrative for layers of sedimentary rocks as experienced in the field (Orion, Ben-Chaim, & Kali, 1997; Riggs & Tretinjak, 2003).

Kali and Orion (1996) characterized the specific spatial abilities required for the study of basic structural geology. To do this they developed a geologic spatial ability test (GeoSAT), in which students were required to draw two-dimensional cross sections of geological structures that were represented as block diagrams. Their outcomes indicate that the problem solving involved in GeoSAT requires a special type of spatial visualization, which they named VPA (Visual Penetration Ability). Spatial visualization is defined as the ability to create a mental image from a "pictorially presented object" and to operate different mental manipulations on those images. The manipulations usually referred to are mental rotation and mental translation. In contrast, the manipulations involved in VPA are to visually penetrate into a three-dimensional mental image in order to envision two-dimensional cross sections.

Based on their findings about VPA, Kali and Orion developed Geo3D, a software package designed to assist high school students in developing their VPA and in acquiring the skills needed for understanding basic structural geology (Kali & Orion, 1997). Using four case studies, they showed that even with a short-term interaction with the software, students significantly improved their ability to solve the problems involved in GeoSAT. Hsi, Linn, and Bell (1997) have also demonstrated the advantage of virtual worlds and computer tools in improving learners' capability to solve problems that require spatial skills. They found that students acquired spatial skills in relatively short time with the use of technological tools.

The NSF-funded Hidden Earth Project (Reynolds et al., 2002) successfully investigated the role of spatial visualization in an introductory geology course. This project developed web-based versions of three standard visualization tests (Cube Rotation, Spatial Visualization, and Hidden Figures) and a geospatial test, containing items of the more visual aspects of geology, such as visualization of topography from contour maps. Reynolds and others developed innovative instructional modules for (1) Visualizing Topography and (2) Interactive 3D Geologic Blocks. An experimental group used these modules, and the control group did not. Although all subjects profited from both the control and the experimental conditions, the effectiveness of the treatment experienced by the experimental group was confirmed by Analysis of Variance and a comparison of normalized gain scores. Very powerful gender effects have also been demonstrated, with the experiment equalizing the performance of males and females in a case where the performance of males was initially superior to that of females. The experiment also was very effective at improving scores and lowering times to completion on the spatial visualization test.

As part of the Hidden Earth Curriculum Project, Reynolds, Piburn, and Clark (2004) conducted a detailed investigation of college student's pre-instructional knowledge, skills, and misconceptions about visualizing topography from contour maps. Students completed pre-tests and post-tests, and selected students were interviewed to assess what their initial skills and strategies were. These interviews exposed several previously unrecognized misconceptions about topographic maps, and a Topographic Visualization Instrument was developed to see how prevalent these misconceptions were in a broader sample of students.

Spatial cognition in a geoscientific problem-solving context must address more than two-dimensional representations of three-dimensional objects. In a geoscientific problem, students inspect three-dimensional objects and infer temporal histories from spatial features.

Studies in geoscience education for Native American students show that students from certain cultural backgrounds more readily learn geoscience in a field setting than do others (Riggs, 2003; Riggs & Semken, 2001). There is probably some robust connection between place-based, indigenous cultures and their success in field-based learning spatial reasoning. Clearly, experience plays an essential role in developing spatial reasoning ability.

Temporal Thinking

In the history of geology two discoveries, plate tectonics and geological time, have determined how geologists view the Earth. Geological time means the understanding (aptly referred to by John McPhee in 1980 as "deep time") that the universe has existed for countless millennia, and that humanity's earthly dominion is confined to the last milliseconds of a metaphorical geological clock.

The understanding of geological time has shaped numerous disciplines, especially geology, cosmology, and evolutionary biology (Dodick & Orion, 2003c). Roseman (1992) noted in a review of the literature of science education that there "was next to nothing about . . . how kids' understanding of notions of systems, scale or models develop over time" (p. 218). Since that time, there have been several large-scale studies of how students understand this concept. They divide roughly into two groups: "event-based studies" and "logic-based studies."

Event-based studies include all research that surveys student understanding of the vast duration of "deep time" (that is, time beginning with the formation of the Earth or the universe). In such studies, the general task is sequencing a series of events (for example, the first appearance of life on Earth) absolutely, along a time line, or relatively, using picture-sorting tasks. Often the subject is asked to justify his or her reasons for the proposed temporal order. Such studies include: Noonan-Pulling and Good's (1999) research on the understanding of the origins of Earth and life among junior high students; a similar study by Marques and Thompson (1997a) with Portuguese students; and Trend's studies on the conception of geological time among 10–11-year-old children (Trend, 1997, 1998), 17-year-old students (Trend, 2001b), and primary teacher trainees (Trend 2000, 2001a).

Qualitative research (structured interviews) with small sample groups dominates the literature. There has never been a large-scale, quantitative study of older students' (junior high to senior high) understanding of geological time.

In logic-based studies, the researcher is interested in the cognitive processes undergone by students when they are confronted with problems of geologic time. It might be added that such studies are more concerned with probing the subject's logical processes rather than his or her knowledge of earth science.

This approach is seen in the work of Ault (1981, 1982) and Dodick and Orion (2003a, 2003b). Ault interviewed a group of 40 students from grades kindergarten, two, four, and six, using a series of puzzles that tested how they understood (and could reconstruct) a series of geological strata. Based on Zwart's (1976) suggestion that the development of people's temporal understanding lies in the before and after relationship, Ault (1981) theorized that children organize geological time relationally.

Based on his findings, Ault (1981, 1982) claimed that young (grade 2–6) children's concept of conventional time in a logical sense (reasoning about before and after) was no impediment to their understanding of geologic events. Many of the children in his test group were successful at solving puzzles involving skills necessary to understanding the logic, though not the extent, of geological time. Nonetheless, in the field, these same children had difficulties in solving similar types of problems, indicating that there was little transfer from classroom problems to authentic geological settings. Children believed rock layers in the field to be old, based upon their being dark or crumbly—not based upon their position in a series of strata.

Piaget's (1969) work on time cognition influenced and restricted Ault's (1981) research design. According to Piaget, a young child's understanding of time is tightly bound to his or her concept of motion; thus, the research problems he used were taken from physics. However, geological science builds its knowledge of time through visual interpretation of *static* entities (formations, fossils; Frodeman, 1995, 1996). Indeed, there is no reason to suggest that an understanding of the (logical) relationships among strata should necessarily allow one to both conceptualize and internalize the entirety of geological time.

Dodick and Orion (2003a, 2003b) conducted a large-scale study with junior high and high school students using validated, reliable quantitative tools. In this study, geological time was divided into two different concepts:

1. A (passive) temporal framework in which large-scale geological events occur. Such understanding depends upon building connections between events and time. In the cognitive literature this is comparable to Friedman's (1982) associative networks, a system of temporal processing used for storing information on points in time. By this reasoning, an understanding of geological time should be mitigated by a person's knowledge of such events.

2. A logical understanding of geological time used to reconstruct past environments and organisms based on a series of scientific principles. This is similar to the work done in logic-based studies, noted above. Based on this definition, it might seem that students unfamiliar with geology might be unable to reconstruct a depositional system; however, in structure, geo-logic is comparable to Montagnero's (1992, 1996) model of "diachronic thinking." He defines diachronic thinking as the capacity to represent transformations over time; such thinking is activated, for example, when a child attempts to reconstruct the growth (and decay) cycle of a tree.

Montagnero (1996) argues that there are four schemes, which are activated when one attempts to reconstruct transformational sequences. Dodick and Orion translated three of these schemes into the logical skills needed to solve temporal problems about geological strata:

1. *Transformation*: This scheme defines a principle of change, whether qualitative or quantitative. In geology it is understood through the principle of actualism (i.e., the present as key to the past).

2. *Temporal Organization*: This scheme defines the sequential order of stages in a transformational process. In geology, principles based on the three-dimensional relationship among strata (ex: superposition) are used in determining temporal organization.

3. *Interstage Linkage*: The connections between the successive stages of transformational phenomena. In geology such stages are reconstructed via the combination of actualism and causal reasoning.

For the purposes of this research, Montagnero designed a specialized (validated) instrument, the GeoTAT, consisting of a series of open puzzles that tested the subject's understanding of diachronic schemes as applied to geological settings.

In addition, two other questionnaires were distributed to subunits of this population to answer questions that arose through the use of the GeoTAT: (a) a Time-Spatial Test (or TST), which tested the possibility that spatial thinking influences temporal thinking and (b) a Stratigraphic Factors Test (SFT), which tested the influence of (geological strata) dimensions on students' temporal understanding. In addition, researchers pursued qualitative research in the classroom and field by studying and interviewing students who were studying geology and paleontology as part of their matriculation studies.

From this study Montagnero constructed a model of temporal thinking. This model identified abilities needed to reconstruct geological features in time:

1. The transformation scheme, which influences the other two diachronic schemes.
2. Knowledge, most importantly empirical knowledge (such as the relationship between environment and rock type) and organizational knowledge (i.e., dimensional change).
3. Extracognitive factors, such as spatial-visual ability, that influence how a subject temporally organizes three-dimensional structures such as geological strata.

Among students who were not taking geology as part of their school program, it was seen that there was a significant difference between samples composed of high school and ninth-grade students (on the one hand) and seventh-grade students (on the other) in their ability to understand geological phenomena with the use of diachronic thinking. This suggests that somewhere between grades 7 and 8 it should be possible to start teaching some of the logical principles permitting one to reconstruct geological structures. These include complex superposition (consisting of tilted strata) and correlation (two outcrop problems), which rely on the use of isolated diachronic schemes, as well the integrated use of all the diachronic schemes to solve complex problems of deposition.

Moreover, this research shows that the ability to think diachronically can be improved if practiced in the context of learning earth sciences. A comparison of high school (grade 11–12) geology and non-geology majors indicated that the former group held a significant advantage over the latter in solving problems involving diachronic thinking. This relationship was especially strengthened by the second year of geological study (grade 12), with the key factor in this improvement (probably) being exposure to fieldwork. Fieldwork both improved students' ability to understand the three-dimensional factors influencing temporal organization and provided them with experience in learning about the types of evidence that are critical in reconstructing a transformational sequence.

The work of Riggs and Tretinjak (2003) supports this finding. Riggs and Tretinjak studied a non-majors course in earth science for pre-service elementary school teachers. They were able to show that integrated field investigations enhance higher-order content knowledge in geoscience, specifically the understanding of environmental change through time as read from the sedimentary rock record. Prior to the field trip students could identify past environments from sedimentary rock, but only after completing the fieldwork unit were they able to understand these rocks as a dynamic temporal/historical record. This is consistent with the findings of Dodick and Orion (2003a, 2003b), who found a correlation between the understanding of geologic time and spatial ability, which in turn implies that well-designed geologic fieldwork will enhance both, even for non-majors. There currently is no comparable data of this nature for geoscience majors, nor do we fully understand the reasons for this correlation among temporal/spatial/and field abilities.

In addition to the studies mentioned above, one might add the small body of research that catalogues general misconceptions in geology and includes within its parameters problems related to geological time (Happs, 1982a,b; Marques, 1988; Oversby, 1996; Schoon, 1989). Finally, one might note those works that have focused on the practical elements of teaching the scale of time (Everitt, Good, & Pankiewicz, 1996; Hume, 1978; Metzger, 1992; Ritger & Cummins, 1991; Rowland, 1983; Spencer-Cervato & Day, 2000). Unfortunately, these teaching models have never been critically evaluated, so they are of untested value to the pedagogic literature.

Systems Thinking

Current earth science education is characterized by a shift toward a systems approach to teaching and curriculum development (Mayer, 2002). Earth science educators call for reexamination of the teaching and learning of traditional earth science in the context of the many environmental and social issues facing the planet (IGEO, 1997). Orion (1998, 2002) claimed that since the natural environment is a system of interacting natural subsystems, students should understand that any manipulation in one part of this complex system might cause an effect in another part, sometimes in ways that are quite unexpected.

Systems thinking is regarded as a type of higher order thinking required in scientific, technological, and everyday domains. Therefore, researchers in many fields have studied systems thinking extensively, for example, in the social sciences (e.g., Senge, 1998), in medicine (e.g., Faughnan & Elson, 1998), in psychology (e.g., Emery, 1992), in decision making (e.g., Graczyk, 1993), in project management (e.g., Lewis, 1998), in engineering (e.g., Fordyce, 1988), and in mathematics (e.g., Ossimitz, 2000). However, little is known about systems thinking in the context of science education.

During the late 1990s and the beginning of this decade three studies were conducted at the Weizmann Institute of Science in relation to system thinking as part of the field of learning earth sciences. Gudovitch and Orion (2001) studied systems thinking in high school students and developed a system-oriented curriculum in the context of the carbon cycle. Kali, Orion, and Elon (2003) studied the effect of a knowledge integration activity on junior high school students' systems thinking, characterizing students' conceptions of the rock cycle as an example of systems thinking. Ben-zvi-Assaraf and Orion (2004) explored the development of system thinking skills at the junior high school level in the context of the hydro (water) cycle.

Gudovitch (1997) examined students' prior knowledge and perceptions concerning global environmental problems in general and the role of people among natural systems in particular. Importantly, the curriculum in this study provided a means of stimulating students to explore the carbon cycle system. Gudovitch found that students' progress with systems thinking consisted of four stages:

1. The first stage includes an acquaintance with the different Earth systems and an awareness of the material transformation between these systems.
2. The second stage includes an understanding of specific processes causing this material transformation.

3. The third stage includes an understanding of the reciprocal relationships between the systems.
4. The fourth stage includes a perception of the system as a whole.

Ault (1998) referred to drawing conclusions about past events as "retrodiction" (a term drawn from Kitts, 1977) as opposed to prediction. Often retrodictions follow from observations of phenomena in present time presumed to sample what has happened through time. The challenge is "to hypothesize an arrangement by stages for what is observed" (p. 196). Stages stand for periods of time; retrodiction and stage inference go hand in hand. Coral atolls, arc volcanoes, and river basins are often explained as developing through stages over time. Examples of a volcano, coral atoll, or river basin at any stage of development exist in the present. Hence, place substitutes for time in order to make retrodictions; one example is another's future.

Kali, Orion, and Elon (2003) claimed that understanding the rock cycle is exactly such a challenge and that such a challenge requires systems thinking. They studied seventh-grade students who participated in learning a 40-hour unit. The main challenge was to assist students in understanding the rock cycle as a system, rather than a set of facts about the Earth's crust.

Kali, Orion, and Elon (2003) reported that while answering an open-ended questionnaire about the rock cycle, students expressed a systems-thinking continuum, ranging from a completely static view of the system to an understanding of the system's cyclic nature. They suggested placing dynamic thinking (which is a critical aspect of systems thinking) on a continuum, in which one side represents a static view and the opposite side represents a highly dynamic view of the system. On top of this continuum they superimposed a dimension of interconnectedness. In the case of the rock cycle, they based higher, more dynamic understanding upon making connections between parts of the system. At the low end of this continuum they located students who expressed a lack of connectedness between parts of the system, indicated poor dynamic thinking, and represented a completely static view of the rock cycle system. At the opposite end of the continuum there were the students who thought dynamically about material transformation within the rock cycle and therefore demonstrated a rich understanding of the interconnectedness between parts of the system. With such a view students were able to grasp the holistic idea that any material in a system can be a product of any other material and apply this insight to novel situations.

It is important to note that students' alternative incorrect models of the rock cycle described above were not interpreted as misconceptions, or naive theories, about the Earth's crust. Rather, placing these models on a continuum reflects the view that such models can serve as the basis for developing more sophisticated models, until the highest level of understanding the cyclic nature of the system is reached.

Ben-zvi-Assaraf and Orion (2005) used a large battery of qualitative and quantitative research tools in order to explore the development of systems-thinking skills of junior high school students who studied the water cycle as part of the "Blue Planet" program. The pre-test findings indicated that most of the students sampled experienced substantial difficulties in all aspects of systems thinking. They even struggled to identify basic system components. They entered the eighth grade holding an incomplete and naive perception of the water cycle and were only acquainted with the atmospheric component of the cycle (i.e., evaporation, condensation, and rainfall). They ignored the groundwater, biospheric, and environmental components. Moreover, they lacked the dynamic and cyclic perceptions of the system and the ability to create a meaningful relationship among the system components as stages linked through processes. Ben-zvi-Assaraf and Orion (2005) found the same phenomenon of disconnected "islands of knowledge" that Kali, Orion, and Elon (2003) reported in reference to how students conceived of the rock cycle. Most of the students were not able to link the various components of the water cycle together into a coherent network of processes and stages. Some of them demonstrated an ability to create a relationship between several components, but even those students were not able to draw a complete network of relationships.

The post-test findings indicated that most of the students shifted from a fragmented conception of the water cycle toward a more holistic view. About 70% of the students who initially grasped only the atmospheric component of the water cycle significantly increased their familiarity with the other stages and processes of the water cycle. For about half of the students, this knowledge improved their ability to identify relationships among the stages and processes of the water cycle. The classification of students' achievements indicated that the development of systems thinking in the context of the earth systems consists of several sequential stages arranged in a hierarchical pyramid structure. The findings of a hierarchical notion and the interrelationships between dynamic perception and cyclic perception are in accordance with the studies of Kali, Orion, and Elon (2003) and Gudovitch (1997). Thus, it suggested that these findings might be generalized to the study of the earth systems. In light of the findings and conclusions of the above studies, it is suggested that the following aspects might contribute to improvement of students' abilities to develop systems thinking:

1. Focusing on inquiry-based learning.
2. Using the outdoor learning environment for the construction of a concrete model of a natural system.
3. Using knowledge integration activities throughout the learning process.

There are interesting connections among the several cognitive studies mentioned above. For example, Dodick and Orion (1993a) reported an interrelationship between temporal thinking ability and spatial thinking ability. Orion, Ben-Chaim, and Kali (1997) and Riggs and Tretinjak (2003) determined that geological outdoor experiences tended to increase students' spatial thinking abilities. Ben-zvi-Assaraf and Orion (1994) found systems thinking about the Earth to be related to temporal thinking (retrospective thinking) and spatial perception (the ability to perceive the hidden parts of a system). Here again, the outdoor learning environment turned out to be a very effective tool for developing a concrete, realistic perception of nature serving as a cognitive bridge for the development of abstract thought: temporal, spatial, and systems thinking. Moreover, all of the above studies acknowledged the significance of alternative frameworks and experiences that most students bring to earth science classes (no matter what age), thus indicating the need to respond to preconceptions and misconceptions with appropriate instruction, whether in the laboratory, the outdoors, or the classroom, or when working with computers.

Despite the limited amount of research about learning earth sciences, a holistic framework has emerged to guide teachers who work within an earth systems approach. Holism in this sense refers not only to the systems approach, but also to the interconnectedness of spatial reasoning and temporal thinking and the cultivation of environmental insight.

The Integration of Learning Environments within the Earth Sciences

An important characteristic of earth science education (and other sciences as well) is the potential to conduct formal teaching in a variety of learning environments: the classroom, the laboratory, the outdoors (field site, museum, or industrial site), and the virtual worlds of computers.

The outdoor learning environment. Review of the proceedings of the three International Geosciences Education Organization international conferences on geoscience education (IGEO, 1997, 2000, 2003) indicates worldwide agreement on the central place of the outdoor learning environment within earth science education.

Orion (1993a) suggested a holistic model that connects the outdoor and the indoor learning environments. The guiding principle of this model is a gradual progression from the concrete levels of the curriculum toward its more abstract components. This model can be used for designing a whole curriculum, a course, or a small set of learning activities (Orion, 1986, 1991).

Orion's holistic model combines indoor and outdoor environments. In this model the learning process begins with a "meaning construction" session. In this session, students converse, with guidance by the teacher, to discover what interests them about a particular subject. Depending on the subject and the school's location, this stage takes place in a relevant outdoor environment or in a versatile indoor space.

According to Orion (1993), the main role of an outdoor learning activity in the learning process is to offer direct experience with concrete phenomena and materials. Familiarity with properties and possibilities is the principal outcome—the raw material for forming concepts and posing questions. Kempa and Orion (1996) add that the outdoor learning environment may introduce the methodology of field research from disciplines such as biology, ecology, and geology. Thus, the goal of the outdoor learning environment includes two main objectives: (a) learning basic concrete concepts through direct interaction with the environment and (b) learning field investigation methodology.

One point is most crucial to understand: the outdoor learning environment addresses phenomena and processes that *cannot be cultivated indoors*. The outdoors, however, is a very complicated learning environment and includes a large number of stimuli that can easily distract students from meaningful learning.

Consider a location where students find that an outcrop reveals an anticline. They begin to infer geological processes that might have produced this structure. Are they ready to approach this task? Or is the challenge too novel? Many of the concepts useful to drawing conclusions about the anticlinal structure (sedimentation, superposition, and initial horizontality) can be better explained through lab observations and simulations. Following the understanding of these concepts, students who arrive at this specific outcrop can conclude that the layers are not located in their original setting. Then, through a field observation they might decipher the anticline structure. From this point, a better understanding of the three-dimensional nature of a folded structure as well as the folding mechanism can be effectively achieved through the use of computer software and hand-held models (Kali & Orion, 1997).

The main aim of the initial indoor phase is to prepare the students for their outdoor learning activities. This preparation reduces what Orion and Hofstein (1994) term the "novelty space" of an outdoor setting (Fig. 23.1). Novelty space consists of three factors: cognitive, geographical, and psychological. The cognitive novelty depends on the concepts and skills that students are asked to deal with throughout the outdoor learning experience. The geographical novelty reflects the acquaintance of the students with the outdoor physical area. The psychological novelty is the gap between the students' expectations and the reality that they face during the outdoor learning event.

The novelty space concept has a very clear implication for planning and conducting outdoor learning experiences. It defines the scope of preparation required for an educational field trip. Preparation that considers the three novelty factors reduces the novelty space to a minimum, thus facilitating meaningful learning during the field trip. Working with the materials that the students will meet in the field and conducting simulations of geological processes through laboratory experiments directly reduces cognitive novelty. To reduce the geographic and psychological novelty of the outdoor learning experience, teachers may turn first to slides, films, and maps, and second to detailed information about the event. Students should know the purpose of outdoor learning, the learning method, the number of learning sta-

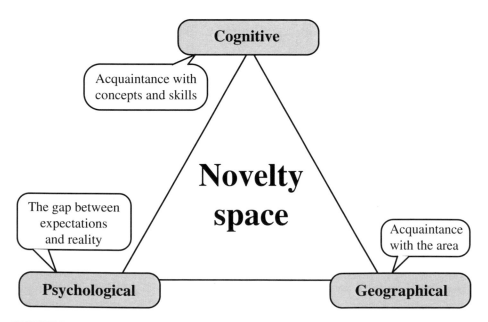

FIGURE 23–1. The three dimensions, which identify the novelty space of an outdoor learning activity.

tions, the length of time, the expected weather conditions, the expected difficulties along the route, etc. Safety briefing is a must as well.

The next phase in this cycle is the outdoor learning activity. The curriculum materials for the outdoor learning experience should lead students to interact directly with the phenomenon and only secondarily, if at all, with the teacher. The teacher's role is to act as a mediator between the students and the concrete phenomena. Some of the students' questions can be answered on the spot, but only those that might be answered according to the evidence uncovered at the specific outdoor site. Otherwise time and resources, including the students' attention, are wasted on activities that might be done elsewhere. Lectures, discussions, and long summaries should be postponed until the next phase, which is better conducted in an indoor environment.

Marques, Paria, and Kempa (2003) explored Orion's model within the Portuguese earth sciences curriculum. Their study supported the importance of preparation for the outdoor learning experience. Furthermore, they found a positive influence of this learning environment on students' learning. However, their study also highlighted the difficulties teachers faced in adapting to the novel, outdoor learning environment.

Geo3D software (Kali & Orion, 1996) clearly illustrates an example of the indoor-outdoor cycle. The design of this software fosters the development of spatial visualization skill. Most geological outcrops hide elements of the three-dimensional configuration of geological structure. Even having observed a structure such as an anticline in the field, most students have difficulty perceiving its three-dimensional form. Thus, the outdoors is not as suitable a learning environment as a computer simulation for the development of spatial visualization (Kali & Orion, 1996). However, without previous concrete outdoors experience with geological structures, such software loses much of its relevance for many students.

Integrating inquiry and the laboratory learning environment.   Although there are many laboratory-based earth science units for various age levels all over the world, little has been published concerning the role of the laboratory learning environment within earth science education.

A review of many such lab-based units indicates that the main role of the laboratory is to demonstrate or simulate the Earth's processes. However, little has been published concerning the influence of simulations on the development of misconceptions among school students.

The earth science laboratory environment has great potential to contribute to the development of the skills of scientific inquiry reasoning. Inquiry in the geosciences has a unique characteristic: its "experiments" in the grandest sense have already been conducted by nature. They are unfundable and unreplicable. No one can send glacial ice across a continent or carve a Grand Canyon. Consequently, many geological inquiries are of a retrospective type—trying to unravel what happened in the past, using "fingerprints" left on the Earth.

Frodeman (1995) describes geology as an interpretive and historical science that "embodies distinctive methodology within the sciences." He further argues that "the geologist picks up on the clues of past events and processes in a way analogous to how the physician interprets the signs of illness or the detective builds a circumstantial case against a defendant" (p. 963). Edelson, Gordin, and Pea (1999) describe the geosciences as "observational sciences" that emphasize comparisons and contrasts among features of the Earth in different times and places. Inference based upon comparison and contrast, especially when considered across different scales in time and place, differs from inference based upon the results of experimentation (Ault, 1998). Both approaches are empirical, quantitative, and subject to scrutiny by rules of logic. They offer different milieus for illustrating the meaning of some of the most basic constructs of scientific thinking: for example, observations, hypotheses, and conclusions.

A traditional method for categorizing inquiry curricula is to analyze the degree of structure or openness of the activities they include (Schwab, 1962; Herron, 1971; German et al., 1996). With such methods, inquiry-based curricula can be placed anywhere on a continuum extending from completely structured curricula on one side to completely open curricula on the other.

Those who advocate inquiry in the science curricula for all accept that the educational system ought to enable students to design, conduct, and analyze their own investigations, then communicate their findings. However, the appropriate stages for engaging students in open inquiry are not clear, nor are the means for bringing students to a stage in which they will be able autonomously to design and conduct their own experiments. While some researchers suggest designing a variety of activities to suit a diversity of cognitive developmental stages in a classroom (e.g., Germann, 1989), others suggest preparing students for open inquiry by engaging them with well-structured investigations (e.g., Edelson et al., 1999).

One of the rarely asked questions regarding inquiry learning concerns the cognitive prerequisites necessary for using open inquiry methods. Elshout and Veenman (1992) claim that "In unguided-discovery learning, one expects high metacognitive skill and intellectual ability to be essential requisites to keep the learning process going" (p. 135). It is therefore reasonable to claim that students should understand the meaning of some of the most basic concepts used in scientific methodologies before they can begin an independent inquiry process. Such understanding provides the means for making hypotheses, designing experiments, collecting and analyzing data, and reporting their findings. Unfortunately, evidence exists indicating that students in junior and senior high schools have severe difficulties in understanding the essence of the scientific method. They have, in effect, failed to learn scientific method as a content with its own concepts and principles. Zohar (1998) reported that junior high school students had difficulties in understanding the difference between their experimental results and their conclusions. Solomon, Duveen, and Hall (1994) reported that high school students had difficulties in distinguishing between descriptions and causal explanations. Tamir (1989) claims that "Students do not understand the concepts that underlie the processes of scientific investigations. These concepts (e.g., hypothesis, control) are not easy to understand" (p. 61).

Learning earth sciences has a role to play in remedying this situation. Orion and Kali (2005) suggest that earth sciences education has the potential to provide students, at beginning stages of their science education, with basic inquiry skills that are required for further open-ended inquiry endeavors. They developed a 34-hour lab-based curriculum unit for junior high school students, focusing on geological processes that transform the materials within the crust of the Earth—"The Rock Cycle"—and organized this curriculum into nine structured inquiry modules. To foster students' awareness of the different inquiry routes embedded in the inquiry modules, each of the modules was followed by a MIR (Metacognitive Inquiry Reconstruction) assignment. In these activities linguistic terms were used as organizing schemes. Students examined their investigation with "scientific inquiry spectacles" and categorized different stages of the inquiry with terms such as *observations, hypotheses,* and *conclusions.*

Orion and Kali (2005) tested the influence of learning an inquiry-based "Rock Cycle" curriculum and its accompanying MIR activities on student ability to distinguish between observations, hypotheses, and conclusions on a sample of 582 students in seventh and eighth grade from 21 classes sharing 14 teachers at 8 junior high schools in Israel. The schools represented urban, suburban, and rural societies. The study used a large battery of qualitative and quantitative research tools in a pre-test/post-test structure.

The pre-test outcomes indicated that the seventh- and eighth-grade students included in this study had considerable difficulty in understanding concepts underlying the scientific method. The large and significant pre-post differences found in many of the classes indicated the high potential for an inquiry-based "Rock Cycle" program to develop and distinguish among three basic elements of scientific thinking (observations, hypotheses, conclusions).

The large improvement in students' scientific thinking skills, found in many of the classes, might have been a result of students' engagement with the unique inquiry methods of geoscience. Students focused their tangible observations on materials of the Earth. They drew conclusions from "experiments" that were conducted by nature in the past and did not design their own investigations.

However, Orion and Kali also found no improvement among classes taught by teachers who did not properly adopt the inquiry-based teaching strategy. These teachers taught the "Rock Cycle" unit in their traditional manner. Appropriate curriculum materials are not sufficient in themselves for inducing cognitive development among students. Sometimes teachers are the limiting factor in students' ability to exploit the potential of "The Rock Cycle" in developing scientific thinking skills.

Research and the Development of Curriculum Materials

The main goal of earth science education is to improve the way students learn about and understand our planet. In this section we report in detail about a curriculum for teaching the water cycle from an earth systems and environmental insight perspective. The curriculum "The Blue Planet" emerged from a "design research" effort.

Edelson, Gordin, and Pea (2004) advocate for "design research" as a powerful model for the development of effective learning tools. They used this model to develop inquiry-based software for the study of climatology through visualization. In design research, the study of learning takes place in the context of designing and revising curriculum materials based upon careful study of student response to these materials.

Orion's (2002) helical model of research, curriculum development, and implementation is similar. In this model, each curriculum development effort starts with a pre-development study to identify misconceptions, preconceptions, and learning difficulties associated with the specific subject. The findings from this stage serve as a basis for the first curriculum development phase. An implementation phase follows curriculum development. The implementation phase involves in-service training for a small number of teachers who will teach the curriculum to their classes.

An evaluation study follows the implementation stage. The results of the evaluation inform the second iteration of curriculum development. In turn, this phase is followed by a wider implementation cycle.

Pre-development of "The Blue Planet" Curriculum

Based upon Orion's helical model, research preceded and followed development for eighth-grade students of an earth systems unit on the hydrosphere, "The Blue Planet." In order to examine students' prior knowledge and understanding in relation to the water cycle, a "zoom-in" analysis was conducted. Quantitative research tools were used with a large sample in order to obtain a general picture of students' knowledge and perceptions. Later, qualitative research tools were used with a smaller, randomly selected sample in order to gain insight into student misconceptions and to validate the quantitative tools.

Review of the literature concerning the predevelopment phase revealed that in spite of the crucial importance of water from the environmental perspective, most of the studies that have been conducted in this area have concentrated on students' perceptions of the physical aspects of the water cycle, namely, changes in the water state (Bar, 1989; Bar & Travis, 1991). An ERIC search in 2002 revealed only a few published studies that focused on children's perceptions of the water cycle in the environmental context of the Earth. Agelidou, Balafoutas, and Gialamas (2001) reported that students do not perceive how human activities are related to water problems and their consequences. Specifically, they do not recognize the principal factors responsible for these problems. Fetherstonhaugh and Bezzi (1992) reported that after 11 years of schooling, students could only present simplistic and naïve conceptions of the water cycle. Moreover, the students showed a poor and inadequate scientific understanding of groundwater as a part of the water cycle.

Brody (1994) conducted a meta-analysis study of about 30 articles published between 1983 and 1992 that dealt with difficulties of middle and high-school students in understanding different subjects connected with water. Only a few of those articles dealt with the environmental aspects of water, whereas at least 80% of them focused on the following three areas of difficulty:

1. Understanding chemical and physical processes such as condensation, evaporation, and the molecular structure of water.
2. Understanding the significance of water for processes that take place in living organisms.
3. Understanding interdisciplinary subjects such as water resources, and the social and scientific linkages of these topics.

Taiwo, Ray, Motswiri, and Masene (1999) confirmed that students' perceptions of the water cycle were influenced by their cultural beliefs and to a large extent by their pseudoscientific knowledge about cloud formation and rainfall. Barker (1998) reported that in spite of the fact that about 90% of the water absorbed by the roots is lost by evaporation, mainly through the leaves, 50% of the students in his study claimed that plants retain all the water that they absorb.

Transcription and qualitative analysis of the questionnaires from the predevelopment study for the Blue Planet curriculum indicated that most of the students demonstrated an incomplete picture of the water cycle and held many misconceptions about it. Children who drew the water cycle usually represented the upper part of the water cycle (evaporation, condensation, and rainfall) and ignored the groundwater system. More than 50% of the students could not identify components of the groundwater system even when they were familiar with the associated terminology. In their mind, underground water was a static, subsurface lake. Furthermore, they imagined that water chemistry was constant throughout the entire water cycle (no purification by evaporation). Presumably, environmental insight regarding water pollution and water conservation requires connecting the stages of the water cycle to the processes that modify water quality and abundance. The water cycle alterative frameworks held by more than 50% of the students do not bode well for learning environmental insights.

Cyclic thinking correlated significantly with drawing the water cycle to include its groundwater component. A student who drew the underground water system held the following concept about the cyclic nature of the water cycle: "I absolutely disagree. There is no starting point and no end point in the water cycle. It is a continuous process."

Development and Evaluation of the "The Blue Planet" Curriculum

The findings of the pre-development study served as a basis for the development of an interdisciplinary program named "The Blue Planet." This program focused on the water cycle as an example of the relationships seen among the various earth systems. Students were asked to create concept maps at the beginning and end of the learning process. Comparison of the number and type of items between the concept maps served as a measure of changes in students' knowledge and understanding of processes. The number of connections within the concept map served as an indication of students' understanding of the relationship between the components of the water cycle (Edmondson, 1999). In addition, regular observations were conducted in the classes.

Observations indicated that teachers concentrated primarily on scientific principles and only very little on the cognitive aspects of the connections between the water cycle and other earth systems, or between the water cycle and environmental case studies. In addition, most teachers tended to ignore the constructivist activities developed in light of the findings of the pre-development study. These were activities intended to correct students' misconceptions and to develop a broader, more coherent conception of the water cycle within an earth systems context.

A significant improvement was found in the student's level of knowledge, namely acquaintance with the components of the water cycle. A significant improvement was found in relation to students' understanding of the evaporation process. However, in relation to all the other processes, only a minor improvement was found.

The analysis of the cyclic and systemic thinking questionnaires showed some improvements in students' understanding of interrelationship among earth systems. However, even after completing The Blue Planet program, poor understanding of the systemic nature of the water cycle dominated student thinking. Most of the students demonstrated a fragmented conception of the water cycle and made no connections between the atmospheric stages of the water cycle and the geospheric (underground) stages of the water cycle.

These findings indicate that improvement in knowledge falls short of the development of environmental insight. For environmental insight, students must develop cyclic and systemic thinking about what happens to water in the air, on the Earth's surface, and underground. Teachers should not overlook activities developed directly for this purpose. Although such activities were provided, teachers tended to ignore them. They need to understand that simply gaining knowledge about the components of the water cycle does not contribute to progress in the development of environmental insight.

PEDAGOGICAL INERTIA AND THE STRUGGLE FOR PARADIGM SHIFT

The science for all paradigm holds promise around the globe. However, its implementation will take decades—perhaps until the return of Haley's Comet in 2061. For learning earth sciences, science for all means cultivating environmental insight through the study of earth systems.

For teachers to move from traditional science teaching to proper earth systems teaching, they must change their goals for student learning, the contents of their curricula, and their approaches to instruction. Clearly, this shift constitutes a major change in philosophy, from reductionism and disciplinary-driven schooling toward holism and attention to educating students for lives of social responsibility within democratic societies. The shift demands something more: that properly trained teachers actually teach earth science subjects, an area in which many science teachers in many countries have little or no scientific background (King, 2003; Orion, 2003b). Furthermore, students learn these subjects best—and often can only learn field methodologies of investigation—when teachers make use of the outdoor learning environment. Most traditional science teaching ignores this environment.

The task to be accomplished exceeds what we might expect of professional development. It requires participation and commitment on many levels, from community and school to business and academia.

Orion (2003b) has reported on the outcome of a long-term (10 years) study within the "storm's eye" of the new Israeli "Science for All" curricula for junior high and high school. This intensive work included participating in the committees that designed the new "Science for All" curricula for junior high and high school; taking a central role in a team that has developed learning materials for these two programs; and leading and taking a practical role in hundreds of in-service training hours in each of the 10 years, both in in-service training centers and in the teachers' schools and classes.

This decade of investigation has produced four Ph.D. dissertations (Kali & Orion, 2003; Dodick & Orion, 2003b; Ben-zvi-Assaraf & Orion, 2005; Kapulnick,

Orion, & Gniel, 2004) and one master's thesis (Midyan, 2003). Altogether, these different studies examined the practice of science teaching and learning for about 1000 science teachers and their students. Most of the studies were conducted at the junior high school level but also included teachers and students from the elementary and the high school levels. In addition to observing teachers and evaluating student learning, these studies addressed systemic reform from the points of view of principals, superintendents, curriculum developers, academic scientists, the ministry of education, as well as in-service training and pre-service education programs for teachers.

From each of these studies came the conclusion that despite their participation in long-term, in-service training programs, the vast majority of the teachers did not undergo genuine professional development. Professional inertia was the rule. Results indicated a clear gap between teachers' perceptions of their development as expressed through questionnaires and interviews and their actual teaching practice.

In addition to teachers' reluctance to implement new teaching methods and incorporate new scientific topics, the interviews uncovered four additional factors preventing them from genuinely implementing reform. They felt, in general, apprehension toward change and that professional training institutes did not provide them with the practical tools needed to overcome their apprehension. Teachers believed that school administrators failed to provide them with the resources necessary for reform, such as laboratory equipment, smaller class sizes in the laboratory, computers, and access to outdoor learning environments. Reform placed, in their judgment, inordinate demands upon their time. Finally, teachers faulted the Ministry of Education and its science education inspectors for a double standard. On the one hand, the Ministry initiated reform and inspectors encouraged participation. On the other hand, resources were not forthcoming and the Ministry called upon the inspectors to implement a national testing regime. The focus of testing tended to institutionalize objectives antithetical to the Science for All paradigm and the earth systems approach.

The world is complicated and diverse, and the Israeli example is that of just one nation. Movement toward an earth systems approach in keeping with the spirit of the Science for All paradigm is a change many teachers cannot or do not really want to undergo. Yet the conflict between reform efforts and testing priorities is worrisome and is certainly experienced elsewhere. Most importantly, the Israeli case illustrates the need for research in science education to address many contexts, from integrating curriculum to changing teaching paradigms.

CONCLUSION

The first decade of the twenty-first century finds earth science education in a more central place in science curricula than a decade before. The progress of earth science in schools all over the world is closely related to its central role in the development of environmental insight among future citizens. However, the ability of educators to establish earth science as a sustainable course of study in schools is highly dependent on the ability of science teachers to overcome many barriers, including their own lack of background and the persistently low stature of the field. This low stature is a function of the failure to understand "what's so special about learning earth sciences."

Learning earth sciences offers the distinct potential of seeing through the landscape and through time. Its many subjects unite to conceive of the world as dynamic, interacting systems, themselves composed of stabilizing cycles. These systems operate on many scales in time and place, some so vast as to challenge the limits of imagination. The earth sciences represent phenomena of interest in visual forms: contour maps, block diagrams, and virtual worlds of the interior earth, its surface features, its motion in space, and its changing climate. These representations place distinctive demands on the cognitive capacities of learners. Making sense of Earth's processes and patterns, structures and changes, and systems and cycles depends upon visualization and spatial reasoning as well as recognizing bias in the human-scale perception of events.

Understanding how the Earth works requires retrospection and retrodiction—making inferences about the past. By interpreting the present as the outcome of natural experiments on vast scales and sleuthing out its causal history, earth sciences set the stage for making extrapolations about possible futures. These extrapolations inform our actions with information about risks, from seismic to atmospheric. On local, regional, and global scales humans interact with earth's natural systems, becoming agents of geologic, climatic, and evolutionary change. This power carries heavy responsibility; learning earth sciences offers lessons students need in order to develop their capacity to exercise this responsibility as environmental insight.

This chapter presents a holistic view of earth sciences education and a holistic perspective for achieving meaningful learning of the earth sciences. This perspective combines an educational vision (development of environmental insight through adopting the earth systems approach) together with a research agenda (curriculum development for outdoor and indoor, laboratory and computer, as well as classroom, learning environments). This vision and agenda acknowledge the challenge of preparing teachers for the implementation of new curriculum materials and adoption of teaching strategies and tactics appropriate for each learning environment.

The vision encompasses how learning earth sciences may contribute to gaining insight into the nature of scientific investigation and scientific reasoning in several contexts. Nevertheless, the conclusion remains that depending upon the earth science disciplines in isolation, either from each other or from the humanities and social sciences, to set the agenda for learning earth sciences will fail to serve the public good. We need to respect students, their families, and their communities as sources of ideas, issues, and problems to solve through application of knowledge about earth systems.

Research has a central role in this holistic plan. It should provide an understanding of students' difficulties with the learning process and identify the appropriate learning and teaching strategies for overcoming cognitive barriers to spatial and temporal thinking, to retrospection, to understanding phenomena across scales, to integrating several subjects, and to developing the cognitive capacity for systems thinking. In addition, the research agenda should provide the basis for the development of curriculum materials, the sequencing of learning, and productive paths for teachers to follow in overcoming internally and externally imposed barriers to reform. We know much too little from a research perspective about thoroughly contextualized, fully integrated, earth systems thinking linked to environmental studies and centered on students' personal and social lives. If we are to have curricula that do these things, then we must understand better what the obstacles are and how to overcome them.

The good news that emerges from this chapter is that there are sound studies that demonstrate the way for progress. The better news is that these studies are still few, and there is room for many young researchers to join the groundswell and make their mark in earth science education and on the future of humankind on Earth.

ACKNOWLEDGMENTS

Thanks to Eugene Chiappetta and Gerald Krockover, who reviewed this chapter.

REFERENCES

Agelidou, E., Balafoutas, G., & Gialamas, V. (2001). Interpreting how third grade junior high school students represent water. *International Journal of Education and Information, 20*, 19–36.

American Association for the Advancement of Science (AAAS). (1990). *Science for All Americans.* New York: Oxford University Press.

American Association for the Advancement of Science (AAAS). (1993). *Benchmarks for science literacy.* New York: Oxford University Press.

Ault, C. R., Jr. (1981). *Children's concepts about time no barrier to understanding the geologic past.* Unpublished doctoral dissertation, Cornell University, Ithaca.

Ault, C. R., Jr. (1982). Time in geological explanations as perceived by elementary school students. *Journal of Geological Education, 30*, 304–309.

Ault, C. R., Jr. (1984). The everyday perspective and exceedingly unobvious meaning. *Journal of Geological Education, 32*, 89–91.

Ault, C. R., Jr. (1994). Research on problem solving: earth science. In D. L. Gabel (Ed.), *Handbook of research on science teaching and problem solving.* New York: Macmillan.

Ault, C. R., Jr. (1998). Criteria of excellence for geological inquiry: The necessity of ambiguity. *Journal of Research in Science Teaching, 35*, 189–212.

Bar, V. (1989). Children's views about the water cycle. *Science Education, 73*, 481–500.

Bar, V., & Travis, A. S. (1991). Children's views concerning phase changes. *Journal of Research in Science Teaching, 28*, 363–382.

Barker, M. (1998). Understanding transpiration—more than meets the eye. *Journal of Biological Education, 33*, 17–20.

Beilfuss, M., Dickerson, D. L., Boone, W., & Libarkin, J. (2004). *Exploring conceptual understandings of groundwater through students' interviews and drawings.* Proceedings of the 77th Annual Meeting of the National Association for Research in Science Teaching, Vancouver, BC.

Ben-zvi-Assaraf, O., & Orion, N. (2005). The development of system thinking skills in the context of Earth System education. *Journal of Research in Science Teaching, 42*, 1–43.

Bezzi, A. (1995). Personal construct psychology and the teaching of petrology at undergraduate level. *Journal of Research in Science Teaching, 33*, 179–204.

Bezzi, A., & Happs, J. C. (1994). Belief systems as barriers to learning in geological education. *Journal of Geological Education, 42*, 134–140.

Bloom, B. S. (1956). *Taxonomy of educational objectives: Handbook I. Cognitive Domain* (pp. 196). New York: David McKay.

Brandon, R. (1994). Theory and experiment in evolutionary biology. *Synthese, 99*, 59–73.

Brody, M. J. (1994). Student science knowledge related to ecological crises. *International Journal of Science Teaching, 16*, 421–435.

Bruner, J. (1960). *The process of education.* New York: Vintage Books.

Bybee, R. W. (1993). *Reforming science education—Social perspectives & personal reflections.* New York: Teachers College Press, Columbia University.

Bybee, R. W., & Deboer, G. E. (1994). Research on goals for the science curriculum. In D. L. Gabel (Ed.), *Handbook of research in science teaching and learning* (pp. 357–388). New York: Macmillan.

Carpenter, J. R. (1996). Models for effective instruction of Earth science teachers in the USA. In D. A. Stow, & G. J. McCall (Eds.), *Geosciences education and training in schools and universities, for industry and public awareness.* AGID special publication series No 19. Rotterdam: Balkema.

Chadwick, P. (1978). Some aspects of the development of geological thinking. *Journal of Geological Teaching, 3,* 142–148.

Chang, C. Y. (2004). Could a laptop plus the liquid crystal display projector amount to improved multimedia geoscience instruction? *Journal of computer Assisted Learning, 20,* 4–10.

Cleland, C. (2002). Methodological and epistemic differences between historical science and experimental science. *Philosophy of Science, 69,* 474–496.

De Jong, T., & van Joolingen, W. R. (1998). Scientific discovery learning with computer simulations of conceptual domains. *Review of Educational Research, 68,* 179–201.

DeLaughter, J., Stein, S., Stein, C., & Bain, K. (1998). Preconceptions about earth science among students in an introductory course. *Eos, 79,* 429.

Department of Education and Science/Welsh Office. (1989). *Science in the national curriculum.* London: Her Majesty's Stationery Office.

Dickerson, D. L. (2003, March). *Naïve conceptions about groundwater among pre-service science teachers and secondary students.* Paper presented at the Annual Conference of the North Carolina Association for Research in Education, Holly Springs, NC.

Dodick, J. T., & Orion, N. (2003a). Cognitive factors affecting student understanding of geological time. *Journal of Research in Science Teaching, 40*(4), 415–442.

Dodick, J. T., & Orion, N. (2003b). Measuring student understanding of "deep time." *Science Education, 87*(5), 708–731.

Dodick, J. T., & Orion, N. (2003c). Geology as an historical science: Its perception within science and the education system. *Science and Education, 12*(2), 197–211.

Dori, Y. J., & Barak, M. (2001). Virtual and physical molecular modeling: Fostering model perception and spatial understanding. *Educational Technology & Society, 4*(1), 61–74.

Dove, J. E. (1997). Student ideas about weathering and erosion. *International Journal of Science Education, 19*(8), 971–980.

Dove, J. E. (1999). Exploring a hydrological concept through children's drawings. *International Journal of Science Education, 21*(5), 485–497.

Driver, R., Asoko, H., Leach, J., Mortimer, E., & Scott, P. (1994). Constructing scientific knowledge in the classroom. *Educational Researcher, 23*(7), 5–12.

Driver, R., Guesne, E., & Tiberghien, A. (1985). *Children's ideas in science.* Milton Keynes, UK: Open University Press.

Driver, R., Squires, A., Rushworth, P., & Wood-Robinson, V. (1994). *Making sense of secondary science: Research into children's ideas.* London: Routledge.

Edelson, D. C., Gordin, D. N., & Pea, R. D. (1999). Addressing the challenges of inquiry based learning through technology and curriculum design. *Journal of the Learning Sciences, 8,* 391–449.

Edmondson, K. M. (1999). Assessing science understanding through concept maps. In J. J. Mintzes, J. H. Wandersee, & J. D. Novak (Eds.), *Assessing science understanding: A human constructivist view.* San Diego: Academic Press.

Elshout, J., & Veenman, M. (1992). Relations between intellectual ability and working method as predictors of learning. *Journal of Educational Research, 85,* 134–143.

Emery, R. E. (1992). Parenting in context: Systemic thinking about parental conflict and its influence on children. *Journal of Consulting and Clinical Psychology, 60,* 909–912.

Everitt, C. L., Good, S. C., & Pankiewicz, P. R. (1996). Conceptualizing the inconceivable by depicting the magnitude of geological time with a yearly planning calendar. *Journal of Geoscience Education, 44*, 290–293.

Faughnan, J. G., & Elson, R. (1998). Information technology and the clinical curriculum: Some predictions and their implications for the class of 2003. *Academic Medicine, 73*, 766–769.

Fetherstonhaugh, A., & Bezzi, A. (1992, August–September). *Public knowledge and private understanding: Do they match? An example with the water cycle.* Paper presented at the 29th International Geological Congress, Kyoto, Japan.

Fordyce, D. (1988). The development of systems thinking in engineering education: An interdisciplinary model. *European Journal of Engineering Education, 13*, 283–292.

Fortner, R. W., & Mayer, V. J. (Eds.). (1998, August). Learning about the Earth as a system. *Proceedings of the 2nd International Conference on Geoscience Education.* Columbus, OH: Earth Systems Education, the Ohio State University. ERIC Document ED422163.

Friedman, W. (1982). Conventional time concepts and children's structuring of time. In W. Friedman (Ed.), *The developmental psychology of time.* New York: Academic Press.

Frodeman, R. L. (1995). Geological reasoning: Geology as an interpretive and historical science. *Geological Society of America Bulletin, 107*(8), 960–968.

Frodeman, R. L. (1996). Envisioning the outcrop. *Journal of Geoscience Education, 44*, 417–427.

Geosciences Professional Services. (Eds.). (2001). *EarthScope: A new view into earth (project plan).* Washington, DC: EarthScope. Report accessed July 30, 2004 at http://www.earthscope.org/links_pubs/index.html.

Germann, P. J., Haskins, S., & Auls, S. (1996). Analysis of nine high school biology laboratory manuals: Promoting scientific inquiry. *Journal of Research in Science Teaching, 33*, 475–499.

Gibson, J. J. (1966). *The senses considered as perceptual systems* (p. 335). Boston: Houghton Mifflin.

Gilbert, J., Osborne, R., & Fensham, P. (1982). Children's science and its consequences for teaching. *Science Education, 66*, 623–633.

Glasersfeld, E. von. (1987). *The construction of knowledge—Contributions to conceptual semantics.* Salinas, CA: Intersystems Publications.

Gobert, D. J. (2000). A typology of casual models for plate tectonics: Inferential power and barriers to understanding. *International Journal of Science Education, 22*, 937–977.

Gobert, J., & Clement, J. (1998). Effects of student-generated diagrams versus student-generated summaries on conceptual understanding of causal and dynamic knowledge in plate tectonics. *Journal of Research in Science Teaching, 36*, 39–53.

Gould, S. J. (1986). Evolution and the triumph of homology, or why history matters. *American Scientist, 74*, 60–89.

Gowin, D. B. (1981). *Educating.* Ithaca, New York: Cornell University Press.

Graczyk, S. L. (1993). Get with the system: General systems theory for business officials. *School Business Affairs, 59*, 16–20.

Greeno, J., Collins, A., & Resnick, L. (1996). Cognition and learning. In *Handbook of Educational Psychology.* New York: Macmillan.

Gudovitch, Y., & Orion, N. (2001, July). The carbon cycle and the Earth systems—Studying the carbon cycle in an environmental multidisciplinary context. *Proceedings of the First IOSTE Symposium in Southern Europe, Paralimni, Cyprus.*

Hanson, N. R. (1965). *Patterns of discovery: An inquiry into the conceptual foundations of science.* Cambridge, UK: Cambridge University Press.

Happs, J. C. (1982a). Some aspects of student understanding of two New Zealand landforms. *New Zealand Science Teacher, 32*, 4–12.

Happs, J. C. (1982b). *Some aspects of student understanding of rocks and minerals.* Working paper of the Science Education Research Unit, University of Waikato, New Zealand.

Happs, J. C. (1985). *Some aspects of student understanding of glaciers and mountains.* Working paper of the Science Education Research Unit, University of Waikato, New Zealand.

Herron, M. D. (1971). A critical look at practical work in school science. *School Science Review, 71*, 33–40.

Hsi, S., Linn, M. C., & Bell, J. (1997). The role of spatial reasoning in engineering and the design of spatial instruction. *Journal of Engineering Education, 86*(2), 151–158.

Hume, J. D. (1978). An understanding of geological time. *Journal of Geological Education, 26,* 141–143.

IGEO. (1997). Learning about the Earth as a system. R. W. Fortner & V. J. Mayer (Eds.). *Proceedings of the Second International Conference on Geoscience Education (1998, August).* Columbus, OH: Earth Systems Education, the Ohio State University. ERIC Document ED422163.

IGEO. (2000, January). *Conference proceedings of the 2nd meeting of the International Geosciences Education Organization, Sydney, Australia.* I. Clark (Ed.).

IGEO. (2003, August). *Conference proceedings of the 3rd meeting of the International Geosciences Education Organization, Calgary, Canada.*

Kali, Y., & Orion, N. (1996). Relationship between Earth science education and spatial visualization. *Journal of Research in Science Teaching, 33,* 369–391.

Kali, Y., & Orion, N. (1997). Software for assisting high school students in the spatial perception of geological structures. *Journal of Geoscience Education, 45,* 10–21.

Kali, Y., & Orion, N. (2005). The effect of an Earth science learning program on students' scientific thinking skills. *Journal of Geoscience Education, 53,* 387–393.

Kali, Y., Orion, N., & Elon, B. (2003). A situative approach for assessing the effect of an Earth-science learning program on students' scientific thinking skills. *Journal of Research in Science Teaching, 40,* 545–565.

Kapulnick, E., Orion, N., & Ganiel, U. (2004). *In-service "science & Technology" training programs: What changes do teachers undergo?* Paper accepted for publication in the NARST annual meeting, Vancouver, USA.

King, C. (2000). The Earth's mantle is solid: Teachers' misconceptions about the Earth and plate tectonics. *School Science Review, 82*(298), 57–65.

Kitts, D. B. (1977). *The structure of geology.* Dallas: Southern Methodist University Press.

Krajcik, J., Blumenfeld, P. C., Marx, R. W., Kristin M. B., & Fredricks, J. (1998). Inquiry in project-based science classrooms: Initial attempts by middle school students. *The Journal of the Learning Sciences* (7), 313–350.

LeGrand, H. (1991). *Drifting continents and shifting theories.* Cambridge, UK: Cambridge University Press.

Leighton, J., & Bisanz, G. L. (2003). Children's and adults' knowledge and reasoning about the ozone layer and its depletion. *International Journal of Science Education, 25,* 117–139.

Lewis, J. P. (1998). *Mastering project management: Applying advanced concepts of systems thinking, control and evaluation, resource allocation.* New York: McGraw-Hill.

Libarkin, J. C., Anderson, S., Dahl, J., Beilfuss, M., & Boone, W. (2005). Qualitative analysis of college students' ideas about earth: Interviews and open-ended questionnaires. *Journal of Geoscience Education, 53,* 17–26.

Lillo, J. (1994). An analysis of the annotated drawings of the internal structure of the Earth made by students aged 10–15 from primary and secondary schools in Spain. *Teaching Earth Sciences, 19*(3), 83–89.

Lovelock, J. (1991). *Healing Gaia—Practical medicine for the planet* (p. 192). New York: Harmony Books.

Marques, L., Paria, J., & Kempa, R. (2003). A study of students' preconceptions of the organization and effectiveness of fieldwork in earth sciences education. *Research in Science and Technological Education, 21,* 265–278.

Marques, L. F., & Thompson, D. B. (1997a). Portuguese students' understanding at age 10/11 and 14/15 of the origin and nature of the Earth and the development of life. *Research in Science and Technology Education, 15,* 29–51.

Marques, L. F., & Thompson D. (1997b). Misconceptions and conceptual changes concerning continental drift and plate tectonics among Portuguese students aged 16–17. *Research in Science and Technological Education, 15*(2), 195.

Mayer, V. J. (1995). Using the Earth system for integrating the science curriculum. *Science Education, 79*, 375–391.

Mayer, V. J. (Ed.). (2002). *Global science literacy*. Dordrecht, the Netherlands: Kluwer.

Mayer, V. J. (Ed.). (2003). *Implementing global science literacy*. Columbus, OH: Ohio State University.

Mayer, V. J., & Armstrong, R. E. (1990). What every 17 year old should know about planet earth: The report of a conference of educators and geoscientists. *Science Education, 74*(2), 155–165.

Mayer, V. J., & Fortner, R. W. (1995). *Science is a study of earth*. Columbus, OH: Earth Systems Education Program, the Ohio State University.

Mayer, V. J., & Fortner, R. W. (2002). A case history of science and science education policies. In V. J. Mayer (ed.), *Global science literacy*. Dordrecht, the Netherlands: Kluwer.

McAuliffe, C., Hall-Wallace, M., Piburn, M., Reynolds, S., & Leedy, D. E. (2000). Visualization and Earth science education. *GSA Abstracts with Programs, 32*, A-266.

McPhee, J. (1980). *Basin and range*. New York: Farrar, Straus & Giroux.

Metzger, E. P. (1992). The strategy column for pre-college science teachers: Lessons on time *Journal of Geological Education, 40*, 261–264.

Meyer, W. (1987). Venacular American theories of earth science. *Journal of Geological Education, 35*, 193–196.

Midyan, Y. (2003). The effect of in-service training on science teachers' attitudes and practical use of the outdoor as a learning environment. Unpublished MSc thesis, Weizmann Institute of Science, Israel.

Mintzes, J. J., Wandersee, J. H., & Novak, J. D. (1998). Research in science teaching and learning: a human constructivist view. In J. J. Mintzes, J. H. Wandersee, & J. D. Novak (Eds.), *Teaching science for understanding: A human constructivist view*. San Diego: Academic Press.

Montagnero, J. (1992). The development of the diachronic perspective in children. In F. Macar (Ed.), *Time action and cognition* (pp. 55–65). Amsterdam: Kluwer Academic.

Montagnero, J. (1996). *Understanding changes in time*. London: Taylor & Francis.

National Research Council. (1996). *National science education standards*. Washington, DC: National Academy Press.

Noonan-Pulling, L. C., & Good, R. G. (1999). *Deep time: Middle school students' ideas on the origins of earth and life on earth*. Paper presented at the National Association for Research in Science Teaching Annual Meeting, Boston.

Nottis, K., & Ketter, K. (1999). Using analogies to teach plate tectonics concepts. *Journal of Geoscience Education, 47*(5), 449–454.

Orion, N. (1993). A practical model for the development and implementation of field trips, as an integral part of the science curriculum. *School Science and Mathematics, 93*(6), 325–331.

Orion, N. (1996). An holistic approach to introduce geoscience into schools: The Israeli model— from practice to theory. In D. A. Stow & G. J. McCall (Eds.), *Geosciences education and training in schools and universities, for industry and public awareness*. AGID special publication series No 19. Rotterdam: Balkema.

Orion, N. (1998, July). Earth science education + environmental education = Earth systems education. In R. W. Fortner & V. J. Mayer (Eds.), *Learning about the Earth as a system. Proceedings of the second International Conference on Geoscience Education* (pp. 134–137). Columbus, OH: Earth Systems Education, the Ohio State University. ERIC Document ED422163.

Orion, N. (2002). An earth systems curriculum development model. In V. Mayer (Ed.), *Global science literacy* (pp. 159–168). Dordecht, the Netherlands: Kluwer.

Orion, N. (2003a). The outdoor as a central learning environment in the global science literacy framework: From theory to practice. In V. Mayer (Ed.), *Implementing global science literacy* (pp. 33–66). Columbus, OH: Ohio State University.

Orion, N. (2003b). Teaching global science literacy: a professional development or a professional change. In V. Mayer (Ed.), *Implementing global science literacy* (pp. 279–286). Columbus, OH: Ohio State University.

Orion, N., Ben-Chaim, D., & Kali, Y. (1997). Relationship between Earth science education and spatial visualization. *Journal of Geoscience Education, 45,* 129–132.

Orion, N., Dubowski, Y., & Dodick, J. (2000). The educational potential of multimedia authoring as a part of earth science curriculum—A case study. *Journal of Research in Science Teaching, 37,* 1121–1153.

Orion, N., & Fortner, W. R. (2003). Mediterranean models for integrating environmental education and earth sciences through earth systems education. *Mediterranean Journal of Educational Studies, 8*(1), 97–111.

Orion, N., & Hofstein, A. (1994). Factors that influence learning during scientific field trips in a natural environment. *Journal of Research in Science Teaching, 31*(10), 1097–1119.

Orion, N., & Kali, Y. (2005). The effect of an Earth-science learning program on students' scientific thinking skills. *Journal of Geosciences Education, 53,* 387–393.

Osborne, R., & Wittrock, M. (1985). The generative learning model and its implications for learning science. *Studies in Science Education, 5,* 1–14.

Ossimitz, G. (2000). *Development of systems thinking skill.* Web site: http:www-sci.uni-klu.ac.at/~gossimit.

Oversby, J. (1996). Knowledge of earth science and the potential for its development. *School Science Review, 78,* 91–97.

Pallrand, G. J., & Seeber, F. (1984). Spatial ability and achievement in introductory physics. *Journal of Research in Science Teaching, 21,* 507–516.

Piaget, J. (1970). *Structuralism.* New York: Basic Books.

Pickering, K., & Owen, L. (1994). *An introduction to global environmental issues.* London and New York: Routledge.

Posner, G. J., Strike, K. A., Hewson, P. W., & Gertzog, W. (1982). Accomodation of a scientific conception: toward a theory of conceptual change. *Science Education, 66*(2), 211–227.

Pribyl, J. R., & Bodner, G. M. (1987). Spatial ability and its role in organic chemistry: A study of four organic courses. *Journal of Research in Science Teaching, 24,* 229–240.

Reynolds, S. J., Piburn, M. D., Leedy, D. E., McAuliffe, C. M., Birk, J. P., & Johnson, J. K. (2002, April). *The hidden Earth: Visualization of geologic features and their subsurface geometry.* Paper presented at the National Association for Research in Science Teaching annual meeting, New Orleans.

Riggs, E. M. (2003). Field-based education and indigenous knowledge: Essential components of geoscience education for native American communities. *Science Education, 89,* 296–313.

Riggs, E. M., & Semken, S. C. (2001). Earth science for Native Americans. *Geotime, 49*(9), 14–17.

Riggs, E. M., & Tretinjak, C. A. (2003). *Evaluation of the effectiveness of a classroom and field-based curriculum in sedimentation and change through time for pre-service elementary school teachers.* Paper presented at the Geological Society of American annual meeting, Seattle.

Ritger, S. D., & Cummins, R. H. (1991). Using student created metaphors to comprehend geological time. *Journal of Geological Education, 39,* 9–11.

Roseman, J. (1992). Project 2061 and evolution. In R. Good, J. E. Trowbridge, S. Demastes, J. Wandersee, M. Hafner, & C. Cummins (Eds.), *Proceedings of the 1992 evolution education research conference* (pp. 214–229). Baton Rouge: Louisiana State University.

Ross, K., & Shuell, T. (1993). Children's beliefs about earthquakes. *Science Education, 77*(2), 191–205.

Roth, W. M., & Roychoudhury, A. (1993). The development of science process skills in authentic contexts. *Journal of Research in Science Teaching, 30,* 127–152.

Rowland, S. M. (1983). Fingernail growth and time-distance rates in geology. *Journal of Geological Education, 31,* 176–178.

Schoon, K. J. (1989, April). *Misconceptions in the earth sciences: A cross-age study.* Paper presented at the 62nd Annual Meeting of the National Association for Research in Science Teaching, San Francisco.

Schumm, S. A. (1991). *To interpret the earth: Ten ways to be wrong.* Cambridge, UK: Cambridge University Press.

Schwab, J. J. (1962). The teaching of science as inquiry. In J. J. Schwab & P. F. Brandweine (Eds.), *The teaching of science.* Cambridge, MA: Harvard University Press.

Senge, P. M. (1998). The practice of innovation. *Leader to Leader, Summer.*

Shymansky, J. A., & Yore, L. D. (1980). A study of teaching strategies, student cognitive development, and cognitive style as they relate to student achievement in science. *Journal of Research in Science Teaching, 5,* 369–382.

Slattery, W., Mayer, V., & Klemm, B. (2002). Using the Internet in earth science systems courses. In V. J. Mayer (Ed.), *Global science literacy* (pp. 93–107). London: Kluwer Academic.

Smith, E. L. (1991). Students' conceptual frameworks: Consequences for learning science. In S. M. Glynn, R. H. Yeany, & B. K. Britton (Eds.), *The psychology of learning science* (pp. 65–85). Hillsdale, NJ: Lawrence Erlbaum Associates.

Solomon, J., Duveen, J., & Hall, S. (1994). What's happened to biology investigations? *Journal of Biological Education, 28*(4), 261.

Spencer-Cervato, C., & Daly, J. F. (2000). Geological time: An interactive team-oriented introductory geology laboratory. *Teaching Earth Sciences, 25*(1), 19–22.

Staver, J. R., & Small, L. (1990). Toward a clearer representation of the crisis in science education. *Journal of Research in Science Teaching, 27,* 79–89.

Stofflett, R. (1994). Conceptual change in elementary school teacher candidate knowledge of rock cycle processes. *Journal of Geological Education, 42,* 494–500.

Stow, D. A., & McCall, G. J. (Eds.). (1993, August). Geosciences education and training in schools and universities, for industry and public awareness. *Proceedings of the conference on geosciences education, Southampton, UK, 1993.* AGID special publication series No 19. Rotterdam: Balkema.

Taiwo, A., Motswiri, M., Ray, H., & Masene, R. (1999). Perceptions of the water cycle among primary school children in Botswana. *International Journal of Science Education, 21*(4), 413–429.

Tamir, P. (1989). Training teachers to teach effectively in the laboratory. *Science Education, 73,* 59–69.

Tank, R. (1983). *Environmental geology* (p. 549). New York: Oxford University Press.

Tomorrow 98. (1993). *Report of the superior committee on science, mathematics and technology education in Israel* (p. 115). Jerusalem: Ministry of Education of Israel.

Toulmin, S. E. (1972). *Human understanding.* Princeton, NJ: Princeton University Press.

Trend, R. D. (1997, July). *An investigation into understanding of geological time among 10 and 11-year old children, with a discussion of implications for learning of other geological concepts.* Paper presented at 1st International Conference on Geoscience Education and Training, Hilo, Hawaii.

Trend, R. D. (1998). An investigation into understanding of geological time among 10- and 11-year old children. *International Journal of Science Education, 20*(8), 973–988.

Trend, R. D. (2000). Conceptions of geological time among primary teacher trainees, with reference to their engagement with geosciences, history and science. *International Journal of Science Education, 22*(5), 539–555.

Trend, R. D. (2001a). Deep time framework: A preliminary study of UK primary teachers' conceptions of geological time and perceptions of geoscience. *Journal of Research in Science Teaching, 38*(2), 191–221.

Trend, R. D. (2001b). An investigation into the understanding of geological time among 17-year-old students, with implications for the subject matter knowledge of future teachers. *International Research in Geographical and Environmental Education, 10,* 298–321.

Trend, R. D. (2002). Developing the concept of deep time. In V. J. Mayer (Ed.), *Global science literacy* (pp. 187–202). London: Kluwer Academic.

Wandersee, J. H., Mintzes, J. J., & Novak, J. D. (1994). Research on alternative conceptions in science. In D. L. Gabel (Ed.), *Handbook of research on science teaching and learning.* New York: Macmillan.

Welch, W. W., Klopfer, L. E., Aikenhead, G. S., & Robinson, J. T. (1981). The role of inquiry in science education: Analysis and recommendation. *Science Education, 65,* 33–50.

Zohar, A. (1998). Result or conclusion? Students' differentiation between experimental results and conclusions. *Journal of Biological Education, 32,* 53–59.

Zwart, P. J. (1976). *About time: A philosophical inquiry into the origin and nature of time.* Amsterdam: North-Holland.

CHAPTER 24

Environmental Education

Paul Hart
University of Regina, Canada

The field of environmental education and associated research activities are experiencing a period of rapid growth as we settle into the new millennium. Many reasons are claimed to explain this relatively new focus, including increasingly more pervasive and global environmental issues, changing societal expectations, and educational reform. Societies are searching for new narratives that give guidance and inspiration to people and purpose to schooling. Within these narratives, that range from teaching young people to accept the world as it is, to those that encourage critical thinking more distanced from conventional wisdom and intended to change what is wrong, is one that insists on our moral obligation to the planet. It is a narrative of extraordinary potential, says Postman (1995), because it is a story of human beings as stewards of the Earth, caretakers with a global consciousness and a sense of educational responsibility.

The purpose of this chapter is to engage the thought and practice of environmental education research in debates about "Our Common Future," debates that are occurring in many established curriculum fields. Because research within environmental education is characterized by both unity and diversity, the field is introduced, first, in terms of the contextual complexity of social, political, and cultural influences within which research in this field is situated. Second, environmental education research is described in terms of a variety of approaches to inquiry, with the use of example cases that illustrate the breadth and depth of research activity. Third, this requisite variety is situated within recent developments and current trends of both methodological and substantive issues in environmental education research. Finally, issues of quality in this field of inquiry are characterized within the politics of research that inscribe each of the research areas of the social sciences, including science education.

Although recent literature reviews have served to both characterize and provide substantive legitimacy to environmental education research (see, for example, Andrew & Malone, 1995; Hart & Nolan, 1999; Palmer, 1998; Posch, 1993; Rickinson, 2001; Williams, 1996), this chapter challenges researchers to regard these forms of inquiry as political. This means taking seriously issues of epistemology/ontology that necessitate reconsideration about what counts as legitimate. For example, attempts to prescribe global research agendas have seldom led to change in practice because they are not well attuned to contextual needs, values, and cultures. Yet local issues often cannot be understood except in the global frame. Thus, tensions between powerful localizing and globalizing forces necessitate more comprehensive understandings of methodologies that may strain the boundaries of inquiry. Challenges for research in environmental education imply a need for broadened conceptions of research as well as innovative and sensitive responses if such meanings of research are to be understood.

Meaning in research is related to purpose. Environmental educators envision caring, responsible people who construct, for themselves, the values that underpin wise judgments and competent actions relating to their environment, whether physical or social (Smyth, 2002). This seemingly simple vision becomes complex because education involves people and organizations at many levels—international and national, governmental and nongovernmental, formal and nonformal, public and private. Together they form a cluster of systems interacting with each other and the societies to which they belong. According to Smyth (2002), although those not directly involved in environmental education may think of it as a formal subject to be taught as a distinct part of the curriculum, it might better be regarded as a competence, as a permeating quality extending from personal and social values and emerging as ways of thinking, acting, or being.

WHAT IS ENVIRONMENTAL EDUCATION?

Arguably the largest of many networks of professionals and people working worldwide to promote environmental education, the North American Association for Environmental Education (see NAAEE, n.d.) represents some of the ideals that can be traced to definitions of environmental education resulting from international agreements at significant conferences such as those held in Stockholm in 1972, Belgrade in 1975, and Tbilisi in 1977 (Palmer, 1998). Along with counterparts in many countries, NAAEE rhetoric from the current website is reminiscent of the following classic definition of environmental education drafted as a result of the international working meeting on environmental education in the school curriculum sponsored by the World Conservation Union (IUCN) and the United Nations Educational, Scientific, and Cultural Organization (UNESCO): "Environmental education is the process of recognizing values and clarifying concepts in order to develop skills and attitudes necessary to understand and appreciate the inter-relatedness among man, his culture, and his biophysical surroundings. Environmental education also entails practice in decision-making and self-formulation of a code of behavior about issues concerning environmental quality" (IUCN, 1970).

However, definitions of environmental education most often referenced are from drafts of the Belgrade Charter and the Tbilisi Declaration. According to these documents, the goals of environmental education are:

(i)   To foster clear awareness of, and concern about, economic, social, political, and ecological inter-dependence in urban and rural areas.

(ii)   To provide every person with opportunities to acquire the knowledge, values, attitudes, commitment, and skills needed to protect and improve the environment.

(iii) To create new patterns of behavior of individuals, groups, and society as a whole, towards the environment. (UNESCO, 1977)

These early statements continue to capture the sentiments of increasingly large educational associations globally, as evidenced by the recent rhetoric of sustainable development originating with the World Conservation Strategy (IUCN, 1980), which, according to Greenall (1987), is becoming more specific and focused:

> Ultimately, the behavior of entire societies towards the biosphere must be transformed if the achievement of conservation objectives is to be assured. A new ethic, embracing plants and animals as well as people, is required for human societies to live in harmony with the natural world on which they depend for survival and wellbeing. The long term task of environmental education is to foster or reinforce attitudes and behavior compatible with this new ethic. (IUCN, 1980, section 13)

The essence of this strategy was reinforced and expanded by the World Conference on Environment and Development (WCED), widely known as the Brundtland Commission Report and published as *Our Common Future* (WCED, 1987).

Environmental Education and Sustainable Development

The term *sustainable development* first gained widespread attention as a result of Brundtland in the run-up to the United Nations Conference on Environment and Development (UNCED) held in Rio de Janeiro in 1992 (Huckle, 2003). The concept was endorsed by 149 countries as Agenda 21, in the global action plan for sustainable development. Chapter 36 recommended that education in each country be reoriented to include environment and development education. This rhetoric has continued to dominate the language of recent international conferences at Thessaloniki in 1997 and Johannesburg in 2003.

Although sustainable development could take different forms in different societies, it is generally defined to mean development that meets the needs of the present without compromising the ability of future generations to meet their own needs. It is widely acknowledged that sustainable development has ecological, economic, social, cultural, and personal dimensions, as a dynamic process that enables all people to realize their potential and improve the quality of life in ways that simultaneously protect and enhance the Earth's life-support systems (Huckle, 2003). The term is not uncontested, however, and although *environmental education* continues as the commonly used term, other concepts, such as environmental literacy, ecological citizenship, or learning for sustainability, have also been proposed (see *EER, 8*(1); Bonnett, 2002; Elliott, 1999; Jickling, 1992; McKeown & Hopkins, 2003; Stables, 1998; Stables & Scott, 2002).

According to Huckle (2003), all such definitions of environmental education or sustainable development rest on ethical foundations that are assumed to be about balancing four sets of values—environmental protection, quality of life, intergenerational equity, and intragenerational equity. These values are subsumed in a global ethic for living sustainably as part of the Earth Charter (2000), which urges the world's people to live as global citizens with a sense of universal responsibility. Its 16 principles are based on respect and caring for the community of life, ecological integrity, social and environmental justice, and democracy through political processes. Although there is no consensus on how these ethics and values should be translated into action, a number of discourses operate to shape our thinking on environment and development issues. These discourses on environmental education need to be made visible to pupils so they can learn to critique its underpinning social values and beliefs. This kind of education for critical thinking represents a challenge to curriculum developers and teachers not unlike new visions proposed for science education (see Cobern, 1991, 2000a, 2000b; Coble & Koballa, 1996; Donnelly, 2002).

Foundations of Environmental Education

It is worth considering whether the philosophical basis for environmental education or education for sustainable development in schools has been adequately conceptualized. It is worth the effort, according to Huckle (2003), because the cultural turn associated with the rise of postmodernism means that educators must now pay greater attention to ways in which social and ecological processes construct nature and environment. For, once constructed and represented, nature, environment, and environmental issues act as resources for identity formation, and, once formed, identity determines how we understand and evaluate social and environmental issues (Payne, 2001). Research in environmental education and in the social sciences has just begun to focus on identity formation in relation to young people's experiences in early and middle childhood (see Corsaro, 1997; Hutchison, 1998; Lee, 2001; Lewis & Lindsay, 2000; Panter-Brick, 1998; Pollard, Thiessen, & Filer, 1997).

As environmental education for sustainable development continues to grow and evolve, an active research community has emerged and has raised questions about education, which, like environmental education itself, often run counter to the dominant social paradigm. Whereas environmental education was once viewed as a conglomerate of nature study, conservation, and outdoor education groups, these tributaries have somehow merged into a stream of professional practice supported by research that seeks to investigate personal intents and values, and social structures that are believed necessary to organize understandings and actions that improve the quality and sustainability of natural and social environments (Palmer, 1998). Thus, research efforts have been directed toward examining which experiences might contribute to the creation of informed, active citizens capable of playing a part in creating societies that are caring about all living things and directed against forms of social and ecological injustice. Such aims and purposes, according to Fien (1993, 2000a, 2000b), are tantamount to a change in worldview from the dominant social paradigms of twentieth century industrial societies toward a new environmental paradigm of postmodern societies.

Given that these ideas are contestable presents practitioners and researchers with a curriculum problem (see, for example, Bowers, 1991, 2001, 2002). Environmental education brings into sharp relief the notion that education is not value-free: all teaching is embedded in an ideological background (see also Cobern, 1996, 2000b). However, only when the ideology strays from the taken-for-granted assumptions of the dominant social paradigm does this become problematic. Whereas a liberal orientation tacitly approves the reproduction of existing social relations, many orientations to environmentalism cannot be understood except within the ideas and values of wider paradigms of social beliefs (see Dunlap & Van Liere, 1978, 1984; Lalonde & Jackson, 2002; Milbrath, 1984, 1989). These ideas and values may challenge major beliefs about concepts of economic growth and current forms of politics.

Socially critical environmental educators argue, for example, that education should seek to promote a vision of a just and sustainable world, thus acknowledging the express political purposes of environmental education. This claim begs the curriculum/pedagogical question of whether ideological critique should be integrated into education. Although the WCED (1987) recognized that environmental education is clearly aimed at transforming the dominant social paradigm through changes in national and international systems of politics, economics, and technology, an idea that has been sustained in more recent international forums in Rio de Janeiro (1992), Thessoliniki (1997), and Johannesberg (2002), it is not at all clear that this rhetoric informs current school practices. Whether mainstream education is ready for such change represents a genuine dilemma, according to many environmental educators. The real issue is ontological that is, whether mainstream education itself can be transformed.

Goals and Directions

One way to view this dilemma from the perspective of science educators is to interpret the goals of environmental education in terms of those characteristics that coincide with Bybee and Deboer's (1994) description. The debate about goals in science education also relates to the priority and emphasis given certain goals in the historical structure of the science curriculum (Roberts, 2000; Roberts & Chastko, 1990). Although there has always been some tension between curriculum models that emphasize knowledge/skills acquisition and those that emphasize personal/social development, it was, according to Hurd (1969, 1970, 1998, 2000), social/environmental realities of the late twentieth century that resulted in a shifting of the goals toward humanism (see Donnelly, 2002). This new conceptualization of science education as a means to scientific literacy, defined more broadly to cohere with societal and technological issues, was reaffirmed by the 1980s in National Science Teachers Association (NSTA) goal statements that provided strong reaffirmation of the personal/social goal emphasis. These goals were operationalized, by the mid-1980s, as a science education research literature actively investigating science-technology-society (STS) approaches to science education, approaches that were overtly humanistic, values-oriented, and relevant to a wide range of social/environmental concerns (see also AAAS, 1993).

According to Bybee and Deboer (1994), one of the greatest forces behind the STS movement within science education was the tremendous growth in environmental awareness. A more aware public was beginning to associate environmental issues, energy conservation, and use of natural resources as well as global concerns about ozone depletion and greenhouse gases as ultimately tied to science and technology. Virtually every writer who advocated for scientific literacy within an STS context raised environmental/ecological concerns as potential subject matter for school science. However, at that time, although recognized as a separate entity within the wider field of education, environmental education remained problematic as a curriculum organizer, arguably because it forced science educators to reexamine priorities as well as older arguments about cognitive, social, and political aspects of the field. While scientific literacy has remained a central goal for science education in the 1990s and 2000s (Hurd, 1998; Roberts & Östman, 1998; Ryder, 2001), the new, large-scale curriculum projects of the American Association for the Advancement of Science (AAAS) (Project 2061), the NSTA, and the National Center for Improving Science Education (NCISE) attempt to balance traditional goals of learning scientific conceptual knowledge and process skills with the study of personal/social/environmental issues. Thus, environmental education remains an issue in science education precisely because the social/environmental realities described by Bybee (1997), Hurd (2000), and others since the 1970s have not gone away.

It should not be assumed that environmental educators necessarily agree on matters of purpose and form. There is a rich diversity of opinions about goals and directions, as in science education, but perhaps more demanding of educational reform (see Jickling, 2001; Stables, 2001). Because environmental education aims at the construction of environmental ethics, it is inherently focused on the personal/social emphasis. Even so, environmental educators differ over the ideological ends served by adopting a values pluralism approach as well as on claims to the neutrality of liberal approaches to the incorporation of values within education. For example, critical environmental educators argue that a liberal orientation fails to recognize education and schooling as already embedded within a system of values that are taken-for granted, and therefore are unexamined and unquestioned (Fien, 1993). Similar cases have been advanced by teachers advocating for consideration of competing perspectives through critical discourse with regard to religious or multicultural education.

In practice, many educators have developed professional strategies that have safeguarded students from forms of indoctrination or unethical teaching practices (Harris, 1990; Huckle, 1985a; Kelly, 1986; Richardson, 1982). Huckle (1983, 2003), for example, argues for approaches that link environmental concerns to wider political agendas, thus viewing environmental education as a form of political (i.e., citizenship) education. Such an approach could provide students with understandings and skills of political literacy and democracy through active citizen participation—those critical thinking and decision-making skills that, along with attention to human intentionality, inscribe forms of environmental education that go beyond behaviorist objectives and toward what Jensen and Schnack (1994) describe as action competence.

There is nothing that should be considered subversive, coercive, or heavy-handed about teachers who adopt institutional guidelines toward student understanding of a wide range of intellectual, action, and communication skills that enable active involvement in human decision making. In respect of environmental learning, Huckle (1985b, 2003) outlines development of critical environmental consciousness, critical thinking skills, environmental ethics, and processes of political literacy (i.e., environmental citizenship) as necessary to understand how current political systems work, appreciate variety in beliefs and policies, and evaluate alternatives. It should be possible to nurture and strengthen democratic values such as freedom of choice, tolerance, fairness, and so on, through learning how to adopt a critical stance, articulate reasons for particular views, assess evidence within political opinion, engage multiple perspectives, and tolerate diversity of ideas, beliefs, interests, and values (see Aikenhead, 1996; Crick, 1978; Porter, 1981). At its most basic level, environmental education is essentially about creating the conditions for citizen participation whereby citizens are educated to take responsibility for shaping and managing their own environments (see Breiting, 1988; Brubaker, 1972; Bull et al., 1988; Fien, 1993; Greenall-Gough, 1990; Hungerford, Peyton, & Wilke, 1980; Ryder, 2002; Wals, 1990).

Whereas earlier movements in nature study, conservation and outdoor education, did not challenge the socioeconomic fabric of society, environmental education has the potential, and some would argue the intent, to do so. The environmental movement signals fundamental changes in social consciousness, as environmental education does for educational consciousness. Socially critical and political action goals of environmental education stand in stark contrast to more conservative goals of science education (see Jenkins, 1994; Millar, 1989; Millar & Osborne, 1998). Thus, it should not be surprising that by the 1980s environmental education researchers began to observe what Stevenson (1987) described as pronounced discrepancies between the contemporary philosophy of environmental education and those of traditional educational programs (see, for example, Fien, 1993; Greenall, 1981; Lowe, 1998; Robottom, 1982; Sterling, 2001; Volk, Hungerford, & Tomera, 1984). Historically, schools were not intended to develop critical thinkers or encourage active participation in social/environmental decision making. Yet the goals of environmental education continue to emphasize critical thinking, problem solving, and decision making as a basis for active involvement in the resolution of environmental problems (Davis, 2003). That these goals are not easily accommodated in the goals and organization of schools poses challenges to existing subject area curricula such as science.

Quite recently there are some indications that pressures to reform curriculum areas such as science are tending, once again, to reduce the grip on rigid adherence to one set of goals (i.e., knowledge and skills) at the expense of others (i.e., personal/ social development). Reasons have been articulated for more constructivist approaches as organizers for science curricula (e.g., Cobern, 1998b; Leach & Scott, 2002). These tendencies, though not uncontested (see Matthews, 1998, 2000; Solomon, 1994), may be more likely to align with the social constructivist inclinations among the goals of environmental education. Thus, the recognition that the relevance of one dominant conception of scientific knowledge as authoritative, objective, discipline-centered, and technical is once again being tempered by the recognition of other, equally legitimate ways of knowing (see Duschl & Osborne, 2002).

ENVIRONMENTAL EDUCATION RESEARCH

Recognition of multiple epistemologies within the research community of science education would seem to create some space for more constructive consideration of commonsense knowledge of everyday experience in science courses, transfer some control for learning to students, and provide openings for more in-depth studies of relevant social/environmental issues and problems (see Jenkins, 1994; Ryder, 2001, 2002). Parallel developments in research in both science and environmental education engage new methodological approaches and new research foci on, for example, the ideas, interests, and thinking of practitioners as important in school pedagogies. The following sections illustrate how environmental education research may represent challenges to traditional conceptions of (science) education research in ways that parallel those just described in pedagogical theory and practice.

Research as Inquiry into the Theory and Practice of Environmental Education—Early Research

Any discussion of research in environmental education must account for perspectives on both its theory and its practice. Increasingly, researchers in environmental education have begun to acknowledge their differences as a sign of health in inter-subjective inquiry. Evolving understandings of even the most fundamental terms such as environmental education itself, as well as sustainability and sustainable development, makes inquiry far from straightforward (see, for example, Gough & Scott, 2003; Palmer, 1998; Scott & Gough, 2003; Scott & Oulton, 1992; Smyth, 2002). Problems of definition surrounding terms such as *environmentalism, deep ecology,* and *ecocentrism* that have been debated in philosophy-oriented journals such as *Environmental Ethics* and *Trumpeter* over many years remain interesting because they constitute broad ontological and epistemological frames for environmental education research.

It should not be surprising, then, when journal editors such as Gough and Scott (2003) attempt to sort through some matters of definition surrounding not only environmental education but education for sustainable development. In so doing they raise questions about educational perspectives as framed by larger goals of education in ways that enable the process of dealing with uncertainty, complexity, and risk, that is, by taking a position yet remaining open to, even encouraging, critique (see Rauch, 2002). Given the notion that problems of definition will and should remain problematic provides new perspectives on the relationships between theory and practice in both environmental education and environmental education research.

Although a rhetoric-reality gap remains an underpinning for research in environmental education (as it does for science education), linking these contested goals to the complex pedagogical tasks associated with classroom contexts represents a new challenge. Whereas attention in the early years of environmental education research was focused on establishing connections between knowledge, attitude, and behavior within traditional school practices, more recent work expands this focus methodologically and philosophically. As Reason (1988) suggests, our basic philosophical stance for new approaches to human inquiry follow from worldviews that merge systems thinking, ecological concerns, feminism, and education in ways that are critical of overreliance on reductionist applied science methods. Such a stance is characterized by research that questions how and why reality comes to be constructed in particular ways. Given that educational systems tend to sustain sets of social values that can be influenced by self-interests, these questions remain largely unscrutinized (Robottom, 1987).

It was Robottom's (1987) contention that the early research agenda in environmental education was shaped by an instrumentalist view of educational change. As a consequence, center-periphery research strategies retained characteristics of objective-based rationalist inquiry that served to reinforce, rather than reconstruct, key features of institutional education. Control over the language of the goals (e.g., through UNESCO-sponsored international forums) influenced decision making, resources, and research practices. By the late 1980s, however, forms of control over the research agenda were openly questioned and contrasted with alternative views of interpretive, participatory, community-based inquiry based on more socially critical forms of environmental education. Such challenges to dominant perspectives in environmental education research were responsible for exposing contradictions in environmental education practices (in schools) as incapable of meeting their socially critical charter. Although subsequently challenged from poststructuralist perspectives, these critiques of existing orthodoxies in environmental education research represented a turning point in how research was considered in environmental education (see Hart & Robottom, 1990; Robottom & Hart, 1993).

The 1990s—Debating Perspectives in Environmental Education Research

By the early 1990s several research symposia and conference workshops were organized to debate perspectives in environmental education research (see Mrazek, 1993). Forums such as these raised questions of epistemology and philosophy that followed wider debates in the field of education. Reviews of environmental education research prior to that time lacked the influences of a broadened consideration of methodological perspectives. For example, according to Palmer (1998), the majority of research studies in the 1970s and 1980s reflected positivist characteristics and a concern for congruence between goals and outcomes, legitimated by the use of applied science methods. Published studies, primarily in the U.S.-based *Journal of Environmental Education*, sought to derive cognitive and affective factors (variables) as determinants of responsible environmental behavior (see, for example, Hungerford, Peyton, & Wilke, 1980, 1983; Hungerford & Volk, 1990; Ramsey & Hungerford, 1989). Meta-analytic studies that posited up to 15 variables associated with environmental behavior resulted in the construction of models of responsible environmental behavior (see Hines, Hungerford, & Tomera, 1986/87). Despite limitations raised in critiques of positivist-based research, reviews by Palmer (1998), Williams (1996), and others recognize the contributions made by these researchers within the context of the times, and, as others have argued, as forms of inquiry that continue to inform our understandings in environmental education research (see Connell, 1997; Oulton & Scott, 2000; Palmer, 1998; Walker, 1997).

Science education is not immune to these debates about research philosophy and methodology, given its educational roots in the social sciences. According to Fien and Hillcoat (1996), the paradigm upon which research methodology is based is often neglected when one paradigm is so dominant that it is viewed as independent of ideology. However, arguments for a meta-research agenda in science education are reflective of growing interpretive and critical movements in education that frame research based on alternative epistemologies and worldviews (see Robottom & Hart, 1993). The importance of these debates is not in the distinctiveness of research methods (i.e., the tools in the researcher's toolkit), but in the assumptions that prefigure what is to count as legitimate ways of knowing and of knowledge (i.e., epistemological distinctiveness) as well as legitimate ways of finding out (i.e., methodologies and methods). Trends toward more humanistic approaches are evident in recent forms of environmental education research (Williams, 1996) and science education research (Donnelly, 2002). The significance of this epistemological shift is that educational researchers are now obliged to ground their work philosophically within several research perspectives and methodologically beyond only technical efficiencies of method.

Educational researchers now have considerably more scope in framing research questions. Perspectives ranging from feminist (including ecofeminist), gendered, race-based, and cultural studies overlie philosophically distinctive interpretive, critical, and poststructural approaches in ways that are often "blurred" (see Denzin & Lincoln, 2000). That this diversity is manifested in environmental education research is reflected in recent reviews of research (Hart & Nolan, 1999; Rickinson, 2001), in articles in an expanding array of journals that report environmental education research in North America, the United Kingdom, Australia, and southern Africa, for example, as well as in special editions of science education [e.g., *International Journal of Science Education (IJSE) 15(5), Studies in Science Education (SSE) 25*] and education journals [e.g., *Cambridge Journal of Education (CJE) 29(3), Journal of Curriculum Studies (JCS) 34(5), Prospects xxx(1)*, and *Educational Philosophy and Theory 33(2)*].

Expansion of research perspectives in environmental education has been accompanied by an elaboration of different views of knowledge within social science and educational research. While environmental education has been concerned about investigating empirical questions posed by environmental problems within educational settings, its distinctive concern, according to Robottom (2000), is with political, sociocultural, and ethical implications of environmental change. Unlike most science education (see, for example, Millar, Leach, & Osborne, 2000; Solomon & Thomas, 1999), environmental education sees the role of education as a post-empiricist concern with social and philosophical forms of inquiry. Knowledge is generated not only by scientific inquiry, but also by addressing philosophical issues about people's intentions and predispositions as subjective, interpretive constructions of the democratic process. Accordingly, professional dilemmas associated with the philosophical and contextual nature of environmental issues remain significant for teachers (Robottom, 2000).

Palmer's (1998) review is useful in consolidating political aspects of these shifts in thinking about what counts as environmental education research. For example, juxtaposing Robertson's (1994) examination of constructivism in science education with interpretivist forms of environmental education research illustrates how representation, implicated in both forms of inquiry, builds on earlier work by Driver and Oldham (1986) in eliciting students' personal conceptualizing and understandings of scientific principles and natural phenomena (see also Driver, Leach, Millar, & Scott, 1996). Given her own work in eliciting and interpreting children's emergent environmentalism, Palmer acknowledges a need for incorporation of growing bodies of research in ethnography, phenomenology, and narrative forms of inquiry in environmental education research.

Examination of critical perspectives in such projects as Environment and School Initiatives (ENSI) (Elliott, 1995; Posch, 1988, 1990, 1996) and in Fien and Hillcoat (1996) generates additional issues. For example, Posch (1996) and Elliott (1995) describe ENSI as action research involving a theory of learning related to active engagement in relevant, real-life problems. As such, the approach has struggled to overcome existing curriculum and school structures. Evaluative criteria, drawn from socially critical theory, are quite formidable, particularly those involving children in social action and social critique (see Walker, 1996). Thus, despite widespread success of the ENSI Project, particularly in European countries, practical pedagogical application, involved in the process of uncovering and making explicit the values and interests of individuals and groups who adopt certain positions with respect to social/environmental issues as a means to individual emancipation or social transformation, has proved challenging.

Ideas underpinning critical education *for* the environment (in contrast to education *about*, or *in*, or *through* environment), built up through the 1980s, have exerted extensive influence in environmental education research, particularly outside the United States. Although critical theory has been useful in overcoming limitations of positivist and interpretivist inquiry, Oulton and Scott (2000) see contradictions in the so-called politics for emancipation. If such a position involves proffering specific and specified values, then critical theory is simply the means to yet another orthodoxy. However, if viewed as a means of self-reflection and social scrutiny without particular ends, then environmental education researchers may in fact be engaged in methodological debates that are more characteristic of poststructuralist than critical forms of educational inquiry, involving more sophisticated philosophical arguments about social constructions of social science research. Obviously, no one research perspective is appropriate to environmental or science education research, and debates about intersubjectivity are as necessary among one group of researchers as another. The point, according to Oulton and Scott (2000), is to look beyond various interests if we are genuinely interested in finding ways—multiple and contextual ways—of resolving problems faced by teachers and schools in implementing environmental education. Such strategies are necessarily multiparadigmatic, reflexive, and iterative.

Recent Research in Environmental Education—Diversity and Critique

Whereas environmental education was virtually unknown until the late 1960s, the last 30 years, according to Rickinson (2001, 2003), have seen growing recognition that environmental challenges have important implications for education. Virtually unknown and frequently misinterpreted in earlier years, environmental education research has gained recognition globally, forming the basis of national frameworks and international policy agreements (Fensham, 1978; Tilbury & Walford, 1996). The research community that drives this activity has expanded so rapidly since Posch's (1993) review of research that it almost defies review, if indeed reviews can be viewed as appropriate forms of reporting the literature (see *EER, 9*(2); Hart, 2003a). This expansion has been complicated by the increasing variety in forms of inquiry that are now viewed as legitimate within the social sciences.

Although the case for diverse forms of inquiry, capable of responding to complex questions of human intention and social relations, has been taken up by environmental education researchers, the nature of this endeavor is difficult to describe.

At this point, it seems that research in environmental education can be characterized by requisite variety, but also by debate about the relative adequacy of several genres of inquiry. Thus, current research in environmental education reflects the need to develop a more reflexive posture toward meta-theorizing in environmental education so that respective methodological assumptions and political theories can be rendered more transparent and open to appraisal (O'Donoghue & McNaught, 1991; Robottom & Hart, 1993).

Rickinson's (2001) portrayal of research on environmental learning illustrates how important methodological critique becomes, given a rapidly expanding evidence base within a methodologically diverse field of inquiry. His findings reveal the need for more sophisticated conversations about the nature and direction of such inquiries as well as the integrity of different theoretical perspectives and methodological applications. Reminiscent of reviews of research that once filled entire volumes of *Science Education*, Rickinson's (2001) review serves to integrate multiple perspectives as a representation of research foci and methodological variety in ways that challenge existing conceptions of learning in complex environments (see Barron, 1995; Bonnett & Williams, 1998: Keliher, 1997; Payne, 1998a, 1998b; Wals, 1994a, 1994b).

First, the Rickinson (2001) review provides evidence that recent studies are likely to be qualitative, often with interests in poststructural forms of interpretive or critical understanding. Claims tend not to be expressed as generalizations but as situational, descriptive, and tentative, reflecting postmodernist sensibilities (see Ballantyne, Connell, & Fien, 1998a, 1998b; Jensen, Kofoed, Uhrenholdt, & Vognsen, 1995). Second, a strong science education influence persists, related particularly to studies of science-based knowledge in environmental issues (see Simmons, 1998) and to studies of environmental education found within science-based school programs (see Bogner, 1998). Common to these types of studies is evidence of inadequacies and misconceptions in students' understanding of environmental issues across many countries (Gambro & Switzky, 1999). This evidence is reflected in the disciplinary background not only of science teachers who primarily engage in this activity, particularly in middle and secondary schools, but of environmental education researchers themselves. However, there is also evidence that this trend may be weakening, given new methodological foci on the nature of students learning experiences and student perceptions rather than on learning outcomes.

Third, a rapid expansion of the geographical base of environmental education research is evident in Rickinson's (2001) review. Although environmental education research has tended to concentrate in North America, Europe/UK, southern Africa, and Southeast Asia, the recent First World Environmental Education Congress (FWEEC) (Azeiteiro et al., 2003) testifies to concentrations of activity in many other countries and regions such as Brazil and Central America. It is interesting that marked variations in methodological approach appear to be somewhat regional and that the dominance of quantitative approaches in certain areas has limited the range and scope of these inquiries in this area of learning (Rickinson, 2001). Other reviews of environmental education research reflect increasing concern about the appropriateness of methodology in areas such as environmental knowledge, attitude, and behavior (see Zelezny, 1999); learning outcomes (Leeming, Dwyer, Porter, & Cobern, 1993); outdoor experiences (Keighley, 1997); environmental sensitivity (Chawla, 1998); and student understanding of global environmental issues (Boyes

& Stanisstreet, 1996). This concern with methodology is also reflected in more comprehensive and in periodic reviews of the research literature in environmental education (see Andrew & Malone, 1995; Iozzi, 1981, 1989; Marcinkowski & Mrazek, 1996; Wagner, 1997).

Although review studies of particular areas of environmental education research have provided indications of, for example, students' weak knowledge or misconceptions of environmental issues, these results are often contested, as they have been in science education (see Brody, 1996; Clark, 1996; Ivy, Lee, & Chuan, 1998; Koulaidis & Christidou, 1999; Wylie, Sheehy, McGuinnes, & Orchard, 1998). Methodologically, the concern is that most of these studies were short-term and did not seek to investigate *why* respondents viewed environmental issues in particular ways. The weakness of this evidence was magnified when the knowledge-attitude relationship was extended to attempts to quantitatively connect knowledge and attitude with behavior (Chan, 1996; Connell et al., 1998). Evidence based on questionnaire or self-reported data varied so greatly that it remains difficult to suggest that this line of inquiry can help us understand what motivates young people to participate in proenvironmental behavior or how this is connected to cognition or affect (see, e.g., Leal Filho, 1996; Kahn & Friedman, 1995; Prelle & Solomon, 1996).

Questions about the quality of evidence from large numbers of these studies, as well as several methodological critiques, remain (see Hungerford, 1996; Smith-Sebasto, 1998a). Despite claims of positive learning outcomes and, in a few cases, behavioral change (see Bogner, 1998; Emmons, 1997; Leeming, Porter, Dwyer, Cobern, & Oliver, 1997; Uzzell et al., 1995), a number of researchers have begun to focus on questions about the nature of student thinking, using metaphors and more robust models of student understanding (see Boyes & Stanisstreet, 1997; Boyes, Stanisstreet, & Papantiniou, 1999). Increasingly researchers are exploring how and why certain processes such as role-modeling and collaborative, community, or direct outdoors experiences bring about positive learning outcomes (Rickinson, 2001, 2003).

Reviews of this literature also provide evidence that researchers can vary their research strategies, given a much wider array of legitimate methodologies (see Hart & Nolan, 1999). For example, in recent studies of students' ideas and perceptions of nature, evidence of learning is often more descriptive, reflecting phenomenological or narrative inquiries as opposed to explanations (see Barron, 1995; Bonnett & Williams, 1998; Keliher, 1997; Palmer & Suggate, 1996; Payne, 1998a, 1998b; Wals, 1994a, 1994b). Although it remains unclear whether these investigations will provide meaningful directions for teachers, researchers were encouraged by the complexity and richness of data about young people's views of nature. These research findings appear to correspond to research with teachers who trace environmental sensitivities and sensibilities to significant life experiences, often from middle childhood, with important adult mentors (see Chawla, 1994, 1998; Kaufman, Ewing, Hyle, Montgomery, & Self, 2001; Palmer, Suggate, Bajd, et al., 1998; Palmer, Suggate, Robottom, & Hart, 1999). Although somewhat speculative, such studies into the nature of these conceptions and about how young people socially construct their ideas and images of nature and of environment appear to warrant further investigation.

Given recent trends in education toward more interpretive forms of inquiry, Hart and Nolan's (1999) review of environmental education research illustrates how epistemological/ontological broadening has, on the one hand, opened inquiry methodologically and raised questions of representation, legitimacy, and quality on the other. Inquiry in environmental education is now a complex, multiparadigmatic array of methodological thought and practice. New forms of research are emerging as researchers' identities are altered to include participatory action as well as perspectives of women, people of color, gays and lesbians, and differently abled people of many kinds. These theoretical perspectives form part of the responsibility of new research texts that together with emergent critical and poststructural theory are changing the face of inquiry in education. As Crotty (1998) suggests, the idea of inquiry is not in adopting an existing paradigm, but in articulating the epistemological and theoretical perspectives that have influenced, rather than determined, their work. New languages are needed so that we can engage more sophisticated discussions about the meanings and purposes of our work, embedded as it is, within a politics of method.

Looking beyond correspondence in knowledge-attitude-behavior relationships involves a complex of perceptions that implicates people's reasons and feelings, reciprocally and dialectically, with their actions. A number of studies in environmental education research are beginning to conceptualize human "actions" as more complex subjective explorations of thought, meaning, and understanding attached to certain ways of being in the world (i.e., ontologies) (see Hicks, 1993; Payne, 1999) These arguments have been extended to include issues of gender, class, race, and cultural identities and relations (see Lousley, 1999).

Smith-Sebasto (1998) contrasts these perspectives with research in science education, where demands are for more rigor in the application of existing behavioral measurements rather than a questioning of the goals of such endeavors themselves. Whatever the reasons, environmental education researchers have concerns that we may have persisted in asking the wrong questions, or questions that do not warrant answers (Scott, 2003). Journal editors and publishers are now obliged to address the politics of publications characterized by methodological diversity, evaluative criteria appropriate to genre as a means of maintaining quality, and justification not only of methods but of philosophical perspective. Suffice it to say that environmental education journals have diverged from their science education prototypes.

Soltis (1984) has argued that a useful way of viewing tensions within a research community is to place them within the broader context of philosophical perspectives. That is to say, different approaches to research are always underpinned by different assumptions about what counts as knowledge or as reality (May, 2001). In Eisner's (1990) terms, there is more than one way to partition reality. Mixing methods is now a matter of methodology that requires addressing issues at theoretical conceptual levels. Whereas object-based inquiries attempt to overcome uncertainty through detachment and analytic procedure, subject-based research seeks to transcend the subject/object binary by acknowledging narratives of primary subjective experience as legitimate knowledge within certain boundaries of credibility and authenticity. Journals such as *EER* have been active in raising meta-theoretical and meta-methodological issues of open engagement and debate. Special editions have examined issues related to research on significant life experiences [*EER* 4(4), 5(4)], qualitative methods [6(1)], language of sustainability [7(2) and 8(1)], reviews of research [9(1)], and case study research (forthcoming). Special issues of the *CJEE* have focused on issues of research involved in narrative approaches [7(2)] and cultural awareness [7(1)]. Educational journals such as *Educational Philosophy and Theory* (see Stables & Scott, 2001), the *CJE* (see Bonnett & Elliott, 1999), and *IJSE* have addressed environmental education for various reasons, including its relevance to educational thought and practice, the adequacy of current approaches, and its significance for education as a whole.

Inquiry in environmental education is finding a place within educational research because researchers are using methods that address questions and issues that the positivist paradigm failed to address. Narrative forms of inquiry (Bruner, 1990, 1996; Polkinghorne, 1995) and analysis (Cortazzi, 1993) grounded in epistemological arguments about the value of storied forms of understanding teachers' philosophies are now forming a niche within environmental education research (see *CJEE* 7(2); Chenhansa & Schleppegrell, 1998; Gibson, 1996; Monroe & DeYoung, 1996; Wirth, 1996). Williams's (1996) review of the role of research in geographical and environmental education includes chapters on interpretive approaches (Gerber, 1996), critical research (Fien & Hillcoat, 1996), grounded theory (Tilbury & Walford, 1996), discourse analysis (Bennett, 1996), and case study research (Roberts, 1996).

Beyond these reviews, a number of exemplary dissertations have established precedents for new approaches to inquiry. For example, Malone (1996) described her study as critical ethnography, Mahony (1994) as ethnography, Brody (1996) as phenomenology, and Rentel (1997) as hermeneutic phenomenology. Various forms of participatory (action) research provide cases of active engagement of participants, intellectually and practically, in critical inquiries within their own contexts (e.g., Andrew, 1997; Elliott, 1991; Kyburz-Graber, Rigendinger, Hirsch, & Werner, 1997; O'Donoghue & McNaught, 1991; Papadimitriou, 1995; Posch, 1994; Robottom, 1987; Wals & Alblas, 1997). As is the case with all forms of qualitative inquiry, these approaches are subject to critique. Thus, researchers have the added task of addressing demands of critical reflexivity and intersubjective scrutiny (see Davis, 2003; N. Gough, 1999; Payne, 1999).

Case study has also been used extensively across various genres of research to represent environmental education activity (see Emmons, 1997; Gayford, 1995; O'Connor, 1997; Page, 1997). Wals and Alblas (1997) describe a case study of curriculum reform through an action research process, where teachers openly reflected on their struggles to incorporate an environmental dimension into their practices (see also Payne & Riddell, 1999). Andrew's (1997) historical case study research exemplifies Robottom's (1987) concern that community-based case-study research, as inclusive of the enactment and consequence of economic rationality as well as context, does not define the research approach that is generated through both the researchers' assumptions and the case experience itself. In other words, the case merely determines the form of a particular study, which is why it can exist within a number of contemporary research forms and discourses, including feminist, critical, and poststructural methodology.

Although many case studies of environmental education programs tend to use participatory research (e.g., Turner, 1998; Walker, 1996), action research (e.g., Schreuder, 1994), critical action research (e.g., Fien & Rawling, 1996), or community-based action research (e.g., Pace, 1997; Peel, Robottom & Walker, 1997), many others remain as basic descriptive evaluations of environmental education programs that struggle for methodologies that can identify crucial dimensions (i.e., factors) in the development of community-based programs. These positivist tendencies, while understandable, remain a concern among interpretive and critical researchers who are more interested in the uniqueness of individual context-sensitive cases.

How we "make sense" of these large numbers of descriptive "reports" that address curriculum issues ranging from integrating environmental education into formal school subjects (e.g., Randall, 1997; Shin, 1997) or art and literature (e.g., Soetaert, Top, & Eeckhout, 1996), drama (e.g., Cabral, 1998), or special education (e.g., Lock, 1998) across many regions and countries (e.g., Adedayo & Olawepo, 1997; Lee, 1997) remains to be determined.

The environmental education research literature also contains examples of out-of-school integrated programs that involve outdoor education (e.g., Nelson, 1996; Richardson & Simmons, 1996; Yerkes & Haras, 1997), experiential education (e.g., Luckman, 1996), or global education (e.g., Selby, 1999). Within these programs, students have explored ecological concepts and environmental issues by using a wide variety of curriculum areas and nonformal approaches, including agriculture (e.g., Miller, 1997), ecotourism (e.g., Cork, 1996), botanical gardens (e.g., Spencer, 1995), parks (e.g., Darlington & Black, 1996), or nature centers (e.g., Wilson, 1993a, 1993b) or by using special topics as foci for these experiences, such as water issues (e.g., Goodwin & Adkins, 1997; Ho, 1997) or endangered species (e.g., Martinez Rivera, 1997).

As the field of environmental education has matured, research has assumed a role in the reporting of large-scale status studies intended to provide more comprehensive "measures" of, for example, science learning achievements, program evaluations, and teacher education. Many of these reports use multiple methods to evaluate formal and informal programs such as Project WILD or Project Learning Tree (e.g., Collins & Romjue, 1995) or the Great Lakes Program (e.g., Nevala, 1997). Studies of specialized programs in many countries have contributed to a more globalized portrait of the nature of environmental education worldwide [e.g., Scotland (Smyth, 1999), Guyana (Leal Filho & Bynoe, 1995), Korea (Sang-Joon, 1995), Germany (Bolscho, 1990), England and Wales (Reid & Scott, 1998); Uganda (Mucunguzi, 1995); the South Pacific (Taylor & Topalian, 1995), New Zealand (Springett, 1992), and southern/eastern Africa (Taylor, 1998)]. These reports and those in the newsletter *Connect* (UNESCO-UNEP) reveal many variations and stages of development in environmental education programs related to local issues. They are valuable in encouraging researchers to consider their research in terms of "western" goals, ideals, and evaluative criteria as part of a "politics of transfer" issue in cultural terms. Justification of programs has often resulted in positivist evaluation models that may be inappropriate in different cultures and contexts (see Courtenay-Hall & Lott, 1999; Fien et al., 2001; Sauvé, 1999).

Research in environmental education is also characterized by inquiries focused on personal and social issues related to environmental education programs and experiences. For example, studies centered around teacher thinking include studies of teacher beliefs aboout and/or perceptions of nature, environment, or social/environmental issues (e.g., Ajiboye, Audu, & Mansaray, 1998; Bachiorri, 1995; Kasper, 1998; Nando Rosales, 1995). Increasingly, it seems, these studies go beyond quantitative comparisons among measured variables using fixed instruments in search of connections related to teachers' beliefs, perceptions, and predispositions/assumptions that may result from life history (e.g., Stocker, 1996), early life experiences (Hart, 2003b; Todt, 1995), sense of place (e.g., Chawla, 1994; Hug, 1998; Stephens, 1998), autobiographical memory (e.g., Conway, 1990), and children's concern for the environment (Chawla & Hart, 1995; P. Hart, 1999; R. Hart, 1997). Motivation for provision of environmental education is also the interest in explorations of significant life experiences (SLE) (e.g., Corcoran, 1999; Elliott, 2002; Palmer, 1998; Palmer & Suggate,

1996; Tanner, 1998a, 1998b; Wilson, 1996). As an instance of memory work, this inquiry has generated some useful critical commentary [see *EER* 5(1)] that has informed subsequent discussions such as AERA's research interest group in environmental education and environmental education research.

As an example of focused critical discourse, the SLE debate has raised important methodological issues that affect all areas of post-positivist inquiry (see N. Gough, 1999; Payne, 1999). This research debate has led to suggestions for explorations, for example, that seek to explain how the structuring and continuity of embodied experience (or inner nature) are immersed and embedded in the historical, social, and ecological environment (or external nature) and, thus, how individuals actively construct experiences, and their significance, in the face of equally problematic social constructions of the environment and nature (Payne, 1999b). This active debate has also led to methodological developments, including the use of certain post-structural understandings of human subjectivity and agency in environmental education research (see A. Gough, 1999). In turn, this debate reiterates the epistemological distinction, in research in the social sciences and education, between inquiry as a neutral technical process and inquiry as engagement in the social construction of knowledge. As well, it considers the ontological distinction whereby a mode of inquiry is incumbent upon the assumptions and practices not only of the research paradigm but the worldview, in this case the ecophilosophical worldview of environmental education (Robottom & Hart, 1993).

Environmental education research has also focused on children's ideas, perceptions, or perspectives, with particular emphasis on the role of nature (e.g., Keliher, 1997; Payne, 1999), early experience (e.g., Hart, 2000; Wilson, 1995, 1996, 2000), story, sense of place (Chawla, 1998; Sobel, 1997), and curriculum/school experiences (e.g., Eagles & Demare, 1999; St. Maurice, 1996) in informing children's emerging ecological and social ontology (see R. Hart, 1997; Palmer, 1995; Peters & Wilson, 1996). Numerous studies have sought to understand children's perspectives and ideas about environment and a variety of environmental issues (e.g., Boyes & Stanisstreet, 1997; Hillcoat, 1995; Williams & Bonnett, 1998). Specific issues such as air pollution (Wylie et al., 1998), the greenhouse effect (Fisher, 1998; Mason & Santi, 1998), the ozone layer (Christidou, Kouladis, & Christidis, 1997), municipal waste (Glazer, Vrtacnik, & Bacnik, 1998), endangered species (Ashworth, 1995), and radon gas (Thrall, 1996) appear to be widespread, internationally, depending on local/regional circumstances.

Research focused more specifically on student thinking as a result of course-based experiences (e.g., Mangas, Martinez & Pedauye, 1997; Tyler-Wood, Cass, & Potter, 1997), as well as experiential courses/programs (e.g., James, 1997; Leeming, 1997), has resulted in questionable findings (see Cobiac, 1995; Kuo, 1994). Thus researchers have begun to look more holistically at students' values and beliefs (e.g., Ballantyne & Clacherty, 1990; Greaves, Stanisstreet, Boyes, & Williams, 1993; Wals, 1992). Jurin (1995) and Fason (1996) report disparities between quantitative and qualitative findings in mixed-method studies, speculating, with Boyes & Stanisstreet (1998), that mixed-belief structures may exist simultaneously and that such disparities in student thinking of this complexity cannot be addressed adequately through short-term, one-shot measures.

This research literature on students thinking illustrates a concern to probe for deeper understanding about how we come to know and think about social/environmental issues in ways that reflect more sentivity to gender (e.g., Barron, 1995;

Mansaray & Ajiboye, 1997; Yeung, 1998) and culture (e.g., Chan, 1998; McIlveene, 1996). Payne (1997, 1998a) argues that it is these forms of inquiry, involving contexts and life experiences research, that are essential to understanding children's minds, ontologically, as being "in" environment, as opposed to belief structures attached to particular personality factors or environmental issues.

WHY SCIENCE EDUCATION RESEARCHERS SHOULD ATTEND TO RESEARCH ISSUES IN ENVIRONMENTAL EDUCATION

So, what is distinctive about inquiry in environmental education? Why should science educators be interested in what environmental education research is saying or in how it is engaged critically and reflexively? Perhaps it is a function of the age of a discipline or of its place in society, or its natural association with dominant forms of inquiry that led to N. Gough's (1999) comment about research in science education that makes little acknowledgment of the limits to scientific explanations within the complexity of decision-making in real-world events such as environmental issues resolution. "Environmental educators," he says, "do not have the science educator's mandate (or excuse) for privileging 'scientific' knowledge and methods. Thus, environmental education researchers need to recognize the contested nature of epistemology . . . and problematize the cultural construction of scientific knowledge" (p. 39). The point is that, within environmental education research, as in educational research generally, considerable space is now devoted not only to issues of methodology, but to issues of epistemology and ontology. Thus, where research in science education hastened to focus on method and to relegate these arguments to the philosophy of science, environmental education research has raised theoretical issues that necessitate serious philosophical consideration by researchers themselves (see Osborne, 2002; Warwick & Stephenson, 2002).

According to Robottom (2000), recent developments at levels of policy, practice, and organization raise new issues for environmental education and render past characterizations of the field as problematic. For example, the policy perspective provided by UNCED's Agenda 21 (UNCED, 1992) has asserted a distinct social change agenda for environmental education that challenges the field's historical disciplinary relationships. If Agenda 21 is taken seriously, then education is critical for promoting sustainable development and improving society's capacity to address social/environmental issues. Robottom (2000) views this emphasis as the basis of arguments for forms of education that address fundamental questions of ethics and values, and encourages public participation in citizen decisions about social/environmental issues as well as cooperation in redressing existing economic, social, racial, and gender inequities. These issues involve philosophical questions (of the "ought" and "should be" kind) that are not exclusively scientific and can only be resolved through considerations of intergenerational equity, health, peace, human rights, ethnicity, gender, age, and class matters concerning democratic process, social justice, and quality of life (Robottom, 2000).

Implied in the consideration of philosophical dimensions to forms of environmental (and science) education, with an interest in individual and collective issues of ecologically sustainable development, are challenges to existing research practices. These challenges foreshadow deeper ontological/epistemological concerns that have been neglected within mainstream education (see R. Hart, 1997; Rivkin, 1995, 1997; Smith, 1998). They require active engagement of methodological considerations about forms of inquiry available to educational researchers (see Ahlberg & Leal Filho, 1998; Greenall-Gough, 1994; Groves, Jane, Robottom, & Tytler, 1998; Huckle & Sterling, 1996; Jensen, Schnack, & Simovska, 2000; Jickling, 1993; Kollmuss & Agyeman, 2002; Mrazek, 1993; Oulton & Scott, 2000; Palmer, 1998; Robertson, 1994; Williams, 1996; and recent issues of *EER* and *CJEE*). Although environmental education researchers have begun to address these challenges at various conference forums of NAAEE and special research seminars, fundamental issues remain unresolved. What seems to be evolving is a critical sociology of environmental education research that continues to problematize the assumptions, values, theories, and practices upon which research activities in this field are grounded. Continuing such engagements will immerse the field in critical and poststructural conversations that appear to be necessary for its survival.

What is interesting about this notion of functioning within multiple perspectives, beyond the essentially contested nature of key conceptualizations of environmental education or philosophical debates about ideas that drive theory and practice, is the rich ground they provide for researchers who can base inquiry in several perspectives and can construct positions on their own grounds (including practical experiences, say, as a teacher). Cases have been established, for example, for forms of environmental literacy (e.g., Disinger & Roth, 2003; Stables, 1998; Stables & Bishop, 2001; Stables & Scott, 1999), education for sustainability (e.g., Huckle & Sterling, 1996), sustainable development (Gough & Scott, 2003), sustainable futures (Turner & Tilbury, 1997), or learning and sustainability (Government of Canada, 2002) where each is contested (e.g., Jickling, 1992; Oulton & Scott, 1998; Plant, 1995). Cases have also been made for particular dimensions of research, including historical (e.g., Andrew, 1998; Marsden, 1998; Morgan, 1998) and constructivist (e.g., Hoffman, 1994; Robertson, 1994b) approaches and action competence (e.g., Breiting & Nielsen, 1996; Jensen & Schnack, 1997; Schnack, 2000). Centers for environmental education research activity and debate of such issues operate in several countries, including Denmark (Royal Danish University), England (University of Bath), Australia (Deakin University and Griffith University), and the United States (University of Michigan, Southern Illinois University, the Ohio State University). Researchers are also active in many other places in areas such as nonformal education (e.g., Heimlich, 1993), technology (e.g., Dillon, 1997), adult education (e.g., Clover, Follen, & Hall, 1998), cross-cultural education (e.g., Armstrong, 1997; Chou & Roth, 1995; Corcoran & Fien, 1996; Kyburz-Graber, et al., 1997), and teacher education (Scott & Oulton, 1995).

Although just a decade ago Posch (1993) identified an absence of viable alternative visions as one of the key obstacles to effective environmental education research, the opposite may be true today. Environmental education researchers have turned their attention from a "search for solutions" to a "search for causes" and have begun to search for answers beyond positivist approaches in order to address issues of value assumptions, social visioning, and mosaics of personal and social qualities, that is, toward a broadened view of learning as action-oriented. Yet concerns remain about educational systems not attuned to the social complexities and environmental uncertainties that threaten established decision-making processes. Thus, environmental education researchers continue to raise questions about education, learning, and how to prepare students to cope with insecurity, decision making with incomplete data, and the contradictory demands of a plurality of values, or how to become citizens who participate in their various forms of government. It seems that environmental education is at a crucial point between destabilization, as prerequisite for incorporation of new elements, and stability, as a condition necessitating vigilance and skepticism. While these tensions create new opportunities for research, there are political aspects to change in subject-based curricula that make problematic the stability of systematic knowledge transmission and involve themselves in school-based initiatives full of uncertainty and risk.

The Politics of Environmental Education Research

Although recognition of the political nature of environmental education research has allowed researchers and practitioners to reconstruct relationships and to reconsider some assumed binaries such as objectivity/subjectivity and expert/novice in a new light, these new modes of knowledge generation are always subject to challenge, as they should be. Developments in the theory and practice of education can be shown to underlie these challenges as part of a politics of inquiry. The context for such challenges becomes more acute when certain forms of inquiry are marginalized because they do not conform to traditions. Viewed as a series of sociocultural processes, however, environmental education research has contested many taken-for-granted assumptions about theory and about practice in educational research.

At the level of theory, a key research issue is how we come to value alternative ways of generating knowledge. Whereas researchers in the natural sciences use objective means to justify their research, knowledge in the social sciences is less clearly defined and is subject to problems of interpretation and representation. Addressing aspects of human behavior such as intents, motives, and values involves levels of indeterminacy that traditional researchers find difficult to comprehend, often leading to misinterpretations, misunderstandings, and unfair accusations. Because education as a human endeavor resists efforts by researchers to establish causal claims that are verifiable, definitive, and cumulative, researchers are left to try to understand sociopolitical processes that reflect sociocultural purposes embedded with contradictions, as well as conflicting criteria for appraisal of success (Larabee, 1997a, 1997b).

As Rickinson (2001) argues, impacts of teaching and curriculum on learning rely on human dimensions that shape outcomes in indeterminate ways that are irreducibly normative. Knowledge generated in one context may or may not apply to another, and even particular contextualized applications depend on perspectives of practitioners and researchers. Thus, constructed knowledge is not bound by foundational constraints. So, while methodological diversity is now valued, this position carries different responsibilities for ensuring quality and accountability. Hence, the new politics of educational research is organized around new debates characterized by attempts to justify methodologies rather than methods. For example, debates within interpretivism are no longer argued as a response to positivist critique (i.e., as paradigm wars), but as differing underlying philosophies about what counts as knowledge and about how reality is perceived.

Environmental education research is characterized by increasingly active debates about the form and content of its inquiry. Questions have been raised, for example, about the legitimacy of various forms of inquiry, thus implicating the politics of methodology. Methodological approaches such as ethnography, phenomenology, and various participatory and poststructuralist perspectives are based on assumptions reflected in the languages and conceptual meanings of various philosophical discourses such as interpretivism, criticalism, and postmodernism (see Denzin & Lincoln, 2000). Unlike the past, when the dominance of positivism relegated such debates to the philosophy of science, questions of subjectivist epistemology and social constructivist ontology now challenge environmental education researchers to justify their narrative-based accounts of research in terms of what counts as legitimate knowledge or as adequate forms of representation in terms of what makes them seem credible, trustworthy, and authentic beyond subjective judgment. Several issues of *EER* and *CJEE* have attempted to raise such issues as we learn to negotiate our interpretations based on shared, intersubjective understandings among the community of interested researchers and practitioners. These discussions are recognized as political when inscribing legitimacy involves authority of a dominant discourse or perceived hierarchy of legitimacy. Those who do not conform may feel alienated or coerced into playing by certain rules. New methodologies that threaten existing orthodoxies may cause resistances and tacit or explicit sanctions from journal editors or granting councils. More deeply, however, the politics of methodology implicates language, sources of evidence, methods, and, ultimately, the ways in which we construct our thinking about research methodology.

At the methodological level, resistances or reactions to fields of inquiry outside our own may result in misinterpretation and misrepresentation of alternative positions whose justification depends on unfamiliar criteria. Statements that appear clear and coherent within one research genre may not be intelligible within another. The problem, according to Lather (1996), is in the assumption that it is acceptable for educational researchers to critique methodology without having studied the underlying philosophy. Thus, pleas for intelligence in debate about methodology can now be found in those special editions of *EER* that focus on helping researchers to rethink their methods within their methodologies without simplifying the complexities of research in practice. The idea is not to defuse debate so much as to engage the space over words as unstable as our clearly bounded territory, divided perhaps by theories and discourses, but centered by struggles to ground our work both theoretically and practically.

As a representational practice, environmental education research is always embedded in methodological commitments that are necessarily political. Researchers speak through particular discourses that understand and close the world in particular ways. Given this embeddedness within theory and the micropolitics of research practice, there are no best practices or superordinate methodologies. Thus, researchers are responsible for becoming more conscious of this politics of methodology as a means of addressing the values and beliefs that underpin our understandings and provide reasons for our research decisions. The methodology question then becomes one of how to account for our subjectivities as researchers and participants. According to N. Gough (1999), if we are to escape the automatic imprint of our own experience, we need to surpass our personal histories through acts of critical reflection, that is, to make more explicit that underlying frame of ideas, assumptions, and beliefs that guide our practices. Once articulated, and subject to critique, we may become more conscious of our values, motives, biases, and unexamined, taken-for-granted assumptions—those personal and social dimensions through which our research practices become intelligible.

Environmental education research in this sense can only be understood as an activity of interpretation where representation is always reflexively problematic. Because reality is constructed through representation, and thus is fictional, reflexivity becomes an issue of problematizing methodology by surfacing preconceptions, finding out how meanings were constructed, and how understanding is bound up in language and writing. In other words, research accounts can no longer function unproblematically as "true" representations, and grounding for accounts of research must be approached through political judgment about whether the interpretation is adequate (in contrast to reliance on foundational criteria). However, reflexivity by itself, as an issue of overcoming blind spots through a kind of self-consciousness, may be far from a neutral process. If constituted as an ability to mobilize across gender, race, and culture, critics can apply this capacity unevenly in inscribing new reflexive hierarchies of speaking positions hidden by claims that critical reviews are progressive within the politics of methodology. The irony is that critical responses to particular lines of inquiry may consciously or unconsciously privilege certain lines of inquiry through critique of others, thus engendering forms of exclusivity in the very act of denying it.

In environmental education research, we continue to search for critically reflexive approaches. In my own work with teachers who struggle to construct stories of their environmental education practice, the point is not that such narratives are true but that they may become truthful fictions through frequent repetitions across a range of contexts and through their credibility to practitioners of all sorts. Research accounts become reasonable in their resonances with broader collectives of meaning (see Hart, 2003). Without such attempts to interpret affect, emotions, feelings, and motivations as meaningful dimensions of human identity and place, we have virtually no way of understanding people's lived experiences as they exist in their imperfect, partial, historical, and contextual accounts of their experiences, full of contradictions, and as imposed fictions in memory as well as the exigencies of everyday life. We believe, as researchers, that our accounts of lived experience may ring true, however fragmented, contingent, and multiple within the social contexts inhabited. And our research will always be confronted by such anxieties and by the politics of intersubjectivity, so we had better get used to it. Rather than recoil in some fit of existential angst, we know that some stories are important and must be told, even as we, as researchers, learn how to accept critique warranted by our necessarily subjective process.

What we need to do, according to Skeggs (2002), is to use reflexivity as a way of sensitizing our research process as we learn to live responsibly in privileged positions; that is, we must try to ensure that our epistemological authority does not compromise our moral authority. Learning to see research as political (as well as multiple, historical, and contextual) involves more than casual appropriation of philosophical concepts or methodological approaches, but rather the serious study of the roots of our ontological/epistemological perspectives. Removal of the notion of certainty in research does not mean anything goes, but that we learn to acknowledge multiple truths and multiple ways of knowing. Environmental education research (as environmental education itself), in affirming that we cannot provide an ultimate rationale (foundation) for any given system of values, does not imply that one considers all views to be equal (i.e., relative). The question is not whether one position is right so much as why we have come to occupy and defend it. Our responsibility is to read widely and deeply and to engage in discussions and debates that expose our ideas and research practices to forms of reflexivity and to become more conscious of the politics of methodology, and of knowing and being, toward improved research praxis.

END NOTE

Those who regard science teaching as engaging in the disciplines of science and education where the serious processes of knowing are stressed and "the virtue of instrumental content knowledge" is valued may have at best a passing interest in examples of environmental "science" that provide relevance to their activities. However, those science educators who understand science from a wider, more encompassing perspective, and particularly those who value the virtue of social values and adopt a pluralist nature of science, may share considerably more philosophical ground with environmental educators. For example, Cobern (1998a), from the perspective of science education, argues that science as a social endeavor should be informed by constructivist epistemology and that the image of science portrayed to students should represent a variety of perspectives, such as cultural, political, economic, critical theory, and theological. This position counters the older view of science as culturally neutral and of science education that uncritically reproduces western or modern versions of universal truths in schools (see N. Gough, 1999).

According to Bybee (1993), Bybee and Deboer (1994), and Hurd (1969, 1970, 1998, 2000), the history of science education is one of oscillations among espoused goals that sometimes include an emphasis on the social aspects of science and sometimes eschew them. These arguments aside, constructivism and social constructivism, as theoretical constructs that provide perspective, seem to encourage a dialogue among science and environmental educators who accept that science is a socially mediated and value-laden activity and that social constructivism allows a more authentic version of science to be represented to students. If science is understood to be part of the social world in dialectical relationship with the natural world, then environmental and science educators have more to talk about, as do researchers in both arenas. With an underlying social constructivist epistemology in common, the scope of a research activity can expand to encompass constructivist/interpretivist, critical, and postmodern ways of knowing and the creation of knowledge, not only in scientific but in educational research, recognized as a social endeavor as well as a cognitive construction. This means science educators' views of research must include conceptions of knowing and understanding as socially/culturally influenced. It also means conceiving of inquiry in science and education as subjective as well as political.

The point is, from research perspectives encountered by many environmental educators, although science is not totally explainable in social, political, or cultural terms, neither is it the pristine, monistic, acultural, ahistorical way of knowing it is purported to be by many devout interpreters of science education (Benson, 2001). The problem has been, in taking a social constructivist position to teaching, that teachers often do not know the presuppositions of teaching from that position. And the same is true for researchers who have not understood the epistemological/ ontological presuppositions among the various ways of knowing. Benson's (2001) explanation of social constructivism, as rooted in the sociology of knowledge, where construction of meaning is rooted in social settings, is instructive for researchers who work beyond positivist methods. The way an individual interprets the world and creates personal understanding, he says, is influenced by five features: knowledge of history (as learned in culture), the particular social context of the research, the researcher's personal life history, the purposes attached to the research (as a sense-making process), and the research act itself (as an act of creating meaning). Thus, we can have similar understandings, but they may be created individually and contextually in ways that influence how we understand this knowledge/understanding.

Extended to social science and to educational research, the suggestion is that researchers use a socially based interpretive method to account for methodological choice and to establish evaluative criteria according to that choice. So conceived, it is absolutely crucial that the researchers lay out epistemological/ontological and methodological assumptions from which their arguments are constructed. This obligates researchers to know why they are researching from a social constructivist, critical, poststructuralist, or any other perspective or combination of perspectives. If research in science education and environmental education is to be recognized and justified as a human creation influenced by social/cultural issues, it implies that science education researchers who maintain a strict realist view of research might be ignoring developments in educational/social science research, as illustrated by the requisite variety in environmental education. More seriously, such researchers may be ignoring recent developments in the philosophy of science and how the nature of research (and of science) is interpreted. It is necessary to engage in these discussions in any attempt to portray a field of research as distinct from science education, but also to engage in the politics of research that this engagement entails. To do less would be to abrogate our responsibilities as social science researchers to theorize our practices, a matter as serious as the failure to ground our theories in practice.

ACKNOWLEDGMENTS

Thanks to Joe Heimlich and Ian Robottom, who reviewed this chapter.

REFERENCES

Adedayo, A., & Olawepo, J. (1997). Integration of environmental education in social science curricula at the secondary school level in Nigeria: Problems and prospects. *Environmental Education Research, 3*(1), 83–93.

Ahlberg, M., & Leal Filho, W. (Eds.). (1998). *Environmental education for sustainability: Good environment, good life.* New York: Peter Lang.

Aikenhead, G. (1996). Science education: Border crossing into the subculture of science. *Studies in Science Education, 27,* 1–52.

Ajiboye, J., Audu, U., & Mansaray, A. (1998). Environmental knowledge and attitudes of some Nigerian secondary school teachers. *Environmental Education Research, 4*(3), 329–339.

American Association for the Advancement of Science. (1993). *Benchmarks for science literacy.* New York: Oxford University Press.

Andrew, J. (1997). *Community-based environmental education: Government and community; economics and environment.* Unpublished doctoral dissertation, Deakin University, Geelong, Victoria. Australia.

Andrew, J. (1998). History and environmental education research. In S. Groves, B. Jane, I. Robottom, & R. Tytler (Eds.), *Contemporary approaches to research in mathematics, science, health, and environmental education.* Geelong, Victoria: Deakin University.

Andrew, J., & Malone, K. (1995). The first ten years: A review of the *Australian Journal of Environmental Education. Australian Journal of Environmental Education, 11,* 131–162.

Armstrong, C. (1997). Social metaphors and their implications for environmental education. *Environmental Education Research, 3*(1), 29–42.

Ashworth, S. (1995). Conservation of endangered species: What do children think? *Environmental Education and Information, 14*(3), 229–244.

Azeiteiro, U., Pereira, M., Bacelar-Nicolau, P., Caieiro, S., Torres Soares, J., & Gonçalves, F. (2003). *First world environmental education congress: Programme.* Espinho, Portugal: FWEEC.

Bachiorri, A. (1995). Environmental education in the Italian school context: Some considerations. *International Journal of Environmental Education and Information, 14*(4), 377–84.

Ballantyne, R., & Clacherty, A. (1990). Understanding student experiences of environmental education programmes: The value of a phenomenological approach. *Environmental Education and Information, 9*(1), 29–42.

Ballantyne, R., Connell, S., & Fien, J. (1998a). Factors contributing to intergenerational communication regarding environmental programs: Preliminary research findings. *Australian Journal of Environmental Education, 14,* 1–10.

Ballantyne, R., Connell, S., & Fien, J. (1998b). Students as catalysts of environmental change: A framework for researching intergenerational influence through environmental education. *Environmental Education Research, 4*(3), 285–298.

Barron, D. (1995). Gendering environmental education reform: Identify the constitutive power of environmental discourses. *Australian Journal of Environmental Education, 11,* 107–120.

Bennett, S. (1996). Discourse analysis: A method for deconstruction. In M. Williams (Ed.), *Understanding geographical and environmental education: The role of research* (pp. 150–161). London: Cassell.

Benson, G. (2001). Science education from a social constructivist position: A worldview. *Studies in Philosophy and Education, 20,* 443–452.

Bogner, F. (1998). The influence of short-term outdoor ecology education on long-term variables of environmental perspective. *Journal of Environmental Education, 29*(4), 17–29.

Bolscho, D. (1990). Environmental education in practice in the Federal Republic of Germany: An empirical study. *International Journal of Science Education, 12*(2), 133–146.

Bonnett, M. (2002). Education for sustainability as a frame of mind. *Environmental Education Research, 8*(1), 9–20.

Bonnett, M., & Elliott, J. (1999). Editorial. *Cambridge Journal of Education, 29*(3), 309–311.

Bonnett, M., & Williams, J. (1998). Environmental education and primary children's attitudes toward nature and the environment. *Cambridge Journal of Education, 28*(2), 159–174.

Bowers, C. (1991). The anthropocentric foundations of educational liberalism: Some critical concerns. *Trumpeter, 8*(3), 102–107.

Bowers, C. (2001). How language limits our understanding of environmental issues. *Environmental Education Research, 7*(2), 141–153.

Bowers, C. (2002). Toward an eco-justice pedagogy. *Environmental Education Research, 8*(1), 21–34.

Boyes, E., & Stanisstreet, M. (1996). Threats to the global atmospheric environment: The extent of pupil understanding. *International Research in Geographical and Environmental Education, 5*(3), 186–195.

Boyes, E., & Stanisstreet, M. (1997). Children's models of understanding of two major global environmental issues (ozone layer and greenhouse effect). *Research in Science and Technological Education, 15*(1), 19–28.

Boyes, E., & Stanisstreet, M. (1998). High school students' perceptions of how major global environmental effects might cause skin cancer. *Journal of Environmental Education, 29*(2), 31–36.

Boyes, E., Stanisstreet, M., & Papantiniou, V. (1999). The ideas of Greek high school students about the "ozone layer." *Science Education, 83*(6), 724–737.

Breiting, S. (1988). Sustainable development and the ideological formation of environmental education. In C. Christensen & K. Nielsen (Eds.), *Environmental education: International contributions 1988, Proceedings of the Research Centre for Environmental and Health Education, No. 5.* Copenhagen: Royal Danish School of Educational Studies.

Breiting, S., & Nielsen, K. (Eds.) (1996). *Environmental education research in the Nordic countries.* Copenhagen: Research Centre of Environmental and Health Education, Royal Danish School of Educational Studies.

Brody, M. (1996). An assessment of 4th, 8th-, and 11th-grade students' environmental science knowledge related to Oregon's marine resources. *Journal of Environmental Education, 27*(3), 21–27.

Brubaker, S. (1972). *To live on earth: Man and his environment in perspective.* Baltimore: Johns Hopkins.

Bruner, J. (1990). *Acts of meaning.* Cambridge, MA: Harvard University Press.

Bruner, J. (1996). *The culture of education.* Cambridge, MA: Harvard University Press.

Bull, J., Cromwell, M., Cwikiel, W., Di Chiro, G., Guarina, J., Rathje, R., et al. (1988). *Education in action: A community problem solving program for schools.* Dexter, MI: Thomson-Shore.

Bybee, R. (1997). *Achieving scientific literacy: From purposes to practices.* Portsmouth, NH: Heinemann.

Bybee, R., & DeBoer, G. (1994). Research on goals for the science curriculum. In D. Gabel (Ed.), *Handbook of research on science teaching and learning* (pp. 357–386). New York: Macmillan.

Cabral, B. (1998). Shells: Awareness of the environment through drama. *NADIE Journal, 22*(1), 27–31.

Chan, K.-K. (1996). Environmental attitudes and behavior of secondary school students in Hong Kong. *The Environmentalist, 16*(4), 297–306.

Chan, K.-K. (1998, July). *Mass media and environmental cognition in Hong Kong.* Paper presented at the Joint Conference of the National Communication Association/International Communication Association's "Communication: Organizing for the Future," Rome.

Chawla, L. (1994). *In the first country of places: Nature, poetry, and childhood memory.* Albany, NY: SUNY Press.

Chawla, L. (1998). Significant life experiences revisited: A review of research on sources of environmental sensitivity. *Journal of Environmental Education, 29*(3), 11–21.

Chawla, L., & Hart, R. (1995.) The roots of environmental concern. *The MAMTA Journal, 20*(1), 148–157.

Chenhansa, S., & Schleppegrell, M. (1998). Linguistic features of middle school environmental education texts. *Environmental Education Research, 4*(10), 53–66.

Chou, J., & Roth, R. (1995). Exploring the underlying constructs of basic concepts in environmental education. *Journal of Environmental Education, 26*(2), 36–43.

Christidou, V., Kouladis, V., & Christidis, T. (1997). Children's use of metaphors in relation to their mental models: The case of the ozone layer and its depletion. *Research in Science Education, 27*(4), 541–552.

Clark, B. (1996). Environmental attitudes and knowledge of year 11 students in a Queensland high school. *Australian Journal of Environmental Education, 12*, 19–26.

Clover, D., Follen, S., & Hall, B. (1998). *The nature of transformation: Environmental, adult and popular education.* Toronto: Transformative Learning Centre and Ontario Institute for Studies in Education/University of Toronto.

Cobern, W. (1991). *Worldview theory and science education research.* Manhattan, KS: National Association for Research in Science Teaching.

Cobern, W. (1996). Worldview theory and conceptual change in science education. *Science Education, 80*(5), 579–610.

Cobern, W. (1998a). Science and a social constructivist view of science education. In W. Cobern (Ed.), *Socio cultural perspectives on science education: An international dialogue* (pp. 7–23). Dordrecht, the Netherlands: Kluwer Academic.

Cobern, W. (Ed.). (1998b). *Socio-cultural perspectives on science education: An international dialogue.* Dordrecht, the Netherlands: Kluwer Academic.

Cobern, W. (2000a). *Everyday thoughts about nature: A worldview investigation of important concepts students use to make sense of nature with specific attention to science.* Dordrecht, the Netherlands: Kluwer Academic.

Cobern, W. (2000b). The nature of science and the role of knowledge and belief. *Science and Education, 9*(3), 219–246.

Cobiac, S. (1995). *Empowerment through critical teaching.* Unpublished master's thesis, University of South Australia.

Colbe, C., & Koballa, T., Jr. (1996). Science education. In J. Sikula (Ed.), *Handbook of research in teacher education* (2nd ed., pp. 459–484). New York: Macmillan.

Collins, L., & Romjue, M. (1995). Evaluation of an environmental science distance education project. *Journal of Educational Media and Library Sciences, 32*(3), 264–81.

Connell, S. (1997). Empirical-Analytical methodological research in environmental education: Response to a negative trend in methodological and ideological discussions. *Environmental Education Research, 3*(2), 117–132.

Connell, S., Fien, J., Sykes, H., & Yencken, D. (1998). Young people and the environment in Australia: Beliefs, knowledge, commitment and educational implications. *Australian Journal of Environmental Education, 14,* 39–48.

Conway, M. (1990). *Autobiographical memory: An introduction.* Milton Keynes, England: Open University Press.

Corcoran, P. (1999). Formative influences in the lives of educators in the United States. *Environmental Education Research, 5*(2), 207–220.

Corcoran, P., & Fien, J. (1996). Learning for a sustainable environment: Professional development and teacher education in environmental education in the Asia-Pacific region. *Environmental Education Research, 2*(2), 227–236.

Cork, C. (1996). *Community-managed ecotourism: A feasibility survey in Phnom Baset, Cambodia.* Unpublished master's thesis, University of Calgary.

Corsaro, W. (1997). *The sociology of childhood.* Thousand Oaks, CA: Pine Forge Press.

Cortazzi, M. (1993). *Narrative analysis.* London: Falmer.

Courtenay-Hall, P., & Lott, S. (1999). Issues of inclusion in developing environmental education policy: Reflections on B.C. experiences. *Canadian Journal of Environmental Education, 4,* 83–102.

Crick, B. (1978). Procedural values in political education. In B. Crick & A. Porter (Eds.), *Political education and political literacy.* London: Longman.

Crotty, M. (1998). *The foundations of social research: Meaning and perspective in the research process.* Thousand Oaks, CA: Sage.

Darlington, P., & Black, R. (1996). Helping to protect the earth—the Kosciusko National Park Education Program. *Australian Journal of Environmental Education, 12,* 3–8.

Davis, J. (2003). *Innovation through action research in environmental education: From project to praxis.* Unpublished doctoral dissertation, Griffith University.

Denzin, N., & Lincoln, Y. (Eds.). (2000). *Handbook of qualitative research* (2nd ed.). Thousand Oaks, CA: Sage.

Dillon, P. (1997). Conducting research over the internet: An interactive, image-based instrument for investigations in environmental education. *Journal of Information Technology for Teacher Education, 6*(2), 147–156.

Disinger, J., & Roth, C. (2003). *Environmental literacy.* Retrieved February 5, 2004 from http://www.ericse.org/digests/dse92–1html

Donnelly, J. (2002). Instrumentality, hermeneutics and the place of science in the school curriculum. *Science and Education, 11*(2), 135–153.

Driver, R., Leach, J., Millar, R., & Scott, P. (1996). *Young peoples' images of science.* Philadelphia: Open University Press.

Driver, R., & Oldham, V. (1986). A constructivist approach to curriculum development in science. *Studies in Science Education, 13*, 105–122.

Dunlap, R., & Van Liere, K. (1978). The new environmental paradigm: A proposed measuring instrument and preliminary results. *Journal of Environmental Education, 9*(4), 10–19.

Dunlap, R., & Van Liere, K. (1984). Commitment to the dominant social paradigm and concern for environmental quality. *Social Science Quarterly, 65*(4), 1013–1028.

Duschl, R., & Osborne, J. (2002). Supporting and promoting argumentation discourse in science education. *Studies in Science Education, 38*, 39–72.

Eagles, P., & Demare, R. (1999). Factors influencing children's environmental attitudes. *Journal of Environmental Education, 30*(4), 33–37.

Earth Charter. (2000). The Earth Charter Initiative. Retrieved June 1, 2003, from http://www.earthcharter.org/earthcharter/charter.htm

Eisner, E. (1990). The meaning of alternative paradigms for practice. In E. Guba (Ed.), *The paradigm dialogue.* Newbury Park, CA: Sage.

Elliott, J. (1991). *Action research for education change.* Milton Keynes, England: Open University Press.

Elliott, J. (1995). Environmental education action research and the role of the school. In *Environmental learning for the 21st century.* Paris: OECD.

Elliott, J. (1999). Sustainable society and environmental education: Future perspectives and demands for the educational system. *Cambridge Journal of Education, 29*(3), 325–340.

Elliott, S. (2002). *A review of early childhood environmental education: Patches of green.* Unpublished manuscript, Sydney, Australia.

Emmons, K. (1997). Perceptions of the environment while exploring the outdoors: A case study in Belize. *Environmental Education Research, 3*(3), 327–344.

Fason, J. (1996). *An assessment of attitudes, knowledge and beliefs of global warming: A comparison between twelfth grade students in Lansing, Michigan and Valdosta, Georgia.* Unpublished doctoral dissertation, Michigan State University.

Fensham, P. (1978). Stockholm to Tbilisi—the evolution of environmental education. *Prospects, VIII*(4), 446–465.

Fien, J. (1993). *Education for the environment: Critical curriculum theorizing and environmental education.* Geelong, Victoria, Australia: Deakin University Press.

Fien, J. (2000a). Education for a sustainable consumption: Towards a framework for curriculum and pedagogy. In B. Jensen, K. Schnack, & V. Simovska (Eds.), *Critical environmental and health education.* Copenhagen: Research Centre for Environmental and Health Education, Danish University of Education.

Fien, J. (2000b). "Education for the environment: A critique"—an analysis. *Environmental Education Research, 6*(2), 179–193.

Fien, J., & Hillcoat, J. (1996). The critical tradition in research in geographical and environmental education. In M. Williams (Ed.), *Understanding geographical and environmental education.* London: Cassell.

Fien, J., & Rawling, R. (1996). Reflective practice: A case study of professional development for environmental education. *Journal of Environmental Education, 27*(3), 11–20.

Fien, J., Scott, W., & Tilbury, D. (2001). Education and conservation: Lessons from an evaluation. *Environmental Education Research, 7*(4), 379–396.

Fisher, B. (1998). There's a hole in my greenhouse effect. *School Science Review, 79*(288), 93–99.

Gambro, J., & Switzky, H. (1999). Variables associated with American high school students' knowledge of environmental issues related to energy and pollution. *Journal of Environmental Education, 39*(2), 15–22.

Gayford, C. (1995). Science education and sustainability: A case study in discussion-based learning. *Research in Science and Technological Education, 13*(2), 135–145.

Gerber, R. (1996). Interpretive approaches to geographical and environmental education research. In M. Williams (Ed.), *Understanding geographical and environmental education.* London: Cassell.

Gibson, G. (1996). *The landcare and environment action program for unemployed young people in the ACT: Enhancing self-concept, learning and teaching for the environment.* Bruce, ACT: University of Canberra.

Glazer, S., Vrtacnik, M., & Bacnik, A. (1998). Primary school children's understanding of municipal waste processing. *Environmental Education Research, 4*(3), 299–308.

Goodwin, D., & Adkins, J. (1997). Problem-solving environmental science on the Chesapeake Bay. *School Science Review, 78*(284), 49–55.

Gough, A. (1999). Recognizing women in environmental education pedagogy and research: Toward an ecofeminist poststructuralist perspective. *Environmental Education Research, 5*(2), 143–161.

Gough, N. (1999). Rethinking the subject: (De)constructing human agency in environmental education research. *Environmental Education Research, 5*(1), 35–48.

Gough, S., & Scott, W. (2003). *Sustainable development: Matters of definition.* Unpublished paper. Bath, UK: University of Bath, Centre for Research in Education and Environment.

Government of Canada. (2002). *A framework for environmental learning and sustainability in Canada.* Ottawa, Canada: Author.

Greaves, E., Stanisstreet, M., Boyes, E., & Williams, T. (1993). Children's ideas about animal conservation. *School Science Review, 75*(271), 51–60.

Greenall, A. (1981). Environmental education: A case study in national curriculum action. *Environmental Education and Information, 1*(4), 285–294.

Greenall, A. (1987). A political history of environmental education in Australia: Snakes and ladders. In I. Robottom (Ed.), *Environmental education: Practice and possibility* (pp. 3–21). Geelong, Victoria, Australia: Deakin University Press.

Greenall-Gough, A. (1990). Environmental education. In K. McRae (Ed.), *Outdoor and environmental education: Diverse purposes and practices.* Melbourne, Australia: Macmillan.

Greenall-Gough, A. (1994). *Fathoming the fathers in environmental education: A feminist poststructuralist analysis.* Unpublished doctoral dissertation, Deakin University, Geelong, Victoria.

Groves, S., Jane, B., Robottom, I., & Tytler, R. (Eds.). (1998). *Contemporary approaches to research in mathematics, science, health, and environmental education.* Geelong, Victoria: Deakin University.

Harris, K. (1990). Empowering teachers: Towards a justification for intervention. *Journal of Philosophy of Education, 24*(2), 171–183.

Hart, P. (1999). *Environmental education in Canadian elementary schools: Teaching children to care.* Invited lecture in the Distinguished Scholars Lecture Series, University of Regina, April 7.

Hart, P. (2000). Searching for meaning in children's participation in environmental education. In B. Jensen, K. Schnack, & V. Simovska (Eds.), *Critical environmental and health education—Research issues and challenges.* Copenhagen: Research Centre for Environmental and Health, Danish University of Education.

Hart, P. (2003a). Reflections on reviewing educational research: (Re)searching for value in environmental education. *Environmental Education Research, 9*(2), 241–257.

Hart, P. (2003b). *Teachers' thinking in environmental education: Consciousness and responsibility.* New York: Peter Lang.

Hart, P., & Nolan, K. (1999). A critical analysis of research in environmental education. *Studies in Science Education, 34*, 1–69.

Hart, P., & Robottom, I. (1990). The science-technology-society movement in science education: A critique of the reform process. *Journal of Research in Science Teaching, 27*(6), 575–588.

Hart, R. (1997). *Children's participation: The theory and practice of involving young citizens in community development and environmental care.* London: Earthscan.

Heimlich, J. (1993). *Nonformal environmental education: Toward a working definition. The environmental outlook.* Columbus, OH: ERIC Clearinghouse for Science, Mathematics, and Environmental Education.

Hicks, W., Jr. (1993). *Effects of environmental action oriented lessons on environmental knowledge, attitudes, and behavior of high school students.* Unpublished doctoral dissertation, Pennsylvania State University.

Hillcoat, J. (1995). "I think it's really great that someone is listening to us . . ." Young people and the environment. *Environmental Education Research, 1*(2), 159–171.

Hines, J., Hungerford, H., & Tomera, A. (1986/87). Analysis and synthesis of research on responsible environmental behavior: A meta-analysis. *Journal of Environmental Education, 18*(2), 1–8.

Ho, R. (1997). River water, well water . . . but environmental problems have no national borders: Environmental education and environmental management for China and Hong Kong after 1997. *Environmental Education and Information, 16*(3), 251–268.

Hoffman, N. (1994). Beyond constructivism: Geothean approach to environmental education. *Australian Journal of Environmental Education, 10*(1), 71–90.

Huckle, J. (1983). Values education through geography: A radical critique. *Journal of Geography, 82*(2), 59–63.

Huckle, J. (1985a). Geography and schooling. In R. Johnston (Ed.), *The future of geography*. London: Methuen.

Huckle, J. (1985b). Ecological crisis: Some implications for geographical education. *Contemporary Issues in Geography and Education, 2*(2), 2–13.

Huckle, J. (2003). *Education for sustainable development: A draft briefing paper for the Teacher Training Agency.* Unpublished paper.

Huckle, J., & Sterling, S. (Eds.). (1996). *Education for sustainability.* London: Earthscan.

Hug, W. (1998). *Learning and teaching for an ecological sense of place: Toward environmental/science education praxis.* Unpublished doctoral dissertation, Pennsylvania State University.

Hungerford, H. (1996, November). *Comments made during "EE: A panel discussion of its past, its, present, and its future,"* 25th Annual Conference of the North American Association for Environmental Education, San Francisco.

Hungerford, H., Peyton, R., & Wilke, R. (1980). Goals for curriculum development in environmental education. *Journal of Environmental Education, 11*(3), 42–47.

Hungerford, H., Peyton, R., & Wilke, R. (1983). Editorial: Yes EE does have a definition and structure. *Journal of Environmental Education, 14*(3), 1–2.

Hungerford, H., & Volk, T. (1990). Changing learner behavior through environmental education. *Journal of Environmental Education, 21*(3), 8–21.

Hurd, P. (1969). *New directions in teaching secondary school science.* Chicago: Rand-McNally.

Hurd, P. (1970). Scientific enlightenment for an age of science. *Science Teacher, 37,* 13.

Hurd, P. (1998). Scientific literacy: New minds for a changing world. *Science Education, 82,* 407–416.

Hurd, P. (2000). Science education for the 21st century. *School Science and Mathematics, 100*(6), 282–288.

Hutchison, D. (1998). *Growing up green: Education for ecological renewal.* New York: Teachers College Press.

Iozzi, L. (1981). *Research in environmental education 1971–1980.* (ED214762). Columbus, OH: ERIC Clearinghouse for Science, Mathematics, and Environmental Education.

Iozzi, L. (1989). What research says to the educator: Part one: Environmental education and the affective domain. *Journal of Environmental Education, 20*(3), 3–9.

IUCN. (1970). *International working meeting on environmental education in the school curriculum: Final report.* Gland, Switzerland: IUCN.

IUCN. (1980). *World conservation strategy: Living resource conservation for sustainable development.* Gland, Switzerland: IUCN.

Ivy, T., Lee, C., & Chuan, G. (1998). A survey of environmental knowledge, attitudes, and behavior of students in Singapore. *International Research in Geographical and Environmental Education, 7*(3), 181–202.

James, P. (1997). The development of problem-solving skills in environmental education. *International Journal of Environmental Education and Information, 16*(4), 417–426.

Jenkins, E. (1994). Public understanding of science and science education for action. *Journal of Curriculum Studies, 26*(6), 601–611.

Jenkins, E. (2000). Research in science education: Time for a health check? *Studies in Science Education, 35*, 1–26.

Jensen, B., & Schnack, K. (1994). Action competence as an educational challenge. In B. Jensen & K. Schnack (Eds.), *Action and action competence* (pp. 5–8). Copenhagen: Royal Danish School of Educational Studies.

Jensen, B., & Schnack, K. (1997). The action competence approach in environmental education. *Environmental Education Research, 3*(2), 163–178.

Jensen, B., Kofoed, J., Uhrenholdt, G., & Vognsen, C. (1995). *Environmental education in Denmark—the Jægerspris project*, Publication No. 31. Copenhagen: Royal Danish School of Educational Studies, Research Centre for Environmental and Health Education.

Jensen, B., Schnack, K., & Simovska V. (Eds.). (2000). *Critical environmental and health education—Research issues and challenges.* Copenhagen: Research Centre for Environmental and Health, Danish University of Education.

Jickling, B. (1992). Why I don't want my children to be educated for sustainable development. *Journal of Environmental Education, 23*(4), 5–8.

Jickling, B. (1993). Research in environmental education: Some thoughts on the need for conceptual analysis. *Australian Journal of Environmental Education, 9*, 85–94.

Jickling, B. (2001). Environmental thought, the language of sustainability, and digital watches. *Environmental Education Research, 7*(2), 167–180.

Jurin, R. (1995). *College students' environmental belief and value structures, and relationship of these structures to reported environmental behavior.* Unpublished doctoral dissertation, the Ohio State University.

Kahn, P., & Friedman, B. (1995). Environmental views and values of children in an inner-city black community. *Child Development, 66*(5), 1403–1417.

Kasper, M. (1998). *Factors affecting elementary principals' and teachers' decisions to support outdoor field trips.* Unpublished doctoral dissertation, University of Texan at Austin.

Kaufman, J., Ewing, M., Hyle, A., Montgomery, D., & Self, P. (2001). Women and nature: Using memory-work to rethink our relationship to the natural world. *Environmental Education Research, 7*(4), 359–378.

Keighley, P. (1997). The impact of experiences out-of-doors on personal development and environmental attitudes. *Horizons, 2*, 27–29.

Keliher, V. (1997). Children's perceptions of nature. *International Research in Geographical and Environmental Education, 6*(3), 240–243.

Kelly, T. (1986). Discussing controversial issues: Four perspectives on the teacher's role. *Theory and Research in Social Education, 14*(2), 113–138.

Kollmuss, A., & Agyeman, J. (2002). Mind the gap: Why do people act environmentally and what are the barriers to pro-environmental behavior? *Environmental Education Research, 8*(3), 239–260.

Koulaidis, V., & Christidou., V. (1999). Models of students' thinking concerning the greenhouse effect and teaching implications. *Science Education, 83*(5), 559–576.

Kuo, L. (1994). *Students' values, attitudes and behaviors towards environmental issues.* Unpublished doctoral dissertation, Murdoch University, Perth.

Kyburz-Graber, R., Rigendinger, L., Hirsch, G., & Werner, K. (1997). A socio-ecological approach to interdisciplinary environmental education in senior high schools. *Environmental Education Research, 3*(1), 17–28.

Labaree, D. (1997a). Public goods, private goods: The American struggle over educational goals. *American Educational Research Journal, 34*, 39–81.

Labaree, D. (1997b). *How to succeed in school without really learning: The credentials race in American education.* New Haven, CT: Yale University Press.

Lalonde, R., & Jackson, E. (2002). The new environmental paradigm scale: Has it outlived its usefulness? *Journal of Environmental Education, 33*(4), 28–36.

Lather, P. (1996, April). *Methodology as subversive repetition: Practices toward a feminist double science.* Paper presented at the annual meeting of the American Educational Research Association, New York, NY.

Leach, J., & Scott, P. (2002). Designing and evaluating science teacher sequences: An approach drawing upon the concept of learning demand and a social constructivist perspective on learning. *Studies in Science Education, 38,* 115–142.

Leal Filho, W. (1996). Eurosurvey: An analysis of current trends in environmental education in Europe. In G. Harris & C. Blackwell (Eds.), *Environmental Education: Vol. 1. Monitoring change in education.* Aldershot: Arena.

Leal Filho, W., & Bynoe, P. (1995). Current trends in environmental education and public awareness in Guyana. *Environmental Education and Information, 14*(4), 351–360.

Lee, J. (1997). Environmental education in schools in Hong Kong. *Environmental Education Research, 3*(3), 359–371.

Lee, N. (2001). *Childhood and society: Growing up in an age of uncertainty.* Buckingham, UK: Open University Press.

Leeming, F. (1997). Effects of participation in class activities on children's environmental attitudes and knowledge. *Journal of Environmental Education, 28*(2), 33–42.

Leeming, F., Dwyer, W., Porter, B., & Cobern, M. (1993). Outcome research in environmental education: A critical review. *Journal of Environmental Education, 24*(4), 8–21.

Leeming, F., Porter, B., Dwyer, W., Cobern, M., & Oliver, D. (1997). Effects of participation in class activities on children' environmental attitudes and knowledge. *Journal of Environmental Education, 28*(2), 33–42.

Lewis, A., & Lindsay, G. (Eds.). (2000). *Researching Children's perspectives.* Buckingham, UK: Open University Press.

Lock, R. (1998). Environmental education and hearing-impaired pupils. *School Science Review, 79*(288), 101–104.

Lousley, C. (1999). De(poliliticizing) the environment club: Environmental discourses and the culture of schooling. *Environmental Education Research, 5*(3), 293–304.

Lowe, I. (1998). Environmental education: The key to a sustainable future. In N. Graves (Ed.), *Education and the environment* (pp. 95–104). London: World Education Fellowship.

Luckman, C. (1996). Defining experiential education. *Journal of Experiential Education, 19*(1), 6–7.

Mangas, V., Martinez, P., & Pedauye, R. (1997). Analysis of environmental concepts and attitudes among biology degree students. *Journal of Environmental Education, 29*(1), 28–33.

Mahony, D. (1994). *An ethnographic field study of positions regarding the environment held by landowners of the Wollombi Valley, and implications for environmental education.* Newcastle, NSW: University of Newcastle.

Malone, K. (1996). *School and community partnerships in socially critical environmental education: Research as environmental activism.* Geelong, Victoria, Australia: Deakin University.

Mansaray, A., & Ajiboye, J. (1997). Environmental education and Nigerian students' knowledge, attitudes and practices (KAP): Implications for curriculum development. *International Journal of Environmental Education and Information, 16*(3), 317–24.

Marcinkowski, T., & Mrazek, R. (Eds.). (1996). *Research in environmental education 1981–1990.* Troy, OH: North American Association for Environmental Education.

Marsden, W. (1998). "Conservation education" and the foundations of national prosperity: Comparative perspectives from early twentieth-century North America and Britain. *History of Education, 27*(3), 345–362.

Martinez Rivera, C. (1997). *Environmental education: A hands-on approach to explore environmental issues in Puerto Rico with emphasis on endangered species.* Unpublished doctoral dissertation, University of Massachusetts.

Mason, L., & Santi, M. (1998). Discussing the greenhouse effect: Children's collaborative discourse reasoning and conceptual change. *Environmental Education Research, 4*(1), 67–85.

Matthews, M. (1998). *Constructivism and science education: A philosophical examination.* Dordrecht, the Netherlands: Kluwer Academic.

Matthews, M. (2000). Constructivism and science education: An evaluation: Editorial. *Science and Education, 9,* 6.

May, T. (2001). *Social research: Issues, methods and process.* Buckingham, UK: Open University Press.

McIlveene, M. (1996). *A comparison of Russian and American students' concerns about environmental issues: Implications for environmental education curriculum.* Unpublished doctoral dissertation, Georgia State University.

McKeown, R., & Hopkins, C. (2003). EE≠ESD: Defusing the worry. *Environmental Education Research, 9*(1), 117–128.

Milbrath, L. (1984). *Environmentalists: Vanguard for a new society.* Albany, NY: SUNY.

Milbrath, L. (1989). *Envisioning a sustainable society: Learning our way out.* Albany, NY: SUNY.

Millar, R. (1989). Constructive criticisms. *International Journal of Science Education, 2,* 587–596.

Millar, R., & Osborne, J. (Eds.). (1998). *Beyond 2000: Science education for the future.* London: King's College.

Millar, R., Leach, J., & Osborne, J. (Eds.). (2000). *Improving science education: The contribution of research.* Buckingham, UK: Open University Press.

Miller, J. (1997). *Plant trees in other people's yards: An investigation into the perspectives forming seventh-graders' understanding of an ecological and sustainable worldview, and possibilities for a curriculum to broaden these perspectives.* Unpublished master's thesis, Pacific Lutheran University.

Monroe, M., & DeYoung, R. (1996). Some fundamentals of engaging stories. *Environmental Education Research, 2*(2), 171–187.

Morgan, J. (1998). *Liberty Hyde Bailey: Pioneer and prophet of an ecological philosophy of education.* Unpublished doctoral dissertation, Columbia University.

Mrazek, R. (Ed.). (1993). *Alternative paradigms in environmental education research.* Troy, OH: North American Association for Environmental Education.

Mucunguzi, P. (1995). A review of non-formal environmental education in Uganda. *Environmental Education Research, 1*(3), 337–344.

NAAEE. (n.d.). *Excellence in EE—guidelines for learning (K–12).* Rock Spring, GA: NAAEE.

Nando Rosales, J. (1995). *Primary education teachers' attitudes and beliefs in the Valencia community in regard to environmental education as an element of criticism for its implementation in the curriculum.* Unpublished doctoral dissertation, Universitat do Valencia, Spain.

Nelson, W. (1996). *Environmental literacy and residential outdoor education programs.* Unpublished doctoral dissertation, University of La Verne.

Nevala, A. (1997). *An evaluation of educators' participation in the Great Lakes Education Program.* Unpublished master's thesis, Michigan State University.

O'Connor, T. (1997). *Creating effective environmental education: A case study utilizing an integrative teaching methodology to develop positive environmental attitudes and behaviors in the secondary general science curriculum.* Unpublished doctoral dissertation, Temple University.

O'Donoghue, R., & McNaught, C. (1991). Environmental education: The development of a curriculum through "grass-roots" reconstructive action. *International Journal of Science Education, 13*(4), 391–404.

Osborne, J. (2002). Science without literacy: A ship without a sail? *Cambridge Journal of Education, 32*(2), 203–218.

Oulton, C., & Scott, W. (1998). Environmental values education: An exploration of its role in the school curriculum. *Journal of Moral Education, 27*(2), 209–224.

Oulton, C., & Scott, W. (2000). Environmental education: A time for re-visioning. In B. Moon, S. Brown, & M. Ben-Peretz (Eds.), *Routledge international companion to education.* London: Routledge.

Pace, P. (1997). Environmental education in Malta: Trends and challenges. *Environmental Education Research, 3*(1), 69–82.

Page, S. (1997). *A case study of an outdoor environmental learning center at an elementary school.* Unpublished doctoral dissertation, Indiana University.

Palmer, J. (1995). Environmental thinking in the early years: Understanding and misunderstanding of concepts related to waste management. *Environmental Education Research, 1*(1), 35–45.

Palmer, J. (1998). *Environmental education in the 21st century: Theory, practice, progress and promise.* London: Routledge.

Palmer, J., & Suggate, J. (1996). Influences and experiences affecting the pro-environmental behaviour of educators. *Environmental Education Research, 2*(1), 109–121.

Palmer, J., Suggate, J., Bajd, B., Hart, P., Ho, R., Ofwono-Orecho, J., et al. (1998). Significant life experiences and formative influences on the development of adults' environmental awareness in nine countries. *Environmental Education Research, 4*(4), 445–464.

Palmer, J., Suggate, J., Robottom, I., & Hart, P. (1999). Significant life experiences and formative influences on the development of adults' environmental awareness in the UK, Australia, and Canada. *Environmental Education Research, 5*(2), 181–200.

Panter-Brick, C. (Ed.). (1998). *Biosocial perspectives on children.* Cambridge, UK: Cambridge University Press.

Papadimitriou, V. (1995). Professional development of in-service primary teachers in environmental education: An action research approach. *Environmental Education Research, 1*(1), 85–97.

Payne, P. (1997). Embodiment and environmental education. *Environmental Education Research, 3*(2), 133–153.

Payne, P. (1998a). Children's conceptions of nature. *Australian Journal of Environmental Education, 14*, 19–26.

Payne, P. (1998b). The politics of nature: Children's conceptions, constructions and values. In M. Ahlberg & W. Leal Filho (Eds.), *Environmental education for sustainability: Good environment, good life.* Frankfurt: Peter Lang.

Payne, P. (1999). Postmodern challenges and modern horizons: Education "for being for the environment." *Environmental Education Research, 5*(1), 5–34.

Payne, P. (2001). Identity and environmental education. *Environmental Education Research, 7*(1), 67–88.

Payne, P., & Riddell, K. (1999) Thinking the environment: The written epistemology of enquiry. *Canadian Journal of Environmental Education, 4*, 243–261.

Peel, G., Robottom, I., & Walker, R. (1997). *Environmental education and self-interest: The educative role of community, government and private environmental agencies and groups.* Geelong, Victoria: Centre for Studies in Mathematics, Science and Environmental Education.

Peters, A., & Wilson, R. (1996). Networking for the environment. *Early Childhood Education Journal, 24*(1), 51–53.

Plant, M. (1995). The riddle of sustainable development and the role of environmental education. *Environmental Education Research, 1*(3), 253–266.

Polkinghorne, D. (1995). Narrative configuration in qualitative analysis. In J. Hatch & R. Wisniewski (Eds.), *Life history and narrative.* London: Falmer.

Pollard, A., Thiessen, D., & Filer, A. (Eds.). (1997). *Children and their curriculum: The perspectives of primary and elementary school children.* London: Falmer.

Porter, A. (1981). Political literacy. In D. Heater & J. Gillespie (Eds.), *Political education in flux.* SAGE annual reviews of social and educational change (Vol. 3). London: SAGE.

Posch, P. (1988). The project environment and school initiatives. In OECD (Ed.), *Environment and school initiatives: International conference, Linz, Austria, September 1988.* Paris: OECD.

Posch, P. (1990). Educational dimensions of environmental school initiatives. *Australian Journal of Environmental Education 6*, 79–91.

Posch, P. (1993). Research issues in environmental education. *Studies in Science Education, 21*, 21–48.

Posch, P. (1994). Changes in the culture of teaching and learning and implications for action research. *Educational Action Research, 2*, 153–160.

Posch, P. (1996). Curriculum change and school development. *Environmental Education Research, 2*(3), 347–362.

Postman, N. (1995). *The end of education.* New York: Vintage Books.

Prelle, S., & Solomon, J. (1996). Young people's "general approach" to environmental issues in England and Germany. *Compare, 26*(1), 91–101.

Ramsey, J., & Hungerford, H. (1989). The effects of issue investigation and action training on environmental behavior in seventh grade students. *Journal of Environmental Education, 20*(4), 29–34.

Randall, J. (1997). Integrating high school chemistry with environmental studies and research. *Journal of Chemical Education, 74*(12), 1409–1411.

Rauch, F. (2002). The potential of education for sustainable development for reform in schools. *Environmental Education Research, 8*(1), 43–52.

Reason, P. (Ed.). (1988). *Human inquiry in action.* London: Sage.

Reid, A., & Scott, W. (1998). The revisioning of environmental education: A critical analysis of recent policy shifts in England and Wales. *Educational Review, 50*(3), 213–223.

Rentel, J. (1997). *Interpreting democracy by decree: A hermeneutic phenomenological study of Paraguayan teachers' experiences with educational reform.* Unpublished doctoral dissertation, University of Minnesota.

Richardson, R. (1982). Now listen children . . . ! *New Internationalist, 115,* 18–19.

Richardson, M., & Simmons, D. (1996). *Recommended competencies for outdoor educators* (ED391624). Charleston, WV: ERIC/CRESS.

Rickinson, M. (2001). Special issue: Learners and learning in environmental education: A critical review of evidence. *Environmental Education Research, 7*(3), 208–318.

Rickinson, M. (2003). Reviewing research evidence in environmental education: Some methodological reflections and challenges. *Environmental Education Research, 9*(2), 257–272.

Rivkin, M. (1995). *The great outdoors: Restoring children's right to play outside.* Washington, DC: National Association for the Education of Young Children.

Rivkin, M. (1997). The schoolyard habitat movement: What it is and why children need it. *Early Childhood Education Journal, 25*(3), 199–201.

Roberts, D. (2000). Achieving scientific literacy: From purposes to practices. *Science Education, 84*(1), 123–126.

Roberts, D., & Östman, L. (1998). *Problems of meaning in science curriculum.* New York: Teachers College Press.

Roberts, D., & Chastko, A. (1990). Absorption, refraction, reflection: An exploration of beginning science teacher thinking. *Science Education, 74,* 555–587.

Roberts, M. (1996). Case study research. In M. Williams (Ed.), *Understanding geographical and environmental education: The role of research* (pp. 135–149). London: Cassell.

Robertson, A. (1994). Toward constructivist research in environmental education. *Journal of Environmental Education, 25*(2), 21–31.

Robottom, I. (1982). *What is: Environmental education as education about the environment.* Paper presented at the Second National Conference of the Australian Association for Environmental Education, Brisbane.

Robottom, I. (Ed.). (1987). *Environmental education: Practice and possibility.* Geelong, Victoria, Australia: Deakin University Press.

Robottom, I. (2000). Environmental education in changing times. In B. Moon, S. Brown, & M. Ben-Peretz (Eds.). *Routledge international companion to education* (pp. 502–512). London: Routledge.

Robottom, I., & Hart, P. (1993). Towards a meta-research agenda in science and environmental education. *International Journal of Science Education, 15*(5), 591–605.

Ryder, J. (2001). Identifying science understanding for functional scientific literacy. *Studies in Science Education, 36,* 1–44.

Ryder, J. (2002). School science education for citizenship: Strategies for teaching about the epistemology of science. *Journal of Curriculum Studies, 34*(6), 637–658.

Sang-Joon, N. (1995). Environmental education in primary and secondary schools in Korea: Current developments and future agendas. *Environmental Education Research, 1*(1), 109–122.

Sauvé, L. (1999). Environmental education between modernity and postmodernity: Searching for an integrating educational framework. *Canadian Journal of Environmental Education, 4,* 9–35.

Schnack, K. (2000). Action competence as a curriculum perspective. In B. Jensen, K. Schnack, & V. Simovska (Eds.), *Critical environmental and health education: Research issues and challenges* (pp. 107–126). Copenhagen: Research Centre for Environmental and Health Education, Danish University of Education.

Schreuder, D. (1994). The Schools Water Project (SWAP): A case study of an action research and community problem solving approach to curriculum innovation. *Australian Journal of Environmental Education, 10*(1), 35–46.

Scott, W. (2002). Personal communication, May 28, 2002.

Scott, W., & Gough, S. (2003). *Sustainable development and learning—Framing the issues.* London: Taylor & Francis.

Scott, W., & Oulton, C. (1992). The inter-dependence of environmental education, economic and industrial understanding, and the other cross-curricular themes within the school curriculum. *Environmental Education and Information, 11*(1), 1–10.

Scott, W., & Oulton, C. (1995). The "environmentally educated teacher": An exploration of the implications of UNESCO-UNEP's ideas for pre-service teacher education programmes. *Environmental Education Research, 1*(2), 213–231.

Selby, D. (1999). Global education: towards a quantum model of environmental education. *Canadian Journal of Environmental Education, 4,* 125–141.

Shin, D. (1997). Environmental earth science course development for preservice secondary school science teachers in the Republic of Korea. Unpublished doctoral dissertation, Columbia University Teachers College.

Simmons, M. (1998). *A study of high school students' attitudes toward the environment and completion of an environmental science course* (ED 423 119). Washington, DC: U.S. Department of Education, Educational Resources Information Centre.

Skeggs, B. (2002). Techniques for telling the reflexive self. In T. May (Ed.), *Qualitative research in action.* London: Sage.

Smith, S. (1998). Playgrounds for learning. *Every Child, 4*(4), 10–11.

Smith-Sebasto, N. (1998). Potential guidelines for conducting and reporting environmental education research: Qualitative methods of inquiry. *Environmental Education Research, 6*(1), 9–26.

Smyth, J. (1999). Is there a future for education consistent with Agenda 21? *Canadian Journal of Environmental Education, 4,* 69–82.

Smyth, J. (2002). *Are educators ready for the next earth summit?* Millennium Papers: Issue 6. London: Stakeholders Forum for Our Common Future.

Sobel, D. (1997). Sense of place education for the elementary years. In *Coming home: Developing a sense of place in our communities and schools. Proceedings of the 1997 forum.* ERIC Document ED421312.

Soetaert, R., Top, L., & Eeckhout, B. (1996). Art and literature in environmental education: Two research projects. *Environmental Education Research, 2*(1), 63–70.

Solomon, J. (1994). The rise and fall of constructivism. *Studies in Science Education, 23,* 1–19.

Solomon, J., & Thomas, J. (2000). Science education for the public understanding of science. *Studies in Science Education, 33,* 61–90.

Soltis, J. (1984). On the nature of educational research. *Educational Researcher, 13*(10), 5–10.

Spencer, D. (1995). *Adult education at botanic gardens: Planning environmental education.* Unpublished doctoral dissertation, Cornell University.

Springett, D. (1992). Environmental education: A view from Aotearoa, New Zealand. *Annual Review of Environmental Education, 5,* 42–45.

Stables, A. (1998). environmental literacy: Functional, cultural, critical. The case of the SCAA guidelines. *Environmental Education Research, 4*(2), 155–164.

Stables, A. (2001). Language and meaning in environmental education: An overview. *Environmental Education Research, 7*(2), 121–128.

Stables, A., & Bishop, K. (2001). Strong and weak conceptions of environmental literacy. *Environmental Education Research, 7*(1), 89–97.

Stables, A., & Scott, W. (1999). Environmental education and the discourses of humanist modernity: Redefining critical environmental literacy. *Educational Philosophy and Theory, 31*(2), 145–155.

Stables, A., & Scott, W. (2001). Editorial. *Educational Philosophy and Theory, 33*(2), 133–135.

Stables, A., & Scott, W. (2002). The quest for holism in education for sustainable development. *Environmental Education Research, 8*(1), 53–60.

Stephens, C. (1998). *Environmental education: A vehicle for integrating community members of all abilities and discovering a sense of place.* Unpublished master's thesis, Prescott College.

Sterling, S. (2001). *Education and learning in change.* Bristol, UK: Green Books.

Stevenson, R. (1987). Schooling and environmental education: Contradictions in purpose and practice. In I. Robottom (Ed.), *Environmental education: Practice and possibility* (pp. 69–82). Geelong, Victoria, Australia: Deakin University Press.

St. Maurice, H. (1996). Nature's nature: Ideas of nature in curricula for environmental education. *Environmental Education Research, 2*(2), 141–48.

Stocker, A. (1996). *Teacher beliefs about the goals and objectives of an environmental studies center program: A cross-case analysis of teacher thinking about the development of responsible environmental behavior.* Unpublished doctoral dissertation, Florida Institute of Technology.

Tanner, T. (1998a). Choosing the right subjects in significant life experiences research. *Environmental Education Research, 4*(4), 399–417.

Tanner, T. (1998b). On the origins of SLE research, questions outstanding, and other research traditions. *Environmental Education Research, 4*(4), 419–428.

Taylor, C. (1998). Environmental education in primary education: Status and trends in southern and eastern Africa. *Environmental Education Research, 4*(2), 201–215.

Taylor, N., & Topalian, T. (1995). Environmental education in the South Pacific: An evaluation of progress in three countries. *Environmentalist, 15*(3), 159–69.

Thrall, D. (1996). *Radon testing: A study of scitech and life science students' environmental knowledge and attitudes.* Unpublished doctoral dissertation, University of New Mexico.

Tilbury, D., & Walford, R. (1996). Grounded theory: Defying the dominant paradigm in environmental education research. In M. Williams (Ed.), *Understanding geographical and environmental education: The role of research* (pp. 51–64). London: Cassell.

Todt, D. (1995). *An investigation of the environmental literacy of teachers in south-central Ohio using the Wisconsin environmental literacy survey, concept mapping and interviews.* Unpublished doctoral dissertation, Ohio State University.

Turner, K., & Tilbury, D. (1997). Environmental education for sustainability in Europe: Philosophy into practice. *Environmental Education and Information, 16*(2), 123–140.

Turner, S. (1998). Redevelopment—a local environmental issue. *Primary Teaching Studies, 10*(1), 0–42.

Tyler-Wood, T., Cass, M., & Potter, L. (1997). Effects of an outdoor science laboratory program on middle school students. *ERS Spectrum, 15*(3), 30–33.

UNCED. (1992). *Agenda 21, The United Nations programme of action from Rio.* New York: United Nations.

UNESCO. (1977). *First intergovernmental conference on environmental education: Final Report.* Paris: UNESCO.

UNESCO-UNEP. (1992). UNCED: The earth summit. *Connect, 17*(2), 1–7.

Uzzell, D. L., Rutland, A., & Whistance, D. (1995). Questioning values in environmental education. In Y. Guerrier, N. Alexander, J. Chase, & M. O'Brien (Eds.), *Values and the environment: A social science perspective.* Chichester: John Wiley.

Volk, T., Hungerford, H., & Tomera, A. (1984). The national survey of curriculum needs as perceived by professional environmental educators. *Journal of Environmental Education, 16*(1), 10–19.

Wagner, E. (1997). *Environmental attitudes in the elementary grades: A bibliographic essay* (ED 412 075). Altanta, GA: Emory University.

Walker, K. (1996). *Improving the learning and teaching of environmental education in the primary school curriculum: A problem-based approach.* Unpublished doctoral dissertation, University of Technology, Sydney.

Walker, K. (1997). Challenging critical theory in environmental education. *Environmental Education Research, 3*(2), 155–162.

Wals, A. (1990). Caretakers of the environment: A global network of teachers and students to save the earth. *Journal of Environmental Education, 21*(3), 3–7.

Wals, A. (1992). Young adolescents' perceptions of environmental issues: Implications for environmental education in urban settings. *Australian Journal of Environmental Education, 8*, 45–58.

Wals, A. (1994a). Nobody planted it, it just grew! Young adolescents' perceptions and experiences of nature in the context of urban environmental education. *Children's Environments, 11*(3), 177–193.

Wals, A. (1994b). *Pollution stinks! Young adolescents' perceptions of nature and environmental issues with implications for education in urban settings.* DeLier, the Netherlands: Academic Book Center.

Wals, A., & Alblas, A. (1997). School-based research and development of environmental education: A case study. *Environmental Education Research, 3*(3), 253–267.

Warwick, P., & Stephenson, P. (2002). Editorial article: Reconstructing science in education: Insights and strategies for making it more meaningful. *Cambridge Journal of Education, 32*(2), 143–156.

WCED. (1987). *Our common future.* New York: Oxford University Press.

Williams, J., & Bonnett, M. (1998). Environmental education and primary children's attitudes towards nature and the environment. *Cambridge Journal of Education, 28*(2), 159–174.

Williams, M. (1996). Positivism and the quantitative tradition in geographical and environmental education. In M. Williams (Ed.), *Understanding geographical and environmental education: The role of research* (pp. 6–11). London: Cassell.

Wilson, R. (1993a). Educators for earth: A guide for early childhood instruction. *Journal of Environmental Education, 24*(2), 15–21.

Wilson, R. (1993b). The importance of environmental education at the early childhood level. *Environmental Education and Information, 12*(1), 15–24.

Wilson, R. (1995). Environmentally appropriate practices. *Early childhood Education Journal, 23*(2), 107–110.

Wilson, R. (1996). Healthy habitats for children. *Early Childhood Education, 28*(4), 235–238.

Wilson, R. (2000). The wonders of nature: Honoring children's ways of knowing. *Early Childhood News, 1997*(March–April), 6–9, 16–19.

Wirth, D. (1996). *Environmental ethics made explicit through situated narrative: Implications for agriculture and environmental education.* Unpublished doctoral dissertation, Iowa State University.

Wylie, J., Sheehy, N., McGuinness, C., & Orchard, G. (1998). Children's thinking about air pollution: A systems theory analysis. *Environmental Education Research, 4*(2), 117–137.

Yerkes, R., & Haras, K. (1997). *Outdoor education and environmental responsibility.* Charleston, WV: ERIC/CRESS.

Yeung, S. P.-M. (1998). Environmental consciousness among students in senior secondary schools: The case of Hong Kong. *Environmental Education Research, 4*(3), 251–268.

Zelezny, L. (1999). Educational interventions that improve environmental behaviors: A meta-analysis. *Journal of Environmental Education, 31*(1), 5–14.

PART IV

Curriculum and
Assessment in Science

CHAPTER 25

Scientific Literacy/ Science Literacy

Douglas A. Roberts
University of Calgary

The title of this chapter deliberately includes two terms—*scientific literacy* and *science literacy*, abbreviated together as SL. The literature on SL has mushroomed in the past two decades. The concept has come to be used more and more extensively, in many countries, to express what should constitute the science education of all students—to the point where one author claims (perhaps overenthusiastically) that SL now enjoys "worldwide cachet" (McEneaney, 2003). At the same time, it is well known in the science education community that no consensus exists about the definition of SL.

In fact, there is a veritable deluge of definitions for SL. The term is used in research studies, in discussions and analyses of science education goals, in assessment programs, and in curriculum embodiments such as policies, programs, and teaching resources. Closely related literature, which cannot be ignored in a review of international scope, uses three other terms as well. In the context of analyzing European science education, Solomon (1998) uses the terms *scientific culture* and *la culture scientifique* (the latter term is also used in francophone Canada, for example). Public understanding of science (PUS—such an unfortunate acronym) is a phrase widely used in England (e.g., Durant, 1994; Hunt & Millar, 2000) and increasingly elsewhere (e.g., Miller, 1992). Incidentally, a colleague informs me that the term *public understanding of science* is becoming less popular because it "assumes a homogeneity of publics and of understandings"; hence the term *public engagement with science* is being used (J. Osborne, personal communication, July 19, 2004).

I shall argue that all of this diverse literature can be better understood if one comes to grips with a continuing political and intellectual tension that has always been inherent in science education itself. I refer to the role of two legitimate but potentially conflicting curriculum sources: science subject matter itself and situations in which science can legitimately be seen to play a role in other human affairs. These two sources have long been used to generate components of science learning—whether in pre-collegiate formal schooling or informal science education in museums and the like. At issue is the question of balance. What has become increasingly noticeable in the SL literature is a growing polarization between advocacy positions that argue for pressing these two sources to the extremes. That is, there seem to be two *visions* of SL that recently have come to represent the extremes on a continuum. I shall call them, simply, *Vision I* and *Vision II*, where a vision is a much broader analytical category than, say, a definition.

Vision I gives meaning to SL by looking inward at the canon of orthodox natural science, that is, the products and processes of science itself. At the extreme, this approach envisions literacy (or, perhaps, thorough knowledgeability) *within science.* I shall argue that the approach taken in producing *Benchmarks for Science Literacy* (American Association for the Advancement of Science, 1993) approximates what I intend by identifying Vision I. Against that, Vision II derives its meaning from the character of situations with a scientific component, situations that students are likely to encounter as citizens. At the extreme, this vision can be called *literacy* (again, read *thorough knowledgeability*) *about science-related situations* in which considerations other than science have an important place at the table. The recent volume *Rethinking Scientific Literacy*, by Roth and Barton (2004), exemplifies Vision II. Whereas that volume comes from North American experience and scholarship, Vision II has older roots in England. Layton, Davey, and Jenkins (1986) introduced and exemplified the concept of "science for specific social purposes" nearly two decades ago. The same concept was presented later in elaborated form, in a slim and oft-cited volume titled *Inarticulate Science?* (Layton, Jenkins, Macgill, & Davey, 1993), whose title signifies that often the science taught in schools does not mesh, or articulate, with the science needed to come to grips with science-related situations.

Although the two visions have quite different starting points and ends in view, it should be kept in mind that these are, in my construction, idealized extremes developed as a heuristic device. Assessment programs and curriculum embodiments partake of these two visions in a kind of mating dance wherein they complement one another. Vision I, rooted in the products and processes of science, has historically been the starting point for defining SL, which has then been exemplified by reaching out to situations or contexts in which science can be seen to have a role. Recently, however, an increasing number of voices have stressed the importance of starting with Vision II, that is, with situations, then reaching into science to find what is relevant.

The scope of the review is broad. Following the completion of this introduction, three major sections analyze approaches to defining SL, and a further section examines how assessment programs affect, and are affected by, the influence of the two visions. A sixth section, on implications of the review, completes the chapter.

WHAT'S IN A TITLE?

The chapter title is intended to be broadly inclusive. *Scientific literacy* is the more familiar term for many science educators. The term is predominant in the literature, and it has widespread current use in a number of countries. *Science literacy* is also familiar—especially to American science educators—as the term used in materials and publications of Project 2061 (American Association for the Advancement of Science [AAAS], 1990 and subsequently). For some authors the distinction seems to be unimportant (e.g., Hurd, 1958, compared with Hurd, 1998; Shen, 1975; Carson, 1998). For others it is significant (e.g., Mayer, 2002; Marshall, Scheppler, & Palmisano, 2003).

It is interesting that Project 2061 used the term *scientific literacy* at the outset, when *Science for All Americans* (AAAS, 1989), or SFAA, was first published. Then, when the Oxford University Press edition of SFAA was published (AAAS, 1990), the term was changed to *science literacy*, and it has remained so in subsequent AAAS publications. I found this puzzling. At the suggestion of Project 2061 staff (J. E. Roseman, personal communication, January 9, 2003), I contacted the project's director emeritus to inquire about the reasons for the change (F. J. Rutherford, personal communications, January 16 and May 12, 2003). Here is his response. ". . . 'science literacy' refers to literacy with regard to science, while 'scientific literacy' properly refers to properties of literacy, namely literacy that is scientifically sound no matter what content domain it focuses on. . . . As far as I know, you are the only one who has raised the question, and most people seem satisfied with either construction." Actually, Champagne and Kouba (1997) did raise a point about this matter. They comment that AAAS "uses the adjectival form science," while the equally prominent (in the United States) *National Science Education Standards* (National Research Council, 1996) "uses the adjectival form scientific"—yet "the organizations have not publicly stated that the difference is significant" (p. 89). Strictly speaking, the word *science* is not an adjective, so the terms are not exactly parallel. Nonetheless, for purposes of this review I shall use the abbreviation SL, except where there is reason to distinguish the terms.

SL ON THE SCIENCE EDUCATION RADAR SCREEN

In devoting a full chapter to research on SL, the present handbook departs from the approach taken in earlier, similar handbooks. Hence the remainder of this introductory section is devoted to surfing previous handbooks and some other milestone collections, to document the noticeable increase in the amount of attention to SL in recent years. This will also serve as an overview of one particular subset of the SL literature—one that reveals the extent to which SL has been on the collective radar screen and research agenda of science educators, whether in a handbook or in a collection that reports on a forum, a symposium, or a research conference.

Seven Handbooks

In the past 10 years, two handbooks were devoted entirely to science education research. In one of them, Bybee and DeBoer (1994) included a brief section on the origins of SL (two pages) in their chapter about goals for the science curriculum. In the other, SL is mentioned at eight spots (12 pages in all), the most significant of which are in chapters by van den Akker (1998) and Bybee and Ben-Zvi (1998)—once again, on aspects of the science curriculum. *Science literacy*, as an independent term, does not appear in the index of either handbook.

The American Educational Research Association (AERA) has sponsored four versions, or editions, of a handbook of research on teaching and one handbook of research on curriculum, each of which has a chapter devoted to science education. Watson (1963) did not mention SL at all in his review. In the review by Shulman and Tamir (1973), the term is mentioned in passing in two places: one alludes to objectives for science education and the other concerns assessment. The term SL does not appear at all in the review by White and Tisher (1986); the handbook index shows no SL entries.

In the most recent edition of these AERA handbooks, White (2001) took quite a different tack from previous reviewers. He presents a picture of a revolution in research on science teaching by attending to such features of published research as questions, topics, method, etc., and showing how these features have shifted since Watson's review was published in 1963. White analyzed the ERIC science education summaries, in five-year increments spanning 1966 through 1995, according to their topics (the indicator of most interest here), as well as other features. He devised a very clever means for comparing the *proportions* (not the absolute number) of summaries devoted to different topics. In the case of scientific literacy (p. 459), the trend is as follows: *94* for 1966–70, *58* for 1971–75, *76* for 1976–80, *142* for 1981–85, *252* for 1986–90, and *209* for 1991–95. White did not discuss the substance of these summaries concerning SL, but it is clear that the topic has been active in the literature to varying degrees in the past 40 years—peaking in the 1986–90 period but remaining still quite robust in 1991–95. The index to this most recent AERA handbook does contain a reference to SL, but it refers to a chapter on assessment. No index entries appear for science literacy, as a separate term, in any of these handbooks.

There is almost casual mention of SL in the four AERA handbooks on teaching, and then only as a topic. In the AERA handbook on curriculum, by contrast, Fensham (1992) essentially—without explicitly saying so—used SL as one of the backbone concepts around which his chapter is built. The scope of Fensham's review includes both science education and technology education. For the science curriculum, he presents a major section about influences that have changed its substance internationally during two periods he labels "1950s/1960s" and "1980s and Onward" (p. 790 and p. 792, respectively). Noting the two "distinct targets" of school science, namely "a scientifically based work force" and "a more scientifically literate citizenry," he points out that "At first sight it can appear that the achievement of either of these two targets . . . will also be a contribution to the other" (p. 793). He uses the 1960s reform projects to illustrate how "the apparent even-handedness" of statements of intent about serving both groups "gave way in practice to the interests the first target represents. . . . By giving priority to the curricula for these students [the specialist work force], the projects were explicitly rejecting the interests of the larger target group in scientific literacy" (p. 794). Despite Fensham's substantial discussion of SL, the index for this handbook contains no entries for either scientific literacy or science literacy.

Five Research Volumes from Europe, One Forthcoming

In April 1995, the European Science Education Research Association (ESERA) was formed at a European Conference on Research in Science Education held at the University of Leeds (Retrieved April 18, 2005, from http://www.esera.net). In the compilation of selected papers from that conference, there are no index entries for SL, but there is passing mention of the concept in the paper by Ratcliffe (1996, p. 126). ESERA has sponsored four biennial conferences since then. (The fifth is planned for Barcelona in August 2005). From the first conference in Rome, in 1997, there are no index entries for SL in the published volume (Bandiera, Caravita, Torracca, & Vicentini [1999]). The volume based on the second conference, held at Kiel in 1999, contains two substantial papers on SL—one by Harlen (2001a) and one by Gräber, Nentwig, Becker, et al. (2001)—both in an entire section (one of six) devoted to SL, suggesting that SL had a relatively high profile at the conference. The third conference was held in Thessaloniki in 2001. The index to the volume of published papers (Psillos, Kariotoglou, Tselfes, et al., 2003) contains a single reference to SL, which Robin Millar discussed briefly in his Presidential Address. A published volume is forthcoming from Kluwer, based on the fourth ESERA conference at Noordwijkerhout in 2003.

Another volume on science education research in Europe reports an earlier conference in Malente, Germany, in late 1976, under the aegis of IPN (Institut für die Pädagogik der Naturwissenschaften) and the Council of Europe. I could find no mention of SL in this report (Frey, Blänsdorf, Kapune, et al., 1977). It is interesting from a historical viewpoint that the volume contains concrete proposals for establishing a European journal of science education and a European society for research in science education.

Four European Symposium Proceedings

In June 1989, the Royal Swedish Academy of Sciences organized a symposium, as one event to mark its 250th anniversary, with the title *Science Education for the 21st Century*. Torsten Husén chaired the symposium, and there were participants from Australia, England, France, Germany, Hungary, Japan, Sweden, USSR, and the United States. In his Preface to the proceedings, Husén notes that three questions were mentioned as major problems for science education, and the first is of most interest here. "What do we mean by 'science literacy,' the common core of science knowledge that citizens in a highly technological society ought to possess? How have the school systems in various countries been able to achieve this goal as evidenced by the IEA surveys of outcomes of science teaching?" (Husén & Keeves, 1991, p. vii).

In September 1996, an international symposium devoted entirely to the concept of SL was held at IPN. In their summary of the symposium, Gallagher and Harsch (1997) report that 30 participants from Germany, England, and the United States "examined the meaning of scientific literacy as an educational goal for secondary school students, its current status in secondary school science classes, impediments to achievement of scientific literacy, and what can be done to help more secondary school students achieve higher levels of scientific literacy" (pp. 13–14). In total, 25 papers were published in the symposium proceedings. To the best of my knowledge, this symposium was the first in science education research history to be devoted exclusively to SL as a research topic.

In November 1996, a symposium was convened in Oslo on "converging research interests in the issues of 'public understanding of science and technology' (PUST) and 'scientific and technological literacy' (STL)" (Sjøberg & Kallerud 1997, p. 5). The relationships among SL, PUS, PUST, and STL are of particular interest for this review. The published volume consists of seven papers by participants from Norway, England, and the United States.

"In the autumn of 2000, the 2nd Utrecht/ICASE [International Council of Associations for Science Education] Symposium brought together a variety of European colleagues to discuss about Teaching for Scientific Literacy." So wrote Eijkelhof (2001) in the Preface to the proceedings. Twelve papers make up the published volume, produced by symposium participants from The Netherlands, England, Northern Ireland, Estonia, and Portugal. Other countries represented by the 40 participants were Belgium, Cyprus, Germany, and Poland.

Three Multi-national Initiatives: UNESCO, ICASE, and OECD

The sixth volume of the series *Innovations in Science and Technology Education* is introduced by Edgar Jenkins with the comment that the series (Jenkins is the current editor) was launched when the International Network for Information in Science and Technology Education (INISTE) was established by UNESCO in 1984. *Volume 6*, devoted to STL, is noteworthy for purposes of this review on two counts. First, Jenkins (1997) provides a thorough and most interesting review of "meanings and rationales" for STL in Part I. This serves to set the stage for Parts II and III, which are, respectively, about "theoretical perspectives" for STL and "realizing" STL. The conflation of meanings of scientific literacy (SL) and technological literacy (TL), a relative newcomer to the literacy literature, has a distinct embodiment in the purposes and substance of school programs in a number of countries, as described in the papers in Part III.

The STL theme appears also in the title of an international project—*Project 2000+: Scientific and Technological Literacy for All*—co-sponsored by UNESCO and ICASE. The first phase of this project included an international forum held in Paris in 1993. "400 participants from more than 80 countries enthusiastically demonstrated their commitment to the task of achieving scientific and technological literacy for the peoples of all nations" (Retrieved April 18, 2005, from http://nerds.unl.edu.icase/I_2000+.htm). In preparation for the forum, Penick (1993) prepared an annotated bibliography on SL containing "more than 250 published and unpublished sources" (p. ii). This item, a book based on "every article we could find that had something to do with scientific literacy," was produced in limited quantity, but it remains available from the ICASE website (J. E. Penick [personal communication, November 25, 2003]). An augmented and updated version of Penick's bibliography was compiled for the third phase of the project (Layton, Jenkins, & Donnelly, 1994).

An initiative begun in 1989 by the Centre for Educational Research and Innovation of OECD concentrated on science, mathematics, and technology education, resulting in the volume titled *Changing the Subject* (Black & Atkin, 1996). This volume is based on a set of 23 case studies of innovation in 13 OECD countries, and I mention it because of the periodic reference to SL in some of its chapters on science education case studies. Based on the OECD initiative, there is a subsequent three-volume set on the case studies in the United States, called *Bold Ventures;* this review will draw from Volume 2 (Raizen & Britton, 1997).

Reflections and a Current Indicator

As White's (2001) review indicated, SL has become much more prominent as a concept on the science education landscape in the past 20 years. That the concept has also become more significant within the science education research community is indicated by its inclusion as one of 12 major themes and topics in the *SciEd Resource Assistant*, initially produced by ERIC. According to the successor to the ERIC website (Educational Realms), the list of research strands used for organizing NARST conference programs "was modified slightly for our purposes to reflect what we felt were the topics of most immediate interest to education professionals and the scope of the ERIC collection" (Retrieved April 14, 2005, from http://www.stemworks .org/CD–1/). Actually, SL is not mentioned in the current NARST program strand titles and descriptors. Nevertheless, the CD contains 15 titles of available full-text ERIC documents and a further 15 recent research journal articles, all dealing with SL (Retrieved April 18, 2005, from http://www.stemworks.org/CD–1/CD/topics-sciliteracy.htm).

DEFINING SL, PART I: FOR WHOM, TYPES-AND-LEVELS, JUSTIFICATION ARGUMENTS

With very few exceptions, definitions of SL have concentrated on identifying what is of value for students over the long haul of a lifetime, irrespective of their career preferences and aspirations. The term was used initially in the late 1950s and early 1960s to call attention to the need to specify science curriculum appropriate for students not planning to pursue further science studies (see, e.g., Fitzpatrick, 1960; Johnson, 1962). Thus from its beginning SL has signified a curriculum orientation intended to be different from pre-professional preparation for scientifically oriented careers—the distinction to which Fensham (1992, p. 793) alludes. More recently, the familiar term science for all has come to be equated with SL appropriate for all students, whether they intend further science-related studies or not.

Two General Observations

The definitional literature for SL is anything but straightforward and focussed, yet two aspects of this literature became clear as I reviewed it. It is worth summarizing these at the outset, to provide the reader with some signposts for the three sections of the chapter that deal with definitions.

My first observation is this. There is no consensus about the meaning, or even the constituent parts, of SL—with one exception: everyone agrees that students can't be scientifically literate if they don't know any science subject matter. The literature contains many expressions of frustration about implications of the lack of consensus for both research and practice. On the face of it, that is a fair complaint. It is difficult to communicate about research results, such as international student assessments of SL, or to compare programs and teaching approaches that claim to advance SL, in the absence of a common definition. Yet, it is a simple statement of fact, in the practical world of policy formation, that a selected definition of SL is very much a function of the educational context in which the policy is to take effect. Once a definition has been selected, specified, and announced as an anchoring basis, the work of program development can go forward. In the case of SL, one of the best examples of tracing the conceptual flow entailed by this fact is Bybee's comprehensive treatment of "purpose, policy, program, and practice" (1997a, p. 1) as integrated and interdependent components of educational planning. Thus, for reasons of context dependence especially, perhaps consensus about one definition throughout the worldwide science education community is a goal not worth chasing.

DeBoer (2000) expresses that very point thus, at the close of his recent review of SL: "instead of defining scientific literacy in terms of specifically prescribed learning outcomes, scientific literacy should be conceptualized broadly enough for local school districts and individual classroom teachers to pursue the goals that are most suitable for their particular situations" (p. 582). McEneaney (2003, p. 217) allows that there is no consensus on defining the specifics of SL. She describes its "worldwide cachet" in terms of a "scientific literacy approach" that, in her view, enjoys worldwide attention as a science education goal. Her analysis is based on examples from curricular statements, textbooks, and assessment materials in a variety of countries.

My second general observation is that the literature can be grasped more easily by considering the approaches, or conceptual methodologies, that authors have used. Five of these are discernible, and they are used to organize the material that follows. One cluster of literature is historical, embedded in the discourse of professional science educators who have tried to synthesize and make sense of the multitude of definitions between about 1960 and 1980. Another concentrates on "types" and "levels" of SL in terms of justification arguments based on presumed learners' needs. A third cluster seeks meaning for SL by concentrating on the word literacy, and a fourth seeks its meaning by focussing on science and scientists. Finally, there is the approach that draws on situations or contexts in which aspects of science are presumed and/or demonstrated to be valuable for students' everyday lives. In the course of presenting the definitional literature according to these five categories, I shall weave in the substance of some quite different critiques of SL—by Shamos (1995); by Sjøberg (1997); by Garrison and Lawwill (1992); by Eisenhart, Finkel, and Marion (1996); and by Roth and Lee (2002, 2004) extended in Roth and Barton (2004).

Historical Development of SL as a Term in Science Education

Some 20 years ago I did an analysis of early historical development of the term SL, based on science education literature published in North America from the late 1950s until the early 1980s, in order to make sense of the diversity of definitions (Roberts, 1983). The starting point of this approach was to examine discussion of the term from the point of view of the logic of educational slogans. SL was introduced in professional science educators' discourse as a slogan—a way to rally support for re-examining the purposes of school science (see, e.g., Hurd, 1958). At first, the SL discourse was primarily (although not entirely) on behalf of curriculum planning for the "90% of students" who are not "potential scientists" and who should therefore experience a "scientific literacy stream" (Klopfer, 1969).

From Slogan to Multiple Definitions

Slogans don't help professional science educators get on with their research and the practical work of specifying policy, planning programs, organizing teaching, and designing assessment. Definitions are needed instead. Between the late 1950s and the early 1980s, a very large number of writers in North America expressed their views about the definition of SL. In my analysis, I drew attention to a characteristic feature of the logic of educational slogans. Slogans must be interpreted, thus anyone moving (in the logical sense) from slogan to definition provides his or her own interpretation—within reasonable bounds. It is therefore not surprising that definitions appeared in abundance, and in considerable variety.

Striving for Consensus

Several authors have attempted to consolidate the definitions of this era into a synthesis that represented the meaning of SL for the science education community. I have selected three illustrative papers, all based on science education in the United States. (See Bybee [1997a, chapters 3 and 4] for a more extensive review and analysis of the consensus-building character of the American literature of this era, including the statements of professional associations such as NSTA, the [US] National Science Teachers Association.)

In 1966, Milton Pella and his colleagues in the Scientific Literacy Center at the University of Wisconsin in Madison reported a study of the "referents" authors had made to SL. On the basis of a comprehensive literature analysis, they identified 100 papers for further analysis and characterized SL with a composite picture based on six referents: "The scientifically literate individual presently is characterized as one with an understanding of the basic concepts in science, nature of science, ethics that control the scientist in his [sic] work, interrelationships of science and society, interrelationships of science and the humanities, [and] differences between science and technology" (Pella, O'Hearn, & Gale, 1966, p. 206).

Building on Pella's analysis and continuing the theme of consolidation, eight years later Michael Agin expressed the following concern. "Many individuals use the term 'scientific literacy' but fail to give it an adequate meaning. . . . A frame of reference should be established to help consolidate and summarize the many definitions" (Agin, 1974, p. 405). Agin used Pella's six categories to organize his own paper, drawing on even more literature (much of it post–1966) to embellish the categories by adding "selected dimensions" from among "the concerns and opinions of scientists and science educators" (p. 407).

The most exhaustive example of consensus seeking I have found is the doctoral study by Lawrence Gabel (1976). Gabel developed a theoretical model of SL based for the most part on statements of, or suggestions about, science education objectives related to interpretations of SL. His model expanded (refined, actually) Pella's six categories to eight, which constituted one dimension of a matrix. The other dimension included the six major categories of cognitive objectives and three categories of affective objectives from Bloom's taxonomies. Gabel reported that from the literature he was able to find examples for all but 16 of the 72 cells in this matrix (p. 92). He provided examples of the missing ones himself, to complete a consolidated picture of all of the possible objectives associated with SL—which, of course, is why it is a theoretical model, despite its substantial empirical basis for 56 of the cells (the complete matrix is shown in Gabel, 1976, p. 93). Thus did SL become an umbrella concept with a sufficiently broad, composite meaning that it meant both everything, and nothing specific, about science education.

A related but slightly different approach to analyzing the history of SL is to start with significant events in the educational history and culture of science education, especially the changing societal demands on the curriculum. The purpose of this approach is to understand how events have made a difference in science education policy statements over time, with specific reference to SL. DeBoer (1991, chapter 6) provides an excellent example of such analysis in the United States. (See also Bybee & DeBoer, 1994, and Matthews, 1994, chapter 3). Mayer (2002, chapter 2) has taken a similar approach, analyzing the history and place of Earth science education in the United States. He used for his book the inviting title "Global Science Literacy" to emphasize the point that he sees SL about the science of the globe itself as a viable curriculum platform for SL around the world. (See the review by Roberts, 2003.) Along the same conceptual and methodological lines, Jenkins (1990) presents a picture of the evolution of the SL concept in England.

Returning about a decade later to the historical events approach, DeBoer (2000) used as the significant event for his analysis the recent onset of contemporary standards-based reform efforts in the United States. He presents nine summary statements of science education goals that represent "a wide range of meanings of scientific literacy" (p. 591), essentially echoing Gabel's finding of a quarter century earlier to the effect that SL has now come to mean one, all, or some combination of the major goals to which science educators subscribe. DeBoer comments as follows, in a manner somewhat reminiscent of the initial intent of the SL slogan, "The one specific thing we can conclude is that scientific literacy has usually implied a broad and functional understanding of science for general education purposes and not preparation for specific scientific and technical careers" (p. 594).

Reflections on the History-of-Usage Approach

There is something comforting about a historical synthesis of definitions for an educational slogan such as SL. One gets a sense that despite the diversity of its definitions, SL did after all express a unity of purpose and meaning for science education by the beginning of the 1980s. In one sense, that is accurate. The focus of SL in the science education literature shifted from an image of curriculum appropriate solely for non-science-oriented students to aspects of science education appropriate for all students.

Definitional activity did not cease, however. Bybee (1997a) points out that during the 1980s, in the United States, "the term [SL] began to take on a symbolic value distinct from its past conceptual development because individuals used it in a variety of ways" (p. 59). This resulted in a substantial increase in the definitional literature—but that should not surprise us, as proliferation of definitions is to be expected in the case of educational slogans. Particular impetus for proliferation came from a variety of challenges to science education worldwide, during the 1980s. Fensham (1992) offers the example that many countries had begun retaining a higher percentage of young people in school for a longer time. As these students reached senior levels of schooling, it became increasingly imperative to pay attention to a curriculum in science that made provision for a "scientifically literate citizenry" as well as a "scientifically based work force" (pp. 793–795). (The reader can refer to Bybee [1997a] and DeBoer [2000] for accounts of further elaboration of the SL concept into the 1990s.)

The consolidation efforts of such writers as Pella, Agin, and Gabel show the manner in which Vision II of SL originated. For example, of the six categories of Pella's composite definition, science itself is the appropriate source for three of them (basic concepts in science, nature of science, and ethics that control the scientist's work). Those are based on Vision I. The other three (interrelationships of science and society, interrelationships of science and the humanities, and differences between science and technology), are based on Vision II—science-related situations.

Types and Levels of SL Needed by the Learner: Distinctions, Not Consensus

This approach takes a different starting point, concentrating on differences instead of consensus. Its purpose is the invention of categories that specify different types of SL according to what learners will be able to do with their SL. A number of writers cite Shen (1975) as their inspiration for this methodological approach. What did Shen actually say? "We may define science literacy as an acquaintance with science, technology, and medicine, popularized to various degrees, on the part of the general public and special sectors of the public through information in the mass media and education in and out of schools" (pp. 45–46). He defined three types of SL. (1) *Practical* —"possession of the kind of scientific knowledge that can be used to help solve practical problems . . . [such as] health and survival" (pp. 46–47). (2) *Civic*—"to enable the citizen to become more aware of science and science-related issues so that he and his [sic] representatives would [bring] common sense to bear upon such issues and thus participate more fully in the democratic processes of an increasingly technological society" (p. 48). (3) *Cultural*—"motivated by a desire to know something about science as a major human achievement. . . . It is to science what art appreciation is to art" (p. 49).

Types and Levels in a Curriculum Sequence

Shen's three categories represent qualitatively different types of SL, but I did not detect any suggestion that he placed them in a hierarchical arrangement. By contrast, the next two authors who take the types-and-levels approach (Shamos and Bybee) are talking about types and levels of SL for learners advancing through a curriculum.

Shamos (1995) proposed that different amounts of science are necessary for achieving Shen's three types of scientific literacy, thus converting them to levels in a hierarchy. His own three levels, a clear example of Vision I, "build upon one another in degree of sophistication as well as in the chronological development of the science-oriented mind" (p. 87).

- "1. *Cultural* scientific literacy. Clearly the simplest form of literacy is that proposed several years ago by Edward Hirsch, . . . by which he means a grasp of certain background information that communicators must assume their audiences already have" (p. 87). The reference is to Hirsch (1987). Related works along the same line are those by Hazen and Trefil (1991), and by Brennan (1992).

- "2. *Functional* scientific literacy. Here we . . . [require that] the individual not only have command of a science lexicon, but also be able to converse, read, and write coherently, using such science terms in perhaps a non-technical but nevertheless meaningful context" (p. 88).
- "3. *'True'* scientific literacy. At this level the individual actually knows something about the overall scientific enterprise . . . the major conceptual schemes . . . of science, how they were arrived at, and why they are widely accepted, how science achieves order out of a random universe, and the role of experiment in science. This individual also appreciates the elements of scientific investigation, the importance of proper questioning, of analytical and deductive reasoning, of logical thought processes, and of reliance upon objective evidence" (p. 89).

About his third level, Shamos comments that it is a "demanding" definition. "But it only means that the term itself, 'scientific literacy,' has been used too loosely in the past and that, when viewed realistically, true scientific literacy, as defined here, is unlikely to be achieved in the foreseeable future" (p. 90). He goes on to estimate the number of individuals in the US and England who are truly scientifically literate to be on the order of 7%, respectively: approximately the number of professional scientists and engineers in each country. (This estimate cites the work of Jon Miller, discussed later in this review.)

It is unfortunate that Shamos used his analysis to attempt to discredit the idea of using SL as a way to express an overall orientation of science education goals. Much of what is otherwise a highly informative and thoughtful piece of work might be lost or neglected if readers react negatively to this apparent desecration of a current science education icon—i.e., dismissing SL as a "myth." Essentially, Shamos sequesters "true" SL as an appropriate goal for science-oriented students only, but later in the book he drops the other shoe in a section titled "Science Awareness: A New Scientific Literacy." There, he presents "three guiding principles for presenting science to the general (nonscience) student" (p. 217, emphasis original). Notice that these map directly onto Shen's three categories.

- "1. Teach science mainly to develop appreciation and awareness of the enterprise, that is, as a *cultural* imperative, and not primarily for content. . . .
- 2. . . . focus on technology as a *practical* imperative for the individual's personal health and safety, and on an awareness of both the natural and man-made environments. . . .
- 3. For developing social (civic) literacy, emphasize the *proper* use of scientific experts, an emerging field that has not yet penetrated the science curriculum."

This last point is presented as an alternative to what Shamos sees as the "impossible task" of "educating all Americans in science to the point where they can reach *independent* judgments on [socioscientific] issues" (p. 216, emphasis original).

In a similar vein, Bybee (1997a, 1997b) has derived a framework that "presents scientific and technological literacy as a continuum in which an individual develops greater and more sophisticated understanding of science and technology" (Bybee, 1997a, p. 84; see also Bybee & Ben-Zvi, 1998, p. 490). (More is said about the conflation of science and technology later in this review.) This is a four-level framework.

- "In *nominal* literacy, the individual associates names with a general area of science and technology. . . . the relationship . . . [to] acceptable definitions is small and insignificant" (Bybee, 1997a, p. 84). Bybee includes misconceptions, naïve theories, and inaccurate concepts as features of this level of SL.
- "Individuals demonstrating a *functional* level of literacy respond adequately and appropriately to vocabulary, . . . they can read and write passages with simple scientific vocabulary . . . [They] may also associate vocabulary with larger conceptual schemes . . . but have a token understanding of these associations" (pp. 84–85).
- "*Conceptual and procedural* literacy occurs when individuals demonstrate an understanding of both the parts and the whole of science and technology as disciplines. . . . At this level, individuals understand the structure of disciplines and the procedures for developing new knowledge and techniques" (p. 85).
- "*Multidimensional* literacy consists of understanding the essential conceptual structures of science and technology as well as the features that make that understanding more complete, for example, the history and nature of science. In addition, individuals at this level understand the relationship of disciplines to the whole of science and technology and to society" (p. 85). Bybee points out that his multidimensional SL reflects the composite definitions and frameworks for SL as described by Pella et al. (1966) and Agin (1974), among others.

Reflections on Types and Levels of SL

Shamos has made a sharp distinction between science education for science-bound students and non-science-bound students. That is, neither "true" SL nor "science awareness" has been defined as a broad curriculum goal appropriate for all students. This approach is at odds with the majority of the science education community's efforts, yet at the same time it is a stark and forthright acknowledgment that science education has to somehow resolve the problems associated with educating two very different student groups (at least two). It is tempting to think that Vision I (looking inward to science itself) could serve as the sole source or generator of curriculum for science-bound students, while Vision II (looking inward from situations to science) has emerged as the appropriate source of planning for non-science-bound, or general, students. This would be wrong-headed. Even Shamos doesn't think so. He notes the importance of Vision I for all students in the following terms: "Every science curriculum, regardless of its professed goals, should at least make clear to students what science is and how it is practiced" (p. 224). Similarly, he remarks on the importance of Vision II for the science-bound student, when he details the contents of a "curriculum guide for scientific awareness." He points out that the science-bound student "might well be exposed to such topics early in his or her educational career" (p. 223).

Bybee does not differentiate between SL for science-bound and non-science-bound students. Indeed, his framework and his entire discussion is about making

SL possible for all students, but he freely admits that "no one could possibly achieve full scientific and technological literacy" (p. 85), that "some [students] will develop further than others at all levels or within one, depending on their motivation, interests, and experiences" (p. 85). Bybee's framework is very much an idealized, complete and comprehensive universe of meanings from which curriculum developers can choose.

Justification Arguments

Closely associated with the methodology of identifying types and levels of SL is Millar's (1996) review and critique of several arguments (Thomas & Durant, 1987) promoting the public understanding of science, a term closely related to SL and used frequently in England (cf. Durant, 1994, p. 83). Noting that "The science curriculum functions as: first stages of a training in science, for a minority, and access to basic scientific literacy, for the majority" (p. 10), Millar raises two questions: "What would a science curriculum designed to promote scientific literacy for the majority look like?" and "Later, as a separate question, we might wish to ask: would such a curriculum also be a reasonable preparation for further study in science for the minority who so chose?" (p. 10). He clustered the arguments into four groups: economic, utility, democratic, and cultural/social.

Justification According to Situation

Ryder (2001), building on Millar's analysis and critique, identified *functional* scientific literacy as "science knowledge needed by individuals to enable them to function effectively in specific settings" (p. 3). Among Millar's groups of arguments, this notion of SL emphasizes "the utility, democratic and (to a lesser extent) the social arguments for why people should know something of science" (p. 3). Ryder analyzed 31 "published case studies of individuals not professionally involved with science interacting with scientific knowledge and/or science professionals" (p. 5) in such settings and activities as public inquiries, parental discussions with health care workers, media reporting, and judicial proceedings.

The analysis is developed around six main areas of science understanding featured in the studies: subject matter knowledge, collecting and evaluating data, interpreting data, modelling in science, uncertainty in science, and science communication in the public domain. Ryder reports extensively on the issues concerning individuals' understanding associated with each area. Granting that "An understanding of subject matter knowledge is necessary for individuals to engage in many science issues," he goes on to point out that "Overall, much of the science knowledge relevant to individuals in the case studies was knowledge about science, i.e., knowledge about the development and use of scientific knowledge rather than scientific knowledge itself" (p. 35).

Ryder concludes with implications of the notion of *functional* SL for compulsory science curriculum. It is important to keep in mind that he reported these implications at a time when the English National Curriculum for Science was being reviewed in rather fundamental ways—especially in terms of the possibility of instituting a compulsory course on SL for students at Key Stage 4 (14 to 16 years old). Some of the implications, then, were already being realized in changes underway as a result of the recommendations put forward in *Beyond 2000: Science Education for the Future* (Millar & Osborne, 1998). Ryder reminds the reader that two of Millar's justification arguments are missing from his (Ryder's) *functional* SL concept: "science for cultural purposes, and science as a preparation for future science professionals," and he comments also about "the conceptual challenge of communicating about many of the issues . . . to school age students"—suggesting that for some of his findings the concepts and issues may be "beyond the level of compulsory science education" (p. 38). He cites a new post-compulsory course called "Science for Public Understanding" as having already identified many of these more difficult concepts and issues. (See the student text *AS Science for Public Understanding* [Hunt & Millar, 2000] for this most interesting development. "AS" is the designation for an "Advanced Subsidiary" GCE qualification.)

Three further implications round out the paper, two of which have to do with the content of a compulsory course that would facilitate "the process of learning to engage with science as an adult." These deal with important conceptual ideas of science (but not the usual more-than-needed packaging of typical science curricula) and "some coverage of social and epistemological issues." The final implication has to do with encouraging in all students "a sense that science is a subject that they are capable of interacting with in later life" (pp. 38–39). All of Ryder's implications further buttress the recommendations for a compulsory course in SL for English schools, as presented in Millar and Osborne (1998). The latter document is discussed in more detail later in this review.

Christensen (2001) echoes many of the points in Ryder's paper. Because "science education has a crucial role to play in preparing future citizens to make personal and collective decisions on socio-scientific issues," her argument goes, "new conceptions and approaches to scientific literacy are needed" (pp. 142–143). She points to "a shift over the past fifty years from a focus on content knowledge towards placing more importance on, and making more specific, the aspects of science by which it is involved with society and with individual lives" (p. 145), yet "this shift is only a beginning towards defining scientific literacy in ways appropriate for future citizens in a 'knowledge/risk' society" (p. 146). Citing "consistent findings of recent research into public understanding of science," she finds a gap: "dimensions of scientific knowledge not usually considered in school science are foregrounded: [including] the uncertainty of much scientific knowledge, the evaluation of evidence, the use of experts and an entirely pragmatic conception of content knowledge" (p. 146). Christensen draws on the way literacy is framed in such disciplines as language education—more in terms of literacy as language practice (reading, writing) and as social practice, embedded in social situations and contexts—as she sketches a view of SL that is appropriate for (adult) PUS, "including proper understanding of the social construction of scientific knowledge and a critical ability to evaluate sources of scientific knowledge" (p. 152).

Justifying Science, or Technology?

Sjøberg (1997) also used a set of four clustered categories similar to Millar's, listing and describing them for the purpose of asking "the impertinent question: Are these sound, well-founded and valid arguments—or do they just constitute a convenient ideology for scientists and science educators?" (p. 17). He does not cite either Millar's article, or the one by Thomas and Durant on which it is based, but the four clusters are readily recognizable from Sjøberg's description. He presents them as follows.

- "The *economic* argument: science for preparation for work
- The *utilitarian* or practical argument: science for mastery of daily life
- Science for *citizenship* and democratic participation
- Science for *cultural literacy*, science as a major human product" (p. 17).

In a lively and very interesting discussion of counter-arguments for each of the four, Sjøberg draws attention to the significance of technology (more than science) in the first two, and the complexity of the science needed to deal intelligently with socioscientific issues in the third (reminiscent of Shamos). He notes his "sympathy" with the fourth (p. 22), recounting several problems with the idea. In the summary of his critique he returns to the conflation of S and T, thus. "[The] distinction between Science and Technology [is] important . . . because some of the arguments that are questionable for having science in the curriculum (and for the entire adult population) are indeed very valid arguments for including *technology!*" (p. 23, emphasis original). Thereafter, he returns to the question "What do we mean by 'scientific literacy'?" and he, too, opts for specifying *functional* scientific literacy—although he does so "to draw attention to the culture- and context-dependency" of the term (p. 24).

Broader Justification through STL

The conflation of scientific and technological literacy (STL) is also a theme in the paper by Jenkins (1997), mentioned earlier. He notes that "The arguments for [STL] can be categorized in ways which reflect the different views of stakeholders" (p. 14). His categories for the arguments have much in common with those used by Millar and by Sjøberg. He begins with three, and identifies the stakeholders: "reference to national economic prosperity, raising the quality of decision-making or enriching the life of individuals, arguments which Layton has associated respectively with economic instrumentalists, with the defenders of participatory democracy and with liberal educationists (Layton, 1994, pp. 15–16)," (cited in Jenkins, 1997, pp. 14–15).

To these, Jenkins adds a fourth; no extrinsic justification is needed because S and T "are themselves important cultural activities" (p. 17). That is, "science offers a distinct and powerful way of understanding the natural world which justifies its claim to a seat at the table of those who would profess to be liberally educated" (p. 17). Similarly, "the history and philosophy of technology . . . offers some support to the claim that technology, as a unique and irreducible form of cognition, also has [an equal] seat at the same table" (p. 18). Finally, a fifth argument is noted. "[STL] offers . . . a means of redressing some social, economic or other injustices and imbalances . . . [and] an opportunity for a radical overhaul of scientific and technological education" (p. 18). Jenkins' paper sets the stage for the rest of the volume, yet he brings it to a close with a cautionary note. "Although much of modern science and technology constitute an integrated system with research socially rather than theory driven, scientific and technological literacy are not the same and there is a need to explore distinctions and establish such common ground as may exist" (p. 33).

Reflections: Justification Arguments and Curricular Arrangements

Arguments justifying SL are used in two different ways. The first has reference to students and/or adults, in terms of the attributes that characterize a scientifically literate person. These we can call student-centered justifications. Invariably, such arguments have to be plausible from a student's point of view. The second has reference to system-wide (national, regional, local) curriculum policies. These we can call policy-centered justifications. Such arguments justify the arrangement of curricular offerings, so that systems can provide SL for students.

Among the most noticeable student-centered justifications is the argument behind the original SL slogan, to the effect that a special kind of program is needed for the large number of students who do not intend to pursue further study in science-related fields (cf. Klopfer, 1969; Fensham, 1992). In a similarly student-centered way, Shamos's "true" SL is reserved for science-bound students, and his "scientific awareness" refers to the non-science-bound. Shamos proposed a different kind of program for each group, as did Klopfer (1969) a quarter century earlier.

More recently, the phrase science for all has come to be equated increasingly with SL for all (regardless of future plans). Implications for curricular arrangements that could advance SL for all are seen in two very different approaches to curricular arrangements.

The first arrangement is the establishment of a separate, compulsory course that concentrates on SL. Hints of this development in England were seen above in the review of Ryder's paper, where reference was made to the report titled *Beyond 2000* (Millar & Osborne, 1998). The second of that report's ten recommendations deals specifically with SL for 14- to 16-year-olds (Key Stage 4): half of their science time would be devoted to a mandatory (statutory) course on SL. (Options would be provided in the other half, for diversified interests in future general and applied science study.) The basis for this curricular arrangement is specified in the recommendation itself. "At Key Stage 4, the structure of the science curriculum needs to differentiate more explicitly between those elements designed to enhance 'scientific literacy', and those designed as the early stages of a specialist training in science, so that the requirement for the latter does not come to distort the former" (p. 10). In other words, the intent is to "unhook" students' development of SL from pre-professional science education. The justification argument for SL in this particular case draws on "the cultural and democratic justifications for an understanding of science" (p. 11); the reader will recognize this language from Millar (1996). The definition of SL embodied in this recommendation is found in the description of the experimental project called *21st Century Science*.

"We would expect a scientifically literate person to be able to:

- appreciate and understand the impact of science and technology on everyday life;
- take informed personal decisions about things that involve science, such as health, diet, use of energy resources;
- read and understand the essential points of media reports about matters that involve science;
- reflect critically on the information included in, and (often more important) omitted from, such reports; and

- take part confidently in discussions with others about issues involving science." (Retrieved April 14, 2005, from http://www.21stcenturyscience.org).

The project has been developing a Core Science course on SL for all Key Stage 4 students, and Additional Science courses, both Applied and General. (These courses are experimental and developmental at this time.) It is clear that the mandatory course on SL is based on Vision II, in that the overall learning outcomes flow from situations, not from the formal structure of science itself. The science content for the course is presented in "science explanations," and students develop skills and background to reflect on science itself through a set of "ideas about science," within which the content is contextualized. Along the same lines, a textbook has been developed for a post-compulsory course on public understanding of science (Hunt & Millar, 2000). So far as I can tell, the only other example of a separate, compulsory course on SL is the one developed in The Netherlands (De Vos & Reiding, 1999) for all grade 10 students. Further discussion of that course is reserved for a later section of this review.

The second curricular arrangement flowing from policy-centered justifications is to use an all inclusive collection of justification arguments as the basis for the overall goals of a science curriculum. In this way, science curriculum policy can incorporate possibilities that accommodate all students—whatever their abilities, interests, and future plans—but do not necessarily provide every student with the same exposure to SL (as a compulsory course would do). In one sense, then, the intent is that SL permeates the entire science curriculum. The composite definitions that evolved in the North American science education community by the late 1970s are examples of this approach to specifying the basis for an SL curriculum policy. Other sources of a composite definition include the collection of five stakeholder arguments on behalf on STL, as stated by Jenkins, the totality of the argument clusters in Millar's paper, and Bybee's sequence of types of SL, to which I shall return in a moment. All of these composites define the universe that a whole curriculum has to incorporate. In other words, the policy is rich and comprehensive enough to allow for varying degrees of development of SL by students with different abilities, motivation, and future plans.

An example of combining justification arguments, which actually predates the publication of Millar's (1996) paper, is found in a policy advisory document released by the Science Council of Canada (1984). There it was recommended that: "the goal of scientific literacy for all can be achieved through a balanced curriculum in which science is taught with four broad aims in mind:

- To encourage full participation in a technological society;
- To enable further study in science and technology;
- To facilitate entry to the world of work;
- To promote intellectual and moral development of individuals (p. 10).

The document is the final report of a three-year study of science education in Canada (see Orpwood, 1985; Orpwood & Souque, 1985), and it has influenced science curriculum revision in Canada for the past two decades. Notice that the justification arguments do not apply in equal measure to every student. That is what makes such a stipulated definition of SL policy-centered, rather than student-centered.

Bybee's sequence of types of SL is an important conceptual basis for the approach taken to SL in the United States. The Call to Action at the beginning of the US *National Science Education Standards* (National Research Council, 1996)—hereafter *NSES*—begins with "This nation has established as a goal that all students should achieve scientific literacy" (p. ix). SL is defined as follows. "Scientific literacy is the knowledge and understanding of scientific concepts and processes required for personal decision making, participation in civic and cultural affairs, and economic productivity. It also includes specific types of abilities. In the [*NSES*], the content standards define scientific literacy" (p. 22). The elaboration of the definition includes the following points:

- "a person can ask, find, or determine answers to questions derived from curiosity about everyday experiences
- a person has the ability to describe, explain, and predict natural phenomena
- entails being able to read with understanding articles about science in the popular press and to engage in social conversation about the validity of the conclusions
- implies that a person can identify scientific issues underlying national and local decisions and express positions that are scientifically and technologically informed
- [as] a citizen, should be able to evaluate the quality of scientific information on the basis of its source and the methods used to generate it
- implies the capacity to pose and evaluate arguments based on evidence and to apply conclusions from such arguments appropriately" (p. 22).

This definition has a strong Vision II flavor (as in Bybee's *multidimensional* SL). It is a policy framework that must be flexible enough to accommodate curriculum and course development for all students, so it is to be expected that students with different career goals ("different types of abilities," noted above) will experience different kinds of courses. Nevertheless, there is no distinction in the SL definition for students who wish to pursue science-related careers and those who do not.

Seven "content standards" define SL, in this document. They are presented in clusters according to grade levels, namely K–4, 5–8, and 9–12, and there is an eighth (K–12) that is superimposed on all of the others, dealing with such overarching ideas as systems, models, change, equilibrium, etc. (pp. 115–119). Within each grade cluster, the seven topics are the same:

- Science as inquiry
- Physical science
- Life science
- Earth and space science
- Science and technology
- Science in personal and social perspectives
- History and nature of science (pp. 121–207).

There is an intended relationship between the three traditional subject matter standards (physical science, life science, Earth and space science) and the four context standards (inquiry, science-technology, personal/social perspectives, and history/nature of science). The intent is that subject matter is to blended with contexts. However, having elevated the context standards to the status of content, *NSES* is open to implementation problems, in my view. That is, one reading of the standards suggests that, in each year of a student's experience, a seventh of the time will be spent on the content and skills of each of the seven standards—meaning 3/7 on traditional science subject matter and 4/7 on the contexts. Elsewhere I have commented on this potential problem (Roberts, 2000), but it is clear to me that the approach to be taken in accomplishing all seven standards is to blend the traditional subject matter with the context standards. In fact, that point is stated clearly in the document (*NSES*, p. 113).

DEFINING SL, PART II: FOCUS ON LITERACY, FOCUS ON SCIENCE AND SCIENTISTS

The Focus-on-Types-of-Literacy Approach

In what has been presented so far, there have been some brief forays into exploring adult SL. By and large, however, the preceding approaches to sorting out the definitional deluge reflect the preoccupations of science educators and science education policy makers, typically for primary and secondary school systems. Laugksch's (2000) review includes three other groups that have an interest in defining SL. A second group, "social scientists and public opinion researchers concerned with science and technology policy issues," has an interest in such matters as public support for science and technology, and the public's attention to science and technology policy. A third, "sociologists of science and science educators employing a sociological approach to scientific literacy," concentrates on individuals' everyday interpretation and negotiation of scientific knowledge. The fourth group is "the informal and nonformal . . . science education community, and those involved in general science communication" (through science museums, science centers, botanical gardens, and zoos, e.g.), including "science journalists and writers, and relevant personnel involved in science radio programs and television shows" (p. 75).

Laugksch reminds us that the four interest groups direct their attention at different populations. The science education group (the first named) focuses largely on the SL of children and adolescents, while the social science approach of the second and third groups targets the SL of out-of-school individuals (i.e., adults). The "general science communication" (fourth) interest group, however, concentrates on promoting the SL of a combination of the three audiences—"that is, children, adolescents, as well as adults" (p. 76). According to Laugksch, it is important to specify the different audiences because a different conception of literacy is being used by each of the interest groups. "Three different interpretations and uses of 'literate' are considered here: literate as *learned*; literate as *competent*; and literate as *able to function minimally in society*" (p. 82, my emphasis).

Laugksch comments on the three conceptions as follows. Regarding the *learned* category, "interpretations appeared to be proposed only for the intellectual value of being scientifically literate" (p. 83). Shen's *cultural* SL and Shamos's *true* SL qualify. This is the only conception that is clearly Vision I. The *competent* category is described thus: "when a context was suggested in which a scientifically literate individual needed to operate . . ., or if a particular activity was required to be performed . . . . Competent relates . . . to the extent of the ability to carry out such tasks" (p. 83). Laugksch included the Project 2061 concept of SL and Shamos's *cultural* and *functional* SL in this category. The *able to function* category "was used if the suggested definition required the scientifically literate individual to play a particular role in society, such as, for example, that of a consumer . . . or citizen" (p. 83). In this category are Shen's *practical* and *civic* SL, as well as Jon Miller's SL (discussed below); the Project 2061 concept of SL is included here also. The significance of Laugksch's work, in my view, is its link to general conceptions of literacy.

Bailey (1998) has reported an analysis based also on conceptions of literacy in a more general sense. She used Scribner's (1986) three metaphors of literacy as a basis: Literacy as *Adaptation*, Literacy as *Power*, and Literacy as a *State of Grace*. Literacy as Adaptation refers to "the pragmatic value of literacy skills. Scribner links this metaphor to discussions of functional literacy or the level of literacy skills required to function effectively in a range of everyday situations in our society . . . a degree of acceptance of the status quo" (Bailey, 1998, p. 53). By contrast, "the Literacy as Power metaphor has an emancipatory interest. . . . the possession of literacy skills has been a powerful tool of elite groups within some societies, employed to maintain their relative position of advantage. Conversely, development of literacy skills is viewed as a means for poor or politically disempowered individuals to claim their place in society" (p. 53). Finally, "State of Grace is a very old [concept]. Scribner links this metaphor to the tendency of many societies to attribute special virtues to the literate person. . . . to be literate is considered synonymous with being cultured. . . . the literate person derives meaning for his or her life from participation in humankind's accumulated knowledge, available through reading and writing" (p. 53). Bailey used these three conceptions of literacy as the basis for an analytical framework to review a Canadian curriculum document (Council of Ministers of Education, Canada [CMEC], 1997). She concluded that it portrays Literacy as *Adaptation*, on the basis that "the document reflects a concern for preparing students to work in science- and technology-related jobs [and links] this effort to the improvement of Canada's relative place in the global economy" (p. 58).

The kind of SL conception Bailey developed for Scribner's Literacy as Adaptation metaphor had earlier attracted quite a drubbing in a critique by Garrison and Lawwill (1992), in light of their interpretation of reform efforts at that time in the US. After examining a variety of influential documents about educational reform, they conclude: "With notable exceptions much of the current call to reform science education and achieve something called 'scientific literacy' seems directed toward [the] *end* [of 'economic competitiveness']" (p. 338, emphasis original). Their critique calls special attention to morality. "Frequently educational reform, especially in mathematics and science education, is intended to improve human capital. There is something very chilling about describing human beings . . . in such an exclusively quantitative and reductionistic way. . . . Chaining science and science education to the goal of maximizing the economic production function . . . is immoral . . . because it treats students as means to the pecuniary ends of others" (p. 343).

Reflections on the Types-of-Literacy Approach

Until recently it has been unusual to find constructs and insights from the study of literacy in the literature on SL. The literature has tended to concentrate on specifying the details of two components of science curriculum that are closer to home, so to speak. Typically, learning outcomes or goals have been specified *within* science (scientific knowledge) and *about* science ("companion meanings"—i.e., meanings derived from such focus areas as the nature of science and STS [Roberts, 1998]). The following brief comments are about literacy's links to SL—first to Vision I, then to Vision II.

In their case study of AAAS Project 2061, Atkin, Bianchini, and Holthuis (1997) point out that "Use of the word 'literacy' . . . is noteworthy," as the term "was not generally employed during the 1960s round of science curriculum reform." They offer an explanation to the effect that the 1970s emphasized the "basics," stressing "core skills, traditionally associated with subjects like reading, computation, and communication." They suggest that "Many of those interested in promoting and improving science education began to . . . talk about scientific *literacy*," implying that to know about science is as necessary "as to know how to read, compute, and communicate" (p. 191).

That explanation comes, obviously, from the perspective of curriculum politics, yet the meaning of literacy in the SL concept itself is left as something of a black box. Opening that black box from the point of view of Vision I has been the agenda of a significant strand of more recent research and writing. For example, Norris and Phillips (2003) begin by distinguishing between a fundamental sense of SL—"reading and writing when the content is science"—and a derived sense of the term—"being knowledgeable, learned, and educated in science" (p. 224). They argue that conceptions of SL "typically attend to the derived sense of literacy and not to the fundamental sense" and contrast the fundamental sense (which they link closely to understanding text) against "a simple, word-recognition-and-information-location view of reading that remains prominent in literacy instruction" (pp. 224–225). One of the most significant implications of their distinction has to do with the distortion of meaning that can come from assessment programs, and they comment specifically about Jon Miller's work (discussed in a later section of this review). They point out that "his vocabulary dimension risks equating successful reading with knowing the meaning of the individual terms" and that it "appears to assume that only scientific constructs need to be known to understand scientific text" (p. 227). As well, "focussing upon the derived sense of literacy as knowledgeability in science has . . . created a truncated and anemic view of scientific knowledge as facts, laws, and theories in isolation from their interconnections" (p. 233).

A more elaborate framework for literacy in Vision I SL—particularly the educational implications—is found in a recent editorial description (Hand, Alvermann, Gee, et al., 2003) of an international conference held in September, 2002, on Vancouver Island, Canada. (The participants, including Norris and Phillips, refer to themselves as the "Island Group.") They maintain that research and practice in all of the recognized language arts (including reading, writing, speaking, listening, and representing) are highly significant for understanding and realizing SL in the fundamental sense just described. Researchers in cognitive science, linguistics, language education, and science education informed one another and addressed "key issues not normally emphasized by the science education research community" (p. 609). They present the structure of their discussions according to four perspectives: students' formal and informal literacies, vernacular language, reading in science, and writing in science.

In this review, it is Laugksch's work that sets the stage for recognizing literacy in a Vision II sense. His *learned* category acknowledges Vision I. The *competent* and *able to function* senses of literacy reflect the broader picture of situations (Vision II) in which SL is being promoted as important for purposes other than those of the academic science culture.

The Focus-on-Science-and-Scientists Approach

Mining the Scientific Canon

The Project 2061 term *science literacy* is now common parlance among science educators in the United States. I have identified this term as Vision I on the basis of two considerations: the substance of the definition itself, and the source of its legitimation in the orthodox scientific canon.

The Project 2061 conception of SL was established initially on the basis of five reports developed in the period 1985–1989 (Phase I) under the aegis of "the National Council on Science and Technology Education—a distinguished group of scientists and educators appointed by the American Association for the Advancement of Science—on what understandings and habits of mind are essential for all citizens in a scientifically literate society" (AAAS, 1989, p. 3). "Five independent scientific panels" developed the reports, and the council solicited broad consultation and review. All told, the process involved "hundreds of individuals" and culminated in the sixth report of the collection, the familiar *Science for All Americans* (SFAA), which was unanimously approved by the AAAS Board of Directors (p. 3). The definition of SL is presented thus, in SFAA:

the scientifically literate person is one who

- is aware that science, mathematics, and technology are interdependent human enterprises with strengths and limitations;
- understands key concepts and principles of science;
- is familiar with the natural world and recognizes both its diversity and unity; and
- uses scientific knowledge and scientific ways of thinking for individual and social purposes. (p. 4, my bullets; not changed in OUP edition)

(The details of this definition were not changed in the OUP edition of SFAA although, as noted earlier, the term *scientific literacy* was changed to *science literacy*.)

Two aspects of this process and its resulting definition of SL are significant for the present review. The first is the impressive sense of authority that results from a process of consulting so many scientific experts, and subsequently obtaining the endorsement and continuing support of one of the world's premiere scientific organizations. The second is the unusual breadth of the subject matter considered to be science. The scope of Phase I included technology, information sciences, engineering, social sciences, health sciences, and mathematics, in addition to the attention typically paid in such ventures to the more familiar cluster of natural sciences, such as physics, chemistry, biology, and geology. To be sure, the panels were not given free rein to include every single concept from their disciplines, or even their favorite ones. On the contrary, the "national council" was under a tight rein. The curriculum had been characterized for them as already "overstuffed and undernourished" as a result of growing over the years "with little restraint" (p. 15). These aspects of Project 2061, and many others, are examined in great and very interesting detail in the case study mentioned previously (Atkin, Bianchini, & Holthuis [1997]). My comments about each will therefore be brief, rather than comprehensive.

(1) Asking scientists to define, or at least suggest, the essential subject matter content for school science has often been a part of science education, to varying degrees. Nevertheless, the sheer investment of time and resources in Phase I of Project 2061 is staggering to contemplate, until one reflects on what is involved in a thoroughgoing delineation of Vision I. The impetus for the project is total, systematic reform of science education K–12, over decades, which requires enormous commitment from a society. An expressed and repeatedly confirmed endorsement by such an organization as AAAS can be seen, then, as a way of garnering lasting support for the effort as well as reaching a clear understanding of what constitutes SL—at least, in the eyes of the scientific community. The cornerstone of Phase I is the belief that we can have enough confidence in science itself to make it worthwhile to see the reform through to its distant conclusion. Such confidence is expressed in this way: "Science, energetically pursued, can provide humanity with the knowledge of the biophysical environment and of social behavior that it needs to develop effective solutions to its global and local problems; without that knowledge, progress toward a safe world will be unnecessarily handicapped" (AAAS, 1989, p. 12).

(2) It was certainly unusual to include such a broad array of disciplines in the early stages of defining SL. That is, the five panel reports developed as the basis for SFAA are *Physical and Information Sciences and Engineering, Biological and Health Sciences, Mathematics, Technology,* and *Social and Behavioral Sciences*. Other definitions of SL have incorporated understandings from some of these "outlying" disciplines, such as engineering and social sciences, but have done so as components of the contexts or "companion meanings" (Roberts, 1998) within which natural science subject matter itself is to be studied. In the case of AAAS, such understandings—as well as understandings from such disciplines as history and philosophy of science—appear to be part of the subject matter base of science education, all under the umbrella of scientific knowledge and "habits of mind." As a consequence, the subsequent documents *Benchmarks for Science Literacy* (AAAS, 1993) and *Atlas of Science Literacy* (AAAS, 2001) provide quite specific academic content requirements for understanding such aspects of SL as the nature of science, human society (including decision-making), and nature of technology (including its interdependence with science and society).

Thus, for example, the "map" for Social Decisions in *Atlas* (AAAS, 2001) shows the following understanding in the group of 9–12 benchmarks: "In deciding among alternatives, a major question is who will receive the benefits and who (not necessarily the same people) will bear the costs" (p. 103). The implication is that understanding the statement (among others) makes one an informed decision-maker. This is decidedly a Vision I approach to SL. By contrast, other definitions (e.g., Ryder's

[2001] *functional* SL) take socioscientific situations as a starting point (Vision II) and inquire about what understandings people actually use when they make a decision, not what they understand about scientists' understanding of the decision-making process. To be sure, Project 2061 has separated issues of defining SL from curriculum and implementation issues, as elaborated in *Designs for Science Literacy* (AAAS, 2000). Nevertheless, this feature of their definition of SL is noteworthy for its focus on scientists' academic understanding of such endeavors as societal decision-making, to the exclusion of such considerations as morality and values. (By contrast, a recent volume [Zeidler, 2003] is devoted entirely to examining the role of moral reasoning about socioscientific issues in science education discourse.)

The Scientists Communicate

Another view of what scientists have to say about SL displays the sense of science as a cultural product—a thing of beauty and elegance in its own right. In this genre of writing about SL, one example is the recent volume titled *Science Literacy for the Twenty-First Century* (Marshall, Scheppler, & Palmisano, 2003). This collection of essays includes contributions by prominent, articulate scientists who describe— often eloquently—their experience in science (frequently, as well, the joy they find in teaching it). Scientists who prepare essays and books of this sort do not so much try to define SL as try to express their sense of it. This genre is probably the oldest writing about SL we have—it is no doubt the kind of thing C.P. Snow was writing about in his famous "two cultures" essay. It may also be reflective of the *true* SL Shamos described, and the sense of SL as a *State of Grace* noted by Bailey/Scribner. The best of this writing is highly cultured and inspiring through its elegance.

Similarly, an emerging field of studies called science communication rests on a multi-faceted message about SL and PUS—multi-faceted because it appears to be motivated both intellectually and politically. Professionals in this field concentrate on analysis of what and how scientists, journalists, and others should and do communicate about science to the general public. In a recent collection of essays about science communication, the editors begin their introduction and overview with the assertion that "It is widely accepted that the importance of the communication of science to the public can be summarised under five headings . . . economic, utilitarian, democratic, cultural, and social" (Stocklmayer, Gore, & Bryant, 2001, p. ix). Although the source of those categories—Millar (1996) and Thomas & Durant (1987)—is not explicitly acknowledged at this point, the categories themselves are by now familiar to the reader. The editors review and critique the five arguments, but their vantage point is not the same as Millar's—nor do they reach the same conclusions. Their interest is in the consequences of having an impact on the public's understanding of science, rather than in justifying the arguments for shaping school science.

The collection itself is wide-ranging. SL, as a concept, is mentioned seldom in its 18 chapters. Overall, the discourse has an aura of proselytizing, of transmitting the scientist's message to the public, from the scientist's point of view.

Those of us who find scientists' reflective writings eloquent and informative are already educated in science. The discourse belongs to the academic science culture, to borrow a term from Joan Solomon (1998). If the intention of such writing is to increase public understanding of science, surely it is important to recognize a distinction Solomon makes between two kinds of scientific cultures. "One, 'popular' scientific culture, refers to the concerns of the public, so important within their own local culture and often having a scientific and technological basis. Against that, a culture of academic science is much more restrictive" (p. 170). The distinction has its counterpart in different kinds of school science offerings. Noting that STS courses "have popular scientific culture as one of their objectives," she points out that classroom discussions based on moral positions and value judgments take place and create "an element of full-blooded popular communication with all its moral and political elements of argumentation" (p. 170). (Solomon's [1992] account of the Discussion of Issues in School Science [DISS] Project provides informative examples of, and insights about, 16- to 18-year old students' deliberations on socioscientific issues.)

Solomon (1998) continues, "Academic science itself bids to be . . . common across the invisible college that unites professional scientists from around the world." This comparison leads her to raise two questions. "Can science be taught so that it connects with attitudes, personal values, and political issues? This would indeed make science a part of popular culture. But would it still be science?" (pp. 170–171). Such questions express the crux of the tensions between Vision I and Vision II.

In further discussion of the culture concept as it applies to European science education, Solomon distinguishes the French term *la culture scientifique* from both Public Understanding of Science in the United Kingdom and Scientific Literacy in North America. "The European nations pride themselves on their long history of prestigious knowledge. It includes such venerable subjects as philosophy and the arts, without which a person in previous ages might not have been considered fit to take an honorable place in educated discourse. Culture, in this sense, holds a more elitist place in general estimation than does literacy" (pp. 171–172). Granting that the concept of culture itself applies in many contexts and does not represent only some elitist self-contained reality, Solomon concludes her paper by distinguishing three purposes for school science education (p. 176).

- "'Academic' scientific culture . . . must be cultivated [for] those who may become the next generation of science scholars."
- "vocational preparation in science-related fields . . . for example, engineering, medicine, and computer technology. It is harder to identify these with any particular 'kind' of school science program."
- "'Popular' scientific culture is just as significant: the promotion of a wide scientific and technical culture . . . in order that everyone can appreciate new developments and can evaluate them for their own and others' styles of living."

Reflections on the Focus-on-Science-and-Scientists Approach

The AAAS definition of "science literacy" focuses on the way science views all aspects of the natural world and of human behavior, excluding from consideration such societal concerns as morality, values, and politics. The science communication enterprise is strikingly similar in its effort to put across the message that science, and a scientific perspective, is the preferred way to think about the objects and events of experience, and by extension about decision making with regard to socioscientific issues. Both of these are distinctly Vision I. By contrast, Solomon's description of popular science culture, and its counterpart in STS courses, embodies much more than scientific understanding and a scientific perspective on situations. Her phrase "full-blooded popular communication with all its moral and political elements of argumentation" captures the essence of Vision II.

DEFINING SL, PART III: FOCUS ON SITUATIONS

Questioning Vision I

Eisenhart, Finkel, and Marion (1996) have questioned in some detail whether the Project 2061 definition of SL—Vision I—is appropriate. They also question the results, in their view, of implementation of the US *National Science Education Standards*. Even acknowledging that the vision of SL in *NSES* is "democratic, socially responsible uses of science," they characterize current implementation in the US as concentrating "narrowly on key content: specifying what facts, concepts, and forms of inquiry should be learned and how they should be taught and evaluated" (p. 266). The authors point out that, in the implementation efforts, there seems to be an assumption "that producing citizens who can use science responsibly and including more people in science will naturally *follow from* teaching a clearly defined set of scientific principles and giving students opportunities to experience 'real' science" (p. 268, emphasis original). Their paper includes interesting examples of teaching approaches and materials designed to foster what they call "socially responsible science use" (p. 283)—a concept that entails learning science in situations where it will actually be used (Vision II of SL).

The focus-on-situations approach to SL has a familiar ring, for anyone acquainted with the work of David Layton and his colleagues on Science for Specific Social Purposes (discussed below). In two recent articles, Roth and Lee (2002, 2004) follow up on the line of thinking expressed by Eisenhart et al., and take it further on theoretical grounds. They assert that "reformers [an unidentified group] have consistently used a limited view of what scientific literacy might be; that is, they always maintained the scientists' version of science while disregarding the version of others. Consequently, . . . [science] in high school and university textbooks [is] said to be the prerequisite for appropriately coping in a modern world." This view of SL amounts, then, to requiring "a certain amount of scientific knowledge *on the part of the individual*" (Roth & Lee, 2002, p. 34, emphasis original). Against that, the authors "conceive of scientific literacy as a property of collective activity rather than individual minds" (p. 33).

The two articles report on a number of aspects of a three-year study centered on an environmental problem in a community in the Pacific Northwest ("Oceanside," a pseudonym). Middle school children participate with other community members to develop the knowledge base appropriate for taking action about a local creek, in which water quality has been seriously compromised over time. "Parents, activists, aboriginal elders, scientists, graduate students, and other Oceanside residents . . . constituted the relevant community in the context of which our seventh-graders learned" (Roth & Lee, 2004, p. 273). From these two richly detailed accounts, the authors describe an alternative perspective on SL that emphasizes its collective (rather than individual) quality, the idea that in a democratic society "all forms of knowledge that contribute to a controversial or urgent issue are to be valued" (science being but one of many), and the point that experiencing an everyday situation as a learning context can mean that the students "could continue this participation along their entire life spans" (p. 284).

Roth and Barton (2004) continue exemplifying and promoting consideration of Vision II SL, in their presentation of case studies of project-based successes of marginalized persons—poor, female, minorities, homeless, aboriginal, and "coded" (e.g., ADHD). Roth's chapters in the book draw on further analysis of the Oceanside study. Barton's chapters concentrate on two different settings: working with children and teenagers in after-school programs at homeless shelters in New York City, and narrative accounts of the working lives of three female science educators in an urban area of Pakistan. The authors argue for a broad definition of SL in these situations, sometimes straining the reader's credulity to accept that the several kinds of knowledge exemplified can actually be said to fall under the SL umbrella. It is the real-ness of the situations and the participants' experience (a familiar feature of project-based work) that prompts the authors to raise questions about science curriculum policy and planning. School science activities are said to be artificial, disconnected from the real purpose of participation in (genuine) community affairs. Even "school-based mock activities . . . designed to empower students to deal with science and scientific experts on emerging socio-scientific issues" are deemed to be inadequate, because "students have to *play* the roles of scientists, environmental activists, or local residents in a pretend activity" (p. 176, emphasis original).

Science for Specific Social Purposes (SSSP)

Pre-dating Roth and Barton by roughly two decades, Layton, Davey, and Jenkins (1986) presented a picture of situated knowledge—motivated especially by their concerns about the inadequacy of assessment programs. Basic to their argument is the point that PUS and civic (public, adult) SL are manifest in specific situations, hence the scientific knowledge people employ in those situations is contextualized according to what the situation requires. This is, of course, Vision II. Nevertheless, they point out, many testing programs for adult SL (and student SL also, I would add) incorporate a set of decontextualized knowledge items selected on some arbitrary basis. Thus there is something of a strained connection between a correct response to such items as "Which travels faster, sound or light?" and the extent to which an individual can be said to understand and/or engage intelligently in debate about a socioscientific issue. In a word, as noted earlier, the scientific knowledge being tested does not articulate or mesh well with the contexts in which one might expect learners to use it. Layton et al. (1986) introduced the term *science for specific social purposes (SSSP)* to capture the point that the context or situation of a socioscientific issue (or even an explanation) has a strong influence on the knowledge people bring to bear on it.

To clarify and exemplify the SSSP concept, the authors present a most engaging overview of adult SL in England during the nineteenth century, which suggests that "different social groups saw in science an instrumentality for the fulfillment of their specific intents" (Layton et al., 1986, p. 32). For example, "Chemistry for precious metal prospectors . . . was different from chemistry for agriculturalists and again from chemistry for public health officials" (p. 30). In commenting on the importance of SSSP to the assessment of public SL, Jenkins (1997) notes that "any estimation is likely to be most useful when it relates to a particular group of citizens addressing a specific issue of common concern to that group, for instance, . . . a community exploring how best to provide and maintain a supply of clean drinking water" (p. 23, and cf. Roth & Lee [2002, 2004]). Obviously, to use that issue and situation in an assessment program, one would have to contextualize reasonable and pertinent items about water chemistry, water biology, ecology, etc, in the situation.

The impact of re-framing the vision of adult SL and civic SL in this way is to get away from the idea that a generalized test of "cognitive deficit" in scientific knowledge is a meaningful way to make a connection to SL at all. Jenkins continues, "Fundamental to the notion of science for specific social purposes is a rejection of the so-called 'cognitive deficit' understanding of scientific literacy in favour of a more interactive model (Layton et al., 1993)" (Jenkins, 1997, p. 23). The differences, laid out in tabular form by Jenkins (p. 24), are described in terms of adult SL, or PUS. I want to single out two of those differences just to provide a flavor of the two models.

The cognitive deficit model sees PUS as highly dependent on science itself (Vision I of SL)—i.e., "central to decisions about practical action in everyday life"—whereas in the interactive model science "is often marginalized or 'off-centred' when integrated with other kinds of knowledge relevant to such decisions." (That's Vision II.) Also, "Scientific thought is the proper yardstick with which to measure the validity of everyday thinking" in the cognitive deficit model, while the interactive model holds that "everyday thinking and 'knowledge in action' are more complex and less well understood than is scientific thinking." This is not to say that scientific knowledge is unimportant. It is, however, to point out the significance of taking the situation as a starting point, rather than the scientific canon itself, when planning assessment. One is, after all, assessing a reasoning pattern that resembles Aristotelian *praxis* in these situations, and knowledge premises are a significant part of the logic and coherence of the practical syllogisms that characterize the *praxis* thinking pattern. The knowledge has to be carefully selected, however, and integrated with other features of the situations such as value premises. Layton (1991) explores these matters further.

A Third Curricular Arrangement: Recognizing the Significance of Vision II

Science curriculum revision that recognizes and mandates embedding science subject matter in situational contexts has been underway in Canada for the past decade. This curricular arrangement obviously differs from the approach taken by 21st Century Science. It also differs from the arrangement of the *NSES* framework, where the contexts are identified, but inclusion of them in local curriculum development would have to be mandated at the state level.

Canada does not have a national curriculum. Jurisdiction over educational matters resides with the governments of the ten provinces and three territories. The most recent science curriculum revision has been based on a nation-wide "framework" (Council of Ministers of Education, Canada [CMEC], 1997) to which provincial ministers of education subscribed in hopes of providing common ground and more consistency in learning outcomes for science across the country. The framework "is guided by the vision that all Canadian students, regardless of gender or cultural background, will have an opportunity to develop scientific literacy." SL is defined as "an evolving combination of the science-related attitudes, skills, and knowledge students need to develop inquiry, problem-solving, and decision-making abilities, to become lifelong learners, and to maintain a sense of wonder about the world around them" (p. 4).

The definition is made operational by specifying four "foundation statements," one each for skills, knowledge, and attitudes, and a fourth for "science, technology, society, and the environment (STSE)" (p. 6). Acquisition of science-related skills, knowledge, and attitudes, according to the document, "is best done through the study and analysis of the interrelationships among science, technology, society, and the environment (STSE)" (p. iii). Implicit in that statement, and more explicit in several provincially mandated curricula based on it, are two important features of the meaning of SL. First, the "science-related skills, knowledge, and attitudes" specified in the respective foundation statements for those three areas are to be developed through the STSE situations and challenges comprising the fourth. That is, the expectation is that curricula and textbooks will provide opportunities for students to learn about STSE interrelationships at the same time they are learning science subject matter, skills, and attitudes. This simultaneous learning is envisioned as happening through contextual communication, in which units of science subject matter are organized to stress three (one at a time, essentially) "broad areas of emphasis:

- a science inquiry emphasis, in which students address questions about the nature of things, involving broad exploration as well as focussed investigations [this is an emphasis on the nature of science];
- a problem-solving emphasis, in which students seek answers to practical problems requiring the application of their science knowledge in new ways [this is an emphasis on science and technology];
- a decision-making emphasis, in which students identify questions or issues and pursue scientific knowledge that will inform the question or issue [this is an emphasis on socioscientific issues]" (p. 8).

Second, although this is not stated explicitly in the document, these three areas of emphasis correspond to the Aristotelian trilogy (*theoria, techne, praxis*) that classifies three different human purposes, namely seeking warranted knowledge, making beautiful and useful things, and arriving at defensible decisions, respectively. A different pattern of reasoning is used in each, and the skill set associated with each emphasis is identified accordingly. Hence SL is operationally defined as the student's grasp of the way science itself permeates human affairs across this broad trilogy of purposes. (Predating the Pan-Canadian framework, this organization of a science curriculum policy was implemented in the province of Alberta, as described by Roberts, 1995.)

Reflections on the Focus-on-Situations Approach

Writers who advocate Vision II SL raise three serious challenges for science education, in my view. I shall comment very briefly on these, according to the topics of assessment, curriculum planning, and the character of science classroom discourse.

Assessment programs—especially if cross-national—are made much more complex, if Vision II SL is taken into account. This matter is pursued in the section immediately following. Two points are important here. First, students' experience of situations, especially as described in Roth and Barton (2004), is local and virtually one-of-a-kind. This feature of Vision II creates significant problems for cross-national, or even national, comparisons. Second, a related concern is the daunting challenge of getting away from the "cognitive deficit model" of assessment in science, as discussed by Jenkins (1997).

Curriculum planning and implementation are complicated by the fact that Vision II takes as its starting point a context, rather than a formal knowledge structure. In the case of Canada's framework (CMEC, 1997) and provincial curricula based on it, the most likely chance of success has been to mandate that certain units of study (e.g., Heat) be taught in a selected context or emphasis (e.g., science and technology). Instructional resources that are approved follow suit. Supporting materials often recommend (in some cases, mandate) that teachers use the familiar learning cycle approach to planning, in order to ensure that situations receive attention and that subject matter is integrated as required for understanding the situation.

The increasing attention to inclusiveness in science education is part of what animates discussion about Vision II. It is imperative, in Vision II SL, that situations be an important focus of science classroom discourse, yet such discussions require teachers to embrace "discourse universes" that are unfamiliar—such as the aboriginal oral history that was an important part of the Oceanside case study (Roth & Lee, 2002, 2004). A number of writers cite Jean Lave's work on situated cognition as an important source for understanding (e.g., Lave & Wenger, 1991). Others concentrate on the character and quality of argumentation in classroom discussions about socioscientific issues (e.g., Zeidler, Osborne, Erduran, et al., 2003). Wynne (1995) describes one research approach based on "the reconstruction of the 'mental models' that laypeople appear to have of the processes that are the object of scientific knowledge" (p. 364). He cites, for example, lay models of home heating to illustrate how knowledge based on such mental models differs from "theoretical knowledge, handed down from science as the 'correct' knowledge against which to measure public understanding" (p. 372). All such matters as these are challenges to science educators, if Vision II is taken seriously.

WHAT IS BEING ASSESSED, IN THE NAME OF SL?

This section concentrates on the meaning of SL used as a basis for measurement in four prominent assessment programs. Two of these are independent of professional science education: the work of Jon Miller in the US and increasingly in other countries, and that of John Durant in England. The other two are used in international testing programs and have involved science educators worldwide: the mathematics and science literacy (MSL) component of the Third International Mathematics and

Science Study (TIMSS) and the OECD-sponsored *Programme for International Student Assessment* (PISA). In each case, the conceptualization of SL is described first, and a commentary follows.

Jon Miller's Assessments of Scientific Literacy

There is good reason to go into a bit of detail about Miller's estimates of SL, whether or not one agrees with them. Miller maintains a high profile as a commentator on SL especially in the US but increasingly around the world, since his methodology has now been used for replication studies in more than 20 countries. He is Director of the International Center for the Advancement of Scientific Literacy, founded by the Chicago Academy of Sciences in 1991, now located at Northwestern University (Retrieved April 13, 2005, from http://www.cmb.northwestern.edu./faculty/jon_miller.htm). For more than two decades, he has designed and conducted the periodic national studies *Science and Engineering Indicators*, polled regularly by the (US) National Science Board. The results of these assessments play a role in his estimates of SL among both adults and students in schools and colleges. In the US, such results are potentially a direct reflection on the school system—especially now that his *Longitudinal Study of American Youth* (LSAY) results have generated equations that "predict" SL on the basis of a large number of curriculum-related (as well as home-related) factors (see Miller, 2000).

The Definition Shifts

Miller's work is based on Vision I, but initially it was planned to embrace Vision II as well. The paper most frequently cited in the literature (Miller, 1983) appeared in an issue of the journal *Daedalus* that was devoted entirely to SL (American Academy of Arts & Sciences, 1983). In that paper, SL is presented as a construct with three components. The first two are defined in terms of the history of assessment in science education, as two separate strands: "definition and measurement of the scientific attitude" by science educators in the US starting in the 1930s, and assessment of "the level of cognitive scientific knowledge" among various groups in the school population as part of the postwar (WWII) growth of standardized testing, also in the US. These two strands were combined in the (US) National Assessment of Educational Progress (NAEP) studies beginning in the mid–1960s—"the first to measure systematically both the understanding of the norms, or processes, of science and the cognitive content of the major disciplines." To these Miller added a third component—one that essentially reaches out to embrace Vision II: "awareness of the impact of science and technology on society and the policy choices that must inevitably emerge" (p. 31).

The assessment procedure specified that an individual must achieve minimal competence on all three dimensions, or components, in order to be declared scientifically literate. Here are examples of the results. In a 1979 survey, the instrument "included all of the items necessary to measure each of the three dimensions of scientific literacy" (Miller, 1983, p. 36). "On the basis of this measure, only 7 percent of the respondents [$N = 1635$]—primarily males, individuals over thirty-five, and college graduates—qualified. . . . But even among holders of graduate degrees, only a quarter could be called scientifically literate" (Miller, 1983, p. 41; cf. Shamos, 1995, p. 90). Later, he reported "approximately 7 percent of American adults qualified as scientifically literate in the 1992 study. . . . [This] estimate . . . shows no significant change from the results of previous studies in 1979, 1985, 1988, and 1990" (Miller, 1996, pp. 193–194).

In three later, related publications, Miller (1997, 1998, 2000) took a different tack in two ways. First, the studies described are more elaborate and include longitudinal student data based on a more comprehensive methodology. Two of the articles (Miller 1997 and 2000) tell essentially the same story, but the later one is more complete, has a larger database, and represents a refinement of the earlier one, so it is the basis for the following discussion. Second, the original third dimension of SL (awareness of the impact of science and technology on individuals and society) is called into question on the following basis. "In more recent cross-national studies of civic scientific literacy, Miller found the third dimension—the impact of science and technology on individuals and society—to vary substantially in content among different nations and adopted a two-dimensional construct for use in cross-national analyses" (Miller, 1998, p. 206; he cites Miller, Pardo, & Niwa [1997] as the basis for this point.) In other words, no significant factor loaded for the third dimension, when the factor analysis was performed. Miller (1997) pointed out that it is "difficult to construct accurate cross-national measures of this dimension because science and technology may be experienced differently, depending on the emergence of public policy issues in a given country" (p. 124). He also expressed the view that an understanding of scientific knowledge and scientific inquiry items is sufficient for declaring that a respondent comprehends the impact dimension (Miller, 2000, pp. 27–29).

Commentary on Miller's Contribution

From a measurement standpoint, Miller had no choice about dropping the third dimension from his original construct of SL. Quite simply, no third factor emerged from the factor analysis. However, the impact on defining SL is more significant: the definition has been squeezed and distorted. In the process, any gestures in the direction of Vision II have been lost. Miller claims "There is general agreement among scholars engaged in national surveys . . . that a reliable two-dimensional measure of civic scientific literacy would be useful in a wide range of national and cross-national research (Miller, 2000, p. 26). As well, he equates "scientifically literate" with "well informed," in that same paper (p. 29). From a conceptual standpoint, it appears that he is downplaying the significance of educational experience related to an understanding of the impact of science and technology on individuals and society. One interpretation would be that Miller truly believes that understanding science and science inquiry somehow prepares individuals for understanding the impact of science and technology. He would not be alone; that seems to be the cornerstone of Vision I.

There are two further implications of Miller's marginalization of Vision II. First, there is the point that cross-national comparisons, and even cross-national discourse about SL, run the risk of talking at cross-purposes if the "impact" dimension is included in a testing program. Science educators involved in PISA and the MSL component of TIMSS are well aware of this point. Second, Miller asserts in two publications intended for science educators that "issue-oriented" courses are not conducive to developing SL (Miller 1996, p. 201, and 2000, p. 44). That claim surely merits further empirical investigation. It would be difficult for many in the science education community to swallow, since analysis of controversial issues is held to be an important instructional context in which students learn the science needed to understand an issue, and simultaneously develop their grasp of decision-making processes about socio-scientific issues in a democracy.

A final point is in order. The decontextualized nature of the probes used in Miller's assessment items (e.g., the Earth goes around the Sun once a year—True or False?) raises issues about validity of the measurements. In turn, questionable validity about claims of SL makes assessments such as his questionable as a component of curriculum policy deliberation (cf. Norris & Phillips [2003]). Nevertheless, in the US but increasingly in other countries as well, Miller's contribution is one to be reckoned with politically.

Asscooing Public Understanding of Science as SL: John Durant and Colleagues

As noted earlier, the term public understanding of science is used more frequently in England than the term SL. In some of John Durant's work the two terms are nevertheless linked explicitly. Durant is no stranger to informal science education. His academic credentials include a Visiting Professorship in the History and Public Understanding of Science at Imperial College of the University of London. He has also held posts as Assistant Director of the Science Museum in London and, currently, as Chief Executive of At-Bristol, a science and discovery center bringing to the general public an increased access to science, technology, natural history, and the environment. I wish to explore three papers for which he was either sole author or co-author.

Wavering on the Vision

Thomas and Durant (1987) examined the relationship between PUS and SL in the first issue of a publication by the Scientific Literacy Group in the University of Oxford Department of External Studies. At the conclusion of the paper, they point out that their "preliminary account of the nature of the public understanding of science in terms of the concept of scientific literacy" rests on the relationship between science and the rest of society, "promoting the public understanding of science which is concerned with decision-making about science-related issues in a democratic society" (p. 13). The vision of SL expressed here is Vision II.

In 1988, the year after that paper was published, an empirical study was launched to test a hypothesis about the relationship between PUS and levels of support for science (Evans & Durant, 1995). Despite professing Vision II in the paper just discussed, Durant and his colleague used Vision I almost exclusively to define PUS for this study. Two of the independent variables are generated directly from Vision I: familiarity with products and processes of science. There is a vague nod in the direction of Vision II. The third independent variable is called "interest in science," measured on the basis of TV and magazine consumption and a self-reported estimate of how likely respondents were to read headlines with scientific content (p. 58). The authors use the phrase "attitudes towards science" to signify a conceptually related group of dependent variables that are taken to indicate "more or less support for, or a more or less positive evaluation of, science, scientists, and scientific activities" (p. 59).

Following discussion of the results of their regression analysis, Evans and Durant conclude that (1) "measures of general attitudes [toward science] are inadequate as a guide to what the public may think of specific areas of scientific research," (2) "there is some evidence that higher levels of knowledge are associated with more supportive attitudes for science in general and for 'useful science' [probably thought to be socially relevant]," (3) "the well informed are more strongly opposed to morally contentious and non-useful areas of research than are the less well informed," and (4) "interest in science may predict attitudes better than scientific understanding will" (p. 70). They bring the paper to a close with the caution that for anyone promoting greater PUS in order to mobilize public support for science, "the results presented in this paper suggest that such attempts cannot always be relied upon to be straightforwardly beneficial" (p. 71).

Durant (1994) returned to defining SL in the following way: "what is it reasonable to hope and expect that ordinary citizens will know about science in order to equip them for life in a scientifically and technologically complex culture?" (p. 83). He structures the argument around three possibilities for defining SL: "knowing a lot of science, knowing how science works, knowing how science really works" (p. 84). The contrast between the second and third is deliberate, of course. The definition is Vision I. In concluding his paper, Durant contrasts the SL of scientists and the SL of the general public. He points out that scientists have first-hand experience of the checks and balances of knowledge production, while most members of the general public do not have any experience of scientific research at all. Allowing that formal science education about the nature of science ameliorates this situation somewhat, he notes that "informal science education has attempted to convey something of the spirit of scientific inquiry through, for example, hands-on exhibits that foster curiosity and the sense of discovery among children" (p. 89).

Commentary on Durant and Visions of SL

The vision of SL inherent in these three papers is not uniform. In the defining article of 1987, it is Vision II, yet Vision I predominates in the 1995 study and in the 1994 article (which is Durant's alone), but the latter is an elaborated form to include some institutional characteristics of science. Regarding this elaborated form of Vision I, Miller, Pardo, and Niwa (1997) comment in the following way. "In recent work [the 1994 article], Durant discusses a three-dimensional model (a comprehension of basic scientific concepts, an understanding of scientific methodology, and an understanding of the institutional dimension of science) but has used for analysis [in another study, namely Bauer, Durant, & Evans (1994)] only a single summated scale that merges the vocabulary and process dimensions" (p. 39).

The shifts between Vision I and Vision II are a significant matter for anyone concerned about the validity of SL and PUS assessments such as Miller's and Durant's.

The concern of these two researchers is more for reliability in cross-national measures than in validity of the definition of SL or in the character of science education.

SL in the Third International Mathematics and Science Study (TIMSS)

At about the same time Miller (1997 ff.) was withdrawing from the use of the impact dimension in his assessments of SL, TIMSS was developing and incorporating items from just such a dimension in a mathematics and science literacy (MSL) component. (Readers will be aware that the "T" in TIMSS has recently begun to stand for "Trends in . . ." rather than its original "Third." This discussion relates to the original meaning.)

Unlike other components of TIMSS, MSL testing was not curriculum-bound. For this component, students were tested in their final year of secondary school. "These students may have studied mathematics and science in their final years of school or they may not have; they may regard themselves as specialists in mathematics and science, in other subjects, or in none; they may be entering occupations or further education related to mathematics and science, or they may have no intention of doing so. . . . The role of the literacy study within TIMSS . . . is to ask whether school leavers can remember the mathematics and science they have been taught and can therefore apply this knowledge to the challenges of life beyond school" (Orpwood & Garden, 1998, pp. 10–11).

In addition to Vision I dimensions in the MSL test (mathematics and science content, and "Reasoning in Mathematics, Science, and Technology"), the distinctively Vision II dimension is called "Social Impacts of Mathematics, Science, and Technology." For testing purposes, the third and fourth dimensions were combined into one grouping known as "RSU"—"reasoning and social utility in mathematics, science, and technology" (pp. 30–31). This became the working framework for developing test items. In the end, the item pool contained 12 RSU items—five multiple choice, three short answer, and four extended response, for a total testing time of 31 minutes out of 121 (Orpwood, 2000, p. 55).

In reflecting on the development of the items, Orpwood commented, "many draft items that went beyond strict knowledge of science or mathematics content were either eliminated on psychometric grounds or on the grounds of unacceptability to participating countries" (p. 56). These two reasons will not surprise the reader at this point, since these problems reflect some of the same concerns that Miller claims to be his reasons for retreating from the inclusion of an impact dimension in his assessments. Orpwood's account provides many more pertinent details for science education than we find in Miller's work. Indeed, in a later paper Orpwood (2001) presents a convincing case for paying serious attention to the lag between major curriculum changes in science education, which he terms "curriculum revolutions" (p. 137), and the development of assessment techniques that are appropriate for evaluating the impact of the changes. Commenting on the 1960s curriculum revolution to incorporate goals related to the nature of science and the acquisition of science inquiry skills, he notes that "teachers and national/international assessment projects continued to use traditional assessment measures—measures that, in the main, called for recall of memorised scientific knowledge" (p. 143). About the delay in shifting assessment techniques to those that match the change, he noted "It was the 1980s before performance assessment even made its first significant appearance and the 1990s before it became at all widespread" (pp. 143–144).

"The second period of revolutionary change," as Orpwood described it, "began slowly in the early 1980s and has now (in the late 1990s) gathered significant momentum . . . outward [from science itself] towards society and the complex relationships among science, technology, society, and the environment" (p. 139). Yet, at this time, "assessment of the curriculum goals . . . for the STS revolution in science curriculum has barely surfaced at all beyond the research level" (p. 144). He describes RSU items from the MSL component of TIMSS, presenting sample items and commenting on both their structure and some of the issues associated with their acceptance or rejection by the project committee and/or participating countries. He also describes items from his experience with another assessment program, in the Canadian province of Ontario, related to goals for a science-technology curriculum. The overall thrust of the article is to express concern that lack of appropriate assessment procedures can distort and stifle curriculum innovation, and the examples give point and substance to Orpwood's argument.

SL in the OECD Programme for International Student Assessment (PISA)

This assessment is planned to test 15-year-old students in participating countries, on a three-yearly basis, in three domains: reading literacy, mathematical literacy, and scientific literacy. This review is concerned only with the conceptualization of SL inherent in the science assessment. The conceptualization initially adopted for PISA states the following: "Scientific literacy is the capacity to use scientific knowledge, to identify questions and to draw evidence-based conclusions in order to understand and help make decisions about the natural world and the changes made to it through human activity" (OECD, 1999, p. 60). The meaning of, and the purpose for including, particular phrases in the definition, such as "scientific knowledge" and "evidence-based conclusions," are elaborated in the OECD document and, as well, in two very informative papers by Harlen (2001a, 2001b).

The following points about the conceptualization paraphrase Harlen (2001b).

- This conceptualization of SL is about what learners should achieve in terms of their needs as citizens—"understanding that will improve their future lives" (p. 87). This suggests a view that future scientists also need such understanding.
- The roots of SL are in school experience, even though it can be "developed throughout life" (p. 87), which is a recognition of the significance of informal science education.
- SL is not equated with vocabulary, but connotes "general competence or being 'at ease' with scientific ways of understanding" (p. 87). This also suggests a broader, different kind of understanding than suggested by knowing how to "do science."

- A key feature of a student's SL is skilfulness at relating evidence to claims: how evidence is used and collected in science, "what makes some evidence more dependable than other, what are its shortcomings and where it can and should be applied" (p. 87).
- This SL conceptualization contextualizes scientific knowledge and scientific thinking in relation to problems, issues, and situations "in the real world" (p. 91)—thus students can apply what they learn in laboratory settings to non-school settings.

Assessments were conducted in 2000 and 2003, and a third is planned for 2006. All three domains of literacy are tested in each assessment, but one is a major feature and the other two are minor: reading literacy was the major domain in 2000, mathematical literacy was major in 2003, and science is the major domain for the 2006 assessment. The conceptualization of SL used in the 2003 assessment is the same as stated above for 2000 (OECD, 2003, p. 133. Retrieved April 13, 2005, from http://www.pisa/oecd.org).

The PISA Governing Board has approved the framework for the 2006 assessment (R.W. Bybee [personal communication April 19, 2005]). The Science Forum, responsible for advising, and the Science Expert Group, responsible for developing specific aspects of the framework, have revised the 2000/2003 framework. The 2006 conceptualization of SL is as follows. (This is taken from a document prepared for the Science Forum and Science Expert Group Meetings held in Warsaw, July 12–15, 2004, and is reproduced here by permission of R.W. Bybee [personal communication April 19, 2005.)

Scientific literacy refers to an individual's:

- Scientific knowledge and use of that knowledge to identify questions, to acquire new knowledge, to explain scientific phenomena, and to draw evidence-based conclusions about science-related issues;
- Understanding of the characteristic features of science as a form of human knowledge and enquiry;
- Awareness of how science and technology shape our material, intellectual, and cultural environments; and
- Willingness to engage in science-related issues, and with the ideas of science, as a reflective citizen.

This conceptualization is clearly specifying Vision II as the basis for PISA in 2006. From the beginning, this project has concentrated on assessment within situations. The 2006 framework emphasizes and strengthens that intention.

The story of SL in PISA is an amazing tale of deliberation and consensus seeking in an area of science education policy formation, namely student assessment, which is not known for wasting time on deciding about what goals of science education to test. Harlen (2001b) notes that "What PISA assesses is what participating countries have agreed are desirable outcomes, whether or not they reflect the current curriculum of a particular country" (p. 85). The implications of that statement are astonishing, and some of the sample test items presented in Harlen's paper, as well as on the OECD/PISA website, are most interesting. Although any more specifics about the assessment program itself are beyond the scope of this review (and are more appropriate elsewhere in this handbook), this is a venture well worth watching from the standpoint of the thoughtfulness that has gone into conceptualizing and measuring SL—especially the challenges of taking Vision II seriously in an assessment framework.

IMPLICATIONS

The most challenging aspect of this literature is trying to get clear on what is actually being claimed, in the name of SL. To be sure, a definition of SL is always provided when a research article, an assessment program, or a curriculum policy is described, discussed, or advocated. The variety among the many definitions pales in significance, though, in comparison to the fundamental differences we can see between Vision I and Vision II. Conclusions and implications of this review are clustered according to four areas. Special attention is paid to implications for further research.

- We can, logically speaking, expect differences in outcomes for students from SL programs and teaching based on Vision I, compared to Vision II.
- We can identify three types of curricular arrangements to make provision for SL and PUS to develop. Is any one arrangement better than the other(s)?
- Vision I and Vision II give rise to different assessment frameworks for making claims about students' and adults' SL and PUS. What are the implications for our discourse with each other, as science educators?
- Different combinations of "discourse universes" are appropriate for inclusion in Vision I and Vision II embodiments. What are the consequences of taking that statement seriously, for teachers, students, and teacher education?

The General Character of Vision I and Vision II Program Outcomes

The identification of Vision I and Vision II of SL/PUS has been presented as a heuristic device intended to highlight the most significant conceptual divide in the literature reviewed here. What are the implications of adopting one vision or the other for program development?

The most serious problem with adopting Vision I is narrowing the student's experience with the breadth of science as a human endeavor. Between Vision I and Vision II, the most obvious distinction has to do with a student's way of conceptualizing and experiencing the character of controversial socioscientific issues and problems. As indicated in my earlier example based on the *Atlas of Scientific Literacy* (AAAS, 2001), Vision I would have students understand an issue as a scientist would. That is well and good, for one perspective on the issue. In several Canadian provinces, science curriculum policy requires that several other perspectives (e.g., economic, aesthetic, political, ethical, social) also be taken into consideration and used in deliberation about socioscientific issues. Roth and Barton are particularly scathing in their comments about the inadequacy of a single perspective. "Just imagine, every individual taking the same ('scientific') perspective on GMO's, genetic manipulation of the human genome, or use of drugs (such as those used to dope certain kinds of children, labelled with [ADHD], to make them compliant)" (p. 3). Eisenhart et al. (1996) seem to be making a similar point. "We disagree with the implicit assumption . . . that teaching students key concepts and scientific methods of inquiry will necessarily lead to socially responsible use [of science] or to a larger and more diverse citizenry who participate in discussion and debate of scientific issues . . . no clear conceptual connections, strategies to achieve, or empirical support are offered . . ." (pp. 268–269).

There are actually two points here. One is an empirical claim that implementation efforts in the US are over-emphasizing Vision I—or, at least, the portion of it contained in the "Science as Inquiry" standard of *NSES* (the other portion is contained in the "History and Nature of Science" standard). I'm not sure sufficient evidence is presented for that claim. The second point probably is more accurate. The assertion that students don't automatically develop a Vision II grasp of SL if they are exposed only to Vision I is based on a logical point. It has to do with the variety of discourses included in each vision. A curriculum based on Vision II discourses potentially encompasses all four of the *NSES* context standards. Similarly, the "ideas about science" in the Vision II project 21st Century Science include "the practices that have produced it; the kinds of reasoning that are used in developing a scientific argument; and on the issues that arise when scientific knowledge is put to practical use." These are grouped into six broad categories: "data and its limitations; correlation and cause; theories; the scientific community; risk; and making decisions about science and technology" (Retrieved April 19, 2005 from http://www.21stcentury science.org).

A Vision I curriculum, though, can be developed in the absence of some of the Vision II discourses, namely the substance of the *NSES* standard on "Science in Personal and Social Perspectives" and, perhaps as well, the standard on "Science and Technology" (NRC, 1996, p. 113). In brief, Vision II subsumes Vision I, but the converse is not necessarily so.

How Visions of SL Materialize

Visions of SL materialize from the contexts in which science subject matter is taught. No science curriculum, textbook, or lesson is "context-free." The contexts for science education are (1) expressions of the reasons students are expected to learn the subject matter and, therefore, in a classroom or textbook, (2) sets of coherent messages (discourse universes, essentially) about the purpose for learning it. I have dubbed these contexts *curriculum emphases* (Roberts, 1982, 1988). Curriculum emphases can be communicated either explicitly, by what is said in the classroom, or implicitly, by what is implied or excluded.

Seven distinct curriculum emphases can be discerned in science curriculum history during the past century. Even a syllabus of subject matter topics has a curriculum emphasis, which I have dubbed "Solid Foundation." This is a default emphasis—meaning it is communicated implicitly. The contextual message it communicates to students is "The reason for learning this material is to get ready for next year, and the year after that." In other words, it is a purpose based on the orderliness of a recognizable sequence. A closely related default emphasis I called

"Correct Explanations." This one communicates that the purpose of learning science is to get your world-view right. Although examples of these two can be found in science education curriculum history, they are not of much interest to the present discussion.

Vision I incorporates two of the emphases I identified. One is called "Scientific Skill Development" and the other "Structure of Science." Together, I would say these two make up two US *NSES* context standards—Science as Inquiry, and History and Nature of Science. Vision II partakes of those, and also the remaining three: "Personal Explanation," "Science, Technology, Decisions," and "Everyday Coping/Applications." The first two of these are found in the *NSES* standards as Personal and Social Perspectives on Science, and the third is found in Science and Technology.

The Potential Effects of Over-emphasizing One Curriculum Emphasis

Science curriculum history is littered with examples of throwing out the baby with the bathwater. Major changes in science curriculum have been due to changes in curriculum emphasis, although of course there have been changes to subject matter as well. When a curriculum emphasis changes, for whatever reason, the rhetoric usually cries out "Stop doing *any of that*, and start doing *all of this*!" Neither Vision I nor Vision II is immune from this possibility.

Vision I programs run the risk of including situation-oriented material (Science and Technology and/or Personal and Social Perspectives on Science) in a token fashion, only as a source for motivating students in lessons. By the same token (pardon the pun), Vision II programs run the risk of paying insufficient attention to science. Aikenhead (1994) presents an analysis of materials development, research, and teaching approaches in STS according to eight categories that show different blends of science content and attention to situations, or "STS content" (pp. 55–56). At one extreme is "Motivation by STS Content," described as "Traditional school science, plus a mention of STS content in order to make a lesson more interesting. Not normally taken seriously as STS instruction. . . . Students are not assessed on the STS content." At the other extreme is "STS Contents," described thus: "A major technology or social issue is studied. Science content is mentioned but only to indicate an existing link to science. . . . Students are not assessed on pure science content to any appreciable degree." There is a message here, as well as an analytical scheme, about what can happen in implementation efforts involving both Vision II and Vision I.

Roth and Lee (2002, 2004) and Roth and Barton (2004) have pushed Vision II to the extreme by redefining SL as "collective praxis"—as if there is no such thing as "individual" SL. All of their case studies, so far as I can determine, are based on teaching science through the same single context: Personal and Social Perspectives on Science. There is a comment in a "Coda" (Roth & Lee 2004, p. 288) that "Much research remains to be done to study the forms distributed and situated cognition take in the approach we propose." Indeed. More research is also needed on whether, and how well, students can shift from one context to another as appropriate in different situations. For example, suppose students learn about water chemistry in the context of a Personal and Social Perspectives on Science. Would that inhibit, contribute to, or have no effect on their understanding of appropriate features of the Scientific Inquiry and/or History and Nature of Science context, such as the system-theory character of ecological inquiry? I would submit we don't have enough research to answer questions of this sort. To be sure, we have substantial research on the impacts of teaching science within a single context, or curriculum emphasis (e.g., the research on learning about the nature of science, about STS, etc.). The point here is about multiple contexts and how those affect learners, therefore feeding back implications for the way SL is defined in curriculum policies and implemented in instructional materials. There are risks in over-emphasizing either Vision II or Vision I.

Curricular Arrangements to Deliver SL and PUS

This review identified three approaches to organizing curriculum in order to achieve SL and/or PUS. I shall summarize them first. The most direct approach—a special course on SL or PUS mandated for all students—is, so far as I can tell, also the most rare. The two examples I have found are the course in England known as 21st Century Science, which is clearly based on Vision II, and a grade 10 course in the Netherlands that began with the intention to embody Vision II.

The second approach, by far the most common, is to work from an overall curriculum framework that is permeated by SL and, generally speaking, identifies SL as its potential outcome for all students. I would say that the approach taken by *NSES* in the US reflects this approach. Another example is a recent report from Australia. According to Rennie, Goodrum, and Hackling (2001), the current curriculum framework emerged from a recent large-scale research project examining the quality of science teaching and learning in Australian schools. Their paper draws from the full report of the study (Goodrum, Hackling, & Rennie, 2000). Most significant for purposes of this review is the conception of SL expressed as the "ideal" approach to science curriculum in the several states (the eight states and territories of Australia do not have a single mandatory or official national curriculum). All of the recommendations of the study are based on five premises, including one that specifies the purpose of science education as developing SL. "Scientifically literate persons are interested in and understand the world around them, are sceptical and questioning of claims made by others about scientific matters. They participate in the discourses of and about science, identify questions, investigate and draw evidence-based conclusions, and make informed decisions about the environment and their own health and well-being" (Rennie, Goodrum, & Hackling, 2001, p. 494).

Such frameworks as *NSES* and the Australian example typically reflect elements of both Vision I and Vision II, just because they are broad, idealized, multi-purpose, and intended to be enabling and facilitating. That is, as Bybee expressed about his types-and-levels definition of SL, not everyone is expected to develop the same degree, or the same kind, of SL. Curriculum frameworks of this sort must accommodate some students who want and/or need pre-professional training in science, as well as preparing students for citizenship.

The third arrangement, used by a number of Canadian provinces, is to ensure that objectives related to Vision II are mandated through the requirement to teach certain units of study according to curriculum emphases (typically called program emphases, in Canadian provinces) that take Vision II situations (technological problem solving and societal decision making) as their starting point.

The Potential for Retreating from Vision II to Vision I

Vision I and Vision II express broadly different views of what it means to be scientifically literate, or to have developed knowledge, skills, and attitudes consistent with public understanding of science. What is important to recognize is that advocates of Vision II stress that all students in democratic societies—regardless of their career plans—need to develop SL that is appropriate to situations other than conducting scientific inquiry. Thus, for example, an understanding of scientific inquiry is not only important for potential scientists, in Vision II thinking. It is a vital component of a citizen's ability to keep a scientific perspective in balance with others. Thus, students need classroom experience with situations in which different perspectives are deliberately brought to bear on socio-scientific issues. Indeed, Roth and Barton (2004) argue that even classroom simulations are not adequate for such learning, but in any event, to paraphrase Eisenhart et al., an approach to SL based on Vision I does not, clearly does not, provide the opportunity to learn what is involved in Vision II. As noted earlier, Jon Miller believes the reverse is also true.

I think this is an area where empirical evidence is needed on two matters. One is the claim by Roth and Barton, to the effect that vicarious, in-class experience with issue analysis is phoney—that students do not learn from simulations, but instead need the real thing, immersion in real socioscientific problems in the community. The second is the claim advanced by Jon Miller that STS courses are not the way to develop an understanding of science. Both of these are sweeping claims, each one sure to create a stir among some science educators (not necessarily the same ones). At very least, such claims should be qualified. Do some students learn better from simulations? Do no students learn science in STS courses? What kinds of STS courses (cf. Aikenhead, 1994)? Shouldn't such claims be qualified at least in terms of specific instances of opportunity to learn?

There is a more insidious problem, whenever curriculum arrangements do not mandate Vision II outcomes. Fensham (1998) has discussed three Australian cases in which proposals to mount courses with a Vision II thrust have been defeated in curriculum committees by academic scientists. Blades (1997) has analyzed a similar phenomenon in the Canadian province of Alberta. In these two examples, the retreat from Vision II to Vision I occurred as a result of power politics within curriculum committees. In the case of the mandatory course on public understanding of science in The Netherlands, there was evidence of a retreat during the implementation. De Vos and Reiding (1999) describe the teaching materials developed for the course as turning out to have "a 'science-plus,' or science-oriented approach" consisting of "fragments of a science curriculum with added information on history, philosophy, society or economics" (p. 717). The nature of the teaching materials is presented as one factor that interfered with establishing a separate identity for the course. "The experience in The Netherlands shows that once a science-oriented approach is adopted, it becomes extremely difficult to escape from the shadows of the science teaching tradition" (p. 718).

Talking to Each Other About the Meaning of SL Assessments

Both Jon Miller and John Durant retreated from Vision II to Vision I, as the basis for their assessments of SL and PUS, respectively. Yet, in the other two assessment programs discussed in this review—namely, the TIMSS MSL assessment and PISA—there is a continuing effort to define SL in a manner that respects the importance of context and situation in Vision II. It seems to me the jury is out, on the matter of whether Vision II can be assessed satisfactorily in international comparisons. I don't mean to be facile about this. It won't be easy. (See papers by Bybee and others on 2003 results in the US context [BSCS, 2005], and the insightful volume *Learning from Others: International Comparisons in Education* [Shorrocks-Taylor & Jenkins, 2000].) However, I think this matter is sufficiently significant that it is worth following the development of PISA 2006 and waiting for the results and some further research on the process.

At issue for cross-national studies is the concern that assessment items might be situated in contexts that are more familiar to students in some nations than in others. This is a valid concern, if an assessment item requires that the situation itself either be understood, or viewed in the same way culturally, in order for students across nations to have a "fair" chance when they respond. Orpwood (2001) provides a detailed account of the measurement problems encountered with TIMSS MSL items that were designed to incorporate situations, and concludes his paper with some serious concerns about the relationship between assessment procedures and curriculum change. "Leadership is therefore required from all quarters to ensure that innovations such as performance assessment and STS assessment are not allowed to be regarded as 'second-class' or entirely 'optional' ways of assessing achievement in science education" (p. 149). My point is that this state of affairs—namely the potential for a retreat from Vision II—is hauntingly familiar. It is just what Miller did, and for the same reason, namely measurement issues.

Expanding Our View of Legitimate Discourse Universes for SL/PUS

One of the most striking differences between Vision I and Vision II is the nature and content of the discourse appropriate and legitimate for each. Curriculum policy statements, assessment items, and instructional resources and activities acknowledge and privilege some discourses and ignore or marginalize others. The discourse of orthodox science and scientific inquiry is the most familiar, of course. Others that have been identified in this review include discourse about moral reasoning (cf. Zeidler, 2003); the oral history provided by the aboriginal elders, as part of the community-based stream study in the Oceanside case study (Roth & Lee, 2002, 2004; Roth & Barton, 2004); the discourse about technological reasoning and problem solving, which is a vital part of STL; and the discourse with which members of different occupations think and talk about the tasks they perform, as displayed in the SSSP work by Layton, Davey, and Jenkins (1986).

Which Discourse Universes are to be Legitimate?

A discourse universe always has situated legitimacy in its own right. Sometimes legitimacy comes from recognized status as a discipline. Technological reasoning and problem solving, for example, are the bread and butter discourses of engineering. Again, the discourse of moral reasoning and ethics is recognized and accepted in philosophy. There is nothing inherently better or worse about such discourses. The decision to include or exclude them from science education is a matter of deliberation and choice.

For illustrative purposes, here is an example of a curriculum policy document that explicitly acknowledges the significance of a discourse universe other than that of orthodox science. A recent version of South Africa's national curriculum policy for natural sciences states that "The Natural Sciences Learning Area deals with the promotion of scientific literacy. It does this by:

- the development and use of science process skills in a variety of settings;
- the development and application of scientific knowledge and understanding; and
- appreciation of the relationships and responsibilities between science, society and the environment" (Department of Education, Pretoria, 2002, p. 4).

The document elaborates on each of these three aspects of SL, synthesizes their intended meaning in three broad learning outcomes, and provides an extended discussion of how the three components can be assessed. The third outcome, described as "challenging, with potential to broaden the curriculum and make it distinctively South African" (p. 10), is of special interest because it includes attention to relationships between science, on one hand, and traditional practices and technologies as these relate to traditional wisdom and knowledge systems, on the other. "One can assume that learners in the Natural Sciences Learning Area think in terms of more than one world-view. Several times a week they cross from the culture of home, over the border into the culture of science, and then back again. How does this fact influence their understanding of science and their progress in the Learning Area? Is it a hindrance to teaching or is it an opportunity for more meaningful learning and a curriculum which tries to understand both the culture of science and the cultures of home?" (p. 12). This curriculum document, as well as others related to South African science education, is in a state of flux. In the corresponding version of the document for Physical Science 10–12, "scientific literacy is a clearly stated purpose" and, while it is not an explicitly stated aim in the Life Science 10–12 document, "it is clear that the attainment of scientific literacy is most definitely a tacit goal" (R.C. Laugksch [personal communication, June 6, 2003]).

Discourse: How Visions of SL Materialize (Or Do Not) in Classrooms

Discourse is the basis for creating meaning in classrooms. A curriculum policy decision to embrace one or the other vision of SL entails making it both necessary and possible for appropriate discourses to come to life in classrooms. For example, arguing on behalf of the importance of moral reasoning as a component of SL, Zeidler and Lewis (2003) put it this way. "Arming our students with improved understandings of nature of science and scientific inquiry does not provide a complete picture of the scientifically literate individual. Moral development and ethical reasoning play an important role as students consider what is best for the common good of society or whether the 'common good' is relevant to the issue at hand" (p. 290). Put another way, the extent to which students can create a meaningful grasp of moral and ethical reasoning depends on whether or not the appropriate discourse is even present in the classroom at all. Some discourses, such as the ones to which Zeidler and Lewis allude, are simply not present in the education of science teachers. As well, such discourses may not be part of a science teacher's image of what is appropriate for a science classroom, and/or the teacher may not feel competent or comfortable teaching such material. The implications for research on implementing curriculum focussed on Vision I, compared to Vision II, of SL are as interesting to contemplate as they are daunting.

An acquaintance of mine once commented to the effect that a substantial change of the dominant curriculum emphasis for science education makes everyone a novice teacher again. There is some truth in that assertion, in the sense that teachers (and teacher educators) have to learn and come to accept new types of discourse—not only to understand the discourse and grasp its significance, but also to comprehend and experience how to teach it. Even some aspects of the nature of science within Vision II (e.g., uncertainty, risk)—which one would consider closer to home for science teachers—present serious challenges in understanding, planning, and actually conducting classroom activities. These matters, and others, are illuminated in detail in a recent study about teaching the "ideas-about-science" domain within the 21st Century Science project. The authors "explore the factors that afforded or inhibited the [11] teachers' pedagogic performance in this domain" (Bartholomew, Osborne, & Ratcliffe 2004, p. 655). Of special interest here is the way the authors link their findings to discussion and implications associated with the characteristics of summative assessment used in science education, and the characteristics of the school science culture (pp. 678–679).

Research of the kind just presented must follow development, rather than lead it, in the sense that a classroom practice has to be instituted before there are any phenomena to study. In a more theoretical vein, one other area of research about discourse is presented, namely on the topic of how discourse produces meaning and, inevitably, learning. Using teaching vignettes and excerpts from Swedish science textbooks, Östman (1998) analyzed the way discourse provides "companion meanings" (including curriculum emphases) in science education. All such analyses are, of course, based on theoretical frameworks (e.g., the use of Toulmin's argument-pattern in the study of discourse about socioscientific issues by Zeidler, Osborne, Erduran, et al. [2003]). In Östman's work, the framework is "grounded in poststructural theory, and it depends on having available some alternative possibilities (about what could have been said and how)" (p. 55). One important outcome of the analysis is the documentation, in specific terms, of differences in discourse about several different companion meanings. An extension of the framework was used in a later, related study by Wickman and Östman (2002). There, the discourse of two students is analyzed, in a laboratory situation in which students had pinned insects in front of them, instructions to reflect on the relationship between structure and function, and the expectation that they "should find out the morphology of insects by observation" (pp. 606–607). The analysis is a fascinating fine-grained ("high-resolution," in the authors' words) documentation of a point that cuts to the heart of discourse about one view of the nature of science: "laboratory work in school is often based on inductive epistemology, as if theory would become evident from the observations students make during laboratory work" (p. 621).

These examples show that discourse is what makes visions of SL come to life in science classrooms. The same can be said for written discourse—in textbooks, in curriculum policy statements, and in assessment programs. Clearly, more research is warranted about the development of SL and PUS through an examination of how discourse is understood, enacted by teachers and students, taken up in student learning, measured, and discussed in the science education community and beyond.

AFTERWORD

The literature on SL cries out for clarity of expression and meaning, as we discuss issues in our professional capacity. In working my way through this literature, I was repeatedly reminded of Humpty Dumpty's scornful admonition to Alice, in Lewis Carroll's *Through the Looking Glass*. "When *I* use a word, it means just what I choose it to mean—neither more nor less." I found it helpful to identify Vision I and Vision II, in an effort to reduce the Humpty Dumpty effect surrounding definitions of, and proposals about, SL and PUS. I trust the reader will find that heuristic device helpful as well.

ACKNOWLEDGMENTS

Thanks to Rodger Bybee and Jonathan Osborne, who reviewed this chapter. Additional thanks to Edgar Jenkins, Rudi Laugksch, Graham Orpwood, Senta Raizen, and Léonie Rennie, for their advice on earlier drafts.

REFERENCES

Agin, M. L. (1974). Education for scientific literacy: A conceptual frame of reference and some applications. *Science Education, 58,* 403–415.

Aikenhead, G. (1994). What is STS science teaching? In J. Solomon & G. Aikenhead (Eds.), *STS education: International perspectives on reform* (pp. 47–59). New York: Teachers College Press.

American Academy of Arts and Sciences. (1983). Scientific literacy. *Daedalus, 112*(2).

American Association for the Advancement of Science. (1989). *Science for all Americans.* Washington, DC: Author.

American Association for the Advancement of Science. (1990). *Science for all Americans.* New York: Oxford University Press.

American Association for the Advancement of Science. (1993). *Benchmarks for science literacy.* Washington, DC: Author.

American Association for the Advancement of Science. (2000). *Designs for science literacy.* Washington, DC: Author.

American Association for the Advancement of Science. (2001). *Atlas of science literacy.* Washington, DC: Author.

Atkin, J. M., Bianchini, J. A., & Holthuis, N. I. (1997). The different worlds of Project 2061. In S. A. Raizen & E. D. Britton (Eds.), *Bold ventures volume 2: Case studies of U.S. innovations in science education* (pp. 131–246). Dordrecht, the Netherlands: Kluwer Academic.

Bailey, P. (1998). Conceptions of scientific literacy: Making sense of a proposed national science curriculum framework. *Alberta Science Education Journal, 30*(2), 52–59.

Bandiera, M., Caravita, S., Torracca, E., & Vicentini, M. (Eds.). (1999). *Research in science education in Europe*. Dordrecht, the Netherlands: Kluwer Academic.

Bartholomew, H., Osborne, J., & Ratcliffe, M. (2004). Teaching students "ideas-about-science": Five dimensions of effective practice. *Science Education, 88*, 655–682.

Black, P., & Atkin, J. M. (1996). *Changing the subject: Innovations in science, mathematics and technology education*. London: Routledge.

Blades, D. (1997). *Procedures of power and curriculum change: Foucault and the quest for possibilities in science education*. New York: Peter Lang.

Bauer, M., Durant, J., & Evans, G. (1994). European public perception of science. *International Journal of Public Opinion Research, 6*, 163–186.

Brennan, R. P. (1992). *Dictionary of scientific literacy*. New York: John Wiley & Sons.

BSCS. (2005). *The Natural Selection: The Journal of BSCS, Winter*. Colorado Springs, CO: Author.

Bybee, R. W. (1997a). *Achieving scientific literacy: From purposes to practices*. Portsmouth, NH: Heinemann.

Bybee, R. W. (1997b). Toward an understanding of scientific literacy. In W. Gräber & C. Bolte (Eds.), *Scientific literacy* (pp. 37–68). Kiel: IPN.

Bybee, R. W., & Ben-Zvi, N. (1998). Science curriculum: Transforming goals to practices. In B. J. Fraser & K. G. Tobin, *International handbook of science education* (pp. 487–498). Dordrecht, the Netherlands: Kluwer Academic.

Bybee, R. W., & DeBoer, G. E. (1994). Research on goals for the science curriculum. In D. L. Gabel (Ed.), *Handbook of research on science teaching and learning* (pp. 357–387). New York: Macmillan.

Carson, R. N. (1998). Science and the ideals of liberal education. In B. J. Fraser & K. G. Tobin (Eds.), *International handbook of science education* (pp. 1001–1014). Dordrecht, the Netherlands: Kluwer Academic.

Champagne, A. B., & Kouba, V. L. (1997). Communication and reasoning in science literacy. In S. Sjøberg & E. Kallerud (Eds.), *Science, technology and citizenship* (pp. 75–92). Oslo: NIFU Rapport 7/97.

Christensen, C. (2001). Scientific literacy for a risky society. In P. Singh & E. McWilliam (Eds.), *Designing educational research: Theories, methods and practices* (pp. 141–154). Flaxton, Queensland, Australia: Post Pressed.

Council of Ministers of Education, Canada. (1997). *Common framework of science learning outcomes K to 12: Pan-Canadian protocol for collaboration on school curriculum for use by curriculum developers*. Toronto: Author.

DeBoer, G. E. (1991). *A history of ideas in science education: Implications for practice*. New York: Teachers College Press.

DeBoer, G. E. (2000). Scientific literacy: Another look at its historical and contemporary meanings and its relationship to science education reform. *Journal of Research in Science Teaching, 37*, 582–601.

Department of Education, Pretoria. (2002). *Revised national curriculum statement for grades R–9 (schools): Natural sciences*. Pretoria: Author.

De Vos, W., & Reiding, J. (1999). Public understanding of science as a separate subject in secondary schools in the Netherlands. *International Journal of Science Education, 21*, 711–719.

Durant, J. (1994). What is scientific literacy? *European Review, 2*, 83–89.

Eijkelhof, H. (2001). Preface. In O. de Jong, E. R. Savelsbergh, and A. Alblas (Eds.), *Teaching for scientific literacy: Context, competency, and curriculum* (p. I). CD-ß Series Vol. 38. Utrecht: CD-ß Press, Utrecht University.

Eisenhart, M., Finkel, E., & Marion, S. F. (1996). Creating the conditions for scientific literacy: A re-examination. *American Educational Research Journal, 33*, 261–295.

Evans, G., & Durant, J. (1995). The relationship between knowledge and attitudes in the public understanding of science. *Public Understanding of Science, 4*, 57–74.

Fensham, P. J. (1992). Science and technology. In P. W. Jackson (Ed.), *Handbook of research on curriculum* (pp. 789–829). New York: Macmillan.

Fensham, P. J. (1998). The politics of legitimating and marginalizing companion meanings: Three Australian case stories. In D. A. Roberts & L. Östman (Eds.), *Problems of meaning in science curriculum*. New York: Teachers College Press.

Fitzpatrick, F. L. (Ed.). (1960). *Policies for science education*. New York: Bureau of Publications, Teachers College, Columbia University.

Frey, K., Blänsdorf, K., Kapune, T., Schaefer, G., & Archenhold, F. (Eds.). (1977). *Research in science education in Europe: Perspectives, structural problems and documentation 1976*. Strasbourg: The Council of Europe; Kiel: IPN; Amsterdam: Swets & Zeitlinger.

Gabel, L. L. (1976). *The development of a model to determine perceptions of scientific literacy*. Doctoral dissertation, The Ohio State University.

Gallagher, J. J., & Harsch, G. (1997). Scientific literacy: Science education and secondary school students: A report of an international symposium. In W. Gräber & C. Bolte (Eds.), *Scientific literacy* (pp. 13–34). Kiel: IPN.

Garrison, J. W. & Lawwill, K. S. (1992). Scientific literacy: For whose benefit? In S. Hills (Ed.), *Proceedings of the second international conference on the history and philosophy of science and science education* (Vol. I, pp. 337–349). Kingston, Ontario, Canada: Queen's University.

Goodrum, D., Hackling, M., & Rennie, L. (2000). *The status and quality of teaching and learning of science in Australian schools: A research report*. Canberra: Department of Education, Training and Youth Affairs.

Gräber, W., Nentwig, P., Becker, H., Sumfleth, E., Pitton, A., Wollweber, K., et al. (2001). Scientific literacy: From theory to practice. In H. Behrendt, H. Dahncke, R. Duit, W. Gräber, M. Komorek, & A. Kross (Eds.), *Research in science education—Past, present, and future* (pp. 61–70). Dordrecht, the Netherlands: Kluwer Academic.

Hand, B. M., Alvermann, D. E., Gee, J., Guzzetti, B. J., Norris, S. P., Phillips, L. M., et al. (2003). Guest editorial: Message from the "Island Group": What is literacy in science literacy? *Journal of Research in Science Teaching, 40*, 607–615.

Harlen, W. (2001a). The assessment of scientific literacy in the OECD/PISA project. In H. Behrendt, H. Dahncke, R. Duit, W. Gräber, M. Komorek, & A. Kross (Eds.), *Research in science education—past, present, and future* (pp. 49–60). Dordrecht, the Netherlands: Kluwer Academic.

Harlen, W. (2001b). The assessment of scientific literacy in the OECD/PISA project. *Studies in Science Education, 36*, 79–104.

Hazen, R. M., & Trefil, J. (1991). *Science matters: Achieving scientific literacy*. New York: Doubleday.

Hirsch, E. D. (1987). *Cultural literacy: What every American needs to know*. Boston: Houghton Mifflin.

Hunt, A., & Millar, R. (Eds.). (2000). *AS Science for public understanding*. Oxford: Heinemann Educational.

Hurd, P. D. (1958). Science literacy for American schools. *Educational Leadership, 16*, 13–16.

Hurd, P. D. (1998). Scientific literacy: New minds for a changing world. *Science Education, 82*, 407–416.

Husén, T., & Keeves, J. (1991). *Issues in science education: Science competence in a social and ecological context*. Oxford: Pergamon Press.

Jenkins, E. W. (1990). Scientific literacy and school science education. *School Science Review, 71*(256), 43–51.

Jenkins, E. W. (1997). Scientific and technological literacy: Meanings and rationales. In E. W. Jenkins (Ed.), *Innovations in science and technology education* (Vol. VI, pp. 11–42). Paris: UNESCO.

Johnson, P. G. (1962). The goals of science education. *Theory into Practice, 1*, 239–244.

Klopfer, L. E. (1969). Science education in 1991. *The School Review, 77*, 199–217.

Laugksch, R. C. (2000). Scientific literacy: A conceptual overview. *Science Education, 84*, 71–94.

Lave, J., & Wenger, E. (1991). *Situated learning: Legitimate peripheral participation*. Cambridge: Cambridge University Press.

Layton, D. (1991). Science education and praxis: The relationship of school science to practical action. *Studies in Science Education, 19,* 43–79.

Layton, D. (1994). A school subject in the making? The search for fundamentals. In D. Layton (Ed.), *Innovations in science and technology education* (Vol. V, 11–28). Paris: UNESCO.

Layton, D., Davey, A., & Jenkins, E. (1986). Science for specific social purposes (SSSP): Perspectives on adult scientific literacy. *Studies in Science Education, 13,* 27–52.

Layton, D., Jenkins, E., & Donnelly, J. (1994). Scientific and technological literacy: Meanings and rationales, an annotated bibliography. Leeds: Centre for Studies in Science and Mathematics Education, University of Leeds; and Paris: UNESCO.

Layton, D., Jenkins, E. W., Macgill, S., & Davey, A. (1993). Inarticulate science? Perspectives on the public understanding of science and some implications for science education. Nafferton, Driffield, East Yorkshire YO25 0JL, England: Studies in Education Ltd.

Marshall, S. P., Scheppler, J. A., & Palmisano, M. J. (Eds.). (2003). *Science literacy for the twenty-first century.* Amherst, NY: Prometheus Books.

Matthews, M. R. (1994). *Science teaching: The role of history and philosophy of science.* New York: Routledge.

Mayer, V. J. (Ed.). (2002). *Global science literacy.* Dordrecht, the Netherlands: Kluwer Academic.

McEneaney, E. H. (2003). The worldwide cachet of scientific literacy. *Comparative Education Review, 47(2),* 217–237.

Millar, R. (1996). Towards a science curriculum for public understanding. *School Science Review, 77(280),* 7–18.

Millar, R., & Osborne, J. (Eds.). (1998). *Beyond 2000: Science education for the future.* King's College London, School of Education. www.kcl.ac.uk/education

Miller, J. D. (1983). Scientific literacy: A conceptual and empirical review. *Daedalus, 112(2),* 29–48.

Miller, J. D. (1992). Toward a scientific understanding of the public understanding of science and technology. *Public Understanding of Science, 1,* 23–26.

Miller, J. D. (1996). Scientific literacy for effective citizenship. In R. E. Yager (Ed.), *Science/technology/society as reform in science education* (pp. 185–204). Albany: State University of New York Press.

Miller, J. D. (1997). Civic scientific literacy in the United States: A developmental analysis from middle school through adulthood. In W. Gräber and C. Bolte (Eds.), *Scientific literacy* (pp. 121–142). Kiel: IPN.

Miller, J. D. (1998). The measurement of civic scientific literacy. *Public Understanding of Science, 7,* 1–21.

Miller, J. D. (2000). The development of civic scientific literacy in the United States. In D. D. Kumar and D. E. Chubin (Eds.), *Science, technology, and society: A sourcebook for research and practice* (pp. 21–47). New York: Kluwer Academic/Plenum.

Miller, J. D., Pardo, R., and Niwa, F. (1997). *Public perceptions of science and technology: A comparative study of the European Union, the United States, Japan, and Canada.* Madrid: BBV Foundation.

National Research Council. (1996). *National science education standards.* Washington, DC: National Academy Press.

Norris, S. P., & Phillips, L. M. (2003). How literacy in its fundamental sense is central to scientific literacy. *Science Education, 87,* 224–240.

Organisation for Economic Co-operation and Development (1999). Measuring student knowledge and skills: A new framework for assessment. Paris: Author.

Orpwood, G. W. F. (1985). Toward the renewal of Canadian science education. I. Deliberative inquiry model. *Science Education, 69,* 477–489.

Orpwood, G. (2000). Diversity of purpose in international assessments: Issues arising from the TIMSS tests of mathematics and science literacy. In D. Shorrocks-Taylor and E. W. Jenkins (Eds.), *Learning from others: International comparisons in education* (pp. 49–62). Dordrecht, the Netherlands: Kluwer Academic.

Orpwood, G. (2001). The role of assessment in science curriculum reform. *Assessment in Education, 8,* 135–151.

Orpwood, G., & Garden, R. A. (1998). *Assessing mathematics and science literacy.* TIMSS Monograph No. 4. Vancouver: Pacific Educational Press.

Orpwood, G. W. F., & Souque, J.-P. (1985). Toward the renewal of Canadian science education. II. Findings and recommendations. *Science Education, 69,* 626–636.

Östman, L. (1998). How companion meanings are expressed by science education discourse. In D. A. Roberts & L. Östman (Eds.), *Problems of meaning in science curriculum* (pp. 54–70). New York: Teachers College Press.

Pella, M. O., O'Hearn, G. T., & Gale, C. W. (1966). Referents to scientific literacy. *Journal of Research in Science Teaching, 4,* 199–208.

Penick, J. E. (1993). *Scientific literacy: An annotated bibliography.* Paris: UNESCO.

Psillos, D., Kariotoglou, P., Tselfes, V., Hatzikraniotis, E., Fassoulopoulos, G., & Kallery, M., (Eds.). (2003). *Science education research in the knowledge-based society.* Dordrecht, the Netherlands: Kluwer Academic.

Raizen, S. A., & Britton, E. D. (Eds.). (1997). *Bold ventures, Volume 2: Case studies in U.S. innovations in science education.* Dordrecht, the Netherlands: Kluwer Academic.

Ratcliffe, M. (1996). Adolescent decision-making, by individuals and groups, about science-related societal issues. In G. Welford, J. Osborne, & P. Scott (Eds.), *Research in science education in Europe: Current issues and themes* (pp. 126–140). London: Falmer Press.

Rennie, L., Goodrum, D., & Hackling, M. (2001). Science teaching and learning in Australian schools: Results of a national study. *Research in Science Education, 31,* 455–498.

Roberts, D. A. (1982). Developing the concept of "curriculum emphases" in science education. *Science Education, 66,* 243–260.

Roberts, D. A. (1983). *Science in the schools: Seven alternatives: Vol. 2. Scientific literacy: Towards balance in setting goals for school science programs.* Toronto, Ontario, Canada: Guidance Centre, University of Toronto (originally published as a discussion paper for the Science Council of Canada, ERIC # ED231673).

Roberts, D. A. (1988). What counts as science education? In P. Fensham (Ed.), *Development and dilemmas in science education* (pp. 27–54). Philadelphia: Falmer Press.

Roberts, D. A. (1995). Junior high school science transformed: Analysing a science curriculum policy change. *International Journal of Science Education, 17,* 493–504.

Roberts, D. A. (1998). Analyzing school science courses: The concept of companion meaning. In D. A. Roberts & L. Östman (Eds.), *Problems of meaning in science curriculum* (pp. 5–12). New York: Teachers College Press.

Roberts, D. A. (2000). Review of *Achieving scientific literacy: From purposes to practices. Science Education, 84,* 123–127.

Roberts, D. A. (2003). Scientific literacy: Around and about the globe. *Canadian Journal of Science, Mathematics and Technology Education, 3,* 287–292.

Roth, W.-M., & Barton, A. C. (2004). *Rethinking scientific literacy.* New York: RoutledgeFalmer.

Roth, W.-M., & Lee, S. (2002). Scientific literacy as collective praxis. *Public Understanding of Science, 11,* 33–56.

Roth, W.-M., & Lee, S. (2004). Science education as/for participation in the community. *Science Education, 88,* 263–291.

Ryder, J. (2001). Identifying science understanding for functional scientific literacy. *Studies in Science Education, 36,* 1–44.

Science Council of Canada. (1984). *Science for every student.* Hull, Quebec: Supply and Services Canada.

Scribner, S. (1986). Literacy in three metaphors. In N. Stein (Ed.), *Literacy in American schools: Learning to read and write* (pp. 7–22). Chicago: University of Chicago Press.

Shamos, M. (1995). *The myth of scientific literacy.* New Brunswick, NJ: Rutgers University Press.

Shen, B. S. P. (1975). Science literacy and the public understanding of science. In S. B. Day (Ed.), *Communication of scientific information* (pp. 44–52). Basel, Switzerland: S. Karger AG.

Shorrocks-Taylor, D., & Jenkins, E. W. (Eds.). (2000). *Learning from others: International comparisons in education.* Dordrecht, the Netherlands: Kluwer Academic.

Shulman, L. S., & Tamir, P. (1973). Research on teaching in the natural sciences. In R. M. W. Travers (Ed.), *Second handbook of research on teaching* (pp. 1098–1148). Chicago: Rand McNally.

Sjøberg, S. (1997). Scientific literacy and school science—Arguments and second thoughts. In S. Sjøberg & E. Kallerud (Eds.), *Science, technology and citizenship* (pp. 9–28). Oslo: NIFU Rapport 10/97.

Sjøberg, S., & Kallerud, E. (Eds.). (1997). *Science, technology and citizenship.* Oslo: NIFU Rapport 10/97.

Solomon, J. (1992). The classroom discussion of STS issues: Public understanding of science in the making. In R. E. Yager (Ed.), *The status of science-technology-society reform efforts around the world: ICASE Yearbook 1992* (pp. 67–80). International Council of Associations for Science Education.

Solomon, J. (1998). The science curricula of Europe and the notion of scientific culture. In D. A. Roberts & L. Östman (Eds.), *Problems of meaning in science curriculum* (pp. 166–177). New York: Teachers College Press.

Stocklmayer, S. M., Gore, M. M., & Bryant, C. (Eds.). (2001). *Science communication in theory and practice.* Dordrecht, the Netherlands: Kluwer Academic.

Thomas, G., & Durant, J. (1987). Why should we promote the public understanding of science? *Scientific literacy papers 1,* 1–14 (University of Oxford, Department of External Studies).

van den Akker, J. (1998). The science curriculum: Between ideals and outcomes. In B. J. Fraser & K. G. Tobin (Eds.), *International handbook of science education* (pp. 421–447). Dordrecht, the Netherlands: Kluwer Academic.

Watson, F. G. (1963). Research on teaching science. In N. L. Gage (Ed.), *Handbook of research on teaching* (pp. 1031–1059). Chicago: Rand McNally.

White, R. (2001). The revolution in research on science teaching. In V. Richardson (Ed.), *Handbook of research on teaching* (4th ed., pp. 457–471). Washington, DC: American Educational Research Association.

White, R. T., & Tisher, R. P. (1986). Research on natural sciences. In M. C. Wittrock (Ed.), *Handbook of research on teaching* (3rd ed., pp. 874–905). New York: Macmillan.

Wickman, P.-O., & Östman, L. (2002). Learning as discourse change: A sociocultural mechanism. *Science Education, 86,* 601–623.

Wynne, B. (1995). Public understanding of science. In S. Jasanoff, G. E. Markle, J. C. Petersen, and T. Pinch (Eds.), *Handbook of science and technology studies* (pp. 361–388). Thousand Oaks, CA: Sage.

Zeidler, D. L. (Ed.). (2003). *The role of moral reasoning on socioscientific issues and discourse in science education.* Dordrecht, the Netherlands: Kluwer Academic.

Zeidler, D. L., & Lewis, J. (2003). Unifying themes in moral reasoning on socioscientific issues and discourse. In D. L. Zeidler (Ed.), *The role of moral reasoning on socioscientific issues and discourse in science education* (pp. 289–306). Dordrecht, the Netherlands: Kluwer Academic.

Zeidler, D. L., Osborne, J., Erduran, S., Simon, S., & Monk, M. (2003). The role of argument during discourse about socioscientific issues. In D. L. Zeidler (Ed.), *The role of moral reasoning on socioscientific issues and discourse in science education* (pp. 97–116). Dordrecht, the Netherlands: Kluwer Academic.

CHAPTER 26

History of Science Curriculum Reform in the United States and the United Kingdom

J Myron Atkin
Stanford University

Paul Black
King's College London, United Kingdom

This chapter examines the history of curriculum reform in science education in the United States and the United Kingdom. For the United States, it identifies several periods of marked change from the mid-1700s to the 1980s and highlights some emblematic features of each one; more recent American curriculum developments are examined in all the other chapters in this section of the *Handbook*. In the case of the United Kingdom, the scope extends into the twenty-first century.

While certain parallels are evident in the development of science education in the two countries, educational change is influenced by both national culture and indigenous organizational structures. Thus there are noteworthy differences. The United Kingdom is a "unity" of England, Northern Ireland, Wales, and Scotland. For all except Scotland, government legislation in education emanated from the London Parliament until devolution of power was introduced in the 1990s. Scotland has always been different, but nevertheless was controlled from London until recently. For most of the twentieth century, about 90 percent of the schools (secular and denominational) were supported by central government, and pupils paid no fees. Yet, until 1988, these schools had a great deal of individual freedom to choose what they taught, the textbooks they used, and the teachers they recruited.

In the United States, the Constitution does not mention education, which means (by provision of the Tenth Amendment) that responsibility for schools resides exclusively in the individual states. Nevertheless, funds have been provided since 1917 by the federal government to meet special national priorities (initially to improve vocational education for industry and agriculture). Such was the case in 1959, for example, when Congress appropriated funds to improve science and mathematics education after the launch of Sputnik I by the Soviet Union. At the present time, about 7 percent of total education expenditures come from the federal government, mostly to assist "special-needs" students and those in low-income neighborhoods. As with many federal programs, however, the influence on the states is often disproportionate to the amount of money provided. "Unfunded mandates" from Washington are a continuing source of tension in the federal system. Historically, and on balance, however, there has been considerable latitude at the state level with respect to schools—and rhetorically at least, the principle of local control is unchallenged.

Two distinctive features have limited such latitude in the United Kingdom. One has been the influence of the universities: they established several examining boards that assigned, through their tests, school-leaving certificates. These have been the main requirement for university entrance, so they acquired status sought by parents and employers. Schools were constrained to ensure pupils' success in those tests, and the curricula became more uniform. Moreover, because they were driven by the needs of the professors for well-qualified freshmen, the aims that dominated the testing in science were to prepare future scientists.

The other feature has been the class structure of British society, reflected in the disproportionate power of a small number of fee-charging and independent schools. The upper classes sent their children to such institutions and expected them to be prepared for the best universities and for the professions. In the government-maintained schools, a system of selection at age 11 supplied an upper tier of academic secondary schools with the high attainers, predominantly middle-class children whose parents also wanted education to secure the most favorable life chances for their children. Between them, these selective schools and the independent schools had the best teachers. Reform tended to be biased in their interests because they had both political power and the people most competent to fashion changes.

From the beginning, the United States had more egalitarian principles, and its social class structures were more fluid. With heavy immigration, "common schools" were created in the nineteenth century to help all children become "Americans." Test scores did not become a significant factor in college admission until the latter half of the twentieth century. Some of the greatest American universities, especially in the Midwest, had been public since the creation of the land-grant colleges during the Civil War (Michigan, Ohio, Illinois, Wisconsin, and Indiana, for example). Through World War II, they accepted *all* high school graduates—despite the fact that about 80 percent did not remain after the freshman year. The principle, fully honored in practice in the land-grant institutions until the late 1950s, was that any high school graduate should have a chance to earn a college degree.

In both countries, the most significant initiatives in science education began in the nineteenth century and first affected primarily institutions of mass education: the schools for young children. Since then, development in these schools has been driven, until very recently, by forces quite different from those of external certification and the elite professions that were dominant at the secondary level (especially in Britain). For this reason, the account of the United Kingdom begins with an examination of primary-school science, and this educational level is also singled out for special description and special analysis in the American section.

THE UNITED STATES: THE EARLY YEARS

European education at the time of the American colonial period emphasized classical languages for older children and skills in reading and arithmetic for the younger ones. This curriculum was the starting point for education in what was to become the United States. But even before the American Revolution, there were seeds of something educationally different from a focus on language study alone: an emphasis on more practical work. This development was led and epitomized by Benjamin Franklin's creation of the Philadelphia Academy in 1750. The new subjects Franklin introduced focused on fields like agriculture, navigation, and surveying. Although the classics were still taught, his aim was to broaden schooling for those who may not have been preparing for the clergy. The idea of preparing students for a broader world of work struck a responsive chord in a developing country, and such schools proliferated rapidly and continued to grow in number for more than 100 years.

Science and science-related practical subjects thereby entered the American education scene early and on a relatively large scale. They began to compete with the subjects featured in the Latin grammar schools. (The new subjects gradually entered the colleges, as students sought a curriculum of greater usefulness at that level, too.) This is not to suggest that science in the academies was taught well. "The teachers [in the academy] were poorly prepared. . . . The courses were primarily book-taught, with the recitation of memorized texts the mode of instruction" (DeBoer, 1991, p. 20).

The picture for younger children was different. At this level, children's literature for the purposes of instruction began to appear in the late eighteenth century. Many of them were full of first-hand science experiences and featured directed observation of and contact with natural phenomena. They seem to have been intended initially to be read at home, but they soon were recommended for use in schools. Frequently they were reviewed and advertised in education journals (Underhill, 1941).

Typically a book would tell a story set in a family, in which the focus of the activities and conversation among children and adults was about subjects like the planets, or the water cycle, or the structure of a housefly. Writing about these books decades later, one authority commented, "Sometimes the learned tutor takes his pupils for a walk and discourses on all they see; or else Harry, thirsting for knowledge, extracts it by questions from a remarkably accurate and omniscient mamma" (Field, 1891, p. 256, cited in Underhill).

Although these children's books were rich in science content, it is far from clear that the teaching of science was their main purpose. Early formal education in western societies centered on piety and moral instruction, in addition to classical languages. It is true that the introduction of science in these books was intended to encourage children to learn more about natural phenomena. The science, however, was to be put in the service of a larger purpose, that of moral uplift and religious reverence. Although education was becoming more secular in the early 1800s—with natural history and geography replacing fables in books for children—the emphasis was usually on the moral virtues and the wonders of the Deity. ". . . [T]he sciences may be taught not only experimentally, but religiously. The pupil may be led to God through the material world, after having once become acquainted with the nature of the divine mind. . . . When the natural sciences can be taught in this manner, there can be no doubt of their beneficial effects" (American Journal of Education, 1828, authorship not ascribed).

In one story for young children drawn from children's literature of the period, a family is sitting around the kitchen table, and the daughter observes a cloud of steam over the water kettle. (Girls seemed in these books to ask questions as often as boys.) Her observation stimulates the father to deliver a short lecture and demonstration about vaporization and condensation by placing a cool metal sheet in the cloud of steam. In another book, the family comes across a compound flower during a walk. Using a hand lens, the father identifies the parts with precision—then emphasizes that the flower surpasses the ingenuity of man, thus proving the existence of God. When his son trips, father spends several pages on the matter of untied shoestrings. The point is that if he had obeyed his mother by being more careful, he might have avoided a bloody knee. Thus, using science as a vehicle, the aim was to promote moral virtues like obedience, modesty, courtesy, and even thrift—along with religious awe (Hughs, 1818; Alfred, or the Youthful Inquirer, 1824).

DEVELOPING THE MIND

Thus, by the mid-nineteenth century, there was significant attention in American elementary schools and in the academies to common objects and events within the experience of the students. The development was loosely unified by a range of principles enunciated by education philosophers and theoreticians like Rousseau, Pestalozzi, Froebel, and Herbart. Though different from one another, all of the theories were based on some form of sense realism, that true learning comes through experience. Methods of teaching emphasized principles like the importance of children being active participants in their own learning, a focus on the individuality of the pupil, and learning proceeding from the simple to the complex and from the proximate to the distal. Additionally, the learning process should be enjoyable.

Principles like these were often considered to be in harmony with nature, and a "natural method" was seen as uplifting and harmonious. "The postulation of a natural method rests on the assumption that there is a unity in nature and that nature is purposive and has direction. *Man* must work *with* nature rather than *against* nature . . . Nature becomes exalted and even deified" (Underhill, p. 31, emphasis in original).

By about 1860, a new theory of learning had emerged called faculty psychology. It was built on the belief that the mind is composed of faculties, and that the function of the school subjects was to develop one or another of the faculties, to train the mind. The faculties included observation, memorization, generalization, and reasoning. In the case of science for children in elementary schools, faculty psychology was grafted onto the science-of-common-experiences enunciated by Rousseau and others, which had become popular by the time of the Civil War. In the case of the secondary schools, the result was often the opposite—an education less related to immediacy and practicality, more dependent on reading and reciting, and more focused on mental discipline as an end in itself.

For the elementary schools, Object Teaching was introduced. Imported from England, it took firm root in the United States by the 1870s. Children studied and described objects brought to class: different rocks, metal wire, a piece of wax, camphor, ivory, a mustard seed, leaves, india rubber, various household chemicals, and much more. Theory in faculty psychology stated that although elementary school children are not capable of "reasoning" or "generalization," they can observe and memorize. If the Object Teaching manuals for teachers that were published at the time are any indication of classroom activity, the nine-year-old students were expected to demonstrate their growing ability to observe by accurately using adjectives like the following (not wrenched terribly out of context): *argillaceous, farinaceous, astringent, acidulated, chalybeate, iridescent, ligneous, oleaginous, malleable, vitrifiable, unctuous*, and many more (Mayo, 1876). The faculty of memorization was honed when the children were asked to recall the adjectives that were appropriate for the various objects. In the history of science teaching, the Object Teaching curriculum may be the one most pervasively influenced by a particular theory of learning, namely faculty psychology. Although very popular at the time, and actively promoted in teacher preparation programs, Object Teaching declined rapidly in the late nineteenth century because it was increasingly seen as sterile and remote from the lives of children. The objects were concrete, and many senses were employed by students in studying them, but there was little connection to matters of consequence in children's lives.

THE COMMITTEE OF TEN

The most influential development at the high school level at the end of the nineteenth century was the report of the Committee of Ten (National Education Association, 1893). This seminal document was intended to give consistent form to the high school curriculum and standardize college admission requirements. Charles Eliot, president of Harvard University, chaired the group, which was composed of university presidents, high school principals, and the U.S. Commissioner of Education. James Baker, principal of Denver High School at the start of the study (and president of the University of Colorado at the end), was chair of the coordinating group that synthesized the reports of nine, separate subject-based "conferences": Latin; Greek; English; other modern languages; mathematics; physics, astronomy, and chemistry; natural history (biology, including botany, zoology, and physiology); history, civil government, and political economy; and geography. The conferences consisted of professors, high school principals, and teachers. (Woodrow Wilson, then a professor at the College of New Jersey—later Princeton—was a member of the conference on history, government, and political economy.)

Recommendations were made about the age at which each subject was to be introduced, the number of years it should be taught (and the number of hours each week), the topics to be included at the secondary-school level, the form in which the subject should be factored into college admission requirements, and whether or not the subject matter should be different for those headed for college as compared with others and (if so) at what age.

The recommendations were extensive and detailed. Four sample programs were listed to offer some flexibility, particularly with respect to the study of classical languages (National Education Association, 1893, pp. 264–265). Perhaps the most provocative recommendation was that all students should study many of the same subjects and topics, the only difference being the number of years that students of different abilities and interests should pursue those studies. A close second was the diminished role of the classical languages and the recommendation that a relatively new subject, (the sciences (including geography) constitute 25 percent of the high school curriculum.

NATURE STUDY

The late nineteenth century saw the continued ascendancy of educational theories that focused on links with nature. Louis Agassiz, a charismatic Harvard biologist well known to the public for his attempts to popularize science (and for his opposition to Darwinian theories of evolution) was often credited by his many followers with the slogan "Nature not Books." The ideas he espoused are easily traced to Rousseau, Herbart, Pestalozzi, and others. G. Stanley Hall, a noted psychologist and educator, extolled the virtues of studying nature, though he expanded the scope to include all human relationships—possibly because he was one of earliest of the psychologists who saw the field as a science and themselves as scientists (Holder, 1893, chapter xv; Underhill, 1941, p. 107).

The broader canvas against which these developments played out was one in which emphasis on connections between education in the schools and the broader community were in the ascendancy. From the days of Franklin's Philadelphia Academy, there were steady pressures to relate work in school to the world in which students lived. By the 1890s and particularly in elementary schools, the emphasis shifted from utility in a narrow sense of personal living and individual advancement to one that encompassed broader social purposes, particularly the conditions in which people lived, and the requirements of good citizenship.

This emphasis took many forms, including the introduction of materials that taught about the dangers of alcohol, stimulated by the growing influence of the Women's Temperance Union. By 1895, 41 of the 44 states had passed laws about teaching temperance (U.S. Commissioner of Education, 1902). However, it was at Cornell University in the early 1900s that Nature Study took definitive shape as a defined subject for elementary-school students. It reflected a social movement, as well as a curriculum—and it originated in Cornell University's College of Agriculture.

A key purpose of Nature Study was to glorify the rural life. As America entered the twentieth century, the citizenry was associating major societal problems with rapid urbanization. The early 1900s the saw the rise of the "muckrakers," people like Upton Sinclair (1906) and Lincoln Steffens (1904), who wrote fact and fiction about corruption, exploitation, and disease in the rapidly growing cities. Cities were seen as evil, dirty, and sinful, the country as pure and beautiful. How are people to be kept on the farm?

Led by the Cornell College of Agriculture, materials were developed for children to instill a love of nature, so that they would resist the migration away from farms. During the first two decades of the twentieth century, the movement was led by professors at Cornell like Anna Botsford Comstock and Liberty Hyde Bailey, both respected biologists. Bailey frequently emphasized that the love of nature he valued so highly is deepened through intellectual understanding. "The best thing in life is sentiment; and the best sentiment is that which is born of the most accurate knowledge" (Bailey, 1903).

The College of Agriculture established a Department of Education to promulgate the new curriculum, both inside and outside New York State. (The Department resides in the College of Agriculture to this day, though not to promote the virtues of the country life.) The *Cornell Leaflets* (later the *Cornell Rural School Leaflets*) represented one of the first attempts at broad-scale and systematic dissemination of an educational philosophy and technique. Four issues per year were distributed, and the publication continued until the 1970s.

In much of the Nature Study literature for children, especially in the early decades of the movement, there was direct appeal to children's feelings to generate a deep sympathy with nature. The emotion-laden approach is illustrated by this excerpt from an article intended to help laypeople understand Nature Study in the schools: "Take for instance, the very common subject of trees. . . . One short sentence alive with love and inspiration, spoken concerning an oak tree for instance, will live on. The children will remember, if not the words, the idea or emotion that came when the burning word was spoken. Therein lies the secret of success—the word spoken must be a burning word" (Morely, 1901, cited in Underhill, p. 175).

It was only a short step to anthropomorphism. To elicit sympathy for and love of nature in children, mature flowers in the books began to talk to flower buds, and birds began to talk to trees. The conversations were almost always about their respective parts, and in that way many detailed aspects of taxonomic botany and zoology were conveyed to children. To introduce one typical story, the author asks, "We are going to hear a story about a little tree that did not like its leaves." The children are asked about the kinds of leaves they collected that fall. "Do you think of any tree whose leaves you slighted; one whose leaves you never thought of calling pretty? How do you suppose it felt, then, when it saw that its leaves were so different from those of the other trees?" The story of "The Discontented Pine Tree" then emphasizes that non-deciduous trees also have a special and valued function (McMurry, 1895).

Teaching of science came to focus on the biological world during the Nature Study period, altering the balance between biological and physical science that had existed for more than 100 years. But the same general approach was taken to physical science. At the Oswego Normal School in New York, an institution that had been particularly influential in spreading object teaching, the prospective teachers were taught about questioning and sequencing of ideas in a lesson. The following was cited as a laudable example of definite, clear, and sequential statements, beginning with experiments and observations and ending with conclusions and generalizations:

EVAPORATION

We put some water in a cup on Friday.

We put the cup in the window.

Monday there was not so much in the cup.

The water went into the air.

Who took the water?

The air fairies took the water.

The water evaporated.

Friday we put a cup of water on the window and on the radiator.

The air fairies took the water from both cups.

Which cup had the least water in it on Monday?

The cup in the warm place had the least water in it on Monday.

Why did the cup in the warm place have the least water in it?

The heat fairies helped the air fairies to take the water from the cup in the warm place.

If the heat fairies help the air fairies, the water goes away quicker. (Scott, 1900)

Advocates claimed that such an approach enlists students' interests and cultivates their imaginations. Often in human history, it was said, myths were the accepted explanation of natural phenomena and therefore were acceptable for young children at a certain level of development (Fistiam, 1908, cited in Underhill, p. 199). There were critics of the approach, of course, including no less a figure than Theodore Roosevelt, who called it "nature faking" (Sullivan, 1930). While the Nature Study movement, with its strong emphasis on children's emotions and commitment gradually atrophied after the first decade of the twentieth century, the emphasis on curricula that stressed students' interests did not.

APPLICATIONS OF SCIENCE; GENERALIZATIONS; PROBLEM SOLVING; ATTITUDES

The yearbooks of the National Society for the Study of Education (NSSE) are dependable benchmarks for understanding how experts in a field view promising and desirable developments at a particular time. The committees responsible for developing the yearbooks are chosen from among those who represent forward-looking perspectives in a given period, and the committee composition itself generally serves to produce a volume that proffers a consensual view.

Yearbook publication began in 1902 and has continued ever since, usually with two volumes a year. There was one on nature study in 1904, then nothing on science until the publication of *A Program for Teaching Science* 28 years later (NSSE, 1932). S. Ralph Powers of Teachers College, Columbia University, chaired the committee.

The authors of the 31st *Yearbook* captured many of the issues that concerned science educators during the first part of the twentieth century. They strove to ground their analysis and recommendations within an overall conception of schooling, including theories about learning and the development of children. They were attentive also to the fact that increasing numbers and percentages of students were entering and completing programs of secondary education and that a relatively new institution, the junior high school, had been created to facilitate transition from elementary to high schools.

They took pains to separate themselves from the kinds of psychological theories (G. Stanley Hall's, for example) and educational practices (Nature Study, for example) that had preceded those that shaped their own thinking. All of Chapter II was devoted to a critique of such approaches to science education. The authors of the 31st *Yearbook* found their intellectual foundations in the writing of such figures as William James, John Dewey, and Edward Thorndike, all of whom stressed the centrality of experience and social context. At the elementary-school level, Nature Study drew especially harsh criticism from the authors, primarily for emphasizing facts over principles and for expounding a theory of discontinuous intellectual development that claimed that intellectual processes in children are different from those in adults. The authors stated that Nature Study had inherited from faculty psychology the view that younger children could not generalize, for example.

At the secondary-school level, the 31st *Yearbook* drew heavily from *The Cardinal Principles of Education* published more than a decade earlier (U.S. Bureau of Education, 1918), a landmark report commissioned by the National Education Association, pointing out that "the manner in which the needs of society and . . . the schools that were purporting to meet these needs were out of harmony" (NSSE, 1932, p. 18). *The Cardinal Principles* had recommended a continuous program from kindergarten to university, greater attention to individual differences in students' intellectual ability and interests, and that educational objectives recognize the needs of individuals and of the society. It also outlined and elaborated upon what it defined as the main objectives of secondary education: fostering good health, gaining command of fundamental processes (reading, writing, elements of oral and written expression), learning to participate in "worthy home membership," preparing for a vocation, participating in civic affairs, fostering in students the worthy use of leisure time (something relatively new in America), and developing of ethical character (U.S. Bureau of Education, 1918, pp. 5–10).

Associated with awareness of the increasing usefulness of science to society was an interest in and respect for the methods that were used to produce scientific ideas and their application. Thus secondary-school science programs were advocated that helped students understand that science is a "problem-solving" kind of inquiry, as well as a body of basic "generalizations" about the natural world. In the Yearbook Committee's words,

> The search for objectives will be one that seeks to determine the major generalizations and the associated scientific attitudes that have come from the field. . . . This Committee stresses the importance of subject matter and recognizes the responsibility for selection of subject matter which shall be functional for . . . . a more satisfactory adjustment of the individual to the society of which he must be a part. In this society man must meet and solve problems. The schools will prepare children for their responsibilities by providing experiences with a body of subject matter (1) that has been tested for truthfulness, (2) that exercises methods that have been used in solving problems, (3) that furnishes practice in these methods—in short, with subject matter that contributes to the ultimate comprehension of major generalizations and the development of associated scientific attitudes. (NSSE, 1932, p. 40)

The first two decades of the twentieth century ushered in a period in which Americans became increasingly aware of the impressive impact of science in daily life. The methods of science were powerful. Led largely by the science education group at Columbia University Teachers College, the goal of science teaching gradually became one of helping students to understand the applications of science, especially in technology. Electrification and central heating were emphasized. Science texts also described how refrigerators and automobiles worked. Every student learned how a gasoline engine works in an automobile, including the names of the four strokes in each cycle. There were demonstrations of how how fuses work. Models were built to illustrate the wiring of houses.

At the same time, there was an underlying conviction that "the program for curriculum work in science for the public schools [should] be directed toward the determination of those major generalizations and associated scientific attitudes which together define the field" (NSSE, 1932, p. 43). For example, in the course of providing a detailed description of how students might study the age of the Earth, two major generalizations that frame their respective topics are offered: 1. The Earth seems very old when its age is measured in ordinary units of time, and (2) The surface of the Earth has not always had its present appearance and is constantly changing (p. 48).

AFTER WORLD WAR II:
SCIENCE FOR SCIENCE'S SAKE

Changes in science education during the 25-year period after World War II were a sharp departure from the science-in-everyday-life focus of the 31st *Yearbook* and were characterized primarily by a dramatic increase in active participation in curriculum matters by outstanding scientists, primarily those from the academic research community. The programs that were developed from the 1950s and into the 1970s are often characterized as the "post-Sputnik reforms" because of major new infusions of federal funds in the years immediately following the Soviet Union's launch of the first artificial earth satellite, *Sputnik I*, in October 1957.

However, the new curriculum movement actually had begun in the early 1950s. It focused on mathematics. Max Beberman at the University of Illinois pointed out that the mathematics curriculum commonly used in schools at that time contained few mathematical ideas developed after 1700. Consistent with the science curriculum of the 1920s, 1930s, and 1940s, the mathematics program in the early 1950s stressed applications—mathematics in daily life. Students in elementary and junior high schools balanced checkbooks, calculated compound interest, and noted differences among different retail discounts, for example. In high school, as preparation for calculus and college, they were introduced to Euclidian geometry, algebra, and trigonometry. Beberman and his colleagues developed a program that introduced "new" mathematics—number theory and set theory, for example (Beberman and Vaughn, 1964). These were topics, among others, that corresponded more closely to ideas that contemporary mathematicians, particularly those engaged in research, found important.

A few years later, in 1955, proposals similar to Beberman's were made for high school physics. Scientists newly interested in curriculum for the schools said that it may or may not be interesting for students in physics to learn about the principles of refrigeration, the four-stroke-cycle gasoline engine, or the Bernoulli effect—topics commonly found in the textbooks—but these ideas hardly reflected those that university-based researchers in physics considered interesting. And so, in 1955, the Physical Science Study Committee, a group centered at the Massachusetts Institute of Technology, developed a course that began with an examination of the ways in which light could be viewed as both wave-like and particulate (Physical Science Study Committee, 1960), a topic considered much more characteristic of the kinds of issues that matter to research-oriented physicists. For the first time, the country moved into a period wherein the teaching of science, as identified by the most advanced scholars in the field, became an end in itself.

Offering something of a counter-example, there was a project across the Charles River in which a physics curriculum was developed that depended somewhat less than the one at MIT on contemporary university-based research. Harvard Project Physics included modern topics, to be sure, but it focused also on how ideas in science develop over the centuries (Harvard Project Physics, 1968). In focusing somewhat more on historical perspectives, the Harvard group was more explicit about the human elements that are integral to the generation of scientific ideas.

A key factor in the marked influence of the country's outstanding research scientists on the curriculum was the extraordinary prestige the group had acquired in helping to win the war. Seemingly arcane and abstract theory had been shown to have extraordinary consequences. Radar and the atom bomb were seen not only as shortening the war but as making victory possible. Just as important, many scientists involved in wartime projects turned their attention to matters of improving science education—several of them never to return to research in science.

This movement led by research scientists crystallized conceptually at a conference in Woods Hole, Massachusetts, in 1959. Thirty-five scientists, psychologists, and curriculum developers were convened under the auspices of the National Academy of Sciences to discuss and try to unify their work, which by that time was receiving impressive support from the National Science Foundation. (The Foundation had been created by the Congress in 1950 and assigned two broad missions: to support basic scientific research and to improve American science education.)

Jerome Bruner, an eminent psychologist, was given the responsibility of preparing the conference report (Bruner, 1960). The report pivoted around the concept of "structure." Each field of intellectual study has a general framework that helps its practitioners understand a relatively small number of major ideas (about patterns, about overarching concepts, about modes of inquiry), which in turn can be used to scaffold new observations and facts. Furthermore, "Mastery of the fundamental ideas of a field involves not only the grasping of general principles, but also the development of an attitude toward learning and inquiry, toward guessing and hunches, toward the possibility of solving problems on one's own" (Bruner, 1960, p. 20). Only those deeply knowledgeable about a field are capable of identifying those principles and habits of mind. "It is a task that cannot be carried out without the active participation of the ablest scholars and scientists" (p. 32). And, capturing what many saw as the essence of the report, "[T]he argument for such for such an approach is premised on the assumption that there is a continuity between what a scholar does on the forefront of his discipline and what a child does in approaching it for the first time" (p. 28).

With support primarily from the National Science Foundation, projects were launched in biology, chemistry, and earth sciences at the high school level. There were also several at the elementary-school level during the 1960s undertaken on the same convictions and assumptions. No other curriculum movement in science so centrally involved the nation's most accomplished scientists in work at elementary- and secondary-school levels as those that flowered from 1955 to the early 1970s. Never had so much public money been devoted to the task of developing new curricula for the schools.

But by the 1970s, however, new curriculum priorities arose that began to edge out those of the research scientists. Since the pre-war year of 1939, the percentage of the 20-year-old cohort that had completed four years of high school had jumped from 25 to 75 percent. In many ways, the major story of American education after World War II was its rapidly growing inclusiveness. At the same time, the U.S. by the 1970s had been the first country to put a person on the Moon. These facts, and the steepening decline of the Soviet Union, eased the country's concern about its military strength. Now the balance of trade and the country's competitiveness were sources of alarm. As with the panic after Sputnik, the education system had to respond. Education policy conversations began to center on educating *all* students, partly because they were now coming to school and partly because they were the future workforce. Better education was one crucial way to stem the perceived decline in the country's economic competitiveness (National Commission on Excellence in Education, 1983). A decades-long focus on "standards" began.

THE UNITED KINGDOM: THE PRIMARY PHASE

In Britain, universal elementary education was achieved in the latter half of the nineteenth century. This period also marks the beginnings of science education in schools. Impetus was given by two ordained Cambridge academics: Dawes, a mathematics fellow, and Henslow, a professor of botany, who moved to country parishes and started schools in which they developed the teaching of a science of everyday things (Layton, 1973). However, the scientific ideas that were at the core of their work tended to be lost in the hands of most teachers. One important approach in elementary science classrooms was the use of "object lessons" (deBoo, 2001), each centered on a common object such as a snail or a lump of coal; these were similar to the object lessons used in the United States, but they gave more emphasis to exercises in observation and classification skills only. There was also much emphasis on nature study, but the aim here was confused: some "naturalists" were interested in the understanding of nature, and others taught only the identification and naming of natural objects. Moves to link physical science concepts to everyday observation (e.g., by measuring the velocities of different rivers) made little progress.

The movements to teach a science of everyday things lost momentum because many reacted by objecting to the time being given to science, both in schools and in teachers' training. Influential scientists also pressed for a much sharper focus on the main ideas of science, arguing for science as a training of the mind and against trapping children in the very restricted view of the science of everyday objects and phenomena. Although such views prevailed, they helped to create a tension, between the pure and conceptual on the one hand, and the applied and everyday on the other. This tension has continued to bedevil school science to this day.

As elementary schooling grew in the 1850s and 1860s, concern to justify the escalating costs led a system of the state grants for primary schools to be based on their performance in inspectors tests limited to the 3Rs; science then shrank, since it did not feature in the payable results. There were few funds to provide apparatus, so that some districts appointed peripatetic demonstrators, who went from school to school with a handcart of apparatus to present demonstrations. The scientists in the British Association for the Advancement of Science (BAAS) recommended in

1908 that this use of demonstrations be abandoned, as it led to superficial presentations that teachers ignorant of science were not able to follow up.

Progress with reforms promoted by the BAAS was halted by the 1914–18 war, with its dire effects in the loss of teachers on the battlefields and in the 1920s recessions in the economy. A further inhibition was the growth in the importance of examinations at the end of primary schooling. These would determine whether or not a pupil could proceed to the "academic" grammar schools, or to the lower status and more vocationally oriented secondary. Since the examination tested only arithmetic and English, science was neglected.

In the same decade, the influence of such thinkers as Montessori, Dewey, and Froebel began to take effect, so that official reports called for a new emphasis on the physical, mental, and emotional development of children (Hadow/Board of Education, 1931, 1933). However, World War II impeded progress, as facilities were damaged, all schooling was disrupted by mass evacuation of pupils out of cities, large numbers of teachers were conscripted for military service, and few were being trained. A nearly bankrupt country could afford little until the 1950s. Although signs of change, from teacher-dominated lessons to child-centered activity, began to be evident, the main obstacle was the lack of training in science of most teachers, so that many primary schools did not feel able to teach science at all: even up to the early 1960s courses for primary teachers taught only biology. Both the national inspectorate and the ministry supported moves to reform, which aimed to develop pupils' interests in the physical sciences and to involve them in their own science investigations. Yet one of the leaders of reform in Scotland stated that "the aim of teaching science in a primary school is not really to lay the foundations of scientific knowledge, still less to offer elementary introductions to different sciences" (Blackie, 1967), so expressing a belief that the aim was to teach only such processes as observation and pattern seeking in order to develop general reasoning.

The child-centered movement of the 1950s and 1960s did lead to excesses in that children often came to be engaged in unguided play. As one observer put it, "the ripples of change moving out from the centres of quality became distorted with distance and repetition" (Wastnedge, 2001, p. 43). Wastnedge became a leading figure when he was appointed to lead a Junior Science Teaching Project in 1964, funded by a private charity, the Nuffield Foundation. The aim was to foster a child-centered approach to teaching, with the children observing, asking questions, and making and testing hypotheses. Given the poor training in science of primary teachers, it was judged that the stress should be on an approach that depended less on scientific knowledge (i.e., a process approach).

In consequence, as Wastnedge explained (2001, p. 50), "At present we must concern ourselves more with how children learn than with what they learn," even though this was often interpreted as "it doesn't matter if they don't learn anything." However, this project, and its successors, were only adopted by about 20% of schools, schools being free at that time to choose the curriculum approach that they preferred.

The general approach was consistent with the growth of a child-centered philosophy of education, which was canonized as national policy backed by a government-sponsored report on primary education, the Plowden Report (Central Advisory Council, 1967). In the 1980s two developments countered this combination of child-centered and process-only approach. One was unease expressed by several science educators about the neglect of content, on the grounds that to present science as a set of commonsense processes was a travesty, and that pupils needed to begin to engage with subtle and apparently unnatural concepts (e.g., that moving objects, if left to themselves, will go on moving forever) that had been the basis of the power of scientific thought (Black, 1983). This thinking led, in 1987, to the Nuffield research project titled the Science Processes and Concept Explorations project (SPACE) (Black and Harlen, 1989), which led to a curriculum development project with a strong basis in new research about the levels of concept that young children could understand (Osborne et al. 1993; Nuffield Primary Science—see Nuffield, 2003).

The other source of change was the belief of the Conservative government that primary education had been undermined by the child-centered ideology—the influence of Dewey, Plowden, and the like had to be destroyed, together with other malign influences of the "educational establishment" (Lawton, 1994). Such thinking was one of the motivations for the setting up in 1988–89 of the Unnited Kingdom's first National Curriculum. Primary science was established as one of only three subjects with national tests at ages 7 and 11, with three content targets and a fourth target on experimental investigations. This stimulated an increase in the effort devoted to helping teachers deal with science. The tests for content were so dominant, that investigations were given low status and low priority. In the late 1990s new requirements to spend designated teaching time each day on prescribed schemes for literacy and numeracy undermined yet again the time given to science education.

SECONDARY SCHOOL SCIENCE

Science at the secondary level was first developed in the late nineteenth century in the elite private schools. For some pupils, the study of science was an alternative for those who could not manage a classical-literary education, but positive impetus came from two sources. One was the changes in medical education, the other was the need for civil engineers, particularly for the military. Both of these professions called for a stronger scientific basis, so higher education, where these professions were trained, required their main providers, the private schools, to teach science at school. The curriculum innovations that were a response to these pressures were largely led by chemistry educators, with some also promoting geology. Biology, having a weaker science basis, was justified by the intrinsic value accorded to the study of nature. Physics suffered because it was not a well-defined subject, and the ownership by mathematicians of the teaching of mechanics curtailed its scope.

Expansion outside the small group of private schools came more slowly. The growing status of science and scientists in the latter half of the nineteenth century, and the evidence that the country's industrial lead over others was fast being eroded, led to pleas for more science education. In response, in 1904 new government regulations, which applied to the schools that were maintained by government funding rather than by collection of fees, required at least seven hours per week to be devoted to mathematics and science and that the science being taught should be taught without bias toward technical or vocational needs. Yet 12 years later a report deplored the fact that in the private schools many pupils were not studying science, while others studied only general science, which had a low status as a school subject for many years (Waring, 1979).

The coordination of the various school leaving examinations, which were provided by several university-led agencies, developed from the setting up by the government of a Secondary Schools Examinations Council in 1917, gave support to the government's new requirements to teach mathematics and science, but it remained possible for candidates to choose between mathematics and science despite pressures to make science compulsory. Over the next 25 years, controversy focused on the choice between having three separate science subjects in biology, chemistry, and physics, and having a single general science course (Jenkins, 1979). The latter eventually became the course for the less able; later still, it became a course for all at ages 11 to 13, with the separate subjects taught by separate subject specialists from 14 to 16. However, despite pleas that schools give more time to science, most required the more able pupils to choose only one or two of the three science subjects for their examination courses, while the general science courses for the less able were constrained by the time allocation for only a single subject.

At the same time, many reports pressed for science education to develop understanding of the nature of science, although this was understood in terms of a "commonsense" model in which principles arose from the data by induction. There were also pleas by the BAAS that the "broader aspects of scientific discovery and investigation as human achievements and applications by which mankind is benefiting" should find a place in the curriculum (Waring, 1979, p. 37). Yet a teacher trainer writing in 1918 painted a gloomy view: "It is disturbing to discover how many young people . . . find their school science uninspiring and even boring . . . [teachers and examiners] . . . both attach too much importance to the formal and theoretical aspects of science, and too little to those which give the subject value in the eyes of boys and girls" (Nunn, 1918, p. 162).

Nunn's priority was to make pupils interested in science as the finding of new knowledge as an end in itself, but he pointed out, with a criticism which has continued to be relevant up to the present day, that "This is an uncomfortable doctrine to two very different types of persons. One is the 'practical man' who supports the teaching of science in schools because he believes in its cash value. The other is the 'high-browed' person who assesses all educational effort in terms of 'mental discipline'" (p. 162).

Practical work was also subject to change and counter-change in this period. The first outstanding influence in Britain was a chemistry professor, Henry Armstrong, who used his status as a university scientist to argue, strongly and effectively, for its importance as an exercise in "guided heurism" (van Praagh, 1973). As the scientific journal *Nature* put it at the time (in 1901): "Two things are essential for Professor Armstrong's plan, first that the pupils should perform experiments with their own hands, and second that these experiments should not be the mere confirmation of something previously learned on authority, but the means of elucidating something previously unknown, or of elucidating something previously uncertain" (quoted in Woolnough and Allsop, 1985, p. 16).

This approach became widespread in schools in the early years of the century, the emphasis being on practical work as experience of enquiry rather than for developing subject knowledge. However, the impact was blunted in 1918 by a report that criticized the approach as inefficient use of pupils' time. It argued that experimental work should be restricted, with a focus on experiments that could establish links with general scientific principles and with everyday life, and that careful demonstrations could often be the most efficient way of using lesson time. So there developed a convergent "cookbook" approach to school laboratory work, with an emphasis on practical skills, following instructions, and confirming well-established results.

It was inevitable that when recovery from the after-effects of the 1939–45 world war allowed serious debate about education to re-open in the United Kingdom, the position of school science education was still problematic. A 1960 report of the national inspectorate called for a new integration of practical work with the central task of learning, and for an end to "cookbook" experiments:

> There is nothing as a rule to correspond to the clear formulation of a question by the pupil himself; this is provided for him and no value is placed on curiosity. Nor is there any necessity to construct a plan of investigation, to design or make ad hoc experimental devices or to modify them in the light of experience. Nor again, if the answer comes out 'right', is there much inducement to consider the results, to estimate their validity or to discuss their further improvements. Finally there is missing the ultimate satisfaction of having really found something out. (Ministry of Education, 1960, p. 38)

The Association for Science Education (ASE), which had a strong membership and support among school science teachers, attempted to foster improvements by the collaborative efforts of their own members, but soon found that its resources were inadequate to the task. The government was sympathetic, but its stance at that time was that it should not play any part in specifying the curriculum.

The outcome was that in 1962 the Nuffield Foundation agreed to fund, but also to direct itself, large-scale curriculum development projects, starting with courses in physics, chemistry, and biology designed for study from ages 11 to 16 for the most able pupils. The steering bodies for these projects were led by eminent professional scientists, and the ASE had hardly any part to play. However, the teams recruited to do the work were composed largely of practicing science teachers. The reform plan was comprehensive, involving extensive school trials, commercial publication, negotiations with equipment manufacturers to provide new apparatus, and arrangements with the examination agencies to provide tailor-made school-leaving examinations and the linked certificates, and with teacher training institutions to provide in-service training for the new courses.

Schools were free at that time to chose whether or not to replace their traditional courses with these offerings, and although no more than about 20% of schools decided to implement them in full, they had widespread influence on many aspects of school teaching. The teams in the three subjects were allowed a fairly free hand, so the styles that emerged were quite different: the physics scheme was tightly prescriptive (the oft-quoted slogan was "if you cut it, it bleeds"), whereas the chemistry course was described as "a sample scheme" to emphasize that schools should feel free to pick and choose the parts that they liked. All gave new emphasis to teaching for understanding rather than rote learning, while also calling for the pupil to be "a scientist for the day." However, the emphasis on the conceptual structure of pure science was strong: applications of science and social implications were given scant attention. With all the Nuffield innovations, the influence of Bruner's dictum was explicit: "The schoolboy [sic] learning physics is a physicist, and it is easier for him to learn physics behaving like a physicist than doing something else" (Bruner, 1960, p. 60).

Thus, for the new physics course, the ideal was that all lessons be conducted in a laboratory so that pupils could move to and fro in a coordinated way between practical exploration and theory development. However, partly because of the stress on this link, the practical investigations of pupils were largely constrained to "illustrate" theory, and the first introduction to this course attempts to make clear that Armstrong's heurism was not being adopted. The new chemistry course laid more stress on "open investigation," whereas biology showed a mixed economy, with some work designed for confirmation, and some for genuinely open exploration.

These three projects for students aged 11 to 16 were followed by projects for the advanced study of sciences from ages 16 to 18, projects to devise courses in general science for the "less able," and courses for all in the age range 11 to 13. These last two types of course gave more emphasis to applications of science and to themes likely to be of interest to pupils. A government decision in the 1970s to ban selection of pupils by ability at the transition from primary to secondary schools implied that all schools had to teach across the full ability range. This change made the division, between pure science for the most able and applied everyday science for the rest, problematic, and when separate examinations for different "ability" bands were replaced by a single system, these curricula had to be revised. The revisions were a compromise between the different aims of science education, but many saw that "academic science" still prevailed.

As ever, the messages of reform for science teaching that underpinned the new Nuffield curricula were weakened in dissemination: one evaluation judged that many "Nuffield" teachers had not "thought through the full implications of changes in philosophy and method presented by the Project team" (West, 1974—quoted in Waring, 1979, p. 207). A study of classroom teaching styles found that most Nuffield teachers used an approach characterized by teacher direction, presenting science as a problem-solving activity and telling pupils to make hypotheses and predictions, but not relinquishing control to the extent required for pupils to personally engage in problem-solving (Eggleston et al., 1976).

Nevertheless, school science in general still defied efforts at improvement. Although experimental work became a more salient part of pupils' experience, it was, with a few notable exceptions, still largely fixed in the "cookbook" mold, and the national inspectorate was again hinting in a 1979 report that more time should be spent on demonstration lessons and less on class practical work (DES, 1979, p. 184). A review written in 1985 concluded that there had been no significant development in practical work in secondary schools since the Nuffield innovations in the 1960s (Woolnough and Allsop, 1985, p. 28). A report by the ASE expressed a more general criticism: "Science appears to exist outside any valid social context. It is objective, value free and totally aseptic" (ASE, 1979, p. 24).

At the same time, a government report drew attention to the failure of schools to require, or make provision for, students to study more than one of the three science subjects: "No school was found, however, which provided balanced science courses for all pupils up to the age of 16-plus. The majority of pupils in secondary schools of all types were taking either no science or only one science in the fourth and fifth years" (DES, 1979, p. 196).

Such dissatisfactions led to a project in the 1980s, the Secondary Science Curriculum Review (SSCR; see West, 1982), which was jointly sponsored by the government agency responsible for curriculum matters (the Schools Council) and the professional association of science teachers (the ASE). This project had two main outcomes. One was the fostering of numerous teacher-led initiatives to improve science education, for the leaders set their face against any centralized curriculum development in the belief that the only way to secure reform lay through the professional development of teachers who would initiate and own their own reforms. The second outcome was quite different. The project conducted a campaign to establish a single science course for the age range 11 to 16, which would have the lesson time and the examination value of a double subject, and which would cover in a combined and comprehensive manner all of the main aims hitherto pursued in the separate subjects of biology, chemistry, and physics. The point was to replace the situation in which the pupil had to choose between a low-status single-subject science course and high-status courses in the separate sciences: with the latter choice it was almost impossible for a pupil to take more than two of the three science courses. An existing "integrated science" course had already attempted to establish a double-subject and comprehensive science course, but had run into fierce opposition from parents who thought that their children were being offered a course of low market value. The SSCR project therefore worked to gain support for a new "double-subject" scheme from leading scientists, educators, government, and the teaching profession. This campaign was successful, and "double-subject" science became a viable option for schools. Most new courses within this framework did not attempt the controversial label of "integrated" (Black, 1986), and in most schools the "double-subject" was taught in separate sections by specialist teachers of the three subjects.

New directions for change also arose from national sample surveys of science performance set up by the government's Assessment of Performance Unit (APU; Black, 1990). The government brief for these was biased in favor of "science process skills" rather than on science content. Of the six main areas to be assessed, two, one on practical skills and one on conducting open-ended investigations, concerned pupils' work with equipment, and a third assessed capacity to design investigations using written tests. The findings established that short open-ended investigations could be so composed that pupils could work through them in a one-hour assessment session, and that standards of performance on written exercises were far lower than on matched exercises in which pupils could actually explore the phenomena with equipment.

Everything was changed with the establishment for the first time, by a law passed in 1988, of a national curriculum for the United Kingdom. Science was one of the mandatory subjects in this curriculum, required to be studied by all from ages 5 to 16, with progress tested by national tests at ages 7, 11, 14, and 16. The task of drawing up the specification for this curriculum was given to a group composed of teachers, teacher trainers, and academics in science education. Their recommendations were quite radical in both structure and content, based on a set of 22 sets of learning goals, expressed in a scheme of progression in learning from ages 5 to 16. These 22 "attainment targets" were grouped as four "profile components." Of these, 16 were grouped under the profile component Knowledge and Understanding, reflecting the established content areas, but adding astronomy and new topics titled Information Transfer and Human Influences on the Earth. A second profile component, Exploration in Science, had two more targets, one for carrying out investigations and one for working in groups. The third profile component was titled

Communication and included the targets Reporting and Responding and Using Secondary Sources. The fourth profile component, titled Science in Action, combined Technological and Social Aspects and The Nature of Science. Taken together, these called for a significant broadening of the science curriculum and one that would have linked it more closely with other school subjects. A final recommendation was for a single double-subject requirement to take 20 percent of curriculum time at the secondary level.

The government minister could not accept these proposals. He asked for an extra proposal for an optional alternative—a subject having single rather than double-subject weight, and in both options for more weight to be given to knowledge and understanding, and for the number of profile components to be reduced. The proposals were sent out for consultation. Only 10 percent of replies supported provision of a single subject option, only 10 percent supported the reduction in the number of profile components, and 80 percent opposed the recommendation to change the weightings (Boyle, 1990). Nevertheless, the single-subject option, a reduction to two profile components—Knowledge and Understanding and Exploration in Science—and an increase in the weighting, in teaching time spent and in mark assignments in examinations, for knowledge and understanding at secondary level from the 40 percent recommended to between 65 and 70 percent, were all put into effect in the final government orders. Five of the original targets were removed, leaving 17: 16 in Knowledge and Understanding and one in the Exploration of Science. The attempt of the profession to reform its subject had failed, probably because of the right-wing government's suspicion of the educational establishment, fueled by lobbying from conservative teachers in the influential private schools.

It turned out that within three years the curriculum had to be revised, because of widespread teacher opposition to the excessive load of the contents of the new curriculum, and the number of the content attainment targets was then reduced to three, covering the conventional areas of biology, chemistry, and physics respectively, and losing the last of the novel topics, The Nature of Science (Black, 1995). The curriculum was revised again in 1995 (DfE, 1995) and yet again in 2000, but without further radical change.

Practical work, as required in the fourth attainment target, now called Experimental and Investigative Science (profile components were now abandoned), was particularly problematic. The requirement was that the work should:

> . . . encourage the ability to plan and carry out investigations in which pupils:
>
> (i)   ask questions, predict and hypotheses;
>
> (ii) observe, measure and manipulate variables;
>
> (iii) interpret their results and evaluate scientific evidence. (Black, 1995, p. 171)

Many teachers were disoriented by this requirement, which went well ahead of current practice and experience (Jenkins, 1995). Even those who did experimental investigations valued them for motivation, not for the learning of concepts (Simon et al., 1992), reflecting a bias that was also evident in the earlier tests of experimental work established by the APU, which had influenced the target's formulation. Many used comparative exercises as used by agencies testing retail products to advise consumers about the "best buy," which usually involved no application of science concepts. Evaluations also reported that too little time was being given to this activity (NCC, 1991) and that some teachers conducted investigations as isolated exercises designed only for assessment purposes (Russell et al., 1995) while having difficulty in conducting the assessments of this work that they were required to make (OFSTED, 1993a, b; Buchan, 1992; Buchan and Jenkins, 1992).

An overarching problem was still the impact of testing. The testing agencies had to set up a system for including scores for practical investigations in the assessment for school-leaving certificates, and this system had to require exercises that the pupils' own teachers could conduct and assess in normal laboratory time. To secure reliability and comparability, the agencies set up very strict rules about the choice and conduct of such assessments. Teachers, under pressure to secure maximum scores, could not afford to take risks, so many specified for their pupils the same stereotyped exercises year after year and thereby made the work yet again into the old cookbook type of exercise. Ways out of this dilemma have yet to be found.

Although several agencies produced guidance material to help teachers with this new area (Jones et al., 1992; Solomon et al., 1994) and others began to research the problems involved (Millar et al., 1994), there were groups who argued that the target should be abandoned, leading others to publish affirmations of support (Hannon, 1994). However, when the curriculum was again revised in 1995, the investigation's target survived, although the stated aims moved it in the direction of more traditional work.

Foreseeing the revision planned for the year 2000, a group of science educators obtained a grant from the Nuffield Foundation to support a set of expert seminars, followed by consultation including open meetings, to reconsider the science curriculum, and hopefully to influence the revision. Their report (Millar & Osborne, 1998) attracted wide attention. Their main plea was that the science curriculum, from ages 5 to 16, should have the main aim of enhancing a broad and general education in science to meet the needs of all citizens, represented by the title "scientific literacy"; only in years from 14 to 16 should there be an aspect devoted to the early stages of specialist training in science, which should not be allowed to distort the primary aim of promoting scientific literacy.

The report also developed an argument that science education had focused too much on detail, so that pupils had lost sight of the major ideas. This was to be offset by organizing the curriculum in a new way, deploying the power of the narrative form to make ideas "coherent, memorable and meaningful." Stories should be organized around such major themes as "the particle model of chemical reactions" or "the earth and beyond." Examples of questions that could form the basis of particular explanatory stories would be How do we catch diseases? or How old is the Earth and how did it come to be? The report also stressed, "Young people need some understanding of the social processes internal to science itself, which are used to test and scrutinize knowledge claims before they can become widely accepted" (p. 20).

Ironically, the government's anxiety about the low morale and decline in numbers in the teaching profession, due largely to the burdens of frequent change in the curriculum and testing rules, made it reluctant to make any significant changes when it was revised in 2000, so the report's ideas, despite the widespread support that they had evoked, produced only a limited response. The investigation's target was renamed as "Scientific Enquiry." The earlier prescription for investigative skills remained but was accompanied by a second section on "Ideas and Evidence in Science." This latter section includes study of:

- how scientific ideas are presented, evaluated and disseminated
- how scientific ideas can arise
- how scientific work is affected by the context in which it takes place
- the power and limitations of science, including social environmental and ethical questions

However, there are other signs of change that can clearly be seen as outcomes of the report. A wholly new course, Science for the 21st Century, has been developed and has gained official sanction, in that its trials can be supported by tailor-made examinations leading to nationally approved certificates (Nuffield, 2003). Its proposal is to divide the double-subject science into two components. One, Core Science, is for all, based on current issues, bringing in moral and social implications, and leading to a single-subject examination certificate. For the second, there is a choice between Applied Additional Science, which should provide a basis for technical, pre-vocational, and vocational courses involving science, and General Additional Science, which should provide a basis for further advanced study in the sciences. Either of these options is to lead to a second single-subject examination certificate. If this scheme succeeds, it will at last help the science curriculum to address themes of interest and concern to the young, rather than to require all of them to undertake studies fashioned only in the image and structures of established pure science.

SOME CONCLUDING COMMENTS ABOUT THE UNITED STATES AND THE UNITED KINGDOM: THE DRIVE OF SOCIAL AND TECHNOLOGICAL CHANGE

The changes described in our histories are driven in part by social and technological change, although the influences are often indirect. The movement toward education for all, first at the primary/middle level, then at the high school level, and now toward college level, has meant that science education, like all features of formal schooling, has had to expand from serving only future specialists at the upper level to serving the needs of all.

The change from agrarian to mainly industrial economies has meant that the contexts in which pupils learn and into which they carry their learning at the end of their education have changed. Rural-oriented science now has split into the high-tech needs of a far smaller number of agricultural producers, and the quite different needs of all citizens who need to understand how to protect the environment. Similarly, an aim of helping young people to understand how things work in a technological world is being transformed because the objects that are produced are losing transparency as they gain sophistication. The self-sufficient adult who used to be able to fix things for him- or herself now has changed into one who knows how to read the instructions and when to throw the artifact away.

Aims of Science Education

Above all the other external pressures, the increasingly powerful influence of science and technology on all societies makes judgments about the aims of science education more complex and yet more critically important. As it is realized that "scientists' science," oriented toward the painstaking construction of conceptual frameworks that explain how the world works, is of limited use to the vast majority, new ways of enabling the citizenry to comprehend and operate in a scientific and technological culture have to be sought. Education must be fashioned in ways that are evocative for young people who are being shaped by rapidly changing societal influences. Indeed, one overarching problem is whether science education can keep up, given that educational change often appears glacial.

Such a change of aims could develop in several directions. A recasting of a "love-of-nature" orientation, so prevalent at the turn of the twentieth century, into the context of preserving the future of the planet, a growing international concern in the twenty-first, would lead to an emphasis on interactions in complex systems. It thus might offset the drive to reductionist analysis that has characterized many of the sciences. And a focus on social influences, if it is not to be unrealistic, must introduce moral questions, values, and clashes of belief into the science classroom. The particular attraction of science as a training in dispassionate judgment based on evidence will then have to be protected within carefully delineated boundaries if it is to continue to be a contribution to education. In all of this, studies of the lessons of history, particularly of contexts that are not too dissimilar from those of the present, might be valuable.

All of these possibilities make clear that the changes in aims that are being, or ought to be, pursued now create new problems for the teaching profession. Any discussion of the effects of scientific and technological change has to confront issues of conflicting social priorities. Many events in the last century have made it clear that the idea of a value-free and unbiased science is a dangerous myth. Yet many science teachers, themselves educated in the shadow of this myth, feel uneasy in confronting controversy. It may be that alliances with teachers of humanities and social science will be the best way forward, for conflicting values are often at the heart of these studies.

Who Has the Power of Control?

In the United Kingdom, the teaching profession has highly qualified science teachers at the secondary level—the majority possessing university degrees in the separate disciplines of physics, chemistry, or biology. The most influential of these have been in the elite schools. The heads of those schools always have had the ear of the government minister and of other private institutions, as well as having the most highly qualified science teachers to formulate and carry through changes.

The picture in the United States is different. Many high school teachers of physical science are not credentialed in the subjects they teach. School districts in most states can assign any credentialed teacher to teach physics or chemistry. They also can award "emergency" credentials to people with no regular license in any subject field. It is not unusual to find a biology teacher, or even a physical education teacher, teaching chemistry or physics. Consequently there has not often been a recognized cadre of science teacher-leaders. One may be emerging, however. In recent years, a system of National Board certification has been established, along the lines of specialty board certification in medicine. There is a rigorous and expensive assessment system, with those who earn national certification receiving extra pay, and influence, in many states.

Reform movements in the United Kingdom have been fashioned mainly by inspiring the teachers. Although academic scientists had oversight on behalf of the funding agencies, they entrusted most of the work to the best practicing school teachers, and to professors whose main interest and experience was in science education. The efforts focused on the professional development of teachers. The new curricula were given a strong framework by providing tailor-made tests that were not limited by any tradition of inexpensive multiple-choice testing. For example, one Nuffield 16-to-18 curriculum led to nationally recognized certificates with their own tests that comprised two three-hour written tests, each with separate parts in a variety of question styles, together with a test in a laboratory and teacher assessment of experimental projects. The cost of running this centrally for 30,000 candidates was of course high but was seen as acceptable. There was no serious attempt to make new curricula "teacher-proof." Heavy emphasis was not placed on the textbook as the instrument to implement the reform; indeed, one Nuffield curriculum had no pupils' textbook and advised that pupils might consult several as the needs arose.

In the United States, the picture was more mixed. Curriculum revision in the post-Sputnik era was undertaken mostly by university-based scientists, with only modest involvement by teachers. Considerable emphasis was placed on writing new textbooks, sometimes with the explicit intention of limiting the latitude of teachers to make changes. There were few external examinations in science until late in the twentieth century.

There is no single answer that emerges from the histories of the two countries to the question of who has special policy influence in the field of science education. At various times, industry and the professions, the academies of the sciences, the academies of education, the teaching profession, and governments have exerted pressures to produce changes. It would not be easy to judge, even in hindsight, whether or not the influence of any of these has been benign or malign, for in the end the judgment would often come down to a choice among core values—as will any prognosis for the future.

Two trends in the power struggles seem important at the moment. One is that education researchers are now developing more powerful tools (in their theories of cognition and of affect, for example) and can therefore claim credibility in attempting to influence curriculum and teaching. Indeed, they are developing more effective relationships in collaborative reform with teachers and school administrators. It is no accident that the scientific academies now recognize this point, as can be seen in the ways in which the U.S. National Academies of Science and the UK Royal Society involve leaders in science education, including researchers from universities, in their deliberations about education. The second trend is that the move to mass education has made the education budget such a large part of all national economies that governments can hardly leave education alone: what matters then is whom politicians choose to listen to. These two trends could be in harmony, but equally well come into conflict.

The Student Perspective

At the secondary-school level in both countries, there have been few influential voices with the power to speak and act for the needs of the majority who were not going to be scientists. That concern has increased in recent decades, but only modestly. Two forces are influencing the scientific community to now speak to these needs. One is that the pupils have been voting with their feet: The numbers of those choosing to continue to study science after age 16 and so become qualified for degree training in science and engineering has declined. The other is that the new public distrust of scientists is seen by many in the scientific community to reflect the weakness of science education in not preparing the young to fully appreciate and use the accomplishments of science.

The feature here that now commands the most attention is that of connecting school science with the broader world. It is assumed that such an approach is more likely to engage the preponderance of students who are not likely to choose scientifically oriented careers. Therefore curricula grounded in contemporary problems of importance to young people have been developed in many countries, including the two highlighted here. Close engagement with the science embedded in these contemporary issues might be shifting toward somewhat less activity in the school laboratory and more in the street, the home, industry, and the countryside.

To attract students who now are uninterested in science will not be enough, however. There clearly is danger of superficiality when students engage in real-world problems. The challenge—for curriculum, design, pedagogy, and assessment—will be to build from the initial enticement to develop sustained and serious work by students in arenas hitherto considered unappealing. The particular power of the discipline of scientific inquiry must be made evident in the way that problems are explored. And the extraordinary intellectual heritage of science must emerge for students as the power of its tools and concepts is made evident. Embedded in this purpose is development in students of a sense of wonder, even awe, at the structures and processes to be seen in the natural world. The histories in this chapter have demonstrated that this goal of science education goes back more than 250 years. It is sometimes subdued, but in one form or another seems to arise for each educational generation. It will do so again as the twenty-first century unfolds, perhaps in ways that will be more comprehensible with a knowledge of the history of these aims and challenges in the eighteenth, nineteenth, and twentieth.

ACKNOWLEDGMENTS

Thanks to George DeBoer and Graham Orpwood, who reviewed this chapter.

REFERENCES

Alfred, or the youthful inquirer. (1824). In which many operations of nature and art are familiarly explained, and adapted to the comprehension of children. London: Baldwin, Cradock, & Joy.

American Journal of Education. (1828). Early education. *American Journal of Education*, 3 (December), 712.

ASE. (1979). *Alternatives for science education*. Hatfield, UK: Association for Science Education.

Bailey, L. H. (1903). *The nature study idea*. New York: Macmillan.

Beberman, M., & Vaughn, H. (1964). *High-school mathematics, Course 1*. Boston: D. C. Heath & Co.

Black, P. J. (1983). Why hasn't it worked? In C. Richards & D. Holford (Eds.), *The Teaching of primary science: Principles, policy and practice* (pp. 29–36). London: Falmer Press.

Black, P. J. (1986). *Integrated or co-ordinated science?* Presidential Address given to Association for Science Education January 1986. *School Science Review, 67*(241), 669–681.

Black, P. J. (1990). APU science—the past and the future. *School Science Review, 72*(258), 13–28.

Black, P. J. (1995). 1987 to 1995—The struggle to formulate a national curriculum for science in England and Wales. *Studies in Science Education, 26,* 159–188.

Black, P. J., & Harlen, W. (1989, December 29). SPACE Probe. *Times Educational Supplement,* No. 3835 (Supplement), p. 24.

Blackie, J. (1967). *Inside the primary school.* London: Her Majesty's Stationary Office.

Boyle, A. (1990). Science in the national curriculum. *The Curriculum Journal, 1*(1), 25–37.

Bruner, J. (1960). *The process of education.* Cambridge: Harvard University Press.

Buchan, A. S. (1992). Practical assessment in GCSE science. *School Science Review, 73*(265), 19–28.

Buchan, A. S., & Jenkins, E. W. (1992). The internal assessment of practical skills in science in England and Wales, 1960–1991; some issues in historical perspective. *International Journal of Science Education, 14*(40), 367–380.

Central Advisory Council for Education (England). (1967). *Children and their primary schools (the Plowden Report).* London: Her Majesty's Stationary Office.

DeBoer, G. E. (1991). *A history of ideas in science education: implications for practice.* New York: Teachers College Press.

De Bóo, M. (2001). Setting the scene. In M. De Bóo & A. Randall (Eds.), *Celebrating a century of primary science* (pp. 1–17). Hatfield, UK: Association for Science Education.

DES. (1979). *Aspects of secondary education in England: A survey by HM inspectors of schools.* London: Her Majesty's Stationary Office.

D.f.E. (1995). Science in the national curriculum. London: Her Majesty's Stationery Office for the Department for Education.

Eggleston, J. F., Galton, M. J., & Jones, M. E. (1976). *Processes and products of science teaching.* London: Macmillan.

Field, E. M. (1891). *The child and his book.* London: Wells Gardner, Darton & Co.

Fistiam, F. A. (1908). *The kindergarten room.* London: Blackie & Son.

Hadow/Board of Education. (1931). *Report of the consultative committee on the primary school.* London: Her Majesty's Stationary Office.

Hadow/Board of Education. (1933). *Report of the consultative committee on infant and nursery schools.* London: Her Majesty's Stationary Office.

Hannon, M. (1994). The place of investigations in science education. *Education in Science, 156,* 167–168.

Harvard Project Physics. (1968). *An introduction to physics.* New York: Holt, Rinehart & Winston.

Holder, C. (1893). *Louis Aggassiz.* New York: Putnam.

Hughs, M. R. (1818). *The alchemist.* London: William Darton.

Jenkins, E. W. (1979). *From Armstrong to Nuffield: Studies in twentieth-century science education in England and Wales.* London: John Murray.

Jenkins, E. W. (1995). Central policy and teacher response? Scientific investigation in the national curriculum of England and Wales. *International Journal of Science Education, 17*(4), 471–480.

Jones, A. T., Simon, S., Black, P. J., Fairbrother, R. W., & Watson, J. R. (1992). *Open work in science: Development of investigations in schools.* Hatfield, UK: Association for Science Education.

Layton, D. (1973). *Science for the people.* London: George Allen & Unwin.

Lawton, D. (1994). *The tory mind on education 1979–94.* London: Falmer Press.

Mayo, E. (1876). *Lessons on objects: As given to children between the ages of six and eight.* San Francisco: A. Roman.

McMurry, F. (1895). Concentration. *Herbart Society, 1st Yearbook,* p. 40.

Millar, R., Lubben, F., Gott, R., & Duggan, S. (1994). Investigating in the school science laboratory: Conceptual and procedural knowledge and their influence on performance. *Research Papers in Education, 9*(2), 207–248.

Millar, R., & Osborne, J. (1998). *Beyond 2000: Science education for the future*. London: King's College.

Ministry of Education. (1960). *Science in secondary schools. Pamphlet no. 38*. London: Her Majesty's Stationary Office.

Morely, M. W. (1901). Nature study and its influence. *Outlook, 68*, 737–739.

National Commission on Excellence in Education. (1983). *A nation at risk: The imperative for educational reform: A report to the Nation and the Secretary of Education*. Washington, DC: Government Printing Office.

National Society for the Study of Education. (1932). *A program for teaching science. Thirty-first Yearbook, Part I*. Bloomington, IN: Public School Publishing Company.

NCC. (1991). *Report on monitoring the implementation of the national curriculum core subjects 1989–1990*. York, UK: National Curriculum Council.

Nuffield Foundation. (2003). *Nuffield Primary Science* and *21st Century Science. Available at* curriculum@<nuffieldfoundation.org

Nunn, T. P. (1918). Science. In J. Adams (Ed.), *The New Teaching* (pp. 154–198). London: Hodder & Stoughton.

OFSTED. (1993a). *Assessment, Recording and Reporting: Key stages 1, 2 and 3: Fourth Year, 1992–3. Report from the Office for Standards in Education*. London: Her Majesty's Stationery Office.

OFSTED. (1993b). *Science. Key stages 1, 2 and 3. Fourth Year, 1992–3. Report from the Office for Standards in Education*. London: Her Majesty's Stationery Office.

Osborne, J. F., Black, P. J., Meadows, J., & Smith, M. (1993). Young children's (7–11) ideas about light and their development. *International Journal for Science Education, 15*(1), 83–93.

Physical Science Study Committee. (1960). *Physics*. Boston: D. C. Heath.

Russell, T., Qualter, A., & McGuigan, L. (1995). Reflections on the implementation of national curriculum science policy for the 5–14 age range: Findings and interpretation from a national evaluation study in England. *International Journal of Science Education, 17*(4), 481–492.

Scott, C. B. (1900). *Nature study and the child*. Boston: D. C. Heath.

Simon, S., Jones, A. T., Fairbrother, R. W., Watson, J. R., & Black, P. J. (1992). *Open work in science; a review of existing practice*. London: C.E.S. King's College.

Sinclair, U. (1906; 2003). *The jungle*. Author, 1906; New York: Norton, 2003.

Solomon, J., Duveen, J., Scott, L., & Hall, S. (1994). *Science through Sc1 investigations: Teaching, learning and assessing as you go*. Hatfield, UK: Association for Science Education.

Steffens, L. (1904). *The shame of the cities*. New York: McClure, Phillips & Co.

Sullivan, M. (1930). *Our times: Pre-war America*. New York: Charles Scribner's Sons.

Underhill, O. E. (1941). *The origins and development of elementary-school science*. Chicago: Scott, Foresman & Co.

U.S. Bureau of Education. (1928 [1918]). *Cardinal principles of secondary education*. A Report of the Commission on the Reorganization of Secondary Education, appointed by the National Education Association. *Bulletin*, 1918, No. 35. Washington, DC: Government Printing Office.

U.S. Office of Education. (1893). *Report of the committee on secondary school studies (Committee of Ten), appointed by the National Education Association*. U.S. Office of Education, Whole Number 205. Washington, DC: U.S. Government Printing Office.

U.S. Office of Education. (1902). Temperence instruction. In *Report of the commissioner* (Chapter 21). Washington, DC: Government Printing Office.

Van Praagh, G. (Ed.). (1973). *H. E. Armstrong and science education: Selections from Armstrong's papers on science education*. London: John Murray.

Waring, M. (1979). *Social pressures and curriculum innovation*. London: Methuen.

Wastnedge, R. (2001). A revolutionary project. In M. De Bóo & A. Randall (Eds.). *Celebrating a century of primary science*. Hatfield, UK: Association for Science Education.

West, R. W. (1982). The secondary science curriculum review. *Education in Science, 99*, 29–31.

Woolnough, B., & Allsop, T. (1985). *Practical work in school science*. Cambridge, UK: Cambridge University Press.

CHAPTER 27

Inquiry as an Organizing Theme for Science Curricula

Ronald D. Anderson
University of Colorado, Boulder

Inquiry has been a prominent theme of science curriculum improvement efforts ever since the post-Sputnik era NSF-funded science education endeavors appeared in the headlines of the late 1950s. By the beginning of the next decade, inquiry was a big idea in science education, as is well illustrated by the work of the Biological Sciences Curriculum Study (BSCS), including their rationale statements prepared by Joseph Schwab and their materials themselves, their *Invitations to Inquiry* being an especially good exemplar. With a certain amount of ebb and flow, inquiry has persisted as a major science education theme ever since, with its current relevance well illustrated by the *National Science Education Standards* (1996) and a more recent National Research Council (NRC) publication, *Inquiry and the National Science Education Standards* (2000).

The prominence of inquiry has persisted for nearly half a century, with no indication that it will soon disappear. Recognizing that its popularity does not prove its merits, there is reason to ask for evidence-based answers to many questions that can be raised about the place of inquiry in science curriculum improvement. Just what is inquiry? Does it mean the same thing to everyone? Does it mean the same thing in varied contexts? When someone talks about science as inquiry, learning through inquiry, or teaching by inquiry, are they talking about the same inquiry? What are the goals of science instruction that go under this label? Does it result in increased learning? Is it realistic for the average teacher? In summary, does it make sense to use inquiry as an organizing theme for science curricula?

The answer to this summary question that you will get here is yes, but it is a very nuanced affirmation. So much depends on what understandings you have of inquiry, and more specifically on your understanding of the nature of science, how people learn, the nature of society and its schools, and the process of teaching.

Inquiry has become a catch phrase encompassing many aspects of science education, but it is also a useful label that summarizes many important ideas and can serve to integrate various facets of educational practice. The many aspects of science education to which the label is applied are among its most important dimensions. So, even though using inquiry to describe an approach to science education can be a tricky exercise in communication, it is worth doing. Other labels could be used; it would be easy to talk about quality science education without ever using the word *inquiry*. The word is in widespread usage, however, and for broad public discussions, it probably is essential to make use of it in any conversation about contemporary science education.

Such conversation will be much more profitable, however, if we recognize that *inquiry* is an imprecise word. Using the word in a conversation about science education is a bit like using the word *romance* in a conversation about human relationships. It has different meanings in varied contexts, and is hard to guess what particular meaning a given speaker has in mind when the word is used. If the word is to continue to be useful we will have to press for clarity when the word enters a conversation and not assume we know the intended meaning.

INQUIRY IN THE NATIONAL SCIENCE
EDUCATION STANDARDS

Current discussion of inquiry is shaped by the *National Science Education Standards* (NSES), the common baseline for defining what quality science instruction should be in contemporary U.S. education. If one reads this landmark publication with care, it is apparent that *inquiry* is not only widely used in the book, it is used in different ways. Three main usages stand out: there is discussion of scientific inquiry, inquiry learning, and inquiry teaching. These three versions are fairly distinct from each other, even though they also have many connections. In addition, each of the three has various nuances and may be applied somewhat differently, depending on the context (Anderson, 1998).

Scientific Inquiry

"Scientific inquiry refers to the diverse ways in which scientists study the natural world and propose explanations based on the evidence derived from their work" (p. 23). The work of scientists, the nature of their investigations, and the abilities and understandings required to do this work are at the heart of this usage of the word *inquiry*. These scientific endeavors are considered as independent of our schooling enterprises, although an understanding of them is a goal of education.

If we wish to move beyond the discussion of scientific inquiry as found in the NSES and address it in more depth, the extensive literature on the nature of science becomes relevant (see Chapter 29 of this *Handbook*). We are dealing with scientific inquiry and the nature of science as curriculum content or goals of instruction.

Inquiry Learning

As used in the NSES, inquiry learning refers to an *active* process of learning— "something that students do, not something that is done to them" (p. 2). Although used to describe a learning process, the NSES generally portrays this inquiry process as having some relationship to scientific inquiry; it is suggested that inquiry learning should reflect the nature of inquiry in the scientific context. Within the formal school context, this active learning process is expected to be one that "encompasses a range of activities" (p. 33) with multiple stages, including "oral and written discourse" (p. 36).

Although the NSES connects its rationale for inquiry learning to scientific inquiry—undoubtedly a valuable approach in communicating with a science-oriented audience—we need to understand inquiry learning more deeply. Studies of human learning give us understandings an earlier generation did not have—well portrayed in *How People Learn* (Bransford et al., 1999)—and we need to utilize these understandings. Although the term *constructivist* is not used in the NSES, it is clear that what is called inquiry learning is very similar to what others call constructivist learning.

As with inquiry, the constructivist label can be applied to the nature of science, learning and teaching, but it has even greater potential for misunderstanding. In contemporary discussions of the nature of science, for example, there are opposing positions—in what is sometimes referred to as the "science wars"—and *constructivist* is a "good" word in one camp, but not in the other. Thus, *inquiry* has more potential for being a useful word that can be applied in these three contexts without undue miscommunication, which is probably one reason why *inquiry* is used in the NSES but *constructivism* is not. Nevertheless, in a discussion of learning, *constructivist* is probably the more useful word, in that it has some generally understood meanings in the context of learning—as distinct from the contexts of science and teaching. Note, however, as used here to discuss learning, *constructivism* is not the same *constructivism* used in discussions of the nature of science and which is the subject of debate there. It is the same word, but it used in different contexts to make different distinctions.

As used in this chapter, constructivist learning—as well as inquiry learning—is understood to carry with it the following four elements:

1. Learning is an active process of individuals constructing meaning for themselves; significant understandings are not just received.
2. The meanings each individual constructs are dependent upon the prior conceptions this individual already has. In the process, these prior conceptions may be modified.
3. The understandings each individual develops are dependent upon the contexts in which these meanings are engaged. The more abundant and varied these contexts are, the richer are the understandings acquired.
4. Meanings are socially constructed; understanding is enriched by engagement of ideas in concert with other people.

Obviously, this four-part characterization includes perspectives that resonate with both cognitive and sociocultural views of knowledge construction. Differences between these and other varying theoretical perspectives are not the focus of our attention here. This four-part characterization, however, describes elements that generally are understood to be included in the learning process by those using constructivist/inquiry terminology.

Inquiry Teaching

When used to describe teaching in the NSES, inquiry is employed in quite varied ways. As noted earlier, the NSES writers' understanding of learning is such that "inquiry is central to science learning," (p. 2) and as a result it must be central to teaching as well. They note, however, that this focus on inquiry learning "does not imply that all teachers should pursue a single approach to teaching science"(p. 2). Even so, they expect that, "Inquiry into authentic questions generated from student experiences is the central strategy for teaching science" (p. 31). Given their inquiry-based understanding of learning, moreover, it is not surprising that when referring to teaching, they use a broad, process-oriented definition that includes significant attention to inquiry as a learning activity (p. 13). It "refers to the activities of students in which they develop knowledge and understandings of scientific ideas, as well as an understanding of how scientists study the natural world." (p. 23) They acknowledge that all inquiry is not the same by distinguishing between a "partial inquiry" and a "full inquiry" (p. 143). Inquiry is part of their picture of assessment as well, and they see it in the context of teaching. "Any boundary between assessment and teaching is lost" (p. 202).

In summary, as a form of teaching, inquiry has multiple manifestations and the NSES generally does not make careful distinctions between these varied forms of teaching, although it does have an entire section devoted to science teaching standards. At the end of the section on inquiry learning above, a four-part explanation was given of what was meant by inquiry or constructivist learning as used in this chapter. It is not possible to give such a concise description of inquiry teaching. It takes an abundance of forms, and the process of inquiry teaching is not as well understood as the desired product of these transactions, namely inquiry learning. It also is probably fair to say that a belief in the value of inquiry teaching probably carries with it a belief in inquiry learning. On the other hand, it probably is less certain that someone who understands inquiry learning as an accurate picture of how learning occurs also has equally strong convictions about the merits of inquiry teaching. In my judgment, belief in the merits of inquiry teaching among science teachers is not as strong as their belief in inquiry learning. Furthermore, common understandings of just what inquiry teaching is in practice are much more varied than understandings of inquiry learning. For further consideration of inquiry learning and inquiry teaching, including lots of examples, see Minstrell and van Zee (2000).

Other Views of Inquiry

The three categories of inquiry described above were identified initially by a careful reading of the NSES. Inquiry has been defined in many other ways in the science education literature. Huffman (2002), for example, conceptualizes inquiry as having "three key components: abilities, procedures, and philosophy. The three different components are represented by concentric circles with abilities at the center, procedures encompassing abilities, and philosophy encompassing both procedures and abilities" (p. 225). Lederman and Niess (2000) contend that the NSES and Project 2061 present inquiry as having three different perspectives. "Inquiry is viewed as a teaching approach, as process skills, and as content" (p. 113). Different category systems may have varied utility, depending upon the context. For our purposes here, neither of these definitional sets seems to have an appropriate place for inquiry as a form of learning.

As noted earlier, the NSES does not set out clear definitions of what constitutes inquiry in various contexts. Possibly in response to a failure to provide clear operational definitions of inquiry in the NSES, the National Research Council released a follow-up publication in 2000 titled *Inquiry and the National Education Standards: A Guide for Teaching and Learning.* In this book, the focus is largely on the activities and transactions of people in classrooms, both students and teachers. It is a pragmatic book that addresses the real world of classrooms; as with the NSES itself, depth of understanding about the nature of learning in a more theoretical sense is not featured.

We need both the practical and theoretical. In general, the NSES and the more recent NRC book reflect an appropriate understanding of the underlying theoretical issues, even though their focus is on the pragmatic, and the theoretical is not explicitly developed. The NSES was informed, of course, by the earlier work of Project 2061, and the theoretical was given explicit attention there, for example, in the chapter on learning and teaching in *Science for All Americans* (AAAS, 1989). We will need to go beyond the NSES and the later companion publication, however, not as a corrective, but as an extension to make more explicit the underlying issues and develop the ideas needed in considering the place of inquiry in developing science curricula.

Although some may prefer to avoid using the word *inquiry*, because of the lack of clarity in its meaning, it is employed here because of its value in making connections between content, learning, and teaching and because it would be difficult to avoid it. In addition to its many meanings, its use seems to be ubiquitous. The choice being made here is to use the word and make the effort required to clarify what is meant in a given context. In the process one is addressing many of the fundamental issues in science education.

HOW IS CURRICULUM UNDERSTOOD?

As we have seen, *inquiry* has many meanings, but it does not get any easier to define when we get to curriculum. Professional conceptions of curriculum are markedly diverse. The goal of this chapter is to address in depth the potential of inquiry as an organizer for curriculum. If we are to do so, we also must come to some understanding of what is meant by various individuals and groups when they talk about curriculum.

Schubert (1986) has presented a set of categories for describing alternative conceptions of curriculum. Although there are substantial differences among these categories, there also is considerable overlap in the sense that they may pursue similar goals. At the same time it must be noted that the form of instruction implied in these different characterizations of curriculum could lead to quite different forms of education. A brief summary of these images or characterizations of the curriculum is presented below. After examining them we can consider their implications for using inquiry as a guiding theme for curriculum.

Curriculum as Content or Subject Matter

This image equates curriculum with the subjects taught: "Educators who use this image intend to explicate clearly the network of subjects taught, interpretations given to those subjects, prerequisite knowledge for studying certain subjects, and a rationale for the ways in which all subjects at a particular level of school fit together and provide what is needed at that level" (Schubert, 1986, p. 26).

Curriculum as a Program of Planned Activities

In this image the curriculum is characterized as a collection of planned activities: "The end of planning is to see that certain desired activities are delivered to students. Granted, all these plans have purposes for which the activities are vehicles. Yet it is the activity—what students do—that is the curriculum" (Schubert, 1986, p. 28).

Curriculum as Intended Learning Outcomes

In this case, the curriculum is defined in terms of intended learning outcomes. The focus is ends, with lesser consideration of the means of reaching them. Purpose is specified by the intended outcomes. The current focus on various forms of standards and the growing use of standardized tests obviously is compatible with this orientation to the curriculum.

Curriculum as Cultural Reproduction

This image of the curriculum focuses on perpetuating the extant culture, thus the curriculum is expected to reflect that culture: "The community, state, or nation takes the lead in identifying the skills, knowledge, and appreciations to be taught" (Schubert, 1986, p. 29).

Curriculum as Experience

A curricular focus on student experiences has been prominent in much discourse about education. It has been commonly associated with John Dewey and his writings, but it can take varied forms: "This position holds that educational means and ends are inseparable parts of a single process: experience. To attend to one's experience reflectively and to strive continuously to anticipate and monitor the consequences of one's thought and action relative to the good that they bring is a continuously evolving curriculum. The teacher is a facilitator of personal growth, and the curriculum is the process of experiencing the sense of meaning and direction that ensues from teacher and student dialogue" (Schubert, 1986, p. 30).

Curriculum as Discrete Tasks and Concepts

Yet another way of conceptualizing the curriculum is as tasks and concepts students should acquire: "The curriculum is seen as a set of tasks to be mastered, and they are assumed to lead to a prespecified end. Usually that end has a specific behavioral interpretation such as learning a new task or performing an old one better. This approach derives from training programs in business, industry, and the military" (Schubert, 1986, p. 31).

Curriculum as an Agenda for Social Reconstruction

Rather than personal development, the focus in this image of the curriculum is social ends. A quite radical curricular view, it promotes the idea of students becoming agents of societal change: "This view of curriculum holds that schools should provide an agenda of knowledge and values that guides students to improve society and the cultural institutions, beliefs, and activities that support it" (Schubert, 1986, p. 32).

Curriculum as "Currere"

The emphasis here, as with curriculum as experience, is personal growth:

> One of the most recent positions to emerge on the curriculum horizon is to emphasize the verb form of *curriculum,* namely *currere.* . . . [It] emphasizes the individual's own capacity to reconceptualize his or her autobiography. . . . [T]he individual seeks meaning amid the swirl of present events, moves historically into his or her own past to recover and reconstitute origins, and imagines and creates possible directions of his or her own future. [T]he curriculum becomes a reconceiving of one's perspective on life . . . [and] . . . a social process whereby individuals come to greater understanding of themselves, others, and the world through mutual reconceptualization. The mutuality involves not only those who are in immediate proximity but occurs through the acquisition of extant knowledge and acquaintance with literary and artistic expression. The central focus, however, is autobiographical. The curriculum is the interpretation of lived experiences" (Schubert, 1986, p. 33).

It involves more than transmitting knowledge, skills, and cultural values; it centers on self-understanding. It depends upon a high level of students' empowerment and students' responsibility for their own learning.

Schubert's characterizations of the curriculum are expressed in fairly concrete terms that, in the majority of cases, are relatively easy to visualize and understand; they are largely expressed in the practical language of schooling. As a result they are good companion categories for our discussion of inquiry in its more pragmatic form, such as found in the NSES. Embedded within Schubert's different characterizations of the curriculum, however, are varied purposes of education, understandings of the nature of learning, perspectives on teaching, and more. And a bit like in our discussion of inquiry, we could introduce more subtleties and nuances if we left this practical language and probed more deeply for underlying conceptual and theoretical frameworks. To do so here is beyond the scope of this chapter, but I would encourage the interested reader to refer to a chapter by Elliot Eisner in the *Handbook of Research on Curriculum* (Jackson, 1992) titled "Curriculum Ideologies." In it Eisner claims that in any given school there is an ideology or "value matrix" that justifies choices made and gives direction to the curriculum. He notes that in some ways these ideologies are rooted in underlying worldviews. Eisner describes six major ideologies that he finds in American education. Schubert and Eisner are not in conflict with each other; they operate at somewhat different levels.

Two words—*inquiry* and *curriculum*—each of which has so many different meanings—have been conjoined as the focus of this chapter. We will address them together at the more practical level of language found in the NRC publications and in Schubert's curriculum writing, but in the process will attempt to go deep enough to seriously attend to matters of educational purpose, the nature of learning, and approaches to teaching. Without this depth of analysis we cannot accomplish the purposes at hand.

THE LITERATURE ON EDUCATIONAL CHANGE

In addition to the literatures on inquiry and curriculum, there is a third area that needs attention before we can attend more directly to the role of inquiry in developing science curricula, namely the extensive literature on educational change. Implied in most discussions of inquiry in science education is the notion that there should be more of it, that is, that our current science education practices are not up to par and we need to change them to include more inquiry, whether that be inquiry as content, learning, or teaching. Assuming this notion as part of our operating perspective here, it is essential that we attend to understandings found in the literature on educational change because they strongly influence how we can expect to connect inquiry and curriculum.

The literature on educational change is extensive and rich. It includes work done from many different perspectives and offers many insights into school practice. For the reader wanting a one-stop overview, the best source probably is the third edition of Michael Fullan's landmark book, *The Meaning of Educational Change* (2001). Of his many books, this one stands out as a good overview of what the research has to say. Other scholars who stand out among the many who have shaped the field include Seymor Sarason (e.g., 1990, 1996), Larry Cuban and David Tyack (1997), and Matt Miles (1993). It is interesting to note that the field has been influenced by scholars who have approached their work from a variety of theoretical and methodological perspectives, for example, social psychology, organizational development, and history. In addition to this work, which has addressed educational change in a general sense, there is literature that is specific to particular subject fields, such as science and mathematics.

For purposes of this chapter, some highlights of this literature need to be identified. To begin with, we need to recognize that changes of the kind under consideration here are not easy. What may seem simple to the uninitiated is in reality a very complex matter. Individual learning itself is complex, and we are addressing it here in the complex social context of a classroom, which in turn is located within the broader context of a school, which furthermore is profoundly shaped by its franchising society, with its many social, political, and economic forces. Failure to recognize this complexity is rampant not only among the public and politicians, but among practitioners and professionals. The educational landscape is strewn with the wreckage of educational innovations that foundered on the misconception of simple solutions.

This complexity may be better understood if we consider the situation from multiple perspectives. A diagram employed in a journal article on this complexity (Anderson, 1992) may be helpful at this point (see Fig. 27.1).

As portrayed here, processes intended to produce changes in educational practice must include both curricular and instructional aspects, and they occur in a broader social context. To understand fully these arenas of action, we need to view them from multiple theoretical perspectives, including philosophical, psychological, sociocultural, economic, and subject matter (in our case, science). The importance of recognizing this complexity and the futility of pursuing simple solutions has never been more obvious than it is now in this day of mandated changes based on the results of standardized tests.

This complexity leads to a second fundamental point—to be successful, change efforts must be systemic in nature. Changing curriculum materials by itself will not bring successful change. New teaching approaches are not the answer. Professional development has not evidenced significant results. Site-based management will not

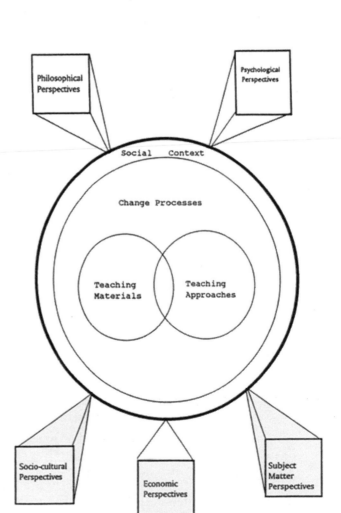

FIGURE 27–1. A model of complexity (Anderson, 1992).

do the job. The list goes on. Even doing all of these together will not work unless it is the right mix of initiatives done in the context of just the right climate and support.

Providing a full picture of what such a successful systemic approach would be is beyond the scope of this chapter, but it may be helpful to point out a few elements of what such a systemic approach would address. What follows are a half-dozen key elements of what research tells us about the complex situation we are facing. Describing these elements may tend toward a reductionist outlook that does damage to the very notion of a systemic approach, so it is done here with caution. Recognize that this description of key elements from the research literature is not intended to imply a list of initiatives which, if successfully pursued, will result in the systemic approach being advocated here. With this caution, some detail is provided about these important facets of the situation.

Teachers Face Many Dilemmas

Case studies of teachers attempting to move to more inquiry-oriented science education (Anderson, 1995, 1996) show many of the dilemmas science teachers face situations in which all of the alternative actions available seem to have undesirable consequences, along with what is desired. Teachers experience a tension between alternatives. Although some of these dilemmas may be more perceived than real, they are nevertheless a part of the teacher's reality. Among these dilemmas are the following:

1. *Time.* There is never enough time to do everything a teacher thinks should be done, and the changes promoted in the *National Science Education Standards* only make the situation more difficult. Inquiry (however you chose to define the term) takes more time, and the teacher wanting to give more emphasis to inquiry faces a dilemma of significant proportions.

2. *Ideal vs. reality.* From the perspective of the teacher in the science classroom it generally appears that the NSES portrays an ideal that is in conflict with the realities of the classroom. This tension highlights the fact that change that introduces more inquiry is not easy.

3. *Changing roles and work.* The school culture has deeply ingrained within it expectations for both students and teachers. It is hard for teachers to change their roles, not just because of the school culture, but because it is difficult for people to change such roles in any context and because the process of learning new roles is more complicated and time consuming than generally thought. And these changes in teacher roles probably are essential if the fundamental desired change is to be achieved, that is, changes in the roles played by students and the nature of the work they do.

4. *The preparation ethic.* The culture of schools, especially among science teachers, is permeated with the idea that preparation for the next level of schooling is the driving value for their work. As a result, science teachers find it difficult to devote significant efforts to a more inquiry-oriented form of science education because they fear preparation will suffer. Teachers feel that this is a real dilemma, even though empirical research shows these fears to be largely groundless.

5. *Equity*. Consideration of the preparation ethic leads to yet another dilemma science teachers perceive—what does it mean to provide "science for all"? Many teachers see a tension between providing a strong education for the able and willing students and at the same time providing for the uninterested or less able students.

Significant Changes in Educational Practice Require Changes in Teachers' Beliefs and Values

Many of the above teacher dilemmas are grounded in beliefs about science, students, and teaching and in values concerning what is important. The influence of teachers' values and beliefs is well grounded in the research literature and is well illustrated in the case studies cited above (Anderson, 1996), as is the relationship between changes in these values and beliefs and changes in classroom practice. Some of these beliefs are related to the nature of high school subjects (Grossman & Stodolsky, 1995) and to teachers' understanding of the nature of science. The potential relationship between teachers' beliefs about the nature of science and classroom transactions and what students learn has been explored in the literature (Lederman, 1992; Duschl & Wright, 1989; Brickhouse, 1990; Russell & Munby, 1989; Koulaidis and Ogborn, 1995). Changes in educational practice related to the preparation ethic are tied to teachers' beliefs (Mitchener & Anderson, 1989), as are teacher decisions related to matters of students' ability, gender, and race (Bianchini, Cavazos, & Helms, 1999).

School Departments Are Important Settings for Change

Although a large proportion of the research on educational change addresses whole school change (Fullan, 2001), the research indicates that deep and lasting change requires intensive department-level efforts. The previously cited case studies illustrate this point (Anderson, 1996), and Talbert (1994) shows that the department is primary among the various embedded contexts where professional identities are formed. Other research pointing to the centrality of the department as the context for educational change has been reported by Grossman and Stodolsky (1994), Little (1993), and McLaughlin (1993). The importance of this context may be related to the next point emerging from the literature, the power of collaboration.

Teacher Collaboration in the Work Context Is a Powerful Influence on Teacher Values and Beliefs

Working together with fellow teachers on day-to-day educational actions—not just in an in-service education context—can be powerful. Talking about the issues raised in the National Science Education Standards is not the same as working together to put ideas into practice. Case studies have shown that this is a setting in which teachers have to come to grips with their values, beliefs, and assumptions and find themselves challenged in this regard as they work with others to develop instruction (Anderson, 1995, 1996). Even though all of the science teachers in a given group may not have the same philosophical perspectives, this sort of collaborative context is where such internal changes emerge. Although new forms of assessment are often presented today as the most influential means of fostering educational change, the research points elsewhere. For further detail on collaboration as an influence on teacher values and beliefs, see Little (1994) and Helms (1995). See also Groarke, Ovens, and Hargreaves (1986); Nolffke and Zeichner (1987); and Tikunoff, Ward, and Griffin (1979); all cited in Richardson (1994).

Parental Support of Reforms Is Essential

Parental support—or probably more important, the absence of resistance—is essential for initiating significant educational reforms. The case studies mentioned above provide striking examples of this situation, with portrayals of changes started in response to new national standards in science and mathematics being seriously restrained by parental opposition. This situation has been studied thoroughly in the field of mathematics (e.g., Peressini, 1996; Romagnano, 1994), with evidence that the assumptions and beliefs of parents are an important part of the overall context in which reform efforts operate.

New Student Roles and New Forms of Student Work Are the Real Indicators of Meaningful Change

This is the moment of truth; if inquiry science education has been installed, it will be evident in new roles played by students and new forms of student work. Even if a number of meaningful changes have been introduced—collaboration among teachers and new roles for them, for example—many reforms seem to fall short when it comes to this "bottom line" of results. Case studies show the possibilities of such significant change, as well as the frequent failure to reach them (Anderson, 1996).

Teachers are at the center of most of the aspects of educational change discussed above. A professional status for teachers that enhances professional decision making clearly is an essential (although by itself not sufficient) element of meaningful educational change.

CONNECTING INQUIRY, CURRICULUM, AND CHANGE

From this description of key elements of the research on educational change, it may be obvious that reforming science education toward a more prominent presence for inquiry will demand a multifaceted approach. It will be essential to have new instructional approaches, revised teaching materials, substantial means of implementation including teacher support and contexts for collaboration, and careful attention to the social context, among others. The issue at hand is how to do it with full attention to the particular forms of inquiry being sought, the understandings of curriculum selected, and the nature of the educational change processes that prevail in the given context. Making these connections is the focus of the remainder of this chapter.

To avoid possible confusion, it is important to relate this discussion to contemporary political events that often carry a label of educational reform. The "standards movement," with its focus on specified expectations—in the case of science, what is the equivalent of selected portions of the content (only) standards from the NSES—coupled with standardized testing and the imposition of penalties for the failure of schools to reach predetermined levels, is far from an adequate expression of what the research on educational change suggests that we do. Such efforts are not systemic in character. Although such standards and testing may be of some help within a broader endeavor, by themselves they have little potential. Furthermore, these contemporary efforts include little attention to inquiry, in any of the various senses that the word is being used here. In fact, anecdotal information and comments from school personnel lead me to conclude that if anything, these efforts are reducing inquiry as science content, inquiry learning, and inquiry teaching.

In pursuing the goal of relating our understandings of inquiry, curriculum, and educational change, the remainder of this chapter is organized in terms of the three notions of inquiry, that is, inquiry as an expression of the nature of science, inquiry learning, and inquiry teaching. Each form of inquiry is explored as a potential guiding theme for positive science curriculum change.

Inquiry as an Aspect of Science Content

In one sense, adding inquiry to the *content* of a science course is relatively easy. Abstractions about the nature of science can be put into text materials, student tests, and teacher presentations, in the same manner as any other knowledge. In other ways, the task is far from easy. To what extent can words in a book capture an understanding of the nature of science inquiry? To what extent must it be experienced?

To address these questions we need to return to our various definitions of curriculum. For discussion purposes, I will set aside Schubert's characterizations of curriculum as cultural reproduction and as an agenda for social reconstruction and divide his other six characterizations of curriculum into two clusters. The first cluster includes curriculum as content, program of planned activities, intended learning outcomes, and discrete tasks and concepts. I am giving it the label of *external,* since in these characterizations of the curriculum the goals and choice of student experiences have origins largely external to the students. In contrast, the other two images of curriculum—curriculum as experience and as currere—are more personal and have origins more internal to the student—hence the label *internal*. Obviously there are many ways to categorize these images, but this particular dichotomy may be useful to us in our consideration of inquiry as science content, as well as when we consider inquiry learning and teaching.

Whichever of these two views of curriculum are employed—*internal* or *external*—science as inquiry can be placed in the curriculum, but one cluster of curricular images may be more useful that the other for the purpose at hand. If a full understanding of the nature of science is dependent upon personal experience—including attention to the emotional aspects of the experience of being engaged in science inquiry—and related intellectual transactions, the *internal* understandings of curriculum may be more helpful. Rather than having these experiences predetermined, there is value in having student choice of hypotheses tested, means of doing such testing, and interpretations to be placed on the results. As with actual scientific experimentation, the student can experience the frustrations and excitement inherent in the endeavor, even though in some senses it is a simulated rather than "real" engagement in science. There is a value in students reflecting on this experience and monitoring the outcomes of their personal thoughts and actions, or—to take it a step further—seeking meaning in past related experiences and re-conceiving their perspectives on life and what they are projecting for themselves in the future.

While personally favoring the *internal* cluster of curriculum images, I recognize that students can experience science inquiry to a considerable degree in curricula whose image is found within the *external* cluster as well. It is of interest to note, in particular, that Schubert's characterization of curriculum as planned activities appears to be quite congruent with the portrayal of inquiry learning and teaching found in the NRC publication *Inquiry and the National Science Education Standards*. Upon reflection, I do not find this surprising, in that the publication is written for practitioners, with an apparent motivation to communicate with them without becoming unduly involved in debates over the nature of the curriculum. Whether one has an external view of the curriculum as determined largely independently of the student, or a view that gives more consideration to the internal dimensions of student interests and prior experiences, the portrayal of the curriculum as planned activities is useful and practical. Descriptions of planned activities can be used to communicate both internal and external conceptions of learning as well as teaching. Furthermore, practitioners with varied understandings of the nature of learning and teaching can engage in meaningful discussion of classroom transactions without foundering on what may seem to be abstract issues.

On the other hand, it may be possible to have such discussions without uncovering fundamental differences among the participants that are truly important to clarity of communication. What is the nature of learning and teaching that is assumed? What understanding of the nature of science do the various participants have? Can practitioners really collaborate with each other in classrooms without getting to these underlying issues? Although I think this publication, *Inquiry and the National Science Education Standards*, is an important and useful tool for practitioners, I would urge dialogue among fellow teachers about its meaning that reaches to the deepest theoretical levels possible.

This deeper understanding on the part of teachers is important if they are to facilitate deep and personal student engagement with the intellectual dimensions of inquiry that students should have. This intellectual engagement generally demands the aid of a teacher who is knowledgeable of the nature of both science and student intellectual development.

Inquiry as science content in the curriculum is well established. It appeared in a rich form in the biology materials of the Biological Sciences Curriculum Study (BSCS) in the early 1960s, with considerable influence coming from Joseph Schwab (Sarther, 1991). It is apparent, however, that there is no one particular understanding of the nature of this science to put into the curriculum (Rudolph, 2003; Lederman, 1992) and that what can be captured in the school curriculum is only a partial portrayal (Rudolph, 2003). The understanding of the nature of science that students acquire through an appropriate curriculum can be rich, intellectually challenging, and emotionally fulfilling, but it must be experienced in significant ways for this to be possible (Magnusson & Palincsar, 1995). The nature of the learning experience is a crucial consideration if this goal is to be attained.

Inquiry Learning

In the sense used here, inquiry learning is foundational and essential for a first-rate education. As noted earlier, it is viewed here as synonymous with what is generally called constructivist learning; that is, learners construct meaning for themselves, such meanings are dependent upon prior constructions, the understandings are context dependent, and they are socially constructed. Although some people may view this statement as an ideal, to a much larger extent it is simply a description of how research tells us learning actually occurs. For optimum learning, curriculum and pedagogical practices should be created that enhance this learning process.

Two clusters of curriculum images were identified above—*external* ones where the origins of the curriculum were largely independent of the students and *internal* ones where the learners themselves significantly shape the curriculum. Inquiry learning can be incorporated into any of Schubert's eight characterizations of the curriculum, but it is not inherent in the *external* versions to the same extent that it is in the *internal* portrayals of curriculum. Inquiry learning is not as easy to add to the former as it is to add the latter. A full flowering of inquiry learning is more feasible in the *internal* versions because students are more likely to shape their own learning in a direct manner.

A fuller explanation of this point will be easier if it can be made more concrete through a means such as Table 27.1. This table describes two orientations to teaching found among teachers in a series of case studies done of schools engaged in curriculum reform of the kind espoused in the NSES (Anderson, 1996). The schools were selected for the case studies because they were successfully implementing such approaches, but within these schools there was a range of approaches. This table describes a continuum where the extremes were labeled *old orientation* and *new orientation*, with the new end of the continuum being consistent with the NSES and constructivist forms of learning. No teacher was totally on one extreme end or the other, but generally teachers displayed a predominance of one or the other. The differences here are described in terms of teacher role, student role, and student work. Because our focus at this point is student learning, our attention is on the latter two. Later we will attend to teaching and what is described in the table as teacher role.

In Table 27.1, the new student orientation is described as a student role as self-directed learner—in contrast to passive receiver—and student work that is student-directed as well—in contrast to student work that is teacher-prescribed activities. Under the new orientation, students process information, not just record it; interpret and explain information, not just memorize it; design their own activities, not just follow teacher directions; and form their own interpretations of data (such as from a laboratory investigation), not just depend upon the teacher's understandings. In addition to this role change, they do different forms of student work. To a considerable extent they direct their own work rather than just complete worksheets, engage in tasks that vary from student to student, design tasks for themselves rather than depend upon teacher-directed tasks, and do work that emphasizes reading and writing for meaning, solving problems, building from existing cognitive structures, and explaining complex problems.

Determiners of the nature of both student role and student work include the nature of the curriculum as well as the role of the teacher. Comment on the teacher's role will be saved for the section on inquiry teaching below. The nature of the cur-

TABLE 27.1
Traditional–Reform Pedagogy Continuum

Predominance of Old Orientation	Predominance of New Orientation
Teacher role	
As dispenser of knowledge	*As coach and facilitator*
Transmits information	Helps students process information
Communicates with individuals	Communicates with groups
Directs student actions	Coaches student actions
Explains conceptual relationships	Facilitates student thinking
Teacher's knowledge is static	Models the learning process
Directed use of textbook, etc.	Flexible use of materials
Student role	
As passive receiver	*As self-directed learner*
Records teacher's information	Processes information
Memorizes information	Interprets, explains, hypothesizes
Follows teacher directions	Designs own activities
Defers to teacher as authority	Shares authority for answers
Student work	
Teacher-prescribed activities	*Student-directed learning*
Completes worksheets	Directs own learning
All students complete same tasks	Tasks vary among students
Teacher directs tasks	Design and direct own tasks
Absence of items on right	Emphasizes reasoning, reading and writing for meaning, solving problems, building from existing cognitive structures, and explaining complex problems

Note: From Anderson (1996).

riculum is the matter at hand. As noted previously, the new orientation to student role and work is possible in any image of the curriculum, but it is more likely in the *internal* cluster of orientations.

As in the case of inquiry as science content, our discussion of inquiry learning deserves special attention to one particular image of the curriculum, curriculum as planned activities. As noted earlier, the NRC publication *Inquiry and the National Education Standards* portrays inquiry in concrete terms through an emphasis on planned activities. A curriculum based on planned activities has the potential of fostering inquiry learning, but realization of this potential is highly dependent upon the teacher's ability to occupy various roles and commitment to particular values and beliefs about such matters as students' capabilities and how they learn. It may be particularly useful to examine curriculum as planned activities here because it is compatible with the above NRC publication and the NSES, and it has the potential of being conducted in a manner that fosters either inquiry learning or its alternatives. Thus, we need to attend closely to the topic of inquiry teaching.

Inquiry Teaching

As noted earlier, inquiry learning is better understood than inquiry teaching. Inquiry learning can be described in the terms provided for us by cognitive science research or in more pragmatic language, such as that used in Table 27.1 to describe student roles and work. Inquiry teaching is more ambiguous. The description of teaching in this table contrasts a teaching orientation that is predominantly dispenser of information with an orientation as coach and facilitator. The distinction is valuable but not sufficient to distinguish between teachers who foster inquiry learning and those who do not. It is possible to play a teaching role as a coach and facilitator—as described in the table—and not foster inquiry learning among students. There is a strong correlation between the teacher role described in the *new orientation* and the student role and work found there, but it is not a perfect correlation. A teacher role that looks to be what is described there may not yield the indicated student role and work. The only real test of the presence of inquiry teaching is whether or not students are engaged in inquiry learning.

If we again use the curriculum as planned activities image, and put it into practice in the sense advocated in *Inquiry and the National Science Education Standards*, we are well on the way to inquiry teaching. But it must be operationalized in a manner that really results in inquiry learning. The teacher so engaged is actively reflective about questions such as the following: Are the students actively constructing understandings rather than memorizing the constructions of others? To what extent are they interpreting and explaining information that comes their way and developing hypotheses about relationships within data sets? Do the students have an opportunity to design and direct some of their own activities rather than just engage in carefully scripted planned activities? Do they have the opportunity to develop—and defend—conclusions they personally draw from the information at hand? Do they engage in activities chosen individually or by a small group, or are they rather consistently engaged in the same tasks as everyone else in the class? Does the students' work in the class emphasize reasoning, include reading and writing that focus on developing meaning and understanding, stress problem solving of varied types, and address complex problems that provide a context for building understandings from existing cognitive structures?

It is possible to employ a curriculum image from the *external* cluster—in particular, curriculum as planned activities—and implement it in a fashion that has many of the characteristics of an *internal* curriculum image, such as curriculum as experience. The most basic issue is not the particular choice of a curriculum image, but whether or not it is put into practice in a manner that fosters inquiry learning; in other words, is something that is called "inquiry teaching" really deserving of this label? A partial basis for answering this question is whether or not it fosters inquiry learning.

Obviously, inquiry teaching is a major topic on its own and an active area of research. It is certainly more than actively reflecting on questions such as the above. In-depth treatment of inquiry teaching, however, is beyond the scope of this chapter. We have touched on it as it pertains to using inquiry as an organizing theme for the curriculum. Research on inquiry teaching, in turn, of course, must attend to context and address many of the matters included in this chapter, such as curriculum content, the nature of the curriculum, and student learning.

Putting It into Practice

As noted earlier, inquiry in its various forms has been put into the science curriculum in various ways for decades. In more recent years—both before and after publication of the NSES—a variety of initiatives have gone in this direction, often in ways that attend to inquiry in its many forms, that is, as science, learning, and teaching. A prime example is project-based science (Blumenfeld, 1994; Krajcik et al., 1994; Marx et al., 1994), a form of instruction that potentially can foster inquiry learning and can bring students in touch with science understood as inquiry. Zuckerman et al. (1998) describe a Vygotskian approach to developing "students' ability to engage in persistent and systematic inquiry." It is an elaboration of an instructional approach; inquiry is defined here as an instructional process that includes an elaboration of a learning cycle of inquiry. The goal here is for students to acquire a certain mode of learning, that is, to be able to do inquiry, in contrast to a goal of having students understand the nature of inquiry in science itself. On the other hand, Ahlgren and Wheeler (2002) describe the foundation of the Project 2061 *Atlas of Science Literacy*, with its many maps, and how the portion on inquiry can be used to teach something about science itself. Cartier and Stewart (2000) provide another example of how science as inquiry is built into a science curriculum, in this case, a high school genetics curriculum. There are a number of examples, but there is still the question of how to put it into wide practice.

CHANGING TOWARD INQUIRY

Inquiry is a viable guiding theme for science curriculum in terms of content, learning, and teaching, but we still face the issue of how to change teaching practices in classrooms to attain the desired inquiry orientation. Whether one is approaching this task as an individual teacher, a science department within a school, or a school system, it is a difficult task; our brief review of the literature on educational change is clear on this point. It also is apparent that beyond an individual teacher, any change endeavor must be systemic, that is, it must attend to many aspects of the situation and it must be done in a manner that attends to the interrelationships among these many facets. Among these many aspects, two stand out—the curricular materials and the teacher. We will address each of them before moving on to the overall systemic situation.

Materials

Curriculum materials have been given highly varied degrees of importance at different times and in different contexts. The attempts to introduce inquiry science education in the 1960s, for example, were centered on innovative new curriculum materials. Although they may not have been billed as such, they often were viewed as teaching materials that should be "teacher proof." In other words, they were developed with the expectation that most any teacher could use them rather easily in his or her classroom in a manner that would result in inquiry learning and student understanding of science as inquiry. In general, the materials did not live up to this expectation.

On the other hand, the particular materials selected are sometimes thought to be of little importance, at least in the hands of a good teacher. It is assumed that what happens in the classroom depends upon the teacher, and if the teacher is competent, it doesn't make much difference what materials are used.

Neither of these extremes is a good grounding for introducing positive educational change. Quality inquiry science materials are of major importance and influence in classrooms; they can be the foundation of quality education. On the other hand, the materials themselves will not do the job independently of a well-qualified teacher. In an analysis of the role that curriculum materials can play—and their relationship to individual teachers, professional development, and school culture—Powell and Anderson (2002) concluded that an answer to questions about the place of materials is dependent upon the given context and situation. Professionals who ignore the value of good materials typically find that an important element of their attempts at educational reform is missing. There are multiple reasons for seeking out the best available inquiry-oriented materials.

The desired materials reflect the vision of science education found in the standards of such documents as the *National Science Education Standards* (NRC, 1996) and *Benchmarks for Scientific Literacy* (AAAS, 1993). In particular, these curriculum materials should have four distinguishing characteristics as follows:

1. are standards-based in that the science content, instructional strategies, and assessment tools optimize student learning as reflected in current research on teaching and learning.

2. are inquiry-based, which includes support for inquiry as a teaching strategy as well as the inclusion of content that addresses the abilities to do inquiry and the understandings about science as inquiry.

3. are based on a carefully developed conceptual framework that reflects the science disciplines and connects factual information to larger ideas, themes, and concepts.

4. are revised as a result of thoughtful and comprehensive field testing, which provides developers with data about the effectiveness of the materials used by teachers and students. (Powell & Anderson, 2002, p. 114)

Good curriculum materials have been presented here as an important vehicle for facilitating inquiry-oriented science education. But some may ask if it would not be possible—maybe even preferable— for a teacher to enter the classroom without such well-developed materials and use one's teaching competence to develop a particular image of the curriculum into reality in the lives of students. This teacher could, for example, begin with a conception of the curriculum as experience (following the tradition of John Dewey), build on student experiences with science-related matters, and facilitate the students' growth in inquiry, science, and applications of this science to personal and social applications. Yes, I think it is possible, but within the reality of the public school context I also think that literally only one in a hundred teachers has the competences required to do it and do it well. Widespread educational change toward inquiry is not possible without appropriate materials.

Furthermore, I think even the teacher with this desired vision and the necessary competences would find such materials helpful in the typical school context. In the early 1990s I conducted a case study over a period of two years, of a high school science department that was developing and implementing a new inquiry-oriented science program that integrated content from the full range of natural sciences. They had found no published materials with which they were satisfied and had decided to write their own. In an interview near the end of the case study with the science department chair—the leader of the innovative effort and writer of the majority of the materials—we discussed the materials and their development. His firm opinion was if he had to do it over again, he would have purchased the best materials available—even though they were highly unsatisfactory from his standpoint—and adapted them as they went along. Personally, I favor the *internal* cluster of curriculum images and am attracted to pursuing curriculum as experience or as currere. Even so, in teaching a secondary school science class I would prefer to start with the best inquiry-oriented materials available and use them as a foundation in a classroom that is more "freewheeling" and individually adapted than the materials developers had in mind. Materials are of major importance, even though, by themselves, they do not come close to doing the job.

A Teacher Focus

Assuming quality materials—such as one would expect from a process with the four characteristics given above—the materials themselves are making demands on teachers that are both substantial and meaningful. The best materials are asking teachers to conduct their classes in a manner that is far from routine, introduce multiple forms of inquiry, and lead to student engagement and empowerment. As a result, teachers are being encouraged to move out of their comfort zone, attempt new practices, and challenge some of their personal values and beliefs. Most teachers find such a venture to be very challenging. Teachers have to be the focal point of a move toward more inquiry-oriented science education.

It is inevitable that teachers who move out of their comfort zone to attempt more inquiry-oriented teaching practices find challenges to their values and beliefs. To what extent are these new educational experiences valuable to my students? Are they valuable for all kinds of students? What is most important for them to learn? Will my students miss certain important knowledge if I use this inquiry approach instead of my usual approach? Do I have enough time to use inquiry? These questions are only samples from the many issues that pass through teachers' consciousness as they attempt innovation. Changing educational practice is not just a matter of learning some new techniques. It is a process of reassessing one's entire understanding of the educational process (Anderson, 1995, 1996; Keys & Bryan, 2001)

Professional development is an important aspect of this process of change, but of necessity it must be a transformative process; routine inservice education is not sufficient. Among characteristics of such in-depth professional development are the following (Thompson & Zeuli, 1999):

1. Cognitive dissonance is created, which disturbs the existing equilibrium between the practices and beliefs of teachers and their experiences with the subject matter, learning, and teaching.
2. Discussion, reading, writing, and revised thinking can lead to resolution of such dissonance when teachers are given the appropriate context, time, and support.
3. The professional development experiences are connected to the teachers' particular context and their own students.

4. A means is provided for the teachers to develop new classroom practices that are consistent with the new understandings they are developing.

5. As new issues and problems arise, teachers are given the support needed to understand them and put these new understandings into classroom practice.

A bit of reflection makes it apparent that professional development of this sort requires more than creating and scheduling an inservice education class. It must be tied to the inquiry materials being used, have an intimate connection with the participants' day-to-day work in their own classrooms, and have strong connections to their fellow teachers and the support system provided by their school. It is not an isolated endeavor.

Research makes it clear that collaboration among colleagues is a powerful part of such an initiative, not just in the context of a professional development experience *per se*, but in the ongoing work context. Collaborative work among teachers can be a powerful influence with a transformative result (Anderson, 1995, 1996). In this context there is a real opportunity for teachers' beliefs to change as they have reason to think deeply about what scholarship about learning and teaching (e.g., Lambert & McCombs, 1998; Bransford et al, 1999; Mayer, 2002) means as applied to their own "real world" situations. They can become dissatisfied with past beliefs, find viable alternative practices, and connect new beliefs with previous understandings. They can become convinced that new approaches will result in improved student learning (Prawat, 1992; Berlin & Jensen, 1989).

Systemic Support

There is abundant evidence that educational change (whether toward inquiry or anything else new) will go nowhere without systemic support, that is, multifaceted support that addresses all aspects of what is obviously a loosely coupled system of interconnecting components. This generalization has been well established in the field of science education in a cost-effectiveness analysis of interventions to improve educational practice (Anderson, 1990) and in case studies of curriculum reform (Anderson, 1995, 1996). With respect to education in general, it has been shown throughout the general literature on educational reform (e.g., Fullan, 2001; Sarason, 1996). Systemic support means support for teachers' professional growth as described above and a lot more.

With respect to inquiry-oriented science education, this systemic support must be centered on this vision of education, including the various understandings of inquiry regarding content, learning, and teaching. At its center must be the professional growth of teachers built on multifaceted means of support, including appropriate materials, collaborative work contexts, suitable forms of coaching, empowerment, and a supportive work environment. As noted earlier, however, it is far more and includes appropriate initiatives in many spheres of influence, including those of parents, the public in general, policymakers, and various administrative levels.

Finally, with respect to systemic support, it should be emphasized that it must be contextual. There is no gold-standard, all-purpose way of providing systemic support for changing toward inquiry-oriented science education. It must be situated in a particular time and designed for a given situation and for the people and place at hand.

Structures as Well as Culture Must Change

Much of what has been described above with respect to systemic support addresses school culture and changes in teachers' values and beliefs. But that should not be the limit of our thinking. If we want to put in place a full new vision of science education, that is, inquiry science education in its many manifestations, something must be done to alter the prevailing patterns of school structures (Cuban, 1995). The literature on reform shows that even such seemingly simple changes as putting in place a common planning period for science teachers who are collaborating on their teaching or block scheduling for science classes (neither of which is presented here as a panacea) is very difficult. But structural changes of many kinds may be in order, and they need to be open for consideration, as must any deliberation about what constitutes inquiry science education and how it can be put in place.

This chapter opened with the assertion that it made sense to use inquiry as an organizing theme for science curricula, but that this assertion had many qualifications. It should be apparent at this point not only that these qualifications are many, but that they have to be considered in concert. The vision of inquiry science contained in the *National Science Education Standards* is powerful, has great merit, and is viable in the practical world of schools. In addition, however, it is a lofty goal that is difficult to attain. It deserves the careful attention and concentrated effort that research tells us will be required to put it into practice.

ACKNOWLEDGMENTS

Thanks to Larry Flick and Jim Minstrell, who reviewed this chapter.

REFERENCES

Ahlgren, A., & Wheeler, S. (2002). Mapping the steps toward basic understanding of scientific inquiry. *Science & Education, 11*, 217–230.

American Association for the Advancement of Science. (1989). *Science for all Americans: A Project 2061 report on literacy goals in science, mathematics, and technology*. Washington, DC: AAAS.

Anderson, R. D. (1990). Policy decisions on improving science education: A cost-effectiveness analysis. *Journal of Research in Science Teaching, 27*(6), 553–574.

Anderson, R. D. (1992). Perspectives on complexity: An essay on curricular reform, *Journal of Research in Science Teaching, 29*(8), 861–876.

Anderson, R. D. (1995). Curriculum reform: Dilemmas and promise. *Phi Delta Kappan, 77*, 33–36.

Anderson, R. D. (1996). *Study of curriculum reform*. (Volume I of the final report of research conducted under contract no. RR91182001 with OERI, U.S. Department of Education). Washington, DC: U.S. Government Printing Office.

Anderson, R. D. (1998). *The research on teaching as inquiry*. A commissioned paper prepared for the Center for Science, Mathematics and Engineering Education at the National Research Council.

Anderson, R. D. (2002). Reforming science teaching: What research says about inquiry. *Journal of Science Teacher Education, 13*(1), 1–12.

Anderson, R. D., & Helms, J. V. (2001). The ideal of standards and the reality of schools: Needed research. *Journal of Research in Science Teaching, 38*(1), 3–16.

Anderson, R. D., et al. (1994). *Issues of curriculum reform in science, mathematics and higher order thinking across the disciplines*. Washington, DC: U.S. Government Printing Office.

Berlin, B. M., & Jensen, K. (1989). Changing teachers. *Education and urban society, 22*(1), 115–120.

Bianchini, J. A., Cavazos, L. M., & Helms, J. V. (1999). *From professional lives to inclusive practice: Science educators' views of gender, ethnicity, and science.* Paper presented at the American Educational Research Association conference in Montreal.

Blumenfeld, P. C. (1994). Lessons learned: How collaboration helped middle grade science teachers learn project-based instruction. *The Elementary School Journal, 94*(5), 539–551.

Bransford, J. D., Brown, A. L., & Cocking, R. (Eds). (1999). *How people learn: Brain, mind, experience, and school.* Washington, DC: National Academy Press.

Brickhouse, N. W. (1990). Teachers beliefs about the nature of science and their relationship to classroom practice. *Journal of Teacher Education, 41,* 53–62.

Cartier, J. L., & Stewart, J. (2000). Teaching the nature of inquiry: Further developments in a high school genetics curriculum. *Science and Education, 9,* 247–267.

Cuban, L. (1995). The hidden variable: How organizations influence teacher responses to secondary science curriculum reform. *Theory into Practice, 34*(1), 4–11.

Duschl, R., & Wright, E. (1989). A case study of high school teachers' decision making models for planning and teaching science. *Journal of Research in Science Teaching, 26,* 467–501.

Eisner, E. W. (1992). Curriculum ideologies. In Philip W. Jackson (Ed.), *Handbook of research on curriculum* (pp. 302–326). New York: Macmillan.

Fullan, M. G. (2001). *The new meaning of educational change.* New York: Teachers College Press, Columbia University.

Groarke, J., Ovens, P., & Hargreaves, M. (1986). Towards more open classrooms. In D. Hustler, A. Cassidy, & E. C. Cuff (Eds.), *Action research in classrooms and schools.* London: Allen & Unwin.

Grossman, P. L., & Stodolsky, S. S. (1995). Content as context: the role of school subjects in secondary school teaching. *Educational Researcher, 24,* 5–11.

Helms, J. V. (1995). *Speaking of the subject: Science teachers reflect on the nature of science, science teaching, and themselves.* Unpublished dissertation.

Huffman, D. (2002). Evaluating science inquiry: A mixed-method approach. In J. W. Altschuld and D. D. Kumar (Eds.), *Evaluation of science and technology education at the dawn of a new millennium.* New York: Kluwer Academic/Plenum.

Keys, C. W., & Bryan, L. A. (2001). Co-constructing inquiry-based science with teachers: Essential research for lasting reform. *Journal of Research in Science Teaching, 38*(6), 631–645.

Koulaidis, V., & Ogborn, J. (1995). Science teachers' philosophical assumptions: How well do we understand them? *International Journal of Science Education, 17,* 273–283.

Krajcik, J. S., et al. (1994). A collaborative model for helping middle grade science teachers learn project-based instruction. *The Elementary School Journal, 94*(5), 483–497.

Lambert, N. M., & McCombs, B. L. (1998). *How students learn: Reforming schools through learner-centered education.* Washington, DC: American Psychological Association.

Lederman, N. G. (1992). Students' and teachers' conception of the nature of science: A review of research. *Journal of Research in Science Teaching, 29,* 331–359.

Lederman, Norman G., & Niess, Margaret L. (2000). Problem solving and solving problems: Inquiry about inquiry. *School Science and Mathematics, 100*(3), 113–116.

Little, J. (1993). Professional community in comprehensive high schools: The two worlds of academic and vocational teachers. In J. W. Little and M. W. McLaughlin (Eds.), *Teachers' work: Individuals, colleagues, and contexts* (pp. 137–163). New York: Teachers College Press

Magnusson, S. J., & Palincsar, A. S. (1995). The learning environment as a site of science education reform. *Theory into Practice, 34*(1), 43–50.

Marx, R. W., et al. (1994). Enacting project-based science: Experiences of four middle grade teachers. *The Elementary School Journal, 94*(5), 517–538.

Mayer, R. E. (2002). *The promise of educational psychology: Vol. II. Teaching for meaningful learning.* Upper Saddle River, NJ: Pearson Education.

McLaughlin, M. W. (1993). What matters most in teachers' workplace context? In J. W. Little and M. W. McLaughlin (Eds.), *Teachers' work: Individuals, colleagues, and contexts.* (pp. 79–103). New York: Teachers College Press.

Miles, M. (1993). Forty years of change in schools: Some personal reflections. *Educational Administration Quarterly, 29,* 213–248.

Minstrell, J., & van Zee, E. (Eds.). (2000). *Inquiry into inquiry learning and teaching in science.* Washington, DC: American Association for the Advancement of Science.

Mitchener, C. P., & Anderson, R. D. (1989). Teachers' perspective: Developing and implementing an STS curriculum. *Journal of Research in Science Teaching, 26,* 351–369.

National Research Council. (1996). *National science education standards.* Washington, DC: National Academy Press.

National Research Council. (2000). *Inquiry and the national science education standards.* Washington, DC: National Academy Press.

Noffke, S. E., & Zeichner, K. M. (1987). *Action research and teacher thinking: The first phase of the AR project at the University of Wisconsin, Madison.* Paper presented at the annual meeting of the American Educational Research Association, Washington, DC.

Peressini, D. (1996). Parents, power, and the reform of mathematics education: An exploratory analysis of three urban high schools. *Urban Education, 31,* 3–28.

Powell, J. C., & Anderson, R. D. (2002). Changing teachers' practices: Curriculum materials and science education reform in the USA. *Studies in Science Education, 37,* 107–136.

Prawat, M. F. (1992). Teachers' beliefs about teaching and learning: A constructivist perspective. *American Journal of Education, 100,* 354–395.

Project 2061. (2001). *Atlas of science literacy.* Washington, DC: American Association for the Advancement of Science.

Richardson, V. (1994). Teacher inquiry as professional staff development. In S. Hollingsworth & H. Sockett (Eds.), *Teacher research and educational reform* (pp. 186–203). Ninety-third Yearbook of the National Society for the Study of Education. Chicago: University of Chicago Press.

Romagnano, L. S. (1994). *The dilemmas of change: A tale of two mathematics teachers.* Portsmouth, NH: Heinemann.

Rudolph, J. L. (2003). Portraying epistemology: School science in historical context. *Science Education, 87,* 64–79.

Russell, T., & Munby, H. (1989). Science as a discipline, science as seen by students and teachers' professional knowledge. In R. Millar (Ed.), *Doing science: Images of science in science education* (pp. 107–125). London: Falmer Press.

Sarason, S. B. (1990). *The predictable failure of educational reform.* San Francisco: Jossey-Bass.

Sarason, S. B. (1996). *Revisiting "The culture of the school and the problem of change."* New York: Teachers College Press.

Sarther, C. M. (1991). Science curriculum and the BSCS revisited. *Teaching Education, 3*(2), 101–108.

Schubert, W. H. (1986). *Curriculum: Perspective, paradigm, and possibility.* New York: Macmillan.

Talbert, J. (1994). Boundaries of teachers' professional communities in U.S. high schools: power and precariousness of the subject department. Paper prepared for Leslie Santee Siskin & Judith Warren Little (Eds.), *The High School Department: Perspectives on the Subject Organization of Secondary Schools.* New York: Teachers College Press.

Thompson, C. L., & Zeuli, J. S. (1999). The frame and the tapestry. In L. Darling-Hammond & G. Sykes (Eds.), *Teaching as the learning profession.* San Francisco: Jossey-Bass.

Tikunoff, W. J., Ward, B., & Griffin, G. (1979). *Interactive research and development on teaching study: Final report.* San Francisco: Far West Laboratory.

Tyack, D., & Cuban, L. (1997). *Tinkering toward Utopia.* Cambridge, MA: Harvard University Press.

Zuckerman, G. A., Chudinova, E. V., & Khavkin, E. E. (1998). Inquiry as a pivotal element of knowledge acquisition within the Vygotskian paradigm: Building a science curriculum for the elementary school. *Cognition and Instruction, 16*(2), 201–233.

CHAPTER 28

Nature of Science:
Past, Present, and Future

Norman G. Lederman
Illinois Institute of Technology

CONCEPTUALIZING THE CONSTRUCT

The construct "nature of science" (NOS) has been advocated as an important goal for students studying science for approximately 100 years (Central Association of Science and Mathematics Teachers, 1907). Most recently, NOS has been advocated as a critical educational outcome by various science education reform documents worldwide (e.g., Australia, Canada, South Africa, United Kingdom, United States). To be blunt, when it comes to NOS, one is hard pressed to find rhetoric arguing against its importance as a prized educational outcome. Still, detractors do exist (Winchester, 1993). The observation that NOS has been a perennial goal of science education, and is now receiving increased emphasis, can be construed to mean that high school graduates, and the general citizenry, do not possess (and never have possessed) adequate views of NOS. The research reviewed later in this chapter provides clear support for such a notion. That said, has anything been lost? Is it really important for students and the general citizenry to understand NOS? What have we not accomplished because our students do not have good understandings of NOS? What can we make of the obsession with NOS?

At a general level, understanding NOS is often defended as being a critical component of scientific literacy (NSTA, 1982). This just begs the question of what it means to be scientifically literate. Perhaps the most concise way of answering the question of why understanding NOS is important is to consider the five arguments provided by Driver, Leach, Millar, and Scott (1996). Their arguments were as follows:

> *Utilitarian*: Understanding NOS is necessary to make sense of science and manage the technological objects and processes in everyday life.
>
> *Democratic*: Understanding NOS is necessary for informed decision-making on socioscientific issues.
>
> *Cultural*: Understanding NOS is necessary to appreciate the value of science as part of contemporary culture.

Moral: Understanding NOS helps develop an understanding of the norms of the scientific community that embody moral commitments that are of general value to society.

Science learning: Understanding NOS facilitates the learning of science subject matter.

Certainly, these are all important and noble reasons for why science educators value NOS as an instructional outcome. However, at this point, the arguments are primarily intuitive, with little empirical support. Much like the general goal of scientific literacy, until we reach a critical mass of individuals who possess adequate understandings of NOS, we have no way of knowing whether achievement of the goal has accomplished what has been assumed. If we become generally more successful at teaching NOS to our students, will they become better decision-makers? Will their science achievement improve? My goal is not to contradict or cheapen my life's work. Rather, my goal is to emphasize that the jury is still out. Most important questions are still left to be answered, and there are most assuredly many questions that have yet to arise. Students' and teachers' understandings of NOS remain a high priority for science education and science education research. As mentioned before, it has been an objective in science education (American Association for the Advancement of Science [AAAS], 1990, 1993; Klopfer, 1969; National Research Council [NRC], 1996; National Science Teachers Association [NSTA], 1982) for almost 100 years (Central Association of Science and Mathematics Teachers, 1907; Kimball, 1967–68; Lederman, 1992). Indeed, "the longevity of this educational objective has been surpassed only by the longevity of students' inability to articulate the meaning of the phrase 'nature of science,' and to delineate the associated characteristics of science" (Lederman & Niess, 1997, p. 1).

WHAT IS AND WHAT IS NOT NATURE OF SCIENCE

With all the support NOS has in the science education and scientific community, one would assume that all stakeholders possess adequate understandings of the construct. Even though explicit statements about the meaning of NOS are provided in well-known reform documents (e.g., NRC, 1996), the pages of refereed journals and the conference rooms at professional meetings are filled with definitions that run contrary to the consensus reached by the *National Science Education Standards* (1996) and other reform documents. Some would argue that the situation is direct support for the idea that there is *no* agreement on the meaning of NOS (Alters, 1997). More recently, Hipkins, Barker, and Bolstad (2005) have expressed concerns about the lack of consensus about NOS in New Zealand curricula. However, counterarguments by others (Smith, Lederman, Bell, McComas, & Clough, 1997; Smith & Scharmann, 1999) point out that more consensus exists than disagreement. Others (Lederman, 1998) are quick to note that the disagreements about the definition or meaning of NOS that continue to exist among philosophers, historians, and science educators are irrelevant to K–12 instruction. The issue of the existence of an objective reality as compared with phenomenal realities is a case in point. There is an acceptable level of generality regarding NOS that is accessible to K–12 students and relevant to their daily lives that can be found in the writings of the aforementioned authors as well as the more recent comments of Elby and Hammer (2001) and Rudolph (2003). Moreover, at this level, little disagreement exists among philosophers, historians, and science educators. Among the characteristics of scientific knowledge corresponding to this level of generality are that scientific knowledge is tentative (subject to change), empirically based (based on and/or derived from observations of the natural world), and subjective (involves personal background, biases, and/or is theory-laden); necessarily involves human inference, imagination, and creativity (involves the invention of explanations); and is socially and culturally embedded. Two additional important aspects are the distinction between observations and inferences, and the functions of and relationships between scientific theories and laws.

Before attempting to review the research on NOS it is important to provide some general parameters for the meaning of the construct. What is NOS? It might help to back up to the proverbial question, What is science? The most common answer to this question in the literature is: 1) body of knowledge, 2) method, and 3) way of knowing. NOS typically refers to the epistemology of science, science as a way of knowing, or the values and beliefs inherent to scientific knowledge and its development (Lederman, 1992). What follows is a brief consideration of these characteristics of science and scientific knowledge related to what students should know. It is important to note that the aspects of NOS described below are not meant as a comprehensive listing. There are other aspects that some researchers include or delete (Osborne, Collins, Ratcliffe, Millar, & Duschl, 2003; Scharmann & Smith, 1999). And any of these lists that consider what students can learn, in addition to a consideration of the characteristics of scientific knowledge, are of equal validity. The primary purpose here is not to emphasize one listing versus another, but to provide a frame of reference that helps delineate NOS from scientific inquiry (and processes of science) and the resulting body of knowledge.

First students should understand the crucial distinction between observation and inference. Observations are descriptive statements about natural phenomena that are "directly" accessible to the senses (or extensions of the senses) and about which several observers can reach consensus with relative ease (e.g., descriptions of the morphology of the remnants of a once living organism). Inferences, on the other hand, go beyond the senses. For example, one may develop explanations about the observed morphology in terms of its possible contributions to function. At a higher level, a scientist can infer models or mechanisms that explain observations of complex phenomena (e.g., models of weather, evolution).

Second, closely related to the distinction between observations and inferences is the distinction between scientific laws and theories. Individuals often hold a simplistic, hierarchical view of the relationship between theories and laws whereby theories become laws, depending on the availability of supporting evidence. It follows from this notion that scientific laws have a higher status than scientific theories. Both notions, however, are inappropriate because, among other things, theories and laws are different kinds of knowledge, and one does not develop or become transformed into the other. Laws are *statements or descriptions of the relationships* among observable phenomena. Boyle's law, which relates the pressure of a gas to its volume at a constant temperature, is a case in point. Theories, by contrast, *are inferred explanations* for observable phenomena (e.g., kinetic molecular theory provides an explanation for what is observed and described by Boyle's law). Scientific models are common examples of theory and inference in science. Moreover, theories are as legitimate a product of science as laws. Scientists do not usually formulate theories in the hope that one day they will acquire the status of "law."

Third, even though scientific knowledge is, at least partially, based on and/or derived from observations of the natural world (i.e., empirical), it nevertheless involves human imagination and creativity. Science, contrary to common belief, is not a totally lifeless, rational, and orderly activity. Science involves the *invention* of explanations, and this requires a great deal of creativity by scientists. This aspect of science, coupled with its inferential nature, entails that scientific concepts, such as atoms, black holes, and species, are functional theoretical models rather than faithful copies of reality.

Fourth, scientific knowledge is subjective and/or theory-laden. Scientists' theoretical commitments, beliefs, previous knowledge, training, experiences, and expectations actually influence their work. All these background factors form a *mind-set* that *affects* the problems scientists investigate and how they conduct their investigations, what they observe (and do not observe), and how they make sense of, or interpret their observations. It is this (sometimes collective) individuality or mind-set that accounts for the role of subjectivity in the production of scientific knowledge. It is noteworthy that, contrary to common belief, science rarely starts with neutral observations (Chalmers, 1982). Observations (and investigations) are motivated and guided by, and acquire meaning in reference to, questions or problems. These questions or problems, in turn, are derived from within certain theoretical perspectives. Often, hypothesis or model testing serves as a guide to scientific investigations.

Fifth, science as a human enterprise is practiced in the context of a larger culture, and its practitioners (scientists) are the product of that culture. Science, it follows, affects and is affected by the various elements and intellectual spheres of the culture in which it is embedded. These elements include, but are not limited to, social fabric, power structures, politics, socioeconomic factors, philosophy, and religion. The practice of acupuncture, for example, was not accepted by western science until western science explanations for the success of acupuncture could be provided.

Sixth, it follows from the previous discussions that scientific knowledge is never absolute or certain. This knowledge, including "facts," theories, and laws, is tentative and subject to change. Scientific claims change as new evidence, made possible through advances in *theory* and technology, is brought to bear on existing theories or laws, or as old evidence is reinterpreted in the light of new theoretical advances or shifts in the directions of established research programs. The construct of punctuated equilibrium was developed through an interpretation of the fossil record from a different perspective. Rather than taking a Darwinian view of gradual change, the lack of transitional species, among other observations, led to a reinterpretation of classic evolutionary theory. It should be emphasized that tentativeness in science not only arises from the fact that scientific knowledge is inferential, creative, and socially and culturally embedded. There are also compelling logical arguments that lend credence to the notion of tentativeness in science. Some have taken issue with the use of the word "tentative" to describe scientific knowledge. Descriptors such as "revisionary" or "subject to change" are preferred by those who feel "tentative" implies that the knowledge is flimsy and not well founded. Whatever word is used, the intended meaning is that the knowledge of science, no matter how much supported evidence exists, may change in the future for the reasons just discussed.

Finally, it is important to note that individuals often conflate NOS with science processes or scientific inquiry. Although these aspects of science overlap and interact in important ways, it is nonetheless important to distinguish between the two. Scientific processes are activities related to collecting and analyzing data, and drawing conclusions (AAAS, 1990, 1993; NRC, 1996). For example, observing and inferring are scientific processes. More complex than individual processes, scientific inquiry involves various science processes used in a cyclical manner. On the other hand, NOS refers to the epistemological underpinnings of the activities of science and the characteristics of the resulting knowledge. As such, realizing that observations are necessarily theory-laden and are constrained by our perceptual apparatus belongs within the realm of NOS. Distinguishing NOS from scientific inquiry for the purpose of providing focus to this chapter should in no way be construed to mean that NOS is considered more important for students to learn about. Certainly, both constructs are important and inquiry and NOS, although different, are intimately related. For this reason, a separate chapter in this Handbook is devoted to scientific inquiry (Chapter 27). Making a distinction between NOS and scientific inquiry was in no way meant to imply that the two constructs are distinct. Clearly, they are intimately related. Furthermore, there is much evidence that NOS is best taught within a context of scientific inquiry or activities that are reasonable facsimiles of inquiry. That is, inquiry experiences provide students with foundational experiences upon which to reflect about aspects of NOS.

The conflation of NOS and scientific inquiry has plagued research on NOS from the beginning and, perhaps, could have been avoided by using the phrase "nature of scientific knowledge" as apposed to NOS. However, the damage has already been done. Hence, the reader will note that many of the earlier studies (and even continuing to the present) are actually more focused on inquiry than NOS. These studies are nevertheless reviewed, rather than excluded, since they have become an accepted part of the history of research on NOS. The definition used by these studies for NOS is just not consistent with current usage of the construct. Again, the aspects of NOS presented here are not meant to be exhaustive. Other listings certainly exist. However, what has been presented is directly consistent with what current reform documents state students should know about NOS and is consistent with the perspective taken by an overwhelming majority of the research literature.

THE CHANGING FACE OF NATURE OF SCIENCE

One of the most vexing issues for those who do research on the teaching and learning of NOS is that NOS can be a moving target. If one considers the differences among the works of Popper (1959), Kuhn (1962), Lakatos (1970), Feyerabend (1975), Laudan (1977), and Giere (1988), it becomes quite clear that perceptions of NOS are as tentative, if not more so, than scientific knowledge itself. In short, NOS is analogous to scientific knowledge. As a consequence, some individuals have dwelled too heavily on such differing perceptions (e.g., Alters, 1997). The recognition that our views of NOS have changed and will continue to change is not a justification for ceasing our research until total agreement is reached, or for avoiding recommendations or identifying what we think students should know. We have no difficulty including certain theories and laws within our science curricula, even though we recognize that these may change in the near or distant future. What is important is that students understand the evidence for current beliefs about natural phenomena, and the same is true with NOS. Students should know the evidence that has led to our current beliefs about NOS, and, just as with "traditional" subject matter, they should realize that perceptions may change as additional evidence is collected or the same evidence is viewed in a different way.

Regardless of the various "problems" associated with reaching consensus on the various aspects of nature of science, and issues created by the tentativeness of the construct itself, the nature of science has been the object of systematic educational research for approximately 50 years. Prior to this review, there were three reviews of research related to the teaching, learning, and assessment of the nature of science (Abd-El-Khalick & Lederman, 2000a; Lederman, 1992; Meichtry, 1992). In addition to revisiting the contents of previous reviews, this review builds on these prior works and, it is hoped, provides some guidance for future research in the field. For practical reasons, the research reviewed is restricted to published reports and to those studies with a primary focus on NOS. These studies have been divided into obvious thematic sections and are presented in a general chronological sequence within each section.

RESEARCH ON STUDENTS' CONCEPTIONS

Considering the longevity of objectives related to students' conceptions of the nature of science, it is more than intriguing that the first formal instrument to assess students' conceptions was developed about 50 years ago (Wilson, 1954). The development of instruments to assess NOS has a long history and is extensive enough to constitute separate treatment in this review. Although it can be argued that placing the discussion of assessment first would provide an important context for the review of the research, it can be equally argued that a discussion of the varied assessments would be too abstract without the context of the specific research investigations. Consequently, the review of NOS assessment has been placed at the end of the review. However, this should not impede those who wish to read the section on assessment first. In Wilson's (1954) investigation, which was primarily an attempt to validate an instrument known as the Science Attitude Questionnaire, a sample of 43 Georgia high school students was found to believe that scientific knowledge is absolute and that scientists' primary objective is to uncover natural laws and truths. The most extensive early attempt to assess students' conceptions of the nature of science (Mead & Metraux, 1957) involved a nationwide sample of 35,000 student essays on the topic "What Do You Think About Science and Scientists?" Mead and Metraux drew a randomized sample that was representative with respect to age, gender, geographic distribution, and socioeconomic status. Their qualitative analysis of the data yielded findings that were consistent with Wilson's (1954) findings on both attitude toward science and students' understandings of the nature of science. It is interesting to note that the earliest studies related to the nature of science often included assessments of attitudes or conflated the nature of science with attitude toward science.

In 1961, Klopfer and Cooley developed the Test on Understanding Science (TOUS), which was to become the most widely used paper-and-pencil assessment of students' conceptions. Using the TOUS and a comprehensive review of several nationwide surveys, Klopfer and Cooley concluded that high school students' understandings of the scientific enterprise and of scientists was inadequate. Miller (1963), also using the TOUS, found student conceptions that were considered totally inadequate. As research began to document that students possessed less than adequate views of nature of science, research in the field began to proliferate (National Science Teachers Association [NSTA], 1962). Early assessments of students' understandings were not limited to the United States. Mackay (1971) pre- and posttested 1,203 Australian secondary students spanning grades 7–10, using the TOUS instrument. He concluded that students lacked sufficient knowledge of (a) the role of creativity in science; (b) the function of scientific models; (c) the roles of theories and their relation to research; (d) the distinctions among hypotheses, laws, and theories; (e) the relationship between experimentation, models and theories, and absolute truth; (f) the fact that science is not solely concerned with the collection and classification of facts; (g) what constitutes a scientific explanation; and (h) the interrelationships among and the interdependence of the different branches of science. Similar findings resulted from the investigations of Korth (1969), Broadhurst (1970), and Aikenhead (1972, 1973).

Bady's (1979) work differed from early efforts in that he focused on a particular aspect of students' understanding of nature of science. Specifically, he investigated students' understandings of the logic of hypothesis testing. His sample included 20 9th-grade students and 20 11th-grade students from a large urban school, as well as 33 9th-grade and 41 12th-grade students from a small private boys' school. Using the Johnson-Laird and Wason (1972) task to assess subjects' understandings of hypothesis testing, he found that most students, regardless of school or grade level, believed that hypotheses can be adequately tested and proved by verification. He concluded that such students are likely to have a simplistic and naively absolutist view of the nature of scientific hypotheses and theories. Similarly, during the development of the Nature of Scientific Knowledge Scale, Rubba (Rubba, 1977; Rubba & Andersen, 1978) found that 30 percent of the high school students surveyed believed that scientific research reveals incontrovertible and necessary absolute truth. Additionally, most of Rubba's sample believed that scientific theories, with constant testing and confirmation, eventually mature into laws. With a sample of 102 high-ability 7th- and 8th-grade students, Rubba, Horner, and Smith (1981) attempted to assess students' adherence to the ideas that laws are mature theories and that laws represent absolute truth. The results indicated that the students, on the whole, tended to be "neutral" with respect to both of these ideas. The authors were particularly concerned about the results, because the sample consisted of students who were considered to be the most capable and interested in science.

During the past two decades a decreasing number of studies have limited themselves to the assessment of students' conceptions (Lederman, 1986a, 1986b; Lederman & O'Malley, 1990) at the secondary level and at the university level (Cotham & Smith, 1981; Gilbert, 1991), with no attempt to identify or test causal factors. However, a few notable studies are described here to illustrate the consistency of findings across the decades of research on students' understandings. Most recently, Kang, Scharmann, and Noh (2004) examined the views of 6th-, 8th-, and 10th-grade students in South Korea. With the use of a multiple-choice test, the views of 1702 students were assessed. Consistent with prior research, the South Korean students were found to have an empiricist/absolutist view of science. Zeidler, Walker, Ackett, and

Simmons (2002) investigated the relationships between students' conceptions of NOS and their reactions to evidence that challenged their beliefs about socioscientific issues. A total of 82 students from 9th- and 10th-grade general-science classes, 11th- and 12th-grade honors biology, physics classes and college-level preservice teachers comprised the sample. Although the authors did not clarify how many of the students in the sample adhered to the array of beliefs presented, it was clear that a significant number of students did not understand scientific knowledge to be tentative and partially subjective, and involve creativity. Although their primary purpose was to investigate relationships between NOS and students' handling of socioscientific issues, the understandings of NOS found are consistent with prior research. Overall, there were no clear differences in the understandings of students with respect to grade level.

In an interesting departure from the usual focus of assessments of students' views, Sutherland and Dennick (2002) investigated conceptions of NOS in students with clearly different worldviews. Historically, research on NOS has failed to consider the influence that world views may have on students' conceptions. The sample consisted of 72 7th-grade Cree students and 36 7th-grade Euro-Canadian students. Although all assessments were done in English, a significant portion of the Cree students spoke English as well as Cree at home. Data were collected with both quantitative (Nature of Scientific Knowledge Scale) and qualitative (interviews) techniques. Although the two groups differed on various aspects of NOS, both groups held views that are considered less than adequate with respect to the following aspects of NOS: tentativeness, creativity, parsimony, unified nature of knowledge, importance of empirical testing, and amoral nature of scientific knowledge. They also found that both language and culture affected students' views, in addition to those factors that affect western students' views. Certainly, the potential influence of worldviews, culture, and language may have on understandings of NOS is important in and of itself and is an area of much-needed research. However, the critical point here is that the findings in this study corroborate what has been found throughout the history of studies that simply aim to assess students' conceptions.

Obviously, all studies cannot be reviewed here, but doing so would simply confirm what the cited assessments of students' conceptions have indicated. As will be seen later, studies that have attempted to change students' views also document students' "starting points" as consistent with what has just been described.

Research on students' conceptions of science was a natural extension of the agreement among educators and scientists that promoting accurate students' understandings of NOS should be a primary objective of science education. The overwhelming conclusion that students did not possess adequate conceptions of the nature of science or scientific reasoning is considered particularly significant when one realizes that a wide variety of assessment instruments were used throughout the aforementioned research. Although evidence does exist that casts some doubt on the validity and reliability of some of the instruments used (Hukins, 1963), it is significant that all investigations yielded the same findings. A detailed analysis of these assessment instruments is included in a subsequent section of this review.

RESEARCH ON TEACHERS' CONCEPTIONS

In general, researchers turned their attention to teaching the nature of science (which will be discussed in a later section) and teachers' conceptions as data emerged, indicating that students did not possess what were considered adequate conceptions of NOS. The logic was simple: a teacher must possess an adequate knowledge of what he/she is attempting to communicate to students. Interestingly, however, the first assessment of teachers' conceptions (Anderson, 1950) was conducted prior to any assessment of students' conceptions. Fifty-six Minnesota high school teachers, including 58 biology teachers and 55 chemistry teachers, constituted the sample to be surveyed. Teachers were asked to answer a total of eight questions on scientific method, and it was revealed that both groups of teachers possessed serious misconceptions.

Behnke (1961) used a 50-statement questionnaire to assess the understandings of scientists and science teachers. Using a three-option response format (i.e., favoring, opposing, and neutral), the questionnaire attempted to assess four categories of information: (a) the nature of science, (b) science and society, (c) the scientist and society, and (d) the teaching of science. The teacher sample consisted of 400 biology teachers and 600 physical science teachers. The scientist sample was 300, but there was no differentiation based upon specific discipline. Although a number of differences were found between scientists and science teachers, only the data concerning the nature of science are relevant here. Over 50 percent of the science teachers felt that scientific findings were not tentative. Even more surprising was that 20 percent of the scientists felt the same way.

Miller's (1963) comparison of TOUS scores of secondary biology teachers and secondary students is one of the most often cited studies of teachers' conceptions of NOS. Five student groups consisted of prospective biology students, as well as those who had just completed a course in general biology. The student groups spanned grades 7–12. The 87 11th- and 12th-grade students were of high ability. Sixty-three 10th-grade biology students, 52 9th-grade, 328 8th-grade, and 205 7th-grade students constituted the remaining portion of the student sample. The sample of teachers consisted of 51 biology teachers from 20 Iowa high schools. Overall, a surprising percentage (ranging from 11 percent to 68 percent) of students in grades 9–12 scored higher on the TOUS than 25 percent of the science teachers. Of particular concern was the finding that 68 percent of the high-ability grade 11–12 students scored higher than 25 percent of the teachers. Although the students were considered as a group (and not specifically compared with their own teachers), Miller concluded that many teachers do not understand science as well as their students, much less understand science well enough to teach it effectively.

Replication studies are not common in science education, but Schmidt (1967) attempted to replicate Miller's findings several years later. A disconcerting proportion of students in grades 9 and 11–12 were found to score higher (14 percent and 47 percent, respectively) than 25 percent of the teacher sample. Schmidt concluded that the problem identified by Miller four years earlier still existed. A year later, Carey and Stauss (1968) attempted to determine whether 17 prospective secondary science teachers being prepared at the University of Georgia possessed a philosophy of science that exhibited an understanding of NOS. The Wisconsin Inventory of Science Processes (WISP) was used to assess NOS. In addition to attempting an initial assessment of the conceptions possessed by the preservice teachers, an attempt was made to investigate the effectiveness of a science methods course in improving such conceptions. Pretest scores on the WISP indicated that the science teachers, as a group, did not possess adequate conceptions of the nature of science. Correlations of WISP scores with academic variables such as high school science credits, college science credits, specific science courses taken, grade-point average, and mathematics grades did not yield any significant relationships. Based on WISP posttest scores, it was concluded that a methods course "specifically oriented toward NOS" could significantly improve teachers' viewpoints.

Carey and Stauss (1970a) continued their line of research by now assessing experienced teachers' conceptions of NOS. Once again, they used the WISP exam. The results were consistent with their previous study: (a) teachers of science, in general, did not possess adequate conceptions of NOS; (b) science methods courses produce a significant pre- to posttest improvement of WISP scores; and (c) academic variables such as grade-point average, math credits, specific courses, and years of teaching experience are not significantly related to teachers' conceptions of science. They recommended that courses in the history and philosophy of science be included in teacher preparation programs.

Kimball (1968), using his own Nature of Science Scale (NOSS), compared understandings of NOS of scientists and science teachers. In no case were significant differences found between the groups. Kimball concluded that there is no difference in understandings of NOS held by scientists and by qualified science teachers when their academic backgrounds are similar. At the time, the results of Kimball's research were used to discredit public criticisms of teacher education programs as the cause of science teachers' poor understandings. Although research focused on teachers' conceptions of NOS (with no attempts to change such conceptions) proliferated during the period from 1950 to 1970, there have been several notable, more recent, assessments.

Beginning teachers' and preservice science teachers' views about scientific knowledge were described and compared by Koulaidis and Ogborn (1989). A 16-item, multiple-choice questionnaire was administered to 12 beginning science teachers and 11 preservice science teachers. The questionnaire items focused on scientific method, criteria for demarcation of science and nonscience, change in scientific knowledge, and the status of scientific knowledge. Based on their responses, the subjects were categorized into four predetermined categories of philosophical belief. The high frequency of individuals possessing eclectic views is consistent with previous research, which has indicated that teachers do not generally possess views that are consistently associated with a particular philosophical position. Overall, the authors concluded that although science teachers place value on scientific method, they see the procedures involved as contextually situated. King (1991) investigated beginning teachers' knowledge of the history and philosophy of science. Thirteen beginning students in Stanford's teacher-education program completed a questionnaire on the first day of their introductory course in curriculum and instruction in science. Eleven of the 13 were interviewed at the end of the course and after they had been student teaching for at least one week. Background information from the questionnaires indicated that only 3 of the 13 preservice teachers had taken formal courses in the history or philosophy of science. Additionally, evaluations of the introductory curriculum course (where the nature of science was discussed) indicated that most of the students felt it was more important to learn the nuts and bolts (e.g., lesson planning, evaluation, etc.) of teaching as opposed to the history and philosophy of science. Data from the interviews indicated that although most of the teachers felt that the history and philosophy of science were important, their lack of education in these areas left them lacking with respect to how such topics could be integrated within instruction. The author concluded that the lack of science teachers' background in the history and philosophy of science clearly influences the teaching of science.

Using a case-study approach, Aguirre, Haggerty, and Linder (1990) assessed 74 preservice secondary science teachers' conceptions of NOS, teaching, and learning. Subjects were asked to respond to 11 open-ended questions about science, teaching of science, and learning of science. Qualitative analysis of the responses yielded the following general conclusions. Most individuals believed that science was either a body of knowledge consisting of a collection of observations and explanations or of propositions that have been proved to be correct. Subjects were evenly divided among the "dispenser of knowledge" and "guide/mediator of understanding" conceptions of science teaching. The authors concluded that these preservice teachers (even though they all possessed undergraduate science degrees) did not possess adequate conceptions of the nature of science. The authors further concluded that there could be some connection between teachers' views of NOS and their conceptions of learning and teaching (although observations of actual instruction were not attempted).

Research on teachers' conceptions of NOS is not limited in focus to secondary teachers. Bloom (1989) assessed preservice elementary teachers' understanding of science and how certain contextual variables contribute to this understanding. Using a sample of 80 preservice elementary teachers (86 percent female), enrolled in three methods courses, Bloom administered a questionnaire that contained six questions related to knowledge of science, theories, and evolution. Additionally, a 21-item rating scale pertaining to prior experiences with science, the nature of science, science teaching, and evolution/creationism was administered. A qualitative analysis of questionnaire responses revealed that the preservice teachers believed science is people centered, with its primary purpose being for the benefit of humankind. Much confusion concerning the meaning and role of scientific theories (e.g., theories are related to belief in one's own thoughts apart from empirical observation) was also noted. Of most significance was the finding that beliefs significantly affect preservice teachers' understandings of science. In this particular case, the anthropocentric nature of the subjects' beliefs significantly influenced their conceptualizations of science, the theory of evolution, and how one would teach evolution.

Finally, there have been some attempts to compare understandings of U.S. preservice teachers with those of other nations. Cobern (1989) used Kimball's Nature of Science Scale (NOSS) to compare the understandings of 21 U.S. preservice science teachers with 32 preservice Nigerian teachers. Two significant differences were noted between the groups. Nigerian preservice teachers were more inclined to view science as a way to produce useful technology. This result is consistent with the findings of Ogunniyi (1982) in his study of 53 preservice Nigerian science teachers. This viewpoint is different from that typically desired in the Western hemisphere, which distinguishes theoretical from applied science. However, an applied view regarding science should not be unexpected in a developing nation. (The author expressed an appropriate concern about the future rejection of science in such societies when it eventually fails to deliver solutions to emerging societal problems.) A second difference between the two samples was the Nigerians' view that scientists were nationalistic and secretive about their work.

At its beginning, research on NOS was fairly descriptive and served to establish that neither teachers nor students possessed what were considered adequate understandings of NOS. Although such research makes no attempt to solve the problem, it did establish that a problem existed. Perhaps it is for this reason that virtually all of the research completed in recent years has made at least some attempt to either explain the impact of teachers' conceptions or effect change in students' and teachers' conceptions.

TEACHING AND LEARNING OF NATURE OF SCIENCE (THE EARLY YEARS)

Research on Students

Klopfer (Klopfer & Cooley, 1963) developed the first curriculum designed to improve students' conceptions of NOS. The curriculum was called "History of Science Cases for High Schools" (HOSC). The rationale for the curriculum was that the use of materials derived from the history of science would help to convey important ideas about science and scientists. A sample of 108 geographically representative science classes, including biology, chemistry, and physics (2,808 students), was used to assess the effectiveness of the HOSC curriculum as measured by the TOUS instrument. After a five-month treatment period, students receiving the HOSC curriculum exhibited significantly greater gains on the TOUS than the control groups. This result was consistent across disciplines. In addition, HOSC students showed significant gains on the TOUS subscales (i.e., the scientific enterprise, the scientist, and the methods and aims of science) as well as on the overall test. It was concluded that the HOSC instructional approach was an effective way to improve students' conceptions of NOS. The large sample size used in this investigation gave it much credibility, and it was followed by widespread curriculum development. Jones (1965) successfully "replicated" Klopfer and Cooley's results with a curriculum similar to HOSC and with a traditional physical science course at the college level. Crumb (1965) compared the Physical Science Study Curriculum (PSSC) with traditional high school physics with respect to gains on the TOUS exam. The PSSC program is a laboratory-centered, experimental approach to physics that is designed to emphasize process as opposed to simply science content. Using a sample of 1,275 students from 29 high schools, Crumb found that PSSC students showed greater gains on the TOUS than students exposed to the traditional physics curriculum.

In addition to the aforementioned research, several studies investigated the effectiveness of the 1960s curriculum projects. These curricula were supposedly designed, regardless of specific science discipline, to promote inquiry and process skills. The curricula were laboratory centered, as opposed to the long-lived tradition of lecture/demonstration (Ramsey & Howe, 1969). Yager and Wick (1966) investigated the effects of various curriculum emphases on students' understandings of NOS as measured by the TOUS. Three approaches were used, all of which revolved around the Biological Sciences Curriculum Study (BSCS) Blue Version. The textbook-laboratory approach (TL) utilized only the textbook and accompanying laboratory materials. The multi-referenced laboratory approach (MRL) utilized materials from the TL group as well as additional paperbacks, texts, references, and excerpts from original scientific works. The multi-referenced laboratory and ideas approach (MRLI) resembled the MRL group, but with the added dimension of attention given to the historical development of the major concepts and principles in science. Experiments and their results were always viewed with respect to how they would have been viewed in various historical contexts. For all three groups an attempt was made to control the effect of teacher variation. The results indicated that the MRLI group exhibited the largest gains on the TOUS, with the MRL group placing second, and the TL group showing the smallest gains. Yager and Wick concluded that the MRL was superior to the more common TL approach. Increased emphasis on ideas and their development (MRLI group) was viewed as maximizing the effects of the MRL approach. The similarity of the MRLI approach, with its emphasis on historical development of ideas, to Klopfer and Cooley's (1963) HOSC program is obvious. Gennaro (1964) and Sorensen (1966) also found success with the MRL and MRLI approaches. Thus, it was accepted that a multi-referenced, laboratory-focused approach to the teaching of biology would produce increased student growth in understanding the nature of the scientific enterprise (Ramsey & Howe, 1969).

Aikenhead (1979) developed and field tested a curriculum titled "Science: A Way of Knowing." The primary goals of the curriculum were to have students develop (a) a realistic, nonmythical understanding of the nature, processes, and social aspects of science; (b) a variety of inquiry skills and a realistic feeling of personal competence in the areas of interpreting, responding to, and evaluating their scientific and technological society; and (c) insight into the interaction of science and technology and, in turn, into the interaction of these with other aspects of society. Using the Science Process Inventory (Welch, 1967) and the Test on the Social Aspects of Science (Korth, 1969), grade 11 and grade 12 students were found to make significant pre- to posttest gains on both instruments.

The findings related to the effectiveness of curriculum specifically designed to teach NOS effects were not all positive. Trent (1965) investigated the relative value of the PSSC course and traditional physics (as did Crumb, 1965). A sample consisting of 52 California high schools was used, and the TOUS exam was used to assess students' conceptions of science. Half of the students in the PSSC classes and half of those in traditional courses were not pretested on the TOUS, and the remaining students were. This methodological approach helped to ascertain the influence of any testing effect. No such effort was made in Crumb's (1965) study. At the end of the school year all students were given a posttest. When prior science understanding and student ability were statistically controlled, no differences were found between the students in the traditional and PSSC courses, as measured by the TOUS. Troxel (1968) compared "traditional" chemistry instruction with both CHEM Study and the Chemical Bond Approach (CBA). In theory, CHEM Study and CBA stress inquiry and are laboratory centered, which theoretically should promote better understandings NOS. However, when teacher background in terms of teaching within the discipline, experience in teaching the course, general philosophy, and student background relative to school size were held constant, no significant differences were found in students' conceptions of NOS.

Two other studies using the 1960s curricula were conducted with Israeli high school students. Jungwirth (1970) attempted to investigate the effectiveness of the BSCS Yellow Version, which was first introduced in Israel in 1964. A total of 693 10th-grade students (from 25 schools) comprised the sample. Scores on both the TOUS and the Processes of Science Test (Biological Sciences Curriculum Study [BSCS], 1962) were used to assess students' understandings of scientific knowledge.

Students were given pre- and posttests over the course of one academic year. No significant differences were found between those students studying BSCS biology and those in the comparison group. Thus, Jungwirth concluded, the curriculum was not any more effective with respect to the enhancement of students' conceptions of science. He concluded that pupil achievement in this area could best be enhanced through "redirected teacher effort and emphases." Tamir (1972) compared the relative levels of effectiveness of three curriculum projects with each other as well as with "traditional" instruction. Using the BSCS Yellow Version, CHEM Study, PSSC, and traditional instructional approaches, Tamir assessed changes in students' conceptions of the nature of science on the Science Process Inventory (Welch, 1967). A total of 3,500 students in grades 9–12 were randomly selected from the four types of Israeli high schools (i.e., city academic, cooperation settlement, agricultural, and occupational) so as to allow comparisons among the different school types. The results indicated no significant differences among students studying any of the curriculum projects and those following traditional courses of study. Comparisons among the four school types did not show any differences either. However, comparisons of the relative levels of effectiveness of curriculum projects showed that of the three, BSCS biology had significantly greater effects upon student conceptions of science than either CHEM Study or PSSC.

Durkee (1974) assessed the effectiveness of a special secondary science program, a six-week institute with content similar to that of PSSC. In short, this six-week summer institute was directly aimed at increasing students' scores on the TOUS exam. The sample consisted of 29 high-ability high school students. The students were given pre- and posttests on the TOUS, and the results did not indicate that the specially designed program significantly changed students' conceptions. More recently, Carey, Evans, Honda, Jay, and Unger (1989) assessed the effectiveness of a unit specifically designed to introduce the constructivist view of science on 7th-graders' epistemological views. Their instructional unit was designed to emphasize theory building and reflection on the theory-building process. All classes, in the three-week unit, were taught by the regular teacher, and each lesson was observed by one or two research assistants. Twenty-seven of the students were randomly selected to be interviewed prior to and after being exposed to the instructional unit. Interviews were selected, as opposed to existing instruments, so that assessments of students' understandings would not be limited by the inherent nature of the instrument format/design. The transcripts of the half-hour clinical interviews were qualitatively analyzed blindly with respect to whether the interview was conducted before or after instruction. In general, the pre-instruction interview indicated that most students thought scientists seek to discover facts about nature by making observations and trying things out. However, post-instruction interviews showed many students understood that inquiry is guided by particular ideas and questions and that experiments are tests of ideas. In short, the instructional unit appeared to have been at least partially successful in enabling students to differentiate ideas and experiments.

There was an implicit assumption that clearly guided research that focused solely on the development of curricula and/or instructional materials. It was assumed that student conceptions could be improved if a concerted effort was made in that direction. Certainly, few would deny the logic of this approach. Unfortunately, for the most part, the teacher's interpretation and enactment of the curriculum were ignored. The following statement from two of the earliest investigators of the curriculum development movement (Klopfer & Cooley, 1963, p. 45) did little to establish the importance of the teacher: "The relative effectiveness of the History of Science Cases Instruction Method, in teaching TOUS-type understandings does *not* depend upon whether the teacher rates 'high' or 'low' in his initial understanding." The implication of this statement is clear. That is, a teacher could promote understandings of certain concepts without having an adequate understanding of the same concepts. Fortunately, others, such as Trent (1965), felt that the equivocal findings with respect to the effectiveness of NOS-oriented curricula could only mean that the instructional approach, style, rapport, and personality of the teacher are important variables in effective science teaching. After all, he reasoned, if the same curriculum is effective for one teacher and ineffective for another, and the variable of student ability is controlled, a significant factor must be the teacher.

Research on Teachers

The rather equivocal results concerning the effectiveness of curricula designed to improve students' conceptions of NOS perhaps motivated other researchers to focus their attentions on the teacher as a significant variable, as opposed to the curriculum being used by the teacher. In the 1960s, the distinction between implementation and enactment of a curriculum had not taken hold in the science education community. Yager (1966) selected eight experienced teachers to use the same inquiry-oriented curriculum (BSCS Blue Version). All teachers utilized the same number of days of discussion, laboratories, examinations, and instructional materials. All extraneous variables were held constant, as nearly as possible, with the exception of teacher-student rapport. Students were pre- and posttested on the TOUS exam. An analysis of covariance indicated that differences in students' TOUS scores could not be completely explained by initial differences in mean TOUS scores for each class. It was concluded that there are significant differences in students' abilities to understand NOS when taught by different teachers. Further direct confirmation of the important influence of teachers upon students' conceptions came from Kleinman's (1965) study of teachers' questioning. When one considers the influence of the individual teacher on student learning, there are at least two directions that can be pursued. One would be to study what a teacher does that affects students' understandings of NOS. The other can be a focus on teachers' knowledge. Few would argue against the notion that a teacher must have an understanding of what he/she is expected to teach. Unfortunately, initially the latter was pursued in the research to the exclusion of attention to the former.

Carey and Stauss (1970b) had 35 prospective secondary science teachers and 221 prospective elementary teachers complete the WISP. Scores were correlated with background variables such as high school science courses, college science courses, college grade-point average, and science grade-point average. No relationship was found between either secondary or elementary teachers' conceptions of science, as measured by WISP, and any of the academic background variables. Thus, it was concluded that none of the academic variables investigated could be used to improve science teachers' conceptions of the nature of science. Gruber (1963) surveyed 314 participants of an NSF summer institute designed to improve teachers' understandings of NOS and found little success. During the validation of the NOSS, Kimball (1968) noted that philosophy majors actually scored higher than either science teachers or professional scientists. He intuitively concluded that inclusion of a philosophy of science course as part of the undergraduate science major curriculum might improve the situation. Carey and Stauss (1968) had previously made such a recommendation. Welch and Walberg (1968) did find success in a summer institute designed for 162 physics teachers at four institute sites. The teachers at all four sites showed significant gains on both the TOUS and Science Process Inventory. No documentation of the specific activities at each of the various institutes was available. Thus, it was not possible to establish what goals and activities led to the differential gains in the understanding of the nature of science.

Lavach (1969) attempted to expand on the success that Klopfer and Cooley (1963) had documented with a historical approach. Twenty-six science teachers participated; 11 constituted the experimental group and 15 served as the control group. The experimental group received instruction in selected historical aspects of astronomy, mechanics, chemistry, heat, and electricity. Each three-hour class was divided into two hours of lecture/demonstration, followed by a one-hour laboratory in which an attempt was made to replicate or perform an experiment conducted by the scientist under discussion. The teachers in the control group did not receive lectures or laboratories presented from a historical perspective. All teachers were pre- and posttested on the TOUS. The teachers in the experimental group exhibited statistically significant gains in their understanding of NOS. Further analysis indicated that these gains were not related to overall teaching experience, subjects taught, undergraduate major, previous in-service participation, or length of teaching experience in the same subject.

Six years later Billeh and Hasan (1975) attempted to identify those factors that affect any increase in the understanding of nature of science by science teachers. Their sample consisted of 186 secondary science teachers in Jordan. The teachers were divided into four groups: biology, chemistry, physical science, and physics. A four-week course for the chemistry, physical science, and physics teachers consisted of lectures and demonstrations in methods of teaching science, laboratory investigations emphasizing a guided-discovery approach, enrichment activities to enhance understanding of specific science concepts, and 12 lectures specifically related to the nature of science. The biology group did not receive any formal instruction on the nature of science, thus establishing a reference group with which the other groups could be compared. The Nature of Science Test (NOST) was used to assess understanding of the nature of science. Those lectures that stressed the nature of science were not oriented toward the specific content of the NOST. Each group of teachers were administered pre- and posttests on the NOST, and an analysis of covariance showed significant increases in the mean scores of the chemistry, physical science, and physics groups. The biology group did not show a significant gain, a finding consistent with that of Carey and Stauss (1968). A second result was that there was no significant relationship between teachers' gain scores on NOST and their educational qualifications, a finding in agreement with previous research (Carey & Stauss, 1970a; Lavach, 1969). Additionally, teachers' gain scores were not significantly related to the subjects they taught. Finally, science teaching experience was not significantly related to NOST gain scores. The conclusion that teaching experience does not contribute to a teacher's understanding of NOS was also consistent with previous research (Carey & Stauss, 1970b; Kimball, 1968; Lavach, 1969).

Trembath (1972) assessed the influence of a "small" curriculum project on prospective elementary teachers' views of NOS. The curriculum project focused on participants' understandings of the ways in which hypotheses are developed and tested, the logical structure of theories and laws, and the ways in which theories and laws can be used to make different types of explanations. The program presented prospective teachers with a set of narratives. Each narrative put forth a certain situation and was divided into a set of "frames." Each frame required students to read several paragraphs and provide a short answer in the form of a hypothesis, prediction, or inference. Trembath (1972) seemed to have assumed that participants would develop adequate understandings of the targeted NOS aspects by simply "going through" the program activities. Trembath reported a statistically significant difference between the mean pretest and posttest score for the experimental group, but noted that this score only increased from 7.0 to 10.7 points out of 18 possible points.

Barufaldi, Bethel, and Lamb (1977) argued that "a major affective goal of science teacher education should be the enhancement of the philosophical viewpoint that science is a tentative enterprise and that scientific knowledge is not absolute" (p. 289). The study assessed the influence of elementary science methods courses on junior and senior elementary education majors' understandings of the tentativeness of science. The courses had no components that were specifically geared toward enhancing participants' views of the tentative NOS. Rather, consistent with the authors' view of NOS as an "affective" outcome, an implicit approach was used. Thus, Barufaldi et al. (1977) noted, in these courses: "Students were presented with numerous hands-on, activity-centered, inquiry-oriented science experiences . . . [and] . . . many problem-centered science activities . . . The uniqueness and the variety of the learning experiences in the courses provided the students with many opportunities to understand the tentativeness of scientific findings" (p. 291).

Barufaldi et al. (1977) thus concluded that a methods course that "stresses inquiry methods and procedures, emphasizing a hands-on approach integrated with individual problem solving, develops, alters, and enhances . . . preservice teachers' . . . philosophical view . . . toward the tentative nature of scientific knowledge" (p. 293). The authors, however, did not present enough evidence to support this rather sweeping generalization. Barufaldi et al. (1977) did not report the pretest mean VOST scores or the mean gain scores for the various groups. However, if we assume that the groups did not differ appreciably on their pretest VOST scores and that the control group mean score did not change appreciably from the pretest to the posttest, then the gains achieved can be assessed. The mean posttest VOST score for the control group was 141. The corresponding scores for the three treatment groups were 153, 149, and 148. As such, the approximate gains achieved were very small and ranged between 3.5 and 6 percentage points. It is difficult to conclude that the reported gains reflect a meaningful improvement in participants' understanding of the tentative nature of scientific knowledge.

Spears and Zollman (1977) assessed the influence of engagement in scientific inquiry on students' understandings of the process of science. Participants were randomly assigned to the four lecture sections and associated laboratory sections of a physics course. Data from only about 50 percent of the original sample were used in the final analysis. The authors, however, did not provide any data to indicate that the remaining participants were representative of the original population. Two types of laboratory instructional strategies served as the treatments. The "structured" approach emphasized verification, whereas the "unstructured" approach stressed inquiry or discovery. Both approaches asked students to investigate problems related to physical principles discussed in the lectures and informed them about the available equipment. Beyond this point the two approaches differed in a major way. In the "structured" laboratory, students were provided with explicit procedures with which they attempted to verify the physical principles concerned. Students in the "unstructured" laboratory, however, were free to investigate the problem in whatever way they deemed appropriate. They made their own decisions regarding what data to collect, how to collect these data, how to treat the data, and how to interpret and present their results.

Data analyses controlled for participants' major, years in college, and course lecture and laboratory grades, as well as the type of lecture presentation in each of the four sections. These analyses indicated that there were no statistically significant differences between the adjusted scores of the two groups on the Assumptions, Nature of Outcomes, and Ethics and Goals components of the SPI Form D (Welch & Pella, 1967–68).

Riley (1979) argued that teachers' understandings of and attitudes toward science would improve as a result of first-hand, manipulative experiences and enhanced proficiency in the processes of science. Riley, like Barufaldi et al. (1977), explicitly labeled an understanding of NOS as an "affective" outcome and attempted to teach about NOS by involving teachers in "doing science." The study investigated the influence of hands-on versus non-manipulative training in science process skills on, among other things, preservice elementary teachers' understandings of NOS. The study had a 3×3 factorial design, with the treatment and science grade point average as independent variables. The treatment had three levels: active-inquiry (hands-on), vicarious-inquiry (non-manipulative), and control. Participants were divided into three groups according to their grade-point average (high, medium, or low), and 30 students from each group were randomly selected and assigned to one of the three treatment levels. The four 1.5-hour-session treatment involved activities that focused on various science process skills, such as observing, classifying, inferring, predicting, communicating, measuring and the metric system, and using space/time relationships. The only difference between the aforementioned levels of treatment was student involvement. In the active-inquiry treatment, participants were trained in science process skills by a hands-on, manipulative approach. Participants in the vicarious-inquiry treatment group did not manipulate any materials. They were trained in science process skills by a demonstration approach where the instructor exclusively manipulated all materials. The control-group participants viewed science-related films for approximately the same amount of time. Data analyses indicated that there were no significant differences between the groups mean TOUS (Cooley & Klopfer, 1961) scores related to the treatments. As such, participants in the active-inquiry, vicarious inquiry, and control groups did not differ in their understandings of NOS.

Haukoos and Penick (1983) investigated the effects of classroom climate on community college students' learning of science process skills and content achievement. The authors replicated their study two years later (Haukoos & Penick, 1985). They argued that gains in the development of students' inquiry skills and science process skills might be related to aspects of the classroom environment, such as the extent to which instruction is directive or non-directive. Implicit in this argument is the assumption that students learn about NOS implicitly through certain aspects related to the classroom environment. The studies featured two treatments: A Discovery Classroom Climate (DCC) treatment and a Non-discovery Classroom Climate (NDCC) treatment. In both studies, participants were enrolled in intact sections of an introductory biology course. Throughout the duration of the course, students in both groups received instruction on the same content. The only difference between the two treatments was the classroom climate that was determined by the extent to which the instructor used direct or indirect verbal behaviors. In the lecture/discussion sessions, students in the NDCC were presented with the content in a manner "that conveyed the impression that science was complete and final, and seldom did the students question it" (Haukoos & Penick, 1983, p. 631). With the DCC group, the instructor assumed a low profile, elicited student questions, and encouraged discussion of the lecture material. All student responses and interpretations were accepted and were not judged as right or wrong. In the laboratory portion of the course, students carried out the same experiments with the same materials. However, during laboratory sessions, students in the NDCC group were told exactly how to manipulate materials. Their results were either accepted or rejected by the instructor. Students in the DCC laboratory were alternatively encouraged to select and explore their own questions and to manipulate the available materials in whatever ways they deemed fit for answering their questions. The instructor kept explicit directions and judgments to a minimum. In this regard, the two laboratory environments were similar to the "structured" and "unstructured" or traditional and inquiry-based treatments that were employed by Spears and Zollman (1977). Data analyses in the first study (Haukoos & Penick, 1983) indicated that the DCC group had a significantly higher mean SPI score than the NDCC group. The reported difference was about eight percentage points. The authors concluded that the classroom climate influenced students' learning of science processes. However, Haukoos and Penick (1985) were not able to replicate these results. Analyses in the second study revealed no statistically significant differences, at any acceptable level, between the DCC and NDCC groups.

Akindehin (1988) argued that attempts to help science teachers develop adequate conceptions of NOS need to be *explicit*. The author assessed the influence of an instructional package, the *Introductory Science Teacher Education* (ISTE) package, on prospective secondary science teachers' conceptions of NOS. The package comprised nine units that included lectures, discussions, and laboratory sessions.

A statistically significant result was obtained for the experimental group. Out of 58 possible points on the NOSS, the grand mean score was 51.84. This mean score, it should be noted, was the highest reported NOSS score among the studies reviewed here. It should be noted, however, that the author did not report the mean pretest and posttest scores. As such, it was difficult to assess the practical significance of the gains achieved by the student teachers.

Scharmann (1990) aimed to assess the effects of a diversified instructional strategy (versus a traditional lecture approach) on freshmen college students' understandings of the nature of scientific theories, among other things. Participants were first given 30 minutes to individually respond in writing to four questions that asked about their feelings and beliefs concerning the evolution/creation controversy. Next, students were randomly assigned to discussion groups of three to five students. They were asked to share their responses to the above questions and then respond to four new questions. These latter questions asked each group to provide reasons that would support teaching only evolution, teaching creation origins in addition to evolution, and teaching neither evolution nor creation origins in science classes. Students were also asked to decide whether, and explain why, one set of reasons was more compelling than another set. Ninety minutes were allocated for this phase of the treatment, during which the author did not interfere in the course of the discussions. For the next 30 minutes, spokespersons shared their groups' concerns, differences, and points of agreement with the whole class. Following a break, the author led a 90-minute interactive lecture/discussion that was intended to resolve any misconceptions that arose as a result of the group discussions and were evident in their presentations. Finally, during the last 30 minutes participants were given the opportunity to reflect on the discussion activity. Scharmann (1990) reported a significant difference between the pretest and posttest scores for both the experimental and control groups. Students in both groups achieved statistically significant gains in their understandings of NOS. Scharmann concluded that both classes provided students with opportunities to grow in their understandings of NOS, but that the diversified instructional strategy was superior in this respect. The author, however, did not provide any evidence to support this claim.

Scharmann and Harris (1992) assessed the influence of a three-week NSF-sponsored summer institute on, among other things, participants' understandings of NOS. The authors noted that "changes in an understanding of the nature of science can be . . . enhanced through a more indirect and applied context . . . and through a variety of readings and activities" that help participants to discuss their NOS views (p. 379). The NOSS (Kimball, 1967–68) was used to assess participants' understandings of the "philosophical" NOS, and an instrument developed by Johnson and Peeples (1987) was used to assess participants' "applied" understandings of NOS. The authors did not elucidate the distinction between "philosophical" and "applied" understandings of NOS. During the first two weeks of the institute, participants were presented with biological and geological content relevant to evolutionary theory. In addition, various instructional methods and teaching approaches, including lectures, small-group and peer discussions, field trips, and other inquiry-based approaches, were taught and modeled by the authors. The authors noted that the "theme" of promoting participants' conceptions of NOS pervaded all the aforementioned activities. However, no direct or explicit NOS instruction was used. Data analyses did not reveal significant differences between pretest and posttest mean NOSS scores. However, statistically significant differences were obtained in the case of the Johnson and Peeples (1987) instrument. The authors thus concluded that even though participants' conceptions of the "philosophical" NOS were not changed, their understandings of the "applied" NOS were significantly improved. Scharmann and Harris (1992), however, did not comment on the practical significance of the gain achieved by the participants. Out of 100 possible points for the latter instrument, the pretest and posttest mean scores were 61.74 and 63.26, respectively.

Shapiro (1996) reported on the changes in one prospective elementary teacher's thinking about the nature of investigation in science during her involvement in designing a study to answer a simple research question. This case study emerged from a larger research project that investigated the ways in which elementary student teachers' thinking and feelings about the nature of investigation in science could be studied. The project was also intended to assess the changes in elementary student teachers' thinking and feelings about the nature of scientific investigation as a result of their involvement in independent investigations.

More than 210 elementary student teachers in four cohorts were involved in the study. During their science methods class, each cohort of student teachers worked on an assignment intended to help them develop an in-depth understanding of science and scientific procedures of investigation. Over the course of about seven weeks devoted to the assignment, student teachers were asked to pose a simple genuine problem, generate a research question, and then design a systematic procedure to answer their question. Throughout the assignment, student teachers kept journals of the various stages of their investigations. Twenty-one (out of the 38) fourth-cohort participants completed a repertory grid at the beginning of the science methods class and again after the conclusion of the investigation. Participants were interviewed following the second administration of the grid. The interviews focused on the changes that students made in their grids.

The repertory grid had two dimensions. The first comprised personal constructs and the second elements related to conducting scientific investigations. Ratings were given along a five-point scale between the opposite poles of each construct. Changes in student teachers' thinking about the nature of scientific investigations were assessed by comparing the grids completed prior to and after the independent investigations were conducted.

Shapiro (1996) only reported in detail on three "themes of change" that were evident in the case of one prospective elementary teacher. The first change theme was related to ideas about the nature of the steps and procedures of investigation in science. The teacher indicated that she often thought of doing science as being synonymous with following rules and checklists. After participating in the investigation, she came to appreciate the role of original thinking and imagination in devising ways to come up with answers to a research question. The second change theme was in the teacher's thinking about what science is. At the beginning of the methods class, Jan indicated that science is a body of information that has been tested and retested so that it now achieved the status of facts. After the completion of the investigation, the teacher came to view science more as a process of inquiry and less as a mere collection of facts. She also indicated that her experience helped her to appreciate the complexity of inquiring into everyday occurrences and the difficulty of drawing conclusions from the generated data. Finally, in the third identified change theme, there was a shift from an objectivist view of science to one that emphasized the role of researchers in creating new knowledge. Perhaps the most important features of the present study were its emphasis on reflection and its explicitness. Shapiro noted that students were often encouraged to reflect on their experiences. Moreover, the author emphasized the reflective nature of the interviews that allowed student teachers to have insights into changes in their thinking about science.

Looking at research investigations that attempted to change teachers' conceptions from an alternative perspective can be enlightening. Overall, these studies took one of two approaches. The first approach was advocated by science educators such as Gabel, Rubba, and Franz (1977), Haukoos and Penick (1983, 1985), Lawson (1982), and Rowe (1974). This approach is labeled the "implicit approach" for this review, as it suggests that an understanding of NOS is a learning outcome that can be facilitated through process skill instruction, science content coursework, and "doing science." Researchers who adopted this implicit approach utilized science process skills instruction and/or scientific inquiry activities (Barufaldi et al., 1977; Riley, 1979; Trembath, 1972) or manipulated certain aspects of the learning environment (Haukoos & Penick, 1983, 1985; Scharmann, 1990; Scharmann & Harris, 1992; Spears & Zollman, 1977) in their attempts to enhance teachers' NOS conceptions. Researchers who adopted the second approach to enhancing teachers' understandings of NOS (Akindehin, 1988; Billeh & Hasan, 1975; Carey & Stauss, 1968, 1970; Jones, 1969; Lavach, 1969; Ogunniyi, 1983) utilized elements from history and philosophy of science and/or instruction focused on various aspects of NOS to improve science teachers' conceptions. This second approach is labeled the "explicit approach" for this review and was advanced by educators such as Billeh and Hasan (1975), Hodson (1985), Kimball (1967–68), Klopfer (1964), Lavach (1969), Robinson (1965), and Rutherford (1964).

TEACHING AND LEARNING OF NATURE OF SCIENCE (CONTEMPORARY YEARS— A SHIFT IN PERSPECTIVE)

During the past 15 years, research on the teaching and learning of NOS has experienced a gradual but drastic change in perspective. This change in perspective has influenced how we attempt to change the conceptions of both teachers and students.

Research on Teachers

The results of the initial research on NOS (which are supported by more recent investigations) may be summarized as follows: (a) science teachers do not possess adequate conceptions of NOS, irrespective of the instrument used to assess understandings; (b) techniques to improve teachers' conceptions have met with some success when they have included either historical aspects of scientific knowledge or direct, explicit attention to nature of science; and (c) academic background variables are not significantly related to teachers' conceptions of nature of science. Two underlying assumptions appear to have permeated the research reviewed thus far. The first assumption has been that a teacher's understanding of NOS affects his/her students' conceptions. This assumption is clear in all the research that focused on improvement of teachers' conceptions with no expressed need or attempt to do anything further. This rather intuitive assumption remained virtually untested, with the exception of two studies that only referred to the assumption in an ancillary manner. Unfortunately, both of these research efforts (Klopfer & Cooley, 1963; Rothman, 1969) contained significant methodological flaws. Klopfer and Cooley (1963) failed to properly monitor teachers' conceptions of NOS throughout the investigation, whereas Rothman (1969) created a ceiling effect by sampling only high-ability students.

The second assumption underlying the research reviewed thus far is closely related to the first. If it is assumed that teachers' conceptions of science affect students' conceptions, some method of influence must exist; naturally the influence must be mediated by teacher behaviors and classroom ecology. In short, initial research concerned with teachers' and students' conceptions of NOS assumed that a teacher's behavior and the classroom environment are necessarily and directly influenced by the teacher's conception of NOS. Although this assumption was explicitly stated by many, including Hurd (1969) and Robinson (1969), it remained an untested assumption into the early 1980s.

As can be seen from the research reviewed thus far, several decades of research on NOS focused on student and teacher characteristics or curriculum development to the exclusion of any direct focus on actual classroom practice and/or teacher behaviors. Although research designed to assess students' and teachers' conceptions continues to the present day, there is clearly less willingness to accept the assumptions that guided earlier research, and the focus is moving toward the realities of daily classroom practice.

The presumed relationships between teachers' conceptions of science and those of their students as well as that between teachers' conceptions and instructional behaviors were finally directly tested and demonstrated to be too simplistic, relative to the realities of the classroom, as a result of a series of investigations (Brickhouse, 1989, 1990; Duschl & Wright, 1989; Lederman, 1986a; Lederman & Druger, 1985; Lederman & Zeidler, 1987; Zeidler & Lederman, 1989). Using a case-study approach, Brickhouse investigated three secondary science teachers' views on the relationship between science and technology, the influence of such views on classroom practice (1989), and the relationship between the same teachers' conceptions of NOS and classroom practice (1990). Two of the three teachers (who were also the experienced teachers) exhibited classroom practices that were consistent with their personal views and philosophy, whereas the beginning teacher's classroom practices were not congruent with his beliefs. Duschl and Wright (1989) observed and interviewed 13 science teachers in a large urban high school. Their results convincingly indicated that the nature and role of scientific theories are not integral components in the constellation of influences affecting teachers' educational decisions. NOS was not being considered or taught to students as a consequence of perceived students' needs, curriculum guide objectives, and accountability.

Lederman and Zeidler's investigation (1987) involved a sample of 18 high school biology teachers from nine schools. The data clearly indicated that there was no significant relationship between teachers' understandings of NOS and classroom practice. Several variables have been shown to mediate and constrain the translation of teachers' NOS conceptions into practice. These variables include pressure to cover content (Abd-El-Khalick, Bell, & Lederman, 1998; Duschl & Wright, 1989; Hodson, 1993), classroom management and organizational principles (Hodson, 1993; Lantz & Kass, 1987; Lederman, 1995), concerns for student abilities and motivation (Abd-El-Khalick et al., 1998; Brickhouse & Bodner, 1992; Duschl & Wright, 1989; Lederman, 1995), institutional constraints (Brickhouse & Bodner, 1992), teaching experience (Brickhouse & Bodner, 1992; Lederman, 1995), discomfort with understandings of NOS, and the lack of resources and experiences for assessing understandings of NOS (Abd-El-Khalick et al., 1998).

Recently, Lederman (1999) attempted to finally put to rest (old habits die hard) the assumption that teachers' conceptions of NOS directly influenced classroom practice. In a multiple case study involving five high school biology teachers with varying experience, Lederman collected data on teachers' conceptions of NOS and classroom practice. All teachers were former students of the author and all possessed informed understandings of NOS. Over the course of a full academic year, data were collected from questionnaires, structured and unstructured interviews, classroom observations, and instructional materials. Data were also collected on students' conceptions of NOS through questionnaires and interviews. The author was unable to find any clear relationship between teachers' conceptions and classroom practice. The two most experienced teachers (14 and 15 years of experience) did exhibit behaviors that seemed consistent with their views of NOS, but interview and lesson plan data revealed that these teachers were not attempting to teach NOS. Data from students in all teachers' classes indicated that none of the students had developed informed understandings of NOS. The results of the investigation indicated that, although the teachers possessed good understandings of NOS, classroom practice was not directly affected. Furthermore, the importance of teachers' intentions relative to students' understandings was highlighted. Even in the classrooms that exhibited some similarity with teachers' understandings, students did not learn NOS, because the teachers did not explicitly intend to teach NOS. Overall, the research was consistent with emerging findings about the relationship between teachers' understandings and classroom practice, as well as the research indicating the importance of explicit instructional attention to NOS. Although it is now clear that teachers' conceptions do not generally translate into classroom practice, concern about teachers' conceptions persists. As was previously mentioned, the past 15 years have been marked by a slow but definite shift in perspective related to how we go about changing teachers' conceptions of NOS. In short, there has been a shift to more explicit instructional approaches in research related to teachers' conceptions of NOS.

Hammrich (1997) used a conceptual change approach to influencing teacher candidates' conceptions of NOS. Students were asked to confront their own beliefs and the beliefs of classmates in cooperative group discussions. The rationale for the approach was that differences of opinions about NOS are inevitable among preservice teachers, and these individuals need opportunities to reflect on what they actually believe and/or know. Although the author claimed her approach to be successful, no documentation of specific understandings was provided, nor was the number of individuals involved mentioned. In addition, Hammrich was more interested in promoting change in students' views rather than having them change toward any particular views. Consequently, it is possible (although no data were provided) that some changes were in directions different from what reform documents have advocated.

In another study of preservice teachers' conceptions of NOS, Bell, Lederman, and Abd-El-Khalick (2000) looked at teachers' translation of knowledge into instructional planning and classroom practice. The subjects were 13 preservice teachers. The teachers' views of NOS were assessed with an open-ended questionnaire before and after student teaching. Throughout the student teaching experience, daily lesson plans, classroom videotapes, portfolios, and supervisors' clinical observation notes were analyzed for explicit instances of NOS in either planning or instruction. Following student teaching, all subjects were interviewed about their questionnaire responses and factors that influenced their teaching of NOS. Although all of the preservice teachers exhibited adequate understandings of NOS, they did not consistently integrate NOS into instruction in an explicit manner. NOS was not evident in these teachers' objectives, nor was any attempt made to assess students' understandings of NOS. The authors concluded that possessing an understanding of NOS is not automatically translated into a teacher's classroom practice. They further concluded that NOS must be planned for and included in instructional objectives, like any other subject matter content.

Akerson, Abd-El-Khalick, and Lederman (2000) were concerned solely with developing elementary teachers' understandings of NOS and not with the translation of this knowledge into classroom practice. The subjects were 25 undergraduate and 25 graduate preservice elementary teachers enrolled in two separate methods courses. Before and after the courses teachers' views about the empirical, tentative, subjective, creative, and social/cultural embeddedness of scientific knowledge were assessed. In addition, the preservice teachers' views on the distinction between observation/inference and between theories and laws were assessed. The courses explicitly addressed these aspects of NOS with a reflective, activity-based approach. The results indicated that explicit attention to NOS was an effective way to improve teachers' understandings of NOS. However, taken in the context of studies such as the previous one (Bell, Lederman, & Abd-El-Khalick, 2000), the authors were quick to point out that mere possession of adequate understandings will not automatically change classroom practice.

Abell, Martini, and George (2001) monitored the views of 11 elementary education majors during a science methods course. The particular context was a Moon investigation in which the authors targeted the following aspects of NOS: empirically based, involves invention and explanations, and is socially embedded. Students were asked to observe the Moon each night during the course and record their observations. An attempt was made by the instructors to be explicit as possible with respect to NOS. After the investigation, students realized that scientists make observations and generate patterns, but they did not realize that observations could precede or follow the development of a theory. Students were able to distinguish the processes of observing from creating explanations, but they could not discuss the role of invention in science. In various other instances, students were capable of articulating aspects of NOS, but were unable to see the connection between what they learned in the activity and the scientific community. The authors recognized the importance of being explicit in the teaching of NOS. They also recognized that their students' failure to apply what they learned beyond the learning activities themselves, to the scientific community in general, was a consequence of not making an explicit connection between what scientists do and the activities completed in class.

Abd-El-Khalick (2001) used an explicit, reflective approach to teach about NOS in a physics course designed for prospective elementary teachers at the American University of Beirut. Data were collected through pre- and posttests on open-ended surveys about NOS. The author reported significant improvement in the aspects of NOS providing focus for the investigation: tentative, empirically based, theory-laden, inferential, imaginative, and creative characteristics of scientific knowledge. In addition, the relationship between theory and law, and the distinction between observation and inference were investigated. The author definitely concluded that the explicit, reflective approach to instruction was successful. However, the conclusions were tempered by the author's concern that understandings of NOS are more easily applied to familiar contexts than to unfamiliar contexts within science.

The use of the history of science has long been advocated as a means to improve students' conceptions of science. Lin and Chen (2002) extended this logic to a program designed to improve preservice teachers' understanding of NOS. Sixty-three prospective chemistry teachers in Taiwan were divided into experimental and control groups. The teachers in the experimental group were exposed to a series of historical cases followed by debates and discussions that highlighted how scientists developed knowledge. The historical cases were promoted as a way for these prospective teachers to teach science. Different from previous attempts to use the history of science to achieve outcomes related to NOS, the historical materials explicitly addressed NOS. The results clearly showed significant improvement in understandings of NOS by the experimental group relative to the control group. In particular, teachers in the experimental group showed significant improvement of their knowledge of creativity in science, the theory-bound nature of observations, and the functions of scientific theories. The authors claimed that helping teachers learn how to use the history of science in science instruction positively influenced the teachers' understandings of NOS.

Schwartz and Lederman (2002) looked at the improvement of two beginning teachers' understandings of the nature of science as well as their integration of such understandings into classroom practice. Two teachers were studied during their student teaching experience and throughout their first year of full-time teaching. These two teachers were part of a larger cohort, but the authors chose to focus more closely on these two teachers because of the differences in their subject matter knowledge. The results showed that the depth of NOS understanding, subject matter knowledge, and the perceived relationship between NOS and science subject matter affected the teachers' learning and teaching of NOS. The teacher with more extensive subject matter background, who also held a more well-developed understanding of NOS, was better able to address NOS throughout his teaching. This teacher's extensive subject matter background enabled him to address NOS throughout his teaching regardless of science topic. The teacher with less extensive subject matter knowledge was limited with respect to where she could integrate NOS. In addition, this teacher seemed more wedded to the examples of NOS integration provided in her preservice education program. This investigation illustrated for the first time that knowledge of subject matter was a mediating factor in the successful teaching of NOS. Prior to this study correlational studies on the relationship between NOS and subject matter knowledge showed little relationship. Of course, the relationship investigated here was with respect to the teaching of NOS.

Abd-El-Khalick and Akerson (2004) studied 28 preservice elementary teachers in a science methods course. In particular, they investigated the effectiveness of an explicit, reflective instructional approach related to NOS on these prospective teachers' views of various aspects of NOS. Data were collected from a combination of questionnaires, interviews, and reflection papers. As expected, participants initially held naïve views of NOS; however, over the course of the investigation substantial and favorable changes in the preservice teachers' views were evident.

Using a combination of authentic research experiences, seminars, and reflective journals, Schwartz, Lederman, and Crawford (2004) studied changes in secondary preservice teachers' conceptions of NOS. Prior research had indicated that providing teachers with authentic research experiences did not affect understandings of NOS. Consequently, the researchers supported such research experiences with explicit attention to NOS through seminars and a series of reflective journal assignments. The participants were 13 master of arts in teaching (MAT) students. Data were collected via questionnaires and interviews. Most of the interns showed substantial changes in their views of NOS. Participants identified the reflective journal writing and seminars as having the greatest impact on their views, with the actual research internship just providing a context for reflection.

Abd-El-Khalick (2005) considered the perennial recommendation that teachers' should take courses in philosophy of science if we want to affect that knowledge of NOS. The sample was 56 undergraduate and graduate preservice secondary science teachers enrolled in a two-course sequence of science methods. Participants received explicit, reflective NOS instruction. Ten of the participants were also enrolled in a graduate philosophy of science course. The Views of Nature of Science—Form C (VNOS-C) was used to assess understandings of NOS at the beginning and end of the investigation. Participants were also interviewed about their written responses. Other data sources included lesson plans and NOS-specific reflection papers. Results indicated that the students who were enrolled in the philosophy of science course developed more in-depth understandings of NOS than those just enrolled in the science methods course. The author did not take the position that the philosophy of science course was more effective than the methods course for teaching NOS. Rather, the methods course, with explicit instruction about NOS, was seen as providing a framework that the 10 students enrolled in the philosophy of science course could use to significantly benefit from the philosophy course. In short, the methods course provided a lens with which learning of NOS could be maximized. Most recently, Scharmann, Smith, James, and Jensen (2005) used an explicit, reflective approach to teaching NOS within the context of a secondary teaching methods course. Nineteen preservice teachers were the subjects. Overall, the authors decided that the instructional approach was successful and supported the emerging literature on the value of an explicit approach to teaching NOS.

In addition to the typical studies investigating ways to change and improve teachers' conceptions of NOS, there is a slowly emerging attention to the rationales that have been used to justify the importance of teaching NOS to K–12 students. One justification for teaching NOS has been that an understanding of NOS will contribute to informed decisions on scientifically based societal and personal issues. Bell and Lederman (2003) tested this assumption, using a group of 21 highly educated individuals. These individuals were faculty members from various universities. Some were scientists and some were from areas outside of science. Individuals completed an open-ended questionnaire, followed by an interview, designed to assess decision-making on science and technology-related issues. A second questionnaire was used to assess participants' understandings of NOS, and an interview followed the completion of the questionnaire. Participants were separated into two groups based on the adequacy of their understanding of NOS. The two groups' decisions, decision-influencing factors, and decision-making strategies were compared. No differences were found between the two groups. Both groups used personal values, morals/ethics, and social concerns when making decisions, but NOS was not used. The authors concluded that decision-making is complex, and the data did not support the assumption that an understanding of NOS would contribute prominently to one's decisions. The authors also speculated that NOS may not have been considered because individuals need to have instruction on how NOS understandings could be used in aiding the decision-making process.

Research on Students

It is safe to assume that teachers cannot possibly teach what they do not understand (Ball & McDiarmid, 1990; Shulman, 1987). Research on the translation of teachers' conceptions into classroom practice, however, indicates that even though teachers' conceptions of NOS can be thought of as a *necessary* condition, these conceptions, nevertheless, should not be considered *sufficient* (Lederman, 1992). At least one implication for research related to NOS is apparent. Research efforts, it is argued, should "extend well beyond teachers' understandings of nature of science, as the translation of these understandings into classroom practice is mediated by a complex set of situational variables" (Lederman, 1992, p. 351). Clearly, complex issues surround the possible influence of teachers' understandings of NOS on classroom practice and have yet to be resolved. It is safe to say, however, that there is general agreement among researchers concerning the strong influence of curriculum constraints, administrative policies, and teaching context on the translation of teachers' conceptions into classroom practice. Although there is a clear pattern in the research that compares teachers' conceptions with classroom practice, it is not uncommon to find a small minority of studies that continue to claim a direct relationship between teachers' conceptions and classroom practice (e.g., Kang & Wallace, 2005). In addition to investigations that assessed the relationship between teachers' conceptions and classroom practice, efforts to identify those factors that do influence students' conceptions have also been pursued.

In a comprehensive study of 18 high school biology teachers (Lederman, 1986a; Lederman & Druger, 1985), a set of 44 teacher behaviors and/or classroom climate variables was identified as being related to specific changes in students' understandings of NOS, as measured by the Nature of Scientific Knowledge Scale (Rubba & Andersen, 1978). In general, the classes of the most effective teachers were typified by frequent inquiry-oriented questioning, active participation by students in problem-solving activities, frequent teacher-student interactions, infrequent use of independent seat work, and little emphasis on rote memory/recall. With respect to classroom climate, classes of the more effective teachers were more supportive, pleasant, and "risk free," with students expected to think analytically about the subject matter presented. Although this investigation was correlational, the findings were supported by an experimental study conducted in junior college biology classes (Haukoos & Penick, 1983). A quasi-experimental design was used with two different instructional approaches (discovery-oriented and non-discovery-oriented) in general biology classes. Students in the discovery-oriented classes were found to make significant gains in the understanding of NOS as measured by the Science Process Inventory. The important point here is that the description of the discovery-oriented classes is consistent with the teaching approaches and classroom climate documented as "effective" in Lederman's correlational studies (Lederman, 1986a; Lederman & Druger, 1985). The significance of teacher-student interactions to conceptual changes in students' views of science motivated a follow-up study with 18 high school biology teachers and 409 students (Zeidler & Lederman, 1989). In this investigation, specific attention was focused on the nature of teacher-student interactions and the specific language used. In general, when teachers used "ordinary language" without qualification (e.g., discussing the structure of an atom without stressing that it is a model), students tended to adopt a realist conception of science.

Alternatively, when teachers were careful to use precise language with appropriate qualifications, students tended to adopt an instrumentalist conception. At the time, this investigation provided clear empirical support for Munby's thesis (1976) that implicit messages embedded in teachers' language provide for varied conceptions of NOS. Indeed, although the recent literature (past 10 years) predominantly indicates otherwise, some investigators (Craven, Hand, & Prain, 2002) still cling to the value of using implicit instruction for the teaching of NOS.

Inclusion of the history of science has often been touted as being a way to improve students' understandings of NOS. The value of history of science, however, has been held mostly as an intuitive assumption as opposed to being an idea having empirical support. Abd-El-Khalick and Lederman (2000b) assessed the influence of three history of science courses on college students' and preservice teachers' conceptions of NOS. The subjects were 166 undergraduate and graduate students and 15 preservice secondary science teachers at Oregon State University. All subjects were pre- and posttested with an open-ended questionnaire. A representative sample of students was also interviewed in an effort to establish face validity for the questionnaires. The results showed that most individuals entered the history of science courses with inadequate views of NOS, and there was little change after they completed the course. When change was noted, it was typically with respect to some explicit attention to NOS in one of the courses. In addition, there was some evidence that the preservice teachers learned more about NOS from the history of science courses than the other students. This was attributed to the possible benefits of having entered the course with a perceptual framework for NOS provided in their science methods course.

The use of "hands-on" activities has often been recommended as a way to improve students' understandings of NOS. Moss (2001) studied five volunteers from a class of 20 students. The volunteers were 11th- and 12th-grade students in a projects-based Conservation Biology class. Using a participant-observation approach, the author observed students, interviewed them six times during the academic year, and collected various artifacts of work. Over the course of the year, students' views did not change. They entered the course with adequate views on at least half of the eight tenet model of NOS used by the researcher, but little change was noted in any of the tenets. Although the author intuitively felt that students' views would change simply by exposure to a problem-based course, he did recognize that making NOS explicit was necessary. Several students made slight changes in response to implicit messages, which led to the conclusion that there is still a valuable place for implicit learning.

Liu and Lederman (2002) studied 29 gifted Taiwanese middle school students during a one-week summer science camp. The focus of the science instruction was scientific inquiry and NOS. A Chinese version of the Views of Nature of Science (VNOS) scale was developed to assess students in their native language. One question was added that was concerned with western medicine and eastern medicine to see if the students' cultural background influenced their views in any way. Instruction was provided in English, unless students clearly needed additional explanation. Liu presented all of the lessons. On the pretest, the students possessed good understandings of the tentative, subjective, empirical, and social/cultural embeddedness of science. Although all instruction was explicit, no changes were noted in students' understandings on the posttest. The authors explained the lack of change in students' views as a possible consequence of a very short instructional period and a ceiling effect. After all, the authors argued, the students did fairly well on the pretest. No evidence was found to support the notion that cultural background may interact with students' understandings of NOS.

Few studies have studied the effectiveness of explicit, reflective approaches to teaching NOS relative to implicit approaches with K–12 students. One such study was completed by Khishfe and Abd-El-Khalick (2002) in Lebanon. A total of 62 6th-grade students in two intact groups ($n = 29$ and 32) experienced inquiry-oriented instruction related to energy transformation and sedimentary rocks. One group was taught with an approach that explicitly addressed the tentative, empirical, inferential, imaginative, and creative aspects of scientific knowledge, whereas in the other class only implicit attention to NOS was included. The same teacher taught both classes. Students' knowledge of NOS was assessed through a combination of an open-ended questionnaire and semistructured interviews. The two groups entered the investigation with naïve, and equivalent, views on the various aspects of NOS. After instruction, the implicit group showed no changes in views of NOS, whereas students in the explicit group all exhibited improvement in their understandings of one or more aspects of NOS. Again, this particular study is important in that it demonstrated the relative effectiveness of explicit instructional approaches with a sample of K–12 students as opposed to preservice and inservice teachers.

Tao (2003) initially was interested in eliciting secondary students' understandings of NOS through a combination of peer collaboration and the use of science stories designed to illustrate aspects of NOS. The investigation showed that many students held empiricist views about scientific investigations and believed scientific theories to be absolute truths about reality. The author noticed that students' views were affected by group discussion about the stories. Instead of developing more informed understandings about NOS, however, the author noted that students moved from one inadequate view to another. In short, Tao felt that students simply looked for aspects of NOS that confirmed their views in the stories and ignored those aspects that ran contrary to their views.

Dhingra (2003) recognized that students learn about NOS through many sources, not just classroom instruction. The sample consisted of 63 female students from two single-sex high schools in New York City. Data were collected in response to a variety of television shows. The primary finding relative to NOS was that students reacted differently to shows that presented science as a collection of facts and those that presented science as more uncertain. Students had virtually no questions or comments about the science in shows that presented final-form science, but had numerous comments and questions in response to shows that presented science otherwise. A critical point here is that the television shows' depictions of science were explicit, and this explicitness appears to have had an impact on student learning.

Science apprenticeship programs have been a popular approach to engaging high-ability students in science, with an eye to promoting their interest in future careers in science. A commonly stated goal of such apprenticeship programs is that students will develop improved conceptions of NOS. Bell, Blair, Crawford, and Lederman (2003) systematically tested this assumed benefit of an apprenticeship program. The apprenticeship program was eight weeks long during the summer. Ten high-ability high school students (juniors and seniors) were pre- and posttested on their understandings of NOS and scientific inquiry before and after the apprenticeship. Both students and their mentor scientists were interviewed after the program. Although the scientists were of the opinion that their students had learned a lot about inquiry and NOS, student data (from interviews and questionnaires) indicated that changes occurred only in students' abilities to do inquiry. Of importance here is that students' conceptions of NOS on the pretest were not consistent with current reform efforts and, after the apprenticeship, with only one exception, remained the same. The authors ultimately concluded that students' conceptions of NOS (and knowledge about inquiry) remained unchanged because there was no explicit instruction about either associated with the apprenticeship. At least in practice, it appears to have been assumed that students would learn about NOS and inquiry simply by doing inquiry. As can be expected, not all studies involving explicit instruction related to NOS have met with success (Leach, Hind, & Ryder, 2003). In this particular investigation, the explicit instructional approach was not effective in promoting improved student views.

Among the volumes of research that focus on effecting change in conceptions of NOS, a small minority of studies focus on the impact that one's conceptions of NOS has on other variables of interest. Sadler, Chambers, and Zeidler (2004) focused on how students' conceptions of NOS affected how they interpreted and evaluated conflicting evidence on a socioscientific issue. Eighty-four high school students were asked to read contradictory reports related to global warming. A subsample of 30 students was interviewed in order to corroborate their written responses. The participants displayed a range of views on three aspects of NOS: empiricism, tentativeness, and social embeddedness. The authors claimed that how the students reacted to conflicting evidence was at least partially related to their views on NOS. This finding would appear to support the claim that an understanding of NOS is important because it contributes to an individual's decision-making.

ASSESSING CONCEPTIONS OF NATURE OF SCIENCE

The development and assessment of students' and teachers' conceptions of nature of science have been concerns of science educators for over 40 years and, arguably, constitute a line of research in their own right. Although there have been numerous criticisms of the validity of various assessment instruments over the years, students' and teachers' understandings have consistently been found lacking. This consistent finding, regardless of assessment approach, supports the notion that student and teacher understandings are not at the desired levels. It is important to note, however, that during the early development of assessment instruments there was more of a focus on what we would currently describe as scientific inquiry as opposed to nature of science.

The history of the assessment of nature of science mirrors the changes that have occurred in both psychometrics and educational research design over the past few decades. The first formal assessments, beginning in the early 1960s, emphasized quantitative approaches, as was characteristic of the overwhelming majority of science education research investigations. Prior to the mid-1980s, with few exceptions, researchers were content to develop instruments that allowed for easily "graded" and quantified measures of individuals' understandings. In some cases, standardized scores were derived. Within the context of the development of various instruments, some open-ended questioning was involved in the construction and validation of items. More recently, emphasis has been placed on providing an expanded view of an individual's beliefs regarding the nature of science. In short, in an attempt to gain more in-depth understandings of students' and teachers' thinking, educational researchers have resorted to the use of more open-ended probes and interviews. The same has been true with the more contemporary approaches to assessment related to the nature of science.

A critical evaluation of assessment instruments has recently been provided elsewhere (Lederman, Wade, & Bell, 1998). Therefore, the purpose here is to summarize the various instruments and identify trends in the assessment of NOS. Table 28.1 presents a comprehensive list of the more formal instruments constructed and validated to assess various aspects of NOS. Most of the instruments address only cer-

TABLE 28.1
Nature of Science Instruments

Date	Instrument	Author(s)
1954	Science Attitude Questionnaire	Wilson
1958	Facts About Science Test (FAST)	Stice
1959	Science Attitude Scale	Allen
1961	Test on Understanding Science (TOUS)	Cooley & Klopfer
1962	Processes of Science Test	BSCS
1966	Inventory of Science Attitudes, Interests, and Appreciations	Swan
1967	Science Process Inventory (SPI)	Welch
1967	Wisconsin Inventory of Science Processess (WISP)	Scientific Literacy Research Center
1968	Science Support Scale	Schwirian
1968	Nature of Science Scale (NOSS)	Kimball
1969	Test on the Social Aspects of Science (TSAS)	Korth
1970	Science Attitude Inventory (SAI)	Moore & Sutman
1974	Science Inventory (SI)	Hungerford &Walding
1975	Nature of Science Test (NOST)	Billeh & Hasan
1975	Views of Science Test (VOST)	Hillis
1976	Nature of Scientific Knowledge Scale (NSKS)	Rubba
1978	Test of Science-Related Attitudes (TOSRA)	Fraser
1980	Test of Enquiry Skills (TOES)	Fraser
1981	Conception of Scientific Theories Test (COST)	Cotham & Smith
1982	Language of Science (LOS)	Ogunniyi
1987	Views on Science-Technology-Society (VOSTS)	Aikenhead, Fleming, & Ryan
1990	Views of Nature of Science A (VNOS-A)	Lederman & O'Malley
1992	Modified Nature of Scientific Knowledge Scale (MNSKS)	Meichtry
1995	Critical Incidents	Nott & Wellington
1998	Views of Nature of Science B (VNOS-B)	Abd-El-Khalick, Bell, & Lederman
2000	Views of Nature of Science C (VNOS-C)	Abd-El-Khalick & Lederman
2002	Views of Nature of Science D (VNOS-D)	Lederman & Khishfe
2004	Views of Nature of Science E (VNOS-E)	Lederman & Ko

tain aspects of NOS and often inappropriately confuse the issue by addressing areas other than NOS, including science process skills and attitudes toward science. Instruments considered to have poor validity have the following characteristics:

1. Most items concentrate on a student's ability and skill to engage in the process of science (e.g., to make a judgment and/or interpretation concerning data).
2. Emphasis is on the affective domain (the realm of values and feelings) rather than knowledge (i.e., over 50 percent of items deal with attitude toward or appreciation of science and scientists).
3. Primary emphasis is placed upon science as an institution, with little or no emphasis placed upon the epistemological characteristics of the development of scientific knowledge.

As mentioned before, the validity of many of these instruments is questionable because their primary focus is on areas beyond the scope of the nature of science. Those instruments with questionable validity (as measures of NOS) include the Science Attitude Questionnaire (Wilson, 1954), Facts About Science Test (Stice, 1958), Science Attitude Scale (Allen, 1959), Processes of Science Test (BSCS, 1962), Inventory of Science Attitudes, Interests, and Appreciations (Swan, 1966), Science Support Scale (Schwirian, 1968), Test on the Social Aspects of Science (Korth, 1969), Science Attitude Inventory (Moore & Sutman, 1970), Science Inventory (Hungerford & Walding, 1974), Test of Science-Related Attitudes (Fraser, 1978), the Test of Enquiry Skills (Fraser, 1980), and the Language of Science (Ogunniyi, 1982).

The remaining instruments have generally been considered to be valid and reliable measures of NOS by virtue of their focus on one or more ideas that have been traditionally considered under the label of "nature of science," as well as their reported validity and reliability data. These instruments have been used in numerous studies, and even the more traditional instruments (e.g., TOUS) continue to be used, even though there is a significant movement away from such types of paper-and-pencil assessments. The validity of some of the assessment instruments listed and briefly described below has been severely criticized (and justifiably so) in the past few years. However, they are presented here as being the most valid (in terms of assessment focus) attempts to assess understandings of NOS using a written response format. Following is a brief discussion of each instrument.

Test on Understanding Science (TOUS) (Cooley & Klopfer, 1961). This instrument has been, by far, the most widely used assessment tool in NOS research. It is a four-alternative, 60-item multiple-choice test. In addition to an "overall" or "general" score, three subscale scores can be calculated: (I) understanding about the scientific enterprise; (II) the scientist; (III) the methods and aims of science. During the past few decades, the content of the *TOUS* has been criticized and has fallen into disfavor (Aikenhead, 1973; Hukins, 1963; Welch, 1969; Wheeler, 1968).

Wisconsin Inventory of Science Processes (WISP) (Scientific Literacy Research Center, 1967). The WISP consists of 93 statements that the respondent evaluates as "accurate," "inaccurate," or "not understood." However, in scoring the exam, "inaccurate" and "not understood" responses are combined to represent the opposite of "accurate." With the exception of the TOUS exam, this instrument has been used more than any other assessment instrument. The WISP was developed and validated for high school students. Although this instrument has excellent validity and reliability data, a few concerns should be considered prior to its use. Of primary concern is its length. The 93-item test takes over an hour to administer, which precludes it from use in a single class period. In addition, this instrument does not possess discrete subscales, which means, unfortunately, that only unitary scores can be calculated.

Science Process Inventory (SPI) (Welch, 1967). This instrument is a 135-item forced-choice inventory (agree/disagree) purporting to assess an understanding of the methods and processes by which scientific knowledge evolves. The content of the SPI is almost identical to that of WISP and TOUS subscale III. The validation of SPI was achieved in the usual manner for such instruments: literature review, devising a model, employing the judgment of "experts," getting feedback from pilot studies, and testing the instrument's ability to distinguish among different groups of respondents. The length (135 items) is a concern, as is its forced choice format. Students are unable to express "neutral" or uncertain answers. Finally, like the WISP, the SPI does not possess subscales.

Nature of Science Scale (NOSS) (Kimball, 1968). This instrument was developed to determine whether science teachers have the same view of science as scientists. It consists of 29 items, which the respondent may answer with "agree" or "disagree" or register a "neutral" response. Kimball's model of NOS is based upon the literature of the nature and philosophy of science and is consistent with the views of Bronowski (1956) and Conant (1951). The specific content of NOSS was validated by nine science educators, who judged whether the items were related to the model. The development, validation, and reliability measures were carried out with college graduates. Thus, it lacks reliability and validity data with respect to high school populations. Another concern is that the instrument lacks subscales and is, therefore, subject to the same criticism as WISP or any other unitary measure of the nature of science.

Nature of Science Test (NOST) (Billeh & Hasan, 1975). This instrument consists of 60 multiple-choice items addressing the following components of NOS: Assumptions of science (8 items), Products of science (22 items), Processes of science (25 items), and Ethics of science (5 items). The test consists of two types of items. The first type measures the individual's knowledge of the assumptions and processes of science, and the characteristics of scientific knowledge. The second type of question presents situations that require the individual to make judgments in view of his/her understanding of the nature of science. The major shortcoming of this instrument is not its content, but rather, that no subscales exist. Thus, only a global or unitary score can be calculated.

Views of Science Test (VOST) (Hillis, 1975). This instrument was developed specifically to measure understanding of the tentativeness of science. It consists of 40 statements that are judged to imply that scientific knowledge is tentative or absolute. Respondents express their agreement with either view, using a five-option Likert scale response format. The instrument is considered too focused by some because it is restricted to a single attribute of scientific knowledge.

Nature of Scientific Knowledge Scale (NSKS) (Rubba, 1976). This instrument is a 48-item Likert scale response format consisting of five choices (*strongly agree, agree, neutral, disagree, strongly disagree*). The test is purported to be an objective measure of secondary students' understanding of NOS. The NSKS and its subscales are based upon the nine factors of NOS specified by Showalter (1974). Rubba (1977) listed these nine factors as tentative, public, replicable, probabilistic, humanistic, historic, unique, holistic, and empirical. He noted a certain amount of shared overlap between the factors and proceeded to collapse them into a six-factor or six-subscale model of the nature of science. These six factors are: amoral, creative, developmental (tentative), parsimonious, testable, and unified. The instrument was developed, validated, and found to be reliable for high school-level students. The five-option Likert scale response format affords maximum freedom of expression to the respondent. The NSKS has generally been viewed positively by the research community; however, there is reason for some concern about its face validity. Many pairs of items within specific subscales are identical, except that one item is worded negatively. This redundancy could encourage respondents to refer back to their answers on previous, similarly worded items. This cross-checking would result in inflated reliability estimates, which could cause erroneous acceptance of the instrument's validity.

Conceptions of Scientific Theories Test (COST) (Cotham & Smith, 1981). The structure of this instrument was dictated by the developers' concern that previously existing instruments were based on single (supposedly enlightened) interpretations of NOS. Thus, the COST supposedly provides for nonjudgmental acceptance of alternative conceptions of science. The instrument is an attitude inventory consisting of 40 Likert scale items (with four options) and four subscales, each corresponding to a particular aspect of scientific theories. These include (I) ontological implications of theories; (II) testing of theories; (III) generation of theories; and (IV) choice among competing theories. The COST provides a theoretical context for four item-sets by prefacing each set with a brief description of a scientific theory and some episodes drawn from its history. The items following each theory description refer to that description. The four theoretical contexts are 1) Bohr's theory of the atom, 2) Darwin's theory of evolution, 3) Oparin's theory of abiogenesis, and 4) the theory of plate tectonics. A fifth context contains items that refer to general characteristics of scientific theories and is, therefore, not prefaced by a description. Two concerns must be addressed prior to the use of COST as an instrument to assess high school students' understandings of the nature of science. The first of these is the cognitive level of the instrument. It was designed for teachers and validated with undergraduate college students. The four theory descriptions used to provide context for the items are presented at a level that may be above the capabilities of many high school students.

A second concern with the COST instrument rests with the authors' claim that it, as opposed to all extant instruments, is sensitive to alternative conceptions of science. Cotham and Smith feel that it is extremely important for education to promote the view that scientific knowledge is tentative and revisionary. In their commitment to this concern, however, they actually specify which subscale viewpoints are consistent with the tentative and revisionary conception. Thus, although they claim to place no value judgments upon the various conceptions of science, Cotham and Smith actually do just that by linking certain viewpoints to the "highly prized" tentative and revisionary conception of scientific knowledge.

Views on Science-Technology-Society (VOSTS) (Aikenhead, Fleming, & Ryan 1989). The VOSTS was developed to assess students' understanding of the nature of science, technology, and their interactions with society. It consists of a "pool" of 114 multiple-choice items that address a number of science-technology-society (STS) issues. These issues include Science and Technology, Influence of Society on Science/Technology, Influence of Science/Technology on Society, Influence of School Science on Society, Characteristics of Scientists, Social Construction of Scientific Knowledge, Social Construction of Technology, and Nature of Scientific Knowledge. The VOSTS was developed and validated for grade 11 and 12 students. A fundamental assumption underlying the development of this instrument was that students and researchers do not necessarily perceive the meanings of a particular concept in the same way. Aikenhead and Ryan (1992) recognized the importance of providing students with alternative viewpoints based upon student "self-generated" responses to avoid the "constructed" responses offered by most of the previous nature of science assessment instruments. Unlike most other instruments, the VOSTS does not provide numerical scores; instead it provides a series of alternative "student position" statements. These statements were obtained from extensive open-ended student "argumentative" paragraphs in which students defended their stated position on a STS issue or topic. The extensive work developing and validating the VOSTS instrument took approximately six years to complete and is reported in a series of re search articles published in a special edition of the journal *Science Education* (Volume 71, 1987).

Views of Nature of Science, Form A (VNOS-A) (Lederman & O'Malley, 1990). In an attempt to ameliorate some of the problems noted by Aikenhead et al. (1987) during the development of the VOSTS and those noted in the use of the NSKS (Rubba, 1976) relative to the use of paper-and-pencil assessments, Lederman and O'Malley developed an open-ended survey consisting of seven items. This instrument was designed to be used in conjunction with follow-up interviews, and each of the seven items focuses on different aspects of tentativeness in science. Several problems were noted in the wording of some of the questions resulting in responses that did not necessarily provide information on students' views of "tentativeness." While these difficulties were alleviated by subsequent interviews, they served to reinforce the problems associated with attempting to interpret students' understandings solely from their written responses to researcher-generated questions.

Modified Nature of Scientific Knowledge Scale (M-NSKS) (Meichtry, 1992). This instrument is a modified NSKS instrument with 32 statements from four of the NSKS subscales. These subscales are: (I) creative, (II) developmental, (III) testable, and (IV) unified. M-NSKS was developed, with reliability and validity reported, for use with 6th-, 7th-, and 8th-graders.

Critical Incidents (Nott & Wellington, 1995). The use of "critical incidents" to assess teachers' conceptions of NOS was a significant departure from the usual paper-and-pencil assessment. In particular, Nott and Wellington are of the opinion that teachers do not effectively convey what they know about the nature of science in "direct response to abstract, context-free questions of the sort, 'What is science?'" (Nott & Wellington, 1995). Instead, they created a series of "critical incidents" that are descriptions/scenarios of actual classroom events. Teachers are expected to respond to the incidents by answering the following three questions: 1) What would you do? 2) What could you do? and 3) What should you do? So, for example, the teacher may be confronted with a situation in which a demonstration or laboratory activity does not yield the desired data. How the teacher responds to the aforementioned questions is believed to communicate what the teacher believes about NOS.

Although the use of critical incidents appears to be an excellent instructional tool to generate meaningful discussions in preservice and inservice courses, whether the teachers' responses are related to their views about NOS is still questionable. In short, the approach is based on the assumption that teachers' views of the nature of science automatically and necessarily influence classroom practice, an assumption that is simply not supported by the existing literature.

Views of Nature of Science B,C,D (VNOS B,C,D,E). This series or buffet of instruments has stemmed from the same research group and was meant to offer variations and improvements upon the original VNOS-A (Lederman & O'Malley, 1990). In particular, each instrument contains open-ended questions that focus on various aspects of NOS, with the differences being either the additional context-specific questions in forms B and C, or the developmental appropriateness and language of VNOS-D. From a practical standpoint, VNOS-B and VNOS-C are too lengthy to be administered easily during a regular class period. Teachers often take as long as 1.5 hours to complete VNOS-C. Consequently, VNOS-D and VNOS-E were created with the aid of focus groups of secondary ($n = 10$) and elementary ($n = 10$) teachers and their students. The resulting instruments are easily administered in less than one hour and yield the same results as the longer VNOS-B and VNOS-C. VNOS-E is the most recently developed instrument, and it has been designed for very young students (grades K–3). The items can also be used with students who cannot read or write (using a focus group format), and it represents the first measure of NOS designed for such a young audience. The particular authors credited for the development of each instrument are noted in the table of NOS instruments. A thorough description of the development of the VNOS A, B, and C instruments can be found in Lederman, Abd-El-Khalick, Bell, and Schwartz (2002).

SOME THOUGHTS ABOUT ASSESSING NOS

The validity of instruments purporting to assess NOS has long been criticized on the grounds that each instrument assumes its interpretation of science to be the correct view (Cotham & Smith, 1981). This criticism is derived from the often discussed lack of consensus concerning NOS among scholars from various fields. As previously discussed, however, when one considers the developmental level of the target target audience (K–12 students), the aspects of NOS stressed are at a level of generality that is not at all contentious. Nevertheless, if one is not willing to let go of the idea that the various aspects of NOS lack consensus and assessment of NOS is, therefore, problematic, the "problem" is easily handled. The issue lies not within the test, but rather in the interpretations of those scoring the test. If one interprets test scores simply as a measure of an individual's adherence to a particular conception of science, then no implicit value judgments are made. In short, the inherent bias in the scoring system of any assessment can be avoided if researchers simply use the scores to construct profiles of beliefs and knowledge.

Overall, there are two critical issues that have surrounded the "traditional" paper-and-pencil assessments of NOS: 1) assessment instruments are interpreted in a biased manner, and 2) some assessment instruments appear to be poorly constructed. These criticisms notwithstanding, it is interesting to note that research conclusions based on these instruments have been unusually uniform. That is, teachers and students generally score at levels considered to be less than adequate.

Thus, although the various instruments suffer from specific weaknesses, if these were significant, it would seem improbable that the research conclusions would be so consistent.

There is a more critical concern, however, about the "traditional" paper-and-pencil approach to the assessment of an individual's understanding of NOS. Although not a new insight, Lederman and O'Malley's (1990) investigation clearly highlighted the problem of paper-and-pencil assessments. They documented discrepancies between their own interpretations of students' written responses and the interpretations that surfaced from actual interviews of the same students. This unexpected finding (i.e., the purpose of the interviews was to help validate the paper-and-pencil survey that was used) was quite timely, as it occurred when educational researchers were making a serious shift toward more qualitative, open-ended approaches to assess individuals' understanding of any concept. Although the VNOS-A was created to avoid some of the concerns about "traditional" assessments (as were the subsequent series of VNOS forms), the problem of researchers interpreting responses differently than intended by the respondent remains to this day. The problem exists at all age levels (K–adult), with increasing levels of uncertainty as the age of the respondent decreases. It is for this reason that researchers should not abandon the interviewing of individuals about their written responses. Throughout the history of NOS assessment there has been a clear movement from traditional convergent assessments to more open-ended assessments. Most researchers realize how difficult it is to assess a construct as complex as NOS with multiple-choice and Likert scale items. Within all of us, however, is this "inherent" need to make our lives easier. Interviews and open-ended assessments are time-consuming to conduct and score. However, a quick perusal of the program from the Annual Meeting of the National Association for Research in Science Teaching in 2003–2005 indicates that attempts to create a "better" traditional assessment are alive and well. The desire to create an instrument that can be mass administered and scored in a short period of time continues. It is hoped that the need to collect valid data as opposed to large data sets will prevail.

Finally, there remains a small minority of individuals (e.g., Sandoval, 2005) who insist that students' and teachers' understandings of NOS are best assessed through observations of behavior during inquiry activities (i.e., knowledge in practice). Such a view is a remnant of the previously discussed assumption that a teacher's understanding of NOS is necessarily reflected in his/her behavior. It is déjà vu all over again. The literature clearly documents the discrepancies that often exist between one's beliefs/knowledge and behavior. More concretely, if an individual believes that scientific knowledge is tentative (subject to change) and another individual believes the knowledge to be absolute/static, how would this be evident in their behavior during a laboratory activity? If a student recognizes that scientific knowledge is partly subjective, how would this student behave differently during a laboratory investigation than a student with differing beliefs? Certainly, many similar questions could be asked in relation to other aspects of NOS. In short, this methodology of assessment adds an unnecessary layer of inference to one's research design. Please do not misinterpret these comments about assessing through observation. Observations of behavior can be valuable if the behavior is what a student **says specifically** about NOS. Those supporting the "observation" approach also think that asking students to answer questions such as What is an experiment? is too abstract and unrelated to the student's practical world. This view ignores the fact that the nature of an experiment is included in most curricula, and it is related to the work that students do. The idea is far from being too much of an abstraction. However, if one insists that direct observations of student or teacher behaviors be pursued, then assessments of the subject's views of NOS should be made after observations and document analysis have been completed by the researcher, or the results of the assessments should be hidden until observations are completed. This is analogous to the "blind" studies often used in medical studies to reduce the impact of the researcher's and subject's bias on the results.

FUTURE DIRECTIONS

After approximately 50 years of research related to students' and teachers' conceptions of NOS, a few generalizations can be justified:

- K–12 students do not typically possess "adequate" conceptions of NOS.
- K–12 teachers do not typically possess "adequate" conceptions of NOS
- Conceptions of NOS are best learned through explicit, reflective instruction as opposed to implicitly through experiences with simply "doing" science.
- Teachers' conceptions of NOS are not automatically and necessarily translated into classroom practice.
- Teachers do not regard NOS as an instructional outcome of equal status with that of "traditional" subject matter outcomes.

At this point in the history of research on the nature of science, the research has been relatively superficial in the sense of an "input-output" model with little known about the in-depth mechanisms that contribute to change in teachers' and students' views. Even the more recent efforts that have documented the efficacy of explicit, reflective approaches (Abd-El-Khalick & Lederman, 2000) to instruction are superficial in the sense that students and/or teachers are pretested and posttested relative to an instructional activity or set of activities. The specific mechanisms of change and/or the dynamics of change have yet to be explored in depth. We have simply discovered the situations under which change has occurred in the desired direction. Clearly, much more work is needed before we, as a research community, can feel confident in making large-scale recommendations to teachers and professional developers.

Regardless of the "holes" that one can find in the existing research literature, the past 50 or so years of research on NOS does provide us with some clear direction in terms of future research and teaching. What follows is just a few of the critical lines of research that need to be pursued.

How do teachers' conceptions of NOS develop over time? What factors are important, and are certain factors more related to certain aspects of nature of science than others?

We need more in-depth knowledge of how views on NOS change over time. Certainly, change in such views must be similar to the change that one sees with other science concepts. Shifts in viewpoints are most likely gradual, and certain aspects of NOS may be more easily altered than others. It is just as likely that those factors of importance have a differential influence on the various aspects of NOS. To date, the available research simply identifies whether an individual's views have changed from "naïve" to "adequate."

What is the influence of one's worldview on conceptions of nature of science?

Although much research on individuals' worldviews has been pursued, such research has rarely been directly and systematically related to views on NOS. One notable exception has been Cobern's work (2000). It seems that NOS may be a subset of one's worldview, or is at least affected by one's worldview. Of primary importance is the relevance of this line of research for the teaching of NOS across cultures. What happens when there is a clash between one's cultural views and the views expressed in western-influenced depictions of science and NOS?

What is the relative effectiveness of the various interventions designed to improve teachers' and students' conceptions? Is one better than another, or is a combination needed?

Although there is strong emerging evidence that an explicit approach to the teaching of NOS is more effective than implicit approaches, there has been virtually no research that compares the relative effectiveness of the various explicit approaches. Are the various approaches equally effective? For example, is explicit instruction in the context of a laboratory investigation more or less effective than explicit reflection within the context of an historical case study? Is a combination of the two approaches more effective than either approach alone?

Is the nature of science learned better by students and teachers if it is embedded within traditional subject matter or as a separate "pull-out" topic? Should the nature of science be addressed as both a separate "pull-out" as well as embedded?

Similar to the issue of the relative effectiveness of various instructional approaches, is the issue of the curriculum context of NOS instruction. There is an existing assumption that when NOS is embedded within the context of lessons on other aspects of subject matter, student learning is enhanced. There is little published research specifically related to this issue. Even the most superficial perusal of the recent research on explicit instruction, however, shows that explicit teaching of NOS has supporters for embedded and non-embedded approaches. Systematic research that compares the relative effectiveness of these instructional approaches alone and in combination is needed.

How do teachers develop PCK for the nature of science? Is it related to their knowledge structures for traditional science content?

The relationship between one's views of NOS, subject matter, and pedagogy remains uncertain. If we are to assume that NOS is analogous to other aspects of subject matter that teachers teach and, it is hoped, students learn, it also stands to reason that teachers can and should develop PCK for NOS. Virtually no research has used the PCK perspective, which was so heavily researched during the 1990s, as a lens for research on the teaching of NOS. Such research would provide critical information for the planning and quality of professional development activities that focus on NOS. After all, it is one thing to teach teachers about NOS; it is a totally different endeavor to teach them how to teach NOS to their students.

How are teachers' conceptions of the nature of science affected during translation into classroom practice? To what extent is the act of teaching an independent variable?

Anyone who has ever attempted to enhance teachers' understandings of NOS is aware that the "newly developed" views resulting from a methods course or professional development workshop are fragile at best. Given what is known about how science is typically presented in various curriculum materials, there is the possibility that the curriculum may influence a teacher's views of NOS. Within the literature on PCK, there is some recognition that how one uses his/her subject matter (e.g., teaching) can influence the individual's subject matter structure (Hauslein, Good, & Cummins, 1992). Consequently, it is quite possible that the teaching of science may have an impact on how a teacher views the epistemology of science.

Does the difficulty of the subject matter within which the nature of science is embedded influence student learning?

Unless NOS is taught independently of other science subject matter, it represents an additional outcome that students are expected to learn during science instruction. That is, for example, students would be expected to learn that scientific knowledge is tentative while at the same time learning the details of the model of the atom. It is quite possible that the difficulty level of the subject matter may interfere with the learning of NOS. Should NOS be withheld for situations in which relatively concrete science topics are being addressed?

Does knowledge of the nature of science improve students' learning of other science subject matter?

One of the original rationales for teaching NOS has been the belief that an understanding of NOS will enhance students' subsequent learning of science subject matter. This assumption, as is true with other assumptions related to the purported value of NOS as an instructional outcome, has yet to be systematically tested. Should students learn to view the subject matter they are being asked to learn through a lens of NOS? This line of research would inform the placement and role of NOS within the science curriculum

Does understanding of the nature of science significantly influence the nature and quality of decisions students make regarding scientifically based personal and social issues?

A second rationale for the teaching of NOS has been that such understandings would enhance decision-making on scientifically based personal and social issues. Other than Bell and Lederman's (2003) investigation of university faculty members (scientists and non-scientists), this assumption has remained untested. The results of that investigation did not support the long-held assumption about the value of NOS as an instructional outcome. In general, the assumptions that have been used as advocacies for the teaching of NOS need to be systematically tested. It may very well be that the only value in teaching NOS is that it gives students a better understanding of science as a discipline.

Are the nature of science and scientific inquiry universal, or are conceptions influenced by the particular scientific discipline?

Although NOS has been treated in the research literature as "generic" across all scientific disciplines, there appears to be a growing belief in the view that different disciplines may have different "definitions" of NOS. For example, is NOS in biology the same as it is in physics? Intuitively, it seems that there would be differences. Indeed, the phrase "natures of science" is starting to be heard in the halls of professional meetings. The published research literature, however, does not contain a test of this assumption. At this point, all that exists is the unpublished work of Schwartz (2005), and the results, as usual, do not support our intuitive assumptions. The implications this line of research has for teaching NOS in schools are clearly significant. Should NOS be characterized differently in the different science classes? Clearly, we need much more research that compares the views of nature of science (and scientific inquiry) of individuals viewed to have strong understandings of each. It cannot be overemphasized that researchers should carefully consider the developmental appropriateness of conceptions of inquiry and NOS they consider for use with K–12 students.

How do teachers come to value NOS as having status equal to or greater than that of "traditional" subject matter?

The last bulleted item at the beginning of this section noted that teachers do not value NOS at a level equal to that of "traditional" subject matter. The existing research clearly indicates that teachers can be taught NOS, and it clearly shows that teachers can be taught how to teach NOS to students. However, the research is lacking when it comes to providing guidance for how to develop teachers' valuing of NOS as an important instructional outcome. Few would argue with the notion that teachers spend less time teaching what they don't value or value less than other material. Even teachers who understand NOS and how to teach it may not actually attempt to teach NOS to students. This was illustrated in Lederman's (1999) case study of five biology teachers quite knowledgeable about NOS. One reason teachers may not teach NOS, even though they are capable, is that NOS is typically not assessed on local, national, or international tests. However, if we hope to improve teachers' instructional attention to NOS in a more creative way than just putting it on the test, a concerted effort must be made to unearth what it takes to get teachers to value NOS relative to other instructional outcomes.

At the beginning of this review, some attention was given to the question, Why teach NOS? A pessimistic answer might focus on the observation that each time one of the perennial reasons for teaching NOS is systematically studied, empirical support for our intuitive claims is nowhere to be found. Hence, all of the reasons we have always used for advocating NOS as an instructional outcome may be false. On a more positive note, it can always be argued that an understanding of NOS provides students with an understanding of science as a discipline, and it provides a meaningful context for the subject matter we expect students to learn. In this sense, NOS is advocated because of its inherent educational value in understanding science as a discipline, as opposed to its being anything of concrete instrumental value. Whether one ultimately decides to be an optimist or pessimist can only be derived from our continued research on teaching and learning of NOS. Although systematic research on NOS has existed for approximately 50 years, we are far from any definitive answers. And, of course, none of the answers we will eventually arrive at will be absolute, and they will always be subject to change!

ACKNOWLEDGMENTS

I gratefully acknowledge Rola Khishfe, Byoung-Sug Kim, and Judith Lederman for their assistance in searching the literature and providing critical and productive feedback on earlier drafts of this chapter. Thanks also to Cathleen Loving and Lawrence Scharmann, who reviewed this chapter.

REFERENCES

Abd-El-Khalick, F. (2001). Embedding nature of science instruction in preservice elementary science courses: Abandoning scientism, but . . . *Journal of Science Teacher Education, 12*(3), 215–233.

Abd-El-Khalick, F. (2005). Developing deeper understandings of nature of science: The impact of a philosophy of science course on preservice teachers' views and instructional planning. *International Journal of Science Education, 27*(1), 15–42.

Abd-El-Khalick, F., & Akerson, V. (2004). Learning as conceptual change: Factors mediating the development of preservice teachers' views of nature of science. *Science Education, 88*(5), 785–810.

Abd-El-Khalick, F., Bell, R. L., & Lederman, N. G. (1998). The nature of science and instructional practice: Making the unnatural natural. *Science Education, 82*(4), 417–437.

Abd-El-Khalick, F., & Lederman, N. G. (2000a). Improving science teachers' conceptions of the nature of science: A critical review of the literature. *International Journal of Science Education, 22*(7), 665–701.

Abd-El-Khalick, F., & Lederman, N. G. (2000b). The influence of history of science courses on students' views of nature of science. *Journal of Research in Science Teaching, 37*(10), 1057–1095.

Abell, S., Martini, M., & George, M. (2001). "That's what scientists have to do": Preservice elementary teachers' conceptions of the nature of science during a moon investigation. *International Journal of Science Education, 23*(11), 1095–1109.

Aguirre, J. M., Haggerty, S. M., & Linder, C. J. (1990). Student-teachers' conceptions of science, teaching and learning: A case study in preservice science education. *International Journal of Science Education, 12*(4), 381–390.

Aikenhead, G. (1972). The measurement of knowledge about science and scientists: An investigation into the development of instruments for formative evaluation. *Dissertations Abstracts International, 33*, 6590A (University Microfilms No. 72-21, 423).

Aikenhead, G. (1973). The measurement of high school students' knowledge about science and scientists. *Science Education, 57*(4), 539–549.

Aikenhead, G. (1979). Science: A way of knowing. *The Science Teacher, 46*(6), 23–25.

Aikenhead, G. (1987). High-school graduates' beliefs about science-technology society. II. Characteristics and limitations of scientific knowledge. *Science Education, 71*(4), 459–487.

Aikenhead, G., Ryan, A. G., & Fleming, R. W. (1987). High-school graduates beliefs about science-technology-society: Methods and issues in monitoring student views. *Science Education, 71*, 145–161.

Akerson, V. L., Abd-El-Khalick, F., & Lederman, N. G. (2000). Influence of a reflective activity-based approach on elementary teachers' conceptions of nature of science. *Journal of Research in Science Teaching, 37*(4), 295–317.

Akindehin, F. (1988). Effect of an instructional package on preservice science teachers' understanding of the nature of science and acquisition of science-related attitudes. *Science Education, 72*(1), 73–82.

Allen, H., Jr. (1959). *Attitudes of certain high school seniors toward science and scientific careers*. New York: Teachers College Press.

Alters, B. J. (1997). Whose nature of science? *Journal of Research in Science Teaching, 34*(1), 39–55.

American Association for the Advancement of Science. (1990). *Science for all Americans*. New York: Oxford University Press.

American Association for the Advancement of Science. (1993). *Benchmarks for science literacy: A Project 2061 report*. New York: Oxford University Press.

Anderson, K. E. (1950). The teachers of science in a representative sampling of Minnesota schools. *Science Education, 34*(1), 57–66.

Bady, R. A. (1979). Students' understanding of the logic of hypothesis testing. *Journal of Research in Science Teaching, 16*(1), 61–65.

Ball, D. L., & McDiarmid, G. W. (1990). The subject-matter preparation of teachers. In W. R. Houston (Ed.), *Handbook of research on teacher education* (pp. 437–465). New York: Macmillan.

Barnes, B. (1974). *Scientific knowledge and sociological theory*. London: Routledge & Kegan Paul.

Barufaldi, J. P., Bethel, L. J., & Lamb, W. G. (1977). The effect of a science methods course on the philosophical view of science among elementary education majors. *Journal of Research in Science Teaching, 14*(4), 289–294.

Behnke, F. L. (1961). Reactions of scientists and science teachers to statements bearing on certain aspects of science and science teaching. *School Science and Mathematics, 61*, 193–207.

Bell, R. L., Blair, L., Crawford, B., & Lederman, N. G. (2003). *Journal of Research in Science Teaching,* 40(5), 487–509.

Bell, R. L., & Lederman, N. G. (2003). Understandings of the nature of science and decision making in science and technology based issues. *Science Education,* 87(3), 352–377.

Bell, R. L., Lederman, N. G., & Abd-El-Khalick, F. (2000). Developing and acting upon one's conception of the nature of science: A follow-up study. *Journal of Research in Science Teaching,* 37(6), 563–581.

Billeh, V. Y., & Hasan, O. E. (1975). Factors influencing teachers' gain in understanding the nature of science. *Journal of Research in Science Teaching,* 12(3), 209–219.

Biological Sciences Curriculum Study. (1962). *Processes of science test.* New York: The Psychological Corporation.

Bloom, J. W. (1989). Preservice elementary teachers' conceptions of science: Science, theories and evolution. *International Journal of Science Education,* 11(4), 401–415.

Brickhouse, N. W. (1989). The teaching of the philosophy of science in secondary classrooms: Case studies of teachers' personal theories. *International Journal of Science Education,* 11(4), 437–449.

Brickhouse, N. W. (1990). Teachers' beliefs about the nature of science and their relationship to classroom practice. *Journal of Teacher Education,* 41(3), 53–62.

Brickhouse, N. W., & Bodner, G. M. (1992). The beginning science teacher: Classroom narratives of convictions and constraints. *Journal of Research in Science Teaching,* 29, 471–485.

Broadhurst, N. A. (1970). A study of selected learning outcomes of graduating high school students in South Australian schools. *Science Education,* 54(1), 17–21.

Bronowski, J. (1956). *Science and human values.* New York: Harper.

Carey, R. L., & Stauss, N. G. (1968). An analysis of the understanding of the nature of science by prospective secondary science teachers. *Science Education,* 52(4), 358–363.

Carey, R. L., & Stauss, N. G. (1970a). An analysis of the relationship between prospective science teachers' understanding of the nature of science and certain academic variables. *Georgia Academy of Science,* 148–158.

Carey, R. L., & Stauss, N. G. (1970b). An analysis of experienced science teachers' understanding of the nature of science. *School Science and Mathematics,* 70(5), 366–376.

Carey, S., Evans, R., Honda, M., Jay, E., & Unger, C. (1989). An experiment is when you try it and see if it works: A study of grade 7 students' understanding of the construction of scientific knowledge. *International Journal of Science Education,* 11, 514–529.

Central Association for Science and Mathematics Teachers. (1907). A consideration of the principles that should determine the courses in biology in secondary schools. *School Science and Mathematics,* 7, 241–247.

Chalmers, A. F. (1999). *What is this thing called science?* Indianapolis: Hackett.

Cobern, W. W. (1989). A comparative analysis of NOSS profiles on Nigerian and American preservice, secondary science teachers. *Journal of Research in Science Teaching,* 26(6), 533–541.

Cobern, W. W. (2000). *Everyday thoughts about nature.* Dordrecht, the Netherlands: Kluwer Academic.

Conant, J. B. (1951). *Science and common sense.* New Haven, CT: Yale University Press.

Cooley, W. W., & Klopfer, L. E. (1961). *Test on understanding science.* Princeton, NJ: Educational Testing Service.

Cooley, W., & Klopfer, L. (1963). The evaluation of specific educational innovations. *Journal of Research in Science Teaching,* 1(1), 73–80.

Cotham, J., & Smith, E. (1981). Development and validation of the conceptions of scientific theories test. *Journal of Research in Science Teaching,* 18(5), 387–396.

Craven, J. A., Hand, B., & Prain, V. (2002). Assessing explicit and tacit conceptions of the nature of science among preservice elementary teachers. *International Journal of Science Education,* 24(8), 785–802.

Crumb, G. H. (1965). Understanding of science in high school physics. *Journal of Research in Science Teaching,* 3(3), 246–250.

Dhingra, K. (2003). Thinking about television science: How students understand the nature of science from different program genres. *Journal of Research in Science Teaching,* 40(2), 234–256.

Driver, R., Leach, J., Millar, R., & Scott, P. (1996). *Young peoples's images of science*. Buckingham, UK: Open University Press.

Durkee, P. (1974). An analysis of the appropriateness and utilization of TOUS with special reference to high-ability students studying physics. *Science Education, 58*(3), 343–356.

Duschl, R. A., & Wright, E. (1989). A case study of high school teachers' decision making models for planning and teaching science. *Journal of Research in Science Teaching, 26*(6), 467–501.

Elby, A., & Hammer, D. (2001). On the substance of a sophisticated epistemology. *Science Education, 85*(5), 554–567.

Feyerabend, D. (1975). *Against method*. London: Verso.

Fraser, B. J. (1978). Development of a test of science-related attitudes. *Science Education, 62*, 509–515.

Fraser, B. J. (1980). Development and validation of a test of enquiry skills. *Journal of Research in Science Teaching, 17*, 7–16.

Gabel, D. L., Rubba, P. A., & Franz, J. R. (1977). The effect of early teaching and training experiences on physics achievement, attitude toward science and science teaching, and process skill proficiency. *Science Education, 61*, 503–511.

Gennaro, E. O. (1964). A comparative study of two methods of teaching high school biology-BSCS Yellow Version and laboratory blocks with collateral reading. *Dissertations Abstracts International, 25*, 3996 (University Microfilms No. 64-13, 878).

Giere, R. N. (1988). *Explaining science: A cognitive approach*. Chicago: University of Chicago Press.

Gilbert, S. W. (1991). Model building and a definition of science. *Journal of Research in Science Teaching, 28*(1), 73–80.

Gruber, H. E. (1963). Science as doctrine or thought? A critical study of nine academic year institutes. *Journal of Research in Science Teaching, 1*(2), 124–128.

Hammrich, P. (1997). Confronting teacher candidates' conceptions of the nature of science. *Journal of Science Teacher Education, 8*(2), 141–151.

Haukoos, G. D., & Penick, J. E. (1983). The influence of classroom climate on science process and content achievement of community college students. *Journal of Research in Science Teaching, 20*(7), 629–637.

Haukoos, G. D., & Penick, J. E. (1985). The effects of classroom climate on college science students: A replication study. *Journal of Research in Science Teaching, 22*(2), 163–168.

Hauslein, P. L., Good, R. G., & Cummins, C. (1992). Biology content cognitive structure: From science student to science teacher. *Journal of Research in Science Teaching, 29*(9), 939–964.

Hillis, S. R. (1975). The development of an instrument to determine student views of the tentativeness of science. In *Research and Curriculum Development in Science Education: Science Teacher Behavior and Student Affective and Cognitive Learning* (Vol. 3). Austin, TX: University of Texas Press.

Hipkins, R., Barker, M., & Bolstad, R. (2005). Teaching the "nature of science": Modest adaptations or radical reconceptions? *International Journal of Science Education, 27*(2), 243–254.

Hodson, D. (1985). Philosophy of science, science and science education. *Studies in Science Education, 12*, 25–57.

Hukins, A. (1963). *A factorial investigation of measures of achievement of objectives in science teaching*. Unpublished doctoral thesis, University of Alberta, Edmonton.

Hungerford, H., & Walding, H. (1974). *The modification of elementary methods students' concepts concerning science and scientists*. Paper presented at the Annual Meeting of the National Science Teachers Association.

Hurd, P. D. (1969). *New directions in teaching secondary school science*. Chicago: Rand-McNally.

Johnson, R. L., & Peeples, E. E. (1987). The role of scientific understanding in college: Student acceptance of evolution. *American Biology Teacher, 49*(2), 96–98.

Johnson-Laird, P. N., & Wason, P. C. (1972). *Psychology of reasoning*. Cambridge, MA: Harvard University Press.

Jones, K. M. (1965). The attainment of understandings about the scientific enterprise, scientists, and the aims and methods of science by students in a college physical science course. *Journal of Research in Science Teaching, 3*(1), 47–49.

Jungwirth, E. (1970). An evaluation of the attained development of the intellectual skills needed for 'understanding of the nature of scientific enquiry' by BSCS pupils in Israel. *Journal of Research in Science Teaching, 7*(2), 141–151.

Kang, N. H., & Wallace, C. S. (2005). Secondary science teachers' use of laboratory activities: Linking epistemological beliefs, goals, and practices. *Science Education, 89*(1), 140–165.

Kang, S., Scharmann, L., & Noh, T. (2004). Examining students' views on the nature of science: Results from Korean 6th, 8th, and 10th graders. *Science Education, 89*(2), 314–334.

Khishfe, R., & Abd-El-Khalick, F. (2002). Influence of explicit and reflective versus implicit inquiry-oriented instruction on sixth graders' views of nature of science. *Journal of Research in Science Teaching, 39*(7), 551–578.

Kimball, M. E. (1967–68). Understanding the nature of science: A comparison of scientists and science teachers. *Journal of Research in Science Teaching, 5*, 110–120.

King, B. B. (1991). Beginning teachers' knowledge of and attitudes toward history and philosophy of science. *Science Education, 75*(1), 135–141.

Kleinman, G. (1965). Teachers' questions and student understanding of science. *Journal of Research in Science Teaching, 3*(4), 307–317.

Klopfer, L. E. (1964). The use of case histories in science teaching. *School Science and Mathematics, 64*, 660–666.

Klopfer, L. E. (1969). The teaching of science and the history of science. *Journal of Research in Science Teaching, 6*, 87–95.

Klopfer, L., & Cooley, W. (1961). *Test on understanding science, Form W*. Princeton, NJ: Educational Testing Service.

Klopfer, L. E., & Cooley, W. W. (1963). The history of science cases for high schools in the development of student understanding of science and scientists. *Journal of Research in Science Teaching, 1*(1), 33–47.

Korth, W. (1969). *Test every senior project: Understanding the social aspects of science*. Paper presented at the 42nd Annual Meeting of the National Association for Research in Science Teaching.

Koulaidis, V., & Ogborn, J. (1989). Philosophy of science: An empirical study of teachers' views. *International Journal of Science Education, 11*(2), 173–184.

Kuhn, T. S. (1962). *The structure of scientific revolutions*. Chicago: University of Chicago Press.

Lakatos, I. (1970). Falsification and the methodology of scientific research programs. In I. Lakatos & A. Musgrave (Eds.), *Criticism and the growth of knowledge*. Cambridge, UK: Cambridge University Press.

Lantz, O., & Kass, H. (1987). Chemistry teachers' functional paradigms. *Science Education, 71*, 117–134.

Laudan, L. (1977). *Progress and its problems*. Berkeley: University of California Press.

Lavach, J. F. (1969). Organization and evaluation of an inservice program in the history of science. *Journal of Research in Science Teaching, 6*, 166–170.

Lawson, A. E. (1982). The nature of advanced reasoning and science instruction. *Journal of Research in Science Teaching, 19*, 743–760.

Leach, J., Hind, A., & Ryder, J. (2003). *Designing and evaluating short teaching interventions about the epistemology of science in high school classrooms*. Science Education, 87(6), 831–848.

Lederman, J. S., & Khishfe, R. (2002). *Views of nature of science, Form D*. Unpublished paper. Chicago: Illinois Institute of Technology, Chicago.

Lederman, J. S., & Ko, E. K. (2003). *Views of scientific inquiry-elementary school version*. Unpublished paper. Illinois Institute of Technology, Chicago.

Lederman, J. S., & Ko, E. K. (2004). *Views of nature of science, Form E*. Unpublished paper. Illinois Institute of Technology, Chicago.

Lederman, N. G. (1986a). Relating teaching behavior and classroom climate to changes in students' conceptions of the nature of science. *Science Education, 70*(1), 3–19.

Lederman, N. G. (1986b). Students' and teachers' understanding of the nature of science: A reassessment. *School Science and Mathematics, 86*(2), 91–99.

Lederman, N. G. (1992). Students' and teachers' conceptions of the nature of science: A review of the research. *Journal of Research in Science Teaching, 29*(4), 331–359.

Lederman, N. G. (1995, January). *Teachers' conceptions of the nature of science: Factors that mediate translation into classroom practice*. Paper presented at the annual meeting of the Association for the Education of Teacher in Science, Charleston, WV.

Lederman, N. G. (1998, December). The state of science education: Subject matter without context. *Electronic Journal of Science Education* [On-Line], 3(2). Available at http://unr.edu/homepage/jcannon/ejse/ejse.html.

Lederman, N. G. (1999). Teachers' understanding of the nature of science and classroom practice: Factors that facilitate or impede the relationship. *Journal of Research in Science Teaching, 36*(8), 916–929.

Lederman, N. G., Abd-El-Khalick, F., Bell, R. L., & Schwartz, R. S. (2002). Views of nature of science questionnaire: Toward valid and meaningful assessment of learners' conceptions of nature of science. *Journal of Research in Science Teaching, 39*(6), 497–521.

Lederman, N. G., & Druger, M. (1985). Classroom factors related to changes in students' conceptions of the nature of science. *Journal of Research in Science Teaching, 22*(7), 649–662.

Lederman, N. G., & Niess, M. L. (1997). The nature of science: Naturally? *School Science and Mathematics, 97*(1), 1–2.

Lederman, N. G., & O'Malley, M. (1990). Students' perceptions of tentativeness in science: Development, use, and sources of change. *Science Education, 74*, 225–239.

Lederman, N. G., Schwartz, R. S., Abd-El-Khalick, F., & Bell, R. L. (2001). Preservice teachers' understandings and teaching of the nature of science: An intervention study. *Canadian Journal of Science, mathematics, and Technology Education, 1*(2), 135–160.

Lederman, N. G., Wade, P. D., & Bell, R. L. (1998). Assessing understanding of the nature of science: A historical perspective. In W. McComas (Ed.), *The nature of science and science education: Rationales and strategies* (pp. 331–350). Dordrecht, the Netherlands: Kluwer Academic.

Lederman, N. G., & Zeidler, D. L. (1987). Science teachers' conceptions of the nature of science: Do they really influence teacher behavior? *Science Education, 71*(5), 721–734.

Lin, H. S., & Chen, C. C. (2002). Promoting preservice teachers' understanding about the nature of science through history. *Journal of Research in Science Teaching, 39*(9), 773–792.

Liu, S. Y., & Lederman, N. G. (2002). Taiwanese students' views of nature of science. *School Science and Mathematics, 102*(3), 114–122.

Mackay, L. D. (1971). Development of understanding about the nature of science. *Journal of Research in Science Teaching, 8*(1), 57–66.

Mead, M., & Metraux, R. (1957). Image of the scientist among high school students. *Science, 126*, 384–390.

Meichtry, Y. J. (1992). Influencing student understanding of the nature of science: Data from a case of curriculum development. *Journal of Research in Science Teaching, 29*, 389–407.

Miller, P. E. (1963). A comparison of the abilities of secondary teachers and students of biology to understand science. *Iowa Academy of Science, 70*, 510–513.

Moore, R., & Sutman, F. (1970). The development, field test and validation of an inventory of scientific attitudes. *Journal of Research in Science Teaching, 7*, 85–94.

Moss, D. M. (2001). Examining student conceptions of the nature of science. *International Journal of Science Education, 23*(8), 771–790.

Munby, H. (1976). Some implications of language in science education. *Science Education, 60*(1), 115–124.

National Research Council. (1996). *National science education standards*. Washington, DC: National Academic Press.

National Science Teachers Association. (1962). The NSTA position on curriculum development in science. *The Science Teacher, 29*(9), 32–37.

National Science Teachers Association. (1982). *Science-technology-society: Science education for the 1980s* (An NSTA position statement). Washington, DC: Author.

Nott, M., & Wellington, J. (1995). Probing teachers' views of the nature of science: How should we do it and where should we be looking? *Proceedings of the Third International History, Philosophy, and Science Teaching Conference*, pp. 864–872.

Ogunniyi, M. B. (1982). An analysis of prospective science teachers' understanding of the nature of science. *Journal of Research in Science Teaching, 19*(1), 25–32.

Osborne, J., Collins, S., Ratcliffe, M., Millar, R., & Duschl, R. (2003). What "ideas-about-science" should be taught in school science? A Delphi study of the expert community. *Journal of Research in Science Teaching, 40*(7), 692–720.

Popper, K. R. (1959). *The logic of scientific discovery.* New York: Harper & Row.

Ramsey, G., & Howe, R. (1969). An analysis of research on instructional procedures in secondary school science. *The Science Teacher, 36*(3), 62–68.

Riley, J. P., II (1979). The influence of hands-on science process training on preservice teachers' acquisition of process skills and attitude toward science and science teaching. *Journal of Research in Science Teaching, 16*(5), 373–384.

Robinson, J. T. (1965). Science teaching and the nature of science. *Journal of Research in Science Teaching, 3*, 37–50.

Rothman, A. I. (1969). Teacher characteristics and student learning. *Journal of Research in Science Teaching, 6*(4), 340–348.

Rowe, M. B. (1974). A humanistic intent: The program of preservice elementary education at the University of Florida. *Science Education, 58*, 369–376.

Rubba, P. (1976). *Nature of scientific knowledge scale.* School of Education, Indiana University, Bloomington, IN.

Rubba, P. A. (1977). The development, field testing and validation of an instrument to assess secondary school students' understanding of the nature of scientific knowledge. *Dissertations Abstracts International, 38*, 5378A (University Microfilms No. 78-00, 998).

Rubba, P. A., & Andersen, H. (1978). Development of an instrument to assess secondary school students' understanding of the nature of scientific knowledge. *Science Education, 62*(4), 449–458.

Rubba, P., Horner, J., & Smith, J. M. (1981). A study of two misconceptions about the nature of science among junior high school students. *School Science and Mathematics, 81*, 221–226.

Rudolph, J. L. (2003). Portraying epistemology: School science in historical context. *Science Education, 87*(1), 64–79.

Rutherford, J. F. (1964). The role of inquiry in science teaching. *Journal of Research in Science Teaching, 2*(2), 80–84.

Sadler, T. D., Chambers, F. W., & Zeidler, D. (2004). Student conceptualizations of the nature of science in response to a socioscientific issue. *International Journal of Science Education, 26*(4), 387–409.

Sandoval, W. A. (2005). Understanding students' practical epistemologies and their influence on learning through inquiry. *Science Education, 89*(5), 634–656.

Scharmann, L. C. (1990). Enhancing the understanding of the premises of evolutionary theory: The influence of diversified instructional strategy. *School Science and Mathematics, 90*(2), 91–100.

Scharmann, L. C., & Harris, W. M., Jr. (1992). Teaching evolution: Understanding and applying the nature of science. *Journal of Research in Science Teaching, 29*(4), 375–388.

Scharmann, L. C., & Smith, M. U. (2001). Defining versus describing the nature of science: A pragmatic analysis for classroom teachers and science educators. *Science Education, 85*(4), 493–509.

Scharmann, L. C., Smith, M. U., James, M. C., & Jensen, M. (2005). Explicit reflective nature of science instruction: Evolution, intelligent design, and umbrellaology. *Journal of Science Teacher Education, 16*(1), 27–41.

Schmidt, D. J. (1967). Test on understanding science: A comparison among school groups. *Journal of Research in Science Teaching, 5*(4), 365–366.

Schwartz, R. S. (2004). *Epistemological views in authentic science practice: A cross-discipline comparison of scientists' views of nature of science and scientific inquiry.* Unpublished doctoral dissertation, Department of Science and Mathematics Education, Oregon State University, Corvallis, OR.

Schwartz, R. S., & Lederman, N. G. (2002). "It's the nature of the beast": The influence of knowledge and intentions on learning and teaching nature of science. *Journal of Research in Science Teaching, 39*(3), 205–236.

Schwartz, R. S., Lederman, N. G., & Crawford, B. (2004). Developing views of nature of science in an authentic context: An explicit approach to bridging the gap between nature of science and scientific inquiry. *Science Education, 88*(4), 610–645.

Schwirian, P. (1968). On measuring attitudes toward science. *Science Education, 52*, 172–179.

Scientific Literacy Research Center. (1967). *Wisconsin inventory of science processes*. Madison, WI: University of Wisconsin.

Shapiro, B. L. (1996). A case study of change in elementary student teacher thinking during an independent investigation in science: Learning about the "face of science that does not yet know." *Science Education, 80*(5), 535–560.

Showalter V. M. (1974). What is united science education? Program objectives and scientific literacy. *Prism, II*, 2.

Shulman, L. S. (1987). Knowledge and teaching: Foundations of the new reform. *Harvard Educational Review, 57*(1), 1–22.

Smith, M. U., Lederman, N. G., Bell, R. L., McComas, W. F., & Clough, M. P. (1997) How great is the disagreement about the nature of science: A response to Alters. *Journal of Research in Science Teaching, 34*(10), 1101–1103.

Sorensen, L. L. (1966). Change in critical thinking between students in laboratory-centered and lecture-demonstration-centered patterns of instruction in high school biology. *Dissertation Abstracts International, 26*, 6567A (University Microfilms No. 66-03, 939).

Spears, J., & Zollman, D. (1977). The influence of structured versus unstructured laboratory on students' understanding the process of science. *Journal of Research in Science Teaching, 14*(1), 33–38.

Stice, G. (1958). *Facts about science test*. Princeton, NJ: Educational Testing Service.

Sutherland, D., & Dennick, R. (2002). Exploring culture, language and perception of the nature of science. *International Journal of Science Education, 24*(1), 25–36.

Swan, M. D. (1966). Science achievement as it relates to science curricula and programs at the sixth grade level in Montana public schools. *Journal of Research in Science Teaching, 4*, 102–123.

Tamir, P. (1972). Understanding the process of science by students exposed to different science curricula in Israel. *Journal of Research in Science Teaching, 9*(3), 239–245.

Tao, P. K. (2003). Eliciting and developing junior secondary students' understanding of the nature of science through peer collaboration instruction in science stories. *International Journal of Science Education, 25*(2), 147–171.

Trembath, R. J. (1972). The structure of science. *The Australian Science Teachers Journal, 18*(2), 59–63.

Trent, J. (1965). The attainment of the concept "understanding science" using contrasting physics courses. *Journal of Research in Science Teaching, 3*(3), 224–229.

Troxel, V. A. (1968). *Analysis of instructional outcomes of students involved with three sources in high school chemistry*. Washington, DC: U.S. Department of Health, Education, and Welfare, Office of Education.

Welch, W. W. (1967). *Science process inventory*. Cambridge, MA: Harvard University Press.

Welch, W. W., & Pella, M. O. (1967–68). The development of an instrument for inventorying knowledge of the processes of science. *Journal of Research in Science Teaching, 5*(1), 64.

Welch, W. W., & Walberg, H. J. (1967–68). An evaluation of summer institute programs for physics teachers. *Journal of Research in Science Teaching, 5*, 105–109.

Wheeler, S. (1968). *Critique and revision of an evaluation instrument to measure students' understanding of science and scientists*. University of Chicago.

Wilson, L. (1954). A study of opinions related to the nature of science and its purpose in society. *Science Education, 38*(2), 159–164.

Winchester, I. (1993). Science is dead. We have killed it, you and I—How attacking the presuppositional structures of our scientific age can doom the interrogation of nature. *Interchange, 24*, 191–197.

Yager, R. E., & Wick, J. W. (1966). Three emphases in teaching biology: A statistical comparison of the results. *Journal of Research in Science Teaching, 4*(1), 16–20.

Zeidler, D. L., & Lederman, N. G. (1989). The effects of teachers' language on students' conceptions of the nature of science. *Journal of Research in Science Teaching, 26*(9), 771–783.

Zeidler, D. L., Walker, K. A., Ackett, W. A., & Simmons, M. L. (2002). Tangled up in views: Beliefs in the nature of science and responses to socioscientific dilemmas. *Science Education, 86*(3), 343–367.

CHAPTER 29

Humanistic Perspectives in the Science Curriculum

Glen S. Aikenhead
University of Saskatchewan

Probably the most pervasive alternative to the traditional science curriculum has been a humanistic approach to school science that is intended to prepare future citizens to critically and rationally assess science and technology. This goal views science as a human endeavor embedded within a social milieu of society and carried out by various social communities of scientists. The purpose of this chapter is to synthesize the research that has investigated humanistic perspectives in the school science curriculum, perspectives that would significantly alter the tenor of school science.

Any perspective on the science curriculum, be it humanistic or solely scientific, expresses an ideological point of view explicitly or implicitly (Cross, 1997; Fensham, 2000b; Fourez, 1989). This chapter's ideology gives priority to a student-centered point of view and to citizens as consumers of science and technology in their everyday lives, as opposed to a scientist-centered view aimed at scientific or science-related careers. In the political arena defined by Spencer's (1859, p. 5) question, "What knowledge is [should be] of most worth?" the research literature expresses essentially two contrary positions, often in combination: educationally driven propositions about what is best for students and society, and politically driven realities supported by de facto arguments supporting the status quo. For instance, although empirical evidence overwhelmingly speaks to the *educational* failure of traditional school science (described below), the continuous survival and high status enjoyed by traditional school science attest to its *political* success. The research reviewed in this chapter reflects the tension between educational soundness and political reality.

We must not forget that curriculum decisions are first and foremost political decisions (Brickhouse & Bodner, 1992; Fensham, 1992; Roberts, 1988; Rudolph, 2003; Young, 1971). Research can *inform* curriculum decision making, but the rational, evidence-based findings of research tend to wilt in the presence of ideologies, as curriculum choices are made within specific school jurisdictions, most often favoring the status quo (Blades, 1997; Carlone, 2003; Cross & Price, 2002; Fensham, 1993, 1998; Gaskell, 1992, 2003; Hart, 2002; Hurd, 1991; Roberts, 1995).

Humanistic perspectives in the science curriculum have been described in various ways, including values, the nature of science, the social aspects of science, and the human character of science revealed through its sociology, history, and philosophy. Since the 1970s, a humanistic perspective has often been identified with science-technology-society (STS) curricula.

Humanistic perspectives have a long history, dating back to the early nineteenth century, when natural philosophy was sporadically taught in some schools. This history, particularly events following World War II, provides a context for appreciating both the educationally and politically driven agendas that motivate the research found in the science education literature and for understanding the literature's conceptualization of humanistic perspectives in the curriculum.

This chapter synthesizes pertinent research studies concerning the formulation of curriculum policy; clarifies different research methods employed; and draws conclusions concerning the strengths, weaknesses, and gaps in the research literature. The chapter unfolds in the following sequence: history of humanistic perspectives in science education, curriculum policy, and a discussion of the research with implications for future research studies.

A humanistic perspective is not the only innovation to challenge the status quo of school science. Other chapters in the *Handbook* are related to humanistic content in the science curriculum (e.g., Chapters 8, 10, 12, 24, and 28), and consequently their topics are not given much attention here, but are cross-referenced.

This chapter restricts itself to the intended school science curriculum that serves 11-year-old and older students. (For a review of research into the taught and the learned curricula of humanistic school science, see Aikenhead [2006].) This chapter excludes literature that simply offers a rationale for a humanistic science curriculum.

A SHORT HISTORY OF HUMANISTIC PERSPECTIVES IN THE SCIENCE CURRICULUM

School subjects are grounded implicitly on the historical process through which they arose (Sáez & Carretero, 2002). The ideology of the traditional science curriculum is easily understood when placed in the historical context of its nineteenth century origin, an origin that emerged within the ongoing evolution of science itself.

Research into the history of the school curriculum provides a framework for the conceptualizations of humanistic perspectives in the science curriculum. Based on Chapter 26 (this volume), DeBoer (1991), Donnelly (2002), Fuller (1997), Hurd (1991), Kliebard (1979), Layton (1986, 1991), MacLeod (1981), Mendelsohn (1976), and Orange (1981), the following outline is offered: (1) The name *science* was chosen to replace *natural philosophy* during the birth of a new organization in 1831, the British Association for the Advancement of Science (BAAS). (2) In a speech to the third annual meeting in 1834, Whewell, the president of the BAAS and natural philosopher, coined the term *scientist* to refer to the cultivators of the new science. (3) The professionalization of natural philosophy into science was completed in England by 1850, by distancing itself from technology and ensconcing itself within the cloisters of university academia, where it could control access to its various disciplines. (4) English education reformers in 1867, directed by a BAAS committee, produced a science curriculum that marginalized practical utility and eschewed utilitarian issues and values related to everyday life. At the same time their "mental training" argument helped squeeze the new science disciplines into an already crowded school curriculum. (5) Meanwhile in the United States, the BAAS served as a model for establishing the American Association for the Advancement of Science (AAAS) in 1848. (6) In 1894 critics of the U.S. National Education Committee of Ten erroneously accused it of imposing college entrance expectations on the high school curriculum, a criticism that college science faculty then embraced as an actual Committee recommendation. (7) By 1910, the American school science mirrored England's. (8) Many events, but particularly World War II, caused science and technology to form a new social institution called research and development (R&D), which is still called "science" today.

WW II
↓
research +
development

By contemplating the historical origins of today's traditional science curriculum, we recognize it as essentially a nineteenth century curriculum in its educational intent. As well, we can better appreciate the powerful ideologies that guide and sustain school science today (i.e., moving students through "the pipeline"; Frederick, 1991). These same ideologies cause most science teachers to teach in very similar ways toward very similar goals (Cross, 1997; Gallagher, 1998). The traditional ideologies of pre-professional scientific training, mental training, and screening for college entrance challenge any attempt to reform school science into a subject that embraces a humanistic perspective (Fensham, 1992).

Obstacle
to
humanistic
perspective

There have always been educators who promoted school science as a subject that connects with everyday society. Different eras have brought different social, economic, political, and educational forces to bear on reforming the science curriculum into a humanistic type of curriculum (Hurd, 1991). Recent historical and case-study research shows how innovative humanistic proposals in the United Kingdom and Australia contravened the social privilege and power that benefited an elite student enrolled in a traditional science curriculum (Fensham, 1998; Hodson, 1994; Layton, 1991; Solomon, 1994a). Accordingly, attempts at reforming the traditional school curriculum into a humanistic one have largely been unsuccessful. This indicates that political and social power is involved in reaching curriculum decisions, an issue revisited throughout this chapter.

A Recent Humanistic Science Curriculum Movement

The empirical research reviewed in this chapter is framed by several post–World War II humanistic conceptions of school science often associated with the STS movement (Ziman, 1980). Details of its particular history can be found elsewhere (Aikenhead, 2003; Bybee, 1993; Cheek, 1992; Fensham, 1992; Solomon, 2003b; Solomon & Aikenhead, 1994; Yager, 1996a) but can be summarized as follows.

Many proposals for a humanistic alternative to school science were inspired by university programs formally initiated in the late 1960s, in the United States, the United Kingdom, Australia, and the Netherlands. Some were highly academic history and philosophy of science programs that eschewed sociological perspectives on science. Others embraced sociology, economics, and politics and gave themselves the label STS. The university STS programs responded to perceived crises in responsibility related to, for instance, the environment and nuclear energy. Thus, social responsibility for both scientist and citizen formed one of the major conceptions on a humanistic perspective in school science (Aikenhead, 1980; Bybee, 1993; Cross & Price, 1992, 2002; Kortland, 2001). For instance, a societal issue-oriented science curriculum project evolved from the integration of social studies and science at the University of Iowa (e.g., Cossman, 1969) and a decade later in Colorado (McConnell, 1982).

A second major conception to emerge from post–World War II academia was the poststructuralist analysis of science itself, often associated with Kuhn's *The Structure of Scientific Revolutions* in 1962. This analysis tended to challenge the positivism and realism inherent in traditional science courses (Abd-El-Khalick & Lederman, 2000; Kelly, Carlsen, & Cunningham, 1993).

Interest in humanistic content in the science curriculum enjoyed a renaissance at several university centers after World War II. At Harvard, for instance, President J. B. Conant (1947) encouraged his faculty to give serious attention to the history, philosophy, and sociology of science. He influenced Ph.D. student Leo Klopfer, who produced the *History of Science Cases* (Klopfer & Watson, 1957) and who critically researched their impact in schools (Klopfer & Cooley, 1963). Similarly influenced was Jim Gallagher (1971), who presciently articulated a blueprint for an STS science curriculum (echoed in Hurd's 1975 seminal publication). It rationalized teaching scientific concepts and processes embedded in the sociology, history, and philosophy of science; relevant technology; and social issues. Probably the most influential science education project to emerge from Harvard was Harvard Project Physics, a historical and philosophical perspective on physics aimed at increasing student enrolment in high school physics (Cheek, 2000; Walberg, 1991; Welch, 1973). It stimulated many other humanistic curriculum innovations worldwide (Aikenhead, 2003; Irwin, 2000).

The integration of two broad academic fields, (1) the interaction of science and scientists with social issues and institutions *external* to the scientific community and (2) the social interactions of scientists and their communal, epistemic, and ontological values *internal* to the scientific community, produced a major conceptual framework for STS (Aikenhead, 1994c; Ziman, 1984). In practice, however, some STS projects narrowly focused on just one of these domains. Other important conceptual frameworks for humanistic school science have been articulated in the research literature:

1. The degree to which a humanistic perspective supports or challenges a traditional positivist and realist view of science (Bingle & Gaskell, 1994).

2. Whether a humanistic perspective advocates being aware of an issue, or making a decision on the issue, or taking social action on the issue (Roth & Désautels, 2004; Rubba, 1987; Solomon, 1994b), a framework particularly salient to environmental education (Chapter 24, this volume) and to social responsibility (Cross & Price, 1992, 2002).

3. The degree to which humanistic content is combined with canonical science content (Aikenhead, 1994b; Bartholomew, Osborne, & Ratcliffe, 2002).

4. The degree to which the content and processes of technology are integrated into the humanistic perspective (Cheek, 2000; Fensham, 1988).

5. The degree to which school science is *integrated*—the integration of scientific disciplines, and the integration of school science with other school subjects (Chapter 19, this volume).

6. The degree to which schooling is expected to reproduce the status quo or be an agent of social change and social justice (Chapter 12, this volume; Apple, 1996; Cross & Price, 1999).

Slogans for a humanistic science curriculum, such as STS, can change from country to country and over time. In every era, slogans have rallied support for fundamental changes to school science (Chapter 25, this volume). Today, there are a number of slogans for humanistic science curricula worldwide, for instance: science-technology-citizenship, science for public understanding, citizen science, functional scientific literacy, public awareness of science, *Bildung*, cross-cultural school science, and variations on science-technology-society-environment. These humanistic science programs are often seen as vehicles for achieving science for all girls' participation in science (Chapter 10), scientific literacy (Chapter 25), and understanding the nature of science (Chapter 28).

Just as science had to compete in the 1860s with the classics and religion to get a foothold in the school curriculum, today a humanistic perspective must compete with the preprofessional training of elite students (moving through the pipeline) to earn a place in the school science curriculum. This reflects a competition between two ideologies: on the one hand, promoting practical utility, human values, and a connectedness with societal issues to achieve inclusiveness and a student-centered orientation, while on the other hand, promoting professional science associations, the rigors of mental training, and academic screening to achieve exclusiveness and a scientist-centered orientation.

Humanistic perspectives are represented by a variety of conceptual frameworks defined in the literature on research into the intended science curriculum, that is, curriculum policy.

CURRICULUM POLICY

Four areas of research address an educationally sound curriculum policy for humanistic perspectives in the science curriculum: major failures of the traditional curriculum, successes of learning science in non-school contexts, the relevance of curriculum content, and the processes for formulating curriculum policy itself. Each area is discussed in turn.

Major Failures of the Traditional Science Curriculum

Deficiencies in the traditional science curriculum have been the cornerstone of arguments supporting a humanistic perspective. At least three major failures are documented in research studies.

The first failure concerns the chronic declines in student enrollment (Dekkers & Delaeter, 2001; Hurd, 1991; Osborne & Collins, 2000; Welch & Walberg, 1967) due to students' disenchantment with school science (Hurd, 1989; SCC, 1984). This failure of school science threatens its primary goal: to produce knowledgeable people to go into careers in science, engineering, and related jobs; or at least to support those who do. It is instructive to examine the pipeline data from a 15-year longitudinal study (beginning in 1977 with grade 10 students) conducted by the U.S. Office of Technology Assessment (Frederick, 1991). Of the initial sample of four million grade 10 students, 18 percent expressed an interest to continue toward university science and engineering courses. Of these interested students, 19 percent lost interest during high school (i.e., they moved out of the pipeline), and then during university undergraduate programs, 39 percent of first-year science and engineering students lost interest, *twice* the proportion than in high school. These quantitative data support in-depth qualitative research that concluded: the problem of qualified students moving out of the pipeline resides much more with universities than with high schools, especially for young women (Astin & Astin, 1992; Seymour, 1995; Tobias, 1990).

Another substantial reduction in the pipeline population occurred between high school graduation and first-year university, a transition that showed a 42 percent loss in the number of students interested in pursuing science and engineering courses (Frederick, 1991; Sadler & Tai, 2001). These data are partly explained by studies that discovered that highly capable A-level science students, particularly young women and minority students, switched out of science as soon as they received their school science credentials, because the curriculum *discouraged* them from studying science further (Gardner, 1998; Oxford University Department of Educational Studies, 1989).

Most research into the science curriculum concluded that school science transmits content that is socially sterile, impersonal, frustrating, intellectually boring, and/or dismissive of students' life-worlds (Hurd, 1989; Lee & Roth, 2002; Osborne & Collins, 2001; Osborne, Driver, & Simon, 1998; Reiss, 2000; SCC, 1984). This perception prevails even for science-proficient students who enroll in senior science courses in high school (Lyons, 2003). One major reason for advocating humanistic content in school science has been to reverse this chronic loss of talented students (Eijkelhof & Lijnse, 1988; Ziman, 1980). Evidence suggests that humanistic perspectives in the science curriculum can improve the recruitment of students (Solomon, 1994a; Welch, 1973; Welch & Rothman, 1968).

A second, and related, major educational failure of the traditional science curriculum concerns the dishonest and mythical images about science and scientists that it conveys (Chapter 28, this volume; Aikenhead, 1973; Gallagher, 1991; Gaskell, 1992; Larochelle & Désautels, 1991; Milne & Taylor, 1998). As a consequence, some strong science students lose interest in taking further science classes, some students become interested in science for the wrong reasons, and many students become citizens who are illiterate with respect to the nature and social aspects of the scientific enterprise. One major reason for offering humanistic content has been to correct these false ideas (Ziman, 1980).

A third documented major failure dates back to the 1970s research into student learning: *most students tend not to learn science content meaningfully* (Anderson & Helms, 2001; Gallagher, 1991; Hart, 2002; Osborne, Duschl, & Fairbrother, 2003; White & Tisher, 1986). Research suggests that the goal of learning canonical science meaningfully is simply not achievable for the majority of students in the context of traditional school science (Aikenhead, 1996; Cobern & Aikenhead, 1998; Costa, 1995; Hennessy, 1993; Layton, Jenkins, Macgill, & Davey, 1993; Osborne et al., 2003; Shapiro, 2004). As a result, alternative science curriculum policies have been proposed to radically change the meaning of school science, a controversial idea to be sure (e.g., Chapters 8 and 12, this volume; Aikenhead, 2000a; Fensham, 2000b, 2002; Jenkins, 2000; Millar, 2000; Roth & Désautels, 2002, 2004).

An important consequence of this third *educational* failure of the traditional science curriculum is the reaction of most students and many teachers to the *political* reality that science credentials must be obtained in high school or a student is screened out of post-secondary opportunities. Empirical evidence demonstrates how students and many teachers react to being placed in the political position of having to play school games to make it appear as if significant science learning has occurred (Bartholomew et al., 2002; Costa, 1997; Loughran & Derry, 1997; Larson, 1995; Meyer, 1998; Roth, Boutonné, McRobbie, & Lucas, 1999). The many rules to these school games are captured by the term "Fatima's rules" (Larson, 1995). Playing Fatima's rules, rather than achieving meaningful learning, constitutes a highly significant *learned curriculum* of students and a ubiquitous *hidden curriculum* of school science (Aikenhead, 2000a). A curriculum policy that inadvertently but predictably leads students and teachers to play Fatima's rules is a policy that is difficult to defend educationally from a humanistic perspective, even though the policy flourishes for political reasons.

Learning and Using Science in Other Contexts

Although the goal of meaningful learning of canonical science is largely unattainable for many students in the context of traditional school science, it seems to be attained in other contexts in which people are personally involved in a science-related everyday task (Davidson & Schibeci, 2000; Dori & Tal, 2000; Goshorn, 1996; Michael, 1992; Roth & Désautels, 2004; Tytler, Duggan, & Gott, 2001; Wynne, 1991). Thirty-one different case studies of this type of research were reviewed by Ryder (2001), who firmly concluded: *When people need to communicate with experts and/or take action, they usually learn the science content required.*

Even though people seem to learn science content in their everyday world as required, this learning is not often the "pure science" (canonical content) transmitted by a traditional science curriculum. Research has produced one clear and consistent finding: *most often, canonical science content is not directly usable in science-related everyday situations*, for various reasons (Furnham, 1992; Gee, 2001; Jenkins, 1992; Layton, 1991; Layton et al., 1993; Ryder, 2001; Solomon, 1984; Wynne, 1991). In other words, the empirical evidence contradicts scientists' and science teachers' hypothetical claims that science content is directly applicable to a citizen's everyday life. What scientists and science teachers probably mean is that scientific concepts can be used to abstract meaning from an everyday event. The fact that this type of intellectual abstraction is only relevant to those who enjoy explaining everyday experiences this way attests to the observation that most students perceive science as having no personal or social relevance.

How well do science teachers apply science content outside the classroom? When investigating an everyday event for which canonical science content was directly relevant, Lawrenz and Gray (1995) found that science teachers with science degrees did not use science content to make meaning out of the event, but instead used other content knowledge, such as values (i.e., humanistic content).

This research result, along with the 31 cases reviewed by Ryder (2001), can be explained by the discovery that canonical science content must be *transformed* (i.e., deconstructed and then reconstructed according to the idiosyncratic demands of the context) into knowledge that is very different in character from the "pure science" knowledge of the science curriculum, as one moves from pure science content for explaining or describing, to "practical science" content for action (Jenkins,

1992, 2002; Layton, 1991). "This reworking of scientific knowledge is demanding, but necessary as socio-scientific issues are complex. It typically involves science from different sub-disciplines, knowledge from other social domains, and of course value judgements and social elements" (Kolstø, 2000, p. 659). When the science curriculum does not include this reworking or transformation process, pure science remains unusable outside of school for most students (Layton et al., 1993). When students attempt to master unusable knowledge, most end up playing Fatima's rules instead. This empirical evidence supports the educational policy of incorporating everyday action-oriented science content (citizen science; Irwin, 1995); for instance, researchers Lawrence and Eisenhart (2002, p. 187) concluded, "science educators and science education researchers are misguided not to be interested in the kinds of science that ordinary people use to make meaning and take action in their lives."

Given these research conclusions that question the efficacy of teaching for meaningful learning in the context of the traditional science curriculum, there would seem to be little educational advantage for a teacher "to cover" the entire science curriculum but, instead, greater advantage to teaching fewer canonical science concepts chosen because of their relevance to a humanistic perspective (Eijkelhof, 1990; Kortland, 2001; Häussler & Hoffmann, 2000; Walberg & Ahlgren, 1973). The latter approach is supported by a plethora of comparison studies, based on standardized achievement tests of canonical science, that showed no significant effect on students' scores when instruction time for the canonical content was reduced to make room for the history of science, the nature of science, or the social aspects of science (Aikenhead, 1994b, 2003b; Bybee, 1993; Eijkelhof & Lijnse, 1988; Irwin, 2000; Klopfer & Cooley, 1963; Pedersen, 1992; Welch, 1973); and on occasion, students in a humanistic science course appeared to fair significantly better on achievement tests of canonical science (Häussler & Hoffmann, 2000; Mbajiorgu & Ali, 2003; Rubba & Wiesenmayer, 1991; Solomon, Duveen, Scot & McCarthy, 1992; Sutman & Bruce, 1992; Wang & Schmidt, 2001; Wiesenmayer & Rubba, 1999; Winther & Volk, 1994; Yager & Tamir, 1993).

In summary, a recurring evidence-based criticism of the traditional science curriculum has been its lack of relevance for the everyday world (Millar & Osborne, 1998; Osborne & Collins, 2000; Reiss, 2000), a problem dating back at least 150 years. The issue of relevance is at the heart of most humanistic science curricula.

Research on Relevance

Humanistic approaches to school science represent many different views on relevance (Chapters 7, 8, & 28, this volume; Bybee, 1993; Cheek, 1992; Irwin, 1995; Kortland, 2001; Kumar & Chubin, 2000; Millar, 2000; Solomon & Aikenhead, 1994; Yager, 1996b). "Relevance" is certainly an ambiguous term. Mayoh and Knutton (1997) characterized relevance as having two dimensions: Relevant to whom? and Relevant to what? In this chapter, however, the multidimensional character of relevance is defined by a more political question (Häussler & Hoffmann, 2000; Roberts, 1988): *Who* decides? Research into humanistic curriculum policies is reviewed here according to seven types of relevance, a scheme developed in part from Fensham's (2000b) views about *who* decides what is relevant. These seven heuristic categories overlap to varying degrees.

Wish-they-knew science.   This type of relevance is typically embraced by academic scientists, education officials, and many science educators when asked: What would make school science relevant? (AAAS, 1989; Fensham, 1992; Walberg, 1991). The usual answer, canonical science content, moves students through the pipeline for success in university programs.

But how relevant is this wish-they-knew content for success by science-oriented students in first-year university courses? Research evidence suggests it is not as relevant as one might assume and, on occasion, not relevant at all (Champagne & Klopfer, 1982; McCammon, Golden, & Wuensch, 1988; Stuart, 1977; Tanaka & Taigen, 1986; Yager & Krajcik, 1989; Yager, Snider, & Krajcik, 1988). First-year university students who had not studied the prerequisite physical science course in high school achieved as well as their counterparts who did enroll in the prerequisite. Sadler and Tai's (2001, p. 111) more recent survey research claims, "Taking a high school physics course has a modestly positive relationship with the grade earned in introductory college physics." An endorsement of "modestly positive" would seem to be faint praise indeed. These research studies might rationally assuage science teachers' fear that time spent on humanistic content and citizen-science content will diminish students' chances of success at university. Although the *educational* arguments favoring wish-they-knew science are particularly weak, political realities favoring it are overwhelming (Fensham, 1993, 1998; Gaskell, 2003).

Need-to-know science.   This type of relevance is defined by people who have faced a real-life decision related to science and technology: for example, parents dealing with the birth of a Down's syndrome child, or town councilors dealing with the problem of methane generation at a landfill site (Layton, 1991; Layton et al., 1993). Curriculum policy researchers ask: What science content was helpful to the people when they were making decisions? Ryder (2001) in his analysis of 31 case studies of need-to-know science concluded, "Much of the science knowledge relevant to individuals in the case studies was *knowledge about science*, i.e. knowledge about the development and use of scientific knowledge rather than scientific knowledge itself" (p. 35, emphasis in the original). In other words, the curriculum must expand to include knowledge *about* science and scientists (humanistic content). One reason that people tend not to use canonical science content in their everyday world (in addition to it not being directly usable, as described above) is quite simple: canonical science content is the wrong type of content to use in most everyday action-oriented settings; instead need-to-know science (humanistic content) turns out to have greater practical value.

Functional science.   This is science content that is deemed relevant primarily by people with careers in science-based industries and professions. The category includes "workplace science" (Chin, Munby, Hutchinson, Taylor, & Clark, 2004).

Coles (1998) surveyed UK employers and higher education specialists in science who were asked to identify scientific content thought to be essential to school science. Unexpectedly, these respondents thought that students' understanding of science ideas was least important, compared with a myriad of other, more favored capabilities. Similar research findings emerged from broad studies into economic development within industrialized countries (e.g., Bishop, 1995; David, 1995; Drori, 1998). Consistently the research indicated that economic development depends on factors other than a population literate in canonical science and on factors beyond the influence of school science, for example: emerging technologies, industrial restructuring, poor management decisions, and government policies that affect military development, monetary exchange rates, wages, and licensing agreements

By conducting research *on the job* with science graduates, Duggan and Gott (2002) in the United Kingdom, Law (2002) in China, and Lottero-Perdue and Brickhouse (2002) in the United States discovered that the canonical science content used by science graduates was so context specific it had to be learned on the job, and that high school and university science content was rarely drawn upon. On the other hand, Duggan and Gott's findings suggested that procedural understanding (ideas about how to do science) was essential across most science-related careers. More specifically, they discovered one domain of concepts, "concepts of evidence," that was generally and directly applied by workers in science-rich occupations to critically evaluate scientific evidence, for instance, concepts related to the validity and reliability of data, and concepts of causation versus correlation. Similar findings arose in their research with an attentive public involved in a science-related societal issue. Duggan and Gott spoke for many researchers (e.g., Fensham, 2000a; Ryder, 2001) when they concluded, "Science curricula cannot expect to keep up to date with all aspects of science but can only aspire to teach students how to access and critically evaluate such knowledge" (p. 675).

The humanistic perspective germane here concerns a correct understanding of concepts of evidence when dealing with social implications, for instance: Is the scientific evidence credible enough to risk investing in a particular industrial process? or Is the scientific evidence good enough to warrant the social action proposed? In these contexts, it is useful for a person to understand the ways in which scientific evidence is technically and socially constructed (Bingle & Gaskell, 1994; Kelly et al., 1993; Cunningham, 1998; McGinn & Roth 1999), that is, humanistic content for the science curriculum. However, when "vocational science" courses are only concerned with vocational technology, they lose their humanistic perspective.

In a project that placed high school students in science-rich workplaces (e.g., veterinary and dental clinics), Chin and colleagues (2004) ethnographically investigated two issues: the relationship between school science and workplace science (a type of functional science) and the participants' perceptions of that relationship. The fact that students saw little or no connection between school science and workplace science was explained by the researchers this way: school science (canonical content) in the workplace was not central to the *purposes* of the workplace, and, therefore, school science was not overtly apparent in the workplace. In short, knowing canonical science content was not relevant to one's accountability in a science-rich workplace (a conclusion very similar to the results of research into need-to-know science, reviewed above).

Surveys and ethnographic research methods are not the only ways to substantiate functional science content. The Delphi research technique used by Häussler and Hoffmann (2000) in Germany was an educationally rational, in-depth method for establishing a physics curriculum policy by consensus among diverse stakeholders over "What should physics education look like so it is suitable for someone living in our society as it is today and as it will be tomorrow" (p. 691). Their 73 stakeholders represented people associated with wish-they-knew science (e.g., physicists and physics teachers) and with functional science (e.g., personnel officers in physics-related industries and general educationalists). Häussler and Hoffmann did not initially group their stakeholders into these two categories, but instead used a hierarchical cluster analysis statistic to tease out like-minded stakeholders. This analysis produced two coherent groups: Group 1 generally favored "scientific knowledge and methods as mental tools" and "passing on scientific knowledge to the next generation" significantly more than Group 2, who favored "physics as a vehicle to promote practical competence" (p. 693). These statistical results lend credence to the two categories of relevance that distinguish between wish-they-knew and functional science. Interestingly, however, Häussler and Hoffmann found that both groups gave *highest* priority to topics related to "physics as a socio-economic enterprise" that show "physics more as a human enterprise and less as a body of knowledge and procedures" (p. 704).

Enticed-to-know science.   By its very nature, enticed-to-know science excels at its motivational value. This is science content encountered in the mass media and on the internet, both positive and negative in its images of science and both sensational and sometimes dishonest in its quest to entice a reader or viewer to pay closer attention. Fensham (2000a, p. 75) reports that the OECD's Performance Indicators of Student Achievement project is using enticed-to-know science "to see how well their science curricula are equipping [15-year old] students to discern, understand and critique the reporting of science in newspapers and the Internet." Millar (2000) in the United Kingdom and Dimopoulos and Koulaidis (2003) in Greece described how a longitudinal analysis of the content of science-related articles in their respective national newspapers led to identifying the science and technology knowledge that would be most useful in making sense of these articles and the stories they presented. Millar's analysis stimulated a revision of the AS-level syllabus in the United Kingdom and eventually culminated in Hunt and Millar's (2000) high school textbook, *AS Science for Public Understanding*, which provides a humanistic perspective.

Moral issues and public risk are often associated with enticed-to-know science because the media normally attend to those aspects of events (Cross & Price, 1992, 2002; Eijkelhof, 1990; Nelkin, 1995; Osborne et al., 2003). Moreover, the more important everyday events in which citizens encounter science involve risk and environmental threats (Chapter 24, this volume; Irwin, 1995).

Have-cause-to-know science.   This is science content suggested by experts who interact with the general public on real-life matters pertaining to science and technology and who know the problems the public encounters when dealing with these experts (Law, Fensham, Li, & Wei, 2000). This empirical approach to developing curriculum policy is being tested in China, where the societal experts were drawn from the following domains: home and workplace safety; medical, health, and hygiene problems; nutrition and dietary habits; consumer savvy; and leisure and entertainment (Fensham, 2002; Law, 2002; Law et al., 2000). The approach assumes that societal experts are better situated than academic scientists to decide what knowledge is worth knowing in today's changing scientific and technological world.

Have-cause-to-know science is a feature of the Science for the Public Understanding of Science Project (SEPUP) in the United States (Thier & Nagle, 1994,

1996). Societal experts in industry, the sciences, and education provided the curriculum developers with elements of a relevant issues-based curriculum that led to STS chemistry modules and three STS textbooks (SEPUP, 2003): *Science and Life Issues; Issues, Evidence and You;* and *Science and Sustainability.*

In the Netherlands, Eijkelhof (1990, 1994) used the Delphi research technique to gain a consensus among *societal experts* to establish the humanistic and canonical science content for an STS physics module, "Ionizing Radiation." The 35 Delphi participants in Eijkelhof's study were carefully selected to represent a variety of fields and opinions on the risks of ionizing radiation (a group purposefully more homogeneous than the stakeholders in Häussler and Hoffmann's [2000] study discussed above). After the normal three rounds in the Delphi procedure, Eijkelhof's radiation experts pointed to suitable societal contexts of application and concomitant scientific content that the public had cause to know. Eijkelhof (1990) warned, however, that policy research by itself should not *prescribe* the final curriculum. A curriculum development team must also consider educational issues, for example, learning difficulties of students, available instruction time, and pedagogical factors. He attended to those issues by drawing upon a decade or more of research by the PLON humanistic physics project (Eijkelhof & Lijnse, 1988; Ratcliffe et al., 2003).

In contrast, an Australian chemistry curriculum committee could not reach a consensus on a balance between societal contexts of application and scientific content, and as a result the committee's writers tended to promote the status quo wish-they-knew science rather than the intended have-cause-to-know science (Fensham & Corrigan, 1994).

The National Curriculum in the United Kingdom calls for humanistic content to be taught but does not specify the content. In a study focused entirely on humanistic content, Osborne and colleagues (2001) employed the Delphi technique to establish a consensus on what "ideas about science" should be taught in school science. During three rounds of the Delphi procedure, 23 experts (professional and academic people notable for their contributions to the clarification of science for the public) produced 18 ideas, nine of which showed sufficient stability and support (the top three were: "scientific methods and critical testing," "creativity," and "historical development of scientific knowledge"). These nine ideas about science informed the development of classroom teaching materials (Bartholomew et al., 2002). These materials were then embedded in a large-scale research project, "Evidence-Based Practice in Science Education" (IPSE). The have-cause-to-know science, elucidated by the IPSE project, addressed humanistic content; the canonical science content had been established by the National Curriculum's wish-they-knew science.

A disadvantage of the Delphi procedure is evident in the ambiguous or "motherhood" statements that sometimes emerge (e.g., creativity). This disadvantage likely results from participants not meeting face to face to clarify and articulate the meaning of each statement.

Curriculum policy research has also included surveys of experts to determine which social issues (and therefore, which have-cause-to-know science) they valued most in a humanistic science curriculum. The experts included (Bybee, 1993) scientists and engineers, citizens, science teachers, and science educators in the United States and around the world. The relevant contexts for have-cause-to-know science were identified, but their actual influence on curriculum policy has not been noticeable (Cheek, 2000). This survey research was perhaps more politically successful at raising awareness of STS than developing specific curriculum policies.

Personal-curiosity science.   When students themselves decide on the topics of interest for school science, relevance takes on a personal though perhaps idiosyncratic meaning, as students' hearts and minds are captured (Gardner, 1988; Osborne & Collins, 2000; Reiss, 2000). Based on a humanistic curriculum policy principle that one builds on the interests and experiences of the student, Sjøberg (2000) surveyed over 9,000 13-year-old students in 21 countries to discover (among other things) their past experiences related to science, their curiosity toward certain science topics, their attitude to science, their perception of scientists at work, and their self-identity as a future scientist. Based on the same curriculum policy principle, Häussler and Hoffmann (2000) surveyed over 6,000 German students, aged 11 to 16 years, to determine their interest in various physics topics. Sjøberg (2000) and Häussler and Hoffmann (2000) offer insights into students' differential interests; for instance, "music" was much more interesting than "acoustics and sounds," and "the rainbow and sunsets" much more than "light and optics." In other words, concrete themes embedded in student experiences were much more relevant than science discipline topics, a finding supported by three decades of research by the Dutch PLON project team (Kortland, 2001). In Sjøberg's study, students in non-Western countries had a significantly more positive image of scientists (heroic figures helping the poor and underprivileged) than their counterparts in Western countries, a finding that points to the importance of culture in a student's everyday world (a topic discussed below). In the Häussler and Hoffmann (2000) study, two outcomes are pertinent here: students' views were congruent with stakeholders who advocated a humanistic perspective in the physics curriculum, but discordant with the status quo. Häussler and Hoffmann pointed out that a curriculum policy founded on their Delphi research with stakeholders (reviewed above) would look very similar to a curriculum policy founded on student interests alone (i.e., personal-curiosity science).

Science-As-Culture

A more holistic yet abstract concept of relevance in school science was advanced by Weinstein's (1998) research concerning the enculturation of students *into everyday society*, an approach to science education that stands in stark contrast to the enculturation of students *into scientific disciplines*. Culture decides, de facto, what is relevant for science-as-culture. For instance, in school culture, "Students constantly are being measured, sorted, and turned into objects of scrutiny. They learn science up close and personal but not as scientists; rather, they learn it as objects of science" (p. 493). Weinstein identified a network of communities in students' everyday lives: health systems, political systems, the media, environmental groups, and industry, to name a few. Each community interacts with communities of science professionals, resulting in a *cultural commonsense notion of science*.

Science-as-culture is more than just pop culture (Solomon, 1998). As a category of relevance, science-as-culture serves in part as a superordinate category to the need-to-know, functional, enticed-to-know, have-cause-to-know, and personal-curiosity science categories. Its relevance resides in the student's community's culture (a commonsense notion of science) and in the student's home and peer cultures (Chapter 8, this volume; Costa, 1995; Solomon, 1994b, 1999, 2003a). Science's role in society is also embedded in science-as-culture, as evidenced by roles such as setting environmental standards, regulating commerce, providing legal evidence, announcing medical breakthroughs, creating novel ethical dilemmas, and requiring financial support for research and development (Dhingra, 2003; Jenkins, 2000; Stocklmayer, Gore, & Bryant, 2001).

Future research into students' science-as-culture may reveal useful ideas for a humanistic science policy, particularly for the enculturation of students into their local, national, and global communities. Prelle and Solomon (1996), for instance, provide a rich account of the differences between students' orientation to an environmental issue and their scientific knowledge on the subject. The researchers explored students' science-as-culture by investigating those differences in three settings: the science classroom, students' homes, and on holidays. Nelkin's (1995) and Stocklmayer et al.'s (2001) seminal research into science and the media raises an important researchable policy question: What understandings of science and journalism are of critical value to consumers of the mass media?

Science-as-culture can also be captured by project-based learning in which local science-related real-life problems are addressed by students in an interdisciplinary way (e.g., Chapters 12 and 24, this volume; Dori & Tal, 2000; Jenkins, 2002; Lee & Roth, 2002; Roth & Désautels, 2004). This approach draws upon community resources and local culture to stimulate need-to-know, functional, and have-cause-to-know science, as well as science-as-culture, in short, citizen science. The presence of a humanistic perspective in a project-based curriculum depends, however, on the degree to which its humanistic content is made explicit in the instruction and assessment of students (Chapter 28, this volume; Aikenhead, 1973; Kortland, 2001; Ratcliffe, 1997).

Conclusion

These seven heuristic categories of relevance, based on who decides what is relevant, can help describe the content and contexts found in a humanistic perspective of a particular science curriculum. More often than not, a curriculum will embrace several categories simultaneously (e.g., Aikenhead, 1994a; Eijkelhof & Kortland, 1988).

Ideologies inherent in any science curriculum can be explained in terms of two mutually exclusive presuppositions of school science (Aikenhead, 2000a; Rudolph, 2003; Weinstein, 1998): (1) the enculturation of students into their *local, national, and global communities*, communities increasingly influenced by advances in science and technology, and (2) the enculturation of students into the *disciplines of science*. These presuppositions represent two fundamentally different axiomatic views of relevance. Therefore, relevance precipitates a policy dilemma. Depending on the humanistic science curriculum, relevance will be fundamentally framed by an allegiance to scientific disciplines or to students' cultural communities. In an attempt to resolve the dilemma by integrating the two positions into the same curriculum, educators risk confusing and alienating students (Egan, 1996). The research reviewed in this chapter suggests that any science curriculum, humanistic or purely scientific, dedicated to the enculturation of all students into scientific ways of thinking will constantly be undermined by Fatima's rules.

Processes of Formulating Curriculum Policy

Throughout this chapter's review of research, educationally driven research findings conflicted with political realities. These political realities intensify when we examine research into the processes by which people have formulated curriculum policy. For example, researchers have explored such questions as: Who has the sociopolitical power to set policy? and How do they assert and maintain that power? However, the paucity of research in this domain (Kortland, 2001; Roberts, 1988) may speak to the unease felt by research participants when political events come under public scrutiny, exposing the natural tension between maintaining the status quo of preprofessional training in the pipeline, and innovating a humanistic perspective for equity and social justice (Chapter 12, this volume; Apple, 1996; Fensham, 1998; Lee, 1997; Roth & McGinn, 1998).

Historical events, summarized earlier in the chapter, revealed the political context in which the first formal science curriculum policy emerged in 1867, a context characterized by the cultural values, conventions, expectations, and ideologies at that time, all of which determined what school science would be. Because context is paramount for policy inquiry, researchers have often employed qualitative methods such as case studies or vignettes to interpret and understand processes that led to a humanistic science curriculum policy. This was certainly the case for research into power conflicts over curriculum policy reported by Aikenhead (2002), Blades (1997), Fensham (1993, 1998), Gaskell (1989, 2003), Hart (2002), Roberts (1988, 1995), and Solomon (2002, 2003b). Each study revealed the various power dynamics adopted by different groups of stakeholders. When deciding what knowledge is of most worth, people usually negotiate by using both rational criteria and political power in an attempt to limit or enhance the influences of various stakeholders. Each educational jurisdiction has its own story to tell about how curriculum policy is formulated.

Two research studies are mentioned here to illustrate this type of research. In his book *Procedures of Power & Curriculum Change* (a research study into the temporary defeat of a humanistic science curriculum policy in Alberta, Canada), Blades (1997) allegorically described the intense clashes between newly aligned interest groups who organized a network of relationships (actor-networks; Carlone, 2003; Foucault, 1980; Gaskell & Hepburn, 1998) to serve their own self-interests, and who enacted "rigor" as a power ploy in their discourse. Blades discovered that one very powerful stakeholder-group altered its alliances, thereby reversing its original policy position. A second study by Gaskell (1989) in British Columbia, Canada, showed how science teachers' allegiances to different professional organizations and to their own professional self-identities undermined an emerging humanistic science curriculum policy (Rowell & Gaskell, 1987).

Although each case study and vignette found in the literature was unique, all reached the same conclusion (with some unique exceptions): local university science professors have a self-interest in maintaining their discipline and will boldly crush humanistic initiatives in school science policy (Aikenhead, 2002; Blades, 1997; Fensham, 1992, 1993, 1998; Fensham & Corrigan, 1994; Gaskell, 1989; Hart, 2002; Pandwar & Hoddinott, 1995; Roberts, 1988; Shymansky & Kyle, 1988), resulting in what Gaskell (2003, p. 140) called "the tyranny of the few." If local science professors become marginalized and lose their power to control policy decisions, they tend to realign their actor-networks into international alliances to defeat a local humanistic curriculum policy (Rafea, 1999).

Science curriculum policy is normally formulated more smoothly through consultation with different stakeholders (Orpwood, 1985), for instance: government officials, the scientific community, science teachers, university science educators, students, parents, business, labor groups, industry, and other groups and institutions. Government ministries of education generally rely on the advice of curriculum committees variously composed of some of these stakeholders. Because government committee meetings are almost always held out of the view of an inquisitive researcher, their confidentiality has prevented research into the early stages of formulation of government policy (De Vos & Reiding, 1999; Roberts, 1988).

Consultative research has also taken the form of research and development (R&D) studies that produced STS classroom materials (e.g., textbooks) as a means to influence or articulate a humanistic curriculum policy. Researchers have collaborated with ministries of education, selected teachers, students, and experts who furnished "functional" and "have-cause-to-know" science (among other types of relevance) for the science curriculum (Aikenhead, 1994a; Eijkelhof & Lijnse, 1988; Eijkelhof & Kapteijn, 2000; Kortland, 2001).

More rigorously systematic policy studies have used the Delphi research method to inform humanistic curriculum policy, for instance (as described above), the research by Eijkelhof (1990), Häussler and Hoffmann (2000), and Osborne and colleagues (2001). Their experts were able to reach a consensus, more or less, on the relevant contexts and associated knowledge for an educationally sound, humanistic science curriculum policy.

The most elaborate, theory-based, consultative methodology to produce curriculum policy is deliberative inquiry. Inspired by Schwab's (1974) "deliberative enquiry," it offers a combination of "top-down" central control by government bureaucrats and "grass-roots" populist control by other stakeholders. Deliberative inquiry is a structured and informed dialogic conversation among stakeholders who, face to face, help government officials reach a decision on curriculum policy by discussing and reexamining their own priorities (i.e., values) along with their reading of relevant research (Orpwood, 1985). Because science teachers will be central to implementing a humanistic science curriculum (Chapter 26, this volume; Roberts, 1988) and because curriculum evaluation research consistently shows that the teacher has more influence on student outcomes than the choice of curriculum taught (Aikenhead, 2006; Welch, 1995), the science teacher is a key stakeholder and usually holds a central role during deliberative inquiry meetings. The process of deliberation encompasses both educational and political dimensions to formulating curriculum policy.

The Science Council of Canada (SCC) used deliberative inquiry to produce a national science curriculum policy that embraced a humanistic perspective (Orpwood, 1985; SCC, 1984). The SCC study ensured that significant problems in science education were identified, that appropriate evidence was collected, and that the problems and evidence were considered by diverse stakeholders attending one of the 11 two-day deliberative conferences held across Canada. Stakeholders included high school students (science-proficient and science-shy students); teachers (elementary and secondary); parents; elected school officials; the scientific community; university science educators; and representatives of the business, industry, and labor communities. The students' contributions were pivotal to recommendations related to student assessment. As Schwab (1978) predicted, "Deliberation is complex and arduous . . . . [it] must choose, not the *right* alternative, for there is no such thing, but the *best* one" (pp. 318–319, emphasis in the original). The "best" science curriculum policy for Canada was published as *Science for Every Citizen* (SCC, 1984). Inspired by the success of this deliberative inquiry, two other Canadian provinces conducted similar research, but on a smaller scale. Drawing upon the SCC's national study, Alberta resolved the problems identified by Blades (1997) (described above) by holding a series of deliberative conferences that gave science teachers a political voice (Roberts, 1995). Saskatchewan almost replicated the SCC study during the renewal of its science curriculum and yielded a strong teacher consensus on a humanistic perspective (Hart, 1989).

A different method of policy formulation, illustrated by the AAAS's (1989) *Project 2061* and the National Research Council's (NRC, 1996) *Standards* in the United States, utilizes consultation with stakeholders on a grand yet narrow scale. After conducting a complex series of inclusive national surveys and committee meetings, a "consensus panel of leading scientists" (Walberg, 1991, p. 57) determined the content of *Project 2061*, content critiqued as conveying a positivist, non-contemporary view of science by Bingle & Gaskell (1994) and Fourez (1989) and as ignoring student relevancy by Settlage and Meadows (2002). Thus the final say in the curriculum was greatly influenced by people who generally espouse the conventional wish-they-knew science. This exclusivity, plus the lack of published research on the consultation process itself, suggests that the national agencies may have prioritized political realism over educational soundness and have repeated their predecessors' 1867 policy decision. A humanistic perspective loses significance in the predominant wish-they-knew science of *Project 2061* and *Standards*.

DISCUSSION OF THE RESEARCH

Contexts of Research

Four themes can be identified in the research literature on curriculum policy: scale, the effect on classroom practice, school culture, and research paradigms. Each theme represents a different context related to the research reviewed in this chapter.

Scale.   As plenary speaker at the 2003 NARST annual meeting, Richard Elmore, drew upon a great deal of research and experience with school innovation undertaken at Harvard University when he cryptically characterized a typical science education innovation study as follows: a gathering of "the faithful" (e.g., a few humanist science educators) to show that the innovation can work on a small scale and then leave "the virus" (i.e., the innovative idea) to populate the system on its own because the innovation is such a good idea (i.e., it is educationally sound). This approach to changing school science through new curricula has continually failed, mostly because of a scaling-up problem: moving from a small-scale preliminary study to a large-scale full implementation study. As an alternative, Elmore (2003) counseled researchers to treat a school jurisdiction as the unit of analysis through enacting larger scale projects.

However, the research synthesized in this chapter clearly indicates that a change to humanistic school science requires a broader context for research than a school system. Significant change demands a multidimensional context of scale that also includes teacher education programs, state curricula, and a host of diverse stakeholders of social privilege and power who provide support over a long period of time (Anderson & Helms, 2001; Fensham, 1992; Sjøberg, 2002). The most effective curriculum research would encompass a scale as broad as the interaction of research, political power, policy, and practice (Alsop, 2003).

The effect of research on classroom practice.   As suggested by Elmore (2003) and Hurd (1991), noticeably absent from the research literature is evidence of a pervasive influence of science education research on practice. This was recently investigated by Ratcliffe and colleagues (2003, p. 21), who concluded: "Unless research evidence, including that from highly regarded studies, is seen to accord with experience and professional judgement [and ideology] it is unlikely to be acted on." However, research is more influential on the "development of national policy on science education." Again, the educationally sound defers to the political reality of teachers' knowledge, beliefs, self-identities, and ideologies (Section V, this volume, Aikenhead, 2006).

School culture.   Elmore (2003) pointed out that school culture must be changed in order to nurture and sustain any significant innovation, a view broadly shared among researchers of humanistic school science (Aikenhead, 2000a; Brickhouse & Bodner, 1992; Carlone, 2003; Medvitz, 1996; Munby, Cunningham, & Lock, 2000; Solomon, 1994c, 2002; Tobin & McRobbie, 1996; Vesilind & Jones, 1998). If research into a humanistic curriculum is to be more than an academic exercise acted out on a small scale, it must reformulate itself into a framework of cultural change, because a humanistic perspective would significantly alter the culture of school science.

Research paradigms.   It is convenient to discuss research in terms of three paradigms: quantitative, interpretive (qualitative), and critical-theoretic (Ryan, 1988). A science educator trained in the natural sciences may feel comfortable in the role of disinterested observer (quantitative paradigm), but most of the research reviewed in this chapter emphasizes the role of a curious empathetic collaborator (interpretive paradigm). Yet, if curriculum researchers expect to effect significant changes in school culture and classroom practice, they will also need to be seen as passionate liberators (critical-theoretic paradigm) generating emancipatory knowledge/practice in the face of seemingly unchangeable organizational structures, relationships, and social conditions.

Most of the research literature reviewed in this chapter reported on preliminary small-scale studies comprising a few volunteer science teachers to initiate or participate in a novel humanistic project, studies without sufficient resources to expand in scale or over time. One exception was the research on Harvard Project Physics (Welch, 1973), but it occurred in the 1960s at a time when a good science curriculum was deemed to be a teacher-proof curriculum (Solomon, 1999), when in-service programs simply transmitted the new curriculum's philosophy to passive teachers (White & Tisher, 1986), and when research strictly conformed to the quantitative research paradigm. This paradigm emphasized measurement of outcomes evaluated against expert judgments or against criteria from academic theoretical frameworks.

In contrast, research into humanistic science curricula has evolved dramatically since the 1960s. It is encouraging to see teachers and now students collaborate in the development of curriculum policy (e.g., Aikenhead, 1994a; Orpwood, 1985; Roberts, 1995), along with stakeholders other than university science professors and professional science organizations (e.g., Eijkelhof, 1990; Häussler & Hoffmann, 2000; Law, 2002). In-service programs now tend to be transactional (e.g., the Iowa Chautauqua Project; Yager & Tamir, 1993) and transformational (typically action research). Today research into humanistic science curricula most often follows the interpretive research paradigm, in which researchers attempt to clarify and understand the participants' views and convey them to others or incorporate them into a curriculum (e.g., Eijkelhof & Lijnse, 1988; Gallagher, 1991; Häussler & Hoffmann, 2000; Orpwood, 1985).

The four themes—scale, effect of research on classroom practice, school culture, and research paradigms—help clarify the contexts for past and future research agendas.

Past Research Agendas

Since World War II, the renaissance of humanistic school science has led researchers to produce new knowledge in the attempt to establish the *credibility* of a humanistic perspective among science teachers and policy makers. Their educationally sound prepositional knowledge, however, was almost insignificant in the arena of political reality. For the intended curriculum (this chapter) and for the taught and learned curricula (Aikenhead, 2006), strong evidence supports the educational soundness of a humanistic perspective. Hence, the issue of credibility need not monopolize research agendas in the future. We do not need more research to show that humanistic school science is educationally sound.

Other agendas have emerged to create classroom change, for instance, agendas associated with action research that combines educationally sound knowledge with politicization (Hodson, 1994; Keiny, 1993). Examples of action research include: Chapter 12, this volume; Bencze, Hodson, Nyhof-Young, and Pedretti (2002); Ogborn (2002); Pedretti and Hodson (1995); Solomon et al. (1992); and Tal, Dori, Keiny and Zoller (2001). However, Solomon (1999) recognized its limitation as only involving a tiny proportion of excellent teachers.

Research agendas associated with classroom change have explored the interaction between political power and practice at the school level (e.g., Carlone, 2003) and have extended this interaction into policy formulation (e.g., Gaskell, 2003; Gaskell & Hepburn, 1998) and into community practice (Calabrese Barton & Yang, 2000; Roth & Désautels, 2004). These studies penetrated the political core of curriculum policy and hold promise for future R&D and developmental research.

Future Research Agendas

To investigate the interaction of research, political power, policy, and practice, with the expressed purpose of changing school culture, researchers must address the politics of school science currently encased in nineteenth-century ideologies. As they do so, one fundamental dilemma must be resolved explicitly and continuously within each research project: does the curriculum aim to enculturate students into their local, national, and global communities (as other school subjects such as English do), or does it aim to enculturate students into a scientific discipline? The prospects of achieving the latter are extremely limited, according to the research synthesized in this chapter.

Politically motivated research in science education by itself may be necessary from time to time to reinvent the discovery that the traditional science curriculum fails most students, for various reasons (e.g., Reiss, 2000), or that humanistic school science can be credible. Of particular interest would be research into Fatima's rules played by various types of students and science teachers, and related to high-stakes testing, educational politics, and ideologies. Future research into humanistic science curricula will best be served by amalgamating the educational with the political, because educationally sound research by itself has had little impact in schools, although its influence is apparent in some official curriculum policies.

To achieve an amalgamation of the educational and political, research into consensus making on curriculum policy promises to be fruitful. Of all the studies into policy formulation reviewed in this chapter, the process of deliberative inquiry holds the greatest potential for devising an educationally sound, politically feasible, humanistic perspective in the science curriculum. Deliberative inquiry provides a political forum to hold negotiations among various stakeholders. During a deliberative inquiry meeting, research concerning major failures of the traditional curriculum can be scrutinized, research concerning successes at learning science in non-school settings can be debated, and research on relevance can help clarify the participants' values. For instance, new research on relevance might include: (1) studies of potential content for science-as-culture (e.g., Who is engaged with science and technology in the community? and How?); (2) studies of science-related knowledge/practice that local workers learn in science-related occupations (e.g., What knowledge do nurses actually use day to day on their job?); (3) studies of how science-proficient students use canonical science in their everyday lives (if at all), compared with how science-shy students cope with similar situations; and (4) studies of how professional scientists actually use canonical science in their everyday lives. An example of this last point is Bell and Lederman's (2003) work that showed how university scientists made decisions on everyday socio-scientific issues primarily on values rather than primarily on scientific ideas and evidence; thus creating a rational evidenced-based expectation for students' socio-scientific decision making in humanistic science courses (i.e., students should not be expected to use science content in situations where scientists do not). Future research projects will be more politically effective if they involve clusters of science teachers and other stakeholders. This research will gain politically potency according to the diversity of the research team and the social privilege of it members.

Deliberative inquiry (i.e., consensus-making R&D) will have greater impact on classroom practice: the larger the project's scale (e.g., SCC, 1984), the more culturally transformational it is (e.g., Chapter 12, this volume; Leblanc, 1989), and the more it embraces all three research paradigms appropriately (a feature of scale). Future research could investigate the influence of stakeholders involved in the consensus-making process: who they represent, their selection, their assigned versus their enacted roles (i.e., the dynamics of deliberative inquiry), and the actor-networks they bring into the deliberation and that develop as a result of the deliberation (e.g., Gaskell & Hepburn, 1998). R&D on actor-networks themselves could be a primary focus of a deliberative inquiry, forging networks to enhance a clearer and more politically endorsed humanistic perspective.

In the future, preliminary small-scale research studies can still be worthwhile: "Rather than viewing the powerful sociohistorical legacy of science as an oppressive structure that limits the potential of reform, we can view the meanings of science in local settings as partially fluid entities, sometimes reproducing and sometimes contesting sociohistorical legacies" (Carlone, 2003, p. 326); but small-scale studies will lose significance unless they explicitly embed themselves in a larger, articulated, politico-educational agenda for humanistic school science (Fensham, 2002).

Future research programs will be strengthened by forging of alliances with researchers in other fields, such as educational cultural anthropology (Chapter 8, this volume), gender studies (Chapter 10), and transformative education studies (Chapters 12 and 24).

Caution is advised, however, against becoming sidetracked by some new research methods such as "design-based research" (Design-Based Research Collective, 2003) or "developmental research" (Lijnse, 1995), because their ultimate aim is to refine theories of learning and didactical structures, respectively. Rather than focus on the question, *How* do students learn best? the fundamental issues to be sorted out first are: *Why* would students want to learn it? and *Who* will allow them to learn it?

These two questions matter critically. The first (Why learn it?) speaks to educationally sound propositions, and the second (Who will allow it to happen?) speaks to the political reality in which all science education research resides.

ACKNOWLEDGMENTS

Thanks to Joan Solomon and Robert Yager, who reviewed this chapter.

REFERENCES

Abd-El-Khalick, F., & Lederman, N. G. (2000). Improving science teachers' conceptions of nature of science: A critical review of the literature. *International Journal of Science Education, 22*, 665–701.

Aikenhead, G. S. (1973). The measurement of high school students' knowledge about science and scientists. *Science Education, 51*, 539–549.

Aikenhead, G. S. (1980). *Science in social issues: Implications for teaching.* Ottawa: Science Council of Canada.

Aikenhead, G. S. (1994a). Collaborative research and development to produce an STS course for school science. In J. Solomon & G. Aikenhead (Eds.), *STS education: International perspectives on reform* (pp. 216–227). New York: Teachers College Press.

Aikenhead, G. S. (1994b). Consequences to learning science through STS: A research perspective. In J. Solomon & G. Aikenhead (Eds.), *STS education: International perspectives on reform* (pp. 169–186). New York: Teachers College Press.

Aikenhead, G. S. (1994c). What is STS teaching? In J. Solomon & G. Aikenhead (Eds.), *STS education: International perspectives on reform* (pp. 47–59). New York: Teachers College Press.

Aikenhead, G. S. (1996). Science education: Border crossing into the subculture of science. *Studies in Science Education, 27*, 1–51.

Aikenhead, G. S. (2000a). Renegotiating the culture of school science. In R. Millar, J. Leach, & J. Osborne (Eds.), *Improving science education: The contribution of research* (pp. 245–264). Birmingham, UK: Open University Press.

Aikenhead, G. S. (2000b). STS science in Canada: From policy to student evaluation. In D. D. Kumar & D. E. Chubin (Eds.), *Science, technology, and society: A sourcebook on research and practice* (pp. 49–89). New York: Kluwer Academic/Plenum.

Aikenhead, G. S. (2002). The educo-politics of curriculum development. *Canadian Journal of Science, Mathematics and Technology Education, 2,* 49–57.

Aikenhead, G. S. (2003). STS education: A rose by any other name. In R. Cross (Ed.), *A vision for science education: Responding to the work of Peter Fensham* (pp. 59–75). New York: RoutledgeFalmer.

Aikenhead, G. S. (2005). Science-based occupations and the science curriculum: Concepts of evidence. *Science Education, 89,* 242–275.

Aikenhead, G. S. (2006). *Science education for everyday life: Evidence-based practice.* New York: Teachers College Press.

Alsop, S. (2003). Pupils, science, research, practice, and politics: Musing on the emergence of a pre-paradigmatic field. *Canadian Journal of Science, Mathematics and Technology Education, 3,* 281–285.

American Association for the Advancement of Science. (1989). *Project 2061: Science for all Americans.* Washington, DC: Author.

Anderson, R. D., & Helms, J. V. (2001). The ideal of standards and the reality of schools: Needed research. *Journal of Research in Science Teaching, 38,* 3–16.

Astin, A., & Astin, H. (1992). *Undergraduate science education: The impact of different college environments on the educational pipeline in the sciences: Final report.* Los Angeles: Higher Education Research Institute, Graduate School of Education, University of California, Los Angeles.

Apple, M. (1996). *Cultural politics and education.* New York: Teachers College Press.

Bartholomew, H., Osborne, J., & Ratcliffe, M. (2002, April). *Teaching pupils "ideas-about-science": Case studies from the classroom.* Paper presented at the annual meeting of the National Association for Research in Science Teaching, New Orleans.

Bell, R. L., & Lederman, N. G. (2003). Understandings of the nature of science and decision making on science and technology based issues. *Science Education, 87,* 352–377.

Bencze, L., Hodson, D., Nyhof-Young, J., & Pedretti, E. (2002). Towards better science: What we learned about science education through action research. In D. Hodson, L. Bencze, J. Nyhof-Young, E. Pedretti, & L. Elshof (Eds.), *Changing science education through action research: Some experiences from the field.* (pp. 233–269). Toronto: University of Toronto Press.

Bingle, W. H., & Gaskell, P. J. (1994). Scientific literacy for decisionmaking and the social construction of scientific knowledge. *Science Education, 72,* 185–201.

Bishop, J. M. (1995). Enemies of promise. *The Wilson Quarterly, 19*(3), 61–65.

Blades, D. (1997). *Procedures of power & curriculum change.* New York: Peter Lang.

Brickhouse, N. W., & Bodner, G. M. (1992). The beginning science teacher: Classroom narratives of convictions and constraints. *Journal of Research in Science Teaching, 29,* 471–485.

Bybee, R. W. (1993). *Reforming science education.* New York: Teachers College Press.

Calabrese Barton, A., & Yang, K. (2000). The case of Miguel and the culture of power in science. *Journal of Research in Science Teaching, 37,* 871–889.

Carlone, H. B. (2003). Innovative science within and against a culture of "achievement." *Science Education, 87,* 307–328.

Champagne, A. B., & Klopfer, L. E. (1982). A causal model of students' achievement in a college physics course. *Journal of Research in Science Teaching, 19,* 299–309.

Cheek, D. W. (1992). *Thinking constructively about science, technology, and society education.* Albany, NY: SUNY Press.

Cheek, D. W. (2000). Marginalization of technology within the STS movement in American K–12 education. In D. D. Kumar & D. E. Chubin (Eds.), *Science, technology, and society: A sourcebook on research and practice* (pp. 167–192). New York: Kluwer Academic/Plenum.

Chin, P., Munby, H., Hutchinson, N. L., Taylor, J., & Clark, F. (2004). Where's the science? Understanding the form and function of workplace science. In E. Scanlon, P. Murphy, J. Thomas, & E. Whitelegg (Eds.), *Reconsidering science learning.* (pp. 118–134). London: RoutledgeFalmer.

Cobern, W. W., & Aikenhead, G. S. (1998). Cultural aspects of learning science. In B. J. Fraser & K. G. Tobin (Eds.), *International handbook of science education* (pp. 39–52). Dordrecht, the Netherlands: Kluwer Academic.

Coles, M. (1998). Science for employment and higher education. *International Journal of Science Education, 20*, 609–621.

Cossman, G. W. (1969). The effects of a course in science and culture for secondary school students. *Journal of Research in Science Teaching, 6*, 274–283.

Costa, V. (1995). When science is "another world": Relationships between worlds of family, friends, school, and science. *Science Education, 79*, 313–333.

Costa, V. (1997). How teacher and students study "all that matters" in high school chemistry. *International Journal of Science Education, 19*, 1005–1023.

Cross, R. T. (1997). Ideology and science teaching: Teachers' discourse. *International Journal of Science Education, 19*, 607–616.

Cross, R. T., & Price, R. F. (1992). *Teaching science for social responsibility*. Sydney: St. Louis Press.

Cross, R. T., & Price, R. F. (1999). The social responsibility of science and public understanding. *International Journal of Science Education, 21*, 775–785.

Cross, R. T., & Price, R. F. (2002). Teaching controversial science for social responsibility: The case of food production. In W.-M. Roth & J. Désautels (Eds.), *Science education as/for sociopolitical action* (pp. 99–123). New York: Peter Lang.

Cunningham, C. M. (1998). The effect of teachers' sociological understanding of science (SUS) on curricular innovation. *Research in Science Education, 28*, 243–257.

David, E. E. (1995). A realistic scenario for U.S. R&D. *Bulletin of Science, Technology & Society, 15*, 14–18.

Davidson, A., & Schibeci, R. (2000). The consensus conference as a mechanism for community responsive technology policy. In R. T. Cross & P. J. Fensham (Eds.), *Science and the citizen for educators and the public* (pp. 47–59). Melbourne: Arena Publications.

DeBoer, G. E. (1991). *A history of ideas in science education*. New York: Teachers College Press.

Dekkers, J., & Delaeter, J. (2001). Enrolment trends in school science education in Australia. *International Journal of Science Education, 23*, 487–500.

Design-Based Research Collective. (2003). Design-based research: An emerging paradigm for educational inquiry. *Educational Research, 32*(1), 5–8.

De Vos, W., & Reiding, J. (1999). Public understanding of science as a separate subject in secondary schools in the Netherlands. *International Journal of Science Education, 21*, 711–719.

Dhingra, K. (2003). Thinking about television science: How students understand the nature of science from different program genres. *Journal of Research in Science Teaching, 40*, 234–256.

Dimopoulos, K., & Koulaidis, V. (2003). Science and technology education for citizenship: The potential role of the press. *Science Education, 87*, 241–256.

Donnelly, J. F. (2002). The "humanist" critique of the place of science in the curriculum in the nineteenth century, and its continuing legacy. *History of Education, 31*, 535–555.

Dori, Y. J., & Tal, R. T. (2000). Formal and informal collaborative projects: Engaging in industry with environmental awareness. *Science Education, 84*, 95–113.

Drori, G. S. (1998). A critical appraisal of science education for economic development. In W. W. Cobern (Ed.), *Socio-cultural perspectives on science education* (pp. 49–74). Boston: Kluwer Academic.

Duggan, S., & Gott, R. (2002). What sort of science education do we really need? *International Journal of Science Education, 24*, 661–679.

Egan, K. (1996). Competing voices for the curriculum. In M. Wideen & M. C. Courtland (Eds.), *The struggle for curriculum: Education, the state, and the corporate sector* (pp. 7–26). Burnaby, BC, Canada: Institute for Studies in Teacher Education, Simon Fraser University.

Eijkelhof, H. M. C. (1990). *Radiation and risk in physics education*. Utrecht, the Netherlands: University of Utrecht Press.

Eijkelhof, H. M. C. (1994). Toward a research base for teaching ionizing radiation in a risk perspective. In J. Solomon & G. Aikenhead (Eds.), *STS education: International perspectives on reform* (pp. 205–215). New York: Teachers College Press.

Eijkelhof, H. M. C., & Kapteijn, M. (2000). A new course on public understanding of science for senior general secondary education in the Netherlands. In R. T. Cross & P. J. Fensham (Eds.), *Science and the citizen for educators and the public* (pp. 189–199). Melbourne: Arena Publications.

Eijkelhof, H. M. C., & Kortland, K. (1988). Broadening the aims of physics education. In P. J. Fensham (ed.), *Development and dilemmas in science education.* (pp. 282–305). New York: Falmer Press.

Eijkelhof, H. M. C., & Lijnse, P. (1988). The role of research and development to improve STS education: Experiences from the PLON project. *International Journal of Science Education, 10*, 464–474.

Elmore, R. F. (2003, March). *Large-scale improvement of teaching and learning: What we know, what we need to know.* Paper presented at the annual meeting of the National Association for Research in Science Teaching, Philadelphia.

Fensham, P. J. (1988). Approaches to the teaching of STS in science education. *International Journal of Science Education, 10*, 346–356.

Fensham, P. J. (1992). Science and technology. In P. W. Jackson (Ed.), *Handbook of research on curriculum* (789–829). New York: Macmillan.

Fensham, P. J. (1993). Academic influence on school science curricula. *Journal of Curriculum Studies, 25*, 53–64.

Fensham, P. J. (1998). The politics of legitimating and marginalizing companion meanings: Three Australian case stories. In D. A. Roberts & L. Östman (Eds.), *Problems of meaning in science curriculum* (178–192). New York: Teachers College Press.

Fensham, P. J. (2000a). Issues for schooling in science. In R. T. Cross & P. J. Fensham (Eds.), *Science and the citizen for educators and the public* (pp. 73–77). Melbourne: Arena Publications.

Fensham, P. J. (2000b). Providing suitable content in the "science for all" curriculum. In R. Millar, J. Leach, & J. Osborne (Eds.), *Improving science education: The contribution of research* (pp. 147–164). Birmingham, UK: Open University Press.

Fensham, P. J. (2002). Time to change drivers for scientific literacy. *Canadian Journal of Science, Mathematics and Technology Education, 2*, 9–24.

Fensham P. J., & Corrigan, D. (1994). The implementation of an STS chemistry course in Australia: A research perspective. In J. Solomon & G. Aikenhead (Eds.), *STS education: International perspectives on reform* (194–204). New York: Teachers College Press.

Foucault, M. (1980). *Power/knowledge: Selected interviews and other writings.* New York: Pantheon Books.

Fourez, G. (1989). Scientific literacy, societal choices, and ideologies. In A. B. Champagne, B. E. Lovitts, & B. J. Calinger (Eds.), *Scientific literacy* (pp. 89–108). Washington, DC: American Association for the Advancement of Science.

Frederick, W. A. (1991). Science and technology education: An engineer's perspective. In S. K. Majumdar, L. M. Rosenfeld, P. A. Rubba, E. W. Miller, & R. F. Schmalz (Eds.), *Science education in the United States: Issues, crises and priorities.* (pp. 386–393). Easton, PA: Pennsylvania Academy of Science.

Fuller, S. (1997). *Science.* Minneapolis: University of Minnesota Press.

Furnham, A. (1992). Lay understanding of science: Young people and adults' ideas of scientific concepts. *Studies in Science Education, 20*, 29–64.

Gallagher, J. J. (1971). A broader base for science education. *Science Education, 55*, 329–338.

Gallagher, J. J. (1991). Prospective and practicing secondary school science teachers' knowledge and beliefs about the philosophy of science. *Science Education, 75*, 121–133.

Gallagher, J. J. (1998). Science teaching as shared culture: An international perspective. *NARST News, 41*(3), 4.

Gardner, P. L. (1998). Students' interest in science and technology: Gender, age and other factors. In L. Hoffmann, A. Krapp, K. A. Renninger, & J. Baumert (Eds.), *Interest and learning. Proceedings of the Seeon conference on interest and gender.* (pp. 41–57). Kiel, Germany: IPN, University of Kiel.

Gaskell, P. J. (1989). Science and technology in British Columbia: A course in search of a community. *Pacific Education, 1*(3), 1–10.

Gaskell, P. J. (1992). Authentic science and school science. *International Journal of Science Education, 14*, 265–272.

Gaskell, P. J. (2003). Perspectives and possibilities in the politics of science curriculum. In R. Cross (Ed.), *A vision for science education: Responding to the work of Peter Fensham.* (pp. 139–152). New York: RoutledgeFalmer.

Gaskell, P. J., & Hepburn, G. (1998). The course as token: A construction of/by networks. *Research in Science Education, 28*, 65–76.

Gee, J. P. (2001). Identity as an analytic lens for research in education. *Review of Research in Education, 25*, 99–125.

Goshorn, K. (1996). Social rationality, risk, and the right to know: Information leveraging with the toxic release inventory. *Public Understanding of Science, 5*, 297–320.

Hart, C. (2002). Framing curriculum discursively: Theoretical perspectives on the experience of VCE physics. *International Journal of Science Education, 24*, 1055–1077.

Hart, E. P. (1989). Toward renewal of science education: A case study of curriculum policy development. *Science Education, 73*, 607–634.

Hart, E. P., & Robottom, I. M. (1990). The science-technology-movement in science education: A critique of the reform process. *Journal of Research in Science Teaching, 27*, 575–588.

Häussler, P., & Hoffmann, L. (2000). A curricular frame for physics education: Development, comparison with students' interests, and impact on students' achievement and self-concept. *Science Education, 84*, 689–705.

Hennessy, S. (1993). Situated cognition and cognitive apprenticeship: Implications for classroom learning. *Studies in Science Education, 22*, 1–41.

Hodson, D. (1994). Seeking directions for change: The personalisation and politicisation of science education. *Curriculum Studies, 2*, 71–98.

Hunt, A., & Millar, R. (2000). *AS science for public understanding*. Oxford: Heinemann.

Hurd, P. D. (1975). Science, technology and society: New goals for interdisciplinary science teaching. *The Science Teacher, 42*(2), 27–30.

Hurd, P. (1989). Science education and the nation's economy. In A. B. Champagne, B. E. Lovitts, & B. J. Calinger (Eds.), *Scientific literacy* (pp. 15–40). Washington, DC: AAAS.

Irwin, A. R. (1995). *Citizen science: A study of people, expertise and sustainable development*. New York: Routledge.

Irwin, A. R. (2000). Historical case studies: Teaching the nature of science in context. *Science Education, 84*, 5–26.

Jenkins, E. (1992). School science education: Towards a reconstruction. *Journal of Curriculum Studies, 24*, 229–246.

Jenkins, E. (2000). "Science for all": Time for a paradigm shift? In R. Millar, J. Leach, & J. Osborne (Eds.), *Improving science education: The contribution of research*. (pp. 207–226). Buckingham, UK: Open University Press.

Jenkins, E. (2002). Linking school science education with action. In W.-M. Roth & J. Désautels (Eds.), *Science education as/for sociopolitical action* (pp. 17–34). New York: Peter Lang.

Keiny, S. (1993). School-based curriculum development as a process of teachers' professional development. *Educational Action Research, 1*, 65–93.

Kelly, G. J., Carlsen, W. S., & Cunningham, C. M. (1993). Science education in sociocultural context: Perspectives from the sociology of science. *Science Education, 77*, 207–220.

Kliebard, H. M. (1979). The drive for curriculum change in the United States, 1890–1958. I. The ideological roots of curriculum as a filed of specialization. *Journal of Curriculum Studies, 11*, 191–202.

Klopfer, L. E., & Cooley, W. W. (1963). "The history of science cases" for high school in the development of student understanding of science and scientists. *Journal of Research in Science Teaching, 1*, 33–47.

Klopfer, L. E., & Watson, F. G. (1957). Historical materials and high school science teaching. *The Science Teacher, 24*, 264–293.

Kolstø, S. D. (2000). Consensus projects: Teaching science for citizenship. *International Journal of Science Education, 22*, 645–664.

Kortland, J. (2001). *A problem posing approach to teaching decision making about the waste issue*. Utrecht, the Netherlands: University of Utrecht Press.

Kumar, D. D., & Chubin, D. E. (Eds.). (2000). *Science, technology, and society: A sourcebook on research and practice*. New York: Kluwer Academic/Plenum.

Larochelle, M., & Désautels, J. (1991). "Of course, it's just obvious": Adolescents' ideas of scientific knowledge. *International Journal of Science Education, 13*, 373–389.

Larson, J. O. (1995, April). *Fatima's rules and other elements of an unintended chemistry curriculum.* Paper presented to the American Educational Research Association Annual Meeting, San Francisco.

Law, N. (2002). Scientific literacy: Charting the terrains of a multifaceted enterprise. *Canadian Journal of Science, Mathematics and Technology Education, 2,* 151–176.

Law, N., Fensham, P. J., Li, S., & Wei, B. (2000). Public understanding of science as basic literacy. In R. T. Cross & P. J. Fensham (Eds.), *Science and the citizen for educators and the public* (pp. 145–155). Melbourne: Arena Publications.

Lawrence, N., & Eisenhart, M. (2002). The language of science and the meaning of abortion. In W.-M. Roth & J. Désautels (Eds.), *Science education as/for sociopolitical action* (pp. 185–206). New York: Peter Lang.

Lawrenz, F., & Gray, B. (1995). Investigation of worldview theory in a South African context. *Journal of Research in Science Teaching, 32,* 555–568.

Layton, D. (1986). Science education and values education—an essential tension. In J. Brown, A. Cooper, T. Horton, F. Toates, & D. Zeldin (Eds.), *Science in schools* (pp. 110–120). Milton Keynes: Open University Press.

Layton, D. (1991). Science education and praxis: The relationship of school science to practical action. *Studies in Science Education, 19,* 43–79.

Layton, D., Jenkins, E., Macgill, S., & Davey, A. (1993). *Inarticulate science? Perspectives on the public understanding of science and some implications for science education.* Driffield, East Yorkshire, UK: Studies in Education.

Leblanc, R. (1989). *Department of education summer science institute.* Halifax, Canada: Ministry of Education.

Lee, O. (1997). Scientific literacy for all: What is it, and how can we achieve it? *Journal of Research in Science Teaching, 34,* 219–222.

Lee, S., & Roth, W.-M. (2002). Learning science in the community. In W.-M. Roth & J. Désautels (Eds.), *Science education as/for sociopolitical action* (pp. 37–66). New York: Peter Lang.

Lijnse, P. (1995). "Developmental research" as a way to an empirically based didactical structure of science. *Science Education, 79,* 189–199.

Lottero-Perdue, P. S., & Brickhouse, N. W. (2002). Learning on the job: The acquisition of scientific competence. *Science Education, 86,* 756–782.

Loughran, J., & Derry, N. (1997). Researching teaching for understanding: The students' perspective. *International Journal of Science Education, 19,* 925–938.

Lyons, T. S. (2003). *Decisions by "science proficient" year 10 students about post-compulsory high school science enrolment: A sociocultural exploration.* Unpublished doctoral dissertation. Armidale, NSW, Australia: University of New England.

MacLeod, R. (1981). Introduction: On the advancement of science. In R. MacLeod & P. Collins (Eds.), *The parliament of science* (pp. 17–42). Northwood, Middlesex, UK: Science Reviews.

Mayoh, K., & Knutton, S. (1997). Using out-of-school experience in science lessons: Reality or rhetoric? *International Journal of Science Education, 19,* 849–867.

Mbajiorgu, N. M., & Ali, A. (2003). Relationship between STS approach, scientific literacy, and achievement in biology. *Science Education, 87,* 31–39.

McCammon, S., Golden, J., & Wuensch, K. L. (1988). Predicting course performance in freshman and sophomore physics courses: Women are more predictable than men. *Journal of Research in Science Teaching, 25,* 501–510.

McConnell, M. C. (1982). Teaching about science, technology and society at the secondary school level in the United States: An education dilemma for the 1980s. *Studies in Science Education, 9,* 1–32.

McGinn, M. K., & Roth, W.-M. (1999). Preparing students for competent scientific practice: Implication of recent research in science and technology studies. *Educational Researcher, 28*(3), 14–24.

Medvitz, A. G. (1996). Science, schools and culture: The complexity of reform in science education. In K. Calhoun, R. Panwar, & S. Shrum (Eds.), *Proceedings of the 8th symposium of IOSTE* (Vol. 2, pp. 158–163). Edmonton, Canada: Faculty of Education, University of Alberta.

Mendelsohn, E. (1976). Values and science: A critical reassessment. *The Science Teacher, 43*(1), 20–23.

Meyer, K. (1998). Reflections on being female in school science: Toward a praxis of teaching science. *Journal of Research in Science Teaching, 35*, 463–471.

Michael, M. (1992). Lay discourses of science, science-in-general, science-in-particular and self. *Science Technology & Human Values, 17*, 313–333.

Millar, R. (2000). Science for public understanding: Developing a new course for 16–18 year old students. In R. T. Cross & P. J. Fensham (Eds.), *Science and the citizen for educators and the public* (pp. 201–214). Melbourne: Arena Publications.

Millar, R., & Osborne, J. (Eds.). (1998). *Beyond 2000: Science education for the future.* London: King's College, School of Education.

Milne, C. E., & Taylor, P. C. (1998). Between myth and a hard place. In W. W. Cobern (Ed.), *Sociocultural perspectives on science education* (pp. 25–48). Boston: Kluwer Academic.

Munby, H., Cunningham, M., & Lock, C. (2000). School science culture: A case study of barriers to developing professional knowledge. *Science Education, 84*, 193–211.

National Research Council. (1996). *National science education standards.* Washington, DC: National Academy Press.

Nelkin, D. (1995). *Selling science: How the press covers science and technology* (rev. ed.). New York: Freeman.

Ogborn, J. (2002). Ownership and transformation: Teachers using curriculum innovations. *Physics Education, 37*, 142–146.

Orange, A. D. (1981). The beginnings of the British Association, 1831–1851. In R. MacLeod & P. Collins (Eds.), *The parliament of science* (pp. 43–64). Northwood, Middlesex, UK: Science Reviews.

Orpwood, G. (1985). Toward the renewal of Canadian science education. I. Deliberative inquiry model. *Science Education, 69*, 477–489.

Osborne, J., & Collins, S. (2000). *Pupils' and parents' views of the school science curriculum.* London: Kings College.

Osborne, J., & Collins, S. (2001). Pupils' views of the role and value of the science curriculum: A focus group study. *International Journal of Science Education, 23*, 441–467.

Osborne, J., Collins, S., Ratcliffe, M., Millar, R., & Duschl, R. (2001, November). *What "ideas-about-science" should be taught in school science? A Delphi study of the expert community.* Paper presented at the History, Philosophy and Science Teaching Conference, Denver.

Osborne, J., Driver, R., & Simon, S. (1998). Attitudes to science: Issues and concerns. *School Science Review, 79*(288), 27–33.

Osborne, J., Duschl, R., & Fairbrother, B. (2003, March). *Breaking the mould? Teaching science for public understanding—lessons from the classroom.* Paper presented at the annual meeting of the National Association for Research in Science Teaching, Philadelphia.

Oxford University Department of Educational Studies. (1989). *Enquiry into the attitudes of sixth-formers towards choice of science and technology courses in higher education.* Oxford, UK: Department of Educational Studies.

Panwar, R., & Hoddinott, J. (1995). The influence of academic scientists and technologists on Alberta's science curriculum policy and programme. *International Journal of Science Education, 17*, 505–518.

Pedersen, J. E. (1992). The jurisprudential model of study for STS issues. In R. E. Yager (Ed.), *The status of STS: Reform efforts around the world. ICASE 1992 Yearbook.* Knapp Hill, South Harting, Petersfield, UK: International Council of Associations for Science Education.

Pedretti, E., & Hodson, D. (1995). From rhetoric to action: Implementing STS education through action research. *Journal of Research in Science Teaching, 32*, 463–485.

Prelle, S., & Solomon, J. (1996). Young people's "general approach" to environmental issues in England and Germany. *Compare, 26*, 91–103.

Rafea, A. M. (1999). *Power, curriculum making and actor-network theory: The case of physics, technology and society curriculum in Bahrain.* Unpublished doctoral dissertation, University of British Columbia, Canada.

Ratcliffe, M. (1997). Pupil decision-making about socio-scientific issues within the science curriculum. *International Journal of Science Education, 19,* 167–182.

Ratcliffe, M., Bartholomew, H., Hames, V., Hind, A., Leach, J., Millar, R., et al. (2003, March). *Evidence-based practice in science education: The research-user interface.* Paper presented at the annual meeting of the National Association for Research in Science Teaching, Philadelphia.

Reiss, M. J. (2000). *Understanding science lessons: Five years of science teaching.* Milton Keynes, UK: Open University Press.

Roberts, D. A. (1988). What counts as science education? In P. J. Fensham (Ed.), *Development and dilemmas in science education* (pp. 27–54). New York: Falmer Press.

Roberts, D. A. (1995). Junior high school science transformed: Analysing a science curriculum policy change. *International Journal of Science Education, 17,* 493–504.

Roth, W.-M., Boutonné, S., McRobbie, C. J., & Lucas, K. B. (1999). One class, many worlds. *International Journal of Science Education, 21,* 59–75.

Roth, W.-M., & Désautels, J. (Eds.). (2002). *Science education as/for sociopolitical action.* New York: Peter Lang.

Roth, W.-M., & Désautels, J. (2004). Educating for citizenship: Reappraising the role of science education. *Canadian Journal of Science, Mathematics and Technology Education, 4,* 149–168.

Roth, W.-M., & McGinn, M. K. (1998). >unDELETE science education:/lives/work/voices. *Journal of Research in Science Teaching, 35,* 399–421.

Rowell, P. M., & Gaskell, P. J. (1987). Tensions and realignments: School physics in British Columbia 1955–1980. In I. Goodson (Ed.), *International perspectives in curriculum history* (pp. 74–106). London: Croom Helm.

Rubba, P. A. (1987). The current state of research in precollege STS education. *Bulletin of Science, Technology & Society, 7,* 248–252.

Rubba, P. A., & Wiesenmayer, R. L. (1991). Integrating STS into school science. In S. K. Majumdar, L. M. Rosenfeld, P. A. Rubba, E. W. Miller, & R. F. Schmalz (Eds.), *Science education in the United States: Issues, crises and priorities* (pp. 186–194). Easton, PA: Pennsylvania Academy of Science.

Rudolph, J. L. (2003). Portraying epistemology: School science in historical context. *Science Education, 87,* 64–79.

Ryan, A. G. (1988). Program evaluation within the paradigm: Mapping the territory. *Knowledge: Creation, Diffusion, Utilization, 10,* 25–47.

Ryder, J. (2001). Identifying science understanding for functional scientific literacy. *Studies in Science Education, 36,* 1–42.

Sadler, P. M., & Tai, R. H. (2001). Success in introductory college physics: The role of high school preparation. *Science Education, 85,* 111–136.

Sáez, M. J., & Carretero, A. J. (2002). The challenge of innovation: The new subject "natural sciences" in Spain. *Journal of Curriculum Studies, 34,* 343–363.

Science Council of Canada. (1984). *Science for every student: Educating Canadians for tomorrow's world* (Report No. 36). Ottawa: Science Council of Canada.

Schwab, J. J. (1974). Decision and choice: The coming duty of science teaching. *Journal of Research in Science Teaching, 11,* 309–317.

Schwab, J. J. (1978). *Science, curriculum, and liberal education.* Chicago: University of Chicago Press.

SEPUP. (2003). *SEPUP News.* Berkeley, CA: Lawrence Hall of Science, University of California at Berkeley (www.sepup.com).

Settlage, J., & Meadows, L. (2002). Standards-based reform and its unintended consequences: Implication for science education within America's urban schools. *Journal of Research in Science Teaching, 39,* 114–127.

Seymour, E. (1995). The loss of women from science, mathematics, and engineering undergraduate majors: An explanatory account. *Science Education, 79,* 437–473.

Shapiro, B. L. (2004). Studying lifeworlds of science learning: A longitudinal study of changing ideas, contests, and personal orientations in science learning. *Canadian Journal of Science, Mathematics and Technology Education, 4,* 127–147.

Shymansky, J. A., & Kyle, W. C. (1988). A summary of research in science education—1986. *Science Education, 72,* 245–373.

Sjøberg, S. (2000). Interesting all children in "science for all." In R. Millar, J. Leach, & J. Osborne (Eds.), *Improving science education: The contribution of research* (pp. 165–186). Birmingham, UK: Open University Press.

Sjøberg, S. (2002). Science and technology education in Europe: current challenges and possible solutions. *Connect* (UNESCO), *27*(3–4), 1–5.

Solomon, J. (1984). Prompts, cues and discrimination: The utilization of two separate knowledge systems. *European Journal of Science Education, 6,* 277–284.

Solomon, J. (1994a). Conflict between mainstream science and STS in science education. In J. Solomon & G. Aikenhead (Eds.), *STS education: International perspectives on reform* (pp. 3–10). New York: Teachers College Press.

Solomon, J. (1994b). Learning STS and judgments in the classroom: Do boys and girls differ? In J. Solomon & G. Aikenhead (Eds.), *STS education: International perspectives on reform* (pp. 141–154). New York: Teachers College Press.

Solomon, J. (1994c). Towards a notion of home culture: Science education in the home. *British Educational Research Journal, 20,* 565–577.

Solomon, J. (1998). The science curricula of Europe and notion of scientific culture. In D. A. Roberts & L. Östman (Eds.), *Problems of meaning in science curriculum* (pp. 166–177). New York: Teachers College Press.

Solomon, J. (1999). Meta-scientific criticisms, curriculum and culture. *Journal of Curriculum Studies, 31,* 1–15.

Solomon, J. (2002). The evolution of cultural entities. *Proceedings of the British Academy, 112,* 183–200.

Solomon, J. (2003a). Home-school learning of science: The culture of homes, and pupils' difficult border crossing. *Journal of Research in Science Teaching, 40,* 219–233.

Solomon, J. (2003b). The UK and the movement for science, technology, and society (STS) education. In R. Cross (Ed.), *A vision for science education: Responding to the work of Peter Fensham* (pp. 76–90). New York: RoutledgeFalmer.

Solomon, J., & Aikenhead, G. S. (Eds.). (1994). *STS education: International perspectives on reform.* New York: Teachers College Press.

Solomon, J., Duveen, J., Scot, L., & McCarthy, S. (1992). Teaching about the nature of science through history: Action research in the classroom. *Journal of Research in Science Teaching, 29,* 409–421.

Spencer, H. (1859). *Education: Intellectual, moral and physical.* New York: John B. Alden.

Stocklmayer, S. M., Gore, M. M., & Bryant, C. (Eds.) (2001). *Science communication in theory and practice.* Boston: Kluwer Academic.

Stuart, T. C. (1977). A comparison of high school and college chemistry courses in New Mexico. *Journal of Chemical Education, 54,* 373–374.

Sutman, F. X., & Bruce, M. H. (1992). Chemistry in the community: A five year evaluation. *Journal of Chemical Education, 69,* 564–567.

Tal, R. T., Dori, Y. J., Keiny, S., & Zoller, U. (2001). Assessing conceptual change of teachers involved in STES education and curriculum development—the STEMS project approach. *International Journal of Science Education, 23,* 247–262.

Tanaka, J., & Taigen, J. (1986, July/August). *Predictability of college chemistry grades based on high school variables.* Paper presented at the 9th Biennial Conference on Chemical Education, Montana State University, Bozeman, MT.

Thier, H. D., & Nagle, B. W. (1994). Developing a model for issue-oriented science. In J. Solomon & G. Aikenhead (Eds.), *STS education: International perspectives on reform* (pp. 75–83). New York: Teachers College Press.

Thier, H. D., & Nagle, B. W. (1996). Development and assessment of an issue-oriented middle school science course. In K. Calhoun, R. Panwar, & S. Shrum (Eds.), *Proceedings of the 8th symposium of IOSTE* (Vol. 3, pp. 265–271). Edmonton, Canada: Faculty of Education, University of Alberta.

Tobias, S. (1990). *They're not dumb, they're different*. Tucson, AZ: Research Corporation.

Tobin, K., & McRobbie, C. J. (1996). Cultural myths as constraints to the enacted science curriculum. *Science Education, 80*, 223–241.

Tytler, R., Duggan, S., & Gott, R. (2001). Public participation in an environmental dispute: Implications for science education. *Public Understanding of Science, 10*, 343–364.

Vesilind, E., & Jones, M. (1998). Gardens or graveyards: Science educational reform and school culture. *International Journal of Science Education, 21*, 231–247.

Walberg, H. J. (1991). Improving school science in advanced and developing countries. *Review of Educational Research, 61*, 25–69.

Walberg, H. J., & Ahlgren, A. (1973). Changing attitudes toward science among adolescents. *Nature, 245*, 187–190.

Wang, H. A., & Schmidt, W. H. (2001). History, philosophy and sociology of science in science education: Results from the third internal mathematics and science study. *Science & Education, 10*, 51–70.

Weinstein, M. (1998). Playing the paramecium: Science education from the stance of the cultural studies of science. *Educational Policy, 12*, 484–506.

Welch, W. W. (1973). Review of the research and evaluation program of Harvard Project Physics. *Journal of Research in Science Teaching, 10*, 365–378.

Welch, W. W. (1995). Student assessment and curriculum evaluation. In B. J. Fraser & H. J. Walberg (Eds.), *Improving science education* (pp. 90–116). Chicago: National Society for the Study of Education (University of Chicago Press).

Welch, W. W., & Rothman, A. I. (1968). The success of recruited students in a new physics course. *Science Education, 52*, 270–273.

Welch, W. W., & Walberg, H. J. (1967). Are the attitudes of teachers related to declining percentages of enrollments in physics? *Science Education, 51*, 422–436.

White, R., & Tisher, R. (1986). Research on natural science. In M. C. Wittrock (Ed.), *Third handbook of research on teacher* (pp. 874–905). New York: Macmillan.

Wiesenmayer, R. L., & Rubba, P. A. (1999). The effects of STS issue investigation and action instruction versus traditional life science instruction on seventh grade students' citizenship behaviors. *Journal of Science Education and Technology, 8*, 137–144.

Winther, A. A., & Volk, T. L. (1994). Comparing achievement of inner-city high school students in traditional versus STS-based chemistry courses. *Journal of Chemical Education, 71*, 501–505.

Wynne, B. (1991). Knowledge in context. *Science, Technology & Human Values, 16*, 111–121.

Yager, R. E. (1996a). History of science/technology/society as reform in the United States. In R. E. Yager (Ed.), *Science/technology/society as reform in science education* (pp. 3–15). Albany, NY: SUNY Press.

Yager, R. E. (Ed.). (1996b). *Science/technology/society as reform in science education*. Albany, NY: SUNY Press.

Yager, R. E., & Krajcik, J. (1989). Success of students in a college physics course with and without experiencing a high school course. *Journal of Research in Science Teaching, 26*, 599–608.

Yager, R. E., Snider, B., & Krajcik, J. (1988). Relative success in college chemistry for students who experienced a high school course in chemistry and those who had not. *Journal of Research in Science Teaching, 25*, 387–396.

Yager, R. E., & Tamir, P. (1993). STS approach: Reasons, intentions, accomplishments, and outcomes. *Science Education, 77*, 637–658.

Young, M. (1971). *Knowledge and control: New directions in the sociology of education*. London: Collier-Macmillan.

Ziman, J. (1980). *Teaching and learning about science and society*. Cambridge, UK: Cambridge University Press.

Ziman, J. (1984). *An introduction to science studies: The philosophical and social aspects of science and technology*. Cambridge, UK: Cambridge University Press.

CHAPTER 30

Systemic Reform: Research, Vision, and Politics

Jane Butler Kahle
Miami University

> Systemic: of a system; specifically, in physiology, of or affecting the entire bodily system. (*Webster's New World Dictionary*, p. 1481)
>
> Reform: v. to make better by removing faults and defects; n. an improvement; correction of faults or evils. (Ibid., p. 1222)

Combining the above definitions provides a basic definition of systemic reform, that is, to make better an entire system by removing faults and defects. Although that basic definition applies to systemic reform of science education, it does not define what is a "system" in educational reform, nor does it address the issue of the time required for systemic reform. This chapter addresses that definition by limiting its discussion of systemic reform to large-scale reforms that affect multiple parts of the education system. In addition, it discusses reform in terms of time, that is, long-term reforms. Obviously these two parameters limit the contents of the chapter by eliminating many regional or local reforms, both in the United States and internationally.[1] But it can be argued that such limitations are necessary to both focus the discussion and to include a historical perspective.

It takes time to change any system, especially one as complex and entrenched as public education. Lee (2002) documented that changes in student achievement, the desired outcome of any educational reform, may require up to 30 years. When one

---

1. For the purposes of this chapter systemic reform has been defined as large-scale, long-term reforms that are intended to improve science education by affecting many parts of an educational system. Furthermore, an educational system is defined as one governed by the equivalent of a state or province. Therefore, although many larger (i.e., nations) or smaller (i.e., cities, districts, schools) entities have enacted reforms of science education and many reforms have focused only on one part of the educational system (i.e., curriculum only, assessment only, etc.), the chapter limits its discussion to research stemming from large-scale reforms affecting multiple parts of the educational system of a state, province, or territory. With these restrictions, a thorough search of the relevant and available literature using ERIC and Educational Abstracts located more than 300 document titles suggesting relevance to systemic science education reform internationally. However, only a handful of documents proved suitable and available, and most were descriptive, not research-oriented. Therefore, the decision was made to limit this chapter to U.S. reforms that fit the definitions above.

expands reform to include a whole system, the issue of time becomes paramount. Therefore, this chapter presents a historical overview of large-scale reform efforts in U.S. science education from the end of World War II to the present. Across the 60 years discussed, three themes have emerged in the United States: *Texts* and *Teaching*, *Courses* and *Competencies*, and *Excellence* and *Equity*. Those themes drove the systemic reforms that occurred in three waves: from Sputnik through *Man, A Course of Study (MACOS)*; from *A Nation at Risk* through national standards; and from the National Science Foundation's systemic initiative program to the No Child Left Behind legislation.

Although the launch of Sputnik in 1957 is commonly accepted as the catalyst for the first wave of systemic science education reform, both Dow (1991) and Jackson (1983) argue that it began earlier, and it focused on educating the scientific and technical workforce that was needed to out-compete the Russians in the race to space. The first wave of reform primarily addressed two parts of the educational system, *texts* and *teaching*. It involved federal support for the development of new curricula and Teacher Training Institutes focused on upgrading the content knowledge of teachers through graduate courses at colleges and universities across the nation. However, because of the public paranoia concerning a national curriculum, the Teacher Training Institutes were not ostensibly tied to the new curricula.

A second wave of reform was catalyzed by the publication of *A Nation at Risk* in 1983. This time the impetus was the need to improve the scientific literacy of all citizens in the new technological age. The U.S. Secretary of Education appointed a commission that had 18 months to report on the quality of America's education. The report focused on high schools and was devastating in its description of weaknesses (Goodlad, 2003; Sizer, 2003). Although it stopped short of calling for comprehensive, systemic reform, many states began to regulate education in ways intended to change the system. During the second wave of reform (approximately 1983 to 1991), another theme emerged, that is, *courses* and *competencies*. State policies were directed toward increasing scientific literacy and using science to improve the quality of life by ensuring that all students graduated from high school with adequate *courses* and *competencies*. The political context of the time involved issues of economic security within the emerging global economy.

The third wave of reform differed from the two previous ones, because it was based on theoretical insights. O'Day and Smith defined systemic reform as an effort "to upgrade significantly the quality of the curriculum and instruction delivered to all children . . . [requiring] major changes in the way states and local school systems make and implement policy" (1993, pp. 250–251). Their thinking and that of others[2] were taken up by the newly reorganized science education directorate at the National Science Foundation (NSF) and its director, Luther Williams. Indeed, the focus of the third wave of reform, as presented in this chapter, is reform of a state's educational system, and it was catalyzed by the NSF's Statewide Systemic Initiative (SSI) program. Although systemic reforms in the third wave addressed a variety of components in the educational system, the themes that focused activities and policies at several levels were *excellence* and *equity*.

It has been impossible to review the research on systemic reform without placing both the reforms and the studies of them in educational and political contexts;

---

2. In addition to O'Day and Smith (1993), Clune (1993), Fuhrman (1993, 1994), and Kirst (1984), among others, identified components and requirements for systemic reform.

1945	*Science-The Endless Frontier*
1950	National Science Foundation
1954	Physical Science Study Committee Funded
1957	Sputnik Launched
1958	National Defense Education Act
1963	*Man: a Course of Study* (MACOS) Funded
1969	Apollo Moon Walk
1975	Congressional Review of *Man: a Course of Study*
1981	NSF Education Directorate Disbanded
1983	*Nation at Risk* and NSF Education Directorate Reestablished
1984	Education for Economic Security Act (Title II)
1989	NCTM Mathematics Education Standards, and AAAS *Benchmarks*
1990	NSF Statewide Systemic Initiatives
1996	NRC Science Education Standards
2000	NCTM Standards Revized
2002	*No Child Left Behind*

FIGURE 30–1.   Timeline of systemic science education reforms in the U.S.

for both contexts have affected the nature of the research. However, a comprehensive review of the literature revealed that the research base is uneven and most of it is evaluative in nature. The first three sections of the chapter address each wave of systemic reform and the research associated with it. A time line to guide the reader through the U.S. reforms is provided in Fig. 30–1. There is a common term used among those who participate in systemic reform, that is, *lessons learned*. The chapter concludes with a consideration of what lessons have been learned through research about systemic reform in science education.

WAVE I: TEXTS AND TEACHING—
(FROM SPUTNIK TO MACOS)

The three full decades after World War II are an intriguing period in the history of American education, for it was during those years—the 1950s through the 1970s, roughly speaking—that the federal government made an extraordinary effort, unprecedented in scale, to involve itself in educational affairs for the purpose of improving the quality of schooling for a significant portion, if not all, of our nation's youth. (Jackson, 1983, p. 143)

Although the launching of *Sputnik* in 1957 is credited with starting the first wave of systemic reform in the United States, Dow (1991) suggests that "Long before *Sputnik*, postwar criticism of American schooling had been gaining momentum both within and outside the education profession" (p. 1). For example, Vannevar Bush's 1945 report to President Truman, "Science—The Endless Frontier," provided the basis for founding the National Science Foundation (NSF) in 1950 (Bush in Jackson, 1983).[3] The report articulated an urgent need to improve mathematics and science education. NSF responded by initiating Teacher Training Institutes and, in

---

3. The report was commissioned by President Roosevelt in 1944.

1954, funding the first curriculum project, the Physical Science Study Committee (PSSC) (Jackson, 1983). Both initiatives were accelerated and expanded after Sputnik, with Congress passing the National Defense Education Act in 1958, which provided funds for local districts to build laboratories and to sponsor teacher education in science, math, and foreign languages. Concurrently, Congress increased funding for education at the National Science Foundation to the point where education was apportioned about one-half of the NSF's budget (Office of Technology Assessment [OTA], 1988). In order to compare the extent of funding, those monies are translated into current dollars in Table 30.1.

Teaching

The first wave of science education reform did not address all parts of the system, but it did address two aspects that were seen both educationally and politically as weaknesses, that is, the quality of the science teaching force and outdated science texts. From 1954 to 1974, NSF focused on *teaching* by funding Teacher Training Institutes at a total cost of $500 million (OTA, 1988). Because the consensus at the time was that the teaching force was deficient in content knowledge about science, institutes focused on increasing content knowledge by developing graduate, degree-granting programs in the individual sciences.

If judged by the numbers of teachers reached, the institutes were very successful. At their peak in the early 1960s, about 1,000 institutes were offered annually, involving the participation of over 40,000 teachers each year (about 15 percent of the math and science teaching force). Although more supervisors (80 percent in mathematics and science) and upper secondary school teachers (37 percent in mathematics and 47 percent in science) attended, 5 percent of early elementary teachers also were involved (OTA, 1988). At the time, NSF judged that the program had reached about as many teachers as any voluntary program could. For example, in the late 1980s (second wave), all of NSF's programs reached only 2 to 3 percent of secondary math and science teachers (OTA, 1988), whereas in the third wave (the 1990s) the statewide systemic initiative program reached only 8 percent of the science and math teachers in the 25 states/territories involved (Zucker, Shields, Adelman, Corcoran, & Goertz, 1998).

TABLE 30.1
NSF's Curriculum Development Funds

	*Actual dollars**	*Equivalent 2003 dollars***
1954	$ 1,725	$ 11,815
1955	$ 5,000	$ 34,247
1957	$ 500,000	$ 3,267,974
1959	$ 5,500,000	$34,810,127
1968	$12,250,000	$64,814,815

Note: *From "The reform of science education: A cautionary tale," P. W. Jackson, (1983) *Daedalus, 112,* 147–148.
**Calculated using: oregonstate.edu/Dept/pol_sci/fac/sahr/cv2003.xls

Although there is little research about the institutes or evaluation of their success, the Office of Technical Assistance reviewed their efficacy in the late 1980s. The OTA report is one of the few documents that include research and evaluation findings on the institute program. It reports, for example, that a General Accounting Office review of research on the NSF-funded institutes "found little or no evidence that such institutes had improved student achievement scores" (OTA, 1988, p. 120). However, the OTA review identified the following important effects of the Teacher Training Institute program.

- It brought teachers up to date with current scientific developments.
- It brought teachers closer to the actual processes of science, thereby improving their sense of competence in science.
- It provided a network of peers who provided professional support long after the institutes ended.
- It allowed teachers to do experimental work in science and encouraged them to replicate such experiences with their students.
- It helped define leaders for the science education community.
- It recognized the importance of the work of science teachers.
- It inspired and invigorated teachers to continue teaching.

In retrospect, many science educators agree that the two outcomes with the most lasting effects were the *development of a network of peers* and the *defining of leaders*. Both of these effects substantively changed the nature of the science teaching force through the next several decades (Helgeson, 1974).

Because NSF did not require evaluations of the institutes, little information other than the OTA (1988) report is available. However, in 1976, Willson and Garibaldi examined the results of a large-scale independent evaluation of five NSF Comprehensive Teacher Training Institutes to determine if there were evidence that the cognitive achievement of junior and senior high students increased because their teachers participated in an NSF-sponsored institute. According to Willson and Garibaldi, previous findings indicating that students benefited from their teachers attending NSF institutes were confounded by differences between institute and non-institute teachers. They also were compromised because the process of assigning students to teachers in schools was nonrandom.[4]

For their analysis, Willson and Garibaldi (1976) identified the most theoretically relevant factors affecting student achievement and examined each with respect to any observed differences in student achievement in classes of institute and non-institute teachers. For example, they examined the possible differential assignment of institute teachers to higher-ability classes and found that the distribution of teacher assignment by student ability was independent of NSF institute participation. As they sum-

---

4. A typical published study on teacher institute attendance and student achievement did not randomly assign teachers or students to experimental and control groups; did not provide the control group of teachers with any substantive professional development; did not control for differences in teacher characteristics such as type of degree, experience, etc.; and used student achievement tests that were oriented toward the content of the institute. Because of these problems, some research concerning institute effectiveness is not included in this review (for an example, see Thelen and Litsky, 1972).

marize, "Thus, it appears unlikely that students of institute attending teachers would do better than students of nonattending teachers because of differential ability" (Willson & Garibaldi, 1976, p. 433). They also examined the possibility that institute teachers might teach in larger cities but rejected this factor because urban representation in the study was small.[5] After controlling for student ability and school location, they found that institute participation was a positive and significant factor affecting student achievement. As they summarized, "[T]eacher attendance at institutes is associated with higher student achievement than no attendance, and . . . students of teachers with high institute attendance perform better than students of teachers who have attended only one or two institutes" (Willson & Garibaldi, 1976, p. 437).

Texts

The second focal point of the first wave of reform was *texts*. Science textbooks in the 1950s were woefully out of date with current scientific advances. In 1954, Jerrold Zacharias and a group of physicists in Cambridge formed the Physical Science Study Committee (PSSC) and began to develop the first course in the NSF curriculum development program. It was soon followed by curricula in mathematics, chemistry, biology, and finally social science. Collectively, these curricula were known as the *alphabet soup* curricula (*BSCS, CHEM Study, CBA, SCIS, ESC*, etc.). By 1975, NSF had funded 53 curriculum projects at a cost of over $117 million. In all cases, teams of scientists, science teachers, and science educators worked on the materials. According to Nelkin (1977), the materials were designed to be "teacher-proof" in that they presented current scientific knowledge and concepts regardless of local norms. The innovative curricula of the 1960s not only updated content; they also focused on the methods of inquiry and stressed individual judgment. Welch and Wahlberg's (1972) analysis of the differences between *Project Physics*, one of the NSF-funded curricula, and traditional physics texts provides insight into the education vision at that time:

> The developers of *Project Physics* were originally concerned about the continuing drop in the proportion of students who take physics in high school. To attract students who are not bound for mathematical, scientific, or technical careers, and without compromising on the physics content, they attempted to develop an interest-awakening, module system of course components using a variety of media and methods for learning. . . . Perhaps the most distinctive aspect of *Project Physics* is its humanistic orientation . . . (Welch & Wahlberg, 1972, pp. 373, 374)

Indeed, the texts developed in the first wave of reform differed from traditional texts in many ways. But all were directed toward improving and enlarging the scientific, mathematical, and technical workforce for the nation, the political necessity of the day.

Two curriculum projects merit discussion because they expanded the scope of the curricula efforts and illustrate how politics, not research findings, affect educational reform. In 1958, the Biological Sciences Curriculum Study (BSCS), initiated

---

5. They reported that "the majority of the schools sampled were in small towns and cities under 50,000 population (81 percent in science, 91 percent in mathematics)" (Willson & Garibaldi, 1976, p. 433).

by the American Institute of Biological Sciences, was the first group to address the needs of a diverse student body by developing three versions of an introductory high school biology text. The need was great. High school biology texts were at least 20 years behind developments in the discipline, hampering especially the teaching of evolution.

Considering the politics of the day, it was not surprising that field testing and marketing of the BSCS books ran into trouble. In 1961 a field test in Dade County, Florida, was stopped because the books contained diagrams of the human reproductive system. Although BSCS refused to remove the offending diagrams, Dade County school officials blackened out the offending ones before allowing the field test to continue (Nelkin, 1977). In addition, state boards of education in both Texas and New Mexico objected to the inclusion of evolution. BSCS stood its ground, and its books—with evolution—were included on their state adoption lists. However, the publicity generated ensured political conflicts in both states and local districts.

The second curriculum project affected by political reality was *Man: a Course of Study* (*MACOS*). Although NSF had approached curriculum development in the social sciences cautiously, in 1963 it funded a year-long program for fifth- and sixth-graders that used an ethnographic approach to studying human behavior. *MACOS* did not avoid controversial issues and urged students to cultivate independent attitudes and to raise questions. Although *MACOS* clearly was treading on sensitive ground, it was successfully field tested in over 300 classrooms before commercial publishers pulled out. After NSF provided a supplement to offset publishing and distribution costs, the books were finally published in 1970. In 1974 *MACOS* was used in over 1,700 schools in 47 states. However, a year later sales plummeted because of an epidemic of community disputes. The congressional hearings that followed not only put the death seal on *MACOS* but also on NSF's curriculum development efforts and, in 1981, on its education directorate. A quote from congressional hearings during that time illustrates the political environment: "You [*MACOS*] are not suggesting the philosophy . . . that is being taught. [That] is a local option of the school district" (Senator Talcott, 1976, in Nelkin, 1977, p. 24). Although generally the *MACOS* controversy is seen as ending the first wave of reform, Peter Dow, one of its authors, credits the Apollo moon walk in July of 1969 with its end. According to him, after that success in space, "the so-called 'education gap' seemed as ephemeral as the 'missile gap,' and federal support for curriculum reform began to wane" (1991, p. 7).

Although NSF was more or less comfortable with supporting projects to develop curricular materials, it approached the implementation of those materials with trepidation. Furthermore, NSF did not endorse or claim responsibility for the educational value of the curricula. It was hoped that by supporting several choices in different subject areas, the Foundation would not be accused of sponsoring a national curriculum. NSF was sensitive to any claims of "federal intervention" and was under constant congressional pressure to avoid such "interference." As Nelkin stated, "[NSF's] role was to make materials available but not to mandate their use" (1977, p. 27). However, Senator Allott put it more forcefully, saying, "I don't want these things rammed down the throat of educators" (Senator Allott, 1964, in Nelkin, 1977, p. 24).

Unlike the situation with the Teacher Training Institutes, there was considerable research on the efficacy of the NSF-supported curriculum materials. At the time, one study summarized the situation in the following way: "After the urgency and excitement of the early years of this new curriculum movement had passed, many individuals and groups, including the Congress of the United States, demanded objective evidence of the value of the new courses" (Walker & Schaffarzick, 1974, p. 83). Research focused on student achievement and overall program impact is summarized next. However, it is important to note that student achievement research was clouded by controversy over the type of test used to obtain the data. Therefore, two studies that specifically addressed the issue of test bias are discussed in detail. The findings of other studies are included in major meta-analytical and qualitative syntheses from the 1970s, which are discussed also.

Some researchers attempted to overcome test content bias by using two achievement tests, one based on the innovative curriculum used and the other based on a comparable traditional curriculum (Heath, 1964; Heath & Stickell, 1963; Lisonbee & Fullerton, 1964; Rainey, 1964; Wallace, 1963). Others examined test content to determine if scores on subscales reflected patterns of emphasis present in the curricula (Herron, 1966; Wasik, 1971). However, findings were mixed, and the concern about test bias continued to cloud research done on student achievement and the NSF-supported curricula.

Two studies, one of *CHEM Study* and the other of *Project Physics*, were unique in that both controlled for test bias and one, *Project Physics*, used an experimental design. In 1966, Herron compared the cognitive ability of students who had a class using *CHEM Study* with those who used a conventional chemistry text.[6] He carefully constructed a chemistry test that measured cognitive ability—without regard to the actual content studied. He administered the test to chemistry students in four suburban schools and analyzed results by three student ability levels as measured by the *Iowa Tests of Educational Development*. Although there were differences in findings among the three ability groups, he found that at all ability levels *CHEM Study* students scored significantly higher on *Application* items than did students using conventional texts (Herron, 1966).

Welch and Wahlberg (1972) also addressed the need for controlled, experimental studies to assess student achievement with NSF-supported curricula. From a national list of 16,911 physics teachers, 136 were randomly selected to participate in this study. Of that number, 72 agreed to participate and were randomly assigned to either the experimental group (attended a six-week briefing session on *Project Physics*) or the control group (participated in a two-day physics workshop at Harvard University). Within the classes of both groups, students were randomly assigned to take one of two instruments that together assessed the following factors: cognitive, affective, learning environment, course reaction, semantic differential, and physics perception. Controlling for student ability, Welch and Wahlberg concluded that *Project Physics* students performed as well as students in other courses on cognitive measures and that they enjoyed their text and found physics less difficult that those in other physics courses. In addition, *Project Physics* had a special appeal to students in the middle-range IQ group (112 to 119), students who, they

---

6. Cognitive ability in Herron's (1966) study referred to any of the abilities described by the *Taxonomy of Educational Objectives* (knowledge, comprehension, application, analysis, synthesis, and evaluation) as well as to critical thinking as measured by the *Watson-Glaser Critical Thinking Appraisal.*

noted, had increasingly tended to elect not to take high school physics (Welch & Wahlberg, 1972).

In response to what many researchers, policy makers, and educators interpreted as a lack of substantive research on the quality of the curriculum and its influence on student learning, researchers began to use synthesis techniques, both qualitative and quantitative, to analyze findings across studies. One synthesis by Walker and Schaffarzick (1974) examined studies "in which an attempt was made to discriminate finer and more subtle differences between innovative and traditional curricula than a single score on an achievement test" (p. 94). They reviewed research since 1957 that compared the achievement of students using innovative curricula with the achievement of students using traditional curricula. The review included studies in science, mathematics, social studies, and English. Of the 23 stud ies that allowed for direct comparison of their results, a majority (12) were in science. Walker and Schaffarzick's (1974) review revealed an advantage for students using innovative curricula, compared with students using traditional curricula. They concluded that "[t]he innovative groups were superior about four times as often as the traditional groups in these comparisons" (p. 90). However, they continued to report that "innovative students do better when the criterion is well-matched to the innovative curriculum, and traditional students do better when the criterion is matched to the traditional curriculum" (p. 94). According to their synthesis, "different curricula produce different patterns of achievement, not necessarily greater overall achievement" (Walker & Schaffarzick, 1974, p. 97).

Boulanger (1981) synthesized research published between 1963 and 1978 that addressed science education for grades 6–12. The findings of over 50 studies were synthesized to determine the impact on student learning of certain aspects of instruction. Boulanger's synthesis "provides some insight into the effectiveness of systematic innovation in instruction" (p. 319). For example, the use of pre-instructional strategies (i.e., behavioral objectives, set induction, advanced organizers) was found to improve student conceptual learning. Training on scientific thinking, increased structure in the verbal content of materials, and increased realism or concreteness in adjunct materials also were aspects of science instruction found to improve cognitive outcomes. He also synthesized research on the quantity of time on topic, reporting that "simply expanding the amount of time spent on a given unit of material holds no special relationship to amount learned" (Boulanger, 1981, p. 321).

In order to provide a quantitative treatment of the research and reduce the potential for investigator bias, Shymansky, Kyle, and Alport (1983) synthesized 25 years (from 1955 to 1980) of experimental and quasi-experimental research regarding the effects of new science curricula on student performance. They used meta-analytic procedures to examine 105 studies, representing a total sample size of 45,626 students and 27 of the new science curricula. They measured the effect of 18 criteria on student performance individually, in combinations called criterion clusters (i.e., analytic skills, process skills, achievement, etc.), and by subject area. [7]

Shymansky and his colleagues found that the average student studying the new materials exceeded the performance of 63 percent of the students in traditional

---

7. Shymansky, Kyle, and Alport's (1983) study was part of a large meta-analysis project conduced by Anderson et al. (1982). The data were reanalyzed in 1990 and involved 81 studies (Shymansky, Hedges, & Woodworth, 1990).

science courses on the aggregate criterion variable (i.e., general achievement, process skills, analytic skills, and attitudes toward science).[8] The greatest gains were in process skills, attitudes, and achievement. They also reported that overall performance scores were more positive for mixed student samples than for samples that were predominantly male (less than 25 percent females) or for ones that were predominately female (more than 75 percent females). When analyzed by subject area, they found the biology curricula, developed in the BSCS, not only had the most positive impact on student performance but also had the most research supporting them. Furthermore, students using the new biology and physics programs showed the greatest gains across the 18 criteria measured, whereas students using the new chemistry and earth science materials showed the least gains.

As Shymansky and his colleagues note, their findings concerning overall improvements in achievement were especially important because much of the criticism of the new curricula assumed that improvements in process skills (a focus of all the new materials) could only be achieved at the expense of content knowledge (Shymansky, Kyle, & Alport, 1983).

Bredderman's (1983) meta-analysis of 57 controlled studies on three activity-based elementary science programs (*Elementary Science Study, ESS; Science—A Process Approach, S-APA;* and *Science Curriculum Improvement Study, SCIS*) found that 32 percent of the 400 comparisons favored the activity-based programs at least at the .05 level of significance. As he concluded,

> The results of this meta-analysis of program effects help in estimating what the impact would be if activity-based programs were adopted across a wide variety of districts. Performance on tests of science process, creativity, and perhaps intelligence would show increases of 10 to 20 percentile units. Reading and math scores might be positively affected, and attitudes toward science and science classes would probably show a small improvement. Student performance on standardized achievement tests in science content, if affected at all, might go up slightly when averaged across all student populations. (p. 511)

On the other hand, Bredderman cautioned that gains from using the activity-based curricula were not sustained unless similar types of materials were used in subsequent grades.

In 1982, Weinstein and colleagues reported on a meta-analysis of 33 studies, involving over 19,000 junior and high school students in the United States, Britain, and Israel that was designed to assess the impact of the U.S. innovative secondary science curricula on achievement since 1960. They found a ratio of approximately 4:1 in favor of outcomes related to the use of the innovative materials (Weinstein, Boulanger, & Walberg, 1982). In 1986, Blosser synthesized many of these studies, concluding that "Data exist to support the idea that the science curriculum improvement project materials developed after 1955 were successful in promoting student

---

8. Shymansky and his colleagues defined traditional science curriculum and contrasted it with the new science curriculum. Traditional science curriculum emphasizes knowledge of scientific facts, laws, and theories. In it, laboratories are verification exercises. In contrast, the new science curricula, developed after 1954, were characterized by their emphasis on higher cognitive skills and the processes of science. In it, laboratories are integrated with the text and extend concepts introduced in the text (Shymansky, Kyle, & Alport, 1983).

TABLE 30.2
Estimates of Percentages of U.S. High School Physics Students Enrolled in PSSC

Source	1962–63	1964–65
U.S. Office of Education	12.6 (50,300)**	20.6 (99,900)
National Science Foundation	25.0 (125,000)	50.0 (200,000)
College Entrance Examination Board	19.6	29.6

Note: **The figures in parentheses are the estimated total PSSC enrollments. From "The impact of national curriculum projects—the need for accurate assessment" by W. W. Welch, 1968, *School Science and Mathematics, 68,* 230.

achievement in the use of science process skills, in creativity, in higher cognitive skills at both the elementary and secondary school levels" (Blosser, 1986, p. 517).

In summary, much of the research concerning the effectiveness of the NSF-supported curricula in improving student achievement was compromised by two issues: first, the problem of test bias, and second, the lack of random sampling. Most of the evidence for improved student achievement is based on secondary analyses, conducted after the period of funding. However, in general, the research indicates that many curriculum projects were successful in improving student achievement.

Another line of research involved the impact of the NSF-supported curricula. By 1970, approximately a quarter of all secondary students in the United States used NSF-funded materials in their science courses (Nelkin, 1977).[9] Together, the curricula spanned all levels of mathematics and science education, including the college level, and, at times, extended across levels and areas. According to Schlessinger and Helgeson (1969), the science curriculum projects were more numerous, but less comprehensive, than those in mathematics. However, both the science and the mathematics programs fell short in their attempts to reach the total school population. Schlessinger and Helgeson (1969) described the situation in the following way: "Varying with the new course content projects, we are reaching only from twenty to about fifty percent of the students within our classrooms. This is true even where the teachers have been given special institutes in preparation for teaching these courses" (pp. 639–640).

Using the Physical Science Study Committee (PSSC), the first NSF-supported project, as a case study, Welch (1968) described how three separate studies produced three different sets of percentages estimating the enrollment of students in PSSC courses (see Table 30.2). Welch concluded that discrepancy among the data sets "leads one to doubt the accuracy of any of the reported figures" (p. 231). As he wrote, "Thus it becomes apparent that an assessment of the impact of the course content improvement program, even at the gross level of counting heads, is not reliable" (p. 234).

In spite of varying estimates of the use of the NSF-supported curriculum, it was a massive effort that updated science content, changed instruction, and influenced

---

9. Use varied greatly across the projects, and type of data collected caused confusion and misunderstandings. For example, the OTA report (1988) states that BSCS materials were estimated to have been used in approximately half of all U.S. biology classes in the late 1980s, and one-quarter of those who graduated with a baccalaureate degree in physics in 1983–84 had studied PSSC physics in high school.

more traditional texts. For example, in biology, although only 50 percent of American secondary schools eventually used BSCS materials, the BSCS books influenced change in nearly 70 percent of the content of the most widely used text at that time, *Modern Biology* (Quick, in Jackson, 1983, p. 149). However, the success of the curricular reform in wave one also had a political pitfall. As Nelkin wrote, "By improving the public school curriculum, the NSF, despite its denial of responsibility, found itself involved not in an isolated neutral research endeavor but in a major social intervention filled with political implications" (1977, p. 27).

Summary

Although the term *systemic reform* was not used in the 1960s and 1970s, the United States embarked on large-scale reform efforts that addressed two major parts of the educational system, *text* and *teaching*. Both efforts substantively changed science education, and the synergy between the two foci enhanced their separate effects. However, evaluation was not required of the various projects, and, particularly for the teacher training institutes, there are few research studies. Although more research exists for the curriculum projects, most studies were done after a project's completion. That is, results were not used to refine or continue the reform. The research usually used synthesis techniques, and findings generally supported the effectiveness of the new curricula to improve student attitudes, process skills, and achievement levels in science. The reforms of the 1960s and 1970s were national in scope; they reflected a shared vision of improved science education; but, in the end, they were limited by political issues and concerns.

WAVE II: COURSES AND COMPETENCIES

> The 1980s produced two distinct approaches to educational reform. One was a 'top-down' strategy that sought to change schools through state programs and regulatory activity. The other has been a 'bottom-up' reform movement in the form of school-based 'restructuring.' Both strategies have proved inadequate in substantial part because of the fragmentation of the current education system. (Smith, O'Day, & Fuhrman, 1992, p. 31)

The next wave of reform was signaled by the release of *A Nation at Risk* in 1983, which stated: "If an unfriendly foreign power had attempted to impose on America the mediocre educational performance that exists today, we might well have viewed it as an act of war" (National Commission on Excellence in Education, 1983, p. 5). Indeed, one researcher referred to reform efforts in the 1980s as "[attempts] to forcefully repair the sinking vessel" (Hawley, 1988, p. 418). Although the nation was aroused, the report did not address the dollars needed to change the educational system. However, in 1984, Congress passed the Education for Economic Security Act (EESA), which was designed to promote the teaching of mathematics, science, and foreign languages. Title II of that act directed the U.S. Department of Education to provide grants to school districts to address the shortfalls highlighted in *A Nation at Risk*. A second impetus for the reforms of the 1980s was the growing national awareness that the United States no longer dominated the global marketplace.

Although reform efforts occurred at both local and state levels, this section focuses on changes that were state, or top-down, efforts, because they were more systemic in their approach and effect.[10] Two major changes occurred at the state level. First, states assumed the responsibility for determining high school graduation requirements; and, second, states mandated competency tests to ensure that graduating students had the skills and knowledge to be effective citizens in a global economy. The themes of the second wave of reform, therefore, are *courses* and *competencies*.

Courses

In total, states enacted more rules and regulations affecting education in the three- to four-year period following the release of *A Nation at Risk* than at any time since the early 1960s (Timar & Kirp, 1989). Between 1983 and 1985, approximately 700 new policies were legislated (Darling-Hammond & Berry, 1988), and much of the activity focused on trying to ensure that all students reached high school graduation standards and, in many states, passed competency tests. In order to reach those goals, states increased the number of academic units or credits needed for graduation while concomitantly reducing the number and type of electives that would count toward graduation. In addition, states mandated passage of competency tests, added "pass to play" provisions (Texas), and developed grade-to-grade promotion standards (Wilson & Rossman, 1993).

The impetus for increasing course requirements was based on research, particularly in mathematics, indicating that student achievement as measured by standardized tests is improved by increased course taking (Alexander & Pallas, 1984; Schmidt, 1983a, b). Changes also were influenced by the National Commission on Excellence in Education's (1983) delineation of minimum high school graduation requirements. Those requirements included four year-long courses in English, three in mathematics, three in science, three in social science, and a semester course in computer science. Furthermmore, a foreign language was recommended for college-bound students. In 1980, 37 states defined minimal graduation requirements, but a decade later, 43 states had assumed that responsibility (Wilson & Rossman, 1993). Math or science requirements were increased in 32 of those states, and 25 raised graduation requirements in both math and science. One result of increased graduation requirements was a proliferation of science courses. Indeed, in the four years between 1982 and 1986, the largest enrollment increases were in science and foreign languages. Furthermore, to ensure that all students passed competency tests, schools offered more remedial courses.

Most of the research on course offerings relied on large national databases, providing profiles of course offerings, and/or state assessments of change. Researchers at the Educational Testing Service used the High School and Beyond database to analyze course-taking patterns across the nation, with the 1982–83 school year providing baseline data. According to Wilson and Rossman, "One topic of high interest in several of the studies was student enrollment in mathematics and science and

---

10. The school-based, "bottom up" reform that approached a systemic effort was *Success for All*, a comprehensive program designed to restructure elementary schools that served many students at risk of academic failure (Slavin, Madden, Karweit, Dolan, & Wasik, 1992). First piloted in Baltimore in 1987, by 1994 the program was implemented in approximately 200 schools in 59 districts in 20 states. Its expansion was primarily to high-poverty schools with substantial Chapter I resources, because schools/districts had to commit $100,000 of their own funds to participate (Madden, Slavin, Dolan, & Wasik, 1993).

whether there was systemic variation by track, race, gender, socioeconomic status, or other demographic variables" (1993, pp. 36, 37). As expected, analyses found that enrollments differed by school characteristics.

Clune, White, and Patterson (1989) collected interview data in six states, 24 districts, and 32 high schools in order to analyze any effects of new graduation requirements. They found that slightly more than a quarter of students enrolled in an additional math class, and a third took an additional science class. They concluded that the increased graduation requirements both succeeded and failed, stating, "They succeeded in getting a lot more students into basic academic courses; . . . they failed in getting students into the most rigorous possible courses, in producing a reasonably uniform education for all students, and, probably, in conveying the higher-order skills necessary for a competitive economy" (p. 47).

Another study analyzed the effects of state policies on teachers' content decisions in elementary mathematics (Schwille et al., 1986, July). The seven states involved in the study ranged from ones with high direct state control (New York and South Carolina) to ones with a mix of direct and indirect control (Florida and California) to ones where control of school policies was at the district level or there was indirect control (Ohio, Indiana, and Michigan). Although differences were found between direct and indirect control states, the authors concluded that in both types of states, teachers had little autonomy over policies on instructional objectives, student testing, student placement, textbook selection, time allocation, and teacher qualifications. Indeed, the top-down component of the second wave of reform did not involve teachers in decision-making.

Retrospectively, Porter and his associates analyzed reforms during the 1980s from the perspective of opportunities to learn (Porter, 1994). The analysis focused on three aspects of the reform during the 1980s. First, did increased graduation requirements lead to higher dropout rates? Second, did schools accommodate students by offering more remedial courses? And, third, was instruction weakened in standard courses? Porter cites a study by the U.S. Department of Education that indicated that dropout rates, particularly among poor and/or minority students, did not increase (U.S. Department of Education, in Porter, 1994). The second question was answered by Clune and White's (1992) analysis of high school course-taking patterns. Using schools that enrolled mostly low-achieving students in four states, they concluded that course-taking patterns had not been affected by increased graduation requirements. That is, the additional academic credits were earned in courses of varying levels of difficulty, not only in basic or remedial courses. Porter focused on answering the third questions. As he wrote, "[N]o evidence was found that requiring more students to take more advanced mathematics and science resulted in compromising the curricula of the courses experiencing the increased enrollments. . . . The required Chemistry/Physics course looked as challenging in terms of topics covered as did the college prep Physical Science course, and the actual quality of instruction looked better" (Porter, 1994, p. 6).

The second wave of reform was characterized by a proliferation of graduation requirements by states that spawned new courses and varied types of instruction. However, the dire predictions that such top-down reform would lead to increased dropout rates or watered-down courses are not supported by the available research. The second characteristic of the second wave of systemic reform was an increase in state mandatory testing or *competencies*.

Competencies

In addition to increasing academic course requirements, state reform policies addressed competencies by increasing the number and importance of state-mandated tests. Although state-mandated testing was intended to drive changes in the curriculum, it often resulted in narrowing the curriculum; thereby "[creating] adverse conditions for reform" (Fullan & Miles, 1992, p. 747). For example, a study by Corbett and Wilson (1990) found that new statewide testing requirements in Maryland and Pennsylvania resulted in narrowing of the curriculum by aligning subjects taught to a specific test. Similarly, a study of the impact of state-mandated assessments in mathematics in two states (Maine and Maryland) found that the new testing mandates resulted in teachers focusing their teaching activities on the tests, especially when testing was combined with high-stake conditions (Firestone, Mayrowetz, & Fairman, 1998).

Wilson and Rossman (1993) summarize the findings concerning the effects of competency testing on student enrollments stating, "What stands out, however, are the low levels of enrollment in mathematics and science courses relative to vocational courses and the suggestion that competency testing pushes students toward basic or remedial courses, at least in mathematics" (pp. 37, 38). Furthermore, they state that "one main effect of the reform of graduation requirements was . . . a redistribution of course offerings and staffing patterns across departments within schools" (p. 41). For example, although math enrollments remained fairly stable, there was a substantial redistribution of types of courses offered and enrollments in various courses.

Porter (1983, January-February) examined the research concerning testing and school effectiveness. He cites multiple studies that support testing as one of five factors contributing to effective schools, writing, "Within the context of the debate on testing, the effective schools literature must be seen as aligned squarely with the advocates of testing" (p. 25). Other analyses, such as the one discussed next, concurred that testing was effective in improving student achievement and in closing achievement gaps among subgroups of students.

A comprehensive analysis of three decades of math and reading scores from NAEP and SAT provides other evidence of the combined effects of increased graduation requirements (leading to diverse course offerings within a subject) and competency testing (Lee, 2002). Although the analyses do not include science, the results are pertinent. Using NAEP data, Lee reports that "During the period from 1978 to 1986, greater academic improvement of lower performing students across all racial and ethnic groups was observed" (p. 4). This change resulted in narrowing achievement gaps between Black/White and Hispanic/White students. Similar results were found with SAT scores. As Lee summarized, "It appears that low-performing students gained more than high-performing students when minimum competency was emphasized during the 1970s and early 1980s" (2002, p. 5).

Summary

In looking back over the 1980s, two issues were paramount in affecting large-scale educational reforms. First, states increased graduation requirements while simultaneously restricting the types of elective courses that could be used to meet those requirements. Second, states began to institute high-stakes tests, which defined the skills and knowledge students should have after successfully completing the courses required. However, many state policies were mandated without substantive input from teachers, resulting in the establishment of unrealistic timelines (Fullan & Miles, 1992; Schwille et al., 1986, July). Furthermore, states often reversed policies before achievement could be affected.[11] As noted in one report, "The 'top-down' mandates of the 1980s did little . . . to change the content of instruction (especially its focus on basic skills) or to alter the reigning notions of teaching and learning because, as some argued, fragmented and contradictory policies diverted teachers' attention and provided little or no support for the type of professional learning necessary" (Goertz, Floden, & O'Day, 1996, p. xi). As the decade drew to a close, the concept of a systemic approach to reforming science and mathematics education began to emerge in the literature (Horizon Research, 1994). Reform programs previously referred to as "comprehensive" were considered less extensive, and researchers and policy makers began to define the ways in which reform could address an entire educational system.

WAVE III: EXCELLENCE AND EQUITY

Systemic education reform, in theory and practice, is at its heart: (a) ambitious—in that it establishes new learning standards for all students, (b) comprehensive—in that it simultaneously targets many pieces of the educational system for change toward a common goal, and (c) coherent—in that it supports mutually reinforcing practices and policies that send a strong, consistent message to students, educators, and society about what is important in education. (Fuhrman, 1994, in Heck, 1998, p. 162)

In 1990, the National Science Foundation (NSF) acknowledged the need to address whole state educational systems by establishing the Statewide Systemic Initiative (SSI) program. The SSI program marked the beginning of the third wave of reform in science education. The program's goal was to improve classroom practice and, ultimately, student achievement through major systemic change in science and mathematics education (Fuhrman et al., 1995). As noted in one report, "In framing its solicitation for proposals, NSF emphasized the need for states to deal comprehensively with the key factors that shape instructional practice, the policies governing education, and the economic and political contexts in which science and mathematics education must operate" (Horizon Research, 1994, p. 3). Between 1991 and 1993, NSF entered into five-year cooperative agreements with 24 states and the Commonwealth of Puerto Rico to carry out standards-based systemic reform in mathematics and science education.

The path for systemic reform was paved by the publication of standards in mathematics (National Council of Teachers of Mathematics [NCTM], 1989) and in science by the American Association for the Advancement of Science's (AAAS)

---

11. Ohio, for example, developed a model curriculum in mathematics and provided a timeline for local districts to implement it. Failure to implement would affect district funding. However, after pressure from state legislators, the State Board of Education removed the penalty clause.

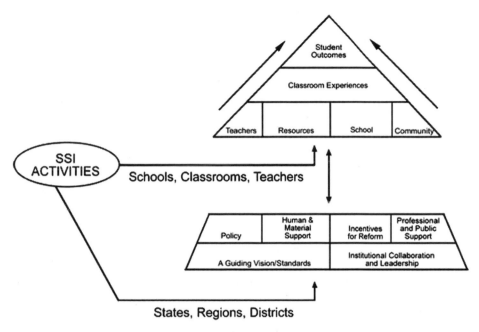

Note: From *A report on the evaluation of the National Science Foundation's Statewide Systemic Initiatives (SSI) Program*, by A. A. Zucker, P. M. Shields, N. E. Adelman, T. B. Corcoran, & M. E. Goertz, 1998, (Report No. NSF 98-147) p. viii. Arlington, VA: National Science Foundation.

FIGURE 30–2.   A model of systemic reform.

Benchmarks for Scientific Literacy (AAAS, 1993). The *Benchmarks* were used by the state systemic initiatives as standards for science education until the publication of the *National Science Education Standards* (National Research Council [NRC], 1996). All three documents stress both *excellence* and *equity*. For example, the *National Science Education Standards* (1996) state, "[t]he intent of the Standards can be expressed in a single phrase: science standards for all students. The phrase embodies both excellence and equity" (p. 2). Furthermore, both the NCTM and the NRC standards are based on the premise that common, minimum standards do not promote equity; on the other hand, common, high standards of excellence do. NSF embraced that premise, and *excellence* and *equity* became cornerstones of systemic reform in science and mathematics in the 1990s.

Perhaps learning from the reforms of the 1960s and 1970s, NSF made comprehensive evaluations a cornerstone of its systemic initiative program. Several groups were contracted to evaluate the reforms through multiple studies that used both quantitative and qualitative methods.[12] In addition, a model of systemic reform was developed that helped focus evaluation and research questions (Zucker, Shields, Adelman, Corcoran, & Goetz, 1998). Figure 30–2 illustrates components of state

---

12. SRI International, Abt Associates Inc., and the Consortium for Policy Research (CPRE) were among the groups providing the NSF with evaluations of the SSIs.

educational systems in the United States. With the overall goal of improving student achievement in mathematics and science, the SSI reforms generally entered the system at two levels, as shown in Fig. 30–2. The majority of the reform activities entered in the middle and worked up through local classrooms, students, and teachers to improve student achievement. However, other activities began at the state, region, or district level to affect policies and public support for the reforms.

At the classroom level, the SSIs' primary focus was on teacher professional development (20 states), on developing instructional materials (initially 6 states but, by 1997, 13 states), and on supporting model schools (7 states). The states involved in systemic reform mainly used five strategies to affect state and district levels. Twenty-two states created an infrastructure to support systemic reform, 13 addressed teacher education, 14 mobilized public opinion, nine funded local systemic initiatives, and three attempted to align state policy as a primary target of the reform effort (Zucker, Shields, Adelman, Corcoran, & Goertz, 1998).[13]

Zucker and Shields (1995, 1998a, 1998b) conducted school-level case studies in 12 of the SSI states from 1992 through 1997 in order to assess the SSI program's impact on classroom practice and to identify characteristics of successful SSI strategies. Wherever possible, data from an SSI's internal evaluation were incorporated into the study. There was general agreement among the SSIs on what the problems were in mathematics and science classrooms and on the kinds of reforms needed to address the problems. The SSIs recognized the need for new, integrated forms of assessing student progress (e.g., portfolios, exhibitions) and the need for instructional strategies that focused more on active and interactive learning. Collectively, the SSIs called for new curriculum materials that placed increased emphasis on learning of all students, conceptual understanding of fundamental mathematical and scientific concepts, applications of mathematics and science to real-life situations, and interrelatedness across disciplines. Another study found that, overall, the SSIs' professional development stressed opportunities for teachers to enhance their content knowledge (Shields, Marsh, & Adelman, 1997).

Although the NSF-funded evaluations of the systemic initiatives are available, to date little research on the SSIs has been published. This is due partly to location of the initiatives within state departments of education (7), state higher education councils (3), or private groups (7), some of which were developed to run the initiatives. Only three SSIs were housed at universities. Much of the research focused on the two aspects of the third wave of reform that both the national standards and the NSF program addressed, *excellence* and *equity*. The review of research for the third wave of systemic reform traces both themes.

Excellence

Because improved student achievement was the overall goal of the program, *excellence* and *equity* are addressed in relation to changes in student achievement. Although the ultimate goal of systemic reforms of the 1990s was to improve student learning, the SSIs varied in both the type and amount of student achievement data collected. Heck (1998) characterized the gathering of student achievement data by the SSIs as "problematic," because the measures of achievement did not fully reflect

---

13. Initiatives could select more than one category, so totals are more than 25.

the standards the initiative had adopted, were not given at the grade levels the initiative had targeted, did not aggregate and report scores at the level of the system the initiative primarily addressed, were given infrequently or changed too frequently to provide stable longitudinal data, or simply did not include science and/or mathematics.

A comprehensive review of the SSIs' impact on student achievement in science limited its findings to seven states "that were likely to generate the most credible evidence that student achievement has risen" (Laguarda, 1998, p. 1).[14] In spite of varying methodological and logistical problems, there was evidence of gains in achievement in science in Louisiana, Montana, Ohio, and Puerto Rico. In addition, findings in Ohio and Louisiana indicated that the reforms particularly benefited African American students. Laguarda (1998) concluded that student achievement gains were most likely to be found in states that focused their reform activities primarily at the school, classroom, and teacher level, as shown in Fig. 30–2. She stated:

> Of the seven SSIs that were reviewed, the four with the most credible evidence of changes in student achievement—Louisiana, Montana, Ohio, and Puerto Rico—were those with the most intensive interventions aimed directly at classrooms. . . . [T]hose SSIs that invested most heavily in activities directed at state-level policy alignment (such as New Mexico and Vermont) or concentrated on building a state-level infrastructure to support change or on building local capacity to reform instruction (such as Kentucky and Vermont) . . . found it much more difficult to produce evidence of changes in student achievement that could be attributed directly to the SSI. (Laguarda, 1998, pp. 5, 6)

Laguarda's conclusion is supported by Zucker, Shields, Adelman, Corcoran, and Goertz's (1998) study. Although Zucker and his colleagues' evidence is based upon findings from four states, they concurred that improved student achievement in science occurred when a state-level reform focused at the school, classroom, and teacher levels.

Clune (1998) synthesized data across nine SSI states to test his theory of systemic reform; that is, *systemic reform* (SR) leads to *systemic policy* (SP) that leads to a *rigorous implemented curriculum* (SC) that results in *higher student achievement* (SA). He posited that those components could be represented as a *continuous causal sequence:*

$$SR \rightarrow SP \rightarrow SC \rightarrow SA$$

In testing his theory, he included several indicators of student achievement; such as overall achievement gains, gains in equity (closing any achievement gaps), gains in course enrollments, and achievement levels in subsequent courses. Using two dimensions to test his theory, breadth of change (number of students) and depth of change (size of change and quality of the data) and the nine case-study states, Clune found that, on a five-point scale, the nine states averaged 2.3 points on both breadth and depth of student achievement gain.[15] The results of his study suggest

---

14. The states and their initiatives were: Kentucky (PRISM), Louisiana (LaSIP), Montana (SIMMS), New Mexico (SIMSE), Ohio (*Discovery*), Puerto Rico (PR-SSI), and Vermont (VISMT).

15. Clune used the Case Studies, commissioned by NSF, as his data source (Zucker & Shields, 1995, 1998a, 1998b). The states included were: Connecticut, Maine, Montana, Louisiana, Michigan, California, Arkansas, Delaware, and New York.

that the goal of excellence, as indicated by overall achievement gains, was not reached in the five years of NSF support.

Near the end of the decade, NSF funded RAND to conduct a study of teaching practices and student achievement in six states and urban districts that had participated in the systemic initiative program (Klein, Hamilton, McCaffrey, Stecher, Robyn, & Burroughs, 2000). The research design included: (a) a measure of instructional practices, (b) an assessment of student achievement, and (c) an analysis of any relationship between them after controlling for student demographics. There are several concerns with the design. First, although large samples of teachers at each site responded to questionnaires, there was no effort to identify teachers who had participated with the SSI and those who had not. Second, there was no effort to link student responses with those of the teachers.[16] And, third, in order to reduce testing burden, scores from existing statewide or district-wide tests were used when available. The study included grades three through seven, and over 300 teachers and approximately 9000 students were included in the data analyses. Klein and his colleagues report, "After controlling for student background characteristics, we found a generally weak but positive relationship between the frequency with which a teacher used the reform practices and student achievement. This relationship was somewhat stronger when achievement was measured with open-ended response tests than with multiple-choice tests" (2000, p. xiv). They note that the findings may be compromised by inaccurate teacher reporting of frequency of use of various instructional practices, lack of alignment between tests and reform curricula, differences in student groups (unrelated to frequency of teacher use of reform practices), and length of time students were taught by teachers using reform practices. However, they suggest that the consistency of findings across sites, despite differences among the sites, is encouraging.

A carefully controlled, smaller study focused on student achievement in eight urban junior-high/middle schools in one SSI (Kahle, Meece, & Scantlebury, 2000). In this study, frequency of use of reform teaching practices was reported by both students and teachers, with student responses validating those of the teachers. Student and teacher data were linked, and teachers were identified as participating (or not) in the SSI's professional development. Furthermore, only one measure of achievement was used, and it was aligned with standards-based science content. However, results were reported only for African American students, because the number of European American students in the schools was too low to use in statistical analyses. Kahle and her colleagues reported that "students of teachers who participated in the SSI professional development, compared with students whose teachers had not participated, scored higher on the science achievement test. Second, students of SSI teachers rated their teachers as more frequently using standards-based teaching practices than did students in non-SSI teachers' classes" (Kahle, Meece, & Scantlebury, 2000, p. 1034). However, participation in the SSI's professional development was not a significant predictor of student achievement; rather the use of standards-based teaching practices was predictive.[17]

---

16. It is not clear if the student sample was limited to students with teachers in the teacher sample.

17. Fifteen percent of the variance in students' science achievement scores was due to teacher differences. Between-teacher variation was largely due to two factors: teacher gender and frequency of use of standards-based teaching practices, including inquiry and problem solving (Kahle, Meece, & Scantlebury, 2000).

Huffman and Lawrenz (2003) investigated the extent to which one state's systemic initiative reformed science education. Eighth-grade science teachers were involved in an ex post facto comparative study that assessed impacts on teachers' instructional practices, external relations, professional communities, school policies, and family involvement. They compared schools with high or low participation in the SSI, matching them on demographic characteristics, such as geographical location (urban/rural/etc.), size of school, and socioeconomic and ethnic characteristics of the students. In schools with high participation, they found that the use of standards-based instructional techniques increased and that external groups had more influence over science instruction. However, no differences were found for (1) teachers' influence on school policy (low in both types of schools), (2) teachers' involvement in professional communities (high in both), or (3) family involvement with the reform (low in both). From their findings, they concluded, "Perhaps comprehensive systemic reform is an unrealistic goal, but it does suggest we need to better understand systemic reform and use research to help design future reform efforts" (p. 376).

Although individual research studies identified successful components of the state systemic initiatives, Anderson, Brown, and Lopez-Ferrao (2003) synthesized official evaluation reports to analyze the effectiveness of the program. They concluded that the systemic initiative program contributed in three significant ways to the improvement of science and mathematics education. First, it led to the broad acceptance of a systemic approach in addressing education problems; second, it made improvement of mathematics and science education a priority nationally; and, third, the systemic reform efforts made serving all students a national mandate.

Equity

Although NSF officially defined equity as the "reduction in attainment difference between those traditionally underserved and their peers" (Zucker, Shields, Adelman, Corcoran, & Goertz, 1998, p. 37), states approached equity in different ways. For example, most states focused on elementary and middle school science and mathematics, because all children would benefit from improvements in instruction and curriculum—improvements that might lead to more equitable enrollments in elective courses (Kahle, 1997). In addition, many states found that leadership both in the SSI and at the state and regional levels was not representative, and some took measures to expand the pool of effective leaders. Furthermore, states addressed the lack of minority teachers of science and mathematics. Overall states reported that 28 percent of teachers served by the SSIs' professional development activities were nonwhite—over double the proportion of minority science and math teachers in the workforce (Zucker, Shields, Adelman, & Powell, 1995).

However, most of the research on equity focused on reducing achievement gaps among identifiable subgroups of students. States varied in relation to the subgroups addressed. For example, ethnic/racial were the focus of 21 states, females of 19, and/or low-income students of four.[18] The different equity emphasis, in most cases, reflected population or achievement differences across the states; for example, Vermont, with few racial/ethnic minorities, did not have that focus, whereas

---

18. States could identify more than one group, so totals are more than 25.

Puerto Rico—with girls achieving higher than boys—did not focus on females. States also differed in the strategies used to improve equity, although the two most commonly identified ones were professional development and targeted funds. Professional development involved specific equity workshops (Georgia, Louisiana, and Ohio), whereas targeted funds were directed to low-performing schools (Connecticut, Michigan, New York, Louisiana, South Dakota, and Puerto Rico) (Zucker, Shields, Adelman, & Powell, 1995).

Much has been written about the "equity challenge" for the SSIs and for standards-based education in general (Boone, 1998; Kahle, 1998). For example, Massell, Kirst, and Hoppe (1997) conducted research on standards-based systemic reform in nine states. Their findings are based on in-depth interviews with policy makers and educators at state and district levels in California, Connecticut, Florida, Georgia, Kentucky, Minnesota (a non-SSI state), New Jersey, South Carolina, and Texas. They concluded, "[F]or the most part, attention to equity issues within the context of standards-based reform remained episodic and weak. With few notable exceptions [Kentucky], desegregation and school finance policies were pursued as separate, independent initiatives" (p. 9).

In 1996, the Office of Educational Research and Improvement (OERI) of the U.S. Department of Education funded 12 studies of different aspects of current education reform, including a study of the systemic reform movement (Goertz, Floden, & O'Day, 1996). The systemic reform study focused on math and reading and was conducted in three stages: first, a comprehensive review of the literature; second, intensive case studies of 12 reforming schools in six districts of three SSI states (California, Michigan, and Vermont); and, third, analyses of the findings in the context of state policies and sustainability. The study focused on all parts of the education system, analyzing capacity for change, governance structures, and teaching practices. It also included a section on equity, noting that both California and Michigan targeted some of their funds for schools and districts with large concentrations of low-performing and/or minority students. Incentives were offered to entice such schools to participate. Goertz and her colleagues reported that both districts and schools were restructured to be more responsive to diverse social, cultural, and educational needs of their students. Furthermore, they noted many examples of restructured curricula across the sites, particularly introducing curricula that embraced state and national standards and providing for bilingual education. Last, they reported that academic tracking declined.

Individual studies also addressed equity. Using Hierarchical Linear Modeling, Kahle, Meece, and Scantlebury (2000) concluded that the standards-based teaching, advocated by Ohio's SSI and promulgated through its sustained professional development programs, improved the attitudes and achievement levels of urban, African American youth. Furthermore, the gender gap in achievement between African American girls and boys (favoring girls) was narrowed in SSI classes, compared with non-SSI classes in the same schools. Their findings are supported by Laguarda (1989), who states, "Special analyses conducted by both of these SSIs [Louisiana and Ohio] show that the gains demonstrated by students in SSI classrooms were greatest among African American students, students who received free or reduced-price lunches, and girls" (p. 3).

Fenster's (1998) study of the New Jersey SSI probed three questions: (a) Do students learn more because of the SSI? (b) Are they better equipped to apply what they learn to everyday problems? and (c) Have inequities in performance among different groups of students been reduced? Using scores on state-mandated assessments, he found that students in NJSSI schools did not learn more than their counterparts in schools without NJSSI affiliation, that the evidence for question (b) was too limited to draw conclusions, and that inequities in performance had widened between underserved school districts and the rest of the state on the required eighth-grade assessment.

Lee (2002) researched changes in racial and ethnic achievement gaps across 30 years. He assessed trends in both NAEP and SAT data for mathematics and reading. Although his study did not include science scores, other analyses suggest that his findings for NAEP mathematics are similar to those for science (Kahle, 2004). His synthesis did not separate SSI states from non-SSI states. His overall finding— that achievement gaps between Black/White as well as between Hispanic/White students widened in the 1990s—reinforces the importance of some systemic initiatives' success in narrowing similar gaps.

Summary

The SSIs were designed to improve all parts of state educational systems; in so doing it was assumed that changes would enhance student achievement in science and mathematics (Weiss & Webb, 2003). The extensive NSF evaluations of the program as well as a smattering of research studies, however, suggest that the overall goal of excellence (as defined by improved student achievement) was not reached in the five years of NSF funding. Lee's (2002) comprehensive review of achievement changes indicates that 30 years are needed for widespread improvement in achievement. Individual research studies as well as case studies of selected SSI states, however, provide indications that the reforms of the 1990s strove for excellence and achieved it, albeit in small increments at various parts of the educational system.

In summary, Heck (1989) notes that *excellence* and *equity* were both mandated by NSF's systemic reforms of science and mathematics. He writes, "Equity, as NSF has conceived it and asserted it in the SSI program, is not a concept reserved for the traditionally underserved and underachieving groups" (p. 169). Rather, the SSIs were directed toward changing the entire system so that all children were able to reach their full potential. Heck recommended that research questions address both *excellence* and *equity* at all levels of the educational system, shown in Fig. 30–2. Clearly, in the third wave, evaluation and research concerning *excellence* and *equity* was needed to address changes in multiple parts of the system. However, the published literature primarily addresses improved student achievement, the ultimate goal of systemic reform.

LESSONS LEARNED

Systemic reform is an extremely complex process, and it is not clear whether systemic reform is even possible. (Huffman and Lawrenz, 2003, p. 358)

So, across 50 years, what has been learned about systemic reform? In each wave of reform—from Sputnik to MACOS, from *A Nation at Risk* to the math standards and science benchmarks, from the SSIs to *No Child Left Behind*—interactions between educational vision and political realities have shaped the reforms as well as the research about them. As research has documented, the vision of improved curricula in the first wave of reform was compromised by several political as well as educational realities. First, some of the new materials did not adhere to local norms concerning human behavior, evolution, and other topics; and, second, research concerning their effectiveness was seriously compromised by the lack of independent tests aligned with the goals of the curricula. Furthermore, although the first wave addressed two major components of the education system—*texts* and *teaching*—the politics of the day prevented articulation between those two massive efforts to improve science education, and each was weakened by that reality. In retrospect, there is a considerable body of research suggesting that the new curricula improved both student attitudes and achievement. However, there is little evidence of the effect of the Teacher Training Institutes on either classroom practice or on student achievement. Positive gains from that program were identified, on the other hand, by changes in the science teaching profession.

It is arguable whether the second wave of reform was systemic. However, authors have identified it as a time of major educational reform, and it involved both top-down strategies and bottom-up reforms (e.g., comprehensive school reform at the local level). The research reviewed focused on state-level, or top-down, reforms during the 1980s, assessing any effects of increased courses in science as well as competency testing on student skills and achievement. Lee (2002) found that the achievement gap between subgroups of students narrowed in the 1980s, a finding based on increases in minority scores while majority scores remained flat. Generally, a review of the research suggests that course proliferation was primarily at the basic level, and that competency testing, rather than raising the bar lowered it, pushing "students toward basic or remedial courses" (Wilson & Rossman, 1993, p. 38).

Indeed, the proliferation of science courses in the 1980s may have contributed to what was, in effect, tracking in science, the elimination of which was one of the goals of the NSF's systemic initiative program. The third wave of large-scale reform, discussed here in relation to the statewide systemic initiatives, had a theoretical underpinning, was driven by an educational vision that excellence for all leads to equity, and was supported politically at the national and state levels. Although much can be learned from multiple and broad-scale evaluations of the SSIs, research concerning the third wave is somewhat elusive. The published literature is mixed concerning achievement of the dual goals of *excellence* and *equity*. There are several reasons for the lack of research concerning the third wave: first, there is the issue of time (the lag between collecting data and publishing results); second, there was more emphasis (at the state level) on doing the reforms than on studying their effectiveness; and, third, the driving vision of systemic reform as articulated through the SSIs was changed dramatically by the politics of the new century, and science education researchers may have shifted their focus before definitive studies were completed.

Across the three waves of reform, two basic lessons have been learned: first, large-scale reform of science education takes time; and, second, systemic reforms must include both top-down and bottom-up approaches. Research supports those lessons. McLaughlin (1990) reviewed a RAND study of 293 local projects in 18 states from 1973 to 1978. All of the projects involved significant federal funds. McLaughlin drew the following conclusions:

- Adoption of a project consistent with federal goals does not ensure successful implementation.
- Successful implementation does not predict long-run continuation.
- Success depends primarily on local factors, not federal guidelines or funding levels.
- Local factors enhancing or distracting from success include commitment of district leadership, the project's scope, and the project's implementation strategy.

Likewise, a summary of research concerning systemic reform provides insights into prerequisites for success as well as for sustainability of systemic reform within and across schools (Carpenter et al., 2004, February). The authors identify the following factors:

- Learning communities through which teachers can articulate and examine new ideas about mathematics, science, student learning, and instructional practice.
- Professional development that enables and supports teachers' inquiry into subject matter, student learning, and teaching practice.
- Infusions of material and human resources from outside the school or the educational system, which are necessary to initiate and sustain reform

Synergy across various levels in the educational system, indeed, leads to sustained change. This synergy is articulated by the findings of the OERI review of research on systemic reform (Goertz, Floden, & O'Day, 1996). Those findings are summarized in Fig. 30–3. Systemic or large-scale reform across the last half-century has attempted changes at both local and state levels. Success has come (in terms of student outcomes) when it has been guided by vision and supported by politics of the day. Research across the past 50 years has probed to understand systemic reform, to develop models to guide it, and to provide findings to guide it. However, both the type of research as well as the type of questions asked have been affected by the politics of the day.[19]

EPILOGUE

One reviewer of this chapter suggested that I include insights that I gained about systemic reform as a principal investigator of one of the initial Statewide Systemic Initiatives—one that continues with state funding. Although I studiously avoided personal thoughts in the chapter, the longer I thought about her suggestion, the more I liked it; for too few researchers are actively involved in systemic reform, and the field suffers from their absence. So, if my personal reflections can entice other scholars to the fray; then, I will modestly add them.

---

19. NSF, under political pressure, switched from qualitative to quantitative studies of SSIs in the mid-1990s.

- Coherence among state policies and a guiding vision is needed.
- Communication about the reform must reach parents, students, and teachers as well as policy makers.
- Reform takes time—time to learn new content and new skills, time to change instruction, time to enhance learning.
- Goals of the reform may have to strike a balance between current and desired practice.
- Deliberate, consistent, and pervasive strategies are needed to infuse equity into the reforms.
- Capacity building must include individual as well as organizational and systemic needs.
- Consistency, alignment, and coherence are needed across and throughout the system.
- Teachers and administrators need to be involved in multiple levels, not only at the school/classroom level.
- Capacity building strategies must pay attention to diversity at all levels of the system.
- Outside stakeholders and supporters must be involved if the reform is to be sustained.

Note. From *Systemic Reform* [*Volume I: Findings and conclusions.] Studies of education reform,* by M. E. Goertz, R. E. Floden, and J. A. O'Day, 1996, (ERIC Document Reproduction Service No. ED397553). East Lansing, MI: National Center for Research on Teacher Learning.

FIGURE 30–3.   Findings of OERI review on systemic reform.

As I wrote in a Performance Effectiveness Review for NSF, the basic problem we faced was trying to do systemic reform while simultaneously learning how to evaluate it, which included the development of the skills and strategies to do large-scale assessments across a period of time. Furthermore, the practicalities of working in multiple districts (in Ohio there were 614 independent school districts during the SSI) with limited budgets were a challenge. In fact, we constantly juggled research design against research practicalities. For those of us who collected student achievement data, the issue of attribution was continuous. In Ohio, we collected various types of achievement information and looked for patterns that supported the SSI. Politically—both in Ohio and at NSF—we could not conduct controlled experiments.

One of the most useful exercises I have ever undertaken was responding to a question, posed by Ohio's evaluator, Iris Weiss, president of Horizon Research Institute. She asked all members of the SSI Coordinating Council what each hoped the reform would look like five years after NSF funds ended—in Ohio's case in 2000. One aspect with which I had had little direct involvement—after its initial implementation—was a regional support system. Regional Councils largely controlled the way SSI funds were expended, public relations, teacher support, etc. I realized that it was critical that the regionalization be sustained to provide services to schools and teachers. Furthermore, I knew that the model of professional development that we had adapted from Reading Recovery was key to our success in changing teacher practice and improving student learning. I hoped that not only teachers and administrators but also parents and policy makers would support that model (sustained, content-based, rigorous, and expensive). I speculated that teacher licensure would change to ensure adequate preparation in math and science for middle school teachers.

Reflecting over the 15 years, there have been some wins and some almost-wins. Regionalization remains, although the Ohio Department of Education now funds and manages the regions. The regional centers support all disciplines, not only math and science, with much less funding. So, regionalization is only a partial win. The professional development model promulgated by the SSI continues, albeit enrolling many fewer teachers, but its basic strengths—content-based, sustained, and rigorous—remain. And, with few exceptions, the model is accepted and supported by administrators as well as by politicians and the public. Last, Ohio moved to middle school licensure (formerly it was K–8 or 7–12 certification) with specialties in math and science. Do I think programs leading to the new licenses have adequate math or science content for today's teachers? No, but they are a giant leap forward.

At the state level, the systemics were to address all parts of the state's educational system; yet, none of the SSIs were staffed by people with expertise in all of the areas needed. Most of us were either science or mathematics educators, so we focused on what we knew best—professional development. But we learned. We learned that appropriate texts were needed, so Montana and Nebraska developed curricula; we learned that the public needed to value what we were trying to do, so Ohio developed free booklets of science activities for each state park; we learned that state personnel were relatively fluid, so Connecticut and New Mexico formed independent agencies to guide their reform; we learned that visible units of change were important, so Maine and Michigan focused on model schools.

In spite of all that has been written about systemic reform, the research base is still shallow. Perhaps it is too soon after the last of the systemics, or, perhaps, we (the researchers) have lost interest in this grand experiment. In any case, two analyses of doctoral programs—one in mathematics education and one in science education—indicated that doctoral education has not changed in ways that will provide researchers with the tools and skills (including people skills) to do and to evaluate large-scale reform. In his recent book, Peter Fensham (2004) makes the distinction between research for its own sake and research to improve/change practice. He notes that for many of the science educators whom he interviewed, "the research process itself bound the purposes they saw as important for their research" (p. 163). Clearly, systemic reform is involved in change and improvement, and researchers with those interests are needed.

For me, the opportunity to be involved in the grand experiment—both as an educator and as a researcher—was the opportunity of a lifetime. To have the resources (both human and fiscal) to affect even some parts of a state's educational system in order to make learning science and mathematics more equitable was important. It was worth all of the political skills that I painfully learned, all of the setbacks along the way, and all of the sleepless nights when I worried about logistics as well as about experimental design!

ACKNOWLEDGMENTS

I would like to thank Dr. Mary Kay Kelly for her thoughtful suggestions and careful editing of this chapter. Her questions provided valuable insights and her suggestions improved it. Thanks also to Deborah Tomanek and Patricia Campbell, who reviewed this chapter.

REFERENCES

Alexander, K. L., & Pallas, A. M. (1984). Curriculum reform and school performance: An evaluation of the new basics. *American Journal of Education, 92*, 391–420.

American Association for the Advancement of Science. (1993). *Benchmarks for science literacy: Project 2061.* New York: Oxford University Press.

Anderson, B. T., Brown, C. L., & Lopez-Ferrao, J. (2003). Systemic reform: Good educational practice with positive impacts and unresolved problems and issues. In D. D. Kumar & J. W. Altschuld (Eds.), *Science and technology education policy*, a symposium issue of *Policy Studies Review, 20*, 617–627.

Anderson, R. D., Kahl, S. R., Glass, G. V., Smith, M. L., Fleming, M. I., & Malone, M. R. (1982). *Science meta-analysis: Final report of NSF project no. SED 80-12310.* Boulder, CO: Laboratory for Research in Science and Mathematics Education, University of Colorado.

Blosser, P. E. (1986). What research says: Research related to instructional materials for science. *School Science and Mathematics, 86*, 513–517.

Boone, W. J. (1998). Assumptions, cautions, and solutions in the use of omitted test data to evaluate the achievement of underrepresented groups in science—implications for long-term evaluation. *Journal of Women and Minorities in Science and Engineering, 4*, 183–194.

Boulanger, F. D. (1981). Instruction and science learning: A quantitative synthesis. *Journal of Research in Science Teaching, 18*, 311–327.

Bredderman, T. (1983). Effects of activity-based elementary science on student outcomes: A quantitative analysis. *Review of Educational Research, 53*, 499–518.

Carpenter, T. P., Blanton, M. L., Cobb, P., Franke, M. L., Kaput, J., & McClain, K. (2004). *Scaling up innovative practices in mathematics and science.* Research Report, National Center for Improving Student Learning and Achievement in Mathematics and Science, University of Wisconsin–Madison.

Clune, W. H. (1993). Systemic educational policy: A conceptual framework. In S. H. Fuhrman (Ed.), *Designing coherent education policy* (pp. 125–140). San Francisco: Jossey-Bass.

Clune, W. H. (1998). *Toward a theory of systemic reform: The case of nine NSF statewide systemic initiatives.* Research Monograph no. 16. Madison: University of Wisconsin, National Institute for Science Education.

Clune, W. H., & White, P. A. (1992). Education reform in the trenches: Increased academic course taking in high schools with lower achieving students in states with higher graduation requirements. *Education Evaluation and Policy Analysis, 14*(1), 2–20.

Clune, W. H., White, P., & Patterson, J. (1989). *The Implementation and effects of high school graduation requirements: First steps toward curricular reform.* New Brunswick, NJ: Center for Policy Research in Education.

Corbett, H. D., & Wilson, B. (1990). *Testing reform and rebellion.* Norwood, NY: Ablex.

Darling-Hammond, L., & Berry, B. (1988). *The evolution of teacher policy.* Santa Monica, CA: Center for Policy Research in Education (ERIC Document Reproduction Service no. ED298599).

Dow, P. B. (1991). *Schoolhouse politics: Lessons from the Sputnik era.* Cambridge, MA: Harvard University Press.

Fensham, P. J. (2004). *Defining an identity: The evolution of science education as a field of research.* Dordrecht, the Netherlands: Kluwer Academic.

Fenster, M. J. (April, 1998). *Evaluating the impact of science, math and technology initiatives on student achievement: The case of the New Jersey Statewide Systemic Initiatives (NJSSI).* Paper presented at the annual meeting of the American Educational Research Association, San Diego (ERIC Document Reproduction Service no. ED424292).

Firestone, W. A., Mayrowetz, D., & Fairman, J. (1998). Performance-based assessment and instructional change: The effects of testing in Maine and Maryland. *Educational Evaluation and Policy Analysis, 20*(2), 95.

Fuhrman, S. H. (Ed.). (1993). *Designing coherent education policy: Improving the system*. San Francisco: Jossey-Bass.

Fuhrman, S. H. (1994). *Politics and systemic education reform*. CPRE Policy Brief. New Brunswick, NJ: Consortium for Policy Research in Education.

Fuhrman, S. H., Odden, A. R., Clune, W. H., Cohen, D. K., Elmore, R. F., & Kirst, M. W. (1995). *Reforming science, mathematics, and technology education: NSF's state systemic initiatives*. CPRE Policy Brief. New Brunswick, NJ: Consortium for Policy Research in Education.

Fullan, M., & Miles, M. (1992). Getting reform right: What works and what doesn't. *Phi Delta Kappan, 73*, 745–752.

Goertz, M. E., Floden, R. E., & O'Day, J. A. (1996). *Systemic reform: Vol. I. Findings and conclusions. Studies of education reform*. East Lansing, MI: National Center for Research on Teacher Learning (ERIC Document Reproduction Service no. ED397553).

Goodlad, J. I. (2003, April 23). A nation in wait. *Education Week*, pp. 24–25, 36.

Hawley, W. D. (1988). Missing pieces of the educational reform agenda: Or, why the first and second waves. *Educational Administration Quarterly, 24*, 416–437.

Heath, R. W. (1964). Curriculum, cognition, and educational measurement. *Educational and Psychological Measurement, 24*, 239–253.

Heath, R. W., & Stickell, D. W. (1963). CHEM and CBA effects on achievement in chemistry. *Science Teacher, 30*, 45–46.

Heck, D. J. (1998). Evaluating equity in statewide systemic initiatives: Asking the right questions. *Journal of Women and Minorities in Science and Engineering, 4*, 161–181.

Helgeson, S. (1974). *Impact of the National Science Foundation teacher institute program*. Research Paper no. 16. University of Minnesota, Minnesota Research and Evaluation Project.

Herron, J. (1966). Evaluation and the new curricula. *Journal of Research in Science Teaching, 4*, 159–170.

Horizon Research. (1994). *Reflections from Wingspread: Lessons learned about the National Science Foundation's systemic initiative*. A report on the March 1994 Wingspread conference. Chapel Hill, NC: Author.

Huffman, D., & Lawrenz, F. (2003). The impact of a state systemic initiative on U.S. science teachers and students. *International Journal of Science and Mathematics Education, 1*, 357–377.

Jackson, P. W. (1983). The reform of science education: A cautionary tale. *Daedalus, 112*, 2, 142–166.

Kahle, J. B. (1997). Systemic reform: Challenges and changes. *Science Educator, 6*(1), 1–6.

Kahle, J. B. (1998). Equitable systemic reform in science and mathematics: Assessing progress. *Journal of Women and Minorities in Science and Engineering, 4*(2–3), 91–112.

Kahle, J. B. (2004). Will girls be left behind? Gender differences and accountability. *Journal of Research in Science Teaching, 41*(10), 961–969.

Kahle, J. B., Meece, J., & Scantlebury, K. (2000). Urban, African American, middle school science students: Does standards-based teaching make a difference? *Journal of Research in Science Teaching, 37*(9), 1019–1041.

Kirst, M. W. (1984). *Who controls our schools? American values in conflict*. New York: W. H. Freeman.

Klein, S. P., Hamilton, L. S., McCaffrey, D., Stecher, B. M., Robyn, A., & Burroughs, D. (2000). *Teaching practices and student achievement: First-year findings from Mosaic study of systemic initiatives in mathematics and science*. Santa Monica, CA: Rand.

Laguarda, K. (1998). *Assessing the SSIs' impacts on student achievement: An imperfect science*. Menlo Park, CA: SRI International.

Lee, J. (2002). Racial and ethnic achievement gap trends: Reversing the progress toward equity? *Educational Researcher, 31*(1), 3–12.

Lisonbee, L., & Fullerton, B. J. (1964). The comparative effects of BSCS and traditional biology on student achievement. *School Science and Mathematics, 64*, 594–598.

Madden, N. A., Slavin, R. E., Karweit, N. L., Dolan, L. J., & Wasik, B. A. (1993). Success for all: Longitudinal effects of a restructuring program for inner-city elementary schools. *American Educational Research Journal, 30*, 123–148.

Massell, D., Kirst, M., & Hoppe, M. (1997). *Persistence and change: Standards-based systemic reform in nine states.* CPRE Policy Briefs. Philadelphia: Consortium for Policy Research in Education.

McLaughlin, M. (1990). The RAND change agent study revisited: Macro perspectives and micro realities. *Educational Researcher, 19,* 11–16.

National Commission on Excellence in Education. (1983). *A nation at risk: The imperative for educational reform: A report to the nation and the Secretary of Education, U.S. Department of Education* (Publication no. ED 1.2:N21). Washington, DC: U.S. Government Printing Office.

National Council of Teachers of Mathematics. (1989). *Curriculum and evaluation standards for school mathematics.* Reston, VA: Author.

National Research Council. (1996). *National science education standards.* Washington, DC: National Academy Press.

Nelkin, D. (1977). *Science textbook controversies and the politics of equal time.* Cambridge, MA: Massachusetts Institute of Technology Press.

O'Day, J. A., & Smith, M. S. (1993). Systemic reform and educational opportunity. In S. H. Furhman (Ed.), *Designing coherent education policy* (pp. 250–312). San Francisco: Jossey-Bass.

Office of Technology Assessment. (1988). *Elementary and secondary education for science and engineering—A technical memorandum* (OTA-TM-SET-41). Washington, DC: U.S. Government Printing Office.

Porter, A. (1983, January–February). The role of testing in effective schools: How can testing improve school effectiveness? *American Education,* 25–28.

Porter, A. (1994). *Reform of high school mathematics and science and opportunity to learn* (CPRE Policy Brief RB-013-9/94). Philadelphia: University of Pennsylvania, Consortium for Policy Research in Education.

Rainey, R. G. (1964). A comparison of the CHEM study curriculum and a conventional approach in teaching high school chemistry. *School Science and Mathematics, 64,* 539–544.

Schlessinger, F. R., & Helgeson, S. L. (1969). National programs in science and mathematics education. *School Science and Mathematics, 69,* 633–643.

Schmidt, W. H. (1983a). Content biases in achievement tests. *Journal of Educational Measurement, 20,* 165–178.

Schmidt, W. H. (1983b). High school course-taking: Its relationship to achievement. *Journal of Curriculum Studies, 15,* 311–332.

Schwille, J. R., Porter, A., Alford, L., Floden, R., Freeman, D., Irwin, S., et al. (1986, July). *State policy and the control of curriculum decisions: Zones of tolerance for teachers in elementary school mathematics.* East Lansing, MI: Institute for Research on Teaching, Michigan State University.

Shields, P. M., Marsh, J., & Adelman, N. (1997). *Evaluation of NSF'S statewide systemic initiatives (SSI) program: The SSI's impacts on classroom practice.* Menlo Park, CA: SRI International.

Shymansky, J. A., Hedges, L. V., & Woodworth, G. (1990). A reassessment of the effects of inquiry-based science curricula of the 60s on student achievement. *Journal of Research in Science Teaching, 27,* 127–144.

Shymansky, J. A., Kyle, W. C., & Alport, J. M. (1983). The effects of new science curricula on student performance. *Journal of Research in Science Teaching, 20,* 387–404.

Sizer, T. R. (2003, April 23). Two reports. *Education Week, 36,* 24–25.

Slavin, R. E., Madden, N. A., Karweit, N. L., Dolan, L., & Wasik, B. A. (1992). *Success for all: A relentless approach to prevention and early intervention in elementary schools.* Arlington, VA: Educational Research Service.

Smith, M. S., O'Day, J., & Fuhrman, S. H. (1992). State policy and systemic school reform. *Educational Technology, 32,* 31–36.

Thelen, L. J., & Litsky, W. (1972). Teacher attendance at a summer institute and high school student achievement. *Science Education, 56,* 293–302.

Timar, T. B., & Kirp, D. L. (1989). Education reform in the 1980's: Lessons from the states. *Phi Delta Kappan, 70,* 502–511.

Walker, D. F., & Schaffarzick, J. (1974). Comparing curricula. *Review of Educational Research, 44,* 83–111.

Wallace, W. (1963). The BSCS 1961–62 evaluation program: A statistical report. *BSCS Newsletter, 19*, 22–24.

Wasik, J. L. (1971). A comparison of cognitive performance of PSSC and non-PSSC physics students. *Journal of Research in Science Teaching, 8*, 85–90.

Webster's New World Dictionary (College Edition). (1966). Cleveland, OH: The World Publishing Company.

Weinstein, R., Boulanger, D., & Walberg, H. J. (1982). Science curriculum effects in high school: A quantitative synthesis. *Journal of Research in Science Teaching, 19*, 511–522.

Weiss, I. R., & Webb, N. (2003). *Study of the impact of the statewide systemic initiatives program: Lessons learned.* Chapel Hill, NC: Horizon Research.

Welch, W. W. (1968). The impact of national curriculum projects—the need for accurate assessment. *School Science and Mathematics, 68*, 225–234.

Welch, W. W., & Walberg, H. J. (1972). A national experiment in curriculum evaluation. *American Educational Research Journal, 9*, 373–383.

Willson, V. L., & Garibaldi, A. M. (1976). The association between teacher participation in NSF institutes and student achievement. *Journal of Research in Science Teaching, 13*, 431–439.

Wilson, B. L., & Rossman, G. B. (1993). *Mandating academic excellence: High school responses to state curriculum reform* (Sociology of Education Series). New York: Teachers College Press.

Zucker, A. A., & Shields, P. M. (1995). *Second-year case studies: Connecticut, Delaware, and Montana.* Menlo Park, CA: SRI International.

Zucker, A. A., & Shields, P. M. (1997). *SSI strategies for reform: Preliminary findings from the evaluation of NSF's SSI program.* Menlo Park, CA: SRI International.

Zucker, A. A., & Shields, P. M. (1998a). *SSI case studies, Cohort 1: Connecticut, Delaware, Louisiana, and Montana.* Menlo Park, CA: SRI International.

Zucker, A. A., & Shields, P. M. (1998b). *SSI case studies, Cohort 3: Arkansas and New York.* Menlo Park, CA: SRI International.

Zucker, A. A., Shields, P. M., Adelman, N. E., Corcoran, T. B., & Goertz, M. E. (1998). *A report on the evaluation of the National Science Foundation's Statewide Systemic Initiatives (SSI) program* (Report No. NSF 98-147). Arlington, VA: National Science Foundation.

Zucker, A. A., Shields, P. M., Adelman, N., & Powell, J. (1995). *Evaluation of the National Science Foundation's Statewide Systemic Initiatives (SSI) program: Second year report* (Report No. NSF 96-48). Arlington, VA: National Science Foundation.

CHAPTER 31

Review of Science Education Program Evaluation

Frances Lawrenz
University of Minnesota

The purpose of this chapter is to review the field of science education program evaluation. To accomplish that purpose the chapter begins by defining evaluation, outlining the broad types of evaluation that can be undertaken and the philosophies that underlie the different approaches, and distinguishing evaluation from research. The chapter goes on to explicate the relationships between science education program funding and science education program evaluation through a historical approach, where the history of science education is juxtaposed with the history of evaluation and examples of the types of science education program evaluation that were implemented. Following this historical examination of the development process, different models of evaluation are discussed, and examples of how these apply to science education program evaluation are provided. This discussion contrasts the strengths and limitations of the different approaches and specifies the types of questions that the different models are able to address. Within the discussion of models, different methodological approaches are also contrasted. Finally the chapter concludes with some thoughts about the future of science education program evaluation.

With the passage of the No Child Left Behind Act our nation is committed to accountability for its schools. Accountability, being held answerable for accomplishing goals, can be considered a subset of the larger concept of evaluation. Evaluation is based on the notion of valuing and includes a variety of perspectives in addition to accomplishing goals. The idea of evaluation is not a new one. Perhaps one of the first implementations of evaluation in the United States was Joseph Rice's 1897–1898 comparative study of student's spelling performance (Rice, 1900). The next landmark was "The Eight Year Study" by Tyler and Smith (1942). This longitudinal study of thirty high schools made use of a wide variety of tests, scales, inventory questionnaires, check lists, pupil logs, and other measures to gather information about the achievement of curricular objectives. The major impetus for science education program evaluation, however, arose out of the National Science Foundation funding of large curriculum development projects and teacher institutes and the Elementary and Secondary Education Act of 1965. This was the first time legislated programs were required to have evaluations. This cemented the reciprocal arrangement between funding and evaluation and led to significant development of the field of educational evaluation.

Extensive literature searches were conducted to provide the background for this chapter. There is an enormous amount of material available, because science education program evaluation crosses discipline areas. For example, keyword searches for documents published between the years 1980 and 2003 on "Program Evaluation" produced 51,660 hits; "Science Education" produced 65,796 hits; and "Science Program Evaluation" 4,213 hits. The majority of articles are geared toward teacher assessment of content with a teacher and administrator audience in mind, not necessarily technical researchers or policy makers. Testing conducted within classrooms by teachers is only one component of science program evaluation, so the majority of the articles are not relevant to this review. The available materials about science education program evaluation are generally descriptions of the evaluation processes and the programs evaluated, again not directly useful for a review of science program evaluation. Also the range of programs is very wide, with references running the gambit from health science programs in universities to effects of using incubators in a fourth-grade classroom. Ultimately there is little direct research about how to conduct program evaluation. The references included in this chapter are meant to be exemplary of the range of material available, not an exhaustive set. Examples are drawn mainly from NSF-funded projects and programs.

WHAT IS EVALUATION?

The Joint Committee on Standards for Educational Evaluation first presented standards for educational evaluation in 1981, and the second edition of the standards (1994) defined *evaluation* as the systematic investigation of the worth or merit of an object. Objects of evaluations include educational and training programs, projects, and materials and are sometimes described as *evaluands*. Michael Scriven in his *Evaluation Thesaurus* (1991) agreed with this definition and went on to say that the process normally involves "some identification of relevant standards of merit, worth, or value; some investigation of the performance of evaluands on these standards; and some integration or synthesis of the results to achieve an overall evaluation" (p. 139).

One of the first definitions of educational evaluation was provided by Daniel Stufflebeam and the Phi Delta Kappan National Study Committee on Evaluation in *Educational Evaluation and Decision-Making* (1971). In this book the authors say "the purpose of evaluation is not to prove but to improve" (p. v). They define *evaluation* as the systematic process of delineating, obtaining, and providing useful information for judging decision alternatives. This definition is particularly useful in that it highlights that evaluation includes determining what type of information should be gathered, how to gather the determined information, and how to present the information in usable formats. Evaluation is often divided into summative and formative aspects. A summative evaluation approach identifies how valuable an object is by demonstrating whether it is successful or not to various stakeholders. Formative evaluation is designed to help improve the object.

The field of evaluation and educational evaluation in particular has expanded quite a bit since the 1970s, although some of the original texts have kept pace through new editions and additional authors and continue to be the leading sources of evaluation information. The first edition of Weiss's *Evaluation Research* was published in 1972, the second, *Evaluation*, in 1998. Rossi and Freeman's *Evaluation: A Systematic Approach* (1979) is now in its sixth edition, with an additional author (Rossi, Freeman, & Lipsey, 1999). The original Worthen and Sanders text, *Educational Evaluation: Theory and Practice* (1973), is now in a fourth rendition with an additional author as *Program Evaluation: Alternative Approaches and Practical Guidelines* (Fitzpatrick, Sanders, & Worthen, 2003). The National Science Foundation has also provided an evolving set of User Friendly Handbooks to help principal investigators evaluate their projects. These began with the Stevens, Lawrenz, Ely, and Huberman (1993) text and culminated recently in the 2002 rendition by Frechtling.

As part of the expanding definitions of evaluation, Patton in his book *Utilization-Focused Evaluation* (1997) reiterates and extends usefulness by making it clear that the receivers of the evaluation information need to be substantively involved in the evaluation process so that the resulting information will be used effectively. Fetterman's empowerment evaluation was introduced in 1994 (Fetterman, 1994) and expanded in his text *Foundations of Empowerment Evaluation* (2001). Fetterman views empowerment evaluation as a shift from the previously exclusive focus on merit and worth alone to a commitment to self-determination and capacity building. In other words, empowerment evaluation is evaluation conducted by participants with the goal of continual improvement and self-actualization.

The different approaches to evaluation are grounded in different philosophies. House (1983) has categorized these differing philosophies along two continua: the objectivist-subjectivist epistemologies and the utilitarian-pluralist values. Objectivism requires evidence that is reproducible and verifiable. It is derived largely from empiricism and related to logical positivism. Subjectivism is based in experience and related to phenomenologist epistemology. The objectivists rely on reproducible facts, whereas the subjectivists depend upon accumulated experience. In the second continuum, utilitarians assess overall impact, whereas pluralists assess the impact on each individual. In other words, the greatest good for utilitarians is that which will benefit the most people, whereas pluralism requires attention to each individual's benefit. Often utilitarianism and objectivism operate together, and pluralism and subjectivism operate together, although other combinations are possible.

Collectively, approaches that engage the evaluand in the evaluation process are identified as participatory approaches to evaluation. Different approaches include stakeholder evaluation (Mark & Shotland, 1985), democratic evaluation McTaggart, (1991), or developmental evaluation (Patton, 1994). Cousins and Whitmore's (1998) framework categorizes participatory evaluation along three dimensions: control of the evaluation process, selection of participants, and the depth of participation. Positions along these different dimensions are indicative of different approaches to participatory evaluation.

Cousins and Whitmore (1998) suggest that there are two philosophies undergirding participatory evaluation. Practical participatory evaluation is one that is common in the United States and Canada and "has as its central function the fostering of evaluation use with the implicit assumption that evaluation is geared toward program, policy, or organizational decision making" (p. 6). Transformative participatory evaluation "invokes participatory principles and actions in order to democratize social change" (p. 7).

Another underlying movement in evaluation is termed responsive evaluation. The legacy of the philosophy of responsiveness in evaluation is discussed by Greene and Abma (2001). This philosophical perspective informed Guba and Lincoln's (1989) influential book, *Fourth Generation Evaluation*. This is an approach to evaluation that rests on a relativist rather than a realist ontology and on a monistic subjective, rather than dualistic objective, epistemology. It therefore recommends evaluations that are important and meaningful within the context and frames of references of the people involved. In terms of the discussion above, responsive evaluation is in the pluralism and subjectivism sphere.

Another way to help define something is to explain what it is not. Therefore it is important to point out that assessment can be considered a subset of evaluation and that although there are many similarities, evaluation and research are not the same. Generally assessment is considered the process of measuring an outcome, whereas evaluation employs assessment information in its determination of merit or worth.

Weiss (1998) suggests that what distinguishes evaluation from other research is not method or subject matter, but intent. In other words, evaluations are conducted for purposes than other research. Worthen, Sanders, and Fitzpatrick (1997) expand the distinction to point out that evaluation and research differ in the motivation of the inquirer, the objective of the inquiry, the outcome of the inquiry, the role played by explanation, and generalizability. In terms of motivation, evaluators are almost always asked to conduct their evaluations and therefore are constrained by the situation. On the other hand, although researchers may apply for grants to conduct their research, they are generally the ones who make the decisions about why and how to conduct it. The objectives and outcomes in the two types of inquiry are also slightly different. Research is generally conducted to determine generalizable laws governing behavior or to form conclusions. Evaluation, on the other hand, is more likely to be designed to provide descriptions and inform decision making. Finally, evaluation is purposefully tied to a specific object in time and space, whereas research is designed to span these dimensions.

These distinctions are important because they affect the type and appropriateness of evaluation designs. Because of their tie to specific situations, evaluations are both less and more constrained than research. They are less constrained because their results do not have to be universally generalizable, but they are more constrained because the results have to address a specific context.

THE RELATIONSHIP OF EVALUATION TO SCIENCE EDUCATION

Evaluation is applied, disciplined inquiry. As suggested above, evaluations are generally commissioned in response to a specific need and operate across various power structures and in different contexts. In science education, evaluations have closely followed the funding priorities and requirements of the federal government. For example, as the government provided funds for science curriculum development, evaluations of science curricula were conducted. Naturally not all evaluation was directly tied to federal funding, but since the federal agendas reflect the priorities of the citizens, the issues of interest to the general public and science educators were included. To help clarify this relationship, this section includes a look at the history of funding in science education with a parallel history of science education evaluation.

Many reviews have been provided on science education research (e.g., Welch, 1985; Finley, Heller, & Lawrenz, 1990); however, these reviews may include only one type of evaluation or may not include evaluations at all (Welch, 1977).

As explained earlier, assessment is a subset of evaluation; a comprehensive review of the history of assessment in science is provided by Doran, Lawrenz, and Helgeson (1994). That review highlights work in instrument development and validity. As they point out, the 1960s laid the groundwork for science education program evaluation with the beginning of the National Assessment of Educational Progress (NAEP) and the ESEA Act. The 1970s were a time of concern about fairness in testing and of advances in testing procedures, such as matrix sampling and item response theory. The first international science study was conducted during the 1969–70 school year by the International Association for the Evaluation of Educational Achievement. The 1980s showed consolidation and growing interest in gathering data on various indicators. Interest in international comparisons and authentic testing grew through the 1990s along with interest in trends analysis because longitudinal data were now becoming available. Currently the emphasis in assessment is on assessing student in-depth understanding of science content through authentic measures (Newman, 1996; Wiggins, 1998).

Status data provide a unique type of evaluation evidence. Generally status data are not tied to specific situations or stakeholders except in a very general way, so they are not evaluations in their own right. They are used, however, as comparison data for many individual programs and can be used to examine trends over time. NAEP, TIMSS, and the science and mathematics teaching surveys by Weiss at Horizon Research, Inc. are classic examples of status-type evaluation evidence. The Weiss reports began in 1977 and have continued at intervals through 2002. These reports contain information on the amount of time spent on science and mathematics, the objectives for science and mathematics, classroom activities, types of students in various types of classes, teachers' views of education, and their opinions about the environments in which they teach. NAEP and TIMSS show state, national, and international levels of student achievement in various areas of science, as well as some data on the teachers and classroom environments. These types of data have been synthesized into large reports outlining indicators of science education (Suter, 1993, 1996) as well as additional pieces such as comparing indicators with standards (Weiss, 1997).

Considering the history of the NAEP science tests provides some insight into the contextual and political changes that have worked to shape science education program evaluation. NAEP was born in a sea of controversy over whether or not the federal government should be collecting any national data. In response to the desire for local autonomy and privacy, the first NAEP reports provided information about only large regions of the country and were very careful to not suggest that any national standards or requirements were included in the data. Today, the pendulum has shifted to acceptance of national standards and openness in reporting, so notonly are individual state data reported, but they are expected. Furthermore, they are tied to standards, and the collection of ever more data is being required

(No Child Left Behind Act, 2001). These types of status data are also being collected internationally; the TIMSS-R (U.S. National Research Center, 2003) is but the latest step in this process.

Another historical example is the evolution of the Joint Dissemination and Review Panel of the Department of Education, which was established in 1972. It began as a group of research experts who judged the quality of educational programs requesting dissemination funds based on evidence the program provided. The panel was strict in its assessment of causality, and very few programs were designated as "programs that work." In 1987 the panel was reconstituted and renamed the Program Effectiveness Panel (Cook, 1991). This panel was instructed to include a variety of evidence in its deliberations, including qualitative data and implementation costs. Educational programs were expected to provide proof that their claims were met, and these claims were judged based on the data provided. In 1994 the Educational Research, Development, Dissemination and Improvement Act directed the establishment of panels of appropriately qualified experts and practitioners to evaluate educational programs and designate them as promising or exemplary. Multiple panels were created (e.g., the Math and Science Education Expert Panel), with several different criteria and several subpanels. Subject matter experts and users determined the quality of the materials. Evaluation experts commented on only one of the criteria—the extent to which the program made a measurable difference in student learning. Programs received overall ratings as promising as well as effective. These panels were phased out recently, but new panels for determining quality programs are being formed.

As an exemplar of evolution at the federal level, Table 31.1 outlines the major activities of the Science Education Directorate at the National Science Foundation, along with evaluation emphases. The accompanying Fig. 31–1 shows the history of funding at the National Science Foundation by directorate. Figure 31–1 clearly shows the changing levels of funding supporting the Education Directorate activities described in Table 31.1 and the proportion of the funding that was allotted to education.

In the 1960s, with the advent of Sputnik, the National Science Foundation began to focus on curriculum development. People believed that the United States would win the race for space if our children had better science and mathematics curricula. Many different curricular projects were undertaken. Evaluation concentrated on the effectiveness of these curricula in helping students learn science.

In the 1970s curriculum development continued, but the emphasis shifted toward how to get these new curricula implemented in the schools. Evaluation was focused on delivery systems and accomplishing change within classrooms, schools, and districts. There was also an emphasis on enhancing teachers' science knowledge so that they would be better prepared to deliver the new curricula. Evaluations of these teacher institutes focused on perceived quality. The "Man: A Course of Study" curriculum caused a great furor across the country. Many people did not believe their children should be studying about different cultural practices, such as Eskimo elders going out on the ice to die. As shown in Fig. 31–1, funding for the Science Education Directorate was essentially wiped out by the political aftermath. It was rebuilt, however, through funding of smaller local programs, often summer institutes, designed to enhance teacher understanding of science and mathematics and teacher pedagogical skills. The small local nature of the programs guaranteed local acceptance. Evaluation of these programs was individualized to the needs of

TABLE 31.1
History of NSF Education Directorate Funding Initiatives
and Science Education Program Evaluation

Date	Major NSF Education Directorate Funding Initiatives	Science Education Program Evaluation
60s	Curriculum development	Focused on improving the individual curricula being developed. National Assessment of Education Progress begins.
70s	Comprehensive curriculum implementation and teacher institutes	Extent of implementation and gains in teacher content knowledge in individual projects. An Office of Program Integration related to evaluation of programs was established. First international science study and first status survey of science teaching.
80s	Precipitous drop in funding and then rebuilding. Funding of small and varied projects in graduate and undergraduate education and K–12 teacher inservice	Evaluation tied to individual projects. Focus on science teacher perceptions of professional development. Status studies continue.
90s	Systemic initiatives	Comprehensive evaluations of many aspects of projects. Centralized requirements for projects to meet program evaluation needs. An office of evaluation was formed and expanded into the Division of Research, Evaluation and Dissemination. Government Performance and Results Act required agency accountability.
00s	Partnerships	Evaluations focusing on K–12 student achievement and institutional climate. RFPs to conduct program evaluations, provide expert assistance to large project evaluators, expand evaluation capacity, and conduct research about evaluation.

the program and their stakeholders. This time also witnessed a growth in commitment to diversity in the pool of science and mathematics professionals. Evaluation of these programs focused more on social activism and facilitation of movement across power barriers.

The 1990s were characterized by systemic initiatives. The idea was that all parts of a system needed to be focused on the same goals in order to achieve success. The systemics included statewide programs, urban programs, and local programs. Evaluation was much more complex and assessed how to change cultures as well as interactions and what results those changes might produce. This produced the beginnings of national data bases to track the status information, centralized or pooled approaches to conducting evaluations, and the realization that this sort of evaluation takes a good deal of time and money. The systemics met with mixed success, and in particular it was difficult for the larger initiatives to "go to scale." The systemics

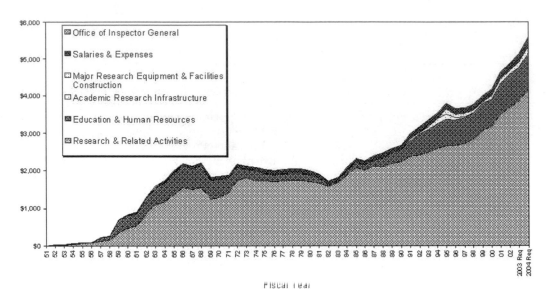

FIGURE 31–1.   Funding levels for the NSF directorates over time (in millions of constant FY 2003 dollars).

were successful in some ways or at some locations, but that success did not seem to spread across the entire system.

The present emphasis in funding is partnerships. These focus on changing various institutions so that they will better interact with others. Evaluation of partnerships is complex, like it was for the systemics, but the approaches are more restricted in some ways. There is a heavy emphasis on accountability and direct ties to state-based testing systems. In contrast, how to measure organizational change and promote interaction is viewed as complex, and several technical assistance evaluation projects are being funded to assist the partnerships with their evaluations.

Today science education evaluation is quite complex. It functions at both the individual project and the state or national program level. The terms *project* and *program* are often used by federal or state funding agencies and their evaluators in a distinct way. The term *program* is used to mean the overall funding initiative across the state or nation, and the term *project* is used to mean the sites that were funded. Therefore program evaluation would be of all of the projects related to or funded under a particular plan or funding initiative. Project evaluation is a smaller and more coherent endeavor with fewer categories of stakeholders. Take, for example, the NSF materials development program, which funds several individual curriculum development projects. Each project would be responsible for conducting an evaluation of itself. The program evaluation would examine the value of all of the projects as a set. Projects can range in size from a single school's attempts to improve its science curriculum to a large math science partnership working with several school districts and multiple institutions, including higher education, informal science settings, and business and industry. With these sorts of large projects the distinctions between program and project evaluations blur somewhat. Sometimes smaller types of project evaluations can be combined in a technique called cluster evaluation, where a cluster of projects work together to obtain evaluation help and comparable data that might be used in a program evaluation (Barley & Jenness, 1993).

Project evaluations are generally quite varied and unique to the specific project. They can follow diverse philosophies and use the full range of evaluation methods, so they are difficult to characterize. The following examples help to illustrate the range of project evaluations. One example is the evaluation of the teaching and learning of Hispanic students in a solar energy science curriculum which showed that the approach increased the student retention rate (Hadi-Tabassum, 1999). Another example is a school district that was concerned about the quality of its K–12 science curriculum. The evaluation consisted of a series of focus group sessions with parents; elementary; middle and high school teachers; and middle school, high school, and recently graduated students. The focus groups discussed visions for excellence and strengths and limitations of the existing curriculum, which revealed a need for stronger communication about goals and closer articulation across schools and grade levels (Huffman & Lawrenz, 2003). Another example is the Desimone, Porter, Garet, Yoon, and Birman (2002) evaluation of the effects of science and mathematics teacher professional development. That evaluation showed that professional development focused on specific instructional practices increases teachers' use of those practices in the classroom. Furthermore, specific features, such as active learning opportunities, increased the effect. It is clear from these examples that the range of issues, styles, and goals is very broad.

The Science Education Directorate at the National Science Foundation provides an exemplar of the current state of affairs in program evaluation. Evaluations being funded can be categorized along a continuum based on the level of participation of the projects: exterior evaluation, centrally prescribed evaluation, consensus evaluation, and pooled evaluation (Lawrenz & Huffman, 2003). At one end of the continuum are evaluations conducted by an entity separate from the projects, with the external entity collecting the data and making the decisions to address the needs of NSF. This type of evaluation is exemplified by the evaluation of the Advanced Technician Education program. The evaluation is funded through a different division of NSF than the program and employs its own instruments and collects its own data independently from the funded projects and centers. It is directly tied to the needs and questions of NSF through matching of survey and site visit instruments to a logic model. This evaluation project produces yearly reports, which are posted on the program evaluation web site (Hanssen, Gullickson, & Lawrenz, 2003). The results have shown that the projects engage in a wide variety of activities related to technician education, that significant amounts of cost sharing have been provided to the projects, that a random subset of the materials developed by the projects is perceived by external experts as of good quality, and that the number of technicians produced has increased.

Another example of an external program evaluation is COSMOS Corporation's evaluation of the statewide systemic reform initiative (SSI) (Yin, 2002). This evaluation examines the status of statewide reform in seven states and one territory through intensive case studies that provide an inventory of district policies and curriculum practices, and an analysis of student achievement trends over time. The interim findings suggest that across the eight sites much reform progress only occurred in the late 1990s and is still occurring. Interestingly, it appears that school finance rulings by state supreme courts may be an important reform influence. Successful reform processes do not necessarily follow a top-down format. The case studies show that successful states may need to make a sustained commitment to the reform process. Finally it appears that SSIs can pursue both catalytic and direct service roles in support of reform.

Moving on toward the middle of the continuum are program evaluations with mandated procedures that each of the sites must follow but which allow the sites to collect their own data and turn it in to the central external evaluator. These are exemplified by the Local Systemic Change (LSC) program evaluation. In that program each funded project is required to gather specific information with the use of pre-designed evaluation instruments. Each project may also add its own evaluation components. The data from all of the different projects are synthesized into program evaluation reports. An extension of this type of evaluation is the status data collection required of projects in several NSF education programs. This status information includes information such as numbers and characteristics of participants.

The LSC evaluation reports are provided yearly (Weiss, Banilower, Crawford, & Overstreet, 2003). The outcomes for 2003, like those for other years, show mixed results. Thirty-five percent of the teachers participating nationally rated the LSC professional development they received as excellent or very good. Professional development sessions show high ratings on appropriateness of the mathematics/science content, the climate of respect for and collegial interactions among participants, and for encouraging active participation. Weaknesses include questioning about conceptual understanding and providing adequate wrap-up. Survey data show significant positive impact on teacher attitudes and beliefs about mathematics/science education. In addition, participants are becoming more confident in their content knowledge and more likely to use standards-based instructional strategies. Classroom observations show that the quality of the lessons taught improved, with increased participation in LSC activities.

Toward the participatory end of the continuum are evaluations where the projects determine the evaluation procedures and what data to collect. The Collaboratives for Excellence in Teacher Preparation (CETP) program evaluation is an example. The CETP program evaluation is one where sites collect some similar data, using centrally developed instruments. The procedures and instruments were developed by the projects, and projects decide which data they wish to provide. The program evaluation or core team provides leadership, a communication hub, instruments, data analysis, and incentives for collecting core data. Evaluation reports are provided yearly (Lawrenz, Michlin, Appeldoorn, & Hwang, 2003). The results show that the CETP projects have had a positive impact on the establishment and institutionalization of reformed courses and on interactions within and among STEM and education schools and K–12 schools. Over time, it appears that all higher education classes used more standards-based instructional strategies. Results from the K–12 classrooms show that CETP and non-CETP teachers were reporting the same frequencies of use of instructional strategies in their classrooms. Students, however, reported that their CETP teachers more frequently used real-world problems, technology, and more complicated problems in their teaching. Students of non-CETP teachers, on the other hand, were more likely to report doing activities involving writing, making presentations, and using portfolios. Moreover, external observers rated CETP classes higher.

MODELS FOR SCIENCE EDUCATION
PROGRAM EVALUATION

Stufflebeam (2001) provides a descriptive and evaluative review of the different evaluation models that have been used over the past 40 years. He describes 22 different approaches and then recommends nine for continued use. He bases this recommendation on how well these approaches meet the Program Evaluation Standards of utility, feasibility, propriety, and accuracy. These nine include three improvement or accountability-oriented approaches, four social agenda or advocacy-oriented approaches, and two method-oriented approaches. The models are defined below and listed in Table 31.2, along with an example of how each could be operationalized in science education.

The three accountability-oriented approaches are Decision/Accountability, Consumer Orientation, and Accreditation. Decision/Accountability evaluation provides information that can be used to help improve a program as well as to judge its merit and worth (Stufflebeam, 1971). Consumer Orientation evaluation provides conclusions about the various aspects of the quality of the objects being evaluated, so that the consumers will know what will be of use in their situations (Scriven, 1974). Accreditation evaluation studies institutions, institutional programs, and personnel to determine the fit with requirements of a given area and what needs to be changed in order to meet these requirements.

TABLE 31.2
Science Education Examples of Evaluation Models

Model of Evaluation	Science Education Example
Decision/accountability	Determining the strengths and weaknesses of a science teacher training program to make decisions about what to do in the coming year
Consumer-oriented	Rating all of the existing high school science curricula using a specific set of criteria
Accreditation Utilization-focused	Certifying that a middle school's science program was acceptable
	Providing a timely report to a school district contrasting the two science curricula they were considering using criteria they felt were important
Client-centered/responsive	Working with a school district as they develop a new science curricula gathering different data about different questions as needs evolve
Deliberative democratic	Having all of the science teachers in the school district debate and vote on the evaluation questions, the data and the interpretation
Constructivist	Providing descriptions of the different perspectives different groups of science teachers have of a new assessment procedure
Case study	Providing a school board with an in depth description of the AP chemistry class
Outcome/value added assessment	Looking at school level student science assessment results over time and examining the change of slope in schools using a new science program.

The four social agenda approaches are Utilization-Focused, Client-centered/ Responsive, Deliberative Democratic, and Constructivist. Utilization-Focused evaluation is a process for making choices about an evaluation study in collaboration with a targeted group of priority users, in order to focus effectively on their intended uses of the evaluation (Patton, 2000). Client-centered evaluation requires that the evaluator interact continuously with the various stakeholders or clients and be responsive to their needs (Stake, 1983). Deliberative Democratic evaluation operates within a framework where democratic principles are used to reach conclusions (House & Howe, 2000). Constructivist evaluation works within a subjectivist framework and requires that the evaluators advocate for all participants, particularly the disenfranchised, to help emancipate and empower everyone (Guba & Lincoln, 1989; Fetterman, 2001).

The two method-oriented approaches are Case Study and Outcome/Value Added Assessment. Case study evaluations are in-depth, holistic descriptions and analyses of evaluands (Merriam, 1998). Outcome/Value Added Assessment evaluation involves determining what changes have occurred in the patterns of data collected over time as the result of program or policy changes (Sanders & Horn, 1994)

Stufflebeam's categorization of evaluation models is in addition to other models that have been proposed for the evaluation of science education. Early models were provided by Welch (1979a,b), Welch (1985), and Knapp, Shields, St. John, Zucker, and Stearns (1988). A more recent model was provided by Altschuld and Kumar in the 1995 issue of *New Directions for Program Evaluation* edited by Rita O'Sullivan. Their model is a synthesis of models of evaluation applied to science programs before 1994. They review several different types of science evaluation at what they call the micro developmental or formative level and the macro system or contextual level. They then provide a model with the main stages of program or product development, defined as Need, Conceptualization, Development, Tryout, Formal Use, and Long-Term Use and Impact. These stages are informed by contextual and supportive factors and intermediate outcomes. Their intent is that the main stages are embedded in specific contexts and that the contexts will have profound effects on the implementation and results of the stages. Synthesis of the stages and factors results in an evaluation of overall effectiveness. They say, "Carefully evaluating development, studying process variables, evaluating outcomes along the way rather than just at the end of product development, and analyzing supportive and contextual variables generates a comprehensive understanding of the overall effectiveness of science education programs and to a degree, the interface between levels" (p. 13).

In 2001 the National Research Council's Committee on Understanding the Influence of Standards in K–12 Science, Mathematics and Technology Education presented *A Framework for Research in Mathematics, Science and Technology Education* (NRC, 2001). The committee's Framework used two main questions: How has the system responded to the introduction of nationally developed mathematics, science, and technology standards? and What are the consequences for student learning? The Framework "provides conceptual guideposts for those attempting to trace the influence of nationally developed mathematics, science, and technology standards and to gauge the magnitude or direction of that influence on the education system, on teachers and teaching practice and on student learning" (p. 3). Undergirding the first question are contextual forces such as politicians and policy makers, the public, business and industry members, and professional organizations. These forces are viewed as operating through channels of influence, including curriculum, teacher development, and assessment and accountability. The context funneled through the channels results in teachers and teaching practice in the classroom and the school context, which ultimately leads to student learning. The Framework goes on to provide examples of hypothetical studies that could address the evaluation questions. In conjunction with this, the Council of Chief State School Officers (1997) has a Tool Kit for evaluating the development and implementation of standards.

METHODS FOR SCIENCE EDUCATION PROGRAM EVALUATION

Despite the differences between research and evaluation, they use similar methodologies and are subject to the considerations of rigor applied to all forms of disciplined inquiry. There is an ongoing debate about what constitutes rigor, which was highlighted by the National Research Council (2003) report *Scientific research in education*. The report articulates the nature of scientific research in education and offers a framework for the future of a federal educational research agency charged with supporting high-quality scientific work. The report considers several different methodological approaches to research, and consequently evaluation, with an emphasis on rigor and matching the methods to the questions. Many of the research questions in education are evaluation-oriented, such as, is this curriculum better than the one we have, or what is happening or how is it happening? A special class of questions is questions of causality, which the NRC report suggests are best answered by randomized experiments. Various researchers have raised several issues, such as how to have a culture of rigor and how to educate professionals to operate within such a culture (Pellegrino and Goldman, 2002). Additionally, issues such as random assignment, the uniqueness of each site, and the potential endorsement of an evidence-based social engineering approach to educational improvement need to be considered (Berliner, 2002; Erickson & Gutierrez, 2002).

There is a good deal of information available on what constitutes rigor in quantitative evaluations. There are fairly clear guidelines on how to calculate appropriate sample sizes, which statistical tests are appropriate for what types of data, and what constitutes a meaningful result. The guidelines for rigor in more interpretive or qualitative evaluation are no less strong, but they are different. Lincoln and Guba (1985) provide an informative contrast of terms related to rigor from the quantitative and qualitative perspectives. They say that in quantitative work there is validity as determined by an evaluation's internal validity, external validity, reliability, and objectivity. In contrast, in qualitative work there is trustworthiness, as determined by an evaluation's credibility, transferability, dependability, and confirmability. Anfara, Brown, and Mangione (2002) suggest making the qualitative research process more public to help ensure rigor. They discuss different techniques that would help to increase trustworthiness (e.g., triangulation, member checks, prolonged field work) and go on to suggest that all qualitative research (or evaluation) should include documentation tables that show how the different techniques were used. Suggestions include specifically linking interview questions to research questions, providing tables of how individual codings of narratives were synthesized, and having matrices of triangulation showing findings and sources.

Another rich methodological source for science education program evaluation is design experiments. This type of evaluation attempts to support arguments constructed around the results of active innovation and intervention in classrooms (Kelly, 2003). It is aimed at understanding learning and teaching processes when the researcher or evaluator is active as an educator. This approach ties into the participatory evaluation literature as well as the evaluation capacity-building literature, because the people involved in the innovation are the evaluators, and through the experience they gain expertise, which will enhance the educational enterprise (Stockdill, Baizerman, & Compton, 2002). It also dovetails with the action research or teacher-as-researcher movements.

Most science education evaluations employ mixed methods. In other words, a variety of data-gathering and interpretation techniques are incorporated into a single evaluation. The issues involved in mixing methods are complex because the methods are often embedded in an overarching philosophy that informs how the method should be interpreted. For example, Greene and Caracelli (1997) suggest three stances to mixing methods: purist, pragmatic, and dialectical. The purist stance uses methods embedded within a philosophical paradigm. The pragmatic stance puts methods together in ways that produce an evaluation result that is the most useful to the stakeholders in the evaluation. The dialectical stance is synergistic in that it plays the different methodologies off against each other to produce an evaluation that transcends any of the individual methods. Caracelli and Greene (1997) go on to discuss how these different stances can be formulated into different mixed method evaluation designs. These include component designs where different methods could be used to triangulate findings, to complement findings from another more dominant method, or to address different aspects of the science education program being evaluated. There are also integrated, mixed-method designs where the use of different methods could be iterative, nested, holistic, or transformative (giving primacy to the value and action oriented aspects of the program). Lawrenz and Huffman (2003) combined these ideas into another mixed-method model they termed the archipelago approach.

The mixed approaches to evaluation are grounded in methodological advances across the qualitative and quantitative continuum. There have been significant advances in quantitative analyses, especially in the area of modeling, such as linear models (Moore, 2002), hierarchical models (Byrk & Radenbush, 1992), longitudinal models (Moskowitz & Hershberger, 2002), and structural equation modeling (Maruyama, 1998). There has also been significant work in measurement and sampling theory, including matrix sampling and Rasch modeling (Wright, 1979). In the middle of the quantitative-qualitative continuum there have been advances in survey design to encompass the new capabilities inherent in web-based settings (Dillman, 2002). On the qualitative side there have been new approaches and new insights, including, for example, interpretive interactionism (Denzin, 2001) and interpreting the unsayable (Budick, 1989).

Table 31.3 lists some science education areas, selected methods that could be used, and the evaluation questions each method would allow the evaluator to answer. The intent is to show the direct tie between the evaluation questions and the

TABLE 31.3
Science Education Area by Evaluation Method and Questions

Science Education Area	Evaluation Method	Questions the Method Addresses
A science education program focused on institutional culture	Case study	How can the nature of the institution be described?
	Opinion surveys of institutional members and persons from other institutions who interact with the primary institution with retrospective items	What do people within the institution think the culture is? How do they think it has changed? What do people who interact with the institution think the culture is? How do they think it has changed?
	Pre and post observations by external experts or participant observers	How do observers characterize the culture of the institution before and after the program?
	Artifact analysis of policies, procedures and public statements during the course of the program	What changes have occurred in the policies, procedures and expressed public image during the program?
A teacher development workshop on participating teachers	Pre and post testing of content knowledge, attitudes, teaching philosophies.	What immediate changes have occurred in teacher content knowledge, attitudes and teaching philosophies?
	Phenomenological study	How do the teachers perceive the lived experience of the workshop?
	Observations of the workshop by external experts or participant observers	What are observers' opinions of the quality of the workshop?
A new curriculum on science classroom environment	Ethnography	What is the culture of the classroom and how is it evolving?
	Pre and post assessment of student perception of the classroom environment	How do students perceive the classroom environment before and after using the curriculum?
	Observations of the classroom by experts	What are observers' opinions of the characteristics of the classroom environment
	Discourse analysis	What verbal interaction patterns are heard within the classroom and how do these reflect on the classroom environment?
Effect of standards based science instruction on students throughout a district	Phenomenological studies	How do selected students view the lived experience of participating in standards based instruction?
	Assessment of student knowledge and attitude and application of HLM analyses	Which student variables are predictive of student achievement and attitude and how much do classrooms and schools contribute to this relationship?
	Value added analysis of student scores over time	What changes have occurred in the longitudinal patterns of student achievement and attitudes across the district since the implementation of the new science instruction?

methods. Methods are not good or bad (assuming they are implemented proficiently), but they can only be used to answer specific types of questions.

CONCLUSION

This review has documented the significant growth experienced by the field of science program evaluation since its solidification in the early 1960s. Science program evaluation is also shown as closely tied to political agendas through public and private funding initiatives. The literature reveals that most published work has focused on practical applications and descriptions of approaches. Philosophical underpinnings have become more clearly articulated, and diverse models and approaches have been developed and implemented. The variety of methods available to use has expanded, and connections between methods and questions have become more explicit. Despite this growth there has been very little research on science program evaluation practices per se. The work has been mainly theoretical. The literature provides extensive examples of procedures and approaches and suggestions of when to use them, but little direct research about which of these might be more effective.

Research comparing the strengths and weaknesses of different science program evaluation approaches and methods would be beneficial to the field. This type of research, however, would be expensive because more than one evaluation would have to be funded for any project. Also research comparing different approaches would have to be carried out in multiple settings, such as different grade levels, different content areas, or different types of students. Also as is clear from the existing theoretical and practical work, different types of evaluation provide different types of information. This information might be differentially valuable to different stakeholders in determining the merit or worth of a science education program. Therefore the value of science program evaluation approaches would have to be determined in terms of the needs and opinions of different stakeholders. One possible cost-effective manner of addressing some of the issues would be through consideration of the evaluation results of similar programs obtained through different methods. This idea is similar to the one suggested by the National Research Committee to assess standards-based reform. However, those recommendations are related to using evaluation results to understand standards-based reform, not to answering questions about how to conduct evaluation. The distinction between researching the value of evaluation and researching the value of the programs being evaluated needs to be kept in mind.

Experience and expertise in science education program evaluation is growing but is still scarce. Educational programs designed to provide qualified science education program evaluators should be continued and perhaps expanded. Increasing the capacity of the evaluation field to deal with science program evaluation has pursued several avenues, such as direct grants, indirect training programs, graduate-level programs, short courses, and intensive workshops. Additionally, although there has been work identifying the essential competencies required of an evaluator, there is no clear indication of what skills might be expressly needed for science program evaluation (King, Stevahn, Ghere, & Minnema, 2001). Furthermore, there is little evidence available about which sort of educational programs would produce the best science program evaluators. Capacity building then is another fruitful area for research. Currently the Research Evaluation and Communication division of NSF has a yearly competition for proposals to increase the capacity of science program evaluators. Coordinating and pooling evidence from these projects might provide valuable information about improving capacity.

The field of science education program evaluation continues to mature and expand. At present evaluations encompass a variety of methodologies, underlying social values, and philosophies. Recent emphases in funding tend toward large projects that require complex evaluations. It is likely that new techniques and devices designed to evaluate system-wide reforms, partnerships, and collaborations will be developed to meet this need. The diversity within science program evaluation contributes to a rich literature and the opportunity for the field to debate and discuss issues and perspectives. These interactions provide fertile ground for the field of science education evaluation to grow and evolve. Without the various perspectives the field could easily become sterile and barren.

The new federal emphasis on accountability, specifically student assessment, may significantly narrow the diversity of methods and perspectives existing in science education evaluation. Currently evaluations use a variety of information to judge program value. Student achievement, as defined by a score on a particular test, is only one of many valuable outcomes hoped for in science education. Science education evaluations are designed to serve the many stakeholders involved in the object being evaluated. This responsiveness to evaluating a program to address the needs and ideals of all people concerned about or affected by it, appears to be the process most likely to produce the most valid indication of the value of the science education programs. Science educators should advocate for diversity of perspectives and methods, as well as high quality and rigor, in evaluations of science education projects.

ACKNOWLEDGMENTS

Thanks to James Alhtshied and William Boone, who reviewed this chapter.

REFERENCES

Altschuld, J. W., & Kumar, D. (1995). Program evaluation in science education: The model perspective. In R. O'Sullivan (Vol. Ed.), *New directions for program evaluation: No. 35. Emerging roles of evaluation in science education reform* (Spring, pp. 5–18). San Francisco: Jossey-Bass.

Anfara, V. A., Brown, K. M., & Mangione, T. L. (2002, October). Qualitative analysis on stage: Making the research process more public. *Educational Researcher, 31*(7), 28–38.

Barley, Z. A., & Jeness, M. (1993, June). Cluster evaluation: A method to strengthen evaluation in smaller programs with similar purposes. *Evaluation Practice, 14*(2), 141–147.

Berliner, D. C. (2002, November). Educational research: The hardest science of all. *Educational Researcher, 31*(8), 18–20.

Budick, S., & Iser, W. (Eds.). (1989). *Languages of the unsayable.* New York: Columbia University Press.

Byrk, A. S., & Radenbush, S. W. (1992). *Hierarchical linear models.* Newbury Park, NJ: Sage.

Caracelli, V. J., & Green, J. C. (1997). Crafting mixed-method evaluation designs. In J. C. Green & V. J. Caracelli (Vol. Eds.), *New directions for evaluation: No. 74. Advances in mixed-method evaluation:*

The challenges and benefits of integrating diverse paradigms (Summer, pp. 19–32). San Francisco: Jossey-Bass.

Cook, N. R., Dwyer, M. C., & Stalford, C. (1991). Evaluation and validation: A look at the program effectiveness panel. New Hampshire: U.S. Government (ERIC Document Reproduction Service no. ED333045).

Council of Chief State School Officers. (1997). *Tool kit: Evaluating the development and implementation of standards*. Washington, DC: Author.

Cousins, J. B., & Whitmore, E. (1998). Framing participatory evaluation. In E. Whitmore (Vol. Ed.), *New directions for evaluation: No. 80. Understanding and practicing participatory evaluation* (Winter, pp. 5–24). San Francisco: Jossey-Bass.

Denzin, N. K. (2001). *Interpretive interactionism* (2nd ed.). Thousand Oaks, CA: Sage.

Desimone, L., Porter, A., Garet, M., Yoon, K., & Birman, B. (2002). Effects of professional development on teachers' instruction: Results from a three-year longitudinal study. *Educational Evaluation and Policy Analysis, 24*(2), 81–112.

Dillman, D. A. (2002). *Mail and internet survey: The tailored design method* (2nd ed.). New York: John Wiley & Sons.

Doran, R., Lawrenz, F., & Helgeson, S. (1994). Research assessment in science. In D. Gabel (Ed.), *Handbook for research teaching and learning* (pp. 388–442). New York: Macmillan.

Educational Research, Development, Dissemination and Improvement Act of 1994. Public Law 103-227, H.R. 856, 103rd Congress, March 31, 1994.

Elementary and Secondary School Act of 1965. Public Law 89-10, 89th Congress, 1st Session, April 11, 1965.

Erickson, F., & Gutierrez, K. (2002, November). Culture, rigor, and science in educational research. *Educational Researcher, 31*(8), 21–24.

Fetterman, D. M. (1994). Empowerment evaluation. *Evaluation Practice, 15*(1), 1–15.

Fetterman, D. M. (2001). *Foundations of empowerment evaluation*. Thousand Oaks, CA: Sage.

Finely, F., Heller, P., & Lawrenz, F. (1990). *Review of research in science education*. Pittsburgh: Science Education.

Fitzpatrick, J. L., Sanders, J. R., & Worthen, B. R. (2003). *Program evaluation: Alternative approaches and practical guidelines* (3rd ed.). New York: Pearson Allyn & Bacon.

Frechtling, J. (2002). *User friendly handbook for project evaluations*. Prepared under contract REC99-12175. Arlington, VA: National Science Foundation, Directorate for Education and Human Resources, Division of Research, Evaluation and Communication.

Greene, J. C., & Abma, T. A. (Eds.). (2001). Editor's notes. In *New directions for evaluation: Responsive evaluation: No. 92* (Winter, pp. 1–5). San Francisco: Jossey-Bass.

Green, J. C., & Caracelli, V. J. (1997). Defining and describing the paradigm issue in mixed-method evaluation. In J. C. Green & V. J. Caracelli (Vol. Eds.), *New directions for evaluation, advances in mixed-method evaluation: No. 74. The challenges and benefits of integrating diverse paradigms* (Summer, pp. 5–18). San Francisco: Jossey-Bass.

Guba, E. G., & Lincoln, Y. S. (1989). *Fourth generation evaluation*. Newbury Park, CA: Sage.

Hadi-Tabassum, S. (1999). Assessing students' attitudes and achievements in a multicultural and multilingual science classroom. *Multicultural Education, 7*(2), 15–20.

Hanssen, C., Gullickson, A., & Lawrenz, F. (2003). *Assessing the impact and effectiveness of the Advanced Technological Education (ATE) Program*. Kalamazoo, MI: The Evaluation Center.

House, E. R. (1983). Assumptions underlying evaluation models. In G. F. Madaus, M. Scriven, & D. L. Stufflebeam (Eds.), *Evaluation models*. Boston, MA: Kluwer-Nijhoff.

House, E. R., & Howe, K. R. (2000). Deliberative democratic evaluation in practice. In D. L. Stufflebeam, G. F. Madaus, & T. Kellaghan (Eds.), *Evaluation models: Viewpoints on educational and human services evaluation* (2nd ed.). Boston, MA: Kluwer Academic.

Huberman, A. M., & Miles, M. B. (Eds.). (2002). *The qualitative researcher's companion*. Thousand Oaks, CA: Sage.

Huffman, D., & Lawrenz, F. (2003). Vision of science education as a catalyst for reform. *Journal for Elementary/Middle Level Science Teachers, 36*(2), 14–22.

Joint Committee on Standards for Educational Evaluation. (1981). *Standards for evaluations of educational programs, projects and materials* (1st ed.). New York: McGraw-Hill.

Joint Committee on Standards for Educational Evaluations. (1994). *The program evaluation standards: How to assess evaluations of educational programs* (2nd ed.). Thousand Oaks, CA: Sage.

Kelly, A. E. (2003). Research as design. *Educational Researcher, 32*(1), 3–4.

King, J., Stevahn, L., Ghere, G., & Minnema, J. (2001). Toward a taxonomy of essential evaluator competencies. *American Journal of Evaluation, 22*(2), 229–247.

Knapp, M. S., Shields, P. M., St. John, M., Zucker, A. A., & Stearns, M. S. (1988). *Recommendations to the National Science Foundation. An approach to assessing initiatives in science.* (ERIC Document Reproduction Service no. ED299145). Menlo Park, CA: SRI International.

Lawrenz, F., & Huffman, D. (2002). The archipelago approach to mixed method evaluation. *American Journal of Evaluation, 23*(3), 331–338.

Lawrenz, F., & Huffman, D. (2003). How can multi-site evaluations be participatory? *American Journal of Evaluation, 24*(4), 331–338.

Lawrenz, F., & Jeong, I. (1993). Science and mathematics curricula. In *Indicators of science and mathematics education.* Washington, DC: National Science Foundation.

Lawrenz, F., Michlin, M., Appeldoorn, K., & Hwang, E. (2003). CETP core evaluation: 2001–2002 results. Minneapolis, MN: Center for Applied Research, University of Minnesota.

Lawrenz, F., Weiss, I., & Queitzsch, M. (1996). The K–12 learning environment. In *Indicators of science and mathematics education,* Washington, DC: National Science Foundation.

Lincoln, Y., & Guba, E. (1985). *Naturalistic inquiry.* Beverly Hills, CA: Sage.

Mark, M. M., & Shotland, L. R. (1985). Stakeholder-based evaluation and value judgments: The role of perceived power and legitimacy in the selection of stakeholder groups. *Evaluation Review, 9,* 605–626.

Maruyama, G. (1998). *Basic structural equation modeling.* Thousand Oaks, CA: Sage.

McTaggart, R. (1991b). When democratic evaluation doesn't seem democratic. *Evaluation Practice, 12*(1), 168–187.

Merrian, S. B. (1998). *Qualitative research and case study applications in education* (rev. ed.). San Francisco: Jossey-Bass.

Moore, S. D. (2002). *The basic practice of statistics* (2nd ed.). New York: W. H. Freeman.

Moskowitz, D. A., & Hershberger, S. L. (Eds.). (2002). *Modeling intraindividual variability with repeated measures data.* Mahwah, NJ: Lawrence Erlbaum Associates.

National Research Council. (2001). I. Weiss, M. Knapp, K. Hollweg, & G. Burrell (Eds.), *Investigating the influence of standards: A framework for research in mathematics science and technology education.* Washington, DC: Committee on Understanding the Influence of Standards in K-12 Science Mathematics and Technology Education.

National Research Council. (2002). R. J. Shavelson & L. Towne (Eds.), *Scientific research in education.* Washington, DC: Committee on Scientific Principles of Educational Research, National Academy Press.

Newman, F. M. (1996). *Authentic achievement: Restructuring schools for intellectual quality* (1st ed.). San Francisco: Jossey-Bass.

No Child Left Behind Act of 2001. Public Law 107-110. H.R. 1. 107th Congress, 2nd Session (2001).

Patton, M. Q. (1978). *Utilization-focused evaluation* (1st ed.). Beverly Hills, CA: Sage.

Patton, M. Q. (1986). *Utilization-focused evaluation* (2nd ed.). Beverly Hills, CA: Sage.

Patton, M. Q. (1994). Developmental evaluation. *Evaluation Practice, 5*(3), 311–319.

Patton, M. Q. (1997). *Utilization-focused evaluation: The new century text* (3rd ed.). Thousand Oaks, CA: Sage.

Patton, M. Q. (2000). Utilization-focused evaluation. In D. L. Stufflebeam, G. F. Madaus, & T. Kellaghan (Eds.). *Evaluation models: Viewpoints on educational and human services evaluation* (2nd ed.). Boston: Kluwer Academic.

Pellegrino, J. W., & Goldman, S. R. (2002, November). Be careful what you wish for—you may get it: Educational research in the spotlight. *Educational Researcher, 31*(8), 15–17.

Rice, J. M. (1898). *The rational spelling book.* New York, NY: American Book Company.

Rossi, P. H., & Freeman, H. E. (1985). *Evaluation: A systematic approach* (3rd ed.). Beverly Hills, CA: Sage.

Rossi, P. H., & Freeman, H. E. (1989). *Evaluation: A systematic approach* (4th ed.). Newbury Park, CA: Sage.

Rossi, P. H., & Freeman, H. E. (1993). *Evaluation: A systematic approach* (5th ed.). Newbury Park, CA: Sage.

Rossi, P. H., Freeman, H. E., & Lipsey, M. W. (1999). *Evaluation: A systematic approach* (6th ed.). Thousand Oaks, CA: Sage.

Rossi, P. H., Freeman, H. E., & Rosenbaum, S. (1982). *Evaluation: A systematic approach* (2nd ed.). Beverly Hills, CA: Sage.

Rossi, P. H., Freeman, H. E., & Wright, S. R. (1979). *Evaluation: A systematic approach* (1st ed.). Beverly Hills, CA: Sage.

Sanders, W. L., & Horn, S. P. (1994). The Tennessee value-added assessment system (TVAAS): Mixed model methodology in educational assessment. *Journal of Personnel Evaluation in Education, 8*(3), 299–311.

Scriven, M. (1974). Evaluation perspectives and procedures. In W. J. Popham (Ed.), *Evaluation in education: Current applications.* Berkeley, CA: McCutchen.

Scriven, M. (1991). *Evaluation thesaurus* (4th ed.). Newbury Park, CA: Sage.

Smith, E. R., & Tyler, R. W. (1942). *Appraising and recording student progress.* New York: McGraw-Hill.

Stake, R. E. (1967). The countenance of educational evaluation. *Teachers College Record, 68,* 523–540.

Stake, R. E. (1983). Program evaluation, particularly responsive evaluation. In G. F. Madaus, M. Scriven, & D. L. Stufflebeam (Eds.), *Complementary methods for research in education* (pp. 253–300). Boston: Kluwer-Nijhoff.

Stevens, F., Lawrenz, F., Ely, D., & Huberman, M. (1993). *The user friendly handbook for project evaluation.* Washington, DC: National Science Foundation.

Stockdill, S., Baizerman, M., & Compton, D. (2002). Toward a definition of the ECB process: A conversation with the ECB literature. In D. W. Compton, M. Baizerman, & S. H. Stockdill (Vol. Eds.), *New directions for evaluation: No. 93. The art, craft, and science of evaluation capacity building* (Spring, pp. 27–26). San Francisco: Jossey-Bass.

Stufflebeam, D. L. (1971). The relevance of the CIPP evaluation model for educational accountability. *Journal of Research and Development in Education, 5*(1), 19–25.

Stufflebeam, D. L. (Vol. Ed.). (2001). Evaluation models. In *New directions for evaluation* (No. 89, Spring). San Francisco: Jossey-Bass.

Stufflebeam, D. L., Foley, W. J., Gephart, W. J., Guba, E. G., Hammond, R. L., Merriman, H. O., & Provus, M. M. (1971). *Educational evaluation and decision-making in education.* Itasca, IL: Peacock (copyright 1971 by Phi Delta Kappa, Bloomington, IN).

Stufflebeam, D. L., & Welch, W. W. (1986). Review of research on program evaluation in United States school districts. *Educational Administrators Quarterly, 22*(3), 150–170.

Suter, L. (1993). *Indicators of science and mathematics education, 1992* (1st ed.). Washington, DC: National Science Foundation.

Suter, L. (1996). *Indicators of science and mathematics education, 1995* (2nd ed.). Washington, DC: National Science Foundation.

U.S. National Research Center for Third International Mathematics and Science Study (TIMMS). Retrieved May 27, 2003 from Michigan State University, College of Education Web site: http://ustimss.msu.edu/

Weiss, C. H. (1972). *Evaluation research: Methods for assessing program effectiveness* (1st ed.). Englewood Cliffs, NJ: Prentice-Hall.

Weiss, C. H. (1998). *Evaluation research: Methods for studying program and policies* (2nd ed.). Upper Saddle River, NJ: Prentice-Hall.

Weiss, I. R. (1997). The status of science and mathematics teaching in the United States: Comparing teacher views and classroom practice to national standards. *ERS Spectrum,* (Summer), 34–39.

Weiss, I., Banilower, E., Crawford, R., & Overstreet, C. (2003). *Local systemic change through teacher enhancement: Year eight cross-site report.* Chapel Hill, NC: Horizon Research.

Welch, W. W. (1969). Curriculum evaluation. *Review of Educational Research, 39*(4), 429–443.

Welch, W. W. (1972). Review of research 1968–69, secondary level science. *Journal of Research in Science Teaching, 9*(2), 97–122.

Welch, W. W. (1979a). Five years of evaluating federal programs: Implications for the future. *Science Education, 63*(2), 335–344.

Welch, W. W. (1979b). Twenty years of science curriculum development: A look back. In F. M. Berliner & R. M. Gagne (Eds.), *Review of research in education* (pp. 282–306). Washington, DC: American Educational Research Association.

Welch, W. W. (1985). Research in science education: Review and recommendations. *Science Education, 69*(3), 421–448.

Welch, W. W. (1995). Student assessment and curriculum evaluation. In B. J. Fraser & H. J. Walberg (Eds.), *Improving science education: What do we know.* Chicago: National Society for the Study of Education.

Wiggins, G. P. (1998). *Educative assessment: Designing assessments to inform and improve student performance* (1st ed.). San Francisco: Jossey-Bass.

Worthen, B. R., & Sanders, J. R. (1973). *Educational evaluation: Theory and practice.* Worthington, OH: Charles A. Jones.

Worthen, B. R., & Sanders, J. R. (1987). *Educational evaluation: Alternative approaches and practical guidelines* (1st ed.). New York: Addison Wesley Longman.

Wright, B. D., & Stone, M. H. (1979). *Best test design: Rasch measurement.* Chicago: Mesa Press.

Yin, R. (2002). Study of statewide systemic reform in science and mathematics education: Interim report. Bethesda, MD: Cosmos.

CHAPTER 32

Classroom Assessment of Science Learning

Beverley Bell
University of Waikato, New Zealand

In this chapter, classroom assessment of science learning is taken as that assessment done by the teacher of science, in the classroom, for formative and summative purposes, for use by the teacher and student. Other chapters are reviewing the research on assessment in science education for the purposes of accountability and international comparisons, for summative assessment for reporting to others outside the classroom and for external qualifications, and for program evaluation. In other words, classroom assessment is viewed as teacher assessment for the participants of the classroom—the teacher and students.

Classroom assessment is an important part of science teaching and learning. Its importance is indicated by the extensive and valuable reviews of classroom assessment of science learning in two previous handbooks of science education (Black, 1998a; Doran, Lawrenz, & Helgeson, 1993; Gitomer & Duschl, 1998; Parker & Rennie, 1998; Tamir, 1998). This review builds on these and other seminal reviews of classroom assessment research in education generally (Black & Wiliam, 1998a; Crooks, 1988; Natriello, 1987) to highlight the continuing as well as new trends in research on classroom assessment of science learning.

The importance of classroom assessment is also indicated in that classroom assessment is viewed as a highly skilled and complex task that is a major component of classroom teacher practice (Bell & Cowie, 2001b; Doran et al., 1993). Hattie and Jaeger (1998) assert that the factors that are most effective at improving student learning are clearly in the hands of teachers and include the giving of feedback during some assessment tasks. Most assessments of science learning are carried out by teachers of science in classrooms, it is the teacher who is responsible for either initiating or implementing changes in assessment in the classroom, and it is the teacher who has to ultimately judge the educational worth, significance, and use of different assessment practices.

This chapter reviews the literature in classroom assessment of learning in general, as well as that in science education, science education being a subset of education. The two bodies of literature form the structure of this integrative review, as does the work in early childhood, primary, secondary, and tertiary science education.

By way of an overview, the two main trends in assessment of science learning (as well as assessment of learning in general) are the following:

1. Assessment in education is moving from being viewed as using only traditional psychometric testing and psychological measurement based on a unitary trait view of intelligence and true score theory (Black, 2001), to *educational assessment*, that is, from assessment to prove learning to assessment to improve learning (Gipps, 1994a, 1994b). This move requires a different view of the learner; a different relationship between the pupil and assessor; an acknowledgment that context, pupil motivation, and the characteristics of the task will affect the performance (the demonstration of the competence on a particular occasion or under particular circumstances) as distinct from the competence (the basic ability to perform); and different notions of quality (Gipps, 1994b).

2. Educational assessment is being "perceived less [as] a technical matter of measurement and more a human act of judgment, albeit based on sound evidence" (Broadfoot, 2002; Harlen & James, 1997, p. 378). This concurs with Eisner's notion of "connoisseurship" (Eisner, 1985). Hence, assessment in classrooms is being seen as a *teacher and student practice embedded in political, historical, social, and cultural contexts* (Broadfoot, 2002).

It is acknowledged that psychometric testing and measurement and their associated technical considerations still have a place in assessment (Black, 2001; Hattie & Jaeger, 1998), and as Black (2001) stated, "the apparatus of psychometric statistics will still be needed, but in the service of new endeavours, not as keeper and promoter of the old traditions" (p. 80).

Hence, this review specifically focuses on these two new more recent and developing trends of educational assessment and assessment as a sociocultral practice of teachers and students. These two trends are evident in the political contexts of assessment, the multiple purposes for assessment, the assessment of multiple goals, assessment for formative and summative purposes, the notion of quality in assessment, and theorizing of assessment. Each of these aspects of assessment of science learning is discussed in this review.

ASSESSMENT AND ITS POLITICAL CONTEXTS

One trend evident in assessment in science classrooms (as in other classrooms) is that it continues to be determined as much by politics as it is by educational theorizing (linking assessment with learning) or psychometrics (the measuring of individual differences) (Donnelly & Jenkins, 2001; Tamir, 1998; Torrance, 2000). Assessment is a part of the political enterprise that is education (Apple, 1982, 1996; Delpit, 1995; Gipps, 1998). In other words, a researcher's findings indicating a need for change will not automatically be accepted by politicians, teachers, students, or the community. Research of itself does not necessarily instigate change. All shareholders in the practice called assessment need to be convinced of the necessity for change. What a researcher values in assessment may not be what is valued by other shareholders.

In the last 20 years, an increasing number of political views are being given voice and demanding attention in educational developments. An increasing number of different stakeholders/shareholders with legitimate interests in the purposes for which the assessments are carried out seek to influence the assessment purposes, practices, and reporting of assessment in classrooms. Shareholders may be government officials seeking to develop and implement government policy, teachers, parents, employers, and discipline authorities. Their influence is particularly visible when the assessments are high stakes; that is, there is much riding on the outcomes, such as teacher appraisals, curriculum evaluations, school funding based on the outcomes, student career paths, or student entry to further education. Accounts are given in the literature of the context of national or local requirements for certification and accountability exerting a powerful influence on the practice of assessment in classrooms in the New Zealand context (Bell, Jones, & Carr, 1995; Codd, McAlpine, & Poskitt, 1995; Crooks, 2002b; Gilmore, 2002; Hill, 1999), English context (Black, 1995a, 1995d, 1998b, 2000; Donnelly & Jenkins, 2001; Reay & Wiliam, 1999), Scottish context (Harlen, 1995a), Canadian context (Doran et al., 1993; Mawhinney, 1998; Orphwood, 1995), Korean context (Han, 1995), Australian context (Butler, 1995), and U.S. context (Atkin, Black, Coffey, & National Research Council [U.S.], Committee on Classroom Assessment and the National Science Education Standards, 2001; Berlak, 2000; Collins, 1995, 1998; Doran et al., 1993; Johnston, Guice, Baker, Malone, & Michelson, 1995).

Increasingly, teachers' professional voice and assessment judgment making, if they are included at all, are negotiated with other shareholders, in the political process that is education (Atkin, 2002). The importance of the values held by the politicians cannot be underrated. An example would be politicians' view of the professionalism of teachers—is this to be fostered to improve the quality of education or a barrier to be removed if quality is to be increased (Atkin et al., 2001; Atkin, 2002; Donnelly & Jenkins, 2001)? Politics can also be viewed in the post-structural sense as the discourses and grand narratives of a society or culture, and the micro-politics of the classroom (Bell, 2000; Torrance, 2000; Torrance & Pryor, 1998). In this view, all human practices and actions can be seen to have a dimension of power and hence a political aspect.

Hence, assessment policies, practices, and issues will vary from country to country or state to state, in accordance with the social, political, and historical contexts in which the assessments are done (for examples see Doran et al., 1993). Therefore, this review discusses the larger trends evident in the research literature, with the details of the debates specific to an individual country or state given in the cited references. Some or all of these trends may or may not be relevant in the country of each reader.

ASSESSMENT OF SCIENCE LEARNING FOR MULTIPLE PURPOSES

The second broad trend, derived from the first, is that the research confirms what science teachers (and other teachers) already know: that they are increasingly being asked to do assessment in their classrooms for multiple purposes. And the number of these purposes has increased with the number of different shareholders wishing to use the assessment information generated by teachers and students in classrooms for different purposes. These purposes are linked not only to the goals of education, but also to the political nature of assessment.

This international trend, of multiple purposes for classroom assessment, was brought into sharp focus in the 1990s, when politicians and others wanting to hold educationalists accountable looked to assessment to provide the information required for the accountability process, for example, to audit teacher effectiveness (Bell & Cowie, 2001b). This added to the existing demands for assessment information by people who operate outside the classroom, for example, care-givers, principals, school governing bodies, local or national government officials, awarders of national qualifications, selection panels for tertiary education programs, and employers. These multiple purposes can include auditing of schools, national monitoring, school leaver documentation, awarding of national qualifications, appraisal of teachers, curriculum evaluation, and the improvement of teaching and learning. While these purposes are often mandated by people who operate outside the classroom, the assessments themselves are often done by teachers on their behalf. There are three cornerstones of this education accountability process—a prescribed set of standards, an auditing and monitoring process to ascertain if the standards have been attained, and a way of raising standards if low standards have been indicated in the audits (Bell & Cowie, 2001b). Classroom assessment of (science) learning is seen as a way of raising standards (Atkin et al., 2001; Ministry of Education, 1993).

This more recent addition of assessment for accountability purposes is reflected in this statement of the three main purposes for assessment in education:

> Assessment has multiple purposes. One purpose is to monitor educational progress or improvement. Educators, policymakers, parents and the public want to know how much students are learning compared to the standards of performance or to their peers. This purpose, often called *summative assessment*, is becoming more significant as states and school districts invest more resources in educational reform.
>
> A second purpose is to provide teachers and students with feedback. The teachers can use the feedback to revise their classroom practices, and the students can use the feedback to monitor their own learning. This purpose, often called *formative assessment*, is also receiving greater attention with the spread of new teaching methods.
>
> A third purpose of assessment is to drive changes in practice and policy by holding people accountable for achieving the desired reforms. This purpose, called *accountability assessment*, is very much in the forefront as states and school districts design systems that attach strong incentives and sanctions to performance on state and local assessments. (National Research Council, 1999)

The multiple purposes for which classroom assessment is done give rise to several issues of interest to the science education research community:

1. There can be confusion about the use of terms *formative* and *summative* assessment (Black & Wiliam, 1998a; Brookhart, 2001; Harlen & James, 1997). The terms *formative* and *summative* were first used by Scriven (1967, 1990) to distinguish between the two roles that evaluation may play in education, but the current use of these terms is as adjectives to describe the different *purposes* of assessment, not evaluation or assessment tasks. There is often a confusion reported in the literature over the

terms *formative, summative,* and *continuous summative assessment* (Bell & Cowie, 2001b; Glover & Thomas, 1999; Harlen & James, 1997; Scriven, 1990). For example, teacher assessments, which are collected mainly for summative purposes, usually over the course of the year, are often aggregated into a single score or grade for reporting purposes. This assessment practice is called "continuous assessment" (Nitko, 1995), and although the assessments may have a weak formative role, the main purpose for the assessment information being generated is summative. In the same way, assessment for accountability purposes may have a weak formative purpose informing future teaching and learning, but the time delay is extended when compared with classroom assessments undertaken primarily for formative purposes. Harlen (1998) suggested the use of a continuum from procedures and purposes of assessment that are strongly formative through to those that have a strong summative focus.

2. The terms *summative, formative,* and *accountability* describe the purpose for which the assessment is done, not the task itself, as one assessment task might be used for both formative and summative purposes. For example, a concept-mapping task may be used for formative purposes during the teaching unit, or summatively after the teaching (Francisco, Nakhleh, Nurrenbern, & Miller, 2002; Toth, Suthers, & Lesgold, 2002), as can portfolios (Childers & Lowry, 1997; Treagust, 1995; Tripp, Murphy, Stafford, & Childers, 1997) and demonstration assessments (Deese, Ramsey, Walczyk, & Eddy, 2000). Although it is acknowledged that teachers do assessment for both formative and summative purposes (Biggs, 1998; Black, 1993, 1995b, 2002) and that the two purposes overlap, the issue arises as to whether the information collected by a teacher for formative purposes (that is, to inform the learning and teaching) can be used at a later time for summative purposes (that is, at the end of the teaching and learning) or accountability purposes. Similarly, can assessment information collected for summative purposes be used by others for accountability purposes, given concerns of ethics; quality such as reliability, validity, fairness; manageability; and the tensions between the dual roles of the teacher of advisor and adjudicator? Harlen (1998) highlighted these problems in that "assessment for formative purposes is pupil-referenced and judgments are made by pupils and teachers about next steps, whilst assessment for summative purposes requires judgments to be made by teachers against public standards or criteria" (p. 9). In the United Kingdom, as in New Zealand, the teacher judgments are often used to allocate students' achievement to a curriculum "level." Harlen saw no problem in using the raw information, but not the judgments, collected for formative purposes for later summative purposes. Hence, she advocated using the *evidence* of pupil learning but not the *results* (emphasis in original). A growing number of authors are arguing that the interaction of all three purposes is both possible and desirable, given the burdens of assessment on teachers and students (Biggs, 1998; Black, 1993; Gilmore, 2002; Harlen & James, 1997). A note of caution was given by Bell & Cowie (1997, 2001b), who presented research findings to indicate that the students in research science classrooms were able to determine the purpose of the assessment as being formative or summative, even if the teacher had not been explicit. Moreover, their performance was influenced by the level of disclosure they felt comfortable with, given the level of trust that existed, thereby influencing the quality of the assessment.

3. In the classroom, the practices of curriculum, pedagogy, learning, and assessment are connected, interdependent, and in tension (Carr et al., 2000), as are the purposes for doing assessment. Changes to the assessment practices in a classroom will affect the other practices and vice versa. For example:

- curriculum change can influence assessment practices (Black & Wiliam, 1998b; Gitomer & Duschl, 1995; Orpwood, 2001);
- assessment practices will affect curriculum, learning, and pedagogy (Buchan & Welford, 1994; Carr et al., 2000; Crooks, 2002a; Hill, 2001; Mavrommatis, 1997; Smith, Hounshell, Copolo, & Wilkerson, 1992), for example, the impact of high-stakes, standardized national testing on school learning (Black & Wiliam, 1998a);
- for assessment practices to change, curricula and pedagogoy must change also (Black & Wiliam, 1998b; Cheng & Cheung, 2001; Dori, 2003; Treagust, Jacobowitz, Gallagher, & Parker, 2001).

In the same way, the three key purposes of assessment, formative, summative, and accountability, are interdependent and interactive:

- Some classroom assessments for school summative purposes may be used for accountability purposes if schools are required to produce evidence that they are making a difference to audit agencies (Hill, 1999). This strong emphasis on assessment for summative and accountability purposes, and especially the high-stakes assessment, may decrease the assessment for formative purposes that teachers feel able to do (Cowie & Bell, 1999).
- There is a tension between classroom assessments (for formative and summative purposes) and national assessment for accountability and monitoring purposes, with opportunities for doing assessment for formative purposes declining with the straitjacket of national assessment (Black & Harrison, 2001a, 2001b; Black & Wiliam, 1998a; Broadfoot, 1996; Daws & Singh, 1996; Eley & Caygill, 2001, 2002; Gipps, Brown, Mccallum, & McAlister, 1995; Keiler & Woolnough, 2002; Preece & Skinner, 1999; Smith et al., 1992; Swain, 1996, 1997). A strong emphasis on national or state assessment for accountability purposes may lead to teaching to the test or increased teaching time on the school work assessed by such tests (Gipps et al., 1995) or even less teaching time available (Gipps et al., 1995). However, the primary teachers (of science) in the Gipps et al. (1995) study on the impact of national testing became more knowledgeable in assessment; redirected the focus of their teaching, with resulting improvements in national assessments of basic skills; undertook more detailed planning; made more use of a systematic approach to collecting evidence from the students and written records than intuition; gained a better understanding of an individual's progress; and developed increased levels of discussion and collegiality with other staff.
- Multiple purposes for assessment means that there are multiple audiences, and it raises the issue of whether one assessment task can provide information for several assessment purposes and audiences (Black, 1998a).

Research on assessment for accountability purposes is reviewed in Chapters 31 and 33. The multiple purposes of classroom assessment of science learning are seen as giving rise to two broad categories of assessment: assessment for formative (including diagnostic) and summative purposes. These two purposes are discussed in the fourth and fifth sections.

ASSESSMENT AND MULTIPLE GOALS OF SCIENCE LEARNING

What is assessed? is an important question, as it links assessment strategies, learning goals, and curriculum together and is part of what is called "validity inquiry in the psychometric literature" (Messick, 1989, 1994). In the 1993 review of assessment of science learning, the list of what is assessed was given as knowledge of facts and concepts, science process skills, higher order science thinking skills, problem-solving skills, skills needed to manipulate laboratory equipment, and attitudes of science (Doran et al., 1993). A strong criticism of assessment in the past has been that only learning goals that could be readily assessed, say by use of recall to answer multiple-choice tests, were assessed with a subsequent negative impact of the curriculum, pedagogy, learning, and learners in the classroom (Crooks, 1988). There is now the recognition that all learning goals need to be assessed, and not just recall and understanding of science concepts because they are easy to test for (Osborne & Ratcliffe, 2002). The additional science learning goals to be assessed include:

- the nature of science views held by students (Aikenhead, 1987; Lederman, Abd-El-Khalick, Bell, & Schwartz, 2002);
- what matters in the discipline of science (Gitomer & Duschl, 1995): knowledge and skills that are deemed important within the discipline, that is, knowledge and science experiences through investigation procedures similar to those scientists employ; the changing nature of scientific knowledge being acquired from an investigation; the accepted rules of practice that guide scientific practice; meanings and background knowledge of the scientific discipline;
- knowing that science is culturally and historically embedded, and contextualized (Fusco & Barton, 2001);
- the ideas and evidence—the processes and practices—of science, that is, *how* we know as well as *what* we know (Osborne & Ratcliffe, 2002);
- learning dispositions (habits of mind), such as resilience, playfulness, reciprocity, curiosity, friendliness, being bossy; confidence, curiosity, intentionality, self-control, relatedness, communication, cooperation, courage, playfulness, perseverance, responsibility, selectivity, experimentation, reflection, opportunism, and conviviality (Allal, 2002; Carr, 2001; Carr & Claxton, 2002), as well as effective learning skills in the learning-to-learn literature (Baird & Northfield, 1992).

In the next section, the research on assessment of science learning for formative purposes is reviewed.

ASSESSMENT OF SCIENCE LEARNING
FOR FORMATIVE PURPOSES

Another trend in the research on classroom assessment is the increasing emphasis on assessment for formative purposes. This trend has arisen because of recent political demands for increased accountability of teachers for learning outcomes, the research on the role of feedback in learning and teaching, and the research on teaching and assessment for conceptual development in science education (Bell & Cowie, 2001b; Treagust et al., 2001).

Definitions and Characteristics

Formative assessment is increasingly being used to refer only to assessment that provides feedback to students (and teachers) about the learning that is occurring, during the teaching and learning, and not after (Cowie, 1997). The feedback or dialogue is seen as an essential component of formative assessment interaction, where the intention is to support learning (Black, 1995b; Black & Wiliam, 1998a; Gipps, 1994a; Hattie, 1999; Hattie & Jaeger, 1998; Perrenoud, 1998; Ramaprasad, 1983; Sadler, 1989). And assessment can be considered formative only if it results in action by the teacher and students to enhance student learning (Black, 1993). These components are reflected in various definitions of formative assessment, for example, "The process used by teachers and students to recognise and respond to student learning in order to enhance that learning, during the learning" (Bell & Cowie, 2001b, p. 8). It is through the teacher-student interactions during learning activities (Newmann, Griffin, & Cole, 1989) that formative assessment is done and that students receive feedback on what they know, understand, and can do and receive teaching to learn further. Formative assessment is at the intersection of teaching and learning (Gipps, 1994a), and, in this way, teaching, learning, and assessment are integrated in the curriculum (Hattie & Jaeger, 1998). The term *formative interaction* (Jones, Cowie, & Moreland, 2003; Moreland, Jones, & Northover, 2001) may be used instead of *formative assessment* to highlight this interactive nature of formative assessment—that teacher-student interactions are the core of formative assessments. Assessment for diagnostic purposes, for example (Barker & Carr, 1989; Feltham & Downs, 2002; Simpson, 1993), is therefore included, as is embedded assessment (Treagust et al., 2001; Volkmann & Abell, 2003). Harlen and James (1997), in a review of literature, summarized that the characteristics of formative assessment, to distinguish it from summative assessment, are that it is positive, is a part of teaching, takes into account the progress of students, can elicit inconsistencies that can provide diagnostic information, places more value on validity and usefulness than reliability, and requires the students to be actively involved in monitoring their own progress and improving their learning. Harlen (1998) describes assessment for formative purposes as that which is "embedded in a pedagogy of which it is an essential part; shares learning goals with students; involves students in self-assessment; provides feedback which leads to students recognizing 'the gap' and closing it; underpinned by confidence that every student can improve; and involves reviewing and reflecting on assessment data" (p. 3).

Bell and Cowie (1997, 2001b), in reporting the findings of a major research project, summarized the characteristics of formative assessment on the basis of the qualitative data generated by the 10 teachers of year 7–8 students (aged 10–14) in a two-year research project into classroom assessment and science education. Over the two years, the teachers were asked to describe what it was that they were doing, when they were doing assessment for formative purposes. Their ability to articulate and make explicit this often tacit practice increased over the two years as a shared understanding and use of a shared language also grew. The nine characteristics of formative assessment discussed by the teachers were that it was responsive (that is, dynamic and progressive, informal, interactive, unplanned as well as planned, proactive as well as reactive, responding with individuals and with the whole class, involves uncertainty and risk taking, and has degrees of responsiveness); uses written, oral, and nonverbal sources of evidence; is a tacit process; uses professional knowledge and experiences; is an integral part of teaching and learning; is done by both teachers and students to improve teaching as well as learning; is highly contextualized; and involves managing dilemmas (Bell & Cowie, 1997, 2001a, 2001b).

A descriptive and interpretive account of some characteristics of formative assessment was also given by Treagust et al. (2001). In this study, the classroom practices of an acknowledged exemplary U.S. middle-school teacher of 23 grade 8 students studying sound were researched with an interpretive research methodology over a period of 3 weeks. The researchers explored and documented how the teacher incorporated assessment tasks as an integral component of her teaching about the topic sound. They reported that the teacher used "the information to inform her teaching, nearly every activity had an assessment component integrated into it, that students had a wide range of opportunities to express their knowledge and understanding through writing tasks and oral questioning, and that individual students responded to and benefited from the different assessment techniques in various ways" (p. 137).

Importance of Formative Assessment

Formative assessment, like assessment in general, does influence learning (Crooks, 2002a; Gipps & James, 1998). The case for formative assessment was made in a report commissioned by the British Educational Research Association to argue the case for raising achievement through the use of assessment for formative purposes, rather than through large-scale testing for accountability purposes. This seminal review of the research reported in 578 articles, by Black and Wiliam (1998a, 1998b), states the importance of formative assessment for learning as "The research reported here shows conclusively that formative assessment does improve learning. The gains in achievement appear to be quite considerable, and as noted earlier, amongst the largest ever reported for educational interventions" (p. 61).

The science education research included in the Black and Wiliam review, along with others to provide evidence to back up this knowledge claim, was that of Frederiksen and White (1997). Likewise, Hattie (1999) concluded his meta-analysis to evaluate the relative effects of different teaching approaches and different components of teaching by stating that the single most powerful moderator that enhances achievement is feedback.

Having reviewed the literature to document the evidence that formative assessment can indeed raise standards Black and Wiliam (1998a) then addressed the question, "is there evidence that there is room for improvement?" They concluded that there is research evidence "that formative assessment is not well understood by teachers and is weak in practice; that the context of national or local requirements for certification and accountability will exert a powerful influence on its practice; and that its implementation calls for rather deep changes both in teachers' perceptions of their own role in relation to their students and in their classroom practice" (Black & Wiliam, 1998a, p. 20). The science education literature to support this knowledge claim is found in a number of studies (Black, 1993; Bol & Strage, 1996; Daws & Singh, 1996; Duschl & Gitomer, 1997; Lorsbach, Tobin, Briscoe, & LaMaster, 1992).

Although there has been much advocacy by science educators on the importance of formative assessment to improve learning and standards of achievement (for example, Atkin et al., 2001; Black, 1995b, 1995c, 1998a; Black & Wiliam, 1998a, 1998b; Harlen, 1995b; Harlen & James, 1997; Hunt & Pellegrino, 2002), there have been only a few actual research studies on the process of formative assessment of science learning. These are now reviewed.

Models of Formative Assessment

In addition to the empirical research on formative assessment in the general assessment research literature, for example (Torrance & Pryor, 1998, 2001) with their work on formative assessment in UK primary classrooms (of students aged 4–7), there are three major research studies in science education: Bell and Cowie (2001b), Cowie (2000), and Treagust et al. (2001). The first study sought to research the nature of assessment for formative purposes so as to make the often tacit knowledge of teachers explicit. In this way, the research could help teachers to share their knowledge of this highly skilled pedagogy during teacher development situations. The findings are summarized in a model of formative assessment (Bell, 2000; Bell & Cowie, 2001b; Cowie & Bell, 1999). This model is notable in that it was developed by the teachers involved in the research project (Bell & Cowie, 1999). The 10 teachers were asked to develop a model that would communicate to teachers not involved in the research what it was that they were doing when they were doing formative assessment. The primary teachers in the research by Torrance and Pryor (2001) similarly developed a "practical classroom model." The teachers within the Bell and Cowie study reported that they undertook two forms of formative assessment: planned formative assessment and interactive formative assessment.

The process of *planned formative assessment* was characterized by the teachers eliciting, interpreting, and acting on assessment information. The main purpose for which the teachers said they used planned formative assessment was to obtain information from the whole class about progress in learning science as specified in the curriculum. This assessment was planned in that the teacher had planned to undertake a specific activity (for example, a survey or brainstorming) to obtain assessment information on which some action would be taken. The teachers considered the information collected as a part of the planned formative assessment was "general," "blunt," and concerned their "big" purposes. It gave them information that was valuable in informing their interactions with the class as a whole with respect to "getting through the curriculum." This form of formative assessment was planned by the teacher mainly to obtain feedback to inform her or his teaching. The purpose for doing the assessment strongly influenced the other three aspects of the planned formative assessment process of eliciting information, interpreting, and taking action to enhance the students' learning. Acting on the interpreted information is the essential aspect of formative assessment that distinguishes it from continuous summative assessment. To do this, the teacher needed to plan to have a flexible program and to allow for ways in which she or he could act in response to the information gathered. It also helped to be able to act in a variety of ways in response to that gathered information.

The second form of formative assessment identified by the teachers was *interactive formative assessment*, which can be characterized as the teachers' noticing, recognizing, and responding. Interactive formative assessment was what took place during student-teacher interactions. It differed from the first form—planned formative assessment—in that a specific assessment activity was not planned. The interactive assessment arose out of a learning activity. Hence, the details of this kind of formative assessment were not planned and could not be anticipated. Although the teachers often planned or prepared to do interactive formative assessment, they could not plan for or predict what exactly they and the students would be doing, or when it would occur. As interactive formative assessment occurred during student-teacher interaction, it had the potential to occur any time students and teachers interacted. The teachers and students within the project interacted in whole-class, small-group, and one-to-one situations. The main purpose for which the teachers said they did interactive formative assessment was to mediate in the learning of individual students with respect the intended learning. The teachers' specific purposes for interactive formative assessment emerged in response to what sense they found the students were making. Interactive formative assessment was therefore embedded in and strongly linked to learning and teaching activities. The teachers indicated that through their interactive formative assessment, they refined their short-term goals for the students' learning within the framework of their long-term goals. The teachers indicated that their purposes for learning could be delayed and negotiated between the teacher and the students through formative assessment feedback. The teachers described interactive formative assessment as teacher and student driven rather than curriculum driven. The response to what the teacher had noticed and recognized was the essential aspect of interactive formative assessment. The response by the teachers was similar to the acting in planned formative assessment, except that the time frame was different—it was more immediate. Within the process of interactive formative assessment, the teachers often had to make quick decisions in circumstances in which they did not have all the necessary information, using "teacher wisdom" rather than intuition or instinct (Jaworski, 1994).

The teachers in the study commented that the two kinds of formative assessment were linked through the purposes for formative assessment; that some teachers used interactive formative assessment more than other teachers; and that a teacher moved from planned to interactive and back. The link between the two parts of the model was seen to be centered around the purposes for doing formative assessment. It is of interest to note that the teachers in the Torrance and Pryor (2001) study placed the "making task and quality criteria explicit" in the center of their classroom practice model, which is linked to purpose. The teachers in the new Zealand study indicated that their assessment for formative purposes tended to be decreased if there was too much emphasis on assessment for summative and accountability purposes (Bell & Cowie, 2001b), reflecting the views of Black (1995c), Harlen and James (1997), and Hill (1999).

The key features of the model are now discussed, in association with other research on formative assessment. First, the model of formative assessment developed by the teachers included the notion of *planning*, which has also been highlighted by other researchers (Fairbrother, Black, & Gill, 1995; Harlen, 1995b; Torrance & Pryor, 1995).

A second key feature of the model is that formative assessment is described as a *complex, highly skilled task*, and as it is in other research (Torrance & Pryor, 1998), which relied on the following knowledge bases (Shulman, 1987): content knowledge (for example, knowing the scientific understanding of the concepts being taught); general pedagogical knowledge (for example, of classroom management); curriculum knowledge (for example, of the learning objectives in the curriculum being taught); pedagogical content knowledge (for example, knowing how best to teach atomic theory to a class of 14-year-olds); a knowledge about learners in general and the students in the class; knowledge of educational contexts (for example, the assessment practices in the school); and a knowledge of educational aims and purposes (for example, a possible "science-for-all" emphasis in a national curriculum). To this list, the teachers' knowledge of progression in students' learning of specific concepts can be added (Bell & Cowie, 2001c; Jones et al., 2003). The formative assessment also relied upon the processes of pedagogical reasoning and action (Shulman, 1987), including the transformation of content knowledge into pedagogical knowledge, through preparation, representation, selection, and adaptation. The teachers felt the use of both forms of formative assessment, and switching between them was the hallmark of a competent teacher.

A third key feature of the model is teachers' *interaction skills, and the nature of the relationships* they had established with the students was also seen as important. It was felt that the teachers needed a disposition to carry out interactive formative assessment; that is, the teachers needed to value and want to interact with the students to find out what they were thinking about. Cowie (2000) also commented on the relationships that developed between the teachers and students as individuals, groups, and a class. Mutual trust and respect were identified as the key factors mediating student willingness to disclose their ideas to teachers and peers, and hence enable formative assessment interactions to occur. Hence the findings support the contention by Tittle (1994) that the views and beliefs of the interpreters and users of assessment information (here teachers and students) are an important dimension of any theory of educational assessment.

A fourth key feature of the model is the central role given to *purpose* in both forms of formative assessment by the teachers.

A fifth key feature of the model is the *action* taken as part of both planned and interactive formative assessment, for it distinguishes assessment for formative purposes from that for summative and accountability. The action means that formative assessment can be described as an integral part of teaching and learning and that it is responsive to students. Much of the current literature, for example, Driver, Squires, Rushworth, and Wood-Robinson (1994), on conceptual development in science education involves a consideration of the teacher being responsive to the thinking of students, often phrased as "taking into account students' thinking." To respond to and mediate students' thinking involves the teacher finding out what the thinking is, evaluating the thinking, and responding to it. These are the three components in both planned and interactive formative assessment. The teachers in the research made the claim that they did not think they could promote learning in science unless they were doing formative assessment (Bell & Cowie, 1997). The role of the teacher included *providing* opportunities for formative assessment to be done (for example, having the students discuss in small groups their and scientists' meanings of "electric current," rather than listening only to a lecture by the teacher) and using the opportunity to do formative assessment (for example, interacting with the students while they are doing small-group discussion work about their conceptual understandings of electric currents). In addition, the action taken as part of both planned and interactive formative assessment was seen by the teachers as a part of teaching and by the students as a part of learning. The teachers acted and responded on the assessment information they obtained in science (criterion-referenced), student (ipsative), and care-referenced ways. In the care-referenced actions, the teachers took action to sustain and enhance the quality of interactions and relationships between the students and between themselves and the students. Other research has also noted the dual ipsative and criterion-referenced nature of formative assessment (Harlen & James, 1997) and the care aspect of formative assessment (Treagust et al., 2001). A single action or response might have one or more of these aspects in it. It was the action part of planned and interactive formative assessment that the teachers felt they needed more help with in future teacher development.

One important aspect of the "taking action" is the feedback to the student from the teacher or another student. The feedback is more effective in improving learning outcomes if it is about the substance of the work, not superficial aspects (Crooks, 1988; Harlen, 1999); linked with goal setting (Black & Wiliam, 1998a; Gipps & Tunstall, 1996b; Hattie, 1999; Hattie & Jaeger, 1998); and linked to the students' strengths and weaknesses of the task, rather than to just the self, as in praise (Black & Wiliam, 1998a; Hattie, Biggs, & Purdie, 1996). The quality of the feedback may involve a comparison between the students' achievement or performance and other students' (norm-referenced), standards or learning goals (critierion-referenced), or the student's previous achievements (ipsative). In assessment for formative purposes the ipsative frame of references for feedback is important. Another important aspect of the taking action part of the formative assessment process has become known as "feedforward," to distinguish it from feedback (Bell & Cowie, 2001b). Whereas "feedback" was used to refer to the response given to the student by the teacher (Sadler, 1989) or another student about the correctness of their learning, the term "feedforward" was used to refer to those aspects of formative assessment in which the teacher was helping students to close the gap between what they know and can do, and what is required of them as indicated in the standards or curriculum objectives (Sadler, 1989). Hence, to provide both feedback and feedforward a teacher must know the curriculum content and standards or curriculum objectives, the progression of students' learning, and the scaffolding required for learning in the Zone of Proximal development, after Vygotsky (Allal & Ducrey, 2000; Torrance & Pryor, 1998).

A sixth key feature of the teachers' model of formative assessment was the central role of *self-assessment and self-monitoring*. This is distinct from feedback, which is given by another person (Sadler, 1989). Research on this aspect of assessment for formative purposes was also reviewed in the meta-analysis by Hattie et al. (1996), who concluded that interventions, which are integrated to suit the individual's self-assessment, orchestrated to the demands of the particular task and context, and self-regulated with discretion, were "highly effective in all domains (performance, study skills and affect) over all ages and abilities, but were particularly useful with high-ability and older students" (p. 128). And they were more effective than the typical study skills training packages. To be able to give effective feedback and feed-forward, the research by Jones et al. (2003), Moreland and Jones (2000), and Moreland et al. (2001) with teachers of technology indicated that the pedagogical content knowledge as well as pedagogical approaches of teachers had to be enhanced. This is so the teachers could make a judgment about where the student's learning is in relation to the intended curriculum learning goals, communicate this to the student, and suggest steps for the student to improve his or her learning, based on their knowledge of progression in learning a specific skill or concept.

The following have been suggested for teachers and students, on the basis of the review of the research evidence, as interventions to improve the use of assessment for formative purposes: "feedback to any pupil should be about the particular quality of his or her work, with advice on what he or she can do to improve, and should avoid comparisons with other pupils"; "for formative assessment to be productive, pupils should be trained in self-assessment so that they can understand the main purposes of their learning and thereby grasp what they need to achieve"; "opportunities for pupils to express their understanding should be designed into any piece of teaching, for this will initiate the interaction whereby formative assessment aids learning"; "the dialogue between pupils and a teacher should be thoughtful, reflective, focused to evoke and explore understandings, and conducted so that all pupils have an opportunity to think and to express their ideas"; "tests and homework exercises can be an invaluable guide to learning, but the exercises must be clear and relevant to learning aims. The feedback on them should give each pupil guidance on how to improve, and each must be given opportunity and help to work at the improvement" (Black & Wiliam, 1998b, pp. 9–13). This was later summarized to the following:

> The research indicates that improving learning through assessment depends on five, deceptively simple key factors: the provision of effective feedback to pupils; the active involvement of students in their own learning; adjusting teaching to take account of the results of assessment; a recognition of the profound influence assessment has on the motivation and self-esteem of pupils, both of which are crucial influences on learning; and the need for pupils to be able to assess themselves and understand how to improve. (Assessment Reform Group, 1999) (p. 4), and;
>
> sharing learning goals with pupils; involving pupils in self-assessment; providing feedback which leads to pupils recognizing their next steps and how to take them; underpinned by confidence that every pupil can improve. (Assessment Reform Group, 1999, p. 7)

Publications for teachers, based on the above research reviews, to help them improve the assessment for formative purposes in the classroom, have been produced (Atkin et al., 2001; Clarke, 1998; Clarke, Timperley, & Hattie, 2003). For example, the latter publication has a chapter on each of the components of formative assessment as:

> clarifying learning intentions at the planning stage, as a condition for formative assessment to take place in the classroom; sharing learning intentions at the beginning of

lessons; involving children in self-evaluation against learning intentions; focusing oral and written feedback around the learning intentions of lessons and tasks; organizing individual target setting so that children's achievement is based on previous achievement as well as aiming for the next level up; appropriate questioning; and raising children's self-esteem via the language of the classroom and the ways achievement is celebrated. (Clarke et al., 2003, p. 14)

The last key feature of the model is the *teacher development* that occurred in its development by the teachers (Bell & Cowie, 1997; Bell & Cowie, 2001c), providing some information to answer Black and Wiliam's question, "Is there evidence about how to improve formative assessment?" Information has also been provided by other researchers, using collaborative action-research (Torrance & Pryor, 2001), reflective surveys (Black & Harrison, 2001a, 2001b), and reflection on teachers' knowledge bases (Jones et al., 2003). A notable feature of the literature is that teacher development for assessment for formative purposes also involves changing one's overall pedagogy, not just the assessment aspects (Ash & Levitt, 2003; Bell & Cowie, 2001c; Black & Wiliam, 1998a, 1998b; Treagust et al., 2001).

Research on Students and Assessment for Formative Purposes

Students have considerable agency in the practice of formative assessment. But although feedback, feedforward, and self-assessment position both the teacher and student as taking action during formative assessment, the core activity of formative assessment lies in "the sequence of two actions. The first is the perception *by the learner* of a gap between the desired goal an his or her present state (of knowledge, and/or understanding, and/or skill). The second is the action taken *by the learner* to close that gap in order to attain the desired goal (Ramaprasad, 1983; Sadler, 1989)" (Black & Wiliam, 1998a) (emphases added).

There is a growing interest in the wider education research literature in the views of students on teaching, learning, and assessment (as distinguished from their views on the subject matter content), for example, Heady (2001) and Morgan and Morris (1999). Although there have been reviews on the impact of assessment on students (Crooks, 1988; Hattie & Jaeger, 1998; Natriello, 1987), there has been little research until recently on students' views of assessment (Brookhart, 2001; Gipps & Tunstall, 1996a; Jones et al., 2003). Two studies are worthy of discussion here. In the primary school, Pollard, Triggs, Broadfoot, McNess, and Osborn (2000) reported on the findings of the Primary Assessment, Curriculum and Experience (PACE) project in the United Kiingdom, stating that "the picture of children's experience of classroom assessment that emerges from different sections of the pupil interviews is remarkably consistent. They are aware of assessment only as a summative activity and use criteria of neatness, correctness, quantity and effort when commenting on their own and others work" (p. 152). In the research by Brookhart (2001) the able students did not keep distinct the formative and summative purposes of assessment, but rather these successful students integrated the two. However, there has been research where students have been interviewed on their views of science assessment for formative purposes (Cowie, 2000). In this doctoral research, 75 students (years 7 to 10, or ages 11 to 14) were interviewed in either individual or group situations about their views on classroom assessment. The findings indicate that the students constructed themselves as active and intentional participants in learning, its assessment, and their self-assessment of it. The criteria for judging the success of their learning, reported by students, included the ability to perform a task, gaining good marks or grades, the teacher confirming their ideas were correct, and feelings of completeness and coherence. Another finding was that students viewed formative assessment as embedded in and accomplished through interaction with teachers, peers, and parents. Disclosure was another aspect of students' views of formative assessment. The students were very aware that their questions, actions, and book work had the potential to disclose not only what they knew but also what they did not know, to peers and teachers, who may or may not make positive judgments and actions on the basis of these disclosures. Students indicated that they withheld disclosure if the classroom was not safe, doing so only in a trusting relationship with the teacher and peers. This would influence not just the validity but the essence of formative assessment. Student disclosure is central to formative assessment, and participation in assessment interactions could lead to both benefit and harm in learning, social, and relationship constructions. Torrance and Pryor (1998) described the teacher during formative assessment as using power-with and power-for students in their learning.

Cowie (2000) also detailed the ways in which student perspectives of formative assessment in the classroom contributed to the mutual construction of what it means to be a student and a teacher in that classroom, that is, notions of identity. For example, "student perceptions that time and attention were limited and teachers assessed what was important to them, meant that teacher assessment served to communicate to the students who and what was important to the teacher" (p. 260); "for students, the key feature of formative assessment as a meaning making activity was that it contributed to their identity in the classroom . . . the students contended that disclosing their ideas in an attempt to enhance their understanding could lead their peers and the teacher to perceive them as 'try hards', 'bright' or 'dumb' and to their learning being enhanced or them being embarrassed and feeling stupid. They indicated that for them, assessment and learning were intimately connected and inherently linked with who they were and how they felt" (p. 261). The students and teachers in Cowie's study were seen as actors (that is, taking action) in formative assessment. The students were actors in formative assessment in three ways: their academic and social goals and interests mediated their interactions; they sought to manage the disclosure of their learning by choosing (or not choosing) to ask questions and by acting to restrict teachers' incidental access to their book work; and they assessed the teacher to ascertain how the teacher reacted to their questions and therefore to find out what was seen as important by the teacher. In summary, Cowie (2000) stated that the students were both active in the formative assessment process and profoundly affected by it, as did Reay and Wiliam (1999). The students in the Cowie (2000) study insisted that

> their teachers could only assess their learning through face-to-face interaction with them. Face-to-face interaction was considered to enhance the fidelity (Wiliam, 1992) of teacher formative assessment, because students could negotiate the meaning of teacher questions and because students were more prepared to ask questions, thereby disclosing their views. Teachers were said to provide more useful feedback during one-to-one and small group interactions. (p. 267)

Students' views of assessment are also embedded in use of the questions generated by students as assessment information for diagnostic and formative purposes (Biddulph, 1989; Rop, 2002; Zeegers, 2003).

ASSESSMENT OF SCIENCE LEARNING FOR SUMMATIVE PURPOSES

A fifth trend in classroom assessment of science learning is the ongoing research and development of assessment for summative purposes. Classroom assessment of science learning for summative purposes is that which summarizes the learning achieved after teaching is completed and includes end-of-unit tests, teacher assessments for qualifications, and teacher assessments for reporting to parents, caregivers, and others outside the classroom. Whereas assessment for formative purposes is to improve learning, assessment for summative purposes is assessment of learning (Crooks, 2001). Included in this section is ongoing or continuous summative assessments, in which a series of short summative assessments is aggregated in some way, usually to reduce the assessment information into a single score or grade (Harlen, 1998).

In the past decade, the bulk of the *development* on classroom assessment of science learning has been largely about assessment for summative purposes and has been concerned with developing the summative assessment of both a wider range of science learning outcomes and the use of a wider range of assessment tasks or formats, in order to increase the quality of the summative assessments, especially validity. This trend is noticeable in the handbook-type publications for teachers on classroom assessment (for example, Phye, 1997) and on assessment of science learning (Enger & Yager, 1998; Mintzes, Wandersee, & Novak, 2001, 1999; Shepardson, 2001); exemplars of assessment as curriculum support (Ministry of Education, downloaded 2003); released assessment items and information from assessment for national and international accountability (for example, Crooks & Flockton, 1996; Eley & Caygill, 2001); resource banks (Gilmore & Hattie, 2001; Marston & Croft, 1999); pre-post-assessment items used in research into science learning (Barker & Carr, 1989); and released national/state examinations papers.

The last decade of *research* of science learning for summative purposes has included researching the assessment of a wider range of learning outcomes using performance assessment and researching the use of a wider range of assessment formats, including performance assessment, concept maps, portfolios, interviews, prediction tasks, learning stories, observations, dynamic assessments, experimental and customized challenges, group assessment, and computer-based assessment. These are now discussed.

THE ASSESSMENT OF A WIDER RANGE OF LEARNING OUTCOMES USING PERFORMANCE ASSESSMENT

Performance assessment to assess a wider range of learning goals, in diverse learning situations (Solano-Flores & Shavelson, 1997; Stoddart, Abrams, Gasper, & Canaday, 2000), has been a focus of research on classroom assessment of science learning. It was felt that traditional pen-paper tests, requiring recall and recognition of knowledge "about," did not validly assess the learning of some goals of science education (Fusco & Barton, 2001). Performance assessments were developed to assess production or performance and hence enable the assessment of all the curricula goals, not just those that were readily assessed by multiple choice or short answers. Performance-based assessment has been defined as "the execution of some task or process which has to be assessed through actual demonstration, that is, a productive activity (Wiggins, 1993)" (Cumming & Maxwell, 1999, p. 180). It is the assessment of actual performance showing what a student can do, rather than what a student can skillfully recall. The term may also include an emphasis on the integration of knowledge, practices, holistic applications (that is, to the whole and not just separate parts); multiple opportunities for teaching and learning (Wolfe, Bixby, Glenn, & Gardner, 1991); assessment in contexts that mirror real-life science or science in everyday life (Lubben & Ramsden, 1998); collaborative inquiry, problem solving, co-construction of understandings, and knowledge-building communities (Fusco & Barton, 2001; Rogoff, 1990), and many different kinds of performance, rather than just one kind (Eisner, 1993; McGinn & Roth, 1998). The literature indicates that performance assessments are highly sensitive, not only to the tasks and the occasions sampled, but also to the method (Ruiz-Primo & Shavelson, 1996b) and the kinds of knowledges that students need to access to complete a performance task (Erickson & Meyer, 1998).

The use of performance assessment has been most notable in the assessment for summative purposes of laboratory or "practical" work, not by the use of pencil-and-paper assessment of knowledge-about and knowledge-how-to, but by assessment of performance (Bednarski, 2003; DeTure, Fraser, Giddings, & Doran, 1995; Doran et al., 1993; Erickson & Meyer, 1998; Fairbrother, 1993; Gott, Welford, & Foulds, 1998; Harlen, 1999; Stefani & Tariq, 1996; Tariq, Stefani, Butcher, & Heylings, 1998). Critiques in the research of the use of performance assessments to assess investigative work include the influence of the always-present content and context in the assessment task (Harlen, 1999); the use of the visiting examiner when the classroom performance assessments are being done for national qualifications (Kennedy & Bennett, 2001); the need to select an investigation that could satisfy the assessment criteria, the perceived tension between the assessment and teaching roles of the teacher and the allocation of marks (Lubben & Ramsden, 1998); calls for caution when using performance-based assessments concerning the establishment of their validity and reliability (for example, Hattie & Jaeger, 1998; Shaw, 1997); the need to address "the psychometric findings that have highlighted the importance of effective scoring protocols, the judgments used in setting cut-offs and standards, and the importance of ensuring the construct representation of performance tests particularly given the costs and the hazards of construct under-representation of these tests" (Hattie & Jaeger, 1998); and a need to expand the current visions of performance assessment (Fusco & Barton, 2001) to include three ideals encompassed in critical, inclusive, feminist, and multicultural views of science education: that "performance/assessment addresses the value-laden decisions about what and whose science is learned and assessed and include multiple world-views, that performance assessment in science simultaneously emerges in response to local needs, and that the performance/assessment is a method as well as an ongoing search for method" (Fusco & Barton, 2001, p. 339).

RESEARCHING A WIDER RANGE
OF ASSESSMENT FORMATS

A second aspect of research on classroom assessment of science learning for summative purposes is research on the use of a wider range of assessment task formats, often called alternative assessments, including performance assessments, concept maps, portfolios, interviews including think-aloud protocols, learning stories, observational methods, dynamic assessment, self-assessment, and self-reports (Dori, 2003). The main rationale for widening the range of assessment tasks has been to match the means of generating assessment information with the learning outcomes, or standards, thereby increasing the validity; the wider range of learning goals being assessed requires different assessment tasks to maintain validity and to develop authentic assessments in that they are embedded in the teaching and learning and not disconnected with it. Hence, there has been an increased use of the terms "school-based," "alternative," "embedded," and "authentic" assessments (Dori, 2003), as well as "performance assessments," "problem-based assessments," and "competence-based assessments" under the general umbrella of "authentic assessments" (Cumming & Maxwell, 1999) to describe this wider range of assessment task formats. Their use has not been limited to the classroom; they are also included in nationwide assessments (Dori, 2003). Examples of the research on this wider range of assessment task formats are now discussed.

Concept Maps

Previous reviews of concept mapping as an assessment tool provide a valuable introduction to their use in the classroom assessment of science learning (Edmondson, 1999; Fisher, Wandersee, & Moody, 2000; White & Gunstone, 1992). Concept maps have been researched for use for assessment for diagnostic and formative purposes (for example, Treagust, 1995; Childers & Lowry, 1997; Tripp et al., 1997); as a research tool (for example, Wallace & Mintzes, 1990); and as a tool for assessment for summative purposes (for example, Barenholz & Tamir, 1992; Childers & Lowry, 1997; Kinchin, 2001; Liu & Hinchey, 1996; McClure, Sonak, & Suen, 1999; Mintzes et al., 1999; Rice, Ryan, & Samson, 1998; Roth & Roychoudhury, 1993; Ruiz-Primo & Shavelson, 1996a; Stoddart et al., 2000; Wilson, 1996). Ruiz-Primo and Shavelson (1996a) reviewed the literature on the use of concept maps in science assessment and described a concept map used as an assessment tool as: "(a) a task that elicits evidence bearing on a student's knowledge structure in a domain, (b) a format for the student's response, and (c) a scoring system by which the student's concept map can be evaluated accurately and consistently" (p. 569).

A concern raised in these studies is about the validity and reliability of the concept maps as assessment tools, and in particular the use of a scoring rubric and/or the comparison/correlation between concept map scores and those on conventional tests (Kinchin, 2001; Liu & Hinchey, 1996; McClure et al., 1999; Rye & Rubba, 2002; White & Gunstone, 1992). For example, Stoddart et al. (2000) documented the development and evaluation of concept mapping as an assessment tool for summative purposes. They document in some detail the development of a concept-mapping method for a specific learning activity, using a scoring rubric, which extracts quantitative information about the quality of understanding from each map in three stages: vocabulary review, content scoring, and a content validity check. Hence, they did not use measures of the elaborateness of the maps or the number of links and map components. The core of the rubric was based on three prepositional variables (accuracy, level of explanation, and complexity). Inter-rater agreement and inter-rater reliability found this concept-map scoring rubric to be reliable, valid, and practical.

Portfolios

Portfolios are another assessment task format in the trend toward more authentic assessment and are described as: "a container of collected evidence with a purpose. Evidence is documentation that can be used by one person or groups of persons to infer another person's knowledge, skill, and/or disposition" (Collins, 1992, p. 453). Other descriptions of portfolios may include that they contain a sample of student work, evidence of reflection and self-evaluation as this represents the students' understanding of the assessment criteria and where their achievements are in relation to these, the students' incremental development in their learning of science, and a rich and broad array of evidence of learning (Anderson & Bachor, 1998).

The issues for the teacher are what multiple goals for science learning are being assessed; what counts as evidence of learning—both the progress toward the goals and the achievement of the goals. What might the portfolios be used for? Weekly or yearly assessments? Reporting to parents, the school, or next year's teacher? (Collins, 1992). Other issues include the method of scoring, which needs to be commensurate with the degree of complexity and multifaceted nature of the assessment tasks and the learning. Although a score may not be appropriate to maintain this complexity, the school of state/national assessment system may require a single score or grade. Other ways of "scoring" need to be developed, such as holistic expert judgment.

Anderson and Bachor (1998), when reviewing the Canadian research on the use of portfolios, list the issues with the use of portfolios for assessment as the consistency of portfolio contents between students; the validity of the contents with respect to learning goals; the level of agreement between judges; the stability of estimates of student achievements; the rigor of standards; the reliability of scoring criteria and rubrics used in evaluating the contents of portfolios; the costs and feasibility of portfolio use; and the extent to which students are involved in making judgments, for example, in co-constructing the criteria, selection of the samples of work, and the application criteria in the marking process, in so-called learner-centered pedagogies and curricula. They also explain the fall in usage as students shift to higher grades on the increased subject specialization, larger student loads per teacher, and an increased focus on obtaining marks and grades for reporting student achievement to those outside the classroom. They report that rubrics are being used in two ways: the teacher selects, perhaps in conjunction with his or her students, the criteria to be used in evaluating the portfolio; and the students use the criteria to help them decide what to include in their portfolios. The notions of validity and reliability in the context of the use of portfolios for assessment of student achievement have been reexamined, and the questions asked about the meaning of these terms, once used for large-scale pen-and-paper testing and measurement, are still appropriate here. Are classroom validity and reliability different from those of large-scale testing?

The reported benefits of using portfolios in the literature include: "students taking more responsibility for their own learning by assessing their own work, learning and its assessment being viewed as a developmental process that occurs over extended time periods, and the encouragement of learning activities that are consistent with current notions of how people learn and what is worth learning" (Gitomer & Duschl, 1995, p. 299); a tool for changing instructional practice in fundamental ways (Duschl & Gitomer, 1997); "students . . . engaging in learning activities consistent with current psychological, historical, and sociological conceptions of growth of scientific knowledge . . . teaching is organized to encourage conceptual change, learners are active constructors of meaning . . . and assessment is an invaluable tool that teachers as well as students use to make instructional decisions" (Gitomer & Duschl, 1995); learners successfully organize and integrate newly acquired scientific knowledge; feel less anxious about learning physics; devote considerable time to reading and studying outside class; internalize and personalize the content material and enjoy the learning experience, although there may be no significant difference in learner achievement (Slater, Ryan, & Samson, 1997; Slater, 1997); there is more of a match with learner-centered curricula and pedagogies (Anderson & Bachor, 1998), especially when the learner is involved in the decision making about the identification of relevant learning outcomes, samples of student work and the marking; and portfolios have been used to document from the critical science perspective, a public story of science for community change with homeless youths (Fusco & Barton, 2001).

There is, however, little empirical evidence to support the use of portfolios (Gitomer & Duschl, 1998), and reliability and validity results may be disappointing (Cizek, 1997; Shapley & Bush, 1999). The questions being asked are, Can portfolios show evidence of complex scientific thinking in several domains? Is there any consistency of high performance over all pieces of work, that is, homogeneity?

Interviews and Conversations

Another assessment format is that of interview and conversations. Interviews have been used to assess for summative purposes (Bell, 1995) to elicit student thinking as to whether they have learned the intended science learning outcomes or to elicit what they have learned, whether intended or not. The interview-about-instances and interview-about-events format, initially developed for research purposes (Osborne & Gilbert, 1980), has been adapted for use in classrooms (Bell, Osborne, & Tasker, 1985). Likewise, (Griffard & Wandersee, 2001) used a think-aloud task to diagnose alternative conceptions of photosynthesis, in conjunction with a traditional pen-and-paper test. Lederman et al. (2002) documented research findings on the use of an open-ended instrument, the views of the Nature of Science Questionnaire, which in conjunction with individual interviews aims to provide meaningful assessments of students' nature of science views. They argued against mass assessments of large samples, aimed at describing or evaluating student beliefs using standardized forced-choice pencil-and-paper assessment instruments. Instead they argue for individual classroom interventions aimed at enhancing learners nature of science views and hence assessment for formative purposes.

Predict-and-Explain Situations

Another assessment task format is that of providing the students with a situation or phenomeona, about which they have to make a prediction, and give an explanation for what actually does happen (Lawrence & Pallrand, 2000; White & Gunstone, 1992). The prediction and explanation can provide information for assessment for summative purposes.

Learning Stories

Learning stories (Carr, 2001) have been developed for assessment for summative (as well as formative) purposes in an early childhood setting. Learning stories are described as

> structured observations in everyday or "authentic" settings, designed to provide a cu-
> mulative series of qualitative "snapshots" or written vignettes of individual children
> displaying one or more of the target learning dispositions. . . . Practitioners collect "crit-
> ical incidents" that highlight one or more of these dispositions and a series of learning
> stories over time, for a particular child, can be put together and scanned for what Carr
> has called "learning narratives": what we might call in the present context, "develop-
> mental trajectories" of learning dispositions. Children's stories are kept in a portfolio; of-
> ten they include photographs or photocopies of children's work and children's com-
> ments (Carr & Claxton, 2002, p. 22).

Observational Methods

Observations may be used in the classroom teaching and learning situation as a source of assessment information for formative and summative purposes. For example, (Leat & Nichols, 2000) used "mysteries" as an assessment tool for formative and diagnostic purposes with 13- and 14-year-old UK pupils.

Dynamic Assessments

Dynamic assessments (as distinct from static intelligence tests) have been used as assessment formats for summative purposes (Lidz, 1987). For example, the study of (Grigorenko & Sternberg, 1998) involved "the assessor setting 'examinees' a task too hard for them and observing how they respond and how they make use of standardised prompts and hints they are offered" (Carr & Claxton, 2002, p. 19). Dynamic assessments are linked theoretically to Vygotsky's notion of the Zone of Proximal Development and reportedly measure the "learning power" of the student, what the student is capable of generating through scaffolded interaction with the assessor. Dynamic assessments were also used to investigate students' mental models of chemical equilibrium and the resulting positive influence of tutoring in cognitive apprenticeship, such as coaching, modeling, scaffolding, articulation, reflection, and exploration (Chiu, Chou, & Liu, 2002).

Experimental and Customized Challenges

Experimental and customized challenges (e.g., jig-saws, problem situations; Norris, 1992) are also another way of eliciting assessment information for summative purposes.

Self and Peer Assessments

Self and peer assessments (Claxton, 1995; Gale, Martin, & McQueen, 2002; Stefani & Tariq, 1996; Taras, 2002; Wiediger & Hutchinson, 2002; Zoller, Fastow, Lubezky, & Tsaparlis, 1999) have also been used for assessment of science learning summative purposes and are often an integral component of other assessment task formats, for example, self-reports, journals, questionnaires, interviews, portfolios.

Group Assessment

Group assessment is the assessment of a group's collective learning rather than that of an individual. The use of group work in science education is increasing as the ability to work cooperatively as part of a team (research and development teams) to achieve a common goal is highly valued by employers in the science and technology sector, and is therefore included in the goals of some science curricula. It is also being advocated by the research into learning science from a sociocultural view point (Rogoff, 1990). Lowe and Fisher (2000), as part of doctoral research, studied the effect of year 9 and year 10 New Zealand students being in small cooperative groups, in which the students performed all their assignments, tests, laboratory work and fieldwork, on their motivation and attitudes toward science. "All members of the group received the same mark for any given assessment exercise and students were encouraged to communicate and work co-operatively during these activities" (p. 131). The protocol for group organization regarding assessment was as follows: "For written tests, students were arranged in their groups at the laboratory benches to allow them to work together with a minimum of contact with other groups. Talk within the group was permissible but talk between groups was not. Answers were by consensus and one group member had the task of writing the script, which was handled in and marked. All members received the same grade" (p. 133). The study reported that the students interviewed stated that "they preferred working in groups, especially during tests where they reported they felt they were learning from their peers even as they completed tests. The students stated that they felt less nervous when doing their tests since they were doing it with their friends" (p. 141). The teachers expressed some initial concern about group work mostly in relation to assessment; they reported positively on the formative purposes of the tests in groups; and they spent significantly less time carrying out assessment, particularly marking. No correlation data between group assessments and the usual individual assessments were reported, nor were any measures of the quality of the assessments.

Computer-Based Assessment

The use of computer technology to assess for summative purposes has been documented (Fisher et al., 2000). Sewell, Stevens, and Lewis (1995) used multimedia computer technology as a tool for teaching and assessing biological science with university students. They found a high rank correlation (0.96, Spearman's correlation) between the computer-based assessment of the knowledge base gained from the teaching program and the marks obtained in the sessional written examination.

In summary, alternatives to paper-and-pen testing formats have been developed and researched in science education. However, concerns about the use of a wider range of assessment tasks have been raised and include time constraints, financial constraints, teacher and student knowledge of assessment, the difficulty in creating authentic tasks, the quality of the wider range of tasks, especially validity and reliability (Lester, Lambdim, & Preston, 1997), and the need for professional development (Gitomer & Duschl, 1998; Ruiz-Primo & Shavelson, 1996b).

A parallel aspect of this trend to use alternative assessment tasks has been the trend to move from using norm-referenced and standardized, commercially made (by people external to the classroom) tests, to criterion-referenced, construct-referenced, or ipsative-referenced teacher-made assessments. Norm-referenced assessment is where individuals are compared with the norm of a group, indicating whether they can do something better or less well than others, and not what an individual can or cannot do. Criterion-referenced assessment compares a student's learning with a well-defined objective, that is, the desired learning goals. Ipsative assessment compares a student's performance with her or his previous performance, and construct-referenced assessment is that made within the context of the school and marked by teachers, of a particular idea or construct (Wiliam, 1992). Others have also noted that criterion-referenced assessment has tended to move away from overspecification toward a more holistic approach (Gipps, 1994a; Moss, 1992; Popham, 1987, 2003), allowing for the assessment of more complex skills and processes than can detailed ones. A disadvantage is that it can result in less reliability, but this can be addressed by the use of exemplars of student work at particular levels and group moderation (Gipps et al., 1995).

INCREASING THE QUALITY OF ASSESSMENTS

The sixth of the trends in assessment in science classrooms (and in other classrooms) has been research on the development of high-quality assessment procedures and is based in the debates of the shift from a paradigm of measurement and psychometric approaches based on true score theory (Black, 2001; Cumming & Maxwell, 1999) to a "new paradigm of assessment" (Gipps, 1994a). In educational assessment, quality is just not a technical issue, as assessment involves making and acting on choices and judgments, which are underpinned by social values (Messick, 1994; Berlak et al., 1992; (Gitomer & Duschl, 1998) and discourses of power (Cherryholmes, 1988). Assessment can be seen as a social practice determined by the specific social, historical, and political contexts in which they are undertaken (Gipps, 1999). Given today's social values, for example, on equity, and given the move from psychometric testing and measurement toward educational assessment, quality is no longer thought of in terms of the initial use of the terms *validity* and *reliability* as previously. The notion of quality in educational assessment has been developed to reflect the notions of assessment for educational purposes, that is, formative assessment (Cowie & Bell, 1996), embedded assessment (Treagust et al., 2001), authentic assessment (Cumming & Maxwell, 1999), holistic assessment (Wiliam, 1994), and the use of quality assessment terms such as *validity, equity, trustworthiness, fairness* (Gipps, 1998; Gipps & Murphy, 1994); *inference, generizablity, consequences, social values* (Gitomer & Duschl, 1998); *manageability, facility, discrimination* (Osborne & Ratcliffe, 2002); *reliability, dependability, validity, disclosure, fidelity* (Wiliam, 1992), *confidence* (Black, 1993), and *equity, trustworthiness*, and *appropriateness* (Cowie & Bell, 1996).

Reliability is only a small aspect of the dependability of a test, and therefore traditional statistical techniques of estimating reliability (test-retest, mark-remark, and parallel forms reliability and split-half reliability) are not relevant to classroom assessment of learning. Therefore other indicators of quality are of more use to classroom assessment (Wiliam, 1992).

A key indication of quality of educational assessments is that of validity. In the 1970s and 1980s, there was much criticism of the low validity of summative assessments used by teachers in classroom-based assessment (Doran et al., 1993) and in external testing and examinations, for example, for national qualifications (Gauld, 1980; Keeves & Alagumalai, 1998). The meaning of validity expanded as alternatives to pen-and-paper testing were developed (Crooks, Kane, & Cohen, 1996). Whereas reliability is affirmed by statistical means, validity relies "heavily on human judgment and is therefore harder to carry out, report and defend" (Crooks et al., 1996, p. 266). The initial meaning of validity as "measuring what it purports to measure" in relation to traditional multiple choice and pen-and-paper tests has been expanded as the notion of validity has been developed with respect to the quality of alternative assessments, such as performance assessment (Moss, 1992). Crooks et al. (1996) indicate the breadth of current understandings of validity and threats to the validity in their account of eight different stages of the assessment "chain" and the associated threats to validity. For Crooks et al. (1996) the validity of the entire assessment procedure is constrained by the strength of the weakest of the eight links in the validity chain.

Whereas some view an independence of validity and reliability in some circumstances (Moss, 1994), others see the two notions as interdependent (Crooks et al., 1996; Gitomer & Duschl, 1998), viewing some degree of generalizability (reliability) as essential for validity. For assessment for formative purposes, the validity of the assessments is more important than the reliability (Harlen & James, 1997; Moss, 1994). There is a tension, in devising assessment procedures, between local validity and beyond-local reliability (Carr, 2001; Carr & Claxton, 2002). Cumming & Maxwell (1999) argued for more attention to be given to authentic learning goals or objectives, teaching practices, and assessment tasks as interdependencies. Then "the validity of an assessment can be evaluated in terms of the extent to which the assessment relates to the ascribed educational values, learning theories and teaching theories as well as to the realisation of the desired assessment theory" (p. 193).

Recent studies on the reliability and validity of newly developed assessments of science learning include researching multiple-choice diagnostic instruments to assess high school students' understanding of inorganic chemistry qualitative analysis (Tan, Goh, Chia, & Treagust, 2002); student competence in conducting scientific inquiry (Zachos, Hick, Doane, & Sargent, 2000); ascertaining whether students have attained specific ideas in benchmarks and standards (Stern & Ahlgren, 2002); the sensitivity of close and proximal assessments to the changes in students' pre- and post-test performances (Ruiz-Primo, Shavelson, Hamilton, & Klein, 2002); multiple-choice and open-ended formats to assess students' understanding of protein synthesis (Pittman, 1999); alternative methods of answering and scoring multiple-choice tests (Taylor & Gardner, 1999); nature of science views (Lederman et al., 2002; Aikenhead, 1987; Taylor & Gardner, 1999); concept mapping (Stoddart et al., 2000; Liu & Hinchey, 1996; Ruiz-Primo & Shavelson, 1996a); time-series design in assessments (Lin & Frances, 1999); inconsistency in test grading by teachers of science (Klein, 2002); the use of distractor-driven multiple choice tests to assess children's conceptions (Sadler, 1998); the use of examinations to elicit "misconceptions" in college chemistry (Zoller, 1996); an assessment scheme for practical science in Hong Kong (Cheung, Hattie, Bucat, & Douglas, 1996); assessment tasks to assess the ideas and evidence—the processes and practices—of science, that is, how we know as well as what we know (Osborne & Ratcliffe, 2002); the use of rubrics (Osborne & Ratcliffe, 2002; Toth et al., 2002); the science achievement outcomes for different subgroups of students using different assessment formats (Lawrenz, Huffman, & Welch, 2001); and the quality of interviews as an assessment tool, in the classroom and in research (Welzel & Roth, 1998).

Researchers have argued that new forms of educational assessment (often called alternative assessments) cannot be fairly appraised unless the older definition of validity is broadened (Linn, Baker, & Dunbar, 1991). Research on the broader notion of quality of assessments of science learning includes those addressing consequences, equity, fairness, cultural validity, trustworthiness, appropriateness, manageability, fidelity, and authenticity. Each of these newer notions of quality is now discussed.

Consequences

Gitomer and Duschl (1998) argued that typically, the validity of assessments has been considered only in terms of *construct validity*—how well the evidence supports the interpretations made on the basis of the assessment. However, Messick (1989) raised the prominence of a second consideration of validity, the consequences of an assessment, that is, consequential validity, which is centrally important to assessment of formative purposes, given that the definition of formative assessment is based on the taking of action to improve learning (Black, 1993; Cowie & Bell, 1996; Crooks, 2001) and given that the appraisal is made in relation to its effectiveness in improving learning. In considering the concept of consequences, Cowie (2000) asserted that the consequences of formative assessment—cognitive, social, and emotional—cannot be separated out, and "therefore adequate and appropriate (valid) ways of generating, interpreting and responding to information gained from students and their learning, are those that benefit and not harm student learning, identity, feelings and relationships with others" (Cowie, 2000, p. 281).

Equity and Fairness

Equity is an important factor in considering the quality of an assessment and is associated with issues of moral and social justice (Darling-Hammond, 1994) and the equitable and inclusive practice and production of science, multiple worldviews, and science assessment across diversity (Fusco & Barton, 2001; Roth & McGinn, 1998). It implies practices and interpretation of results that are fair and just to all groups, and a definition of achievement which applies to all students, not just a subgroup (Gipps & Murphy, 1994); equal opportunity to sit and achieve within an exam (Wiliam, 1994); and providing opportunities for all students to participate in communication and particularly in the classroom interactions that are the heart of assessment for formative purposes (Cowie & Bell, 1996; Torrance, 1993; Crooks, 1988), even if different modes of communication and task formats have to be used (Kent, 1996; Lawrenz et al., 2001).

Fairness is an aspect of equity and validity. Students do not come to school with identical experiences, nor do they have identical experiences at school. Therefore, multiple opportunities for assessment might be needed to provide fairness and comparable treatment for all students in a class—students who will have differing educational experiences—to demonstrate their achievement if they are disadvantaged by any one assessment in a program (Gipps, 1998). The notion of fairness can be viewed as having three aspects: in the sense of assessing students on a fair basis, in the sense of not jeopardizing students' chances to learn the subject matter while they were being assessed, and in the sense of not depriving students of opportunities of receiving an all-around education (Yung, 2001). Equity and fairness may be in terms of gender (Gipps, 1998; Gipps & Murphy, 1994) or ethnicity (Darling-Hammond, 1994; Gipps, 1998; Lawrenz et al., 2001; Lee, 1999, 2001). The two main messages here are that where differences in performance are ignored and not monitored, patterns of inequality will increase, and that to ensure assessments are as fair as possible, we need to address the curriculum content (the constructs) being taught and assessed, teacher attitudes toward different groups of students, and the assessment mode and item format (Gipps, 1998).

Cultural Validity

Cultural validity has been suggested as an indication of quality in science assessment (Klein et al., 1997; Lokan, Adams, & Doig, 1999; Solano-Flores & Nelson-Barber, 2001). To attain cultural validity, development of the assessments must consider how the sociocultural context in which students live influences the ways in which they make sense of science items and the ways in which they solve them. These sociocultural influences include the values, beliefs, experiences, communication patterns, teaching and learning styles, and epistemologies inherent in the students' cultural backgrounds, as well as the socioeconomic conditions prevailing in their cultural groups. They contend that current approaches to handling student diversity in assessment (e.g., adapting or translating tests, providing assessment accommodations, estimating test cultural bias) are considered to be limited and lacking a sociocultural perspective. Solano-Flores and Nelson-Barber (2001) asserted that there are five aspects to cultural validity: "student epistemology, student language proficiency, cultural world views, cultural communication and socialization styles and student life context and values" (Solano-Flores & Nelson-Barber, 2001, p. 566).

Trustworthiness

Trustworthiness relates to whether something or someone can be trusted in the classroom setting and is based on the perceptions of both teachers and students and is an essential element of teaching, learning, and assessment, particularly formative assessment (Bell & Cowie, 1997; Cowie & Bell, 1996). Teachers must trust students to provide them with reasonably honest and representative information about their understandings and misunderstandings. Students must trust teachers to provide them with learning opportunities, to show interest in and support for their ideas and questions, to act on what they find out in good faith, and have faith and trust in the assessment practices. Trust in the relationship between a student and teacher in the practice of formative assessment also effects the disclosure by the students of what they know and can do (Cowie, 2000). Cowie stated that from a student perspective, a valid formative assessment is trustworthy, one in which students can have trust in the process as well as the person, where both support and the process do not undermine student understanding, affect, and relationships; give all students access to opportunities to participate in formative assessment; and encourage them to participate in and respond to formative feedback.

Appropriateness

To be judged appropriate by teachers and students, assessment must be beneficial and not harmful to student learning (Crooks, 1988). Hence, appropriate formative assessment, for example, is that which is first equitable and trustworthy but also supportive of learning (Black, 1995c), is indicative of what counts as learning (Crooks, 1988), is matching of the views of teaching and learning used in the classroom (Gipps, 1994a; Torrance, 1993), and addresses the importance of students' views and the ongoing interactive nature of the practice of assessment for formative purposes (Bell & Cowie, 1997; Cowie & Bell, 1996). Validity concerns are raised when students do not give the fullest responses they are capable of (Eley & Caygill, 2001, 2002; Gauld, 1980; Kent, 1996; Shaw, 1997).

Manageability

An aspect of quality that is of great concern for teachers is that of manageability, that the assessment can be managed within the busy classroom life of teachers and students, and not take time away from teaching and learning the set curriculum (McClure et al., 1999; Stoddart et al., 2000).

Fidelity and Disclosure

Wiliam (1992) identified two issues, disclosure and fidelity, which may limit the information teachers have to notice and recognize in interactive formative assessment. The disclosure of an assessment strategy is the extent to which it produces evidence of attainment (or nonattainment) from an individual in the area being assessed (Cowie & Bell, 1996). Wiliam (1992) defined *fidelity* as the extent to which evidence of attainment, which has been disclosed, is observed faithfully. He claimed that fidelity is undermined if evidence of attainment is disclosed but not observed.

For example, the teacher may not hear a small-group discussion in which the students demonstrate they understand a concept. Fidelity is also undermined if the evidence is observed but incorrectly interpreted. For example, if the teacher did not understand the student's thinking, it is possible that there is insufficient commonalty in the teacher and the students' thinking.

Authenticity

Another aspect of quality is that of authentic assessment (a term used mostly in the United States), for example (Brown, 1992; Kamen, 1996). It includes a construct of the teaching, learning, and assessment that is contextualized and meaningful for students; holistic rather than extremely specific (Erickson & Meyer, 1998); representative of activities actually done in out-of-school settings (Atkin et al., 2001); interacting with/in the world in informed, reflective, critical, and agentic ways (Fusco & Barton, 2001; Rodriguez, 1998); and includes authentic learning goals and including of performance assessments of complex tasks, problem-based assessments, and competence-based assessments (Cumming & Maxwell, 1999; Darling-Hammond, 1995; Darling-Hammond & Snyder, 2000; Doran et al., 1993). An assessment is authentic (and of sufficient quality) if the form and criteria for success are explicit and public; it involves collaboration (which is not seen as cheating); it is contextualized; it represents realistic and fair practices in the discipline; it uses scoring commensurate with the complexity and multifaceted nature of the assessments; it identifies strengths; it is multipurpose; it enables the integration of knowledge and skills learned from different sources; it is dynamic, as evidence can be added or removed during its development; and it encourages metacognition and reflection along with peer and self-evaluation (Collins, 1992; Wiggins, 1989). Concerns about authentic assessment include "camouflage," which Cumming and Maxwell (1999) describe as occurring "when a traditional form of assessment is 'dressed up' to appear authentic, often by the introduction of 'real world' elements or tokenism" (p. 188). The extra reading demands of the camouflage may not facilitate a solution and in fact may even add to the literacy demands of the task for some students. Another concern is that the assessment task will invariably be in a context, as will the teaching. If the context is familiar, it may be measuring only recall and comprehension, not higher order cognitive skills such as argumentation, that examine evidence critically. If the context is too unfamiliarand demands too high a level of literacy, the wording of the contextual information may be a distraction for students answering the question, add a reading comprehension problem, or confuse the students' interpretation of the demands of the assessment (Osborne & Ratcliffe, 2002; Eley & Caygill, 2001).

THEORIZING ASSESSMENT

A seventh trend in research and development in assessment of science classrooms (as of other classrooms) has been to consider pedagogy, learning, assessment, and curriculum together, rather than individually in an analytical, reductionist approach. Hence, a discussion on assessment cannot be divorced from a discussion of teaching and learning, or from its curriculum and political contexts (Carr et al., 2000). If teaching, learning, assessment, and curriculum are considered in an integrated and interdependent way, one might theorize them in similar ways, and therefore assessments should create a "learning environment in which students are engaging in learning activities consistent with current psychological, philosophical historical, and sociological conceptions of the growth of scientific knowledge" (Gitomer & Duschl, 1995, p. 300). This match/mismatch between theorizing, and between practices and theorizing is discussed by Bol and Strage (1996) and Hickey and Zuiker (2003).

As theorizing about learning and teaching has developed from a behaviorist to cognitive science to sociocultural views (Bell & Gilbert, 1996; Duit & Treagust, 1998), so too has theorizing of assessment.

For example, there has been the development of views of assessment to match the constructivist views of learning (Berlak et al., 1992; Gipps, 1994a; Wiliam, 1994), and a growing number of studies theorize assessment as a sociocultural practice (Bell & Cowie, 2001b; Broadfoot, 1996; Carr, 2001; Chiu et al., 2002; Filer, 1995; Filer, 2000; Filer & Pollard, 2000; Gipps, 1999; Keys, 1995; McGinn & Roth, 1998; Roth & McGinn, 1997; Welzel & Roth, 1998; Cowie, 2000; Fusco & Barton, 2001; Hickey & Zuiker, 2003; Pryor & Torrance, 2000; Solano-Flores & Nelson-Barber, 2001; Torrance & Pryor, 1998), and with discursive, post-structuralist theorizing (Bell, 2000; Fusco & Barton, 2001; Gipps, 1999; Sarf, 1998; Torrance, 2000). As Berlak (2000) stated, "there is an overwhelming body of research conducted over the last two decades documenting that, beyond a shadow of a doubt, that the school context, the particularities of its history, the immediate and wider socio-economic context, the language, the race and social class of the students and their families, and the culture of the school itself have an enormous bearing students' interest in and performance on all school tasks, including taking standardised test, and examinations" (p. 193). To view assessment as a sociocultural practice is to view it as value laden, socially constructed, and historically, socially, and politically situated. That is, one can never do assessment separate from one's own history (individual or social) or outside of its contexts. As Gipps (1999) said, "to see assessment as a scientific, objective activity is mistaken; assessment is not an exact science" (p. 370). Assessment may be viewed as a purposeful, intentional, responsive activity involving meaning making and giving feedback to students and teachers, to improve learning; an integral part of teaching and learning; a situated and contextualized activity; a partnership between teacher and students; and involving the use of language to communicate meaning (Bell, 2000; Bell & Cowie, 2001b).

Theorizing assessment as a sociocultural practice raises several issues for researchers. One is the issue of whose theorizing and the purpose of the theorizing (Bell, 2000; Bell & Cowie, 2001b, 2001c; Torrance & Pryor, 1998, 2001). In both of these major research studies, the teachers and university researchers involved have been encouraged to theorize their own assessment practices and to develop classroom practice models, using their own shared vocabulary. This theorizing was identified by the teachers as an important aspect of their teacher development practices. Another is the unit of analysis, which is "the *event*, rather than the individual is the primary unit of analysis for evaluating learning environments from a socio-cultural perspective. . . . The key issue in studying innovative curricula is the knowledge practices in which learners collectively participate" (Hickey & Zuiker, 2003, p. 548). This is evident in the use of cameos (Bell & Cowie, 1997, 2001b) and "incidents" (Torrance & Pryor, 1998) in research on formative assessment.

If assessment is theorized in terms of a sociocultural view of mind, the implications (Gipps, 1999) include that assessment can only be fully understood if the social, cultural, and political contexts in the classroom are taken into account; the practices of assessment reflect the values, culture of the classroom, and, in particular, those of the teacher; assessment is a social practice, constructed within social and cultural norms of the classroom; what is assessed is what is socially and culturally valued; the cultural and social knowledge of the teacher and students will mediate their responses to assessment; assessments are value-laden and socially constructed; a distinction needs to be made between what a student can typically do (without mediational tools) and best performance (with the use of mediational tools); assessments need to give feedback to students on the assessment process itself to enable them to do self and peer formative assessment; and teachers and students need to negotiate the process of assessment to be used, the criteria for achievement, and what counts as acceptable knowledge.

FURTHER RESEARCH ON CLASSROOM ASSESSMENT OF SCIENCE LEARNING

Despite the wealth of research reviewed in this chapter, there are many opportunities for further research, including professional development, pre- and inservice, higher education for teachers of science on classroom assessment of science learning (Bell & Cowie, 2001c; Campbell & Evans, 2000; Higgins, Hartley, & Skelton, 2002; Yorke, 2003); online teaching and assessment, especially that using web-based sites (Buchanan, 2000; Peat & Franklin, 2002), where feedback and feedforward are given to students without face-to-face contact; group assessment (Black, 2001); students' views of assessment practices, as well as teaching practices; and a critique of the research paradigms and methods used to date, including action research, case studies, cameos, incidents, classroom observations, interviews, pre- and post-testing; the progression in students' learning and how this research findings might be used in assessment for formative and summative purposes (Osborne & Ratcliffe, 2002); the quality of assessment for summative purposes, given the trend from normative to criterion, construct and ipsative referenced assessment; and the interaction between classroom assessments for formative and summative purposes.

Further research on the quality of assessments will continue as new assessment task formats are developed, particularly on the effect of context on performance and construct validity (Gipps, 1998).

ACKNOWLEDGMENTS

Thanks to Audrey Champagne and John Pryor, who reviewed this chapter.

REFERENCES

Aikenhead, G. (1987). *Views on science-technology-society (question book and Canadian standard responses)*. Saskatchewan: Department of Curriculum Studies, University of Saskatchewan.

Allal, L. (2002). The assessment of learning dispositions in the classroom. *Assessment in Education, 9*(1), 55.

Allal, L., & Ducrey, G. P. (2000). Assessment of—or in—the zone of proximal development. *Learning and Instruction, 10*(2), 137–152.

Anderson, J. O., & Bachor, D. (1998). A Canadian perspective on portfolio use in student assessment. *Assessment in Education, 5*(3), 327, 353.

Apple, M. (1982). *Education and power*. Boston: Routledge & Kegan Paul.

Apple, M. (1996). *Cultural politics and power*. Buckingham, UK: Open University Press.

Ash, D., & Levitt, K. (2003). Working within the zone of proximal development: Formative assessment as professional development. *Journal of Science Teacher Education, 14*(1), 23.

Assessment Reform Group. (1999). *Assessment for learning: beyond the black box*. Cambridge, UK: University of Cambridge.

Atkin, J. M., Black, P., Coffey, J., & National Research Council (U.S.). Committee on Classroom Assessment and the National Science Education Standards. (2001). *Classroom assessment and the National Science Education Standards*. Washington, DC: Center for Education National Research Council, National Academy Press.

Atkin, M. (2002). How science teachers lose power. *Studies in Science Education, 37*, 163–171.

Baird, J., & Northfield, J. (Eds.). (1992). *Learning from the PEEL experience*. Melbourne, Australia: Monash University.

Barenholz, H., & Tamir, P. (1992). A comprehensive use of concept mapping in design, instruction and assessment. *Research in Science and Technology Education, 10*, 37–52.

Barker, M., & Carr, M. (1989). Teaching and learning about photosynthesis. Part 1: an assessment in terms of students prior knowledge. *International Journal of Science Education, 11*(1), 49–56.

Bednarski, M. (2003). Assessing performance tasks. *The Science Teacher, 70*(4), 34.

Bell, B. (1995). Interviewing: a technique for assessing science knowledge. In R. Duit (Ed.), *Learning science in the schools: Research reforming practice*. Mahwah, NJ: Lawrence Erlbaum Associates.

Bell, B. (2000). Formative assessment and science education: modelling and theorising. In R. Miller, J. Leach, J. Osborne (Eds.), *Improving science education: the contribution of research*. Buckingham, UK: Open University Press.

Bell, B., & Cowie, B. (1997). *Formative assessment and science education: Research report of the Learning in Science Project (Assessment)*. Hamilton, New Zealand: Centre for Science Mathematics Technology Education Research, University of Waikato.

Bell, B., & Cowie, B. (1999). Researching teachers doing formative assessment. In J. Loughran (Ed.), *Researching teaching*. London: Falmer Press.

Bell, B., & Cowie, B. (2001a). The characteristics of formative assessment in science education. *Science Education, 85*(5), 536–553.

Bell, B., & Cowie, B. (2001b). *Formative assessment and science education*. Dordrecht and Boston: Kluwer Academic.

Bell, B., & Cowie, B. (2001c). Teacher development and formative assessment. *Waikato Journal of Education, 7*, 37–50.

Bell, B., & Gilbert, J. (1996). Views of learning to underpin teacher development. In *Teacher development: A model from science education* (pp. 38–69). London: Falmer Press.

Bell, B., Jones, A., & Carr, M. (1995). The development of the recent national New Zealand Science Curriculum. *Studies in Science Education, 26*.

Bell, B. F., Osborne, R., & Tasker, R. (1985). Finding out what children think. In P. Freyberg (Ed.), *Learning in science: the implications of children's science*. Auckland, New Zealand: Heinemann.

Berlak, H. (2000). Cultural politics, the science of assessment and democratic renewal of public education. In A. Filer (Ed.), *Assessment: social practice and social product*. London: Routledge-Falmer.

Berlak, H., Newmann, E., Adams, E., Archbald, D., Burgess, T., Raven, J., et al. (Eds.). (1992). *Toward a New Science of Educational Testing and Assessment*. Albany: State University of New York Press.

Biddulph, F. (1989). *Children's questions; their place in primary science education*. Unpublished D.Phil. thesis, University of Waikato, Hamilton.

Biggs, J. (1998). Assessment and classroom learning: A role for summative assessment? *Assessment in Education, 5*(5), 103–110.

Black, P. (1993). Formative and summative assessment by teachers. *Studies in Science Education, 21*, 49–97.

Black, P. (1995a). 1987–1995—The struggle to formulate a national science curriculum for science in England and Wales. *Studies in Science Education, 26*, 159–188.

Black, P. (1995b). Assessment and feedback in science education. *Studies in Educational Evaluation, 21*(3), 257.

Black, P. (1995c). Can teachers use assessment to improve learning? *British Journal of Curriculum and Assessment, 5*(2), 7–11.

Black, P. (1995d). Curriculum and assessment in science education: The policy interface. *International Journal of Science Education, 17*, 453.

Black, P. (1998a). Assessment by teachers and the improvement of students' learning. In K. Tobin (Ed.), *International handbook of science education* (pp. 811–822). London: Kluwer Academic.

Black, P. (1998b). Learning, league tables and national assessment: Opportunity lost or hope deferred? *Oxford Review of Education, 24*(1), 57–68.

Black, P. (2000). Research and the development of educational assessment. *Oxford Review of Education, 26*(3–4), 407–419.

Black, P. (2001). Dreams, strategies and systems: portraits of assessment past, present and future. *Assessment in Education, 8*(1), 65–85.

Black, P. (2002). *Report to the Qualifications Development Group, Ministry of Education, New Zealand, on the proposals for development of the National Certificate of Educational Achievement*. London: King's College London.

Black, P., & Harrison, C. (2001a). Feedback in questioning and marking: the science teacher's role in formative assessment. *School Science Review, 82*(301), 55–61.

Black, P., & Harrison, C. (2001b). Self- and peer-assessment and taking responsibility. *School Science Review, 83*(302).

Black, P., & Wiliam, D. (1998a). Assessment and classroom learning. *Assessment in Education, 5*(1), 7–74.

Black, P., & Wiliam, D. (1998b). Inside the black box—Raising standards through classroom assessment. *Phi Delta Kappan, 80*(2), 139.

Bol, L., & Strage, A. (1996). The contradictions between teachers' instructional goals and their assessment practices in high school biology courses. *Science Education, 80*(2), 145–163.

Broadfoot, P. (1996). *Education, assessment and society*. Buckingham, UK: Open University Press.

Broadfoot, P. (2002). Editorial. Dynamic versus arbitrary standards: recognising the human factor in assessment. *Assessment in Education, 9*(2), 157–159.

Brookhart, S. M. (2001). Successful students' formative and summative uses of assessment information. *Assessment in Education, 8*(2), 153–169.

Brown, R. (Ed.). (1992). *Authentic assessment: A collection*. Melbourne: Hawker Brownlow Education.

Buchan, A., & Welford, G. (1994). Policy into practice: the effects of practical assessment on the teaching of science. *Research in Science & Technological Education, 12*(1), 21, 29.

Buchanan, T. (2000). The efficacy of a World-Wide Web mediated formative assessment. *Journal of Computer Assisted Learning, 16*(3), 193–200.

Butler, J. (1995). Teachers judging standards in senior science subjects: Fifteen years of the Queensland Experiment. *Studies in Science Education, 26*, 135–157.

Campbell, C., & Evans, J. A. (2000). Investigation of preservice teachers' classroom assessment practices during student teaching. *Journal of Educational Research, 93*(6), 350–355.

Carr, M. (2001). *Assessment in early childhood: Learning stories in learning places*. London: Paul Chapman.

Carr, M., & Claxton, G. (2002). Tracking the development of learning dispositions. *Assessment in Education, 9*(9), 9–37.

Carr, M., McGee, C., Jones, A., McKinley, E., Bell, B., Barr, H., et al. (2000). *Strategic research: Initiative literature review: The effects of curricula and assessment on pedagogical approaches and on educational outcomes*. Wellington, New Zealand: Ministry of Education.

Cheng, M. H., & Cheung, F. W. M. (2001). Science and biology assessment in relation to the recently proposed education reform in Hong Kong. *Journal of Biological Education, 35*(4), 170.

Cherryholmes, C. (1988). Construct validity and discourses of research. *American Journal of Education, 96*, 421–457.

Cheung, D., Hattie, J., Bucat, R., & Douglas, G. (1996). Measuring the degree of implementation of school-based assessment schemes for practical science. *Research in Science Education, 26*(4), 375–389.

Childers, P. B., & Lowry, M. (1997). Engaging students through formative assessment in science. *The Clearing House, 71*(2), 97.

Chiu, M.-H., Chou, C.-C., & Liu, C.-J. (2002). Dynamic processes of conceptual change: Analysis of constructing mental models of chemical equilibrium. *Journal of Research in Science Teaching, 39*(8), 688.

Cizek, G. J. (1997). Learning, achievement and assessment: constructs at the crossroads. In G. D. Phye (Ed.), *Handbook of classroom assessment: learning, adjustment and achievement*. San Diego: Academic Press.

Clarke, S. (1998). *Targeting assessment in the primary classroom*. London: Hodder & Stoughton.

Clarke, S., Timperley, H., & Hattie, J. (2003). *Unlocking formative assessment: practical strategies for enhancing students' lerning in the primary and intermediate classroom. New Zealand version.* Auckland: Hodder Moa Beckett.

Claxton, G. (1995). What kind of learning does self-assessment drive? *Assessment in Education, 2*(3), 335, 339.

Codd, J., McAlpine, D., & Poskitt, J. (1995). Assessment policies in New Zealand: Educational reform or political agenda. In B. Tuck (Ed.), *Setting the standards*. Palmerston North, New Zealand: Dunmore Press.

Collins, A. (1992). Portfolios for science education: Issues in purpose, structure, and authenticity. *Science Education, 76*(4), 451.

Collins, A. (1995). National Science Education Standards in the United States: A process and a product. *Studies in Science Education, 26*, 7–37.

Collins, A. (1998). National science education standards: A political document. *Journal of Research in Science Teaching, 35*(7), 711.

Cowie, B. (1997). Formative assessment and science classrooms. In B. a. B. Bell (Ed.), *Developing the science curriculum in Aotearoa New Zealand*. Auckland: Addison Wesley Longman.

Cowie, B. (2000). *Formative assessment in science classrooms*. Unpublished Ph.D. thesis, University of Waikato, Hamilton, New Zealand.

Cowie, B., & Bell, B. (1996). *Validity and formative assessment in the classroom*. Paper presented at the International Symposium on Validity in Educational Assessment, University of Otago, Dunedin, New Zealand, June 28–30, 1996.

Cowie, B., & Bell, B. (1999). A model of formative assessment in science education. *Assessment in Education, 6*(1), 102–116.

Crooks, T. (1988). The impact of classroom evaluation practices on students. *Review of Educational Research, 58*(4), 438–481.

Crooks, T. (2001). *The validity of formative assessments*. Paper presented at the paper presented to the Annual Meeting of the British Educational Research Association, Leeds, UK, September 13–15, 2001.

Crooks, T. (2002a). *Assessment, accountability and achievement—Principles, possibilities and pitfalls*. Paper presented at the annual conference of the New Zealand Association for Research in Education, Palmerston North, New Zealand, December 5–8, 2002.

Crooks, T. (2002b). Educational assessment in New Zealand schools. *Assessment in Education, 9*(2), 217, 237.

Crooks, T., & Flockton, L. (1996). *National Education Monitoring Report 1: Science assessment results 1995*. Dunedin, New Zealand: Educational Assessment Research Unit, University of Otago.

Crooks, T., Kane, M., & Cohen, A. (1996). Threats to the valid use of assessments. *Assessment in Education, 3*(3), 265–285.

Cumming, J., & Maxwell, G. (1999). Contextualising authentic assessment. *Assessment in Education, 6*(2), 177–194.

Darling-Hammond, L. (1994). Performance-based assessment and educational equity. *Harvard Educational Review, 64*(1), 5–30.

Darling-Hammond, L. (1995). *Authentic assessment in action.* New York: Teachers' College Press.

Darling-Hammond, L., & Snyder, J. (2000). Authentic assessment of teaching in context. *Teaching and Teacher Education, 16*(5–6), 523–545.

Daws, N., & Singh, B. (1996). Formative assessment: to what extent is its potential to enhance student learning being relaised? *School Science Review, 77*(281), 93–100.

Deese, W. C., Ramsey, L. L., Walczyk, J., & Eddy, D. (2000). Using demonstration assessments to improve learning. *Journal of Chemical Education, 77*(11), 1511.

Delpit, L. (1995). *Other people's children: Cultural conflict in the classroom.* New York: The New Press.

DeTure, L., Fraser, B. J., Giddings, J., & Doran, R. L. (1995). Assessment and investigation of science laboratory skills among year 5 students. *Research in Science Education, 25*(3), 253–266.

Donnelly, J. F., & Jenkins, E. W. (2001). *Science education. Policy, professionalism and change.* London: Paul Chapman.

Doran, R. L., Lawrenz, F., & Helgeson, S. (1993). Research on assessment in science. In D. Gabel (Ed.), *Handbook of research in science teaching and learning* (pp. 388–442). New York: Macmillan.

Dori, Y. (2003). From nationwide standardised testing to school-based alternative embedded assessment in Israel: Students' performance in the Matriculation 2000 Project. *Journal of Research in Science Teaching, 40*(1), 34–52.

Driver, R., Squires, A., Rushworth, P., & Wood-Robinson, V. (1994). *Making sense of secondary science: Research into children's ideas.* London: Routledge.

Duit, R., & Treagust, D. F. (1998). Learning in science—From behaviorism towards social constructivism and beyond. In K. Tobin (Ed.), *International handbook of science education.* Dordrecht, the Netherlands: Kluwer Academic.

Duschl, R., & Gitomer, D. H. (1997). Strategies and challenges to changing the focus of assessment and instruction in science classrooms. *Educational Assessment, 4,* 37–73.

Edmondson, K. (1999). Assessing science understanding through concept maps. In J. Novak (Ed.), *Assessing science understanding: a human constructivist view.* San Diego: Academic Press.

Eisner, E. (1985). *The educational imagination: On the design and evaluation of school programs.* New York: Macmillan.

Eisner, E. (1993). Reshaping assessment in education: some criteria in search of practice. *Journal of Curriculum Studies, 25,* 219–233.

Eley, L., & Caygill, R. (2001). Making the most of testing: Examination of different assessment formats. *SET: Research Information for Teachers, 2,* 20–23.

Eley, L., & Caygill, R. (2002). One test fits all? An examination of differing assessment task formats. *New Zealand Journal of Educational Studies, 37*(1), 27–38.

Enger, S. K., & Yager, R. (1998). *The Iowa assessment handbook.* Iowa City: Science Education Center, University of Iowa.

Erickson, G., & Meyer, K. (1998). Performance assessment tasks in science: What are they measuring? In K. Tobin (Ed.), *International handbook of science education.* London: Kluwer Academic.

Fairbrother, B. (1993). Problems in the assessment of scientific skills. In D. West (Ed.), *Teaching, learning and assessment in science education.* London: Paul Chapman.

Fairbrother, B., Black, P., & Gill, P. (Eds.). (1995). *Teachers assessing pupils.* London: Association of Science Education.

Feltham, N. F., & Downs, C. T. (2002). Three forms of assessment of prior knowledge, and improved performance following an enrichment programme, of English second language biology students within the context of a marine theme. *International Journal of Science Education, 24*(2), 157–184.

Filer, A. (1995). Teacher Assessment: social process and social product. *Assessment in Education, 2*(1).

Filer, A. (Ed.). (2000). *Assessment: social practice and social product.* London: RoutledgeFalmer.

Filer, A., & Pollard, A. (2000). *The social world of pupil assessment: Processes and contexts of primary schooling.* London: Continuum.

Fisher, K., Wandersee, J. H., & Moody, D. (2000). *Mapping biology knowledge*. Dordrecht, the Netherlands: Kluwer Academic.

Francisco, J. S., Nakhleh, M. B., Nurrenbern, S. C., & Miller, M. L. (2002). Assessing student understanding of general chemistry with concept mapping. *Journal of Chemical Education, 79*(2), 248.

Frederiksen, J., & White, B. (1997). *Reflective assessment of students' research within an inquiry-based middle school science curriculum*. Paper presented at the annual meeting of the AERA, Chicago.

Fusco, D., & Barton, A. C. (2001). Representing student achievements in science. *Journal of Research in Science Teaching, 38*(3), 337–354.

Gale, K., Martin, K., & McQueen, G. (2002). Triadic assessment. *Assessment and Evaluation in Higher Education, 27*, 557–567.

Gauld, C. (1980). Subject orientated test construction. *Research in Science Education, 10*, 77–82.

Gilmore, A. (2002). Large-scale assessment and teachers' assessment capacity: Learning opportunities for teachers in the National Monitoring Project in New Zealand. *Assessment in Education, 9*(3), 319.

Gilmore, A., & Hattie, J. (2001). Understanding usage of an Internet based information resource for teachers: The assessment resource banks. *New Zealand Journal of Educational Studies, 36*(2), 237–257.

Gipps, C. (1994a) *Beyond testing: Towards a theory of educational assessment*. London: The Falmer Press.

Gipps, C. (1994b). Developments in educational assessment or what makes a good test? *Assessment in Education, 1*(3).

Gipps, C. (1998). *Equity in education and assessment*. Paper presented at the annual conference of the New Zealand Association for Research in Education, Dunedin, December 1998.

Gipps, C. (1999). Socio-cultural aspects of assessment. *Review of Research in Education, 24*, 355–392.

Gipps, C., Brown, M., Mccallum, B., & McAlister, S. (1995). *Intuition or evidence?* Buckingham, UK: Open University Press.

Gipps, C., & James, M. (1998). Broadening the basis of assessment to prevent the narrowing of learning. *The Curriculum Journal, 9*(3), 285–297.

Gipps, C., & Murphy, P. (1994). *A fair test?* Buckingham, UK: Open University Press.

Gipps, C., & Tunstall, P. (1996a). "How does your teacher help you to make your work better?" Children's understanding of formative assessment. *Curriculum Journal, 7*(2), 185–203.

Gipps, C., & Tunstall, P. (1996b). Teacher feedback to young children in formative assessment: A typology. *British Educational Research Journal, 22*(4), 389–404.

Gitomer, D. H., & Duschl, R. (1995). Moving towards a portfolio culture in science education. In R. Duit (Ed.), *Learning science in schools: Research reforming practice*. Hillsdale, NJ: Lawrence Erlbaum Associates.

Gitomer, D. H., & Duschl, R. (1998). Emerging issues and practices in science assessment. In K. Tobin (Ed.), *International handbook of science education*. London: Kluwer Academic.

Glover, P., & Thomas, R. (1999). Coming to grips with continuous assessment. *Assessment in Education, 6*(1), 111, 117.

Gott, R., Welford, G., & Foulds, K. (1998). *The assessment of practical work in science*. Oxford: Blackwell.

Griffard, P. B., & Wandersee, J. H. (2001). The two-tier instrument on photosynthesis: What does it diagnose? *International Journal of Science Education, 23*(10), 1039–1052.

Grigorenko, E. L., & Sternberg, R. J. (1998). Dynamic testing. *Psychological Bulletin, 124*(1), 75–111.

Han, J.-J. (1995). The quest for national standards in science education in Korea. *Studies in Science Education, 26*, 59–71.

Harlen, W. (1995a). Standards and science education in Scottish schools. *Studies in Science Education, 26*, 107–134.

Harlen, W. (1995b). To the rescue of formative assessment. *Primary Science Review, 37*, 14–16.

Harlen, W. (1998). *Classroom assessment: A dimension of purposes and procedures*. Paper presented at the annual conference of the New Zealand Association of Educational Research, Dunedin, December 1998.

Harlen, W. (1999). Purposes and procedures for assessing science process skills. *Assessment in Education, 6*(1), 129.

Harlen, W., & James, M. (1997). Assessment and learning. *Assessment in Education, 4*(3), 365.

Hattie, J. (1999). *Influences on student learning.* Paper presented at the Inaugural Professorial lecture, University of Auckland. Retrieved 1 August 2003 from http://www.arts.auckland.ac.nz/edu/staff/jhattie/Inaugural.html.

Hattie, J., Biggs, J., & Purdie, N. (1996). Effects of learning skills interventions on student learning: A meta-analysis. *Review of Educational Research, 66,* 99–136.

Hattie, J., & Jaeger, R. (1998). Assessment and classroom learning: a deductive approach. *Assessment in Education, 5*(5), 111.

Heady, J. E. (2001). Gauging students' learning in the classroom. *Journal of College Science Teaching, 31*(3), 157.

Hickey, D. T., & Zuiker, S. J. (2003). A new perspective for evaluating innovative science programs. *Science Education, 87*(4), 539–563.

Higgins, R., Hartley, P., & Skelton, A. (2002). The conscientious consumer: Reconsidering the role of assessment feedback in student learning. *Studies in Higher Education, 27*(1), 53–64.

Hill, M. (1999). Assessment in self-managing schools: Primary teachers balancing learning and accountability demands in the 1990s. *New Zealand Journal of Educational Studies, 34*(1), 176–185.

Hill, M. (2001). Dot, slash, cross: How assessment can drive teachers to ticking instead of teaching. *SET: Research information for teachers, 1,* 21–25.

Hunt, E., & Pellegrino, J. (2002). Issues, examples, and challenges of formative assessment. *New Directions for Teaching & Learning, 89,* 73.

Jaworski, B. (1994). *Investigating mathematics teaching: A constructivist enquiry.* London: The Falmer Press.

Johnston, P., Guice, S., Baker, K., Malone, J., & Michelson, N. (1995). Assessment of teaching and learning in "literature-based" classrooms. *Teaching and Teacher Education, 11*(4), 359–371.

Jones, A., Cowie, B., & Moreland, J. (2003). *Enhancing formative interactions in science and technology: a synthesis of teacher student perspectives.* Paper presented at the NARST Annual Conference, Philadelphia, March 23–26, 2003.

Kamen, M. (1996). A teacher's implementation of authentic assessment in an elementary science classroom. *Journal of Research in Science Teaching, 33*(8), 859–877.

Keeves, J., & Alagumalai, S. (1998). Advances in measurement in science education. In K. Tobin (Ed.), *International handbook of science education.* London: Kluwer Academic.

Keiler, L., & Woolnough, B. (2002). Practical work in school science: The dominance of assessment. *School Science Review, 83*(304), 83–88.

Kennedy, D., & Bennett, J. (2001). Practical work at the upper high school level: The evaluation of a new model of assessment. *International Journal of Science Education, 23*(1), 97–110.

Kent, L. (1996). *How shall we know them? Comparison of Maori student responses for written and oral assessment tasks.* Unpublished M.Ed. thesis, University of Waikato, Hamilton, New Zealand.

Keys, C. W. (1995). An interpretive study of students' use of scientific reasoning during a collaborative report writing intervention in ninth grade general science. *Science Education, 79*(4), 415.

Kinchin, I. M. (2001). If concept mapping is so helpful to learning biology, why aren't we all doing it? *International Journal of Science Education, 23*(12), 1257–1269.

Klein, J. (2002). The failure of a decision support system: Inconsistency in test grading by teachers. *Teaching and Teacher Education, 18*(8), 1023.

Klein, S., Jovanovic, J., Stecher, B., McCaffrey, D., Shavelson, R., Haertel, E., et al. (1997). Gender and racial/ethnic differences on performance assessments in science. *Educational Evaluation and Policy Analysis, 19,* 83–97.

Lawrence, M., & Pallrand, G. (2000). A case study of the effectiveness of teacher experience in the use of explanation-based assessment in high school physics. *School Science and Mathematics, 100*(1), 36.

Lawrenz, F., Huffman, D., & Welch, W. (2001). The science achievement of various subgroups on alternative assessment formats. *Science Education, 85*(3), 279–290.

Leat, D., & Nichols, A. (2000). Brains on the table: Diagnostic and formative assessment through obsevation. *Assessment in Education, 7*(1), 103.

Lederman, N. G., Abd-El-Khalick, F., Bell, R. L., & Schwartz, R. S. (2002). Views of nature of science questionnaire: Toward valid and meaningful assessment of learners' conceptions of nature of science. *Journal of Research in Science Teaching, 39*(6), 497–521.

Lee, O. (1999). Equity implications based on the conceptions of science achievement in major reform documents. *Review of Educational Research, 69*(1), 83.

Lee, O. (2001). Culture and language in science education: what do we know and what do we need to know? *Journal of Research in Science Teaching, 38*(5), 499.

Lester, F., Lambdim, D., & Preston, R. (1997). A new vision of the nature and purposes of assessment in the mathematics classroom. In G. D. Phye (Ed.), *Handbook of classroom assessment: learning, adjustment and achievement.* San Diego: Academic Press.

Lidz, C. S. (1987). *Dynamic assessment: An interactional approach to evaluating learning potential.* New York: Guilford Press.

Lin, H. S., & Frances, L. (1999). Using time-series design in the assessment of teaching effectiveness. *Science Education, 83*(4), 409.

Linn, R. L., Baker, E., & Dunbar, S. (1991). Complex, peformance-based assessment: expectations and validity criteria. *Education Researcher, 20,* 15–21.

Liu, X., & Hinchey, M. (1996). The internal consistency of a concept mapping scoring scheme and its effect on prediction validity. *International Journal of Science Education, 18*(8), 921–937.

Lokan, J., Adams, R., & Doig, B. (1999). Broadening assessment, improving fairness? Some examples from school science. *Assessment in Education, 6*(1), 83.

Lorsbach, A., Tobin, K., Briscoe, C., & LaMaster, S. (1992). An interpretation of assessment methods in middle school science. *International Journal of Science Education, 14,* 305–317.

Lowe, P., & Fisher, D. L. (2000). Peer power: The effect of group work and assessment on student attitudes in science. *SAMEpapers 2000,* 129–147.

Lubben, F., & Ramsden, J. B. (1998). Assessing pre-university students through extended individual investigations: teachers' and examiners' views. *International Journal of Science Education, 20*(7), 833–848.

Marston, C., & Croft, C. (1999). What do students know in science? Analysis of data from the assessment resource banks. *SET: Research Information for Teachers, 12*(2), 1–4.

Mavrommatis, Y. (1997). Understanding assessment in the classroom: Phases of the assessment process—the assessment episode. *Assessment in Education, 4*(3), 381.

Mawhinney, H. B. (1998). Patterns of social control in assessment practices in Canadian frameworks for accountability in education. *Educational Policy, 12*(1–2), 98–109.

McClure, J. R., Sonak, B., & Suen, H. K. (1999). Concept map assessment of classroom learning: Reliability, validity, and logistical practicality. *Journal of Research in Science Teaching, 36*(4), 475–492.

McGinn, M. K., & Roth, W. M. (1998). Assessing students' understanding about levers: Better test instruments are not enough. *International Journal of Science Education, 20*(7), 813–832.

Messick, S. (1989). Validity. In R. L. Linn (Ed.), *Educational measurement in education.* Washington, DC: American Council on Education and National Council on Measurement in Education.

Messick, S. (1994). The interplay of evidence and consequences in the validation of performance assessment. *Educational Researcher, 23*(2), 13–23.

Ministry of Education. (1993). *The New Zealand curriculum framework.* Wellington: Learning Media.

Ministry of Education. (2003). *Assessment exemplars.* Wellington, NZ: Ministry of Education. Retrieved from http://www.tki.org.nz/e/community/ncea/

Mintzes, J., Wandersee, J. H., & Novak, J. (Eds.). (1999). *Assessing science understanding: A human constructivist view.* San Diego: Academic Press.

Mintzes, J., Wandersee, J. H., & Novak, J. (2001). Assessing understanding in biology. *Journal of Biological Education, 35*(3), 118–124.

Moreland, J., & Jones, A. (2000). Emerging assessment practices in an emergent curriculum: Implications for technology. *International Journal of Technology and Design Education, 10*(3), 283–305.

Moreland, J., Jones, J., & Northover, A. (2001). Enhancing teachers' technological knowledge and assessment practices to enhance stuent learning in technology: A two year classroom study. *Research in Science Education, 31*(1), 155–176.

Morgan, C., & Morris, G. (1999). *Good teaching and learning: Pupils and teachers speak*. Buckingham, UK: Open University Press.

Moss, P. A. (1992). Shifting conceptions of validity in educational measurement: Implications of performance assessment. *Review of Educational Research, 62*(3), 229–258.

Moss, P. A. (1994). Can there be validity without reliability? *Educational Researcher, 23*(2), 5–12.

National Research Council. (1999). *The assessment of science meets the science of assessment*. Washington, DC: National Academy Press.

Natriello, G. (1987). The impact of evaluation processes on students. *Educational Psychologist, 22*, 155–175.

Newmann, D., Griffin, P., & Cole, M. (1989). *The construction zone: Working for cognitive change in school*. Cambridge, UK: Cambridge University Press.

Nitko, A. (1995). Curriculum-based continuous assessment: a framework for concepts, procedures and policy. *Assessment in Education, 2*(3), 321.

Norris, S. P. (1992). Testing for the disposition to think critically. *Informal Logic, 2/3*, 157–164.

Orphwood, G. (1995). Juggling educational needs and political realities in Canada: National standards, provincial control and teachers' professionalism. *Studies in Science Education, 26*, 39–57.

Orpwood, G. (2001). The role of assessment in science curriculum reform. *Assessment in Education, 8*(2), 135.

Osborne, J., & Ratcliffe, M. (2002). Developing effective methods of assessing ideas and evidence. *School Science Review, 83*(305), 113–123.

Osborne, R., & Gilbert, J. (1980). A method for the investigation of concept understanding in science. *European Journal of Science Education, 2*(3), 311–321.

Parker, J., & Rennie, L. (1998). Equitable assessment issues. In K. Tobin (Ed.), *International handbook of science education* (Vol. 2, pp. 897–910). London: Kluwer Academic.

Peat, M., & Franklin, S. (2002). Supporting student learning: the use of computer-based formative assessment modules. *British Journal of Educational Technology, 33*(5), 515–523.

Perrenoud, P. (1998). From formative evaluation to a controlled regulation of learning processes. Towards a wider conceptual field. *Assessment in Education, 5*(1), 85–102.

Phye, G. D. E. (1997). *Handbook of classroom assessment: Learning, adjustment and achievement*. San Diego: Academic Press.

Pittman, K. M. (1999). Student-generated analogies: Another way of knowing? *Journal of Research in Science Teaching, 36*(1), 1–22.

Pollard, A., Triggs, P., Broadfoot, P., McNess, E., & Osborn, M. (2000). *What pupils say: Changing policy and practice in primary education*. London: Continuum.

Popham, W. J. (1987). Two decades of educational objectives. *International Journal of Educational Research, 11*(1).

Popham, W. J. (2003). Trouble with testing. *The American School Board Journal, 190*(2), 14.

Preece, P. F. W., & Skinner, N. C. (1999). The national assessment in science at Key Stage 3 in England and Wales and its impact on teaching and learning. *Assessment in Education, 6*(1), 11.

Pryor, J., & Torrance, H. (2000). Questioning the three bears: The social construction of classroom assessment. In A. Filer (Ed.), *Assessment: social practice and social product*. London: Routledge-Falmer.

Ramaprasad, A. (1983). On the definition of feedback. *Behavioural Science, 28*(1), 4–13.

Reay, D., & Wiliam, D. (1999). "I'll be a nothing": Structure, agency and the construction of identity through assessment. *British Educational Research Journal, 25*(3), 343–354.

Rice, D. C., Ryan, J., & Samson, S. (1998). Using concept maps to assess student learning in the science classroom: must different methods compete? *Journal of Research in Science Teaching*, *35*(10), 1103–1127.

Rodriguez, A. J. (1998). Strategies for counterresistence: Toward sociotransformative constructivism and learning to teach science for diversity and for understanding. *Journal of Research in Science Teaching, 35*, 589–622.

Rogoff, B. (1990). *Apprenticeship in thinking*. New York: Cambridge University Press.

Rop, C. J. (2002). The meaning of student inquiry questions: A teacher's beliefs and responses. *International Journal of Science Education, 24*(7), 717.

Roth, W.-M., & McGinn, M. K. (1997). Graphing: Cognitive ability or practice? *Science Education, 81*(1), 91.

Roth, W. M., & McGinn, M. K. (1998). UnDELETE science education: Lives/work/voices. *Journal of Research in Science Teaching, 35*, 399–421.

Roth, W. M., & Roychoudhury, A. (1993). The concept map as a tool for the collaborative construction of knowledge: A microanalysis of high school physics students. *Journal of Research in Science Teaching, 30*(5), 503–534.

Ruiz-Primo, M. A., & Shavelson, R. J. (1996a). Problems and issues in the use of concept maps in science assessment. *Journal of Research in Science Teaching, 33*(6), 569–600.

Ruiz-Primo, M. A., & Shavelson, R. J. (1996b). Rhetoric and reality in science performance assessments: An update. *Journal of Research in Science Teaching, 33*(10), 1045–1063.

Ruiz-Primo, M. A., Shavelson, R. J., Hamilton, L., & Klein, S. (2002). On the evaluation of systemic science education reform: Searching for instructional sensitivity. *Journal of Research in Science Teaching, 39*(5), 369–393.

Rye, J. A., & Rubba, P. A. (2002). Scoring concept maps: An expert map-based scheme weighted for relationships. *School Science and Mathematics, 102*(1), 33.

Sadler, P. (1998). Psychometric models of student conceptions in science: Reconciling qualitative studies and distractor-driven assessment instruments. *Journal of Research in Science Teaching, 35*(3), 265–296.

Sadler, R. (1989). Formative assessment and the design of instructional systems. *Instructional Science, 18*(2), 119–144.

Sarf, A. (1998). On two metaphors for learning and the dangers of choosing just one. *Educational Researcher, 27*(4–13).

Scriven, M. (1967). The methodology of evaluation. In M. Scriven (Ed.), *Perspectives of curriculum evaluation*. Chicago: Rand McNally.

Scriven, M. (1990). Beyond formative and summative evaluation. In K. J. Rehage, M. McLaughlin, and D. Phillips (Eds.), *Evaluation and education: At quarter century. NSSE yearbook*. Chicago: NSSE.

Sewell, R. D. E., Stevens, R. G., & Lewis, D. J. A. (1995). Multimedia computer technology as a tool for teaching and assessment of biological science. *Journal of Biological Education, 29*, 27.

Shapley, K. S., & Bush, M. J. (1999). Developing a valid and reliable portfolio assessment in the primary grades: Building on practical experience. *Applied Measurement in Education, 12*(2), 111–132.

Shaw, J. (1997). Threats to the validity of science performance assessments for English language learners. *Journal of Research in Science Teaching, 34*(7), 721–743.

Shepardson, D. P. (Ed.). (2001). *Assessment in science: A guide to professional development and classroom practice*. Dordrecht, the Netherlands: Kluwer Academic.

Shulman, L. (1987). Knowledge and teaching: foundations of the new reforms. *Harvard Educational Review, 57*, 1–22.

Simpson, M. (1993). Diagnostic assessment and its contribtuion to pupils' learning. In D. West (Ed.), *Teaching, learning and assessment in science education*. London: Paul Chapman Publishing.

Slater, T. F. (1997). The effectiveness of portfolio assessments in science. *Journal of College Science Teaching, 26*(5), 315.

Slater, T., Ryan, J., & Samson, S. (1997). Impact and dynamics of portfolio assessment and traditional assessment in a college physics course. *Journal of Research in Science Teaching, 34*(3), 255–271.

Smith, P. S., Hounshell, P., Copolo, C., & Wilkerson, S. (1992). The impact of end-of-course testing in chemistry on curriculum and instruction. *Science Education, 76*(5), 523–530.

Solano-Flores, G., & Nelson-Barber, S. (2001). On the cultural validity of science assessments. *Journal of Research in Science Teaching, 38*(5), 553–573.

Solano-Flores, G., & Shavelson, R. J. (1997). Development of peformance assessment in science: conceptual, practical and logistical issues. *Educational Measurement, 1997*, 16.24.

Stefani, L. A. J., & Tariq, V. N. (1996). Running group practical projects for first-year undergraduate students. *Journal of Biological Education, 30*, 36.

Stern, L., & Ahlgren, A. (2002). Analysis of students' assessments in middle school curriculum materials: Aiming precisely at benchmarks and standards. *Journal of Research in Science Teaching, 39*(9), 889–910.

Stoddart, T., Abrams, R., Gasper, E., & Canaday, D. (2000). Concept maps as assessment in science inquiry learning—a report of methodology. *International Journal of Science Education, 22*(12), 1221–1246.

Swain, J. (1996). The impact and effect of key stage 3 science tests. *School Science Review, 78*(283), 79–90.

Swain, J. (1997). The impact and effect of key stage 3 science tasks. *School Science Review, 78*(284), 99–104.

Tamir, P. (1998). Assessment and evaluation in science education: Opportunities to learn and outcomes. In K. Tobin (Ed.), *International Handbook of Science Education* (pp. 761–789). London: Kluwer Academic.

Tan, K. C. D., Goh, N. K., Chia, L. S., & Treagust, D. F. (2002). Development and application of a two-tier multiple choice diagnostic instrument to assess high school students' understanding of inorganic chemistry qualitative analysis. *Journal of Research in Science Teaching, 39*(4), 283–301.

Taras, M. (2002). Using assessment for learning and learning from assessment. *Assessment and Evaluation in Higher Education, 27*(6), 501–510.

Tariq, V. N., Stefani, L. A. J., Butcher, A. C., & Heylings, D. J. A. (1998). Developing a new approach to the assessment of project work. *Assessment and Evaluation in Higher Education, 23*(3), 221.

Taylor, C., & Gardner, P. (1999). An alternative method of answering and scoring multiple choice tests. *Research in Science Education, 29*(3), 353–363.

Tittle, C. (1994). Toward an educational psychology of assessment for teaching and learning: Theories, contexts and validation arguments. *Educational Psychologist, 29*(3), 149–162.

Torrance, H. (1993). Formative assessment: Some theoretical problems and empirical questions. *Cambridge Journal of Education, 23*(3), 333–343.

Torrance, H. (2000). Post-modernism and educational assessment. In A. Filer (Ed.), *Assessment; social practice and social product.* London: RoutledgeFalmer.

Torrance, H., & Pryor, J. (1995). Investigating teacher assessment in infant classrooms: Methodological problems and emerging issues. *Assessment in Education, 2*(3), 305–320.

Torrance, H., & Pryor, J. (1998). *Investigating formative assessment: Teaching, learning and assessment in the classroom.* Buckingham, UK: Open University Press.

Torrance, H., & Pryor, J. (2001). Developing formative assessment in the classroom: using action research to explore and modify theory. *British Educational Research Journal, 27*(5), 615–631.

Toth, E. E., Suthers, D. D., & Lesgold, A. M. (2002). "Mapping to know": The effects of representational guidance and reflective assessment on scientific inquiry. *Science Education, 86*(2), 264–286.

Treagust, D. F. (1995). Diagnostic assessment. In R. Duit (Ed.), *Learning science in the schools: Research reforming practice.* Hillsdale, NJ: Lawrence Erlbaum Associates.

Treagust, D. F., Jacobowitz, R., Gallagher, J. L., & Parker, J. (2001). Using assessment as a guide in teaching for understanding: A case study of a middle school science class learning about sound. *Science Education, 85*(2), 137–157.

Tripp, G., Murphy, A., Stafford, B., & Childers, P. B. (1997). Peer tutors and students work with formative assessment. *The Clearing House, 71*(2), 103.

Volkmann, M. J., & Abell, S. K. (2003). Seamless assessment. *Science and Children, 40*(8), 41.

Wallace, J., & Mintzes, J. (1990). The concept map as a research tool: Exploring conceptual change in biology. *Journal of Research in Science Teaching, 27*(10), 1033–1052.

Welzel, M., & Roth, W. M. (1998). Do interviews really assess students' knowledge? *International Journal of Science Education, 20*(1), 25–44.

White, R., & Gunstone, R. (1992). *Probing understanding*. London: The Falmer Press.

Wiediger, S. D., & Hutchinson, J. S. (2002). The significance of accurate student self-assessment in understanding of chemical concepts. *Journal of Chemical Education, 79*(1), 120.

Wiggins, G. (1989). A true test: Toward more authentic and equitable assessment. *Phi Delta Kappan*, 703–713.

Wiggins, G. (1993). *Assessing student performance*. San Franisco: Jossey-Bass.

Wiliam, D. (1992). Some technical issues in assessment: A user's guide. *British Journal of Curriculum and Assessment, 2*(3), 11–20.

Wiliam, D. (1994). *Towards a philosophy for educational assessment*. Paper presented at the Annual Conference of the British Education Research Association, Bath, England.

Wilson, J. (1996). Concept maps about chemical equilibrium and students' achievement scores. *Research in Science Education, 26*(2), 169–185.

Wolfe, D., Bixby, J., Glenn, J. I., & Gardner, H. (1991). To use their minds well: Investigating new forms of student assessment. *Review of Research in Education, 17*, 31–74.

Yorke, M. (2003). Formative assessment in higher education: Moves towards theory and the enhancement of pedagogic practice. *Higher Education, 45*(4), 477–501.

Yung, B. H. W. (2001). Three views of fairness in a school-based assessment scheme of practical work in biology. *International Journal of Science Education, 23*(10), 985–1005.

Zachos, P., Hick, T. L., Doane, W. E. J., & Sargent, C. (2000). Setting theoretical and empirical foundations for assessing scientific inquiry and discovery in educational programs. *Journal of Research in Science Teaching, 37*(9), 938–962.

Zeegers, Y. (2003). *Pedagogical content knowledge or pedagogical reasoning about science teaching and learning*. Paper presented at the Paper presented at the Annual Conference of the Australasian Science Education Research Association, Melbourne, July 2003.

Zoller, U. (1996). The use of examinations for revealing and distinguishing between students' misconceptions, misunderstandings and "no conceptions" in college chemistry. *Research in Science Education, 26*(3), 317–326.

Zoller, U., Fastow, M., Lubezky, A., & Tsaparlis, G. (1999). Students' self-assessment in chemistry examinations requiring higher- and lower-order cognitive skills. *Journal of Chemical Education, 76*(1), 112.

CHAPTER 33

Large-Scale Assessments in Science Education

Edward D. Britton
Steven A. Schneider
WestEd Mathematics, Science and Technology Program
Redwood City, California

This chapter focuses on changes in large-scale assessments in science education, at the international, national, and state levels. Historically, these assessments are for purposes such as international comparisons, accountability, summative assessment for reporting to others outside the classroom, qualification for entry to college, and evaluation of programs. Thus, the term "large-scale assessments" encompasses quite a variety of assessments that differ in their purposes, formats, and other features. It is important to consider the specifics of those features to avoid inappropriate generalizations—ones that imply all large-scale assessments have the same characteristics (Kifer, 2000).

The number and types of large-scale science assessments have grown substantially in recent years at every level of education system, as illustrated by the following facts, which are discussed in this chapter. Since 2000, there have been two international organizations sponsoring international science comparisons on a regular basis, and the number of countries that participate in such studies is growing. At the national level in the United States, the nature of the National Assessment of Education Progress (NAEP) will undergo significant changes beginning in 2009. This chapter includes the just-released framework that will guide the future of NAEP science assessments. The No Child Left Behind (NCLB) legislation is dramatically increasing the number of state science assessments, including increased use of Advanced Placement exams and creation of high school exit examinations (Center on Education Policy, 2005). Many countries have had the latter for some time, but such examinations have been relatively rare in the United States until this decade.

An indicator of how much science assessment has increased is the fact that this Handbook needs to split its treatment of assessment into two chapters. Chapter 32 in this Handbook describes research on classroom assessments—those by teachers for direct use for and with students. The current chapter on large-scale assessment does not revisit classroom assessments, but mentions emerging models for enhancing the relationship between large-scale and classroom assessment. In prior hand-books for science education, only a single chapter had to be devoted to all large-scale assessments. Both Doran, Lawrenz, and Helgeson (1994) and Tamir (1998) provide broad portraits of science assessment that span both classroom assessment and large-scale external assessments. The former review includes considerably more discussion of large-scale assessments than the latter. The current chapter builds on these prior reviews by focusing more on recent developments rather than also recounting the considerable history of science assessment already provided, particularly by Doran, Lawrenz, and Helgeson (1994).

We must further delimit the large body of work that could be in the purview of a chapter on large-scale assessment. Research in large-scale assessment cuts across many subject-area disciplines and resides in several fields of educational research. Although such literatures are as relevant to science education as any other subject area, we generally emphasize literature that is targeted at science education, while still noting some seminal publications that address a broader context. Also, a rendering in detail of the results from each major large-scale assessment is beyond the scope of the following discussion, as are the psychometric or other technical issues involved, even those specific to science assessments (e.g., Quellmalz et al., 2005; Welch, Huffman, & Lawrenz, 1998).

This chapter elaborates the following recent trends and prospects for the future of large-scale assessment of science:

- The increased potential benefits as well as risks of large-scale assessments in science education, should the increasingly prevalent assessments become more of the same.
- Both the frequency and types of international comparisons of student understanding in science, which are increasing.
- Aspects of national science assessment in upcoming administrations of NAEP are about to change.
- The number if not the nature of state science assessments is changing because of requirements of the No Child Left Behind (NCLB) legislation for implementation beginning in 2007. The chapter ends by reporting a model for creating coherent systems of large-scale and classroom assessments.

OVERVIEW OF ISSUES IN LARGE-SCALE SCIENCE ASSESSMENT

Certain prevailing characteristics of large-scale assessments present significant benefits and risks to science education. This section gives an overview of four issues that will grow if the upcoming, increased number of assessments continue mostly to have the same characteristics as ones currently in use. First, attaching increasingly high stakes to assessments can increase the amount of science instruction occurring in classrooms and provide some policy guidance, but the policy implications drawn and resulting science instruction can be at odds with research on some aspects of how students learn. This section begins by framing and elaborating on such tensions.

Second, this barrier to congruence stems from emphasizing use of multiple-choice and short open-ended items (also referred to as constructed or free response items), because the former type of item cannot adequately interrogate the whole spectrum of science standards held by the science education community. For example, multiple-choice items are limited for assessing students' ability to conduct scientific investigations, particularly through the use of inquiry approaches. This section describes research on alternative types of items for science assessment.

Third, just as the science education community continues its quest to reach all students, large-scale assessments need to be designed in ways such that all kinds of students have equivalent opportunities to succeed at taking them. This section briefly notes research on accommodating students with disabilities and addressing problems in creating and translating tests for students of different languages and cultures.

Fourth, using assessments that are not adequately aligned with standards for science education cannot provide adequate guidance to teachers on what to do differently. This section discusses the alignment of state science assessments with state science standards, which would be a significant incremental enhancement of the state of large-scale assessment.

Benefits and Risks of More of the Same

Increased large-scale science assessment offers both great opportunity and substantial risk for science education. Requiring science assessment helps ensure that science gets attention in school. This is particularly true for the elementary grades, where teachers must balance and choose the amount of attention to all subjects, but it also has implications for secondary levels of schooling.

In the United States, the initial NCLB requirement of assessment in mathematics and reading but not in science has had a dampening effect on elementary teachers' inclusion of science instruction. This is common knowledge in the science education community, and the first author has encountered examples of analogous effects at the middle and even high school levels during field work in recent years. He encountered more than one high school where students who, because they were failing at mathematics, were required to double up their number of mathematics courses. The concern is that this was being accomplished by dropping their formerly required general science classes. By requiring that science join reading and mathematics as annual subjects of states' standards-based assessment by the year 2007, NCLB pushes science to the center stage of public attention and helps to ensure that it gets the priority it deserves in the school curriculum.

Particular kinds of assessment can help to promote more effective teaching and learning of science for all students. But there is also the danger of assessment pushing teaching and learning in undesirable directions that are counterproductive to the goals of scientific literacy. There is danger too of missed opportunities to push the current state of the art to the new levels required to have assessment systems that truly support accountability and classroom assessment purposes.

Ample research suggests that accountability systems can be powerful in communicating expectations and stimulating teachers and schools to modify their teaching and work to attain established performance goals. Studies conducted in numerous states using a variety of quantitative and qualitative methodologies have shown quite consistent results, described below [Arizona (Smith & Rottenberg, 1991), California (McDonnell & Choisser, 1997; Herman & Klein, 1996), Kentucky (Koretz, Barron, Mitchell, & Stecher, 1996; Stecher, Barron, Kaganoff, & Goodwin, 1998; Borko & Elliott, 1998; Wolf & McIver, 1999), Maine (Firestone, Mayrowetz, & Fairman, 1998), Maryland (Lane, Stone, Parke, Hansen, & Cerrillo, 2000; Firestone et al., 1998; Goldberg & Rosewell, 2000), New Jersey (Firestone, Camilli, Yurecko, Monfils, & Mayrowetz, 2000), North Carolina (McDonnell & Choisser, 1997), Vermont (Koretz, McCaffrey, Klein, Bell, & Stecher, 1993), and Washington (Stecher, Barron, Chun, & Ross, 2000; Borko & Stecher, 2001)]:

1. Accountability tests serve to focus instruction. Teachers and principals indeed pay attention to what is tested and adapt their curriculum and teaching accordingly.

2. Teachers model what is assessed. They tend to model the pedagogical approach reflected on high-visibility tests. When a state or district assessment is composed of multiple-choice tests, teachers tend to rely heavily on multiple-choice worksheets in their classroom instruction. However, when the assessments use open-ended items and/or extended writing and rubrics to judge the quality of student work, teachers prepare students for the test by incorporating these same types of activities into their classroom practice.

3. Test scores show initial increases. In state after state, when new assessments and accountability provisions are put into place, student scores show an increase, at least for the first few years. Such sustained attention to test content and format tends to show up in test performance.

Although these first points demonstrate some of the benefits of assessment, other research showed unintended consequences:

4. Schools focus on the test rather than the standards. With sanctions and incentives riding on test performance, educators appear to give their primary attention to what is tested and how it is tested, rather than to the standards underlying the test. Teachers shift how much classroom instruction time is accorded to core curriculum subjects, depending on whether or not a particular subject is tested at their grade levels (Stecher & Barron, 1999).

5. What is not tested becomes invisible. As a corollary, focusing on the test rather than the standards also means that that which is not tested tends to get less attention or may be ignored altogether. Both the broader domain of the tested disciplines and important subjects that are not tested may get short shrift. That a number of studies have found that state tests tend to give relatively little attention to complex thinking and problem solving and instead tend to focus on lower levels of student performance thus has strong implications for what is likely to be taught. Moreover, when tests and standards are not well aligned, it seems clear that the test and not the standards will be the focus of attention.

6. Test score increases appear to be inflated. If teachers teach only to the test and not to the larger domain that the test is intended to represent, the test score

results may represent just that—higher scores on a specific test and not genuine learning that generalizes to other domains of science instruction. Research findings showing disparities between student performance on state accountability tests and that on other achievement measures that are intended to measure similar areas of learning raise questions about the meaning of increasing test scores. For example, Bob Linn (1998) has shown dramatic drops in performance when school districts or states change from one standardized test to another. Dan Koretz and colleagues (Koretz & Barron, 1998) have found limited correspondence between gains on state tests and those on the National Assessment of Educational Progress.

Use of More Varied Types of Assessment Items

Multiple-choice and short-answer-type items tend to dominate in large-scale accountability tests for several reasons. Many of them can be included within the testing time available, permitting assessment of as many domains of science content as possible. Furthermore, this type of item can be more inexpensively scored than open-ended items. However, large-scale assessments certainly have employed other types of items, for example: several international comparisons have included performance-based science assessments as an option for participating countries; and NAEP science examinations have included practical skills tests for subsets of the sample—even as far back as 1972 (NAEP, 1975). Israel and some regional examination boards in England and Wales have historically used laboratory practicals as part of large-scale high school exit examinations (Britton & Raizen, 1996; Tamir, 1974).

Multiple-choice and short-answer items can be different or more complex than the routine fare. Sadler (1998) is developing science assessments where the distractors in multiple-choices items are based on research about students' misconceptions rather than mostly being based on the psychometric analysis of whether they adequately discriminate between high- and low-performing students. Figure 33.1 is a Japanese multiple-choice item in biology for students who are applying for college. The item requires applicants to make two sequential choices from among 13 response options instead of the more typical four or five choices. Figure 33.2 presents a short-answer item in biology from an Israeli matriculation examination. It provides students with a multiple-choice item and identifies the correct answer, but then asks students to explain why that response is the correct one. Other, similar items require students to identify the correct answer first, before asking them to explain their answer.

However, the multiple-choice and short-answer items that most commonly are employed in large-scale assessments can go only so far in tapping the complex thinking, communication, and problem-solving skills that students will need for future success. Rather, multiple measures are needed to address the full depth and breadth of our expectations for student learning (Herman, 1997).

In addition to multiple-choice and short open-ended items, large-scale assessments can include such item types as more extended constructed-response items (varying from responses involving sentences or paragraphs to full essays), concept maps, and performance-based science tasks, involving hands-on problems with ma-

Read the following descriptions, and select one correct answer from Group A and *two* correct answers from Group B. Write your answer from Group A first. List your answers from Group B in the order of the photosynthesis process, such as "1,4,5."

Group A:
1)   Oxygen is discharged during photosynthesis in chlorophytes or during photosynthesis by photosynthetic bacteria.
2)   Oxygen is discharged during photosynthesis in chlorophytes but not during photosynthesis by photosynthetic bacteria.
3)   Oxygen is discharged during photosynthesis by photosynthetic bacteria but not during photosynthesis in chlorophytes.

Group B:
4)   Oxygen, which is discharged during photosynthesis in chlorophytes or photosynthesis by photosynthetic bacteria, derives from the water.
5)   Oxygen, which is discharged during photosynthesis by photosynthetic bacteria, derives from the water.
6)   Oxygen, which is discharged during photosynthesis in chlorophytes, derives from the water.
7)   Oxygen, which is discharged during photosynthesis in chlorophytes or photosynthesis by photosynthetic bacteria, derives from the carbon dioxide.
8)   Oxygen, which is discharged during photosynthesis by the photosynthetic bacteria, derives from the carbon dioxide.
9)   Oxygen, which is discharged during photosynthesis in cholorophytes, derives from the carbon dioxide.
10)   Glucose is produced from a reaction between water and carbon in carbon dioxide.
11)   Glucose is produced from a reduction of carbon dioxide by hydrogen in the water.
12)   Glucose is produced through oxidation of the carbon dioxide by oxygen in the water.
13)   Glucose is produced from a reaction between hydroxide ions in water and carbon dioxide.

Note. Reproduced by permission from Britton & Raizen, 1996, p. 64.

FIGURE 33–1.   Japanese multiple-choice item in biology for students who are applying for college.

terials or computer-based simulations of phenomena or data. Berg and Smith (1994) examined differences in multiple-choice items and free-response items in assessing graphing abilities.

Science performance assessments can address aspects of knowledge that multiple-choice items cannot, but they bring their own challenges, such as not always tapping higher-order thinking, and they are expensive to develop, administer, and score (Collins, 1993; Ruiz-Primo & Shavelson, 1996a; Solano-Flores & Shavelson, 1997). Doran et al. (1993) tried a large-scale, performance-based assessment of science laboratory skills in Ohio and found that more refinements would be needed. It is challenging to devise performance tasks that adequately probe cognitive complexities (Baxter & Glaser, 1997; Sugrue, 1994). Science items involving concept maps pre-

In the next question, the correct answer is noted. Copy the answer into your notebook and explain briefly why it is correct.

   2. An accurate measurement was made between the amounts of dry substance in corn plants at two different times: at noon on a hot summer day and at night after that day. It is reasonable to assume that the amount of dry substance is

<u>1.</u>   larger at noon.
2.   larger at midnight.
3.   identical at the two times.
4.   in some of the plants, larger at noon, whereas larger at midnight in others.

Note. Reproduced by permission from Britton & Raizen, 1996, p. 66.

FIGURE 33–2.   Short answer item in biology from an Israeli matriculation examination.

sent problems as well as advantages (Ruiz-Primo & Shavelson, 1996b). Computer-simulated and hands-on science performance assessments are not interchangeable, and several possible sources of variation can explain this (Huff & Sireci, 2001; Rosenquist, Shavelson, & Ruiz-Primo, 2000).

Assessment for All

The science education community has for some time adopted the goal of reaching all students with science instruction. There are related issues in devising and administering large-scale assessments for which all kinds of students have equivalent opportunities to demonstrate their learning. Researchers have investigated gender differences in large-scale science assessments (e.g., Lee & Burkam, 1996; Walding et al., 1994). Assessments historically have not accommodated well the needs of students with disabilities. Korenz and Hamilton (1999) conducted an analysis of the effects of accommodations and test formats in science and other subjects for students with disabilities taking the Kentucky state assessment. Abedi et al. (2001) looked at NAEP math test accommodations for students with limited English proficiency, and similar studies are envisioned for NAEP in science and other school subjects.

   Research is revealing more challenges than were recognized in the recent past for producing tests originally developed in English for use by students of other languages and from different cultures. This issue is of critical importance in international U.S. assessments. Research has shown that test translation for science and other subjects does not guarantee full test equivalence (e.g., Sireci, 1997). International and some national assessments now employ a process of back-translation to reveal differences in meaning. Developers of large-scale assessments have for some time been on the lookout for cultural bias during item development. However, studies of how cultural differences as well as language differences generate variation between translated and untranslated versions of science tests in both Spanish-speaking and Native American communities reveal more complexity to the issue (Solano-Flores & Nelson-Barber, 2001; Solano-Flores, Trumbull, & Nelson-Barber, 2002). Assumptions about the experiences and cultures of English learners, combined with test developers' limited experiential knowledge about students' home and community lives, led to greater than anticipated inadequacies in test development. These emerging results suggest that different test development methods may need to be considered in the future if such sources of variation are to be fully addressed.

Alignment of Large-Scale Assessments with Standards

Alignment is the lynchpin of standards-based reform. If assessment results are to be used to provide feedback that helps schools and the teachers and students within them attain understanding described in state standards, then it is essential that the standards and assessments be aligned. Although the vagueness and lack of specificity of standards in many states can make any determination difficult, available evidence suggests that the alignment of current tests is problematic.

Studies have been conducted by several research teams on the alignment of state or local assessments with corresponding curriculum frameworks, for science and several other subjects. Results from more than 10 states by each of the teams led by the Achieve organization, Norm Webb (Webb model), and Andrew Porter and John Smithson (Surveys of Enacted Curriculum or SEC model) reach similar overarching conclusions. Existing state tests do not fully cover intended science standards. A common omission in state assessments is attention to scientific inquiry. Furthermore, state assessments tend to emphasize levels of knowledge and skills that are lower than those exhorted by the state standards (Porter, 2002; Rothman et al., 2002; Webb, 1997, 2002). What is tested instead seems to be at least as much a function of the items that particular item writers are most adept at producing and those that survive psychometric field-testing—such as items that are at appropriate levels of item difficulty and that relate in empirically coherent ways to other items—as it is a function of what sets of items will provide the most comprehensive and balanced view of how students are achieving relative to standards (Herman, Webb, & Zuniga, 2003).

MORE AND DIFFERENT INTERNATIONAL SCIENCE ASSESSMENTS

The frequency of cross-national assessments in science has escalated over time to the point where it is now hard to keep track of them all. Table 33.1 provides a chronology of the major assessments conducted or planned through 2007. The biggest jump occurs in 2000. Until then, the Netherlands-based International Association for the Evaluation of Educational Achievement (IEA) had been the only main sponsor of cross-national comparisons. The Educational Testing Service (ETS) briefly entered the terrain during a time period between two administrations by the IEA. That is, the International Assessment of Educational Progress (IAEP), which borrows its name and some concepts from the ETS administration of the U.S. NAEP, occurred between IEA's first and second international studies of science (LaPointe, Mead, & Phillips, 1989; LaPointe, Askew, & Mead, 1992).

In 2000, the Paris-based Organisation for Economic Co-Operation and Development (OECD) launched a line of cross-national comparisons that has important differences from the IEA studies, which are discussed in a following section. Both IEA

TABLE 33.1
Chronology of International Large-Scale Assessments in Science

Year	Org.[1]	Short Name[2]	Subjects	Ages/Grades[5]	Size[7]	Results, Select Publications[8]
1969–70	IEA	FISS	Science	10, 14, end sec[6]	19	Comber & Keeves, 1973
1983–86	IEA	SISS	Science	10,14 end sec	17	IEA 1988; Postlethwaite & Wiley, 1992
1988	ETS	IEAP	Science, math	13	6	LaPointe, Mead & Phillips, 1989
1992	ETS	IEAP	Science, math	9, 13	20	LaPointe et al., 1992
1994–95	IEA	TIMSS[3]	Science, math	3–4, 7–8, end of sec	42	Beaton et al., 1996; Martin et al., 1997; Mullis et al., 1998
1999	IEA	TIMSS-R[3]	Science, math	8	39	Martin et al., 2000
2000	OECD	PISA	Reading[4], (science/math)	4, 8	39	OECD, 2001, 2003
2003	IEA	TIMSS[3]	Science, math	4, 8	48	Martin et al., 2004
2003	OECD	PISA	Math[4], (read, science)	4, 8	41	OECD, 2004a, 2004b
2006	OECD	PISA	Science[4] (math, reading)	4, 8	—	—
2007	IEA	TIMSS[3]	Science, math	TBA	—	—
2007	IEA	TEDS[9]	Teachers, math	TBA	—	IEA, 2005

Notes:

(1) Sponsoring organizations: International Associations for the Evaluation of Educational Achievement (IEA); Educational Testing Service (ETS); Organisation for Economic Co-Operation and Development (OECD)

(2) Short names of acronyms stand for the following full names of the studies: First Interational Science Study (FISS); Second International Science Study (SISS); International Assessment of Educational Progress (IAEP); Third International Mathematics and Science Study (TIMSS); Programme for International Student Assessment (PISA).

(3) The naming of the TIMSS evolved after the original TIMSS in 1995. The 1999 version became TIMSS-repeat, or TIMSS-R for short. Beginning in 2003, the full name was changed to *Trends* in Mathematics and Science Study, which still has the short name of TIMSS.

(4) PISA assesses three subjects each time (reading, mathematics, science). In a given year, however, one subject is fully tested while only partial tests are given for the other two subjects. The lead subject has been rotated, and the first main administration of science will be in 2006.

(5) International Assessments have used two similar means of setting the target populations of students to be assessed. Some studies target students of a particular age, while others target students in a particular grade. These two strategies lead to different sampling strategies and have implications for study studies.

(6) End Sec stands for End of Secondary. Since the last year of schooling varies among countries (e.g., some end at grade 12, others at 13), the international study does not set a uniform age or grade level for the targeted secondary population.

(7) Size refers to number of participating countries. The number provided here is for the number of countries that participated in at least one test population (age/grade). Typically, a number of countries elect to participate in some rather than all populations.

(8) These sample reports are limited to those reporting international comparisons for international audiences, versus U.S. or any other nation's perspective on its performance relative to other countries (e.g., Schmidt, McKnight & Raizen, 1997). The reports selected also are limited to results of student achievement in science. Many studies report on other aspects of the study, such as accompanying analyses of the countries' science curricula (Schmidt et al., 1997).

(9) The Teachers Education and Development Study (TEDS) will be the first IEA study with a principal focus on data collection about teachers rather than students. The 2007 administration will be for mathematics teachers, and study organizers hope to conduct a similar investigation about science teachers in the future.

and OECD studies occur every three years now. The two studies occurred in the same year recently (2003), and a number of countries participated in both of them.

Notice the following characteristics that can help distinguish among studies:

1. All of the listed studies assessed science, but some studies assessed science only (FISS, SISS), whereas others assessed both mathematics and science fairly equally (the TIMSS and IEAP series); and the PISA series emphasizes one of three subjects (reading, mathematics, or science) in any given year, limiting the assessment of the other two subjects in that year.

2. The studies use either ages or grades to identify target populations of students to be assessed. Studies vary in the number of target populations they include. See notes 5 and 6 in Table 33.1.

3. There is wide variation in the number of countries that participated, and a participating country may decide to assess only some of the target populations. See note 7 in Table 33.1.

4. This table lists only international publications of cross-national results for science achievement. All studies measure students' science achievement, which is the original focus and a continuing hallmark of such studies. The table does not list U.S. or other countries' reports that give a national perspective on cross-national achievement results. See note 8 of Table 33.1.

However, all studies, in addition to achievement tests, include to varying extents some data collection from other sources, such as national, school, teacher, or student questionnaires. Furthermore, many tests offer additional student assessment options; for example, study organizations offer a performance-based science assessment that countries can elect to add to their administration. Some assessments go further and include an optional or required analysis of participating countries' science curriculum, accompanying qualitative case studies of nations' science education, or video studies of classroom teaching in select countries. Using the above characteristics, the largest international science assessment to date remains the first TIMSS study (1995), as explained below.

Notice that IEA has recently authorized a quite different kind of international large-scale study during 2005–2009—a comparison of how different countries prepare and induct beginning teachers for mathematics at both the elementary and secondary levels (Teacher Education and Development Study, TEDS). Study organizers are interested in a similar, future study of science teachers. These studies are the first systematic, extensive investigations for IEA where the principal study focus is on teacher rather than student information.

The following sections further discuss the IEA and OECD series of studies in science. As mentioned in the chapter introduction, the authors describe the characteristics of each study and point readers to the published results. However, it is beyond the confines of this chapter to provide the actual results from each study.

IEA Studies

The International Association for the Evaluation of Student Achievement (IEA), with administrative offices in Amsterdam and a technical data-processing center in Hamburg, is an independent research organization comprising members from national and government research institutions and agencies. It began in 1958 at the UNESCO Institute for Education at Hamburg as a discussion and consultation among psychologists, sociologists, and psychometricians around issues of schools and student achievement and what constituted the proper evaluation of these. A Pilot Twelve-Country Study, conducted in 1959–1962, evaluated five areas: science, mathematics, reading comprehension, geography, and nonverbal ability. IEA studies are most widely known for assessing science content (including the nature of science), but they also are designed to assess students' performance expectations in science and perspectives toward science. As an example of the latter, the study framework for science in the TIMSS called for investigation of students' understanding; theorizing, analyzing, and solving problems; use of tools, routine procedures, and science processes (performance expectations); and attitudes, careers, and participation by underrepresented groups (perspectives) (Robitaille et al., 1993).

A hallmark of IEA studies has been their emphasis on students' opportunity to learn the subject matter. Opportunity to Learn (OTL) has had a pragmatic focus on what is actually done in classrooms with respect to the subject assessed as opposed to what may be intended to occur in classrooms according to official standards or textbooks. This emphasis may also be seen as a natural development from the goal shared by all IEA studies to illuminate the factors that explain or cause differences in educational achievement (Postlethwaite, 1995). The IEA tripartite curriculum model defines curriculum at three different levels: the *Intended*—what a system intends students to study and learn; the *Implemented*—what is taught in classrooms; and the *Attained*—what students are able to demonstrate that they know (Travers & Westbury, 1989).

The First International Science Study (FISS) was conducted by the IEA from 1966 through 1973, part of a larger Six Subject Survey that was designed to apply what had been learned in the First International Mathematics Study to other subjects. IEA studies routinely target one or more of three student populations: 10-year-olds, 14-year-olds, and those in the last year of secondary education. For FISS, only 10-year-olds were assessed in earth science, whereas only the older two student populations were assessed in the areas of the nature and methods of science and understanding science. All three student populations were assessed in the areas of biology, chemistry, and physics. Nineteen national education systems participated in the assessments of the older two student populations; 17 participated in the study of 10-year-olds (Comber & Keeves, 1973).

The Second International Science Study (SISS), conducted in 1983–1986, sought to apply what had been learned from FISS as well as from the Second International Mathematics Study (SIMS), which had recently been conducted. There was an interest in examining achievement differences between countries and gathering some information that could suggest explanations for these differences, as well as in making an attempt to explain the source of achievement differences *within* any one country. The number of countries that participated in SISS again varied according to the student population of interest. Fifteen national systems participated in the assessment of 10-year-olds (grade 5 in the United States); 17 systems in the assessment of 14-year-olds (U.S. grade 9); and 14 systems in the assessment of students in their last year of secondary education (U.S. grade 12) (Jacobsen & Doran, 1988). For assessment purposes, four groups of students were defined for the oldest group: those who were studying biology, those studying chemistry, those studying physics, and those not studying any science at the time of assessment (IEA, 1998; Postlethwaite & Wiley, 1992). A report by Keeves (1992) discusses changes in achievement among the 10 countries that participated in both FISS and SISS over the 14 years between the two studies.

Third International Mathematics and Science Study

"[T]he Third International Mathematics and Science Study [1995] is the largest, most comprehensive, and most rigorous study of schools and students ever." These remarks by Pascal Forgione, the Commissioner of Education Statistics, were the opening words in the first U.S. report coming from the U.S. participation in the TIMSS (National Center for Education Statistics, 1996, p. 3). Subsequent versions of the TIMSS have enlisted comparable or greater numbers of countries than the 1995 TIMSS, and PISA studies by the OECD have attracted similar country participation (see Table 33.1). Table 33.2 shows the varying numbers of countries participating in versions of the TIMSS over the years and, within a given year, the large differences in numbers of countries participating at the various target populations (ages/grades).

What remains unprecedented today is the scope and depth of the information gathered in the first TIMSS. One of the goals of the original Third International Mathematics and Science Study (TIMSS), conducted in 1993–95, was to collect data on mathematics and science education at the *same time* and with the *same students*, so that relationships between these two school subjects might be more easily explored. In addition to assessments in both mathematics and science, students completed a background survey. The teachers of the students participating in the assessments were also asked to complete an extensive survey, as was the principal (or other school official) in the schools where students were assessed.

A pioneering in-depth analysis of curriculum standards and textbooks contributed a unique facet to the study and is likely to be one of the main reasons it will remain unparalleled for years to come. Most of countries were trained to analyze the science topics and student performance expectations found in their science textbooks, line by line, page by page (McKnight & Britton, 1992; Schmidt, Jakwerth, & McKnight, 1998). Some prior IEA studies included curriculum analyses; for example, Rosier and Keeves (1991) reported the curriculum analysis in SISS. However, none of them employed such extensive data collection and analyses.

While the TIMSS 1995 collected data from the three standard IEA student populations, a more complex and demanding means of doing so was utilized: the two adjacent grade levels in which the most nine-year-olds were enrolled (grades 3 and 4 in the United States); the two adjacent grade levels in which the most 13-year-olds were enrolled (U.S. grades 7 and 8); and students in their last year of secondary school (U.S. grade 12). Subsequent editions of TIMSS and PISA assessments have not assessed all of these student populations. One of the challenges in interpreting international comparative research is the differences between countries in when students begin formal schooling. Differences among countries in this educational policy create difficulties in defining a consistent population of students to study. Does one want to study and compare students who are of a particular age but will have had varying numbers of years of formal schooling from one country to another,

TABLE 33.2
Countries Participating in TIMSS Assessments

	TIMSS 1995							TIMSS-R	TIMSS 2003								
	3rd Grade	4th Grade	4th Grade Performance Assmt	7th Grade	8th Grade Performance Assmt	8th Grade	End of secondary school	8th Grade	4th Grade	8th Grade	95 & 99	99 & 03	ALL 3 8th grade time points	1995 3rd grade	1995 7th grade	All 5 1995 grades	1995 A+
Argentina				X		X		X		X	TRUE	TRUE	TRUE		X	FALSE	
Armenia								X	X	X	FALSE	FALSE	FALSE			FALSE	
Australia	X	X	X	X	X	X	X	X	X	X	TRUE	TRUE	TRUE	X	X	TRUE	
Austria	X	X		X		X	X			X	FALSE	FALSE	FALSE	X	X	TRUE	
Bahrain										X	FALSE	FALSE	FALSE			FALSE	
Belgium (Flemish)				X		X		X	X	X	TRUE	TRUE	TRUE		X	FALSE	
Belgium (French)				X		X					FALSE	FALSE	FALSE		X	FALSE	
Botswana										X	FALSE	FALSE	FALSE			FALSE	
Bulgaria				X		X		X		X	TRUE	TRUE	TRUE		X	FALSE	
Canada	X	X	X	X	X	X	X	X			TRUE	FALSE	FALSE	X	X	TRUE	
Chile								X		X	FALSE	TRUE	FALSE			FALSE	
Chinese Taipei								X	X	X	FALSE	TRUE	FALSE		X	FALSE	
Colombia				X	X	X					FALSE	FALSE	FALSE		X	FALSE	
Cyprus	X	X	X	X	X	X	X	X	X	X	TRUE	TRUE	TRUE	X	X	TRUE	
Czech Republic	X	X		X	X	X	X	X			TRUE	FALSE	FALSE	X	X	TRUE	X
Denmark				X		X	X				FALSE	FALSE	FALSE		X	FALSE	
Egypt										X	FALSE	FALSE	FALSE			FALSE	
England	X	X		X	X	X		X	X	X	TRUE	TRUE	TRUE	X	X	FALSE	
Estonia										X	FALSE	FALSE	FALSE			FALSE	
Finland								X			FALSE	FALSE	FALSE			FALSE	
France				X		X	X				FALSE	FALSE	FALSE		X	FALSE	
Germany				X		X	X				FALSE	FALSE	FALSE		X	FALSE	
Ghana										X	FALSE	FALSE	FALSE			FALSE	
Greece	X	X	X	X	X	X	X				FALSE	FALSE	FALSE	X	X	TRUE	
Hong Kong SAR	X	X	X	X	X	X		X	X	X	TRUE	TRUE	TRUE	X	X	FALSE	
Hungary	X	X		X	X	X	X	X	X	X	TRUE	TRUE	TRUE	X	X	TRUE	
Iceland	X	X		X		X	X				FALSE	FALSE	FALSE	X	X	TRUE	
Indonesia								X		X	FALSE	TRUE	FALSE			FALSE	
Iran, Islamic Republic	X	X	X	X	X	X		X	X	X	TRUE	TRUE	TRUE	X	X	FALSE	
Ireland	X	X		X		X					FALSE	FALSE	FALSE	X	X	FALSE	
Israel		X	X		X	X		X		X	TRUE	TRUE	TRUE			FALSE	
Italy	X	X		X		X		X	X	X	TRUE	TRUE	TRUE		X	FALSE	
Japan	X	X		X	X	X		X	X	X	TRUE	TRUE	TRUE	X	X	FALSE	X
Jordan								X		X	FALSE	TRUE	FALSE			FALSE	
Korea, Republic of	X	X		X	X	X		X	X	X	TRUE	TRUE	TRUE	X	X	FALSE	X
Kuwait		X				X					FALSE	FALSE	FALSE			FALSE	
Latvia	X	X		X		X		X	X	X	TRUE	TRUE	TRUE	X	X	**FALSE**	
Lebanon										X	FALSE	FALSE	FALSE			FALSE	
Lithuania				X		X	X	X	X	X	TRUE	TRUE	TRUE		X	FALSE	
Macedonia, Republic of								X		X	FALSE	TRUE	FALSE			FALSE	
Malaysia								X		X	FALSE	TRUE	FALSE			FALSE	
Moldova								X	X	X	FALSE	TRUE	FALSE			FALSE	
Morocco								X	X	X	FALSE	TRUE	FALSE			FALSE	
Netherlands	X	X	X	X	X	X	X	X	X	X	TRUE	TRUE	TRUE	X	X	TRUE	
New Zealand	X	X	X	X	X	X	X	X	X	X	TRUE	TRUE	TRUE	X	X	TRUE	
Norway	X	X		X	X	X	X			X	FALSE	FALSE	FALSE	X	X	TRUE	
Palestinian Authority										X	FALSE	FALSE	FALSE			FALSE	
Philippines								X	X	X	FALSE	TRUE	FALSE			FALSE	
Portugal	X	X	X	X	X	X					FALSE	FALSE	FALSE	X	X	FALSE	
Romania				X	X	X		X		X	TRUE	TRUE	TRUE		X	FALSE	
Russian Federation				X		X	X	X	X	X	TRUE	TRUE	TRUE		X	FALSE	
Saudi Arabia										X	FALSE	FALSE	FALSE			FALSE	
Scotland	X	X		X	X	X				X	FALSE	FALSE	FALSE	X	X	FALSE	
Serbia										X	FALSE	FALSE	FALSE			FALSE	
Singapore	X	X		X	X	X		X	X	X	TRUE	TRUE	TRUE	X	X	FALSE	X
Slovak Republic				X		X		X		X	TRUE	TRUE	TRUE		X	FALSE	
Slovenia	X	X	X	X	X	X	X	X	X	X	TRUE	TRUE	TRUE	X	X	TRUE	
South Africa				X	X	X	X	X		X	TRUE	TRUE	TRUE		X	FALSE	
Spain				X	X	X				*	FALSE	FALSE	FALSE		X	FALSE	
Sweden				X	X	X	X			X	FALSE	FALSE	FALSE		X	FALSE	
Switzerland				X	X	X	X				FALSE	FALSE	FALSE		X	FALSE	
Syria										X	FALSE	FALSE	FALSE			FALSE	
Thailand	X	X		X		X		X			TRUE	FALSE	FALSE	X	X	FALSE	
Tunisia								X	X	X	FALSE	TRUE	FALSE			FALSE	
Turkey								X			FALSE	FALSE	FALSE			FALSE	
United States	X	X	X	X	X	X	X	X	X	X	TRUE	TRUE	TRUE	X	X	TRUE	
Yemen										X	FALSE	FALSE	FALSE			FALSE	
Total	25	27	10	41	21	43	22	39	26	48	27	34	24	24	42	13	4

or does one want to study and compare students who have all had the same number of years of formal schooling but may differ in age by a year or more, thus confounding developmental maturity with educational exposure? In an attempt to proceed down a middle path, TIMSS defined the two younger student populations as the combination of both age and years of schooling: the two adjacent grades in which the majority of 9-year-olds (population 1) or 13-year-olds (population 2) were enrolled. Wiley and Wolfe (1992) discuss the additional kinds of analyses that such methods permit.

Twenty-seven national systems participated in the assessment of 9-year-olds (grade 3 for the lower grade and grade 4 for the upper grade in the United States and many other systems) and 43 systems in the assessment of 13-year-olds (grade 7 for the lower grade and grade 8 for the upper grade in the United States and many other countries). All but two countries (Israel and Kuwait) that assessed students in the upper of the two adjacent grades for 9- and 13-year-old students also assessed students in the lower grades (see Martin et al., 1997; Beaton et al., 1996). Two student populations were defined for assessment of the end-of-secondary student population: all students who were completing the last year of secondary education in their program and those students who were in their last year of secondary education and had specialized in science. The general population was administered a science literacy assessment designed to measure what experts considered to be the level of scientific knowledge required to function as a science-literate citizen of the twenty-first century. Science specialists were given an assessment in physics. Twenty-two countries participated in the assessment of mathematics and science literacy, and only 16 countries participated in the physics assessment (Mullis et al., 1998).

Another aspect of TIMSS unique to the original 1995 study was the inclusion of an optional performance assessment component for both mathematics and science for students in the fourth and eighth grades (Harmon et al., 1997). Far fewer countries participated in this aspect of the study (10 at fourth grade; 21 at eighth grade). These performance tasks required students to use materials and apparatus to solve a multistep practical problem such as designing and constructing a box to hold four plastic balls.

In conjunction with the U.S. participation in TIMSS 1995, the U.S. government, through the National Center for Education Statistics, funded two supplementary international projects: the videotape classroom study and three case studies (Stigler et al., 1999; Stevenson, 1998). Both studies focused on mathematics at the eighth-grade level in Germany, Japan, and the United States. For TIMSS 1999, a more extensive video study included science, and results were released early in 2006 (National Center for Education Statistics, 2006).

Results.   In addition to an overall score for science, the TIMSS international science report included the average percentage correct in five broad science areas: earth science, life science, physics, chemistry, and environmental issues and the nature of science (Beaton et al., 1996). A later analysis of TIMSS grade 8 data identified a group of A+ countries as those countries significantly outperforming the majority of TIMSS countries (Valverde & Schmidt, 2000). These A+ or highest performing countries for science were Singapore, the Czech Republic, Japan, and Korea. There was great consistency in the relative rankings of these four countries—and indeed for nearly all countries—across the five broad content areas in the international report. Singapore was the top-ranked country in all five areas, and Korea was in the top four ranked countries in all areas.

Overall science rankings by country can mask significant differences within particular science areas. For example, even the highest overall performers had areas of science in which their performance was not as strong. One of the books published by the U.S. National Research Center for TIMSS contained a more detailed analysis of student achievement that reflected greater variation (Schmidt et al., 1999). The authors argued that this greater variation was a reflection of the variation in the science curriculum found across the participating countries. Considering the 17 eighth-grade curricular areas of science presented, one can see that each of the highest performing countries ranked first in at least one of these categories. However, among these four countries, Singapore had the lowest rank in any one area (21st in the area of Life Cycles and Genetics), and each country had ranks of 10th or lower in four of the 17 curricular areas.

The extensive curriculum analysis, which was a unique aspect of TIMSS 1995, provided an in-depth analysis of these issues through an examination of official curriculum standards and textbooks (Schmidt et al., 1997). An examination of the curriculum in the highest performing countries found that across these four countries (Singapore, the Czech Republic, Japan, and Korea) the five most emphasized science topics accounted for about 80 percent of the eighth-grade science textbook. These five most emphasized topics were electricity; the chemical properties of matter; chemical changes; energy, types, sources, and conversions; and organs and tissues. This represents one biology topic, two physics topics, and two chemistry topics.

The Teacher Questionnaire in TIMSS provided two more indicators of the science curriculum in countries: the percentage of teachers who taught specific topics during the school year in which the student assessment was conducted and the relative proportion of instructional time devoted to specific topics. Several reports have combined these two curricular indicators from teachers with the two curricular indicators of content standards and textbooks to provide a multifaceted perspective on what constitutes eighth-grade science across the world from the perspective of the TIMSS countries (Cogan, Wang, & Schmidt, 2001; Schmidt et al., 2001). Comparing the five most emphasized eighth-grade science topics according to each of the indicators—content standards, textbooks, percentage of teachers teaching a topic, and relative amount of instruction time devoted to a topic—the topic of "human biology" is the only topic present in all four. Aspects of energy ("electricity," "energy processes," and "energy types, sources, conversions") were also well represented.

Not all countries intended to begin science instruction as soon as children entered school. In fact, three of the four top-performing countries at eighth grade—Singapore, Japan, and the Czech Republic—did not intend science instruction to begin until grade 3 (see Schmidt et al., 1997, pp. 83–84). The number of topics intended to be taught and learned at each grade, the emphasis afforded topics within a year, and the pattern of sequencing topics across the years of schooling have been identified as important indicators of the coherence, focus, and rigor of any country's curriculum (Schmidt, McKnight, & Raizen, 1997). Nonetheless, two of the highest achieving countries at eighth grade were also the top performers on the fourth-grade student assessment: Korea and Japan; Singapore ranked 10th and the Czech Republic ranked 6th (Martin et al., 1997).

The Czech Republic was the only highest achieving country at eighth grade that also participated in the end-of-secondary student assessments but did not demonstrate comparable outstanding performance, ranking only 13th out of 21 participating countries on the science literacy assessment and 14th out of 16 on physics (Mullis et al., 1998). Students in Sweden ranked first in science literacy and second in physics. Norway ranked first on the physics assessment and fourth on the science literacy assessment.

Many participating countries generate national reports that show how their students performed in TIMSS and discuss implications for national issues in science education. Researchers also have done analyses to compare science performance between particular countries (e.g., Wang, 1998). In the United States, TIMSS garnered so much attention that states and consortia of school districts have done special, more intensive sampling in order to relate their local student science or mathematics performance to international results (e.g., Kimmelman, 1999).

TIMSS 1999 and 2003

Although items from each of these assessments were released into the public domain, similar items were written and included in the subsequent assessments to maintain a very similar emphasis in the broad areas of science. Across the three eighth-grade student assessment times—TIMSS (1995), TIMSS-R (1999), and TIMSS 2003—the emphasis on earth science was 16 percent, 15 percent, and 16 percent, respectively. Life science emphasis was 30 percent, 27 percent, and 29 percent; physics was 30 percent, 27 percent, and 24 percent; chemistry was 14 percent, 14 percent, and 16 percent. Environmental issues and the nature of science was the focus of 10 percent, 17 percent, and 14 percent of the items on the respective assessments.

The number of countries involved in each assessment and the differences in the items comprising each assessment preclude drawing any conclusions from direct comparisons. Furthermore, because the scaled scores are formed each time on the basis of the participating students, the scaled scores for any two assessments, such as TIMSS 1995 and TIMSS 2003, are not directly comparable. One report uses revised scale scores for each of the assessments to enable more appropriate comparisons (Gonzales et al., 2004). Only seven countries have participated in all assessments at each of the three TIMSS time points: Australia, Cyprus, Hungary, the Netherlands, New Zealand, Slovenia, and the United States. Although the report does note some statistically significant differences in the performance of some countries from one assessment to another, the magnitudes of these differences do not suggest major shifts in student performance (see Gonzales et al., p. 17, Table 11).

OECD-PISA

The Organisation for Economic Co-operation and Development (OECD) launched a new cross-national assessment of science in 2000. The OECD is a Paris-based organization of industrialized countries that historically is most widely known for its cross-national reports on economics, such as comparisons of per capita spending on education. Within OECD, the Center for Education Research and Innovation (CERI) has since 1968 organized occasional studies of the educational aspects of education, including science education (e.g., Black & Atkin, 1996; Raizen & Britton, 1997).

The new regularly scheduled assessment by OECD is known as the Programme for International Student Achievement (PISA). This assessment emphasized science for the first time in 2006. It focuses only on 15-year-olds and includes assessment of three subject areas every year it is offered—literacy, mathematics, and science. In each cycle, however, one subject receives dominant attention: literacy in 2000 (OECD 2001), mathematics in 2003 (OECD 2004a), and science in 2006. The IEA's TIMSS series occurs every four years, and the PISA cycle is three years. PISA has attracted strong international interest, as indicated by the participation of over 40 countries in the first two administrations. The TIMSS and PISA test specifications give comparable emphasis to life sciences, whereas PISA has emphasized earth sciences more than TIMSS, and TIMSS has more strongly emphasized physical science.

The characteristic of PISA that distinguishes it from TIMSS is the nature of science that it seeks to evaluate, and this affects the nature of the test items in PISA versus TIMSS. Whereas TIMSS primarily focuses on the formal content of the scientific disciplines, PISA emphasizes students' application of science in real-life contexts. Gauging these multifaceted aspects of science requires more open-ended than defined-response items (Nohara, 2001). Neidorf et al. (2004) reports that typical PISA items make more complex cognitive demands on students. Scott and Owen (2005) contrast the purposes, construction, and uses of NAEP, PISA, and TIMSS.

The PISA 2006 specification of scientific literacy has four interconnected aspects. *Context* involves recognizing life situations involving science and technology. *Knowledge* is understanding the natural world, including technology, on the basis of scientific knowledge that includes both knowledge of the natural world as well as knowledge *about* science itself. The latter includes interactions among science and technology and the material, intellectual, and cultural environments. The first criterion for choosing knowledge to be assessed is its relevance to real-life situations. The second criterion is that the selected knowledge should represent important scientific concepts. The TIMSS design typically reverses these priorities. The *attitude* aspect includes interest in science, support for scientific inquiry, and motivation to act responsibly (e.g., toward natural resources and the environment).

The PISA framework gives priority to a fourth related aspect, *competencies*: identifying scientific questions; describing, predicting, or explaining phenomena based on scientific knowledge; interpreting evidence and conclusions; and using scientific evidence to make and communicate decisions. In other words, solving science-based problems is a central student activity in PISA assessments (OECD, 2004b).

The PISA 2006 science framework gives significant attention to technology education. A number of countries have for more than 10 years included technology as an additional school subject, separate in the school day from science (Britton, De Long-Cotty, & Levenson, 2005), but technology education does not have as strong a foothold to date in the United States (Meade & Dugger, 2004). The National Academy of Engineering and the National Research Council describe technology as follows:

> In its broadest sense, technology is the process by which humans modify nature to meet their needs and wants. However, most people think of technology only in terms of its artifacts: computers, aircraft, . . . , to name a few. But technology also is the knowledge and processes necessary to create and operate those products, such as engineering know-how and design, manufacturing expertise, various technical skills, and so on. (NAE & NRC, 2002, pp. 2–3)

Both the AAAS and NRC standards documents clearly include attention to technology (AAAS, 1993; NRC, 1996). Additionally, the technology education community has its own national curriculum standards (International Technology Education Association, ITEA, 2000). Development of the technology standards was funded by both the NSF and the National Aeronautics and Space Agency (NASA), and they were vetted by NAE and NRC.

The PISA results to date have received significantly less attention than TIMSS results in the United States, perhaps because of the current policymaker emphasis on the formal disciplinary knowledge that is more strongly assessed by TIMSS.

CHANGES IN NAEP SCIENCE

More than 35 years ago, NAEP began gathering information on student achievement in selected academic subjects (Johnson, 1975). That first administration included practical skills tests in science (NAEP, 1975). It has grown in scope several times over the years. The third assessment added items to assess student attitudes toward science (NEAP 1978). The 1986 NAEP science investigated students' home environments and the kinds of science instruction they received in school (Mullis & Jenkins, 1998). Also in 1986, an experimental assessment was developed to test higher order thinking skills, and students interacted with a computer simulation for an item (NAEP, 1987). Originally, assessments were of students 9, 13, and 17 years old; beginning in 1983, the assessment has sampled students in grades 4, 8, and 12. During the late 1980s, the Educational Testing Service (ETS), the contractor that conducts NAEP, made a brief, analogous foray into international assessments (LaPointe, Mead, & Phillips, 1989; LaPointe, Askew, & Mead, 1992).

Each administration of NAEP has become an important and continuing source of information on what U.S. students know and are able to do at that time. In addition, NAEP provides information on how student performance has changed over time in reading, mathematics, science, U.S. history, writing, and other subjects (e.g., NAEP, 1992; Campbell, Voelkl, & Donahue, 1998). NAEP data are publicly available, so that researchers can conduct secondary analysis of the science assessment (e.g., Linn et al., 1987; Welch, Walberg, & Fraser, 1986).

Since the mid-1990s, in addition to the national-level assessments, NAEP has conducted and reported state-level assessments at grades 4 and 8 in reading, mathematics, writing, and science (Hudson, 1990). State-level science assessments were conducted in 1996, 2000, and 2005. The resulting data on student knowledge and performance have been accompanied by background information that allows analyses of a number of student demographic and instructional factors related to achievement. The assessments have been designed to allow comparisons of student performance over time and among subgroups of students according to region, parental education, gender, and race/ethnicity. In 2002, NAEP began a Trial Urban District Assessment (TUDA) in districts that volunteered to participate. The TUDA continued through 2005, when 10 districts took part in NAEP assessments that produce district-level results.

The National Assessment Governing Board (NAGB) is responsible for the NAEP program. This included the development in 1993 of three levels of achievement—basic, proficient, and advanced. *Basic* denotes partial mastery of prerequisite knowledge and skills that are fundamental for proficient work at each grade. *Proficient* represents solid academic performance for each grade assessed. Students reaching this level have demonstrated competency over challenging subject matter, including subject-matter knowledge, application of such knowledge to real-world situations, and analytical skills appropriate to the subject matter. *Advanced* signifies superior performance. These levels are the primary means of reporting NAEP results to the general public and policymakers regarding what students should know and be able to do on NAEP assessments.

The framework that guided the last three NAEP science assessments was developed 15 years ago. The NAGB in late 2005 approved the next framework that will guide administrations of NAEP science from 2009 through 2021.

Science Content

The 2009 NAEP science content domain is defined by a series of content statements that describe key principles, concepts, and facts in three broad content areas: physical science, life science, and earth and space science (see Table 33.3).

As measured by student response time, the distribution of items by content area should be as follows: roughly equal across physical, life, and earth and space science at grade 4; more emphasis on earth and space science at grade 8; a shift to more emphasis on physical and life science at grade 12.

Some content cuts across the areas of physical, life, and earth and space science. Some instances of cross-cutting content are identified and described below.

Uses and transformations of energy and energy conservation.   To demonstrate an understanding of energy uses, transformations, and conservation, students must be able to do so in the context of different types of systems. These systems include biological organisms, earth systems, ecosystems (combining both life forms and

TABLE 33.3
Science Content, NAEP Science 2009–2021

Physical Science Major and Minor Topics for Grades 4, 8, and 12
Matter
    Properties of Matter
    Changes in Matter
Energy
    Forms of Energy
    Energy Conversions and Conservation
Motion
    Motion at the Macroscopic and Molecular Levels
    Forces Affecting Motion

Life Science Content Topics for Grades 4, 8, and 12
Structures and Functions of Living Systems
    Organization and development of living systems
    Matter and energy transformations in living systems
    Interdependence of living systems
Changes in Living Systems
    Heredity and reproduction of living systems
    Evolution and diversity of living systems

Earth and Space Science Content Topics for Grades 4, 8, and 12
Earth in Space and Time
    Objects in the Universe
    History of Earth
Earth Structures
    Properties of Earth Materials
    Tectonics
Earth Systems
    Energy in Earth Systems
    Climate and Weather
    Biogeochemical Cycles

their physical environment), the solar system and other systems in the universe, and human-designed systems.

Biogeochemical cycles.   To demonstrate an understanding of biogeochemical cycles, students must draw on their knowledge of matter and energy (physical science), structures and functions of living systems (life science), and Earth systems (earth and space science). Fixed amounts of chemical atoms or elements cycle within the Earth system; energy drives this movement of matter, which includes water and nutrient cycles; and human use of Earth's finite resources affects the land, oceans, and atmosphere, as well as plant and animal populations.

Science Practices

The second dimension of the framework is defined by four practices: identifying science principles, using science principles, scientific inquiry, and technological design. By crossing any science content statement above with the four practices, it is possible to generate specific performance expectations on which assessment items can be based. Therefore, neither content statements nor practice statements will be assessed in isolation; all assessment items will be derived from a combination of the two. Observed student responses to these items can then be compared with expected student responses in order to make inferences about what students know and can do.

Table 33.4 summarizes general performance expectations for each of the four practices. Certain ways of knowing and thinking—cognitive demands—underpin the four science practices. Four such cognitive demands are as follows: *knowing what, knowing how, knowing why,* and *knowing when and where to apply knowledge.* The set of four cognitive demands can be used as a lens to analyze student responses, thereby checking expectations regarding what content and practice(s) are being tapped by a given assessment item.

Item Formats

Item formats for the 2009 NAEP science assessment fall into two broad categories: 1) selected-response items comprise individual multiple-choice items, cluster multiple-choice items, and Predict-Observe-Explain (POE) multiple-choice items; 2) constructed-response items comprise short constructed-response items, extended constructed-response items, concept maps, hands-on performance tasks, and interactive computer tasks. As measured by student response time, roughly no more than 50 percent of the assessment items at each grade level should be selected-response items; the remainder should be made up of constructed-response items. In order to further probe students' abilities to combine their understandings with the investigative skills reflective of practices, a subsample of students should receive an additional 20–30 minutes of response time to complete hands-on performance and interactive computer tasks. There should be at least a total of four of these tasks at each grade; of these four tasks, there should be at least one hands-on *and* one interactive computer task per grade; the number of hands-on tasks should not exceed the number of interactive computer tasks.

TABLE 33.4
General Performance Expectations for Practices, NAEP Science 2009–2021

Identifying Science Principles	Using Science Principles	Scientific Inquiry	Technological Design
State correct science principles	Explain specific observations or phenomena	Design and critique scientific investigations	Design and critique technological solutions to given problems
Connect different representations of science principles and patterns in data	Predict specific observations or phenomena	Conduct scientific investigations using appropriate tools and techniques	Identify scientific tradeoffs in design decisions and choose among alternative solutions
Make connections among closely related content statements	Propose, analyze, and evaluate alternative predictions or explanations	Find patterns in data. Relate patterns in data to theoretical models	Apply science principles or data to anticipate effects of technological design decisions
Describe, measure, or classify observations	Suggest examples of observations that illustrate a science principle	Use empirical evidence to draw valid conclusions about explanations and predictions	
	← Communicate accurately and effectively →		

In hands-on performance tasks, students manipulate selected physical objects and try to solve a scientific problem involving the objects. NAEP hands-on performance tasks should provide students with a concrete, well-contextualized task (problem) along with "laboratory" equipment and materials. However, the response format should give students the freedom to determine scientifically justifiable procedures for addressing the problem and arriving at a solution. Students' scores should be based on both the solution and the procedures created for carrying out the investigation and the solution.

Interactive computer tasks should be of four types: 1) information search and analysis, 2) empirical investigation, 3) simulation, and 4) concept maps. Information search and analysis items pose a scientific problem and ask students to query an information database to bring conceptual and empirical information to bear, through analysis, on the problem. Empirical investigation items put hands-on performance tasks on the computer and invite students to design and conduct a study to draw inferences and conclusions about a problem. Simulation items model systems (e.g., food chains), pose problems of prediction and explanation about changes in the system, and permit students to collect data and solve problems in the system. Concept-map items probe aspects of the structure or organization of students' scientific knowledge by providing concept terms and having students build concept maps on the computer. A concept map is a network whose nodes are concept terms (e.g., *density, buoyancy, mass*). The nodes are connected by directed, labeled lines. A directed line shows the relationship between a pair of concept terms; the label on the line describes the relationship.

COHERENT STATE SYSTEMS OF LARGE-SCALE
AND CLASSROOM ASSESSMENT

Better alignment between large-scale science assessments and science standards, discussed earlier, enhances the assessment enterprise in educational systems. Shepard (1993) discusses the difficulties in making large-scale assessments relevant to student learning. However, experts in assessment now argue for more substantial changes in both classroom assessment and large-scale assessments to forge them into coherent, articulated assessment systems. The National Research Council has released a model for doing this, *Systems for State Science Assessment* (Wilson & Bertenthal, 2005). Although few if any states currently or will soon be able to have systems that are mostly consistent with this model, the NRC publication at a minimum is a good lens for examining the explosion of state science assessments being driven by the NCLB requirement that states must be assessing science no later than 2007.

The NRC model particularly draws upon some prior NRC work, for example: Committee on Assessment in Support of Instruction on Learning (2003) led by Atkin, the Committee on the Foundations of Assessment (*Knowing What Students Know; Science and Design of Educational Assessment*, NRC, 2001) led by Pellegrino, and How People Learn (Bransford, Brown, & Cocking, 1999). Another prominent influence on the 2005 NRC model is ongoing work at the NSF-funded Center for the Assessment and Evaluation of Student Learning (CAESL), which includes work at the Berkeley Evaluation and Assessment Research Center (BEAR).

Three kinds of coherence are envisioned (Wilson & Bertenthal, 2005, p. 4). Horizontal coherence is where curriculum, instruction, and assessment are all aligned with the standards, as described previously. Vertical coherence exists when all levels of the educational system—classroom, school, district, state—are based on a shared vision of the goals for science education, the purposes of assessment, and a definition of competent performance. The system is developmentally coherent when it attends to how students' science understanding develops over time.

The CAESL model, shown in Fig. 33.3, proposes a systems view of assessment that serves top-down policy needs for sound assessment information for accountability purposes, but is also built bottom up so that it is responsive to teachers' needs for ongoing, formative information to support their students' learning. As designed, the system also would support needs at intermediate levels (e.g., school/department, district) for periodic monitoring and evaluation of student performance.

The CAESL model starts with specified standards and uses a theory-based model of student cognition to derive a coordinated set of large-scale and classroom-based assessment tools. The large-scale assessments incorporate on-demand, multiple-choice, open-ended, concept-map, performance, and explanation items, which are intended to provide comparable and generalizable information on the status of students' attainment. Such information is appropriate for determining whether learning goals have been achieved—at the individual, classroom, school, or district levels—and is a source of needs assessment information for program and instructional planning at an annual or semiannual interval, depending on when such results are available.

Historically, most external assessments in the United States have been administered at the end of the school year, timed to capture what students have mastered

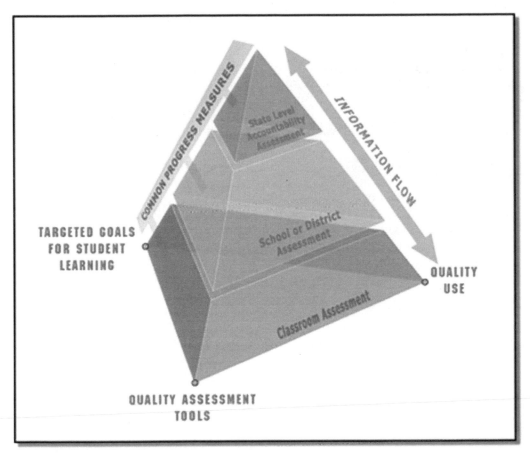

FIGURE 33–3   Assessment model, Center for Assessment and Evaluation of Student Learning (CAESL, www.caesl.org).

during the school year. Teachers can only use such information to inform what they might do differently next school year, so the tested students do not get a direct benefit from the time that they had to spend on the assessments. As a result, today we find that although students are tested in the spring for national or state purposes, districts may also be testing them at the beginning of the year to produce data to guide teachers' instruction. During the 1980s, France instituted an assessment system where national examinations were administered in grades 3 and 6 at the beginning of the school year and quickly scored so that teachers could have the results. Policy makers accepted that for external purposes, they had to make different inferences about what the results could mean. However, many teachers became enthusiastic about the examinations because they served as a diagnostic that could immediately inform their instruction (Black & Atkin, 1996, pp. 103–107).

In the CAESL model, the classroom or curriculum-embedded tools are more ongoing and performance-oriented and provide the smaller grain size and instructionally sensitive information needed to diagnose whether and how students are making progress on key science content. Results from these classroom tools are intended to be the basis for immediate instructional action for individuals, subgroups, and/or the class as a whole, drawing on strengths and addressing learning needs that may be revealed by the assessments.

Both the large-scale and classroom measures reflect common continuums of expected learning progress relative to core areas of scientific knowledge and skills that are subject to assessment—for example, fundamental ideas, core principles, and/or key aspects of inquiry. Based in a model of cognition (Shavelson, 2003; Li & Shavelson, 2001; Shavelson & Ruiz-Primo, 1999), each of these progress continuums forms a "progress variable" in the CAESL model and are the basis for the consistent measurement system linking all educational levels (Masters, Wilson, & Adams, 1992; Wilson, 2005).

That all measures are developed to reveal students' progress relative to a consistent, cognitively based measurement scale means that the *classroom assessments have potential to be aggregated beyond the classroom level*. Such aggregated data have potential for monitoring student progress at the school and/or district levels and may even serve accountability purposes, possibly reducing or eliminating the need for traditional, on demand assessments (Wilson, 1992, 2004).

The emphasis on student progress has other implications as well. It connotes CAESL's commitment to measures that assess and support the development of students' depth of understanding, as progress implies movement from naïve to sophisticated understanding and applications. Because dealing with science content in depth necessarily limits the range of science content that can be taught and because coordinating classroom and large-scale assessment requires advance planning, the model thus advocates assessment of a limited but powerful set of science understandings and applications. To derive the most power from a limited but rich set of assessments, the CAESL model focuses its assessment targets on key unifying ideas and inquiry skills of science.

Note that the CAESL model also includes explicit attention to the *use* of assessment information. Having sound tools integrated into a coordinated system of assessment provides essential precursors but does not ensure that the results of such a system will be used to promote students' learning. In fact, there is considerable evidence that most teachers do not currently have the capacity to use assessment for such purposes well.

While laying out these multiple pathways through which assessment can enhance teaching and learning, recent research also acknowledges the sophisticated content and pedagogical knowledge required to implement this vision: knowledge of standards and their conceptual underpinnings, knowledge of the instructional content and sequences that are most likely to achieve aims, knowledge of optimal and varied ways to support student progress, knowledge of ways to capitalize on students' background knowledge and provide access for all students, and knowledge of likely stumbling blocks and misconceptions, etc.

Moreover, the model recognizes that its view of assessment implies a dramatic shift in how teachers see themselves as teachers and as professionals who truly are responsible for their students' learning progress and for their attainment of standards. Substantial professional development and support are needed to build teachers' capacity and guiding perspectives in this domain (Atkin, Black, & Coffey, 2001). The CAESL model is mindful of the role and challenges in building teacher capacity to use assessment well, including teachers' knowledge of science, their knowledge of assessment, and their teaching and assessment practices.

All stakeholders in a coherent assessment system will have to make significant efforts in forging an assessment system from the fractured collection of assessments that is typical today. A substantial investment is needed in professional development to help practitioners understand the relationships possible between large-scale and classroom assessment, and to empower them to incorporate classroom assessment strategies that will produce versions of the former that can be aggregated into or articulated with external assessments. State policy makers, assessment experts, scientists, and educators who oversee development of state science tests along with practitioners will need to collaborate very much more than typically is the case.

Sample State Assessment Systems

The NCLB legislation requires all states to test the progress of all students in science once during grades 3–5, 6–9, and 10–12, beginning in 2007. To meet the NCLB requirement, states only need to report student scores and not necessarily establish a comprehensive assessment system that meets the current recommendations of the National Academy of Science's Board on Testing and Assessment (BOTA). These recommendations encompass a broad range of ideas for a systems approach to assessment that stresses ideas of *vertical coherence* and *horizontal coherence* (Wilson & Bertenthal, 2005). Vertical coherence indicates the importance of having shared goals for assessments at the classroom, district, and state levels. Horizontal coherence emphasizes the need for consistency between standards, assessments, curricula, and instructional practice.

The implications of science literacy on assessment are also discussed, as states are encouraged to align their assessment systems to accurately measure the following components: knowledge of science content, understanding science as a way of knowing, and understanding and conducting scientific inquiry. States are urged to develop detailed content standards, generate guidelines for all users, allow for independent reviewers, and maintain regular cycles of revision of the standards. The report also advises states to consult research and professionals in the design of their assessments to ensure that test items bring to light student progress and understanding.

Many suggestions for both the implementation and support of assessments are elaborated. States should form advisory committees, develop plans and strategies for the entire assessment system, align assessment plans with science standards, ensure analysis and usability of score reports, provide staff development in the use of the assessments, and certify teachers who are competent in their subject and assessing student understanding of it. States must also be conscious of issues of equity and adequacy. Assessments systems should collect information on opportunities for a wide range of students to learn the necessary material. At the same time, systems should include alternative assessments for those with significant cognitive disabilities. States should set aside resources for the revision of these assessments. Finally, it is recommended that states rigorously monitor and evaluate their science assessment systems to ensure that all parts of their systems are aligned with corresponding goals.

There are a number of states moving beyond NCLB compliance toward the kinds of assessment systems envisioned by the NRC. We provide here four examples of current state systems that have incorporated components of the recommendations.

The state of Connecticut has established a statewide testing program that includes both the Connecticut Mastery Test (CMT) and the Connecticut Academic Performance

Test (CAPT), the latter of which includes a science assessment (Connecticut State Board of Education, 2001, 2005). Connecticut has also developed a CAPT Skills Checklist for students identified with cognitive disabilities. The state has been building this assessment system for almost two decades. English language learners are provided with accommodations as needed, ensuring equality in testing. The CAPT goes beyond traditional multiple-choice testing to include a variety of assessment techniques, such as performance tests, which not only indicate what students know, but what they can do. The tests were designed to assess not only knowledge of scientific facts, but also the application of concepts, the use of experimentation, and the understanding of scientific reasoning. The science portion of CAPT includes a hands-on laboratory activity that is to be completed in the weeks prior to the written portion of the test.

The CAPT produces vertical coherence, as educational priorities from the classroom level to the state level are set and reinforced by the content of the assessment. Results of the test provide feedback to educators at all levels of the system for the reevaluation of their work and priorities. Results of the CAPT are provided to students and educators, along with an interpretive guide and software for data analysis. In the development of CAPT, advisory committees are utilized, as are testing companies and curriculum and assessment specialists. Aware of the need for staff development and training, Connecticut provides various initiatives to enhance the use of assessment results and subsequent instructional change, including annual test coordinator workshops, instructional workshops with curriculum consultants, and alternativee assessment workshops for the CAPT Skills Checklist. The state has also set long-term plans for its assessments, as the testing program is viewed in terms of "generations," allowing for periodic and systematic review and revision of assessments.

The Delaware Student Testing Program (DSTP) employs a systems approach to assessment (see Delaware Department of Education, 2005, n.d.). Assessments are linked to the state content standards and are intended to measure student progress. Assessment results are reported at the state, district, school, and individual student levels. Delaware teachers are involved in the entire process of developing the DSTP, from writing, reviewing, and editing test questions to recommending cutoff points for performance levels. This encourages horizontal coherence by giving guidance for instructional change and provides vertical coherence in serving as the state's overarching accountability system.

Delaware has content standards that reflect current thinking in the scientific community, regarding science literacy as not only knowledge of content but also as a way of understanding the world. Delaware's science assessment employs both multiple-choice and constructed-response items. Students identified as having cognitive disabilities are given the Delaware Alternate Portfolio Assessment. A Bias Committee, a Content Advisory Committee, and several other specialists and advisors ensure the reliability, validity, and unbiased nature of the test. Delaware also uses test results to form Individual Improvement Plans for students who may need extra support, advising, extra tutoring, extra classes, or summer school. Results of the DSTP are also used to inform districts and schools of specific content areas that may need improvement.

Maine's approach to assessment is quite systematic (see Maine Department of Education, n.d.). Each component of the system has its specific purpose and process for enhancing teaching and learning, monitoring and holding educators accountable to state standards, and ensuring student achievement of standards. Maine has established a Comprehensive Assessment System comprising an interconnected web of state and local components. The Maine Educational Assessment is the statewide assessment aligned to Maine's "Learning Results" or standards. Maine also has a Local Assessment System, which is perhaps the most important component of Maine's larger Comprehensive Assessment System.

This Local Assessment System allows individual districts to develop their own comprehensive systems of assessment that can be tailored to the needs of their students. However, districts are also expected to ensure that assessments are aligned to state standards and are valid, reliable, and equitable. Going beyond traditional multiple-choice tests, Maine has developed the Maine Assessment Portfolio Project, which provides another option for local assessments whereby students are able to demonstrate proficiency on standards and performance indicators. Maine's Comprehensive Assessment System is vertically coherent in its structure of including everything from NAEP to classroom assessments developed by individual teachers. The system is also horizontally coherent in its focus on local assessments that have been developed and scored by individual districts and teachers.

This structure provides educators with detailed knowledge of the material being assessed and may result in corresponding instructional changes. The state recognizes its responsibilities in maintaining such a system of assessment and therefore provides assistance to districts in clarifying their system standards, in monitoring and evaluating performance tasks and student portfolios, in disseminating information to and from individual districts regarding best practices, and providing alternative assessment frameworks to ensure equality.

The Washington State Assessment System (WSAS) has three components: statewide standardized testing, classroom-based assessments, and professional development for teachers about assessment (see Washington Department of Education, n.d.). Washington has developed its own content standards (Essential Academic Learning Requirements, or EALRs), which provide vertical coherence in having achievement indicators for the state, the districts, schools, and individual students. Additionally, curriculum specialists are consulted in the design of assessments that are distributed to districts. Horizontal coherence is incorporated into the state's use of classroom-based assessments that are linked to the content standards and which affect instructional practice. Washington also has a staff development assessment program in which teams of trainers provide instruction and materials to classroom teachers and principals to aid the improvement of reliable assessment practices. The state has developed its own assessment, the Washington Assessment of Student Learning (WASL), a criterion-reference test incorporating multiple-choice questions, short constructed response items, and extended constructed response items. Each item is individually aligned to a state content standard, as well as to a component of science literacy.

The entire statewide testing program includes three components: the WASL, the Iowa Tests of Basic Skills (ITBS) or the Iowa Tests of Education Development (ITED), and the National Assessment of Educational Progress (NAEP). The performance standards for the WASL are based on research from an outside professional testing service, the Iowa tests provide data on basic skills, and NAEP acts as a national base of comparison as well as an indicator of the validity of the WASL.

An assessment system that provides feedback to all major stakeholders in the educational system is very demanding and costly. This type of system has to clearly demonstrate the "value added" to the educational enterprise to justify effort and cost. The state systems described above illustrate how best practice in the field can address the National Academy's guidance. However, a number of states that previously had complex assessment systems had to scale them back when they were perceived as creating unacceptable burdens at various levels of the educational system.

HIGH SCHOOL EXIT EXAMS

The chapter concludes by briefly mentioning a kind of exam that historically was rare in the United States but has spread quickly in recent years—the high school exit exam. For years in many other countries, there have been examinations in science and other subjects given at the end of secondary school, either as part of matriculation, or for college-bound students to gain entry to college. In a companion study to the TIMSS, the National Center for Improving Science Education (NCISE) conducted an item-by-item content analysis of such science examinations (Britton & Raizen, 1996). In collaboration with the American Federal of Teachers (AFT), the exams themselves were published to make U.S. audiences more aware of them (AFT & NCISE, 1994, 1995, 1996).

In the United States, 26 states now have exit exams or are preparing to implement them, including 19 states that currently require students to pass exit exams and 7 states that plan to phase in mandatory exit exams during the next 7 years (Center on Education Policy, 2005). Historically, only a few states, such as California and New York, had such examinations (Golden State Exams and New York Regents Exams, respectively). Although only a bare majority of the states even now have exams, this is not an accurate representation of the number of students affected. By 2012, about 72 percent of all American public school students will attend school in states with required exit exams. An estimated 82 percent of minority students, 71 percent of special education students, and 87 percent of English language learners will have to pass exit exams in coming years.

There are three kinds of exams: minimum competency exams, standards-based exams, and end-of-course exams (such as Advanced Placement). States are moving away from the reputedly easier minimum competency tests toward the more challenging standards-based and end-of-course exams. Only three of the 25 states that are now using or plan to implement exit exams will use minimum competency exams, 17 will be using standards-based, and five will use end-of-course exams.

Currently, 10 states have exit exams in science: Alabama, Georgia, Louisiana, Mississippi, New Mexico, New York, Ohio, Tennessee, Texas, and Virginia. By 2010, the states of Maryland, Nevada, New Jersey, and Washington also will have science examinations. By 2007, 11 states plan to use the same science exam to award diplomas and meet the NCLB requirement for testing high school science.

ACKNOWLEDGMENTS

Lee Cogan at Michigan State University provided substantial text for the section on the TIMSS. The NAEP section draws upon work by the NAEP framework development committee, co-chaired by Richard Shavelson and Senta Raizen. Joan Herman at CRESST, Mike Timms at WestEd, and others provided substantial text for the section on CAESL. Stephen Zuniga at CRESST contributed to the literature review for several sections, and Cindy Lee contributed to the section on exemplar state science examinations. Thanks to Audrey Champagne and Angelo Collins, who reviewed this chapter.

REFERENCES

Abedi, J., Hofstetter, C., Baker, E., & Lord, C. (2001). NAEP math performance and test accommodations: interactions with student language background. *CSE Technical Report 536.* Los Angeles: CRESST/UCLA.

American Association for the Advancement of Science. (1993). *Benchmarks for science literacy.* New York: Oxford University Press.

American Federation of Teachers. (1995). *What secondary students abroad are expected to know: Gateway exams taken by average-achieving students in France, Germany, and Scotland.* Washington, DC: American Federation of Teachers.

American Federation of Teachers & National Center for Improving Science Education. (1994). *What college-bound students abroad are expected to know about biology: Exams from England and Wales, France, Germany and Japan.* Washington, DC: American Federation of Teachers.

American Federation of Teachers & National Center for Improving Science Education. (1996). *What college-bound students abroad are expected to know about chemistry and physics: Exams from England and Wales, France, Germany and Japan.* Washington, DC: American Federation of Teachers.

Atkin, J. M., Black, P., & Coffey, J. (Eds.). (2001). *Classroom assessment and the national science education standards.* Washington, DC: National Academies Press.

Baxter, G., & Glaser, R. (1997). An approach to analyzing the cognitive complexity of science performance assessments. *CSE Technical Report 452.* Los Angeles: CRESST/UCLA.

Beaton, A. E., Mullis, I. V. S., Martin, M. O., Gonzalez, E. J., Kelly, D. L., & Smith, T. A. (1996). *Science achievement in the middle school years: IEA's Third International Mathematics and Science Study.* Chestnut Hill, MA: Center for the Study of Testing, Evaluation, and Educational Policy, Boston College.

Berg, C., & Smith, P. (1994). Assessing students' abilities to construct and interpret line graphs: Disparities between multiple-choice and free-response instruments. *Science Education, 78,* 527–554.

Black, P., & Atkin, J. M. (Eds.). (1996). *Changing the subject: Innovations in science, mathematics and technology education.* London: Routledge.

Borko, H., & Elliott, R. (1998). Tensions between competing pedagogical and accountability commitments for exemplary teachers of mathematics in Kentucky. *CSE Technical Report 495.* Los Angeles: CRESST/UCLA.

Borko, H., & Stecher, B. M. (2001, April). *Looking at reform through different methodological lenses: Survey and case studies of the Washington state education reform.* Paper presented as part of a symposium at the annual meeting of the American Educational Research Association, Seattle.

Bransford, J. D., Brown, A. L., & Cocking, R. R. (Eds.). (1999). *How people learn: Brain, mind, experience, and school.* Washington, DC: National Academy Press.

Britton, E., De Long-Cotty, B., & Levenson, T. (2005). *Bringing technology education into K–8 classrooms: A guide to curricular resources about the designed world.* Arlington, VA: NSTA Press.

Britton, E., & Raizen, S. A. (Eds.). (1996). *Examining the examinations: An international comparison of science and mathematics examinations for college-bound students.* Boston: Kluwer Academic.

Campbell, J. R., Voelkl, K. E., & Donahue, P. L. (1998). *NAEP 1996 trends in academic progress, addendum.* Washington, DC: National Center for Education Statistics.

Center on Education Policy. (2005). *States try harder, but gaps persist: High school exit exams 2005.* Washington, DC: Author.

Cogan, L. S., Wang, H. A., & Schmidt, W. H. (2001). Culturally specific patterns in the conceptualization of the school science curriculum: Insights from TIMSS. *Studies in Science Education, 36,* 105–134.

Collins, A. (1993). Performance-based assessment of biology teachers: Promise and pitfalls. *Journal of Research in Science Teaching, 30,* 1103–1120.

Comber, L. C., & Keeves, J. P. (1973). *Science education in nineteen countries: An empirical study.* New York: Wiley.

Committee on Assessment in Support of Instruction and Learning. (2003). *Assessment in support of instruction and learning: Bridging the gap between large-scale and classroom assessment.* Washington, DC: National Academies Press.

Connecticut State Board of Education. (2001). *Connecticut academic performance test: Second generation, science handbook.* Retrieved January 31, 2006, from http://www.state.ct.us/sde/dtl/curriculum/currsci_publ_capt.htm

Connecticut State Board of Education. (2005). *Connecticut academic performance test: Second generation.* Retrieved January 31, 2006, from http://www.csde.state.ct.us/public/cedar/assessment/capt/resources/misc_capt/2005_capt_program_overview_part1.pdf and http://www.csde.state.ct.us/public/cedar/assessment/capt/resources/misc_capt/2005_capt_program_overview_part2.pdf

Delaware Department of Education. (n.d.). *About the DSTP.* Retrieved January 31, 2006, from http://www.doe.k12.de.us/aab/DSTP_intro.html

Delaware Department of Education. (2005). *Delaware student testing program: Frequently asked questions.* Retrieved January 31, 2006, from http://www.doe.k12.de.us/aab/DSTP%20FAQs.pdf

Doran, R. L., Boorman, J., Chan, F., & Hejaily, N. (1993). Alternative assessment of high school laboratory skills. *Journal of Research in Science Teaching, 30,* 1121–1132.

Doran, R. L., Lawrenz, F., & Helgeson, S. (1994). Research on assessment in science. In D. L. Gabel (Ed.), *Handbook of research on science teaching and learning* (pp. 388–442). New York: Macmillan.

Doran, R. L., & Tamir, P. (1992). An international assessment of science practical skills. *Studies in Educational Evaluation, 18*(3), 263–406.

Firestone, W. A., Camilli, G., Yurecko, M., Monfils, L., & Mayrowetz, D. (2000). State standards, socio-fiscal context and opportunity to learn in New Jersey [electronic version]. *Educational Policy Analysis Archives, 8*(35).

Firestone, W. A., Mayrowetz, D., & Fairman, J. (1998). Performance-based assessment and instructional change: The effects of testing in Maine and Maryland. *Educational Evaluation and Policy Analysis, 20*(2), 95–114.

Goldberg, G. L., & Rosewell, B. S. (2000). From perception to practice: The impact of teachers' scoring experience on performance based instruction and classroom practice. *Educational Assessment, 6*(4), 257–290.

Harmon, M., Smith, T. A., Martin, M. O., Kelly, D. L., Beaton, A. E., Mullis, I., et al. (1997). *Performance Assessment in IEA's Third International Mathematics and Science Study.* Chestnut Hill, MA: Center for the Study of Testing, Evaluation, and Educational Policy, Boston College.

Herman, J. (1997). Large-scale assessment in support of school reform: lessons in the search for alternative measures. *CSE Technical Report 446.* Los Angeles: CRESST/UCLA.

Herman, J. L., & Klein, D. (1996). Evaluating equity in alternative assessment: An illustration of opportunity to learn issues. *Journal of Educational Research, 89*(9), 246–256.

Hudson, L. (1990). National initiatives for assessing science education. In A. Champagne, B. Lovitts, & B. Calinger (Eds.), *Assessment in the service of instruction.* Washington, DC: American Association for the Advancement of Science.

Huff, K. L., & Sireci, S. G. (2001). Validity issues in computer based testing. *Educational Measurement: Issues and Practice, 20,* 16–25.

International Association for the Evaluation of Educational Achievement (IEA). (1988). *Science achievement in seventeen countries: A preliminary report.* New York: Pergamon.

International Technology Education Association. (2000). *Standards for technological literacy: Content for the study of technology.* Reston, VA: International Technology Education Association.

Jacobson, W. J., & Doran, R. L. (1988). *Science achievement in the United States and sixteen countries: A report to the public.* Washington, DC: National Science Teachers Association.

Johnson, S. (1975). *Update on education: A digest of the National Assessment of Educational Progress.* Denver, CO: Educational Commission of the States.

Jones, L., Mullis, D., Raizen, S., Weiss, I., & Weston, E. (1992). *The 1990 science report card: NAEP's assessment of fourth, eighth and twelfth graders* (Library of Congress No. 92-60173). Washington, DC: Educational Testing Service and National Center for Educational Statistics.

Keeves, J. P. (1992). *The IEA study of science III: Changes in science education and achievement 1970 to 1984.* Oxford, England: Pergamon.

Kifer, E. (2000). *Large-scale assessment: Dimensions, dilemmas, and policy.* Thousand Oaks, CA: Corwin Press.

Kimmelman, P., Kroeze, D., Schmidt, W., van der Ploeg, A., McNeely, M., & Tan, A. (1999). *A first look at what we can learn from high performing school districts: An analysis of TIMSS data from the First in the World Consortium.* Washington, DC: National Center for Education Statistics.

Koretz, D. M., & Barron, S. I. (1998). *The validity of gains in scores on the Kentucky Instructional Results Information System (KIRIS).* Santa Monica, CA: Rand.

Koretz, D. M., Barron, S., Mitchell, K. J., & Stecher, B. M. (1996). *Perceived effects of the Kentucky Instructional Results Information System (KIRIS).* Santa Monica, CA: Rand.

Koretz, D. M., & Hamilton, L. (1999). Assessing students with disabilities in Kentucky: The effects of accommodations, format, and subject. *CSE Technical Report 498.* Los Angeles: CRESST/UCLA.

Koretz, D. M., McCaffrey, D., Klein, S., Bell, R., & Stecher, B. M. (1993). The reliability of scores from the 1992 Vermont Portfolio Assessment Program. *CSE Technical Report 355.* Los Angeles: CRESST/UCLA.

Lane, S., Stone, C. A., Parke, C. S., Hansen, M. A., & Cerrillo, T. L. (2000, April). *Consequential evidence for MSPAP from the teacher, principal and student perspective.* Paper presented at the annual meeting of the National Council of Measurement in Education, New Orleans.

LaPointe, A., Askew, J., & Mead, N. (1992). *Learning science: IAEP.* Princeton, NJ: Educational Testing Service.

LaPointe, A., Meade, N., & Phillips, G. (1989). *A world of differences: An international assessment of mathematics and science.* Princeton, NJ: Educational Testing Service.

Lee, V., & Burkam, D. (1996). Gender differences in middle grade science achievement: Subject domain, ability level, and course emphasis. *Science Education, 80,* 613–650.

Linn, M., DeBenedictis, T., Delucchi, K., Harris, A., & Stage, E. (1987). Gender differences in National Assessment of Educational Progress science items: What does "I don't know" really mean? *Journal of Research in Science Teaching, 24*(3), 267–278.

Linn, R. (1998). Assessments and accountability. *CSE Technical Report 490.* Los Angeles: CRESST/UCLA.

Maine State Department of Education. (n.d.). *Assessment System Q & A.* Retrieved January 31, 2006, from http://www.maine.gov/education/lsalt/Assessment%20QA.htm

Martin, M. O., Mullis, I. V. S., Beaton, A. E., Gonzalez, E. J., Kelly, D. L., & Smith, T. A. (1997). *Science achievement in the primary school years: IEA's Third International Mathematics and Science Study.* Chestnut Hill, MA: Center for the Study of Testing, Evaluation, and Educational Policy, Boston College.

Martin, M. O., Mullis, I. V. S., Gonzalez, E. J., & Chrostowski, S. J. (2004). *TIMSS 2003 International Science Report.* Chestnut Hill, MA: TIMSS & PIRLS International Study Center, Lynch School of Education, Boston College.

Martin, M. O., Mullis, I. V. S., Gonzalez, E. J., Gregory, K. D., Smith, T. A., Chrostowski, S. J., et al. (2000). *TIMSS 1999 international science report: Findings from IEA's repeat of the Third International Mathematics and Science Study at the eighth grade.* Chestnut Hill, MA: International Study Center, Lynch School of Education, Boston College.

McDonnell, L. M., & Choisser, C. (1997). *Testing and teaching: Local implementation of new state assessments*. Los Angeles: CRESST/UCLA.

McKnight, C., & Britton, E. (1992). *Methods for analyzing curricular materials*. East Lansing: Michigan State University, Survey of Mathematics and Science Opportunities, Technical Report Series.

Meade, S. D., & Dugger, W. E., Jr. (2004, October). Reporting on the status of technology education in the U.S. *The Technology Teacher*, 29–35.

Mullis, I. V. S., & Jenkins, L. B. (1988). *The science report card: Elements of risk and recovery. Trends and achievement based on the 1986 national assessment*. Princeton, NJ: Educational Testing Service.

Mullis, I. V. S., Martin, M. O., Beaton, A. E., Gonzalez, E. J., Kelly, D. L., & Smith, T. A. (1998). *Mathematics and science achievement in the final year of secondary school: IEA's Third International Mathematics and Science Study*. Chestnut Hill, MA: Center for the Study of Testing, Evaluation, and Educational Policy, Boston College.

National Assessment of Educational Progress. (1975). *Selected results from the national assessments of science: Scientific principles and procedures* (Report no. 04-5-02). Princeton, NJ: National Assessment of Educational Progress.

National Assessment of Educational Progress. (1978). *The national assessment in sciences: Changes in achievement, 1969–72*. Denver: Educational Commission of the States.

National Assessment of Educational Progress. (1907). *Learning by doing—a manual for teaching and assessing higher order skills in science and mathematics* (Report no. 17, HOS-80). Princeton, NJ: Educational Testing Services.

National Assessment of Educational Progress. (1992). *Trends in academic progress: Achievement of U.S. students in science 1969–70 to 1990, mathematics 1973 to 1990, reading 1971 to 1990, and writing 1984 to 1990*. Princeton, NJ: Educational Testing Services.

National Center for Education Statistics (NCES). (1996). *Pursuing excellence: A study of U.S. eighth-grade mathematics and science teaching, learning, curriculum, and achievement in international context* (no. NCES 97-198). Washington, DC: U.S. Department of Education, National Center for Education Statistics.

National Center for Education Statistics (NCES). (2006). *Highlights from the TIMSS 1999 video study of eighth-grade science teaching*. Washington, DC: Author.

National Research Council. (1996). *National science education standards*. Washington, DC: National Academy Press.

Nohara, D. (2001). *A comparison of the National Assessment of Educational Progress (NAEP), the Third International Mathematics and Science Study Repeat (TIMSS-R), and the Programme for International Student Assessment (PISA)* (Working Paper no. 2001-07). Washington, DC: National Center for Education Statistics.

Pellegrino, J. W., Chudowsky, N., & Glaser, R. (Eds.). (2001). *Knowing what students know: The science and design of educational assessment*. Washington, DC: National Academy Press.

Porter, A. C. (2002, October). Measuring the content of instruction: Uses in research and practice. *Educational Researcher, 31*(7), 3–14.

Postlethwaite, T. N. (1995). International empirical research in comparative education: An example of the studies of the International Association for the Evaluation of Educational Achievement (IEA). *Journal für Internationale Bildungsforschung, 1*(1), 1–19.

Postlethwaite, T. N., & Wiley, D. E. (1992). *The IEA study of science II: Science achievement in twenty-three countries*. Oxford, England: Pergamon.

Programme for International Student Assessment (PISA). (2000). *Measuring student knowledge and skills: The PISA 2000 assessment of reading, mathematical, and science literacy*. Paris: OECD.

Quellmalz, E. S., Haertel, G. D., DeBarger, A., & Kreikemeier, P. (2005). *A study of evidence of the validities of assessments of science inquiry in the National Assessment of Educational Progress (NAEP), Trends in Mathematics and Science Survey (TIMSS), and the New Standards Science Reference Exam (NSSRE) in science* (Validities Technical Report no. 1). Menlo Park, CA: SRI International.

Robitaille, D. F., Schmidt, W. H., Raizen, S., McKnight, C., Britton, E., & Nicol, C. (1993). *Curriculum frameworks for mathematics and science* (TIMSS Monograph no. 1). Vancouver: Pacific Educational Press.

Rosenquist, A., Shavelson, R., & Ruiz-Primo, M. (2000). On the "exchangeability" of hands-on and computer-simulated science performance assessments. *CSE Technical Report 531*. Los Angeles: CRESST/UCLA.

Rosier, M. J., & Keeves, J. (Eds.). (1991). *The IEA study of science I: Science education and curricula in twenty-three countries.* Oxford, England: Pergamon.

Rothman, R., Slattery, J., Vranek, J., & Resnick, J. (2002). Benchmarking and alignment of standards and testing. *CSE Technical Report 566*. Los Angeles, CA: CRESST/UCLA.

Ruiz-Primo, M. A., & Shavelson, R. J. (1996a). Problems and issues in the use of concept maps in science assessment. *Journal of Research in Science Teaching, 33*(6), 569–600.

Ruiz-Primo, M. A., & Shavelson, R. J. (1996b). Rhetoric and reality in science performance assessments: An update. *Journal of Research in Science Teaching, 33*(10), 1045–1064.

Sadler, P. (1998). Psychometric models of student conceptions in science: Reconciling qualitative studies and distractor-driven assessment instruments. *Journal of Research in Science Teaching, 35*, 265–296.

Schmidt, W. H., Jakwerth, P. M., & McKnight, C. C. (1998). Curriculum-sensitive assessment: Content *does* make a difference. *International Journal of Educational Research, 29*, 503–527.

Schmidt, W. H., Jorde, D., Cogan, L. S., Barrier, E., Gonzalo, I., Moser, U., et al. (1996). *Characterizing pedagogical flow: An investigation of mathematics and science teaching in six countries.* Dordrecht, the Netherlands: Kluwer Academic.

Schmidt, W. H., McKnight, C. C., Cogan, L. S., Jakwerth, P. M., & Houang, R. T. (1999). *Facing the consequences: Using TIMSS for a closer look at U.S. mathematics and science education.* Dordrecht, the Netherlands: Kluwer Academic.

Schmidt, W. H., McKnight, C. C., Houang, R. T., Wang, H. A., Wiley, D. E., Cogan, L. S., et al. (2001). *Why schools matter: A cross-national comparison of curriculum and learning.* San Francisco: Jossey-Bass.

Schmidt, W. H., McKnight, C. C., & Raizen, S. A. (1997). *A splintered vision: An investigation of U.S. science and mathematics education.* Dordrecht, the Netherlands: Kluwer Academic.

Schmidt, W. H., Raizen, S. A., Britton, E. D., Bianchi, L. J., & Wolfe, R. G. (1997). *Many visions, many aims, Volume II: A cross-national investigation of curricular intentions in school science.* Dordrecht, the Netherlands: Kluwer Academic.

Scott, E., & Owen, E. (2005). *Brief: Comparing NAEP, TIMSS and PISA results.* Washington, DC: National Center for Education Statistics.

Shepard, L. A. (2003). Reconsidering large-scale assessment to heighten its relevance to learning. In J. M. Atkin & J. E. Coffey (Eds.), *Everyday assessment in the science classroom* (pp. 121–146). Arlington, VA: NSTA Press.

Sireci, S. G. (1997). Problems in linking assessments across languages. *Educational Measurement: Issues and Practice, 17*, 12–29.

Smith, M. L., & Rottenberg, C. (1991). Unintended consequences of external testing in elementary schools. *Educational Measurement: Issues and Practice, 10*(4), 7–11.

Solano-Flores, G., & Nelson-Barber, S. (2001). On the cultural validity of science assessments. *Journal of Research in Science Teaching, 38*, 1–21.

Solano-Flores, G., & Shavelson, R. (1997). Development of performance assessments in science: Conceptual, practical, and logistical issues. *Educational Measurement: Issues and Practice, 17*, 16–24.

Solano-Flores, G., Trumbull, E., & Nelson-Barber, S. (2002). Concurrent development of dual language assessments: An alternative to translating tests for linguistic minorities. *International Journal of Testing, 2*(2), 107–129.

Spruce, M. (n.d.). *Grand ideas and practical work: The Maine local assessment system resource guide.* Retrieved January 31, 2006, from http://mainegov-images.informe.org/education/lres/mlss.pdf

Stecher, B., & Barron, S. (1999, April). *Test based accountability: The perverse consequences of milepost testing*. Paper presented at the annual meeting of the American Educational Research Association, Montreal, Canada.

Stecher, B. M., Barron, S. L., Chun, T., & Ross, K. (2000). The effects of the Washington state education reform on schools and classroom. *CSE Technical Report 525*. Los Angeles: CRESST/UCLA.

Stecher, B. M., Barron, S. L., Kaganoff, T., & Goodwin, J. (1998). The effects of standards- based assessment on classroom practices: Results of the 1996–1997 RAND survey of Kentucky teachers of mathematics and writing. *CSE Technical Report 482*. Los Angeles: CRESST/UCLA.

Stevenson, H. W. (1998). A study of three cultures: Germany, Japan, and the United States—an overview of the TIMSS Case Study Project. *Phi Delta Kappan, 79*(7), 524–529.

Stigler, J., Gonzales, P., Kawanaka, T., Knoll, S., & Serrano, A. (1999). *The TIMSS videotape classroom study: Methods and findings from an exploratory research project on eighth-grade mathematics instruction in Germany, Japan, and the United States* (no. NCES 99-074). Washington, DC: U.S. Department of Education, National Center for Education Statistics.

Sugrue, B. (1994). Specifications for the design of problem-solving assessments in science. *CSE Technical Report 387*. Los Angeles: CRESST/UCLA.

Sullivan, P., Yeager, M., Chudowsky, N., Kober, N., O'Brien, E., & Gayler, K. (2005). *States try harder, but gaps persist: High school exit exams 2005*. Washington, DC: Center on Education Policy.

Tamir, P. (1974). An inquiry oriented laboratory examination. *Journal of Educational Measurement, 11*, 25–33.

Tamir, P. (1998). Assessment and evaluation in science education: Opportunities to learn and outcomes. In B. J. Fraser & K. G. Tobin (Eds.), *International handbook of science education* (pp. 761–789). London: Kluwer Academic.

Travers, K. J., & Westbury, I. (1989). *The IEA study of mathematics I: Analysis of mathematics curricula* (Vol. 1). Oxford, England: Pergamon Press.

Valverde, G. A., & Schmidt, W. H. (2000). Greater expectations: Learning from other nations in the quest for "world-class standards" in US school mathematics and science. *Journal of Curriculum Studies, 32*(5), 651–687.

Walding, R., Fogliani, C., Over, R., & Bain, J. (1994). Gender differences in response to questions on the Australian National Chemistry Quiz. *Journal of Research in Science Teaching, 31*, 833–846.

Wang, J. (1998). Comparative study of student science achievement between United States and China. *Journal of Research in Science Teaching, 35*, 329–336.

Washington State Department of Education. (n.d.). *Assessment*. Retrieved January 31, 2006, from http://www.k12.wa.us/assessment/default.aspx

Webb, N. L. (1997). Determining the alignment of expectations and assessments in mathematics and science education. *National Center for Improving Science Education, 1*, 1–8.

Welch, W. W., Huffman, D., & Lawrenz, F. (1998). The precision of data obtained in large-scale science assessments: An investigation of bootstrapping and half-sample replication methods. *Journal of Research in Science Teaching, 3*, 697–704.

Welch, W. W., Walberg, H., & Fraser, B. (1986). Predicting elementary science learning using national assessments data. *Journal of Research in Science Teaching, 23*, 699–706.

Wiley, D. E., & Wolfe, R. G. (1992). Major survey design issues for the IEA Third International Mathematics and Science Study. *Prospects, 22*(3), 297–304.

Wilson, M. R. (2004). *Constructing measures: An item response modeling approach*. Mahwah, NJ: Lawrence Erlbaum Associates.

Wilson, M. R., & Bertenthal, M. W. (Eds.). (2005). *Systems for state science assessment*. Washington, DC: National Academies Press.

Wolf, S. A., & McIver, M. C. (1999). When process becomes policy: the paradox of Kentucky state reform for exemplary teachers of writing. *Phi Delta Kappan, 80*, 401–406.

PART V

Science Teacher Education

CHAPTER 34

Science Teacher as Learner

J. John Loughran
Monash University, Australia

Research into learning to teach was initially based on ideas associated with a developmental model of teacher learning (Fuller, 1969; Fuller & Bown, 1975), a model that could be construed as portraying student teachers progressing along a predetermined path in the development of their competence as teachers. Over time, however, this interpretation has been challenged. For example, teacher thinking (Clark & Peterson, 1986) brought new ways of researching practice to the fore as it focused on the complexity of teachers' knowledge and expertise. Likewise, the resurgence of Dewey's (1933) articulation of reflection through the work of Schön (1983, 1987) led to views of good teaching being aligned with the notion of reflective practice (Clarke, 1995; Clift, Houston & Pugach, 1990; Grimmett & Erickson, 1988; Loughran, 1996; Russell & Munby, 1991). And, reflective practice became an entrée into studies of teachers learning about teaching through researching their own practice (Cochran-Smith & Lytle, 1993).

Hand in hand with these developments was the growth in understanding of constructivism (e.g., Cobb, 1994; Gunstone, 2000), which, as Clarke and Erickson (2004) have noted, reflected a shift in views of the nature of learning from a predominantly behaviorist model to more cognitive and phenomenological models. Thus, through developments in approaches to examining teachers' practice and a sharper focus on the need for greater congruence between the purposes and practices of teaching and learning, the limitations of transmissive teaching approaches (Barnes, 1975) were called into question. Not surprisingly, then, the notion of teacher as learner has emerged as an important construct in extending perceptions of quality in (science) teaching and learning.

Science teacher as learner is a seductive descriptor, as it captures the essence of the necessary challenge to the long tradition of science teaching as telling that has been so pervasive in schools, characterized by the stereotypical view of the transmission of science as propositional knowledge. Science teacher as learner suggests that practice carries an ongoing commitment to teaching science for understanding. Hence, science teacher as learner offers one way of exploring the uneasy tensions of practice that emerge as science teachers attempt to better align their teaching with their expectations for their students' science learning, partly derived from understandings of constructivism. So, just as views about the nature of learning have changed over time, so too have views of, and the subsequent expectations for, teaching. In reviewing research literature within these two fields, this chapter attempts to build a case for the centrality of the notion of science teacher as learner in the quest to better align science teaching with science learning.

STRUCTURE AND PURPOSE OF THE CHAPTER

In this chapter, four general areas (preservice science teacher as learner, elementary science teacher as learner, secondary science teacher as learner, and science teacher educator as learner) have been designated in order to highlight some of the distinguishing features of science teachers as learners. Interestingly, much of the teacher as learner literature tends to focus on the development of understanding and knowledge of teaching generally, rather than being content specific. Hence, a literature search with the science designation offers diminished returns. Yet, this result can be viewed as a challenge for science teaching and learning researchers, as it highlights the need for a more concentrated effort in this area. Another positive aspect to this outcome is that the studies that inform the field are generally richly descriptive and offer interesting insights into the work of science teachers as learners. Furthermore, the personal perspective germane to much of this work also highlights a clear bifurcation between studies *on* science teachers as learners as opposed to studies *of* science teachers as learners.

In this chapter, studies of science teachers as learners, or studies that at least carry the voice of science teachers as learners, were selected for review so that a concentration on what had been learned and why was considered in concert with how it was learned from the participants' perspective. Inevitably, then, the particular exemplars cited in this chapter are examined in more detail than is common in a Handbook. This strong attention to exemplars is also important in drawing attention to that which research efforts have perhaps overlooked in the past and to therefore help set an agenda for the future so that science teaching and learning research might push the boundaries of that which is understood to be meaningful, applicable, and useful in the world of practice.

PRESERVICE SCIENCE TEACHER AS LEARNER

Student-teachers' experiences of school science influence their understanding of science teaching (per Lortie's (1975) apprenticeship of observation), and, as successful graduates of the "system," they often teach in ways similar to how they were taught (Sarason, 1990). Not surprisingly, many student teachers expect to learn the "script" for science teaching and can be quite resistant to alternative perspectives (Britzman, 1991; Hayward, 1997; Richardson, 1996). This issue is important in shaping what it means to challenge student teachers' prior experiences in order to influence their own practice of science teaching.

Research into teachers' beliefs (Pajares, 1992) and the relationship between beliefs and practice has drawn much attention (Bandura, 1986; Brickhouse, 1990; Bryan &

Abell, 1999; Hashweh, 1996), largely because challenging an individual's beliefs may be a powerful way of encouraging a restructuring of understanding of both learning and teaching. Hence, by challenging beliefs, one's prior experiences may be questioned rather than remain as taken-for-granted assumptions for practice (Brookfield, 1995).

Challenging beliefs has been a common beginning point for reshaping student teachers' views of, and approaches to, practice (Gunstone, Slattery, Baird, & Northfield, 1993). However, strong examples of preservice science teachers as learners are not easy to find, because many studies focus on the big picture of the intent of such a challenge, rather than highlighting specific instances of participants' personal shifts in understanding. With this in mind, the studies selected in this section of the chapter illustrate that, in science teacher preparation programs, clear examples of student teacher as learner exist, but the field itself is one that begs more involvement of the participants themselves—as co-authors and authors of their own experiences of teaching and learning science. This then is a major challenge for the science teacher education research community, so that new ways of accessing understandings of what student teachers are confronted by might be more readily identified—so that responses to learning outcomes might be appropriately implemented.

Challenging Conceptions and Beliefs

The children's science and conceptual change literature (e.g., Driver, Guesne, & Tiberghien, 1985; Gunstone, 1990; Hewson, Beeth, & Thorley, 1998; Osborne & Freyburg, 1985; West & Pines, 1985) has illustrated how important it can be for students to experience cognitive dissonance, so that their existing conceptions might not only be personally recognized, but also restructured as a result of the experience. Dana, McLoughlin, and Freeman (1998) reported on a long-term project that studied changes in conceptions and beliefs of prospective teachers while learning to teach science in a preservice teacher education program based around the use of dissonance. Their study paid particular attention to the ways in which prospective science teachers made sense of teaching science for understanding and the program features that helped them to do so.

By focusing on the student teachers themselves, the authors built on Borko and Putnam's (1996) view that what and how student teachers learn in their teacher preparation program is strongly influenced by their existing knowledge and beliefs; therefore, challenging these through *creating* dissonance as one way of *generating* opportunities for new learning. They outlined how the program was purposely designed to "support the prospective teachers' conceptual development around ideas connected to teaching science for understanding" and how "certain aspects of the course appeared to be especially helpful in creating dissonance, challenging beliefs, and fostering the reconstruction of science pedagogies, stimulating professional growth" (p. 7).

Dana et al. (1998) also illustrated how they created a *need to know* for student teachers that encouraged a reconsideration of the teacher as teller role so strong in many student teachers. They also highlighted how the recognition of an unanticipated classroom problem was the catalyst for change. A strength of the data they offered was in student teachers' voices and how participants personally detailed situations with which they were confronted, and how their ensuing sense of dissonance caused them to learn about aspects of teaching and learning science that they had not explicitly questioned previously.

These authors described the principles that guided their program and offered ways of conceptualizing how to create opportunities for student teachers to be learners by confronting their taken-for-granted assumptions of teaching as telling and learning as memorization. They also noted that the "learning to teach process is generative" (p. 14). Lederman, Gess-Newsome, and Latz (1994) also illustrated evidence of student teachers as learners in their study of secondary preservice science teachers' content and pedagogical knowledge structures, whereby pedagogical knowledge stood out as a primary influence on instructional decisions.

These studies are illustrative of student-teachers as learners, because an overt focus on their experiences was adopted as a guiding principle in teacher preparation. Furthermore, van Driel and de Jong's (1999) investigation of preservice chemistry teachers' pedagogical content knowledge (PCK) (Shulman, 1986, 1987) highlighted the importance of listening to students as an impetus for recognizing and responding to differences between beliefs and practices. While van Driel and de Jong focused on the question, "Is a development in the preservice teachers' PCK observable, and if so, what is the influence of specific factors on this development?" their study illustrated how these student teachers recognized that "their usual way of reasoning cause[d] problems for [their] students, who . . . became confused . . . [as] the different activities and events during [their] classroom teaching affected their knowledge of specific learning difficulties of students" (p. 5). Thus the primacy of experience emerged as in important factor in the promotion of a preservice science teacher as learner stance.

Veal (1999), another researcher interested in the PCK of preservice science teachers, also paid careful attention to student teachers' voices. Veal's participants questioned the use of language as an important shaping force in the implicit messages of teaching about science in ways that they had not previously recognized in their own learning of science. They also responded to their own sense of dissonance when confronted by difficulties in (re)learning chemistry and physics and began to make meaningful links to the ways in which they might then teach those concepts themselves. For example, one student teacher (Randi), in responding to a consideration of the abstract nature of chemistry, focused attention on the importance of concrete representations—a learning breakthrough that affected Randi's view of teaching. However, Veal made clear that just because student teachers recognized the need for particular approaches to practice, it did not necessarily follow that changes were automatically implemented. This point is a reminder of the interplay between beliefs and practice and the role of dissonance as a catalyst for meaningful learning from experience for student teachers.

Like many others (e.g., Cochran & Jones, 1998; Gunstone & Northfield, 1994; Hoban, 2003; Northfield, 1998; Vander Borght, 2003), Veal (1999) also noted how the influence of classroom teaching experience and participants' interactions with students tended to raise new issues for teaching and learning that could only really be apprehended through the experiences of student teachers. Therefore, Veal further supported the view that, to encourage student teachers as learners, their existing belief structures need to be sufficiently (and consistently) challenged in ways that will cause them to reconsider their taken-for-granted assumptions of science teaching and learning.

Learning from Experience

Munby and Russell (1994) offered an analysis of detailed feedback from physics methods students enrolled in a preservice education program at Queen's University, Canada, and used these messages to develop the notion of the "authority of experience" to explain the unease many student teachers felt about their transition from being "under authority" to being "in authority" as they moved through student teaching. The development of "authority of experience" was a salutary reminder of the ongoing conflict between teaching as telling and teaching for understanding as it highlighted how some student teachers wanted to be *told* how to teach while others wanted to *learn* how to teach. Through a desire to explicitly develop student teachers' authority of experience, Russell (1997) sought new ways of empowering his student teachers as learners through a sustained concentration on, and analysis of, *their* teaching experiences (see Featherstone, Munby, & Russell, 1997; Russell & Bullock, 1999). Russell therefore worked with his student teachers (Featherstone and Bullock) to help them reflect upon, and research, their own experiences of learning to teach.

Featherstone documented how his views of teaching and learning changed as he gathered feedback from his students about their learning, and how he listened to his students to *really* hear what they were saying. In so doing, he better aligned both his teaching and learning intents in explicit and meaningful ways. Following a series of lessons on "natural succession" and his purposeful attention to his students' views, he noted that, "I have been reminded just how important it is that one does not underestimate the value of creating a forum for listening to students' voices . . . there is something special about being able to say that my decision [about how to further develop his teaching] is based on what I have learned from my students" (Featherstone et al., p. 136).

In a similar way, Bullock highlighted his learning through experience by documenting his practice. Having spent some time thinking about the differences between his views of science learning and his actual science teaching, Bullock was encouraged to take risks in his practice. Eventually, even though his instincts told him to act differently, he came to see value in allowing his students to explore science for themselves, not unlike the way he was learning to explore teaching himself, by discovery and risk, not through "being told." His big-picture breakthrough highlighted how his learning about teaching was based on valuing experience:

> I would argue that the nature of science is to construct your own reality of how the world works. . . . We as educators should remember that although it is apparent to us that, say, all objects undergo the same acceleration due to gravity near the Earth's surface, it remains a mystery to most high school students. "Experience first" allows people to discover science rather than be information sponges. (Bullock in Russell & Bullock, 1999, p. 137)

Featherstone and Bullock's reports lend further weight to the call (see Lederman et al., 1994) for more importance to be placed on better integration of subject-specific pedagogy courses in preservice teacher preparation programs. If subject-specific pedagogy is to be recognized and developed by preservice science teachers as learners, then they need opportunities to pursue their learning about practice in more meaningful ways (per Geddis's [1993] study of student teachers' learning about isotopes), rather than simply as task-driven activities. In so doing, the possibilities for preservice science teachers as learners would be enhanced through the creation of possibilities for effective reflective practice (Loughran, 2002), whereby their own experiences are the basis for personally identifying the value in framing practice in intelligible, plausible, and fruitful ways (Posner, Strike, Hewson, & Gertzog, 1982) for their own conceptual development. If this were the case, then de Jong, Korthagen, and Wubbels' (1998) concern for better linking of student teachers' conceptions and actions in classroom practice might be realized.

ELEMENTARY SCIENCE TEACHER AS LEARNER

Elementary science teachers' need for a strong science knowledge base has been raised many times in the literature (Appleton, 1992; Appleton & Symington, 1996; Carr & Symington, 1991; DEET, 1989; Harlen, Holroyd, & Byrne, 1995; Skamp, 1991; Welch, 1981) and is often interpreted as simply meaning that more science content knowledge equates with better science teaching. This interpretation, though, has been challenged (Bennett, Summers, & Askew, 1994). In fact, Schibeci and Hickey (2000) noted that "there is no place, in our view, for a 'cognitive deficit' model in providing assistance to elementary teachers to improve their content backgrounds" (p. 1168). They stated this as a result of their experience in organizing and conducting a professional development program[1] designed to help elementary science teachers become meaningful learners of science. However, what they came to learn was that such development was dependent on three salient dimensions: a scientific dimension—to promote change in teachers' concepts and support development of more sophisticated ideas, theories, and principles; a professional dimension—based on content to be taught in elementary classes thus having high relevance and purpose to teachers; and a personal dimension—related to everyday life and providing a motivation for teachers to learn and understand (p. 1168).

Schibeci and Hickey (2000) conceptualized these three dimensions because their involvement with elementary teachers highlighted for them that content alone did not necessarily lead to more effective teaching. What this suggests is that the general predominance of the scientific dimension as a focus for the development of elementary science teachers' practice has perhaps masked the importance of the other two dimensions in learning about science teaching and learning. However, finding real examples in the literature of the professional and personal dimensions of science teachers as learners (in the teachers' voice) is difficult; perhaps it could also be argued that a strong science knowledge base itself is important in encouraging the necessary risk-taking to publicly explore the professional and personal dimensions of science teacher as learner in research reports.

Confidence in Science Teaching

Appleton and Kindt (1999) offered another way of viewing the development of these three dimensions through a consideration of "science activities that work."

---

1. Similar learning through organizing professional development for elementary teachers is also reported by Pearson and Wallace (1997).

They noted how science content was sometimes perceived as being well taught if the "activities" for the students were fun, hands-on, and/or thematically developed. They also highlighted how some elementary teachers' lack of confidence in science led them to avoid teaching science.

The need to place more emphasis on elementary science teachers as learners has been apparent for some time but is perhaps a part of the science education research agenda that has not garnered sufficient attention in the mainstream research literature. Yet, the seeds for such development have long been planted. For example, Smith and Neale (1989) offered strong indicators of the value of concentrating on personally and professionally meaningful shifts in perspectives and practices in science teaching as an invitation for science education researchers to work *with* rather than *on* teachers.

Geddis (1996), working with teachers, and exploring two experienced elementary teachers' efforts to make science a more significant part of their teaching, drew attention to the fact that a concentration on teaching science disrupted elementary teachers' views of themselves as teachers. In Geddis' case studies, the participating teachers appeared to have developed new perspectives on science teaching and learning. For these elementary science teachers as learners, their actions created a sense of unease in "intervening in [their] students' learning" (p. 263). Yet, in many instances, intervention was necessary if science teaching was to begin to address students' alternative conceptions. What Geddis's work highlighted was how elementary teachers' "professional identities have often been associated with a variety of slogans whose central message is essentially, I teach *children*, not *subjects*" (p. 264). Adopting a science teaching and learning frame for practice may well cause a sense of unease among teachers because it challenges their traditional view of themselves as teachers. Addressing this unease is congruent with Schibeci and Hickey's (2000) suggestions about the need for personal and professional change as opposed to that of science knowledge alone. But how might this be done in ways that are responsive to the real needs and expectations of elementary teachers?

Science Learning Through a Community of Practice

Summers and Kruger (1994), through a two-year longitudinal study of the development of elementary teachers' subject matter knowledge in science, illustrated that through well-designed in-service education, participants' understanding of science concepts could be substantially enhanced. Yet despite the best intentions, education systems and providers often fail to develop and implement ongoing, well-organized, and conceptually coherent science education programs.

Fleer and Grace (2003) responded to this situation in their study of the professional commitment to teacher as learner through the development of a community of practice (Wenger, 1998). In their account, the voice of the teachers and students was particularly strong and illustrated how the professional and personal dimensions of learning about practice, and the subsequent changes in actions, blossomed through collegial leadership. They paid attention to their community of practice through full participation and the collective (rather than individual) accumulation of experiences. Their study illustrated how children's science experiences were deliberately broadened as more teachers joined their quest for learning. It also made clear how, by centering on children and their learning, classroom teachers could be drawn into an evolving community of science practice. This work challenges some of the barriers to teaching and learning science raised in many previous studies by addressing the situation holistically—in the typical elementary approach of an integrated curriculum—rather than focusing solely on the science itself.

Grace offered a series of case studies that illustrated the development of the community of practice in which the involvement of others in the students' study of the Enhanced Greenhouse Effect positively influenced approaches to science teaching and learning. The teachers themselves were genuinely involved in the children's learning journey and were activated to join the growing community of learners.

The development of a community of science practice created a context in which the boundaries for learning were not defined by a single classroom, but were deliberately broad. The evolving community of practice included the staff in the school, the families of the children, community members, and local, regional, and international contexts (Fleer & Grace, 2003, p. 132).

The majority of research into elementary teachers' practice of science adopts an individualistic approach whereby the unit of study is the teacher. In such situations, the community in which the teacher exists is perhaps less likely to be accorded sufficient importance as a research focus. The framing of the research may simply overlook aspects of science teaching and learning that are embedded in the community rather than the individual. Fleer and Grace's overt focus on the community illustrated how teaching and learning in science can respond to many of the concerns and issues raised in much of the literature. However, such responses require researchers to be active participants within the elementary school environment itself, and such practice no doubt challenges more "traditional" research practices. Perhaps the unease felt by elementary teachers (as noted by Geddis, 1996) is equally apparent in the "practice" of researchers (in that traditional research is seen as distinct from the work of practice) and helps to account for the small number of strong alternative perspectives on elementary science teacher as learner available in the mainstream science education literature. Fleer and Grace clearly offer one way of challenging such a situation.

SECONDARY SCIENCE TEACHER AS LEARNER

The literature shows a clear distinction between beginning and experienced secondary science teachers as learners. Obviously, beginning and experienced science teachers are two ends of a continuum. However, the distinction between them can be somewhat blurry. For example, White, Russell, and Gunstone (2002) and Lockard (1993) illustrated how, when experienced science teachers changed schools or taught unfamiliar content, they became beginning science teachers again. In this case, for ease of distinction and analysis, I define a beginning science teacher as someone in the first five years of teaching.

Beginning Science Teachers as Learners

Adams and Krockover (1997) studied science teachers moving from preservice into the early years of teaching. They found that the initial shifts from didactic teaching practices toward conceptual/constructivist teaching and learning practices were encouraged through reflection, and that seeds for the development of PCK were incorporated into the schema of beginning teachers. Loughran (1994), following a cohort in a similar fashion, outlined a model to account for beginning science teachers' search for a better alignment of their teaching and learning intents. Carlsen (1991), in his year-long study of four new high school biology teachers, attempted to quantify subject matter knowledge and how that knowledge affected novices' teaching. However, what he recognized was what McNeil (1986) described as a "contradiction of control" whereby the "social and institutional concerns act at cross-purposes with goals like promoting inquiry through discourse" (Carlsen, 1991, p. 646), affecting these beginning science teachers' approach to teaching. This contradiction of control was also noted by Munby, Cunningham, and Locke (2000) in their detailed case study of a year 9 science teacher, highlighting how the nature of the school in which she worked set up barriers to the development of her professional knowledge.

Through this period of transition from student teacher to beginning teacher, much learning occurs as the search for time to reflect on practice as well as the need to develop professionally satisfying approaches to practice are continually buffeted by the day-to-day concerns and expectations of the role. Trumbull's (1999) longitudinal study of six beginning biology teachers in her book, *The New Science Teacher*, is one study that strongly illustrated this transition through the participants' own voices.

Trumbull (1999) followed six of her student teachers through their teacher preparation program and out into their first three years of teaching science. Through insightful interview data, she allowed each participant to tell the story of his or her development and learning over time. The first participant, Fred, learned about the contradiction between teaching for understanding and teaching to pass examinations; his learning was about his realization of the ongoing dilemma associated with choosing to teach for understanding by trying to help his students get "excited" about the topics they were investigating.

Pat Green learned about the importance of a personal connection to content by responding to the serendipitous nature of learning and, in so doing, came to see how central that was to her growth in understanding of science teaching and learning. Sylvie Andrews learned about how taking risks in her teaching required a confidence to pursue teaching approaches that were initially discomforting for both the teacher and the learners. Yet, Elaine Spring grew in confidence sufficiently to be more responsive to the need to modify her existing teaching materials and to develop a more coherent view of the courses she was teaching. In so doing, she learned how to "react more immediately when her students brought up important topics spontaneously" (p. 76).

Being involved in the research with Trumbull was helpful in Maggie Deering's development, as she came to see aspects of her practice that she needed to adjust in order to capitalize on her teaching and learning intents in practical ways. She noted the need for explicit instruction in higher level thinking and explanatory writing for her students to become more independent and responsible learners. This was also mirrored in her recognition of the same thing occurring in her learning through the research project. "As I read your [Trumbull's] case study about me, I wondered if my involvement in the project helped me be more reflective in my practice" (p. 91).

The final participant, George Frage, was interested in "biology for its own sake and for the complex reasoning involved in research and experimentation" (p. 103). However, his learning was centered on the frustration he felt about the perceived need to cover the content as opposed to learning some concepts in depth. This frustration was something with which he struggled. His level of concern was more closely linked to his developing notions of PCK; his strength of content knowledge appeared to influence his concern for teaching in ways that enhanced his understanding of practice. It could well be argued that George was beginning to learn that content knowledge alone was not sufficient for good teaching, and that the development of his students' learning in ways that would satisfy him professionally would be the teaching and learning challenge he might come to name for his future development.

Anderson and Mitchener (1994) described the transition from pre-service to in-service education as an induction phase whereby the beginning teacher is confronted by: "(1) the isolated nature of teaching, (2) the abrupt nature of the transition into teaching, (3) the documented attrition rate of beginning teachers, and (4) the personal and professional well-being of the beginning teachers" (pp. 31–32). What the beginning science teacher as learner literature illustrates is that, in this induction phase, there is a need for genuine support and guidance so that these science teachers can learn to frame and name the nature of their concerns in order to actively decide what they personally need to pursue to enhance their own learning about teaching and learning in science. It seems that when personal and professional well-being is well managed, the beginning science teacher as learner begins to emerge as a result of a growth in confidence through the associated risk-taking and experimenting with practice necessary in addressing the differences between teaching intents and learning outcomes (see Trumbull's cases).

The challenge, though, is to manage this induction phase in such a way as to encourage the sharing of learning so that the sometimes contradictory messages of socialization do not reinforce the very teaching behaviors that have so shaped many beginning teachers' views of science teaching. Professionalization rather than socialization for the beginning science teacher is encouraged most through the modeling of a science teacher as learner approach by the experienced science teachers who comprise the community in which the beginning teachers work.

Experienced Science Teachers as Learners

Klopfer's (1991) *summary of science education to 1989* highlights not only the approach to research in science education to that point in time (largely instrumental and generally work on teachers rather than with teachers), but also that "some researchers found that teachers had difficulty translating their knowledge into practice or that teachers believed that they had implemented more good practice into their classroom than observations supported" (p. 352). This point about translating knowledge into practice highlights an issue indicative of science teacher as learner—making the tacit explicit.

Articulation

One common external mechanism that encourages science teachers to see a need to make the tacit explicit is involvement with science education researchers (often through enrolment in postgraduate programs) and the subsequent development of a language for sharing understandings of the complex nature of science teaching and learning. Geelan (1996) illustrated this point when his "newfound" need to read about educational theories and practices offered him tools to reflect on his own teaching and to grow and develop as a science teacher. Geelan's study showed how, when a teacher is placed in the position of learner, the need to articulate understandings of teaching and learning is catalyzed.

Maor (1999) described such a situation through a professional development program designed to place teachers in the role of learners in an attempt to challenge their use of multimedia and to influence their use of constructivist teaching approaches in their classrooms. The need for a vocabulary to share their knowledge of practice was an important issue and has been central to much of the debate about teaching as a profession—it is seen as crucial to teachers valuing the knowledge that underpins their practice.

As a high school chemistry teacher, Ian Mitchell became well aware of the value of a language for discussing teaching and learning. The cofounder of PEEL (Project for the Enhancement of Effective Learning; see Baird & Mitchell, 1986; Baird & Northfield, 1992; Loughran, 1999), Mitchell was responsible for an ongoing, largely unfunded professional development project that hinged on teachers' using a language for learning and the extensive development of teaching procedures to enhance students' metacognition. Yet, when he found himself facing an impending absence from his science class, the crucial information that he needed to pass on to the teacher who was going to cover for him did not carry the understanding necessary for that teacher to perform her function in the way Mitchell had intended. Mitchell soon discovered that,

> I had no idea that I had omitted in my advice [to the other teacher] such a huge part of what I did. I was astounded to discover this. Identifying the frame of "maintain a sense of progress" was very important for lesson sequences that have a focus on restructuring or constructing understanding of key ideas rather than completing tasks . . . however, part of the crucial wisdom that I had also developed about how to maximize the prospect by overtly maintaining a sense of progress of success was only revealed [to me] by the sequence of events just reported. (Mitchell, 1999, pp. 60–61)

What Mitchell came to recognize was that, despite his exemplary teaching practice and overt focus on developing students' metacognitive skills through teaching for understanding, he did not explicitly recognize the key features of the information he needed to pass on to another teacher to continue with his class commensurate with the ideas and approaches he was using. Only by being confronted by the situation in which he found himself did he learn how "seriously [he] underestimated the highly tacit nature of so many crucial aspects of teacher knowledge" (p. 63).

Drawing further on PEEL, Zwolanski (1997) and McMaster (1997) highlighted how their focus on students' learning gave them a powerful language for discussing issues of teaching and learning that directly related to changes in their science teaching practice. Zwolanski noted, "I am more aware of my teaching style and am constantly evaluating the lessons and content taught . . . the students have a say in the direction of the lesson" (p. 133). For Zwolanski, this was quite a shift in her approach to teaching, something that she had to learn about in order to do, not something she could just simply employ. Similarly, McMaster described how he began to learn how to bring his practices more into line with his beliefs about teaching and learning: "It is of no use to admit that children have prior views of topics if you don't let them approach the 'scientist's view' by their own learning skills. The method of acknowledging their views only to systematically knock them down would not shift them as much as by letting them review their own ideas or check their own understanding" (McMaster, 1997, p. 143).

The PEEL project is replete with examples of science teachers as learners whereby the need to articulate features of practice drives a learning about practice in very real and tangible ways. However, change itself is invariably problematic.

Science Teaching and Learning: A Problematic Adventure

Viewing teaching and learning as problematic is important, for were it not problematic, it would surely be a simple task to apply the correct approach to resolving any prescribed learning difficulty. If one accepts that teaching is problematic, then one way of understanding this perspective is through the notion of dilemmas. A dilemma by definition is something that is managed, not resolved; hence, a teacher who is learning to manage a dilemma is learning about practice rather than solving a problem with practice. This is not to suggest that there is a lack of progress or development in the knowledge and skills of teaching. Rather, that which is being better understood is itself an indication of development and progress and is a sign of a professional approach to understanding the ongoing tensions, frustrations, and concerns associated with better linking of teaching and learning.

In the edited book *Dilemmas of Science Teaching: Perspectives on Problems in Practice* (Wallace & Louden, 2002) this very point of practice being problematic is the basis for insights into science teachers as learners. The understandings that emerged through the careful examination of teachers' dilemmas led to a questioning of the taken-for-granted assumptions of practice that guided these teachers' development in new understandings of teaching and learning in science. For example, when McGuiness, Roth, and Gilmer (2002) reconsidered laboratory work and questioned what it did, how it was performed, and the value of the associated tasks, assessing practical work emerged as an issue that had not seriously been considered in the past. In a similar way, the Krueger, Barton, and Rennie (2002) examination of group work led to a confrontation with the exclusionary approaches of some students that limited the learning possibilities for others. Furthermore, Gribble, Briggs, Black, and Abell (2002) reconsidered the use of questioning and began to see things in classroom discourse that had not been so apparent (if at all) in the past. Overall, the examination of dilemmas highlights how attempting to teach, not tell, continually emerges as a challenge for those who perceive practice as being problematic.

Northfield, in *Opening the Classroom Door: Teacher, Researcher, Learner* (Loughran & Northfield, 1996), his year-long examination of his teaching of a year 7 class of high school students, left no doubt about his learning as a science teacher. Through extensive accounts of classroom situations and his reflections on practice through conversations with others and his journal entries, he came to a point whereby he was able to synthesize and categorize his learning.

Northfield's categories highlighted principles that shaped his approach to practice; however, the differences he articulated between his expectations for teaching and learning and his students were disconcerting. Northfield explored these differences by contrasting his teacher view, "Learning requires learner consent," and his students' view, that "Learning is done to students and teachers have a major responsibility for achieving learning" (p. 137). Northfield's account offered interesting insights into the world of the teacher as learner and raised issues about the theory-practice gap. And it is through appropriate explorations of the theory-practice gap that the science education community's knowledge and understanding of practice might be enhanced. However, in some cases, neither world pays sufficient attention to the other, despite the efforts of those who try to bridge this gap in thoughtful ways.

Theory-Practice Gap: Practice-Theory Bridge

Pekarek, Krockover, and Shepardson (1996) drew attention to the oft-cited theory-practice gap as an issue in terms of addressing concerns about changes in the pedagogy of science. McGoey and Ross (1999), in response to the lament about "the lack of teachers' application of research in informing their day-to-day practice" (p. 117), discussed their use of conceptual change pedagogy and offered a "report to the research community [about] where advances in research ha[d] taken [them], and where [they] would appreciate future research to be directed" (p. 117).

In an interesting slant on the theory-practice gap (so often reported from the research perspective), McGoey and Ross (1999) outlined what they saw as the important difference between technical information (the "how to" of teacher journals) and theoretical frameworks (the "how come" and "what if" of research journals) that influences what is sought and what is useful in the worlds of theory and practice. In so doing, they approached the theory-practice gap from a teaching perspective. Although they stated that they represented a minority of teachers, they offered a bridge into theory from practice by making clear what had been helpful to them and, therefore, what they looked for in their learning about science teaching and learning. Their approach illustrated the difference between what many researchers might pursue and make available to practitioners and what they, as teachers, do pursue. They rightly expected that the explication of their perspective might encourage a shift in research focus as they "look[ed] forward to a day when collaboration between the academy and the classroom teacher [would be] a commonplace of [the] profession [of] science teaching" (p. 120). The hope was that the two would work together so that research and practice might inform one another in meaningful ways.

There has been a great deal of research into aspects of the nature of teachers' beliefs, knowledge, and practice (see chapters by Lederman, Abell, Jones, & Carter) designed to elucidate factors that might genuinely help to improve the quality of science teaching (in ways commensurate with the hopes of Goodrum & Hackling, 1997). Many of these efforts have been professional development projects (Johanna, Lavonen, Koponen, & Kurki-Suonio, 2002; Radford, 1998; Shymansky et al., 1993; van Driel, Verloop, & de Vos, 1998) aimed at addressing many of the research findings (noted above). However, the difficulty has often been that although these projects are sympathetic to the work of science teachers, and the researchers are concerned for the development of quality in science teaching and learning,[2] the teachers

---

2. Particularly evident in the work of Clark (2003) in his study of a South African teacher attempting to teach for understanding while struggling with a major lack of resources and support. Clark's account is one that reflects, in a very powerful way, the concerns, issues and difficulties of teaching science for understanding when the lack of expectations and conditions for such practice are overwhelming.

themselves have not necessarily been the initiators or sustainers of the research effort. When teachers are the initiators and sustainers of the work (as reported by Hoban, 2003), the focus and results are considerably different.

Briscoe (1991), for example, followed an experienced secondary science teacher considered exemplary by his peers, for a year. The teacher wanted to make changes to his teaching practice, but the paper illustrated how such a purpose was continually under attack because of the conflict between his goals for learning and his actions as a teacher. The study illustrated how difficult it can be for a teacher to actually make the changes being sought, even though the expectation is clear. Nelson (2001) also followed an experienced teacher with an extensive understanding of oceanography as she transformed her teaching from a more traditional form into an inquiry-based approach. She found that changes in the teacher's practice occurred, and were encouraged, as a result of her strong content knowledge in conjunction with reflection on her students' learning.

Both of these studies are examples of research into science teaching and learning from the practice perspective and illustrate the shift in research focus, data, and results that accompany such a shift. Both researchers appeared sympathetic to the teachers' world; what they uncovered was no doubt helpful to other teachers in similar situations. However, the work of Fitzpatrick (1996), a science teacher and head of his school's science department, took this process one step further. He described what happened when he and his colleagues decided to "throw away" the existing year 8 curriculum and replace it with a new course structure and new teaching and learning approaches because, "after years of stagnation . . . [he was] very quickly convinced of the benefits of adopting a constructivist philosophy" (p. 1). Fitzpatrick (1996) gave reasons for deciding to change and described how their work led to the development of new pedagogical skills.

However, few studies responded to the McGoey and Ross (1999) agenda to the extent of that described by Berry and Milroy (2002). Having decided to pay careful attention to their students' learning about atomic theory, Berry and Milroy were confronted by a realization:

> We asked students to expose their thinking and did not know how to help them . . . when we turned to the research literature to find a context for teaching about atomic structure, or practical classroom assistance for dealing with the particular conceptions we had uncovered and wanted to challenge, we found little . . . We needed a user-friendly guide (where the users were teachers like us) for dealing with the variety of individual conceptions—how to challenge; what to do with those students who already had a coherent view of the phenomenon. (Berry & Milroy, 2002, pp. 200–201)

Because they were unable to find the research knowledge and help they required for the task they had set themselves, they became active science teacher learners, collaborating in a learning about science teaching experience that was certainly much more demanding and challenging than they had anticipated. The nature of their work, the daily demands of teaching, and the need to make real progress (for their students and themselves) created a research agenda (and a report) very different from that generally found in the literature, especially when such work is portrayed from a traditional research perspective. Their account was constructed around 10 powerful "snapshots" of their learning about science teaching and presented issues and concerns that were developed and analyzed in ways that other teachers would readily identify with and likely find helpful and informative in their own practice. Their study was one that has helped to set a new agenda for what research into science teaching and learning might pursue in seriously challenging the theory-practice gap. These science teachers as learners illustrated that there are real ways of responding to McGoey and Ross's (1999) call as they began to build a bridge from practice into theory that invited travelers to traverse from both sides.

SCIENCE TEACHER EDUCATOR AS LEARNER

Over the past decade, self-study of teacher education practices (Hamilton, 1998) has become increasingly influential in shaping approaches to teaching and research in teacher education, partly as a result of a shift in focus toward teacher educators' desire to learn more about their own practice (Adler, 1993; Korthagen & Russell, 1995; Mueller, 2003; Munby, 1996; Nicol, 1997; Pereira, 2000) and partly in response to teacher educators' growing interest in the knowledge base of teaching and learning about teaching (e.g., Berry & Loughran, 2002; Loughran & Russell, 1997; Mayer-Smith & Mitchell, 1997; Trumbull, 1996; Trumbull & Cobb, 2000).

Science methods teaching in teacher preparation programs is the context in which much of the science teacher educator as learner studies are located. For example, Russell (1997), through his physics methods teaching, considered his learning about science teaching specifically in terms of how his knowledge of practice could be made more accessible to his student teachers, so that their learning of science teaching would encourage them to challenge the status quo of science teaching as the delivery of facts. Chin (1997) similarly pursued an understanding of his teaching about chemistry teaching as he "articulate[d] some significant experiences that informed [his] beliefs about teaching and learning within the teacher education context" (p. 117). In so doing he made clear how, as a science teacher educator, he was also a learner. Both of these teacher educators illustrated how their learning about their own science teaching substantially informed their practice in teaching about science teaching and that their learning was continually being challenged as they sought honest and constructive feedback about the impact of their practice on their student teachers' learning.

Segal (1999) pursued her learning about teaching science by taking the risk of placing herself in the learner's position as she struggled with how to teach in a three-part learning and teaching model (cooperative groups, learners' questions, and a techno-science context). Her paper examined the differences between being a learner of science teaching and a learner of science learning and showed how she came to better understand the dilemmas of practice that were important in shaping the situations through which the teaching approach (the three-part model above) affected the learning of her students:

> I did not realize until I was a full participant in their [student-teachers'] explorations that my own understanding was tenuous. . . . In genuinely seeking to understand how they were learning, I was involved in the appropriation process myself. . . . After a positive boost to my confidence, I was probably keen that students should experience this type of inner satisfaction through the learners' questions part of the learning model. (Segal, 1999, pp. 17–18)

Segal's efforts were extended by collaboration with a colleague, following their student teachers through teacher preparation and into their first year of teaching (see Schuck & Segal, 2002). They learned a great deal about their teacher education practices and how their own assumptions about student teachers' learning of science were challenged when they sought evidence of meaningful change. Having specifically taught science in ways designed to create student-centered, activity-based, small-group learning, Segal came to see that she needed to "employ multiple strategies in class to challenge the assumption . . . that as long as the children are having fun, they are developing conceptual science understanding" (p. 95). She found using first-hand experiences with student teachers did not lead to student teachers using the same practices when they were full-time teachers.

Schuck and Segal (2002) found that, although they could create powerful learning experiences for their student teachers at the university, in many cases these experiences created an impression for their student teachers that such approaches were "seamless and unproblematic" (p. 96). Hence, when their student teachers were challenged by the reality of teaching in those ways themselves, many retreated to the very teaching approaches they had experienced and been dissatisfied with as school students.

Hoban's (1997) investigation of his teaching about elementary science focused on helping his student teachers understand their own learning of science in order to counter the transmissive model of teaching about teaching so predominant in teacher preparation programs. His study showed that, although many elementary student teachers lacked "a solid knowledge base about science and many ha[d] negative attitudes about the subject, . . . providing them with large amounts of science content in courses [was] not the way to address this difficulty" (p. 146). His study illustrated how enhancing student teachers' self-awareness of their own beliefs and practices led them to make meaningful shifts in their own practice. In his teaching about teaching, modeling was important to him: "This is risky business; you are exposing yourself to criticism from your own students. But [how can] trainee teachers take seriously your recommendations about being a reflective teacher [if] you do not do it yourself?" (p. 147).

Modeling what one expects of one's students is a crucial feature of science teacher educator as learner. Tobin (2003) accepted this challenge when he found his previous science education knowledge and experiences less than helpful in a new and demanding situation. In his study, not only did he reconceptualize what it meant to be a science teacher educator, but he also placed the same expectations on himself as a teacher as he had for his student teachers by student-teaching in a local urban high school:

> I regarded myself as a strong teacher and never considered that the knowledge gleaned from a long career of teaching, research, and teacher education would fail to carry me through even the stiffest of challenges. . . . I moved to the University of Pennsylvania where I taught a science education course for prospective science teachers . . . all of the new teachers were assigned to urban high schools for a year-long field experience. The problems they were experiencing were profound and my suggestions, though grounded in research and theory, were of little use to them. Most of what I knew seemed inapplicable to their problems and the contexts in which they taught . . . [I took a teaching position in an urban high school similar to that which my student-teachers were experiencing] . . . I was to realize all too quickly that I needed to re-learn to teach in urban schools . . . I failed to understand teaching as praxis. For too long I had regarded teaching as

knowledge that could be spoken, written, and thought. But words could not be turned into teaching to mediate the learning of students. (Tobin, 2003, p. 34)

Tobin's learning experiences could not help but dramatically affect his teaching about science teaching. The sense of dissonance, the inability to convey meaning to his student teachers, and then being confronted by the same problems as his student teachers were experiencing helped him understand and know about practice in new and different ways, ways that he did not understand before genuinely adopting a science teacher and science teacher educator as learner stance.

CONCLUSION

Clarke and Erickson (2004) noted how the literature on student as learner and that on teacher as learner have converged through common links to constructivism and how the search for "universal type laws" of learning that apply equally well to all contexts have been abandoned because of the inherent situated and contextually bound nature of learning. Following from this, the notion of science teacher as learner is then clearly bound up in understandings of contemporary theoretical perspectives on learning and concerns for the improvement of teaching practices—especially so from a teacher's perspective. Wallace (2003) extended this view through his articulation of three conceptual themes: (a) that learning about teaching is situated, and as a consequence, the development of teachers' understanding and knowledge requires a focus on authentic activities; (b) that learning about teaching is social and that "creating rich opportunities for diverse groups of teachers to participate in, and to shape, discourse communities" is critical (p. 10); and (c) that learning about teaching is distributed, and, hence, collaboration is central to change.

I suggest that a major unaddressed challenge facing the science education community is to purposefully pursue research that is meaningful, applicable, and appropriate for teachers in the development of *their* pedagogy of science, so that ultimately students' learning of science is enhanced. As I trust this review illustrates, addressing such a challenge demands a concentration on the science teacher as learner in conjunction with that of science teacher educator as learner—the two cannot be divorced. A science teacher as learner stance must be taken seriously at all levels of teaching about science, and doing so requires an understanding of teaching as being problematic.

Fundamental to responding appropriately to this challenge is the need for science teachers to consistently: (a) challenge the taken-for-granted in their practice; (b) examine, articulate, and disseminate their learning through experience; and (c) seek to continually ensure that practice and theory inform one another. To do this requires a conceptualization of professional practice that explicitly values a science teacher as learner stance. The science education community can no longer excuse (science) teachers or teacher educators who espouse constructivist views of learning while continuing to practice transmissive approaches to teaching. For the expectations of the science education community in general to shift, individuals must respond. This chapter has offered insights into some of the approaches to, and experiences of, science teachers as learners who have approached their research and practice in ways that have helped to genuinely rejuvenate and shape the world of science teaching and learning. More than ever, your personal response matters.

ACKNOWLEDGMENTS

Thanks to Gary Hoban and John Wallace, who reviewed this chapter.

REFERENCES

Adams, P. E., & Krockover, G. H. (1997). Beginning science teacher cognition and its origins in the preservice secondary science teacher program. *Journal of Research in Science Teaching, 34*, 633–653.

Adler, S. A. (1993). Teacher education: Research as reflective practice. *Teaching and Teacher Education, 9*, 159–167.

Anderson, R. D., & Mitchener, C. P. (1994). Research on science teacher education. In D. L. Gabel (Ed.), *Handbook of research on science teaching and learning* (pp. 3–44). New York: Macmillan.

Appleton, K. (1992). Discipline knowledge and confidence to teach science: Self-perceptions of primary teacher education students. *Research in Science Education, 22*, 11–19.

Appleton, K., & Kindt, I. (1999, March). *How do beginning elementary teachers cope with science: Development of pedagogical content knowledge in science.* Paper presented at the Annual Meeting of the National Association for Research in Science Teaching, Boston (Eric Document Reproduction Service no. ED488990).

Appleton, K., & Symington, D. (1996). Changes in primary science over the past decade: Implications for the research community. *Research in Science Education, 26*, 299–316.

Baird, J. R., & Mitchell, I. J. (Eds.). (1986). *Improving the quality of teaching and learning: An Australian case study—the PEEL project.* Melbourne: Monash University Printing Services.

Baird, J. R., & Northfield, J. R. (Eds.). (1992). *Learning from the PEEL experience.* Melbourne: Monash University.

Bandura, A. (1986). *Social foundations of thought and action: A social cognitive theory.* Englewood Cliffs, NJ: Prentice-Hall.

Barnes, D. (1975). *From communication to curriculum.* Harmondsworth, UK: Penguin.

Bennett, N., Summers, M., & Askew, M. (1994). Knowledge for teaching and teaching performance. In A. Pollard (Ed.), *Look before you leap? Research evidence for the curriculum at key stage two* (pp. 23–36). London: Tufnell Press.

Berry, A., & Loughran, J. J. (2002). Developing an understanding of learning to teach in teacher education. In J. Loughran & T. Russell (Eds.), *Improving teacher education practices through self-study* (pp. 13–29). London: RoutledgeFalmer.

Berry, A., & Milroy, P. (2002). Changes that matter. In J. Loughran, I. Mitchell, & J. Mitchell (Eds.), *Learning from teacher research* (pp. 196–221). New York: Teachers College Press.

Borko, H., & Putnam, R. (1996). Learning to teach. In D. Berliner & R. Calfee (Eds.), *Handbook of educational psychology* (pp. 673–708). New York: Macmillan.

Brickhouse, N. W. (1990). Teachers' beliefs about the nature of science and their relationship to classroom practice. *Journal of Teacher Education, 41*, 53–62.

Briscoe, C. (1991). The dynamic interactions among beliefs, role metaphors, and teaching practices: A case study of teacher change. *Science Education, 75*, 185–199.

Britzman, D. (1991). *Practice makes practice.* Albany, NY: SUNY Press.

Brookfield, S. D. (1995). *Becoming a critically reflective teacher.* San Francisco: Jossey-Bass.

Bryan, L. A., & Abell, S. K. (1999). Development of professional knowledge in learning to teach elementary science. *Journal of Research in Science Teaching, 36*, 121–140.

Carlsen, W. S. (1991). Effects of new biology teachers' subject matter-knowledge on curricular planning. *Science Education, 75*, 631–647.

Carr, M., & Symington, D. (1991). The treatment of science disciplinary knowledge in primary teacher education. *Research in Science Education, 21*, 39–46.

Chin, P. (1997). Teaching and learning in teacher education: Who is carrying the ball? In J. Loughran & T. Russell (Eds.), *Teaching about teaching: Purpose, passion and pedagogy in teacher education* (pp. 117–130). London: Falmer Press.

Clark, C. M., & Peterson, P. L. (1986). Teachers' thought processes. In M. C. Wittrock (Ed.), *Handbook of research on teaching* (3rd ed., pp. 255–298). New York: Macmillan.

Clark, J. (2003). Challenges to practice, constraints on change: Managing innovation in a South African township science classroom. In J. Wallace & J. Loughran (Eds.), *Leadership and professional development in science education: New possibilities for enhancing teacher learning* (pp. 63–77) London: RoutledgeFalmer.

Clarke, A. (1995). Professional development in practicum settings: Reflective practice under scrutiny. *Teaching and Teacher Education, 11*, 243–262.

Clarke, A., & Erickson, G. (2004). The nature of teaching and learning in self-study. In J. Loughran, M. L. Hamilton, V. LaBoskey, & T. Russell (Eds.), *The international handbook of self-study of teaching and teacher education practices* (pp. 41–67). Dordrecht, the Netherlands: Kluwer Academic.

Clift, R., Houston, W., & Pugach, M. (Eds.). (1990). *Encouraging reflective practice in education*. New York: Teachers College Press.

Cobb, P. (1994). Where is the mind? Constructivist and sociocultural perspectives on mathematical development. *Educational Researcher, 23*(7), 13–20.

Cochran, K. F., & Jones, L. L. (1998). The subject matter knowledge of preservice science teachers. In B. Fraser & K. Tobin (Eds.), *International handbook of science education* (pp. 707–718). Dordrecht, the Netherlands: Kluwer Academic.

Cochran-Smith, M., & Lytle, S. L. (1993). *Inside/outside: Teacher research and knowledge*. New York: Teachers College Press.

Dana, T. M., McLoughlin, A. S., & Freeman, T. B. (1998, April). *Creating dissonance in prospective teachers' conceptions of teaching and learning science*. Paper presented at the annual meeting of the National Association for Research in Science Teaching, San Diego (Eric Document Reproduction Service no. ED446929).

de Jong, O., Korthagen, F., & Wubbels, T. (1998). Research on science teacher education in Europe: Teacher thinking and conceptual change. In B. Fraser & K. Tobin (Eds.), *International handbook of science education* (pp. 745–758). Dordrecht, the Netherlands: Kluwer Academic.

Department of Employment, Education & Training. (1989). *Discipline review of teacher education in mathematics and science*. Canberra: Australian Government Printing Service.

Dewey, J. (1933). *How we think*. New York: Heath & Company.

Driver, R., Guesne, E., & Tiberghien, A. (Eds.). (1985). *Children's ideas in science*. Milton Keynes, UK: Open University Press.

Featherstone, D., Munby, H., & Russell, T. (1997). *Finding a voice while learning to teach*. London: Falmer Press.

Fitzpatrick, B. (1996). The application of constructivist learning strategies to the redesign of the lower secondary science curriculum. In M. Hackling (Ed.), *Proceedings of the 21st Annual Conference of the Western Australian Science Education Association* (pp. 59–64). Perth, Western Australia: Department of Science Education, Edith Cowan University.

Fleer, M., & Grace, T. (2003). Building a community of science learners through legitimate collegial participation. In J. Wallace & J. Loughran (Eds.), *Leadership and professional development in science education: New possibilities for enhancing teacher learning* (pp. 116–133). London: RoutledgeFalmer.

Fuller, F. F. (1969). Concerns of teachers: A developmental conceptualization. *American Educational Research Journal, 6*, 207–226.

Fuller, F. F., & Bown, O. H. (1975). Becoming a teacher. In *Teacher Education 74th Yearbook of the National Society for the Study of Education* (pp. 25–52). Chicago: National Society for the Study of Education.

Geddis, A. N. (1993). Transforming content knowledge: Learning to teach about isotopes. *Science Education, 77*, 575–591.

Geddis, A. N. (1996) Science teaching and reflection: Incorporating new subject-matter into teachers' classroom frames. *International Journal of Science Education, 18*, 249–65.

Geelan, D. R. (1996). Learning to communicate: Developing as a science teacher. *Australian Science Teachers Journal, 42*(1), 30–43.

Goodrum, D., & Hackling, M. W. (1997). The secondary science investigations project: preliminary findings. In R. Schibeci & R. Hickey (Eds.), *Proceedings of the 22nd Annual Conference of the Western Australian Science Education Association* (pp. 110–117). Perth, Western Australia: School of Education, Murdoch University.

Gribble, J., Briggs, S., Black, P., & Abell, S. K. (2002). Questioning. In J. Wallace & W. Louden (Eds.), *Dilemmas of science teaching: Perspectives on problems in practice* (pp. 143–157). London: RoutledgeFalmer.

Grimmett, P. P., & Erickson, G. L. (1988). *Reflection in teacher education.* New York: Teachers College Press.

Gunstone, R. F. (1990). "Children's science": A decade of developments in constructivist views of science teaching and learning. *Australian Science Teachers Journal, 36*(4), 9–19.

Gunstone, R. F. (2000). Constructivism and learning research in science education. In D. Phillips (Ed.), *Constructivism in education: Opinions and second opinions on controversial issues* (99th Annual Yearbook of the National Society for the Study of Education, Part I, pp. 254–280). Chicago: University of Chicago Press.

Gunstone, R. F., & Northfield, J. R. (1994). Metacognition and learning to teach. *International Journal of Science Education, 16*, 523–537.

Gunstone, R. F., Slattery, M., Baird, J. R., & Northfield, J. R. (1993). A case study exploration of development in preservice science teachers. *Science Education, 77*, 47–73.

Hamilton, M. L. (Ed.). (1998). *Reconceptualizing teaching practice: Self-study in teacher education.* London: Falmer Press.

Harlen, W., Holroyd, G., & Byrne, M. (1995). *Confidence and understanding in teaching science and technology in primary schools.* Edinburgh: Scottish Council for Research in Education.

Hashweh, M. Z. (1996). Effects of science teachers' epistemological beliefs in teaching. *Journal of Research in Science Teaching, 33*, 47–64.

Hayward, G. (1997). Principles for school focused initial teacher education: Some lessons from the Oxford Internship Scheme. In T. Allsop & A. Benson (Eds.), *Mentoring for science teachers* (pp. 11–26). Buckingham, UK: Open University Press.

Hewson, P. W., Beeth, M. E., & Thorley, R. (1998). Teaching for conceptual change. In B. Fraser & K. Tobin (Eds.), *International handbook of science education* (pp. 199–218). Dordrecht, the Netherlands: Kluwer Academic.

Hoban, G. (1997). Learning about learning in the context of a science methods course. In J. Loughran & T. Russell (Eds.), *Teaching about teaching: Purpose, passion and pedagogy in teacher education* (pp. 133–149). London: Falmer Press.

Hoban, G. (2003). Changing the balance of a science teacher's belief system. In J. Wallace & J. Loughran (Eds.), *Leadership and professional development in science education: New possibilities for enhancing teacher learning* (pp. 19–33). London: RoutledgeFalmer.

Johanna, J., Lavonen, J., Koponen, I., & Kurki-Suonio, K. (2002). Experiences from long-term in-service training for physics teachers in Finland. *Physics Education, 37*, 128–134.

Klopfer, L. E. (1991). A summary of research in science education—1989. *Science Education, 75*, 255–402.

Korthagen, F., & Russell, T. (Eds.). (1995). *Teachers who teach teachers: Reflections on teacher education.* London: Falmer Press.

Krueger, B., Barton, A., & Rennie, L. J. (2002). Equity. In J. Wallace & W. Louden (Eds.), *Dilemmas of science teaching: Perspectives on problems in practice* (pp. 73–85). London: RoutledgeFalmer.

Lederman, N. G., Gess-Newsome, J., & Latz, M. S. (1994). The nature and development of preservice science teachers' conceptions of subject matter and pedagogy. *Journal of Research in Science Teaching, 31*, 129–146.

Lockard, D. L. (1993). Secondary science teachers' knowledge base when teaching science courses in and out of their area of certification. *Journal of Research in Science Teaching, 30*, 723–736.

Lortie, D. (1975). *Schoolteacher.* Chicago: University of Chicago Press.

Loughran, J. J. (1994). Bridging the gap: An analysis of the needs of second year science teachers. *Science Education, 78*, 365–386.

Loughran, J. J. (1996). *Developing reflective practice: Learning about teaching and learning through modeling*. London: Falmer Press.

Loughran, J. J. (1999). Professional development for teachers: A growing concern. *The Journal of In-Service Education, 25*, 261–272.

Loughran, J. J. (2002). Effective reflective practice: In search of meaning in learning about teaching. *Journal of Teacher Education, 53*, 33–43.

Loughran, J. J., & Northfield, J. R. (1996). *Opening the classroom door: Teacher, researcher, learner*. London: Falmer Press.

Loughran, J. J., & Russell, T. L. (1997). Meeting student teachers on their own terms: Experience precedes understanding. In V. Richardson (Ed.), *Constructivist teacher education: Building a world of new understandings* (pp. 164–181). London: Falmer Press.

Maor, D. (1999). Teachers-as-learners: The role of multimedia professional development program in changing classroom practice. *Australian Science Teachers Journal, 45*(3), 45–50.

Mayer-Smith, J. A., & Mitchell, I. J. (1997). Teaching about constructivism: Using approaches informed by constructivism. In V. Richardson (Ed.), *Constructivist teacher education: Building a world of new understandings* (pp. 129–153). London: Falmer Press.

McGoey, J., & Ross, J. (1999). Guest editorial: Research, practice, and teacher internship. *Journal of Research in Science Teaching, 36*, 121–139.

McGuiness, B., Roth, W. M., & Gilmer, P. J. (2002). Laboratories. In J. Wallace & W. Louden (Eds.), *Dilemmas of science teaching: Perspectives on problems in practice* (pp. 36–55). London: RoutledgeFalmer.

McMaster, J. (1997). Theory into practice. In J. R. Baird & I. J. Mitchell (Eds.), *Improving the quality of teaching and learning: An Australian case study—the PEEL project* (3rd ed., pp. 135–143). Melbourne: Monash University.

McNeil, L. M. (1986). *Contradictions of control*. New York: Routledge.

Mitchell, I. (1999). Bridging the gulf between research and practice. In J. J. Loughran (Ed.), *Researching teaching: Methodologies and practices for understanding pedagogy* (pp. 44–64). London: Falmer Press.

Mueller, A. (2003). Looking back and looking forward: Always becoming a teacher educator through self-study. *Reflective Practice 4*(1), 67–84.

Munby, H. (1996). Being taught by my teaching: Self-study in the realm of educational computing. In J. Richards & T. Russell (Eds.), *Empowering our future in teacher education*. Proceedings of the First International Conference of the Self-Study of Teacher Education Practices, Herstmonceux Castle, East Sussex, England (pp. 62–66). Kingston, Ontario: Queen's University.

Munby, H., Cunningham, M., & Locke, C. (2000). School science culture: A case study of barriers to developing professional knowledge. *Science Education, 84*, 193–211.

Munby, H., & Russell, T. (1994). The authority of experience in learning to teach: Messages from a physics methods course. *Journal of Teacher Education, 45*, 86–95.

Nelson, T. H. (2001, April). *A science teacher's wisdom of practice in teaching inquiry-based oceanography*. Paper presented at the annual meeting of the American Educational Research Association, Seattle, WA (Eric Document Reproduction Service no. ED455099).

Nicol, C. (1997). Learning to teach prospective teachers to teach mathematics: The struggles of a beginning teacher educator. In J. Loughran & T. Russell (Eds.), *Teaching about teaching: Purpose, passion and pedagogy in teacher education* (pp. 95–116). London: Falmer Press.

Northfield, J. R. (1998). Teacher educators and the practice of science teacher education. In B. Fraser & K. Tobin (Eds.), *International handbook of science education* (pp. 695–706). Dordrecht, the Netherlands: Kluwer Academic.

Osborne, R. J., & Freyburg, P. (1985). *Learning in science: The implications of children's science*. Auckland, New Zealand: Heinemann.

Pajares, M. F. (1992). Teachers' beliefs and educational research: Cleaning up a messy construct. *Review of Educational Research, 62*, 307–332.

Pearson, J., & Wallace, J. (1997). Reflection: A tool for experienced teachers. In R. Schibeci & R. Hickey (Eds.), *Proceedings of the 22nd Annual Conference of the Western Australian Science Education Association* (pp. 70–76). Perth, Western Australia: School of Education, Murdoch University.

Pekarek, R., Krockover, G. H., & Shepardson, D. P. (1996). The research-practice gap in science education. *Journal of Research in Science Teaching, 33*, 111–113.

Pereira, P. (2000). Reconstructing oneself as a learner of mathematics. In J. J. Loughran & T. L. Russell (Eds.), *Exploring myths and legends of teacher education*. Proceedings of the Third International Conference of the Self-Study of Teacher Education Practices, Herstmonceux Castle, East Sussex, England (pp. 204–207). Kingston, Ontario: Queen's University.

Posner, G. J., Strike, K. A., Hewson, P. W., & Gertzog, W. A. (1982). Accommodation of a scientific conception: Toward a theory of conceptual change. *Science Education, 66*, 211–227.

Radford, D. L. (1998). Transferring theory into practice: A model for professional development for science education reform. *Journal of Research in Science Teaching, 35*, 73–88.

Richardson, V. (1996). The role of attitudes and beliefs in learning to teach. In J. Sikula (Ed.), *Handbook of research on teacher education* (pp. 102–119). New York: Macmillan.

Russell, T. (1997). Teaching teachers: How I teach IS the message. In J. Loughran & T. Russell (Eds.), *Teaching about teaching: Purpose, passion and pedagogy in teacher education* (pp. 32–47). London: Falmer Press.

Russell, T., & Bullock, S. (1999). Discovering our professional knowledge as teachers: Critical dialogues about learning from experience. In J. Loughran (Ed.), *Researching teaching: Methodologies and practices for understanding pedagogy* (pp. 132–151). London: Falmer Press.

Russell, T., & Munby, H. (1991). Reframing: The role of experience in developing teachers' professional knowledge. In D. A. Schön (Ed.), *The reflective turn: Case studies in and on educational practice* (pp. 164–187). New York: Teachers College Press.

Sarason, S. (1990). *The predictable failure of educational reform: Can we change course before it is too late?* San Francisco: Jossey-Bass.

Schibeci, R., & Hickey, R. (2000). Is it natural or processed? Elementary school teachers and conceptions about materials. *Journal of Research in Science Teaching, 37*, 1154–1170.

Schön, D. A. (1983). *The reflective practitioner: How professionals think in action*. New York: Basic Books.

Schön, D. A. (1987). *Educating the reflective practitioner*. San Francisco: Jossey-Bass.

Schuck, S., & Segal, G. (2002). Learning about our teaching from our graduates, learning about our learning with critical friends. In J. Loughran & T. Russell (Eds.), *Improving teacher education practices through self-study* (pp. 88–101). London: RoutledgeFalmer.

Segal, G. (1999, April). *Collisions in a science education reform context: Anxieties, roles and power*. Paper presented at the annual meeting of the American Educational Research Association, Montreal, Canada (Eric Document Reproduction Service no. ED431733).

Shulman, L. S. (1986). Those who understand: Knowledge growth in teaching. *Educational Researcher, 15*(2), 4–14.

Shulman, L. (1987). Knowledge and teaching: Foundations of the new reform. *Harvard Educational Review, 57*(1), 1–22.

Shymansky, J. A., Woodworth, G., Norman, O., Dunkhase, J., Mathews, C., & Liu, C. T. (1993). A study of changes in middle school teachers' understanding of selected ideas in science as a function of an in-service program focusing on student perceptions. *Journal of Research in Science Teaching, 30*, 737–55.

Skamp, K. (1991). Primary science and technology: How confident are teachers? *Research in Science Education, 21*, 290–299.

Smith, D. S., & Neale, D. C. (1989). The construction of subject matter knowledge in primary science teaching. *Teaching and Teacher Education, 5*, 1–20.

Summers, M., & Kruger, C. (1994). A longitudinal study of a constructivist approach to improving primary school teachers' subject matter knowledge in science. *Teaching and Teacher Education, 10*, 499–519.

Tobin, K. (2003). The challenges of attaining a transformative science education in urban high schools. In J. Wallace & J. Loughran (Eds.), *Leadership and professional development in science education: New possibilities for enhancing teacher learning* (pp. 34–47). London: RoutledgeFalmer.

Trumbull, D. (1996). Using students' responses to my journal to understand my teaching in a preservice teacher education course. In J. Richards & T. Russell (Eds.), *Empowering our future in teacher education*. Proceedings of the First International Conference of the Self-Study of Teacher Education Practices, Herstmonceux Castle, East Sussex, England (pp. 143–146). Kingston, Ontario: Queen's University.

Trumbull, D. J. (1999). *The new science teacher: Cultivating good practice*. New York: Teachers College Press.

Trumbull, D., & Cobb, A. (2000). Comments to students and their effects. In J. J. Loughran & T. L. Russell (Eds.), *Exploring myths and legends of teacher education*. Proceedings of the Third International Conference of the Self-Study of Teacher Education Practices, Herstmonceux Castle, East Sussex, England (pp. 243–246). Kingston, Ontario: Queen's University.

van Driel, J. H., & de Jong, O. (1999, March). *The development of preservice chemistry teachers' pedagogical content knowledge*. Paper presented at the annual meeting of the National Association for Research in Science Teaching, Boston (Eric Document Reproduction Service no. ED444841).

van Driel, J. H., Verloop, N., & de Vos, W. (1998). Developing science teachers' pedagogical content knowledge. *Journal of Research in Science Teaching, 35*, 673–695.

Vander Borght, C. (2003). Developing leadership in science teacher trainees for upper secondary schools: Changing orientations and examples of implementation. In J. Wallace & J. Loughran (Eds.), *Leadership and professional development in science education: New possibilities for enhancing teacher learning* (pp. 177–197). London: RoutledgeFalmer.

Veal, W. R. (1999, March). *The TTF model to explain PCK in teacher development*. Paper presented at the annual meeting of the National Association for Research in Science Teaching, Boston (Eric Document Reproduction Service no. ED 443690).

Wallace, J. (2003). Learning about teacher learning: reflections of a science educator. In J. Wallace & J. Loughran (Eds.), *Leadership and professional development in science education: New possibilities for enhancing teacher learning* (pp. 1–16). London: RoutledgeFalmer.

Wallace, J., & Louden, W. (Eds.). (2002). *Dilemmas of science teaching: Perspectives on problems of practice*. London: RoutledgeFalmer.

Welch, W. (1981). Inquiry in school science. In N. Harms & R. Yager (Eds.), *What research says to the science teacher* (Vol. 3, pp. 53–72). Washington, DC: National Science Teachers Association.

Wenger, E. (1998). *Communities of practice: Learning, meaning and identity*. Cambridge, UK: Cambridge University Press.

West, L., & Pines, A. (Eds.). (1985). *Cognitive structure and conceptual change*. Orlando, FL: Academic Press.

White, G., Russell, T., & Gustone, R. F. (2002). Curriculum change. In J. Wallace & W. Louden (Eds.), *Dilemmas of science teaching: Perspectives on problems of practice* (pp. 231–244). London: RoutledgeFalmer.

Zwolanski, S. (1997). Theory into practice. In J. R. Baird & I. J. Mitchell (Eds.), *Improving the quality of teaching and learning: An Australian case study—the PEEL project* (3rd ed., pp. 121–134). Melbourne: Monash University.

CHAPTER 35

Science Teacher Attitudes and Beliefs

M. Gail Jones
Glenda Carter
North Carolina State University

When Janice, a biology teacher, enters the classroom each day, her beliefs and attitudes about science, science learning, and science teaching influence virtually every aspect of her job, including lesson planning; teaching; assessment; interactions with peers, parents, and students; as well as her professional development and the ways she will implement reform. Although this influence is not necessarily linear or obvious, attitudes and beliefs play significant roles in shaping teachers' instructional practices.

This chapter examines the complex constructs of science teacher beliefs and attitudes and how beliefs and attitudes influence instructional practices. According to Keys and Bryan (2001), virtually every aspect of teaching is influenced by the complex web of attitudes and beliefs that teachers hold, including knowledge acquisition and interpretation, defining and selecting instructional tasks, interpreting course content, and choices of assessment. Advances in cognitive psychology have integrated attitudes and beliefs into conceptual change models as significant influences on conceptual growth and change. Putnam and Borko (1997) suggested that teachers learn as they "construct new knowledge and understandings based on what they already know and believe" (p. 1125). Although teacher attitudes and beliefs are key to understanding and reforming science education, these areas are poorly understood. Research that can unravel the complexities of teacher attitudes and belief systems is needed.

In this chapter, we summarize the historical perspectives and early research on science teacher attitudes and beliefs and present a sociocultural model. Using this model, we describe recent research studies on beliefs and attitudes. One of the consistent research findings discussed is the link between science teachers' epistemological beliefs and their instruction. Pajares (1992) maintains that "beliefs teachers hold influence their perceptions and judgments, which, in turn affect their behavior in classrooms" (p. 307). These beliefs have been called theories of action; Kane, Sandretto, and Heath (2002) maintained that teachers' "espoused theories of action impacts their theories-in-use" (p.188). In the sections that follow, we describe teachers' epistemologies about science, science teaching, and science learning. This is accompanied by a discussion of the relationships of these to prior experiences, other beliefs, self-efficacy, expectancies, perceived environmental constraints, motivation, and, ultimately, instructional behaviors. In addition, we include new advances in research that document the role of the larger culture in shaping science teachers' beliefs systems.

WHAT ARE ATTITUDES AND BELIEFS?

Emerging Constructs

Although social psychology and the study of attitudes first emerged as an investigative area in the early 1900s, theory in this area lacked cohesiveness until the 1930s. It was during the 1930s that L. L. Thurstone and G. W. Allport laid the groundwork for the emergence of this branch of psychology that focused on attitudes (Kiesler, Collins, & Miller, 1969). Allport, in his 1935 *Handbook of Social Psychology*, synthesized the definitions and theories of attitude into a relatively cohesive construct. Thurstone provided a rationale as well as a method for measuring attitudes; thus attitudinal studies became a way to predict and understand social change (Ostrum, 1968).

Despite Allport's attempt to unite the definitions of attitude, a universal definition was never adopted. Throughout the research literature there reside multiple definitions for the construct of attitude and several theories of attitude construction. This makes interpreting the body of literature related to teacher attitudes problematic, and the issue is compounded by the interchangeable use of the term *belief* with *attitude*.

Defining Attitudes and Beliefs

Attitude as a construct has been defined in a myriad of ways by philosophers, psychologists, researchers, and practitioners. Simpson, Koballa, Oliver, and Crawley (1994) defined an attitude as "a predisposition to respond positively or negatively to things, people, places, events, or ideas" (p. 212). In a similar fashion, Jaccard, Litardo, and Wan (1999) stated, "[A]n attitude is traditionally viewed as how favorable or unfavorable an individual feels about performing a behavior" (p. 103).

Ernest (1989) included not only positive and negative affect, but also added other characteristics, "attitudes include liking, enjoyment and interest . . . or their opposites . . . teacher's confidence . . . the teachers' self-concept . . . valuing" (p. 24).

As researchers moved from identifying attitudes to examining beliefs as a separate construct, the distinctions became problematic. Table 35.1 shows the wide range of definitions and attributes that are used throughout the literature. Fishbein (1967) delineated *attitudes* from *beliefs* by identifying attitudes as affective constructs and beliefs as cognitive constructs. While this distinction seems to be generally accepted, the relationship between knowledge and beliefs is viewed from multiple perspectives. Smith and Siegel (2004) identified five distinct relationships of beliefs

TABLE 35.1
Definitions of Belief

Definition	Source
"Individuals' thoughts are equated with belief." (p. 331)	Southerland, Sinatra, & Mathews, 2001
"lay theories . . . images . . . metaphors, and webs" (p. 254)	Bird, Anderson, Sullivan, & Swidler, 1993
"both evidential and nonevidential, static, emotionally-bound, organized into systems, and develop(ed) episodically" (p. 55)	Gess-Newsome, 1999
"affective and subjective" (p. 335)	Southerland, Sinatra, & Mathews, 2001
"deeply personal, stable, lie beyond individual control or knowledge, and are usually unaffected by persuasion." (p. 786)	Haney & McArthur, 2002
"attitudes, judgments, axioms, opinions, ideology, perceptions, conceptions, conceptual systems, preconceptions, dispositions, implicit theories, explicit theories, personal theories, internal mental processes, action theories, rules of practice, practical principles, perspectives, repertories of understanding, and social strategy" (p. 309)	Pajares, 1992
"personal constructs" (p. 1) "propositions considered to be true by the individual . . . non-evidential as they are based on personal judgment and evaluation" (p. 2)	Luft, Roehrig, Brooks, & Austin, 2003
"espoused theories of action" (p. 178)	Kane, Sandretto, & Heath, 2002
"person's understanding of himself and his environment" (p. 131)	Fishbein & Ajzen, 1975
"psychologically held understandings, premises or propositions about the world that are felt to be true" (p. 103)	Richardson, 1996
"subjective, private opinion" (p. 227)	Coburn, 2000

and knowledge by research communities and described them as follows. One, knowledge and beliefs are separate constructs with reciprocal impact. Two, beliefs are viewed as an integral part of schema and beliefs are subsumed in the knowledge construct. Three, knowledge and beliefs are inseparable, as they do not represent separate entities and therefore no attempt is made to distinguish between them. Four, the term *belief* is used to identify naïve conceptions, and the term *knowledge* implies the presence of scientifically accepted constructs. Five, the terms are used interchangeably with the tacit assumption that the difference will be interpreted within context of the research.

Regardless of the knowledge/belief perspective adopted, the cognitive and developmental views of beliefs precipitated a shift in the research focus in teacher education from attitudes to beliefs. This shift, beginning in the 1980s, is attributed to the shift in social psychology from an affective orientation to a developmental and cognitive orientation (Kane et al., 2002; Richardson, 1996). Until this time, attitude research studies were more prevalent in the science education literature than studies that focused on beliefs.

In this chapter, we situate attitudes as a component of an individual's belief system. As Fishbein (1967) noted, attitudes have an affective dimension. Beliefs, however, are integral to larger belief systems that include self-efficacy, epistemologies, attitudes, and expectations. These are all intertwined and embedded in the sociocultural context. For example, a teacher's beliefs about using cooperative learning in the science classroom cannot be separated from her beliefs about science, science teaching, science learning, her motivation, her self-efficacy, her knowledge of constraints, her knowledge of cooperative learning, her skills using cooperative learning, prior experiences, the class and school context, as well as the larger cultural contexts. Thus beliefs are part of belief systems and attitudes are components of this larger system.

HISTORICAL PERSPECTIVES

Early Research on Attitudes and Beliefs

The initial interest in researching teachers' attitudes was based on the underlying premise that attitudes could be used to predict teaching behavior, and that changes in attitude would result in changes in behavior. A review of the science education research literature from the 1940s through the 1970s reveals three bodies of literature related to science teacher attitudes. One body of attitude literature reported prevailing teacher attitudes about science and teaching science, and science curriculum. Elementary teachers were the focus of most of the research on teacher attitudes toward science and teaching science. Although Dutton and Stephens (1963) reported that preservice elementary teachers' attitudes toward science were generally positive, many other surveys concluded that elementary teachers generally did not feel positive about teaching science. The sources of elementary teachers' negative attitudes were identified as a lack of interest in science, perceived difficulty of science, lack of content and/or pedagogical content knowledge, and lack of time (Lammers, 1949; Soy, 1967; Victor, 1962; Washton, 1961; Wytias, 1962). Needs surveys during the early years revealed that elementary school teachers were also concerned about management of materials and how to excite students about science, whereas secondary school teachers reported needing to know how scientists work and the latest advances in the field (Stronk, 1974). Both elementary and secondary school teachers reported negative attitudes about having students memorize information as the emphasis of science teaching (Stronk, 1974). Other informational needs reported by secondary science teachers included where to get materials, how to motivate students, and how to select appropriate pedagogy for science teaching (Moore, 1978).

Sputnik Reform: Testing Variables

The pre-Sputnik/post-Sputnik years provide the line of demarcation in studies of teachers' attitudes toward science curricula. Though comparably few in number, attitudes toward using "innovative practices" during the pre-Sputnik years revealed underlying concerns similar to those espoused toward the post-Sputnik curricula. Teachers cited lack of equipment and time as well as a preference for traditional curricula as reasons for negative attitudes toward change in practice (Lampkin, 1944; Sadler, 1967).

The onslaught of the National Science Foundation alphabet curricula of the late 1960s contributed to an increase in the number of studies on attitudes toward new curricula. Certain personal characteristics were found to be linked with a tendency to accept and implement the new curricula. Open-mindedness (Strawitz, 1977; Symington & Fensham, 1976), a preference for indirect and inductive teaching (James, 1971), and independent thought and action were linked to positive attitudes toward nontraditional curricula (Blankenship, 1965; Hoy & Blankenship, 1972). Less rigid control was aligned with practices advocated by Biological Sciences Curriculum Study (Jones & Blankenship, 1970). Conflicting research findings were reported on the effect of using the new curriculum on teaching practices. Hall (1970) reported that using a nontraditional curriculum did not affect teaching behaviors, whereas Orgren (1974) found that teachers changed their teaching behaviors as a result of using a new curriculum.

The second body of attitude research focused on identifying variables such as self-concept, coursework, age, cooperating teachers' attitudes, and knowledge related to teacher attitudes about teaching science. Self-concept was found to be directly related to teacher attitudes (Campbell & Martinez-Perez, 1977). Butts and Raun (1969a, 1969b) reported that the number of science courses taken was linked to attitudes toward teaching inquiry science with fewer courses linked to more positive attitudes, whereas Douglass (1979) found that more courses were linked to more positive attitudes. Other studies examined the correlation of age with attitudes. Schwirian (1969) reported that younger teachers were more positive, whereas Shrigley and Johnson (1974) found no relationship. Cooperating teacher attitudes were not found to influence student teachers' attitudes (James, 1971). Low correlation between teacher attitudes and knowledge was reported (Shrigley, 1974).

The third body of attitude research examined the effectiveness of interventions in affecting attitudes toward a number of variables. Role playing was used to improve attitudes toward teaching science (Hughes, 1971); essay writing generated positive attitudes toward using Bloom's taxonomy (Kauchak, 1977). Teaching process skills improved teachers' attitudes toward using a process approach (Butts & Raun, 1969a), as well as toward teaching science (Kennedy, 1973). Recognition of the importance of process skills led elementary teachers to change their teaching practices (Bradley, Earp, & Sullivan, 1966), and modeling recommended practices produced positive attitudes toward the practices modeled (Bratt, 1977). Researchers found that preservice teacher preparation programs could affect preservice teachers' attitudes toward teaching science (Gabel & Rubba, 1977), toward student-centered classrooms (Downs & DeLuca, 1979), and toward inquiry (Barufaldi, Huntsberger, & Lazarowitz, 1976). Using inquiry-based curricula was also found to improve attitudes toward inquiry (Lazarowitz, 1976). Researchers reported that early field experiences did not affect preservice teachers' attitudes (Weaver, Hounshell, & Coble, 1979). Inservice workshops improved attitudes toward teaching science (Moore, 1975), toward teaching environmental education (Jaus, 1978), and toward a new curriculum (Ost, 1971) and could affect teaching practices (Mayer, Disinger, & White, 1975; Welch & Walberg, 1967). Jaus (1977) reported that microteaching was found to improve inservice teachers' attitudes about teaching science, but Bergel (1977) found that microteaching had no effect on the attitudes of preservice teachers. In general, most of the studies indicated that planned interventions positively affected teacher attitudes, at least in the short term.

ASSESSING ATTITUDES AND BELIEFS

Quantitative Assessments

Traditional measurements of attitudes in the early research literature relied almost exclusively on quantitative methods. The most popular method of quantitatively measuring attitude was survey instruments with Likert scales where subjects ranked their level of agreement to statements with the use of a five-point scale (Behnke, 1961; Bratt, 1977; Golman, 1975; Sutman, 1969). Semantic differentials were also used to measure intensity of feeling about a statement (Butts & Raun, 1969a; Sunal, 1980). These scales were constructed by generating a series of adjective antonym pairs and placing each pair on opposite sides of a marked continuum. Respondents indicated relative attitude about a construct by placing a mark on each continuum closer to the adjective that described their feelings about the construct. Common examples of adjective antonyms used were *happy-sad, interesting-dull*, and *harmful-helpful*. Sentence completion and word associations were also used to assess teacher attitudes (Hovey, 1975; Lowery, 1966; Moyer, 1977). A few examples of qualitative methodologies for assessing attitudes, such as interviewing, were found in the literature but were used in conjunction with quantitative methodologies (Soy, 1967; Thomson & Thompson, 1975). See Pearl (1974) for a comprehensive review and critique of early attitude measurement techniques.

Qualitative Assessments

About the time research on teachers' attitudes declined in favor of examining teachers' beliefs, qualitative methodologies gained acceptance. This shift in research methodology reflected a movement away from a behaviorist view of the teaching-learning process and toward a more individualized and context-based approach. These qualitative assessments of attitudes and beliefs sought to *understand* the complex relationships among beliefs, experiences, and practices, with less emphasis on predicting and controlling teachers. Even with the growing use of qualitative methods, quantitative methodologies such as semantic differentials (DeSouza & Czerniak, 2003) were occasionally used, and Likert scale instruments (Aikenhead & Otsuji, 2000; Brown, 2000; Pedersen & McCurdy, 1992) remained a popular way for measuring attitudes and beliefs. [For examples of Likert scale instruments used to measure science teachers' attitudes and beliefs see the following: Science Teaching Efficacy Beliefs Instrument for preservice science teachers (Enochs & Riggs, 1990), Science Attitude Scale (Thompson & Shrigley, 1986), Science Support Scale (Schwirian, 1968), Test of Science-Related Attitudes (Fraser, 1981), and Context Beliefs about Teaching Science (Lumpe, Haney, & Czerniak, 2000)].

Whereas attitude researchers have generally favored quantitative techniques, belief research methodologies have tended to be primarily qualitative. There has also been an increase in the number of research studies applying multiple data collection methods (Simmons et al., 1999; Yerrick & Hoving, 1999), though qualitative traditions have dictated selection of methodologies. Interviews have become one of the most popular ways to examine individuals' beliefs and attitudes (Appleton & Kindt, 1999; Duffee & Aikenhead, 1992; Skamp, 2001; Tsai, 2002). Teacher biographies and journaling (Stuart & Thurlow, 2000), open-ended questions (Plucker, 1996; Windschitl, 2000), and case studies (Abell & Roth, 1992; Briscoe, 1991; Zahur, Barton, & Upadhyay, 2002) are also widely used as methods to assess attitudes and beliefs. These latter research tools have enabled researchers to go beyond simply identifying attitudes and beliefs to documenting the complex system of beliefs while shedding light on the development of belief systems within individuals. For a thorough review of the history of research on teachers' beliefs and attitudes, see Richardson's chapter in the 1996 *Handbook on Research in Teacher Education.*

THEORETICAL MODELS

Predicting Behavior

Initial interest in teacher attitudes was based on a fairly simple linear model that predicted that positive attitudes toward a behavior were sufficient for implementation of that behavior. Over time, increasingly complex models have been developed to account for the multiple variables affecting decisions to engage in certain behaviors. A behaviorist frame for early attitude/belief research provided a linear model with a stimulus eliciting an attitude that in turn produced an observable response. However, research employing this model indicated a weak to modest correlation of attitudes with behavior; models grew in complexity to encompass other variables. One widely used model, the Theory of Reasoned Action (Ajzen & Fishbein, 1980; Fishbein & Ajzen, 1975), suggests that behavior can be predicted from an examination of an individual's intent to perform the behavior. Intent is dependent on personal attitude toward the behavior and social influences (subjective norm) in favor of or against performing the behavior.

Another widely used model is the Theory of Planned Behavior. Whereas the Theory of Reasoned Action is limited to behaviors over which the individual has volitional control, the Theory of Planned Behavior takes into account the degree to which an individual perceives control (Ajzen, 1985, 1988; Zint, 2002). This model includes perceived behavioral control as a predictor. This variable represents the perception that an individual holds about the opportunities and resources available to perform the behavior. For example, applying this theory to environmental risk education suggests that teachers would teach environmental risk education when they have a favorable disposition toward the instruction, when they perceive social pressure to teach environmental risk education, and when they are confident that they can successfully accomplish the instruction (Zint, 2002).

SOCIOCULTURAL MODEL OF EMBEDDED
BELIEF SYSTEMS

Figure 35–1 illustrates a blended theoretical framework developed by reviewing science teacher attitude and belief literature and by borrowing heavily from theoretical models of social psychology (Jaccard, Litardo, & Wan, 1999). We will use this

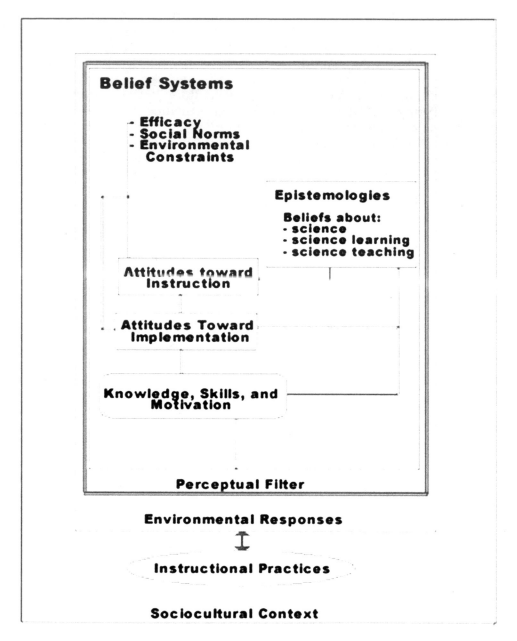

FIGURE 35–1.   Sociocultural model of embedded belief systems.

model, the *Sociocultural Model of Embedded Belief Systems*, as a basis for framing recent research on science teacher attitudes and beliefs and as a tool for understanding the construction and development of beliefs and attitudes.

Although the two-dimensional restrictions on illustrating the model may imply linearity of the components, this is not the intention; we acknowledge multiple reciprocal interactions. It is important to note that this model is bound by the sociocultural context of the teacher (peers, students, culture, etc.). The cyclical nature of the model denies a point of origin, but we will begin the explanation with motivation, knowledge, and skills. Here it is illustrated that knowledge and skills, as well as motivation, are prerequisites for engaging in a particular instructional practice. Although facilitating construction of knowledge and skills is complex, changing existing belief and attitude structures that underpin the motivation to engage in a set of behaviors is a daunting task.

In this model, motivation is affected by two sets of attitudes, one related to the attitudes about the instructional practice, the other related to attitudes toward implementing the practice. Each attitude set incorporates related belief systems; the relative strengths of the systems determine the strength and direction (positive or negative) of the resultant attitude. The direction and relative strength of each attitude set, defined as a disposition to act, will contribute to the strength of the motivation toward the instructional practice.

As shown in the model, science teachers' attitudes are strongly influenced by epistemological beliefs. From an epistemological viewpoint, knowledge is socially constructed, but beliefs are individually constructed. Thus, a personal epistemology is made up of belief systems that form the perspectives with which one views a particular behavior. Science teachers' epistemologies—which include beliefs about science, beliefs about teaching science, and beliefs about learning science—affect the type of instructional behaviors that occur in science classrooms (van Driel, Verloop, & de Vos, 1998). That is, science teachers' epistemologies frame their teaching paradigms. Preservice teachers enter professional development programs with these core beliefs firmly in place (Cobern & Loving, 2002). Therefore, regardless of a teacher's place along the professional continuum, an instructional strategy perceived as incongruent with that teacher's teaching paradigm will generate a negative attitude response toward that strategy.

The level of motivation is influenced by attitudes toward instructional practices. Attitudes *toward* performing particular instructional practices may have a direction and a strength that are different from attitudes *about* these practices. For example, a study comparing the attitudes of elementary teachers in self-contained classrooms and attitudes of elementary science resource teachers revealed that although resource teachers had a more favorable attitude toward teaching science, there was no difference between the two groups in attitudes about science (Earl & Winkeljohn, 1977). Although having a positive attitude about a behavior and a negative attitude toward implementing a behavior may be interpreted as resulting from conflicts within belief systems, this model emphasizes the highly contextualized nature of instructional practices. Here the relative weights of the beliefs are highly dependent on interactions of a number of factors (Lederman, 1992; Ritchie, 1999; Strage & Bol, 1996), factors that may be overlooked in the research literature (McGuiness & Simmons, 1999). Although we acknowledge that this model of belief systems has multiple components, we have included only those variables that have been repeatedly substantiated in the research literature, including self-efficacy, perceived social norms, and context.

Self-efficacy, or beliefs about one's ability to successfully implement an instructional strategy, has been identified in several studies as a major component in the instructional decision-making process (discussed later in this chapter). Lumpe et al. (2000) outlined the multiple contributions that emerge from the possible interactions of content and efficacy beliefs and showed that decisions about practice are influenced by the relative weights of the components of the belief system.

Perceived social norms, that is, what a teacher believes is expected by others in terms of the teaching and learning process, also influence attitudes about implementing an instructional practice. Perceived environmental constraints, or physical factors that can impede success, such as lack of resources or lack of time, have been identified as underpinning this belief. Strong belief systems that lead to strong teacher identities have been shown to lessen the influence of environmental constraints (Hawkey, 1996).

The relative strengths of all these components at any given time, in any given context, can shift, producing a negative or positive attitude toward implementing the instructional practice. That is, the sociocultural environment as perceived by the teacher ultimately determines whether the instructional practice is enacted, by affecting the relative weights of the major determinants.

Once instructional behaviors are enacted, responses to teachers' actions affect their beliefs, just as beliefs affect actions (Haney, Lumpe, Czerniak, & Egan, 2002). For example, students' epistemologies can affect how they respond to a teacher's instruction (Laplante, 1997). If students have a traditional view of what it means to learn science, they may respond negatively to a teacher's attempt to implement a nontraditional strategy. In turn this response is filtered back through the teacher's perceptions. Whether or not the response will have an impact on a teacher's decision to continue to implement the strategy will depend on the strength of the students' responses as well as the strength of the teacher's beliefs about the practice.

If both attitude sets are negative, then there is no motivation to implement the instructional practice, whether or not the knowledge and skills to do so are present. If one attitude is positive and the other is negative, the relative strengths of attitudes will determine whether there is motivation to undertake the task. Perceived environmental constraints, weak content background, and weak instructional skills all eliminate the possibility of alignment of practice with beliefs (King, Shumow, & Lietz, 2001). If motivation is present but knowledge and skills are not, the instructional practice will either not be enacted or will not be realized in the way it was intended (Sequeira, Leite, & Duarte, 1993).

Recent Attitude and Belief Research

The following sections describe the attitude/belief research from the 1980s to the present day. Although we made no attempt to review every research article on science teacher attitudes and beliefs over the last two decades, a cross section of studies representing research on the major mediators of teaching behavior is included. The research methodologies of the last two decades are distinctly different from earlier research. The knowledge claim shift in attitude/belief research from post-positivist to social constructivist required a shift to qualitative methodologies more suited to examining the complexity and individuality of teaching (Creswell, 2003). Data collection methods in the last two decades have centered on observations and interviews, which are most appropriate for revealing the nature of teachers' thinking and worldviews (Richardson, 1996). Although the evaluative nature of attitudes is still acknowledged, the dynamic nature of the system in context has moved to the forefront.

The *Sociocultural Model of Embedded Belief Systems* frames the sections that follow. The first sections review literature on teachers' epistemologies, sets of beliefs that contribute to the decisions teachers make about their practice. These sections are followed by sections reviewing literature on the personal and environmental constraints perceived by teachers as affecting their instructional decisions.

SCIENCE TEACHERS' EPISTEMOLOGICAL BELIEFS

Epistemologies are sets of beliefs about knowing and learning that play a mediating role in the processing of new information. Teachers' personal epistemologies emerge from formal and informal learning experiences and serve as mental exemplars for constructing and evaluating their own teaching practices. The research reviewed includes studies examining the origins of beliefs, the influence of belief systems on practice, epistemological shifts, and factors that contribute to belief and practice inconsistencies.

ORIGINS OF EPISTEMOLOGIES

Prospective teachers enter teacher education programs with images and models of teaching that they experienced as students (Eick & Reed, 2002; Laplante, 1997; Lortie, 1975; Southerland & Gess-Newsome, 1999). As they move through their teacher education programs, these beliefs serve as filters for new ideas (Meyer, Tabachnick, Hewson, Lemberger, & Park, 1999). That is, prospective teachers make sense of practices promoted by the preservice education curriculum in terms of their personal epistemologies. If students' personal epistemologies are not aligned with those of the program, the outcome of instruction may be different from what had been promoted and anticipated (Bird, Anderson, Sullivan, & Swidler, 1993).

Adams and Krockover (1997) investigated the origin of the teaching and learning beliefs of four beginning science teachers. They found that one student adopted a model of teaching based on his own high school experiences. Another student's foundational experience was teaching horseback riding. The other two borrowed primarily from their experiences as teaching assistants, and all borrowed quite heavily from experiences in science content courses.

Smith (2003) examined the prior experiences of two elementary teachers who had similar backgrounds, teaching experience, and time spent teaching science and found that teachers' experiences of learning directly affected their beliefs and practices as science teachers. For example, one of the teachers, Vicki, was not allowed to work on the farm where she grew up or spend much time out of doors. Vicki preferred learning through expository teaching and listening to information transmitted by a teacher. She learned science through courses where teachers taught with lecture and discussion and became successful at memorizing science content. The other teacher, Hannah, used constructivist practices and described her interest in science as beginning with participation in science fairs. Hannah and her family spent time together reading science tradebooks, learning to use microscopes and telescopes, and exploring the geology along a river. Hannah described her best science experiences in learning science in school as those that involved "real life"

(p. 29) applications and deepened her understanding of science. Smith argued that early experiences outside of formal education may have a greater impact on teachers' beliefs about teaching and learning science than their formal education.

This significant link between prior experiences and beliefs about teaching practices has been shown in other studies. Stuart and Thurlow (2000) examined preservice teachers' beliefs during a science and mathematics methods course and found that preservice teachers filtered their developing beliefs about teaching through their prior experiences. "I arrived at these beliefs of how students learn because . . . I've witnessed it in my classroom, and more importantly I've experienced it myself as a student" (p. 118). This relationship was also documented by Skamp (2001) in a study of Canadian preservice teachers who reported that their prior experiences as learners in university undergraduate science classes as well as science methods classes formed their images of good science teaching. However, Skamp observed that this changed once they began to teach in the schools. At this point, teacher education field experiences were most influential in shaping beliefs about good teaching as they saw what worked with their students.

EPISTEMOLOGIES AND SCIENCE INSTRUCTIONAL PRACTICES

Despite the latest reform efforts, most science teachers in the United States tend to hold epistemological beliefs aligned with a behaviorist tradition. Although professional development workshops have successfully encouraged the adoption of some constructivist strategies, the adoption of these practices does not necessarily affect the teachers' epistemologies. For example, in 1996 a survey of K–12 teachers ($N =$ 148) indicated that although many had adopted instructional practices aligned with constructivism, the majority did not believe that students learned by constructing their own understanding (Czerniak & Lumpe, 1996).

Taiwanese teachers have also been found to hold a traditional or transmission view of the nature of science, learning science, and teaching science. Tsai (2002) interviewed physical science teachers and found that more than half of the teachers believed that learning science is acquiring knowledge, that science provides correct answers (nature of science), and science is taught best by transferring knowledge from the teacher to the students. Less than 15 percent of the Taiwanese teachers in the study held constructivist views of learning science, teaching science, or the nature of science.

Several research studies have clearly indicated the influence of epistemologies on practice. Hashweh (1985) examined the relationship between being a constructivist teacher and the types of teaching strategies used. He found that teachers who held constructivist beliefs had a larger repertoire of teaching strategies and used strategies that would promote conceptual change.

Benson (1989) reported that epistemological beliefs at odds with a constructivist curriculum inhibited the implementation of a constructivist curriculum. A case study of two middle-grades teachers implementing a curriculum on wildlife species revealed that beliefs about learning science as a body of facts inhibited the implementation of the discovery-oriented curriculum (Cronin-Jones, 1991).

Brickhouse (1990) found that teachers' views about how scientists construct knowledge were consistent with how they believed students should learn science.

For example, one of the teachers in the study believed that scientists use scientific theories to make sense of observations and therefore believed that students should use theories to explain their observations within the science classroom. Furthermore, teachers' beliefs about science influenced explicit lessons about the nature of science as well as the implicit curriculum about the nature of scientific knowledge. Gallagher (1991) reported that science teachers who hold positivist views of science tended to emphasize the scientific method and the objective nature of science.

Hashweh (1996) studied 35 Palestinian science teachers who described themselves as either constructivist or empiricist (as defined by a questionnaire). He found that the constructivist teachers were more likely to recognize students' alternative conceptions and to indicate they would use a variety of teaching strategies than did empiricist teachers. Hashweh argued that constructivist teachers view the development of knowledge as residing at the student level and as a result view science as a process of conceptual change. Thus, the teachers in this study selected instructional strategies that were congruent with their beliefs about science and science learning.

A case study by Richmond and Anderson (2003) of three secondary science teacher candidates clearly revealed the influence of their epistemologies on practice. One teacher's beliefs about science as a body of facts shaped his planning and teaching. Furthermore, his focus on science as facts led him to assess low-level understanding rather than conceptual development. Another teacher viewed her primary role as a science teacher as helping students appreciate science. As a result, she spent her planning time creating an engaging instructional setting and much less time on determining if students had developed the targeted scientific understandings.

Zipf and Harrison (2003) conducted a qualitative study of two Australian elementary science teachers and examined the relationship between these teachers' beliefs and their teaching practices. Patty, a more traditional teacher, tended to use worksheets and emphasize content in her teaching. She used the textbook in her planning to map out the content and stated, "I'm happy for the text to choose what we teach . . . the textbook has to be not only a student reference but the main resource for the lesson" (p. 7). Furthermore, Patty believed the textbook was the tool that allowed her to meet the wide variation in her students' abilities: "[We need a textbook] that's got a bit of everything in it for all learners, low, middle, high ability" (p. 7). In contrast, Tina wanted to use a textbook that would support her belief in teaching relationally and would allow her "students to experience and actively participate in science" (p. 9). The differences in these two teachers' beliefs about teaching and learning were further translated into their assessment practices. Tina used open-ended formative assessments in her instructional unit to provide her with continuous feedback on student learning, whereas Patty "favored end-on marks-based assessment techniques focusing on science content and felt that she 'must have marks'" (p. 6).

EPISTEMOLOGICAL BELIEF
SYSTEMS AND CHANGE

Teachers' epistemological beliefs tend to be relatively stable and resistant to change (Pajares, 1992). This is particularly true of experienced teachers. Luft (2001) found that an inservice program designed to promote inquiry teaching changed the beliefs of induction teachers, but changed only the practices of experienced teachers. BouJaoude (2000) used metaphors to assess preservice science teachers' beliefs as they progressed through their teacher education program and found that the program was successful in affecting beliefs. The types of metaphors the prospective teachers used showed that 75 percent of the preservice teachers held a transmission view of teaching at the beginning of the year; this number dropped to 34 percent by the end of the year. The number of teachers who held constructivist-based views grew from 1 percent at the beginning of the year to 50 percent at the end of the year. BouJaoude also found that biology teachers were more likely to hold a transfer model of teaching than chemistry or physics teachers throughout the course of the study. Teachers' metaphors have been used in many studies to elicit teachers' epistemological views, because metaphors can reveal the subtle assumptions and frames that teachers apply to their practices.

Although preservice and induction teachers' beliefs tend to be more malleable (Salish I Research Project, 1997), research has indicated that the belief systems of these groups may remain virtually unchanged, despite the constructivist traditions of their teacher education programs. Cronin Jones and Shaw (1992) reported that preservice teachers' beliefs remained relatively unchanged by participation in a science education program. These researchers found that their elementary and secondary preservice teachers had similar clusters of beliefs about teaching and learning both before and after their participation in a methods class.

Even if a teacher education program is successful in moving students toward a constructivist epistemology, the stability of this change is dependent on the sociocultural context. Stofflett (1994) reported that a preservice teacher education program had successfully moved preservice science teachers from a traditional epistemology to a constructivist epistemology. However, Stofflett found that classroom practice during student teaching was not likely to be constructivist unless the cooperating teacher supported the classroom practice. In another example of sociocultural influences on instruction, Haney and McArthur (2002) conducted a case study with four preservice science teachers, examining their beliefs about constructivist practices and how consistent these beliefs were with classroom practices. They identified central or core beliefs (those that are both stated and enacted) and peripheral beliefs (those that are stated but not enacted). During student teaching, the preservice teachers whose beliefs were a mismatch with those held by their cooperating teachers had the most difficulty incorporating new beliefs into changes in teaching practices. At times, peripheral beliefs moved into core beliefs when preservice teachers felt supported by the cooperating teacher. When peripheral beliefs were not supported, they did not move from stated beliefs to implemented beliefs.

In a large-scale research project on beginning teachers' beliefs and practices, Simmons et al. (1999) indicated that although beginning teachers espoused a student-centered approach, perhaps as a result of their undergraduate programs, their practices were not aligned with their beliefs. They found that beginning teachers held many beliefs about science teaching and learning, and that these beliefs were not always aligned with any one belief system. The study also revealed the vacillation between beliefs that many teachers articulated in the early years, as well as the articulation of beliefs that contradicted their practices. However, by the third year, many teachers espoused the teacher-centered beliefs that aligned with their teacher-centered practices.

A survey of nine teacher education programs found that the characteristics of the program determined whether graduates of the program adopted the advocated philosophy (Tatto, 1998). The more successful programs in achieving this alignment had the following characteristics: a consistent philosophy promoted throughout the program, faculty who maintained and espoused a consistent vision, context-relevant experiences, learning cohorts, and personalized programs.

Moss and Kaufman (2003) surveyed preservice science teachers' beliefs about classroom organization, management, and rules and found that teachers hold complex views about class management that were not supported by their philosophical and theoretical stances. Although preservice teachers may have held progressive ideas about teaching, they felt unable to implement these views in their teaching and instead focused on control and maintaining order.

Yerrick and Hoving (2003) examined preservice teachers' beliefs about teaching and learning that the teachers held while enrolled in a field-based course that focused on culturally diverse students. Prospective teachers who made changes in their instruction were reflective and engaged in the production of new knowledge of teaching. Other teachers, who were unable to make changes, tended to filter their perspectives through their own prior educational experiences. This latter group of teachers Yerrick and Hoving called "reproducers" (p. 404) because they sought to reenact their own recollected science experiences with new groups of students. These reproducers rarely mentioned student learning in their reflections and tended to focus on management of student behavior as a measurement of their success in teaching. Other prospective teachers, designated as "producers," saw themselves as learners and recognized the need to change. These producers altered their beliefs and changed their instruction to more effective strategies.

Yerrick, Parke, and Nugent (1997) found that inservice teachers participating in a professional development workshop held traditional views on entering the workshop and left the workshop with many of these views intact. The researchers observed that teachers changed the way they talked about teaching and did indeed incorporate some of the ideas from the workshop into practice. However, the researchers noted that the participants had "rooted out" strategies that conflicted less with existing belief systems and had incorporated those ideas into their existing belief structures.

Summary

Recent attitude/belief research has revealed how individuals' epistemological systems are constructed through their formal and informal experiences as students. These systems are extremely stable because new information is filtered through these systems and because the enactment of this system has been modeled for a number of years.

Preservice teachers' systems seem less resistant to change, although lack of content and pedagogical knowledge may inhibit change. Inservice programs have been successful in getting teachers to assimilate new practices, but without a corresponding change in beliefs. Preservice and inservice programs should be cognizant of existing belief systems, should assist teachers with recognizing their beliefs, and should provide long-term support to newly born epistemological practices. Researchers have argued that significant changes in teachers' instructional practices come only after there are fundamental changes in teachers' belief systems and that these changes are not necessarily linear. Therefore, there may be a lag time between changes in beliefs and changes in practices that may not be captured by the research project. What is clear from some research is that the process of making epistemological and personal beliefs explicit is critical for professional development. Teachers may not recognize the contradiction between their beliefs and practices (Tobin & LaMaster, 1995). According to Kagan (1992), "If a program is to promote growth among novices, it must require them to make their preexisting personal beliefs explicit; it must challenge the adequacy of those beliefs; and it must give novices extended opportunities to examine, elaborate, and integrate new information into their existing belief systems" (p. 77).

BELIEF AND PRACTICE MISMATCH: CONSTRAINTS TO PRACTICE

In the previous section on epistemological change, belief-practice mismatch seemed to be a result of either the stability of the initial epistemological system or lack of support for the enacted constructivist epistemology. Many studies have substantiated belief-practice inconsistencies in other contexts, and other factors that may contribute to this mismatch have emerged.

Justi and Gilbert (2002) investigated teachers' beliefs about the use of models and modeling for teaching science phenomena. The researchers argued that to learn science, students need to know major scientific models; to learn about science, students should understand the nature of scientific models and role of models in scientific inquiry; and to understand how to do science, students must be able to create and test their own models. Through the use of a semistructured interview with 39 Brazilian teachers (four different grade levels from primary to university), Justi and Gilbert explored teachers' beliefs about the status and value of models in science as well as how these beliefs were translated into instructional practices. Teachers in the study noted that they believed that models could (a) make science more interesting; (b) provide a framework for explanations of phenomena; (c) make abstract concepts more understandable; (d) promote conceptual change; and (d) promote learning about the nature of science. Although the teachers in the study valued using models to help students learn science, they did not widely report using models in practice.

Part of the developmental process of moving from student to teacher involves a shift in focus from self to one's students (Jones & Vesilind, 1995). Regardless of belief systems, there is evidence that novice teachers make instructional decisions for their students based on their own needs and not their students' needs. Peacock and Gates (2000) examined newly qualified United Kingdom teachers' perceptions of textbook selection and use. They found that these teachers did not base their decisions about textbook use on their students' needs but instead made decisions based on their beliefs about the demands that would be placed on them as teachers.

In a study of preservice teachers' beliefs, Lotter (2003) examined teachers enrolled in a secondary science methods course and found that preservice teachers expressed the most concern about issues related to themselves rather than their students. These same teachers expressed positive attitudes about the value of inquiry teaching as a way to increase students' critical thinking, motivation, ownership of science, and comprehension.

SOCIAL NORMS

Teacher beliefs are situated in the contexts of the existing social norms of the school community. Social norms influence how teachers believe their enacted practices will be perceived. For science teachers, this tension between beliefs and practices may arise when they are teaching about controversial issues such as evolution.

Elementary and secondary teachers' beliefs about teaching science-technology-society (STS) as part of the science curriculum were investigated by Lumpe, Haney, and Czerniak (1998).Through the use of both open and closed questionnaires, teachers' beliefs about STS were assessed within Ajzen and Madden's (1986) Theory of Planned Behavior. The questionnaires were designed to elicit teachers' beliefs about the advantages and disadvantages of implementing STS, beliefs about who might approve or disapprove of their implementation of STS in their classroom, and factors that might encourage or discourage them from STS implementation. Teachers indicated that they believed STS would help students learn science and would assist students in applying science to their everyday lives. However, teachers were concerned about the time it takes to implement STS as part of the science curriculum. Other concerns about STS centered on teaching controversial issues as well as concerns about religious groups' reactions to STS instruction.

ENVIRONMENTAL CONSTRAINTS

Teachers may state that they hold one set of beliefs about teaching and learning while revealing their perceptions of constraints to enacting their beliefs. Collison (1993) found, as have many researchers, that teachers who reported that they did not use hands-on science indicated they could not because they lacked the materials and supplies needed.

In many cases, the contradictions between beliefs and practices arise from the perceived sociocultural context. An in-depth look at the beliefs and actions of an experienced high school science teacher revealed beliefs about teaching science that were at odds with beliefs about how students learn. Although this dichotomy in thinking was revealed to the science teacher, the teacher felt that his beliefs were aligned with practice. He explained that he was acting out his belief systems as well as he could in the *context* in which he was teaching (Lyons, Freitag, & Hewson, 1997). In contrast, a case study of a novice middle-grades science teacher indicated that he was aware that his beliefs about science were not aligned with his beliefs about learning science, but he felt that institutional constraints left him little time to reflect on this misalignment (Brickhouse & Bodner, 1992).

A study of Chinese teachers' and teacher educators' epistemological beliefs about inquiry-based learning showed that although Chinese teachers believed that inquiry-based teaching was a good way to teach science, these teachers believed there were significant barriers to implementing inquiry teaching (Zhang et al., 2003). In this study, 220 teachers and teacher educators completed a questionnaire about their constructivist and traditional views of science and science education, and 12 individual interviews were conducted to obtain more in-depth data. The Chinese science educators indicated that barriers to implementing inquiry-based teaching included the need to prepare students for the college entrance examination, which did not assess inquiry, the need for different curricular frameworks and materials for inquiry, large class size (including issues with class management), and concerns about a lack of teacher preparation to teach with inquiry.

DeSouza and Czerniak (2003) explored teachers' intent to collaborate with other teachers to address their students' needs and found that their perceived behavioral control was more significant than their attitudes toward the behavior. The teachers believed that collaboration to provide instruction for students from diverse backgrounds would not occur unless there was more time to collaborate, good facilities and technology, and support from colleagues.

Summary

Research has shown that teachers can believe that an instructional practice is important but, for any number of reasons, resist engaging in the practice. This contradiction may emerge as a result of lack of knowledge or because other instructional issues, such as discipline, take precedence. Also, teachers may feel that some practices are controversial and the risk of engaging in a particular instructional strategy outweighs the perceived benefits. In addition, science teachers consistently note that there are insufficient time and materials to support new practices. However, the contradictory nature of a belief/practice system may not be totally negative. Constraints, which may have appeared insurmountable, may be viewed differently if belief systems are changed (Tobin, Briscoe, & Holman, 1990). This conflict between belief and practice may produce the disequilibrium needed for change to occur.

EFFICACY, EPISTEMOLOGIES, AND TEACHING PRACTICES

Research indicates that teaching efficacy is a complex construct influenced by a number of variables. Desouza, Boone, and Yilmaz (2003) assessed 300 teachers from India, with the use of the Science Teaching Efficacy Belief Instrument (STEBI-A) developed by Riggs and Enochs (1990). They found higher teaching efficacy for teachers who held a science degree and who spent more time teaching science each week. Interestingly, teachers with more experience were less confident of their students' achievement (outcome expectancy) than those teachers with less experience.

There is research evidence that teachers who lack confidence about teaching a subject will give it minimal emphasis within the curriculum. This pattern is painfully evident in elementary science instruction. Jones and Levin (1994) examined elementary teachers' attitudes toward science and science teaching and found that preservice teachers had significantly more confidence about science teaching than inservice teachers, and males had more confidence than females. The researchers also found that there was a positive relationship between the number of science courses teachers had completed and their attitudes about teaching science. Teachers who had completed three or more science courses ranked science as a higher instructional priority than teachers with fewer science courses.

Woolfolk and Hoy (1990) suggested that teaching efficacy (in a general sense) is related to teachers' experiences managing and motivating students. Furthermore, beginning teachers' success or failure in acting on their beliefs about student management may influence the development of a sense of efficacy. The researchers assessed 182 preservice teachers' teaching efficacy, personal teaching efficacy, pupil control ideology, and motivational orientation (controlling or autonomous). They found that preservice teachers possessed teaching efficacy independently of personal efficacy. Personal efficacy included beliefs about responsibility for positive student outcomes and beliefs about responsibility for negative student outcomes. Woolfolk and Hoy reported that prospective teachers who had high teaching efficacy were more humanistic in relation to pupil control than those prospective teachers who were low in teaching efficacy. However, the authors noted that this was true only for prospective teachers who also had high personal efficacy and believed that they could make a difference in student achievement.

Cakiroglu and Boone (2000) explored the relationships between elementary preservice teachers' self-efficacy and their conceptions of photosynthesis and inheritance. Teachers who had relatively high personal science teaching efficacy held fewer alternative conceptions related to photosynthesis. Surprisingly, the study failed to find any relationship between the number of high school and college courses completed and the number of alternative conceptions held by the prospective teachers.

Affecting Self-Efficacy

Students' responses to instructional practices can alter teachers' beliefs about teaching and learning science. A recent study (Sweeney, Bula, & Cornett, 2001) elucidated the change in the personal practice theories of a first-year chemistry teacher from a goal of preparing future scientists to a belief that this job meant preparing scientifically literate citizens.

For teachers to believe that changes in instruction will make a difference, Bandura (1986) suggested that teachers need to have feedback, experience success, observe models of success that are credible, and be persuaded that the concerns can be overcome with positive benefits. Bandura also suggested that affective feelings that arise from success will affect the teacher's self-efficacy. Evidence for the relationship between attitudes, beliefs, and affect was found in a set of case studies of prospective elementary teachers conducted by Palmer (2002). He reported that elementary teacher candidates' attitudes changed when they had external validation for their work, experienced success teaching children, and had a confident and supportive teacher who modeled teaching behaviors and used simple, understandable language. These factors increased the preservice teachers' positive interest and self-efficacy.

As beginning teachers experience success, the type of support they receive may affect their self-efficacy. Luft, Roehrig, and Patterson (2003) studied three types of induction programs (general support, science-focused support, and no support) and found that teachers who participated in a science-focused induction program were more likely to implement student-centered inquiry lessons, believe in student-centered practices, and feel fewer constraints within their teaching than teachers who participated in either the general support group or did not participate in an induction group. In addition, the science-focused support group participants were more likely to use laboratories and to implement standards-based lessons than teachers in the other groups. Teachers in the no induction group held significantly more didactic beliefs about teaching than teachers in the science-focused support group. This study provided evidence that beliefs can be shaped and scaffolded by appropriate support during the early stages of learning to teach.

Knowledge and Skills

One obvious reason for the conflict between beliefs and practices as indicated in the *Sociocultural Model of Embedded Belief Systems* (Fig. 35–1) is a lack of knowledge and skills needed to implement the preferred practice. Not knowing how to implement a specific teaching behavior is an insurmountable roadblock to engaging in the strategy, regardless of strength of beliefs about its effectiveness. Atwater, Gardner, & Kight (1991) studied primary (K–3) urban teachers' attitudes toward physical science and found that early-grade teachers believe that using hands-on approaches is the best way to teach physical science (100 percent), that they feel insecure about attempting to teach physical science (60 percent), and that it makes them nervous to even think about having to do a physical science experiment (84 percent). Tosun (2000) assessed prospective elementary teachers' prior science coursework, achievement in science courses, and science teaching self-efficacy and found that prospective elementary teachers had overwhelmingly negative attitudes toward science, using terms such as "boring," "meaningless," "scared," and "impossible" (p. 376) to describe their previous science coursework.

According to Tobin et al. (1990), teachers may have a misalignment of beliefs and practice without knowing how to address the mismatch. One teacher was dissatisfied with her practice and believed that science teaching should be other than what she was doing, but had no vision of practice. Through intervention she was gradually able to align her belief and practices.

In a case study of a preservice elementary teacher, Bryan and Abell (1999) observed that inconsistencies between teacher practice and vision emerged during the student teaching experience. The resulting tension between the beliefs and practice led to professional growth. The authors stated that professional knowledge emerges as a result of experience, not before experience.

Environmental Response

The link between professional growth and the belief-practice mismatch was also examined by Guskey (1986). He proposed that changes in teachers' beliefs come only after teachers have changed their teaching practices, which results in changes in their students' learning (the environmental response seen in the *Sociocultural Model of Embedded Belief Systems*, Fig. 35–1). Guskey suggested that staff development leads to changes in teachers' classroom practices, which change students' learning outcomes. Changes in teachers' beliefs and attitudes follow changes in behavior. Guskey stated, "Evidence of improvement (positive change) in the learning outcomes of students generally precedes and may be a prerequisite to significant change in the beliefs and attitudes of most teachers" (p. 7). The model is based on observations that teachers believe a strategy can be successful only after they have seen it successfully work in their own classroom.

Summary

Research suggests that teachers with more science content knowledge spend more time teaching science; teachers who lack confidence tend to teach content less. In addition, teachers with greater teaching efficacy tend to be more humanistic in relation to pupil control, and teachers with high science teaching efficacy may hold fewer alternative conceptions than teachers with less science self-efficacy. A teacher's self-efficacy is influenced by responses of others to her teaching practices. Therefore, the sociocultural context may inhibit change as cooperating teachers, colleagues, administrators, parents, and students challenge practices that do not align with their vision of teaching and learning.

Teachers' Beliefs and Educational Reform

A systems view of beliefs.   As the *Sociocultural Model of Embedded Belief Systems* (Fig. 35–1) shows, instructional practices are influenced by a complex set of belief systems, prior knowledge, epistemologies, attitudes, knowledge, and skills. Many efforts to reform science education have come and gone with minimal impact because they failed to conceptualize reform as situated within this complex system. The emerging research on attitudes and beliefs sheds light on why reform movements have failed to have a lasting impact.

In a survey of 1000 elementary teachers (Bayer Corporation, 1995), a majority of the teachers reported that they were not knowledgeable about recommendations for the reform of science education. Only 56 percent of the respondents indicated that they were well qualified to teach science. Only a third of the teachers reported that they were scientifically literate enough to understand stories about science on TV, in newspapers, or in magazines. A majority of the teachers believed the emphasis on science education should increase and that teachers should use more hands-on science instruction and experimentation. When teachers were asked about their perceptions about obstacles to teaching hands-on science, 73 percent indicated lack of time, 70 percent indicated a lack of equipment, 51 percent felt they lacked an understanding of science, 30 percent believed their administrators did not place a priority on teaching science, and 38 percent noted they lacked interest in teaching more hands-on science.

Intent to reform: The theory of planned behavior.   Feldman (2002) found that the degree to which reform curricula in physics were implemented varied greatly from teacher to teacher. To investigate this phenomenon, he compared two physics teachers with similar teaching situations and backgrounds, but with different degrees of experience in implementing the new curriculum. Both teachers indicated that they had concerns about how much time was needed to implement the new curriculum to allow for student investigation, and both indicated that they saw the potential of the new curriculum to intellectually engage and develop students' understandings. Despite these similarities, one teacher enthusiastically embraced the new curriculum, and the other did not. Feldman concluded that many factors trigger teachers' acceptance of a new curriculum, including epistemological stances, situational contexts, and knowledge of the epistemological basis of the curriculum.

Concerns about Reform

Haney, Czerniak, and Lumpe (1996) examined teachers' beliefs about the state of Ohio's competency-based science model and their intent to implement the reform strands (scientific inquiry, scientific knowledge, conditions for learning science, and applications for science learning) by applying Ajzen's (1985) Theory of Planned Behavior. This theory suggests that attitude toward the behavior, the subjective norm, and the perceived behavioral control (primarily variables), accompanied by salient beliefs can predict whether a person will behave in a particular way. Salient beliefs, according to the Theory of Planned Behavior, include the extent to which an individual believes the behavior will lead to a favorable outcome, the belief that other people think the behavior should be performed, and the beliefs about the extent to which internal (ability, skill, and knowledge) and external (opportunity, cooperation, and resources) factors exist. This theory has been applied to students' learning in science (Allen & Crawley, 1993; Crawley & Black, 1992; Crawley & Koballa, 1992) and to teachers' intentions to engage in reflective teaching (Desouza, 1994). Haney et al. (1996) surveyed 100 teachers and found that teachers' attitudes about implementing the reform model significantly influenced their intent to implement the model into their classroom practices. Furthermore, they found that the resources teachers believed were available (obstacles and enablers) were less important to them than their beliefs about whether the reform would have positive or negative outcomes. The teachers surveyed did not believe that significant people in their teaching environment would support their efforts to implement the Ohio reform effort, or that the available support was valuable. Female teachers in the study indicated they were more likely to implement the reform model than male teachers, and elementary teachers were more likely than middle or high school teachers.

Beck, Czerniak, and Lumpe (2000) examined Ohio elementary, middle, and high school teachers' beliefs about implementing components of constructivism (personal relevance, crucial voice, shared control, scientific uncertainty, and student negotiation) within the Theory of Planned Behavior. Teachers who held bachelor's and master's degrees had more positive attitudes toward teaching for personal relevance than teachers who had doctoral degrees. Not surprisingly, attitude toward teaching for critical voice was a significant predictor in the study of teachers' intent to implement critical voice in their classroom. Teachers expressed concern about the amount of time it takes to prepare and teach for personally relevant instruction as well as concerns about having to cover less content in order to teach for personal relevance. Although teachers believed that teaching for shared control can "help students take a vested interest in and ownership of their learning" (p. 336), they were concerned about students' immaturity and inexperience in the use of shared control in learning contexts. Across grade levels, teachers were concerned about classroom management but held positive attitudes about teaching for student negotiation. Teachers believed that a lack of planning and class time was a barrier to implementing constructivist practices. Some felt that planning for constructivist teaching took too long and that it took too long for students to develop understandings of concepts.

Haney et al. (2002) selected six teachers from a National Science Foundation systemic change project in Ohio and analyzed their teaching practices in terms of self-efficacy. With the exception of one subject, teachers with higher self-efficacy tended to engage more frequently in constructivist teaching practices such as inquiry, collaborative projects, and preassessments.

Perceptions of constraints are often contextualized and situation specific, as shown in a study by Yerrick and Hoving (1999) that examined teachers' perceptions of obstacles to their implementation of new technology. In particular, the researchers focused on teachers' perceived behavioral control and social support. Teachers in the study received the same resources, including financial and curricular support, but differed in their implementation of the project based on their specific context. For example, one group of teachers used the new technology for real-time data collection and inquiry, whereas another group of teachers used the technology to complete traditional tasks such as looking up information or preparing presentations. Differences in implementation were accompanied by differences in perceived control and support. For example, the teachers who used technology with inquiry viewed obstacles as problems to be solved and believed their school culture supported their efforts to meaningfully implement new instructional technology. The more traditional teachers perceived obstacles as reinforcement for their beliefs that change within the school context was impossible; as a result they were unable to successfully overcome barriers for the implementation of the new technology.

Summary

Teachers have distinct beliefs about efforts to reform science education, and these beliefs shape the subsequent implementation of new innovations and reform efforts. Studies have shown that elementary teachers believe they lack time, equipment, administrative support, interest in science, as well as knowledge of science. Efforts to introduce an innovation are filtered through teachers' beliefs about the goals and purposes of the innovation as well as the amount of time teachers perceive an innovation will require. Other studies have shown that there are differences in the implementation of reform by gender and the amount of professional preparation that a teacher has completed. Concerns about specific classroom contexts as well as beliefs about class management influence how reform is perceived by teachers. Finally, the degree to which teachers believe the school culture supports their efforts to be innovative can affect the success of reform implementation.

BELIEFS ABOUT SCIENCE EDUCATION AS A ROAD TO EMPOWERMENT AND SOCIAL JUSTICE

During the 1980s, an interest in teaching for social justice emerged from constructivist research (Creswell, 2003). Social justice researchers proposed that the primary goal of research should be the development of action agendas to address the lives of marginalized groups. The sections that follow describe the influence of teacher beliefs on teaching practices from a social/political point of view.

Controversial Issues

Teachers' beliefs about the role of science and science instruction in the future of their students' lives affect the topics they teach and how topics are framed within the curriculum. The teaching of controversial issues is one way that teachers pro-mote democratic participation and social justice. An international study of teachers' beliefs about the role of controversial issues in the teaching of science found that all of the teachers reported teaching about controversial topics in science, such as nu-clear energy or global warming. Furthermore, teachers indicated that they believed this was an important part of their job, "as responsible citizens—we teachers are charged with the education of the future citizens and leaders of this country—we have an obligation, so we have to (teach) . . . issues such as global warming, defor-estation, and rain forest" (Cross & Price, 1996, pp. 323–324). The teachers surveyed indicated that they recognized the political and economic aspects of science related to social justice, and some of the teachers felt the need to provide their students with information so they could participate democratically in the debate over contro-versial issues. Teachers varied in their beliefs about whether or not teachers should express their own positions in discussions of controversial issues.

Environmental education used with preservice elementary teachers has been shown to improve prospective teachers' attitudes about science. Brown (2000) mea-sured preservice teachers' attitudes before and after an environmental science course and found that the course had a positive impact on preservice teachers' attitudes about the social benefits of science and the problems that accompany scientific progress.

Empowerment through the History of Science

One way that science educators have promoted social justice and empowerment is through the inclusion of the history of science in science instruction. This position is based on beliefs that for students to become scientifically literate and capable of participating in democratic decision-making, they need to be able to understand the past complexities of science and society (Conant, 1951) as well as the concep-tual, procedural, and contextual aspects of science (Klopfer, 1969). Wang and Marsh (2002) surveyed and interviewed elementary and secondary teachers to determine their beliefs about the value of the history of science and their practice in using it in their science teaching. Teachers at both elementary and secondary levels indicated that they did not believe the history of science was appropriate for elementary sci-ence instruction. The teachers who included the history of science in their teaching believed that teaching the history of science is a way to show that science is a hu-man endeavor and helps students understand how social factors or political power are tied to science. Furthermore, some teachers used the history of science as a way to show the contributions of different cultures and to teach students about cultural heritage and diverse role models. Teachers indicated that the curriculum was over-crowded and as a consequence only incorporated history of science topics when they could be blended into the existing curriculum.

In another study, Wang and Cox-Peterson (2002) reported that elementary teach-ers, more than high school teachers, placed emphasis within the history of science on helping students understand the role of science in society, developing positive attitudes toward the study of science, and as a way to bring role models or diversity to students' conceptions of science. High school teachers tended to use the history of science as a way to help students understand science content, the nature of sci-ence, and science process skills. In addition, Wang and Cox-Peterson found that al-though elementary, middle, and high school teachers expressed beliefs about the importance of teaching the history of science, this belief was not congruent with their instructional practices. An earlier study by King (1991) examined preservice teachers' beliefs about teaching and learning the history and philosophy of science. She found that the majority of preservice teachers thought that history and philosophy of science are important, but they "did not have a clue how to teach this way, or even enough knowledge to (in one student's words) 'ask the right questions'" (p. 238).

Social and Community Change

Other teachers go beyond teaching a few topics to promote social change to framing their overall teaching role within the larger goal of promoting student empowerment and social change within the community. A case study of one science educator in Pakistan found that this teacher believed that science education "ought to be about empowering students to make physical and political changes in the community" (Zahur et al., 2002, p. 899). The case study showed that this Pakistani teacher believed that students' low levels of achievement were tied to poor children's families' lack of power and influence over the processes of schooling, and that one way to address social inequities is to provide students with knowledge of health and environmental issues. The purpose of science education for this teacher was to bring students and families together to make changes for the improvement of the society (including addressing garbage, sewage, clean water, and pollution control).

Summary

There is increasing research that explores how teachers use science teaching as a mechanism for social justice and empowerment. Teachers who view their profession as a way to make the lives of the students better use their teaching to evoke change. Studies have shown that teachers report that they believe teaching the history of science can teach students about science as a human endeavor, the social and political factors related to science, and the impact culture can have on science investigations. Other studies have shown that some teachers believe they can promote social change within the community by teaching students to address social inequities related to health and the environment.

CULTURE/CONTEXT

Some of the most insightful studies in the area of beliefs and attitudes conducted in the last decade have examined how belief systems differ across contexts and cultures. Within the *Sociocultural Model of Embedded Belief Systems* that we have presented (Fig. 35–1), the sociocultural context undergirds belief systems and is tied to attitudes, motivation, knowledge, and skills. By examining commonalities and differences for teachers in different instructional settings, we can better understand the situated nature of belief systems.

The High School/College Divide

Razali and Yager (1994) examined how perceptions of the importance of knowledge and skills needed by students when they enter college chemistry differed for high school and college chemistry teachers. College teachers identified students' personal attributes as significantly more important than specific knowledge and skills. High school teachers indicated that knowledge and skills were more important for college preparation than personal attributes. Razali and Yager speculated that high school teachers have traditionally viewed the goal of secondary science as preparing students to take examinations over a prescribed syllabus, whereas the college professors seek independent learners who have attributes such as study skills, imagination, interest, creativity, and inquisitiveness.

Sociocultural Factors and Attitudes

Context emerged as the critical factor in a study of teachers' attitudes toward the philosophy of science (Gwimbi & Monk, 2003). Teachers' responses to a questionnaire designed to measure teachers' views of the philosophy of science were analyzed by school affluence. The attitudes of teachers from poorer schools were significantly different from those of teachers from wealthier schools. Teachers from richer schools had more relativist and deductionist attitudes, whereas teachers from poorer schools were more positivist and inductivist. Gwimbi and Monk noted that, although the richer schools were able to hire better qualified teachers, the school context reinforced the differential distribution of attitudes. The researchers maintained that teachers teach the way they do not because of how they think, but instead because of where they work.

Cross-Country Contexts

Studies of teachers from different countries have shown that the impact of teacher education is influenced by the beliefs and values of the larger culture. Through the use of questionnaires and interviews, Thompson and Orion (1999) compared preservice teachers' attitudes and perceptions from Israel and England/Wales during and at the end of the teacher education programs. Teachers from both regions initially had similar reasons for wanting to teach, and both groups changed their views about science education after the program. The British teachers held a more pupil-oriented approach to teaching science and management than the Israeli teachers. However, the Israeli teachers held a more progressive view of the socializing aspects of education than the British teachers. Both groups were overconfident and underestimated the complexity of skills needed to be a successful teacher. Thompson and Orion noted that teaching is held in higher status in England and Wales than in Israel. In addition, approximately 75 percent of Israeli teachers were female, whereas only 40 percent of English teachers were female. Salaries were also lower in Israel, where teaching is sometimes viewed as a secondary wage for women whose spouses provide the primary support for the family.

Egyptian, Korean, and United Kingdom teachers' attitudes about the aims of practical work in science education were studied by Swain, Monk, and Johnson (1999). When UK teachers were compared with Korean teachers, the Korean teachers valued practical work for finding facts and arriving at new principles, as a creative activity, to verify facts, to elucidate theoretical work, and to help remember facts and principles more than UK teachers. The UK teachers rated practical work as more important for seeing problems and seeking new ways to solve them, promoting a logical reasoning method of thought, developing an ability to cooperate, and developing a critical attitude. The Korean teachers viewed the practical as content-focused and fact-oriented. The UK teachers viewed science as more focused on investigating problems and manufacturing new knowledge. Egyptian teachers, when compared with UK teachers, tended to view practical work as important as a creative activity focused on developing self-reliance and giving students experience with standard techniques. Overall, Korean teachers tended to have a positivistic approach to science. The researchers linked the teachers' attitudes to their work conditions and suggested that the Egyptian teachers' large classes, limited equipment, and restrictive curriculum affected their views of practical experiences. For the Korean teachers, the researchers suggested that the habit of competition and emphasis on factual knowledge dominated their perspectives on practical work. According to the researchers, the UK teachers' perspectives were shaped by their concerns about doing investigations. For these teachers from three different countries, their attitudes appeared to be shaped by their cultural context and conditions of work.

Aikenhead and Otsuji (2000) examined Canadian and Japanese teachers' perceptions of science, science and culture, everyday knowledge, and teaching and learning science. Using a Likert scale assessment instrument, the researchers found that Canadian teachers held a more reductionist view of science than their Japanese counterparts, who viewed science and nature as one entity, including themselves as part of nature. Furthermore, more Japanese teachers than Canadian teachers believed school science was reflected in the local culture. Aikenhead and Otsuji found that neither set of teachers seemed aware of the cultural clashes that students experience in the typical science classroom. Similarly, Plucker (1996) found that although teachers were concerned about gender inequity for their students, they were generally not familiar with the range of possible causes (including their own behavior).

Religion, Beliefs, and Instructional Practices

A teacher's religious beliefs as well as the cultural beliefs of the society affect how instruction is framed and interpreted. Haidar (1999) examined United Arab Emirates preservice and inservice teachers' beliefs about the nature of science through the use of a questionnaire in which participants responded to items on a continuum from traditional to constructivist views. Traditional views were held by teachers for the role of a scientist, constructivist views were held for scientific knowledge, and mixed perspectives were held about scientific theories, scientific method, and scientific laws. Haidar speculated that the mixed views emerge from the teachers' Islamic beliefs: "The purpose of science is to discover God's wisdom in the universe; knowledge can be acquired by the scientific method as well as by other means . . . truth is not absolute, we see only what God permits us to see; and the only absolute truth is what God knows" (Haidar, 1999, p. 808).

The teachers' Islamic beliefs were also influenced by historical perspectives from the 1960s and 1970s, when government officials viewed science as a way to fight ignorance, imperialism, and underdevelopment and officials encouraged citizens to adopt science as a way to promote development. According to Haidar, teachers' constructivist views were congruent with Islamic views, suggesting that the scientific method is not the only way to gain knowledge and knowledge is "only humanity's best effort to understand the world" (p. 818).

Summary

The growing research that examines belief systems across cultures and contexts has highlighted the power of contextual influences on teachers' beliefs. Contexts, such as level of schooling (high school versus higher education) or wealth of the school community, have been associated with differences in teachers' attitudes and beliefs. Other studies compared beliefs of teachers from different countries and have shown that culture plays a powerful role in shaping beliefs about teaching strategies and approaches. Finally, a teacher's religious beliefs may frame a teacher's views of the goals and nature of science. These cultural and contextual studies have begun to provide a richer view of teachers' attitudes and beliefs while highlighting differences across teachers in different contexts.

CONCLUSIONS

There has been consistent acknowledgment of the importance of science teachers' attitudes and beliefs over the decades. However, the initial model for examining attitudes was a simplistic cause-and-effect model. Situated in a behaviorist framework, this research noted relationships between variables without gaining insight into the development of attitudes across time and without understanding how the larger cultural context influenced the development of attitudes. Over the years, the model has become more complex as research findings have elucidated the myriad of variables likely to affect a teacher's instructional practices.

The vast majority of research has focused only on one particular aspect of the decision-making process, making it difficult to construct a cohesive picture of the research. Significant to understanding teachers' instructional practices is the sociocultural context, the importance of which has recently been recognized. The research to date provides evidence of the complexity of the decision-making process in instructional settings and the critical role of teacher beliefs in reforming science education.

Much of the current research about beliefs has focused on individual teachers or small groups of teachers in case-study or ethnographic formats. Although these have been valuable in informing the science education community about the complexity of belief systems, future research is needed that can include larger samples, such as the study by Simmons et al. (1999). There is emerging evidence that patterns in belief systems can be identified across cultures and contexts. Further research is needed that examines beliefs across subcultures, as well as developmental trends as teachers move along the novice-to-expert continuum. Studies that can cross the boundaries of different countries to explore commonalities across teachers have the potential to inform us about the underlying structures of teacher belief systems as well as strategies that can be effective in promoting teacher development across subpopulations. This new generation of research on teacher belief studies is crucial to promoting growth and sustaining reform within science education.

Research highlighted in this chapter has shown that teachers' belief systems influence their attitudes. Studies have shown that teachers' content knowledge, confidence, self-efficacy, experience, and social context are linked to belief systems and practices. Teachers' epistemological beliefs about the nature of science, science learning, and science teaching further affect these belief systems, attitudes, and practices.

Furthermore, research has shown that these complex belief systems influence how teachers interact with students, the strategies they use for instruction, their classroom management systems, their selection of topics and subtopics, and their assessment practices. As teachers try new instructional methods, the responses of those in the educational environment further influence their perceptions and their belief systems. It is becoming increasingly clear that teachers' belief systems are embedded in the larger sociocultural environment, which includes students, peer teachers, parents, administrators, families, communities, and political/government environments.

FUTURE RESEARCH

The study of teachers' beliefs is in its infancy, and there are numerous areas yet to be researched. It is not clear how epistemological assumptions and patterns of reasoning may differ for individuals across content domains, and whether there is a developmental relationship between epistemologies and beliefs within a domain (Hofer & Pintrich, 1997).

The differences in elementary and secondary teachers' views about science and science teaching persist across programs and contexts. What experiences contribute to these differences across teachers? What factors influence an individual to enter elementary education versus secondary education? Are there dispositions or abilities that encourage a teacher to select one area over another? How do attitudes and belief systems influence dispositions or abilities (or vice versa) if they do exist? Are there differences in biology and chemistry teachers' attitudes, as BouJaoude (2000) has suggested? If content differences exist, what contributes to the development of these differences?

The growing diversity of student populations necessitates an understanding of how teachers' beliefs about culturally diverse students affect their interactions and instruction (Bryan & Atwater, 2002). How can we make teachers' beliefs about culturally diverse students explicit to become a tool for professional and personal growth?

There is only limited research that explores whether teachers' and students' attitudes and beliefs differ. If teachers hold beliefs and attitudes that are different from those of their students, does this difference affect student learning? In one of the few studies in this area, Cary and Smith (1993) explored the challenges of teachers' use of a constructivist approach to science that were at odds with students' objectivist views of science. If teachers' and students' views of science differ year after year, how does this affect students' development?

Pajares (1992) and DeSouza and Czerniak (2003) have suggested that confidence involves both personal and social components—including classrooms, teacher teams, schools, and school districts—and that together these contribute to a sense of collective efficacy. We know that attitudes and beliefs are influenced by significant other people in our environments. How systems of beliefs situated within individuals and the greater sociocultural context contribute to teachers' attitudes about teaching and learning can inform the teacher development process has yet to be researched.

Although most researchers accept that there is a strong link between teachers' beliefs and teaching practices, research that documents how changes in beliefs subsequently affect teaching behaviors is limited (Hashweh, 1996). Where in the complex model of beliefs do changes make the most impact in instructional practice? Ediger (2002) argued for measuring preservice teachers' attitudes toward science as a way to ensure that teachers have the qualifications to be good science teachers. What would these types of assessments look like? Can we really measure attitudes and beliefs in a valid way? What are the ethical implications of making decisions about teacher education candidates based on their beliefs?

For decades, despite reform efforts, traditional teaching has maintained a strong foothold in our science classrooms. The literature suggests that some teachers believe that traditional methods are most effective for teaching science. However, a great number of teachers hold a vision of science teaching that is aligned with national standards, but do not enact this vision in the classroom. Some lack content knowledge and so avoid teaching science. Some lack pedagogical skills, such as maintaining classroom discipline, which limits their ability to effectively teach science. Others lack pedagogical content knowledge and are unsure about how to implement an inquiry lesson or how to lead a class discussion to make sense of data. The task of addressing these issues seems easier than addressing the attitudes and beliefs which inhibit student-centered practices. The most significant contribution of attitude/belief research would lead to developmentally sequenced preservice, induction, and professional development programs, so that knowledge and skills are given sufficient time and support to develop. Additionally, these programs would be structured to acknowledge and address environmental constraints. And most importantly, these programs would make salient for teachers their own attitude beliefs systems as well as the complex factors that contribute to the development of these systems.

Our definitions of ourselves as science teachers (and learners) is bound to our belief systems, epistemologies, prior experiences, motivation, knowledge, and skills. These factors are all linked to each other with reciprocal influence and are embedded in the larger sociocultural environment. Only through further research that can take a systems view of attitudes and beliefs can we truly understand how attitudes and beliefs shape instructional practice and use this knowledge to achieve reform.

ACKNOWLEDGMENTS

Thanks to Lynn Bryan and J. M. Shireen DeSouza, who reviewed this chapter.

REFERENCES

Abell, S. K., & Roth, M. (1992). Constraints to teaching elementary science: A case study of a science enthusiast student teacher. *Science Education, 76*, 581–595.

Adams, P. E., & Krockover, G. H. (1997). Beginning secondary teacher cognition and its origins in the preservice secondary science teacher program. *Journal of Research in Science Teaching, 34*, 633–653.

Aikenhead, G. S., & Otsuji, H. (2000). Japanese and Canadian science teachers' views on science and culture. *Journal of Science Teacher Education, 11*, 277–299.

Ajzen, I. (1985). From intentions to actions: A theory of planned behavior. In J. Kuhl & J. Beckmann (Eds.), *Action control: From cognition to behavior* (pp. 11–39). New York: Springer-Verlag.

Ajzen, I. (1988). *Attitudes, personality and behavior*. Chicago: Dorsey.

Ajzen, I., & Fishbein, M. (1980). *Understanding attitudes and predicting social behavior*. Englewood Cliffs, NJ: Prentice Hall.

Ajzen, I., & Madden, T. (1986). Prediction of goal-directed behavior: Attitudes, intentions, and perceived behavioral control. *Journal of Experimental Social Psychology, 22*, 453–474.

Allen, N., & Crawley, F. (1993, April). *Understanding motivation to achieve in science using rational decision-making, motivation, and choice-framing theories.* Paper presented at the annual meeting of the National Association for Research in Science Teaching, Atlanta.

Appleton, K., & Kindt, I. (1999). Why teach primary science? Influences on beginning teachers' practices. *International Journal of Science Education, 21,* 155–168.

Atwater, M., Gardner, C., & Kight, C. (1991). Beliefs and attitudes of urban primary teachers toward physical science and teaching physical science. *Journal of Elementary Science Education, 3,* 3–12.

Bandura, A. (1986). *Social foundations of action and thought: A social cognitive theory.* Englewood Cliffs, NJ: Prentice-Hall.

Barufaldi, J. P., Huntsberger, J. P., & Lazarowitz, R. (1976). Changes in attitudes of preservice elementary education majors toward inquiry teaching strategies. *School Science and Mathematics, 76,* 420–424.

Bayer Corporation. (1995). *The Bayer facts of science education: An assessment of elementary school parent and teacher attitudes toward science education: An executive summary.* Pittsburgh: Bayer Corporation.

Beck, J., Czerniak, C., & Lumpe, A. (2000). An exploratory study of teachers' beliefs regarding the implementation of constructivism in their classroom. *Journal of Science Teacher Education, 11,* 323–343.

Behnke, F. L. (1961). Reactions of scientists and science teachers to statements bearing on certain aspects of science and science teaching. *School Science and Mathematics, 61,* 193–207.

Benson, G. D. (1989). Epistemology and science curriculum. *Journal of Curriculum Studies, 21,* 329–344.

Bergel, S. P. (1977). *The effects of microteaching on the attitudes of preservice elementary teachers towards teaching science.* Unpublished doctoral dissertation, Pennsylvania State University.

Bird, T., Anderson, L. M., Sullivan, B. A., & Swidler, S. A. (1993). Pedagogical balancing acts: A teacher educator encounters problems in an attempt to influence prospective teachers' beliefs. *Teacher and Teacher Education, 9,* 253–267.

Blankenship, J. W. (1965). Biology teachers and their attitudes concerning BSCS. *Journal of Research in Science Teaching, 3,* 54–60.

BouJaoude, S. (2000). Conceptions of science teaching revealed by metaphors and by answers to open-ended questions. *Journal of Science Teacher Education, 11,* 173–186.

Bradley, R. C., Earp, N. W., & Sullivan, T. (1966). A review of fifty years of science teaching and its implications. *Science Education, 50,* 152–155.

Bratt, H. M. (1977). An investigation of two methods of science instruction and teacher attitudes toward science. *Journal of Research in Science Teaching, 14,* 533–538.

Brickhouse, N. (1990). Teachers' beliefs about the nature of science and their relationship to classroom practice. *Journal of Teacher Education, 41,* 53–62.

Brickhouse, N., & Bodner, G. (1992). The beginning science teacher: Classroom narratives of convictions and constraints. *Journal of Research in Science Teaching, 29,* 471–486.

Briscoe, C. (1991). The dynamic interactions among beliefs, role metaphors, and teaching practices: A case study of teacher change. *Science Education, 75,* 185–199.

Brown, F. (2000). The effect of an inquiry-oriented environmental science course on preservice elementary teachers' attitudes about science. *Journal of Elementary Science Education, 12(2),* 1–6.

Bryan, L. A., & Abell, S. K. (1999). The development of professional knowledge in learning to teach science. *Journal of Research in Science Teaching, 36,* 121–139.

Bryan, L. A., & Atwater, M. M. (2002). Teacher beliefs and cultural models: A challenge for science teacher preparation programs. *Science Education, 86,* 821–839.

Butts, D., & Raun, C. E. (1969a). A study in teacher attitude change. *Science Education, 53,* 101–104.

Butts, D., & Raun, C. E. (1969b). A study of teacher change. *Science Education, 53,* 3–8.

Cakiroglu, J., & Boone, W. (2000). Preservice elementary teachers' self-efficacy beliefs and their conceptions of photosynthesis and inheritance. *Journal of Elementary Science Education, 14,* 1–14.

Campbell, R. L., & Martinez-Perez, L. (1977). Self concept and attitude as factors in the achievement of preservice teachers. *Journal of Research in Science Teaching, 14*, 455–460.

Cary, S., & Smith, C. (1993). On understanding the nature of scientific knowledge. *Educational Psychologist, 28*, 235–251.

Cobern, W. W., & Loving, C. C. (2002). Investigation of preservice elementary teachers' thinking about science. *Journal of Research in Science Teaching, 39*, 1016–1031.

Coburn, W. (2000). The nature of science and the role of knowledge and belief. *Science and Education, 9*, 219–246.

Collison, G. E. (1993). *Teacher attitudes toward hands-on science instruction versus traditional teaching methods* (Eric Document Reproduction Service no. ED380271).

Conant, J. (1951). *On understanding science: An historical approach.* New York: New American Library.

Crawley, F., & Black, C. (1992). Causal modeling of secondary science students' intentions to enroll in physics. *Journal of Research in Science Teaching, 29*, 585–599.

Crawley, F., & Koballa, T. (1992, March). *Attitude/behavior change in science education: Part I—models and methods.* Paper presented at the annual meeting of the National Association of Research in Science Teaching, Boston.

Creswell, J. W. (2003). *Research design: Qualitative, quantitative, and mixed methods approaches.* Thousand Oaks, CA: Sage

Cronin-Jones, L. L. (1991). Science teacher beliefs and their influence on curriculum implementation: Two case studies. *Journal of Research in Science Teaching, 28*, 235–250.

Cronin-Jones, L. L., & Shaw, L. E., Jr. (1992). The influence of methods instruction on the beliefs of prospective elementary and secondary science teachers: Preliminary comparative analysis. *School Science and Mathematics, 92*, 14–22.

Cross, R. T., & Price, R. F. (1996). Science teachers' social conscience and the role of controversial issues in the teaching of science. *Journal of Research in Science Teaching, 33*, 319–333.

Czerniak, C., & Lumpe, A. (1996). Relationship between teacher beliefs and science education reform. *Journal of Science Teacher Education, 7*, 247–266.

DeSouza, J., Boone, W., & Yilmaz, O. (2003, March). *Science teaching self-efficacy and outcome expectancy beliefs of teachers in southern India.* Paper presented at the annual meeting of the National Association for Research in Science Teaching, Philadelphia.

DeSouza, J., & Czerniak, C. (2003). Study of science teachers' attitudes toward beliefs about collaborative reflective practice. *Journal of Science Teacher Education, 14*, 75–96.

Desouza, S. (1994). *Do science teachers intend to engage in collaborative reflective practice?* Paper presented at the annual meeting of the National Association for Research in Science Teaching, Anaheim, CA.

Douglass, C. B. (1979). Differences in attitude and ability of biology majors, nonmajors, and preservice teachers. *Improving College and University Teaching, 27*(3), 110–113.

Downs, G. E., & DeLuca, F. P. (1979). Effect of a four-year elementary teacher preparation program on undergraduates' preferences for teaching science. *Science Education, 63*, 45–52.

Duffee, L., & Aikenhead, G. (1992). Curriculum change, student evaluation, and teacher practical knowledge. *Science Education, 76*, 493–506.

Dutton, W. H., & Stephens, L. (1963). Measuring attitudes toward science. *School Science and Mathematics, 63*, 43–49.

Earl, R. D., & Winkeljohn, D. R. (1977). Attitudes of elementary teachers toward science and science teaching. *Science Education, 61*, 41–45.

Ediger, M. (2002). Assessing teacher attitudes in teaching science. *Journal of Instructional Psychology, 29*(1), 25–29.

Eick, C. J., & Reed, C. J. (2002). What makes an inquiry-oriented science teacher? The influence of learning histories on student teacher role identity and practice. *Science Education, 86*, 401–416.

Enochs, L., & Riggs, I. (1990). Further development of an elementary science teaching efficacy beliefs instrument: A preservice elementary scale. *School Science and Mathematics, 90*, 695–706.

Ernest, P. (1989). The knowledge, beliefs and attitudes of the mathematics teacher: A model. *Journal of Education for Teaching, 15*, 13–33.

Feldman, A. (2002). Multiple perspectives for the study of teaching: Knowledge, reason, understanding, and being. *Journal of Research in Science Teaching, 39*, 1032–1055.

Fishbein, M. (1967). A consideration of beliefs and their role in attitude measurement. In M. Fishbein (Ed.), *Readings in attitude theory and measurement* (pp. 257–266). New York: John Wiley & Sons.

Fishbein, M., & Ajzen, I. (1975). *Belief, attitude, intention and behavior.* Reading, MA: Addison-Wesley.

Fraser, B. J. (1981). *Test of science-related attitudes.* Melbourne: Australian Council for Educational Research.

Gabel, D. L., & Rubba, P. A. (1977). The effect of early teaching and teaching experience on physics achievement, attitude toward science and science teaching and process skill efficiency. *Science Education, 61*, 503–511.

Gallagher, J. J. (1991). Prospective and practicing secondary school science teachers' knowledge and beliefs about the philosophy of science. *Science Education, 75*, 121–133.

Gess-Newsome, J. (1999). Teachers' knowledge and beliefs about subject matter and its impact on instruction. In J. Gess-Newsome & N. G. Lederman (Eds.), *Examining pedagogical content knowledge: The construct and its implication for science education* (pp. 51–94). Dordrecht, the Netherlands: Kluwer Academic.

Golman, M. E. (1975). Assessing teaching opinions of pre-service science teachers. *School Science and Mathematics, 75*, 338–342.

Guskey, T. (1986). Staff development and the process of teacher change. *Educational Researcher, 15*, 5–12.

Gwimbi, E., & Monk, M. (2003). A study of the association of attitudes to the philosophy of science with classroom contexts, academic qualification and professional training, amongst A level biology teachers in Harare, Zimbabwe. *International Journal of Science Education, 25*, 469–488.

Hairdar, A. (1999). Emirates pre-service and in-service teachers' views about the nature of science. *International Journal of Science Education, 21*, 807–822.

Hall, G. E. (1970). Teacher-pupil behaviors exhibited by two groups of second grade teachers using science—A process approach. *Science Education, 54*, 325–334.

Haney, J. J., Czerniak, C. M., & Lumpe, A. T. (1996). Teacher beliefs and intentions regarding the implementation of science education reform strands. *Journal of Research in Science Teaching, 33*, 971–993.

Haney, J. J., Lumpe, A. T., Czerniak, C. M., & Egan, V. (2002). From beliefs to actions: The beliefs and actions of teachers implementing change. *Journal of Science Teacher Education, 13*, 171–187.

Haney, J. J., & McArthur, J. (2002). Four case studies of prospective science teachers' beliefs concerning constructivist teaching practices. *Science Education, 86*, 783–802.

Hashweh, M. Z. (1985). *An exploratory study of teacher knowledge and teaching: The effects of science teachers' knowledge of subject-matter and their conceptions of learning on their teaching.* Unpublished doctoral dissertation, Stanford University.

Hashweh, M. Z. (1996). Effects of science teachers' epistemological beliefs in teaching. *Journal of Research in Science Teaching, 33*, 47–64.

Hawkey, K. (1996). Image and the pressure to conform in learning to teach. *Teaching and Teacher Education, 12*, 99–108.

Hofer, B. K., & Pintrich, P. R. (1997). The development of epistemological theories: Beliefs about knowledge and knowing and their relation to learning. *Review of Educational Research, 67*, 88–140.

Hovey, L. M. (1975). Design of an instrument to measure teachers' attitudes toward experimenting. *School Science and Mathematics, 75*, 167–172.

Hoy, W. K., & Blankenship, J. W. (1972). A comparison of the ideological orientations and personality characteristics of teacher acceptors and rejecters. *Science Education, 56*, 71–77.

Hughes, E. F. (1971). Role playing as a technique for developing a scientific attitude in elementary teacher trainees. *Journal of Research in Science Teaching, 8*, 113–122.

Jaccard, J., Litardo, H. A., & Wan, C. K. (1999). Subjective culture and social behavior. In J. Adamopoulos & Y. Kashima (Eds.), *Social psychology and cultural context* (pp. 95–106). Thousand Oaks, CA: Sage.

James, H. (1971). Attitudes and attitude change: Its influence upon teaching behavior. *Journal of Research in Science Teaching, 8*, 351–356.

Jaus, H. H. (1977). Using microteaching to change elementary teachers' attitudes toward science instruction. *School Science and Mathematics, 77*, 402–406.

Jaus, H. H. (1978). The effect of environmental education instruction on teachers' attitudes toward teaching environmental education. *Science Education, 62*, 79–84.

Jones, C., & Levin, J. (1994). Primary/elementary teachers' attitudes toward science in four areas related to gender differences in students' performance. *Journal of Elementary Science Education, 6*, 46–66.

Jones, M. G., & Vesilind, E. M. (1995). Preservice teachers' development of a cognitive framework for class management. *Teacher Education, 11*, 313–330.

Jones, P., & Blankenship, J. W. (1970). A correlation of biology teachers' pupil control ideology and their classroom teaching practices. *Science Education, 54*, 263–265.

Justi, R. S., & Gilbert, J. K. (2002). Science teachers' knowledge about and attitudes towards the use of models and modeling in learning science. *International Journal of Science Education, 24*, 1273–1292.

Kagan, D. (1992). Implications of research on teacher belief. *Educational Psychologist, 27*, 65–90.

Kane, R., Sandretto, S., & Heath, C. (2002). Telling half the story: A critical review of research on the teaching beliefs and practices of university academics. *Review of Educational Research, 72*, 177–228.

Kauchak, D. P. (1977). The effect of essay writing on the attitudes of undergraduate methods students. *Journal of Research in Science Teaching, 14*, 139–143.

Kennedy, T. G. (1973). The effect of process approach instruction upon changing pre-service elementary teachers' attitudes toward science. *School Science and Mathematics, 73*, 569–574.

Keys, C. W., & Bryan, L. A. (2001). Co-constructing inquiry-based science with teachers: Essential research for lasting reform. *Journal of Research in Science Teaching, 38*, 631–645.

Kiesler, C. A., Collins, B. E., & Miller, N. (1969). *Attitude change: A critical analysis of theoretical approaches.* New York: John Wiley & Sons.

King, B. (1991). Beginning teachers' knowledge of and attitudes toward history and philosophy of science. *Science Education, 75*, 135–141.

King, K., Shumow, L., & Lietz, S. (2001). Science education in an urban elementary school: Case studies of teachers' beliefs and classroom practices. *Science Education, 85*, 89–110.

Klopfer, L. (1969). The teaching of science and the history of science. *Journal of Research in Science Teaching, 6*, 87–95.

Lammers, T. J. (1949). One hundred interviews with elementary school teachers concerning science education. *Science Education, 33*, 292–295.

Lampkin, R. H. (1944). Do teachers consider suggestions for teaching. *Science Education, 28*, 219–222.

Laplante, B. (1997). Teachers' beliefs and instructional strategies in science: Pushing analysis further. *Science Education, 81*, 277–294.

Lazarowitz, R. (1976). Does use of curriculum change teachers' attitudes toward inquiry? *Journal of Research in Science Teaching, 13*, 547–552.

Lederman, N. G. (1992). Students' and teachers' conceptions on the nature of science: A review of the research. *Journal of Research in Science Teaching, 29*, 331–360.

Lortie, D. (1975). *Schoolteacher: A sociological study.* Chicago: University of Chicago Press.

Lotter, C. (2003, March). *Preservice science teachers' concerns through classroom observations and student teaching.* Paper presented at the annual meeting of the National Association for Research in Science Teaching, Philadelphia.

Lowery, L. F. (1966). Development of an attitude measuring instrument for science education. *School Science and Mathematics, 66,* 494–502.

Luft, J. A. (2001). Changing inquiry practices and beliefs: The impact of an inquiry-based professional development programmed on beginning and experienced secondary teachers. *International Journal of Science Education, 23,* 517–534.

Luft, J., Roehrig, G., Brooks, T., & Austin, B. (2003, March). *Exploring the beliefs of secondary science teachers through interview maps.* Paper presented at the meeting of the National Association of Research in Science Teaching, Philadelphia.

Luft, J., Roehrig, G., & Patterson, N. (2003). Contrasting landscapes: A comparison of the impact of different induction programs on beginning secondary science teachers' practices, beliefs, and experiences. *Journal of Research in Science Teaching, 40,* 77–97.

Lumpe, A., Haney, J., & Czerniak, C. (1998). Science teacher beliefs and intentions to implement science-technology-society (STS) in the classroom. *Journal of Science Teacher Education, 9,* 1–24.

Lumpe, A., Haney, J. J., & Czerniak, C. (2000). Assessing teachers' beliefs about their science teaching context. *Journal of Research in Science Teaching, 37,* 275–292.

Lyons, L. L., Freitag, P. K., & Hewson, P. W. (1997). Dichotomy in thinking: Researcher and teacher perspectives on a chemistry teaching practice. *Journal of Research in Science Teaching, 34,* 239–254.

Mayer, V. J., Disinger, J. F., & White, A. L. (1975). Evaluation of an inservice program for earth science teachers. *Science Education, 59,* 145–153.

McGuiness, J. R., & Simmons, P. (1999). Teachers' perspectives of teaching science-technology-society in local cultures: A sociocultural analysis. *Science Education, 83,* 179–212.

Meyer, H., Tabachnick, B. R., Hewson, P. W., Lemberger, J., & Park, H.-J. (1999). Relationships between prospective elementary teachers' classroom practice and their conceptions of biology and of teaching science. *Science Education, 83,* 323–346.

Moore, K. (1978). An assessment of secondary science teacher needs. *Science Education, 62,* 339–348.

Moore, R. (1975). A two-year study of a CCSS group's attitudes toward science and science teaching. *School Science and Mathematics, 75,* 288–290.

Moss, D. M., & Kaufman, D. (2003, March). *Examining preservice science teachers' conception of classroom management.* Paper presented at the annual meeting of the National Association for Research in Science Teaching, Philadelphia.

Moyer, R. (1977). Environmental attitude assessment: Another approach. *Science Education, 61,* 347–356.

Orgren, J. (1974). Using an interaction analysis instrument to measure the effect on teaching behavior of adopting a new science curriculum. *Science Education, 58,* 431–436.

Ost, D. H. (1971). An evaluation of an institute for teachers of secondary school biology. *American Biology Teacher, 33,* 546–548.

Ostrum, T. M. (1968). The emergence of attitude theory: 1930–1950. In A. G. Greenwald, T. C. Brock, & T. M. Ostrum (Eds.), *Psychological foundations of attitudes* (pp. 1–28). New York: Academic Press.

Pajares, M. F. (1992). Teachers' beliefs and educational research: Cleaning up a messy construct. *Review of Educational Research, 62,* 307–332.

Palmer, D. (2002). Factors contributing to attitude exchange amongst preservice elementary teachers. *Science Education, 86,* 122–138.

Peacock, A., & Gates, S. (2000). Newly qualified primary teachers' perceptions of the role of text material in teaching science. *Research in Science & Technology, 18,* 155–170.

Pearl, R. E. (1974). The present status of science attitude measurement: History, theory and availability of measurement instruments. *School Science and Mathematics, 74,* 375–379.

Pedersen, J. E., & McCurdy, D. W. (1992). The effects of hands-on, minds-on teaching experiences on attitudes of preservice elementary teachers. *Science Education, 76,* 141–146.

Plucker, J. A. (1996). Secondary science and mathematics teachers and gender equity: Attitudes and attempted interventions. *Journal of Research in Science Teaching, 33,* 737–751.

Putnam, R., & Borko, H. (1997). Teacher learning: Implications of new views of cognition. In B. J. Biddle, T. L. Good, & I. F. Goodson (Eds.), *International handbook of teachers and teaching* (pp. 1223–1296). Amsterdam: Kluwer Academic.

Razali, S. N., & Yager, R. E. (1994). What college chemistry instructors and high school chemistry teachers perceive as important for incoming college students. *Journal of Research in Science Teaching, 31,* 735–747.

Richardson, V. (1996). The role of attitudes and beliefs in learning to teach. In J. Sikula (Ed.), *Handbook of research on teacher education* (pp. 102–119). New York: Simon & Schuster and Macmillan.

Richmond, G., & Anderson, C. (2003, March). *The nature of tensions between educator and teacher candidate beliefs about science teaching practice.* Paper presented at the National Association for Research in Science Teaching, Philadelphia.

Riggs, I., & Enochs, L. (1990). Toward the development of an elementary science teachers' science teaching efficacy belief instrument. *Science Education, 74,* 625–635.

Ritchie, S. M. (1999). The craft of intervention: A personal practical theory for a teacher's within-group interactions. *Science Education, 83,* 213–232.

Sadler, P. M. (1967). Teacher personality characteristics and attitudes concerning PSSC Physics. *Journal of Research in Science Teaching, 5,* 28–29.

Salish I Research Project. (1997). *Secondary science and mathematics teacher preparation programs: Influences on new teachers and their students.* Final Report to the Department of Education, Science Education Center, University of Iowa, Iowa City.

Schwirian, P. M. (1968). On measuring attitudes toward science. *Science Education, 52,* 172–179.

Schwirian, P. M. (1969). Characteristics of elementary teachers related to attitudes toward science. *Journal of Research in Science Teaching, 6,* 203–213.

Sequeira, M., Leite, L., & Duarte, M. (1993). Portuguese science teachers' education, attitudes, and practice relative to the issue of alternative conceptions. *Journal of Research in Science Teaching, 30,* 845–856.

Shrigley, R. L. (1974). The correlation of science attitudes and science knowledge of preservice elementary teachers. *Science Education, 58,* 143–151.

Shrigley, R. L., & Johnson, T. M. (1974). The attitude of inservice elementary teachers toward science. *School Science and Mathematics, 74,* 437–446.

Simmons, P., Emory, A., Carter, T., Coker, T., Finnegan, B., Crockett, D., et al. (1999). Beginning teachers: Beliefs and classroom actions. *Journal of Research in Science Teaching, 36,* 930–954.

Simpson, R. D., Koballa, T. R., Oliver, J. S., & Crawley, F. (1994). Research on the affective dimension of science learning. In D. Gable (Ed.), *Handbook of research on science teaching and learning* (pp. 211–234). New York: Macmillan.

Skamp, K. (2001). A longitudinal study of the influences of primary and secondary school, university and practicum on student teachers' images of effective primary science practice. *International Journal of Science Education, 23,* 227–245.

Smith, L. (2003, April). *The impact of early life history on teachers' beliefs: In-school and out-of-school experiences as learners and knowers of science.* Paper presented at the American Educational Research Association Annual Meeting, Chicago.

Smith, M. U., & Siegel, H. (2004). *Knowing, believing, and understanding: The goals of science education? Science Education, 13,* 553–582.

Southerland, S. A., & Gess-Newsome, J. (1999). Preservice teachers' views of inclusive science teaching as shaped by images of teaching, learning and knowledge. *Science Education, 83,* 131–150.

Southerland, S., Sinatra, G., & Mathews, M. (2001). *Educational Psychology Review, 133,* 325–351.

Soy, E. M. (1967). Attitudes of prospective elementary teachers toward science as a field of specialty. *School Science and Mathematics, 67,* 507–517.

Stofflett, R. T. (1994). The accommodation of science pedagogical knowledge: The application of conceptual change constructs to teacher education. *Journal of Research in Science Teaching, 31,* 787–810.

Strage, A., & Bol, L. (1996). High school biology: What makes it a challenge for teachers? *Journal of Research in Science Teaching, 33,* 753–772.

Strawitz, B. (1977). Open-mindedness and attitudes about teaching science. *Journal of Research in Science Teaching, 14,* 545–549.

Stronk, D. R. (1974). The attitudes and needs of inservice science teachers. *Science Education, 58,* 505–508.

Stuart, C., & Thurlow, D. (2000). Making it their own: Preservice teachers' experiences, beliefs, and classroom practices. *Journal of Teacher Education, 51,* 113–121.

Sunal, D. W. (1980). Relationship of affective measures and preservice teaching behavior. *Science Education, 64,* 337–347.

Sutman, F. X. (1969). The development, field test and validation of an inventory of scientific attitudes. *Journal of Research in Science Teaching, 7,* 85–93.

Swain, J., Monk, M., & Johnson, S. (1999). A comparative study of attitudes to the aims of practical work in science education in Egypt, Korea and the UK. *International Journal of Science Education, 21,* 1311–1324.

Sweeney, A. E., Bula, O. A., & Cornett, J. W. (2001). The role of personal practice theories in the professional development of a beginning high school chemistry teacher. *Journal of Research in Science Teaching, 38,* 408–441.

Symington, D. J., & Fensham, P. J. (1976). Elementary school teachers' close mindedness, attitude toward science and congruence with a new curriculum. *Journal of Research in Science Teaching, 13,* 441–447.

Tatto, M. T. (1998). The influence of teacher education on teachers' experiences, beliefs, and classroom practices. *Journal of Teacher Education, 49,* 66–77.

Thompson, C. L., & Shrigley, R. (1986). What research says: Revising the science attitude scale. *School Science and Mathematics, 86,* 331–343.

Thompson, D., & Orion, N. (1999). Changes in perceptions and attitudes of pre-service postgraduate secondary science teachers: A comparative study of programs in Israel, England and Wales. *Research in Science and Technological Education, 17,* 165–192.

Thomson, R. G., & Thompson, A. G. (1975). Building attitudes toward science for pre-service teachers: An experiment. *School Science and Mathematics, 75,* 213–216.

Tobin, K., Briscoe, C., & Holman, J. R. (1990). Overcoming constraints to effective elementary science teaching. *Science Education, 74,* 409–420.

Tobin, K., & LaMaster, S. U. (1995). Relationships between metaphors, beliefs, and actions in the context of science curriculum change. *Journal of Research in Science Teaching, 32,* 225–242.

Tosun, T. (2000). The beliefs of preservice elementary teachers toward science and science teaching. *School Science and Mathematics, 100,* 374–379.

Tsai, C. (2002). Nested epistemologies: Science teachers' beliefs of teaching, learning, and science. *International Journal of Science Education, 24,* 771–783.

van Driel, J. H., Verloop, N., & de Vos, W. (1998). Developing science teachers' pedagogical content knowledge. *Journal of Research in Science Teaching, 35,* 673–695.

Victor, E. (1962). Why are our elementary school teachers reluctant to teach science? *Science Education, 46,* 185–192.

Wang, H., & Cox-Peterson, A. (2002). A comparison of elementary, secondary and student teachers' perceptions and practices related to history of science instruction. *Science & Education, 11,* 69–81.

Wang, H. A., & Marsh, D. D. (2002). Science instruction with a humanistic twist: Teachers' perception and practice in using the history of science in their classrooms. *Science & Education, 11,* 169–189.

Washton, N. S. (1961). Improving elementary teachers education in science. *Science Education, 45,* 33–34.

Weaver, H. M., Hounshell, P. B., & Coble, C. B. (1979). Effects of science methods courses with and without field experiences on attitudes of preservice elementary teachers. *Science Education, 63,* 655–664.

Welch, W. W., & Walberg, H. J. (1967). An evaluation of summer institute programs for physics teachers. *Journal of Research in Science Teaching, 5*, 105–109.

Windschitl, M. (2000). *Pre-service science teachers and the independent inquiry experience* (Eric Document Reproduction Service no. ED 441703).

Woolfolk, A., & Hoy, W. (1990). Prospective teachers' sense of efficacy and beliefs about control. *Journal of Educational Psychology, 82*, 81–91.

Wytias, P. L. (1962). A study of attitudes of 5th grade teachers of Cumberland County New Jersey toward science and their preparation for teaching it in elementary school. *Science Education, 46*, 151–152.

Yerrick, R., & Hoving, T. (1999). Obstacles confronting technology initiatives as seen through the experience of science teachers: A comparative study of science teachers' beliefs, planning, and practice. *Journal of Science Education and Technology, 8*, 291–307.

Yerrick, R., & Hoving, T. (2003). One foot on the dock and one foot on the boat: Differences among preservice science teachers' interpretations of field-based science methods in culturally diverse contexts. *Science Education, 87*, 390–418.

Yerrick, R., Parke, H., & Nugent, J. (1997). Struggling to promote deeply rooted change: The "filtering effect" of teachers' beliefs on understanding transformational views of teaching science. *Science Education, 81*, 137–159.

Zahur, R., Barton, A. C., & Upadhyay, B. R. (2002). Science education for empowerment and social change: A case study of a teacher educator in urban Pakistan. *International Journal of Science Education, 24*, 899–917.

Zhang, B., Krajcik, J., Wang, L., Hu, J., Wu, J., Qiang, Y., et al. (2003, April). *Opportunities and challenges of China's inquiry-based education reform in middle and high school: Perspectives of science teachers and teacher educators.* Paper presented at the American Education Research Association, National Conference, Chicago.

Zint, M. (2002). Comparing three attitude-behavior theories for predicting science teachers' intentions. *Journal of Research in Science Teaching, 39*, 819–844.

Zipf, R., & Harrison, A. (2003, April). *The terrarium unit: A challenge to teachers' concepts of what is science teaching.* Paper presented at the American Educational Research Association Annual Meeting, Chicago.

CHAPTER 36

Research on Science Teacher Knowledge

Sandra K. Abell
University of Missouri, Columbia

It is commonly held that the teacher is the most important factor in student learning (Committee on Science and Mathematics Teacher Preparation, 2001). We who educate future and practicing teachers assume the veracity of this statement. However, what characteristics of teachers are crucial to student learning? Do teachers who know more science make better science teachers? If this were true, surely the best science teaching would take place at the university level by individuals who possess a Ph.D. in their science field. Yet we know that this is not necessarily so; university science students cite poor teaching as one of the main reasons for dropping out of science majors (National Science Foundation, 1996). What should science teachers know in addition to subject matter knowledge? What do future and practicing science teachers know and how do they come to know it? How does their knowledge interact with beliefs, goals, and values? How does their knowledge affect their practice and their students' learning? Such questions have generated a plethora of research in science education.

Although science education researchers have been studying science teacher knowledge since the 1960s, the theoretical foundations and methodological strategies have changed greatly over the years. This chapter begins with a historical overview of teacher knowledge research, including the variety of terms and approaches that have been applied. I then describe the model of teacher knowledge that frames the review. This theoretical foundation leads into a review of the research literature on science teacher knowledge. The chapter ends with implications for science teacher education and recommendations for future research.

FOUNDATIONS OF THIS REVIEW

Historical Views of Teacher Knowledge

Teacher knowledge has assumed a number of meanings in educational research over the past 50 years. Fenstermacher (1994) examined the epistemological aspects of various research programs about teacher knowledge and developed a classification scheme. In his scheme, he distinguished knowledge about teaching (TK/F or formal knowledge) from knowledge derived from teachers participating in teaching (TK/P or practical knowledge). Research in the 1960s and 1970s, for the most part, did not make explicit mention of teacher knowledge. These process-product studies aimed to define effective teaching based on studying the relationships among particular variables and treatments. In the science education literature, teacher knowledge was defined as a static component (a qualification or competency) of the broader category of teacher characteristics that was then compared with teacher practice (Bruce, 1971; Smith & Cooper, 1967) or student outcomes (Northfield & Fraser, 1977; Rothman, Welch, & Walberg, 1969). In such studies, teachers were the objects of research, what Fenstermacher called the "known," and the emphasis was on producing a "knowledge base" (Reynolds, 1989) to summarize the TK/F that was needed for teaching.

In the 1980s, a new set of research programs arose that changed the face of teacher knowledge research. In these programs, teachers were seen as the "knowers," and the focus shifted to examining their practical knowledge (TK/P). Fenstermacher (1994) outlined four such research programs: Clandinin and Connelly's work on personal practical knowledge through teacher narrative (e.g., Clandinin & Connelly, 1996); Schön's notions of reflective practice for professional development (Schön, 1983, 1987); Cochran-Smith and Lytle's leadership in the teacher researcher movement (Cochran-Smith & Lytle, 1993, 1999); and Shulman's research program on teacher knowledge types (e.g., Shulman, 1986). These research programs shifted the perspective from knowledge about teaching produced by others to teacher knowledge residing within teachers, from teachers as objects of research to teachers as co-researchers.

Although differing in epistemological details (see Fenstermacher, 1994), the first three research programs were similar in their focus on teachers producing and possessing their own knowledge. The Shulman program was substantially different. Shulman and his colleagues attempted to answer the question "What knowledge is essential for teaching?" by studying teachers from different subject areas (e.g., English, science, social studies). This work differed from earlier attempts to develop a knowledge base for teaching in that it derived from studies of what teachers know about their subject and about teaching, assuming teacher as "knower," not from studies of effective teaching where the teacher was the "known." In the United States, Shulman's model served as the foundation for the development of teaching standards for beginning teachers (e.g., *Standards for Science Teacher Preparation*, National Science Teachers Association, 1998). The model has also catalyzed scores of studies concerning teacher knowledge. This review uses Shulman's theoretical model, explained in more detail in the next section, as its organizational base.

Shulman's Model of Teacher Knowledge

In 1986, Shulman proposed a model for understanding the specialized knowledge for teaching that distinguishes teachers from subject matter specialists. Shulman and his colleagues (Hashweh, 1985; Grossman, 1990; Shulman, 1986, 1987; Wilson, Shulman, & Richert, 1987) defined pedagogical content knowledge (PCK) as the knowledge that is developed by teachers to help others learn. Teachers build PCK as they teach specific topics in their subject area. PCK is influenced by the transformation of three other knowledge bases: subject matter knowledge (SMK), pedagogical knowledge (PK), and knowledge of context (KofC) (Grossman) (see Fig. 36–1).

Shulman's view of SMK was derived from the work of Schwab (1964), who defined two types of subject matter knowledge: substantive and syntactic. The substantive structure of a discipline is the organization of concepts, facts, principles, and theories, whereas syntactic structures are the rules of evidence and proof used to generate and justify knowledge claims in the discipline. Shulman and colleagues added two other categories of subject matter knowledge: knowledge of content (facts,

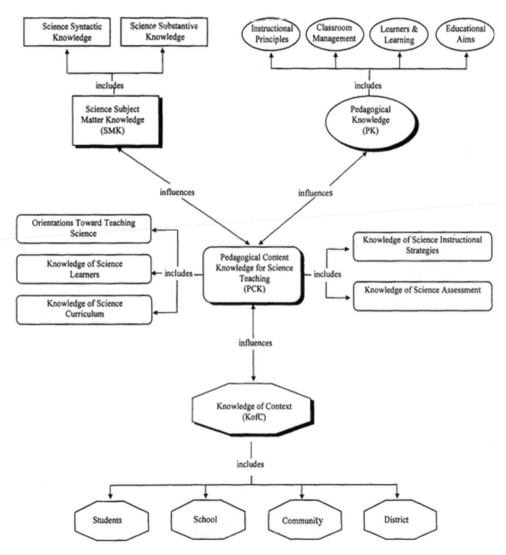

FIGURE 36–1. A model of science teacher knowledge (modified from Grossman, 1990 and Magnusson, Krajcik, & Borko, 1999).

concepts, and procedures) and beliefs about the discipline (Grossman, Wilson, & Shulman, 1989). Carlsen (1991c) criticized this scheme, claiming that in science it is difficult to determine whether knowing a particular concept or principle is an example of substantive knowledge or content knowledge. For the purpose of this review, I examine studies of science SMK that could be considered either substantive knowledge in Schwab's terms or knowledge of content in Grossman's. For the most part, I leave a discussion of research on teacher knowledge of the syntactic structure of science and beliefs about the discipline to Lederman's chapter in this volume.

Pedagogical knowledge (PK) includes the general, not subject-specific, aspects of teacher knowledge about teaching, such as learning theory, instructional principles, and classroom discipline. Knowledge of context (KofC) was formalized by Grossman (1990) to account for the knowledge of communities, schools, and student backgrounds that teachers use in their teaching. For the most part, this review does not concentrate on these types of knowledge, since they are not specific to science teachers. Together SMK, PK, and KofC influence and are translated by a teacher's PCK into instruction.

Magnusson, Krajcik, and Borko (1999) defined PCK as consisting of five components: (a) orientations toward science teaching, which include a teacher's knowledge of goals for and general approaches to science teaching; (b) knowledge of science curriculum, including national, state, and district standards and specific science curricula; (c) knowledge of assessment for science, including what to assess and how to assess students; (d) knowledge of science instructional strategies, including representations, activities, and methods; and (e) knowledge of student science understanding, which includes common conceptions and areas of difficulty (see Fig. 36–1). These components represent a broader view of PCK than the original conceptualization, which focused on topic-specific case knowledge, or what Hashweh (1985) called subject-matter pedagogical knowledge. Since its introduction, Shulman's model has been translated, explicated, revised, and extended by numerous science educators (Appleton, 2002; Barnett & Hodson, 2001; Carlsen, 1991c; Gess-Newsome & Lederman, 1999; Magnusson et al., 1999; Tamir, 1988; Veal, 1997), and the model has formed the theoretical framework for much research on science teacher knowledge. However, a full discussion of the different views of PCK is beyond the scope of this chapter. Admitting the problematic nature of the Magnusson et al. model, I maintain it is a useful heuristic for organizing the research on science teacher knowledge.

Situating This Review

The research on teacher knowledge has been reviewed a number of times in the past 15 years (Ball & McDiarmid, 1996; Borko & Putnam, 1996; Calderhead; 1996; Carter, 1990; Grimmett & MacKinnon, 1992; Munby, Russell, & Martin, 2001). These reviews are immensely informative accounts of the theoretical and empirical bases of teacher knowledge in general. However, because they are not science education specific, they are of limited use to science education researchers.

Previous reviews of science teacher knowledge research exist, but cannot claim the comprehensive nature of the present project. The Anderson and Mitchener chapter in the Gabel handbook (1994) focused on preservice and inservice science teacher education with only passing attention to research on science teacher thinking; the authors reported nothing related to teacher knowledge. The chapter on alternative conceptions by Wandersee, Mintzes, and Novak in the same volume devoted a one-page section to teachers' alternative conceptions in science. The Fraser and Tobin handbook (1998) acknowledged the topic of science teacher knowledge in two chapters. The de Jong, Korthagen, and Wubbels chapter reviewed only the European research on teacher knowledge about teaching. The Cochran and Jones chapter on SMK reported only on research with preservice science teachers, and a chapter by de Jong, Veal, and van Driel (2002) reviewed teacher SMK about chemistry. In the volume on PCK edited by Gess-Newsome and Lederman (1999), the Gess-Newsome (1999) review of SMK encompassed research on mathematics, social studies, and English teacher knowledge in addition to science.

The current chapter provides an integrative review of the research on *science teacher knowledge*, including SMK, PK, and PCK. The review includes studies of both preservice and practicing teachers at all levels of instruction. I systematically reviewed the science education research since 1960 reported in dissertations and published internationally in journals and book chapters. For these reasons, this chapter is a comprehensive review of science teacher knowledge research.

Selecting research to review for this chapter was problematic. First of all, teacher knowledge goes by a variety of designations, partly as an artifact of the theoretical orientation of the time. For example, teacher knowledge has been reported as *craft knowledge, personal practical knowledge, wisdom of practice, practitioner knowledge, knowledge in action*, and *event-structured knowledge* (see Carter, 1990). Are these categories mutually exclusive renderings of teacher knowledge, outside of Shulman's model? I also debated how to review research on teachers' beliefs, conceptions, perspectives, ideologies, and theories. When do such studies belong here versus in a chapter on teacher attitudes and beliefs (see Chapter 35, this volume)? The distinction between knowledge and beliefs is not always clear in the research or agreed upon by the researchers (see Fenstermacher, 1994). Numerous studies concern teacher thinking (e.g., planning, decision making, reflecting, reasoning). Should such studies be included in a chapter on teacher knowledge? Shulman (1999) made his point of view clear, that teacher cognition is not the same as teacher knowledge. However, I was not ready to dismiss science-specific studies in this realm.

With these issues in mind, I selected studies that were about science teacher subject matter, pedagogical, or pedagogical content knowledge. In some cases, studies that referred to "beliefs" were also included, when I could interpret them as referring to part of a comprehensive "knowledge and beliefs" system (see Magnusson et al., 1999) rather than to the domain of "attitudes and beliefs." I reported studies of teacher thinking and studies that used different terms for teacher knowledge within the category of PCK when they were specifically about knowledge and reasoning in science classrooms, but omitted studies of teacher attitudes (Chapter 35, this volume), teacher knowledge of the nature of science (Chapter 28), and teacher views of learners from various backgrounds or with special needs/talents (see Section 2). I also avoided studies where teacher knowledge development was reported as a teacher learning outcome influenced by teacher preparation (Chapter 37), professional development (Chapter 38), or teacher research (Chapter 39), when the teacher education "treatment" appeared the more salient subject of study. In addition to ERIC searches using teacher knowledge key words, the contents of 22 science education and educational research journals were scanned by hand for relevant articles. I also mined the bibliographies of existing reviews and relevant studies for additional research reports.[1] Although I am sure that my decisions about what to include and exclude from this chapter were far from perfect, and some studies that could arguably be included do not appear, I believe that what follows is a comprehensive review of science teacher knowledge research.

RESEARCH ON SCIENCE TEACHER SUBJECT MATTER KNOWLEDGE

Most early studies in science education equated the number of science courses taken, and in a few case grade point average in those courses, to teacher SMK. A few researchers administered tests of science knowledge, usually in true/false or multiple-choice formats. An interesting exception was a study by Jena (1964) in which the researcher inferred SMK through observations of the teaching errors made by secondary student teachers while teaching. Later, Kennedy (1998) clarified the character of SMK needed by teachers as going beyond the "recitational" to include understanding of central ideas, relationships, elaborated knowledge, and reasoning ability. As the characterization of teacher knowledge shifted from a "quantity" view to a conceptual understanding view, methods for assessing teacher knowledge also changed. Written tests included open-ended items and requested explanations in addition to answers (e.g., Ginns & Watters, 1995). Concept mapping emerged as a useful tool for examining the subject matter structures held by teachers (Ferry, 1996; Jones, Rua, & Carter, 1998; Willson & Williams, 1996). Researchers also administered individual interviews, where they asked participants to explain phenomena, sort concept cards, and respond to hypothetical teaching situations (e.g., Hashweh, 1985). A few studies examined SMK *in situ*, while teachers worked to solve a science task (Moscovici, 2001) or taught science lessons to students (Veiga, Costa Pereira, & Maskill, 1989). Do varying epistemological and methodological assumptions guiding studies of SMK lead to different conclusions? The following sections review studies of science teacher SMK in part to answer this question.

General Science Subject Matter Knowledge

Early science education research defined teacher knowledge from a "quantity" perspective, claiming that prospective and practicing science teachers did not have enough (Mallinson & Sturm, 1955; Raina, 1967; Swann, 1969; Uselton, Bledsoe, & Koelsche, 1963). Often SMK was defined by the number of science courses taken. The study of teachers' SMK via understanding their conceptions in science became a popular field in the 1980s, on the heels of the work with student science ideas.

1. I would like to acknowledge the contributions of Abdulkadir Demir in performing library searches, requesting and copying books and articles, and constructing the final bibliography for this chapter. His work was invaluable to me.

However, understanding teachers' misconceptions[2] in science can be traced back much earlier (Blanchett, 1952; Ralya & Ralya, 1938). Using a true/false written test, researchers found that prospective elementary[3] teachers (Ralya & Ralya) and practicing teachers (Blanchett) held a large number of misconceptions about science and science-related issues. The Ralya and Ralya study is interesting in that misconceptions they identified for a significant number of teachers became key targets for research on both student and teacher science conceptions 50 years later (e.g., causes of the seasons, force and motion, heat and temperature).

In their 1994 review of research on alternative conceptions, Wandersee et al. claimed that the research in the 1980s on teachers' science conceptions demonstrated that "teachers often subscribe to the same alternative conceptions as their students" (p. 189), a claim that they described as not "particularly surprising." The examination of teacher SMK continues to the present and includes studies of a mixture of life and physics science concepts as well as discipline-specific studies of conceptions in biology, chemistry, earth and space science, or physics. By far the most studied group has been preservice elementary teachers, although preservice secondary teachers and practicing teachers at all levels have been subjects of study.

Several studies in the 1980s expanded the work of the New Zealand Learning in Science Project by examining teachers' science concept understanding. Among New Zealand elementary student teachers, Hope and Townsend (1983) found that biology concepts (plant, animal, living) were relatively well understood, whereas performance on physics concepts (force, friction, gravity) was similar to that of fourth-form students. Ameh and Gunstone (1985, 1986) examined preservice secondary teachers in Australia and Nigeria with the Learning in Science survey. Contrary to the observations of Hope and Townsend, they found evidence of misconceptions in both life and physical science: only 26 percent of their teachers held the scientific view of animal, 71 percent of living, 30 percent of force, 66 percent of gravity, and 40 percent of current. Furthermore, they found no evidence of cultural influences in the responses. Other researchers developed written instruments for collecting data on a variety of science concepts. Working with science teachers in the United Kingdom (Carré, 1993; Lloyd et al., 1998; Smith, 1997), Singapore (Lloyd et al.), Estonia (Kikas, 2004), and the United States (Schoon & Boone, 1998; Wenner, 1993), researchers consistently found that misconceptions or alternative conceptions that had been reported for children persisted into adulthood.

Going beyond the limitations of survey data that were focused on defining correct/incorrect conceptions, Harlen (1997; Harlen & Holroyd, 1997) designed a two-phase study of SMK among practicing primary teachers in the United Kingdom. In the first phase, the researchers sent written surveys to 514 teachers to evaluate their knowledge and confidence on a variety of concepts. In the second phase, they interviewed a smaller sample of 57 teachers, from which they defined three groups of concepts: (a) concepts already understood by most teachers (e.g., water exists in different states, bones move at joints because of muscles); (b) concepts in which understanding developed during the interview itself (e.g., water from air condenses on

---

2. Although I recognize the problematic nature of the term, and am aware of possible alternatives, I use *misconceptions* when the authors of these studies do.

3. For convenience and clarity, I use the American *elementary* throughout to refer to this grade range.

cool surfaces; muscles pull, not push); and (c) concepts less commonly understood and resistant to change (e.g., reflection of light; energy flow in circuits). They also determined sources of teachers' inaccuracies (e.g., inappropriate analogy, everyday language; mechanisms without evidence). This approach provided a value added to studies that merely catalogued misconceptions, including clear implications for science teacher education—designating concepts to which to devote time and describing how to help teachers overcome various inappropriate ways of reasoning.

Few studies have examined the development of science teacher SMK over time. Arzi and White (2004) investigated SMK in a 17-year longitudinal study of secondary science teachers. They found that the school science curriculum was "the most powerful determinant of teachers' knowledge, serving as both knowledge organizer and knowledge source" (p. 2). This study is significant both for the rarity of its longitudinal methods as well as the resulting phase model of teacher SMK development that could be a useful tool in science teacher education.

Several studies examined teacher syntactic SMK in science, such as teachers' ability to control variables (Aiello-Nicosia, Sperandeo-Mineo, & Valenza, 1984), understanding of assumptions (Yip, 2001), hypothesizing skills (Baird & Koballa, 1988), knowledge of modeling (Justi & Gilbert, 2002b, 2003; van Driel & Verloop, 1999), conceptions of scientific evidence (Taylor & Dana, 2003), and use of data representation (Roth, McGinn, & Bowen, 1998). Lawson (2002) studied preservice biology teachers' arguments in response to a set of hypotheses. He found that the future teachers were more successful when the hypothesized causal agent was observable and made many errors when the hypothesis involved nonobservable entities. (Other studies of teacher syntactic SMK as related to the nature of science are reported in Chapter 28.)

In another group of studies, researchers sought to correlate general science substantive SMK with other teacher characteristics—confidence, attitude, and self-efficacy. In the United Kingdom, several research programs were interested in future elementary teachers' subject matter confidence and competence as related to the National Curriculum (Carter, Carré, & Bennett, 1993; Harlen, 1997; Russell et al., 1992; Shallcross, Spink, Stephenson, & Warwick, 2002; Sorsby & Watson, 1993). Harlen found that, in general, science background and confidence to teach are related. Studies from other parts of the world have been less definitive. Appleton (1992, 1995) claimed that factors other than increased science study affected confidence to teach science but admitted that teachers who experienced success in learning science content did become more confident. Appleton also warned science educators not to confuse confidence with competence. Waldrip, Knight, and Webb (2002) reported a significant correlation between preservice elementary teachers' perceived ability to explain scientific language and their perceived competence to teach science concepts, but no correlation between their actual explanations and perceived competence to teach. Shrigley (1974) noted low positive correlation between SMK and attitude on the part of preservice teachers. Studies attempting to correlate SMK with measures of teacher self-efficacy have been inconclusive (Schoon & Boone, 1998; Stevens & Wenner, 1996; Wenner, 1993, 1995). The question of the relation of general science SMK to various teacher characteristics remains open for study.

The studies reviewed so far investigated teachers' SMK within a number of different concept areas across two or more science disciplines. The remaining review of SMK is organized within the major science disciplines in which the research was conducted. Furthermore, a number of studies have attempted to understand the relationship between SMK and teaching practice. I consider these studies at the end of this section.

Teachers' SMK in Chemistry

Teacher SMK in chemistry[4] has been a subject of study since 1987, when Gabel, Samuel, and Hunn examined preservice elementary teachers' ideas about the particulate nature of matter. Using the Nature of Matter Inventory, they asked teachers to draw pictures of atomic/molecular arrangements, given certain scenarios. Teachers ignored conservation and orderliness of particles in over 50 percent of the answers. Furthermore, only 4 percent of the variance in performance was accounted for by the number of chemistry courses taken. In a cross-cultural study of preservice elementary teachers in Spain and the United Kingdom, Ryan, Sanchez Jimenez, and Onorbe de Torre (1989) examined understanding of conservation of mass via a two-part questionnaire that included a definition and a task to solve. More Spanish teachers could give an acceptable definition of mass and conservation of mass, but all teachers had trouble solving the problems, regardless of nationality. The researchers hypothesized that the more term-focused Spanish curriculum led to better performance on the definition question but did not improve understanding. Contrary to Gabel et al.'s findings, the more science-experienced teachers in both groups performed better. Roth (1992) conducted an experimental study of preservice elementary teachers' ideas about the particulate nature of matter in which participants explained changes in water and ice when heated. Prior to the treatment, involving the use of concrete models to explain activity results, all 17 teachers explained phase change at a phenomenological level. Two weeks later, the treatment group used the particle model to explain melting and evaporation, but not to discuss volume changes. Similarly, Kruger and Summers (1989) and Kruger, Palacio, and Summers (1992) found that practicing elementary teachers did not refer to molecules or energy to explain changes in materials. Martin del Pozo (2001) asked prospective elementary teachers to evaluate the concept map of a hypothetical 13-year-old about the composition of matter. Teachers confused the relationship among topics such as substance/element, mixture/compound, element/atom, and compound/molecule. Birnie (1989) compared the conceptions about particle theory in gases held by elementary students, teachers, and parents. He found that elementary teachers and parents performed at the same level as ninth-grade students, whereas intermediate and secondary teachers performed better. These findings and others (e.g., Ginns & Watters, 1995) concerning preservice and practicing elementary teachers' SMK in chemistry are, in the words of Wandersee et al. (1994), not particularly surprising.

However, college students other than preservice elementary teachers also demonstrate poor understanding in chemistry. Kokkotas, Vlachos, and Koulaidis (1998) asked prospective secondary teachers in Greece to evaluate children's answers to items involving understanding of the particulate nature of matter. They found that preservice teachers lacked the SMK necessary to accurately score the answers. In a study of college student understanding of the greenhouse effect (Groves & Pugh,

---

4. Some topics could be reasonably classified as either physics or chemistry. I chose to include studies of SMK of the particulate nature of matter and conservation of mass under chemistry, while placing studies of SMK of thermal properties of materials under physics.

1999), students across disciplines, including preservice teachers, gave incorrect answers about the causes and consequences associated with this phenomenon. Indeed, problems in understanding college chemistry are not limited to prospective elementary teachers.

Another group of studies examined chemistry SMK among practicing high school chemistry teachers around the world. The results of these studies are perhaps more troubling than the studies with future elementary teachers, given the discrepancy in formal subject matter preparation. Widespread misconceptions have been found among chemistry teachers in the United Arab Emirates about the concepts of atomic mass, mole, conservation of atoms, and conservation of mass (Haidar, 1997); in Singapore about chemical reactions (Lee, 1999); in India about chemical equilibrium, Le Chatelier's principle, rate and equilibrium, and acid-based and ionic solutions (Banerjee, 1991); in Spain about Le Chatelier's principle (Quílez-Pardo & Solaz-Portolés, 1995); and in Sweden about the mole (Strömdahl, Tulberg, & Lybeck, 1994). Some studies compared practicing chemistry teachers' SMK with student knowledge. Teachers had a better understanding of the mole concept than their students, but some ambiguities in their thinking were still apparent (Gorin, 1994; Tulberg, Strömdahl, & Lybeck, 1994). Teachers and students held similar alternative conceptions about gases and displayed similar misuses of the gas laws (Lin, Cheng, & Lawrenz, 2000). A review of the research on teacher SMK about chemistry (de Jong et al., 2002) corroborates the observation that even teachers who have strong preparation in chemistry lack understanding of concepts fundamental to their field.

Teachers' SMK in Earth and Space Science

The examination of teachers' views of earth and space science concepts has occurred more recently in the history of SMK research. These studies have been conducted largely with elementary teachers (preservice and practicing) about concepts that have also been studied with students: day/night (Atwood & Atwood, 1995; Mant & Summers, 1993; Parker & Heywood, 1998), seasons (Atwood & Atwood, 1996; Kikas, 2004; Mant & Summers; Parker & Heywood; Schoon, 1995), moon phases (Mant & Summers; Parker & Heywood; Schoon; Suzuki, 2003; Trundle, Atwood, & Christopher, 2002), geological time (Trend, 2000; 2001), the solar system (Mant & Summers), and atmospheric phenomena (Aron, Francek, Nelson, & Bisard, 1994). These studies documented that preservice teachers lack scientific views in earth and space science, but more so in astronomy topics than in geology (Schoon, 1995). The Aron et al. study compared preservice earth/physical science teachers with students and prospective elementary teachers and found that, although the future secondary teachers performed better than the elementary teachers and students, they still held many misconceptions. Preservice teachers in this study performed better on a question about the seasons than in other studies involving this topic, which is most likely a function of method: the researchers used a multiple-choice survey as opposed to the other studies that assessed SMK with a combination of open-ended questionnaires and interviews requiring teachers to generate causal explanations. For example, in the Mant and Summers (1993) study, interviewees demonstrated 13 distinguishable models of astronomical phenomena, with only 4 of the 20 participants holding the scientific model.

Two other studies of SMK in earth and space science (Barba & Rubba, 1992; 1993) were substantially different in that they adopted an expert/novice theoretical framework to study inservice/preservice and novice/veteran teachers' declarative and procedural knowledge about a variety of earth and space science topics. Aligned with their theoretical frame, they found that expert teachers had better content knowledge structures, gave more accurate answers, used information chunks in solving problems, solved problems in fewer steps, and generated more solutions. Novice teachers moved between declarative and procedural knowledge more often and were less fluent in solving earth/space science tasks overall.

Teachers' SMK in Biology

Unlike the majority of studies of SMK in other disciplines, the research in biology education includes both studies of substantive and syntactic knowledge, or what the researchers have called "subject matter structures." Only a few researchers in biology education have been interested in finding out teachers' conceptions of specific concepts. For example, Sanders (1993) studied South African teachers' conceptions about respiration, Gayford (1998) examined British teachers' understanding of the concept of sustainability, and Greene (1990) researched U.S. preservice elementary teachers' understanding of natural selection. Jungwirth (1975) and Barass (1984) pointed out the misconceptions perpetrated by biology textbooks and the teachers who used them about cells, respiration, gas exchange, and homeostasis. More researchers have been concerned with uncovering the teachers' understanding of relations among biological concepts. For example, Douvdevany, Dreyfus, and Jungwirth (1997) studied Israeli junior high biology teachers' conceptions of living cell by asking them to link topics via two activities—a card sort and a lotto game. Hoz, Tomer, and Tamir (1990) used concept mapping to determine biology (and geography) teachers' knowledge structures. Tamir (1992) asked preservice and practicing teachers to organize biology topics and comment on their perception of their own knowledge and topic importance. In most areas, perceived knowledge lagged behind perceived importance.

The study of biology teachers' subject matter structures (SMSs) was marked in the 1990s by two research groups. In her dissertation, Hauslein (Hauslein, 1989; Hauslein, Good, & Cummins, 1992) studied five groups: biology majors, preservice teachers, novice teachers, experienced teachers, and scientists, using a card-sort task of 37 terms. Finding that veteran teachers and scientists had a deep-versus-surface understanding of subject matter structure, the researchers claimed that teachers restructure their thinking about biology as they gain more teaching experience. In the second research program, Lederman and his students (Gess-Newsome & Lederman, 1993; 1995; Lederman, Gess-Newsome, & Latz, 1994; Lederman & Latz, 1995) examined the subject matter structures of preservice and practicing secondary teachers, primarily in biology. For example, Gess-Newsome and Lederman studied 10 preservice biology teachers. Rather than provide the terms used in the card sort, the researchers asked teachers to first generate their own terms and then diagram the relationships. Data collection occurred at several times throughout the preservice program and during student teaching, culminating with a final interview. Teachers typically chose topics derived directly from their college biology course titles. Their subject matter structures changed over time with the addition of more terms and greater integration of topics. The researchers concluded, "It does not appear that preservice biology teachers are cognizant of their SMSs or that these SMSs are stable" (p. 42). Both of these research programs lend support to the commonly held notion that teachers improve their SMK through teaching.

Other research concerning biology teachers' SMK has been concerned with the relationship between SMK and teaching practice (e.g., Carlsen, 1991a, 1991b, 1993; Gess-Newsome & Lederman, 1995; Hashweh, 1987). I review these studies in a later section.

Teachers' SMK in Physics

By far the most research on teachers' SMK in science has taken place in the domain of physics. These studies have examined both preservice and practicing teachers, elementary through secondary, around the globe (including Australia, Canada, Estonia, Hong Kong, India, Israel, Italy, Nigeria, Pakistan, Portugal, South Africa, the United Kingdom, and the United States). Topics that have been studied with children have also received attention in studies of teachers. This line of research commenced in the 1980s with the Lawrenz (1986) study of inservice elementary teachers. Using a multiple-choice test, she found that teachers understood some concepts (over 50 percent of teachers gave correct answers for items about atomic structure, off-center balancing, density, and stars) and did not understand others (less than 50 percent gave correct answers for electric current, mixture of gases, temperature, motion, and light). About the same time in the United Kingdom, a research program devoted to understanding elementary teachers' SMK in physics was under way. In response to the British National Curriculum and the increased role for science content in primary schools, Kruger and colleagues (e.g., Kruger, 1990; Kruger, Palacio, & Summers, 1992; Kruger & Summers, 1988; Summers & Kruger, 1994) undertook the Primary School Teachers and Science Project. They studied teachers' ideas about energy, forces, gravity, and materials, first through interviews and later via large-scale surveys. Finally they developed teacher education materials based on their findings (Summers, 1992). Golby, Martin, and Porter (1995) criticized this research program, questioning the "orthodoxy of the deficiency model" (p. 298) that they claimed supported a transmission view of teaching and learning, a claim debunked by Summers and Mant (1995) in response.

From the 1980s until the present, a host of studies have examined teacher SMK for the following concepts:

1. Light and shadows (Bendall, Goldberg, & Galili, 1993; Feher & Rice, 1987; Jones, Carter, & Rua, 1999; Smith, 1987; Smith & Neale, 1989);
2. Electricity (Daehler & Shinohara, 2001; Heller, 1987; Heywood & Parker, 1997; Jones et al., 1999; Pardhan & Bano, 2001; Stocklmayer & Treagust, 1996; Webb, 1992; Yip, Chung, & Mak, 1998);
3. Sound (Jones et al., 1999; Linder & Erickson, 1989);
4. Force and motion (Ginns & Watters, 1995; Kikas, 2004; Kruger, Palacio et al., 1992; Kruger, Summers, & Palacio, 1990b; Mohaptra & Bhattacharyya, 1989; Preece,

1997; Summers & Kruger, 1994; Trumper; 1999; Trumper & Gorsky, 1997; Yip et al., 1998);

5. Energy (Kruger, 1990; Kruger et al., 1992; Nottis & McFarland, 2001; Summers & Kruger, 1992; Trumper, 1997; Yip et al., 1998);

6. Heat and temperature (Frederik, Valk, Leite, & Thorén, 1999; Jasien & Oberem, 2002; Veiga et al., 1989);

7. Thermal properties of materials (Sciarretta, Stilli, & Vicente Missoni, 1990);

8. Sinking/floating (Ginns & Watters, 1995; Parker & Heywood, 2000; Stepans, Dyche, & Beiswenger, 1988);

9. Air pressure (Ginns & Watters, 1995; Rollnick & Rutherford, 1990);

10. Gravity (Ameh, 1987; Kruger et al., 1990a; Smith & Peacock, 1992).

The overall finding from these studies of teacher SMK in physics is that teachers' misunderstandings mirror what we know about students. This finding holds regardless of the method used to assess teacher knowledge: true/false (Yip et al., 1998), multiple choice (e.g., Lawrenz, 1986), open-ended surveys (Mohaptra & Bhattacharyya, 1989), interviews (Linder & Erickson, 1989; Smith, 1987), and observation techniques (Daehler & Shinohara, 2001; Pardhan & Bano, 2001). Several studies also included strategies and materials for science teacher educators to improve teacher SMK (Bendall et al., 1993; Heywood & Parker, 1997; Jones et al., 1999; Summers, 1992). Unlike studies in chemistry SMK, researchers have not examined the relation of number of courses taken to physics SMK, most likely because the amount of formal coursework in physics typically taken in high school or university is lower than the amount of coursework completed for other science subjects. Unlike the biology SMK studies, most researchers of physics have been more interested in teacher understanding of specific concepts rather than their subject matter structures (see Abd-El-Khalick & BouJaoude, 1997, for one exception). Understanding how physics teachers understand the structure of the discipline and the relation among concepts remains a largely unmapped field of study.

Relation of SMK to Teaching

The studies reviewed up to this point have focused on describing, and in some cases treating, science teacher SMK. Another body of literature has attempted to uncover the relationships between SMK and science teaching. In general, these researchers wanted to know if teachers with better SMK were also better science teachers. The connection between SMK and teaching has been of interest among science educators for many years. Early attempts often correlated a teacher's science background (usually in the form of the number of science courses taken) with some measure of teaching effectiveness. According to Dobey (1980), studies conducted before the post-Sputnik wave of science curriculum reform supported a "positive correlation between the amount of science background and various teaching competencies" (p. 13). In a meta-analysis of 28 studies conducted between 1957 and 1977 of science teacher characteristics by teaching behavior, Druva and Anderson (1983) found a small but significant positive relation between "science training" and "teaching effectiveness."

However, a closer examination of selected studies relating science background to teaching proves less conclusive. Some researchers found no or a negative relationship between science background and teaching. Bruce (1971), in a study of elementary teachers using *Science Curriculum Improvement Study* materials, found no relationship between a teacher's formal science background and the use of higher level questioning. Butts and Raun (1969) found no evidence of a relationship between course hours in science and classroom practices among elementary teachers using *Science—A Process Approach*. Perkes (1975) found that, among prospective elementary teachers, the number of college science courses was negatively related to both preference for and sense of adequacy to teach science. In Stalheim's (1986) study of secondary biology teachers, the number of science courses was not a predictor of the use of classroom inquiry, but the year of the most recent course was. Because these researchers operationalized effective teaching differently in these studies, their findings are difficult to compare.

Other researchers who correlated formal science background with teaching found a positive relationship. For example, Wish (in Dobey, 1980) tried to explain the teaching behaviors of elementary science student teachers in terms of the number of college courses taken and found that formal science background was significantly and positively correlated with teaching science processes. Smith and Cooper (1967) surveyed 1,504 elementary teachers about their use of eight teaching techniques and correlated these with a set of teacher characteristics, including formal study in science. They found a positive relationship between science background and use of demonstration, pupil-conducted experiments, pupil recording and reporting, and individual and group projects. Furthermore, the use of textbooks "decreased steadily with increased amounts of formal study in science" (p. 562). In an observational study of elementary science teachers, Anderson (1979) provided convincing evidence that, "Lack of science content . . . made it virtually impossible for them to structure the information in lessons in ways preferred by science educators" (p. 226); the teachers avoided spontaneous questions from students, emphasized minor details in discussion, and failed to develop important concepts.

In the 1980s, researchers began to define SMK in new ways. Dobey, in his dissertation (Dobey, 1980; Dobey & Schafer, 1984), studied 22 preservice elementary teachers' SMK and level of inquiry teaching via their planning and teaching of a pendulum unit to fifth graders. The researchers measured SMK, not by the number of college science courses taken, but by performance and training on topic-specific tasks. The findings were mixed. Teachers in the "no knowledge" group were more teacher-directed than those with "intermediate knowledge," but not more so than the "knowledge" group teachers. The "no knowledge" teachers did not pursue new avenues of investigation during the lesson and allowed the least number of student ideas. The "no knowledge" group did not give out pendulum information in the lesson, and one-half of the "knowledge" group lectured at some point. This study demonstrates the complexities of correlating SMK with teaching.

It was followed by others that measured SMK with methods other than counting the number of science courses and assessed teaching effectiveness in a variety of ways. One of the most heavily cited studies in the area is Hashweh's dissertation (1985, 1987). He studied three biology and three physics teachers' SMK on a physics topic (simple machines) and a biology topic (photosynthesis) with the use of free recall, concept map line labeling, and sorting tasks. He also assessed their "preactive" and "simulated interactive" teaching of each topic. The teachers had a strong SMK base in their field of expertise, which affected their simulated teaching behaviors. "When activities were provided by the textbook, unknowledgeable teachers followed them closely. Knowledgeable teachers made many modifications. . . . When no activities were provided, only knowledgeable teachers could generate activities on their own" (Hashweh, 1985, p. 247). Furthermore, knowledgeable teachers asked higher level questions on tests and were more able to detect student misconceptions. Hashweh demonstrated that SMK was related to another kind of knowledge for science teaching.

In a series of articles derived from his dissertation, Carlsen (1988, 1991a, 1991b, 1993) examined the SMK and teaching behavior of four novice biology teachers. He measured SMK via a card sort task of 15 topics, interviews about sources of knowledge, and analysis of the teachers' undergraduate science course records. Identifying high-knowledge and low-knowledge topics for each of the teachers, he analyzed lesson plans and observed actual lessons taught by the teachers for both kinds of topics. The results are complex and not easily summarized. Teachers used lectures, quizzes, and tests more with high-knowledge topics and group work more with low-knowledge topics. Three of the four teachers asked more questions on low-knowledge topics; all teachers asked higher level questions with high-knowledge topics. Teachers talked more in laboratories when they were knowledgeable, but labs on high-knowledge topics were less "cookbooky," and teacher talk in these labs was more responsive than initiative. Carlsen concluded that teacher SMK influenced their instructional decisions, but failed to recognize other types of teacher knowledge that might have been involved.

A host of other studies have examined connections between SMK and actual classroom practice. In a conceptually rich study, Sanders, Borko, and Lockard (1993) observed three experienced secondary science teachers as they taught disciplines for which they were certified and noncertified. Although the teachers acted similarly in terms of general pedagogical knowledge, they differed in their planning, interactive teaching, and reflection based on SMK; within their certification area, teachers talked less, chose more "conversationally risky" activities, and involved students more. In her dissertation study of five experienced biology teachers, Gess-Newsome (Gess-Newsome & Lederman, 1995) compared the teachers' subject matter structures with their classroom practice, concluding that the "level of content knowledge had a significant impact on how content was taught" (p. 317). Newton and Newton (2001) found that elementary teachers with less SMK (based on formal science background) interacted less, asked fewer causal questions, and spent more time lecturing. According to Smith (1987), elementary teachers' difficulties with the physics of light affected their ability to focus on the conceptual understanding of light in science activities and limited their use of examples and metaphors. Abell and Roth (1992) found that when Roth, an elementary student teacher, taught a low-knowledge topic, she started lessons late and ended early, used fewer hands-on activities, and relied more on text-based lessons. Lee (1995) found similar results in a case study of a middle-level science teacher whose limited SMK was associated with heavy reliance on the textbook and seatwork and avoidance of whole class discussion.

Researchers have also correlated SMK to teaching behaviors of preservice teachers with the use of simulated teaching activities. Smith (1997), in attempting to relate preservice teachers' success on class assignments such as lesson planning with their SMK, claimed that "knowledge of science does enhance teaching, but not in a straightforward manner" (p. 151). Lloyd et al. (1998) tested preservice elementary teachers on their SMK and pedagogical content knowledge, and although teachers held misconceptions in both areas, the researchers did not find a direct relationship between SMK and PCK. Symington (1980) found that preservice elementary teachers who were given a scientific explanation of a phenomenon did not generate more teaching options in response to written cases, but did demonstrate reduced teacher directiveness. Examining preservice elementary teachers as they planned a science lesson, Symington and Hayes (1989) demonstrated that inadequate SMK led to limitations in planning, and that future teachers had few strategies for coping with their lack of science understanding. However, in another study, Symington (1982) found no direct relationship of SMK to a preservice teacher's ability to plan appropriate materials for student investigation. According to Symington, there must be other kinds of knowledge and abilities that "compensate for a lack of scientific knowledge" (p. 70). In an interesting twist on studying the relation between SMK and teaching, Shugart and Hounshell (1995) examined the relation between SMK (as measured on standardized tests) and teacher retention among 83 secondary science teachers; they found that the higher the science test scores, the more likely teachers were to leave teaching by the 9th or 10th year.

The studies of the relationship between SMK and science teaching represent a variety of participants (preservice and practicing teachers at the elementary, middle, and high school levels) and a variety of methods for assessing SMK (courses taken, surveys, interviews) and teaching behaviors (indirect methods such as responses to hypothetical teaching situations and direct observations of teaching). Despite this mixture of settings and methods, the evidence does support a positive relationship between SMK and teaching. Although Lederman and Gess-Newsome (1992) were less enthusiastic about this claim, their evidence included studies of teachers' views of the nature of science, studies that are not considered here. Could it be, as Lederman and Gess-Newsome suggested, that some minimal SMK is necessary, but that studies at different grades, or with preservice versus practicing teachers, cannot be compared fairly? Or could it be that SMK does have an effect on science teaching, but that this effect is mediated by other types of teacher knowledge? This was implied in many of the studies reported. Perhaps SMK is necessary, but not sufficient, for effective teaching. A review of studies of PK and PCK could be instructive.

SCIENCE TEACHER PEDAGOGICAL KNOWLEDGE

Grossman's (1990) formalization of Shulman's model of teacher knowledge included a component of pedagogical knowledge separate from PCK that she labeled general pedagogical knowledge (PK). PK includes knowledge of instructional principles, classroom management, learners and learning, and educational aims that are not subject-matter-specific. Theoretically, these types of knowledge interact with PCK for teaching of a particular topic in a discipline (see Fig. 36–1). In the science education literature, most of the research on teacher pedagogical knowledge logically falls into the category of PCK, pedagogical knowledge for teaching science topics (see next section). Some studies that claimed to be about PK actually cited science-specific teacher knowledge (see Gustafson, Guilbert, & MacDonald, 2002) and are better placed in the PCK category. However, the few studies that examined the PK of science teachers in particular are reviewed here.

Science teachers' generic meaning of learning (Aguirre & Haggerty, 1995) and their metacognitive knowledge of higher order thinking (Zohar, 1999) have been investigated. Another group of studies focused on science teachers' knowledge of classroom management. Three studies examined "pupil control ideologies" with a written instrument developed for the purpose (Harty, Andersen, & Enochs, 1984; Jones & Blankenship, 1970; Jones & Harty, 1981). As is all too familiar in the science education literature, researchers coined a new term for a hypothetical construct, developed a measurement tool, and used the tool in a few studies. Then the construct and the tool disappeared from the literature. In another study of classroom management, Latz (1992) used an open-ended questionnaire to learn about pre-service teachers' knowledge of management and discipline. He suggested a link between instructional approaches and teachers' "preventative" view of classroom management.

One interesting outcome of several case studies of science teachers has been that a majority of assertions have concerned PK rather than PCK (Gallagher, 1989; Mills, 1997; Treagust, 1991). For the most part, the findings of such studies could relate to teachers of any discipline; what makes these studies significant to the science education community? Could it be that the influence of PK on PCK needs to be better articulated? I believe that more attention must be paid to the interaction of PK with PCK—for example, the role of caring, classroom management, or general learning views—in how teachers teach science.

SCIENCE TEACHER PEDAGOGICAL CONTENT KNOWLEDGE

Frameworks and Methods of Representation

Pedagogical content knowledge (PCK) has been defined as "the transformation of subject-matter knowledge into forms accessible to the students being taught" (Geddis, 1993, p. 675). Grossman (1990) and later Magnusson et al. (1999) defined separate components of PCK, including orientations, knowledge of learners, curriculum, instructional strategies, and assessment. Yet, the PCK literature in science education is not nearly as tidy as the SMK literature. Some researchers directly studied PCK, but only a small portion explicitly discussed a particular kind of PCK. Most use PCK as a generic term across several of the subsections. Others did not mention PCK at all, either because they preceded Shulman's work in the mid-1980s, or used frameworks other than Shulman's to interpret the findings. Still other researchers who used the PCK framework introduced new constructs into the literature, including "activities that work" (Appleton, 2002), "pedagogical content concerns" (de Jong,

2000; de Jong & van Driel, 2001), and "pedagogical context knowledge" (Barnett & Hodson, 2001). Moreover, the words researchers used for "knowledge" have been conflated within and across studies, and included terms such as *conceptions, perceptions, theories, concerns,* and *beliefs,* in addition to *knowledge.* For example, Porlán and Martín del Pozo (2004) studied teachers' *"conceptions* about science teaching and learning" (p. 43) by using the Inventory of Science Pedagogical *Beliefs.*

For these reasons, the science education PCK literature lacks coherence (for example, there are few common citations) and is difficult to categorize. However, I felt compelled to impose some order on this large literature. I tried to fit studies, without forcing, into the five PCK categories (see Fig. 36–1), whether the researchers were explicit about such a categorization or not. Other studies that did not fit neatly into one type of PCK are discussed in this introductory section. Here I also discuss some of the common methods for representing teacher PCK that have been used.

Several lines of research used frameworks other than Shulman's to understand science teacher knowledge. For example, science education researchers have used Schön's theory of reflective practice to understand the development of "professional knowledge" (Abell, Bryan, & Anderson, 1998; Anderson, Smith, & Peasley, 2000; Munby, Cunningham, & Lock, 2000; Munby & Russell, 1992; Russell & Munby, 1991). These studies demonstrated how teacher knowledge develops over time with respect to various inputs and perturbations, but did not classify teacher knowledge as Shulman did.

Another line of science teacher research concerned itself with teacher planning. Although this research typically did not mention Shulman or PCK, being more often framed by a teacher cognition perspective, notions of teacher knowledge were often implicit. The planning literature in teacher education is rich (see Clark & Peterson, 1986; So, 1997), but science education is not well represented. Science education studies on teacher planning have examined both preservice (Davies & Rogers, 2000; Morine-Dershimer, 1989; Roberts & Chastko, 1990) and practicing (Aikenhead, 1984; Sanchez & Valcárcel, 1999; So, 1997) science teachers in an attempt to understand how teachers plan and what knowledge and beliefs influence their planning. Peterson and Treagust (1995) used Shulman's model of pedagogical reasoning to study the stages of science teacher reasoning while planning. While planning, preservice teachers relied on SMK and curricular knowledge, but during instruction, their reasoning "considered the teaching sequence, the science content and curriculum knowledge, the prior knowledge of the learner, and the explanations they would use for the activities to be discussed" (p. 300). The "Lesson Preparation Method" (Valk & Broekman, 1999) was introduced as a strategy to uncover science teacher PCK, and lesson planning has been used in other studies of science teacher knowledge (de Jong, 2000; de Jong, Ahtee, Goodwin, Hatzinikita, & Koulaidis, 1999). However, the findings of Peterson and Treagust lend some degree of skepticism to the method of representing PCK solely by planning activities and suggest that studies of PCK during teaching need to simultaneously occur.

Another method of representing teacher PCK has been via metaphors (Bradford & Dana, 1996; Briscoe, 1991; Hand & Treagust, 1997; Munby 1986; Tobin & LaMaster, 1995). Munby claimed that "metaphorical figures can be studied with a view to comprehending a teacher's construction of professional reality" (p. 206). Although none of these studies used Shulman's views of teacher knowledge as their theoretical framework, their findings do help in understanding the knowledge/orientations of science teachers.

Loughran and colleagues (Loughran, Gunstone, Berry, Milroy, & Mulhall, 2000; Loughran, Mulhall, & Berry, 2004; Loughran, Milroy, Berry, Gunstone, & Mulhall, 2001) developed a system for representing science teacher PCK. Their work began by writing cases of PCK, a process they called "classroom window" methodology. Finding deficits in this method of representation, they next developed PaP-eRs, Pedagogical and Professional-experience Repertoires. The PaP-eR characterizes teacher knowledge around a specific science topic and is an amalgam of types of PCK. The researchers called this mode of representation a breakthrough in capturing a teacher's PCK. At this writing, it is too soon to tell if the PaP-eR will find a more widespread use among researchers and science teacher educators.

A host of other methods, including expert/novice studies (MacDonald, 1992; Pinnegar, 1989), interviews (Fernández-Balboa & Stiehl, 1995; Koballa, Gräber, Coleman, & Kemp, 1999), classroom observations (van Driel, Verloop, & de Vos, 1998), and analysis of teacher study group discussions (Daehler & Shinohara, 2001; Geddis, 1993) have been employed to understand science teacher PCK. Given the complexity of representing PCK, studies that use multiple methods over time to understand teacher knowledge seem to be the richest. For example, Bellamy (1990) observed and interviewed high school biology teachers teaching genetics. The teachers demonstrated similarities in their PCK for genetics teaching through the use of common teaching sequences and activities. Sanders, Borko, et al. (1993) observed and interviewed three secondary science teachers as they planned, taught, and reflected on their science teaching both within and outside of their certification area. Their study generated a rich data set from which they made numerous claims concerning SMK, PK, and PCK. van Driel, de Jong, and Verloop (2002) studied preservice chemistry teachers' PCK via questionnaires, interviews, and workshop session conversations over one semester and were able to describe teachers' PCK and its development.

Research on science teacher PCK resides in a formative phase, where researchers continue to define the terms and methods that guide their work. The research has raised several questions. For example, Peterson and Treagust (1995) suggested that the knowledge a teacher uses for teaching may not be the same as that represented in written surveys or instruments. What forms of represented PCK are most trustworthy? What research designs are most viable? Appleton (2002) reported that elementary teachers of science consider "activities that work" the basis of their science instruction, and he claimed that this notion is the centerpiece of elementary teachers' science PCK. Should PCK be defined differently for teachers at different grade levels? Other researchers cause us to question Shulman's model itself—do we need to add new terms such as *pedagogical context knowledge* and *pedagogical content concerns* to our research lexicon? Science educators have embraced Schulman's work as a useful theoretical framework. The PCK framework has been used to understand science teacher knowledge across grade levels and career spans. It has also been suggested as a viable model for thinking about the knowledge that science teacher educators hold, or should develop, to be effective (Abell, Smith, Schmidt, & Magnusson, 1996; Smith, 2000). However, we must continue to ask if the theoretical construct of PCK is supported, disconfirmed, or in need of expansion, using evidence derived through empirical research. The following sections examine empirical research within the five components of PCK shown in Fig. 36–1.

Orientations toward Science Teaching

Anderson and Smith (1987) introduced the term "orientation" as a way to categorize disparate approaches to science teaching (activity-driven, didactic, discovery, and conceptual-change). Grossman's (1990) model of PCK included the category "conceptions of purposes for teaching subject matter" (p. 5), for which Magnusson et al. (1999) substituted the label "orientation." They used the label to represent teacher knowledge of the purposes and goals for teaching science at a particular grade level, after Grossman, but also called an orientation a "general way of viewing or conceptualizing science teaching" (p. 97). They expanded Anderson and Smith's list of four orientations to nine. The inclusion of "orientations" in the PCK model is problematic. First of all, an orientation is theorized as a generalized view of science teaching, not topic-specific knowledge. Second, these general views of science teaching and learning are often studied as an interaction among knowledge, beliefs, and values, not strictly as knowledge structures. Furthermore, these general views have been called by a number of different names in the literature. Although some will undoubtedly question the inclusion of some of the studies in this section, I believe their presence in the literature must be acknowledged, so that we can understand the field and develop a more cohesive research agenda.

Very few studies set out to explicitly understand teachers' orientations to teaching science. Studies by Greenwood (2003) and Friedrichsen (2002; Friedrichsen & Dana, 2003, 2005) are notable exceptions. Friedrichsen called orientations "a messy concept" (p. 11) because either researchers provided no clear definition, or they introduced new terms into the mix. For example, researchers have used labels such as "conceptions of science teaching" (Hewson & Hewson, 1987; Porlán & Martín del Pozo, 2004), "functional paradigms" (Lantz & Kass, 1987), "world images" (Wubbels, 1992), "preconceptions of teaching" (Weinstein, 1980), and "approaches to teaching" (Trigwell, Prosser, & Taylor, 1994) to study what appears to be teaching orientations. For this section, I selected studies that examined teacher knowledge of guiding purposes and frameworks for science teaching and left studies of teacher views of curricular goals and instructional models to later sections.

One line of research on orientations followed the work of Anderson and Smith (1987). Roth (1987) studied 13 experienced junior high life science teachers and found three groups of teaching orientations: fact acquisition, conceptual development, and content understanding. Smith and Neale (1989, 1991) imposed four orientations on their data: discovery, processes, didactic/content mastery, and conceptual change. Hollon, Roth, and Anderson (1991) examined the cases of two middle-level science teachers and claimed that teacher practice was governed not only by SMK, but also by "deeply held patterns of thought and action that have developed over many years" (p. 176). Anderson et al. (2000), using interviews as primary data sources, described the development of five preservice teachers' "conceptions" across one year of teacher education. The authors claimed that the students entered the teacher education program along a particular trajectory and focused their learning on aspects of teaching congruent with these conceptions. However, one student, Mindy, experienced a more dramatic change: from a teacher-centered conception of science teaching to a view where students took center stage. Bryan and Abell (1999), although not studying orientations directly, found a similar progression in one student teacher's thinking. Barbara began student teaching with a teacher-centered view that blamed students for their inability to learn and progressed to a deeper understanding of the requirements for learning. This line of research changed over time from a concern with labeling specific teaching orientations to understanding how these orientations develop.

Another line of research on orientations introduced the term "conceptions of teaching" as "the set of ideas, understandings, and interpretations of experience" concerning teaching, learning, and the nature of science that teachers use to make decisions (Hewson & Hewson, 1989, p. 194). Hewson and Hewson (1987) defended the construct and then designed an interview task (1989) for identifying teacher conceptions of teaching science. In subsequent studies, they refined the protocol and used it to study the conceptions of teaching held by both preservice and practicing science teachers (Hewson, Kerby, & Cook, 1995; Lemberger, Hewson, & Park, 1999; Lyons, Freitag, & Hewson, 1997; Meyer, Tabachnick, Hewson, Lemberger, & Park, 1999). In particular, they were interested in how teachers built their understanding of conceptual change science teaching.

Other than these two lines of research, studies of teacher orientations have not formed a coherent line of thought, often because researchers introduced their own terms rather than building on the existing literature. Several studies categorized teaching orientations. Lantz and Kass (1987) studied how three chemistry teachers translated curriculum materials into practice. They interpreted teacher comments to represent three views of teaching: pedagogical efficiency, academic rigor, and motivating students. They used the term "functional paradigm" to describe the teachers' views of chemistry, teaching, students, and the school setting and claimed that a teacher's functional paradigm (or what Shulman might call PK or Magnusson et al. (1999) would call orientation) influenced how curriculum materials were interpreted and implemented. Freire and Sanches (1992) used both "orientations" and "conceptions of teaching" to describe Portuguese physics teachers' views. They derived five conceptions of teaching physics—traditional, experimentalist, constructivist, pragmatist, and social—but did not find them demonstrated in practice. Huibregtse, Korthagen, and Wubbels (1994) identified goals and approaches to teaching held by Dutch physics teachers. They found that the teachers favored approaches to teaching that fit their own learning preference, but had limited conceptions of teaching overall. In one of the few studies on college science teacher PCK, Trigwell et al. (1994) found 24 chemistry and physics professors to hold one of five "approaches to teaching": (a) teacher-centered to transmit information (13 instructors); (b) teacher-centered so students acquire concepts (6 instructors); (c) teacher-student interaction so that students acquire concepts (3 instructors); (d) student-centered so students develop conceptions (1 instructor); and (e) student-centered aimed at students changing their conceptions (1 instructor). Huston (1975) measured the "values orientations" of chemistry teachers and students in Canada and found that students were more highly oriented to the humanistic and technological aspects of chemistry, whereas teachers were oriented to the more abstract and theoretical. Cheung and Ng (2000) defined five curriculum orientations: academic, cognitive processes, society-centered, humanistic, and technological, and asked secondary science teachers in Hong Kong which orientations they most valued. They found that teachers were most enthusiastic about the cognitive processes orientation but valued all of the orientations. These findings resonate with Friedrichsen's (2002) study of secondary biology teachers. Orientations shifted based on which course the teacher was teaching and the "perceived needs of a particular group of students" (p. 143). Thus a teacher's orientation is not a single static entity with neat boundaries, but a fluid set of components influenced by a host of issues.

Attempting to categorize and understand orientations by the use of common terms from the literature is not the only approach that has been used to study this component of PCK. Some studies used open-ended questionnaires to ask teachers about their conceptions of science teaching and learning (Aguirre, Haggerty, & Linder, 1990; Gurney, 1995; Parsons, 1991) or a survey to find out their "conceptions of purposes" for science teaching (Zeitler, 1984). Another strategy for studying teaching orientations has been to examine teacher views of good science teaching (Brickhouse, 1993; Guillaume, 1995; Skamp, 1995; Skamp & Mueller, 2001; Stofflett & Stefanon, 1996). Other researchers adopted a case-study methodology as a way to understand science teachers' frameworks (Adams & Krockover, 1997; Cornett, Yeotis, & Terwilliger, 1990; Feldman, 2002; Geddis & Roberts, 1998; Johnston, 1991; Maor & Taylor, 1995; Ritchie, 1999; Sweeney, Bula, & Cornett, 2001). Mellado (1998) constructed cases of four Spanish student teachers—elementary and secondary— and their conceptions of teaching and learning science. All four teachers demonstrated an "apparent constructivist orientation" (p. 204) toward learning, but they assigned different values to student ideas. Furthermore, their classroom practices were closer to traditional models of teaching than to the orientation they espoused.

Orientation is indeed a messy construct. Some researchers adopt PCK as their theoretical perspective, some use theories other than Shulman's to guide their work, and others appear to be atheoretical in their approach. Researchers need to come to a clear consensus about what they are studying in this realm. Rather than introduce new terms, it would benefit the field to more deeply understand the existing constructs. Nevertheless, a few conclusions seem reasonable based on the literature: (a) orientations influence teacher learning and practice, although that influence is not direct (Anderson et al., 2000; Lantz & Kass, 1987; Lemberger et al., 1999); (b) orientations (or whatever they are termed) are much less coherently held and much more context-specific than the theoretical literature led us to believe (Cheung & Ng, 2000; Friedrichsen, 2002; Friedrichsen & Dana, 2005); (c) teachers often do not possess a tacit knowledge of their conceptual framework (Gallagher, 1989); (d) although teachers possess or value a range of orientations that guide practice, their set of teaching strategies is much more narrow (Freire & Sanches, 1992; Gallagher, 1989; Huibregtse et al., 1994; Mellado, 1998); and (e) orientations can change over time (Anderson et al., 2000; Bryan & Abell, 1999; Feldman, 2002; Sweeney et al., 2001). However, much more work is needed to understand the frameworks that guide science teachers in their planning and enactment of instruction.

Knowledge of Science Learners

This category of PCK pertains to knowledge teachers have about student science learning: requirements for learning certain concepts, areas that students find difficult, approaches to learning science, and common alternative conceptions (Magnusson et al., 1999). The research in this area has concentrated on teacher knowledge of alternative conceptions, teacher images of the ideal science student, and more general views of science learning.

A logical extension of the research on children's and teachers' science conceptions was to examine teacher knowledge of student science ideas. As early as 1981, Nussbaum asked biology and chemistry student teachers to respond to hypothetical students' science explanations about the structure of matter that contained three major misconceptions. Although 45 percent of the teachers detected one misconception, only 7 percent found all three and 22 percent found none. The chemistry student teachers performed no better than the biology student teachers. In a similar study, Kokkotas et al. (1998) found that preservice secondary teachers could not identify student problems in thinking about the particulate nature of matter. Deficiencies in teacher knowledge of student ideas about heat and temperature (Frederik et al., 1999) and electricity (Stocklmayer & Treagust, 1996) have also been found.

Survey methods were used in some studies to determine teacher knowledge about student science ideas. Pine, Messer, and St. John (2001) surveyed 122 elementary science teachers in the United Kingdom. When asked to give examples of common ideas held by students, 90 of the teachers produced 130 responses, in all areas of the science curriculum. The researchers concluded that teachers had a strong awareness of student alternative ideas. This finding stands in stark contrast to the results of other studies. For example, McNay (1991) asked a small group of Canadian elementary teachers to read several research articles about students' science ideas. Some teachers did not believe what they read until they interviewed their own students and heard the ideas firsthand. In a study of secondary physical science teachers in Portugal (Sequeira, Leite, & Duarte, 1993), only 45 percent stated they had heard about alternative conceptions, even though 80 percent of university instructors claimed it was part of the preservice program. Of the teachers who had heard of alternative conceptions, most recognized them from a list and stated that such ideas can be hard to change. In Malaysia, Halim and Meerah (2002) asked 12 prospective physics teachers how they thought students would respond to a set of questions. The researchers found that many teachers were unaware of students' likely misconceptions and had inadequate SMK. In an interview setting, Berg and Brouwer (1991) asked 20 high school physics teachers to predict student responses to questions about force and gravity. In addition to demonstrating several alternative conceptions themselves, the teachers underestimated the number of students who would hold various conceptions and overestimated the number of students who would respond with the correct answer.

Several studies examined teacher knowledge of student conceptions within the context of teaching. de Jong and van Driel (2001) asked prospective chemistry teachers to discuss their concerns before teaching a lesson in grade 9 and then to discuss the difficulties they had after teaching. Prior to the lesson, only 3 of the 8 students mentioned any concerns about student learning. After the lesson, a few more discussed student learning difficulties in their reflection. Jones et al. (1999) engaged elementary and middle-level teachers in interviewing students and teaching lessons and assessed their pre/post SMK and knowledge of teaching. They found that teachers were "shocked" by the science concepts revealed by students and that student concepts served as catalysts for the teachers to reevaluate both their SMK and their pedagogical practices. Geddis, Onslow, Beynon, and Oesch (1993) found that two chemistry student teachers, in the context of teaching about isotopes, did not realize the difficulties students would encounter in learning weighted averages, given their familiarity with simple averages. The veteran teacher, in contrast, was able to predict and plan around these difficulties. Likewise, Akerson, Flick, and Lederman (2000) found a big difference between how two veteran elementary teachers and a student teacher dealt with student ideas. The veterans viewed children's ideas as perceptually dominated, structured, coherent, experience-based, and resistant to change and repeatedly tried to elicit student ideas. The student teacher, on the other hand, discouraged student expression of their science ideas, and focused on eliminating student ideas so she could proceed with her instruction. Morrison and Lederman (2003) found that the four secondary science teachers in their study valued diagnosis of student preconceptions, but had varying degrees of understanding of possible preconceptions.

A host of other studies have attempted to understand teacher knowledge of students with the use of various frameworks. For example, Pinnegar (1989) used an expert/novice frame and a repeated interview technique to study high school science teachers' knowledge of students. She found that teachers' knowledge of students came mostly from classroom observations and interactions, and that their knowledge increased over time. Experienced teachers were able to provide evidence to support their interpretations of students. Two studies examined teacher views of excellent science students (Bailey, Boylan, Francis, & Hill, 1986; Raina, 1970). Teachers often mentioned traits of good students (e.g., obedience, good listener, completing tasks), as well as personality traits (organized, neat), as opposed to traits associated with scientific or creative thinking.

As views of science learning broadened, so did attempts to understand teacher knowledge of science learning. In a study of exemplary secondary science teachers in Australia (Gallagher, 1989), teachers characterized learning as driven by motivation. Several studies of preservice teachers (Geddis & Roberts, 1998; Gustafson & Rowell, 1995; Lemberger et al., 1999; Zembal-Saul, Blumenfeld, & Krajcik, 2000) described teacher views of science learning as part of an overall orientation to science teaching. Others related teachers' views of learning to their views of the nature of science (Abell & Smith, 1994; Flores, Lopez, Gallegos, & Barojas, 2000; Hashweh, 1996a, 1996b). These researchers claimed a connection between a positivist epistemology and a behaviorist or discovery-oriented view of science learning. Hashweh demonstrated that teachers holding what he called "empirical" beliefs of knowledge and learning were more apt to judge student alternative conceptions as acceptable than were teachers holding "constructivist" views. The research on teacher knowledge of science learning has employed a broad range of methods and lacks cohesion in terms of the research questions addressed. Overall it appears that teachers lack knowledge of student science conceptions, but that this knowledge improves with teaching experience.

Knowledge of Science Curriculum

Magnusson et al. (1999) defined two types of science curriculum knowledge: (a) knowledge of mandated goals and objectives (e.g., state and national standards) and (b) knowledge of specific curriculum programs and materials. Few studies attempted to directly study teacher knowledge of science curriculum, or cited Shulman's model as a theoretical foundation for the research. One notable exception is Peterson and Treagust (1995), who found that knowledge of curriculum was an essential component of preservice teacher pedagogical reasoning around lesson planning and instruction.

Science teacher knowledge of curricular goals has been researched, but studies typically asked teachers to rank the relative importance of the goals, rather than examine teacher knowledge directly. Tamir and Jungwirth (1972) asked Israeli biology teachers familiar with the BSCS biology curriculum to rank 18 teaching objectives. A majority ranked "developing critical thinking" as most important, and 54 percent assigned bottom rank to "accumulation of biological knowledge." However, there was not agreement about objectives such as "understanding the role of science in everyday life" or "understanding the nature and aims of science." In 1982, Finley, Stewart, and Yarroch surveyed 400 U.S. science teachers in four science disciplines about their perceptions of the difficulty and importance of 50 topics in their discipline. Teachers rated a number of topics important, but not difficult, for students to learn (e.g., cell theory, periodic table, energy and energy conservation, Earth/Moon system). Finley and colleagues made no attempt to link teacher perceptions with local or state curricular goals. Science teachers' goals have been studied around the world, with the use of terms such as "goal conceptions," "goal orientations," and "views of goals," in Australia (Schibeci, 1981), Finland (Hirvonen & Viiri, 2002), France (Boyer & Tiberghien, 1989), Israel (Hofstein, Mandler, Ben-Zvi, & Samuel, 1980), Spain (Furio, Vilches, Guisasola, & Romo, 2002), the United Kingdom (Carrick, 1983), and the United States (McIntosh & Zeidler, 1988). Although science teachers recognize a variety of goals for science teaching, they tend to emphasize content goals over attitudinal or process goals.

In a study of teaching goals in action, Geddis et al. (1993) examined the curricular knowledge that comes into play in the teaching of a particular topic. The researchers introduced the term "curricular saliency," to explain how veteran teachers cope with a curriculum full of concepts and decide what is important to teach. Teacher rankings of goals is only a small part of the knowledge that comes into play when curricular decisions are made.

In the wake of the standards-based science education reforms of the 1990s, it is surprising that so little attention has been paid to understanding teacher knowledge of science standards. A few studies have addressed this (Fischer-Mueller & Zeidler, 2002; Furió et al., 2002; Lynch, 1997), but more are needed. Although educators often bemoan the lack of reform-minded science teaching, researchers have not contributed an understanding of the curriculum knowledge that is necessary for the reforms to be effective.

Science teacher knowledge of curriculum programs and materials (the second type of knowledge of science curriculum defined by Magnusson and her colleagues (1999)) likewise suffers from a dearth of research attention. One of the earliest studies of this type of knowledge looked at teacher awareness and use of population education materials (O'Brien, Huether, & Philliber, 1978) and found that 60–70 percent of U.S. population education teachers were not familiar with a range of curriculum materials. Schriver and Czerniak (1999) compared U.S. middle school science teachers to those in junior high settings on a number of variables, including self-efficacy and knowledge of developmentally appropriate curriculum. Knowledge of developmentally appropriate curriculum was higher for the middle school teachers, positively correlated with level of outcome expectancy, but unrelated to self-efficacy. Peacock and Gates (2000) examined the perceptions of 23 newly qualified elementary teachers in the United Kingdom regarding the role of the textbook in science learning. Teachers thought of the text as peripheral to science activities and as needing to be adapted before use. Textbook selection was based on surface features and was not related to a teacher's SMK. Although several tools have been generated in the United States for teacher use in curriculum analysis (Kesidou & Roseman, 2002; National Research Council, 1999), we know little about the knowledge teachers bring to bear on the analysis, selection, or design of science curriculum materials. One recent study (Lynch, Pyke, & Jansen, 2003) offers insight into this process.

Knowledge of Science Instructional Strategies

This type of teacher knowledge includes subject-specific strategies (e.g., learning cycle, use of analogies or demos or labs) and topic-specific teaching methods and strategies, including representations (examples, models, metaphors), demonstrations, and activities (labs, problems, cases) (Magnusson et al., 1999). The research has examined both categories of teacher knowledge but is lacking in studies of teacher representations of science content.

A small group of researchers has studied teacher understanding of science teaching approaches (Jones, Thompson, & Miller, 1980), including the learning cycle (Marek, Eubanks, & Gallagher; 1990; Marek, Laubach, & Pedersen, 2003; Odom & Settlage, 1996; Settlage, 2000), the Generative Learning Model (GLM) (Flick, 1996), and STS instruction (Tsai, 2001). Flick found that U.S. elementary teachers could not completely distinguish between the GLM and direct instruction teaching models. Olson (1990) found a similar confusion among UK teachers: "They tended to think of discovery teaching approaches as if they were variants of more familiar teacher directed forms" (p. 210). Settlage and colleagues reported a lack of understanding of the learning cycle among preservice elementary teachers after instruction but found no relation between this knowledge and anxiety about teaching science. Marek and colleagues found that both elementary and secondary science teachers who demonstrated a sound understanding of a Piagetian view of learning also had a deeper understanding of the learning cycle. Hashweh (1996a) related teachers' epistemological views to their knowledge of conceptual change teaching strategies and found that teachers holding constructivist views possessed richer repertoires of such strategies.

Although we emphasize inquiry-based teaching and instructional models such as the learning cycle in science teacher education programs, we have little empirical knowledge of what teachers learn. According to Keys and Bryan (2001), research on teacher knowledge of inquiry-based instructional strategies has not been sufficiently developed. More science education research should be devoted to examining what teachers understand about classroom inquiry strategies and science teaching models, and how they translate their knowledge into instruction.

Other studies have looked at PCK related to strategies for teaching specific topics within chemistry (de Jong, Acampo, & Verdonk, 1995; de Jong & van Driel, 2001; Geddis et al., 1993; Tulberg et al., 1994; van Driel et al., 1998, 2002; see also de Jong et al., 2002, for a review), biology (Mastrilli, 1997; Treagust, 1991), and physics (Halim & Meerah, 2002). Geddis and colleagues compared the teaching of isotopes between two novices and a veteran teacher. Both of the novices taught procedural knowledge—calculating average atomic masses—with the use of accurate examples. The veteran, however, was more concerned with conceptual understanding and used inaccurate examples to scaffold student learning. The researchers claimed that this is a clear instance of a teacher transforming SMK by using instructional strategies that take student learning into account. In contrast, de Jong, Acampo, and Verdonk observed the teaching of redox reactions by two experienced chemistry teachers and found that the teachers had many difficulties developing viable instructional strategies.

Researchers have also studied teacher knowledge and use of general science instructional strategies. Enochs, Oliver, and Wright (1990) found that one-third or more of Kansas science teachers never used teaching strategies such as demonstrations, cooperative learning, or laboratories. Others examined the use of strategies such as analogies (Mastrilli, 1997; Nottis & McFarland, 2001), models (Justi & Gilbert, 2002a, 2002b; van Driel & Verloop, 2002), and demonstrations (Clermont, Borko, & Krajcik, 1994; Clermont, Krajcik, & Borko, 1993). Clermont and his colleagues found differences in the PCK for chemical demonstrations between experienced and novice demonstrators. The experienced teachers discussed more alternative chemical demonstrations for each topic and provided more detail about their alternatives than the novices. They also generated more variations on the demonstration presented. Novices occasionally discussed inappropriate content or pedagogically unsound demonstrations. These studies demonstrate that knowledge of instructional strategies is linked to SMK and knowledge of learners, but also demands understanding of the subtleties of the strategy in use.

A conceptually rich study of the content representations of two elementary student teachers as they engaged in two cycles of planning, teaching, and reflecting (Zembal-Saul et al., 2000) provides a window into the development of teacher knowledge of instructional strategies. In an initial teaching cycle, these preservice teachers were able to plan many scientifically accurate content representations but included too many topics that were not sequenced well. Furthermore, during teaching, they had difficulty in helping students make connections among the topics. In a second cycle, the teachers again planned multiple and accurate representations of the content, but were more selective and better able to connect activities and representations during class discussions. Following these teachers into student teaching, the researchers found that although one of the teachers was able to maintain and enhance content representations in science, the second teacher was not (Zembal-Saul, Krajcik, & Blumenfeld, 2002). These studies demonstrate the complexity of science teaching in terms of the interplay of SMK and PCK. They also illustrate how future teachers can learn from the authority of experience (Munby & Russell, 1994) and how context affects a student teacher's content representations.

Knowledge of Science Assessment

According to Magnusson et al. (1999), this type of teacher knowledge includes knowledge of what to assess in science as well as methods for assessing. A few studies have attempted to directly study teacher assessment knowledge by a variety of methods. Pine, Messer, and St. John (2001) described the methods UK elementary teachers used to find out what students know, which included discussion, brainstorming, past records, questioning, testing, and predicting. Duffee and Aikenhead (1992) interviewed six 10th-grade urban science teachers regarding student evaluation decisions within an STS curriculum. Although teachers used a variety of techniques, tests and lab assignments were weighted most heavily to determine final grades. How and what the teachers chose to assess were mediated by their beliefs and values. For example, the four teachers who integrated STS and the nature of science into their teaching assessed students' abilities to solve problems and reason, and the two teachers who thought of science as factual relied more on objectively scored items with one right answer.

However, knowing what assessment methods teachers use does not provide insight into how assessment is enacted. In attempting to understand science teacher assessment knowledge in action, Sanders (1993) asked 136 South African biology teachers to mark student answers about respiration. The teachers used different criteria to mark the answers, resulting in a wide distribution of final scores. Many teachers looked for correct statements only, ignored wrong answers, and failed to provide feedback to students. The majority of positive feedback referred to the logical structure of the essay (34 percent) or neatness (22 percent), and 11 percent gave general positive comments even when student ideas were wrong. Kokkotas et al. (1998) attributed Greek preservice secondary teachers' inability to identify problems in student answers about the particulate nature of matter to their lack of SMK. In addition, teachers scored answers too strictly or leniently based on factors other than student responses, including their perceptions of the difficulty of the topic and their attitude toward the need to encourage students. Morrison and Lederman (2003) found that the science teachers in their study did not use any assessment tools to diagnose student preconceptions, even though they recognized the importance of student prior knowledge. Bol and Strage (1996) found a similar contradiction between biology teacher goals and assessment practices.

Two case studies of science teachers emphasized assessment knowledge and practices. Kamen (1996) found that a third-grade teacher was able to shift her assessment practices when her image of science instruction changed from hands-on to minds-on, supported by learning new assessment methods. Briscoe (1993) claimed that Brad, a veteran high school chemistry teacher, viewed assessment as rewards and punishments and equated assessment to testing, thus was resistant to change. According to Briscoe, a teacher's ability to change his/her assessment practices is "influenced by what the teacher already knows or understands about teaching, learning, and the nature of schooling" (p. 983). These studies of teacher knowledge of assessment in science provide rich research models that demonstrate a link between PCK for assessment and science teaching orientation. More studies are needed to better understand what teachers know about assessment, and how they design, enact, and score assessments in their science classes.

DISCUSSION

The science education research on teacher knowledge rests on firm theoretical and empirical foundations, yet continues to develop both conceptually and methodologically. The research on SMK is cohesive, partly because definitions of SMK are commonly shared even when research methods differ. In contrast, the research on PCK is less cohesive. Researchers do not agree about what constitutes PCK, or do not evenly apply their meanings to their research. In addition, frames other than PCK have been used to ground research on teacher pedagogical knowledge. Nevertheless, I believe we can use this review of this literature to derive implications both for science teacher education and for further research.

Implications for Science Teacher Education

Science educators have recognized the value of Shulman's model of teacher knowledge as an organizer for science teacher education. Cochran, DeRuiter, and King (1993) proposed a revision to Shulman's model that combined SMK and PCK, claiming that all teacher knowledge is pedagogical. They also posited that, because knowledge is not a static state but an active process, PCK should be changed to PCKg, pedagogical content knowing, and that such a model could inform teacher education programs. However, this idea has not been pursued in the literature.

Several science educators have used the PCK framework to design teacher preparation programs for elementary (Mellado, Blanco, & Ruiz, 1998) and middle-level (Doster, Jackson, and Smith, 1997) science teacher education. Zembal-Saul, Haefner, Avraamidou, Severs, & Dana (2002) demonstrated how to employ the PCK framework not only to structure learning goals and teaching methods, but also to design performance-based tools for evaluating teacher learning. Although Shulman's model is useful for practice in science teacher education, the teacher knowledge framework is necessary, but not sufficient. Windschitl (2002) reminds us that, although teacher knowledge is essential in what he calls constructivist instruction, considerations of cultural and political dilemmas are also necessary if a teacher is to be successful. Science teacher education must honor not only formal teacher knowledge, but also the local and practical knowledge of teachers in the field and the sociocultural contexts that frame their work.

Understanding the development and interaction of science teacher SMK and PCK is critical for our success in science teacher education. It also has implications for teacher education policy. Teacher certification in many countries is governed by accrediting agencies that define necessary SMK and PCK in terms of university coursework and/or teaching standards. Policy makers decide how much SMK, PCK, and other kinds of knowledge are needed for beginning teachers. Current U.S. federal policy implies that only SMK is needed to produce highly qualified teachers (U.S. Department of Education, 2002). This review provides evidence to the contrary.

Recommendations for Future Research

Science education researchers are often queried by our scientist colleagues about the value of educational research. Within our own research community, we wonder if progress has been made. Have we built on the work of earlier research to generate a viable knowledge base about science teacher knowledge?

In the area of science teacher SMK, much "normal science" (Kuhn, 1996) has occurred. Landmark studies are commonly cited, research methods are fairly consistent, and findings confirm theory, perhaps because science conceptual understanding for all learners has an agreed-upon meaning. Although researchers are unlikely to turn up anything revolutionary here, they fit a few more pieces into the puzzle with each study. The area in which the SMK literature is less clear is the relation of SMK to other forms of teacher knowledge, to teacher beliefs and values, and to classroom practice. We need more studies that take place within the teaching context to examine how SMK develops, how it plays out in teaching, and how it is related to other kinds of teacher knowledge (see Ball & McDiarmid, 1996).

The research on science teacher PCK is markedly different from the SMK literature. It is more like what Kuhn (1996) would call pre-science. Researchers do not yet agree about terminology or methodology. The research as a whole is less coherent; and researchers do not build on previous studies or reference a common body of literature. As researchers continue to sort out the viability of Shulman's framework and introduce new variations into it, we must ask ourselves if these new terms are conceptually necessary to understand science teacher knowledge. It would benefit the research if conceptual frameworks were made explicit. Furthermore, it would behoove researchers in this area to become more familiar with the literature and attempt to build a coherent conceptualization of PCK. More studies need to focus on the essence of PCK—how teachers transform SMK of specific science topics into viable instruction (see van Driel et al., 1998).

The research in both SMK and PCK has predominantly been at the level of description. In the current area of standards-based education and accountability for student learning, science education researchers should make more efforts to connect what we know about teacher knowledge to student learning. Although we have a good understanding of the kinds of knowledge that teachers bring to bear on science teaching, we know little about how teacher knowledge affects students. Answering this question will require more work in classroom settings of all kinds (see Fernández-Balboa & Stiehl, 1995; Keys & Bryan, 2001) and more complex research designs. The ultimate goal for science teacher knowledge research must be not only to understand teacher knowledge, but also to improve practice, thereby improving student learning.

ACKNOWLEDGMENTS

Thanks to Maher Hashweh and Jan van Driel for reviewing this chapter.

REFERENCES

Abd-El-Khalick, F., & BouJaoude, S. (1997). An exploratory study of the knowledge base for science teaching. *Journal of Research in Science Teaching, 34*, 673–699.

Abell, S. K., Bryan, L. A., & Anderson, M. A. (1998). Investigating preservice elementary science teacher reflective thinking using integrated media case-based instruction in elementary science teacher preparation. *Science Education, 82*, 491–510.

Abell, S. K., & Roth, M. (1992). Constraints to teaching elementary science: A case study of a science enthusiast student teacher. *Science Education, 76*, 581–595.

Abell, S. K., & Smith, D. C. (1994). What is science? Preservice elementary teachers' conceptions of the nature of science. *International Journal of Science Education, 16*, 475–487.

Abell, S. K., Smith, D. C., Schmidt, J. A., & Magnusson, S. J. (1996, April). *Building a pedagogical content knowledge base for elementary science teacher education.* Paper presented at the National Association for Research in Science Teaching, St. Louis.

Adams, P. E., & Krockover, G. H. (1997). Beginning science teacher cognition and its origins in the preservice secondary science teacher program. *Journal of Research in Science Teaching, 34,* 633–653.

Aguirre, J. M., & Haggerty, S. M. (1995). Preservice teachers' meaning of learning. *International Journal of Science Education, 17,* 119–131.

Aguirre, J. M., Haggerty, S. M., & Linder, C. J. (1990). Student-teachers' conceptions of science, teaching and learning: A case study in preservice science education. *International Journal of Science Education, 12,* 381–390.

Aiello-Nicosia, M. L., Sperandeo-Mineo, R. M., & Valenza, M. A. (1984). The relationship between science process abilities of teachers and science achievement of students: An experiential study. *Journal of Research in Science Teaching, 21,* 853–858.

Aikenhead, G. S. (1984). Teacher decision-making: The case of Prairie High. *Journal of Research in Science Teaching, 21,* 167–186.

Akerson, V. L., Flick, L. B., & Lederman, N. G. (2000). The influence of primary children's ideas in science on teaching practice. *Journal of Research in Science Teaching, 37,* 363–385.

Ameh, C. (1987). An analysis of teachers' and their students' views of the concept of "gravity." *Research in Science Education, 17,* 212–219.

Ameh, C., & Gunstone, R. (1985). Teachers' concepts in science. *Research in Science Education, 15,* 151–157.

Ameh, C., & Gunstone, R. (1986). Science teachers' concepts in Nigeria and Australia. *Research in Science Education, 16,* 73–81.

Anderson, C. W. (1979). An observational study of classroom management and information structuring in elementary school science lessons. *Dissertation Abstracts International, 40* (11), 5810A (UMI no. 8009823).

Anderson, C. W., & Smith, E. L. (1987). Teaching science. In V. Richardson-Koehler (Ed.), *Educators' handbook: A research perspective* (pp. 84–111). New York: Longman.

Anderson, L. M., Smith, D. C., & Peasley, K. (2000). Integrating learner and learning concerns: Prospective elementary science teachers' paths and progress. *Teaching and Teacher Education, 16,* 547–574.

Anderson, R. D., & Mitchener, C. P. (1994). Research on science teacher education. In D. L. Gabel, (Ed.), *Handbook of research on science teaching and learning* (pp. 3–44). New York: Macmillan.

Appleton, K. (1992). Discipline knowledge and confidence to teach science: Self-perceptions of primary teacher education students. *Research in Science Education, 22,* 11–19.

Appleton, K. (1995). Student teachers' confidence to teach science: Is more science knowledge necessary to improve self-confidence. *International Journal of Science Education, 17,* 357–369.

Appleton, K. (2002). Science activities that work: Perceptions of primary school teachers. *Research in Science Education, 32,* 393–410.

Aron, R. H., Francek, M. A., Nelson, B. D., & Bisard, W. J. (1994). Atmospheric misconceptions: How they cloud our judgment. *The Science Teacher, 61*(1), 30–33.

Arzi, H. J., & White, R. T. (2004, April). *Seeking change in teachers' knowledge of science: A 17-year longitudinal study.* Paper presented at the American Educational Research Association, San Diego.

Atwood, R. K., & Atwood, V. A. (1996). Preservice elementary teachers' conceptions of the causes of seasons. *Journal of Research in Science Teaching, 33,* 553–563.

Atwood, V. A., & Atwood, R. K. (1995). Preservice elementary teachers' conceptions of what causes night and day. *School Science and Mathematics, 95,* 290–294.

Bailey, J., Boylan, C., Francis, R., & Hill, D. (1986). Constructs used by science teachers to describe able students: A pilot study. *Research in Science Education, 16,* 111–118.

Baird, W. E., & Koballa, T. R., Jr. (1988). Changes in preservice elementary teachers' hypothesizing skills following group or individual study with computer simulations. *Science Education, 72,* 209–223.

Ball, D. L., & McDiarmid, G. W. (1996). The subject-matter preparation of teachers. In W. R. Houston (Ed.), *Handbook of research on teacher education* (pp. 437–449). New York: Macmillan.

Banerjee, A. C. (1991). Misconceptions of students and teachers in chemical equilibrium. *International Journal of Science Education, 13*, 487–494.

Barass, R. (1984). Some misconceptions and misunderstandings perpetuated by teachers and textbooks in biology. *Journal of Biological Education, 18*, 201–206.

Barba, R. H., & Rubba, P. A. (1992). A comparison of preservice and in-service earth and space science teachers' general mental abilities, content knowledge, and problem-solving skills. *Journal of Research in Science Teaching, 29*, 1021–1035.

Barba, R. H., & Rubba, P. A. (1993). Expert and novice, earth and space science: Teachers' declarative, procedural and structural knowledge. *International Journal of Science Education, 15*, 273–282.

Barnett, J., & Hodson, D. (2001). Pedagogical context knowledge: Toward a fuller understanding of what good science teachers know. *Science Education, 85*, 426–453.

Bellamy, M. L. (1990). Teacher knowledge, instruction, and student understandings: The relationship evidenced in the teaching of high school Mendelian genetics. *Dissertation Abstracts International, 51*(12), 4079A (UMI no. 9110272).

Bendall, S., Goldberg, F., & Galili, I. (1993). Prospective elementary teachers' prior knowledge about light. *Journal of Research in Science Teaching, 30*, 1169–1187.

Berg, T., & Brouwer, W. (1991). Teacher awareness of student alternate conceptions about rotational motion and gravity. *Journal of Research in Science Teaching, 28*, 3–18.

Birnie, H. H. (1989). The alternative conceptions of a particle theory of air possessed by year 1–5 primary students, their parents, and their teachers. *Research in Science Education, 19*, 25–36.

Blanchet, W. W. E. (1952). Prevalence of belief in science misconceptions among a group of in-service teachers in Georgia. *Science Education, 36*, 221–227.

Bol, L., & Strage, A. (1996). The contradiction between teachers' instructional goals and their assessment practices in high school biology courses. *Science Education, 80*, 145–163.

Borko, H., & Putman, R. T. (1996). Learning to teach. In D. C. Berliner & R. C. Caffee (Eds), *Handbook of educational psychology* (pp. 673–708). New York: Macmillan.

Boyer, R., & Tiberghien, A. (1989). Goals in physics and chemistry education as seen by teachers and high school students. *International Journal of Science Education, 11*, 297–308.

Bradford, C. S., & Dana, T. M. (1996). Exploring science teacher metaphorical thinking: A case study of a high school science teacher. *Journal of Science Teacher Education, 7*, 197–211.

Brickhouse, N. W. (1993). What counts as successful instruction? An account of a teacher's self-assessment. *Science Education, 77*, 115–129.

Briscoe, C. (1991). The dynamic interactions among beliefs, role metaphors, and teaching practices: A case study of teacher change. *Science Education, 75*, 185–199.

Briscoe, C. (1993). Using cognitive referents in making sense of teaching: A chemistry teacher's struggle to change assessment practices. *Journal of Research in Science Teaching, 30*, 971–987.

Bruce, L. R. (1971). A study of the relationship between the SCIS teachers' attitude toward the teacher-student relationship and question types. *Journal of Research in Science Teaching, 8*, 157–164.

Bryan, L. A., & Abell, S. K. (1999). The development of professional knowledge in learning to teach elementary science. *Journal of Research in Science Teaching, 36*, 1221–139.

Butts, D. P., & Raun, C. E. (1969). A study of teacher change. *Science Education, 53*, 3–8.

Calderhead, J. (1996). Teachers: Beliefs and knowledge. In D. C. Berliner & R. C. Chaffee (Eds.), *Handbook of educational psychology* (pp. 709–725). New York: Simon & Schuster Macmillan.

Carlsen, W. S. (1988). The effects of science teacher subject-matter knowledge on teacher questioning and classroom discourse. *Dissertation Abstracts International, 49*(06), 1421A (UMI no. 8814986).

Carlsen, W. S. (1991a). Effect of new biology teachers' subject-matter knowledge on curricular planning. *Science Education, 75*, 631–647.

Carlsen, W. S. (1991b). Saying what you know in the biology laboratory. *Teaching Education, 3*(2), 17–29.

Carlsen, W. S. (1991c). Subject-matter knowledge and science teaching: A pragmatic perspective. In J. Brophy (Ed.), *Advances in research on teaching: Vol. 2. Teachers' knowledge of subject matter as it relates to their teaching practice* (pp. 115–144). Greenwich, CT: JAI Press.

Carlsen, W. S. (1993). Teacher knowledge and discourse control: Quantitative evidence from novice biology teachers' classrooms. *Journal of Research in Science Teaching, 30*, 471–481.

Carré, C. (1993). Performance in subject-matter knowledge in science. In N. Bennett & C. Carré (Eds.), *Learning to teach* (pp. 18–35). London: Routledge.

Carrick, T. (1983). Some biology teachers' goals for advanced level teaching. *Journal of Biological Education, 17*, 205–214.

Carter, D. S. G., Carré, C. G., & Bennett, S. N. (1993). Students teachers' changing perceptions of their subject matter competence during an initial teacher training program. *Educational Research, 35*, 89–95.

Carter, K. (1990). Teachers' knowledge and learning to teach. In W. R. Houston (Ed.), *Handbook of research on teacher education* (pp. 291–310). New York: Macmillan.

Cheung, D., & Ng, P. (2000). Science teachers' beliefs about curriculum design. *Research in Science Education, 30*, 357–375.

Clandinin, D. J., & Connelly, F. M. (1996). Teachers' professional knowledge landscapes: Teachers stories-stories of teachers-school stories-stories of schools. *Educational Researcher, 25*(3), 24–30.

Clark, C., & Peterson, P. (1986). Teachers' thought processes. In M. C. Wittrock (Ed.), *Handbook of research on teaching* (3rd ed., pp. 255–296). New York: Macmillan.

Clermont, C. P., Borko, H., & Krajcik, J. S. (1994). Comparative study of the pedagogical content knowledge of experienced and novice chemical demonstrators. *Journal of Research in Science Teaching, 31*, 419–441.

Clermont, C. P., Krajcik, J. S., & Borko, H. (1993). The influence of an intensive in-service workshop on pedagogical content knowledge growth among novice chemical demonstrators. *Journal of Research in Science Teaching, 30*, 21–43.

Cochran, K. F., DeRuiter, J. A., & King, R. A. (1993). Pedagogical content knowing: An integrative model for teacher preparation. *Journal of Teacher Education, 44*, 263–272.

Cochran, K. F., & Jones, L. L. (1998). The subject matter knowledge of preservice science teachers. In B. J. Fraser & K. G. Tobin (Eds.), *International handbook of science education* (pp. 707–718). Dordrecht, the Netherlands: Kluwer Academic.

Cochran-Smith, M., & Lytle, S. L. (1993). *Inside/outside: Teacher research and knowledge.* New York: Teachers College Press.

Cochran-Smith, M., & Lytle, S. L. (1999). The teacher research movement: A decade later. *Educational Researcher, 28*(7), 15–25.

Committee on Science and Mathematics Teacher Preparation. (2001). *Educating teachers of science, mathematics, and technology: New practices for the new millennium.* Washington, DC: National Academy Press.

Cornett, J. W., Yeotis, C., & Terwilliger, L. (1990). Teacher personal practical theories and their influence upon teacher curricular and instructional actions: A case study of a secondary science teacher. *Science Education, 74*, 517–529.

Daehler, K. R., & Shinohara, M. (2001). A complete circuit is a complete circle: Exploring the potential of case materials and methods to develop teachers' content knowledge and pedagogical content knowledge of science. *Research in Science Education, 31*, 267–288.

Davies, D., & Rogers, M. (2000). Pre-service primary teachers' planning for science and technology activities: Influences and constraints. *Research in Science and Technological Education, 18*, 215–225.

de Jong, O. (2000). The teacher trainer as researcher: Exploring the initial pedagogical content concerns of prospective science teachers. *European Journal of Teacher Education, 23*, 127–137.

de Jong, O., Acampo, J., & Verdonk, A. (1995). Problems in teaching the topic of redox reactions. Actions and conceptions of chemistry teachers. *Journal of Research in Science Teaching, 32*, 1097–1110.

de Jong, O., Ahtee, M., Goodwin, A., Hatzinikita, V., & Koulaidis, V. (1999). An international study of prospective teachers' initial teaching conceptions and concerns: The case of teaching "combustion." *European Journal of Teacher Education, 22*, 45–59.

de Jong, O., Korthagen, F., & Wubbels, T. (1998). Research on science teacher education in Europe: Teacher thinking and conceptual change. In B. J. Fraser & K. G. Tobin (Eds.), *International handbook of science education* (pp. 745–758). Dordrecht, the Netherlands: Kluwer Academic.

de Jong, O., & Van Driel, J. (2001). The development of prospective teachers' concerns about teaching chemistry topics at a macro-micro-symbolic interface. In H. Behredt, H. Dahncke, R. Duit, W. Gräber, M. Komorek, A. Kross, & P. Reiska (Eds.), *Research in science education: Past, present and future* (pp. 271–276). Dordrecht, the Netherlands: Kluwer Academic.

de Jong, O., Veal, W. R., & van Driel, J. H. (2002). Exploring chemistry teachers' knowledge base. In J. K. Gilbert, O. de Jong, R. Justi, D. F. Treagust, & J. H. van Driel (Eds.), *Chemical education: Towards research-based practice* (pp. 369–390). Dordrecht, the Netherlands: Kluwer Academic.

Dobey, D. C. (1980). The effects of knowledge on elementary science inquiry teaching. *Dissertation Abstracts International, 41*(09), 3973A (UMI no. 8104519).

Dobey, D. C., & Schafer, L. E. (1984). The effects of knowledge on elementary science inquiry teaching. *Science Education, 68*, 39–51.

Doster, E. C., Jackson, D. F., & Smith, D. W. (1997). Modeling pedagogical content knowledge in physical science for prospective middle school teachers: Problems and possibilities. *Teacher Education Quarterly, 24*(4), 51–65.

Douvdevany, O., Dreyfus, A., & Jungwirth, E. (1997). Diagnostic instrument for determining junior high-school science teachers' understanding of functional relationships within the "living cell." *International Journal of Science Education, 19*, 593–606.

Druva, C. A., & Anderson, R. D. (1983). Science teacher characteristics by teacher behavior and by student outcome: A meta-analysis of research. *Journal of Research in Science Teaching, 20*, 467–479.

Duffee, L., & Aikenhead, G. (1992). Curriculum change, student evaluation, and teacher practical knowledge. *Science Education, 76*, 493–506.

Enochs, L., Oliver, S., & Wright, E. L. (1990). An evaluation of the perceived needs of secondary science teachers in Kansas. *Journal of Science Teacher Education, 1*, 74–79.

Feher, E., & Rice, K. (1987). A comparison of teacher-student conceptions in optics. In J. D. Novak (Ed.), *Proceedings of the Second International Seminar on Misconceptions and Education Strategies in Science and Mathematics* (Vol. II, pp. 108–117). Ithaca, NY: Department of Education, Cornell University.

Feldman, A. (2002). Multiple perspectives for the study of teaching: Knowledge, reason, understanding, and being. *Journal of Research in Science Teaching, 39*, 1032–1055.

Fenstermacher, G. D. (1994). The knower and the known: The nature of knowledge in research on teaching. In L. Darling-Hammond (Ed.), *Review of research in education* (Vol. 20, pp. 3–56). Washington, DC: American Educational Research Association.

Fernández-Balboa, J.-M., & Stiehl, J. (1995). The generic nature of pedagogical content knowledge among college professors. *Teaching & Teacher Education, 11*, 293–306.

Ferry, B. (1996). Probing personal knowledge: The use of a computer-based tool to help preservice teachers map subject matter knowledge. *Research in Science Education, 26*, 233–245.

Finley, F. N., Stewart, J., & Yarroch, W. L. (1982). Teachers' perceptions of important and difficult science content. *Science Education, 66*, 531–538.

Fischer-Mueller, J., & Zeidler, D. L. (2002). A case study of teacher beliefs in contemporary science education goals and classroom practices. *Science Educator, 11*, 46–57.

Flick, L. B. (1996). Understanding a generative learning model of instruction: A case study of elementary teacher planning. *Journal of Science Teacher Education, 7*, 95–122.

Flores, F., Lopez, A., Gallegos, L., & Barojas J. (2000). Transforming science and learning concepts of physics teachers. *International Journal of Science Education, 22*, 197–208.

Fraser, B. J., & Tobin, K. G. (Eds.). (1998). *International handbook of science education.* Dordrecht, The Netherlands: Kluwer Academic.

Frederik, I., van der Valk, T., Leite, L., & Thorén, I. (1999). Pre-service physics teachers and conceptual difficulties on temperature and heat. *European Journal of Teacher Education, 22,* 61–74.

Freire, A. M., & Sanches, M. (1992). Elements for a typology of teachers' conceptions of physics teaching. *Teaching & Teacher Education, 8,* 497–507.

Friedrichsen, P. (2002). A substantive-level theory of highly-regarded secondary biology teachers' science teaching orientations *Dissertation Abstracts International, 63*(07), 2496A (UMI No. 3060018).

Friedrichsen, P. M., & Dana, T. M. (2003). Using a card-sort task to elicit and clarify science-teaching orientations. *Journal of Science Teacher Education, 14,* 291–309.

Friedrichsen, P. M., & Dana, T. M. (2005). Substantive-level theory of highly regarded secondary biology teachers' science teaching orientations. *Journal of Research in Science Teaching, 42,* 218–244.

Furio, C., Vilches, A., Guisasola, J., & Romo, V. (2002). Spanish teachers' views of the goals of science education in secondary education. *Research in Science and Technological Education, 20,* 39–52.

Gabel, D. L., Samuel, K. V, & Hunn, D. (1987). Understanding the particulate nature of matter. *Journal of Chemical Education, 64,* 695–697.

Gallagher, J. J. (1989). Research on secondary school science teachers' practices, knowledge, and beliefs: A basis for restructuring. In M. Matyas, K. Tobin, & B. Fraser (Eds.), *Looking into windows: Qualitative research in science education* (pp. 43–57). Washington, DC: American Association for the Advancement of Science.

Gayford, C. (1998). The perspectives of science teachers in relation to current thinking about environmental education. *Research in Science & Technological Education, 16,* 101–113.

Geddis, A. N. (1993). Transforming subject-matter knowledge: The role of pedagogical content knowledge in learning to reflect on teaching. *International Journal of Science Education, 15,* 673–683.

Geddis, A. N., Onslow, B., Beynon, C., & Oesch, J. (1993). Transforming content knowledge: Learning to teach about isotopes. *Science Education, 77,* 575–591.

Geddis, A. N., & Roberts, D. A. (1998). As science students become science teachers: A perspective on learning orientation. *Journal of Science Teacher Education, 9,* 271–292.

Gess-Newsome, J. (1999). Secondary teachers' knowledge and beliefs about subject matter and their impact on instruction. In J. Gess-Newsome & N. G. Lederman (Eds.), *Examining pedagogical content knowledge: The construct and its implications for science education* (pp. 51–94). Boston: Kluwer.

Gess-Newsome, J., & Lederman, N. G. (1993). Preservice biology teachers' knowledge structures as a function of professional teacher education: A year-long assessment. *Science Education, 77,* 25–45.

Gess-Newsome, J., & Lederman, N. G. (1995). Biology teachers' perceptions of subject matter structure and its relationship to classroom practice. *Journal of Research in Science Teaching, 32,* 301–325.

Gess-Newsome, J., & Lederman, N. G. (Eds.). (1999). *Examining pedagogical content knowledge: The construct and its implications for science education.* Boston: Kluwer.

Ginns, I. S., & Watters, J. J. (1995). An analysis of scientific understanding of preservice elementary teacher education students. *Journal of Research in Science Teaching, 32,* 205–222.

Golby, M., Martin, A., & Porter, M. (1995). Some researchers' understanding of primary teaching: Comments on Mant and Summers' "Some primary-school teachers' understanding of the Earth's place in the universe." *Research Papers in Education, 10,* 297–302.

Gorin, G. (1994). Mole and chemical amount: A discussion of the fundamental measurements of chemistry. *Journal of Chemical Education, 71,* 114–116.

Greene, E. D., Jr. (1990). The logic of university students' misunderstanding of natural selection. *Journal of Research in Science Teaching, 27,* 875–885.

Greenwood, A. M. (2003). Factors influencing the development of career-change teachers' science teaching orientation. *Journal of Science Teacher Education, 14,* 217–234.

Grimmett, P. P., & MacKinnon, A. M. (1992). Craft knowledge and the education of teachers. *Review of Research in Education, 18*, 385–456.

Grossman, P. L. (1990). *The making of a teacher: Teacher knowledge and teacher education.* New York: Teachers College Press.

Grossman, P. L., Wilson, S. M., & Shulman, L. S. (1989). Teachers of substance: Subject matter knowledge for teaching. In M. C. Reynolds (Ed.), *Knowledge base for the beginning teacher* (pp. 23–36). New York: Pergamon.

Groves, F. H., & Pugh, A. F. (1999). Elementary pre-service teacher perceptions of the greenhouse effect. *Journal of Science Education and Technology, 8*, 75–81.

Guillaume, A. M. (1995). Elementary student teachers' situated learning of science education: The big, Big, BIG picture. *Journal of Science Teacher Education, 6*, 89–101.

Gurney, B. F. (1995). Tugboats and tennis games: Preservice conceptions of teaching and learning revealed through metaphors. *Journal of Research in Science Teaching, 32*, 569–583.

Gustafson, B., Guilbert, S., & MacDonald, D. (2002). Beginning elementary science teachers: Developing professional knowledge during a limited mentoring experience. *Research in Science Education, 32*, 281–302.

Gustafson, B. J., & Rowell, P. M. (1995). Elementary preservice teachers: Constructing conceptions about learning science, teaching science and the nature of science. *International Journal of Science Education, 17*, 589–605.

Haidar, A. H. (1997). Prospective chemistry teachers' conceptions of the conservation of matter and related concepts. *Journal of Research in Science Teaching, 34*, 181–197.

Halim, L., & Meerah, S. M. (2002). Science trainee teachers' pedagogical content knowledge and its influence on physics teaching. *Research in Science and Technological Education, 20*, 215–225.

Hand, B., & Treagust, D. F. (1997). Monitoring teachers' referents for classroom practice using metaphors. *International Journal of Science Education, 19*, 183–192.

Harlen, W. (1997). Primary teachers' understanding in science and its impact in the classroom. *Research in Science Education, 27*, 323–337.

Harlen, W., & Holroyd, C. (1997). Primary teachers' understanding of concepts of science: Impact on confidence and teaching. *International Journal of Science Education, 19*, 93–105.

Harty, H., Andersen, H. O., & Enochs, L. G. (1984). Science teaching attitudes and class control ideologies of preservice elementary teachers with and without early field experiences. *Science Education, 68*, 53–59.

Hashweh, M. Z. (1985). An exploratory study of teacher knowledge and teaching: The effects of science teachers' knowledge of subject-matter and their conceptions of learning on their teaching. *Dissertation Abstracts International, 46*(12), 3672A (UMI no. 8602482).

Hashweh, M. Z. (1987). Effects of subject-matter knowledge in the teaching of biology and physics. *Teaching and Teacher Education, 3*, 109–120.

Hashweh, M. Z. (1996a). Effects of science teachers' epistemological beliefs in teaching. *Journal of Research in Science Teaching, 33*, 47–63.

Hashweh, M. Z. (1996b). Palestinian science teachers' epistemological beliefs: A preliminary survey. *Research in Science Education, 26*, 89–102.

Hauslein, P. (1989). The effect of teaching upon the biology content cognitive structure of teachers. *Dissertation Abstracts International, 50*(08), 2369A (UMI no. 9002148).

Hauslein, P. L., Good, R. G., & Cummins, C. L. (1992). Biology content cognitive structure: From science student to science teacher. *Journal of Research in Science Teaching, 29*, 939–964.

Heller, P. (1987). Use of core propositions in solving current electricity problems. In J. D. Novak (Ed.), *Proceedings of the second international seminar on misconceptions and educational strategies in science and mathematics* (Vol. III, pp. 225–235). Ithaca, NY: Department of Education, Cornell University.

Hewson, P. W., & Hewson, M. G. A'B. (1987). Science teachers' conceptions of teaching: Implications for teacher education. *International Journal of Science Education, 9*, 425–440.

Hewson, P. W., & Hewson, M. G. A'B. (1989). Analysis and use of a task for identifying conceptions of teaching science. *Journal of Education for Teaching, 15*, 191–209.

Hewson, P. W., Kerby, H. W., & Cook, P. A. (1995). Determining the conceptions of teaching science held by experienced high school science teachers. *Journal of Research in Science Teaching, 32*, 503–520.

Heywood, D., & Parker, J. (1997). Confronting the analogy: Primary teachers exploring the usefulness of analogies in the teaching and learning of electricity. *International Journal of Science Education, 19*, 869–885.

Hirvonen, P. E., & Viiri, J. (2002). Physics student teachers' ideas about the objectives of practical work. *Science & Education, 11*, 305–316.

Hofstein, A., Mandler, V., Ben-Zvi, R., & Samuel, D. (1980). Teaching objectives in chemistry: A comparison of teachers' and students' priorities. *European Journal of Science Education, 2*, 61–66.

Hollon, R. E., Roth, K. J., & Anderson, C. W. (1991). Science teachers' conceptions of teaching and learning. In J. Brophy (Ed.), *Advances in research on teaching: Vol. 2. Teachers' knowledge of subject matter as it relates to their teaching practice* (pp. 145–186). Greenwich, CT: JAI Press.

Hope, J., & Townsend, M. (1983). Student teachers' understanding of science concepts. *Research in Science Education, 13*, 177–183.

Hoz, R., Tomer, Y., & Tamir, P. (1990). The relations between disciplinary and pedagogical knowledge and the length of teaching experience of biology and geography teachers. *Journal of Research in Science Teaching, 27*, 973–985.

Huibregtse, I., Korthagen, F., & Wubbels, T. (1994). Physics teachers' conceptions of learning, teaching and professional development. *International Journal of Science Education, 16*, 539–561.

Huston, P. H. (1975). A study of value orientations as a characteristic of secondary school students and teachers of chemistry. *Journal of Research in Science Teaching, 12*, 25–30.

Jasien, P. G., & Oberem, G. E. (2002). Understanding of elementary concepts in heat and temperature among college students and K–12 teachers. *Journal of Chemical Education, 79*, 889–895.

Jena, S. B. P. (1964). An analysis of errors of pupil teachers teaching general science in criticism lessons. *Science Education, 48*, 488–490.

Johnston, K. (1991). High school science teachers' conceptualizations of teaching and learning: Theory and practice. *European Journal of Teacher Education, 14*, 65–78.

Jones, D. R., & Harty, H. (1981). Classroom management—Pupil control ideologies before and after secondary school science student teaching. *Science Education, 65*, 3–10.

Jones, H. L., Thompson, B., & Miller, A. H. (1980). How teachers perceive similarities and differences among various teaching models. *Journal of Research in Science Teaching, 17*, 321–326.

Jones, M. G., Carter, G., & Rua, M. J. (1999). Children's concepts: Tools for transforming science teachers' knowledge. *Science Education, 83*, 545–557.

Jones, M. G., Rua, M. J., & Carter, G. (1998). Science teachers' conceptual growth within Vygotsky's zone of proximal development. *Journal of Research in Science Teaching, 35*, 967–985.

Jones, P. L., & Blankenship, J. W. (1970). A correlation of biology teachers' pupil control ideology and their classroom teaching practices. *Science Education, 54*, 263–265.

Jungwirth, E. (1975). Preconceived adaptation and inverted evolution: A case of distorted concept-formation in high-school biology. *Australian Science Teachers Journal, 21*(1), 95–100.

Justi, R., & Gilbert, J. (2002a). Modelling, teachers' views on the nature of modelling, and implications for the education of modellers. *International Journal of Science Education, 24*, 369–387.

Justi, R. S., & Gilbert, J. K. (2002b). Science teachers' knowledge about and attitudes towards the use of models and modeling in learning science. *International Journal of Science Education, 24*, 1273–1292.

Justi, R. S., & Gilbert, J. K. (2003). Teachers' views on the nature of models. *International Journal of Science Education, 25*, 1369–1386.

Kamen, M. (1996). A teacher's implementation of authentic assessment in an elementary science classroom. *Journal of Research in Science Teaching, 33*, 859–877.

Kennedy, M. M. (1998). Education reform and subject matter knowledge. *Journal of Research in Science Teaching, 35*, 249–263.

Kesidou, S., & Roseman, J. E. (2002). How well do middle school science programs measure up? Findings from Project 2061's curriculum review. *Journal of Research in Science Teaching, 39*, 522–549.

Keys, C. W., & Bryan, L. A. (2001). Co-constructing inquiry-based science with teachers: Essential research for lasting reform. *Journal of Research in Science Teaching, 38*, 631–645.

Kikas, E. (2004). Teachers' conceptions and misconceptions concerning three natural phenomena. *Journal of Research in Science Teaching, 41*, 432–448.

Koballa, T. R., Jr., Gräber, W., Coleman, D., & Kemp, A. C. (1999). Prospective teachers' conceptions of the knowledge base for teaching chemistry at the German gymnasium. *Journal of Science Teacher Education, 10*, 269–286.

Kokkotas, P., Vlachos, I., & Koulaidis, V. (1998). Teaching the topics of the particulate nature of matter in prospective teachers' training courses. *International Journal of Science Education, 20*, 291–303.

Kruger, C. (1990). Some primary teachers' ideas about energy. *Physics Education, 25*, 86–91.

Kruger, C., Palacio, D., & Summers, M. (1992). Surveys of English primary school teachers' conceptions of force, energy, and materials. *Science Education, 76*, 339–351.

Kruger, C., & Summers, M. (1988). Primary school teachers' understanding of science concepts. *Journal of Education for Teaching, 14*, 259–265.

Kruger, C., & Summers, M. (1989). An investigation of some primary school teachers' understanding of changes in materials. *School Science Review, 71*, 17–27.

Kruger, C., Summers, M., & Palacio. (1990a). An investigation of some English primary school teachers' understanding of the concepts force and gravity. *British Educational Research Journal, 16*, 383–397.

Kruger, C., Summers, M., & Palacio, D. (1990b). A survey of primary school teachers' conceptions of force and motion. *Educational Research, 32*, 83–95.

Kuhn, T. S. (1996). *The structure of scientific revolutions* (3rd ed.). Chicago: University of Chicago Press.

Lantz, O., & Kass, H. (1987). Chemistry teachers' functional paradigms. *Science Education, 71*, 117–134.

Latz, M. (1992). Preservice teachers' perceptions and concerns about classroom management and discipline: A qualitative investigation. *Journal of Science Teacher Education, 3*, 1–4.

Lawrenz, F. (1986). Misconceptions of physical science concepts among elementary school teachers. *School Science and Mathematics, 86*, 654–660.

Lawson, A. E. (2002). Sound and faulty arguments generated by preservice biology teachers when testing hypotheses involving unobservable entities. *Journal of Research in Science Teaching, 39*, 237–252.

Lederman, N. G., & Gess-Newsome, J. (1992). Do subject matter knowledge, pedagogical knowledge, and pedagogical content knowledge constitute the ideal gas law of science teaching? *Journal of Science Teacher Education, 3*, 16–20.

Lederman, N. G., Gess-Newsome, J., & Latz, M. S. (1994). The nature and development of preservice science teachers' conceptions of subject matter and pedagogy. *Journal of Research in Science Teaching, 31*, 129–146.

Lederman, N. G., & Latz, M. S. (1995). Knowledge structures in the preservice science teacher: Sources, development, interactions, and relationships to teaching. *Journal of Science Teacher Education, 6*, 1–19.

Lee, K. L. (1999). A comparison of university lecturers' and pre-service teachers' understanding of a chemical reaction at the particulate level. *Journal of Chemical Education, 76*, 1008–1012.

Lee, O. (1995). Subject matter knowledge, classroom management, and instructional practices in middle school science classrooms. *Journal of Research in Science Teaching, 32*, 423–440.

Lemberger, J., Hewson, P. W., & Park, H. (1999). Relationships between prospective secondary teachers' classroom practice and their conceptions of biology and of teaching science. *Science Education, 83*, 347–371.

Lin, H., Cheng, H., & Lawrenz, F. (2000). The assessment of students' and teachers' understanding of gas laws. *Journal of Chemical Education, 77*, 235–238.

Linder, C. J., & Erickson, G. L. (1989). A study of tertiary physics students' conceptualizations of sound. *International Journal of Science Education, 11*, 491–501.

Lloyd, J. K., Smith, R. G., Fay, C. L., Khang, G. N., Kam Wah, L. L., & Sai, C. L. (1998). Subject knowledge for science teaching at primary level: A comparison of pre-service teachers in England and Singapore. *International Journal of Science Education, 20*, 521–532.

Loughran, J., Gunstone, R., Berry, A., Milroy, P., & Mulhall, P. (2000, April). *Science cases in action: Developing an understanding of science teachers' pedagogical content knowledge.* Paper presented at the National Association for Research in Science Teaching, New Orleans.

Loughran, J., Milroy, P., Berry, A., Gunstone, R., & Mulhall, P. (2001). Documenting science teachers' pedagogical content knowledge through PaP-eRs. *Research in Science Education, 31*, 289–307.

Loughran, J., Mulhall, P., & Berry, A. (2004). In search of pedagogical content knowledge in science: Developing ways of articulating and documenting professional practice. *Journal of Research in Science Teaching, 41*, 370–391

Lynch, S. (1997). Novice teachers' encounter with national science education reform: Entanglements or intelligent interconnections? *Journal of Research in Science Teaching, 34*, 3–17.

Lynch, S., Pyke, C., & Jansen, J. (2003). Deepening understanding of science and mathematics education reform principles: Novice teachers design web-based units using Project 2061's curriculum analysis. *Journal of Science Teacher Education, 14*, 193–216.

Lyons, L. L., Freitag, P. K., & Hewson, P. W. (1997). Dichotomy in thinking, dilemma in actions: Researcher and teacher perspectives on a chemistry teaching practice. *Journal of Research in Science Teaching, 34*, 239–254.

MacDonald, D. (1992). Novice science teachers learn about interactive lesson revision. *Journal of Science Teacher Education, 3*, 85–91.

Magnusson, S., Krajcik, J., & Borko, H. (1999). Nature, sources and development of pedagogical content knowledge for science teaching. In J. Gess-Newsome & N. G. Lederman (Eds.), *Examining pedagogical content knowledge: The construct and its implications for science education* (pp. 95–132). Boston: Kluwer.

Mallinson, G. G., & Sturm, H. E. (1955). The science backgrounds and competencies of students preparing to teach in the elementary school. *Science Education, 39*, 398–405.

Mant, J., & Summers, M. (1993). Some primary school teachers' understanding of the Earth's place in the universe. *Research Papers in Education, 8*(1), 101–129.

Maor, D., & Taylor, P. C. (1995). Teacher epistemology and scientific inquiry in computerized classroom environments. *Journal of Research in Science Teaching, 32*, 839–854.

Marek, E. A., Eubanks, C., & Gallagher, T. H. (1990). Teachers' understanding and the use of the learning cycle. *Journal of Research in Science Teaching, 27*, 821–834.

Marek, E. A., Laubach, T. A., & Pedersen, J. (2003). Preservice elementary school teachers' understanding of theory based science education. *Journal of Science Teacher Education, 14*, 147–159.

Martín del Pozo, R. M. (2001). Prospective teachers' ideas about the relationships between concepts describing the composition of matter. *International Journal of Science Education, 23*, 353–371.

Mastrilli, T. M. (1997). Instructional analogies used by biology teachers: Implications for practice and teacher preparation. *Journal of Science Teacher Education, 8*, 187–204.

McIntosh, W. J., & Zeidler, D. L. (1988). Teachers' conceptions of the contemporary goals of science education. *Journal of Research in Science Teaching, 25*, 93–102.

McNay, M. (1991). Teachers' responses to original research in children's science. *Journal of Science Teacher Education, 2*, 57–60.

Mellado, V. (1998). The classroom practice of preservice teachers and their conceptions of teaching and learning science. *Science Education, 82*, 197–214.

Mellado, V., Blanco, L. J., & Ruiz, C. (1998). A framework for learning to teach science in initial primary teacher education. *Journal of Science Teacher Education, 9*, 195–219.

Meyer, H., Tabachnick, B. R., Hewson, P. W., Lemberger, J., & Park, H. (1999). Relationship between prospective elementary teachers' classroom practice and their conceptions of biology and of teaching science. *Science Education, 83*, 323–346.

Mills, R. A. (1997). Expert teaching and successful learning at the middle level: One teacher's story. *Middle School Journal, 29*, 30–39.

Mohapatra, J. K., & Bhattacharyya, S. (1989). Pupils, teachers, induced incorrect generalization and the concept of "force." *International Journal of Science Education, 11*, 429–436.

Morine-Dershimer, G. (1989). Preservice teachers' conceptions of content and pedagogy: Measuring growth in reflective, pedagogical decision-making. *Journal of Teacher Education, 40*(5), 46–52.

Morrison, J. A., & Lederman, N. G. (2003). Science teachers' diagnosis and understanding of students' preconceptions. *Science Education, 87*, 849–867.

Moscovici, H. (2001). Task dynamics in a college biology course for prospective elementary teachers. *School Science and Mathematics, 101*, 372–379.

Munby, H. (1986). Metaphor in the thinking of teachers: An exploratory study. *Journal of Curriculum Studies, 18*, 197–209.

Munby, H., Cunningham, M., & Lock, C. (2000). School science culture: A case study of barriers to developing professional knowledge. *Science Education, 84*, 193–211.

Munby, H., & Russell, T. (1992). Transforming chemistry research into teaching: The complexities of adopting new frames for experience. In T. Russell & H. Munby (Eds.), *Teachers and teaching: From classroom to reflection* (pp. 9–108). London: Falmer Press.

Munby, H., & Russell, T. (1994). The authority of experience in learning to teach: Messages from a physics methods class. *Journal of Teacher Education, 45*(2), 86–95.

Munby, H., Russell, T., & Martin, A. K. (2001). Teachers' knowledge and how it develops. In V. Richardson (Ed.), *Handbook of research on teaching* (4th ed., pp. 877–904). Washington, DC: American Educational Research Association.

National Research Council. (1999). *Selecting instructional materials*. Washington, DC: National Academy Press.

National Science Foundation. (1996). *Shaping the future: New expectations for undergraduate education in science, mathematics, engineering, and technology*. Arlington, VA: Author.

National Science Teachers Association. (1998). *Standards for science teacher preparation*. Arlington, VA: Author. Retrieved August 28, 2003 from http://www.nsta.org/main/pdfs/nsta98standards.pdf

Newton, D. P., & Newton, L. D. (2001). Subject content knowledge and teacher talk in the primary science classroom. *European Journal of Teacher Education, 24*, 369–379.

Northfield, J. R., & Fraser, B. J. (1977). Teacher characteristics and pupil outcomes in secondary science classrooms. *Research in Science Education, 7*, 113–121.

Nottis, K. E. K., & McFarland, J. (2001). A comparative analysis of pre-service teacher analogies generated for process and structure concepts. *Electronic Journal of Science Education, 5*. Retrieved April 15, 2003, from http://unr.edu/homepage/crowther/ejse/ejse5n4.html

Nussbaum, J. (1981). Towards the diagnosis by science teachers of pupils' misconceptions: An exercise with student teachers. *European Journal of Science Education, 3*, 159–169.

O'Brien, P. J., Huether, C. A., & Philliber, S. G. (1978). Teacher knowledge and use of population education materials: Report from national surveys. *Science Education, 62*, 429–442.

Odom, A. L., & Settlage, J., Jr. (1996). Teachers' understandings of the learning cycle as assessed with a two-tier test. *Journal of Science Teacher Education, 7*, 123–142.

Olson, J. K. (1990). Teachers' conceptions of their subject and laboratory work in science. In E. Hegarty-Hazel (Ed.), *The student laboratory and the science curriculum* (pp. 201–220). London: Routledge.

Pardhan, H., & Bano, Y. (2001). Science teachers' alternative conceptions about direct-currents. *International Journal of Science Education, 23*, 301–318.

Parker, J., & Heywood, D. (1998). The earth and beyond: Developing primary teachers' understanding of basic astronomical events. *International Journal of Science Education, 20*, 503–520.

Parker, J., & Heywood, D. (2000). Exploring the relationship between subject knowledge and pedagogic knowledge in primary teachers' learning about forces. *International Journal of Science Education, 22*, 89–111.

Parsons, S. (1991). Preservice secondary science teachers making sense of constructivism. *Research in Science Education, 21*, 271–280.

Peacock, A., & Gates, S. (2000). Newly qualified primary teachers' perceptions of the role of text material in teaching science. *Research in Science and Technological Education, 18*, 155–171.

Perkes, V. A. (1975). Relationships between a teacher's background and sensed adequacy to teach elementary science. *Journal of Research in Science Teaching, 12*, 85–88.

Peterson, R., & Treagust, D. (1995). Developing preservice teachers' pedagogical reasoning ability. *Research in Science Education, 25*, 291–305.

Pine, K., Messer, D., & St. John, K. (2001). Children's misconceptions in primary science: A survey of teachers' views. *Research in Science and Technological Education, 19*, 79–96.

Pinnegar, S. E. (1989). Teachers' knowledge of students and classrooms. *Dissertation Abstracts International, 51*(01), 0142A (UMI no. 9014676).

Porlán, R., & Martín del Pozo, R. (2004). The conceptions of in-service and prospective primary school teachers about the teaching and learning of science. *Journal of Science Teacher Education, 15*, 39–62.

Preece, P. F. W. (1997). Force and motion: Pre-service and practicing secondary science teachers' language and understanding. *Research in Science and Technological Education, 15*, 123–128.

Quílez-Pardo, J., & Solaz-Portolés, J. J. (1995). Students' and teachers' misapplication of Le Chatelier's principle: Implications for the teaching of chemical equilibrium. *Journal of Research in Science Teaching, 32*, 939–957.

Raina, M. K. (1970). Prospective science teachers' perception of the ideal pupil. *Journal of Research in Science Teaching, 7*, 169–172.

Raina, T. N. (1967). How well prospective teachers know general science? *Science Education, 51*, 234–239.

Ralya, L. L., & Ralya, L. L. (1938). Some misconceptions in science held by prospective elementary teachers. *Science Education, 22*, 244–251.

Reynolds, M. C. (Ed.). (1989). *Knowledge base for the beginning teacher*. Oxford, England: Pergamon.

Ritchie, S. M. (1999). The craft of intervention: A personal practical theory for a teacher's within-group interactions. *Science Education, 83*, 213–231.

Roberts, D. A., & Chastko, A. M. (1990). Absorption, refraction, reflection: An exploration of beginning science teacher thinking. *Science Education, 74*, 197–224.

Rollnick, M., & Rutherford, M. (1990). African primary school teachers—what ideas do they hold on air and air pressure? *International Journal of Science Education, 12*, 101–113.

Roth, K. J. (1987, April). *Helping science teachers change: The critical role of teachers' knowledge about science and science learning*. Paper presented at the annual meeting of the American Educational Research Association, Washington, DC.

Roth, W.-M. (1992). The particulate theory of matter for preservice elementary teachers. *Journal of Science Teacher Education, 3*, 115–122.

Roth, W.-M., McGinn, M. K., & Bowen, M. G. (1998). How prepared are preservice teachers to teach scientific inquiry? Levels of performance in scientific representation practices. *Journal of Science Teacher Education, 9*, 25–48.

Rothman, A. I., Welch, W. W., & Walberg, H. J. (1969). Physics teacher characteristics and student learning. *Journal of Research in Science Teaching, 6*, 59–63.

Russell, T., Bell, D., McGuigan, L., Qualter, A., Quinn, J., & Schilling, M. (1992). Teachers' conceptual understanding in science: Needs and possibilities in the primary phase. In L. D. Newton (Ed.), *Primary science* (pp. 69–83). Clevedon, UK: Multilingual Matters.

Russell, T., & Munby, H. (1991). Reframing: The role of experience in developing teachers' professional knowledge. In D. Schön (Ed.), *The reflective turn: Case studies in and on educational practice* (pp. 164–187). New York: Teachers College Press.

Ryan, C., Sanchez Jimenez, J. M., & Onorbe de Torre, A. M. (1989). Scientific ideas held by intending primary teachers in Britain and Spain. *European Journal of Teacher Education, 12,* 239–251.

Sanchez, G., & Valcárcel, M. V. (1999). Science teachers' views and practices in planning for teaching. *Journal of Research in Science Teaching, 36,* 493–513.

Sanders, L. R., Borko, H., & Lockard, J. D. (1993). Secondary science teachers' knowledge base when teaching science courses in and out of their area of certification. *Journal of Research in Science Teaching, 30,* 723–736.

Sanders, M. (1993). Erroneous ideas about respiration: The teacher factor. *Journal of Research in Science Teaching, 30,* 919–934.

Schibeci, R. A. (1981). Do teachers rate science attitude objectives as highly as cognitive objectives? *Journal of Research in Science Teaching, 18,* 69–72.

Schön, D. A. (1983). *The reflective practitioner.* New York: Basic Books.

Schön, D. A. (1987). *Educating the reflective practitioner: Toward a new design for teaching and learning in the professions.* San Francisco: Jossey-Bass.

Schoon, K. J. (1995). The origin and extent of alternative conceptions in the earth and space sciences: A survey of pre-service elementary teachers. *Journal of Elementary Science Education, 7*(2), 27–46.

Schoon, K. J., & Boone, W. J. (1998). Self-efficacy and alternative conceptions of science of preservice elementary teachers. *Science Education, 82,* 553–568.

Schriver, M., & Czerniak, C. M. (1999). A comparison of middle and junior high science teachers' levels of efficacy and knowledge of developmentally appropriate curriculum and instruction. *Journal of Science Teacher Education, 10,* 21–42.

Schwab, J. J. (1964). The structure of disciplines: Meanings and significance. In G. W. Ford & L. Pugno (Eds.), *The structure of knowledge and the curriculum.* Chicago: Rand McNally.

Sciarretta, M. R., Stilli, R., & Vicentini Missoni, M. (1990). On the thermal properties of materials: Common-sense knowledge of Italian students and teachers. *International Journal of Science Education, 12,* 369–379.

Sequeira, M., Leite, L., & Duarte, M. D. C. (1993). Portuguese science teachers' education, attitudes, and practice relative to the issue of alternative conceptions. *Journal of Research in Science Teaching, 30,* 845–856.

Settlage, J. (2000). Understanding the learning cycle: Influences on abilities to embrace the approach by preservice elementary school teachers. *Science Education, 84,* 43–50.

Shallcross, T., Spink, E., Stephenson, P., & Warwick, P. (2002). How primary trainee teachers perceive the development of their own scientific knowledge: Links between confidence, content and competence? *International Journal of Science Education, 24,* 1293–1312.

Shrigley, R. L. (1974). The correlation of science attitude and science knowledge of preservice elementary teachers. *Science Education, 58,* 143–151.

Shugart, S. S., & Hounshell, P. B. (1995). Subject matter competence and the recruitment and retention of secondary science teachers. *Journal of Research in Science Teaching, 32,* 63–70.

Shulman, L. S. (1986). Those who understand: Knowledge growth in teaching. *Educational Researcher, 15*(2), 4–14.

Shulman, L. S. (1987). Knowledge and teaching: Foundations of the new reform. *Harvard Educational Review, 57*(1), 1–22.

Shulman, L. S. (1999). Foreword. In J. Gess-Newsome & N. G. Lederman (Eds.), *Examining pedagogical content knowledge: The construct and its implications for science education* (pp. ix–xii). Boston: Kluwer

Skamp, K. (1995). Student teachers' conceptions of how to recognize a "good" primary science teacher: Does two years in a teacher education program make a difference? *Research in Science Education, 25,* 395–429.

Skamp, K., & Mueller, A. (2001). Student teachers' conceptions about effective primary science teaching: A longitudinal study. *International Journal of Science Education, 23,* 331–351.

Smith, D. C. (1987). Primary teachers' misconceptions about light and shadows. In J. D. Novak (Ed.), *Proceedings of the second international seminar on misconceptions and educational strategies in science and mathematics* (Vol. II, pp. 461–476). Ithaca, NY: Department of Education, Cornell University.

Smith, D. C. (2000). Content and pedagogical content knowledge for elementary science teacher educators: Knowing our students. *Journal of Science Teacher Education, 11*, 27–46.

Smith, D. C., & Neale, D. C. (1989). The construction of subject matter knowledge in primary science teaching. *Teaching & Teacher Education, 5*, 1–20.

Smith, D. C., & Neale, D. C. (1991). The construction of subject-matter knowledge in primary science teaching. In J. Brophy (Ed.), *Advances in research on teaching: Vol. 2. Teachers' knowledge of subject matter as it relates to their teaching practice* (pp. 187–244). Greenwich, CT: JAI Press.

Smith, D. M., & Cooper, B. (1967). A study of various techniques in teaching science in the elementary school. *School Science and Mathematics, 67*, 559–566.

Smith, R. G. (1997). "Before teaching this I'd do a lot of reading." Preparing primary student teachers to teach science. *Research in Science Education, 27*, 141–154.

Smith, R. G., & Peacock, G. (1992). Tackling contradictions in teachers' understanding of gravity and air resistance. *Evaluation and Research in Education, 6*, 113–127.

So, W. W. (1997). A study of teacher cognition in planning elementary science lessons. *Research in Science Education, 27*, 71–86.

Sorsby, B. D., & Watson, E. (1993). Students' and teachers' confidence about their own science knowledge and skills in relation to the science national curriculum. *British Journal of In-service Education, 19*(3), 43–49.

Stalheim, W. (1986). Teacher characteristics and characteristics of the teaching environment as predictors of the use of inquiry laboratory activities by high school biology teachers. *Dissertation Abstracts International, 47*(07), 2530A (UMI no. 8624669).

Stepans, J., Dyche, S., & Beiswenger, R. (1988). The effects of two instructional models in bringing about a conceptual change in the understanding of science concepts by prospective elementary teachers. *Science Education, 72*, 185–195.

Stevens, C., & Wenner, G. (1996). Elementary preservice teachers' knowledge and beliefs regarding science and mathematics. *School Science and Mathematics, 96*, 2–9.

Stocklmayer, S. M., & Treagust, D. F. (1996). Images of electricity: How do novices and experts model electric current? *International Journal of Science Education, 18*, 163–178.

Stofflett, R. T., & Stefanon, L. (1996). Elementary teacher candidates' conceptions of successful conceptual change teaching. *Journal of Elementary Science Education, 8*(2), 1–20.

Strömdahl, H., Tulberg, A., & Lybeck, L. (1994). The qualitatively different conceptions of 1 mol. *International Journal of Science Education, 16*, 17–26.

Summers, M. (1992). Improving primary school teachers' understanding of science concepts: Theory into practice. *International Journal of Science Education, 14*, 25–40.

Summers, M., & Kruger, C. (1992). Research into English primary school teachers' understanding of the concept of energy. *Evaluation and Research in Education, 6*, 95–111.

Summers, M., & Kruger, C. (1994). A longitudinal study of a constructivist approach to improving primary science teachers' subject matter knowledge in science. *Teaching & Teacher Education, 10*, 499–519.

Summers, M., & Mant, J. (1995). A misconceived view of subject-matter knowledge in primary science education: A response to Golby *et al.* "Some researchers' understanding of primary teaching." *Research Papers in Education, 10*, 303–307.

Suzuki, M. (2003). Conversations about the moon with prospective teachers in Japan. *Science Education, 87*, 892–910.

Swann, A. H. (1969). Qualification of Mississippi public high school teachers of physics, chemistry, and physical science survey. *Science Education, 53*, 135–136.

Sweeney, A. E., Bula, O. A., & Cornett, J. W. (2001). The role of personal practice theories in the professional development of a beginning high school chemistry teacher. *Journal of Research in Science Teaching, 38*, 408–441.

Symington, D. (1980). Primary school teachers' knowledge of science and its effect on choice between alternative verbal behaviors. *Research in Science Education, 10*, 69–76.

Symington, D. (1982). Lack of background in science: Is it likely to always adversely affect the classroom performance of primary teachers in science lessons? *Research in Science Education, 12*, 64–70.

Symington, D., & Hayes, D. (1989). What do you need to know to teach science in the primary school? *Research in Science Education, 19*, 278–285.

Tamir, P. (1988). Subject matter and related pedagogical knowledge in teacher education. *Teaching & Teacher Education, 4*, 99–110.

Tamir, P. (1992). High school biology teachers' image of subject matter: An exploratory study. *American Biology Teacher, 54*, 212–217.

Tamir, P., & Jungwirth, E. (1972). Teaching objectives in biology: Priorities and expectations. *Science Education, 56*, 31–39.

Taylor, J. A., & Dana, T. M. (2003). Secondary school physics teachers' conceptions of scientific evidence: An exploratory case study. *Journal of Research in Science Teaching, 40*, 721–736.

Tobin, K., & LaMaster, S. U. (1995). Relationships between metaphors, beliefs, and actions in a context of science curriculum change. *Journal of Research in Science Teaching, 32*, 225–242.

Treagust, D. F. (1991). A case study of two exemplary biology teachers. *Journal of Research in Science Teaching, 28*, 329–342.

Trend, R. D. (2000). Conceptions of geological time among primary teacher trainees with reference to their engagement with geoscience, history and science. *International Journal of Science Education, 22*, 539–555.

Trend, D. R. (2001). Deep time framework: A preliminary study of U.K. primary teachers' conceptions of geological time and perceptions of geoscience. *Journal of Research in Science Teaching, 38*, 191–221.

Trigwell, K., Prosser, M., & Taylor, P. (1994). Qualitative differences in approaches to teaching first year university science. *Higher Education, 27*, 75–84.

Trumper, R. (1997). A survey of conceptions of energy of Israeli pre-service high school biology teachers. *International Journal of Science Education, 19*, 31–46.

Trumper, R. (1999). A longitudinal study of physics students' conceptions of force in pre-service training for high school teachers. *European Journal of Teacher Education, 22*, 247–258.

Trumper, R., & Gorsky, P. (1997). A survey of biology students' conceptions of force in pre-service training for high school teachers. *Research in Science and Technological Education, 15*, 133–147.

Trundle, K. C., Atwood, R. K., & Christopher J. E. (2002). Preservice elementary teachers' conceptions of moon phases before and after instruction. *Journal of Research in Science Teaching, 39*, 633–658.

Tsai, C. (2001). A science teacher's reflections and knowledge growth about STS instruction after actual implementation. *Science Education, 86*, 23–41.

Tulberg, A., Strömdahl, H., & Lybeck, L. (1994). Students' conceptions of 1 mol and educators' conceptions of how they teach "the mole." *International Journal of Science Education, 16*, 145–156.

U.S. Department of Education. (2002). *Meeting the highly qualified teachers challenge: The Secretary's annual report on teacher quality*. Washington, DC: U.S. Department of Education, Office of Postsecondary Education, Office of Policy, Planning, and Innovation.

Uselton, H. W., Bledsoe J. C., & Koelsche, C. L. (1963). Factors related to competence in science of prospective elementary teachers. *Science Education, 47*, 506–508.

van der Valk, T., & Broekman, H. (1999). The lesson preparation method: A way of investigating pre-service teachers' pedagogical content knowledge. *European Journal of Teacher Education, 22*, 11–22.

van Driel, J. H., de Jong, O., & Verloop, N. (2002). The development of preservice chemistry teachers' pedagogical content knowledge. *Science Education, 86*, 572–590.

van Driel, J. H., & Verloop, N. (1999). Teachers' knowledge of models and modeling in science. *International Journal of Science Education, 21*, 1141–1153.

van Driel, J. H., & Verloop, N. (2002). Experienced teachers' knowledge of teaching and learning of models and modeling in science education. *International Journal of Science Education, 24*, 1255–1272.

van Driel, J. H., Verloop, N., & de Vos, W. (1998). Developing science teachers' pedagogical content knowledge. *Journal of Research in Science Teaching, 35,* 673–695.

Veal, W. R. (1997). *The evolution of pedagogical content knowledge in chemistry and physics prospective secondary teachers.* Unpublished doctoral dissertation, University of Georgia, Athens.

Veiga, M., Costa Pereira, D., & Maskill, R. (1989). Teachers' language and pupils' ideas in science lessons: Can teachers avoid reinforcing wrong ideas? *International Journal of Science Education, 11,* 465–479.

Waldrip, B. G., Knight, B. A., & Webb, G. (2002). "Science words and explanations": What do student teachers think they mean? *Electronic Journal of Literacy Through Science, 1.* Retrieved April 15, 2003, from http://sweeneyhall.sjsu.edu/ejlts/current_issue/articles/index.html

Wandersee, J. H., Mintzes, J. J., & Novak, J. D. (1994). Research on alternative conceptions in science. In D. L. Gabel (Ed.), *Handbook of research on science teaching and learning* (pp. 177–210). New York: Macmillan.

Webb, P. (1992). Primary science teachers' understanding of electric current. *International Journal of Science Education, 14,* 423–429.

Weinstein, C. S. (1989). Teacher education students' preconceptions of teaching. *Journal of Teacher Education, 40*(2), 53–60.

Wenner, G. (1993). Relationship between science knowledge levels and beliefs toward science instruction held by preservice elementary teachers. *Journal of Science Education and Technology, 2,* 461–468.

Wenner, G. (1995). Science knowledge and efficacy beliefs among preservice elementary teachers: A follow-up study. *Journal of Science Education and Technology, 4,* 307–315.

Willson, M., & Williams, D. (1996). Trainee teachers' misunderstandings in chemistry: Diagnosis and evaluation using concept mapping. *School Science Review, 77,* 107–113.

Wilson, S., Shulman, L., & Richert, A. (1987). "150 different ways" of knowing: Representations of knowledge in teaching. In J. Calderhead (Ed.), *Exploring teachers' thinking* (pp. 104–124). London: Cassell.

Windschitl, M. (2002). Framing constructivism in practice as the negotiation of dilemmas: An analysis of the conceptual, pedagogical, cultural, and political challenges facing teachers. *Review of Educational Research, 72,* 131–175.

Wubbels, T. (1992). Taking account of student teachers' preconceptions. *Teaching & Teacher Education, 8,* 137–149.

Yip, D. Y. (2001). Assessing and developing the concept of assumptions in science teachers. *Journal of Science Education and Technology, 10,* 173–179.

Yip, D. Y., Chung, C. M., & Mak, S. Y. (1998). The subject matter knowledge in physics related topics of Hong Kong junior secondary science teachers. *Journal of Science Education and Technology, 7,* 319–328.

Zeitler, W. R. (1984). Science backgrounds, conceptions of purposes, and concerns of preservice teachers about teaching children science. *Science Education, 68,* 505–520.

Zembal-Saul, C., Blumenfeld, P., & Krajcik, J. (2000). Influence of guided cycles of planning, teaching, and reflection on prospective elementary teachers' science content representations. *Journal of Research in Science Teaching, 37,* 318–339.

Zembal-Saul, C., Haefner, L. A., Avraamidou, L., Severs, M., & Dana, T. (2002). Web-based portfolios: A vehicle for examining prospective elementary teachers' developing understandings of teaching science. *Journal of Science Teacher Education, 13,* 283–302.

Zembal-Saul, C., Krajcik, J., & Blumenfeld, P. (2002). Elementary student teachers' science content representations. *Journal of Research in Science Teaching, 39,* 443–463.

Zohar, A. (1999). Teachers' metacognitive knowledge and the instruction of higher order thinking. *Teaching and Teacher Education, 15,* 413–429.

CHAPTER 37

Learning to Teach Science

Tom Russell
Andrea K. Martin
Queen's University, Canada

We write as teacher educators who are passionate about improving teacher education. As teaching becomes increasingly complex, those learning to teach science deserve all the help we can provide. We argue here that such help involves much more than the transfer of insights derived from research on science teaching and science teacher education. Teacher education is also becoming more complex, and therein lies part of our challenge. In this chapter we draw on our experiences as teacher educators to inform our accounts and interpretations of research related to learning to teach science.

One of the most striking observations we can offer concerns the extent to which science education research appears *not* to be extended and extrapolated to programs of science teacher education. Research appears to confirm what our own experiences as teacher educators tell us: *A fundamental challenge resides in the prior teaching and learning beliefs and experiences of those learning to teach,* just as a fundamental challenge of teaching science resides in students' prior beliefs about phenomena. The research associated with constructivism and conceptual change reminds us that beliefs and experiences are deeply intertwined. Just as children in elementary, middle, and secondary schools tend to be unaware of their initial beliefs about phenomena and unaware of how personal experiences shape and constrain those beliefs, so those who are learning to teach science tend to be unaware of their initial beliefs about what and how they will learn in a program of science teacher education. In our experience, many prospective teachers assume that they know very little about teaching, that they will learn teaching ideas in university classes, and that they will apply what they learn in classes during their school practicum experiences. Is this really very different from children's assumptions in a science class? Do they not assume that they know little about science, that they will be taught science concepts, and that they will apply what they learn when given opportunities by their teachers? *"Science separates knowledge from experience"* (Franklin, 1994). Similarly, school and university alike often treat students in ways that imply that experience has little to do with knowledge. Those learning to teach tend to be unaware that they may have learned more about *how* to teach science than about science and scientific concepts while they were studying science in school and university classes.

Northfield (1998) tackles this theme in a discussion of how science teacher education is *practiced.* He begins by quoting an unnamed individual's provocative comment about teacher education: "Teacher preparation is necessary and worthwhile, but it is generally conducted in the wrong place, at the wrong time, for too little time" (p. 695). Northfield's concern is one that we share: *How does school experience influence an individual's learning to teach?* And he immediately offers a challenging answer: "If experience is seen as a place to *apply* the ideas and theories of the course, then the campus program could be seen to be out of step with the demands and concerns of the new teacher (the wrong time, the wrong place and too little time)" (p. 696).

Northfield makes the following assertions that help us frame our task in this chapter:

> As a starting point, consider the proposition that teacher educators could overestimate what they can teach new teachers, while also underestimating their ability to provide appropriate conditions for them to learn about teaching. Such a proposition serves to shift the teacher education task (at both preservice and inservice levels) from one of delivering what has to be known by teachers to one of providing better conditions for learning about teaching. (p. 698)

Whether in the science classroom or in the science teacher education program, how individuals learn from experience remains a poorly understood phenomenon.

Chapters in research handbooks often attempt to provide comprehensive surveys of published research. While we are attentive to such research, our major goal in this chapter is to stimulate new perspectives for thinking about the values and actions that occur in preservice programs for those who are learning to teach science. We summarize our overall argument in the following points:

1. Calls for change to how science is taught in schools and universities can be traced to the 1960s and even earlier in the twentieth century. Dewey's (1938) contrast between traditional and progressive education shows just how little the fundamentals of school culture have changed (Sarason, 1996).

2. Teaching for conceptual development and change has been a dominant theme in the science education research literature for several decades, and only a small fraction of that research considers how individuals learn to teach science in preservice programs.

3. Teaching practices are far more stable (Sarason, 1996) than those who call for change (see Handelsman et al., 2004) seem to realize. Logic alone cannot change teaching practices that were initially learned indirectly and unintentionally from one's own teachers.

4. Conceptual change research indicates that achieving more complete conceptual understanding (and the significant epistemological change that must accompany that understanding; see Elby, 2001) requires dramatic changes in how we teach (Knight, 2004, pp. 42–45).

5. Learning from experience is an undervalued and neglected aspect of science teaching and learning that is similarly undervalued in programs where individuals learn to teach science. This undervaluation is rooted in the value that the university associates with rigorous argument and positivist epistemology.

While learning from experience is being recognized as an element of teachers' professional development (Russell & Bullock, 1999) as attention is given to teacher research and action research, these tend to be undervalued as inferior forms of research.

6. Learning to teach science must *model* conceptual change approaches both for teaching fundamental concepts of science and for teaching fundamental concepts of teaching and learning.

One of this chapter's major contributions involves highlighting the need for explicit attention to epistemological issues associated with teaching science and learning to teach science. As long as the university's dominant epistemology is fundamentally positivist, we conclude that breakthroughs in how science is taught and learned are unlikely to be achieved.

To acknowledge, at least modestly, the need for attention to narrative as well as propositional knowledge, we include a number of "narrative boxes" that document some of Tom Russell's personal learning from experience over a quarter-century of teaching individuals how to teach science. Each narrative box ends with an italicized question related to learning from one's own teaching and learning experiences.

THE COMPLEX CHALLENGE OF CONCEPTUAL CHANGE

Venturing into the literature of conceptual change is daunting but absolutely essential to learning to teach science. Pfundt and Duit (1994) refer to approximately 3500 studies related to students' alternative conceptions in science. Research on this topic has moved from simply identifying conceptual changes and bringing students' beliefs more in line with scientists' to mapping how conceptions are developed (White, 2001). The nomenclature itself is varied, and the labels used include *misconceptions, alternative conceptions, preconceptions, naïve conceptions, intuitive science,* or *alternative frameworks* (Guzzetti, Snyder, Glass, & Gamas, 1993). Whatever the label, conceptual change is central to learning and teaching science (see Chapter 2, this volume) and to learning to teach science.

Narrative Box 37–1
Is Experience Important for Learning?

I began teaching as a Peace Corps Volunteer in northern Nigeria. For two years, with my students' help and patience, I taught myself to teach—learning from experience as best I could. During a master's program in which I gained certification as a physics teacher, I noticed that I had many more questions than most people in my classes. Experience generates questions, both for teachers and for students.

Were your own science classes rich in hands-on experiences that stimulated your personal interest in understanding science concepts? How important is experience for motivating you to understand a topic more fully and completely?

As Duschl and Hamilton (1998) point out, conceptual change involves the restructuring of both declarative and procedural knowledge. Prospective science teachers need to reframe their own understanding of science learning to recognize the inherent challenges associated with subjecting prevailing concepts to scrutiny and validation. Unless new teachers understand why conceptual change is so complex, they are unlikely to be able to effect changes in patterns of classroom interaction.

Teaching Conceptual Change

The extensive work of Novak (1987, 1989, 1993) provides a framework both for understanding why conceptual change is so critical if students are to *learn how to learn* in science and for understanding why instruction often fails. Novak builds on Ausubel's (1968) hypothesis that the single most important factor influencing learning is prior knowledge and Kelly's (1955) personal construct theory that emphasizes the view that knowledge is constructed and is highly personal, idiosyncratic, and socially negotiated. Novak and Gowin (1984) advance a set of three knowledge claims about the preconceptions that students carry into their science classes, with subsequent effects on their learning (Wandersee, Mintzes, & Novak, 1994).

1. Learners are not "empty vessels" but bring with them a finite but diverse set of ideas about natural objects and events, which are often inconsistent with scientific explanations.
2. Students' alternative conceptions are tenacious and resistant to extinction by conventional teaching strategies. Wandersee (1986) suggests that the similarities between students' ideas and ideas that science has discarded can provide a worthwhile heuristic opportunity as students struggle with their own conceptual shortcomings.
3. Alternative conceptions are the product of a diverse set of personal experiences that include direct observation of natural objects and events, peer culture, everyday language, the mass media, as well as teachers' explanations and instructional materials.

Novak and his group also advance three claims regarding successful science learners: (a) the process of constructing meanings relies on the development of elaborate, strongly hierarchical, well-differentiated, and highly integrated frameworks of related concepts; (b) conceptual change requires knowledge to be restructured by making and breaking interconnections between concepts and replacing or substituting one concept with another; and (c) successful science learners regularly use strategies that enable them to be metacognitive and to plan, monitor, control, and regulate their own learning (Mintzes, Wandersee, & Novak, 1997).

Posner, Strike, Hewson, and Gertzog's (1982) theory of conceptual change makes a valuable contribution to understanding its complexity and the conditions necessary for change to occur. Duit and Treagust (1998) describe it as the most influential theory on conceptual change in science education, with wide-ranging applications in other fields as well. Posner et al. propose that conceptual change will not occur unless learners experience some level of dissatisfaction with their current beliefs or understandings. For a new idea to be accepted, it must meet three conditions: *intelligibility* (understandable), *plausibility* (reasonable), and *fruitfulness* (useful). Learners need to understand what an idea means, what its potential or actual utility is, and why scientists are concerned with coherence and internal consistency. If an idea is plausible, then learners need to be able to reconcile the idea with their own beliefs and to be able to make sense of it. Hodson (1998) points out that "making sense" in scientific terms may be very different from a commonsense point of view. If an idea is fruitful, then learners will gain something of value as a result.

Dissatisfaction with current beliefs or understandings is built on *cognitive conflict* where students' conceptions and scientific conceptions are at odds. Central in the Posner et al. (1982) framework are the issues of status and conceptual ecology. Status is determined by the conditions of intelligibility, plausibility, and fruitfulness, and "the *status* that an idea has for the person holding it is an indication of the degree to which he or she knows and accepts it" (Hewson, Beeth, & Thorley, 1998, pp. 199–200). Yet ideas cannot be considered in isolation, for each learner has a *conceptual ecology* that deals with all the knowledge that a person holds, recognizes that it consists of different kinds, focuses attention on the interactions within this knowledge base, and identifies the role that these interactions play in defining niches that support some ideas (raise their status) and discourage others (reduce their status). Learning something, then, means that the learner has raised its status within the context of his or her conceptual ecology (Hewson et al., p. 200).

Thus teachers need to incorporate multiple opportunities for classroom discourse that explores students' conceptual ecologies explicitly. Kagan (1992) summarizes the recommendations of Posner et al. for how teachers can promote students' conceptual change. Teachers must (a) help students make their implicit beliefs explicit, (b) confront students with the inadequacies of their beliefs, and (c) provide extended opportunities for integrating and differentiating old and new knowledge, eliminating brittle preconceptions that impede learning and elaborating anchors that facilitate learning. By extension, similar efforts are required of teacher educators working in science teacher education programs.

Any discussion of conceptual change must include Piagetian ideas, specifically *assimilation, accommodation, disequilibrium,* and *equilibration* (Duit & Treagust, 1998). Clearly, Piagetian notions have been incorporated into the conceptual change literature and into constructivist approaches to learning and teaching. Cognitive conflict, built on disequilibrium and equilibration, plays a predominant role in the work of Posner et al. (1982), and the themes of active learning and constructivism feature prominently in the work of Novak and colleagues, as already discussed.

Central to Vygotskyian theory is the influence of sociocultural factors on cognitive development. Duschl and Hamilton (1998) credit Vygotsky's work with stimulating research that addresses the social context of cognition and learning. This includes work in the areas of reciprocal teaching, collaborative learning, guided participation, and authentic approaches to teaching, learning, and assessment. Constructs such as situated cognition, apprenticeships, cognitive apprenticeships, and the social construction of meaning can be linked to Vygotskyian theory. Each of these involves the contextual nature of learning and the interrelation of individual, interpersonal, and cultural-historical factors in development (Tudge & Scrimsher, 2003). Putnam and Borko (2000) have summarized the major arguments and implications of situated cognition for teacher learning. Science teacher educators will do well to consider carefully the themes associated with the situative perspective: "that cognition is (a) situated in particular physical and social contexts; (b) social in nature; and (c) distributed across the individual, other persons, and tools" (Putnam & Borko, p. 4).

Teaching for Conceptual Change

Misconceptions are persistent and highly resistant to change (Duit & Treagust, 1998; Guzzetti et al., 1993; Mintzes et al., 1997). During the 1970s and 1980s, the predominant assumption was that students' misconceptions had to be extinguished before they could be replaced by the correct scientific view; however, there appears to be no study that confirms that a particular student's conception could be totally extinguished and then replaced (Duit & Treagust). Most studies reveal that the preexisting idea stays "alive" in particular contexts (Duit & Treagust), a phenomenon that diSessa (1993) describes as refinement, rather than replacement, of concepts.

The essence of teaching *for* conceptual change is restructuring of knowledge (Mintzes et al., 1997). This is far easier said than done, given the range and variability of students' responses to cognitive restructuring. Hodson (1998) provides a helpful overview of students' resistant responses. Some students may look for evidence to confirm rather than disconfirm their existing ideas. Often, their original notion prevails. Hodson points to variations in personality traits that may make some students more receptive to new ideas, whereas others may be reluctant to pursue alternatives because what they know (or think they know) is consistent with their own cognitive schema. If they hold on to what they know, they avoid the anxiety of the unknown or uncertain.

The work of the Children's Learning in Science (CLIS) group at the University of Leeds (e.g., Driver, 1989; Scott, Asoko, & Driver, 1992; Scott & Driver, 1998) is seminal in the area of constructivist approaches to conceptual change. CLIS suggests that certain commonalities extend across scientific disciplines and support reconceptualizations. These can be characterized as instructional activities that involve a teaching approach designed to address a particular learning demand (Scott et al.; Scott & Driver). These are sequenced as follows: (a) orientation or "messing about," which uses students' prior knowledge and existing conceptions as a starting point; (b) an elicitation phase where conceptions that are global and ill-defined are differentiated (e.g., heat and temperature, weight and mass); (c) restructuring, where experiential bridges are built to a new conception; and (d) constructing new conceptions through practice or application. If students' preconceptions are incommensurate with scientific conceptions, then Scott and Driver recommend that the teacher acknowledge and discuss students' ideas, indicate that scientists hold an alternative view, and present that model. They caution that the sequence should not be construed as a recipe, given that teaching for conceptual change requires learning activities in a variety of forms (e.g., reading, discussion, practical activity, teacher presentation). In contrast to the typical question-and-answer interchanges focused on "right" answers, discussion needs to be based on supporting and evaluating differing views in the light of evidence. Small-group discussions, poster presentations, and student learning diaries can provide students with valuable opportunities for sharing their understandings.

There is a growing body of work on strategies to support students' learning of science in ways that challenge their conceptual frameworks. Novak and Gowin's

(1984) work on concept mapping is helpful in assessing students' conceptual problems in science learning and in promoting metacognition. Originally developed as a science education research tool, concept maps are now widely used as a learning tool, as well as for curriculum design and instructional planning, implementation, and evaluation. As an example, Mason's (1992) two-year study looked at the operationalization of concept maps in preservice science teacher education. She concluded that the science majors in her study had acquired verbal information (declarative knowledge) in their undergraduate science courses but lacked a conceptual understanding of science. "These students did not exhibit an inability to enter the phase of learning required for understanding and application, but simply had been programmed to memorize terms and learn algorithms" (Mason, pp. 59–60).

> [Without fostering conceptual restructuring that would sensitize the prospective teach ers to] their lack of comprehension of the body of scientific knowledge and its origin, they would present a misinterpretation of the nature of science and perpetuate, in their own students, the inability to transfer conceptual understanding to novel situations. As a result, these teachers would tend to continue the cycle of science classroom environments which develop negative student attitudes toward science. (p. 60)

Mason found that her participants were able to develop maps that were less linear and term-oriented. They learned to produce maps that demonstrated the interrelatedness of scientific concepts and, in so doing, restructured information that had been presented to them discretely in previous undergraduate courses. One of the students wrote that concept mapping "gave the knowledge a fluid character, not simply a number of facts to outline and remember" (p. 57).

In addition to concept mapping, strategies such as concept webs, concept circle diagrams, Vee diagrams, and semantic networks can serve as conceptual tools that "fill different niches in meta-cognition" (Mintzes et al., 1997, p. 436). Because of their graphic organization and representation of concepts, there is an opportunity for students to "see" science, to better understand the interconnections between and among concepts, and to more actively engage in the construction and reconstruction of knowledge. Other approaches use student drawings and diagrams as a springboard to encourage and support the development of scientific discourse within the classroom community (e.g., Driver, 1989; Hayes, Symington, & Martin, 1994; Nussbaum & Novick, 1982). Tobin (1997) describes this as re-presentations, where students can use their visual representation as a basis for framing questions for their peers and their teacher. By incorporating a public accounting where students explain the science behind their drawings (Nussbaum & Novick), they can be initiated into the process of learning how to set forth a knowledge claim, justify it, and respond to challenges.

Creating conditions for cognitive conflict where teachers challenge students to look for limitations in their views or deliberately provide examples of discrepant or surprising events, often through hands-on demonstrations or activities, can spur reconceptualization (Hodson, 1998). However, we question the extent to which preservice teacher education anchors science courses within a conceptual change framework, explores conceptual change theory, probes the concepts that teacher candidates hold about science and learning science, provokes cognitive conflict, and exposes candidates to instructional approaches and strategies to support conceptual change. Unless prospective teachers are *directly* challenged to confront their own alternative conceptions and work through the process of conceptual change, it is highly unlikely that they will be able to support their own students in doing so.

Teaching for Conceptual Change in Preservice Science Teacher Education

Elby (2001) signals the potential significance of epistemological issues when teaching for conceptual change in physics, and we would extend Elby's insights to the significance of epistemological issues associated with concepts of teaching and learning. The following excerpt from Elby's report signals that attention to epistemological development must be explicit: "Many of the best research-based reformed physics curricula, ones that help students obtain a measurably deeper conceptual understanding, generally fail to spur significant epistemological development. Apparently, students can participate in activities that help them learn more effectively *without* reflecting upon and changing their beliefs about how to learn effectively" (p. S54). Elby concludes that "even the best reform curricula, however, have not been very successful at helping students develop more sophisticated epistemological beliefs" (p. S64).

We immediately extend Elby's conclusion to the context of learning to teach science by declaring that significant attention must be given to the epistemological beliefs of prospective science teachers, both in terms of the science concepts they will teach and in terms of the educational concepts they bring to a preservice program. Here we draw on an argument by McGoey and Ross (1999), both secondary science teachers, in which they provide a vivid account of student resistance to conceptual change and the complex teaching skills needed to negotiate it:

> We suspect that almost every teacher who has used a CC [conceptual change] model in the classroom has borne the brunt of student anger, frustration, and criticism. Students do not like having their ideas elicited in a nonjudgmental manner, only to have those ideas revealed as inadequate (whether it be mere seconds or days later). Some students eventually just stop giving their ideas. . . . Dealing with this without disaffecting students emotionally and intellectually requires delicate, precise, and theoretically sound skills of the teacher. (p. 118)

The challenges continue when students respond in ways that confirm that they do hold significant epistemological beliefs:

> The really messy stuff appears when the teacher gets a range of different (though adequate) models from the students. Now the fat is really in the fire. If the teacher refuses to give a single answer, positivist-minded students demand the right answer. Give a single answer and you may promote positivism. Give them a few rules (beware logical empiricism!) and the students interpret it as carte blanche for relativism or conventionalism. Another response of students is to challenge the teacher's practice outright. These attacks assert that since everybody knows that science is simply a universal body of facts and methods, just give us the recipe and tell us the answer so we can study for the test. (pp. 118–119)

These two teachers then extend their discussion to teacher education and to the stress that candidates experience when they sense cognitive conflict associated with relying extensively on content knowledge. Again, we see that epistemological assumptions about teaching and learning are implicit:

> Teacher interns are often deeply troubled to have their content knowledge questioned. They are already nervous enough about whether they can get in front of 30 adolescents for 80 minutes. . . . Content knowledge is often their major life-saving device. When student teachers engage in action research activities that undermine overreliance upon content knowledge, they experience considerable distress. The experience is extremely unsettling. (p. 119)

In this extended discussion of conceptual change in the context of learning to teach science, we have provided an overview of major arguments with respect to conceptual change in science teaching as a prelude to extending the topic of conceptual change to learning to teach science. In both contexts we believe that Elby's (2001) attention to epistemological beliefs is essential for making productive changes to how science is taught. We turn next to another issue with significant epistemological overtones: learning from experience and the associated authority of experience.

LEARNING FROM EXPERIENCE
AND THE AUTHORITY OF EXPERIENCE

The Authority of Experience

In our culture, we speak easily of "learning from experience" in everyday life, and yet we also hear many stories in which people seem not to have learned from experience. Just as propositional knowledge claims are easily forgotten and links are not always made from one context to another, so it is with learning from experience, which seems to be a marginal feature of many classrooms in the formal learning contexts of schools and universities. Science teachers are often credited with an advantage of being able to use everyday materials, yet laboratory experiences are rarely described by students as major contributing activities in their learning of concepts. Because learning from experience is not a significant feature of many classrooms, when those learning to teach science begin a professional preparation program, the role of learning from experience may never have been considered. Quite universally, student teachers report that the practicum is the most significant element of their preparation for teaching, yet this does not mean that new science teachers understand how they learn from experience or that they are proficient in learning from experience. Munby and Russell (1994) addressed this issue when they introduced the phrase "the authority of experience":

> Listening to one's own experience is not the same as listening to the experience of others, and the [physics method] students seem to indicate that they still place much more authority with those who have experience and with those who speak with confidence about how teaching should be done. They seem reluctant to listen to or to trust their own experiences as an authoritative source of knowledge about teaching. We wonder how and to what extent they will begin to hear the voice of their own experiences as they begin their teaching careers.
>
> The basic tension in teacher education derives for us from preservice students wanting to move from being under authority to being in authority, without appreciating the

potential that the authority of experience can give to their learning to teach. The challenge for teacher education is to help new teachers recognize and identify the place and function of the authority of experience. (pp. 93–94)

Action Research and a New Scholarship

In recent years there has been a small but significant shift in teachers' continuing professional development toward learning from experience. After 1990, we began to read much more about "teacher research" and "action research," two closely related fields in which individual teachers attempt to learn from their firsthand classroom experiences (see Chapter 39, this volume). Often such inquiry begins with questions such as: How can I help my students improve the quality of their learning? Research by teachers in their own classrooms represents a major shift from the cultural norms of our schools and universities, and it is in the university that such research would most readily be challenged for being subjective, for not being generalizable, and for lacking in rigor. Schön (1995) saw this problem in the context of a "new scholarship" and framed the challenge in terms of introducing an alternative to the university's standard epistemology:

> The problem of changing the universities so as to incorporate the new scholarship must include, then, how to introduce action research as a legitimate and appropriately rigorous way of knowing and generating knowledge. . . . If we are prepared to take [this task] on, then we have to deal with what it means to introduce an epistemology of reflective practice into institutions of higher education dominated by technical rationality. (pp. 31–32)

Within the very large community of teacher educators, there is a subset of individuals who have addressed this epistemological issue by focusing on the study of their own teaching practices within preservice teacher education programs. By working collectively in conferences, books, and journal articles, the self-study of teacher education practices has achieved significant levels of recognition for an "epistemology of reflective practice." A two-volume international handbook (Loughran, Hamilton, LaBoskey, & Russell, 2004) illustrates in many ways their individual and collective efforts to learn from experience.

The issue of experience in relation to education was explored extensively by Dewey (1938), and Schön's (1995) work emerged directly from that of Dewey. One of Dewey's many points is that familiar educational patterns persist as tradition, not on their rationale. Bringing the authority of experience into programs for learning to teach science will involve all the familiar challenges of learning from experience: "There is no discipline in the world so severe as the discipline of experience subjected to the tests of intelligent development and direction. . . . The road of the new education is not an easier one to follow than the old road but a more strenuous and difficult one. . . . The greatest danger that attends its future is, I believe, the idea that it is an easy way to follow" (Dewey, p. 90).

We find it interesting that the issue of learning from experience and the associated epistemological issues tend not to be raised in the conceptual change literature, and here we call attention to the issue of learning from experience because it represents an important, perhaps essential, perspective for helping individuals learn to teach science.

A strong case for recognizing the authority of experience in the science classroom appears in the findings and recommendations reported in a book intended for those who teach first-year undergraduate courses in physics. Knight (2004) summarizes 25 years of physics education research on students' concepts and problem-solving strategies with three conclusions that have direct implications not only for teaching science *but also for learning to teach science*:

1. Students enter our classroom not as 'blank slates,' *tabula rasa*, but filled with many prior concepts.
2. Students' prior concepts are remarkably resistant to change.
3. Students' knowledge is not organized in any coherent framework. (p. 25)

These statements remind us that, in contrast to what is learned from textbooks, that which is learned from experience can be powerful without being coherently organized. Knight closes his analysis with five "lessons" for teachers:

1. "Keep students actively engaged and provide rapid feedback" (p. 42).
2. "Focus on phenomena rather than abstractions" (p. 42).
3. "Deal explicitly with students' alternative conceptions" (p. 43).
4. "Teach and use explicit problem-solving skills and strategies" (p. 44).
5. "Write homework and exam problems that go beyond symbol manipulation to engage students in the qualitative and conceptual analysis of physical phenomena" (p. 44).

The first four lessons can be translated directly from teaching science to learning to teach science. The fifth lesson could easily be reshaped to "engage students in the qualitative and conceptual analysis of educational phenomena." In "traditional" preservice teacher education programs, one might view these as research findings to include in the "knowledge base" to be transmitted to preservice science teachers. Our analysis of the research literature confirms that it is *entirely counterproductive* to simply transmit such lessons to teachers as content. Rather, preservice science teacher education programs *must* explore the implications of these lessons through all the learning experiences created in teacher education classrooms (see Segall, 2002).

Reflection by a Teacher Educator

To illustrate learning from experience in the context of preservice science teacher education, we recount briefly Russell's personal learning from experience as a teacher educator trying to understand how experience helps those learning to teach. In both 1991 and 1992, he arranged to teach one class of physics in a local high school; in return the school's regular physics teacher helped teach the physics method course at Queen's. Building on the 1991 experience, he arranged for one of his physics method classes in 1992 to be held each week in the room where he taught physics, with an invitation to preservice teachers to observe his class if they wished. Despite being in the physics classroom himself and holding some of his classes in the school rather than at the university, the impact on the preservice teachers seemed minimal. A series of interviews with some of the preservice teachers led Russell to develop a list of potential barriers to learning from experience that the preservice teachers seemed to bring to their efforts to learn to teach. Just as Knight (2004) reports, the future physics teachers did not arrive as blank slates; they had strong views that did not change easily. Five years later, when the preservice program at Queen's changed dramatically to begin with 14 weeks of teaching experience, the barriers implicit in the 1993 candidates were replaced by more constructive "frames" generated by their learning from experience (see Table 37.1).

Reflection by those Learning to Teach

Two recent papers report on significant efforts to understand and improve learning to teach science at the elementary level, with special reference to learning from teaching experience. These papers emphasize the importance of reflection in relation to learning from experience, and we value their attention to structuring and supporting reflection by those learning to teach. Early in Bryan and Abell's (1999) case study of a student teacher named "Barbara," the authors declare their perspective on the role of experience in learning to teach: "The heart of knowing how to teach cannot be learned from coursework alone. The construction of professional knowledge requires experience. . . . Experience influences the frames that teachers employ in identifying problems of practice, in approaching those problems and implementing solutions, and in making sense of the outcomes of their actions" (pp. 121–122).

The case of Barbara begins with an account of what Barbara believed about science teaching and learning and moves on to describe her vision for teaching elementary science as well as the tensions within her thinking about her professional responsibilities. Of particular interest is Barbara's initial premise that a teacher should

TABLE 37.1
Barriers to Learning to Teach and Frames for Learning to Teach

Barriers to learning to teach: Prior views of preservice science teachers who gained teaching experience gradually during an eight-month program.	Frames for learning to teach: Views of preservice science teachers who began a nine-month program with 14 weeks of teaching experience.
Teaching can be told.	Teaching cannot be told.
Learning to teach is passive.	Learning to teach is active.
Discussion and opinion are irrelevant.	Discussion, opinion and sharing of experiences are crucial.
Personal reactions to teaching are irrelevant.	Personal reactions to teaching are the starting point.
Goals for future students do not apply personally.	Goals for future students definitely must apply personally.
Theory is largely irrelevant.	Theory is relevant.
Experience cannot be analyzed or understood.	Experience can be analyzed and understood.

Note: From Russell (2000, pp. 231–232, 238–239).

continue to teach a scientific concept until all children show that they understand it. Once the process of reflection became apparent, "Barbara began to shift her perspective and reframe the tension between her vision and practice. Her professional experience provided feedback that forced her to confront the idea that in teaching science, teachers need to consider more than students getting it" (Bryan & Abell, p. 131). This case study could help new science teachers anticipate the challenges and prospects of student teaching, although the real help would probably be realized *during* rather than *before* the student teacher assignment. The implications for further study of learning from experience are clear:

> Barbara's case implicitly underscores the fallacy of certain assumptions underlying traditional teacher education programs: (a) that propositional knowledge from course readings and lectures can be translated directly into practice, and (b) that prospective teachers develop professional knowledge before experience rather than in conjunction with experience. . . . Teacher educators are challenged to coach prospective teachers to purposefully and systematically inquire into their own practices, encouraging them to make such inquiry a habit. (Bryan & Abell, p. 136)

Just as a conceptual change approach to teaching science begins with students' experiences, so Bryan and Abell conclude that "the genesis of the process of developing

---

Narrative Box 37–2
Narrowing the Gap between Practice
and Theory, Actions and Values

In 1983, in my sixth year of teaching a preservice science course and visiting candidates in their practicum classrooms, I was feeling acutely aware of the gaps between educational theory and practice. Many of the strategies I promoted in my classes could not be observed in my students' classes in the practicum setting. A colleague loaned me a copy of Schön's (1983) *The reflective practitioner: How professionals think in action*. My first sabbatical leave later that year provided an opportunity to study this book and prepare a research proposal that would let me explore this new perspective in the context of preservice teacher education. Years of work with the ideas have led me to conclude that Schön's terminology is more readily adopted than it is understood. I see Schön arguing two main points:

1. Learning from teaching experience involves finding new frames or perspectives (perhaps from the research literature) to better understand surprising and puzzling events of practice.
2. Improving as a teacher involves deliberately narrowing the inevitable gaps between our values as teachers and the effects of our teaching actions on those we teach.

How do you react when asked to "reflect"? Do you have enough experiences to reflect about? Would it help if someone undertook to teach you how to reflect?

professional knowledge should be seen as inherent in experience" (p. 136). "A pre-eminent goal of science teacher education should be to help prospective teachers challenge and refine their ideas about teaching and learning science and learn how to learn from experience" (Bryan & Abell, p. 137).

The paper by Zembal-Saul, Krajcik, and Blumenfeld (2002) focuses on representation of science content to children during teaching experiences. Three case studies describe the context in which individuals taught, their representations of science content, and the support provided for learners. The authors build on the earlier conclusion of Bryan and Abell (1999) that "experience plays a significant role in developing professional knowledge" (p. 121). To this they add their own conclusion that "what we do know . . . is that experience alone is not enough. It needs to be coupled with thoughtful reflection on action" (Zembal-Saul et al., p. 460). Their overall conclusions make important points that remind science teacher educators yet again of the importance of the cooperating teacher in supporting (implicitly, if not explicitly) the student teacher's professional learning: "There is evidence that cooperating teachers who facilitate students' meaningful learning in general and support student teachers in their efforts to continue to emphasize science content representation can positively influence the territory student teachers attempt to master" (p. 460). Reminding us that our collective understanding of how experience contributes to learning to teach still requires attention and development, the authors conclude: "There is an urgent need to understand better the role of experience in learning to teach, in particular the aspects of teaching experiences that support or hinder new teachers' continuing development in the often fragile domain of science content knowledge and its representations" (p. 461).

This material on learning from experience and on reflection, both in science classrooms and in science teacher education settings, completes our introduction of perspectives on conceptual change and the authority of experience. We turn next to an earlier review of research on learning to teach science.

DOMINANT THEMES IN EARLIER RESEARCH ON LEARNING TO TEACH SCIENCE

Anderson and Mitchener's (1996) extensive review of research on science teacher education provides a strong foundation for the issues of learning to teach science that are explored and developed in this chapter. They describe a "traditional model" of preservice science teacher education that seems very much with us a decade after their review. The model has three familiar elements—educational foundations, methods courses, and field experiences and student teaching. Anderson and Mitchener conclude their review with statements that bear repeating:

> Looking back, this three-pronged traditional model of preservice teacher education has survived relatively intact since its birth in the normal school. . . . The challenge facing science teacher educators today is this: how will you address in a coherent, comprehensive manner such emerging issues as new views of content knowledge, constructivist approaches to teaching and learning, and a reflective disposition to educating teachers. In addition, thoughtful science teacher educators need to attend to the theoretical orientation of their programs and how important professional issues are addressed within these orientations. (p. 19)

> ### Narrative Box 37–3
> ### Can Reflection Be Taught?
>
> In 2001, one of my classes included an individual who knew that he would never be a teacher. He had to wait 18 months to begin a training program, and his future employers were willing to support his time in a preservice education program. As a result, he had more time than most to critique the various elements of the program. At the end of the year, we revisited a series of weekly practicum reports that he had volunteered to send me (and to which I replied quickly). He suggested that our corresponding about his practicum experiences had done more than any other program element to teach him how to reflect. He offered advice to my colleagues and me: "Don't tell people to reflect. Instead, teach them how to reflect and then show them that that is what you have done." Subsequent attempts to follow this advice have paid positive dividends.
>
> *What specific meanings do you associate with the words "reflect" and "reflection"? Do you see reflection as something that can be taught? Is it possible to reflect during teaching as well as after?*

These reviewers went on to identify six dominant themes in research on the preservice curriculum in the twentieth century: an "established preservice model," "inadequate subject matter preparation," "haphazard education preparation," the "importance of inquiry," "reliance on the laboratory," and "valued educational technologies" (Anderson & Mitchener, pp. 21–22). We find little to indicate that these dominant themes have changed. Anderson and Mitchener describe criticisms directed at the traditional model and then offer important conclusions:

> Considering the longevity and volume of such efforts, one would expect a review of preservice science teacher education programs to portray a rich landscape, complete with diverse views, cohesive images, and defined detail. Research on these programs, however, is neither accessible nor diverse.
>
> Indeed, there is a dearth of literature describing preservice science teacher education programs. . . . Actual portrayals of comprehensive programs—including conceptual and structural components—are rare. . . .
>
> Differences that do exist among programs are most often found at the course level. Innovative efforts in reforming science teacher preparation usually are directed at changing one or two isolated components within a program, as opposed to the program as a whole. (p. 23)

Our review of literature on the development of teachers' knowledge (Munby, Russell, & Martin, 2001) and our examination of research available since Anderson and Mitchener's review lead us to the conclusion that the six dominant themes they identified continue to appear in research related to learning to teach science, despite repeated calls for change and reform in science education and in preservice teacher education.

SCIENCE TEACHER EDUCATION PROGRAMS THAT WORK TO MAKE A DIFFERENCE

We have already noted Anderson and Mitchener's (1996) observation that detailed accounts of preservice teacher education programs are uncommon. Here we consider two such accounts, one from Monash University in Australia and one from the University of Wisconsin–Madison in the United States. Each is an account of efforts to achieve coherence around a focused set of understandings related to how and why students learn science.

Monash University

In theory, coherence and a set of guiding principles within a preservice science teacher education program should be valuable and productive. Gunstone, Slattery, Baird, and Northfield (1993) present seven propositions underlying the program at Monash University in Australia that we summarize as follows: A program must consider the needs of teacher candidates and recognize that needs change as development occurs. Collaboration with other candidates is essential, and candidates construct new views based on previous experiences and perceptions. Teacher educators need to model the principles they are teaching as they strive to enact a program seen as worthwhile yet inevitably and necessarily incomplete because it precedes full teaching responsibilities. Finally, teacher educators need to demonstrate to candidates the reflective practice that they expect of those learning to teach.

The authors speak bluntly about the challenges of creating and enacting an effective program of preservice science teacher education:

> After at least 16 years' experience as learners, students come to programs with well-developed but often simplistic views of teaching and learning. . . . These views are very persistent and often at odds with the views we hope to cultivate. Failure to respond to this issue can result in student teachers either reconstructing what they encounter in the program so as to leave their initial views unchanged, or simply rejecting what does not fit the initial views. . . . Hence the views need to be identified, discussed, and evaluated by student teachers by means of carefully managed teaching/learning experiences. (pp. 51–52)

Gunstone et al. see two types of managed experiences for student teachers: "revealing and challenging perceptions of one's own learning" and exploring "perceptions of teaching and pupil learning" (p. 52). They are quick to emphasize the complex nature of these activities: "Most graduates in teacher education programs require considerable assistance and support to even begin to take control of their own learning in this constructivist way. . . . The assistance and support must be in the context of what is seen to be learning of value by the learner; that is, it must be woven through the usual course as an ongoing influence on the pedagogy adopted by those teaching the course" (p. 52).

The authors go on to discuss the issue of preservice science teachers' understanding of their science subjects, reminding us that teachers trained in one science may benefit from opportunities to study topics in other sciences. Attention also turns to the complex issue of how well study of a science subject prepares one for the demands of teaching that subject to others.

It is relatively common for [student teachers] to hold naïve, alternative and erroneous conceptions in areas they have studied intensively. . . . This issue must be handled with considerable sensitivity, as much of the self-esteem which student teachers possess on commencing teacher preparation is derived from their successful academic study. The identification of alternative conceptions should occur in the context of personal experience of constructivist views of learning and teaching. (p. 53)

In the second half of their paper, Gunstone and his colleagues consider the propositions they have set forth in light of the experiences of one seminar group in the 1987 academic year. This study is essential reading for any group of teacher educators intending to study the impact of their own program on prospective teachers. The study also provides valuable insights into what is possible in a coherent program that seeks to foster a conceptual change approach to the teaching of science.

The authors acknowledge and illustrate the importance of views brought by prospective teachers, just as science teachers committed to conceptual change must work with the views their students bring to their classrooms. Finally, keeping the familiar parallels between conceptual change and reflective practice, the Monash group stresses the importance of modeling the principles they teach and of ensuring that new teachers are aware of the principles and limitations of their program.

University of Wisconsin–Madison

A set of papers from University of Wisconsin–Madison (UW-Madison) (*Science Education, 83*(3), 1999) contrasts with the paper from Monash University in interesting ways. The UW-Madison researchers worked with elementary or secondary science methods courses and an action research seminar, whereas the Monash researchers were able to work with the entire preservice program. Significantly, teacher educators subjecting their own practices to scrutiny is far more apparent in the Monash study than in the UW-Madison study, even though the UW-Madison researchers allude to the importance of such scrutiny. The UW-Madison experience also merits close examination for its rich array of hypotheses.

The researchers offer an excellent summary of the task facing all science teacher educators who would challenge their students to move beyond the truism that "we teach as we were taught":

These prospective teachers' understanding of the nature of knowledge was a critical factor in their teaching. . . . There were almost no indications that, upon graduation from the program, these prospective teachers thought it was necessary to give class time for their students to consider the relative status of alternative conceptions. We suggest that this is not surprising from a positivist perspective in which the truth of scientific information is not at issue. (Hewson, Tabachnick, Zeichner, & Lemberger, 1999, p. 378)

The array of evidence gathered in the UW-Madison study points to a fundamental problem that lies outside the domain of teacher education: the way that science is taught and assessed in universities:

It appears that prospective teachers were inadequately prepared by their content courses to do anything more than the mostly transmissionist teaching we observed. . . . We suggest that this is the result of the teaching and assessment strategies of college science courses that do little to emphasize the integration of course content. Lectures seldom encourage students to think about and relate concepts to each other, and multiple choice testing procedures ask for information in a piecemeal fashion. (Hewson et al., pp. 379–380)

This paper set concludes with a range of valuable but familiar comments about the need for school placements that support student teachers working for conceptual change as well as the need for communication and collaboration between university and school personnel.

As Anderson and Mitchener (1996) observed, the science education and teacher education communities devote far more time and effort to studies in science classrooms than to studies in science teacher education classrooms (where all who are learning to teach science must spend time before moving into their own classrooms). As the reports of the Monash and Wisconsin programs indicate, theoretical and empirical insights about learning science in classrooms can be extended to learning to teach science in teacher education classrooms. Important progress in programs where individuals learn to teach science seems unlikely to occur until coherent frameworks are extended to programs as a whole rather than to individual program elements (Russell, McPherson, & Martin, 2001), with sound research studies that make conceptual and structural gains available to those learning to teach and to those who teach them.

The Project for Enhancing Effective Learning

The Project for Enhancing Effective Learning (PEEL) (see http://peelweb.org) is a unique example of a teacher-directed, teacher-sustained collaborative action research. PEEL is a comprehensive school-based program for improving the quality of teaching in schools. With supportive links to nearby universities, PEEL began in 1985 in one school in the western suburbs of Melbourne, Australia. The key issues were deceptively simple:

> The major aim of PEEL is to improve the quality of school learning and teaching. Training for this improvement is centered on having students become more willing and able to accept responsibility and control for their own learning. Training has three aspects: increasing students' knowledge of what learning is and how it works; enhancing students' awareness of learning progress and outcome; improving students' control of learning through more purposeful decision making. (Baird & Mitchell, 1986, p. iii)

Thus PEEL is a comprehensive program of inservice professional development for teachers as well as a project for enhancing effective student learning.

A central element of PEEL involves *reframing* the activities of teachers *and* the activities of students within the classroom context. The power of PEEL resides in its extensive array of specific, practical procedures for the various steps that are inevitably involved in helping students develop a metacognitive stance toward their own learning. To present specific PEEL approaches to a beginning teacher with no teaching experience is to accomplish nothing at all. To use PEEL approaches to help beginning teachers interpret early teaching experiences in relation to their own goals and beliefs is to facilitate conceptual change. To practice PEEL approaches in teacher

---

Narrative Box 37–4
Do Students Notice Your Major Goals For Teaching?

When I began teaching preservice candidates in 1977, my three years of work with experienced teachers had a major impact. I had just finished working with a group of history teachers in a program that taught them how to analyze their own teaching. As a group, their overall reactions to their analysis can be summarized in two conclusions: (1) "We talk far more than we realized we did," and (2) "It is extremely difficult to change how much talking we do." Imagine how confused my first teacher education classes were when I tried to teach by talking less than most of my colleagues, a strategy that I attempted because I wanted to try for myself the challenge that the history teachers had identified. One early issue became "How do I model doing LESS of something?"

What major values do you hold for your teaching that will require you, as a teacher, to act in ways that differ from the norms of teacher behavior?

---

education classrooms as well as in school classrooms is to begin to realize the need for epistemological reframing in both contexts.

To extend our earlier references to the importance of epistemological considerations both in teaching science and in learning to teach science, we turn now to perspectives on knowledge acquisition and on knowledge construction in learning to teach.

ACQUIRING AND CONSTRUCTING KNOWLEDGE

We find it helpful to link the work of the PEEL project to Chinn and Brewer's (1998) framework for "understanding and evaluating theories of knowledge acquisition" (p. 97). There is a strong parallel between this framework and the practical knowledge developed within PEEL: each account is driven by constructive logical analysis of the domain of interest. Of eight questions posed by Chinn and Brewer, we here focus particularly on question 5: "What is the fate of the old knowledge and the new information after knowledge change occurs?" (p. 97). Chinn and Brewer make it clear that conceptual change can be of at least five types:

1. B replaces A, with A being forgotten or ignored.
2. A is reinterpreted within the framework of B.
3. B is reinterpreted within the framework of A.
4. A is incorporated into B.
5. A and B are compartmentalized. (p. 106)

Teaching may be conducted most easily by assuming that the first fate —simple replacement—will occur, but if it did, we would hardly need research on conceptual change. Compartmentalization is something most teachers wish to avoid, for it seems counterproductive to restrict the application of more complex and complete explanations for phenomena. The territory suggested by the other three "fates" indicates the breadth and complexity of the work of teachers and reminds us of the challenges of planning for teaching. The procedures constructed and organized by PEEL over nearly two decades of teacher collaboration provide potential support for teachers concerned about what happens to "old knowledge." Making this process explicit is a powerful initial step in the reframing that we argue is critical to conceptual change. As a venture in collaborative action research, PEEL is specifically committed to fostering students' change from nonawareness to awareness and then using that awareness to support conceptual change itself.

Knowledge Construction in Learning to Teach

Oosterheert and Vermunt (2003) present an intriguing addition to the literature of reflection in learning to teach. Schön (1983) gave considerable impetus to the "teacher as reflective practitioner" movement with his distinction between problem-solving and problem-setting. Reframing problems to develop and enact new approaches became an attractive image for teachers thinking professionally about their work. The argument has intrinsic appeal in the context of teacher education and learning to teach, and it readily extends to the conceptual change approaches so often advocated in the science education community.

Oosterheert and Vermunt (2003) distinguish between "external" and "internal" sources of regulation in constructing knowledge. External sources (which would include experience with phenomena of science and practicum teaching experiences) provide information from outside the learner (whether child or adult). Internal sources of regulation refer to the capacities of the brain "to process information and to reconstruct existing knowledge" (Oosterheert & Vermunt, p. 159). To the familiar idea of "active" internal sources of regulation, the authors add the category of "dynamic" internal sources of regulation and argue that these are essential in learning to teach. In doing so, they build on Iran-Nejad's (1990) challenge of the assumption that learning involves incremental internalization in response to external sources. Whereas active processing is "slow," "deliberate," and "sequential," dynamic processing is "rapid," "non-deliberate," and "simultaneous" (Oosterheert & Vermunt, p. 160).

Teacher educators who have employed reflective practice perspectives may quickly recognize these contrasts as similar to Schön's (1983) contrast between *solving* problems and *reframing* problems. We are particularly interested in the implications of seeing internal sources of regulation as both "active" *and* "dynamic." Whereas "active" self-regulation appears to capture the familiar tasks of *schooling*, including note-taking, homework, reviewing, quizzes, and tests, "dynamic" self-regulation appears to lead to the conceptual changes that science teachers often take as goals and genuine indicators of their success in teaching. Similarly, whereas "active" self-regulation appears to capture the familiar tasks of *learning to teach*, including class participation, preparing and presenting practicum lessons, and completing assigned work, "dynamic" self-regulation appears to lead to the shifts of understanding and perspective that teacher educators often take as genuine indicators of their success in helping individuals learn to teach. Oosterheert and Vermunt (2003) suggest that "dynamic self-regulation is a prerequisite in constructive learning. Active self-regulation may be helpful, but is never sufficient nor always necessary" (pp. 160–161).

This complex paper draws to a close with an important conclusion: "Active self-regulation can be very helpful, but never sufficient in conceptual change. In learning to teach as well as in academic learning, dynamic sources should be more involved" (Oosterheert & Vermunt, 2003, p. 167). Oosterheert and Vermunt's overall contribution involves recognizing that learning involves more than activities in which students proceed "deliberately and intentionally" (p. 170). In their view, learning also involves "non-deliberate processing strategies" (p. 170), which we take to be essential to conceptual change. These ideas merit consideration in the teacher education classroom as well as in the science classroom.

One of the key features of "dynamic" self-regulation, as introduced by Oosterheert and Vermunt (2003), is that it is characterized by "rapid, spontaneous, non-deliberate, simultaneous" processing of "sensorial" information leading with "ease" to "reconceptualization" and "understanding" (p. 160). These are not qualities that we typically associate with learning. At first we found it puzzling that the authors speak of student teachers relying on dynamic sources when teaching, when "most of their decisions and actions require no deliberate thought" (Oosterheert & Vermunt, p. 165). Later they use a term that we have also found very helpful with respect to learning to teach. They suggest that student teachers may rely on a "default teaching repertoire" that they associate with dynamic regulation. We take this to refer to the "default" (do-it-without-thinking) style that every individual is capable of after more than 15 years of schooling, a style learned spontaneously, nondeliberately,

---

Narrative Box 37–5
Identifying One's Default Teaching Style

In 1997–1998, the preservice program at Queen's University changed dramatically. After registration and brief introductions to professors and fellow students, candidates began their practicum experiences on the first day of school. Only during a two-week return to the university after eight weeks of teaching did individuals begin to get to know each other. The intensity of discussions was unlike anything I had ever experienced. I was challenged to assist people who would be returning to the same classes in the same schools and who sought answers and insights appropriate to very pressing questions of engagement, motivation, planning and discipline. For the first time I began speaking of "default" teaching styles—the teaching moves we make based on reflex, not on thought, the teaching moves we make that are comfortable and familiar because our own teachers used them when teaching us. This prompted the conclusion that each new teacher needs to identify and understand her or his own default teaching style before being able to modify that style to include deliberately chosen teaching behaviors.

Do you find it helpful to think of your own teaching behaviors in terms of default styles and deliberate efforts to modify them to enact teaching moves that will enhance the quality of student learning?

simultaneously, sensorially, and unintentionally by observation of one's own teachers, typically without understanding. Here again, the parallel to learning science is strong, for children acquire "default" understandings of the phenomena of science from their everyday experiences, and these can readily accumulate without deliberate processing.

This concludes our account of important arguments about acquiring and constructing knowledge in the context of learning to teach. Programs for learning to teach continue to operate on patterns guided more by tradition than by arguments such as these. Thus we turn next to the issue of whether teacher education programs can move beyond the rhetoric of reform.

MOVING BEYOND THE RHETORIC OF REFORM

White (2001) contends that the last two decades have produced a revolution in research on science teaching. "The change in the amount of research is sufficient alone to warrant the term *revolution*, but even more significant is its nature" (White, p. 457). Against a background of revolution, the foreground offers clarion calls for reform and the improvement of science education (e.g., American Association for the Advancement of Science, 1989, 1993, 2001; Council of Ministers of Education, Canada, 1997; Curriculum Corporation, 1994a, 1994b; National Research Council, 1996). Prominent among the recommendations are changes in science classrooms whereby instruction is situated in a context that supports students' explorations of questions that develop deeper understandings of science content and processes and encourages learners to share developing ideas and information (Crawford, Krajcik, & Marx, 1999).

More broadly, reform efforts urge closer attention to students' conceptions of the nature of science and scientific inquiry (see Chapter 29, this volume). Lederman (1998) makes the case that, unless teachers have a functional understanding of these concepts, there is little hope of achieving the vision of science teaching and learning that is detailed in the reform literature. It is but a small step to argue that these understandings must be embedded appropriately in teacher education programs if prospective teachers are to move beyond the rhetoric of reform, become scientifically and pedagogically capable themselves, and then enable their students to do likewise.

Learning What Science Is: Beyond Facts to Concepts and Discipline

Duit and Treagust (1998) relate learning science to the conceptions held by students and teachers of science content, conceptions of the nature of science, the aims of science instruction, the purpose of teaching events, and the nature of the learning process. The complexity of the construct "learning science," with its multiple components, points to many of the issues that confound science teacher education. These include the tenacity of students' conceptions about science and scientific inquiry as well as the tenacity of their experiences learning science—the procedural aspects in addition to the propositional, the pedagogy they were exposed to in their science classes, and the (subconscious) interpretation they attached to it.

Challenges to Science Teachers and Science Teacher Educators

The complexity of learning to teach science for comprehension and understanding is obvious, and the agenda for successful science teachers is full: teaching about the nature and limitations of scientific knowledge, helping students to understand and apply scientific laws and theories, and enabling them to participate in scientific discourse and inquiry processes. For teacher educators, the agenda is doubly full because, in addition to the above, teacher education also requires a better understanding of the demands placed on teachers as they introduce their students to the nature of science, as they engage them in classroom discourse, and as they enable them to pursue scientific inquiry (Anderson, 2000). *How* we teach must be a major focal point for all who are concerned with teaching and learning science and with how individuals learn to teach science.

The Significance of Discourse

Often teacher candidates entering classrooms are ill-prepared for the fallout from students' years of exposure to an alienating discourse: "We hardly do anything except copy notes that the teacher has written (not our own words) and do experiments that the teacher does for us. All we do is sit there and watch demonstrations and listen to the teacher talk. Everyone just sits there and looks like they're listening. I hate science" (Baird, Gunstone, Penna, Fensham, & White, 1990, p. xx).

How, if at all, do teacher educators address the discourse of science and its myriad representations and effects? How do they ready prospective teachers for less than enthusiastic responses from students, and how do they deconstruct those responses? When science is presented as a series of knowledge claims verified by others, it becomes no more than a compendium of facts to be warehoused, and

---

Narrative Box 37–6
The Importance of Coherence in Teaching

As we were completing this chapter, I was teaching two online courses for physics teachers. The courses had just been rewritten to focus on recent research findings (Knight, 2004), the significance of students' prior views, teaching strategies for fostering metacognition and the role of choice and motivation. The highly positive responses demonstrated the power of a coherent set of perspectives on learning to teach science. Where teaching to "cover the curriculum" typically involves teachers looking only for right answers, teaching to foster understanding necessarily involves looking for conceptual change. Exposing students' prior views of phenomena is crucial.

How coherent are the many messages conveyed by teacher educators to those learning to teach science?

learning entails stockpiling "prefabricated knowledge that then is stored in memory" (Duit & Treagust, 1998, p. 6).

Baird and Mitchell (1986) link the familiar transmission model of learning to students' conceptions of what, for them, counts as schoolwork and what does not. Essentially, whatever is not presented in this mode is not considered real work, and discussions where alternative perspectives are advanced or meanings negotiated are perceived as time wasting and counterproductive. This perspective is not exclusive to students and may (unwittingly) be shared by teachers and teacher educators. Thus the discourse of the classroom, be it elementary, secondary, or post-secondary, reveals much about *how* students learn science and *what* their conceptions of scientific knowledge and inquiry are. Discourse is pivotal to understanding the resistance teacher educators encounter when alternative frameworks and conceptualizations are introduced. Thus we see changes in classroom discourse at all levels as central to moving beyond the rhetoric of reform.

CONCLUSION

Our examination of literature about learning to teach science suggests that, in general, science teacher educators continue to be reluctant to practice in their own teaching what their research suggests that new and experienced teachers should do. Just as teachers are learning that action research is a way to explore in practice the challenges of teaching for conceptual change, so teacher educators must explore those challenges as they work with those learning to teach science. It continues to be easy to pin the hopes for improved teaching of science on those who are just entering the teaching profession; this approach seems fundamentally flawed. Experienced teachers and teacher educators who ask of new teachers what they have not attempted themselves are ignoring the reality that we learn to teach more by what is modeled than by what is told.

Anderson's (2000) introduction to a series of papers on the challenges facing science teacher education identified a central issue for the development of the profession: "We need to develop teacher education programs that promote the qualities of practice that we value" (p. 294). The Narrative Boxes included in this chapter posed questions about the practice of science teacher education. Here we revisit those boxes to suggest a course for future research on learning to teach science.

1. Experience is important for learning science and for learning to teach science. How can science education researchers help teachers and teacher educators understand the many challenges involved in giving credence to students' first-hand experiences within classroom learning activities?

2. The gap between practices and values in education goes back much further than Dewey and Schön, who were major twentieth-century figures calling attention to this gap. How can science education researchers help teachers and teacher educators navigate the tensions between theory and practice, finding the courage to think in new ways about learning and then weave the resulting insights into practice?

3. The call for more and more critical reflection by those learning to teach has been evident for more than 20 years, since Schön (1983) stressed the role of

reflection-in-action in professional learning. There is little public evidence that reflection is actually being taught, and there is little public evidence that teacher educators are themselves engaging in reflection-in-action. Can researchers find ways to address this lack of evidence and expose the complexities of making reflection-in-action a meaningful element of professional development?

4. Can researchers help teachers find productive ways to rethink the familiar background of teaching in our schools and universities? We hope that those learning to teach science will go on to improve how science is taught, yet how science is taught does not seem to change. Can researchers help teacher educators prepare new teachers who realize the profound challenges that accompany efforts to improve the practices of science teaching?

5. Science teacher education naturally seeks to inspire new teachers to develop best practices supported by research evidence. Yet research evidence also shows the importance of addressing explicitly students' prior views. Can science education researchers move beyond the studies of conceptual change in science classrooms to document the parallel complexity of conceptual change in prior views of teaching and learning that are evident in new teachers' earliest teaching moves, or default styles?

6. Schools and universities are often expected to be "all things to all learners," and this generates a significant risk that the result will be many fragmented pieces rather than a clear and interconnected picture. Can researchers help us develop coherent perspectives in our teaching and document the effects of messages that interact and support each other?

Methodologically, research on learning to teach science that explores the issues we have raised in this chapter will use predominantly qualitative methods. After all, we are concerned here about the *quality* of the learning experiences of those learning to teach. Action research and self-study are two prominent methodologies that are well illustrated in the research literature (Loughran et al., 2004). The field of science teacher education research has much to learn from the methods that have moved teacher research forward since 1990.

Many people are not optimistic about the prospect of actually moving beyond the rhetoric of reform. In this chapter we have endeavored to show that moving forward requires an epistemological revolution, a reframing of not just how we think about teaching science, but also how we think about learning to teach science. Progress demands that perspectives that move us forward in teaching science be extended to the context of learning to teach science. Science education research has produced compelling insights that must be developed coherently as those learning to teach science move through their initial teaching experiences.

We concur with Schön's (1995) call for a new epistemology that must be developed both in universities and in schools. Thus we must consider conceptual change not just as change in how students—*and* prospective teachers—think about phenomena but also as change in how students—*and* prospective teachers—think about education. Conceptual changes happen not just to students but also to prospective teachers, experienced teachers, and teacher educators—to teachers in schools and in universities. The entire argument always needs to complete the circle of reasoning about theory and practice. In the process, we must find ways to recognize and develop the authority of experience within our teaching and learning practices.

ACKNOWLEDGMENTS

Thanks to Peter Aubusson and Gaalen Erickson, who reviewed this chapter.

REFERENCES

American Association for the Advancement of Science. (1989). *Science for all Americans.* New York: Oxford University Press.

American Association for the Advancement of Science. (1993). *Benchmarks for science literacy.* New York: Oxford University Press.

American Association for the Advancement of Science. (2001). *Designs for science literacy.* New York: Oxford University Press.

Anderson, C. W. (2000). Challenges to science teacher education. *Journal of Research in Science Teaching, 37,* 293–294.

Anderson, R. D., & Mitchener, C. P. (1996). Research on science teacher education. In D. Gabel (Ed.), *Handbook of research on science teaching and learning* (pp. 3–44). New York: Macmillan.

Ausubel, D. (1968). *Educational psychology: A cognitive view.* New York: Holt, Rinehart & Winston.

Baird, J. R., Gunstone, R. F., Penna, C., Fensham, P. J., & White, R. T. (1990). Researching balance between cognition and affect in science teaching and learning. *Research in Science Education, 20,* 11–20.

Baird, J. R., & Mitchell, I. M. (Eds.). (1986). *Improving the quality of teaching and learning: An Australian case study—The PEEL project.* Melbourne, Australia: Monash University.

Bryan, L. A., & Abell, S. K. (1999). The development of professional knowledge in learning to teach elementary science. *Journal of Research in Science Teaching, 36,* 121–139.

Chinn, C. A., & Brewer, W. F. (1998). Theories of knowledge acquisition. In B. J. Fraser & K. G. Tobin (Eds.), *International handbook of science education* (pp. 97–113). Dordrecht, The Netherlands: Kluwer Academic.

Council of Ministers of Education, Canada. (1997). *Pan-Canadian protocol for collaboration on school curriculum: Common framework of science learning outcomes K–12 (draft).* Toronto: Author.

Crawford, B. A., Krajcik, J. S., & Marx, R. W. (1999). Elements of a community of learners in a middle school science classroom. *Science Education, 83,* 701–723.

Curriculum Corporation. (1994a). *Science—A curriculum profile for Australian schools.* Carlton, Victoria, Australia: Curriculum Corporation.

Curriculum Corporation. (1994b). *A statement on science for Australian schools.* Carlton, Victoria, Australia: Curriculum Corporation.

Dewey, J. (1938). *Experience and education.* New York: Macmillan.

DiSessa, A. (1993). Toward an epistemology of physics. *Cognition and Instruction, 10,* 105–225.

Driver, R. (1989). Changing conceptions. In P. Adey, J. Bliss, J. Head, & M. Shayer (Eds.), *Adolescent development and school science* (pp. 79–99). Lewes, UK: Falmer Press.

Duit, R., & Treagust, D. F. (1998). Learning in science—from behaviourism towards social constructivism and beyond. In B. J. Fraser & K. G. Tobin (Eds.), *International handbook of science education* (pp. 3–26). Dordrecht, The Netherlands: Kluwer Academic.

Duschl, R. A., & Hamilton, R. J. (1998). Conceptual change in science and in the learning of science. In B. J. Fraser & K. G. Tobin (Eds.), *International handbook of science education* (pp. 1047–1065). Dordrecht, The Netherlands: Kluwer Academic.

Elby, A. (2001). Helping physics students learn how to learn. *American Journal of Physics, Physics Education Research Supplement, 69*(7), S54–S64.

Franklin, U. (1994, November). *Making connections: Science and the future of citizenship.* Paper presented at the meeting of the Science Teachers Association of Ontario, Toronto.

Gunstone, R. F., Slattery, M., Baird, J. R., & Northfield, J. R. (1993). A case study exploration of development in pre-service science students. *Science Education, 77,* 47–73.

Guzzetti, B. J., Snyder, T. E., Glass, G. V., & Gamas, W. S. (1993). Promoting conceptual change in science: A comparative meta-analysis of instructional interventions from reading education and science education. *Reading Research Quarterly, 28*(2), 117–154.

Handelsman, J., Ebert-May, D., Beichner, R., Bruns, P., Chang, A., DeHaan, R., et al. (2004). Scientific teaching. *Science, 304*, 521–522.

Hayes, D., Symington, D., & Martin, M. (1994). Drawing during science activity in the primary school. *International Journal of Science Education, 16*, 265–277.

Hewson, P. W., Beeth, M. E., & Thorley, N. R. (1998). Teaching for conceptual change. In B. J. Fraser & K. G. Tobin (Eds.), *International handbook of science education* (pp. 199–218). Dordrecht, The Netherlands: Kluwer Academic.

Hewson, P. W., Tabachnick, B. R., Zeichner, K. M., & Lemberger, J. (1999). Educating prospective teachers of biology: Findings, limitations, and recommendations. *Science Education, 83*, 373–384.

Hodson, D. (1998). *Teaching and learning science: Towards a personalized approach.* Buckingham, UK. Open University Press.

Iran-Nejad, A. (1990). Active and dynamic self-regulation of learning processes. *Review of Educational Research, 60*, 573–602.

Kagan, D. M. (1992). Implications of research on teacher belief. *Educational Psychologist, 27*, 65–90.

Kelly, G. (1955). *The psychology of personal constructs.* New York: Norton.

Knight, R. D. (2004). *Five easy lessons: Strategies for successful physics teaching.* San Francisco: Addison-Wesley.

Lederman, N. G. (1998). The state of science education: Subject matter without context [electronic version]. *Electronic Journal of Science Education, 3*(2), 1–12.

Loughran, J. J., Hamilton, M. L., LaBoskey, V. K., & Russell, T. (Eds.). (2004). *International handbook of self-study of teaching and teacher education practices.* Dordrecht, The Netherlands: Kluwer Academic.

Mason, C. L. (1992). Concept mapping: A tool to develop reflective science instruction. *Science Education, 76*, 51–63.

McGoey, J., & Ross, J. (1999). Research, practice, and teacher internship. *Journal of Research in Science Teaching, 36*, 117–120.

Mintzes, J. J., Wandersee, J. H., & Novak, J. D. (1997). Meaningful learning in science: The human constructivist perspective. In G. D. Phye (Ed.), *Handbook of academic learning: Construction of knowledge* (pp. 404–447). San Diego: Academic Press.

Munby, H., & Russell, T. (1994). The authority of experience in learning to teach: Messages from a physics method class. *Journal of Teacher Education, 45*, 86–95.

Munby, H., Russell, T., & Martin, A. K. (2001). Teachers' knowledge and how it develops. In V. Richardson (Ed.), *Handbook of research on teaching* (4th ed., pp. 877–904). Washington, DC: American Educational Research Association.

National Research Council. (1996). *National science education standards.* Washington, DC: National Academy Press.

Northfield, J. (1998). Teacher education and the practice of science teacher education. In B. J. Fraser & K. G. Tobin (Eds.), *International handbook of science education* (pp. 695–706). Dordrecht, The Netherlands: Kluwer Academic.

Novak, J. (1987). Human constructivism: Toward a unity of psychological and epistemological meaning making. In J. D. Novak (Ed.), *Proceedings of the second international seminar on misconceptions and educational strategies in science and mathematics* (Vol. 1, pp. 349–360). Ithaca, NY: Cornell University Department of Education.

Novak, J. (1989). The use of metacognitive tools to facilitate meaningful learning. In P. Adey (Ed.), *Adolescent development and school science* (pp. 227–239). London: Falmer Press.

Novak, J. (1993). Human constructivism: A unification of psychological and epistemological phenomena in meaning making. *International Journal of Personal Construct Psychology, 6*, 167–193.

Novak, J., & Gowin, D. B. (1984). *Learning how to learn.* New York: Cambridge University Press.

Nussbaum, J., & Novick, S. (1982). Alternative frameworks, conceptual conflict and accommodation. *Instructional Science, 11,* 183–208.

Oosterheert, I. E., & Vermunt, J. D. (2003). Knowledge construction in learning to teach: The role of dynamic sources. *Teachers and Teaching: Theory and Practice, 9,* 157–173.

Pfundt, H., & Duit, R. (1994). *Students' alternative frameworks and science education.* Kiel, Germany: Institute for Science Education, University of Kiel.

Posner, G. J., Strike, K. A., Hewson, P. W., & Gertzog, W. A. (1982). Accommodation of a scientific conception: Toward a theory of conceptual change. *Science Education, 66,* 211–227.

Putnam, R. T., & Borko, H. (2000). What do new views of knowledge and thinking have to say about research on teacher learning? *Educational Researcher, 29*(1), 4–15.

Russell, T. (2000). Teaching to build on school experiences. In R. Upitis (Ed.), *Who will teach? A case study of teacher education reform* (pp. 227–240). San Francisco: Caddo Gap Press.

Russell, T., & Bullock, S. (1999). Discovering our professional knowledge as teachers: Critical dialogues about learning from experience. In J. Loughran (Ed.), *Researching teaching: Methodologies and practices for understanding pedagogy* (pp. 132–151). London: Falmer Press.

Russell, T., McPherson, S., & Martin, A. K. (2001). Coherence and collaboration in teacher-education reform. *Canadian Journal of Education, 26,* 37–55.

Sarason, S. B. (1996). *Revisiting "the culture of the school and the problem of change."* New York: Teachers College Press.

Schön, D. A. (1983). *The reflective practitioner: How professionals think in action.* New York: Basic Books.

Schön, D. A. (1995). The new scholarship requires a new epistemology. *Change, 27,* 27–34.

Scott, P., Asoko, H., & Driver, R. (1992). Teaching for conceptual change: A review of strategies. In R. Duit, F. Goldberg, & H. Neidderer (Eds.), *Research in physics learning: Theoretical issues and empirical studies* (pp. 310–329). Kiel, Germany: Schmidt & Klannig.

Scott, P. H., & Driver, R. H. (1998). Learning about science teaching: Perspectives from an action research project. In B. J. Fraser & K. G. Tobin (Eds.), *International handbook of science education* (pp. 67–80). Dordrecht, The Netherlands: Kluwer Academic.

Segall, A. (2002). *Disturbing practice: Reading teacher education as text.* New York: Peter Lang.

Tobin, K. (1997). The teaching and learning of elementary science. In G. D. Phye (Ed.), *Handbook of academic learning: Construction of knowledge* (pp. 369–403). San Diego: Academic Press.

Tudge, J., & Scrimsher, S. (2003). Lev S. Vygotsky on education: A cultural-historical, interpersonal, and individual approach to development. In B. J. Zimmerman & D. H. Schunk (Eds.), *Educational psychology, a century of contributions* (pp. 207–228). Mahwah, NJ: Lawrence Erlbaum Associates.

Wandersee, J. (1986). Can the history of science help science educators anticipate students' misconceptions? *Journal of Research in Science Teaching, 23,* 581–597.

Wandersee, J., Mintzes, J., & Novak, J. (1994). Research on alternative conceptions in science. In D. Gabel (Ed.), *Handbook of research on science teaching and learning* (pp. 177–210). New York: Macmillan.

White, R. (2001). The revolution in research on science teaching. In V. Richardson, (Ed.), *Handbook of research on teaching* (4th ed., pp. 457–471). Washington, DC: American Educational Research Association.

Zembal-Saul, C., Krajcik, J., & Blumenfeld, P. (2002). Elementary student teachers' science content representations. *Journal of Research in Science Teaching, 39,* 443–463.

CHAPTER 38

Teacher Professional Development in Science

Peter W. Hewson
University of Wisconsin-Madison

Professional development for science teachers is of considerable current importance. This is an era in which, around the world, a new vision of learner-centered instruction is being developed. This grows out of a major, extended research enterprise over the past quarter-century. The focus of attention on what learners know and can do when they enter classrooms, and how this influences the instruction that they receive, has led to significant advances in our understanding of student learning and the implications this has for teaching. In parallel with these reforms, there has been a major push to develop new curricula and to identify explicit standards that together represent significant changes in what it is that students are expected to learn and do. A third circumstance of considerable importance is the increasing recognition of the systemic nature of the educational enterprise, arising in part from the difficulties experienced by reformers who sought to introduce new curricula and new teaching approaches. Aligning different components of educational systems is not a straightforward matter and has led to the investment of large amounts of resources for systemic reform. A notable example in the United States is the large number of Systemic Initiatives funded by the National Science Foundation (NSF) throughout the last decade of the twentieth century (see Chapter 30, this volume): a considerable portion of their budgets funded teacher professional development activities. Another circumstance that has considerable implications for teacher professional development is the growth of more extensive testing of students at all levels. Most, if not all, states in the United States have instituted their own proficiency tests and use these to judge the quality of schools and teachers. Furthermore, the No Child Left Behind legislation in the United States extended these testing requirements throughout the country. In part, these initiatives have been driven by international studies, such as the Third International Mathematics and Science Study and the Programme for International Student Assessment, that have raised issues of national performance. In a number of countries, the perception of inadequate performance has been a driving force for reform.

There are several arguments to be made to support the idea that responses to these national and international circumstances should necessarily, if not exclusively, focus on practicing teachers and their professional development. The first argument addresses the question, why focus on teachers? There is currently a broad consensus that teachers play a central, key role in any model of educational improvement. We are long past the era of so-called teacher-proof curricula. We have also tried, and found wanting, the assumption that teachers could be replaced by computers. Much of this recognition has come from recent research into the nature of a teacher's practice and expertise. What teachers do is not a formulaic following of rules, but nuanced, professional practice in which teachers constantly make important decisions and judgments in how they interact with their students to facilitate their learning. What this means is that if teachers are not involved, educational reform will not happen.

A second argument addresses the question, why not put our efforts into initial teacher education? If the teaching profession as a whole has to change its practices, this cannot happen solely through the introduction of new teachers into the profession. There are several reasons for this. If a teacher's effective teaching life is 25 to 30 years, the proportion of new teachers entering the profession each year is a small subset of the total teaching force. In other words, it will take a long time to change the teaching force if this is the sole means by which it is done. It is also the case that new teachers enter the profession without much power. Their veteran colleagues have experience and expertise that they do not have, and the likelihood that new teachers will be able to teach in different ways and perhaps influence their colleagues is small.

A related argument is that it is an optimistic assumption that all teacher preparation institutions will certify teachers who are fully capable of teaching in ways that are consistent with current reforms. Another argument is that internationally there are many countries where the current teaching force is poorly qualified. This may be due to a lack of resources for teacher education, or the country may have only recently moved to expand its education to all children, thereby creating the need to produce many teachers very rapidly. Under the circumstances, it is clear that the quality of new teachers will be severely compromised.

A final argument addresses the question, why focus on teacher professional development for practicing teachers? This is necessary because in the current climate of reform, teachers' practices, even when they were highly effective at an earlier stage, may be in need of reconsideration and updating. In other words, as the educational context changes, teachers' existing practices and beliefs may not be well matched with the revised demands of new reform efforts.

The focus, then, of this chapter is teacher professional development in science. First, I identify the meaning of teacher professional development in science as used in this chapter, followed by several comments on the specific boundaries of the term as it is adopted in this chapter. Then, I consider some general comments on the difficulty of doing research in this area. Next, I outline three different perspectives on teacher professional development in science; these focus respectively, though not exclusively, on the various aspects of teachers' personal, social, and professional development; what it is that teacher professional developers attend to and do; and the enactment of teachers' professional development in their classrooms. Then, I review specific studies that connect professional development activities on the one hand with the teacher participants in these activities, and on the other hand with learning outcomes of students in the classrooms of teacher participants. The chapter concludes with a discussion of issues raised by the review.

DIMENSIONS OF TEACHER PROFESSIONAL DEVELOPMENT IN SCIENCE

What is teacher professional development in science? First, it is about teachers and their teaching activities involving curriculum, instruction, and assessment; about their students and their learning; and about the educational system in which they practice. Second, it is about teachers being professionals who have an extensive knowledge base of conceptions, beliefs, and practices that they bring to bear on the unique complexities of their daily work lives, a knowledge base that is shared within a professional community. Third, it is about teachers as adult learners who have an interest in and control over the continuing development of their professional practice throughout their working lives, a process that is greatly facilitated by working in community with their peers. Finally, it is about science and the epistemologies, methodologies, and bodies of knowledge about the natural world that give scientific disciplines their distinctive character.

What are the boundaries of teacher professional development in science as used in this chapter? Focusing first on professional development, an obvious answer would be to include only professional development activities themselves and the teachers who participate in them. An alternative viewpoint is to recognize that the ultimate purpose in providing professional development is the improvement of student learning. This, then, leads to the conclusion that the connection between professional development activities themselves and student learning should also be included. The problem with such a perspective is that this connection is lengthy and complicated; it is also difficult to separate it out from many other issues. Increasingly, however, professional developers are being called upon to evaluate their programs in terms of student learning. For these reasons it is necessary to expand the domain of professional development from a tidy, focused, coherent perspective on professional development activities and participants to include the complex, intertwined connection to student learning.

I have included only those research studies that focus on practicing teachers, as distinct from those involved in initial teacher education. Studies of prospective teachers involved in initial teacher education are examined elsewhere in this volume (see Chapter 37). Although this is a convenient division that reflects the reality that initial teacher education and inservice teacher professional development are most commonly different enterprises, it cuts through the important principle that teacher learning should be a continuum, something that happens across the whole professional life of a teacher (Feiman-Nemser, 2001). Although the emphasis and intensity of teacher learning change as teachers move from initial certification to their first teaching positions, there are important common features across these two phases that need to be preserved.

Next, I included only those studies that explicitly described a professional development program. This means that I excluded studies that only consider teacher learning and, possibly, its outcomes in teaching and student learning, or that consider teachers who are their own professional developers. In identifying this limitation it is necessary to recognize, but reject, a possible implication of the distinction this makes between programs and teachers, that is, that programs and the professional developers who run them are active providers, and the teachers who are participants in these programs are passive recipients. On the contrary, it is of the utmost importance to recognize that the focus of any professional development program is the teacher, and that it is teachers themselves who are responsible for their own professional development (Kennedy, 1999; Shapiro & Last, 2002; Wilson & Berne, 1999). Any activity should have the purpose of supporting teachers in taking responsibility for their own learning, in making the topics of teacher professional development their own, and in being active learners.

Finally, included studies needed to have an explicit focus on teachers of science. This requirement arises from the nature of this volume. It also has the practical effect of limiting the number of studies to be reviewed. It goes without saying that the specific character of science is an essential ingredient of student learning, of teacher practice, of teachers' professional development, and thus of programs designed to facilitate these outcomes. That being said, it is also the case that there are many aspects of professional development that are shared across disciplinary contexts, and thus there is much to be learned from literature that makes no reference to the subject matter of science. While not explicitly addressing this literature might be regarded as a significant limitation of this chapter, its influence is apparent, however, in many of the studies included.

Research on Teacher Professional Development in Science

What can be said about the nature of research on teacher professional development in science? The short answer is that it is complicated and difficult, because the object of study—teacher professional development in science—is itself inherently complex, consisting as it does of a number of interrelated components. Therefore it is necessary for research to focus on the nature of relationships between these components, while it concurrently explores each of these components in its own right.

Conceptually, research in this area is very difficult. Although the immediate focus is on the professional development activity itself and the teachers who participate in it, the ultimate purpose of professional development is the improvement of student learning. The pathways of influence of professional development from the original activity to student learning proceed through the intervening variables of teacher learning and classroom enactment. These pathways are complicated, not only by the time it takes for teachers to clarify their learning from professional development activities and translate this into effective curriculum and instruction, but also by everything else that is happening concurrently in the lives of students, teachers, schools, and the community; teacher learning in professional development activities, teachers teaching in classrooms, and student learning are not isolated from the educational and social environments of schools and communities.

There are also practical difficulties in conducting research in this area. Because of the number of components involved, the length of time it takes for teaching practice to mature, and the amount of detail and intensive research techniques required to provide understanding of what is happening at each stage of the process, the cost of effective research on and evaluation of teacher professional development can be substantial. Inevitably there is a trade-off between the costs of the evaluation and the value of the information that is obtained. A valuable approach adopted by the NSF in the United States has been to contract with one organization, Horizon Research, Inc., to develop a set of evaluation instruments that can be used across many projects that NSF has funded to reform the teaching of mathematics and science (Weiss, 1999).

A final comment is that, as always, there is a close relationship between research into a topic and evaluation of that topic, even though they are inherently different activities. This is particularly so because of the complexity of teacher professional development. Thus, in this chapter clear distinctions are not made between research and evaluation, and in some cases these terms will be used interchangeably.

Perspectives on Teacher Professional Development in Science

It is necessary to recognize two essential focal points when considering teacher professional development in science. One essential focus is on the *people* who are experiencing professional development—teachers of science—and the processes through which they are going. This is encapsulated in the language that teachers use—they talk about developing professionally. The question that arises from this focal point is: How do teachers develop professionally? The second essential focus is on the *programs* that have an explicit purpose of providing professional development to teachers. In most cases this means that one or more persons can be identified as professional developers whose purpose is to plan and implement activities for science teachers that are designed to further their professional development. Professional developers, likewise, use characteristic language: they talk about the professional development they are providing. The question that arises from this second focal point is: What is it that good professional developers do? As previously argued, however, it is necessary to follow the influence of programs into teachers' classrooms. Thus a third question to consider is: What is the relationship between teachers and professional development programs? These questions were addressed respectively in three studies that specifically considered the teaching of science, all of which produced theoretical frameworks that conceptualize these essential focal points.

How Do Teachers Develop Professionally?

This question was addressed in a three-year research project, the Learning in Science Project (Teacher Development), in New Zealand (Bell & Gilbert, 1996). In the project, teachers of science learned about and implemented teaching approaches designed with students' thinking and ideas in mind. During this time they experienced development of different kinds that were interwoven with each other. Bell and Gilbert modeled this in terms of personal, professional, and social development, and argued that, if development is to happen, teacher development programs must address all three of these components. In the project, a total of 48 teachers of science, both elementary and secondary, participated in four teacher development programs. Each program consisted of two-hour weekly after-school meetings over one or two school terms. In the meetings teachers shared their experiences of implementing new teaching activities that explicitly took account of students' thinking. The researchers collected multiple forms of data. In addition to that obtained in program meetings, the data included interviews, surveys, and classroom observations. Bell and Gilbert's model of teacher development is detailed in the following paragraphs.

In the initial phase, *Personal Development* involves teachers coming to realize that some *aspects of their practice are problematic*. This could be a slow process, starting with an inarticulate awareness that requires time to take shape. It could also be sparked by a specific event that crystallizes dissatisfaction. This realization then becomes the spur for teachers to seek ways to address the problem. There are, of course, many cases in which teachers get involved with programs even though they do not see their practice as problematic (e.g., a department chair has recommended attendance). Bell and Gilbert (1996) suggested that no progress happens without this phase of personal development. However, they pointed out that this is more likely to happen if teachers feel that overall their teaching is competent, with only a limited aspect being problematic. Related to this is *Social Development*, in which teachers become *aware of their professional isolation* from their peers and recognize that this, too, is problematic. This, then, helps to create a willingness to find ways of discussing their practice with others. A key element of this is the need to be able to trust that their peers will be supportive colleagues who offer critique in a nonjudgmental fashion. These developments support the initial phase of their *Professional Development* in which teachers are *prepared to try out new activities* in their classrooms. In doing so, they take on the role of teacher-as-learner, in which they become aware of the process of change and development; this is seen as a positive progression, the anticipated outcomes of which are better student learning and feeling better about themselves as teachers.

In the next phase, *Personal Development* involves *coping with the restraints inherent in teaching*. When new teaching activities and approaches are introduced, particularly if these give students more opportunities for input, the personal concerns include fear of losing control and not knowing when and how to intervene, uncertainty of the demands on their knowledge of the subject, worries about covering the curriculum and meeting assessment requirements, and concerns about dealing with students, parents, and others who may object to these changes. In this phase, *Social Development* involves teachers coming to *see the value of collaborating with their colleagues*. As trust in each other grows, teachers become more ready to share their experiences with each other, listen openly to their colleagues' suggestions and critiques, and offer their own ideas about ways to address questions, problems, and concerns. In the process, their own self-confidence and ability to reflect critically on their own practice grows. In effect, their collaboration involves their "renegotiating and reconstructing their shared knowledge about *what it means to be a teacher of science*" (Bell & Gilbert, 1996, p. 26, emphasis added). Their *Professional Development* in this phase manifests itself in *developing a more coherent practice*. Their conceptions of teaching science become more articulated, more nuanced, and more reflective. Their classroom practice becomes more flexible, more responsive, and more able to accommodate changes in appropriate ways. More importantly, they see the need to integrate their conceptions with their practice and thus to reconstruct what it means to be a teacher of science.

In the final phase in Bell and Gilbert's (1996) model of teacher development, *Personal Development* entails teachers *feeling more empowered* with respect to their own development. They come to trust that what they are doing will produce the outcomes they hope for, and that students will not let them down when they hand over control. Feelings of empowerment also extend to interactions with their colleagues: teachers feel good about contributing ideas and volunteering their time and energy. In this phase, *Social Development* takes place as teachers begin to initiate activities and relationships with their colleagues, thereby *fostering collaborative ways of working*. Closely related is the *Professional Development* they experience by seeking out or *initiating different development opportunities* beyond the programs in which they are involved.

The scenario outlined in the previous paragraphs is a plausible narrative of how the various phases of the three forms of development might be interwoven with each other. There is a progression through these phases as teachers initially see themselves as competent professionals who nevertheless have room for growth in some aspects of their practice. Next, as they learn new ideas, approaches, and activities, and become more self-aware, they reconstruct aspects of the practice, and they develop a new sense of being a teacher of science within their collegial group. A natural outcome of this development is that they feel empowered to take the initiative with respect to all three types of development. Bell and Gilbert (1996), however, emphasized that their model of teacher development is not a stage model. In other words, there are no requirements that teachers complete one phase before proceeding to the next, or that they have to go through each phase in their developmental journey.

What Is It That Good Professional Developers Do?

This question was addressed by the professional development team of the National Institute for Science Education in the United States. The team explored the nature of professional development practice through a process of collaborative reflection over the period of a year with five accomplished professional developers in science and mathematics (Loucks-Horsley, Hewson, Love, & Stiles, 1998). Rather than thinking of their practice as the refinement and use of models of professional development that others could easily adopt, these professional developers felt that their practice was more complex. Instead, it combined components of different models in programs that were changing over time and tailored to the particular circumstances in which they were working. In other words, they agreed that the practice of professional development is a process of design. On the one hand, professional developers have a set of purposes that they want to achieve. On the other hand, they are working in a particular context, with a particular group of teachers, in a set of circumstances that are unique to this particular project. The process of design requires that purposes be matched with context. Although this inevitably will require compromises, the intent is that these decisions will be made in order to maximize desirable outcomes. These reflections were summarized, albeit greatly simplified, in the form of a framework for the design of teacher professional development in science and mathematics. The specific components of the most recent version of the design framework for professional development in science and mathematics (Loucks-Horsley, Love, Stiles, Mundry, & Hewson, 2003) are elaborated in the following paragraphs.

The design framework has several major elements. First, there is a generic *planning process*, the steps of which are likely to be familiar to readers. These steps start with a commitment to a vision and a set of standards, and an analysis of student learning data; move on to the setting of goals, the planning and doing, or implementing, of professional development; and conclude with evaluation. Second, there are a series of *inputs* into the steps of the planning process. These inputs represent the knowledge and expertise about professional development that developers bring to the process of designing programs. They include *knowledge and beliefs* about all aspects of the process and participants of professional development, knowledge of the specific *context* in which the specific project will be implemented, knowledge and awareness of the range of *critical issues* that any professional development project needs to address, and a knowledge of the range of possible *strategies* that can be used within a professional development project to achieve its particular purposes. Third, these inputs are most salient for different steps of the planning process. For example, knowledge and beliefs will strongly influence the step at which professional developers commit to a vision of professional development, whereas it is only at the planning step that professional developers will be making decisions about which strategies to use. This is not to say, of course, that these inputs will be exclusively considered at these different steps. Rather, once inputs have entered the planning process, they will be considered in subsequent steps. Finally, there is feedback from the reflective evaluation of the project not only to the process of the project, thereby leading to improvements in the design itself, but also to the various inputs into the process that are as a result extended, deepened, and enriched. In other words, this is a dynamic framework.

The first of the four inputs into the professional development design process are the *knowledge and beliefs* that professional developers hold. There are five major knowledge bases that all professional developers are likely to consider when they are designing any professional development project. Of course, it is not the case that this will lead to identical designs. On the contrary, the outcome of the design will be strongly influenced by the specific content of these knowledge bases, and this will change as different theoretical orientations are adopted and further research with respect to each is carried out. The first two concern the principal players at the heart of an educational system and the activities that they are involved in. Thus, professional developers use knowledge of *learners and learning* on the one hand, and *teachers and teaching* on the other, in the design process. The third knowledge base concerns the substance, the content of what is being taught; in this handbook the focus is on the *nature of science*. The final two knowledge bases are directly related to the process of professional development itself: the *nature of professional development* and the *change process*. Current thinking in the field with respect to these five knowledge bases is considered in detail in Loucks-Horsley et al. (2003, Chapter 2).

The second of the four inputs into the professional development design process is the set of *context* factors influencing professional development. If design is the process of marrying theory with reality, and the knowledge and beliefs that professional developers bring with them are theory, then the reality of the particular project to be designed is rooted in the local context. Thus professional developers need to know the teachers that they will be working with and their learning needs, and these teachers' students, the standards they are expected to achieve, and what they currently know. They also need to know what the local curriculum is, the forms of instruction that teachers use, their assessment practices, and the learning environment in their classrooms. Professional developers will also need to know about the larger context in which these teachers' classrooms are situated. What is the organizational structure and culture in the school? Who are the leaders and what support do they give to education reform? What are the local, state, and national policies that influence education in the school? What resources are available to schools and teachers? What history of professional development is there in the school, district, or state? Who are the parents of the students in the school, and what is the nature of the community and its commitment to education? A detailed consideration of these context factors is contained in Loucks-Horsley et al. (2003, Chapter 3).

A third major input into the process of designing professional development is that of the *critical issues* that any professional development project will face. Although these may not be front and center for all projects, professional developers ignore them at their peril. First, there is the need to find *time* for professional development, either within the existing structures, or by influencing policies and practices to create more time. Next is the question of ensuring *equity*. In societies that are increasingly diverse, and needing a greater array of scientific expertise, specific attention needs to be given to ensuring access for all to science education. Another critical issue is the building of a *professional culture* for teachers that recognizes that teachers should be lifelong learners. Closely related to this is the issue of developing *leadership*, particularly with respect to ensuring an environment that facilitates teachers' transforming professional development experiences into classroom practice. A related critical issue is the need to build capacity for *sustainability*. A major failing of much professional development is the lack of sustainability: when a project ends, teachers and schools return to the status quo. Even if a project is successful in sustaining itself, however, another critical issue is *scaling up*. Will the new professional practice only be maintained or will it grow? A final critical issue is that of garnering *public support*. Professional developers need not only to build awareness of science initiatives in schools, but also to engage the public in supporting these initiatives. These critical issues are discussed in depth in Loucks-Horsley et al. (2003, Chapter 4).

The final major input into professional development design is that of *strategies* for professional learning. Even though Loucks-Horsley et al. (2003) documented a large number of potential strategies, they pointed out that strategies are the means of achieving ends that should already have been specified, rather than ends in themselves. It is for this reason that the design process should be quite advanced before suitable strategies are chosen. Any one project is likely to employ a number of different strategies to achieve its various purposes. One set of strategies focuses on the processes of *aligning and implementing curriculum*. When new curriculum materials are available, this is an obvious choice. Another set of strategies looks at a different part of classroom experience by *examining teaching and learning*. Teachers might focus on their own practice through action research, or on their students' thinking and work. A third set of strategies focuses on ways of teachers' *immersion* in the science content that they teach, either through inquiry and problem-solving in science, or by spending time in the world of scientists. A fourth set of strategies focuses on *teaching* itself through strategies such as coaching, mentoring, and demonstration lessons. Another set of strategies focuses more on the ways in which teachers *collaborate* with one another than on the content of their collaborations. Examples of these are partnerships with scientists, professional networks, and study groups. A final set of strategies includes the *vehicles and mechanisms* that professional developers use in their projects: developing professional developers, technologies for professional development, and various structures such as workshops, institutes, courses, and seminars. Strategies for professional learning are considered in detail in Loucks-Horsley et al. (2003, Chapter 5).

What Is the Relationship Between Teachers and Professional Development Programs?

Fishman, Marx, Best, and Tal (2003) explored the relationship between professional development programs and science teachers' practice and developed a model of teacher learning from professional development. In common with Loucks-Horsley et al. (2003), they viewed professional development as a process of design, in which professional developers consider a broad array of issues in order to design all the activities that constitute an effective professional development program. In considering professional development practice, they specifically focused on the issues that professional developers have control over, or "*design elements*," and categorize these in four ways that have much in common with the design framework proposed by Loucks-Horsley et al. (2003). Content is the first design element; this refers to the learning outcomes for teachers who participate in professional development. This might be pedagogical knowledge (e.g., assessment knowledge) or subject matter knowledge. The second design element is strategy, used much as Loucks-Horsley et al. (2003) did. The third design element is sites: these are the settings in which teacher learning happens. This element pays attention to aspects of context, format, and place. Media are the final design element. This pays attention to the means through which professional development might be carried out (e.g., video, computers, face-to-face interactions).

Fishman et al. (2003) focused explicitly on teacher practice as an outcome of professional development programs, going beyond Loucks-Horsley et al. (2003) in the process. For them, the primary criterion for deciding program effectiveness was teacher learning: the *knowledge, beliefs, and attitudes* that teachers acquire as a result of participating in *professional development activities*. However, they did not stop with teacher learning. Rather, they adopted from Richardson (1996) the viewpoint that one has to consider teachers' knowledge, beliefs, and attitudes as an interactive entity with their classroom *enactment* in which each influences the other. Thus, they saw a need to consider how teachers' knowledge, beliefs, and attitudes are enacted in classroom settings, and how enactment influences student learning, as evidenced in *student performance*. They also recognized a reciprocal, interactive relation in which student learning influences teacher learning, mediated through enactment. A final node in the framework is *curriculum*, about which they made two arguments. On the one hand, they saw curriculum influencing, and being involved in, professional development activities. On the other hand they argued that curriculum materials themselves may be educative.

This framework is valuable in the emphasis that it gives to tracking the influence of teacher learning, through its enactment in the classroom, and on to student learning. This emphasis gives explicit attention to various aspects that need to be considered in evaluating teacher professional development. Their illustration of this point in terms of a project that they evaluate is considered elsewhere in this review.

Summary

The three frameworks provide perspectives on teacher professional development in science that are complementary of each other. Together, they illuminate the many different components of the complex enterprise of professional development. Professional development programs have the goal of facilitating changes toward more effective teacher practices that ultimately are intended to improve students' science learning. Bell and Gilbert's (1996) model of teacher development focused on the teacher participants in professional programs and the interrelated strands of their personal, social, and professional development. Loucks-Horsley et al. (2003) high-lighted the need for professional developers to pay explicit attention to a range of knowledge bases, to the wide variety of strategies for professional development, to the context of their particular programs, and to critical issues that arise for any program as they design their programs. Finally, Fishman et al. (2003) stressed the importance of being explicit about the connections between program, teacher practice, and student learning.

RESEARCH STUDIES

While there are considerable numbers of research studies that focus on individual components of these frameworks of programs, teachers and their practice, and students, and many that consider the relationship between classroom practice and student performance, the number of studies that consider the effect of programs on other components of these frameworks, with specific reference to science, was considerably smaller. The only previous review of professional development that explicitly considered professional development in science (and mathematics) was that conducted by Kennedy (1999). She included studies if they considered benefits to students. Four of the 10 studies included in Kennedy's review focused on science.

One other review, by Wilson and Berne (1999), discussed a small number of professional development projects. Their criteria for inclusion required that projects also conducted research, thought about both the content and process of professional development, and conceptualized professional teaching knowledge in terms of knowledge of subject matter, of individual students, of cultural differences across groups, of learning, and of pedagogy. Only one of these studied the teaching of science.

One reason why there are so few studies of professional development in science is likely to be the complexity of what is being studied. Consider the question of how student learning is related to professional development activity. The first link is between the professional development activities, for which some relevant variables are their nature, content, and extent, and the teachers who participate in them. Next, the outcomes from teachers' engagement in these activities will be mediated by their knowledge, beliefs, attitudes, and skills, as well as by the contexts in which they work. These outcomes could include learning further knowledge and skills, and developing different beliefs and attitudes; they could lead to the planning and implementation of revised curriculum and instruction that through reflection become more coherent. The next link, then, is between teachers, their professional practice, and their students' participation in classroom activities. Finally, as with teachers, students' learning outcomes are mediated by their knowledge, beliefs, attitudes, and skills, as well as by the contexts of school, home, and community. In other words, the connection is complex and involved. This conclusion is supported by Guskey's (2000) identification of five levels of professional development evaluation: participants' reaction, participants' learning, organizational support and change, participants' use of new knowledge and skills, and student learning outcomes.

Before considering studies in some detail, it is useful to address who should be considered as professional developers. Professional developers are people who are likely to play different but complementary roles, depending on their primary places of employment. Boyd, Banilower, Pasley, and Weiss (2003) identified a broad array of people who served as professional development providers for U.S. Local Systemic Change projects funded by the NSF. Their data demonstrated that teachers can be professional developers, as can their colleagues, heads of departments in schools, curriculum specialists in the school or in the district, staff development personnel in the district, personnel drawn from independent educational organizations, and/or people employed at tertiary-level institutions such as colleges or universities. Within this range, teachers released full-time from their teaching assignments constituted the largest group. Although teachers can be, and often are, their own personal professional developers, articles that focus on teachers' own self-study and development are not considered in this chapter, since this important group of studies is considered elsewhere in this volume (see Chapter 34). For the purposes of this chapter, a professional developer will be regarded as someone who is concerned with the professional development of others.

All of the research studies reviewed include descriptions of professional development programs with teachers of science. These studies are grouped in two ways. First, there are those that only consider the influence of these programs on the teachers who were participants in them. Second, there are those that include student outcomes from classes taught by teachers who participated in professional development programs. Within each group, studies are ordered, depending on the size of the study in terms of teacher participants: case studies of one or two teachers, studies of coherent groups of teachers, and large-scale samples of teachers.

Professional Development and Teachers of Science

The first three studies reviewed are case studies of one or two teachers. This allowed the researchers to spend extended periods of time with each teacher and thus to consider in some depth a variety of aspects of the teachers themselves, the professional development activities they were engaged in, and their enactment of ideas and approaches considered in these activities. Because of the concentrated nature of the research, the data-gathering methods produced loosely structured, thick descriptions, and these were analyzed with qualitative techniques.

Appleton and Asoko (1996) presented a case study of an elementary teacher in the United Kingdom who taught a science unit in which he sought to implement his understanding of a constructivist view of learning. The teacher, Robert, taught the unit for nearly a year (10 months) after attending an inservice program whose primary focus was a constructivist view of learning and its implications for instruction.

The program consisted of four blocks of five days each over a period of 10 weeks. Teachers in the program learned key principles of learning and were given examples of teaching approaches derived from these principles. They also had opportunities within the program to plan lessons using these approaches and were encouraged to try them out in their classrooms between the blocks. Robert had been enthusiastic about the ideas in the program and had reported success in using them in his classroom. In the period between the end of the program and the case study, Robert had had no formal support in putting these ideas into practice. The case study itself took place over a three-week period, during which Robert implemented a science topic he had planned on his own in a class of 10-year-olds. While he maintained overall control of the unit, one researcher was a participant observer in the classroom and provided some support for the teacher, both in helping out in small groups and making suggestions about the teaching of the unit. Data sources included observational field notes, audiotapes of teacher talk and pupil discussion, interviews with Robert, and samples of pupils' work. Analysis showed that Robert implemented some of the principles of constructivist learning more effectively than others. Although he provided an encouraging classroom atmosphere that facilitated his being able to elicit pupils' prior knowledge, he was not able to articulate clearly defined conceptual goals for the unit (focusing more on classroom process than content), he did not consistently use teaching strategies that challenged pupils to develop new ideas, and he provided no opportunities for pupils to use new ideas in different contexts. The researchers noted that Robert held prior beliefs about teaching and learning that facilitated his assimilation of some of the principles, while hampering the assimilation of other principles. They concluded that Robert would have benefited from inservice programs that modeled the principles they are teaching more effectively and that provided regular ongoing support, since teacher change is difficult and incremental, particularly if it involves a teacher's core beliefs about teaching and learning.

Rosebery and Puttick (1998) presented a case study of a single science teacher in the United States involved in an intensive professional development project that extended for nearly two years. The project advocated a view that both learning science and practicing science teaching are socially and historically constituted sensemaking practices. Consistent with this viewpoint was a perspective that, even for the most experienced teachers, their daily teaching would always involve challenges, dilemmas, and uncertainties. The teacher, Liz, was videotaped while she learned science in workshops and taught science in her sixth-grade classroom, and was interviewed about both her learning and her teaching. During the project, data were gathered as Liz taught the same unit twice and planned the way she would teach it a third time. The extensive, detailed data gathering demonstrated a strong connection between key aspects of her science learning and her classroom practice. Specifically, Liz valued the opportunities she had to explore her ideas in an environment that supported her struggle to learn, while challenging her thinking, and sought to construct her elementary science practice along similar lines. Critical colleagues and a set of resources (e.g., videotape) to facilitate reflection on both her science learning and her teaching of science were essential features in her journey toward teaching in ways that she had experienced as a science learner.

Hand and Prain (2002) detailed an extended case study of two science teachers' participation in an ongoing inservice program in Australia to develop pedagogical practices to support writing-to-learn strategies. The inservice program was set up in response to the concerns of "a group of science teachers about the role of language in science . . . to generate strategies to diversify the types of writing used for learning science in each class" (p. 745). Eight junior secondary science teachers participated in the program. The article reported on two of these teachers, Alan and Chris, who were most open to innovation. The program's goal was to facilitate reflection on teachers' changing concerns arising from ongoing classroom practice, through an equal partnership between researchers and teachers. Although teacher ownership of the program remained high throughout the four-year time frame of the study, at times teachers assumed a cognitive apprenticeship role when researchers introduced and modeled different approaches in regular inservice sessions. Data sources included audiotapes of these inservice sessions, field notes of classroom observations, and interviews with teachers. Analysis of the data identified three issues that were central to the two teachers' concerns. The first issue was assessment, with teachers primarily seeing writing in science as an excellent assessment technique. Initially, they saw it as summative, but in time realized its many formative uses. The second issue was planning and setup of writing tasks in order to incorporate them into normal classroom practice. More specifically, they needed to develop strategies that supported students completing and, in time, planning writing tasks. The final issue concerned their changing roles as classroom teachers. They came to see that they needed to move from being a "wisdom-giver" (Hand & Prain, p. 750) to being a facilitator if students were to maximize the benefits they gained from writing-to-learn tasks. Critical features of this professional development experience were its long-term support for the teachers and the balance between the teachers' ownership and apprenticeship roles.

These studies understandably have strong similarities in their data-gathering and data-analysis techniques. They are, however, quite different from one another in the design of the professional development programs; there were differences with respect to the explicit content focus of the programs, the strategies that were used (examining teaching and learning, and immersion in inquiry), the extent to which teachers had input into the programs, and whether programmatic professional development overlapped with teacher enactment. The specifics of each program understandably carried through quite directly into the teachers' classrooms. Of particular interest is the considerable difference between the first study, where Robert's teaching was observed nearly a year after formal professional development activity concluded, and the latter two, in which teachers' implementation of different teaching approaches was interspersed with continuing interactions with professional developers and peers. On the one hand, Robert only adopted aspects that he could assimilate to his core beliefs about teaching (which he did not examine). On the other hand, there is evidence that the teachers in the other two studies became more aware of, and in some cases reconsidered, their core beliefs about teaching, as enacted in their classrooms.

The next two studies focus on larger groups of teachers who participated in a single professional development program. Briscoe and Peters (1997) in the United States explored how collaboration among elementary teachers from several schools, and with university researchers, supported them as they attempted change in their practices. Twenty-four teachers (mostly volunteers, with some specifically recruited) participated in a three-week summer workshop (four hours a day, four days a week) on problem-centered learning in science. The agenda implemented in the workshop was negotiated between teachers and researchers. During the following semester, a researcher visited each teacher twice a month to observe him or her teaching science, and once a month all teachers and researchers held a day-long meeting. Data sources included initial structured interviews with teachers, field notes of classroom observations, transcripts of discussions, and collections of artifacts created by each teacher, representing respectively the implementation of problem-centered activities and the nature of teaching and learning. Analysis of the data showed that, as a result of the professional development, many teachers were thinking about changing their practices. Doing so was, however, difficult. Case studies of six teachers showed that having someone with whom to brainstorm ideas and discuss successes and failures was key to their learning both content and pedagogical knowledge, and sustaining their commitment to and enthusiasm for problem-centered learning.

Luft and Pizzini (1998) reported on a program designed to teach a structured model of problem solving in science (the Search-Solve-Create-Share (SSCS) model). Thirteen elementary teachers in the United States, all volunteers, attended a four-day workshop on the model, including information on the model, being a student in a model cycle, and planning implementation. During the following school year, they were encouraged to implement the model in their classrooms, to observe an experienced teacher demonstrating the model (up to four times), and to repeat the implementation. Seven of the teachers completed all of these phases and were the focus of the study. All implementations were observed by a researcher, and the teachers' use of the problem-solving model was assessed with a specially designed instrument, the SSCS Implementation Assessment Instrument, which focused on key categories of the problem-solving model, such as learning group performance, student participation, and the teacher's role in supporting a student-centered classroom. The level of SSCS implementation on each category before and after observing demonstration lessons was compared. Of eight categories, there were significant increases in three (time in groups, group cohesiveness, and active participation) at the 0.05 level, and two (teacher role and students generating problems and action plans) at the 0.10 level.

These two studies have strong similarities with the first group of studies with respect to similar, intensive data-gathering procedures and the differences in program structures and strategies. In both studies, program support structures and classroom implementation overlapped to provide the opportunity for the reflective cycles that are an essential part of effective teacher enactment (Fishman et al., 2003). Although to varying degrees, both studies stressed the value of collegial interaction in supporting this process. Finally, in both studies there was evidence that there were changes in teachers' classroom practices toward those advocated in the programs, though not as extensively as the professional developers had hoped for. A reasonable conclusion is that it is still an open question whether these changes will be embedded in teachers' continuing practice.

The final group of studies connecting professional development programs and teachers involved large numbers of teachers who participated in a broad range of different programs. Supovitz and Turner (2000) examined the relationship between professional development and teaching practice and classroom culture. The data were gathered, by means of a survey, from teachers in the United States involved with the Local Systemic Change initiative of the NSF. The survey was completed by nearly 3500 K–8 teachers in 24 diverse localities around the country, who had received varying amounts of professional development, ranging from none to more than 160 hours. The professional development was assumed to be of high quality, with characteristics such as immersion in inquiry, intensive and sustained, embedded in classroom realities, focused on teachers' subject matter knowledge, consistent with standards for professional development, and connected to other aspects of school reform. These teachers reported on the extent and nature of the professional development they received, their teaching practices in science classrooms, and their classroom and school culture. Analysis showed that there was a strong relationship between the extent of teachers' professional development on the one hand, and their self-reported adoption of reform-oriented teaching practices (e.g., "design or implement their own investigation") and classroom culture of investigation (e.g., "encourage students to explain concepts to one another") on the other hand. The level of teachers' content preparation was also a strong influence on their teaching practice and classroom culture.

Garet, Porter, Desimone, Birman, and Yoon (2001) researched the effects of different characteristics of professional development on teacher outcomes in the United States. These characteristics, or structural features, included form of activity, duration (contact hours), and degree of collective participation, these being identified as elements of "best practice" in the professional development literature. Teacher outcomes focused on teacher knowledge and skills, and change in classroom teaching practice. These outcomes were determined by a survey of a national probability sample of teachers of science and mathematics who were involved in professional development provided through state and local institutions using national Eisenhower funding. The study showed that there were significant positive effects on teachers' self-reported increases in knowledge and skills and changes in classroom practices by core features from professional development activities. Mediating between structural features of professional development and teacher outcomes were content knowledge, active learning (observing and being observed; planning for classroom implementation; reviewing student work; and presenting, leading, and writing), and coherence of the professional development programs (being integrated into the daily life of the school).

Because of the large numbers of teachers involved, these studies differ from those previously discussed in this section in several ways. The sampling techniques together with the large numbers sampled provide assurances that the samples studied are representative of the whole population and the results can thus be generalized. The necessary use of surveys to gather information from teachers means, however, that the data gathered about classroom enactment, in particular, are qualitatively quite different. Data on teaching practices come from teacher self-reports in terms of categories provided by the researchers rather than from classroom observations.

Professional Development, Teaching, and Students' Science Learning

The first four studies reviewed below focus on relatively small, coherent groups of teachers and their students. The groups, all with fewer than 20 teachers, were coherent because within each group teachers participated in the same professional development program, and, in the first two of these studies, the teachers taught in the same school.

Parke and Coble (1997) conducted a study in the United States that connected professional development, teachers' instruction, and student achievement. Professional development sessions for middle school science teachers were built around a strategy of curriculum development. Prior to focusing on curriculum, however, teachers were introduced to research on teaching and learning, as well as reform goals and standards, and, through dialogue, articulated their personal beliefs about teaching, learning, and assessment. They also worked to align their curriculum with the demands and constraints of their school and community environments through conversations with peers, administrators, and parents, and explored the implications of their revised curricula for assessment. Data were gathered in the same school from 19 teachers who participated in the project, and 11 control teachers who did not, and from 205 project students and 120 control students. Teachers were individually interviewed about their teaching practices and their perceptions of student attitudes toward learning science, and students were surveyed about their teachers' teaching practices and their attitudes toward science. Analysis of these data indicated statistically significant differences with respect to the frequency of in-class experiments and student collaboration (both higher for project teachers), and students' attitudes toward science class (more positive in project classrooms). There were, however, no significant differences between project and control classroom students on a state-mandated science test that emphasized factual information recall. The test was developed in 1960 and thus predated current reform efforts.

Barak and Pearlman-Avnion (1999) reported on a two-year case study of a junior high school in Israel aiming to integrate the teaching of science and technology. The primary mechanism for achieving this was intensive and extended professional development for the school's eight science teachers and three technology teachers. Information on implementation of an integrated unit was gained from interviews with professional development providers, administrators, and teachers; from school visits; and from an achievement test and an attitude questionnaire (specifically designed for the study) at the end of the first year to assess pupil performance on a science-technology project. Geared to the quite different backgrounds of science teachers and technology teachers, the professional development opportunities were intensive in nature and extended over time. First, teachers were released for half a day each week throughout the school year to attend inservice courses offered by higher education institutions to improve relevant content knowledge of science for technology teachers, and vice versa, based on instructional materials specially prepared for integrating science and technology. Second, teachers attended individual, nonevaluative tutoring sessions about once every two weeks that focused on class activities, pupil achievement, and relationships with administrators and different subject area teachers. A key factor in the first-year implementation was the reluctance and, in one or two cases, the refusal of science teachers to teach the technical aspects of science-technology projects (e.g., combining the physics of sound with designing and constructing an audio amplifier). It should be noted that pupil achievement scores were noticeably higher on technology items. The authors concluded that a more realistic professional development goal was to develop awareness of the different field of study rather than expect teachers to teach both science and technology.

Fishman et al. (2003) illustrated their approach to linking teacher and student learning with professional development previously discussed in this chapter, in their report on a study with eight middle school science teachers in a large urban school district in the United States. The study was guided by their iterative model for evaluation of professional development that specifies that the design of professional development should be based on evidence of students' performance with respect to particular content standards. The implementation of the professional development should be evaluated by teachers who, in turn, enact ideas explored in the professional development. This enactment should be observed and student performance evaluated. This should then lead to redesign of the professional development, leading to a reiteration of the same cycle. In the study, the professional development was redesigned after an initial lack of student success on map reading and watershed concepts. Conducted in four Saturday workshops of six hours' duration held once a month, the professional development activities used strategies of curriculum review, peer information exchanges, and the examination of student work and consisted of an overview of the unit, modeling of a particular activity from the unit, and practice with a software tool used for building student understanding of watersheds. Teachers reported that their confidence in being able to support student learning had increased as a result of these workshops. Observations of their teaching showed that they used several strategies developed in the workshop. An evaluation of student learning, in this case with 755 students, showed that there was a statistically significant improvement in responses to water quality test items from the previous year.

A statewide NSF-funded systemic initiative (SSI) in the United States was the context for a study connecting professional development and student learning (Kahle, Meece, & Scantlebury, 2000). Ohio's SSI focused on middle school science and mathematics in urban districts through intensive teacher professional development activities. Teachers attended six-week summer institutes with six follow-up seminars throughout the course of the subsequent year. The institutes addressed teachers' lack of content knowledge and modeled inquiry teaching in science and mathematics, with a particular emphasis on standards-based teaching practices such as cooperative groups, open-ended questioning, extended inquiry, and problem-solving. Kahle et al.'s (2000) study was based on a subset of the data gathered in this project.[1] These data, gathered in two ways from students, included student achievement tests, prepared by the SSI from National Assessment of Educational Progress public-release items, and student questionnaires. The latter had subscales on student attitudes, standards-based teaching strategies used by their teachers, parents' involvement in science homework, and peers' participation in science activities. The data reported were gathered in eight middle schools, in each of which teachers who had participated in the SSI's professional development program were matched with one or more teachers teaching similar classes who had not. The data reported in this study were gathered in the science classrooms of eight SSI teachers and 10 non-SSI teachers. Analysis showed that there was a positive relationship between the SSI's standards-based professional development and students' science achievement and attitudes, especially for boys. This relationship was mediated by the reported use of standards-based teaching practices that were positively related with teachers' participation in the SSI's professional development.

---

1. At least 30 percent of the students in all schools in this study were minorities. The data reported were for African American students. Although this was a significant aspect of the published study, the ethnicity of students is not considered further in this chapter.

It is instructive to compare how the three components—professional develop-ment, teaching practice, and student outcomes—played out across these studies. First, the professional development provided to teachers in each of these studies had several commendable characteristics. In each case, professional development in-cluded intensive sessions where teachers had opportunities to build knowledge of new approaches and explore implications for teaching, followed by opportunities to teach using these approaches that were interspersed with follow-up—reflective sessions to talk through aspects of their implementation in the specific circum-stances of their classrooms. Different professional development strategies were used, some in combination with each other; these included aligning and implementing curriculum, immersion experiences, and examining teaching and learning (Loucks-Horsley et al., 2003). Data on classroom teaching strategies were gathered in differ-ent ways, including classroom observations, interviews with teachers about their teaching, and student surveys of teaching strategies. The inclusion of students in these studies provided a further opportunity to gather data about teaching that was not provided by the teacher. Next, these studies reported different ways of gather-ing student achievement data, varying from the proximal to the distal. In two stud-ies, tests were prepared by the researchers themselves, in one study tests specifi-cally targeted to the purposes of the study were constructed from available national test banks (Kahle et al., 2000), and in another study (Parke & Coble, 1997), an inde-pendent, statewide assessment test was used. Finally, there were variations in how closely the relationships among these three components were followed, flowing in part from the data-gathering methods employed. The study by Fishman et al. (2003) is noteworthy in this respect. Guided by an iterative model for the evaluation of professional development, the authors were able to track the influence of profes-sional development explicitly and directly through teachers' enactment to student performance on tests specifically designed for the study.

One large-scale study reported connections among types of professional de-velopment, classroom activities, and student achievement. Huffman, Thomas, and Lawrenz (2003) conducted an external evaluation of a large-scale, statewide profes-sional development project in science and mathematics in the southern United States.[2] The professional development provided by the state was extensive and di-verse, consisting of coordinated workshops in the summer, with extended follow-up through the school year. It utilized all five general categories of professional development strategies proposed by Loucks-Horsley et al. (1998). Across all of the sites at which the project was implemented, there were many opportunities for teachers to engage in long-term, intensive professional development. Because the teachers were free to decide in which opportunities they would engage, there were variations in the type and duration of professional development. The authors sur-veyed 94 eighth-grade science teachers about, first, the type and duration of profes-sional development they had experienced, and, second, the type and frequency of use of standards-based instructional methods they used. Student achievement was measured with the existing state achievement test, "part of a criterion-referenced state assessment system designed to measure student achievement of the state stan-dards" (Huffman et al., p. 381). The test included multiple-choice and short-answer

---

2. Only the science results are reported in this chapter.

questions and a comprehensive scientific inquiry task. Regression analyses were conducted with the independent variable being the type and duration of professional development. The dependent variables used were, first, the reported frequency of use of standards-based instructional methods, and, second, class mean scores on the state achievement test. The professional development strategies of curriculum development and examining practice were the only ones predictive of the use of standards-based instructional methods. Finally, there were no significant statistical relationships between any of the professional development strategies and students' achievement scores.

DISCUSSION

The frameworks for considering teacher professional development in science adopted in this chapter include programs that provide professional development to teachers of science, the people—teachers—who participate in these programs, the classroom practices that emanate from this participation, and the people—students—who are the participants in these practices. Research studies reviewed in this chapter explicitly addressed professional development programs for teachers of science. Some were primarily concerned with the effect of these programs on teacher practice, and others sought to connect student performance to programs through classroom practice.

How has research been conducted on programs, teachers, classroom practice, and students in the studies reviewed in this chapter? First, the research on programs is largely descriptive. In most studies these descriptions focus on project design, including its purpose, the pattern and duration of professional development activities, the professional development strategies used in these activities, the focus of these activities (science content, teaching strategies, etc.), and the teachers who participate in these activities. In only a few cases were data gathered during program activities and from participants, and in only one case was the research focused on program activities themselves (Fishman et al., 2003). The intent, for the most part, was to treat the programs as contextual constraints on the professional development of the teachers. Second, the research on teachers is both descriptive and evaluative, rooted, as it is, in a large, growing body of literature on teachers of science and other disciplines that detail what teachers know and believe, how they teach, and how they learn to teach. Thus it uses the same variety of data-gathering procedures used in the larger literature, including surveys, interviews, and observations of teaching and, in a few studies, participation in program sessions. It is no surprise, therefore, that these studies provide a much clearer picture of the teachers and their teaching, than they do of their learning as a result of their participation in professional development programs. A few studies, such as that of Rosebery and Puttick (1998), paid close attention to teacher learning within professional development programs. Others, such as Parke and Coble (1997) and the large-scale studies, relied on implicit assumptions about how and what teachers learned as a result of the programs in which they participated. Finally, the research on students largely focused on student outcomes, as measured by scores on achievement tests. The tests used in these studies varied with respect to their proximity to program, from those specifically designed within the context of the study, such as Barak and Pearlman-Avnion (1999), to those that used existing, distal measures such as state tests, such as Huffman et al. (2003).

How have the ideas in the theoretical frameworks considered in this chapter been addressed in the studies that have been reviewed? First, consider the model of teacher development outlined in terms of three different components—personal, social, and professional—by Bell and Gilbert (1996). Although none of the studies reviewed used this framework, the case studies that gathered detailed data from teachers provided an opportunity to consider teacher development in these terms. For the most part, these teachers engaged in the first two phases of personal development: they implicitly accepted aspects of their teaching as problematic as they were dealing with aspects of the restraints of their classrooms and schools, with some rethinking their core beliefs about teaching. Barak and Pearlman-Avnion (1999) provided a counterexample that strengthens the importance of personal development: some science teachers saw no need for the professional development program provided (to integrate science and technology) and refused to change their practice. In terms of professional development, most teachers in these studies tried out new activities and were engaged in developing their classroom practice. There was also social development through their expressions of seeing the value of collaborative ways of working. Of interest, however, is that there was little evidence presented to decide whether any of these teachers moved into the third phases of development: feeling personally empowered and initiating other activities and collaborative ways of working.

Second, consider the professional development design framework outlined by Loucks-Horsley et al. (2003). Derived from a consideration of the practice of professional developers, the framework considers the process of design as being informed by knowledge and beliefs about various aspects of professional development, the context in which professional development occurs, various critical issues that all professional developers need to consider, and a catalog of professional development strategies. Only one study (Huffman et al., 2003) explicitly used any components of this framework, categorizing strategies of professional development across a broad array of professional development programs. Few studies explicitly considered the knowledge and beliefs underlying professional development. Other studies, to varying degrees, considered some aspects of the framework—case studies generally included context and some discussion of critical issues, and most studies gave some indication of the professional development strategies used, such as Luft's and Pizzini's (1998) consideration of demonstration classrooms. No studies, however, used the framework in a systematic fashion in planning, or in formative or summative assessments of professional development programs.

Finally, consider the emphasis on enactment as an interactive entity involving teachers, their classroom practice, and student performance provided by Fishman et al. (2003). Only a few studies considered these interactions in the larger context of professional development programs. One obvious reason is the difficulty of keeping a detailed focus on the different components of enactment as an interactive entity; across the studies that attempted to do so, classroom practice and student assessment were components that were addressed in a distant or indirect fashion. Another reason is that, although there are persistent calls to assess the effectiveness of professional development programs in terms of student achievement, there are other more proximal goals that professional developers might like to achieve, such as finding ways to reduce the out-of-class workload of teachers.

Kennedy's (1999) review of professional development in science and mathematics concluded that, based on evidence of benefits to students, the content of professional development (what to teach and how students learn it) is more important than its form and structure (its duration, whether it is interspersed with teaching, whether it advocates prescriptive or discretionary approaches). Kennedy also concluded that it was important to treat teachers as professionals. The studies reviewed in this chapter do not support Kennedy's conclusion that the content of professional development is more important than form and structure. On the contrary, the various case studies demonstrate that without continuing support during the critical phases of planning, implementing, and reflecting on instruction, teachers are unlikely to make major changes in their teaching, particularly if these changes require reconsideration of their core beliefs about science, teaching, learning, instruction, and/or assessment. Content is still important: the studies reviewed here largely included it in ways similar to the most effective studies in Kennedy's review. The conclusion about the importance of treating teachers as professionals is also relevant; it is a reminder that the role of program structure is facilitative and not causative. Teachers themselves are responsible for changing their practice and, in the process, empowering themselves. In this regard, the questions that Bobrowsky, Marx, and Fishman (2001) posed about whether participants in professional development programs are volunteers or not, and how to design effective professional development for non-volunteers who may need it most are clearly relevant.

Because of the complexity of professional development programs and their effects on teachers and students, it is not surprising that the variations across the studies reviewed in this chapter are extensive; with a finite amount of resources to devote to studies of these issues, trade-offs are necessary. Consider the number of participants in a study. By limiting the study to one or a few teachers, it is possible to focus in depth on a broad array of factors that influence a teacher's learning, practice, and influence on students. Although this leads to a rich, nuanced description of a teacher and a deep understanding of the complexities of his or her world, it does not provide pictures of the breadth, extent, and variation of teachers' professional development experiences across schools, districts, regions, or nations. In studies with large numbers of teachers, choices need to be made to limit the number of issues to focus on, and to choose efficient methods of data-gathering. For example, in order to reach over 3,500 teachers, Supovitz and Turner (2000) used teacher self-reports for information about their professional development experiences and their teaching practices, rather than data gathered by independent observers. Trade-offs also need to be made with respect to the components that are studied. Deciding to include programs, teachers and their practices, and student outcomes in a single study requires other limitations. For example, Parke and Coble (1997) relied on a state-mandated science test, developed some 30 years prior to their study, for information on student achievement. In contrast, Fishman et al. (2003) designed the achievement tests used in their study, but limited the study to a tightly constrained content area and a few teachers. In other words, in studying teacher professional development in science, trade-offs are inevitable. This means that it is essential that there be a broad array of different methods and data that complement one another in providing an overall picture of the field. While the studies reviewed in this chapter illustrate the diversity of possible approaches, they also illustrate that many more studies are needed to paint a coherent picture of the field.

CONCLUDING REMARKS

The complexity of teacher professional development in science points to its systemic nature and suggests that research consider not only the people involved in professional development, but also the systems in which these programs are embedded. A metaphor that provides some insight into this issue is that of pathways. In considering professional development programs, it is necessary to consider not only the outcomes that the programs seek to achieve but also the means, the processes, the pathways by which those outcomes will be achieved. It is seldom that outcomes are ignored; much more frequently, however, it is only when desired outcomes are not achieved that the pathways by which they might be achieved are considered. However, the likelihood of programs being successful is greatly enhanced if the pathways are explicitly included in the program design. The pathway metaphor itself is valuable because it suggests several important issues. First, it draws attention to the starting point, the endpoint, and the various ways by which they might be connected. Without knowing where one starts from, and identifying reasonable connections between various points along the way, the possibility exists of finding oneself on the wrong side of a chasm to be bridged that requires more resources than are available. Next, the pathway metaphor suggests the need to pay careful attention to the journey and the resources that are likely to be available along the way. In other ways it is necessary to understand the system components that facilitate progress along the pathway. Finally, the idea of a pathway draws attention to the time that will be needed to complete the journey. It does not happen instantaneously; specifying milestones along the way reminds us that this is the case.

Thinking systemically also highlights a particular aspect of the relationship between people and systems. Frequently, what makes sense to individual participants is at odds with what makes sense at the organizational level. If a system and the people who work within it are to work effectively, there are different conditions that need to be met. On the one hand, at an individual level, each person needs to believe that she or he is an important part of the enterprise, that his or her contributions are valued and respected, and that she or he has a measure of autonomy in carrying out his or her responsibilities. This means that each person needs to develop an understanding of the many facets of his or her job and become committed to the belief that it is fair, equitable, and worthwhile. The organization needs to be responsive to the needs and ideas of its members, and to be trusting of their abilities. In other words, each person needs to be able to take ownership of the position to which she or he is appointed, and the work that this entails. On the other hand, at an organizational level, if the system itself is to operate effectively, there needs to be coherency in its vision, a concerted working together to achieve common goals, and a lack of different groups working at cross purposes to one another. This requires leadership to create a vision, set goals to be achieved, and developing strategies for reaching those goals. One of the key strategies needs to be the effective communication of the vision to all participants in the system. Individuals, then, can come to see that their efforts are responsive to, contributing to, and fitting in with an overall vision.

Bringing a system together such that what makes sense for the participants is coherent with what makes sense for the system does not happen of its own accord. There need to be strategies in place that allow reconciliation of these different perspectives to occur as a normal part of the functioning of the system, whether it be a classroom, a school district, or teacher professional development.

ACKNOWLEDGMENTS

Thanks to Ian Mitchell and Kathleen O'Sullivan, who reviewed this chapter.

REFERENCES

Appleton, K., & Asoko, H. (1996). A case study of a teacher's progress toward using a constructivist view of learning to inform teaching in elementary science. *Science Education, 80,* 165–180.

Barak, M., & Pearlman-Avnion. (1999). Who will teach an integrated program for science and technology in Israeli junior high schools? A case study. *Journal of Research in Science Teaching, 36,* 239–253.

Bell, B., & Gilbert, J. (1996). *Teacher development: A model from science education.* London: Falmer Press.

Bobrowsky, W., Marx, R. W., & Fishman, B. J. (2001, March). *The empirical base for professional development in science education: Moving beyond volunteers.* Paper presented at the annual meeting of the National Association for Research in Science Teaching, St. Louis.

Boyd, S. E., Banilower, E. R., Pasley, J. D., & Weiss, I. R. (2003). *Progress and pitfalls: A cross-site look at local systemic change through teacher enhancement.* Chapel Hill, NC: Horizon Research.

Briscoe, C., & Peters, J. (1997). Teacher collaboration across and within schools: Supporting individual change in elementary science teaching. *Science Education, 81,* 51–65.

Feiman-Nemser, S. (2001). From preparation to practice: Designing a continuum to strengthen and sustain teaching. *Teachers College Record, 103,* 1013–1055.

Fishman, B. J., Marx, R. W., Best, S., & Tal, R. T. (2003). Linking teacher and student learning to improve professional development in systemic reform. *Teaching and Teacher Education, 19,* 643–658.

Garet, M. S., Porter, A. C., Desimone, L., Birman, B. F., & Yoon, K. S. (2001). What makes professional development effective? Results from a national sample of teachers. *American Educational Research Journal, 38,* 915–945.

Guskey, T. R. (2000). *Evaluating professional development.* Thousand Oaks, CA: Corwin.

Hand, B., & Prain, V. (2002). Teachers implementing writing-to-learn strategies in junior secondary science: A case study. *Science Education, 86,* 737–755.

Huffman, D., Thomas, K., & Lawrenz, F. (2003). Relationship between professional development, teachers' instructional practices, and the achievement of students in science and mathematics. *School Science and Mathematics, 103,* 378–387.

Kahle, J. B., Meece, J., & Scantlebury, K. (2000). Urban African-American middle school science students: Does standards-based teaching make a difference? *Journal of Research in Science Teaching, 37,* 1019–1041.

Kennedy, M. M. (1999). Form and substance in mathematics and science professional development. *NISE Brief, 3*(2), 1–8.

Loucks-Horsley, S., Hewson, P. W., Love, N., & Stiles, K. E. (1998). *Designing professional development for teachers of science and mathematics education.* Thousand Oaks, CA: Corwin.

Loucks-Horsley, S., Love, N., Stiles, K. E., Mundry, S., & Hewson, P. W. (2003). *Designing professional development for teachers of science and mathematics* (2nd ed.). Thousand Oaks, CA: Corwin.

Luft, J. A., & Pizzini, E. L. (1998). The demonstration classroom inservice: Changes in the classroom. *Science Education, 82,* 147–162.

Parke, H., & Coble, C. R. (1997). Teachers designing curriculum as professional development: A model for transformational science teaching. *Journal of Research in Science Teaching, 34,* 773–789.

Richardson, V. (1996). The role of attitudes and beliefs in learning to teach. In J. Sikula & T. J. Buttery & E. Guyton (Eds.), *Handbook of research on teacher education* (2nd ed., pp. 102–119). New York: Macmillan.

Rosebery, A. S., & Puttick, G. M. (1998). Teacher professional development as situated sense-making: A case study in science education. *Science Education, 82,* 649–677.

Shapiro, B. L., & Last, S. (2002). Starting points for transformation: Resources to craft a philosophy to guide professional development in elementary science. In P. Fraser-Abder (Ed.), *Professional development of science teachers: Local insights with lessons for the global community* (pp. 1–20). New York: RoutledgeFalmer.

Supovitz, J. A., & Turner, H. M. (2000). The effects of professional development on science teaching practices and classroom culture. *Journal of Research in Science Teaching, 37,* 963–980.

Weiss, I. R. (1999). *Evaluating science and mathematics professional development programs.* Chapel Hill, NC: Horizon Research.

Wilson, S. M., & Berne, J. (1999). Teacher learning and the acquisition of professional knowledge: An examination of research on contemporary professional development. In I.-N. Asghar & P. D. Pearson (Eds.), *Review of research in education* (Vol. 24, pp. 173–209). Washington, DC: American Educational Research Association.

CHAPTER 39

Science Teachers as Researchers

Kathleen J. Roth
LessonLab Research Institute

It is a statement about the growing interest in teacher research that this volume includes a separate chapter addressing science teacher research. The 1994 *Handbook of Research on Science Teaching and Learning* did not review different research approaches (Gabel, 1994). And although the 1998 *International Handbook for Science Education* did address these topics, teacher research or teacher action research was mentioned only briefly in chapters about qualitative research, science teacher education, and grassroots equity initiatives (Fraser & Tobin, 1998).

This lack of attention to science teacher research might reflect the relatively late entry of science teachers into the teacher researcher movement. Teacher research, which dates back to the late nineteenth and early twentieth centuries, initially investigated teaching and schooling in ways that cut across disciplinary boundaries, rather than with specific subject matter lenses. The re-emergence of the teacher research movement in the 1980s, however, was spearheaded by teacher inquiry groups focused on the literacy curriculum, especially in the area of writing (Atwell, 1987; Bissex & Bullock, 1987; Mohr, 1987; Myers, 1985; Wells, 1994). Investigations around issues of social justice and social change also played a prominent role (Beyer, 1988; Carr & Kemmis, 1986; Kemmis & McTaggart, 1988; Stenhouse, 1983). More recently the teacher researcher movement has gained momentum in other subject matter areas, including science.

In this chapter I describe the status of teacher research in science education, examine the advantages and pitfalls of science teacher research, and consider possibilities for the role of science teacher research in the future. In particular, how might science teacher research contribute to the professional development of teachers and the development of a knowledge base for science teaching and learning?

In the U.S. context, this is a particularly interesting moment in time to examine the contributions and potentials of science teacher research. On the one hand, the science education community, as well as the education community more broadly, is driven by content standards (American Association for the Advancement of Science [AAAS], 1993; National Research Council [NRC], 1996) and standardized tests.

Federal funding through the No Child Left Behind Act of 2001 (NCLB) is dependent on evidence from standardized tests that students are meeting high content standards and requires that federal grantees use their funds on "evidence-based" teaching strategies. NCLB guidelines define large-scale, randomized controlled trials as the kind of educational research that provides such rigorous evidence (U.S. Department of Education, Institute of Education Sciences, 2003). Thus, like the students, the field of educational research is challenged to reach new standards. By definition, teacher research, where teachers examine issues in their own classrooms, does not meet the standard of large-scale randomized trials. What is the role for teacher research in this climate?

Although the standards and testing movement as well as the debate about what counts as evidence in educational research (Burkhardt & Schoenfeld, 2003; Feuer, Towne, & Shavelson, 2002) seem to minimize or ignore the importance of the teacher research movement, there are at least two bodies of current educational research that suggest an important role for science teacher research. Research about teacher learning and research about the relationship between research and practice both point to the importance of teacher-conducted studies, especially studies of teaching about particular subject matter (e.g., science) content.

First, the research on teacher learning suggests that teacher research is likely an effective professional development activity for teachers. There is an increased recognition of the importance of teacher learning across a career span as well as a growing consensus about the kinds of professional development activities that best support such teacher learning. Although more studies examining the impact of professional development programs on teachers' science teaching practice and on their students' learning are needed (Kennedy, 1998), there is evidence that effective professional development activities (a) engage teachers actively in collaborative, long-term problem-based inquiries, (b) treat content as central and intertwined with pedagogical issues, (c) enable teachers to see these issues as embedded in real classroom contexts, and (d) focus on the content and curriculum teachers will be teaching (Ball & Cohen, 1999; Carpenter, Fennema, Peterson, Chiang, & Loef, 1989; Cobb et al., 1991; Cohen & Barnes, 1993; Cohen & Hill, 1998; Darling-Hammond & Sykes, 1999; Elmore, 2002; Garet, Porter, Desimone, Birman, & Yoon, 2001; Kennedy, 1998; Lewis & Tsuchida, 1997, 1998; Loucks-Horsley, Love, Stiles, Mundry, & Hewson, 2003; National Staff Development Council, 2001; Shimahara, 1998; Steiner, 1999; Stigler & Hiebert, 1999; Takemura & Shimizu, 1993; Whitehurst, 2002; Yoshida, 1999; Zeichner, Klehr, & Caro-Bruce, 2000). These features of effective professional development (see also Chapter 38, this volume) point to the need for ongoing, collaborative, and content-specific inquiry into practice. Most of the science teacher research studies reviewed in this chapter involved teachers who were engaged in these types of activities—analyzing their practice in terms of specific content learning goals and in collaboration with other teacher researchers.

Second, there continues to be a gap between research knowledge and science teaching practice. Science teacher research might help close this gap. Advocates of action research "claim that action research can lead to praxis, a position in which theory and practice are dialectically related" (Goodnough, 2003, p. 60) and that through action research the theory-practice gap can be bridged (Carr & Kemmis,

1986; Grundy, 1987). For example, although the traditional university-based research community has built a large body of knowledge about students' ways of thinking about specific science topics and phenomena, there is still much to be learned about how to best utilize that knowledge in teaching (Berry & Milroy, 2002; K. J. Roth, 2002). This is one example of a type of research that teachers are uniquely situated to explore. In order to understand what is possible in terms of student learning, the science education community can benefit from teachers' investigations into their attempts to give students' ideas a prominent role in teaching about specific content ideas and phenomena. In this way, teacher research can play an important role in contributing to the knowledge base in science education and in making links between the worlds of practice and research.

These two bodies of research suggest two important but different roles for science teacher research: to support teacher learning and professional growth, and to contribute to the research knowledge base about science teaching and learning. Much of the early work in action research or teacher research focused on its value as a strategy for teacher professional development. However, at least as early as Dewey, there was also the idea that teacher research could provide more than an avenue of professional development for the teacher involved in the research. In addition, it could contribute knowledge to the education community. To what extent has science teacher research played these two different roles?

I have organized this review into the following sections:

1. Part One: Definitions and Historical Context
2. Part Two: Science Teacher Research Supports Teacher Learning
3. Part Three: Science Teacher Research Produces Knowledge
4. Part Four: Issues in Science Teacher Research

In Part One, I provide a background context including definitions and descriptions of different types of teacher research and highlights of the history of the science teacher research movement. In Part Two, I describe examples of science teacher research, starting with teacher research conducted as part of preservice and inservice teacher education or professional development programs, where the focus is on the role of teacher research in supporting science teacher learning and professional growth. I consider the impact of these programs on preservice and inservice teacher learning. In Part Three, I consider the contributions of science teacher research to the knowledge base for science teaching. Examples of published teacher research studies are described and categorized to characterize the kinds of issues science teachers are investigating, the kinds of methodologies they are using, and the kinds of knowledge they are generating. In what ways do these studies contribute knowledge of interest to the larger science education community? In Part Four, I turn my attention to three important issues in teacher research: the benefits and pitfalls of teacher research, the criteria for quality in teacher research, and new directions in science teacher research: What role will science teacher research play in a standards and high-stakes testing environment? What new directions look promising? How might teacher research be both better nurtured and better studied? How can teacher research become more integral in building knowledge for science teaching?

PART ONE: DEFINITIONS
AND HISTORICAL CONTEXT

Definition of Teacher Research

Teacher research, in its many forms, shares with other forms of research a goal of understanding educational practice. However, teacher research is distinct from other forms of educational research in its emphasis on "changing practice as a result of study and changing practice to better understand it" (Zeichner & Noffke, 2001, p. 306). This emphasis on change and improvement of practice plays out in different ways in different forms of teacher research, with teachers entering into teacher research for a variety of purposes—to know more about how students learn, to understand a particular aspect of one's teaching practice, to improve a particular aspect of one's teaching, to try out a new teaching approach, to become a more reflective practitioner, to document successful teaching approaches, and so forth (Fischer, 1996; Zeichner, 1997).

Teacher research is defined in this chapter using the definition provided by Cochran-Smith and Lytle (1993, 1999) in their seminal works about the teacher research movement in North America in the last two decades. They defined teacher research in the broadest possible sense to encompass all forms of practitioner inquiry that involve "systematic, intentional inquiry by teachers about their own school and classroom work" (Cochran-Smith & Lytle, 1993, pp. 23–24). Included in this definition are inquiries that are referred to as action research, practitioner inquiry, teacher inquiry, first-person research, and so forth. It does not include reflection on one's own educational practice or being thoughtful about one's work unless that reflection is intentional and systematic.

The teacher research studies reviewed in this chapter share an additional feature: the teacher research was done with the intention of being shared in some way. The work was shared both locally with a group of collaborators in a teacher inquiry group or class, and more widely through presentations at professional conferences or teacher research festivals and through publication in a variety of professional formats. Thus, all of the studies reviewed in this chapter were made available for public scrutiny. This is consistent with Stenhouse's (1975) definition of research as "systematic critical inquiry made public."

Teacher research comes in many forms, but all forms focus on issues of teaching practice. Teacher research is distinguished from other forms of research in the deliberate fusing of the work of teaching and the work of inquiry (Ball, 2000): "What most clearly distinguishes first-person inquiry from other approaches to the study of teaching and learning is that it deliberately uses the position of the teacher to ground questions, structure analysis, and represent interpretation" (Ball, 2000, p. 365).

Shafer (2000) described three forms of teacher research placed on a continuum from reflective practice to action research to qualitative inquiry (teacher research). This continuum reflects the historical development of these forms of teacher research, with each successive form incorporating features of the previous one while adding new features.

Reflective practice is most closely tied to the ongoing work of teaching and does not require any special research plan or design. The goal is to heighten awareness and deliberation about teaching (Abell & Bryan, 1997; G. Erickson & MacKinnon, 1991; Grimmett & Erickson, 1988; Schön, 1983, 1988). To be considered as teacher research by Cochran-Smith and Lytle's (1993) definition, reflective practice must have some intentional element. Teacher narratives written after a process of reflection on teaching represent teacher research where the intentional element arose after the teaching act.

Action research is more planned and, as its name suggests, has traditionally had a goal of improving practice (Carr & Kemmis, 1986; Loucks-Horsley et al., 2003; Reason, 2001). Teachers identify a problem of practice that they want to understand and address, develop a method to study the problem, collect data to inform the problem, and analyze the data to generate ideas for improving practice. The learning from the research is documented and shared. In some settings, action research is seen as a cycle, with results informing changes in practice and the generation of new questions to investigate (Corey, 1953; Loucks-Horsley et al.). However, in practice, action research studies are often carried out as stand-alone studies, using a more linear set of steps from question to results (Taba & Noel, 1957; Zeichner & Noffke, 2001). Most proponents of action research encourage a collaborative process in order to help individual practitioners develop inquiry and reflection skills (Miller, 1990; Reason & Bradbury, 2002).

Action research projects have been used as central activities within science professional development programs delivered by universities and other providers outside of school districts (*Colorado College Integrated Science Teacher Enhancement Project*, 2004; *Continuous Assessment in Science Project*, WestEd, 2005; *Project to Enhance Effective Learning*, Baird & Northfield, 1992; Baird & Mitchell, 1986; *Florida State University and Dade County Public Schools*, Sweeny & Tobin, 2000). However, action research projects are also initiated and supported by schools and school districts (Love, 2002; Zeichner et al., 2000).

Some action research takes on a critical, activist stance that has goals of bringing about a more just and humane society and understanding social forces so that practitioners can gain access to processes for change and overcome oppressive situations (Carr & Kemmis, 1986). *Participatory action research* is a variant of action research that is intended to reclaim the common person's knowledge and wisdom by involving them in the action research process (Kemmis & McTaggart, 2000). This form of research has occurred in developing countries as well as Europe, Australia, and North America (Fals-Borda 1997; Park, Brydon-Miller, Hall, & Jackson, 1993; Rosas, 1997). In science education, Barton's work as a science teacher and researcher collaborating with parents and community members in an after-school science program in a homeless shelter in New York City fits the description of participatory action research (Barton, 2003; Barton, Johnson, & the students in Ms. Johnson's Grade 8 science classes, 2002).

Teacher research emerged as distinct from action research in the 1980s, and, according to Zeichner and Noffke (2001), teacher research differs from action research in at least four ways. First, teacher research does not have the "action" emphasis of action research; understanding practice and documenting knowledge held by expert teachers are valid goals of teacher research that do not necessitate change in practice. Second, teacher research incorporates more qualitative methods than was typical of action research prior to the 1980s. Thus, teacher research includes case studies and conceptual research, such as the teacher essays by Karen Gallas (Cochran-

Smith & Lytle, 1993; Gallas, 1995, 1997). Third, and reflective of the qualitative research methodology, a teacher researcher's questions change and evolve during the inquiry process. Thus, the path from question to data to interpretations is not as linear and prescribed as in traditional action research projects. And finally, the teacher research movement included a new focus on the value of teacher-generated knowledge as having unique contributions to make to the field of educational research because of its insider status (C. W. Anderson, Butts, Lett, Mansdoerfer, & Raisch, 1995; G. Anderson, Herr, & Nihlen, 1994; Cochran-Smith & Lytle, 1993; Northfield, 1996). Thus, teacher research is as much about empowering teachers and making teacher voices a part of knowledge generation efforts as it is about teacher professional development and improving the practice of individual teacher researchers.

Lesson study, a process originating in Japan where teacher groups develop, teach, analyze, revise, and publish lesson plans, is a special type of teacher research focusing on collaborative analysis of practice (Fernandez & Yoshida, 2004; Lewis & Tsuchida 1997, 1998). In the United States, lesson study groups with a science teaching focus are a recent development (Hedman, 2003). For the purposes of this review, lesson study groups as well as study groups that meet to analyze artifacts of practice (student work, lesson videos) are considered as "first person" teacher research only if the teachers are intentionally studying their *own* lessons or artifacts of practice. This excludes teachers who participate in seminars or courses where they examine lessons and artifacts of practice from other teachers.

Teacher research takes place in the university setting as well as in P–12 schools. Two variants of teacher research carried out by university faculty have had a significant impact on the way educational research is defined in academia. The first is what Ball names *"researcher teacher"* (Ball, 2000). In this form of teacher research, university-based academics trained in research conduct research on their own teaching in P–12 school settings. The pioneering researcher-teacher work of Magdalene Lampert and Deborah Ball in elementary school mathematics classrooms stimulated a series of such studies in mathematics education (Chazen, 2000; Heaton, 2000; Lampert & Ball, 1998). In science education, university-based researchers such as Sandi Abell, Elaine Howes, Jim Minstrell, Jeff Northfield, Margery Osborne, Kathleen Roth, Wolf-Michael Roth, and David Wong have studied their own P–12 science teaching practice (Abell, 2000; Abell, Anderson, & Chezem, 2000; Howes, 2002; Loughran & Northfield, 1996; Osborne, 1993; Rosaen & Roth, 2001; K. J. Roth, 1993, 1994, 2000, 2002; W.-M. Roth & Boyd, 1999; W.-M. Roth & Tobin, 2004; Wong, 1995).

University professors also engage in research on their university-level teaching. Such *self-study research* has been growing in acceptance as a valid form of scholarship, especially among teacher educators, at colleges and universities. In the field of science education, Abell, Martini, and George (2001), Bianchini and Solomon (2003), Duckworth (1987), Feldman (1995), Loughran and Russell (1997), Munby (1996), Northfield (1998), Russell (1997), Smith (2001), and van Zee (1998a, 1998b, 2000) provide examples of such self-study research.

Whereas Cochran-Smith and Lytle (1990, 1993, 1999) considered teacher educators doing self-study on their own teaching as teacher researchers, I focus in this chapter on P–12 science teacher research in all of its various forms. (John Loughran discusses examples of university teachers' self-study in Chapter 34, this volume).

Historical Context

Excellent reviews of the literature regarding the history of the action research and teacher research movements can be found in a chapter written by Mary Olson (1990) and in Zeichner and Noffke's (2001) chapter in the *Handbook of Research on Teaching*. Articles by Cochran-Smith and Lytle (1990, 1999), Hall, Campbell, and Miech (1997), and Huberman (1996) also contribute to the story of the history of teacher research. In this section, I focus on the extension of teacher research from an early focus in the areas of literacy education and equity issues into the subject matter areas of mathematics and science.

Prior to the 1990s, teacher research in the United States focused mainly on the literacy and writing curricula or on issues of social justice in schooling. During the late 1980s and 1990s, teacher research began to move into other areas of educational interest. Of particular interest to science educators was the development of a movement toward subject matter investigations by teacher researchers. In the late 1980s Magdalene Lampert and Deborah Ball taught elementary school mathematics each day as part of their teaching load at Michigan State University. In the early 1990s, Lampert and Ball received funding to document their elementary school mathematics teaching over the course of a year. The products from this research played an important role in making concrete the potential contributions of subject-matter-focused teacher research. The products included descriptions of their analyses of mathematics teaching dilemmas (Ball, 1993; Lampert, 1990, 2001; Lampert & Ball, 1998), as well as videotapes of lessons and associated lesson artifacts (student work, teacher logs, etc.). These multimedia products captured the interest of researchers, teacher educators, teachers, as well as mathematicians and suggested the power of new technologies to enhance the impact and reach of teacher research studies. This work also inspired teacher research doctoral dissertations in mathematics (Heaton, 2000), writing (Lensmire, 1997), and science (Osborne, 1993).

The 1980s also marked some pioneering efforts in science teacher research. During the early part of the decade, Jim Minstrell, a high school physics teacher, initiated a productive line of research in his own classroom. Influenced by his mentor, Arnold Arons at the University of Washington, and by his participation in the development of the *Project Physics* curriculum and in the *Project for Assessing Conceptual Development*, Jim began to study his students' learning and his own teaching. Over the years, he was successful in getting research grant money to release himself from some of his teaching responsibilities to allow time for more in-depth research activities, using analysis of audio- and videotaped lessons and student interviews to uncover student misconceptions and develop methods for helping students develop conceptual understanding of physics concepts. The insights he gained about his students' thinking and learning, and the results of his efforts to design, implement, and study teaching strategies that would better help students develop deep understandings of science content, had a tremendous impact on the science education community. His teacher research work was well received both in the world of science teachers (Minstrell, 1982b, 1983) and in the world of academic research (Minstrell, 1984, 1989). In fact, although Minstrell retired from the classroom in 1993 (to focus full time on research and development projects), videotapes of his teaching still provide useful sources of data that inform teaching practice and influence the policymaking world. For example, Schoenfeld's development of a "theory of teaching-in-context" was based, in part, on a close analysis of Minstrell's teaching practice (Schoenfeld, 1998). In addition, Minstrell's teacher researcher work was highlighted as an example of research on effective teaching in the widely cited National Research Council book, *How People Learn* (Bransford, Brown, & Cocking, 2000).

Influenced by the teacher research work of Jim Minstrell, Deborah Ball, and Magdalene Lampert, I began my own line of teacher research in the late 1980s. After finishing my doctorate in science education in 1985, I was eager to return to my classroom roots to find out what might be possible if I focused my teaching practice on students' thinking and learning. The knowledge I brought from my doctoral studies and my dissertation study convinced me that students had the potential to develop much deeper understandings of science than science teaching was typically tapping. During the 1988–1989 school year, I taught science and social studies to 29 fifth graders and traced their thinking and understanding of science content and the nature of science across the school year. The experience transformed my science teaching practice, my thinking about the teacher role, and my vision of research on science teaching and led to a line of teacher research in elementary school classrooms throughout the 1990s (Hazelwood & Roth, 1992; Rosaen & Roth, 1995; K. J. Roth, 1993, 1994, 1996, 2000, 2002; K. J. Roth et al., 1992). I was particularly interested in the usefulness of the videotapes that I had collected for research purposes, so I also explored the usefulness of creating video products from my work (K. J. Roth, 1998).

The teacher research and action research movements became more active and visible in the science education community during the 1990s when some teacher education, master's degree, and teacher professional development programs began to require teachers to conduct inquiries into their practice. Multiple events are likely to have contributed to this movement.

For example, such requirements came at a time when both research on science teaching and learning and the development of standards for science teaching at state and national levels had made clear the complexity of teaching science effectively (AAAS, 1993; Mintzes, Wandersee, & Novak, 1998; NRC, 1996; West & Pines, 1985). Research on students' personal experiences and ideas about specific phenomena and topics in the science curriculum suggested that teachers needed more than knowledge about the science content and generic science teaching strategies. In addition, they needed knowledge about students' ways of thinking about key ideas in the science curriculum and pedagogical strategies for addressing students' personal theories and supporting them in learning about specific science ideas (C. W. Anderson & Smith, 1987; Driver, 1989; Driver, Osoko, Leach, Mortimer, & Scott, 1994; Hewson, Beeth, & Thorley, 1998; Hewson & Hewson, 1984; Hollon, Anderson, & Roth, 1991; Posner, Strike, Hewson, & Gertzog, 1982). Shulman (1987) named this type of knowledge "pedagogical content knowledge"—knowledge of teaching strategies that are specific to key ideas within the curriculum rather than generic science teaching strategies. For example, a teacher needs to know specific strategies to support students in changing and deepening their personally constructed ideas about how light helps you see, why coats keep you warm, how plants get their food, and the source of water that appears on the outside of cold drink containers. According to

Loucks-Horsley et al. (2003), "To succeed in such a complex environment, teachers need opportunities to develop their pedagogical content knowledge through critical reflection on their own and others' classroom practice" (p. 41).

In addition, this was a period when research documented the limitations of preservice science teacher education programs (Feiman-Nemser & Buchmann, 1985, 1989; Howey & Zimpher, 1989; Rosaen, Roth, & Lanier, 1988), science curriculum materials (C. W. Anderson & Smith, 1987; Eichinger & Roth, 1991; Kesidou & Roseman, 2002; K. J. Roth, Anderson, & Smith, 1987), and the traditional "one-shot" workshop approach to teacher professional development in preparing effective science teachers (Loucks-Horsley, 1996; Loucks-Horsley, Hewson, Love, & Stiles, 1998). At this time, many researchers were also convinced that research had some compelling ideas to inform science teaching but that, despite the apparent usefulness of the research, the research-to-practice gap was not narrowing (C. W. Anderson & Smith, 1987; Pekarek, Krockover, & Shepardson, 1996; Penick, 1986). In addition, studies of teaching practice revealed how little science teaching reflected the kinds of teaching recommended by research (K. J. Roth et al., 2005; SALISH I Project, 1997; Simmons et al., 1999; Weiss, Pasley, Smith, Banilower, & Heck, 2003).

The professional development school movement that started in the early 1990s also contributed to a view of teaching as inquiry by supporting collaborative inquiries among K–12 school-based teachers and university-based researchers and teacher educators (Holmes Group, 1990). As a result of these collaborations, more teachers in these sites (and the preservice teachers working with them) became involved in carrying out classroom research, making presentations at conferences, and participating in the publication process (K. J. Roth et al., 1992).

In response to one or more of these trends, as well as the growth of teacher research in other subject matter areas (especially literacy), preservice and inservice programs for teachers sought to develop reflective science teachers who could make research-based decisions to support their efforts to help students meet the new science standards developed at state and national levels. These program requirements acknowledged the complexity of teaching science for understanding for all students and the limits of existing teacher education programs, professional development programs, and curriculum materials in supporting such teaching.

Another event that stimulated interest in teacher inquiry was the release of the first *TIMSS Video Study* (Stigler & Hiebert, 1999), which brought attention to the unique Japanese lesson study approach to teacher professional development. In the United States, this led to a growing interest in using or adapting the Japanese lesson study model to support teacher inquiries into some of their practice (Fernandez, Chokshi, Cannon, & Yoshida, in press; Fernandez & Yoshida, 2004; Lewis, 2002; Lewis & Tsuchida, 1997, 1998). In the area of science, the statewide *California Science Project* incorporated lesson study activities into some of their professional development programs (see http://csmp.ucop.edu/csp/resources/lessonstudy.html).

One of the results of these various science teacher research efforts was modest but increased attendance of K–12 practitioners at research conferences such as the National Association for Research in Science Teaching (NARST). This challenged the NARST research community and other organizations to acknowledge the lack of teacher voices in science education research. Although a teacher research special interest group had been established in the American Educational Research Association in 1989, it was not until 2000 that a similar interest group was established at NARST. That same year, NARST began an annual practice of including a teacher researcher reception at the annual meeting.

Another indication of the increased interest in science teacher research was the December 2000 Conference on Teacher Research in Science and Mathematics, funded by the Spencer Foundation, the National Science Foundation, and the U.S. Department of Education Office of Educational Research and Improvement. Thirty-five teacher researchers, including newcomers as well as experienced teachers from established groups such as the Brookline Teacher Research Group, the ChecheKonnen Collaborative, the Fairfax County Teacher Researcher Group, the Philadelphia Teachers' Learning Cooperative, and the Prospect Archives and Center for Education and Research, joined five university-based researchers to explore children's classroom talk and work in science and mathematics (Ballenger & Rosebery, 2003). One reason given for the focus on science and mathematics was the growing number of teacher researchers expressing an interest in moving outside of the language and literacy area to examine science and mathematics learning issues.

PART TWO: SCIENCE TEACHER RESEARCH SUPPORTS TEACHER LEARNING

After a brief review of different perspectives about the role of science teacher research in supporting teacher learning, I describe in this section examples of science teacher research efforts embedded in teacher education and teacher professional development programs. I focus first on science teacher research inquiries that occurred within preservice teacher education programs. I next consider programs for inservice teachers, starting with descriptions of science teacher research within degree-awarding programs and then turning to science teacher research within non-degree-awarding professional development programs.

Perspectives on Teacher Research and Teacher Learning

In 1996, Pekarek et al. stated that the idea of teachers as researchers "ought to be incorporated in science teacher preparation and professional development programs" (p. 112). Others agree that teacher research can play an important role in enhancing science teacher learning, and a variety of rationales are used to support this view. Research on teacher reflection, for example, makes a strong case that reflection is a central and critical part of a professional educator's responsibility, requiring the teacher's consideration of many factors in deciding how to act in a particular situation (Abell & Bryan, 1997; Grimmett & Erickson, 1988; Schön, 1983). The importance of the role of reflection in teaching is underscored by the growing body of research knowledge about how difficult and complex it is to teach science (and other subject matters) so that all students, including those at risk for academic failure, develop meaningful understandings of central concepts and scientific ways of knowing (C. W. Anderson & Roth, 1989; Mintzes et al., 1998). There is wide agreement in the science education community that science teaching cannot be reduced to a set of techniques and knowledge that can be quickly given to teachers (NRC, 1996).

Thus the complexity of the teaching environment in the twenty-first century suggests that learning to teach science is a lifelong undertaking and that teachers need to learn how to learn from experience (Akerson & McDuffie, 2002; NRC). As Stenhouse suggested in 1975, and Duckworth elaborated in 1987, teaching should be viewed as a form of inquiry, experimentation, or research.

There are other arguments supporting the case for teacher research as a way to improve science teacher learning. For example, van Zee (1998a) suggested that teachers who are attempting to put new reform approaches to science teaching into their practice may receive better support from administrators, parents, and colleagues if they have clearly articulated and studied their intentions and practices. Others point to the motivational value of learning in the context of practice. By studying their own practice rather than simply reading research about other teachers' practices, teachers are more likely to be engaged in their learning and personal growth (Hewson, Tabachnick, Zeichner, Blomker, et al., 1999). Still others suggest that inquiry into practice provides an opportunity for teachers to experience the kinds of inquiry that characterize science itself (Akerson & McDuffie, 2002; McGoey & Ross, 1999). McGoey and Ross argued that, just as science is the construction of new knowledge representations and new understandings, so science teaching should involve construction of new knowledge about teaching science. "In order for science teachers to demonstrate authentic inquiry, we must be engaged in authentic research ourselves. Researching our practice is a natural fit" (McGoey & Ross, p. 118).

Because of the potential for teacher research to enhance teacher learning, various forms of teacher research have been incorporated into preservice and inservice science teacher education and professional development programs. Examples of these efforts and their findings are presented next, beginning with preservice teacher education efforts, and then we turn to inservice teacher professional development programs.

Preservice Programs and Science Teacher Research

Both teachers and teacher educators suggest that preservice teacher education programs should include teacher research experiences. In an editorial in the *Journal of Research on Science Teaching*, McGoey and Ross (1999), two high school science teachers working with student teachers, argued that "the way to deal with the research-practice gap is to engage new teachers in action research from the very beginning of their own practice" (p. 118). Teacher educators Abell and Bryan (1997) concurred, challenging teacher educators to "coach prospective teachers to purposefully and systematically inquire into their own practice, encouraging them to make such inquiry a habit that will become increasingly valuable throughout their careers" (p. 136). Loughran (2002) noted that the possibilities for preservice teacher learning could be enhanced through effective reflective practice. Kyle, Linn, Bitner, Mitchner, and Perry (1991) went so far as to claim that "the process of recognizing the role of teachers-as-researchers should permeate every teacher education course" (p. 416).

Examples of efforts to carry out and study this view of preservice science teacher education are summarized in Table 39.1. The examples differ in their target preservice teacher population (elementary versus secondary, post-baccalaureate versus undergraduate) and in the length of the teacher research projects. In some programs

TABLE 39.1

Teacher as Researcher in Preservice Science Teacher Education Programs

Citations	Participants	Context	Length	Description of project	Results
Featherstone, Munby, & Russell, 1997; Russell & Bullock, 1999	Preservice secondary science teachers	Bachelor's of Education; Queens University	One semester action research project in conjunction with teaching practicum and field-related course	Teacher educators sought to develop student teachers' "authority of experience" by engaging them in in sustained analyses of their student teaching experiences. They supported two student teachers, Featherstone and Bullock, in publishing the story of their learning through inquiry into their own practice.	Preservice teacher Featherstone's ideas about science teaching and learning changed as a result of his efforts to listen to students and be responsive to students' ideas in his teaching. Preservice teacher Bullock identified a conflict between his vision of science teaching and his practice, studied these contradictions, and changed his teaching practice to allow student exploration with less teacher direction.
Tillotson, Ochanji, & Diana, 2004	Preservice secondary science teachers	Syracuse University Science Teacher Education Program	2-year program with data collected during a 12-week student teaching experience	Prior to student teaching, students developed a research-based rationale paper describing how they will teach science. During a 12-week student teaching period, they examined one aspect of this rationale in an action research project carried out in collaboration with the host teacher.	Surveys showed high levels of satisfaction with the research-based rationale paper experience. Effectiveness of the action research might have been due to: 1) Students were required to revisit their research-based rationales,

			The study and rationale were presented in a final portfolio session at the end of the program.	2) Studying teaching rationales in the context of teaching gave credibility to the research review process Additional benefit: Research collaboration with the host teacher allowed research results to reach the inservice teacher audience. Students gave high ratings of the course in its success in addressing most of the national science education teaching standards. Students expressed frustration with the clash between the inquiry orientation of the class and their expectations that they would be told how to teach science.
van Zee 1998b	Preservice elementary teachers	University of Maryland teacher education program	1 semester course	In an elementary science methods course, van Zee engaged preservice elementary teachers in doing research while learning how to teach science. In addition to a science inquiry project (phases of the Moon), students conducted an inquiry into teaching practice. The teaching inquiries included interviewing students and adults about a science topic, engaging students in conversations about the topic, assessing student learning, writing reflections on students' learning and their own learning, and participating in a research festival with experienced teacher researchers.	

teacher research activities were embedded in single courses, while in others teacher research projects developed across both course and student teaching experiences. The programs also differed in the extent to which they studied their preservice teachers' learning from the experience. In many cases, such examinations of preservice teacher learning were limited to student self-report; in contrast, the study of teacher learning in the University of Wisconsin–Madison program was studied rigorously with the use of interviews and observations of preservice teachers. The results of these various efforts to integrate teacher research into preservice teacher education programs highlight the successes, challenges, and limitations of our knowledge about the relationship between teacher research and preservice teacher learning.

Impact on Preservice Teacher Learning

All of the preservice programs described in Table 39.1 were studied by the faculty members who developed and taught them. Thus, all of these researchers were conducting self-study in one way or another. Both van Zee and Tabachnick and Zeichner made this self study aspect of their work explicit in their writing. What do we learn from this set of self-studies in science teacher education? What evidence do they provide that teacher research can enhance preservice teacher learning about science teaching? Although these studies represent only a subset of similar studies, they provide important insights about what we know and do not know about teacher research and preservice teacher learning.

First of all, these studies provide evidence that teacher research conducted during a student teaching experience is possible and that preservice teachers can find it valuable. Many preservice teachers and teacher educators wonder whether a novice teacher can simultaneously learn how to teach and learn how to conduct research on teaching: It is not a trivial matter to be able to act in the classroom and to step outside of that action to observe and analyze. However, in these programs preservice teachers were able to do this at some level and to value the process.

Second, the studies showed some impact on preservice teachers' awareness, beliefs, and knowledge. Most commonly, preservice teachers became much more aware of and oriented to students' ideas and ways of thinking. In some cases, they became aware of conflicts between their beliefs and visions and their teaching practice.

Finally, although some preservice teachers reported changes in their teaching as a result of the action research (e.g., Featherstone, Munby, & Russell, 1997), there is little evidence that the teacher research components of these programs had much impact on the teaching practices of the preservice teachers. This is not surprising, given the short time frame of the programs (one course to two years) and the many demands placed on the preservice teachers, especially during their student teaching experiences, which typically lasted 8–12 weeks. It is not realistic to expect that preservice teachers' conceptions of science teaching will undergo significant change in such a short time period. In addition to developing a new concept of teaching, they are also challenged to translate that vision into action without many models of what the new practice might look like. However, this finding suggests possibilities for future exploration, including longer-term studies of preservice teachers and the development of more robust teacher research experiences within teacher education programs.

The reports of these programs also highlight the need to collect more in-depth data about the development of preservice teachers' knowledge about science teaching and the role that teacher research projects play in that learning process. Most of the studies reported here relied predominantly on end-of-program surveys filled out by the preservice teachers. To better understand the role of teacher research in the teacher learning process, we need studies that trace the unfolding impact of these activities on preservice teachers' thinking and actions. In addition, follow-up studies that examine these prospective teachers' views toward teacher research during their initial years of teaching would provide important data about impact.

Inservice Programs and Science Teacher Research

Degree-awarding inservice programs. There are many degree-awarding programs for practicing teachers that now include teacher research or action research as a core component. Teacher research is built into these programs primarily because of its potential to support teacher learning that will lead to changes in teaching practice rather than contribute to the science education community's knowledge base. Many of these programs are not targeted only to science teachers, whereas others are designed specifically to support teacher research in science classrooms. Examples of three programs are summarized in Table 39.2.

Non-degree-awarding inservice programs. Teacher research is also a component of a variety of professional development activities that occur outside of degree-awarding programs. Some of these activities are local, state, or federally funded professional development programs (Hedman, 2003; Reardon & Saul, 1996; Saul, 1993, 2002), research collaborations initiated and supported by university faculty (Goodnough, 2001a, 2001b, 2001c; Lehrer & Schauble 2002), school district initiatives or school-university collaborations, university-sponsored programs, and more grass-roots teacher research study groups. In some of these programs, teacher research is more than an opportunity to support teacher learning; it is also a vehicle for bringing teachers' voices into the larger science education research community. Thus, these programs and teacher groups vary in their relative emphasis on the goals of teacher professional development or the generation of knowledge for the wider science education community. Examples of these programs are described Table 39.3.

Impact on inservice teacher learning. As these examples suggest, science teachers are becoming involved in teacher research, and some in teacher research programs that have continued over time. These indicators and others, such as teachers' participation in conference presentations and publications of their work, suggest that teachers find value in teacher research. In fact, most of the programs presented in Table 39.3 claim positive outcomes of teacher research on inservice teacher learning. Most are careful, however, to limit the claims to changes in teacher beliefs, knowledge, and analytical abilities, rather than to changes in teachers' practice and their students' learning. Tabachnick and Zeichner (1999) referred to "a voluminous literature representing work in several countries (that) has consistently reported that teachers who engage in action research generally become more aware of their own practices, of the gaps between their beliefs and their practices, and of what their pupils are thinking, feeling, and learning" (p. 310).

TABLE 39.2
Teacher as Researcher in Inservice, Degree-awarding Programs

Program and Citations	Participants	Degree	Length	Description of Program	Results
Science for Early Adolescence Teachers (FEAT), Florida State University; McDonald & Gilmer, 1997	65 Teachers, grades 5–9	Master's Degree	3 years	The program included three 5-week summer academic sessions and associated activities during the intervening academic years. An action research project during the second year was a core part of the program. Questions for inquiry grew out of analysis of videotapes of the teachers' own teaching during the first year. Results were presented in written form and at a research colloquium.	65 of 72 teachers who started the program completed it. Twelve teachers' action research reports were published (McDonald & Gilmer, 1997; Spiegel, Collins, & Lappert, 1995). For example: Graham, 1995; Joanos, 1997; Thompson, 1995; Veldman, 1997.
Florida State University–Dade County Distance learning program in science education; Sweeney & Tobin, 2000	250 elementary and middle school science and mathematics teachers	Master's or specialist degree	3 years (3 summers and 2 academic years)	In a synchronous, web-based program, inservice teachers were introduced to research from the outset of the program in a summer course on interpretive methodology. They became teacher researchers right away, undertaking inquires into their own practice during both academic years of the program. The action research part of the program was further developed within each of the science education courses.	Twelve of these teacher inquiries were published in a monograph (Sweeney & Tobin, 2000). For example: Bagley, 2000; Britton, 2000; Fink, 2000; Ormes, 2000. Tobin emphasizes the benefit of the studies to the participating teachers and their students.
Nottingham Trent University, UK; Ovens, 2000	Primary teachers	Certificate in Science Teaching	2.5 terms	The year-long course engaged teachers in three core activities: (a) developing science knowledge and investigative ways of learning, (b) developing ideas about students' development of science knowledge and skills, and (c) investigating some aspect of one's science teaching. Teachers took the lead in identifying areas of inquiry.	Ovens wrote 6 case studies of the of the teacher researchers and their development in this program. Commonalities across the 6 included: 1. Increased science knowledge, 2. Increased confidence in teaching science and guiding their own development, 3. Increased understanding of students' science learning, and 4. Appreciation of and skill in carrying out action research.

TABLE 39.3

Teacher as Researcher in Inservice, Non-degree-awarding Programs

Program and Citations	Participants	Longevity	Focus	Description of Program	Results
Action Research Laboratory, Highland Park High School, Highland Park, Illinois; Senese, n.d.; Senese, Fagel, Gorleski, & Swanson, 1998.	High school teacher researchers	Ongoing since 1995	Constructivist approach to both student and teacher learning Interdisciplinary collaboration among teachers	Teachers work in cross-disciplinary teams of 3 to investigate ways to apply research to their practice. Each team picks a theme that will cut across disciplinary areas—such as assessment or gender equity. Results of the action research projects are shared in writing with building and district administrators, faculty, and the school board. Some are shared on local cable television, in local newspapers, and through professional publications.	The program documents both teacher growth and student achievement gains, using a variety of research strategies. Evidence of impact includes: 1. increased communication and collaboration among departments, 2. increased experimentation and risk-taking, and 3. more awareness of research about best teaching practices. 4. online publications (e.g., McDaniel Hill, 1996; Gapinski, Hill, & Solis, 2000).
ChecheKonnen Center at TERC, Cambridge MA; Ballenger & Rosebery, 2003	Elementary and middle school teacher researchers	Ongoing since 1987	Urban science teaching Science learning for language minority students, issues of language and discourse	The Center conducts long-term, intensive partnerships with 13 public school districts to develop self-sustaining, inquiry-based programs of teacher professional development. The Center uses a professional development model of teaching as inquiry where teachers engage in science inquiries and in inquiries of their teaching practice. Teachers focus their analyses on what "puzzling children" in their classrooms say and do. They read relevant literatures and question their assumptions about children, science, language, culture, learning and teaching.	A focus on children's ideas and questions typically "leads both teacher and students deeper into the conceptual territory of the scientific phenomenon they are studying" (Ballenger & Rosebery, 2003, p. 297). The Center has published research reports about both teacher and student learning. The Center hosted two conferences for teacher researchers that centered on teaching cases in mathematics and science. Teacher researchers have published (e.g., DiSchino, 1998).

(continued)

TABLE 39.3
(Continued)

Program and Citations	Participants	Longevity	Focus	Description of Program	Results
Classroom Action Research Madison Metropolitan School District, Madison, Wisconsin; Caro-Bruce & Zeichner, 1998	K–12 teacher researchers	Ongoing since 1990	Supporting teachers of all subject areas in conducting action research as a district-wide professional development strategy	This school-district sponsored action research professional development program involves teachers, principals, and other staff. Teachers participate for a school year, with the option to continue a second year. Teachers meet once a month for a full or half day in small groups supported by two experienced action researchers. The group facilitators are supported in seminars held about every six weeks. Teacher researchers write reports of their work that are published and circulated within the school district.	Reports of teachers' inquiries are posted online and include 20 that focus on science teaching (e.g., Field, 2001; Schoenemann, 2003). Study of the program has identified critical features, common obstacles (most are related to time), how useful the research is to others in the district, and how the program influenced teachers' thinking about their practice. Teachers report an increased sense of control, increased professionalism, a stronger disposition to be analytical about their teaching decisions, and an increased focus on student thinking and learning.
CRESS Center Teacher Research Program, University of California, Davis; http://education.ucdavis.edu/cress/	K–12 teacher researchers	Ongoing since 1992	Supporting teachers of all subject areas in conducting systematic inquiries about how their students learn	A year-long set of seminars supports teacher researchers. At twice-monthly, small-group meetings, teachers learn various approaches to classroom research, discuss logs of their classes with other teachers, and share research questions, plans, and data. Some groups are discipline-based; most are school-based. Teachers write a report of their research.	Some teacher research reports are published in *Windows on Our Classrooms*, a collection of 7 volumes produced by the CRESS Center (e.g., Carlton, 1996). An annual Spring conference, "Voices from the Classroom," brings teacher researchers together.
Elementary Science Integration Project; University of Maryland—Baltimore County; Saul, 2002, 1993; Reardon & Saul, 1996	Elementary teacher researchers		Applying whole-language approaches to the teaching of inquiry science	Teachers are supported in integrating literacy activities in their teaching of inquiry-based science. In parallel to this activity, they support each other in developing and carrying out inquiries about their efforts to change their science teaching practice.	Three edited volumes have been published by these teachers (e.g., Blackwood, 1993, 1999; Dieckman, 2002a, 2000b; Pearce, 1993; Reardon, 2002)

Goodnough action research group; Goodnough, 2001a, 2001b, 2001c, 2003	Elementary, middle, and high school science teachers	1998–99	Use of multiple intelligence theory in the context of science teaching	Five teachers (2 elementary, 1 middle, and 1 high school) formed an action research group with Goodnough as facilitator. The teachers wanted to improve their own science teaching and were interested in ways in which multiple intelligence theory might help them. Goodnough was interested in developing more empirical data regarding the use of multiple intelligence theory in science teaching.	Teachers reported positive outcomes such as: 1. becoming more reflective in planning, 2. being more sensitive to the diverse learning needs of students, 3. learning about multiple intelligences theory, 4. gaining confidence in teaching science. Goodnough attributes these positive outcomes to the supportive learning community within the group. Generated preliminary empirical evidence regarding the challenges and benefits of using multiple intelligences theory in science teaching at different grade levels.
Language Minority Teacher Induction Program, George Mason University and Washington, DC Metropolitan Schools; http://gse/gmu.edu/research/index.htm	Elementary, middle, and high school teacher researchers	Ongoing since 1998	New teachers who are working with language minority students	A partnership between George Mason University and 12 high-impact schools in the metropolitan DC area (5 high schools, 3 middle schools, and 4 elementary schools) supports new teachers. Action research is a core component. Beginning teachers meet in small groups to examine the challenges of teaching language minority students and to design research projects. Their written reports are published (currently there are 4 volumes).	The program has served 200 teachers. There are 149 papers published online; 11 of these studies focus on science teaching (e.g., Cucchiarelli, 2001; DeSouze-Wyatt, 2002; Dougherty, 2000; Gaither, 2000; Gonzalez, 1999; Hermann, 2002; Hicok, 2000; Jinks & Stanton, 2002; Tracy, 2002; McGee, 2000). Program evaluation shows an impact on beginning teachers' development as reflective practitioners who focus on meeting students' needs. However, the quality of the action research projects varies and needs to be strengthened. The teachers' studies document student improvement in literacy, academic achievement, cross-cultural understanding, and attitudes toward learning.

(continued)

TABLE 39.3
(Continued)

Program and Citations	Participants	Longevity	Focus	Description of Program	Results
Modeling in Mathematics and Science Program, University of Wisconsin and schools in Verona, WI (Lehrer & Schauble, 2002)	Elementary teacher researchers	Ongoing since 1998	Understanding students' thinking about important ideas in mathematics and science, such as data modeling.	Elementary teachers work in a cross-grade forum to improve and study student learning in mathematics and science. The work was initiated by a collaboration between teachers and researchers at the University of Wisconsin and has been subsequently sustained by teacher governance. The goal of the group is to improve teaching and learning by developing a public and sharable field of knowledge about the long-term development of student thinking in important ideas in mathematics and science, such as data modeling.	Teachers report that understanding student thinking supports teaching decisions in action. Teachers have published their findings as chapters in a book edited by Lehrer and Schauble, 2002 (e.g., Clement, 2002; Curtis, 2002; DiPerna, 2002; Gavin, 2002; Putz, 2002; Wainwright, 2002)
Physics Teachers Action Research Group (PTARG), San Francisco Bay Area, California; Feldman, 1994b, 1996	High school and community college physics teachers	Ongoing since 1990	Physics teaching	The group began as an occasional meeting of high school and community-college physics teachers in the Bay area who gathered to discuss the teaching of physics and to hear presentations from physicists on current research. A new focus on collaborative, systematic inquiry into their teaching evolved.	Feldman analyzed the group's meetings and noted that knowledge about physics, teaching, learning, and pedagogical content knowledge was generated and shared by the group. In addition, teachers began to see themselves as researchers as well as teachers. They have made presentations at national conferences and published in *The Physics Teacher*.
Project for Enhancing Effective Learning (PEEL), Melbourne, Australia; Baird & Mitchell, 1986	Grew from one small group of high school teacher researchers to many, multi-grade level groups	Ongoing since 1985	Promoting more metacognitive learning across the curriculum	This teacher-initiated program started at a high school in Melbourne, Australia where Mitchell was interested in using Baird's research about students' poor learning strategies to improve his science teaching. Teachers formed collaborative action research groups and received support and resources from university-based participants.	PEEL teachers contributed chapters to a book that was well received by teachers. The PEEL project and now includes groups in Canada, New Zealand, Sweden, and Denmark as well as Australia.

Name	Participants	Date	Focus	Description	Outcomes
Perspective and Voice of the Teacher Project (PAVOT); Loughran, Mitchell, & Mitchell, 2002	Primary and secondary teacher researchers	Started in 1994	Closer collaboration with academic researchers to carry out more systematic research across the curriculum	This began initially as an unfunded offshoot of the PEEL project. The PAVOT teachers wanted to be more systematic about their research. Teachers received support in conducting research, writing for publication, and making public presentations of their research. Funding from two 3-year Australian Research Council grants provided teachers with short-term classroom release for writing and attending PAVOT meetings as well as funding to support presentations of their findings at educational conferences.	It remains an active community of action research teachers despite being unfunded and voluntary. Concurrent with geographic expansion, there was a drop in the percentage of teachers involved at the level of presenting findings to outside audiences. PAVOT teachers published a book that includes reports of 15 teacher research studies (Loughran, Mitchell, & Mitchell, 2002), including one that is science focused (Berry & Milroy, 2002).
Sacramento Area Science Project, Lesson Study Group, Natomas High School	High school science teacher researchers	Ongoing since 2001	Lesson study approach in high school science teaching	Following a variant of the Japanese lesson study model, teachers meet in small groups to choose a student learning goal and deliberate together to develop, teach, analyze, and revise a lesson plan that addresses this learning goal. Video technology enhances deeper analysis of lessons than is possible with observations.	The group has grown in size and is now interested in developing a model of effective science teaching to inform their planning. The group's writing about their lesson study inquiry is limited to progress reports that are not widely available.

(continued)

TABLE 39.3
(Continued)

Program and Citations	Participants	Longevity	Focus	Description of Program	Results
Science Inquiry Group (SING), Maryland; D. Roberts, 2000; van Zee, 2000; van Zee, Iwaskyk, Kurose, Simpson, & Wild, 2001	Elementary teacher researchers	Ongoing since 1996	Documenting things that are working well in science teaching Collaborations between preservice and inservice teachers	This group focuses on collecting data to communicate to others what is working well rather than to guide actions for improving problematic situations. Experienced teachers meet in small groups in monthly after-school meetings. The group develops case studies which start with written abstracts presented at Research Festivals where experienced teachers discuss their ongoing research with preservice teachers. The Research Festivals serve as a basis for writing proposals for presentations at conferences as well as a place to rehearse conference presentations.	Teachers in this group have been active in making presentations at conferences, and some of the participating teachers have refined their conference papers into published pieces (e.g., Kwan, 2000; Lay, 2000; Nissley, 2000; D. Roberts, 1999, 2000). The teachers report favorably on their interactions with preservice teachers.

They also pointed to studies that show that action research sharpens teachers' reasoning capabilities and supports the development of the disposition to monitor one's own practice (Biott, 1983; Feldman 1994b, 1996; Noffke & Zeichner, 1987; Ruddick 1985; Zeichner 1993).

Akerson and McDuffie (2002) found that several elementary teachers and teacher educators improved their science teaching with a reflective teacher approach (Akerson, Abd-El-Khalick, & Lederman, 2000; Dickinson, Burns, Hagen, & Locker, 1997). Other researchers demonstrated the importance of action or teacher research in developing teachers' abilities to reflect on and improve their own science teaching (Chandler, 1999; Fueyo & Neves, 1995; Scott 1994; Stanulis & Jeffers, 1995; van Zee, 1998a, 1998b; Winograd & Evans, 1995). In his work with physics teachers, Feldman (1996) found that action research played an important role in helping teachers identify and reflect on their underlying assumptions about science and teaching, but that this growth in knowledge and understanding led to only modest changes in teaching practice, which he described as "enhanced normal practice" (Feldman & Minstrell, 2000).

Regarding teacher research as a mode of professional development, teacher researchers often testify to the power of the research process in changing their way of thinking about their teaching practice and their students' thinking and learning (Aladro & Suarez, 2000; Osler & Flack, 2002; Valverde, 2000). Despite the challenges, those who persist report positive learning outcomes: "As I reflect on my research, I see that I have learnt much more than I ever anticipated . . . There are many things that this first attempt at teacher research has taught me" (Boyle, 2002, p. 86).

Beyond teacher researchers' self-reports, however, there is limited evidence—from either teacher research or larger-scale studies of teacher researcher learning—about the impact of teacher research on changes in teaching practice that result in improved student learning outcomes. Do teacher researchers use research findings to change and improve their practice, or do their findings simply confirm their expectations and justify their current practices? Does teacher research stimulate professional learning and growth and help teachers scrutinize their practice more rigorously (Kennedy, 1996a)? Or does teacher research lead to stagnation and even self-delusion as the status of research is used to justify and maintain current teaching practices (Hodgkinson, 1957, as cited in Zeichner & Noffke, 2001; Huberman, 1996)?

One of the few attempts to make teacher researchers the subjects of a research study was conducted by Kennedy (1996a). This teacher researcher learning study examined 78 teachers involved in conducting research in their own classrooms. Kennedy found that these first-time teacher researchers, whose participation came as a result of either a master's program requirement or a district-sponsored action research program, clearly believed that what they learned through the research process was important. Most mentioned positive emotional or intellectual benefits, and many expressed interest in doing another research project. However, most of the teachers also reported that their study validated the teaching approach under study rather than challenging it ("I did interactive writing with my students, and this reinforced to me that it needs to be part of the classroom curriculum" (p. 5)). Only a small fraction of the teachers reported that their research challenged them to revise their thinking about their teaching.

In another study, Kennedy (1998) examined professional development programs in science and mathematics that looked at program impact in terms of changes in teaching practice and student learning outcomes. She identified only four such studies in science, and none of these programs was organized around teacher research. Clearly, more research is needed to assess the impact of teacher research on science teaching and on student learning.

PART THREE: SCIENCE TEACHER RESEARCH PRODUCES KNOWLEDGE

What kind of knowledge is being produced by science teacher research? In what ways might this knowledge be of interest beyond the individual teacher researcher and her/his immediate collaborative group or school?

To address these questions, I reviewed 78 examples of science teacher research. In order to represent the broad range of teacher researchers, I included in this analysis all studies that I was able to access in print format, but limited my review to only one representative study from each teacher researcher. Many, but not all, of the selected studies were developed as part of programs summarized in Tables 39.1, 39.2, and 39.3, and are cited there. The studies were selected from a variety of sources, including research journals (*American Educator, Educational Action Research, Journal for Teacher Research, Journal of Curriculum Studies, Journal of Research in Science Education, Teachers College Record, Teaching and Change*), ERIC documents, books (Barton, 2003; Doris, 1991; Gallas, 1995; Howes, 2002; Loughran & Northfield, 1996), edited collections of teacher research (Atkinson & Fleer, 1995; Lehrer & Schauble, 2002; Loughran et al., 2002; McDonald & Gilmer, 1997; Minstrell & van Zee, 2000; Saul, 1993, 2002; Spiegel, Collins, & Lappert, 1995; Sweeney & Tobin, 2000), online publications (*Networks: An Online Journal for Teacher Research*), and teacher research web sites (e.g., Brookline Teacher Research Group, Cheche Konnen Center, CRESS Center at University of California–Davis, Fairfax County Public Schools, Highland Park High School, Language Minority Teacher Induction Program at George Mason University, Madison Metropolitan School District Classroom Action Research). Additional studies that I reviewed but did not list in Tables 39.1 through 39.3 include one of my own teacher research studies (K. J. Roth, 2002) and the following: Barnes, Hamilton, Hill, Sullivan, & Witcher (2003); Donoahue (2000); Elliot (1995); Genovese (2003); Hayton (1995); Irwin (1997); Jesson (1995); Joseph (2002); Lin (1998); McGlinchey (2002); Minstrell (1982a); Osborne (1997); Painter (1997); Pinkerton (1994); A. Roberts (1999); W.-M. Roth (2000); and Stahly, Krockover, and Shepardson (1999).

Of the 78 studies, 45 focused on elementary science teaching and 30 focused on secondary science teaching (13 at the middle school level and 17 at the high school level). The remaining three studies spanned multiple grade levels, including the college level.

Issues Addressed in the Science Teacher Research Studies

One way of describing the knowledge produced by these studies is to examine the issues addressed in the teacher inquiries. As shown in Table 39.4, 71 percent of the studies focused primarily on the use of particular science teaching strategies or approaches. These teacher researchers tried out teaching approaches recommended in

TABLE 39.4
Issues Addressed in 78 Science Teacher Research Studies

Issues Addressed	Percentage of Studies
Use of particular teaching strategies	71
Use of science inquiry strategies	24
Use of language-related strategies (journal writing, strategies for English language learners, science talks, trade books, etc.)	29
Other (assessment strategies, group work, multiple intelligences strategies, technology, outdoor environment)	18
Teaching and learning of a particular science concept or topic (sound, light and shadows, the moon, electricity, force and motion, plants and photosynthesis, water cycle, nutrition, rocks, particulate nature of matter)	14
Equity issues in science teaching	5
Other (teacher researcher role, becoming a teacher researcher, dilemmas of science teaching, theoretical analyses)	10

the research literature or in national science education documents and considered their impact. For example, 24 percent of teachers explored their efforts to use inquiry approaches to science teaching or a "science workshop" approach where students are encouraged to ask questions and to act as scientists in investigating their questions. Twenty-nine percent of the studies explored language issues such as engaging students in science talks, using journal writing, and so forth. Within this group of studies, there was a particular interest in strategies to support English language learners.

Fourteen percent of the studies focused primarily on a particular topic or concept in the science curriculum with the goal of examining students' activities and learning related to that topic. These studies described the teaching of a particular topic or idea and usually focused heavily on student thinking and learning: How were students making sense of this science content? These topic- or concept-focused studies used a variety of strategies to examine student thinking and learning, including student interviews and videotapes of focus students, but the majority of them examined students' thinking and learning in the context of instruction, primarily through analysis of classroom talk and student work. Within this group, there was some (although limited) focus on analyzing what Ballenger and Rosebery (2003) refer to as "puzzling students."

Only 5 percent of the reviewed studies looked directly at equity issues in science teaching. Ten percent of the studies were classified as "other."

Data Types

What kinds of data did the science teacher researchers in these studies use? Table 39.5 summarizes the commonly used sources of data.

A common feature of the studies was at least some attention to student learning, thinking, and actions. However, the types and quality of evidence used to support claims about student learning varied widely. Most of the studies presented

TABLE 39.5
**Types of Data Used in 78 Science Teacher Research Studies
to Provide Evidence of Student Learning**

Types of Data	Percentage of Studies*
Student work	56
Transcripts of classroom talk	28
Student interviews	25
Teacher journal/logs	25
Videotapes	12
Pre-post measures of student learning	12
Quantitative measures—elementary teachers	9
Quantitative measures—secondary teachers	32

Note: *Percentages do not sum to 100 percent because studies used more than one data type.

examples of students' work to support evidence of student learning, but these examples were used in different ways, and some provided more insight into student thinking and learning than others. In many cases, the examples of student work were presented as exemplars, showing what is possible without addressing how other students or groups of students performed the same task. In a much smaller number of studies, teacher researchers presented student work illustrating "puzzling students"; these studies revealed students' alternative ways of thinking about the science content rather than those intended by the teacher. Still other teacher researchers attempted to show a range of student work. This was sometimes accomplished by describing a particular assessment task and then reporting students' scores on the task, usually reported as a percentage of correct answers rather than an analysis of the facets or features of students' understandings and misunderstandings. Rarely did the studies present a sequence of student work to illustrate changes in student thinking over time.

Other methods for providing evidence of student thinking and learning and the effectiveness of the teaching strategies were used less frequently. As with the use of student work, transcripts of classroom interactions were more often used to demonstrate exemplars of the quality of student thinking and questioning that is possible rather than to demonstrate student understanding of particular content, to explore student confusions and difficulties, or to raise dilemmas of teaching. Both student interviews and teacher journals/logs were used in 25 percent of the studies, but in many cases data from these sources were not presented in the published report.

Pre-post measures or other indicators of change in student thinking and learning over time were used in only 12 percent of the studies. These assessment strategies were usually given to all students in the class, rather than focusing on case studies of individual students (as might be expected, given teachers' responsibility for teaching all students). The type of pre-post measures varied and ranged from yes/no questions about students' attitudes toward particular topics or aspects of doing science to standardized multiple-choice test questions to teacher-designed questions designed to assess student understanding, such as concept mapping tasks or application questions. Pre-post measures were not always written tasks; for example, one teacher researcher compared students' discussion of the same question before and after a unit of instruction. Other data sources that might provide evidence of change in student thinking over time, such as case studies of individual students or student interviews across time, were evident in only a few of these studies.

Secondary teacher researchers were more likely than elementary teacher researchers to use quantitative measures (32 percent of students in secondary versus 9 percent of elementary school studies), to conduct surveys of their students, and to set up experimental comparisons of different conditions. Secondary teachers' interaction with a larger number of students might explain their interest in more quantitative methods, and their work with multiple groups of students in a school day might create a more natural condition for comparing different teaching approaches.

Videotaping was used in only 12 percent of studies. This is a surprisingly low percentage, given the wide availability of this technology and its potential for enabling teachers to examine their own practice (Hiebert, Gallimore, & Stigler, 2002). This issue is revisited in the section on new directions for science teacher research.

Knowledge Contribution

What contributions might this group of 78 teacher researcher studies make to the larger science education community? What contributions do they make to teachers, to the research community, and to the knowledge base for science teaching?

As a group, the studies do not provide sufficient evidence of impact on student thinking, learning, and actions to use them to make any recommendations about effective science teaching. Larger-scale studies and closer analyses of changes in student learning over time are needed to make such claims. However, the studies do provide valuable insights into how science education research and reform recommendations are being implemented in classrooms, what makes such implementation challenging within real classrooms, teachers' assessment of the value and usefulness of these recommendations, and what issues science teacher researchers are and are not studying.

For example, there are a considerable number of studies that examined teachers' efforts to teach science with an inquiry orientation (e.g., Doris, 1991; Hayton, 1995; Iwasyk, 2000; Kurose, 2000; Kwan, 2000; Lay, 2000; Nissley, 2000; Pearce, 1993, 1999; Reardon, 2002; D. Roberts, 2000). Each of these studies provides a portrait of how such inquiry teaching was interpreted and implemented in one classroom. Descriptions of these teaching efforts give other teachers concrete and varying images of what inquiry science teaching might look like and how students might respond. The studies are for the most part inspirational, presenting captivating images of students engaged in scientific inquiry. Such images are necessary to help teachers translate the rhetoric of reform into a reality in the classroom. In this sense, teacher researchers are the pioneers, the ones who are willing to not only try new approaches in their science teaching, but to also make that effort visible for others. These pioneering inquiries provide valuable images for other teachers and provide important knowledge to the larger research community.

The research community can examine these studies to ascertain which features of inquiry teaching are being implemented and which are not and use this knowledge to develop future research agendas. Keys and Bryan (2001) reviewed many of the same studies reviewed for this chapter and used them (along with other studies) to develop a proposal for a science education research agenda that examines research on inquiry in diverse classrooms with a special focus on modes of inquiry-based instruction that are designed by teachers.

Another interesting finding from the review of these studies of science inquiry is the emphasis on addressing authentic student questions (studying a local oil spill, local traffic flow, family recycling bins, and so forth). In contrast, teacher researcher studies of inquiry science teaching less frequently looked at inquiry within the context of addressing the development of the canonical science knowledge that is the focus of many science standards, benchmarks, and state or local learning goals and objectives. Such an observation could be used to stimulate discussion and debate within the science education community about the possible need for more studies of inquiry teaching that include a focus on canonical knowledge development.

Science teacher researchers' emphasis on student inquiry and relative inattention to the large body of research about students' naive conceptions, alternative frameworks, or misconceptions also provides important knowledge for the science education research community. Is this an important gap to be addressed in future teacher research? Or is "conceptual change" science teaching, and the development of understandings of science canonical ideas viewed as incompatible with inquiry teaching? This is an important issue for the science education community that the teacher research studies place before us.

While teacher research does not lend itself to making quantitative claims and generalizations about student learning or about which strategy works better than another, teacher research does provide a rich context for exploring what's possible and what's difficult in teaching a given topic, concept, or inquiry skill. For example, a group of teachers in Wisconsin provided rich descriptions of their efforts to help first-through third-grade students learn how to organize and interpret data in various representations (Clement, 2002; Curtis, 2002; DiPerna, 2002; Gavin, 2002; Putz, 2002; Wainwright, 2002). These teachers were exploring new ground in terms of challenging young students to use rather sophisticated data organization and reasoning strategies. These teachers explored curricular territory that is usually reserved for much older students who are more able to think abstractly, and their efforts challenge our assumptions of what's possible for young students to understand.

Berry and Milroy's study (2002) of their efforts to use a conceptual change approach to the teaching of the particulate nature of matter to year 10 students in Australia provides important insights about "what's difficult" in implementing research-based, theoretical perspectives in the classroom. They successfully identified their students' thinking that matter is continuous rather than particulate, but then struggled to figure out how to help students understand the scientific view of matter as particulate. They drew from the research literature to help identify the students' conceptual difficulties, but found that the research literature was largely silent about how to help students reconcile their ideas with scientific concepts. As Berry wrote in her journal: "This is so frustrating! I can find probes of students' conceptions all over the place [in the research literature] but there's nothing really that says what to do next!! Bits and pieces, nothing more" (Berry & Milroy, 2002, p. 200). Their efforts to develop a curriculum to address students' naive ideas represent a first step in building the knowledge that they could not find. But their efforts also communicate the need to the larger research community that this kind of knowledge is needed by classroom teachers.

The results of this review of science teacher research in many ways parallel Dressman's (2000) review of 61 examples of classroom research published in *Language Arts*. He found that the most common teacher research genre was the "good practice narrative" in which teachers reported their largely successful efforts to instantiate theory into practice. The same can be said of the majority of the studies in this review. Science teacher researchers are creating interesting learning contexts where there is much to report about student thinking and learning that is exciting and holds promise for the future. But there is an underrepresentation of studies that examine problems, learning difficulties, and discontinuities between intended and actual learning outcomes.

Both Dressman (2000) and Ballenger and Rosebery (2003) challenged teacher researchers to reveal more of the factors that "give teaching and learning their texture, their contour, and all too often, their outcome" (Dressman, p. 57). Fecho and Allen (2003) agreed, suggesting that the teacher researcher should reveal, embrace, and interrogate dissonances within his or her practice. Ballenger and Rosebery emphasized the importance of scrutinizing moments of confusion and "puzzling students," viewing this activity as the core of their teacher research practice. The idea is to delve into something that is confusing, perhaps unsuccessful, and to try to understand it better. This approach is at the core of the Brookline Teacher Research Group and the Cheche Konnen Center. This approach is evident in some of the published science teacher research, but it is the exception rather than the rule. For example, Judy Wild (2000) described how much difficulty her fourth-grade students had in understanding the basic idea of a complete electric circuit. She examines the discontinuities between students' abilities to build circuits and their difficulties in predicting whether given circuits will allow a light bulb to light. Many teachers might assume that the successful building of a circuit represents evidence of understanding circuits, but Wild's examples challenge this assumption and encourage teachers to take a deeper look at student understanding. In another example, Margery Osborne (1997) considered the dilemmas she faced in addressing the needs of the group and the needs of the individual when using a constructivist approach in her first-grade science teaching.

PART FOUR: ISSUES IN SCIENCE TEACHER RESEARCH

Part Four addresses the benefits and pitfalls of science teacher research and the debate about criteria for judging quality of teacher research, and considers new directions for the future.

Benefits and Pitfalls of Science Teacher Research

Is teacher research an effective model for teacher learning and professional development? Can teacher research make valuable contributions to the knowledge base for science teaching? Clearly, more research is needed to understand the impact of teacher research on teacher learning, on teaching practice, and on knowledge development in the science education research community. Science teacher research is in its infancy, and there are many unanswered questions about its effectiveness in supporting teacher professional development and in contributing to the knowledge base for science teaching. Given this context, there is debate about the effectiveness and usefulness of science teacher research. Both teacher researchers and academic researchers point to a number of potential benefits and pitfalls of teacher research. Many of the benefits and pitfalls relate to the standards of quality of teacher research, which are further discussed in the next section.

Teacher Is Both Teacher and Researcher

Teacher research provides an insider view of teaching that is often invisible to outside observers (Ball, 2000; Cochran-Smith & Lytle, 1993; Zeichner & Noffke, 2001). Approaches to research that use the personal view of the teacher as a resource offer the possibility of new insights that an outsider could not see and might not think to ask about. Only the teacher, for example, knows what she was thinking when a class discussion veered off in an unanticipated direction (see Abell & Roth, 1995). Only the teacher knows the kinds of thinking that went on during the planning process. Although an outsider can try to tap into this knowledge through interviews and other research strategies, it is difficult for an outsider to ask the right question at the right moment and to build the level of trust needed for the teacher to reveal critical information. "Teachers offer special insights into the knowledge-production process that those studying someone else's teaching are unable to provide" (Zeichner & Noffke, 2001, p. 299).

But it is difficult—and essential—that teacher researchers step outside their own assumptions and preconceptions and maintain a healthy skepticism about their observations of themselves and their students (Ball, 2000). Huberman (1996) and Hodgkinson (1957) questioned the ability of teachers to bracket their preconceptions and to "avoid distortions and self-delusion" (as cited in Zeichner & Noffke, 2001, p. 299). "Understanding events when one is a participant in them is excruciatingly difficult if not impossible" (Cochran-Smith & Lytle, 1999, p. 20; Huberman). Ball was more optimistic, but highlighted the challenge of this role: teacher researchers must remain open and curious, defending against the natural urge to defend against questions raised by others without silencing the interior voice that provides the unique and critical insights. Unless the insider perspective can be balanced by this outsider perspective, there is the danger that the research will become too personal, resulting in products that are useless and sometimes even embarrassing (Behar, 1996).

Research Questions

Teacher research can address questions that take advantage of the teacher's insider status and would be difficult for outsiders to pursue with as much insight (Ball, 2000). For example, the teacher researcher is uniquely positioned to examine her efforts to implement a new science teaching strategy. The teacher has unique access to knowledge about the full scope of the thinking and planning that took place before, during, and after her teaching and about how teaching with the new strategy was more or less difficult than strategies used in the past. In addition, the teacher has a special vantage point for understanding the variety of influences that contributed to her experience using the new teaching strategy: What role did curriculum materials play? Were interactions with colleagues important? What about professional development experiences? How did the students' reactions to the new instructional approach influence her decision-making?

Ball (2000) suggested that teacher research focus on such questions where a first-person account can contribute to making visible knowledge that is less likely to be accessed by outsiders, and she cautioned teacher researchers to avoid questions that are best examined by outsiders. For example, teacher researchers sometimes ask questions that are best explored through in-depth case studies of individual students in their classrooms: *How are mainstreamed special education students experiencing the inquiry science teaching in my classroom?* Such questions require special observations and interviews with individual students, whereas the teachers' responsibilities as teacher require her to attend to all students in the classroom. An outside observer would be better suited to carry out this kind of research. Similarly, teacher researchers sometimes develop questions designed to develop generalizations or comparisons that are difficult if not impossible to make within the classroom context, such as: *Do students develop better understandings of the nature of science in an inquiry-oriented science classroom or in a conceptual change science classroom?* While a middle school science teacher could set up such a comparison between two of his classes, it would be difficult for him to set up and maintain the two contrasting conditions, and the student learning results would not have the same weight as a larger-scale study. However, the teacher's knowledge about what it was like to implement the two different approaches would provide a valuable insider perspective that might not be revealed in a larger-scale study.

Research Context

The science teacher researcher has daily access to a rich data set about students, teaching, teacher thinking and planning, and student learning that provides unique opportunities for research. Unlike teacher researchers, researchers who watch other teachers rarely have access to the daily unfolding of instruction, and they can tap into teacher thinking and planning only on an occasional basis. This rich context enables the teacher researcher to examine classroom events with much more knowledge relevant to the situation than can an outside researcher. Thus, teacher research provides the opportunity to explore the many particulars of teaching and their interactions (Akerson & McDuffie, 2002; Ball, 2000).

The rich context can also be problematic, however. The environment is so dense with information and events that it may be difficult for the teacher researcher to focus the area of inquiry (Baird & Northfield, 1992; Northfield, 1996). Knowing too much about the particulars can make it difficult to see patterns and to make any kind of claims that might be of interest to the consumers of the research (Ball, 2000).

Collaboration

Those involved in teacher research commonly emphasize the importance and value of collaboration among teacher researchers, which challenges the prevailing norm of teaching as an isolated activity (Cochran-Smith & Lytle, 1990, 1999; Goodnough, 1991a; Northfield, 1996; Ovens, 2000; Zeichner & Noffke, 2001; Zeichner et al., 2000).

The opportunity to work with other teacher researchers plays a central role in helping teachers make sense of the particulars of their own classroom, it provides insights into other teachers' practices, and it can support teachers in learning to be more analytical about teaching by challenging their assumptions and preconceptions. Teacher researchers frequently comment on the valuable role collaboration played in their growth as a teacher and a teacher researcher (Berry & Milroy, 2002; Mohr et al., 2004).

Although collaboration certainly contributes to making teaching more visible, it is not always easy to establish norms of interaction that focus on analysis and criticism. Teachers have not been trained in research techniques, and they are not experienced in having evidence-based conversations about teaching. Scientific norms of skepticism, precision, and demands for evidence are not typically part of teachers' professional interactions. The science teacher researcher community needs to support the development of collaborative norms that challenge teacher researchers' analyses and lead to insights that will be more transformative for the teachers themselves and that will be of more interest to the larger science education community.

Teacher Voice, Professionalism, and Satisfaction

Since the 1980s, increasing numbers of academic researchers have called for the valuing of teachers as producers of knowledge (Carr & Kemmis, 1986; Cochran-Smith & Lytle, 1993; F. Erickson, 1986; Richardson, 1994; Russell & Munby, 1994). They have argued that teachers' knowledge has too often been dismissed by the research community as anecdotal and that teacher voices should be more prominent in educational research. Teachers should gain more faith in their own experience and knowledge instead of relying primarily on outside authority. Self-reports from teacher researchers suggest that they do gain professional satisfaction and a new respect for their own knowledge and ability to learn and grow. But they also acknowledge the demands and frustrations of conducting research and teaching. Both teaching and research are time-consuming and intellectually challenging endeavors, and only a few teachers find the wherewithal to make both activities a part of their professional lives. Although some teacher researchers get financial support from grants or school districts to provide time to work on research-related activities (e.g., writing, attending conferences), most teacher researcher groups meet during after-school hours. They spend these hours learning to carry out research tasks that academic researchers acquired as part of doctoral studies. Is it realistic to expect that teachers can learn to do meaningful research within this structure, and is it fair to teachers to ask them to take on this new role without any accommodations to their regular teaching load?

Teacher Learning

As noted earlier in this chapter, one of the major goals of teacher research is to stimulate and deepen teacher learning and to promote changes in teaching practice. However, there is also the danger that teacher research can be used to justify the status quo (Ball, 2000; Hodgkinson, 1957, as cited in Zeichner & Noffke, 2001; Kennedy, 1996a; Zeichner & Noffke, 2001). In fact, Kennedy's review of 78 teacher researcher studies found that most of these teacher researchers found evidence to support their current practice; challenging current practice or raising problematic situations was an uncommon feature of these studies. Teacher researchers must be wary about their claims; the fact that something is stated from a first-person perspective and experience does not necessarily make it true (Ball, 2000).

Usefulness of Knowledge for Teachers

As noted in the historical context section of Part One, there has been much concern over the years about the failure of educational research to affect teaching practice. Teacher research, with its focus on the particulars of teaching described in teachers' voices, offers the promise of providing research knowledge that will be useful to teachers. But are teachers any more likely to read each others' research than they are to read academic research? Is the research too specific to the situation to be of interest to other teachers? A study by Kennedy found that teachers did not always rate teacher research studies as more meaningful to them than more traditional academic research. They found that it was the persuasiveness and relevance of the research and whether or not it influenced their thinking that determined its value to them, rather than whether the source was an academic researcher or a teacher researcher (Kennedy, 1996b, 1997).

Quality of Knowledge Produced

One of the biggest areas of debate concerning teacher research is the quality of the research knowledge that is produced. Some argue that teacher research is a new genre of research that will improve the knowledge base for science teaching by building on academic research and linking it more closely to practice. Teacher research builds the bridge linking academic research and practice. Teacher research, in this view, can extend academic research knowledge by exploring it in the context of real classrooms. For example, teacher researchers can examine specific teaching strategies that have been recommended based on preliminary research, studying questions such as: What is possible in terms of student learning when you use these strategies? What makes these teaching strategies/recommendations difficult to enact? What is it like for a teacher to try to change his teaching practice in these ways? What discrepancies emerge between what was intended and what occurs?

Skeptics question whether knowledge produced by teacher researchers meets the criteria of quality that will enable it to be integrated with academic research (Hodgkinson, 1957, as cited in Zeichner & Noffke, 2001; Huberman, 1996). In this sense, teacher research is also viewed as a new genre of research, but it is separate and not equal to traditional academic research because of limitations in its standards of validity, reliability, evidence, claims, and generalizability. These debates about quality are examined in the next section.

The Debate about Criteria for Quality

The history of action research and teacher research includes much debate about the standards for quality of such research: Are there special criteria needed for judging the quality of teacher research, or should the same standards used in academic research be used? And who should set the standards of quality for teacher research?

In its early days, educational action research in the U.S. context was judged by traditional, positivistic research standards, resulting in severe criticisms of the quality of the research. Hodgkinson (1957) described teacher research as "hobby games for little engineers" and asserted that "research is no place for an amateur" (as cited in Zeichner & Noffke, 2001, p. 299). Despite the efforts of Stephen Corey (1953) and others to defend action research as a legitimate form of inquiry, action research was ridiculed from the perspective of the conventional research standards of the day, and it largely disappeared from the U.S. literature until the late 1970s (Zeichner & Noffke, 2001).

The development of qualitative research standards in education, and the growing recognition of these standards as respectable and legitimate, contributed to the reemergence of the teacher research movement in the United States in the late 1970s and 1980s (Zeichner & Noffke, 2001). Since then, various researchers have attempted to define standards for quality in teacher research, drawing largely from standards developed for qualitative research. Although there is wide agreement that the qualitative standards are useful in teacher research, many researchers assert that traditional standards of reliability, validity, and generalizability are not appropriate for judging the quality of teacher research, especially given the wide variety of forms and purposes of teacher research (Altrichter, 1993; G. Anderson et al., 1994; Dadds, 1995; Feldman 1994a; Jacobson, 1998; Lomax, 1994; Munby, 1995; Stevenson, 1996; Zeichner & Noffke). Instead, they argue for new standards of quality that are designed specifically for teacher research. Others argue that teacher research should be held to the same standards as other types of research.

In the latter group, Huberman (1996) asserts that teacher researchers should be held to the same classic standards that are applied to all qualitative research, including "evidence, consistency, freedom from obvious bias and perceptions of the people involved" (p. 128) and minimally reliable methods to minimize "delusion and distortion" (p. 132). Eisenhart and Howe (1992) and Eisenhart and Borko (1993) propose a master set of criteria for all forms of classroom research, including both qualitative and quantitative teacher research.

Those who argue for special standards of quality for teacher research highlight issues unique to teacher research. After reviewing arguments made by a variety of researchers on this issue, I selected five proposed standards for teacher research that seem to me to address issues that are specific to teacher research: (a) insider-outsider stance, (b) trustworthiness, (c) collaboration and public dialogue, (d) complexity of context and triangulation, and (e) impact on teacher/student learning. I believe that careful attention to these criteria would improve the quality of the science teacher research reviewed in this chapter.

Insider-Outsider Stance

This criterion is at the heart of teacher research and is the feature of teacher research that most sets it apart from other forms of research. It is also the most challenging criterion to practice effectively as a teacher researcher.

Because the teacher researcher role involves self-study, many emphasize standards of quality related to the teacher researcher's stance toward his or her study.

Ball (2000) describes the need for teacher researchers to step back and view their own work as teachers as matters for scrutiny while also being caught up inside the day-to-day actions of teaching. They must assume a stance of inquiry and curiosity, instead of defending one's actions against questions that others might raise. The teacher researcher must value and listen to the insider voice while also adopting an outsider perspective: "This kind of research requires both an unusual concentration on, and use of, self, combined with an almost unnatural suspension of the personal" (Ball, pp. 392–393). Northfield (1996) described the need for the teacher researcher to reframe classroom situations, to suspend judgment rather than rely on preconceptions, and to regard their assumptions as problematic. O'Dea (1994) drew from the field of literary criticism to describe the need for teacher researchers to be authentic, true to themselves, and self-critical. Lather (1993), working from a feminist perspective, called for the disclosure and self-scrutiny of the teacher researcher's preconceptions and experiences.

I believe that the quality of science teacher research will improve as the teacher research community develops guidelines and other supports to help teachers adopt this challenging insider-outsider stance. Strategies, guiding questions, or routines can be developed to challenge and support teacher researchers as they try to be aware of both perspectives and to examine each from a critical stance.

Trustworthiness: Evidence-based Reasoning and Worthwhile Questions

At the center of the debate about quality in teacher research are the issues of validity and generalizability. In defining standards in qualitative research more generally, Lincoln and Guba (1985) and F. Erickson (1986) asserted that conventional notions of validity and generalizability cannot be applied to research that does not fall within the positivist experimental design paradigm. Lincoln and Guba suggested abandonment of the idea of validity, to be replaced by a notion of trustworthiness. Zeichner and Noffke (2001) nominated the term *trustworthiness* as a replacement for *validity* in the context of teacher research. They argued that the term *trustworthiness* "better captures the need for practitioner research to justify its claims to know in terms of the relationships among knowers and knowledges" (pp. 314–315). A standard of trustworthiness challenges researchers to develop arguments that persuade the reader that their findings are worthy of attention.

I find the term *trustworthiness* interesting, because it captures both the importance of having "trustworthy" data and the importance of exploring questions that are "worthy" of investigation and of interest beyond the individual teacher researcher's classroom. In constructing a list of criteria to guide teacher researcher work, I would prefer to highlight these different meanings by creating two separate categories. The new categories might be named "evidence-based reasoning" and "worthwhile questions." The "evidence-based reasoning" criterion points to the need for justifying claims and developing arguments based on specific pieces of evidence that can come in a variety of forms. Under the category of "worthwhile questions," I would emphasize that in addition to being of interest to the teacher researcher, research questions in high-quality teacher research are also linked to the work of others and/or to theoretical perspectives. I believe that if teacher researchers learn about and connect with the work of others, the quality of their research will improve.

In addition, this process will help them in developing the outsider stance described in the previous criterion.

Collaboration and Public Dialogue

Collaboration is important and critical to the success of many different kinds of research projects, and I would argue that it is an essential criterion of quality in teacher research. Partly because of the difficulties involved in analyzing a situation in which one is a participant and taking an outsider stance (Huberman 1996), collaboration is a crucial element in teacher research (G. Anderson et al., 1994; Northfield, 1996; Stevenson, 1996). It provides teacher researchers access to outside perspectives and knowledge and challenges their assumptions. Because teachers are typically isolated in their classrooms and are not trained in research, collaboration is necessary to gain research skills and to connect their personal research with others' situations and concerns. Anderson et al. defined a standard of dialogic validity that assesses the degree to which the research promotes reflective dialogue among the participants in the research. Related to this but coming from a feminist perspective, Lather (1993) and Dadds (1995) described the quality of relationships among the participants as a key criterion of quality research. Stevenson emphasized the importance of making results public and engaging in dialogue about them beyond the research group.

In my experiences with teacher research, I have observed that high-quality teacher researcher collaboration is difficult to achieve. And yet this difficulty is not made visible in most of the science teacher research accounts reviewed for this chapter. Collaboration that challenges teacher researchers to reveal their own practices and to consider outside perspectives is often uncomfortable in school cultures where teachers do not say things that might appear critical or "challenging" of someone else's practice. It is easier to collaborate in supportive ways than in challenging ways. And yet, I would argue that the quality and usefulness of science teacher research will not develop and flourish unless teacher research groups can develop strategies and norms for challenging as well as supporting each other.

Because so many of the studies reviewed in this chapter were made possible because of collaborations initiated by academic researchers, I am convinced that collaborations between teacher researchers and academic researchers provide one excellent avenue for developing norms of "challenging" collaboration. But this kind of collaboration can also be precarious. Academic researchers have the experience and expertise to bring the language of argumentation and "challenge" to the table, but they can easily do this in a way that is alienating to some teacher researchers. On the other hand, academic researchers can be so fearful of alienating teacher researchers that they refrain from bringing new norms of interaction to the group, and an important opportunity for growth within the group is lost. Discussing differences in norms openly and frequently in teacher researcher groups is necessary, and the development of materials, guidelines, and research stories that help teacher researchers and academic researchers learn how to communicate in both challenging and supportive ways will support progress in this arena.

Complexity of Context and Triangulation

A key criterion of quality for teacher research is the examination of the complexity of the classroom context and the use of triangulation to make sense of this complexity (Feldman & Minstrell, 2000; Northfield, 1996; Stevenson, 1996). This criterion is important for at least two reasons. First, a unique strength of teacher research is the deep and broad insider knowledge held by the teacher researcher; good teacher research uses the richness of this knowledge to provide insights unavailable to an outside observer (Ball, 2000). Triangulation, which involves collecting data from several different views of the same situation, enables teacher researchers to mine the wealth of this complexity. Along with collaboration, such triangulation also supports the teacher researcher in looking at classroom events from multiple perspectives, not just the teacher perspective.

The complexity of context criterion is also important in addressing issues of external validity, providing readers with sufficient detail to understand similarities and differences with his or her own context. Teacher researchers need to provide enough detail to convince others that "what they have learned is true in the particular case of their teaching in their classrooms" (Feldman & Minstrell, 2000, p. 6).

Many of the science teacher research studies reviewed for this chapter did not reveal the complexities of the situation through such methods as proposing alternative explanations, considering various sources of data, or examining conflicting evidence. In part, this might be explained by the expectations of traditional educational research publications and expectations of readers/audiences who are looking for a nice, clean story told in a certain number of pages/minutes. In contrast, teacher researchers need to figure out how to tell a "messy" (complex) story in a certain number of pages/minutes and to have the story be compelling and meaningful to audiences. This is a challenge, but a worthwhile one to take on: How can a report of teacher research reveal the complexities and yet still reveal a clear story that is meaningful to the teacher and to others?

Impact on Teacher/Student Learning

A criterion that is at the core of action research and of many other forms of teacher research is the degree to which the research has been transformative, leading to a change in the researcher's understandings and/or practice (Stevenson, 1996). This was described by Lather (1991) and G. Anderson et al. (1994) as catalytic validity—to what extent does the research energize the teacher researcher to better understand and transform the teaching situation? Dadds (1995) identified improvements in teacher researchers' practice and teacher researchers' professional learning and growth as two different categories for judging the quality of teacher research.

Although some teacher researchers specifically focus on documenting and analyzing their practice rather than improving it, I would argue that high-quality inquiries and analyses should also prompt the teacher researcher to develop new understandings that have implications for his or her teaching. In addition, I propose that the best quality teacher research transforms teaching practice in ways that improve student learning. This is a high bar to hold up for quality teacher research, but what is the value of teacher understanding and learning if it has no implications for student growth? Good teacher research, therefore, should ultimately transform the teacher researcher's knowledge and understanding, the teacher researcher's teaching practice, and his or her students' learning.

Who Decides?

Many of those engaged in the debate about standards for quality in teacher research, including myself, are university-based academic researchers. Although teacher researchers themselves discuss and raise issues of quality (e.g., Threatt et al., 1994), publications in print about these issues are dominated by academic researcher voices. Zeichner and Noffke (2001) and Evans, Stubbs, Frechette, Neely, and Warner (1987) criticized this situation as a silencing of the voices of teachers: "P–12 educators need to assume a central role in formulating and applying standards for assessing the quality of their own work" (p. 322). The field would be well served by public discussion of these issues across teacher researcher groups.

New Directions for Science Teacher Research
in an Era of Standards and High-Stakes Testing

Cochran-Smith and Lytle (1999) described the future of teacher research in the standards movement era to be uncertain. They noted that pressures for accountability are likely to make research-based whole-school improvement models more widespread, with the voices of outside authoritative experts dominating over teachers' voices in educational research. Since Cochran-Smith and Lytle wrote of this concern in 1999, the high-stakes testing environment in the United States has only intensified with the federal No Child Left Behind legislation (NCLB, 2001). The NCLB legislation not only mandates extensive testing; it also explicitly states that teachers should implement teaching practices that are shown to be effective by high-quality research. The "gold standard" of high-quality research is defined as large-scale, randomized controlled trials.

Will the teacher researcher movement continue to grow and flourish in this environment? Teacher researchers will have to wrestle with both the accountability demands and the demands of teaching and research. Can they continue their inquiries and collaborations in ways that will be supported and valued in their schools? Can the changes they are making in their teaching as a result of their inquiries be linked to the kinds of improvement in their students' learning that will show up on high-stakes tests?

What Cochran-Smith and Lytle said in 1999 about the standards movement is even more valid with regard to the NCLB environment: "These and many other challenges undoubtedly will influence the direction, and perhaps the continued existence, of the teacher research movement in the years to come" (p. 22). They pointed to the history of teacher research as a compelling reason for optimism, noting how valuable teacher research is and has been to many teachers, teacher educators, and researchers.

However, science teacher research as a movement and a force in the research and policy communities is in its infancy. Cochran-Smith and Lytle's experiences with teacher research are in the literacy curriculum area, where there is a longer history of teacher research and a much larger body of published materials compared with science teacher research. Among science teacher researchers, there is less history and less momentum to sustain. Science teacher research is at a stage where it needs to be supported and nurtured in order to understand its potential contributions to teachers' professional growth and to the research knowledge base about science teaching and learning. What new directions might provide such support?

Studies about Teacher Research

It may be that larger-scale studies conducted by academics about teacher research and its impact can contribute to the future flourishing of science teacher research. From the professional development perspective, for example, studies that examine the impact of teacher research on teacher learning and on teachers' practice could provide additional evidence to support the value of teacher research. Do teachers change their teaching practice as a result of their inquiries? Do these changes result in improvements in student learning? Two teacher researchers, McGoey and Ross (1999), pointed to a need for such formal studies in their guest editorial in the *Journal for Research in Science Teaching*: "We suspect that research-based initiatives in education reform will not thrive outside a community of professionals capable of sustaining an action research ethos, but we are unable to conduct formal studies. An answer to this question could significantly reduce wasted effort" (p. 119). They argued that such research knowledge would support the efforts of teacher researchers in communicating with their peers, school administrators, and parents.

Teacher Research Syntheses

From the production of knowledge perspective, syntheses of science teacher research might make teachers' knowledge more accessible to other teacher researchers, to teachers who are not researchers, and to academic researchers. Research reviews or meta-analyses that synthesize science teacher research studies about particular aspects of science teaching might help make science teacher research more accessible as well as contribute to addressing the generalizability issue in teacher research. This might nurture the science teacher research movement by making more visible the value of the knowledge generated by teacher researchers.

Searchable Online Libraries

The current body of science teacher research is not easy to access and search. Articles are published most frequently on web sites and in edited book volumes, which are usually organized as a collection of articles by teacher researchers within a given group rather than by topic, grade level, or issue. The production of an easily searchable, centralized teacher research online library that is organized not just by key words and authors, but also by grade level, curriculum materials, learning goals, and so forth, is another strategy that could make teacher research more accessible and valuable to both teachers and researchers. For example, a teacher who is preparing to teach a unit or conduct an inquiry about electricity could access other teachers' studies that took place in the context of teaching this topic. Or a teacher who is struggling to implement language activities to support English-language learners could access research studies relevant to this issue. Research studies about patterns of use of such a library could assess the usefulness of the knowledge that is being generated by teacher researchers and contribute to establishing the value of teacher research.

A National/International Science Teacher Research Community

But such tasks are not likely to be taken on by an individual teacher researcher or teacher research group. It is an effort that needs to be undertaken by organized professional communities or by collaborative teams of academic researchers and teacher researchers. The teacher research special-interest group at NARST might be a place to begin building such collaborations.

One debate within teacher researcher groups is the extent to which teacher researchers and more traditional academic researchers should partner. There is a fear among some teacher researchers that academic voices might drown out teacher voices and force teacher research to adopt the same norms and criteria of quality as academic research (Threatt et al., 1994). However, much of the science teacher research to date has been initiated through research grants or master's programs developed by academic researchers. Thus, there is active support for teacher research among academic researchers. This group of academic researchers can play an important role in the further development of science teacher research, and their opportunities to collaborate and meet with teacher researchers might help nurture the science teacher research movement.

Funding Opportunities

Funding opportunities to support teacher research and to promote communications across science teacher research groups would also help nurture science teacher research. However, the teacher research movement faces a paradox in the funding situation. In order to make the case for the importance of teacher research, the teacher research community needs opportunities to grow and develop and especially to communicate across groups about standards for high quality in teacher research. Funding is needed to support such communication of science teacher research groups with each other and with teacher research groups with longer histories in other subject matter areas. But funding will be difficult to obtain until funding sources are convinced that science teacher research is likely to result in improved science teaching and learning.

New Modes of Representation of Teacher Research

To date, science teacher research has been shared with the science education community through traditional publication and presentation routes, with a special emphasis on online publication. We do not yet know the extent to which such representations of teacher research provide useful knowledge to other teachers and researchers. Dadds (1995) suggested that a larger variety of representations of teacher research might better reflect the needs and contexts of different teacher researchers. She argued for broadening what counts as legitimate forms of representing teacher research: "If we continue to limit our view of 'text' to the more conventional academic research genre . . . we may ignore the appropriateness of other forms of communication, written or spoken, that may have greater potential for shaping and communicating meaning, for putting the action in action research, for acting as catalysts for institutional action and change" (Dadds, 1995, p. 132).

Criteria for judging quality need to take into account the possibility of such alternative forms of representation, which might include educational actions, drama, photography, film, and poetry (Lomax & Parker, 1995; McNiff, Lomax, & Whitehead, 1996).

There has been little experimentation with alternative modes of representation of teacher research, but one mode that seems particularly suited to communicating about teaching is video (Hiebert et al., 2002; Stigler, Gallimore, & Hiebert, 2000). Surprisingly, only 12 percent of the science teacher research studies reviewed for this chapter reported that they used video methodology in collecting data. One reason for its limited use might be the risks involved in making video images of teachers and students publicly available. In this digital age, this risk is even more important to address, and procedures and policies to minimize such risks to teachers and students need to be carefully developed and rigorously implemented.

Perhaps another reason for the limited use of video in these studies is a narrow vision of how such video might be used by teacher researchers. If video is considered only as a data collection strategy that must then be painstakingly analyzed, the use of video might seem too time consuming to be useful in the teacher research genre. But video could also be viewed as an alternative publication strategy that might better suit many teachers than writing research articles.

Videocases could be developed by teachers to be shared with other teachers, with preservice teachers, and with academic researchers. Videocases of teaching could be shared at any stage in the inquiry process, especially if they are presented in an online, digital format that allows for time-linked commentary by the teacher researcher. The teacher researcher could make the videocase available through an indexed and searchable online, digital video library. Other teachers, teacher researchers, and academic researchers could be invited to view the videocase and add their own comments, which could also be time-linked to specific places in the video. In this way, the "product" of a teacher's inquiry is actually still part of his or her inquiry process, providing outsider perspectives that can challenge and deepen the teacher researcher's study.

The video artifact from the inquiry process could also be useful as a teaching tool in preservice and inservice teacher education programs as well as a research data source for additional studies carried out by other investigators. For example, if the many studies about inquiry science teaching reviewed in this chapter had made teaching video available online, it would be feasible to build on the work of each individual teacher researcher by analyzing and comparing various instantiations of inquiry teaching.

The use of such video products over time could help the science education community develop a shared language for talking about science teaching that would be closely matched to visual images of what the ideas might look like in action in the classroom. This would be a tremendous contribution of teacher research to the knowledge base for science teaching.

CONCLUDING REMARKS

Science teacher research holds much promise for enhancing science teacher learning within preservice and inservice teacher education programs and teacher researcher inquiry groups. It has been used in a variety of teacher education and teacher professional development programs as a strategy for developing reflective, inquiring science teachers. Although there is evidence that science teacher research contributes to teachers' professional dispositions, learning, and growth, there is less evidence that it affects science teachers' practice in ways that result in improved student learning. Further research is needed to examine the impact of teacher research on science teachers' practice.

Science teacher research also holds promise for making important contributions to the knowledge base for science teaching. Although there are many pitfalls in science teacher research, it does offer a unique insider perspective that might help bridge the gap between traditional academic research and science teaching practice. But science teacher research is in its infancy as a movement within the science education research community. There are debates about the standards of quality for science teacher research, and it is unclear whether and how science teacher research will become widely accessible and usable within the science education community. Supports of various kinds, including funding and tools such as online, searchable text and video libraries, and collaborations between teacher researchers and academic researchers are needed to nurture the movement in order to explore its potential: "The partnership between researchers and practitioners is in its infancy. . . . We look forward to a day when collaboration between the academy and the classroom teacher is a commonplace of professional science teaching" (McGoey and Ross, 1999, p. 120).

ACKNOWLEDGMENTS

Thanks to Deborah Trumbull, who reviewed this chapter.

REFERENCES

Abell, S. K. (2000). From professor to colleague: Creating a professional identity as collaborator in elementary science. *Journal of Research in Science Teaching, 37,* 548–562.

Abell, S. K, Anderson, G., & Chezem, J. (2000). Science as argument and explanation: Exploring concepts of sound in third grade. In J. Minstrell & E. van Zee (Eds.), *Inquiring into inquiry learning and teaching in science* (pp. 65–79). Washington, DC: American Association for the Advancement of Science.

Abell, S. K., & Bryan, L. A. (1997). Reconceptualizing the elementary science methods course using a reflection orientation. *Journal of Science Teacher Education, 8,* 153–166.

Abell, S. K., Martini, M., & George, M. D. (2001). "That's what scientists have to do": Preservice elementary teachers' conceptions of the nature of science during a moon investigation. *International Journal of Science Education, 23,* 1095–1109.

Abell, S. K., & Roth, M. (1995). Reflections on a fifth grade life science lesson: Making sense of children's understanding of scientific models. *International Journal of Science Education, 17,* 59–74.

Akerson, V. L., Abd-El-Khalick, F. S., & Lederman, N. G. (2000). The influence of a reflective activity-based approach on elementary teachers' conceptions of the nature of science. *Journal of Research in Science Teaching, 3*, 295–317.

Akerson, V. L., & McDuffie, A. R. (2002, January). *The elementary science teacher as researcher.* Paper presented at the meeting of the Association for the Education of Teachers of Science, Charlotte, NC.

Akins, A., & Akerson, V. L. (2002). Connecting science, social studies, and language arts: An interdisciplinary approach. *Educational Action Research, 10*, 479–497.

Aladro, L, & Suarez, O. (2000). How do LEP students acquire and develop the language of science? In A.E. Sweeney & K. Tobin (Eds.), *Language, discourse, and learning in science: Improving professional practice through action research* (pp. 105–116). Tallahassee, FL: SouthEastern Regional Vision for Education (SERVE).

Altrichter, H. (1993). The concept of quality in action research: Giving practitioners a voice in educational research. In M. Schratz (Ed.), *Qualitative voices in educational research* (pp. 40–55). London: Falmer Press.

American Association for the Advancement of Science. (1993). *Benchmarks for science literacy.* New York: Oxford University Press.

Anderson, C., Butts, J., Lett, P., Mansdoerfer, S., & Raisch, M. (1995). Voices in unison: Teacher research and collaboration. *Teacher Research, 2*(2), 117–135.

Anderson, C. W., & Roth, K. J. (1989). Teaching for meaningful and self-regulated learning of science. In J. Brophy (Ed.), *Advances in research on teaching* (Vol. 1, pp. 265–309). Greenwich, CT: JAI Press.

Anderson, C. W., & Smith, E. L. (1987). Teaching science. In V. Richardson-Koehler (Ed.), *Educators' handbook: A research perspective* (pp. 84–111). White Plains, NY: Longman.

Anderson, G., Herr, K, & Nihlen, A. (1994). *Studying your own school: An educator's guide to qualitative practitioner research.* Thousand Oaks, CA: Corwin Press.

Atkinson, S., & Fleer, M. (1995). *Science with reason.* Portsmouth, NH: Heinemann.

Atwell, N. (1987). *In the middle: Writing, reading, and learning with adolescents.* Portsmouth, NH: Boynton/Cook-Heinemann.

Bagley, R. (2000). Does teaching science to LEP students through cooperative learning and hands-on activities increase language proficiency? In A. E. Sweeney & K. Tobin (Eds.), *Language, discourse, and learning in science: Improving professional practice through action research* (pp. 45–52). Tallahassee, FL: SouthEastern Regional Vision for Education (SERVE).

Baird, J. R., & Mitchell, I. J. (1986). *Improving the quality of teaching and learning: An Australian case study—the PEEL Project.* Melbourne, Australia: Monash University Printery.

Baird, J. R., & Northfield, J. R. (1992). *Learning from the PEEL experience.* Melbourne, Australia: Monash University Printery.

Ball, D. L. (1993). Halves, pieces, and twoths: Constructing representational contexts in teaching fractions. In T. Carpenter, E. Fennema, & T. Romberg (Eds.), *Rational numbers: An integration of research* (pp. 157–196). Hillsdale, NJ: Lawrence Erlbaum Associates.

Ball, D. L. (2000). Working on the inside: Using one's own practice as a site for studying teaching and learning. In A. Kelly & R. Lesh (Eds.), *Handbook of research design in mathematics and science education* (pp. 365–402). Mahwah, NJ: Lawrence Erlbaum Associates.

Ball, D. L., & Cohen, D. K. (1999). Developing practice, developing practitioners: Toward a practice-based theory of professional education. In G. Sykes & L. Darling-Hammond (Eds.), *Teaching as the learning profession: Handbook of policy and practice* (pp. 3–332). San Francisco: Jossey-Bass.

Ballenger, C., & Rosebery, A. (2003). What counts as teacher research?: Continuing the conversation. *Teachers College Record, 105*, 297–314.

Barnes, B., Hamilton, M., Hill, C., Sullivan, C., & Witcher, P. (2002). *Science investigations: Hands on . . . minds on.* Fairfax, VA: Fairfax County Public Schools.

Barton, A. C. (2003). *Teaching science for social justice.* New York: Teachers College Press.

Barton, A. C., Johnson, V., & The students in Ms. Johnson's Grade 8 science classes. (2002). Truncating agency: Peer review and participatory research. *Research in Science Education, 32*, 191–214.

Behar, R. (1996). *The vulnerable observer: Anthropology that breaks your heart.* Boston: Beacon Press.

Berry, A., & Milroy, P. (2002). Changes that matter. In J. Loughran, I. Mitchell, & J. Mitchell (Eds.), *Learning from teacher research* (pp. 196–221). New York: Teachers College Press.

Beyer, L. (1988). *Knowing and acting: Inquiry ideology and educational studies.* London: Falmer Press.

Bianchini, J. A., & Solomon, E. M. (2003). Constructing views of science tied to issues of equity and diversity: A study of beginning science teachers. *Journal of Research in Science Teaching, 40,* 53–76.

Biott, C. (1983). The foundations of classroom action research in initial teacher training. *Journal of Education for Teaching, 9,* 152–160.

Bissex, G., & Bullock, R. (1987). *Seeing ourselves: Case study research by teachers of writing.* Portsmouth, NH: Heinemann.

Blackwood, D. (1993). Connecting language and science assessment. In W. Saul (Ed.), *Science workshop: A whole language approach* (pp. 95–118). Portsmouth, NH: Heinemann.

Bohrman, M. L., & Akerson, V. L. (2001). A teacher's reflections on her actions to improve her female students' self-efficacy toward science. *Journal of Elementary Science Education, 13,* 41–45.

Boyle, L. (2002). Disasters and metacognition in the SOSE classroom. In J. Loughran, I. Mitchell, & J. Mitchell (Eds.), *Learning from teacher research* (pp. 74–88). New York: Teachers College Press.

Bransford, J. D., Brown, A. L., & Cocking, R. R. (Eds.). (2000). *How people learn: Brain, mind, experience, and school.* Washington, DC: National Academy Press.

Britton, D. (2000). Facilitating conceptual change in science: A case study. In A. D. Swooney & K. Tobin (Eds.), *Language, discourse, and learning in science: Improving professional practice through action research* (pp. 21–31). Tallahassee, FL: SouthEastern Regional Vision for Education (SERVE).

Burkhardt, H., & Schoenfeld, A. H. (2003). Improving educational research: Toward a more useful, more influential, and better-funded enterprise. *Educational Researcher, 32*(9), 3–14.

Carlton, W. (1996). Grades that have meaning! In P. Castori (Ed.), *Windows on our classrooms.* Retrieved February 26, 2004, from http://education.ucdavis.edu/cress/projects/satellites/teach research/papers/carlton.html

Caro-Bruce, C., & Zeichner, K. (1998). *The nature and impact of an action research professional development program in one urban school district: Final Report.* Retrieved December 15, 2004, from http://www.madison.k12.wi.us/sod/car/carspencerreport.html

Carpenter, T. P., Fennema, E., Peterson, P. L., Chiang, C. P., & Loef, M. (1989). Using knowledge of children's mathematical thinking in classroom teaching: An experimental study. *American Educational Research Journal, 26,* 499–453.

Carr, W., & Kemmis, S. (1986). *Becoming critical: Education, knowledge and action research.* London: Falmer Press.

Chandler, K. (1999). Working in her own context: A case study of one teacher researcher. *Language Arts, 77,* 27–33.

Chazen, D. (2000). *Beyond formulas in mathematics and teaching: Dynamics of the high school algebra classroom.* New York: Teachers College Press.

Clement, J. (2002). Graphing. In R. Lehrer & L. Schauble (Eds.), *Investigating real data in the classroom* (pp. 63–74). New York: Teachers College Press.

Cobb, P., Wood, T., Yackel, E., Nicholls, J., Wheatley, G., Trigatti, B., et al. (1991). Assessment of a problem-centered second-grade mathematics project. *Journal for Research in Mathematics Education, 22,* 13–29.

Cochran-Smith, M., & Lytle, S. L. (1990). Research on teaching and teacher research: The issues that divide. *Educational Researcher, 19*(2), 2–11.

Cochran-Smith, M., & Lytle, S. L. (Eds.). (1993). *Inside/outside: Teacher research and knowledge.* New York: Teachers College Press.

Cochran-Smith, M., & Lytle, S. L. (1999). The teacher researcher movement: A decade later. *Educational Researcher, 28*(7), 15–25.

Cohen, D. K., & Barnes, C. A. (1993). Pedagogy and policy. In D. K. Cohen, M. W. McLaughlin, & J. E. Talbert (Eds.), *Teaching for understanding: Challenges for policy and practice* (pp. 207–239). San Francisco: Jossey-Bass.

Cohen, D. K., & Hill, H. C. (1998). *Instructional policy and classroom performance: The mathematics reform in California (RR-39)*. Philadelphia: Consortium for Policy Research in Education.

Colorado College Integrated Science Teacher Enhancement Project. (2004). *Integrated science teacher enhancement project* (ISCEP). Retrieved February 26, 2004, from http://equinox.unr.edu/homepage/crowther/iscep.html

Continuous Assessment in Science Project, WestEd. (2005). *Supporting high quality science teaching, learning, and continuous assessment*. Retrieved February 27, 2005, from http://www.wested.org/cs/we/view/serv/18

Corey, S. M. (1953). *Action research to improve school practices*. New York: Teachers College Press.

Cucchiarelli, D. (2001). *The use of inquiry-based education in the science classroom*. Retrieved December 15, 2004, from http://gse.gmu.edu/research/lmtip/arp/vol2.htm

Curtis, C. (2002). What's typical: A study of the distributions of items in recycling bins. In R. Lehrer & L. Schauble (Eds.), *Investigating real data in the classroom* (pp. 49–53). New York: Teachers College Press.

Dadds, M. (1995). *Passionate enquiry and school development*. London: Falmer Press.

Darling-Hammond, L., & Sykes, G. (Eds.). (1999). *Teaching as the learning profession: Handbook of policy and practice*. San Francisco: Jossey-Bass.

DeSouze-Wyatt, B. (2002). *A multi-strategy approach to increase ESOL student performance on the high-stakes Virginia end-of-course biology standards of learning assessment*. Retrieved December 12, 2004, from http://gse.gmu.edu/research/lmtip/arp/vol2.htm

Dickinson, V. L., Burns, J., Hagen, E. R., & Locker, K. M. (1997). Becoming better primary science teachers: A description of our journey. *Journal of Elementary Science Education, 8*, 295–311.

Dieckman, D. (2002a). Reading as scientists. In W. Saul (Ed.), *Science workshop: Reading, writing, thinking like a scientist* (pp. 74–85). Portsmouth, NH: Heinemann.

Dieckman, D. (2002b). Inquiring into assessment. In W. Saul (Ed.), *Science workshop: Reading, writing, thinking like a scientist* (pp. 101–114). Portsmouth, NH: Heinemann.

DiPerna, E. (2002). Data models of ourselves: Body self-portrait project. In R. Lehrer & L. Schauble (Eds.), *Investigating real data in the classroom* (pp. 81–98). New York: Teachers College Press.

DiSchino, M. (1998). Why do bees sting and why do they die afterward? In A. Rosebery & B. Warren (Eds.), *Boats, balloons, and classroom video: Science teaching as inquiry* (pp. 109–133). Portsmouth, NH: Heinemann.

Donoahue, Z. (2003). Science teaching and learning: Teachers and children plan together. *Networks: An Online Journal for Teacher Research, 6*(1). Retrieved November 15, 2004, from http://education.ucsc.edu/faculty/gwells/networks/

Doris, E. (1991). *Doing what scientists do: Children learn to investigate their world*. Portsmouth, NH: Heinemann.

Dougherty, L. A. (2000). *Peer tutoring: Can it have an affect on science in the content area?* Retrieved December 13, 2004, from http://gse.gmu.edu/research/lmtip/arp/vol2.htm

Dressman, M. (2000). Theory into practice? Reading against the grain of good practice narratives. *Language Arts, 78*(1), 50–59.

Driver, R. (1989). Students' conceptions and the learning of science. *International Journal of Science Education, 11*, 481–490.

Driver, R., Osoko, H., Leach, J., Mortimer, E., & Scott, P. (1994). Constructing scientific knowledge in the classroom. *Educational Researcher, 23*(7), 5–12.

Duckworth, E. (1987). *"The having of wonderful ideas" and other essays on teaching and learning*. New York: Teachers College Press.

Eichinger, D., & Roth, K. J. (1991). *Analysis of an elementary science curriculum: Bouncing around or connectedness?* (Research Series No. 32). East Lansing: Michigan State University, Institute for Research on Teaching, Center for the Learning and Teaching of Elementary Subjects.

Eisenhart, M., & Borko, H. (1993). *Designing classroom research: Themes, issues, and struggles.* Boston: Allyn & Bacon.

Eisenhart, M., & Howe, K. (1992). Validity in qualitative research. In M. LeCompte, W. Milroy, & J. Preissie (Eds.), *The handbook of qualitative research in education* (pp. 643–680). San Diego: Academic Press.

Elliot, J. (1995). Exploring telephones. In S. Atkinson & M. Fleer (Eds.), *Science with reason* (pp. 82–89). Portsmouth, NH: Heinemann.

Elmore, R. F. (2002). *Bridging the gap between standards and achievement: The imperative for professional development in education.* Washington, DC: Albert Shanker Institute.

Erickson, F. (1986). Qualitative methods in research on teaching. In M. Wittrock (Ed.), *Handbook of research on teaching* (3rd ed., pp. 119–161). New York: Macmillan.

Erickson, G., & MacKinnon, A. M. (1991). Seeing classrooms in new ways: On becoming a science teacher. In D. A. Schön (Ed.), *The reflective turn: Case studies in and on educational practice* (pp. 15–36). New York: Teachers College Press.

Evans, C., Stubbs, M., Frechette, P., Neely, C., & Warner, J. (1987). *Educational practitioners: Absent voices in the building of educational theory* (Working Paper no. 170). Wellesley, MA: Center for Research on Women.

Fals-Borda, O. (1997). Participatory action research in Colombia: Some personal feelings. In R. McTaggart (Ed.), *Participatory action research: International contexts and consequences* (pp. 107–124). Albany, NY: State University of New York Press.

Featherstone, D., Munby, H., & Russell, T. (1997). *Finding a voice while learning to teach.* London: Falmer Press.

Fecho, B., & Allen, J. (2003). Teacher inquiry into literacy, social justice, and power. In J. Flood, D. Lapp, J. R. Squire, & J. M. Jensen (Eds.), *Handbook of research on teaching the English language arts* (2nd ed., pp. 232–246). Mahwah, NJ: Lawrence Erlbaum Associates.

Feiman-Nemser, S., & Buchmann, M. (1985). Pitfalls of experience in teacher preparation. *Teachers College Record, 87,* 53–65.

Feiman-Nemser, S., & Buchmann, M. (1989). Describing teacher education: A framework and illustrative findings from a longitudinal study of six students. *Elementary School Journal, 89,* 365–377.

Feldman, A. (1994a). Erzberger's dilemma: Validity in action research and science teachers' need to know. *Science Education, 78,* 83–101.

Feldman, A. (1994b, April). *Teachers learning from teachers: Knowledge and understanding in collaborative action research.* Paper presented at the meeting of the American Educational Research Association, New Orleans.

Feldman, A. (1995). The institutionalization of action research: The California "100 schools" project. In S. Noffke & R. Stevenson (Eds.), *Educational action research: Becoming practically critical* (pp. 180–196). New York: Teachers College Press.

Feldman, A. (1996). Enhancing the practice of physics teachers: Mechanisms for the generation and sharing of knowledge and understanding in collaborative action research. *Journal of Research in Science Teaching, 33,* 513–540.

Feldman, A., & Minstrell, J. (2000). Action research as a research methodology for the study of teaching and learning of science. In A. E. Kelly & R. A. Lesh (Eds.), *Handbook of research design in mathematics and science education* (pp. 429–456). Mahwah, NJ: Lawrence Erlbaum Associates.

Fernandez, C., Chokshi, S., Cannon, J., & Yoshida, M. (in press). Learning about lesson study in the US. In M. Beauchamp (Ed.), *New and old voices on Japanese education.* Armonk, NY: M. E. Sharpe.

Fernandez, C., & Yoshida, M. (2004). *Lesson study: Improving mathematics teaching and learning—A Japanese approach to improving mathematics teaching and learning.* Mahwah, NJ: Lawrence Erlbaum Associates.

Feuer, M. J., Towne, L., & Shavelson, R. J. (2002). Scientific culture and educational research. *Educational Researcher, 31*(8), 4–14.

Field, J. (2001). *Science is life: How does using the outdoors as an extension of my classroom influence students' perspectives of their world?* Madison, WI: Teacher Action Research Project, Madison Metropolitan Public Schools.

Fink, L. C. (2000). Middle school students' perspectives on collaborative learning, group size, and conceptual change. In A. E. Sweeney & K. Tobin (Eds.), *Language, discourse, and learning in science: Improving professional practice through action research* (pp. 33–43). Tallahassee, FL: South Eastern Regional Vision for Education (SERVE).

Fischer, J. (1996). Open to ideas: Developing a framework for your research. In G. Burnaford, J. Fischer, & D. Hobson (Eds.), *Teachers doing research: Practical possibilities* (pp. 33–50). Mahwah, NJ: Lawrence Erlbaum Associates.

Fraser, B. J., & Tobin, K. G. (Eds.). (1998). *International handbook of science education.* Dordrecht, the Netherlands: Kluwer Academic.

Fueyo, V., & Neves, A. (1995). Pre-service teacher as researcher: A research context for change in the heterogeneous classroom. *Action in Teacher Education, 14*, 39–49.

Gabel, D. (Ed.). (1994). *Handbook of research on science teaching and learning.* New York: Simon & Schuster Macmillan.

Gaither, V. P. (2000). *Interactive software as a tool for increasing student comprehension of basic chemistry concepts.* Retrieved December 10, 20004, from http://gse.gmu.edu/research/lmtip/arp/vol2.htm

Gallas, K. (1995). *Talking their way into science: Hearing children's questions and theories and responding with curricula.* New York: Teachers College Press.

Gallas, K. (1997). Arts as epistemology: Enabling children to know what they know. In I. Hall, C. H. Campbell, & E. J. Miech (Eds.), *Class acts: Teachers reflect on their own classroom practice* (pp. 93–106). Cambridge, MA: Harvard Educational Review.

Gapinski, R., Hill, C., & Solis, S. (2000). *How girls learn: Three case studies.* Retrieved October 24, 2004, from http://www.d113.lake.k12.il.us/hphs/action/table_of_contents.htm

Garet, M. S., Porter, A. C., Desimone, L., Birman, B. F., & Yoon, K. S. (2001). What makes professional development effective? Results from a national sample of teachers. *American Educational Research Journal, 38*, 915–945.

Gavin, J. (2002). How much traffic? Beep! Beep! Get that car off the number line! In R. Lehrer & L. Schauble (Eds.), *Investigating real data in the classroom* (pp. 39–47). New York: Teachers College Press.

Genovese, C. (2003). Can computer-based instruction improve molecular biology comprehension among general education students? *Networks: An Online Journal for Teacher Research, 6*(2), 1–7. Retrieved September 12, 2004, from http://education.ucsc.edu/faculty/gwells/networks/

Gonzalez, J. (1999). *Failure and success rates of language minority students in a biology class.* Retrieved September 12, 2004 from http://gse.gmu.edu/research/lmtip/arp/vol2.htm

Goodnough, K. (2001a). Teacher development through action research: A case study of an elementary teacher. *Action in Teacher Education, 23*, 37–46.

Goodnough, K. (2001b). Implementing multiple intelligences theory in a grade nine science classroom: The experiences of a high school teacher. *Canadian Journal of Science, Mathematics and Technology Education, 1*, 419–436.

Goodnough, K. (2001c). Multiple intelligences theory: A framework for personalizing science curricula. *School Science and Mathematics, 101*, 180–193.

Goodnough, K. (2003). Facilitating action research in the context of science education: Reflections of a university researcher. *Educational Action Research, 11*(1), 41–63.

Graham, E. (1995). What patterns of teacher-student verbal communication exist in my classroom? In S. A. Spiegel, A. Collins, & J. Lappert (Eds.), *Action research: Perspectives from teachers' classrooms. Science FEAT (Science for Early Adolescent Teachers, Section 4).* Retrieved January 24, 2003, from http://www.enc.org/resources/records/full/0,1240,002432,00.shtm

Grimmett, P. P., & Erickson, G. L. (Eds.). (1988). *Reflection in teacher education.* New York: Teachers College Press.

Grundy, S. (1987). *Curriculum: Product or praxis.* London: Falmer Press.

Hall, I., Campbell, C. H., & Miech, E. J. (Eds.). (1997). *Class acts: Teachers reflect on their own classroom practice.* Cambridge, MA: Harvard Educational Review.

Hayton, M. (1995). Talking it through: Young children thinking science. In S. Atkinson & M. Fleer (Eds.), *Science with reason* (pp. 32–41). Portsmouth, NH: Heinemann.

Hazelwood, C., & Roth, K. J. (1992). *Gender and discourse: The unfolding "living text" of a science lesson* (Research Series no. 60). East Lansing: Michigan State University, Institute for Research on Teaching, Center for the Learning and Teaching of Elementary Subjects.

Heaton, R. M. (2000). *Teaching mathematics to the new standards: Relearning the dance.* New York: Teachers College Press.

Hedman, R. (2003). *Lesson study 2002–2003: Natomas High School.* Sacramento, CA: Sacramento Area Science Project.

Hermann, K. (2002). *Teaching science to high school students who have limited formal schooling.* Retrieved November 09, 2004, from http://gse.gmu.edu/research/lmtip/arp/vol2.htm

Hewson, P. W., Beeth, M. E., & Thorley, N. R. (1998). Teaching for conceptual change. In B. J. Fraser & K. G. Tobin (Eds.), *International handbook of science education* (pp. 199–218). Dordrecht, the Netherlands: Kluwer Academic.

Hewson, P. W., & Hewson, M. G. (1984). The role of conceptual conflict in conceptual change and the design of science instruction. *Instructional Science, 13,* 1–13.

Hewson, P. W., Tabachnick, B. R., Zeichner, K. M., Blomker, K. D., Meyer, H., Lemberger, J., et al (1999). Educating prospective teachers of biology: Introduction and research methods. *Science Education, 83,* 247–273.

Hewson, P. W., Tabachnick, B. R., Zeichner, K. M., & Lemberger, J. (1999). Educating prospective teachers of biology: Findings, limitations, and recommendations. *Science Education, 83,* 373–384.

Hicok, S. (2000). *How does the use of reading strategies improve achievement in science for language minority students?* Retrieved November 09, 2004, from http://gse.gmu.edu/research/lmtip/arp/vol2.htm

Hiebert, J., Gallimore, R., & Stigler, J. (2002). A knowledge base for the teaching profession: What would it look like and how can we get one? *Educational Researcher, 31*(5), 3–15.

Hodgkinson, H. L. (1957). Action research—a critique. *Journal of Educational Sociology, 31*(4), 137–153.

Hollon, R., Anderson, C. W., & Roth, K. J. (1991). Science teachers' conceptions of teaching and learning. In J. Brophy (Ed.), *Advances in research on teaching: Vol. 2. Teachers' knowledge of subject matter as it relates to their teaching practice* (pp. 145–185). Greenwich, CT: JAI Press.

Holmes Group. (1990). *Tomorrow's schools: Principles for the design of professional development schools.* East Lansing, MI: The Holmes Group.

Howes, E. (2002). *Connecting girls and science: Constructivism, feminism, and science education reform.* New York: Teachers College Press.

Howey, K., & Zimpher, N. (1989). *Profiles of preservice teacher education.* Albany: SUNY Press.

Huberman, M. (1996). Moving mainstream: Taking a closer look at teacher research. *Language Arts, 73*(2), 124–140.

Irwin, O. E. (1997). *How much information from the textbook can grade 11 chemistry students read and process on their own?* Retrieved November 09, 2004, from http://educ.queensu.ca/~ar/liz-i.htm

Iwasyk, M. (2000). Kids questioning kids: "Experts" sharing. In J. Minstrell & E. van Zee (Eds.), *Inquiring into inquiry learning and teaching in science* (pp. 130–138). Washington, DC: American Association for the Advancement of Science.

Jacobson, W. (1998). Defining the quality of practitioner research. *Adult Education Quarterly, 48*(3), 125–139.

Jesson, J. (1995). Rock week. In S. Atkinson & M. Fleer (Eds.), *Science with reason* (pp. 135–146). Portsmouth, NH: Heinemann.

Jinks, S., & Stanton, K. (2002). *Reinforcing biology.* Retrieved November 09, 2004, from http://gse.gmu.edu/research/lmtip/arp/vol2.htm

Joanos, L. G. (1997). First graders' beliefs and perceptions of "what is science?" and "who is a scientist?" In J. B. McDonald & P. Gilmer (Eds.), *Science in the elementary school classroom:*

Portraits of action research (pp. 25–36). Tallahassee, FL: SouthEastern Regional Vision for Education (SERVE).

Joseph, C. H. (2002). Using concept maps to aid reading comprehension in a high school biology classroom. *Networks: An Online Journal for Teacher Research, 5*(1). Retrieved November 09, 2004, from http://education.ucsc.edu/faculty/gwells/networks/

Kemmis, S., & McTaggart, R. (1988). *The action research planner* (3rd ed.). Geelong, Australia: Deakin University Press.

Kemmis, S., & McTaggart, R. (2000). Participatory action research. In N. K. Denzin & Y. S. Lincoln (Eds.), *Handbook of qualitative research* (2nd ed., pp. 567–605). Thousand Oaks, CA: Sage.

Kennedy, M. M. (1996a). *Teachers conducting research.* East Lansing, MI: National Center for Research on Teacher Learning.

Kennedy, M. M. (1996b). *Teachers' responses to educational research.* East Lansing, MI: National Center for Research on Teacher Learning.

Kennedy, M. M. (1997). The connection between research and practice. *Educational Researcher, 26*(7), 4–12.

Kennedy, M. M. (1998). *Form and substance in inservice teacher education.* Madison: University of Wisconsin–Madison, National Institute for Science Education.

Kesidou, S., & Roseman, J. E. (2002). How well do middle school science programs measure up? Findings from Project 2061's curriculum review. *Journal of Research in Science Teaching, 39,* 522–549.

Keys, C. W., & Bryan, L. A. (2001). Co-constructing inquiry-based science with teachers: Essential research for lasting reform. *Journal of Research in Science Teaching, 38,* 631–645.

Kurose, A. (2000). Eyes on science: Asking questions about the moon on the playground, in class, and at home. In J. Minstrell & E. van Zee (Eds.), *Inquiring into inquiry learning in science* (pp. 139–147). Washington, DC: American Association for the Advancement of Science.

Kwan, R. (2000). How can I tap into children's curiosity in science? In J. Minstrell & E. van Zee (Eds.), *Inquiring into inquiry learning in science* (pp. 148–150). Washington, DC: American Association for the Advancement of Science.

Kyle, W. C., Linn, M. C., Bitner, B. L., Mitchner, C. P., & Perry, B. (1991). The role of research in science teaching: An NSTA theme paper. *Science Education, 75,* 413–418.

Lampert, M. (1990). When the problem is not the question and the solution is not the answer: Mathematical knowing and teaching. *American Educational Research Journal, 27,* 29–63.

Lampert, M. (2001). *Teaching problems and problems of teaching.* New Haven, CT: Yale University Press.

Lampert, M., & Ball, D. L. (1998). *Teaching, multimedia, and mathematics: Investigations of real practice.* New York: Teachers College Press.

Lather, P. (1991). *Getting smart: Feminist research and pedagogy with/in the postmodern.* New York: Routledge.

Lather, P. (1993). Fertile obsession: Validity after poststructuralism. *Sociological Quarterly, 34,* 673–693.

Lay, D. (2000). Science inquiry conference—a better way. In J. Minstrell & E. van Zee (Eds.), *Inquiring into inquiry learning in science* (pp. 164–168). Washington, DC: American Association for the Advancement of Science.

Lehrer, R., & Schauble, L. (Eds.). (2002). *Investigating real data in the classroom: Expanding children's understanding of math and science.* New York: Teachers College Press.

Lensmire, T. (1997). Writing workshop as carnival: Reflections on an alternative learning environment. In I. Hall, C. H. Campbell, & E. J. Miech (Eds.), *Class acts: Teachers reflect on their own classroom practice* (pp. 127–149). Cambridge, MA: Harvard Educational Review.

Lewis, C. (2002). Everywhere I looked—levers and pendulums: Research lessons bring studies to life and energize teaching. *Journal of Staff Development, 23*(3), 59–65.

Lewis, C., & Tsuchida, I. (1997). Planned educational change in Japan: The shift to student-centered elementary science. *Journal of Educational Policy, 12,* 313–331.

Lewis, C., & Tsuchida, I. (1998). A lesson is like a swiftly flowing river. *American Educator, 22*(4), 12–17, 50–52.

Lin, W.-J. (1998, April). *The effects of restructuring biology teaching: An action research.* Paper presented at the meeting of the National Association for Research in Science Teaching, San Diego.

Lincoln, Y., & Guba, E. (1985). Emerging criteria for quality in qualitative and interpretive research. *Qualitative Inquiry, 1,* 275–289.

Liu, Z., & Akerson, V. L. (2002). Science and language links: A fourth grade intern's attempt to increase language skills through science. *Electronic Journal of Literacy Through Science, 1,* Article 4. Retrieved August 11, 2004, from http://sweeneyhall.sjsu.edu/ejlts/vol1–2.htm

Lomax, P. (1994). Standards, criteria and the problematic of action research within an award-bearing course. *Educational Action Research, 2*(1), 113–126.

Lomax, P., & Parker, Z. (1995). Accounting for ourselves: The problematic of representing action research. *Cambridge Journal of Education, 25*(3), 301–314.

Loucks-Horsley, S. L. (1996). Professional development for science education: A critical and immediate challenge. In R. W. Bybee (Ed.), *National standards and the science curriculum: Challenges, opportunities, and recommendations* (pp. 83–95). Dubuque, IA: Kendall/Hunt.

Loucks-Horsley, S. L., Hewson, P. W., Love, N., & Stiles, K. E. (1998). *Designing professional development for teachers of science and mathematics.* Thousand Oaks, CA: Corwin.

Loucks-Horsley, S. L., Love, N., Stiles, K. E., Mundry, S., & Hewson, P. W. (2003). *Designing professional development for teachers of science and mathematics* (2nd ed.). Thousand Oaks, CA: Corwin.

Loughran, J. J. (2002). Effective reflective practice. In search of meaning in learning about teaching. *Journal of Teacher Education, 53*(1), 33–43.

Loughran, J. J., Mitchell, I., & Mitchell, J. (2002). *Learning from teacher research.* New York: Teachers College Press.

Loughran, J. J., & Northfield, J. R. (1996). *Opening the classroom door: Teacher, researcher, learner.* London: Falmer Press.

Loughran, J. J., & Russell, T. (1997). *Teaching about teaching: Purpose, passion and pedagogy in teacher education.* London: Falmer Press.

Love, N. (2002). *Using data/getting results: A practical guide for school improvement in mathematics and science.* Norwood, MA: Christopher Gordon.

McDaniel Hill, C. (1996). *Project-based education in freshman chemistry/physics.* Retrieved December 17, 2004, from http://www.d113.lake.k12.il.us/hphs/action/table_of_contents.htm

McDonald, J. B., & Gilmer, P. J. (Eds.). (1997). *Science in the elementary school classroom: Portraits of action research.* Tallahassee, FL: SouthEastern Regional Vision for Education (SERVE).

McGee, K. C. (2000). *Reading road maps or reading guides: Which reading strategy helps students comprehend science textbook reading?* Retrieved December 17, 2004, from http://gse.gmu.edu/research/lmtip/arp/vol2.htm

McGlinchey, A. (2002). *Nutrition information in the fifth grade classroom: Does knowledge affect eating habits?* Fairfax County, VA: Fairfax County Public Schools.

McGoey, J., & Ross, J. (1999). Guest editorial: Research, practice, and teacher internship. *Journal of Research in Science Teaching, 36,* 121–130.

McNiff, J., Lomax, P., & Whitehead, J. (1996). *You and your action research project.* London: Routledge.

Miller, J. (1990). *Creating spaces and finding voices: Teachers collaborating for empowerment.* Albany, New York.

Minstrell, J. (1982a). Conceptual development research in the natural setting of a secondary school science classroom. In M. B. Rowe & W. S. Higuchi (Eds.), *Education in the 80's: Science.* Washington, DC: National Education Association.

Minstrell, J. (1982b). Explaining the "at rest" condition of an object. *The Physics Teacher, 20,* 10–14.

Minstrell, J. (1983). Getting the facts straight. *The Science Teacher, 50*(1), 52–54.

Minstrell, J. (1984). Teaching for the development of ideas: Forces on moving objects. In C. Anderson (Ed.), *AETS yearbook: Observing science classrooms: Observing perspectives from research and practice* (pp. 55–73). Columbus, OH: ERIC Clearinghouse for Science, Mathematics, and Environmental Education.

Minstrell, J. (1989). Teaching science for understanding. In L. B. Resnick & L. E. Klopfer (Eds.), *Toward the thinking curriculum: Current cognitive research. 1989 yearbook of the association for supervision and curriculum development* (pp. 129–149). Alexandria, VA: ASCD.

Minstrell, J., & van Zee, E. H. (Eds.). (2000). *Inquiring into inquiry learning and teaching in science.* Washington, DC: American Association for the Advancement of Science.

Mintzes, J. J., Wandersee, H. H., & Novak, J. D. (1998). *Teaching science for understanding: A human constructivist view.* New York: Academic Press, Elsevier Science.

Mohr, M. M. (1987). Teacher researchers and the study of the writing process. In D. Goswami & P. R. Stillman (Eds.), *Reclaiming the classroom: Teacher research as agency for change* (pp. 94–106). Upper Montclair, NJ: Boynton/Cook.

Mohr, M. M., Rogers, C., Sanford, B., Nocerino, M. A., MacLean, M. S., & Clawson, S. (2004). *Teacher research for better schools.* New York: Teachers College Press.

Munby, H. (1995, April). *Gazing in the mirror: Asking questions about validity in self-study research.* Paper presented at the meeting of the American Educational Research Association, San Francisco.

Munby, H. (1996). Being taught by my teaching: Self-study in the realm of educational computing. In J. Richards & T. Russell (Eds.), *Proceedings of the First International Conference of the Self-Study of Teacher Education Practices: Empowering our future in teacher education* (pp. 62–66). Herstmonceux Castle, East Sussex, England.

Myers, M. (1985). *The teacher researcher: How to study writing in the classroom.* Urbana, IL: National Council of Teachers of English.

National Research Council. (1996). *National science education standards.* Washington, DC: National Academy Press.

National Staff Development Council. (2001). *National staff development standards.* Retrieved October 13, 2004, from http://www.nsdc.org/standards/datadriven.cfm

Nissley, C. (2000). Giving children a chance to investigate according to their own interests. In J. Minstrell & E. van Zee (Eds.), *Inquiring into inquiry teaching in science* (pp. 151–156). Washington, DC: Association for the Advancement of Science.

No Child Left Behind Act of 2001, Pub. L. No. 107-110.

Noffke, S., & Zeichner, K. (1987, April). *Action research and teacher development.* Paper presented at the meeting of the American Educational Research Association, Washington, DC.

Northfield, J. (1996, November). *The nature and quality of teacher research.* Paper presented at the conference hosted jointly by the Singapore Educational Research Association and the Australian Association for Research in Education, Singapore.

Northfield, J. R. (1998). Teacher educators and the practice of science teacher education. In B. Fraser & K. Tobin (Eds.), *International handbook of science education* (pp. 695–706). Dordrecht, the Netherlands: Kluwer Academic.

Northfield, J., & Mitchell, I. (1995, April). *Bringing a research focus into the teaching role.* Paper presented at the meeting of the American Educational Research Association, San Francisco.

O'Dea, J. (1994). Pursuing truth in narrative research. *Journal of Philosophy of Education, 28*(2), 161–171.

Olson, M. W. (1990). The teacher as researcher: A historical perspective. In M. W. Olson (Ed.), *Opening the door to classroom research* (pp. 1–20). Newark, DE: International Reading Association.

Ormes, C. (2000). Science teaching and learning as a vehicle for literacy of Hispanic illiterate children at risk. In A. E. Sweeney & K. Tobin (Eds.), *Language, discourse, and learning in science: Improving professional practice through action research* (pp. 151–160). Tallahassee, FL: South Eastern Regional Vision for Education (SERVE).

Osborne, M. D. (1993). *Teaching with and without mirrors: Examining science teaching in elementary school from the perspective of teacher and learner.* Unpublished doctoral dissertation, Michigan State University, East Lansing.

Osborne, M. D. (1997). Balancing individual and the group: A dilemma for the constructivist teacher. *Journal of Curriculum Studies, 29,* 183–196.

Osler, J., & Flack, J. (2002). Tales from the poppy patch. In J. Loughran, I. Mitchell, & J. Mitchell (Eds.), *Learning from teacher research* (pp. 222–245). New York: Teachers College Press.

Ovens, P. (2000). *Reflective teacher development in primary science*. London: Falmer Press.

Painter, D. deM. (1997). *A journey through the solar system*. Fairfax County, VA: Deer Park Elementary School, Fairfax Public Schools.

Park, P., Brydon-Miller, M., Hall, B., & Jackson, T. (Eds.). (1993). *Voices of change: Participatory research in the US and Canada*. Westport, CT: Bergin & Garvey.

Pearce, C. R. (1993). What if . . . .? In W. Saul (Ed.), *Science workshop: A whole language approach* (pp. 53–77). Portsmouth, NH: Heinemann.

Pearce, C. R. (1999). *Nurturing inquiry: Real science for the elementary classroom*. Portsmouth, NH: Heinemann.

Pekarek, R., Krockover, G. H., & Shepardson, D. P. (1996). The research-practice gap in science education. *Journal of Research in Science Teaching, 33*, 111–113.

Penick, J. E. (1986, January/February). Science education research: Why don't we believe it? *Curriculum Review, 23*(3), 67–70.

Pinkerton, K. (1994). Using brain-based techniques in high school science. *Teaching and Change, 2*(1), 44–61.

Posner, G. J., Strike, K. A., Hewson, P. W., & Gertzog, W. A. (1982). Accommodation of a scientific conception: Toward a theory of conceptual change. *Science Education, 66*, 211–227.

Putz, A. (2002). How children organize and understand data. In R. Lehrer & L. Schauble (Eds.), *Investigating real data in the classroom* (pp. 27–38). New York: Teachers College Press.

Reardon, J. (2002). Science workshop. Capturing the essence of scientific inquiry. In W. Saul (Ed.), *Science workshop: Reading, writing, thinking like a scientist* (pp. 17–38). Portsmouth, NH: Heinemann.

Reardon, J., & Saul, W. (Eds.). (1996). *Beyond the science kit: Inquiry in action*. Portsmouth, NH: Heinemann.

Reason, P. (2001). Learning and change through action research. In J. Henry (Ed.), *Creative management* (pp. 182–194). London: Sage.

Reason, P., & Bradbury, H. (2002). *Handbook of action research: Participative inquiry and practice*. London: Sage.

Richardson, V. (1994). Teacher inquiry as professional staff development. In S. Hollingsworth & H. Sockett (Eds.), *Teacher research and educational reform* (pp. 186–203). Chicago: University of Chicago Press.

Roberts, A. (1999). Taming the monsters: Practical intimacies in a third grade Costa Rican classroom. *Educational Action Research, 7*, 345–363.

Roberts, D. (1999). The sky's the limit. *Science and Children, 37*(1), 33–37.

Roberts, D. (2000). Learning to teach science through inquiry: A new teacher's story. In J. Minstrell & E. van Zee (Eds.), *Inquiring into inquiry learning and teaching in science* (pp. 120–129). Washington, DC: Association for the Advancement of Science.

Rosaen, C. R., & Roth, K. J. (1995). Similarities and contrasts between writing during a writer's workshop and writing in science: Examining the teacher's role. In J. Brophy (Ed.), *Advances in research on teaching* (Vol. 5, pp. 291–355). Greenwich, CT: JAI Press.

Rosaen, C. R., Roth, K. J., & Lanier, P. E. (1988, February). *Learning to teach subject matter: Cases in English, mathematics and science*. Paper presented at the Midwest regional meeting of the Holmes Group, Chicago.

Rosas, C. (1997). Using participatory action research for the reconceptualization of educational practice. In S. Hollingsworth (Ed.), *International action research: A casebook for educational reform* (pp. 219–224). London: Falmer Press.

Roth, K. J. (1993). *What does it mean to understand science? Changing perspectives from a teacher and her students* (Elementary Subjects Center Research Series no. 96). East Lansing: Center for the Learning and Teaching of Elementary Subjects, Michigan State University.

Roth, K. J. (1994). Second thoughts about interdisciplinary curricula. *American Educator, 18*(1), 44–48.

Roth, K. J. (1996). *The role of writing in creating a science learning community* (Research Series 62). East Lansing, MI: Elementary Subjects Center.

Roth, K. J. (1998). *I listened to the kids' ideas, now what? A conceptual change model of science teaching.* East Lansing: Michigan State University and Future Media.

Roth, K. J. (2000). The photosynthesis of Columbus: Exploring interdisciplinary curriculum from the students' perspectives. In S. Wineburg & P. Grossman (Eds.), *Interdisciplinary curriculum: Challenges to implementation* (pp. 112–133). New York: Teachers College Press.

Roth, K. J. (2002). Talking to understand science. In J. Brophy (Ed.), *Advances in research on teaching* (Vol. 6, pp. 197–262). Boston: JAI Press.

Roth, K. J. Anderson, C. W., & Smith, E. L. (1987). *Curriculum materials, teacher talk, and student learning: Case studies in fifth grade science teaching* (Research Series no. 171). East Lansing: Institute for Research on Teaching, Michigan State University.

Roth, K. J., Druker, S. L., Garnier, H., Lemmens, M., Chen, C., Kawanaka, T., et al. (2005). *Teaching science in five countries: Results from the TIMSS 1999 video study.* Washington, DC: U.S. Department of Education, National Center for Education Statistics.

Roth, K. J., Hasbach, C., Hazelwood, C., Hoekwater, E., Ligett, C., Lindquist, B., et al. (1992). *Entryways into science and science teaching: Teacher and researcher development in a professional development school* (Elementary Subjects Center Series no. 84). East Lansing: Michigan State University, Institute for Research on Teaching, Center for the Learning and Teaching of Elementary Subjects.

Roth, K. J., Peasley, K., & Hazelwood, C. (1992). *Integration from the student perspective: Constructing meaning in science* (Research Series no. 63). East Lansing: Michigan State University, Institute for Research on Teaching, Center for the Learning and Teaching of Elementary Subjects.

Roth, W.-M. (2000, April). *Being and becoming in the science classroom.* Paper presented at the meeting of the National Association for Research in Science Teaching, New Orleans.

Roth, W.-M., & Boyd, N. (1999). Coteaching, as colearning, in practice. *Research in Science Education, 29,* 51–67.

Roth, W.-M., & Tobin, K. (2004). Coteaching: From praxis to theory. Teachers and teaching. *Theory and Practice, 10*(2), 161–179.

Ruddick, J. (1985). Teacher research and research-based teacher education. *Journal of Education for Teaching, 11,* 281–289.

Russell, T. (1997). Teaching teachers: How I teach IS the message. In J. Loughran & T. Russell (Eds.), *Teaching about teaching: Purpose, passion and pedagogy in teacher education* (pp. 32–47). London: Falmer Press.

Russell, T., & Bullock, S. (1999). Discovering our professional knowledge as teachers: Critical dialogues about learning from experience. In J. Loughran (Ed.), *Researching teaching: Methodologies and practices for understanding pedagogy* (pp. 132–151). London: Falmer Press.

Russell, T., & Munby, H. (1994). The authority of experience in learning to teach: Messages from a physics methods class. *Journal of Teacher Education, 4*(5) 86–95.

Salish I Research Project. (1997). *Secondary science and mathematics teacher preparation programs: Influences on new teachers and their students.* Iowa City: University of Iowa.

Saul, W. (Ed.). (1993). *Science workshop: A whole language approach.* Portsmouth, NH: Heinemann.

Saul, W. (Ed.). (2002). *Science workshop: Reading, writing, thinking like a scientist.* Portsmouth, NH: Heinemann.

Schoenemann, A. (2003). *How can I assess what students understand about key science concepts?* Madison, WI: Teacher Action Research Project, Madison Metropolitan Public Schools.

Schoenfeld, A. H. (1998). Toward a theory of teaching-in-context. *Issues in Education, 4,* 1–94.

Schön, D. (1983). *The reflective practitioner: How professionals think in action.* New York: Basic Books.

Schön, D. (1988). Educating teachers as reflective practitioners. In P. Grimmett & G. Erickson (Eds.), *Reflection in teacher education* (pp. 19–29). New York: Teachers College Press.

Scott, C. A. (1994). Project-based science: Reflections of a middle school teacher. *Elementary School Journal, 95,* 75–94.

Senese, J. (n.d.). *The action research laboratory: A model of professional development for teachers.* Retrieved November 10, 2004, from http://www.d113.lake.k12.il.us/hphs/action/table_of_contents.htm

Senese, J., Fagel, L, Gorleski, J., & Swanson, P. (1998, August). *Teacher self study: Classroom practitioners' perspectives on the merits of the action research laboratory experience.* Paper presented at the meeting of the Second International Conference on Self-Study of Teacher Education Practices, Herstmonceux Castle, UK.

Shafer, L. (2000). *Teacher research continuum chart.* Retrieved September 13, 2004, from http://gse.gmu.edu/research/tr/Trprofessional.shtml

Shimahara, N. K. (1998). The Japanese model of professional development: Teaching as craft. *Teaching and Teacher Education, 14,* 451–462.

Shulman, L. (1987). Knowledge and teaching: Foundations of the new reform. *Harvard Educational Review, 57,* 1–22.

Simmons, P. E., Emory, A., Coker, T., Finnegan, B., Crockett, D., Richardson, L., et al. (1999). Beginning teachers: Beliefs and classroom actions. *Journal of Research in Science Teaching, 36,* 930–954.

Smith, D. (2001). *Making a new song about science.* Retrieved July 15, 2004, from http://gallery.carnegiefoundation.org/dsmith/index2.html

Spiegel, S. A., Collins, A., & Lappert, J. (1995). *Action research: Perspectives from teachers' classrooms.* Tallahassee, FL: SouthEastern Regional Vision for Education Math/Science Consortium (SERVE).

Stahly, L. L., Krockover, G. H., & Shepardson, D. P. (1999). Third grade students' ideas about the lunar phases. *Journal of Research in Science Teaching, 36,* 159–177.

Stanulis, R. N., & Jeffers, L. (1995) Action research as a way of learning about teaching in a mentor/student teacher relationship. *Action in Teacher Education, 16,* 14–21.

Steiner, L. (1999). What the research says about professional development that works. In E. Hassel, *Professional development: Learning from the best* (pp. 93–100). Oak Brook, IL: North Central Regional Educational Laboratory.

Stenhouse, L. (1975). *An introduction to curriculum research and development.* London: Heinemann.

Stenhouse, L. (1983). *Authority, education, and emancipation.* London: Heinemann Educational Books.

Stevenson, R. (1996, February). *What counts as "good" action research?* Paper presented at the meeting of the Ethnography in Educational Research Forum, Philadelphia.

Stigler, J., Gallimore, R., & Hiebert, J. (2000). Using video surveys to compare classrooms and teaching across cultures: Examples and lessons from the TIMSS video studies. *Educational Psychologist, 35*(2), 87–100.

Stigler, J., & Hiebert, J. (1999). *The teaching gap: Best ideas from the world's teachers for improving education in the classroom.* New York: Free Press.

Sweeney, A. E., & Tobin, K. (Eds.) (2000). *Language, discourse, and learning in science: Improving professional practice through action research.* Tallahassee, FL: SouthEastern Regional Vision for Education (SERVE).

Taba, H., & Noel, E. (1957). *Action research: A case study.* Washington, DC: Association for Curriculum and Supervision.

Tabachnick, B. R., & Zeichner, K. M. (1999). Ideas and action: Action research and the development of conceptual change teaching of science. *Science Education, 83,* 309–322.

Takemura, S., & Shimizu, K. (1993). Goals and strategies for science teaching as perceived by elementary teachers in Japan and the US. *Peabody Journal of Education, 14*(1), 25–40.

Thompson, S. (1995). Equality in the classroom: An attempt to eliminate bias in my classroom. In S. A. Spiegel, A. Collins, & J. Lappert (Eds.), *Action research: Perspectives from teachers' classrooms. Science FEAT (Science for Early Adolescent Teachers, Section 6).* Retrieved January 24, 2003, from http://www.enc.org/professional/learn/research/journal/science/document.shtm?input=ENC-002432-2432

Threatt, S., Buchanan, J., Morgan, B., Strieb, L. Y., Sugarman, J., Swenson, J., Teel, K., & Tomlinson, J. (1994). Teachers' voices in the conversation about teacher research. In S. Hollingsworth & H. Sockett (Eds.), *Teacher research and educational reform* (pp. 222–233). Chicago: University of Chicago Press.

Tillotson, J. W., Ochanji, M. K., & Diana, T. J. (2004). Reflecting on the game: Action research in science education . In J. Weld (Ed.). *The game of science education.* Boston: Allyn & Bacon.

Tracy, C. O. (2002). *Assessment: A new science teacher's attempt to use assessment as a form of conversation*. Retrieved October 16, 2004, from http://gse.gmu.edu/research/lmtip/arp/vol2.htm

U.S. Department of Education, Institute of Education Sciences. (2003). *Identifying and implementing educational practices supported by rigorous evidence: A user friendly guide*. Washington, DC: Coalition for Evidence-Based Policy.

Valverde, R. M. (2000). Children's literature: An integrative strategy for teaching elementary scientific concepts and vocabulary. In A.E. Sweeney & K. Tobin (Eds.), *Language, discourse, and learning in science: Improving professional practice through action research* (pp. 85–93). Tallahassee, FL: SouthEastern Regional Vision for Education (SERVE).

van Zee, E. H. (1998a). Fostering elementary teachers' research on their science teaching practices. *Journal of Teacher Education, 49*(4), 1–10.

van Zee, E. H. (1998b). Preparing teachers as researchers in courses on methods of teaching science. *Journal of Research in Science Teaching, 35*, 7 91–809.

van Zee, E. H. (2000). Ways of fostering teachers' inquiries into science learning and teaching. In J. Minstrell & E. van Zee (Eds.), *Inquiring into inquiry learning and teaching in science* (pp. 100–119). Washington, DC: American Association for the Advancement of Science.

van Zee, E. H., Iwasyk, M., Kurose, A., Simpson, D., & Wild, J. (2001). Student and teacher questioning during conversations about science. *Journal of Research in Science Teaching, 38*, 159–190.

Veldman, P. M. (1997). Changing a teacher's role to evoke meaningful learning behaviors. In J. B. McDonald & P. Gilmer (Eds.), *Science in the elementary school classroom: Portraits of action research* (pp. 49–58). Tallahassee, FL: SouthEastern Regional Vision for Education (SERVE).

Wainwright, S. (2002). Shadows. In R. Lehrer & L. Schauble (Eds.), *Investigating real data in the classroom* (pp. 55–62). New York: Teachers College Press.

Weiss, I. R., Pasley, J. D., Smith, P. S., Banilower, E. R., & Heck, D. J. (2003). *Looking inside the classroom: A study of K–12 mathematics and science education in the US*. Chapel Hill, NC: Horizon Research.

Wells, G. (1994). *The meaning makers: Children learning language and using language to learn*. Portsmouth, NH: Heinemann.

West, L. H. T., & Pines, A. L. (1985). *Cognitive structure and conceptual change*. New York: Academic Press.

Whitehurst, G. J. (2002, March). *Research on teacher preparation and professional development*. Paper presented at the meeting of the White House Conference on Preparing Tomorrow's Teachers, Washington, DC.

Wild, J. (2000). How does a teacher facilitate conceptual development in the intermediate classroom? In J. Minstrell & E. van Zee (Eds.), *Inquiring into inquiry learning and teaching in science* (pp. 157–163). Washington, DC: American Association for the Advancement of Science.

Winograd, K., & Evans, T. (1995). Pre-service elementary teachers' perceptions of an action research assignment. *Action in Teacher Education, 17*, 13–22.

Wong, E. D. (1995). Challenges confronting the researcher/teacher: Conflicts of purpose and conduct. *Educational Researcher, 24*, 22–28.

Yoshida, M. (1999). *Lesson study: An ethnographic investigation of school-based teacher development in Japan*. Unpublished doctoral dissertation, University of Chicago.

Zeichner, K. M. (1993). Action research: Personal renewal and social reconstruction. *Educational Action Research, 1*, 199–219.

Zeichner, K. M. (1997, October). *Action research as a tool for educational and social reconstruction*. Paper presented at the meeting of the Brazilian National Association of Postgraduate Education and Educational Research, Caxambu, Brazil.

Zeichner, K. M, Klehr, M., & Caro-Bruce, C. (2000). Pulling their own levers: The control aspect of action research helps Madison project succeed. *Journal of Staff Development, 21*(4), 36–39.

Zeichner, K. M., & Noffke, S. E. (2001). Practitioner research. In V. Richardson (Ed.), *Handbook of research on teaching* (4th ed., pp. 298–330) Washington, DC: American Educational Research Association.

Author Index

Numbers in *italics* indicate pages with complete bibliographic information.

A

Abd-El-Khalick, F., 408, 410, *434*, 510, *531*, 605, 606, *624*, 836, 853, 854, 855, 856, 857, 859, 860, 867, 869, *872, 873, 874, 876, 877*, 884, *901*, 971, *1002*, 1117, *1134*, 1227, *1247*

Abedi, J., 181, 190, *191*, 1013, *1035*

Abell, S. K., 65, *72, 439*, 454, *464*, 514, *527*, 855, *873*, 972, *1006*, 1045, 1054, *1060, 1062*, 1073, 1086, *1096*, 1119, 1122, 1123, 1126, 1128, *1134, 1135, 1136*, 1162, 1163, 1164, *1176*, 1209, 1210, 1214, 1215, 1234, *1246*

Abma, T. A., 946, *960*

Abraham, L. M., 131, 132, *163*

Abraham, M., 385, *390*

Abraham, M. R., 384, 385, 386, *386, 389*, 404, *434*, 645, *652*

Abrams, R., 507, 509, 526, *533*, 981, *1005*

Acampo, J., 634, *649*, 1130, *1137*

Ackerman, C., 84, *102*

Ackett, W. A., 837, *879*

Adams, D., 152, *160*

Adams, E., *996*

Adams, M., *157*, 1388

Adams, P. E., 1050, *1060*, 1077, *1096*, 1126, *1135*

Adams, R., 991, *1002*

Adamson, G., 272, *282*

Adedayo, A., 704, *712*

Adelman, L. M., 140, *157*

Adelman, N. E., 914, 927, 928, 929, 931, 932, *940, 941*

Adey, P., 33, 39, *51*, 59, *70*

Adkins, C. R., 214, 215, 218, *225*

Adkins, J., 704, *717*

Adler, S. A., 1057, *1060*

Adolphe, G., 109, 116, *119*

Agar, M., 173, *191*

Agelidou, E., 662, 676, *681*

Agin, M. L., 737, 741, *775*

Agrest, B., 587, *595*

Aguirre, J. M., 841, *873*, 1121, 1126, *1135*

Agyeman, J., 707, *719*

Ahern, J., 541, 542, 545, *556, 558*

Ahlberg, M., 707, *712*

Ahlgren, A., 540, *558*, 824, *828*, 888, *910*, 990, *1005*

Ahtee, M., 633, 637, 648, *649*, 1122, *1138*

Aiello-Nicosia, M. L., 1112, *1135*

Aikenhead, G., 82, *96*, 177, 178, *192*, 204, 206, 207, 208, 209, 210, 212, 213, 215, 216, 217, 219, 220, *221, 224*, 231, *255, 434, 595, 687*, 695, *712*, 769, 771, *775*, 837, 843, 863, 865, 866, *873*, 882, 883, 884, 886, 887, 888, 894, 896, 898, 899, *901, 902, 903, 909*, 971, 990, *995*, 1072, 1073, 1093, *1096, 1098*, 1122, 1132, *1135, 1138*

Ainscow, M., 300, *311*

Ainsworth, S. E., 381, *386*

Aisabie, J., 209, 215, *225*

Ajiboye, J., 704, 706, *712, 720*

Ajzen, I., 78, 80, 84, *96*, 1073, 1083, 1088, *1096, 1099*

Akaygun, S., 645, *649*

Akerson, V. L., 499, 506, *527*, 541, 542, *554*, 855, 856, 873, *873*, 898, 1128, *1135*, 1215, 1227, 1235, *1247, 1248, 1254*

Akindehin, F., 849, 852, *873*

Akins, A., *1247*

Al-Shualili, 406, *437*

Aladro, L., 1227, *1247*

Alagumalai, S., 989, *1001*

Alblas, A., 703, *726*
Aldridge, J., 109, 112, 113, 114, 116, *119, 122*
Aldridge, J. M., 105, 107, 108, 109, 110, 112, 113, 114,
    115, 118, *119, 122, 123*
Alexander, G., 564, *595*
Alexander, K. L., 923, *938*
Alexopoulou, E., 457, *464*
Alford, L., *940*
Alfred, 784, *804*
Ali, A., 888, *906*
Allal, L., 971, 977, *995, 996*
Allday, J., 153, *157*
Allen, C. S., 545, *556*
Allen, H., Jr., 863, *873*
Allen, J., *1250*
Allen, N., 1088, *1097*
Allen, N. J., 178, *192*, 216, *221*
Allen, S., 137, 138, *157*
Allman, V., 583, *595*
Allsop, T., 795, 797, *806*
Allsopp, D. H., 296, *314*
Almazroa, H., 408, *438*
Alport, J. M., 919, 920, *940*
Alsop, S., 76, 78, 79, 94, *96*, 508, *534*, 898, *902*
Alt, M. B., 135, 136, *157, 163*
Altermatt, E., 278, *279*
Alters, B. J., 832, 835, *873*
Alton-Lee, A., 509, *532*
Altrichter, H., 1238, *1247*
Altschuld, J. W., *959*
Alvermann, D. E., 457, 458, 459, 460, 463, *466, 469*,
    750, *777*
Alves, F., 138, *160*
Amaral, O., 180, 184, *192*, 346, *366*
Ameh, C., 1111, 1117, *1135*
Amir, R., 591, *596*
Amouroux, R., 639, *649*
Amsel, E., 33, 38, *53*
Ana, G., *387*
Anderman, E. M., 91, *96*
Andersen, H., 858, *878*
Andersen, H. O., 1121, *1140*
Anderson, B. T., 931, *938*
Anderson, C., 263, *280*, 1079, *1102*
Anderson, C. W., 5, 13, 20, 27, *28, 29*, 183, 184, *193*,
    450, 451, *464*, 496, 521, 522, *527, 531*, 1118, 1124,
    1135, 1141, 1173, 1174, *1176*, 1210, 1212, 1214, *1247,
    1252, 1257*
Anderson, D., 126, 127, 128, 129, 130, 134, 141, 142,
    154, *157, 159*
Anderson, D. R., 151, *167*
Anderson, G., 454, *464*, 1210, 1238, 1240, 1241,
    1246, 1247
Anderson, G. J., 105, *123*
Anderson, J., *435*
Anderson, J. O., 984, 985, *996*
Anderson, J. R., 88, *96*

Anderson, K. E., 837, 839, *873*
Anderson, L. M., 1077, 1122, 1124, 1126, *1135*
Anderson, M., 504, 510, 515, *528*
Anderson, M. A., 1122, *1134*
Anderson, M. L., 150, *157*
Anderson, O. R., 66, *70*
Anderson, R. D., 373, *387*, 622, *624*, 808, 815, 816,
    817, 818, 821, 825, 826, 827, *828, 830*, 886, *902, 938*,
    1052, *1060*, 1117, *1135, 1138*, 1164, 1165, 1166, 1168
Anderson, S., 125, 130, 156, *157, 684*
Andersson, B., 33, *51*, 633, *649*
Andre, T., 83, *96*
Andrew, J., 689, 701, 703, 707, *713*
Anfara, V. A., 956, *959*
Aoki, T. T., 204, *221*
Appeldoorn, K., 952, *961*
Apple, M., 264, *279*, 884, 895, *902*, 966, *996*
Appleton, K., 497, 502, 503, 504, 505, 511, 515, 516,
    521, 523, 524, *527, 530*, 1048, *1060*, 1073, *1097*, 1108,
    1112, 1121, 1123, *1135*, 1190, *1202*
Arafeh, S., 472, *489*
Archbald, D., *996*
Archenhold, F., *777*
Ardac, D., 645, *649*
Armitage, M., 514, *528*
Armstrong, C., 707, *713*
Armstrong, R. E., 658, *685*
Arnot, M., 258, 262, *279*
Aron, R. H., 1114, *1135*
Arons, A., 599, 606, *624*
Aronson, E., 383, *387*, 572, *595*
Arredondo, D. E., 549, *555*
Arzi, H. J., 1111, *1135*
Asch, A., 296, *312*
Ash, D., 130, 143, *157*, 384, *387*, 979, *996*
Ashcroft, B., 201, 202, *221*
Ashmann, S., 13, *28*, 183, 184, *193*
Ashworth, S., 705, *713*
Askew, J., 1014, 1024, *1037*
Askew, M., 1048, *1060*
Asoko, H., 36, *52, 55*, 502, 504, *527*, 657, 659, *682*,
    1156, 1190, *1202*
Astin, A., 886, *902*
Astin, H., 886, *902*
Astrin, C., 142, *157*
Atkin, J. M., 734, 752, *776*, 967, 968, 978, 993, *996*,
    1022, 1029, 1030, *1035*
Atkin, M., 967, *996*
Atkinson, J. W., 90, *96*
Atkinson, S., 1228, *1247*
Atwater, M., 214, 219, *221, 222*, 1086, 1095, *1097*
Atwater, M. M., 176, 178, 182, 189, *192, 1097*
Atwell, N., 1205, *1247*
Atwood, R. K., 295, *310*, 1114, *1135, 1148*
Atwood, V. A., *1135*
Au, K. H., 61, 66, *70*
Aubusson, P., 524, *528*

Audu, U., 704, *712*
August, D., 180, 183, *192*
Auls, S., 586, *596*, 674, *683*
Ault, C. R., Jr., 156, *157*, 322, 323, 324, *342*, 656, 662, 665, 674, *681*
Austin, B., *1101*
Austin, J. R., 88, *102*
Ausubel, D. P., 33, 35, *51*, 1154, *1176*
Avery, L. D., 307, *316*
Avraamidou, L., 1133, *1149*
Azeiteiro, U., 700, *713*

B

Bacelar-Nicolau, P., 700, *713*
Bachelard, G., 43, *52*
Bachiorri, A., 704, *713*
Bachor, D., 984, 985, *996*
Bacnik, A., 705, *717*
Bady, R. A., *873*
Baeriswy, F. J., 624, *628*
Bagley, R., *1247*
Bahr, M. A., 521, *533*
Bailey, J., 1128, *1135*
Bailey, L. H., 787, *804*
Bailey, P., 749, *776*
Bailey, S., 521, *527*
Bain, J., *1040*
Bain, K., 662, *682*
Baird, J., 971, *996*
Baird, J. H., 583, *595*
Baird, J. R., 374, *387*, 1045, 1053, *1060, 1062*, 1112, 1166, 1168, 1174, *1176*, 1209, 1224, 1235, *1247*
Baird, W. E., 80, *101*, 353, 356, 365, *366, 1135*
Baizerman, M., 956, *962*
Bajd, B., 701, *722*
Baker, D., 259, 260, 263, 264, 265, 269, 270, 275, 276, 277, *279, 283*, 456, *464*
Baker, D. R., 79, 80, 82, *100*, 608, *624*
Baker, E., 296, 297, *310*, 990, *1002, 1035*
Baker, J. M., 296, *310*
Baker, K., 967, *1001*
Baker, M., 199, 218, *221, 223*
Baker, R., 199, *223*
Baker, S. D., 589, *596*
Bakhtin, M. M., 42, *52*
Bakken, J. P., 299, *315*
Balafoutas, G., 662, 676, *681*
Ball, D., 475, *489*
Ball, D. L., 858, *873*, 1108, 1134, *1136*, 1206, 1208, 1210, 1211, 1234, 1235, 1236, 1239, 1241, *1247, 1253*
Ballantyne, R., 700, 705, *713*
Ballenger, C., 179, 188, *192, 197*, 329, *341, 343*, 456, *464*, 496, *534*, 1214, 1221, 1233, *1247*
Balling, J. D., 143, *161*, 422, *436*
Bandiera, M., 609, *629*, 733, *776*

Bandura, A., 92, *96*, 1044, *1060*, 1085, *1097*
Banerjee, A. C., 1114, *1136*
Banilower, E., 396, *441*, 522, *531*, 952, *963*, 1190, *1202*, 1213, *1259*
Bano, Y., 1116, 1117, *1144*
Bar, V., 676, *681*
Barab, S., 483, 484, *489*
Barab, S. A., 546, *555*
Barak, M., 663, *682*, 1195, 1199, *1202*
Barass, R., *1136*
Barba, R., 455, 456, 457, *464*, 1115, *1136*
Barber, B., 508, *534*
Barenhoz, H., 983, *996*
Barker, M., 676, *681*, 832, *875*, 972, 981, *996*
Barker, V., 635, 636, 640, 641, 642, 644, *649*
Barley, Z. A., 951, *959*
Barman, C., 523, *528*
Barnes, B., *873*, 1228, *1247*
Barnes, C. A., 1206, *1249*
Barnes, D., 1043, *1060*
Barnett, J., 1108, 1122, *1136*
Barnett, M., 483, 484, *489*, 507, 512, 513, 517, *528*
Barnhardt, C., 203, *221*
Barojas, J., 1128, *1138*
Barr, H., *997*
Barrett, R. E., 141, *157*
Barriault, C., 130, *157*
Barrier, E., *1039*
Barron, B. J. S., 406, *434*
Barron, D., 700, 701, 705, *713*
Barron, S., 1010, *1039*
Barron, S. I., 1011, *1037*
Barron, S. L., *1040*
Barrow, L. H., 85, *100*, 346, 353, *366*
Bartholomew, H., 774, *776*, 884, 887, 892, *902, 908*
Barton, A., 1054, *1062*, 1073, 1209, 1228
Barton, A. C., 21, 22, 23, 24, 25, *28*, 272, 279, 457, *464*, 730, 736, 756, 759, 769, 771, 772, 779, 971, 981, 982, 985, 991, 993, 994, *1000, 1104, 1247*
Barufaldi, J. P., 847, 848, 852, *873*, 1071, *1097*
Basista, B., 548, *555*
Bass, G., 307, *311, 316*
Bass, K. M., 15, *29*, 452, *467*, 518, *528*
Bates, G. R., 395, 397, 398, *434*
Battiste, M., 203, 204, 205, 217, 220, *221*
Bauer, M., 763, *776*
Baum, S. M., 307, *314*
Baumert, J., 605, 624, *624, 627*
Baumgärtner, T., 638, 639, *651*
Bauwens, J., 294, *311*
Baxter, G., 1012, *1035*
Baxter, G. P., 518, *528*
Bazerman, C., 57, 67, 70, 444, 453, 455, 458, *465, 466*
Beach, K. R., 94, *97*
Beane, J. A., 537, 539, 540, 542, 543, 545, 552, *555*
Beardsley, D. G., 141, *157*

Beaton, A. E., 236, *254, 255*, 262, *279*, 604, *625*, 1015, 1020, *1035, 1036, 1038*
Beaver, J. B., 363, *367*
Beberman, M., 790, *804*
Beck, J., 1088, *1097*
Becker, H., 733, *777*
Becker, J., 328, *343*, 498, 510, 518, *534*
Bednarski, M., 982, *996*
Bedsole, B., 506, *528*
Beeth, M. E., 36, *53*, 500, 512, 516, 517, 524, *528, 530*, 1045, *1062*, 1155, *1177*, 1212, *1252*
Behar, R., 1234, *1248*
Behnke, F. L., 839, *873*, 1072, *1097*
Beichner, R., 609, 617, *625, 1177*
Beilfuss, M., 662, *681*
Beiswenger, R., 1117, *1147*
Bell, B., 34, *52*, 128, *159*, 199, 200, 212, *223, 225*, 377, *387*, 507, 509, *528*, 965, 967, 968, 970, 971, 972, 973, 974, 976, 977, 979, 985, 989, 990, 991, 992, 993, 994, 995, *996*, 997, *998*, 1183, 1184, 1185, 1189, 1199, *1202*
Bell, D., *1145*
Bell, J., 664, *684*
Bell, P., 453, *465*, 473, *490*
Bell, R., 1010, *1037*
Bell, R. L., 408, *438*, 605, 606, *624*, 832, 853, 855, 857, 860, 862, 867, 871, *873, 874, 877, 879*, 900, *902, 1002*
Bellamy, M. L., 1123, *1136*
Ben-Chaim, D., 663, 670, *685*
Ben-Zvi, N., 731, 740, *776*
Ben-Zvi, R., 398, 399, 434, *436, 438*, 1129, *1141*
Ben-Zvi-Assaraf, O., 662, 668, 669, 670, 678, *681*
Bencze, L., 374, *388*, 899, *902*
Bendall, S., 608, 609, *626*, 1116, 1117, *1136*
Benenson, G., 507, *528*
Benke, G., 608, *629*
Bennett, A. E., 232, *254*
Bennett, J., 80, 81, 82, *96, 97*, 153, *157*, 414, 418, *434*, 643, *649*, 982, *1001*
Bennett, N., 1048, *1060*, 1112
Bennett, S., 703, *713*
Bennett, S. N., *1137*
Benson, G., 711, 712, *713*
Benson, G. D., 1078, *1097*
Bentz, B., 322, 323, 324, *342*
Beoku-Betts, J., 276, *279*
Bereiter, C., 87, *100*, 376, *387*, 460, *465*, 474, 484, *490*
Berg, C., *1035*
Berg, T., 1127, *1136*
Bergel, S. P., 1072, *1097*
Berger, C. F., 541, *555*
Berger, I., 474, *489*
Berger, P. L., 43, *52*
Bergman, J. I., 288, *315*
Berkovitz, B., 39, *56*
Berlak, H., 967, 988, 994, *996*
Berlin, B. M., 827, *829*
Berlin, D., 537, 538, 539, 540, 542, 543, 546, 552, *555*

Berliner, D. C., 955, *960*
Berlyne, D., 88, *96*
Berne, J., 1182, 1189, *1203*
Bernstein, B., 66, *70*
Berry, A., 400, *436*, 1056, 1057, *1060*, 1123, *1143*, 1207, 1232, 1236, *1248*
Berry, B., 923, *938*
Berry, J., 59, *73*
Berryman, C., *196*
Bertenthal, M. W., 1028, *1040*
Best, S., 1188, *1202*
Bethel, J. L., 573, *595*
Bethel, L. J., 847, *873*
Bethge, T., 618, 620, *625*
Beyer, L., 1205, *1248*
Beynon, C., 1128, *1139*
Bezzi, A., 659, 662, 676, *681, 683*
Bhabbha, H. K., 201, *221*
Bhattacharyya, S., 1116, 1117, *1144*
Bianchi, L. J., *1039*
Bianchini, J. A., 182, *192*, 451, 456, 457, 463, *465*, 505, 522, 528, 730, 752, 776, 817, 820, 1210, 1248
Bibby, P. A., 381, *386*
Biddulph, F., 524, 525, *528*, 981, *996*
Biemans, H. J. A., 507, 517, *528*
Biggs, J., 969, *997, 1001*
Billeh, V. Y., 846, 852, 864, *874*
Bingle, W. H., 884, 890, 897, *902*
Biott, C., 1227, *1248*
Bird, T., 1077, *1097*
Birk, J. P., 664, *686*
Birman, B. F., 951, *960*, 1194, *1202*, 1206, *1251*
Birney, B. A., 142, *157*
Birnie, H. H., 385, *390*, 1113, *1136*
Bisanz, G. L., 58, *74*, 149, 154, *160, 162*, 377, *391*, 444, *469, 684*
Bisanz, J., 154, *162*
Bisard, W. J., 1114, *1135*
Biscoe, C., *1202*
Bishop, J. M., 889, *902*
Bishop, K., 707, *724*
Bishop, N., 301, *312*
Bishop, R., 213, 218, *222*
Bissex, G., 1205, *1248*
Bitgood, S., 126, 127, 136, 141, *157, 158*
Bitner, B. L., 1215, *1253*
Bixby, J., 982, *1006*
Black, C., 1088, *1098*
Black, C. B., 78, *97*
Black, P., 507, *528*, 734, *776*, 794, 798, 799, *805, 806*, 965, 966, 967, 968, 969, 970, 972, 973, 974, 976, 977, 978, 979, 988, 989, 990, 992, 995, *996, 997, 999*, 1022, 1029, 1030, *1035*, 1054, *1062*
Black, R., 704, *715*
Blackie, J., 793, *805*
Blackmore, J., 258, 276, *281*
Blackwood, D., *1248*

Blades, D., 219, 222, 771, *776*, 881, 895, 897, *902*
Blair, G., 259, 260, 261, *280*
Blair, L., 860, *874*
Blake, A., 504, *532*
Blanchet, W. W. E., 1111, *1136*
Blanco, L. J., 1133, *1143*
Blaney, N., 383, *387*, 572, *595*
Blank, L. M., 508, 517, 523, *528*
Blank, R. K., 5, *28*
Blankenship, J. W., 1071, *1097, 1099, 1100*, 1121, *1141*
Blänsdorf, K., 733, *777*
Blanton, M. L., 63, *70, 938*
Bledsoe, J. C., 1110, *1148*
Bleicher, M., 607, *627*
Bleicher, R., 444, 452, *465*
Bleschke, M., 610, *629*
Bloch, I., 594, *595*
Blomker, K. B., 1215, *1252*
Bloom, B. S., 76, *96*, 578, *595, 681*
Bloom, J. W., 841, *874*
Blosser, P., 397, *434*, 921, *938*
Blumenfeld, B., 401, 412, *437*
Blumenfeld, P., 15, *29*, 90, 91, *99*, 183, 186, *192, 193*,
    452, *467, 684*, 824, *829*, 1128, 1131, *1149*, 1164, *1178*
Blunck, S., 365, *366*
Bobrowsky, W., 1200, *1202*
Boddy, N., 524, *528*
Bodner, G. M., 663, *686*, 853, *874*, 881, 898, *902*,
    1083, *1097*
Bodzin, A. M., 150, *158*
Boehme, C., 154, *162*
Boenig, R. W., 348, 349, *367*
Bogner, F., 700, 701, *713*
Bohrman, M. L., *1248*
Boix-Mansilla, V., 538, 550, *556*
Bol, L., 974, 994, *997*, 1075, *1103*, 1132, *1136*
Bolscho, D., 704, *713*
Bolstad, R., 140, 142, 143, *166*, 199, *223*, 832, *875*
Bong, M., 92, *96, 98*
Bonnett, M., 691, 700, 701, 702, 705, *713, 726*
Bonnstetter, R. J., 426, *439*
Boone, W., 118, *123*, 274, *280*, 662, *681, 684*, 1084,
    1085, *1097, 1098*, 1111, 1112
Boone, W. J., 496, 497, *533*, 932, *938, 1146*
Boorman, J., *1036*
Booth, T., 300, *311*
Borg, W. R., 430, *436*
Borko, H., 1010, *1035*, 1045, *1060*, 1067, *1102*, 1107,
    1108, 1119, 1123, 1131, *1136, 1137, 1143, 1146*, 1155,
    1156, *1178*, 1238, *1250*
Borun, M., 130, 143, 144, *158*
Boshuizen, H. P. A., 380, 381, *387, 390*
Bouillion, L., 186, *192*, 327, 333, 335, 340, *341*
BouJaoude, S., 1080, 1095, *1097*, 1117, *1134*
Boulanger, D., 920, *941*
Boulanger, F. D., 919, *938*
Boulter, C., 377, 379, *388*, 514, *528*

Bourdieu, P., 173, *192*
Bourque, S., 266, *280*
Boutonné, S., 375, *390*, 452, 462, *468*, 887, *908*
Bowen, G. M., 46, *55*, 62, 66, *70, 73*
Bowen, M. G., 1112, *1145*
Bowers, C., 692, *713*
Bowers, J., 45, *52*
Bowman, J. K., 547, *557*
Bown, O. H., 1043, *1061*
Boyce, L. N., 307, *311*
Boyd, N., 1210, *1257*
Boyd, S. E., 1190, *1202*
Boyer, R., 1129, *1136*
Boyes, E., 700, 701, 705, *713, 714, 717*
Boylan, C., 1128, *1135*
Boyle, A., 799, *805*
Boyle, L., 1227, *1248*
Boyle, R. A., 38, *55*, 76, *100*, 607, *628*
Bradburne, J. M., 139, 150, *158*
Bradbury, H., 1209, *1265*
Brader-Araje, L., 522, *531*
Bradford, B., 150, *158*
Bradford, C. S., 354, *367*, 1122, *1136*
Bradley, R. C., 1071, *1097*
Bragg, J., 182, *194*
Bragow, D., 546, *555*
Brake, M., 155, *158*
Bramanti, B., 474, *489*
Brandon, R., 656, *681*
Brandt, C., 220, *223*
Brandt, G., 474, *489*
Brandwein, P., 308, *311, 597*
Brannigan, A., 67, *70*
Bransford, J. D., 288, *311*, 401, 405, *434*, 473, 481, 485,
    488, *489, 490*, 809, 827, *829*, 1028, *1035*, 1212, *1248*
Bratt, H. M., 1071, 1072, *1097*
Brazee, E. N., 540, *555*
Bredderman, T., 920, *938*
Breier, B. R., 288, *315*
Breiting, S., 695, 707, *714*
Brekelmans, M., 106, 115, *119, 124*
Brennan, R. P., 739, *776*
Brewer, R. D., 296, *314*
Brewer, W. F., 1169, *1176*
Brickhouse, N. W., 177, *196*, 206, 211, *226*, 272, 274,
    280, 339, *342*, 515, *528*, 817, *829*, 853, *874*, 881,
    889, 898, *902, 906*, 1044, *1060*, 1078, 1083, *1097*,
    1126, *1136*
Briggs, S., 1054, *1062*
Brigham, F. J., 299, *315*
Briscoe, C., 547, *555*, 974, *1002*, 1056, *1060*, 1073,
    1084, *1097*, 1122, *1136*, 1192
Britner, S. L., 91, *96*
Britsch, S. J., 518, 519, *533*
Britton, B. K., 87, 90, *98*
Britton, D., *1248*
Britton, E., 734, *779*, 1011, 1018, 1022, *1035, 1038, 1039*

Britzman, D., 1044, *1060*
Broadfoot, P., 966, 970, 979, 994, *997, 1003*
Broadhurst, N. A., 837, *874*
Broadway, F. S., 259, 277, *284*
Brody, M., 140, *158*, 701, 703, *714*
Brody, M. J., 658, 662, 676, *681*
Broekman, H., 1122, *1148*
Bronowski, 864
Brookfield, S. D., 1045, *1060*
Brookhart, S. M., 968, 979, *997*
Brooks, J. G., 537, *555*
Brooks, M. G., 537, *555*
Brooks, T., *1101*
Brophy, J., 87, 89, 93, *96, 98, 99*
Brophy, S., 481, *490*
Brouwer, W., 1127, *1136*
Brown, A., 39, *52*
Brown, A. L., 87, *96*, 288, *311*, 384, *387*, 401, 405, *434*,
    473, 485, 488, *489*, 809, 827, *829*, 1028, *1035*, 1043,
    1212, *1248*
Brown, B., 275, 276, *285*
Brown, C., 63, *71*, 143, *158*, 448, *465, 167, 499, 531*
Brown, C. L., 931, *938*
Brown, D. E., 522, *533*
Brown, F., 1072, 1090, *1097*
Brown, J. S., 19, *28*, 45, *52*, 128, *158*, 405, *434*
Brown, K., 504, *532*
Brown, K. M., 956, *959*
Brown, L. R., 355, *367*
Brown, M., 970, *1000*
Brown, R., 993, *997*
Brown, S. K. M., 151, *160*
Brown, W. R., 544, *555*
Brubaker, S., 695, *714*
Bruce, L. R., 1106, 1118, *1136*
Bruce, M. H., 888, *909*
Bruckerhoff, C., 356, *367*
Bruckman, A., 485, *489*
Bruner, J., 132, *166*, 485, *491*, 654, *682*, 703, *714*, 791,
    796, *805*
Bruns, P., *1177*
Bryan, L. A., 182, 189, *192*, 214, *222*, 826, *829*, 1044,
    1060, 1067, 1086, 1095, *1097, 1100*, 1122, 1126, 1130,
    1134, *1134, 1136, 1142*, 1162, 1163, 1164, *1176*, 1209,
    1214, 1215, 1231, *1246, 1253*
Bryant, C., 753, *780*, 894, *909*
Bryant, M., 295, *316*
Bryce, T. G. K., 413, *434*
Brydon-Miller, M., 1209, *1256*
Bryk, A. S., 111, *119*
Bucat, R., 990, *998*
Buchan, A., 800, *805*, 970, *997*
Buchanan, A. M., 506, *528*
Buchanan, J., *1258*
Buchanan, T., 995, *997*
Buchmann, M., 1213, *1250*
Budde, M., 621, *625*

Budick, S., 958, *960*
Bula, O. A., *1103*, 1126, *1147*
Bull, J., 695, *714*
Bullock, R., 1205, *1248*
Bullock, S., 1047, *1064*, 1153, *1178*, 1216, *1257*
Bulmahn, N., 269, *280*
Bunce, D. M., 633, *650*
Bunch, G., 303, *315*
Burchett, B. M., 346, 353, *366*
Burden, R. L., 117, *123*
Burgess, T., *996*
Burkam, D., 1013, *1037*
Burke, K., 425, *434*
Burkhardt, H., 1206, *1248*
Burns, J., 1227, *1249*
Burroughs, D., 930, *939*
Burruss, J. D., 307, *311*
Bursuck, W. D., 292, 301, *312*
Bush, M. J., 913, 985, *1004*
Buss, R. R., 548, *555*
Bustillo, I., 266, *280*
Butcher, A. C., 982, *1005*
Butler, J., *967, 997*
Butler, M. B., 84, *96*
Butler Kahle, J., 118, *123*
Butts, B., 641, *649*
Butts, D., 1071, 1072, *1097*
Butts, D. P., 504, 510, 515, *528*, 1118, *1136*
Butts, J., 1210, *1247*
Buty, C., 400, *440*, 609, *628*
Buxton, C. A., 506, *529*
Byard, M., 381, *388*
Bybee, R. W., 127, 155, 156, *158*, 401, 404, *434*, 524,
    529, 582, 583, *595*, 600, 607, *625*, 659, *682*, 693, 694,
    711, *714*, 731, 735, 737, 738, 740, 741, 742, 766, *776*,
    883, 888, 892, *902*
Bynoe, P., 704, *720*
Byrd, T., 276, *282*
Byrk, A. S., 956, *960*
Byrne, M., 1048, *1062*
Byrne, P. F., 150, *158*

C

Cabral, B., 704, *714*
Cacioppo, J. T., 78, 93, *96, 100*
Caieiro, S., 700, *713*
Caillods, F., 243, *254*
Cajete, G., 205, 216, *222*
Cakiroglu, J., 1085, *1097*
Calabrese Barton, A., 179, 186, *192*, 321, 327, 330,
    335, 338, 339, 341, *342*, 899, *902*
Calderhead, J., 1108, *1136*
Callanan, M. A., 130, 143, *159*
Callen, B. W., 545, *556*
Cameron, D., 444, *465*

Cameron, J., 86, *97*
Camilli, G., 1010, *1036*
Camione, J. C., 384, *387*
Camp, B. D., 156, *162*
Camp, C., 617, *625*
Campbell, B., 61, *72*
Campbell, C., 995, *997*
Campbell, C. H., 1211, *1252*
Campbell, J. R., 175, *192*, 1024, *1035*
Campbell, P. B., 148, *163*
Campbell, R. L., 1071, *1098*
Campione, J. C., 87, *96*
Canaday, D., 66, *74*, 184, *196*, 507, 509, 526, *533*, 981, *1005*
Canady, R., 552, 553, *555*
Candela, A., 59, *70*, 503, *529*
Cannon, J., 1213, *1250*
Cantonwine, D., 425, *434*
Cantor, J., 151, *162*
Capelluti, J., 540, *555*
Caracelli, V. J., 129, *161*, 956, *960*
Carambo, C., 347, *369*
Caravita, S., 511, 517, *529*, 733, *776*
Carboni, L. W., 522, *531*
Cardinale, L., 456, 457, *464*
Carey, R. L., 839, 840, 845, 846, 852, *874*
Carey, S., 36, 38, 52, 844, *874*
Carillo, R., 178, *195*, 331, 332, 333, *342*
Carlisle, R., 452, *468*
Carlone, H. B., 881, 895, 898, 901, *902*
Carlsen, W. S., 14, *28*, 60, 62, 63, 64, *70*, 71, *74*, 353, *367*, 444, 446, 447, 453, *465*, 884, *905*, 1051, *1060*, 1108, 1116, 1119, *1136*, *1137*
Carlton, W., *1248*
Caro-Bruce, C., 1206, 1222, *1248*
Carpenter, J. R., 660, *682*
Carpenter, T. P., 935, *938*, 1206, *1248*
Carr, J., 540, 545, *558*
Carr, M., 645, *649*, 967, 970, 971, 972, 981, 986, 989, 994, 996, 997, 1048, *1060*
Carr, W., 1205, 1206, 1209, 1236, *1248*
Carré, C., 1111, 1112, *1137*
Carretero, A. J., 882, *908*
Carrick, T., 1129, *1137*
Carrillo, R., 15, 16, 17, 18, 19, 24, *29*, 66, *72*, 444, 462, *468*, 511, *532*
Carroll, J. B., 497, *532*
Carson, G. A., *99*
Carson, R. N., 730, *776*
Carter, C., 273, *283*
Carter, D. S. G., 1112, *1137*
Carter, G., 63, *70*, 508, 509, 512, 522, *529*, *531*, 1110, 1116, *1141*
Carter, J. C., 131, *158*
Carter, K., 1108, 1109, *1137*
Carter, L., 220, *222*
Carter, N. P., 213, *222*

Carter, T., *1102*
Cartier, J. L., 824, *829*
Cary, S., 1095, *1098*
Caseau, D., 296, *314*
Cass, M., 705, *725*
Cassady, J. C., 88, *97*
Castellano, M. B., 203, 209, 210, *222*
Castillo, R. N., 288, *315*
Caswell, B., 519, *529*
Cates, W. M., 150, *158*
Cavallo, A., 85, *97*, 635, 636, *649*
Cavazos, L. M., 182, *192*, 817, *829*
Cawley, J. F., 297, 302, *311*
Caygill, R., 970, 981, 992, 993, *999*
Cazden, C., 384, *387*, 445, 450, *465*
Cazelli, S., 138, *160*
Celis, W., 346, *367*
Cerrillo, T. L., 1010, *1037*
Chabbott, C., 253, *254*
Chadwick, P., 663, *682*
Chaiklin, S., 61, *70*
Chalmers, A. F., 834, *874*
Chambers, F. W., 861, *878*
Chambers, M. B., 130, 143, 144, *158*
Chambers, S., 83, *96*
Champagne, A. B., 375, *387*, 403, 422, 427, *434*, *436*, 731, *776*, 889, *902*
Champagne, D. W., 138, 139, *158*
Chan, F., *1036*
Chan, K.-K., 701, 706, *714*
Chandler, K., 1227, *1248*
Chandrasekhar, M., 85, *100*
Chang, A., 1114, 1125, *1177*
Chang, C. Y., *682*
Chang, P. J., 203, *222*
Charen, G., 77, *97*, 398, *435*
Charness, N., 305, *312*
Charnitski, C. W., 59, *71*
Charron, E. H., 355, 356, 365, *367*
Chase, C., *98*
Chastko, A., 693, *723*, 1122, *1145*
Chastrette, M., 639, *649*
Chatterji, M., xiii, *xiv*
Chawla, I., 700, 701, 704, 705, *714*
Chazen, D., 1210, *1248*
Cheek, D. W., 883, 884, 888, *902*
Chen, C., 63, *72*, 445, 453, 463, *467*, *1257*
Chen, C. C., 108, 115, *119*, 855, *877*
Chen, L., 151, *160*
Chen, M., 126, 136, 151, *158*
Chen, M. J., 362, 363, *367*
Cheney, C., 299, *311*
Cheng, H., *1143*
Cheng, M. H., 970, *998*
Cheng, Y. C., 234, *254*
Chenhansa, S., 703, *714*
Cherryholmes, C., 988, *998*

Cheung, D., 990, *998*, 1125, 1126, *1137*
Cheung, F. W. M., 970, *998*
Chew, F., 152, *158*
Chezem, J., 454, *464*, 1210, *1246*
Chi, M. T. H., 33, 37, 49, *52*, 617, *625*
Chia, L. S., 990, *1005*
Chiang, C. P., 1206, *1248*
Childers, P. B., 969, 983, *998*, *1006*
Childress, R., 506, *528*
Chin, C., 508, 524, *529*
Chin, C.-C., 155, *158*
Chin, P., 889, 890, *902*, 1057, *1060*
Chinn, C., 498, 503, 524, *529*
Chinn, C. A., 1169, *1176*
Chinn, P. W. U., 461, *465*
Chionh, Y.-H., 109, 112, 113, *120*
Chittleborough, G., 382, *390*, 607, 618, *629*
Chiu, M.-H., 987, 994, *998*
Cho, H., 85, *97*
Cho, J. I., 112, *119*
Choi, H. J., 92, *98*
Choi, K., 85, *97*
Choi, M. Y., 141, 143, *165*
Choisser, C., 1010, *1038*
Chokshi, S., 1213, *1250*
Chomsky, N., 65, *71*
Chou, C.-C., 987, *998*
Chou, J., 707, *714*
Christensen, C., *776*
Christenson, S., 297, *317*
Christidis, T., 705, *714*
Christidou, V., 701, 705, *714*, *719*
Christie, M. J., 212, *222*
Christopher, J. E., 1114, *1148*
Chrostowski, S. J., *255*, *1037*
Chuan, G., 701, *718*
Chubin, D. E., 888, *906*
Chudinova, E. V., 824, *830*
Chudowsky, N., *1038*, *1040*
Chun, T., 1010, *1040*
Chung, C. M., 1116, *1149*
Chung, S., 295, *313*
Chye, Y. O., *440*
Cilley, M., 293, *316*
Ciskszentmihalyi, M., 89, *97*
Cizek, G. J., 985, *998*
Clacherty, A., 705, *713*
Clair, R., 261, *280*
Clandinin, D. J., 1106, *1137*
Clark, B., 701, *714*
Clark, C., 1122, *1137*
Clark, C. M., 1043, *1061*
Clark, D. A. T., 220, *222*
Clark, F., 889, *902*
Clark, J., *1061*
Clark, R. E., 92, *96*

Clarke, A., 1043, 1059, *1061*
Clarke, C. O., 352, *367*
Clarke, S., 978, 979, *998*
Clawson, S., *1255*
Claxton, G., 512, *529*, 971, 986, 987, 989, *997*, *998*
Cleary, B., 145, *159*
Cleghorn, A., 130, 143, 144, *158*
Cleland, C., 656, *682*
Cleland, J. V., 548, *555*
Clement, J., 39, *52*, 613, 617, *625*, 662, *683*, 1232, *1248*
Clement, J. J., 514, *530*
Clermont, C. P., 1131, *1137*
Clift, R., 1043, *1061*
Clough, M. P., 408, 411, 422, 423, 427, *435*, *438*, 832, *879*
Clover, D., 707, *714*
Clune, W. H., 924, 929, *938*, *939*
Cobb, A., 1057, *1065*
Cobb, P., 45, *52*, 454, *938*, 1043, *1061*, 1206, *1248*
Cobbs, G., 545, 551, *557*
Cobern, M., 700, 701, *720*
Cobern, W. W., 178, *192*, 210, 212, 220, 222, 232, *254*, 499, 529, 692, 695, 711, *714*, *715*, 841, 870, 871, 886, *903*, 1075, *1098*
Cobiac, S., 705, *715*
Coble, C. B., 1071, *1103*
Coble, C. R., 1195, 1197, 1198, 1200, *1203*
Coburn, C. E., 185, *192*
Coburn, W., *1098*
Cochran, K. F., 1046, *1061*, 1133, *1137*
Cochran-Smith, M., 182, *192*, 1043, *1061*, 1106, *1137*, 1208, 1209, 1210, 1211, 1234, 1235, 1236, 1242, *1248*
Cocking, R. R., 288, *311*, 401, 405, *434*, 473, 485, 488, 489, 809, 827, *829*, 1028, *1035*, 1212, *1248*
Codd, J., 967, *998*
Coffey, J., 967, *996*, 1030, *1035*
Cogan, L. S., 5, *29*, 1021, *1036*, *1039*
Cohen, A., *998*
Cohen, D., 475, *489*
Cohen, D. K., 13, *28*, *939*, 1206, *1247*, *1249*
Cohen, P., 267, *280*, 537, *556*
Cohen, S., 37, *56*
Coker, T., *1102*, *1258*
Colbe, C., *715*
Cole, D. A., 296, *311*
Cole, M., 14, *28*, *29*, 972, *1003*
Coleman, D., 1123, *1142*
Coleman, L. J., 308, *311*
Coles, G., 289, 304, *311*
Coles, M., 889, *903*
Coley, R., 273, *280*
Colinvaux, D., 138, *160*
Coll, R. K., 140, 142, 143, *166*, 380, *387*, 642, 646, *649*
Collazo, C., 511, *532*
Collazo, T., 15, 16, 17, 18, 19, 24, *29*, 66, *72*, 178, *195*, 444, 462, *468*

Collins, A., 19, *28*, 45, *52, 128, 158, 311*, 405, *434, 683,* 967, 984, 993, *998*, 1012, *1036*
Collins, A. M., 87, *98*
Collins, B. E., 1068, *1100*, 1228
Collins, L., 704, *715*
Collins, P. A., 151, *167*
Collins, S., 67, *72*, 78, 95, *99*, 272, *283*, 833, *878*, 885, 886, 888, 893, *907*
Collison, G. E., 1083, *1098*
Comber, C., 507, *530*
Comber, L. C., 1015, 1017, *1036*
Compton, D., 956, *962*
Conant, F., 179, 180, *196*, 456, *468, 469*, 864, 884
Conant, J., 864, 874, 1090, *1098*
Conant, P. R., 19, *29*
Conçalves, F., 700, *713*
Connell, M. C., 588, 596
Connell, S., 697, 700, 701, *713, 715*
Connelly, F. M., 1106, *1137*
Connolly, T. R., 296, *314*
Conway, J., 266, *280*
Conway, M., 704, *715*
Cook, N. R., 948, *960*
Cook, P. A., 1125, *1141*
Cooley, W. W., 842, 843, 845, 846, 848, 852, 863, *874, 876*, 884, 888, *905*
Cooper, B., 1106, 1118, *1147*
Copley, A., 262, *280*
Copolo, C., 970, *1005*
Corbett, H. D., 925, *938*
Corcoran, P., 704, 707, *715*
Corcoran, T. B., 914, 927, 928, 929, 931, *941*
Cordell, L. S., 156, *158*
Cordova, R., 462, *468*
Corey, C., 61, *71*, 332, *342*
Corey, S. M., 1209, 1238, *1249*
Cork, C., 704, *715*
Cornett, J. W., *1103*, 1126, *1137, 1147*
Corno, L., 75, 79, *101*
Corrigan, D., 892, 895, *904*
Corsaro, W., 692, *715*
Corsiglia, J., 177, 178, *196*, 205, 206, 208, 211, *222, 226*
Cortazzi, M., 703, *715*
Cossman, G. W., 884, *903*
Costa, V., 178, *192*, 886, 887, 894, *903*
Costa Pereira, D., 1110, *1149*
Costello, C., 296, *311*
Cotham, J., 837, 865, 867, *874*
Coulson, D., 128, 130, 133, *160*
Coulthard, M., 445, *468*
Coupland, N., 444, *466*
Courtnay-Hall, P., 704, *715*
Cousins, J. B., 946, *960*
Covington, M. V., 90, *97*
Covotsos, T., 66, *70*
Cowan, E., 452, *465*

Cowie, B., 507, 509, *528*, 965, 968, 969, 970, 972, 973, 974, 976, 977, 979, 980, 989, 990, 991, 993, 994, 995, *996, 998, 1001*
Cox-Petersen, A., 142, 156, *158*
Cox-Peterson, A., 1090, *1103*
Crandall, B., *366*
Crane, S., 540, *556*
Crane, V., 126, 136, *158*
Crasco, L., 185, *193*
Crasco, L. M., 5, *29*
Craven, J. A., 859, *874*
Crawford, B., 416, *441*, 453, 454, 463, *469*, 856, 860, *874, 878*, 1172, *1176*
Crawford, R., 952, *963*
Crawford, T., 63, *71*, 448, 451, 452, 462, *465, 467*, 499, *531*
Crawley, F., 1068, 1088, *1097, 1098, 1102*
Crawley, F. E., 77, 78, 79, 82, 93, *97, 98, 101*, 178, *192*, 216, *221*
Cremin, L., 539, *556*
Creswell, J. W., 1076, 1089, *1098*
Crick, B., 695, *715*
Crockett, D., 214, 219, *221*, 346, *367, 1102, 1258*
Croft, C., 981, *1002*
Cromer, A., 408, *435*
Cromwell, M., 695, *714*
Cronin, M., 297, *314*
Cronin-Jones, L. L., 1078, 1080, *1098*
Croninger, J. B., 184, *194*
Crooks, T., 965, 967, 970, 971, 973, 977, 979, 981, 989, 990, 991, 992, *998*
Cros, D., 639, *649*
Crosby, A., 202, *222*
Cross, C. T., 290, *311*
Cross, R. T., 447, *465*, 881, 883, 884, *903*, 1090, *1098*
Cross, T. L., 308, *311*
Crotty, M., 702, *715*
Crow, L. W., 426, *439*
Crowley, K., 128, 130, 143, *159, 162*
Crumb, G. H., 842, 843, *874*
Csikzentmihályi, M., 138, *159*
Cuban, L., 472, 473, *489*, 814, 827, *829, 830*
Cucchiarelli, D., *1249*
Cuevas, P., 183, *194*
Cumming, J., 982, 983, 988, 989, 993, *999*
Cummins, C. L., 871, *875*, 1115, *1140*
Cummins, R. H., 668, *686*
Cunningham, C. M., 14, *28*, 60, *71*, 884, 890, 898, *903, 905*
Cunningham, M., *907*, 1051, *1063*, 1122, *1144*
Curtis, C., 1232, *1249*
Curtis, F. D., 348, 349, 350, 351, *367*
Curtis, S., 65, *71*, 180, *192*
Cwikiel, W., 695, *714*
Czerniak, C., 505, *529*, 542, 545, 549, *556, 557, 558*, 1072, 1076, 1078, 1083, 1084, 1088, 1095, *1097, 1098, 1099, 1101*, 1129, *1146*

D

Dadds, M., 1238, 1240, 1241, 1245, *1249*
Daehler, K. R., 1116, 1117, 1123, *1137*
Dagher, Z., 380, *387*, *390*, 449, *465*
Dahl, J., *684*
Dahncke, H., 600, *625*
Daly, J. F., 668, *687*
Damasio, A., 79, 80, 93, *97*
Dana, T., 354, *367*, 1045, *1061*, 1112, 1122, 1124, 1133, *1136*, *1139*, *1148*, *1149*
Daniels, J. D., 278, *280*
Darkside, *335*, *342*
Darling-Hammond, L., 303, *311*, 323, *342*, 923, *938*, 991, 993, *999*, 1206, *1249*
Darlington, P., 704, *715*
Davey, A., 153, *162*, 730, 756, 757, 772, *778*, 886, *906*
David, E. E., 889, *903*
David, M., 258, 262, *279*
Davidson, A., 887, *903*
Davier, M. V., 610, *629*
Davies, 325, *342*
Davies, D., 185, *193*, 1122, *1137*
Davis, B., 474, *490*
Davis, C. O., 350, *367*
Davis, E., 473, 486, *489*, *490*
Davis, E. A., 413, *435*
Davis, J., 274, *280*, 651, 695, 703, *715*
Davison, D. M., 215, *222*, 542, 544, 550, *556*
Daws, N., 970, 974, *999*
Dawson, C., 83, *97*
Dawson, C. R., 39, *55*
De Baz, T., 85, *97*
De Bóo, M., 792, *805*
De Jong, O., 633, 634, 646, 648, *649*, *650*, 1046, 1048, *1061*, *1065*, 1109, 1114, 1121, 1122, 1127, 1130, *1137*, *1138*, *1148*
De Jong, T., 380, *390*, *682*
de Leeuw, N., 37, 49, *52*, 617, *625*
De Long-Cotty, B., *1035*
de Montellano, B. R. O., 206, 211, 215, *224*
De Torre, A. M. O., 647, *651*
De Vos, W., 634, 636, *650*, 746, 771, *776*, 896, *903*, 1055, *1065*, 1075, *1103*, 1123, *1149*
De Vries, D. L., 383, *387*
DeBacker, T. K., 91, *97*
DeBarger, A., *1038*
DeBenedictis, T., *1037*
DeBoer, G. E., 260, *280*, *311*, 452, 457, *465*, 659, *682*, 693, 711, *714*, 731, 736, 738, *776*, 783, *805*, 882, *903*
DeCarlo, C. L., 407, *435*
Deci, E. L., 86, 87, 89, 95, *97*, *100*, *102*
Deeds, D. G., 545, *556*
Deel, O. R., 507, 517, *528*
Deese, W. C., 969, *999*
DeFranco, T. C., 544, 547, 551, *557*
DeGisi, L. L., 586, *595*

DeGroot, E. V., 91, *100*
DeHaan, R., *1177*
DeHart Hurd, P., 563, 571, 588, *595*, *596*
Dei, G. J. S., 209, 210, *222*
Dekkers, J., 885, *903*
Del Pozo, R. M., 647, *650*
Delaeter, J., 885, *903*
DeLaughter, J., 662, *682*
Delpit, L., 20, 25, *28*, 171, 178, *193*, 966, *999*
DeLuca, F. P., 1071, *1098*
Delucchi, K., *1037*
Demare, R., 705, *716*
den Brock, P., 115, *119*
Denby, D., 417, *435*
Denicolo, P., 291, *312*
Denig, S. J., 85, *99*
Dennick, R., 215, *226*, 838, *879*
Denzin, N., 698, 709, *715*, 958, *960*
Derry, N., 887, *906*
DeRuiter, J. A., 1133, *1137*
Désautels, J., 46, *55*, 884, 886, 887, 894, 899, *906*, *908*
Desimone, L., *951*, *960*, 1191, *1203*, 1206, *1251*
DeSouza, J., 1072, 1084, 1095, *1098*
Desouza, S., 1088, *1098*
DeSouze-Hammond, L., *1249*
DeSouze-Wyatt, B., *1249*
DeTure, L., 982, *999*
Deutsch, G. K., *316*
Dewandre, N., 268, 269, *280*
Dewey, J., 77, *97*, 1043, *1061*, 1152, 1160, *1176*
Deyhle, D., 501, *530*
Deylitz, S., 609, 621, *628*
DeYoung, R., 703, *721*
Dhingra, K., 152, 155, *159*, 860, *874*, 894, *903*
Di Chiro, G., 695, *714*
Diamond, J., 132, 143, 145, 156, *159*, *160*, 184, 185, *196*, 326, *343*, 499, 501, *533*
Diana, T. J., 1216, *1258*
Dickerson, D. L., 662, *681*, *682*
Dickinson, D., 1227, *1249*
Dickinson, V. L., 541, *556*
Dickson, M. W., *367*
Dieckman, D., *1249*
Dierking, L. D., 126, 127, 128, 129, 130, 134, 136, 138, 141, 142, 143, 144, 154, 156, *157*, *159*, *160*, *162*, *164*
Dika, S., 84, *101*
Dillman, D. A., 956, *960*
Dillon, J., 141, 143, *165*
Dillon, J. S., 637, *652*
Dillon, P., 707, *715*
Dimitrakopoulou, A., 512, 515, *534*
Dimopoulos, K., 891, *903*
DiPerna, E., 1232, *1249*
DiSchino, M., *1249*
DiSessa, A., 37, 38, *52*, 512, 529, 616, *625*, 1156, *1176*
Disinger, J., 707, *715*, 1071, *1101*
Dixon, C. N., 48, *53*

Doane, W. E. J., 990, *1006*
Dobey, D. C., 1117, 1118, *1138*
Dodick, J. T., 662, 663, 665, 667, 670, 678, *682, 685*
Doig, B., 991, *1002*
Dolan, L., *940*
Dolan, L. J., *939*
Domin, D. S., 403, *435*
Donahoe, K., 302, *311*
Donahue, P. L., 1024, *1035*
Donald, N., 289, *311*
Donaldson, M., 33, *52*
Donnelly, J., 692, 693, 697, *716, 778*
Donnelly, J. F., 882, *903*, 966, 967, *999*
Donoahue, Z., 1228, *1249*
Donovan, M. S., 288, *311*
Donovan, S. M., 290, *311*
Doolittle, F., 322, *343*
Doran, R., 947, *960*, 965, 967, 971, 982, 989, 993, 1008, 1012, 1017
Doran, R. L., *440, 999, 1036, 1037*
Dori, Y., 412, *435*, 663, *682*, 887, 894, 899, *903, 909*, 970, 983, *999*
Doris, E., 1228, 1231, *1249*
Dorman, J. P., 109, 115, 118, *119*
Dormedy, D. F., *99*
Dörries, M., 67, *71*
Doster, E. C., 1133, *1138*
Dougherty, L. A., *1249*
Douglas, G., 990, *998*
Douglass, C. B., 1071, *1098*
Douvdevany, O., 1115, *1138*
Dove, J. E., 662, *682*
Dovidio, J. F., 94, *97*
Dow, P. B., 912, *938*
Dowdy, C. A., 292, 293, 300, *315*
Downing, J. E., 296, *315*
Downs, C. T., 972, *999*
Downs, G. E., 1071, *1098*
Drake, C., 341, *342*
Dressman, M., 1233, *1249*
Dreves, C., 85, *98*
Drew, C. J., 287, 305, *312*
Dreyfus, A., 1115, *1138*
Dritsas, J., 143, *143, 158*
Driver, R., 7, *28*, 33, 34, 36, 39, 41, 46, 49, *52, 54, 55*, 62, *71*, 78, 83, *99*, 128, *159*, 230, 232, *254*, 381, *388*, 405, 410, 414, 427, *435, 438*, 453, 457, *464, 465*, 605, 615, 617, *625*, 646, *650*, 656, 657, 659, *682*, 698, *716*, 831, *875*, 886, *907*, 976, *999*, 1045, *1061*, 1156, 1157, *1176, 1178*, 1212, *1249*
Drori, G. S., 889, *903*
Drucker, S., 453, *467*
Druger, M., 853, 858, *877*
Druker, S., *467, 1257*
Druva, C. A., 1117, *1138*
Dryden, M., 108, *120*
Duarte, M., 1076, *1102*, 1127

Duarte, M. D. C., *1146*
Dubowski, Y., *685*
Duckworth, E., 1210, *1249*
Ducrey, G. P., 977, *996*
Duffee, L., 1073, *1098*, 1132, *1138*
Dugan, T., 66, *71*, 180, *193*
Duggan, S., 519, *530, 805*, 887, 890, *903, 910*
Dugger, W. E., Jr., 1023, *1038*
Duguid, P., 45, *52*, 128, *158*, 405, *434*
Duit, R., 7, 12, 15, *28*, 34, *54*, 87, *98*, 128, *159, 254*, 373, *387*, 514, 599, 602, 605, 606, 607, 608, 610, 611, 618, 623, 624, *625, 626, 629*, 994, *999*, 1153, 1154, 1155, 1156, 1172, 1174, *1176, 1178*
Dukepoo, F., 214, 216, *222*
Dunbar, S., 990, *1002*
Duncan, R., 474, *490*
Dunkel, J., *366*
Dunlap, R., 693, *716*
Dunn, R., 85, *99*
Dunwoody, S., 149, *166*
Dupin, J. J., 612, *628*
Duran, B. J., 66, *71*, 180, *193*
Durant, J., 729, 742, 753, 762, 763, *776, 777, 780*
Durie, M. H., 203, 210, 211, *222*
Durkee, P., 844, *875*
Durrant, J., 742, 763, *776*
Duschl, R., 401, 406, 408, 409, 410, 414, *435, 436*, 453, 454, 462, *465, 466*, 508, 509, *530*, 695, *716*, 817, *829*, 833, 853, *875, 878*, 886, *907*, 965, 970, 971, 974, 985, 988, 989, 990, 994, *999, 1000*, 1154, 1155, *1176*
Dutton, W. H., 1070, *1098*
Duveen, J., 674, 687, *806*, 888, *909*
Dwyer, M. C., *960*
Dwyer, W., 385, *387*, 700, 701, *720*
Dyche, S., 1117, *1147*
Dyck, L., 203, *222*
Dzama, E. N. N., 203, *222*

E

Eagles, P., 705, *716*
Earl, R. D., 1075, *1098*
Earp, N. W., 1071, *1097*
Easley, J., 34, *52*
Ebert-May, D., *1177*
Eccles, J., 93, *101*, 148, *159*
Eddy, D., 969, *999*
Edelson, D. C., 407, 412, 413, *435, 438, 489, 490*, 673, 674, 675, *682*
Edens, K. M., 507, 514, 519, 526, *529*
Edgeworth, M., 394, *435*
Edgeworth, R. L., 394, *435*
Ediger, M., 1095, *1098*
Edmondson, K., 677, *682*, 983, *999*
Edmunds, J., *531*
Edwards, D., 44, *53*

Eeckhout, B., 704, *724*
Egan, K., 894, *903*
Egan, M. W., 287, 305, *312*
Egan, V., 1076, *1099*
Eggleston, J. F., 797, *805*
Eglen, J. R., *435*
Eichinger, D., 1213, *1250*
Eick, C. J., 64, *74*, 1077, *1098*
Eide, K. Y., 177, *193*
Eijkelhof, H. M. C., 734, *776*, 886, 888, 891, 892, 894, 896, 899, *903, 904*
Eisele, M. R., 296, *314*
Eisenhart, M., 172, *193*, 736, 755, 768, *776*, 888, *906*, 1238, *1250*
Eisner, E., 302, *311*, 402, *435*, 702, *716*, 813, *829*, 966, 982, *999*
Elby, A., 463, *466*, 833, *875*, 1152, 1157, 1159, *1176*
Eley, L., 992, 993, *999*
Ellenbogen, K. M., 126, 127, 128, 136, 143, 144, 154, *159*
Elliot, J., 1228, *1250*
Elliott, E. J., 253, *254*
Elliott, J., 691, 698, 702, 703, *713, 716*
Elliott, R., 1010, *1035*
Elliott, S., 704, *716*
Ellis, J., 82, *97*
Elmer, R., 377, 379, *388*
Elmesky, R., 329, 330, *342*
Elmore, R., 185, *193*
Elmore, R. F., 13, *28*, 897, 898, *904, 939*, 1206, *1250*
Elon, B., 662, 668, 669, 670, *684*
Elshout, J., 674, 682
Elson, R., 668, *683*
Ely, D., 945, *962*, 970, 981
Emery, R. E., 668, *682*
Emmons, K., 701, 703, *716*
Emory, A., *1102, 1258*
Enersen, D. L., 307, *311*
Engelhard, P., 616, 617, *626*
Enger, S. K., 981, *999*
Enochs, L., 353, 356, 363, 364, *367, 369*, 1072, 1084, *1098, 1102*, 1121, 1131, *1138, 1140*
Entwistle, N. J., 230, *254*
Enyeart, M., 308, *314*
Epps, S., 296, *312*
Erb, T. O., 540, *556*
Erduran, S., 403, *439*, 759, 774, *780*
Erickson, F., 61, 66, *71, 73*, 955, *960*, 1236, 1239, *1250*
Erickson, G., 32, *53*, 404, *435*, 982, 993, *999*, 1043, 1059, *1061, 1062*, 1116, 1117, *1143*, 1209, 1214, *1250, 1251*
Ericsonn, K. A., 305, *312*
Ermine, W. J., 217, *223*
Ernest, P., 1068, *1099*
Escalada, L. T., 85, *97*
Espinoza, C., *437*
Estrin, E. T., 217, *225*
Eubanks, C., 1130, *1143*

Evans, C., 1242, *1250*
Evans, G., 762, 763, *776, 777*
Evans, J. A., 995, *997*
Evans, R., 844, *874*
Evans, T., 1227, *1259*
Everitt, C. L., 668, *683*
Ewing, M., 701, *719*
Eybe, H., 638, 639, *651*
Eylon, B., 403, *435*

F

Fagel, L., 1221, *1258*
Fairbrother, B., 886, *907*, 976, 982, *999*
Fairbrother, R., 452, *465*, 799, *805, 806*
Fairclough, N., 444, 446, *465*
Fairman, J., 925, *938*, 1010, *1036*
Falcão, D., 138, *160*
Falk, J. H., 126, 127, 128, 129, *129*, 130, *130*, 133, 134, 136, *136*, 138, 140, 143, *143*, 144, 154, 156, *157, 159, 160, 161, 122, 136*
Fals-Borda, O., 1209, *1250*
Fan, X., 362, 363, *367*
Fara, P., 139, *160*
Farenga, S. J., 499, *529*
Farmer, W. A., 593, *596*
Farrell, J. J., 386, *387*
Farrell, M. A., 593, *596*
Fason, J., 705, *716*
Fassinger, R., 270, *284*
Fassoulopoulos, G., *779*
Fastow, M., 987, *1006*
Faughnan, J. G., 668, *683*
Fay, C. L., *1143*
Fayol, M., 639, *649*
Featherstone, D., 1047, *1061*, 1216, 1218, *1250*
Fecho, B., *1250*
Feher, E., 136, 143, 154, *160, 164*, 1116, *1138*
Fehn, B., 307, *312*
Feiman-Nemser, S., 1181, *1202*, 1213, *1250*
Feldhusen, J., 309, *313*
Feldman, A., 1087, *1099*, 1126, *1138*, 1210, 1224, 1227, 1238, 1241, *1250*
Feldman, N. G., 135, *163*
Fellows, N., 512, 514, 520, 521, *529*
Feltham, N. F., 972, *999*
Fennema, E., 1206, *1248*
Fensham, P. J., 50, *53*, 232, *254*, 287, *312*, 374, *387*, 601, 602, *626*, 633, 637, *650, 683*, 699, *716*, 732, 735, 738, 745, 771, *777*, 881, 883, 884, 886, 890, 891, 892, 895, 898, 901, *904, 906, 938*, 1071, *1103*, 1173, *1176*
Fenster, M. J., *938*
Fenstermacher, G. D., 357, *367*, 1105, 1106, 1109, *1138*
Ferguson, D. L., 296, *312*
Ferguson, P., 296, *312*
Fernandez, C., 1210, 1213, *1250*

Fernández-Balboa, J.-M., 1123, 1134, *1138*
Ferreira, M., 85, *97*
Ferry, B., 1110, *1138*
Fetherstonhaugh, A., 662, 676, *683*
Fetterman, D. M., 945, 954, *960*
Fetters, M. K., 505, *529*
Feuer, M. J., 1206, *1251*
Feurzeig, W., 4, *28*
Feyerabend, D., 835, *875*
Field, E. M., 783, *805*
Field, J., *1251*
Field, T., 262, *280*
Fien, J., 692, 694, 695, 697, 698, 700, 703, 704, 707,
    713, 715, 716
Fierros, E. G., *255*
Fifield, S., 259, 276, *280*
Filer, A., 692, 722, 994, *1000*
Finely, F., 947, *960*
Fink, L. C., *1251*
Finkel, E., 172, *193*, 736, 755, *776*
Finley, F., 591, *596, 1138*
Finnegan, B., *1102, 1258*
Finson, K. D., 82, *97*, 353, 363, *366, 367*
Finster, D. C., 642, *650*
Firbas, F., *596*
Firestone, W. A., 925, *938*, 1010, *1036*
Fisch, S. M., 151, *160*
Fischer, H. E., 604, 606, 609, *628*
Fischer, J., 1208, *1251*
Fischer-Mueller, J., 1129, *1138*
Fischler, H., 620, 621, *626*
Fish, L., 505, *529*
Fishbein, M., 78, 80, 84, *96*, 1070, 1073, *1096, 1099*
Fisher, B., 705, *716*
Fisher, D., 107, 115, *119, 120*, 324, *343*, 399, *436*
Fisher, D. L., 84, *102*, 104, 105, 106, 107, 108, 109, 110,
    111, 112, 113, 114, 115, 116, 117, *120, 121, 122, 123,*
    987, *1002*
Fisher, K., 983, 988, *1000*
Fisher, K. M., 65, *71*
Fisher, M. K., 594, *596*
Fisher, N., 142, *157*
Fishman, B. J., 183, 186, *192, 193*, 1188, 1189, 1193,
    1195, 1197, 1198, 1199, 1200, *1202*
Fistiam, F. A., 788, *805*
Fitzpatrick, B., 1056, *1061*
Fitzpatrick, F. L., 351, *368*, 735, *777*
Fitzpatrick, J. L., 945, 946, *960*
Flack, J., 1227, *1255*
Fleer, M., 524, 527, *529*, 1049, 1050, *1061*, 1228, *1247*
Fleming, M. I., *938*
Fleming, R. W., 865, *873*
Fletcher, J. M., 288, *315*
Flick, L. B., 499, 510, *527, 529*, 1128, *1135, 1138*
Flockton, L., 981, *998*
Floden, R. E., 926, 932, 935, *939, 940*
Flores, F., 1128, *1138*

Florio, S., 66, *73*
Fogliani, C., *1040*
Foley, D. E., 187, *194*
Follen, S., 707, *714*
Foorman, E. M., 288, *315*
Forbes, J., 139, *164*
Fordyce, D., *683*
Forgasz, H., 275, 276, *280*
Forman, E. A., 384, *387*
Forster, P., 474, *489*
Fort, D. C., 307, *312*
Fortner, R. W., *683, 685*
Fortner, W. R., 660, *685*
Foucault, M., 20, *28*, 895, *904*
Foulds, K., 982, *1000*
Fourez, G., 881, 897, *904*
Fournier, J. F., 355, *367*
Fradd, S. H., 61, 72, 178, 180, 188, *193, 194*, 331, 332,
    342, 455, *467*, 661
Francek, M. A., 1114, *1135*
Frances, L., 990, *1002*
Francis, L. J., 80, 81, *97*, 152, *160*
Francis, R., 1128, *1135*
Francis, R. W., 544, 545, *556*
Francisco, J. S., 969, *1000*
Franke, M. L., *938*
Franklin, S., 995, *1003*
Franklin, U., 1151, *1176*
Franz, J. R., 851, *875*
Fraser, B. J., 84, *97*, 103, 104, 105, 106, 107, 108, 109,
    110, *110*, 111, 112, 113, 114, 115, 116, 117, 118, *119,*
    120, 121, 122, 123, 124, 263, *283*, 384, *387*, 399, 418,
    436, 507, *529*, 599, *628*, 863, *875*, 982, *999*, 1024,
    1040, 1072, 1106, 1109, *1138, 1144*, 1205, *1251*, x, *xiv*
Frechette, P., 1242, *1250*
Frechtling, J., *960*
Frederick, W. A., 883, 885, 886, *904*
Frederik, I., 1117, 1127, *1139*
Frederiksen, J., 4, *30*, 484, 488, *491*, 507, *533*, 973, *1000*
Fredricks, J., 15, *29*, 452, *467*, 684
Freedman, M., 85, *97*, 273, *280*, 399, *436*
Freeman, D., *940*
Freeman, H. E., 945, *962*
Freeman, T. B., 1045, *1061*
Freiberg, H. J., 87, *100*
Freidman, T. L., 472, *489*
Freire, A. M., 1125, 1126, *1139*
Freire, P., 25, *28*
Freitag, P. K., 1083, *1101*, 1125, *1143*
Fretz, E., 474, *490*
Freudenrich, C. C., 155, *160*
Frey, K., 733, *777*
Freyberg, P., 34, *54*, 230, 232, *256*, 404, *439*, 522, *534*
Freyburg, P., 1045, *1063*
Fridler, Y., *440*
Friedel, A. W., 380, *388*
Friedl, A. E., 523, *529*

Friedler, Y., 412, *436*, 591, *596*
Friedman, A. J., 139, *160*
Friedman, B., 701, *719*
Friedman, W., 666, *683*
Friedrichsen, P., 416, *441*, 453, 454, 463, *469*, 1124, 1126, *1139*
Friend, H., 546, *556*
Friend, M., 292, 301, *312*
Frodeman, R. L., 666, *683*
Fry, R., 259, 260, *280*
Fuß, S., 607, *627*
Fuchs, D., 293, 296, 300, 301, *312*
Fuchs, L. S., 206, 293, 300, 301, *312*
Fueyo, V., 1227, *1251*
Fuhrman, S. H., 922, 926, *939, 940*
Fulbright, R. K., *315*
Fullan, M., 817, 827, *829*, 925, 926, *939*
Fuller, F. F., 573, 576, *596*, 1043, *1061*
Fuller, S., 882, *904*
Fullerton, B. J., 918, *939*
Furio, C., 1129, *1139*
Furnham, A., 887, *904*
Fusco, D., 186, *193*, 327, 335, *342*, 971, 981, 982, 985, 991, 993, 994, *1000*

G

Gabel, D. L., 85, 98, 373, 380, *388*, 493, *529*, 633, 647, *650*, 851, *875*, 1071, *1099, 1139*, 1205, I1251, x, *xiv*
Gabel, L. L., 737, *777*
Gagne, R. M., 565, *596*
Gaither, V. P., *1251*
Galco, J., 130, 143, *159*
Gale, C. W., 737, 741, *779*
Gale, K., 987, *1000*
Galili, I., 605, *626*, 1116, *1136*
Gall, J. P., 430, *436*
Gall, M. D., 430, *436*
Gallagher, J. J., 263, *280*, 306, *312*, 733, *777*, 883, 884, 886, 899, *904*, 1079, *1099*, 1121, 1126, 1128, *1139*
Gallagher, J. L., 970, *1006*
Gallagher, T. H., 1130, *1143*
Gallard, A. J., 377, *390*
Gallas, K., 448, 462, *466*, 524, *529*, 1210, 1228, *1251*
Gallegos, L., 1128, *1138*
Gallgher, J. T., 571, *596*
Gallimore, R., 1231, 1245, *1252*
Galton, M. J., *805*
Gamas, W. S., 459, *466*, 1153, *1177*
Gambro, J., 700, *716*
Gammon, B., 130, 138, *160*
Gamoran, A., 13, *28*, 183, 184, *193*
Ganiel, U., 678, *684*
Gapinski, R., *1251*
Garden, R. A., 764, *779*
Gardner, C., 1086, *1097*
Gardner, C. M., 176, *192*

Gardner, F., Jr., 64, *74*
Gardner, H., 138, *160*, 538, 550, *556*, 982, *1006*
Gardner, P., 990, *1005*
Gardner, P. L., 886, 893, *904*
Gardner, R., 456, 457, 462, *467*
Garet, M., 951, *960*, 1194, *1202*, 1206, *1251*
Garibaldi, A. M., 915, 916, *941*
Garner, M. S., 151, *160*
Garner, R., *89, 98*
Garnett, P., 404, *440*, 641, 644, *650, 651*
Garnett, R., 146, *160*
Garnier, H., *1257*
Garrison, J. W., 736, 749, *777*
Garrison, L., 180, *192*, 346, *366*
Gartner, A., 292, 293, 296, 297, 301, 303, *312, 313*
Garvey, C., 132, *160*
Gascoigne, T., 147, *160*
Gaskell, J., 259, 260, 261, 278, *280, 282*
Gaskell, J. P., 881, 884, 886, 889, 890, 899, *904, 905*
Gaskell, P. J., 895, 897, 899, 900, *902, 908*
Gaskins, S., 143, *164*
Gasper, E., 507, 509, 526, *533*, 981, *1005*
Gates, S., 504, *532*, 1002, *1101*, 1130, *1145*
Gauld, C., 989, 992, *1000*
Gavin, J., 1232, *1251*
Gay, G., 182, *193*
Gay, J., 14, *28*
Gayford, C., 703, *717*, 1115, *1139*
Gayler, K., *1040*
Geddis, A. N., 64, *71*, 1048, 1049, 1050, *1061*, 1121, 1123, 1126, 1128, 1129, 1130, *1139*
Gee, J., 15, *28*, 61, *71*, 445, 460, 463, *466*, 750, *777*
Gee, J. P., 14, *28*, 444, 461, *466*, 887, *905*
Geelan, D. R., 1053, *1061*
Gennaro, E. O., 843, *875*
Genova, P., 132, *166*
Genovese, C., 1228, *1251*
George, J., 212, *223*
George, J. M., 207, 209, 216, *223*
George, M., 341, *342*, 855, *873*
George, M. D., 1210, *1246*
George, P. S., 537, 549, *556*
George, R., 83, *98*
Georghiades, P., 511, *530*
Gerber, R., 703, *717*
German, P. J., 586, *596*
Germann, P. J., 674, *683*
Gertzog, W. A., 7, *29*, 35, 36, 38, 48, *55*, 60, 73, 659, *686*, 1048, *1064*, 1154, *1178*, 1212, *1256*
Gess-Newsome, J., 1046, *1062*, 1077, *1099, 1102*, 1108, 1109, 1115, 1116, 1119, 1120, *1139, 1142*
Getzels, J. W., 104, *121*
Ghere, G., 959, *961*
Ghose, A. M., 347, 348, *367*
Gialamas, V., 662, 676, *681*
Gibson, D., 385, *388*
Gibson, G., 703, *717*
Gibson, H. L., *98*

Gibson, H. M., 152, *160*
Gibson, J., 524, 525, *530*
Gibson, J. J., *683*
Giddings, G. J., 107, *120*, 399, 414, 417, *436, 440*
Giddings, J., 982, *999*
Giddings, J. G., 415, *436*
Giere, R. N., 835, *875*
Gilbert, A., 179, 189, *193*, 354, 365, *368*
Gilbert, J., 258, 259, 272, *280*, 377, 379, *388, 683*, 985,
    994, *996, 1003*, 1112, 1131, *1141*, 1183, 1184, 1185,
    1189, 1199, *1202*
Gilbert, J. K., 34, *53*, 130, 134, 137, 138, *138, 160, 166,
    379, 388*, 638, 643, 645, 646, 647, *650*, 1082, *1100*
Gilbert, S. W., 837, *875*
Giles, N. D., 513, *532*
Gill, P., 976, *999*
Gillespie, R. J., 640, *650*
Gillett, G., 34, *53*
Gillilan, S., 152, *160*
Gilmer, P. J., 1054, *1063*, 1220, 1228, *1254*
Gilmore, A., 967, 969, 981, *1000*
Gimmett, P. P., *1139*
Ginns, I. S., 128, 129, 134, 141, 142, *157*, 498, 501, 503,
    511, 521, *532, 534*, 1110, 1113, 1116, 1117, *1139*
Ginorio, A., 275, *280*
Gipps, C., 965, 966, 970, 972, 973, 977, 979, 988, 989,
    991, 992, 994, 995, *1000*
Girwidz, R., 605, *627*
Gitari, W., 139, *164*
Gitomer, D. H., 396, 414, *435, 436*, 508, 509, *530*,
    965, 970, 971, 974, 985, 988, 989, 990, 994,
    999, 1000
Glaser, R., 507, 509, 518, *528, 532*, 1012, *1035, 1038*
Gläser-Zikuda, M., 607, *627*
Glaserfeld, E. von, *683*
Glasgow, J., 212, *223*
Glasgow, K. A., 546, *555*
Glass, G. V., 459, *466, 938*, 1153, *1177*
Glass, H. B., 351, *368*
Glassman, F., 579, *598*
Glazar, S. A., 633, *650*
Glazer, S., 705, *717*
Glenn, E. R., 350, *368*
Glenn, J. I., 982, *1006*
Glick, J. A., 14, *28*
Glover, P., 969, *1000*
Glynn, S., 458, 459, *466*
Glynn, S. M., 87, 88, 90, *98, 99*, 379, 380, 381, *388*,
    513, *530*
Glynn, T., 213, 218, *222*
Gobert, J., 662, *683*
Gobert, J. D., 474, 484, *489*, 514, *530*
Goertz, M. E., 914, 926, 927, 928, 929, 931, 932, 935,
    939, 941
Goes in Center, J., 208, 209, *223*
Goh, N. K., 990, *1005*
Goh, S. C., 104, 105, 106, 110, 111, 113, 116, 118,
    120, 121

Golby, M., 1116, *1139*
Goldberg, A. L., *255*
Goldberg, F., 608, 609, 612, *626, 628*, 1116, *1136*
Goldberg, G. L., 1010, *1036*
Goldberg, H., 546, *556*
Golden, J., 889, *906*
Goldman, S. R., 149, *160*, 377, *391*, 955, *962*
Goldstein, B. A., 293, *316*
Golman, M. E., 1072, *1099*
Golomb, K., 295, *312*
Gomes, M. de F. C., 48, *53*
Gomez, L., 327, 333, 335, 340, *341*, 474, 485, *490*
Gomez, L. M., 186, *192, 438*
Gonzales, P., *1040*
Gonzalez, E. J., 236, *254, 255*, 262, *279*, 604, *625, 1035,
    1037, 1038*
Gonzalez, J., *1251*
Gonzalo, I., *1039*
Good, R., 506, *532*, 541, 552, 553, 554, *558*
Good, R. G., 662, 665, *685*, 871, *875*, 1115, *1140*
Good, S. C., 668, *683*
Good, T. L., 93, *98*
Goodlad, J. I., 402, *436*, 912, *939*
Goodnough, K., 1206, 1219, 1223, 1235, *1251*
Goodrum, D., 496, 497, *530*, 770, *777, 779*,
    1055, *1062*
Goodwin, A., 648, *649*, 1122, *1138*
Goodwin, D., 704, *717*
Goodwin, J., 1010, *1040*
Goodwin, L., 295, *313*
Gordin, D. N., 407, *435*, 673, 675, *682*
Gordon, A., 384, *387*
Gore, M. M., 753, *780*, 894, *909*
Gorin, C., 1114, *1139*
Gorleski, J., 1221, *1258*
Gorsky, P., 1117, *1148*
Goshorn, K., 887, *905*
Gosling, D. C., 135, *163*
Goto, M., 247, *254*
Gott, R., 519, *530*, 805, 887, 890, *903, 910*, 982, *1000*
Gottelmann-Duret, G., 243, *254*
Gottfried, J. L., 141, *160*
Gough, A., 263, 264, 278, *281*, 703, 705, *717*
Gough, N., 703, 705, 706, 709, 711, *717*
Gough, S., 696, 707, *717, 724*
Gould, S. J., 656, *683*
Gowin, D. B., 659, *683*, 1154, 1156, *1178*
Gräber, W., 733, *777*, 1123, *1142*
Grace, T., 1049, 1050, *1061*
Graczyk, S. L., 668, *683*
Graeber, W., 633, *652*
Graham, E., *1251*
Graham, T., 59, *73*
Graham, W. F., 129, *161*
Granville, M., 84, *101*
Graves, J., 140, *158*
Gray, B., 887, *906*
Gray, B. V., 521, *530*

Gray, D., 499, *533*
Gray, D. E., 291, *312*
Grayson, D., 613, *626*
Greaves, E., 705, *717*
Green, G., 80, 81, 82, *96*
Green, J., 445, 451, 452, 462, *466, 467*
Green, J. L., 48, *53*
Greenall, A., 691, 695, *717*
Greenall-Gough, A., 695, 707, *717*
Greenberg, J. B., 186, *196*
Greenbowe, T., 425, *434, 439*
Greene, E. D., Jr., 1115, *1139*
Greene, J. C., 129, *161*, 946, 956, *960*
Greene, L. C., 540, 545, *556*
Greenfield, T. A., 176, *193*
Greeno, J., 87, *98, 683*
Greenwood, A. M., 1124, *1139*
Greer, J. E., 80, 81, *97*
Gregory, K. D., 237, 238, 239, *255, 1037*
Gregory, S., 270, *280*
Gribble, J., 1054, *1062*
Griffard, P., 337, *342*
Griffard, P. B., 985, *1000*
Griffin, G., 818, *830*
Griffin, J., 130, 133, 141, 142, 143, *161, 161* 141, *162*
Griffin, P., 972, *1003*
Griffiths, A. K., 646, *650*
Grifiths, G., 201, 202, *221*
Grigg, W. S., 175, 181, 190, *195*
Grigorenko, E. L., 986, *1000*
Grimberg, I. B., 425, *436*
Grimm, V., 474, *489*
Grimmett, P. P., 1043, *1062*, 1108, 1209, 1214, *1251*
Groarke, J., 818, *829*
Grobman, H., 413, *436*
Groisman, A., 61, *71*
Grolnick, W. S., 95, *100*
Gropengießer, H., 602, *626*
Grossman, P. L., 817, *829*, 1106, 1107, 1108, 1120, 1121, 1124, *1140*
Groves, F. H., 1113, *1140*
Groves, S., 707, *717*
Gruber, H. E., 845, *875*
Gruenberg, B. C., 351, *368*
Grundy, S., 1207, *1252*
Guarina, J., 695, *714*
Guba, E., 946, 954, 955, *960, 961*, 1239, *1254*
Gudovitch, Y., 668, 670, *683*
Guenter, C. E., 547, *557*
Guerra, M. R., 451, *466*
Guesne, E., 34, *52*, 656, 659, *682*, 1045, *1061*
Guice, S., 967, *1001*
Guilbert, S., 1121, *1140*
Guillaume, A. M., 1126, *1140*
Guisasola, J., 1129, *1139*
Gullickson, A., 957, *960*
Gunstone, R. F., 34, *53*, 232, *254*, 374, *375, 387, 388, 391*, 400, 403, 405, 406, 422, 425, 427, *434, 436, 441,*

983, 986, *1006*, 1043, 1045, 1046, 1050, *1062*, 1111, 1123, *1135, 1143*, 1166, 1173, *1176*
Guo, Y., 84, *102*
Gurganus, S., 297, *312*
Gurney, B. F., 1126, *1140*
Guskey, T., 1086, *1099, 1202*
Gustafson, B., 1121, 1128, *1140*
Gustone, R. F., *1065*
Guthrie, J. T., 546, *556*
Gutierrez, K., 955, *960*
Gutiérrez, K. D., 174, *193*
Gutwill, J., 138, *157*
Guzdial, M., 481, 484, *489, 490*
Guzzetti, B. J., 459, 460, 463, *466*, 750, *777*, 1153, 1156, *1177*
Gwimbi, E., 1092, *1099*

H

Haak, W., 474, *489*
Haberman, M., 337, *342*
Hacker, R. G., 308, *312*
Hackling, M., 452, *465*, 496, 497, *530*, 644, *650*, 770, *777, 779*, 1055, *1062*
Hadi-Tabassum, S., 951, *960*
Haedzegeorgiou, Y., 288, *316*
Haefner, L. A., 1133, *1149*
Haertel, E., 110, *121*, 181, *194, 1001*
Haertel, G. D., 110, *121, 1038*
Hagen, E. R., 1227, *1249*
Haggerty, S. M., 841, *873*, 1121, 1126, *1135*
Haidar, A. H., 648, *650*, 1093, 1114, *1140*
Haigh, W., 547, *556*
Hailes, J., 80, *102*
Hain, P., 150, *158*
Hairdar, A., *1099*
Hake, R. R., 618, *626*
Hakuta, K., 180, 183, *192*
Haladyna, T. M., 90, *99*
Halim, L., 1131, *1140*
Hall, B., 707, *714, 1256*
Hall, G. E., 1071, *1099*
Hall, I., 1209, 1211, *1252*
Hall, S., 674, 687, *806*
Hall-Wallace, M., 663, *685*
Hallahan, D. P., 294, *314*
Hallak, J., 234, *254*
Haller, K., 609, *628, 629*
Halliday, M. A. K., 67, *71*, 377, *388*, 444, 458, 460, *466*
Halverson, R., 184, 185, *196*, 326, *343*, 499, 501, *533*
Hames, V., *908*
Hamilton, L., 930, *939*, 990, *1004*, 1013, *1037*
Hamilton, M., 1228, *1247*
Hamilton, M. L., 1057, *1062*, 1160, *1177*
Hamilton, R. J., *465*, 1154, 1155, *1176*
Hamlett, C. L., 300, *312*

Hamlyn, J., 61, *71*
Hamm, D., 89, *100*
Hammeken, P., 295, *312*
Hammelev, D., 609, *629*
Hammer, D., 463, *466*, 833, *875*
Hammond, L., 180, 186, *193, 195*, 220, *223*, 334, 335, *342*
Hammrich, P., 854, *875*
Hampson, B., 507, *533*
Han, J.-J., 967, *1000*
Hand, B., 58, 67, *72, 73, 74,* 377, *391,* 425, *434, 436, 437, 439,* 444, 458, 460, 461, 463, *466, 468, 469,* 750, 777, 859, *874,* 1122, *1140,* 1191, *1202*
Handelsman, J., 1152, *1177*
Haney, J., 1072, 1076, 1080, 1083, 1088, *1101*
Haney, J. J., 542, 549, *556, 1099, 1101*
Hannon, M., 800, *805*
Hanrahan, M., 461, *466*
Hansen, M. A., 1010, *1037*
Hansen, R. A., 88, *98*
Hanson, N. R., 657, *683*
Hanssen, C., 951, *960*
Happs, J. C., 662, 668, *681, 683*
Haras, K., 704, *726*
Haraway, D., 200, *223*
Hard, M. S., 573, *595*
Harder, R., *596*
Harding, J., 608, *626*
Harding, S., 20, *28,* 207, *223*
Hardman, M. L., 287, 305, *312*
Hardy, T., 524, *529*
Hargreaves, L., 507, *530*
Hargreaves, M., 818, *829*
Harlen, W., 496, 497, 498, 501, 504, 508, 516, 525, *530,* 765, 766, *777,* 794, *805,* 966, 967, 968, 969, 972, 974, 976, 977, 981, 982, 989, *1000, 1001,* 1048, *1062,* 1111, 1112, *1140*
Harmon, M., 1020, *1036*
Harms, N. C., 585, *596*
Harré, R., 34, *53*
Harrington, J., 150, *158*
Harris, A., *1037*
Harris, K., 694, *717*
Harris, R. A., 458, *466*
Harris, W. M., R., 850, 852, *878*
Harrison, A., 376, 380, *390,* 638, 639, 640, 643, 645, 646, *650,* 1079, *1104*
Harrison, A. G., 380, 381, *388,* 618, 619, 620, *626*
Harrison, C., 507, *528,* 970, 979, *997*
Harsch, G., 733, *777*
Hart, C., 400, *436,* 881, 886, 895, *905*
Hart, E. P., 897, *905*
Hart, J., 184, *193*
Hart, L. C., *556*
Hart, P., 689, 697, 698, 699, *700,* 701, 704, 705, 710, 717, *722, 723*
Hart, R., 704, 705, 707, *714, 717*
Hartley, P., 995, *1001*

Harty, H., 1121, *1140, 1141*
Harvey, F. A., 59, *71*
Harwell, S., 273, *281*
Harwood, W. S., 85, *98*
Hasan, O. E., 846, 849, 852, 864, *874*
Hasbach, C., *1257*
Hashweh, M. Z., 1045, *1062,* 1078, 1079, 1095, *1099,* 1106, 1108, 1110, 1116, 1118, 1119, 1128, 1130, *1140*
Haskins, S., 586, *596,* 674, *683*
Haslanger, S., 258, *281*
Hassan, F., 266, 267, *281*
Hattie, J., 104, *121,* 965, 966, 972, 973, 977, 978, 979, 981, 982, 990, *998, 1000, 1001*
Hatzikraniotis, E., *779*
Hatzinikita, V., 648, 649, 1122, *1138*
Häußler, P., 605, 608, *626, 627*
Haukoos, G. D., 848, 851, 852, 858, *875*
Hausafus, C. O., 186, *196*
Hauslein, P., 871, *875,* 1115, *1140*
Haussler, P., 85, *98*
Häussler, P., 888, 890, 891, 892, 893, 896, 899, *905*
Hawk, K., 214, *223*
Hawkey, K., 1076, *1099*
Hawkey, R., 150, *161*
Hawkins, D., 133, 138, *161*
Hawley, W. D., 922, *939*
Hay, K., 481, 483, 484, *489, 490*
Hayes, D., 1120, *1148,* 1157, *1177*
Hayes, M. T., 501, *530*
Hayton, M., 1228, 1231, *1252*
Hayward, G., 1044, *1062*
Hazan, A., 605, *626*
Hazelwood, C., 1212, *1252, 1257*
Hazen, R. M., 739, *777*
Heady, J. E., 979, *1001*
Heath, C., 1068, *1100*
Heath, R. W., 918, *939*
Heath, S. B., 19, *28,* 61, *71*
Heaton, R. M., 1210, 1211, *1252*
Heck, D. J., 396, *441,* 926, 928, 933, *939,* 1213, *1259*
Hedman, R., 1210, 1219, *1252*
Heikkinen, M. W., 177, *193*
Heimann, P., 603, *626*
Heimlich, J., 707, *718*
Hein, G. E., 126, 128, 131 135, 136, *161*
Hejaily, N., *1036*
Helgeson, S., 915, 921, *939, 940,* 947, *960,* 965, *999,* 1008, *1036*
Heller, P., 947, *960,* 1116, *1140*
Helms, J. V., 373, *387,* 622, *624,* 817, 818, *828, 829,* 886, 898, *902*
Hemara, W., 216, *223*
Henderson, D., 106, 107, *120,* 399, *436*
Henderson, J. Y., 203, 204, 205, 217, 220, *221*
Hendley, D., 81, *99*
Hendrickson, A., 83, *96*
Henig, J., 274, *281*

Hennesey, M. G., 36, *53*
Hennessy, S., 45, *53*, 374, 381, *388*, 886, *905*
Henwood, F., 259, *281*
Hepburn, G., 895, 900, *905*
Herbert, T., 307, *314*
Herlihy, C., 322, *343*
Herman, J. L., 1010, 1011, 1014, *1036*
Hermann, K., *1252*
Hermanson, K., 138, *159*
Herr, K., 1210, *1247*
Herrenkohl, L. R., 451, *466*
Herrick, J., 156, *157*
Herrmann, F., 617, 621, *626*
Herron, J., 404, *440*, 918, *939*
Herron, M. D., 674, *683*
Herscovitz, O., 412, *435*
Hershberger, S. L., 956, *961*
Hertz, B., 265, 266, *281*
Hertz-Lazarowitz, R., 383, *389*, 583, 594, *597*
Hestenes, D., 617, *626*
Heward, W. L., *312*
Hewitt, N., 275, *284*
Hewson, M. G., 61, *71*, 1124, 1212, *1252*
Hewson, M. G. A'B., 1124, 1125, *1140*
Hewson, P. W., 7, 29, 35, 36, 38, 48, *53*, *55*, 60, *73*, 185,
    193, 325, *342*, 500, 511, 516, 517, *528*, 530, 659, *686*,
    1045, 1048, *1062*, *1064*, 1077, 1083, *1101*, 1124, 1125,
    1140, *1141*, *1142*, *1143*, *1144*, 1154, 1155, 1167, *1177*,
    1178, 1185, *1202*, *1203*, 1206, 1212, 1213, 1215, *1252*,
    1254, *1256*
Heylings, D. J. A., 982, *1005*
Heywood, D., 513, 514, *530*, 1114, 1116, 1117, *1141*,
    1144, *1145*
Hick, T. L., 990, *1006*
Hickey, D. T., 994, *1001*
Hickey, R., 1048, 1049, *1064*
Hicks, W., Jr., 702, *718*
Hicok, S., *1252*
Hiebert, J., 1206, 1213, 1231, 1245, *1252*, *1258*
Higgins, R., 995, *1001*
Hildebrand, G. M., 377, *391*, 460, 461, *466*
Hilgers, T. L., 461, *465*
Hilke, D. D., 143, *161*
Hill, C., 1228, *1247*, *1251*
Hill, D., 1128, *1135*
Hill, D. L., ix, *xiv*
Hill, H. C., 1206, *1249*
Hill, H. G., 13, *28*
Hill, J., 214, *223*
Hill, M., 967, 970, 976, *1001*
Hill, S., 186, *195*
Hillcoat, J., 697, 698, 703, 705, 716, *718*
Hillen, J. A., 546, *555*
Hillis, S. R., 864, *875*
Hilton-Brown, B., 462, *466*
Hinchey, M., 983, 990, *1002*
Hind, A., 861, *876*, 908

Hines, J., 697, *718*
Hipkins, R., 199, 223, 832, *875*
Hirata, S., 105, 112, *121*
Hirsch, E. D., *777*
Hirsch, G., 703, 707, *719*
Hirvonen, P. E., 1129, *1141*
Hmelo, C. E., 406, *441*
Ho, R., 701, 704, *718*, *722*
Hoadley, C., 64, *71*, 484, 485, *489*
Hoban, G., 1046, 1056, 1058, *1062*
Hodder, A. P. W., 127, *161*
Hoddinott, J., 895, *907*
Hodgkinson, 1234, 1252
Hodson, D., 41, 44, *53*, 177, *193*, 219, 223, 374, 377,
    388, 397, 399, 400, 401, 402, *436*, 609, *626*, 852, 853,
    875, 883, 899, *902*, *905*, *908*, 1108, 1122, *1136*, 1155,
    1156, 1157, *1177*
Hodson, J., 41, 44, *53*, 377, *388*
Hoekwater, E., *1257*
Hofer, B. K., 1095, *1099*
Hoffman, L., 85, *98*
Hoffman, N., 707, *710*
Hoffmann, L., 608, *626*, 888, 890, 891, 892, 893, 896,
    899, *905*
Hoffstein, A., 580, 581, 585, *598*
Hofman, H. M., 510, 515, *528*
Hofstein, A., 136, *161*, 374, *388*, 395, 397, 398, 399,
    400, 401, 403, 407, 411, 413, 415, 417, 420, *434*, *436*,
    437, *438*, 672, *685*, 1129, *1141*
Hofstetter, C., *1035*
Hogan, K., 61, 63, 64, 67, *71*, 332, *342*, 451, 462, *466*
Hogg, K., 622, *629*
Holden, C., 268, *281*
Holder, C., 786, *805*
Holland, C., 408, *439*
Holland, D. C., 187, *194*
Holland, J. D., 450, 451, *464*, 522, *527*
Holliday, W. G., 457, 458, 459, *469*
Hollon, R., 1124, 1212, *1252*
Hollon, R. E., *1141*
Hollowood, T., 296, *312*
Holman, J., 643, *649*, 1084, *1103*
Holroyd, C., 496, 504, *530*, 1111, *1140*
Holroyd, G., 1048, *1062*
Holthuis, N. I., 750, 752, *776*
Hombo, C. M., 175, *192*
Honda, M., 844, *874*
Hope, J., 1111, *1141*
Hopkins, C., 691, *721*
Hopkins, K., 545, *558*
Hopmann, S., 600, 601, *629*
Hoppe, M., 932, *940*
Horgan, J., ix, *xiv*
Horn, J., 356, 358, 359, 360, 361, *368*
Horn, J. G., 346, 352, 354, 357, 365, *368*
Horn, S. P., 954, *962*
Horner, J., *878*

Hornig, L. E., *435*
Horwood, R. H., 376, *388*
Houang, R. T., 5, *29, 1039*
Hough, D. L., 551, *558*
Hounshell, P., 970, *1005*, 1071, *1103*, 1120, *1146*
Hourcade, J., 294, *311*
House, E. R., 954, *961*
Houseal, A., 496, 505, *531*
Houston, W., 1043, *1061*
Hovey, L. M., 1072, *1099*
Hoving, T., 1073, 1081, 1089, *1104*
Hoving, T. J., 182, *197*, 363, *369*
Howard, C., 506, *528*
Howe, A., 83, 84, *98*, 272, 273, *281*
Howe, A. C., 41, *53*, 59, *71*, 377, *388*
Howe, K., 1238, *1250*
Howe, K. R., 954, *961*
Howe, R., 842, 843, *878*
Howes, E., 1210, 1228, *1252*
Howey, K., 1213, *1252*
Hoy, W., 1071, 1085, *1099, 1104*
Hoyle, C., 237, 238, 239, *255*
Hoyle, R. H., 90, 91, *99*, 430, *437*
Hoz, R., 1115, *1141*
Hsi, S., 4, *29*, 485, *489*, 664, *684*
Hu, J., *1104*
Huang, T.-C. I., 108, 109, 115, *119*
Huber, R. A., 515, 523, *530*
Huberman, A. M., *961*
Huberman, M., 945, *962*, 1211, 1227, 1234, 1237, 1238, 1240, *1252*
Hucke, L., 609, *628*
Huckle, J., 691, 692, 694, 707, *718*
Hudicourt-Barnes, J., 179, 188, *197*, 329, *343*, 496, *534*
Hudson, A., *101*
Hudson, L., 1024, *1036*
Huether, C. A., 1129, *1144*
Huff, K. L., 1013, *1036*
Huffman, D., 181, *194*, 275, *282*, 810, *829*, 931, 933, *939*, 951, 956, *961*, 990, *1002*, 1008, *1040*, 1197, 1199, *1202*
Hug, B., *437*
Hug, W., 704, *718*
Hughes, E. F., 1071, *1100*
Hughes, G., 444, 457, 462, *466*
Hughs, M. R., 784, *805*
Huibregtse, I., 1125, 1126, *1141*
Huitt, W., 228, 229, *254*
Hukins, A., 863, *875*
Hula, R., 274, *281*
Hume, J. D., 668, *684*
Hungerford, H., 695, 695, 697, 701, *718, 723, 725*, 863, *875*
Hunn, D., 647, *650, 1139*
Hunt, A., 729, 743, 746, *777*, 891, *905*
Hunt, E., 974, *1001*
Hunt, J., 503, 505, *530*

Huntley, B., 215, *221*
Huntley, M. A., 544, 548, 549, 551, *556, 559*
Huntsberger, J. P., 1071, *1097*
Huppert, J., 583, *596*
Hurd, P., 693, 694, 711, *718*
Hurd, P. D., 234, 235, *255*, 538, *556*, 730, 736, *777*, 853, 875, 881, 882, 883, 885, 886, 898, *905*
Hurley, M. M., 505, 506, *530*, 539, 541, 542, 544, 545, 546, 547, 553, *556*
Husén, T., 733, *777*
Huston, A. C., 151, *167*
Huston, P. H., 1125, *1141*
Hutchinson, J. S., 987, *1006*
Hutchinson, N. L., 889, *902*
Hutchison, D., 692, *718*
Hutt, C., 132, 133, *161*
Hwang, E., 952, *961*
Hyle, A., 701, *719*

I

Idol-Maestas, L., 296, *312*
Ilan, M., 247, *255*
Ingersoll, R., 323, *342*
Inhelder, B., 33, *55*
Ioannides, C., 37, *56*, 512, 515, *534*
Iozzi, L., 701, *718*
Iran-Nejad, A., 1170, *1177*
Irvine, J. J., 216, *223*
Irwin, A. R., 884, 888, 891, *905*
Irwin, O. E., 1228, *1252*
Irwin, S., *940*
Irzik, G., 206, *223*
Isaac, S., 430, *437*
Iser, W., *960*
Ivy, T., 701, *718*
Iwasyk, M., 508, 516, 524, 525, *530, 534*, 1226, 1231, *1252, 1259*

J

Jaccard, J., 1068, 1073, *1100*
Jackman, L. E., 385, 386, *388*
Jacknicke, K., 204, *221*
Jackson, D., 75, 79, *101*
Jackson, D. F., 1133, *1138*
Jackson, E., 693, *720*
Jackson, P. W., 912, 913, 914, 922, *939*
Jackson, R., 150, *165*
Jackson, S. A., 299, *312*
Jackson, T., 1209, *1256*
Jacobowitz, R., 970, *1006*
Jacobs, H. H., 543, 544, 552, *556*
Jacobson, L., 92, *100*
Jacobson, W., 1238, *1252*

Jacobson, W. J., 1017, *1037*
Jaeger, R., 965, 966, 972, 977, 979, 982, *1001*
Jakwerth, P. M., 1018, *1039*
Jallad, B., 297, *316*
James, H., 1071, *1100*
James, K., 210, 220, *223*
James, M., 966, 968, 969, 972, 973, 974, 976, 977, 989, *1000, 1001*
James, M. C., 857, *878*
James, P., 705, *719*
James, S., 140, *157*
Jamison, E. D., 141, *161*
Janas, M., 297, *312*
Jane, B., *530*, 707, *717*
Jansen, J., 1130, *1143*
Jantzi, D., 295, *313*
Jarvis, T., 80, 81, *100*, 507, *530*
Jarwan, F. E., 309, *313*
Jasien, P. G., 1117, *1141*
Jaus, H. H., 1071, *1100*
Jaworski, A., 444, *466*
Jaworski, B., *1001*
Jay, E., 844, *874*
Jayaratne, T. E., 85, *98*
Jeffers, L., 1227, *1258*
Jeffryes, C., *366*
Jegede, O., 178, *192*, 206, 210, 212, 213, 215, 216, 217, 220, *223*
Jeltsch, F., 474, *489*
Jena, S. B. P., *1141*
Jeness, M., 951, *959*
Jenkins, E., 153, *162*, 601, *626*, 695, *719*, 730, 738, 744, 756, 757, 759, 772, *778*, 886, 887, 894, *905, 906*
Jenkins, E. W., 734, 757, *777, 779*, 795, 799, 800, *805*, 966, 967, *999*
Jenkins, L. B., 1024, *1038*
Jensen, B., 694, 700, 707, *719*
Jensen, J. H., 350, *368*
Jensen, K., 827, *829*
Jensen, M., 857, *878*
Jeong, I., *961*
Jesson, J., 219, *226*, 1228, *1252*
Jewitt, C., 46, 47, 50, *53, 55*
Jianxiang, Y., 270, *281*
Jickling, B., 691, 694, 707, *719*
Jimenez, S., *1146*
Jimenez-Aleixandre, M. P., 453, 454, *466*
Jiminez, J. M. S., 647, *651*
Jinks, S., *1252*
Jipson, J. L., 130, 143, *159*
Jita, L., 184, 185, *196*, 326, *343*, 499, 501, *533*
Joanos, L. G., *1252*
Jobling, W. M., *530*
Johanna, J., 1055, *1062*
Johnson, B., 308, *313*
Johnson, D. T., 307, *311*
Johnson, D. W., 383, *388*, 407, *437*

Johnson, G., 5, *29*, 185, *193*
Johnson, J., *143, 158*
Johnson, J. K., 664, *686*
Johnson, L. J., 294, 299, 301, *313, 314*
Johnson, P., 633, 637, *650*
Johnson, P. G., 351, *368*, 735, *777*
Johnson, R. B., xiii, *xiv*
Johnson, R. E., 88, *97*
Johnson, R. L., 850, *875*
Johnson, R. T., 383, *388*, 398, 407, *437*
Johnson, S., 1024, *1037*, 1092, *1103*
Johnson, S. L., 499, 500, *530*
Johnson, T. M., 1071, *1102*
Johnson, V., 1209, *1247*
Johnson-Laird, P. N., 837, *875*
Johnson-Laird, P. N., 377, *388*
Johnston, C. C., 182, *192*
Johnston, D., 133, *161*
Johnston, D. J., 128, 133, *164, 165*
Johnston, K., 1126, *1141*
Johnston, P., 967, *1001*
Johnstone, A. H., 382, *388*, 406, 422, *437*, 591, *596*, 631, *650*
Jones, A., 967, 972, 976, 978, 979, *996, 997, 1001, 1003*
Jones, A. T., 799, *805, 806*
Jones, B., 521, *533*
Jones, C., 1084, *1100*
Jones, C. J., 303, *313*
Jones, D. R., 1121, *1141*
Jones, E. E., 76, *98*
Jones, G., 508, 512, 522, *529*
Jones, H. L., 1130, *1141*
Jones, K. M., 842, 852, *875*
Jones, L., 972, 978, *1037*
Jones, L. L., 1046, *1061, 1137*
Jones, L. S., 307, *313*
Jones, M., 898, *910*
Jones, M. C., 134, 138, *160*
Jones, M. E., 800, *805*
Jones, M. G., 83, 84, 91, *98, 99*, 272, 273, *281*, 509, 522, *529, 531*, 1082, *1100*, 1110, 1116, 1117, 1127, *1141*
Jones, P., 1071, *1100*
Jones, P. L., 1121, *1141*
Jones, R., 199, *223*
Jones, S., 152, *163*
Jones, T., 479, 488, *490, 651*
Joo, Y. J., 92, *98*
Jordan, B., 62, *71*
Jordan, L., 296, *314*
Jordan, W., 274, *280*
Jordan-Bychkov, T. G., 345, *368*
Jorde, D., *1039*
Jorgenson, O., 189, *193*
Joseph, C. H., 1228, *1253*
Joseph, R., 322, 324, *343*
Joshua, S., 612, *628*
Jovanovic, J., 85, *98*, 181, *194*, 273, 278, 279, *281, 1001*

Joyce, B. A., 499, *529*
Jung, W., 612, 616, 617, *626, 628*
Jungwirth, E., 572, 576, 579, *598*, 843, *875*, 1115, 1129, *1138, 1141, 1148*
Jurd, E., 83, *98*
Jurin, R., 705, *719*
Jussim, L., 93, *101*
Justi, R., 379, *388*, 638, 643, 645, 646, 647, *650*, 1082, *1100*, 1112, 1131, *1141*

K

Kaberman, Z., 412, *435*
Kaestle, C. F., 600, *626*
Kagan, D., 1082, *1100*, 1155
Kagan, D. M., *1177*
Kaganoff, T., 1010, *1040*
Kahl, S. R., *938*
Kahle, J. B., 183, 185, *193*, 262, 263, 264, 265, 271, 272, 273, 274, 277, 278, *281*, 325, 326, *342, 343*, 456, *466*, 930, 931, 932, *939*, 1196, 1197, *1202*
Kahn, H., 302, *311*
Kahn, P., 701, *719*
Kali, Y., 662, 663, 664, 668, 669, 670, 672, 674, 675, 678, *684, 685*
Kallerud, E., *780*
Kallery, M., *779*
Kam, R., 337, *343*
Kam Wah, L. L., *1143*
Kamen, M., 508, 509, *531*, 993, *1001*, 1132, *1141*
Kane, M., 989, *998*
Kane, R., 1067, 1069, *1100*
Kang, N. H., 858, *876*
Kang, S., 837, *876*
Kannari, Z., 403, 410, *437*
Kanner, B., *317*
Kaplan, A., 90, *99*
Kapteijn, M., 896, *904*
Kapulnick, E., 678, *684*
Kapune, T., 733, *777*
Kaput, J., *938*
Karantonis, A., 5, *29*, 185, *193*
Kardash, C. M., 92, *98*
Kariotoglou, P., 733, *779*
Karns, K., 300, *312*
Karplus, R., 384, *388*, 404, *437*, 523, *531*
Karrqvist, C., 612, *628*
Karsenty, G., *389*, 407, *437*
Karweit, N. L., *939, 940*
Kaskinen-Chapman, A., 296, *313*
Kasper, M., 704, *719*
Kass, H., 853, *876*, 1124, 1125, 1126, *1142*
Kattmann, U., 602, *626*
Katz, P., 148, *161*
Kauchak, D. P., 1071, *1100*
Kaufman, D., 1081, *1101*

Kaufman, J., 701, *719*
Kawagley, A. O., 204, 205, 209, 210, 211, 214, 216, *224*
Kawakami, K., 94, *97*
Kawanaka, T., *1040, 1257*
Kawasaki, K., 218, *224*
Kay, T., *368*
Kayalvizhi, G., 508, 524, *529*
Kearney, M. D., 376, *388*
Kearsey, J., 180, *193*
Keating, D., 276, *284*
Keating, T., 483, 484, *489*
Keeves, J., 231, *255*, 607, *627*, 733, 777, 989, *1001*, 1015, 1017, 1018, *1036, 1037, 1039*
Keighley, P., 700, *719*
Keil, F., 37, *53*
Keiler, L., 970, *1001*
Keiny, S., 899, *905, 909*
Keliher, V., 700, 701, 705, *719*
Keller, E. F., 20, *28*
Kelly, A., 264, 273, 275, 278, *281*
Kelly, A. E., 956, *961*
Kelly, D. A., 604, *625*
Kelly, D. L., 236, *254, 255*, 258, 262, 279, *1035, 1036, 1038*
Kelly, F., 248, *255*
Kelly, G., 262, *281*, 505, *528*, 1154, *1177*
Kelly, G. J., 14, *28*, 60, 63, *71, 72*, 445, 448, 451, 452, 453, 454, 455, 462, 463, *465, 466, 467, 468, 469*, 884, 890, *905*
Kelly, G. J., 499, *531*
Kelly, J., 145, 156, *161, 162*
Kelly, L., 143, *162*
Kelly, P. V., 385, *390*
Kelly, T., 694, *719*
Kelter, P. B., *99*
Kemmis, S., 1205, 1206, 1209, 1236, *1248, 1253*
Kemp, A. C., 1123, *1142*
Kempa, R., 415, *434, 435, 437*, 671, 673, *684*
Kennard-McClelland, A. M., 514, *533*
Kennedy, D., 414, 418, *434, 437*, 982, *1001*, ix, *xiv*
Kennedy, J., 137, *162*
Kennedy, M. M., 1110, *1141*, 1181, 1189, 1200, *1202*, 1227, 1236, 1237, *1253*
Kennedy, T. G., 1071, *1100*
Kent, L., 991, 992, *1001*
Kenway, J., 258, 263, 264, 275, 276, 278, *281*
Kenyon, L., 64, *74*
Keogh, B., 508, 509, 521, 525, *531*
Kerby, H. W., *1141*
Kesidou, S., 396, 400, *437*, 1130, *1142*, 1213, *1253*
Ketter, K., 662, *685*
Key, S., 211, *224*
Keyes, M., 273, *283*
Keys, C., 524, *531*
Keys, C. W., 67, *72*, 425, *437*, 444, 445, 458, 460, *467*, 826, *829*, 994, *1001*, 1067, *1100*, 1130, 1134, *1142*, 1231, *1253*

Keys, P., 549, *557*
Khang, G. N., *1143*
Khavkin, E. E., 824, *830*
Khine, M. S., 104, 107, 109, 112, 113, 114, 117, *121*
Khishfe, R., 510, *531*, 860, *876*
Khoo, H. S., 113, *121*
Kibas, E., *1142*
Kidd, R., 456, 457, 462, *467*
Kiesler, C. A., 1068, *1100*
Kifer, E., 1007, *1037*
Kight, C., 1086, *1097*
Kikas, E., 1111, 1116, *1142*
Killip, A., 82, *97*
Kiluva-ndunda, M., 276, *282*
Kim, D. Y., 107, *122*
Kim, H.-B., 107, 108, 109, 110, 113, *121, 122*
Kim, J. J., 5, *29*, 185, *193*
Kim, S., 152, *158*
Kimball, M. E., 832, 840, 846, 850, 852, 864, *876*
Kimmelman, P., 1022, *1037*
Kincheloe, J. L., 202, 206, 207, *226*
Kinchin, I. M., 983, *1001*
Kindt, I., 497, 503, 504, 521, *527*, 1048, *1060*, 1073, *1097*
King, B., 1091, *1100*
King, B. B., 840, *876*
King, C., 662, 678, *684*
King, J., 959, *961*
King, K., 497, *531*, 1076, *1100*
King, R. A., 1133, *1137*
King, S., 273, *281*
Kinzie, J., 175, *195*
Kipnis, M., 399, 407, *436, 437*
Kircher, E., 605, *627*
Kirp, D. L., 923, *940*
Kirst, M., 932, *939, 940*
Kisiel, J., 142, 156, *158*
Kittleson, J. M., 64, *72*
Kitts, D. B., 656, 669, *684*
Klafki, W., 602, *627*
Klassen, C. W. J. M., 449, *467*
Klehr, M., 1206, *1259*
Klein, D., 1010, *1036*
Klein, J., 990, *1001*
Klein, S., 990, 991, *1004*, 1010, *1037*
Klein, S. P., 181, *194*, 930, *939*
Kleinman, G., 845, *876*
Klemm, B., *686*
Klentschy, M., 180, 184, *192*
Kliebard, H. M., 882, *905*
Klinckman, E., 591, *596*
Klopfer, L. E., 375, *387*, 401, 403, *434, 437*, 687, 736, 745, *777*, 832, 843, 845, 846, 848, 852, 863, *874, 876*, 884, 888, 889, *902, 905*, 1052, *1062*, 1090, *1100*
Klugman, E., 132, *162*
Knapp, M. S., 183, 185, *194, 961*
Knight, B. A., 1112, *1149*, 1152
Knight, R. D., 1161, 1162, *1177*

Knoll, S., *1040*
Knorr-Cetina, K. D., 68, *72*
Knote, H., 618, 620, *627*
Knutson, K., 128, 130, *162*
Knutton, S., 155, *163*, 888, *906*
Ko, E. K., *876*
Koballa, T., 76, 77, 78, 79, 82, 93, *97, 98, 101*, 504, *528*, 1068, 1088, *1098, 1102*, 1112, 1123
Koballa, T., Jr., 692, *715, 1135, 1142*
Kober, N., *1040*
Koch, J., 523, *531*
Koelsche, C. L., 1110, *1148*
Koening, R., 266, *282*
Koestner, R., 86, *97*
Kofod, L. H., 141, *166*
Kofoed, J., 700, *719*
Kohn, A., 301, 302, *313*
Koirala, H. P., 547, *557*
Kokkotas, P., 647, 648, *650*, 1113, 1127, 1132, *1142*
Köller, O., 605, 624, *624, 627*
Kollmuss, A., 707, *719*
Kolstø, S. D., 888, *906*
Komorek, M., 602, 624, *625, 626*
Koosimile, A. T., 155, *162*
Koponen, I., 1055, *1062*
Koran, J. J., Jr., 126, 127, *160*, 589, *596*
Koran, M. L., 589, *596*
Koretz, D. M., 1010, 1011, 1013, *1037*
Korpan, C. A., 154, *162*
Korth, W., 837, 843, 863, *876*
Korthagen, F., 1048, 1057, *1061, 1062*, 1125, *1138, 1141*
Kortland, J., 883, 888, 893, 894, 895, 896, *906*
Kortland, K., *904*
Kosciw, J. G., 259, 276, *282*
Koslow, M. J., 77, *98*
Koslowski, B., 33, *53*
Koster, E. H., 131, 132, *162, 165*
Kotar, M., 547, *557*
Kotte, D., 607, *627*
Kouba, V. L., 731, *776*
Kouffetta-Menicou, C., 378, *389*
Kouladis, V., 647, 648, *649, 650*, 701, 705, *714, 719*, 817, *829*, 840, *876*, 891, *903*, 1113, 1122, *1138, 1142*
Koumaras, P., 609, *629*
Kozma, R. B., 376, 379, 381, *389, 411, 437*, 651
Krajcik, J., 15, *29*, 177, 183, 186, *192, 193, 195*, 333, *343*, 401, 412, *437, 438*, 452, *467*, 474, *490*, 637, 645, *651, 684*, 824, *829*, 889, *910, 1104*, 1107, 1108, 1128, 1130, 1131, *1137, 1143, 1149*, 1164, 1172, *1176, 1178*
Krapas, S., 138, *160*
Kreikemeier, P., *1038*
Kress, G., 44, 46, 47, 50, *53, 54*, 375, *390*
Kristin, M. B., *684*
Krnel, D., 633, *650*
Krockover, G. H., 264, 277, *282*, 1050, 1055, *1060, 1064*, 1077, *1096*, 1126, *1135*, 1213, 1228, *1256, 1258*
Kroeze, D., *1037*

Kroh L. B., 607, *627*
Krueger, B., 1054, *1062*
Kruger, C., 498, 501, 503, 507, 513, *531, 534,* 1049,
   1065, 1113, 1116, 1117, *1142, 1147*
Krugley-Smolska, E., 199, *224*
Kubotta, C. A., 422, *437*
Kuhn, D., 33, 38, *53*
Kuhn, T., 7, *29,* 35, *53,* 206, *224*
Kuhn, T. S., 59, *72,* 835, *876,* 1133, 1134, *1142*
Kuklinski, M. R., 93, *102*
Kumar, D., *959*
Kumar, D. D., 888, *906*
Kuo, L., 705, *719*
Kurdziel, J., *684*
Kurki-Suonio, K., 1055, *1062*
Kurose, A., 508, 516, 524, *534,* 1226, 1231, *1253, 1259*
Kurth, L., 20, *29,* 456, 457, 462, *467,* 496, 521, *531*
Kusimo, P., 273, *283*
Kuwahara, M., 269, *282*
Kwan, R., 1231, *1253*
Kyburz-Graber, R., 703, 707, *719*
Kyle, W. C., 895, *909,* 919, 920, *940,* 1215, *1253*

L

Labaree, D., 708, *719*
LaBoskey, V. K., 1160, *1177*
Labov, W., 173, *194*
Lach, C., 506, *531*
Ladson-Billings, G., 25, *29,* 182, 189, *194*
Laguarda, K., 929, 932, *939*
Lakatos, I., 35, *53,* 835, *876*
Lalonde, R., 693, *720*
LaMaster, S. U., 974, *1002,* 1082, *1103,* 1122, *1148*
Lamb, W. G., 847, *873*
Lambdim, D., 988, *1002*
Lambert, J., 183, *194*
Lambert, N. M., 827, *829*
Lammers, T. J., 1070, *1100*
Lamon, M., 519, *529*
Lampert, M., 45, *53,* 1210, 1211, *1253*
Lampkin, R. H., 1071, *1100*
Land, S., 295, *316,* 407, 413, 416, *437, 441,* 453, 454,
   463, *469,* 485, *491*
Landa, A., 546, 554, *555*
Lane, E., 270, *283*
Lane, H. B., 296, *314*
Lane, S., 1010, *1037*
Lang, H. G., 297, *313*
Langesen, D., 5, *28*
Lanier, P. E., 1213, *1256*
Lantz, O., 853, *876,* 1124, 1125, 1126, *1142*
Laplante, B., 498, *531,* 1076, 1077, *1100*
LaPointe, A., 1014, 1015, 1024, *1037*
Lappert, J., 1228, *1258*
Lararowitz, R., 374, 383, *389*

Larke, P. J., 213, *222*
Larkin, J. H., 381, *389*
Larochelle, M., 886, *906*
Larson, J. O., 887, *906*
Last, S., 1182, *1203*
Latham, G. P., 90, *99*
Lather, P., 200, *224,* 709, *720,* 1239, 1240, 1241, *1253*
Latour, B., 14, *29,* 64, *72*
Latz, M., 1046, *1062,* 1115, 1121, *1142*
Latzke, M., 66, *74,* 184, *196*
Laubach, T. A., 85, *97,* 1130, *1143*
Laudan, L., 835, *876*
Laugksch, R. C., 109, 112, *119, 123,* 748, 773, *777*
Laukenmann, M., 607, *627*
Lauko, M. A., 175, 181, 190, *195*
Lavach, J. F., 846, 852, *876*
Lave, J., 14, 19, *29,* 45, *53,* 61, *70, 72,* 87, *99,* 128, *162,*
   759, *777*
Laverty, D. T., 635, 636, *650*
Lavoie, D. R., 60, *72,* 385, *389*
Lavonen, J., 1055, *1062*
Law, N., 890, 891, *906*
Lawless, D., 66, *73*
Lawlor, E. P., 348, 349, *368*
Lawrence, C., 458, *466*
Lawrence, M., 986, *1002*
Lawrence, N., 888, *906*
Lawrenz, F., 181, *194,* 275, *282,* 887, *906,* 931, 933,
   939, 945, 947, 951, 952, 956, *960, 961, 962,* 965, 990,
   991, *999, 1002,* 1008, *1036, 1040,* 1114, 1116, 1117,
   1142, 1143, 1197, *1202*
Laws, P. W., 608, 618, *627*
Lawson, A., 33, *54*
Lawson, A. E., 384, 385, *389,* 592, 594, *596,* 851, *876,*
   1112, *1142*
Lawton, D., 794, *805*
Lawwill, K. S., 736, 749, *777*
Lay, D., 1231, *1253*
Layton, D., 153, *162,* 730, 744, 756, 757, 772, 778, 792,
   805, 882, 883, 886, 887, 888, 889, *906*
Lazarowitz, R., 397, 399, 400, 407, *437,* 564, 577, 579,
   583, 584, 585, 592, 593, 594, *595, 596, 597, 598,* 1071,
   1097, 1100
Le Marechal, J. F., 400, *440*
Leach, J., 39, 41, 42, 44, 46, 49, *52, 54, 55,* 608, 621,
   625, 627, 646, *650,* 657, 659, *682,* 695, 698, *716, 720,*
   721, 831, 861, *875, 876, 908,* 1212, *1249*
Leal Filho, W., 701, 704, 707, 712, *720*
Leat, D., 986, *1002*
Leavitt, D. J., 5, *29,* 185, *193*
Leber, J., 639, *649*
Leblanc, R., 900, *906*
Ledbetter, C. E., 108, *122*
Leder, G., 275, 276, *280*
Lederman, J. S., 832, *876*
Lederman, N., 605, 606, *624*
Lederman, N. F., 408, *438*

Lederman, N. G., 83, *99*, 156, *162*, 408, 410, *434, 440*, 499, 500, 510, *527, 531, 533*, 542, 543, 550, *557*, 810, 817, 820, *829*, 832, 833, 836, 853, 855, 856, 857, 858, 859, 860, 862, 866, 867, 868, 869, 871, *873, 874*, 876, *876, 877, 878, 879*, 884, 900, *901, 902*, 971, 990, *1002*, 1046, *1062*, 1075, *1100*, 1108, 1115, 1119, 1120, 1128, 1132, *1135, 1139, 1142, 1144*, 1172, *1177*, 1227
Lee, C., 507, *528*, 701, *718*
Lee, C. A., 496, 505, *531*
Lee, D. J., 150, *158*
Lee, H., 337, *343*
Lee, H. S., 177, *196*, 473, 485, *489*
Lee, J., 704, *720*, 911, 925, 933, 934, *939*
Lee, K. L., 648, *651*, 1114, *1142*
Lee, N., 692, *720*
Lee, O., 61, 66, *72*, 89, *99*, 172, 178, 180, 181, 183, 184, 188, 189, *193, 194*, 199, 224, 331, 332, *342*, 455, 456, 457, 462, *467*, 895, *906*, 991, *1002*, 1119, *1142*
Lee, S., 736, 755, 757, 759, 769, 772, *779*, 886, *906*
Lee, S. K., 107, *122*
Lee, S. S., 107, 110, 111, 112, 114, *122*
Lee, S. S. U., 107, 108, 111, 112, 114, *122*
Lee, V., 184, *194*, 276, *282*, 1013, *1037*
Leedy, D. E., 663, 664, *685, 686*
Leeming, F., 700, 701, 705, *720*
Legg, M. L., 425, *439*
LeGrand, H., 656, 659, *684*
Legro, P., 156, *158*
Lehman, J. R., 539, 547, 552, 554, *557*
Lehrer, R., 406, *439*, 513, *532*, 1219, 1224, 1228, *1253*
Leighton, J., *684*
Leinhardt, G., 128, 128, *129*, 130, *162, 165*
Leite, L., 1076, *1102*, 1117, 1127, *1139, 1146*
Leithwood, K., 295, *313*
Lemberger, J., 36, *53*, 1077, *1101*, 1125, 1126, 1128, *1142, 1144*, 1167, *1177, 1252*
Lemerise, T., 141, *162*
Lemke, J. L., 46, 47, 50, *54*, 57, 60, *72*, 377, 378, *389*, 444, 445, 446, 447, 452, 458, 459, 462, 463, *467*
Lemmens, M., *1257*
Lensmire, T., 1211, *1253*
Leone, A. J., 412, 413, *439*
Leontiev, A. N., *54*
LePore, P., 275, *282*
Lepper, M. R., 382, *389*
Lesgold, A. M., 969, *1005*
Lester, F., 988, *1002*
Lett, P., 1210, *1247*
Letts, W. J., 259, 276, *282*
Levenson, T., *1035*
Levi-Nahum, T., 399, *436*
Levin, D., 472, *489*
Levin, J., 1084, *1100*
Levine, J. M., 128, *165*
Levinson, B. A., 187, *194*
Levitt, K., 497, 498, *531*, 979, *996*
Levy, J., 106, *119, 124*

Lewenstein, B. V., 130, *162*
Lewin, K., 103, *122*, 235, 243, *254, 255*
Lewin, T., 275, *282*
Lewis, A., 692, *720*
Lewis, B. F., 206, 207, *224*
Lewis, B. N., 135, *163*
Lewis, C., 1206, 1210, 1213, *1253, 1254*
Lewis, D. J. A., 988, *1004*
Lewis, E. L., 610, *627*
Lewis, J., 774, *780*
Lewis, J. P., 668, *684*
Li, A., 272, *282*
Li, S., 891, *906*
Libarkin, J. C., 662, *681, 684*
Libby, R. D., 385, *389*
Librero, D., 145, *159*
Lichtfeldt, M., 620, 621, *626*
Lidz, C. S., 986, *1002*
Lieberman, P., 289, *313*
Lietz, S., 497, *531*, 1076, *1100*
Liew, C. W., 375, *389*, 426, *438*
Ligett, C., *1257*
Lightburn, M. E., 108, 112, *122*
Lijnse, P., 39, *54*, 449, *467*, 886, 888, 892, 896, 899, 901, *904, 906*
Likert, R., 77, *99*
Lillo, J., 662, *684*
Limón, M., 511, *531*
Lin, H., 1114, *1143*
Lin, H. S., 855, *877*, 990, *1002*
Lin, W.-J., 1228, *1254*
Lin, X., 481, *490*
Lincoln, Y., 698, 709, *715*, 946, 954, 955, *960, 961*, 1239, *1254*
Linder, C. J., 841, *873*, 1116, 1117, 1126, *1135, 1143*
Lindquist, B., *1257*
Lindsay, G., 692, *720*
Linebarger, D. L., 151, *167*
Linfield, R. S., 518, 519, 520, *534*
Linkson, M., 209, *225*
Linn, M., 4, *29*, 403, *435*, 1011, 1024, *1037*
Linn, M. C., 64, 71, 375, *389*, 412, 413, *435, 436, 438*, 453, *465*, 473, 475, *490*, 507, *534*, 610, *627*, 664, *684*, 1215, *1253*
Linn, R., 1011, *1037*
Linn, R. L., 990, *1002*
Linnenbrink, E. A., *99*
Lipsey, M. W., 945, *962*
Lipsky, D., 292, 293, 296, 297, 301, 303, *312, 313*
Lisonbee, L., 918, *939*
Litardo, H. A., 1068, 1073, *1100*
Litsky, W., *940*
Little, E., 506, *531*
Little, J., 818, *829*
Liu, C.-J., 987, *998*
Liu, S. Y., 499, 510, *531*, 859, *877*
Liu, X., 983, 990, *1002*

Liu, Z., *1254*
Llamas, V., 358, 360, *368*
Lloyd, J. K., 1111, 1120, *1143*
Lloyd, P., 511, *532*
Lock, C., 898, *907*, 1122, *1144*
Lock, P., 704, *720*
Lockard, D. L., *1062*
Lockard, J. D., 1119, *1146*
Locke, C., 1051, *1063*
Locke, E. A., 90, *99*
Locker, K. M., 1227, *1249*
Lockheed, M., 276, *282*
Loef, M., 1206, *1248*
Logsdon, S. M., 299, *312*
Loh, B., *438*, 485, *490*
Lokan, J., 991, *1002*
Lomax, P., 1238, 1245, *1254*
Long, M., 152, *162*
Longino, H. E., 68, *72*
Lonning, R. A., 544, 547, 551, *557*
Lopez, A., 1128, *1138*
Lopez, V. E., 385, *387*
Lopez-Ferrao, J., 931, *938*
Lord, C., *1035*
Lorsbach, A., 974, *1002*
Lortie, D., 1044, *1062*, 1077, *1100*
Lott, S., 704, *715*
Lotter, C., 1082, *1100*
Lottero-Perdue, P. S., 890, *906*
Loucks-Horsley, S., 1185, 1186, 1187, 1188, 1197, *1202*,
   1203, 1206, 1209, 1213, *1254*
Louden, W., 1054, *1065*
Loughran, J., 400, *436*, 887, *906*, 1043, 1048, 1051,
   1053, 1054, 1057, *1060*, *1063*, 1123, *1143*, 1160, 1175,
   1177, 1210, 1215, 1225, 1228, *1254*
Lounsbury, J., 540, *558*
Lousley, C., 702, *720*
Love, N., 1185, *1202*, *1203*, 1206, 1209, 1213, *1254*
Lovelock, J., *684*
Loving, C. C., 177, *194*, 206, 210, 211, 215, 222, *224*,
   499, *529*, 1075, *1098*
Lowe, I., 695, *720*
Lowe, P., *1002*
Lowery, L. F., 1072, *1101*
Lowery, P., 272, *280*
Lowry, M., 969, 983, 987, *998*
Lubben, F., 61, *72*, 805, 982, *1002*
Lubezky, A., 987, *1006*
Lucas, A. M., *130*, 136, 140, *162*, *166*
Lucas, K. B., 128, 129, 134, 141, 142, *157*, 375, *389*,
   390, *908*
Lucas, T., 182, *196*
Luckman, C., 704, *720*
Luckmann, T., 43, *52*
Luft, J. A., 182, *194*, 1085, *1101*, 1193, 1199, *1203*
Lujan, J., 210, *224*
Luke, A., 446, 462, *467*

Luke, J., 138, *157*
Luke, J. J., 143, 144, 156, *159*, *162*
Lumpe, A., 542, 549, *556*, 1072, 1075, 1076, 1078,
   1083, 1088, *1097*, *1098*, *1099*, *1101*
Lunetta, V. N., 374, *388*, 394, 395, 397, 398, 400, 401,
   403, 405, 406, 407, 411, 412, 413, 415, 417, 420, *436*,
   438, *440*, 585, *598*, 609, *627*
Luster, B., 328, *343*, 498, 510, 518, *534*
Luykx, A., 183, 189, *194*
Lybeck, L., 1114, *1147*, *1148*
Lynch, M., 444, 449, 450, *467*
Lynch, M. A., 154, *162*
Lynch, P. P., 218, *224*
Lynch, S., 172, *194*, 307, 308, *313*, 1129, 1130, *1143*
Lyons, L. L., 1083, *1101*, 1125, *1143*
Lyons, T. S., *906*
Lytle, S. L., *1043*, *1061*, 1106, *1137*, 1208, 1209, 1210,
   1211, 1234, 1235, 1236, 1242, *1248*

M

Macbeth, D., 444, 449, 450, *467*
MacDonald, D., 1121, 1123, *1140*, *1143*
Macdonald, R. D., 139, *164*
Macgill, S., 153, *162*, 730, *778*, 886, *906*
Machado, A. H., 60, 65, *73*
Mackay, L. D., *877*
MacKinnon, A. M., 1108, *1139*, 1209, *1250*
MacLean, M. S., *1255*
MacLeod, R., 882, *906*
Macpherson, C., 207, 210, *226*
Madaus, G. F., 562, *597*
Madden, N. A., *939*, *940*
Madden, T., 1083, *1096*
Maddock, M. N., 200, 203, *224*
Madison, S. M., 93, *102*
Mael, F., 275, 276, *282*
Maglienti, M., 67, *71*
Magnusson, S., 820, *829*, 1107, 1108, 1109, 1121, 1123,
   1124, 1125, 1127, 1128, 1130, 1131, *1135*, *1143*
Mahaffy, P., 644, *651*
Mahmoud, K., 584, 585, *597*
Mahmoud, N. A., 591, *596*
Mahoney, D., 703, *720*
Majeed, A., 105, 110, *122*
Mak, S. Y., 1116, *1149*
Maker, C. J., 305, *313*, *317*
Malave, C., 84, *102*
Malhotra, B., 498, 503, 524, *529*
Malleus, P., 246, *255*
Mallinson, G. G., 1110, *1143*
Malone, J., 505, *534*, 543, 552, *558*, 967, *1001*
Malone, K., 689, 701, 703, *713*, *720*
Malone, M. R., *938*
Malone, T. W., 382, *389*
Maloney, D. P., 606, *627*

Mamiala, T. L., 607, 618, *629*
Mamlock, R., *437*
Mamlok-Naaman, R., 407, *436*
Mandler, V., 1129, *1141*
Mangas, V., 705, *720*
Mangino, M., 300, *315*
Mangione, T. L., 956, *959*
Mann, D., 132, *162*
Mansaray, A., 704, 706, *712, 720*
Mansdoerfer, S., 1210, *1247*
Mant, J., 498, 501, 507, 513, *534*, 1114, 1116, *1143, 1147*
Mantziopoulos, P., 295, *313*
Maor, D., 1053, *1063*, 1126, *1143*
Marback-Ad, G., 382, *389*
Marcinkowski, T., 701, *720*
Marek, E. A., 362, *369*, 385, *389*, 635, 636, *649*, 1130, *1143*
Mares, K. R., 91, *101*
Mares, M., 151, *162*
Margianti, E. S., 109, 110, 112, 113, 114, *122*
Marion, S. F., 172, *193*, 736, 755, *776*
Mark, M. M., 946, *961*
Markakis, K. M., 95, *102*
Marker, M., 203, *224*
Marks, H., 276, *282*
Marques, L. F., 662, 665, 668, 673, *684*
Marsden, W., 707, *720*
Marsh, D. D., 142, 156, *158*, 1090, *1103*
Marsh, J., 928, *940*
Marshall, B., 507, *528*
Marshall, S., *438*
Marshall, S. P., 730, 753, *778*
Marston, C., 981, *1002*
Martin, A., 1116, *1139*
Martin, A. K., 1108, *1144*, 1165, 1168, *1177, 1178*
Martin, C. L., 278, *283*
Martin, D., 136, 145, *159, 162*
Martin, E., 506, *528*
Martin, I., 375, *390*
Martin, J. R., 67, 71, 277, *282*, 377, 444, 458, 460, *466*
Martin, K., 987, *1000*
Martin, L., 128, 129, *165*
Martin, M., 1157, *1177*
Martin, M. O., 236, 237, 238, 239, *254, 255*, 262, *279*, 604, *625*, 1015, 1020, 1021, *1035, 1036, 1037, 1038*
Martin, P., 211, *224*
Martín del Pozo, R., 1113, 1122, 1124, *1143, 1145*
Martinez, K., 499, *531*
Martinez, P., 705, *720*
Martinez-Perez, L., 1071, *1098*
Martinez Rivera, C., 704, *720*
Martini, M., 855, *873*, 1210, *1246*
Martins, I., 44, 50, *54*
Martins, L., 380, *389*
Maruyama, G., 956, *961*
Marx, N., *651*
Marx, R., 186, *193*, 401, 412, *437*

Marx, R. W., 15, 16, 17, 18, 19, 24, *29*, 38, *55*, 66, 72, 76, *100*, 178, 183, 186, *192, 195*, 331, 332, 333, *342, 343*, 444, 452, 462, *467, 468*, 511, *532*, 607, *628, 684*, 824, *829*, 1172, *1176*, 1188, 1200, *1202*
Masciotra, D., 66, *73*
Masene, R., 662, 676, *687*
Mashhadi, A., 620, *627*
Maskill, R., 1110, *1149*
Maslow, A. H., 87, *99*
Mason, C. L., 1157, *1177*
Mason, C. W., 135, 141, *163*
Mason, J. L., *162*
Mason, J. M., 61, 66, *70*
Mason, L., 512, 520, *531*, 705, *720*
Mason, T. C., 537, 538, 550, 552, 554, *557*
Massell, D., 932, *940*
Masten, W. G., 300, *315*
Mastrilli, T. M., 1131, *1143*
Mastropieri, M., 295, *313*
Mastropieri, M. A., 296, 298, 299, *315*, 502, *531*
Matarasso, F., 146, *162*
Mathews, K., 260, *282*
Mathews, M., *1102*
Mathews, S., 548, 554, *555*
Mathison, S., 129, *162*
Matsumura, S., 474, *489*
Matthews, C. E., 177, *194*
Matthews, D. B., 95, *99*
Matthews, M., 34, 41, *54*, 401, 405, 408, *438*, 695, *721*
Matthews, M. R., 232, *255*, 606, *627*, 738, *778*
Matthews, P. S. C., 38, *54*
Matusov, E., 128, *163*
Mauer, S., 299, *313*
Maurin, M., 639, *649*
Mavrommatis, Y., 970, *1002*
Mawhinney, H. B., 967, *1002*
Maxwell, G., 982, 983, 988, 989, 993, *999*
May, T., 702, *721*
Mayer, R. E., 48, *54*, 827, *829*
Mayer, V. J., 658, 660, 668, *683, 685, 686*, 730, 738, *778*, 1071, *1101*
Mayer-Smith, J. A., 1057, *1063*
Mayo, E., 785, *805*
Mayoh, K., 155, *163*, 888, *906*
Mayring, P., 607, *627*
Mayrowetz, D., 925, *938*, 1010, *1036*
Mazlo, J., *99*
Mazzeo, J., 175, *192*
Mbajiorgu, N. M., 888, *906*
McAlister, S., 970, *1000*
McAlpine, D., 967, *998*
McArthur, J., 1080, *1099*
McAuliffe, C., 663, 664, *685, 686*
McBride, J. W., 538, 551, *557*
McCaffrey, D., 181, *194*, 930, *939, 1001*, 1010, *1037*
McCall, G. J., 660, *687*
Mccallum, B., 970, *1000*

McCammon, S., 889, *906*
McCann, W. S., 296, *313*
McCarthy, S., 888, *909*
McClafferty, T. P., 133, 136, 138, 141, 142, 143, 150, *165*
McClain, K., *938*
McCloskey, M., 33, *54*, 616, *627*
McClure, J. R., 983, 992, *1002*
McCluskey, K. W., 307, *314*
McComas, W. F., 408, *438*, 546, *557*, 600, 604, 605, 606, *627*, 832, *879*
McCombs, B. L., 827, *829*
McConnell, M. C., 884, *907*
McCurdy, D. W., 1072, *1101*
McDaniel Hill, C., *1254*
McDermott, L. C., 616, *629*
McDiarmid, G. W., 858, *873*, 1108, 1134, *1136*
McDill,. E., 20, *29*
McDonald, J., 545, *557*
McDonald, J. B., 1220, 1228, *1254*
McDonald, J. L., 547, *557*
McDonald, J. T., 65, *72*
McDonald, S., 177, *196*
McDonnell, L. M., 1010, *1038*
McDuffie, A. R., 1215, 1227, 1235, *1247*
McEneaney, E. H., 729, 736, *778*
McFarland, J., 1117, 1131, *1144*
McGarvey, J. E. B., 635, 636, *650*
McGee, C., *997*
McGee, K. C., *1254*
McGehee, J. J., 545, 553, *557*
McGhee, R., *437*
McGillicuddy, K., 44, 50, *54*, 375, *390*
McGinn, M. K., 452, 462, *468*, 508, 509, *532*, 890, 895, *907, 908*, 982, 991, 994, *1002, 1004*, 1112, *1145*
McGinnis, J. R., 148, *161*, 291, 294, 295, 298, *313*
McGlinchey, A., 1228, *1254*
McGoey, J., 1055, 1056, 1057, *1063*, 1157, *1177*, 1215, 1243, 1246, *1254*
McGovern, S., 206, *224*
McGuigan, L., 800, *806, 1145*
McGuiness, B., 1054, *1063*
McGuiness, J. R., 1075, *1101*
McGuinness, C., 701, *726*
McIlveene, M., 706, *721*
McIntosh, W. J., 1129, *1143*
McIver, M. C., 1010, *1040*
McKeown, R., 691, *721*
McKie, R., 153, *163*
McKinley, E., 200, 202, 203, 206, 209, 210, 211, 212, 213, 214, 215, 216, 218, 219, 220, *224, 225, 226*, 997
McKnight, C., 1018, 1021, *1038*
McKnight, C. C., 5, *29*, 396, *440, 1039*
McLaren, A., 278, *282*
McLaughlin, H., 139, *164*
McLaughlin, M., 934, *940*
McLaughlin, M. W., 817, *829*
McLean, K., 137, *163*

McLeskey, J., 296, *314*
McLoughlin, A. S., 1045, *1061*
McMahon, M. M., 85, *98*
McManus, D. O., 85, *99*
McManus, P., 130, *162*
McManus, P. M., 131, 136, 137, 138, 143, 144, *163*
McMaster, J., 1053, 1054, *1063*
McMurry, F., 787, *805*
McNaught, C., 700, 703, *721*
McNay, M., 1127, *1143*
McNeely, J. C., 635, 636, *649*
McNeely, M., *1037*
McNeil, J., 1051, *1063*
McNeil, L. M., 171, *195*
McNess, E., 979, *1003*
McNiff, J., 1245, *1254*
McNulty, B. A., 296, *314*
McPhee, J., 664, *685*
McPherson, S., 1168, *1178*
McPherson Waiti, P., 211, *225*
McQueen, G., 987, *1000*
McRobbie, C. J., 107, 108, 110, *120, 121, 122, 180, 196*, 375, *389, 390*, 399, *436*, 887, 898, *908, 910*
McSharry, G., 152, *163*
McTaggart, R., 946, *961*, 1205, 1209, *1253*
Mead, M., 836, *877*
Meade, N., 1014, 1015, 1024, *1037*
Meade, S. D., 1023, *1038*
Meadows, J., 794, *806*
Meadows, L., 185, 190, *196*, 897, *909*
Mechner, F., 589, *597*
Medawar, P., 57, *72*
Medved, M. I., 134, *163*
Medvitz, A. G., 898, *907*
Meece, J., 90, 91, *99*, 183, *193*, 262, 263, 264, 271, 272, 274, *281*, 325, 326, *342*, 456, *466*, 930, 932, *939*, 1196, *1202*
Meerah, S. M., 1131, *1140*
Mehan, H., 63, *72*, 291, *314*, 445, 449, *468*
Meheut, M., 39, *55*
Meichtry, Y. J., 836, 866, *877*
Meier, S. L., 545, 551, *557*
Melber, L. M., 131, 132, 141, 142, 156, *158, 163*
Mellado, V., 1126, 1133, *1143*
Melton, A. W., 135, *163*
Mencl, W. E., *315*
Mendelsohn, E., 882, *907*
Mercer, C. D., 296, *314*
Mercer, N., 44, *53*
Merino, B., 180, *195*
Merrian, S. B., 954, *961*
Merrill, C., 551, *557*
Merrill, R. J., 395, *438*
Mervis, J., 261, *282*
Merzenich, M. M., *316*
Meskimen, L., 322, 323, 324, *342*
Messer, D., 1127, 1132, *1145*

Messick, S., 971, 988, 990, *1002*
Metcalfe, J., 147, *160*
Metheny, D. L., 542, 544, 550, *556*
Metraux, R., 836, *877*
Metz, K., 33, *54*
Metz, K. E., 45, *54*
Metzger, D., 547, *557*
Metzger, E. P., 668, *685*
Meyer, H., 1077, *1101*, 1125, *1144, 1252*
Meyer, K., 452, *468*, 510, 512, 515, 523, *532, 534*, 887, 907, 982, 993, *999*
Meyer, L. H., 296, *311*
Meyer, W., 662, *685*
Meyling, H., 606, *627*
Michael, M., 887, *907*
Michael, W. B., 430, *437*
Michaels, S., 14, 19, *29*
Michelson, N., 967, *1001*
Michie, M., 141, 143, *163*, 209, *225*
Michlin, M., 952, *961*
Middleton, M., 90, *99*
Midgley, C., 90, *99*
Midyan, Y., 679, *685*
Miech, E. J., 1211, *1252*
Mihesuah, D. A., 220, *225*
Milbrath, L., 693, *721*
Miles, M., 814, *830*, 925, 926, *939*
Miles, M. B., *961*
Miles, R. S., 135, *163*
Millar, M. G., 94, *99*
Millar, R., 39, 49, *52, 54*, 65, *71*, 180, *192*, 248, *255*, 400, 403, 410, 414, *437, 438, 440*, 625, 635, 636, 640, 641, 642, 644, 646, *649, 650*, 695, 698, *716, 721*, 729, 742, 743, 745, 746, 753, *777, 778*, 800, *805, 806*, 831, 833, *875, 878*, 886, 888, 891, *905, 907, 908*
Miller, A. H., 1130, *1141*
Miller, D. F., 351, *368*
Miller, J., 704, *721*, 1209, *1254*
Miller, J. D., 729, 760, 761, 762, 763, 764, *778*
Miller, K., 259, *281*, 545, *559*
Miller, K. W., 215, 222, 542, 544, 550, *556*
Miller, M. L., 969, *1000*
Miller, N., 1068, *1100*
Miller, P. E., 839, *877*
Miller, S. L., *316*
Mills, R. A., 1121, *1144*
Millwater, J., 117, *124*
Milne, C. E., 886, *907*
Milner, N., 398, *438*
Milroy, P., 1056, *1060*, 1123, *1143*, 1207, 1232, 1236, *1248*
Minnema, J., 959, *961*
Minstrell, J., 39, 44, *54, 56*, 447, *469*, 512, *529*, 617, *627*, 810, *830*, 1211, 1227, 1228, 1241, *1250, 1254*
Mintzes, J., 34, *56*, 81, *101*, 230, 232, *255, 256*, 599, 606, *627, 629*, 656, 659, *685, 687*, 981, 983, *1003, 1006*, 1149, 1154, 1156, 1157, *1177, 1178*, 1212, 1214, *1255*
Mishler, E. G., 62, *72*

Mistler, M. M., 507, *532*
Mitchell, I., 517, *532, 1063*, 1225, *1254, 1255*
Mitchell, I. J., 1053, 1057, *1060, 1063*, 1209, 1224, 1225
Mitchell, I. M., 1168, 1174, *1176*
Mitchell, J., 517, *532*
Mitchell, K. J., 1010, *1037*
Mitchener, C. P., 817, *830*, 1052, *1060, 1135*, 1164, 1165, 1166, 1168, *1176*, 1215
Mitchner, C. P., *1253*
Mohammed, E., *436*
Mohanram, R., 201, *225*
Mohapatra, J. K., 1116, 1117, *1144*
Mohatt, G., 61, *71*
Mohr, M. M., 1205, 1236, *1255*
Moje, E. B., 15, 16, 17, 18, 19, 24, *29*, 66, 72, 178, *195*, 331, 332, 333, *342*, 444, 446, 462, 463, *468*, 511, 514, *532, 533*
Molella, A. P., 139, *163*
Moll, L. C., 186, *195*
Monfils, L., 1010, *1036*
Monhardt, R. M., 211, *225*
Monk, D. H., 353, *367*
Monk, M., *780*, 1092, *1099, 1103*
Monroe, M., 703, *721*
Montagnero, J., 666, *685*
Montgomery, D., 701, *719*
Moody, D., 983, *1000*
Moody, D. E., 65, *71*
Moody, E. D., 594, *596*
Moody, K. W., 589, *596*
Moog, R. S., 386, *387*
Mooij, W., 474, *489*
Moore, A., 406, *434*
Moore, C. J., 515, 523, *530*
Moore, E. H., 539, *557*
Moore, K., 1070, *1101*
Moore, R., 863, *877*, 1071, *1101*
Moore, S. D., 956, *961*
Moos, R. H., 103, 105, *122*
Moran, J., 640, *651*
Moreland, J., 972, 978, *1001, 1003*
Morell, P. D., 497, *532*
Morely, M. W., 787, *806*
Morgan, B., *1258*
Morgan, C., 979, *1003*
Morgan, J., 707, *721*
Morine-Dershimer, G., 1122, *1144*
Morran, J., 507, 512, 513, 517, *528*
Morrell, P. D., 83, *99*
Morris, G., 979, *1003*
Morris, M., 141, 143, *165*
Morrison, A. P., 296, *315*
Morrison, J. A., 1128, 1132, *1144*
Morrison, K., 64, *73*, 410, *440*
Mortimer, E., *52*, 377, *389*, 657, 659, *682*, 1212, *1249*
Mortimer, E. F., 41, 42, 43, 44, 50, *54*, 60, 65, *73*, 79, 80, 93, *101*, 454, *468*

Moscovici, H., 64, *74*, 338, *342*, 549, *559*, 1110, *1144*
Moser, U., *1039*
Moskowitz, D. A., 956, *961*
Moss, D. M., 859, *877*, 1081, *1101*
Moss, P. A., 988, 989, *1003*
Motswiri, M., 662, 676, *687*
Moussouri, T., 128, 130, 133, 138, *157, 160*
Moyer, R., 1072, *1101*
Moyer, R. H., 355, *367*
Mrazek, R., 697, 701, 707, *720, 721*
Mucunguzi, P., 704, *721*
Mueller, A., *533*, 1057, *1063*, 1126, *1146*
Muir, K., 322, 324, *343*
Mulhall, P., 400, *436*, 1123, *1143*
Mulkay, M., 68, *73*
Müller, C. T., 605, 608, *625*
Muller, P. A., 175, *195*
Müller, R., 620, 621, *627*
Mullis, D., *1037*
Mullis, I., 236, 237, 238, 239, *254, 255*, 262, 279, 604, *625*, 1015, 1020, 1021, 1024, *1035, 1036, 1037, 1038*
Munby, H., 817, *830*, 859, *877*, 889, 898, *902, 907*, 1043, 1047, 1051, 1057, *1061, 1063, 1064*, 1108, 1122, 1131, *1144, 1145*, 1159, 1165, *1177*, 1210, 1216, 1218, 1236, 1238, *1250, 1255, 1257*
Mundry, S., 1185, *1203*, 1206, *1254*
Munford, D., 416, *441*, 453, 454, 463, *469*
Munson, S., 299, *314*
Murphy, A., 969, *1006*
Murphy, P., 989, 991, *1000*
Murray, H. A., 103, *122*
Muth, K., 458, 459, *466*
Muth, K. D., 90, *98*
Myers, M., 1205, *1255*
Myles, B., 295, *314*

N

Nachmias, R., 412, *436*
Nachshon, M., 584, *597*
Nachtigal, P. M., 348, 363, *368*
Nagle, B. W., 891, *909, 910*
Naizer, G. L., 547, *558*
Nakagawa, K., 384, *387*
Nakhleh, M. B., 969, *1000*
Nakiboglu, C., 639, *651*
Nakleh, M. B., 412, *438*, 637, 645, *651*
Namuth, D. M., 150, *158*
Nando Rosales, J., 704, *721*
Nania, P., 299, *317*
Nason, R., 511, *532*
Nassivera, J. W., 141, *166*
Nastasi, B. K., 63, *71*, 451, *466*
Natriello, G., 20, *29*, 965, 979, *1003*
Navon, O., 407, *436*
Nay, M. A., 77, *98*

Naylor, S., 508, 509, 521, 525, *531*
Nazzaro, D., 506, *531*
Neale, D. C., 1049, *1064*, 1116, 1124, *1147*
Neber, H., 91, *99*
Nebergall, R. E., 77, *101*
Neely, C., 1242, *1250*
Neimoth-Anderson, J. D., *99*
Nelkin, D., 891, 894, *907*, 916, 917, 921, *940*
Nelson, B. D., 1114, *1135*
Nelson, R. M., 91, *97*
Nelson, T. H., 1056, *1063*
Nelson, W., 704, *721*
Nelson-Barber, S., 181, *196*, 217, *225*, 991, 992, 994, *1005*, 1013, *1039*
Nentwig, P., 733, *777*
Nesin, G., 540, *558*
Netshisaulu, T., 61, *72*
Neubrand, J., 605, *627*
Nevala, A., 704, *721*
Neves, A., 1227, *1251*
Newman, F. M., *961*
Newman, S., 45, *52*
Newman, S. E., 19, *28*
Newmann, D., 972, *1003*
Newmann, E., 947, *996*
Newton, D. P., 498, 500, 504, *532*, 1119, *1144*
Newton, L. D., 498, 500, 504, *532, 1144*
Newton, P., *435*, 453
Ng, P., 1125, 1126, *1137*
Nicholls, J., *1248*
Nicholls, J. G., 90, *99*
Nichols, A., 986, *1002*
Nicholson, H., 126, 136, *158*
Nicholson, II. J., 148, *163*
Nicol, C., *1038*, 1057, *1063*
Nicol, M., 545, 551, *557*
Niedderer, H., 609, 612, 620, 621, *625, 628, 629*, 640, *651*
Nielsen, K., 707, *714*
Niess, M. L., 156, *162*, 542, 543, 550, *557*, 810, *829*, 832, *877*
Nieswandt, M., 635, 636, *651*
Nihlen, A., 1210, *1247*
Ninnes, P., 177, *195*, 213, 214, 219, 220, *225*
Nissley, C., 1231, *1255*
Nitko, A., 969, *1003*
Niwa, F., 761, 763, *778*
Nix, G., 89, *100*
Nix, R. K., 108, *122*
Nkopodi, N., 218, *226*
Nocerino, M. A., *1255*
Noel, E., 1209, *1258*
Noffke, S., 818, *830*, 1208, 1209, 1211, 1227, 1234, 1235, 1236, 1237, 1238, 1239, 1242, *1255, 1259*
Noh, T., 837, *876*
Nohara, D., 1023, *1038*
Nolan, K., 689, 698, 701, *717*

Nolen, S. B., 90, *99*
Nolet, V., 294, *314*
Nolet, V. W., 294, *314*
Noonan-Pulling, L. C., 662, 665, *685*
Norman, C., ix, *xiv*
Norman, K., 296, *314*
Norman, O., 322, 323, 324, *342*
Normile, D., 270, *282*
Norris, S. P., 457, 460, 463, *466, 468*, 750, 762, *777, 778*, 987, *1003*
Northfield, J., 971, *996*, 1045, 1046, 1053, 1054, *1060, 1062, 1063*, 1106, *1144*, 1152, 1166, *1176, 1177*, 1209, 1210, 1228, 1235, 1239, 1240, 1241, *1247, 1254, 1255*
Northover, A., 972, *1003*
Nott, M., 866, *877*
Nottis, K., 662, *685*, 1117, 1131, *1144*
Novak, J., 34, *54*, 981, *1003*, 1154, 1156, *1177, 1178*, 1212
Novak, J. D., 34, *56*, 230, 232, *255, 256*, 374, *389*, 589, *597*, 599, 606, *627, 629*, 656, *685, 687, 1149, 1177, 1255*
Novick, S., 404, *438*, 1157, *1178*
Nsengiyumva, J.-B., 76, 80, 85, *100*
Nugent, J., 1081, *1104*
Nunn, T. P., 795, *806*
Nurrenbern, S. C., 969, *1000*
Nussbaum, J., 404, *438, 1144*, 1157, *1178*
Nussinuvitz, R., *440*
Nuthall, G., 495, 496, 502, 509, 511, 513, 515, 521, 522, *532*
Nyhof-Young, J., 145, *163*, 899, *902*

O

Oakes, J., 176, 184, *195*, 322, 323, 324, *343*
Oatley, K., 134, *163*
Oberem, G. E., 1117, *1141*
O'Brien, E., *1040*
O'Brien, P. J., 1129, *1144*
Ochanji, M. K., 1216, *1258*
O'Connor, M. C., 14, 19, *29*
O'Connor, T., 703, *721*
O'Day, J. A., 922, 926, 932, 935, *939, 940*
Odden, A. R., *939*
O'Dea, J., 1239, *1255*
Odom, A. L., 1130, *1144*
O'Donoghue, R., 700, 703, *721*
Odum, A. L., 385, *390*
Oesch, J., 1128, *1139*
Ofwono-Orecho, J., 701, 722
Ogawa, M., 210, 212, 213, 216, *225*, 269, *283*
Ogborn, J., 44, 46, 47, 50, *53, 54*, 375, 380, *389, 390*, 817, *829*, 840, *876*, 899, *907*
Ogbu, J. U., 20, *29*
Ogonowski, M., 179, 188, *197*, 329, *343*, 496, *534*
Ogunniyi, M. B., 407, *438*, 841, 852, 863, *877*
Oh, P. S., 111, *122*

Ohadi, M. M., 517, *533*
O'Hearn, G. T., 737, 741, *779*
Okebukola, P. A., 212, *224*, 398, 407, *438*
Olawepo, J., 704, *712*
Oldham, B. R., 295, *310*
Oldham, V., 617, *625*, 698, *716*
Oliver, D., 701, *720*
Oliver, J. S., 78, 79, 93, *101*, 353, 359, 360, 365, *366, 367, 368, 369*, 1068, *1102*
Oliver, S., 1131, *1138*
O'Loughlin, M., 33, 38, *53*, 212, *225*, 264, *283*
Olsen, L., 274, *283*
Olson, J. K., 411, 422, *438, 1144*
Olson, L., 152, *160*
Olson, M. W., 1211, *1255*
Olstad, R. G., 422, *437*
O'Malley, M., 837, 866, 867, 868, *877*
O'Neill, K. D., 474, 485, *490*
Onorbe de Torre, A. M., 1113, *1146*
Onslow, B., 1128, *1139*
Onwuegbuzie, A. J., xiii, *xiv*
Oosterheert, I. E., 1170, 1171, *1178*
Oppenheimer, F., 137, *163*
Oram, S. Y., 182, *192*
Orange, A. D., 882, *907*
Orchard, G., 701, *726*
Orgren, J., 1071, *1101*
Orion, N., 142, *164*, 658, 660, 662, 663, 664, 665, 667, 668, 669, 670, 671, 672, 674, 675, 678, *681, 682, 683, 684, 685*, 1092, *1103*
Ormes, C., *1255*
Orpwood, G., 746, 764, *778*, 896, 899, *907*, 967, 970, *1003*
Orr, M., 274, *281*
Osborn, M., 979, *1003*
Osborne, J., 41, *54*, 78, 83, 95, *99*, 140, *166*, 203, 222, 232, 248, 249, *255, 256*, 272, *283*, 377, *391*, 403, 404, 406, *435, 439*, 453, 459, *469*, 496, *532*, 695, 698, 706, *716, 721*, 729, 743, 745, 759, 774, *776, 778*, 780, 794, 800, *806*, 833, *878*, 884, 885, 886, 888, 891, 892, 893, 896, *902, 907*, 989, 990, 993, 995, *1003*, 9971
Osborne, M. D., 1210, 1211, 1228, 1233, *1255*
Osborne, R., 34, *54*, 230, 232, *256, 439*, 524, 525, *528*, 612, *628*, 659, *683, 686*, 985, *996, 1003*, 1045, *1063*
Oser, F. K., 624, *628*
O'Shea, T., 381, *388*
Osler, J., 1227, *1255*
Osoko, H., 1212, *1249*
Ossimitz, G., 668, *686*
Ost, D. H., 1071, *1101*
Östman, L., *625*, 694, *723*, 774, *779, 780*
Ostrum, T. M., 1068, *1101*
O'Sullivan, C. Y., 175, 181, 190, *195*
Otsuji, H., 1072, 1093, *1096*
Otto, G., 603, *626*
Otto, P. B., 348, *368*
Oulton, C., 696, 697, 699, 707, *721, 724*

Ovens, P., 818, *829*, 1220, 1235, *1256*
Over, R., *1040*
Overholt, J. L., 547, *557*
Oversby, J., 662, 667, *686*
Overstreet, C., 952, *963*
Owen, E., *1039*
Owen, L., 658, *686*
Owens, C. V., 500, 520, *532*

P

Pace, P., 703, *721*
Packard, B. W., 145, 146, *164*
Page, R., 323, *343*
Page, S., 703, *721*
Paige, R. M., 105, *122*
Painter, D. M., de 1228, *1256*
Pajares, F., 91, *96*
Pajares, M. F., 1044, *1064*, 1079, 1095, *1101*
Palacio, D., 1113, 1116, *1142*
Palinscar, A. S., 20, *29*, 450, 451, *464*, 496, 521, *527*, *531*, 820, *829*
Pallant, A., 474, 484, *489*
Pallas, A., 20, *29*, 923, *938*
Pallrand, G., 986, *1002*
Pallrand, G. J., 663, *686*
Palmer, D., 375, *390*, *439*, 508, *532*, 1085, *1101*
Palmer, D. H., 79, 82, 84, *99*
Palmer, E. L., 350, *368*
Palmer, J., 689, 690, 692, 696, 697, 698, 701, 704, 705, 707, *722*
Palmer, S., 152, *158*
Palmisano, M. J., 730, 753, *778*
Palombaro, M., 296, 300, *312*, *315*
Pang, J. S., 506, *532*, 541, 552, 553, 554, *558*
Pankiewicz, P. R., 668, *683*
Panter-Brick, C., 692, *722*
Panwar, R., 895, *907*
Papademetriou, E., 512, 515, *534*
Papadimitriou, V., 703, *722*
Papantiniou, V., 701, *714*
Pardhan, H., 1116, 1117, *1144*
Pardo, R., 761, 763, *778*
Paria, J., 673, *684*
Paris, N. A., *99*
Paris, S. G., 145, 146, *164*
Park, D. Y., 112, *119*
Park, H., 1125, *1142*, *1144*
Park, H.-J., 1077, *1101*
Park, P., 1209, *1256*
Parke, C. S., 1010, *1037*
Parke, H., 1081, *1104*, 1195, 1197, 1198, 1200, *1203*
Parker, J., 513, 514, *530*, 965, 970, *1003*, *1006*, 1114, 1116, 1117, *1141*, *1144*, *1145*
Parker, L., 263, 272, *283*
Parker, L. H., 263, *281*, 599, *628*

Parker, V., 510, *532*
Parker, Z., 1245, *1254*
Parkinson, J., 81, *99*
Parkyn, M., 139, *164*
Parr, C., 479, 488, *490*
Parrot, L., 273, *283*
Parsons, S., 1126, *1145*
Pasley, J. D., 396, *441*, 1190, *1202*, 1213, *1259*
Patterson, E. W., 518, *532*
Patterson, J., 924, *938*
Patterson, N., 1085, *1101*
Patton, J., 297, 299, *314*
Patton, J. R., 292, 293, 300, *314*, *315*
Patton, M. Q., 945, 946, 954, *961*, *962*
Paule, L., 356, *369*
Payne, P., 692, 700, 701, 702, 703, 705, 706, *722*
Pea, R. D., 63, *73*, 407, *435*, 673, 675, *682*
Peacock, A., 504, *532*, 1082, *1101*, 1117, 1130, *1145*
Peacock, G., *1147*
Pearce, C. R., 1231, *1256*
Pearce, U. J., 156, *162*
Pearl, R. E., 1072, *1101*
Pearlman-Avnion, 1195, 1199, *1202*
Pearson, J., *1064*
Peasley, K., 1122, *1135*, *1257*
Peat, M., 995, *1003*
Peck, C., *316*
Pedauye, R., 705, *720*
Pedersen, J., 888, *908*, 1072, *1101*, 1130, *1143*
Pedescleaux, D., *281*
Pedretti, E., 138, 139, 156, *164*, 899, *902*, *908*
Peel, G., 703, *722*
Peeples, E. E., 850, *875*
Peers, C. E., 505, *532*
Pekarek, R., 1055, *1064*, 1213, *1256*
Pell, T., 80, 81, *100*
Pella, M. O., 737, 741, *779*, 848, *879*
Pellegrino, J. W., 288, *311*, 955, *962*, 974, *1001*, *1038*
Pelletier, L. G., 87, 89, *97*
Peng, S., 186, *195*
Penick, J. E., 426, *439*, 734, *779*, 848, 849, 851, 852, 858, *875*, 1213, *1256*
Penna, C., 1173, *1176*
Penner, A., 274, *283*
Penner, D. E., 406, *439*, 513, *532*
Pennington, K., 548, 554, *555*
Penso, S., 592, *597*
Penuel, W. R., 486, *490*
Pereira, M., 700, *713*
Pereira, P., 1057, *1064*
Peressini, D., 818, *830*
Perez, G., 341, *342*
Perkes, V. A., 1118, *1145*
Perkins, D., 538, *558*
Perold, H., 521, *533*
Perrenoud, P., 972, *1003*
Perrier, F., 76, 80, 85, *100*

Perry, B., 1215, *1253*
Perry, D. L., 137, *164*
Perry, M., 278, *279*
Peters, A., 705, 722
Peters, C., 182, *194*
Peters, J., 1192, *1202*
Peters, T., 545, *558*
Peterson, P., 1122, *1137*
Peterson, P. L., 1043, *1061*, 1206, *1248*
Peterson, R., 1123, 1129, *1145*
Peterson, R. F., 641, *651*
Peterson, S., 502, *534*
Petri, J., 620, *628*, 640, *651*
Petrigala, M., 300, *315*
Petrosino, A., 406, *434*
Petty, R. E., 78, 93, *96, 100*
Peyton, R., 695, 697, *718*
Pfundt, H., 34, *54*, 1153, *1178*
Philips, S. U., 64, *73*
Philliber, S. G., 1129, *1144*
Phillips, G., 1014, 1015, 1024, *1037*
Phillips, K. A., 85, *100*
Phillips, L. M., 457, 460, 463, *466, 468*, 750, 762,
    777, 778
Phillips, N., 300, *312*
Phye, G. D. E., 981, *1003*
Piaget, J., 32, 33, *55*, 59, *73*, 511, 523, 532, 665, *686*
Piburn, M., 308, *314*, 663, *685*
Piburn, M. D., 664, *686*
Pickering, K., 658, *686*
Pierce, W. D., 86, *97*
Piirto, J., 305, *314*
Pilburn, M. D., 79, 80, 82, *100*
Pinal, A., 66, *74*, 184, *196*
Pine, K., 1127, 1132, *1145*
Pines, A., 1045, *1065, 1259*
Pinkerton, K., 1228, *1256*
Pinnegar, S. E., 1123, 1128, *1145*
Pintrich, P. R., 38, *55*, 76, 85, 86, 88, 89, 90, 91, 92, 94,
    99, 100, 102, 373, *390*, 607, *628*, 1095, *1099*
Pittman, K. M., 990, *1003*
Pitton, A., *777*
Pizzini, E. L., 424, 425, *439*, 1193, 1199, *1203*
Plant, M., 707, 722
Plecki, M. L., 185, *194*
Plucker, J. A., 1073, 1093, *1101*
Poisson, M., 245, *256*
Poland, D., 307, *316*
Poldrack, R. A., *316*
Polkinghorne, D., 703, 722
Pollard, A., 692, 722, 979, *1003*
Pollard, D. S., 273, *283*
Pollard, R. R., 301, *315*
Polloway, E., 292, 293, 296, 297, 300, *314, 315*
Polman, J. L., 63, *73*, 406, *439*
Polya, G., 379, *390*
Pomeroy, D., 216, *225*

Poock, J., 425, *434*
Poodry, C., 214, *225*
Popham, W. J., 988, *1003*
Popper, K. R., 835, *878*
Porlán, R., 1124, *1145*
Porter, A., 695, 722, 924, 925, *940*, 951, *960*, 1014
Porter, A. C., *1038*, 1194, *1202*, 1206, *1251*
Porter, B., 700, 701, *720*
Porter, M., 1116, *1139*
Posch, P., 689, 698, 703, 707, 722
Poskitt, J., 967, *998*
Posner, G. J., 35, 36, 38, 48, *55*, 60, *73*, 1048, *1064*,
    1154, 1155, *1178*, 1212, *1256*
Posner, J., 7, *29*, 659, *686*
Postlethwaite, T. N., 1015, 1018, *1038*
Postman, N., 419, *439*, 689, 722
Potter, E., 507, 514, 519, 526, *529*
Potter, J., 339, *342*
Potter, J. T., 274, *280*
Potter, L., 705, *725*
Powell, J., 931, 932, *941*
Powell, J. C., 825, 830
Powell-Mikel, A., 145, 156, *162*
Prain, V., 67, 72, 73, 74, 458, 460, 461, *466, 468*, 514,
    528, 859, *874*, 1191, *1202*
Prain, V. R., 425, *437*
Prather, J. P., 141, *164*, 353, 365, *366, 368*
Prawat, M. F., 827, *830*
Preece, P. F. W., 970, *1003*, 1116, *1145*
Prelle, S., 701, *723*, 894, *908*
Prenzel, M., 610, *629*
Pressley, M., 63, *71*, 451, *466*
Preston, K. R., 646, *650*
Preston, R., 988, *1002*
Pribyl, J. R., 663, *686*
Price, R. F., 881, 884, 891, *903*, 1090, *1098*
Priest, M., 130, *160*
Prieto, T., 637, *652*
Proctor, C., 228, *256*
Prosser, M., 1124, *1148*
Prothero, W., 445, 463, *467*
Pryor, J., 967, 974, 975, 976, 977, 979, 980, 994,
    1003, 1005
Psillos, D., 39, *55*, 625, 733, *779*
Puchner, L., 143, *164*
Pugach, M., 294, 299, 301, *313, 314*, 1043, *1061*
Pugh, A. F., 1113, *1140*
Pugh, D., 548, 554, *555*
Pugh, K., 65, *74*
Pugh, K. R., *315*
Punch, K. F., 84, *100*
Purdie, N., 977, *1001*
Purser, R. K., 404, *439*
Pushkin, D., *625*
Putman, R. T., *1136*
Putnam, R., 1045, *1060*, 1067, *1102*, 1108, 1155,
    1156, *1178*

Puttick, G. M., 1191, 1198, *1203*
Putz, A., 1232, *1256*
Pyke, C., 1130, *1143*

Q

Qian, J., 175, 181, 190, *195*
Qiang, Y., *1104*
Qualter, A., 800, *806, 1145*
Queitzsch, M., *961*
Quek, C. L., 113, *122*
Quellmalz, E. S., 1008, *1038*
Querioz, G., 138, *160*
Quilez-Pardo, J., 646, *651*, 1114, *1145*
Quinn, J., *1145*
Quinn, S., 260, *283*
Quintana, C., 474, 485, *490*
Quiroz, P. A., 13, *28*, 183, 184, *193*

R

Raaflaub, C. A., 109, 112, *122*
Radenbush, S. W., 956, *960*
Radford, D. L., 1055, *1064*
Radinsky, J., *438, 490*
Radziewicz, C., 292, *316*
Rafea, A. M., 896, *908*
Raghavan, K., 507, 509, 513, *532*
Raghubir, K. P., 398, *439*
Rahm, J., 186, *195*, 320, 334, 335, 340, *343*
Railsback, S., 474, *489*
Raina, M. K., 1110, 1128, *1145*
Rainey, R., 90, *100*, 918, *940*
Rainforth, B., 296, 300, *312, 315*
Rainson, S., 39, *56*
Raisch, M., 1210, *1247*
Raizen, S., 396, *440*, 734, *779*, 1011, 1021, 1022, *1035, 1037, 1038, 1039*
Rakow, S. J., 176, *195*, 543, *558*
Ralya, L. L., 1111, *1145*
Ramaprasad, A., 972, 979, *1004*
Ramey-Gassert, L., 136, *164*
Ramos, E., 498, *533*
Ramsden, J. B., 982, *1002*
Ramsden, J. M., 78, 93, *100*, 644, *651*
Ramsey, G., 842, 843, *878*
Ramsey, G. A., 397, *439*
Ramsey, J., 697, *723*
Ramsey, L. L., 969, *999*
Randall, J., 704, *723*
Randle, D., 66, *70*
Ranney, M. A., 79, 80, 81, 85, *101*
Rapoport, R., 143, *164*
Raptis, J., 275, *285*

Rasher, S. P., 105, *123*
Ratcliffe, M., 732, 774, *776, 779*, 833, *878*, 884, 892, 894, 898, *902, 907, 908*, 971, 989, 990, 993, 995, *1003*
Rath, A., 522, *533*
Rathje, R., 695, *714*
Rauch, F., 696, *723*
Raudenbush, S., 111, *119*, 475, *489*
Rauhauser, B., 300, *315*
Raun, C. E., 1071, 1072, *1097*, 1118, *1136*
Raven, J., *996*
Ravest, J., 139, *164*
Rawling, R., 703, *716*
Ray, H., 662, 676, *687*
Rayl, A. J. S., 153, *164*
Raynor, J. O., 90, *96*
Raz, G., 7, 8, 10, 11, 12, 13, 18, 24, *29*
Razali, S. N., 1091, *1102*
Reardon, J., 1219, 1222, 1231, *1256*
Reason, P., 696, *723*, 1209, *1256*
Reay, D., 967, 980, *1004*
Rebello, N. S., 622, *629*
Rebello, S., 622, *628*
Redish, E. F., 606, 608, 609, *628*
Reed, C. J., 1077, *1098*
Rees, T., 268, *283*
Reeve, J., 89, *89*, 95, *100, 102*
Reeve, P. T., 294, *314*
Rehfeld, D., 547, *556*
Reid, A., 704, *723*
Reid, N., 83, *100*, 608, *628*
Reiding, J., 746, 771, *776*, 896, *903*
Reimann, P., 380, *390*
Reiser, B., 403, 412, 413, *439*, 474, 486, *489, 490*
Reiser, B. J., 410, 413, *438, 440*
Reiss, M. J., 886, 888, 893, 900, *908*
Renner, J. W., 384, 385, *386, 389, 390*, 404, *439, 440*
Rennie, L., 84, *100*, 126, 127, 128, 133, 134, 136, 138, 139, 141, 142, 143, 146, 149, 150, 154, *159, 160, 161, 164, 165*, 258, 263, 265, 272, 276, 278, *281, 283*, 496, 497, 505, *530, 534*, 543, 552, *558*, 599, *628*, 770, *777, 779*, 965, *1003*, 1054, *1062*
Rentel, J., 703, *723*
Renzulli, J. S., 307, *314*
Resnick, J., *1039*
Resnick, L., 87, *98*, 128, *165, 683*
Rettig, M., 552, 553, *555*
Reveles, J. M., 462, *468*
Revilla, E., 474, *489*
Reyes, M., 178, *195*
Reynolds, M., 297, 301, *314, 317*
Reynolds, M. C., 1106, *1145*
Reynolds, S., 663, *685*
Reynolds, S. J., 664, *686*
Riah, H., 107, 109, 113, *122*
Rice, D., 150, *158*
Rice, D. C., 983, *1004*
Rice, J. M., 943, *962*

Rice, K., 1116, *1138*
Rich, A. C., 257, 258, 275, *283*
Richards, P., 214, 215, 216, 218, *225*
Richardson, L., *1258*
Richardson, M., 704, *723*
Richardson, R., 694, *723*
Richardson, V., 78, *100*, 818, *830*, 1044, *1064*, 1069, 1076, *1102*, 1188, *1203*, 1236, *1256*
Richert, A., 1106, *1149*
Richmond, G., 270, *284*, 453, 454, 457, *468*, 1079, *1102*
Rickards, A., 107, *120*
Rickards, T., 115, 116, *119, 120*
Rickinson, M., 141, 143, *165*, 689, 698, 699, 700, 701, 708, *723*
Riddell, K., 703, *722*
Riddle, O., 351, *368*
Ridgeway, D. W., 395, *438*
Ries, R., 307, *316*
Ries, R. R., 307, *311*
Rigendinger, L., 703, 707, *719*
Riggs, E. M., 663, 664, 667, *686*
Riggs, I., 1072, 1084, 1098, *1102*
Rikihana, T., 208`, *225*
Riley, D., 263, *281*
Riley, J. P. H., 848, 852, 865, *878*
Rillero, P., 548, *555*
Riquarts, K., 600, 601, *629*
Ritchie, S. M., 496, 507, 521, 522, *533*, 1075, *1102*, 1126, *1145*
Ritger, S. D., 668, *686*
Rivard, L. P., 67, *73*, 425, *439*, 444, 445, 458, 460, 461, *468*
Rivet, A. E., 177, *195*
Rivkin, M., 707, *723*
Rizzo, J. V., 302, *316*
Robert, G., 184, *194*
Roberts, A., 1228, *1256*
Roberts, D. A., 693, 694, 703, *723*, 736, 738, 748, 752, 758, 768, *779*, 881, 888, 895, 896, 899, *908*, 1122, 1126, 1128, *1139, 1145*, 1226, 1231, *1256*
Roberts, L., 131, 132, 136, *165*
Roberts, M., 208`, *225, 723*
Roberts, N., 4, *28*
Robertson, A., 698, 707, *723*
Robertson, I. J., 84, *100*, 413, *434*
Robinson, E., 108, *123*
Robinson, E. S., 135, *165*
Robinson, J. T., 588, *596, 687*, 852, 853, *878*
Robitaille, D. F., 1017, *1038*
Robottom, I., 695, 696, 697, 698, 700, 701, 703, 705, 706, 707, *717, 722, 723, 905*
Robyn, A., 930, *939*
Rodriguez, A. B., 453, 454, *466*
Rodriguez, A. J., 172, 175, 179, 182, 185, *195, 196*, 993, *1004*
Roebuck, K. I., 544, 551, 552, *558*
Roehrig, G., 1085, *1101*

Rogers, C., 87, *100, 1255*
Rogers, M., 1122, *1137*
Rogoff, B., 14, 29, 45, *55*, 63, *73*, 128, *163*, 174, *193*, 288, *314*, 982, 987, *1004*
Rojewski, J. W., 301, *315*
Rollnick, M., 80, 81, 82, *96*, 521, *533*, 1117, *1145*
Romagnano, L. S., 818, *830*
Romjue, M., 704, *715*
Romo, V., 1129, *1139*
Ron, S., 593, *597*
Rop, C. J., 93, *100*, 981, *1004*
Rosaen, C. R., 1210, 1213, *1256*
Rosas, C., 1209, *1256*
Roschelle, J., 128, *165*
Roscoe, R. D., 37, *52*
Rose, L. H., 503, *534*
Rose, S., 153, 156, *165*
Rosebery, A., 19, *29*, 179, 180, 188, *196, 197*, 329, *343*, 456, *468, 469*, 496, *534*, 1191, 1198, *1203*, 1214, 1221, 1233, *1247*
Roseman, J., 396, 400, *437*, 665, *686*, 1130, *1142*, 1213, *1253*
Rosen, S. A., 394, *439*
Rosenbaum, S., *962*
Rosenfeld, S., 136, *161*
Rosenman, E. J., 586, 587, *597*
Rosenquist, A., 1013, *1039*
Rosenthal, D. B., 586, *597*
Rosenthal, R., 92, *100*
Rosewell, B. S., 1010, *1036*
Rosiek, J., 179, 189, *196*, 203, *222*
Rosier, M. J., 1018, *1039*
Ross, G., 485, *491*
Ross, J., 1055, 1056, 1057, *1063*, 1157, *1177*, 1215, 1243, 1246, *1254*
Ross, K., 662, *686*, 1010, *1040*
Ross, N. R., 588, *596*
Rosser, S., 270, 271, *283*
Rossi, P. H., 945, *962*
Rossiter, M. W., 275, *283*
Rossman, G. B., 923, 925, 934, *941*
Roth, C., 707, *715*
Roth, K. J., 550, *558*, 1124, *1141, 1145*, 1207, 1210, 1212, 1213, 1214, 1228, *1247, 1250, 1252, 1256, 1257*
Roth, M., 514, *527*, 1073, *1096*, 1119, *1134*, 1234, *1246*
Roth, R., 707, *714*
Roth, W. M., 45, 46, *55*, 60, 62, 66, *70, 73*, 118, *123*, 182, *196*, 291, *315*, 375, *389, 390*, 405, 406, *439*, 452, 462, *468*, 477, 497, 507, 508, 509, *532, 533, 686*, 730, 736, 755, 756, 757, 759, 769, 771, 772, *779*, 884, 886, 887, 890, 894, 895, 899, *906, 907, 908*, 982, 983, 990, 991, 994, *1002, 1004, 1006*, 1054, *1063*, 1112, 1113, *1145*, 1210, 1228, *1257*
Rothman, A. I., 852, *878*, 886, *910*, 1106, *1145*
Rothman, R., 1014, *1039*
Rottenberg, C., 1010, *1039*
Rousseau, M. K., 141, *166*

Rowe, M. B., 377, 378, *390*, 408, *439*, 851, *878*
Rowe, M. J., 308, *312*
Rowe, R. W., 397, 427, *439*
Rowell, J. A., 39, *55*
Rowell, P. M., 518, *533*, 895, *908*, 1128, *1140*
Rowland, P. M., 214, 215, 218, *225*
Rowland, S. M., 668, *686*
Rowlands, S., 59, 64, *73*
Roychoudhury, A., 325, *343*, 406, *439*, *686*, 983, *1004*
Rua, M., 83, 84, *98*, 272, 273, *281*, 508, 509, 512, 522, *529*, *531*, 1110, 1116, *1141*
Rubba, P. A., 353, *369*, 407, *435*, 837, 851, 858, 864, 865, 866, *875*, *878*, 884, 888, *908*, *910*, 983, *1004*, 1071, *1099*, 1115, *1136*
Ruble, D., 278, *283*
Rucinski, T. T., 549, *555*
Rudd, J. A., 425, *439*
Ruddick, J., 1227, *1257*
Rudolph, J. L., 409, *439*, 820, *830*, 833, *878*, 881, 894, *908*
Ruiz, C., 1133, *1143*
Ruiz-Primo, M., 181, *196*, 982, 983, 988, 990, *1004*, 1012, 1013, 1030, *1039*
Rury, J., 260, *283*
Rushworth, P., 7, *28*, 230, 232, *254*, 625, 656, *682*, 976, *999*
Russell, E., *490*
Russell, J. W., 645, *651*
Russell, T., 446, 447, 453, *468*, 800, *806*, 817, *830*, 1043, 1047, 1050, 1057, *1061*, *1062*, *1063*, *1064*, *1065*, 1108, 1112, 1122, 1131, *1144*, *1145*, 1153, 1159, 1160, 1162, 1165, 1168, *1177*, *1178*, 1210, 1216, 1218, 1236, *1250*, *1254*, *1257*
Russell, T. L., 1057, *1063*
Russell, T. L., 63, *73*
Russon, C., 356, 357, 358, 359, 360, 361, *368*
Rutherford, F. J., 565, 570, *597*, 619
Rutherford, J., 540, *558*
Rutherford, J. F., 852, *878*
Rutherford, M., 218, *226*, 384, *387*, 1117, *1145*
Rutland, A., 725
Ryan, A., 82, *96*
Ryan, A. G., 866, *873*, 898, *908*
Ryan, C., 647, *651*, 1113, *1146*
Ryan, F. L., *437*
Ryan, J., 983, 985, *1004*, *1005*
Ryan, R. M., 86, 87, 89, 95, *97*, *100*
Ryder, J., 46, *55*, 694, 695, *723*, 742, 752, *779*, 861, *876*, 887, 889, 890, *908*
Rye, J. A., 983, *1004*
Ryndak, D. L., 296, *315*

S

Sacks, O., 127, *165*
Sadker, D., 258, *283*
Sadker, M., 258, *283*

Sadler, P., 886, 889, *908*, 972, 977, 979, 990, *1004*, 1011, *1039*, 1071, *1102*
Sadler, T. D., 861, *878*
Sáez, M. J., 882, *908*
Saglam, Y., *651*
Sai, C. L., *1143*
Said, E., 202, *226*
Sako, T., 105, 112, *121*
Salisbury, C., 296, 300, *312*, *315*
Säljö, R., 65, *73*
Salvione, P., 300, *315*
Samarapungavan, A., 637, *651*
Sambursky, S., 619, *628*
Sammons, P., 80, *102*
Sampson-Cordle, A. V., 346, *369*
Samson, S., 983, 985, *1004*, *1005*
Samuel, D., 398, 399, *434*, *436*, 1129, *1141*
Samuel, J., 380, *388*
Samuel, K. V., 647, 650, *1139*
Sanches, M., 1125, 1126, *1139*
Sanchez, G., 1122, *1146*
Sanchez Jimenez, J. M., 1113, *1146*
Sander, F., 609, *628*
Sanders, D., 141, 143, *165*
Sanders, J. R., 945, 946, *960*, *963*
Sanders, L. R., 1119, 1123, *1146*
Sanders, M., 1115, 1132, *1146*
Sanders, W. L., 954, *962*
Sandmann, A., 541, 542, 545, *556*, *558*
Sandoval, W. A., 64, *73*, 410, 412, 413, *440*, 454, 463, *468*, 868, *878*
Sandretto, S., 1067, *1100*
Sanford, B., *1255*
Sang-Joon, N., 704, *723*
Santi, M., 705, *720*
Santos, E., 213, *222*
Sapon-Shevin, M., 297, 301, *315*
Sarason, S., 814, 827, *830*, 1044, *1064*, 1152, *1178*
Sarf, A., 994, *1004*
Sargent, C., 990, *1006*
Sarther, C. M., 820, *830*
Sartoris, M. L., 507, 509, *532*
Sasson, I., 412, *435*
Saul, J. M., 609, *628*
Saul, W., 1219, 1222, 1228, *1256*, *1257*
Saumell, L., 297, *316*
Saunders, W. L., 424, *440*
Sauvé, L., 704, *723*
Savage, G., 143, *162*
Scaife, J., 378, *389*
Scantlebury, K., 118, *123*, 183, 185, *193*, 219, *226*, 269, 270, 271, 272, 274, 277, 278, *283*, *284*, 325, 326, *342*, 930, 932, *939*, 1196, *1202*
Scardamalia, M., 87, *100*, 376, *387*, 460, *465*, 474, 484, *490*
Schaefer, G., 777
Schafer, L. E., 1118, *1138*

Schaffarzick, J., 918, 919, *940*

Scharmann, L. C., 832, 833, 837, 849, 850, 852, 857, *876, 878*

Schauble, L., 128, *129, 165*, 406, *439*, 513, *532*, 1219, 1224, 1228, *1253*

Schecker, H., 604, 606, 608, 609, 610, 617, *628*

Scheppler, J. A., 730, 753, *778*

Schibeci, R., 77, 78, *100, 903*, 1048, 1049, *1064*, 1129, *1146*

Schiele, B., 131, *165*

Schilling, M., *1145*

Schleppegrell, M., 703, *714*

Schlessinger, F. R., 921, *940*

Schmidt, D. J., 839, *878*

Schmidt, H.-J., 638, 639, *651*

Schmidt, J. A., 1123, *1135*

Schmidt, W., 1018, 1020, 1021, *1037*

Schmidt, W. H., 396, *440*, 888, *910*, 923, *940, 1038, 1039, 1040*

Schmitt, K. L., 151, *167*

Schmitt, L., 297, *312*

Schnack, K., 694, 707, *719, 724*

Schneider, L. S., 404, *440*

Schneider, R., 333, *343*

Schoenemann, A., *1257*

Schoenfeld, A. H., 1206, 1212, *1248, 1257*

Schommer-Aikins, M., 91, *99*

Schön, D., 1043, *1064*, 1106, *1146*, 1160, 1163, 1170, 1174, 1175, *1178*, 1209, 1214, *1257*

Schoon, K. J., 496, 497, *533*, 656, 662, 667, *686*, 1111, 1112, 1114, *1146*

Schreuder, D., 703, *724*

Schriver, M., 1129, *1146*

Schroeder, H., *437*

Schubeck, K., 545, *558*

Schubert, W. H., 811, 812, 813, *830*

Schuck, S., 1058, *1064*

Schultz, K., 272, *280*

Schulz, W., 603, *626*

Schumacher, W., *596*

Schumm, J., 293, 296, 297, *315, 316*

Schumm, S. A., 656, *686*

Schunk, D. H., 86, 87, 88, 89, 90, 91, *100, 101*

Schwab, J. J., 562, 569, 570, 585, 588, *597*, 674, *686*, 896, *909, 1146*

Schwartz, D. L., 406, *434*, 481, *490*

Schwartz, R. S., 410, *440*, 500, *533*, 856, 867, *877, 878*, 971, *1002*

Schwille, J. R., 924, 926, *940*

Schwirian, P., 863, *879*, 1071, *1102*

Sciarretta, M. R., 1117, *1146*

Sconiers, Z. D., 179, 189, *196*

Scot, L., 888, *909*

Scott, B. J., 300, *315*

Scott, C., 132, 134, 138, *160, 165*

Scott, C. A., 1227, *1257*

Scott, C. B., *806*

Scott, E., *1039*

Scott, J. C., 20, *29*

Scott, L., *806*

Scott, P., 39, 41, 42, 44, 49, 50, *52, 54*, 377, *389*, 621, *625*, 646, *650, 657, 682*, 695, 698, *716, 720*, 831, *875*, 1156, *1178*, 1212, *1249*

Scott, P. H., 36, 41, 44, 47, *55*, 618, *628*

Scott, R. H., 107, 110, *123*

Scott, W., 691, 696, 697, 699, 702, 702, 704, 707, *716, 717, 721, 723, 724, 725*

Screven, C. G., 135, *165*

Scribner, J. P., 364, *369*

Scribner, S., 14, *29*, 45, *55*, 749, *779*

Scrimsher, S., 1155, *1178*

Scriven, M., 135, *165*, 954, *962, 968, 969, 1004*

Scruggs, T. E., 295, 296, 298, 299, *313, 315*, 502, *531*

Sebela, M. P., 108, *123*

Secada, W. G., 13, *28*, 183, 184, *193*

Seeber, F., 663, *686*

Segal, G., *1064*

Segall, A., 1057, 1058, 1161, *1178*

Seller, G., 179, 189, 196, 274, 277, 284, 327, 329, 337, 338, 339, *343*

Selby, D., 704, *724*

Self, P., 701, *719*

Seligman, M. E. P., 90, *101*

Sellers, S., 425, *437*

Semali, L. M., 202, 206, 207, *226*

Semken, S. C., 664, *686*

Semper, R. J., 133, 138, 150, *165*

Senese, J., 1221, *1257, 1258*

Senge, P. M., 668, *686*

Senkbeil, M., 610, *629*

Seo, H. A., 112, *119*

Seopa, M. A., 109, 112, *119, 123i*

Sequeira, M., 1076, *1102*, 1127, *1146*

Sere, G. M., 400, *440*

Serrano, A., *1040*

Serrell, B., 138, *166*

Settlage, J., 185, 190, *196*, 897, *909*, 1130, *1146*

Settlage, J., Jr., *1144*

Severs, M., 1133, *1149*

Sewell, R. D. E., 988, *1004*

Seymour, E., 275, *284*, 886, *909*

Sfard, A., 34, 35, 48, *55*

Shafer, L., 1208, *1258*

Shaffer, S., 57, *73*

Shallcross, T., 1112, *1146*

Shamos, M., 736, 739, 761, *779*

Shann, M. H., 546, *558*

Shapin, S., 57, *73*

Shapiro, B., 61, *71*

Shapiro, B. L., 850, 851, *879*, 886, *909*, 1182, *1203*

Shapka, J., 276, *284*

Shapley, K. S., 985, *1004*

Sharma, A., 5, 27, *29*

Sharp, D. W., 14, *28*

Shavelson, R., 172, 181, *194, 196,* 429, *440,* 981, 982, 983, 988, 990, *1001, 1004, 1005,* 1012, 1013, 1030, *1039,* 1206, *1251*

Shaw, J., 982, 992, *1004*

Shaw, J. M., 181, *196*

Shaw, K. M., 135, 136, *157*

Shaw, L. E., Jr., 1080, *1098*

Shawberry, J., 505, *529*

Shayer, M., 33, 39, *51, 55*

Shaywitz, B. A., 288, *315*

Shaywitz, S. E., 288, *315*

She, H. C., 84, *101,* 115, *123*

Sheehy, N., 701, *726*

Shemesh, M., 592, *597*

Shen, B. S. P., 730, 739, *779*

Shen, C., 237, 238, 239, 255

Shepard, L. A., 1028, *1039*

Shepardson, D. P., 264, 277, *282,* 425, *439,* 513, 514, 515, 516, 518, 519, *533,* 981, *1004,* 1055, *1064,* 1213, 1228, *1256, 1258*

Sher, B. T., 307, *311*

Sher, J. P., 345, 364, *369*

Sherburne, M., 289, *315*

Sherif, C. W., 77, *101*

Sherif, M., 77, *101*

Sherin, B., 37, 38, *52*

Sherwood, S. P., 292, *315*

Shields, C. J., 133, *166*

Shields, P. M., 914, 927, 928, 929, 931, 932, *940, 941,* 954, *961*

Shimahara, N. K., 1206, *1258*

Shimizu, K., 1206, *1258*

Shimoda, T. A., 507, *533*

Shin, D., 704, *724*

Shinohara, M., 1116, 1117, 1123, *1137*

Shipstone, D. M., 612, *628*

Shmidt, W. H., 5, *29*

Shore, R., 399, *436, 437*

Shorrocks-Taylor, D., *779*

Shortland, M., 133, *166*

Shotland, L. R., 946, *961*

Showalter, 865, 879

Shrager, J., 130, 143, *159*

Shrigley, R. L., 77, 78, 84, *101,* 1071, 1072, *1102, 1103,* 1112, *1146*

Shroyer, G., 356, 363, 364, *369*

Shuell, T., 662, *686*

Shugart, S. S., 1120, *1146*

Shulman, L. S., 379, *390,* 497, *533,* 564, 570, *597,* 603, 623, *629,* 731, *780,* 858, *879,* 976, *1004,* 1046, *1064,* 1106, 1108, 1109, *1140, 1146, 1149,* 1212, *1258,* xii, *xiv*

Shultz, J. J., 66, *73*

Shumow, L., 497, *531,* 1076, *1100*

Shymansky, J. A., *686,* 895, *909,* 919, 920, *940,* 1055, *1064*

Siegel, H., 1069, *1102*

Siegel, M. A., 79, 80, 81, 85, *101*

Siegfried, T., ix, *xiv*

Sikes, J., 572, *595*

Silver, A. Z., 144, *166*

Silverman, F. L., 538, 551, *557*

Silverstein, B., 302, *316*

Simchoni, D., 583, *596*

Sime, R. L., 260, *284*

Simmons, D., 704, *723*

Simmons, M., 700, *724*

Simmons, M. L., 837, *879*

Simmons, P., 1073, 1075, 1080, 1094, *1101, 1102,* 1213

Simmons, P. E., *1258*

Simon, H. A., 381, *389*

Simon, S., 78, 83, 95, *99,* 272, *283,* 403, *439,* 496, *532,* 780, 799, *805, 806,* 886, *907*

Simons, P. R., 507, 517, *528*

Simos, P. G., 288, *315*

Simovska, V., 707, *719*

Simpson, D., 508, 516, 524, *534,* 1226, *1259*

Simpson, M., *315.* 308, 972, *1004*

Simpson, R., 295, *314*

Simpson, R. D., 78, 79, 93, *101,* 1068, *1102*

Simpson, W. D., 362, *369*

Sinatra, G., 36, *56,* 373, *390, 1102*

Sinclair, B. B., 109, 117, *123*

Sinclair, J., 445, *468*

Sinclair, U., 786, *806*

Singh, B., 970, 974, *999*

Singh, K., 84, *101*

Singh, R., 105, *123*

Singleton-Taylor, G., 213, *222*

Sinnott, E. W., 351, *368*

Sireci, S. G., 1013, *1036, 1039*

Sizer, T. R., 912, *940*

Sjøberg, S., 233, 242, 244, 245, *256,* 736, 743, *780,* 893, 898, *909*

Skaalvik, E. M., 92, *96*

Skamp, K., 497, *533,* 1048, *1064,* 1073, 1078, *1102,* 1126, *1146*

Skeggs, B., 710, *724*

Skelton, A., 995, *1001*

Skinner, N. C., 970, *1003*

Skryabina, E. A., 83, *100,* 608, *628*

Skudlarski, P., *315*

Slater, T. F., 985, *1005*

Slattery, J., *1039*

Slattery, M., 1045, *1062,* 1166, *1176*

Slattery, W., *686*

Slavin, R. E., 383, *387, 390, 939, 940*

Slotta, J. D., 37, 49, *52, 490,* 617, *625*

Slusher, J., 297, *316*

Small, L., *687*

Smilansky, S., 132, 133, *162, 166*

Smith, A., 93, *101*

Smith, B. L., 412, 413, *439*
Smith, C., 540, *558*, 1095, *1098*
Smith, C. L., 7, 8, 10, 11, 12, 13, 18, 24, *29*
Smith, D., 1210, *1258*
Smith, D. A., 150, *166`*
Smith, D. C., 1116, 1117, 1119, 1122, 1123, 1124, 1128, *1134, 1135, 1146, 1147*
Smith, D. M., 1106, 1118, *1147*
Smith, D. S., 1049, *1064*
Smith, D. W., 1133, *1138*
Smith, E., 546, *555*, 837, 865, 867, *874*
Smith, E. L., 456, 457, 462, *467*, 659, *686*, 1123, 1124, *1135*, 1212, *1257*
Smith, E. R., 943, *962*
Smith, F. M., 186, *196*
Smith, J., 289, *315*
Smith, J. B., 184, *194*
Smith, J. B., 184, *194*
Smith, J. M., *878*
Smith, L., 1077, *1102*
Smith, L. T., 203, 207, 210, 220, *226*
Smith, M., 794, *806*
Smith, M. L., *938*, 1010, *1039*
Smith, M. R., 207, 213, *226*
Smith, M. S., 922, *940*
Smith, M. U., 832, 833, 857, *878, 879*, 1068, *1102*
Smith, P., *1035*
Smith, P. S., 396, *441*, 970, *1005*, 1213, *1259*
Smith, R., 641, *649*
Smith, R., 185, *193*
Smith, R. B., 5, *29*
Smith, R. G., 1111, 1117, 1120, *1143, 1147*
Smith, S., 707, *724*
Smith, T. A., 236, *254, 255*, 262, *279*, 604, *625, 1035, 1036, 1037, 1038*
Smith, T. E., 292, 293, 300, *315*
Smith, W. S., 177, *194*
Smith-Sebasto, N., 701, 702, *724*
Smyth, J., 690, 696, 704, *724*
Snapp, M., 383, *387*, 572, *595*
Sneider, C. I., 517, *533*
Snider, B., 889, *910*
Snipes, J., 322, *343*
Snir, J., 7–13, 18, 24, *29*
Snively, G., 177, 178, *196*, 205, 206, 208, 211, *222, 226*
Snow, C., 183, *197*
Snow, R. E., 75, 79, *101*
Snyder, J., 993, *999*
Snyder, T. E., 459, *466*, 1153, *1177*
Snyder, V. L., 259, 277, *284*
So, W. W., 1122, *1147*
Sobel, D., 705, *724*
Soerjaningsih, W., 107, 109, 114, *123*
Soetaert, R., 703, *724*
Sokolic, J., 337, 338, *343*

Sokoloff, D. R., 617, 618, *629*
Solano-Flores, G., 181, 190, *196*, 981, 991, 992, 994, *1005*, 1012, 1013, *1039*
Solaz-Portolés, J. J., 1114, *1145*
Solis, S., *1251*
Solomon, E. M., 463, *465*, 1210, *1248*
Solomon, J., 43, *56*, 212, *226*, 674, 687, 695, 698, 701, *723, 724*, 729, 753, 754, *780, 800, 806*, 883, 884, 886, 887, 888, 893, 894, 895, 898, 899, *908, 909*
Solomonidou, C., 635, 636, 637, *651*
Soloway, E., 186, *193*, 333, *343*, 412, *437*, 452, *467*, 481, *490*
Soltis, J., 702, *724*
Sonak, B., 983, *1002*
Songer, N. B., 177, *196*, 337, *343*, 473, 479, 485, 487, 488, *489, 490*, 507, *532*, 610, *627*
Soren, B., 129, 139, *164, 166*
Sørensen, H., 141, *166*
Sorensen, L. L., 843, *879*
Sorsby, B. D., 1112, *1147*
Souque, J.-P., 746, *779*
Southerland, S., 61, 72, 1077, *1102*
Soy, E. M., 1070, 1072, *1102*
Soyibo, K., 85, *101*, 399, *440*
Spatig, L., 273, *283*
Spears, J., 847, 849, 852, *879*
Spencer, D., 704, *724*
Spencer, H., 881, *909*
Spencer, J. N., 386, *387*
Spencer-Cervato, C., 668, *687*
Spender, D., 278, *284*
Sperandeo-Mineo, R. M., 1112, *1135*
Sperling, G., 265, 266, *281*
Spiegel, S. A., 1228, *1258*
Spielberger, C. D., 88, *101*
Spillane, J. P., 184, 185, *196*, 326, *343*, 499, 500, 501, *533*
Spink, E., 1112, *1146*
Spivey, R. E., *390*
Springett, D., 704, *724*
Spruce, M., *1039*
Squires, A., 7, *28*, 230, 232, *254, 625*, 656, *682*, 976, *999*
St. Clair, B., 551, *558*
St. John, K., 1127, 1132, *1145*
St. John, M., 145, *159, 166*, 954, *961*
St. Louis, K., 341, *342*
St. Maurice, H., 705, *725*
Stables, A., 81, *99*, 691, 694, 702, 707, *724, 725*
Stadler, H., 608, *629*
Stafford, B., 969, *1006*
Stage, E., *1037*
Stage, F. K., 175, *195*
Stahl, R. J., 383, *390*
Stahley, L. L., 1228, *1258*
Stainback, S., 295, 296, 297, 300, 303, *315*
Stainback, W., 295, 296, 297, 300, 303, *315*

Stake, J. E., 91, *101*
Stake, R. E., 954, *962*
Stalford, C., *960*
Stalheim, W., *1147*
Stamler, S. E., *255*
Stanisstreet, M., 700, 701, 705, *713, 714, 717*
Stanley, W. B., 177, *196*, 206, 211, *226*
Stanton, K., *1252*
Stanulis, R. N., 1227, *1258*
Stark, L., 358, 359, *369*
Stark, R., 499, *533*
Stauss, N. G., 839, 840, 845, 846, 852, *874*
Staver, J. R., *687*
Stavridou, H., 635, 636, 637, *651*
Stavy, R., 37, 38, 39, *56*, 382, *389*
Stearns, M. S., 954, *961*
Stecher, B. M., 181, *194*, 930, *939, 1001, 1010, 1035, 1037, 1039, 1040*
Steele, C. M., 20, *29*
Stefani, L. A. J., 982, 987, *1005*
Stefanich, G., 288, 296, 297, 298, 299, 300, *314, 316*
Stefanon, L., 1126, *1147*
Steffens, L., 786, *806*
Stein, C., 662, *682*
Stein, S., 662, *682*
Steinbach, J. B., 151, *162*
Steinberg, M., 613, *625*
Steinberg, R. N., 609, *628*
Steiner, L., 1206, *1258*
Steinke, J., 152, *162*
Steinmuller, F., 314, 412, *439*
Stenhouse, L., 1205, 1208, *1258*
Stepans, J., 1117, *1147*
Stephan, C., 383, *387*, 572, *595*
Stephens, C., 704, *725*
Stephens, L., 1070, *1098*
Stephenson, P., 500, 509, 518, 519, 520, *534*, 706, *726*, 1112, *1146*
Sterling, S., 695, 707, *718, 725*
Stern, G. G., 104, *123*
Stern, J., 610, *627*
Stern, J. D., 346, *369*
Stern, L., 586, 587, *597*, 990, *1005*
Sternberg, R. J., 986, *1000*
Stetson, R., 145, 156, *162*
Stevahn, L., 959, *961*
Stevens, C., 1112, *1147*
Stevens, F., 945, *962*
Stevens, F. I., 273, *284*
Stevens, R. G., 988, *1004*
Stevenson, C., 540, 545, *558*
Stevenson, H. W., 1020, *1040*
Stevenson, J., 134, *166*
Stevenson, R., 695, *725*, 1238, 1240, 1241, *1258*
Stevenson, S., 150, *166*
Steward, J., 591, *596*, 824, *829*

Steward, J. H., 591, *598*
Stewart, G., 214, 215, 216, 218, *225*
Stewart, J., 409, 439, 824, 829, *1138*
Stice, G., 863, *879*
Stickell, D. W., 918, *939*
Stiehl, J., 1123, 1134, *1138*
Stigler, J., 1020, *1040*, 1206, 1213, 1231, 1245, *1252, 1258*
Stiles, K. E., 1185, *1202, 1203*, 1206, 1213, *1254*
Stilli, R., 1117, *1146*
Stine, P. C., 346, *369*
Stipek, D. J., 91, *101*
Stockdill, S., 956, *962*
Stocker, A., 704, *725*
Stocklmayer, S. M., 130, 134, 138, *166*, 753, *780*, 894, *909*, 1116, 1127, *1147*
Stoddart, T., 66, *74*, 184, *196*, 507, 509, 526, *533*, 981, 983, 990, 992, *1005*
Stodolsky, S. S., 817, *829*
Stofflett, R., 662, *687*, 1080, *1102*, 1126, *1147*
Stone, C. A., 1010, *1037*
Stone, M. H., *963*
Stout, D., 547, *555*
Stow, D. A., 660, *687*
Stow, W., 508, *533*
Strage, A., 974, 994, *997*, 1075, *1103*, 1132, *1136*
Strain, P., *316*
Straub, D., *316*
Straw, S. B., 67, *73*, 444, 445, 458, 461, *468*
Strawitz, B., 1071, *1103*
Streitmatter, J., 276, *284*
Streten, K., 150, *166*
Strieb, L. Y., *1258*
Strike, K. A., 7, *29*, 35, 36, 38, 48, *55*, 60, *73*, 444, *468*, 659, *686*, 1048, *1064*, 1154, *1178*, 1212, *1256*
Striley, J., 453, 454, 457, *468*
Strömdahl, H., 1114, *1147, 1148*
Stronk, D. R., 1070, *1103*
Stuart, C., 1073, 1078, *1103*
Stuart, T. C., 889, *909*
Stubbs, M., 1242, *1250*
Stuessy, C. L., 545, 547, *558*
Stufflebeam, D. L., 229, *256*, 360, *368*, 562, *597*, 945, 953, 954, *962*
Sturgeon, A., 295, *313*
Sturm, H. E., 1110, *1143*
Suarez, O., 1227, *1247*
Suchman, J., 523, *534*
Suen, H. K., 983, *1002*
Sugarman, J., *1258*
Suggate, J., 701, 704, *722*
Sugi, A., 269, 270, *283*
Sugrue, B., 1012, *1040*
Sullivan, B. A., 1077, *1097*
Sullivan, C., 1228, *1247*
Sullivan, M., 788, *806*
Sullivan, P., *1040*

Sullivan, T., 1071, *1097*
Sumfleth, E., *777*
Summers, M., 498, 501, 503, 507, 513, 514, 525, *531, 534*, 1048, 1049, *1060, 1065*, 1113, 1114, 1116, 1117, *1142, 1143, 1147*
Sumrall, J., 503, *534*
Sunal, D. W., 1072, *1103*
Supovitz, J. A., 1193, 1200, *1203*
Suran, B. G., 302, *316*
Suter, L., 948, *962, 963*
Sutherland, D., 215, 216, *226*, 838, *879*
Suthers, D. D., 969, *1005*
Sutman, F., 863, *877*, 888, *909*, 1072, *1103*
Sutton, C., 57, 62, 67, *74*, 377, *390*, 463, *468*
Suzuki, M., 1114, *1147*
Swackhamer, G., 617, *626*
Swain, H., 259, 276, *280*
Swain, J., 970, *1005*, 1092, *1103*
Swan, M. D., 863, *879*
Swann, A. H., 1110, *1147*
Swanson, P., 1221, *1258*
Sweeney, A. E., *1103*, 1126, *1147*, 1209, 1220, 1220, *1250*
Swenson, J., *1258*
Swidler, S. A., 1077, *1097*
Swift, N. J., 348, 349, *369*
Switzky, H., 700, *716*
Sykes, G., 1206, *1249*
Sykes, H., *715*
Sylva, K., 132, *166*
Symington, D., 141, 142, *161*, 1048, *1060*, 1071, *1103*, 1120, *1147, 1148*, 1157, *1177*
Syryca, S., 300, *315*

T

Taba, H., 1209, *1258*
Tabachnick, B. R., 1077, *1101*, 1125, *1144*, 1167, *1177*, 1215, 1219, *1252, 1258*
Tabak, I., 412, 413, *439, 440*
Taber, K. S., 620, *629*, 638, 639, 641, 642, 646, *651*
Tai, R. H., 886, 889, *908*
Taigen, J., 889, *909*
Taiwo, A., 662, 676, *687*
Takahashi, T., 88, *98*, 513, *530*
Takao, A. Y., 454, 455, *467, 469*
Takemura, S., 1206, *1258*
Takes, M. J., 292, *316*
Tal, R. T., 887, 894, 899, *903, 909*, 1188, *1202*
Talbert, J., 817, *830*
Tallal, P., *316*
Tam, K. Y., 141, *166*
Tamir, P., 374, *389*, 395, 397, 399, 400, 403, 414, 415, 417, *437, 438, 440*, 564, 572, 576, 579, 591, 593, 594, *596, 597, 598*, 674, *687*, 731, *780*, 844, *879*, 888, 899, *910*, 965, 966, 983, *996, 1005*, 1008, 1011, *1036, 1040*, 1108, 1115, 1129, *1141, 1148*

Tan, A., *1037*
Tan, K.-C., 641, *652*
Tan, K. C. D., 990, *1005*
Tanaka, J., 889, *909*
Tank, R., 658, *687*
Tannen, D., 14, *30*
Tannenbaum, A. J., 305, *316*
Tanner, H., 81, *99*
Tanner, T., 705, *725*
Tanzer, M., 474, *489*
Tao, P. K., 860, *879*
Taras, M., 987, *1005*
Tariq, V. N., 982, 987, *1005*
Tasker, R., 403, *440*, 522, *534*, 985, *996*
Tatto, M. T., 1081, *1103*
Taylor, B., 142, *157*
Taylor, C., 704, *725*, 990, *1005*
Taylor, J., 889, *902*
Taylor, J. A., 1112, 1124, *1148*
Taylor, N., 207, 210, *226*, 642, 646, *649*, 704, *725*
Taylor, N. A., 299, *312*
Taylor, P., *1148*
Taylor, P. C., 107, 108, 115, *119, 123*, 886, *907*, 1126, *1143*
Teamey, K., 141, 143, *165*
Teasley, S. D., 128, *165*
Tedesco, A., 302, *311*
Teel, K., *1258*
Teh, G., 110, 111, *123*
Teh, G. P. L., 111, *121*
Tehani, C., 331, 332, 333, *342*
Teixeira dos Sanmtos, F. M., 79, 80, 93, *101*
Temple, E., 289, *316*
Templeman, J., 148, *159*
Terry, J. M., 80, *101*
Terwilliger, L., 1126, *1137*
Tesch, M., 605, 608, *625*
Tesser, A., 94, *99*
Their, H. D., 384, *388*
Thelen, H. A., 104, *121*
Thelen, L. J., *940*
Theobald, M., 259, 260, *284*
Thier, H. D., 523, *531*, 891, *909, 910*
Thiessen, D., 692, *722*
Thijs, G. D., 211, *226*
Thirunarayanan, M. O., 155, *166*
Thomas, G., 130, *162*, 742, 753, 762, *780*
Thomas, J., 698, *724*
Thomas, K., 1197, *1202*
Thomas, N. G., 85, *98*
Thomas, R., 969, *1000*
Thompson, A. G., 1072, *1103*
Thompson, B., 1130, *1141*
Thompson, C. L., 826, *830*, 1072, *1103*
Thompson, D., 1092, *1103*
Thompson, D. B., 662, 665, *684*
Thompson, J., 81, 85, *101*, 399, *440*

Thompson, L. D., 592, *596*
Thompson, S., 301, *316, 1258*
Thomsen, P. V., 607, *627*
Thomson, R. G., 1072, *1103*
Thorén, I., 1117, *1139*
Thorley, N. R., 36, *53,* 513, 516, 517, *530, 534,* 1155, *1177,* 1212, *1252*
Thorley, R., 1045, *1062*
Thornton, R., 155, *158,* 617, 618, *629*
Thorp, H., 117, *123*
Thrall, D., 705, *725*
Threatt, S., 1242, 1244, *1258*
Thurlow, D., 1073, 1078, *1103*
Thurlow, M., 297, 299, 302, *316, 317*
Thurstone, L. L., 77, *101*
Tiberghien, A., 34, 39, 42, *52, 56,* 656, 659, *682,* 1045, *1061,* 1129, *1136*
Tibergien, A., 400, *440*
Tiegerman-Farber, E., 292, *316*
Tiffin, H., 201, 202, *221*
Tikunoff, W. J., 818, *830*
Tilbury, D., 699, 703, 707, *716, 725*
Tilgner, P. J., 496, *534*
Tillotson, J. W., 1216, *1258*
Timar, T. B., 923, *940*
Timperley, H., 978, *998*
Tindall, G., 294, 296, *312, 314*
Tinker, R., 471, *490,* 609, *629*
Tippins, D. J., 377, *390*
Tirosh, D., 37, 38, *56*
Tisher, R., 732, *780,* 886, 898, *910*
Tittle, C., 976, *1005*
Tobias, S., 886, *910*
Tobin, K., 62, *73,* 113, 114, 117, 118, *121, 123,* 179, 180, 182, 189, *196,* 231, 232, *256,* 337, 338, *343,* 347, *369,* 377, 385, *390, 397,* 399, 400, 404, 406, 407, *440,* 507, *529,* 898, *910,* 974, *1002,* 1058, 1059, *1065,* 1082, 1084, 1086, *1103,* 1109, 1122, *1138, 1148,* 1157, *1178,* 1205, 1209, 1210, 1220, 1228, *1251, 1257, 1258,* x, *xiv*
Todt, D., 704, *725*
Tofield, S., 140, 142, 143, *166*
Tolley, K., 259, *284*
Tomer, Y., 1115, *1141*
Tomera, A., 695, 697, *718, 725*
Tomkiewicz, W., 140, *158*
Tomkins, S. P., 511, 514, 517, 519, 520, *534*
Tomlin, J., 548, 554, *555*
Tomlinson, J., *1258*
Tonkin, S., 143, *162*
Top, L., 703, *724*
Topalian, T., 704, *725*
Topping, K., 130, 143, *159*
Torracca, E., 733, *776*
Torrance, H., 966, 967, 974, 975, 976, 977, 979, 980, 991, 992, 994, *1003, 1005*
Torres, H. N., 180, *196*

Torres Soares, J., 700, *713*
Torri, G., 145, *166*
Tosun, T., *1103*
Toth, E. E., 969, 990, *1005*
Toulmin, S., 7, *30,* 63, *74,* 408, *440,* 453, 454, *469,* 654, *687*
Tout, A. F., 135, *163*
Towne, L., 172, *196,* 429, *440,* 1206, *1251*
Townsend, M., 1111, *1141*
Tracy, C. O., *1259*
Trautmann, M., 85, *98*
Trautmann, N. M., 64, *74*
Travers, K. J., 1017, *1040*
Travis, A. S., 676, *681*
Traweek, S., 14, *30*
Treagust, D. F., 128, *159, 254,* 373, 375, 376, 376, 377, 380, 381, 382, *387, 388, 388i, 389,* 390, *391,* 426, *438,* 606, 607, 618, 619, 620, *625, 626, 629,* 633, 638, 639, 640, 641, 643, 645, 646, *650, 651, 652,* 969, 970, 972, 973, 977, 979, 983, 989, 990, 994, *999, 1005, 1006,* 1116, 1121, 1122, 1123, 1127, 1129, 1131, *1140, 1145, 1147, 1148,* 1154, 1155, 1156, 1172, 1174, *1176*
Trefil, J., 739, *777*
Tremayne, M., 149, *166*
Trembath, R. J., 847, 852, *879*
Trend, D. R., 1114, *1148*
Trend, R. D., 656, 662, 665, *687,* 1114, *1148*
Trenholm, S., 78, *101*
Trent, J., 843, 845, *879*
Tretinjak, C. A., 663, 667, *686*
Trickett, E. J., 105, *122*
Trigatti, B., *1248*
Triggs, P., 979, *1003*
Trigwell, K., 1124, 1125, *1148*
Tripp, G., 969, 983, *1006*
Trowbridge, D. E., 616, *629*
Troxel, V. A., 843, *879*
Trumbull, D., 1051, 1057, *1065*
Trumbull, E., 181, 190, *196,* 1013, *1039*
Trumper, R., 1117, *1148*
Trundle, K. C., 1114, *1148*
Tsai, C., 1073, 1078, *1103, 1148*
Tsaparlis, G., 640, 647, *652,* 987, *1006*
Tsatsarelis, C., 46, 47, 50, *53*
Tselfes, V., 733, *779*
Tsuchida, I., 1206, 1210, 1213, *1253, 1254*
Tsui, C.-Y., 376, 382, *390*
Tucker, B. P., 293, *316*
Tudge, J., 1155, *1178*
Tulberg, A., 1114, 1130, *1147, 1148*
Tulviste, P., 43, *56*
Tuner, S., 180, *193*
Tunnicliffe, S. D., 140, *166,* 511, 514, 517, 519, 520, *534*
Tunstall, P., 977, 979, *1000*
Turnbull, A. P., 301, *316*
Turnbull, H. R., 301, *316*
Turnbull, R., 293, *316*

Turner, H. M., 1193, 1200, *1203*
Turner, K., 703, *725*
Turner, S., 707, *725*
Turner, S. A., 507, 525, *534*
Turney, J., 149, *166*
Turns, J., 484, *489*
Twigger, D., 381, *388*
Tyack, D., 814, *830*
Tyler, R., 707, *717*
Tyler, R. W., 943, *962*
Tyler, W. R., 561, 562, *598*
Tyler-Wood, T., 705, *725*
Tytler, R., 502, 509, 512, *534*, 887, *910*

U

Udvari-Solner, A., 300, *316*
Uhrenholdt, G., 700, *719*
Underhill, O. E., 783, 786, 787, 788, *806*
Underhill, R., 544, 545, *556, 558*
Unger, C., 844, *874*
Upadhyay, B. R., 1073, *1104*
Ure, J., 308, *315*
Urhahne, D., 610, *629*
Urlacher, T., *99*
Uselton, H. W., 1110, *1148*
Uysal, S., 269, 270, *283*
Uzzell, D., 136, *166*, 701, 725

V

Vahey, P., 471, *490*
Valcárcel, M. V., 1122, *1146*
Valenza, M. A., 1112, *1135*
Valian, V., 271, *284*
Vallerand, R. J., 87, 89, *97*
Valverde, G. A., 1020, *1040*
Valverde, R. M., 1227, *1259*
van de Wiel, W. J., 381, *387*
van den Akker, J., 230, 231, *256*, 731, *780*
van den Berg, E., 211, *226*, 414, *440*
van der Ploeg, A., *1037*
van der Valk, T., 1117, 1122, *1139, 1148*
van Driel, J., 633, 646, 648, *650, 652*, 1046, 1055, *1065*,
    1075, *1103*, 1109, 1112, 1122, 1123, 1127, 1130, 1131,
    1134, *1138, 1148, 1149*
van Joolingen, W. R., *682*
Van Leire, K., 693, *716*
Van Praagh, G., 795, *806*
van Zee, E. H., 44, *56*, 447, 448, 452, *469*, 810, *830*,
    1210, 1215, 1217, 1226, 1227, 1228, *1255, 1259*
van Zee, E. J., 508, 516, 524, *534*
Vander Borght, C., 1046, *1065*
vanSomeren, M. W., 380, *390*
VanTassel-Baska, J., 306, 307, *311, 316*

Varelas, M., 328, *343*, 498, 510, 518, *534*
Varjola, I., 633, 637, *649*
Vars, G. F., 545, *558*
Vasquez, J., 543, *558*
Vaughan, M. N., 503, *534*
Vaughan, S., 640, *651*
Vaughn, H., 790, *804*
Vaughn, S., 293, 296, 297, *315, 316*
Veal, W. R., 1046, *1065*, 1108, 1109, *1138, 1149*
Veenman, M., 674, 682
Veiga, M., 1110, 1117, *1149*
Veillard, L., 400, *440*
Veldman, P. M., *1259*
Vélez-Ibáñez, C. G., 186, *196*
Venville, G., 380, *390*, 505, *534*, 543, 552, *558*
Verdonk, A., 1130, *1137*
Verdonk, A. H., 634, 636, *649, 650*
Verloop, N., 646, *650*, 1055, *1065*, 1075, *1103*, 1112,
    1123, 1131, *1148, 1149*
Vermunt, J. D., 1170, 1171, *1178*
Vesilind, E., 898, *910*, 1082, *1100*
Vicentini, M., 732, 776
Vicentini Missoni, M., 1117, *1146*
Victor, E., 1070, *1103*
Viennot, L., 33, 38, 39, *56*, 606, 616, *629*
Viiri, J., 1129, *1141*
Vilches, A., 1129, *1139*
Villegas, A. M., 182, *196*
Vispoel, W. P., 88, *102*
Vitale, M. R., 300, *315*
Vitale, P., 308, *313*
Vlachos, I., 1113, *1142*
Vlachos, L., 647, 648, *650*
Voelkl, K. E., 1024, *1035*
Vognsen, C., 700, *719*
Volk, T., 695, 697, *718, 725*, 888, *910*
Volkmann, M. J., 972, *1006*
von Denffer, D., *596*
von Rhöneck, C., 607, 610, 611, 612, *625, 627, 628*
VonSecker, C., 546, *556*
Vosniadou, S., 37, 49, *56*, 512, 515, *534*, 617, *629*
Vranek, J., *1039*
Vreeland, P., 141, *166*
Vrtacnik, M., 705, *717*
Vye, N. J., 406, *434*
Vygotsky, L. S., 40, 42, *56*, 58, *74*, 128, *167*, 378, *390*,
    406, *440*
Vyle, B., 140, 142, 143, *166*

W

Wade, P. D., 408, *438*, 862, *877*
Wade, S. E., 88, *102*
Wagner, E., 701, *725*
Wagner-Gershgoren, I., 587, *598*
Wagreich, P., 546, *556*

Wahlberg, H. J., 303, *317*
Wainwright, C. L., 645, *652*
Wainwright, S., *1259*
Waiti, P., 200, 209, 212, 215, *225*
Walberg, H. J., 104, *104*, 105, 110, *121, 123*, 136, *164*, 296, 297, 301, *310, 314*, 399, *436*, 846, *879*, 884, 885, 888, 889, *910*, 916, 918, 919, 920, *941*, 1024, *1040*, 1071, *1104*, 1106, *1145*
Walczyk, J., 969, *999*
Walding, H., 863, *875*
Walding, R., 1013, *1040*
Waldrip, B. G., *558*, 1112, *1149*
Waldron, J. L., 296, *314*
Walford, R., 699, 703, *725*
Walker, D. F., 918, 919, *940*
Walker, K., 697, 699, 703, *725*
Walker, K. A., 837, *879*
Walker, L., 326, *343*
Walker, L. J., 184, 185, *196*, 499, 501, *533*
Walker, R., 703, *722*
Walkerdine, V., 212, *226*
Wall, C. E., 544, *555*
Wallace, C., 425, *436*
Wallace, C. S., 858, *876*
Wallace, J., 505, *534*, 543, 552, *558*, 983, *1006*, 1054, 1059, *1064, 1065*
Wallace, M. L., 92, *98*
Wallace, W., 918, *941*
Walls, E., 337, 338, *343*
Wals, A., 695, 700, 701, 703, 705, *726*
Walter-Thomas, C., 295, *316*
Walton, R., 126, *167*
Wan, C. K., 1068, 1073, *1100*
Wandersee, H. H., 1113, 1212, *1255*
Wandersee, H. J., 594, *596*
Wandersee, J., 337, *342*, 1154, *1178*
Wandersee, J. H., 34, *56*, 65, *71*, 230, 232, *255, 256*, 599, 606, *627, 629*, 656, 659, *685, 687*, 981, 983, 985, *1000, 1003, 1149, 1177*
Wang, H., 5, *29*, 1090, *1103*
Wang, H. A., 546, *557*, 888, *910*, 1021, *1036, 1039, 1103*
Wang, J., 1022, *1040*
Wang, L., *1104*
Wang, M., 296, 297, 301, *310, 314*
Wang, M. C., 297, 303, *317*
Wanner, N., 150, *165*
Ward, B., 818, *830*
Ward, C. R., 404, *440*
Ward, J. F., *437*
Ward, M., 402, 414, *441*
Ward, S. M., 150, *158*
Warden, M. A., 544, 551, 552, *558*
Waring, M., 794, 795, 797, *806*
Warner, J., 1242, *1250*
Warren, B., 19, *29*, 179, 180, 188, *196, 197*, 329, *343*, 456, *468, 469*, 496, *534*
Warren, J., 275, *282*

Warren, J. W., 615, 617, *629*
Warwick, P., 500, 509, 517, 518, 519, 520, *534*, 706, *726*, 1112, *1146*
Washton, N. S., 1070, *1103*
Wasik, B. A., *939, 940*
Wasik, J. L., 918, *941*
Wason, P. C., 837, *875*, 884
Wastnedge, R., 793, *806*
Watanabe, T., 548, 549, 551, *559*
Watson, E., 1112, *1147*
Watson, F. G., 731, *780, 905*
Watson, H., 261, *285*
Watson, J. R., *805*
Watson, K., 524, *528*
Watson, R., 375, *391*, 521, *527*, 633, 637, *650, 652*
Watson, R. W., 799, *806*
Watters, J. J., 498, 501, 503, 505, 521, *532, 534*, 1110, 1113, 1116, 1117, *1139*
Watts, M., 34, *53*, 76, 78, 79, 94, *96*, 508, 524, 525, *534*, 646, *651*
Weaver, A., 275, *285*
Weaver, G. C., 512, *534*
Weaver, H. M., 1071, *1103*
Webb, G., 1112, *1149*
Webb, N., 933, *941*, 1014
Webb, N. L., *1040*
Webb, P., 1116, *1149*
Weber, W., 542, 545, *556, 558*
Webster, B. J., *84, 102*, 324, *343*
Webster, J., 500, 509, 518, 519, 520, *534*
Weffer, R., 66, *71*, 180, *193*
Wei, B., 891, *906*
Weil, S. E., 131, *167*
Weinburgh, M., 83, *102*, 272, *285*
Weiner, B., 87, 91, *102*
Weiner, G., 258, 262, *279*
Weinland, T. P., 544, *557*
Weinstein, C. S., 1124, *1149*
Weinstein, M., 893, 894, *910*
Weinstein, R., 920, *941*
Weinstein, R. S., 93, *102*
Weinstock, H., 77, *102*
Weiss, C. H., *963*
Weiss, F., 148, *163*
Weiss, I., *961, 1037*
Weiss, I. R., 396, *441*, 933, *941*, 945, 946, 948, 952, *963*, 1183, 1190, *1202, 1203*, 1213, *1259*
Weiss, J., 297, *317*
Welch, M., 296, *317*
Welch, W., 181, *194*, 275, *282, 1002*, 1008, 1024, 1048, *1065*, 1071, 1106
Welch, W. W., 104, *121, 123, 687*, 843, 844, 846, 848, 863, 864, *879*, 884, 885, 886, 888, 896, 898, *910*, 916, 918, 919, 921, *941*, 947, 954, *963*, 990, *1040, 1104, 1145*
Welford, G., 970, 982, *997, 1000*
Welicker, M., 593, *598*
Weller, F., *102*

Wellington, J., 127, *167*, 408, *441*, 459, *469*, 866, *877*
Wells, G., 41, 46, *56*, 1205, *1259*
Wells, M., 617, *626*
Welzel, M., 66, *73*, 609, *629*, 990, 994, *1006*
Wenger, E., 14, 19, *29*, 45, *53*, 61, *72*, *74*, 87, *99*, 128, *162*, 406, *441*, 759, *777*, 1049, *1065*
Wenner, G., 1111, 1112, *1147*, *1149*
Wentzel, K. R., 90, *102*
Wenzel, S., 328, *343*, 498, 510, 518, *534*
Werner, C. M., 152, *160*
Werner, K., 703, 707, *719*
Wertsch, J. V., 42, *56*, 59, 63, *74*, *317*, 378, *391*
West, A., 80, *102*
West, L., 1045, *1065*
West, L. H. T., *1259*
West, R. W., 797, *806*
Westbrook, S. L., 63, *70*
Westbury, I., 1017, *1040*
Westbury, L., 600, 601, *629*
Weston, E., *1037*
Wetzel, K. A., 548, *555*
Wham, A. J. B., 422, *437*
Whatley, A., 506, *529*
Wheatley, G., *1248*
Wheeler, S., 824, *828*, 863, *879*
Whigham, M., 83, *96*
Whistance, D., 725
White, A., 538, 540, 542, 543, 552, *555*
White, A. L., 1071, *1101*
White, B., 973, *1000*
White, B. T., 484, 488, *491*
White, B. Y., 4, *30*, 507, *533*
White, G., 1050, *1065*
White, M., 80, 81, 82, *96*
White, P. A., 924, *938*
White, R., 232, *254*, 374, 375, 384, *391*, *780*, 886, 898, *910*, 983, 986, *1006*, 1153, 1172, *1178*
White, R. T., 228, 230, 232, *256*, 374, *387*, *391*, 405, 425, *441*, 732, 734, *780*, 1112, *1135*, *1173*, *1176*
Whitehead, J., 1245, *1254*
Whitehurst, G. J., 1206, *1259*
Whitmore, E., 946, *960*
Whitmore, J. R., 305, *317*
Whorf, B. L., 64, *74*
Wick, J. W., 842, *879*
Wickman, P.-O., 774, *780*
Widodo, A., 605, 608, *625*
Wiediger, S. D., 987, *1006*
Wiener, M. W., 95, *102*
Wieseman, K. C., 549, *559*
Wiesenmayer, R. L., 888, *908*, *910*
Wiesner, H., 604, 606, 616, 617, 620, *626*, *627*, *628*
Wigfield, A., 546, *556*
Wiggins, G., *1006*
Wiggins, G. P., 947, *963*, 982, 993
Wiggins, J., 176, *192*
Wilbers, J., 602, 624, *625*

Wild, J., 508, 516, 524, *534*, 1226, 1233, *1259*
Wiley, D. E., 5, *29*, 1015, 1018, 1020, *1038*, *1039*, *1040*
Wiliam, D., 965, 967, 968, 970, 972, 973, 974, 977, 978, 979, 980, 988, 989, 991, 992, 993, 994, *997*, *1004*, *1006*
Wilke, R., 695, 697, *718*
Wilkenson, J. W., 402, 414, *441*
Wilkerson, S., 970, *1005*
Will, M. C., 293, *317*
Willard-Holt, C., 305, *317*
Willet, J. B., 586, *595*
William, D., 507, *528*
Williams, D., 1110, *1149*
Williams, G. C., 95, *102*
Williams, G. F., 146, *165*
Williams, G. P., 139, *165*
Williams, J., 689, 697, 700, 701, 703, 705, 707, *713*, *726*
Williams, L., 506, *528*
Williams, L. J., 296, *315*
Williams, M., 507, *534*
Williams, N., 268, 269, *285*
Williams, S. M., 406, *441*
Williams, T., 13, *28*, 183, 184, *193*, 705, *717*
Williamson, V. M., 645, *652*
Willinsky, J., 61, *71*
Willis, S., 258, 276, *281*, 541, *559*
Willson, M., 1110, *1149*
Willson, V. L., 915, 916, *941*
Wilson, A. C., 220, *225*
Wilson, B., 925, *938*
Wilson, B. L., 923, 925, 934, *941*
Wilson, J., 983, *1006*
Wilson, J. M., 63, *74*
Wilson, L., 836, 863, *879*
Wilson, M. R., 1028, 1030, *1040*
Wilson, P. G., 296, *314*
Wilson, R., 704, 705, *722*, *726*
Wilson, S., 1106, 1108, *1149*
Wilson, S. M., *1140*, 1182, 1189, *1203*
Wilson, V. L., 84, *102*
Winchester, I., 839, *879*
Windschitl, M., 384, *391*, 427, *441*, 1073, *1104*, 1133, *1149*
Winkeljohn, D. R., 1075, *1098*
Winnicott, D. W., 94, *102*
Winograd, K., 1227, *1259*
Winter, S., 301, 303, *317*
Winther, A. A., 888, *910*
Wirth, D., 703, *726*
Witcher, P., 1228, *1246*
Witenoff, S., 593, *598*
Wittgenstein, L., 63, *74*
Wittrock, M., 659, *686*
Wolf, R. L., 136, *167*
Wolf, S. A., 1010, *1040*
Wolfe, D., 982, *1006*
Wolfe, L. F., 306, *317*
Wolfe, R. G., 1020, *1039*, *1040*

Wolford, F., 351, 365, *369*
Wollman, J., 276, *285*
Wollweber, K., *777*
Wolpert, L., 405, 408, *441*
Wong, A. F. L., 107, 110, 111, 112, 113, 116, *120, 122, 124*
Wong, D., 65, *74*
Wong, E. D., 1210, *1259*
Wong, N. Y., 115, *124*
Wong-Fillmore, L., 183, *197*
Wood, B., 275, 276, *285*
Wood, D., 485, *491*
Wood, D. J., 381, *386*
Wood, K., 299, *317*
Wood, M. W., 545, *556*
Wood, T., 45, *52, 1248*
Wood-Robinson, C., 39, 41, 49, *52, 54*
Wood-Robinson, V., 7, *28,* 230, 232, *254, 625, 656,*
    682, 976, 999
Woodbury, J. M., 497, *534*
Woodruff, E., 510, 512, 515, 523, *532, 534*
Woods, R. K., 513, 516, *534*
Woolf, V., 257, *285*
Woolfolk, A., 1085, *1104*
Woolgar, S., 14, *29,* 64, 67, *72, 74*
Woolnough, B., 84, *102,* 608, *629,* 795, 797, *806,*
    970, *1001*
Worsnop, W. A., 592, *596*
Worthen, B. R., 945, 946, *960, 963*
Woszczyna, C., 452, 462, *468*
Wotruba, J., 299, *317*
Wright, B. D., 956, *963*
Wright, E., 600, *629,* 817, *829,* 853, *875*
Wright, E. L., 353, *367,* 1131, *1138*
Wright, J. C., 151, *167*
Wright, S. R., *962*
Wu, J., *1104*
Wubbels, T., 106, 115, *119, 124,* 1048, *1061,* 1124, 1125,
    1138, 1141, 1149
Wuensch, K. L., 889, *906*
Wykoff, J., *651*
Wylie, J., 701, 705, *726*
Wymer, P., 139, *167*
Wynne, B., 759, *780,* 887, *910*
Wytias, P. L., 1070, *1104*

Y

Yackel, E., 45, *52, 1248*
Yager, R. E., 111, 112, *119, 122,* 366, 579, 580, 581, 585,
    586, 588, *596, 598,* 842, 845, *879,* 883, 888, 889, 899,
    910, 981, 999, 1091, *1102*
Yakabu, J. M., 211, *226*
Yambor, K. M., 145, 146, *164*
Yang, E., 425, *436*
Yang, K., 21, 22, 23, 24, *28,* 338, 339, *342,* 899, *902*
Yanowitz, K. L., 513, *534*

Yarnal, L., 486, *490*
Yarnell, L., *437*
Yaroch, L., 591, *596*
Yarroch, W. L., *1138*
Yarrow, A., 117, *124*
Yates, L., 259, 260, 261, *285*
Yeager, M., *1040*
Yeany, R. H., 87, *98*
Yencken, D., *715*
Yeo, S., 376, *388*
Yeotis, C., 1126, *1137*
Yerkes, R., 704, *726*
Yerrick, R., 179, 182, 189, *193, 197,* 354, 363, 365,
    368, 369, 1073, 1081, 1089, *1104*
Yesseldyke, J. E., 302, *316*
Yeung, S. P.-M., 706, *726*
Yılmaz, Ö., 1084, *1098*
Yin, R., 952, *963*
Yip, D. Y., 1112, 1116, 1117, *1149*
Yoon, K., 951, *960*
Yoon, K. S., 1194, *1202,* 1206, *1251*
Yorath, J., 156, *167*
Yore, L. D., 58, 67, *74,* 377, *391,* 444, 457, 458, 459,
    466, 469, 686
York, D. E., 216, *223*
Yorke, M., 995, *1006*
Yoshida, A., 269, 270, *283*
Yoshida, K. M., 1210, 1213, *1259*
Yoshida, M., 1206, *1250*
Yotive, W., 151, *160*
Young, A. J., 91, *96*
Young, D., 324, *343*
Young, D. J., 105, 111, 118, *121, 124,* 361, 362, *369*
Young, M., 881, *910*
Young, M. F. D., 200, *226*
Young, T. A., 506, *527,* 541, *556*
Ysseldyke, J., 297, 299, 301, *317*
Yung, B. H. W., 414, 417, *441,* 991, *1006*
Yurecko, M., 1010, *1036*

Z

Zachos, P., 990, *1006*
Zadnik, M. G., 376, *388*
Zahur, R., 1073, 1091, *1104*
Zambo, R., 548, *555*
Zandvliet, D. B., 108, *124*
Zaslavsky, C., 206, *226*
Zech, L., 406, *434*
Zeegers, Y., 981, *1006*
Zeichner, K., 818, *830,* 1167, *1177,* 1206, 1208, 1209,
    1211, 1215, 1219, 1222, 1227, 1234, 1235, 1236, 1237,
    1238, 1239, 1242, *1248, 1252, 1255, 1258, 1259*
Zeidler, D. L., 180, *196,* 753, 759, 772, 774, *780,* 837,
    853, 858, 861, *877, 878, 879,* 1129, *1138, 1143*
Zeitler, W. R., 1126, *1149*

Zelezny, L., 700, *726*
Zembal-Saul, C., 407, 412, 413, 416, *437, 441*, 453, 454, 463, *469*, 485, *491*, 1128, 1131, 1133, *1149*, 1164, *1178*
Zembylas, M., 234, *256*
Zepeda, O., 214, *226*
Zeuli, J. S., 826, *830*
Zhang, B., 1083, *1104*
Zhang, J., 175, 181, 190, *195*
Zigmond, N., 296, 302, *310, 311*
Ziman, J., 883, 884, 886, *910*
Zimmerman, A., 182, *196*
Zimmerman, B. J., 91, 95, *101, 102*
Zimmermann, A., 118, *123*
Zimpher, N., 1213, *1252*
Zint, M., 1073, *1104*

Zipf, R., 1079, *1104*
Zohar, A., 674, *687*, 1121, *1149*
Zoller, U., *909*, 987, 990, *1006*
Zollman, D., 85, *97*, 622, *628, 629*, 847, 849, 852, *879*
Zubrowski, B., 501, *534*
Zucker, A. A., *437*, 914, 927, 928, 929, 931, 932, *941*, 954, *961*
Zuckerman, G. A., 824, *830*
Zuiker, S. J., 994, *1001*
Zurub, A. R., 353, *369*
Zusho, A., 85, 92, *102*
Zwart, P. J., 665, *687*
Zwick, T., 545, *559*
Zwolanski, S., 1053, *1065*

Subject Index

A

Access and equity, issues of, 455–457
Accountability assessment, 968–971
Achievement gaps, 174–176
    ideological and methodological limitations, 175
    rural students, 360–361
    science outcomes, 175–176
    urban science, 322–327
Acquisition metaphor, 33–35
Actualizing tendency, 87
Adaptation, Piagetian theory, 32
Advanced Placement (AP) exams, 176
Agency of the material world, in scientific
    literacy, 5
Alphabet soup curriculum, 916
American Association for the Advancement of
    Science (AAAS), 176
    Cooperative Committee, 305
American Association of Museums, 131
American Association of University Women
    (AAUW), 258
American College Test (ACT), 176
Americans with Disabilities Act (ADA), 1975, 293
Analogies and metaphors, 379–380
A Nation at Risk, 912, 922–923, 933
Apprenticeship, 19
Aquaria, learning from, 140
Arousal and anxiety, in motivation, 88
Asia, science education for women, 269–270
Assessment, *see also* specific type
    classroom, *see* Classroom assessment of science
        learning
    ELL students, 181–182
    formative, *see* Formative assessment
    laboratory-related research in science education,
        429–430
    large-scale, in science education, 1007–1040
    scientific literacy, 759–767
    special needs students, 301–303
    student diversity and, 180–181

techniques and strategies in elementary
    science, 509
Atomic physics, teaching of, 618–622, 619–620*f*
Atomic structure, multiple meanings, 637–643
Attitude, 76–85
    achievement and science-related decisions, 84
    attitudes and what influences them, 83
    change intervention, 85
    definition and meaning, 78–79
    drawing, 82
    future research, 93–94
    gender, 83–84
    historical background and theoretical orientations,
        77–78
    implications for policy and practice, 94–96
    instruments, 80–82
    interview, 82–83
    research methods and instruments, 79–80
    summary data for sample instruments, 81*t*
Attitudes and beliefs, teacher
    affecting self-efficacy, 1085–1086
    belief and practice mismatch, 1082–1083
    concerns about reform, 1088–1089
    cross-country contexts, 1092–1093
    culture/context effects, 1091–1094
    definition, 1068–1070, 1069*t*
    early research, 1070
    educational reform and, 1087
    emerging constructs, 1068
    environmental constraints, 1083–1084
    environmental response, 1086
    future research, 1095–1096
    high school/college divide, 1091–1092
    historical perspectives, 1070–1072
    knowledge and skills, 1086
    qualitative assessments, 1072–1073
    quantitative assessments, 1072
    recent research, 1076—1077
    religion, beliefs, and instructional practices, 1093
    science education as a road to empowerment and
        social justice, 1089–1091

Attitudes and beliefs, teacher (*continued*)
science teacher, 1067–1104
social norms, 1083
sociocultural, 1092
sociocultural model of embedded belief systems, 1073–1077, 1074f
Sputnik reform, 1070–1072
theoretical models, 1073
Attitude Toward Science Scale, 80
Augmentation, use of evidence, 453–455
Australian Science Education Project (ASEP), 111
Authority of experience, 1159–1160

B

Behavior prediction, teacher attitudes and beliefs, 1073
Belief and practice mismatch, 1082–1083
Beliefs *versus* knowledge, in concept learning, 34
Belief systems, 1073–1077, 1074f
Benchmarks for Scientific Literacy (AAAS), 920–927
Bildung, 601–603
BioKIDS sequence, 477f, 487, 487f
Biological Science: An Inquiry into Life—The Yellow Version (1968) (BSCS), 568
Biological Science: Molecules to Man—The Blue Version (1968) (BSCS), 568
Biological Science: Patterns and Process (1966), 568
Biological Sciences Curriculum Study (BSCS), 384, 568–569, 807, 916–917
adaptation, *Yellow Version* in Israel, 575–577, 843
Blue Version, 842, 845
curricula, academic achievement, and mastery of inquiry skills, 572
implementation in the U.S., 570–571
Yellow and Green Versions in U.S., 580
Biology, subject matter knowledge, 115–116
Biology curriculum, 561–598
content-oriented, 563, 564, 565f
development in the United States, 567–569
evaluation and grading, 593
inquiry-oriented, 565
new high school science, 565–566
problem-oriented, 580–581
teaching concepts and principles, 588–589
Biology research, 563–564
impact of chemistry and physics, 566–567
Biology textbooks
high schools, 580, 585–593
reasons for choices, 587
teachers' perceptions of, 586–587
Blue Planet curriculum
development and evaluation of, 677–678
pre-development of, 676–677
Botanical gardens, learning from, 140
British Association for the Advancement of Science (BAAS), 1831, 882

C

Center for the Assessment and Evaluation of Student Learning (CAESL), model, 1028–1031, 1029f
Changes in Attitudes about the Relevance of Science (CARS) questionnaire, 79–80
Chemical bonding, multiple meanings, 637–643
Chemical reactions
multiple meanings, 632–635
students' conceptual difficulties, 633–635
Chemistry, subject matter knowledge, 1113–1114
Chemistry curriculum, 631–652
course content structure, 636–637
courses developed from modern teaching and learning perspectives, 635–637
looking forward, 648–649
multiple meanings through contexts, 643–644, 644f
multiple meanings through models, 645–647
multiple meanings through multimedia tools, 644–645
near-future reform, 643–648
potential perspectives, 632f
CHEM Study, 916, 918
Child rearing, in critical research, 22–23
Children's Learning in Science Project (CLISP), Britain, 212
Civil Rights Restoration Act of 1987, 293
Classroom assessment of science learning, 965–1006
appropriateness, 992
authenticity, 993
coherent state systems, 1028–1034
consequences, 990
cultural validity, 991–992
equity and fairness, 991
fidelity and disclosure, 992–993
further research, 995
increasing the quality of, 988–990
manageability, 992
for multiple purposes, 967–971
political contexts, 966–967
theorizing assessment, 993–995
trustworthiness, 992
wider range of research on formats, 983–988
Classroom communities of inquirers, 406–407
Classroom environment
cross-national studies, 115–116
determinants of, 112–113
discourse in, 443–469
evaluation of educational innovations, 111–112
explanations, 376–377
future directions for indigenous students, 219–221
improving IK practice in, 212–213
learning problems worldwide, 249–250
questionnaires for assessment of, 105–109, 106t
research instruments, 109–116
school laboratory, practice and research, 419–426
sociocultural, 272–274
student and teacher perceptions, 112

student outcomes and, 110–111
technology underutilization in, 472–473
use of qualitative research methods, 113–115
using cultural contexts in, 215–216
Classroom Environment Scale (CES), 105
Classroom learning, 103–124
Cognitive Acceleration through Science Education in Britain (Adey & Shayer), 33
Cognitive conflict, in elementary science teaching, 511–512
Cognitively based instruction, student diversity and, 178–179
Cognitive tools
    definition, 476–479, 477f
    versus digital resources, 471–491
    gathering and analyzing data, 486–487
    learning earth sciences, 661–678
    transformation via, 479–482, 480f
Cognitive Tools Framework, 479–487
Collaboration, teachers of students with special needs, 294–295
Committee of Ten, 785—786
Commonplaces, in science learning, 6
Community and government organizations, learning science from, 147–148
Community-based programs, 147–148
Competencies, in systemic reform, 925
Composite culture, learning in urban settings, 332
Computer-based assessment, 988
Computers and the internet, science learning and, 150
Computer software, demonstrations enhanced by, 375–376
Computer Supported Intentional Learning Environment (CSILE), 484
Computer-Supported Intentional Learning Environment (CSILE), 87
Concept development
    biology, 588–590
    earth sciences, 661–662
    laboratory activities, 420–421
Conceptions of Scientific Theories Test (COST), 865
Concept maps, 983–984
Conceptual change
    cold, 38
    different meanings of, 36
    in elementary science teaching, 511
    knowledge, discourse and, 448–450
    learning to teach science, 1153–1159
    physics, 606–607, 606t
    teaching for, 1156–1158
    teaching of, 1154–1156
    what changes during, 36–38
Conceptual change theory (CCT), 4, 7–14, 59–60
    characteristics of, 11–12
    example, 7–8
    junior high level atomic structure, 640
    power and limitations, 12–14

Conceptual conflict, 12
Conceptual learning, 31–56
    as acquisition, 35–39, 40–44
    as addition/replacement, 42–43
    in classroom settings, 48–50
    cognitive approaches, 38–39
    difficulties with atomic structure, 638–639
    difficulties with chemical bonding, 640–642
    difficulties with chemical reactions, 633–635
    future research directions, 50–51
    multimodal approach, 46–47
    as participation, 45–48
    starting points and trends, 32–34
    structuring the review, 33–35
    what changes, 36–38
Conceptual profile, 43
Conceptual tools, in science learning, 49
Concrete models, 379
Congruence, analysis of learning in urban settings, 331–333
Congruent third space, 331
Constructivism, 60
    views of teaching and learning science, 232
Constructivist Learning Environment Survey (CLES), 107–108, 111, 112, 114, 115
Constructs, definition, 75
Content knowledge structure (CKS)
    biology inquiry-oriented curriculum, 568f, 569f
    research in biology, 563–564
Content-specific simulation programs, physics, 608
Contextual Model of Learning, 129
Continuous assessment, laboratory activity, 417
Cooperative learning, 383–384
Courses, in systemic reform, 923–924
Critical consciousness, development of, in critical research, 24
Critical discourse analysis, 446
Critical incidents, 866–867
Critical research tradition, 4, 20–25
    characteristics, 23–25
    culture of power, 21
    discussion and implications, 23
    example, 4, 20–2521
    methods and interpretation, 22–23
    power and limitations, 25
Critical thinking, modeling, visualization, and simulation tools, 483–484
Critiquing peer culture, in critical research, 22
Cross-national studies
    classroom environments, 115–116
    findings, 236–243
    student science learning, 232–233
Cultural, understanding of NOS, 831
Culturally congruent instruction, student diversity and, 178
Cultural toolkits, analysis of learning in urban settings, 329–330

Culture
    classroom practice for indigenous students, 213–219
    in language and science learning, 66
    learning styles and, 216–217
    in meaning-making, 64–65
    scientific education and student diversity, 171–197
Culture of power, 21
Curriculum, *see and the specific subject;* Science
        curriculum
CyberTracker sequence, 478*f*, 486

D

Data types, used in science teacher research studies,
        1229–1231, 1230*t*
Deductive reasoning, 384–386
Degree-awarding inservice programs, 1219
Democratic, understanding of NOS, 831
Demonstrations, 374–376
    computer software enhancement, 375–376
    increase of student cognitive involvement, 375
    for motivation, 375
Developing countries, science education in, 243–244
Digest of Educational Statistics, U.S. Department of
        Education, 289
Digital resources
    versus cognitive tools, 471–491
    definition, 475, 477*f*
Discontinuity of matter, in conceptual change
        research, 7–8
Discourse, 61
    augmentation, explanation and use of evidence,
        453–455
    control of, 62–63
    future directions and challenges, 461–464
    issues of access and equity, 455–457
    knowledge and conceptual change, 448–450
    in science classrooms, 443–469
    spoken, 445–448
    student small-group, 450–453
Discourse community, scientific literacy as
        participation in, 4, 14–20
Docents, role in learning, 142–143
Draw-a-Scientist Checklist, 82
Dropping out of school and science, in critical
        research, 22
Dynamic assessments, 986–987

E

Earth and space science, subject matter knowledge,
        1114–1115
Earth sciences curriculum, 653–687
    Blue Planet curriculum, 676–678
    distinctive characteristics, 654–661

integration of learning environments within,
        671–675
    learning, 661–678
    research and development of materials, 675–676
    shifting profiles, 657–660
    struggle for paradigm shift, 678–679
    systems thinking, 668–671
    temporal thinking, 664–668
    visualization and spatial reasoning, 663–664
Earth systems science, 660–661
Educational evaluation
    definition, 944–947
    relationship to science education, 947–953
Educational Evaluation: Theory and Practice (Worthen
        and Sanders), 945
Educational Evaluation and Decision-Making
        (Stufflebeam), 945
Educational innovations, evaluation of, 111–112
Educational policies, student diversity and, 185–186
Educational practice, learning science outside of
        school, 153–156
Educational Testing Service (ETS), 1014
    chronology of international assessments, 1015*t*
Education for All Handicapped Children Act (1975),
        292–294
Education for Economic Security Act (EESA), 922
Electricity, teaching of, 610–14, 610*f*
Elementary and Secondary Education Act,
        Title IX, 258
Elementary school
    assessment in science, 507–510
    context for teaching and learning science, 495–496
    cross-disciplinary teaching, 505–507
    cultural influences on curriculum, 501
    curriculum, 501–507
    curriculum integration, 539–540
    future research directions, 526–527
    gender trends in science teaching, 499–500
    generalist/specialist science teaching, 500–501
    identifying students' initial ideas, 525–526
    instructional materials used by teachers, 502–504
    metacognition in, 517
    pedagogy for learning in science, 510–526
    research into science teaching, 494–495
    scaffolding, 514–517
    science notebooks, 518–520
    science teacher, 496–501
    science teaching in, 493–535
    specific strategies for science teaching, 521–523
    students' questions as a basis for investigations,
        524–525
    teacher avoidance of science, 496–499
    writing in, 517
Elementary science teacher, 1048–1050
    community practice, 1049–1050
    confidence in science teaching, 1048–1049
Engagement phase, learning model, 404

English language learners (ELL)
   achievement gaps and, 174
   science assessment and, 181–182
   student diversity and, 179–180
   teacher education and, 183–184
Environmental constraints, teacher beliefs, 1083–1084
Environmental education curriculum, 689–726
   foundations, 692–693
   goals, 690–691, 693–695
   politics of research, 708–711
   research, 695–706
   sustainable development and, 691–692
Epistemological underpinning, conceptual tools, 49
Epistemologies
   belief systems and change, 1079–1082
   origins of, 1077–1078
   science instructional practices and, 1078–1079
Equity, in systemic reform, 931–933
Equity Metric (Kahle), 325
ESEA Act, 947
Ethnomethodology, 449
European countries
   science education in, 244–245
   science education for women, 268–269
European Union (EU), on women in science,
      268–269
Evaluands, 944
Evaluation: A Systematic Approach (Rossi and
      Freeman), 945
Evaluation phase, learning model, 404
Evaluation Research (Weiss), 945
Evaluation Thesaurus (Scriven), 944
Evaluation (Weiss), 945
Everyday sense-making, analysis of learning in
      urban settings, 329
Evidence, augmentation, explanation and use of,
      453–455
Evidence-Based Practice in Science Education
      (IPSE), 892
Excellence, in systemic reform, 928–931
Exceptional students, perspectives guiding research
      on, 288–289
Expectancy-value theory of achievement
      motivation, 90
Experimental and customized challenges, 987
Explanatory model, in conceptual change
      research, 7–8
Exploration-invention-discovery, learning cycle
      approach, 384–385

                      F

Family, visits to museums, 143–144
Feedback, teaching elementary science, 520
Field trips, learning science from, 140–142
First International Science Study (FISS), 1017

Formative assessment, 968–971
   definitions and characteristics, 972–973
   in elementary science education, 507–508
   importance of, 973–974
   interactive, 975
   models for, 974–979
   planned, 974–975
   research on students and assessment, 979–981
Framework theories, of concepts, 37
France, science education reform, 246
Free and appropriate public education (FAPE),
      PL94-142
Functional science, 889–891

                      G

Gay, lesbian, bisexual, and transgender (GLBT), 259,
      276–277
Gender, Science and Mathematics (Parker, Rennie, &
      Fraser), 263
Gender and Science and Technology (GASAT), 261
Gender differences
   attitudes towards science, 83–84
   definition, 258–259
   future research directions, 277–279
   high-stakes test-taking patterns, 274–275
   international perspective, 265–270
   participation in science, 262–263
   physics, 607–608
   science education research, 257–285
   single-sex *versus* mixed-sex classes, 275–276
   sociocultural aspects, 271–277
   trends in elementary science teaching, 499–500
   women in science majors and careers, 270–271
Generalists, elementary school teachers, 501
General science, subject matter knowledge, 1110–1113
Generative Learning model, 404
Genres, analysis of learning in urban settings,
      328–329
German *Didaktik* tradition, 601–603, 602f
Gestural mode of representation (actions), 379
Globalization, 233–234
Goal-directed behavior, in motivation, 90–91
Goal theory, 90
Group assessment, 987–988
Group learning, 383–384

                      H

Handbook of Research on Science Teaching and Learning
      (Gabel), 85, ix
Hands On Science Outreach (HOSO), 148
High school
   biology curriculum, 563–585
   biology textbooks, 580, 585–593

High school (*continued*)
  exit exams, 1034
  multiple meanings of atomic structure and
    chemical bonding, 637–643
High School Biology—The Green Version (1968)
  (BSCS), 568
Historical perspective, science education for girls,
  259–261
History of science, empowerment through,
  1090–1091
History of Science Cases for High Schools
  (HOSC), 842
History of Science Cases (Klopfer & Cooley), 884
Horizontal coherence, 1031
Hot-reports, laboratory activity, 417–418
Human health and science, 583
Humanistic perspectives
  conceptual frameworks for school science, 884
  curriculum policy, 885–897
  recent science curriculum movement, 883–885
  short history, 882–885

I

ICASE, scientific literacy project, 734
Ideologies and power relationships, in critical
  research, 24
Image of science and scientists, dishonest and
  mythical, 886
Imperialism, 206–212
Inclusion, teachers of students with special needs,
  295–301
Indigeneity, postcolonialism and, 201–204
Indigenous knowledge (IK)
  as contemporary knowledge, 209–210
  disciplining, 210
  finding a place in science curriculum, 208–209
  no connection to WMS, 210–211
  science and curricula, 206
  traditional ecological knowledge and, 204–206
Indigenous languages, science education and,
  218–219
Indigenous students, 199–226
  culture and learning, 216–217
  future directions, 219–221
  teacher preparation and efficacy, 213–215
Individual interest, 88
Individual plane, in learning, 40
Individuals with Disabilities Education Act (IDEA),
  1997, 293
Inductive reasoning, 384–386
Informal learning, 126–128
Informal Science Education Ad Hoc Committee,
  NARST, 126
Information and communication technology
  advances, 234–235

Information technology, in science teaching, 507
Inform-verify-practice, 385
Inquiry
  changing toward, 824–828
  connecting curriculum and change, 818–824
  in developing science curricula, 814–818, 815*f*
  in elementary science teaching, 510–511
  how is curriculum understood, 811–814
  organizing theme in science curricula, 807–830
  in science content, 819–820
Inquiry empowering technologies, 411–412
Inquiry matriculation examinations, biology in
  Israel, 577–579
Inquiry-oriented curriculum, biology, 565, 568*f*, 570
  heterogeneous student population and, 579
  matriculation exams, 577–578
  summary of implementation, 578–579
Inquiry science teaching, 396
Inservice programs, science teacher research and,
  1219–1228, 1220–1226*t*
Inservice teachers, attitude toward integrated
  curriculum, 540–549
Instructional congruence, 331–332
Instructional methods and strategies, 373–391
Interaction of Experiments and Ideas (2nd ed. 1970), 569
Interdisciplinary science teaching, 537–559
  brief history, 539
  disadvantages, 549–553
  disadvantages of integration, 549–553
  effects on student achievement, 545–546
  integrated curriculum design, 543–544
  national standards, 540–541
  rationale, 538–539
  research on integration, 544–549
  teacher attitude, 547
  unfocused definition, 542–543
Interest and curiosity, in motivation, 88
Interest and extrinsic motivation, 89
International Assessment of Educational Progress
  (IAEP), 1014
  chronology of international assessments, 1015*t*
  studies, 1016–1018
International Association for the Evaluation of
  Educational Achievement (IEA), 947–948, 1014
International Council of Museums (ICOM), 131
International Handbook of Science Education (Sutton),
  57, ix
International Institute for Educational Planning, 243
International Journal of Science Education, articles on
  attitudes, 78
Interpretive centers, learning from, 140
Intervention models, special talent students,
  306–308
Interviews and conversations, 985–986
Introductory Science Teacher Education (ISTE)
  package, 849
Ionizing radiation, 584

Israel, science education reform, 247
Israeli short-answer assessment item, 1013*f*

J

Japan, science education reform, 247
Japanese multiple-choice assessment item, 1012*f*
Jigsaw method, cooperative instruction, 383
Joint Committee on Standards for Educational
    Evaluation, 944
Journal of Research in Science Technology,
    science/diversity topics, 176
Journal of Science Teaching, gender research in science
    education, 263–264

K

Knowledge
    acquiring and constructing, 1169–1172
    discourse and conceptual change, 448–450
Knowledge construction in learning to teach,
    1170–1172
Knowledge of context (KofC), 1108
Knowledge *versus* beliefs, in concept learning, 34

L

Laboratory
    analysis of emerging themes, 401–403
    assessment resources and strategies, 413–418
    communities of inquirers, 406–407
    developing students' understanding if the nature
        of science, 407–410
    as earth sciences learning environment, 673–675
    historical overview, 394–397
    implications for classroom practice and research,
        419–427
    learning and teaching in, 393–441
    learning environment, 399
    learning goals for, 419–420, 419*t*
    looking to the future, 431–434
    minds-on engagement in, 422–424
    models and strategies for teaching, 424–427, 426*t*
    physics experimentation, 608–609
    principal goals for learning, 402*t*
    reports, assessment of lab activity, 415–416
    research in science education, 429–430
    reviews of research, 397–401
    role of teacher, 427–429
    selecting and modifying activities, 422–424, 423*t*
    selecting materials, 421–422
    topics, ideas, and activities for concept
        development, 420–421

Language and learning, 57–74
    changing perspectives, 69*t*
    how it works, 64–66
    indigenous languages and science education, 218–219
    integration of science teaching with, 506
    origins of contemporary research, 58–62
    revised framework, 62–68
    in science, 67–68
    scientific education and student diversity, 171–197
    what a speaker appears to be doing, 62–63
    what listeners think they are doing, 64
Large-scale science assessment
    alignment with standards, 1014
    assessment for all, 1013–1014
    benefits and risks, 1009–1011
    coherent state systems, 1028–1034
    international, 1014–1023, 1015*t*
    overview, 1008–1009
    sample state systems, 1031–1034
    varied types of assessment items, 1011–1013
Latin America, science education for women, 266
Learners as rational but inexperienced thinkers,
        in conceptual change research, 11–12
Learners' culture, language, and practices
    different characteristics, 242
    in sociocultural research, 18–19
Learning, *see also* specific type
    attitudinal and motivational constructs, 75–102
    as conceptual addition/replacement, 42–43
    as conceptual change, 35–36
    context problems worldwide, 251
    as control of multiple discourses, in sociocultural
        research, 18
    group and cooperative, 383–384
    input problems worldwide, 250–251
    inquiry, 808–809, 821–822, 822*t*
    language and, 57–74
    learning to talk science, 46
    over time, 130
    as a personal process, 128–129
    perspectives and research traditions, 3–6
    problems and issues worldwide, 249
    school science laboratory, 393–441
    social constructivist views, 41
    social language of science, 42
    socially contextualized, 129–130
    studies of, 457–461
Learning cycle approach, 384–386
    chemistry courses, 635–637
    elementary science education, 523–524
    three-phase model, 404
Learning difficulties
    in atomic structure, 638–639
    in biology, 591
    in chemical bonding, 640–642
    in chemical reactions, 633–637
    conceptual change tradition, 8–9

Learning dimensions, associated technologies and, 482–483, 483*t*

Learning Environment Inventory (LEI), 105

Learning environments, earth sciences, 671–675

Learning from experience, 1159–1164
    action research and a new scholarship, 1160–1161
    reflection by a teacher educator, 1161–1162
    reflection by those learning to teach, 1162–1164

Learning goals, 90
    conceptual change tradition, 9
    laboratory experiences, 419–420, 419*t*
    laboratory materials to match, 421–422
    multiple goals of science learning, 971

Learning in Science: The Implications of Children's Science (Osborne & Freyberg), 34

Learning in Science Project (LISP), 212
    Teacher Development, 1183

Learning outcomes, performance assessment of, 981–982

Learning process in biology, 591
    students' cognitive stages, 592–593

Learning stories, 986

Learning styles, culture and, 216–217

Learning theory organizers, 403–406

Learning together, cooperative instruction, 383

Learning to participate, urban learners, 338–340

Learning to succeed, urban learners, 337–338

Learning to teach science, 1151–1178, 1162*t*

Least restrictive environment, PL94-142

Legitimate participation, learning science in urban settings, 332–336

Limited English proficient (LEP) students
    achievement gaps and, 175
    science assessment and, 181–182

Literacy, student diversity and, 179–180

Literature, language and science education, 57–58, 58*f*

Local Systemic Change (LSC) program evaluation, 952

M

Macroscopic representation, 382

Mainstream, definition, 173–174

Man, A Course of Study (MACOS), 912, 917

Masculine nature of science, 264–265

Material world, definition, 5

Mathematical mode of representation, 379

Mathematics, integration of science teaching with, 506

Meaningful learning of science, educational failure, 886–887

Meaning-making
    creation of, 63–64
    culture and language, 64–65

Mechanics, teaching of, 614–618, 616*f*

Media, learning science from, 148–153

Metacognition, in elementary science teaching, 517

Micro-based labs, physics, 608

Microorganisms, 584–585

Microscopic representation, 382

Microworlds, physics, 608

Middle East, science education for women, 266–268

Middle school, *see* Elementary school

Model building systems (MBS), physics, 608

Modeling, thinking critically with, 483–484

Models, teaching multiple meanings of chemical reactions, 645–647

Models and analogies
    drama/simulations, 521
    in elementary science teaching, 513–514

Modes of communication, in science learning, 46–47

Modified Nature of Scientific Knowledge Scale (M-NSKS), 866

Monash University, science teacher education program, 1166–1167

Moral, understanding of NOS, 831

Motivated Learning Strategies Questionnaire (Pintrich & DeGroot), 91

Motivation, 85–93
    definition, 85
    demonstrations for, 375
    expectations and strategies, 92–93
    future research, 93–94
    historical background and theoretical orientations, 86–87
    implications for policy and practice, 94–96
    motivational constructs, 87

Multimedia tools
    multiple meanings of chemical reactions, 644–645
    physics instruction, 609–610

Multiple analogies, 381–382

Multiple external representations (MERs), 381–382

Museums
    demolishing myths, 132–135
    family visits, 143–144
    learning from visits, 135–136
    science and science centers, 137–139
    science learning in and from, 131–147

Museum-school-community links, 144–147

My Class Inventory (MCI), 105, 111

N

National Academies Press (NAP), list of international comparative studies, 233

National Assessment of Educational Progress (NAEP), 175, 947, 1007
    changes in, 1024–1027
    great performance expectations for practices, 1027*t*
    item formats, 1026–1027
    science content changes, 1025–1026, 1025*t*
    science practice changes, 1026

National Association of Research in Science Teaching (NARST), ix
   Informal Science Education Ad Hoc Committee, 126
National Center for Improving Science Education (NCISE), 1034
National Education Longitudinal Study (NELS), 176
National Research Council (NRC)
   model for coherent state assessment systems, 1028
   National Science Education Standards, 473, 897, 927
National Research Council Report on Minority Students in Special Education and Gifted Education (Donovan & Cross), 290
National Science Education Standards
   definition of scientific literacy, 473
   emphasis on curriculum integration, 540–541
   inquiry in, 808–811
   what is and what is not NOS, 832–835
National Science Foundation, ix
   curriculum development funds, 914t
   Education Directorate funding initiatives, 949t, 950f
   systemic initiative program, 912
National Society for the Study of Education (NSSEE), history of science curriculum, 788–790
National standards movement, 540–541
National Science Teachers Association (NSTA)
   Position Statement on Informal Science Education, 127–128
   Scope, Sequence and Coordination project, 540
Natural philosopher (scientist), 882
Natural philosophy (science), 882
Nature of science (NOS), 605–606
   assessing conceptions of, 861–867
   assessment thoughts, 867–869
   changing face of, 835–836
   conventional assumptions, 409
   future directions, 869–872
   instruments, 862t
   past, present, and future, 831–879
   research on students' conceptions, 836–838, 842–845, 858–861
   research on teachers' conceptions, 838–842, 845–852, 852–857
   students' understanding of, 407–410
   teaching and learning in contemporary years, 852–861
   understanding the construct, 831–835
Nature of Science Scale (NOSS), 840–841, 864
Nature of Science Test (NOST), 846, 864
Nature of Scientific Knowledge Scale (NSKS), 864
New Zealand, science education reform, 247
No Child Left Behind legislation, 912, 933–934, 1007
Non-mainstream, definition, 173–174
North American Association for Environmental Education (NAAEE), 690
Nuffield Project in Biology, U.K., 573–575

O

Observational methods, 986
OECD, scientific literacy initiative, 734
Office of Technology Assessment (OTA), 914
Online libraries, teacher research, 1243–1244
Online scaffolding tools
   evaluation and communication of scientific ideas, 484–485
   formulating knowledge with, 485–486
Ontology, conceptual tools, 49
Organisation for Economic Co-Operation and Development (OECD), 1014, 1022–1023
   chronology of international assessments, 1015t
Origins of student thinking, in concept learning, 34
Outdoor learning environment, earth sciences, 671–673, 672f
Out-of-school learning, 125–167
   contexts for science, 130–131
   implications for practice and policy, 154–156
   implications for research, 154
   learning in and from museums, 131–147
   meaning of, 126–128

P

Participation metaphor, 33–35
Participative approaches
   conceptual learning, 45–48
   summary and implications, 47–48
Particulate models, 8–9
Pedagogical approach
   BSCS textbooks, 569
   inertia and the struggle for paradigm shift, 678–679
   for learning in science, 510–526
   physics, 610–622
Pedagogical content knowledge (PCK), 379, 515–517, 1106–1107, 1120–1132
   frameworks and methods of representation, 1121–1124
   knowledge of science curriculum, 1128–1130
   knowledge of science instructional strategies, 1130–1132
   knowledge of science learners, 1126–1128
   orientation toward science teaching, 1124–1126
Peer Tutoring in Small Investigative Group (PTSIG), 383
Performance assessment, learning outcomes, 981–982
Performance goals, 90
Personal development, teachers, 1184–1185
Personal Meaning Mapping questionnaire, 128
Perspectives on learning, xii
Physical Science Study Curriculum (PSSC), 842, 916–921
   U.S. high school physics enrolled in, 921t

Physics curriculum, 599–629
    aims of instruction, 604–605
    conceptual change, 606–607, 606t
    desiderata for education research, 622–624
    education research, 600–603, 600f
    interdisciplinary nature, 600
    labwork and multimedia, 608–610
    major fields of research, 603–610
    science processes and nature of science, 605–606
    students' interests and gender issues, 607–608
    subject matter knowledge, 1116–1117
Piagetian theory, in concept learning, 32–34
Pluralism, 206–212
Portfolios, 984–985
    assessment of lab activity, 416
Position Statement on Informal Science Education,
        NSTA, 127–128
Postcolonialism, 199–226
    principle of indigeneity and, 201–204
Practical examinations, laboratory activity, 415
Predict-and-explain situations, 986
Predict-Observe-Explain (POE), 975–976
    laboratory teaching, 425
Preservice science teacher, 1044–1048
    attitude toward integrated curriculum, 547–548
    challenging conceptions and beliefs, 1045–1046
    learning from experience, 1047–1048
    teacher research and, 1215–1218, 1216–1217t
    teacher research impact on learning, 1218–1219
    teaching for conceptual change, 1158–1159
Primary Assessment, Curriculum and Experience
        (PACE) project, 979
Primary school, see Elementary school
Print media, science learning and, 149
Problem-oriented curriculum, biology, 580–581
    matriculation exams and learning units, 581–582
    students not taking a science discipline, 582
Professional developers, 1185–1188
    relationship with teachers, 1188–1189
Professional development, 1179–1203
    dimensions of, 1181–1189
    perspectives on, 1183
    research on, 1182–1183, 1189–1198
    student diversity and, 183
Program Evaluation: Alternative Approaches and
        Practical Guidelines (Fitzpatrick, Sanders &
        Worthen), 945
Programme for International Student Assessment
        (PISA), 232, 1015t, 1022–1023
    findings, 239–241
    physics instruction, 604
Project 2061 (AAAS), 897
Project for Enhancing Effective Learning (PEEL),
        1168–1169
Project Physics, 916, 918
Pygmalion effect, 92–93

Q

Questioning, as an instructional method, 377–378
Questionnaire on Teacher Interaction (QTI), 106–107,
        111, 112, 114, 115
Questionnaires
    assessing classroom environment, 105–109, 106t
    Changes in Attitudes about the Relevance of Science
        (CARS), 79–80
    Motivated Learning Strategies Questionnaire
        (Pintrich & DeGroot), 91
Questions
    laboratory-related research in science education,
        429–430
    students', 524–525

R

Race, ethnicity
    exceptional students and, 290–291
    gender differences in science education, 263–264
    scientific education and student diversity, 171–197
Reading science, 457–461
    research, 460–461
Reflective toss, 447
Rehabilitation Act of 1973 and amendments, 293
Representation, 378–379
    forms of, 382–383
Representing knowledge, 65–66
Research, see also Teacher research
    biology, see Biology research
    change over time, xii
    classroom assessment of learning, 995
    conceptual change
        results and conclusions, 10–11
        for students' conceptions, 12
    curriculum integration, 544–549
    dominant themes in learning to teach science,
        1164–1165
    elementary science teaching, 494–495
    environmental education, 695–706
    exceptional learners, 288–289
    future directions in elementary science education,
        526–527
    gender in science education, 277–279
    high-stakes testing and accountability, 190
    humanistic perspectives, 897–901
    international perspective, 230–231
    laboratory-related, 429
    learning science outside of school, 128–131,
        153–154
    nature of science, 869–872
    physics education, 600–610, 600f, 622–624
    qualitative, classroom environments, 113–115
    recommendations for international studies,
        253–254

school laboratory teaching, 397–401
school science and home/community connection, 190–191
science achievement, 187–188
science teachers as researchers, 1205–1259
shift in focus, 474–482
special learners, 309–310
special needs students, 304–305
student diversity, 187
teacher attitudes and beliefs, 1067–1104
teacher education, 189–190
teacher knowledge, 1105–1149
teacher professional development in science, 1182–1183, 1189–1198
urban science education through, 321–322
Research traditions, 3–6
commonplaces and contrasts, 5–6
core goals and issues, 5
prescriptions for policy and practice, 27
putting issues in perspective, 27
relationship among, 26–27
understanding learners' dialogues with nature, 27
Resources
convergence in rural settings, 360
urban science achievement gap, 323–327
Rural settings
broad support from stakeholders, 360
consistent policy, 359
contrasting rural and non-rural schools, 361–363
convergence of resources, 360
definition in contemporary sense, 354–356
evidence of student achievement, 360–361
historical studies, 349–352
renewed interest in research on, 352–354
Rural Systemic Initiatives in Science, Mathematics, and Technology Education Program (RSI), 356–361
science education, 345–369
science teacher education, 363–364
standards-based curricula, 359

S

Sapir-Whorf hypothesis, 64
Scaffolding
instruction in elementary education, 514–517
tools for evaluation and communication of scientific ideas, 484–485
Scholastic Aptitude Test (SAT), 176
School-based learning, model, 228–230, 229f
School organization, student diversity and, 184–185
School science laboratory, see Laboratory
Science advances, 234–235
Science and Scientists (SAS) study, 232
findings, 242–243

Science as a discourse community, in sociocultural research, 18
Science-as-culture, 893–894
Science as ideological and institutional, in critical research, 23–24
Science as theoretical dialogue with nature, in conceptual change research, 11
Science curriculum
after World War II, 790–792
applications of science, 788–790
Committee of Ten, 785—786
contesting WMS for all peoples, 207–208
contexts of research, 897–899
disadvantages of integration, 549–553
diversity of student experiences and, 188–189
elementary school, 501–507
finding a place for IK, 208–209
future research agendas, 899–901
history of reform in U.S. and U.K., 781–806
humanistic perspectives, 881–910
indigenous knowledge and, 206
inquiry as organizing theme, 807–830
integration, 537–559
major failures of, 885–887
mandated standards and tests, 504–505
moving beyond the rhetoric of reform, 1172–1174
nature study, 786–788
past research agendas, 899
pedagogical content knowledge, 1128–1130
social and technological change, 801–804
special needs students, 294–301
special talent students, 306
standards-based, 359
student diversity and, 177
systemic influences, 502
teacher and other resources, 503–504
technology and societal issues, 566
types of instructional materials, 502–504
U.K.: primary phase, 792–794
U.K.: secondary school science, 794–801
U.S.: development of the mind, 784–785
U.S.: early years, 783–784
Science Curriculum Improvement Study (SCIS) (Andersson), 33, 384, 523–524
Science education
achievement gaps in, 174–176
assessment and multiple goals of learning, 971
assessment for formative purposes, 972
assessment for summative purposes, 981
attitudes/attributes, 77
best practice in, 501–502
classroom assessment of science learning, 965–1006
comparative studies, 572–573
constructivist views of teaching and learning, 232
context for teaching and learning, 495–496
controversial issues, 1089–1090
cross-national studies, 232–233

cultural commonsense notion of science, 893
current conditions in selected countries, 243–249
driving forces, 229*f*
elementary school, 493–535
enticed-to-know science, 891
evaluation relationship to, 947–953
factors influencing rates of participation, 262–263
functional science, 889–891
future directions for indigenous students, 219–221
future directions of discourse, 461–464
future of, xii–xiii
for girls, 259–261
globalization, 233–234
global view in the 21st Century, 251–252
have-cause-to-know science, 891–893
heteronormative, 276–277
history of science, 1090–1091
home/community connection, 186, 190–191
humanistic perspectives, 881–910
indigenous languages and, 218–219
interdisciplinary teaching, 537–559
international assessments, 1014–1023, 1015*t*
international perspective, 227–256
international perspective on gender differences,
    265–270
laboratory-related research, 429–430
large-scale assessments, 1007–1040
learning and use in other contexts, 887–888
major problems and issues worldwide, 249–251
masculine education, 264–265
need-to-know science, 889
outside of school, 125–167
personal-curiosity science, 893
postcolonialism, indigenous students and, 199–226
recommendations for international research
    studies, 253–254
reform documents, 291–292
reforms worldwide, 231–235, 245–249
research issues in environmental education,
    706–711
research on relevance, 888–893
review of literature on special learners, 294–303
as a road to empowerment and social justice,
    1089–1091
rural settings, 345–369
science/diversity topics, 176
scientific literacy/science literacy and, 731–735
single-sex *versus* mixed-sex classes, 275–276
social and community change, 1091
sociocultural aspects, 271–277
special needs and talents in, 287–317
special talents, 305–310
student diversity and, 171–197
systemic reform, 911–941, 913*t*
technology and, 471–491
turn teaching by generalists, 501
understanding of NOS, 831
in urban settings, 319–343

wish-they-knew science, 889
women in science majors and careers, 270–271
Science education program evaluation, 943–963
    methods for, 955–958, 957*t*
    models for, 953–955, 953*t*
*Science for All Americans and Benchmarks for Science
    Literacy* (AAAS), 176
Science for Specific Social Purposes (SSSP), 756–757
Science for the Public Understanding of Science
    Project (SEPUP), 891–893
Science Laboratory Environment Inventory (SLEI),
    107, 110, 112, 114, 399
Science learning, *see* Learning; Science education
Science museums, *see* Museums
Science notebooks, 518–520
Science Process Inventory (SPI), description of, 864
Science specialists, elementary school teachers, 500
Science teachers, *see also* Teachers
    attitudes and beliefs, 1067–1104
    knowledge, *see also* Teacher knowledge
    PCK implications for education, 1133
    as researchers, 1205–1259
    research on knowledge, 1105–1149
Science Writing Heuristic (SWH), for laboratory
    teaching, 425
Scientific literacy/Science literacy (SL), 5, 729–780
    assessment programs, 759–767
    as conceptual understanding, 7–14
    definition by National Science Education
        Standards, 473
    definitions, 729–731
    as empowerment in critical traditions, 20–25
    five research volumes from Europe, one
        forthcoming, 732–733
    focus on literacy, science, or scientists, 748–755
    focus on situations, 755–759
    four European symposium proceedings, 733–734
    implications for further research, 767–775
    justification arguments, 735–748
    multi-national initiatives, 734
    as participation in a discourse community, 4,
        14–20
    reading and science learning, 458–460
    reflections and a current indicator, 734–735
    in science education, 731–735
    seven handbooks, 731–732
    technology role in, 473–474
Search, Solve, Create, and Share (SSCS), for
    laboratory teaching, 424
Secondary science teacher, 1050–1057
    articulation, 1052–1054
    beginning teachers, 1050–1052
    experienced teachers, 1052
Second International Science Study (SISS), 1015*t*,
    1017–1018
Self-actualization, 87
Self and peer assessments, 987
Self-assessment, in elementary science education, 508

Self-determination, 87
in motivation, 89–90
Self-efficacy, in motivation, 92
Self-regulation, in motivation, 91
Self-report instruments, attitude, 80–82
Sex differences, *see* Gender differences
Simulation tools, thinking critically with, 483–484
Situated cognition, 45–46
Situated learning, communities of practice and, 61–62
Situational interest, 88
Small-group interaction, in elementary science
teaching, 512–513, 521–523
Social agency, in scientific literacy, 5
Social and community change, science education
and, 1091
Social constructivist views, 41
summary and implications, 44
Social development, teachers, 1185
Social languages, 42
alternative conceptions and, 43–44
ontological differences, 50
Social norms, teacher beliefs, 1083
Social plane, in learning, 40
Social semiotics, sociocultural considerations and,
60–61
Sociocultural model of embedded belief systems,
1074*f*, 1086–1087, 1091
Sociocultural research tradition, 4, 14–20
characteristics, 17–20
discussion and implications, 17
example of, 15
power and limitations, 19–20
research methods and results, 15–17
social semiotics and, 60–61
theoretical approach, 15
Sociocultural status, urban science achievement gap
and, 322–327
Socioeconomic status (SES)
gender differences in science education, 263–264
scientific education and student diversity, 171–197
Sociopolitical process of instruction, student
diversity and, 178–179
Software tool, helping students achieve their
learning goals, 9
Spatial reasoning, in learning earth sciences, 663–664
Special needs
assessment, 301–303
curriculum and instruction, 294–301
definitions, 289–290, 290*t*
issues of race and, 290–291
legislation affecting rights, 292–293
Special talents, 305–310
curriculum and instruction, 306
identification of learners, 308–309
legislation affecting rights, 305–306
perspectives of learners, 308
review of literature, 306–309
Specific theories, of concepts, 37

Spoken discourse, studies, 445–448
State-Trait Anxiety Inventory (Spielberger), 88
Statewide Systemic Initiative (SSI) program, NSF,
926, 927*f*
Student attitudes
gender differences in, 272
perspective on science curriculum reform, 804
Student diversity
gender issues in science education, 257–285
key findings, 176–186
science education and, 171–197
terminology, 173–174
*Student Engagement at School—A Sense of Belonging
and Participation* (OECD), PISA study, 240
Student enrollment in science, chronic decline in,
885–886
Student learning approaches
demonstrations, 375
predictor of performance, 241
Student outcomes
classroom environments and, 110–111
curriculum integration effects, 545–546
learning approaches and, 241–242
Student perceptions, 31–56
actual and preferred environment, 112
conceptions on NOS, 836–838, 842–845, 858–861
physics, 607–608
Students' Alternative Frameworks and Science Education
(Pfundt & Duit), 34
Students' ideas, identification, 525–526
Student small-group discourse, 450–453
Students with disabilities (SD)
achievement gaps and, 175
science assessment and, 181–182
Student Teams and Achievement Division (STAD), 383
Studying/doing herpetology, in critical research, 22
Subject matter knowledge (SMK), 1107
biology, 1115–1116
chemistry, 1113–1114
earth and space science, 1114–1115
general science, 1110–1113
physics, 1115–1116
relation to teaching, 1117–1120
research on science teachers, 1110–1120
Success and participation, urban learners, 336–337
Success for All (Slavin et al.), 923
Summative assessment, 968–971, 981
in elementary science education, 508–509
Sustainable development, environmental education
and, 691–692
Symbolic model, 379
Symbolic representation, 382
Systemic reform
courses and competencies, 922–926
definition, 911
excellence and equity, 926–933
lessons learned, 933–935, 936*f*
research, vision, and politics, 911–941, 913*t*

Systemic reform (*continued*)
   teaching, 914–*916*
   texts, 916–922
   timeline, 913*f*
Systems for State Science Assessment (Wilson &
    Bertenthal), 1028
Systems thinking, in learning earth sciences, 668–671

T

Talking Science: Language, Learning, and Values
    (Lemke), 46–47, 60, 445
*Talking Their Way into Science: Hearing Children's
    Questions and Theories, Responding with
    Curricula* (Galla), 448
Teacher education and preparation
   avoidance of science, 496–499
   choice of materials, 504
   constructivist views, 232
   cross-disciplinary teaching, 505–506
   curriculum integration and, 511 542
   elementary school science, 496–501
   ELL students, 183–184
   feedback, 520
   gender trends in science, 499–500
   generalist/specialist science teaching, 500–501
   indigenous and minority students, 213–215
   inservice teachers and integrated curriculum,
    548–549
   integration of science with language, 506
   integration of science with mathematics, 506
   integration of science with technology, 506–507
   learning to teach science, 1151–1178
   multiple meanings of chemical topics, 647–648
   perspectives on teacher research and learning,
    1214–1215
   preservice teachers and integrated curriculum,
    547–548
   professional development in science, 1179–1203
   programs that work to make a difference,
    1166–1169
   relationship with professional developers,
    1188–1189
   research, 189–190
   role in laboratory activities, 427–429
   rural science education, 363–364
   science teacher as learner, 1043–1065
   science teacher educator as learner, 1057–1059
   specific strategies for elementary science, 521–523
   student diversity and, 182
   turn teaching by generalists, 501
Teacher knowledge
   historical views of, 1105–1106
   Shulman's model, 1106–1108, 1107*f*
Teacher perceptions
   actual and preferred environment, 112

biology, textbooks' role, 586–587
   perspectives on professional development, 1183
   reason for choice of textbooks, 587
   research on teachers' conceptions of NOS,
    838–842, 845–852, 852–857
Teacher research
   benefits and pitfalls, 1233–1234
   both teacher and researcher, 1234
   collaboration, 1235–1236
   collaboration and public dialogue, 1240
   complexity of context and triangulation, 1241
   context of, 1235
   criteria for quality of, 1237–1238
   definition, 1208–1210
   funding opportunities, 1244
   historical context, 1211–1214
   inservice programs and, 1219–1228, 1220–1226*t*
   insider-outsider research, 1238–1239
   issues addressed in studies, 1228–1233, 1229*t*
   knowledge contribution of, 1231–1233
   national/international community of, 1244
   new directions for, 1242–1243
   new modes of representation, 1244–1246
   preservice programs and, 1215–1218, 1216–1217*t*
   questions addressed, 1234–1235
   searchable online libraries, 1243–1244
   student learning and, 1241
   studies about, 1243
   teacher learning and, 1214–1215, 1236–1237, 1241
   trustworthiness, 1239–1240
   usefulness and quality of knowledge, 1237
   voice, professionalism, and satisfaction, 1236
Teachers Education and Development Study
    (TEDS), 1015*t*
Teacher Training Institutes program, 914–916
Teaching and learning, problematic, 1054–1055
Teaching efficacy, epistemologies and teaching
    practices, 1084–1089
Teaching Integrated Mathematics and Science
    (TIMS), 546
Teaching methods
   assessment techniques and strategies in
    elementary science, 507
   atomic structure courses developed from modern
    perspectives, 639–640
   avoidance of science, 496–499
   chemistry courses developed from modern
    perspectives, 635–637
   concepts and principles in biology, 588–589
   for conceptual change learning, 12
   in critical research, 24–25
   cross-disciplinary, 505–506
   discourse studies in classroom, 445–448
   effects of attitudes and beliefs, 1067–1104
   elementary science curriculum, 496–501, 501–506
   information technology, 507
   inquiry, 810, 822–823

interdisciplinary, 537–559
laboratory models and strategies, 424–427, 426t
laboratory-related research in science education,
   429–430
mandated curricula, standards, and tests, 504–505
resources, 503
school science laboratory, 393–441
in sociocultural research, 19
studies of, 457–461
Teams Games Tournaments (TGT), 383
Technology
   advances, 234–235
   integration of science teaching with, 506–507
   learning science with, 471–491
   relative to Cognitive Tools Framework, 482–487
   role in scientific literacy, 473–474
   underutilization in classrooms, 472–473
Television, science learning and, 151–153
Temporal thinking, in learning earth sciences, 664–668
Testing and accountability, research on, 190
Test of Enquiry Skills (TOES), 110
Test of Science Related Attitudes (TOSRA), 110
Test on Understanding Science (TOUS), 836–838
   description of, 863
   teacher and student comparison, 839
Test-taking patterns, gender differences, 274–275
Texts and teaching (Sputnik to MACOS), 913–922
The End of Education (Postman), 419
Theoretical structures of concepts, 37
Theory-practice gap, 1055–1057
The Pupil as Scientist (Driver), 34
The Structure of Scientific Revolutions (Kuhn), 884
Think-pair-share (TPS), laboratory teaching, 425
Third International Mathematics and Science Study
      (TIMSS), 84, 233, 1018–1022, 1019t
   1999 and 2003, 1022
   chronology of international assessments, 1015t
   findings, 237–239
   physics instruction, 604
   status-type evaluation evidence, 947
Thought and Language (Vygotsky), 40, 59
Traditional ecological knowledge (TEK), indigenous
      knowledge and, 204–206
Transformation, via cognitive tools framework,
      479–482, 480f
Trends of International Mathematics and Science
      Study (TIMSS 1995), 232
   findings, 236
Tyler's Rationale for Curriculum Development, 562

U

U.S. National Science Education Standards, 291–292, 303
UNESCO
   scientific literacy initiatives, 734
   women's access to education, 270

Unified Science and Mathematics for Elementary
      Schools (USMES), 546
United Kingdom, science education reform, 247
United Nations Development Fund for Women
      (UNIFEM), 265–266
Universalism, 206–212
University of Wisconsin—Madison, science teacher
      education program, 1167–1168
Urban settings
   achievement in science, 322–327
   emergent questions in understanding and
      bridging difference, 336
   process of learning, 327–340
   research on education in, 321–322
   science education in, 319–343
   what else students learn, 340
Utilitarian, understanding of NOS, 831
Utilization-Focused Evaluation (Patton), 945

V

Verbal mode of representation, 379
Vertical coherence, 1031
View of Science Test (VOST), 864
Views of Nature of Science, Form A (VNOS0A), 866
Views on Science-Technology-Society (VOSTS),
      865–866
Visualization
   in learning earth sciences, 663–664
   thinking critically with, 483–484
Visual mode of representation, 379
Vygotskian perspective on learning, 40–41, 58–59

W

Western Modern Science (WMS), 201, 206–212
   no place for IK, 210–211
What is Happening in This Class? Questionnaire
      (WIHIC), 108–109, 115
Wisconsin Inventory of Science Processes (WISP),
      839–840
   description of, 863–864
   research on teachers, 845
Worldview, science education research, 212
Writing
   in elementary science teaching, 518
   in language and science learning, 66–67
Writing science, 457–461
   research, 460–461

Z

Zone of proximal development (ZPD), Vygotsky, 59
Zoos, learning from, 140

About the Authors

Sandra K. Abell
Sandra K. Abell is professor of science education at the University of Missouri-Columbia, US, where she directs the university's Science Education Center. Her research interests focus on teacher learning throughout the career span and across the grade levels. She is a past President of the National Association for Research in Science Teaching (NARST).

Glen S. Aikenhead
I have always embraced a humanistic perspective on science, as a research chemist in Canada and as a science teacher at international schools in Germany and Switzerland. This perspective was enhanced during my graduate studies at Harvard University in the late 1960s and has since then guided my research in science education at the University of Saskatchewan, Canada.

Charles W. Anderson
Charles W. (Andy) Anderson has been a Peace Corps volunteer, middle school science teacher, and professor at Michigan State University, US, since 1979. Dr. Anderson's primary research interests are in using conceptual change and sociocultural research on student learning to improve classroom science teaching. He is a past President of NARST.

Ronald D. Anderson
Ronald D. Anderson is professor of education at the University of Colorado at Boulder, US. The author of books and numerous research articles on science education reform, he is a past President of both NARST and the Association for the Education of Teachers in Science.

Ken Appleton
After retiring recently, Ken Appleton was appointed an adjunct associate professor at Central Queensland University, Australia. He has published extensively in international journals in his areas of interest that include elementary science teaching and learning, constructivism, elementary science teacher knowledge, and science teacher professional development.

Hilary Asoko

Hilary Asoko is a senior lecturer at the University of Leeds, UK. She is particularly interested in the teaching and learning of science in primary schools and in science teacher education.

J Myron (Mike) Atkin

J Myron (Mike) Atkin, Professor of Education (Emeritus) at Stanford University, US, is a National Associate of the National Academy of Sciences, where he was a member of the National Committee on Science Education Standards and chair of the Committee on Science Education K-12. His current research and writing center on science education curriculum and assessment.

Charles R. Ault, Jr.

Charles Ault is professor of education at Lewis & Clark College, US, where he teaches science education courses in the Master of Arts in Teaching (M.A.T.) program for elementary and secondary teachers. His teaching emphasizes the interpretation of local landscapes and stems from his scholarly interests in learning earth science, with particular attention to children's conception of time and the nature of geological problem-solving.

Dale Baker

Dale Baker is a professor in the Division of Curriculum and Instruction in the College of Education at Arizona State University, US. She is a former editor of the *Journal of Research in Science Teaching*. Her research focuses on gender equity issues in the teaching and learning of science as well as in engineering education.

Angela Calabrese Barton

Angela Calabrese Barton's research focuses on the science practices of high poverty urban youth and on the role that community-based and case-based learning experiences can play in the development of science teachers' understandings of urban youth and their own science teaching. Her work has been published in numerous venues and her most recent book, *Teaching Science for Social Justice* (Teachers College Press), won the 2003 AESA Critics Choice Award. She is on the faculty of Michigan State University, US.

Beverley Bell

Beverley Bell is an associate professor in the School of Education at the University of Waikato, Hamilton, New Zealand. She has a background in science education conceptual change research for over 20 years, and her current research interests are in pedagogy, learning, assessment, and teacher education.

Paul Black

Paul Black is emeritus professor in the School of Education at King's College in London, UK. He worked as a physicist for 20 years before moving to science education. He has made contributions to curriculum development, and to research into learning and assessment, particularly for teachers' classroom assessments. He has served on advisory groups of the US National Research Council and as visiting professor at Stanford University.

Edward Britton

Edward Britton, is senior research associate in WestEd's Mathematics and Science Program, US. He contributed to the Third International Mathematics and Science Study and co-led an international comparison of high school exit examinations in science.

Glenda Carter

Glenda Carter is an associate professor of science education and the associate director of the Center for Mathematics and Science Education at North Carolina State University, US. Her research focuses on the use of language, gesture and tools as mediators of conceptual understanding. She is a member of the Friday Institute Mathematics and Science Collaboratory and the Middle Grades Academy.

William Carlsen

Bill is a professor of Science Education in Penn State's College of Education, US, and is director of the university's new Center for Science and the Schools. His current research focuses on the use of web-mediated peer review of original scientific research by high school students and preservice science teachers.

Michael P. Clough

Dr. Clough is an Associate Professor at Iowa State University, US where he directs the secondary science teacher education program and teaches courses addressing science learning and teaching and the nature of science and science education. His scholarly work examines learning and teaching the nature of science, laboratory learning and teaching, and the teacher's role in both.

Charlene M. Czerniak

Charlene M. Czerniak is a professor at The University of Toledo, US. She is the co-author of a methods textbook on Project-Based Science, and she has written numerous articles on teachers' beliefs, curriculum integration, teacher professional development, and science education reform.

Onno De Jong

Dr. Onno De Jong is an associate professor in chemical education at Utrecht University, The Netherlands. He has published on education in problem solving, models and modeling, and electrochemistry. His current research interests include the professional development of chemistry teachers.

Reinders Duit

Reinders Duit is a professor of physics education at the Leibniz-Institute for Science Education (IPN) in Kiel (Germany). His research interests include teaching and learning processes from conceptual change perspectives, quality development, teacher professional development and video-based studies on the practice of science instruction.

Barry J. Fraser

Barry J. Fraser is director of the Science and Mathematics Education Centre at Curtin University of Technology in Perth, Australia. He is author/editor of *Learning Environments Research: An International Journal, International Handbook of Science Education, Classroom Environment, and Educational Environments*. A past President of NARST, he was 2003 recipient of that association's Distinguished Contributions to Science Education through Research Award.

Shawn M. Glynn

Shawn M. Glynn is a professor of science education and educational psychology at the University of Georgia, US. His specialization is in the application of psychology to science education, particularly in the areas of cognition and motivation. His books include *The Psychology of Learning Science* and *Learning Science in the Schools*.

Chorng-Jee Guo

Chorng-Jee Guo is a professor and the president of National Taitung University, Taitung, Taiwan. His research interests in science education are students' learning of science, science teaching strategies and materials, professional development of science teachers, and science education policy.

Paul Hart

Paul Hart is a Professor of Science Education at University of Regina in Canada. He is executive editor of the *Journal of Environmental Education* and consulting editor for several journal in environmental education. He has published widely and is the recipient of several research awards including the Jeske Award from the North American Association for Environmental Education.

Peter W. Hewson

Peter Hewson is a professor of science education at the University of Wisconsin-Madison, US. His primary interest is in conceptual change approaches to the learning and teaching of science, and the initial education and professional development of science teachers. He is also interested in fostering international collaborative research opportunities.

Avi Hofstein

Avi Hofstein is Professor and Head of the Department of Science Teaching at the Weizmann Institute of Science, Israel. For more than 30 years he has engaged in science curriculum development, implementation, and evaluation. He holds a B.Sc. in chemistry, M.A. in education, and Ph.D. in science education.

M. Gail Jones

M. Gail Jones is a professor of science education in the Department of Mathematics, Science and Technology Education at North Carolina State University, US, where she prepares middle and high school science teachers. In addition to an interest in teacher beliefs, her research interests include the impacts of high stakes testing policy, gender, and nanotechnology education.

Jane Butler Kahle

Jane Butler Kahle, Condit Professor of Science Education, Miami University, US, is former director of the Elementary, Secondary, & Informal Education division at the US National Science Foundation. In 1991, Miami University awarded her an honorary L.H.D. degree. Her scholarship focuses on gender equity and systemic reform of education. She is a past president of NARST.

Gregory J. Kelly
Gregory Kelly is a professor of science education at Pennsylvania State University, US. He teaches courses on teaching and learning science, qualitative research methods, and uses of history, philosophy, sociology of science in science education. His research examines science learning, classroom discourse, and epistemology in science education.

Thomas R. Koballa, Jr.
Thomas R. Koballa, Jr. is a professor in the Department of Mathematics and Science Education at the University of Georgia, US. His research interests include the science-related attitudes of students and teachers and the induction experiences of beginning science teachers. He is a past President of NARST and co-author of *Science Instruction in the Middle and Secondary Schools*.

Frances Lawrenz
Dr. Lawrenz is Wallace Professor of Teaching and Learning in the Educational Psychology Department at the University of Minnesota, US. Her specialty is science education program evaluation. She has published extensively, received the university's highest award for teaching and has served as department chair and assistant vice president for research.

Reuven Lazarowitz
Reuven Lazarowitz is Emeritus Professor of Science Education in Biology, at the Israeli Institute of Technology, Technion, Haifa, Israel. His research interest is in the structure of high school biology curriculum; teaching and learning biology concepts and principles in individualized, cooperative small groups and computer-assisted learning settings. Recently he was involved in the national committee for developing learning units in the STS approach and educating teachers for teaching those units to the high school students who do not major in science and technology.

John Leach
John Leach is Professor of Science Education and Head of the School of Education at the University of Leeds, UK. His research interests include epistemic aspects of science learning and the use of insights from research in the practice of science teaching.

Norman G. Lederman
Norman G. Lederman is Chair and Professor of Mathematics and Science Education at the Illinois Institute of Technology, US. He is internationally known for his research and scholarship on the development of students' and teachers' conceptions of nature of science and scientific inquiry. He is a former President of NARST and of the Association for the Education of Teachers in Science (AETS). He has also served as Director of Teacher Education for the National Science Teachers Association (NSTA) and as Editor of *School Science and Mathematics*.

Okhee Lee
Okhee Lee is a professor in the School of Education, University of Miami, Florida, US. Her research involves language and culture in science education. One of her

current research projects implements instructional interventions to promote science learning and language development for elementary students from diverse languages and cultures.

J. John Loughran

J. John Loughran is a professor in education and the Foundation Chair in Curriculum and Professional Practice in the Faculty of Education at Monash University in Australia. He has been actively involved in teacher education for the past decade. His research interests include science teacher education, teacher-as-researcher, and reflective practice.

Vincent N. Lunetta

Vincent Lunetta is Professor Emeritus at Penn State University, US. He has received awards for scholarship and leadership in science education and given special attention to: teacher education; goals for science learning; the role of the laboratory, computer technologies, and simulation in learning and teaching; the development of conceptual procedural knowledge; international education; and education policy.

Aurolyn Luykx

Aurolyn Luykx is an anthropologist specializing in ethnography of schooling, bilingual-intercultural education, and language planning and policy. Her book, *The Citizen Factory*, was published in 1999 by SUNY Press. She currently holds a joint appointment in the Departments of Sociology/Anthropology and Teacher Education at the University of Texas at El Paso, US.

Andrea K. Martin

Andrea K. Martin is an adjunct professor in the Faculty of Education, Queen's University, Kingston, Ontario, Canada. Her areas of interest and scholarship include the development of teachers' knowledge, preservice teacher education, special education, and literacy development and interventions.

J. Randy McGinnis

J. Randy McGinnis is professor of science education in the Science Teaching Center at the University of Maryland, College Park, US. His research and writing primarily concern science teacher education and equity. He has served on the executive boards of NARST and the Association for Science Teacher Education. He is co-editor of the *Journal of Research in Science Teaching*.

Elizabeth McKinley

Dr. Elizabeth McKinley currently teaches research methodologies, curriculum and social issues at the University of Auckland, New Zealand. She researches and writes on indigenous people's educational issues, particularly with respect to Maori students in science education. She has had extensive experience teaching science in high schools and in bilingual (Maori/English) science curriculum development.

Hans Niedderer

Hans Niedderer is a retired professor of physics education at the University of Bremen (Germany). His research interests include students' alternative conceptions, learning processes, and curriculum development. Currently he works as guest professor at two Swedish universities in cooperation with the Swedish National Graduate School in Science and Technology Education Research (FoNTD).

J. Steve Oliver
J. Steve Oliver is an associate professor in science education at the University of Georgia, US. His interest in rural education issues began during a childhood spent around the family farms. His current interests include secondary science teacher education as well as teacher knowledge and practices.

Nir Orion
Dr. Nir Orion holds a professorship in the Weizmann Institute of Science in Israel where he heads the Earth Science and Environment Group of the Science Teaching Department. His activity covers all facets of science education: research, curriculum development, implementation, and teacher education from K-12. His main areas of activity are: Earth and Environmental Sciences; the outdoors as a learning environment; science for all; and teachers' professional change.

Léonie J. Rennie
Dr Léonie Rennie is Professor of Science and Technology Education and Dean, Graduate Studies at Curtin University of Technology in Western Australia. Her research interests include adults' and children's learning in science and technology and the communication of science in a range of out-of-school contexts.

Douglas A. Roberts
Doug Roberts, Professor Emeritus of the University of Calgary in Canada, began his science education career in 1957 as a high school science teacher in Pennsylvania. Doug has been a university faculty member at Harvard, Temple, Toronto (OISE), and Calgary. His research interests include science curriculum policy and the development of science teacher thinking.

Kathleen J. Roth
After teaching middle school science and later completing a PhD in science education, Kathy became a teacher-researcher in elementary classrooms while also teaching teachers at Michigan State University. In 1999, Kathy became the director of the TIMSS video study of science teaching at LessonLab Research Institute in the US, where she currently supports and studies elementary teacher-researchers.

Tom Russell
Tom Russell is a professor in the Faculty of Education at Queen's University, Kingston, Ontario, Canada. His research focuses on reflective practice and learning from experience in the context of learning to teach. He teaches preservice physics methods, supervises the preservice practicum, and teaches action research in the graduate program.

Kathryn Scantlebury
Kathryn Scantlebury is an associate professor in the Department of Chemistry and Biochemistry and the Secondary Science Education Coordinator in the College of Arts & Sciences at the University of Delaware, US. Her research focuses on gender and equity issues in science education.

Phil Scott
Phil Scott is professor of science education at the University of Leeds, UK. His main research interests lie in drawing on research findings to plan and implement science instruction and analyzing language, teaching and learning in science classrooms. This research informs a wide range of professional development activities with science teachers.

Horst Schecker
Horst Schecker is a professor of physics education at the University of Bremen (Germany). His research interests include multimedia, learning processes in physics, and curriculum development. One of his current projects is about a standardized test of students' understanding of thermodynamics.

Steven Schneider
Steven Schneider, program director of mathematics, science and technology at WestEd, US, is principal investigator for the NSF-funded Center for Assessment and Evaluation of Student Learning (CAESL) and the National Assessment Governing Board's development project, 2009–2021 US National Assessment of Educational Progress Science Framework and Test Specification.

Nancy Butler Songer
Dr. Songer is a Professor of Science Education and Learning Technologies at the University of Michigan, US. Focusing on students in high-poverty urban settings, Songer's research: a) characterizes children's higher-order thinking in science, b) evaluates simple technologies used as cognitive tools, and c) develops assessment systems to provide developmental evidence of complex reasoning in science.

Gregory P. Stefanich
Dr. Gregory P. Stefanich is professor of science education and former Interim Head of the Department of Curriculum and Instruction at the University of Northern Iowa, US. He joined the faculty at the UNI in 1976. His research over the years has focused on special needs learners and science.

Keith S. Taber
Keith Taber taught science in schools, and a college, before joining the Faculty of Education at Cambridge University, UK. He has been a Teacher Fellow for the Royal Society of Chemistry, is Chair of the Society's Chemical Education Research Group; and serves as Associate Editor of *Chemistry Education: Research and Practice*.

David Treagust
David Treagust is Professor of Science Education at Curtin University in Perth, Western Australia and teaches courses in campus-based and international programs related to teaching and learning science. His research interests are related to understanding students' ideas about science concepts, and how these ideas can be used to enhance the design of curricula and improve teachers' classroom practice. He is past President of NARST and recipient of the association's 2006 Distinguished Contributions to Science Education through Research Award.